AF778836

Individual Income Taxes 2023

General Editors

James C. Young
Ph.D., CPA

Annette Nellen
J.D., CPA, CGMA

William A. Raabe
Ph.D., CPA

Mark B. Persellin
Ph.D., CPA, CFP®

Sharon S. Lassar
Ph.D., CPA

Andrew D. Cuccia
Ph.D., CPA

Bradrick M. Cripe
Ph.D., CPA

Contributing Authors

James H. Boyd
Ph.D., CPA
Arizona State University

Bradrick M. Cripe
Ph.D., CPA
Northern Illinois University

D. Larry Crumbley
Ph.D., CPA
Texas A&M University – Corpus Christi

Andrew D. Cuccia
Ph.D., CPA
University of Oklahoma

Steven C. Dilley
J.D., Ph.D., CPA
Michigan State University

Sharon S. Lassar
Ph.D., CPA
University of Denver

David M. Maloney
Ph.D., CPA
University of Virginia

Annette Nellen
J.D., CPA, CGMA
San Jose State University

Mark B. Persellin
Ph.D., CPA, CFP®
St. Mary's University

William A. Raabe
Ph.D., CPA
Philadelphia, Pennsylvania

Toby Stock
Ph.D., CPA
Ohio University

James C. Young
Ph.D., CPA
Northern Illinois University

Kristina Zvinakis
Ph.D.
The University of Texas at Austin

Cengage

Australia • Brazil • Canada • Mexico • Singapore • United Kingdom • United States

Cengage

South-Western Federal Taxation: Individual Income Taxes, 2023 Edition

James C. Young, Annette Nellen, William A. Raabe, Mark B. Persellin, Sharon S. Lassar, Andrew D. Cuccia, Bradrick M. Cripe

SVP, Product: Erin Joyner

VP, Product: Thais Alencar

Product Director: Joe Sabatino

Product Manager: Jonathan Gross

Product Assistant: Flannery Cowan

Learning Designer: Kristen Meere

Sr. Content Manager: Nadia Saloom

Digital Project Manager: Steven McMillan

VP, Product Marketing: Jason Sakos

Director, Product Marketing: Danae April

Product Marketing Manager: Colin M. Kramer

IP Analyst: Ashley Maynard

IP Project Manager: Nick Barrows

Production Service: Straive

Designer: Chris Doughman

Cover Image Source: Pgiam/E+/Getty Images

Interior Image Source:
- Concept Summary: iStock.com/enot-poloskun
- Global Tax Issues: Enot-Poloskun/ E+/Getty Images
- Ethics & Equity: iStock.com/LdF
- Comprehensive Tax Return Problems: iStock.com/peepo
- Financial Disclosure Insights: Vyaseleva Elena/Shutterstock.com
- Framework 1040: Concept Photo/ Shutterstock.com

Last three editions, as applicable: © 2023, © 2022, © 2021

Copyright © 2023 Cengage Learning, Inc. ALL RIGHTS RESERVED.

No part of this work covered by the copyright herein may be reproduced or distributed in any form or by any means, except as permitted by U.S. copyright law, without the prior written permission of the copyright owner.

Unless otherwise noted, all content is Copyright © Cengage Learning, Inc.

For product information and technology assistance, contact us at **Cengage Customer & Sales Support, 1-800-354-9706** or **support.cengage.com.**

For permission to use material from this text or product, submit all requests online at **www.cengage.com/permissions**.

All tax forms within the text are: Source: Internal Revenue Service
Tax software: Source: Intuit ProConnect Tax
Becker CPA Review: Source: Becker CPA
Excel screenshots: Source: Used with permissions from Microsoft
Intuit ProConnect Tax, Becker, Microsoft and Checkpoint and all Intuit ProConnect Tax, Becker, Microsoft and Checkpoint-based trademarks and logos are registered trademarks of Intuit ProConnect Tax, Becker, Microsoft and Checkpoint in the United States and other countries.

ISSN: 0272-0329
2023 Annual Edition

Student Edition ISBN: 978-0-357-71982-4
Looseleaf Edition ISBN: 978-0-357-71984-8

Cengage
200 Pier 4 Boulevard
Boston, MA 02210
USA

Cengage is a leading provider of customized learning solutions with employees residing in nearly 40 different countries and sales in more than 125 countries around the world. Find your local representative at **www.cengage.com**.

To learn more about Cengage platforms and services, register or access your online learning solution, or purchase materials for your course, visit **www.cengage.com**.

Printed in the United States of America
Print Number: 01 Print Year: 2022

ProConnect™ Tax

intuit
Accountants

Work like a pro.

Get the #1 cloud-based professional tax software for free.[1,2]

Go beyond the basics and connect with the modern tools you need to work efficiently.

- **Work with confidence.**
  Get returns done right the first time with access to all the forms you need, backed by industry-leading calculations and diagnostics.
- **Work smarter.**
  Save time with logical data-entry worksheets instead of traditional forms-based methods. Plus, get quick training resources so it's easy to stay up to speed.
- **Work from anywhere.**
  It's all online, so there's nothing to install or maintain. And whether you're on your mobile phone or laptop, PC or Mac – you're always good to go.

How to Register for/Access Intuit ProConnect Tax Online

1. Visit https://www.intuit.com/partners/education-program/products/proconnect-tax-online/student-signup/ and complete the Student Registration form.
   a. Instructors should use this form: https://www.intuit.com/partners/education-program/products/proconnect-tax-online/educator-signup/
2. Once Intuit verifies student/educator status (via SheerID), registrants will receive instructions on their screen. An e-mail confirmation of verification will also be sent.
3. Students/educators can use their credentials to log in to the educational version of ProConnect at www.taxeducation.intuit.com.

Only one sign-up per student. No special code required. If you have trouble accessing or using the software, reach out to us at taxeducation_support@intuit.com anytime for help.

intuit turbotax quickbooks mint credit karma

[1] Based on Intuit internal data of the number of paid users of ProConnect Tax for Tax Year 2019 compared to publicly available statements from competitors for the same time period.

[2] If you sign-up for the free version of ProConnect Tax for students and educators, you will not have access to certain features, including functionality such as Electronic Filing Services and Intuit Link.

© 2022 Intuit Inc. All rights reserved. Intuit, the Intuit logo, ProConnect and QuickBooks among others, are trademarks or service marks of Intuit Inc. in the United States and other countries. Terms and conditions, features, support, pricing, and service options subject to change without notice.

THOMSON REUTERS

CHECKPOINT™

3 Simple ways Checkpoint Edge helps you make sense of all those taxes

1. Find what you are looking for quickly and easily online with Checkpoint® Edge
2. A comprehensive collection of primary tax law, cases, and rulings, along with analytical insight you simply can't find anywhere else
3. Checkpoint Edge has built-in productivity tools to make research more efficient — a resource tax pros use more than any other

Titles that include Checkpoint Edge Student Edition:

- **Young/Nellen/Raabe/Persellin/Lassar/Cuccia/Cripe,** *South-Western Federal Taxation: Individual Income Taxes, 2023 Edition*
- **Raabe/Young/Nellen/Cripe/Lassar/Persellin/Cuccia,** *South-Western Federal Taxation: Corporations, Partnerships, Estates & Trusts, 2023 Edition*
- **Young/Nellen/Maloney/Persellin/Cuccia/Lassar/Cripe,** *South-Western Federal Taxation: Comprehensive Volume, 2023 Edition*
- **Nellen/Cuccia/Persellin/Young,** *South-Western Federal Taxation: Essentials of Taxation: Individuals and Business Entities, 2023 Edition*
- **Murphy/Higgins/Skalberg,** *Concepts in Federal Taxation, 2022 Edition*

Important information

The purchase of this textbook includes access to Checkpoint Edge Student Edition for a 6-month duration.

To log in, visit **checkpoint.tr.com**, and you will be asked to supply a User ID and Password.

Instructors: please contact your Cengage Account Executive to obtain access for your class.

Students: please work with your instructors to gain access.

For technical support, please visit **cengage.com/support**

©2022 Thomson Reuters TR1273709/2-2022. Checkpoint is a registered trademark of Thomson Reuters (Tax & Accounting) Inc. Other names and trademarks are properties of their respective owners.

THOMSON REUTERS®

Preface

Committed to Educational Success

South-Western Federal Taxation (SWFT) is the most trusted and best-selling taxation series used by colleges and universities. We are focused exclusively on providing the most useful, comprehensive, and up-to-date tax texts, online study aids, tax preparation tools, and research tools to help instructors and students succeed in their tax courses and beyond.

SWFT is a comprehensive package of teaching and learning materials, significantly enhanced with each edition to meet instructor and student needs and to add overall value to learning taxation.

Individual Income Taxes, 2023 Edition provides a dynamic learning experience inside and outside of the classroom. Built with resources and tools that have been identified as the most important, our complete learning system provides options for students to achieve success.

In addition, *Individual Income Taxes*, 2023 Edition provides accessible, comprehensive, and authoritative coverage of the relevant tax code and regulations as they pertain to the individual taxpayer, as well as coverage of all major developments in Federal taxation.

In revising the 2023 Edition, we focused on:

- ***Accessibility. Clarity. Substance.*** The authors and editors made this their focus as they revised the 2023 edition. Coverage has been streamlined to make it more accessible to students, and difficult concepts have been clarified, all without losing the substance that makes up the *South-Western Federal Taxation* series.
- ***Developing professional skills.*** SWFT excels in bringing students to a professional level in their tax knowledge and skills, to prepare them for immediate success in their careers. We include development of written and verbal communication skills, the use of tax preparation and tax research software, orientation toward success on the CPA Exam (including the upcoming CPA Evolution version of the exam), exposure to tax policy and tax law development, consideration of the time value of money in the tax planning process, and experience with advanced spreadsheet applications and data analytics.
- ***CNOWv2 as a complete learning system.*** Cengage Learning understands that digital learning solutions are central to the classroom. Through sustained research, we continually refine our learning solutions in CNOWv2 to meet evolving student and instructor needs. CNOWv2 fulfills learning and course management needs by offering a personalized study plan, video lectures, auto-graded homework, auto-graded tests, and a full eBook with features and advantages that address common challenges.

Learning Tools and Features to Help Students Make the Connection

Full-Color Design: We understand that students struggle with learning difficult tax law concepts and applying them to real-world scenarios. The 2023 edition uses color to bring the text to life, capture student attention, and present the tax law in an understandable and logical format.

- Selected **content is streamlined** to guide students in focusing on the most important concepts for the CPA Exam while still providing in-depth coverage of topics.

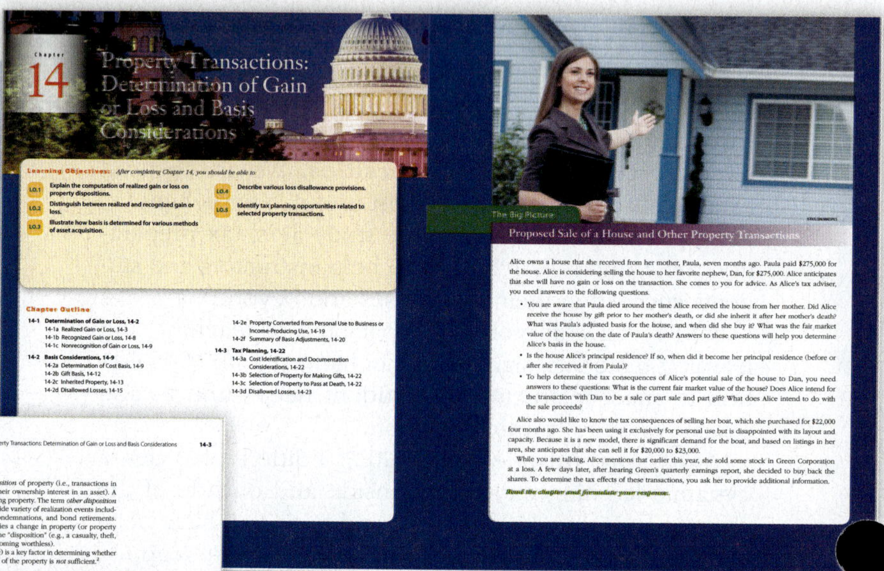

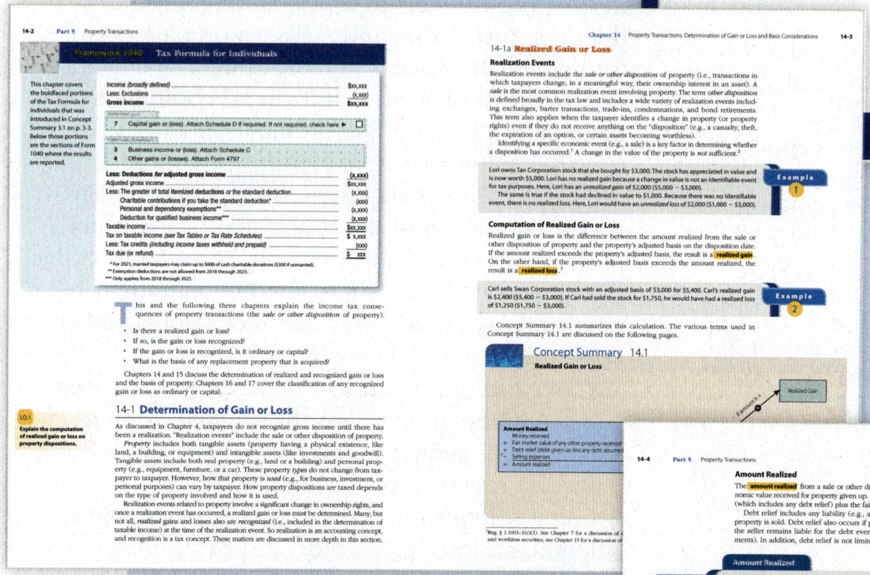

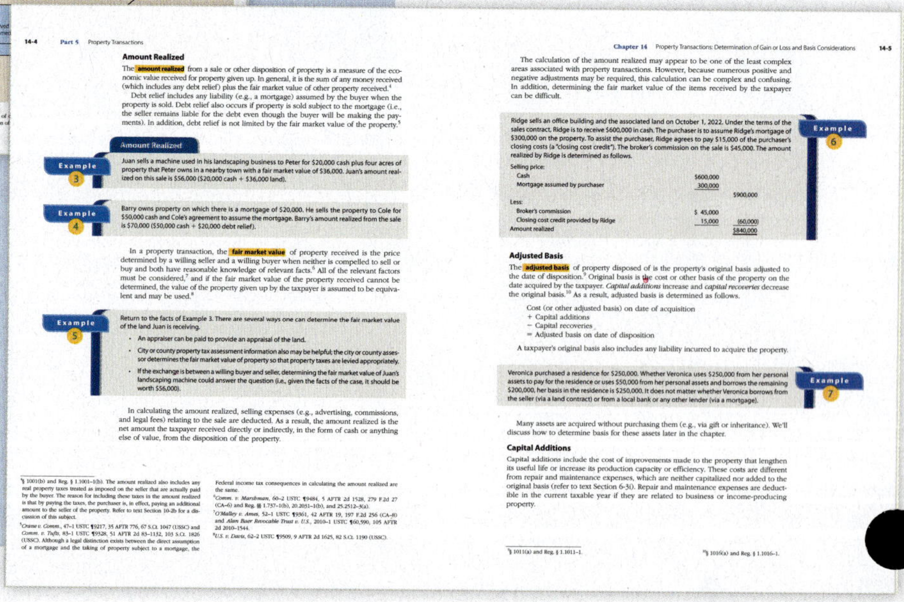

- Examples are clearly labeled and directly follow concepts to assist with student application. An **average of over 40 examples in each chapter** use realistic situations to illustrate the complexities of the tax law and allow students to integrate chapter concepts with illustrations and examples.

Computational Exercises: Students need to learn to apply the rules and concepts covered in each chapter to truly understand them. These exercises, many of which mirror text examples, allow students to practice and apply what they are learning.

- Found in the end-of-chapter sections of the textbook
- CNOWv2 provides algorithmic versions of these problems

Computational Exercises

17. LO.1, 2 Sally owns real property for which the annual property taxes are $9,000. She sells the property to Kate on March 9, 2022, for $550,000. Kate pays the real property taxes for the entire year on October 1, 2022.
    a. How much of the property taxes can be deducted by Sally and how much by Kate?
    b. What effect does the property tax apportionment have on Kate's adjusted basis in the property?
    c. What effect does the apportionment have on Sally's amount realized from the sale?
    d. How would the answers in parts (b) and (c) differ if Sally paid the taxes?
18. LO.1 Melba purchases land from Adrian. Melba gives Adrian $225,000 in cash and agrees to pay Adrian an additional $400,000 one year later plus interest at 5%.
    a. What is Melba's adjusted basis for the land at the acquisition date?
    b. What is Melba's adjusted basis for the land one year later?

Research and Data Analytics Problems:

- Research Problems provide students with vital practice in an increasingly demanded skill area. These end-of-chapter items ask students to find and analyze tax documents, helping them to understand the application of this information in various scenarios. These essential features prepare students for professional tax environments.

Becker Professional Education Review Questions: End-of-chapter CPA Review Questions from Becker PREPARE STUDENTS FOR SUCCESS. Students review key concepts using proven questions from Becker Professional Education®—one of the industry's most effective tools to prepare for the CPA Exam.

- Located in select end-of-chapter sections
- Tagged by concept in CNOWv2
- Questions similar to what students would actually find on the CPA Exam

Becker CPA Review Questions

Becker

1. Jasmin purchased 100 shares of Pinkstey Corporation (publicly traded company) on January 1 of year 1 for $5,000. The FMV of the shares at the end of year 1 was $6,000. On January 1 of year 4, Pinkstey Corporation declared a 2-for-1 stock split when the fair market value of the stock was $65 per share. On January 1 of year 5, Jasmin sold all of her Pinkstey Corporation stock when the fair market value was $40 per share. Which of the following statements is true?
   a. Jasmin reports $6,500 in gross income for the 2-for-1 stock split in year 4.
   b. Jasmin's basis in the Pinkstey Corporation stock at the end of year 4 is $65 per share.
   c. Jasmin has no taxable income for the Pinkstey Corporation stock in year 4.
   d. Jasmin owns 100 shares in Pinkstey Corporation stock at the end of year 4.
2. Alice gifted stock to her son, Bob, in year 5. Alice bought the stock in year 1 for $8,300. The value of the stock on the date of gift was $6,400. Bob sold the stock in year 7 for $15,800. What is Bob's recognized gain or loss on the sale in year 7?
   a. $0
   b. $7,500 gain
   c. $9,400 gain
   d. $15,800 gain

Becker

See how the SWFT series helps students understand the big picture and the relevancy behind what they are learning.

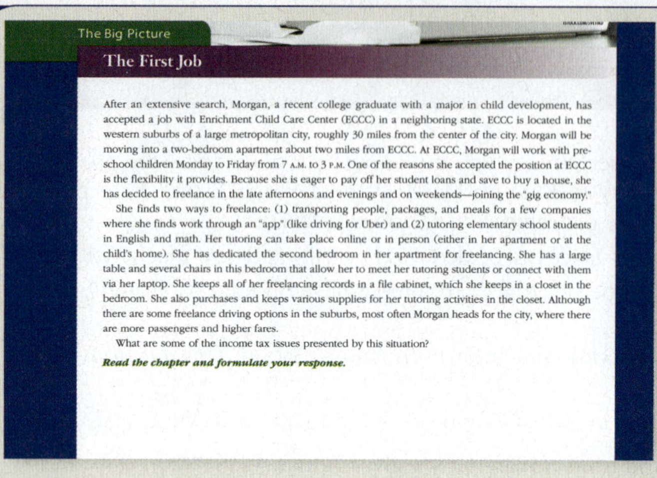

The Big Picture

The First Job

After an extensive search, Morgan, a recent college graduate with a major in child development, has accepted a job with Enrichment Child Care Center (ECCC) in a neighboring state. ECCC is located in the western suburbs of a large metropolitan city, roughly 30 miles from the center of the city. Morgan will be moving into a two-bedroom apartment about two miles from ECCC. At ECCC, Morgan will work with preschool children Monday to Friday from 7 A.M. to 3 P.M. One of the reasons she accepted the position at ECCC is the flexibility it provides. Because she is eager to pay off her student loans and save to buy a house, she has decided to freelance in the late afternoons and evenings and on weekends—joining the "gig economy."

She finds two ways to freelance: (1) transporting people, packages, and meals for a few companies where she finds work through an "app" (like driving for Uber) and (2) tutoring elementary school students in English and math. Her tutoring can take place online or in person (either in her apartment or at the child's home). She has dedicated the second bedroom in her apartment for freelancing. She has a large table and several chairs in this bedroom that allow her to meet her tutoring students or connect with them via her laptop. She keeps all of her freelancing records in a file cabinet, which she keeps in a closet in the bedroom. She also purchases and keeps various supplies for her tutoring activities in the closet. Although there are some freelance driving options in the suburbs, most often Morgan heads for the city, where there are more passengers and higher fares.

What are some of the income tax issues presented by this situation?

Read the chapter and formulate your response.

The Big Picture: **Tax Solutions for the Real World.**

Taxation comes alive at the start of each chapter as The Big Picture examples provide a glimpse into the lives, families, careers, and tax situations of typical taxpayers. Students will follow a family, individual, or other taxpayer throughout the chapter, to discover how the concepts they are learning apply in the real world.

Finally, to solidify student comprehension, each chapter concludes with a **Refocus on The Big Picture** summary and tax planning scenario. These scenarios re-emphasize the concepts and topics from the chapter and allow students to confirm their understanding of the material.

Framework 1040:

Fitting It All Together.

This chapter-opening feature demonstrates how topics within *Individual Income Taxes* fit together, using the Income Tax Formula for Individuals as the framework. The framework helps students organize their understanding of the chapters and topics to see how they relate to the basic tax formula and then identify where these items are reported on the Form 1040. Framework 1040 helps students navigate topics by explaining how tax concepts are organized.

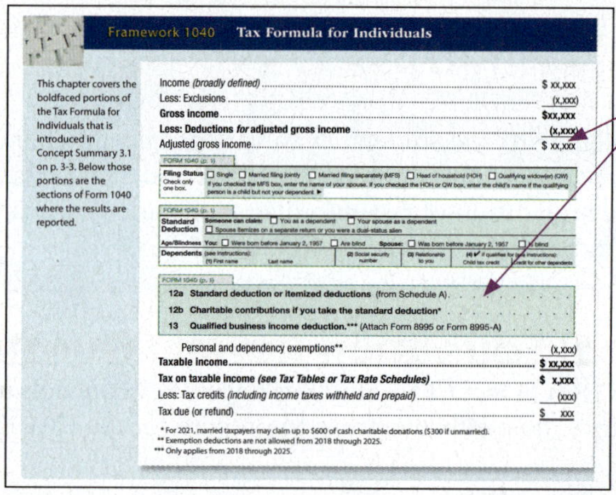

Framework 1040 **Tax Formula for Individuals**

This chapter covers the boldfaced portions of the Tax Formula for Individuals that is introduced in Concept Summary 3.1 on p. 3-3. Below those portions are the sections of Form 1040 where the results are reported.

Income *(broadly defined)*	$ xx,xxx
Less: Exclusions	(x,xxx)
Gross income	**$xx,xxx**
Less: Deductions *for* adjusted gross income	**(x,xxx)**
Adjusted gross income	$ xx,xxx

FORM 1040 (p. 1)

Filing Status (Check only one box.) ☐ Single ☐ Married filing jointly ☐ Married filing separately (MFS) ☐ Head of household (HOH) ☐ Qualifying widow(er) (QW)
If you checked the MFS box, enter the name of your spouse. If you checked the HOH or QW box, enter the child's name if the qualifying person is a child but not your dependent ▶

FORM 1040 (p. 1)

Standard Deduction — Someone can claim: ☐ You as a dependent ☐ Your spouse as a dependent
☐ Spouse itemizes on a separate return or you were a dual-status alien
Age/Blindness — You: ☐ Were born before January 2, 1957 ☐ Are blind Spouse: ☐ Was born before January 2, 1957 ☐ Is blind
Dependents (see instructions): (1) First name Last name (2) Social security number (3) Relationship to you (4) ✔ if qualifies for (see instructions): Child tax credit Credit for other dependents

FORM 1040 (p. 1)

12a Standard deduction or itemized deductions (from Schedule A)
12b Charitable contributions if you take the standard deduction*
13 Qualified business income deduction.*** (Attach Form 8995 or Form 8995-A)

Personal and dependency exemptions**	(x,xxx)
Taxable income	**$ xx,xxx**
Tax on taxable income *(see Tax Tables or Tax Rate Schedules)*	**$ x,xxx**
Less: Tax credits *(including income taxes withheld and prepaid)*	(xxx)
Tax due (or refund)	$ xxx

* For 2021, married taxpayers may claim up to $600 of cash charitable donations ($300 if unmarried).
** Exemption deductions are not allowed from 2018 through 2025.
*** Only applies from 2018 through 2025.

Use this chapter-opening **Framework 1040**, which shows the topics as they appear in the individual tax formula, to understand where on the Form 1040 these chapter topics appear.

Financial Disclosure Insights: Tax professionals need to understand how taxes affect financial statements. **Financial Disclosure Insights**, appearing throughout the text, use current information about existing taxpayers to highlight book-tax reporting differences, effective tax rates, and trends in reporting conventions.

Financial Disclosure Insights — Tax Deferrals from Reserves

The tax law generally applies the all events and economic performance tests in determining when an expense is deductible. Accordingly, the use of reserves for financial accounting purposes does not carry over to the tax return. When a business creates a reserve, for example, to account for warranty obligations to customers or vacation pay for employees, book expenses are allowed, but the corresponding tax deduction usually is delayed until an expenditure is actually incurred. The temporary book-tax difference typically creates or adds to a deferred tax asset on the entity's balance sheet.

On a GAAP balance sheet, all deferred tax assets are deemed to be noncurrent.

Ethics & Equity — Punching the Time Clock at Year-End

As the end of the tax year approaches, Julie, a successful full-time real estate developer and investor, recognizes that her income tax situation for the year could be bleak. Unless she and her spouse, Ralph, are able to generate more hours of participation in one of her real estate rental activities, they will not reach the material participation threshold. Consequently, the tax losses from the venture will not be deductible. To ensure deductibility, Julie suggests the following plan:

- She will document the time she spends "thinking" about her rental activities.
- During the week, Ralph will visit the apartment building to oversee (in a management role) the operations of the rentals.
- On weekends, she and Ralph will visit the same units to further evaluate the operations.
- Also on the weekends, they will be on the lookout for other rental properties to buy and visit open houses of homes they find on the market. Julie plans to count both her and Ralph's weekend hours toward the tally of total participation.

Julie contends that the law clearly allows the efforts of one's spouse to count for purposes of the material participation tests. Likewise, nothing in the tax law requires taxpayers to be efficient in their hours of participation. How do you react?

Ethics & Equity: Ethics & Equity features will spark critical thinking and invite classroom discussion, enticing students to evaluate their own value system. Suggested reactions to Ethics & Equity scenarios appear in the Solutions Manual.

Tax Planning: Chapters include a separate section calling attention to how taxpayers can use the law to reach financial and other goals. Tax planning applications and suggestions also appear throughout each chapter, as pertinent topics are discussed.

LO.11

Suggest tax planning strategies to minimize the effect of the passive activity loss and investment interest limitations and recognize the general impact of the additional tax on net investment income.

11-6 Tax Planning

11-6a Minimizing the Impact of the Passive Activity Loss Limits

Perhaps the biggest challenge individuals face with the passive activity loss rules is to recognize the potential impact of the rules and then to structure their affairs to minimize this impact. If a taxpayer does invest in an activity that produces losses subject to the passive activity loss rules, the following discussion describes strategies that may help minimize the loss of current deductions.

Taxpayers who have passive activity losses should adopt a strategy of buying an interest in an activity that is generating passive activity income that can be offset (or sheltered) by the existing passive activity losses. From a tax perspective, it would be foolish to buy a loss-generating passive activity unless (1) the taxpayer has other passive activity income to shelter, (2) the activity is rental real estate that can qualify for the $25,000 exception, or (3) the activity qualifies for the exception available to real estate professionals.

If money is borrowed to finance the purchase of a passive activity, the associated interest expense is generally treated as part of any passive activity loss. Consequently, by using more available (i.e., not borrowed) cash to purchase the passive investment, the investor will need less debt and will incur less interest expense. By incurring less interest expense, a possible suspended passive activity loss deduction is reduced.

Global Tax Issues — From "All Sources" Is a Broad Definition

When § 61 refers to "income from whatever source derived," the law is reaching far beyond the borders of the United States. Although one interpretation of "source" in this context is type of income (e.g., wages and interest), a broader interpretation revolves around the place where the income is generated. In this context, citizens and residents of the United States are subject to taxation on income earned from sources both inside and outside the country. This "worldwide income" tax base can cause potential double taxation problems, with other countries also taxing income earned within their borders. However, mechanisms such as the foreign tax credit can alleviate these tax burdens.

Over the years, a number of individuals have relocated to other countries and renounced their U.S. citizenship to avoid high U.S. tax rates. Others who have already relocated may renounce their U.S. citizenship to avoid complicated filing and reporting requirements. After hitting a then-record high of 5,411 in 2017, the number of expatriations declined to 2,071 in 2019. However, 6,707 individuals gave up their U.S. citizenship in 2020, a new record. This was in spite of the additional practical challenges in completing the expatriation process caused by the COVID-19 pandemic. Once per quarter, the Department of State publishes the names of U.S. citizens who have renounced their citizenship. Some of these individuals may owe Federal taxes as a result of renouncing. See § 877A.

See "Renouncing American Citizenship Hits All-Time Record" at **forbes.com/sites/robertwood/2021/02/07/renouncing-american-citizenship-hits-all-time-record**.

Global Tax Issues: The **Global Tax Issues** feature gives insight into the ways in which taxation is affected by international concerns and illustrates the effects of various events on tax liabilities across the globe.

Take your students from Motivation to Mastery with CNOWv2

MASTERY
APPLICATION
MOTIVATION

CNOWv2 is a powerful course management tool and online homework resource that elevates student thinking by providing superior content designed with the entire student workflow in mind.

- **Motivation:** engage students and better prepare them for class
- **Application:** help students learn problem-solving behavior and skills to guide them to complete taxation problems on their own
- **Mastery:** help students make the leap from memorizing concepts to actual critical thinking

Motivation —

To help with student engagement and preparedness, CNOWv2 for SWFT offers:

- **"Tax Drills" test students on key concepts and applications.** With three to five questions per learning objective, these "quick-hit" questions help students prepare for class lectures or review prior to an exam.

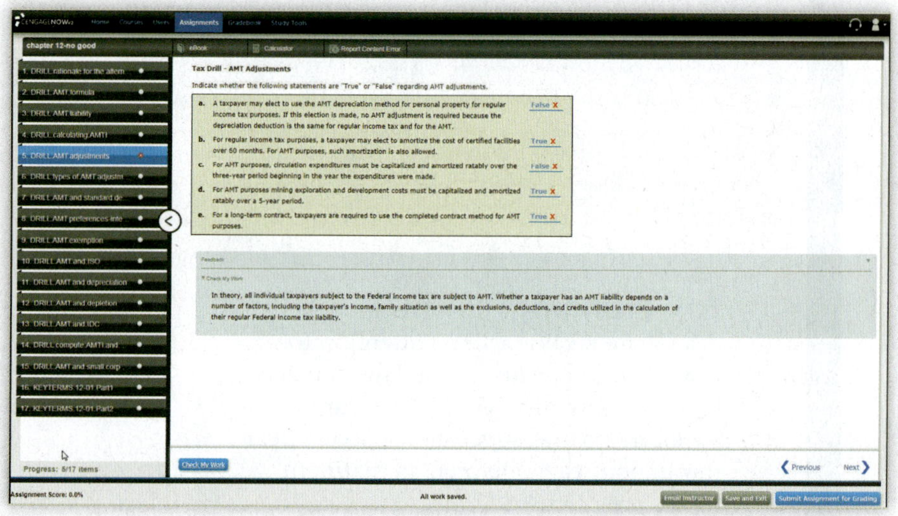

Application —

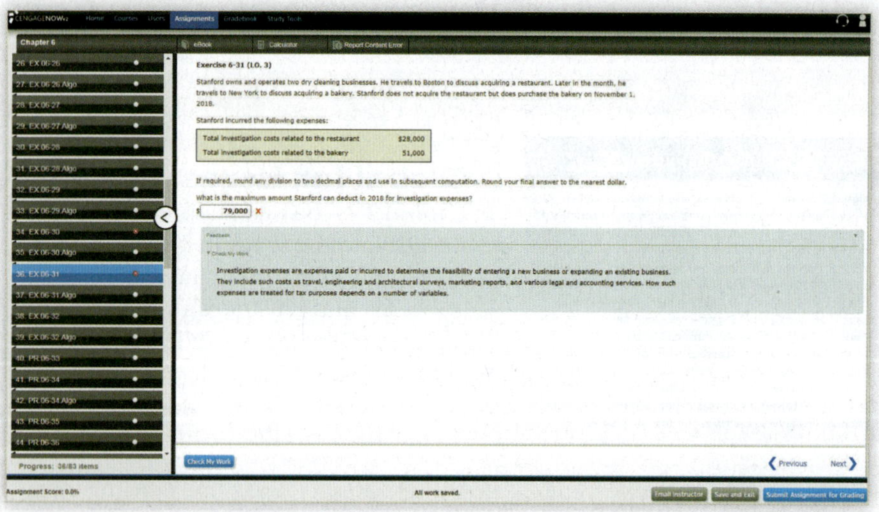

Students need to learn problem-solving behavior and skills, to guide them to complete taxation problems on their own. However, as students try to work through homework problems, sometimes they become stuck and need extra help. To reinforce concepts and keep students on the right track, CNOWv2 for SWFT offers the following:

- **End-of-chapter homework from the text** is expanded and enhanced to follow the workflow a professional would use to solve various client scenarios. These enhancements better engage students and encourage them to think like a tax professional.

- **Algorithmic versions** of end-of-chapter homework are available for computational exercises and at least 15 problems per chapter.
- **"Check My Work" Feedback.** Homework questions include immediate feedback so students can learn as they go. Levels of feedback include an option for "check my work" prior to submission of an assignment.
- **Post-Submission Feedback.** After submitting an assignment, students receive even more extensive feedback explaining why their answers were incorrect. Instructors can decide how much feedback their students receive and when, including the full solution.
- **Built-in Test Bank** for online assessment.

Mastery —

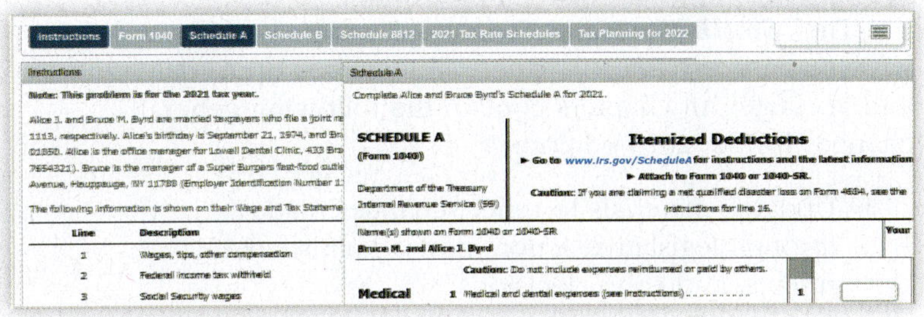

- **Tax Form Problems** give students the option to complete the Cumulative Intuit ProConnect Tax problems and other homework items found in the end-of-chapter material manually or in a digital environment.
- **An Adaptive Study Plan** comes complete with an eBook, practice quizzes, glossary, and flashcards. It is designed to help give students additional support and prepare them for the exam.

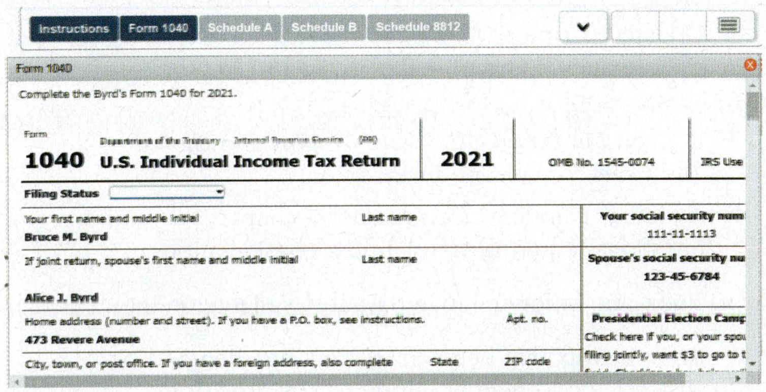

CNOWv2 Instant Access Code ISBN:
978-0-357-71987-9

Contact your Cengage Learning Consultant about different bundle options.

Extensively Revised. Definitively Up to Date.

Each year the ***South-Western Federal Taxation*** series is updated with thousands of changes to each text. Some of these changes result from the feedback we receive from instructors and students in the form of reviews, focus groups, web surveys, and personal e-mail correspondence to our authors and team members. Other changes come from our careful analysis of the evolving tax environment. **We make sure that every tax law change relevant to the introductory taxation course was considered, summarized, and fully integrated into the revision of text and supplementary materials.**

The ***South-Western Federal Taxation*** authors have made every effort to keep all materials up to date and accurate. All chapters contain the following general changes for the 2023 edition:

- Updated materials to reflect changes made through legislative action, new administrative rulings, and court decisions.
- Streamlined chapter content (where applicable) to clarify material and make it easier for students to understand.
- Revised numerous materials as the result of changes caused by indexing of statutory amounts.
- Revised Problem Materials, Computational Exercises, and CPA Exam problems.
- Updated Chapter Outlines to provide an overview of the material and to make it easier to locate specific topics.
- Revised *Financial Disclosure Insights* and *Global Tax Issues* for current developments.
- Added a "Planning" icon to end-of-chapter questions requiring tax planning considerations.

In addition, the following materials are available online:

- An appendix that helps instructors broaden and customize coverage of important tax provisions of the Affordable Care Act. (Instructor Companion Website at **www.cengage.com/login**)
- An appendix that has comprehensive tax return problems for the 2021 tax filing year (Appendix F). (Instructor Companion Website at **www.cengage.com/login**)
- An appendix that covers depreciation and the Accelerated Cost Recovery System (ACRS). (Instructor Companion Website at **www.cengage.com/login**)

Chapter 1

- Expanded discussion on the relevance of taxation to accounting and finance professionals to include the role of a corporate tax director in global growth strategy (added to the planning function), ESG reporting (likely covered in other accounting and business courses and now part of AACSB accreditation standards), and tax advocacy.
- Added information on space travel tax proposals.
- Added information (and a related example) on Preparer Tax Identification Numbers (PTINs).
- Updated figures based on revised IRS data and inflation adjustments.
- Added Research Problem 5 on the data security question tied to the "Safeguards Rule" that is on Form W–12 to obtain or renew a PTIN (ties to the CPA Evolution Model Curriculum).

Chapter 2

- Based on adopter feedback, added 15 basic (simple) research problems involving the legislative sources, administrative sources, and judicial sources of tax law.
- Updated chapter materials (including various references and citations); modified exhibits and concept summaries for new sources (including IRS FAQs).
- Updated end-of-chapter materials as needed.

Chapter 3

- Updated chapter materials to reflect 2021 tax legislation and 2022 inflation adjustments.
- Updated chapter materials to reflect changes in Form 1040 and related schedules; updated various exhibits, including when Form 1040 Schedules 1 through 3 are used and when the 0%, 15%, and 20% break points occur for the alternative tax on net capital gains.
- Revised and clarified materials as needed; updated end-of-chapter materials to reflect 2021 tax legislation and 2022 inflation adjustments.

Chapter 4

- Updated Global Tax Issues feature entitled "From 'All Sources' Is a Broad Definition" for the number of recent expatriations.
- Added an Ethics & Equity feature discussing the discrepancy between alimony deducted on tax returns and that reported as income prior to the TCJA of 2017.

- Revised the discussion of the Applicable Financial Statement (AFS) income inclusion rule and related examples for exceptions included in the Regulations issued since last edition.
- Added a new exercise on the AFS income inclusion rule and available exceptions.

Chapter 5

- Reduced coverage of voluntary death benefit payments by employers (employers are more likely to have group term life insurance for employees).
- Added a brief explanation of the foreign housing exclusion or deduction.
- Added a discussion question involving critical thinking and the need to examine the facts to understand why an individual received funds. This determination is necessary in order to determine whether the funds are excludible from gross income.

Chapter 6

- Revised Concept Summary 6.4 (Classification of Expenses) by focusing on activity type (business; personal; investment/production of income).
- Updated and revised chapter materials to reflect changes in tax law and inflation adjustments.
- Deleted discussion question about legal fees incurred in connection with a divorce; created new discussion about the § 162(m) compensation limitation.
- Updated end-of-chapter materials as needed.

Chapter 7

- Updated chapter materials as needed (including end-of-chapter materials).
- Added new research problem, asking students to gather information on whether to repeal or permanently extend the excess business loss limitation provision [§ 461(l)].

Chapter 8

- Updated chapter materials as needed to reflect changes to § 179 limits (including SUVs) and luxury automobile limits, and updated Form 4562 and Schedule C (Form 1040).
- Added a new Excel problem, asking students to build a spreadsheet to calculate MACRS cost recovery and end-of-year adjusted basis for MACRS 3-, 5-, and 7-year assets.
- Updated balance of end-of-chapter materials as needed.

Chapter 9

- Updated chapter materials for revised standard mileage amounts.
- Updated chapter materials for revised QBI deduction limits and the example illustrating the completion of Form 8995-A and Schedule A (Form 8995-A).
- Revised and clarified materials based on feedback from adopters.
- Updated end-of-chapter materials to reflect revised standard mileage amounts, revised QBI deduction limits, the QBI deduction form completion problem (Form 8995), and other questions/ problems as needed.

Chapter 10

- Added information about Notice 2020-75 and SALT workarounds some states have enacted for pass-through entities and their owners.
- Revised and clarified text as needed; updated end-of-chapter materials as needed.

Chapter 11

- Updated chapter materials based on feedback from adopters and IRS updates; revised end-of-chapter materials as needed.
- Added a new discussion question on the average period of customer use rental exception.
- Added an additional reference to Research Problem 3 (Reg. § 1.163–15) allowing students to include this expanded tracing rule in their research.

Chapter 12

- Updated chapter materials for AMT exemption inflation adjustments.
- Revised AMT research and experimentation text and problems.
- Added new Global Minimum Tax discussion relative to existing AMT provisions.
- Streamlined text discussion regarding AMT and depreciation.
- Added new planning discussion regarding AMT recordkeeping.
- Added new The Big Picture feature and related examples.

Chapter 13

- Changed Learning Objective 7 (now focused on additional Medicare taxes assessed on high-income individuals).
- Removed Premium Tax Credit discussion, which is covered in online appendix on the Affordable Care Act.
- Updated materials for 2021 legislation (including the American Recovery Plan Act) and inflation adjustments to various items (including the 2022 Social Security base amount). Retained 2021 information when needed (for tax return problems).

Chapter 14

- Updated chapter materials as needed to reflect tax law changes and adopter comments (including revision to the unified estate and gift tax exemption amount).
- Converted a computational exercise dealing with the effective interest rate method for amortizing bond premium (which is not discussed in the chapter) to a discussion question.
- Revised/updated end-of-chapter materials as needed [including the tax form problem related to Form 8949 and a Schedule D (Form 1040)].

Chapter 15

- Revised and updated chapter materials as needed.
- Updated end-of-chapter materials as needed; updated end-of-chapter tax form problem (completion of a Form 8824).

Chapter 16

- Updated Exhibit 16.1 summarizing 2022 and 2021 break points for the 0%/15%/20% alternative tax rates on net capital gains and qualified dividend income.
- Updated the chapter tax return example [including the Form 8949, Schedule D (Form 1040), and the capital gains worksheet].
- Updated text materials based on adopter feedback and tax law changes; updated end-of-chapter materials as needed (including new links to websites for tax research problems).

Chapter 17

- Updated the chapter tax return example [Form 4797 and Schedule D (Form 1040)].
- Updated text materials based on feedback from adopters and various tax law changes [including 2022 alternative tax rate brackets (for net capital gains)].
- Updated end-of-chapter materials (including revised forms); updated data analytics tax research problem for new IRS data.

Chapter 18

- Added an example of the 12-month rule of Reg. § 1.263(a)–1(f).
- Reduced coverage of the installment sale method.
- Reduced Exhibit 18.1 to focus on the most common contract and indirect costs.
- Added new tax planning items.

Chapter 19

- Revised introductory materials.
- Provided context and financial information about § 401(k) and IRA participation.
- New Ethics & Equity item added concerning vesting and plan withdrawals.
- Relocated planning ideas relative to NQDC and NQSO plans.
- Added three new Excel solutions.
- Added one new Excel problem using the XLOOKUP function.
- Timeline analysis added to one problem.

Chapter 20

- Added Excel elements to Problem 41.
- Added Research Problem 7 on finding and analyzing IRS data.

Tax Law Outlook

From your SWFT Series Editors:

Legislation related to the COVID-19 pandemic was a vehicle for tax changes in 2021, including a wide variety of tax changes incorporated into the American Rescue Plan Act of 2021. The Biden administration and Congress continue to discuss a wide variety of tax law changes. Although the Build Back Better plan was not enacted, pieces of that proposal are likely to be debated (and possibly adopted) before the end of 2022. In addition, it is likely that Congress will return to its pattern of extending expired and expiring tax provisions sometime in 2022.

Annually, the Joint Committee on Taxation publishes a report of all expired and expiring provisions in the tax law. The report released in January 2022 lists 40 provisions that expired in 2021 (**jct.gov/publications/2022/jcx-1-22/**). This list does not include the change to § 174 for R&D expenditures to be capitalized and amortized (rather than currently expensed) for tax years beginning after 2021. The Build Back Better Act passed by the House in November 2021 extended that date by four years. If that act does not become law, it is likely that Congress will find another way to extend the effective date of this change that originated with the Tax Cuts and Jobs Act of 2017.

Taxpayers and their advisers will need to evaluate how these changes affect their financial planning strategies and adjust their plans appropriately. The SWFT editors will be monitoring these activities and provide updates to adopters as needed.

Supplements Support Students and Instructors

Built around the areas students and instructors have identified as the most important, our integrated supplements package offers more flexibility than ever before to suit the way instructors teach and students learn.

Online and Digital Resources for Students

Cengage CNOWv2

CNOWv2 is a powerful course management and online homework tool that provides robust instructor control and customization to optimize the student learning experience and meet desired outcomes.

CNOWv2 Instant Access Code ISBN:
978-0-357-71987-9

Contact your Cengage Learning Consultant about different bundle options.

the answer company™ THOMSON REUTERS®

Thomson Reuters Checkpoint™ is the leading online tax research database used by professionals. Checkpoint™ helps introduce students to tax research in three simple ways:

- Intuitive web-based design makes it fast and simple to find what you need.
- Checkpoint™ provides a comprehensive collection of primary tax law, cases, and rulings along with analytical insight you simply can't find anywhere else.
- Checkpoint™ has built-in productivity tools such as calculators to make research more efficient—a resource more tax pros use than any other.

Six months' access to Checkpoint™ (after activation) is packaged automatically with every NEW copy of the textbook.*

ProConnect™ Tax

More than software: Put the experience of ProConnect™ Tax on your side.

- Get returns done right the first time with access to all the forms you need, backed by industry-leading calculations and diagnostics.
- Save time with logical data-entry worksheets instead of traditional forms-based methods.
- It's all online, so there's nothing to install or maintain.

Online access to ProConnect™ Tax software is offered with each NEW copy of the textbook—at no additional cost to students.*

www.cengage.com Students can use **www.cengage.com** to select this textbook and access Cengage Learning content, empowering them to choose the most suitable format and giving them a better chance of success in the course. Buy printed materials, eBooks, and digital resources directly through Cengage Learning and save at **www.cengage.com**.

Online Student Resources

Students can go to **www.cengage.com** for free resources to help them study as well as the opportunity to purchase additional study aids. These valuable free study resources will help students earn a better grade:

- Flashcards use chapter terms and definitions to aid students in learning tax terminology for each chapter.
- Online glossary for each chapter provides terms and definitions from the text in alphabetical order for easy reference.
- Learning objectives can be downloaded for each chapter to help keep students on track.
- Tax tables used in the textbook are downloadable for reference.

Cengage Unlimited

The first-of-its-kind digital subscription designed specially to lower costs.

Students get total access to everything Cengage has to offer on demand—in one place. That's 20,000 eBooks, 2,300 digital learning products, and dozens of study tools across 70 disciplines and over 675 courses. **www.cengage.com/unlimited**

Printed Resources for Students

Looseleaf Edition (978-0-357-71984-8)

This version provides all the pages of the text in an unbound, three-hole-punched format for portability and ease of use. Online access to ProConnect™ Tax software is included with every NEW textbook as well as Checkpoint™ from Thomson Reuters.*

*NEW printed copies of the textbook are automatically packaged with access to Checkpoint™ and ProConnect™ Tax software. If students purchase the eBook, they will not automatically receive access to Checkpoint™ and ProConnect™ Tax software.

Comprehensive Supplements Support Instructors' Needs

Cengage CNOWv2

CNOWv2 is a powerful course management and online homework tool that provides robust instructor control and customization to optimize the student learning experience and meet desired outcomes. In addition to the features and benefits mentioned earlier for students, CNOWv2 includes these features for instructors.

- **Learning Outcomes Reporting** and the ability to analyze student work from the gradebook. Each exercise and problem is tagged by topic, learning objective, level of difficulty, estimated completion time, and business program standards to allow greater guidance in developing assessments and evaluating student progress.
- **Built-in Test Bank for online assessment.** The Test Bank files are included in CNOWv2 so that they may be used as additional homework or tests.

Solutions Manual

Written by the ***South-Western Federal Taxation*** editors and authors, the Solutions Manual features solutions arranged in accordance with the sequence of chapter material.

Solutions to all homework items are tagged with their Estimated Time to Complete, Level of Difficulty, and Learning Objective(s), as well as the AACSB's and AICPA's core competencies—giving instructors more control than ever in selecting homework to match the topics covered. The Solutions Manual also contains the solutions to Appendix F: Practice Set Assignments—Comprehensive Tax Return Problems and answers with explanations to the end-of-chapter Becker CPA Review Questions. **Available on Instructor Companion Website at www.cengage.com/login.**

PowerPoint® Lectures with Notes

The Instructor PowerPoint® Lectures contain more than 30 slides per chapter, including outlines and instructor guides, concept definitions, and key points. **Available on Instructor Companion Website at www.cengage.com/login.**

Test Bank

Written by the ***South-Western Federal Taxation*** editors and authors, the Test Bank contains approximately 2,200 items and solutions arranged in accordance with the sequence of chapter material.

Each test item is tagged with its Estimated Time to Complete, Level of Difficulty, and Learning Objective(s), as well as the AACSB's and AICPA's core competencies—for easier instructor planning and test item selection. The 2023 Test Bank is available in Cengage's test generator software, Cognero.

Cengage Learning Testing Powered by Cognero is a flexible, online system that allows you to:

- author, edit, and manage Test Bank content from multiple Cengage Learning solutions
- create multiple test versions in an instant
- deliver tests from your LMS, your classroom, or wherever you want
- create tests from school, home, the coffee shop—anywhere with Internet access (No special installs or downloads needed.)

Test Bank files in Word format as well as versions to import into your LMS are available on the Instructor Companion Website. **Cognero Test Banks are available via single sign-on (SSO) account at www.cengage.com/login.**

Other Instructor Resources

All of the following instructor course materials are available online at www.cengage.com/login. Once logged into the site, instructors should select this textbook to access the online Instructor Resources.

- Instructor Guide
- Edition-to-edition correlation grids by chapter
- An appendix that helps instructors broaden and customize coverage of important tax provisions of the Affordable Care Act
- Depreciation and the Accelerated Cost Recovery System (ACRS) appendix
- Comprehensive Tax Return Problems appendix

Custom Solutions

Cengage Learning Custom Solutions develops personalized solutions to meet your taxation education needs. Consider the following for your adoption of ***South-Western Federal Taxation 2023 Edition***.

- Remove chapters you do not cover or rearrange their order to create a streamlined and efficient text.
- Add your own material to cover additional topics or information.
- Add relevance by including sections from Sawyers/Gill's *Federal Tax Research* or your state's tax laws and regulations.

Acknowledgments

We want to thank all the adopters and others who participated in numerous online surveys as well as the following individuals who provided content reviews and feedback in the development of the ***South-Western Federal Taxation 2023 titles***.

James C. Young / Annette Nellen / William A. Raabe / Mark B. Persellin / Sharon S. Lassar / Andrew D. Cuccia / Bradrick M. Cripe

Ken Abramowicz, *University of Alaska Fairbanks*
Lindsay G. Acker, *University of Wisconsin – Madison*
Deborah S. Adkins, *Nperspective, LLC*
Mark P. Altieri, *Kent State University*
Susan E. Anderson, *Elon University*
Henry M. Anding, *Woodbury University*
Jennifer A. Bagwell, *Ohio University*
George Barbi, *Lanier Technical College*
Terry W. Bechtel, *Texas A&M University – Texarkana*
Chris Becker, *LeMoyne College*
Tamara Berges, *UCLA*
Ellen Best, *University of North Georgia*
Tim Biggart, *Berry College*
Rachel Birkey, *Illinois State University*
Israel Blumenfrecht, *Queens College*
Patrick M. Borja, *Citrus College / California State University, Los Angeles*
Dianne H. Boseman, *Nash Community College*
Cathalene Bowler, *University of Northern Iowa*
Madeline Brogan, *Lone Star College – Montgomery*
Darryl L. Brown, *Illinois Wesleyan University*
Timothy G. Bryan, *University of Southern Indiana*
Robert S. Burdette, *Salt Lake Community College*
Ryan L. Burger, *Concordia University Nebraska*
Lisa Busto, *William Rainey Harper College*
Julia M. Camp, *Providence College*
Al Case, *Southern Oregon University*
Machiavelli W. Chao, *Merage School of Business, University of California, Irvine*
Eric Chen, *University of Saint Joseph*
Christine Cheng, *Louisiana State University*
James Milton Christianson, *Southwestern University and Austin Community College*
Wayne Clark, *Southwest Baptist University*
Ann Burstein Cohen, *University at Buffalo, The State University of New York*
Ciril Cohen, *Fairleigh Dickinson University*
Seth Colwell, *University of Texas – Rio Grande Valley*
Dixon H. Cooper, *University of Arkansas*
John P. Crowley, *Castleton University*
Susan E. M. Davis, *South University*
Dwight E. Denman, *Newman University*
James M. DeSimpelare, *Ross School of Business at the University of Michigan*
John Dexter, *Northwood University*
James Doering, *University of Wisconsin – Green Bay*
Michael P. Donohoe, *University of Illinois at Urbana Champaign*
Deborah A. Doonan, *Johnson & Wales University*
Monique O. Durant, *Central Connecticut State University*
Wayne L. Edmunds, *Virginia Commonwealth University*
Rafi Efrat, *California State University, Northridge*
Frank J. Faber, *St. Joseph's College*
A. Anthony Falgiani, *University of South Carolina, Beaufort*
Jason Fiske, *Thomas Jefferson School of Law*
John Forsythe, *Eagle Gate College*
Alexander L. Frazin, *University of Redlands*
Carl J. Gabrini, *College of Coastal Georgia*
Kenneth W. Gaines, *East-West University, Chicago, Illinois*
Carolyn Galantine, *Pepperdine University*
Sheri Geddes, *Hope College*
Alexander Gelardi, *University of St. Thomas*
Joel Gelb, *Farleigh Dickinson University*
Daniel J. Gibbons, *Waubonsee Community College*
Martie Gillen, *University of Florida*
Charles Gnizak, *Fort Hays State University*
J. David Golub, *Northeastern University*
George G. Goodrich, *John Carroll University*
Marina Grau, *Houston Community College – Houston, TX*
Vicki Greshik, *University of Jamestown College*
Jeffrey S. Haig, *Santa Monica College*
Marcye S. Hampton, *University of Central Florida*
June Hanson, *Upper Iowa University*
Donald Henschel, *Benedictine University*
Kenneth W. Hodges, *Sinclair Community College*
Susanne Holloway, *Salisbury University*
Susan A. Honig, *Herbert H. Lehman College*
Jeffrey L. Hoopes, *University of North Carolina*
Christopher R. Hoyt, *University of Missouri (Kansas City) School of Law*
Marsha M. Huber, *Youngstown State University*
Carol Hughes, *Asheville-Buncombe Technical Community College*
Helen Hurwitz, *Saint Louis University*
Richard R. Hutaff, *Wingate University*
Zite Hutton, *Western Washington University*
Steven L. Jager, *Cal State Northridge*
Janeé M. Johnson, *University of Arizona*
Brad Van Kalsbeek, *University of Sioux Falls*
Carl Keller, *Missouri State University*
Cynthia Khanlarian, *Concord University*
Bob G. Kilpatrick, *Northern Arizona University*
Gordon Klein, *UCLA Anderson School*
Taylor Klett, *Sam Houston State University*
Aaron P. Knape, *Peru State College*
Cedric Knott, *Colorado State University – Global Campus*
Ausher M. B. Kofsky, *Western New England University*
Emil Koren, *Saint Leo University*
Jack Lachman, *Brooklyn College – CUNY*
Adena LeJeune, *Louisiana College*
Gene Levitt, *Mayville State University*
Teresa Lightner, *University of North Texas*
Sara Linton, *Roosevelt University*
Roger Lirely, *The University of Texas at Tyler*
Jane Livingstone, *Western Carolina University*
Heather Lynch, *Northeast Iowa Community College*
Mabel Machin, *Florida Institute of Technology*
Maria Alaina Mackin, *ECPI University*
Anne M. Magro, *George Mason University*
Richard B. Malamud, *California State University, Dominguez Hills*
Harold J. Manasa, *Winthrop University*
Barry R. Marks, *University of Houston – Clear Lake*
Dewey Martin, *Husson University*
Anthony Masino, *East Tennessee State University*
Norman Massel, *Louisiana State University*
Bruce W. McClain, *Cleveland State University*
Jeff McGowan, *Trine University*
Allison M. McLeod, *University of North Texas*
Meredith A. Menden, *Southern New Hampshire University*
Robert H. Meyers, *University of Wisconsin-Whitewater*
John G. Miller, *Skyline College*
Tracie L. Miller-Nobles, *Austin Community College*

Jonathan G. Mitchell, *Stark State College*
Richard Mole, *Hiram College*
David Morack, *Lakeland University*
Lisa Nash, *University of North Georgia*
Mary E. Netzler, *Eastern Florida State College*
Joseph Malino Nicassio, *Westmoreland County Community College*
Mark R. Nixon, *Bentley University*
Garth Novack, *Pantheon Heavy Industries & Foundry*
Claude R. Oakley, *DeVry University, Georgia*
Al Oddo, *Niagara University*
Sandra Owen, *Indiana University – Bloomington*
Vivian J. Paige, *Old Dominion University*
Carolyn Payne, *University of La Verne*
Ronald Pearson, *Bay College*
Thomas Pearson, *University of Hawaii at Manoa*
Nichole L. Pendleton, *Friends University*
Chuck Pier, *Angelo State University*
Lincoln M. Pinto, *DeVry University*
Sonja Pippin, *University of Nevada – Reno*
Steve Platau, *The University of Tampa*
Elizabeth Plummer, *TCU*
Walfyette Powell, *Strayer University*
Darlene Pulliam, *West Texas A&M University*
Thomas J. Purcell, *Creighton University*
John S. Repsis, *University of Texas at Arlington*
Jennifer Hardwick Robinson, *Trident Technical College*
Shani N. Robinson, *Sam Houston State University*
Donald Roth, *Dordt College*
Richard L. Russell, *Jackson State University*
Robert L. Salyer, *Northern Kentucky University*
Rhoda Sautner, *University of Mary*
Bunney L. Schmidt, *Keiser University*
Allen Schuldenfrei, *University of Maryland – Baltimore County*
Eric D. Schwartz, *LaRoche College*
Tony L. Scott, *Norwalk Community College*
Randy Serrett, *University of Houston – Downtown*
Wayne Shaw, *Southern Methodist University*
Paul A. Shoemaker, *University of Nebraska – Lincoln*
Kimberly Sipes, *Kentucky State University*
Georgi Smatrakalev, *Florida Atlantic University*
Randy Smit, *Dordt College*
Leslie S. Sobol, *California State University Northridge*
Eric J. Sommermeyer, *Wartburg College*
Marc Spiegel, *University of California, Irvine*
Teresa Stephenson, *University of Alaska Anchorage*
Beth Stetson, *Oklahoma City University*
Debra Stone, *Eastern New Mexico University*
Frances A. Stott, *Bowling Green State University*
Todd S. Stowe, *Southwest Florida College*
Julie Straus, *Culver-Stockton College*
Martin Stub, *DeVry University*
James Sundberg, *Eastern Michigan University*
Kent Swift, *University of Montana*
Robert L. Taylor, *Lees-McRae College*
Francis C. Thomas, *Richard Stockton College of New Jersey*
Randall R. Thomas, *Upper Iowa University*
Ronald R. Tidd, *Central Washington University*
MaryBeth Tobin, *Bridgewater State University*
James P. Trebby, *Marquette University*
Heidi Tribunella, *University of Rochester*
James M. Turner, *Georgia Institute of Technology*
Anthony W. Varnon, *Southeast Missouri State University*
Adria Palacios Vasquez, *Texas A&M University – Kingsville*
Stanley Veliotis, *Fordham University*
Terri Walsh, *Seminole State College of Florida Marie Wang*
Natasha R. Ware, *Southeastern University*
Mark Washburn, *Sam Houston State University*
Bill Weispfenning, *University of Jamestown (ND)*
Kent Williams, *Indiana Wesleyan University*
Candace Witherspoon, *Valdosta State University*
Sheila Woods, *DeVry University, Houston, TX*
Xinmei Xie, *Woodbury University*
Thomas Young, *Lone Star College – Tomball*

Special Thanks

We are grateful to the faculty members who have diligently worked through the problems and test questions to ensure the accuracy of the ***South-Western Federal Taxation*** homework, solutions manuals, test banks, and comprehensive tax form problems. Their comments and corrections helped us focus on clarity as well as accuracy and tax law currency. We also thank Thomson Reuters for its permission to use Checkpoint™ with the text.

Sandra A. Augustine, (retired) *Hilbert College*
Robyn Dawn Jarnagin, *University of Arkansas*
Kate Mantzke, *Northern Illinois University*
Ray Rodriguez, *Murray State University*
Miles Romney, *Florida State University*
George R. Starbuck, *McMurry University*
Donald R. Trippeer, *State University of New York College at Oneonta*
Raymond Wacker, *Southern Illinois University, Carbondale*
Michael Weissenfluh, *Tillamook Bay Community College*
Marvin Williams, *University of Houston – Downtown*

The South-Western Federal Taxation Series

To find out more about these books, go to www.cengage.com.

Individual Income Taxes, 2023 Edition

(Young, Nellen, Raabe, Persellin, Lassar, Cuccia, Cripe, Editors) provides accessible, comprehensive, and authoritative coverage of the relevant tax code and regulations as they pertain to the individual taxpayer, as well as coverage of all major developments in Federal taxation.

(ISBN 978-0-357-71982-4)

Corporations, Partnerships, Estates & Trusts, 2023 Edition

(Raabe, Young, Nellen, Cripe, Lassar, Persellin, Cuccia, Editors) covers tax concepts as they affect corporations, partnerships, estates, and trusts. The authors provide accessible, comprehensive, and authoritative coverage of relevant tax code and regulations, as well as all major developments in Federal income taxation. This market-leading text is intended for students who have had a previous course in tax.

(ISBN 978-0-357-71996-1)

Comprehensive Volume, 2023 Edition

(Young, Nellen, Maloney, Persellin, Cuccia, Lassar, Cripe, Editors) Combining the number one individual tax text with the number one corporations text, *Comprehensive Volume, 2023 Edition* is a true winner. An edited version of the first two ***South-Western Federal Taxation*** textbooks, this book is ideal for undergraduate or graduate levels. This text works for either a one-semester course in which an instructor wants to integrate coverage of individual and corporate taxation or for a two-semester sequence in which the use of only one book is desired.

(ISBN 978-0-357-71968-8)

Essentials of Taxation: Individuals and Business Entities, 2023 Edition

(Nellen, Cuccia, Persellin, Young, Editors) emphasizes tax planning and the multidisciplinary aspects of taxation. This text is designed with the AICPA Model Tax Curriculum in mind, presenting the introductory Federal taxation course from a business entity perspective. Its **Tax Planning Framework** helps users fit tax planning strategies into an innovative pedagogical framework. The text is an ideal fit for programs that offer only one course in taxation where users need to be exposed to individual taxation, as well as corporate and other business entity taxation. This text assumes no prior course in taxation has been taken.

(ISBN 978-0-357-72010-3)

Federal Tax Research, 12E

(Sawyers and Gill) *Federal Tax Research*, Twelfth Edition, offers hands-on tax research analysis and fully covers computer-oriented tax research tools. Also included in this edition is coverage on international tax research, a review of tax ethics, and many new real-life cases to help foster a true understanding of Federal tax law.

(ISBN 978-0-357-36638-7)

About the Editors

James C. Young is the PwC Professor of Accountancy at Northern Illinois University. A graduate of Ferris State University (B.S.) and Michigan State University (M.B.A. and Ph.D.), Jim's research focuses on taxpayer responses to the income tax using archival data. His dissertation received the PricewaterhouseCoopers/American Taxation Association Dissertation Award, and his subsequent research has received funding from a number of organizations, including the Ernst & Young Foundation Tax Research Grant Program. His work has been published in a variety of academic and professional journals, including the *National Tax Journal, The Journal of the American Taxation Association*, and *Tax Notes*. Jim is a Northern Illinois University Distinguished Professor, received the Illinois CPA Society Outstanding Accounting Educator Award in 2012, and has received university teaching awards from Northern Illinois University, George Mason University, and Michigan State University.

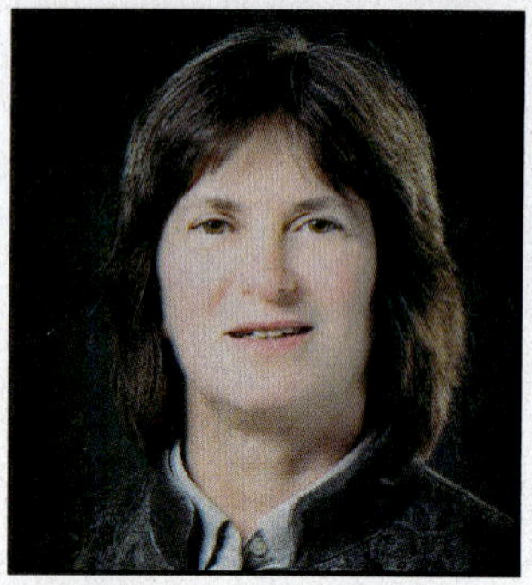

Annette Nellen, J.D., CPA, CGMA, directs San José State University's graduate tax program (MST) and teaches courses in tax research, tax fundamentals, accounting methods, property transactions, employment tax, ethics, leadership, and tax policy. Professor Nellen is a graduate of CSU Northridge, Pepperdine (MBA), and Loyola Law School. Prior to joining SJSU in 1990, she was with a Big 4 firm and the IRS. At SJSU, Professor Nellen is a recipient of the Outstanding Professor and Distinguished Service Awards. Professor Nellen is an active member of the tax sections of the AICPA and American Bar Association. In 2013, she received the AICPA Arthur J. Dixon Memorial Award, the highest award given by the accounting profession in the area of taxation. Professor Nellen is the author of BloombergBNA Tax Portfolio, *Amortization of Intangibles*. She has published numerous articles in the *AICPA Tax Insider, Tax Adviser, Tax Notes State*, and *The Journal of Accountancy*. She has testified before the House Ways & Means and Senate Finance Committees and other committees on Federal and state tax reform. Professor Nellen maintains the 21st Century Taxation Website and blog (21stcenturytaxation.com) as well as Websites on tax policy and reform, virtual currency, and state tax issues (sjsu.edu/people/annette.nellen/).

William A. Raabe, Ph.D., CPA, was the Wisconsin Distinguished Professor of Taxation. He taught at Ohio State, Arizona State, the Capital University (OH) Law School, and the Universities of Wisconsin – Milwaukee and Whitewater. A graduate of Carroll University (Wisconsin) and the University of Illinois, Dr. Raabe has been a visiting tax faculty member for a number of public accounting firms, bar associations, and CPA societies. He has received numerous teaching awards, including the Accounting Educator of the Year award from the Wisconsin Institute of CPAs.

Mark B. Persellin, Ph.D., CPA, CFP®, is the Ray and Dorothy Berend Professor of Accounting at St. Mary's University. He is a graduate of the University of Arizona (B.S.), the University of Texas at Austin (M.P.A. in Taxation), and the University of Houston (Ph.D.). He teaches Personal Income Tax, Business Income Tax, and Research in Federal Taxation. Prior to joining St. Mary's University in 1991, Professor Persellin taught at Florida Atlantic University and Southwest Texas University (Texas State University) and worked on the tax staff of a Big 4 firm. His research has been published in numerous academic and professional journals including *The Journal of the American Taxation Association, The Accounting Educators' Journal, The Tax Adviser, The CPA Journal, Journal of Taxation, Corporate Taxation, The Tax Executive, TAXES—The Tax Magazine, Journal of International Taxation,* and *Practical Tax Strategies*. In 2003, Professor Persellin established the St. Mary's University Volunteer Income Tax Assistance (VITA) site, and he continues to serve as a trainer and reviewer at the site.

Sharon S. Lassar, Ph.D., CPA (Florida), is the John J. Gilbert Professor and Director of the School of Accountancy at The University of Denver. Dr. Lassar earned her Ph.D. at the University of Southern California, her Master of Taxation at Bentley University, and her Bachelor's in Accounting from West Virginia University. Prior to joining the University of Denver, Dr. Lassar was the Director of the School of Accounting at Florida International University and previously served on the faculties of Florida Atlantic University and the University of Arizona. She began her career with a Big 4 firm. Dr. Lassar has served the profession in many ways, most recently as a member of the AICPA Council. Dr. Lassar is a past president of the Accounting Programs Leadership Group and Past Chair of the Colorado Society of CPAs. Dr. Lassar also served on the Accounting Accreditation Task Force of AACSB International whose work resulted in new standards for accreditation, the hallmark of them being fully engaging practitioners in the accreditation process.

Andrew D. Cuccia, Ph.D., CPA, is the Steed Professor of Accounting at the University of Oklahoma. He is a graduate of Loyola University, New Orleans (B.B.A.) and the University of Florida (Ph.D.). Prior to entering academia, Andy practiced as a CPA with a Big 4 accounting firm. Before joining the University of Oklahoma, he was on the faculty at Louisiana State University and the University of Illinois. His research focusses on taxpayer and tax professional judgment and decision making and has been published in several journals including *The Accounting Review*, the *Journal of Accounting Research*, the *Journal of the American Taxation Association*, and *Tax Notes*. He has taught undergraduate and graduate courses in income tax fundamentals as well as graduate courses in corporate tax, tax policy, and tax research. Andy is a past president of the American Taxation Association and a member of the American Accounting Association, the National Taxation Association, and the AICPA.

Bradrick M. Cripe, Ph.D., CPA, is a Presidential Teaching Professor and the Donald E. Kieso Endowed Chair of Accountancy at Northern Illinois University. He is a graduate of New Mexico State University (B.A., B.C.J., and M.Acc.) and the University of Nebraska Lincoln (Ph.D.). Prior to receiving his Ph.D. in 2006, he worked on the tax staff of a Big 4 accounting firm. Professor Cripe teaches courses in taxation and business strategy, corporate taxation, international taxation, and advanced issues in taxation. He has published in *The Accounting Review, Issues in Accounting Education, Journal of Accountancy, Tax Notes*, and other academic and practitioner journals.

Brief Contents

Part 1: Introduction and Basic Tax Model

Chapter 1	An Introduction to Taxation and Understanding the Federal Tax Law	1-1
Chapter 2	Working with the Tax Law	2-1
Chapter 3	Tax Formula and Tax Determination; An Overview of Property Transactions	3-1

Part 2: Gross Income

Chapter 4	Gross Income: Concepts and Inclusions	4-1
Chapter 5	Gross Income: Exclusions	5-1

Part 3: Deductions

Chapter 6	Deductions and Losses: In General	6-1
Chapter 7	Deductions and Losses: Certain Business Expenses and Losses	7-1
Chapter 8	Depreciation, Cost Recovery, Amortization, and Depletion	8-1
Chapter 9	Deductions: Employee and Self-Employed-Related Expenses	9-1
Chapter 10	Deductions and Losses: Certain Itemized Deductions	10-1
Chapter 11	Investor Losses	11-1

Part 4: Special Tax Computation Methods, Tax Credits, and Payment Procedures

Chapter 12	Alternative Minimum Tax	12-1
Chapter 13	Tax Credits and Payment Procedures	13-1

Part 5: Property Transactions

Chapter 14	Property Transactions: Determination of Gain or Loss and Basis Considerations	14-1
Chapter 15	Property Transactions: Nontaxable Exchanges	15-1
Chapter 16	Property Transactions: Capital Gains and Losses	16-1
Chapter 17	Property Transactions: § 1231 and Recapture Provisions	17-1

Part 6: Accounting Periods, Accounting Methods, and Deferred Compensation

Chapter 18	Accounting Periods and Methods	18-1
Chapter 19	Deferred Compensation	19-1

Part 7: Corporations and Partnerships

Chapter 20	Corporations and Partnerships	20-1

Contents

Part 1: Introduction and Basic Tax Model

Chapter 1
An Introduction to Taxation and Understanding the Federal Tax Law **1-1**

The Big Picture: *Family and Taxes—A Typical Year* *1-1*

Approaching the Study of Taxation **1-2**
What Is Taxation? 1-2
Taxation in Our Lives 1-2
The Relevance of Taxation to Accounting and Finance Professionals 1-3
How to Study Taxation 1-5

A Brief History of U.S. Taxation **1-5**
Early Periods 1-5
Concept Summary: *Individuals and Taxes* *1-6*
Revenue Acts 1-6
Trends 1-7

Tax System Design **1-8**
Legal Foundation 1-8
The Basic Tax Formula 1-8
Tax Principles 1-9

Major Types of Taxes **1-10**
Property Taxes 1-12
Transaction Taxes 1-13
Ethics & Equity: *Making Good Use of Out-of-State Relatives* *1-14*
Taxes on Transfers at Death 1-15
Gift Taxes 1-16
Income Taxes 1-17
Employment Taxes 1-19
Other U.S. Taxes 1-20
Concept Summary: *Overview of Taxes in the United States* *1-21*
Proposed U.S. Taxes 1-22
Global Tax Issues: *VAT in USA?* *1-23*

Tax Administration **1-23**
Internal Revenue Service 1-23
The Audit Process 1-24
Statute of Limitations 1-25
Interest and Penalties 1-26
Global Tax Issues: *Outsourcing of Tax Return Preparation* *1-27*
Tax Practice 1-27

Understanding the Federal Tax Law **1-29**
Revenue Needs 1-29
Economic Considerations 1-29
Social Considerations 1-30
Equity Considerations 1-31
Political Considerations 1-33
Influence of the Internal Revenue Service 1-34
Influence of the Courts 1-35
Summary 1-36
Refocus on The Big Picture: *Family and Taxes—A Typical Year* *1-37*

Chapter 2
Working with the Tax Law **2-1**

The Big Picture: *Importance of Tax Research* *2-1*

Tax Law Sources **2-2**
Statutory Sources of the Tax Law 2-2
Administrative Sources of the Tax Law 2-6
Ethics & Equity: *Reporting Tax Fraud* *2-7*
Judicial Sources of the Tax Law 2-10
Concept Summary: *Federal Judicial System: Trial Courts* *2-12*
Concept Summary: *Judicial Sources* *2-15*
Other Sources of the Tax Law 2-17

Working with the Tax Law—Tax Research Tools **2-18**
Commercial Tax Services 2-18
Using Electronic (Online) Tax Services 2-19
Noncommercial Electronic (Online) Tax Services 2-19

Working with the Tax Law—Tax Research **2-20**
Identifying the Problem 2-21
Refining the Problem 2-22
Locating the Appropriate Tax Law Sources 2-22
Assessing the Validity of Tax Law Sources 2-23
Arriving at the Solution or at Alternative Solutions 2-25
Financial Disclosure Insights: *Where Does GAAP Come From?* *2-26*
Communicating Tax Research 2-26

Working with the Tax Law—Tax Planning **2-28**
Nontax Considerations 2-29
Components of Tax Planning 2-29
Tax Avoidance and Tax Evasion 2-30
Follow-Up Procedures 2-30
Tax Planning 2-31

Taxation on the CPA Examination **2-31**
Preparation Blueprints 2-31
Regulation Section 2-31

Chapter 3 Tax Formula and Tax Determination; An Overview of Property Transactions **3-1**

The Big Picture: *A Divided Household* *3-1*

Tax Formula **3-2**
Concept Summary: *Tax Formula for Individuals (Components Integrated into the Text)* *3-3*
Components of the Tax Formula 3-3
Tax Formula—Correlation with Form 1040 3-8

Standard Deduction **3-17**
Basic and Additional Standard Deduction 3-17
Individuals Not Eligible for the Standard Deduction 3-18
Special Limitations on the Standard Deduction for Dependents 3-18

Exemptions **3-19**

Dependents **3-19**
Qualifying Child 3-19
Concept Summary: *Tiebreaker Rules for Claiming Qualified Child* *3-21*
Qualifying Relative 3-21
Other Rules for Determining Dependents 3-25
Comparison of Dependent Categories 3-25
Concept Summary: *Tests for Dependents* *3-26*
Ethics & Equity: *Whose Qualifying Child Is He?* *3-26*
Child and Dependent Tax Credits 3-26

Filing Status and Filing Requirements **3-29**
Filing Status 3-29
Global Tax Issues: *Filing a Joint Return* *3-30*
Ethics & Equity: *Abandoned Spouse?* *3-33*
Filing Requirements 3-33

Tax Determination **3-34**
Tax Rates 3-35
Computation of Net Taxes Payable or Refund Due 3-36
Kiddie Tax—Unearned Income of Dependent Children 3-37

Tax Return Filing Procedures **3-39**
Selecting the Proper Form 3-39
The E-File Approach 3-40
When and Where to File 3-40
Modes of Payment 3-41

Gains and Losses from Property Transactions—In General **3-41**

Gains and Losses from Property Transactions—Capital Gains and Losses **3-42**
Definition of a Capital Asset 3-42
Determination of Net Capital Gain 3-42
Treatment of Net Capital Loss 3-43
Taxation of Net Capital Gain 3-43
Taxation of Virtual Currency 3-44

Tax Planning **3-45**
Maximizing the Use of the Standard Deduction 3-45
Dependents 3-45
Taking Advantage of Tax Rate Differentials 3-46
Income of Certain Children 3-47
Refocus on The Big Picture: *A Divided Household* *3-47*

Part 2: Gross Income

Chapter 4 Gross Income: Concepts and Inclusions **4-1**

The Big Picture: *Calculation of Gross Income* *4-1*

Gross Income **4-3**
Definition 4-3
Recovery of Capital Doctrine 4-3
Global Tax Issues: *From "All Sources" Is a Broad Definition* *4-3*
Economic and Accounting Concepts of Income 4-4
Financial Accounting Income versus Taxable Income 4-5
Form of Receipt 4-6

Timing of Income Recognition **4-6**
Taxable Year 4-6
Accounting Methods 4-7
Special Rules Applicable to Cash Basis Taxpayers 4-9
Ethics & Equity: *Should the Tax Treatment of Government Bonds and Corporate Bonds Be Different?* *4-12*
Special Rules Applicable to Accrual Basis Taxpayers 4-13

General Sources of Income and to Whom They Are Taxed **4-14**
Personal Services 4-14
Income from Property 4-15
Income from Partnerships, S Corporations, Trusts, and Estates 4-17
Concept Summary: *Taxation of Income and Distributions from Partnerships, S Corporations, Trusts, and Estates* *4-18*
Income in Community Property States 4-18

Special Rules Related to Certain Items Included in Gross Income **4-20**
Alimony and Separate Maintenance Payments 4-20
Ethics & Equity: *The Taxation of Alimony and the Alimony Tax Gap* *4-22*
Concept Summary: *Tax Treatment of Payments and Transfers Pursuant to Divorce Agreements and Decrees* *4-23*
Imputed Interest on Below-Market Loans 4-23
Concept Summary: *Effect of Certain Below-Market Loans on the Lender and Borrower* *4-24*
Concept Summary: *Exceptions to the Imputed Interest Rules for Below-Market Loans* *4-26*
Ethics & Equity: *Taxing "Made-Up" Income* *4-26*
Income from Annuities 4-26
Prizes and Awards 4-29
Unemployment Compensation 4-29
Ethics & Equity: *Tax Treatment of Unemployment Compensation* *4-30*
Social Security Benefits 4-30
Income Earned from Foreign Bank and Financial Accounts and FBAR Rules 4-31

Tax Planning **4-32**
Minimize Income Included in Gross Income 4-32
Tax Deferral 4-32
Shifting Income to Other Taxpayers 4-34
Refocus on The Big Picture: *Calculation of Gross Income* *4-35*

Chapter 5
Gross Income: Exclusions **5-1**
The Big Picture: *Exclusions* *5-1*

Income Exclusions **5-2**
Exclusion Defined 5-2
Exclusions versus Non-Income Items 5-3

Gifts and Inheritances **5-3**
Legislative Intent 5-3
Employer Payments to Employees 5-4
Employee Death Benefits 5-4

Life Insurance Proceeds **5-5**
General Rule 5-5
Accelerated Death Benefits 5-5
Ethics & Equity: *Should the Terminally Ill Pay Social Security Taxes?* *5-6*
Transfer for Valuable Consideration 5-6

Scholarships **5-7**
General Information 5-7
Timing Issues 5-8

Compensation for Injuries and Sickness **5-8**
Damages 5-8
Ethics & Equity: *Tax Treatment of Damages Not Related to Physical Personal Injury* *5-9*
Concept Summary: *Taxation of Damages* *5-9*
Ethics & Equity: *Classifying the Amount of the Claim* *5-10*
Wrongful Incarceration 5-10
Workers' Compensation 5-10
Accident and Health Insurance Benefits 5-10

Employer-Sponsored Accident and Health Plans **5-11**
Medical Reimbursement Plans 5-11
Long-Term Care Insurance Benefits 5-12

Meals and Lodging **5-13**
General Rules for the Exclusion 5-13
Other Housing Exclusions 5-14

Employee Fringe Benefits **5-14**
Specific Benefits 5-15
Cafeteria Plans 5-15
Flexible Spending Plans 5-16
General Classes of Excluded Benefits 5-16
Ethics & Equity: *Fringe Benefits* *5-20*
Group Term Life Insurance 5-20

Foreign Earned Income **5-21**
Concept Summary: *Employee Fringe Benefits* *5-22*
Global Tax Issues: *Benefits of the Earned Income Exclusion Are Questioned* *5-22*

Interest on Certain State and Local Government Obligations **5-23**

Educational Savings Bonds **5-24**

Education Savings Programs (§ 529 and § 530 Plans) **5-25**
Qualified Tuition Program 5-26
Coverdell Education Savings Account 5-26

Qualified ABLE Programs (§ 529A Plans) **5-26**

Income from Discharge of Indebtedness **5-27**

Tax Benefit Rule **5-28**

Tax Planning **5-30**
Life Insurance 5-30
Employee Fringe Benefits 5-30
Investment Income 5-31
Refocus on The Big Picture: *Exclusions* *5-32*

Part 3: Deductions

Chapter 6
Deductions and Losses: In General **6-1**
The Big Picture: *Calculation of Deductible Expenses* *6-1*

Classification of Deductible Expenses **6-2**
Classifying Deductions 6-3

Authority for Deductions 6-3
Deduction Criteria for § 162 and § 212 6-5
Personal Expenses 6-6
Business and Nonbusiness Losses 6-6
Deduction for Qualified Business Income 6-7
Reporting Procedures 6-9

Deductions and Losses—Timing of Expense Recognition 6-10
Importance of Taxpayer's Method of Accounting 6-10
Cash Method Requirements 6-10
Accrual Method Requirements 6-10
Prepaid Expenses—The "12-Month Rule" 6-12
Time Value of Tax Deductions 6-12

Disallowance Possibilities 6-13
Public Policy Limitation 6-13
Global Tax Issues: *Overseas Gun Sales Result in Large Fines 6-14*
Ethics & Equity: *State Allowed Marijuana Activity: Do Regular Business Deduction Rules Apply (or Those for Drug Dealers)? 6-15*
Political Contributions and Lobbying Activities 6-15
Excessive Executive Compensation 6-16
Investigation of a Business 6-17
Concept Summary: *Costs of Investigating a Business 6-18*
Hobby Losses 6-18
Concept Summary: *Common Questions from the IRS Concerning Hobbies/Businesses with Losses 6-20*
Rental of Vacation Homes 6-21
Concept Summary: *Vacation/Rental Home 6-22*
Expenditures Incurred for Taxpayer's Benefit or Taxpayer's Obligation 6-25
Disallowance of Personal Expenditures 6-26
Ethics & Equity: *Personal or Business Expenses? 6-26*
Disallowance of Deductions for Capital Expenditures 6-26
Transactions between Related Parties 6-28
Substantiation Requirements 6-29
Expenses and Interest Relating to Tax-Exempt Income 6-29
Other Disallowances 6-30

Tax Planning 6-30
Vacation Homes 6-30
Concept Summary: *Classification of Expenses 6-31*
Hobby Losses 6-32
Do Deduction Limits Affect Executive Compensation? 6-33
Refocus on The Big Picture: *Calculation of Deductible Business Expenses and Tax Planning 6-33*

Chapter 7
Deductions and Losses: Certain Business Expenses and Losses 7-1
The Big Picture: *Losses 7-1*

Bad Debts 7-2
Specific Charge-Off Method 7-3
Concept Summary: *The Tax Treatment of Bad Debts Using the Specific Charge-Off Method 7-4*
Business versus Nonbusiness Bad Debts 7-4
Loans between Related Parties 7-5
Concept Summary: *Bad Debt Deductions 7-5*

Worthless Securities and Small Business Stock Losses 7-6
Worthless Securities 7-6
Small Business Stock (§ 1244 Stock) Losses 7-6

Losses of Individuals 7-7
Events That Are Not Casualties 7-7
Theft Losses 7-8
When to Deduct Casualty Losses 7-8
Measuring the Amount of Loss 7-9
Ethics & Equity: *Is Policy Cancellation an Escape Hatch? 7-10*
Personal Casualty Gains and Losses 7-12
Concept Summary: *Casualty Gains and Losses 7-14*
Statutory Framework for Deducting Losses of Individuals 7-14
Concept Summary: *Statutory Framework for Deducting Losses of Individuals 7-15*

Research and Experimental Expenditures 7-15
Expense Method 7-16
Deferral and Amortization Method 7-16

Excess Business Losses 7-17
Excess Business Loss Defined 7-17
Losses from Partnerships or S Corporations 7-18
Other Rules 7-19

Net Operating Losses 7-19
General Rules 7-20
Computation of the Net Operating Loss 7-20
Concept Summary: *Computation of Net Operating Loss 7-21*
Computation of Taxable Income for Year to Which Net Operating Loss Is Carried 7-23
Calculation of the Remaining Net Operating Loss 7-24

Tax Planning 7-25
Small Business Stock (§ 1244 Stock) Losses 7-25
Casualty Losses 7-25
Refocus on The Big Picture: *Losses 7-25*

Chapter 8
Depreciation, Cost Recovery, Amortization, and Depletion 8-1
The Big Picture: *Calculating Cost Recovery Deductions 8-1*

Depreciation and Cost Recovery 8-2
Nature of Property 8-2

Placed in Service Requirement 8-3
Cost Recovery Allowed or Allowable 8-3
Cost Recovery Basis for Personal Use Assets Converted to Business or Income-Producing Use 8-4

Modified Accelerated Cost Recovery System (MACRS): General Rules 8-4
Concept Summary: *MACRS: Class Lives, Methods, and Conventions 8-4*
Personalty (and Certain Realty): Recovery Periods and Methods 8-5
Financial Disclosure Insights: *Tax and Book Depreciation 8-6*
Concept Summary: *Straight-Line Cost Recovery under MACRS (Personalty vs. Realty) 8-9*
Realty: Recovery Periods and Methods 8-9

Modified Accelerated Cost Recovery System (MACRS): Special Rules 8-10
Election to Expense Assets (§ 179) 8-10
Ethics & Equity: *Section 179 Limitation 8-14*
Additional First-Year Depreciation (Bonus Depreciation) 8-14
Using § 179 and Bonus Depreciation Effectively 8-15
Concept Summary: *Using § 179 and Bonus Depreciation in 2022 8-17*
Business and Personal Use of Automobiles and Other Listed Property 8-18
Alternative Depreciation System (ADS) 8-23

Reporting Procedures 8-24

Amortization 8-25

Depletion 8-28
Intangible Drilling and Development Costs (IDCs) 8-29
Depletion Methods 8-29

Tax Planning 8-31
Cost Recovery 8-31
Amortization 8-32
Cost Recovery Tables 8-32
Refocus on The Big Picture: *Calculating Cost Recovery Deductions 8-36*

Chapter 9 Deductions: Employee and Self-Employed-Related Expenses 9-1

The Big Picture: *The First Job 9-1*

Employee versus Independent Contractor 9-2
Concept Summary: *Employee versus Independent Contractor 9-4*

Self-Employed and Employee-Related Expenses—In General 9-5

Transportation Expenses 9-5
Qualified Expenses 9-5
Computation of Automobile Expenses 9-6

Travel Expenses 9-9
Definition of Travel Expenses 9-9
Away-from-Home Requirement 9-10
Restrictions on Travel Expenses 9-11
Combined Business and Pleasure Travel 9-12

Education Expenses 9-14
General Requirements 9-14
Legal Requirements to Keep a Job 9-14
Maintaining or Improving Existing Skills 9-15
Concept Summary: *Conditions for Deducting Regular Education Expenses 9-15*
What Expenses Are Allowed? 9-15
Other Provisions Dealing with Education 9-16
Concept Summary: *Tax Consequences of Provisions Dealing with Education 9-16*

Other Business Expenses 9-17
Office in the Home 9-17
Moving Expenses 9-21
Entertainment and Meal Expenses 9-21
Ethics & Equity: *Your Turn or Mine? 9-23*
Miscellaneous Employee Expenses 9-24

The Deduction for Qualified Business Income 9-25
General Rule 9-25
The Overall Limitation: Modified Taxable Income 9-26
What Is Qualified Business Income? 9-26
What Is a Qualified Trade or Business? 9-27
Limitations on the QBI Deduction 9-29
Limitation Based on Wages and Capital Investment 9-29
Concept Summary: *An Overview of the 2022 Qualified Business Income Deduction 9-30*
Limitation for "Specified Services" Businesses 9-33
Reporting the Qualified Business Income Deduction 9-42
Aggregation of Qualified Trades or Businesses under the § 199A Regulations 9-43
Treatment of Losses 9-48
Other Items in the § 199A Regulations 9-51

Contributions to Retirement Accounts 9-52
Employee IRAs 9-52
Self-Employed Keogh (H.R. 10) Plans 9-53

Classification of Employee Expenses 9-53
Accountable Plans 9-53
Nonaccountable Plans 9-54

Limitations on Itemized Deductions 9-55
Miscellaneous Itemized Deductions Subject to the 2%-of-AGI Floor 9-55
Miscellaneous Itemized Deductions Not Subject to the 2%-of-AGI Floor 9-56

Tax Planning 9-56
Employment Status 9-56
Implications of Misclassifying Workers 9-56
Transportation and Travel Expenses 9-57
Refocus on The Big Picture: *The First Job* 9-58

Chapter 10
Deductions and Losses: Certain Itemized Deductions 10-1
The Big Picture: *Impact of Itemized Deductions on Major Purchases* 10-1

Medical Expenses 10-3
Medical Expenses Defined 10-3
Capital Expenditures for Medical Purposes 10-4
Medical Expenses Incurred for Spouse and Dependents 10-5
Transportation, Meal, and Lodging Expenses for Medical Treatment 10-6
Amounts Paid for Medical Insurance Premiums 10-6
Year of Deduction 10-7
Reimbursements 10-7
Health Savings Accounts 10-8
Affordable Care Act Provisions 10-10

Taxes 10-10
Deductibility as a Tax 10-10
Property Taxes 10-11
State and Local Income Taxes and Sales Taxes 10-13

Interest 10-14
Allowed and Disallowed Items 10-14
Restrictions on Deductibility and Timing Considerations 10-17
Classification of Interest Expense 10-17
Concept Summary: *Deductibility of Personal, Student Loan, Mortgage, and Investment Interest* 10-18

Charitable Contributions 10-18
Criteria for a Gift 10-18
Qualified Organizations 10-20
Ethics & Equity: *An Indirect Route to a Contribution Deduction* 10-20
Time of Deduction 10-20
Record-Keeping and Valuation Requirements 10-21
Concept Summary: *Documentation and Substantiation Requirements for Charitable Contributions* 10-21
Global Tax Issues: *Choose the Charity Wisely* 10-22
Limitations on Charitable Contribution Deduction 10-22
Concept Summary: *Determining the Deduction for Contributions by Individuals* 10-25

Timing of Payments to Maximize Deductions 10-26

Other Itemized Deductions 10-27

Comprehensive Example of Schedule A 10-27

Tax Planning 10-29
Maximizing the Medical Deduction 10-29
Ensuring the Charitable Contribution Deduction 10-29
Planning to Avoid Nondeductible Treatment 10-31
Refocus on The Big Picture: *Impact of Itemized Deductions on Major Purchases* 10-31

Chapter 11
Investor Losses 11-1
The Big Picture: *Investor Loss Limitations Affect the Viability of Certain Investment Opportunities* 11-1

The Tax Shelter Problem 11-2

At-Risk Limits 11-4
Concept Summary: *Calculation of At-Risk Amount* 11-5

Passive Activity Loss Limits 11-5
Classification and Tax Treatment of Passive Activity Income and Losses 11-5
Taxpayers Subject to the Passive Activity Loss Rules 11-9
Rules for Determining Passive Activities 11-10
Concept Summary: *Tests to Determine Material Participation* 11-14
Interaction of the At-Risk and Passive Activity Loss Limits 11-15
Special Passive Activity Rules for Real Estate Activities 11-16
Concept Summary: *Treatment of Losses Subject to the At-Risk and Passive Activity Loss Limitations* 11-17
Ethics & Equity: *Punching the Time Clock at Year-End* 11-18
Dispositions of Passive Activities 11-20

Investment Interest Limitation 11-21
Limitation Imposed 11-21
Concept Summary: *Passive Activity Loss Rules: Key Issues and Answers* 11-22
Computation of Allowable Deduction 11-23

Other Investment Losses 11-23
Concept Summary: *Common Investment Loss Limitation Rules* 11-24

Tax Planning 11-24
Minimizing the Impact of Passive Activity Loss Limits 11-24
Maximizing the Investment Interest Deduction 11-26
Effect of the Additional Tax on Net Investment Income 11-26
Refocus on The Big Picture: *Investor Loss Limitations Can Affect Investment Returns* 11-27

Part 4: Special Tax Computation Methods, Tax Credits, and Payment Procedures

Chapter 12
Alternative Minimum Tax 12-1
The Big Picture: *The Presence or Absence of the AMT* 12-1

The AMT Calculation Generally 12-2
AMT Formula: Alternative Minimum Taxable Income (AMTI) 12-3

Ethics & Equity: *Who Will Pay the AMT?* 12-4
AMT Formula: Other Components 12-4

AMT Adjustments and Preferences **12-6**
Adjustments 12-6
Global Tax Issues: *A Global Minimum Tax* 12-15
Concept Summary: *Summary of AMT Adjustment Provisions* 12-18
Preferences 12-18
Ethics & Equity: *Incentive Stock Options and the AMT* 12-20
Illustration of the AMT Computation 12-21

AMT Credit **12-21**
Concept Summary: *Summary of AMT Preference Provisions* 12-22

Tax Planning **12-22**
Avoiding Preferences and Adjustments 12-22
Concept Summary: *AMT Adjustments and Preferences for Individuals* 12-23
Controlling the Timing of Preferences and Adjustments 12-24
Other AMT Tax Planning Strategies 12-24
Refocus on The Big Picture: *The Presence or Absence of the AMT* 12-24

Chapter 13
Tax Credits and Payment Procedures **13-1**
The Big Picture: *Education Tax Credits* 13-1

Tax Policy Considerations **13-3**

Overview and Priority of Credits **13-4**
Refundable versus Nonrefundable Credits 13-4
General Business Credit 13-5
Treatment of Unused General Business Credits 13-5

Specific Business-Related Tax Credits **13-6**
Tax Credit for Rehabilitation Expenditures 13-6
Work Opportunity Tax Credit 13-7
Research Activities Credit 13-7
Low-Income Housing Credit 13-9
Disabled Access Credit 13-10
Credit for Small Employer Pension Plan Startup Costs 13-11
Credit for Employer-Provided Child Care 13-11
Credit for Employer-Provided Family and Medical Leave 13-12

Other Tax Credits **13-12**
Earned Income Credit 13-12
Foreign Tax Credit 13-14
Child and Dependent Tax Credits 13-15
Credit for Child and Dependent Care Expenses 13-15
Ethics & Equity: *Is This the Right Way to Use the Credit for Child and Dependent Care Expenses?* 13-17
Education Tax Credits 13-18
Energy Credits 13-19
Credit for Certain Retirement Plan Contributions 13-19
Concept Summary: *Tax Credits* 13-21

Payment Procedures **13-23**
Employers 13-23
Self-Employed Taxpayers 13-25
Additional Medicare Taxes on High-Income Individuals 13-29

Tax Planning **13-31**
Credit for Child and Dependent Care Expenses 13-31
Adjustments to Increase Withholding 13-32
Adjustments to Avoid Overwithholding 13-33
Refocus on The Big Picture: *Education Tax Credits* 13-33

Part 5: Property Transactions

Chapter 14
Property Transactions: Determination of Gain or Loss and Basis Considerations **14-1**
The Big Picture: *Proposed Sale of a House and Other Property Transactions* 14-1

Determination of Gain or Loss **14-2**
Realized Gain or Loss 14-3
Concept Summary: *Realized Gain or Loss* 14-3
Recognized Gain or Loss 14-8
Concept Summary: *Realized and Recognized Gain or Loss* 14-8
Nonrecognition of Gain or Loss 14-9

Basis Considerations **14-9**
Determination of Cost Basis 14-9
Gift Basis 14-12
Inherited Property 14-13
Disallowed Losses 14-15
Concept Summary: *Wash Sale Rules* 14-17
Ethics & Equity: *Washing a Loss Using an IRA* 14-19
Property Converted from Personal Use to Business or Income-Producing Use 14-19
Summary of Basis Adjustments 14-20
Concept Summary: *Adjustments to Basis* 14-21

Tax Planning **14-22**
Cost Identification and Documentation Considerations 14-22
Selection of Property for Making Gifts 14-22
Selection of Property to Pass at Death 14-22
Disallowed Losses 14-23
Refocus on The Big Picture: *Proposed Sale of a House and Other Property Transactions* 14-23

Chapter 15
Property Transactions: Nontaxable Exchanges **15-1**

The Big Picture: *Alternative Uses of Property* *15-1*

Nontaxable Exchanges **15-2**

Like-Kind Exchanges—§ 1031 **15-3**
Like-Kind Property 15-4
Exchange Requirement 15-4
Concept Summary: *Delayed § 1031 Exchange* *15-5*
Boot 15-6
Basis and Holding Period of Property Received 15-7
Reporting Considerations 15-10

Involuntary Conversions—§ 1033 **15-10**
Involuntary Conversion Defined 15-12
Computing the Amount Realized 15-12
Replacement Property 15-13
Concept Summary: *Involuntary Conversions: Replacement Property Tests* *15-14*
Time Limitation on Replacement 15-14
Nonrecognition of Gain 15-15
Reporting Considerations 15-16

Sale of a Residence—§ 121 **15-16**
Principal Residence 15-17
Requirements for Exclusion Treatment 15-17
Calculating the Exclusion 15-19
Exceptions to the Two-Year Rules 15-20

Tax Planning **15-22**
Like-Kind Exchanges 15-22
Involuntary Conversions 15-23
Sale of a Principal Residence 15-23
Refocus on The Big Picture: *Alternative Uses of Property* *15-24*

Chapter 16
Property Transactions: Capital Gains and Losses **16-1**

The Big Picture: *Managing Capital Asset Transactions* *16-1*

General Scheme of Taxation **16-3**

Capital Assets **16-3**
Definition of a Capital Asset (§ 1221) 16-4
Ethics & Equity: *Sculpture as a Capital Asset* *16-6*
Effect of Judicial Action 16-6
Statutory Expansions 16-7

Sale or Exchange **16-8**
Worthless Securities and § 1244 Stock 16-8
Retirement of Corporate Obligations 16-9
Options 16-9
Concept Summary: *Options: Consequences to the Grantor and Grantee* *16-11*
Patents 16-11
Franchises, Trademarks, and Trade Names (§ 1253) 16-12
Concept Summary: *Franchises: Consequences to the Franchisor and Franchisee* *16-14*
Lease Cancellation Payments 16-14

Holding Period **16-15**
General Rules 16-15
Special Holding Period Rules 16-15
Special Rules for Short Sales 16-16
Concept Summary: *Short Sales of Securities* *16-17*

Tax Treatment of Capital Gains and Losses of Noncorporate Taxpayers **16-19**
Capital Gain and Loss Netting Process 16-19
Qualified Dividend Income 16-23
Alternative Tax on Net Capital Gain and Qualified Dividend Income 16-24
Concept Summary: *Income Layers for Alternative Tax on Capital Gain Computation* *16-25*
Treatment of Net Capital Losses 16-27
Concept Summary: *Final Results of the Capital Gain and Loss Netting Process and How They Are Taxed* *16-28*
Reporting Procedures 16-28

Tax Treatment of Capital Gains and Losses of Corporate Taxpayers **16-29**
Global Tax Issues: *Capital Gain Treatment in the United States and Other Countries* *16-35*

Tax Planning **16-35**
Importance of Capital Asset Status 16-35
Planning for Capital Asset Status 16-35
Effect of Capital Asset Status in Transactions Other Than Sales 16-36
Stock Sales 16-37
Maximizing Benefits 16-37
Year-End Planning 16-37
Refocus on The Big Picture: *Managing Capital Asset Transactions* *16-38*

Chapter 17
Property Transactions: § 1231 and Recapture Provisions **17-1**

The Big Picture: *Depreciation Recapture* *17-1*

Section 1231 Assets **17-3**
Relationship to Capital Assets 17-3
Property Included 17-4
Property Excluded 17-4
Special Rules for Certain § 1231 Assets 17-4
General Procedure for § 1231 Computation 17-6
Concept Summary: *Section 1231 Netting Procedure* *17-7*

Section 1245 Recapture **17-10**
Section 1245 Property 17-12
Observations on § 1245 17-12

Section 1250 Recapture **17-13**
Section 1250 Recapture Situations 17-13

Concept Summary: *Comparison of § 1245 and § 1250 Depreciation Recapture* 17-14
Unrecaptured § 1250 Gain (Real Estate 25% Gain) 17-14
Ethics & Equity: *The Sale of a "Cost-Segregated" Building* 17-15

Considerations Common to §§ 1245 and 1250 17-16
Exceptions 17-16
Other Applications 17-17
Concept Summary: *Depreciation Recapture and § 1231 Netting Procedure* 17-18
Global Tax Issues: *Depreciation Recapture in Other Countries* 17-19

Special Recapture Provisions 17-19
Special Recapture for Corporations 17-19
Gain from Sale of Depreciable Property between Certain Related Parties 17-19
Intangible Drilling Costs 17-19

Reporting Procedures 17-20
Ethics & Equity: *Incorrect Depreciation and Recognized Gain* 17-22

Tax Planning 17-27
Timing of § 1231 Gain 17-27
Timing of Recapture 17-27
Postponing and Shifting Recapture 17-28
Avoiding Recapture 17-28
Refocus on The Big Picture: *Depreciation Recapture* 17-28

Part 6: Accounting Periods, Accounting Methods, and Deferred Compensation

Chapter 18 Accounting Periods and Methods 18-1

The Big Picture: *Accounting Period and Method* 18-1

Accounting Periods 18-2
Specific Provisions for Partnerships, S Corporations, and Personal Service Corporations 18-3
Ethics & Equity: *Who Benefits from the Change in Tax Year?* 18-5
Selecting the Tax Year 18-6
Changes in the Accounting Period 18-6
Taxable Periods of Less Than One Year 18-7
Mitigation of the Annual Accounting Period Concept 18-8
Ethics & Equity: *Special Tax Relief* 18-10

Accounting Methods 18-10
Permissible Methods 18-10
Cash Receipts and Disbursements Method 18-11
Accrual Method 18-13
Concept Summary: *Accruals Under the Economic Performance Test (Reg. § 1.461–4)* 18-14
Financial Disclosure Insights: *Tax Deferrals from Reserves* 18-16
Hybrid Method 18-16
Change of Method 18-17
Ethics & Equity: *Change in Accounting Method* 18-19

Special Accounting Methods 18-19
Installment Method 18-19
Long-Term Contracts 18-25

Inventories 18-28
Determining Inventory Cost 18-29
Ethics & Equity: *Preserving the LIFO Reserve* 18-33
The LIFO Election 18-33
Special Inventory Methods Relating to Farming and Ranching 18-34
Inventory of Small Taxpayers 18-34

Tax Planning 18-35
Taxable Year 18-35
Cash Method of Accounting 18-35
Installment Method 18-35
Inventories 18-36
Refocus on The Big Picture: *Accounting Period and Method* 18-36

Chapter 19 Deferred Compensation 19-1

The Big Picture: *A Taxpayer Who Saves* 19-1

Qualified Pension, Profit Sharing, Stock Bonus, and Cash Balance Plans 19-2
Types of Plans 19-2
Concept Summary: *Defined Benefit Plan and Defined Contribution Plan Compared* 19-3
Ethics & Equity: *Switching from Defined Benefit to Defined Contribution Pension Plans* 19-4
Qualification Requirements 19-4
Ethics & Equity: *Vesting and Withdrawal Rules* 19-8
Tax Consequences to the Employee and Employer 19-8
Limitations on Contributions to and Benefits from Qualified Plans 19-9
Section 401(k) Plans 19-10

Retirement Plans for Self-Employed Individuals 19-11
Keogh (H.R. 10) Plans 19-11
Solo § 401(k) Plans 19-12
Savings Incentive Match Plan for Employees (SIMPLE Plans) 19-12
Simplified Employee Pension Plans (SEPs) 19-12
Concept Summary: *Keogh Plan and SEP Compared* 19-13

Individual Retirement Accounts (IRAs) 19-13
General Rules 19-13
Taxation of Benefits 19-16
Rollovers and Conversions 19-17
Concept Summary: *Comparison of IRAs* 19-17

Nonqualified Deferred Compensation Plans 19-18
Underlying Rationale for Tax Treatment 19-18
Tax Treatment to the Employer and Employee 19-18
Ethics & Equity: *The Ethics of Sustainable Investing* 19-19

Stock Options 19-19
Incentive Stock Options 19-19
Financial Disclosure Insights: *Share-Based Compensation* 19-20
Financial Disclosure Insights: *Executive Compensation* 19-22
Nonqualified Stock Options 19-22

Tax Planning 19-23
Qualified Plans 19-23
Self-Employed Retirement Plans 19-23
Individual Retirement Accounts 19-23
Comparison of § 401(k) Plan with IRA 19-24
Nonqualified Deferred Compensation (NQDC) Plans 19-24
Concept Summary: *Section 401(k) Plan and IRA Compared* 19-25
Stock Options 19-25
Concept Summary: *Incentive Stock Options and Nonqualified Stock Options Compared* 19-25
Liquidating Retirement Assets 19-26
Refocus on The Big Picture: *A Taxpayer Who Saves* 19-26

Part 7: Corporations and Partnerships

Chapter 20
Corporations and Partnerships **20-1**
The Big Picture: *Choice of Business Entity* 20-1

Choice of Entity 20-2
Nontax Considerations 20-2
Concept Summary: *Nontax Characteristics of Business Entities* 20-4
General Tax Consequences of Different Forms of Business Entities 20-4
Check-the-Box Election 20-5

Corporations 20-6
Legal Status 20-6
Individuals and Corporations Compared—An Overview 20-6
Specific Provisions Compared 20-8
Deductions Available Only to C Corporations 20-12
Determination of Corporate Tax Liability 20-14
Corporate Filing Requirements 20-15
Reconciliation of Corporate Taxable Income and Accounting Income 20-15
Concept Summary: *Summary of Income Tax Consequences: Individuals Compared with C Corporations* 20-17

Forming the Corporation 20-18
Transfers to Controlled Corporations 20-18
Capital Contributions 20-20
Ethics & Equity: *Selective Incorporation* 20-21

Distributions to Shareholders 20-21
Dividend Distributions 20-21
Constructive Dividends 20-22

S Corporations 20-23
Qualification for S Status 20-23
Operational Rules 20-25
Ethics & Equity: *Income Tax Basis That Does Not Change?* 20-28

Partnerships 20-28
Nature of Partnership Taxation 20-28
Concept Summary: *A Comparison of Some of the Tax Attributes of S and C Corporations* 20-29
Partnership Formation and Basis 20-29
Partnership Operations 20-31

Tax Planning 20-33
Corporate versus Noncorporate Forms of Business Organization 20-33
C Corporation versus S Status 20-35
Income Shifting to Reduce the Family Income Tax Burden 20-35
Refocus on The Big Picture: *Choice of Business Entity* 20-36

Appendices

Tax Formulas, Tax Rate Schedules, and Tables A-1
Tax Forms B-1
Glossary C-1
Table of Code Sections Cited D-1
Present Value and Future Value Tables E-1
Practice Set Assignments—Comprehensive Tax Return Problems F-1
Index I-1

Online Appendices

Depreciation and the Accelerated Cost Recovery System (ACRS)
Affordable Care Act Provisions

Part 1

Introduction and Basic Tax Model

Chapter 1
An Introduction to Taxation and Understanding the Federal Tax Law

Chapter 2
Working with the Tax Law

Chapter 3
Tax Formula and Tax Determination; An Overview of Property Transactions

Part 1 provides an introduction to taxation in the United States. Although this text focuses on income taxation, other types of taxes also are briefly discussed. The purposes of the Federal tax law are examined, and the legislative, administrative, and judicial sources of Federal tax law, including their application to the tax research process, are analyzed. Part 1 concludes by introducing the basic tax model for the individual taxpayer (the tax formula), discussing tax determination, and providing an overview of property transactions.

Chapter 1

An Introduction to Taxation and Understanding the Federal Tax Law

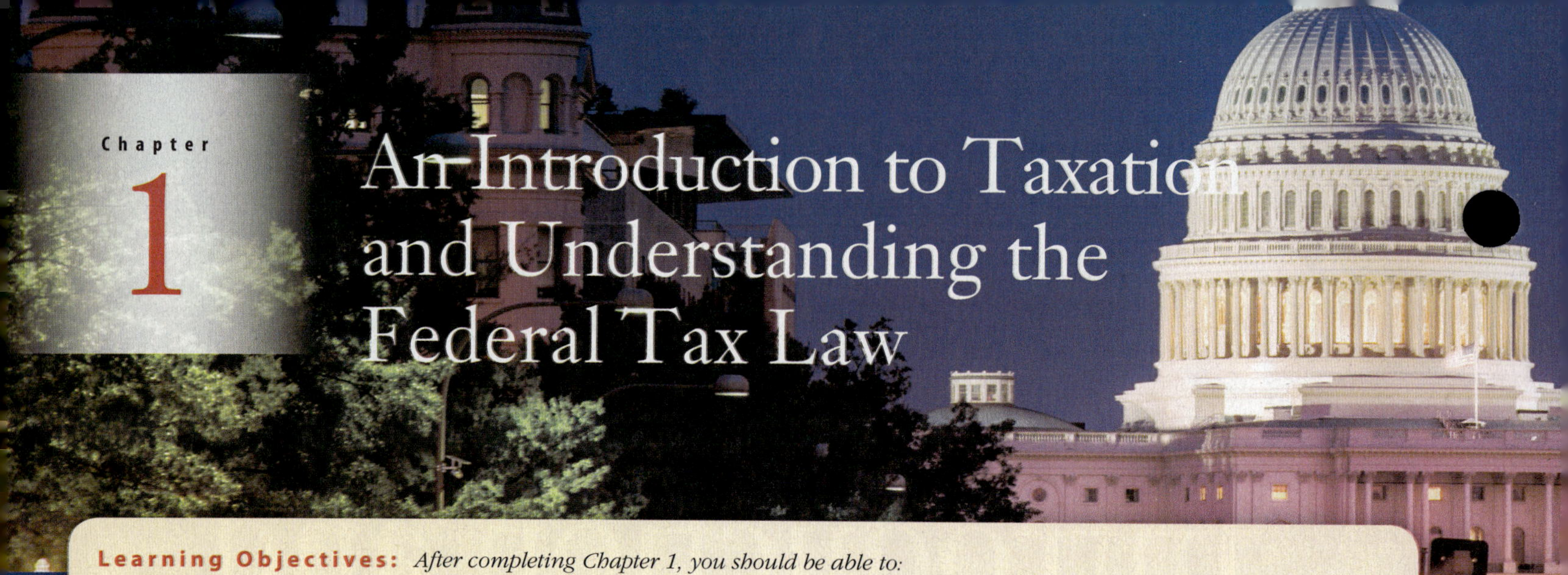

Learning Objectives: *After completing Chapter 1, you should be able to:*

- **LO.1** Explain the importance of taxation and apply methods for studying this topic.
- **LO.2** Describe some of the history and trends of the Federal income tax.
- **LO.3** Describe and apply principles and terminology relevant to the design of a tax system.
- **LO.4** Identify the different taxes imposed in the United States at the Federal, state, and local levels.
- **LO.5** Explain the administration of the tax law, including the audit process utilized by the IRS.
- **LO.6** Evaluate some of the ethical guidelines involved in tax practice.
- **LO.7** Classify tax rules based on their possible economic, social, equity, and political reasons for inclusion in a particular tax system.
- **LO.8** Explain the role played by the IRS and the courts in the evolution of the Federal tax system.

Chapter Outline

1-1 Approaching the Study of Taxation, 1-2
- 1-1a What Is Taxation? 1-2
- 1-1b Taxation in Our Lives, 1-2
- 1-1c The Relevance of Taxation to Accounting and Finance Professionals, 1-3
- 1-1d How to Study Taxation, 1-5

1-2 A Brief History of U.S. Taxation, 1-5
- 1-2a Early Periods, 1-5
- 1-2b Revenue Acts, 1-6
- 1-2c Trends, 1-7

1-3 Tax System Design, 1-8
- 1-3a Legal Foundation, 1-8
- 1-3b The Basic Tax Formula, 1-8
- 1-3c Tax Principles, 1-9

1-4 Major Types of Taxes, 1-10
- 1-4a Property Taxes, 1-12
- 1-4b Transaction Taxes, 1-13
- 1-4c Taxes on Transfers at Death, 1-15
- 1-4d Gift Taxes, 1-16
- 1-4e Income Taxes, 1-17
- 1-4f Employment Taxes, 1-19
- 1-4g Other U.S. Taxes, 1-20
- 1-4h Proposed U.S. Taxes, 1-22

1-5 Tax Administration, 1-23
- 1-5a Internal Revenue Service, 1-23
- 1-5b The Audit Process, 1-24
- 1-5c Statute of Limitations, 1-25
- 1-5d Interest and Penalties, 1-26
- 1-5e Tax Practice, 1-27

1-6 Understanding the Federal Tax Law, 1-29
- 1-6a Revenue Needs, 1-29
- 1-6b Economic Considerations, 1-29
- 1-6c Social Considerations, 1-30
- 1-6d Equity Considerations, 1-31
- 1-6e Political Considerations, 1-33
- 1-6f Influence of the Internal Revenue Service, 1-34
- 1-6g Influence of the Courts, 1-35
- 1-6h Summary, 1-36

CORBIS/SUPERSTOCK

The Big Picture

Family and Taxes—A Typical Year

Travis and Amy Carter are married and live in a state that imposes both a sales tax and an income tax. They have two children, April (age 17) and Martin (age 18). Travis is a mining engineer who specializes in land reclamation. After several years with a mining corporation, Travis established a consulting practice that involves a considerable amount of travel due to work he performs in other states. Amy is a registered nurse who, until recently, was a homemaker. In November of this year, she decided to reenter the job market and accepted a position with a medical clinic. The Carters live only a few blocks from Ernest and Mary Walker, Amy Carter's parents. The Walkers are retired and live on interest, dividends, and Social Security benefits.

Activities during the year with possible tax ramifications are summarized below.

- The ad valorem property taxes on the Carters' residence are increased, whereas those on the Walkers' residence are lowered.
- When Travis registers an automobile purchased last year in another state, he is required to pay a sales tax to his home state.
- As an anniversary present, the Carters gave the Walkers a recreational vehicle (RV).
- Travis employs his children to draft blueprints and prepare scale models for use in his work. Both April and Martin have had training in drafting and topography.
- Early in the year, the Carters are audited by the state on an income tax return filed a few years ago. Later in the year, they are audited by the IRS on a Form 1040 they filed for the same year. In each case, a tax deficiency and interest were assessed.
- The Walkers are audited by the IRS. Unlike the Carters, they did not have to deal with an agent, but settled the matter by mail.

Explain these developments, and resolve the issues raised.

Read the chapter and formulate your response.

This chapter provides an introduction to our Federal tax system to set a foundation for what you'll learn in subsequent chapters. Among the topics discussed are:

- The importance and relevance of taxation and how to study taxation.
- A brief history of the Federal income tax.
- The types of taxes imposed at the Federal, state, and local levels.
- Some highlights of tax law administration.
- Tax concepts that help explain the reasons for various tax provisions.
- The influence the Internal Revenue Service (IRS) and the courts have had in the evolution of current tax law.

1-1 Approaching the Study of Taxation

LO.1

Explain the importance of taxation and apply methods for studying this topic.

1-1a What Is Taxation?

"Taxes are what we pay for civilized society."

This is a famous quote from U.S. Supreme Court Justice Oliver Wendell Holmes, Jr. (1841 to 1935).[1] It is engraved on the government building at 1111 Constitution Avenue in Washington, D.C.—headquarters of the Internal Revenue Service (IRS). This quote eloquently sums up the primary purpose of taxation—to raise revenue for government operations. Governments at all levels—national, state, and local—require funds for defense, protection (police and fire), education, roads, the court system, social services, and more. Various types of taxes provide the resources to pay for government services.

In addition, taxation is often used as a tool to influence the behavior of individuals and businesses. For example, an income tax credit (which reduces a taxpayer's tax bill) may be designed to *encourage* people to purchase a fuel-efficient car. A tobacco excise tax may *discourage* individuals from smoking by increasing the cost of tobacco products. The tax system can also be used to provide direct benefits to taxpayers (e.g., to help pay for health insurance) and indirect benefits (in the form of exclusions, deductions, and credits that reduce a taxpayer's tax liability).

1-1b Taxation in Our Lives

"Nothing is certain, except death and taxes."

Most people attribute this quote to Benjamin Franklin (1706–1790). Taxes permeate our society. Various types of taxes, such as income, sales, property, and excise taxes (discussed in text Section 1-4), come into play in many of the activities of individuals, businesses, nonprofit entities (e.g., charitable organizations), and even governments.

Most directly, individuals are affected by taxes by paying them. Taxes may be paid directly or indirectly. A direct tax is paid to the government by the person who pays the tax. Examples include the personal income tax, which is paid by filing a personal income tax return (Form 1040 at the Federal level), and property taxes on one's home (paid to the local government). Individuals also pay many taxes indirectly. For example, most states impose sales tax on the purchase of tangible goods such as clothes. While this tax is collected and remitted to the government by the seller, the buyer is charged the tax along with the purchase price of the goods or services. Taxes also can be imposed indirectly when embedded in the prices charged by the seller. For example, when you buy gasoline for your car, the price you pay likely includes some of the income taxes and the gasoline excise taxes owed by the oil company. And a renter indirectly pays property taxes assessed on the landlord (who will consider that cost when determining how much rent to charge).

[1] *Compania General De Tabacos De Filipinas v. Collector of Internal Revenue*, 275 U.S. 87, 100 (1927), dissenting opinion.

Ultimately, all taxes are paid by individuals. The corporate income tax, for example, is paid directly by the corporation but is really paid indirectly by individuals in their capacity as customers, investors (owners), or employees. Economists and others often study this topic to estimate the percentage of the corporate income tax borne by individuals in these different capacities. It is not easy to measure, but it is known that taxes are passed along to individuals through higher prices, lower dividends, and/or lower wages.

Taxes also affect the lives of individuals via the ballot box. Federal, state, and local elections often include initiatives that deal with taxation, such as whether state income taxes should be raised (or lowered), whether a new tax should be imposed on soda, or whether the sales tax rate should be changed. Candidates running for office often have positions on tax changes they would like to make if elected.

Given the pervasiveness of taxation—in our roles as both direct and indirect payers of taxes as well as citizens/voters—it is important that we understand how the tax system operates.

1-1c The Relevance of Taxation to Accounting and Finance Professionals

The U.S. corporate income tax rate is 21 percent. State income taxes can easily constitute, on average, an additional 5 percent. So a large corporation such as a Fortune 500 company may have to devote 26 percent or more of its net income to pay income taxes. In addition, businesses are subject to employment taxes, property taxes, sales taxes, and various excise taxes. Corporations with international operations are subject to taxation in other countries. Small businesses are also subject to a variety of taxes that affect profits and cash flows.

Given its significance, taxation is a crucial topic for accounting and finance professionals. They must understand the various types of business taxes to assist effectively with the following:

- *Compliance:* Ensure that the business files all tax returns and makes all tax payments on time. Mistakes and missed due dates will lead to penalties and interest expense.
- *Planning.* Help a business apply favorable tax rules, such as income deferral and tax credits, to minimize tax liability (and maximize owner wealth). The time value of money concept is also important here, as is coordinating tax planning with other business goals to maximize earnings per share.[2]
- *Financial reporting:* Financial statements include a variety of tax information, including income tax expense on the income statement and deferred tax assets and liabilities on the balance sheet. Footnotes to the financial statements report various tax details, including the company's effective tax rate. Computation and proper reporting of this information require knowledge of both tax and financial reporting rules [including the Financial Accounting Standards Board's Accounting Standards Codification (ASC) 740, *Income Taxes*].
- *Environmental, Social, and Governance (ESG) reporting:* A growing trend in corporate reporting is to address various business sustainability and responsibility matters and to report environmental, social, and governance activities and impact. Standard frameworks might be used that include tax metrics such as the Global Reporting Initiative (GRI) Standards or ones generated by the World Economic Forum.[3] This reporting can include taxes paid in each country (part of "country-by-country reporting"), reconciliation between taxes paid and the statutory tax

[2] A corporate tax director or vice president of tax is typically involved in the strategic planning and growth of the company due to the significance of tax liabilities and planning opportunities to the business. For example, a 2021 position announcement for a Tax Director at Roblox stated that the director would lead initiatives to support global growth of the company.

[3] For example, see World Economic Forum, *Toward Common Metrics and Consistent Reporting of Sustainable Value Creation,* Jan. 2020; **www3.weforum.org/docs/WEF_IBC_ESG_Metrics_Discussion_Paper.pdf**.

rate on financial statement profits, financial assistance received from governments via tax deductions and credits, and an explanation of the corporation's tax policy and strategy.[4]

- *Controversy:* This term refers to interaction a taxpayer may have with a tax agency such as the IRS. The IRS and state and local tax agencies regularly audit tax returns that have been filed to verify that taxes were properly computed and paid.
- *Cash management:* Taxes must be paid on time to avoid penalties and interest. Income and self-employment taxes must be estimated and paid quarterly and reconciled on the annual return. Other taxes may be due weekly, monthly, or semiannually. Businesses must be sure they have the funds ready when the taxes are due and have procedures to track due dates.
- *Data analysis:* With a majority, if not all, of a company's records maintained in digital form, there are opportunities to use this information to enhance profits, better understand the customer base, and improve and understand the information from a tax perspective. Tax practitioners often need skills in data analysis and visualization to identify samples for both internal and external audits, find ways to identify the products and services subject to sales tax in different states, and extract tax data to help inform other business functions such as where to locate a new sales office.
- *Tax advocacy:* Taxpayers and tax practitioners can add tremendous value to the improvement and evolution of our tax laws by sharing their knowledge, experiences, and ideas with lawmakers and tax agencies. Some of this work is performed by professional organizations such as the American Institute of CPAs (AICPA), industry associations, and various policy organizations. This input might take the form of comment letters, testimony before legislative committees (delivered in person or submitted for the record), or individual correspondence and meetings.[5]

These tasks are also relevant to professionals such as CPAs who advise business and individual clients.

The level and depth of tax knowledge needed for any accounting or tax professional depends on the specific job. The vice president of tax for a company clearly needs thorough knowledge in all areas of taxation; the same is true of a partner in a CPA firm. In contrast, the corporate treasurer likely focuses more on cash management, while working closely with the company's tax advisers.

Ultimately, much of taxation is transaction-based. How a transaction is structured (e.g., as a sale or a lease) has varying tax consequences that must be considered. Even the purchase of a home can result in significant change—the new mortgage interest and property tax deductions may mean that an individual itemizes her deductions (using Schedule A of Form 1040) rather than using the standard deduction. And life events such as marriage (and divorce) will change an individual's tax situation. Similar "life events" can also affect a corporation (e.g., acquiring a corporation or spinning off a subsidiary).

It is essential in working with taxation to maintain a balanced perspective. A corporation that is deciding where to locate a new factory does not automatically select the city or state that offers the most generous tax benefits. Nor does the person who is retiring to a warmer climate pick Belize over Arizona because the former has no income tax but the latter does. Tax considerations should not control decisions, but they remain one of many factors to be considered (and often one of the most significant).

[4] For examples, see Intel's 2020–21 Corporate Responsibility Report; **csrreportbuilder.intel.com/pdfbuilder/pdfs/CSR-2020-21-Full-Report.pdf**; and The Walt Disney Company's 2020 Corporate Social Responsibility Report; **thewaltdisneycompany.com/app/uploads/2021/02/2020-CSR-Report.pdf**.

[5] For examples of such advocacy, see formal letters submitted by the AICPA (**aicpa.org/advocacy/tax.html**); testimony delivered at tax reform hearings in Congress (**sjsu.edu/people/annette.nellen/website/117th-hearings.htm**); and tax policy activities and reports of various industry and policy organizations such as the U.S. Chamber of Commerce (**uschamber.com/taxes**) and the Center on Budget and Policy Priorities (**cbpp.org/research/topics/federal-tax**).

1-1d How to Study Taxation

The goal of studying taxation is to be able to recognize issues (or transactions) that have tax implications and, when possible, try to understand the justification for them. Suppose, for example, that you come upon a situation that involves a discharge of indebtedness. If you know that forgiveness of debt results in income but that there are exceptions to this rule, you're doing well. The issue has been identified, and the outcome (i.e., when an exception applies) can be resolved through research. A variety of commercial and free tools and resources are available to help you research and reach a conclusion.

You may have heard that tax is a difficult subject because of the many rules, exceptions, and definitions, as well as frequent changes to tax rules. You even may have heard that taxation is boring. Taxation is a challenging topic, but it is certainly not boring. Taxation is an important and exciting topic due to constant change by the three branches of our Federal government (as well as changes by state and local governments), the significance of taxes to the bottom line of a company and an individual's finances, and the impact on our economy and society.

Tax professionals tend to find enjoyment in their chosen field due to the intellectual challenge of dealing with tax rules for compliance and planning purposes, the opportunity to interact with colleagues or clients to help them understand the effect of taxes, and the knowledge that their work affects the financial well-being of individuals and businesses.

In studying taxation, focus on understanding the rules and the why(s) behind them (rather than memorizing the many rules and terms). The rules become more meaningful by thinking about why they exist for the particular type of tax. For example, why does the Federal income tax allow for a casualty loss deduction in certain situations? Why is tax depreciation different from that used for financial reporting? Also consider how the rules apply to different types of taxpayers (like employees, sole proprietors, corporations, investors, children, and retirees). Also think about how the rules apply to taxpayers of varying income levels and sophistication of transactions (a homeowner versus someone who owns assets in several countries). Aiming for understanding rather than memorization will make your journey into the world of taxation interesting and meaningful and will prepare you well for dealing with taxation in your accounting or finance career.

For tax professionals, the study of taxation is an ongoing and intriguing process. When Congress changes the tax law, tax professionals must review the new rules in order to understand how they affect clients or their employer. In addition, decisions rendered by the courts in tax disputes and guidance issued by the Treasury Department and Internal Revenue Service must be understood to ensure correct compliance with the law as well as identification of updated and proper tax planning ideas.

Concept Summary 1.1 illustrates the various ways that individuals deal with, and are affected by, taxes.

1-2 A Brief History of U.S. Taxation

LO.2

Describe some of the history and trends of the Federal income tax.

1-2a Early Periods

An income tax was first enacted in 1634 by the English colonists in the Massachusetts Bay Colony, but the Federal government did not adopt an income tax until 1861. In fact, both the Federal Union and the Confederate States of America used the income tax to raise funds to finance the Civil War.

When the Civil War ended, the need for additional revenue disappeared and the income tax was repealed. Once again the Federal government was able to finance its operations almost exclusively from customs duties (tariffs).

When a new Federal income tax on individuals was enacted in 1894, its opponents were prepared to successfully challenge its constitutionality. In *Pollock v. Farmers' Loan*

Concept Summary 1.1

Individuals and Taxes

The diagram to the right illustrates the many ways individuals interact with taxes. For example, as shown in the outer circle, individuals pay taxes and file tax returns (tax compliance). They also engage in tax planning as part of their desire to maximize after-tax wealth. If their tax return is audited or they do not pay their taxes, taxpayers will deal with the IRS or their state tax agency (tax controversy). Individuals deal with tax rules and planning in their roles as consumers, employees, investors, and business owners. Tax law is designed around these various taxpayer activities. Finally, as shown by the inner circle, individuals have a personal responsibility to comply with tax laws and pay any taxes due. Individuals also have a civic responsibility to understand taxes in their role as citizens and voters. And individuals need to understand how taxes affect their personal cash flows, consumption, and savings.

Use this diagram as you study the materials in this text, considering where in the circle various rules fit.

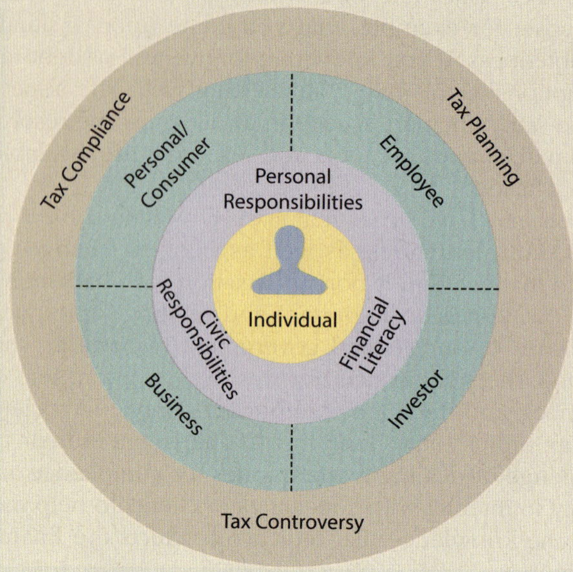

and Trust Co., the U.S. Supreme Court found that taxes on the income of real and personal property were the legal equivalent of a tax on the property involved and, therefore, required apportionment based on the population of the United States, as required by Article I, Section 8 of the Constitution.[6]

A Federal corporate income tax, enacted by Congress in 1909, fared better in the judicial system. The U.S. Supreme Court found this tax to be constitutional because it was treated as an excise tax.[7] In essence, it was a tax on the right to do business in the corporate form. So it was viewed as a form of the franchise tax.[8] Since the corporate form of doing business had been developed in the late nineteenth century, it was unknown to the framers of the U.S. Constitution. Because a corporation is an entity created under law, jurisdictions possess the right to tax its creation and operation. Using this rationale, many states still impose franchise taxes on corporations.

The ratification of the Sixteenth Amendment to the U.S. Constitution in 1913 sanctioned both the Federal individual and corporate income taxes and, as a consequence, neutralized the continuing effect of the *Pollock* decision.

1-2b Revenue Acts

After the Sixteenth Amendment was ratified by the states, Congress enacted the Revenue Act of 1913. Under this Act, the first Form 1040 was due on March 1, 1914. The law allowed various deductions and personal exemptions of $3,000 for a single individual and $4,000 for married taxpayers. These large exemptions excluded all but the more wealthy taxpayers from the new income tax.[9] Rates ranged from a low of 1 percent to a high of 6 percent. The 6 percent rate applied only to taxable income in excess of $500,000.[10]

[6] 3 AFTR 2602, 15 S.Ct. 912 (USSC, 1895). See Chapter 2 for an explanation of the citations of judicial decisions.

[7] *Flint v. Stone Tracy Co.*, 3 AFTR 2834, 31 S.Ct. 342 (USSC, 1911).

[8] See the discussion of state franchise taxes later in text Section 1-4g.

[9] A $3,000 exemption in 1913 would be about $82,000 today, while a $4,000 exemption would be about $109,000.

[10] This should be contrasted with the highest 2022 tax rate of 37%, which applies once taxable income exceeds $539,900 for single taxpayers and $647,850 for married taxpayers filing a joint return.

Various revenue acts were passed between 1913 and 1939. In 1939, all of these revenue laws were codified (arranged in a systematic manner) into the Internal Revenue Code of 1939. In 1954, a similar codification took place. The Internal Revenue Code of 1986, which largely carries over the provisions of the 1954 Code, is our current law. Tax law changes occur almost every year (how this happens is discussed in Chapter 2).

1-2c Trends

The income tax is a major source of revenue for the Federal government. Exhibit 1.1 shows the tax revenue sources[11] and the importance of the income tax. Income tax collections from individuals and corporations amount to 61 percent of the total receipts. One revenue source missing from the Exhibit 1.1 pie chart is borrowing to cover the deficit, which in recent years has represented between 10 to 40 percent of total government revenues.

The need for revenues to finance the war effort during World War II converted the income tax from one that applied mostly to high-income individuals to a *mass tax*. In 1939, less than 6 percent of the U.S. population was subject to the Federal income tax. By 1945, more than 74 percent of the population was subject to the Federal income tax.[12]

Certain tax law changes are important to understand. In 1943, Congress passed the Current Tax Payment Act, which provided for a pay-as-you-go tax system. A pay-as-you-go income tax system requires employers to withhold a specified portion of an employee's wages and remit them to the government to cover the worker's income taxes. Persons with income from other than wages may have to make quarterly payments to the IRS for estimated taxes due for the year.

The increasing complexity of the Federal income tax laws causes concern among many, including lawmakers, taxpayers, and tax practitioners. Congress has added to this complexity by frequently changing the tax laws (e.g., by adding or deleting deductions or tax credits). This complexity forces many taxpayers to seek assistance in preparing their income tax returns. According to estimates, more than one-half of individual taxpayers who file a return pay a preparer and most of these returns are prepared using

Exhibit 1.1 **Federal Tax Revenues (Estimated) in 2022**

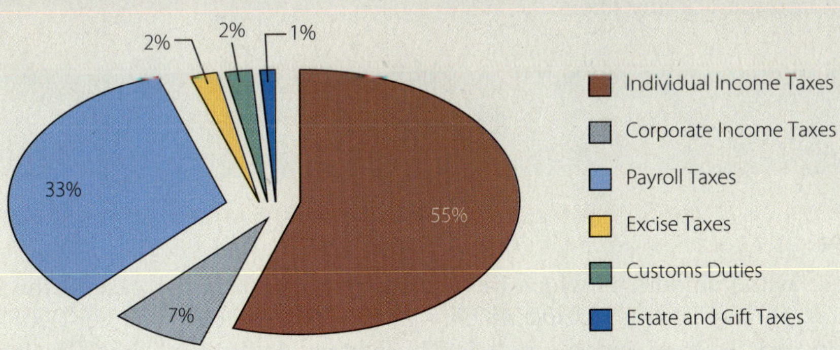

[11]Revenue data can be found at **irs.gov/statistics**, **cbo.gov,** and **whitehouse.gov/omb**. The instruction booklet for Form 1040 includes a revenue pie chart that includes borrowing to cover the deficit, as well as a pie chart that shows government spending in broad categories.

[12]Richard Goode, *The Individual Income Tax* (Washington, D.C.: The Brookings Institution, 1964), pp. 2–4.

tax software.[13] The IRS estimates that the average time spent by individuals to prepare and file their tax return and engage in necessary recordkeeping is 12 hours

New ways of doing business and living often require changes and/or clarifications to the tax law. For example, increased longevity requires a need for more revenues from Social Security taxes (and/or an increase in retirement age). Increased global business activity means modifying a country's tax system to be more in line with other countries to make sure businesses are not impeded when entering the global marketplace. New types of digital assets [e.g., virtual currency (or cryptocurrency) and non-fungible tokens (NFTs)] often require lawmakers or the IRS to clarify how existing tax rules apply to the new assets and related transactions. Ideally, lawmakers should review tax systems periodically to ensure that they continue to be efficient in light of changes in how businesses and individuals function.

LO.3

Describe and apply principles and terminology relevant to the design of a tax system.

1-3 Tax System Design

1-3a Legal Foundation

Article I, Section 8 of the U.S. Constitution states in part: "The Congress shall have power to lay and collect taxes." The Constitution also provided some limits on this taxing power, which led to the enactment of the Sixteenth Amendment to allow for an income tax (discussed in text Section 1-2a). This history lesson is important for a legislature or an electorate that wants to change a tax system. The jurisdiction's underlying governing documents (whether a country, state, or city) must be reviewed to determine whether they impose any restrictions relevant to taxation.

For example, the California Constitution (Article 13A) states that the maximum tax rate for real property taxation is 1 percent. The Florida Constitution (Section 5) specifies limits on the imposition of income taxes on natural persons. Also, state law may impose limitations on the types or amounts of taxes that cities and counties can impose.

Thus, the governing documents of a jurisdiction must be considered as part of any effort to modify that jurisdiction's tax system to make sure the change is permissible. If a change is not permissible but desired, then the governing document must be amended, as was done with the addition of the Sixteenth Amendment to the U.S. Constitution.

1-3b The Basic Tax Formula

The basic formula for any tax is:

Tax base ⓧ **Tax rate** ⊜ **Tax liability**

Tax Base

A tax base is the amount to which the tax rate is applied. In the case of the Federal income tax, the tax base is *taxable income*. As noted later in the chapter (Exhibit 1.3), taxable income is gross income reduced by certain deductions (both business and personal).

Tax Rates

Tax rates are applied to the tax base to determine a taxpayer's liability. Some taxes, like the sales tax and the gasoline excise tax, apply a fixed tax rate to all transactions.

[13] Most IRS instructions for forms and schedules include an estimate of the time needed to prepare the form or schedule.

Example 1

Kansas applies a sales tax rate of 6.5% to all taxable items. In contrast, Illinois applies a sales tax rate of 6.25% for most taxable items but applies a rate of 1% when the tax base consists of food or prescription drugs.

Alternatively, for some taxes, tax rates may vary depending on the details of the tax base. Income taxes tend to use a *progressive* tax rate structure where a higher rate of tax applies as the tax base increases.

Example 2

Bill and Chris, a married couple filing jointly, have taxable income of $15,000. Their Federal income tax rate for 2022 is 10%, which is the rate that applies to the first $20,550 of taxable income for a married couple filing jointly. Their tax liability is $1,500.

If, however, their taxable income is $85,000, their Federal income tax rates progress from 10% to 12% to 22% as their taxable income increases. In this case, their 2022 Federal income tax liability is $9,934. The Federal income tax uses a *progressive* rate structure that applies higher rates to taxable income (the tax base) as that income increases (see Appendix A to confirm these calculations, and note how progressivity is built into the rate structure of the Federal income tax).

The basic tax formula (shown above) is relevant for both computing taxes and planning, as well as for reforming a tax system. For example, if a legislator wants to lower tax rates but generate the same amount of tax revenues, the tax base must be increased. However, if she wants to increase tax revenues, the tax base can be increased *or* tax rates can be increased (or both can be increased). Changes to the tax base will depend on how it is constructed. For example, the income tax base is taxable income (income minus income exclusions minus deductions). To increase this tax base, income exclusions or deductions could be limited or eliminated. The details of the income tax base are discussed in later chapters. Tax system changes also involve canons (or principles) of taxation, discussed next.

1-3c Tax Principles

In the late 1700s, Adam Smith identified the following *canons (or principles) of taxation*, which are still considered today when evaluating a particular tax structure:[14]

- *Equity*. Each taxpayer enjoys fair or equitable treatment by paying taxes in proportion to his or her income level. Ability to pay a tax is one of the measures of how equitably a tax is distributed among taxpayers.
- *Certainty*. A tax should be certain rather than arbitrary. Taxpayers need to be able to understand how tax rules work so that they understand the effect of the rules on various transactions and can comply.
- *Convenience of payment*. Taxes should be imposed in a manner that involves a convenient time for payment. An advantage of the existing withholding system (pay-as-you-go) is its convenience for taxpayers.
- *Economy in collection*. A *good* tax system involves only nominal collection costs by the government and minimal compliance costs on the part of the taxpayer.

[14] *The Wealth of Nations* (New York: Dutton, 1910), Book V, Chapter II, Part II.

The American Institute of Certified Public Accountants (AICPA) has issued suggestions to guide tax reform and policy activities. Titled *Guiding Principles of Good Tax Policy: A Framework for Evaluating Tax Proposals*, the monograph identifies 12 principles that are commonly used as indicators of desirable tax policy. The first four principles are adapted from Adam Smith's *The Wealth of Nations*. The complete list follows:[15]

1. *Equity and Fairness*. Similarly situated taxpayers should be taxed in a similar manner.
2. *Certainty*. Taxpayers should have certainty rather than ambiguity as to when and how a tax is paid as well as how to calculate it.
3. *Convenience of Payment*. A tax should be due at a time and manner that is most convenient for the taxpayer.
4. *Effective Tax Administration*. Tax compliance and administrative costs should be kept to a minimum.
5. *Information Security*. Taxpayer information must be protected from improper disclosure.
6. *Simplicity*. Tax rules should be simple so that taxpayers understand them and can follow them in a cost-efficient manner.
7. *Neutrality*. The effect of tax rules on taxpayer decision making should be kept to a minimum.
8. *Economic Growth and Efficiency*. The tax system should not harm economic growth or distort economic effects among different activities and investments.
9. *Transparency and Visibility*. Taxpayers should know that a tax exists and how and when it applies to them.
10. *Minimum Tax Gap*. A tax should be structured to minimize noncompliance.
11. *Accountability to Taxpayers*. Taxpayers should have access to information on taxes as well as proposed law changes and their rationale.
12. *Appropriate Government Revenues*. Tax rules should enable the government to predict the amount and timing of revenue production.

Exhibit 1.2 provides an application of these principles to a proposed tax law change.

LO.4

Identify the different taxes imposed in the United States at the Federal, state, and local levels.

1-4 Major Types of Taxes

Why does a text devoted primarily to the Federal individual income tax discuss state and local taxes? A simple illustration demonstrates the importance of non-Federal taxes.

Example 3

Rick is employed by Flamingo Corporation in San Antonio, Texas, at a salary of $74,000. Rick's employer offers him a chance to transfer to its New York City office at a salary of $94,000.

Although Rick must consider many nontax factors before he decides on a job change, he should also evaluate the tax climate. How do state and local taxes compare? For example, neither Texas nor San Antonio imposes an income tax, but New York State and New York City do. A quick computation indicates that the additional income taxes (Federal, state, and local) involve approximately $12,000.

continued

[15] AICPA, *Guiding Principles of Good Tax Policy: A Framework for Evaluating Tax Proposals*, 2017. Similarly, see GAO, *Understanding the Tax Reform Debate: Background, Criteria, & Questions*, 2005. As "long-standing criteria," the GAO lists "equity; economic efficiency; and a combination of simplicity, transparency, and administrability."

Consequently, what appears to be a $20,000 pay increase is actually only about $8,000 when the additional $12,000 of income taxes are taken into account. Other taxes and costs (e.g., sales taxes, property taxes, food, utilities, transportation) will also have to be factored into a decision.

Exhibit 1.2 Application of the *Guiding Principles of Good Tax Policy*

The *Guiding Principles of Good Tax Policy* can be applied to evaluate an existing tax rule or a proposed change. Here is an example of how the principles apply to a state's proposal to exempt college textbooks from sales tax.

Principle	Application	Result
Equity and fairness	Although all college students would pay no sales tax on their textbooks, the effect varies among students based on their ability to pay. This proposal provides tax savings not only to lower-income students but also to higher-income students who may not need the tax break to cover school costs. Also, higher-income students might buy full-price new books rather than lower-cost used books, resulting in larger tax savings.	Not fully met
Certainty	College textbooks can be identified, such as by looking at what is listed on a course syllabus.	Met
Convenience of payment	A sales tax exemption generally means that the tax is not owed at the time of purchase. If, instead, the exemption is structured for the student to pay the sales tax and apply for a refund later, convenience of payment would not be met.	Met
Effective tax administration	Sellers will have additional record keeping and reporting requirements to separate tax-exempt textbook sales from taxable sales. Some type of system is needed to prove that the buyer is a student purchasing a book for a college class. The state tax agency will incur additional time and costs in writing rules, modifying tax forms, and auditing compliance with the new rule.	Not met
Information security	If obtaining the exemption requires that students show proof to retailers that they are a student, there should be no need to provide a Social Security number. If students are required to claim the exemption with the state tax agency after purchasing the textbooks, the agency might request a student's Social Security number, which could increase the risk of identity theft.	Likely met
Simplicity	"Textbook" needs to be defined. The intent of the exemption is to benefit students. The seller needs to verify that the book is for use by a student for a class. For example, both students and nonstudents might buy a copy of *Romeo and Juliet*. Only the student purchasing it for a college class is entitled to the sales tax exemption. Complexity exists in the procedures needed to ensure that the exemption is used properly.	Not met
Neutrality	Students purchase textbooks because they are needed for class. The exemption is unlikely to change a student's behavior.	Met
Economic growth and efficiency	The exemption will reduce costs of attending college by a small amount. As a result, the change is unlikely to result in a greater number of college graduates (which might benefit the economy). Savings from not paying sales tax might be spent on other consumables. The impact on the economy is likely minor.	Met
Transparency and visibility	Students and textbook sellers are likely to be aware of the exemption because colleges will promote it as a reduction in the cost of attending college.	Met
Minimum tax gap	Students may abuse the rule by using the exemption for books that are not for class use. Nonstudents may abuse this rule by claiming they are college students.	Not met
Accountability to taxpayers	Were students and universities, particularly those funded by the state, aware of the textbook sales tax exemption proposal? Students and universities could provide information to legislators on whether there is a need for a sales tax exemption or if other financial support would be more helpful. Bookstores would want an opportunity to provide information on the compliance costs and challenges of the exemption.	More information needed
Appropriate government revenue	Existing data on how many textbooks are purchased enable the government to estimate how much tax revenues will decrease due to the new exemption.	Met

***Conclusion*:** Although the majority of the principles are met, the ones that are not met (effective tax administration, simplicity, and minimum tax gap) are significant. If lawmakers believe this tax exemption is necessary to help lower costs for college students, they should consider alternative means of achieving the goal that are less complex. For example, grants could be offered or increased for college students in need of financial assistance.

1-4a Property Taxes

Correctly referred to as **ad valorem taxes** because they are based on value, property taxes are a tax on wealth, or capital. As a result, they have much in common with estate taxes and gift taxes discussed later in the chapter. Although property taxes do not tax income, the income actually derived from the property (or the potential for any income) may be relevant if it affects the value of the property being taxed.

Property taxes fall into *two* categories: those imposed on real property (land and buildings) and those imposed on personal property (assets other than land and buildings). Both have added importance because they often generate a deduction for Federal income tax purposes (see Chapter 10).

Ad Valorem Taxes on Real Property

Property taxes on real property are used exclusively by states and their local subdivisions (such as cities, counties, and school districts). They represent a major source of revenue for *local* governments (and school districts).

How real property is defined can have an important bearing on which assets are subject to tax. This is especially true in jurisdictions that do not impose ad valorem taxes on personal property. Real property, or **realty**, generally includes real estate and any fixtures. A *fixture* is something so permanently attached to the real estate that its removal will cause irreparable damage. A built-in bookcase is likely a fixture, whereas a movable bookcase is not. Electrical wiring and plumbing become realty when they are installed in a building.

Here are some of the characteristics of ad valorem taxes on real property:

- Property owned by the Federal government is exempt from tax. In general, the same is true for property owned by state and local governments and by charitable organizations.
- Some states provide for lower valuations on property used for agriculture or other special uses (e.g., wildlife sanctuaries).
- States may have a homestead exemption, which makes some portion of the value of a personal residence exempt from tax.
- Lower taxes may apply to a residence owned by a taxpayer aged 65 or older.
- When non-income-producing property (e.g., a personal residence) is converted to income-producing property (e.g., a rental house), the appraised value may be increased.

The Big Picture

Example 4

Return to the facts of *The Big Picture* on p. 1-1. Why did the Walkers' property taxes decrease but those of the Carters increase?

A likely explanation is that one (or both) of the Walkers achieved senior citizen status, leading to a reduction of their property taxes. In the case of the Carters, the assessed value of their property might have increased due to property values increasing in their location. Or perhaps they made significant home improvements (e.g., kitchen/bathroom renovation or addition of a deck) that increased the value (tax base) of the home.

Ad Valorem Taxes on Personal Property

Personal property, or **personalty**, can be defined as all property that is not realty. There is a difference between how property is *classified* (realty or personalty) and how it is *used*. Both realty and personalty can be either business use or personal use property. Examples include a residence (realty that is personal use), an office building (realty that is business use), surgical instruments (personalty that is business use), and home furniture (personalty that is personal use).[16]

[16]The distinction, important for ad valorem and for Federal income tax purposes, often becomes confusing when personalty is referred to as "personal" property to distinguish it from "real" property. This designation does not give a complete picture of what is involved. The description "personal" residence, however, is clearer, because a residence can be identified as being realty. What is meant in this case is realty that is personal use property.

Personal property can also be classified as tangible property or intangible property. For ad valorem tax purposes, intangible personalty includes stocks, bonds, and various other securities (e.g., bank shares).

Here are some general rules related to ad valorem taxes on personal property:

- Generally, for individuals, vehicles (e.g., cars and boats) are the only non-realty personal use assets subject to property tax. The value of a vehicle is typically established by a schedule based on its age and make/model (a high-priced car versus a low-priced car). Usually, any vehicle property tax is assessed and collected along with vehicle license or registration fees.
- Generally, businesses are assessed property taxes on equipment and other tangible property, although many states do not tax inventory.
- A few states levy an ad valorem tax on intangibles such as stocks and bonds.

1-4b Transaction Taxes

Transaction taxes, imposed at the manufacturer's, wholesaler's, or retailer's level, cover a wide range of transfers. Transaction taxes can be assessed by any taxing authority (Federal, state, or local government). As the description implies, these taxes cover transfers of property and normally are determined by multiplying the value by a percentage rate.

Federal Excise Taxes

In general, Federal **excise taxes** cover fewer items than in the past. Congress has focused (and substantially increased) the Federal excise taxes on items such as tobacco products, fuel and gasoline sales, and air travel. Other Federal excise taxes include:

- Manufacturers' excise taxes on trucks, trailers, tires, firearms, sporting equipment, and coal and the gas guzzler tax on automobiles.[17]
- Alcohol taxes.
- Miscellaneous taxes (e.g., the tax on wagering and the tax on investment income of certain private colleges and universities).

When reviewing the list of both Federal and state excise taxes, recognize that these taxes may be trying to influence social behavior. For example, the gas guzzler tax is intended as an incentive for an individual to buy (and for the automobile companies to build) fuel-efficient cars.

State and Local Excise Taxes

Many state and local excise taxes parallel the Federal version. For example, all states tax the sale of gasoline, liquor, and tobacco products. However, the rates vary significantly. For gasoline products, for example, compare the 58.7 cents per gallon imposed by the Commonwealth of Pennsylvania with the 19.0 cents per gallon levied by the state of Arizona. For tobacco sales, contrast the 17.0 cents per pack of 20 cigarettes in effect in Missouri with the $4.35 per pack in the state of New York.

Other excise taxes found at some state and local levels include those on admission to amusement facilities, on the sale of playing cards, and on prepared foods. Some counties impose a transaction tax on the transfer of property that requires the recording of documents (e.g., real estate sales).

Over the last few years, two types of excise taxes imposed at the local level have become increasingly popular: the hotel occupancy tax and the rental car "surcharge." The hotel occupancy tax is called a transient occupancy tax (TOT) in some areas. This tax also can apply to short-term rentals of one's home or a room in the home (such as via Airbnb). Because they tax the visitor who cannot vote, they are a political windfall and are often used to finance special projects that generate civic pride (e.g., convention centers and state-of-the-art sports arenas). These levies can be significant, as demonstrated by Houston's hotel tax of 17 percent [6 percent (state) + 7 percent (city) + 2 percent (county) + 2 percent (sports authority)].

[17]The gas guzzler tax is imposed on the manufacturers of automobiles (both domestic and foreign) with fuel economy under 22.5 miles per gallon (mpg). For example, a 2021 Rolls-Royce Dawn gets about 14 mpg in combined city/highway driving and costs about $360,000. The gas guzzler tax on this vehicle is $5,400. The highest gas guzzler tax is $7,700, and the lowest is $1,000. § 4064.

General Sales Taxes

The distinction between an excise tax and a general **sales tax** is easy to make. One is restricted to a particular transaction (e.g., the 18.4 cents per gallon Federal excise tax on the sale of gasoline), whereas the other covers a multitude of transactions (e.g., a 5 percent tax on *all* retail sales). In actual practice, however, the distinction is not always that clear. Some states exempt certain items from the general sales taxes (e.g., groceries, medicines, and drugs). Also, sales tax rates can vary. Many states, for example, allow lower rates for the sale of agricultural equipment or prescription drugs or apply different rates (either higher or lower than the general rate) to the sale of automobiles.

A **use tax** is a complement to the sales tax and is assessed at the same rate as the sales tax. A use tax is owed on property purchased outside the state but used in the state. The purpose of a use tax is to prevent the avoidance of a sales tax. For example, if you purchase clothes online and are not charged sales tax but clothes are subject to sales tax in your state, you owe use tax on the purchase. State rules vary on how use tax is collected. Many states allow individuals to pay it along with their state income tax. Alaska, Delaware, Montana, New Hampshire, and Oregon do not impose sales or use taxes. There is no Federal general sales or use tax.

The Big Picture

Example 5

Return to the facts of *The Big Picture* on p. 1-1. The payment Travis made when he registered the car is probably a use tax.

When the car was purchased in another state, likely no (or a lesser) sales tax was levied. The current payment makes up for the amount of sales tax he would have paid had the car been purchased in his home state.

Ethics & Equity Making Good Use of Out-of-State Relatives

Marcus, a resident of Austin, Texas, has found the ideal gift for his spouse in celebration of their upcoming wedding anniversary—a $22,000 gold watch. However, Marcus is appalled at the prospect of paying the state and local sales tax of $1,815 (combined rate of 8.25 percent). So, he asks his aunt, a resident of Montana, to purchase the watch. The jewelry store lists the aunt as the buyer and ships the watch to her, with no sales tax owed on the transaction. Prior to the anniversary, Marcus receives the watch from his aunt. Is Marcus able to save $1,815 on the present for his spouse? What can go wrong?

Local general sales taxes, over and above state sales taxes, are common. It is not unusual to find taxpayers living in the same state but paying different general sales taxes due to the location of their residence.

Example 6

Pete and Sam both live in a state that has a general sales tax of 3%. Sam, however, resides in a city that imposes an additional general sales tax of 2%. Even though Pete and Sam live in the same state, one is subject to a rate of 3%, whereas the other pays a tax of 5%.

For various reasons, some jurisdictions will suspend the application of a general sales tax for a specified, brief time period. For example, a state may have a "sales tax holiday" in late summer for back-to-school clothing and supplies. Some states use sales tax holidays to encourage the purchase of energy-conserving appliances and hurricane preparedness items.

Severance Taxes

Severance taxes are transaction taxes that are based on the notion that the state has an interest in its natural resources (e.g., oil, gas, iron ore, or coal). Therefore, a tax is imposed when the natural resources are extracted. For some states, severance taxes can be a significant source of revenue.

1-4c Taxes on Transfers at Death

The right to transfer property or to receive property upon the death of the owner may be subject to estate and/or inheritance taxes. Consequently, such taxes fall into the category of excise taxes. An **estate tax** is levied on the estate of the decedent (it is a tax on the right to pass property at death). An **inheritance tax** is levied on the person receiving the property (the heir). The value of the property transferred provides the base for determining the amount of the tax.

The Federal government imposes only an estate tax. Some state governments, however, levy inheritance taxes, estate taxes, or both. Some states (e.g., Florida and Texas) levy neither tax.

Example 7

At the time of her death, Cari lived in a state that imposes an inheritance tax but not an estate tax. Amy, one of Cari's heirs, lives in the same state. Cari's estate is subject to the Federal estate tax, and Amy is subject to the state inheritance tax.

The Federal Estate Tax

The Revenue Act of 1916 incorporated the estate tax into the tax law. The tax was originally intended to prevent large concentrations of wealth from being kept in a family for many generations. Whether this objective has been accomplished is debatable. Like the income tax, estate taxes can be reduced through various planning procedures.

The gross estate includes property the decedent owned at the time of death.[18] It also includes property interests, such as life insurance proceeds paid to the estate. All property included in the gross estate is valued as of the date of death or, if the alternate valuation date is elected, six months later.[19]

Deductions from the gross estate in arriving at the taxable estate include funeral and administration expenses; certain taxes; debts of the decedent; casualty losses[20] incurred during the administration of the estate; transfers to charitable organizations; and, in some cases, the marital deduction. The *marital deduction* is available for amounts actually passing to a surviving spouse (a widow or widower).

Once the taxable estate has been determined and certain taxable gifts made by the decedent during life have been added to it, the estate tax can be computed. From this amount, various credits are subtracted to arrive at the tax, if any, that is due.[21] The most significant credit is the *unified transfer tax credit*. The main reason for this credit is to eliminate or reduce the estate tax liability for certain estates. For 2022, the credit exempts a tax base of up to $12,060,000, meaning that the vast majority of estates pass tax-free to the heirs.

Example 8

Jason made no taxable gifts before his death in 2022. If Jason's taxable estate amounts to $12,060,000 or less, no Federal estate tax is due because of the application of the unified transfer tax credit.

State Taxes on Transfers at Death

As noted earlier, some states levy an inheritance tax, an estate tax, or both. Typically, a state inheritance tax divides the heirs into classes based on their relationship to the decedent. The more closely related the heir, the lower the rates imposed and/or the greater the exemption allowed. Some states allow amounts passing to a surviving spouse to escape taxation.

[18]For further information on these matters, see *South-Western Federal Taxation: Corporations, Partnerships, Estates & Trusts*.

[19]See the discussion of the alternate valuation date in Chapter 14.

[20]For a definition of *casualty losses*, see the Glossary in Appendix C.

[21]For tax purposes, it is crucial to appreciate the difference between a deduction and a credit. A *credit* is a dollar-for-dollar reduction of tax liability. A *deduction*, however, provides a benefit only to the extent of the taxpayer's tax bracket. A taxpayer in a 50% tax bracket, for example, would need $2 of deductions to eliminate $1 of tax liability. In contrast, $1 of credit eliminates $1 of tax liability.

1-4d Gift Taxes

Like taxes on transfers at death, a **gift tax** is an excise tax levied on property transfers made during the owner's life and not at death. If the recipient pays the donor for the property (but at an amount less than its fair market value), the difference is a gift.

Example 9

Carl sells property worth $50,000 to his daughter for $1,000. Although property worth $50,000 has been transferred, only $49,000 represents a gift because this is the portion that was not paid for.

The Federal Gift Tax

First enacted in 1932, the Federal gift tax was intended to complement the estate tax. If lifetime transfers by gift were not taxed, it would be possible to avoid the estate tax and escape taxation entirely.

Only taxable gifts are subject to the gift tax. For this purpose, a taxable gift is measured by the fair market value of the property on the date of transfer less the *annual exclusion per donee* and, in some cases, less the *marital deduction*, which allows tax-free transfers between spouses. In 2022, each donor is allowed an annual exclusion of $16,000 for each donee ($15,000 in 2021).[22]

Example 10

On December 31, 2022, Yasmin (a widow) gives $16,000 to each of her four married children, their spouses, and her eight grandchildren. On January 2, 2023, she repeats the procedure.

Due to the annual exclusion, Yasmin has not made a taxable gift, although she transferred $256,000 [$16,000 (annual exclusion) × 16 (donees)] in 2022 and another $256,000 in 2023, for a total of $512,000 ($256,000 + $256,000).

A married couple may make a special election that allows one-half of the gift made by the donor-spouse to a third party to be treated as being made by the non-donor-spouse. This *gift splitting* effectively allows the annual exclusion to double.

The Big Picture

Example 11

Return to the facts of *The Big Picture* on p. 1-1. Although the value of the RV is not stated, it is likely to exceed the annual exclusion allowed of $60,000 [$15,000 (annual exclusion) × two donees (the Walkers) × two donors (the Carters)].

As a result, a taxable gift results, and a Form 709 (Gift Tax Return) must be filed. Whether any gift tax is due depends on what past taxable gifts the Carters have made and how much of their unified transfer tax credit (see the following discussion) is still available.

The gift tax and estate tax rate schedules are the same. The schedule is commonly referred to as the *unified transfer tax rate schedule*.

The Federal gift tax is *cumulative* in effect. What this means is that the tax base for current taxable gifts includes past taxable gifts. Although a credit is allowed for prior gift taxes, the result of adding past taxable gifts to current taxable gifts could force the donor into a higher tax bracket.[23] Like the Federal estate tax rates, the Federal gift tax rates are progressive (see Example 2 earlier in this chapter).

The unified transfer tax credit is available for all taxable gifts. As was the case with the Federal estate tax, the credit for 2022 is $4,769,800 (which covers taxable gifts up to $12,060,000) and for 2021 is $4,625,800 (which covers taxable gifts up to $11,700,000). There is, however, only one unified transfer tax credit, and it applies to both taxable

[22]The purpose of the annual exclusion is to avoid the need to report and pay a tax on *modest* gifts. Without the exclusion, the IRS could face a real problem of taxpayer noncompliance. The annual exclusion is indexed as the level of inflation warrants. The exclusion was $15,000 from 2018 to 2021, $14,000 from 2013 to 2017, and $13,000 from 2009 through 2012.

[23]For further information on the Federal gift tax, see *South-Western Federal Taxation: Corporations, Partnerships, Estates & Trusts*, Chapter 18.

gifts and the Federal estate tax. Once the unified transfer tax credit has been used up for Federal gift tax purposes, any transfers at death will be subject to the Federal estate tax.

Making lifetime gifts of property carries several tax advantages over passing the property at death. If income-producing property is involved (e.g., marketable securities and rental real estate), a gift may shift subsequent income to donees in a lower income tax bracket. If the gift involves property that is expected to appreciate in value (e.g., life insurance policies, real estate, and artwork), future increases in value will be assigned to the donee and will not be included in the donor's estate. And due to the annual exclusion ($16,000 per donee in 2022; $15,000 per donee in 2021), some of the gift can escape tax (with gift splitting, married donors can double the annual exclusion).

Neither the actual receipt of a gift nor an inheritance will cause income tax consequences to the donee or heir.

1-4e Income Taxes

Income taxes are levied by the Federal government, most states, and some local governments. Income taxes generally are imposed on individuals, corporations, and certain fiduciaries (estates and trusts). Most jurisdictions attempt to ensure the collection of income taxes by requiring pay-as-you-go procedures, including withholding requirements for employees and estimated tax payments for all taxpayers.

Federal Income Taxes

Exhibit 1.3 illustrates the formula for the Federal income tax imposed on individuals. This formula provides a framework for much of the text. Beginning with Chapter 3, each component of the formula is illustrated and explained.

Unlike its individual counterpart, the Federal corporate income tax is not progressive, but instead uses a flat tax rate of 21 percent. Also, it does not include the computation of adjusted gross income (AGI) and does not provide for the standard deduction or the deduction for qualified business income. As a result, a corporation's taxable income is the difference between gross income and deductions. While Chapters 3 through 19 cover

Exhibit 1.3 Formula for Federal Income Tax on Individuals

Income (broadly defined)		$xx,xxx
Less: Exclusions (income that is not subject to tax)		(x,xxx)
Gross income (income that is subject to tax)		$xx,xxx
Less: Certain deductions (usually referred to as deductions *for* adjusted gross income)		(x,xxx)
Adjusted gross income		$xx,xxx
Less: The greater of:		
Certain personal and investment deductions (referred to as *itemized deductions*)		
or		
The standard deduction (including any additional standard deduction)	(x,xxx)	
Less: Personal and dependency exemptions*	(x,xxx)	
Deduction for qualified business income**	(x,xxx)	
Taxable income		$xx,xxx
Tax on taxable income (see the Tax Tables and Tax Rate Schedules in Appendix A)		$ x,xxx
Less: Tax credits (including Federal income tax withheld and other prepayments of Federal income taxes)		(xxx)
Tax due (or refund)		$ xxx

*Exemption deductions are not allowed from 2018 through 2025.
**Only applies from 2018 through 2025.

the Federal income tax applicable to individuals, Chapter 20 discusses the Federal income tax rules that apply to corporations and partnerships.[24]

State Income Taxes

Almost all states impose an income tax on individuals.[25]

Here are some of the characteristics of state income taxes:

- With few exceptions, all states require some form of withholding procedures.
- Most states use as the tax base the income determination made for Federal income tax purposes. This is often referred to as the piggyback approach to state income taxation. Although the term *piggyback* does not lend itself to a precise definition, in this context, it means making use, for state income tax purposes, of what was done for Federal income tax purposes.
- Some states "decouple" from selected Federal tax changes passed by Congress. The purpose of the decoupling is to retain state revenue that would otherwise be lost. For example, some states do not allow "bonus depreciation" allowed for Federal tax purposes.
- Because of the tie-ins to the Federal return, a state may be notified of any changes made by the IRS upon audit of a Federal return (or vice versa).
- Most states allow a deduction for personal and dependency exemptions. Some states substitute a tax credit for a deduction.
- Many state income tax returns provide checkoff boxes for donations to various causes. Many are dedicated to medical research and wildlife programs, but special projects are not uncommon. For example, Wisconsin uses one for maintenance and operating costs of Lambeau Field (home of the Green Bay Packers). These checkoff boxes have been criticized as adding complexity to the returns and misleading taxpayers.[26]
- The objective of most states is to tax the income of residents and those who conduct business in the state (e.g., employees sent to the state to help a client or a professional athlete playing a game in the state).
- Most states allow their residents some form of tax credit for income taxes paid to other states.

The Big Picture

Example 12

Return to the facts of *The Big Picture* on p. 1-1. Travis will need to review the state income tax laws in each state he has clients to determine if he is subject to that state's tax on his consulting income earned in that state. If the income is subject to tax in another state as well as his home state, the home state might provide a credit to negate the double taxation.

- The due date for filing generally is the same as for the Federal income tax (for individuals, the fifteenth day of the fourth month following the close of the tax year; usually April 15 for calendar year taxpayers).
- Some states have occasionally instituted amnesty programs that allow taxpayers to pay back taxes (and interest) on unreported income with no (or reduced) penalty. In many cases, the tax amnesty has generated enough revenue to warrant the authorization of follow-up programs covering future years.[27] Amnesties usually include other taxes as well (e.g., sales, franchise, and severance).

---

[24] For an in-depth treatment of the Federal income tax as it affects corporations, partnerships, estates, and trusts, and owners or beneficiaries of these entities as well as sole proprietors, see *South-Western Federal Taxation: Corporations, Partnerships, Estates & Trusts*, Chapters 2 through 9, 12, and 20. See Chapters 6 and 9 for additional discussion of the deduction for qualified business income.

[25] Alaska, Florida, Nevada, South Dakota, Tennessee, Texas, Washington, and Wyoming do not have an individual income tax. New Hampshire imposes an individual income tax only on interest and dividends.

[26] Many taxpayers do not realize they are paying for the checkoff donation (usually with some of their income tax refund). Unlike the presidential election campaign fund available for Federal income tax purposes ($3 in this case), the contribution is *not made* by the government.

[27] Although the suggestion has been made, no comparable amnesty program has been offered for the Federal income tax. The IRS has, however, offered exemption from certain penalties for taxpayers who disclose offshore bank accounts and participation in certain tax shelters.

- Because many consumers do not pay state and local sales taxes on out-of-state purchases, state income tax returns in some states include a separate line for reporting any use tax that is due. As a result, the income tax return serves as a means of collecting use taxes.

Nearly all states have an income tax applicable to corporations. Other states have a franchise tax (discussed later in the chapter) that can be based in part on corporate income.

Local Income Taxes

Cities imposing an income tax include Baltimore, Cincinnati, Cleveland, Detroit, Kansas City (Missouri), New York, Philadelphia, and St. Louis. The application of a city income tax is not limited to local residents.

1-4f Employment Taxes

Employment taxes are a type of income tax imposed on employers and employees. We concentrate on the two major employment taxes: FICA (Federal Insurance Contributions Act—commonly referred to as the Social Security tax) and FUTA (Federal Unemployment Tax Act). Both taxes can be justified by social and public welfare considerations: FICA offers some measure of retirement security, and FUTA provides a modest source of income in the event of loss of employment.

These employment taxes come into play for employees (*not self-employed* individuals) if the particular work is covered under FICA or FUTA or both.[28]

FICA Taxes

The **FICA tax** rates and wage base have increased steadily over the years. It is difficult to imagine that the initial rate in 1937 was only 1 percent of the first $3,000 of covered wages. Thus, the maximum tax due was only $30.

The FICA tax has two components: Social Security tax (old age, survivors, and disability insurance) *and* Medicare tax (hospital insurance). The Social Security tax rate is 6.2 percent and generally does not change. The base amount usually increases each year. For 2022, the base amount is $147,000 ($142,800 for 2021).

The Medicare portion of FICA is applied at a rate of 1.45 percent and, unlike Social Security, is not subject to any dollar limitation. The Affordable Care Act (ObamaCare) imposes an additional 0.9 percent tax on earned income (including self-employment income) *above* $200,000 (single filers) or $250,000 (married filing jointly). Unlike the Social Security tax of 6.2 percent and the regular Medicare portion of 1.45 percent, an employer does not have to match the employees' 0.9 percent tax.

A spouse employed by another spouse is subject to FICA. However, children under the age of 18 who are employed in a parent's unincorporated trade or business are exempted.

The Big Picture

Example 13

Return to the facts of *The Big Picture* on p. 1-1. Presuming that April and Martin perform meaningful services for Travis (which the facts seem to imply), they are legitimate employees. April is not subject to Social Security tax because she is under the age of 18. However, Martin is 18 and needs to be covered. Furthermore, recall that Amy Carter is now working at a medical clinic and will likewise be subject to Social Security tax. Travis, as an independent contractor, is subject to self-employment tax.

[28]Chapter 13 includes additional coverage of employment taxes for employees, employers, and self-employed persons. See also Circular E, *Employer's Tax Guide*, issued by the IRS as Publication 15.

Taxpayers who are not employees (e.g., sole proprietors and independent contractors) may also be subject to Social Security taxes. Known as the self-employment tax, the rates are 12.4 percent for Social Security and 2.9 percent for Medicare, or twice that applicable to an employee. The additional 0.9 percent Medicare tax also covers situations involving high net income from self-employment. The Social Security tax is imposed on net self-employment income up to the annual base amount ($147,000 for 2022; $142,800 for 2021). The Medicare portion of the self-employment tax is not subject to any dollar limitation.

To help cover the government's cost of medical care, Congress enacted a special tax on investment income.[29] For this purpose, "investment income" is often referred to as "unearned income" because it is not generated by the performance of services. A tax of 3.8 percent is imposed on net investment income when a taxpayer's modified adjusted gross income (MAGI) exceeds certain threshold amounts.[30] The threshold amounts are $250,000 for married taxpayers and $200,000 for single taxpayers. Investment income generally includes passive-type income (e.g., rents, taxable interest, dividends, and capital gains). For further discussion, see Chapter 13 and the online appendix on the Affordable Care Act.

FUTA Taxes

The purpose of the **FUTA tax** is to provide funds the states can use to administer unemployment benefits. This leads to the somewhat unusual situation of one tax being handled by both Federal and state governments. This joint administration means that the employer must observe two sets of rules. State and Federal returns must be filed and payments made to both governmental units.

In 2022, FUTA is 6 percent on the first $7,000 of covered wages paid during the year to each employee. The Federal government allows a credit for FUTA paid (or allowed under a merit rating system) to the state. The credit cannot exceed 5.4 percent of the covered wages. Thus, the amount required to be paid to the Federal government could be as low as 0.6 percent (6.0% − 5.4%).

States reduce the unemployment tax on employers who experience stable employment, since the state pays less unemployment benefits. Thus, an employer with little or no employee turnover might find that the state rate drops to as low as 0.1 percent or, in some states, even to zero.

FUTA, unlike FICA, is paid entirely by the employer. A few states, however, levy a special tax on employees to provide either disability benefits or supplemental unemployment compensation or both.

1-4g Other U.S. Taxes

To complete the overview of the U.S. tax system, some missing links need to be covered that do not fit into the classifications discussed elsewhere in this chapter.

Federal Customs Duties

The tariff on imported goods,[31] also known as customs duties, together with excise taxes, provided most of the revenues needed by the Federal government during the nineteenth century. In view of present times, it is remarkable that tariffs and excise taxes alone paid off the national debt in 1835 and enabled the U.S. Treasury to pay a surplus of $28 million to the states.

In recent years, tariffs have served both as an instrument for carrying out protectionist policies and for generating revenue. By imposing customs duties on the importation of foreign goods that can be sold at lower prices, protectionists contend that the tariff thereby neutralizes the competitive edge held by the producer of the foreign goods. However, history shows that tariffs often lead to retaliatory action on the part of the nation or nations affected.

[29] Enacted as part of the Health Care and Education Reconciliation Act of 2010.

[30] MAGI is adjusted gross income (see Exhibit 1.3 and page 1 of Form 1040) plus any foreign income or excluded foreign housing costs. An online appendix covers the net investment income tax (NIIT) and other Affordable Care Act tax provisions.

[31] Less-developed countries that rely principally on one or more major commodities (e.g., oil or coffee) are prone to favor *export* duties.

Miscellaneous State and Local Taxes

Most states impose a **franchise tax** on corporations for the right to do business in the state.[32] The tax base used varies from state to state but most often is based on the capitalization of the corporation (either with or without certain long-term indebtedness).

Similar to the franchise tax are **occupational fees** that apply to various trades or businesses (e.g., a liquor store license; a taxicab permit; or a fee to practice a profession such as law, medicine, or accounting). Most of these are not significant revenue producers, and the fees are used to fund the costs of regulating the business or profession in the interest of the public good.

The Big Picture

Example 14

Return to the facts of *The Big Picture* on p. 1-1. Although the facts do not mention the matter, both Travis and Amy might owe occupation or license fees—Travis for engineering and Amy for nursing.

Concept Summary 1.2 provides an overview of the major taxes existing in the United States and specifies which political jurisdiction imposes them.

Concept Summary 1.2

Overview of Taxes in the United States

	Imposed by Jurisdiction		
Type of Tax	**Federal**	**State**	**Local**
Property taxes:			
Ad valorem on realty	No	Yes	Yes
Ad valorem on personalty	No	Yes	Yes
Transaction taxes:			
Excise	Yes	Yes	Few*
General sales	No	Most	Some
Severance	Yes**	Most	No
Estate	Yes	Some	No
Inheritance	No	Some	No
Gift	Yes	Few	No
Income taxes:			
Corporations	Yes	Most	Few
Individuals	Yes	Most	Few
Employment taxes:			
FICA	Yes	No	No
FUTA	Yes	Yes	No
Customs duties	Yes	No	No
Franchise taxes	No	Yes	No
Occupational taxes or fees***	Yes	Yes	Yes

* An example of a local excise tax is a tax on hotel occupancy, typically referred to as a transient occupancy tax (TOT).
** For Federal public lands and continental-shelf areas.
*** An example is a fee to operate a beauty salon or barbershop.

[32] Only five states do not impose a franchise tax (Michigan, Nevada, South Dakota, Washington, and Wyoming).

1-4h Proposed U.S. Taxes

The last two major reforms to the U.S. tax system were in 2017 [the Tax Cuts and Jobs Act (TCJA) of 2017] and in 1986 (the Tax Reform Act of 1986). Tax reform discussions over the past few decades also have included use of a consumption tax to replace all or a portion of the income tax or as a new additional tax. Consumption taxes considered include the flat tax, a national sales tax, and a value added tax. Federal tax reform discussions have also included adding a carbon tax or a financial transactions tax. A brief description of these types of taxes follows.

Flat Tax

The **flat tax**, as introduced in 1981 by economists Robert Hall and Alvin Rabushka of the Hoover Institution, is a form of a consumption tax. Their proposal achieves some of the administrative advantages of a value added tax (VAT) relative to a sales tax while also partially addressing concerns that consumption taxes impose a relatively heavier tax burden on lower-income taxpayers. It assesses a "flat" 19 percent tax on all businesses (corporate or otherwise)—identical to the VAT, except that wages, pension contributions, materials costs, and capital investments are deducted from the tax base. Individuals (or households) are assessed a 19 percent flat-rate tax on wages and pension benefits above an exemption of $25,500 for a family of four. No other income is taxable, and no other deductions are allowed. Over the past 35 years, the Hall-Rabushka proposal has served as the blueprint for a number of proposals to reform the Federal tax system.[33]

National Sales Tax

A **national sales tax** would operate similarly to most state sales taxes although the tax base would be larger. The rate would also be higher to generate the revenues needed to replace the Federal income tax.

A frequent proposal for a national sales tax, called the "Fair Tax," would tax all purchases, including food and medicine, real property, and many types of services, at approximately 23 percent. Exempt items include business expenses, used goods, and the costs of education. The Fair Tax would replace the income tax (both individual and corporate), payroll taxes (including the self-employment tax), and the gift and estate taxes. To help address the regressivity of the tax, many individuals would receive a monthly rebate to offset a portion of sales tax paid.

Value Added Tax

A **value added tax (VAT)** is imposed on the value added by each party in a production cycle. For example, a furniture maker is charged VAT on wood purchased to make the furniture. Customers are charged VAT when they buy the furniture. A system of credits results in the VAT ultimately only being paid by the final consumer. This form of VAT—a credit invoice VAT—is similar to a sales tax. It is viewed as more efficient than a sales tax because assessment throughout the production process better ensures collection of the tax. The credit invoice VAT is widely used throughout the world.

A VAT has been considered in the United States various times since the 1960s. In 1984, the Treasury Department released a three-volume tax reform report, with one volume devoted to the VAT.[34] In 2016, Congressman James Renacci (R-OH) introduced a proposal to replace the corporate income tax with a credit invoice VAT as part of his Simplifying America's Tax System (SATS) proposal.[35]

---

[33] Usually, the tax bill carries the number H.R. 1040. See R. E. Hall and A. Rabushka, *The Flat Tax*, Hoover Institution (2007).

[34] U.S. Treasury Department, *Tax Reform for Fairness, Simplicity, and Economic Growth: The Treasury Department Report to the President*, Volume 3, 1984.

[35] Tax Foundation, *Details and Analysis of Rep. Jim Renacci's Tax Reform Proposal*, July 14, 2016.

Global Tax Issues VAT in USA?

The United States is the only country in the OECD (Organization of Economic Cooperation and Development) that does not have a value added tax (VAT). Over 140 countries around the world use a VAT, with rates ranging from 5 percent to 27 percent.

Is the United States out of sync with most other countries by not having a VAT? One advantage of a VAT is that it provides a significant revenue source, allowing for lower individual and corporate income tax rates. Also, unlike the income tax, a VAT is "border-adjustable," meaning that a country can impose it on imports but not exports. These are some considerations for U.S. lawmakers in evaluating the economic effects of the U.S. tax system and tax reform options in a global perspective.

One challenge of implementing a VAT in the United States is that it is a regressive tax (it has a greater impact on lower-income taxpayers relative to higher-income taxpayers). As a result, adjustments need to be implemented to protect lower-income taxpayers (e.g., expanding the earned income tax credit and/or child tax credit; both occur in the SATS proposal). Another challenge is that the Treasury Department (and IRS) will have to learn how to implement and enforce the VAT.

Carbon Tax

A **carbon tax** aims to help reduce carbon emissions (i.e., greenhouse gases). The tax could be applied to fossil fuels based on their level of greenhouse gas emissions. Because a significant fossil fuel is gasoline, some people suggest a higher gasoline excise tax as a simple form of a carbon tax.

Financial Transaction Tax

A **financial transaction tax** can take many forms. For example, it could be imposed on the value of financial instruments purchased (e.g., stocks and bonds). It could be restricted in some way (e.g., only applying to high-frequency trading). It could be imposed on the value of bank assets. Because the tax base is quite large, the tax rate would likely be low, perhaps even less than 1 percent. The primary concern with this type of tax is the possible adverse effects on financial markets.

Space Flight Excise Tax

With the growth of commercial space flight activity and Sir Richard Branson and Jeff Bezos riding on rockets their companies (Virgin Galactic and Blue Origin, respectively) recently launched into space, Congress is evaluating whether to assess specific taxes on these commercial ventures. Just as there is already an excise tax on airline tickets, many think the same should apply to tickets for space flights. In 2021, Congressman Blumenauer (D-OR) announced the Securing Protections Against Carbon Emissions (SPACE) Tax Act proposal. This tax is also intended to help address the externalities of the emissions resulting from rocket launches.

1-5 Tax Administration

LO.5

Explain the administration of the tax law, including the audit process utilized by the IRS.

1-5a Internal Revenue Service

The responsibility for administering the Federal tax laws rests with the Treasury Department. The IRS is part of the Department of the Treasury and is responsible for enforcing the tax laws. The Commissioner of Internal Revenue is appointed by the President with the advice and consent of the Senate. The Commissioner is responsible for establishing policy and supervising the activities of the IRS. Here is the mission statement of the IRS:

> *Provide America's taxpayers top quality service by helping them understand and meet their tax responsibilities and enforce the law with integrity and fairness to all.*

1-5b The Audit Process

Selection of Returns for Audit

Only a small number of tax returns are audited each year. The overall audit rate for individuals is 0.2 percent. The audit rate for corporations is 0.3 percent. Keep in mind, however, that the probability for audit increases for higher-income taxpayers.[36]

Tax returns are selected for audit in different ways. A common technique for individuals is called information matching. For example, the IRS compares information returns it receives (e.g., a Form 1099 interest income statement from a bank related to an individual) to an individual's tax return. If the information is not reported correctly, the IRS sends a notice to the taxpayer indicating the problem and the additional tax owed. Another approach is done through computer scoring. This approach uses mathematical formulas and statistical sampling techniques to select tax returns that are most likely to contain errors and to provide significant amounts of additional tax revenues when audited. The mathematical formula produces what is called a Discriminant Function (DIF) score. It is the DIF score given to a particular return that may lead to its selection for audit. Periodically, the IRS updates the DIF components by auditing a random cross section of returns to determine the most likely areas of taxpayer noncompliance.

Although the IRS does not openly disclose the details of all of its audit selection techniques, here are some general comments about audit selection:

- Certain groups of taxpayers are subject to audit much more frequently than others. These groups include individuals with large amounts of gross income, self-employed individuals with substantial deductions, and taxpayers with prior tax deficiencies. The same is true for businesses that receive a large proportion of their receipts in cash (e.g., cafés and small service businesses) and thus have a high potential for tax avoidance.

Example 15

Jack owns and operates a liquor store on a cash-and-carry basis. Because all of Jack's sales are for cash, he might be a prime candidate for an audit by the IRS. Cash transactions are easier to conceal than those made on credit.

- If information returns (e.g., Form 1099 or Form W–2) are not in substantial agreement with reported income, an audit can be anticipated.
- If an individual's itemized deductions are in excess of averages established for various income levels, the probability of an audit is increased.
- Filing of a refund claim by the taxpayer may prompt an audit of the return.
- Information obtained from other sources (e.g., informants and news items) may lead to an audit.

The IRS pays rewards to persons who provide information leading to the discovery and punishment of those who violate the tax laws. The rewards may not exceed 30 percent of the taxes, fines, and penalties recovered.

Information Leading to an IRS Audit

Example 16

After 15 years of service, Rita is discharged by her employer, Dr. Benjamin Smith. Shortly thereafter, the IRS receives an anonymous letter stating that Dr. Smith keeps two separate sets of books and that the one used for tax reporting substantially understates his cash receipts.

[36] Internal Revenue Service, *Data Book 2020*, Table 17. Examination Coverage and Recommended Additional Tax After Examination, by Type and Size of Return, Tax Year 2018.

Information Leading to an IRS Audit

Example 17

During a divorce proceeding, it is revealed that Leo, a public official, kept large amounts of cash in a shoe box at home. This information is widely disseminated by the news media and comes to the attention of the IRS. Needless to say, the IRS is interested in knowing whether these funds originated from a taxable source and, if so, whether they were reported on Leo's income tax returns.

Types of Audits

Once a return is selected for audit, the taxpayer is notified by mail. If the issue involved is minor, the matter often can be resolved simply by correspondence (a **correspondence audit**) between the IRS and the taxpayer. For fiscal year 2020, approximately 73 percent of audits were handled via correspondence.[37]

Other examinations are generally classified as either office audits or field audits. An **office audit** usually is restricted in scope and is conducted in IRS offices. In contrast, a **field audit** involves an examination of numerous items reported on the return and is conducted at the taxpayer's location (or that of the taxpayer's representative).

The Big Picture

Example 18

Return to the facts of *The Big Picture* on p. 1-1. The audit of the Walkers by the IRS obviously was a correspondence type. The reason for the audit was probably triggered by a minor oversight by the Walkers, such as the omission of some interest or dividend income. The audit of the Carters, however, was more serious—probably a field or office type. Because the Federal audit followed a state audit that was productive (i.e., led to the assessment of a deficiency), there may have been an exchange of information between the two taxing authorities—see p. 1-16 in this chapter.

At the end of an audit, the examining agent issues a Revenue Agent's Report (RAR) that summarizes the findings. The RAR will result in a refund (the tax was overpaid), a deficiency (the tax was underpaid), or a no change (the tax was correct) finding. If during the course of an audit a special agent accompanies (or takes over from) the regular auditor, the IRS suspects fraud. In this case, the taxpayer should retain competent legal counsel.

Settlement Procedures

If an audit results in an assessment of additional tax and no settlement is reached with the IRS agent, the taxpayer may request an appeal within the IRS. The Independent Office of Appeals of the IRS is authorized to settle all disputes based on the *hazards of litigation* (the probability of favorable resolution of the disputed issue or issues if litigated). In some cases, a taxpayer may be able to obtain an overall reduction of the assessment or a favorable settlement of one or more disputed issues.

If a satisfactory settlement is not reached within the IRS, the taxpayer can litigate the case in the Tax Court, a Federal District Court, or the Court of Federal Claims. However, litigation is normally discouraged because of the legal costs involved and the uncertainty of the final outcome. Tax litigation considerations are discussed more fully in Chapter 2.

1-5c Statute of Limitations

A **statute of limitations** is a provision that requires any lawsuit to be brought within a reasonable period of time. Found at the state and Federal levels, such statutes cover a multitude of suits, both civil and criminal.

For the Federal income tax, two categories are involved, which cover time limits on the assessment of additional tax deficiencies by the IRS and time limits related to refund claims by taxpayers.

[37] Internal Revenue Service, *Data Book, 2020*, p. 34.

Assessment by the IRS

In general, the IRS may assess an additional tax liability against a taxpayer within *three years* of the filing of the income tax return. If the return is filed early, the three-year period begins to run from the due date of the return (usually April 15 for a calendar year individual taxpayer). If the taxpayer files the return late (i.e., beyond the due date), the three-year period begins to run on the date filed.

If a taxpayer omits an amount of gross income in excess of 25 percent of the gross income reported on the return, the statute of limitations is increased to six years.

Example 19

For 2022, Amin, a calendar year taxpayer, reported gross income of $400,000 on a timely filed income tax return. If Amin omitted more than $100,000 (25% × $400,000), the six-year statute of limitations would apply to the 2022 tax year.

The six-year provision on assessments by the IRS applies only to the omission of income; it does not cover other factors that might lead to an understatement of tax liability, such as overstatement of deductions and credits.

There is *no* statute of limitations on assessments of tax if *no return* is filed or if a *fraudulent* return is filed.

Limitations on Refunds

If a taxpayer believes that an overpayment of Federal income tax was made, a claim for refund should be filed with the IRS. A *claim for refund* is a request to the IRS that it return a tax overpayment to the taxpayer.[38]

A claim for refund generally must be filed within *three years* from the date the return was filed *or* within *two years* from the date the tax was paid, whichever is later. Income tax returns that are filed early are deemed to have been filed on the date the return was due.

1-5d Interest and Penalties

Interest rates are determined quarterly by the IRS based on the existing Federal short-term rate. Currently, the rates for tax refunds (overpayments) for individual taxpayers are the same as those applicable to assessments (underpayments). For the first quarter (January 1–March 31) of 2022, the rates were 3 percent for refunds and assessments.[39]

For assessments of additional taxes, the interest begins running on the unextended due date of the return. With refunds, however, no interest is allowed if the overpayment is refunded to the taxpayer within 45 days of the date the return is filed. For this purpose, returns filed early are deemed to have been filed on the due date.

In addition to interest, the tax law provides various penalties for lack of compliance by taxpayers. Some of these penalties are summarized as follows:

- For *failure to file* a tax return by the due date (including extension—see Chapter 3), a penalty of 5 percent per month up to a maximum of 25 percent is imposed on the amount of tax shown as due on the return. Any fraction of a month counts as a full month.
- A penalty for *failure to pay* the tax due as shown on the return is imposed in the amount of 0.5 percent per month up to a maximum of 25 percent. Again, any fraction of a month counts as a full month. During any month in which both the failure to file penalty and the failure to pay penalty apply, the failure to file penalty is reduced by the amount of the failure to pay penalty.

[38]Generally, an individual filing a claim for refund should use Form 1040X.

[39]Rev.Rul. 2021–24; the rates for the remainder of 2022 were not available when the text went to press.

Global Tax Issues — Outsourcing of Tax Return Preparation

The use of foreign nationals to carry out certain job assignments for U.S. businesses is an increasingly popular practice. Outsourcing activities such as telemarketing to India, for example, can produce the same satisfactory result as having the work done in the United States but at a lower cost.

Outsourcing is also being applied to the preparation of tax returns. This practice not only can be expected to continue but also is likely to increase in volume. Outsourcing tax return preparation does not violate Federal law and is compatible with accounting ethical guidelines as long as three safeguards are followed: First, the practitioner must make sure client confidentiality is maintained. Second, the practitioner must verify the accuracy of the work that has been outsourced. Third, the practitioner must inform clients, preferably in writing, when any third-party contractor is used to provide professional services.

Practitioners justify outsourcing as a means of conserving time and effort that can be applied toward more meaningful tax planning on behalf of their clients.

Example 20

Adam files his tax return 18 days after the due date of the return. Along with the return, he remits a check for $1,000, which is the balance of the tax he owed. Disregarding the interest element, Adam's total penalties are as follows:

Failure to pay penalty (0.5% × $1,000)		$ 5
Plus:		
Failure to file penalty (5% × $1,000)	$50	
Less failure to pay penalty for the same period	(5)	
Failure to file penalty		45
Total penalties		$50

Note that the penalties for one full month are imposed even though Adam was delinquent by only 18 days. Unlike the method used to compute interest, any part of a month is treated as a whole month.

- A *negligence* penalty of 20 percent is imposed if any of the underpayment was for intentional disregard of rules and Regulations without intent to defraud. The penalty applies to just that portion attributable to the negligence.

Example 21

Cindy underpaid her taxes in the amount of $20,000, of which $15,000 is attributable to negligence. Cindy's negligence penalty is $3,000 (20% × $15,000).

- Various penalties may be imposed in the case of *fraud*. Fraud involves specific intent on the part of the taxpayer to evade a tax. In the case of *civil* fraud, the penalty is 75 percent of the underpayment attributable to fraud. In the case of *criminal* fraud, the penalties can include large fines as well as prison sentences. The difference between civil and criminal fraud is one of degree. Criminal fraud involves the presence of willfulness on the part of the taxpayer. Also, the burden of proof, which is on the IRS in both situations, is more stringent for criminal fraud than for civil fraud. The negligence penalty is not imposed when the fraud penalty applies. For possible fraud situations, refer to Examples 16 and 17.

1-5e Tax Practice

A practitioner who is a member of a profession (e.g., public accounting or law) must abide by certain ethical standards. Furthermore, the Internal Revenue Code imposes penalties on Federal tax return preparers who violate identified acts and procedures.

LO.6

Evaluate some of the ethical guidelines involved in tax practice.

Ethical Guidelines

The American Institute of CPAs has issued its "Statements on Standards for Tax Services" (SSTS), dealing with CPAs engaged in tax practice. These pronouncements are *enforceable* as part of its Code of Professional Conduct. They include the following summarized provisions:

- Do not take questionable positions on a client's tax return in the hope the return will not be selected for audit by the IRS. Any positions taken should be supported by a good-faith belief that they have a realistic possibility of being sustained if challenged. The client should be fully advised of the risks involved and of the penalties that will result if the position taken is not successful.
- A practitioner can use a client's estimates if they are reasonable under the circumstances. If the tax law requires receipts or other verification, the client should be so advised. In no event should an estimate be given the appearance of greater accuracy than is the case. For example, an estimate of $1,000 should not be deducted on a return as $999.
- Every effort should be made to answer questions appearing on tax returns. A question need not be answered if the information requested is not readily available, the answer is voluminous, or the question's meaning is uncertain. The failure to answer a question on a return cannot be justified on the grounds that the answer could prove disadvantageous to the taxpayer.
- Upon learning of an error on a past tax return, advise the client to correct it. Do not, however, inform the IRS of the error. If the error is material and the client refuses to correct it, consider withdrawing from the engagement. This will be necessary if the error has a carryover effect and prevents the current year's tax liability from being determined correctly.

Statutory Penalties Imposed on Tax Return Preparers

In addition to ethical constraints, a tax return preparer may be subject to specific penalties, including the following:

- Penalty for understatement of a tax liability based on a position that lacks substantial authority. If the position has a reasonable basis, the penalty can be avoided by disclosing it on the return.
- Penalty for any willful attempt to understate taxes. This usually results when a preparer disregards or makes no effort to obtain pertinent information from a client.
- Penalty for failure to exercise due diligence in determining eligibility for, or the amount of, an earned income tax credit, the child tax credit, or the American opportunity tax credit.
- Various penalties involving procedural matters. Examples include failing to furnish the taxpayer with a copy of the return, endorsing a taxpayer's refund check, failing to sign the return as a preparer, failing to furnish one's identification number, and failing to keep copies of returns or maintain a client list. The identification number required of preparers of most Federal tax returns is the **Preparer Tax Identification Number (PTIN)**. A PTIN is required by all persons who are paid for preparing or assisting in preparing all or substantially all of a Federal tax return.[40]

Example 22

In a few months, Jaden, an accounting major at State University, will start an internship at Nguyen & Associates, CPAs. He will assist other employees by organizing and analyzing client data for completeness, entering client information into the tax preparation software program used by the firm, and comparing results to the prior year's return. Jaden will not sign any tax returns.

Jaden will need to obtain a PTIN from the IRS because he is assisting in the preparation of the returns. If, instead, Jaden were only entering data provided by his colleagues and making copies, and not exercising any discretion or independent judgment regarding client tax information, he would not need a PTIN.[41]

[40] § 6109(a)(4). Also see IRS website on PTINs that includes an online tool to obtain or annually renew a PTIN (**rpr.irs.gov/datamart/mainMenuUSIRS.do**).

[41] § 6109(a)(4) and Reg. §§ 1.6109–2(d) and (g).

1-6 Understanding the Federal Tax Law

LO.7

Classify tax rules based on their possible economic, social, equity, and political reasons for inclusion in a particular tax system.

The Federal tax law reflects the three branches of our Federal government. It is a mixture of laws passed by Congress, explanations provided by the Treasury Department and the Internal Revenue Service (IRS), and interpretation of the law by the courts. Anyone who has attempted to work with this vast amount of information is familiar with its complexity. For the person who has to sift through this information to find the solution to a tax problem, it is good to know that there are reasons behind the law. Knowing these reasons is the first step toward understanding the Federal tax law.

The *primary objective* of any tax system is to raise the revenue needed to fund government operations. Although the fiscal needs of the government are important, other considerations (economic, social, equity, and political factors) also play a significant role. The Treasury Department, the IRS, and the courts also have significant impacts on the evolution of Federal tax law. The remainder of the chapter focuses on these topics. While the discussion focuses on the Federal tax system, it also applies to any level of government that imposes taxes.

1-6a Revenue Needs

Raising revenues to fund the cost of government operations is the key factor in structuring a tax system. In a perfect world, taxes raised by the government would equal the expenses incurred by government operations. However, this goal is rarely achieved by the U.S. government, but is typically achieved by state and local governments that may face restrictions on borrowing.

When enacting tax legislation, a deficit-conscious Congress often has been guided by the concept of **revenue neutrality** so that changes neither increase nor decrease the net revenues received by the government. With revenue-neutral legislation, there are likely to be both "winners" (taxpayers who see a reduction in taxes paid) and "losers" (taxpayers who see an increase in taxes paid).

In addition to making revenue-neutral changes in the tax law, several other procedures can be taken to mitigate any revenue loss. When tax reductions are involved, the full impact of the legislation can be phased in over a period of years. Or as an alternative, the tax reduction can be limited to a period of years. When the period expires, the prior law is reinstated through a **sunset provision**. For example, at times, Congress has allowed more rapid depreciation treatment for a specified number of years. These sunset (or temporary) provisions move legislation toward revenue neutrality (even though it is not achieved).

1-6b Economic Considerations

Sometimes tax legislation is designed to help control the economy or encourage certain activities and businesses.

Control of the Economy

Congress has used the tax depreciation rules as a means of controlling the economy. Theoretically, shorter asset lives and accelerated methods should encourage additional investment in depreciable property acquired for business use. On the other hand, longer asset lives and use of straight-line depreciation should discourage capital outlays. Congress also uses incentives such as bonus depreciation to stimulate the economy when needed.

A change in tax rates has a more immediate impact on the economy. With lower tax rates, taxpayers retain money that can be used for other purposes (e.g., purchases or savings). If, however, Congress is using the concept of revenue neutrality, these rate reductions may be offset by a reduction or elimination of deductions or credits. As a result, lower tax rates do not always mean lower taxes.

Encouragement of Certain Activities

Congress uses the tax law to encourage certain types of economic activity or segments of the economy. For example, certain research and development expenditures may generate a tax credit that reduces the taxpayer's tax liability. Inventions are also encouraged by tax law. Under certain conditions, the sale of a patent results in long-term capital gain treatment.

Part of the tax law addresses the nation's energy policy—in terms of both our reliance on carbon-based fuels and the need to ease the problem of climate change. For example, a tax credit is available for installation of solar and small wind energy equipment. Residential energy credits are available for home improvements that conserve energy or make its use more efficient (e.g., solar water heaters). Ecological considerations explain why pollution control facilities can be amortized over 60 months (rather than over the 39-year period for most buildings).

Is saving desirable for the economy? Saving can lead to capital formation, making funds available to finance home construction and industrial expansion. The tax law encourages saving by giving private retirement plans preferential treatment. Besides contributions to certain Individual Retirement Accounts (IRAs) and Keogh (H.R. 10) plans being deductible, income from the contributions accumulates tax-free until it is withdrawn.

Encouragement of Certain Industries

Historically, agricultural activities have been favored under Federal tax law. Among the benefits are the election to expense rather than capitalize certain soil and water conservation expenditures and fertilizers and the election to defer the recognition of gain on the receipt of crop insurance proceeds.

The tax law favors the development of natural resources by permitting the use of percentage depletion and a write-off (rather than a capitalization) of certain exploration costs. The railroad and banking industries also receive special tax treatment under Federal tax law.

Encouragement of Small Business

Small business development is also encouraged under the tax law. For example, the shareholders of a small business corporation can make an election that allows the profits (or losses) of the corporation to flow through to its shareholders, avoiding the corporate income tax.[42] Another provision allows non-corporate shareholders of certain small corporations to exclude from income their gain from the sale of the stock if held over five years.

1-6c Social Considerations

Some provisions of the Federal tax law, particularly those dealing with individuals, can be explained by social considerations. Here are some notable examples:

- Certain benefits provided to employees through accident and health plans financed by employers are nontaxable to employees. It is socially desirable to encourage these plans because they provide medical benefits in the event of an employee's illness or injury. In addition, insurance companies are paying for these benefits (rather than the government).
- Most premiums paid by an employer for group term insurance covering the life of the employee are nontaxable to the employee. Life insurance proceeds (which are also nontaxable) provide funds to help the family unit adjust to the loss of wages caused by the employee's death.
- A contribution made by an employer to a qualified pension or profit sharing plan for an employee may receive special treatment. The contribution and any income it generates are not taxed to the employee until the funds are distributed. This arrangement also benefits the employer by allowing a tax deduction for the contribution to the qualified plan. Private retirement plans are encouraged to supplement any Social Security payments.[43]

[42]Known as the S election, it is discussed in Chapter 20.

[43]The same rationale explains the availability of similar arrangements for self-employed persons (e.g., the H.R. 10, or Keogh, plan). See Chapter 19.

- A deduction is allowed for contributions to qualified charities. The deduction shifts some of the financial and administrative burden of socially desirable programs from the public (the government) to the private sector.
- A tax credit is allowed for amounts spent to furnish care for dependents to enable the taxpayer to work. A credit for employers who incur certain child care expenses assists employees indirectly.
- To encourage taxpayers to join the workforce even though their wages may be low, an earned income tax credit can be claimed. The credit varies depending on the number of qualifying children and the level of wages earned.
- Certain credits are made available to individuals aged 65 and older and those with disabilities. Credits also are allowed to businesses that incur expenditures to make their facilities more accessible to the disabled.
- Various tax credits, deductions, and exclusions are designed to encourage taxpayers to obtain additional education.[44]
- A tax deduction is not allowed for certain expenses deemed to be contrary to public policy. Expenses not allowed include fines, penalties, illegal kickbacks, bribes to government officials, and gambling losses in excess of gains. In addition, any business expense (including attorney fees) related to sexual harassment or abuse is not deductible if the settlement or payment is subject to a nondisclosure agreement.

1-6d **Equity Considerations**

The concept of equity (or fairness) is relative. One measure of equity is whether a tax is *regressive or progressive*. The determination is made by calculating the percentage of a taxpayer's income that is used to pay a tax. As noted earlier, the Federal income tax is progressive. In contrast, the gasoline excise tax is regressive.

Example 23

Hanna and Lori are single taxpayers living in the same state. Hanna has income of $100,000, and Lori has income of $10,000. Assume that Hanna pays $5,000 in state income taxes while Lori pays only $100. The state income tax represents 5% of Hanna's income but only 1% of Lori's income. Because the higher-income taxpayer (Hanna) devotes a larger percentage of her income to pay the tax relative to a lower income taxpayer (Lori), this state income tax is *progressive* in its effect on taxpayers.

Alternatively, assume that Hanna and Lori each purchase the same quantity of gasoline during the year and each pays gasoline excise tax of $200. This tax represents less than 0.1% of Hanna's income but 2% of Lori's income. Because the lower-income taxpayer (Lori) devotes a larger percentage of her income to pay the tax relative to a higher-income taxpayer (Hanna), the gasoline excise tax is *regressive* in its effect on taxpayers.

Lawmakers and others often consider whether a tax change is progressive or regressive to understand its impact on taxpayers and whether the change should be made. If a tax represents the same percentage of the income of all taxpayers, it is a *proportional* tax.

Example 24

Eduardo and Sanjay are single taxpayers living in the same state. Eduardo has income of $50,000 and pays $1,500 in state taxes. Sanjay has income of $20,000 and pays $600 in state taxes. In this case, Eduardo and Sanjay are devoting the same percentage of their income to the state tax (3%), making the tax *proportional* in terms of the effect it has on taxpayers.

The concept of equity also appears in tax provisions that alleviate the effect of multiple taxation and postpone the recognition of gain when the taxpayer lacks the ability or wherewithal to pay the tax. Provisions that mitigate the effect of the application of the annual accounting period concept and help taxpayers cope with the eroding results of inflation also reflect equity considerations.

[44]These provisions can also be justified under the category of economic considerations because a better-educated workforce carries a positive economic impact.

Alleviating the Effect of Multiple Taxation

Equity considerations can explain the Federal tax treatment of certain income from foreign sources. Because double taxation results when the same income is subject to both foreign and U.S. income taxes, the tax law permits the taxpayer to choose between a credit and a deduction for the foreign taxes paid.

The Wherewithal to Pay Concept

The **wherewithal to pay** concept recognizes the inequity of taxing a transaction when the taxpayer lacks the means (i.e., funds) to pay the tax. This concept is typically applied to transactions where the taxpayer's economic position has not changed significantly.

An illustration of the wherewithal to pay concept is the tax treatment of an involuntary conversion. An involuntary conversion occurs when property is destroyed by a casualty (e.g., a fire or hurricane) or taken by a public authority through condemnation (e.g., taking land to build a new road). If gain results from the conversion, it is deferred if the taxpayer replaces the property within a specified period of time.

Example 25

Some of the pasture land belonging to Ron, a rancher, is condemned by the state for use as a game preserve. The condemned pasture land cost Ron $120,000, but the state pays him $150,000 (its fair market value). Shortly thereafter, Ron buys more pasture land for $150,000.

In Example 25, Ron has a realized gain of $30,000 [$150,000 (condemnation award) − $120,000 (cost of land)]. It would be inequitable to force Ron to pay a tax on this gain for two reasons. First, without selling the property acquired (the new land), Ron does not have the funds to pay the tax. Second, his economic position has not changed (i.e., he still owns pasture land worth $150,000). If, however, the taxpayer's economic position changes in any way, tax consequences may result.

Example 26

Assume the same facts as in Example 25, except that Ron reinvests only $140,000 of the award in new pasture land. Now Ron has a taxable gain of $10,000. Instead of ending up with only replacement property, Ron has $10,000 in cash.

Mitigating the Effect of the Annual Accounting Period Concept

All taxpayers must report their taxable income to the Federal government at regular intervals. The accounting period used to report taxable income (and settle any tax liability) is one year. Referred to as the annual accounting period concept, its effect is to divide each taxpayer's life, for tax purposes, into equal annual intervals.

The annual accounting period concept can lead to different tax treatment for taxpayers who are in the same economic position. Consider the following example.

Example 27

José and Alicia, both sole proprietors, showed the following results during the past three years:

	Profit (or Loss)	
Year	**José**	**Alicia**
2020	$50,000	$150,000
2021	60,000	60,000
2022	60,000	(40,000)

Although José and Alicia have the same total profit of $170,000 over the three-year period, the annual accounting period concept places Alicia at a definite disadvantage for tax purposes. The net operating loss (NOL) deduction offers Alicia some relief by allowing her to carry forward (but not back) some or all of her 2022 loss to future years. With a net operating loss carryforward, Alicia may apply her 2022 loss to future years' profits (with certain limitations; see Chapter 7).

The reasoning used to support the net operating loss deduction also can explain the special treatment the tax law accords to excess capital losses and excess charitable contributions.[45] Carryback and carryover procedures help mitigate the effect of limiting a loss or a deduction to the accounting period in which it was realized. Using these procedures, a taxpayer can salvage a loss or a deduction that might otherwise be lost.

The installment method of recognizing gain on the sale of property allows a taxpayer to spread tax consequences over the payout period.[46] The installment method is supported by the wherewithal to pay concept; recognition of gain corresponds to the collection of the cash received from the sale of the property. The tax consequences match the seller's ability to pay the tax.

Coping with Inflation

Because of the progressive nature of the income tax, a wage adjustment to compensate for inflation could place the employee in a higher income tax bracket. Known as *bracket creep*, its overall impact is an erosion of purchasing power. Congress recognizes this problem and adjusts various income tax components, such as tax brackets, standard deduction amounts, and a wide variety of other items, through an indexation procedure. **Indexation** is based on the change in the chained consumer price index over the prior year.

1-6e Political Considerations

A large segment of the Federal tax law is made up of statutory provisions. Because these statutes are enacted by Congress, political considerations often influence tax law. The effect of political considerations on the tax law includes special interest legislation, political expediency situations, and state and local government influences.

Special Interest Legislation

There is no doubt that certain provisions of the tax law can largely be explained by the political influence some groups have had on Congress. For example, prepaid subscription and dues income is not taxed until earned, whereas prepaid rents are taxed to the landlord in the year received. This exception was created because certain organizations (e.g., the American Automobile Association) convinced Congress that special tax treatment was needed for multi-year dues and subscriptions.

Another provision, sponsored by a senator from Georgia, suspended the import duties on ceiling fans. The nation's largest seller of ceiling fans is Atlanta-based Home Depot.

Although some special interest legislation can be justified on economic or social grounds, in most cases, it cannot. It is, however, an inevitable product of our political system.

Political Expediency Situations

Various tax changes can be tied to the shifting moods of the American public. That Congress is sensitive to popular feelings is an accepted fact. As a result, certain provisions of the tax law can be explained by the political climate at the time they were enacted.

Measures that deter more affluent taxpayers from obtaining so-called preferential tax treatment have always had popular appeal and, consequently, the support of Congress. Tax provisions like the imputed interest rules and the limitations on the deductibility of interest on investment indebtedness affect affluent taxpayers directly. More subtle are provisions that phase out tax breaks as income rises. These phaseouts are often called *stealth taxes* because the effects are *indirect* (and the taxpayer might not be aware of

[45]The tax treatment of these items is discussed in Chapters 7, 10, and 16.

[46]Under the installment method, each payment received by the seller represents both a recovery of capital (the nontaxable portion) and profit from the sale (the taxable portion). The tax rules governing the installment method are discussed in Chapter 18.

them). The tax law contains several of these phaseout rules. Examples include the phaseout of the child tax credit and education tax credits.

State and Local Government Influences

Political considerations played a major role in the nontaxability of interest received on state and local obligations. Somewhat less apparent has been the influence state law has had in shaping our present Federal tax law. Such was the case with community property systems. The nine states with community property systems are Arizona, California, Idaho, Louisiana, Nevada, New Mexico, Texas, Washington, and Wisconsin. The rest of the states are common law jurisdictions.[47] The difference between common law and community property systems centers around the property rights possessed by married persons. In a common law system, each spouse owns whatever each earns. Under a community property system, one-half of the earnings of each spouse is considered owned by the other spouse.

Example 28

Adam and Fran are married, and their only income is the $80,000 annual salary Adam receives. If they live in New Jersey (a common law state), the $80,000 salary belongs to Adam. If, however, they live in Arizona (a community property state), the $80,000 is divided equally, in terms of ownership, between Adam and Fran.

At one time, the tax position of the residents of community property states was so advantageous that many common law states adopted community property systems. Needless to say, the political pressure placed on Congress to correct the disparity in tax treatment was considerable. To a large extent, this was accomplished in the Revenue Act of 1948, which extended many of the community property tax advantages to residents of common law jurisdictions.

Congress accomplished this by allowing married taxpayers to file joint returns and compute their tax liability as if one-half of the income had been earned by each spouse. This result is automatic in a community property state because half of the income earned by one spouse belongs to the other spouse. The income-splitting benefits of a joint return are now incorporated as part of the tax rates applicable to married taxpayers. See Chapter 3.

LO.8

Explain the role played by the IRS and the courts in the evolution of the Federal tax system.

1-6f Influence of the Internal Revenue Service

The IRS has exerted its influence in many areas of the tax law. As the protector of the national revenue, the IRS has been instrumental in securing the passage of legislation designed to curtail aggressive tax avoidance practices (i.e., closing *tax loopholes*). In addition, the IRS has sought and obtained law changes to make its job easier (to attain administrative feasibility).

The IRS as Protector of the Revenue

Many provisions in the tax law resulted from the direct efforts of the IRS to prevent taxpayers from exploiting a tax loophole. Working within the letter of existing laws, ingenious taxpayers and their advisers devise techniques that accomplish indirectly what cannot be accomplished directly. As a result, Congress passes laws to close the loopholes that taxpayers have located and exploited.

In addition, Congress has passed laws that enable the IRS to make adjustments based on the substance of a transaction (rather than the form chosen by the taxpayer). For example, the IRS can make adjustments to a taxpayer's method of accounting when the method used by the taxpayer does not *clearly reflect income*.[48]

[47] In Alaska, spouses can choose to have the community property rules apply. Otherwise, property rights are determined under common law rules.

[48] See Chapter 18.

Example 29

Tran owns and operates a clothing distribution business with over $26,000,000 of annual gross receipts. The merchandise acquired is charged to the purchases account and written off (expensed) for tax purposes in the year of acquisition. Since this procedure does not clearly reflect income, it would be appropriate for the IRS to require that Tran establish and maintain an ending inventory account.

Administrative Feasibility

Some tax laws are created to simplify the task of the IRS in collecting the revenue and administering the law. As to collecting revenue, the IRS long ago realized the importance of placing taxpayers on a pay-as-you-go basis. Withholding procedures apply to wages, but the tax on other types of income may have to be paid via quarterly estimated payments. The IRS has been instrumental in convincing the courts that accrual basis taxpayers should, in most cases, pay taxes on prepaid income in the year received and not when earned. The approach may be contrary to generally accepted accounting principles, but prepayment is consistent with the wherewithal to pay concept.

To help the IRS collect revenues when due, Congress has passed many provisions that impose interest and penalties on taxpayers if they don't comply with the tax law. Provisions such as the penalties for failure to pay a tax or to file a return that is due, the negligence penalty for intentional disregard of rules and Regulations, and various penalties for civil and criminal fraud are intended to encourage taxpayers to comply with the tax law.

The audit process conducted by the IRS is key to an effective administration of our tax system. To carry out this function, the IRS is aided by provisions that reduce the chance of taxpayer error or manipulation, thus simplifying the audit effort. For example, by increasing the standard deduction amount, the audit function is simplified because fewer returns with itemized deductions need to be checked.[49]

1-6g Influence of the Courts

In addition to interpreting statutory provisions and the administrative pronouncements issued by the Treasury Department and the IRS, the Federal courts have influenced tax law in two other ways.[50] First, the courts have developed a number of judicial concepts and doctrines that help guide how tax provisions are applied. Second, certain key decisions have led to changes in the Internal Revenue Code.

Judicial Concepts and Doctrines Relating to Tax

A leading tax concept developed by the courts deals with the interpretation of statutory tax provisions that operate to benefit taxpayers. The courts have decided that these relief provisions are exceptions to general tax rules so they should be applied narrowly. If a taxpayer wants a relief provision to apply, the taxpayer has the responsibility to meet the provision's requirements (i.e., no exceptions).

The *arm's length* concept is applied in dealings between related parties. Transactions may be tested by asking this question: Would unrelated parties have handled the transaction in the same way?

Example 30

Matt, the sole shareholder of Silver Corporation, leases property to the corporation for a yearly rent of $60,000. To test whether the corporation should be allowed a rent deduction for this amount, the IRS and the courts will apply the arm's length concept. Would Silver Corporation have paid $60,000 a year in rent if it had leased the same property from an unrelated party (rather than from Matt)?

continued

[49] For a discussion of the standard deduction, see Chapter 3. The same justification was given by the IRS when it proposed to Congress the $100 limitation on personal casualty and theft losses. Imposition of the limitation eliminated many casualty and theft loss deductions and, as a consequence, saved the IRS considerable audit time. Later legislation, in addition to retaining the $100 feature, generally limits deductible losses to those in Federally declared disaster areas. In addition, only losses in excess of 10% of a taxpayer's adjusted gross income are allowed. See Chapter 7.

[50] A great deal of case law is devoted to ascertaining congressional intent. The courts, in effect, ask: What did Congress have in mind when it enacted a particular tax provision?

Suppose it is determined that an unrelated third party would have charged an annual rent for the property of only $50,000. Under these circumstances, Silver Corporation will be allowed a deduction of only $50,000. The other $10,000 it paid for the use of the property represents a nondeductible dividend. Accordingly, Matt will be treated as having received rent income of $50,000 and dividend income of $10,000.

A judicial doctrine that must be considered in some transactions is the *substance over form* doctrine. Here, no matter how a transaction is structured, the actual substance of how the transaction is carried out controls.

Example 31

Gold Corporation hired Adam to work as its bookkeeper for six months while the regular bookkeeper is on sick leave. This is a full-time position, and Adam reports to Gold's CFO who directs his assignments. Gold gave Adam a contract that states he is not an employee of Gold, but is instead an independent contractor. Despite the form saying Adam is not an employee, the substance of what he does and the relationship between Gold and Adam will control Adam's employment designation for tax purposes.

Judicial Influence on Statutory Provisions

Some court decisions have been so important that Congress incorporated them into the Internal Revenue Code. For example, many years ago the courts found that stock dividends distributed to the shareholders of a corporation were not taxable as income. This result was largely accepted by Congress, and the Code was modified to reflect the court's position.

On occasion, however, Congress reacts negatively to judicial interpretations of the tax law.

Example 32

Nora leases unimproved real estate to Wade for 20 years. At a cost of $400,000, Wade erects a building on the land. The building is worth $150,000 when the lease terminates and Nora takes possession of the property.

Does Nora have any income either when the improvements are made or when the lease terminates? In a landmark decision, a court held that Nora must recognize income of $150,000 upon the termination of the lease.

Congress believed that the result reached in Example 32 was not consistent with the wherewithal to pay concept. As a result, the tax law was changed to provide that a landlord does not recognize any income either when the improvements are made (unless made in lieu of rent) or when the lease terminates.[51]

1-6h Summary

In addition to raising revenues, other factors have influenced the development of Federal tax law:

- *Economic considerations.* Congress uses the tax law to help regulate the economy and encourage certain activities and types of businesses.
- *Social considerations.* The tax law has been used to encourage (or discourage) certain socially desirable (or undesirable) practices.
- *Equity considerations.* The tax law can be designed to alleviate the effect of multiple taxation, recognize the wherewithal to pay concept, mitigate the effect of the annual accounting period concept, and recognize the eroding effect of inflation.
- *Political considerations.* Some tax law represents special interest legislation, reflects political expediency, or illustrates the effect of state and local law.
- *Influence of the IRS.* Laws are enacted to aid the IRS in the collection of revenue and the administration of the tax law.
- *Influence of the courts.* Court decisions have established a body of judicial concepts relating to tax law and have, on occasion, led Congress to enact laws to either clarify or negate their effect.

These factors help us understand how tax law develops (and why some provisions exist). We also must learn to work with the tax law, which is the subject of Chapter 2.

[51] *M.E. Blatt Co. v. U.S.*, 305 U.S. 267 (1938) and § 109.

Refocus on The Big Picture

Family and Taxes—A Typical Year

The explanation given for the difference in the ad valorem property taxes—the Carters' increase and the Walkers' decrease—seems reasonable (see Example 4). It is not likely that the Carters' increase was solely due to a *general* upward assessment in valuation, because the Walkers' taxes on their residence (located nearby) dropped. More business use of the Carters' residence (presuming that Travis conducts his consulting practice from his home) might be responsible for the increase, but capital improvements appear to be a more likely cause.

The imposition of the use tax when Travis registered the new automobile illustrates one of the means by which a state can preclude the avoidance of its sales tax (see Example 5).

When gifts between family members are material in amount (e.g., an RV) and exceed the annual exclusion, a gift tax return needs to be filed (see Example 11). Even though no gift tax may be due because of the availability of the unified transfer tax credit, the filing of a return starts the running of the statute of limitations.

The Carters must recognize that some of their income is subject to income taxes in more than one state and take advantage of whatever relief is available to mitigate the result of double taxation (see Example 12).

Employment within and by the family group (e.g., children, other relatives, and domestics) has become a priority item in the enforcement of Social Security tax and income tax withholdings. Thus, the Carters must be aware of the need to cover their son, Martin (see Example 13).

Because of the double audit (i.e., both state and Federal) and the deficiency assessed, the Carters need to make sure that future returns do not contain similar errors (see Example 18). As the text suggests, taxpayers with prior deficiencies are among those whose returns may be selected for audit.

CORBIS/SUPERSTOCK

Key Terms

Ad valorem taxes, 1-12
Carbon tax, 1-23
Correspondence audit, 1-25
Employment taxes, 1-19
Estate tax, 1-15
Excise taxes, 1-13
FICA tax, 1-19
Field audit, 1-25
Financial transaction tax, 1-23
Flat tax, 1-22
Franchise tax, 1-21
FUTA tax, 1-20
Gift tax, 1-16
Indexation, 1-33
Inheritance tax, 1-15
National sales tax, 1-22
Occupational fees, 1-21
Office audit, 1-25
Personalty, 1-12
Preparer tax identification number (PTIN), 1-28
Realty, 1-12
Revenue neutrality, 1-29
Sales tax, 1-14
Severance taxes, 1-14
Statute of limitations, 1-25
Sunset provision, 1-29
Use tax, 1-14
Value added tax (VAT), 1-22
Wherewithal to pay, 1-32

Discussion Questions

1. **LO.1** This textbook includes many features beyond the text materials in each chapter. For example, a glossary is included in the appendices and the end of each chapter contains a list of key terms. Skim through the chapters, appendices, and any other supplemental materials required for your course, and identify two special features. For each, explain what it is and how it can help you understand taxation in this tax course.

2. **LO.1, 4** In the following independent situations, is the tax position of the taxpayer likely to change? Explain why or why not.
   a. John started renting out a spare room in his home.
   b. Theresa quit her job as a staff accountant and established her own practice as a CPA.
   c. Paul's employer transferred him from its California office to an office in Florida.

Critical Thinking

3. **LO.1, 4** Marvin is the executor and sole heir of his aunt's estate. The estate includes her furnished home, which Marvin is considering converting to rental property to generate additional cash flow. What are some of the tax considerations Marvin may confront?

4. **LO.2** World War II converted the Federal income tax into a *mass tax*. Explain.

5. **LO.2** How does the pay-as-you-go procedure apply to wage earners? To persons who have income from sources other than wages?

6. **LO.3** Jane, a tax practitioner, has reviewed the law on how a certain state's income tax applies to a client's web-based consulting business but is unable to reach a conclusion for which she has a high level of confidence. Assuming that Jane is a knowledgeable and experienced tax professional, which *Guiding Principles of Good Tax Policy* might not be followed by this state?

7. **LO.3** Distinguish between taxes that are *regressive* and those that are *progressive.*

Critical Thinking

8. **LO.4** Several years ago Ethan purchased the former parsonage of St. James Church to use as a personal residence. To date, Ethan has not received any ad valorem property tax bills from either the city or the county tax authorities.
   a. What is a reasonable explanation for this oversight?
   b. What should Ethan do?

Critical Thinking

9. **LO.4** The Adams Independent School District wants to sell a parcel of unimproved land that it does not need. Its three best offers are as follows: from the state's Department of Public Safety (DPS), $2,300,000; from the Second Baptist Church, $2,200,000; and from Baker Motors, $2,100,000. DPS would use the property for a new state highway patrol barracks, Second Baptist would start a church school, and Baker would open a car dealership. If you are the financial adviser for the school district, which offer would you prefer? Why?

10. **LO.4** The commissioners for Walker County are actively negotiating with Falcon Industries regarding the location of a new manufacturing plant in the area. Since Falcon is considering several other sites, a "generous tax holiday" may be needed to influence the final choice. The local school district is opposed to any "generous tax holiday."
    a. What would probably be involved in a generous tax holiday?
    b. Why would the school district be opposed?

11. **LO.4** Sophia lives several blocks from her parents in the same residential subdivision. Sophia is surprised to learn that her ad valorem property taxes for the year were raised but those of her parents were lowered. What is a possible explanation for the difference?

12. **LO.4** The Morgan family lives in Massachusetts. They moor their sailboat in Rhode Island. What might be a plausible reason for this?

13. **LO.4** Is the breadth and number of Federal excise taxes increasing or decreasing? Explain.

14. **LO.4** After her first business trip to a major city, Jayla is alarmed when she reviews her credit card receipts. Both the hotel bill and the car rental charge are in

excess of the price she was quoted. Was Jayla overcharged, or is there an explanation for the excess amounts?

15. LO.4 What is the difference between an excise tax and a general sales tax?
    a. Do all states impose a general sales tax?
    b. Does the Federal government impose a general sales tax?

16. LO.4 The Garcías live in Clay County, which is adjacent to Jackson County. Although the retail stores in both counties are comparable, the Garcías usually drive a few extra miles to shop in Jackson County. As to why the Garcías might do this, consider the following:
    a. Clay County is in a different state than Jackson County.
    b. Clay County and Jackson County are in the same state.

17. LO.4 During a social event, Muriel and Caleb are discussing the home computer each recently purchased. Although the computers are identical makes and models, Muriel is surprised to learn that she paid a sales tax but Caleb did not. Comment as to why this could happen. Critical Thinking

18. LO.4 Distinguish between an estate tax and an inheritance tax.
    a. Do some states impose both? Neither?
    b. Which, if either, does the Federal government impose?

19. LO.4 Jake (age 72) and Jessica (age 28) were recently married. To avoid any transfer taxes, Jake has promised to leave Jessica all of his wealth when he dies. Is Jake under some misconception about the operation of the Federal gift and estate taxes? Explain.

20. LO.4 Address the following issues:
    a. What is the purpose of the unified transfer tax credit?
    b. Is the same amount available for both the Federal gift tax and the estate tax? Explain.
    c. Does the use of the credit for a gift affect the amount of credit available for the estate tax? Explain.

21. LO.4 Elijah and Anastasia are married and have five married children and nine minor grandchildren. For 2022, what is the maximum amount they can give to their family (including the sons- and daughters-in-law) without using any of their unified transfer tax credit?

22. LO.4 What is the difference between the Federal income tax on individuals and that imposed on corporations?

23. LO.4 As to those states that impose an income tax, comment on the following:
    a. "Piggyback" approach and possible "decoupling" from this approach.
    b. Use of IRS audit results as part of a state tax audit.
    c. Credit for taxes paid to other states.

24. LO.4 In May 2022, Hernando, a resident of California, has his 2020 Federal income tax return audited by the IRS. An assessment of additional tax is made because he inadvertently omitted some rental income. In October 2022, California audits his state return for the same year. Explain the coincidence.

25. LO.4 Mike Barr was an outstanding football player in college and expects to be drafted by the NFL in the first few rounds. Mike has let it be known that he would prefer to sign with a club located in Florida, Texas, or Washington. Mike sees no reason why he should have to pay state income tax on his player's salary. Is Mike under any delusions? Explain. Critical Thinking

Critical Thinking

26. **LO.4, 5** A question on a state income tax return asks the taxpayer if any out-of-state internet or mail-order catalog purchases were made during the year. The question requires a yes or no answer, and if the taxpayer answers yes, the total dollar amount of these purchases is to be provided.
    a. Does this inquiry have any relevance to the state income tax? If not, why is it being asked?
    b. Your client, Hannah, wants to leave the question unanswered. As the preparer of her return, how do you respond?

27. **LO.4** Many state income tax returns contain checkoff boxes that allow taxpayers to make donations to a multitude of local charitable causes. On what grounds has this procedure been criticized?

28. **LO.4** Many states have occasionally adopted amnesty programs that allow taxpayers to pay back taxes with reduced penalties.
    a. Besides the revenue generated, how are these programs advantageous?
    b. Could an amnesty program be used by a state that does not levy an income tax?
    c. Does the IRS utilize this approach?

29. **LO.4** Contrast FICA and FUTA as to the following:
    a. Purpose of the tax.
    b. Upon whom imposed.
    c. Governmental administration of the tax.
    d. Reduction of tax based on a merit rating system.

30. **LO.4** In connection with the Medicare component of FICA, comment on the following:
    a. Any dollar limitation imposed.
    b. The applicability of the 0.9% increase in the 1.45% regular tax rate.

31. **LO.4** One of the tax advantages of hiring family members to work in your business is that FICA taxes are avoided. Do you agree with this statement? Explain.

32. **LO.4** Describe the nature and purpose of the following taxes:
    a. Severance taxes.
    b. Franchise taxes.
    c. Occupational fees.
    d. Customs duties.
    e. Export duties.

33. **LO.4** Regarding the value added tax (VAT), comment on the following:
    a. Popularity of this type of tax.
    b. Nature of the tax.
    c. Effect on government spending.

34. **LO.4** Both a value added tax (VAT) and a national sales tax have been criticized as *regressive* in their effect.
    a. Explain.
    b. How could this shortcoming be remedied?

35. **LO.4, 5** Serena operates a gift shop. To reduce costs of credit card transactions, she offers customers a discount if they pay in cash. For the holiday rush, she hires some short-term workers but pays them cash and does not add them to the payroll.
    a. What are some of the tax problems Serena might have?
    b. Assess Serena's chances of audit by the IRS.

36. **LO.5** With regard to the IRS audit process, comment on the following:
    a. The audit is resolved by mail.
    b. The audit is conducted at the office of the IRS.
    c. A "no change" RAR results.
    d. A special agent joins the audit team.

37. **LO.5** Aldo has just been audited by the IRS. He does not agree with the agent's findings but believes that he has only two choices: pay the proposed deficiency or resort to the courts. Do you agree with Aldo's conclusion? Why or why not?

38. **LO.5** What purpose is served by a statute of limitations? How is it relevant in the case of tax controversies?

39. **LO.5** Regarding the statute of limitations on additional assessments of tax by the IRS, determine the applicable period in each of the following situations. Assume a calendar year individual with no fraud or substantial omission involved.
    a. The income tax return for 2021 was filed on February 19, 2022.
    b. The income tax return for 2021 was filed on June 25, 2022.
    c. The income tax return for 2021 was prepared on April 4, 2022, but was never filed. Through some misunderstanding between the preparer and the taxpayer, each expected the other to file the return.
    d. The income tax return for 2021 was never filed because the taxpayer thought no additional tax was due.

40. **LO.5** Brianna, a calendar year taxpayer, files her income tax return for 2021 on February 3, 2022. Although she makes repeated inquiries, she does not receive her refund from the IRS until May 28, 2022. Is Brianna entitled to interest on the refund? Explain.

41. **LO.5, 6** On a Federal income tax return filed five years ago, Andy inadvertently omitted a large amount of gross income.
    a. Andy seeks your advice as to whether the IRS is barred from assessing additional income tax in the event he is audited. What is your advice?
    b. Would your advice differ if you were the person who prepared the return in question? Explain.
    c. Suppose Andy asks you to prepare his current year's return. Would you do so? Explain.

42. **LO.5** Rita files her income tax return 35 days after the due date of the return without obtaining an extension from the IRS. Along with the return, she remits a check for $40,000, which is the balance of the tax she owes. Disregarding the interest element, what are Rita's penalties for failure to file and for failure to pay?

43. **LO.5** For tax year 2020, the IRS assesses a deficiency against David for $500,000. Disregarding the interest component, what is David's penalty if the deficiency is attributable to:
    a. Negligence?
    b. Fraud?

44. **LO.5, 6** In March 2022, Kuni asks you to prepare his Federal income tax returns for tax years 2019, 2020, and 2021. In discussing this matter with him, you discover that he also has not filed for tax year 2018. When you mention this fact, Kuni tells you that the statute of limitations precludes the IRS from taking any action as to this year.

a. Is Kuni correct about the application of the statute of limitations? Why or why not?

b. If Kuni refuses to file for 2018, should you prepare returns for 2019 through 2021? Explain.

45. **LO.5, 6** The Benson CPA firm is considering utilizing an offshore service provider to prepare many of its tax returns. In this regard, what ethical considerations must be taken into account?

46. **LO.7** In terms of tax policy, what do the following mean?

a. Revenue neutrality.

b. Sunset provision.

c. Indexation.

47. **LO.7** Some tax rules can be justified on multiple grounds (e.g., economic and social). In this connection, comment on the possible justification for the rules governing the following:

a. Pension plans.

b. Education.

c. Home ownership.

Critical Thinking

48. **LO.7, 8** Discuss the probable justification for each of the following aspects of the tax law. Be sure to use concepts and terminology covered in this chapter.

a. A tax credit is allowed for amounts spent to furnish care for minor children while the parent works.

b. Deductions for interest on home mortgage and property taxes on a personal residence.

c. The income-splitting benefits of filing a joint return.

d. Fines and penalties are not deductible.

e. Net operating losses of a current year can be carried forward to profitable years.

f. A taxpayer who sells property on an installment basis can recognize gain on the sale over the period the payments are received.

g. The exclusion from Federal tax of certain interest income from state and local bonds.

h. Prepaid income is taxed to the recipient in the year received and not in the year earned.

49. **LO.7** Mia owns a warehouse that has a cost basis to her of $80,000. The city condemns the warehouse to make room for a new fire station. It pays Mia $400,000 for the property, its agreed-to fair market value. Shortly after the condemnation, Mia purchases another warehouse as a replacement. What is her recognized gain if the new property cost:

a. $280,000?

b. $444,000?

c. $80,000?

d. What, if any, is the justification for deferring the recognition of gain on the involuntary conversion?

50. **LO.8** A mother sells a valuable collection of antiques to her son for $1,000. What judicial concept might the IRS invoke to question this transaction?

Research Problems

Use internet tax resources to address the following questions. Look for reliable websites and blogs of the IRS and other government agencies, media outlets, businesses, tax professionals, academics, think tanks, and political outlets.

Research Problem 1. Using information from this chapter as well as information from the tax agency in your state (likely called the Department of Revenue) and your local government, find all of the taxes to which a sole proprietor is subject. Create a table that lists all of these taxes, the rate(s), and the level(s) of government that imposes each tax.

Research Problem 2. Use **congress.gov** or another reliable website to find a proposal for a carbon tax or a financial transactions tax. Draft a summary of the tax, and analyze it against five of the AICPA's principles of good tax policy. Critical Thinking

Research Problem 3. Find a Federal or state proposal for a soda tax or sweetened beverage tax. Provide the bill number and a brief explanation. Also apply the AICPA's principles of good tax policy to support your recommendation for or against the bill. Critical Thinking

Research Problem 4. Visit the websites of a few public accounting firms to learn how they are using data analytics and visualization in the tax function. In an e-mail to your instructor, explain what you found, provide the source(s) you used, and explain how you think the data analysis helps businesses engage in tax compliance and planning. Communications, Data Analytics

Research Problem 5. Use the IRS website to find Form W–12 (IRS Paid Preparer Tax Identification Number (PTIN) Application and Renewal) and its instructions. Review these documents and focus specifically on Question 11 (related to the data security responsibilities of the paid preparer). One purpose of this question is to remind preparers of their obligations to comply with the "Safeguards Rule" overseen by the Federal Trade Commission. Use IRS Publication 4557, *Safeguarding Taxpayer Data*, to find information on this rule. Prepare an e-mail to your instructor that briefly describes this rule, and lists three actions a preparer could take to help meet this rule. Communications

Chapter

2 Working with the Tax Law

Learning Objectives: *After completing Chapter 2, you should be able to:*

- **LO.1** **Distinguish between the statutory, administrative, and judicial sources of the tax law and understand the purpose of each source.**
- **LO.2** **Locate and work with the appropriate tax law sources.**
- **LO.3** **Develop an awareness of tax research tools.**
- **LO.4** **Describe the tax research process.**
- **LO.5** **Communicate the results of the tax research process in a client letter and a tax file memorandum.**
- **LO.6** **Apply tax research techniques and planning procedures.**
- **LO.7** **Be aware of taxation on the CPA examination.**

Chapter Outline

2-1 Tax Law Sources, 2-2
- 2-1a Statutory Sources of the Tax Law, 2-2
- 2-1b Administrative Sources of the Tax Law, 2-6
- 2-1c Judicial Sources of the Tax Law, 2-10
- 2-1d Other Sources of the Tax Law, 2-17

2-2 Working with the Tax Law—Tax Research Tools, 2-18
- 2-2a Commercial Tax Services, 2-18
- 2-2b Using Electronic (Online) Tax Services, 2-19
- 2-2c Noncommercial Electronic (Online) Tax Services, 2-19

2-3 Working with the Tax Law—Tax Research, 2-20
- 2-3a Identifying the Problem, 2-21
- 2-3b Refining the Problem, 2-22
- 2-3c Locating the Appropriate Tax Law Sources, 2-22
- 2-3d Assessing the Validity of Tax Law Sources, 2-23
- 2-3e Arriving at the Solution or at Alternative Solutions, 2-25
- 2-3f Communicating Tax Research, 2-26

2-4 Working with the Tax Law—Tax Planning, 2-28
- 2-4a Nontax Considerations, 2-29
- 2-4b Components of Tax Planning, 2-29
- 2-4c Tax Avoidance and Tax Evasion, 2-30
- 2-4d Follow-Up Procedures, 2-30
- 2-4e Tax Planning, 2-31

2-5 Taxation on the CPA Examination, 2-31
- 2-5a Preparation Blueprints, 2-31
- 2-5b Regulation Section, 2-31

MONKEY BUSINESS IMAGES/SHUTTERSTOCK.COM

The Big Picture

Importance of Tax Research

Early in November 2022, Fred and Megan Martel scheduled a meeting with you to discuss a potential tax problem. Fred and Megan purchased a 40-acre parcel of property in 2017 for $195,000. On it, they built their "dream home" in 2018. In March 2022, while walking on a remote part of their property, they spotted something shiny on the ground. They started digging and eventually unearthed eight metal cans containing more than 1,400 rare gold coins in $5, $10, and $20 denominations dated from 1846 to 1895. The face value of the gold coins is about $28,000, and many of the coins are in mint condition. Their delay in coming to you for tax advice was due to a state law that required their discovery to be turned over to the state for disposition. The state, for a period of six months, was required to publicize the find and ask if anyone could prove ownership. When no one came forward, the coins were returned to the Martels in October 2022. Since they are now the rightful owners of the coins, they want to know the tax implications (if any) of their discovery.

Read the chapter and formulate your responses.

Federal tax law reflects the three branches of our Federal government. It is a mixture of laws passed by Congress, explanations provided by the Treasury Department and the Internal Revenue Service (IRS), and court decisions. Anyone who has attempted to work with this vast amount of information is familiar with its complexity. The tax research process allows us to understand, evaluate, and apply these sources of tax law to questions that are raised by taxpayers and tax practitioners.

In addition to being able to locate, interpret, and apply tax law, a tax professional also must understand the relative *weight of authority* that each source carries. The tax law is of little significance, however, until it is applied to a set of facts and circumstances. This chapter introduces the statutory, administrative, and judicial sources of tax law and explains how the law is applied to individual and business transactions. It also explains how to apply tax research techniques and use planning procedures effectively. A large part of tax research focuses on determining the intent of Congress.

Frequently, uncertainty in the tax law causes disputes between the Internal Revenue Service (IRS) and taxpayers. Due to these *gray areas* and the complexity of the tax law, a taxpayer may have more than one alternative for structuring a financial transaction. In structuring financial transactions and engaging in other tax planning activities, the tax adviser must be cognizant that the objective of tax planning is not necessarily to minimize the tax liability. Instead, a taxpayer's after-tax wealth should be maximized, which may include maximizing nontax as well as noneconomic benefits.

LO.1

Distinguish between the statutory, administrative, and judicial sources of the tax law and understand the purpose of each source.

2-1 Tax Law Sources

Understanding taxation requires a strong understanding of the sources of tax law. These sources include laws passed by Congress, which are contained in the Internal Revenue Code and congressional Committee Reports, Treasury Department Regulations, other Treasury Department and IRS pronouncements, and court decisions. As a result, the *primary sources* of tax law include information from all three branches of government: legislative (or statutory), executive, and judicial.[1]

2-1a Statutory Sources of the Tax Law

Statutory sources of law include the Constitution (Article I, Sections 7, 8, and 10), the Internal Revenue Code, and tax treaties (agreements between countries to mitigate the double taxation of taxpayers subject to the tax laws of those countries). The Constitution grants Congress the power to impose and collect taxes and authorizes the creation of treaties with other countries. The power of Congress to implement and collect taxes is reflected in the Internal Revenue Code, the official title of U.S. tax law, and the Code is the basis for arriving at solutions to all tax questions.

Origin of the Internal Revenue Code

Before 1939, the statutory provisions relating to Federal taxation were contained in the individual revenue acts enacted by Congress. Because dealing with many separate acts was inconvenient and confusing, Congress codified all of the Federal tax laws in 1939. Known as the Internal Revenue Code of 1939, the codification arranged all Federal tax provisions in a logical sequence and placed them in a separate part of the Federal statutes. A further rearrangement took place in 1954 and resulted in the Internal Revenue Code of 1954, which continued in effect until 1986, when it was replaced by the Internal Revenue Code of 1986. Although Congress did not recodify the law in the Tax Reform Act (TRA) of 1986, the magnitude of the changes made by TRA of 1986 did provide some rationale for renaming the Federal tax law the Internal Revenue Code of 1986.[2]

[1] *Secondary sources* also are used by tax practitioners. These sources are not part of the tax law and include items like tax articles from professional tax journals, newsletters, and textbooks. Commentary contained in various tax research services (such as Thomson Reuters *Checkpoint*) also are secondary sources.

[2] This point is important in assessing judicial decisions interpreting provisions of the Internal Revenue Code of 1939 and the Internal Revenue Code of 1954. If a provision from the 1939 or 1954 Code was included in the Internal Revenue Code of 1986 and has not been subsequently amended, the provision and the related judicial decisions have continuing validity.

The Legislative Process

Exhibit 2.1 illustrates the legislative process for enacting changes to the Internal Revenue Code of 1986. Federal tax legislation generally originates in the House of Representatives, where it is first considered by the House Ways and Means Committee.[3] Once approved by the House Ways and Means Committee, the proposed bill is referred to the entire House of Representatives for approval or disapproval. Approved bills are sent to the Senate, where they are considered by the Senate Finance Committee.[4]

After approval by the Senate Finance Committee, the bill is sent to the entire Senate. Assuming no disagreement between the House and Senate, passage by the Senate results in referral to the President for approval or veto. If the bill is approved or if the President's veto is overridden, the bill becomes law and part of the Internal Revenue Code of 1986.

Exhibit 2.1 Legislative Process for Tax Bills

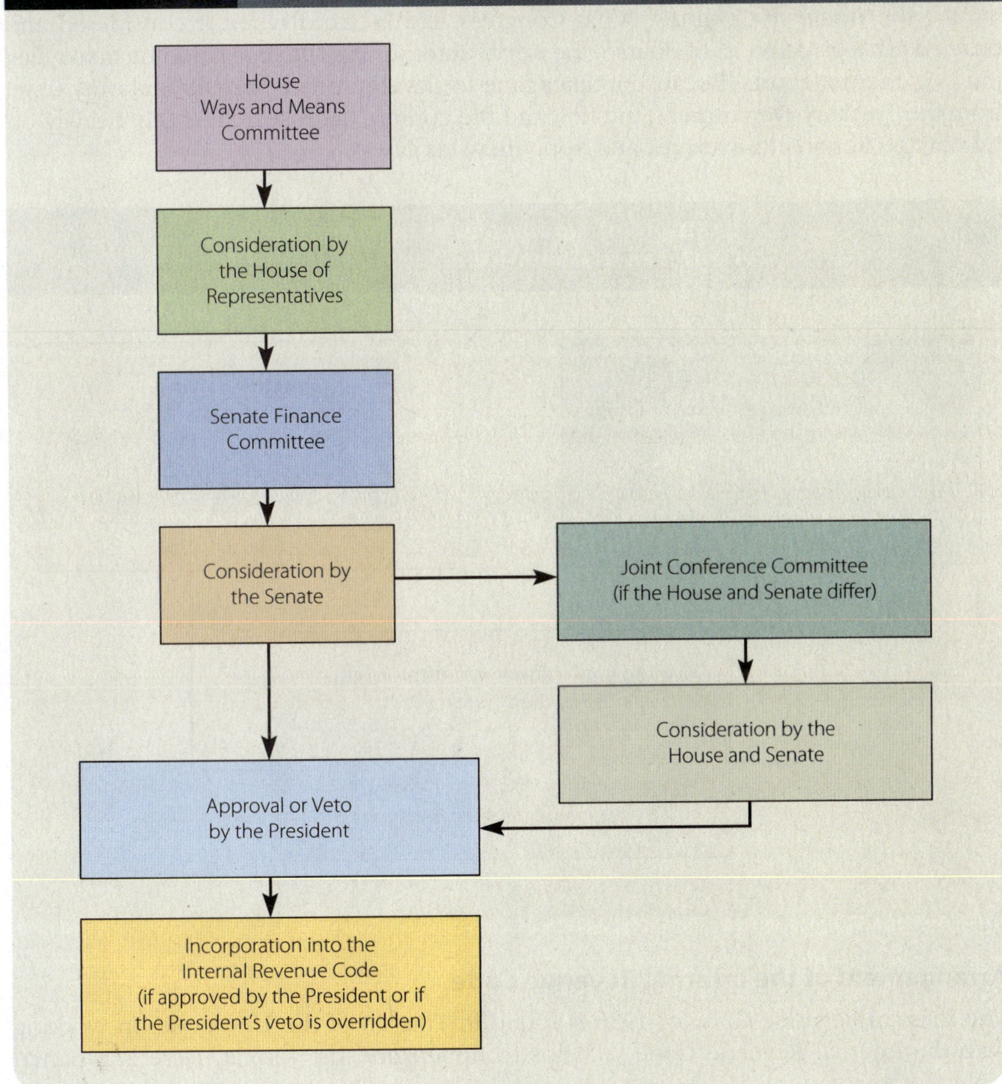

[3]Congress enacts tax legislation virtually every year, and each piece of legislation contains changes to the Internal Revenue Code of 1986.

[4]Although rare, a tax bill can originate in the Senate when it is attached as a rider to a different legislative proposal. The Tax Equity and Fiscal Responsibility Act of 1982 originated in the Senate, and its constitutionality was upheld by the courts.

House and Senate versions of major tax bills frequently differ. One reason bills are often changed in the Senate is that each senator has considerable latitude to make amendments when the Senate as a whole is voting on a bill referred to it by the Senate Finance Committee.[5] In contrast, the entire House of Representatives either accepts or rejects what is proposed by the House Ways and Means Committee, and changes from the floor are rare. When the Senate version of the bill differs from that passed by the House, the Joint Conference Committee, which includes members of both the House Ways and Means Committee and the Senate Finance Committee, resolves the differences. The deliberations of the Joint Conference Committee usually produce a compromise between the two versions, which then is voted on by both the House and the Senate. If both bodies accept the bill, it is referred to the President for approval or veto.

The role of the Joint Conference Committee indicates the importance of compromise in the legislative process. Exhibit 2.2 illustrates what happened with amendments to the child tax credit in the Tax Cuts and Jobs Act (TCJA) of 2017.

The House Ways and Means Committee, the Senate Finance Committee, and the Joint Conference Committee each produce a Committee Report. These Committee Reports explain the provisions of the proposed legislation and are a valuable source for ascertaining the *intent of Congress*. What Congress had in mind when it considered and enacted tax legislation is, of course, the key to interpreting the legislation by taxpayers, the IRS, and the courts. Because it takes time to develop other primary authority (e.g., from the Treasury Department, the IRS, and the courts), tax researchers rely heavily on Committee Reports to interpret and apply new tax laws.

Exhibit 2.2 **Example of Compromise in the Joint Conference Committee**

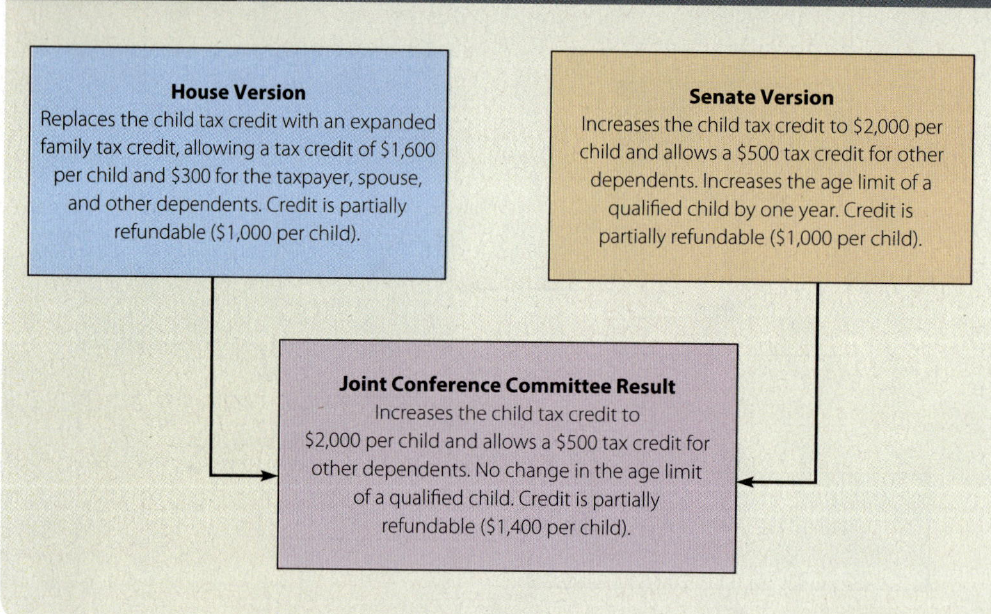

Arrangement of the Internal Revenue Code

The Internal Revenue Code of 1986 is found in Title 26 of the U.S. Code. In working with the Internal Revenue Code, it helps to understand the format. Here is a partial table of contents:

Subtitle A. Income Taxes
  Chapter 11. Normal Taxes and Surtaxes

[5]During the passage of the Tax Reform Act of 1986, Senate leaders tried to make the bill *amendment proof* to avoid the normal amendment process.

Subchapter A. Determination of Tax Liability
Part I. Tax on Individuals
Sections 1–5
Part II. Tax on Corporations
Sections 11–12

In referring to a provision of the Code, the *key* is usually the Section number. In citing a Section number, identifying the related Subtitle, Chapter, Subchapter, and Part is not necessary. Merely mentioning the Section is sufficient because the Section numbers run consecutively and do not begin again with each new Subtitle, Chapter, Subchapter, or Part.[6]

Tax researchers often refer to specific areas of income tax law by their Subchapters. Some of the more common Subchapter designations include Subchapter C ("Corporate Distributions and Adjustments"), Subchapter K ("Partners and Partnerships"), and Subchapter S ("Tax Treatment of S Corporations and Their Shareholders").

Citing the Code

Code Sections often are broken down into subparts.[7] Code § 2(a)(1)(A) serves as an example.

Broken down by content, § 2(a)(1)(A) becomes:

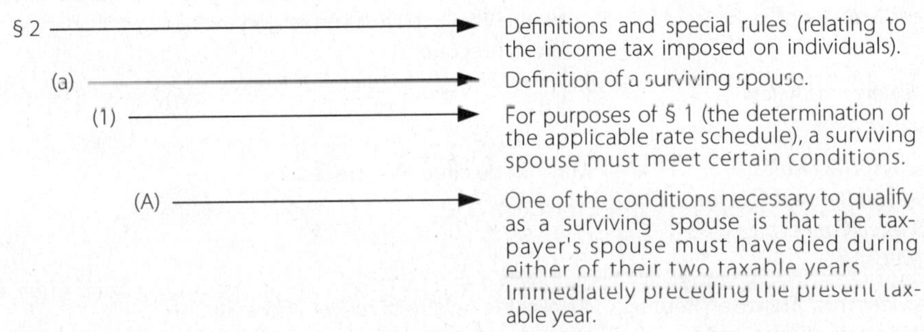

Throughout the text, references to the Code Sections are in the form given above. The symbols "§" and "§§" are used in place of "Section" and "Sections," respectively. The following table summarizes the format that we use:

Complete Reference	Text Reference
Section 2(a)(1)(A) of the Internal Revenue Code of 1986	§ 2(a)(1)(A)
Sections 1 and 2 of the Internal Revenue Code of 1986	§§ 1 and 2
Section 2 of the Internal Revenue Code of 1954	§ 2 of the Internal Revenue Code of 1954
Section 12(d) of the Internal Revenue Code of 1939[9]	§ 12(d) of the Internal Revenue Code of 1939

[6]When the 1954 Code was drafted, some Section numbers were intentionally omitted so that later changes could be incorporated into the Code without disrupting its organization. When Congress does not leave enough space, subsequent Code Sections are given A, B, C, etc., designations. A good example is the treatment of §§ 280A through 280H.

[7]Some Code Sections do not require subparts. See, for example, §§ 211 and 241.

[8]Some Code Sections omit the subsection designation and use the paragraph designation as the first subpart. See, for example, §§ 212(1) and 1222(1).

[9]Code § 12(d) of the Internal Revenue Code of 1939 is the predecessor to § 2 of the Internal Revenue Code of 1954 and the Internal Revenue Code of 1986. Keep in mind that the 1954 Code superseded the 1939 Code and the 1986 Code superseded the 1954 Code. Footnote 2 explains why references to the 1939 or 1954 Code are included.

2-1b Administrative Sources of the Tax Law

The administrative sources of the Federal tax law include Treasury Department Regulations, Revenue Rulings and Revenue Procedures, and various other administrative pronouncements (see Exhibit 2.3). All are issued by either the U.S. Treasury Department or the IRS.

Treasury Department Regulations

Regulations are issued by the U.S. Treasury Department under authority granted by Congress.[10] Interpretive by nature, they provide taxpayers with considerable guidance on the meaning and application of the Code. Regulations, which carry considerable authority as the official interpretation of tax law, may be issued in *proposed*, *temporary*, or *final* form.

Because Regulations interpret the Code, they are arranged in the same sequence as the Code. A number is added at the beginning, however, to indicate the type of tax or administrative, procedural, or definitional matter to which they relate.[11] For example, the prefix 1 designates the Regulations under the income tax law. As a result, the Regulations under Code § 2 are cited as Reg. § 1.2, with subparts added for further identification. The numbering patterns of these subparts often have no correlation with the Code subsections.

Exhibit 2.3 Administrative Sources

Source	Location	Authority
Regulations	*Federal Register*	Force and effect of law.
Temporary Regulations	*Federal Register* *Internal Revenue Bulletin (IRB)* *Cumulative Bulletin**	May be cited as a precedent.
Proposed Regulations	*Federal Register* *Internal Revenue Bulletin* *Cumulative Bulletin**	Preview of Final Regulations. Not yet a precedent.
Revenue Rulings	*Internal Revenue Bulletin* *Cumulative Bulletin**	IRS interpretation only. Items published in the IRB are binding on the IRS. Taxpayers can rely on these items.** Weak precedent.
Revenue Procedures Notices	*Internal Revenue Bulletin* *Cumulative Bulletin**	
Chief Counsel Advice Technical Advice Memoranda Actions on Decisions	Tax Analysts' *Tax Notes;* Thomson Reuters *Checkpoint****; CCH *IntelliConnect;* IRS website	May not be cited as a precedent.
Letter Rulings	Tax services from Thomson Reuters, CCH Wolters Kluwer, and Bloomberg Law; IRS website	Applicable only to taxpayer addressed. May not be cited as precedent by others, but can be used as authority to avoid certain tax penalties on audit.
Frequently Asked Questions (FAQs)	IRS website****	FAQs have no precedential value. However, if relied upon in good faith, a taxpayer will have a "reasonable cause" defense against any negligence penalty or accuracy-related penalty.

Note: All Administrative Sources can be accessed electronically through Thomson Reuters *Checkpoint* (and other commercial tax services).

*Through 2008, the contents of Internal Revenue Bulletins were consolidated semiannually into a Cumulative Bulletin. The IRS no longer produces a Cumulative Bulletin because Internal Revenue Bulletins from mid-2003 are available electronically on the IRS website (**irs.gov/irb**).

**Internal Revenue Manual (IRM) 4.10.7.2.4 (01-10-2018).

***Thomson Reuters *Checkpoint* includes a wide variety of tax resources. The most significant are materials produced by the Research Institute of America (RIA), including the *Federal Tax Coordinator 2d*.

****Starting after October 15, 2021, FAQs on newly enacted tax legislation are announced in a news release and posted on the IRS website as a Fact Sheet. FAQs on other topics are posted on the website and not announced in a news release (IR-2021-202).

[10] § 7805.

[11] The prefix 20 designates estate tax Regulations, 25 covers gift tax Regulations, 31 relates to employment taxes, and 301 refers to procedure and administration.

Ethics & Equity **Reporting Tax Fraud**

Maybe someone in your extended family is driving a luxury car and comments that only fools pay all of their taxes. Or maybe a contractor demands payment in cash. Or perhaps someone at work is not reporting all of their income. If cheating on taxes bothers you, the IRS wants to hear from you (and may make it worthwhile). The IRS has two whistleblower programs. The small-awards program is for situations involving less than $2 million of tax, and the award can be as high as 15% of collections, although it often is less. The large-awards program covers situations involving $2 million or more of tax. Here, the reward can go as high as 30%. The IRS no longer takes tax law violations over the phone, but the appropriate form to report tax fraud is Form 3949–A (Information Referral). Form 211, Application for Award for Original Information, is required to claim an award. Would you turn in someone?

New Regulations and changes to existing Regulations are usually issued in proposed form before they are finalized. The interval between the proposal of a Regulation and its finalization permits taxpayers and other interested parties to comment on the propriety of the proposal. **Proposed Regulations** under Code § 2, for example, are cited as Prop.Reg. § 1.2. The Tax Court indicates that Proposed Regulations carry little weight in the litigation process.[12] **Final Regulations** have the force and effect of law.

Sometimes the Treasury Department issues **Temporary Regulations** where immediate guidance is important. These Regulations are issued without the comment period required for Proposed Regulations. Temporary Regulations, cited as Temp.Reg. §, have the same authoritative value as Final Regulations and may be cited as precedents. However, Temporary Regulations also must be issued as Proposed Regulations and automatically expire within three years after the date of issuance.[13]

Proposed, Temporary, and Final Regulations are published in the *Federal Register*, in the *Internal Revenue Bulletin* (I.R.B.), and by major tax services. Final Regulations are issued as Treasury Decisions (TDs).

Regulations also may be classified as *legislative, interpretive*, or *procedural*. These classifications are discussed in text Section 2-3d (Assessing the Validity of Tax Law Sources) later in the chapter.

Revenue Rulings, Revenue Procedures, and Notices

Revenue Rulings are official pronouncements of the National Office of the IRS.[14] They typically provide one or more examples of how the IRS would apply a law to *specific fact situations*. Like Regulations, Revenue Rulings are designed to provide interpretation of the tax law. Although they do not carry the same legal force and effect as Regulations, because they are focused on a specific fact pattern, they provide a more detailed analysis of the law.

Although letter rulings (discussed below) are not the same as Revenue Rulings, a Revenue Ruling often results from a specific taxpayer's request for a letter ruling. If the IRS believes that a letter ruling request has widespread impact, the letter ruling will be converted into a Revenue Ruling and issued. Revenue Rulings also can be issued in response to technical advice to District Offices of the IRS, court decisions, and suggestions from tax practitioner groups.

Revenue Procedures deal with the internal management practices and procedures of the IRS. For example, Rev.Proc. 2022–1 provides general instructions for taxpayers requesting letter rulings or determination letters from the IRS. A taxpayer's failure to follow a Revenue Procedure can result in unnecessary delay or, in a discretionary situation, can cause the IRS to decline to act.

Notices are issued when immediate guidance is needed by taxpayers and tax practitioners. Typically, this guidance is transitional while the IRS works on permanent guidance on the particular topic. For example, Notice 2021–49 provides guidance

[12] *F. W. Woolworth Co.*, 54 T.C. 1233 (1970); *Harris M. Miller*, 70 T.C. 448 (1978); and *James O. Tomerlin Trust*, 87 T.C. 876 (1986).

[13] § 7805(e).

[14] § 7805(a).

to employers claiming the employee retention credit during the last six months of 2021; the guidance reflects changes to the credit made by the American Rescue Plan Act of 2021.

Revenue Rulings, Revenue Procedures, and Notices serve an important function by providing *guidance* to IRS personnel and taxpayers in handling routine tax matters. Revenue Rulings and Revenue Procedures generally apply retroactively and are binding on the IRS until revoked or modified by subsequent rulings or procedures, Regulations, legislation, or court decisions.

Revenue Rulings, Revenue Procedures, and Notices are published weekly by the U.S. Government in the *Internal Revenue Bulletin* (I.R.B.).

The proper form for citing Revenue Rulings is shown below. Revenue Procedures and Notices are cited in the same manner, except that "Rev.Proc." or "Notice" is substituted for "Rev.Rul."

Rev.Rul. 2021–2, 2021–4 I.R.B. 495.

Explanation: Revenue Ruling Number 2, appearing on page 495 of the 4th weekly issue of the *Internal Revenue Bulletin* for 2021.

Internal Revenue Bulletins can be found at the IRS website: **irs.gov/irb**.[15]

Letter Rulings

Letter rulings are issued for a fee upon a taxpayer's request and describe how the IRS will treat a *proposed* transaction for tax purposes. Issued by the National Office of the IRS, they apply only to the taxpayer who asks for and obtains the ruling.[16] Letter rulings can be useful to taxpayers who want to be certain of how a transaction will be taxed before proceeding with it. Letter rulings also allow taxpayers to avoid unexpected tax costs and may be the most effective way to carry out tax planning. However, the IRS limits the issuance of individual rulings to restricted, preannounced areas of taxation.[17] The IRS issues more than 2,500 letter rulings each year.

The IRS must make individual rulings available for public inspection after identifying details are deleted.[18] Published digests of private letter rulings can be found in a variety of sources, including *IRS Letter Rulings Reports* (published by CCH), Bloomberg BNA's *Daily Tax Reports*, Tax Analysts' *Tax Notes*, and electronic (online) tax research services (such as Thomson Reuters *Checkpoint*).

Letter rulings are issued multi-digit file numbers that indicate the year and week of issuance as well as the number of the ruling during that week. For example, Ltr.Rul. 202129001 holds that contractually obligated payments for part of the cost of acquiring water rights was deductible as an ordinary expense.

2021	29	001
Year 2021	29th week of 2021	1st ruling issued during the 29th week

Other Administrative Pronouncements

Treasury Decisions (TDs) are issued by the Treasury Department to announce new Regulations, amend or change existing Regulations, or announce the position of the

[15]Commercial sources for Revenue Rulings and Revenue Procedures are available, usually requiring a subscription fee. Older Revenue Rulings and Revenue Procedures are often cited as being published in the *Cumulative Bulletin* (C.B.) rather than in the *Internal Revenue Bulletin* (I.R.B.).

[16]Letter rulings differ from Revenue Rulings, which are applicable to *all* taxpayers. A letter ruling may later lead to the issuance of a Revenue Ruling if the holding affects many taxpayers. In its Internal Revenue Manual, the IRS indicates that letter rulings may be used as a guide with other research materials in formulating a District Office position on an issue. The IRS is required to charge a taxpayer a fee for letter rulings, determination letters, etc.

[17]Rev.Proc. 2022–3 contains a list of areas in which the IRS will not issue advance rulings. According to the IRS, the main reason it will not rule in certain areas is that specific fact-oriented situations are involved. As a result, a ruling may not be obtained on many of the problems that are particularly troublesome for taxpayers.

[18]§ 6110.

Government on selected court decisions. Like Revenue Rulings and Revenue Procedures, TDs are published in the *Internal Revenue Bulletin*.

The IRS also publishes other administrative communications on its website, including Announcements, IRs (News Releases), Internal Legal Memoranda (ILMs), Chief Counsel Advice (CCA), and Chief Counsel Notices (CCN).

Like letter rulings, **determination letters** are issued at the request of taxpayers and provide guidance on the application of the tax law. They differ from letter rulings in that the issuing source is an IRS Area Director (rather than the National Office of the IRS). Also, determination letters usually involve *completed* (as opposed to proposed) transactions. Determination letters are not published and are made known only to the party making the request.

The following examples illustrate the distinction between letter rulings and determination letters.

Difference between Letter Rulings and Determination Letters

Example 1

The shareholders of Red Corporation and Green Corporation want assurance that the consolidation of the corporations into Blue Corporation will be a nontaxable reorganization. The proper approach is to request that the National Office of the IRS issue a letter ruling concerning the income tax effect of the proposed transaction.

Example 2

Chris operates a barbershop in which he employs eight barbers. To comply with the rules governing income tax and payroll tax withholdings, Chris wants to know whether the barbers working for him are employees or independent contractors. The proper procedure is to request a determination letter on their status from the IRS.

A variety of internal memoranda that constitute the working law of the IRS also are released. These Chief Counsel Advice (CCAs), Technical Advice Memoranda (TAMs), and Internal Legal Memoranda (ILMs) are not officially published, and the IRS indicates that they may not be cited as precedents by taxpayers.[19] However, these working documents do explain the IRS's position on various issues. In addition, the "Law" section of these documents refers to primary authority (e.g., the Code, Regulations, and court cases) that is being relied on in developing the conclusion(s).

The National Office of the IRS releases **Technical Advice Memoranda (TAMs)** weekly. TAMs resemble letter rulings in that they give the IRS's determination of an issue. However, they differ in several respects. Letter rulings deal with proposed transactions and are issued to taxpayers at their request. In contrast, TAMs deal with completed (rather than proposed) transactions. TAMs are issued by the National Office of the IRS in response to questions raised by taxpayers or IRS field personnel during audits. TAMs are not officially published and may not be cited or used as precedent.[20] They are assigned file numbers according to the same procedure used for letter rulings. For example, TAM 202121010 refers to the 10th TAM issued during the 21st week of 2021.

The Office of Chief Counsel prepares Chief Counsel Advice (CCAs) and Chief Counsel Notices (CCNs) to help IRS employees. These are issued in response to requests for advice, guidance, and analysis on difficult or significant tax issues and are not binding on either the taxpayer to whom they pertain or the IRS. Another form of field guidance are Technical Expedited Advice Memoranda (TEAMs). The purpose of TEAMs is to expedite legal guidance to field agents as disputes are developing.[21]

[19]These are made available by the publishers listed in Exhibit 2.3.

[20]§ 6110(k)(3). PLRs and TAMs may be authority for purposes of avoiding the accuracy-related penalty. Reg. § 1.6662–4(d)(3).

[21]A TEAM guidance differs from a TAM in several ways, including a mandatory presubmission conference involving the taxpayer. In the event of a tentatively adverse conclusion for the taxpayer or the field agent, a conference of right is offered to the taxpayer and to the field agent; once the conference of right is held, no further conferences are offered.

2-1c Judicial Sources of the Tax Law

Five Federal courts have jurisdiction over tax disputes between the IRS and taxpayers: the U.S. Tax Court, the U.S. District Court, the U.S. Court of Federal Claims, the U.S. Court of Appeals, and the U.S. Supreme Court.

The Judicial Process in General

Once a taxpayer has exhausted the remedies available within the IRS (i.e., no satisfactory settlement has been reached at the agent or at the Independent Office of Appeals level), the dispute can be taken to the Federal courts. The trial and appellate court system for Federal tax litigation is illustrated in Exhibit 2.4.

A trial court, also known as a **court of original jurisdiction**, initially hears the case. Appeals (either by the taxpayer or the IRS) are heard by the appropriate appellate court. A taxpayer has a choice of *three trial courts:* a **U.S. District Court**, the **U.S. Court of Federal Claims**, or the **U.S. Tax Court**.

The U.S. Tax Court contains a **Small Cases Division** that only hears cases involving amounts of $50,000 or less. The ruling of the judge is final (no appeal is available), and these rulings are not precedent for any other cases (i.e., they are not primary authority and are not citable as substantial authority). Proceedings of the Small Cases Division are informal, and because there is no requirement that a taxpayer be represented by an attorney, they can be less costly for a taxpayer (the filing fee is only $60). The typical small case lasts one to two hours, and the taxpayer only needs to tell the judge their story and present any supporting evidence. Special trial judges, rather than Tax Court judges, often preside over these hearings. Some of these cases can be found on the U.S. Tax Court website.

American law, following English law, is frequently *created* by judicial decisions. Under the doctrine of *stare decisis* ("let the decision stand"), each case has precedential value for future cases with the same set of facts. Judges are not required to follow judicial precedent beyond their own jurisdiction. For example, the decisions of an appellate court are binding only on the trial courts within its jurisdiction and not on other trial courts. Different appellate courts may reach different opinions about the same issue. Further, the doctrine of *precedential authority* requires a court to follow prior cases only when the issues and material facts of the current case are essentially the same as those involved in the prior decisions.

Exhibit 2.4 Federal Judicial System

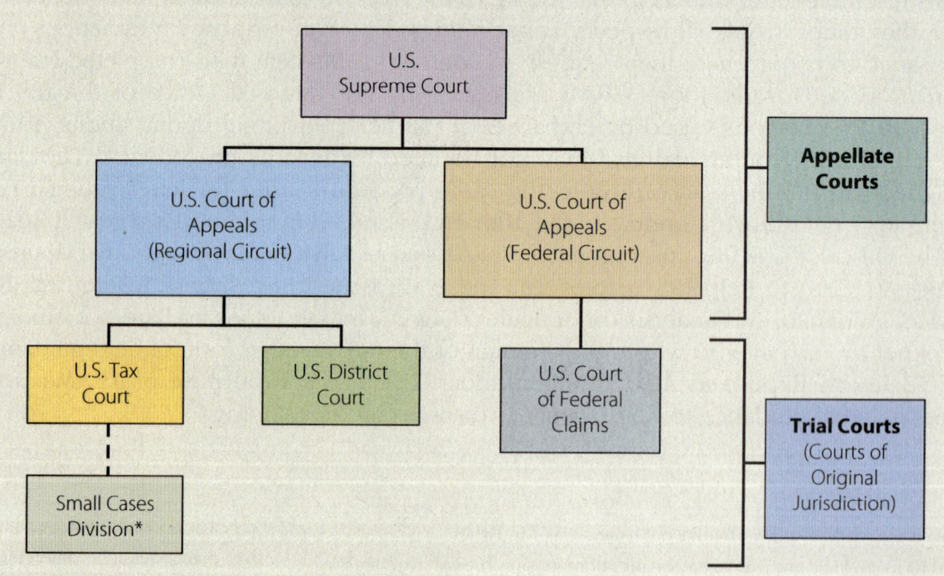

*No appeal from this division of the U.S. Tax Court.

Most Federal and state appellate court decisions and some decisions of trial courts are published. Published court decisions are organized by jurisdiction (Federal or state) and level of court (trial or appellate).[22]

Several other terms are important to understand. The *plaintiff* is the party requesting a hearing, and the *defendant* is the party being challenged. Sometimes a court uses the terms *petitioner* and *respondent* (rather than *plaintiff* and *defendant*). At the trial court level, a taxpayer is normally the plaintiff (or petitioner) and the Government is the defendant (or respondent). If the taxpayer wins and the Government appeals, the Government becomes the petitioner (or appellant), and the taxpayer becomes the respondent.

Trial Courts

Here are some differences between the various trial courts (courts of original jurisdiction):

- *Number of courts.* There is only one Court of Federal Claims and only one Tax Court, but there are many U.S. District Courts. District Courts hear cases based on where the taxpayer lives (so a taxpayer in Atlanta would have her case heard by the Atlanta U.S. District Court).
- *Number of judges.* District Courts have a number of judges, but only one judge hears a case. The Court of Federal Claims has 16 judges, and the Tax Court has up to 19 regular judges. Typically, Tax Court cases are heard and decided by only one of the 19 regular judges. However, if the case is viewed as important or novel tax issues are raised, the entire Tax Court might hear the case. If a case is reviewed by the full Tax Court, such an *en banc* decision has compelling authority.
- *Location.* The Court of Federal Claims meets most often in Washington, D.C. Each state has at least one District Court, and the more populous states have more than one. Although the Tax Court is officially based in Washington, D.C., its judges travel to different parts of the country and hear cases at predetermined locations and dates.
- *Jurisdiction of the Tax Court and District Courts.* The Tax Court hears only Federal tax cases and is the most frequently used forum for tax cases since its judges have more tax expertise; many had careers in the IRS or Treasury Department before being appointed to the Tax Court. The District Courts hear a wide variety of nontax cases as well as tax cases. As a result, District Court judges are viewed as generalists (rather than specialists) in tax law.
- *Jurisdiction of the Court of Federal Claims.* The Court of Federal Claims has jurisdiction over any claim against the United States. As a result, the Court of Federal Claims hears nontax litigation as well as tax cases. Court of Federal Claims judges are tax law generalists. This court is viewed as a stronger option when equity is an issue (as opposed to purely technical issues) or when the case requires extensive discovery of evidence. It is considered by some to have a pro-business orientation.[23]
- *Jury trial.* A jury trial is available only in a District Court. However, because juries can decide only questions of fact (and not questions of law), taxpayers who choose a District Court often do not request a jury trial. In that event, the judge decides all issues in a bench trial. A District Court decision carries precedential value only in its district.
- *Payment of deficiency.* Before the Court of Federal Claims or a District Court will hear a case, the taxpayer must pay any taxes assessed by the IRS and sue for a refund. This is not the case with the Tax Court. Here, a taxpayer may request a hearing without making any payments to the IRS. As a result, whether to pay the

[22]A decision of a particular court is called its holding. Sometimes a decision includes *dicta*, or incidental opinions beyond the current facts. Such passing remarks, illustrations, or analogies are not essential to the current holding. Although the holding has precedential value under *stare decisis*, dicta are not binding on a future court.

[23]T. D. Peyser, "The Case for Selecting the Claims Court to Litigate a Federal Tax Liability," *Tax Executive* (Winter 1988): 149.

tax in advance (and limit further interest and penalties) or wait to pay the tax (and risk additional interest and penalties) becomes part of the decision-making process of selecting a trial court.

- *Appeals*. Appeals from a District Court or a Tax Court decision go to the U.S. Court of Appeals for the circuit where the taxpayer lives. Appeals from the Court of Federal Claims go to the Court of Appeals for the Federal Circuit.
- *Bankruptcy*. When a taxpayer files a bankruptcy petition, the IRS, like other creditors, is prevented from taking action against the taxpayer. Sometimes a bankruptcy court may settle a tax claim.
- *Gray areas*. Because there are "gray areas" in the tax laws, courts may disagree as to the proper tax treatment of an item. With these differences in judicial authority, a taxpayer must consider how a specific court might rule when choosing the most favorable forum to hear the case.

See Concept Summary 2.1 for a summary of various attributes of the Federal trial courts.

Concept Summary 2.1

Federal Judicial System: Trial Courts

Issue	U.S. Tax Court	U.S. District Court	U.S. Court of Federal Claims
Number of judges per court	19*	Varies	16
Payment of deficiency before trial	No	Yes	Yes
Jury trial available	No	Yes	No
Types of disputes	Tax cases only	Most criminal and civil issues	Claims against the United States
Jurisdiction	Nationwide	Location of taxpayer	Nationwide
IRS acquiescence policy	Yes	Yes	Yes
Appeal route	U.S. Court of Appeals	U.S. Court of Appeals	U.S. Court of Appeals for the Federal Circuit

*Some positions may be unfilled at any time. Senior judges and special trial judges may be used to manage the caseload.

Appellate Courts

A trial court decision can be appealed to the appropriate **Circuit Court of Appeals** by the losing party. The 11 geographic circuits, the circuit for the District of Columbia, and the Federal Circuit[24] appear in Exhibit 2.5. Generally, a three-judge panel hears a Court of Appeals case, but occasionally the *full* court decides more controversial cases.

If the Government loses at the trial court level (District Court, Tax Court, or Court of Federal Claims), it may decide not to appeal. However, the fact that the IRS does not appeal does not mean that the IRS agrees with the result (and it may litigate similar issues in the future).

The IRS may decide not to appeal for a number of reasons. First, the IRS may decide that available personnel should be assigned to other more important cases. Second, the IRS may decide that the taxpayer has a sympathetic position or the facts are particularly strong in their favor. In that event, the IRS may wait to test the legal issues with a different taxpayer (who might have a weaker case). Third, the Court of Appeals jurisdiction might matter. Based on past experience and precedent, the IRS may decide that the chance for success on a particular issue might be more promising in a different Court of Appeals.

The Federal Circuit provides the taxpayer with an alternative forum. When a particular Circuit Court of Appeals has issued an adverse decision in a similar case, the taxpayer may prefer the Court of Federal Claims route because any appeal is to the Federal Circuit.

[24]The Court of Appeals for the Federal Circuit was created effective October 1, 1982, by P.L. 97–64 (4/2/82) to hear decisions appealed from the Claims Court (now the Court of Federal Claims).

Exhibit 2.5 The Federal Courts of Appeals

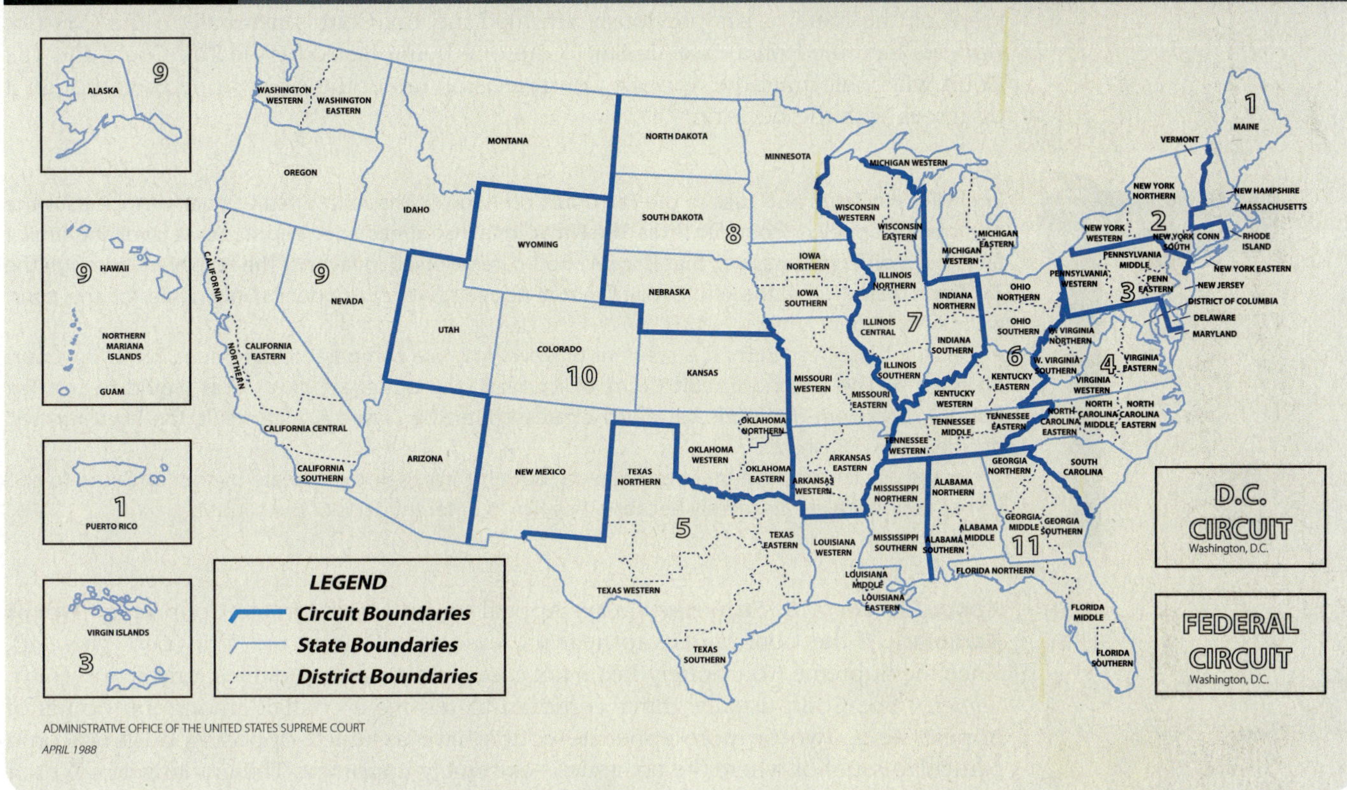

The Appellate Process

The *role* of the appellate court usually is limited to a review of whether the trial court applied the proper law in arriving at its decision. Rarely does an appellate court question a lower court's fact-finding determination. Both the Code and the Supreme Court indicate that Federal appellate courts are bound by findings of facts unless they are clearly erroneous.[25]

An appeal can have a number of possible outcomes. The appellate court may approve (affirm) or disapprove (reverse) the lower court's finding, or it may send the case back to the trial court for further consideration (remand). When many issues are involved, a mixed result is not unusual. As a result, the lower court may be affirmed (*aff'd*) on Issue A and reversed (*rev'd*) on Issue B and Issue C is remanded (*rem'd*) for additional fact finding.

When more than one judge is involved in the decision-making process, disagreements are common. In addition to the majority view, one or more judges may concur (agree with the result reached but not with some or all of the reasoning) or dissent (disagree with the result). In any decision, of course, the majority controls. But concurring and dissenting views can have an influence on future cases or other courts.

Appellate Precedents and the Tax Court District Courts, the Tax Court, and the Court of Federal Claims must abide by the **precedents** set by a Court of Appeals jurisdiction. A particular Court of Appeals need not follow the decisions of another Court of Appeals. All courts, however, must follow the decisions of the **U.S. Supreme Court**.

This pattern of appellate precedents raises an issue for the Tax Court. Because the Tax Court is a national court, it decides cases from all parts of the country. Under a

[25] §§ 7482(a) and (c). *Comm. v. Duberstein*, 60–2 USTC ¶9515, 5 AFTR 2d 1626, 80 S.Ct. 1190 (USSC, 1960). See Rule 52(a) of the Federal Rules of Civil Procedure.

policy known as the *Golsen* rule, the Tax Court decides a case as it believes the law should be applied *only* if the Court of Appeals of appropriate jurisdiction has not yet ruled on the issue or has previously affirmed the Tax Court's rationale. If the Court of Appeals has ruled on a case similar to the one being heard by the Tax Court, the Tax Court will conform to the Appeals Court decision under the *Golsen* rule even though it disagrees with the decision.[26]

Example 3

Emily lives in Texas and sues in the Tax Court on Issue A. The Fifth Circuit Court of Appeals is the appropriate appellate court for Texas. The Fifth Circuit has already decided, in a case involving similar facts but a different taxpayer, that Issue A should be resolved in favor of the taxpayer. Although the Tax Court believes that the Fifth Circuit Court of Appeals is wrong, under its *Golsen* rule, the trial court will rule in favor of Emily.

Shortly thereafter, Rashad, a resident of New York, in a comparable case, sues in the Tax Court on Issue A. The Second Circuit Court of Appeals, the appellate court that would hear a Tax Court appeal from New York, has never expressed itself on Issue A. As a result, the Tax Court will decide against Rashad.

As a result, it is possible for two taxpayers, both having their cases heard by the Tax Court, to end up with opposite results merely because they live in different parts of the country.

Appeal to the U.S. Supreme Court Appeal to the U.S. Supreme Court is by **Writ of Certiorari**. If the Court agrees to hear the case, it will grant the Writ (*Cert. granted*). Since the Supreme Court rarely hears tax cases, most often, it denies jurisdiction (*Cert. denied*). The Court usually grants certiorari to resolve a conflict among the Courts of Appeals (e.g., two or more appellate courts have assumed opposing positions on a particular issue) or where the tax issue is extremely important. The granting of a Writ of Certiorari indicates that at least four of the nine members of the Supreme Court believe that the issue is of sufficient importance to be heard by the full Court.

LO.2

Locate and work with the appropriate tax law sources.

Judicial Citations

Court decisions are an important source of tax law, and the ability to cite and locate a case is a critical skill when working with the tax law. Judicial citations usually follow a standard pattern: case name, volume number, reporter series, page or paragraph number, court (where necessary), and year of the decision (see Concept Summary 2.2). These conventions are based on the legacy of publishing court decisions in books, but they carry on even in today's electronic research environment.

Judicial Citations—The U.S. Tax Court The U.S. Tax Court issues two types of decisions: Regular and Memorandum, based on the Chief Judge's determination. They differ in both substance and form. In terms of substance, *Memorandum* decisions deal with cases that involve only the application of established principles of law. *Regular* decisions involve novel issues not previously resolved by the Tax Court. In actual practice, however, both *Regular* and *Memorandum* represent the position of the Tax Court and, as such, can be relied on.[27]

The Regular and Memorandum decisions issued by the Tax Court also differ in form. Regular decisions are published by the U.S. Government in a series entitled *Tax Court of the United States Reports* (T.C.). Each volume of these *Reports* covers a six-month period (January 1 through June 30 and July 1 through December 31) and is given a succeeding volume number. Usually there is a time lag between the date a decision is rendered and the date it is published. A temporary citation may be necessary to help the researcher locate a recent Regular decision. Consider, for example, the temporary and permanent citations for *Wiley Ramey*, a decision filed on January 14, 2021.

[26] *Jack E. Golsen*, 54 T.C. 742 (1970).

[27] In contrast, U.S. Tax Court Small Cases Division Summary Opinions carry no precedential value. Summary Opinions issued after January 9, 2001, are available on the U.S. Tax Court website.

Concept Summary 2.2

Judicial Sources

Court	Location	Authority
U.S. Supreme Court	S.Ct. Series (West) U.S. Series (U.S. Gov't.) L.Ed.2d (Lawyer's Co-op.) AFTR (RIA) USTC (CCH)	Highest authority
U.S. Courts of Appeal	Federal 3d (West) AFTR (RIA) USTC (CCH)	Next highest appellate court
Tax Court (Regular decisions)	U.S. Gov't. Printing Office RIA/CCH separate services	Highest trial court*
Tax Court (Memorandum decisions)	RIA T.C.Memo. (RIA) TCM (CCH)	Less authority than Regular T.C. decision
U.S. Court of Federal Claims**	Federal Claims Reporter (West) AFTR (RIA) USTC (CCH)	Similar authority as Tax Court
U.S. District Courts	F.Supp.2d Series (West) AFTR (RIA) USTC (CCH)	Lowest trial court
Small Cases Division of Tax Court	U.S. Tax Court website***	No precedent value

Note: All Judicial Sources can be accessed electronically through Thomson Reuters *Checkpoint* (and other commercial tax services).

*Theoretically, the Tax Court, Court of Federal Claims, and District Courts are on the same level of authority. But some people believe that because the Tax Court hears and decides tax cases from all parts of the country (i.e., a national court), its decisions may be more authoritative than a Court of Federal Claims or District Court decision.

**Before October 29, 1992, the U.S. Claims Court.

***Starting in 2001.

Temporary Citation { *Wiley Ramey*, 156 T.C. ____, No. 1 (2021).
Explanation: Page number left blank because not yet known.

Permanent Citation { *Wiley Ramey*, 156 T.C. 1 (2021).
Explanation: Page number now available.

Both citations tell us that the case will ultimately appear in Volume 156 of the *Tax Court of the United States Reports*. But until this volume is made available, the page number must be left blank. Instead, the temporary citation identifies the decision as being the first Regular decision issued by the Tax Court since Volume 155 ended. With this information, the decision can easily be located in the special Tax Court services published by Commerce Clearing House (CCH) and Research Institute of America (RIA). Once Volume 156 is released, the permanent citation can be substituted and the number of the case dropped. Starting in 1995, both Regular decisions and Memorandum decisions are published on the U.S. Tax Court website (**ustaxcourt.gov**). Memorandum decisions, although available on the U.S. Tax Court website, are not published by the U.S. Government.

Before 1943, the Tax Court was called the Board of Tax Appeals, and its decisions were published as the *United States Board of Tax Appeals Reports* (B.T.A.). These 47 volumes cover the period from 1924 to 1942. For example, the citation *Karl Pauli*, 11 B.T.A. 784 (1928), refers to the 11th volume of the *Board of Tax Appeals Reports*, page 784, issued in 1928.

Memorandum decisions are published by both CCH and RIA. Consider, for example, the three different ways the *Nick R. Hughes* case can be cited:

Nick R. Hughes, T.C.Memo. 2009–94

Explanation: The 94th Memorandum decision issued by the Tax Court in 2009.

Nick R. Hughes, 97 TCM 1488

Explanation: Page 1488 of Vol. 97 of the CCH *Tax Court Memorandum Decisions.*

Nick R. Hughes, 2009 RIA T.C.Memo. ¶2009,094

Explanation: Paragraph 2009,094 of the RIA *T.C. Memorandum Decisions.*

Note that the third citation contains the same information as the first. Thus, ¶2009,094 indicates both the year and decision number of the case.[28]

U.S. Tax Court Summary Opinions relate to decisions of the Tax Court's Small Cases Division.[29] These opinions may not be treated as precedent for any other case. For example, *Angela West*, decision entered on July 26, 2021, is cited as follows:

Angela West, T.C. Summary Opinion 2021–21.

If the IRS loses a decision, it may indicate whether it agrees or disagrees with the results reached by the court by publishing an **acquiescence** ("A" or "*Acq.*") or **nonacquiescence** ("NA" or "*Nonacq.*"), respectively. The acquiescence or nonacquiescence is published in the *Internal Revenue Bulletin* (and an *Action on Decision* is issued). The IRS can revoke an acquiescence or a nonacquiescence retroactively.

Most often, the IRS issues nonacquiescences to adverse decisions that are not appealed. In this manner, the Government indicates that it disagrees with the result reached, despite its decision not to seek review of the matter in an appellate court. A nonacquiescence provides a warning to taxpayers that a similar case cannot be settled administratively. A taxpayer will incur fees and expenses while the case moves through the IRS even though the IRS may be unwilling to litigate a fact pattern similar to a nonacquiescence decision.[30]

Judicial Citations—The U.S. District Court, Court of Federal Claims, and Courts of Appeals District Court, Court of Federal Claims, Court of Appeals, and Supreme Court decisions dealing with Federal tax matters are reported in both the CCH *U.S. Tax Cases* (USTC) and the RIA *American Federal Tax Reports* (AFTR) series. U.S. District Court decisions, dealing with *both* tax and nontax issues, also are published by West in its *Federal Supplement Second Series* (F.Supp.2d).[31] The following examples illustrate three different ways of citing a District Court case:

Turner v. U.S., 2004–1 USTC ¶60,478 (D.Ct. Tex., 2004).

Explanation: Reported in the first volume of the *U.S. Tax Cases*, published by Commerce Clearing House, for calendar year 2004 (2004–1) and located at paragraph 60,478 (¶60,478).

Turner v. U.S., 93 AFTR 2d 2004–686 (D.Ct. Tex., 2004).

Explanation: Reported in the 93rd volume of the second series of the *American Federal Tax Reports* (AFTR 2d), published by RIA, and beginning on page 686.

Turner v. U.S., 306 F.Supp.2d 668 (D.Ct. Tex., 2004).

Explanation: Reported in the 306th volume of the *Federal Supplement Second Series* (F.Supp.2d), published by West, and beginning on page 668.

The case name, the reference to the U.S. District Court of Texas (D.Ct. Tex.), and the year the decision was rendered (2004) appear in each of the citations.[32]

[28]In this text, the RIA citation for Memorandum decisions of the U.S. Tax Court is omitted. As a result, *Nick R. Hughes* is cited as 97 TCM 1488, T.C. Memo. 2009–94.

[29]In 2005, the U.S. Supreme Court held that decisions of the Small Cases Division must be made public.

[30]G. W. Carter, "Nonacquiescence: Winning by Losing," *Tax Notes* (September 19, 1988): 1301–1307.

[31]Cases prior to 1999 are found in West's *Federal Supplement Series* (F.Supp.).

[32]In this text, the case is cited in the following form: *Turner v. U.S.*, 2004–1 USTC ¶60,478, 93 AFTR 2d 2004–686, 306 F.Supp.2d 668 (D.Ct. Tex., 2004).

Decisions of the Court of Federal Claims[33] and the Courts of Appeals are published in the USTCs, the AFTRs, and two West reporters. The *Federal Third Series* (F.3d) reports Courts of Appeals decisions, whereas the *Federal Claims Reporter* (abbreviated as Fed.Cl.) reports Court of Federal Claims decisions.[34] The following examples illustrate the different forms:

Estate of Gribauskas v. Comm. (CA–2, 2003)

2003–2 USTC ¶60,466 (CCH citation)
92 AFTR 2d 2003–5914 (RIA citation)
342 F.3d 85 (West citation)

Apollo Computer, Inc. v. U.S. (Fed.Cl., 1994)

95–1 USTC ¶50,015 (CCH citation)
74 AFTR 2d 94–7172 (RIA citation)
32 Fed.Cl. 334 (West citation)

Estate of Gribauskas v. Comm. is a decision rendered by the Second Circuit Court of Appeals in 2003 (CA–2, 2003), and *Apollo Computer, Inc.*, was issued by the Court of Federal Claims in 1994 (Fed.Cl., 1994).

Judicial Citations—The U.S. Supreme Court Supreme Court decisions are published by CCH in the USTCs and by RIA in the AFTRs. The U.S. Government Printing Office also publishes these decisions in the *United States Supreme Court Reports* (U.S.), as does West in its *Supreme Court Reporter* (S.Ct.), and the Lawyer's Co-operative Publishing Company in its *United States Reports, Lawyer's Edition* (L.Ed.). The following illustrates the different ways the same decision can be cited:

U.S. v. The Donruss Co. (USSC, 1969)

69–1 USTC ¶9167 (CCH citation)
23 AFTR 2d 69–418 (RIA citation)
89 S.Ct. 501 (West citation)
393 U.S. 297 (U.S. Government Printing Office citation)
21 L.Ed.2d 495 (Lawyer's Co-operative Publishing Co. citation)

The parenthetical reference (USSC, 1969) identifies the decision as having been rendered by the U.S. Supreme Court in 1969. In this text, Supreme Court decision citations are limited to the CCH (USTC), RIA (AFTR), and West (S.Ct.) versions.

2-1d Other Sources of the Tax Law

Other sources of tax information that a tax professional may need to consult include tax treaties and tax periodicals.

Tax Treaties

The United States signs certain tax treaties (sometimes called tax conventions) with foreign countries to assist in tax enforcement and to avoid double taxation. These treaties affect transactions involving U.S. persons and entities operating or investing in a foreign country, as well as persons and entities of a foreign country operating or investing in the United States. Although these bilateral agreements are not codified in any one source, they are available from the IRS at **tinyurl.com/taxtreaties**, as well as in various commercial tax services.

Neither a tax law nor a tax treaty automatically takes legal precedence. When there is a direct conflict between the Code and a treaty, the most recent item takes precedence. A taxpayer must disclose on the tax return any position where a treaty overrides a tax law.[35]

[33]Before October 29, 1992, the Court of Federal Claims was called the Claims Court. Before October 1, 1982, the Court of Federal Claims was called the Court of Claims.

[34]West's *Federal Second Series* (F.2d) contains cases prior to 1994. Beginning in October 1982, the Court of Federal Claims decisions were published in a different West reporter called the *Claims Court Reporter* (abbreviated Cl.Ct.).

[35]§ 7852(d); there is a $1,000 penalty per failure to disclose for individuals and a $10,000 per failure penalty for corporations. See Reg. §§ 301.6114–1, 301.6712–1, and 301.7701(b)(7).

Tax Periodicals

The use of tax periodicals can often shorten the research time needed to resolve a tax issue. An article relevant to the issue at hand may provide the references needed to locate the primary sources of the tax law that apply (e.g., citations to judicial decisions, Regulations, and other IRS pronouncements).

Several indexes are available for locating tax articles, including CCH's *Federal Tax Articles* (which includes a subject index, a Code Section number index, and an author's index) and the *Index to Federal Tax Articles* (published by Thomson Reuters). Both of these indexes are available by subscription.

Here are some of the more useful tax periodicals:

Journal of Taxation
Journal of International Taxation
Practical Tax Strategies
Estate Planning
Corporate Taxation
Business Entities
Taxation of Exempts
Real Estate Taxation
store.tax.thomsonreuters.com

The Tax Executive
tei.org

The Tax Adviser (AICPA)
thetaxadviser.com

Tax Law Review
law.nyu.edu/tax/taxlawreview/

Journal of the American Taxation Association
aaajournals.org/loi/atax

The ATA Journal of Legal Tax Research
aaajournals.org/loi/jltr

Oil, Gas & Energy Quarterly
faculty.tamucc.edu/dcrumbley/index.html

Trusts & Estates
wealthmanagement.com/trusts-estates

Journal of Passthrough Entities
TAXES—The Tax Magazine
taxna.wolterskluwer.com

Tax Notes
Tax Notes State
Tax Notes International
taxnotes.com

LO.3

Develop an awareness of tax research tools.

2-2 Working with the Tax Law—Tax Research Tools

Tax law consists of a body of legislative (e.g., Code Sections and tax treaties), administrative (e.g., Regulations and Rulings), and judicial (e.g., court cases) pronouncements. Working with the tax law requires being able to locate and use these sources effectively. A major consideration is the time required to find relevant information related to the issues identified.

Unless the problem is simple (e.g., the Code Section is known and there is a Regulation on point), the research process begins with a tax service.

2-2a Commercial Tax Services

In the past, commercial tax services could be classified as *annotated* (i.e., organized by Internal Revenue Code) or *topical* (i.e., organized by major topics). However, as tax research has become electronic, this classification system is no longer appropriate. For example, Thomson Reuters *Checkpoint* includes both the *Federal Tax Coordinator 2d* (topical) and the *United States Tax Reporter* (annotated).

Here is a partial list of the available commercial tax services:

- *CCH IntelliConnect* and CCH *AnswerConnect*, CCH/Wolters Kluwer. Includes the *Standard Federal Tax Reporter* (along with other CCH materials).
- Thomson Reuters *Checkpoint*, Research Institute of America. Includes RIA's *Federal Tax Coordinator 2d* and *United States Tax Reporter*.

- *Practical Tax Expert*, CCH/Wolters Kluwer.
- *Tax Management Portfolios*, Bloomberg BNA.
- *Parker Tax Pro Library*.
- *Mertens Law of Federal Income Taxation*, Thomson Reuters.
- Thomson Reuters *Westlaw* and *WestlawNext*—compilations include access to *Tax Management Portfolios*, *Federal Tax Coordinator 2d*, and *Mertens*.
- LexisNexis *TaxCenter*—a compilation of primary sources and various materials taken from CCH, Matthew Bender, Kleinrock, and Bloomberg BNA.

2-2b Using Electronic (Online) Tax Services

A competent tax professional must become familiar and proficient with electronic research services and be able to use them to complete research projects efficiently. Following certain general procedures can simplify the research process. The following suggestions may be helpful:[36]

- Carefully choose keywords for the search and put quotation marks around the terms. Words with a broad usage, such as *income*, are of limited value. If the researcher is interested in a specific type of dividend income, the search phrase *dividend income* is too broad because it finds a variety of topics including stock dividends, constructive dividends, and liquidating dividends (drawing about 2,000 hits in Thomson Reuters *Checkpoint*). Searching for *qualified dividend income, stock dividend income, cash dividend income*, or *property dividend income* narrows the number of items found.
- Take advantage of *connectors* such as "+" and quotation marks to place parameters on the search and further restrict the output. Although each tax service has its own set of connectors, many are similar. Enclosing words in quotation marks means "exact phrase" in both Thomson Reuters *Checkpoint* and CCH *IntelliConnect* (e.g., "personal service corporation").
- Be selective in choosing the data to search. For example, if the research project does not involve case law, do not include judicial decisions in the search.
- Use a table of contents, an index, or a citation when appropriate. Although the key word approach is used most frequently, electronic databases can be searched in other ways. Using the table of contents or index may narrow the information that needs to be examined. Tax law (including annotations) also can be accessed by a citation: statutory (e.g., Code Section), administrative (e.g., Rev.Rul.), or judicial (e.g., Tax Court).
- Always check for current developments. Tax services are updated several times a day, and tax newsletters often feature highlights of recent tax law developments. In addition, there is no substitute for the original source. Do not base a conclusion solely on a tax service's commentary. If a Code Section, Regulation, or case is vital to the research, read it.

2-2c Noncommercial Electronic (Online) Tax Services

The internet provides a wealth of tax information in several popular forms, sometimes at no cost to the researcher. A tax professional can access a significant amount of information that can assist in the research process.

[36]For a more complete discussion of the use of Thomson Reuters *Checkpoint* and CCH *IntelliConnect* and internet research in taxation, see Sawyer and Gill, *Federal Tax Research*, 12th ed. (Cengage Learning, 2021), Chapters 6 and 7.

- *Websites* are provided by accounting and consulting firms, publishers, tax academics, libraries, and governmental bodies as a means of making information widely available. One of the best sites available to the tax professional is the Internal Revenue Service's home page, illustrated in Exhibit 2.6. This site offers downloadable forms and instructions, interpretations of Regulations, and news update items. Exhibit 2.7 lists some of the websites that may be most useful to tax researchers.
- *Blogs and RSS sites* provide a means by which information related to the tax law can be exchanged among taxpayers, tax professionals, and others who subscribe to the group's services. Individuals can read the exchanges and offer replies and suggestions to inquiries. Discussions address the interpretation and application of existing law, analysis of proposals and new pronouncements, and reviews of tax software.

Although tax information on the internet is plentiful, information in the public domain should not be relied upon without referring to other sources. Anyone can set up a website, and the quality of the information can be difficult for a tax professional to ascertain.

LO.4

Describe the tax research process.

2-3 Working with the Tax Law—Tax Research

Tax research is the process of finding a competent and professional conclusion to a tax problem. The problem may originate from completed or proposed transactions. In the case of a completed transaction, the objective of the research is to determine the tax result of what has already taken place. For example, is a taxpayer expense deductible? When dealing with proposed transactions, tax research has a different objective: effective tax planning by determining the tax consequences of various alternatives. A large part of a tax professional's career is spent on this type of tax research.

Exhibit 2.6 **The IRS's Home Page**

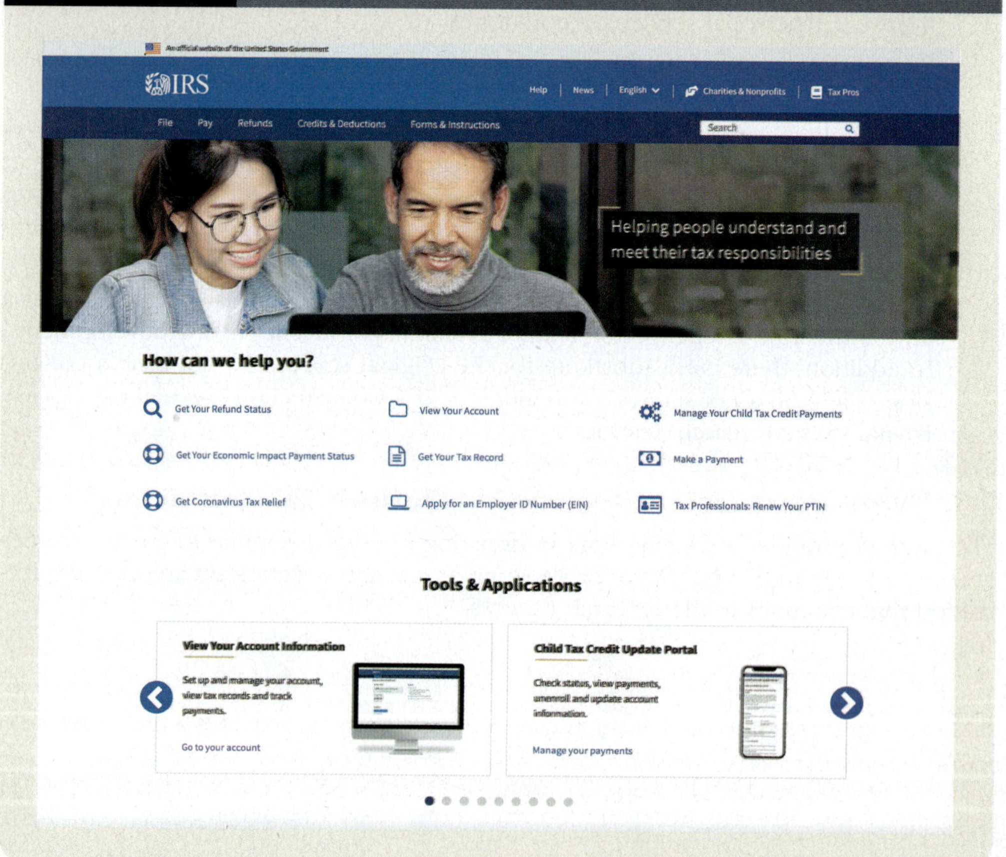

© IRS-Internal Revenue Service

Exhibit 2.7 **Tax-Related Websites**

Website	Web Address	Description
Accounting firms and professional organizations	For instance, the AICPA's page is at **aicpa.org**, Ernst & Young is at **ey.com**, Deloitte is at **deloitte.com**, KPMG is at **kpmg.com**, and PricewaterhouseCoopers is at **pwc.com**	Tax planning newsletters, descriptions of services offered and career opportunities, and exchange of data with clients and subscribers
Cengage Learning	**cengage.com**	Informational updates, newsletters, support materials for students and adopters, and continuing education
Commercial tax publishers	For instance, **taxnotes.com**, **taxna.wolterskluwer.com**, **tax.thomsonreuters.com**, and **pro.bloombergtax.com**	Information about products and services available for subscription and newsletter excerpts
Court opinions	The site at **law.justia.com** covers state, Federal, and Supreme Court decisions (but not Tax Court)	A synopsis of result reached by the court
Federal Register	**federalregister.gov**	Releases from the IRS (e.g., Regulations)
Internal Revenue Service	**irs.gov**	News releases, downloadable forms and instructions, tables, Circular 230, and e-mail
Tax Almanac	**taxalmanac.org**	Smorgasbord of tax research resources
Tax Analysts	**taxnotes.com**	Policy-oriented readings on the tax law and proposals to change it and articles on various tax subjects
	taxnotes.com/research/federal	Tax-related laws, regulations, rulings, procedures, and other documents
Tax Foundation	**taxfoundation.org**	Nonprofit educational organization that promotes sound tax policy and measures tax burdens
Tax laws online	Regulations are at **law.cornell.edu/cfr**, and the Code is at **uscode.house.gov**	
U.S. Tax Court decisions	**ustaxcourt.gov**	Recent U.S. Tax Court decisions

Caution: Web addresses change frequently.

Tax research involves the following steps:

- Identifying and refining the problem.
- Locating the appropriate tax law sources.
- Assessing the validity of the tax law sources.
- Arriving at the solution or at alternative solutions (including consideration of nontax factors).
- Effectively communicating the solution to the taxpayer.
- Updating the solution (where appropriate) in light of new developments.

The tax research process is illustrated in Exhibit 2.8. The broken lines reflect the steps of particular interest when tax research is directed toward proposed, rather than completed, transactions.

2-3a **Identifying the Problem**

Problem identification starts by documenting the relevant facts involved with the issue.[37] *All* of the facts that may have a bearing on the problem must be gathered; if any facts are omitted, the solution provided will likely change. To illustrate, return to the facts of

[37]For an excellent discussion of the critical role of facts in carrying out tax research, see Gardner, Stewart, and Worsham, *Tax Research Techniques*, 10th ed. (New York: The American Institute of Certified Public Accountants, 2017), Chapter 2.

Exhibit 2.8 **Tax Research Process**

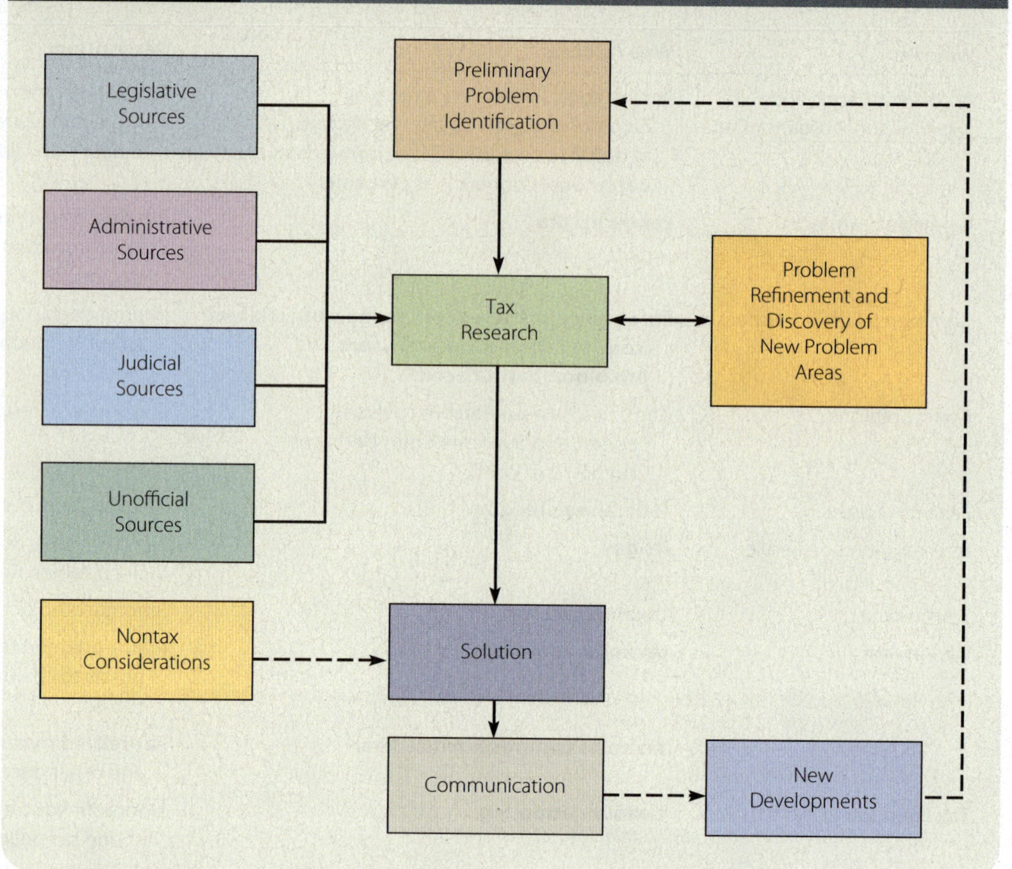

The Big Picture on p. 2-1 and consider the tax implications of the gold coins discovered by Fred and Megan Martel.

2-3b **Refining the Problem**

In the facts of *The Big Picture* on p. 2-1, the question of the tax implications of the Martels' discovery can be determined with some basic research. Internal Revenue Code § 61 defines gross income as "all income from whatever source derived."[38] Further, Treasury Regulation § 1.61–14(a) states that "a treasure trove, to the extent of its value in United States currency, constitutes gross income for the taxable year in which it is reduced to undisputed possession."

Given that the Martels discovered the coins on their property in March 2022 and the state returned the coins to them in October 2022 ("undisputed possession"), their gross income in 2022 will include the "value in United States currency" of the coins. The question of "value" is key to the Martels' situation.

2-3c **Locating the Appropriate Tax Law Sources**

Once a problem is clearly defined, what is the next step? Although the next step is a matter of individual judgment, most tax research begins with a keyword search using an electronic tax service. If the problem is not complex, the researcher may turn directly to the Internal Revenue Code and Treasury Regulations. The Code and Regulations are accessible electronically (and also available in print from a number of publishers).[39]

---

[38] See the related discussion in Chapter 3.

[39] The Internal Revenue Service provides a gateway to the Internal Revenue Code, Treasury Department Regulations, and other items at **irs.gov/tax-professionals/tax-code-regulations-and-official-guidance**.

2-3d Assessing the Validity of Tax Law Sources

Once a source has been located, the next step is to assess it in light of the problem at hand. Proper assessment involves careful interpretation of the tax law with consideration given to its relevance and validity. In connection with validity, an important step is to check for recent changes in the tax law.

Interpreting the Internal Revenue Code

The language of the Code can be extremely difficult to comprehend. Some of this difficulty is due to its structure (the Code follows the structure of all U.S. law), so getting used to reading (and interpreting) the Code can take time.

The Code must be read carefully for restrictive language such as "*at least* 80 percent" and "*more than* 80 percent" or "*less than* 50 percent" and "*exceeds* 50 percent." Whether two or more clauses are connected by *or* or by *and* makes a great deal of difference.

Sometimes the Code directs the researcher elsewhere for the answer. For example, § 162(c) refers to the Foreign Corrupt Practices Act for purposes of determining when payments to foreign officials are deductible.

Definitions vary from one Code Section to another. For example, § 267 disallows losses between related parties. Brothers and sisters are included in this definition of related parties. This is not the case with § 318, which deals with the definition of related parties for certain stock redemptions. Research has shown that in one-third of the conflicts reaching the Tax Court, the court could not discern the intent of Congress by simply reading the statute (the Court had to look to Committee Reports to understand intent).[40]

If an answer is not in the Code, it may be necessary to look to other tax law, including Regulations and judicial decisions.

Assessing the Validity of a Treasury Regulation

Treasury Regulations are the official interpretation of the Code and are entitled to great deference. Occasionally, however, a court invalidates a Regulation (or a portion of it) because the Regulation is contrary to the intent of Congress. Usually, courts do not question the validity of Regulations. Courts believe that "the first administrative interpretation of a provision as it appears in a new act often expresses the general understanding of the times or the actual understanding of those who played an important part when the statute was drafted."[41]

Keep the following things in mind when you assess the validity of a Regulation:

- IRS agents must give the Code and any related Regulations equal weight when dealing with taxpayers and their representatives.
- Proposed Regulations provide a preview of future Final Regulations, but they are not binding on the IRS or taxpayers.
- Taxpayers have the burden of proof to show that a Regulation varies from the language of the statute and is not supported by the related Committee Reports.
- If the taxpayer challenges a Regulation and loses, a 20 percent accuracy-related penalty may apply.[42]

[40] T. L. Kirkpatrick and W. B. Pollard, "Reliance by the Tax Court on the Legislative Intent of Congress," *The Tax Executive* (Summer 1986): 358–359.

[41] *Augustus v. Comm.*, 41–1 USTC ¶9255, 26 AFTR 612, 118 F.2d 38 (CA–6, 1941).

[42] §§ 6662(a) and (b)(1). This accuracy-related penalty applies to any failure to make a reasonable attempt to comply with the tax law and any disregard of rules and Regulations [§ 6662(c)]. The term *reasonable* is not defined in the Code; the IRS looks at all of the facts and circumstances surrounding the effort of the taxpayer to report the correct tax liability.

- Final Regulations can be classified as procedural, interpretive, or legislative. **Procedural Regulations** are *housekeeping-type instructions* indicating information that taxpayers should provide the IRS, as well as information about the internal management and conduct of the IRS itself.
- Some **interpretive Regulations** rephrase or elaborate what Congress stated in the Committee Reports that were issued when the tax legislation was enacted. These Regulations are almost impossible to overturn because they clearly reflect the intent of Congress. Historically, an interpretive Regulation has been given less deference than a legislative Regulation.[43] The Supreme Court has told lower courts to analyze Treasury Regulations carefully before accepting the Treasury's interpretation.[44]
- In some Code Sections, Congress has given the *Treasury Secretary or his delegate* the authority to prescribe Regulations to carry out the details of administration or to otherwise complete the operating rules. In these cases, Congress is delegating its legislative powers to the Treasury Department. Regulations issued under this type of authority possess the force and effect of law and are often called **legislative Regulations**.
- Courts tend to apply a legislative reenactment doctrine. A particular Regulation is assumed to have received congressional approval if the Regulation was finalized many years earlier and Congress has not amended the related Code Section.

Assessing the Validity of Other Administrative Sources of the Tax Law

Revenue Rulings issued by the IRS carry less weight than Treasury Department Regulations. Revenue Rulings are important, however, in that they reflect the position of the IRS on tax matters. IRS agents will follow the results reached in a Revenue Ruling that relates to the research question (or the tax return). A 1986 Tax Court decision, however, indicated that Revenue Rulings "typically do not constitute substantive authority for a position."[45] Most Revenue Rulings apply retroactively unless the ruling indicates otherwise.[46]

Actions on Decisions document the IRS's reaction to certain court decisions. The IRS follows a practice of either acquiescing (agreeing) or nonacquiescing (not agreeing) with selected judicial decisions.

Assessing the Validity of Judicial Sources of the Tax Law

How much reliance can be placed on a particular decision depends on the following variables:

- *The level of court.* A decision rendered by a trial court (e.g., a U.S. District Court) carries less weight than one issued by an appellate court (e.g., the Fifth Circuit Court of Appeals). Unless Congress changes the Code, decisions by the U.S. Supreme Court represent the last word on any tax issue.
- *Residence of the taxpayer.* A decision of the appellate court in the taxpayer's circuit carries more weight than one rendered by an appellate court in a different circuit. If, for example, a taxpayer lives in Texas, a decision of the Fifth Circuit Court of Appeals (which would hear an appeal from a Texas trial court) means more than one rendered by the Second Circuit Court of Appeals.[47]

---

[43] However, see *Mayo Foundation for Medical Education and Research*, 2011–1 USTC ¶50,143, 107 AFTR 2d 2011–341, 103 S.Ct. 704 (USSC, 2011), where the Supreme Court provided greater deference to interpretive Regulations (and appeared to blur the line between legislative and interpretive Regulations).

[44] *U.S. v. Vogel Fertilizer Co.*, 82–1 USTC ¶9134, 49 AFTR 2d 82–491, 102 S.Ct. 821 (USSC, 1982); *National Muffler Dealers Assn., Inc.*, 79–1 USTC ¶9264, 43 AFTR 2d 79–828, 99 S.Ct. 1304 (USSC, 1979).

[45] *Nelda C. Stark*, 86 T.C. 243 (1986). See also *Ann R. Neuhoff*, 75 T.C. 36 (1980). For a different opinion, however, see *Industrial Valley Bank & Trust Co.*, 66 T.C. 272 (1976).

[46] Rev.Proc. 87–1.

[47] Before October 1, 1982, an appeal from the then-named U.S. Court of Claims (the other trial court) was directly to the U.S. Supreme Court.

- *Regular or Memorandum decision.* A Tax Court Regular decision carries more weight than a Memorandum decision because the Tax Court does not consider Memorandum decisions to be binding precedents.[48] A Tax Court *reviewed* decision (where *all* of the Tax Court judges participate) carries even more weight.
- *Circuit Court decision.* A Circuit Court decision heard *en banc* (all of the judges participate) carries more weight than a normal Circuit Court case.
- *Other courts' support.* A decision that is supported by cases from other courts carries more weight than a decision that is not supported by other cases.
- *Status on appeal.* The weight of a decision also can be affected by its status on appeal. For example, was the decision affirmed or overruled?

In connection with the last three variables, the use of a citator is invaluable to tax research.[49] A **citator** provides the history of a case, including the authority relied on (e.g., other judicial decisions) in reaching the result. Reviewing the references listed in the citator discloses whether the decision was appealed and, if so, with what result (e.g., affirmed, reversed, or remanded). The Thomson Reuters *Checkpoint* citator also shows other cases with the same or similar issues and how they were decided. As a result, a citator reflects on the validity of a case and may lead to other relevant judicial material.[50] If one intends to rely on a judicial decision, "citating" the case is imperative.

Assessing the Validity of Other Sources

Primary sources of tax law include the Constitution, legislative history materials, statutes, treaties, Treasury Regulations, IRS pronouncements, and judicial decisions. The IRS considers only primary sources to constitute substantial authority. However, reference to *secondary sources* such as legal periodicals, treatises, legal opinions, IRS publications, and other materials can be useful. In general, secondary sources are not authority.

Although the statement that the IRS regards only primary sources as substantial authority generally is true, there is one exception. For purposes of the accuracy-related penalty in § 6662, the IRS expands the list of substantial authority to include a number of nonprimary sources (e.g., letter rulings, Chief Counsel Advice, and the Bluebook).[51] "Authority" does not include conclusions reached in treatises, legal periodicals, and opinions rendered by tax professionals.

A letter ruling or determination letter is substantial authority *only* for the taxpayer to whom it is issued, except for the accuracy-related penalty.

Once major tax legislation is completed, the staff of the Joint Committee on Taxation (in consultation with the staffs of the House Ways and Means and Senate Finance Committees) often prepares a General Explanation of the Act, commonly known as the Bluebook (because of the color of its cover). The IRS and the courts do not accept this detailed explanation as having legal effect. The Bluebook does, however, provide valuable guidance to tax advisers and taxpayers until Regulations are issued.

2-3e Arriving at the Solution or at Alternative Solutions

The Big Picture on p. 2-1 raises the question of how a "treasure trove" should be taxed. Based on Reg. § 1.61–14(a), the Martels must include in their gross income the "value in United States currency" of the coins once they have "undisputed possession" of the coins.

Does it make any difference that the couple paid $195,000 for the land where the coins were buried? Since the taxpayers found the gold coins on their own property, they could argue that they purchased the coins when they purchased the land. This argument is similar to an individual discovering oil or natural gas on her property. And with

[48] *Severino R. Nico, Jr.*, 67 T.C. 647 (1977).

[49] The major citators are published by CCH, RIA, Westlaw, and Shepard's.

[50] The CCH citator is available online through the CCH *IntelliConnect* service; RIA's citator can be found in Thomson Reuters *Checkpoint*. Westlaw's citator (KeyCite) is part of its online service. Shepard's citator is part of LexisNexis.

[51] Reg. § 1.6661–3(b)(2).

Financial Disclosure Insights — Where Does GAAP Come From?

Tax law is developed by many entities, including Congress, and the legislators of other countries, the courts, and the IRS. Accounting principles also have many sources. Consequently, in reconciling the tax and financial accounting reporting of a transaction, the tax professional needs to know the hierarchy of authority of accounting principles—in particular, the level of importance to assign to a specific GAAP document. The diagram below presents the sources of GAAP arranged in a general order of authority from highest to lowest.

Professional research is conducted to find and analyze the sources of accounting reporting standards in much the same way a tax professional conducts research on an open tax question. In fact, many of the publishers that provide tax research materials also can be used to find GAAP and International Financial Reporting Standards (IFRS) documents. The Financial Accounting Standards Board (FASB) also makes its standards and interpretations available by subscription.

Highest Authority

- Financial Accounting Standards and Interpretations of the FASB.
- Pronouncements of bodies that preceded the FASB, such as the Accounting Principles Board (APB).

- FASB Technical Bulletins.
- Audit and Accounting Guides, prepared by the American Institute of CPAs (AICPA) and cleared by the FASB.
- Practice Bulletins, prepared by the American Institute of CPAs (AICPA) and cleared by the FASB.

- Interpretation Guides of the FASB Staff.
- Accounting Interpretations of the AICPA.
- IASB Accounting Standards.
- FASB Concepts Standards.
- Widely accepted accounting practices, professional journals, accounting textbooks, and treatises.

natural resources, there must be a realization event (e.g., a sale or exchange) before there is income. Would this notion work for this couple? Unfortunately, no. A decision affirmed by the Sixth Circuit Court of Appeals indicates that the *entire value* of the couple's discovery would be included in their income in the year of discovery.[52] In *Cesarini*, the taxpayer purchased a piano that happened to conceal cash. The courts allocated the entire purchase price to the piano, so the "windfall" currency was wholly taxable in the year of discovery. Although the Martels might want to argue that there is no "income" until the coins are sold (i.e., the coins have a zero basis on discovery), Reg. § 1.61–14(a) and *Cesarini* indicate that the treasure trove's value should be included in gross income as soon as the couple has "undisputed possession."

Finally, the "value" is *not* the $28,000 face value of the coins. Rather, it is the *fair market* value of the coins. But how does one *value* the coins? It will likely depend on the appraisal of the coins (and, as you might suspect, there could be differences in appraisals). If the Martels sell any of the coins, they could argue that the best "value" would be the sales price of the coins. But an appraisal will be required to determine the fair market value of the coins, and this amount must be included in the Martels' 2022 gross income.[53]

LO.5

Communicate the results of the tax research process in a client letter and a tax file memorandum.

2-3f Communicating Tax Research

Once the research process has been completed (including checking for any new developments; see Exhibit 2.8), the researcher will need to prepare a memo, a letter, or an oral presentation. The form of communication depends on a number of factors. For example, most firms document the results of a tax research project in a memorandum. Although the

[52] *Cesarini v. U.S.*, 69–1 USTC ¶9270, 23 AFTR 2d 69–997, 296 F.Supp. 3 (D.Ct. N.Oh., 1969), *aff'd* 70–2 USTC ¶9509, 26 AFTR 2d 70–5107, 428 F.2d 812 (CA–6, 1970).

[53] This *Big Picture* example is based on a 2013 discovery made in California; see **en.wikipedia.org/wiki/Saddle_Ridge_Hoard**. For more detail on the tax implications of this discovery, see M. Morris, C. Cheng, and D. L. Crumbley, "The Saddle Ridge Gold Coin Discovery: How the U.S. Should Tax U.S. Currency Under the Treasure Trove Regulations," *Houston Business and Tax Law Journal*, Vol. 17, Issue 2 (2017), pp. 120–145.

format of this memorandum can vary, certain elements appear in all memos. In addition, virtually all memos are reviewed by senior tax professionals to ensure accuracy.

How are results communicated to the client (does the client receive the tax research memo, a letter, or some other form of communication)? If an oral presentation is required, who will be the audience? Whatever form it takes, the following elements will be part of the communication:

- A clear statement of the issue.
- In more complex situations, a short review of the facts that raised the issue.
- A review of the relevant tax law sources (e.g., Code, Regulations, Revenue Rulings, Revenue Procedures, Notices, and judicial authority).
- Any assumptions made in arriving at the solution.
- The solution recommended and the logic or reasoning supporting it.
- The references consulted in the research process.

A good tax research communication should tell the reader what was researched, the results of that research, and the justification for any recommendations.[54]

Exhibits 2.9 and 2.10 present the tax file memorandum (internal to the firm) and the client letter associated with the facts of *The Big Picture*.

Exhibit 2.9 Tax File Memorandum

November 11, 2022

TAX FILE MEMORANDUM

FROM: John J. Jones
SUBJECT: Fred and Megan Martel
Income from Coin Discovery

Today I met with Fred and Megan Martel related to a request for tax assistance. In 2017, the Martels purchased 40 acres of land for $195,000; they built their current residence on the property in 2018. In March 2022, while walking on a remote part of their property, they spotted something shiny on the ground. They started digging and eventually unearthed eight metal cans containing more than 1,400 rare gold coins in $5, $10, and $20 denominations dated from 1846 to 1895. The face value of the gold coins is about $28,000, and the coins are in mint condition. As required by state law, the Martels turned over the coins to the state for disposition. For a period of six months, the state was required to publicize the find and ask if anyone could prove ownership. When no one came forward, the coins were returned to the Martels in October 2022.

ISSUE: What are the tax implications of the Martels' coin discovery?

FINDINGS: Internal Revenue Code § 61 defines gross income as "all income from whatever source derived." Further, Treasury Regulation § 1.61–14(a) states that "a treasure trove, to the extent of its value in United States currency, constitutes gross income for the taxable year in which it is reduced to undisputed possession." The fact that the state returned the coins to the Martels in October 2022 appears to indicate "undisputed possession" as required by Reg. § 1.61–14(a). As a result, their gross income will include "value in United States currency" of the coins. The question of "value" is key to the Martels' situation.

Since the Martels found the gold coins on their own property, the taxpayers could argue that they purchased the coins when they purchased the land. This argument is similar to an individual discovering oil or natural gas on her property. With natural resources, there must be a realization event (e.g., a sale or exchange) before there is income.

Given the findings in *Cesarini* [70–2 USTC ¶9509, 26 AFTR 2d 70–5107, 428 F.2d 812 (CA–6, 1970)], this notion would not appear to work for the Martels. In *Cesarini*, the taxpayer purchased a piano that happened to conceal cash. The court allocated the entire purchase price to the piano, so the "windfall" currency was wholly taxable in the year of discovery. As a result, this decision by the Sixth Circuit Court of Appeals would indicate that the *entire value* of the couple's discovery is to be included in their income in the year of discovery.

Although the Martels might want to argue that there is no "income" until the coins are sold (i.e., the coins have a zero basis on discovery), Reg. § 1.61–14(a) and *Cesarini* indicate that the treasure trove's value should be included in gross income as soon as the couple has "undisputed possession."

Finally, the "value" is *not* the $28,000 face value of the coins. Rather, it is the *fair market value* of the coins. The Martels should engage a qualified appraiser (or appraisers) to value the coins appropriately. Then the appraised value of the coins will be included in their 2022 gross income.

[54] See Chapter 7 of the AICPA publication cited in Footnote 37. For oral presentations, see W. A. Raabe and G. E. Whittenburg, "Talking Tax: How to Make a Tax Presentation," *Tax Adviser* (March 1997): 179–182.

Exhibit 2.10 Client Letter

SWFT, LLP
5191 Natorp Boulevard
Mason, OH 45040

November 18, 2022

Mr. and Mrs. Fred Martel
111 Saddle Ridge Road
Williamsburg, VA 23185

Dear Mr. and Mrs. Martel:

This letter is in response to your request for advice related to your discovery of gold coins on your property in March 2022. Our conclusions are based on the facts discussed during our meeting with you on November 11, 2022. Any change in the facts may affect our conclusions.

In general, the fair market value of the coins you discovered must be included in your 2022 gross income. This conclusion is based on your "undisputed possession" of the coins (as of October 2022) and opinions expressed in U.S. Treasury Department Regulations and court cases (including one from the Sixth Circuit Court of Appeals).

Given the potential value of your discovery, I would encourage you to seek a competent appraiser (or appraisers) to assess the value of the coins. Once a determination of value is made, we can work on a plan to pay the related Federal and state income taxes.

Should you need more information or want to clarify our conclusions, do not hesitate to contact me.

Sincerely yours,

John J. Jones, CPA
Partner

LO.6

Apply tax research techniques and planning procedures.

2-4 Working with the Tax Law—Tax Planning

Tax research and tax planning are inseparable. The *primary* purpose of effective *tax planning* is to maximize the taxpayer's after-tax wealth. The course of action selected might not produce the lowest possible tax under the circumstances. The minimization of tax liability must be considered in context with the nontax goals of the taxpayer.

A *secondary* objective of effective tax planning is to reduce or defer the tax in the current tax year. Specifically, this objective aims to accomplish one or more of the following:

- Eliminating the tax entirely.
- Eliminating the tax in the current year.
- Deferring the receipt of income.
- Converting ordinary income into capital gains.
- Converting active income to passive activity income.
- Converting passive activity expense to active expense.
- Increasing the number of taxpayers (i.e., forming partnerships and corporations or making lifetime gifts to family members).
- Avoiding double taxation.
- Avoiding ordinary income.
- Creating, increasing, or accelerating deductions.

However, this objective should be approached with caution. For example, a tax election in one year may reduce taxes currently but cause future years to have disadvantageous tax positions.

2-4a **Nontax Considerations**

There is a danger that tax considerations may impair the exercise of sound financial planning or business judgment by the taxpayer. As a result, the tax planning process can lead to ends that are economically (or socially) incorrect. Unfortunately, a tendency exists for planning to move toward the opposing extremes of placing either too little or too much emphasis on tax considerations. The goal should be a balance that recognizes the significance of taxes, but not beyond the point where planning detracts from the exercise of good business judgment. In general, if the only reason for pursuing a specific course of action is because of the tax benefits, then one should rethink that decision.

2-4b **Components of Tax Planning**

The popular perception of tax planning often is restricted to the adage "defer income and accelerate deductions." Although this timing approach does hold true and is important, meaningful tax planning involves considerably more.

Preferable to deferring taxable income is complete *avoidance* of taxation. Consider, for example, the employee who chooses nontaxable fringe benefits (e.g., group term life insurance and health insurance coverage) over a fully taxable future pay increase.[55] Complete avoidance of gain recognition also occurs when the owner of appreciated property transfers it by death. Here, the "step-up" (appreciation) in basis to fair market value completely escapes the income tax.[56]

If the recognition of income cannot be avoided, its deferral will postpone income tax consequences. A tax paid in the future costs less than a tax paid today because of the time value of money. *Deferral* of income can take many forms. Besides like-kind exchanges and involuntary conversions, most retirement plans postpone income tax consequences until the benefits are paid. Deferral of gain recognition also can occur when appreciated property is transferred to a newly formed corporation or partnership.[57]

A corollary to the deferral of income is the acceleration of deductions. For example, if an accrual basis, calendar year corporation authorizes a charitable contribution in 2022 and pays it on or before the due date of its tax return in 2023, the deduction can be claimed for 2022.[58] Taxes also can be saved by *shifting* income to lower-bracket taxpayers. Gifts of appreciated property to lower-bracket family members can reduce the related capital gain tax rate on a later sale by 15 percentage points (from 15 percent to 0 percent).[59] For certain high-income taxpayers, the reduction is 20 percentage points.

If income cannot be avoided, deferred, or shifted, the nature of the gain can be *converted*. By changing the classification of property, income taxes can be reduced. As a result, a taxpayer who transfers appreciated inventory to a controlled corporation has converted ordinary income property (the inventory) to a capital asset (stock in the corporation). When the taxpayer's stock is later sold, preferential capital gain rates apply.

The conversion approach also can work in tax planning for losses. Properly structured, a loan to a corporation that becomes worthless can be an ordinary loss rather than a capital loss. Likewise, via § 1244, an investor in qualified small business stock can convert what would be a capital loss into an ordinary loss.[60]

Effective tax planning requires that careful consideration be given to the *choice of entity* used for conducting a business. The corporate form results in double taxation but permits shareholder-employees to be covered by fringe benefit programs. Partnerships and S corporations allow a pass-through of losses and other tax attributes, but transferring ownership interests as gifts to family members may be difficult.[61]

Although the substance of a transaction rather than its form generally controls, this rule is not always the case with tax planning. *Preserving formalities*, with particularly

---

[55]See text Sections 5-6 and 5-8 and Examples 19 and 40 in Chapter 5.

[56]See Example 24 in Chapter 14.

[57]See Examples 27 and 47 in Chapter 20.

[58]See Example 15 in Chapter 20.

[59]See text Section 14-3b in Chapter 14.

[60]See Example 9 in Chapter 7.

[61]See text Sections 20-5, 20-6, and 20-7c in Chapter 20.

clear documentation, often is crucial to the result. Is an advance to a corporation a loan or a contribution to capital? The answer may depend on the existence of a note.

Along with preserving formalities, the taxpayer should keep records that support how a transaction is treated. Returning to the issue of loan versus contribution to capital, how is the advance listed on the books of the borrower? What do the corporate minutes say about the advance?

Finally, effective tax planning requires *consistency* on the part of taxpayers. A shareholder who treats a corporate distribution as a return of capital cannot later avoid a stock basis adjustment by contending that the distribution was really a dividend.

In summary, the key components of tax planning include the following:

- *Avoid* the recognition of income (usually by resorting to a nontaxable source or nontaxable event).
- *Defer* the recognition of income (or accelerate deductions).
- *Convert* the classification of income (or deductions) to a more advantageous form (e.g., ordinary income into capital gain).
- *Choose* the business *entity* with the desired tax attributes.
- Preserve *formalities* by generating and maintaining supporting documentation.
- Act in a manner *consistent* with the intended objective.

2-4c Tax Avoidance and Tax Evasion

A fine line exists between legal tax planning and illegal tax planning—tax avoidance versus tax evasion. **Tax avoidance** is merely tax minimization through legal techniques, which is the proper objective of all tax planning. Tax evasion, although also aimed at the elimination or reduction of taxes, connotes the use of subterfuge and fraud as a means to an end. Popular usage—probably because of the common goals involved—has so linked these two concepts that many individuals are no longer aware of the true distinctions between them. Consequently, some taxpayers may not take advantage of planning possibilities. The now classic words of Judge Learned Hand in *Commissioner v. Newman* reflect the true values the taxpayer should have:

> Over and over again courts have said that there is nothing sinister in so arranging one's affairs as to keep taxes as low as possible. Everybody does so, rich or poor; and all do right, for nobody owes any public duty to pay more than the law demands: taxes are enforced extractions, not voluntary contributions. To demand more in the name of morals is mere cant.[62]

As Denis Healy, a former British Chancellor, once said, "The difference between tax avoidance and tax evasion is the thickness of a prison wall."

The National Taxpayers Union estimates that the annual economic tax compliance costs to taxpayers were $300 billion in 2020, with $84 billion borne by businesses.[63] Youssef Benzarti found that the costs of complying with the Federal individual income tax rose to 1.2 percent of GDP, or around $235 billion, in 2017.[64] For example, the Treasury Department's Final Regulations related to the qualified business income deduction are 248 pages long, and the IRS estimates that they could increase compliance costs by $1.3 billion over the next 10 years. Of course, additional time is spent filing state tax returns each year.

2-4d Follow-Up Procedures

Because tax planning usually involves a proposed (rather than a completed) transaction, being aware of if or when the law changes is critical to the tax planning process. A change in the tax law (legislative, administrative, or judicial) could alter the original conclusion. Additional research may be necessary to test the solution in light of current developments (refer to the broken lines at the right in Exhibit 2.8).

[62] *Comm. v. Newman*, 47–1 USTC ¶9175, 35 AFTR 857, 159 F.2d 848 (CA–2, 1947).

[63] Demian Brady, "Tax Complexity 2021: Compliance Burdens Ease for Third Year in a Row after Tax Reform," National Taxpayers Union, April 15, 2021.

[64] Youssef Benzarti, "How Taxing Is Tax Filing? Using Revealed Preferences to Estimate Compliance Costs," *American Economic Journal: Economic Policy*, 12(4): 38–57. See also, Alex Muresianu, "Simplifying the Tax Code and Reducing the Tax Gap: What Can Be Achieved?," Tax Foundation, July 28, 2021.

2-4e Tax Planning

Throughout this text, each chapter concludes with observations on Tax Planning. These observations are not all-inclusive, but they are intended to illustrate some of the ways in which the material covered in the chapter can be effectively utilized to minimize taxes.

2-5 Taxation on the CPA Examination

LO.7

Be aware of taxation on the CPA examination.

The CPA exam continues to test in the familiar four sections—Auditing and Attestation (AUD), Business Environment and Concepts (BEC), Financial Accounting and Reporting (FAR), and Regulation (REG). However, the exam continues to evolve, placing less emphasis on remembering-and-understanding skills and greater focus on higher-level analysis and evaluation skills.

- Task-based simulations, a highly effective way to assess higher-order skills, are part of each section of the CPA exam. Four task-based simulations appear on the BEC section, and eight task-based simulations appear on the AUD, FAR, and REG sections.
- Total testing time is 16 hours (4 hours per section).
- Multiple-choice questions and task-based simulations each contribute about 50 percent toward the candidate's score in the AUD, FAR, and REG sections. In the BEC section, multiple-choice questions contribute about 50 percent of the scoring, with 35 percent coming from task-based simulations and 15 percent from written communication.
- Using Bloom's taxonomy, the CPA exam tests remembering and understanding, application, analysis, and evaluation. In prior years, the CPA exam only tested for the first two of these items.

2-5a Preparation Blueprints

To prepare for the CPA exam, candidates are able to use AICPA-developed Blueprints that replaced the Content Specification Outline (CSO) and Skill Specification Outline (SSO).[65]

The Blueprints provide candidates with more detail about what to expect on the exam. They contain about 570 representative tasks, which are aligned with the skills required of newly licensed CPAs, across the four exam sections. The Blueprints are designed to provide candidates with clearer information on the material the exam tests and show educators what knowledge and skills candidates need as newly licensed CPAs. In addition, the Blueprints provide candidates with sample tasks that align with both the content and skill level at which the content will be tested.

2-5b Regulation Section

Taxation continues to be tested within the REG section of the CPA exam. Testing within REG is administered in five blocks called testlets, which feature multiple-choice questions (MCQs) and task-based simulations (TBSs). Candidates receive at least one research question (research-oriented TBS) that requires the candidate to search the applicable authoritative literature and find an appropriate reference.

Each of the five topics in REG includes one or more representative tasks that are not necessarily questions on the exam. For example, the exam does not specifically ask

[65]The Blueprints can be accessed at **future.aicpa.org/resources/article/learn-what-is-tested-on-the-cpa-exam**; the Practice Analysis Final Report that details the changes reflected in the Blueprints also is available on this website.

a candidate to "Calculate taxpayer penalties relating to Federal tax returns." However, identifying *situations* where a taxpayer penalty might apply would be appropriate. In addition, tasks are to be inclusive, not exclusive, of exam content. For example, the task "Calculate tax depreciation for a tangible business property..." could include the calculation of additional first-year (bonus) depreciation.

Task-based simulations are case studies that allow candidates to demonstrate their knowledge and skills by generating responses to questions rather than simply selecting an answer. They typically require candidates to use spreadsheets and/or to research authoritative literature provided in the CPA exam (e.g., Internal Revenue Code, Treasury Department Regulations, IRS publications, and Federal tax forms).

There are five content areas in the REG section of the CPA exam:

- Area 1: Ethics, professional responsibilities, and Federal tax procedures (weight: 10 to 20 percent).
- Area 2: Business law (weight: 10 to 20 percent).
- Area 3: Federal taxation of property transactions (weight: 12 to 22 percent).
- Area 4: Federal taxation of individuals (weight: 15 to 25 percent).
- Area 5: Federal taxation of entities (weight: 28 to 38 percent).

Area 1 covers ethics and responsibilities in tax practice, licensing and disciplinary systems, Federal tax procedures, and legal duties and responsibilities of a CPA.

Area 3 covers Federal taxation of property transactions and Federal estate and gift taxation.

Area 4 covers the Federal income taxation of individuals from both a tax preparation and tax planning perspective (e.g., income, exclusions, deductions, and retirement plans).

Area 5 covers the Federal income taxation of entities, including sole proprietorships, partnerships, limited liability companies, C corporations, S corporations, joint ventures, trusts, estates, and tax-exempt organizations from both a tax preparation and tax planning perspective.

Accounting methods and periods and tax elections are included in Areas 3, 4, and 5. Only Area 2 does not involve taxation.

Remembering-and-understanding skills are tested mainly in Areas 1 and 2. Application and analysis skills are tested primarily in Areas 3, 4, and 5. These three areas contain more of the day-to-day tasks that newly licensed CPAs are expected to perform. As a result, they are tested at the higher end of the skill level continuum. Overall, the REG section tests skills in the following way: remembering and learning (25 to 35 percent), application (35 to 45 percent), and analysis (25 to 35 percent). The REG section does not test any content at the evaluation skill level since newly licensed CPAs are not expected to demonstrate that level of skill in regard to the REG content.

Topical coverage in the REG section of the CPA exam is reviewed and updated regularly. For example, beginning in July 2021, the alternative minimum tax, estate taxation, and certain tax-exempt organization topics (obtaining and maintaining tax-exempt status) are no longer covered. In addition, net operating loss and capital loss limitations, unrelated business income of tax-exempt organizations, and bankruptcy and insolvency are being tested on a more simplified level.

The REG section has 76 multiple-choice questions and 8 task-based simulations (TBSs). The TBSs are used by the AICPA to assess the candidate's higher-order skills. In addition, TBSs on the CPA exam provide increased background material and data that require candidates to determine what information is or is not relevant to the question. The scoring weight of multiple-choice questions and TBSs is about 50 percent each on the REG section of the CPA exam.

Depending on the skill level being assessed, well-prepared candidates likely will spend 15 to 20 minutes for each TBS. Certain analysis and/or evaluation-level TBSs could take a well-prepared candidate up to 30 minutes to complete. Several illustrations of task-based simulations are shown in the examples that follow.

CPA Exam Simulation Examples

Example 4

The *tax citation type* simulation requires the candidate to research the Internal Revenue Code and enter a Code Section and subsection.

For example, Amber Company is considering using the simplified dollar-value method of pricing its inventory for purposes of the LIFO method that is available to certain small businesses. What Code Section is the relevant authority in the Internal Revenue Code you should use to determine whether the taxpayer is eligible to use this method? To be successful, the candidate must find § 474.

Example 5

A *tax form completion* simulation requires the candidate to fill out a portion of a tax form. For example, Red Company is a limited liability company (LLC) for tax purposes. Complete the income section of Form 1065 for Red Company using the values found and calculated on previous tabs along with the following data:

Ordinary income from other partnerships	$ 5,200
Net gain (loss) from Form 4797	2,400
Management fee income	12,000

The candidate is provided with page 1 of Form 1065 on which to record the appropriate amounts.

Any field that requires an entry is a shaded rectangular cell. Some white rectangular cells will automatically calculate based on the entries in the shaded cells.

Candidates can learn more about the CPA examination at **aicpa.org/resources/toolkit/cpa-exam**. In addition to accessing the Uniform CPA Examination Blueprints, candidates will find tutorials related to the exam, have the ability to take sample exams, learn how the exam is graded, and discover the requirements needed to sit for the CPA exam in each licensing jurisdiction.

In 2020, the AICPA and the National Association of State Boards of Accountancy (NASBA) announced the start of a modification to the CPA exam expected for 2024 (see **evolutionofcpa.org**). The change aims to ensure that the CPA designation reflects the knowledge and skills expected of a CPA today. The new approach to the CPA exam (and licensure) is a core plus disciplines. The core includes accounting, auditing, tax, and technology; all candidates take this part of the CPA exam. The three disciplines are business analysis and reporting, information systems and controls, and tax compliance and planning, with candidates taking an exam in *one* of these areas. Regardless of the chosen discipline, this model leads to full CPA licensure, and the CPA is not limited to practice only in the discipline selected for testing on the CPA exam.

Key Terms

Acquiescence, 2-16
Circuit Court of Appeals, 2-12
Citator, 2-25
Court of original jurisdiction, 2-10
Determination letters, 2-9
Final Regulations, 2-7
Interpretive Regulations, 2-24
Legislative Regulations, 2-24
Letter rulings, 2-8
Nonacquiescence, 2-16
Notices, 2-7
Precedents, 2-13
Procedural Regulations, 2-24
Proposed Regulations, 2-7
Revenue Procedures, 2-7
Revenue Rulings, 2-7
Small Cases Division, 2-10
Tax avoidance, 2-30
Tax research, 2-20
Technical Advice Memoranda (TAMs), 2-9
Temporary Regulations, 2-7
U.S. Court of Federal Claims, 2-10
U.S. District Court, 2-10
U.S. Supreme Court, 2-13
U.S. Tax Court, 2-10
Writ of Certiorari, 2-14

Discussion Questions

Note: Relevant documents for the end-of-chapter materials can be found by using the Thomson Reuters Checkpoint™ online tax research database (which accompanies this textbook), Tax Notes (taxnotes.com/research/federal), or the IRS website (including irs.gov/irb).

1. **LO.1** A large part of tax research consists of determining what?
2. **LO.1** Why do taxpayers often have more than one alternative for structuring a business transaction?
3. **LO.1** Where does Federal tax legislation generally originate?
4. Communications — **LO.2, 5** Sonja Bishop operates a small international firm named Tile, Inc. A new treaty between the United States and Spain conflicts with a Section of the Internal Revenue Code. Sonja asks you for advice. If she follows the treaty position, does she need to disclose this on her tax return? If she is required to disclose, are there any penalties for failure to disclose? Prepare a letter in which you respond to Sonja. Tile's address is 100 International Drive, Tampa, FL 33620.
5. **LO.1, 2** Interpret this Regulation citation: Reg. § 1.163–10(a)(2).
6. Critical Thinking — **LO.1** A client who is a small independent oil and gas producer asks you to determine whether the business qualifies for percentage depletion. The client is worried that it may be classified as a refiner. Look up and read Code § 613A(d)(4), and prepare a response to your client.
7. **LO.1, 4** Rank the following items from the lowest to highest authority in the Federal tax law system:
    a. Interpretive Regulation.
    b. Legislative Regulation.
    c. Letter ruling.
    d. Revenue Ruling.
    e. Internal Revenue Code.
    f. Proposed Regulation.
8. **LO.1** Interpret each of the following citations:
    a. Temp.Reg. § 1.956–2T.
    b. Rev.Rul. 2012–15, 2012–23 I.R.B. 975.
    c. Ltr.Rul. 200204051.
9. Communications — **LO.1, 5** Sally Andrews calls you on the phone. She says that she has found a 2015 letter ruling that agrees with a position she wants to take on her tax return. She asks you about the precedential value of a letter ruling. Draft a memo for the tax files, outlining what you told Sally.
10. Critical Thinking — **LO.1** Sri is considering writing the IRS to find out whether a possible stock redemption would be a qualified stock redemption. Outline some relevant tax issues Sri faces in determining whether to request a letter ruling.
11. **LO.1** Where may private letter rulings be found?
12. **LO.1** What are the differences between Technical Advice Memoranda (TAMs) and Technical Expedited Advice Memoranda (TEAMs)?
13. Critical Thinking — **LO.1** Sanjay receives a settlement letter from the IRS after his discussion with an IRS appeals officer. He is not satisfied with the $101,000 settlement offer. Identify the relevant issues facing Sanjay if he chooses to contest the settlement offer.
14. **LO.1** List an advantage and a disadvantage of using the U.S. Court of Federal Claims as the trial court for Federal tax litigation.

15. **LO.1, 5** Eddy Falls is considering litigating a tax deficiency of approximately $229,030 in the court system. He asks you to provide him with a short description of his alternatives, indicating the advantages and disadvantages of each. Prepare your response to Eddy in the form of a letter. His address is 200 Mesa Drive, Tucson, AZ 85714. Communications Planning

16. **LO.1** List an advantage and a disadvantage of using the U.S. Tax Court as the trial court for Federal tax litigation.

17. **LO.1** A taxpayer lives in Michigan. In a controversy with the IRS, the taxpayer loses at the trial court level. Describe the appeal procedure under the following different assumptions:
    a. The trial court was the Small Cases Division of the U.S. Tax Court.
    b. The trial court was the U.S. Tax Court.
    c. The trial court was a U.S. District Court.
    d. The trial court was the U.S. Court of Federal Claims.

18. **LO.1** What is meant by the term *petitioner*?

19. **LO.1** An appellate court will often become involved in fact-finding determination. Discuss the validity of this statement.

20. **LO.1** For the U.S. Tax Court, U.S. District Court, and U.S. Court of Federal Claims, indicate the following:
    a. Number of regular judges per court.
    b. Availability of a jury trial.
    c. Whether the deficiency must be paid before the trial.

21. **LO.1** A taxpayer living in the following states would appeal a decision of the U.S. District Court to which Court of Appeals?
    a. Wyoming.
    b. Nebraska.
    c. Idaho.
    d. Louisiana.
    e. Illinois.

22. **LO.1** What precedents must each of these courts follow?
    a. U.S. Tax Court.
    b. U.S. Court of Federal Claims.
    c. U.S. District Court.

23. **LO.1** What determines the appropriate Circuit Court of Appeals for a particular taxpayer?

24. **LO.1, 2, 4** In assessing the validity of a prior court decision, discuss the significance of the following on the taxpayer's issue:
    a. The decision was rendered by the U.S. District Court of Wyoming. Taxpayer lives in Wyoming.
    b. The decision was rendered by the U.S. Court of Federal Claims. Taxpayer lives in Wyoming.
    c. The decision was rendered by the Second Circuit Court of Appeals. Taxpayer lives in California.
    d. The decision was rendered by the U.S. Supreme Court.
    e. The decision was rendered by the U.S. Tax Court. The IRS has acquiesced in the result.
    f. Same as part (e), except that the IRS has issued a nonacquiescence as to the result.

25. **LO.2** In the citation *Schuster's Express, Inc.*, 66 T.C. 588 (1976), *aff'd* 562 F.2d 39 (CA–2, 1977), *nonacq.*, to what do the 66, 39, and *nonacq.* refer?

26. **LO.1** Is there an automatic right to appeal to the U.S. Supreme Court? If so, what is the process?

27. **LO.2** Referring to the citation only, determine which court issued these decisions.
    a. 716 F.2d 693 (CA–9, 1983).
    b. 20 T.C. 734 (1953).
    c. 348 U.S. 426 (1955).
    d. 3 B.T.A. 1042 (1926).
    e. T.C.Memo. 1957–169.
    f. 50 AFTR2d 92–6000 (Ct. Cl., 1992).
    g. Ltr.Rul. 9046036.
    h. 111 F.Supp.2d 1294 (S.D.N.Y., 2000).
    i. 98–50, 1998–1 C.B. 10.

28. **LO.2** Interpret each of the following citations:
    a. 14 T.C. 74 (1950).
    b. 592 F.2d 1251 (CA–5, 1979).
    c. 95–1 USTC ¶50,104 (CA–6, 1995).
    d. 75 AFTR2d 95–110 (CA–6, 1995).
    e. 223 F.Supp. 663 (W.D. Tex., 1963).
    f. 491 F.3d 53 (CA–1, 2007).
    g. 775 F.Supp.2d 765 (D.Ct. V.I., 2011).

29. **LO.2** Give the Commerce Clearing House citation for the following courts:
    a. Small Cases Division of the Tax Court.
    b. U.S. District Court.
    c. U.S. Supreme Court.
    d. U.S. Court of Federal Claims.
    e. Tax Court Memorandum decision.

30. **LO.2** Where can you locate a published decision of the U.S. Court of Federal Claims?

31. **LO.1, 2** Which of the following items probably can be found in the *Internal Revenue Bulletin*?
    a. Action on Decision.
    b. Small Cases Division of the U.S. Tax Court decision.
    c. Letter ruling.
    d. Revenue Procedure.
    e. Finalized Regulation.
    f. U.S. Court of Federal Claims decision.
    g. Acquiescences to Tax Court decisions.
    h. U.S. Circuit Court of Appeals decision.

Critical Thinking

32. **LO.3** For her tax class, Yvonne must prepare a research paper discussing the tax aspects of qualified stock options. Explain to Yvonne how she can research this topic using various tax research resources.

33. **LO.4** Where can a researcher find the current Internal Revenue Code of 1986?

Critical Thinking
Decision Making

34. **LO.2, 3, 4** You inherit a tax problem that was researched five months ago. You believe the answer is correct, but you are unfamiliar with the general area. How would you find recent articles dealing with the subject area? How do you evaluate the reliability of the authority cited in the research report? How do you determine the latest developments pertaining to the research problem?

35. **LO.6** What is the primary purpose of effective tax planning? Explain.

36. **LO.7** Describe the task-based simulations that are part of the CPA exam.

Problems

37. **LO.1** In which Subchapter of the Internal Revenue Code would one find information about corporate distributions?
    a. Subchapter S.
    b. Subchapter C.
    c. Subchapter P.
    d. Subchapter K.
    e. Subchapter M.

38. **LO.1, 2** Identify the general contents of each of the following Internal Revenue Code sections:
    a. § 1.
    b. § 11.
    c. § 61.
    d. § 62.
    e. § 162.
    f. § 212.
    g. § 262.

39. **LO.1, 2** Log on to **waysandmeans.house.gov** (the website for the House Ways and Means Committee of the U.S. House of Representatives) and answer the following questions:
    a. Who is the Chair of the committee? What district does he or she represent?
    b. What is the total number of members on the committee? How many are representatives of each party (Democratic and Republican)?
    c. Locate and summarize the history of the committee.
    d. The Ways and Means Committee has several subcommittees. Identify three of these subcommittees.

40. **LO.1** To locate an IRS Revenue Procedure that was issued during the past month, which source would you consult?
    a. *Federal Register*.
    b. *Internal Revenue Bulletin*.
    c. Internal Revenue Code.
    d. Some other source.

41. **LO.1** Which of the following items can be found in the *Federal Register*?
    a. Letter Ruling.
    b. Action on Decision.
    c. Revenue Procedure.
    d. Temporary Regulation.
    e. Technical Advice Memorandum.

42. **LO.1, 4** Rank the items below from most reliable to least reliable. Decision Making
    a. Letter Ruling.
    b. Legislative Regulation.
    c. Code Section.
    d. Revenue Ruling.
    e. Proposed Regulation.
    f. Interpretive Regulation.
    g. Recent Temporary Regulation.

43. **LO.1, 2** Locate each of the following revenue rulings. What is the subject of each ruling?
    a. Rev.Rul. 2021–1.
    b. Rev.Rul. 2014–17.
    c. Rev.Rul. 77–323.
    d. Rev.Rul. 2005–47.

44. **LO.1, 2** Locate each of the following revenue procedures. What is the subject of each procedure?
    a. Rev.Proc. 2015–48.
    b. Rev.Proc. 2021–31.
    c. Rev.Proc. 2017–60.
    d. Rev.Proc. 86–14.

45. **LO.1, 2** Locate, read, and summarize Announcement 2020-1.

46. **LO.1, 2** Locate, read, and summarize PLR 201450001.

47. **LO.1, 2** Locate the pronouncement at 2019–14 I.R.B. 931.
    a. Identify the pronouncement.
    b. What issue is addressed by the pronouncement?
    c. What is the holding of the pronouncement?

Critical Thinking

48. **LO.1, 2** Sonja and Evan are homeowners with an adjustable rate mortgage. In 2020, they claimed an itemized deduction for interest paid. In 2022, due to an error noted by their mortgage servicer, they receive a refund of a portion of the interest they paid in 2020. Are Sonja and Evan required to include the refund as gross income? Locate and read Announcement 92–172 and formulate a response.

Critical Thinking

49. **LO.1, 2** Leland and Amy are buying their first home. They are considering paying "points" to reduce the interest rate on a Veteran Affairs (VA) or Federal Housing Administration (FHA) loan. If they do this, they would like to know whether this expense can be deducted in the year a house is purchased. Locate Rev. Proc. 92–12 and Rev. Proc. 94–27 and formulate a response.

Critical Thinking
Decision Making

50. **LO.2** A client contacts you and asks if an exchange of different cryptocurrencies qualifies for like-kind exchange treatment (e.g., an exchange of bitcoin for ethereum). In addition, she mines cryptocurrency and would like to know if her activities result in self-employment income. Research these questions in preparation for a meeting with your client.

Critical Thinking

51. **LO.2** A client contacts you and indicates that she would like to obtain a private letter ruling from the IRS. You are not familiar with the process. How do you determine what is required to obtain a private letter ruling?

Critical Thinking
Decision Making

52. **LO.2** Alejandra invites Zach, a business client, to a college football game. Alejandra purchases both tickets and buys Zach's lunch in the alumni tent before the game. The lunch is purchased separately from the tickets. Substantive business discussions occur during lunch and at various times during the football game. Consult § 274, Reg. §§ 1.274–12 and 1.274–11(b)(1), and Notice 2018–76 to determine which of these expenses are deductible (if any).

53. **LO.4** Using the legend provided, classify each of the following tax sources:

Legend
P = Primary tax source
S = Secondary tax source
B = Both
N = Neither

a. Sixteenth Amendment to the U.S. Constitution.
b. Tax treaty between the United States and India.
c. Revenue Procedure.
d. An IRS publication.
e. U.S. District Court decision.
f. *Yale Law Journal* article.
g. Temporary Regulations (issued 2019).
h. U.S. Tax Court Memorandum decision.
i. Small Cases Division of the U.S. Tax Court decision.
j. House Ways and Means Committee report.
k. Notice.

54. **LO.1, 2** Using the legend provided, classify each of the following citations as to publisher:

Legend
RIA = Research Institute of America
CCH = Commerce Clearing House
W = West
U.S. = U.S. Government
O = Others

a. 83–2 USTC ¶9600.
b. 52 AFTR 2d 83–5954.
c. 67 T.C. 293 (1976).
d. 39 TCM 32 (1979).
e. 416 U.S. 938.
f. RIA T.C. Memo. ¶80,582.
g. 89 S.Ct. 501.
h. 40 Fed.Cl. 172.
i. 415 F.2d 488.
j. 592 F.Supp. 18.
k. 77–37, 1977–2 C.B. 568.
l. S. Rep. No. 1622, 83rd Cong., 2d Sess. 42 (1954).

55. **LO.1,2** Locate the court case *Commissioner v. Glenshaw Glass Co.*, 348 U.S. 486. Read the case and answer the following questions: Critical Thinking
a. Which court heard this case?
b. In what year was the case decided?
c. What was the issue (or issues) involved in the case? What was the court's ruling?

56. **LO.1,2** Locate the court case *David H. Hoffman, et ux. v. Commissioner*, T.C. Memo. 2016–69. Use the headnotes to the case to answer the following questions: Critical Thinking
a. What issue (or issues) did the court address?
b. What was the court's ruling?

57. **LO.1,2** Locate the court decision with the following citation: 144 T.C. 279. Critical Thinking
a. What is the name of the case?
b. Which court heard this case?
c. In what year was the case decided?
d. What was the issue (or issues) involved in the case? What was the court's ruling?

58. **LO.6** Using the legend provided, classify each of the following statements:

Legend
A = Tax avoidance
E = Tax evasion
N = Neither

a. Sue writes a $707 check for a charitable contribution on December 26, 2022, but does not mail the check to the charitable organization until January 10, 2023. She takes a deduction in 2022.

b. Sam decides not to report interest income from a bank because the amount is only $19.75.

c. Harry pays property taxes on his home in December 2022 rather than waiting until February 2023.

d. Variet switches her investments from taxable corporate bonds to tax-exempt municipal bonds.

e. Mel encourages his mother to save most of her Social Security benefits so that he will be able to claim her as a dependent.

Research Problems

the answer company™ THOMSON REUTERS®

Note: Solutions to the Research Problems can be prepared by using the Thomson Reuters Checkpoint™ online tax research database, which accompanies this textbook. Solutions can also be prepared by using research materials found in a typical tax library.

Research Problem 1. Determine the missing data in these court decisions and rulings.

a. *Higgens v. Comm.*, 312 U.S. ______ (1941).

b. *Talen v. U.S.*, 355 F.Supp.2d 22 (D.Ct. D.C., ______).

c. Rev.Rul. 2008–18, 2008–13 I.R.B. ______.

d. *Pahl v. Comm.*, 150 F.3d 1124 (CA–9, ______).

e. *Veterinary Surgical Consultants PC*, 117 T.C. ______ (2001).

f. *Yeagle Drywall Co.*, T.C.Memo. 2001______.

Research Problem 2. Can a Tax Court Small Case Decision be treated as a precedent for other cases? Explain.

Partial list of research aids:
IRC § 7463(b).
Maria Antionette Walton Mitchell, T.C. Summ. 2004–160.

Decision Making

Research Problem 3. When Oprah gave away new cars to her TV audience, was the value of the cars taxable? Several years ago, World Furniture Mall in Plano, Illinois, gave away $275,000 of furniture because the Chicago Bears shut out the Green Bay Packers in the team's football season opener at Lambeau Field in Green Bay. Was the free furniture in the form of a discount or rebate taxable, or should the furniture company have handed the customers a Form 1099–MISC?

Decision Making

Research Problem 4. You are interviewing a client before preparing his tax return. He indicates that he did not list as income $96,000 received as a recovery for false imprisonment. What should you do with respect to this significant recovery?

Partial list of research aids:
CCA 200809001.
Daniel and Brenda Stadnyk, T.C.Memo. 2008–289.
Rev.Rul. 2007–14.
§ 104.

Use internet tax resources to address the following questions. Look for reliable websites and blogs of the IRS and other government agencies, media outlets, businesses, tax professionals, academics, think tanks, and political outlets.

Research Problem 5. (1) Use an internet search engine (e.g., Google) to find Internal Revenue Code § 61(a). What is defined in this Code Section? Is the definition broad or narrow? (2) Go to the U.S. Tax Court website (**ustaxcourt.gov**), and find the U.S Tax Court case in which Mark Spitz, the former Olympic gold medalist, is the petitioner. Answer the following questions about the case:

a. What tax years are at issue in the case?
b. In what year was the case decided?
c. Did the court decide in favor of Mr. Spitz or the IRS?
d. Were any penalties imposed on Mr. Spitz? Why or why not?

Research Problem 6. Go to the U.S. Tax Court website (**ustaxcourt.gov**). Communications

a. What different types of cases can be found on the site?
b. What is a Summary Opinion? Find one (and record its citation).
c. What is a Memorandum Opinion? Find one (and record its citation).
d. Find the "Rules of Practice and Procedure." Summarize one (and its citation).
e. Communicate your findings in an e-mail to your instructor. Is the website reader-friendly? If not, e-mail the Tax Court (and copy your instructor).

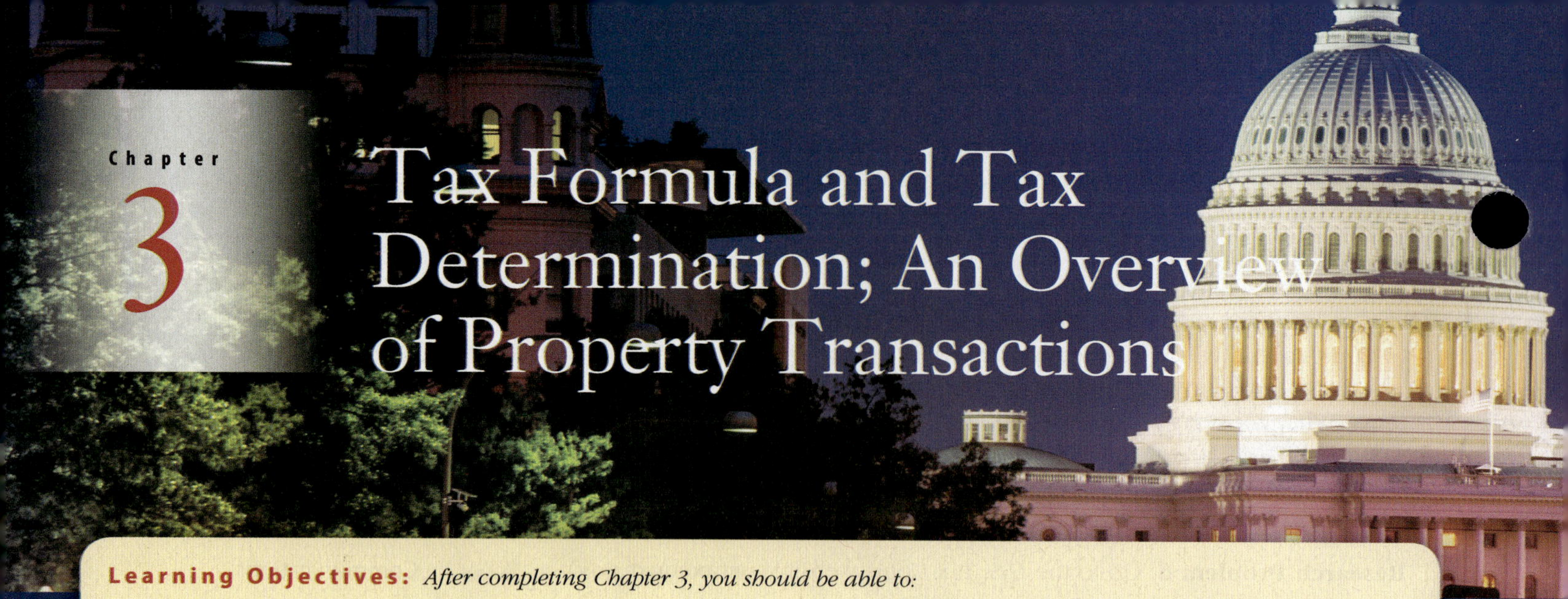

Chapter 3

Tax Formula and Tax Determination; An Overview of Property Transactions

Learning Objectives: *After completing Chapter 3, you should be able to:*

- **LO.1** **Identify and apply the components of the Federal income tax formula.**
- **LO.2** **Explain the standard deduction and evaluate its choice in arriving at taxable income.**
- **LO.3** **Describe the current status of the exemption deduction.**
- **LO.4** **Explain the rules for determining whether someone is a dependent.**
- **LO.5** **Choose the proper filing status and identify the related filing requirements.**
- **LO.6** **Demonstrate the proper procedures for determining the tax liability.**
- **LO.7** **Identify and report the unearned income of dependent children (the kiddie tax).**
- **LO.8** **Explain the fundamentals of property transactions.**
- **LO.9** **Evaluate tax planning opportunities associated with the individual tax formula.**

Chapter Outline

3-1 Tax Formula, 3-2
- 3-1a Components of the Tax Formula, 3-3
- 3-1b Tax Formula—Correlation with Form 1040, 3-8

3-2 Standard Deduction, 3-17
- 3-2a Basic and Additional Standard Deduction, 3-17
- 3-2b Individuals Not Eligible for the Standard Deduction, 3-18
- 3-2c Special Limitations on the Standard Deduction for Dependents, 3-18

3-3 Exemptions, 3-19

3-4 Dependents, 3-19
- 3-4a Qualifying Child, 3-19
- 3-4b Qualifying Relative, 3-21
- 3-4c Other Rules for Determining Dependents, 3-25
- 3-4d Comparison of Dependent Categories, 3-25
- 3-4e Child and Dependent Tax Credits, 3-26

3-5 Filing Status and Filing Requirements, 3-29
- 3-5a Filing Status, 3-29
- 3-5b Filing Requirements, 3-33

3-6 Tax Determination, 3-34
- 3-6a Tax Rates, 3-35
- 3-6b Computation of Net Taxes Payable or Refund Due, 3-36
- 3-6c Kiddie Tax—Unearned Income of Dependent Children, 3-37

3-7 Tax Return Filing Procedures, 3-39
- 3-7a Selecting the Proper Form, 3-39
- 3-7b The E-File Approach, 3-40
- 3-7c When and Where to File, 3-40
- 3-7d Modes of Payment, 3-41

3-8 Gains and Losses from Property Transactions—In General, 3-41

3-9 Gains and Losses from Property Transactions—Capital Gains and Losses, 3-42
- 3-9a Definition of a Capital Asset, 3-42
- 3-9b Determination of Net Capital Gain, 3-42
- 3-9c Treatment of Net Capital Loss, 3-43
- 3-9d Taxation of Net Capital Gain, 3-43
- 3-9e Taxation of Virtual Currency, 3-44

3-10 Tax Planning, 3-45
- 3-10a Maximizing the Use of the Standard Deduction, 3-45
- 3-10b Dependents, 3-45
- 3-10c Taking Advantage of Tax Rate Differentials, 3-46
- 3-10d Income of Certain Children, 3-47

The Big Picture

A Divided Household

Aleha maintains a household in which she lives with her unemployed husband (Trevor), stepdaughter (Paige), and a family friend (Terrah). She provides more than half of the support for both Paige and Terrah. Terrah was fatally injured in an automobile accident in February, and Aleha paid for her hospitalization and funeral expenses. Paige, an accomplished gymnast, graduated from high school last year. Paige has a part-time job but spends most of her time training and looking for an athletic scholarship to the "right" college. In March, Trevor left for parts unknown and has not been seen or heard from since. Aleha was more surprised than distressed over Trevor's unexpected departure. One reaction, however, was to sell her wedding rings to a cousin who was getting married. The rings cost $11,800 and were sold for their approximate value of $9,000.

Based on these facts, what are Aleha's income tax concerns for the current year?

Read the chapter and formulate your response.

Framework 1040 **Tax Formula for Individuals**

This chapter covers the boldfaced portions of the Tax Formula for Individuals that is introduced in Concept Summary 3.1 on p. 3-3. Below those portions are the sections of Form 1040 where the results are reported.

Income *(broadly defined)*	$ xx,xxx
Less: Exclusions	(x,xxx)
Gross income	**$xx,xxx**
Less: Deductions *for* adjusted gross income	**(x,xxx)**
Adjusted gross income	$ xx,xxx

FORM 1040 (p. 1)

Filing Status Check only one box. ☐ Single ☐ Married filing jointly ☐ Married filing separately (MFS) ☐ Head of household (HOH) ☐ Qualifying widow(er) (QW)
If you checked the MFS box, enter the name of your spouse. If you checked the HOH or QW box, enter the child's name if the qualifying person is a child but not your dependent ►

FORM 1040 (p. 1)

Standard Deduction **Someone can claim:** ☐ You as a dependent ☐ Your spouse as a dependent
☐ Spouse itemizes on a separate return or you were a dual-status alien

Age/Blindness **You:** ☐ Were born before January 2, 1957 ☐ Are blind **Spouse:** ☐ Was born before January 2, 1957 ☐ Is blind

Dependents (see instructions): (1) First name Last name	(2) Social security number	(3) Relationship to you	(4) ✔ if qualifies for (see instructions): Child tax credit	Credit for other dependents

FORM 1040 (p. 1)

12a Standard deduction or itemized deductions (from Schedule A)

12b Charitable contributions if you take the standard deduction*

13 Qualified business income deduction.*** (Attach Form 8995 or Form 8995-A)

Personal and dependency exemptions**	(x,xxx)
Taxable income	**$ xx,xxx**
Tax on taxable income *(see Tax Tables or Tax Rate Schedules)*	**$ x,xxx**
Less: Tax credits *(including income taxes withheld and prepaid)*	(xxx)
Tax due (or refund)	$ xxx

* For 2021, married taxpayers may claim up to $600 of cash charitable donations ($300 if unmarried).
** Exemption deductions are not allowed from 2018 through 2025.
*** Only applies from 2018 through 2025.

The tax formula provides a framework for applying the Federal income tax to individuals. It is an integral part of our U.S. tax system (i.e., local, state, and Federal). Chapter 3 presents a summary of its components while providing a detailed discussion of several of its key components—the standard deduction, determination of whether someone is a dependent, and tax determination. In addition, the tax formula establishes the framework for much of the text; its relationship to the chapters that follow are reflected in Concept Summary 3.1.

Chapter 3 also provides an overview of property transactions. When property is sold, a gain or loss results, and this can affect the determination of taxable income. Chapters 14 through 17 discuss property transactions in detail. But understanding the basic rules will help in applying other materials in the text. In addition, we discuss two concepts unique to the income tax: the difference between realized and recognized gain or loss and the classification of gain or loss (as ordinary or capital).

LO.1

Identify and apply the components of the Federal income tax formula.

3-1 Tax Formula

We begin by reviewing the various components of the income tax formula. Then we explore several components in more depth: the standard deduction, exemptions, filing status, and tax determination. The structure of the individual income tax return parallels the tax formula. The 2021 Form 1040 is included on pages 3-9 and 3-10; three schedules to Form 1040 (Schedules 1, 2, and 3) appear on pages 3-11 through 3-16. Review these as you read about the tax formula.

Concept Summary 3.1

Tax Formula for Individuals (Components Integrated into the Text)

		Text Discussion
Income (broadly defined)	$xx,xxx	Chs. 3, 4
Less: **Exclusions**	(x,xxx)	Ch. 5
Gross income	$xx,xxx	Chs. 4, 16, 17
Less: **Deductions *for*** adjusted gross income	(x,xxx)	Chs. 6–9, 11, 16, 17
Adjusted gross income	$xx,xxx	
Less: The greater of—		
Total **itemized deductions** *or* **standard deduction**	(x,xxx)	Chs. 6, 9, 10, 11 Ch. 3
Less: **Personal** and **dependency exemptions***	(x,xxx)	Ch. 3
Less: **Deduction for qualified business income****	(x,xxx)	Chs. 6 and 9
Taxable income	$xx,xxx	Chs. 3, 12, 13
Tax on taxable income	$ x,xxx	Chs. 3, 12, 13
Less: **Taxes withheld/Tax credits**	(xxx)	Ch. 13
Tax due (or refund)	$ xxx	Chs. 3, 12, 13

*Exemption deductions are not allowed from 2018 through 2025.
**Only applies from 2018 through 2025.

Note: For 2021, individuals using the standard deduction also may subtract *from* adjusted gross income, cash charitable contributions of up to $300 ($600 if married, filing jointly).

3-1a Components of the Tax Formula

Income (Broadly Defined)

In the tax formula, *income* is broadly defined and includes all of the taxpayer's income, both taxable and nontaxable. In general, the courts have defined *income* as "any increase in wealth."[1] As a result, it does not include a return of capital or borrowed funds.

Example 1

Dan decides to quit renting and buy a new house. The owner of the apartment building returns to Dan the $600 damage deposit he previously made. To make a down payment on the house, Dan sells stock for $50,000 (original cost of $28,000) and borrows $200,000 from a bank.

Only the $22,000 gain from the sale of the stock is income to Dan. The $600 damage deposit and the $28,000 cost of the stock are a return of capital. The $200,000 bank loan is not income since Dan has an obligation to repay that amount (and it does not increase his wealth).

Exclusions

For various reasons, Congress has chosen to exclude certain types of income from the income tax base. A partial list of these exclusions is shown in Exhibit 3.1. Income exclusions are covered in Chapter 5.

Gross Income

The Internal Revenue Code defines gross income broadly as "except as otherwise provided ..., all income from whatever source derived."[2] The "except as otherwise provided" phrase refers to exclusions. A partial list of items included in gross income

[1] *Comm. v. Glenshaw Glass Co.*, 55–1 USTC ¶9308, 47 AFTR 162, 75 S.Ct. 473. [2] § 61(a).

Exhibit 3.1 Partial List of Exclusions from Gross Income

Accident insurance proceeds	Life insurance paid at death
Alimony (divorces after 2018)	Meals and lodging (if furnished for employer's convenience)
Annuities (cost element)	Military allowances
Bequests	Minister's dwelling rental value allowance
Child support payments	Railroad retirement benefits (to a limited extent)
Cost-of-living allowance (for military)	Scholarship grants (to a limited extent)
Damages for personal injury or sickness	Social Security benefits (to a limited extent)
Gifts received	Veterans' benefits
Group term life insurance, premium paid by employer (for coverage up to $50,000)	Welfare payments
Inheritances	Workers' compensation benefits
Interest from state and local (i.e., municipal) bonds	

Example 2

Beth received the following amounts during the year:

Salary	$30,000
Interest on savings account	900
Gift from her aunt	10,000
Prize won in state lottery	1,000
Alimony from ex-spouse (divorce finalized in 2015)	12,000
Child support from ex-spouse	6,000
Damages for injury in auto accident	25,000
Ten $50 bills in an unmarked envelope found in an airport lounge (airport authorities could not locate anyone who claimed ownership)	500
Federal income tax refund for last year's tax overpayment	120
Increase in the value of stock held for investment	5,000

Review Exhibits 3.1 and 3.2 to determine the amount Beth must include in the computation of taxable income and the amount she may exclude.[3]

appears in Exhibit 3.2. Gross income does not include *unrealized* gains (e.g., stock that has appreciated in value but has not been sold). Gross income is discussed in Chapters 4 and 5.

Deductions *for* Adjusted Gross Income

Individual taxpayers have two categories of deductions: (1) deductions *for* adjusted gross income (deductions from gross income to arrive at adjusted gross income) and (2) deductions *from* adjusted gross income.

Deductions *for* adjusted gross income (AGI) are sometimes called *above-the-line* deductions because on the tax return, they are taken before the "line" designating AGI. Deductions *for* AGI include, but are not limited to, the following:[4]

- Trade or business expenses.
- Part of the self-employment tax.
- Contributions to traditional Individual Retirement Accounts (IRAs) and other retirement plans.

[3]Beth must include $44,400 in computing taxable income ($30,000 salary + $900 interest + $1,000 lottery prize + $12,000 alimony + $500 found property). She can exclude $41,000 ($10,000 gift from aunt + $6,000 child support + $25,000 damages). The $120 Federal income tax refund is excluded because it represents an adjustment (i.e., overpayment) of a nondeductible expenditure made in the previous year. The unrealized gain on the stock held for investment also is not included in gross income.

[4]§ 62(a); many of these deductions are limited in some way. And some of these deductions appear on supporting schedules or forms. For example, the business expenses of a sole proprietor appear on Schedule C (Form 1040).

Exhibit 3.2 Partial List of Gross Income Items

Alimony (divorces before 2019)
Annuities (income element)
Awards
Back pay
Bargain purchase from employer
Bonuses
Breach of contract damages
Business income
Clergy fees
Commissions
Compensation for services
Death benefits
Debts forgiven
Director's fees
Dividends
Embezzled funds
Employee awards (in certain cases)
Employee benefits (except certain fringe benefits)
Estate and trust income
Farm income
Fees
Gains from illegal activities
Gains from sale of property
Gambling winnings
Group term life insurance, premium paid by employer (for coverage over $50,000)
Hobby income
Interest
Jury duty fees
Living quarters, meals (unless furnished for employer's convenience)
Mileage allowance (in certain cases)
Military pay (unless combat pay)
Notary fees
Partnership income
Pension distributions
Prizes
Professional fees
Punitive damages
Rents
Rewards
Royalties
Salaries
Severance pay
Strike and lockout benefits
Supplemental unemployment benefits
Tips and gratuities
Travel allowance (in certain cases)
Treasure trove (found property)
Wages

- Contributions to Health Savings Accounts (HSAs).
- Interest on student loans.
- Excess capital losses.
- Certain alimony payments.

The following example illustrates how deductions *for* AGI affect the computation of AGI.

Example 3

Mason, age 45, earned a salary of $78,000 in 2022. He contributed $4,000 to his traditional Individual Retirement Account (IRA), sold stock held as an investment for a short-term capital loss of $2,000, and paid $4,600 in alimony to his ex-wife (divorce finalized in 2017). His AGI is determined as follows:

Gross income		
Salary		$ 78,000
Less: Deductions *for* AGI		
IRA contribution	$4,000	
Capital loss	2,000	
Alimony paid	4,600	(10,600)
AGI		$ 67,400

The principal deductions *for* AGI are discussed in Chapters 6, 7, 8, 9, 11, 16, and 17.

Deductions *from* Adjusted Gross Income

As a general rule, personal expenses are not allowed as deductions in computing taxable income. However, Congress allows some personal expenses as deductions *from* AGI (commonly referred to as **itemized deductions**); see Exhibit 3.3 for a partial list of these deductions.

AGI is an important calculation since it is used to limit certain itemized deductions (e.g., medical expenses, charitable contributions, and casualty losses). For example, medical expenses are deductible only to the extent they exceed 7.5 percent of AGI, and charitable contribution deductions may not exceed 50 percent of AGI (60 percent for cash contributions to public charities; 100 percent in 2021). These limitations can be described as a *floor* under the medical expense deduction and a *ceiling* on the charitable contribution deduction.

Example 4

Assume the same facts as in Example 3, and assume that Mason had medical expenses of $8,000. Medical expenses are included in itemized deductions to the extent they exceed 7.5% of AGI. In computing his itemized deductions, Mason includes medical expenses of $2,945 [$8,000 medical expenses − $5,055 (7.5% × $67,400 AGI)].

In addition, taxpayers are allowed itemized deductions for expenses related to (1) the production or collection of income and (2) the management of property held for the production of income.[5] These expenses, sometimes referred to as *nonbusiness expenses*, are expenses incurred in connection with an income-producing activity that does *not* qualify as a trade or business. The deductions for many of these expenses are suspended from 2018 through 2025.

Example 5

Leo is the owner and operator of a small package delivery service. All allowable expenses that he incurs in connection with the delivery business are deductions *for* AGI. In addition, Leo has an extensive portfolio of stocks and bonds.

Leo's investment activity is not treated as a trade or business. Any allowable expenses that Leo incurs in connection with these investments (e.g., subscriptions to investment publications, financial planning fees, safety deposit box rental) are itemized deductions. These are "miscellaneous itemized deductions" and are not deductible from 2018 through 2025.

Itemized deductions are discussed in Chapters 9 and 10.

Exhibit 3.3 Partial List of Itemized Deductions

Medical expenses in excess of 7.5% of AGI
State and local income or sales taxes*
Real estate taxes*
Personal property taxes*
Interest on home mortgage (subject to certain limitations)
Investment interest (up to the amount of net investment income)
Charitable contributions (within specified percentage limitations)
Casualty and theft losses in excess of 10% of AGI

*Only $10,000 of combined state and local taxes is deductible.

[5] § 212.

Nondeductible Expenses

Many expenses are not deductible and, therefore, provide no tax benefit. Here are some examples:

- Personal living expenses.
- Employee business expenses (unless reimbursed by employer).*
- Most investment expenses (e.g., investment counsel fees, safe deposit box rental, and publications).*
- Tax return preparation fees.*
- Losses on the sale of personal use property (e.g., the furniture you own).
- Hobby expenses.*
- Life insurance premiums.
- Gambling losses (in excess of gains).
- Child support payments.
- Fines and penalties.
- Political contributions.
- Funeral expenses.
- Capital expenditures.

*Prior to 2018, these "miscellaneous itemized deductions" were allowed as *from* AGI deductions, subject to a 2%-of-AGI floor. These deductions are not allowed from 2018 through 2025.

Many of these items are discussed in Chapters 6, 9, and 10.

Standard Deduction

Instead of claiming itemized deductions, taxpayers can use the **standard deduction**. As discussed later in the chapter, the standard deduction varies depending on filing status, age, and blindness. The standard deduction is adjusted each year for inflation.

Cash Charitable Contributions

For 2021, individuals who use the standard deduction are allowed to claim a *from* AGI deduction of up to $300 for charitable contributions made in cash ($600 for married couples filing jointly). This deduction is in addition to the taxpayer's standard deduction.[6]

Personal and Dependency Exemptions

Prior to 2018, exemption deductions were allowed for the taxpayer, the taxpayer's spouse, and each dependent of the taxpayer. Exemption deductions are suspended from 2018 through 2025.

Deduction for Qualified Business Income

From 2018 through 2025, a deduction for qualified business income is allowed. In general, this deduction relates to business income generated by *noncorporate* businesses (e.g., proprietorships, S corporations, partnerships, and LLCs). In general, the deduction allowed is the *lesser* of (1) 20 percent of qualified business income or (2) 20 percent of modified taxable income. This deduction is introduced in Chapter 6 and discussed extensively in Chapter 9.

Taxable Income

The determination of taxable income is illustrated in Example 6.

---

[6] § 170(p).

Example 6

Grace, age 25, is not married and has her disabled and dependent mother living with her during 2022. This qualifies Grace for head-of-household filing status and a standard deduction of $19,400. In 2022, Grace earned a $44,000 salary as a high school teacher. Her other income consisted of $1,100 interest on a certificate of deposit (CD) and $500 interest on nontaxable municipal bonds that she had received as a graduation gift in 2015. During 2022, she sold stock that resulted in a $1,000 deductible capital loss. Her itemized deductions are $11,000. Grace's taxable income for the year is computed as follows:

Income (broadly defined)	
Salary	$ 44,000
Interest on a CD	1,100
Interest on municipal bonds	500
	$ 45,600
Less: Exclusion—Interest on municipal bonds	(500)
Gross income	$ 45,100
Less: Deduction *for* adjusted gross income—capital loss	(1,000)
Adjusted gross income	$ 44,100
Less: The greater of total itemized deductions ($11,000) *or* the standard deduction for head of household ($19,400)	(19,400)
Less: Deduction for qualified business income	(–0–)
Taxable income	$ 24,700

The exclusion of $500 (i.e., interest from municipal bonds) is subtracted in determining gross income, and the capital loss of $1,000 is classified as a deduction *for* AGI. Grace chose to use the standard deduction as her *from* AGI deduction since it exceeded her total itemized deductions. We will determine Grace's income tax liability later in the chapter (in Example 52).

Tax Due (or Refund)

The last step in applying the tax formula is the determination of tax due (or refund). Tax rates (which differ based on filing status) are applied to taxable income to determine the tax liability.[7] Once the tax is computed, this amount is reduced by any taxes withheld and tax credits allowed to arrive at the additional tax due or overpayment (i.e., refund). Filing status and the tax computation are discussed later in this chapter; tax credits are the subject of Chapter 13.

3-1b Tax Formula—Correlation with Form 1040

Now that you understand the definitions used in the tax formula, review the Form 1040 (and related Schedules 1, 2, and 3) included on the following pages. The 2021 Form 1040 is included in the text because the 2022 Form 1040 was not available when we went to press. As you can see, the structure of the individual income tax return parallels the tax formula in Concept Summary 3.1. In arriving at gross income (referred to as *total income*), *most* exclusions are *not* reported on the tax return. Form 1040 (page 1) includes the most common gross income items (e.g., wages, interest, dividends, retirement distributions, and Social Security benefits). Less common income items (including net income from sole proprietorships and rental activities and gains and losses from property transactions) are reported on Schedule 1 (Form 1040); the total of these amounts is reported on line 8 of Form 1040. Deductions *for* AGI also are summarized on (Schedule 1) Form 1040 and used to determine the taxpayer's AGI (see line 11 of Form 1040).

A taxpayer's "itemized deductions" (a *from* AGI deduction) are carried over from Schedule A (Form 1040) to page 1, line 12a of Form 1040, where the choice between the standard deduction and itemized deductions is made. This is followed by the deduction for qualified business income to arrive at taxable income. Page 2 of Form 1040 contains the tax computation and reductions for tax credits and withholdings. The format of Form 1040 and its connections to the various supporting schedules containing tax formula information is illustrated in Exhibit 6.2 of Chapter 6.

[7] § 1. Tax Rate Schedules can be found in Appendix A. Tax Tables, developed by the IRS, are used if taxable income is less than $100,000 (the 2021 Tax Tables can be found in Appendix A; 2022 Tax Tables are available on the IRS website).

Form **1040** Department of the Treasury—Internal Revenue Service (99)
U.S. Individual Income Tax Return **2021** OMB No. 1545-0074 IRS Use Only—Do not write or staple in this space.

Filing Status ☐ Single ☐ Married filing jointly ☐ Married filing separately (MFS) ☐ Head of household (HOH) ☐ Qualifying widow(er) (QW)
Check only one box.
If you checked the MFS box, enter the name of your spouse. If you checked the HOH or QW box, enter the child's name if the qualifying person is a child but not your dependent ▶

Your first name and middle initial	Last name	**Your social security number**
If joint return, spouse's first name and middle initial	Last name	**Spouse's social security number**

Home address (number and street). If you have a P.O. box, see instructions.		Apt. no.	**Presidential Election Campaign** Check here if you, or your spouse if filing jointly, want $3 to go to this fund. Checking a box below will not change your tax or refund. ☐ **You** ☐ **Spouse**
City, town, or post office. If you have a foreign address, also complete spaces below.	State	ZIP code	
Foreign country name	Foreign province/state/county	Foreign postal code	

At any time during 2021, did you receive, sell, exchange, or otherwise dispose of any financial interest in any virtual currency? ☐ **Yes** ☐ **No**

Standard Deduction **Someone can claim:** ☐ You as a dependent ☐ Your spouse as a dependent
☐ Spouse itemizes on a separate return or you were a dual-status alien

Age/Blindness **You:** ☐ Were born before January 2, 1957 ☐ Are blind **Spouse:** ☐ Was born before January 2, 1957 ☐ Is blind

Dependents (see instructions):
If more than four dependents, see instructions and check here ▶ ☐

(1) First name	Last name	(2) Social security number	(3) Relationship to you	(4) ✔ if qualifies for (see instructions): Child tax credit	Credit for other dependents
				☐	☐
				☐	☐
				☐	☐
				☐	☐

Attach Sch. B if required.

Standard Deduction for—
- Single or Married filing separately, $12,550
- Married filing jointly or Qualifying widow(er), $25,100
- Head of household, $18,800
- If you checked any box under *Standard Deduction*, see instructions.

Line	Description				
1	Wages, salaries, tips, etc. Attach Form(s) W-2			1	
2a	Tax-exempt interest	2a	b Taxable interest	2b	
3a	Qualified dividends	3a	b Ordinary dividends	3b	
4a	IRA distributions	4a	b Taxable amount	4b	
5a	Pensions and annuities	5a	b Taxable amount	5b	
6a	Social security benefits	6a	b Taxable amount	6b	
7	Capital gain or (loss). Attach Schedule D if required. If not required, check here ▶ ☐			7	
8	Other income from Schedule 1, line 10			8	
9	Add lines 1, 2b, 3b, 4b, 5b, 6b, 7, and 8. This is your **total income** ▶			9	
10	Adjustments to income from Schedule 1, line 26			10	
11	Subtract line 10 from line 9. This is your **adjusted gross income** ▶			11	
12a	**Standard deduction or itemized deductions** (from Schedule A)	12a			
b	Charitable contributions if you take the standard deduction (see instructions)	12b			
c	Add lines 12a and 12b			12c	
13	Qualified business income deduction from Form 8995 or Form 8995-A			13	
14	Add lines 12c and 13			14	
15	**Taxable income.** Subtract line 14 from line 11. If zero or less, enter -0-			15	

For Disclosure, Privacy Act, and Paperwork Reduction Act Notice, see separate instructions. Cat. No. 11320B Form **1040** (2021)

Form 1040 (2021) Page **2**

	16	**Tax** (see instructions). Check if any from Form(s): 1 ☐ 8814 2 ☐ 4972 3 ☐			16
	17	Amount from Schedule 2, line 3			17
	18	Add lines 16 and 17			18
	19	Nonrefundable child tax credit or credit for other dependents from Schedule 8812			19
	20	Amount from Schedule 3, line 8			20
	21	Add lines 19 and 20			21
	22	Subtract line 21 from line 18. If zero or less, enter -0-			22
	23	Other taxes, including self-employment tax, from Schedule 2, line 21			23
	24	Add lines 22 and 23. This is your **total tax** ▶			24
	25	Federal income tax withheld from:			
	a	Form(s) W-2		25a	
	b	Form(s) 1099		25b	
	c	Other forms (see instructions)		25c	
	d	Add lines 25a through 25c			25d
If you have a qualifying child, attach Sch. EIC.	26	2021 estimated tax payments and amount applied from 2020 return			26
	27a	Earned income credit (EIC)		27a	
		Check here if you were born after January 1, 1998, and before January 2, 2004, and you satisfy all the other requirements for taxpayers who are at least age 18, to claim the EIC. See instructions ▶ ☐			
	b	Nontaxable combat pay election	27b		
	c	Prior year (2019) earned income	27c		
	28	Refundable child tax credit or additional child tax credit from Schedule 8812		28	
	29	American opportunity credit from Form 8863, line 8		29	
	30	Recovery rebate credit. See instructions		30	
	31	Amount from Schedule 3, line 15		31	
	32	Add lines 27a and 28 through 31. These are your **total other payments and refundable credits** ▶			32
	33	Add lines 25d, 26, and 32. These are your **total payments** ▶			33
Refund	34	If line 33 is more than line 24, subtract line 24 from line 33. This is the amount you **overpaid**			34
	35a	Amount of line 34 you want **refunded to you.** If Form 8888 is attached, check here ▶ ☐			35a
Direct deposit? See instructions.	▶ b	Routing number ▶ c Type: ☐ Checking ☐ Savings			
	▶ d	Account number			
	36	Amount of line 34 you want **applied to your 2022 estimated tax** ▶		36	
Amount You Owe	37	**Amount you owe.** Subtract line 33 from line 24. For details on how to pay, see instructions ▶			37
	38	Estimated tax penalty (see instructions) ▶		38	

Third Party Designee

Do you want to allow another person to discuss this return with the IRS? See instructions ▶ ☐ **Yes.** Complete below. ☐ **No**

Designee's name ▶ | Phone no. ▶ | Personal identification number (PIN) ▶

Sign Here

Under penalties of perjury, I declare that I have examined this return and accompanying schedules and statements, and to the best of my knowledge and belief, they are true, correct, and complete. Declaration of preparer (other than taxpayer) is based on all information of which preparer has any knowledge.

Joint return? See instructions. Keep a copy for your records.

Your signature	Date	Your occupation	If the IRS sent you an Identity Protection PIN, enter it here (see inst.) ▶
Spouse's signature. If a joint return, **both** must sign.	Date	Spouse's occupation	If the IRS sent your spouse an Identity Protection PIN, enter it here (see inst.) ▶
Phone no.	Email address		

Paid Preparer Use Only

Preparer's name	Preparer's signature	Date	PTIN	Check if: ☐ Self-employed
Firm's name ▶			Phone no.	
Firm's address ▶			Firm's EIN ▶	

Go to *www.irs.gov/Form1040* for instructions and the latest information. Form **1040** (2021)

SCHEDULE 1 (Form 1040)

Department of the Treasury
Internal Revenue Service

Additional Income and Adjustments to Income

▶ Attach to Form 1040, 1040-SR, or 1040-NR.
▶ Go to *www.irs.gov/Form1040* for instructions and the latest information.

OMB No. 1545-0074

2021

Attachment Sequence No. **01**

Name(s) shown on Form 1040, 1040-SR, or 1040-NR | **Your social security number**

Part I Additional Income

1	Taxable refunds, credits, or offsets of state and local income taxes		1	
2a	Alimony received		2a	
b	Date of original divorce or separation agreement (see instructions) ▶ ______			
3	Business income or (loss). Attach Schedule C		3	
4	Other gains or (losses). Attach Form 4797		4	
5	Rental real estate, royalties, partnerships, S corporations, trusts, etc. Attach Schedule E		5	
6	Farm income or (loss). Attach Schedule F		6	
7	Unemployment compensation		7	
8	Other income:			
a	Net operating loss	8a ( )		
b	Gambling income	8b		
c	Cancellation of debt	8c		
d	Foreign earned income exclusion from Form 2555	8d ( )		
e	Taxable Health Savings Account distribution	8e		
f	Alaska Permanent Fund dividends	8f		
g	Jury duty pay	8g		
h	Prizes and awards	8h		
i	Activity not engaged in for profit income	8i		
j	Stock options	8j		
k	Income from the rental of personal property if you engaged in the rental for profit but were not in the business of renting such property	8k		
l	Olympic and Paralympic medals and USOC prize money (see instructions)	8l		
m	Section 951(a) inclusion (see instructions)	8m		
n	Section 951A(a) inclusion (see instructions)	8n		
o	Section 461(l) excess business loss adjustment	8o		
p	Taxable distributions from an ABLE account (see instructions)	8p		
z	Other income. List type and amount ▶ ______	8z		
9	Total other income. Add lines 8a through 8z		9	
10	Combine lines 1 through 7 and 9. Enter here and on Form 1040, 1040-SR, or 1040-NR, line 8		10	

Schedule 1 (Form 1040) 2021 Page **2**

Part II Adjustments to Income

11	Educator expenses			11	
12	Certain business expenses of reservists, performing artists, and fee-basis government officials. Attach Form 2106			12	
13	Health savings account deduction. Attach Form 8889			13	
14	Moving expenses for members of the Armed Forces. Attach Form 3903			14	
15	Deductible part of self-employment tax. Attach Schedule SE			15	
16	Self-employed SEP, SIMPLE, and qualified plans			16	
17	Self-employed health insurance deduction			17	
18	Penalty on early withdrawal of savings			18	
19a	Alimony paid			19a	
b	Recipient's SSN ▶				
c	Date of original divorce or separation agreement (see instructions) ▶				
20	IRA deduction			20	
21	Student loan interest deduction			21	
22	Reserved for future use			22	
23	Archer MSA deduction			23	
24	Other adjustments:				
a	Jury duty pay (see instructions)	24a			
b	Deductible expenses related to income reported on line 8k from the rental of personal property engaged in for profit	24b			
c	Nontaxable amount of the value of Olympic and Paralympic medals and USOC prize money reported on line 8l	24c			
d	Reforestation amortization and expenses	24d			
e	Repayment of supplemental unemployment benefits under the Trade Act of 1974	24e			
f	Contributions to section 501(c)(18)(D) pension plans	24f			
g	Contributions by certain chaplains to section 403(b) plans	24g			
h	Attorney fees and court costs for actions involving certain unlawful discrimination claims (see instructions)	24h			
i	Attorney fees and court costs you paid in connection with an award from the IRS for information you provided that helped the IRS detect tax law violations	24i			
j	Housing deduction from Form 2555	24j			
k	Excess deductions of section 67(e) expenses from Schedule K-1 (Form 1041)	24k			
z	Other adjustments. List type and amount ▶	24z			
25	Total other adjustments. Add lines 24a through 24z			25	
26	Add lines 11 through 23 and 25. These are your **adjustments to income.** Enter here and on Form 1040 or 1040-SR, line 10, or Form 1040-NR, line 10a			26	

Schedule 1 (Form 1040) 2021

SCHEDULE 2 (Form 1040) Department of the Treasury Internal Revenue Service	**Additional Taxes** ▶ Attach to Form 1040, 1040-SR, or 1040-NR. ▶ Go to *www.irs.gov/Form1040* for instructions and the latest information.	OMB No. 1545-0074 **2021** Attachment Sequence No. **02**
Name(s) shown on Form 1040, 1040-SR, or 1040-NR		**Your social security number**

Part I Tax

1	Alternative minimum tax. Attach Form 6251	1	
2	Excess advance premium tax credit repayment. Attach Form 8962	2	
3	Add lines 1 and 2. Enter here and on Form 1040, 1040-SR, or 1040-NR, line 17	3	

Part II Other Taxes

4	Self-employment tax. Attach Schedule SE			4	
5	Social security and Medicare tax on unreported tip income. Attach Form 4137	5			
6	Uncollected social security and Medicare tax on wages. Attach Form 8919	6			
7	Total additional social security and Medicare tax. Add lines 5 and 6			7	
8	Additional tax on IRAs or other tax-favored accounts. Attach Form 5329 if required			8	
9	Household employment taxes. Attach Schedule H			9	
10	Repayment of first-time homebuyer credit. Attach Form 5405 if required			10	
11	Additional Medicare Tax. Attach Form 8959			11	
12	Net investment income tax. Attach Form 8960			12	
13	Uncollected social security and Medicare or RRTA tax on tips or group-term life insurance from Form W-2, box 12			13	
14	Interest on tax due on installment income from the sale of certain residential lots and timeshares			14	
15	Interest on the deferred tax on gain from certain installment sales with a sales price over $150,000			15	
16	Recapture of low-income housing credit. Attach Form 8611			16	

(continued on page 2)

For Paperwork Reduction Act Notice, see your tax return instructions. Cat. No. 71478U **Schedule 2 (Form 1040) 2021**

Schedule 2 (Form 1040) 2021 Page **2**

Part II Other Taxes *(continued)*

17	Other additional taxes:		
a	Recapture of other credits. List type, form number, and amount ▶ ________	**17a**	
b	Recapture of federal mortgage subsidy. If you sold your home in 2021, see instructions	**17b**	
c	Additional tax on HSA distributions. Attach Form 8889	**17c**	
d	Additional tax on an HSA because you didn't remain an eligible individual. Attach Form 8889	**17d**	
e	Additional tax on Archer MSA distributions. Attach Form 8853 .	**17e**	
f	Additional tax on Medicare Advantage MSA distributions. Attach Form 8853	**17f**	
g	Recapture of a charitable contribution deduction related to a fractional interest in tangible personal property	**17g**	
h	Income you received from a nonqualified deferred compensation plan that fails to meet the requirements of section 409A . . .	**17h**	
i	Compensation you received from a nonqualified deferred compensation plan described in section 457A	**17i**	
j	Section 72(m)(5) excess benefits tax	**17j**	
k	Golden parachute payments	**17k**	
l	Tax on accumulation distribution of trusts	**17l**	
m	Excise tax on insider stock compensation from an expatriated corporation	**17m**	
n	Look-back interest under section 167(g) or 460(b) from Form 8697 or 8866	**17n**	
o	Tax on non-effectively connected income for any part of the year you were a nonresident alien from Form 1040-NR	**17o**	
p	Any interest from Form 8621, line 16f, relating to distributions from, and dispositions of, stock of a section 1291 fund	**17p**	
q	Any interest from Form 8621, line 24	**17q**	
z	Any other taxes. List type and amount ▶ ________	**17z**	
18	Total additional taxes. Add lines 17a through 17z	**18**	
19	Additional tax from Schedule 8812	**19**	
20	Section 965 net tax liability installment from Form 965-A . . .	**20**	
21	Add lines 4, 7 through 16, 18, and 19. These are your **total other taxes.** Enter here and on Form 1040 or 1040-SR, line 23, or Form 1040-NR, line 23b	**21**	

Schedule 2 (Form 1040) 2021

SCHEDULE 3 (Form 1040)
Department of the Treasury Internal Revenue Service

Additional Credits and Payments

▶ Attach to Form 1040, 1040-SR, or 1040-NR.
▶ Go to *www.irs.gov/Form1040* for instructions and the latest information.

OMB No. 1545-0074
2021
Attachment Sequence No. **03**

Name(s) shown on Form 1040, 1040-SR, or 1040-NR	**Your social security number**

Part I Nonrefundable Credits

1	Foreign tax credit. Attach Form 1116 if required			1	
2	Credit for child and dependent care expenses from Form 2441, line 11. Attach Form 2441			2	
3	Education credits from Form 8863, line 19			3	
4	Retirement savings contributions credit. Attach Form 8880			4	
5	Residential energy credits. Attach Form 5695			5	
6	Other nonrefundable credits:				
a	General business credit. Attach Form 3800	6a			
b	Credit for prior year minimum tax. Attach Form 8801	6b			
c	Adoption credit. Attach Form 8839	6c			
d	Credit for the elderly or disabled. Attach Schedule R	6d			
e	Alternative motor vehicle credit. Attach Form 8910	6e			
f	Qualified plug-in motor vehicle credit. Attach Form 8936 . . .	6f			
g	Mortgage interest credit. Attach Form 8396	6g			
h	District of Columbia first-time homebuyer credit. Attach Form 8859	6h			
i	Qualified electric vehicle credit. Attach Form 8834	6i			
j	Alternative fuel vehicle refueling property credit. Attach Form 8911	6j			
k	Credit to holders of tax credit bonds. Attach Form 8912 . . .	6k			
l	Amount on Form 8978, line 14. See instructions	6l			
z	Other nonrefundable credits. List type and amount ▶ ____________	6z			
7	Total other nonrefundable credits. Add lines 6a through 6z			7	
8	Add lines 1 through 5 and 7. Enter here and on Form 1040, 1040-SR, or 1040-NR, line 20			8	

(continued on page 2)

Schedule 3 (Form 1040) 2021 Page **2**

Part II Other Payments and Refundable Credits

9	Net premium tax credit. Attach Form 8962			9	
10	Amount paid with request for extension to file (see instructions)			10	
11	Excess social security and tier 1 RRTA tax withheld			11	
12	Credit for federal tax on fuels. Attach Form 4136			12	
13	Other payments or refundable credits:				
a	Form 2439	13a			
b	Qualified sick and family leave credits from Schedule(s) H and Form(s) 7202 for leave taken before April 1, 2021	13b			
c	Health coverage tax credit from Form 8885	13c			
d	Credit for repayment of amounts included in income from earlier years	13d			
e	Reserved for future use	13e			
f	Deferred amount of net 965 tax liability (see instructions)	13f			
g	Credit for child and dependent care expenses from Form 2441, line 10. Attach Form 2441	13g			
h	Qualified sick and family leave credits from Schedule(s) H and Form(s) 7202 for leave taken after March 31, 2021	13h			
z	Other payments or refundable credits. List type and amount ▶ ______	13z			
14	Total other payments or refundable credits. Add lines 13a through 13z			14	
15	Add lines 9 through 12 and 14. Enter here and on Form 1040, 1040-SR, or 1040-NR, line 31			15	

Schedule 3 (Form 1040) 2021

3-2 Standard Deduction

LO.2

Explain the standard deduction and evaluate its choice in arriving at taxable income.

The effect of the standard deduction is to exempt part of a taxpayer's income from Federal income tax liability. Congress has indicated that the standard deduction, when coupled with the child tax credit and dependent tax credit, should be roughly equal to the poverty level.[8]

3-2a Basic and Additional Standard Deduction

The standard deduction is the sum of two components: the *basic* standard deduction and the *additional* standard deduction.[9] Exhibit 3.4 lists the basic standard deduction allowed for taxpayers in each filing status. Certain taxpayers, however, are not allowed to claim *any* standard deduction, and the standard deduction is *limited* for others.

A taxpayer who is age 65 or over *or* blind in 2022 qualifies for an *additional standard deduction* of $1,400 or $1,750, depending on filing status (see amounts in Exhibit 3.5). Two additional standard deductions are allowed for a taxpayer who is age 65 or over *and* blind. The additional standard deduction provisions also apply for a qualifying spouse who is age 65 or over or blind, but not for a dependent.

To determine whether to itemize, the taxpayer compares the *total* standard deduction (the sum of the basic standard deduction and any additional standard deductions) with total itemized deductions. Taxpayers are allowed to deduct the *greater* of itemized deductions or the standard deduction. The choice is elective each year. For example, a taxpayer who buys a home may change from using the standard deduction to itemizing

Exhibit 3.4 **Basic Standard Deduction Amounts**

	Standard Deduction Amount	
Filing Status	**2021**	**2022**
Single	$12,550	$12,950
Married, filing jointly	25,100	25,900
Surviving spouse	25,100	25,900
Head of household	18,800	19,400
Married, filing separately	12,550	12,950

Exhibit 3.5 **Additional Standard Deduction Amounts**

Filing Status	**2021**	**2022**
Single	$1,700	$1,750
Married, filing jointly	1,350	1,400
Surviving spouse	1,350	1,400
Head of household	1,700	1,750
Married, filing separately	1,350	1,400

[8]S.Rep. No. 92-437, 92nd Cong., 1st Sess., 1971, p. 54, discusses the combination of the standard deduction and exemption deductions. Congress expanded the child tax credit and added a dependent tax credit to offset the suspension of the dependency exemption deductions from 2018 through 2025. Another purpose of the standard deduction, discussed in Chapter 1, is to reduce the number of taxpayers who itemize their deductions. Reducing the number of taxpayers who itemize also reduces the audit effort required from the IRS.

[9]§ 63(c)(1).

deductions (because of mortgage interest and property tax deductions). The taxpayer's age also can make a difference. In recent years, between 85 and 90 percent of individual tax returns filed use the standard deduction (rather than itemized deductions).

Using Itemized Deductions or Standard Deduction

Example 7

Juan and Lisa, married taxpayers filing a joint return, have been renting an apartment while saving money for a down payment on a house. Early in 2022, they purchased a house. Interest paid on their home mortgage in 2022 amounted to $9,800, and they paid property taxes of $5,500. In addition, they had charitable contributions of $8,000 and paid state income taxes of $4,000.

In total, their itemized deductions amount to $27,300, and they will compute their taxable income using this amount rather than the $25,900 standard deduction.

Example 8

Prior to 2022, Sara, who is single, had always chosen to itemize. In 2022, however, she reaches age 65. Her itemized deductions for 2022 are $13,800, but her total standard deduction is $14,700 [$12,950 (basic standard deduction) + $1,750 (additional standard deduction)].

Sara should compute her taxable income for 2022 using the standard deduction ($14,700) because it exceeds her itemized deductions ($13,800).

3-2b Individuals Not Eligible for the Standard Deduction

Some individuals are not allowed to use the standard deduction. The following individual taxpayers must itemize their deductions:[10]

- A married individual filing a separate return where either spouse itemizes deductions.
- An individual who is neither a U.S. citizen nor a U.S. resident (the Internal Revenue Code refers to these individuals as "nonresident aliens").

If an individual dies during a year, a full standard deduction is available for the final tax return; the deduction is not reduced because the return only covers a portion of the calendar year.

Example 9

Sandy (age 80 and single) died on January 14, 2022. Her itemized deductions for 2022 amounted to $2,400. On her final income tax return, covering the period from January 1 to January 14, 2022, a standard deduction of $14,700 can be claimed (the $12,950 basic standard deduction plus the $1,750 age-related standard deduction).

3-2c Special Limitations on the Standard Deduction for Dependents

Special rules apply to the standard deduction of an individual who can be claimed as a dependent on another person's tax return.

When a dependent files a tax return, the *dependent's* basic standard deduction in 2022 is limited to the greater of $1,150 or the sum of the individual's earned income for the year plus $400.[11] However, if the sum of the individual's earned income plus $400 exceeds the basic standard deduction, the basic standard deduction is used (see Exhibit 3.4). A dependent who is 65 or over or blind or both also is allowed the additional standard deduction amount on his or her return (refer to Exhibit 3.5). These provisions are illustrated in Examples 10 through 13.

[10] § 63(c)(6); also ineligible is an individual filing a return for a period of less than 12 months because of a change in the annual accounting period.

[11] § 63(c)(5). Both the $1,100 amount and the $350 amount are subject to adjustment for inflation each year. In 2021, the amounts were $1,100 and $350.

Dependent Standard Deduction

Example 10

Gabrielle, who is 17 years old and single, is a dependent of her parents. During 2022, she received $1,200 interest (unearned income) on a savings account. She also earned $450 from a part-time job. When Gabrielle files her own tax return, her standard deduction is $1,150 [the greater of $1,150 or $850 (the sum of earned income of $450 plus $400)].

Example 11

Assume the same facts as in Example 10, except that Gabrielle is 67 years old and is a dependent of her son. In this case, when Gabrielle files her own tax return, her standard deduction is $2,900 [$1,150 (see Example 10) + $1,750 (the additional standard deduction allowed because Gabrielle is 65 or older)].

Example 12

Aleshia, who is 16 years old and single, earned $800 from a summer job and had no unearned income during 2022. She is a dependent of her parents. Her standard deduction is $1,200 [the greater of $1,150 or $1,200 (the sum of $800 earned income plus $400)].

Example 13

Javier, a 20-year-old, single, full-time college student, is a dependent of his parents. He worked as a musician during the summer of 2022, earning $12,750. Javier's standard deduction is $12,950 [the greater of $1,150 or $12,950 (the sum of $12,750 earned income plus $400, but limited to the $12,950 basic standard deduction for a single taxpayer)].

3-3 Exemptions

LO.3

Describe the current status of the exemption deduction.

Historically, the use of exemptions in the tax system has been based in part on the idea that a taxpayer with a small amount of income should be exempt from income taxation. Two types of exemptions have been allowed— **personal exemptions** and **dependency exemptions**. Beginning in 2018, however, Congress suspended the deduction for exemptions through 2025 (and increased the standard deduction amount for taxpayers).

Even though the exemption deduction has been suspended through 2025, understanding the definitions and the exemption amount remains important. For example, the *exemption amount* is used to determine whether certain taxpayers are dependents. In addition, the *definition of a "dependent"* is used for a variety of purposes in the Internal Revenue Code. Personal exemptions are granted to the taxpayer and spouse. Dependency exemptions are allowed for a qualifying child or a qualifying relative. The exemption amount in 2022 is $4,400 (it was $4,300 in 2021). Dependent status is discussed in the following section.

3-4 Dependents

LO.4

Explain the rules for determining whether someone is a dependent.

Under the Internal Revenue Code, there are two types of dependents—a *qualifying child* and a *qualifying relative*. Unique tests apply to each type of dependent; these tests are discussed next.

3-4a Qualifying Child

Congress has adopted a uniform definition of a qualifying child. The definition applies to the following tax provisions:

- Head-of-household filing status.
- Earned income tax credit.
- Child tax credit.
- Credit for child and dependent care expenses.

A **qualifying child** must meet the relationship, residence, age, and support tests (discussed below). A qualifying child must *also* satisfy the joint return test and the citizenship or residency test (discussed later).

Relationship Test

The relationship test includes a taxpayer's child (son or daughter), adopted child, stepchild, eligible foster child, brother, sister, half brother, half sister, stepbrother, stepsister, or a *descendant* of any of these parties (e.g., grandchild, nephew, niece). *Ancestors* of any of these parties (e.g., uncles and aunts) and in-laws (e.g., son-in-law and brother-in-law) *are not included.*

An adopted child includes a child placed with the taxpayer even though the adoption is not final. An eligible foster child is a child who is placed with the taxpayer by an authorized placement agency or by a court order.

Example 14

Maureen's household includes her mother, grandson, stepbrother, stepbrother's daughter, uncle, and sister. All meet the relationship test for a qualifying child *except* the mother and uncle.

Residence Test

A qualifying child must live with the taxpayer for more than half of the year. Temporary absences (e.g., school, vacation, medical care, military service, detention in a juvenile facility) are ignored. Special rules apply in the case of certain kidnapped children.[12]

Age Test

A qualifying child must, by the end of the tax year, be (1) under age 19 or (2) under age 24 *and* a full-time student. A full-time student is a child who was in school during any part of five months of the year.[13] The age test does not apply to a child who is disabled during any part of the year.[14] Also, a qualifying child must be younger than the taxpayer claiming the child (e.g., a brother cannot claim his older sister as a qualifying child).

The Big Picture

Example 15

Return to the facts of *The Big Picture* on p. 3-1. Does Paige meet the requirements of a qualifying child as to Aleha? Paige satisfies the relationship and residence tests, but the answer to the age test remains unclear. Because she is not a full-time student or disabled, she must be under 19 to meet the age test.

Support Test

To be a qualifying child, the individual must not be self-supporting (i.e., provide more than half of the individual's own support). Support includes food, shelter, clothing, medical and dental care, education, recreation/toys, transportation, and similar items.[15] In the case of a child who is a full-time student, scholarships are not considered to be support.[16]

[12] § 152(f)(6).

[13] §§ 152(c)(3)(A) and (f)(2).

[14] § 152(c)(3)(B). Within the meaning of § 22(e)(3). Concept Summary 13.1 contains a brief discussion of the elderly and disabled tax credit.

[15] A worksheet for determining support is provided in IRS Publication 501 (*Dependents, Standard Deduction, and Filing Information*).

[16] § 152(f)(5).

Example 16

Shawn, age 23, is a full-time student and lives with his parents and an older cousin. During 2022, Shawn receives his support from the following sources: 30% from a part-time job, 30% from a scholarship, 20% from his parents, and 20% from the cousin.

Shawn is not self-supporting and is a dependent of his parents even though they contribute only 20% of his support. (Note: Shawn cannot be his cousin's qualifying child due to the relationship test.)

Tiebreaker Rules

In some situations, a child may be a qualifying child to more than one person. In this event, the tax law specifies which person has priority in claiming the child as a dependent.[17] Called "tiebreaker rules," these rules are summarized in Concept Summary 3.2 and are illustrated in the examples that follow.

Concept Summary 3.2

Tiebreaker Rules for Claiming Qualified Child

Persons Eligible to Claim Qualified Child as Dependent	Person Prevailing
One of the persons is the parent.	Parent
Both persons are the parents, and the child lives longer with one parent.	Parent with the longer period of residence
Both persons are the parents, and the child lives with each the same period of time.	Parent with the higher adjusted gross income (AGI)
None of the persons is the parent.	Person with highest AGI

Qualified Child—Tiebreaker Rules

Example 17

Tim, age 15, lives in the same household with his mother and grandmother. As the parent, the mother has priority to claim Tim as a dependent.

Example 18

Jennifer, age 17, lives in the same household with her parents during the entire year. If her parents file separate returns, the one with the higher AGI has priority to claim Jennifer as a dependent.

Example 19

Assume the same facts as in Example 18, except that the father moves into an apartment in November (Jennifer remains with her mother). The mother has priority to claim Jennifer as a dependent (see Concept Summary 3.2).

3-4b Qualifying Relative

In addition to a qualifying child, a **qualifying relative** can be a dependent. A qualifying relative must meet the relationship, gross income, and support tests.[18]

[17] § 152(c)(4).

[18] § 152(d).

Relationship Test

The relationship test for a qualifying relative is more expansive than for a qualifying child. Also included are the following relatives:

- Lineal ascendants (e.g., parents and grandparents).
- Collateral ascendants (e.g., uncles and aunts).
- Certain in-laws (e.g., son-, daughter-, father-, mother-, brother-, and sister-in-law).[19]

Children who do not satisfy the qualifying child definition (e.g., a 25-year-old daughter) may meet the qualifying relative criteria.

The relationship test also includes individuals who are "members of the household" (i.e., live with the taxpayer for the *entire year*). These individuals can be related or unrelated. For example, cousins are not "qualifying relatives" (cousins are not included in the list above). But a cousin can meet the relationship test if the cousin is a "member of the household." Member-of-the-household status is not available for anyone who was a spouse during any part of the year.[20] However, an ex-spouse can qualify as a member of the household in a year following the year of the divorce.

As the relationship test indicates, the category designation of "qualifying relative" is somewhat misleading, since persons *other than relatives* can qualify as dependents. And not all relatives will qualify (although relatives who are not listed could be a "member of the household").

The Big Picture

Example 20

Return to the facts of *The Big Picture* on p. 3-1. Although Terrah is unrelated to Aleha, she qualifies as Aleha's dependent by being a member of the household. Because Terrah is a dependent, Aleha also can claim the medical expenses she paid on Terrah's behalf. The funeral expenses are not deductible.

Gross Income Test

A dependent's gross income must be *less* than the exemption amount—$4,400 in 2022 ($4,300 in 2021). Gross income is determined by any income that is taxable. In the case of scholarships, for example, include the taxable portion (e.g., amounts received for room and board) and exclude the nontaxable portion (e.g., amounts received for books and tuition).

Gross Income Test

Example 21

Haylie provides more than half of the support of her son, Tom, who does not live with her. Tom, age 26, is a full-time student in medical school, earns $3,000 from a part-time job, and receives a $12,000 scholarship covering his tuition.

Tom is Haylie's dependent because he meets the gross income test and is a qualifying relative. (Note: Tom is *not* a qualifying child; he fails both the residence and age tests.)

Example 22

Aaron provides more than half of the support of his widowed aunt, Myrtle, who does not live with him. Myrtle's income for the year is as follows: dividend income of $1,100, earnings from pet sitting of $1,200, nontaxable Social Security benefits of $6,000, and nontaxable interest from City of Milwaukee bonds of $8,000.

Because Myrtle's gross income is only $2,300 ($1,100 + $1,200), she meets the gross income test and is Aaron's dependent.

[19] Reg. § 1.152–2(d). Once established by marriage, in-law status continues to exist and survives divorce.

[20] §§ 152(d)(2)(H) and (f)(3); also excluded is anyone whose relationship to the taxpayer violates local law.

The Big Picture

Example 23

Return to the facts of *The Big Picture* on p. 3-1. Assuming that Paige is not a qualifying child (see Example 15), can she be a qualifying relative? She meets the relationship and support tests, but what about the gross income test?

If her income from her part-time job is less than $4,400 (the 2022 exemption amount), she does qualify and would be Aleha's dependent.

Support Test

The taxpayer must furnish over half of the qualifying relative's support. As with a qualifying child, support includes food, shelter, clothing, medical and dental care, education, recreation, transportation, and similar items. If a child is being evaluated as a qualifying relative (and is a full-time student), a scholarship received by the child is *not included* for purposes of computing whether the taxpayer furnished more than half of the child's support. Any other relative being evaluated must include a scholarship as support in making this determination.

Example 24

Waleed contributed $3,400 (consisting of food, clothing, and medical care) toward the support of his nephew, Aroosa, who lives with him. Aroosa earned $1,300 from a part-time job and received $2,000 from a student loan to attend a local university. Assuming that the other dependency tests are met, Waleed can claim Aroosa as a dependent because he contributed more than half of Aroosa's support.

If the individual does not spend funds that have been received from any source, the unexpended amounts are *not* counted for purposes of the support test.

Example 25

Emily contributed $3,000 to her father's support during the year. In addition, her father received $2,400 in Social Security benefits, $200 of interest, and wages of $600. Her father deposited the Social Security benefits, interest, and wages in his own savings account and did not use any of the funds for his support. Thus, the Social Security benefits, interest, and wages are not considered as support provided by Emily's father. Emily's father is her dependent if the other tests are met.

An individual's own funds, however, must be taken into account if applied toward support. The source of the funds is not relevant.

Example 26

Dominic contributes $8,000 toward his parents' total support of $20,000. The parents, who do not live with Dominic, obtain the other $12,000 from savings and a home equity loan on their residence. Although the parents have no income, their use of savings and borrowed funds are counted as part of their support. Because Dominic does not satisfy the support test, he cannot claim his parents as dependents.

Capital expenditures for items like furniture, appliances, and automobiles are included in total support if the item does, in fact, constitute support.

Example 27

Tebin purchased a television set costing $950 and gave it to his mother who lives with him. The television set was placed in his mother's bedroom and was used exclusively by her. Tebin should include the cost of the television set in determining the support of his mother.

Multiple Support Agreements An exception to the support test involves a **multiple support agreement**. A multiple support agreement allows a group of taxpayers—none of whom provide more than 50 percent of the support of a taxpayer—to designate one member of the group to claim the individual as a dependent. All taxpayers in the group must satisfy the other dependency requirements (e.g., the relationship test), and, collectively, the group must provide more than 50 percent of the support. Any taxpayer in the group who contributed *more than 10 percent* of the support is entitled to claim the individual as a dependent. This provision is often used by the children of aged dependent parents when none of the children meet the support test.

Example 28

Wanda, who resides with her son, Adam, received $12,000 from various sources during the year. This constituted her entire support for the year. She received support from the following:

	Amount	Percentage of Total
Adam, a son	$ 5,760	48%
Bob, a son	1,200	10
Carol, a daughter	3,600	30
Diane, a friend	1,440	12
	$12,000	100%

If Adam and Carol file a multiple support agreement, either may claim Wanda as a dependent. Bob may not claim Wanda because he did not contribute *more than 10%* of her support. Bob's consent is not required for Adam and Carol to file a multiple support agreement. Diane does not meet the relationship or member-of-the-household test and cannot be a party to the agreement. The decision as to who claims Wanda rests with Adam and Carol. It is possible for Carol to claim Wanda even though Adam furnished more of Wanda's support.

Form 2120 (Multiple Support Declaration) must be completed and filed by the individual claiming the dependent. In addition, every other person who qualifies under the more-than-10% rule must provide a signed statement agreeing not to claim the individual as a dependent.

Children of Divorced or Separated Parents Another exception to the support test applies when parents with children are divorced or separated. Unmarried parents living apart for the last six months of the year also are covered by these rules. This exception applies if the parents meet the following conditions:

- They would have been entitled to claim the individual(s) as a dependent had they been married and filed a joint return.
- They have custody (either jointly or singly) of the child (or children) for more than half of the year.

In general, the parent having custody of the child (children) for the greater part of the year (i.e., the custodial parent) is entitled to claim the dependent(s).[21] However, the custodial parent can sign a waiver that allows the noncustodial parent to claim the child as a dependent.[22]

The waiver, Form 8332 (Release/Revocation of Release of Claim to Exemption for Child by Custodial Parent), can apply to a single year, a number of specified years, or all future years. Form 8332 must be attached to the noncustodial parent's tax return.

[21] Reg. § 1.152–4; the general rule does not apply if a multiple support agreement is in effect.

[22] § 152(e)(2).

3-4c Other Rules for Determining Dependents

In addition to fitting into either the qualifying child or the qualifying relative category, a dependent must meet the joint return and citizenship tests.

Joint Return Test

In general, a taxpayer cannot claim as a dependent a married individual who files a joint return with his or her spouse.[23] The joint return rule does not apply, however, if the reason for filing is to claim a refund for tax withheld (and no tax liability exists).[24]

Example 29

Paul provides over half of the support of his son, Quinn. He also provides over half of the support of Vera, who is Quinn's wife. During the year, both Quinn and Vera had part-time jobs. To recover the taxes withheld, they file a joint return. If Quinn and Vera are not required to file a return, both are dependents of Paul.

Citizenship Test

To be a dependent, the individual must be a U.S. citizen, a U.S. resident, or a resident of Canada or Mexico for some part of the calendar year in which the taxpayer's tax year begins. However, from 2018 through 2025, a taxpayer may not claim a dependent tax credit unless the individual is a U.S. citizen or a U.S. resident.[25]

Under an exception, an adopted child need not be a citizen or resident of the United States (or a contiguous country) as long as the child's principal residence is with a U.S. citizen.

Example 30

Alexis is a U.S. citizen who lives and works in Spain. She has adopted Benito, a four-year-old Italian national, who lives with her and is a member of her household.

Although Benito does not meet the citizenship test, he is covered by the exception. Benito is a qualifying child and a dependent of Alexis.

3-4d Comparison of Dependent Categories

Concept Summary 3.3 identifies the tests for the two categories of dependents. In contrasting the two categories, here are some observations:

- As to the relationship tests, the qualifying relative category is considerably more expansive. In addition to including those identified under the qualifying child grouping, other relatives are added. Nonrelated persons who are members of the household also are included.
- The support tests are entirely different. In the case of a qualifying child, the key is that the child is *not* self-supporting.
- The qualifying child category has no gross income limitation; the qualifying relative category has no age restriction.

---

[23] § 152(b)(2).

[24] Prop.Reg. § 1.152–1(a)(2)(ii) and Rev.Rul. 54–567.

[25] §§ 152(b)(3) and 24(h)(4)(B). See text Section 3-4e.

Concept Summary 3.3

Tests for Dependents

Test	Qualifying Child	Qualifying Relative
Relationship:		
• Children (natural, step, or adopted) and their *descendants*, and siblings and stepsiblings and their *descendants*.	X	
• Children (natural, step, or adopted) and their *descendants*, siblings and their children, parents and their *ascendants*, uncles and aunts, stepparents and stepsiblings, and certain in-laws.		X
• Member of the household (live with taxpayer for *entire* year; relative or non-relative)		X
Residence	X	
Age	X	
Support:		
• Not self-supporting ("child" furnishes half or less of his or her support)	X	
• Taxpayer furnishes over half of the support of potential dependent		X
Gross income less than the exemption amount		X
Joint return (potential dependent cannot file joint return)	X	X
Citizenship (potential dependent must meet test)	X	X

Ethics & Equity **Whose Qualifying Child Is He?**

The Rands are successful professionals and have combined AGI of approximately $450,000. Their household includes two children: Henry (age 16) and Belinda (age 22). Belinda is not a student and has a job where she earns $15,000 a year. After a short family meeting in early April 2022, the parties decide that Belinda should claim Henry as her qualifying child. As a result, Belinda is able to claim a child tax credit and an earned income tax credit yielding significant tax savings (more than $4,600, much of which is refundable). Had the Rands claimed Henry as their dependent, no child tax credit or earned income credit would have been available (these credits are phased out for higher-income taxpayers). Has the Rand family acted properly?

3-4e Child and Dependent Tax Credits

The **child tax credit** and **dependent tax credit** are provided to individual taxpayers based on the *number* of their qualifying children and dependents. With the suspension of the exemption deductions from 2018 through 2025, Congress increased the amount of the child tax credit, expanded its scope, and made it available to more taxpayers during the same time frame.[26] Congress also created a dependent tax credit.

A $2,000 child tax credit is allowed for each qualifying child (including stepchildren and foster children). To be eligible for the credit, the child must be under age 17 at the end of the year (under age 18 for 2021), must be a U.S. citizen, and must be a dependent of the taxpayer.[27] A Social Security number must be provided for any qualifying child.[28]

Due to the COVID-19 pandemic, Congress provided a temporary increase in the child tax credit. For 2021, the amount of the child tax credit was increased to $3,000 ($3,600 for a qualifying child under age 6 at the end of the year).[29]

In addition, a $500 tax credit is allowed for each dependent of the taxpayer (other than a qualifying child).[30] Examples of qualifying relatives for purposes of the dependent tax credit include children over age 16 (over age 17 in 2021), including full-time students

[26] § 24(h).

[27] §§ 24(c) and 24(i)(2).

[28] § 24(h)(4)(7).

[29] § 24(i)(3). During the last half of 2021, taxpayers received half of their available 2021 child tax credit in advance via monthly payments from the IRS unless they used the IRS website to opt out of receiving the payments in advance. These payments began in July and ended in December 2021. Any remaining child tax credit was claimed when the 2021 tax return was filed. § 7527A.

[30] § 24(h)(4)(A).

under age 24, children without a Social Security number, parents of the taxpayer, and "members of the household" (see text Section 3-4b). For purposes of the dependent tax credit, these qualifying relatives must be a U.S. citizen, a U.S. national, or a U.S. resident.[31]

The child tax credits (the $2,000 general credit and the 2021 additional credits) and the dependent tax credit are subject to specific phaseout rules based on a taxpayer's adjusted gross income.

Child and Dependent Tax Credits Phaseout

The available $2,000 child tax credit and $500 dependent tax credit both begin to phase out when AGI reaches $400,000 for married taxpayers filing jointly ($200,000 for all other taxpayers). These credits are phased out by $50 for each $1,000 (or part thereof) of AGI above the $400,000 (or $200,000) amount.[32] Because the maximum credit amount depends on the *number* of qualifying children and dependents, the income level at which these credits are phased out completely also depends on the *number* of qualifying children and dependents.

If married taxpayers filing a joint return have one qualifying child, the child tax credit is completely phased out if their AGI exceeds $439,000. If those taxpayers have two qualifying children, the child tax credit is completely phased out if their AGI exceeds $479,000. For all other taxpayers, these amounts would be $239,000 and $279,000, respectively. The allowed tax credit can be determined using the following steps:

1. AGI − Threshold amount = Excess amount.
2. Excess amount ÷ $1,000 = Reduction factor (round up to next whole number; for example, 18.2 = 19).
3. Reduction factor × $50 = Child and dependent tax credit reduction.
4. Maximum child and dependent tax credit amount − Child and dependent tax credit reduction = Child and dependent tax credit allowed.

The 2021 additional child tax credits [$1,000 for a qualifying child ($1,600 if the child is under age 6)] are subject to a separate phaseout rule.[33] Any additional child tax credit is phased out as AGI exceeds $150,000 (married, filing jointly), $112,500 (head of household), or $75,000 (other taxpayers). These credits are reduced by $50 for each $1,000 (or part thereof) of AGI over the applicable threshold amount. This phaseout does not reduce the $2,000 child tax credit amount, which has its own phaseout rule (discussed above).

Child and Dependent Tax Credit and Phaseout

Example 31

In 2021, Juanita and Alberto are married and file a joint tax return. They have two dependent children, ages 4 and 7. Their AGI is $85,400. Juanita and Alberto's maximum child tax credit is $6,600 ($3,600 + $3,000). Because Juanita and Alberto's AGI is less than the $150,000 threshold, they will be allowed a child tax credit of $6,600.

If, instead, the year is 2022, Juanita and Alberto will be allowed a $4,000 child tax credit ($2,000 × 2).

Example 32

Assume the same facts as Example 31, except that Juanita and Alberto's 2021 AGI is $165,400. Since their AGI does not exceed $400,000, Juanita and Alberto will receive a $4,000 child tax credit ($2,000 × 2 children). However, since their AGI is over the $150,000 threshold that relates to the additional 2021 child tax credits, the additional 2021 amounts ($2,600 in total; $1,600 + $1,000) must be reduced by $50 for every $1,000 (or portion of $1,000) above the $150,000 threshold. Their total child tax credit allowed is $5,800, computed as follows:

1. $165,400 (AGI) − $150,000 (Threshold amount) = $15,400 (Excess amount).
2. $15,400 (Excess amount) ÷ $1,000 = Reduction factor (15.4, rounded up to 16).
3. 16 (Reduction factor) × $50 = $800 (Additional child tax credit reduction).
4. $2,600 (Maximum additional child tax credit amount) − $800 (Additional child tax credit reduction) = $1,800 (Additional child tax credit allowed).
5. Total child tax credit: $5,800; $1,800 additional 2021 child tax credit + $4,000 general child tax credit.

If Juanita and Alberto's AGI exceeded $201,000, their additional 2021 child tax credit would be eliminated [($201,001 − $150,000 = $51,001; $51,001 ÷ $1,000 = 51.001, rounded up to 52; 52 × $50 = $2,600).

If, instead, the year was 2022, Juanita and Alberto would be allowed a $4,000 child tax credit ($2,000 × 2).

[31] § 24(h)(4)(B).

[32] § 24(b), as modified by § 24(h)(3). AGI is modified for this purpose; the threshold amounts are *not* indexed for inflation.

[33] § 24(i)(4).

Child and Dependent Tax Credit and Phaseout

Example 33

Assume the same facts as Example 31, except that Juanita and Alberto's 2021 AGI is $412,400. Since their AGI exceeds $201,000, the 2021 additional child tax credits have been eliminated (see Example 32). Since their AGI is over the $400,000 threshold, the maximum child tax credit ($4,000) must be reduced by $50 for every $1,000 (or portion of $1,000) above the $400,000 threshold. The child tax credit allowed is $3,350, computed as follows:

1. $412,400 (AGI) − $400,000 (Threshold amount) = $12,400 (Excess amount).
2. $12,400 (Excess amount) ÷ $1,000 = Reduction factor (12.4, rounded up to 13).
3. 13 (Reduction factor) × $50 = $650 (Child and dependent tax credit reduction).
4. $4,000 (Maximum child and dependent tax credit amount) − $650 (Child and dependent tax credit reduction) = $3,350 (Child and dependent tax credit allowed).

If, instead, the year is 2022, the outcome is the same as in 2021; Juanita and Alberto would qualify for a $3,350 child tax credit.

Example 34

Assume the same facts as Example 33, but also assume that Juanita's mother (age 88) is living with Juanita and Alberto and is a qualifying relative.

Since Juanita's mother is a qualifying relative, Juanita and Alberto will receive a $500 dependent tax credit. Their maximum combined child and dependent tax credit is $4,500 ($4,000 child tax credit + $500 dependent tax credit). This maximum amount is reduced by $650 (the child and dependent tax credit reduction; see Example 33). So their allowed child and dependent tax credit is $3,850 ($4,500 − $650).

Refundable Portion of Child Tax Credit

In 2021, for all taxpayers with qualifying children (regardless of how many), the child tax credit is fully refundable.[34] In 2022, absent a legislative change, any child tax credit is refundable to the extent of the *lesser* of:

1. $1,500 of the child tax credit for each qualifying child, or
2. 15 percent of the taxpayer's earned income in excess of $2,500.

The $1,500 amount is adjusted for inflation each year (it may increase in 2023); the $2,500 amount is not inflation-adjusted. The $500 dependent tax credit is *nonrefundable.*

Example 35

Return to the facts of Example 31. In 2022, assume that Juanita and Alberto have $82,000 of earned income and their taxable income is $58,600. Their child tax credit will be $4,000 ($2,000 × 2 children). The refundable portion of their child tax credit is $3000, computed as follows:

1. $3,000 (2 qualifying children × $1,500), or
2. $11,925 [15% × ($82,000 – $2,500)].

However, since their 2022 tax liability exceeds $4,000, they will claim the full amount of their child tax credit ($4,000).

Based on the computations in Example 35, one can see that the *refundability* of the child tax credit is aimed at lower-income taxpayers with earned income.

Example 36

In 2022, Tom and Cindy are married (filing jointly) and have two qualifying children. Their AGI is $18,000 (entirely earned income). With their standard deduction, Tom and Cindy will have no taxable income (and no Federal tax liability). Because the child tax credit is partially refundable, Tom and Cindy will receive a refund related to the child tax credit of $2,325, computed as follows:

1. $3,000 (2 qualifying children × $1,500), or
2. $2,325 [15% × ($18,000 – $2,500)]

If a taxpayer has three or more qualifying children, an alternative formula is available to determine the refundable portion.[35] In this case, the refundable portion is equal to the amount by which a taxpayer's Social Security (or self-employment) taxes exceed the earned income tax credit. The earned income tax credit, which also is partially refundable, is discussed in Chapter 13.

[34] § 24(i)(1); taxpayers must have a principal place of abode in the United States for more than one half of the taxable year.

[35] § 24(d)(1)(B)(ii).

3-5 Filing Status and Filing Requirements

LO.5

Choose the proper filing status and identify the related filing requirements.

Individuals must know their *filing status* to correctly compute both taxable income and the related income tax liability. In addition, individuals need to understand the tax return filing process. Text Sections 3-5 through 3-7 cover these important tax compliance points:

- Determination of filing status and whether a tax return must be filed (text Section 3-5).
- Computation of tax liability and adjustment for available tax credits (text Section 3-6; also see Concept Summary 3.1 and the tax formula).
- Selection of the appropriate tax form and how to file it with the IRS (text Section 3-7).

3-5a Filing Status

Every year, taxpayers must determine their **filing status**. The taxpayer's filing status is important because it is used to determine:

- The taxpayer's standard deduction (see Exhibits 3.4 and 3.5);
- Whether the taxpayer must file a tax return;
- The taxpayer's tax liability;
- Reductions of itemized deductions and certain tax credits; and
- Eligibility for certain provisions (e.g., some credits are not available when the married, filing separately status is used).

There are five filing statuses, and all taxpayers will file a return based on the filing status selected.

- Single.
- Married, filing jointly.
- Married, filing separately.
- Surviving spouse (qualifying widow or widower).
- Head of household.

The amount of tax varies considerably depending on which filing status is used. Consider the following example.

Example 37

The following amounts of tax are computed using the 2022 Tax Rate Schedules for a taxpayer (or taxpayers in the case of a joint return) with $60,000 of taxable income (see Appendix A).

Filing Status	Amount of Tax
Single	$8,817
Married, filing jointly	6,789
Married, filing separately	8,817
Surviving spouse	6,789
Head of household	7,317

These sample calculations are intended to illustrate the rate schedule differences for these filing statuses. To qualify for head-of-household status, the taxpayer would also have a child or dependent tax credit that would reduce the tax liability.

Single Taxpayers

A taxpayer who is unmarried (including a taxpayer who is legally separated or divorced) and does not qualify for head-of-household status (discussed below) will file as a single taxpayer.

Example 38

Phil was divorced in March and is unmarried at the end of the year. Phil has no dependents. As a result, Phil's filing status is single.

Global Tax Issues **Filing a Joint Return**

John is a U.S. citizen and resident, but he spends much of his time in London, where his employer sends him on frequent assignments. John is married to Victoria, a citizen and resident of the United Kingdom.

Can John and Victoria file a joint return for U.S. Federal income tax purposes? Although § 6013(a)(1) specifically precludes the filing of a joint return if one spouse is a nonresident alien, another Code provision permits an exception. Under § 6013(g), the parties can elect to treat the nonqualifying spouse as a "resident" of the United States. This election would allow John and Victoria to file jointly.

But should John and Victoria make this election? If Victoria has considerable income of her own (from non-U.S. sources), the election could be ill-advised. As a nonresident alien, Victoria's non-U.S. source income *would not* be subject to the U.S. income tax. If she is treated as a U.S. resident, however, her non-U.S. source income *will be subject to U.S. tax*. Under the U.S. global approach to taxation, all income (regardless of where earned) of anyone who is a *resident* or *citizen* of the United States is subject to tax.

Married Taxpayers

Married couples can file tax returns together (married, filing jointly) or apart (married, filing separately). In general, marital status is determined on the last day of the year. As mentioned above, when one spouse dies during the year, the surviving spouse is considered to be married to the spouse who died at the end of the year. Most married couples will find it beneficial to file a joint return.

Married, Filing Jointly The joint filing status was originally enacted in 1948 to establish equity between married taxpayers in common law states and those in community property states. Before the joint filing status was established, taxpayers in community property states were in an advantageous position relative to taxpayers in common law states because they could split their income. For instance, in a community property state, if one spouse earned $100,000 and the other spouse was not employed, each spouse could report $50,000 of income. Splitting the income in this manner caused the total income to be subject to lower marginal tax rates; each spouse would start at the bottom of the rate structure.

Taxpayers in common law states did not have this income-splitting option, so their taxable income was subject to higher marginal rates. This inconsistency in treatment was remedied by the joint filing status. The joint return Tax Rate Schedule is constructed based on the assumption that income is earned equally by the two spouses.

A legally married same-sex couple is treated as married for Federal tax purposes no matter where they live. Registered domestic partners, however, are not "spouses" under Federal law. Therefore, they cannot file Federal tax returns using married, filing jointly or married, filing separately status. The same rule applies to same-sex partners in civil unions.[36]

Marital status is determined as of the last day of the tax year, except when a spouse dies during the year. In that case, marital status is determined as of the date of death.

Example 39

Return to the facts of Example 38. Would things be different if, rather than getting a divorce, Phil's spouse passed away during the year? Yes. In this case, Phil would still be "married" for tax purposes at the end of the year.

What if Phil remarried during the year? In this case, Phil and his new spouse are a married couple (and they would file joint or separate returns). Phil's deceased spouse's filing status is married, filing separately.

Filing a joint return carries the potential disadvantage of joint and several liability.[37] This means that the IRS can pursue the collection of the tax due for that year against either spouse.

[36] Reg. § 301.7701–18 and *U.S. v. Windsor*, 2013–2 USTC ¶50,400, 111 AFTR 2d 2013–2385, 133 S.Ct. 2675; **irs.gov/newsroom/Answers-to-Frequently-Asked-Questions-for-Registered-Domestic-Partners-and-Individuals-in-Civil-Unions**.

[37] § 6013(d)(3).

Once a joint return has been filed and the due date has passed, the spouses cannot switch to separate returns for that year. However, if married persons file separately, they can change later to a joint return.

Married, Filing Separately If married individuals file separate returns, each reports only their own income, deductions, and credits, and each must use the married, filing separately tax rates. In a community property state, each individual must report half of the community property income.[38] Most married couples file a joint return, because the combined amount of tax is lower. However, special circumstances (e.g., significant medical expenses incurred by one spouse subject to the 7.5%-of-AGI limitation) may lead a married couple to file separate returns.

The Internal Revenue Code places some limitations on married persons who file separate returns. Here are some examples:

- If either spouse itemizes deductions, the other spouse also must itemize.
- The earned income credit and the credit for child and dependent care expenses cannot be claimed (see Chapter 13).
- No deduction is allowed for interest paid on qualified education loans (see Chapter 10).
- Only $1,500 of excess capital losses can be claimed by each spouse (see Chapter 16).

Surviving Spouse A special filing status applies for two years following the death of one spouse if the surviving spouse maintains a household for a dependent child. The child must be a son, stepson, daughter, or stepdaughter who qualifies as a dependent of the taxpayer (the gross income and joint return tests are waived for this purpose). This is referred to as **surviving spouse** status.[39] While surviving spouse is a distinct filing status, taxpayers filing as a surviving spouse use the married, filing jointly tax rates and standard deduction amounts.

Example 40

Dylan dies in 2022, leaving Jennifer with a dependent child. For the year of Dylan's death (2022), Jennifer files a joint return with Dylan. For the next two years (2023 and 2024), Jennifer, as a surviving spouse, may use the married, filing jointly tax rates. Beginning in 2025, Jennifer may use the head-of-household rates if she continues to maintain a household for her dependent child.

Marriage Penalty When Congress enacted the rate structure available to those filing joint returns, it generally favored married taxpayers. In certain situations, however, the parties would incur less tax if they were not married and filed as single taxpayers. The additional tax that a joint return caused, commonly called the **marriage penalty**, usually occurs when *both* spouses have substantial income. Long aware of the inequity of the marriage penalty, Congress reduced its effect on couples by increasing the standard deduction available to married filers to 200 percent of that applicable to single persons and doubling the size of the married filer tax brackets below 35 percent. However, the marriage penalty still exists for couples who itemize their deductions and have substantial amounts of income beyond the 32 percent tax bracket.

Head of Household

Unmarried individuals who maintain a household for a dependent (or dependents) can use the **head-of-household** filing status.[40] The tax liability using the head-of-household rates falls between the tax liabilities for married taxpayers filing jointly and single taxpayers.

To qualify for the head-of-household filing status, a taxpayer must pay more than half the cost of maintaining a household where the taxpayer lives. The household also must be the principal home of a dependent. Except for temporary absences (e.g., school, hospitalization), the dependent must live in the taxpayer's household for over half the year.

A dependent must be either a qualifying child or a qualifying relative who meets the relationship test (other than someone who qualifies under the member-of-the-household test).

[38] Form 8958 (Allocation of Tax Amounts Between Certain Individuals in Community Property States) is used for this purpose.

[39] § 2(a)(1). The IRS term for surviving spouse status is "qualifying widow(er) with dependent child."

[40] § 2(b).

The Big Picture

Example 41

Return to the facts of *The Big Picture* on p. 3-1. Assuming that Aleha can be treated as single (i.e., not married), can Terrah qualify Aleha for head-of-household filing status? The answer is no. Even though Terrah can be claimed as Aleha's dependent (see Example 20), she does not meet the relationship test for head-of-household status (Terrah qualified as a dependent under the member-of-the-household test).

Example 42

Kohsei, a widow, maintains a household in which she and her aunt live. If the aunt qualifies as a dependent, Kohsei may file as head of household. Note that an aunt meets the relationship test.

A special rule allows taxpayers to avoid having to live with their parents. Head-of-household status is allowed if a taxpayer maintains a *separate home* for the taxpayer's *parent or parents* if at least one parent qualifies as a dependent of the taxpayer.[41]

Example 43

Melissa, an unmarried individual, lives in New York City and maintains a household in Detroit for her dependent parents. Melissa may use the head-of-household filing status even though her parents do not reside in her New York home.

Head-of-household status is not changed during the year by the death of the dependent. As long as the taxpayer provided more than half of the cost of maintaining the household prior to the dependent's death, head-of-household status is preserved.

Abandoned Spouse Rules

When married persons file separate returns, several unfavorable tax consequences result. For example, the taxpayer must use the married, filing separately tax rates. But what about a taxpayer who is abandoned by his or her spouse? Since the taxpayer is married, absent a special rule, the taxpayer would likely have no choice but to file separately (a harsh result). To mitigate this outcome, Congress enacted the **abandoned spouse** rules. Under these rules, the taxpayer is treated as *not married* and qualifies for head-of-household status if the following conditions are met:[42]

- The taxpayer does not file a joint return.
- The taxpayer paid more than half the cost of maintaining a home for the tax year.
- The taxpayer's spouse did not live in the home during the last six months of the tax year.
- The home was the principal residence of the taxpayer's son, daughter, stepson, stepdaughter, foster child, or adopted child for more than half the year, and the child can be claimed as a dependent.[43]

The Big Picture

Example 44

Return to the facts of *The Big Picture* on p. 3-1. Can Aleha qualify as an abandoned spouse?

Yes, if she can claim Paige as a dependent—either as a qualifying child (see Example 15) or as a qualifying relative (see Example 23). If so, Aleha can use head-of-household filing status. If not, her filing status is married, filing separately.

[41] § 2(b)(1)(B).

[42] § 7703(b).

[43] §§ 7703(b)(1) and 152(e). The dependency requirement does not apply, however, if the taxpayer could have claimed the child as a dependent except for the fact that the child was claimed as a dependent by the noncustodial parent under a written agreement.

Ethics & Equity Abandoned Spouse?

Bob and Carol have been in and out of marital counseling for the past few years. Early in 2022, they decide to separate. However, because they are barely able to get by on their current incomes, they cannot afford separate housing or the legal costs of a divorce. So Bob moves out of their house in March and takes up residence in their detached garage (which has an enclosed workshop and bathroom). Carol stays in the house with their two children and pays more than half of the costs of maintaining their residence. Bob does not enter the house for the remainder of the year. Can Carol qualify as an abandoned spouse?

3-5b Filing Requirements

General Rules

In general, an individual must file a tax return if gross income equals or exceeds the applicable standard deduction.[44] A married taxpayer filing a separate return is required to file a return if *any* amount of gross income must be reported. Because the standard deduction amounts are subject to an annual inflation adjustment, the gross income amounts for determining whether a tax return must be filed normally change each year.[45] For example, a single taxpayer under age 65 must file a tax return in 2022 if gross income equals or exceeds $12,950 (the amount of the standard deduction). Exhibit 3.6 lists the income levels that require tax returns under the general rule and under certain special rules.

The additional standard deduction for being age 65 or older is considered in determining the gross income filing requirements. For example, the 2022 filing requirement for a single taxpayer age 65 or older is $14,700 ($12,950 basic standard deduction + $1,750

Exhibit 3.6 Filing Requirements for Most Taxpayers

Filing Status	2021 Gross Income	2022 Gross Income
Single		
Under 65	$12,550	$12,950
65 or older	14,250	14,700
Married, filing jointly		
Both spouses under 65	$25,100	$25,900
One spouse 65 or older	26,450	27,300
Both spouses 65 or older	27,800	28,700
Married, filing separately		
All	$ *	$ *
Head of household		
Under 65	$18,800	$19,400
65 or older	20,500	21,150
Qualifying widow(er)		
Under 65	$25,100	$25,900
65 or older	26,450	27,300

*Any amount of gross income will require a return to be filed.

[44] § 6012(f), modifying § 6012(a)(1) from 2018 through 2025; in years prior to 2018, an individual was required to file a return if gross income equaled or exceeded the sum of the exemption amount plus the applicable standard deduction.

[45] See §§ 1(f), 63(c)(4), and 151(d)(3).

additional standard deduction). Except in the case of dependents, the additional standard deduction for blindness is not taken into account in determining whether a taxpayer must file a tax return (see Filing Requirements for Dependents below).

A self-employed individual with net earnings of $400 or more from a business or profession must file a tax return regardless of the amount of gross income.

Even though an individual has gross income below the filing level amounts and therefore does not owe any tax, the individual must file a return to obtain a tax refund of amounts withheld. A return is also necessary to obtain the benefits of the earned income credit (see Chapter 13).

Filing Requirements for Dependents

Computation of the gross income filing requirement for an individual who can be claimed as a dependent on another person's tax return is subject to more complex rules. These rules are tied to the amount of a dependent's standard deduction (see text Section 3-2c). For 2022, a dependent with *any* of the following must file a return:

- Earned income only and gross income that is more than the total standard deduction (including any additional standard deduction).
- Unearned income only and gross income of more than $1,150 plus any additional standard deduction.
- Both earned and unearned income and gross income of more than the larger of $1,150 or the sum of earned income plus $400 (but limited to the basic standard deduction) plus any additional standard deduction.

Dependent Filing Requirements

Example 45

Tom is an unmarried dependent child who works part-time at the neighborhood pool as a lifeguard. During 2022, Tom earns $4,800 and has no other income. Must Tom file a return?

Answer: No. He had earned income only, and his gross income is less than his standard deduction of $12,950. However, if income taxes were withheld from his earnings, Tom will want to file a return to get a refund of any income taxes withheld.

Example 46

Martha is a widow, age 68, who lives with her son (and is his dependent). In 2022, her only source of income is interest income from her bank account ($450) and tax-exempt interest income of $200. Must Martha file a return?

Answer: No. She has unearned income only and gross income of only $450 (which is less than $2,900; $1,150 plus her $1,750 additional standard deduction).

Example 47

Return to the facts of Example 45. Tom also has $150 of interest income from his savings. Must Tom file a return?

Answer: No. He has earned income of $4,800 and gross income of $4,950. His standard deduction is $5,200 (earned income plus $400). As in Example 45, Tom will want to file a return to get a refund of any income taxes withheld.

If Tom had $450 of interest income, he would need to file a return. Now his gross income of $5,250 exceeds his $5,200 standard deduction (earned income plus $400).

LO.6

Demonstrate the proper procedures for determining the tax liability.

3-6 Tax Determination

The computation of income tax due (or refund) involves applying the proper set of tax rates to taxable income and then adjusting for available credits. In certain cases, however, the application of the kiddie tax will change how the tax is determined (see text Section 3-6c).

3-6a Tax Rates

The basic tax rate structure is progressive, with current rates ranging from 10 percent to 37 percent.[46] By way of comparison, the lowest rate structure, which was in effect in 1913–1915, ranged from 1 to 7 percent, and the highest, in effect during 1944–1945, ranged from 23 to 94 percent.

Tax Table Method

The tax liability is computed using either the Tax Table method or the Tax Rate Schedule method. Most taxpayers compute their tax using the **Tax Table**. Eligible taxpayers compute taxable income (as shown in Concept Summary 3.1) and *must* determine their tax by reference to the Tax Table. The following taxpayers, however, may *not* use the Tax Table method:

- Individuals whose taxable income exceeds the maximum (ceiling) amount in the Tax Table. In 2021, the Tax Table applies to taxable income below $100,000 for Form 1040.
- An estate or a trust.

The IRS does not release the Tax Tables until late in the year to which they apply. So the 2022 Tax Tables will be available at the end of 2022. The 2022 Tax Rate Schedules were released at the end of 2021.[47] For purposes of estimating tax liability and making quarterly estimated tax payments, the Tax Rate Schedules normally are used. Because it is available, the 2021 Tax Table is used to illustrate the tax computation using the Tax Table method.

Although the Tax Table is derived from the Tax Rate Schedules (discussed next), the tax calculated using the two methods may vary slightly. This is because the tax for a particular income range in the Tax Table is based on the midpoint amount.

Example 48

Liang is single and has taxable income of $30,000 for calendar year 2021. To determine Liang's tax using the Tax Table (see Appendix A), find the $30,000 to $30,050 income line. Liang's tax is $3,404. This amount is actually the tax the Tax Rate Schedule for 2021 would yield on taxable income of $30,025 (i.e., the midpoint amount between $30,000 and $30,050).

Tax Rate Schedule Method

Taxpayers who do not use the Tax Tables use the **Tax Rate Schedules**. The 2022 Tax Rate Schedule for single taxpayers is reproduced in Exhibit 3.7.[48] This schedule is used to illustrate the tax computations in Examples 49 and 50.

Example 49

Pat is single and had $5,810 of taxable income in 2022. His tax, based on the Tax Rate Schedule, is $581 ($5,810 × 10%).

Pat's tax, based on the Tax Table, is $583. This tax is based on taxable income of $5,825 (the midpoint between $5,800 and $5,850). Because his taxable income is less than $100,000, Pat must use the Tax Table.

Several terms are used to describe tax rates. The rates in the Tax Rate Schedules are often referred to as *statutory* (or nominal) rates. The *marginal* rate is the tax rate that would be assessed on the next dollar of income for a particular taxpayer. In Example 49, the statutory rate and the marginal rate are both 10 percent.

---

[46] Rev.Proc. 2021–45.

[47] The 2021 Tax Tables and the 2022 and 2021 Tax Rate Schedules are reproduced in Appendix A; 2022 Tax Tables will be available on the IRS website in late 2022. For quick reference, the Tax Rate Schedules also are reproduced inside the front cover of this text.

[48] § 1(i), as modified by § 1(j).

Exhibit 3.7 2022 Tax Rate Schedule for Single Taxpayers

If Taxable Income Is			
Over	**But Not Over**	**The Tax Is:**	**Of the Amount Over**
$ -0-	$ 10,275	10%	$ -0-
10,275	41,775	$ 1,027.50 + 12%	10,275
41,775	89,075	4,807.50 + 22%	41,775
89,075	170,050	15,213.50 + 24%	89,075
170,050	215,950	34,647.50 + 32%	170,050
215,950	539,900	49,335.50 + 35%	215,950
539,900		162,718.00 + 37%	539,900

Example 50

Jocelyn is single and had taxable income of $102,000 in 2022. Her tax is $18,315.50 [$15,213.50 + 24%($102,000 – $89,075)].

The *average* rate is equal to the tax liability divided by taxable income. In Example 50, Jocelyn has statutory rates of 10 percent, 12 percent, 22 percent, and 24 percent. Jocelyn's average rate is 17.96 percent ($18,315.50 tax liability ÷ $102,000 taxable income); her marginal rate is 24 percent.

A tax is *progressive* (or graduated) if a higher rate of tax applies as the tax base increases. The progressive nature of the Federal income tax on individuals is illustrated by computing the tax in Example 50 using each rate bracket.

Tax on first $10,275 at 10%	$ 1,027.50
Tax on $41,775 − $10,275 at 12%	3,780.00
Tax on $89,075 − $41,775 at 22%	10,406.00
Tax on $102,000 − $89,075 at 24%	3,102.00
Total tax on taxable income of $102,000	$18,315.50

A special computation (see text Section 3-9d) limits the effective tax rate on qualified dividends (see Chapter 4) and net long-term capital gain (see Chapter 16).

3-6b Computation of Net Taxes Payable or Refund Due

The pay-as-you-go feature of the Federal income tax system requires payment of all or part of the taxpayer's income tax liability during the year. These payments take the form of Federal income tax withheld by employers or estimated tax paid by the taxpayer or both.[49] The payments are applied against the tax liability to determine whether the taxpayer will get a refund or pay additional tax.

Employers are required to withhold income tax on compensation paid to their employees and to pay this tax to the government. The employer must provide each employee a Form W–2 (Wage and Tax Statement), which documents wages and taxes withheld (including income, Social Security, and Medicare taxes). An employee should receive a 2022 Form W–2 no later than January 31, 2023.

If taxpayers receive income that is not subject to withholding or income from which not enough tax is withheld, they may have to pay estimated tax. Form 1040–ES (Estimated Tax for Individuals) is used for these payments, and estimates are due quarterly (see Chapter 13 for a thorough discussion).

[49] § 3402 for withholding; § 6654 for estimated payments.

The income tax liability is reduced by any available tax credits (which are different from tax deductions). Tax credits reduce the tax liability dollar for dollar. Tax deductions reduce taxable income on which the tax liability is based.

Example 51

In 2022, Gail is a single taxpayer in the 24% tax bracket. As a result of incurring $1,000 in child care expenses, she is entitled to a $200 child care credit ($1,000 child care expenses × 20% credit rate; see Chapter 13 for details). She also contributed $1,000 to the American Cancer Society and included this amount in her itemized deductions.

The child care credit results in a $200 reduction of Gail's tax liability for the year. The contribution to the American Cancer Society reduces taxable income by $1,000 and results in a $240 reduction in Gail's tax liability ($1,000 reduction in taxable income × 24% tax rate).

Tax credits (other than the child and dependent tax credits; see text Section 3-4e) are discussed in Chapter 13. Some of the more common credits include:

- Earned income credit.
- Credit for child and dependent care expenses.
- Education tax credits.
- Premium tax credit.

The computation of net taxes payable or refund due can be illustrated by returning to the facts of Example 6.

Example 52

Grace is not married and has her disabled and dependent mother living with her. This qualifies Grace for head-of-household filing status. Recall that Example 6 established that Grace has taxable income of $24,700. In addition, assume that you have the following information: income tax withheld, $2,000; estimated tax payments, $600; and dependent tax credit, $500. Grace's net taxes payable is computed as follows:

Income tax (from 2022 Tax Rate Schedule, for head of household, Appendix A)		$2,671
Less: Tax credits and prepayments—		
Dependent tax credit	$ 500	
Income tax withheld	2,000	
Estimated tax payments	600	(3,100)
Net taxes payable or (refund due)		($ 429)

Grace's tax was computed using the Tax Rate Schedules rather than the Tax Tables because the 2022 Tax Tables were not available when this textbook was published (they are not available until the end of 2022).

3-6c Kiddie Tax—Unearned Income of Dependent Children

LO.7

Identify and report the unearned income of dependent children (the kiddie tax).

At one time, a dependent child could claim an exemption deduction (along with a standard deduction) on his or her own return even if claimed as a dependent by the parents. This enabled a parent to shift investment income (like interest and dividends) to a child by transferring income-producing assets. The child would pay no tax on the income to the extent that it was sheltered by the child's exemption and standard deduction amounts. And if the child did pay any tax, that tax was at the child's (lower) rates rather than the parents' (higher) rates.

To reduce the tax savings that result from shifting income from parents to children, the net **unearned income**[50] (commonly called investment income) of certain children is taxed using special rules. This provision, commonly referred to as the **kiddie tax**, applies to any child who is under age 19 (or under age 24 if a full-time student) and has unearned income of more than $2,300 in 2022 ($2,200 in 2021).[51]

[50] Unearned income includes taxable interest, dividends, capital gains, rents, royalties, the taxable portion of scholarships, pension and annuity income, and income (other than earned income) received as the beneficiary of a trust.

[51] § 1(g)(2). The kiddie tax does not apply if the child has earned income that exceeds half of the support received, if the child is married and files a joint return, or if both parents are deceased.

Net Unearned Income

In 2022, net unearned income of a dependent child is computed as follows:[52]

Unearned income

Less: $1,150

Less: The greater of:

- $1,150 of the standard deduction, *or*
- The amount of allowable itemized deductions directly connected with the production of the unearned income

Equals: Net unearned income

If net unearned income is zero (or negative), the child's tax is computed using the appropriate Tax Rate Schedule (likely single). If net unearned income is positive, this amount is taxed at the parents' rate. The child's remaining taxable income (known as nonparental source income) is taxed at the child's rate.

Tax Determination

If a child is subject to the kiddie tax, there are two options for computing the tax on the income. A separate return may be filed for the child, or the parents may elect to report the child's income on their own return.

If a separate return is filed for the child, the tax on net unearned income (referred to as the *allocable parental tax*) is computed as though the income had been included on the parents' return. Form 8615 (Tax for Certain Children Who Have Unearned Income) is used to compute the tax. The steps required in this computation are illustrated in Example 53.

Example 53

Olaf and Olga have a child, Hans (age 10). In 2022, Hans received $3,400 of interest income and had no earned income. Olaf and Olga had $70,000 of taxable income, not including their child's investment income. The parents have no qualified dividends or capital gains. Olaf and Olga do not make the parental election (discussed below).

1. Determine Hans's net unearned income	
Gross income (unearned)	$ 3,400
Less: $1,150	(1,150)
Less: The greater of	
• $1,150 or	
• Investment expense ($200)	(1,150)
Equals: Net unearned income	$ 1,100
2. Determine allocable parental tax	
Parents' taxable income	$70,000
Plus: Hans's net unearned income	1,100
Equals: Revised taxable income	$71,100
Tax on revised taxable income	$ 8,121
Less: Tax on parents' taxable income	(7,989)
Allocable parental tax	$ 132
3. Determine Hans's nonparental source tax	
Hans's AGI	$ 3,400
Less: Standard deduction	(1,150)
Less: Personal exemption	(–0–)
Equals: Taxable income	$ 2,250
Less: Net unearned income	(1,100)
Nonparental source taxable income	$ 1,150
Nonparental source tax ($1,150 × 10% rate)	$ 115
4. Determine Hans's total tax liability	
Nonparental source tax (Step 3)	$ 115
Allocable parental tax (Step 2)	132
Total tax	$ 247

Without the kiddie tax, Hans's tax liability would have been $225 ($2,250 taxable income × 10% rate); as a result, the kiddie tax results in an increased tax liability of $22 ($247 – $225) for Hans.

[52] The $1,150 amounts in the net unearned income computation are adjusted each year for inflation. The amounts were $1,100 in 2021.

Election to Claim Certain Unearned Income on Parent's Return

A parent may elect to report the child's unearned income that exceeds $2,300 ($2,200 in 2021) on the parent's own tax return if the child meets *all* of the following requirements:

- Gross income is from interest and dividends only.
- Gross income is more than $1,150 but less than $11,500 (for 2021, these amounts are $1,100 and $11,000).
- No estimated tax has been paid in the name and Social Security number of the child, and the child is not subject to backup withholding (see Chapter 13).

If this election is made, the child is treated as having no gross income and is not required to file a tax return. In this case, Form 8814 (Parents' Election to Report Child's Interest and Dividends) must be filed as part of the parents' tax return. The parent(s) also must pay an additional tax equal to the smaller of $115 or 10 percent of the child's gross income over $1,150.[53]

Other Rules

Here are a few other rules that apply to the kiddie tax:[54]

- If parents have more than one child subject to the tax on net unearned income, the tax for the children is computed as shown in Example 53 and then allocated to the children based on their relative amounts of income.
- For children of divorced parents, the taxable income of the custodial parent is used to determine the allocable parental tax. This parent is the one who may elect to report the child's unearned income.
- For married individuals filing separate returns, the individual with the greater taxable income is the applicable parent.

3-7 Tax Return Filing Procedures

3-7a Selecting the Proper Form

Because the 2022 tax forms had not been released when this text was published, the following comments apply to the 2021 forms.[55]

All taxpayers use Form 1040 as a starting point. Then depending on their various activities (e.g., business, investment, personal), supplemental schedules may be required.

If the taxpayer:	File:
Has additional income to report (e.g., business income or loss, unemployment compensation, prize or award money, or gambling winnings). *OR* Has any deductions *for* AGI to claim (e.g., student loan interest, self-employment tax, individual retirement account contributions, or educator expenses).	Schedule 1 (Form 1040)
Owes the alternative minimum tax or needs to make an excess advance premium tax credit repayment. *OR* Owes other taxes (e.g., the self-employment tax, household employment taxes, or additional taxes on IRAs or other qualified retirement plans and tax-favored accounts).	Schedule 2 (Form 1040)

[53] § 1(g)(7). Parents who have substantial itemized deductions based on AGI (see Chapter 10) may find that making the parental election increases total taxes for the family unit. Taxes should be calculated both with and without the parental election to determine the appropriate choice.

[54] See IRS Publication 17 (*Your Federal Income Tax*) and Form 8615 (Tax for Certain Children Who Have Unearned Income).

[55] Draft tax forms are available from the IRS at **apps.irs.gov/app/picklist/list/draftTaxForms.html**.

If the taxpayer:	File:
Can claim a nonrefundable credit other than the child tax credit or the dependent tax credit (e.g., the foreign tax credit, education credits, or the general business credit). *OR* Can claim a refundable credit other than the earned income credit, American Opportunity credit, or additional child tax credit (e.g., the net premium tax credit, health coverage tax credit, or qualified sick and family leave credits). *OR* Has other payments to report (e.g., an amount paid with an extension to file or excess Social Security tax withheld).	Schedule 3 (Form 1040)

Schedules 1, 2, and 3 are reproduced on pages 3-11 through 3-16. The other schedules are available on the IRS website (**irs.gov**). Other forms and schedules may be needed to supplement Form 1040 and Schedules 1 through 3. For example, a self-employed taxpayer will need to complete Schedule C (Form 1040) as a supplement to Schedule 1 while also computing any self-employment tax liability by completing Schedule SE (Form 1040) as a supplement to Schedule 2. Taxpayers who want to itemize deductions *from* AGI need to complete Schedule A (Form 1040) to document those deductions.

The IRS has developed a tax return (Form 1040-SR) for taxpayers who are age 65 by the last day of the year. Form 1040-SR is very similar to Form 1040.[56]

3-7b The E-File Approach

The **e-file** program is used by the vast majority of individual taxpayers (and is mandatory for most tax return preparers). The required tax information is transmitted to the IRS electronically either directly from the taxpayer (i.e., an "e-file online return") or indirectly through an "Authorized *e-file* Provider." These Providers are tax professionals who have been accepted into the electronic filing program by the IRS. Providers often are the preparers of the return as well.

Taxpayers also can use IRS Free File (with online fillable forms) or use commercial software to file a tax return at no cost. A number of software providers offer free e-filing services. These services are generally available only to taxpayers who have AGI of $73,000 or less. Eligibility requirements and a list of the software providers are available on the IRS website: **irs.gov/filing/e-file-options**.

All taxpayers and tax return preparers must attest to the returns they file. For most taxpayers, this is done through an electronic return signature using a personal identification number (a Self-Select PIN). Or the taxpayer can authorize a tax preparer to generate a PIN by signing Form 8879 (IRS *e-file* Signature Authorization). If certain paper documents must be submitted, a one-page form must be completed and filed when the return is e-filed. Form 8453 (U.S. Individual Income Tax Transmittal for an IRS *e-file* Return) is used to submit required attachments for both self- and practitioner-prepared electronic returns.

The *e-file* approach has two major advantages over paper filing. First, it eliminates many reporting errors. Second, it reduces the time required for processing a refund.

3-7c When and Where to File

Tax returns of individuals are due on or before the fifteenth day of the fourth month following the close of the tax year. For the calendar year taxpayer, the usual filing date is on or before April 15 of the following year.[57] When the due date falls on a Saturday, Sunday, or legal holiday, the filing deadline is the next business day. If the return is mailed to the proper address with sufficient postage and is postmarked on or before the due date, it is deemed timely filed.[58] The return should be sent or delivered to the IRS Regional Service Center listed in the instructions for each type of return or contained in software applications.[59]

[56]Created by Sec. 41106 of P.L. 115–123, the Bipartisan Budget Act of 2018.

[57]§ 6072(a); Rev.Rul. 2015–13 provides filing deadline guidance when there are unique state holidays.

[58]The Code allows the IRS to prescribe rules when taxpayers use FedEx, UPS, or a similar delivery service [§ 7502(f)]. See Notice 2016–30 for the current list of "designated private delivery services" that, if used, will meet the timely filed rules.

[59]The appropriate IRS Regional Service Center address can be found at **irs.gov/filing/where-to-file-addresses-for-taxpayers-and-tax-professionals-filing-form-1040**.

If a taxpayer is unable to file the return by the return's due date, a six-month extension of time can be obtained by filing Form 4868 (Application for Automatic Extension of Time to File U.S. Individual Income Tax Return) by the return's due date. Members of the U.S. Armed Forces also are allowed additional time for filing their Federal income tax returns.[60]

Although an extension provides additional time to file a return, it does not extend the deadline for paying any taxes due. If more tax is owed, it should be paid when the Form 4868 is filed. If a taxpayer does not obtain an extension of time to file and/or pay any tax due, the failure to file and failure to pay penalties can be assessed (these are discussed in Chapter 1).

If an individual taxpayer needs to file an amended return (e.g., because of a failure to report income or to claim a deduction or tax credit), Form 1040X is filed. The form generally must be filed within three years of the filing date of the original return or within two years from the time the tax was paid, whichever is later.

3-7d Modes of Payment

Payments of any taxes due can be made in a variety of ways, including check or money order (with payment made to "United States Treasury"), IRS Direct Pay (electronic funds withdrawal from a bank account), or the Electronic Federal Tax Payment System (EFTPS). In addition, the IRS has approved the use of MasterCard, American Express, Discover, and Visa to pay Federal taxes using a payment processor (fees will apply to these transactions).

3-8 Gains and Losses from Property Transactions—In General

LO.8

Explain the fundamentals of property transactions.

Gains and losses from property transactions are discussed in detail in Chapters 14 through 17. But an overview is relevant for topics that are discussed in the intervening chapters.

When property is sold (or otherwise disposed of), a gain or loss results. This gain or loss has a tax effect on the seller when the *realized* gain or loss is *recognized* for tax purposes. Without a transaction generating realized gain or loss, there generally can be no recognized gain or loss. Realized gain or loss is computed as follows:

Amount realized from the sale − **Adjusted basis of the property** = **Realized gain (or loss)**

The amount realized is the selling price of the property less any costs of disposition (e.g., brokerage commissions) incurred by the seller. The adjusted basis of the property is determined as follows:

	Cost (or other original basis) at date of acquisition[61]
Add:	Capital additions
Subtract:	Depreciation (if appropriate) and other capital recoveries (see Chapter 8)
Equals:	Adjusted basis at date of sale or other disposition

In general, all realized gains are recognized (taxable). However, the tax law provides some exceptions (see, for example, Chapter 15 dealing with certain nontaxable exchanges). Realized losses may or may not be recognized (deductible) for tax purposes. For example, losses realized from the sale of personal use property (e.g., a residence, home furnishings, clothing, sports equipment) are not recognized.

Example 54

During the current year, Ted sells his sailboat (adjusted basis of $4,000) for $5,500. Ted also sells one of his personal automobiles (adjusted basis of $8,000) for $5,000.

Ted's realized gain of $1,500 from the sale of the sailboat is recognized. On the other hand, the $3,000 realized loss on the sale of the automobile is not recognized and will not provide Ted with any deductible tax benefit.

[60] Reg. § 1.6081–4. See also IRS Publication 17 (*Your Federal Income Tax*), Chapter 1.

[61] Cost usually means purchase price plus expenses related to the acquisition of the property and incurred by the purchaser (e.g., brokerage commissions). For the basis of property acquired by gift or inheritance and other basis rules, see Chapter 14.

In terms of the tax formula, recognized gains from property transactions are included in gross income. If the gain is deferred (e.g., like-kind exchanges or involuntary conversions—see Chapter 15) or not recognized (e.g., sale of a residence—see Chapter 15), there is no immediate tax effect. Recognized losses from property transactions are treated as deductions *for* adjusted gross income (AGI).

If a property disposition results in a recognized gain or loss, the gain or loss must be *classified* as capital or ordinary. Although ordinary gain is fully taxable and ordinary loss is fully deductible, the same is often not true for capital gains and capital losses.

3-9 Gains and Losses from Property Transactions—Capital Gains and Losses

Capital gains and losses are treated uniquely in the Federal income tax system. Capital gains are included in the determination of taxable income and may be taxed at lower (preferential) tax rates. Capital losses, on the other hand, may not be fully deductible when determining taxable income (if limited, the amount not allowed can be carried over and used in subsequent years).

3-9a Definition of a Capital Asset

Capital assets are defined in the Code as any property held by the taxpayer *other than* certain items including inventory, accounts receivable, and depreciable property or real estate used in a business (see Chapter 16 for a complete discussion). As a result, the sale or exchange of these assets normally results in ordinary income or loss (see Chapter 17).

Example 55

Kelly owns a pizza parlor. During the current year, he sells an automobile that had been used as a delivery car for three years. The sale resulted in a loss of $1,000. Because this automobile is property used in his business, Kelly has an ordinary loss deduction of $1,000 rather than a capital loss deduction.

The principal capital assets held by an individual taxpayer include (1) assets held for personal (rather than business) use (e.g., a personal residence or an automobile) and (2) assets held for investment purposes (e.g., corporate securities or land). Capital assets generally include collectibles, which are subject to somewhat unique tax treatment. **Collectibles** include art, antiques, gems, metals, stamps, some coins and bullion, and alcoholic beverages that are held as investments.

3-9b Determination of Net Capital Gain

To arrive at a net capital gain, capital losses must be taken into account. First, capital gains and losses are categorized based on their holding period: *short term* (held for one year or less) and *long term* (held for more than one year). Then gains and losses in each category are netted together. If excess losses result, they are applied to the category carrying the *highest* tax rate. A *net capital gain* occurs if the net long-term capital gain (NLTCG) exceeds the net short-term capital loss (NSTCL).

Example 56

In the current year, Colin has the following capital transactions and resulting gains (losses):

Penguin Corporation stock (held for 8 months)	$ 1,000
Owl Corporation stock (held for 10 months)	(3,000)
Cardinal Corporation stock (held for 5 years)	2,000
Land (held as an investment for 3 years)	4,000

The Penguin Corporation short-term capital gain (STCG) of $1,000 is offset by the Owl Corporation short-term capital loss (STCL) of $3,000, resulting in a net STCL of $2,000. The Cardinal Corporation long-term capital gain (LTCG) and the land LTCG are combined, resulting in a net LTCG of $6,000. The net STCL offsets the net LTCG, resulting in a net capital gain of $4,000.

3-9c Treatment of Net Capital Loss

For individual taxpayers, net capital loss can be used to offset ordinary income of up to $3,000 ($1,500 for married persons filing separate returns). If a taxpayer has both short- and long-term capital losses, short-term losses are used first. Any remaining net capital loss is carried over indefinitely until used up (subject to the annual $3,000 limit). When carried over, the excess capital loss retains its classification as short- or long-term.

Example 57

In 2022, Tina has a short-term capital loss of $2,000, a long-term capital loss of $2,500, and no capital gains. She can deduct $3,000 ($2,000 short-term + $1,000 long-term) of this amount as an ordinary loss. The remaining $1,500 is carried over to 2023 as a long-term capital loss.

The Big Picture

Example 58

Return to the facts of *The Big Picture* on p. 3-1. Aleha's sale of her wedding rings resulted in a realized capital loss of $2,800 [$9,000 (selling price) − $11,800 (cost basis)]. However, because they were personal use property, Aleha cannot deduct the loss.

3-9d Taxation of Net Capital Gain

Net capital gains are classified and taxed as follows:

Classification	Maximum Rate*
Short-term gains (held for one year or less)	37%
Long-term gains (held for more than one year):	
Collectibles	28%
Certain depreciable property used in a trade or business (known as unrecaptured § 1250 gain and discussed in Chapter 17)	25%
All other long-term capital gains	20%, 15%, or 0%

*Does not include additional Medicare taxes on high-income taxpayers.

The special tax rates for long-term capital gains (called the alternative tax computation) are used when the taxpayer's regular tax rate *exceeds* the alternative tax rate. When tax liability is determined, long-term capital gains are taxed last. As a result, the tax rate applied to a long-term capital gain will depend on the taxpayer's regular tax rate on other income and the size of the long-term capital gain (a large long-term capital gain may cross marginal rates brackets and, theoretically, could be taxed at 0%, 15%, and 20% rates). The alternative rates are applied based on the taxpayer's filing status and taxable income (see Exhibit 3.8).[62] Special rates apply to collectibles and certain types of depreciable realty. If losses are used to offset gains, the losses are first used to offset gains with the *highest* tax rates.[63] These special tax rates also apply to qualified dividend income (see Chapter 4). Chapter 16 provides a detailed discussion of these tax computations.

Exhibit 3.8 2022 Alternative Tax Rates on Net Capital Gains (NCG) (Based on Filing Status and Taxable Income)

FILING STATUS								
Single		Married, Filing Jointly		Married, Filing Separately		Head of Household		NCG Tax Rate
Taxable Income		Taxable Income		Taxable Income		Taxable Income		
Greater Than	No More Than	Greater Than	No More Than	Greater Than	No More Than	Greater Than	No More Than	
$ -0-	$ 41,675	$ -0-	$ 83,350	$ -0-	$ 41,675	$ -0-	$ 55,800	0%
41,675	459,750	83,350	517,200	41,675	258,600	55,800	488,500	15%
459,750		517,200		258,600		488,500		20%

[62] In 2021, the 0% rate applies when taxable income does not exceed $80,800 (married, filing jointly), $54,100 (head of household), or $40,400 (single and married, filing separately). The 20% rate applies only when the taxpayer's taxable income exceeds $501,600 (married, filing jointly), $250,800 (married, filing separately), $473,750 (head of household), or $445,850 (single).

[63] § 1(h)(1).

Net Capital Gain Tax Computation

Example 59

During 2022, Marco is single, has taxable income of $35,000, and has the following capital gains for the year:

Robin Corporation stock (held for 6 months)	$1,000
Crow Corporation stock (held for 13 months)	1,000

Although both transactions yield a $1,000 capital gain, the tax effects are quite different. Marco pays a tax of $120 ($1,000 × 12%) on the Robin stock gain but $0 ($1,000 × 0%) on the Crow stock gain (his taxable income does not exceed $41,675).

Example 60

Assume the same facts as in Example 59, except that Marco's taxable income for the year is $170,000 (rather than $35,000). Marco's taxable income puts him in the 32% tax bracket. In addition, his taxable income is above $41,675 (where the 0% rate would apply to long-term capital gains) and does not exceed $459,750 (where the 20% rate would apply to long-term capital gains).

Marco now pays a tax of $320 ($1,000 × 32%) on the Robin stock gain and $150 ($1,000 × 15%) on the Crow stock gain.

Example 61

In 2022, Colin is single, has taxable income of $195,000, and has the following capital transactions and resulting gains (losses):

Penguin Corporation stock (held for 8 months)	$ 1,000
Owl Corporation stock (held for 10 months)	(3,000)
Stamp collection (held for 5 years)	2,000
Land (held as an investment for 3 years)	4,000

The Penguin Corporation short-term capital gain (STCG) of $1,000 is offset by the Owl Corporation short-term capital loss (STCL) of $3,000, resulting in a net STCL of $2,000. This $2,000 net STCL is then applied against the stamp collection gain—a collectible long-term capital gain (LTCG) with the highest tax rate (28%). Because there is no remaining STCL, Colin has a net LTCG of $4,000 from the land sale. Because Colin's taxable income exceeds $41,675 and does not exceed $459,750, the net LTCG is taxed at a 15% rate.

3-9e Taxation of Virtual Currency

Over 6,000 types of virtual currency exist. The first and best-known virtual currency is bitcoin, which had its first real-world transaction in 2010 (to purchase two pizzas).[64] In 2014, the IRS issued guidance on the tax treatment of convertible virtual currency used to pay for goods or services.[65] Convertible means that the virtual currency can be exchanged for real (sovereign) currency in that it acts as a substitute for real currency, such as the U.S. dollar. The key point of this IRS guidance is that virtual currency is treated as *property* rather than as a *foreign currency*. As a result, if an employee is paid in bitcoin, her wages are equal to the value of the bitcoin when received. When a holder of virtual currency uses it to acquire goods, services, or a different virtual currency, the transaction is treated as a barter transaction with tax consequences to the holder.

Example 62

Neha acquired $500 of bitcoin from a virtual currency exchange in 2020 to hold for investment. In 2022, when its value was $1,650, Neha used all of her bitcoin to pay for repairs to her car (the repair business accepted bitcoin from customers).

Neha must report a long-term capital gain of $1,150 ($1,650 fair market value less $500 basis; her holding period is more than one year). She is treated as having sold her bitcoin for $1,650 when she exchanged it for services worth $1,650. Neha will also answer "yes" to the virtual currency question on page one of her Form 1040 (discussed next).

[64] **en.bitcoinwiki.org/wiki/Bitcoin_history**. Other virtual currencies include Ethereum and Litecoin.

[65] Notice 2014–21.

The 2021 Form 1040 includes a specific question about virtual currency (see the last line in the partial Form 1040 presented below).

Form **1040** Department of the Treasury—Internal Revenue Service (99) **U.S. Individual Income Tax Return** **2021** OMB No. 1545-0074 IRS Use Only—Do not write or staple in this space.

Filing Status Check only one box. ☐ Single ☐ Married filing jointly ☐ Married filing separately (MFS) ☐ Head of household (HOH) ☐ Qualifying widow(er) (QW)
If you checked the MFS box, enter the name of your spouse. If you checked the HOH or QW box, enter the child's name if the qualifying person is a child but not your dependent ▶

Your first name and middle initial	Last name		**Your social security number**
If joint return, spouse's first name and middle initial	Last name		**Spouse's social security number**
Home address (number and street). If you have a P.O. box, see instructions.		Apt. no.	**Presidential Election Campaign** Check here if you, or your spouse if filing jointly, want $3 to go to this fund. Checking a box below will not change your tax or refund. ☐ **You** ☐ **Spouse**
City, town, or post office. If you have a foreign address, also complete spaces below.	State	ZIP code	
Foreign country name	Foreign province/state/county	Foreign postal code	

At any time during 2021, did you receive, sell, exchange, or otherwise dispose of any financial interest in any virtual currency? ☐ **Yes** ☐ **No**

Since most individuals do not own virtual currency, most Form 1040 filers will answer "no." The purpose of the question is to remind taxpayers about the need to report taxable virtual currency transactions, like the sale of virtual currency for cash or other virtual currency, the receipt of virtual currency for performance of services, or the use of virtual currency to buy goods or services. According to the IRS, the purchase of virtual currency with cash, the holding of virtual currency in a wallet or an account, or the transfer of virtual currency from one wallet or account to another (owned by the same taxpayer) is *not* a "transaction" for purposes of responding to this question. To assist taxpayers in complying with these rules, the IRS also maintains a comprehensive "*frequently asked questions*" page on its website.[66]

3-10 Tax Planning

LO.9

Evaluate tax planning opportunities associated with the individual tax formula.

3-10a Maximizing the Use of the Standard Deduction

In some cases, the difference between using the standard deduction and itemizing may not be a significant amount. Here, taxes might be saved by alternating between the two options. The taxpayer does this by using the cash method to concentrate multiple years' deductions in a single year (e.g., church pledges for several years can be paid in one year). Then the standard deduction is used in alternate years.

3-10b Dependents

The Joint Return Test

A married person can be claimed as a dependent only if that individual does not file a joint return with his or her spouse. If a joint return has been filed, the damage may be undone if separate returns are substituted on or before the due date of the return.

Example 63

While preparing a client's 2021 income tax return on April 3, 2022, the tax professional discovered that the client's daughter had filed a joint return with her spouse in late January 2022. Presuming that the daughter otherwise qualifies as the client's dependent, her dependency status is not lost if she and her spouse file separate returns on or before April 15, 2022.

If the daughter and her spouse attempt to file separate returns after April 15, 2022, the returns will not be accepted (the joint return election is binding).[67]

Keep in mind that the filing of a joint return will not affect dependency status if the parties are filing solely to recover all income tax withholdings and no tax liability exists.

[66] **irs.gov/individuals/international-taxpayers/frequently-asked-questions-on-virtual-currency-transactions**.

[67] Reg. § 1.6013–1(a)(1).

Support Considerations

The support of a qualifying child becomes relevant only if the child is self-supporting. In cases where the child has an independent source of funds, planning could help prevent an undesirable result. When a qualifying relative is involved, meeting the support test is essential.

Example 64

In 2022, Cheryl maintains a household that she shares with her son and mother. The son, Barry, is 23 years old and a full-time student in law school. The mother, Gladys, is 68 years old and active in charitable causes. Barry works part-time for a local law firm, and Gladys has income from investments. In resolving the support issue (or self-support in the case of Barry), Cheryl's contribution must be compared with that made by Barry and Gladys.[68]

What Barry and Gladys do with their funds becomes crucial. Funds that are used for nonsupport purposes (e.g., purchase of investments) or not used at all (e.g., deposited in a bank) are not considered. Limiting how much Barry and Gladys contribute to their own support enhances Cheryl's chances of claiming them as dependents. Records should be maintained showing the amount of support and its source.

Example 64 does not mention the possible application of the gross income test. Presuming that Barry is a qualifying child, the amount he earns does not matter, since the gross income test does not apply. Gladys, however, comes under the qualifying relative category, where the gross income test applies. In 2022, for her to be claimed as a dependent, her gross income must be less than $4,400.

Community Property Ramifications

In certain cases, state law can have an effect on dependent status.

Dependents: State Law Implications

Example 65

During the year, Mitch provides more than half of the support of his son, Ross, and daughter-in-law, Connie, who live with him. Ross, age 22, is a full-time student, and Connie earns $5,000 from a part-time job. Ross and Connie do not file a joint return. All parties live in New York, a common law state. Mitch can claim Ross as a dependent since he is a qualifying child. Connie is not a dependent because she does not meet the gross income test under the qualifying relative category.

Example 66

Assume the same facts as in Example 65, except that all parties live in Arizona, a community property state. Now Connie also qualifies as a dependent. Because Connie's gross income is only $2,500 (half of the community income), she satisfies the gross income test.

3-10c Taking Advantage of Tax Rate Differentials

It is natural for taxpayers to be concerned about the taxes they are paying. How does a tax professional communicate information about tax rates to clients? There are several possibilities.

The *marginal rate* (refer to Examples 49 and 50) provides information that can help a taxpayer evaluate a particular course of action or structure a transaction in the most advantageous manner. For example, a taxpayer who is in the 12 percent bracket this year and expects to be in the 24 percent bracket next year should, if possible, defer payment of deductible expenses until next year to maximize the tax benefit of the deduction.

However, Congress understands these tax planning possibilities and has enacted many provisions to limit them. Some income-shifting limitations are discussed in Chapters 4, 5, and 18. Limitations that affect a taxpayer's ability to shift deductions are discussed in Chapters 6 through 11 and in Chapter 18.

[68] As part of her support contribution to Barry and Gladys, Cheryl can count the fair market value of the meals and lodging she provides.

A taxpayer's *effective rate* can be an informative measure of the effectiveness of tax planning. The effective rate is computed by dividing the taxpayer's tax liability by the total amount of income. A low effective rate can be considered an indication of effective tax planning.

One way of lowering the effective rate is to exclude income from the tax base. For example, a taxpayer might consider investing in tax-free municipal bonds rather than taxable corporate bonds. Although pretax income from corporate bonds is usually higher, after-tax income may be higher if the taxpayer invests in tax-free municipals.[69]

Another way of lowering the effective rate is to make sure the taxpayer's expenses and losses are deductible. For example, losses on investments in passive activities may not be deductible (see Chapter 11). Therefore, a taxpayer who plans to invest in an activity that will produce a loss in the early years should take steps to ensure that the business is treated as active rather than passive. Active losses are deductible, but passive activity losses are not.

3-10d **Income of Certain Children**

Taxpayers can use several strategies to avoid or minimize the effect of the rules that tax the unearned income of certain children. Parents should consider giving a younger child assets that defer taxable income until the child reaches 19 (or 24 for full-time students). For example, U.S. government Series EE savings bonds can be used to defer income until the bonds are cashed in (see Chapter 4).

Growth stocks, which typically pay little in the way of dividends, are another option. If the child holds the stock and then sells it at a profit once the child reaches a safe age, the profit is taxed at the child's low rates.

Taxpayers who own a business can employ their children. The child's earned income is sheltered by the standard deduction, and the parents' business is allowed a deduction for the wages.

Refocus on The Big Picture

A Divided Household

ISTOCK.COM/ATNOYDUR

Of major concern to Aleha is her filing status. If she qualifies as an abandoned spouse, she is entitled to file as head of household. If not, she is considered to be a married person filing separately. Moreover, to be an abandoned spouse, Aleha must be able to claim Paige as a dependent. To be a dependent, Paige must meet the requirements of a qualifying child *or* a qualifying relative.

For qualifying child purposes, Paige must meet either the age (i.e., under age 19) or the full-time student (under age 24) test. (A disabled child exception seems highly unlikely.) Because Paige currently is not a full-time student, is she under age 19? If so, she is a qualifying child (see Example 15). If Paige is not a qualifying child, is she a qualifying relative? Here, the answer depends on meeting the gross income test (see Example 23). How much did Paige earn from her part-time job? If her earnings are under $4,300, she satisfies the gross income test. As a result, if Paige can be claimed as a dependent under either the qualifying child or the qualifying relative category, Aleha is an abandoned spouse entitled to head-of-household filing status (see Example 44). If not, she is a married person filing separately.

Terrah can be claimed as Aleha's dependent because she is a member of the household. It does not matter that she died in February. Because Terrah is her dependent,

continued

[69] Investment in tax-free bonds also will reduce the net investment income tax (§ 1411) if the individual is subject to this additional tax (see Chapter 13).

Aleha can claim the medical expenses she paid on Terrah's behalf. The funeral expenses, however, are not deductible (see Example 20).

Does Terrah qualify Aleha for head-of-household filing status? No—although she is a dependent, Terrah does not meet the relationship test (see Example 41).

The sale of the wedding rings results in a capital loss of $2,800 ($9,000 – $11,800). Because the loss is for personal use property, it cannot be claimed for tax purposes (see Example 58).

What If?

Assume that Trevor left for parts unknown in *August* (not March). Now Aleha cannot qualify as an abandoned spouse. Her spouse lived in the home during part of the last six months of the year. Since Aleha is married, she cannot qualify for head-of-household filing status. She must file as a married person filing separately. The change in when Trevor left will not affect the dependency issue regarding Paige, however.

Key Terms

Abandoned spouse, 3-32
Child tax credit, 3-26
Collectibles, 3-42
Dependency exemptions, 3-19
Dependent tax credit, 3-26
E-file, 3-40
Filing status, 3-29
Head-of-household, 3-31
Itemized deductions, 3-6
Kiddie tax, 3-37
Marriage penalty, 3-31
Multiple support agreement, 3-24
Personal exemptions, 3-19
Qualifying child, 3-20
Qualifying relative, 3-21
Standard deduction, 3-7
Surviving spouse, 3-31
Tax Rate Schedules, 3-35
Tax Table, 3-35
Unearned income, 3-37

Discussion Questions

Critical Thinking

1. **LO.1, 5, 8, 9** During the year, Addison is involved in the following transactions:
   a. Lost money gambling on a recent trip to a casino.
   b. Helped pay for her neighbor's dental bills. The neighbor is a good friend who is unemployed.
   c. Received from the IRS a tax refund due to Addison's overpayment of last year's Federal income taxes.
   d. Paid a traffic ticket received while double parking to attend a business meeting.
   e. Contributed to the mayor's reelection campaign. The mayor had promised Addison to have some of her land rezoned. The mayor was reelected and got Addison's land rezoned.
   f. Borrowed money from a bank to make a down payment on an automobile.
   g. Sold a houseboat and a camper on eBay. Both were personal use items, and the gain from one offset the loss from the other.
   h. Paid for dependent grandfather's funeral expenses.
   i. Paid premiums on her dependent son's life insurance policy.

   What are the possible income tax ramifications of these transactions?

2. **LO.1** Which of the following items are *inclusions* in gross income?
   a. During the year, stock that the taxpayer purchased as an investment doubled in value.
   b. Amount an off-duty motorcycle police officer received for escorting a funeral procession.
   c. While his mother was in the hospital, the taxpayer sold some of her jewelry to help pay for the hospital bills.
   d. Child support payments received.
   e. A damage deposit the taxpayer recovered when he vacated the apartment he had rented.
   f. Interest received by the taxpayer on an investment in general purpose bonds issued by IBM.
   g. Amounts received by the taxpayer, a baseball "Hall of Famer," for autographing sports equipment (e.g., balls and gloves).
   h. Tips received by a bartender from patrons. (Taxpayer is paid a regular salary by the cocktail lounge that employs him.)
   i. Taxpayer sells his Super Bowl tickets for three times what he paid for them.
   j. Taxpayer receives a new BMW from his grandmother when he passes the CPA exam.

3. **LO.1** Which of the following items are *exclusions* from gross income?
   a. Alimony payments received (relates to a divorce settlement in 2016).
   b. Damages award received by the taxpayer for personal physical injury—none were for punitive damages.
   c. A new golf cart won in a church raffle.
   d. Amount collected on a loan previously made to a college friend.
   e. Insurance proceeds paid to the taxpayer on the death of her uncle—she was the designated beneficiary under the policy.
   f. Interest income on City of Chicago bonds.
   g. Jury duty fees.
   h. Stolen funds the taxpayer had collected for a local food bank drive.
   i. Reward paid by the IRS for information provided that led to the conviction of the taxpayer's former employer for tax evasion.
   j. An envelope containing $8,000 found (and unclaimed) by the taxpayer in a bus station.

4. **LO.1, 8, 9** In late 2022, the Polks come to you for tax advice. They are considering selling some stock investments for a loss and making a contribution to a traditional IRA. In reviewing their situation, you note that they have large medical expenses and a casualty loss (in a Federally declared disaster area), neither of which is covered by insurance. What advice would you give the Polks? Critical Thinking Decision Making Planning

5. **LO.2** In choosing between taking the standard deduction and itemizing deductions *from* AGI, what effect, if any, does each of the following have? Critical Thinking
   a. The age of the taxpayer(s).
   b. The health (i.e., physical condition) of the taxpayer.
   c. Whether taxpayers rent or own their residence.
   d. Taxpayer's filing status (e.g., single, married, filing jointly).
   e. Whether married taxpayers decide to file separate returns.
   f. The taxpayer's uninsured personal residence that was recently destroyed by a wildfire (the region was declared a disaster area by the Federal government).
   g. The number of dependents the taxpayer can claim.

6. **LO.2, 3, 5** In 2022, David is age 78, is a widower, and is being claimed as a dependent by his son. How does this situation affect the following?
   a. David's own individual filing requirement.
   b. The standard deduction allowed to David.
   c. The availability of any additional standard deduction.

Critical Thinking

7. **LO.4** Magda maintains a household that includes a son (age 30) and a cousin (age 28). She can claim the cousin as a dependent but not her son. Explain.

8. **LO.4** Heather, age 12, lives in the same household with her mother, grandmother, and uncle.
   a. Who can claim Heather as a dependent?
   b. Who takes precedence?

9. **LO.4** Caden and Lily are divorced on March 3, 2021. For financial reasons, however, Lily continues to live in Caden's apartment and receives her support from him. Caden does not claim Lily as a dependent on his 2021 Federal income tax return but does so on his 2022 return. Explain.

10. **LO.4** Isabella, Emma, and Jacob share equally in the support of their parents. Jacob tells each of his sisters to claim one of their parents as a dependent. Explain what Jacob means.

Critical Thinking

11. **LO.4** Mark and Lisa were divorced in 2021. In 2022, Mark has custody of their children, but Lisa provides nearly all of their support. Who is entitled to claim the children as dependents?

Critical Thinking

12. **LO.4** Mario, who is single, is a U.S. citizen and resident. He provides almost all of the support of his parents and two aunts, who are citizens and residents of Guatemala. Mario's parents and aunts are seriously considering moving to and becoming residents of Mexico. Would such a move have any impact on Mario? Why or why not?

13. **LO.5** Casey is a U.S. citizen employed by a multinational corporation at its London office. Casey is married to Michael, a British citizen, and they reside in England. Michael receives substantial rent income from real estate he owns in western Europe.
    a. Must Casey file a U.S. income tax return?
    b. Under what circumstances might Michael be considered a resident of the United States? Would such a classification be advantageous? Disadvantageous? Explain.

14. **LO.4, 5** Comment on the availability of head-of-household filing status for 2022 in each of the following independent situations:
    a. Taxpayer lives alone but maintains the household of his parents. In July 2022, the parents use their savings to purchase a new BMW for $62,000.
    b. Taxpayer maintains a home in which she and her dependent father live. The father enters a nursing facility for treatment of a mental disorder.
    c. Taxpayer, a single parent, maintains a home in which she and her unmarried son live. The son, age 18, earns $5,000 from a part-time job.
    d. Assume the same facts as in part (c), except that the son is age 19 (not 18), is not a full-time student, and is not disabled.
    e. Taxpayer is married and maintains a household in which he and his dependent stepson live.
    f. Taxpayer lives alone but maintains the household where her dependent daughter lives.
    g. Taxpayer maintains a household that includes an unrelated friend who qualifies as his dependent.

15. **LO.5** In many cases, a surviving spouse ultimately becomes a head of household for filing status purposes. Explain this statement.

16. **LO.6** Jayden calculates his 2022 income tax by using both the Tax Tables and the Tax Rate Schedules. Because the Tax Rate Schedules yield a slightly lower tax liability, he plans to pay this amount.
   a. Why is there a difference?
   b. Is Jayden's approach permissible? Why or why not?

17. **LO.7** In connection with the application of the kiddie tax, comment on the following:
   a. The child has only earned income.
   b. The child has a modest amount of unearned income.
   c. The child is age 20, is not a student, and is not disabled.
   d. The child is married.
   e. Effect of the parental election.
   f. The result when the parental election is made and the married parents file separate returns.

18. **LO.8** During the year, Hernando has the following transactions:
   - Gain on the sale of stock held as an investment for 10 months.
   - Gain on the sale of land held as an investment for 4 years.
   - Gain on the sale of a houseboat owned for 2 years and used for family vacations.
   - Loss on the sale of a reconditioned motorcycle owned for 3 years and used for recreational purposes.

   How should Hernando treat these transactions for income tax purposes?

19. **LO.8** During the year, Brandi had the following transactions: a long-term capital gain from the sale of land, a short-term capital loss from the sale of stock, and a long-term capital gain from the sale of a gun collection.
   a. How are these transactions treated for income tax purposes?
   b. Does this treatment favor the taxpayer or the IRS? Explain.

Computational Exercises

20. **LO.2** Brett and Abby are dependents of their parents, and each has income of $2,100 for the year. Brett's standard deduction for the year is $1,150, and Abby's is $2,500. Because their income is the same, what causes the difference in the amount of the standard deduction? Critical Thinking

21. **LO.2** Compute the 2022 standard deduction for the following taxpayers.
   a. Ellie is 15 and claimed as a dependent by her parents. She has $800 in dividend income and $1,400 in wages from a part-time job.
   b. Ruby and Woody are married and file a joint tax return. Ruby is age 66, and Woody is 69. Their taxable retirement income is $10,000.
   c. Shonda is age 68 and single. She is claimed by her daughter as a dependent. Her earned income is $500, and her interest income is $125.
   d. Frazier, age 55, is married but is filing a separate return. His wife itemizes her deductions.

22. **LO.5, 9** Paul and Sonja, who are married, had itemized deductions of $13,200 and $400, respectively, during 2022. Paul suggests that they file separately—he will itemize his deductions *from* AGI, and she will claim the standard deduction. Critical Thinking
   a. Evaluate Paul's suggestion.
   b. What should they do?

23. **LO.6** Compute the 2022 tax liability and the marginal and average tax rates for the following taxpayers (use the 2022 Tax Rate Schedules in Appendix A for this purpose):
   a. Chandler, who files as a single taxpayer, has taxable income of $94,800.
   b. Lazare, who files as a head of household, has taxable income of $57,050.

24. **LO.7** In 2022, Jack, age 12, has interest income of $4,900 on funds he inherited from his aunt and no earned income. He has no investment expenses. Christian and Danielle (his parents) have taxable income of $82,250 and file a joint return. Assume that no parental election is made. Determine Jack's net unearned income, allocable parental tax, and total tax liability.

25. **LO.8** Madeline sells her personal scooter for $550. She purchased the scooter for $700 three years ago. She also sells a painting for $1,200 that she acquired five years ago for $900. What are the tax implications of these sales?

26. **LO.8** During the year, Tamara had capital transactions resulting in gains (losses) as follows:

Sold stock in ABC Company (acquired two years ago)	($1,500)
Sold collectible coins (held for more than one year)	2,000
Sold stock in XYZ Company (acquired six months ago)	(4,100)
Sold stock in LMN Company (acquired three years ago)	500

Determine Tamara's net capital gain or loss as a result of these transactions.

Problems

27. **LO.1** Compute the taxable income for 2022 in each of the following independent situations:
   a. Aaron and Michele, ages 40 and 41, respectively, are married and file a joint return. In addition to four dependent children, they have AGI of $125,000 and itemized deductions of $27,000.
   b. Sybil, age 40, is single and supports her dependent parents who live with her, as well as her grandfather who is in a nursing home. She has AGI of $80,000 and itemized deductions of $8,000.
   c. Scott, age 49, is a surviving spouse. His household includes two unmarried stepsons who qualify as his dependents. He has AGI of $75,000 and itemized deductions of $10,100.
   d. Amelia, age 33, is an abandoned spouse who maintains a household for her three dependent children. She has AGI of $58,000 and itemized deductions of $10,650.
   e. Chang, age 42, is divorced but maintains the home in which he and Lei, his daughter, live. Lei is single and qualifies as Chang's dependent. Chang has AGI of $64,000 and itemized deductions of $9,900.

Note: Problems 28 and 29 can be solved by referring to Concept Summary 3.1, Exhibits 3.1 through 3.5, *and the discussion under* Deductions *for* Adjusted Gross Income *in this chapter.*

28. **LO.1, 8** Compute the taxable income for 2022 for Emily on the basis of the following information. Her filing status is single.

Salary	$85,000
Interest income from bonds issued by Xerox	1,100
Alimony payments received (divorce occurred in 2014)	6,000
Contribution to traditional IRA	6,000
Gift from parents	25,000
Short-term capital gain from stock investment	2,500
Amount lost in football office pool	500
Age	40

29. **LO.1** Compute the taxable income for 2022 for Aiden on the basis of the following information. Aiden is married but has not seen or heard from his wife since 2020.

Salary	$ 80,000
Interest on bonds issued by City of Boston	3,000
Interest on CD issued by Wells Fargo Bank	2,000
Cash dividend received on Chevron common stock	2,200
Life insurance proceeds paid at death of aunt (Aiden was the designated beneficiary of the policy)	200,000
Inheritance received at death of aunt	100,000
Jackson (a cousin) repaid a loan Aiden made to him in 2016 (no interest was provided for)	5,000
Itemized deductions (state income tax, property taxes on residence, interest on home mortgage, and charitable contributions)	9,700
Number of dependents (children, ages 17 and 18, and mother-in-law, age 70)	3
Age	43

30. **LO.2** Determine the amount of the standard deduction allowed for 2022 in the following independent situations. In each case, assume that the taxpayer is claimed as another person's dependent.
    a. Curtis, age 18, has income as follows: $700 interest from a certificate of deposit and $12,800 from repairing cars.
    b. Mattie, age 18, has income as follows: $600 cash dividends from investing in stock and $4,700 from working as a lifeguard at a local pool.
    c. Jason, age 16, has income as follows: $675 interest on a bank savings account and $800 for painting a neighbor's fence.
    d. Ayla, age 15, has income as follows: $400 cash dividends from a stock investment and $500 from grooming pets.
    e. Sarah, age 67 and a widow, has income as follows: $500 from a bank savings account and $3,200 from babysitting.

31. **LO.4** Analyze each of the characteristics in considering the indicated test for dependency as a qualifying child or qualifying relative. In the last two columns, after each listed test (e.g., Gross income), state whether the particular test is Met, Not Met, or Not Applicable (NA).

	Characteristic	Qualifying Child Test	Qualifying Relative Test
a.	Taxpayer's son has gross income of $7,000.	Gross income	Gross income
b.	Taxpayer's niece has gross income of $3,000.	Gross income	Gross income
c.	Taxpayer's uncle lives with him.	Relationship	Relationship
d.	Taxpayer's daughter is 25 and disabled.	Age	Age
e.	Taxpayer's daughter is age 18, has gross income of $8,000, and does not live with him.	Residence Gross income	Gross income
f.	Taxpayer's cousin does not live with her.	Relationship Residence	Relationship
g.	Taxpayer's brother does not live with her.	Residence	Relationship
h.	Taxpayer's sister has dropped out of school, is age 17, and lives with him.	Relationship Residence Age	Relationship
i.	Taxpayer's older nephew is age 23 and a full-time student.	Relationship Age	Relationship
j.	Taxpayer's grandson lives with her and has gross income of $7,000.	Relationship Residence	Relationship Gross income

32. **LO.3, 4** For tax year 2022, determine the number of dependents in each of the following independent situations:
    a. Ben and Molly (ages 48 and 46, respectively) are married and furnish more than 50% of the support of their two children, Libby (age 18) and Sam (age 24). During the year, Libby earns $4,500 providing transportation for older persons with disabilities, and Sam receives a $5,000 scholarship for tuition at the law school he attends.
    b. Audry (age 45) was divorced this year. She maintains a household in which she, her ex-husband (Clint), and his mother (Olive) live and furnishes more than 50% of their support. Olive is age 91 and blind.
    c. Crystal, age 45, furnishes more than 50% of the support of her married son, Andy (age 18), and his wife, Paige (age 19), who live with her. During the year, Andy earned $9,000 from a part-time job. All parties live in Iowa (a common law state).
    d. Assume the same facts as in part (c), except that all parties live in Washington (a community property state).

33. **LO.3, 4** Determine the number of dependents in each of the following independent situations:
    a. Reginald, a U.S. citizen and resident, contributes 100% of the support of his parents who are citizens of Canada and live there.
    b. Pablo, a U.S. citizen and resident, contributes 100% of the support of his parents, who are citizens of Panama. Pablo's father is a resident of Panama, and his mother is a legal resident of the United States.
    c. Gretchen, a U.S. citizen and resident, contributes 100% of the support of her parents, who are U.S. citizens but residents of Germany.
    d. Elena is a U.S. citizen and a resident of Italy. Her household includes Carlos, a four-year-old adopted son who is a citizen of Spain.

34. **LO.3, 4** Determine the number of dependents in each of the following independent situations, and identify whether the dependent is a qualifying child or a qualifying relative.
    a. Andy maintains a household that includes a cousin (age 12), a niece (age 18), and a son (age 26). All are full-time students. Andy furnishes all of their support, and all are "members of the household."
    b. Mandeep provides all of the support of a family friend's son (age 20) who lives with her. She also furnishes most of the support of her stepmother, who does not live with her.
    c. Raul, a U.S. citizen, lives in Costa Rica. Raul's household includes a friend, Mariana, who is age 19 and a citizen of Costa Rica. Raul provides all of Mariana's support.
    d. Karen maintains a household that includes her ex-spouse, her mother-in-law, and her brother-in-law (age 23 and not a full-time student). Karen provides more than half of all of their support. Karen is single and was divorced last year.

35. **LO.4** During 2022, Jenny, age 14, lives in a household with her father, uncle, and grandmother. The household is maintained by the uncle. The parties, all of whom file separate returns, have AGI as follows: father ($30,000), uncle ($50,000), and grandmother ($40,000).
    a. Who is eligible to claim Jenny as a dependent?
    b. Who has precedence to claim Jenny as a dependent?

36. **LO.4, 9** Wesley and Camilla (ages 90 and 88, respectively) live in an assisted care facility and for 2021 and 2022 received their support from the following sources:

	Percentage of Support
Social Security benefits	16%
Son	20
Niece	29
Cousin	12
Brother	11
Family friend (not related)	12

a. Which persons are eligible to claim Wesley and Camilla as dependents under a multiple support agreement?
b. Must Wesley and Camilla be claimed as dependents by the same person(s) for both 2021 and 2022? Explain.
c. Who, if anyone, can claim their medical expenses?

37. **LO.3, 7** Taylor, age 18, is claimed as a dependent by her parents. For 2022, she has the following income: $6,250 wages from a summer job, $800 interest from a money market account, and $300 interest from City of Chicago bonds.
a. What is Taylor's taxable income for 2022?
b. What is Taylor's tax for 2022? [Her parents file a joint return and have taxable income of $135,000 (no dividends or capital gains).]

38. **LO.4, 9** Walter and Nancy provide 60% of the support of their daughter (age 18) and son-in-law (age 22). The son-in-law (John) is a full-time student at a local university, and the daughter (Stella) holds various part-time jobs from which she earns $11,000. Walter and Nancy engage you to prepare their tax return for 2022. During a meeting with them in late March 2023, you learn that John and Stella have filed a joint return. What tax advice would you give based on the following assumptions?

Critical Thinking
Decision Making

a. All parties live in Louisiana (a community property state).
b. All parties live in New Jersey (a common law state).

39. **LO.1, 2, 3, 4, 5, 6** Charlotte (age 40) is a surviving spouse and provides all of the support of her four minor children (ages 4, 8, 11, and 14) who live with her. She also maintains the household in which her parents live and furnished 60% of their support. Besides interest on City of Miami bonds in the amount of $5,500, Charlotte's father received $2,400 from a part-time job. Charlotte has a salary of $80,000, a short-term capital loss of $2,000, a cash prize of $4,000 from a church raffle, and itemized deductions of $10,500. Using the Tax Rate Schedules, compute Charlotte's 2022 tax liability and any available child and dependent tax credits.

40. **LO.1, 2, 3, 4, 5, 6** Morgan (age 45) is single and provides more than 50% of the support of Tammy (a family friend), Jen (a niece, age 18), and Jerold (a nephew, age 18). Both Tammy and Jen live with Morgan, but Jerold (a French citizen) lives in Canada. Morgan earns a salary of $96,000, contributes $6,000 to a traditional IRA, and receives sales proceeds of $15,000 for an RV that cost $60,000 and was used for vacations. She has $8,200 in itemized deductions. Using the Tax Rate Schedules, compute Morgan's 2022 tax liability and any available child and dependent tax credits.

41. **LO.5** Which of the following individuals are required to file a tax return for 2022? Should any of these individuals file a return even if filing is not required? Why or why not?
    a. Patricia, age 19, is a self-employed single individual with gross income of $5,200 from an unincorporated business. Business expenses amounted to $4,900.
    b. Mike is single and is 67 years old. His gross income from wages was $12,750.
    c. Ronald is a dependent child under age 19 who received $6,800 in wages from a part-time job.
    d. Sam is married and files a joint return with his spouse, Lana. Both Sam and Lana are 67 years old. Their combined gross income was $24,250.
    e. Quinn, age 20, is a full-time college student who is claimed as a dependent by his parents. For 2022, Quinn has taxable interest and dividends of $2,500.

Critical Thinking
Decision Making

42. **LO.5, 6, 9** Sarah and Brandi are engaged and plan to get married. During 2022, Sarah is a full-time student and earns $9,000 from a part-time job. With this income, student loans, savings, and nontaxable scholarships, she is self-supporting. For the year, Brandi is employed and has wages of $61,000. How much income tax, if any, can Brandi save if she and Sarah marry in 2022 and file a joint return?

43. **LO.5** In each of the following independent situations, determine Winston's filing status for 2022. Winston is not married.
    a. Winston lives alone, but he maintains a household in which his parents live. The mother qualifies as Winston's dependent, but the father does not.
    b. Winston lives alone but maintains a household in which his married daughter, Karin, lives. Both Karin and her husband (Winston's son-in-law) qualify as Winston's dependents.
    c. Winston maintains a household in which he and a family friend, Ward, live. Ward qualifies as Winston's dependent.
    d. Winston maintains a household in which he and his mother-in-law live. Winston's wife died in 2021.
    e. Same as part (d), except that Winston's wife disappeared (i.e., she did not die) in 2020.

44. **LO.4, 5** Christopher died in 2020 and is survived by his wife, Chloe, and their 18-year-old son, Dylan. Chloe is the executor of Christopher's estate and maintains the household in which she and Dylan live. All of their support is furnished by Chloe, and Dylan saves his earnings. Dylan's earnings and student status for 2020 to 2022 are as follows:

Year	Earnings	Student Status
2020	$5,000	Yes
2021	7,000	No
2022	6,000	Yes

What is Chloe's filing status for:
a. 2020?
b. 2021?
c. 2022?

45. **LO.3, 4, 5** Nadia died in 2021 and is survived by her husband, Jerold (age 44); her married son, Travis (age 22); and her daughter-in-law, Macy (age 18). Jerold is the executor of his wife's estate. He maintains the household where he, Travis, and Macy live and furnishes all of their support. During 2021 and 2022, Travis is a full-time student, and Macy earns $7,000 each year from a part-time job. Travis and Macy do not file jointly during either year. What is Jerold's filing status for 2021 and 2022 if all parties reside in:
    a. Idaho (a community property state)?
    b. Kansas (a common law state)?

46. **LO.1, 3, 7** Paige, age 17, is a dependent of her parents. Her parents report taxable income of $120,000 on their joint return (no qualified dividends or capital gains). During 2022, Paige earned $3,900 pet sitting and $4,300 in interest on a savings account. What are Paige's taxable income and tax liability for 2022?

47. **LO.1, 3, 7** Terri, age 16, is a dependent of her parents. During 2022, Terri earned $5,000 in interest income and $3,000 from part-time jobs.
    a. What is Terri's taxable income?
    b. How much of Terri's income is taxed at her rate? At her parent's rate?
    c. Can the parental election be made? Why or why not?

48. **LO.8** During 2022, Inez (a single taxpayer) had the following transactions involving capital assets:

Gain on the sale of unimproved land (held as an investment for 3 years)	$ 6,000
Loss on the sale of a camper (purchased 2 years ago and used for family vacations)	(5,000)
Gain on the sale of ADM stock (purchased 9 months ago as an investment)	2,450
Gain on the sale of a fishing boat and trailer (acquired 18 months ago at an auction and used for recreational purposes)	1,000

    How much income tax results from these capital asset transactions if:
    a. Inez has taxable income of $188,450?
    b. Inez has taxable income of $32,250?

49. **LO.8** During 2022, Chester (a married taxpayer filing a joint return) had the following transactions involving capital assets:

Gain on the sale of an arrowhead collection (acquired as an investment at different times but all pieces have been held for more than 1 year)	$ 6,000
Loss on the sale of IBM Corporation stock (purchased 11 months ago as an investment)	(3,500)
Gain on the sale of a city lot (acquired 5 years ago as an investment)	2,000

    How much income tax results from these capital asset transactions if:
    a. Chester has taxable income of $378,400?
    b. Chester has taxable income of $74,125?

50. **LO.9** Each year, Tom and Cindy Bates normally have itemized deductions of $22,000 (which includes a $4,000 pledge payment to their church). On the advice of a friend, they do the following: in early January 2022, they pay their pledge for 2021; during 2022, they pay their pledge for 2022; and in late December 2022, they prepay their pledge for 2023.
    a. Explain what the Bateses are trying to accomplish.
    b. What will be the tax savings if their marginal tax bracket is 24% for all three years? (Assume that the standard deduction amounts for 2022 and 2023 are the same.)
    c. Write a letter to Tom and Cindy Bates (8212 Bridle Court, Reston, VA 20194) summarizing your analysis.

Communications
Critical Thinking
Decision Making
Planning

Tax Return Problems

Tax Forms Problem

ProConnect™ Tax

51. Lance H. and Wanda B. Dean are married and live at 431 Yucca Drive, Santa Fe, NM 87501. Lance works for the convention bureau of the local Chamber of Commerce, and Wanda is employed part-time as a paralegal for a law firm.

During 2021, the Deans had the following receipts:

Salaries ($60,000 for Lance, $42,000 for Wanda)		$102,000
Interest income—		
City of Albuquerque general purpose bonds	$1,000	
Ford Motor company bonds	1,100	
Ally Bank certificate of deposit	400	2,500
Child support payments from John Allen		7,200
Annual gifts from parents		26,000
Settlement from Roadrunner Touring Company		90,000
Lottery winnings		600
Federal income tax refund (for tax year 2020)		400

Wanda was previously married to John Allen. When they divorced several years ago, Wanda was awarded custody of their two children, Penny and Kyle. (Note: Wanda has never issued a Form 8332 waiver.) Under the divorce decree, John was obligated to pay alimony and child support—the alimony payments were to terminate if Wanda remarried.

In July, while going to lunch in downtown Santa Fe, Wanda was injured by a tour bus. Because the driver was clearly at fault, the owner of the bus, Roadrunner Touring Company, paid her medical expenses (including a one-week stay in a hospital). To avoid a lawsuit, Roadrunner also transferred $90,000 to her in settlement of the personal injuries she sustained.

The Deans had the following expenditures for 2021:

Medical expenses (not covered by insurance)		$7,200
Taxes—		
Property taxes on personal residence	$3,600	
State of New Mexico income tax (includes amount withheld from wages during 2021)	4,200	7,800
Interest on home mortgage (First National Bank)		6,000
Charitable contributions (cash)		3,600
Life insurance premiums (policy on Lance's life)		1,200
Contribution to traditional IRA (on Wanda's behalf)		6,000
Traffic fines		300
Contribution to the reelection campaign fund of the mayor of Santa Fe		500
Funeral expenses for Wayne Boyle		6,300

The life insurance policy was taken out by Lance several years ago and designates Wanda as the beneficiary. As a part-time employee, Wanda is excluded from coverage under her employer's pension plan. Consequently, she provides for her own retirement with a traditional IRA obtained at a local trust company. Because the mayor is a member of the local Chamber of Commerce, Lance felt compelled to make the political contribution.

The Deans' household includes the following, for whom they provide more than half of the support:

	Social Security Number	Birth Date
Lance Dean (age 42)	123-45-6786	12/16/1979
Wanda Dean (age 40)	123-45-6787	08/08/1981
Penny Allen (age 19)	123-45-6788	10/09/2002
Kyle Allen (age 16)	123-45-6780	05/03/2005
Wayne Boyle (age 75)	123-45-6785	06/15/1946

Penny graduated from high school on May 9, 2021, and is undecided about college. During 2021, she earned $8,500 (placed in a savings account) playing a harp in the lobby of a local hotel. Wayne is Wanda's widower father who died on December 20, 2021. For the past few years, Wayne qualified as a dependent of the Deans.

Federal income tax withheld is $3,900 (Lance) and $1,800 (Wanda). The proper amount of Social Security and Medicare tax was withheld. The Deans received the appropriate coronavirus recovery rebates (economic impact payments); related questions in ProConnect Tax should be ignored.

Determine the Federal income tax for 2021 for the Deans on a joint return by completing the appropriate forms. They do not own and did not use any virtual currency during the year, and they do not want to contribute to the Presidential Election Campaign Fund. If an overpayment results, it is to be refunded to them. Suggested software: ProConnect Tax.

Communications
Decision Making
Planning
Tax Forms Problem

ProConnect™ Tax

52. Logan B. Taylor is a widower whose wife, Sara, died on June 6, 2019. He lives at 4680 Dogwood Lane, Springfield, MO 65801. He is employed as a paralegal by a local law firm. During 2021, he had the following receipts:

Salary		$ 80,000
Interest income—		
Money market account at Omni Bank	$ 300	
Savings account at Boone State Bank	1,100	
City of Springfield general purpose bonds	3,000	4,400
Inheritance from Daniel		60,000
Life insurance proceeds		200,000
Amount from sale of St. Louis lot		80,000
Proceeds from estate sale		9,000
Federal income tax refund (for 2020 tax overpayment)		700

Logan inherited securities worth $60,000 from his uncle, Daniel, who died in 2021. Logan also was the designated beneficiary of an insurance policy on Daniel's life with a maturity value of $200,000. The lot in St. Louis was purchased on May 2, 2016, for $85,000 and held as an investment. Because the neighborhood has deteriorated, Logan decided to cut his losses and sold the lot on January 5, 2021, for $80,000. The estate sale consisted largely of items belonging to Sara and Daniel (e.g., camper, boat, furniture, and fishing and hunting equipment). Logan estimates that the property sold originally cost at least twice the $9,000 he received and has declined or stayed the same in value since Sara and Daniel died.

Logan's expenditures for 2021 include the following:

Medical expenses (including $10,500 for dental)		$13,500
Taxes—		
State of Missouri income tax (includes withholdings during 2021)	$4,200	
Property taxes on personal residence	4,500	8,700
Interest on home mortgage (Boone State Bank)		5,600
Contribution to church (paid pledges for 2021 and 2022)		4,800

While Logan and his dependents are covered by his employer's health insurance policy, he is subject to a deductible, and dental care is not included. The $10,500 dental charge was for Helen's implants. Helen is Logan's widowed mother, who lives with him (see below). Logan normally pledges $2,400 ($200 per month) each year to his church. On December 5, 2021, on the advice of his pastor, he prepaid his pledge for 2022.

Logan's household, all of whom he supports, includes the following:

	Social Security Number	Birth Date
Logan Taylor (age 48)	123-45-6787	08/30/1973
Helen Taylor (age 70)	123-45-6780	01/13/1951
Asher Taylor (age 23)	123-45-6783	02/18/1998
Mia Taylor (age 22)	123-45-6784	07/16/1999

Helen receives a modest Social Security benefit. Asher, a son, is a full-time student in dental school and earns $4,500 as a part-time dental assistant. Mia, a daughter, does not work and is engaged to be married.

Part 1—Tax Computation
Using the appropriate forms and schedules, compute Logan's income tax for 2021. Federal income tax of $4,200 was withheld from his wages. If Logan has any overpayment on his income tax, he wants the refund sent to him. Assume that the proper amounts of Social Security and Medicare taxes were withheld. Logan received the appropriate coronavirus recovery rebates (economic impact payments); related questions in ProConnect Tax should be ignored. Logan does not own and did not use any virtual currency during the year, and he does not want to contribute to the Presidential Election Campaign Fund. Suggested software: ProConnect Tax.

Part 2—Follow-Up Advice
In early 2022, the following take place:

- Helen decides that she wants to live with one of her daughters and moves to Arizona.
- Asher graduates from dental school and joins an existing practice in St. Louis.
- Mia marries, and she and her spouse move in with his parents.
- Using the insurance proceeds he received on Daniel's death, Logan pays off the mortgage on his personal residence.

Logan believes that these events may have an effect on his tax position for 2022. Therefore, he requests your advice.

Write a letter to Logan explaining in general terms the changes that will occur for tax purposes. Assume that Logan's salary and other factors not mentioned (e.g., property and state income taxes) will remain the same.

Research Problems

the answer company™ THOMSON REUTERS®

Note: Solutions to the Research Problems can be prepared by using the Thomson Reuters Checkpoint™ online tax research database, which accompanies this textbook. Solutions can also be prepared by using research materials found in a typical tax library.

Communications

Research Problem 1. Kathy and Brett Ouray married in 2004. They began to experience marital difficulties in 2018 and, in the current year, although they are not legally separated, consider themselves completely estranged. They have contemplated getting a divorce. However, because of financial concerns and because they both want to remain involved in the lives of their three sons, they have not yet filed for divorce. In addition, their financial difficulties have meant that Kathy and Brett cannot afford to live in separate residences. So although they consider themselves emotionally estranged, they and their three sons all reside in a single-family home in Chicago, Illinois.

Although Brett earns significantly more than Kathy, both contribute financially to maintaining their home and supporting their teenage sons. In one of their few and brief conversations this year, they determined that Brett had contributed far more than Kathy to the maintenance of their home and the support of their sons. Thus, Brett has decided that for the current tax year, they will file separate Federal income tax returns and that he will claim head-of-household filing status. Although they live under the same roof, Brett believes that he and Kathy should maintain separate households. Given this fact and the fact that he provides significantly more for the support of their sons, he believes that he is eligible for head-of-household filing status. Advise Brett on which filing status is most appropriate for him in the current year. His address is 16 Lahinch, Chicago, IL 60608.

Research Problem 2. John and Janet Baker are married and maintain a household in which the following persons live: Calvin and Florence Carter and Darin, Andrea, and Morgan Baker. Decision Making

- Calvin and Florence are Janet's parents, who are retired. During the year, they receive $19,000 in nontaxable funds (e.g., disability income, interest on municipal bonds, and Social Security benefits). Of this amount, $8,000 is spent equally between them for clothing, transportation, and recreation (e.g., vacation) and the balance of $11,000 is invested in tax-exempt securities. Janet paid $1,000 for her mother's dental work and the $1,200 premium on an insurance policy her father owned on his own life. Calvin also had medical expenses, but he insisted on paying for them with his own funds.
- Darin is the Bakers' 18-year-old son, who is not a student but operates a pool-cleaning service on a part-time basis. During the year, he earns $14,000 from the business, which he places in a savings account for later college expenses.
- Andrea is the Bakers' 19-year-old daughter, who does not work or go to school. Tired of the inconvenience of borrowing and sharing the family car, during the year, she purchased a Camaro for $21,000. Andrea used funds from a savings account she had established several years ago with an inheritance from her paternal grandfather.
- Morgan is the Bakers' 23-year-old daughter. To attend graduate school at a local university, she applied for and obtained a student loan of $20,000. She uses the full amount to pay her college tuition.

The Bakers' fair rental value of their residence, including utilities, is $14,000, and their total food expense for the household is $10,500.

a. How many dependents are the Bakers entitled to claim for the year? Explain your answer.

b. From a planning standpoint, how might the Bakers have improved the tax result?

Partial list of research aids:
Reg. §§ 1.152–1(a) and –1(c).
IRS Publication 17 (*Your Federal Income Tax*), Chapter 3.

Use internet tax resources to address the following questions. Look for reliable websites and blogs of the IRS and other government agencies, media outlets, businesses, tax professionals, academics, think tanks, and political outlets.

Research Problem 3. How do U.S. individuals generate their income? Does it vary by size of income (AGI)? Go to the IRS tax statistics website (**irs.gov/statistics**), and download a recent tax year's information on "sources of income." Compare the following types of income by size of AGI: (1) wages, (2) capital gain distributions, Communications Data Analytics

(3) sales of capital assets, and (4) sales of property other than capital assets. Cluster the data into no more than six AGI categories. Present your findings in a visual (e.g., bar chart), and summarize your findings in a one-page memo to your instructor.

Research Problem 4. Locate IRS Form 2120 (at **irs.gov**), and answer the following questions.

a. Who must sign the form?

b. Who must file the form?

c. Can it be used for someone who is not related to the taxpayer? Explain.

Research Problem 5. What purpose is served by Form 8857? Read the directions for the form, and see IRS Publication 971 for additional information.

Research Problem 6. A nonresident alien earns money in the United States that is subject to Federal income tax. What guidance does the IRS provide about what tax form needs to be used and when it should be filed? In terms of the proper filing date, does it matter whether the earnings were subject to income tax withholding? Explain.

Research Problem 7. Research the following questions regarding virtual currency, and write your answers in the form of a set of "frequently asked questions" (FAQs) suitable for the website of your CPA firm. As part of your research, consider the IRS's FAQs on virtual currency transactions (**irs.gov/individuals/international-taxpayers/frequently-asked-questions-on-virtual-currency-transactions**) and Rev.Rul. 2019–24.

a. Since taxpayers want to easily track virtual currency and use it to acquire goods and services, how do taxpayers typically "hold" their virtual currency?

b. Janice acquired bitcoin in 2018 and 2020. This year, she used a portion of her bitcoin holdings to acquire 100 litecoin. What are the tax implications of this transaction? What do you recommend Janice do to help track her acquisition and use of virtual currency (in order to have records readily available about these investments and their tax consequences)?

c. Rajiv acquired $20 worth of bitcoin in 2017 using an automatic teller machine that converted cash to bitcoin. He has never used any of this currency. How should Rajiv answer the virtual currency question on Form 1040 this year? Why? Consider the possibility that there was a "hard fork" or an "airdrop" associated with Rajiv's bitcoin (also explain these terms in your FAQs).

Becker CPA Review Questions

1. Bob provides more than half of his mother's support. His mother earns $6,000 per year as a hairdresser. She lives in an apartment across town. Bob is unmarried and has no children. What is Bob's most advantageous filing status?

   a. Single
   b. Head of household
   c. Qualifying single
   d. Supporting single

2. Jane is 20 years old and is a sophomore at Lake University. She is a full-time student and does not have any gross income. Jane spends the holidays and summers at home with her parents. Her total support for the current tax year is $30,000, including a scholarship for $5,000 to cover her tuition. Jane used $12,000 of her savings, and her grandparents provided $13,000. Which of the following statements regarding the dependency rules for Jane is true?

   a. If Jane's parents (rather than her grandparents) provided the $13,000, then they would not be able to claim Jane as a dependent because Jane provided more than half of her own support.

b. Jane's grandparents can claim her as a dependent because Jane did not provide more than half of her own support.

c. Jane's grandparents cannot claim her as a dependent because Jane provided more than half of her own support.

d. Jane does not qualify as a dependent for either her parents or grandparents.

3. In the current tax year, Blake Smith provided more than half of the support for his cousin, his niece, and a close family friend. Blake lives alone and sends a monthly support check to each person. None of the individuals whom Blake supports has any income or files a tax return. All three individuals are U.S. citizens. Which of the three people Blake supports can he claim as a dependent on his tax return?

a. Cousin
b. Niece
c. Family friend
d. None

4. Jeff and Rhonda are married and have two children, Max and Jen. Max is 20, attends college in the Los Angeles area full-time, and works as a stunt double for a television show while he is in school. Max earns $15,000 per year as a stunt double and lives at home when school is not in session. Jeff and Rhonda pay for Max's tuition and all of his living expenses. Jen, who lives at home, is 18 years old and makes $18,000 per year working full-time as an office administrator. Jeff and Rhonda pay for 65% of Jen's living expenses. In addition, Rhonda's mother, Joanne (a widow), resides with the family, earns $3,000 per year in taxable interest and dividends from her investments, and receives $9,000 per year in nontaxable Social Security benefits. Jeff and Rhonda receive no rent from Joanne and provide all the support she needs for the year. Everyone mentioned is a U.S. citizen. How many people qualify as dependents for Jeff and Rhonda's income tax return?

a. Two
b. Three
c. Four
d. Five

5. Katherine and Bill Grant have two children. Kelly is 22 years old and is a full-time student. She lives on campus at an out-of-state university but will return home for the summer. Kelly earns $5,000 a year working part-time. Her parents provide her with $15,000 of support, and her grandparents provide her with $15,000 of support. Jake is 15 years old and lives at home. He is fully supported by his parents. Jake's friend Luke also lives with the Grants. Luke is 15 years old and moved into the Grant home in April. The Grants pay all of Luke's support. How many total dependents may Katherine and Bill Grant claim for the current year?

a. One
b. Three
c. Two
d. Zero

6. Bill and Anne Chambers are married and file a joint return. They have no children. Their college friend, Ryan, lived with them for the entire current tax year. Ryan is 40 years old and earned $2,000 at a part-time job and received $25,000 in municipal bond interest. Ryan is a citizen of the United States and is unmarried. Which of the following statements is true regarding claiming Ryan as a dependent on the Chambers' tax return?

a. If Ryan earns $15,000 in self-employment income in addition to the part-time job and municipal bond interest, he will qualify as a dependent on the Chambers' tax return.

b. Ryan qualifies as a dependent for the Chambers under the qualifying child rules.

c. As long as Ryan does not provide more than half of his own support, he qualifies as a dependent for the Chambers under the qualifying relative rules because he lived with them for the entire year.

d. As long as the Chambers provide more than half of Ryan's support, he qualifies as a dependent for the Chambers under the qualifying relative rules.

7. Susie, John, Luke, and Will provide support for their 80-year-old mother, Joyce. Joyce lives by herself in an apartment in Miami, Florida. Joyce earned $5,000 this year working at her church. Joyce provides 5% of her own support. Susie provides 30% of Joyce's support, John provides 10% of Joyce's support, Luke provides 15% of Joyce's support, and Will provides 40% of Joyce's support. Under a multiple support agreement, who may claim Joyce as a dependent?
   a. Susie, Luke, John, and Will
   b. Susie, Luke, and Will
   c. Susie and Will
   d. Will

8. Heather is single and has one son, Rhett, who is 19 years old. Rhett lived at home for four months of the current tax year before moving away to take a full-time job in another city. Heather provided more than half of Rhett's support for the taxable year. Rhett earned $20,000 in gross income and is unmarried. Which of the following statements regarding the dependency rules for Rhett is true?
   a. Heather may claim Rhett as a dependent because he is a qualifying child.
   b. Heather may claim Rhett as a dependent because he is a qualifying relative.
   c. Rhett fails the age limit test for a qualifying child.
   d. Rhett must live with Heather for the entire year to meet the qualifying relative test.

9. Jonathan Jones is a 19-year-old full-time college student at the local community college. He lives in an apartment near campus during the school year and returns home for the summer break and holidays. Jonathan earned $5,000 this year working at the campus bookstore. His parents gave him $20,000 and his grandparents gave him $10,000 this year in support. Which of the following statements is true?
   a. Jonathan does not qualify as a dependent for his parents because his gross income is too high.
   b. Jonathan does not meet the residency test for a qualifying child.
   c. Jonathan's grandparents can claim him as a dependent.
   d. Jonathan's parents can claim him as a dependent.

10. In 2022, Madison and Nick Koz have two children, ages 8 and 10. Both children meet the definition of qualifying child. The Koz family has adjusted gross income of $300,000. What is the amount of the child tax credit on the couple's income tax return?
    a. $1,000
    b. $2,000
    c. $3,000
    d. $4,000

11. The Tiller family has an adjusted gross income of $200,000 in 2022. The Tillers have two children, ages 12 and 13, who qualify as dependents. All of the Tillers' income is from wages. What is the Tillers' child tax credit, and what portion of their child tax credit is refundable?

	Child Tax Credit	Refundable Portion
a.	$4,000	$0
b.	$4,000	$2,800
c.	$2,000	$1,400
d.	$2,000	$0

Part 2

Gross Income

Chapter 4
Gross Income: Concepts and Inclusions

Chapter 5
Gross Income: Exclusions

Part 2 presents information related to the income component of the basic tax model. The determination of what is income and the statutory exclusions that are permitted in calculating gross income are discussed. Because the taxpayer's accounting method and accounting period affect when income is reported, a basic discussion of these topics is also provided.

Chapter

4 Gross Income: Concepts and Inclusions

Learning Objectives: *After completing Chapter 4, you should be able to:*

LO.1 **Explain the differences between the economic, accounting, and tax concepts of gross income.**

LO.2 **Identify and describe the taxable years and tax accounting methods generally available to taxpayers and other tax reporting entities.**

LO.3 **Identify the general sources of income and to whom they are taxed.**

LO.4 **Recognize and apply the special tax rules related to alimony, loans made at below-market interest rates, annuities, prizes and awards, unemployment compensation, Social Security benefits, and foreign bank accounts.**

LO.5 **Identify tax planning strategies for minimizing gross income and the present value of the related tax.**

Chapter Outline

4-1 Gross Income, 4-3
- 4-1a Definition, 4-3
- 4-1b Recovery of Capital Doctrine, 4-3
- 4-1c Economic and Accounting Concepts of Income, 4-4
- 4-1d Financial Accounting Income versus Taxable Income, 4-5
- 4-1e Form of Receipt, 4-6

4-2 Timing of Income Recognition, 4-6
- 4-2a Taxable Year, 4-6
- 4-2b Accounting Methods, 4-7
- 4-2c Special Rules Applicable to Cash Basis Taxpayers, 4-9
- 4-2d Special Rules Applicable to Accrual Basis Taxpayers, 4-13

4-3 General Sources of Income and to Whom They Are Taxed, 4-14
- 4-3a Personal Services, 4-14
- 4-3b Income from Property, 4-15
- 4-3c Income from Partnerships, S Corporations, Trusts, and Estates, 4-17
- 4-3d Income in Community Property States, 4-18

4-4 Special Rules Related to Certain Items Included in Gross Income, 4-20
- 4-4a Alimony and Separate Maintenance Payments, 4-20
- 4-4b Imputed Interest on Below-Market Loans, 4-23
- 4-4c Income from Annuities, 4-26
- 4-4d Prizes and Awards, 4-29
- 4-4e Unemployment Compensation, 4-29
- 4-4f Social Security Benefits, 4-30
- 4-4g Income Earned from Foreign Bank and Financial Accounts and FBAR Rules, 4-31

4-5 Tax Planning, 4-32
- 4-5a Minimize Income Included in Gross Income, 4-32
- 4-5b Tax Deferral, 4-32
- 4-5c Shifting Income to Other Taxpayers, 4-34

Bob Daemmrich/Alamy Stock Photo

The Big Picture

Calculation of Gross Income

In 2022, Dr. Cliff Payne, age 27, opened his dental practice as a sole proprietorship with a December 31 year-end. By the beginning of February, construction on his medical building was completed. He also leased a separate office building and entered into a contract to make improvements to it. In addition, early in the year, he invested $12,000 in the stock of an unrelated corporation.

The following financial information shows the results of Dr. Payne's first year of operation:

Revenues (amounts billed patients for dental services throughout the year)	$385,000
Accounts receivable: January 1	–0–
Accounts receivable: December 31	52,000

During the year, Sam Jones, a contractor who owed Dr. Payne $4,000 for dental services, satisfied his account by installing solar panels on the roof of Dr. Payne's new medical building.

As an undergraduate student, Dr. Payne took an accounting course in which he learned that the accrual method of accounting provides a good measure of the income and expenses of a business. Based on this knowledge and the above financial information, Dr. Payne concludes that the gross income for Federal income tax purposes is the $385,000 he billed his patients for the dental services rendered.

Has Dr. Payne correctly calculated the gross income of his dental practice in its first year of operations? Is there an alternative method of accounting that would result in less taxable income in this first year?

Read the chapter and formulate your response.

Framework 1040 **Tax Formula for Individuals**

This chapter covers the boldfaced portions of the Tax Formula for Individuals that was introduced in Concept Summary 3.1 on p. 3-3. Below those portions are the sections of Form 1040 where the results are reported.

Income *(broadly defined)*	$xx,xxx
Less: Exclusions	(x,xxx)
Gross income	$xx,xxx

FORM 1040 (p. 1)

1	Wages, salaries, tips, etc. Attach Form(s) W-2			1
2a	Tax-exempt interest	2a	b Taxable interest	2b
3a	Qualified dividends	3a	b Ordinary dividends	3b
4a	IRA distributions	4a	b Taxable amount	4b
5a	Pensions and annuities	5a	b Taxable amount	5b
6a	Social security benefits	6a	b Taxable amount	6b

FORM 1040 (Schedule 1)

2a	Alimony received
b	Date of original divorce or separation agreement (see instructions) ▶
3	Business income or (loss). Attach Schedule C
8	Other income:

Less: Deductions *for* adjusted gross income	(x,xxx)
Adjusted gross income	$xx,xxx
Less: The greater of total itemized deductions *or* the standard deduction	(x,xxx)
Charitable contributions if you take the standard deduction*	(xxx)
Personal and dependency exemptions**	(x,xxx)
Deduction for qualified business income***	(x,xxx)
Taxable income	$xx,xxx
Tax on taxable income *(see Tax Tables or Tax Rate Schedules)*	$ x,xxx
Less: Tax credits *(including income taxes withheld and prepaid)*	(xxx)
Tax due (or refund)	$ xxx

* For 2021, married taxpayers may claim up to $600 of cash charitable donations ($300 if unmarried).
** Exemption deductions are not allowed from 2018 through 2025.
*** Only applies from 2018 through 2025.

This chapter addresses the first step in the computation of taxable income—the determination of gross income. Questions that are addressed include the following:

- What is gross income?
- When is gross income recognized?
- To whom is gross income taxable?

As you will see, the Code starts with a comprehensive definition of gross income that includes all income regardless of its source or type. However, as discussed in Chapter 5, the Code goes on to identify a variety of income items that are specifically excluded from gross income (called exclusions). When gross income is recognized, or taxable, is determined by the tax accounting periods and methods used by a taxpayer. Finally, income is generally recognized by, or taxable to, the taxpayer who has the legal right to the income, although exceptions and special rules may sometimes apply. These issues are addressed in more depth below.

4-1 Gross Income

LO.1

Explain the differences between the economic, accounting, and tax concepts of gross income.

4-1a Definition

Code § 61(a) of the Internal Revenue Code defines the term **gross income** as follows:

> Except as otherwise provided in this subtitle, gross income means all income from whatever source derived.

This definition, taken from the Sixteenth Amendment to the Constitution, provides perhaps the broadest definition of gross income possible. It clearly requires that all income be included in a taxpayer's gross income unless it is explicitly excluded elsewhere in the Code. However, neither the Sixteenth Amendment nor the Code provides a definition of income itself. Rather, Congress left it to the judicial and administrative branches to specifically determine the meaning of *income*. Some of the most important issues related to the meaning of income are discussed below.

4-1b Recovery of Capital Doctrine

Although gross income is clearly defined to include all income, the Supreme Court has held that gross income is not synonymous with gross receipts. Rather, a taxpayer does not have income until recovering any amount of capital that might have been invested in an item that is sold.[1] This concept, known as the **recovery of capital doctrine**, prevents income from being taxed more than once. The rationale is that "capital" is the accumulation of previously taxed income.

In its simplest application, this doctrine means that sellers can reduce their gross receipts (selling price) by the adjusted basis of the property sold in determining their gross income.[2]

The Big Picture

Example 1

Return to the facts of *The Big Picture* on p. 4-1. Assume that Dr. Payne receives $15,000 when he sells the common stock he had purchased for $12,000. Although he has $15,000 of gross receipts, $12,000 represent a recovery of capital, leaving him with $3,000 of gross income.

Global Tax Issues — From "All Sources" Is a Broad Definition

When § 61 refers to "income from whatever source derived," the law is reaching far beyond the borders of the United States. Although one interpretation of "source" in this context is type of income (e.g., wages and interest), a broader interpretation revolves around the place where the income is generated. In this context, citizens and residents of the United States are subject to taxation on income earned from sources both inside and outside the country. This "worldwide income" tax base can cause potential double taxation problems, with other countries also taxing income earned within their borders. However, mechanisms such as the foreign tax credit can alleviate these tax burdens.

Over the years, a number of individuals have relocated to other countries and renounced their U.S. citizenship to avoid high U.S. tax rates. Others who have already relocated may renounce their U.S. citizenship to avoid complicated filing and reporting requirements. After hitting a then-record high of 5,411 in 2017, the number of expatriations declined to 2,071 in 2019. However, 6,707 individuals gave up their U.S. citizenship in 2020, a new record. This was in spite of the additional practical challenges in completing the expatriation process caused by the COVID-19 pandemic. Once per quarter, the Department of State publishes the names of U.S. citizens who have renounced their citizenship. Some of these individuals may owe Federal taxes as a result of renouncing. See § 877A.

See "Renouncing American Citizenship Hits All-Time Record" at **forbes.com/sites/robertwood/2021/02/07/renouncing-american-citizenship-hits-all-time-record.**

[1] *Doyle v. Mitchell Bros. Co.*, 1 USTC ¶17, 3 AFTR 2979, 38 S.Ct. 467 (USSC, 1916).

[2] Reg. § 1.61–3. For a definition of *adjusted basis*, see the Glossary in Appendix C.

4-1c Economic and Accounting Concepts of Income

Even after clarifying that **income** did not include recoveries of capital, the courts were nonetheless required to interpret "the commonly understood meaning of the term [income] which must have been in the minds of the people when they adopted the Sixteenth Amendment to the Constitution."[3] Early in the development of the income tax law, a choice had to be made between two competing models: economic income and accounting income.

Economists measure income (**economic income**) as the sum of (1) the value of goods and services consumed during a period and (2) the change in the value of net assets (assets minus liabilities) from the beginning to the end of the period. Importantly, the change in the value of net assets is not dependent on the sale or exchange of those assets: economic income is derived by a mere change in the value of assets held. Similarly, economic income includes in consumption the imputed value of personally provided items such as the rental value of an owner-occupied home and the value of food grown for personal consumption.[4]

Example 2

Sharon has economic income as follows:

Consumption			
Food, clothing, and other personal expenditures	$ 25,000		
Imputed rental value of the home Sharon owns and occupies	12,000		
Total consumption			$37,000
Fair market value of Sharon's assets on December 31, 2022	$220,000		
Less liabilities on December 31, 2022	(40,000)		
Net worth on December 31, 2022		$180,000	
Fair market value of Sharon's assets on January 1, 2022	$200,000		
Less liabilities on January 1, 2022	(80,000)		
Net worth on January 1, 2022		(120,000)	
Increase in net worth			60,000
Economic income for 2022			$97,000

The need to value assets annually would make compliance with the tax law burdensome and would cause numerous controversies between the taxpayer and the IRS over valuation. In addition, including changes in the value of assets in income for tax purposes could result in liquidity problems. The taxpayer's assets may increase in value even though they are not readily convertible into the cash needed to pay the tax (e.g., commercial real estate). For these reasons, the courts have rejected the economic concept of income as impractical.[5]

In contrast, the accounting concept of income is founded on the realization principle: **accounting income** is not recognized until it is realized.[6] Realization requires (1) an exchange of goods or services to take place between the accounting entity and some independent, external party and (2) the accounting entity to receive in the exchange something that is capable of being objectively valued. For example, income is not recognized merely due to the appreciation of assets held by the taxpayer or when an individual or a business creates an asset for its own use. Income is realized, however, whenever a taxpayer enters into any transaction that results in an accession to wealth.[7]

---

[3] *Merchants Loan and Trust Co. v. Smietanka*, 1 USTC ¶42, 3 AFTR 3102, 41 S.Ct. 386 (USSC, 1921).

[4] See Henry C. Simons, *Personal Income Taxation* (Chicago: University of Chicago Press, 1933), Chapters 2–3.

[5] *Eisner v. Macomber*, 1 USTC ¶32, 3 AFTR 3020, 40 S.Ct. 189 (USSC, 1920).

[6] See the American Accounting Association Committee Report on the "Realization Concept," *The Accounting Review* (April 1965): 312–322.

[7] *Glenshaw Glass Co.*, 348 U.S. 426, 429–430, 75 S.Ct. 473, 99 L.Ed. 483 (1955); Reg. § 1.61–14.

4-1d Financial Accounting Income versus Taxable Income

As discussed above, the measurement of taxable income is much closer to accounting income than it is to economic income. However, due to the different purposes they serve, several differences exist between accounting and taxable income. The purpose of financial reporting is to provide information to investors and creditors relevant to predicting a business's future cash flows. To better predict future cash flows, financial accounting income will sometimes stray from the realization principle, valuing assets at their net realizable value with any appreciation recognized as income. For example, an increase in the value of marketable securities is recognized as income for financial accounting purposes. Conversely, taxable income is primarily intended to capture taxpayers' relative abilities to pay tax. As a result, the determination of taxable income seldom strays from the realization principle. For example, the same appreciation of marketable securities that leads to the recognition of income for financial reporting purposes will not result in taxable income. Similarly, to better predict future cash flows and to better match expenses with the revenues they generate, financial accounting is amenable to the use of estimates. For example, estimates of receivables that will not be collected and future costs that will be incurred to honor warranties on products sold during the current period reduce financial accounting income, but have no impact on taxable income.

The Supreme Court, in a decision involving inventory and bad debt adjustments, provided an explanation for some of the variations between accounting and taxable income:

> The primary goal of financial accounting is to provide useful information to management, shareholders, creditors, and others properly interested; the major responsibility of the accountant is to protect these parties from being misled. The primary goal of the income tax system, in contrast, is the equitable collection of revenue.... Consistently with its goals and responsibilities, financial accounting has as its foundation the principle of conservatism, with its corollary that 'possible errors in measurement [should] be in the direction of understatement rather than overstatement of net income and net assets.' In view of the Treasury's markedly different goals and responsibilities, understatement of income is not destined to be its guiding light.
>
> ... Financial accounting, in short, is hospitable to estimates, probabilities, and reasonable certainties; the tax law, with its mandate to preserve the revenue, can give no quarter to uncertainty.[8]

Finally, because the tax law is used by the government to achieve several social and economic goals, taxable income is impacted by several things that do not impact accounting income and vice versa. For example, although income earned by foreign subsidiaries, the appreciation of property donated to charity, and the payment of fines and penalties all impact financial accounting income, none are included in the determination of taxable income. Conversely, although taxable income may be reduced for a portion of income earned on sales to customers in foreign countries, there is no corresponding reduction of financial accounting income. For these reasons, the taxable income reported by corporations in their financial statements may differ significantly from their taxable income (see text Section 20-2g). Many of these differences between accounting and taxable income will be discussed in greater detail throughout this text.

---

[8] *Thor Power Tool Co. v. Comm.*, 79–1 USTC ¶9139, 43 AFTR 2d 79–362, 99 S.Ct. 773 (USSC).

4-1e Form of Receipt

As discussed above, income is not taxable until it is realized. Realization, however, does not require the receipt of cash. "Gross income includes income realized in any form, whether in money, property, or services. Income may be realized [and recognized], therefore, on the receipt of services, meals, accommodations, stock or other property, as well as in cash."[9]

Form of Receipt

Example 3

Ostrich Corporation allows Bill, an employee, to use a company car for his vacation. Bill realizes income equal to the rental value of the car.

Example 4

Khalil owes $10,000 on a mortgage. The creditor accepts $8,000 in full satisfaction of the debt. Khalil realizes income of $2,000 from retiring the debt, the amount of the debt that is forgiven.[10]

Example 5

Sam, a practicing attorney, owns a personal residence in need of repairs. Sam decided to list his services on a barter exchange. He offered to provide an hour of legal services in exchange for home repairs.

A qualified carpenter performed the repairs in eight hours. The carpenter normally charges $50 an hour. Sam formed a corporation for the carpenter in exchange for the carpenter's services. Sam realized $400 (8 hours × $50) in gross income for his services.

LO.2

Identify and describe the taxable years and tax accounting methods generally available to taxpayers and other tax reporting entities.

4-2 Timing of Income Recognition

4-2a Taxable Year

As in financial reporting, taxable income must be measured and reported on a periodic basis. The annual accounting period, or **taxable year**, is a basic component of our tax system. As a general rule, a taxpayer may use as a taxable year either a calendar year or a fiscal year (a period of 12 months ending on the last day of any month other than December) as long as adequate books and records based on that year are maintained.[11] Although it is not required, most individuals use a calendar year as their taxable year. As discussed in Chapter 18, the fiscal year option generally is not available to partnerships, S corporations, and personal service corporations.[12]

It is important that income be recognized in the proper year for several reasons. For example, a taxpayer's tax rate may vary across years. This may occur for one or more of the following reasons:

- Given the progressive rates applicable to individual taxpayers, a taxpayer's marginal tax rate can change from year to year.
- Congress may change the tax rates.
- The rates that apply to a specific taxpayer may change because of a change in the taxpayer's status (e.g., a person may marry or a business may be incorporated).

Even when the rates do not change between tax years, deferring the recognition of income and, therefore, the payment of tax to a future tax year reduces the present value of the tax. Finally, several provisions in the Code are dependent on the taxpayer's gross

[9] Reg. § 1.61–1(a).

[10] Reg. § 1.61–12. See *U.S. v. Kirby Lumber Co.*, 2 USTC ¶814, 10 AFTR 458, 52 S.Ct. 4 (USSC, 1931). Exceptions to this general rule are discussed in Chapter 5.

[11] § 441.

[12] §§ 441(i), 706, and 1378.

income for the year (e.g., a deduction or credit might not be available if the taxpayer's income exceeds a specified amount). Therefore, the proper determination of several items of income and deduction will depend on other items being recognized in the proper year.

4-2b Accounting Methods

The year an item of gross income is recognized depends on which acceptable **accounting method** the taxpayer regularly employs.[13] The two primary methods of accounting allowed are (1) the cash receipts and disbursements method and (2) the accrual method. Most individuals and many small businesses may use either of these allowable methods, although most choose to use the cash method. In general, large corporations are required to use the accrual method. Generally, the tax law also requires larger taxpayers to use the accrual method for determining sales and the cost of goods sold when inventory is an income-producing factor.[14] However, taxpayers may also use a hybrid method that is a combination of the cash and accrual methods of accounting (e.g., the accrual method for sales and cost of goods sold and the cash method for all other items of income and expenses).

In addition to these overall accounting methods, taxpayers may be allowed or required to use special accounting methods in specific situations. For example, a taxpayer may choose to spread the gain from a sale of eligible property over the collection period by using the *installment method* of income recognition. Taxpayers who are parties to certain long-term contracts may either spread the profits from the contract over the periods in which the work is done (the *percentage of completion method*) or defer all profit until the year in which the project is completed (the *completed contract method*).[15]

The availability of any accounting method is dependent on its ability to clearly reflect the taxpayer's income. Section 446(b) grants the IRS broad powers to determine whether a taxpayer's accounting method *clearly reflects income*:

> If no method of accounting has been regularly used by the taxpayer, or *if the method used does not clearly reflect income, the computation of taxable income shall be made under such method as, in the opinion of the Secretary . . . does clearly reflect income.*

Unless a taxpayer is required to use a particular accounting method, an accounting method generally is selected by a taxpayer simply by using it the first time income is calculated and reported. A change in accounting method, however, generally requires the advance consent of the IRS.[16]

Cash Receipts Method

Under the **cash receipts method**, income is recognized in the year it is actually or constructively received by the taxpayer or the taxpayer's agent, regardless of whether the income was earned in that year.[17] Further, in spite of the method's name, the taxpayer need not receive cash to be required to recognize income under the cash receipts method. Rather, the receipt of anything that can be valued in terms of money, or that has a cash equivalent, is includible in income under the cash receipts method.[18] As a result, a cash basis taxpayer who receives a note in payment for services has income equal to the value of the note in the year the note is received. However, a creditor's mere promise to pay (e.g., an account receivable), with no supporting note, usually is not considered to have a fair market value and therefore is not a cash equivalent.[19] As a result, a cash basis taxpayer who receives an account receivable in return for goods or services defers income recognition until the receivable is collected.

[13] See Accounting Methods in Chapter 18.

[14] Reg. § 1.446–1(c)(2)(i) and § 471(c). Other circumstances in which the accrual method must be used are presented in Chapter 18.

[15] §§ 453 and 460. See Chapter 18 for limitations on the use of the installment method and the completed contract method. See Appendix C for definitions of *installment method* and *completed contract method.*

[16] § 446(e).

[17] *Julia A. Strauss*, 2 B.T.A. 598 (1925). See the Glossary in Appendix C for a discussion of the terms *cash equivalent doctrine* and *constructive receipt.*

[18] Reg. §§ 1.446–1(a)(3) and (c)(1)(i).

[19] *Bedell v. Comm.*, 1 USTC ¶359, 7 AFTR 8469, 30 F.2d 622 (CA–2, 1929).

Example 6

Dana, an accountant, reports her income using the cash method. In 2022, she performed an audit for Orange Corporation and billed the client for $5,000, which was collected in 2023. In 2022, Dana also performed an audit for Blue Corporation. Because of Blue's precarious financial position, Dana required Blue to issue an $8,000 secured negotiable note in payment of the fee. The note had a fair market value of $6,000. Dana collected $8,000 on the note in 2023. Dana's gross income for the two years is as follows:

	2022	2023
Fair market value of note received from Blue	$6,000	
Cash received		
From Orange on account receivable		$ 5,000
From Blue on note receivable		8,000
Less: Recovery of capital (Blue's note receivable)		(6,000)
Total gross income	$6,000	$ 7,000

Generally, a check is considered a cash equivalent and must be recognized as income when received by a cash basis taxpayer. An exception to this rule applies if the person paying with the check requests that the check not be cashed until a subsequent date. In this case, the income is deferred until that later date.[20]

The tax law restricts the availability of the cash receipts method for several reasons. For example, the cash receipts method could distort taxable income as income and expenses from the same activity may be recognized in different tax years. Moreover, a taxpayer using the cash receipts method has some degree of control over when income is recognized (e.g., by delaying the sending of invoices to customers). One important restriction requires most corporations with average annual gross receipts greater than $27 million over the preceding three-year period to use the accrual method. Other businesses with average annual gross receipts in excess of $27 million, whether or not they are corporations, are required to account for their inventory under the accrual method.[21]

Accrual Method

Under the **accrual method**, income is generally included in gross income in the year in which it is earned, regardless of when it is collected. Income is earned when (1) all events have occurred that fix the right to receive such income and (2) the amount to be received can be determined with reasonable accuracy.

Generally, a taxpayer's right to income accrues when title to property being sold passes to the buyer or services are performed for the customer or client.[22] If the rights to the income have accrued but are subject to a potential refund claim (e.g., under a product warranty), the income is reported in the year of sale and a deduction is allowed in subsequent years when actual claims accrue.[23]

Where a taxpayer's right to income is contested (e.g., when a customer claims that a contractor has failed to meet the specifications of a construction contract), the year in which the income is subject to tax depends on whether payment has been received. If payment has not been received, no income is recognized until the claim is settled. Only then is the right to the income established.[24] However, if the payment is received before the dispute is settled, the **claim of right doctrine** requires the taxpayer to recognize the income in the year of receipt.[25]

[20] *Charles F. Kahler*, 18 T.C. 31 (1952); *Bright v. U.S.*, 91–1 USTC ¶50,142, 67 AFTR 2d 91–673, 926 F.2d 383 (CA–5).

[21] §§ 448, 471(c), and 263A(i). Code § 448, which requires certain taxpayers to use the accrual method, does not apply to individuals, partnerships without a C corporation partner, S corporations, estates, and trusts. In general, these types of taxpayers may use the cash receipts method regardless of their gross receipts level (unless the entity is a tax shelter per § 448(d)(3)). Additional analysis as to accounting methods is required if these taxpayers have inventory as well as gross receipts above the $27 million threshold. The $27 million threshold is adjusted annually for inflation. See further discussion in Chapter 18.

[22] *Lucas v. North Texas Lumber Co.*, 2 USTC ¶484, 8 AFTR 10276, 50 S.Ct. 184 (USSC, 1930). See also Rev.Rul. 84–31, 1984–1 C.B. 127.

[23] *Brown v. Helvering*, 4 USTC ¶1222, 13 AFTR 851, 54 S.Ct. 356 (USSC, 1933).

[24] *Burnet v. Sanford and Brooks*, 2 USTC ¶636, 9 AFTR 603, 51 S.Ct. 150 (USSC, 1931).

[25] *North American Oil Consolidated Co. v. Burnet*, 3 USTC ¶943, 11 AFTR 16, 52 S.Ct. 613 (USSC, 1932).

The Big Picture

Example 7

Return to the facts of *The Big Picture* on p. 4-1. Assume that on completing the construction improvements to Dr. Payne's medical office building in 2022, the contractor, who uses the accrual method, submitted a bill. Dr. Payne refused to pay the bill, however, claiming that the contractor had not met specifications. The contractor did not reach a settlement with Dr. Payne until 2023. No income is taxable to the contractor until 2023. If Dr. Payne had paid for the work and then filed suit for damages, the contractor could not defer the income (the income would be taxable in 2022).

Under the accrual method, the amount of income that must be included in gross income is the amount the taxpayer has earned and, therefore, has the right to receive. Unlike the cash basis, the value of a customer's obligation is irrelevant in measuring accrual basis income. The ability to defer income that is earned but not yet received is a distinct advantage of the cash method over the accrual method. However, as discussed above, most larger corporations are required to use the accrual method.[26]

Example 8

Assume the same facts as in Example 6, except that Dana is an accrual basis taxpayer. Dana must recognize $13,000 ($8,000 + $5,000) of gross income in 2022, the year her rights to the income accrued.

Hybrid Method

The **hybrid method** is a combination of the accrual method and the cash method. Generally, a taxpayer using the hybrid method is in the business of buying and selling inventory but not otherwise required to use the accrual method. As a result, a taxpayer using the hybrid method would account for the sale of goods and cost of goods sold using the accrual method and use the cash method for other income and expense items (e.g., services and interest income). Because most small businesses can use the cash method for sales and cost of goods sold, the hybrid method is not commonly used.

4-2c Special Rules Applicable to Cash Basis Taxpayers

Constructive Receipt

In general, a cash basis taxpayer does not recognize income until it is received. Income that has not actually been received by the taxpayer is nonetheless taxed as though it had been received—the income is considered constructively received—if the amount is made readily available to the taxpayer and not subject to substantial limitations or restrictions.[27] The purpose of the **constructive receipt** doctrine is to prevent a cash basis taxpayer from deferring the recognition of income that, although not yet received, has been made practically available to the taxpayer. For instance, a taxpayer is not permitted to defer income earned in December simply by refusing to accept payment until January. Conversely, if an employee receives a paycheck on December 31 that is dated for January 8, the constructive receipt doctrine would allow the employee to defer recognizing the income until January. Whether income is *readily available* and whether *substantial limitations or restrictions exist* is determined by all the facts and circumstances surrounding a situation.[28] Following are some examples of the application of the constructive receipt doctrine.

[26] §§ 448(c) and 471(c) and Reg. § 1.446–1(c)(2).

[27] Reg. § 1.451–2(a).

[28] *Baxter v. Comm.*, 87–1 USTC ¶9315, 59 AFTR 2d 87–1068, 816 F.2d 493 (CA–9).

Constructive Receipt

Example 9

Ted is a member of a barter club. In 2022, Ted performed services for other club members and earned 1,000 points. Each point entitles him to $1 in goods and services provided by other members of the club; the points can be used at any time. In 2023, Ted exchanged his points for a new high-definition TV. Ted must recognize $1,000 gross income in 2022 when the 1,000 points were credited to his account.[29]

Example 10

Brianna has a savings account with Eagle Savings and Loan Association. Under the terms of the account, interest accrues monthly and the depositor can withdraw the funds (including accrued interest) at any time. The interest accrued during the year is constructively received by Brianna even though she does not withdraw the funds.[30]

The Big Picture

Example 11

Return to the facts of *The Big Picture* on p. 4-1. On December 31, Dr. Payne has $10,000 in patients' checks that have not been deposited. They include a check for $3,000 from a patient who asked Dr. Payne not to deposit the check until after January 4 of next year because her account did not contain sufficient funds to pay the debt.

Under the cash method, Dr. Payne must recognize $7,000 of income from the $7,000 in checks on hand in the current year because the checks are a cash equivalent that is actually received. The income from the $3,000 check is neither actually nor constructively received in the current year because an insufficient account means that the funds are not available.[31]

The constructive receipt doctrine does not apply to income the taxpayer is not yet entitled to receive even though the taxpayer could have contracted to receive the income at an earlier date.[32]

The Big Picture

Example 12

Return to the facts of *The Big Picture*. Assume that Dr. Payne adopted the cash basis of accounting. On December 15, Dr. Payne sees a new patient in need of extensive dental work at a cost of $2,000. The patient indicates she may be willing to pay for the services before they are performed if they are scheduled before the end of the year. However, before the services are performed, the parties agree to a payment plan that requires payment to be made within 30 days after services are performed. The services are performed on December 28, and the patient pays on January 15.

Dr. Payne is not in constructive receipt of the $2,000 at the end of the year. Although Dr. Payne could have collected the fee prior to year-end, he was not yet entitled to the fee when he contracted to receive payment at a later date.[33]

Even income set apart or made available to the taxpayer is not constructively received if the ultimate right to it is subject to *substantial restrictions*. For example, employees sometimes receive from their employers property subject to substantial restrictions, such as stock or stock options. Generally, no income is recognized until the restrictions lapse.[34]

---

[29] Rev.Rul. 80–52.

[30] Reg. § 1.451–2(a).

[31] *L. M. Fischer*, 14 T.C. 792 (1950).

[32] *Baxter v. Comm.*, 816 F.2d 493, 59 AFTR 2d 87–1068, 87–1 USTC ¶9315 (CA–9, 1997).

[33] *Cowden v. Comm.*, 61–1 USTC ¶9382, 7 AFTR 2d 1160, 289 F.2d 20 (CA–5).

[34] § 83(a). See also Restricted Property Plans in Chapter 19.

Example 13

Carlos is a key employee of Red, Inc. The corporation gives stock with a value of $10,000 to Carlos. The stock cannot be sold, however, for five years. Carlos is not required to recognize income until the restrictions lapse at the end of five years.

The life insurance industry has used substantial restrictions as a cornerstone for designing life insurance contracts with favorable tax features. Ordinary life insurance policies provide (1) current protection—an amount payable in the event of death—and (2) a savings feature—a cash surrender value payable to the policyholder if the policy is terminated during the policyholder's life. The annual increase in cash surrender value is not taxable because the policyholder must cancel the policy to actually receive the increase in value. Because the cancellation requirement is a substantial restriction, the policyholder does not constructively receive the annual increase in cash surrender value.[35]

Income Received by an Agent

Income received by the taxpayer's agent is considered to be received by the taxpayer. Therefore, a cash basis principal must recognize the income at the time it is received by the agent.[36]

Example 14

Jack, a cash basis taxpayer, delivered cattle to the auction barn in late December. The auctioneer, acting as Jack's agent, sold the cattle and collected the proceeds in December. The auctioneer did not pay Jack until the following January. Jack must include the sales proceeds in his gross income for the year the auctioneer received the funds.

Original Issue Discount

Lenders frequently make loans that require a payment at maturity of more than the amount of the original loan. The difference between the original amount of the loan and the amount due at maturity, or the **original issue discount**, is actually interest. In such an arrangement, the original issue discount must be reported as it is earned, regardless of the taxpayer's accounting method.[37] The interest "earned" is calculated using the effective interest rate method.

Example 15

On January 1, 2022, Mark, a cash basis taxpayer, pays $90,703 to a bank for a 24-month certificate of deposit (i.e., Mark loaned $90,703 to the bank). The certificate is priced to yield 5% (the effective interest rate) with interest compounded annually. No interest is paid until maturity, when Mark receives $100,000.

As a result, Mark's gross income from the certificate is $9,297 ($100,000 − $90,703). Mark's income earned each year is calculated as follows:

2022 (5% × $90,703)	$4,535
2023 [5% × ($90,703 + $4,535)]	4,762
	$9,297

The original issue discount rules do not apply to U.S. savings bonds (discussed in the following paragraphs) or to obligations with a maturity date of one year or less from the date of issue.[38] See Chapter 16 for additional discussion of the tax treatment of original issue discount.

Series E and Series EE Bonds

Certain U.S. government savings bonds (Series E before 1980 and Series EE after 1979) are issued at a discount. No interest payments are actually made. Instead, the difference between the purchase price and the amount received on redemption is the bondholder's interest income from the investment.

[35] *Theodore H. Cohen*, 39 T.C. 1055 (1963).

[36] Rev.Rul. 79–379.

[37] §§ 1272(a)(3) and 1273(a).

[38] § 1272(a)(2).

As mentioned above, although these bonds are issued at a discount, they are not subject to the rules generally applicable to original issue discount. Instead, the income from these savings bonds is generally deferred until the bonds are redeemed or mature. As a result, U.S. savings bonds have attractive income deferral features not available with corporate bonds and certificates of deposit issued by financial institutions.

Of course, the deferral feature of government bonds issued at a discount is not an advantage if the investor has insufficient income to be subject to tax as the income accrues. In fact, the deferral may work to the investor's disadvantage if the investor will face a higher tax rate at the time of redemption than they do as the income accrues or if the bunching of the bond interest into one tax year moves the investor to a higher tax bracket than they would otherwise be in. To avoid this possibility, a cash basis taxpayer may elect to include in gross income the interest on Series E and EE bonds annually as it accrues.[39] This election can be especially valuable for a child whose current income is below the available standard deduction but anticipates higher income when the bond is redeemed.

Example 16

Kate purchases Series EE U.S. savings bonds for $500 (face value of $1,000) on January 2 of the current year. If the bonds are redeemed during the first six months, no interest is paid. At December 31, the redemption value is $519.60.

If Kate makes no election, she will report no interest income for the current year. However, she may elect to report the interest income annually, requiring her to report income of $19.60 in the current year.

When the bond matures, Kate may receive a Form 1099 indicating that she should include as income all of the interest that accrued over the life of the bond. If she elects to report the income as it accrues, she should keep good records to prove that she did so.

When a taxpayer elects to report the income from the bonds on an annual basis, the election applies to all such bonds the taxpayer owns at the time of the election and to all such securities acquired subsequent to the election. A change in the method of reporting the income from the bonds requires permission from the IRS.

Ethics & Equity **Should the Tax Treatment of Government Bonds and Corporate Bonds Be Different?**

Taxpayers are permitted to defer the original issue discount earned on U.S. Government Series EE bonds until the bonds mature, but the original issue discount on a corporate bond must be taken into gross income each year the bond is held. Is this difference in the tax treatment of income earned on government and corporate bonds defensible in terms of equity? Why or why not?

Amounts Received under an Obligation to Repay

The receipt of funds with an obligation to repay those funds in the future is the essence of borrowing. Because the taxpayer's assets and liabilities increase by the same amount, no income is realized when the borrowed funds are received. This same concept extends to the receipt by a taxpayer of any funds that carry an obligation for repayment.

Example 17

A landlord receives a damage deposit from a tenant. The landlord does not recognize income unless and until the deposit is forfeited because the landlord has an obligation to repay the deposit if no damage occurs.[40] However, if the deposit is in fact a prepayment of rent, it is taxed in the year of receipt.

[39] § 454(a).

[40] *John Mantell*, 17 T.C. 1143 (1952) and *Indianapolis Power & Light Co.*, 90–1 USTC ¶50,007, 65 AFTR2d 90–394, 110 S.Ct. 589 (USSC).

4-2d Special Rules Applicable to Accrual Basis Taxpayers

The All Events Test and Financial Reporting

Under the accrual method of accounting, income generally is not included in gross income until all the events have occurred that fix the taxpayer's right to that income. Conversely, for financial reporting purposes, income is recognized as an entity performs those obligations that are necessary to earn the income, even if all the obligations necessary to fix the entity's right to the income have not been met.

Example 18

E&I Company contracts with a customer to install new equipment so that it is integrated efficiently into the customer's production process. The contract calls for E&I to bill the customer after the installation and integration are complete. As of the end of E&I's year, it has completed the installation but not the integration.

E&I must provide certified GAAP financial statements to its bank for credit purposes. For financial reporting purposes, E&I has met one of its obligations under its contract with the customer and, therefore, recognizes the income from the installation of the equipment but not the system integration.

Under the financial statement inclusion rule, if an accrual method taxpayer issues certified GAAP financial statements, the all-events test is generally considered satisfied no later than when the income is included in those financial statements.[41] However, an exception to this rule prevents a taxpayer from having to recognize additional gross income based on their financial statements if the taxpayer does not have an enforceable right to the income by the end of the year. Whether such a right exists is determined by the terms of the contract between the taxpayer and their customer or client.[42]

Example 19

Return to the facts of Example 18. Because E&I has not legally met all the requirements necessary to be entitled to the income from its contract with the customer by the end of the year, the all events test would generally not be considered met and the company would recognize no gross income for tax purposes. However, assume that E&I has an enforceable right to the income from the installation (e.g., it would be contractually entitled to the revenue if the customer were to cancel the contract before the integration). In this case, the all events test would be considered met and E&I would be required to recognize in its gross income the revenue related to the installation and included in its financial statements. If, however, E&I did not have an enforceable right to the income (e.g., it would receive no income if it did not complete the integration), no gross income would be recognized related to the installation regardless of it being reported in the financial statements.

If E&I did not issue GAAP certified financial statements, it would not recognize any income for tax purposes until the all events test was met (i.e., it both delivered the equipment and completed the system integration as required by the contract).

Unearned Income

For financial reporting purposes, advance payments received from customers are initially reflected in the financial statements of the seller as a liability and recognized as income over the period in which the income is earned. However, for tax purposes, even accrual basis taxpayers generally must include unearned income in their gross income in the year of receipt.

Example 20

In December 2022, a tenant pays his January 2023 rent of $1,000. The accrual basis landlord must include the $1,000 in her 2022 gross income for tax purposes, although the unearned rent income is reported as a liability on the landlord's December 31, 2022 financial accounting balance sheet.

[41] § 451(b).

[42] § 1.451–3(b).

However, accrual basis taxpayers who receive advance payments for goods or services may elect to include in gross income in the year of receipt only the amount that would be recognized as income in their financial statements with the remaining amount recognized in the subsequent year.[43] The special deferral rule for accrual method taxpayers is a method of accounting that must be properly adopted (discussed further in Chapter 18). This special method will result in differences in the timing of the reporting of revenue when financial reporting rules require the revenue to be reported over three or more years, as illustrated in the following example.

Example 21

Yellow Corporation, an accrual basis calendar year taxpayer, sells its services under 12-month, 24-month, and 36-month contracts. The corporation provides services to each customer every month. On May 1, 2022, Yellow Corporation sold the following customer contracts:

Length of Contract	Total Proceeds
12 months	$3,000
24 months	4,800
36 months	6,300

Yellow may defer until 2023 all of the income that will be earned after 2022.

Length of Contract	Income Recorded in 2022	Income Recorded in 2023
12 months	$2,000 ($3,000 × 8/12)	$1,000 ($3,000 × 4/12)
24 months	1,600 ($4,800 × 8/24)	3,200 ($4,800 × 16/24)
36 months	1,400 ($6,300 × 8/36)	4,900 ($6,300 × 28/36)

The special election generally is available for advance payments for goods and services. It is not available, however, for unearned rent, interest, insurance premiums, and certain other advance payments. Advance payments for these items are taxed in the year of receipt.

4-3 General Sources of Income and to Whom They Are Taxed

LO.3

Identify the general sources of income and to whom they are taxed.

Gross income is often described as including that coming from labor (i.e., personal services) and capital (i.e., property). This section examines several issues generally related to income from personal services and property, including when and to whom this income is taxable.

4-3a Personal Services

It is a well-established principle of taxation that income from personal services must be included in the gross income of the person who performs the services. This principle was first established in a Supreme Court decision, *Lucas v. Earl*.[44] Mr. Earl entered into a binding agreement with his wife under which Mrs. Earl was to receive one-half of Mr. Earl's salary. Justice Holmes used the celebrated **fruit and tree metaphor** to explain that the fruit (income) must be attributed to the tree from which it came (Mr. Earl). A mere **assignment of income** does not shift the liability for the tax.

Services of an Employee

As discussed above, the income from personal services generally is taxable to the person performing the services. However, services performed by an employee for an employer's customers or clients are considered performed by the employer. So the employer is taxed on the income from the services provided, and the employee is taxed on any compensation received from the employer.[45]

[43] § 451(c).

[44] 2 USTC ¶496, 8 AFTR 10287, 50 S.Ct. 241 (USSC, 1930).

[45] *Sargent v. Comm.*, 91–1 USTC ¶50,168, 67 AFTR 2d 91–718, 929 F.2d 1252 (CA–8).

The Big Picture

Example 22

Return to the facts of *The Big Picture* on p. 4-1. Assume that instead of operating his dental practice as a sole proprietorship, Dr. Payne incorporated his dental practice in an attempt to limit his liability. He entered into an employment contract with his corporation and was to receive a salary. All patients contract to receive their services from the corporation, and those services are provided by the corporation's employee, Dr. Payne.

As a result, the corporation earned the income from patients' services and must include the patients' fees in its gross income. Dr. Payne must include his salary in his gross income. The corporation is allowed a deduction for the reasonable salary paid to Dr. Payne. (See the discussion of unreasonable compensation in Chapter 6.)

Services of a Child

In the case of a child, the Code specifically provides that amounts earned from personal services must be included in the child's gross income. This result applies even though the income may be paid to other persons (e.g., the child's parents).[46]

4-3b Income from Property

The courts have used the fruit and tree metaphor also to determine who should pay the tax on the income from property. In this context, the "tree" is the property and income is its "fruit." The owner of the tree has control over the fruit; therefore, the owner of the property should pay tax on the income the property produces. For example, if a father gives his daughter the right to collect the rent from his rental property, the father will nonetheless be taxed on the rent because he retains ownership of the property.[47] The fact that he can grant the right to the income to his daughter is evidence that he has control over the income. On the other hand, if a father gives his daughter the property, she is taxed on all the income earned after ownership of the property is transferred to her.

Interest

Because income from property is taxable to the owner of the property when the income is generated, it is important to determine when that income is deemed generated, especially when ownership of the property may be transferred during the year. Interest is considered to accrue daily regardless of when it is paid. Therefore, the interest on an obligation for the period that includes a transfer of ownership is allocated between the transferor and transferee based on the number of days during the period that each owned the obligation.

Example 23

Floyd, a cash basis taxpayer, gave his son, Ethan, corporate bonds with a face amount of $12,000 and a 5% stated annual interest rate. The gift was made on February 28, 2022, and the interest was paid on the last day of each quarter. Floyd must recognize $100 of interest income (5% × $12,000 × 2/12) accrued at the time of the gift.

For the transferor, the timing of the recognition of the income from the property depends on the accounting method and the manner in which the property was transferred. In the case of a gift of income-producing property, the transferor must recognize their share of the accrued income at the time it would have been recognized had the property not been transferred.[48]

Example 24

Return to the facts of Example 23. Assume that Floyd is a cash basis taxpayer. Because he transferred the bonds to his son as a gift, he must recognize the $100 of interest income as of March 31, the date he would have received the interest had he retained ownership of the bonds.

---

[46] § 73. For treatment of the child's unearned income, see Kiddie Tax—Unearned Income of Dependent Children in text Section 3-6c.

[47] *Galt v. Comm.*, 54–2 USTC ¶9457, 46 AFTR 633, 216 F.2d 41 (CA–7); *Helvering v. Horst*, 40–2 USTC ¶9787, 24 AFTR 1058, 61 S.Ct. 144 (USSC).

[48] Rev.Rul. 72–312.

If the property transfer is the result of a sale, the sale proceeds must include any income accrued prior to the sale. Because the transferor has indirectly received the income, the accrued income is recognized immediately on the sale of the property.

Example 25

Mia purchased a corporate bond at its face amount of $10,000 on July 1, 2022. The bond pays 5% interest on each June 30. On September 30, 2022, Mia sold the bond for $10,600. Mia must recognize $125 of interest income in 2022 (5% × $10,000 × 3/12). She must also recognize a $475 capital gain from the sale of the bond:

Amount received from sale	$ 10,600
Less accrued interest income	(125)
Selling price of bond excluding interest	$ 10,475
Less cost of the bond	(10,000)
Capital gain on sale	$ 475

Dividends

As a separate taxable entity, a corporation is taxed on its earnings, with those earnings taxed again as dividends when distributed to shareholders. Therefore, corporate earnings distributed as dividends are subject to double taxation. Partial relief from this double taxation is provided by taxing qualified dividends received by individuals at the same rate as capital gains ranging from 0 to 20 percent based on the taxpayer's taxable income (see text Section 3-9d).[49]

To be eligible for the special rates, stock must have been held for more than 60 days during the 121-day period beginning 60 days before the ex-dividend date.[50] The purpose of this requirement is to prevent taxpayers from buying stock shortly before a dividend is paid, receiving the preferentially-taxed dividend, and then selling the stock at a loss (a short-term capital loss) after the stock goes ex-dividend (a stock's price often declines after the stock goes ex-dividend).

Note that qualified dividends are *not* capital gains; as a result, they cannot be used to recognize capital losses. Qualified dividend income is merely taxed at the rates that would apply to taxpayers if they had an excess of net long-term capital gain over net short-term capital loss.

Stock Holding Period

Example 26

In June 2022, Green Corporation pays a dividend of $1.50 on each share of its common stock. Madison and Daniel, two unrelated shareholders, each own 1,000 shares of the stock. Consequently, each receives a dividend of $1,500 (1,000 shares × $1.50). Assume that Daniel satisfies the 60/121-day holding period rule but Madison does not.

The $1,500 that Daniel receives is subject to preferential 0%/15%/20% treatment in 2022. The $1,500 that Madison receives, however, is not. Because Madison did not comply with the holding period rule, her dividend is not a *qualified dividend* and is taxed at ordinary income rates.

Example 27

Assume that both Madison and Daniel in Example 26 are in the 32% tax bracket. Consequently, Madison pays a tax of $480 (32% × $1,500) on her dividend, whereas Daniel pays a tax of $225 (15% × $1,500) on his. The $255 savings that Daniel enjoys underscores the advantages of qualified dividend treatment.

Unlike individuals, corporations are not granted special tax rates for capital gains or dividends. However, corporations are permitted a dividends received deduction ranging from 50 percent to 100 percent of the dividends received from another domestic corporation. This deduction is discussed in text Section 20-2d.

[49] §§ 1(h)(11) and (j).

[50] The ex-dividend date is the date before the record date on which the corporation finalizes the list of shareholders who will receive the dividends.

Although interest generally accrues on a daily basis, dividends do not because the declaration of a dividend is at the discretion of the corporation's board of directors. Generally, dividends are taxed to the person who is entitled to receive them—the shareholder on the record date.[51] As a result, if a taxpayer sells stock after a dividend has been declared but before the record date, the dividend generally will be taxed to the purchaser.

This rule differs in the case of a gift of stock. If a donor makes a gift of stock to someone (e.g., a family member) after the declaration date but before the record date, the Tax Court has held that the dividend must be included in the gross income of the donor, not the donee. The *fruit* has sufficiently ripened as of the declaration date to tax the dividend income to the donor of the stock.[52] However, where a taxpayer gave stock to a qualified charity (a charitable contribution) after the declaration date and before the record date, the Fifth Circuit Court of Appeals concluded that the dividend income should be included in the gross income of the donee (the owner at the record date). As a result, dividends declared on stock gifted to a charity and stock gifted to family members are treated differently.[53]

Example 28

On June 20, the board of directors of Black Corporation declares a $10 per share dividend. The dividend is payable on June 30 to shareholders of record on June 25. As of June 20, Maria owned 200 shares of Black Corporation's stock. On June 21, Maria sold 100 of the shares to Norm for their fair market value and gave 100 of the shares to Sam (her son). Both Norm and Sam are shareholders of record as of June 25.

Norm (the purchaser) will be taxed on $1,000 because he is entitled to receive the dividend. However, Maria (the donor) will be taxed on the $1,000 received by Sam (the donee) because the gift was made after the declaration date but before the record date of the dividend.

Some payments are frequently referred to as dividends but are *not* considered dividends for tax purposes, although they are included in gross income:

- Dividends received on deposits with savings and loan associations, credit unions, and banks are actually interest (an amount paid for the use of money).
- Patronage dividends paid by cooperatives (e.g., for farmers) are rebates made to the users and are considered reductions in the cost of items purchased from the association. The rebates usually are made after year-end (after the cooperative has determined whether it has met its expenses) and are apportioned among members on the basis of their purchases.
- Mutual insurance companies pay dividends on unmatured life insurance policies that are considered rebates of premiums.
- Shareholders in a mutual investment fund are allowed to report as capital gains their proportionate share of the fund's gains realized and distributed. The capital gain and ordinary income portions are reported on the Form 1099 that the fund supplies to its shareholders each year.

4-3c Income from Partnerships, S Corporations, Trusts, and Estates

Unlike a corporation, a **partnership** is not a separate taxpaying entity for Federal income tax purposes. Rather, the income of a partnership is included in the taxable income of its partners. A partnership merely files an information return (Form 1065) that serves to provide the data necessary for determining the amount and character of each partner's distributive share of the partnership's income and deductions. Partners must each report their distributive share of the partnership's income and deductions for the partnership's tax year ending in or with the partner's tax year. The income must be reported by each

[51] Reg. § 1.61–9(c). The record date is the cutoff for determining the shareholders who are entitled to receive the dividend.

[52] *M. G. Anton*, 34 T.C. 842 (1960).

[53] *Caruth Corp. v. U.S.*, 89–1 USTC ¶9172, 63 AFTR 2d 89–716, 865 F.2d 644 (CA–5).

partner in the year it is recognized by the partnership, even if such amounts are not actually distributed to the partners. Because a partner pays tax on partnership income as the partnership earns it, a distribution by the partnership to the partner generally is treated as a tax-free recovery of capital.[54]

Example 29

Tara owns a one-half interest in the capital and profits of T & S Company (a calendar year partnership). For tax year 2022, the partnership earned revenue of $150,000 and had operating expenses of $80,000. During the year, Tara withdrew from her capital account $2,500 per month (for a total of $30,000).

For 2022, Tara must report $35,000 as her share of the partnership's profits [½ × ($150,000 − $80,000)] even though she received distributions of only $30,000. The $30,000 distribution is a recovery of capital and has no impact on Tara's taxable income.

Contrary to the general rule that a corporation must pay tax on its income, a *small business corporation* may elect to be taxed, under Subchapter S of the Internal Revenue Code, similarly to a partnership. As a result, the shareholders rather than the corporation pay the tax on the corporation's income.[55] The electing corporation is commonly referred to as an **S corporation**. Similar to partners in a partnership, the shareholders report their proportionate shares of the corporation's income and deductions for the year, regardless of whether the corporation actually makes any distributions to the shareholders.

Unlike partnerships and S corporations, estates and trusts generally are not business entities. Rather, they are intended to care for assets on behalf of their beneficiaries until those assets are distributed. However, because those assets are often income-generating (e.g., investments), estates and trusts often earn income while caring for and administering their assets. The *beneficiaries of estates and trusts* generally are taxed on the income earned by the estates or trusts that is actually distributed or required to be distributed to them.[56] Any income not taxed to the beneficiaries is taxable to the estate or trust.

The taxation of income and distributions of partnerships, S corporations, and estates and trusts is compared in Concept Summary 4.1.

Concept Summary 4.1

Taxation of Income and Distributions from Partnerships, S Corporations, Trusts, and Estates

	Partnership	S Corporation	Estate or Trust
Share of the income for the year	Taxable to partner when earned by the partnership.	Taxable to stockholder when earned by the S corporation.	Undistributed income taxed to the estate or trust.
Distributions	Recovery of capital, which reduces basis in the partnership.	Recovery of capital, which reduces basis in the stock.	Taxable to beneficiary when distributed.

4-3d Income in Community Property States

General

State law in Arizona, California, Idaho, Louisiana, Nevada, New Mexico, Texas, Washington, and Wisconsin is based on a community property system. In Alaska, spouses can choose to have the community property rules apply. All other states have a common law property system. The basic difference between common law and community property systems centers around the property rights of married persons. Questions about the taxation of income from community property most frequently arise when spouses file separate returns.

Under a **community property** system, all property owned by a married individual is deemed either to be separately owned by one spouse or to belong to the marital community. Property may be owned separately by a spouse if it was acquired before marriage or received by gift or inheritance following marriage. Otherwise, property is deemed to be community property.

[54] § 706(a) and Reg. § 1.706–1(a)(1). For further discussion, see Chapter 20.

[55] §§ 1361(a) and 1366. For further discussion, see Chapter 20.

[56] §§ 652(a) and 662(a). For further discussion of the taxation of income from partnerships, S corporations, trusts, and estates, see *South-Western Federal Taxation: Corporations, Partnerships, Estates & Trusts*, Chapters 10, 11, 12, and 20.

The Federal income taxation of income generated by property in community property states generally is based on who has the right to the income. Any income generated by community property is taxable equally to each spouse. The taxation of income from separate property, however, differs across community property states. The laws of Idaho, Louisiana, Texas, and Wisconsin distinguish between separate property and the income it produces. In these states, the income from separate property belongs to the community. As a result, for Federal income tax purposes, each spouse is taxed on one-half of the income. In the remaining community property states, separate property produces separate income that the owner-spouse must report on his or her Federal income tax return.

What appears to be income, however, may really represent a recovery of capital. A recovery of capital and gain realized on separate property retain their identity as separate property. Items such as nontaxable stock dividends, royalties from mineral interests, and gains and losses from the sale of property take on the same classification as the assets to which they relate.

Example 30

Bob and Jane are married and reside in California. Among other transactions during the year, the following occurred:

- A nontaxable stock dividend was received by Jane on stock that was given to her by her mother after Jane's marriage.
- A gain of $10,000 was realized on the sale of unimproved land purchased by Bob before the marriage.
- Oil royalties of $15,000 were received from a lease Jane acquired with her separate funds after the marriage.

Because the stock dividend was distributed on stock held by Jane as separate property, it also is her separate property. The same result occurs for the oil royalties Jane receives. All of the proceeds from the sale of the unimproved land (including the gain of $10,000) are Bob's separate property.

In all community property states, income from personal services (e.g., salaries, wages, and income from a professional partnership) is generally treated as if one-half is earned by each spouse.

Example 31

Fred and Wilma are married but file separate returns. Fred received $25,000 of salary and $300 of taxable interest on a savings account he established in his name. All deposits to the savings account were made from Fred's salary that he earned since the marriage. Wilma collected $2,000 taxable dividends on stock she inherited from her father.

Wilma's gross income is computed as follows under three assumptions as to the state of residency of the couple:

	California	Texas	Common Law States
Dividends	$ 2,000	$ 1,000	$2,000
Salary	12,500	12,500	–0–
Interest	150	150	–0–
	$14,650	$13,650	$2,000

Note that the savings account is a community asset because it was created with community funds (i.e., Fred's salary).

Because they have community property income and are filing separately, both Fred and Wilma must include Form 8958, Allocation of Tax Amounts Between Certain Individuals in Community Property States, with their Form 1040.

Community property should not be confused with jointly owned property. There are several differences between the two. For example:

- Jointly owned property (i.e., property owned by tenants in common or joint tenants) is not limited to married couples.
- More than two owners can own property jointly. For example, three siblings or two or more unrelated individuals can be joint owners of a tract of land.
- Ownership interests in jointly owned property need not be equal. For example, one sibling can hold a one-half interest while two others own a one-quarter interest each.

Community Property Spouses Living Apart

The general rules for taxing the income from services performed by residents of community property states can create complications and even inequities for spouses who are living apart.

Example 32

Mason and Lily, a married couple, have always lived in a community property state. After a bitter argument in December 2021, Lily moves in with her parents, where she remains for all of 2022. During 2022, Lily receives none of Mason's income. Nor is she sure how much income Mason earned. When Lily files her separate return for 2022, must she include one-half of Mason's salary?

Congress has developed a simple solution to this problem. A spouse (or former spouse) is taxed only on his or her actual earnings from personal services if all of the following conditions are met:[57]

- The spouses (or former spouses) live apart for the entire year.
- They do not file a joint return with each other.
- No portion of the earned income is transferred between the individuals.

As a result, in the prior example, Lily will not include any of Mason's salary in her gross income for the year.

LO.4

Recognize and apply the special tax rules related to alimony, loans made at below-market interest rates, annuities, prizes and awards, unemployment compensation, Social Security benefits, and foreign bank accounts.

4-4 Special Rules Related to Certain Items Included in Gross Income

Although § 61 makes it clear that all income is taxable unless explicitly excluded, Congress has deemed it necessary to clarify and provide specific rules for several types of income. Some of these special rules appear in §§ 71–91 of the Code.

4-4a Alimony and Separate Maintenance Payments

There are several financial consequences that result when a married couple divorce or become legally separated. For example, when a divorce occurs, state law generally requires a division of the property accumulated during the marriage. In addition, one spouse may have a legal obligation to support the other spouse. The Code has treated property divisions and support payments (alimony or separate maintenance) differently from each other with those differences changing over time. Because the tax treatment of a divorce arrangement and any subsequent payments are generally determined as of the date of the divorce, the current tax treatment of divorced couples will differ depending on when they were divorced.

Property Settlements

A transfer of property other than cash owned prior to divorce to a former spouse under a divorce decree or agreement is not a taxable event. The transferor is not entitled to a deduction and does not recognize gain or loss on the transfer. The transferee does not recognize income and has a basis equal to the transferor's basis.[58]

---

[57] § 66. See Form 8958.

[58] § 1041, added to the Code in 1984 to repeal the rule of *U.S. v. Davis*, 62–2 USTC ¶9509, 9 AFTR 2d 1625, 82 S.Ct. 1190 (USSC). Under the *Davis* rule, which applied to pre-1985 divorces, a property transfer incident to divorce was a taxable event.

Example 33

Paul transfers stock to Rob as part of a divorce settlement. The cost of the stock to Paul is $12,000, and the stock's value at the time of the transfer is $15,000. Rob later sells the stock for $16,000. Neither Paul nor Rob recognizes any gain or income from the transfer of the stock to Rob. Rob has a realized and recognized gain of $4,000 ($16,000 − $12,000) when he sells the stock.

Support Payments

Alimony and separate maintenance payments made under a divorce agreement executed after 2018 are neither taxable to the recipient nor deductible by the payor.[59] Payments made under an agreement entered into on or before December 31, 2018, are *includible* in the gross income of the party receiving the payments and *deductible for* AGI by the party making the payments. For payments related to these pre-2019 agreements, income is shifted from the income earner to the income beneficiary, who has a legal right to the income and is better able to pay the tax on the amount received.

Example 34

Pete and Tina were divorced in 2018. Pete is required to pay Tina $15,000 of alimony each year. Pete earns $61,000 a year. Tina has the ultimate legal right to the $15,000 and is better able than Pete to pay the tax on it. Therefore, Tina must include the $15,000 in her gross income. Pete is required to include the $61,000 in his gross income but is allowed to deduct $15,000 from his gross income.

If the divorce occurred in 2022, Tina would not be required to include the alimony in her income and Pete would not be allowed a deduction for the alimony paid.

Requirements for Alimony

Because a payor may face a higher marginal tax rate than a payee, parties entering into divorce agreements before 2019 may have had an incentive to have payments treated as support obligation (alimony) rather than as part of a property settlement. To clarify the appropriate treatment of payments between former spouses subsequent to a divorce, Congress developed the following objective rules. Payments made under pre-2019 agreements and decrees are *classified as alimony* only if the following conditions are satisfied:

- The agreement or decree does not specify that the payments are not alimony. (This allows the parties to determine by agreement whether the payments will be alimony.)
- The payments are in cash. Payments other than cash are likely to be part of a property division.
- There is no liability to make the payments for any period after the death of the payee. (Payments due after death would be a property interest that could be transferred to the heirs.)
- The payor and payee are not members of the same household at the time the payments are made. (This ensures that the payments are for maintaining two households.)

Front-Loading

As an additional safeguard against a pre-2019 property settlement being disguised as alimony, special rules apply if payments are front-loaded (i.e., if the payments in the first two years of the arrangement are significantly higher than in subsequent years). If the payments meet the requirements laid out above, they are treated as alimony during the first two years of the agreement. However, if the annual payments decrease after the second year of the agreement by more than a statutory amount, the **alimony recapture** rules require that the payor include the excess payments made in years 1 and 2 as income in year 3 to the extent they were deducted previously. Similarly, the payee may deduct in year 3 the excess payments from years 1 and 2 that were included in income previously. The mechanics involved in computing recapture are complex and beyond the scope of this text. Worksheets for computing the recapture are provided in *Divorced or Separated Individuals* (IRS Publication 504).

[59]§§ 71 and 215.

Child Support

As the consequence of a divorce, one former spouse also may be required to make payments to the other with the express purpose of supporting a child. A taxpayer does not realize income from the receipt of child support payments since the money received must be used for the child's benefit. Similarly, the payor is not allowed to deduct the child support payments because the payments are made to satisfy the payor's legal obligation to support the child.

In many cases, it may be difficult to determine whether payments subject to pre-2019 agreements are intended to be alimony or child support. The tax law generally treats any payments that would be reduced on the happening of a contingency related to a child (e.g., the child attains age 21 or dies) as child support. In addition, if the total payments actually made during the year are less than legally required, the payments that are made are considered first to cover the required child support with any excess treated as the required alimony payments. These rules are applied even though the divorce agreement specifies other amounts for the support of the child.[60]

Example 35

Under a divorce agreement entered into in 2017, Matt is required to make periodic payments of $500 per month to Grace. However, when Matt and Grace's child reaches age 21, marries, or dies (whichever occurs first), the payments will be reduced to $300 per month. Grace has custody of the child. Because the required payments will be reduced by $200 per month once the child reaches age 21, $200 of the monthly payments will be considered child support for Federal tax purposes regardless of how they are labeled in the agreement. Only $300 of the monthly payment will be considered alimony.

If Matt makes payments of only $350 per month, $200 is treated as child support with the remaining $150 considered to be alimony.

Ethics & Equity — The Taxation of Alimony and the Alimony Tax Gap

Prior to 2019, alimony payments were deductible by payors and taxable to recipients. This was consistent with the assignment of income doctrine, the idea that income is taxable to the party who has the right to that income. To ensure that recipients properly reported alimony payments as income, payors were required to report the Social Security numbers of the recipient on their tax returns. For divorce agreements reached after 2018, alimony is no longer deductible by payors, nor taxable to recipients, leaving those who earn, but are legally obligated to transfer, income subject to tax on amounts they directly receive but have no right to keep.

Of course, assuming the recipient of alimony is generally in a lower tax bracket than is the payor, placing the tax burden of amounts transferred as alimony on recipients lowers overall tax revenues. However, transferring the burden to recipients may lower tax revenues for other reasons as well. A 2019 examination of 2016 individual tax returns found that the amount by which total deductions for alimony exceeded the amount reported by recipients had grown to more than $3.2 billion, a 38% increase over the amount determined in 2010. Approximately half of the 2016 discrepancy related to differences in the amounts reported by payors and the recipients whose identity had been reported, resulting in $248 million of unpaid taxes. Nearly half of the discrepancy related to amounts reported by payors for which the corresponding recipient's tax return could not be identified. Nearly $40 million related to amounts claimed by payors who reported invalid Social Security numbers. Of the nearly 285,000 tax returns resulting in a reporting discrepancy, nearly half of all returns reporting alimony deductions, the IRS previously had selected only 7,500 for audit.

Should those who are legally required to transfer their income in the form of alimony to another party be required to pay tax on that income? What role, if any, should the potential loss in tax revenue, whether due to the differences in the tax rates of payors and recipients or the potential overreporting of alimony by payors, play in the decision? Are there other factors that should be considered?

Data source: Treasury Inspector General for Tax Administration (TIGTA) Report 2019-40-048 at **treasury.gov/tigta/auditreports/2019reports/201940048fr.pdf**.

[60] §§ 71(c)(2) and (3), and *Allen H. Johnson*, 107 TCM 1358, T.C.Memo. 2014–67.

The tax rules relating to divorce settlements are reviewed in Concept Summary 4.2.

Concept Summary 4.2

Tax Treatment of Payments and Transfers Pursuant to Divorce Agreements and Decrees

	Payor	Recipient
Property settlement	No income or deduction.	No income or deduction; basis for the property is the same as the transferor's basis.
Alimony pursuant to divorce after 2018	Not deductible.	Not taxable.
Alimony pursuant to a divorce prior to 2019	Deductible *for* AGI in year paid.	Included in gross income in year received.
Alimony recapture	Included in gross income of the third year.	Deducted from gross income of the third year.
Child support	Not deductible.	Not taxable.

4-4b Imputed Interest on Below-Market Loans

The overall tax on income can be reduced if the taxation of the income can be shifted to a taxpayer in a lower tax bracket. As discussed above, shifting the taxation of income from services is difficult given the assignment of income doctrine. Although shifting the taxation of the income from property can be accomplished by shifting the ownership of the property, this might be a high price to pay. However, lending income-producing property to another taxpayer without charging interest on the loan, as illustrated in the following example, could allow such shifting without requiring the taxpayer to give up ownership of the income-producing property.

Example 36

Kareem is in the 50% (combined Federal and state) marginal tax bracket, while his daughter, Veneia, is in the 20% marginal tax bracket. Kareem has $400,000 available to invest. He plans to use the income from the investment to help support Veneia. Rather than invest the money himself, Kareem decides to loan the money to Veneia in exchange for a non-interest-bearing demand note. Veneia could invest the cash, and the income would be taxed at her 20% tax rate. In addition, Kareem retains control over the principal because he could demand payment on the note at any time.

Although this was a common tax planning technique at one time, the imputed interest rules now reduce the benefits of the income shifting illustrated in the example. Even when no interest is charged on a loan, the lender and borrower may be required to calculate their income as if it had been. If the rules are applicable, lenders are treated as if they had earned interest on the loan and are required to recognize this **imputed interest** in their gross income. Likewise, borrowers are treated as if they had incurred interest expense, although whether the interest expense is deductible will depend on several factors (see Chapters 10 and 11).[61]

Example 37

Returning to Example 36, Kareem would be treated as if he had earned interest on the loan and be required to recognize the imputed interest in his gross income. Veneia would be treated as if she had incurred interest expense. Veneia's interest may be deductible as investment interest if she itemizes her deductions.

Imputed interest is calculated using the rate the Federal government pays on new borrowings, compounded semiannually. This Federal rate is adjusted monthly and is published by the IRS.[62] There are three Federal rates: short-term (applicable to loans not over three years, including demand loans), mid-term (applicable to loans over three years but not over nine years), and long-term (applicable to loans over nine years).[63]

[61] § 7872(a)(1).

[62] §§ 7872(b)(2) and (f)(2).

[63] § 1274(d).

Example 38

Assume that the Federal rate applicable to the loan in Example 36 is 3.5% through June 30 and 4% from July 1 through December 31. Kareem makes the loan on January 1, and the loan is still outstanding on December 31. Kareem must recognize interest income of $15,140, and Veneia has interest expense of $15,140.

Imputed interest calculations:	
January 1–June 30: 3.5% × $400,000 × ½ year	$ 7,000
July 1–December 31: 4% × ($400,000 + $7,000) × ½ year	8,140
	$15,140

If interest is charged on the loan at less than the Federal rate, the imputed interest is the difference between the amount that would have been charged at the Federal rate and the amount actually charged.

Example 39

Assume the same facts as in Example 38, except that Kareem charged 3% interest, compounded annually.

Interest at the Federal rate	$ 15,140
Less interest charged (3% × $400,000)	(12,000)
Imputed interest	$ 3,140

Although a lender may be required to recognize imputed interest as income for tax purposes, the lender nonetheless has realized no economic benefit. To better capture the economic positions of the parties involved, the lender is deemed to transfer back to the borrower an amount of money equal to the imputed interest. The nature of this transfer (and its Federal tax consequences) is determined by the relation of the parties to each other.

Example 40

Return to Example 38. Kareem is deemed to transfer back to Veneia $15,140, the same amount he is deemed to have received in interest. Assuming that Kareem's only relation to Veneia is as a family member, the transfer from Kareem to Veneia is deemed to be a gift. Since gifts are not subject to income taxes (see Chapter 5), this transfer has no income tax consequences for either Kareem or Veneia. However, it may have gift tax consequences for Kareem (see Chapter 1).

The imputed interest rules apply to most below-market rate loans including the following:[64]

- Gift loans (loans made out of love, affection, or generosity, as in Example 36).
- Compensation-related loans (loans made by an employer to an employee).
- Corporation-shareholder loans (loans made by a corporation to a shareholder).

The effects of these loans on the borrower and lender are summarized in Concept Summary 4.3.

Concept Summary 4.3

Effect of Certain Below-Market Loans on the Lender and Borrower

Type of Loan	Lender	Borrower
Gift loans	Interest income	Interest expense
	Gift made	Gift received
Compensation-related loans	Interest income	Interest expense
	Compensation expense	Compensation income
Corporation to shareholder loans	Interest income	Interest expense
	Dividend paid	Dividend income

[64] § 7872(c).

Exceptions and Limitations

No interest is imputed on total outstanding *gift loans* of $10,000 or less between individuals unless the loan proceeds are used to purchase income-producing property.[65] This exception eliminates loans that do not result in material shifts of income. However, if total gift loans between individuals exceed $10,000 or the proceeds of such a loan are used to purchase income-producing property, this exception does not apply.

It is unlikely that income shifting was the motivation of a below-market rate loan if the borrower has no investment income. On gift loans of $100,000 or less between individuals, the interest that must be imputed is limited to the borrower's net investment income for the year (gross income from all investments less the related expenses).[66] In addition, if the borrower's net investment income for the year does not exceed $1,000, no interest is imputed. However, these limitations for loans of $100,000 or less do not apply if a principal purpose of a loan is tax avoidance.[67]

Example 41

Vicki made interest-free gift loans as follows:

Borrower	Amount	Borrower's Net Investment Income	Purpose
Susan	$ 8,000	$ -0-	Education
Dan	9,000	500	Purchase of stock
Bonnie	25,000	-0-	Purchase of a business
Megan	90,000	15,000	Purchase of a residence
Olaf	120,000	-0-	Purchase of a residence

Assume that tax avoidance is not a principal purpose of any of the loans. The loan to Susan is not subject to the imputed interest rules because the $10,000 exception applies. The $10,000 exception does not apply to the loan to Dan because the proceeds were used to purchase income-producing assets. However, under the $100,000 exception, the imputed interest is limited to Dan's investment income ($500). Because the $1,000 threshold also applies to this loan, no interest is imputed.

No interest is imputed on the loan to Bonnie because the gift loan is less than $100,000 and Bonnie has no investment income. The $100,000 exception also applies to the loan made to Megan. Although interest must be imputed, the amount imputed will be no more than Megan's investment income. None of the exceptions apply to the loan to Olaf because the loan was for more than $100,000.

Assume that the relevant Federal rate is 5% and that the loans were outstanding for the entire year. Vicki would recognize interest income, compounded semiannually, as follows:

Loan to Megan:	
First 6 months (5% × $90,000 × ½ year)	$ 2,250
Second 6 months (5% × $92,250 × ½ year)	2,306
	$ 4,556
Loan to Olaf:	
First 6 months (5% × $120,000 × ½ year)	$ 3,000
Second 6 months (5% × $123,000 × ½ year)	3,075
	$ 6,075
Total imputed interest ($4,556 + $6,075)	$10,631

As with gift loans, there is a $10,000 exemption for *compensation-related loans* and *corporation-shareholder loans*. However, the $10,000 exception does not apply to compensation-related or corporation-shareholder loans if tax avoidance is one of the principal purposes of the loan.[68] This vague tax avoidance standard makes practically all compensation-related and corporation-shareholder loans suspect. Nevertheless, the $10,000 exception should apply when an employee's borrowing was necessitated by personal needs (e.g., to meet unexpected expenses) rather than tax considerations.

[65] § 7872(c)(2).

[66] § 7872(d).

[67] *Deficit Reduction Tax Act of 1984: Explanation of the Senate Finance Committee* (April 2, 1984), p. 484.

[68] § 7872(c)(3).

These exceptions to the imputed interest rules are summarized in Concept Summary 4.4.

Concept Summary 4.4

Exceptions to the Imputed Interest Rules for Below-Market Loans

Exception	Eligible Loans	Ineligible Loans and Limitations
De minimis—aggregate loans of $10,000 or less	Gift loans	Proceeds are used to purchase income-producing assets.
	Employer-employee	Principal purpose is tax avoidance.
	Corporation-shareholder	Principal purpose is tax avoidance.
Aggregate loans of $100,000 or less	Gift loans	Principal purpose is tax avoidance. For all other loans, interest is imputed to the extent of the borrower's net investment income if that income exceeds $1,000.

Ethics & Equity Taxing "Made-Up" Income

Under the imputed interest rules, a taxpayer who makes a below-market loan may be required to recognize income not actually received. For example, assume that Christiana loans $200,000 to Max, her son, to start a business.

Christiana does not charge interest because Max needs the funds to operate a struggling startup business. Why should Christiana be required to pay tax on interest she did not collect? On one hand, she received no interest income. On the other hand, interest would have been charged by Christiana in an arm's length loan made to any other borrower or by any other lender on a loan to Max. Christiana's choice not to charge interest is really an indirect gift to Max. Should Christiana be able to avoid tax on the income she assigned to Max? This type of income is sometimes referred to as "phantom" income.

4-4c Income from Annuities

Annuity contracts generally involve a purchaser (the annuitant) paying a fixed amount for the right to receive a future stream of payments. Typically, the issuer of the contract is an insurance company. The insurance company invests the amounts received from the annuitant, and the income earned serves to increase the cash value of the annuity. If the annuitant cancels the contract early, the issuer will pay the annuitant the cash value of the annuity.

Generally, the increase in the cash value of the contract is not immediately taxable because it is subject to substantial restrictions (the contract must be canceled to realize the benefit). However, if the contract is canceled early, the amount received over the cost of the contract must be recognized as income.

Example 42

Jean, age 50, pays $30,000 for an annuity contract that is to pay her $500 per month beginning when she reaches age 65 and continuing until her death. A year after purchasing the contract, its cash value increases to $30,200. If Jean should cancel the policy after one year, she would include $200 ($30,200 − $30,000) in her gross income. However, if she does not cancel the policy, the $200 increase in value is not includible in her gross income.

The tax accounting problem associated with receiving periodic payments under an annuity contract is one of apportioning the amounts received between recovery of capital (the original investment in the contract) and income.

Computing the Exclusion Amount

The annuitant can exclude from income the portion of each payment that represents a recovery of capital. The *exclusion amount* is calculated as follows:

$$\frac{\text{Investment}}{\text{Expected return}} \times \text{Annuity payment} = \text{Exclusion amount}$$

The taxpayer's *investment* in the annuity contract is the total amount paid by the taxpayer for the annuity. The *expected return* is the annual amount to be paid to the annuitant multiplied by the number of years the payments will be received. The payment period may be fixed (a *term certain*) or may be for the life of one or more individuals. When payments are for life, the taxpayer generally must use an annuity table published by the IRS to determine the expected return (see Exhibit 4.1).[69] The expected return is calculated by multiplying the appropriate multiple (life expectancy) by the annual payment.

Exhibit 4.1 Ordinary Life Annuities: One Life—Expected Return Multiples

Age	Multiple	Age	Multiple	Age	Multiple
5	76.6	42	40.6	79	10.0
6	75.6	43	39.6	80	9.5
7	74.7	44	38.7	81	8.9
8	73.7	45	37.7	82	8.4
9	72.7	46	36.8	83	7.9
10	71.7	47	35.9	84	7.4
11	70.7	48	34.9	85	6.9
12	69.7	49	34.0	86	6.5
13	68.8	50	33.1	87	6.1
14	67.8	51	32.2	88	5.7
15	66.8	52	31.3	89	5.3
16	65.8	53	30.4	90	5.0
17	64.8	54	29.5	91	4.7
18	63.9	55	28.6	92	4.4
19	62.9	56	27.7	93	4.1
20	61.9	57	26.8	94	3.9
21	60.9	58	25.9	95	3.7
22	59.9	59	25.0	96	3.4
23	59.0	60	24.2	97	3.2
24	58.0	61	23.3	98	3.0
25	57.0	62	22.5	99	2.8
26	56.0	63	21.6	100	2.7
27	55.1	64	20.8	101	2.5
28	54.1	65	20.0	102	2.3
29	53.1	66	19.2	103	2.1
30	52.2	67	18.4	104	1.9
31	51.2	68	17.6	105	1.8
32	50.2	69	16.8	106	1.6
33	49.3	70	16.0	107	1.4
34	48.3	71	15.3	108	1.3
35	47.3	72	14.6	109	1.1
36	46.4	73	13.9	110	1.0
37	45.4	74	13.2	111	0.9
38	44.4	75	12.5	112	0.8
39	43.5	76	11.9	113	0.7
40	42.5	77	11.2	114	0.6
41	41.5	78	10.6	115	0.5

[69] The life expectancies in Exhibit 4.1 apply for annuity investments made on or after July 1, 1986. See *General Rules for Pensions and Annuities*, IRS Publication 939 (Rev. Dec. 2018), p. 26. See also *Pension and Annuity Income*, IRS Publication 575.

Example 43

A taxpayer, age 60, purchases an annuity from an insurance company for $90,000. In return, she is to receive $500 per month for life. Her life expectancy (from Exhibit 4.1) is 24.2 years from the annuity starting date. As a result, her expected return is $500 × 12 × 24.2 = $145,200, and the exclusion amount is $3,719 [($90,000 investment ÷ $145,200 expected return) × $6,000 annual payment]. On an annual basis, $3,719 is treated as a nontaxable return of capital and $2,281 ($6,000 − $3,719) is included in gross income.

The *exclusion ratio* (investment ÷ expected return) applies until the annuitant has recovered their entire investment in the contract. Once the investment is recovered, the entire amount of subsequent payments is taxable. If the annuitant dies before recovering the investment, the unrecovered cost (adjusted basis) is deductible in the year the payments cease (usually the year of death).[70]

Example 44

Assume that the taxpayer in Example 43 receives annuity payments for 25.2 years (302 months). For the last 12 months [302 − (12 × 24.2) = 12], the taxpayer will include $500 (the total amount received) each month in gross income. If instead the taxpayer dies after 36 months, she is eligible for a $78,843 deduction on her final tax return.

Cost of the contract	$ 90,000
Cost previously recovered [$90,000 ÷ $145,200 × 36($500)]	(11,157)
Deduction	$ 78,843

Simplified Method for Annuity Distributions from Qualified Retirement Plans

A simplified method is required for allocating basis to the annuity payments received under a qualified retirement plan.[71] The portion of each annuity payment that is excluded as a return of capital is the employee's investment in the contract, if any, divided by the number of anticipated monthly payments determined in accordance with Exhibit 4.2 rather than the annuity table illustrated in Exhibit 4.1.[72]

Example 45

Andrea, age 62, receives an annuity distribution of $500 per month for life from her qualified retirement plan beginning in January 2020. Her investment in the contract is $100,100. The excludible amount of each payment is $385 ($100,100 investment ÷ 260 monthly payments). As a result, $115 ($500 − $385) of each annuity payment is included in Andrea's gross income.

The rules for annuity payments received after the basis has been recovered by the annuitant and for the annuitant who dies before the basis is recovered are the same as under the exclusion ratio method discussed earlier.

Exhibit 4.2 Number of Anticipated Monthly Annuity Payments under the Simplified Method

Age	Number of Anticipated Monthly Payments
55 and under	360
56–60	310
61–65	260
66–70	210
71 and over	160

[70] § 72(b).

[71] See Chapter 19.

[72] § 72(d).

4-4d Prizes and Awards

Gross income includes the fair market value of any prizes and awards (other than scholarships exempted under § 117; see text Section 5-4) received by a taxpayer.[73] For example, TV giveaway prizes, magazine publisher prizes, door prizes, and awards from an employer to an employee in recognition of performance are fully taxable to the recipient.

A narrow exception permits a prize or an award to be excluded from gross income if *all* of the following requirements are satisfied:

- The prize or award is received in recognition of religious, charitable, scientific, educational, artistic, literary, or civic achievement (e.g., Nobel Prize, Pulitzer Prize, or faculty teaching award).
- The recipient was selected without any action on his or her part to enter the contest or proceeding.
- The recipient transfers the prize or award to a qualified governmental unit or nonprofit organization.
- The recipient is not required to render substantial future services as a condition for receiving the prize or award.[74]

The transfer of the property to a qualified governmental unit or nonprofit organization ordinarily would be a deductible charitable contribution (an itemized deduction as explained in Chapter 10). The exclusion produces beneficial tax consequences in the following situations:

- The taxpayer does not itemize deductions and so would receive no tax benefit from the charitable contribution.
- The taxpayer's charitable contributions exceed the annual statutory ceiling on the deduction.
- Including the prize or award in gross income would reduce the amount of deductions for which the taxpayer would otherwise qualify because of gross income limitations (e.g., the adjusted gross income limitation in calculating the medical expense deduction).

Another exception allows an exclusion for certain *employee achievement awards* made in the form of tangible personal property (e.g., a gold watch) but not cash or cash equivalents (e.g., gift certificates, meals, lodging, or tickets to theater or sporting events). To qualify for the exclusion, the award must be made in recognition of an employee's length of service or safety achievement. Generally, the ceiling on the excludible amount for an employee is $400 per taxable year. However, if the award is made as a part of a tax qualified plan, the ceiling on the exclusion is $1,600 per taxable year.[75]

A third exception allows certain participants in the Olympic and Paralympic Games to exclude the value of any medal and cash award received. The exclusion is only available to those with income of $1 million or less. The rationale offered for this tax preference is that the athletes "perform a valuable patriotic service."[76]

Finally, a taxpayer also can avoid including prizes and awards in gross income by simply refusing to accept the prize or award.[77]

4-4e Unemployment Compensation

The unemployment compensation program is sponsored and operated by the states and Federal government to provide a source of income for people who have been employed and are temporarily (hopefully) out of work. In a series of rulings over a period of 40 years, the IRS had exempted unemployment benefits from tax. These payments were considered social benefit programs for the promotion of the general welfare. After experiencing dissatisfaction with the IRS's treatment of unemployment compensation, Congress amended the Code to make the benefits taxable.[78]

---

[73] § 74.

[74] § 74(b).

[75] § 74(c). Qualified plan awards are defined in § 274(j) and explained in *Business Expenses*, Chapter 2 (IRS Publication 535).

[76] P.L. 114-239 (10/7/16), adding § 74(d) effective for awards received after 2015. Also see H.R. Rep. No. 114–762 (9/20/16).

[77] See Rev.Rul. 57–374 and Rev.Proc. 87–54.

[78] § 85. In 2020, households with AGI less than $150,000 were allowed to exclude up to $10,200 of unemployment compensation received (American Rescue Plan Act of 2021; P.L. 117–2).

Ethics & Equity Tax Treatment of Unemployment Compensation

The unemployment insurance program is a joint Federal-state program designed to replace a portion of wages for workers who have lost their jobs. Prior to the COVID-19 pandemic, those who left a job voluntarily were not covered. Nor were the self-employed, including independent contractors and gig workers. Although eligibility requirements and benefits differed by state, most states required workers to have a minimum amount of time worked or earnings to qualify. Qualified workers generally were eligible for coverage for up to 26 weeks. On average, benefits replaced half of a worker's previous earnings or $387 per week. Any benefits received were taxable, as was the income they replaced.

In response to the COVID-19 pandemic and the resulting recession, the 2020 Coronavirus Aid and Economic Security (CARES) Act made several temporary changes to the unemployment system. It eliminated prior work requirements and extended coverage to part-time workers, independent contractors, and the self-employed through the end of 2020. Along with the pandemic itself, this significantly increased the number of taxpayers receiving unemployment benefits. The Act also extended benefits an additional 13 weeks and initially increased payments by $600 per week over existing benefits.

Estimates suggest that the enhanced benefits resulted in covered individuals receiving, on average, 90 percent of their previous earnings with approximately two-thirds making more than they did when employed and 20 percent receiving more than twice their prior earnings. Although most agreed that it was appropriate to adjust unemployment benefits in response to the pandemic, some believed it was inconsistent to require some of the economic assistance to be repaid through income taxes. Conversely, some worried that the increased benefits would discourage people from returning to work when able, hindering any economic recovery.

The American Rescue Plan Act of 2021 extended Federal unemployment benefits through August 2021 at a reduced rate of $300 per week. It also allowed households with AGI less than $150,000 to exclude up to $10,200 of unemployment compensation received during 2020.

However, fearing the increased benefits were preventing people from reentering the workforce, many states discontinued the benefits early. Do you think unemployment compensation should be taxable? Why or why not?

More information may be found at **taxfoundation.org/unemployment-compensation-taxable-income/** and **usatoday.com/story/money/2021/07/09/unemployment-benefits-jobs-worker-shortage/7826616002/**.

4-4f Social Security Benefits

The amount of Social Security benefits included in a taxpayer's gross income is based on two factors: (1) the taxpayer's ability to pay and (2) the amount of benefits considered to be a recovery of the taxpayer's contributions, or a recovery of capital. In this context, ability to pay is based on *modified adjusted gross income* (MAGI). MAGI is equal to the taxpayer's adjusted gross income from all sources other than Social Security benefits, increased by any tax-exempt income including the foreign earned income exclusion.

If a taxpayer's MAGI plus 50 percent of Social Security benefits received, often referred to as *provisional income*, does *not exceed* a threshold amount ($32,000 for married taxpayers filing a joint return or $25,000 for single taxpayers), the taxpayer need not include any Social Security benefits in gross income. If provisional income *exceeds* this threshold, the taxpayer must include a portion of the Social Security benefits in gross income, determined as follows:

1. The amount included in gross income is equal to 50 percent of the amount by which the provisional income exceeds the threshold, limited to 50 percent of the benefits themselves.
2. If the taxpayer's provisional income also exceeds a second threshold ($44,000 for a married couple filing a joint return or $34,000 for a single taxpayer), the amount included in gross income is equal to 85 percent of the amount that provisional income exceeds the higher threshold, plus the *smaller* of the following:
   - The amount determined in 1, above, or
   - 50 percent of the difference between the two threshold amounts (i.e., $6,000 for a married taxpayer filing jointly or $4,500 for a single taxpayer).

In general, the threshold amounts for married taxpayers filing separately are set at zero.

Regardless of a taxpayer's MAGI, or ability to pay, the total amount included in gross income is limited to 85 percent of the benefits themselves.[79]

[79] § 86. The rationale for taxing 85% of the Social Security benefits is as follows: For the average Social Security recipient, 15% of the amount received is a recovery of amounts that the individual paid into the program, and the remainder of the benefits is financed by the employer's contribution and interest earned by the Social Security trust fund.

Taxation of Social Security Benefits

Example 46

A married couple with adjusted gross income of $30,000, no tax-exempt income, and $11,000 of Social Security benefits who file jointly must include $1,750 of the benefits in gross income. This is determined as follows:

1. 50% × [$30,000 + ½($11,000) − $32,000] = $1,750
2. Limited to 50% × $11,000 = $5,500

If instead the couple had adjusted gross income of $15,000, none of the benefits would be taxable because provisional income [$15,000 + (50% × $11,000)] does not exceed $32,000.

Example 47

A married couple who file jointly have adjusted gross income of $72,000, no tax-exempt income, and $12,000 of Social Security benefits. Their includible Social Security benefits are $10,200, determined as follows:

1. 85% × [$72,000 + ½($12,000) − $44, 000] = $28, 900
   Plus the lesser of:
   50% × [$72,000 + ½($12,000) − $32, 000] = $23, 000
   50% × ($44,000 − $32,000) = $6,000
2. All limited to 85% × $12,000 = $10,200

Because 85% of the Social Security benefits received is less than $34,900 ($28,900 + $6,000), $10,200 is included in the couple's gross income.[80]

4-4g Income Earned from Foreign Bank and Financial Accounts and FBAR Rules

Given the broad definition of gross income, income earned outside the United States by a U.S. taxpayer generally is included in gross income (although limited exclusions are available, as discussed in Chapter 5). However, because it has historically been difficult for the IRS to get information regarding this income and its sources from international payers, taxpayers with a foreign bank account, brokerage account, or similar financial account generally are required to file an annual report with the Treasury Department. If the aggregate value of their foreign accounts exceeds $10,000 at any time during the calendar year, FinCEN Form 114, **Report of Foreign Bank and Financial Accounts (FBAR)**, must be filed electronically with the Treasury Department. This form is due by April 15 (with an automatic extension until October 15) for the preceding tax year. The form is filed separately from the account holder's income tax return. Schedule B of Form 1040 includes questions that also must be answered for individuals with foreign accounts. The penalty for failure to comply with the FBAR reporting requirements can be substantial: as much as 50 percent of the value of the foreign accounts.[81]

Example 48

Jane, an employee of Maple Corporation, travels frequently for her work. She learned that it is easier to handle rent and other payments while working abroad if she has banking arrangements in these countries. In June and July of this year, during her trips, she opened an account in Canada and an account in France. Each started with a deposit of $6,000. Because on at least one day this year Jane had over $10,000 in foreign financial accounts, she must file FinCEN Form 114 (FBAR) to report the accounts. In addition, any interest earned on the accounts is included in calculating her Federal income tax liability.

[80] To help taxpayers compute taxable benefits, a worksheet is provided in the instructions to Form 1040, as well as in *Social Security and Equivalent Railroad Retirement Benefits* (IRS Publication 915).

[81] See **fincen.gov/resources/filing-information**. FinCEN is the Financial Crimes Enforcement Network and is part of the U.S. Department of the Treasury.

LO.5

Identify tax planning strategies for minimizing gross income and the present value of the related tax.

4-5 Tax Planning

The topics covered in this chapter have focused on the following questions:

- What is gross income?
- When is gross income recognized?
- To whom is gross income taxable?

Planning strategies suggested by these questions include the following:

- Minimize the economic benefits that are included in gross income.
- Defer the recognition of gross income.
- Shift the taxability of income to taxpayers who are in a lower marginal tax bracket.

Some specific techniques for accomplishing these strategies are discussed in the following paragraphs.

4-5a Minimize Income Included in Gross Income

Given the broad definition of gross income included in the Code, most items of income are included in gross income. However, a taxpayer may be able to restructure a transaction so that an item is not considered income. For example, a lessor may be able to structure a lease such that some amounts received under the contract are considered deposits. Given the requirement that the amount be repaid under certain circumstances, the receipt would not be considered income.[82] Of course, this could also result in the taxpayer forfeiting their right to the amount that is reclassified. Conversely, in situations in which more than one taxpayer is involved, taxpayers may find it advantageous to have transfers between the parties considered income. For example, before 2019, it was often advantageous to structure divorce agreements such that payments between former spouses would qualify as taxable alimony rather than child support or a property settlement. Assuming that the payor was in a higher tax bracket than the recipient, alimony payments could reduce the joint tax liability of the parties.

In spite of the broad general definition of gross income, several types of income are specifically excluded from gross income. Several of these are discussed in Chapter 5.

4-5b Tax Deferral

General

Because deferring the recognition of income and the payment of the related tax reduces the net present value of the tax liability, the deferral of taxes is a primary goal of the tax planner. In fact, a significant amount of tax planning deals with when taxes are owed rather than how much is owed. As discussed in text Section 4-2, the timing of income recognition generally is determined by the taxpayer's accounting method. The cash method provides the taxpayer with more deferral opportunities than does the accrual method. For example, under the cash method, income derived from services can be deferred until it is collected rather than recognized when the services are provided as required under the accrual method. Although taxpayers are somewhat constrained by the constructive receipt doctrine (they cannot turn their backs on income), seldom will customers and clients offer to pay before they are asked. The usual lag between billings and collections (e.g., December's billings collected in January) will result in a continuous deferral of some income until the last year of operations.

Regardless of a taxpayer's method of accounting, no income is recognized and no tax is due on a property transaction until a gain has been realized. Therefore, the law favors investments that appreciate in value over ones that provide regular cash payments.

Example 49

Vera can buy a corporate bond or an acre of land for $10,000. The bond pays $500 of interest (5%) each year, and Vera expects the land to increase in value 5% each year for the next 10 years. She is in the 40% (combined Federal and state) tax bracket. Assuming that the bond would mature or the land would be sold in 10 years and Vera would reinvest the interest at a 5% before-tax return, she would accumulate the following amount at the end of 10 years:

continued

[82]See *Commissioner v. Indianapolis Power and Light*, 90–1 USTC ¶50,007, 65 AFTR 2d 90–394, 110 S.Ct. 589 (USSC).

		Bond	Land
Original investment		$10,000	$10,000
Annual income	$ 500		
Less tax	(200)		
	$ 300		
Compound amount reinvested for 10 years at 3% [5% × (1 − 0.4)] after-tax return	× 11.46	3,438	
		$13,438	
Compound amount, 10 years at 6%			× 1.79
			$17,900
Less tax on sale: 40%($17,900 − $10,000)			(3,160)
			$14,740

Therefore, the value of the deferral that results from investing in the land rather than in the bond is $1,302 ($14,740 − $13,438). The advantage of investing in the land may be increased further by the availability of the lower rates applicable to long-term capital gains.

Of course, a taxpayer can often defer the recognition of income from appreciated property by postponing the event triggering realization (the final closing on a sale or exchange of property). If the taxpayer needs cash, obtaining a loan by using the appreciated property as collateral may be a less costly alternative than selling the property. The need to sell an appreciated asset to purchase a new investment will practically increase the return available on the new asset necessary to make it preferable to the old.

Example 50

Ira owns 100 shares of Pigeon Company common stock with a cost of $20,000 and a fair market value of $50,000. Although the stock's value has increased substantially in the past three years, Ira thinks future appreciation will be much less. Ira is considering selling the Pigeon stock and investing the proceeds from the sale in other common stock. Assuming that Ira's marginal tax rate on the sale is 15%, he will have only $45,500 [$50,000 − 15%($50,000 − $20,000)] to reinvest. Therefore, if considered as competing alternatives, Ira will have to earn approximately 10% more ($50,000 ÷ $45,500) on a new investment to make it as profitable as his current investment in the Pigeon stock.

As discussed in text Section 4-2c, Series EE bonds offer taxpayers the unusual opportunity of long-term deferral of interest income until the maturity of the bond. In situations where the taxpayer's goal is merely to shift income one year into the future, bank certificates of deposit are useful tools. If the maturity period is one year or less, all interest is reported in the year of maturity. Bank certificates of deposit are especially useful for taxpayers who find themselves in an unusually high tax bracket in one year (perhaps due to a nonrecurring gain on the sale of property) but expect their gross income to be less the following year.

Generally, the timing of income recognition under the accrual method is not impacted by when cash is received. However, even accrual basis taxpayers may be able to defer the recognition of income by deferring when payment is received. Recall that an accrual basis taxpayer who receives unearned income need only recognize for tax purposes in the year of receipt what is recognized in their financial statements, but cannot defer recognition of the remainder beyond the year following the year of receipt. In some cases, deferring receipt from a year prior to when income would first be recognized to a subsequent year may result in a valuable tax deferral.

Example 51

NerdSquad, Inc., sells three-year computer service agreements for $15,000, requiring the customer to prepay for the service when a contract is signed. In December 2022, NerdSquad will sell several three-year contracts covering the period from January 2023 to December 2025. It is considering whether to require customers to pay in December 2022 or January 2023. As illustrated below, NerdSquad will recognize in its financial statements $5,000 of income from each contract in each year from 2023 through 2025. However, by deferring receipt of the revenue for only a short period, the company will defer the tax on a significant portion of it.

continued

	Financial Statement Income	Taxable Income: If payments are received December 30, 2022	Taxable Income: If payments are received January 2, 2023
2022	$ -0-	$ -0-	$ -0-
2023	5,000	15,000	5,000
2024	5,000		10,000
2025	5,000		

Of course, the tax planner must also consider the tax rates for the years the income is shifted from and to. For example, a one-year deferral of income from a year in which the taxpayer's tax rate is 24 percent to a year in which the tax rate will be 35 percent would not be advisable unless the taxpayer could earn an after-tax return of approximately 45 percent on the deferred tax.

4-5c Shifting Income to Other Taxpayers

The benefits of income are often shared among multiple individuals regardless of who earns it. For example, the earnings of one family member may be used to support his or her spouse, children, and parents. The tax liability of a family who may be directly or indirectly sharing income can be minimized by shifting the taxability of that income from higher- to lower-bracket family members. This can be accomplished through gifts of income-producing property. Furthermore, in many cases, income can be shifted with no negative effect on the family's spending or investment plans.

Income Shifting

Example 52

Adam, who is in the 24% tax bracket, helps support his father, Mike, who is a widower. Mike's main source of income is Social Security. Rather than simply transferring part of his income to Mike, Adam could transfer to Mike income-producing property. Some of the income would be offset by Mike's standard deduction with the rest subject to tax at Mike's tax rate, which is likely lower than Adam's.

Example 53

Adam, from Example 52, also would like to save for his children's education. All of his children are under 19 years of age and are dependents of Adam. Adam could transfer income-producing properties to the children as well. However, in this case, the kiddie tax may negate the benefits of shifting more than $1,100 of income to each child (see text Section 3-6c).

The Uniform Gifts to Minors Act, a model law adopted by all states (but with some variations among the states), facilitates such income shifting. Under the Act, a gift of intangibles (e.g., bank accounts, stocks, bonds, and life insurance contracts) can be made to a minor but with an adult serving as custodian. Usually, the parent who makes the gift is also named as custodian. State laws allow the custodian to sell or redeem and reinvest the principal and to accumulate or distribute the income, practically at the custodian's discretion provided there is no commingling of the child's income with the parent's property. By giving appreciated securities to the child, and having the donor custodian sell the securities and reinvest the proceeds, the parent shifts both the gain and the annual income to the child. Such planning is limited by the kiddie tax (refer to text Section 3-6c).

U.S. savings bonds provide another opportunity for income shifting. As discussed above, taxpayers may defer the interest (original issue discount) earned on U.S. government (Series EE) bonds. However, if and when this income is shifted to children, it may be beneficial to elect to recognize the interest early while the child has little or no other income. When this is done, the children generally should file a return and elect to report the income on the accrual basis.

Example 54

Abby pays $7,500 for Series EE bonds in 2022 and registers them in her son's name. Her son, Wade, will enter college the year of original maturity of the bonds. The bonds have a maturity value of $10,000. Wade elects to report the annual increment in redemption value as income for each year the bonds are held. The first year the increase is $250, and Wade includes that amount in his gross income. If Wade has no other income, no tax will be due on the $250 bond interest because such an amount will be more than offset by his available standard deduction. The following year the increment is $260, and Wade includes this amount in income. As a result, over the life of the bonds, Wade will include $2,500 in income ($10,000 − $7,500), none of which will result in a tax liability, assuming that he has no other income.

However, if the election had not been made, Wade would have been required to include $2,500 in income on the bonds in the year of original maturity if they had been redeemed as planned. This amount of income might result in a tax liability.

Refocus on The Big Picture

Calculation of Gross Income

Bob Daemmrich/Alamy Stock Photo

Dr. Cliff Payne has correctly calculated the gross income of his sole proprietorship based on the accrual method of accounting. He will report $385,000, including the $4,000 he received in the form of the solar panels, on his tax return (Schedule C of Form 1040).

What If?

From a tax planning perspective, what can Dr. Payne do to decrease his gross income from the first year of operating his dental practice and thereby produce better financial results for him?

Rather than adopt the accrual method of accounting, Dr. Payne could instead adopt the cash method of accounting. His gross income for Federal income tax purposes under the cash method is calculated as follows:

Revenues	$385,000
Plus: Accounts receivable: January 1	–0–
Less: Accounts receivable: December 31	(52,000)
Gross income	$333,000

The cash method of accounting enables Dr. Payne to defer paying Federal income taxes on the accounts receivable he has yet to collect. Furthermore, each year that Dr. Payne has accounts receivable at the end of the tax year, that income is continuously deferred. As a result, if his accounts receivable remain at $52,000 at the end of each tax year, by using the cash method of accounting rather than the accrual method, he will defer that amount of income until he terminates his practice.

Key Terms

Accounting income, 4-4
Accounting method, 4-7
Accrual method, 4-8
Alimony and separate maintenance payments, 4-21
Alimony recapture, 4-21
Annuity, 4-26
Assignment of income, 4-14
Cash receipts method, 4-7
Claim of right doctrine, 4-8
Community property, 4-18
Constructive receipt, 4-9
Economic income, 4-4
Fruit and tree metaphor, 4-14
Gross income, 4-3
Hybrid method, 4-9
Imputed interest, 4-23
Income, 4-4
Original issue discount, 4-11
Partnership, 4-17
Recovery of capital doctrine, 4-3
Report of Foreign Bank and Financial Accounts (FBAR), 4-31
S corporation, 4-18
Taxable year, 4-6

Discussion Questions

1. **LO.1** According to the Supreme Court, would it be good tax policy to use income as computed by financial accounting principles as the correct measure of income for Federal income tax purposes? Explain.

2. **LO.1** Compare and contrast the economist's concept of income with the concept employed in measuring taxable income.

Critical Thinking

3. **LO.1** Allen visits Reno, Nevada, once a year to gamble. This year his gambling loss was $25,000. He commented to you, "At least I didn't have to pay for my airfare and hotel room. The casino paid that because I am such a good customer. That was worth at least $3,000." What are the relevant tax issues for Allen?

4. **LO.1** Hana lost her job in 2022 when her employer moved its plant. During the year, she collected unemployment benefits for three months, a total of $1,800. While she was waiting to hear from prospective employers, she painted her house. If Hana had paid someone else to paint her house, the cost would have been $3,000. The cost of the paint Hana used was $800. What is Hana's 2022 gross income for tax purposes from the above events?

Critical Thinking

5. **LO.1** Howard buys wrecked cars and stores them on his property. Recently, he purchased a 1991 Ford Taurus for $400. If he can sell all of the usable parts, his total proceeds from the Taurus will be over $2,500. As of the end of the year, he has sold only the radio for $75 and he does not know how many, if any, of the remaining parts will ever be sold. What are Howard's income recognition issues?

6. **LO.2** On December 29, 2022, an employee received a $5,000 check from her employer's client. The check was payable to the employer. The employee did not remit the funds to the employer until December 30, 2022. The employer deposited the check on December 31, 2022, but the bank did not credit the employer's bank account until January 2, 2023. When is the cash basis employer required to include the $5,000 in gross income?

7. **LO.2** What is the purpose of the constructive receipt doctrine?

Planning

8. **LO.2** A taxpayer is considering two alternative investments. A Series EE U.S. government savings bond accrues 3.5% interest each year. The bond matures in three years, at which time the principal and interest will be paid. Alternatively, a bank will pay the taxpayer a 3.5% interest rate each year if he agrees to leave money on deposit for three years. What tax advantage does the Series EE bond offer that is not available with the bank deposit?

Planning

9. **LO.2** A taxpayer performs services for customers with payment due within 30 days. All customers pay within the time limit. What would be the benefit to the taxpayer using the cash method of accounting rather than the accrual method?

10. **LO.3, 5** Wade paid $7,000 for an automobile that needed substantial repairs. He worked nights and weekends to restore the car and spent $2,400 on parts for it. He knows that he can sell the car for $13,000, but he is very wealthy and does not need the money. On the other hand, his daughter, who has very little income, needs money to make the down payment on a house.

    a. Would it matter, after taxes, whether Wade sells the car and gives the money to his daughter or whether he gives the car to his daughter and she sells it for $13,000? Explain.

    b. Assume that Wade gave the car to his daughter after he had arranged for another person to buy it from his daughter. The daughter then transferred the car to the buyer and received $13,000. Who is taxed on the gain?

11. **LO.3** Anita, a cash basis taxpayer, sued her former employer for wage discrimination. Her attorney agreed to pursue the case on a contingent fee basis—the attorney would receive one-third of any settlement or court award. The parties reached a settlement, and the attorney for Anita's former employer wrote a check payable to Anita for \$320,000 and a check payable to her attorney for \$160,000. Anita reasons that she and the attorney were partners in the lawsuit who shared profits two-thirds and one-third, respectively. Therefore, she includes \$320,000 in her gross income. Is Anita's analysis correct? Explain.

12. **LO.3** Rex purchased a 30% interest in a partnership for \$200,000. In 2022, the partnership generated \$400,000 of taxable income and Rex withdrew \$100,000. In 2023, the partnership earned \$600,000 of taxable income and Rex withdrew \$200,000. What is Rex's gross income from the partnership in 2022 and 2023?

13. **LO.4** A divorce agreement entered into in 2017 requires Alice to pay her former spouse \$50,000 a year for the next 10 years. Will the payments qualify as alimony? Why or why not?

14. **LO.4, 5** William and Abigail, who live in San Francisco, have been experiencing problems with their marriage. They have a three-year-old daughter, April, who stays with William's parents during the day because both William and Abigail are employed. Abigail worked to support William while he attended medical school, and now she has been accepted by a medical school in Mexico. Abigail has decided to divorce William and attend medical school. April will stay in San Francisco because of her strong attachment to her grandparents and because they can provide her with excellent day care. Abigail knows that William will expect her to contribute to the cost of raising April. Abigail also believes that to finance her education, she must receive cash for her share of the property they accumulated during their marriage. In addition, she believes that she should receive some reimbursement for her contribution to William's support while he was in medical school. She expects the divorce proceedings to take several months. Identify the relevant tax issues for Abigail. Critical Thinking

15. **LO.4, 5** Patrick and Eva are planning to divorce in 2022. Patrick has offered to pay Eva \$12,000 each year until their 11-year-old daughter reaches age 21. Alternatively, Patrick will transfer to Eva common stock that he owns with a fair market value of \$100,000. What factors should Eva and Patrick consider in deciding between these two options? Decision Making Planning

16. **LO.4** In the current year, Madero Corporation made a \$400,000 interest-free loan to Francisco Madero, the corporation's controlling shareholder. Mr. Madero is also the corporation's chief executive officer and receives a salary of \$300,000 a year. What are the tax consequences of classifying the loan as a compensation-related loan rather than as a corporation-shareholder loan?

17. **LO.4** Connor purchased an annuity that was to pay him a fixed amount each month for the remainder of his life. He began receiving payments in 2005, when he was 65 years old. In 2022, Connor was killed in an automobile accident. What are the effects of the annuity on Connor's final tax return?

18. **LO.4** Carlos is retired and receives Social Security benefits. During the year, Carlos appeared on a television game show and won \$5,000. By how much will the prize increase his gross income? Critical Thinking

19. **LO.4** In January 2022, Sonja deposited \$20,000 in a bank in the Bahamas. She earned \$500 interest income. She closed the account in December 2022.
    a. Is Sonja subject to the FBAR reporting requirement? Explain.
    b. Is the interest income taxable in the United States? Explain.

Computational Exercises

20. **LO.2** On January 1, 2022, Kunto, a cash basis taxpayer, pays $46,228 for a 24-month certificate of deposit. The certificate is priced to yield 4% (the effective interest rate) with interest compounded annually. No interest is paid until maturity, when Kunto receives $50,000.

    a. Compute Kunto's gross income from the certificate for 2022.

    b. Compute Kunto's gross income from the certificate for 2023.

    Round all calculations to the nearest dollar.

21. **LO.2** Bigham Corporation, an accrual basis calendar year taxpayer, sells its services under 12- and 24-month contracts. The corporation provides services to each customer every month. On July 1, 2022, Bigham sold the following customer contracts:

Length of Contract	Total Proceeds
12 months	$14,000
24 months	$24,000

Determine the income to be recognized in taxable income in 2022 and 2023.

Length of Contract	2022 Income	2023 Income
12 months	a. ____________	c. ____________
24 months	b. ____________	d. ____________

22. **LO.3** Simba and Zola are married but file separate returns. Simba received $80,000 of salary and $1,200 of taxable dividends on stock he purchased in his name with the salary he earned since the marriage. Zola collected $900 in taxable interest on a certificate of deposit she inherited from her aunt. Compute Zola's gross income under two assumptions as to the state of residency of the couple. If an amount is zero, enter "$0."

	Idaho (Community Property State)	South Carolina (Common Law State)
Dividends	a. ____________	d. ____________
Interest	b. ____________	e. ____________
Salary	c. ____________	f. ____________

23. **LO.4** Casper and Cecile divorced in 2018. As part of the divorce settlement, Casper transferred stock to Cecile. Casper purchased the stock for $25,000, and it had a market value of $43,000 on the date of the transfer. Cecile sold the stock for $40,000 a month after receiving it. In addition, Casper is required to pay Cecile $1,500 a month in alimony. He made five payments to her during the year.

    What are the tax consequences for Casper and Cecile regarding these transactions?

24. **LO.4** Elizabeth made the following interest-free loans during the year. Assume that tax avoidance is not a principal purpose of any of the loans. Assume that the relevant Federal rate is 5% and that the loans were outstanding for the last six months of the year.

Borrower	Amount	Borrower's Net Investment Income	Purpose of Loan
Richard	$ 5,000	$800	Gift
Woody	8,000	600	Purchase stock
Irene	105,000	–0–	Purchase residence

What are the effects of the imputed interest rules on these transactions? Compute Elizabeth's gross income from each loan.

a. Richard

b. Woody

c. Irene

25. **LO.4** A taxpayer, age 64, purchases an annuity from an insurance company for $50,000. She is to receive $300 per month for life. Her life expectancy is 20.8 years from the annuity starting date. Assuming that she receives $3,600 this year, how much is included in her gross income? Round any percentages to two decimal places. Round the final answer for the income to the nearest dollar.

26. **LO.4** Compute the taxable Social Security benefits in each of the following situations:

a. Tyler and Candice are married and file a joint tax return. They have adjusted gross income of $46,000 before considering their Social Security benefits, no tax-exempt interest, and $12,400 of Social Security benefits.

b. Tyler and Candice have adjusted gross income of $12,000 before considering their Social Security benefits, no tax-exempt interest, and $16,000 of Social Security benefits.

c. Tyler and Candice have adjusted gross income of $85,000 before considering their Social Security benefits, no tax-exempt interest, and $15,000 of Social Security benefits.

Problems

27. **LO.1** Determine the taxpayer's current-year (1) economic income and (2) gross income for tax purposes from the following events:

a. Ja-ron's employment contract as chief executive of a large corporation was terminated, and he was paid $500,000 not to work for a competitor of the corporation for five years.

b. Elliot, a six-year-old child, was paid $5,000 for appearing in a television commercial. His parents put the funds in a savings account for the child's education.

c. Valery found a suitcase that contained $100,000. She could not determine who the owner was.

d. Winn purchased a lottery ticket for $5 and won $750,000.

e. Larry spent $1,000 to raise vegetables that he and his family consumed. The cost of the vegetables in a store would have been $2,400.

f. Dawn purchased an automobile for $1,500 that was worth $3,500. The seller was in desperate need of cash.

28. **LO.1, 2, 5** Harper is considering three alternative investments of $10,000. Assume that the taxpayer is in the 24% marginal tax bracket for ordinary income and 15% for qualifying capital gains in all tax years. The selected investment will be liquidated at the end of five years. The alternatives are: Decision Making Planning

- A taxable corporate bond yielding 5.333% before tax and the interest can be reinvested at 5.333% before tax.
- A Series EE bond that will have a maturity value of $12,200 (a 4% before-tax rate of return).
- Land that will increase in value.

The gain on the land is classified and taxed as a long-term capital gain. The income from the bonds is taxed as ordinary income. How much must the land increase in value to yield a greater after-tax return than either of the bonds? For this analysis, ignore the effect of property taxes on the land.

Use the future value tables in Appendix E as needed for your calculations and comparisons. Present your answers using spreadsheet software such as Microsoft Excel.

29. **LO.1** Determine Amos's gross income in each of the following cases:
    a. In the current year, Amos purchased an automobile for $25,000. As part of the transaction, Amos received a $1,500 rebate from the manufacturer.
    b. Amos sold his business. In addition to the selling price of the stock, he received $50,000 for a covenant not to compete—an agreement that he will not compete with his former business for five years.
    c. Amos owned some land he held as an investment. As a result of a change in the zoning rules, the property increased in value by $20,000.

30. **LO.1,2** Determine the taxpayer's gross income for tax purposes in each of the following situations:
    a. Deb, a cash basis taxpayer, traded a corporate bond with accrued interest of $300 for corporate stock with a fair market value of $12,000 at the time of the exchange. Deb's cost of the bond was $10,000. The value of the stock had decreased to $11,000 by the end of the year.
    b. Deb needed $10,000 to make a down payment on her house. She instructed her broker to sell some stock to raise the $10,000. Deb's cost of the stock was $3,000. Based on her broker's advice, instead of selling the stock, she borrowed the $10,000 using the stock as collateral for the debt.
    c. Deb's boss gave her two tickets to the Rabid Rabbits rock concert because she met her sales quota. At the time she received the tickets, each ticket had a face price of $200 and was selling on eBay for $300. On the date of the concert, the tickets were selling for $250 each. Deb and her son attended the concert.

Decision Making
Planning

31. **LO.2, 5** Al is a medical doctor who conducts his practice as a sole proprietor. During 2022, he received cash of $280,000 for medical services. Of the amount collected, $40,000 was for services provided in 2021. At the end of 2022, Al had accounts receivable of $60,000, all for services rendered in 2022. In addition, at the end of the year, Al received $12,000 as an advance payment from a health maintenance organization (HMO) for services to be rendered in 2023. Compute Al's gross income for 2022:
    a. Using the cash basis of accounting.
    b. Using the accrual basis of accounting.
    c. Advise Al on which method of accounting he should use.

32. **LO.2** Selma operates a contractor's supply store. She maintains her books using the cash method. At the end of 2022, her accountant computes her accrual basis income that is used on her tax return. For 2022, Selma had cash receipts of $1,400,000, which included $200,000 collected on accounts receivable from 2021 sales. It also included the proceeds of a $100,000 bank loan. At the end of 2022, she had $250,000 in accounts receivable from customers, all from 2022 sales.
    a. Compute Selma's accrual basis gross revenues for 2022.
    b. Selma paid cash for all of the purchases. The total amount paid for merchandise in 2022 was $1,300,000. At the end of 2021, she had merchandise on hand with a cost of $150,000. At the end of 2022, the cost of merchandise on hand was $300,000. Compute Selma's gross income from merchandise sales for 2022.

33. **LO.2** Trip Garage, Inc. (459 Ellis Avenue, Harrisburg, PA 17111), is an accrual basis taxpayer that repairs automobiles. In late December 2022, the company repaired Samuel Mosley's car and charged him $1,000. Samuel did not think the problem had been fixed and refused to pay; as a result, Trip refused to release the automobile. In early January 2023, Trip made a few adjustments and convinced Samuel that the automobile was working properly. At that time, Samuel agreed to pay only $900 because he did not have the use of the car for a week. Trip said "fine," accepted the $900, and released the automobile to Samuel. An IRS agent thinks Trip, as an accrual basis taxpayer, should report $1,000 of income in 2022, when the work was done, and then deduct a $100 loss in 2023. Prepare a memo to Susan Apple, the treasurer of Trip, with the recommended treatment for the disputed income. Communications

34. **LO.2** Determine the effects of the following on a cash basis taxpayer's gross income for 2022 and 2023:

    a. On the morning of December 31, 2022, the taxpayer received a $1,500 check from a customer. The taxpayer did not cash the check until January 3, 2023.

    b. The same as part (a), except that the customer asked the taxpayer not to cash the check until January 3, 2023, after the customer's salary check could be deposited.

    c. The same as part (a), except that the check was not received until after the bank had closed on December 31, 2022.

35. **LO.2** Marlene, a cash basis taxpayer, invests in Series EE U.S. government savings bonds and bank certificates of deposit (CDs). Determine the tax consequences of the following on her 2022 gross income:

    a. On September 30, 2022, she cashed in Series EE bonds for $10,000. She purchased the bonds in 2012 for $7,090. The yield to maturity on the bonds was 3.5%.

    b. On July 1, 2021, she purchased a 24-month CD for $10,000. The CD matures on June 30, 2023, and will pay $10,816, yielding a 4% annual return.

    c. On July 1, 2022, she purchased a 12-month CD for $10,000. The maturity date on the CD was June 30, 2023, when Marlene will receive $10,300.

36. **LO.2** Drake Appliance Company, an accrual basis taxpayer, sells home appliances and service contracts. Determine the effect of each of the following transactions on the company's 2022 gross income assuming that the company uses any available options to defer its taxes.

    a. In December 2021, the company received a $1,200 advance payment from a customer for an appliance that Drake special-ordered from the manufacturer. The appliance did not arrive from the manufacturer until January 2022, and Drake immediately delivered it to the customer. The sale was reported in 2022 for financial accounting purposes.

    b. In October 2022, the company sold a 6-month service contract for $240. The company also sold a 36-month service contract for $1,260 in July 2022.

    c. On December 31, 2022, the company sold an appliance for $1,200. The company received $500 cash and a note from the customer for $700 and $240 interest, to be paid at the rate of $10 a month for 24 months. Because of the customer's poor credit record, the fair market value of the note was only $600. The cost of the appliance was $750.

37. **LO.2** In 2022, Wright's, Inc., signs a contract to design and deliver 100 laptop computers customized to perform certain functions required by a customer. Wright's will be paid $300 per computer but must deliver all 100 laptops to fulfill the contract. At the end of 2022, Wright's has completed and delivered 75 laptops and recognizes $22,500 (75 × $300) in revenues in its audited financial statements.

a. Assuming Wright's is an accrual basis taxpayer, how much gross income must it recognize in its 2022 taxable income?

b. (How) would your answer change if the contract allowed the customer to cancel the contract prior to delivery of the 100 computers but required them to pay for any computers completed prior to cancellation?

38. **LO.2, 5** Freda is a cash basis taxpayer. In 2022, she negotiated her salary for 2023. Her employer offered to pay her $21,000 per month in 2023 for a total of $252,000. Freda countered that she would accept $10,000 each month for the 12 months in 2023 and the remaining $132,000 in January 2024. The employer accepted Freda's terms for 2023 and 2024.

a. Did Freda actually or constructively receive $252,000 in 2023?

b. What could explain Freda's willingness to spread her salary over a longer period of time?

Decision Making
Planning

39. **LO.2, 5** The Bluejay Apartments, a new development, is in the process of structuring its lease agreements. The company would like to set the damage deposits high enough that tenants will keep the apartments in good condition. The company is actually more concerned about damage than about tenants not paying their rent.

a. Discuss the tax effects of the following alternatives:
   - $1,000 damage deposit with no rent prepayment.
   - $500 damage deposit and $500 rent for the final month of the lease.
   - $1,000 rent for the final two months of the lease and no damage deposit.

b. Which option do you recommend? Why?

40. **LO.3** Rusty has been experiencing serious financial problems. His annual salary was $100,000, but a creditor garnished his salary for $20,000 [i.e., the employer paid the creditor (rather than Rusty) the $20,000]. To prevent creditors from attaching his investments, Rusty gave his investments to his 21-year-old daughter, Rebecca. Rebecca received $5,000 in dividends and interest from the investments during the year. Rusty transferred some cash to a Swiss bank account that paid him $6,000 interest during the year. Rusty did not withdraw the interest from the Swiss bank account. Rusty also hid some of his assets in his wholly owned corporation that received $150,000 rent income but had $160,000 in related expenses, including a $20,000 salary paid to Rusty. Rusty reasons that his gross income should be computed as follows:

Salary received	$ 80,000
Loss from rental property ($150,000 – $160,000)	(10,000)
Gross income	$ 70,000

Determine Rusty's gross income for the year, and explain any differences between your calculation and Rusty's.

41. **LO.2** Troy, a cash basis taxpayer, is employed by Eagle Corporation, also a cash basis taxpayer. Troy receives a salary of $60,000 per year. He also receives a bonus equal to 10% of all collections from clients he serviced during the year. Determine the tax consequences of the following events to the corporation and to Troy:

a. On December 31, 2022, Troy was visiting a customer. The customer gave Troy a $10,000 check payable to the corporation for appraisal services Troy performed during 2022. Troy did not deliver the check to the corporation until January 2023.

b. The facts are the same as in part (a), except that the corporation is an accrual basis taxpayer and Troy deposited the check on December 31, but the bank did not add the deposit to the corporation's account until January 2023.

c. The facts are the same as in part (a), except that the customer told Troy to hold the check until January 2023 when the customer could make a bank deposit that would cover the check.

42. **LO.3** Faye, Gary, and Heidi each have a one-third interest in the FGH Partnership. The following information is available with respect to the partnership for the year and the amount allocable to each partner.

	Faye	Gary	Heidi	Total
Withdrawals	(20,000)	(35,000)	(10,000)	(65,000)
Additional contributions	–0–	–0–	5,000	5,000
Allocable share of profits	90,000	90,000	90,000	270,000

Compute each partner's gross income from the partnership for the tax year.

43. **LO.3, 5** During the year, Alva received dividends on her stocks as follows:

Amur Corporation (a French corporation whose stock is traded on an established U.S. securities market)	$60,000
Blaze, Inc., a Delaware corporation	40,000
Grape, Inc., a Virginia corporation	22,000

a. Alva purchased the Grape stock three years ago, and she purchased the Amur stock two years ago. She purchased the Blaze stock 18 days before it went ex-dividend and sold it 20 days later at a $5,000 loss. Alva had no other capital gains and losses for the year. She is in the 32% marginal tax bracket. Compute Alva's tax on her dividend income for the year.

b. Alva's daughter, who is 25 and not Alva's dependent, had taxable income of $6,000, which included $1,000 of dividends on Grape, Inc. stock. The daughter had purchased the stock two years ago. Compute the daughter's tax liability on the dividends.

c. Alva can earn 4.5% before-tax interest on a corporate bond or a 4% dividend on a preferred stock. Assuming that the appreciation in value is the same, which investment produces the greater after-tax income?

d. The same as part (c), except that Alva's daughter is to make the investment.

44. **LO.3** Imani and Doug were divorced on December 31, 2022, after 10 years of marriage. Their current year's income received before the divorce was as follows:

Doug's salary	$41,000
Imani's salary	55,000
Rent on apartments purchased by Imani 15 years ago	8,000
Dividends on stock Doug inherited from his mother 4 years ago	1,900
Interest on a savings account in Imani's name funded with her salary	2,400

Determine Imani's and Doug's separate gross incomes assuming that they live in:

a. California.

b. Texas.

45. **LO.4** Nell and Kirby are in the process of negotiating their divorce agreement, to be finalized in 2022. What should be the tax consequences to Nell and Kirby if the following, considered individually, became part of the agreement?

a. In consideration for her one-half interest in their personal residence, Kirby will transfer to Nell stock with a value of $200,000 and $50,000 of cash. Kirby's cost of the stock was $150,000, and the value of the personal residence is $500,000. They purchased the residence three years ago for $300,000.

b. Nell will receive $1,000 per month for 120 months. If she dies before receiving all 120 payments, the remaining payments will be made to her estate.

c. Nell is to have custody of their 12-year-old son, Bobby. She is to receive $1,200 per month until Bobby (1) dies or (2) attains age 21 (whichever occurs first). After either of these events occurs, Nell will receive only $300 per month for the remainder of her life.

Decision Making

46. **LO.4** Alicia and Rafel are in the process of negotiating a divorce agreement to be finalized in 2022. They both worked during the marriage and contributed an equal amount to the marital assets. They own a home with a fair market value of $400,000 (cost of $300,000) that is subject to a mortgage of $250,000. They have lived in the home for 12 years. They also have investment assets, all held more than one year, with a cost of $160,000 and a fair market value of $410,000. As a result, the net worth of the couple is $560,000 ($400,000 − $250,000 + $410,000). Alicia would like to continue to live in the house. Therefore, she has proposed that she receive the residence subject to the mortgage, a net value of $150,000. In addition, she would receive $17,600 each year for the next 10 years, which has a present value (at 6% interest) of $130,000. Rafel would receive the investment assets. If Rafel accepts this plan, he must sell one-half of the investments so that he can purchase a home. Assume that you are counseling Alicia. Explain to Alicia whether the proposed agreement would be "fair" on an after-tax basis.

Decision Making

47. **LO.4, 5** Roy decides to buy a personal residence and goes to the bank for a $150,000 loan. The bank tells him that he can borrow the funds at 4% if his father will guarantee the debt. Roy's father, Hal, owns a $150,000 CD currently yielding 3.5%. The Federal rate is 3%. Hal agrees to either of the following:
   - Roy borrows from the bank with Hal's guarantee to the bank.
   - Hal cashes in the CD (with no penalty) and lends Roy the funds at 2% interest.

   Hal is in the 32% marginal tax bracket. Roy, whose only source of income is his salary, is in the 12% marginal tax bracket. The interest Roy pays on the mortgage will be deductible by him. Which option will maximize the family's after-tax wealth?

48. **LO.2, 4** Your client, Aldridge, is a generous individual. During the year, he made interest-free loans to various family members when the Federal rate was 3%. What are the tax consequences of the following loans by Aldridge:
   a. On June 30, 2022, Aldridge loaned $12,000 to his cousin, Jim, to buy a used truck. Jim's only source of income was his wages on various construction jobs during the year.
   b. On August 1, 2022, Aldridge loaned $8,000 to his niece, Sonja. The loan was to enable her to pay her college tuition. Sonja had $1,200 interest income from CDs her parents had given her.
   c. On September 1, 2022, Aldridge loaned $25,000 to his brother, Al, to start a business. Al had $220 of dividends and interest for the year.
   d. On September 30, 2022, Aldridge loaned $150,000 to his mother so that she could enter a nursing home. His mother's only income was $9,000 of Social Security benefits and $500 of interest income.

49. **LO.4** Indicate whether the imputed interest rules should apply in the following situations. Assume that all of the loans were made at the beginning of the tax year unless otherwise indicated.
   a. Mike loaned his sister $90,000 to buy a new home. Mike did not charge interest on the loan. The Federal rate was 5%. Mike's sister had $900 of investment income for the year.
   b. Nico's employer maintains an emergency loan fund for its employees. During the year, Nico's wife was very ill and he incurred unusually large medical

expenses. He borrowed $8,500 from his employer's emergency loan fund for six months. The Federal rate was 5.5%. Nico and his wife had no investment income for the year.

c. Jody borrowed $25,000 from her controlled corporation for six months. She used the funds to pay her daughter's college tuition. The corporation charged Jody 4% interest. The Federal rate was 5%. Jody had $3,500 of investment income for the year.

d. Kait loaned her son, Jake, $60,000 for six months. Jake used the $60,000 to pay off college loans. The Federal rate was 5%, and Kait did not charge Jake any interest. Jake had dividend and interest income of $2,100 for the tax year.

50. **LO.4** Vito is the sole shareholder of Vito, Inc. He also is employed by the corporation. On June 30, 2022, Vito borrowed $8,000 from Vito, Inc., and on July 1, 2023, he borrowed an additional $10,000. Both loans were due on demand. No interest was charged on the loans, and the Federal rate was 4% for all relevant dates. Vito used the money to purchase a boat, and he had $2,500 of investment income. Determine the tax consequences to Vito and Vito, Inc., in each of the following situations:

a. The loans are considered employer-employee loans.

b. The loans are considered corporation-shareholder loans.

51. **LO.4** Pam retires after 28 years of service with her employer. She is 66 years old and has contributed $42,000 to her employer's qualified pension fund, all of which was taxable when earned. She elects to receive her retirement benefits as an annuity of $3,000 per month for the remainder of her life.

a. Assume that Pam retired in June 2021 and collected six annuity payments that year. What is her gross income from the annuity payments in the first year?

b. Assume that Pam lives 25 years after retiring. What is her gross income from the annuity payments in the twenty-fourth year?

c. Assume that Pam dies after collecting 160 payments. She collected eight payments in the year of her death. What are Pam's gross income and deductions, if any, from the annuity contract in the year of her death?

52. **LO.4** For each of the following, determine the amount that should be included in gross income:

a. Peyton was selected the most valuable player in the Super Bowl. In recognition of this, he was awarded an automobile with a value of $60,000. Peyton did not need the automobile, so he asked that the title be put in his parents' names.

b. Jacob was awarded the Nobel Peace Prize. When he was presented the check for $1,400,000, Jacob said, "I do not need the money. Give it to the United Nations to use toward the goal of world peace."

c. Linda appeared on a television game show during the year, winning $6,000 of cash and $4,000 of furniture and appliances.

53. **LO.2, 4** Herbert was employed for the first six months of 2022 and earned $90,000 in salary. During the next six months, he collected $8,800 of unemployment compensation, borrowed $12,000 (using his personal residence as collateral), and withdrew $2,000 from his savings account (including $60 of interest). He received dividends of $550. His luck was not all bad; in December, he won $1,500 in the lottery on a $5 ticket. Calculate Herbert's gross income.

Decision Making
Planning

54. **LO.4, 5** Linda and Don are married and file a joint return. In 2022, they received $12,000 in Social Security benefits and $35,000 in taxable pension benefits and interest.

a. Compute the couple's adjusted gross income on a joint return.

b. Don would like to know whether they should sell for $100,000 (at no gain or loss) a corporate bond that pays 8% in interest each year and use the proceeds to buy a $100,000 nontaxable State of Virginia bond that will pay $6,000 in interest each year. Assume that their marginal tax rate is 12%.

c. If Linda in part (a) works part-time and earns $30,000, how much will Linda and Don's adjusted gross income increase?

55. **LO.3, 4, 5** Donna does not think she has an income tax problem but would like to discuss her situation with you just to make sure there is no unexpected tax liability. Base your suggestions on the following relevant financial information:

a. Donna's share of the SAT Partnership income is $150,000, but none of the income can be distributed because the partnership needs the cash for operations.

b. Donna's Social Security benefits totaled $8,400, but Donna loaned the cash received to her nephew.

c. Donna assigned to a creditor the right to collect $1,200 of interest on some bonds she owned.

d. Donna and her husband lived together in California until September, when they separated. Donna has heard rumors that her husband had substantial gambling winnings since they separated.

Tax Return Problems

Communications
Decision Making
Tax Forms Problem

ProConnect™ Tax

56. Daniel B. Butler and his spouse Freida C. Butler file a joint return. The Butlers live at 625 Oak Street in Corbin, KY 40701. Dan's Social Security number is 111-11-1112, and Freida's is 123-45-6780. Dan was born on January 15, 1970, and Freida was born on August 20, 1971.

During 2021, Dan and Freida furnished over half of the total support of each of the following individuals, all of whom still live at home:

a. Gina, their daughter, age 22, a full-time student, who married on December 21, has no income of her own and did not file a joint return with her husband, Casey, who earned $10,600 during 2021. Gina's Social Security number is 123-45-6788.

b. Willie, their son, age 19, graduated high school in May 2021. He is taking a leap year and will not begin college until 2022. He had gross income of $6,300 in 2021. Willie's Social Security number is 123-45-6787.

c. Ben, their oldest son, age 26, is a full-time graduate student with gross income of $5,200. Ben's Social Security number is 123-45-6786.

Dan was employed as a manager by WJJJ, Inc. (employer identification number 11-1111111, 604 Franklin Street, Corbin, KY 40702), and Freida was employed as a salesperson for Corbin Realty, Inc. (employer identification number 98-7654321, 899 Central Street, Corbin, KY 40701). Selected information from the W–2 forms provided by the employers is presented below. Dan and Freida use the cash method.

Line	Description	Dan	Freida
1	Wages, tips, other compensation	$74,000	$86,000
2	Federal income tax withheld	11,000	12,400
17	State income tax withheld	2,960	3,440

Freida sold a house on December 30, 2021, and will be paid a commission of $3,100 (not included in the $86,000 reported on the W–2) on the January 10, 2022, closing date.

Other income (as reported on 1099 forms) for 2021 consisted of the following:

Dividends on CSX stock (qualified)	$4,200
Interest on savings at Second Bank	1,600
Interest on City of Corbin bonds	900
Interest on First Bank CD	382

The $382 from First Bank was an original issue discount. Dan and Freida collected $16,000 on the First Bank CD that matured on September 30, 2021. The CD was purchased on October 1, 2018, for $14,995, and the yield to maturity was 3.3%. Dan participated on a game show and won a cash prize of $7,000.

In addition to the above information, Dan and Freida's itemized deductions included the following:

Paid on 2021 Kentucky income tax	$ 700
Personal property tax paid	600
Real estate taxes paid	1,800
Interest on home mortgage (Corbin S&L)	4,900

Sales tax from the sales tax table is $1,860. Dan and Freida made Federal estimated tax payments of $8,000. They have never owned or used any virtual currency, and they do not wish to contribute to the Presidential Election Campaign. For 2021, they received the correct amount of economic impact payments (2021 recovery credits). The Kentucky income tax rate is 4%.

Compute Dan and Freida's 2021 Federal income tax payable (or refund due), and complete their 2021 tax return using the appropriate forms and schedules. Suggested software: ProConnect Tax.

57. Cecil C. Seymour is a 64-year-old widower. He had income for 2022 as follows: Tax Computation Problem

Pension from former employer	$39,850
Interest income from Alto National Bank	5,500
Interest income on City of Alto bonds	4,500
Dividends received from IBM stock held for over one year	2,000
Collections on annuity contract he purchased from Great Life Insurance	5,400
Social Security benefits	14,000
Rent income on townhouse	9,000

The cost of the annuity was $46,800, and Cecil was expected to receive a total of 260 monthly payments of $450. Cecil has received 22 payments through 2022.

Cecil's 40-year-old daughter, Sarah C. Seymour, borrowed $60,000 from Cecil on January 2, 2022. She used the money to start a new business. Cecil does not charge her interest because she cannot afford to pay it, but he does expect to collect the principal eventually. Sarah is living with Cecil until the business becomes profitable. Except for housing, Sarah provides her own support from her business and $1,600 in dividends on stocks that she inherited from her mother.

Other relevant information is presented below.

- Expenses on rental townhouse:

Utilities	$2,800
Maintenance	1,000
Depreciation	2,000
Real estate taxes	750
Insurance	700

- State income taxes paid: $3,500
- County personal property taxes paid: $3,100
- Payments on estimated 2022 Federal income tax: $5,900
- Charitable contributions of cash to Alto Baptist Church: $7,400
- Federal interest rate: 4%
- Sales taxes paid: $912

Compute Cecil's 2022 Federal income tax payable (or refund due).

Research Problems

the answer company™ THOMSON REUTERS®

Note: Solutions to the Research Problems can be prepared by using the Thomson Reuters Checkpoint™ online tax research database, which accompanies this textbook. Solutions can also be prepared by using research materials found in a typical tax library.

Communications

Research Problem 1. Tranquility Funeral Home, Inc., your client, is an accrual basis taxpayer that sells preneed funeral contracts. Under these contracts, the customer pays in advance for goods and services to be provided at the contract beneficiary's death. These payments are refundable at the contract purchaser's request, pursuant to state law, anytime until the goods and services are furnished. Tranquility, consistent with its financial accounting reporting, includes the payments in income for the year the funeral service is provided. The IRS agent insists that the payments be prepaid income subject to tax in the year of receipt. Your client believes that the amounts involved are customer deposits. Write a letter to Tranquility that contains your advice about how the issue should be resolved. The client's address is 400 Rock Street, Memphis, TN 38152.

Research Problem 2. Your client was the beneficiary of an annuity contract purchased by her stepmother. When the stepmother died, the insurance company paid the client $400,000 and sent her a Form 1099 indicating that the taxable portion (i.e., the amount in excess of the investment in the contract) was $50,000. However, according to the client, her father fraudulently convinced her that he was the intended beneficiary. She gave her father a check equal to the amount she had received from the insurance company. She did not report any of the annuity proceeds in her income tax return. She later discovered the fraud and filed a lawsuit to collect from her father. The IRS has examined your client's return and has taken the position that she must include the $50,000 in her gross income.

Evaluate the IRS's position.

Research Problem 3. Your client owns a life insurance policy on his life. He has paid $6,800 in premiums, and the cash surrender value of the policy is $30,000. He borrowed $30,000 from the insurance company, using the cash surrender value as collateral. He is considering canceling the policy in payment of the loan. He would like to know the tax consequences of canceling his policy.

Research Problem 4. Your client is a new retailer who often issues store gift (debit) cards to customers in lieu of a cash refund. You recall that a special rule allows accrual method taxpayers to defer all or a portion of advance payments received. Conduct research to determine if this rule applies to the gift cards issued as refunds for product returns.

Use internet tax resources to address the following questions. Look for reliable websites and blogs of the IRS and other government agencies, media outlets, businesses, tax professionals, academics, think tanks, and political outlets.

Research Problem 5. Lottery winnings are taxable for Federal income tax purposes. What many lottery hopefuls forget to factor into their tax considerations are that lottery winnings are also taxable in many states. Search the internet to see if you can determine whether lottery winnings are taxable for California residents.

Research Problem 6. Go to the web page of a consulting firm that offers counseling services to individuals as they negotiate the terms of a divorce. What specific tax-related services do these firms offer? Suggest a new tax-related service the consulting firm could offer. Communications

Becker CPA Review Questions

Becker

1. Which of the following statements is true regarding the taxation of Social Security benefits?
   a. 85% is the maximum amount of taxable Social Security benefits.
   b. 50% is the maximum amount of taxable Social Security benefits.
   c. If a taxpayer's only source of income is $10,000 of Social Security benefits, then 50% of the benefits are taxable.
   d. If a taxpayer's only source of income is $10,000 of Social Security benefits, then 85% of the benefits are taxable.

2. Fred and Wilma were divorced in year 1 (before 2019). Fred is required to pay Wilma $12,000 of alimony each year until their child turns 18. At that time, the payment will be reduced to $10,000 per year. In year 3, in accordance with the divorce agreement, Fred paid $6,000 directly to Wilma and $6,000 directly to the law school Wilma is attending. What amount of the payments received in year 3 is income to Wilma?
   a. $6,000
   b. $10,000
   c. $12,000
   d. $0

3. Bill and Jane Jones were divorced on January 1, 2018. They have no children. In accordance with the divorce decree, Bill transferred the title of their house over to Jane. The home had a fair market value of $250,000 and was subject to a $100,000 mortgage. Under the divorce agreement, Bill is to make $1,000 monthly mortgage payments on the home for the remainder of the mortgage. In the current year, Bill made 12 mortgage payments. What amount is taxable to Jane in the current year?
   a. $12,000
   b. $250,000
   c. $100,000
   d. $0

4. Jake pays the following amounts to his former spouse during the current year:

Regular alimony payments	$ 12,000
Child support	10,000
Residence as part of a property settlement	115,000

   What amount can Jake deduct as alimony for the current year? Assume that the divorce occurred before 2019.
   a. $0
   b. $12,000
   c. $22,000
   d. $137,000

5. Mary purchased an annuity that pays her $500 per month for the rest of her life. She paid $70,000 for the annuity. Based on IRS annuity tables, Mary's life expectancy is 16 years. How much of the first $500 payment will Mary include in her gross income (round to two decimals)?
   a. $0
   b. $135.42
   c. $364.58
   d. $500.00
6. Which of the following is taxable as gross income?
   a. Child support received based on a divorce agreement executed in 2015.
   b. Alimony received based on a divorce agreement executed in 2015.
   c. Child support received based on a divorce agreement executed in 2019.
   d. Alimony received based on a divorce agreement executed in 2019.
7. Parents lend $2,000,000 to their child to start a business. The loan is interest-free and is payable on demand. The imputed interest is subject to:
   a. The gift tax only in the year the parents lend the money.
   b. The gift tax only in the year the loan is repaid.
   c. The gift tax each year the loan is outstanding.
   d. An excise tax.

Chapter 5

Gross Income: Exclusions

Learning Objectives: *After completing Chapter 5, you should be able to:*

- **LO.1** Explain the difference between exclusions and items that are not income.
- **LO.2** Discuss commonly encountered income exclusions.
- **LO.3** Determine the extent to which receipts can be excluded under the tax benefit rule.
- **LO.4** Identify tax planning strategies for obtaining the maximum benefit from exclusions.

Chapter Outline

5-1 Income Exclusions, 5-2
- 5-1a Exclusion Defined, 5-2
- 5-1b Exclusions versus Non-Income Items, 5-3

5-2 Gifts and Inheritances, 5-3
- 5-2a Legislative Intent, 5-3
- 5-2b Employer Payments to Employees, 5-4
- 5-2c Employee Death Benefits, 5-4

5-3 Life Insurance Proceeds, 5-5
- 5-3a General Rule, 5-5
- 5-3b Accelerated Death Benefits, 5-5
- 5-3c Transfer for Valuable Consideration, 5-6

5-4 Scholarships, 5-7
- 5-4a General Information, 5-7
- 5-4b Timing Issues, 5-8

5-5 Compensation for Injuries and Sickness, 5-8
- 5-5a Damages, 5-8
- 5-5b Wrongful Incarceration, 5-10
- 5-5c Workers' Compensation, 5-10
- 5-5d Accident and Health Insurance Benefits, 5-10

5-6 Employer-Sponsored Accident and Health Plans, 5-11
- 5-6a Medical Reimbursement Plans, 5-11
- 5-6b Long-Term Care Insurance Benefits, 5-12

5-7 Meals and Lodging, 5-13
- 5-7a General Rules for the Exclusion, 5-13
- 5-7b Other Housing Exclusions, 5-14

5-8 Employee Fringe Benefits, 5-14
- 5-8a Specific Benefits, 5-15
- 5-8b Cafeteria Plans, 5-15
- 5-8c Flexible Spending Plans, 5-16
- 5-8d General Classes of Excluded Benefits, 5-16
- 5-8e Group Term Life Insurance, 5-20

5-9 Foreign Earned Income, 5-21

5-10 Interest on Certain State and Local Government Obligations, 5-23

5-11 Educational Savings Bonds, 5-24

5-12 Education Savings Programs (§ 529 and § 530 Plans), 5-25
- 5-12a Qualified Tuition Program, 5-26
- 5-12b Coverdell Education Savings Account, 5-26

5-13 Qualified ABLE Programs (§ 529A Plans), 5-26

5-14 Income from Discharge of Indebtedness, 5-27

5-15 Tax Benefit Rule, 5-28

5-16 Tax Planning, 5-30
- 5-16a Life Insurance, 5-30
- 5-16b Employee Fringe Benefits, 5-30
- 5-16c Investment Income, 5-31

VM/E+/GETTY IMAGES

The Big Picture

Exclusions

Paul is a graduate student in the last semester of the accounting program at State University. This past summer he was an intern with a CPA firm, working in the compliance area. Paul was paid well enough for his work as an intern that he was able to pay for his meals and lodging and to save some for school. The CPA firm was so pleased with Paul's work that at the conclusion of his internship, he was given a bonus of $1,500 more than the firm had agreed to pay him. The extra amount was intended to help with his graduate school expenses. The CPA firm offered him a full-time job after he completes his graduate program in December.

Because of his excellent academic record, the university awarded Paul a graduate assistantship that waives his tuition of $6,000 per semester and pays him $400 per month. Paul is required to teach a principles of accounting course each semester. Paul has used the $400 per month for books and for room and board.

In November, Paul was crossing a street in the pedestrian crosswalk when a delivery van struck him. The driver of the truck was found to be driving under the influence of alcohol. Paul suffered a severe injury to his right arm that delayed his starting date for work by three months. The delivery company's insurance company settled the case by paying the following damages:

Compensatory damages:	
Medical expenses	$ 30,000
Injury to Paul's right arm	100,000
Pain and suffering	50,000
Loss of income	15,000
Legal fees	25,000
Punitive damages	160,000
	$380,000

Paul's mother was with him in the crosswalk. Fortunately, the van did not hit her, and she was not physically injured. But she did suffer emotional distress and received $25,000 in the settlement.

Besides being Paul's friend, you also are a senior accounting major and have a keen interest in taxation. You tell Paul that you will look into the tax consequences of the payments made by the insurance company.

Read the chapter and formulate your response.

Framework 1040 **Tax Formula for Individuals**

This chapter covers the boldfaced portions of the Tax Formula for Individuals that was introduced in Concept Summary 3.1 on p. 3-3. Below those portions are the sections of Form 1040 where the results are reported.

Income *(broadly defined)*	$xx,xxx
Less: Exclusions	**(x,xxx)**

FORM 1040 (p. 1)

2a Tax-exempt interest . . . **2a**   **b** Taxable interest **2b**

Gross income	**$xx,xxx**

FORM 1040 (Schedule 1)

1 Taxable refunds, credits, or offsets of state and local income taxes . . . .
7 Unemployment compensation . . . .
8 Other income: ▶

Less: Deductions *for* adjusted gross income	(x,xxx)
Adjusted gross income	$xx,xxx
Less: The greater of total itemized deductions *or* the standard deduction	(x,xxx)
Charitable contributions if you take the standard deduction*	(xxx)
Personal and dependency exemptions**	(x,xxx)
Deduction for qualified business income***	(x,xxx)
Taxable income	$xx,xxx
Tax on taxable income *(see Tax Tables or Tax Rate Schedules)*	$ x,xxx
Less: Tax credits *(including income taxes withheld and prepaid)*	(xxx)
Tax due (or refund)	$ xxx

* For 2021, married taxpayers may claim up to $600 of cash charitable donations ($300 if unmarried).
** Exemption deductions are not allowed from 2018 through 2025.
*** Only applies from 2018 through 2025.

Chapter 4 discussed the concepts and judicial doctrines that affect the determination of gross income. If an income item is within the all-inclusive definition of gross income, the item can be excluded only if the taxpayer can locate specific authority for doing so. Chapter 5 focuses on the exclusions Congress has authorized. The chapter begins by defining exclusions and distinguishing them from items that are not income.

LO.1

Explain the difference between exclusions and items that are not income.

5-1 Income Exclusions

5-1a Exclusion Defined

Code §§ 101 through 140 provide the authority for excluding specific items from gross income. Exclusion means that something that should be in the tax base is removed per provisions in the tax law. Each exclusion has its own reason for enactment.

Some exclusions are intended as tax relief measures, such as the exclusion on up to $500,000 of gain from sale of a principal residence.[1] Others are to encourage and support certain activities, such as higher education. Some exclusions relate to design of the income tax. For example, damages received for physical injury are excluded under the premise that they are restoring damage to one's body rather than increasing one's personal wealth.[2]

At times, Congress responds to specific events. For example, in 2001, Congress enacted § 139, Disaster Relief Payment, to ensure that victims of a *qualified disaster* (disaster resulting from a terrorist attack, Presidentially declared disaster, or common carrier accident of a catastrophic nature) could exclude from gross income payments received for living expenses, funeral expenses, and property damage resulting from the disaster.

[1] § 121. See Chapter 15.

[2] Other examples include § 117 on certain scholarships and § 104 on physical injury; each is discussed in more detail later in this chapter.

For some types of transactions, the IRS does not tax what is in fact income because the revenue involved is not worth the collection effort or it is too difficult to measure the income. For example, the IRS has decided that it will not attempt to tax the value of frequent flier miles earned on airline tickets purchased for business use.

5-1b Exclusions versus Non-Income Items

Exclusions apply to specified income items. That is, the item must constitute income to possibly warrant an exclusion. For example, a gift you receive from your grandmother is *income* because it is a realized increase in your wealth. However, you'll learn in this chapter that a statutory *exclusion* is related to gifts—making it non-taxable for income tax purposes. A gift is income, but it is excluded (and not part of gross income).

In contrast, when a business borrows money from the bank, that money is not income because there is an offsetting liability to repay the amount. Here, there is no increase in wealth. No exclusion is needed because the loan proceeds are not income in the first place. A return of capital (e.g., a specific type of distribution a shareholder receives from a corporation) is another example of something that is not income.

Corporate Distributions

Corporate distributions are payments to shareholders with respect to their stock (see Chapter 4).

- Distributions are taxed as dividends to shareholders only to the extent the payments are made from *either* the corporation's *current earnings and profits* (similar to net income per books) or its *accumulated earnings and profits* (similar to retained earnings per books).[3]
- Distributions that exceed earnings and profits are treated as a nontaxable recovery of capital and reduce the shareholder's basis in the stock. These distributions are not considered income.
- Once the shareholder's basis is reduced to zero, any subsequent distributions are taxed as capital gains (see Chapters 14 and 20).[4]

When a corporation issues a simple stock dividend (e.g., common stock issued to common shareholders), the shareholder has received additional shares but maintains the same total investment. As a result, the shareholder does not realize income; instead, the per share basis is reduced.[5]

However, if the shareholder has the *option* of receiving either cash or stock in the corporation, the individual realizes gross income whether they receive stock or cash.[6] A taxpayer who elects to receive the stock values the stock dividend by determining the value of the stock received (which could be different from the cash rejected).[7] See Chapter 14 for a discussion of stock dividends.

5-2 Gifts and Inheritances

LO.2

Discuss commonly encountered income exclusions.

5-2a Legislative Intent

From the beginning of the Federal income tax in 1913, Congress has allowed the recipient of a gift to exclude its value from gross income. The exclusion applies to gifts made during the life of the donor (*inter vivos* gifts) and transfers that take effect upon the death of the donor (bequests and inheritances).[8] However, as discussed in Chapter 4, when income-producing property is gifted, the recipient is subject to tax on the income subsequently earned from the property. Also, as discussed in Chapter 1, gift or estate taxes on the transfer might apply.

In many cases, gifts are made in a business setting. For example, a salesperson gives a purchasing agent free samples, an employer gives cash to an employee on retirement,

---

[3] § 316(a). Refer to the discussion of the beneficial tax rates for qualified dividends in Chapter 4.

[4] § 301(c). See Chapter 5, *South-Western Federal Taxation: Corporations, Partnerships, Estates & Trusts*, for a detailed discussion of corporate distributions.

[5] *Eisner v. Macomber*, 1 USTC ¶32, 3 AFTR 3020, 40 S.Ct. 189 (1920); § 305(a).

[6] § 305(b).

[7] Refer to the discussion of constructive receipt in Chapter 4.

[8] § 102.

or a corporation makes payments to employees who were victims of a natural disaster. In these and similar instances, it is frequently unclear whether the payment was a gift or represents compensation for past, present, or future services.

The courts have defined a gift as "a voluntary transfer of property by one to another without adequate [valuable] consideration or compensation therefrom."[9] If the payment is intended to be for services rendered, it is *not* a gift, even though the payment is made without legal or moral obligation and the payor receives no economic benefit from the transfer. To qualify as a gift, the payment must be made "out of affection, respect, admiration, charity or like impulses."[10] As a result, these cases have been decided by looking at the donor's intent.

In a landmark case, *Comm. v. Duberstein*,[11] the taxpayer (Duberstein) received a Cadillac from a business acquaintance. Duberstein had supplied the businessman with the names of potential customers with no expectation of compensation. The Supreme Court concluded:

> ... despite the characterization of the transfer of the Cadillac by the parties [as a gift] and the absence of any obligation, even of a moral nature, to make it, it was at the bottom a recompense for Duberstein's past service, or an inducement for him to be of further service in the future.

As a result, Duberstein was required to include the fair market value of the car in gross income.

5-2b Employer Payments to Employees

In the case of cash or other property *received by an employee* from an employer, Congress has eliminated any ambiguity. Transfers from an employer to an employee cannot be excluded as a gift.[12]

The Big Picture

Example 1

Return to the facts of *The Big Picture* on p. 5-1. The $1,500 bonus paid to Paul by his summer employer was compensation for his services rather than a gift, even though the employer had not contracted to pay this additional amount. This results because the payment was most likely not motivated by the employer's generosity, but rather was made as a result of business considerations. Even if the payment had been made out of generosity, because the payment was received from his employer, Paul could not exclude the "gift."

5-2c Employee Death Benefits

An employer may make payments (**death benefits**) to a deceased employee's surviving spouse, children, or other beneficiaries. If the decedent had a nonforfeitable right to the payments (e.g., the decedent's accrued salary), the amounts are generally taxable to the recipient as if the employee had lived and collected the payments. Many employers provide group-term life insurance for employees in order to provide assistance to the deceased employee's family. If the employer makes voluntary payments (not accrued wages, a late paid bonus, or life insurance proceeds) to the family of the deceased employee, the facts and circumstances must be evaluated to determine if the payments are a nontaxable gift or additional compensation attributable to the deceased employee.[13]

---

[9] *Estate of D. R. Daly*, 3 B.T.A. 1042 (1926).

[10] *Robertson v. U.S.*, 52–1 USTC ¶9343, 41 AFTR 1053, 72 S.Ct. 994.

[11] 60–2 USTC ¶9515, 5 AFTR 2d 1626, 80 S.Ct. 1190.

[12] § 102(c). But see § 139 for qualified disaster situations.

[13] Rev.Rul. 62–102, *Estate of Sydney J. Carter v. Comm.*, 72–1 USTC ¶9129, 29 AFTR 2d 332, 453 F.2d 61 (CA–2), and *Simpson v. U.S.*, 58–2 USTC ¶9923, 2 AFTR 2d 6036, 261 F.2d 497 (CA–7), *cert. denied* 79 S.Ct. 724 (1959).

Income earned by an employee that was not received by the employee prior to their death is not an employee death benefit. These earnings are referred to as "income in respect of a decedent"[14] and are generally taxable income to the decedent's beneficiary. This is another rare instance where the beneficiary of the income, rather than the person who earned the income, is subject to tax.

5-3 Life Insurance Proceeds

5-3a General Rule

Life insurance proceeds paid to the beneficiary because of the death of the insured are excluded from gross income.[15]

Example 2

Linda purchases an insurance policy on her life and names her husband, Tyler, as the beneficiary. Linda pays $45,000 in premiums. When she dies, Tyler collects the insurance proceeds of $200,000. The $200,000 is excluded from Tyler's gross income (and exempt from Federal income tax).

Congress believed it was good tax policy to exclude life insurance proceeds for the following reasons:

- For family members, life insurance proceeds serve much the same purpose as a nontaxable inheritance.
- In a business context (as well as in a family situation), life insurance proceeds replace an economic loss suffered by the business.

Example 3

Gold Corporation purchases a life insurance policy to cover its CEO (a key employee). If the proceeds were taxable, the corporation would require more insurance coverage to pay the tax as well as to cover the economic loss of the employee.

5-3b Accelerated Death Benefits

Generally, if the owner of a life insurance policy cancels the policy and receives the cash surrender value, the taxpayer must recognize gain equal to the excess of the amount received over premiums paid on the policy (a loss is not deductible). The gain is recognized because the proceeds were *not* paid on the death of the insured. If the taxpayer cancels the policy and receives the cash surrender value, the life insurance policy is treated as an investment by the insured.

In a limited circumstance, however, the insured is permitted to receive the benefits of the life insurance contract without having to include the gain in gross income. Under the **accelerated death benefits** rules, an exclusion is available for insured taxpayers who are either terminally ill or chronically ill.[16] A terminally ill taxpayer can collect the cash surrender value of the policy from the insurance company or assign the policy proceeds to a qualified third party. The resulting gain, if any, is excluded from the insured's gross income. A person is *terminally ill* if a medical doctor certifies that death is likely to occur within 24 months.

In the case of a chronically ill patient, no gain is recognized if the proceeds of the policy are used for the patient's long-term care. A person is *chronically ill* if they are

[14] § 691.

[15] § 101(a).

[16] § 101(g); reporting may be required per § 6050Y.

certified as needing assistance to perform certain activities of daily living. These exclusions for the terminally ill and the chronically ill are available only to the insured. A person who purchases a life insurance policy from the insured does not qualify.

Accelerated Death Benefits

Example 4

Tom owned a term life insurance policy at the time he was diagnosed as having a terminal illness. After paying $5,200 in premiums, he sold the policy to Amber Benefits, Inc., a company that is authorized by the state of Virginia to purchase such policies. Amber paid Tom $50,000. When Tom died six months later, Amber collected the face amount of the policy, $75,000. Tom is not required to include the $44,800 gain ($50,000 − $5,200) on the sale of the policy in his gross income.

Example 5

Assume that Amber Benefits, Inc., in Example 4 paid additional premiums of $4,000 during the six months it owned the policy. When Amber collects the life insurance proceeds of $75,000, it must include the $21,000 gain [$75,000 proceeds − ($50,000 cost + $4,000 additional premiums paid)] in gross income.

Ethics & Equity **Should the Terminally Ill Pay Social Security Taxes?**

The rationale for excluding accelerated death benefits from the gross income of the terminally ill is that they often use the funds to pay medical expenses and other costs associated with dying and do not have the ability to pay tax on the gain from the accelerated receipt of the life insurance proceeds. Yet the wages of a terminally ill person who is employed (or profits of a self-employed person) are subject to Social Security taxes. The Social Security taxes are intended to pay for retirement benefits, but a terminally ill person is unlikely to collect any Social Security benefits.

Bills have been introduced in Congress to exempt the terminally ill from the Social Security tax. Evaluate the equity of the current tax treatment versus that in the proposed legislation.

5-3c Transfer for Valuable Consideration

A life insurance policy (other than one associated with accelerated death benefits) may be transferred after it is issued by the insurance company. If the policy is *transferred for valuable consideration*, the insurance proceeds are includible in the gross income of the purchaser to the extent the proceeds received exceed the amount paid for the policy plus any subsequent premiums paid.

Example 6

Adam pays premiums of $4,000 for an insurance policy that has a face amount of $10,000 on the life of Brianna and subsequently transfers the policy to Carol for $6,000. Upon Brianna's death, Carol receives the proceeds of $10,000.

The amount Carol can exclude from gross income is limited to $6,000 plus any premiums she paid subsequent to the transfer.

The Code, however, provides five exceptions to the rule illustrated in Example 6. Exclusion treatment is allowed for transfers to the following:

1. The insured under the policy.
2. A partner of the insured.
3. A partnership in which the insured is a partner.
4. A corporation in which the insured is an officer or a shareholder.
5. A transferee whose basis in the policy is determined by reference to the transferor's basis.

The fifth exception applies to policies that were transferred in a tax-free exchange or were received by gift.[17]

[17] § 101(a)(2). See the discussion of gifts in Chapter 14 and tax-free exchanges in Chapters 15 and 20. In the case of a gift, the donor's basis becomes the donee's basis.

Example 7

When Logan's daughter Emily was born, he purchased an insurance policy on her life. Twenty-four years later after Emily graduated from college and married, Logan sold her the policy for its fair value. When Emily dies, the transfer for consideration rules will not apply.

Because the transfer was to the insured, the policy proceeds paid to Emily's beneficiaries will be excluded from the recipient's gross income. The results would be the same if Logan gave (rather than sold) the policy to Emily.

Investment earnings arising from the reinvestment of life insurance proceeds are generally subject to income tax. Often the beneficiary will elect to collect the insurance proceeds in installments. The annuity rules (discussed in text Section 4-4c) are used to apportion the installment payment between the principal element (excludible) and the interest element (includible).[18]

5-4 Scholarships

5-4a General Information

Payments or benefits received by a student at an educational institution may be (1) compensation for services, (2) a gift, or (3) a scholarship. If the payments or benefits are received as compensation for services (past or present), the fact that the recipient is a student generally does not render the amounts received nontaxable.[19] A university teaching or research assistant is generally considered an employee, and a stipend is taxable compensation. On the other hand, athletic scholarships generally are nontaxable when the individual is expected (but not required) to participate in the sport.[20] Unless received from family members, amounts received for educational purposes cannot be excluded as gifts because conditions usually attached to the funds mean that the payments were not made out of "detached generosity."

The **scholarship** rules are intended to provide exclusion treatment for education-related benefits that cannot qualify as gifts but are not compensation for services. To be excluded from income, the scholarship must be used for qualified tuition and related expenses (e.g., books and supplies).[21] The recipient must be a candidate for a degree at an educational institution.[22]

Example 8

Aliyah enters a contest sponsored by a local newspaper. Each contestant is required to submit an essay on local environmental issues. The prize is one year's tuition at State University. Aliyah wins the contest. The newspaper has a legal obligation to Aliyah (as contest winner). As a result, the benefits are not a gift. However, because the tuition payment aids Aliyah in pursuing her studies, the payment is a scholarship.

If a nonprofit educational institution provides tuition reductions for its employees, the employees can exclude these amounts from their gross income. The exclusion also applies to tuition reductions granted to the employee's spouse and the employee's dependent children. In general, the exclusion applies only to education below the graduate level. However, tuition reductions for graduate students who are engaged in teaching or research activities at the educational institution also qualify for the exclusion.[23]

The Big Picture

Example 9

Return to the facts of *The Big Picture* on p. 5-1. Paul was paid $400 a month by the university for teaching. This is reasonable compensation for his services. Although he received the assistantship because of his excellent academic record, the monthly payment of $400 must be included in his gross income because it is compensation for his services. However, the $6,000 graduate tuition reduction can be excluded from gross income.

[18] Reg. §§ 1.72–7(c)(1) and 1.101–7.

[19] Reg. § 1.117–2(a). See *C. P. Bhalla*, 35 T.C. 13 (1960), for a discussion of the distinction between a scholarship and compensation. See also *Bingler v. Johnson*, 69–1 USTC ¶9348, 23 AFTR 2d 1212, 89 S.Ct. 1439. For potential exclusion treatment, see the subsequent discussion of qualified tuition reductions.

[20] Rev.Rul. 77–263.

[21] § 117(b).

[22] § 117(a).

[23] § 117(d).

The exclusion for qualified scholarships does not apply to room and board.[24] The NCAA allows athletic scholarships to include a "cost of attendance" amount. In addition to tuition, fees, books, and room and board, an athletic scholarship can include expenses like academic-related supplies, transportation, and other similar items. The value of these benefits may differ from campus to campus. However, only the amounts received for tuition, books, and supplies can be excluded from gross income.

Example 10

Kelly received an athletic scholarship from State University. The scholarship pays her tuition of $9,000 and books and supplies of $2,400. She also receives $4,500 a year for costs of attendance, which she uses to pay for housing, food, laundry, and transportation.

The tuition and the cost of books and supplies are excluded from gross income as a qualified scholarship. The $4,500 received as costs of attendance does not qualify for the scholarship exclusion, and Kelly must include that amount in her gross income.

Some employers make scholarships available solely to the children of key employees. The tax objective of these plans is to provide a nontaxable fringe benefit to the executives by making the payment to the child in the form of an excludible scholarship. However, the IRS has ruled that the payments are generally includible in the gross income of the parent-employee.[25]

5-4b Timing Issues

Frequently, the scholarship recipient is a cash basis taxpayer who receives the money in one tax year but pays the educational expenses in a subsequent year. The amount eligible for exclusion may not be known at the time the money is received. In that case, the transaction is held *open* until the educational expenses are paid.[26]

Example 11

In August 2022, Sanjay received a $10,000 scholarship for the 2022–2023 academic year. Sanjay's expenditures for tuition, books, and supplies were as follows:

August–December 2022	$3,000
January–May 2023	4,500
	$7,500

Sanjay's gross income for 2023 includes $2,500 ($10,000 − $7,500) that is not excludible as a scholarship. None of the scholarship is included in his gross income in 2022.

5-5 Compensation for Injuries and Sickness

5-5a Damages

A person who suffers harm caused by another is often entitled to compensatory damages. The tax consequences of the damages awarded depend on the type of harm the taxpayer experienced. The taxpayer may seek recovery for (1) a loss of income, (2) expenses incurred, (3) property destroyed, or (4) personal injury.

Generally, reimbursement for a loss of income is taxed the same as the income replaced (see the exception under Personal Injury below). The recovery of an expense is not income unless the expense was deducted; if the expense was deducted, the damages generally are taxable under the tax benefit rule, discussed later in this chapter.

A payment for damaged or destroyed property is treated as an amount received in a sale or exchange of the property. As a result, the taxpayer has a realized gain if the damages received exceed the property's basis. Damages for personal injuries receive special treatment under the Code.

[24] § 117(b). See also **irs.gov/newsroom/tax-benefits-for-education-information-center**.

[25] Rev.Rul. 75–448; *Richard T. Armantrout*, 67 T.C. 996 (1977).

[26] Prop.Reg. § 1.117–6(b)(2).

Personal Injury

The legal theory of personal injury damages is that the amount received is intended "to make the plaintiff [the injured party] whole as before the injury."[27] It follows that if the damages payments received were subject to tax, the after-tax amount received would be less than the actual damages incurred and the injured party would not be "whole as before the injury." In terms of personal injury damages, a distinction is made between compensatory damages and punitive damages.

Ethics & Equity — Tax Treatment of Damages Not Related to Physical Personal Injury

An individual who prevails in a personal injury claim for something other than a physical injury or sickness must include the amount of the award or settlement in gross income. In contrast, an award or a settlement for a physical personal injury or sickness can be excluded (except for punitive damages) from gross income. Should damages awarded for a physical personal injury or sickness be treated more favorably than damages awarded for emotional distress or other nonphysical personal injuries such as age and sex discrimination?

Compensatory damages are intended to compensate the taxpayer for the damages incurred. Only those compensatory damages received for *physical personal injury or physical sickness* can be excluded from gross income.[28] This includes amounts received for loss of income associated with the physical personal injury or physical sickness.[29] Compensatory damages awarded for emotional distress cannot be excluded (except to the extent of any amount received for medical care) from gross income. Likewise, any amounts received for age discrimination or injury to one's reputation cannot be excluded.

Punitive damages are amounts the person who caused the harm must pay to the victim as punishment for the bad conduct. Punitive damages are not intended to compensate the victim, but rather to punish the party who caused the harm. So amounts received as punitive damages may actually place the victim in a better economic position than before the harm was experienced. As a result, punitive damages are included in gross income.

These rules are summarized in Concept Summary 5.1.

Concept Summary 5.1

Taxation of Damages

Type of Claim	Taxation of Award or Settlement
Breach of contract (generally loss of income)	Taxable.
Property damages	Gain to the extent damages received exceed basis. A loss is deductible for business property and investment property to the extent of basis over the amount realized. In certain cases, a loss may be deductible for personal use property (see discussion of casualty losses in Chapter 7).
Personal injury	
Physical	All compensatory amounts are excluded unless previously deducted (e.g., medical expenses). Amounts received as punitive damages are included in gross income.
Nonphysical	Compensatory damages and punitive damages are included in gross income.

[27] *C. A. Hawkins*, 6 B.T.A. 1023 (1927).

[28] § 104(a)(2).

[29] Rev.Rul. 85–97.

The Big Picture

Example 12

Return to the facts of *The Big Picture* on p. 5-1. The damages Paul received were awarded as a result of a physical personal injury. As a result, all of the compensatory damages can be excluded. Note that even the compensation for the loss of income of $15,000 can be excluded. The punitive damages Paul received, however, must be included in his gross income.

Paul's mother did not suffer a personal physical injury or sickness. So the $25,000 she received must be included in her gross income.

Ethics & Equity — Classifying the Amount of the Claim

Lee was injured in an automobile accident caused by a negligent driver of a commercial vehicle. Lee threatened to file a lawsuit against the company for $100,000 in damages for his physical injury and $100,000 for punitive damages. The company's insurer would not pay punitive damages. As a result, the company advised Lee to revise his claim for $150,000 in physical damages and no punitive damages. Should Lee accept the offer?

5-5b Wrongful Incarceration

Code § 139F exempts amounts received as damages for being wrongfully incarcerated. The exclusion applies to an individual convicted of a Federal or state crime who is later exonerated.

5-5c Workers' Compensation

State workers' compensation laws require the employer to pay fixed amounts for specific job-related injuries. The state laws were enacted to allow the employee to recover the damages without suing the employer. Although the payments are intended, in part, to compensate for a loss of future income, Congress has specifically excluded workers' compensation benefits from gross income.[30]

5-5d Accident and Health Insurance Benefits

The income tax treatment of accident and health insurance benefits depends on whether the policy providing the benefits was purchased by the taxpayer or the taxpayer's employer. Benefits collected under an accident and health insurance policy *purchased by the taxpayer* are excludible even though the payments are a substitute for income.[31]

Tax-Exempt Benefits

Example 13

Quynh purchases a medical and disability insurance policy. The insurance company pays Quynh $1,000 per week to replace wages she loses while in the hospital. Although the payments serve as a substitute for income, the amounts received are tax-exempt benefits collected under Quynh's insurance policy.

Example 14

Joe's injury results in a partial paralysis of his left foot. He receives $20,000 for the injury from his accident insurance company under a policy he had purchased. The $20,000 accident insurance proceeds are tax-exempt.

[30] § 104(a)(1).

[31] § 104(a)(3).

A different set of rules applies if the accident and health insurance protection was *purchased by the individual's employer*, as discussed in the following section.

5-6 Employer-Sponsored Accident and Health Plans

Congress encourages employers to provide employees, retired former employees, and their dependents with **accident and health benefits**, disability insurance, and long-term care plans. The *premiums* are deductible by the employer and excluded from the employee's income.[32] Although § 105(a) provides the general rule that the employee has includible income when they collect the insurance *benefits*, two exceptions are provided.

Code § 105(b) generally excludes payments received for medical care of the employee, spouse, and dependents. However, if the payments are for expenses that do not meet the Code's definition of medical care,[33] the amount received must be included in gross income. In addition, the taxpayer must include in gross income any amounts received for medical expenses that were deducted by the taxpayer on a prior return.

Example 15

In 2022, Branden's employer-sponsored health insurance plan pays $4,000 for hair transplants that do not meet the Code's definition of medical care. Branden must include the $4,000 in his gross income for 2022.

Code § 105(c) excludes payments for the permanent loss or the loss of the use of a member or function of the body or the permanent disfigurement of the employee, the spouse, or a dependent. Payments that are a substitute for salary (e.g., related to the period of time absent) are includible.

Example 16

Jill loses an eye in an automobile accident unrelated to her work. As a result of the accident, Jill incurs $2,000 of medical expenses, which she deducts on her return. She collects $100,000 from an accident insurance policy carried by her employer. The benefits are paid according to a schedule of amounts that vary with the part of the body injured (e.g., $100,000 for loss of an eye and $150,000 for loss of a hand).

Because the payment is for loss of a *member or function of the body*, the $100,000 is excluded from gross income. Jill is absent from work for several weeks as a result of the accident. Her employer provides her with insurance for the loss of income due to illness or injury. Jill collects $7,500, and this amount is includible in her gross income.

5-6a Medical Reimbursement Plans

As discussed above, amounts received through the insurance coverage (insured plan benefits) are excluded from income under § 105 or § 106. Instead of providing the employee with insurance coverage for hospital and medical expenses, the employer may agree to reimburse the employee for these expenses (a self-insured arrangement). Generally, the benefits received under a self-insured plan can be excluded from the employee's income if the plan does not discriminate in favor of highly compensated employees.[34]

[32] § 106, Reg. § 1.106–1, and Rev.Rul. 82–196.

[33] See the discussion of medical care in Chapter 10.

[34] § 105(h). Also see § 106 and Rev.Rul. 61–146. Employers should make sure such reimbursement plans fall within the requirements of the Affordable Care Act to avoid an excise tax. See § 4980D, Notice 2013–54 and Notice 2015–17. Also see rules on Qualified Small Employer Health Reimbursement Arrangements (QSEHRA) at § 9831(d) and Notice 2017–67.

There is also an alternative means of accomplishing a medical reimbursement plan. The employer can purchase a medical insurance plan with a high deductible (e.g., the employee is responsible for the first $2,800 of the family's medical expenses) and then make contributions to the employee's **Health Savings Account (HSA)**.[35] The employer can make contributions each month up to the maximum contribution of 100 percent of the deductible amount. The monthly deductible amount is limited to one-twelfth of $3,650 under a high-deductible plan for self-only coverage. The monthly amount for an individual who has family coverage is limited to one-twelfth of $7,300 under a high-deductible plan. Withdrawals from the HSA must be used to reimburse the employee for the medical expenses paid by the employee that are not covered under the high-deductible plan. The employee is not taxed on the employer's contributions to the HSA, the earnings on the funds in the account, or the withdrawals made for medical expenses.[36]

5-6b Long-Term Care Insurance Benefits

Generally, **long-term care insurance**, which covers expenses such as the cost of care in a nursing home, is treated the same as accident and health insurance benefits. As a result, the employee does not recognize income when the employer pays the premiums. Also, the individual who purchases his or her own policy can exclude the benefits from gross income. However, the Code specifies limits (annually indexed for inflation) for the following amounts:

- Premiums paid by the employer.
- Benefits collected under the employer's plan.
- Benefits collected from the individual's policy.

The employer or insurance company generally provides the employee with information on the amount of his or her taxable benefits. The maximum amount excluded must be reduced by any amount received from third parties (e.g., Medicare, Medicaid).[37]

Example 17

Hazel, who suffers from Alzheimer's disease, is a patient in a nursing home for the last 30 days of 2022. While in the nursing home, she incurs total costs of $8,400. Medicare pays $3,800 of the costs. Hazel receives $8,400 from her long-term care insurance policy, which pays benefits while she is in the nursing home. In 2022, $390 per day of long-term care benefits is excludible from gross income.

The amount Hazel may exclude is calculated as follows:

Greater of:		
Daily excludible amount in 2022 ($390 × 30 days)	$11,700	
Actual cost of the care	8,400	$11,700
Less: Amount received from Medicare		(3,800)
Available exclusion amount		$ 7,900

As a result, Hazel must include $500 ($8,400 − $7,900) of the long-term care benefits received in her gross income.

The exclusion for long-term care insurance is not available if it is provided as part of a cafeteria plan or a flexible spending plan (explained later in the chapter).

[35] §§ 106(d) and 223. See additional coverage in Chapter 10.

[36] §§ 106(d), 223(b), and 223(d). The 2022 inflation-adjusted amounts are published in Rev.Proc. 2021–25. The amounts for 2021 were $3,600 and $7,200.

[37] §§ 7702B and 213(d)(10). See IRS Publication 525 for the taxable and nontaxable amounts that the employer is required to report on the employee's W–2.

5-7 Meals and Lodging

5-7a General Rules for the Exclusion

As discussed in Chapter 4, income can take any form, including meals and lodging. However, § 119 excludes from income the value of meals and lodging provided to the employee and the employee's spouse and dependents under the following conditions:[38]

- The meals and/or lodging are *furnished* by the employer on the employer's *business premises* for the *convenience of the employer*. From 2018 through 2025, the employer may only deduct 50 percent of the cost of the meals provided.[39] After 2025, employers may not claim any deduction for these meals. If the employer continues to provide such meals, their value remains as an exclusion for the employees.
- In the case of lodging, the *employee is required* to accept the lodging as a condition of employment.

The courts have interpreted these requirements strictly.

Furnished by the Employer

The following two questions have been raised with regard to the *furnished by the employer* requirement:

- Who is considered an *employee*?
- What is meant by *furnished*?

The IRS and some courts have reasoned that because a partner is not an employee, the exclusion does not apply to a partner. However, the Tax Court and the Fifth Circuit Court of Appeals disagree with this conclusion.[40]

The Supreme Court held that a cash meal allowance was ineligible for the exclusion because the employer did not actually furnish the meals. Similarly, one court denied the exclusion where the employer paid for the food and supplied the cooking facilities but the employee prepared the meal.[41]

On the Employer's Business Premises

The *on the employer's business premises* requirement, applicable to both meals and lodging, has resulted in much litigation. The Regulations define business premises as simply "the place of employment of the employee."[42] The Sixth Circuit Court of Appeals held that a residence, owned by the employer and occupied by an employee, two blocks from the motel that the employee managed was *not* part of the business premises.[43] However, the Tax Court considered an employer-owned house across the street from the hotel that was managed by the taxpayer to be on the business premises of the employer.[44] Apparently, the closer the lodging is to the business operations, the more likely the convenience of the employer is served.

---

[38] § 119(a). The value of the meals and lodging is also excluded from FICA and FUTA tax. *Rowan Companies, Inc. v. U.S.*, 81–1 USTC ¶9479, 48 AFTR 2d 81–5115, 101 S.Ct. 2288.

[39] For 2021 and 2022, taxpayers can deduct 100% of meals provided by a restaurant. § 274(n)(2)(D).

[40] Rev.Rul. 80; *Comm. v. Doak*, 56–2 USTC ¶9708, 49 AFTR 1491, 234 F.2d 704 (CA–4); but see *G. A. Papineau*, 16 T.C. 130 (1951); *Armstrong v. Phinney*, 68–1 USTC ¶9355, 21 AFTR 2d 1260, 394 F.2d 661 (CA–5).

[41] *Comm. v. Kowalski*, 77–2 USTC ¶9748, 40 AFTR 2d 6128, 98 S.Ct. 315; *Tougher v. Comm.*, 71–1 USTC ¶9398, 27 AFTR 2d 1301, 441 F.2d 1148 (CA–9).

[42] Reg. § 1.119–1(c)(1).

[43] *Comm. v. Anderson*, 67–1 USTC ¶9136, 19 AFTR 2d 318, 371 F.2d 59 (CA–6, 1966).

[44] *J. B. Lindeman*, 60 T.C. 609 (1973).

For the Convenience of the Employer

The *convenience of the employer* test is intended to focus on the employer's motivation for furnishing the meals and lodging rather than on the benefits received by the employee. If the employer furnishes the meals and lodging primarily to enable the employee to perform any required duties properly, the "convenience" test is met.

The Regulations give the following examples where the "convenience" test is met:[45]

- A restaurant requires its service staff to eat their meals on the premises during the busy lunch and breakfast hours.
- A bank furnishes meals on the premises for its tellers to limit the time the employees are away from their booths during the busy hours.
- A worker is employed at a construction site in a remote part of Alaska. The employer must furnish meals and lodging due to the inaccessibility of other facilities.

Required as a Condition of Employment

The *required as a condition of employment* test applies only to lodging. If the employee's use of the housing would serve the convenience of the employer but the employee is not required to use the housing, the exclusion is not available.

Example 18

Khalid is the manager of a large apartment complex. The employer requires Khalid to live on the premises but does not charge him rent. The rental value of his apartment is $9,600 a year. Although Khalid considers the rent-free housing a significant benefit, he is not required to include the value of the housing in his gross income.

5-7b Other Housing Exclusions

An employee of an educational institution may be able to exclude the value of campus housing provided by the employer. If the employee pays annual rents equal to or greater than 5 percent of the appraised value of the facility, the housing benefit may be excluded. If the rent payments are less than 5 percent of the value of the facility, the deficiency must be included in gross income.[46]

Ministers of the gospel and other religious leaders can exclude (1) the rental value of a home furnished as compensation; (2) a rental allowance paid to them as compensation, to the extent the allowance is used to rent, buy, or provide a home; or (3) the rental value of a home owned by the minister.[47] The housing or housing allowance must be provided as compensation for the conduct of religious worship, the administration and maintenance of religious organizations, or the performance of teaching and administrative duties at theological seminaries.

Military personnel are allowed housing exclusions under various circumstances. Authority for these exclusions generally is found in Federal laws that are not part of the Internal Revenue Code.[48]

5-8 Employee Fringe Benefits

Benefits other than wages and salary that are provided to employees by the employer are often referred to as **fringe benefits**. Generally, Congress decided that the availability of these benefits serves social goals. In addition, providing an income tax

[45] Reg. § 1.119–1(f).

[46] § 119(d).

[47] § 107 and Reg. § 1.107–1.

[48] H. Rep. No. 99–841, 99th Cong., 2d Sess., p. 548 (1986). See § 134 and *Armed Forces Tax Guide* (IRS Publication 3).

exclusion provides an incentive for employees to bargain for these nontaxable fringe benefits instead of taxable compensation. For example, if the employee is in the 22 percent marginal tax bracket, $100 of nontaxable fringe benefits is equivalent to $128 [$\$100 \div (1-0.22) = \$128$] in taxable compensation. From the employer's perspective then, it costs only $100 to provide $128 in value to that employee in the form of a tax-favored fringe benefit.

In Chapter 4 and earlier in this chapter, various fringe benefits were discussed (e.g., accident and health insurance and meals and lodging). Other employee benefits are discussed below.

5-8a **Specific Benefits**

Congress has dealt specifically with some other fringe benefits, which are summarized below.

- An employee does not have to include in gross income the value of child and dependent care services paid for by the employer and incurred to enable the employee to work. In 2022, the exclusion cannot exceed $5,000 per year ($2,500 if married and filing separately); these amounts were $10,500 and $5,250, respectively, in 2021. For a married couple, the annual exclusion cannot exceed the earned income of the spouse with the smaller amount of earned income. For an unmarried taxpayer, the exclusion cannot exceed the taxpayer's earned income.[49]
- The value of the use of a gymnasium or other athletic facilities by employees, their spouses, and their dependent children may be excluded from an employee's gross income. The facilities must be on the employer's premises, and substantially all of the use of the facilities must be by employees and their family members.[50]
- Qualified employer-provided educational assistance (tuition, fees, books, and supplies) at the undergraduate and graduate levels is excludible from gross income. Through 2025, eligible assistance includes principal and interest on a student loan. An employee can exclude a maximum of $5,250 per year.[51] The exclusion does not cover meals, lodging, and transportation costs. In addition, it does not cover educational payments for courses involving sports, games, or hobbies.
- If an employer has a qualified adoption assistance program, an employee can exclude up to $14,890 of adoption expenses that are paid or reimbursed by the employer.[52] If the child has special needs (is not physically or mentally capable of caring for themselves), the $14,890 exclusion from gross income applies even if the actual adoption expenses are less than that amount. For 2022, the exclusion is phased out as adjusted gross income increases from $223,410 to $263,410.

5-8b **Cafeteria Plans**

Generally, if an employee is offered a choice between cash and some other form of compensation, the employee is deemed to have constructively received the cash even when the noncash option is elected. As a result, the employee has gross income regardless of the option chosen.

An exception to this constructive receipt treatment is provided under the **cafeteria plan** rules. Under these plans, the employee can choose between cash and nontaxable benefits (e.g., group term life insurance, health and accident protection, child care). If the employee chooses nontaxable benefits, the cafeteria plan rules enable the benefits

[49] § 129. The exclusion applies to the same types of expenses that, if paid by the employee (and not reimbursed by the employer), would be eligible for the credit for child and dependent care expense discussed in Chapter 13.

[50] § 132(j)(4).

[51] § 127.

[52] § 137. A credit is also available under § 23, as discussed in Chapter 13.

to remain nontaxable.[53] Cafeteria plans provide tremendous flexibility in tailoring the employee pay package to fit individual needs. Some employees (usually younger employees) prefer cash, while others (usually older employees) will opt for the fringe benefit program.

Example 19

Hawk Corporation offers its employees (on a nondiscriminatory basis) a choice of any one or all of the following benefits:

Benefit	Cost
Group term life insurance	$ 200
Hospitalization insurance for family members	2,400
Child care payments	1,800
	$4,400

If a benefit is not selected, the employee receives cash equal to the cost of the benefit. Kay, an employee, has a spouse who works for another employer that provides hospitalization insurance but no child care payments. Kay elects to receive the group term life insurance, the child care payments, and $2,400 of cash. Only the $2,400 must be included in Kay's gross income.

5-8c Flexible Spending Plans

Flexible spending plans (often referred to as flexible benefit plans) operate much like cafeteria plans. Under these plans, the employee accepts lower cash compensation in return for the employer agreeing to pay certain costs that would normally be excludible from the employee's income. An annual inflation-adjusted cap applies to these plans ($2,850 in 2022).

For example, assume that the employer's health insurance policy does not cover dental expenses. Under a flexible spending plan, an employee estimates any dental expenses for the upcoming year and agrees to a salary reduction equal to the estimated dental expenses. The employer then pays or reimburses the employee for the actual dental expenses incurred, with a ceiling of the amount of the salary reduction. If the employee's actual dental expenses are less than the reduction in cash compensation, the employee cannot recover the difference. As a result, these plans are often called *use or lose* plans. To avoid the loss of unpaid amounts, the IRS allows a payment until two and a half months after the end of the plan year to count (March 15 for calendar year plans). Flexible spending plans cannot be used to pay long-term care insurance premiums (this is also the case for cafeteria plans).

5-8d General Classes of Excluded Benefits

An employer can provide many forms and types of economic benefits to employees. Under the all-inclusive concept of income, the benefits are taxable unless the Code specifically excludes the item from gross income. The amount of the income is the fair market value of the benefit.

Example 20

Ryan is employed in New York as a ticket clerk for Trans National Airlines. He has a sick mother in Miami, Florida, but has no money for plane tickets. Trans National has daily flights from New York to Miami that often leave with empty seats. The cost of a round-trip ticket is $400.

In general, if Trans National allows Ryan to fly without charge to Miami, Ryan has income equal to the value of a ticket ($400). However, as discussed below, this is one of several classes of excluded benefits allowed under the tax law.

[53] § 125.

Because Congress believed that taxing fringe benefits often yielded harsh results, § 132 was enacted to provide gross income exclusions for eight broad classes of employee benefits:[54]

- No-additional-cost services.
- Qualified employee discounts.
- Working condition fringes.
- *De minimis* fringes.
- Qualified transportation fringes.
- Qualified moving expense reimbursements.
- Qualified retirement planning services.
- Qualified military base realignment and closure fringes.

No-Additional-Cost Services

The value of the services that the employer provides its employees is nontaxable under certain circumstances. Example 20 above illustrates the reason for the **no-additional-cost service** type of fringe benefit. The services are excludible from the employee's gross income if all of the following conditions are satisfied:

- The employee receives services, as opposed to property.
- The employer does not incur substantial additional cost, including forgone revenue, in providing the services to the employee.
- The services are offered to customers in the ordinary course of the business in which the employee works.[55]

Example 21

In Example 20, although the airplane may burn slightly more fuel because Ryan is on board and he may receive the same snacks as paying customers, the additional costs to the airline are *not* substantial. As a result, the flight qualifies as a no-additional-cost service, and the value of Ryan's flight is excluded from his gross income.

The no-additional-cost exclusion extends to the employee's spouse and dependent children and to retired and disabled former employees.[56] However, the exclusion is not allowed to highly compensated employees unless the benefit is available on a nondiscriminatory basis.

Qualified Employee Discounts

When the employer sells goods or services (other than no-additional-cost benefits just discussed) to the employee for a price that is less than the price charged regular customers, the employee realizes income equal to the discount. However, the discount, referred to as a **qualified employee discount**, can be excluded from the employee's gross income, subject to the following conditions and limitations:

- The exclusion is not available for real property (e.g., a house) or for personal property commonly held for investment (e.g., common stock).
- The property or services must be from the same line of business in which the employee works.
- In the case of *property*, the exclusion is limited to the *gross profit component* of the customer price.
- In the case of *services*, the exclusion is limited to 20 percent of the customer price.

[54] See, generally, § 132.

[55] § 132(b) and Reg. § 1.132–2.

[56] § 132(h) and Reg. § 1.132–1(b).

Example 22

Silver Corporation, which operates a department store, sells a television to a store employee for $300. The regular customer price is $500, and the gross profit rate is 25%. The corporation also sells the employee a service contract for $120; the regular customer price for the contract is $150. The employee must include $75 in gross income ($75 for the television; $0 for the service contract).

Customer price for property (television)	$ 500
Less: Gross profit (25%)	(125)
	$ 375
Employee price	(300)
Income	$ 75
Customer price for service contract	$ 150
Less: 20% (maximum exclusion)	(30)
	$ 120
Employee price	(120)
Income	$ -0-

As in the case of no-additional-cost benefits, the exclusion applies to employees (including service partners), employees' spouses and dependent children, and former employees who left due to retirement or disability.

Working Condition Fringes

Generally, an employee is not required to include in gross income the cost of property or services provided by the employer if the employee could deduct the cost of those items if they had actually paid for them. These benefits are called **working condition fringes**.

Example 23

Jayden is a CPA employed by an accounting firm. The employer pays Jayden's annual dues to professional organizations. Jayden is not required to include the payment of the dues in gross income because it is an allowable business expense to Jayden (as discussed in text Section 9-9).[57]

Unlike the other fringe benefits discussed previously, working condition fringes can be made available on a discriminatory basis and still qualify for the exclusion.

De Minimis Fringes

As the term suggests, ***de minimis* fringe** benefits are so small that accounting for them is impractical. The House Report contains the following examples of *de minimis* fringes:

- Occasional personal use of a company copying machine, occasional company cocktail parties or picnics for employees, occasional supper money or taxi fare for employees because of overtime work, and certain holiday gifts of property with a low fair market value are excluded.
- Subsidized eating facilities (e.g., an employees' cafeteria) operated by the employer are excluded if located on or near the employer's business premises, if revenue equals or exceeds direct operating costs, and if nondiscrimination requirements are met. This exclusion applies regardless of whether the employer can deduct any of the facility's costs.

When taxpayers venture beyond the specific examples contained in the House Report and the Regulations, there can be room for disagreement as to what is *de minimis*. According to the IRS, cash or gift cards are not considered *de minimis*.[58]

The value of a cell phone can be excluded if it is provided for business reasons (e.g., to enable the employee to be in contact with clients when the employee is away from the office). When the primary purpose test is satisfied, any personal use of the employer-provided cell phone will be excluded as a *de minimis* fringe benefit.[59]

[57] In many cases, this exclusion merely avoids reporting income and using an off-setting deduction. The TCJA of 2017 suspends the deduction for unreimbursed employee business expenses for 2018 through 2025. So if Jayden paid the dues on his own, he could not deduct them. IRS Publication 15B, *Employer's Tax Guide to Fringe Benefits*, states that the payment continues to be a nontaxable fringe benefit for the employee.

[58] TAM 200437030 (9/10/04) and IRS Publication 15B, *Employer's Tax Guide to Fringe Benefits*.

[59] Notice 2011–72, 2011–38 I.R.B. 407.

Qualified Transportation Fringes

The exclusion for **qualified transportation fringes** is intended to encourage the use of mass transit for commuting to and from work. Qualified transportation fringes include the following benefits provided by the employer to the employee:

1. Transportation in a commuter highway vehicle between the employee's residence and the place of employment.
2. A transit pass.
3. Qualified parking.

These exclusions have annual limits. For 2022, the inflation adjusted limit is $280 per month ($270 in 2021).[60]

A *commuter highway vehicle* is any highway vehicle with a seating capacity of at least six adults (excluding the driver). In addition, at least 80 percent of the vehicle's use must be for transporting employees between their residences and place of employment.

Qualified parking includes the following:

- Parking provided to an employee on or near the employer's business premises.
- Parking provided to an employee on or near a location from which the employee commutes to work via mass transit, in a commuter highway vehicle, or in a carpool.

Qualified transportation fringes may be provided directly by the employer or may be in the form of cash reimbursements.

Example 24

Gray Corporation's offices are located in the center of a large city. The company pays for parking spaces to be used by the company officers. Steve, a vice president, receives $300 of such benefits each month during 2022. The parking space rental qualifies as a qualified transportation fringe. Of the $300 benefit Steve received each month, $280 is excludible from gross income. The balance of $20 is included in his gross income. The same result would occur if Steve paid for the parking and was reimbursed by his employer.

The TCJA of 2017 generally prohibits employers from *deducting* their expenses of qualified transportation fringe benefits provided to employees [§ 274(a)(4)]. If the employer provides the benefit, though, the employee may exclude it from income within the limits stated above.

Qualified Moving Expense Reimbursements

Prior to the TCJA of 2017, qualified moving expenses reimbursed or paid by the employer were excludible from gross income. A qualified moving expense would be deductible under § 217. For 2018 through 2025, the exclusion only applies to members of the Armed Forces on active duty. See the discussion of moving expenses in text Section 9-6b.

Qualified Retirement Planning Services

Qualified retirement planning services include any retirement planning advice or information that an employer who maintains a qualified retirement plan provides to an employee or the employee's spouse. Congress decided to exclude the value of these services from gross income because they are a key part of retirement income planning and they may serve as motivation for more employers to provide retirement planning services to their employees.

Qualified Military Base Realignment and Closure Fringe

Payments made under the Demonstration Cities and Metropolitan Development Act of 1966 are generally excluded from income.

[60] Prior to 2018, qualified transportation fringes included qualified bicycle commuting reimbursement up to $20 per month. For 2018 through 2025, this benefit is not treated as a qualified transportation fringe benefit. As a result, if an employer provides this benefit, it is taxable to the employee and deductible by the employer.

Ethics & Equity Fringe Benefits

The TCJA of 2017 changed the tax treatment of certain fringe benefits to better tie an employer's deduction for employee compensation with the amount employees report as wage income. The approach taken, such as for meals provided for the convenience of the employer and qualified transportation fringe benefits, was to retain the exclusion for the employee receiving these benefits but to repeal or reduce the deduction for the employer. Did Congress take the right approach? Or should Congress instead have allowed employers to deduct the cost of the benefits provided to employees with the employees including the benefits in wage income?

Nondiscrimination Provisions

For no-additional-cost services, qualified employee discounts, and qualified retirement planning services that are discriminatory in favor of highly compensated employees, exclusion treatment is denied. However, for the discriminatory plans, the exclusion treatment for non-highly compensated employees remains.[61]

Example 25

Dove Company's officers are allowed to purchase goods from the company at a 25% discount. All other employees are allowed only a 15% discount. The company's gross profit margin on these goods is 30%. Because the officers receive more favorable discounts, the plan is discriminatory in favor of the officers. In regard to all other employees, the discount is "qualified" because it is available to all employees (other than the officers who receive a more favorable discount) and the discount is less than the company's gross profit.

Peggy, an officer in the company, purchased goods from the company for $750 when the price charged to customers was $1,000. Peggy must include $250 in gross income because the plan is discriminatory.

Mason, an employee of the company who is not an officer, purchased goods for $850 when the customer price was $1,000. Mason is not required to recognize gross income because he received a qualified employee discount.

De minimis (except in the case of subsidized eating facilities) and working condition fringe benefits can be provided on a discriminatory basis. The *de minimis* benefits are not subject to tax because the accounting problems that would be created are out of proportion to the amount of additional tax that would result.

A review of employee fringe benefits is provided in Concept Summary 5.2.

5-8e Group Term Life Insurance

For many years, the IRS did not attempt to tax the value of life insurance protection provided to an employee or former employee by the employer. Some companies took undue advantage of the exclusion by providing large amounts of insurance protection for executives. As a result, Congress enacted § 79, which created a limited exclusion for **group term life insurance**. The premiums on the first $50,000 of group term life insurance protection are excludible from the employee's and former employee's gross income.

The benefits of this exclusion are available only to employees. Proprietors and partners are not considered employees. The Regulations generally require broad-scale coverage of employees to satisfy the *group* requirement (e.g., shareholder-employees would not constitute a qualified group). The exclusion applies only to term insurance (protection for a period of time but with no cash surrender value) and not to ordinary life insurance (lifetime protection plus a cash surrender value that can be drawn upon before death).

As mentioned, the exclusion applies to the first $50,000 of group term life insurance protection. For each $1,000 of coverage in excess of $50,000, the employee must include the amounts indicated in Exhibit 5.1 in gross income.[62]

[61] §§ 132(j)(1) and (m)(2).

[62] Reg. § 1.79–3(d)(2).

Exhibit 5.1 Uniform Premiums for $1,000 of Group Term Life Insurance Protection

Attained Age on Last Day of Employee's Tax Year	Cost per $1,000 of Protection for One-Month Period*
Under 25	$0.05
25–29	0.06
30–34	0.08
35–39	0.09
40–44	0.10
45–49	0.15
50–54	0.23
55–59	0.43
60–64	0.66
65–69	1.27
70 and above	2.06

*Reg. § 1.79–3, effective for coverage after June 30, 1999.

Example 26

Finch Corporation has a group term life insurance policy with coverage equal to the employee's annual salary. Keith, age 52, is president of the corporation and receives an annual salary of $350,000. Keith must include $828 in gross income from the insurance protection for the year.

$$\frac{\$350{,}000 - \$50{,}000}{\$1{,}000} \times \$0.23 \times 12 \text{ months} = \$828$$

Generally, the amount that must be included in gross income, computed from Exhibit 5.1, is much less than the price an individual would pay an insurance company for the same amount of protection. As a result, even the excess coverage provides some tax-favored income for employees when group term life insurance coverage exceeds $50,000.

If the plan discriminates in favor of certain key employees (e.g., officers), the key employees are not eligible for the exclusion. In such a case, the key employees must include in gross income the *greater* of actual premiums paid by the employer or the amount calculated from the Uniform Premiums in Exhibit 5.1. The other employees are still eligible for the $50,000 exclusion and continue to use the Uniform Premiums table to compute the income from excess insurance protection.[63]

5-9 Foreign Earned Income

For individuals, the United States uses a global (or citizen-based) tax system as opposed to a territorial system. Under this global system, U.S. citizens generally are subject to tax on their income regardless of its economic origin. Some other countries use a territorial system; that is, a person's income is taxed only in the country in which the income was earned. Under a global system, a U.S. citizen who earns income in another country could experience double taxation—the same income would be taxed in the United States and in the foreign country. Out of a sense of fairness and to encourage U.S. citizens to work abroad (so that exports might be increased), Congress has provided alternative forms of relief from taxes on foreign earned income. Taxpayers can elect *either* (1) to include the foreign earned income in their taxable income and then claim a credit for foreign taxes paid or (2) to exclude up to $112,000 of foreign earned income from their U.S. gross income (the **foreign earned income exclusion**).[64] As will be apparent from the following discussion, most taxpayers choose the exclusion.

[63] § 79(d).

[64] § 911(a). The exclusion for 2021 was $108,700.

Concept Summary 5.2

Employee Fringe Benefits

Type of Benefit	Exclusion
Group term life insurance (§ 79)	Premiums on up to $50,000 of protection
Employee achievement awards (§ 74)	Up to $1,600 in a year
Accident, health, and long-term care insurance and medical reimbursement (§§ 105 and 106)	Insurance premiums paid by the employer and benefits collected
High-deductible health insurance and contributions to employee's Health Savings Account (§§ 106 and 223)	Employer premiums on high-deductible medical insurance plus contributions to Health Savings Account (statutory limits, indexed for inflation)
Meals and lodging furnished for the convenience of the employer (§ 119)	Value of meals and lodging on the employer's premises
Child care provided by the employer or reimbursement for employee's cost (§ 129)	Services provided or reimbursement of expenses up to $5,000 a year
Athletic facilities on the employer's premises (§ 132)	Value of services
Educational assistance for tuition, fees, books, and supplies (§ 127)	Limited to $5,250 per year
No-additional-cost services [e.g., use of employer's facilities (§ 132)]	Value of the use
Employee discount on purchase of goods from employer at employer's cost (§ 132)	Employer's normal profit margin
Employee discount for purchases of employer's services (§ 132)	Maximum of 20% of employer's normal price
Working condition fringes [e.g., a mechanic's tools (§ 132)]	Employer's cost
De minimis items so small that the accounting effort is not warranted [e.g., use of employer telephone (§ 132)]	Value of the goods or services
Qualified transportation [e.g., transit passes and parking (§ 132)]	Statutory amounts, adjusted for inflation
Moving expense reimbursement for members of the Armed Forces on active duty (§ 132)	Reimbursement to the extent otherwise deductible by employee
Retirement planning services (§ 132)	Reasonable cost of services

Foreign earned income consists of the earnings from the individual's personal services rendered in a foreign country (other than as an employee of the U.S. government). To qualify for the exclusion, the taxpayer must be either:

- A bona fide resident of the foreign country (or countries), or
- Present in a foreign country (or countries) for at least 330 days during any 12 consecutive months.[65]

The following rules apply in calculating the exclusion and tax owed:

- The exclusion must be computed on a daily basis when the exclusion period straddles two years.
- The tax on the income in excess of the excluded amount is taxed at the marginal rate that would apply without the exclusion (i.e., as though the excluded income were included in taxable income).

Global Tax Issues — Benefits of the Earned Income Exclusion Are Questioned

The foreign earned income exclusion is intended to be a means to increase exports. But a GAO study questioned whether the $6 billion of lost revenue is money well spent. The report was inconclusive. It is clear that repealing the exclusion would make it more costly for U.S. companies to send their employees abroad, but there is no evidence that the benefits to the United States, in general, are worth the cost.

Source: Economic Benefits of Income Exclusion for U.S. Citizens Working Abroad Are Uncertain GAO-14-387: Published: May 20, 2014, available at **gao.gov/products/GAO-14-387**.

[65] § 911(d). For the definition of *resident*, see Reg. § 1.871–2(b). Under the Regulations, a taxpayer is not a resident if they are there for a definite period (e.g., until completion of a construction contract).

Calculating the Exclusion and Tax

Example 27

Sandra's trips to and from a foreign country in connection with her work were as follows:

Arrived in Foreign Country	Returned to United States
March 11, 2021	February 16, 2022

During the 12 consecutive months ending on March 11, 2022, Sandra was present in the foreign country for at least 330 days (365 days less the 12 days remaining in February 2022 and 11 days in March 2022 equals 342 days). As a result, the income earned in the foreign country through March 11, 2022, is eligible for the exclusion.

Example 28

Keith qualifies for the foreign earned income exclusion. He was present in France for all of 2022. Keith's salary for 2022 is $120,000. Because all of the days in 2022 are qualifying days, Keith can exclude $112,000 of his $120,000 salary.

Assume instead that only 342 days were qualifying days. Then Keith's exclusion is limited to $104,942, computed as follows:

$$\$112{,}000 \times \frac{342 \text{ days in foreign country}}{365 \text{ days in the year}} = \$104{,}942$$

Example 29

In 2022, Alejandra, who is not married, had taxable income of $30,000 after excluding $112,000 of foreign earned income. Without the benefit of the exclusion, Alejandra's taxable income would have been $142,000 ($30,000 + $112,000). The tax on the taxable income of $30,000 is calculated using the marginal rate applicable to income between $112,000 and $142,000, which is 24%. As a result, Alejandra's tax liability is $7,200 ($30,000 × 24%).

As previously mentioned, the taxpayer may elect to include the foreign earned income in gross income and claim a credit (an offset against U.S. tax) for the foreign tax paid. The credit alternative may be advantageous if the individual's foreign earned income exceeds the excludible amount so that the foreign taxes paid exceed the U.S. tax on the amount excluded. However, once an election is made, it applies to all subsequent years unless affirmatively revoked. A revocation is effective for the year of the change and the four subsequent years.

In addition to the foreign earned income exclusion, the employee also can exclude or deduct a foreign housing amount if certain requirements are met. To qualify, the employer must pay for all or a portion of the housing costs.

5-10 Interest on Certain State and Local Government Obligations

At the time the Sixteenth Amendment was ratified by the states, there was some question as to whether the Federal government possessed the constitutional authority to tax interest on state and local government obligations. Taxing this interest was thought to violate the doctrine of intergovernmental immunity in that the tax would impair the state and local governments' ability to finance their operations.[66] As a result, interest on state and local government obligations was specifically exempted from Federal income

[66] *Pollock v. Farmer's Loan & Trust Co.*, 3 AFTR 2602, 15 S.Ct. 912 (1895).

taxation.[67] However, the Supreme Court concluded that there is no constitutional prohibition against levying a nondiscriminatory Federal income tax on state and local government obligations.[68] Congress, however, has shown no inclination to eliminate this exclusion.

Obviously, the exclusion of the interest reduces the cost of borrowing for state and local governments. A taxpayer in the 35 percent tax bracket requires only a 3.9 percent yield on a tax-exempt bond to obtain the same after-tax income as a taxable bond paying 6 percent interest [$3.9\% \div (1 - 0.35) = 6\%$].

The current exempt status applies solely to state and local government bonds. Income received from the accrual of interest on a condemnation award or an overpayment of state income tax is fully taxable.[69] In addition, the exemption does not apply to gains on the sale of tax-exempt securities.

Example 30

Megan purchases State of Virginia bonds for $10,000 on July 1, 2021. The bonds pay $300 interest each June 30 and December 31. On March 31, 2022, Megan sells the bonds for $10,500 plus $150 for accrued interest. Megan must recognize a $500 gain ($10,500 − $10,000), but the $150 accrued interest is exempt from taxation.

Although the Internal Revenue Code excludes from Federal gross income the interest on state and local government bonds, the interest on U.S. government bonds is *not* excluded from the Federal tax base. Congress decided, however, that if the Federal government does not tax state and local bond interest, state and local governments should not tax interest on U.S. government bonds.[70] However, state and local governments are free to tax each other's obligations. As a result, some states exempt the interest on the bonds they issue but tax the interest on bonds issued by other states.[71]

5-11 Educational Savings Bonds

The cost of a college education has risen dramatically during the past few decades. According to U.S. Department of Education estimates, the cost of attending a publicly supported university for four years now commonly exceeds $60,000. For a private university, the cost often exceeds $200,000. As a result, Congress has passed a variety of legislation to assist low- to middle-income parents in paying for their children's college education.

One of the ways the Federal government assists these families is through an interest income exclusion on **educational savings bonds**.[72] The interest on Series EE U.S. government savings bonds may be excluded from gross income if the bond proceeds are used to pay qualified higher education expenses. The bonds must be issued to a taxpayer age 24 or older.

---

[67] § 103(a).

[68] *South Carolina v. Baker III*, 88–1 USTC ¶9284, 61 AFTR 2d 88–995, 108 S.Ct. 1355.

[69] *Kieselbach v. Comm.*, 43–1 USTC ¶9220, 30 AFTR 370, 63 S.Ct. 303; *U.S. Trust Co. of New York v. Anderson*, 3 USTC ¶1125, 12 AFTR 836, 65 F.2d 575 (CA–2, 1933).

[70] 31 U.S.C.A. § 742.

[71] The practice of a state exempting interest on its bonds from tax but taxing the interest on bonds issued by other states has been upheld by the Supreme Court. See *Department of Revenue of Kentucky v. Davis*, 128 S.Ct. 1801 (2008).

[72] § 135.

Qualified higher education expenses consist of tuition and fees paid to an eligible educational institution for the taxpayer, spouse, or dependent. If the redemption proceeds (both principal and interest) exceed the qualified higher education expenses, only a pro rata portion of the interest will qualify for exclusion treatment.

Example 31

Tracy's redemption proceeds from qualified savings bonds during the taxable year are $6,000 (principal of $4,000 and interest of $2,000). Tracy's qualified higher education expenses are $5,000. Because the redemption proceeds exceed the qualified higher education expenses, only $1,667 [($5,000 ÷ $6,000) × $2,000] of the interest is excludible.

Once a taxpayer's modified adjusted gross income exceeds a threshold amount, the exclusion is phased out. *Modified adjusted gross income (MAGI)* is adjusted gross income prior to the foreign earned income exclusion and the educational savings bond exclusion. The threshold amounts are adjusted for inflation each year. For 2022, the phaseout begins at $85,800 ($128,650 on a joint return).[73] The phaseout is completed when MAGI exceeds the threshold amount by more than $15,000 ($30,000 on a joint return). The otherwise excludible interest is reduced by the amount calculated as follows:

$$\frac{\text{MAGI} - \$85{,}800}{\$15{,}000} \times \text{Excludible interest before phaseout} = \text{Reduction in excludible interest}$$

On a joint return, $128,650 is substituted for $85,800 (in 2022) and $30,000 is substituted for $15,000.

Example 32

Assume the same facts as in Example 31, except that Tracy's MAGI for 2022 is $87,000. The phaseout results in Tracy's interest exclusion being reduced by $133 {[($87,000 − $85,800) ÷ $15,000] × $1,667}. As a result, Tracy's exclusion is $1,534 ($1,667 − $133).

5-12 Education Savings Programs (§ 529 and § 530 Plans)

The Federal tax law provides two types of programs to help individuals and families save for education costs. These savings programs are referred to as the qualified tuition program (§ 529 plans) and Coverdell education savings accounts (§ 530 plans). Earnings in these accounts are not taxable if distributions are used for qualified education expenses. Also, rules govern the type of account that can be used for these savings programs, and specific rules exist regarding contributions, distributions, rollovers, and other transfers. In addition, the benefits of these plans must be coordinated with other educational tax provisions, such as nontaxable scholarships. Distributions from these accounts are reported on Form 1099–Q, Payments from Qualified Education Programs. Taxable distributions (generally those not used for qualified purposes) may be subject to an additional 10 percent tax [reported on Form 5329, Additional Taxes on Qualified Plans (Including IRAs) and Other Tax-Favored Accounts].

There are income limits on contributions to Coverdell accounts as well as a dollar limit on the annual contribution per beneficiary. A beneficiary may have both § 529 and § 530 plans.

[73]The indexed amounts for 2021 were $83,200 and $124,800.

5-12a Qualified Tuition Program

Nearly all states have created programs whereby parents can in effect prepay their child's college tuition. The prepayment serves as a hedge against future increases in tuition. Generally, if the child does not attend college, the parents are refunded their payments plus interest. Although these prepaid tuition programs resemble the below-market loans (discussed in text Section 4-4b), Congress has created an exclusion provision for these programs.

Under a **qualified tuition program (§ 529 plan)**, the amounts contributed must be used for qualified higher education expenses. These expenses include tuition, fees, books, supplies, room and board, and equipment required for enrollment or attendance at a college, a university, or certain vocational schools. Allowable expenses also include computers and peripheral equipment, software, and internet access used primarily by the beneficiary while enrolled at an eligible educational institution. Qualified higher education expenses also include the expenses for special needs services that are incurred in connection with the enrollment and attendance of special needs students. Tuition paid to public, private, and religious K–12 schools, as well as certain apprenticeship programs, are also allowable expenses. In addition, a lifetime maximum of $10,000 of funds in a § 529 account may be used to pay principal or interest on a qualified education loan.

The earnings of the contributed funds, including the discount on tuition charged to participants, are not included in Federal gross income provided the contributions and earnings are used for qualified higher education expenses. Some states also exclude these educational benefits from state gross income.

Example 33

Angie paid $20,000 into a qualified tuition program to be used for her son's college tuition. When her son graduated from high school, the fund balance had increased to $30,000 as a result of interest credited to the account. The interest was not included in Angie's gross income. During the current year, $7,500 of the balance in the fund was used to pay the son's tuition and fees. None of this amount is included in either Angie's or the son's gross income.

If the parent receives a refund (e.g., child does not attend college), the excess of the amount refunded over the amount contributed by the parent is included in the parent's gross income. A special rule applies to refunded amounts recontributed to a qualified tuition program of the beneficiary.

5-12b Coverdell Education Savings Account

A **Coverdell education savings account (§ 530 plan)** may be used to save for K–12 education as well as postsecondary education expenses. The contributions to the plan are limited to $2,000 in any year, and the beneficiary must be under 18 or must be a special needs beneficiary in the year the contribution is made. As with the § 529 plan, contributions are nondeductible, but the income to the beneficiary is nontaxable provided the funds are used for qualified education expenses.

5-13 Qualified ABLE Programs (§ 529A Plans)

The **qualified ABLE program** was created to assist individuals who become blind or disabled before age 26. The program allows for § 529A plans, or ABLE (Achieving a Better Life Experience) plans, similar in concept to § 529 plans described earlier. The program must be established by a state. The ABLE account must be for the benefit of a designated beneficiary's disability expenses, and the beneficiary must have a disability certification from the government.

Contributions to the account must be in cash and may not, in total, exceed the annual gift tax exclusion for the year ($16,000 for 2022; $15,000 for 2021). Contributions to the account are not deductible. The tax benefit of an ABLE account is that its earnings are not taxable. Distributions from the account also are not taxable provided they do not exceed the qualified disability expenses of the designated beneficiary. Certain rollovers from a § 529 account to an ABLE account are permitted for 2018 through 2025.

5-14 Income from Discharge of Indebtedness

When a person is relieved of a debt for less than the amount owed, the debtor's net worth increases. This increase in net worth must be included in gross income unless one of the exceptions discussed below applies.[74]

Example 34

Kayla is unable to make her credit card payments and has negotiated a settlement with the credit card issuer. Her $40,000 debt will be settled for $25,000. Kayla must recognize income of $15,000 from the discharge of debt.

When property serves as security for debt, the creditor may foreclose on the property. The foreclosure is treated as a sale.[75]

Example 35

Juan owns land that serves as security for a $60,000 mortgage held by State Bank. Juan does not have personal liability for the mortgage (it is nonrecourse debt). When Juan's basis in the land is $20,000 and the land's fair market value is $50,000, the bank forecloses on the loan and takes title to the land. Juan must recognize a $40,000 gain on the foreclosure, as though he sold the land for $60,000 (the amount of the nonrecourse debt). No income from discharge of indebtedness is generated in this transaction.

If property serves as security for the debt and the taxpayer is personally liable for the difference between the value of the property and the amount of the debt (i.e., the debt is "with recourse"), the taxpayer may have income from the discharge of the debt in addition to gain or loss from the foreclosure.

Example 36

Assume the same facts in Example 35, except that Juan's debt is recourse. Juan is treated as selling the property for its fair market value ($50,000) resulting in a gain or loss. His gain is $30,000 ($50,000 sales price − $20,000 basis). In addition, Juan has $10,000 of income from discharge of indebtedness because the lender accepted the $50,000 sales price in discharging the $60,000 debt. Juan will want to determine whether any exclusion applies to his income from discharge of indebtedness (discussed next).

[74] § 61(a)(11) and Reg. § 1.1001–2(a).

[75] *Estate of Delman*, 73 T.C. 15 (1979).

The following discharge of indebtedness situations are subject to special exclusion treatment:[76]

1. Creditors' gifts.
2. Discharges under Federal bankruptcy law.
3. Discharges that occur when the debtor is insolvent (the exclusion is limited to the amount of insolvency).
4. Discharge of the farm debt of a solvent taxpayer.
5. Discharge of **qualified real property business indebtedness**.
6. A seller's cancellation of the buyer's indebtedness.
7. A shareholder's cancellation of the corporation's indebtedness.
8. Forgiveness of certain loans to students.
9. Discharge of indebtedness on the taxpayer's principal residence that occurs between January 1, 2007, and January 1, 2026, and is the result of the financial condition of the debtor.[77]

If the creditor reduces the debt as an act of *love*, *affection*, or *generosity*, the debtor has simply received a nontaxable gift (situation 1). Rarely will a gift be found to have occurred in a business context. A businessperson may settle a debt for less than the amount due, but as a matter of business expediency (e.g., high collection costs or disputes as to contract terms) rather than generosity.[78]

In situations 2, 3, 4, 5, and 9, the Code allows the debtor to reduce the related asset's basis by the realized income from the discharge.[79] As a result, the realized income is merely deferred until the assets are sold (or depreciated). Similarly, in situation 6 (a price reduction), the debtor reduces the basis in the specific assets financed by the seller.[80]

A shareholder's cancellation of the corporation's indebtedness to them (situation 7) usually is considered a tax-free contribution of capital to the corporation by the shareholder. As a result, the corporation's paid-in capital is increased, and its liabilities are decreased by the same amount.[81]

Many states make loans to students on the condition that the loan will be forgiven if students practice a profession in the state upon completing their studies. The amount of the loan that is forgiven (situation 8) is excluded from gross income.[82] In addition, any portion of a student loan forgiven after December 31, 2020, and before January 1, 2026, is excludible from gross income. This exclusion applies to all loans made by the Federal or state governments, as well as loans made by private lenders and educational institutions. However, the exclusion does not apply to debt forgiven in exchange for services rendered by the student to the lending organization.[83]

LO.3

Determine the extent to which receipts can be excluded under the tax benefit rule.

5-15 Tax Benefit Rule

Often a person will incur a cost or an expense in one year but receive a refund or recovery in a subsequent year. Effectively, this refund or recovery reduces the original cost. For example, the taxpayer may purchase an item from a retailer and then receive a rebate from the manufacturer. The rebate is generally a purchase price adjustment. If the item purchased did not result in a tax deduction (e.g., the purchase of a personal automobile), the rebate does not affect taxable income. However, if the original payment resulted in a tax deduction in one year and the rebate is received in a subsequent year,

[76] § 108. See Rev.Proc. 2020–11 for special debt discharge exclusions under the U.S. Department of Education's "Defense to Repayment" program.

[77] When Congress extended this exclusion for 2021 through 2025, it lowered the maximum exclusion from $2,000,000 to $750,000 to match the debt limit for the home mortgage interest deduction (see text Section 10-3); Consolidated Appropriations Act of 2021 (P.L. 116–260).

[78] *Comm. v. Jacobson*, 49–1 USTC ¶9133, 37 AFTR 516, 69 S.Ct. 358.

[79] §§ 108(a), (c), (e), and (g). Note that § 108(b) provides that other tax attributes (e.g., net operating loss) will be reduced by the realized gain from the debt discharge prior to the basis adjustment unless the taxpayer elects to apply the basis adjustment first. See § 1017 for the basis reduction rules.

[80] § 108(e)(5).

[81] § 108(e)(6).

[82] § 108(f).

[83] § 108(f)(5), as modified by the American Rescue Plan Act of 2021 (P.L. 117–2).

the tax benefit rule will apply. Generally, if a taxpayer claims a deduction for an item in one year and in a later year recovers all or a portion of the prior deduction, the recovery is included in gross income in the year received.[84]

Example 37

An accrual basis taxpayer deducted as a loss a $1,000 receivable from a customer when it appeared the amount would never be collected. The following year, the customer paid $800 on the receivable. The taxpayer must report the $800 as gross income in the year it is received.

However, the § 111 **tax benefit rule** provides that no income is recognized upon the recovery of a deduction, or the portion of a deduction, that did not yield a tax benefit in the year it was taken. If the taxpayer in Example 37 had no tax liability in the year of the deduction (e.g., itemized deductions exceeded adjusted gross income), the recovery would be partially or totally excluded from gross income in the year of the recovery.[85]

A common situation that leads to consideration of the tax benefit rule occurs when individuals who itemize their deductions (on Schedule A of Form 1040) get part of their state income tax back as a refund the next year. The TCJA of 2017 added a new wrinkle to this situation. For 2018 through 2025, individuals may only deduct up to $10,000 of state and local taxes as part of their itemized deductions. This is often referred to as the "SALT" deduction. This new limitation raises the question of how the tax benefit rule works when individuals who itemize their deductions (1) paid state and local taxes (SALT) greater than the $10,000 allowable deduction and (2) receive a state income tax refund the next year.

The IRS has issued guidance on how the tax benefit rule applies to state income tax refunds in light of the $10,000 SALT cap.[86] Basically, taxpayers need to determine what their tax return would have looked like if they had known the actual state income tax amount when the return was prepared (factoring in the later refund). This analysis leads to one of the following:

1. *All or part of the refund is taxable:* If the amount of the refund causes the actual SALT amount for the year to drop below $10,000, then the individual obtained a tax benefit from the SALT deduction and all or part of that refund is taxable under the tax benefit rule. The individual also must determine if the refund results in total itemized deductions totaling less than the standard deduction amount. See Example 38.
2. *The refund is not taxable:* If the individual had a SALT amount greater than $10,000 and the SALT amount equals or exceeds $10,000 even when considering the refund, then no income results under the tax benefit rule. See Example 39.

Tax Benefit Rule and the SALT Cap

Example 38

Ali filed his 2021 income tax return as a single individual. His AGI for 2021 was $78,000. He had $13,100 in itemized deductions, including $6,200 in state income tax and no other state or local taxes. In 2022, he received a $700 refund of the state income taxes that he paid in 2021.

continued

[84]§ 111(a).

[85]Itemized deductions are discussed in Chapter 10.

[86]Rev.Rul. 2019–11.

Because the standard deduction in 2021 was $12,550, Ali's $6,200 of state income tax deduction in 2021 yielded a tax benefit of only $550 ($13,100 itemized deductions − $12,550 standard deduction). Under the tax benefit rule, only $550 of the state income tax refund is included in gross income in 2022.

Example 39

Julie filed her 2021 return as a single individual. Her AGI for 2021 was $170,000, and she reported $22,000 of itemized deductions. In 2021, Julie paid property taxes on her home of $8,000 and state income taxes of $15,000, for total SALT of $23,000. Due to the SALT cap, she could only deduct $10,000 of this amount on her 2021 return.

After filing her 2021 state income tax return in early 2022, Julie received a state income tax refund of $1,250. Under the tax benefit rule and IRS guidance on the TCJA of 2017, none of this refund is includible in Julie's 2022 gross income; even if the refund was received in 2021, Julie would still be subject to the SALT cap of $10,000. As a result, she received no tax benefit from the $1,250 state income taxes paid in 2021 that were refunded to her in 2022.

LO.4

Identify tax planning strategies for obtaining the maximum benefit from exclusions.

5-16 Tax Planning

The present law excludes certain types of economic gains from taxation. As a result, taxpayers may find tax planning techniques helpful in obtaining the maximum benefits from the exclusion of such gains. Following are some of the tax planning opportunities made available by the exclusions described in this chapter.

5-16a Life Insurance

Life insurance offers several favorable tax attributes. As discussed in Chapter 4, the annual increase in the cash surrender value of the policy is not taxable (because no income has been actually or constructively received). By borrowing on the policy's cash surrender value, the owner can actually receive the policy's increase in value in cash without recognizing income.

5-16b Employee Fringe Benefits

Generally, employees view accident and health insurance, as well as life insurance, as necessities. Employees can obtain group coverage at much lower rates than individuals would have to pay for the same protection. Premiums paid by the employer can be excluded from the employees' gross income. Because of the exclusion, employees will have a greater after-tax and after-insurance income if the employer pays a lower salary but also pays the insurance premiums.

Example 40

Pat receives a salary of $30,000. The company has group insurance benefits, but Pat is required to pay his own premiums as follows:

Hospitalization and medical insurance	$1,400
Term life insurance ($30,000 coverage)	200
Disability insurance	400
	$2,000

To simplify the analysis, assume that Pat's tax rate on income is 24%. After paying taxes of $7,200 ($30,000 × 24%) and $2,000 for insurance, Pat has $20,800 remaining ($30,000 − $7,200 − $2,000) for his other living needs.

continued

If Pat's employer reduced Pat's salary by $2,000 (to $28,000) but paid his insurance premiums, Pat's tax liability would be only $6,720 ($28,000 × 24%). As a result, Pat would have $21,280 ($28,000 − $6,720) to meet his other living needs. The change in the compensation plan would save Pat $480 ($21,280 − $20,800).

Similarly, employees often incur expenses for child care and parking. The employee can have more income for other uses if the employer pays these costs but reduces the employee's salary by the cost of the benefits.

The use of cafeteria plans has increased dramatically in recent years. These plans allow employees to tailor their benefits to meet their individual situations. As a result, where both spouses are working, duplication of benefits can be avoided and other needed benefits can often be added. If less than all of the employee's allowance is spent, the employee can receive cash.

The meals and lodging exclusion enables employees to receive from their employer what they ordinarily must purchase with after-tax dollars. Although the employee must live on the employer's premises in order to exclude the value of the lodging, the exclusion is an important factor in the employee's compensation in certain situations (e.g., hotels, motels, restaurants, farms, and ranches). The meals and lodging are clearly a benefit to the employee but are also for the convenience of the employer; as a result, they are excluded from income.

The employees' discount provision is especially important for manufacturers and wholesalers. Employees of manufacturers can avoid tax on the manufacturer's, wholesaler's, and retailer's markups. The wholesaler's employees can avoid tax on an amount equal to the wholesale and retail markups.

The exclusion of benefits is generally available only to employees. Proprietors and partners must pay tax on the same benefits their employees receive tax-free. By incorporating and becoming an employee of the corporation, the former proprietor or partner also can receive these tax-exempt benefits. As a result, the availability of employee benefits is a consideration in the decision to incorporate.

5-16c Investment Income

Tax-exempt state and local government bonds are logical investments for high-income taxpayers, who may be subject to a 37 percent regular tax rate plus a 3.8 percent rate on their net investment income. To realize the maximum benefit from the exemption, the investor can purchase zero-coupon bonds. Like Series EE U.S. government savings bonds, these investments pay interest only at maturity. The advantage of the zero-coupon feature for a tax-exempt bond is that the investor can earn tax-exempt interest on the accumulated principal and interest. If the investor purchases a bond that pays the interest each year, the interest received may be such a small amount that an additional tax-exempt investment cannot be made. In addition, reinvesting the interest may entail transaction costs (brokers' fees). The zero-coupon feature avoids these problems.

Series EE U.S. government savings bonds can earn tax-exempt interest if the bond proceeds are used for qualified higher education expenses. Many taxpayers can foresee these expenditures being made for their children's educations. In deciding whether to invest in the bonds, however, the investor must take into account the income limitations for excluding the interest from gross income.

Refocus on The Big Picture

Exclusions

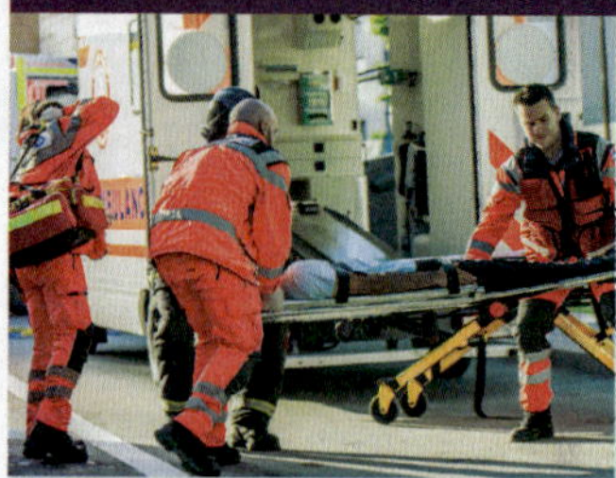

You have looked into Paul's tax situation and have the following information for him:

- *Compensation.* The amount Paul was paid for his internship is compensation for services rendered and must be included in his gross income. This includes both his base pay and the $1,500 bonus (Example 1).
- *Graduate assistantship.* The tuition waiver of $6,000 is excluded from Paul's gross income. The related payments of $400 per month are intended as a form of compensation. So Paul must include the $400 per month in his gross income (Example 9).
- *Damages.* Damages awards that relate to personal physical injury or sickness can be excluded from gross income if the payments are for compensatory damages. So all of the compensatory damages of $220,000 can be excluded from gross income. The punitive damages of $160,000 must be included in Paul's gross income. Likewise, the compensatory damages of $25,000 received by Paul's mother must be included in her gross income because emotional distress does not qualify as personal physical injury or sickness (Example 12).

What If?

From a tax planning perspective, can Paul do anything to reduce the amount of the punitive damages settlement that he must include in his gross income?

As things now stand (i.e., a completed settlement), Paul cannot reduce the $160,000 punitive damages amount he must include in gross income. However, proper tax planning might have enabled Paul to reduce the amount includible in gross income. Note that both the amount of the damages and the labels attached to the damages are negotiated. If a larger portion of the settlement had been assigned to compensatory damages rather than punitive damages, Paul could have reduced the amount he must include in his gross income.

VM/E+/GETTY IMAGES

Key Terms

Accelerated death benefits, 5-5
Accident and health benefits, 5-11
Cafeteria plan, 5-15
Compensatory damages, 5-9
Coverdell education savings account (§ 530 plan), 5-26
De minimis fringe, 5-18
Death benefits, 5-4
Educational savings bonds, 5-24
Flexible spending plans, 5-16
Foreign earned income exclusion, 5-21
Fringe benefits, 5-14
Group term life insurance, 5-20
Health Savings Account (HSA), 5-12
Life insurance proceeds, 5-5
Long-term care insurance, 5-12
No-additional-cost service, 5-17
Punitive damages, 5-9
Qualified ABLE program, 5-26
Qualified employee discount, 5-17
Qualified real property business indebtedness, 5-28
Qualified transportation fringes, 5-19
Qualified tuition program (§ 529 plan), 5-26
Scholarship, 5-7
Tax benefit rule, 5-29
Working condition fringes, 5-18

Discussion Questions

1. **LO.1, 2** Fred specified in his will that his nephew John should serve as executor of Fred's estate. John received $10,000 for serving as executor. John inherited $100,000 of cash from his uncle as well. He also borrowed $5,000 when he bought a new car this year. Classify each of the amounts received by John using terminology covered in this chapter. Explain the rationale for each classification.

2. **LO.2** Leonard's home was damaged by a fire. He also had to be absent from work for several days to make his home habitable. Leonard's employer paid Leonard his regular salary, $2,500, while he was absent from work. In Leonard's pay envelope was the following note from the employer: To help you in your time of need. Leonard's fellow employees also took up a collection and gave him $900. Leonard spent over $4,000 repairing the fire damage.

   Based on the above information, how much is Leonard required to include in his gross income?

3. **LO.2** Megan is a college student who works as a part-time server in a restaurant. Her usual tip is 20% of the price of the meal. A customer ordered a piece of pie and said that he would appreciate prompt service. Megan abided by the customer's request. The customer's bill was $8, but the customer left a $100 bill on the table and did not ask for a receipt. Megan gave the cashier $8 and pocketed the $100 bill (so Megan ends up with $92). Megan concludes that the customer thought that he had left a $10 bill, although the customer did not return to correct the apparent mistake. The customer had commented about how much he appreciated Megan's prompt service. Megan thinks that a $2 tip would be sufficient and that the excess is like "found money." How much should Megan include in her gross income?

4. **LO.2** Carey is a waiter at a restaurant that pays a small hourly amount plus tips. Customers are not required to tip the waiter. Carey is especially attentive and friendly, and her tips average 25% of the restaurant charges. Is Carey required to include any of her tips in gross income when the customer has no legal obligation to make the payment? Explain the basis for your conclusion.

5. **LO.2** Lime Finance Company requires its customers to purchase a credit life insurance policy associated with the loans it makes. Lime is the beneficiary of the policy to the extent of the remaining balance on the loan at the time of the customer's death. In 2021, Lime wrote off as uncollectible a $5,000 account receivable from Wally, which included $1,500 of accrued interest. When Wally died in 2022, the life insurance policy was still in force and Lime received $3,500. Is the $3,500 of life insurance proceeds received by Lime included in its gross income? Explain.

6. **LO.2** Billy fell off a bar stool and hurt his back. As a result, he was unable to work for three months. He sued the bar owner and collected $100,000 for the physical injury and $50,000 for the loss of income. Billy also collected $15,000 from an income replacement insurance policy he purchased. Amber was away from work for three months following heart bypass surgery. Amber collected $30,000 under an income replacement insurance policy purchased by her employer. Are the amounts received by Billy and Amber treated the same under the tax law? Explain.

7. **LO.2** Wes was a major league baseball pitcher who earned $10,000,000 for his 20 wins this year. Sam was also a major league baseball pitcher before a career-ending injury caused by a negligent driver. Sam sued the driver and collected $6,000,000 as compensation for lost estimated future income as a pitcher and $4,000,000 as punitive damages. Do the amounts that Wes and Sam receive have the same effect on their gross income? Explain.

8. **LO.2** Holly was injured while working in a factory and received $12,000 as workers' compensation while she was unable to work because of the injury. Jill, who was self-employed, was also injured and unable to work. Jill collected $12,000 on an

insurance policy she had purchased to replace her loss of income while she was unable to work. How much are Holly and Jill each required to include in their gross income?

Decision Making 9. **LO.2, 4** Casey is in the 12% marginal tax bracket, and Mei is in the 35% marginal tax bracket. Their employer is experiencing financial difficulties and cannot continue to pay for the company's health insurance plan. The annual premiums are approximately $8,000 per employee. The employer has proposed to either (1) require the employee to pay the premiums or (2) reduce each employee's pay by $10,000 per year with the employer paying the premium. Which option is less objectionable to Casey, and which is less objectionable to Mei?

10. **LO.2** Anh suffered injuries when she fell out of her bed while hospitalized. She sued the hospital for $90,000 (for her physical injuries). She lost the case and brought a lawsuit against the lawyer who represented her in the hospital litigation, alleging malpractice. Anh won a judgment of $100,000 from the law firm. What is the tax treatment of this $100,000 judgment for Anh?

11. **LO.2** Ted works for Azure Motors, an automobile dealership. All employees can buy a car at the company's cost plus 2%. The company does not charge employees the $300 dealer preparation fee that nonemployees must pay. Ted purchased an automobile for $29,580 ($29,000 + $580). The company's cost was $29,000. The price for a nonemployee would have been $33,900 ($33,600 + $300 preparation fee). What is Ted's gross income from the purchase of the automobile?

Planning 12. **LO.2, 4** Wilbur has been offered a job at a salary that would put him in the 24% marginal tax bracket. In addition to his salary, he would receive health insurance coverage. Another potential employer does not offer health insurance but has agreed to match the first offer on an after-tax and insurance basis. The cost of health insurance comparable to that provided by the other potential employer is $9,000 per year. How much more in salary must the second potential employer pay so that Wilbur's financial status will be the same under both offers?

13. **LO.2, 4** Eagle Life Insurance Company pays its employees $0.30 per mile for driving their personal automobiles to and from work. The company reimburses each employee who rides the bus $100 a month for the cost of a pass. Tom collected $100 for his automobile mileage, and Mason received $100 as reimbursement for the cost of a bus pass.

a. What are the effects of the above on Tom's and Mason's gross income?

b. Assume that Tom and Mason are in the 24% marginal tax bracket and the actual before-tax cost for Tom to drive to and from work is $0.30 per mile. What are Tom's and Mason's after-tax costs of commuting to and from work?

Critical Thinking 14. **LO.2** Several of Egret Company's employees have asked the company to create a hiking trail that employees could use during their lunch hours. The company owns vacant land that is being held for future expansion but would have to spend approximately $50,000 if it were to make a trail. Nonemployees would be allowed to use the facility as part of the company's effort to build strong community support. What are the relevant tax issues for the employees?

15. **LO.2** The Sage Company has the opportunity to purchase a building located next to its office. Sage would use the building as a day care center for the children of its employees and an exercise facility for the employees. Occasionally, portions of the building could be used for employees' family events such as reunions, birthday parties, and anniversaries. The company would like to know if the planned uses of the building would fit into a beneficially taxed employee compensation plan.

Decision Making
Planning 16. **LO.2, 4** Katie, a resident of Virginia, is considering purchasing a North Carolina bond that yields 4.6% before tax. She is in the 35% Federal marginal tax bracket and the 5% state marginal tax bracket. She is aware that State of Virginia bonds of comparable risk are yielding 4.5%. However, the Virginia bonds are exempt from Virginia tax, but the North Carolina bond interest is taxable in Virginia. Which of the two options will provide the greater after-tax return to Katie? Katie can deduct

any state taxes paid on her Federal income tax return. In your analysis, assume that the bond amount is $100,000.

17. **LO.2** Andrea entered into a § 529 qualified tuition program for the benefit of her daughter, Joanna. Andrea contributed $15,000 to the fund. The fund balance had accumulated to $25,000 by the time Joanna was ready to enter college. However, Joanna received a scholarship that paid for her tuition, fees, books, supplies, and room and board. So Andrea withdrew the funds from the § 529 plan and bought Joanna a new car.
    a. What are the tax consequences to Andrea of withdrawing the funds?
    b. Assume instead that Joanna's scholarship did not cover her room and board, which cost $7,500 per academic year. During the current year, $7,500 of the fund balance was used to pay for Joanna's room and board. The remaining amount was left in the § 529 plan to cover her room and board for future academic years. What are the tax consequences to Andrea and to Joanna of using the $7,500 to pay for the room and board?

18. **LO.2** Ralph has experienced financial difficulties as a result of his struggling business. He has been behind on his mortgage payments for the last six months. The mortgage holder, who is a friend of Ralph's, has offered to accept $80,000 in full payment of the $100,000 owed on the mortgage and payable over the next 10 years. The interest rate of the mortgage is 7%, and the market rate is now 8%. What tax issues are raised by the creditor's offer? Critical Thinking

19. **LO.3** Dolly is a cash basis taxpayer. In 2022, she filed her 2021 South Carolina income tax return and received a $2,200 refund. Dolly took the standard deduction on her 2021 Federal income tax return but will itemize her deductions in 2022. Molly, a cash basis taxpayer, also filed her 2021 South Carolina income tax return in 2022 and received a $600 refund. She deducted no other state or local taxes. Molly had $16,000 in itemized deductions on her 2021 Federal income tax return but will take the standard deduction in 2022. How does the tax benefit rule apply to Dolly's and Molly's situations? Explain.

Computational Exercises

20. **LO.2** Valentino is a patient in a nursing home for 45 days of 2022. While in the nursing home, he incurs total costs of $13,500. Medicare pays $8,000 of the costs. Valentino receives $15,000 from his long-term care insurance policy, which pays while he is in the facility. Assume that the Federal daily excludible amount for Valentino is $390.

    Of the $15,000, what amount may Valentino exclude from his gross income?

21. **LO.2** Mio was transferred from New York to Germany. He lived and worked in Germany for 340 days in 2022. Mio's salary for 2022 is $190,000. In your computation, round any division to four decimal places before converting to a percentage. For example, 0.473938 would be rounded to 47.39%.

    What is Mio's foreign earned income exclusion?

22. **LO.2** Ellie purchases an insurance policy on her life and names her brother, Jason, as the beneficiary. Ellie pays $32,000 in premiums for the policy during her life. When she dies, Jason collects the insurance proceeds of $500,000.

    As a result, how much gross income does Jason report?

23. **LO.2** Alfred owned a term life insurance policy at the time he was diagnosed with a terminal illness. After paying $18,300 in premiums, he sold the policy to a company that is authorized by the state of South Carolina to purchase such policies. The company paid Alfred $125,000. When Alfred died 18 months later, the company collected the face amount of the policy, $150,000.

    As a result of the sale of the policy, how much is Alfred required to include in his gross income?

24. **LO.1, 2** Leland pays premiums of $5,000 for an insurance policy in the face amount of $25,000 upon the life of Caleb and subsequently transfers the policy to Tyler for $7,500. Over the years, Tyler pays subsequent premiums of $1,500 on the policy. Upon Caleb's death, Tyler receives the proceeds of $25,000.

    As a result, what amount is Tyler required to include in his gross income?

25. **LO.1, 2** Jarrod receives a scholarship of $18,500 from East State University to be used to pursue a bachelor's degree. He spends $12,000 on tuition, $1,500 on books and supplies, $4,000 for room and board, and $1,000 for personal expenses.

    How much may Jarrod exclude from his gross income?

26. **LO.3** Apply the tax benefit rule to determine the amount of the state income tax refund included in gross income in 2022.
    a. Myrna and Geoffrey filed a joint tax return in 2021. Their AGI was $85,000, and itemized deductions were $25,800, which included $7,000 in state income tax and no other state or local taxes. In 2022, they received a $1,800 refund of the state income taxes they paid in 2021. The standard deduction for married filing jointly in 2021 was $25,100.
    b. Veronica filed as a single taxpayer in 2021. Her AGI was $230,000, and itemized deductions were $42,000. Her local property taxes were $13,000, and her state income taxes were $17,000. In 2022, Veronica received a $2,100 refund of the state income taxes she paid in 2021. The standard deduction for single filers in 2021 was $12,550.

Problems

27. **LO.2** Ed, an employee of the Natural Color Company, suffered from a rare disease that was very expensive to treat. The local media ran several stories about Ed's problems, and the family created a website that generated more than $10,000 in gifts from individuals to help pay the medical bills. Ed's employer provided hospital and medical insurance for its employees, but the policy did not cover Ed's illness. When it became apparent that Ed could not pay all of his medical expenses, the hospital canceled the $25,000 Ed owed at the time of his death. After Ed's death, his former employer paid Ed's widow $12,000 in "her time of need." Ed's widow also collected $50,000 on a group term life insurance policy paid for by Ed's employer. What are Ed's and his widow's gross income?

28. **LO.2** Determine the gross income of the beneficiaries in the following cases:
    a. Justin's employer was downsizing and offered employees an amount equal to one year's salary if the employee would voluntarily retire.
    b. Trina contracted a disease and was unable to work for six months. Because of her dire circumstances, her employer paid her one-half of her regular salary while she was away from work.
    c. Coral Corporation collected $1,000,000 on a key person life insurance policy when its chief executive died. The corporation had paid the premiums on the policy of $77,000, which were not deductible by the corporation.
    d. Juan collected $40,000 on a life insurance policy when his husband, Leon, died in 2022. The insurance policy was provided by Leon's employer, and the premiums were excluded from Leon's gross income as group term life insurance. In 2022, Juan also collected the $3,500 accrued salary owed to Leon at the time of his death.

Decision Making
Planning

29. **LO.2, 4** As a result of a cancer diagnosis in early 2022, Laura has begun chemotherapy treatments. A cancer specialist has stated that Laura has less than one year to live. She has incurred many medical bills and other general living expenses and is in need of cash. So she is considering selling stock that cost $35,000 and has a fair market

value of $50,000. This amount would be sufficient to pay her medical bills. However, she has read about a company (the Vital Benefits Company) that would purchase her life insurance policy for $50,000. She has paid $30,000 in premiums on the policy.

a. Considering only the tax effects, would selling the stock or selling the life insurance policy result in more beneficial tax treatment?

b. Assume that Laura is a dependent child and that her mother owns the stock and the life insurance policy, which is on the mother's life. Which of the alternative means of raising the cash would result in more beneficial tax treatment?

30. **LO.2** What is the taxpayer's gross income in each of the following situations?

a. Darrin received a salary of $50,000 from his employer, Green Construction.

b. In July, Green gave Darrin an all-expense-paid trip to Las Vegas (value of $3,000) for exceeding his sales quota.

c. Marta received $10,000 from her employer to help her pay medical expenses not covered by insurance.

d. Blake received $15,000 from his deceased spouse's employer as compensation for a bonus earned prior to death.

e. Clint collected $50,000 as the beneficiary of a group term life insurance policy when his wife died. The premiums on the policy were paid by his deceased wife's employer.

31. **LO.2** Donald was killed in an accident while he was on the job. Darlene, Donald's wife, received several payments as a result of Donald's death. What is Darlene's gross income from the items listed below?

a. Donald's employer paid Darlene an amount equal to Donald's three months' salary ($60,000), which is what the employer does for all widows and widowers of deceased employees.

b. Donald had $20,000 in accrued salary that was paid to Darlene.

c. Donald's employer had provided Donald with group term life insurance of $480,000 (twice his annual salary), which was payable to his widow in a lump sum. Premiums on this policy totaling $12,500 had been included in Donald's gross income under § 79.

d. Donald had purchased a life insurance policy (premiums totaled $250,000) that paid $600,000 in the event of accidental death. The proceeds were payable to Darlene, who elected to receive installment payments as an annuity of $30,000 each year for a 25-year period. She received her first installment this year.

32. **LO.2** Ray and Carin are partners in an accounting firm. The partners have entered into an arm's length agreement requiring Ray to purchase Carin's partnership interest from Carin's estate if she dies before Ray. The price is set at 120% of the book value of Carin's partnership interest at the time of her death. Ray purchased an insurance policy on Carin's life to fund this agreement. After Ray had paid $45,000 in premiums, Carin was killed in an automobile accident and Ray collected $800,000 of life insurance proceeds. Ray used the life insurance proceeds to purchase Carin's partnership interest.

a. What amount should Ray include in his gross income from receiving the life insurance proceeds?

b. The insurance company paid Ray $16,000 interest on the life insurance proceeds during the period Carin's estate was in administration. During this period, Ray had left the insurance proceeds with the insurance company. Is this interest taxable?

c. When Ray paid $800,000 for Carin's partnership interest, priced as specified in the agreement, the fair market value of Carin's interest was $1,000,000. How much should Ray include in his gross income from this bargain purchase?

33. **LO.2** Sally was an all-state soccer player during her junior and senior years in high school. She accepted an athletic scholarship from State University. The scholarship provided the following:

Tuition and fees	$15,000
Housing and meals	6,000
Books and supplies	1,500
Transportation	1,200

a. Determine the effect of the scholarship on Sally's gross income.

b. Sally's brother, Willy, was not a gifted athlete, but he received $8,000 from their father's employer as a scholarship during the year. The employer grants the children of all executives a scholarship equal to one-half of annual tuition, fees, books, and supplies. Willy also received a $6,000 scholarship (to be used for tuition) as the winner of an essay contest related to bioengineering, his intended field of study. Determine the effect of the scholarships on Willy's and his father's gross income.

34. **LO.2** Adrian was awarded an academic scholarship to State University for the 2022–2023 academic year. He received $6,500 in August and $7,200 in December 2022. Adrian had enough personal savings to pay all expenses as they came due. Adrian's expenditures for the relevant period were as follows:

Tuition, August 2022	$3,700
Tuition, January 2023	3,750
Room and board	
August–December 2022	2,800
January–May 2023	2,500
Books and educational supplies	
August–December 2022	1,000
January–May 2023	1,200

Determine the effect on Adrian's gross income for 2022 and 2023.

35. **LO.2** Leigh sued an overzealous bill collector and received the following settlement:

Damage to her automobile that the collector attempted to repossess	$ 3,300
Physical damage to her arm caused by the collector	15,000
Loss of income while her arm was healing	6,000
Punitive damages	80,000

a. What effect does the settlement have on Leigh's gross income?

b. Assume that Leigh also collected $25,000 of damages for slander to her personal reputation caused by the bill collector misrepresenting the facts to Leigh's employer and other creditors. Is this $25,000 included in Leigh's gross income? Explain.

36. **LO.2** Determine the effect on gross income in each of the following cases:

a. Eloise received $150,000 in settlement of a sex discrimination case against her former employer.

b. Nell received $10,000 for damages to her personal reputation. She also received $40,000 in punitive damages.

c. Orange Corporation, an accrual basis taxpayer, received $50,000 from a lawsuit filed against its auditor who overcharged for services rendered in a previous year.

d. Beth received $10,000 in compensatory damages and $30,000 in punitive damages in a lawsuit she filed against a tanning parlor for severe burns she received from using its tanning equipment.

e. Joanne received compensatory damages of $75,000 and punitive damages of $300,000 from a cosmetic surgeon who botched her nose job.

37. **LO.2** Rex, age 55, is an officer of Blue Company, which provides him with the following nondiscriminatory fringe benefits in 2022:

- Hospitalization insurance premiums for Rex and his dependents. The cost of the coverage for Rex is $2,900 per year, and the additional cost for his dependents is $3,800 per year. The plan has a $3,000 deductible, but his employer contributed $1,500 to Rex's Health Savings Account (HSA). Rex withdrew only $800 from the HSA, and the account earned $50 of interest during the year.
- Insurance premiums of $840 for salary continuation payments. Under the plan, Rex will receive his regular salary in the event he is unable to work due to illness. Rex collected $4,500 on the policy to replace lost wages while he was ill during the year.
- Rex is a part-time student working on his bachelor's degree in engineering. His employer reimbursed his $5,200 tuition under a plan available to all full-time employees.

Determine the amount Rex must include in gross income.

38. **LO.2** The UVW Union and HON Corporation are negotiating contract terms. Assume that the union members are in the 24% marginal tax bracket and that all benefits are provided on a nondiscriminatory basis. Write a letter to the UVW Union members, explaining the tax consequences of the options discussed below. The union's address is 905 Spruce Street, Washington, DC 20227. Communications Planning

    a. The company would eliminate the $250 deductible on medical insurance benefits. Most employees incur more than $250 each year in medical expenses.
    b. Employees would get an additional paid holiday with the same annual income (the same pay but less work).
    c. An employee who did not need health insurance (because the employee's spouse works and receives family coverage) would be allowed to receive the cash value of the coverage.

39. **LO.2, 4** Mauve Corporation has a group hospitalization insurance plan that has a $200 deductible amount for hospital visits and a $15 deductible for doctor visits and prescriptions. The deductible portion paid by employees who have children has become substantial for some employees. The company is considering adopting a medical reimbursement plan or a flexible benefits plan to cover the deductible amounts. Either of these plans can be tailored to meet the needs of the employees. What are the cost considerations to the employer that should be considered in choosing between these plans? Decision Making

40. **LO.2** Belinda spent the last 60 days of 2022 in a nursing home. The cost of the services provided to her was $18,000 ($300 per day). Medicare paid $8,500 toward the cost of her stay. Belinda also received $7,500 of benefits under a long-term care insurance policy she purchased. Assume that the Federal daily excludible amount is $390. What is the effect on Belinda's gross income?

41. **LO.2** Tim is the vice president of western operations for Maroon Oil Company and is stationed in San Francisco. He is required to live in an employer-owned home, which is three blocks from his company office. The company-provided home is equipped with high-speed internet access and several telephone lines. Tim receives telephone calls and e-mails that require immediate attention any time of day or night because the company's business is spread all over the world. A full-time administrative assistant resides in the house to assist Tim with the urgent business matters. Tim often uses the home for entertaining customers, suppliers, and employees. The fair market value of comparable housing is $9,000 per month. Tim is also provided with free parking at his company's office. The value of the parking is $370 per month. Calculate the amount associated with the company-provided housing and free parking that Tim must include in his gross income for 2022.

42. **LO.2** Does the taxpayer recognize gross income in the following situations?

a. Ava is a filing clerk at a large insurance company. She is permitted to leave the premises for lunch, but she usually eats in the company's cafeteria because it is quick and she is on a tight schedule. On average, she pays $2 for a lunch that would cost $12 at a restaurant and it cost her employer $10 to prepare. However, if the prices in the cafeteria were not so low and the food was not so delicious, she would probably bring her lunch at a cost of $3 per day.

b. Scott is an executive for an international corporation located in New York City. Often he works late, taking telephone calls from the company's European branch. Scott often stays in a company-owned condominium when he has a late-night work session. The condominium is across the street from the company office and has the technology needed to communicate with employees and customers throughout the world.

c. Ira recently moved to take a job. For the first month on the new job, Ira was searching for a home to purchase or rent. During this time, his employer permitted Ira to live in an apartment the company maintains for customers during the buying season. The month that Ira occupied the apartment was not during the buying season, and the apartment would not otherwise have been occupied.

Decision Making
Planning

43. **LO.2, 4** Bertha is considering taking an early retirement offered by her employer. She would receive $3,000 per month, indexed for inflation. However, she would no longer be able to use the company's health facilities, and she would be required to pay her hospitalization insurance premiums of $8,000 each year. Bertha and her husband will file a joint return and take the standard deduction. She currently receives a salary of $55,000 a year. If she retires, she will spend approximately $300 less each month for commuting and clothing. Bertha and her husband have other sources of income and are in and will remain in the 22% marginal tax bracket. Her income tax for the current year was $8,875. She currently pays Social Security and Medicare taxes of 7.65% on her salary, but her retirement pay would not be subject to this tax. According to Bertha, she and her husband could live well if her after-tax retirement income was at least 50% of her current income. Provide Bertha with information she will need to make her decision.

Communications

44. **LO.2, 4** Finch Construction Company provides the carpenters it employs with all of the required tools. However, the company believes that this practice has led to some employees not taking care of the tools and to the mysterious disappearance of some tools. The company is considering requiring all of its employees to provide their own tools. Each employee's salary would be increased by $1,500 to compensate for the additional cost. Write a letter to Finch's management explaining the tax consequences of this plan to the carpenters. Finch's address is 300 Harbor Drive, Vermillion, SD 57069.

Critical Thinking
Planning

45. **LO.2, 4** Bluebird, Inc., does not provide its employees with any tax-exempt fringe benefits. The company is considering adopting a hospital and medical benefits insurance plan that will cost approximately $9,000 per employee. To adopt this plan, the company may have to reduce salaries and/or lower future salary increases. Bluebird is in the 25% (combined Federal and state rates) bracket. Bluebird is also responsible for matching the Social Security and Medicare taxes withheld on employees' salaries (at the full 7.65% rate). The hospital and medical benefits insurance plan will not be subject to the Social Security and Medicare taxes, and the company is not eligible for the small business credit for health insurance. The employees generally fall into two marginal tax rate groups:

Income Tax	Social Security and Medicare Tax	Total
12%	7.65%	19.65%
24%	1.45%	25.45%

The company has asked you to assist in its financial planning for the hospital and medical benefits insurance plan by computing the following:

a. How much taxable compensation is the equivalent of $9,000 of exempt compensation for each of the two classes of employees?

b. What is the company's after-tax cost of the taxable compensation computed in part (a)?

c. What is the company's after-tax cost of the exempt compensation?

d. Briefly explain your conclusions from the preceding analysis.

46. **LO.2, 4** Rosa's employer has instituted a flexible benefits program. Rosa will use the plan to pay for her daughter's dental expenses and other medical expenses that are not covered by health insurance. Rosa is in the 24% marginal tax bracket and estimates that the medical and dental expenses not covered by health insurance will be within the range of $2,000 to $3,000. Her employer's plan permits her to set aside as much as $2,850 in the flexible benefits account. Rosa does not itemize her deductions. Decision Making

a. Rosa puts $1,850 into her flexible benefits account, and her actual expenses are $2,850. What is her cost of underestimating the expenses?

b. Rosa puts $2,850 into her flexible benefits account, and her actual expenses are only $1,850. What is her cost of overestimating her expenses?

c. What is Rosa's cost of underfunding as compared with the cost of overfunding the flexible benefits account?

d. Does your answer in part (c) suggest that Rosa should fund the account closer to the low end or to the high end of her estimates?

47. **LO.2** Sparrow Corporation would like you to review its employee fringe benefits program with regard to the tax consequences of the plan for the company's president (Polly), who is also the majority shareholder.

a. The company has a qualified retirement plan. The company pays the cost of employees attending a retirement planning seminar. The employee must be within 10 years of retirement, and the cost of the seminar is $1,500 per attendee.

b. The company owns a parking garage that is used by customers, employees, and the general public, but primarily by the employees. Only the general public is required to pay for parking. The charge to the general public for Polly's parking for the year would have been $3,600 (a $300 monthly rate).

c. All employees are allowed to use the company's fixed charge long-distance telephone services, as long as the privilege is not abused. Although no one has kept track of the actual calls, Polly's use of the telephone had a value (what she would have paid on her personal telephone) of approximately $600.

d. The company owns a condominium at the beach, which it uses to entertain customers. Employees are allowed to use the facility without charge when the company has no scheduled events. Polly used the facility 10 days during the year. Her use had a rental value of $1,000.

e. The company is in the household moving business. Employees are allowed to ship goods without charge whenever there is excess space on a truck. Polly purchased a dining room suite for her daughter. Company trucks delivered the furniture to the daughter. Normal freight charges would have been $750.

f. The company has a storage facility for household goods. Officers are allowed a 20% discount on charges for storing their goods. All other employees are allowed a 10% discount. Polly's discounts for the year totaled $900.

48. **LO.2** George is a U.S. citizen who is employed by Hawk Enterprises, a global company. Beginning on June 1, 2022, George began working in London. He worked there until January 31, 2023, when he transferred to Paris. He worked in Paris the remainder of 2023. His salary for the first five months of 2022 was

$100,000, and it was earned in the United States. His salary for the remainder of 2022 was $175,000, and it was earned in London. George's 2023 salary from Hawk was $300,000, with part being earned in London and part being earned in Paris. What is George's gross income in 2022 and 2023? (Assume that the foreign earned income exclusion amount is the same in both 2022 and 2023.)

49. **LO.2, 3** Determine Hazel's gross income from the following receipts for the year:

Gain on sale of Augusta County bonds	$800
Interest on U.S. government savings bonds	400
Interest on state income tax refund	200
Interest on Augusta County bonds	700
Patronage dividend from Potato Growers Cooperative	350

The patronage dividend was received in March of the current year for amounts paid for her (nondeductible) garden and lawn supplies.

50. **LO.1** In January 2022, Ezra purchased 2,000 shares of Gold Utility Mutual Fund for $20,000. In June, Ezra received an additional 100 shares as a dividend, in lieu of receiving $1,000 in cash dividends. In December, the company declared a two-for-one stock split. Ezra received an additional 2,100 shares, but there was no option to receive cash. At the time of the stock dividend in December and at the end of the year, the fund shares were trading for $5 per share. Also, at the end of the year, the fund offered to buy outstanding shares for $4.50. Ezra did not sell any shares during the year.
    a. What is Ezra's gross income from the 100 shares received in June?
    b. What is Ezra's gross income from the receipt of the 2,100 shares as a two-for-one stock split in December?
    c. Should Ezra be required to recognize gross income in 2022 even though the fair market value of his investment at the end of the year was less than the fair market value at the beginning of the year? Explain.

Decision Making
Planning

51. **LO.2** Tonya, who lives in California, inherited a $100,000 State of California bond in 2022. Her marginal Federal tax rate is 35%, she itemizes deductions on her Federal tax return, and her marginal state tax rate is 5%. The California bond pays 3.3% interest, which is not subject to California income tax. She can purchase a corporate bond of comparable risk that will yield 5.2% or a U.S. government bond that pays 4.6% interest. Which investment will provide the greatest after-tax yield?

Communications
Decision Making
Planning

52. **LO.2** Lynn Swartz's husband died three years ago. Her parents have income of over $200,000 a year and want to ensure that funds will be available for the education of Lynn's eight-year-old son, Eric. Lynn is currently earning $45,000 a year. Lynn's parents have suggested that they start a savings account for Eric. They have calculated that if they invest $4,000 a year for the next 8 years, at the end of 10 years, sufficient funds will be available for Eric's college expenses. Lynn realizes that the tax treatment of the investments could significantly affect the amount of funds available for Eric's education. She asked you to write a letter to her advising about options available to her parents and to her for Eric's college education. Lynn's address is 100 Myrtle Cove, Fairfield, CT 06824.

53. **LO.2** Starting in 2011 Chuck and Luane have been purchasing Series EE bonds in their name to use for the higher education of their daughter Susie, who currently is age 18. During the year, they cash in $12,000 of the bonds to use for freshman year tuition, fees, and room and board. Of this amount, $5,000 represents interest. Of the $12,000, $8,000 is used for tuition and fees and $4,000 is used for room and board. Chuck and Luane's AGI, before the educational savings bond exclusion, is $132,200. Review § 135, and answer the following questions.
    a. Determine the tax consequences for Chuck and Luane, who will file a joint return, and for Susie.
    b. Assume that Chuck and Luane purchased the bonds in Susie's name. Determine the tax consequences for Chuck and Luane and for Susie.

54. **LO.2** Albert established a qualified tuition program for each of his twins, Kim and Jim. He started each fund with $20,000 when the children were five years old. Albert made no further contributions to his children's plans. Thirteen years later, both children have graduated from high school. Kim's fund has accumulated to $45,000, and Jim's has accumulated to $42,000. Kim decides to attend a state university, which will cost $60,000 for four years (tuition, fees, room and board, and books). Jim decides to go to work instead of going to college. During the current year, $7,500 is used from Kim's plan to pay the cost of her first semester in college. Because Jim is not going to college now or in the future, Albert withdraws the $42,000 plan balance and gives it to Jim to start his new life after high school.

   a. During the period since the plans were established, should Albert or the twins have been including the annual plan earnings in gross income? Explain.

   b. What are the tax consequences to Kim and Albert of the $7,500 being used for the first semester's higher education costs?

   c. Because of her participation in the qualified tuition program, Kim received a 10% reduction in tuition charges; so less than $7,500 was withdrawn from her account. Is either Albert or Kim required to include the value of this discount in gross income? Explain.

   d. What are the tax consequences to Albert and Jim of Jim's qualified tuition program being closed?

55. **LO.3** How does the tax benefit rule apply in the following cases?

   a. In 2020, the Orange Furniture Store, an accrual method sole proprietorship, sold furniture on credit for $1,000 to Sammy. The cost of the furniture was $600. In 2021, Orange took a bad debt deduction for the $1,000. In 2022, Sammy inherited some money and paid Orange the $1,000 he owed. Orange's owner was in the 35% marginal tax bracket in 2020, the 12% marginal tax bracket in 2021, and the 35% marginal tax bracket in 2022.

   b. In 2021, Marvin, a cash basis taxpayer, took a $2,000 itemized deduction for state income taxes paid; the deduction was not limited by the SALT cap. This increased his itemized deductions to a total that was $800 more than the standard deduction. In 2022, Marvin received a $1,500 refund when he filed his 2021 state income tax return. Marvin was in the 12% marginal tax bracket in 2021 but was in the 35% marginal tax bracket in 2022.

   c. In 2021, Barb, a cash basis taxpayer, was in an accident and incurred $8,000 in medical expenses, which she claimed as an itemized deduction for medical expenses. Because of the 7.5%-of-AGI reduction, the expense reduced her taxable income by only $3,000. In 2022, Barb successfully sued the person who caused the physical injury and collected $8,000 to reimburse her for the cost of her medical expenses. Barb was in the 22% marginal tax bracket in 2021, 12% in 2022.

56. **LO.2** Vic, who was experiencing financial difficulties, was able to adjust his debts as follows:

   a. Vic is an attorney. Vic owed his uncle $25,000. The uncle told Vic that if he serves as the executor of the uncle's estate, Vic's debt will be canceled in the uncle's will.

   b. Vic borrowed $80,000 from First Bank. The debt was secured by land that Vic purchased for $100,000. Vic was unable to pay, and the bank foreclosed when the liability was $80,000, which was also the fair market value of the property.

   c. The Land Company, which had sold land to Vic for $80,000, reduced the mortgage on the land by $12,000.

   Determine the tax consequences to Vic.

Tax Return Problems

Critical Thinking
Decision Making
Tax Forms Problem
ProConnect™ Tax

57. Alfred E. Old and Beulah A. Crane, each age 42, married on September 7, 2019. Alfred and Beulah will file a joint return for 2021. Alfred's Social Security number is 111-11-1109. Beulah's Social Security number is 123-45-6780, and she has chosen to use "Old" as her married name. They live at 211 Brickstone Drive, Atlanta, GA 30304.

    Alfred was divorced from Sarah Old in March 2017. Under the divorce agreement, Alfred is to pay Sarah $1,250 per month for the next 10 years or until Sarah's death, whichever occurs first. Alfred paid Sarah $15,000 in 2021. In addition, in January 2021, Alfred paid Sarah $50,000, which is designated as being for her share of the marital property. Also, Alfred is responsible for all prior years' income taxes. Sarah's Social Security number is 123-45-6788.

    Alfred's salary for 2021 is $150,000. He is an executive working for Cherry, Inc. (Federal I.D. No. 98-7654321). As part of his compensation package, Cherry provides him with group term life insurance equal to twice his annual salary. His employer withheld $24,900 for Federal income taxes and $8,000 for state income taxes. The proper amounts were withheld for FICA taxes.

    Beulah recently graduated from law school and is employed by Legal Aid Society, Inc. (Federal I.D. No. 11-1111111), as a public defender. She received a salary of $42,000 in 2021. Her employer withheld $7,500 for Federal income taxes and $2,400 for state income taxes. The proper amounts were withheld for FICA taxes.

    Alfred and Beulah received taxable interest income of $500. They received a $1,900 refund on their 2020 state income taxes; they claimed the standard deduction on their 2020 Federal income tax return. Alfred and Beulah paid $4,500 interest and $1,450 property taxes on their personal residence in 2021. They paid sales taxes of $1,400, for which they maintain the receipts. Alfred and Beulah have never owned or used any virtual currency, and they do not want to contribute to the Presidential Election Campaign. Alfred and Beulah received the appropriate coronavirus recovery rebates (economic impact payments); related questions in ProConnect Tax should be ignored.

    Compute the Olds' net tax payable (or refund due) for 2021. Suggested software: ProConnect Tax.

Communications
Decision Making
Planning
Tax Computation Problem

58. Martin S. Albert (Social Security number 111-11-1111) is 39 years old and is married to Michele R. Albert (Social Security number 123-45-6789). The Alberts live at 512 Ferry Road, Newport News, VA 23601. They file a joint return and have two dependent children, Charlene, age 16, and Jordan, age 18. Charlene's Social Security number is 123-45-6788, and Jordan's Social Security number is 123-45-6787. In 2022, Martin and Michele had the following transactions:

    a. Michele received $120,000 in salary from Red Steel Corporation, where she is a construction engineer. Withholding for Federal income tax was $10,750. The amounts withheld for FICA taxes were as follows: $7,440 ($120,000 × 6.2%) for Social Security and $1,740 ($120,000 × 1.45%) for Medicare. Michele worked in Mexico from January 1, 2021, until February 15, 2022. Her $120,000 salary for 2022 includes $18,000 she earned for January and one-half of February 2022 while working in Mexico.
    b. Martin and Michele received $400 interest on Montgomery County (Virginia) school bonds.
    c. Martin received $2,300 interest from a Bahamian bank account.
    d. Michele received 50 shares of Applegate Corporation common stock as a stock dividend. The shares had a fair market value of $2,500 at the time Michele received them, and she did not have the option of receiving cash.
    e. Martin and Michele received a $1,200 refund on their 2021 Virginia income taxes. Their itemized deductions in 2021 totaled $34,000 and included state taxes of $7,400.
    f. Michele paid $6,600 alimony to her former husband, Benjamin P. Morgan (Social Security number 123-45-6786). The divorce was finalized in March 2016.

g. Martin and Michele kept the receipts for their sales taxes paid of $1,100.

h. Martin and Michele's itemized deductions were as follows:

- State income tax paid and withheld totaled $5,100.
- Real estate taxes on their principal residence were $3,700.
- Mortgage interest on their principal residence was $2,500.

Part 1—Tax Computation

Compute the Alberts' net tax payable (or refund due) for 2022.

Part 2—Tax Planning

The Alberts are considering buying another house. Their house mortgage payments would increase by $500 (to $1,500) per month, which includes a $250 increase in interest and a $100 increase in property tax. The Alberts would like to know how much the mortgage payments would increase net of any change in their income tax. Write a letter to the Alberts that contains your advice.

Research Problems

Note: Solutions to the Research Problems can be prepared by using the Thomson Reuters Checkpoint™ online tax research database, which accompanies this textbook. Solutions can also be prepared by using research materials found in a typical tax library.

the answer company™ THOMSON REUTERS®

Research Problem 1. Your client Murray reported to the Environmental Protection Agency that his employer was illegally dumping chemicals into a river. His charges were true, and Murray's employer was fined. In retaliation, Murray's employer fired him and made deliberate efforts to prevent Murray from obtaining other employment. Murray sued the employer, claiming that his reputation had been damaged. Murray won his lawsuit and received an award for "damages to his personal and professional reputation and for his mental suffering." Murray has asked you whether the award is taxable. He argues that he was awarded damages as a recovery of his human capital and that a recovery of capital is not income. Is Murray's logic correct?

Research Problem 2. The employees of the city of Greenville must make mandatory contributions to the city's postretirement health benefit plan. The employees' contributions are placed in a trust and are used exclusively for the employees' benefits. The employees believe that because they are required to make the contributions from their base salaries, the result should be the same as if the employer made the contribution and had reduced their salaries by the amount of the contributions. As a result, the employees believe they should be permitted to exclude the payments from gross income. The employees have asked you to research the issue.

Research Problem 3. Your client, Simon Che, is an avid Texas Rangers fan. Last March at the Rangers' home opener, as a result of a random drawing of those in attendance at the game, Simon won 300 Shipley Do-Nut coupons. Each coupon entitled him to a cup of coffee and a free doughnut or a dozen doughnut holes.

Simon used some of the coupons (approximately 20), but he found that eating so many doughnuts directly conflicted with his goal of losing weight. The unused coupons expired on January 1, 2023. As a result, Simon was surprised when he received a Form 1099 in February 2023 that valued his prize at $900. Simon would like to know whether the value of the doughnut coupons should be included in income and asks you to research his question. If you conclude that their value should be included in income, Simon also would like to know if he can reduce his gross income by including in income only the value of the coupons that he used. He has the unused coupons as documentation that neither he nor anyone else used them.

Research Problem 4. Aubrey Brown is a decorated veteran. As a result of a significant injury sustained in combat, Aubrey is unable to work. He received $12,000 of Social Security disability payments in the current year. He reasons that the payments should be excluded from his gross income because the payments are compensation for the physical injury he suffered as a result of his service in the armed forces. Is Aubrey correct? Explain.

Partial list of research aids:
Rev.Rul. 77–318.
Reimels v. Comm., 2006–1 USTC ¶50,147, 97 AFTR 2d 2006–820, 436 F.3d 344 (CA–2).

Use internet tax resources to address the following questions. Look for reliable websites and blogs of the IRS and other government agencies, media outlets, businesses, tax professionals, academics, think tanks, and political outlets.

Communications
Data Analytics

Research Problem 5. Use information about individual income tax returns available at the IRS Tax Stats website (**irs.gov/statistics/soi-tax-stats-individual-income-tax-returns**) to find data on the number of individuals who report tax-exempt interest income on their tax return and the amount of that exempt income. The data you find should show this information for individuals at different ranges of adjusted gross income (AGI). Use the data to create pie charts (or similar visuals) of the percent of AGI represented by the tax-exempt interest income exclusion as well as the number of individuals claiming this exclusion at different AGI levels. Analyze the IRS data, draw conclusions from it, and summarize your findings in a two- to three-paragraph e-mail sent to your instructor. Be sure your conclusions are explained and supported by the data.

Research Problem 6. Employers often use the internet as a means of attracting applications from potential employees. Locate an internet site offering employment opportunities, ideally one provided by a well-known corporation. How does the employer promote its fringe benefit and cafeteria plan packages? Compare and contrast three such sites.

Research Problem 7. One income exclusion that some states allow but the Federal government does not is for lottery winnings. Does your state have an exclusion for lottery winnings? If so, how does it work? Why do you think a state might allow winnings from its own state lottery to be excluded from state income taxes?

Becker CPA Review Questions

Becker

1. Stephen is a graduate student at West University. He works part-time at the campus coffee shop earning $5,000 this year. Stephen also receives a $25,000 scholarship that pays for his tuition, fees, and books. What amount does Stephen include in his gross income?

   a. $25,000 c. $30,000
   b. $5,000 d. $0

2. Jeffrey Dean, a Master's Degree candidate at North State Central University, was awarded a $15,000 scholarship from North State Central in the current year. During the current year, he paid the following expenses:

Tuition	$12,000
Books	1,000
Fees	500
Room and board	1,500

   In addition, he received $6,000 for teaching two undergraduate accounting courses. What amount must be included in Dean's gross income?

   a. $0 c. $7,500
   b. $6,000 d. $21,000

3. Linda is an employee of JRH Corporation. Which of the following would be included in Linda's gross income?
   a. Premiums paid by JRH Corporation for a group term life insurance policy for $50,000 of coverage for Linda.
   b. $1,000 of tuition paid by JRH Corporation to State University for Linda's master's degree program.
   c. A $2,000 trip given to Linda by JRH Corporation for meeting sales goals.
   d. $1,200 paid by JRH Corporation for an annual parking pass for Linda.

4. Kim was seriously injured at her job. As a result of her injury, she received the following payments:
   - $5,000 reimbursement from employer-provided health insurance for medical expenses paid by Kim. The premiums this year paid by Kim's employer totaled $6,000.
   - $15,000 disability pay. Kim has disability insurance provided by her employer as a nontaxable fringe benefit. Kim's employer paid $6,000 in disability premiums this year on behalf of Kim.
   - $10,000 received for damages for personal physical injury.
   - $200,000 for punitive damages.

   What amount is taxable to Kim?

   a. $215,000
   b. $225,000
   c. $236,000
   d. $0

5. Danny received the following interest and dividend payments this year. What amount should Danny include in his gross income?

Source Amount	
City of Atlanta bond interest	$1,200
U.S. Treasury bond interest	500
State of Georgia bond interest	1,000
Ellis Company common stock dividend	400
Row Corporation bond interest	600

   a. $2,500
   b. $1,500
   c. $3,700
   d. $2,200

6. Elizabeth received the following sources of income in the current year:

U.S. Treasury bond certificates interest	$500
Interest on state tax refund (paid by state government for late payment of tax refund to Elizabeth)	200
Corporate bond interest	600
Amount received for opening a new savings account at a local bank	50
Puerto Rico bond interest	350

   What amount must Elizabeth include in gross income on her Federal income tax return?

   a. $650
   b. $1,150
   c. $1,350
   d. $1,700

Part 3

Deductions

Chapter 6
Deductions and Losses: In General

Chapter 7
Deductions and Losses: Certain Business Expenses and Losses

Chapter 8
Depreciation, Cost Recovery, Amortization, and Depletion

Chapter 9
Deductions: Employee and Self-Employed-Related Expenses

Chapter 10
Deductions and Losses: Certain Itemized Deductions

Chapter 11
Investor Losses

Part 3 presents information related to the deduction component of the basic tax model. Deductions are classified as business versus nonbusiness, "for" AGI versus "from" AGI, employee versus employer, active versus passive, and reimbursed versus unreimbursed. The effect of each of these classifications is analyzed. The deduction for qualified business income, deduction limitations, and deduction disallowances are also covered. A separate chapter examines the special tax treatment affecting losses from investment activities.

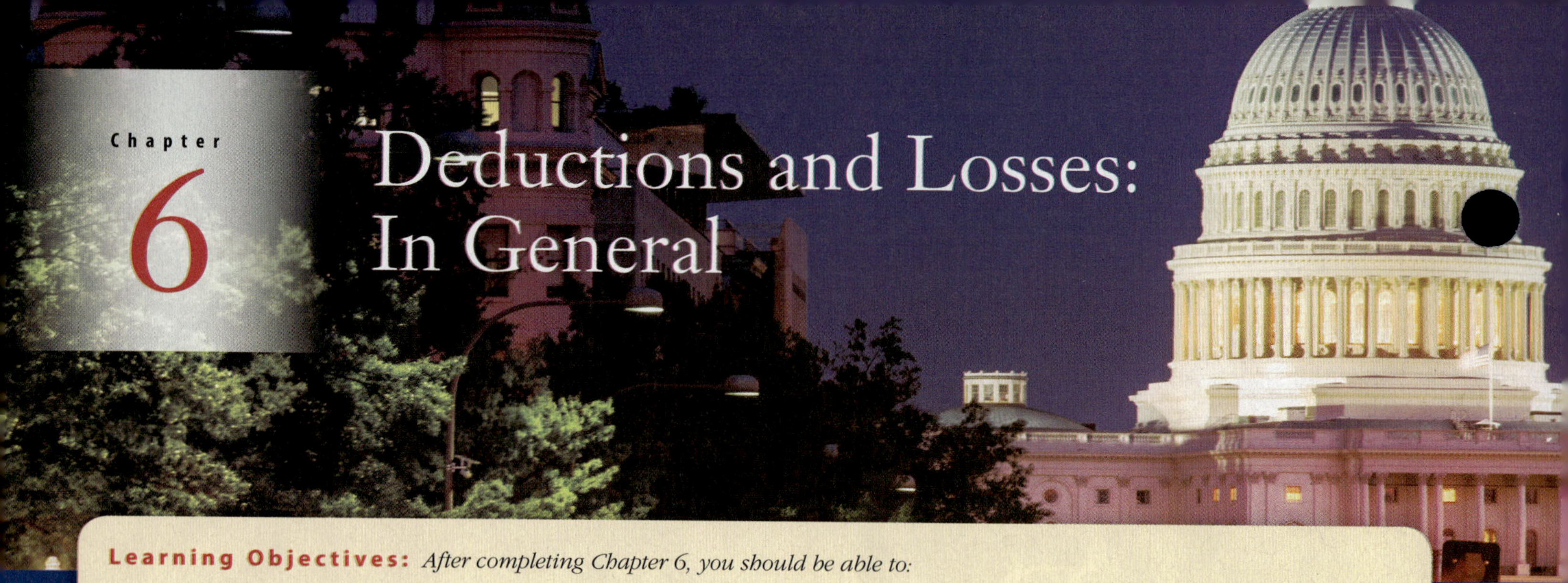

Chapter 6

Deductions and Losses: In General

Learning Objectives: *After completing Chapter 6, you should be able to:*

LO.1 Differentiate between deductions *for* and *from* adjusted gross income and describe the relevance of the differentiation.

LO.2 Describe the cash and accrual methods of accounting with emphasis on the deduction aspects.

LO.3 Apply some of the most common Internal Revenue Code deduction disallowance provisions.

LO.4 Identify tax planning opportunities for maximizing deductions and minimizing the disallowance of deductions.

Chapter Outline

6-1 Classification of Deductible Expenses, 6-2
- 6-1a Classifying Deductions, 6-3
- 6-1b Authority for Deductions, 6-3
- 6-1c Deduction Criteria for § 162 and § 212, 6-5
- 6-1d Personal Expenses, 6-6
- 6-1e Business and Nonbusiness Losses, 6-6
- 6-1f Deduction for Qualified Business Income, 6-7
- 6-1g Reporting Procedures, 6-9

6-2 Deductions and Losses—Timing of Expense Recognition, 6-10
- 6-2a Importance of Taxpayer's Method of Accounting, 6-10
- 6-2b Cash Method Requirements, 6-10
- 6-2c Accrual Method Requirements, 6-10
- 6-2d Prepaid Expenses—The "12-Month Rule," 6-12
- 6-2e Time Value of Tax Deductions, 6-12

6-3 Disallowance Possibilities, 6-13
- 6-3a Public Policy Limitation, 6-13
- 6-3b Political Contributions and Lobbying Activities, 6-15
- 6-3c Excessive Executive Compensation, 6-16
- 6-3d Investigation of a Business, 6-17
- 6-3e Hobby Losses, 6-18
- 6-3f Rental of Vacation Homes, 6-21
- 6-3g Expenditures Incurred for Taxpayer's Benefit or Taxpayer's Obligation, 6-25
- 6-3h Disallowance of Personal Expenditures, 6-26
- 6-3i Disallowance of Deductions for Capital Expenditures, 6-26
- 6-3j Transactions between Related Parties, 6-28
- 6-3k Substantiation Requirements, 6-29
- 6-3l Expenses and Interest Relating to Tax-Exempt Income, 6-29
- 6-3m Other Disallowances, 6-30

6-4 Tax Planning, 6-30
- 6-4a Vacation Homes, 6-30
- 6-4b Hobby Losses, 6-32
- 6-4c Do Deduction Limits Affect Executive Compensation?, 6-33

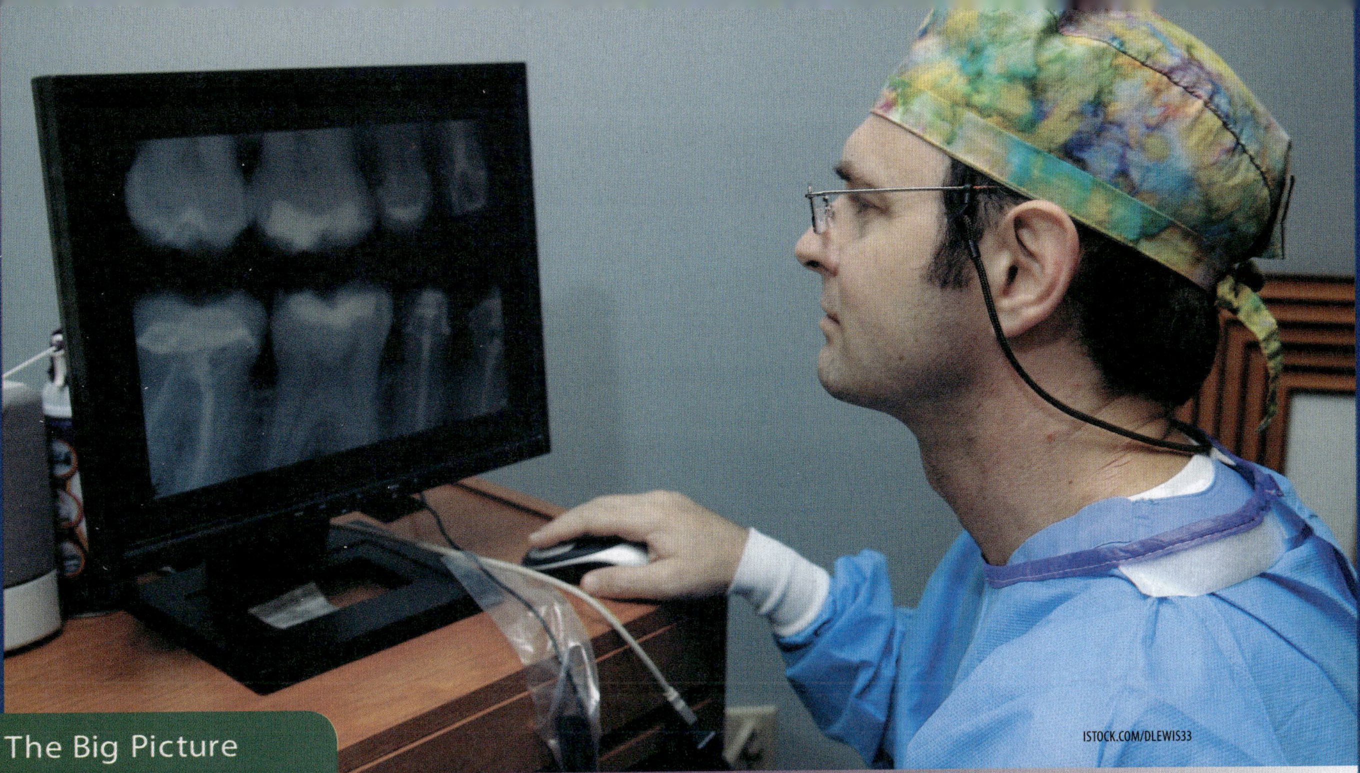

The Big Picture

Calculation of Deductible Expenses

Dr. Cliff Payne determines that the deductible expenses associated with his dental practice (a sole proprietorship) are as follows:

Salaries including FICA ($5,000 are unpaid at year-end)	$120,000
Building rent	24,000
Depreciation of dental equipment and office furnishings and equipment	52,000
Insurance (malpractice, dental equipment, and office furnishings and equipment)	22,000
Dental supplies	16,000
Office supplies	3,000
Investigation expenses	6,000
Contribution to the State Senate campaign fund of Tom Smith	1,000
Contribution to the State Senate campaign fund of Virginia White	1,000
Legal expenses associated with patient lawsuit	4,000
Fine imposed by city for improper disposal of medical waste	3,000
Dues paid to The Dental Society	10,000
Draw by Dr. Payne for living expenses ($5,000 monthly)	60,000

Has Dr. Payne correctly calculated the deductible business expenses for his dental practice?

Read the chapter and formulate your response.

Framework 1040 **Tax Formula for Individuals**

This chapter covers the boldfaced portions of the Tax Formula for Individuals that was introduced in Concept Summary 3.1 on p. 3-3. Below those portions are the sections of Form 1040 where the results are reported.

Income *(broadly defined)*	$ xx,xxx
Less: Exclusions	(x,xxx)
Gross income	**$xx,xxx**
Less: Deductions *for* adjusted gross income	**(x,xxx)**

FORM 1040 (Schedule 1)

3 Business income or (loss). Attach Schedule C . . . .

Adjusted gross income	$ xx,xxx
Less: The greater of total itemized deductions *or* the standard deduction	(x,xxx)

FORM 1040 (p. 1)

12a **Standard deduction or itemized deductions** (from Schedule A) . . . .

Charitable contributions if you take the standard deduction*	(xxx)
Personal and dependency exemptions**	(x,xxx)
Deduction for qualified business income***	(x,xxx)
Taxable income	$ xx,xxx
Tax on taxable income *(see Tax Tables or Tax Rate Schedules)*	$ x,xxx
Less: Tax credits *(including income taxes withheld and prepaid)*	(xxx)
Tax due (or refund)	$ xxx

* For 2021, married taxpayers may claim up to $600 of cash charitable donations ($300 if unmarried).
** Exemption deductions are not allowed from 2018 through 2025.
*** Only applies from 2018 through 2025.

The tax law has an all-inclusive definition of income; that is, income from whatever source derived is includible in gross income. Income cannot be excluded unless there is a specific statement to that effect in the tax law.

The opposite approach is used for deductions. A deduction is allowed only if there is a specific provision in the tax law that permits it. The inclusive definition of income and the exclusive definition of deductions may not seem fair to taxpayers, but it is the structure of the tax law. The courts agree with this structure, holding that any exclusions from income and all deductions are gifts from Congress.[1]

LO.1

Differentiate between deductions *for* and *from* adjusted gross income and describe the relevance of the differentiation.

6-1 Classification of Deductible Expenses

It is important to classify deductible expenses as **deductions *for* adjusted gross income** (AGI) or **deductions *from* adjusted gross income**. Deductions *for* AGI can be claimed whether or not the taxpayer itemizes. With the exception of the deduction for qualified business income, deductions *from* AGI result in a tax benefit only if, collectively, they exceed the taxpayer's standard deduction. If itemized deductions (*from* AGI) are less than the standard deduction, they provide no tax benefit. As Example 1 illustrates, whether a deduction is classified as *for* AGI or *from* AGI can affect the benefit the taxpayer receives from the deduction.

[1]The courts refer to this as "legislative grace"; see *New Colonial Ice Co. v. Helvering*, 4 USTC ¶1292, 13 AFTR 1180, 54 S.Ct. 788 (1934).

Example 1

Steve is a self-employed CPA. Ralph is one of Steve's employees. During the year, Steve and Ralph incur the following expenses:

	Steve	Ralph
Dues to American Institute of CPAs and State Society of CPAs	$ 400	$ 300
Subscriptions to professional journals	500	200
Registration fees for tax conferences	800	800
	$1,700	$1,300

Steve does not reimburse any of his employees for dues, subscriptions, or educational programs.

Steve's expenses are classified as deductions *for* AGI because they are business expenses of a sole proprietor. As a result, he can deduct the $1,700 on his Federal income tax return. Ralph's unreimbursed employee business expenses are classified as deductions *from* AGI. However, these expenses are miscellaneous itemized deductions and, from 2018 through 2025, are not deductible.

Deductions *for* AGI may affect the *amount* of itemized deductions directly because some itemized deductions are limited to amounts in excess of specified percentages of AGI. Itemized deductions that have AGI limitations include medical expenses (7.5% of AGI) and personal casualty losses (10% of AGI).

Example 2

Tina, age 36, earns a salary of $90,000 and has no other income. She itemizes her deductions during 2022. Unreimbursed medical expenses for the year are $12,000. Tina's medical expense deduction is $5,250, as computed below.

Alternatively, assume that Tina receives a $10,000 bonus from her employer in 2022. Her AGI would then be $100,000 ($90,000 + $10,000), and her medical expense is reduced by $750 to $4,500.

	Without Bonus	With Bonus
Qualified medical expenses	$12,000	$12,000
Reduction: AGI × 7.5%	(6,750)	(7,500)
Deductible medical expenses	$ 5,250	$ 4,500

When Tina's income increased by $10,000, this reduced her medical expense deduction by $750; so the total effect on taxable income is an increase of $10,750.[2]

6-1a Classifying Deductions

Two key issues must be resolved for any potential deduction. First, it must be determined whether the item is deductible, as discussed in text Section 6-1b. If the item is deductible, then the second issue is to determine if the deduction is classified as *for* AGI or *from* AGI. Deductions *for* AGI are listed in § 62. If a deduction is not listed in § 62, it is an itemized deduction. Exhibit 6.1 provides a partial list of the items classified as deductions *for* AGI.

6-1b Authority for Deductions

The specific authority for deductions is provided in many different Code sections. However, two of the most important are § 212 and § 162. To determine the proper authority

[2]See Chapter 10 for additional discussion of medical expenses.

Exhibit 6.1 Common Deductions *for* Adjusted Gross Income

Deduction	Chapter
Alimony payments (divorce decrees before 2019)	4
Expenses attributable to property held for the production of rents and royalties	6
Expenses attributable to a trade or business	9
Employee business expenses (reimbursed)	9
Professional development and supplies [up to $300 in 2022 ($250 in 2021)] for elementary and secondary school teachers	9
Student loan interest	9 and 10
Contributions to retirement plans	9 and 19
Medical insurance premiums paid by a self-employed taxpayer	10
Self-employment taxes	13
Losses on the sale or exchange of property	14 and 16
Penalty on premature withdrawal of funds from time savings accounts	19

for claiming a deduction, first determine what type of activity the expenditure relates to. All activities can be divided into one of the following mutually exclusive categories:

1. Investment/production of income (§ 212).
2. Trade or business (§ 162).
3. Personal (various Code sections).

For example, are legal expenses deductible? To make that determination, first determine whether the legal expense relates to an investment, a trade or business, or a personal activity.

Example 3

Darryl pays $400 to an attorney for her advice. If this payment relates to his business, it is a § 162 business expense. If the payment relates to the purchase of land that he intends to hold for profit, it is a § 212 investment/production of income expense. If the payment relates to the development of an estate plan, it is a nondeductible personal expense (§ 262).

Section 212 Expenses

Code § 212 allows deductions for ordinary and necessary expenses paid or incurred for:

- The production or collection of income.
- The management, conservation, or maintenance of property held for the production of income.
- Expenses paid in connection with the determination, collection, or refund of any tax.

Expenses related to rent and royalty income (reported on Schedule E) are § 212 expenses, and these expenses are deductible *for* AGI. All other § 212 expenses are itemized deductions (deductions *from* AGI). For example, investment interest expense and investment-related state and local taxes are deductible *from* AGI (but subject to specific limitations discussed in Chapters 10 and 11). Any remaining § 212 expenses (e.g., safe deposit box rentals and investment advisory fees) are miscellaneous itemized deductions and, from 2018 through 2025, are not deductible.[3]

Section 162 Trade or Business Expenses

Code § 162(a) permits a deduction for all ordinary and necessary expenses paid or incurred in carrying on a trade or business. These include reasonable salaries paid for services, expenses for the use of business property, and one-half of self-employment taxes paid (see Chapters 9 and 13). These expenses are deducted *for* AGI.

[3] § 62(a)(4) and Reg. § 1.212–1(g).

It is sometimes difficult to determine whether an expense is deductible as a trade or business expense. The term *trade or business* is not defined in the Code or Regulations, and the courts have not provided a satisfactory definition. One key determination is to ensure that the activity is not a hobby. If the taxpayer's operations are not extensive enough to indicate that a trade or business exists, expenses related to the activity are deductible only to the extent of the activity's income (see text Section 6-3e).

Code § 162 *excludes* the following items from classification as trade or business expenses:

- Charitable contributions or gifts.
- Illegal bribes and kickbacks and certain treble damage payments.
- Fines and penalties.

6-1c Deduction Criteria for § 162 and § 212

Expenses under § 162 and § 212 must be **ordinary and necessary** to be deductible. In addition, compensation for services must be "reasonable" in amount.

An expense is *necessary* if a prudent businessperson would incur the same expense and the expense is expected to be appropriate and helpful in the taxpayer's business.[4] An expense is *ordinary* if it is normal, usual, or customary in the type of business conducted by the taxpayer and is not capital in nature.[5] However, an expense need not be recurring to be deductible as ordinary. For example, a business may be in a situation that is a very rare occurrence and incur an expense. If other businesses in a similar situation are likely to incur a similar expense, then the expense can be ordinary even though it is not recurring.

Example 4

Nisha engaged in a mail-order business. The post office judged that her advertisements were false and misleading. Under a fraud order, the post office stamped "fraudulent" on all letters addressed to Nisha's business and returned them to the senders. Nisha spent $30,000 on legal fees in an unsuccessful attempt to force the post office to stop.

The legal fees (although not recurring) were ordinary business expenses because they were normal, usual, or customary in the circumstances.[6]

To be deductible, an expense must be both ordinary *and* necessary.

Example 5

Pat purchased a business that had just been adjudged bankrupt. Because the business had a poor financial rating, Pat wanted to restore its financial reputation. Consequently, he paid off some of the debts owed by the former owners that had been canceled by the bankruptcy court.

Because Pat had no legal obligation to make these payments, the U.S. Supreme Court found that he was trying to generate goodwill. Although the payments were necessary (i.e., appropriate and helpful), they were *not* ordinary and their deduction *was not* allowed.[7]

The Code refers to **reasonableness** solely with respect to salaries and other compensation for services.[8] But the courts have held that for any business expense to be ordinary and necessary, it also must be reasonable in amount.[9] Example 6 illustrates the reasonableness concept for an investment expense.

Example 6

Danielle is a retired pilot who owns a small portfolio of investments, including 10 shares of Robin, Inc., a publicly traded company, worth $1,000. She incurred $350 in travel expenses to attend the annual shareholders' meeting where she voted her 10 shares against the current management group.

No deduction is permitted because a 10-share investment is insignificant in value in relation to the travel expenses incurred.[10]

What constitutes reasonableness is a question of fact. If an expense is unreasonable, the excess amount is not allowed as a deduction.

---

[4] *Welch v. Helvering*, 3 USTC ¶1164, 12 AFTR 1456, 54 S.Ct. 8 (1933).

[5] *Deputy v. DuPont*, 40–1 USTC ¶9161, 23 AFTR 808, 60 S.Ct. 363.

[6] *Comm. v. Heininger*, 44–1 USTC ¶9109, 31 AFTR 783, 64 S.Ct. 249 (1943).

[7] *Welch v. Helvering*, cited in Footnote 4.

[8] § 162(a)(1).

[9] *Comm. v. Lincoln Electric Co.*, 49–2 USTC ¶9388, 38 AFTR 411, 176 F.2d 815 (CA–6).

[10] *J. Raymond Dyer*, 36 T.C. 456 (1961).

The question of reasonableness generally arises with respect to closely held corporations since there is no separation of ownership and management. Transactions between the shareholders and the closely held company may result in the disallowance of deductions for excessive salaries and rent expense paid by the corporation to the shareholders. An unusually large salary will often be challenged by the IRS, but the courts may conclude that it is reasonable given the facts that surround a particular business.[11] If excessive payments for salaries and rents are closely related to the percentage of stock owned by the recipients, the payments are generally treated as dividends.[12] Because dividends are not deductible by the corporation, the disallowance results in an increase in the corporate taxable income.

Example 7

Sparrow Corporation, a closely held corporation, is owned equally by Lupe, Carlos, and Ramon. The company has been highly profitable for several years and has not paid dividends. Lupe, Carlos, and Ramon are key officers of the company, and each receives a salary of $200,000. Salaries for similar positions in comparable companies average only $100,000.

Amounts paid to the owners in excess of $100,000 may be deemed unreasonable; if so, a total of $300,000 in salary deductions by Sparrow is disallowed. The disallowed amounts are treated as dividends rather than salary to Lupe, Carlos, and Ramon because the payments are proportional to stock ownership. Salaries are deductible by the corporation, but dividends are not.

Note that the shareholders may benefit from this reclassification. Salaries would be taxed at ordinary income rates and are subject to payroll taxes. However, dividend income would be taxed at long-term capital gains rates if qualified and would not be subject to payroll taxes.

6-1d Personal Expenses

Expenditures that are incurred in one's personal life are deductible only if a specific Code section authorizes the deduction. These expenses are usually deductions *from* AGI. Some of the more common deductions in this category include the following:

- Contributions to qualified charitable organizations.
- Mortgage interest expense.
- State and local taxes.
- Medical expenses.
- Personal casualty losses.

Many of these deductions are limited in some way [e.g., only amounts in excess of a specific percentage of AGI; a specific cap on the deduction (for example, the deduction for state and local taxes is capped at $10,000)]. Casualty losses are discussed in Chapter 7; itemized deductions are discussed in Chapter 10.

Example 8

Yolanda paid her doctor $650 for a medical procedure this year. She also made a charitable contribution to the United Way for $1,000. She spent $400 on uniforms for her children to wear to school.

The Code specifically provides for deducting medical expenses and qualified charitable contributions, so these are deductible. Since the Code does not provide a deduction for clothing worn for personal use, the uniforms are not deductible.

6-1e Business and Nonbusiness Losses

Code § 165 provides for a deduction for losses not compensated for by insurance. As a general rule, deductible losses of individual taxpayers are limited to those incurred in a trade or business or in a transaction entered into for profit. Individuals also are allowed to deduct losses that are the result of a casualty, but only if the casualty occurs in a Federally declared disaster area. Casualty losses include, but are not limited to, those caused by fire, storm, shipwreck, and theft (see Chapter 7). A deductible personal casualty loss is an itemized deduction (i.e., *from* AGI).

[11] *Kennedy, Jr. v. Comm.*, 82–1 USTC ¶9186, 49 AFTR 2d 82–628, 671 F.2d 167 (CA–6).

[12] Reg. § 1.162–8.

Example 9

During the current year, Kareem encountered a series of unfortunate events. A tornado hit his personal residence in March, and he incurred a loss of $30,000; due to the widespread damage, his county was declared a Federal disaster area. In June, he sold his car to generate cash to pay his bills. The loss on the car sale was $3,500. In October, he sold 100 shares of stock in MMM Company at a loss of $2,000.

Since the tornado is a casualty that occurred in a Federal disaster area, the $30,000 loss is potentially deductible on Schedule A (but subject to limitations). The car is a personal use asset, and the loss was not caused by a casualty, so the $3,500 loss is not deductible. The $2,000 stock loss is from an investment activity, so this is deductible as a capital loss.

6-1f Deduction for Qualified Business Income

An individual can deduct up to 20 percent of **qualified business income (QBI)** from a sole proprietorship, a partnership, or an S corporation. This *from* AGI deduction reduces the tax on income from proprietorships and flow-through businesses.[13] The deduction does *not* reduce self-employment income. The QBI deduction is discussed in detail in text Section 9-7; a brief overview is provided here.

In general, the deduction for QBI is the *lesser of* 20 percent of:

1. Qualified business income, or
2. Modified taxable income (taxable income before the QBI deduction, reduced by any net capital gain).[14]

Qualified business income is defined as the ordinary income less ordinary deductions a taxpayer earns from a "qualified trade or business" (e.g., from a sole proprietorship, an S corporation, or a partnership). QBI does not include any wages earned as an employee, any capital gains or losses, any dividend income, or any interest income. In determining QBI, all deductions attributable to a trade or business are taken into account. Relevant deductions include the self-employment tax deduction [§ 164(f)], the self-employed health insurance deduction [§ 162(l)], and any deduction for contributions to qualified retirement plans [§ 404].[15] If a taxpayer has a qualified business loss in one year, no QBI deduction is allowed and the loss is carried over to the next year to reduce QBI (but not below zero).

Example 10

Trevor, a single taxpayer, has modified taxable income of $150,000. His sole proprietorship reports $108,000 of net income [on Schedule C (Form 1040)]. As a result, Trevor's self-employment tax liability is $15,260 ($108,000 × 0.9235 × 15.3%). He is allowed a *for* AGI deduction for one-half of his self-employment tax liability ($7,630; $15,260 × 1/2). Trevor's QBI is $100,370 ($108,000 − $7,630).

Since Trevor's QBI is less than his modified taxable income, his QBI deduction is $20,074 ($100,370 × 20%).

Limit on the QBI Deduction Based on Wages and Capital Investment

In 2022, if taxable income before the QBI deduction is greater than $340,100 (married, filing jointly) or $170,050 (all other taxpayers), the QBI deduction cannot exceed (i.e., is limited to) the *greater of*:[16]

1. 50 percent of the W–2 wages relating to the qualified trade or business, or
2. The sum of:
   a. 25 percent of the W–2 wages relating to the qualified trade or business, and
   b. 2.5 percent of the unadjusted basis (immediately after acquisition) of all qualified property.

This limit is phased in over $100,000 (married, filing jointly) or $50,000 (all other taxpayers) of taxable income. Once a married couple has taxable income in 2022 over $440,100 ($220,050 for all other taxpayers), the W–2 wages and capital investment limitation will be completely in play. Exhibit 6.2 summarizes the limitations that may reduce or eliminate the QBI deduction.

[13] § 199A.

[14] § 199A(a).

[15] § 199A(c) and Reg. § 1.199A–3(b)(1)(vi).

[16] In 2021, the threshold amounts were $329,800 (married taxpayers filing a joint return), $164,925 (married taxpayers filing separately), and $164,900 (all other taxpayers).

Exhibit 6.2 — 2022 QBI Limitations

Filing Status*	Taxable Income Before the QBI Deduction		
Married, Filing Jointly	$340,100 or less	More than $340,100 and less than $440,100	$440,100 or more
Single and Head of Household	$170,050 or less	More than $170,050 and less than $220,050	$220,050 or more
Wage/Asset Limitation	Does not apply	Limitation phased in	Limitation applies in full
Specified Services Limitation	Does not apply	QBI deduction partially allowed	QBI deduction not allowed
Does 20% of Modified Taxable Income Limitation Apply?	Yes	Yes	Yes

* In 2022, married taxpayers filing separately have a threshold amount of $170,050.

QBI Deduction Limitation

Example 11

Simone, a married taxpayer, operates a business as a sole proprietor. The business has one employee, who is paid $80,000 during 2022. Assume that the business has no significant assets. During 2022, Simone reports qualified business income of $500,000 and taxable income before the QBI deduction of $600,000. Because Simone's taxable income before the QBI deduction exceeds $440,100, her QBI deduction is $40,000, the lower of:

- $100,000 (20% × $500,000), or
- $40,000 (50% of W–2 wages of $80,000).

Example 12

Assume the same facts as in Example 11, except that Simone's taxable income before the QBI deduction is $380,100.

Because Simone's taxable income before the QBI deduction exceeds $340,100 but is less than $440,100, the W–2 limit is partially phased in. Her taxable income before the QBI deduction exceeds $340,100 by $40,000. So Simone must reduce her "normal" QBI deduction ($100,000) by 40% ($40,000 ÷ $100,000) of the difference between the "normal" QBI deduction and the "limited" QBI deduction (based on W–2 wages; $40,000). As a result, Simone's QBI deduction is $76,000, computed as follows:

Normal QBI deduction	$100,000
Less: 40% × $60,000 ($100,000 – $40,000)	(24,000)
QBI deduction	$ 76,000

Qualified Trade or Business

A qualified trade or business means any trade or business *other than* a "specified service trade or business."[17] Specified services include the following:

- Health.
- Law.
- Accounting.
- Actuarial Science.
- Performing Arts.
- Consulting.
- Athletics.
- Financial Services.
- Brokerage Services.

Special rules apply to specified service businesses. In general, a trade or business is *not* a specified service trade or business if the trade or business has gross receipts of

[17] §§ 199A(d)(1) and (2).

$25 million or less in a taxable year and *less than 10 percent* of its gross receipts relates to a "specified service." For a trade or business with gross receipts greater than $25 million in a taxable year, the test is *less than 5 percent* (rather than less than 10 percent).[18] And if taxable income is below the thresholds identified, a taxpayer is still allowed a partial (or full) QBI deduction. These rules are discussed in more depth in Chapter 9.

6-1g Reporting Procedures

All deductions *for* AGI are ultimately reported on Schedule 1 (Form 1040). Most of the deductions *for* AGI originate on supporting schedules. Examples include business expenses (Schedule C); rent, royalty, partnership, and fiduciary deductions (Schedule E); and farming expenses (Schedule F). Other deductions *for* AGI, such as contributions to traditional IRAs and Keogh retirement plans and alimony payments, are entered directly on Schedule 1 (Form 1040).

Adjusted gross income appears on page 1 of Form 1040. Deductions *from* AGI (itemized deductions) are reported on Schedule A (Form 1040). The total of all itemized deductions is subtracted *from* AGI (unless the standard deduction is greater). Then the qualified business income deduction is subtracted to arrive at taxable income.

Exhibit 6.3 summarizes the reporting and flow of deductions on the taxpayer's return (Form 1040). See Concept Summary 6.4 later in the chapter for the classification of deductions as *for* AGI or *from* AGI.

Exhibit 6.3 Format of Form 1040

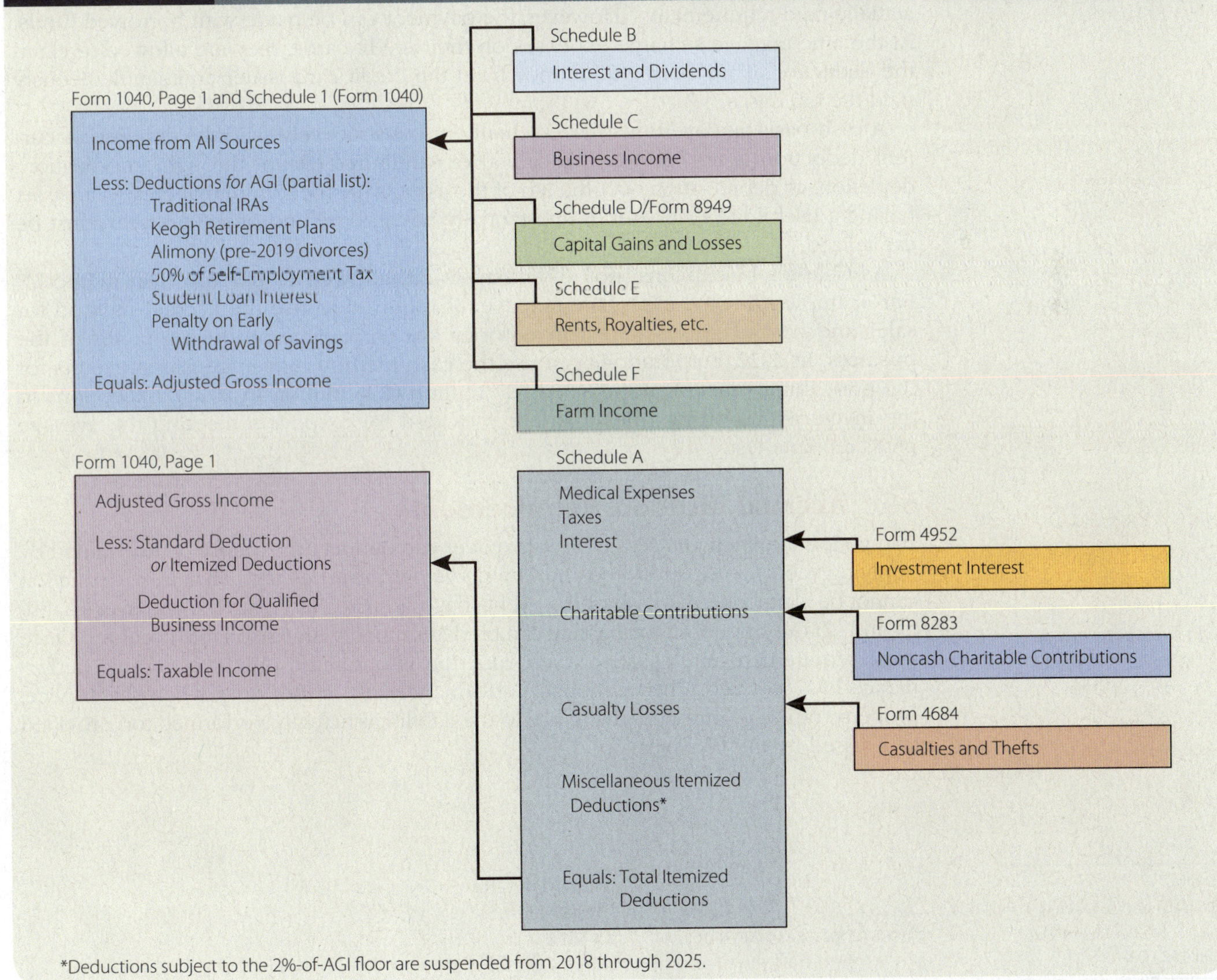

*Deductions subject to the 2%-of-AGI floor are suspended from 2018 through 2025.

[18] Reg. § 1.199A–5(c)(1).

LO.2

Describe the cash and accrual methods of accounting with emphasis on the deduction aspects.

6-2 Deductions and Losses—Timing of Expense Recognition

6-2a Importance of Taxpayer's Method of Accounting

A taxpayer's **accounting method** is a major factor in determining taxable income. The method used determines when an item is includible in income and when an item is deductible on the tax return. Usually, the taxpayer's normal method of record keeping is used for income tax purposes.[19] The taxing authorities require that the method used clearly reflect income and that items be handled consistently.[20] The most common methods of accounting are the cash method and the accrual method. If a taxpayer owns multiple businesses, it may be possible to use the cash method for some and the accrual method for others.

Throughout the portions of the Code dealing with deductions, the phrase *paid or incurred* is used. *Paid* refers to the cash basis taxpayer who gets a deduction only in the year of payment. *Incurred* concerns the accrual basis taxpayer who obtains the deduction in the year in which the liability for the expense becomes certain (refer to Chapter 4).

6-2b Cash Method Requirements

The expenses of cash basis taxpayers are deductible only when they are actually paid with cash or other property. Promising to pay or issuing a note does *not* satisfy the actually paid requirement.[21] However, the payment can be made with borrowed funds. At the time taxpayers charge expenses on their credit cards, they are allowed to claim the deduction. They borrowed money from the credit card issuer and simultaneously paid the expenses.[22]

A cash basis taxpayer must have actually or constructively paid the expense. A current deduction is not allowed for capital expenditures except through amortization, depletion, or depreciation over the life of the asset. An expenditure that creates an asset having a useful life that extends substantially beyond the end of the tax year must be capitalized.[23]

As Chapter 18 explains, not all taxpayers are allowed to use the cash method.[24] For example, in some cases, the taxpayer is required to use the accrual method for sales and cost of goods sold if inventories are an income-producing factor of the business. In 2022, corporations can use the cash method if average gross receipts for the prior three years do not exceed $27 million ($26 million in 2021). Exceptions to the inventory reporting rules also are provided for taxpayers meeting the average gross receipts test.

6-2c Accrual Method Requirements

The period in which an accrual basis taxpayer can deduct an expense is determined by applying the *all events test* and the *economic performance test*. That is, a deduction cannot be claimed until (1) all of the events have occurred to create the taxpayer's liability and (2) the amount of the liability can be determined with reasonable accuracy. Once these requirements are satisfied, the deduction is permitted only if economic performance has occurred. The economic performance test is met only when the service, property, or use of property giving rise to the liability is actually performed for, provided to, or used by the taxpayer.[25]

---

[19] § 446(a).

[20] §§ 446(b) and (e); Reg. § 1.446–1(a)(2).

[21] *Page v. Rhode Island Trust Co., Exr.*, 37–1 USTC ¶9138, 19 AFTR 105, 88 F.2d 192 (CA–1).

[22] Rev.Rul. 78–39. See also Rev.Rul. 80–335, which applies to pay-by-phone arrangements.

[23] Reg. § 1.461–1(a).

[24] §§ 448 and 448(c)(1).

[25] § 461(h).

Example 13

Greg's entertainment business sponsored a jazz festival in a rented auditorium at a local college. His business is responsible for cleaning up after the festival, which took place on December 22, 2022, and reinstalling the auditorium seats. Because the college is closed over the Christmas holidays, the company hired by Greg to perform the work did not begin these activities until January 3, 2023. Greg's business cannot deduct the related costs until 2023, when the services are performed.

An exception to the economic performance requirements allows certain *recurring items* to be deducted immediately if all of the following conditions are met:

- The item is recurring in nature and is treated consistently by the taxpayer.
- Either the accrued item is not material or accruing it in the current period results in better matching of income and expenses.
- All of the events have occurred that determine the existence of the liability, and the amount of the liability can be determined with reasonable accuracy.
- Economic performance occurs within a reasonable period (but not later than 8½ months after the close of the taxable year).[26]

The Third Circuit Court of Appeals has ruled that accrual basis taxpayers who award points to customers to use for future purchases can deduct the value of the points when awarded to the customers.[27] The IRS and Tax Court had taken the position that the deduction could not be recorded until the points were redeemed and used. In addition, the Third Circuit noted that the points are recurring items and can qualify for this exception to the economic performance test if the requirements listed above have been met.

Exceptions to Economic Performance Rules

Example 14

Marco, an accrual basis, calendar year taxpayer, entered into a monthly maintenance contract during the year. He makes a monthly accrual at the end of every month for this service and pays the fee sometime between the first and fifteenth of the following month when services are performed. The amount involved is immaterial, and all of the other tests are met.

The December 2022 accrual is deductible in 2022 even though the service is performed on January 12, 2023.

Example 15

Rita, an accrual basis, calendar year taxpayer, shipped merchandise sold on December 30, 2022, via Greyhound Van Lines on January 3, 2023, and paid the freight charges at that time.

Because Rita reported the sale of the merchandise in 2022, the shipping charge also should be deductible in 2022. This procedure results in a better matching of income and expenses.

Reserves for estimated expenses such as warranties and bad debts are often deducted for financial accounting purposes before the specific expense is identified. Generally, these reserves are not allowed for tax purposes because the economic performance test cannot be satisfied.

Example 16

Blackbird Airlines is required by Federal law to test its engines after 3,000 flying hours. Aircraft cannot return to flight until the tests have been conducted. An unrelated aircraft maintenance company does all of the company's tests for $1,500 per engine.

For financial reporting purposes, the company accrues an expense based upon $0.50 per hour of flight and credits an allowance account. The actual amounts paid for maintenance are offset against the allowance account.

For tax purposes, the economic performance test is not satisfied until the work has been done. Therefore, the reserve method cannot be used for tax purposes.

[26] § 461(h)(3)(A).

[27] *Giant Eagle, Inc.*, 2016–1 USTC ¶50,274, 117 AFTR 2d 2016–1476, 822 F.3d 666 (CA–3). Also see IRS Action on Decision 2016–03.

6-2d Prepaid Expenses—The "12-Month Rule"

A taxpayer doesn't have to capitalize amounts paid to create a benefit that doesn't extend beyond the earlier of (1) 12 months after the first date on which the taxpayer realized the benefit or (2) the end of the tax year following the tax year in which the payment was made (the "12-month rule").[28] Although this rule applies to both cash and accrual method taxpayers, accrual method taxpayers cannot claim a deduction unless economic performance has occurred.[29]

"12-Month Rule"

Example 17

On November 1, 2022, Nada, a calendar year and cash basis taxpayer, pays $6,000 for a one-year premium on a catastrophic liability policy that takes effect December 15, 2022. Nada will receive a benefit from this policy from December 15, 2022, through December 14, 2023. Her benefit does not extend beyond 12 months after the benefit begins on December 15. It also does not extend beyond the end of 2023. Therefore, this payment satisfies the requirements of the 12-month rule and Nada can deduct the $6,000 in 2022.

Example 18

Assume the same facts as in Example 17, except that the benefit from the policy runs from February 1, 2023, through January 31, 2024. Nada's benefit now extends beyond the end of the tax year following the tax year in which the payment was made (December 31, 2023), so the 12-month rule requirements are not met. Nada must capitalize the $6,000 payment in 2022 and amortize it over the benefit period.

6-2e Time Value of Tax Deductions

Both the time value of money and marginal tax rate changes must be considered when an expense can be paid and deducted in either of two years. Cash basis taxpayers often have the choice to pay expenses at the end of the current year or at the beginning of the following year. In view of the time value of money, a tax deduction this year may be worth more than the same deduction next year. However, accelerating the payment may not be advantageous if the taxpayer's marginal tax rate is higher in the following year. Before accelerating a payment, the taxpayer also needs to forecast future cash flow to ensure that an early payment makes sense.

Example 19

Rita pledged $50,000 to her church's special building fund. She can make the contribution on December 31, 2022, or January 1, 2023. Rita is in the 24% tax bracket in 2022 and in the 35% bracket in 2023. She itemizes her deductions in both years. Assume that Rita's discount rate is 5%. If she takes the deduction in 2023, she saves $4,667 ($16,667 − $12,000). Even though the tax savings from a January 1, 2023 contribution won't be realized until her 2023 tax return is filed, the increase in her deduction due to her increased marginal tax rates overcomes the time value of money consequences. See Table E-2 in Appendix E.

	2022	2023
Contribution	$50,000	$50,000
Tax bracket	× 0.24	× 0.35
Tax savings	$12,000	$17,500
Discounted @ 5%	×1.0000	×0.9524
Savings in present value	$12,000	$16,667

If tax rates are changing between two years, there are several areas in which taxpayers may have discretion as to which year to make a payment to achieve tax savings. Examples include certain alimony payments (see Chapter 4), assets purchased and expensed under § 179 or additional first-year (bonus) depreciation (see Chapter 8), home mortgage interest, and charitable contributions (see Chapter 10). Always remember to consider the time value of money in the analysis.

[28] Reg. § 1.263(a)–4(f).

[29] Reg. § 1.263(a)–4(f)(6).

6-3 Disallowance Possibilities

LO.3

Apply some of the most common Internal Revenue Code deduction disallowance provisions.

Certain types of expenses are disallowed by the tax law. Without these restrictions, taxpayers might attempt to deduct items that, in reality, are personal expenditures. For example, specific tax rules are provided to determine whether an expense is for trade or business purposes or is related to a personal hobby.

6-3a Public Policy Limitation

Payments considered to be in violation of public policy are not deductible. In addition, any payment to a governmental entity is not deductible. This provision does not apply to payments that are restitution for damage caused by the taxpayer or payments for taxes paid.[30]

Justification for Denying Deductions

The courts developed the principle that a payment in violation of public policy is not a necessary expense and is not deductible.[31] Allowing a deduction would, in effect, be indirectly subsidizing a taxpayer's wrongdoing. The following expenses, which are considered contrary to public policy, are not deductible:

- Bribes and kickbacks, including those associated with Medicare or Medicaid (in the case of foreign bribes and kickbacks, only if the payments violate the U.S. Foreign Corrupt Practices Act of 1977).
- Fines and penalties paid to a government for violation of law.
- Two-thirds of the treble damage payments made to claimants resulting from violation of the antitrust law.[32]

The Big Picture

Example 20

Refer to the facts of *The Big Picture* on p. 6-1. Dr. Payne had not instituted proper procedures for disposing of medical waste from his laboratory. During the current tax year, he was fined $3,000 by the city. Dr. Payne believes the fine should be deducted as an ordinary business expense.

However, because the fine was due to a violation of public policy, the $3,000 is not deductible.

To be disallowed, a bribe or kickback must be illegal under either Federal or state law and also must subject the payor to a criminal penalty or the loss of a license or privilege to engage in a trade or business. For a bribe or kickback that is illegal under state law, a deduction is denied if the state law is generally enforced.

Example 21

During the year, Jean-Paul, an insurance salesperson, paid $5,000 to Karen, a real estate broker. The payment represented 20% of the commissions Jean-Paul earned from customers referred by Karen. Under state law, the splitting of commissions by an insurance salesperson is an act of misconduct that could warrant a revocation of the salesperson's license.

Jean-Paul's $5,000 payments to Karen are not deductible if the state law is generally enforced.

Legal Expenses Incurred in Defense of Civil or Criminal Penalties

To deduct legal expenses, the taxpayer must be able to show that the origin and character of the claim are related directly to (1) a trade or business or (2) an income-producing activity. Personal legal expenses are not deductible. As a result, legal fees incurred in connection with a criminal defense are deductible only if the crime is associated with the taxpayer's trade or business or income-producing activity.[33]

[30] § 162(f)(1).

[31] *Tank Truck Rentals, Inc. v. Comm.*, 58–1 USTC ¶9366, 1 AFTR 2d 1154, 78 S.Ct. 507.

[32] §§ 162(c), (f), and (g).

[33] *Comm. v. Tellier*, 66–1 USTC ¶9319, 17 AFTR 2d 633, 86 S.Ct. 1118.

Global Tax Issues — Overseas Gun Sales Result in Large Fines

The Foreign Corrupt Practices Act (FCPA) is intended to punish taxpayers who make illegal payments to foreign officials to obtain economic advantages. Besides such payments (usually improperly recorded as business expenses) being nondeductible for income tax purposes, serious and consistent violations can lead to the imposition of fines. Severe consequences can result from violating the bribery provisions of the FCPA, as Smith & Wesson discovered.

Smith & Wesson is a Massachusetts-based firearms manufacturer that wanted to begin selling firearms in India, Pakistan, and other foreign countries. As a small player in this international market, company officials decided to provide gifts to government officials in these countries to encourage them to do business with Smith & Wesson. This turned out to be a costly mistake. Smith & Wesson had profits of only $100,000 from this scheme before it was uncovered, and in 2014, it agreed to pay the Securities and Exchange Commission fines of more than $2 million. Of course, the fines are not deductible because they are a violation of public policy [§ 162(f)].

Source: **sec.gov/news/press-release/2014-148.**

Example 22

Debra, a financial officer of Blue Corporation, incurs legal expenses in connection with her defense in a criminal indictment for evasion of Blue's income taxes.

Debra's legal expenses relate to her role as an employee because she is deemed to be in the trade or business of being an executive. The legal action impairs her ability to conduct this business activity.[34] However, since these legal expenses are employee business expenses, they are classified as a miscellaneous itemized deduction (and not deductible from 2018 through 2025).

The following legal expenses are deductible *for* AGI:

- Ordinary and necessary expenses incurred in connection with a trade or business.
- Ordinary and necessary expenses incurred in conjunction with rental or royalty property held for the production of income.

Legal expenses for tax advice relative to the preparation of an individual's income tax return are a miscellaneous itemized deduction (and not deductible from 2018 through 2025). On the other hand, legal fees for tax advice relative to the preparation of the portion of the tax return for a sole proprietor's trade or business (Schedule C) or an individual's rental or royalty income (Schedule E) are a *for* AGI deduction.

Example 23

Gabriela received an invoice from MJY LLC (a law firm) for $5,000 for the following services performed in 2022:

- $1,200 (advising on a lawsuit filed against her sole proprietorship)
- $800 (advising on a dispute with a tenant who lives in a duplex she owns and rents)
- $1,300 (fees related to preparing and filing her Form 1040)
- $1,700 (fees for preparing a will)

The $1,700 in fees for preparing her will is a personal expense and is not deductible. The $1,300 for preparing and filing her Form 1040 is a miscellaneous itemized deduction (and currently is not deductible). The balance of the legal fees ($2,000) is deductible when paid.

The $1,200 for the sole proprietorship is deducted on Schedule C (Form 1040) as a *for* AGI deduction. The $800 related to the duplex is a rental expense and is deducted on Schedule E as a *for* AGI deduction.

Expenses Relating to an Illegal Business

The ordinary and necessary expenses of operating an illegal business (e.g., a gambling operation) are deductible.[35] Although allowing deductions for illegal activity may seem inappropriate, this is necessary because the law taxes net income from a business

[34] Rev.Rul. 68–662.

[35] *Comm. v. Sullivan*, 58–1 USTC ¶9368, 1 AFTR 2d 1158, 78 S.Ct. 512.

operation, not gross revenue. However, § 162 disallows a deduction for fines, bribes to public officials, illegal kickbacks, and other illegal payments whether these payments are part of a legal or illegal business.

Example 24

Sam owns and operates an illegal gambling establishment. In connection with this activity, he has the following expenses during the year:

Rent	$ 60,000
Payoffs to the police	40,000
Depreciation on equipment	100,000
Wages	140,000
Interest	30,000
Criminal fines	50,000
Illegal kickbacks	10,000
Total	$430,000

All of the usual expenses (rent, depreciation, wages, and interest) are deductible; payoffs, fines, and kickbacks are not deductible. Of the $430,000 spent, $330,000 is deductible and $100,000 is not.

An exception applies to expenses incurred in illegal trafficking in drugs.[36] *Drug dealers* are not allowed a deduction for ordinary and necessary business expenses incurred in their business, except for cost of goods sold.[37]

Example 25

Assume in Example 24 that instead of an illegal gambling business, Sam was operating an illegal drug business. Also assume that the $100,000 was not for depreciation, but for the cost of the drugs sold.

Of the $430,000 spent, only $100,000 (the cost of goods sold) is deductible. Also note that to claim the cost of goods sold as a deduction, Sam will need documentation supporting the purchases.

Ethics & Equity **State Allowed Marijuana Activity: Do Regular Business Deduction Rules Apply (or Those for Drug Dealers)?**

Cole England operates Herbal Center in Sacramento, California, as a sole proprietorship. The distribution of marijuana for medical purposes as well as nonmedical use by adults is legal in California.

This is Cole's first year of business operations, and he reports the following tax information:

Revenues	$200,000
Cost of goods sold	120,000
Other business expenses	50,000

Cole reported $30,000 of net income on Schedule C this year for Herbal Center. Is this reporting appropriate?

6-3b Political Contributions and Lobbying Activities

Generally, no business deduction is allowed for direct or indirect payments for political purposes.[38] The government has been reluctant to allow these deductions since it might encourage abuses and enable businesses to have undue influence on the political process.

[36] § 280E.

[37] Reg. § 1.61–3(a). Gross income is defined as sales minus cost of goods sold. Thus, although § 280E prohibits any deductions for drug dealers, it does not modify the normal definition of gross income.

[38] § 276.

The Big Picture

Example 26

Refer to the facts of *The Big Picture* on p. 6-1. Dr. Payne had made political contributions to the State Senate campaigns of Tom Smith and Virginia White. Dr. Payne made these contributions to encourage these senators to support a new bill that is beneficial to the state's dental profession. Therefore, he assumed that these would be deductible business expenses.

However, political contributions are not deductible, so he will receive no tax benefit from them.

Lobbying expenses incurred in attempting to influence local, state, or Federal legislation or the actions of certain high-ranking public officials are not deductible.[39] The disallowance also applies to a pro rata portion of the membership dues of trade associations and other groups that are involved in lobbying activities.

The Big Picture

Example 27

Refer to the facts of *The Big Picture* on p. 6-1. Dr. Payne had made contributions to The Dental Society, a trade association for dentists. The trade association estimates that 70% of its dues are allocated to lobbying activities. As a result, his deduction on Schedule C is limited to $3,000 ($10,000 × 30%).

There are two exceptions to the disallowance of lobbying expenses. First, the disallowance provision does not apply to activities devoted solely to monitoring legislation. Second, a *de minimis* exception is provided for annual in-house expenditures (lobbying expenses other than those paid to professional lobbyists or any portion of dues used by associations for lobbying) if such expenditures do not exceed $2,000. If the in-house expenditures exceed $2,000, none of the in-house expenditures can be deducted.

Example 28

The city of Florence, Tennessee, is considering spending $1,000,000 to build a sports complex that will host youth baseball and softball tournaments. Julie, who owns a local hotel, spends $1,500 on lobbying (not paid to a professional lobbyist) to persuade the five members of the Florence City Council to support the project.

The $1,500 is deductible as a lobbying expense since it meets the *de minimis* exception.

6-3c Excessive Executive Compensation

The deduction of executive compensation normally is subject to two limitations. As discussed earlier, the compensation of shareholder-employees of closely held corporations is subject to the reasonableness requirement. The second limitation, known as the millionaires' provision, applies to publicly held corporations, including foreign corporations traded on U.S. exchanges.[40]

The millionaires' provision does not limit the amount of compensation that can be paid to an employee. Instead, it limits the amount the employer can deduct for the taxable compensation of a covered executive to $1 million annually. Covered employees are anyone serving as the chief executive officer (CEO) or the chief financial officer (CFO) during the year and the next three most highly compensated executives. Designation as a covered employee is permanent even if the employee takes a different position in the company. As a result, the compensation deduction for any of these covered employees will be permanently capped at $1 million per year.

In general, the $1 million maximum applies to compensation, commissions based on individual performance, and performance-based compensation tied to overall company performance. Before 2018, the $1 million limit *excluded* commissions and performance-based compensation. Contracts in place on November 2, 2017, are grandfathered into pre-2018 law as long as there are no material changes to the contract.

[39] § 162(e).

[40] § 162(m). For taxable years beginning after December 31, 2026, this provision will also apply to a second group of employees: the five highest compensated employees that are not included in the first group of covered employees. This second group of covered employees—not limited to officers—does not permanently retain this status in subsequent tax years.

Example 29

Yvette became CEO of Lowe's Depot, a home supply store and a publicly traded corporation on May 1, 2022 (the date her contract was signed by Yvette and the Board of Lowe's Depot). For 2022, her compensation package consists of the following:

Cash compensation	$1,800,000
Taxable fringe benefits	100,000
Bonus from a qualified bonus plan tied to company performance	5,000,000

Lowe's Depot can deduct only $1,000,000 of her compensation.

6-3d Investigation of a Business

Investigation expenses are expenses paid or incurred to determine the feasibility of entering a new business or expanding an existing business. They include such costs as travel, engineering and architectural surveys, marketing reports, and various legal and accounting services. How such expenses are treated for tax purposes depends on a number of variables, including the following:

- The current business, if any, of the taxpayer.
- The nature of the business being investigated.
- The extent to which the investigation has proceeded.
- Whether the acquisition actually takes place.

If the taxpayer is in a business that is the *same as or similar to* that being investigated, all investigation expenses are deductible in the year paid or incurred. The tax result is the same whether or not the taxpayer acquires the business being investigated.[41]

The Big Picture

Example 30

Refer to the facts of *The Big Picture* on p. 6-1. Dr. Payne believes that his administrative and business skills can be used to turn around dental practices whose revenues have been declining. He investigates Teeth Restoration LLC, a local dental practice that is for sale. Expenses paid to consultants and accountants as part of this investigation totaled $6,000. He determined that Teeth Restoration would not be a good investment, so he did not buy it.

The $6,000 spent to investigate this business is deductible as a business expense because Dr. Payne is already in the dental business. Expenses incurred to investigate new business opportunities in one's current trade or business are deductible as ordinary and necessary business expenses.

When the taxpayer is *not* in a business that is the same as or similar to the one being investigated, the tax result depends on whether the new business is acquired. If the business is not acquired, all investigation expenses generally are nondeductible.[42]

Example 31

Lynn, a retired merchant, incurs expenses in traveling from Rochester, New York, to California to investigate the feasibility of acquiring several auto care centers.

If no acquisition takes place, none of the expenses are deductible.

If the taxpayer is *not* in a business that is the same as or similar to the one being investigated and actually acquires the new business, the expenses must be capitalized as **startup expenditures**. Startup expenses are not deductible under § 162 because they are incurred *before* a business begins rather than in the course of carrying on a trade or business. The first $5,000 of the expenses is immediately deducted. Any excess over $5,000 is amortized over a period of 180 months (15 years). In arriving at the $5,000

[41] § 195. *York v. Comm.*, 58–2 USTC ¶9952, 2 AFTR 2d 6178, 261 F.2d 421 (CA–4).

[42] Rev.Rul. 57–418; *Morton Frank*, 20 T.C. 511 (1953); and *Dwight A. Ward*, 20 T.C. 332 (1953).

immediate deduction allowed, a dollar-for-dollar reduction must be made for those expenses in excess of $50,000.[43] An election can be made by the taxpayer not to deduct or amortize any portion of the startup costs. In that case, this intangible asset will remain on the balance sheet until the business is sold.

Example 32

Dasha owns and operates 10 restaurants located in various cities throughout the Southeast. She travels to Atlanta to discuss the acquisition of an auto dealership. In addition, she incurs legal and accounting costs associated with the potential acquisition. After incurring total investigation costs of $52,000, she acquires the auto dealership on October 1, 2022.

Dasha may immediately deduct $3,000 [$5,000 − ($52,000 − $50,000)] and amortize the balance of $49,000 ($52,000 − $3,000) over a period of 180 months. For calendar year 2022, therefore, Dasha can deduct $3,817 [$3,000 + ($49,000 × 3/180)].

Concept Summary 6.1 depicts the tax rules related to the costs involved in investigating a business.

Concept Summary 6.1

Costs of Investigating a Business

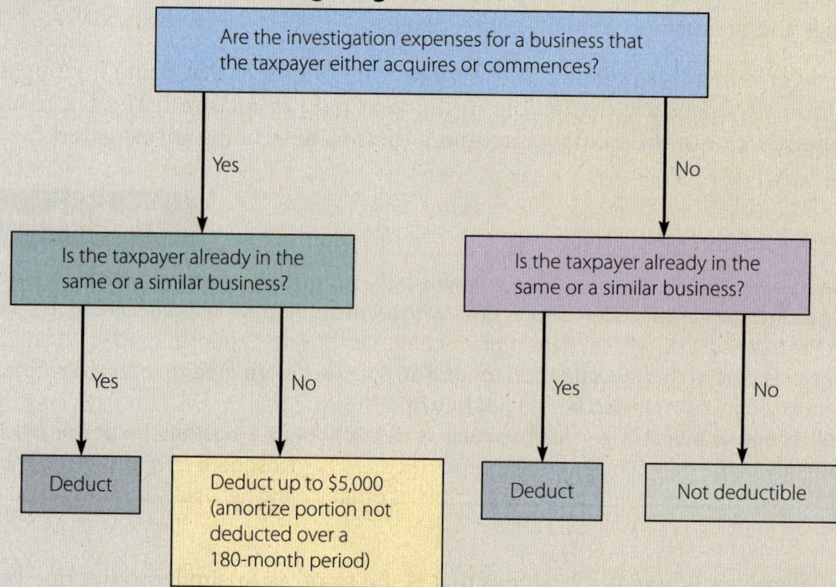

6-3e **Hobby Losses**

Business or investment expenses are deductible only if the taxpayer can show that the activity was entered into for the purpose of making a profit. Certain activities can have attributes that make it difficult to determine if the primary motivation for the activity is to make a profit or is for personal pleasure. Examples include raising horses and operating a farm used as a weekend residence.

Although personal losses are not deductible, losses attributable to profit-seeking activities may be deducted and used to offset a taxpayer's other income. Activities that have both personal and profit-seeking motives are classified as hobbies, and the tax law limits the deductibility of **hobby losses**.

The income and deductions from a hobby are reported separately on the tax return. The revenue for the hobby is always reported as other income [line 8i of Schedule 1 (Form 1040)]. The deductions (and how they are reported) are discussed in more detail below.

[43]§ 195(b).

General Rules

If an individual can show that an activity has been conducted with the intent to earn a profit, losses from the activity are fully deductible (and reported, along with any income, on Schedule C). The hobby loss rules apply only if the activity is *not* engaged in for profit. Hobby expenses are deductible only to the extent of hobby income.[44]

The Regulations indicate that the following nine factors should be considered in determining whether an activity is profit-seeking or is a hobby:[45]

- Whether the activity is conducted in a businesslike manner.
- The expertise of the taxpayers or their advisers.
- The time and effort expended.
- The expectation that the assets of the activity will appreciate in value.
- The taxpayer's previous success in conducting similar activities.
- The history of income or losses from the activity.
- The relationship of profits earned to losses incurred.
- The financial status of the taxpayer (e.g., if the taxpayer does not have substantial amounts of other income, this may indicate that the activity is engaged in for profit).
- Elements of personal pleasure or recreation in the activity.

Whether an activity is profit-seeking or a hobby does not depend on the presence or absence of one of these factors. Rather, the decision is a subjective one that is based on an analysis of all of the facts and circumstances. Exhibit 6.4 provides a list of the common activities that may be treated as hobbies. Concept Summary 6.2 provides more details on the nature of the nine factors identified in the Regulations.

Presumptive Rule of § 183

The Code provides a rebuttable presumption that an activity is profit-seeking if the activity shows a profit in at least three of the previous five tax years.[46] If the activity involves horses, a profit in at least two of the previous seven tax years meets the presumptive rule. If these profitability tests are met, the activity is presumed to be a trade or business rather than a personal hobby. If this is the case, the IRS must prove that the activity is personal rather than trade- or business-related. In all circumstances, the history of profits and losses is just one of the factors used in determining whether the activity is a hobby or business.

Example 33

Camille and Walter are married taxpayers who enjoy a busy lifestyle. Camille, who is an executive for a large corporation, is paid a salary of $800,000. Walter is a collector of antiques. Several years ago he opened an antique shop in a local shopping center and spends most of his time buying and selling antiques. He occasionally earns a small profit from this activity but more frequently incurs substantial losses. If Walter's losses are business-related, they are fully deductible against Camille's salary income on a joint return. In resolving this issue, consider the following:

- Initially determine whether Walter's antique activity has met the three-out-of-five years profit test.
- If the presumption is not met, the activity may nevertheless qualify as a business if Walter can show that the intent is to engage in a profit-seeking activity. It is not necessary to show actual profits.
- Determine if the operation is for profit, using the nine factors identified in the Regulations.

---

[44] § 183(b)(2).

[45] Reg. §§ 1.183–2(b)(1) through (9).

[46] § 183(d).

Exhibit 6.4 Common Activities Classified as Hobbies

Airplane Charter	Entertainers	Photography
Artists	Farming	Rentals
Auto Racing	Fishing	Stamp Collecting
Bowling	Gambling	Writing
Craft Sales	Horse Breeding	Yacht Charter
Direct Sales	Horse Racing	
Dog Breeding	Motorcross Racing	

Source: Internal Revenue Service Audit Technique Guide: IRC § 183: Activities Not Engaged in For Profit (Revised June 2009).

Concept Summary 6.2

Common Questions from the IRS Concerning Hobbies/Businesses with Losses

Whether the activity is conducted in a businesslike manner.

- Is there a written business plan?
- Is there business insurance? Is it covered in the company name?
- Are books and records maintained for the business?
- Is there a business license to operate?

The expertise of the taxpayers or their advisers.

- Does the taxpayer have any relevant education?
- Did the taxpayer prepare for the activity by conducting research or an extensive study of its accepted business, economic, and scientific practices?

The time and effort expended.

- How many hours are spent on this activity per week? Per month? Per year? Per season?
- Who is involved with the day-to-day business operations?

The expectation that the assets of the activity will appreciate in value.

- Were the assets held prior to starting the business?
- Has anyone ever offered to buy any of the assets?

The taxpayer's previous success in conducting similar activities.

- In what other activities has the taxpayer had previous success?
- Was the business ultimately profitable?

The history of income or losses from the activity.

- Is there a trend toward profitability?
- Did the taxpayer change operating methods, adopt new techniques, or abandon nonprofitable methods in a manner consistent with intent to improve profitability?

The relationship of profits earned to losses incurred.

- Is this a highly speculative business?
- What amount of investment has the taxpayer made in the business?

The financial status of the taxpayer.

- Does the taxpayer have substantial income or capital (e.g., investments) from other sources?
- Are there other economic reasons for the taxpayer to be engaged in the activity (e.g., reduced property taxes for farmland, low-interest loans, or federal grants)?

Elements of personal pleasure or recreation in the activity.

- Are elements of fun or recreation generally associated with it by the taxpayer, by members of the taxpayer's family, or by the taxpayer's friends?
- If there are any personal benefits to being in this business, are they substantial?

Source: Internal Revenue Service Audit Technique Guide: IRC § 183: Activities Not Engaged in For Profit (Revised September 2021).

Determining the Amount of the Deduction

If an activity is a hobby, any gross income (sales less cost of goods sold) generated is taxable. Other expenses are deductible only to the extent of the gross income from the hobby. These expenses must be deducted in the following order:

1. Amounts deductible under other Code sections without regard to the nature of the activity, such as property taxes and home mortgage interest.

2. Amounts deductible under other Code sections if the activity had been engaged in for profit, but only if those amounts do not affect adjusted basis (e.g., maintenance and utilities).
3. Amounts for depreciation, amortization, and depletion.[47]

Expenses included in items 2 and 3 are miscellaneous itemized deductions. From 2018 through 2025, *miscellaneous itemized deductions are not deductible.* Since property taxes and mortgage interest are deductible without the hobby revenue, the net effect is that the taxpayer is taxed on all of the gross income from the hobby.

Example 34

Stefan, the vice president of an oil company, has AGI of $180,000. He decides to pursue painting in his spare time. He uses a home studio exclusively for his painting; it comprises 10% of the home's square footage. During the current year, Stefan incurs the following expenses:

Frames	$ 2,800
Art supplies	900
Home studio expenses:	
Total home property taxes	2,000
Total home mortgage interest	10,000
Total home maintenance and utilities	4,600
Calculated depreciation on 10% of home	500

During the year, Stefan sold paintings for a total of $5,660. His cost of goods sold is $3,700 (the cost of the frames and art supplies) and his gross income is $1,960. If the activity is held to be a hobby, Stefan would determine his potential deductions under the hobby loss rules as follows:

Gross income	$ 1,960
Deduct: Property taxes and mortgage interest (10% of $12,000)	(1,200)
Remainder	$ 760
Deduct: Maintenance and utilities (10%)	(460)
Remainder	$ 300
Deduct: Depreciation ($500, but limited to $300)	(300)
Net income	$ -0-

Outcome: Stefan includes the $1,960 of gross income in AGI, making his AGI $181,960. The taxes and interest are itemized deductions, deductible in full. The remaining $760 of expenses are *miscellaneous itemized deductions and currently not deductible.*

Because the property taxes and home mortgage interest are deductible even without the hobby and no deduction is allowed for the other expenses, Stefan is taxed on his $1,960 of gross income.

6-3f Rental of Vacation Homes

Restrictions on the deductions allowed for part-year rentals of personal **vacation homes** prevent taxpayers from deducting essentially personal expenses as rental losses. Many taxpayers who own vacation homes use the property for personal use during a portion of the year and rent the property at other times. For example, assume that a summer cabin is rented for two months per year, used for a family vacation for one month, and left vacant the rest of the year. The issue is how to treat expenses during the nine months the cabin is vacant. If these expenses are allowed as rental expenses, a rental loss is likely to result (otherwise, personal expenses have been converted to rental expenses). Code § 280A

[47] Reg. § 1.183–1(b)(1).

eliminates this treatment by not allowing a loss for property that is not used primarily for rental purposes. Deductions are only allowed to the extent of income received.

There are three possible tax treatments for residences used for both personal and rental purposes. The treatment depends upon the *relative time* the residence is used for personal purposes versus rental use. These rules are summarized in Concept Summary 6.3.

Primarily Personal Use

If the residence is *rented* for *fewer than 15 days* in a year, it is treated as a personal residence. The rent income is excluded from gross income, and mortgage interest and real estate taxes are allowed as itemized deductions, as with any personal residence.[48] No other expenses (e.g., depreciation, utilities, and maintenance) are deductible.

Concept Summary 6.3

Vacation/Rental Home

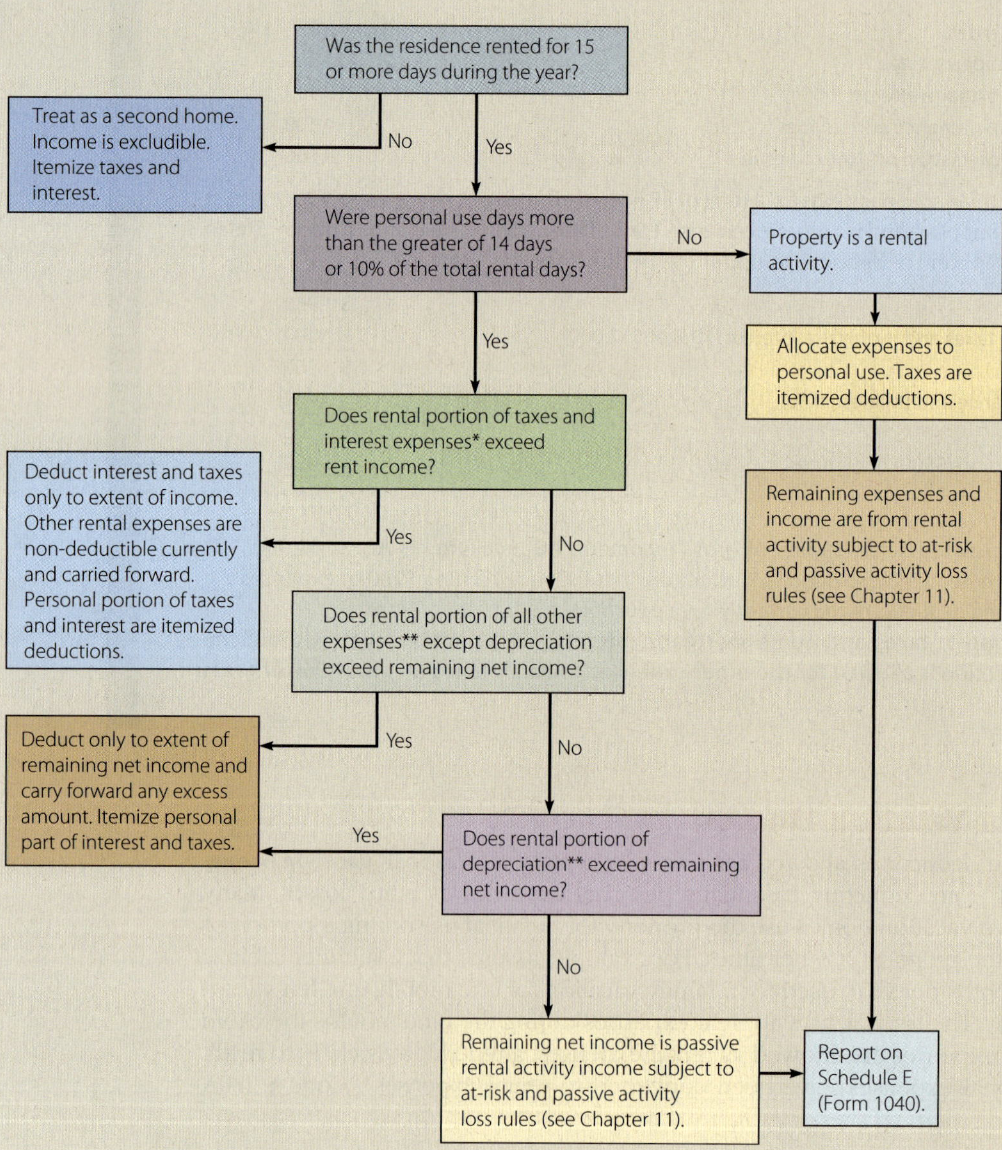

*Allocated on the basis of 365 (366 in a leap year) days (court decisions) or total days of use (IRS); see Examples 38 and 39.
**Allocated on the basis of total days of use.

[48] § 280A(g).

Example 35

Catherine owns a vacation cottage on the lake. During the current year, she rented it for $1,600 for two weeks, lived in it two months, and left it vacant the remainder of the year. The year's expenses amounted to $6,000 mortgage interest expense, $500 property taxes, $1,500 utilities and maintenance, and $2,400 depreciation.

Because the property was not rented for at least 15 days, the income is excluded, the mortgage interest and property tax expenses are itemized deductions, and the remaining expenses are nondeductible personal expenses.

Primarily Rental Use

If the residence is *rented* for 15 days or more in a year and is *not used* for personal purposes for more than the greater of (1) 14 days or (2) 10 percent of the total days rented, the residence is treated as rental property.[49] The expenses must be allocated between personal and rental days if there are any personal use days during the year. The real estate taxes allocated to the personal days are deductible as an itemized deduction. However, the mortgage interest allocated to the personal days cannot be deducted because the property is not a qualified residence. The deduction of the expenses allocated to rental days can exceed rent income and result in a rental loss. The loss may be deductible, subject to the at-risk and passive activity loss rules (discussed in Chapter 11).

Example 36

Assume instead that Catherine in Example 35 used the cottage for 12 days and rented it for 48 days for $4,800. The threshold for personal use is 14 days—the greater of (1) 14 days or (2) 4.8 days (10% × 48 rental days). Because she rented the cottage for 15 days or more but did not use it for more than 14 days, the cottage is treated as rental property. The expenses must be allocated between personal and rental days.

	Percentage of Use	
	Rental 80%	**Personal 20%**
Income	$4,800	$ -0-
Expenses		
Mortgage interest ($6,000)	($4,800)	($1,200)
Property taxes ($500)	(400)	(100)
Utilities and maintenance ($1,500)	(1,200)	(300)
Depreciation ($2,400)	(1,920)	(480)
Total expenses	($8,320)	($2,080)
Rental loss	($3,520)	$ -0-

Catherine deducts the $3,520 rental loss *for* AGI on Schedule E (assuming that she satisfies the at-risk and passive activity loss rules, discussed in Chapter 11). She also has an itemized deduction for property taxes of $100 associated with the personal use. The mortgage interest of $1,200 associated with the personal use is not deductible as an itemized deduction because the cottage is not a qualified residence (qualified residence interest) for this purpose (see Chapter 10). The portion of utilities and maintenance and depreciation attributable to personal use is not deductible.

Personal/Rental Use

If the residence is rented for 15 days or more in a year *and* is used for personal purposes for more than the greater of (1) 14 days or (2) 10 percent of the total days rented, it is treated as a personal/rental use residence. The expenses must be allocated between personal days and rental days. Expenses are allowed only to the extent of rent income.[50]

[49] § 280A(d) and Prop.Reg. § 1.280A–3(c).

[50] A related issue is whether a taxpayer's primary residence is subject to the preceding rules if it is converted to rental property. If the vacation home rules apply, a taxpayer who converts a personal residence to rental property during the tax year, without any tax-avoidance motive, could have the allowable deductions limited to the rent income. To prevent this from occurring, the personal use days will not cause the property to be treated as personal/rental if once the rental period begins, the property is rented for at least 12 consecutive months at a fair rental price (a qualified rental period).

Example 37

Assume instead that Catherine in Example 35 rented the property for 30 days and lived in it for 30 days. The threshold for personal use is 14 days—the greater of (1) 14 days or (2) 3 days (10% × 30 rental days).

The residence is classified as personal/rental use property because she used it more than 14 days and rented it for 15 days or more. The expenses must be allocated between rental use and personal use, and the rental expenses are allowed only to the extent of rent income.

If a residence is classified as personal/rental use property, the expenses that are deductible anyway (e.g., real estate taxes and mortgage interest) must be deducted first. If a positive net income results, expenses, other than depreciation, that are deductible for rental property (e.g., maintenance, utilities, and insurance) are allowed next. Finally, if any positive balance remains, depreciation is allowed. Any disallowed expenses allocable to rental use are carried forward and used in future years subject to the same limitations. Note that these ordering rules for deductions are the same as for hobby expenses.

Expenses must be allocated between personal and rental days before the limits are applied. The courts have held that real estate taxes and mortgage interest, which accrue ratably over the year, are allocated on the basis of 365 days (366 days in a leap year).[51] The IRS, however, disagrees and allocates real estate taxes and mortgage interest on the basis of total days of use.[52] Other expenses (e.g., utilities, maintenance, depreciation) are allocated on the basis of total days used.

Personal/Rental: IRS vs. Courts

Example 38

Jason rents his vacation home for 60 days and lives in the home for 30 days. The property is classified as personal/rental because it is rented for 15 days or more, and personal use (30 days) is greater than 14 [greater of 14 days or 6 days (10% × 60 rental days)]. Jason's gross rent income is $10,000. For the entire year, the real estate taxes are $2,190, his mortgage interest expense is $10,220, utilities and maintenance expense equals $2,400, and depreciation is $9,000.

Using the IRS approach, these amounts are deductible in this specific order:

Gross income	$10,000
Deduct: Taxes and interest ($^{60}/_{90}$ × $12,410)	(8,273)
Remainder to apply to rental operating expenses and depreciation	$ 1,727
Deduct: Utilities and maintenance ($^{60}/_{90}$ × $2,400)	(1,600)
Balance	$ 127
Deduct: Depreciation ($^{60}/_{90}$ × $9,000 = $6,000 but limited to above balance)	(127)
Net rent income	$ -0-

The nonrental use portion of real estate taxes and mortgage interest ($4,137 in this case) is deductible if the taxpayer elects to itemize (see Chapter 10). The personal use portion of utilities, maintenance, and depreciation is not deductible in any case.

Jason has a carryover of $5,873 ($6,000 − $127) of the unused depreciation, which he may be able to deduct in future years. Also note that the basis of the property is only reduced by the $127 depreciation allowed because of the above limitation. (See Chapter 14 for a discussion of the reduction in basis for depreciation allowed or allowable.)

[51] *Bolton v. Comm.*, 82–2 USTC ¶9699, 51 AFTR 2d 83–305, 694 F.2d 556 (CA–9).

[52] Prop.Reg. § 1.280A–3(d)(4).

Personal/Rental: IRS vs. Courts

Example 39

Using the court's approach in allocating real estate taxes and mortgage interest, Jason, in Example 38, would have this result:

Gross income	$10,000
Deduct: Taxes and interest ($^{60}/_{365}$ × $12,410)	(2,040)
Remainder to apply to rental operating expenses and depreciation	$ 7,960
Deduct: Utilities and maintenance ($^{60}/_{90}$ × $2,400)	(1,600)
Balance	$ 6,360
Deduct: Depreciation ($^{60}/_{90}$ × $9,000 but limited to above balance)	(6,000)
Net rent income	$ 360

Jason can deduct $10,370 ($12,410 paid − $2,040 deducted as expense in computing net rent income) of personal use mortgage interest and real estate taxes as itemized deductions.

Note the contrasting results in Examples 38 and 39. The IRS's approach (Example 38) results in no rental gain or loss and an itemized deduction for real estate taxes and mortgage interest of $4,137. In Example 39, Jason has net rent income of $360 and $10,370 of itemized deductions. The court's approach decreases his taxable income by $10,010 ($10,370 itemized deductions less $360 net rent income). The IRS's approach reduces his taxable income by only $4,137.

6-3g Expenditures Incurred for Taxpayer's Benefit or Taxpayer's Obligation

To be deductible, an expense must be incurred for the taxpayer's benefit or arise from the taxpayer's obligation. An individual cannot claim a tax deduction for the payment of the expenses of another individual.

Example 40

During the current year, Carlos pays the property taxes on his son Jayden's home. Neither Carlos nor Jayden can take a deduction for the amount paid for Jayden's property taxes. Carlos is not entitled to a deduction because the property taxes are not his obligation. Jayden cannot claim a deduction because he did not pay the property taxes.

The tax result would have been more favorable had Carlos made a cash gift to Jayden and let him pay the property taxes. Then Jayden could have deducted the property taxes.

One exception to this disallowance rule is the payment of medical expenses for a dependent. These expenses are deductible by the payor subject to the normal rules that limit the deductibility of medical expenses (see Chapters 3 and 10).[53] The Tax Court has provided a different exception to this disallowance rule in the case of a mother who paid medical expenses and property taxes for her adult daughter, who was not her dependent.[54] The mother, who was not legally obligated to do so, paid medical providers and the city government directly on behalf of her daughter. The Tax Court ruled that the mother had, in substance, made a gift to her daughter in the amounts of the payments and deemed that the daughter had then paid the related medical expenses and property taxes. As a result, the daughter was permitted to take a deduction for these expenses on her return. Although this case provides substantial authority for these deductions, when planning with taxpayers, it is better to have the donor make the gift directly to the donee and then have the donee pay the expenses.

[53] § 213(a).

[54] *Judith F. Lang*, 100 TCM 603, T.C.Memo. 2010–286.

6-3h Disallowance of Personal Expenditures

In general, no deduction is allowed for personal, living, or family expenses.[55] To justify a deduction, an individual must be able to identify a particular section of the Code that permits the deduction (e.g., charitable contributions and medical expenses).

Ethics & Equity **Personal or Business Expenses?**

For the last eight years, Jaynice and her family have lived in a large Victorian house in New England. In the current year, Jaynice and her husband decide to convert the home into a bed-and-breakfast. The family (including the two children and the dog) moves into the basement, which accounts for 30 percent of the square footage of the house. The basement has two bedrooms, two baths, a den, and a small kitchen. The upper two floors of the house are used for the bed-and-breakfast, which is operated as a sole proprietorship.

Jaynice hires two employees to help her run the business. Total expenses for the first year of operation are as follows:

Mortgage interest	$18,000
Real estate taxes	3,000
Salaries for two employees	40,000
Groceries for breakfast and snacks	7,000
Depreciation	10,000

For breakfast, all of the family members eat the same food that is prepared for the guests. They usually also share in the homemade cookies and cakes in the evening.

On Jaynice's Schedule C for the business, she deducts $78,000 of expenses for the current tax year. Discuss whether these deductions are appropriate.

6-3i Disallowance of Deductions for Capital Expenditures

A deduction is not allowed for amounts paid for new buildings or for permanent improvements or betterments that increase the value of any property.[56] Incidental repairs and maintenance of the property are not capital expenditures and can be deducted as ordinary and necessary business expenses. Repairing a roof is a deductible expense, but replacing a roof is a capital expenditure subject to depreciation deductions over its recovery period. The tune-up of a delivery truck is an expense; a complete engine overhaul probably is a capital expenditure. Adding new gravel to a gravel parking lot is a repair, but paving the parking lot is a capital expenditure because this is doing more than restoring the asset to its original condition.

All costs incurred in acquiring or producing a unit of property (UOP) are included in its cost, except for employee compensation and overhead costs. The taxpayer can elect to capitalize employee compensation and overhead costs (can elect separately or both). The cost includes all related expenditures incurred before the date the asset is placed in service, even if these expenditures would be repairs if incurred after the asset was placed in service. The cost of a UOP includes costs incurred to obtain a clean title and investigation costs.[57] Material or supplies that cost $200 or less can generally be deducted in the first tax year they are used or consumed.[58]

Capitalize or Expense

Example 41

In year 1, Corporation Biz purchases 100 cell phones for its employees to use, each phone costing $130. Each cell phone is considered to be a unit of property. During year 1, 60 of the phones are put into use. The remaining phones are not used until year 2.

Since the cell phones cost less than $200, they are considered to be material and supplies. As a result, 60 of the phones can be expensed in year 1 ($7,800). The remaining 40 phones cannot be expensed until they are put into use in year 2.

[55] § 262.

[56] § 263(a)(1).

[57] Reg. § 1.263(a)–3(e)(1).

[58] Reg. § 1.162–3(a)(1).

Capitalize or Expense

Example 42

Jared owns a building that has 10 apartments. During the current year, one of the apartments needed a new stove. Jared paid $800 for the stove, including $75 of sales tax. He also paid $50 for the stove to be delivered and an extra $60 for it to be installed.

The stove is considered to be a unit of property, and all of these costs are included in its basis. Therefore, $910 ($800 + $50 + $60) is capitalized for the stove and this amount will be depreciated.

A single UOP includes all components that are functionally interdependent. Thus, a building includes, for example, the walls, floors, ceilings, roof, windows, doors, electrical systems, plumbing, and heating and air systems. The major exception to this rule is that if a component is treated separately for depreciation purposes, it will not be grouped into another UOP.[59]

Taxpayers can elect under the *de minimis* safe harbor election to expense outlays for lower-cost items. The election is irrevocable. This safe harbor applies if the taxpayer:

- Has written procedures in place at the beginning of the tax year that provide for the expensing of amounts below a specified dollar amount or that have a useful life of 12 months or less,
- Also expenses the items for its accounting/book records, and
- Ensures that items costing more than $5,000 are capitalized [$2,500 if the company does not have acceptable (generally meaning audited) financial statements].

The *de minimis* safe harbor election cannot be made for inventory, land, and certain types of spare parts.[60]

Example 43

Freight Car Unlimited builds railroad cars and has adopted a written policy providing that any item purchased for $5,000 or less will be expensed for both financial reporting and tax purposes. Freight Car has audited financial statements.

During the current tax year, Freight Car purchases 120 laptop computers that cost $2,700 each. These computers do not have to be capitalized and will be expensed in Freight Car's current-year tax return.

Routine maintenance to keep UOPs operating efficiently is expensed, such as testing, cleaning, inspecting, and replacing parts. To be routine, the expectation is that the expenditure will be needed more than once during the asset's life. An expense cannot be treated as routine maintenance if it improves a UOP (treated as a betterment). A cost is treated as a betterment if it:

- Enlarges or increases the capacity of a UOP, or
- Materially increases the productivity, efficiency, or quality of the UOP.[61]

Qualifying small taxpayers (those with $10 million or less of average annual gross receipts in the three preceding tax years) can deduct improvements made to an eligible building property (one with an unadjusted basis of $1 million or less). The safe harbor election applies only if the total amount paid during the tax year for repairs, maintenance, improvements, and similar activities performed on the eligible building does not exceed the lesser of $10,000 or 2 percent of the building's unadjusted basis.[62]

Capitalization versus Expense

When an expenditure is for a tangible asset that has an ascertainable life, it is capitalized and may be deducted as depreciation (or cost recovery) over its depreciable life. Land is not subject to depreciation (or cost recovery) because it does not have an ascertainable life. [See Chapter 8 for a discussion of depreciation (cost recovery).]

[59]Reg. § 1.263(a)–3(e).

[60]Reg. § 1.263(a)–1(f)(1).

[61]Reg. § 1.263(a)–3(i)(1).

[62]Reg. § 1.263(a)–3(h)(1); Rev.Proc. 2015–14.

Example 44

Stan purchased a prime piece of land located in an apartment-zoned area. Stan paid $500,000 for the property, which had an old but usable apartment building on it. He immediately had the building demolished at a cost of $100,000.

The $500,000 purchase price and the $100,000 demolition costs must be capitalized, and the basis of the land is $600,000. Because land is a nondepreciable asset, no deduction is allowed.

If the expenditure is for an intangible asset (e.g., copyright, patent, covenant not to compete, and goodwill), the capitalized expenditure can be amortized regardless of whether the intangible asset has an ascertainable life. Intangible assets, referred to as § 197 intangibles, are amortized over a 15-year statutory period using the straight-line method. See Chapter 8 for additional discussion of the amortization of intangibles.

Example 45

Elite Fireworks purchased all of the assets of Interstate Fireworks for $2,000,000. The fair market value of Interstate's assets is $1,400,000.

The additional $600,000 paid is allocated to goodwill. The goodwill is a § 197 intangible asset and will be amortized over 15 years.

6-3j Transactions between Related Parties

The Code places restrictions on the recognition of losses from **related-party transactions**. Without these restrictions, relationships created by birth, marriage, and business would provide endless possibilities for engaging in financial transactions that produce tax savings with no real economic substance or change. For example, to create an artificial loss, a wife could sell investment property to her husband at a loss and deduct the loss on their joint return. Her husband could then hold the asset indefinitely, and the family would sustain no real economic loss. A complex set of rules has been designed to eliminate these possibilities.

Relationships and Constructive Ownership

Before reviewing the tax consequences of related-party sales, it is important to know the individuals and business entities that are considered to be related parties. *Related parties* include the following:

- Brothers and sisters (whether whole, half, or adopted), spouse, ancestors (parents and grandparents), and lineal descendants (children and grandchildren) of the taxpayer.
- A corporation that is owned more than 50 percent (directly or indirectly) by the taxpayer.
- Two corporations that are members of a controlled group.
- A series of other complex relationships between trusts, corporations, partnerships, and individual taxpayers.

Constructive ownership provisions are applied to determine whether the taxpayers are related. Under these provisions, stock owned by certain relatives or related entities is *deemed* to be owned by the taxpayer for purposes of applying the loss disallowance provisions. For example, a taxpayer is deemed to own not only his or her stock but also the stock owned by lineal descendants, ancestors, brothers and sisters or half-brothers and half-sisters, and spouse.

Example 46

The stock of Sparrow Corporation is owned 20% by Ted, 30% by Ted's father, 30% by Ted's mother, and 20% by Ted's sister. Although Ted actually owns only 20% of Sparrow Corporation, he is *deemed* to own the stock owned by his father (30%), mother (30%), and sister (20%).

As a result, Ted directly and indirectly owns 100% of Sparrow Corporation, and Ted and Sparrow are related parties. The same outcome (100% direct and indirect ownership) results for all of the shareholders in this example.

Losses

Losses are disallowed from sales or exchanges of property between related parties.[63] A right of offset is created equal to the disallowed loss. When the property is subsequently sold to a nonrelated party, any gain recognized is reduced by the right of offset. However, the right of offset cannot create or increase a loss. Any right of offset is permanently lost if it is not used by the related-party buyer to offset some or all of the recognized gain on a subsequent sale or exchange to an unrelated party.

Use of Right of Offset

Example 47

Ming sells common stock with a basis of $10,000 to her son, Jin, for its fair market value of $8,000. The $2,000 realized loss is not recognized, which creates a $2,000 right of offset. Jin sells the stock several years later for $11,000.

Ming's $2,000 loss is disallowed on the sale to Jin, and only $1,000 of gain ($11,000 selling price − $8,000 basis − $2,000 right of offset) is recognized by Jin on the subsequent sale.

Example 48

Assume the same facts as in Example 47, except that Jin sells the stock for $9,500. Jin's gain of $1,500 ($9,500 selling price − $8,000 basis) is not recognized because of the right of offset of $2,000 from Ming's sale. The remaining $500 right of offset is permanently lost.

Note that the offset may result in only partial tax benefit on the subsequent sale (as in this case). If Ming had sold the stock to an unrelated party rather than to Jin, she could have recognized a $2,000 loss. However, as a family unit, Ming and Jin recognized only $1,500 of loss.

6-3k Substantiation Requirements

The tax law is built on a voluntary compliance system. Taxpayers file their tax returns, report income and take deductions to which they are entitled, and pay their taxes through withholding or estimated tax payments during the year. The taxpayer has the burden of proof for substantiating expenses deducted on the returns and must retain adequate records. Upon audit, the IRS can disallow any undocumented or unsubstantiated deductions. These requirements have resulted in numerous conflicts between taxpayers and the IRS.

For example, *specific* and *more stringent* rules apply for deducting travel, entertainment, and gift expenses, which are discussed in Chapter 9. Certain mixed-use (both personal and business use) assets also are subject to more stringent documentation rules (see Chapter 8).

Substantiation is also important for establishing the basis of an asset (see Chapter 14). An asset's basis includes all costs incurred to place an asset in service, which includes transportation, sales tax, setup, testing, unpaid property taxes of the previous owner, and other purchase costs. Basis is used to determine gain or loss on a sale of the asset and to compute depreciation for depreciable assets. The taxpayer must document all expenses included in basis.

6-3l Expenses and Interest Relating to Tax-Exempt Income

Certain income, such as interest on municipal bonds, is tax-exempt.[64] The law also allows the taxpayer to deduct expenses incurred for the production of income.[65] However, expenses related to the production of tax-exempt income are not deductible.[66] Interest on debt used to purchase or hold tax-exempt financial instruments also is disallowed.

[63] § 267(a)(1).

[64] § 103.

[65] § 212.

[66] § 265.

Expenses Related to Tax-Exempt Income

Example 49

Sandy, a taxpayer in the 35% bracket, purchased $100,000 of 6% municipal bonds. At the same time, she used the bonds as collateral on a bank loan of $100,000 at 8% interest. A positive cash flow would result from the tax benefit as follows:

Cash paid for interest expense on loan	($8,000)
Cash received as interest income from bonds	6,000
Net negative cash flow	($2,000)

Had the deduction of $8,000 been allowed for interest expense, this would have resulted in a tax benefit of $2,800 (35% × $8,000). In that case, a positive cash flow of $800 ($6,000 + $2,800 − $8,000) would have resulted.

Example 50

In January of the current year, Alan borrowed $100,000 at 8% interest. He used the loan proceeds to purchase 5,000 shares of stock in White Corporation. In July, he sold the stock for $120,000 and reinvested the proceeds in City of Denver bonds, the income from which is tax-exempt.

Assuming that the $100,000 loan remained outstanding throughout the entire year, Alan cannot deduct the interest attributable to the period in which he held the tax-exempt bonds.

6-3m Other Disallowances

The following expenditures also are disallowed:

- Settlements or payments, including attorney's fees, related to sexual harassment or sexual abuse if subject to a nondisclosure disagreement.[67]
- Payments for qualified transportation fringe benefits, including mass transit and qualified parking.[68]
- Net interest expense, which is limited to business interest income plus 30 percent of adjusted taxable income. Any disallowed interest is carried forward indefinitely. The limitation does not apply to businesses that have annual average gross receipts of $27 million or less during the prior three taxable years.[69]

Example 51

For 2022, Corporation NFL has $50,000,000 of adjusted taxable income, $1,000,000 of business interest income, and $20,000,000 of business interest expense. Interest expense is limited to $16,000,000, the sum of its $1,000,000 of business interest income plus 30% of its adjusted taxable income (30% × $50,000,000 = $15,000,000). The $4,000,000 of disallowed interest expense is carried forward to future tax years.

The classification of various expenses in terms of their deductibility and nondeductibility is reflected in Concept Summary 6.4.

LO.4

Identify tax planning opportunities for maximizing deductions and minimizing the disallowance of deductions.

6-4 Tax Planning

6-4a Vacation Homes

As discussed previously in this chapter, homes that are used for both personal and rental use can fall into one of three categories, all of which have different tax consequences. Therefore, careful tax planning often ensures that the home is classified into the category that provides the optimal tax result. For example, if a taxpayer is

[67] § 162(q).

[68] § 274(a)(4).

[69] § 163(j); § 448(c).

Concept Summary 6.4

Classification of Expenses

Expense Item	Deductible: For AGI	Deductible: From AGI	Not Deductible	Applicable Code Section
Business				
Employee				
Reimbursed expenses	X			§§ 162(a) and 62(a)(2)(A)
Teacher professional development and supplies	X			§ 62(a)(2)(D)
Commuting expenses			X	§ 262
Moving expenses			X	§ 217(k)
Meals and entertainment[1]			X[2]	§ 162(a)
Travel and transportation[1]			X[2]	§ 162(a)(2)
All other employee expenses[1]			X[2]	§ 162(a)
Self employed				
Entertainment			X	§ 274(a)(1)(A)
Meals[3]	X			§ 274(n)
Taxes	X			§§ 162, 164, and 62(a)(1)
Interest	X			§§ 162, 163, and 62(a)(1)
Bad debt	X			§§ 166 and 62(a)(1) or (3)
Casualty losses	X			§ 165(c)(1)
Rent	X			§§ 162 and 62(a)(1) or (4)
Other	X			§§ 162 and 62(a)(1)
Qualified Business Income (QBI) deduction		X		§ 199A
Investigation of a business	X			§§ 195, 162, and 62(a)(1)
Certain expenses of performing artists	X			§ 62(a)(2)(B)
Personal				
Medical		X		§ 213
Taxes				
Real property		X		§ 164(a)(1)
Personal property		X		§ 164(a)(2)
State and local income *or* sales tax		X		§§ 164(a)(3) and (b)(5)
Interest				
Qualified residence		X		§ 163(h)(3)
Student loan	X			§ 221
Other			X	§ 163(h)(1)
Qualified tuition and related expenses	X			§§ 62(a)(18) and 222
Charitable contributions		X		§ 170
Casualty losses		X		§ 165(c)(3)
All other personal expenses			X	§ 262
Investment/Production of Income				
Rent and royalty producing property investment expenses	X			§§ 212 and 62(a)(4)
Other income producing investment expenses				
Interest		X		§§ 212 and 163(d)(3)
Taxes		X		§§ 212 and 164
All other investment expenses			X[2]	§ 212

[1]Deduction for AGI if reimbursed, an adequate accounting is made, and employee is required to repay excess reimbursements.

[2]From 2018 through 2025, miscellaneous itemized deductions are not deductible.

[3]50% of meals related to business related activities are deductible. A 100% deduction is allowed for food and beverages provided by a restaurant in calendar years 2021 and 2022

Note: A number of expenses listed above are subject to limitations that are discussed in subsequent chapters.

planning to rent a home for 15 or more days, this will subject the net income from the rental activity to taxation. If the homeowner could rent the home for 14 days or less (possibly just one less day), then all of the rental income received would escape taxation. This strategy is particularly attractive to individuals who live in areas where major sporting or entertainment events are held if there is a lack of hotel accommodations in the area.

In addition, assume that a taxpayer intends to use a home for 150 rental days and 16 personal days. Because the personal days exceed 15 (the greater of 14 days or 10% × the number of rental days), the property will be classified as *rental/personal* and a rental loss will not be allowed. However, if the owner can reduce the personal use days by only one day to 15, then the property will be classified as *rental*, and a rental loss can be allowed (subject to the passive activity loss rules).

6-4b **Hobby Losses**

To demonstrate that an activity has been entered into for the purpose of making a profit, a taxpayer should treat the activity as a business. The business should engage in advertising, use business letterhead stationery, and maintain a business phone.

If a taxpayer's activity earns a profit in three out of five consecutive years, the presumption is that the activity is engaged in for profit. It may be possible for a cash basis taxpayer to meet these requirements by timing the payment of expenses or the receipt of revenues. The payment of certain expenses incurred before the end of the year might be made in the following year. The billing of year-end sales might be delayed so that collections are received in the following year.

Keep in mind that the three-out-of-five-years rule under § 183 is not absolute. All it does is shift the burden of proof. If a profit is not made in three out of five years, the losses still may be allowed if the taxpayer can show that they are due to the nature of the business. For example, success in artistic or literary endeavors can take a long time, so losses for several years in a row could occur even for a legitimate business. Also, depending on the state of the economy, full-time farmers and ranchers may have losses for several consecutive years.

Merely satisfying the three-out-of-five-years rule does not guarantee that a taxpayer is automatically home free. If the three years of profits are insignificant relative to the losses of other years or if the profits are not from the ordinary operation of the business, the taxpayer is vulnerable. The IRS may still be able to establish that the taxpayer is not engaged in an activity for profit.

Example 52

Ashley had the following gains and losses in an artistic endeavor:

2018	($50,000)
2019	(65,000)
2020	400
2021	200
2022	125

Under these circumstances, the IRS might try to overcome the presumption that this is a business because it has profits in three of the last five years. To do this, the IRS would focus on the nine factors from the Regulations discussed in text Section 6-3e.

On the other hand, if Ashley could show conformity with the factors enumerated in the Regulations or could show evidence of business hardships (e.g., injury, death, or illness), the government might have difficulty overriding the presumption.[70]

[70] *Faulconer, Sr. v. Comm.*, 84–2 USTC ¶9955, 55 AFTR 2d 85–302, 748 F.2d 890 (CA–4).

6-4c Do Deduction Limits Affect Executive Compensation?

Only $1 million of compensation can be deducted for the CEO, the CFO, and the three other highest compensated executives of publicly traded companies. However, this limitation did not apply to performance-based compensation before 2018. This exception was removed because it was broad enough to allow publicly traded companies to pay substantial compensation to executives and still receive a tax deduction.

For example, in 2014, the CEO of Microsoft received a base salary of $918,917, which was just under the $1 million limitation. However, he received bonuses and stock incentives of over $80 million, which qualified to be deducted under the performance-based exception.

The *Wall Street Journal* recently reported that the median pay for the CEOs of 322 major companies in 2020 was nearly $14 million, an increase of almost a million over the prior year and a new record. Pay climbed as companies modified compensation plans in response to the COVID pandemic. Base salary accounted for only 10 percent of the compensation. The remainder consisted primarily of performance incentives.[71] The removal of the exception for performance-based compensation seems to have had no effect on the amount and type of executive compensation.

Refocus on The Big Picture

Calculation of Deductible Business Expenses and Tax Planning

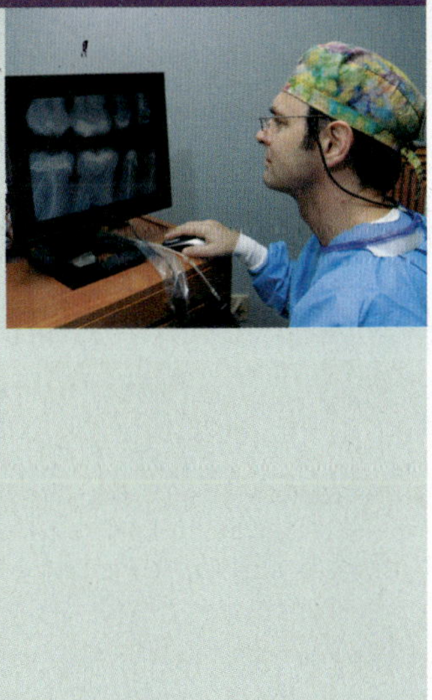

ISTOCK.COM/DLEWIS33

Of the expenses incurred by Dr. Payne, several comments need to be made. Being personal in nature, none of the $5,000 monthly draw is deductible. Nor is the amount involved subject to the reasonableness test (see Example 7). Dr. Payne is a sole proprietor and not in an employment relationship. The fine paid for violating waste control rules comes under the public policy limitations (see Example 20) and is specifically made nondeductible by § 162(f). Along the same line, the political contributions (Example 26) are made nondeductible by § 162(e). However, Dr. Payne's investigation of the practice of another dental firm (Example 30) appears reasonable and the expense incurred is deductible. The dues paid to The Dental Society are not 100 percent deductible because 70 percent of the Society's efforts relate to lobbying activities (Example 27). Although not specifically discussed in the text, his legal fees incurred in connection with a lawsuit filed by a patient appear related to his practice (Example 22). As a result, they are deductible because they are ordinary and necessary to his trade or business.

What If?

From a tax planning perspective, should Dr. Payne calculate his deductible business expenses using the accrual method of accounting or the cash method?

In Chapter 4, we concluded that Dr. Payne could minimize his Federal income tax liability if he used the cash method of accounting. If the cash method is used for reporting the gross income of a Schedule C business, the cash method also must be used for reporting the deductible business expenses that will appear on Schedule C of Form 1040.

[71] Theo Francis and Kristen Broughton, "CEO Pay Climbs in Year of Vast Upheaval," *Wall Street Journal*, April 12, 2021, page A1.

Key Terms

Accounting method, 6-10
Deductions *for* adjusted gross income, 6-2
Deductions *from* adjusted gross income, 6-2
Hobby losses, 6-18
Ordinary and necessary, 6-5
Qualified business income (QBI), 6-7
Reasonableness, 6-5
Related-party transactions, 6-28
Startup expenditures, 6-17
Vacation homes, 6-21

Discussion Questions

1. LO.1 "All income must be reported, and all deductions are allowed unless specifically disallowed in the Code." Discuss.

2. LO.1 Michael earned $20,000 at the K-M Resort Golf Club during the summer prior to his senior year in college. He wants to make a contribution to a traditional IRA, but the amount is dependent on whether it reduces his taxable income. If Michael is going to claim the standard deduction, will a contribution to a traditional IRA reduce his taxable income? Explain.

3. LO.1 Classify each of the following expenditures paid in 2022 as a deduction *for* AGI, a deduction *from* AGI, or not deductible:
   a. Roberto gives cash to his father as a birthday gift.
   b. Sandra gives cash to her church.
   c. Albert pays Dr. Dafashy for medical services rendered.
   d. Mia pays alimony to Bill according to a divorce decree entered the previous year.
   e. Rex, who is self-employed, contributes to his pension plan.
   f. Bonita pays expenses associated with her rental property.

4. LO.1 Classify each of the following expenditures paid in 2022 as a deduction *for* AGI, a deduction *from* AGI, or not deductible:
   a. Barak contributes to his H.R. 10 plan (i.e., a retirement plan for a self-employed individual).
   b. Keith pays child support to his former wife, Renee, for the support of their son, Chris.
   c. Judy pays professional dues that are *not* reimbursed by her employer.
   d. Ted pays $500 as the monthly mortgage payment on his personal residence. Of this amount, $100 represents a payment on principal and $400 represents an interest payment.
   e. Oni pays a moving company for moving her household goods to Detroit, where she is starting a new job. She is not reimbursed by her employer.
   f. Ralph pays $6,000 of property taxes on his personal residence and $5,000 of state income taxes.

Critical Thinking

5. LO.1 In 2022, Larry and Susan each invest $10,000 in separate investment activities. They each incur deductible expenses of $800 associated with their respective investments. Explain why Larry's expenses might not be deductible and Susan's expenses might be appropriately classified as deductions *for* AGI.

6. LO.1 Nanette, a single taxpayer, is a first-grade teacher. Potential deductions are charitable contributions of $800, personal property taxes on her car of $240,

and various supplies purchased for use in her classroom of $225 (none reimbursed by her school). How will these items affect Nanette's Federal income tax return for 2022?

7. **LO.1** In the determination of whether a business expense is deductible, the reasonableness requirement applies only to salaries. Evaluate this statement.

8. **LO.1** Dave uses the second floor of a building for his residence and the first floor for his business. The uninsured building is destroyed by fire. Are the tax consequences the same for each part of the building? Explain. Critical Thinking

9. **LO.1** Monique owns a building that she leases to an individual who operates a grocery store. Rent income is $10,000, and rental expenses are $6,000. On what Form 1040 schedule or schedules are the income and expenses reported?

10. **LO.2** What is the "actually paid" requirement for the deduction of an expense by a cash basis taxpayer? Does actual payment ensure a deduction? Explain.

11. **LO.2** Aubry, a cash basis and calendar year taxpayer, decides to reduce his taxable income for the current year by buying $65,000 worth of supplies for his business on December 27, 2022. Aubry thinks it will take more than a year to use up the supplies.
    a. Can Aubry deduct the expenditure for 2022? Explain.
    b. Would your answer in part (a) change if Aubry bought the supplies because the seller was going out of business and offered a large discount on the price? Explain.

12. **LO.3** Clear, Inc., is a bottled water distributor. Clear's delivery trucks frequently are required to park in no-parking zones to make their deliveries. If the trucks are occasionally ticketed, can Clear deduct the fines that it pays? Explain.

13. **LO.3** Angelo, an agent for an airline manufacturer, is negotiating a sale with a representative of the U.S. government and with a representative of a developing country. Angelo's company has sufficient capacity to handle only one of the orders. Both orders will have the same contract price. Angelo believes that if his employer authorizes a $500,000 payment to the representative of the foreign country, he can guarantee the sale. He is not sure that he can obtain the same result with the U.S. government. Identify the relevant tax issues for Angelo. Critical Thinking

14. **LO.3** Stuart, an insurance salesperson, is arrested for allegedly robbing a convenience store. He hires an attorney who is successful in getting the charges dropped. Is the attorney's fee deductible? Explain.

15. **LO.3** Linda operates an illegal gambling operation. Which of the following expenses that she incurs can reduce taxable income?
    a. Bribes paid to city employees.
    b. Salaries to employees.
    c. Security cameras.
    d. Kickbacks to police.
    e. Rent on an office.
    f. Depreciation on office furniture and equipment.
    g. Tenant's casualty insurance.
    h. Utilities.

16. **LO.3** Gordon anticipates that being positively perceived by the individual who is elected mayor will be beneficial for his business. Therefore, he contributes to the campaigns of both the Democratic and Republican candidates. The Republican candidate is elected mayor. Can Gordon deduct any of the political contributions he made?

Critical Thinking

17. **LO.3** Melissa, the owner of a sole proprietorship, does not provide health insurance for her 20 employees. She plans to spend $1,500 lobbying in opposition to legislation that would require her to provide such insurance. Discuss the tax advantages and disadvantages of paying the $1,500 to a professional lobbyist rather than spending the $1,500 on in-house lobbying expenditures.

18. **LO.3** What limits exist on the deductibility of executive compensation? Do the limits apply to all types of business entities? Are there any exceptions to the limitations? Explain.

Critical Thinking

19. **LO.3** Blaze operates a restaurant in Cleveland. He travels to Columbus to investigate acquiring a business. He incurs expenses as follows: $1,500 for travel, $2,000 for legal advice, and $3,500 for a market analysis. Based on the different tax consequences listed below, describe the circumstances that were involved in Blaze's investigation of the business.
    a. Blaze deducts the $7,000 of expenses.
    b. Blaze cannot deduct any of the $7,000 of expenses.
    c. Blaze deducts $5,000 of the expenses and amortizes the $2,000 balance over a period of 180 months.

Critical Thinking
Planning

20. **LO.3** Karen and Andy own a beach house. They have an agreement with a rental agent to rent it up to 200 days per year. For the past three years, the agent has been successful in renting it for 200 days. Karen and Andy use the beach house for one week during the summer and one week during Thanksgiving. Their daughter, Sarah, a college student, has asked if she and some friends can use the beach house for the week of spring break. Advise Karen and Andy on how they should respond, and identify any relevant tax issues.

21. **LO.3** Hank was transferred from Arizona to North Dakota on March 1 of the current year. He immediately put his home in Phoenix up for rent. The home was rented May 1 to November 30 and was vacant during the month of December. It was rented again on January 1 for six months. What expenses related to the home, if any, can Hank deduct on his return? Which deductions are *for* AGI, and which ones are *from* AGI?

Critical Thinking
Decision Making
Planning

22. **LO.3** Ray loses his job as a result of a corporate downsizing. Consequently, he falls behind on the mortgage payments on his personal residence. His friend Sahar would like to make the delinquent mortgage payments for him.
    a. Could the payments be structured so that Ray can deduct the mortgage interest?
    b. Could the payment arrangement deny both Ray and Sahar a mortgage interest deduction?
    c. Could the payments be structured so that Sahar can deduct the mortgage interest?

Critical Thinking
Planning

23. **LO.3** Ella owns 60% of the stock of Peach, Inc. The stock has declined in value since she purchased it five years ago. She is going to sell 5% of the stock to a relative. Ella also is going to make a gift of 10% of the stock to another relative. Identify the relevant tax issues for Ella.

24. **LO.3** Jarret owns City of Charleston bonds with an adjusted basis of $190,000. During the year, he receives interest payments of $3,800. Jarret partially financed the purchase of the bonds by borrowing $100,000 at 5% interest. Jarret's interest payments on the loan this year are $4,900, and his principal payments are $1,100.
    a. What is Jarret's gross income from the interest income this year? Explain.
    b. Can Jarret deduct any interest expense this year? Explain.

25. **LO.3** In 2022, Blair Corporation paid its CEO base compensation of $700,000 and a performance bonus of $500,000; the CEO was hired in January 2020. How much of the compensation can Blair deduct? Discuss.

Computational Exercises

26. **LO.2** Shanna, a calendar year and cash basis taxpayer, rents property to be used in her business from Janice. As part of the rental agreement, Shanna pays $8,400 rent on April 1, 2022, for the 12 months ending March 31, 2023.
    a. How much is Shanna's deduction for rent expense in 2022?
    b. Assume the same facts, except that the $8,400 is for 24 months' rent ending March 31, 2024. How much is Shanna's deduction for rent expense in 2022?

27. **LO.2** Falcon, Inc., paid salaries of $500,000 to its employees during its first year of operations. At the end of the year, Falcon had unpaid salaries of $45,000.
    a. Calculate the salary deduction if Falcon is a cash basis taxpayer.
    b. Calculate the salary deduction if Falcon is an accrual basis taxpayer.

28. **LO.2** Meghan, a calendar year taxpayer, is the owner of a sole proprietorship that uses the cash method. On February 1, 2022, she leases an office building to use in her business for $120,000 for an 18-month period. To obtain this favorable lease rate, she pays the $120,000 at the inception of the lease. How much rent expense may Meghan deduct on her 2022 tax return?

29. **LO.3** Vella owns and operates an illegal gambling establishment. In connection with this activity, he has the following expenses during the year:

Rent	$ 24,000
Bribes	40,000
Travel expenses	4,000
Utilities	18,000
Wages	230,000
Payroll taxes	13,800
Property insurance	1,600
Illegal kickbacks	22,000

What are Vella's total deductible expenses for tax purposes?

30. **LO.3** Printer Company pays a $25,000 annual membership fee to a trade association for paper wholesalers. The trade association estimates that 60% of its dues are allocated to lobbying activities.
    a. What are Printer's total deductible expenses for tax purposes?
    b. Assume the same facts as above, except that the $25,000 was incurred for in-house lobbying expenses. What are Printer's total deductible expenses for tax purposes?

31. **LO.3** Stanford owns and operates two dry cleaning businesses. He travels to Boston to discuss acquiring a restaurant. Later in the month, he travels to New York to discuss acquiring a bakery. Stanford does not acquire the restaurant but does purchase the bakery on November 1, 2022.

    Stanford incurred the following expenses:

Total investigation costs related to the restaurant	$28,000
Total investigation costs related to the bakery	51,000

What is the maximum amount Stanford can deduct in 2022 for investigation expenses?

32. **LO.3** Tobias has a brokerage account and buys on the margin, which resulted in an interest expense of $20,000 during the year. Income generated through the brokerage account was as follows:

Municipal interest	$ 50,000
Taxable dividends and interest	350,000

How much investment interest can Tobias deduct?

Problems

33. **LO.1** Amos is a self-employed tax attorney. He and Monica, his employee, attend a tax conference in Dallas sponsored by the American Institute of CPAs. The following expenses are incurred during the trip:

	Amos	Monica
Conference registration	$ 900	$900
Airfare	1,200	700
Taxi fares	100	–0–
Lodging in Dallas	750	300

a. Amos pays for all of these expenses. Calculate the effect of these expenses on Amos's AGI.

b. Would your answer to part (a) change if the American Bar Association had sponsored the conference? Explain.

Critical Thinking
Decision Making

34. **LO.1** Daniel, age 38, is single and has the following income and expenses in 2022:

Salary income	$65,000
Net rent income	6,000
Dividend income	3,500
Payment of alimony (divorce finalized in March 2020)	12,000
Mortgage interest on residence	9,900
Property tax on residence	1,200
Contribution to traditional IRA	6,000
Contribution to United Church	2,100
Loss on the sale of real estate (held for investment)	2,000
Medical expenses	3,250
State income tax	2,300
Federal income tax	5,800

a. Calculate Daniel's AGI.

b. Should Daniel itemize his deductions *from* AGI or take the standard deduction? Explain.

Critical Thinking
Planning

35. **LO.1** María, age 32, earns $60,000 working in 2022. She has no other income. Her medical expenses for the year total $6,000. During the year, she suffers a casualty loss of $9,500 when her apartment is damaged by flood waters (part of a Federally declared disaster area). María contributes $6,000 to her church and pays $4,000 of state income taxes. On the advice of her friend, María is trying to decide whether to contribute $5,000 to a traditional IRA. What effect would the IRA contribution have on María's itemized deductions?

36. **LO.1** A list of the items that Faith sold and the losses she incurred during the current tax year is as follows:

Yellow, Inc. stock	$ 1,600
Faith's personal use SUV	8,000
Faith's personal residence	10,000
City of Newburyport bonds	900

She also had a theft loss of $1,500 on her uninsured business use car. Calculate Faith's deductible losses.

37. **LO.1** Suzanne, a single taxpayer, operates a printing business as a sole proprietor. The business has two employees who are paid a total of $90,000 during 2022.

Assume that the business has no significant assets. During 2022, the business generates $150,000 of income and Suzanne's taxable income before the QBI deduction is $155,000.

a. What is Suzanne's qualified business income deduction?

b. What is Suzanne's qualified business income deduction if the facts are the same except that the business income is $250,000 and Suzanne's taxable income before the QBI deduction is $270,000?

38. **LO.2** Duck, an accrual basis corporation, sponsored a rock concert on December 29, 2022. Gross receipts were $300,000. The following expenses were incurred and paid as indicated: Critical Thinking Planning

Expense		Payment Date
Rental of coliseum	$ 25,000	December 21, 2022
Cost of goods sold:		
Food	30,000	December 30, 2022
Souvenirs	60,000	December 30, 2022
Performers	100,000	January 5, 2023
Cleaning of coliseum	10,000	February 1, 2023

Because the coliseum was not scheduled to be used again until January 15, the company with which Duck had contracted did not perform the cleanup until January 8–10, 2023.

a. Calculate Duck's net income from the concert for tax purposes for 2022.

b. Using the present value tables in Appendix E, what is the true cost to Duck if it had to defer the $100,000 deduction for the performers until 2023? Assume a 5% discount rate and a 21% marginal tax rate in 2022 and 2023.

39. **LO.3** Fynn incurred and paid the following expenses during 2022:

- $50 for a ticket for running a red light while he was commuting to work.
- $100 for a ticket for parking in a handicapped parking space.
- $200 to an attorney to represent him in traffic court as to the two tickets.
- $500 to an attorney to draft an agreement with a tenant for a one-year lease on an apartment that Fynn owns.
- $1,000 to an attorney to negotiate a reduction in his child support payments.
- $2,500 to an attorney to negotiate a reduction in his alimony payments to a former spouse.

Calculate the amount of Fynn's deductible expenses.

40. **LO.3** Trevor, a friend of yours from high school, works as a server at the ST Café. He asks you to help him prepare his Federal income tax return. When you inquire about why his bank deposits substantially exceed his tip income, he confides to you that he is a bookie on the side. Trevor then provides you with the following documented income and expenses for the year:

Tip income	$16,000
Gambling income	52,000
Gambling expenses	
Payouts to winners	29,000
Employee compensation	8,000
Bribe to police officer who is aware of Trevor's bookie activity	7,500

a. How will these items affect Trevor's AGI (ignore the impact of self-employment taxes)?

b. His taxable income (ignore the impact of self-employment taxes)?

Communications
Critical Thinking
Decision Making
Planning

41. **LO.3, 4** Ascend, a publicly held corporation, currently pays its president an annual salary of $900,000. As a means of increasing company profitability, the board of directors increased the president's compensation effective January 1, 2017, with a performance-based compensation program. This program increased the president's compensation by $600,000 in 2017, $650,000 in 2018, $750,000 in 2019, $800,000 in 2020 and 2021. Her compensation under this performance-based compensation program is expected to be $850,000 in 2022. Prepare a letter to Ascend's board of directors that identifies the amount of compensation that will be deductible by Ascend in 2022 and explains whether any changes should be made to the president's compensation plan in 2022. Address the letter to the board chairperson, Angela Riddle, whose address is 150 Erieview Tower, Cleveland, OH 44106.

42. **LO.3** Henrietta, the owner of a very successful hotel chain in the Southeast, is exploring the possibility of expanding the chain into a city in the Northeast. She incurs $35,000 of expenses associated with this investigation. Based on the regulatory environment for hotels in the city, she decides not to expand. During the year, she also investigates opening a restaurant that will be part of a national restaurant chain. Her expenses for this are $53,000. She proceeds with opening the restaurant, and it begins operations on September 1. Determine the amount that Henrietta can deduct in the current year for investigating these two businesses.

43. **LO.3** Terry traveled to a neighboring state to investigate the purchase of two hardware stores. His expenses included travel, legal, accounting, and miscellaneous expenses. The total was $52,000. He incurred the expenses in June and July 2022. Under the following circumstances, what can Terry deduct in 2022?
   a. Terry was in the hardware store business and did not acquire the two hardware stores.
   b. Terry was in the hardware store business and acquired the two hardware stores and began operating them on October 1, 2022.
   c. Terry did not acquire the two hardware stores and was not in the hardware store business.
   d. Terry acquired the two hardware stores but was not in the hardware store business when he acquired them. Operations began on October 1, 2022.

44. **LO.3** Jamari Peters (Social Security number 123-45-6789) operates a business with the following results in 2022:

Revenue	$20,000
Depreciation on car	3,960
Operating expenses of car	3,100
Rent	6,000
Wages	8,200
Amortization of intangibles	680

Jamari estimates that due to a depressed real estate market, the value of land owned by the business declined by $5,200.
   a. Calculate the effect of Jamari's business on his AGI.
   b. How would your answer in part (a) change if the activity was a hobby?

45. **LO.3** Alex, who is single, conducts an activity in the current year that is appropriately classified as a hobby. The activity produces the following revenues and expenses:

Revenue	$18,000
Property taxes	3,000
Materials and supplies	4,500
Utilities	2,000
Advertising	5,000
Insurance	750
Depreciation	4,000

Without regard to this activity, Alex's AGI is $62,000. Determine the amount of income Alex must report and the amount of the expenses he is permitted to deduct.

46. **LO.3** Piper owns a vacation cabin in the Tennessee mountains. Without considering the cabin, she has gross income of $65,000. During the year, she rents the cabin for two weeks for $2,500 and uses it herself for four weeks. The total expenses for the year are $10,000 mortgage interest; $1,500 property tax; $2,000 utilities, insurance, and maintenance; and $3,200 depreciation.

    a. What effect does the rental of the vacation cabin have on Piper's AGI?

    b. What expenses can Piper deduct, and how are they classified (i.e., *for* or *from* AGI)?

47. **LO.3** Adelene, who lives in a winter resort area, rented her personal residence for 14 days while she was visiting Brussels. Rent income was $5,000. Related expenses for the year were as follows:

Real property taxes	$ 3,800
Mortgage interest	7,500
Utilities	3,700
Insurance	2,500
Repairs	2,100
Depreciation	15,000

Determine the effect on Adelene's AGI.

48. **LO.3** During the year (not a leap year), Anna rented her vacation home for 30 days, used it personally for 20 days, and left it vacant for 315 days. She had the following income and expenses:

Rent income	$ 7,000
Expenses	
Real estate taxes	2,500
Interest on mortgage	9,000
Utilities	2,400
Repairs	1,000
Roof replacement (a capital expenditure)	12,000
Depreciation	7,500

    a. Compute Anna's net rent income or loss and the amounts she can itemize on her tax return, using the court's approach to allocating property taxes and interest.

    b. How would your answer in part (a) differ using the IRS's method of allocating property taxes and interest?

49. **LO.3** How would your answer to Problem 48 differ if Anna had rented the house for 87 days and had used it personally for 13 days? Use the IRS's method of allocating property taxes and interest.

50. **LO.1, 3** Chee, single, age 40, had the following income and expenses during 2022: Critical Thinking

Income	
Salary	$43,000
Rental of vacation home (rented 60 days, used personally 60 days, vacant 245 days)	4,000
Municipal bond interest	2,000
Dividend from General Electric	400
Expenses	
Interest on home mortgage	8,400
Interest on vacation home	4,758
Interest on loan used to buy municipal bonds	3,100
Property tax on home	$2,200
Property tax on vacation home	1,098

State income tax	3,300
State sales tax	900
Charitable contributions	1,100
Tax return preparation fee	300
Utilities and maintenance on vacation home	2,600
Depreciation on rental portion of vacation home	3,500

Calculate Chee's taxable income for the year. If Chee has any options, choose the method that maximizes his deductions.

Critical Thinking
Decision Making

51. **LO.1, 3, 4** Elisa and Clyde operate a retail sports memorabilia shop. For the current year, sales revenue is $75,000 and expenses are as follows:

Cost of goods sold	$30,000
Advertising	1,000
Utilities	2,000
Rent	4,500
Insurance	1,500
Wages to Boyd	9,000

Elisa and Clyde pay $9,000 in wages to Boyd, a part-time employee. Because this amount is $1,000 below the minimum wage, Boyd threatens to file a complaint with the appropriate Federal agency. Although Elisa and Clyde pay no attention to Boyd's threat, Chelsea (Elisa's mother) gives Boyd a check for $1,000 for the disputed wages. The retail shop is the only source of income for Elisa and Clyde.

a. Calculate Elisa and Clyde's AGI.

b. Can Chelsea deduct the $1,000 payment on her tax return? Explain.

c. How could the tax position of the parties be improved?

Communications
Decision Making
Planning

52. **LO.3, 4** Brittany Callihan sold stock (basis of $184,000) to her son, Ridge, for $160,000, the fair market value.

a. What are the tax consequences to Brittany?

b. What are the tax consequences to Ridge if he later sells the stock for $190,000? For $152,000? For $174,000?

c. Prepare your solution using spreadsheet software such as Microsoft Excel. The spreadsheet should compute the gain or loss for Ridge for all scenarios. Use the IF function to compute the right of offset.

d. Write a letter to Brittany in which you inform her of the tax consequences if she sells the stock to Ridge for $160,000. Explain how a sales transaction could be structured that would produce better tax consequences for her. Brittany's address is 32 Country Lane, Lawrence, KS 66045.

53. **LO.3** For each of the following independent transactions, calculate the recognized gain or loss to the seller and the adjusted basis to the buyer.

a. Kiera sells Parchment, Inc. stock (adjusted basis $17,000) to Phillip, her brother, for its fair market value of $12,000.

b. Darnell sells land (adjusted basis $85,000) to his nephew, Boyd, for its fair market value of $70,000.

c. Susan sells a tax-exempt bond (adjusted basis $20,000) to her wholly owned corporation for its fair market value of $19,000.

d. Sinbad sells a business truck (adjusted basis $20,000) that he uses in his sole proprietorship to his cousin, Agnes, for its fair market value of $18,500.

e. Martha sells her partnership interest (adjusted basis $175,000) in Pearl Partnership to her adult daughter, Kim, for $220,000.

54. **LO.1, 3, 4** During the current year, Robert pays the following amounts associated with his own residence:

Communications
Critical Thinking
Decision Making
Planning

Property taxes	$3,000
Mortgage interest	8,000
Repairs	1,200
Utilities	2,700
Replacement of roof	4,000

In addition, Robert paid $1,500 of property taxes on the home that is owned and used by Anne, his daughter.

a. Which of these expenses can Robert deduct?

b. Can Anne deduct the $1,500 of property taxes?

c. Are the deductions *for* AGI or *from* AGI (itemized)?

d. How could the tax consequences be improved? Summarize your recommendation in an e-mail, and send it to your instructor.

55. **LO.3** For 2022, MSU Corporation has $500,000 of adjusted taxable income, $22,000 of business interest income, and $120,000 of business interest expense. It has average annual gross receipts of more than $27,000,000 over the prior three taxable years.

a. What is MSU's interest expense deduction?

b. How much interest expense can be deducted if MSU's adjusted taxable income is $300,000?

Tax Return Problems

Tax Forms Problem

ProConnect™ Tax

56. Roberta Santos, age 41, is single and lives at 120 Sanborne Avenue, Springfield, IL 62701. Her Social Security number is 123-45-6780. Roberta has been divorced from her former husband, Wayne, for two years. She has a son, Jason, who is 17, and a daughter, June, who is 18. Jason's Social Security number is 111-11-1112, and June's is 123-45-6788. Roberta has never owned or used any virtual currency. She does not want to contribute $3 to the Presidential Election Campaign Fund. Roberta received the appropriate recovery rebates (economic impact payments); related questions in ProConnect Tax should be ignored.

Roberta, an advertising executive, earned a salary from ABC Advertising of $136,000 in 2021. Her employer withheld $16,000 in Federal income tax and $4,400 in state income tax.

Roberta has legal custody of Jason and June. The divorce decree provides that Roberta is to receive the dependency deductions for the children. Jason lives with his father during summer vacation. Wayne indicates that his expenses for Jason are $5,500. Roberta can document that she spent $8,500 for Jason's support during 2021. In prior years, Roberta gave a signed Form 8332 to Wayne regarding Jason. For 2021, she has decided not to do so. Roberta provides all of June's support.

Roberta's mother died on January 7, 2021. Roberta inherited assets worth $625,000 from her mother. As the sole beneficiary of her mother's life insurance policy, Roberta received insurance proceeds of $300,000. Her mother's cost basis for the life insurance policy was $120,000. Roberta's favorite aunt gave her $13,000 for her birthday in October.

On November 8, 2021, Roberta sells for $22,000 Amber stock that she had purchased for $24,000 from her first cousin, Walt, on December 5, 2016. Walt's cost basis for the stock was $26,000. On December 1, 2021, Roberta sold Falcon stock for $13,500. She had acquired the stock on July 2, 2017, for $8,000.

An examination of Roberta's records reveals that she received the following:

- Interest income of $2,500 from First Savings Bank.
- Groceries valued at $750 from Kroger Groceries for being the 100,000th customer.
- Qualified dividend income of $1,800 from Amber.
- Interest income of $3,750 on City of Springfield school bonds.
- Alimony of $16,000 from Wayne; divorce finalized in May 2019.
- Distribution of $4,800 from ST Partnership (Employer Identification Number: 46-4567893). Her distributive share of the partnership passive taxable income was $5,300. She had no prior passive activity losses. Assume that the qualified business income deduction applies and the W–2 wage limitation does not.

From her checkbook records, she determines that she made the following payments during 2021:

- Charitable contributions of $4,500 to First Presbyterian Church and $1,500 to the American Red Cross (proper receipts obtained).
- Payment of $5,000 to ECM Hospital for the medical expenses of a friend from work.
- Mortgage interest on her residence of $7,800 to Peoples Bank.
- Property taxes of $3,200 on her residence and $1,100 (ad valorem) on her car.
- $800 for landscaping expenses for residence.
- Estimated Federal income taxes of $2,800 and estimated state income taxes of $1,000.
- Medical expenses of $5,000 for her and $800 for Jason. In December, her medical insurance policy reimbursed $1,500 of her medical expenses.
- A $1,000 ticket for parking in a handicapped space.
- Attorney's fees of $500 associated with unsuccessfully contesting the parking ticket.
- Contribution of $250 to the campaign of a candidate for governor.

Because she did not maintain records of the sales tax she paid, she calculates the amount from the sales tax table to be $1,808.

Calculate Roberta's net tax payable or refund due for 2021. Use the appropriate forms and schedules. Suggested software: ProConnect Tax.

Communications
Critical Thinking
Decision Making
Planning
Tax Computation Problem

57. John and Mary Jane Diaz are married, filing jointly. Their address is 204 Shoe Lane, Blacksburg, VA 24061. John is age 35, and Mary Jane is age 30. They are expecting their first child in early 2023. John's salary in 2022 was $125,000, from which $22,800 of Federal income tax and $5,700 of state income tax were withheld. Mary Jane made $62,000 and had $5,600 of Federal income tax and $3,100 of state income tax withheld. The appropriate amounts of FICA tax and Medicare tax were withheld for John and for Mary Jane. John's Social Security number is 111-11-1111, and Mary Jane's Social Security number is 123-45-6789.

Both John and Mary Jane are offered medical insurance by their employers with 80% of the premiums being paid by the employers. Mary Jane declines coverage by her employer. The premium paid by John's employer for the family plan he receives is $21,350. Mary Jane received medical benefits of $7,300 under the plan. John was not ill during 2022. Mary Jane paid noncovered medical expenses of $1,300.

John makes child support payments of $15,000 for his son, Rod, who lives with Jill, John's former spouse, except for two months in the summer when he visits John and Mary Jane. At the time of the divorce, John worked for a Fortune 500 company and received a salary of $225,000. As a result of corporate downsizing, he lost his job.

Mary Jane's father lived with them until his death in November. His only sources of income were salary of $3,800, unemployment compensation benefits of $3,500, and Social Security benefits of $4,100. Of this amount, he deposited $6,000 in a savings account. The remainder of his support of $11,000, which included funeral expenses of $4,500, was provided by John and Mary Jane.

Other income received by the Diazes was as follows:

Interest on certificates of deposit	$3,500
Share of S corporation taxable income (distributions from the S corporation to Mary Jane were $1,100; assume no wage limitation for qualified business income deduction)	4,500
Award received by Mary Jane from employer for an outstanding suggestion for cutting costs	4,000

John has always wanted to operate his own business. In October 2022, he incurred expenses of $15,000 in investigating the establishment of a retail computer franchise. With the birth of their child expected next year, however, he decides to forgo self-employment for at least a couple of years.

John and Mary Jane made charitable contributions of $8,700 during the year and paid an additional $1,800 in state income taxes in 2022 upon filing their 2021 state income tax return. Their deductible home mortgage interest was $9,800, and their property taxes came to $4,800. They paid sales taxes of $2,000, for which they have receipts. They paid a ticket of $150 that Mary Jane received for running a red light (detected by a red light camera).

Part 1—Tax Computation
Calculate John and Mary Jane's tax (or refund) due for 2022.

Part 2—Tax Planning
Assume that the Diazes come to you for advice in December 2022. John has learned that he will receive a $40,000 bonus. He wants to know if he should take it in December 2022 or in January 2023. Mary Jane will quit work on December 31 to stay home with the baby. Their itemized deductions will decrease by $3,100 because Mary Jane will not have state income taxes withheld. Mary Jane will not receive the employee award in 2023. She expects the medical benefits received to be $9,000. The Diazes expect all of their other income items to remain the same in 2023. Write a letter to John and Mary Jane that contains your advice, and prepare a memo for the tax files.

Research Problems

Note: Solutions to the Research Problems can be prepared by using the Thomson Reuters Checkpoint™ online tax research database, which accompanies this textbook. Solutions can also be prepared by using research materials found in a typical tax library.

the answer company™ THOMSON REUTERS®

Communications
Critical Thinking

Research Problem 1. Gray Chemical Company manufactured pesticides that were toxic. Over the course of several years, the toxic waste contaminated the air and water around the company's plant. Several employees suffered toxic poisoning, and the Environmental Protection Agency cited the company for violations. In court, the judge found Gray guilty and imposed fines of $15 million. The company voluntarily set up a charitable fund for the purpose of bettering the environment and funded it with $8 million. The company incurred legal expenses in setting up the foundation and defending itself in court. The court reduced the fine from $15 million to $7 million.

Gray Chemical Company deducted the $8 million paid to the foundation and the legal expenses incurred. The IRS disallowed both deductions on the grounds that the payment was, in fact, a fine and in violation of public policy.

Gray's president, Ted Jones, has contacted you regarding the deductibility of the $7 million fine, the $8 million payment to the foundation, and the legal fees. Write a letter to Mr. Jones that contains your advice, and prepare a memo for the tax files. Gray's address is 200 Lincoln Center, Omaha, NE 68182.

Partial list of research aids:
§§ 162(a) and (f).
Reg. § 1.162–21(b).

Critical Thinking **Research Problem 2.** Rex and Agnes Harrell purchased a beach house at Duck, North Carolina, in early 2022. Although they intended to use the beach house occasionally for recreational purposes, to help pay the mortgage payments, property taxes, and maintenance costs, they also planned to rent it through the realty agency that had handled the purchase. Rex is a surgeon, and Agnes is a counselor.

The beach house was in need of substantial repairs. Rather than hiring a contractor, Rex and Agnes decided they would make the repairs themselves. During both high school and college, Rex had worked summers in construction. In addition, he had taken an advanced course in woodworking and related subjects from a local community college several years ago.

During 2022, according to a log maintained by the Harrells, they occupied the beach house 38 days and rented it 49 days. The log also indicated that on 24 of the 38 days they occupied the beach house, one or both of them were engaged in work on the beach house. Their two teenage children were with them on all of these days but did not help with the work being done. On their 2022 income tax return, Rex and Agnes, who filed a joint return, treated the beach house as a rental property and deducted a pro rata share of the property taxes, mortgage interest, utilities, maintenance and repairs, and depreciation in determining their net loss from the beach home. In the current year, after examining their return, an IRS agent has limited the deductions to the rent income. He contends that the 14-day personal use provision was exceeded and that many of the alleged repairs were capital expenditures. Advise the Harrells on how they should respond to the IRS.

Critical Thinking **Research Problem 3.** Mona viewed herself as a creative individual who had chosen to go to law school for economic reasons. Mona's undergraduate majors were creative writing and American Indian studies.

Mona was very successful as an attorney and eventually was admitted to partnership in her law firm, having an expertise in negotiating settlements involving Indian water rights.

While practicing law, Mona continued her interest in the arts. She had directed plays in high school and maintained her involvement in the theater, even during law school. She belonged to local theater organizations while she practiced law. She took several courses in filmmaking and read extensively in the area. She even took several months off from her legal practice to enroll in NYU's filmmaking program. Her enrollment in the program provided her with hands-on experience and taught her about the technical aspects of filmmaking and allowed her to meet individuals who would later work with her on her documentary.

When she discovered that her husband had similar interests, she decided to create a documentary about Way to Sing America. After acquiring the rights to all of the archival footage of Way to Sing America, she hired a video production company to film interviews that she conducted with Way to Sing America alumni (over 400 hours of such interviews). She spent weekends and nights over a three-year period working on the documentary.

Once the documentary was completed, Mona began marketing it at film festivals. At some of these festivals, her documentary received awards. At the same time, she developed a business plan, hired a bookkeeper to manage the finances, and hired an accounting firm to provide tax advice.

During this three-year period, she reported the following losses:

2019	$ 30,000
2020	400,000
2021	200,000

On her tax returns for the three-year period, in each year, she offset these amounts against her law firm income of approximately $1,000,000.

Upon audit by the IRS, the agent concluded that her filmmaking activity is a hobby and therefore the losses cannot be deducted except to the extent of the income generated.

Who is correct? Explain.

Use internet tax resources to address the following questions. Look for reliable websites and blogs of the IRS and other government agencies, media outlets, businesses, tax professionals, academics, think tanks, and political outlets.

Research Problem 4. Isabelle was contemplating making a contribution to her traditional IRA in 2021. She determined that she would contribute $6,000 in December 2021, but forgot about making the contribution until she was preparing her 2021 tax return in February 2022. Use the website of any well-known IRA provider (e.g., Fidelity, Vanguard, T. Rowe Price) to determine if Isabelle can make a 2021 contribution to her IRA after the tax year has ended.

Research Problem 5. The $1 million maximum compensation deduction does not seem to have deterred large corporations from remunerating their executives at very high levels. What techniques are being used to work around the millionaires' provision? Are executives taking pay cuts, or are their salaries being deferred or changed in nature due to § 162(m)? How do you think companies should respond to the changes made to this area by the TCJA of 2017?

Research Problem 6. A qualified expense is not deductible unless there is appropriate substantiation to document it. Find two websites and/or articles that provide (1) guidance on the types of substantiation required for business expenses and (2) suggestions for taxpayers on how to collect this information and organize it.

Becker CPA Review Questions

Becker

1. Which of the following is a deduction *for* AGI?
   a. Charitable contributions of property.
   b. Alimony paid pursuant to a 2015 divorce agreement.
   c. State income taxes.
   d. Mortgage interest paid on your primary residence.

2. Which of the following is *not* a deduction *for* AGI?
   a. Alimony paid for a divorce finalized in 2018.
   b. Business rent on a self-employed business.
   c. Property taxes paid on your primary residence.
   d. One half of self-employment tax.

3. David is a CPA and enjoys playing the lottery. This year David won $10,000 in lottery scratch-off tickets. He spent $200 purchasing the tickets. Which statement is true regarding David's winnings?
   a. David must include $9,800 in gross income.
   b. David must include the $10,000 in gross income and can deduct $200 as an itemized deduction.
   c. David must include $10,000 in gross income and can deduct $200 as an adjustment to AGI.
   d. David's winnings are not taxable.

4. Bob is a farmer and is required to use the accrual method. At the beginning of the year, Bob has inventory, including livestock held for resale, amounting to $10,000. During the year, Bob purchased livestock totaling $3,000. Bob's ending inventory was $4,000. Bob's net sales for the year totaled $17,000. What is Bob's gross profit for the current year?
   a. $9,000
   b. $17,000
   c. $8,000
   d. $13,000

5. The Griffins own a mountain cabin that is used for both personal and rental purposes. In the current year, the Griffins rented the cabin out for 150 days and used it personally for 50 days. Assume that the Griffins itemize their deductions. Which of the following statements regarding the treatment of the mountain cabin on the Griffins' tax return is true?
   a. 100% of the utilities for the mountain cabin for the entire year are deductible.
   b. Depreciation is deductible under all rental circumstances.
   c. Real estate taxes are deductible under all rental circumstances.
   d. The rental income received is not included in gross income.

6. The Groves own a beach house as a second home. This year, the Groves used the beach house personally for 4 months. For 14 days during the summer, the Groves rented out their beach house for $5,000 total to friends. Which statement is true regarding the taxability of the Groves' beach house?
   a. $5,000 is included in gross income.
   b. Mortgage interest paid on the beach house is deductible.
   c. All repair expenses on the beach house are deductible.
   d. Depreciation expense on the beach house is deductible.

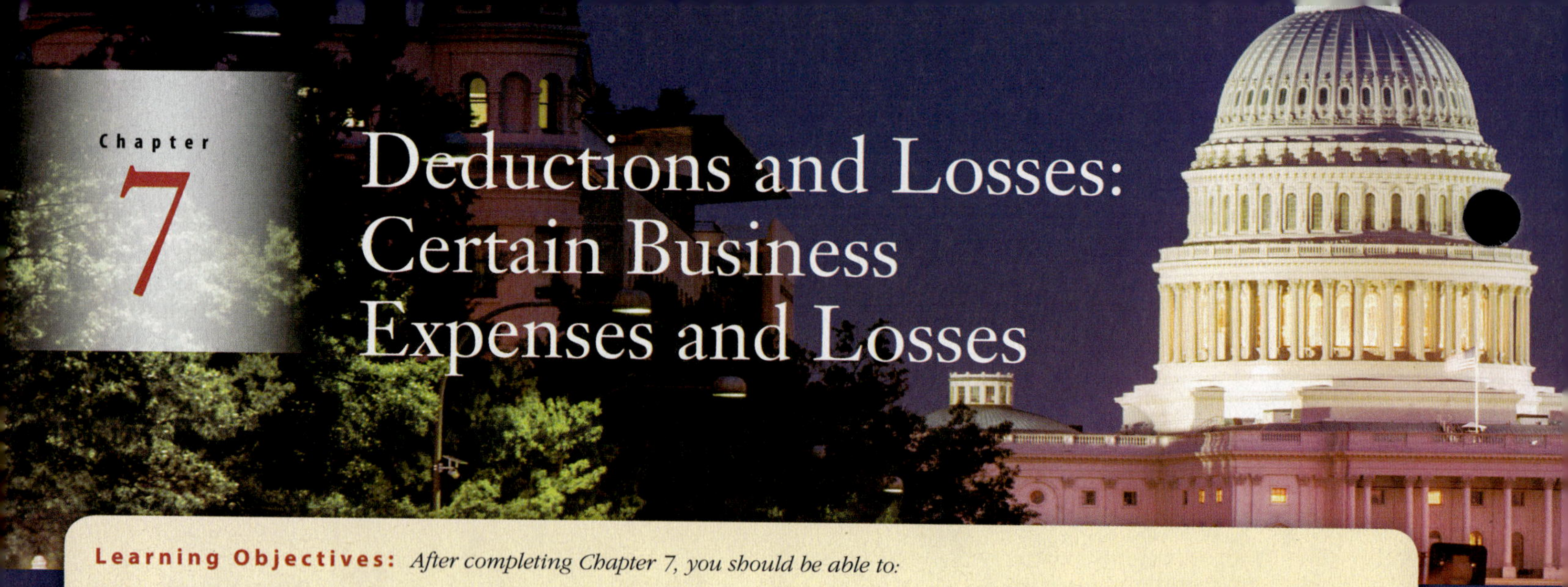

Chapter 7

Deductions and Losses: Certain Business Expenses and Losses

Learning Objectives: *After completing Chapter 7, you should be able to:*

- **LO.1** Determine the amount, classification, and timing of the bad debt deduction.
- **LO.2** Illustrate the tax treatment of worthless securities, including § 1244 stock.
- **LO.3** Distinguish between deductible and nondeductible losses of individuals.
- **LO.4** Identify a casualty and determine the amount, classification, and timing of casualty and theft losses.
- **LO.5** Apply the alternative tax treatments for research and experimental expenditures.
- **LO.6** Apply the excess business loss limitation rules.
- **LO.7** Determine the amount of the net operating loss and review the effect of the carryover provisions on previous and subsequent years' taxable income.
- **LO.8** Identify tax planning opportunities in deducting certain business expenses, business losses, and personal losses.

Chapter Outline

7-1 Bad Debts, 7-2
- 7-1a Specific Charge-Off Method, 7-3
- 7-1b Business versus Nonbusiness Bad Debts, 7-4
- 7-1c Loans between Related Parties, 7-5

7-2 Worthless Securities and Small Business Stock Losses, 7-6
- 7-2a Worthless Securities, 7-6
- 7-2b Small Business Stock (§ 1244 Stock) Losses, 7-6

7-3 Losses of Individuals, 7-7
- 7-3a Events That Are Not Casualties, 7-7
- 7-3b Theft Losses, 7-8
- 7-3c When to Deduct Casualty Losses, 7-8
- 7-3d Measuring the Amount of Loss, 7-9
- 7-3e Personal Casualty Gains and Losses, 7-12
- 7-3f Statutory Framework for Deducting Losses of Individuals, 7-14

7-4 Research and Experimental Expenditures, 7-15
- 7-4a Expense Method, 7-16
- 7-4b Deferral and Amortization Method, 7-16

7-5 Excess Business Losses, 7-17
- 7-5a Excess Business Loss Defined, 7-17
- 7-5b Losses from Partnerships or S Corporations, 7-18
- 7-5c Other Rules, 7-19

7-6 Net Operating Losses, 7-19
- 7-6a General Rules, 7-20
- 7-6b Computation of the Net Operating Loss, 7-20
- 7-6c Computation of Taxable Income for Year to Which Net Operating Loss Is Carried, 7-23
- 7-6d Calculation of the Remaining Net Operating Loss, 7-24

7-7 Tax Planning, 7-25
- 7-7a Small Business Stock (§ 1244 Stock) Losses, 7-25
- 7-7b Casualty Losses, 7-25

The Big Picture

Losses

Martha, a cash basis and calendar year taxpayer, is nearing the end of a year she would like to forget. Several years ago she loaned $25,000 to her friend Janice to enable her to start a business. Janice had made scheduled payments of $7,000 ($1,000 of this was interest) when she unexpectedly died in January. At the time of her death, Janice was insolvent. Martha's attempts to collect on the debt were fruitless.

On October 1, 2021, Martha invested $50,000 in the stock of a pharmaceutical company that previously had been profitable. However, as a result of losing a patent infringement suit, the company declared bankruptcy on May 31, 2022. The bankruptcy trustee has informed shareholders that they should not expect to receive anything from the company.

Martha has owned and operated a bookstore as a sole proprietorship for the past 10 years. The bookstore previously produced annual profits of about $75,000. Due to the continued growth of online vendors and e-books, Martha's bookstore sustained a net loss of $180,000 this year.

On September 28, 2022, a hurricane caused a large oak tree to blow over onto Martha's house. In the aftermath of the hurricane, Martha's county was designated a Federal disaster area by the President. The cost of removing the tree and making repairs was $32,000. Martha received a check for $25,000 from her insurance company in final settlement of the claim. Her adjusted basis for the house was $280,000.

On March 8, 2021, Martha purchased what she believed to be "small business stock" (§ 1244 stock) from her friend Peter for $20,000. The stock's value began to decline significantly soon after its purchase. On November 2, 2022, Martha sold the stock for $12,000.

Can you help relieve Martha's feeling of despair by making her aware of beneficial loss provisions in the tax law?

Read the chapter and formulate your response.

Framework 1040 **Tax Formula for Individuals**

This chapter covers the boldfaced portions of the Tax Formula for Individuals that was introduced in Concept Summary 3.1 on p. 3-3. Below those portions are the sections of Form 1040 where the results are reported.

Income *(broadly defined)*	$ xx,xxx
Less: Exclusions	(x,xxx)
Gross income	$ xx,xxx
Less: Deductions *for* adjusted gross income	**(x,xxx)**
FORM 1040 (Schedule 1)	
3 Business income or (loss). Attach Schedule C	
Adjusted gross income	$ xx,xxx
Less: The greater of total itemized deductions *or* the standard deduction	**(x,xxx)**
FORM 1040 (p. 1)	
12a Standard deduction or itemized deductions (from Schedule A)	
Charitable contributions if you take the standard deduction*	(xxx)
Personal and dependency exemptions**	(x,xxx)
Deduction for qualified business income***	(x,xxx)
Taxable income	$ xx,xxx
Tax on taxable income *(see Tax Tables or Tax Rate Schedules)*	$ x,xxx
Less: Tax credits *(including income taxes withheld and prepaid)*	(xxx)
Tax due (or refund)	$ xxx

* For 2021, married taxpayers may claim up to $600 of cash charitable donations ($300 if unmarried).
** Exemption deductions are not allowed from 2018 through 2025.
*** Only applies from 2018 through 2025.

Individual deductions must be properly classified as either *for* adjusted gross income (AGI) or *from* AGI (e.g., itemized deductions). Business expenses and losses, along with expenses and losses related to rent and royalty activities (entered into for profit), are deducted *for* AGI. Most other investment expenses are deducted *from* AGI. The determination of the taxpayer's activity (i.e., whether the taxpayer is engaged in a trade or business, an investment, or a personal activity) is crucial in this classification process.[1]

Deductible losses on personal use property are deductions *from* AGI (as itemized deductions). Casualty and theft losses on personal use property are discussed in this chapter; other itemized deductions are discussed in Chapter 10.

In determining the amount and timing of the deduction for bad debts, proper classification is again important. A business bad debt is classified as a deduction *for* AGI, and a nonbusiness bad debt is classified as a short-term capital loss.

Other topics discussed in Chapter 7 are research and experimental expenditures, the limitation on excess business losses, and the net operating loss deduction.

LO.1

Determine the amount, classification, and timing of the bad debt deduction.

7-1 Bad Debts

If a taxpayer sells goods or provides services on credit and, later, the account receivable becomes worthless, a **bad debt** deduction is allowed only if the income related to the account receivable was previously included in income.[2] No deduction is allowed, for example, for a bad debt related to the sale of a product or service when the taxpayer is on the cash basis because no income is reported until the cash has been collected.

[1]See, for example, *Groetzinger v. Comm.*, 85–2 USTC ¶9622, 56 AFTR 2d 85–5683, 771 F.2d 269 (CA–7), *aff'd* in 87–1 USTC ¶9191, 59 AFTR 2d 87–532, 107 S.Ct. 980.

[2]Reg. § 1.166–1(e).

Example 1

Daniela, a sole proprietor, operates a business named Executive Accounting and Tax Services. Last year Pat hired Daniela to help him with the accounting for his small business. Daniela also prepared the S corporation income tax return for the business and Pat's personal income tax return. Daniela billed Pat $8,000 for the services she performed. Pat has never paid the bill, his business no longer exists, and his whereabouts are unknown.

If Daniela is an *accrual basis taxpayer*, she includes the $8,000 in income when the services are performed. When she determines that Pat's account will not be collected, she deducts the $8,000 as a bad debt expense.

If Daniela is a *cash basis taxpayer*, she does not include the $8,000 in income until payment is received. When she determines that Pat's account will not be collected, she cannot deduct the $8,000 as a bad debt expense because it was never recognized as income.

The Big Picture

Example 2

Return to the facts of *The Big Picture* on p. 7-1. Because Martha is a cash basis taxpayer, she cannot take a bad debt deduction for any unpaid accrued interest on the loan to Janice (her friend) because the interest was never recognized as income.

A bad debt also can result from the nonrepayment of a loan made by the taxpayer or from purchased debt instruments.

7-1a Specific Charge-Off Method

In general, the **specific charge-off method** must be used for tax purposes when accounting for bad debts. Certain financial institutions are allowed to use the **reserve method** for computing deductions for bad debts.

A taxpayer using the specific charge-off method may claim a deduction in the year when a specific business debt becomes either partially or wholly worthless. A nonbusiness debt must be wholly worthless to claim a deduction.[3] The taxpayer must be able to document the fact that the debt is either partially or completely worthless. This is one of the more difficult tasks facing a taxpayer. Legal proceedings against the debtor are not required as long as the taxpayer can demonstrate that collection is unlikely.

In the case of a business debt, partial worthlessness can result in a deduction. If, in a later year, the balance of the debt is deemed uncollectible, it can be deducted. In the case of a nonbusiness debt, a deduction is only allowed in the year the debt becomes completely worthless.

Example 3

In 2020, Ross loaned $1,000 to Josh, who agreed to repay the loan in two years. In 2022, Josh disappeared after the note became delinquent. If a reasonable investigation by Ross indicates that he cannot find Josh or that a suit against Josh would not result in collection, Ross can deduct the $1,000 in 2022.

Bankruptcy is generally an indication of at least partial worthlessness of a debt. Bankruptcy may create worthlessness before the settlement date. If this is the case, the deduction may be taken in the year of worthlessness.

Example 4

In Example 3, assume that Josh filed for personal bankruptcy in 2021 and that the debt is a business debt. At that time, Ross learned that unsecured creditors (including Ross) were ultimately expected to receive 20 cents on the dollar.

In 2022, settlement is made, and Ross receives only $150. He should deduct $800 ($1,000 loan − $200 expected settlement) in 2021 and $50 in 2022 ($200 balance − $150 proceeds).

[3] §§ 166(a) and (d).

If a receivable is written off (deducted) as uncollectible and then collected in a later tax year, income will result if the deduction yielded a tax benefit in the year it was taken. See the discussion and examples in text Section 5-15.

Concept Summary 7.1 provides a summary of the tax treatment of bad debts using the specific charge-off method.

Concept Summary 7.1

The Tax Treatment of Bad Debts Using the Specific Charge-Off Method

	Business Bad Debts	Nonbusiness Bad Debts
Timing of deduction	A deduction is allowed when the debt becomes either partially or wholly worthless.	A deduction is allowed *only* when the debt becomes wholly worthless.
Character of deduction	The bad debt is deducted as an ordinary loss.	The bad debt is classified as a short-term capital loss, subject to the $3,000 net capital loss limitation for individuals.
Recovery of amounts previously deducted	If the account recovered was written off during the current tax year, the write-off entry is reversed. If the account was written off in a previous tax year, income is created subject to the tax benefit rule.	If the account recovered was written off during the current tax year, the write-off entry is reversed. If the account was written off in a previous tax year, income is created subject to the tax benefit rule.

7-1b Business versus Nonbusiness Bad Debts

Whether a debt is business or nonbusiness depends on the role of the lender. How the borrower uses the funds is of no consequence. A **nonbusiness bad debt** is unrelated to the lender's trade or business either when it was created or when it became worthless. Loans to relatives or friends are the most common type of nonbusiness bad debt.

The Big Picture

Example 5

Return to the facts of *The Big Picture* on p. 7-1. Martha loaned her friend Janice $25,000. Janice used the money to start a business, which subsequently failed. When Janice died after having made payments of $7,000 on the loan, she was insolvent.

Even though the proceeds of the loan were used in a business, the loan is a nonbusiness bad debt because the business was Janice's, not Martha's, and Martha is not in the business of lending money.

The distinction between a business bad debt and a nonbusiness bad debt is important. A **business bad debt** is treated as an ordinary deduction in the year incurred. In contrast, a nonbusiness bad debt is always treated as a short-term capital loss. Since net capital loss deductions are limited to no more than $3,000 per year, a taxpayer's nonbusiness bad debt deduction could have a limited benefit (see Chapter 16 for a detailed discussion). It is assumed that any loans made by a business are related to its trade or business. Credit sales to customers are a common example. Any bad debts that occur from these transactions are business bad debts.

The following example is an illustration of business bad debts adapted from the Regulations.[4]

Example 6

In 2021, Leif sold his business but retained a claim (note or account receivable) against Bob. The claim became worthless in 2022.

Leif's loss is treated as a business bad debt because the debt was created in the conduct of his former trade or business. Leif is accorded business bad debt treatment even though he was holding the note as an investor and was no longer in a trade or business when the claim became worthless.

[4] Reg. § 1.166–5(d).

7-1c Loans between Related Parties

Loans between related parties (especially family members) raise the issue of whether the transaction was a *bona fide* loan or a gift. The Regulations indicate that individual circumstances must be examined to determine whether advances between related parties are gifts or loans. Some considerations are these:

- Was a note properly executed?
- Was there a reasonable rate of interest?
- Was collateral provided?
- What collection efforts were made?
- What was the intent of the parties?

Example 7

Lana loans $2,000 to her widowed mother for an operation. Lana's mother owns no property and is not employed, and her only income consists of Social Security benefits. No note is issued for the loan, no provision for interest is made, and no repayment date is mentioned. In the current year, Lana's mother dies, leaving no estate.

Assuming that the loan is not repaid, Lana cannot take a deduction for a nonbusiness bad debt because the facts indicate that no debtor-creditor relationship existed.

See Concept Summary 7.2 for a review of the bad debt deduction rules.

Concept Summary 7.2

Bad Debt Deductions

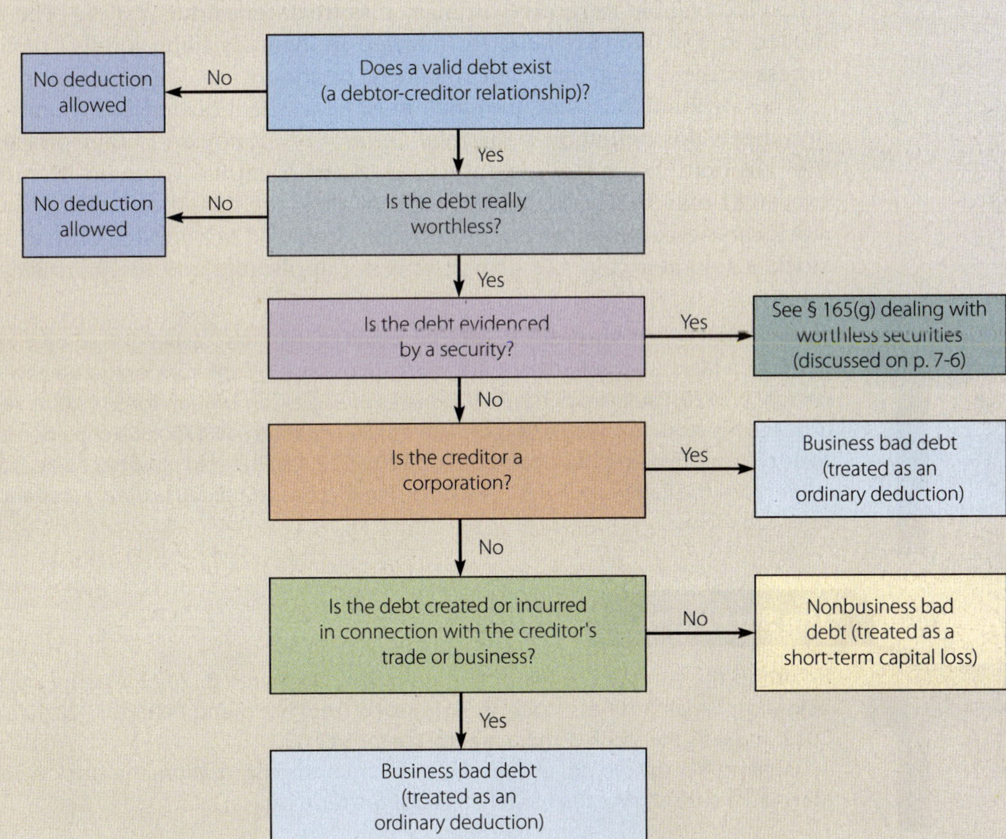

LO.2

Illustrate the tax treatment of worthless securities, including § 1244 stock.

7-2 Worthless Securities and Small Business Stock Losses

7-2a Worthless Securities

A loss is allowed for securities that become *completely* worthless during the year (**worthless securities**).[5] Securities covered by this rule include shares of stock, bonds, notes, or other evidence of indebtedness issued by a corporation or government. The losses generated are treated as capital losses deemed to have occurred on the *last day* of the taxable year. By treating the loss as having occurred on the last day of the taxable year, a loss that would otherwise have been classified as short term (if the date of worthlessness was used) may be classified as a long-term capital loss. Capital losses may be of limited benefit due to the $3,000 net capital loss limitation.[6]

The Big Picture

Example 8

Return to the facts of *The Big Picture* on p. 7-1. Martha owned stock in a pharmaceutical company that she acquired as an investment on October 1, 2021, at a cost of $50,000. On May 31, 2022, the stock became worthless when the company declared bankruptcy.

Because the stock is deemed to have become worthless as of December 31, 2022, Martha has a capital loss from an asset held for 15 months (a long-term capital loss).

7-2b Small Business Stock (§ 1244 Stock) Losses

In general, shareholders receive capital gain or loss treatment when they sell stock. However, it is possible to receive an ordinary loss deduction if the loss relates to **small business stock (§ 1244 stock)**. Only *individuals*[7] who acquired the stock *from* the corporation are eligible to receive ordinary loss treatment under § 1244. The ordinary loss is limited to $50,000 ($100,000 for married individuals filing jointly) per year. Losses in excess of these limits receive capital loss treatment.

The corporation issuing the stock must be a "small business corporation."[8] A corporation meets this definition if the total amount of money and other property received by the corporation for stock as a contribution to capital (or paid-in surplus) does not exceed $1 million. The $1 million test is made at the time the stock is issued. Code § 1244 stock can be common or preferred stock. Code § 1244 applies only to losses. If § 1244 stock is sold at a gain, the provision is not applicable and the gain is capital gain.

Example 9

Paulina, a single individual, was looking for an investment that would give some diversity to her stock portfolio. A friend suggested that she acquire some stock in Eagle Corporation, a new startup company. On July 1, 2020, Paulina purchased 100 shares of Eagle Corporation for $100,000. At the time Paulina acquired her stock from Eagle Corporation, the corporation had $700,000 of paid-in capital. As a result, the stock qualified as § 1244 stock. On June 20, 2022, Paulina sold all of her Eagle stock for $20,000.

Because the Eagle stock is § 1244 stock, Paulina has a $50,000 ordinary loss and a $30,000 long-term capital loss.

The Big Picture

Example 10

Return to the facts of *The Big Picture* on p. 7-1. On March 8, 2022, Martha purchases what she believes is "small business stock" (§ 1244 stock) from her friend Peter for $20,000. On November 2, 2022, she sells the stock in the marketplace for $12,000.

Because Martha did not acquire the stock from the corporation, the stock is *not* § 1244 stock to Martha. As a result, Martha has an $8,000 short-term capital loss.

[5] § 165(g); see *MCM Investment Management, LLC* (118 TCM 437, T.C.Memo. 2019–158) where the Tax Court provides a comprehensive overview of the law in many different contexts (e.g., worthless stock, partnership interests, and other assets).

[6] § 1211(b).

[7] The term *individuals* for this purpose does not include a trust or an estate (but could include a partnership or an LLC). §§ 1244(a) and (d)(4).

[8] § 1244(c)(3).

7-3 Losses of Individuals

LO.3

Distinguish between deductible and nondeductible losses of individuals.

An individual may deduct the following losses under § 165(c):

- Losses incurred in a trade or business (e.g., business loss of a sole proprietor or sale of a business asset at a loss).
- Losses incurred in a transaction entered into for profit (e.g., sale of an asset used in a rental activity at a loss).
- Losses caused by fire, storm, shipwreck, or other casualty or by theft (e.g., a residence damaged in a hurricane).

Although the terms *fire*, *storm*, *shipwreck*, and *theft* are easy to understand, what is meant by *other casualty*? First, it means that events similar to a fire, storm, or shipwreck qualify. In addition, accidental losses also qualify.

Overall, the loss must result from an event that is (1) identifiable; (2) damaging to property; and (3) sudden, unexpected, and unusual in nature.[9] Examples include auto accidents, mine cave-ins, sonic booms, and vandalism. Weather that causes damage (e.g., drought) must be unusual and severe for the particular region. Damage must be to the taxpayer's property to qualify as a **casualty loss**.

In general, losses on personal use property (e.g., a car, furniture, or a residence) are not deductible. The casualty loss rules are an exception. However, from 2018 through 2025, a taxpayer can take a deduction for a *personal* casualty or theft loss only if the loss occurs in a Federally declared disaster area.[10]

Example 11

In May 2022, due to significant rainstorms, the river behind Jiawen's house overflows its banks and floods the basement. After receiving an insurance settlement, Jiawen's remaining loss is $10,000. Although this event results in a casualty loss, Jiawen's loss will not be deductible unless the event is part of a Federally declared disaster.

Assume instead that the flooding affects a rental home owned by Jiawen. Because the rental home is *not* a personal use asset, the loss is deductible.

See text Section 7-3e for an exception to this rule when there are personal casualty gains during the year.

7-3a Events That Are Not Casualties

LO.4

Identify a casualty and determine the amount, classification, and timing of casualty and theft losses.

Not all acts of nature are treated as casualty losses for income tax purposes. Because a casualty must be sudden, unexpected, and unusual, progressive deterioration (e.g., erosion due to wind or rain) is not a casualty because it does not meet the suddenness test.

Examples of nonsudden events that generally do not qualify as casualties include disease and insect damage. When the damage was caused by termites over a period of several years, some courts have disallowed a casualty loss deduction.[11] Other examples of events that are not casualties are losses resulting from a decline in value rather than an actual loss of the property. No loss was allowed where the taxpayer's home declined in value as a result of a landslide that destroyed neighboring homes but did no actual damage to the taxpayer's home.[12] Similarly, a taxpayer was allowed a loss for the actual flood damage to his property but not for the decline in market value due to the property being flood-prone.[13]

[9] Rev.Rul. 72–592.

[10] § 165(h)(5). A Federally declared disaster is a disaster determined by the President of the United States to warrant assistance by the Federal government under the Stafford Disaster Relief and Emergency Assistance Act [§ 165(i)(5)].

[11] *Fay v. Helvering*, 41–2 USTC ¶9494, 27 AFTR 432, 120 F.2d 253 (CA–2); *U.S. v. Rogers*, 41–1 USTC ¶9442, 27 AFTR 423, 120 F.2d 244 (CA–9). The current position of the IRS is that termite damage is not deductible (Rev.Rul. 63–232).

[12] *H. Pulvers v. Comm.*, 69–1 USTC ¶9222, 23 AFTR 2d 69–678, 407 F.2d 838 (CA–9).

[13] *S. L. Solomon*, 39 TCM 1282, T.C.Memo. 1980–87.

7-3b Theft Losses

Theft includes, but is not necessarily limited to, larceny, embezzlement, and robbery.[14] Theft does not include misplaced items.[15]

Theft losses are deducted in the year of *discovery*, which may not be the same as the year of the theft. If an insurance claim exists and there is a reasonable expectation of recovering the adjusted basis of the asset from the insurance company, no deduction is permitted.[16] If in the year of settlement the recovery is less than the asset's adjusted basis, a partial deduction may be available. If the recovery is greater than the asset's adjusted basis, gain may be recognized.

Example 12

Keith's new sailboat, which he uses for business purposes, was stolen from the storage marina in May 2022. He discovered the loss on June 3, 2022, and filed a claim with his insurance company that was settled on January 30, 2023.

Assuming that there is a reasonable expectation of full recovery, no deduction is allowed in 2022 (the year of discovery). A partial deduction may be available in 2023 if the actual insurance proceeds are less than the lower of the fair market value or the adjusted basis of the asset.

If Keith used his sailboat personally (i.e., not for business), no deduction would be allowed. In general, only personal casualty losses in Federally declared disaster areas are deductible.

7-3c When to Deduct Casualty Losses

General Rule

Generally, a casualty loss is deducted in the year the loss occurs. However, no casualty loss is permitted if an insurance claim with a *reasonable prospect of full recovery* exists.[17] If the taxpayer has a partial claim, only part of the loss can be claimed in the year of the casualty, and the remainder is deducted in the year the claim is settled.

Example 13

Brian's new fishing boat, which he uses in his charter fishing business, was completely destroyed by fire in 2022. Its cost and fair market value were $15,000. Brian's only claim against the insurance company was on a $10,000 policy, which was not settled by year-end. The following year, 2023, Brian settled with the insurance company for $8,000.

Brian is entitled to a $5,000 deduction in 2022 ($10,000 − $15,000) and a $2,000 deduction in 2023.

If a taxpayer receives reimbursement for a casualty loss sustained and deducted in a previous year, an amended return is *not* filed. Instead, the taxpayer includes the reimbursement in gross income when it is received to the extent the previous deduction resulted in a tax benefit.

Example 14

Selena had a deductible casualty loss of $4,000 on her 2021 tax return. Selena's taxable income for 2021 was $60,000. In June 2022, Selena is reimbursed $2,750 for the prior year's casualty loss.

Selena includes the entire $2,750 in gross income for 2022 because the deduction in 2021 produced a tax benefit.

Disaster Area Losses

An exception to the general rule for the time of deduction is allowed for **disaster area losses**, which are casualties sustained in an area designated as a disaster area by the President of the United States.[18] In these cases, a taxpayer may *elect* to treat the loss as

[14] Reg. § 1.165–8(d).

[15] *Mary Francis Allen*, 16 T.C. 163 (1951).

[16] Reg. §§ 1.165–1(d)(2) and 1.165–8(a)(2).

[17] Reg. § 1.165–1(d)(2)(i).

[18] § 165(i) refers to Federally declared disasters. Disaster loss treatment also applies if a residence has been rendered unsafe as the result of a disaster within 120 days of the disaster loss designation [§ 165(k)].

having occurred in the taxable year immediately *preceding* the taxable year in which the disaster actually occurred. The rationale for this exception is to provide immediate relief to disaster victims by accelerating the tax refunds related to the loss.

The Big Picture

Example 15

Return to the facts of *The Big Picture* on p. 7-1. On September 28, 2022, Martha's personal residence was damaged when a hurricane caused an oak tree to fall onto the house. The amount of her uninsured loss was $7,000 ($25,000 insurance settlement − $32,000 damages incurred). Because of the extent of the damage in the area, the President of the United States designated the area a disaster area.

Because Martha's loss is a disaster area loss, she may elect to file an amended return for 2021 and take the loss in that year. Alternatively, she may take the loss on her 2022 income tax return.

COVID-19 Losses

On March 13, 2020, the President of the United States issued an emergency declaration in response to the ongoing COVID-19 pandemic. This declaration creates the *opportunity* to claim losses attributable to COVID-19 on the prior year's tax return. If losses are sustained in 2022, the taxpayer can claim the losses on the 2021 tax return; if losses were sustained in 2021, the taxpayer could claim the losses on the 2020 tax return.

In general, the amount of the loss will be the taxpayer's basis in the asset less any amount realized on its disposition. Following are some examples of losses that might qualify if *directly attributable* to the COVID-19 pandemic:

- Inventory scrapped due to spoilage as a result of the economic shutdown;
- Inventory purchased to fulfill a contract when the contract is canceled;
- Closure costs of store and facility locations;
- Termination payments to cancel contracts, leases, or licenses;
- Abandonment of leasehold improvements;
- Permanent retirement of fixed assets;
- Losses from the sale or exchange of property;
- Prepaid items when taxpayer is not provided a refund or credit (e.g., travel, hotel rooms, conference space);
- Costs related to the abandonment of pending business transactions/deals; or
- Worthless securities (but not bad debts).

The taxpayer has the burden of proving the existence of the casualty; here, the taxpayer must be able to prove that the loss was *directly attributable* to the COVID-19 pandemic.

7-3d Measuring the Amount of Loss

Amount of Loss

The rules for determining the amount of a loss depend in part on whether business use, income-producing use, or personal use property was involved. Another factor that must be considered is whether the property was partially or completely destroyed.

If business or rental property is *completely destroyed*, the loss is equal to the adjusted basis of the property at the time of destruction.

Example 16

Zoë's business equipment was destroyed by flood. Zoë had no flood insurance on her business. The fair market value of the equipment was $9,000 at the time of the flood, and its adjusted basis was $10,000.

Zoë is allowed a loss deduction of $10,000 (the basis of the equipment). The $10,000 loss is a deduction *for* AGI.

A different measurement rule applies for *partial destruction* of business or rental property and for *partial* or *complete destruction* of personal use property. In these situations, the loss is the *lesser* of the following:

- The adjusted basis of the property.
- The difference between the fair market value of the property before the event and the fair market value immediately after the event.

Example 17

Wan's uninsured automobile, which was used only for business purposes, was damaged in an accident. On the date of the accident, the fair market value of the automobile was $12,000, and its adjusted basis was $9,000. After the accident, the automobile was appraised at $4,000.

Wan's loss deduction is $8,000 (the lesser of the adjusted basis or the decrease in fair market value). The $8,000 loss is a deduction *for* AGI.

If the property is used for both personal and business/rental use, the loss deduction must be computed separately for the business portion and the personal portion. If a taxpayer has insurance coverage on *personal use* property, an insurance claim must be filed to claim a casualty loss.[19]

Generally, an appraisal before and after the casualty is needed to measure the amount of the loss. However, the *cost of repairs* can be used if the following criteria are met:

- The repairs are necessary to restore the property to its condition immediately before the casualty.
- The amount spent for repairs is not excessive.
- The repairs do not extend beyond the damage suffered.
- The value of the property after the repairs does not, as a result of the repairs, exceed the value of the property immediately before the casualty.[20]

Ethics & Equity **Is Policy Cancellation an Escape Hatch?**

Noah's house is flooded for the third time, and he knows that if he files a claim, the insurance company will cancel his homeowner's policy or impose a prohibitive premium. Noah does not file a claim, yet he deducts the loss on his tax return. Is his loss allowed?

Personal Use Loss Reductions: The $100-per-Event and 10%-of-AGI Floors

The amount of the allowed loss for *personal use* property must be further reduced by a $100-*per-event* floor and a 10%-of-AGI *aggregate* floor.[21] The $100 floor applies separately to each casualty and applies to the entire loss from each casualty (e.g., if a storm damages both a taxpayer's residence and automobile, only $100 is subtracted from the total amount of the loss). The losses are then added together, and the total is reduced by 10 percent of the taxpayer's AGI. The resulting loss is the taxpayer's itemized deduction for casualty and theft losses.

Example 18

Nick, who had AGI of $30,000, lost all the furniture in his apartment as a result of a flood in a Federally declared disaster area in 2022. His furniture had a fair market value of $12,000 and an adjusted basis of $9,000 and was completely destroyed. He received $5,000 from his insurance company.

Nick's casualty loss deduction is $900 [$9,000 basis − $5,000 insurance recovery − $100 floor − $3,000 (10% × $30,000 AGI)]. The $900 casualty loss is an itemized deduction (*from* AGI).

[19] § 165(h)(4)(E).

[20] Reg. § 1.165–7(a)(2)(ii).

[21] § 165(h). For Federally declared disasters from January 1, 2020 through February 25, 2021, taxpayers can deduct casualty losses in excess of $500 (the $100-per-event and 10%-of-AGI floors do not apply to these losses). In addition, taxpayers who do not itemize can increase their standard deduction by the amount of the net disaster loss.

When a personal casualty loss is spread between two taxable years because of an outstanding insurance claim, the loss in the second year is not reduced by the $100 floor (the "$100-per-event" reduction occurred in the first year). However, the loss in the second year is still subject to the 10 percent floor based upon the taxpayer's second-year AGI. For taxpayers who suffer qualified disaster area losses, the 10%-of-AGI floor is determined by using the AGI of the year the deduction is claimed.[22]

Example 19

Brian's new *personal use* sailboat was completely destroyed by a hurricane in 2022 (a Federally declared disaster area). The boat had a $15,000 cost and fair market value, but Brian only had $10,000 of insurance coverage for the boat. He filed an insurance claim and settled with the insurance company in 2023 for $8,000.

Brian is entitled to a $5,000 deduction in 2022 ($10,000 − $15,000) and a $2,000 deduction in 2023. Brian's $5,000 casualty loss deduction in 2022 is reduced first by $100 and then by 10% of his 2022 AGI. The $2,000 deduction in 2023 is reduced by 10% of his 2023 AGI.

Multiple Losses

The rules for computing loss deductions where multiple losses have occurred are explained in Examples 20 and 21.

Multiple Casualty Losses

Example 20

During the year, Kien had the following casualty losses related to assets used in his business:

		Fair Market Value of Asset		
Asset	**Adjusted Basis**	**Before the Casualty**	**After the Casualty**	**Insurance Recovery**
A	$900	$600	$–0–	$400
B	300	800	250	100

The following losses are allowed:

Asset A: $500. The complete destruction of a business asset results in a deduction of the adjusted basis of the property (reduced by any insurance recovery), regardless of the asset's fair market value.

Asset B: $200. The partial destruction of a business (or personal use) asset results in a deduction equal to the lesser of the adjusted basis ($300) or the decline in value ($550), reduced by any insurance recovery ($100).

Both Asset A and Asset B losses are deductions *for* AGI. The $100 floor and the 10%-of-AGI floor do not apply because the assets are business assets.

Example 21

During the year, Emily had AGI of $20,000 and the following personal casualty losses related to a flood in a Federally declared disaster area:

		Fair Market Value of Asset		
Asset	**Adjusted Basis**	**Before the Casualty**	**After the Casualty**	**Insurance Recovery**
A	$1,900	$1,400	$ –0–	$200
B	2,500	4,000	1,000	–0–
C	800	400	100	250

continued

[22] § 165(i).

The loss for each asset is computed as follows:

Asset A:	$1,200. The lesser of the adjusted basis of $1,900 or the $1,400 decline in value, reduced by the insurance recovery of $200.
Asset B:	$2,500. The lesser of the adjusted basis of $2,500 or the $3,000 decline in value.
Asset C:	$50. The lesser of the adjusted basis of $800 or the $300 decline in value, reduced by the insurance recovery of $250.

Since the losses all related to a single casualty, Emily must reduce the sum of the losses by $100 and then apply the 10%-of-AGI floor. Emily's itemized casualty loss deduction for the year is $1,650:

Asset A loss	$ 1,200
Asset B loss	2,500
Asset C loss	50
Total loss	$ 3,750
Less: $100-per-event reduction	(100)
Less: 10% of AGI (10% × $20,000)	(2,000)
Itemized casualty loss deduction	$ 1,650

7-3e Personal Casualty Gains and Losses

If a taxpayer has personal casualty and theft gains as well as losses, a special set of rules applies for determining the tax consequences. Here, an exception to the rule that disallows a deduction for personal casualty losses other than those in Federally declared disaster areas applies.[23] In this case, the taxpayer may use a personal casualty loss (or losses) *not* attributable to a Federally declared disaster to offset any personal casualty gains. After this netting process, if any loss remains, it is not deductible (since it relates to a non-Federally declared disaster area casualty). If, however, a net personal casualty gain remains, it is offset by any Federally declared disaster area casualty losses.

Calculating Personal Casualty Gains and Losses

Example 22

During 2022, Emmanuel has AGI of $50,000 and the following personal casualty gains and losses (after deducting the $100 floor):

Asset	Item	Gain or (Loss)
A	Personal casualty gain	$ 2,500
B	Personal casualty loss (non-Federally declared disaster area)	(2,000)
C	Personal casualty loss (Federally declared disaster area)	(9,000)

Emmanuel first offsets the non-Federally declared disaster area losses against the personal casualty gain, resulting in an excess personal casualty gain of $500, computed as follows:

Personal casualty gain	$ 2,500
Personal casualty loss (non-Federally declared disaster area)	(2,000)
Excess personal casualty gain	$ 500

Next, the excess personal casualty gain offsets the Federally declared disaster area loss. Emmanuel's overall net personal casualty loss is $8,500, computed as follows:

Personal casualty loss (Federally declared disaster area)	($ 9,000)
Less: Excess personal casualty gain	500
Overall net personal casualty loss	($ 8,500)

After this second netting process, because a net personal casualty loss remains, it will be deductible to the extent of the 10%-of-AGI floor. Emmanuel's itemized deduction for casualty losses is $3,500, computed as follows:

Net personal casualty loss	$ 8,500
Less: 10% of AGI (10% × $50,000)	(5,000)
Itemized deduction for casualty loss	$ 3,500

[23] § 165(h)(5)(B); personal casualty gains and losses are defined at § 165(h)(3).

Calculating Personal Casualty Gains and Losses

Example 23

Refer back to the facts of Example 22. How would your answer change if the casualty loss related to Asset B was $4,000 (rather than $2,000)?

Emmanuel would begin by offsetting the non-Federally declared disaster area losses against the personal casualty gain, resulting in an excess personal casualty loss of $1,500, computed as follows:

Personal casualty gain	$ 2,500
Personal casualty loss (non-Federally declared disaster area)	(4,000)
Excess personal casualty loss	($ 1,500)

Since this net loss relates to a non-Federally declared disaster area, the loss is *not* deductible. Emmanuel's itemized deduction for casualty losses is $4,000, computed as follows:

Personal casualty loss (Federally declared disaster area)	$ 9,000
Less: 10% of AGI (10% × $50,000)	(5,000)
Itemized deduction for casualty loss	$ 4,000

One further complication exists—determining the character of the casualty gains and losses. If the gains exceed the losses, the gains and losses are treated as gains and losses from the sale of capital assets.[24] The capital gains and losses are short term or long term, depending on how long the taxpayer held each of the assets (assets held more than one year are long term). In the netting process, personal casualty and theft gains and losses are not netted with the gains and losses on business and income-producing property.

Example 24

During the year, Cliff had the following personal casualty gains and losses (after deducting the $100 floor):

Asset	Holding Period	Gain or (Loss)
A	Three months	($ 300)
B	Three years	(2,400)
C	Two years	3,200

Cliff computes the tax consequences as follows:

Personal casualty gain	$ 3,200
Personal casualty loss ($300 + $2,400)	(2,700)
Net personal casualty gain	$ 500

Cliff treats all of the gains and losses as capital gains and losses:

Short-term capital loss (Asset A)	$ 300
Long-term capital loss (Asset B)	2,400
Long-term capital gain (Asset C)	3,200

If personal casualty losses exceed personal casualty gains, all gains and losses are treated as ordinary items. The gains—and the losses to the extent of gains—are treated as ordinary income and ordinary loss in computing AGI. Losses in excess of gains are deducted as itemized deductions and are deductible only if related to a Federally declared disaster.[25]

[24] § 165(h)(2)(B).

[25] § 165(h).

Example 25

During the year, Hazel had AGI of $20,000 and the following personal casualty gain and loss (after deducting the $100 floor). Neither are related to a Federally declared disaster:

Asset	Holding Period	Gain or (Loss)
A	Three years	($2,700)
B	Four months	200

Hazel computes the tax consequences as follows:

Personal casualty loss	($2,700)
Personal casualty gain	200
Net personal casualty loss	($2,500)

Hazel treats the gain and the loss as ordinary items. The $200 gain and $200 of the loss are included in computing AGI. The remaining net personal casualty loss is not deductible (it is not related to a Federally declared disaster area).

See Concept Summary 7.3 for a review of the tax treatment of casualty gains and losses.

Concept Summary 7.3

Casualty Gains and Losses

	Business Use or Income-Producing Property	Personal Use Property*
Event creating the loss	Any event.	Casualty or theft.
Amount	The lesser of the decline in fair market value or the adjusted basis, but always the adjusted basis if the property is totally destroyed.	The lesser of the decline in fair market value or the adjusted basis.
Insurance	Insurance proceeds received reduce the amount of the loss.	Insurance proceeds received (or for which there is an unfiled claim) reduce the amount of the loss.
$100 floor	Not applicable.	Applicable per event.
Gains and losses	Gains and losses are netted (see detailed discussion in Chapter 17).	Personal casualty and theft gains and losses are netted.
Gains exceeding losses	See Chapter 17.	The gains and losses are treated as gains and losses from the sale of capital assets.
Losses exceeding gains	See Chapter 17.	The gains—and the losses to the extent of gains—are treated as ordinary items in computing AGI. The losses in excess of gains, to the extent they exceed 10% of AGI, are itemized deductions.

*In general, from 2018 through 2025, losses are allowed only if the event is related to a Federally declared disaster; if there are both casualty gains and losses, non-Federally declared casualty losses can be used to offset casualty gains.

7-3f Statutory Framework for Deducting Losses of Individuals

Concept Summary 7.4 provides a summary of the statutory framework of deducting losses of individuals.

Concept Summary 7.4

Statutory Framework for Deducting Losses of Individuals

	Personal Casualty/Theft Losses*		Employee Casualty/Theft Losses	Production of Income Casualty/Theft Losses	Trade or Business Casualty/Theft Losses
	$100-per-Event Rule	10%-of-AGI Rule	Reimbursed Expenses and 2%-of-AGI Rule		
General Application	Reduce each casualty or theft loss by $100 when figuring the potential casualty loss deduction. Apply this rule to personal use property after the amount of the loss has been determined.	Reduce the *total* casualty or theft loss by 10% of adjusted gross income. Apply this rule to personal use property after each loss is reduced by $100 (the "$100-per-event rule").	Casualty and theft losses incurred by an employee in connection with a trade or business are deductible *for* AGI if the loss is reimbursed by the employer (with the net loss being deductible). If the loss is *not* reimbursed, the loss is deductible *from* AGI as an employee business expense (a miscellaneous itemized deduction). Although these losses are not subject to the $100-per-event rule or the 10%-of-AGI rule, miscellaneous itemized deductions are currently not deductible.[26]	Casualty and theft losses incurred by an individual in a transaction entered into for profit are not subject to the $100-per-event and the 10%-of-AGI limitations. If these losses are attributable to rents or royalties, the deduction is *for* AGI.[27] If not, they are deductions *from* AGI (and are *not* a miscellaneous itemized deduction).[28]	Casualty and theft losses incurred by an individual in connection with a trade or business are deductible *for* AGI.[29] These losses are not subject to the $100-per-event and the 10%-of-AGI limitations.
Single Event	Apply this rule only once to each casualty or theft event, even if many pieces of property are affected by the event.	Apply this rule only once, even if many pieces of property are affected.	Apply this rule only once, even if many pieces of property are affected.		
More Than One Event	Apply to the loss from each event.	Apply to the total of all losses from all events.	Apply to the total of all losses from all events.		

*From 2018 through 2025, only personal casualty or theft losses occurring in Federally declared disaster areas are allowed.

7-4 Research and Experimental Expenditures

LO.5

Apply the alternative tax treatments for research and experimental expenditures.

Code § 174 covers the treatment of research and experimental expenditures. The Regulations define **research and experimental expenditures** as follows:

> all such costs incident to the development or improvement of a product (including an experimental or pilot model, a plant process, a product, a formula, an invention, or similar property). The term includes the costs of obtaining a patent, such as attorneys' fees expended in making and perfecting a patent application. Expenditures represent research and development costs in the experimental or laboratory sense if they are for activities intended to discover information that would eliminate uncertainty concerning the development or improvement of a product. The term does not

[26] § 67(b)(3). See Chapter 10; no deduction is allowed for miscellaneous itemized deductions from 2018 through 2025.

[27] § 62(a)(4).

[28] § 67(b)(3).

[29] § 62(a)(1).

include expenditures such as those for the ordinary testing or inspection of materials or products for quality control or those for efficiency surveys, management studies, consumer surveys, advertising, or promotions.[30]

The law permits the following *three alternatives* for the handling of research and experimental expenditures:

- Expensed in the year paid or incurred.
- Deferred and amortized.
- Capitalized.

If the costs are capitalized, a deduction may not be available until the research project is abandoned or is deemed worthless. Because many products resulting from research projects do not have a definite and limited useful life, most taxpayers choose to write off the expenditures immediately or to defer and amortize them.[31]

7-4a Expense Method

A taxpayer can expense all of the research and experimental expenditures incurred provided this method is adopted for the first taxable year in which these expenditures were paid or incurred.[32] Once this method is adopted, the taxpayer must continue to expense all qualifying expenditures unless a request for a change is made to, and approved by, the IRS. As discussed below, the expense method will not be available in taxable years beginning after December 31, 2021.

7-4b Deferral and Amortization Method

Taxable Years Beginning before January 1, 2022

If elected by the taxpayer, research and experimental expenditures may be deferred and amortized ratably over a period of not less than 60 months.[33] A deduction is allowed beginning with the month in which the taxpayer first realizes benefits from the experimental expenditure. The election is binding, and a change requires permission from the IRS.

Example 26

Gold Corporation, a calendar year corporation, decides to develop a new line of adhesives. The project begins in 2019. Gold incurs the following expenses in 2019 and 2020 in connection with the project:

	2019	2020
Salaries	$25,000	$18,000
Materials	8,000	2,000
Depreciation on machinery	6,500	5,700

The benefits from the project are realized starting in March 2021. If Gold Corporation elects a 60-month deferral and amortization period, there is no deduction prior to March 2021, the month benefits from the project begin to be realized. The deduction for 2021 is $10,867, and the deduction for 2022 is $13,040, computed as follows:

Salaries ($25,000 + $18,000)	$43,000
Materials ($8,000 + $2,000)	10,000
Depreciation ($6,500 + $5,700)	12,200
Total	$65,200

Research and experimentation expense in 2021	$10,867	[$65,200 × (10 months ÷ 60 months)]
Research and experimentation expense in 2022	$13,040	[$65,200 × (12 months ÷ 60 months)]

[30] Reg. §§ 1.174–2(a)(1), (2), and (3). Expenses in connection with the acquisition or improvement of land or depreciable property are not research and experimental expenditures. Rather, they increase the basis of the land or depreciable property. However, depreciation on an asset used for research may be a research and experimental expense.

[31] A credit for increasing research expenditures is also available; § 41. See Chapter 13 for a more detailed discussion of this credit.

[32] Deductions are even allowed if incurred before carrying on a trade or business activity as long as incurred in connection with a trade or business; *Snow v. Comm.*, 74–1 USTC ¶9432, 33 AFTR 2d 74–1251, 94 S.Ct. 1876.

[33] § 174(b)(2).

The option to defer and amortize research and experimental expenditures is usually employed when a company does not have sufficient income to offset the expenses.[34] The deferral of research and experimental expenditures also should be considered if the taxpayer expects higher tax rates in the future.

Taxable Years Beginning after December 31, 2021

Research and experimental expenditures paid or incurred in taxable years beginning after December 31, 2021, must be capitalized and amortized. A few other changes also occur. First, amortization begins at the midpoint of the year the expenses are paid or incurred rather than the month in which the taxpayer first realizes benefits. Second, the expenditures are amortized ratably over a five-year period (15 years for foreign research expenses) rather than ratably over a period of not less than 60 months. Finally, if a research project is abandoned, any unamortized expenditures are deducted over the remaining amortization period.[35]

Example 27

Assume the same facts as Example 26, except that Gold Corporation incurs the expenses in 2022 and 2023 (rather than 2019 and 2020) and the benefits from the project will be realized starting in March 2024.

Gold's research and experimentation expenses total $39,500 in 2022 and $25,700 in 2023. Gold will amortize both sets of expenses over a five-year period beginning at the mid-point of the year the expenses are incurred (in this case, July 1 of 2022 or 2023); the year benefits will be realized no longer matters. Gold's research and experimentation deduction in 2022 and 2023 is computed as follows:

2022 Taxable Year	
2022 expenses [$39,500 × (½ year ÷ 5 years)	$ 3,950
2023 Taxable Year	
2022 expenses ($39,500 ÷ 5 years)	$ 7,900
2023 expenses ($25,700 × (½ year ÷ 5 years)	2,570
Total research and experimentation deduction	$ 10,470

7-5 Excess Business Losses

LO.6 **Apply the excess business loss limitation rules.**

If a noncorporate taxpayer has an **excess business loss** for the year, it is not allowed.[36] Instead, it is carried forward and treated as part of the taxpayer's net operating loss (NOL) carryforward in subsequent years (NOLs are discussed in text Section 7-6).

7-5a Excess Business Loss Defined

An *excess business loss* is defined as:[37]

	The aggregate deductions for the year attributable to the taxpayer's businesses
Less:	The sum of aggregate gross income or gains of the taxpayer
Less:	A threshold amount (in 2022, $540,000 for married taxpayers filing a joint return; $270,000 for all other taxpayers)

The threshold amounts are adjusted for inflation each year.[38]

At its core, the purpose of the excess business loss limitation is to limit the amount of nonbusiness income (e.g., salaries, interest, dividends, and capital gains) that can be "sheltered" from tax as a result of business losses.

[34] Another option is to deduct these expenses for regular tax purposes, but elect in any year where helpful, to capitalize and amortize the expenses over 10 years for both regular tax and alternative minimum tax purposes [§ 59(e)]. Chapter 12 includes a discussion of this option.

[35] § 174 as amended by P.L. 115–97.

[36] § 461(l). The provision applies to taxable years beginning after December 31, 2020, and before January 1, 2027.

[37] § 461(l)(3). Originally effective beginning in 2018, the CARES Act [P.L. 116–136 (3/27/20)] retroactively eliminated the excess business loss provision for 2018 through 2020 by deferring its effective date to taxable years beginning after December 31, 2020.

[38] In 2021, the threshold amounts were $524,000 and $262,000, respectively.

Calculating an Excess Business Loss

Example 28

In 2022, Tonya, a single taxpayer, operates a sole proprietorship in which she materially participates. Her proprietorship generates gross income of $320,000 and deductions of $605,000, resulting in a loss of $285,000. The large deductions are due to the acquisition of equipment and the use of immediate expense and additional first-year depreciation to deduct all of the costs associated with the acquisitions. Tonya's excess business loss is $15,000, computed as follows:

Aggregate business deductions	$ 605,000
Less: Aggregate business gross income and gains	(320,000)
Less: Threshold amount	(270,000)
Excess business loss	$ 15,000

So of Tonya's $285,000 proprietorship loss, $270,000 can be used to offset nonbusiness income. The $15,000 excess business loss is treated as part of Tonya's net operating loss carryforward in subsequent years.

Example 29

Assume the same facts as Example 28, except that Tonya is married and files a joint return. In this case, Tonya does not have an excess business loss due to the increased threshold amount.

Aggregate business deductions	$ 605,000
Less: Aggregate business gross income and gains	(320,000)
Less: Threshold amount	(540,000)
Excess business loss	$ None

As a result, Tonya's $285,000 sole proprietorship loss is fully deductible and can be used to offset nonbusiness income (e.g., her spouse's wages and their interest and dividend income).

The excess business loss limitation applies to the aggregate gross income and deductions from all of a taxpayer's trades or businesses.[39] So if a married couple files a joint return, information from all of the couple's trades or businesses must be consolidated. Further, as noted in Example 29, if married taxpayers file a joint return, the losses of one spouse can be used to offset the other spouse's nonbusiness income (up to the $540,000 limit in 2022).

7-5b Losses from Partnerships or S Corporations

For a partnership or an S corporation, the excess business loss limitation applies at the partner or shareholder level.[40] Each partner's or S corporation shareholder's share of items of income, gain, deduction, or loss of the partnership or S corporation is taken into account in applying the limitation for the tax year of the partner or S corporation shareholder.

Example 30

Jayson, a single taxpayer, is an S corporation shareholder and materially participates in the grocery store business. During 2022, the store had a large depreciation deduction causing a substantial loss. Jayson has a flow-through loss of $345,000 from the S corporation. He also received a $78,000 salary from the corporation. At the beginning of the year, Jayson had a $520,000 basis in his S corporation shares—enough to absorb the S corporation loss. Because he materially participates in the business, it is not a passive activity (see Chapter 11 for a discussion of passive activity losses).

However, Jayson's flow-through loss exceeds the $270,000 excess business loss threshold by $75,000 ($345,000 − $270,000). So Jayson can deduct $270,000 (and use it to offset his salary and other nonbusiness income). The $75,000 excess is not deductible in 2022 but carries forward as a net operating loss.

Assume that in 2023, the grocery store business generates a profit and flows through $210,000 of income to Jayson. Jayson can deduct the 2022 excess business loss of $75,000 against this flow-through income.

The excess business loss rules also treat similarly situated owners differently (based on their filing status).

[39] § 461(l)(3)(A).

[40] § 461(l)(4)(A).

Example 31

Maggie leaves her job in 2022 to pursue her dream, a technology startup. Maggie is single and invests $500,000 of capital, as does her business partner Julita, who is married. Together they form TechStart LLC (which reports as a partnership for Federal tax purposes); both materially participate in the business. In 2022, the LLC reports a net loss of $700,000. Each LLC member receives a Schedule K–1 from the LLC indicating a $350,000 ordinary loss; each will report this loss on her 2022 individual income tax return [on Form 1040 (Schedule E)].

Maggie has an excess business loss of $80,000 ($350,000 minus the $270,000 threshold for single taxpayers). This excess business loss is an NOL carryforward for Maggie.[41] Julita can use the full $350,000 loss in 2022 since it is less than the $540,000 threshold that applies to married taxpayers who file jointly.

7-5c Other Rules

The excess business loss limitation is applied *after* the application of the § 469 passive activity loss rules (see Chapter 11 for a discussion of these rules).[42] Given this requirement, losses from *passive* trades or businesses (e.g., a business in which the taxpayer does not materially participate) are limited first by the § 469 passive activity loss rules, and once the losses are allowed under § 469, they are subject to these rules.

The Treasury Department and IRS are to specify reporting requirements necessary to implement these rules.[43] Form 461 (Limitation on Business Losses) is used to calculate and report the loss limitation.

7-6 Net Operating Losses

LO.7

Determine the amount of the net operating loss and review the effect of the carryover provisions on previous and subsequent years' taxable income.

The requirement that every taxpayer file an annual income tax return may result in inequities for taxpayers who experience income fluctuations (and losses in certain tax years) versus taxpayers with stable income levels. A loss in a particular tax year would produce no tax benefit if the Code did not provide for the use of these losses in profitable years.

Example 32

Juanita has a business and realizes $300,000 of taxable income or loss over a five-year period as follows: year 1, $50,000; year 2, ($30,000); year 3, $100,000; year 4, ($200,000); and year 5, $380,000. She is married and files a joint return. Sean also has a business and has a taxable income pattern of $60,000 every year ($300,000 over the five-year period). He, too, is married and files a joint return. Assuming that there is no provision for carryback or carryover of net operating losses (NOLs), Juanita and Sean would pay the following taxes over the five-year period:

Year	Juanita's Tax	Sean's Tax
1	$ 5,589	$ 6,789
2	–0–	6,789
3	13,234	6,789
4	–0–	6,789
5	82,063	6,789
	$100,886	$33,945

Note: The 2022 Tax Rate Schedules are used to compute the tax.

Even though Juanita and Sean realized the same total taxable income over the five-year period, Juanita had to pay taxes of $100,886, while Sean paid taxes of only $33,945.

To provide partial relief from this inequitable tax treatment, a **net operating loss (NOL)** deduction is allowed.[44] NOLs for any one year can be offset against taxable income of other years. In general, only losses from the operation of a trade or business and casualty and theft losses can create an NOL.

[41] Prior to 2021, NOLs could be carried back to prior tax years and used to offset income in those years (a five-year carryback for losses incurred in 2018, 2019, and 2020; a two-year carryback for losses incurred prior to 2018). This carryback allowed taxpayers to immediately "monetize" an NOL by using the NOL to generate an income tax refund in those years. Beginning in 2021, NOL carrybacks are no longer allowed; NOLs can only be carried forward. As a result, in addition to treating similarly situated owners differently based on filing status, the inability to carry back these losses also is detrimental to business owners.

[42] § 461(l)(6).

[43] § 461(l)(5).

[44] § 172(a).

7-6a General Rules

Carryforward Only (with Certain Exceptions)

For taxable years beginning after December 31, 2020, an NOL can be carried forward indefinitely (and cannot be carried back).[45] As a result, beginning in 2021, taxpayers must wait at least one year to receive a tax benefit from the loss.[46]

Example 33

For 2021, the taxpayer and spouse have an NOL of $50,000. The NOL can be carried forward indefinitely (beginning with 2022).

NOL Deduction Limit

For taxable years beginning after December 31, 2020, an NOL deduction is limited to 80 percent of taxable income, determined without regard to the NOL deduction itself.[47] If the NOL carryover is less than the computed limitation, the entire carryover is allowed as a deduction. As a result, the 80 percent of taxable income limit may extend the time over which an NOL is used, making taxpayers wait longer to receive a tax benefit from the NOL (and reducing the present value of the related tax benefit).

Example 34

For 2022, a married couple have an NOL of $25,000 (and no other NOL carryovers exist). The NOL is carried forward to 2023. In 2023, the taxpayers have taxable income of $80,000 before considering the 2022 NOL carryover. The taxpayers' 2023 NOL deduction can be no more than $64,000 ($80,000 × 80%). Since the NOL carryover from 2022 is only $25,000, the entire 2022 NOL carryover can be used to reduce their 2023 taxable income. As a result, their 2023 taxable income is $55,000 ($80,000 − $25,000).

If, instead, the taxpayers had taxable income of $30,000 before considering the 2022 NOL carryover, only $24,000 ($30,000 × 80%) of the carryover could be used. In this case, their 2023 taxable income would be $6,000 ($30,000 − $24,000), and the remaining $1,000 of the 2022 NOL carryover would be carried forward to 2024.

NOLs and the Deduction for Qualified Business Income

The deduction for qualified business income will not create or increase a net operating loss.[48] Losses from qualified businesses are carried over separately and will offset future income from qualified businesses, reducing the related deduction for qualified business income.[49]

NOLs and Self-Employment Taxes

An NOL *cannot* be used to reduce self-employment income. As a result, a taxpayer's self-employment tax liability will not change as the result of an NOL deduction.[50]

7-6b Computation of the Net Operating Loss

Because the NOL provisions apply solely to business-related and casualty losses, individual taxpayers must make adjustments to their taxable income since nonbusiness deductions are allowed (e.g, itemized deductions). To arrive at the NOL for an individual, taxable income must be adjusted as follows:[51]

1. No deduction is allowed for personal and dependency exemptions. From 2018 through 2025, the exemption deduction amount is zero, so there will be no addback during these years for these amounts.
2. The NOL carryover from another year is not allowed in the computation of the current year's NOL.

[45] § 172(b)(1)(A).

[46] A two-year carryback period is available for any NOL resulting from a farming business; § 172(b)(1)(B)(i).

[47] § 172(a)(2).

[48] § 172(d)(8).

[49] § 199A(c)(2).

[50] § 1402(a).

[51] § 172(d); Reg. § 1.172–3(a). Also see *Net Operating Losses (NOLs) for Individuals* (IRS Publication 536).

3. The qualified business income deduction (§ 199A) is not allowed.
4. Capital losses and nonbusiness deductions are limited in determining the current year's NOL. These limits are as follows:
   a. The excess of nonbusiness capital losses over nonbusiness capital gains must be added back.
   b. The excess of nonbusiness deductions over the sum of nonbusiness income and *net* nonbusiness capital gains must be added back. *Net nonbusiness capital gains* are the excess of nonbusiness capital gains over nonbusiness capital losses. *Nonbusiness income* is income that is not related to a taxpayer's trade or business (e.g., dividends, investment interest, alimony received, and Social Security income). *Nonbusiness deductions* are those deductions that are not related to a taxpayer's trade or business [e.g., Individual Retirement Account (IRA) deductions, alimony paid deductions, and most itemized deductions]. Personal casualty and theft losses, losses incurred in a transaction entered into for profit, and employee business expense deductions are allowed.

      A taxpayer who does not itemize deductions computes the excess of nonbusiness deductions over nonbusiness income by substituting the standard deduction for total itemized deductions.
   c. The excess of business capital losses over the sum of business capital gains and the excess of nonbusiness income and net nonbusiness capital gains over nonbusiness deductions must be added back.
   d. The add-back for net nonbusiness capital losses and excess business capital losses does not include net capital losses not included in the current-year computation of taxable income because of the capital loss limitation provisions (discussed in text Section 16-5d).

For a review of the computation of the net operating loss for individuals, see Concept Summary 7.5.

Concept Summary 7.5

Computation of Net Operating Loss

Taxable Income shown on the return

Add back:

1. Personal and dependency exemptions (suspended from 2018 through 2025).
2. Net operating loss carryover from another year.
3. The qualified business income deduction (§ 199A).
4. The excess of nonbusiness capital losses over nonbusiness capital gains.
5. The excess of nonbusiness deductions over the sum of nonbusiness income plus *net* nonbusiness capital gains.
6. The excess of business capital losses over the sum of business capital gains plus the excess of nonbusiness income and *net* nonbusiness capital gains over nonbusiness deductions.

Note: The add-back from the total of items 4 and 6 will not exceed $3,000 because of the capital loss limitation rules.

Equals: The net operating loss

The capital loss and nonbusiness deduction limits are illustrated in Examples 35 through 38.

Capital Loss and Nonbusiness Deduction Limits

Example 35

For 2022, taxpayer and spouse have $6,000 of nonbusiness capital losses and $4,000 of nonbusiness capital gains.

They must add back $2,000 to taxable income ($6,000 − $4,000), which is the excess of nonbusiness capital losses over nonbusiness capital gains.

Capital Loss and Nonbusiness Deduction Limits

Example 36

For 2022, taxpayer and spouse have $2,600 of nonbusiness capital gains, $1,000 of nonbusiness capital losses, $2,000 of interest income, and no itemized deductions.

They must add back $22,300 to taxable income {$25,900 standard deduction − [$2,000 interest income + $1,600 ($2,600 − $1,000) net nonbusiness capital gains]}.

Note that in this example, there is no excess of nonbusiness capital losses over nonbusiness capital gains.

Example 37

For 2022, taxpayer and spouse have $2,600 of nonbusiness capital gains, $1,000 of nonbusiness capital losses, $30,000 of interest income, $29,000 of itemized deductions (none of which are personal casualty and theft losses), $4,000 of business capital losses, and $1,000 of business capital gains.

They must add back $400 to taxable income {$4,000 business capital losses − [$1,000 business capital gains + ($30,000 nonbusiness income + $1,600 net nonbusiness capital gains − $29,000 nonbusiness deductions)]}.

Note that in this example, there is no excess of nonbusiness capital losses over nonbusiness capital gains, nor is there an excess of nonbusiness deductions over the sum of nonbusiness income and net nonbusiness capital gains.

Example 38

For 2022, taxpayer and spouse have $2,600 of nonbusiness capital gains, $3,000 of nonbusiness capital losses, $28,000 of interest income, $30,000 of itemized deductions (none of which are personal casualty and theft losses), $8,000 of business capital losses, and $4,000 of business capital gains.

They must add back $5,000 to taxable income:

(1) $2,000 ($30,000 − $28,000), which is the excess of nonbusiness deductions over nonbusiness income, and

(2) $3,000, the excess of combined capital losses is $4,400, but the capital loss limitation caps the loss at $3,000 in computing taxable income for the year.

Example 39 illustrates the computation of an NOL.

Example 39

James opened a retail store in 2021 and experienced an NOL of $2,000 for that year. James is married, has no dependents, and files a joint return. For 2022, James and his spouse have the following taxable income:

Gross income from the business	$ 67,000	
Less: Business expenses	(73,000)	($ 6,000)
Salary from a part-time job		875
Interest on savings account		525
Nonbusiness long-term capital gain		1,000
NOL carryover from 2021		(2,000)
Net loss on rental property (managed by James)		(100)
Adjusted gross income		($ 5,700)
Less: Itemized deductions		
Interest expense on home mortgage	$ 4,600	
Taxes	7,300	
Casualty loss	2,000	
Total itemized deductions	$ 13,900	
Standard deduction (greater than itemized deductions)		(25,900)
Deduction for qualified business income*		(–0–)
Taxable income		($31,600)

*James has no qualified business income in 2022; the retail store generated a loss of $6,000, and the rental property he manages generated a loss of $100. These losses carry forward to future years and will reduce any qualified business income in those years.

continued

James's 2022 NOL is computed as follows:

Taxable income				($31,600)
Add:				
Net operating loss from 2021			$ 2,000	
Excess of nonbusiness deductions over nonbusiness income				
Standard deduction		$25,900		
Less: Interest income	$ 525			
Less: Long-term capital gain	1,000	(1,525)	24,375	26,375
Net operating loss				($ 5,225)

Effectively, the 2022 NOL is made up of the following amounts:

Business loss	($ 6,000)
Rental loss	(100)
Salary income	875
Net operating loss	($ 5,225)

7-6c Computation of Taxable Income for Year to Which Net Operating Loss Is Carried

When an NOL is carried to a nonloss year, the taxable income for the year is determined by including the NOL as a deduction *for* AGI. Several deductions (such as medical expenses and charitable contributions) are based on the amount of AGI. These deductions must be determined on the basis of the AGI after the NOL has been applied.

Example 40

Continue with the facts from Example 39. Assume that in 2023, James and his spouse report the following information:

Gross income from the business	$ 98,000	
Less: Business expenses	(74,000)	$24,000
Salary (spouse)		32,000
Interest on savings account		310
Net income on rental property (managed by James)		750

In addition, assume that James and his spouse will use the standard deduction. Determine their taxable income for the year and any NOL carryforward to 2024.

Solution: Due to the 80% of taxable income limitation on NOL carryforwards, a multistep process is required: (1) determine taxable income before application of the NOL, (2) determine the NOL deduction, and (3) determine final taxable income.

(1) Determine taxable income before application of the NOL:

Gross income from the business	$ 98,000	
Less: Business expenses	(74,000)	$ 24,000
Salary (spouse)		32,000
Interest on savings account		310
Net income on rental property		750
Adjusted gross income		$ 57,060
Less: Standard deduction*		(25,900)
Less: Deduction for qualified business income:**		
Store [$24,000 − $2,000 (2021 loss) − $6,000 (2022 loss)] × 20%	$ 3,200	
Rental [$750 − $100 (2022 loss)] × 20%	130	(3,330)
Taxable income		$ 27,830

* Because the 2023 standard deduction amount will not be released by the IRS until late 2022, the 2022 standard deduction amount is used.

** According to § 199A, the deduction for qualified business income must be determined separately for each trade or business. This example assumes that a managed rental property qualifies for the deduction. The § 199A(b)(1) "combined qualified business income amount" is $3,330. Taxable income before the QBI deduction is $31,160 ($57,060 − $25,900); this is also modified taxable income. So the QBI deduction is not limited by the overall taxable income limitation (modified taxable income × 20%).

continued

(2) Determine the NOL deduction:

The NOL deduction is limited to the lesser of:

1. The NOL carryforward ($7,225; $2,000 from 2021 and $5,225 from 2022), or
2. 80% of taxable income computed in step 1: $22,264 ($27,830 × 80%).

Because the NOL carryforward is less than the 80% limitation, the entire NOL carryover is allowed as a *for* AGI deduction in 2023.

(3) Determine final taxable income:

Gross income from the business	$ 98,000	
Less: Business expenses	(74,000)	$ 24,000
Salary (spouse)		32,000
Interest on savings account		310
Net income on rental property		750
NOL deduction		(7,225)
Adjusted gross income		$ 49,835
Less: Standard deduction		(25,900)
Less: Deduction for qualified business income:*		
Store [$24,000 − $2,000 (2021 loss) − $6,000 (2022 loss)] × 20%	$ 3,200	
Rental [$750 − $100 (2022 loss)] × 20%	130	(3,330)
Taxable income		$ 20,605

Note: The NOL deduction is a *for* AGI deduction. As a result, if the taxpayers were itemizing their deductions, this recomputation of AGI could have an impact on their itemized deductions (e.g., medical, contributions, or casualty loss).

*Taxable income before the QBI deduction is $23,935 ($49,835 − $25,900); this is also modified taxable income. So the QBI deduction is not limited by the overall taxable income limitation (modified taxable income × 20%).

(4) Determine any NOL carryforward to 2024:

As the 2021 and 2022 NOL carryforwards were entirely used in 2023, there is no NOL carry forward to 2024.

7-6d Calculation of the Remaining Net Operating Loss

After computing taxable income for the initial carryforward year, it is then necessary to determine the extent to which any NOL remains to carry over to future years.[52] The amount of this carryover loss is the excess of the NOL over the taxable income of the year to which the loss is being applied. However, the taxable income of the year to which the loss is being applied must be determined with the following *modifications*:

- No deduction is allowed for excess capital losses over capital gains.
- No deduction is allowed for an NOL that is being carried back. However, deductions are allowed for NOLs occurring before the loss year.
- Any deductions claimed that are based on or limited by AGI must be determined after making the preceding adjustments. However, charitable contributions do not take into account any NOL carryback.
- The qualified business income deduction is not allowed.
- No deduction is allowed for personal and dependency exemptions; from 2018 through 2025, the exemption amount is zero.

Although this computation is somewhat similar to the calculations discussed previously, additional nuances exist, including determining the implications of recent legislative changes to the NOL carryforward computation (e.g., the 80 percent of taxable income limitation on NOLs and the qualified business income deduction). The resulting complexities and lack of current guidance from the Treasury Department and the IRS make this computation challenging (and beyond the scope of this text).

[52]Taxpayers with an NOL carryover must keep records to track its use in carryforward years.

7-7 Tax Planning

LO.8

Identify tax planning opportunities in deducting certain business expenses, business losses, and personal losses.

7-7a Small Business Stock (§ 1244 Stock) Losses

Because § 1244 limits the amount of loss classified as ordinary loss on a yearly basis, a taxpayer might maximize the benefits of § 1244 by selling the stock in more than one taxable year. The result could be that the losses in any one taxable year would not exceed the § 1244 limits on ordinary loss.

Example 41

Mitch, a single individual, purchased small business stock in 2020 for $150,000 (150 shares at $1,000 per share). On December 20, 2022, the stock is worth $60,000 (150 shares at $400 per share). Mitch wants to sell the stock at this time. Mitch earns a salary of $80,000 a year, has no other capital transactions, and does not expect any in the future.

If Mitch sells all of the small business stock in 2022, his recognized loss will be $90,000 ($60,000 − $150,000). The loss will be characterized as a $50,000 ordinary loss and a $40,000 long-term capital loss. In computing taxable income for 2022, Mitch could deduct the $50,000 ordinary loss but could deduct only $3,000 of the capital loss. The remainder of the capital loss could be carried over and used in future years subject to the $3,000 limitation if Mitch has no capital gains.

Instead, if Mitch sells 82 shares in 2022, he will recognize an ordinary loss of $49,200 [82 × ($1,000 − $400)]. If Mitch then sells the remainder of the shares in 2023, he will recognize an ordinary loss of $40,800 [68 × ($1,000 − $400)]. Mitch could deduct the $49,200 ordinary loss in computing 2022 taxable income and the $40,800 ordinary loss in computing 2023 taxable income.

7-7b Casualty Losses

A special election is available for taxpayers who sustain casualty losses in an area designated by the President as a disaster area. This election affects only the *timing*, not the calculation, of the deduction. The benefit, of course, is a faster refund (or reduction in tax). It will also be advantageous to carry the loss back if the taxpayer's tax rate in the carryback year is higher than the tax rate in the year of the loss.

To find out if an event qualifies as a disaster area loss, one can look in any of the major tax services, the Compilation of Presidential Documents (released by the U.S. Government Publishing Office), or the *Internal Revenue Bulletin*.

Refocus on The Big Picture

Losses

TETRA IMAGES/GETTY IMAGES

Martha can receive tax benefits associated with her unfortunate occurrences during the current tax year. Some of the losses, however, will provide a greater tax benefit than others as a result of different tax provisions governing the amount and the classification of the losses.

Bad Debt

Based on the facts provided, it appears that Martha's loan to her friend Janice was a bona fide debt. Otherwise, nothing would be deductible. The amount of the deduction is the unpaid principal balance of $19,000 ($25,000 − $6,000). Unfortunately, because the bad debt is a nonbusiness bad debt, it is classified as a short-term capital loss (see Example 5).

continued

Investment Losses

The $50,000 loss from the pharmaceutical company stock is deductible. However, it appears that the loss should be classified as a long-term capital loss rather than as a short-term capital loss. Although the actual holding period was not greater than one year (October through May), the disposal date for the stock (which qualifies as a worthless security) is deemed to be the last day of the tax year (October of last year through end of December of the current year). Further, the loss does not appear to qualify for ordinary loss treatment under § 1244 (see Example 8).

The stock she purchased from her friend Peter results in an $8,000 short-term capital loss (and does not qualify under § 1244; see Example 10).

Loss from Bookstore

The $180,000 loss from Martha's sole proprietorship (her bookstore) is reported on Schedule C of Form 1040. It is an ordinary loss, and it qualifies for NOL treatment. Martha can carry forward any net loss and offset it against future taxable income. However, the NOL carryforward will be limited (each year) to the lesser of the NOL or 80 percent of taxable income (computed without regard to the NOL carryforward).

Casualty Loss

The loss from the damage to Martha's personal residence is classified as a personal casualty loss. Using the cost of repairs method, the amount of the casualty loss is $7,000 ($25,000 − $32,000). However, this amount must be reduced by the $100-per-event floor and the 10%-of-AGI floor.

Because the President classified the county in which Martha's house is located as a Federal disaster area, Martha has the option of deducting the casualty loss on the prior year's tax return (see Example 15).

Key Terms

Bad debt, 7-2
Business bad debt, 7-4
Casualty loss, 7-7
Disaster area losses, 7-8
Excess business loss, 7-17
Net operating loss (NOL), 7-19
Nonbusiness bad debt, 7-4
Research and experimental expenditures, 7-15
Reserve method, 7-3
Small business stock (§ 1244 stock), 7-6
Specific charge-off method, 7-3
Theft losses, 7-8
Worthless securities, 7-6

Discussion Questions

1. **LO.1** Explain how an account receivable can give rise to a bad debt deduction.
2. **LO.1** Ron, a cash basis taxpayer, sells his business accounts receivable of $100,000 to Felicia for $70,000 (70% of the actual accounts receivable). Discuss the amount and classification of Ron's bad debt deduction.
3. **LO.1** Discuss when a bad debt deduction can be taken for a nonbusiness debt.
4. **LO.1** Discuss the treatment of a business bad debt when the business also has long-term capital gains.

5. **LO.1, 2, 3, 4, 7** Many years ago, Jack purchased 400 shares of Canary stock. During the current year, the stock became worthless. It was determined that the company "went under" because several corporate officers embezzled a large amount of company funds. Identify the relevant tax issues for Jack. Critical Thinking

6. **LO.1, 2** Sean is in the business of buying and selling stocks and bonds. He has a bond of Green Corporation for which he paid $200,000. The bond is currently worth only $50,000. Discuss whether Sean can take a $150,000 loss for a business bad debt or for a worthless security.

7. **LO.2** Discuss the tax treatment of the sale of § 1244 stock at a gain.

8. **LO.3, 4** Jim discovers that his residence has extensive termite damage. Discuss whether he may take a deduction for the damage to his residence.

9. **LO.3, 4** The value of Terrah's personal residence has declined significantly because of a recent forest fire in the area where she lives. The fire was a Federally declared disaster. Terrah's house suffered no actual damage during the fire, but because much of the surrounding area was destroyed, the value of all of the homes in the area declined substantially. Discuss whether Terrah can take a casualty loss for the decline in value of her residence caused by the fire.

10. **LO.4** Discuss at what point in time a theft loss generally is recognized.

11. **LO.4** Discuss the circumstances under which the cost of repairs to the damaged property can be used to measure the amount of a casualty loss.

12. **LO.4** In 2022, Kelsey sustained a loss on the theft of a painting. She had paid $20,000 for the painting, but it was worth $40,000 at the time of the theft. Evaluate the tax consequences of treating the painting as investment property or as personal use property.

13. **LO.2, 4** Kelly decided to invest in Lime, Inc. common stock after reviewing Lime's public disclosures, including recent financial statements and a number of press releases issued by Lime. On August 7, 2020, Kelly purchased 60,000 shares of Lime for $210,000. In May 2021, Lime entered into a joint venture with Cherry, Inc. In November 2021, the joint venture failed, and Lime's stock began to decline in value. In December 2021, Cherry filed a lawsuit against Lime for theft of corporate opportunity and breach of fiduciary responsibility. In February 2022, Lime filed a countersuit against Cherry for fraud and misappropriation of funds. At the end of December 2022, Kelly's stock in Lime was worth $15,000. Identify the relevant tax issues for Kelly. Critical Thinking

14. **LO.3, 4** In 2019, John opened an investment account with Randy Hansen, who held himself out to the public as an investment adviser and securities broker. John contributed $200,000 to the account in 2019. John provided Randy with a power of attorney to use the $200,000 to purchase and sell securities on John's behalf. John instructed Randy to reinvest any gains and income earned. In 2019, 2020, and 2021, John received statements of the amount of income earned by his account and included these amounts in his gross income for these years. In 2022, it was discovered that Randy's purported investment advisory and brokerage activity was in fact a fraudulent investment arrangement known as a Ponzi scheme. In reality, John's account balance was zero, the money having been used by Randy in his scheme. Identify the relevant tax issues for John. Critical Thinking

15. **LO.5** Discuss under what circumstances a company would elect to amortize research and experimental expenditures rather than use the expense method.

Critical Thinking

16. **LO.6, 7** Amos began a business, Silver LLC (a single-member LLC), on July 1, 2019. The business extracts and processes silver ore. During 2022, as a result of a decline in demand for silver ore, Amos expects to generate a large loss. Identify the relevant tax issues for Amos.

17. **LO.6** Discuss the rationale behind the excess business loss provision.

18. **LO.7** Discuss whether unreimbursed employee business expenses can create an NOL for an individual taxpayer.

19. **LO.7** Discuss whether deductions *for* AGI can be treated as nonbusiness deductions in computing an individual's NOL.

Critical Thinking

20. **LO.7** Thomas believes that he has an NOL for the current year and plans to carry it forward, offsetting it against future income. In determining his NOL, Thomas offset his business income by alimony payments he made to his ex-wife and contributions he made to his traditional Individual Retirement Account (IRA). His reason for using these items in the NOL computation is that each item is a deduction *for* AGI. Identify the relevant tax issues for Thomas.

Computational Exercises

21. **LO.1** Last year Aleshia identified $15,000 as a nonbusiness bad debt. In that tax year, before considering the tax implications of the nonbusiness bad debt, Aleshia had $100,000 of taxable income, of which $12,000 consisted of short-term capital gains. This year Aleshia collected $8,000 of the amount she had previously identified as a bad debt. Determine Aleshia's tax treatment of the $8,000 received in the current tax year.

22. **LO.1** Bob owns a collection agency. He purchases uncollected accounts receivable from other businesses at 60% of their face value and then attempts to collect these accounts. During the current year, Bob collected $60,000 on an account with a face value of $80,000. Determine the amount of Bob's bad debt deduction.

23. **LO.2** On May 9, 2020, Calvin acquired 250 shares of stock in Hobbes Corporation, a new startup company, for $68,750. Calvin acquired the stock directly from Hobbes, and it is classified as § 1244 stock (at the time Calvin acquired his stock, the corporation had $900,000 of paid-in capital). On January 15, 2022, Calvin sold all of his Hobbes stock for $7,000. Assuming that Calvin is single, determine his tax consequences as a result of this sale.

24. **LO.4** Determine the treatment of a loss on rental property under the following facts:

Basis	$650,000
FMV before the loss	800,000
FMV after the loss	200,000

25. **LO.4** Belinda was involved in a boating accident in 2022. Her speedboat, which was used only for personal use and had a fair market value of $30,000 and an adjusted basis of $14,000, was completely destroyed. She received $10,000 from her insurance company. Her AGI for 2022 is $37,000. What is Belinda's casualty loss deduction (after any limitations)?

26. **LO.4** During the current year, Tucker had the following personal casualty gains and losses (after deducting the $100 floor):

Asset	Holding Period	Gain or (Loss)
Asset 1	18 months	($1,200)
Asset 2	2 months	750
Asset 3	3 years	1,500

What are the tax consequences of these items to Tucker?

27. **LO.5** Sandstorm Corporation decides to develop a new line of paints. The project begins in 2021. Sandstorm incurs the following expenses in 2021 in connection with the project:

Salaries	$85,000
Materials	30,000
Depreciation on equipment	12,500

The benefits from the project will be realized starting in July 2022. If Sandstorm Corporation chooses to defer and amortize its research and experimental expenditures over a period of 60 months, what are its related deductions in 2021 and 2022?

28. **LO.6** Tim, a single taxpayer, operates a business as a single-member LLC. In 2022, his LLC reports business income of $225,000 and business deductions of $595,000, resulting in a loss of $370,000. What are the implications of this business loss? Can this business loss be used to offset other income that Tim reports? If so, how much? If not, what happens to the loss?

29. **LO.7** Valeria and Trey are married and file a joint tax return. For 2022, they have $4,800 of nonbusiness capital gains, $2,300 of nonbusiness capital losses, $500 of interest income, and no itemized deductions. The standard deduction for married filing jointly is $25,900.

Based on these transactions, to arrive at the NOL, Valeria and Trey's taxable income must be adjusted by what amount?

30. **LO.7** Emily, who is single, sustains an NOL of $7,800 in 2022. The loss is carried forward to 2023. For 2023, Emily's income tax information before taking into account the 2022 NOL is as follows:

Adjusted gross income		$ 48,200
Itemized deductions*:		
Medical [$3,650 – (7.5% × $48,200)]	$ 35	
Taxes	6,100	
Interest expense on home mortgage	11,000	(17,135)
Taxable income		$ 31,065

*The 2022 single standard deduction is $12,950; Emily's itemized deductions will exceed the 2023 single standard deduction (after adjustment for inflation).

How much of the NOL carryforward can Emily use in 2023, and what is her adjusted gross income and her taxable income?

Problems

Communications

31. **LO.1** Several years ago Amy Westbrook, who is in the lending business, loaned Sara Stuart $30,000 to purchase an automobile to be used for personal purposes. In August of the current year, Sara filed for bankruptcy, after paying back $1,000 of the loan to Amy. Amy was notified by the bankruptcy court that she could not expect to receive more than an additional $4,000. Amy has contacted you about the possibility of taking a bad debt deduction for the current year.

    Write a letter to Amy that contains your advice as to whether she can claim a bad debt deduction for the current year. Also prepare a memo for the tax files. Amy's address is 100 Tyler Lane, Erie, PA 16563.

32. **LO.1** Monty loaned his friend Ned $20,000 three years ago. Ned signed a note and made payments on the loan. Last year, when the remaining balance was $11,000, Ned filed for bankruptcy and notified Monty that he would be unable to pay the balance on the loan. Monty treated the $11,000 as a nonbusiness bad debt. Last year, before considering the tax implications of the nonbusiness bad debt, Monty had capital gains of $9,000 and taxable income of $45,000. During the current year, Ned paid Monty $10,000 in satisfaction of the debt. Determine Monty's tax treatment for the $10,000 received in the current year.

33. **LO.1** Sally is in the business of purchasing accounts receivable. Last year Sally purchased an account receivable with a face value of $80,000 for $60,000. During the current year, Sally settled the account, receiving $65,000. Determine the maximum amount of the bad debt deduction for Sally for the current year.

34. **LO.1, 2** Jocelyn and Esteban file a joint return. For the current year, they had the following items:

Salaries	$120,000
Loss on sale of § 1244 stock acquired two years ago	105,000
Gain on sale of § 1244 stock acquired six months ago	20,000
Nonbusiness bad debt	19,000

    Determine their AGI for the current year.

Critical Thinking
Decision Making
Planning

35. **LO.2, 8** Abby, a single taxpayer, purchased 10,000 shares of § 1244 stock several years ago at a cost of $20 per share. In November of the current year, Abby received an offer to sell the stock for $12 per share. She has the option of either selling all of the stock now or selling half of the stock now and half of the stock in January of next year. Abby will receive a salary of $80,000 for the current year and $90,000 next year. Abby will have long-term capital gains of $8,000 for the current year and $10,000 next year. If Abby's goal is to minimize her AGI for the two years, determine whether she should sell all of her stock this year or half of her stock this year and half next year.

Critical Thinking
Decision Making
Planning

36. **LO.3, 4, 8** Olaf lives in the state of Minnesota. In May 2022, a tornado hit the area and damaged his home and automobile. Applicable information is as follows:

Item	Adjusted Basis	FMV before	FMV after	Insurance Proceeds
Home	$350,000	$500,000	$100,000	$280,000
Auto	60,000	40,000	10,000	20,000

    Because of the extensive damage caused by the tornado, the President designated the area a Federal disaster area.

    Olaf and his wife, Anna, always file a joint return. Their 2021 tax return shows AGI of $180,000 and taxable income of $145,000. In 2022, their return shows AGI of $300,000 and taxable income (exclusive of the casualty loss deduction) of $245,000.

    Determine the amount of Olaf and Anna's loss and the year in which they should take the loss.

37. **LO.3, 4** Heather owns a two-story building. The building is used 40% for business use and 60% for personal use. During 2022, a fire caused major damage to the building and its contents. Heather purchased the building for $800,000 and has taken depreciation of $100,000 on the business portion. At the time of the fire, the building had a fair market value of $900,000. Immediately after the fire, the fair market value was $200,000. The insurance recovery on the building was $600,000. The contents of the building were insured for any loss at fair market value. The business assets had an adjusted basis of $220,000 and a fair market value of $175,000. These assets were totally destroyed. The personal use assets had an adjusted basis of $50,000 and a fair market value of $65,000. These assets were also totally destroyed. If Heather's AGI is $100,000 before considering the effects of the fire, determine her itemized deduction as a result of the fire. Also determine Heather's AGI.

38. **LO.3, 4** On July 24 of the current year, Trevor Pickard was involved in an accident with his business use automobile. Trevor had purchased the car for $30,000. The automobile had a fair market value of $20,000 before the accident and $8,000 immediately after the accident. Trevor has taken $20,000 of depreciation on the car. The car is insured for the fair market value of any loss. Because of Trevor's history, he is afraid that if he submits a claim, his policy will be canceled. Therefore, he is considering not filing a claim. Trevor believes that the tax loss deduction will help mitigate the loss of the insurance reimbursement. Trevor's current marginal tax rate is 35%.

Communications
Decision Making
Planning

Write a letter to Trevor that contains your advice with respect to the tax and cash-flow consequences of filing versus not filing a claim for the insurance reimbursement for the damage to his car. Also prepare a memo for the tax files. Trevor's address is 450 Colonel's Way, Warrensburg, MO 64093.

39. **LO.5** Blue Corporation, a manufacturing company, decided to develop a new line of merchandise. The project began in 2019. Blue had the following expenses in connection with the project:

	2019	2020
Salaries	$500,000	$600,000
Materials	90,000	70,000
Insurance	8,000	11,000
Utilities	6,000	8,000
Cost of inspection of materials for quality control	7,000	6,000
Promotion expenses	11,000	18,000
Advertising	–0–	20,000
Equipment depreciation	15,000	14,000
Cost of market survey	8,000	–0–

The new product will be introduced for sale beginning in April 2021. Determine the amount of the deduction for research and experimental expenditures for 2019, 2020, 2021, and 2022 if:

a. Blue Corporation elects to expense the research and experimental expenditures.

b. Blue Corporation elects to amortize the research and experimental expenditures over 60 months.

c. How would your answer change if Blue Corporation incurred the expenses in 2022 and 2023 (rather than 2019 and 2020)?

40. **LO.6** During 2022, Leisel, a single taxpayer, operates a sole proprietorship in which she materially participates. Her proprietorship generates gross income of $142,000 and deductions of $420,000, resulting in a loss of $278,000. The large deductions are due to the acquisition of equipment and the use of immediate expense and additional first-year depreciation to deduct all of the acquisitions. Can Leisel use all of this loss to offset other income she has? Explain.

41. **LO.6** Timothy Gates and Prada Singh decide to form a new company, TGPS LLC (a multimember LLC that will report its operations as a partnership). Timothy is married, and Prada is single. Each contributes $400,000 of capital to begin the business, and both materially participate in the business. In 2022, TGPS reports a net loss of $580,000. What are the implications of this loss for Timothy and Prada?

42. **LO.7** Mario, a single taxpayer with two dependent children, has the following items of income and expense during 2022:

Gross receipts from business	$144,000
Business expenses	180,000
Net capital gain	22,000
Interest income	3,000
Itemized deductions (state taxes, residence interest, and contributions)	24,000

a. Determine Mario's taxable income for 2022.

b. Determine Mario's NOL for 2022.

43. **LO.7** Xinran, who is married and files a joint return, owns a grocery store. In 2022, his gross sales were $276,000 and operating expenses were $320,000. Other items on his 2022 return were as follows:

Nonbusiness capital gains (short term)	$20,000
Nonbusiness capital losses (long term)	9,000
Itemized deductions	18,000
Ordinary nonbusiness income	8,000
Salary from part-time job (spouse)	10,000

In 2023, Xinran provides the following information:

Net business income		$60,000
Salary (spouse)		25,000
Interest income		2,000
Adjusted gross income		$87,000
Itemized deductions*		
Charitable contributions (cash)	$35,000	
Medical expenses of $6,925 [limited to the amount in excess of 7.5% of AGI ($6,925 – $6,525)]	400	
Total itemized deductions		$35,400

*The 2022 married filing jointly standard deduction is $25,900; Xinran's itemized deductions will exceed the 2022 standard deduction (after adjustment for inflation).

a. What is Xinran's 2022 NOL?

b. Determine Xinran's taxable income for 2023.

44. **LO.7** During 2022, Rick and his wife, Sara, had the following items of income and expense to report:

Gross receipts from business	$400,000
Business expenses	525,000
Interest income from bank savings accounts	8,000
Sara's salary	50,000
Long-term capital gain on stock held as an investment	4,000
Itemized deductions	15,000

a. Assuming that Rick and Sara file a joint return, what is their taxable income for 2022?

b. What is the amount of Rick and Sara's NOL for 2022?

c. To what years can Rick and Sara's NOL be carried?

d. Based on your computations, identify the components of their NOL. What is the rationale for excluding the items that do not affect the NOL computation?

45. **LO.1, 2, 3, 4, 7** Jed, age 55, is married with no children. During 2022, Jed had the following income and expense items:

a. Three years ago, Jed loaned a friend $10,000 to help him purchase a new car. In June of the current year, Jed learned that his friend had been declared bankrupt and had left the country. There is no possibility that Jed will ever collect any of the $10,000.

b. In April 2020, Jed purchased some stock for $5,000. In March 2022, the company was declared bankrupt and Jed was notified that his shares of stock were worthless.

c. Several years ago Jed purchased some § 1244 stock for $120,000. This year he sold the stock for $30,000.

d. In July of this year, Jed sold some land that he had held for two years for $60,000. He had originally paid $42,000 for the land.

e. Jed received $40,000 of interest income from State of Minnesota bonds.

f. In September, Jed's home was damaged by an earthquake; Jed's county was declared a Federal disaster area by the President. Jed's basis in his home was $430,000. The value of the home immediately before the earthquake was $610,000. After the earthquake, the home was worth $540,000. Because earthquake damage was an exclusion on Jed's homeowner's insurance policy, he received no insurance recovery.

g. Jed received a salary of $80,000.

h. Jed paid home mortgage interest of $14,000.

If Jed files a joint return for 2022, determine his NOL for the year.

Tax Return Problems

Communications
Critical Thinking
Decision Making
Planning
Tax Forms Problem
ProConnect™ Tax

46. Denise Lopez, age 40, is single and has no dependents. She is employed as a legal secretary by Legal Services, Inc. She owns and operates Typing Services located near the campus of Florida Atlantic University at 1986 Campus Drive, Boca Raton, FL 33434. Denise is a material participant in the business, she is a cash basis taxpayer, and her Social Security number is 123-45-6781. Denise lives at 2020 Oakcrest Road, Boca Raton, FL 33431. Denise wants to designate $3 to the Presidential Election Campaign Fund. She has never owned or used any virtual currency. Denise received the appropriate coronavirus recovery rebates (economic impact payments); related questions in ProConnect Tax should be ignored. During 2021, Denise had the following income and expense items:

a. $100,000 salary from Legal Services, Inc.

b. $20,000 gross receipts from her typing services business.

c. $700 interest income from Third National Bank.

d. $1,000 Christmas bonus from Legal Services, Inc.

e. $60,000 life insurance proceeds on the death of her sister.

f. $5,000 check given to her by her wealthy aunt.

g. $100 won in a bingo game.

h. Expenses connected with Typing Services:

Office rent	$7,000
Supplies	4,400
Utilities and telephone	4,680
Wages to part-time typists	5,000
Payroll taxes	500
Equipment rentals	3,000

i. $9,500 interest expense on a home mortgage (paid to Boca Raton Savings and Loan).

j. $15,000 fair market value of silverware stolen from her home by a burglar on October 12, 2021. Denise had paid $14,000 for the silverware on July 1, 2011. She was reimbursed $10,000 by her insurance company.

k. Denise had loaned $2,100 to a friend, Joan Jensen, on June 3, 2017. Joan declared bankruptcy on August 14, 2021, and was unable to repay the loan. Assume that the loan is a bona fide debt.

l. Legal Services, Inc., withheld Federal income tax of $15,000 and the appropriate amount of FICA tax from her wages.

m. Alimony of $10,000 received from her former husband, Omar Guzman; divorce was finalized on December 2, 2013, and no changes have been made to the divorce decree since that time.

n. Interest income of $800 on City of Boca Raton bonds.

o. Denise made estimated Federal tax payments of $2,000.

p. Sales taxes from the sales tax table of $953.

q. Property taxes on her residence of $3,200.

r. Charitable contribution of $2,500 to her alma mater, Citrus State College.

s. On November 1, 2021, Denise was involved in an automobile accident. At the time of the accident, her automobile's FMV was $45,000. After the accident, the automobile's FMV was $38,000. Denise acquired the car on May 2, 2020, at a cost of $52,000. Denise's car was covered by insurance, but because the policy had a $5,000 deduction clause, Denise decided not to file a claim for the damage.

Part 1—Tax Computation

Compute Denise Lopez's 2021 Federal income tax payable (or refund due), and complete her 2021 Federal tax return using appropriate forms and schedules. Suggested software: ProConnect Tax.

Part 2—Tax Planning

In 2022, Denise plans to continue her job with Legal Services, Inc. As a result, items a, d, and l will recur in 2022. Denise plans to continue her typing services business (refer to item b) and expects gross receipts of $34,000. She projects that all business expenses (refer to item h) will increase by 10%, except for office rent, which, under the terms of her lease, will remain the same as in 2021. Items e, f, g, j, k, and s will not recur in 2022. Items c, i, m, n, p, q, and r will be approximately the same as in 2021.

Based on this information, Denise would like you to provide a tentative computation of her 2022 taxable income. Prepare a memo for her tax files that details this computation.

Tax Computation Problem

47. Mason Phillips, age 45, and his wife, Alyssa, live at 230 Wood Lane, Salt Lake City, UT 84101. Mason's Social Security number is 111-11-1111. Alyssa's Social Security number is 123-45-6789. Mason and Alyssa are cash basis taxpayers and report the following items for 2022:

- Salary of $140,000.
- Collection of unpaid rent from a prior year of $6,000.

- Rental income of $60,000 (not including prior year unpaid rent; the rental property is managed by the Phillips).
- Rental expenses of $33,000.
- Uncollected rent (bad debts) of $4,000.
- Casualty loss on rental property of $10,000.
- Sale of § 1244 stock resulting in a loss of $105,000. The stock was acquired eight months ago.
- Personal casualty loss (from one event) of $3,000; not in a Federally declared disaster area.
- Theft loss of $8,000 on a painting held for investment.
- Other itemized deductions of $21,000.
- Federal income tax withheld of $3,000.

Compute Mason and Alyssa's 2022 Federal income tax payable (or refund due).

Research Problems

Note: Solutions to the Research Problems can be prepared by using the Thomson Reuters Checkpoint™ online tax research database, which accompanies this textbook. Solutions can also be prepared by using research materials found in a typical tax library.

the answer company™ THOMSON REUTERS®

Research Problem 1. During 2022, your client, Kendra Adams, was the chief executive officer and a shareholder of Maze, Inc. She owned 60% of the outstanding stock of Maze. In 2019, Kendra and Maze, as co-borrowers, obtained a $100,000 loan from United National Bank. This loan was secured by Kendra's personal residence. Although Maze was listed as a co-borrower, Kendra repaid the loan in full in 2022. On Maze's Form 1120 tax returns, no loans from shareholders were reported. Discuss whether Kendra is entitled to a bad debt deduction for the amount of the payment on the loan.

Partial list of research aids:
U.S. v. Generes, 92 S.Ct. 827 (1972).
Dale H. Sundby, T.C.Memo. 2003–204.
Arrigoni v. Comm., 73 T.C. 792 (1980).
Estate of Herbert M. Rapoport, T.C.Memo. 1982–584.
Clifford L. Brody and Barbara J. DeClerk, T.C. Summary Opinion, 2004–149.

Research Problem 2. Esther owns a large home on the Southeast Coast. Her home is surrounded by large, mature oak trees that significantly increase the value of her home. In September 2022, a hurricane damaged many of the trees surrounding her home; her region was declared a Federal disaster area as a result of the hurricane's damage. In October 2022, Esther engaged a local arborist to evaluate and treat the trees, but five of the largest trees were seriously weakened by the storm. These trees died from disease in 2023. Esther has ascertained that the amount of the casualty loss from the death of the five trees is $25,000; however, she is uncertain in which year to deduct this loss and has come to you for advice. Discuss whether the casualty loss should be deducted in the calculation of Esther's 2022 or 2023 taxable income. Planning

Partial list of research aids:
Reg. § 1.165–1.
Oregon Mesabi Corporation, 39 B.T.A. 1033 (1939).

Use internet tax resources to address the following questions. Look for reliable websites and blogs of the IRS and other government agencies, media outlets, businesses, tax professionals, academics, think tanks, and political outlets.

Research Problem 3. Find an article that discusses tax planning for casualty losses when a Federal disaster area designation is made. Does the article convey the pertinent tax rules correctly? Then list all of the locations identified by the President as Federal disaster areas in the last two years.

Communications
Data Analytics

Research Problem 4. How many U.S. individuals claim a deduction for casualties? Does it vary by size of income (AGI)? How do casualty loss deductions compare to the amounts of other itemized deductions claimed by taxpayers? Go to the IRS tax statistics website (**irs.gov/statistics**), and download a recent tax year's information on "Individual Income Tax Returns with Itemized Deductions." Cluster the data into no more than six AGI categories. Present your findings in a visual (e.g., a bar chart), and summarize your findings in a one-page memo to your instructor.

Communications

Research Problem 5. Many states have their income tax calculations "piggyback" the Federal income tax calculation. In other words, these states' income tax calculations incorporate many of the Federal calculations and deductions to make both compliance and verification of tax liability easier. However, given the significant legislative changes implemented in late 2017, some state legislatures have passed laws modifying some of these rules for state purposes. How are states reacting to the 2017 legislative changes to personal casualty losses, the excess business loss limitation, and the net operating loss changes (no carryback and 80% of taxable income limitation)? Be sure to state the sources for your answer.

Communications

Research Problem 6. There is significant debate about the excess business loss deduction. Some believe it should be repealed; others (including the President) believe it should be made permanent. Find several articles that summarize this debate, synthesize the articles into a one-page memo, and share the memo with your instructor.

Becker CPA Review Questions

1. Mark and Lucy owned two stocks, Tinker Inc., and Chance Inc., that became worthless during year 8. The adjusted basis in Tinker was $300,000. Tinker was incorporated in year 2, and Mark and Lucy purchased their stock in year 4. Their adjusted basis in Chance was $200,000. Chance was incorporated in year 2, and Mark and Lucy were original stockholders. Both stocks were purchased for cash, and each corporation had total capital of $500,000. How much ordinary loss can Mark and Lucy deduct on their joint year 8 tax return as a result of these transactions?

   a. $0
   b. $100,000
   c. $200,000
   d. $300,000

2. Mark and Lucy owned two stocks, Tinker Inc., and Chance Inc., that became worthless during year 8. The adjusted basis in Tinker was $80,000. Tinker was incorporated in year 2, and Mark and Lucy purchased their stock in year 4. Their adjusted basis in Chance was $20,000. Chance was incorporated in year 2, and Mark and Lucy were original stockholders. Both stocks were purchased for cash, and each corporation had total capital of $500,000. How much ordinary loss can Mark and Lucy deduct on their joint year 8 tax return as a result of these transactions?

   a. $0
   b. $20,000
   c. $80,000
   d. $100,000

3. Chad owned an office building that was destroyed in a tornado. The area was declared a Federal disaster area. The adjusted basis of the building at the time was $890,000. After the deductible, Chad received an insurance check for $850,000. He used the $850,000 to purchase a new building that same year. How much is Chad's recognized loss, and what is his basis in the new building?

	Recognized Loss	New Basis
a.	$0	$850,000
b.	$0	$890,000
c.	$40,000	$850,000
d.	$40,000	$890,000

4. Which of the following is a true statement regarding the carryback and carryforward of a net operating loss (NOL) arising in a calendar tax year after 2020, assuming that there are no NOL carryforwards from previous years?
   a. The NOL can be carried forward and offset 100 percent of taxable income in the following year.
   b. The NOL can be carried forward and offset 80 percent of taxable income in the following year.
   c. The NOL can be carried back and offset 100 percent of taxable income in the previous year.
   d. The NOL can be carried back and offset 80 percent of taxable income in the previous year.

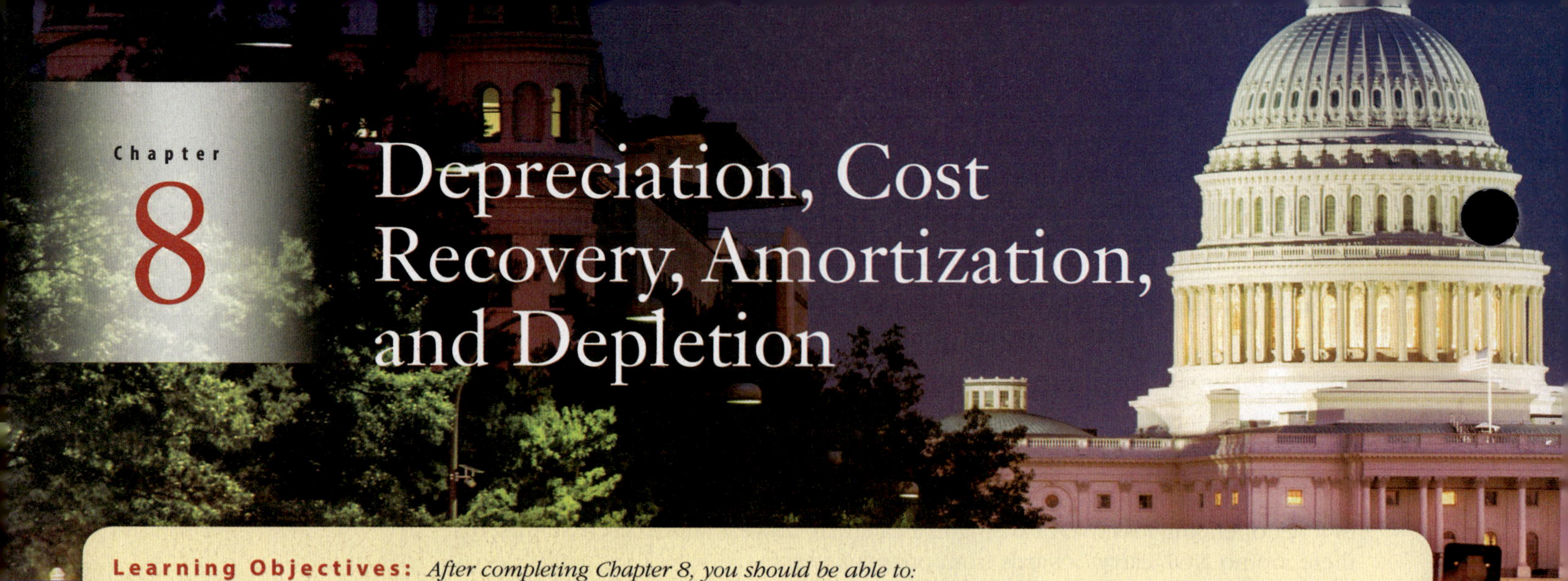

Chapter

8 Depreciation, Cost Recovery, Amortization, and Depletion

Learning Objectives: *After completing Chapter 8, you should be able to:*

LO.1 State the rationale for allowing the cost recovery of an asset.

LO.2 Determine the amount of cost recovery under the Modified Accelerated Cost Recovery System (MACRS).

LO.3 Recognize when and how to make the § 179 expensing election, use additional first-year depreciation, and calculate the amount of these deductions as part of the MACRS calculation.

LO.4 Identify listed property and apply the deduction limitations on listed property and on luxury automobiles.

LO.5 Determine when and how to use the alternative depreciation system (ADS).

LO.6 Report cost recovery deductions appropriately.

LO.7 Identify intangible assets that are eligible for amortization and calculate the amount of the deduction.

LO.8 Determine the amount of depletion expense, including being able to apply the alternative tax treatments for intangible drilling and development costs.

LO.9 Identify tax planning opportunities for cost recovery, amortization, and depletion.

Chapter Outline

8-1 Depreciation and Cost Recovery, 8-2
- 8-1a Nature of Property, 8-2
- 8-1b Placed in Service Requirement, 8-3
- 8-1c Cost Recovery Allowed or Allowable, 8-3
- 8-1d Cost Recovery Basis for Personal Use Assets Converted to Business or Income-Producing Use, 8-4

8-2 Modified Accelerated Cost Recovery System (MACRS): General Rules, 8-4
- 8-2a Personalty (and Certain Realty): Recovery Periods and Methods, 8-5
- 8-2b Realty: Recovery Periods and Methods, 8-9

8-3 Modified Accelerated Cost Recovery System (MACRS): Special Rules, 8-10
- 8-3a Election to Expense Assets (§ 179), 8-10
- 8-3b Additional First-Year Depreciation (Bonus Depreciation), 8-14
- 8-3c Using § 179 and Bonus Depreciation Effectively, 8-15
- 8-3d Business and Personal Use of Automobiles and Other Listed Property, 8-18
- 8-3e Alternative Depreciation System (ADS), 8-23

8-4 Reporting Procedures, 8-24

8-5 Amortization, 8-25

8-6 Depletion, 8-28
- 8-6a Intangible Drilling and Development Costs (IDCs), 8-29
- 8-6b Depletion Methods, 8-29

8-7 Tax Planning, 8-31
- 8-7a Cost Recovery, 8-31
- 8-7b Amortization, 8-32
- 8-7c Cost Recovery Tables, 8-32

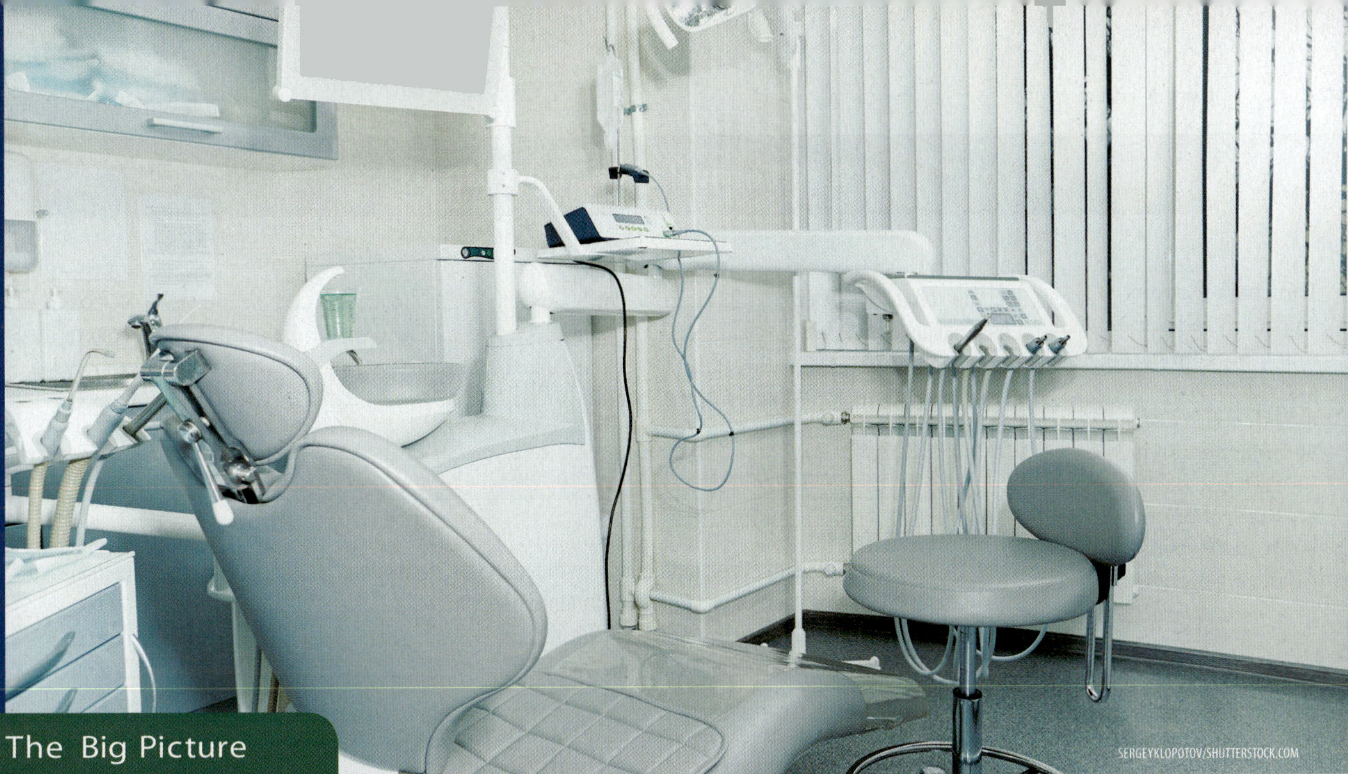

The Big Picture

Calculating Cost Recovery Deductions

Dr. Cliff Payne purchased and placed in service $612,085 of new fixed assets in his dental practice during the current year.

Office furniture and fixtures	$ 70,000
Computers and peripheral equipment	67,085
Dental equipment	475,000

Using his financial reporting system, he concludes that the depreciation expense on Schedule C of Form 1040 is $91,298.

Office furniture and fixtures ($70,000 × 14.29%)	$10,003
Computers and peripheral equipment ($67,085 × 20.00%)	13,417
Dental equipment ($475,000 × 14.29%)	67,878
	$91,298

In addition, this year Dr. Payne purchased a new personal residence for $480,000 and converted his original residence (purchased for $250,000 in 2008) to a rental property.

Has Dr. Payne correctly calculated the depreciation expense for his dental practice? Will he be able to deduct any depreciation expense for his rental property?

Read the chapter and formulate your response.

Framework 1040 **Tax Formula for Individuals**

This chapter covers the boldfaced portions of the Tax Formula for Individuals that was introduced in Concept Summary 3.1 on p. 3-3. Below those portions are the sections of Form 1040 where the results are reported.

Income *(broadly defined)*	$ xx,xxx
Less: Exclusions	(x,xxx)
Gross income	**$ xx,xxx**
Less: Deductions *for* adjusted gross income	**(x,xxx)**

FORM 1040 (Schedule 1)

3	Business income or (loss). Attach Schedule C.

Adjusted gross income	$ xx,xxx
Less: The greater of total itemized deductions *or* the standard deduction	(x,xxx)
Charitable contributions if you take the standard deduction*	(xxx)
Personal and dependency exemptions**	(x,xxx)
Deduction for qualified business income***	(x,xxx)
Taxable income	$ xx,xxx
Tax on taxable income *(see Tax Tables or Tax Rate Schedules)*	$ x,xxx
Less: Tax credits *(including income taxes withheld and prepaid)*	(xxx)
Tax due (or refund)	$ xxx

* For 2021, married taxpayers may claim up to $600 of cash charitable donations ($300 if unmarried).
** Exemption deductions are not allowed from 2018 through 2025.
*** Only applies from 2018 through 2025.

The Internal Revenue Code allows a depreciation, cost recovery, amortization, or depletion deduction based on an asset's cost. These deductions reflect the recovery of capital doctrine (see text Section 4-1b). Cost recovery deductions are based on the idea that the asset acquired (or improvement made) benefits more than one accounting period. If not, the expenditure is deducted in the year incurred.[1]

Taxpayers may "write off" (deduct) the cost of certain assets that are used in a trade or business or held for the production of income. The deduction may take the form of depreciation (or cost recovery), depletion, or amortization. Tangible assets, other than natural resources, are *depreciated*. Natural resources, such as oil, gas, coal, and timber, are *depleted*. Intangible assets, such as copyrights and patents, are *amortized*. Generally, a deduction is allowed for an asset only if it has a determinable useful life.

Congress completely revised the tax **depreciation** rules in 1981 by creating the **accelerated cost recovery system (ACRS)**, which shortened depreciable lives and allowed accelerated depreciation methods. In 1986, Congress made substantial modifications to ACRS, which resulted in the **modified accelerated cost recovery system (MACRS)**, which is the focus of this chapter. Although the terms *depreciation* and **cost recovery** often are used interchangeably, the former normally refers to the allocation of costs to the appropriate period for financial reporting purposes whereas the latter refers to an equivalent concept for tax purposes.[2] A brief discussion of the amortization of intangible property and startup expenditures and the depletion of natural resources concludes the chapter.

8-1 Depreciation and Cost Recovery

8-1a Nature of Property

LO.1

State the rationale for allowing the cost recovery of an asset.

Property includes both realty (real property) and personalty (personal property). *Realty* generally includes land and buildings permanently affixed to the land. *Personalty* is

[1] See the discussion of capitalization versus expense in text Section 6-3i.

[2] § 168. The terms *depreciation* and *cost recovery* are used interchangeably in the text and in § 168. Pre-1986 depreciation rules are covered in the online appendix *Depreciation and the Accelerated Cost Recovery System (ACRS)*.

defined as any asset that is not realty.[3] Personalty includes furniture, machinery, equipment, and any other asset that is movable or not permanently affixed to land. Personalty (or personal property) should not be confused with *personal use* property. Personal use property is any property (realty or personalty) that is held for personal use rather than for use in a trade or business or an income-producing activity. Cost recovery deductions are not allowed for personal use assets.

In summary, both realty and personalty can be either business use/income-producing property or personal use property. Examples include:

- A residence (realty that is personal use),
- An office building (realty that is business use),
- A dump truck (personalty that is business use), and
- Common clothing (personalty that is personal use).

It is critical that the distinction between the *classification* of an asset (realty or personalty) and the *use* to which the asset is put (business/income-producing or personal) be understood.

Assets used in a trade or business or for the production of income are eligible for cost recovery if they are subject to wear and tear, decay or decline from natural causes, or obsolescence (e.g., equipment the taxpayer rents to third parties). Assets that do not decline in value on a predictable basis or that do not have a determinable useful life (e.g., land, stock, and antiques) are not eligible for cost recovery.

8-1b Placed in Service Requirement

Cost recovery begins on the date an asset is placed in service (ready and available for use), *not* the date of purchase. This distinction is particularly important for an asset that is purchased near the end of the tax year but not placed in service until the following tax year.

8-1c Cost Recovery Allowed or Allowable

To prevent the recovery of the same cost more than once (i.e., through periodic cost recovery during the asset's life and via its basis on the sale of the asset), the basis of property is reduced by any cost recovery deducted on a tax return (this is the *allowed* cost recovery). However, the property's basis is reduced by at least the amount of cost recovery that could have been taken using the appropriate cost recovery method (this is the *allowable* cost recovery). As a result, even if the taxpayer does not claim any cost recovery on property during a particular year, the basis of the property still is reduced by the amount of cost recovery that should have been deducted (the allowable cost recovery).

Example 1

On March 15, year 1, Jack purchased a copier, to use in his business, for $10,000. The copier is 5-year property, and Jack elected to use the straight-line method of cost recovery. Jack made the election because the business was a new undertaking and he reasoned that in the first few years of the business, a large cost recovery deduction was not needed.

Because the business was doing poorly, Jack did not deduct any cost recovery in years 3 and 4. In years 5 and 6, Jack deducted the proper amount of cost recovery. The *allowed* cost recovery (cost recovery actually deducted) and the *allowable* cost recovery are computed as follows:

	Cost Recovery Allowed	Cost Recovery Allowable
Year 1	$1,000	$1,000
Year 2	2,000	2,000
Year 3	–0–	2,000
Year 4	–0–	2,000
Year 5	2,000	2,000
Year 6	1,000	1,000

continued

[3]Refer to text Section 1-4a for further discussion.

If Jack sold the copier for $800 in year 7, he would recognize an $800 gain ($800 amount realized − $0 adjusted basis); the adjusted basis of the copier is zero ($10,000 cost − $10,000 total *allowable* cost recovery in years 1 through 6).

8-1d Cost Recovery Basis for Personal Use Assets Converted to Business or Income-Producing Use

If personal use assets are converted to business or income-producing use, the basis for cost recovery and for loss is the *lower* of the adjusted basis or the fair market value at the time the property was converted. This rule ensures that any decline in value that occurred while the property was a personal use asset is not eligible for cost recovery.

The Big Picture

Example 2

Return to the facts of *The Big Picture* on p. 8-1. In 2007, Dr. Payne purchased a personal residence for $250,000. In the current year, Dr. Payne found a larger home that he acquired for his personal residence. Because of the downturn in the housing market, however, he was not able to sell his original residence and recover his purchase price of $250,000. The residence was appraised at $180,000.

Instead of continuing to try to sell the original residence, Dr. Payne converted it to rental property. The basis for cost recovery of the rental property is $180,000 because the fair market value is less than the adjusted basis. The $70,000 decline in value is deemed to be personal (because it occurred while the property was held for personal use by Dr. Payne) and therefore nondeductible.

LO.2

Determine the amount of cost recovery under the Modified Accelerated Cost Recovery System (MACRS).

8-2 Modified Accelerated Cost Recovery System (MACRS): General Rules

Under the modified accelerated cost recovery system (MACRS), the cost of an asset is recovered over a time period that generally is shorter than the economic life of an asset. The MACRS rules were designed to encourage investment, improve productivity, and simplify the tax law and its administration.

MACRS provides separate cost recovery systems for realty and personalty. Based on cost recovery periods (called class lives), methods, and conventions specified in the Internal Revenue Code, the IRS provides tables that identify cost recovery allowances for personalty and for realty. Excerpts from the IRS tables are provided in text Section 8-7c.

Concept Summary 8.1 provides an overview of the class lives, methods, conventions, and deductions in the year of disposition that apply to personalty and realty under MACRS.

Concept Summary 8.1

MACRS: Class Lives, Methods, and Conventions

	Personalty (and Certain Realty)	Realty
Class lives	3 to 20 years	Residential: 27.5 years Nonresidential: 39 years
Method	200% declining balance for property with class lives less than 15 years 150% declining balance for property with 15- or 20-year class lives	Straight-line
Convention	Half-year or mid-quarter	Mid-month
Cost recovery deduction in the year of disposition*	Half-year for year of sale or half-quarter for quarter of sale	Half-month for month of sale

* A disposition can include a sale, an exchange, abandonment, or retirement. For simplicity, we will assume a sale in this chapter.

8-2a Personalty (and Certain Realty): Recovery Periods and Methods

Classification of Property

MACRS provides that the basis of eligible personalty (and certain realty) is recovered over 3, 5, 7, 10, 15, or 20 years. An asset's MACRS recovery period is determined by identifying its Asset Depreciation Range (ADR) midpoint life (determined by the IRS).[4] See Exhibit 8.1 for examples of assets in each class.[5]

Double declining balance is used for the 3-, 5-, 7-, and 10-year classes, with a switchover to straight-line depreciation when appropriate. Cost recovery for the 15- and 20-year classes is based on the 150 percent declining-balance method, with an appropriate straight-line switchover.[6] These methods and conventions are built into the IRS tables. As a result, it is generally not necessary to make these calculations.

To determine an asset's cost recovery deduction for a year, you identify the asset's MACRS class, find the cost recovery percentage for the year using the appropriate IRS table, and multiply this percentage by the asset's cost. The MACRS percentages for personalty appear in Exhibit 8.3 (see text Section 8-7c).

Exhibit 8.1 Cost Recovery Periods: MACRS Personalty (and Certain Realty)

Property Class	Generally Includes Assets with the Following ADR Lives	Examples
3-year	4 years or less	Tractor units for use over the road
		A racehorse that is more than 2 years old, or any other horse that is more than 12 years old, at the time it is placed in service
		Special tools used in the manufacturing of motor vehicles, such as dies, fixtures, molds, and patterns
5-year	More than 4 years and less than 10 years	Automobiles and taxis
		Light and heavy general-purpose trucks
		Calculators and copiers
		Computers and peripheral equipment
		Rental appliances, furniture, carpets
7-year	10 years or more and less than 16 years	Office furniture, fixtures, and equipment
		Agricultural machinery and equipment
10-year	16 years or more and less than 20 years	Vessels, barges, tugs, and similar water transportation equipment
		Assets used for petroleum refining or for the manufacture of grain and grain mill products, sugar and sugar products, or vegetable oils and vegetable oil products
		Single-purpose agricultural or horticultural structures
15-year	20 years or more and less than 25 years	Land improvements
		Qualified improvement property
		Assets used for industrial steam and electric generation and/or distribution systems
		Assets used in the manufacture of cement
20-year	25 years or more	Farm buildings except single-purpose agricultural and horticultural structures
		Water utilities

[4] Personalty is assigned to recovery classes based on Asset Depreciation Range (ADR) midpoint lives (Rev.Proc. 87–56). ADR lives generally represent estimates of an asset's useful economic life.

[5] § 168(e).

[6] § 168(b).

Financial Disclosure Insights — Tax and Book Depreciation

A common book-tax difference relates to the depreciation amounts that are reported for GAAP and Federal income tax purposes. Typically, tax depreciation deductions are accelerated; that is, they are claimed in earlier reporting periods than is the case for financial accounting purposes.

Almost every tax law change since 1980 has included depreciation provisions that accelerate the related deductions relative to the expenses allowed under GAAP. Accelerated cost recovery deductions represent a means by which the taxing jurisdiction infuses the business with cash flow created by the reduction in the year's tax liabilities.

For instance, recently, about one-quarter of General Electric's deferred tax liabilities related to depreciation differences. Ford's depreciation differences amounted to about one-third of its deferred tax liabilities. And for the trucking firm Ryder Systems, depreciation differences accounted for virtually all of the deferred tax liabilities.

Taxpayers may *elect* the straight-line method to compute cost recovery allowances for each of these classes of property. Certain property is not eligible for accelerated cost recovery and must be depreciated under an alternative depreciation system (ADS). Both the straight-line election and ADS are discussed later in the chapter.

Cost recovery for personalty generally incorporates the **half-year convention**; that is, cost recovery in the year the asset is placed in service, as well as the year it is removed from service, is based on the assumption that the asset was used for exactly one half of the year, allowing a half-year of cost recovery.[7] For example, the regular MACRS recovery period for property with a life of three years begins in the middle of the year an asset is placed in service and ends three years later, in the fourth taxable year. In practical terms, this means that an asset's cost is actually recovered over 4, 6, 8, 11, 16, or 21 years.

MACRS Personalty; Half-Year Convention

Example 3

Kareem acquires a 5-year class asset on April 10, 2022, for $30,000. Kareem's cost recovery deduction for 2022 is computed as follows:

MACRS cost recovery [$30,000 × 0.20 (Exhibit 8.3)] $6,000

Example 4

Assume the same facts as in Example 3. Kareem sells the asset on March 5, 2024. Kareem's cost recovery deduction for 2024 is $2,880 [$30,000 × 0.192 (Exhibit 8.3) × ½].

Mid-Quarter Convention

The half-year convention is based on the simplifying presumption that assets generally are acquired at an even pace throughout the tax year. However, Congress was concerned that taxpayers might defeat that presumption by placing large amounts of property in service toward the end of the taxable year (and by doing so, receive a half-year's depreciation on those large end-of-year acquisitions).

[7] § 168(d)(4)(A).

To inhibit this behavior, Congress added the **mid-quarter convention** that applies if more than 40 percent of the cost of property other than real estate (see text Section 8-2b) is placed in service during the last quarter of the year.[8] If the mid-quarter convention applies, property acquisitions are grouped by the quarter of acquisition. Acquisitions made during the first quarter are allowed 10.5 months (three and one-half quarters) of cost recovery in the first year; the second quarter, 7.5 months (two and one-half quarters); the third quarter, 4.5 months (one and one-half quarters); and the fourth quarter, 1.5 months (one-half quarter). The percentages are shown in Exhibit 8.4.

Example 5

Silver Corporation acquires the following new 5-year class property in 2022.

Property Acquisition Dates	Cost
February 15	$ 200,000
July 10	400,000
December 5	600,000
Total	$1,200,000

Because more than 40% ($600,000 ÷ $1,200,000 = 50%) of the acquisitions are in the last quarter, the mid-quarter convention applies. Silver's cost recovery allowances for the first two years are computed below.

2022	Mid-Quarter Convention Depreciation (Exhibit 8.4)	Total Depreciation
February 15	$200,000 × 0.35	$ 70,000
July 10	$400,000 × 0.15	60,000
December 5	$600,000 × 0.05	30,000
		$160,000

2023	Mid-Quarter Convention Depreciation (Exhibit 8.4)	Total Depreciation
February 15	$200,000 × 0.26	$ 52,000
July 10	$400,000 × 0.34	136,000
December 5	$600,000 × 0.38	228,000
		$416,000

Without the mid-quarter convention, Silver's 2022 cost recovery deduction would have been $240,000 [$1,200,000 × 0.20 (Exhibit 8.3)]. As a result, the mid-quarter convention reduces the taxpayer's available cost recovery deductions in the acquisition year (and defers those deductions to later years).

When "mid-quarter" property is sold, the property is treated as though it were sold at the midpoint of the quarter. So in the quarter when sold, cost recovery is allowed for one-half of the quarter.

[8] § 168(d)(3).

Example 6

Assume the same facts as in Example 5, except that Silver Corporation sells the $400,000 asset on November 30, 2023. The cost recovery deduction for 2023 is computed as follows (using Exhibit 8.4):

February 15	$200,000 × 0.26	$ 52,000
July 10	$400,000 × 0.34 × (3.5/4)	119,000
December 5	$600,000 × 0.38	228,000
Total cost recovery deduction		$399,000

The tax adjusted basis of the $400,000 asset when sold is $221,000 [$400,000 (cost) − $60,000 (2022 cost recovery) − $119,000 (2023 cost recovery)].

The Big Picture

Example 7

Return to the facts of *The Big Picture* on p. 8-1. If the placed-in-service date for the office furniture and fixtures and computers and peripheral equipment is September 29 and the placed-in-service date for the dental equipment is October 3, Dr. Payne's total cost recovery deduction is computed as follows:

Office furniture and fixtures:	
MACRS cost recovery $70,000 × 0.1071 (Exhibit 8.4)	$ 7,497
Computers and peripheral equipment:	
MACRS cost recovery $67,085 × 0.15 (Exhibit 8.4)	10,063
Dental equipment:	
MACRS cost recovery $475,000 × 0.0357 (Exhibit 8.4)	16,958
Total cost recovery deduction	$34,518

Note the implications of the mid-quarter convention. If the dental equipment had been placed in service before October 1 (the beginning of the fourth quarter), the total cost recovery deduction would have been $91,298 (as detailed on p. 8-1).

Qualified Improvement Property

Nonresidential realty has a 39-year life, and any improvements made to this property would normally have a 39-year life. An exception to this general rule is provided for **qualified improvement property**. Qualified improvement property is recovered over a 15-year life using the half-year convention and the straight-line method.[9]

Qualified improvement property is any improvement to an interior portion of nonresidential real property made after the property is placed in service, including leasehold improvements. However, it does not include the costs of an elevator or escalator or improvements that enlarge a building or modify its internal framework.

Example 8

Redbud, Inc., finishes construction of an office building in July 2021. It plans to lease the third floor of the building to a tenant. In January 2022, Crimson Enterprises leases the third floor and immediately builds out the rental space to meet its needs. It spends $50,000 on cubicles, shelving, and other nonpermanent additions. These improvements are qualified improvement property and will be recovered over 15 years using the half-year convention and straight-line method.

In 2022, Crimson's cost recovery deduction is $1,667 ($50,000 × 0.03333; see Exhibit 8.5 for cost recovery percentages).

Straight-Line Election

A taxpayer may *elect* to use the straight-line method for personal property.[10] If elected, the property is depreciated using the MACRS life of the asset with a half-year convention

[9] § 168(e)(6).

[10] § 168(b)(5).

or a mid-quarter convention, whichever applies. The election is available on a class-by-class and year-by-year basis (see Concept Summary 8.2). So, for example, a taxpayer could elect the straight-line method for 5-year MACRS assets placed in service during the current year; 5-year MACRS assets placed in service the following year are not bound by this choice. And the choice of having 5-year MACRS assets on the straight-line method would not apply to other personalty (e.g., the 3-year and 7-year MACRS classes) unless elected by the taxpayer. The percentages for the straight-line election with a half-year convention appear in Exhibit 8.5.

Concept Summary 8.2

Straight-Line Cost Recovery under MACRS (Personalty vs. Realty)

	Personalty	**Realty***
Convention	Half-year or mid-quarter	Mid-month
Cost recovery deduction in the year of disposition**	Half-year for year of sale or half-quarter for quarter of sale	Half-month for month of sale
Elective or mandatory	Elective	Mandatory
Breadth of election	Class by class	

*Straight-line method must be used.

**A disposition can include a sale, exchange, abandonment, or retirement. For simplicity, we will assume a sale in this chapter.

The Big Picture

Example 9

Return to the facts of *The Big Picture* on p. 8-1. If Dr. Payne elects the straight-line method of cost recovery, his total cost recovery deduction is computed as follows:

Office furniture and fixtures ($70,000 × 0.0714) (Exhibit 8.5)	$ 4,998
Computers and peripheral equipment ($67,085 × 0.10) (Exhibit 8.5)	6,709
Dental equipment ($475,000 × 0.0714) (Exhibit 8.5)	33,915
Total cost recovery deduction	$45,622

If Dr. Payne does not elect the straight-line cost recovery method, his cost recovery deduction is $91,298 (as detailed on p. 8-1).

The Big Picture

Example 10

Assume the same facts as in Example 9, except that Dr. Payne sells the computers and peripheral equipment on November 21, 2023. His cost recovery deduction for 2023 is $6,709 ($67,085 × 0.20 × ½) (Exhibit 8.5).

8-2b Realty: Recovery Periods and Methods

Under MACRS, the cost of most real property is recovered using the straight-line method. The recovery period for residential rental real estate is 27.5 years. **Residential rental real estate** includes property where 80 percent or more of the gross rental revenues are from residential units (e.g., an apartment building). Hotels, motels, and similar establishments are not residential rental property. Nonresidential real estate is recovered over 39 years.[11]

[11] §§ 168(b), (c), and (e). A 31.5-year life is used for nonresidential real estate placed in service before May 13, 1993.

Some items of real property are not treated as real estate under MACRS. For example, single-purpose agricultural structures are in the 10-year MACRS class. Land improvements are in the 15-year MACRS class.

All MACRS real estate is depreciated using the **mid-month convention**.[12] Under this convention, one-half month's cost recovery is allowed for the month the property is placed in service. So if a calendar year taxpayer places MACRS real estate in service on June 2 of the current tax year, it will be able to deduct six and one-half months of cost recovery (June 15 to December 31). If the property is sold before the end of the recovery period, one-half month's cost recovery is allowed for the month of sale (no matter when the property is sold).

As with personalty, the IRS provides tables to assist taxpayers in computing cost recovery on realty. Cost recovery is computed by multiplying the applicable rate (Exhibit 8.8) by the cost recovery basis.

Real Estate Cost Recovery

Example 11

Alec acquired a building on April 1, 2005, for $800,000. If the building is classified as residential rental real estate, the cost recovery deduction for 2022 is $29,088 (0.03636 × $800,000).

If, instead, the building is sold on October 7, 2022, the cost recovery deduction for 2022 is $23,028 [0.03636 (Exhibit 8.8) × (9.5/12) × $800,000].

Example 12

Marie acquired a building on March 2, 1993, for $1,000,000. If the building is classified as nonresidential real estate, the cost recovery deduction for 2022 is $31,740 (0.03174 × $1,000,000).

If, instead, the building is sold on January 5, 2022, the cost recovery deduction for 2022 is $1,323 [0.03174 (Exhibit 8.8) × (0.5/12) × $1,000,000].

Example 13

Marco acquired a building on November 19, 2022, for $1,200,000. If the building is classified as nonresidential real estate, the cost recovery deduction for 2022 is $3,852 [0.00321 (Exhibit 8.8) × $1,200,000]. The cost recovery deduction for 2023 is $30,768 [0.02564 (Exhibit 8.8) × $1,200,000].

If, instead, the building is sold on May 21, 2023, the cost recovery deduction for 2023 is $11,538 [0.02564 (Exhibit 8.8) × (4.5/12) × $1,200,000].

LO.3

Recognize when and how to make the § 179 expensing election, use additional first-year depreciation, and calculate the amount of these deductions as part of the MACRS calculation.

8-3 Modified Accelerated Cost Recovery System (MACRS): Special Rules

A number of special rules apply under MACRS. To encourage investment in capital assets and reduce the related compliance costs, Congress has implemented two rules: immediate expensing (§ 179) and additional first-year depreciation (also called bonus depreciation). To curb potential taxpayer abuses of certain assets—particularly when the assets are used for both business and personal purposes—Congress established specific rules for "listed property." Finally, Congress also created an alternative depreciation system (ADS) that taxpayers can use instead of MACRS. The ADS must be used in certain settings (e.g., for the alternative minimum tax).

8-3a Election to Expense Assets (§ 179)

Code § 179 (Election to Expense Certain Depreciable Business Assets) permits the taxpayer to deduct up to $1,080,000 in 2022 ($1,050,000 in 2021) of the acquisition cost of specific types of *trade or business* property. Amounts that are expensed under § 179 reduce the asset's basis for additional first-year depreciation (see text Section 8-3b) and MACRS cost recovery (see text Section 8-2a).

[12] § 168(d)(1).

The **§ 179 expensing** election (also known as the immediate expense election) applies to the acquisition cost of property placed in service during a year. Property to which § 179 applies includes tangible personal property, computer software, qualified improvement property, and certain real property (roofs; heating, ventilation, and air conditioning units; fire protection and alarm systems; security systems). In general, the immediate expense election is not available for real property or for property used for the production of income.[13]

Any elected § 179 expense is taken *before* additional first-year depreciation is computed (see text Section 8-3b). Any MACRS deduction is calculated on the basis of the asset net of the § 179 expense and any additional first-year depreciation.

§ 179 Election and Basis

Example 14

Allison acquires and places in service business equipment (a 5-year class asset) on February 1, 2022, at a cost of $80,000. It is the only asset she places in service in 2022. If Allison elects § 179, she can deduct the asset's entire cost in 2022. If not, she will use MACRS to recover the asset's cost over six years.

- If Allison elects § 179:

2022	§ 179 deduction	$80,000

- If Allison uses MACRS (see Exhibit 8.3):

2022	$80,000 × 0.20	$16,000
2023	$80,000 × 0.32	25,600
2024	$80,000 × 0.192	15,360
2025	$80,000 × 0.1152	9,216
2026	$80,000 × 0.1152	9,216
2027	$80,000 × 0.0576	4,608
		$80,000

Example 15

Assume the same facts as in Example 14. Allison sells the asset in 2024 for $50,000.

- If Allison elects § 179, the asset's adjusted basis is zero ($80,000 − $80,000) and she has a realized gain of $50,000.
- If Allison uses MACRS, the asset's adjusted basis is $30,720 and she has a realized gain of $19,280.

Selling price			$ 50,000
Cost		$ 80,000	
Less: Cost recovery			
2022 MACRS	$16,000		
2023 MACRS	25,600		
2024 MACRS ($15,360 × ½)	7,680	(49,280)	(30,720)
Realized gain			$ 19,280

Deduction Limitations

The § 179 expense deduction is subject to three limitations, applied in this order.

1. **Ceiling Amount.** A taxpayer's § 179 deduction cannot exceed an annual ceiling amount ($1,080,000 in 2022; $1,050,000 in 2021).
2. **Property Placed in Service Maximum.** The § 179 deduction ceiling amount ($1,080,000 in 2022) is reduced dollar for dollar when § 179 property placed in

[13]The § 179 amount allowed is per taxpayer, per year. On a joint return, the statutory amount applies to the couple. If the taxpayers are married and file separate returns, each spouse is eligible for 50% of the statutory amount.

The annual expense and phaseout amounts in § 179 ($1,000,000 and $2,500,000, respectively) are adjusted for inflation each year and rounded to the nearest $10,000 multiple.

service during the taxable year exceeds a specified maximum amount ($2,700,000 in 2022; $2,620,000 in 2021). In 2022, a taxpayer who places in service $3,780,000 or more of qualifying property ($1,080,000 + $2,700,000) cannot claim a § 179 deduction.

3. **Business Income Limitation.** The § 179 deduction allowed for a taxable year cannot exceed the taxpayer's business income for the year.

Ceiling Amount. A taxpayer can choose to use *all, part, or none* of the annual § 179 amount. If a business expects its marginal tax rate to increase in the future, it may decide *not* to use the § 179 deduction. In such a situation, it may be better to defer deductions to those later years. As discussed below, the business income limitation also may lead a business owner to choose not to expense assets.

Example 16

In 2022, Sonya places in service $450,000 of 7-year MACRS assets. Although she could immediately expense all of these assets, she would prefer to use § 179 on just $275,000 of the assets. She knows that combining this expense with regular MACRS depreciation effectively reduces her business income to zero, and she wants to defer the remaining deductions to future years when her marginal tax rate will be higher. As a result, Sonya's total cost recovery deduction for 2022 is calculated as follows:

§ 179 expense	$275,000
MACRS depreciation [($450,000 − $275,000) × 0.1429 (Exhibit 8.3)]	25,008
Total cost recovery deduction	$300,008

Property Placed in Service Maximum. This rule effectively restricts the application of the § 179 deduction to smaller businesses. In 2022, a business that places in service more than $2,700,000 of qualifying property will have its § 179 deduction reduced. A business that places in service $3,780,000 or more of qualifying property will have its § 179 deduction eliminated.

§ 179: Property Placed in Service Maximum

Example 17

During 2022, Madison places $1,245,000 of § 179 property in service for use in her engineering consultancy. Madison can take a $1,080,000 § 179 expense election; there is no reduction in the § 179 amount; the property placed in service maximum ($2,700,000) was not reached.

Example 18

During 2022, George places $3,300,000 of § 179 property in service for use in his manufacturing business (all assets are 7-year MACRS assets). Because George placed in service more than the $2,700,000 maximum, he must reduce his § 179 deduction ($3,300,000 − $2,700,000 = $600,000).

As a result, George's maximum § 179 deduction is $480,000 ($1,080,000 − $600,000). This reduction cannot be reclaimed in any way; it is permanently lost. George's total cost recovery deduction for 2022 is calculated as follows:

§ 179 expense	$480,000
MACRS depreciation [($3,300,000 − $480,000) × 0.1429 (Exhibit 8.3)]	402,978
Total cost recovery deduction	$882,978

George also places in service a $1,500,000 office building during 2022. Will this have any effect on the calculation above? No. The building is MACRS *realty*. Only *§ 179 property* is used to determine whether the § 179 ceiling amount ($1,080,000 in 2022) is reduced.

Note: George also can take additional first-year (bonus) depreciation on the 7-year MACRS assets. We will revisit this example after discussing bonus depreciation.

Business Income Limitation. The §179 deduction allowed for a taxable year cannot exceed the taxpayer's business income for the year. For this purpose, business income is calculated by deducting all business expenses except the § 179 deduction. As a result, a taxpayer's § 179 deduction cannot create (or increase) a net operating loss. A taxpayer's "business income" includes income not only from a sole proprietorship but also from wages and any allocated business income from a partnership or an S corporation.

Example 19

During 2022, Lance has a sole proprietorship through which he provides accounting and tax services that generated net income of $68,000. In addition, Lance is a 40% shareholder in a management consultancy operated as an S corporation. The S corporation pays Lance a salary of $40,000, and it recorded taxable income of $50,000. In this case, Lance's business income is $128,000 [$68,000 + $40,000 + $20,000 ($50,000 × 40%)].

Any § 179 amount in excess of business income is carried forward to future taxable years and added to other amounts eligible for expensing. Then the various limitations for that carryforward year are applied (i.e., the ceiling amount, the placed in service maximum amount, and the business income limitation).

Example 20

Jill owns a computer service and operates it as a sole proprietorship. In 2022, taxable income is $138,000 before considering any § 179 deduction. If Jill spends $2,830,000 on new equipment, her § 179 expense deduction for the year is computed as follows:

§ 179 deduction before adjustment	$1,080,000
Less: Dollar limitation reduction ($2,830,000 − $2,700,000)	(130,000)
Remaining § 179 deduction	$ 950,000
Business income limitation	$ 138,000
§ 179 deduction allowed	$ 138,000
§ 179 deduction carryforward ($950,000 − $138,000)	$ 812,000

Additional first-year (bonus) depreciation is *not* limited by a taxpayer's taxable income. Taxpayers who make large capital investments with limited taxable income may choose *not* to make a § 179 election and only take bonus depreciation on these items.

Effect on Basis

The basis of the property for cost recovery purposes is reduced by the § 179 amount after accounting for the current-year amount of property placed in service in excess of the specified maximum amount ($2,700,000 for 2022). This adjusted amount does not reflect any business income limitation.

Example 21

Assume the same facts as in Example 20. Jill's adjusted basis in the equipment for cost recovery purposes is $1,880,000 ($2,830,000 cost less the $950,000 § 179 expense amount before the business income limitation). If any portion of the $812,000 carryover (due to the business income limitation) is not deducted before the equipment is sold, this amount may be added back to the basis of the equipment in determining its adjusted basis.

Section 179 and the Mid-Quarter Convention

The mid-quarter convention generally results in smaller depreciation deductions in the asset's acquisition year. However, the basis of property used to determine whether the mid-quarter convention applies is derived *after* any § 179 immediate expense election.[14] As a result, a taxpayer may be able to avoid the mid-quarter convention by designating § 179 treatment for assets placed in service during the last quarter of the taxable year.

[14] Reg. § 1.168(d)–1(b)(4).

Example 22

Dimond Manufacturing places the following assets in service during 2022. All are 5-year class assets, and they are the only assets Dimond placed in service during the year.

Asset 1 (April 3, 2022)	$ 873,000
Asset 2 (July 17, 2022)	232,000
Asset 3 (October 22, 2022)	1,185,000
Total	$2,290,000

Since Dimond has placed more than 40% of the assets in service during the last quarter of the taxable year, the mid-quarter convention applies ($1,185,000 ÷ $2,290,000 = 51.7%). As a result, Dimond's cost recovery deduction for the year is computed as follows (see Exhibit 8.4).

Asset 1	$ 873,000 × 0.25	$ 218,250
Asset 2	$ 232,000 × 0.15	34,800
Asset 3	$1,185,000 × 0.05	59,250
Total		$ 312,300

However, if Dimond elects to expense $1,080,000 of the October 22 acquisition under § 179, the mid-quarter convention would not apply.

Asset 1 (April 3, 2022)	$ 873,000
Asset 2 (July 17, 2022)	232,000
Asset 3 (October 22, 2022; $1,185,000 − $1,080,000)	105,000
Total	$1,210,000

Now Dimond has placed only 8.7% ($105,000 ÷ $1,210,000) of the assets in service during the last quarter of the taxable year. As a result, the mid-quarter convention does not apply, and Dimond's cost recovery deduction for the year (including the § 179 expense election) is as follows.

MACRS depreciation (1,210,000 × 0.20; Exhibit 8.3)	$ 242,000
Section 179 expense (Asset 3)	1,080,000
Total cost recovery deduction	$1,322,000

As a result of its effective use of § 179, Dimond has increased its 2022 cost recovery deduction and simplified its reporting and record keeping related to these assets.

Conversion to Personal Use

Conversion of the expensed property to personal use at any time results in recapture income (see text Section 17-2). A property is converted to personal use if it is not used predominantly in a trade or business.[15]

Ethics & Equity Section 179 Limitation

Joe Moran worked in the construction business throughout most of his career. In June of the current year, he sold his interest in Ajax Enterprises LLC for a profit of $300,000. Shortly thereafter, Joe started his own business, which involves the redevelopment of distressed residential real estate.

In connection with his new business venture, Joe purchased a dump truck at a cost of $70,000. The new business struggled and showed a net operating loss for the year. Joe is considering expensing the $70,000 cost of the truck under § 179 on this year's tax return. Evaluate Joe's plan.

8-3b Additional First-Year Depreciation (Bonus Depreciation)

Congress often uses the tax system to stimulate the economy. An example is **additional first-year depreciation** (also referred to as bonus depreciation). In 2022, taxpayers are allowed to deduct 100 percent cost recovery of any *qualified property* that is placed in service (80 percent in 2023).[16]

[15] See Reg. § 1.179–1(e) and related examples.

[16] § 168(k). Additional first-year depreciation is allowed for qualified property placed in service after 2011 and before 2027. The additional first-year depreciation percentage (100% from 2018 to 2022) decreases to 80% in 2023, 60% in 2024, 40% in 2025, and 20% in 2026. No bonus depreciation is scheduled for tax years after 2026. Different rules applied between 2008 and 2017 (in general, the bonus depreciation percentage was no more than 50%).

The term *qualified property* includes most depreciable assets other than buildings with a recovery period of 20 years or less.[17] Bonus depreciation applies to both new *and* used property.[18]

The additional first-year depreciation is taken in the year in which the qualifying property is placed in service; it is computed after any immediate expense (§ 179) deduction is claimed. After the additional first-year depreciation is determined, the regular MACRS cost recovery deduction is calculated by multiplying the remaining cost recovery basis (original cost recovery basis less § 179 expense and additional first-year depreciation) by the appropriate MACRS percentage. A taxpayer may elect *not* to take additional first-year depreciation.

Example 23

Kelly acquires equipment (a 5-year class asset) on February 1, 2022, at a cost of $1,345,000 and elects to expense $1,080,000 under § 179. Kelly also chooses to take bonus depreciation. As a result, her total cost recovery deduction for the year is calculated as follows:

§ 179 expense	$1,080,000
Additional first-year depreciation [($1,345,000 − $1,080,000) × 100%]	265,000
Total cost recovery deduction	$1,345,000

Alternatively, Kelly could choose *not* to elect § 179 on the equipment and completely deduct the cost of the equipment using bonus depreciation.

8-3c Using § 179 and Bonus Depreciation Effectively

With 100 percent bonus depreciation available from 2018 through 2022, the majority of taxpayers will be able to completely deduct the cost of any MACRS personalty. However, there may be times when the taxpayer finds it better to defer some of these deductions to future years. This might be the case if the taxpayer expects marginal tax rates to increase over time. In addition, the limitations on excess business losses (see text Section 7-5) or the 80 percent of taxable income limit on net operating losses (see text Section 7-6) might lead a taxpayer not to use § 179 and/or bonus depreciation. In addition, certain assets might not qualify for § 179 expensing or bonus depreciation. If any of these conditions applies, then other considerations come into play.

Deferring MACRS Deductions to Future Years

Taxpayers may find it better not to use § 179 expensing and/or bonus depreciation to completely write off asset acquisitions. If taxpayers expect their marginal tax rates to increase over time (and in some instances, remain the same), it might be best, in present value terms, to defer some MACRS deductions to future years.

[17]Bonus depreciation is available for both "qualified film or television productions" and "qualified live theatrical productions." Bonus depreciation is *not* available to (1) any business that has floor-plan financing (e.g., an auto dealer) if the related interest is deducted in full or (2) regulated public utilities. In addition, bonus depreciation is *not* available on any asset that is required to use ADS depreciation.

[18]Effective for property placed in service after September 27, 2017. Used property will qualify as long as it is the taxpayer's first use of the property. § 168(k)(2)(E)(ii)(I).

Example 24

Aditi is married and operates a small business in Fairfax, Virginia. During 2022, she purchases $550,000 of equipment (5-year MACRS assets) for use in her business. Aditi and her spouse report $586,900 of taxable income before considering any cost recovery related to the equipment. Their marginal tax rate is 35%.

Aditi is confident that her business will grow significantly over the next few years and expects her marginal tax rate to remain at least 35% during that time. As a result, she is wondering whether to use bonus depreciation on the entire 2022 purchase or spread her MACRS deductions over the next few years.

If Aditi takes $550,000 of bonus depreciation in 2022, she and her spouse will have tax savings of $148,904.* However, much of the bonus depreciation will offset income that would have been taxed at rates lower than 35%.

Another option is to take just enough cost recovery (both bonus depreciation and regular MACRS) to reduce the couple's taxable income from $586,900 to $431,900 (the bottom of the 35% rate bracket in 2022). We can determine this combined amount using the following formula:

Bonus depreciation + [($550,000 − Bonus depreciation) × 20% (first-year MACRS)] = $155,000

Solving for bonus depreciation yields $56,250. So we can reduce the couple's taxable income to $431,900 by taking bonus depreciation of $56,250 and the usual MACRS of $98,750 [($550,000 − $56,250) × 20%].

If we assume a 5% discount rate on future tax savings, Aditi and her spouse will save $178,386 in taxes by deferring some of the available cost recovery deductions and using it to offset future income that would otherwise be subject to a 35% tax rate.

	2022	2023	2024	2025	2026	2027
Normal MACRS	$493,750	$493,750	$493,750	$493,750	$493,750	$493,750
MACRS factor	× 0.2000	× 0.3200	× 0.1920	× 0.1152	× 0.1152	× 0.0576
MACRS depreciation	$ 98,750	$158,000	$ 94,800	$ 56,880	$ 56,880	$ 28,440
Bonus depreciation	56,250	−0−	−0−	−0−	−0−	−0−
Total MACRS deduction	$155,000	$158,000	$ 94,800	$ 56,880	$ 56,880	$ 28,440
Marginal tax rate	× 35%	× 35%	× 35%	× 35%	× 35%	× 35%
Tax savings	$ 54,250	$ 55,300	$ 33,180	$ 19,908	$ 19,908	$ 9,954
PV factors @ 5% (Appendix E)	× 1.0000	× 0.9524	× 0.9070	× 0.8638	× 0.8227	× 0.7835
	$ 54,250	$ 52,668	$ 30,094	$ 17,197	$ 16,378	$ 7,799
Net present value	$178,386					

Overall, the combination of $56,250 bonus depreciation in 2022 plus MACRS depreciation in 2022 through 2027 provides a better outcome for Aditi and her spouse, generating $29,482 of tax savings in present value terms over the next six years ($178,386 tax savings by deferring MACRS deductions *less* $148,904 tax savings by using $550,000 of bonus depreciation in 2022).

* Tax on $586,900 = $152,921 {$98,671 + [($586,900 − $431,900) × 35%]}; tax on $36,900 = $4,017 [$2,055 + ($16,350 × 12%)].

Choosing Assets for Immediate Expensing

The § 179 deduction can be allocated to reduce the basis of qualifying assets in any manner the taxpayer chooses. This allows the deduction to be allocated proportionally across all assets acquired during the year or to specific assets identified by the taxpayer. This flexibility is important.

Two general rules might affect this choice. First, taxpayers generally should *not* use the § 179 election on automobiles. Automobiles are subject to special cost recovery rules (and annual limits), which we discuss later in this chapter. Second, given the time value of money, taxpayers should accelerate deductions to the earliest year possible. This is accomplished by expensing the assets with the *longest* MACRS lives first.

Example 25

During 2022, Dexter purchases manufacturing equipment (a 7-year MACRS asset) costing $725,000 and a computer system costing $480,000 (a 5-year MACRS asset). As the total amount of MACRS assets placed in service for the year ($1,205,000; $725,000 + $480,000) is less than $2,700,000, there is no reduction in the $1,080,000 § 179 deduction.

Dexter chooses not to take bonus depreciation. How should Dexter allocate his $1,080,000 § 179 expense election?

Dexter should expense the longest-lived MACRS asset first (the equipment; the 7-year MACRS asset). If he makes this choice, Dexter's total cost recovery deduction in 2022 is $1,105,000, calculated as follows:

Equipment (7-year MACRS asset)	
§ 179 expense	$ 725,000
Computer system (5-year MACRS asset)	
§ 179 expense ($1,080,000 − $725,000)	355,000
MACRS cost recovery [($480,000 − $355,000) × 0.20 (Exhibit 8.3)]	25,000
Total cost recovery deduction	$1,105,000

If Dexter were to allocate the § 179 expense election to the machinery (MACRS 5-year asset), his total cost recovery deduction in 2022 would be only $1,096,434, calculated as follows:

Computer system (5-year MACRS asset)	
§ 179 expense	$ 480,000
Equipment (7-year MACRS asset)	
§ 179 expense ($1,080,000 − $480,000)	600,000
MACRS cost recovery [($725,000 − $600,000) × 0.1429 (Exhibit 8.3)]	17,863
Total cost recovery deduction	$1,097,863

No matter which asset is expensed, after using both § 179 and bonus depreciation, $125,000 is subject to MACRS cost recovery. However, if the 7-year MACRS asset is expensed, this $125,000 is cost recovered over six tax years (here, the $125,000 relates to the 5-year MACRS asset). If the 5-year MACRS asset is expensed, the $125,000 will be recovered over eight tax years (here, the $125,000 relates to the 7-year MACRS asset).

Using the § 179 expense election on the longest-lived asset accelerates overall cost recovery deductions to earlier years, gaining a time-value-of-money advantage for the taxpayer.

Using Both § 179 and Bonus Depreciation

In general, in 2022, a business that places in service $1,080,000 or less of qualifying § 179 property will exclusively use § 179 to immediately expense all of those assets, while a business placing in service $3,780,000 or more of qualifying assets (the point at which the § 179 amount is completely phased out; $1,080,000 + $2,700,000) will qualify only for bonus depreciation. Any business placing in service between $1,080,000 and $3,780,000 of qualifying § 179 property will be able to use a combination of both § 179 and bonus depreciation (see Concept Summary 8.3).[19]

Concept Summary 8.3

Using § 179 and Bonus Depreciation in 2022

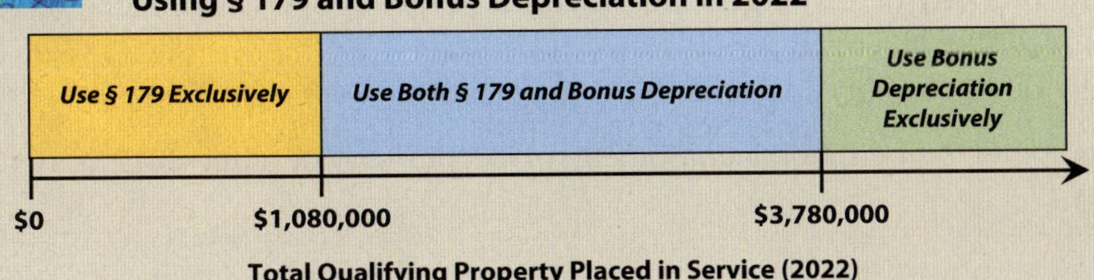

[19]This general rule applies to the vast majority of taxpayers. However, it would not apply if the § 179 taxable income limitation applied or the taxpayer chose to defer deductions to later tax years (e.g., if the taxpayer expects marginal tax rates to increase) to gain a time value of money advantage.

Example 26

Return to the facts of Example 18. Given that George has placed $3,300,000 of 7-year MACRS assets in service during 2022, he can use both § 179 and additional first-year depreciation (see Concept Summary 8.3). If George uses both § 179 and bonus depreciation, his total cost recovery deduction will increase to $3,300,000.

§ 179 expense	$ 480,000
Additional first-year depreciation [($3,300,000 − $480,000) × 100%]	2,820,000
Total cost recovery deduction	$3,300,000

As discussed above, George might choose to use only a portion of the § 179 election and/or choose not to use bonus depreciation. However, it is possible for George to deduct all of his 2022 acquisitions immediately.

The Big Picture

Example 27

Return to the facts of *The Big Picture* on p. 8-1 and assume that the tax year is 2022. Dr. Payne has placed $612,085 of assets in service ($70,000 + $67,085 + $475,000). Because this amount is less than $2,700,000, there is no reduction in the $1,080,000 maximum § 179 deduction.

If Dr. Payne has sufficient business income to avoid § 179's business income limitation, he can use § 179 to expense all of the assets placed in service in 2022 ($612,085).

If § 179's business income limitation comes into play, Dr. Payne can elect out of § 179 and deduct $612,085 using additional first-year depreciation (which has no income limitation). In this case, however, other limitations might affect his decision (including the excess business loss limitation; see text Section 7-5). Or he can apply § 179 or additional first-year depreciation to selected assets, reducing his taxable income this year and deferring some deductions to future years.

If Dr. Payne chooses to use neither § 179 nor additional first-year depreciation, his cost recovery deduction will be $91,298 (as detailed on p. 8-1).

LO.4

Identify listed property and apply the deduction limitations on listed property and on luxury automobiles.

8-3d Business and Personal Use of Automobiles and Other Listed Property

Limits exist on cost recovery deductions for automobiles and other listed property that are used for both personal and business purposes.[20] If listed property is not *predominantly used* for business purposes when placed in service, it is not eligible for the accelerated methods built into MACRS, the immediate expense election (§ 179), or bonus depreciation.

If not *predominantly used* for business when placed in service, the listed property's cost must be recovered using the *straight-line method* (see Exhibit 8.5). Further, the straight-line method must continue to be used even if, at some later date, the property *is* predominantly used for business.

Listed property includes:

- Any passenger automobile.
- Any other property used as a means of transportation.
- Any property of a type generally used for purposes of entertainment, recreation, or amusement.
- Any other property specified in the Regulations.

A computer or peripheral equipment placed in service after 2017 is not listed property.[21]

[20] § 280F.

[21] § 280F(d)(4)(A). A computer or peripheral equipment placed in service before 2018 is subject to the listed property rules.

Automobiles and Other Listed Property Used Predominantly in Business

For listed property to be *predominantly used in business*, its *business use* must exceed 50 percent.[22] The use of listed property for production of income does not qualify as business use for purposes of the more-than-50% test. However, both production of income and business use percentages are used to compute the cost recovery deduction.

Example 28

On September 1, 2022, Emma places in service listed property (MACRS 5-year property). The property cost $10,000. She elects not to take any available additional first-year depreciation.

If Emma uses the property 40% for business and 25% for the production of income, the property is not considered as predominantly used for business. The cost is recovered using straight-line cost recovery. Emma's cost recovery allowance for the year is $650 ($10,000 × 0.10 × 65%).

If, however, Emma uses the property 60% for business and 25% for the production of income, the property is considered as used predominantly for business. As a result, she may use the regular MACRS method. Emma's cost recovery allowance for the year is $1,700 ($10,000 × 0.20 × 85%).

In determining the percentage of business use of listed property, a mileage-based percentage is used for automobiles. For other listed property, one employs the most appropriate unit of time (e.g., hours) for which the property actually is used (rather than its availability for use).[23]

Limits on Cost Recovery for Automobiles

The law places further limits on the annual cost recovery deductions for passenger automobiles. These dollar limits were imposed because of the belief that the tax system was being used to underwrite automobiles whose cost and luxury far exceeded what was needed for the taxpayer's business use.

A *passenger automobile* is any four-wheeled vehicle manufactured for use on public streets, roads, and highways with an unloaded gross vehicle weight (GVW) rating of 6,000 pounds or less.[24] This definition specifically excludes vehicles used directly in the business of transporting people or property for compensation [e.g., taxicabs (including autos used for Uber or Lyft), ambulances, hearses, and trucks and vans].

The following "luxury auto" depreciation limits apply.[25]

Date Placed in Service	First Year	Second Year	Third Year	Fourth and Later Years
2021*	$10,200	$16,400	$9,800	$5,860
2019–2020	$10,100	$16,100	$9,700	$5,760
2018	$10,000	$16,000	$9,600	$5,760

*Because the 2022 indexed amounts were not available when we published, the 2021 amounts are used in the Examples and end-of-chapter problem materials.

In the event a passenger automobile used predominantly for business qualifies for additional first-year depreciation, the first-year recovery limitation is increased by $8,000 for automobiles placed in service before 2027.[26] As a result, for acquisitions made in 2021, the initial-year cost recovery limitation increases from $10,200 to $18,200 ($10,200 + $8,000).[27]

The luxury auto limits must be reduced proportionally for any personal use of the auto. In addition, the limitation in the first year includes any amount the taxpayer elects

[22] § 280F(b)(3).

[23] Reg. § 1.280F–6T(e).

[24] § 280F(d)(5).

[25] § 280F(a)(1); Rev.Proc. 2021–31. Cost recovery limitations for years prior to 2018 are found in IRS Publication 463.

[26] § 168(k)(2)(F)(i).

[27] Different cost recovery limitations apply to trucks and vans and to electric automobiles.

to expense under § 179.[28] If the passenger automobile is used partly for personal use, the personal use percentage is ignored for the purpose of determining the unrecovered cost available for deduction in later years.

Example 29

On July 1, 2022, Dan places in service a new automobile that cost $55,000. He does not elect § 179 expensing, and he elects not to take any available additional first-year depreciation. The car is used 80% for business and 20% for personal use in each tax year. Dan chooses the MACRS 200% declining-balance method of cost recovery (the auto is a 5-year asset).

The depreciation computation for 2022 through 2027 is summarized in the table below. The cost recovery allowed is the lesser of the MACRS amount or the recovery limitation.

Year	MACRS Amount	Recovery Limitation	Depreciation Allowed
2022	$8,800	$8,160	$ 8,160
	($55,000 × 0.2000 × 80%)	($10,200 × 80%)	
2023	$14,080	$13,120	$13,120
	($55,000 × 0.3200 × 80%)	($16,400 × 80%)	
2024	$8,448	$7,840	$ 7,840
	($55,000 × 0.1920 × 80%)	($9,800 × 80%)	
2025	$5,069	$4,688	$ 4,688
	($55,000 × 0.1152 × 80%)	($5,860 × 80%)	
2026	$5,069	$4,688	$ 4,688
	($55,000 × 0.1152 × 80%)	($5,860 × 80%)	
2027	$2,534	$4,688	$ 2,534
	($55,000 × 0.0576 × 80%)	($5,860 × 80%)	

If Dan continues to use the car after 2027, his cost recovery is limited to the lesser of the recoverable basis or the recovery limitation (i.e., $5,860 × business use percentage). For this purpose, the recoverable basis is computed as if the full recovery limitation was allowed even if it was not. As a result, the recoverable basis as of January 1, 2028, is $3,712 ($55,000 − $10,200 − $16,400 − $9,800 − $5,860 − $5,860 − $3,168*).

If Dan takes additional first-year depreciation, the calculated amount of additional first-year depreciation is $44,000 ($55,000 × 100% × 80%). However, the deduction would be limited to $14,560 [($8,000 + $10,200) × 80%].

* $55,000 × 0.0576 × 100%; this is the full 2027 MACRS amount (which is less than the $5,860 recovery limitation for the year).

The cost recovery limitations are maximum amounts. If the regular MACRS calculation produces a smaller amount of cost recovery, the smaller amount is used.

Example 30

On April 2, 2022, Gail places in service a used automobile that cost $10,200. The car is used 70% for business and 30% for personal use. The cost recovery allowance for 2022 is $1,428 ($10,200 × 0.20 MACRS table factor × 70%), not $7,140 ($10,200 passenger auto maximum × 70%).

Special Limitation for Sport-Utility Vehicles (SUVs)

Some sport-utility vehicles (SUVs) are not considered passenger automobiles and, therefore, are not subject to the luxury automobile limitations. However, in 2022, a $27,000 limit applies for the § 179 deduction when the luxury auto limits do not apply ($26,200 in 2021). The limit is in effect for SUVs with an unloaded GVW rating of more than 6,000 pounds and not more than 14,000 pounds.[29]

[28] § 280F(d)(1).

[29] § 179(b)(5).

Example 31

During 2022, Jay acquires and places in service a new SUV that cost $70,700 and has a GVW of 8,000 pounds. Jay uses the vehicle 100% of the time for business use and elects not to use bonus depreciation. The total cost recovery deduction for 2022 with respect to the SUV is computed as follows:

§ 179 expense	$27,000
Regular MACRS calculation [($70,700 − $27,000) × 0.20 (Exhibit 8.3)]	8,740
Total cost recovery deduction	$35,740

If Jay chooses to use bonus depreciation on the SUV, then the entire $70,700 cost will be recovered in 2022 ($27,000 § 179 and $43,700 bonus depreciation).

Automobiles and Other Listed Property Not Used Predominantly in Business

For automobiles and other listed property not used predominantly in business in the year of acquisition (i.e., 50 percent or less), the straight-line method under the alternative depreciation system is required (see text Section 8-3e).[30] Under this system, the straight-line recovery period for automobiles is five years. However, the cost recovery deduction for any passenger automobile cannot exceed the luxury auto limit.

Auto Not Predominantly Used in Business

Example 32

On July 27, 2022, Fred places in service an automobile that cost $20,000. The auto is used 40% for business and 60% for personal use. The cost recovery allowance for 2022 is $800 [$20,000 × 0.10 (Exhibit 8.7) × 40%].

Example 33

Assume the same facts as in Example 32, except that the automobile cost $50,000. The cost recovery allowance for 2022 is $2,000 [$50,000 × 0.10 (Exhibit 8.7) × 40%; $2,000 is less than 40% of the first-year limit].

The straight-line method is used even if, at some later date, the business use of the property increases to more than 50 percent (although the cost recovery allowed will reflect the increase in business use).

Example 34

Assume the same facts as in Example 32, except that in 2023, Fred uses the automobile 70% for business and 30% for personal use. Fred's cost recovery allowance for 2023 is $2,800 [$20,000 × 0.20 (Exhibit 8.7) × 70%], which is less than 70% of the second-year limit.

Change from Predominantly Business Use

If the business use percentage of listed property falls to 50 percent or less after the year the property is placed in service, the property is subject to *cost recovery recapture*. The amount required to be recaptured and included in the taxpayer's ordinary income is the *excess cost recovery*.

Excess cost recovery is the excess of the cost recovery deduction taken in prior years using the regular MACRS method over the amount that would have been allowed if the straight-line method had been used since the property was placed in service.[31]

[30] § 280F(b)(1).

[31] § 280F(b)(2).

Example 35

Seth purchased a new car on January 22, 2022, at a cost of $40,000. Business use was 80% in 2022, 70% in 2023, 40% in 2024, and 60% in 2025. Seth elects not to take any available additional first-year depreciation. Seth's excess cost recovery to be recaptured as ordinary income in 2024 is computed as follows:

2022	
MACRS ($40,000 × 0.20 × 80%, limited to $10,200 × 80%)	$ 6,400
Straight-line ($40,000 × 0.10 × 80%, limited to $10,200 × 80%)	(3,200)
Excess	$ 3,200
2023	
MACRS ($40,000 × 0.32 × 70%, limited to $16,400 × 70%)	$ 8,960
Straight-line ($40,000 × 0.20 × 70%, limited to $16,400 × 70%)	(5,600)
Excess	$ 3,360
2024	
2022 excess	$ 3,200
2023 excess	3,360
Ordinary income recapture	$ 6,560

After the business use of the listed property drops below the more-than-50% level, the straight-line method is used for the remaining life of the property.

Example 36

Assume the same facts as in Example 35. Seth's cost recovery deductions for 2024 and 2025 are:

2024	$3,200 [$40,000 × 0.20 × 40% ($3,200), limited to $9,800 × 40% ($3,920)]
2025	$3,516 [$40,000 × 0.20 × 60% ($4,800), limited to $5,860 × 60% ($3,516)]

Leased Automobiles

Taxpayers who lease rather than purchase a passenger automobile for business purposes are not subject to the luxury auto limits. To prevent taxpayers from circumventing the luxury auto limits by deducting the full amount of rental payments associated with a luxury automobile leased for business, the law requires these taxpayers to report an *inclusion amount* in gross income.

The inclusion amount (determined from an IRS table) is based on the fair market value of the automobile. It must be computed for each taxable year the automobile is leased. Once determined, the inclusion amount is prorated for the number of days the auto is used during the taxable year. The prorated dollar amount then is multiplied by the business and income-producing use percentage.[32] The taxpayer deducts the lease payments, multiplied by the business and income-producing use percentage. In effect, the taxpayer's annual deduction for the lease payment is reduced by the inclusion amount.

[32] Reg. § 1.280F–7(a).

Example 37

On April 1, 2022, Jim leases and places in service a passenger automobile worth $88,600. The lease is to be for a period of five years. During the taxable years 2022 and 2023, Jim uses the automobile 70% for business and 30% for personal use.

Assuming that the dollar amounts from the IRS table for 2022 and 2023 are $12 and $27, respectively, Jim includes in gross income:

2022	$\$12 \times (275/365) \times 70\% = \$6$
2023	$\$27 \times (365/365) \times 70\% = \$19$

In each year, Jim still can deduct 70% of the lease payments made (i.e., the amount related to his business use of the auto).

Substantiation Requirements

The substantiation requirements of § 274 apply to listed property. A taxpayer must be able to prove for any business use the amount of expense or use, the time and place of use, the business purpose for the use, and the business relationship to the taxpayer of persons using the property.

Substantiation requires adequate records or sufficient evidence corroborating the taxpayer's statement. For example, to document business use of an automobile, it is expected that a taxpayer maintain a contemporaneous record of business miles driven (versus other miles), any expenses incurred (e.g., fuel, repairs, business tolls, parking), and the business reason for the auto's use.[33]

8-3e Alternative Depreciation System (ADS)

LO.5 **Determine when and how to use the alternative depreciation system (ADS).**

The **alternative depreciation system (ADS)** must be used:[34]

- To calculate the portion of depreciation treated as an alternative minimum tax (AMT) adjustment for purposes of the individual AMT (see Chapter 12).[35]
- For residential and nonresidential real estate and any qualified improvement property placed in service after 2017 by a "real property trade or business" that opts out of the interest expense limitations of § 163(j). In general, these interest expense limitation rules only apply to businesses with annual gross receipts in excess of $27 million (in 2022; $26 million in 2021).
- To compute depreciation allowances for earnings and profits purposes (see text Section 20-4a).

In general, ADS depreciation is computed using the straight-line method. However, for AMT, depreciation of personal property is computed using the 150 percent declining-balance method with a switch to the straight-line method when appropriate.

The taxpayer must use the half-year or the mid-quarter convention, whichever is applicable, for all property other than real estate. The mid-month convention is used for real estate. Under ADS, personal property (other than qualified improvement property) is depreciated using the appropriate asset class life (e.g., 5- or 7-year) and the 150 percent declining-balance method (see Exhibits 8.6 and 8.7). Under ADS, qualified improvement property has a 20-year life, residential rental real estate has a 30-year life, and nonresidential real estate has a 40-year life; all are depreciated using the straight-line method (see Exhibits 8.5 and 8.9).[36]

[33]§§ 274(d) and (i). These substantiation requirements do not apply to vehicles that, by reason of their nature, are not likely to be used more than a *de minimis* amount for personal purposes.

[34]§ 168(g). ADS also must be used to compute cost recovery for property used predominantly outside the United States, by a tax-exempt entity, and in several other situations.

[35]This AMT adjustment applies for real and personal property placed in service before 1999. However, it also applies for personal property placed in service after 1998 if the taxpayer uses the 200% declining-balance method for regular income tax purposes. See text Section 12-2a.

[36]Residential rental real estate placed in service before 2018 uses an ADS life of 40 years. The class life for certain properties described in § 168(e)(3) is specially determined under § 168(g)(3)(B).

To simplify reporting, taxpayers may *elect* to use the 150 percent declining-balance method to compute cost recovery for the regular income tax (rather than the 200 percent declining-balance method that is available for personal property). If this election is made, there is no difference between the regular income tax and AMT cost recovery.[37]

Example 38

On March 1, 2022, Abby purchases computer-based telephone central office switching equipment for $80,000. Abby elects not to take any available additional first-year depreciation. If Abby uses regular MACRS cost recovery (assuming no § 179 election), her deduction for 2022 is $16,000 [$80,000 × 0.20 (Exhibit 8.3, 5-year class property)].

If Abby elects to use ADS 150% declining-balance cost recovery for the regular income tax (assuming no § 179 election), the cost recovery allowance for 2022 is $12,000 [$80,000 × 0.15 (Exhibit 8.6, 5-year class property)].

Rather than determining depreciation under the regular MACRS method, taxpayers may *elect* straight-line under ADS. One reason for making this election is to defer cost recovery deductions to later years (presuming that marginal tax rates will be higher in those years). Another reason is to simplify record keeping, since the cost recovery deduction will be the same as earnings and profits depreciation.[38]

Example 39

Palladium, Inc., acquires an office building on March 17, 2022, for $1,700,000. It takes the maximum cost recovery allowance for determining taxable income. For 2022, Palladium deducts $34,561 [$1,700,000 × 0.02033 (Exhibit 8.8)].

However, Palladium's cost recovery for computing its earnings and profits is only $33,643 [$1,700,000 × 0.01979 (Exhibit 8.9)].

LO.6

Report cost recovery deductions appropriately.

8-4 Reporting Procedures

Sole proprietors engaged in a business file a Schedule C, Profit or Loss from Business, to accompany Form 1040. A 2021 Schedule C is illustrated; the 2022 Schedule C was not available when we published.

The top part of page 1 requests certain key information about the taxpayer (e.g., name, address, Social Security number, principal business activity, and accounting method used). Part I provides for the reporting of items of income. If the business requires the use of inventories and the computation of cost of goods sold (see text Section 18-2 for when this is necessary), Part III must be completed and the cost of goods sold amount transferred to line 4 of Part I.

Part II allows for the reporting of deductions. Some of the deductions discussed in this chapter and their location on the form are depletion (line 12) and depreciation (line 13). Other expenses (line 27a) include those items not already covered (see lines 8 through 26). An example is research and experimental expenditures.

If depreciation is claimed, Form 4562 should be completed. A 2021 Form 4562 is illustrated; the 2022 Form 4562 was not available when we published. The amount reported on line 22 of Form 4562 is transferred to line 13 of Part II of Schedule C.

[37]For personal property placed in service before 1999, taxpayers making the election use the ADS recovery periods in computing cost recovery for the regular income tax. The ADS recovery periods generally are longer than the regular recovery periods under MACRS.

[38]This straight-line election is made on a year-by-year basis. For property other than real estate, the election is made by MACRS class and applies to all assets in that MACRS class. So, for example, the election could be made for 7-year MACRS property and not for 5-year MACRS property placed in service during the same year. For real estate, the election is made on a property-by-property basis.

Example 40

Thomas Andrews, Social Security number 111-11-1111, was employed as an accountant until May 2021, when he opened his own practice as a CPA (Andrews Accounting Services; business activity code: 541211). His business address is 279 Mountain View, Ogden, UT 84201. Andrews keeps his books on the cash basis and reported the following revenue and business expenses in 2021.

a. Revenue from accounting practice, $192,000.
b. Insurance, $5,000.
c. Office supplies, $4,000.
d. Office rent, $16,000.
e. Copier lease payments, $3,000.
f. Licenses, $2,000.
g. New furniture and fixtures were acquired on May 10 for $142,000. Thomas elects § 179 expensing and uses the regular MACRS cost recovery method.

Thomas reports the above information on Schedule C and Form 4562 as illustrated on the following pages.

8-5 Amortization

LO.7

Identify intangible assets that are eligible for amortization and calculate the amount of the deduction.

Taxpayers can recover the costs of certain intangible assets through an **amortization** deduction. The amount of the deduction is determined by amortizing the adjusted basis of these intangibles ratably over a 15-year period beginning in the month in which the intangible is acquired.[39]

Code § 197 covers the amortization of most intangibles. *Amortizable § 197 intangibles* include most intangibles acquired after August 10, 1993, and acquired in connection with the acquisition of a business, including goodwill, going-concern value, franchises, trademarks, copyrights, patents, and covenants not to compete. Generally, self-created intangibles are *not* § 197 intangibles.

The 15-year amortization period applies regardless of the actual useful life of an amortizable § 197 intangible. No other depreciation or amortization deduction is permitted for these intangibles.

Example 41

On June 1, 2022, Neil purchased and began operating the Falcon Café. Of the purchase price, $90,000 is allocated to goodwill. The 2022 § 197 amortization deduction is $3,500 [($90,000 ÷ 15) × (7/12)].

Startup expenditures are partially amortizable by election.[40] A taxpayer must make this election no later than the due date of the return for the taxable year in which the trade or business begins.[41] If no election is made, the startup expenditures are capitalized.[42]

The amortization election for startup expenditures allows the taxpayer to deduct the smaller of (1) the startup expenditures related to the trade or business or (2) $5,000. The $5,000 maximum is reduced dollar for dollar by the amount of startup expenditures in excess of $50,000. As a result, if startup expenditures equal or exceed $55,000, no immediate deduction is allowed. Any startup expenditures not deducted are amortized ratably over a 180-month period, beginning in the month in which the trade or business begins.[43]

[39] § 197(a).
[40] §§ 195(a) and (b).
[41] § 195(d).
[42] § 195(a).
[43] §§ 195(b)(1)(A) and (B).

Form **4562**

Department of the Treasury
Internal Revenue Service (99)

Depreciation and Amortization

(Including Information on Listed Property)

▶ Attach to your tax return.

▶ Go to *www.irs.gov/Form4562* for instructions and the latest information.

OMB No. 1545-0172

2021

Attachment Sequence No. 179

Name(s) shown on return	Business or activity to which this form relates	Identifying number
Thomas Andrews	*Andrews Accounting Services*	*111-11-1111*

Part I Election To Expense Certain Property Under Section 179

Note: If you have any listed property, complete Part V before you complete Part I.

1	Maximum amount (see instructions)	1	*1,050,000*
2	Total cost of section 179 property placed in service (see instructions)	2	*142,000*
3	Threshold cost of section 179 property before reduction in limitation (see instructions)	3	*2,620,000*
4	Reduction in limitation. Subtract line 3 from line 2. If zero or less, enter -0-	4	*-0-*
5	Dollar limitation for tax year. Subtract line 4 from line 1. If zero or less, enter -0-. If married filing separately, see instructions	5	*142,000*

6 (a) Description of property	(b) Cost (business use only)	(c) Elected cost
Furniture and Fixtures	*142,000*	*142,000*
7 Listed property. Enter the amount from line 29	7	

8	Total elected cost of section 179 property. Add amounts in column (c), lines 6 and 7	8	*142,000*
9	Tentative deduction. Enter the **smaller** of line 5 or line 8	9	*142,000*
10	Carryover of disallowed deduction from line 13 of your 2020 Form 4562	10	*-0-*
11	Business income limitation. Enter the smaller of business income (not less than zero) or line 5. See instructions	11	*142,000*
12	Section 179 expense deduction. Add lines 9 and 10, but don't enter more than line 11	12	*142,000*
13	Carryover of disallowed deduction to 2022. Add lines 9 and 10, less line 12 ▶ 13		

Note: Don't use Part II or Part III below for listed property. Instead, use Part V.

Part II Special Depreciation Allowance and Other Depreciation (Don't include listed property. See instructions.**)**

14	Special depreciation allowance for qualified property (other than listed property) placed in service during the tax year. See instructions	14	
15	Property subject to section 168(f)(1) election	15	
16	Other depreciation (including ACRS)	16	

Part III MACRS Depreciation (Don't include listed property. See instructions.**)**

Section A

17	MACRS deductions for assets placed in service in tax years beginning before 2021	17	
18	If you are electing to group any assets placed in service during the tax year into one or more general asset accounts, check here ▶ ☐		

Section B—Assets Placed in Service During 2021 Tax Year Using the General Depreciation System

(a) Classification of property	(b) Month and year placed in service	(c) Basis for depreciation (business/investment use only—see instructions)	(d) Recovery period	(e) Convention	(f) Method	(g) Depreciation deduction
19a 3-year property						
b 5-year property						
c 7-year property						
d 10-year property						
e 15-year property						
f 20-year property						
g 25-year property			25 yrs.		S/L	
h Residential rental			27.5 yrs.	MM	S/L	
property			27.5 yrs.	MM	S/L	
i Nonresidential real			39 yrs.	MM	S/L	
property				MM	S/L	

Section C—Assets Placed in Service During 2021 Tax Year Using the Alternative Depreciation System

20a Class life					S/L	
b 12-year			12 yrs.		S/L	
c 30-year			30 yrs.	MM	S/L	
d 40-year			40 yrs.	MM	S/L	

Part IV Summary (See instructions.)

21	Listed property. Enter amount from line 28	21	
22	**Total.** Add amounts from line 12, lines 14 through 17, lines 19 and 20 in column (g), and line 21. Enter here and on the appropriate lines of your return. Partnerships and S corporations—see instructions	22	*142,000*
23	For assets shown above and placed in service during the current year, enter the portion of the basis attributable to section 263A costs	23	

For Paperwork Reduction Act Notice, see separate instructions. Cat. No. 12906N Form **4562** (2021)

SCHEDULE C (Form 1040)

Department of the Treasury
Internal Revenue Service (99)

Profit or Loss From Business
(Sole Proprietorship)

▶ Go to *www.irs.gov/ScheduleC* for instructions and the latest information.
▶ Attach to Form 1040, 1040-SR, 1040-NR, or 1041; partnerships must generally file Form 1065.

OMB No. 1545-0074
2021
Attachment Sequence No. **09**

Name of proprietor: *Thomas Andrews*
Social security number (SSN): *111-11-1111*

A Principal business or profession, including product or service (see instructions): *Certified Public Accountant*
B Enter code from instructions ▶ *5 4 1 2 1 1*

C Business name. If no separate business name, leave blank. *Andrews Accounting Services*
D Employer ID number (EIN) (see instr.)

E Business address (including suite or room no.) ▶ *279 Mountain View*
City, town or post office, state, and ZIP code *Ogden, UT 84201*

F Accounting method: (1) ☑ Cash (2) ☐ Accrual (3) ☐ Other (specify) ▶

G Did you "materially participate" in the operation of this business during 2021? If "No," see instructions for limit on losses . ☑ Yes ☐ No

H If you started or acquired this business during 2021, check here ▶ ☐

I Did you make any payments in 2021 that would require you to file Form(s) 1099? See instructions ☐ Yes ☐ No

J If "Yes," did you or will you file required Form(s) 1099? ☐ Yes ☐ No

Part I Income

		Line	Amount
1	Gross receipts or sales. See instructions for line 1 and check the box if this income was reported to you on Form W-2 and the "Statutory employee" box on that form was checked ▶ ☐	1	*192,000*
2	Returns and allowances	2	
3	Subtract line 2 from line 1	3	*192,000*
4	Cost of goods sold (from line 42)	4	
5	**Gross profit.** Subtract line 4 from line 3	5	*192,000*
6	Other income, including federal and state gasoline or fuel tax credit or refund (see instructions)	6	
7	**Gross income.** Add lines 5 and 6 ▶	7	*192,000*

Part II Expenses. Enter expenses for business use of your home **only** on line 30.

		Line	Amount			Line	Amount
8	Advertising	8		18	Office expense (see instructions)	18	*4,000*
9	Car and truck expenses (see instructions)	9		19	Pension and profit-sharing plans	19	
10	Commissions and fees	10		20	Rent or lease (see instructions):		
11	Contract labor (see instructions)	11		a	Vehicles, machinery, and equipment	20a	*3,000*
12	Depletion	12		b	Other business property	20b	*16,000*
13	Depreciation and section 179 expense deduction (not included in Part III) (see instructions)	13	*142,000*	21	Repairs and maintenance	21	
14	Employee benefit programs (other than on line 19)	14		22	Supplies (not included in Part III)	22	
15	Insurance (other than health)	15	*5,000*	23	Taxes and licenses	23	*2,000*
16	Interest (see instructions):			24	Travel and meals:		
a	Mortgage (paid to banks, etc.)	16a		a	Travel	24a	
b	Other	16b		b	Deductible meals (see instructions)	24b	
17	Legal and professional services	17		25	Utilities	25	
				26	Wages (less employment credits)	26	
				27a	Other expenses (from line 48)	27a	
				b	**Reserved for future use**	27b	

		Line	Amount
28	**Total expenses** before expenses for business use of home. Add lines 8 through 27a ▶	28	*172,000*
29	Tentative profit or (loss). Subtract line 28 from line 7	29	*20,000*
30	Expenses for business use of your home. Do not report these expenses elsewhere. Attach Form 8829 unless using the simplified method. See instructions. **Simplified method filers only:** Enter the total square footage of (a) your home: ______ and (b) the part of your home used for business: ______ . Use the Simplified Method Worksheet in the instructions to figure the amount to enter on line 30	30	
31	**Net profit or (loss).** Subtract line 30 from line 29. • If a profit, enter on both **Schedule 1 (Form 1040), line 3,** and on **Schedule SE, line 2.** (If you checked the box on line 1, see instructions). Estates and trusts, enter on **Form 1041, line 3.** • If a loss, you **must** go to line 32.	31	*20,000*

32 If you have a loss, check the box that describes your investment in this activity. See instructions.
• If you checked 32a, enter the loss on both **Schedule 1 (Form 1040), line 3,** and on **Schedule SE, line 2.** (If you checked the box on line 1, see the line 31 instructions.) Estates and trusts, enter on **Form 1041, line 3.**
• If you checked 32b, you **must** attach **Form 6198.** Your loss may be limited.

32a ☐ All investment is at risk.
32b ☐ Some investment is not at risk.

For Paperwork Reduction Act Notice, see the separate instructions. Cat. No. 11334P **Schedule C (Form 1040) 2021**

Startup Expenditures

Example 42

Green Corporation begins business on August 1, 2022. The corporation incurs startup expenditures of $47,000. If Green elects amortization under § 195, the total startup expenditures that Green may deduct in 2022 are computed as follows:

Deductible amount	$5,000
Amortizable amount {[($47,000 − $5,000) ÷ 180] × 5 months}	1,167
Total deduction	$6,167

Example 43

Assume the same facts as in Example 42, except that the startup expenditures total $53,000. The 2022 deduction is computed as follows:

Deductible amount [$5,000 − ($53,000 − $50,000)]	$2,000
Amortizable amount {[($53,000 − $2,000) ÷ 180] × 5 months}	1,417
Total deduction	$3,417

Amortizable startup expenditures generally must satisfy two requirements.[44] First, the expenses must be paid or incurred in connection with:

- Creating a business,
- Investigating the creation or acquisition of a business, or
- Anticipating an activity becoming a business.

Second, the expenses must reflect those that could be deducted in an existing trade or business in the same field (see Investigation of a Business, text Section 6-3d).

The startup costs of creating a new active trade or business could include advertising; salaries and wages; travel and other expenses incurred in lining up prospective distributors, suppliers, or customers; and salaries and fees for executives, consultants, and professional services. Costs that relate to either created or acquired businesses could include expenses incurred for the analysis or survey of potential markets, products, labor supply, transportation facilities, and the like. Startup expenditures do not include allowable deductions for interest, taxes, and research and experimental costs.[45]

Amortization deductions also can be claimed for organizational expenses (see text Section 20-2d) and research and experimental expenditures (see text Section 7-4).

LO.8

Determine the amount of depletion expense, including being able to apply the alternative tax treatments for intangible drilling and development costs.

8-6 Depletion

Natural resources (e.g., oil, gas, coal, gravel, and timber) are subject to **depletion**, a form of cost recovery that applies to natural resources. Land generally cannot be depleted.

Although all natural resources are subject to depletion, oil and gas wells are used as an example in the following paragraphs to illustrate the related costs and issues.

In developing an oil or gas well, the producer typically makes four types of expenditures.

- Natural resource costs.
- Intangible drilling and development costs.
- Tangible asset costs.
- Operating costs.

Natural resources are physically limited, and the costs to acquire them (e.g., oil under the ground) are, therefore, recovered through depletion. Costs incurred in making the

[44] §§ 195(c)(1)(A) and (B).

[45] § 195(c).

property ready for drilling, such as the cost of labor in clearing the property, erecting derricks, and drilling the hole, are **intangible drilling and development costs (IDCs)**. These costs generally have no salvage value and are a lost cost if the well is dry.

Costs for tangible assets such as tools, pipes, and engines are capitalized and recovered through depreciation (cost recovery). Costs incurred after the well is producing are operating costs. These costs include expenditures for such items as labor, fuel, and supplies. Operating costs are deductible as trade or business expenses. Depletable costs and intangible drilling and development costs receive different treatment.

8-6a Intangible Drilling and Development Costs (IDCs)

Intangible drilling and development costs can be handled in one of two ways at the option of the taxpayer. They can be *either* charged off as an expense in the year in which they are incurred *or* capitalized and written off through depletion. The taxpayer makes the election in the first year such expenditures are incurred, either by taking a deduction on the return or by adding them to the depletable basis.

Once made, the election is binding on both the taxpayer and the IRS for all such expenditures in the future. If the taxpayer fails to elect to expense IDCs on the original timely filed return for the first year in which such expenditures are incurred, an irrevocable election to capitalize them has been made.

As a general rule, it is more advantageous to expense IDCs. The obvious benefit of an immediate write-off (as opposed to a deferred write-off through depletion) is not the only advantage. Because a taxpayer can use percentage depletion, which is calculated without reference to basis (see Example 47), the IDCs may be completely lost as a deduction if they are capitalized.

8-6b Depletion Methods

There are two methods of calculating depletion. *Cost depletion* can be used on any wasting asset (and is the only method allowed for timber). *Percentage depletion* is subject to a number of limitations, particularly for oil and gas deposits. Depletion should be calculated both ways, and the method that results in the larger deduction should be used. The choice between cost depletion and percentage depletion is an annual decision; the taxpayer can use cost depletion in one year and percentage depletion in the following year.

Cost Depletion

Cost depletion resembles units-of-production depreciation.[46] The basis is divided by the estimated recoverable units of the asset (e.g., barrels and tons) to arrive at the depletion per unit. This amount then is multiplied by the number of units sold (*not* the units produced) during the year to arrive at the cost depletion allowed.

Example 44

On January 1, 2022, Pablo purchases the rights to a mineral interest for $1,000,000. At that time, the remaining recoverable units in the mineral interest are estimated to be 200,000. The depletion per unit is $5 ($1,000,000 adjusted basis ÷ 200,000 estimated recoverable units).

If 60,000 units are mined and 25,000 are sold this year, the cost depletion is $125,000 ($5 depletion per unit × 25,000 units sold).

If the taxpayer later discovers that the original estimate was incorrect, the depletion per unit for future calculations is redetermined using the revised estimate.[47]

[46] § 612.

[47] § 611(a).

Example 45

Assume the same facts as in Example 44. In 2023, Pablo realizes that an incorrect estimate was made as to the capacity of the mine. The remaining recoverable units now are determined to be 400,000. Based on this new information, the revised depletion per unit is $2.1875 ($875,000 adjusted basis ÷ 400,000 estimated recoverable units). The $875,000 adjusted basis is the original cost ($1,000,000) reduced by the depletion claimed in 2022 ($125,000).

If 30,000 units are sold in 2023, the depletion for the year is $65,625 ($2.1875 depletion per unit × 30,000 units sold).

Percentage Depletion

Percentage depletion uses a specified percentage provided by the Code. The percentage varies according to the type of mineral interest involved. A sample of these percentages is shown in Exhibit 8.2. The rate is applied to the gross income from the property, but in no event may percentage depletion exceed 50 percent of the taxable income from the property before the allowance for depletion.[48]

Example 46

CarrollCo reports gross income of $100,000 and other property-related expenses of $60,000 and uses a depletion rate of 22%. CarrollCo's depletion allowance is determined as follows.

Gross income	$100,000
Less: Other expenses	(60,000)
Taxable income before depletion	$ 40,000
Depletion allowance [the lesser of $22,000 (22% × $100,000) or $20,000 (50% × $40,000)]	(20,000)
Taxable income after depletion	$ 20,000

The adjusted basis of CarrollCo's property is reduced by $20,000, the depletion deduction allowed. If the other expenses had been only $55,000, the full $22,000 could have been deducted, and the adjusted basis would have been reduced by $22,000.

Exhibit 8.2 Selected Percentage Depletion Rates

22% Depletion		
Cobalt	Nickel	Sulfur
Lead	Platinum	Tin
15% Depletion		
Copper	Iron	Oil shale
Gold	Oil and gas	Silver
14% Depletion		
Borax	Limestone	Potash
Granite	Marble	Slate
10% Depletion		
Coal	Lignite and perlite	Sodium chloride
5% Depletion		
Gravel	Peat	Sand

[48] § 613(a). Special rules apply for certain oil and gas wells (e.g., the 50% ceiling is replaced with a 100% ceiling and the percentage depletion may not exceed 65% of the taxpayer's taxable income from all sources before the allowance for depletion). § 613A.

Note that percentage depletion is based on a percentage of the gross income from the property and makes no reference to cost. All other deductions detailed in this chapter are a function of the adjusted basis (cost) of the property. Thus, when percentage depletion is used, it is possible to claim aggregate depletion deductions that exceed the original cost of the property. If percentage depletion is used, however, the adjusted basis of the property (for computing cost depletion in a future tax year) is reduced by any depletion deducted until the basis reaches zero.

Example 47

Melissa reports the following related to her sulfur mine.

Remaining depletable basis	$ 11,000
Gross income (10,000 units)	100,000
Expenses (other than depletion)	30,000

Because cost depletion is limited to the remaining depletable basis of $11,000, Melissa would choose percentage depletion of $22,000 (a 22% depletion rate is used for sulfur). Her basis in the mine then becomes zero. In future years, however, she can continue to take percentage depletion; percentage depletion is computed without reference to the remaining basis.

8-7 Tax Planning

LO.9

Identify tax planning opportunities for cost recovery, amortization, and depletion.

8-7a Cost Recovery

Cost recovery schedules should be reviewed annually for possible retirements, abandonments, and obsolescence.

Example 48

An examination of the cost recovery schedule of Eagle Company reveals the following.

- Asset A was abandoned when it was discovered that the cost of repairs would be in excess of the cost of replacement. Asset A had an adjusted basis of $3,000.
- Asset J became obsolete this year, at which point its adjusted basis was $8,000.

Assets A and J should be written off, resulting in deductions of $11,000.

Another consideration when making decisions related to cost recovery is whether faster (or slower) cost recovery will be more beneficial for the taxpayer. If the taxpayer's goal is to recover the cost of fixed assets as quickly as possible, then using § 179 or additional first-year depreciation is preferable.

If, however, a taxpayer has a new business with little income or a business with a net operating loss carryover, the taxpayer's goal may be to slow down cost recovery. In this situation, the taxpayer generally should do the following.

- Elect not to take additional first-year depreciation, if available.
- Choose the straight-line cost recovery method.
- Elect not to expense assets under § 179.
- Defer placing assets in service in the current tax year or postpone capital outlays until future tax years.

8-7b Amortization

When a business is purchased, goodwill and covenants not to compete are both subject to an amortization period of 15 years. Given that goodwill and covenants not to compete are treated the same from a tax perspective, bargaining for a covenant should be based on legal rather than tax reasons. The seller, however, may have different motives because goodwill is a capital asset whereas a covenant is an ordinary income asset.

Because the amortization period for both goodwill and a covenant is 15 years, the purchaser may want to assign purchase costs to assets with shorter lives (e.g., inventory, receivables, and personalty). If, however, the purchase price will be assigned to assets with longer recovery periods (e.g., realty) or to assets not eligible for cost recovery (e.g., land), the purchaser would likely prefer costs to be assigned to goodwill or a covenant.

8-7c Cost Recovery Tables

Summary of Tables

Exhibit 8.3 Regular MACRS table for personalty.
Depreciation methods: 200 or 150 percent declining-balance switching to straight-line.
Recovery periods: 3, 5, 7, 10, 15, 20 years.
Convention: half-year.

Exhibit 8.4 Regular MACRS table for personalty.
Depreciation method: 200 percent declining-balance switching to straight-line.
Recovery periods: 3, 5, 7 years.
Convention: mid-quarter.

Exhibit 8.5 MACRS optional straight-line table for personalty.
Depreciation method: straight-line.
Recovery periods: 3, 5, 7, 10, 15, 20 years.
Convention: half-year.

Exhibit 8.6 Alternative minimum tax declining-balance table for personalty.
Depreciation method: 150 percent declining-balance switching to straight-line.
Recovery periods: 3, 5, 7, 9.5, 10, 12 years.
Convention: half-year.

Exhibit 8.7 Alternative depreciation system straight-line table for personalty.
Depreciation method: straight-line.
Recovery periods: 5, 10, 12 years.
Convention: half-year.

Exhibit 8.8 Regular MACRS straight-line table for realty.
Depreciation method: straight-line.
Recovery periods: 27.5, 31.5, 39 years.
Convention: mid-month.

Exhibit 8.9 Alternative depreciation system straight-line table for realty.
Depreciation method: straight-line.
Recovery period: 30, 40 years.
Convention: mid-month.

Exhibit 8.3 MACRS Accelerated Depreciation for Personal Property Assuming Half-Year Convention (Percentage Rates)

For Property Placed in Service after December 31, 1986

Recovery Year	3-Year (200% DB)	5-Year (200% DB)	7-Year (200% DB)	10-Year (200% DB)	15-Year (150% DB)	20-Year (150% DB)
1	33.33	20.00	14.29	10.00	5.00	3.750
2	44.45	32.00	24.49	18.00	9.50	7.219
3	14.81*	19.20	17.49	14.40	8.55	6.677
4	7.41	11.52*	12.49	11.52	7.70	6.177
5		11.52	8.93*	9.22	6.93	5.713
6		5.76	8.92	7.37	6.23	5.285
7			8.93	6.55*	5.90*	4.888
8			4.46	6.55	5.90	4.522
9				6.56	5.91	4.462*
10				6.55	5.90	4.461
11				3.28	5.91	4.462
12					5.90	4.461
13					5.91	4.462
14					5.90	4.461
15					5.91	4.462
16					2.95	4.461
17						4.462
18						4.461
19						4.462
20						4.461
21						2.231

*Switchover to straight-line depreciation.

Exhibit 8.4 MACRS Accelerated Depreciation for Personal Property Assuming Mid-Quarter Convention (Percentage Rates)

For Property Placed in Service after December 31, 1986 (Partial Table*)

3-Year

Recovery Year	First Quarter	Second Quarter	Third Quarter	Fourth Quarter
1	58.33	41.67	25.00	8.33
2	27.78	38.89	50.00	61.11

5-Year

Recovery Year	First Quarter	Second Quarter	Third Quarter	Fourth Quarter
1	35.00	25.00	15.00	5.00
2	26.00	30.00	34.00	38.00

7-Year

Recovery Year	First Quarter	Second Quarter	Third Quarter	Fourth Quarter
1	25.00	17.85	10.71	3.57
2	21.43	23.47	25.51	27.55

*The figures in this table are taken from the official tables that appear in Rev.Proc. 87–57. Because of their length, the complete tables are not presented.

Exhibit 8.5 MACRS Straight-Line Depreciation for Personal Property Assuming Half-Year Convention*

For Property Placed in Service after December 31, 1986

MACRS Class	% First Recovery Year	Other Recovery Years: Years	Other Recovery Years: %	Last Recovery Year: Year	Last Recovery Year: %
3-year	16.67	2–3	33.33	4	16.67
5-year	10.00	2–5	20.00	6	10.00
7-year	7.14	2–7	14.29	8	7.14
10-year	5.00	2–10	10.00	11	5.00
15-year	3.33	2–15	6.67	16	3.33
20-year	2.50	2–20	5.00	21	2.50

*The official table contains a separate row for each year. For ease of presentation, certain years are grouped in this table. In some instances, this will produce a difference of .01 for the last digit when compared with the official table.

Note: The last two rows of this table are used for qualified improvement property (15-year normal MACRS; 20-year ADS).

Exhibit 8.6 Alternative Minimum Tax: 150% Declining-Balance Assuming Half-Year Convention (Percentage Rates)

For Property Placed in Service after December 31, 1986 (Partial Table*)

Recovery Year	3-Year 150%	5-Year 150%	7-Year 150%	9.5-Year 150%	10-Year 150%	12-Year 150%
1	25.00	15.00	10.71	7.89	7.50	6.25
2	37.50	25.50	19.13	14.54	13.88	11.72
3	25.00**	17.85	15.03	12.25	11.79	10.25
4	12.50	16.66**	12.25**	10.31	10.02	8.97
5		16.66	12.25	9.17**	8.74**	7.85
6		8.33	12.25	9.17	8.74	7.33**
7			12.25	9.17	8.74	7.33
8			6.13	9.17	8.74	7.33
9				9.17	8.74	7.33
10				9.16	8.74	7.33
11					4.37	7.32
12						7.33
13						3.66

*The figures in this table are taken from the official table that appears in Rev.Proc. 87–57. Because of its length, the complete table is not presented.

**Switchover to straight-line depreciation.

Exhibit 8.7 **ADS Straight-Line for Personal Property Assuming Half-Year Convention (Percentage Rates)**

For Property Placed in Service after December 31, 1986 (Partial Table)*

Recovery Year	3-Year	5-Year	7-Year	10-Year	12-Year
1	16.67	10.00	7.14	5.00	4.17
2	33.33	20.00	14.29	10.00	8.33
3	33.33	20.00	14.29	10.00	8.33
4	16.67	20.00	14.29	10.00	8.33
5		20.00	14.29	10.00	8.33
6		10.00	14.29	10.00	8.33
7			14.29	10.00	8.34
8			7.14	10.00	8.33
9				10.00	8.34
10				10.00	8.33
11				5.00	8.34
12					8.33
13					4.17

*The figures in this table are taken from the official table that appears in Rev.Proc. 87–57. Because of its length, the complete table is not presented. The tables for the mid-quarter convention also appear in Rev.Proc. 87–57.

Exhibit 8.8 **MACRS Straight-Line Depreciation for Real Property Assuming Mid-Month Convention* (Percentage Rates)**

For Property Placed in Service after December 31, 1986: 27.5-Year Residential Real Property

Recovery Year(s)	The Applicable Percentage Is (Use the Column for the Month in the First Year the Property Is Placed in Service):											
	1	2	3	4	5	6	7	8	9	10	11	12
1	3.485	3.182	2.879	2.576	2.273	1.970	1.667	1.364	1.061	0.758	0.455	0.152
2–18	3.636	3.636	3.636	3.636	3.636	3.636	3.636	3.636	3.636	3.636	3.636	3.636
19–27	3.637	3.637	3.637	3.637	3.637	3.637	3.637	3.637	3.637	3.637	3.637	3.637
28	1.970	2.273	2.576	2.879	3.182	3.485	3.636	3.636	3.636	3.636	3.636	3.636
29	0.000	0.000	0.000	0.000	0.000	0.000	0.152	0.455	0.758	1.061	1.364	1.667

For Property Placed in Service after December 31, 1986, and before May 13, 1993: 31.5-Year Nonresidential Real Property

Recovery Year(s)	The Applicable Percentage Is (Use the Column for the Month in the First Year the Property Is Placed in Service):											
	1	2	3	4	5	6	7	8	9	10	11	12
1	3.042	2.778	2.513	2.249	1.984	1.720	1.455	1.190	0.926	0.661	0.397	0.132
2–19	3.175	3.175	3.175	3.175	3.175	3.175	3.175	3.175	3.175	3.175	3.175	3.175
20–31	3.174	3.174	3.174	3.174	3.174	3.174	3.174	3.174	3.174	3.174	3.174	3.174
32	1.720	1.984	2.249	2.513	2.778	3.042	3.175	3.175	3.175	3.175	3.175	3.175
33	0.000	0.000	0.000	0.000	0.000	0.000	0.132	0.397	0.661	0.926	1.190	1.455

For Property Placed in Service after May 12, 1993: 39-Year Nonresidential Real Property

Recovery Year(s)	The Applicable Percentage Is (Use the Column for the Month in the First Year the Property Is Placed in Service):											
	1	2	3	4	5	6	7	8	9	10	11	12
1	2.461	2.247	2.033	1.819	1.605	1.391	1.177	0.963	0.749	0.535	0.321	0.107
2–39	2.564	2.564	2.564	2.564	2.564	2.564	2.564	2.564	2.564	2.564	2.564	2.564
40	0.107	0.321	0.535	0.749	0.963	1.177	1.391	1.605	1.819	2.033	2.247	2.461

*The official tables contain a separate row for each year. For ease of presentation, certain years are grouped in these tables. In some instances, this will produce a difference of .001 for the last digit when compared with the official tables.

Exhibit 8.9 ADS Straight-Line for Real Property Assuming Mid-Month Convention (Percentage Rates)

For Property Placed in Service after December 31, 2017; 30-Year Residential Rental Property

Recovery Year	Month Placed in Service											
	1	**2**	**3**	**4**	**5**	**6**	**7**	**8**	**9**	**10**	**11**	**12**
1	3.194	2.917	2.639	2.361	2.083	1.806	1.528	1.250	0.972	0.694	0.417	0.139
2–30	3.333	3.333	3.333	3.333	3.333	3.333	3.333	3.333	3.333	3.333	3.333	3.333
31	0.139	0.417	0.694	0.972	1.250	1.528	1.806	2.083	2.361	2.639	2.917	3.194

For Property Placed in Service after December 31, 1986; 40-Year Nonresidential Real Property*

Recovery Year	Month Placed in Service											
	1	**2**	**3**	**4**	**5**	**6**	**7**	**8**	**9**	**10**	**11**	**12**
1	2.396	2.188	1.979	1.771	1.563	1.354	1.146	0.938	0.729	0.521	0.313	0.104
2–40	2.500	2.500	2.500	2.500	2.500	2.500	2.500	2.500	2.500	2.500	2.500	2.500
41	0.104	0.312	0.521	0.729	0.937	1.146	1.354	1.562	1.771	1.979	2.187	2.396

*Also used for residential rental property placed in service before 2018.

Refocus on The Big Picture

Calculating Cost Recovery Deductions

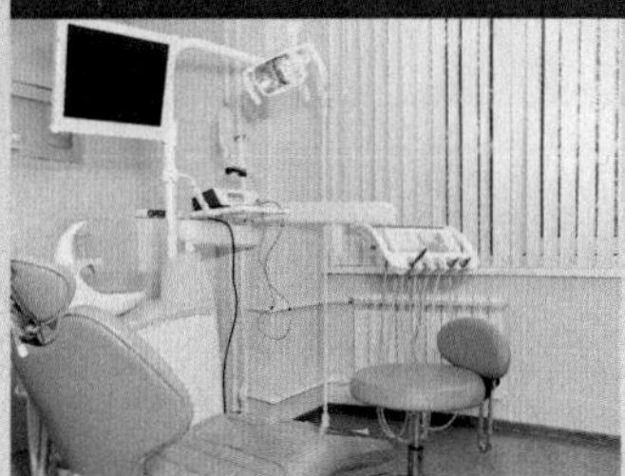

SERGEYKLOPOTOV/SHUTTERSTOCK.COM

Regardless of whether the accrual or cash method of accounting is used, MACRS must be used to calculate the cost recovery of fixed assets for tax purposes. Evidently, Dr. Payne's financial reporting system uses MACRS because $91,298 is the correct amount of cost recovery. The computers and peripheral equipment are 5-year property. The office furniture and fixtures and the dental equipment are 7-year property.

Based on the IRS cost recovery tables, the following percentages are used in calculating depreciation expense for the first year of each asset's life.

5-year property	20.00%
7-year property	14.29%

Dr. Payne can deduct depreciation on the house he converted from personal use to rental use and on the rental house he purchased.

What If?

From a tax planning perspective, Dr. Payne can increase the cost recovery deductions associated with the purchase of these fixed assets and reduce the amount of the business net income reported on Schedule C of Form 1040 for his dental practice by using the § 179 immediate expense election or additional first-year (bonus) depreciation.

Code § 179 applies to personalty, but does not apply to realty (e.g., buildings). The maximum amount that can be deducted under § 179 is subject to several limitations. First, the total amount deducted cannot exceed $1,080,000. Second, the maximum amount is reduced dollar for dollar for any § 179 assets placed in service in excess of $2,700,000. Finally, the § 179 deduction cannot exceed the taxable income from the business. Additional first-year (bonus) depreciation allows 100 percent of qualified property to be deducted.

The sequence of calculating the cost recovery deduction is, in order:

1. § 179 immediate expensing.
2. Additional first-year depreciation.
3. Regular MACRS cost recovery.

continued

If Dr. Payne reports sufficient business income to avoid the § 179 business income limitation, he can use § 179 to expense all of the assets placed in service in 2022 ($612,085).

If § 179's business income limitation comes into play, Dr. Payne can elect out of § 179 and deduct $612,085 using additional first-year depreciation (which has no income limitation). In this case, however, other limitations might affect his decision (including the excess business loss limitation; see text Section 7-5). Or he can apply § 179 or additional first-year depreciation to selected assets, reducing his taxable income this year and deferring some deductions to future years.

Key Terms

Accelerated cost recovery system (ACRS), 8-2
Additional first-year depreciation, 8-14
Alternative depreciation system (ADS), 8-23
Amortization, 8-25
Cost depletion, 8-29
Cost recovery, 8-2
Depletion, 8-28
Depreciation, 8-2
Half-year convention, 8-6
Intangible drilling and development costs (IDCs), 8-29
Listed property, 8-18
Mid-month convention, 8-10
Mid-quarter convention, 8-7
Modified accelerated cost recovery system (MACRS), 8-2
Percentage depletion, 8-30
Qualified improvement property, 8-8
Residential rental real estate, 8-9
Section 179 expensing, 8-11
Startup expenditures, 8-25

Discussion Questions

1. **LO.1** Discuss whether property that is classified as personal use is subject to cost recovery.

2. **LO.1** Discuss the difference between personal property and personal use property.

3. **LO.1** Discuss whether land improvements used in a trade or business are eligible for cost recovery.

4. **LO.2** At the beginning of the current year, Henry purchased a ski resort for $10,000,000. Henry does not own the land on which the resort is located. The Federal government owns the land, and Henry has the right to operate the resort on the land pursuant to Special Use Permits, which are terminable at will by the Federal government, and Term Special Use Permits, which allow the land to be used for a fixed number of years. Critical Thinking

   In preparing the income tax return for the current year, Henry properly allocated $2,000,000 of the purchase price to the costs of constructing mountain roads, slopes, and trails. Since the acquisition, Henry has spent an additional $2,000,000 on maintaining the mountain roads, slopes, and trails. Identify the relevant tax issues for Henry.

5. **LO.2** Identify the three factors reflected in the MACRS tables when the amount of cost recovery is determined.

6. **LO.2** Discuss the computation of cost recovery in the year an asset is placed in service when the mid-quarter convention is being used.

7. **LO.2** Discuss the computation of cost recovery in the year of sale of an asset when the mid-quarter convention is being used.

Critical Thinking

8. **LO.2** Robert purchased and placed in service $100,000 of 7-year class assets on August 10 of the current year. He also purchased and placed in service $500,000 of 5-year class assets on November 15 of the current year. He does not claim any available additional first-year depreciation. If Robert elects to use the MACRS straight-line method of cost recovery on the 7-year class assets, discuss the calculation of cost recovery for the 5-year class assets.

9. **LO.3** Discuss when § 179 expense must be recaptured.

10. **LO.3** Explain how the § 179 immediate expensing deduction affects the computation of MACRS cost recovery.

11. **LO.3** Discuss the treatment of a § 179 expensing carryforward.

12. **LO.3** Discuss the definition of *business income* as it is used in limiting the § 179 expensing amount.

Critical Thinking

13. **LO.2, 3** A professional consulting business sells professional tools and equipment and provides associated services, such as repair and maintenance, to its customer base. The company's employees include technicians who are required to provide and maintain their own tools and equipment for performing the repairs and maintenance work. The company will reimburse a technician for amounts spent to purchase tools and equipment eligible for a § 179 deduction up to a set amount each year. Any costs for tools and equipment that exceed the set amount will not be reimbursed.

    Jiaxu is a technician for the company. During the current year, he purchased equipment that qualifies for the § 179 deduction. Jiaxu paid $50,000 for the equipment and was reimbursed the set amount of $40,000. Identify the relevant tax issues for Jiaxu with respect to § 179 and the computation of his taxable income.

14. **LO.4** Discuss how the limits on cost recovery apply to listed property.

15. **LO.4** Discuss the tax consequences if the business use percentage of listed property falls to 50% or lower after the year the property is placed in service.

Critical Thinking

16. **LO.7** Harold and Bart own 75% of the stock of Orange Motors. The other 25% of the stock is owned by Jeb. Orange Motors entered into an agreement with Harold and Bart to acquire all of their Orange stock.

    In addition, Harold and Bart signed a noncompete agreement with Orange Motors. Under the terms of the noncompete agreement, Orange will pay Harold and Bart $15,000 each per year for four years. Identify the relevant tax issues for Orange Motors.

Critical Thinking

17. **LO.4, 7** In May 2022, Gwen began searching for a trade or business to acquire. In anticipation of finding a suitable acquisition, Gwen hired an investment banker to evaluate three potential businesses. She also hired a law firm to begin drafting regulatory approval documents for a target company. Eventually, Gwen decided to purchase all of the assets of Brash Corporation. Brash and Gwen entered into an acquisition agreement on December 1, 2022. Identify the relevant tax issues for Gwen.

18. **LO.8** Discuss how the cost of mineral rights enters into the calculation of cost depletion.

Computational Exercises

19. **LO.2** Euclid acquires a 7-year class asset on May 9, 2022, for $80,000 (the only asset acquired during the year). Euclid does not elect immediate expensing under § 179. She does not claim any available additional first-year depreciation. Calculate Euclid's cost recovery deduction for 2022 and 2023.

20. **LO.2** Hamlet acquires a 7-year class asset on November 23, 2022, for $100,000 (the only asset acquired during the year). Hamlet does not elect immediate expensing under § 179. He does not claim any available additional first-year depreciation. Calculate Hamlet's cost recovery deductions for 2022 and 2023.

21. **LO.2** Lopez acquired a building on June 1, 2017, for $1,000,000. Calculate Lopez's cost recovery deduction for 2022 if the building is:
    a. Classified as residential rental real estate.
    b. Classified as nonresidential real estate.

22. **LO.2** Andre acquired a computer on March 3, 2022, for $2,800. He elects the straight-line method for cost recovery. Andre does not elect immediate expensing under § 179. He does not claim any available additional first-year depreciation. Calculate Andre's cost recovery deduction for the computer for tax years 2022 and 2023.

23. **LO.2, 3** Diana acquires, for $65,000, and places in service a 5-year class asset on December 19, 2022. It is the only asset that Diana acquires during 2022. Diana does not elect immediate expensing under § 179. She elects additional first-year deprecation. Calculate Diana's total cost recovery deduction for 2022.

24. **LO.3** McKenzie purchased qualifying equipment for his business that cost $212,000 in 2022. The taxable income of the business for the year is $5,600 before consideration of any § 179 deduction.
    a. Calculate McKenzie's § 179 expense deduction for 2022 and any carryover to 2023.
    b. How would your answer change if McKenzie decided to use additional first-year (bonus) depreciation on the equipment instead of using § 179 expensing?

25. **LO.4** On April 5, 2022, Kinsey places in service a new automobile that cost $60,000. He does not elect § 179 expensing, and he elects not to take any available additional first-year depreciation. The car is used 70% for business and 30% for personal use in each tax year.

    Kinsey chooses the MACRS 200% declining-balance method of cost recovery (the auto is a 5-year asset). Assume the following luxury automobile limitations: year 1: $10,200; year 2: $16,400. Compute the total depreciation allowed for 2022 and 2023.

26. **LO.7** On October 1, 2022, Verónica purchased a business. Of the purchase price, $60,000 is allocated to a patent and $375,000 is allocated to goodwill. Calculate Verónica's 2022 § 197 amortization deduction.

27. **LO.8** On March 25, Parscale Company purchases the rights to a mineral interest for $8,000,000. At that time, the remaining recoverable units in the mineral interest are estimated to be 500,000 tons. If 80,000 tons are mined and 75,000 tons are sold this year, calculate Parscale's cost depletion for the year.

28. **LO.8** Jebali Company reports gross income of $340,000 and other property-related expenses of $229,000 and uses a depletion rate of 14%. Calculate Jebali's depletion allowance for the current year.

Problems

29. LO.1, 2 On November 4, 2020, Blue Company acquired an asset (27.5-year residential real property) for $200,000 for use in its business. In 2020 and 2021, respectively, Blue deducted $642 and $5,128 of cost recovery. These amounts were incorrect; Blue applied the wrong percentages (i.e., those for 39-year rather than 27.5-year assets). Blue should have taken $910 and $7,272 cost recovery in 2020 and 2021, respectively.

    On January 1, 2022, the asset was sold for $180,000. Calculate the gain or loss on the sale of the asset for that year.

30. LO.1, 2 In 2019, José purchased a house for $325,000 ($300,000 relates to the house; $25,000 relates to the land). He used the house as his personal residence. In March 2022, when the fair market value of the house was $400,000, he converted the house to rental property. What is José's cost recovery for 2022?

31. LO.2, 3 Orange Corporation acquired new office furniture on August 15, 2022, for $130,000. Orange does not elect immediate expensing under § 179. Orange claims any available additional first-year depreciation.
    a. Determine Orange's cost recovery for 2022.
    b. How would your answer change if Orange decided to use $52,000 of bonus depreciation and use normal MACRS on the balance of the acquisition cost?

32. LO.2 Juan acquires a new 5-year class asset on March 14, 2022, for $200,000. This is the only asset Juan acquired during the year. He does not elect immediate expensing under § 179. He does not claim any available additional first-year depreciation. On July 15, 2023, Juan sells the asset.
    a. Determine Juan's cost recovery for 2022.
    b. Determine Juan's cost recovery for 2023.

33. LO.2 Debra acquired the following new assets during 2022.

Date	Asset	Cost
April 11	Furniture	$40,000
July 28	Trucks	40,000
November 3	Computers	70,000

    Determine Debra's cost recovery deductions for the current year. Debra does not elect immediate expensing under § 179. She does not claim any available additional first-year depreciation.

34. LO.2 On August 2, 2022, Wendy purchased a new office building for $3,800,000. On October 1, 2022, she began to rent out office space in the building. On July 15, 2026, Wendy sold the office building.
    a. Determine Wendy's cost recovery deduction for 2022.
    b. Determine Wendy's cost recovery deduction for 2026.

35. LO.2 On April 3, 2022, Terry purchased and placed in service a building that cost $2,000,000. An appraisal determined that 25% of the total cost was attributed to the value of the land. The bottom floor of the building is leased to a retail business for $32,000. The other floors of the building are rental apartments with an annual rent of $160,000. Determine Terry's cost recovery deduction for 2022.

36. LO.2 On May 5, 2022, Christy purchased and placed in service a hotel. The hotel cost $10,800,000, and the land cost $1,200,000 ($12,000,000 in total). Calculate Christy's cost recovery deductions for 2022 and for 2032.

37. **LO.2** Janice acquired an apartment building on June 4, 2022, for $1,600,000. The value of the land is $300,000. Janice sold the apartment building on November 29, 2028.
    a. Determine Janice's cost recovery deduction for 2022.
    b. Determine Janice's cost recovery deduction for 2028.

38. **LO.2, 3, 9** Lori, who is single, purchased 5-year class property for $200,000 and 7-year class property for $420,000 on May 20, 2022. Lori expects the taxable income derived from her business (before considering any amount expensed under § 179) to be about $550,000. Lori has determined that she should elect immediate § 179 expensing in the amount of $520,000, but she doesn't know which asset she should completely expense under § 179. She does not claim any available additional first-year depreciation. Communications Critical Thinking Decision Making Planning
    a. Determine Lori's total cost recovery deduction if the § 179 expense is first taken with respect to the 5-year class asset.
    b. Determine Lori's total cost recovery deduction if the § 179 expense is first taken with respect to the 7-year class asset.
    c. What is your advice to Lori?
    d. Assume that Lori is in the 24% marginal tax state and Federal income bracket and that she elects § 179 for the 7-year asset. Determine the present value of the tax savings from the cost recovery deductions for both assets. See Appendix E for present value factors, and assume a 6% discount rate.
    e. Assume the same facts as in part (d), except that Lori decides not to use § 179 on either asset. Determine the present value of the tax savings under this choice. In addition, determine which option Lori should choose.
    f. Present your solution to parts (d) and (e) of the problem in a spreadsheet using appropriate Microsoft Excel formulas. E-mail your spreadsheet to your instructor with a two-paragraph summary of your findings.

39. **LO.2, 3** Olga is the proprietor of a small business. In 2022, the business's income, before consideration of any cost recovery or § 179 deduction, is $250,000. Olga spends $620,000 on new 7-year class assets and elects to take the § 179 deduction on them. She does not claim any available additional first-year depreciation. Olga's cost recovery deduction for 2022, except for the cost recovery with respect to the new 7-year assets, is $95,000. Determine Olga's total cost recovery for 2022 with respect to the 7-year class assets and the amount of any § 179 carryforward. Critical Thinking

40. **LO.2, 3, 9** On June 5, 2021, Javier Sanchez purchased and placed in service a new 7-year class asset costing $560,000 for use in his landscaping business, which he operates as a single member LLC (Sanchez Landscaping LLC). During 2021, his business generated a net income of $945,780 before any § 179 immediate expense election.
    a. Rather than using bonus depreciation, Javier would like to use § 179 to expense $200,000 of this asset and then use regular MACRS to cost recover the remaining cost. Given this information, determine the cost recovery deductions that Javier can claim with respect to this asset in 2021 and 2022.
    b. Complete Javier's Form 4562 (page 1) for 2021. His Social Security number is 123-45-6789.

41. **LO.2, 4** On October 15, 2022, Jon purchased and placed in service a used car. The purchase price was $38,000. This was the only business use asset Jon acquired in 2022. He used the car 80% of the time for business and 20% for personal use. Jon used the regular MACRS method. Calculate the total cost recovery deduction Jon may take for 2022 with respect to the car.

42. **LO.4** On June 5, 2021, Leo purchased and placed in service a new car that cost $75,000. The business use percentage for the car is always 100%. Leo does not claim any available additional first-year depreciation. Compute Leo's cost recovery deductions for 2021 and 2022.

43. **LO.2, 3, 4** On March 15, 2022, Helen purchased and placed in service a new Escalade. The purchase price was $62,000, and the vehicle had a rating of 6,500 GVW. The vehicle was used 100% for business.

a. Assuming that Helen does not use additional first-year depreciation, calculate the total depreciation deduction that she can take on the vehicle for 2022.

b. What would your answer be if Helen decided to take additional first-year depreciation?

44. **LO.2, 4** On May 28, 2022, Mary purchased and placed in service a new $60,000 car. The car was used 60% for business, 20% for production of income, and 20% for personal use in 2022. In 2023, the usage changed to 40% for business, 30% for production of income, and 30% for personal use. Mary did not elect immediate expensing under § 179. She did not claim any available additional first-year depreciation. Compute Mary's cost recovery deduction and any cost recovery recapture for 2023.

Decision Making

45. **LO.2, 4, 9** Naya purchased a new computer (5-year property) on June 1, 2022, for $4,000. Naya could use the computer 100% of the time in her business, or she could allow her family to use the computer as well. Naya estimates that if her family uses the computer, the business use will be 45% and the personal use will be 55%.

Determine the tax cost to Naya, in the year of acquisition, of allowing her family to use the computer. Assume that Naya would not elect § 179 immediate expensing and that her marginal income tax rate is 32%. She does not claim any available additional first-year depreciation.

Communications
Critical Thinking
Decision Making
Planning

46. **LO.2, 4, 9** Dennis Harding is considering acquiring a new automobile that he will use 100% for business. The purchase price of the automobile would be $64,500. If Dennis leased the car for five years, the lease payments would be $875 per month. Dennis will acquire the car on January 1, 2022. Assume that the inclusion dollar amounts from the IRS table for the next five years are $63, $140, $208, $251, and $289.

Dennis wants to know the effect on his adjusted gross income of purchasing versus leasing the car for the next five years. He does not claim any available additional first-year depreciation. Write a letter to Dennis summarizing your calculations. Then prepare a memo for the tax files containing your analysis. Dennis's address is 150 Avenue I, Memphis, TN 38112.

47. **LO.2, 5** In 2022, Muhammad purchased a new computer for $16,000. The computer is used 100% for business. Muhammad did not make a § 179 election with respect to the computer. He does not claim any available additional first-year depreciation. If Muhammad uses the regular MACRS method, determine his cost recovery deduction for 2022 for computing taxable income and for computing his alternative minimum tax.

Communications
Critical Thinking
Decision Making
Planning

48. **LO.2, 5, 9** Jamie purchased $100,000 of new office furniture for her business in June of the current year. Jamie understands that if she elects to use ADS to compute her regular income tax, there will be no difference between the cost recovery for computing the regular income tax and the AMT.

a. Jamie wants to know the present value of the *tax cost*, after three years, of using ADS rather than MACRS. Assume that Jamie does not elect § 179 expensing, she does not claim any additional first-year depreciation, and her combined state and Federal income marginal tax rate is 32%. See Appendix E for present value factors, and assume a 6% discount rate.

b. What is the present value of the tax savings/costs that result over the life of the asset if Jamie uses MACRS rather than ADS?

c. Present your solution to part (b) of the problem in a spreadsheet using appropriate Microsoft Excel formulas. E-mail your spreadsheet to your instructor with a one-paragraph explanation.

49. **LO.2, 7, 9** Mike Saxon is negotiating the purchase of a business. The final purchase price ($2,000,000) has been agreed upon, but the allocation of the purchase price to the assets is still being discussed. Appraisals on a warehouse range from $1,200,000 to $1,500,000. If a value of $1,200,000 is used for the warehouse, the remainder of the purchase price, $800,000, will be allocated to goodwill. If $1,500,000 is allocated to the warehouse, goodwill will be $500,000.

Communications
Critical Thinking
Decision Making
Planning

Mike wants to know what effect each alternative will have on cost recovery and amortization during the first year. Under the agreement, Mike will take over the business on January 1 of next year.

Write a letter to Mike in which you present your calculations and recommendation. Then prepare a memo for the tax files, addressing these matters. Mike's address is 200 Rolling Hills Drive, Shavertown, PA 18708.

50. **LO.7** Oleander Corporation, a calendar year entity, begins business on March 1, 2022. The corporation incurs startup expenditures of $64,000. If Oleander elects § 195 treatment, determine the total amount of startup expenditures that it may deduct for 2022.

51. **LO.7** Martha was considering starting a new business. During her preliminary investigations related to the new venture, she incurred the following expenditures.

Salaries	$22,000
Travel	18,000
Interest on short-term note	4,000
Professional fees	13,000

Martha begins the business on July 1 of the current year. If Martha elects § 195 treatment, determine her startup expenditure deduction for the current year.

52. **LO.8** Wes acquired a mineral interest during the year for $10,000,000. A geological survey estimated that 250,000 tons of the mineral remained in the deposit. During the year, 80,000 tons were mined and 45,000 tons were sold for $12,000,000. Other related expenses amounted to $5,000,000. Assuming that the mineral depletion rate is 22%, calculate Wes's lowest taxable income after any depletion deductions.

53. **LO.2, 9** Build an Excel spreadsheet that calculates annual cost recovery and end-of-year adjusted basis for MACRS 3-, 5-, and 7-year assets. Begin by constructing a table that incorporates the relevant MACRS cost recovery percentages from Exhibit 8.3. Then build a table that links to the MACRS cost recovery table, allowing a user to input three data points: (1) Asset cost, (2) Year of acquisition, and (3) MACRS life. Based on these inputs, your spreadsheet should create a schedule that provides annual MACRS cost recovery and end-of-year adjusted basis for that asset. Once completed, e-mail the spreadsheet to your instructor. *Hint*: Your spreadsheet needs to use "IF" functions to create the MACRS cost recovery/adjusted basis schedule. Critical Thinking

Tax Return Problems

54. Janice Morgan, age 24, is single and has no dependents. She is a freelance writer. In January 2021, Janice opened her own office located at 2751 Waldham Road, Pleasant Hill, NM 88135. She called her business Writers Anonymous. Janice is a cash basis taxpayer. She lives at 132 Stone Avenue, Pleasant Hill, NM 88135. Her Social Security number is 123-45-6782. Janice's parents continue to provide health insurance for her under their policy. Janice did not engage in any virtual currency transactions during the year and wants to contribute to the Presidential Election Campaign Fund. Janice received the appropriate coronavirus recovery rebates (economic impact payments); related questions in ProConnect Tax should be ignored.

Tax Forms Problem
ProConnect™ Tax

During 2021, Janice reported the following income and expense items connected with her business.

Income from sale of articles	$95,000
Rent	16,500
Utilities	7,900
Supplies	1,800
Insurance	5,000
Travel (including restaurant meals of $600)	2,900

Janice purchased and placed in service the following fixed assets for her business. Janice wants to elect immediate expensing under § 179, if possible.

- Furniture and fixtures (new) costing $21,000 on January 10
- Computer equipment (new) costing $12,400 on July 28

Janice's itemized deductions include:

State income tax	$2,950
Home mortgage interest paid to First National Bank	8,000
Property taxes on home	2,500
Charitable contribution to her alma mater, State College	1,200

Janice did not keep a record of the sales tax she paid. The amount allowed by the sales tax table is $437.

Janice reports interest income of $4,000 on certificates of deposit at Second National Bank. Janice makes estimated tax payments of $5,000 for 2021.

Compute Janice Morgan's 2021 Federal income tax payable (or refund due), and complete her 2021 tax return using appropriate forms and schedules. Suggested software: ProConnect Tax.

Communications
Decision Making
Planning
Tax Computation Problem

55. John Rivera, age 31, is single and has no dependents. At the beginning of 2022, John started his own excavation business and named it Earth Movers. John lives at 1045 Center Street, Lindon, UT, and his business is located at 381 State Street, Lindon, UT. The Zip Code for both addresses is 84042. John's Social Security number is 111-11-1111, and the business identification number is 11-1111111. John is a cash basis taxpayer. During 2022, John reports the following items in connection with his business.

Fee income for services rendered	$912,000
Building rental expense	36,000
Office furniture and equipment rental expense	9,000
Office supplies	2,500
Utilities	4,000
Salary for secretary	34,000
Salary for equipment operators	42,000
Payroll taxes	7,000
Fuel and oil for the equipment	21,000
Purchase of three new front-end loaders on January 15, 2022	560,000
Purchase of a new dump truck on January 18, 2022	80,000

During 2022, John recorded the following additional items.

Interest income from First National Bank	$10,000
Dividends from ExxonMobil	9,500
Quarterly estimated tax payments	11,500

John wants to maximize his cost recovery deductions (including taking any § 179 expense and any available additional first-year depreciation).

On October 8, 2022, John inherited IBM stock from his Aunt Mildred. John had been her favorite nephew. According to the data provided by the executor of Aunt Mildred's estate, the stock was valued for estate tax purposes at $110,000. John is considering selling the IBM stock for $125,000 on December 29, 2022, and using $75,000 of the proceeds to purchase an Acura ZDX. He would use the car 100% for business. John wants to know what effect these transactions would have on his 2022 adjusted gross income.

Write a letter to John in which you present your calculations. Ignore any Federal self-employment tax implications.

Research Problems

Note: Solutions to the Research Problems can be prepared by using the Thomson Reuters Checkpoint™ online tax research database, which accompanies this textbook. Solutions can also be prepared by using research materials found in a typical tax library.

the answer company™ THOMSON REUTERS®

Research Problem 1. Your client, Dave's Sport Shop, sells sports equipment and clothing in three retail outlets in New York City. During 2022, the CFO decided that keeping track of inventory using a combination of QuickBooks and spreadsheets was not an efficient way to manage the stores' inventories. So Dave's purchased an inventory management system for $9,000 that allowed the entity to keep track of inventory, as well as automate ordering and purchasing, without replacing QuickBooks for its accounting function.

Communications

The CFO would like to know whether the cost of the inventory management program can be expensed in the year of purchase. Write a letter to the CFO, Cassandra Martin, that addresses the tax treatment of purchased software. Cassandra's mailing address is 867 Broadway, New York, NY 10003.

Research Problem 2. In 2018, Jed James began planting a vineyard. The costs of the land preparation, labor, rootstock, and planting were capitalized. The land preparation costs do not include any nondepreciable land costs. In 2022, when the plants became viable, Jed placed the vineyard in service. Jed wants to know whether he can claim a deduction under § 179 on his 2022 income tax return for the 2018 costs for planting the vineyard.

Research Problem 3. Juan owns a business that acquires exotic automobiles that are high-tech, state-of-the-art vehicles with unique design features or equipment. The exotic automobiles are not licensed or set up to be used on the road. Rather, the cars are used exclusively for car shows or related promotional photography. With respect to the exotic automobiles, Juan would like to know whether he can take a cost recovery deduction on his Federal income tax return.

Partial list of research aids:
Bruce Selig, 70 TCM 1125, T.C.Memo. 1995–519.

Use internet tax resources to address the following questions. Look for reliable websites and blogs of the IRS and other government agencies, media outlets, businesses, tax professionals, academics, think tanks, and political outlets.

Research Problem 4. Locate a financial calculator app or program that assesses the wisdom of buying versus leasing a new car. Use it to work through Problem 46 in this chapter.

Research Problem 5. There are significant tax planning opportunities related to fixed asset acquisition (and depreciation). Search out how large public accounting firms are assisting clients in this area. Summarize your findings in an e-mail to your instructor.

Communications

Research Problem 6. Do depreciation deductions vary by entity type or by industry? Go to the IRS Tax Statistics page (**irs.gov/statistics**), and review the spreadsheets containing data for corporations, partnerships, and nonfarm proprietorships by sector or industry. You can find these in the Business Tax Statistics section of the IRS site.

Communications
Critical Thinking
Data Analytics

Evaluate the depreciation deductions by sector (19 sectors are identified in the IRS spreadsheets) and by entity using Microsoft Excel. E-mail the spreadsheet to your instructor along with a brief summary of your findings.

Becker CPA Review Questions

Becker

1. Michael Sima, a sole proprietor craftsman, purchased an amount of equipment in the current year that exceeded the maximum allowable § 179 depreciation election limit by $20,000. Sima's total purchases of property placed in service in the current year did not exceed the § 179 phaseout threshold. All of the personal property (including the equipment) was purchased in November of the current year. Sima elected the maximum § 179 and elected out of bonus depreciation. The § 179 expense election did not create or increase a loss on Sima's Schedule C for the current year. Which method may Sima use to depreciate the remaining equipment in the current year?
   a. Sima may not depreciate any additional equipment other than the § 179 maximum in the current year and must carry forward the excess amount to use in the following taxable year.
   b. MACRS half-year convention for personal property.
   c. MACRS mid-quarter convention for personal property.
   d. Straight-line, mid-month convention for real property.
2. Cox Construction, a company in its 10th year of business, purchased a piece of equipment on April 1, year 9, for $20,000. Cox has used it for business purposes since the initial purchase date. The company depreciated the equipment using the MACRS half-year table for 5-year assets. For tax purposes, what is the amount of accumulated depreciation for the equipment as of December 31, year 10?
   a. $6,000
   b. $10,400
   c. $11,600
   d. $12,800
3. Stem Corp. bought a machine in February of year 7 for $20,000. Then Stem bought furniture in November of year 7 for $30,000. Both machines were placed in service for business purposes immediately after purchase. No other assets were purchased during year 7. What depreciation convention must Stem use for the machine purchased in February year 7?
   a. Mid-month
   b. Half-year
   c. Mid-quarter
   d. Full-year
4. Data, Inc., purchased and placed in service $5,000 of office furniture on August 24, year 3. This is the only asset purchase during the year. Code § 179 expensing and bonus depreciation were not elected. Using the excerpt of the MACRS half-year convention table below, what is the MACRS depreciation in year 3 for the office furniture?

Recovery Period	5-Year	7-Year	10-Year
1	20%	14.29%	10%
2	32%	24.49%	18%
3	19.2%	17.49%	14.4%

   a. $500
   b. $715
   c. $875
   d. $1,000
5. Which statement below is correct?
   a. Real property is depreciated using the half-year convention.
   b. Residential real estate is depreciated over a 39-year life.
   c. One-half month of depreciation is taken for the month real property is disposed of.
   d. Salvage value is considered in MACRS depreciation.
6. Charlie purchased an apartment building on November 16, year 1, for $1,000,000. Determine the cost recovery for year 20.
   a. $36,360
   b. $32,100
   c. $45,500
   d. $331,850

7. Under which of the following tax cost recovery methods can the amount a taxpayer can deduct each year be limited?
   a. MACRS depreciation.
   b. Straight-line depreciation.
   c. § 179 expense.
   d. First-year bonus depreciation.
8. Which statement below is incorrect about the § 179 deduction?
   a. The § 179 deduction is allowed even if there is a loss.
   b. The § 179 deduction may be reduced based on total purchases.
   c. Real property is generally not eligible for the § 179 deduction.
   d. Corporations may elect to take the § 179 deduction.

Chapter 9

Deductions: Employee and Self-Employed-Related Expenses

Learning Objectives: *After completing Chapter 9, you should be able to:*

- **LO.1** Distinguish between employee and self-employed (independent contractor) status.
- **LO.2** Recognize deductible transportation expenses.
- **LO.3** Describe how travel expenses are treated.
- **LO.4** Differentiate between deductible and nondeductible education expenses.
- **LO.5** Identify other business expenses.
- **LO.6** Determine a taxpayer's deduction for qualified business income.
- **LO.7** Compare various deductions for contributions to retirement accounts.
- **LO.8** Demonstrate the difference between accountable and nonaccountable employee plans.
- **LO.9** Recognize the limitations on miscellaneous itemized deductions.
- **LO.10** Identify tax planning ideas related to employee and self-employed business expenses.

Chapter Outline

9-1 Employee versus Independent Contractor, 9-2

9-2 Self-Employed and Employee-Related Expenses—In General, 9-5

9-3 Transportation Expenses, 9-5
- 9-3a Qualified Expenses, 9-5
- 9-3b Computation of Automobile Expenses, 9-6

9-4 Travel Expenses, 9-9
- 9-4a Definition of Travel Expenses, 9-9
- 9-4b Away-from-Home Requirement, 9-10
- 9-4c Restrictions on Travel Expenses, 9-11
- 9-4d Combined Business and Pleasure Travel, 9-12

9-5 Education Expenses, 9-14
- 9-5a General Requirements, 9-14
- 9-5b Legal Requirements to Keep a Job, 9-14
- 9-5c Maintaining or Improving Existing Skills, 9-15
- 9-5d What Expenses Are Allowed?, 9-15
- 9-5e Other Provisions Dealing with Education, 9-16

9-6 Other Business Expenses, 9-17
- 9-6a Office in the Home, 9-17
- 9-6b Moving Expenses, 9-21
- 9-6c Entertainment and Meal Expenses, 9-21
- 9-6d Miscellaneous Employee Expenses, 9-24

9-7 The Deduction for Qualified Business Income, 9-25
- 9-7a General Rule, 9-25
- 9-7b The Overall Limitation: Modified Taxable Income, 9-26
- 9-7c What Is Qualified Business Income?, 9-26
- 9-7d What Is a Qualified Trade or Business?, 9-27
- 9-7e Limitations on the QBI Deduction, 9-29
- 9-7f Limitation Based on Wages and Capital Investment, 9-29
- 9-7g Limitation for "Specified Services" Businesses, 9-33
- 9-7h Reporting the Qualified Business Income Deduction, 9-42
- 9-7i Aggregation of Qualified Trades or Businesses under the § 199A Regulations, 9-43
- 9-7j Treatment of Losses, 9-48
- 9-7k Other Items in the § 199A Regulations, 9-51

9-8 Contributions to Retirement Accounts, 9-52
- 9-8a Employee IRAs, 9-52
- 9-8b Self-Employed Keogh (H.R. 10) Plans, 9-53

9-9 Classification of Employee Expenses, 9-53
- 9-9a Accountable Plans, 9-53
- 9-9b Nonaccountable Plans, 9-54

9-10 Limitations on Itemized Deductions, 9-55
- 9-10a Miscellaneous Itemized Deductions Subject to the 2%-of-AGI Floor, 9-55
- 9-10b Miscellaneous Itemized Deductions Not Subject to the 2%-of-AGI Floor, 9-56

9-11 Tax Planning, 9-56
- 9-11a Employment Status, 9-56
- 9-11b Implications of Misclassifying Workers, 9-56
- 9-11c Transportation and Travel Expenses, 9-57

The Big Picture

The First Job

After an extensive search, Morgan, a recent college graduate with a major in child development, has accepted a job with Enrichment Child Care Center (ECCC) in a neighboring state. ECCC is located in the western suburbs of a large metropolitan city, roughly 30 miles from the center of the city. Morgan will be moving into a two-bedroom apartment about two miles from ECCC. At ECCC, Morgan will work with preschool children Monday to Friday from 7 A.M. to 3 P.M. One of the reasons she accepted the position at ECCC is the flexibility it provides. Because she is eager to pay off her student loans and save to buy a house, she has decided to freelance in the late afternoons and evenings and on weekends—joining the "gig economy."

She finds two ways to freelance: (1) transporting people, packages, and meals for a few companies where she finds work through an "app" (like driving for Uber) and (2) tutoring elementary school students in English and math. Her tutoring can take place online or in person (either in her apartment or at the child's home). She has dedicated the second bedroom in her apartment for freelancing. She has a large table and several chairs in this bedroom that allow her to meet her tutoring students or connect with them via her laptop. She keeps all of her freelancing records in a file cabinet, which she keeps in a closet in the bedroom. She also purchases and keeps various supplies for her tutoring activities in the closet. Although there are some freelance driving options in the suburbs, most often Morgan heads for the city, where there are more passengers and higher fares.

What are some of the income tax issues presented by this situation?

Read the chapter and formulate your response.

Framework 1040 **Tax Formula for Individuals**

This chapter covers the boldfaced portions of the Tax Formula for Individuals that was introduced in Concept Summary 3.1 on p. 3-3. Below those portions are the sections of Form 1040 where the results are reported.

Income *(broadly defined)*	$xx,xxx
Less: Exclusions	(x,xxx)
Gross income	$xx,xxx
Less: Deductions *for* adjusted gross income	**(x,xxx)**

FORM 1040 (Schedule 1)

3	Business income or (loss). Attach Schedule C
11	Educator expenses
12	Certain business expenses of reservists, performing artists, and fee-basis government officials. Attach Form 2106
15	Deductible part of self-employment tax. Attach Schedule SE
16	Self-employed SEP, SIMPLE, and qualified plans
17	Self-employed health insurance deduction
20	IRA deduction

Adjusted gross income	$xx,xxx
Less: The greater of total itemized deductions *or* the standard deduction	(x,xxx)

FORM 1040 (p. 1)

12a	**Standard deduction or itemized deductions** (from Schedule A)
12b	Charitable contributions if you take the standard deduction*
13	Qualified business income deduction from Form 8995 or Form 8995-A***

Personal and dependency exemptions**	(x,xxx)
Taxable income	$xx,xxx
Tax on taxable income *(see Tax Tables or Tax Rate Schedules)*	$ x,xxx
Less: Tax credits *(including income taxes withheld and prepaid)*	(xxx)
Tax due (or refund)	$ xxx

* For 2021, married taxpayers may claim up to $600 of cash charitable donations ($300 if unmarried).
** Exemption deductions are not allowed from 2018 through 2025.
*** Only applies from 2018 through 2025.

Considering the large number of taxpayers affected, the tax treatment of job-related expenses is somewhat complex. To resolve this complexity, a number of key questions must be asked:

- Is the taxpayer an *employee* or *self-employed*?
- What expenses *qualify* as deductions?
- How are the deductible expenses *classified* for tax purposes (*for* AGI or *from* AGI)?
- To the extent the expenses are classified as deductions *from* AGI, are they subject to any *limitation*?

In addition to answering these questions, the chapter also discusses the deduction for qualified business income and some tax planning ideas.

9-1 Employee versus Independent Contractor

LO.1

Distinguish between employee and self-employed (independent contractor) status.

When one person performs services for another, the person performing the service either is an employee or is self-employed (an **independent contractor**). Failure to recognize a person's work status correctly can have serious tax consequences (in addition to Federal and state labor law consequences). Tax deficiencies as well as interest and penalties may result from improper classification.

Unlike employees, self-employed individuals do not have to be included in the employer's various fringe benefit programs (e.g., group term life insurance and retirement plans). Because self-employed individuals are not covered by FICA and FUTA (see Chapter 1), a business also avoids these payroll costs. The IRS is aware of the tendency of some businesses to attempt to classify workers as self-employed rather than as employees.

Employment status also makes a great deal of difference to the person who performs the services. Expenses of self-employed individuals, if deductible, are classified as deductions *for* AGI and are reported on Schedule C (Profit or Loss From Business) of Form 1040.[1] Unless reimbursed under an accountable plan (discussed later in the chapter), employee business expenses are deductions *from* AGI as miscellaneous itemized deductions. However, from 2018 through 2025, the deduction for miscellaneous itemized deductions is suspended. As a result, there is no tax benefit from these deductions during this period.[2]

Most persons classified as employees are common law employees. The common law employee classification originated in the courts and is summarized in various IRS pronouncements.[3] Revenue Ruling 87–41, for example, lists 20 factors to determine whether a worker is a common law employee or an independent contractor (and, thus, self-employed).[4] The IRS has indicated that these 20 factors can be grouped into three broad categories: behavioral control, financial control, and the relationship of the parties.

An employee-employer relationship exists when the employer has the right to control what is to be done and the ways and means by which results are to be attained.[5] In general, this means that a worker is classified as an employee if the employer identifies *what* should be done and *how* it should be done. If an individual is told *what* to do but is allowed to independently determine how to do it, an employee-employer relationship likely does not exist.

If a business provides the following items to a worker, a common law employee-employer relationship likely exists:

- Furnishing tools or equipment and a place to work.
- Providing support services, including the hiring of assistants to help do the work.
- Training the worker for needed job skills.
- Allowing participation in various workplace fringe benefits (e.g., accident and health plans, group life insurance, and retirement plans).
- Paying for services based on time rather than the task performed.

Alternatively, independent contractors are more likely to have unreimbursed business expenses, a significant investment in tools and work facilities, and less permanency in their business relationships. Independent contractors anticipate a profit from their work, make their services available to the relevant marketplace, and are likely to be paid a flat fee on a per-job basis.

In resolving employment status, each case must be tested on its own merits. But the key test is whether the business (service recipient) has the *right to control* the means and methods of accomplishment (both what must be done *and* how it should be done). If this is the case, an employer-employee relationship exists. Concept Summary 9.1 provides an overview of the current IRS position in this area.

Code § 6041(a) requires businesses that pay $600 or more in a calendar year to a contractor to issue Form 1099–NEC (Nonemployee Compensation) to the IRS and the contractor after year-end. While this helps the contractor determine their income tax obligations, it is crucial that this business owner (contractor) maintain proper records of all receipts and expenses to be able to satisfy all of their income and other tax obligations.

---

[1]In simple situations, a Schedule C–EZ can be used. Also, a Schedule SE (Self-Employment Tax) must be filed.

[2]§ 67(g); added by the Tax Cuts and Jobs Act (TCJA) of 2017.

[3]See, for example, IRS Publication 15–A (*Employer's Supplemental Tax Guide*).

[4]Also see IRS Publication 1779 (*Independent Contractor or Employee*).

[5]Reg. § 31.3401(c)–(1)(b).

Concept Summary 9.1

Employee versus Independent Contractor

Although the 20 factors identified by the Internal Revenue Service in Revenue Ruling 87–41 remain relevant, the IRS has grouped these factors into three broad categories in order to provide some clarity to a difficult area, while acknowledging that the 20 factors are not all-inclusive.

Behavioral Control

- Does the business control (or have the right to control) what the worker does and how the worker does their job?
- Facts that show whether the business has **behavioral control** include:
  - *Instructions*. An employee is generally told:
    1. When, where, and how to work.
    2. What equipment, tools, or processes to use.
    3. What workers can be hired to assist with the work.
    4. Where to purchase supplies and services.
    5. What work must be performed by a specified individual.
    6. What order or sequence to follow in performing the work.
  - *Training*. An employee normally receives training to perform work in a particular manner.

Financial Control

- Are the business aspects of the worker's job controlled by the payer?
- Facts that show whether the business has **financial control** include:
  - The extent to which the worker has unreimbursed business expenses.
  - The extent of the worker's investment.
  - The extent to which the worker makes services available to a larger market (e.g., is the worker marketing their services to multiple businesses?).
  - How the business pays the worker (is it the same as or different from how employees are paid?).
  - The extent to which the worker can realize a profit or loss.

The Relationship of the Parties

- A variety of facts and documents can show the **relationship of the parties**:
  - Written contracts describing the relationship the parties intended to create.
  - Whether the worker is provided with employee-type fringe benefits.
  - The permanency of the relationship (e.g., is the work for a specified period of time or indefinite?).
  - How integral the services are to the principal activity of the business.

Summary

1. Businesses must weigh all factors when determining whether a worker is an employee or independent contractor. Some factors might indicate that the worker is an employee, and other factors might indicate that the worker is an independent contractor.
2. No set number of factors "makes" the worker an employee or an independent contractor, and no one factor controls in making this determination. Also, factors that are relevant in one setting may not be relevant in a different setting.
3. Overall, one must look at the entirety of the relationship, consider the degree or extent of the right to direct and control, and document each of the factors used in coming to a decision.

Employee *versus* Independent Contractor

Example 1

Arnold is a lawyer whose major client accounts for 60% of his billings. He does the routine legal work and income tax returns at the client's request. He is paid a monthly retainer in addition to amounts charged for extra work. Arnold is a self-employed individual. Even though most of his income comes from one client, he still has the right to determine how the end result of his work is attained.

Example 2

Ellen is a lawyer hired by Arnold to assist him in the performance of services for the client mentioned in Example 1. Ellen is under Arnold's supervision; he reviews her work and pays her an hourly fee. Ellen is an employee of Arnold.

When one taxpayer holds multiple jobs, it is possible to have dual status as both an employee and an independent contractor (i.e., self-employed).

Example 3

Dr. Stephanie Davis, DDS, is a full-time employee at the Robin University Health Center. In the evenings and on weekends, she shares a practice with another dentist who works the Monday through Friday day-time shifts. Dr. Davis is both employed and self-employed.

Certain workers who *are not* common law employees are treated as employees for employment tax purposes. Known as **statutory employees**, this group includes certain drivers (e.g., nondairy beverage distributors and laundry and dry cleaning pickup service), life insurance sales agents, home workers, and other salespersons. These employees are allowed to claim their business-related expenses as deductions *for* AGI by using Schedule C. The wages or commissions paid to statutory employees are not subject to Federal income tax withholding but are subject to Social Security tax.[6]

To avoid the confusion that might otherwise result in their classification, the tax law categorically treats certain categories of workers as independent contractors. Included in this group are licensed real estate agents and direct sellers. These individuals are treated as self-employed for all Federal purposes, including income and employment taxes.[7]

If a taxpayer wants to know whether employee or independent contractor status exists, the IRS will make a determination if the taxpayer files a Form SS–8 (Determination of Worker Status for Purposes of Federal Employment Taxes and Income Tax Withholding).

9-2 Self-Employed and Employee-Related Expenses—In General

Self-employed and employee expenses fall into one of the following categories:

- Transportation.
- Travel.
- Moving.
- Education.
- Entertainment.
- Other (including office in the home and miscellaneous expenses).

Self-employed deductions are allowed *for* AGI; most employee business expenses are miscellaneous itemized deductions (a *from* AGI deduction and subject to a 2%-of-AGI floor). The Tax Cuts and Jobs Act (TCJA) of 2017 made a significant change in this area by suspending the deduction for miscellaneous itemized deductions (including unreimbursed employee business expenses) from 2018 through 2025. As a result, the only employee business expenses that are currently deductible are those that are *reimbursed by an employer* (and these expenses, once reimbursed, have no effect on an employee's taxable income).

Given the TCJA of 2017 changes to the status of employee business expenses, the materials that follow are focused on the self-employed taxpayer. However, employees incurring these expenses in employer-related activities might be able to seek reimbursement for them. In addition, an employee also might have a separate business (e.g., consulting, rentals, etc.) that would allow these business expenses to be deducted in that activity.

9-3 Transportation Expenses

LO.2

Recognize deductible transportation expenses.

9-3a Qualified Expenses

A deduction is allowed for business transportation expenses. **Transportation expenses** include only the cost of transporting the self-employed taxpayer (or employee) from one place to another in the course of business when the taxpayer is *not in travel status* (discussed in text Section 9-4). Transportation costs include taxi fares, automobile expenses, tolls, and parking.

[6] § 3121(d)(3). See Circular E, *Employer's Tax Guide* (IRS Publication 15), for further discussion of statutory employees.

[7] § 3508. Also see *Employer's Supplemental Tax Guide* (IRS Publication 15–A).

Commuting Expenses

Commuting between home and one's place of employment is a personal, nondeductible expense. The fact that one employee drives 30 miles to work and another employee walks six blocks to work does not matter.

Example 4

Geraldo is employed by Sparrow Corporation. He drives 22 miles each way to work. The 44 miles he drives each workday are nondeductible commuting expenses.

If a taxpayer has a home office that qualifies as a principal place of business, the transportation costs between home and various work locations are deductible (i.e., the costs are *not* a commuting expense).

The Big Picture

Example 5

Return to the facts of *The Big Picture* on p. 9-1. Because Morgan will have an office in her home for her two freelancing businesses, the apartment will be her principal place of business. As a result, any transportation from her home to freelancing sites (e.g., driving to a child's home for tutoring) is *not* a commuting expense.[8] However, Morgan will have commuting expenses for the mileage between her apartment and her job at Enrichment Child Care Center.

9-3b Computation of Automobile Expenses

A taxpayer has two choices in determining automobile expenses: the automatic mileage method and the actual cost method. If an automobile is used for both business and personal purposes (mixed use), only the expenses related to the business use are deductible. The percentage of business use is usually arrived at by comparing the business mileage with total mileage—both business and personal.

Automatic Mileage Method

Also called the standard mileage method, the **automatic mileage method** is convenient in that it simplifies record keeping. The rate allowed per mile takes into account average operating expenses (such as gas and oil, repairs, and depreciation). Consequently, the taxpayer only has to multiply the automatic mileage rate by the business miles driven to compute the deduction.

For 2022, the deduction is based on 58.5 cents per mile for business miles.[9] This represents a two and one-half cent increase from the rate of 56 cents that applied in 2021. Although the mileage rate usually remains constant for an entire year, the IRS occasionally makes mid-year changes to the rate, usually when there is a large change in the cost of fuel. As a result, it is important that the taxpayer keep records to identify when the driving took place.

Example 6

Chad drove his car 20,000 miles for business during 2022. To determine his standard mileage deduction, he simply multiplies his business miles by the appropriate standard mileage rate (58.5 cents per mile in 2022). So his total standard mileage deduction for the year is $11,700 (20,000 miles × 58.5 cents per mile).

The automatic mileage rate for deductible education expenses is the same as for business; 18 cents per mile is allowed for medical purposes, and the rate for the charitable contribution deduction is 14 cents a mile (see Chapter 10 for a discussion of medical

[8] *Walter K. Strohmalter*, 113 T.C. 106 (1999).

[9] Notice 2022–3 and Rev.Proc. 2019–46.

expenses and charitable contributions). Parking fees and tolls are allowed in addition to the deduction computed using the automatic mileage method.

Generally, a taxpayer may elect either method for any particular year. However, the following restrictions apply to the standard mileage method:

- The vehicle must be owned or leased by the taxpayer.
- If five or more vehicles are in use (for business purposes) at the *same* time (not alternately), a taxpayer may not use the automatic mileage method.
- A basis adjustment for depreciation is required if the taxpayer changes from the automatic mileage method to the actual operating cost method. The depreciation adjustment for the business miles is determined using the following schedule:

Year	Rate per Mile
2022	26 cents
2021	26 cents
2020	27 cents
2019	26 cents
2018	25 cents

Example 7

Tim purchased his automobile in 2019 for $36,000. It is used 90% for business purposes. Tim drove the automobile for 10,000 business miles in 2021, 8,500 business miles in 2020, and 6,000 business miles in 2019. At the beginning of 2022, the basis of the business portion of his car is $25,945.

Depreciable basis ($36,000 × 90%)	$32,400
Less depreciation:	
2021 (10,000 miles × 26 cents)	(2,600)
2020 (8,500 miles × 27 cents)	(2,295)
2019 (6,000 miles × 26 cents)	(1,560)
Adjusted business basis 1/1/2022	$25,945

- Use of the automatic mileage method in the first year an auto is placed in service is considered an election to exclude the auto from MACRS cost recovery (discussed in Chapter 8).
- A taxpayer may not switch to the automatic mileage method if the MACRS statutory percentage method or a § 179 expense election has been used.

Actual Cost Method

Under this method, the actual cost of operating the automobile is used to compute the deduction. Actual costs include the following expenses:

- Gas and oil, lubrication.
- Depreciation (or lease payments).
- Insurance.
- Dues to auto clubs.
- Repairs.
- Tires and other parts.
- Licenses and registration fees.
- Parking and tolls.

Example 8

Return to the facts of Example 6. Chad drove his car a total of 25,000 miles in 2022 (20,000 for business and 5,000 for personal use). He incurred the following automobile costs (he has receipts for all of these expenses):

Lease payments ($350 per month)	$ 4,200
Fuel	2,300
Insurance	2,800
Repairs and maintenance	1,200
State registration fee	150
Total expenses	$ 10,650
× Business use percentage (20,000 ÷ 25,000)	× 80%
Actual cost method deduction	$ 8,520

As a result, Chad is better off using the automatic mileage method. Chad's true cost of operating the vehicle is 42.6 cents per mile ($10,650 ÷ 25,000 miles), yet the government is allowing him to deduct 58.5 cents per mile.

As noted in Chapter 8, deductions for depreciation (or lease payments) are subject to limitations when a "mixed use" vehicle is involved (e.g., a vehicle used in both business and personal activities). Interest on a car loan is not deductible if the taxpayer is an employee, but it can qualify as a business expense if the taxpayer is self-employed. Sales taxes paid on the purchase of a car are added to the cost of the car and recovered via the MACRS deduction. In mixed use situations, the portion of the sales tax attributable to personal use may, in some cases, be claimed as a deduction *from* AGI (see Chapter 10 and the choice required between state and local income and sales taxes).

Except for parking and tolls, none of the expenses noted previously can be separately claimed under the automatic mileage method. A deduction for parking tickets and other traffic violations is not allowed under either method because it is a violation of public policy [§ 162(f); see Chapter 6].

The Big Picture

Example 9

Return to the facts of *The Big Picture* on p. 9-1. During Morgan's senior year in college, her parents gave her one of the family cars—a 2018 Toyota Camry. Morgan has no idea as to the car's original cost or the odometer reading at the time the car was registered in her name. She has, however, kept track of the miles driven for business since she accepted her new job. Morgan should use the automatic mileage method in claiming business use of the car.

Which Method Is Best?

Every year the American Automobile Association estimates how much it costs per mile to drive a car in the United States. Its most recent report shows that it costs, on average, anywhere from 48.2 cents to 62.4 cents per mile to drive a sedan for 15,000 miles. Driving a compact SUV for 15,000 miles costs an average of 56.6 cents per mile, and an all-wheel drive SUV costs 66.5 cents per mile.[10]

The difference depends on the size (and cost) of the car and the number of miles driven during the year—the more miles driven, the less one's cost per mile.

In general, taxpayers are better off using the standard mileage rate if they drive a smaller car, particularly if they drive many business miles. And a taxpayer is likely to benefit from using the standard mileage rate if an old or inexpensive car is used. Why? Because the same fixed deduction rate applies no matter how much the car is worth. Because the standard mileage rate factors in depreciation (which does not vary), an inexpensive car might benefit more from using this method than would an expensive vehicle.

[10]American Automobile Association, *Your Driving Costs*, 2021 edition.

The actual cost method will likely provide a larger deduction if the taxpayer drives a more expensive car, an SUV, or a minivan. In addition, the actual cost method will normally result in a larger deduction if fewer business miles are driven.

Yet the only way to know for sure which method is best is to keep careful track of the actual costs and the business mileage driven. Then calculations can be done under both methods, and the larger deduction can be taken.

The Big Picture

Example 10

Return to the facts of *The Big Picture* on p. 9-1. Morgan wants to make sure she documents her business miles appropriately. She knows that the IRS expects her to keep track of her business miles on a regular basis, including where she drove and the business reason for the trip. She wonders whether there are some mobile apps that can help.

Actually, a number of mileage tracking apps are available that would allow Morgan to begin logging miles automatically every time she started a trip. Some use Bluetooth and begin as soon as the car starts moving; others (usually free) require the user to input locations. All of the apps create detailed records of all trips; the user just needs to identify the purpose of the trip. Here are a few apps that are available (with information from the developer's website):

- **MileIQ (mileiq.com)** tracks every trip you take automatically. Then it lets you quickly categorize a trip as business, personal, medical, charity, or a custom category you create. It also lets you log any additional information (like freeway tolls or parking fees). Trip information is backed up automatically using MileIQ's cloud servers, and its data integrates with a number of accounting/tax software programs (including QuickBooks). MileIQ is free if you track fewer than 40 trips per month and about $60 per year with unlimited trip tracking.
- **TripLog (triplogmileage.com)** monitors your mileage via GPS; tracks any parking, tolls, or other expenses; records fuel costs; generates IRS-ready reports; and integrates with QuickBooks. As with MileIQ, you have the option of specifying the nature of the trip (business, charity, medical, etc.), entering notes, and adding any applicable parking or toll costs. TripLog's basic features are free. Advanced features, such as Bluetooth "autostart" and automatic daily cloud backup, cost about $60 per year. You also can use TripLog to estimate your gas mileage and find the best gas prices.
- **QuickBooks Self Employed (quickbooks.intuit.com/self-employed/)** automatically tracks mileage using your phone's GPS and groups the information into trips (allowing you to categorize them as business or personal). This feature, combined with easy expense categorization (via swiping on the phone) and the ability to organize receipts by taking a picture, lets you easily compare whether you should use the standard mileage or actual cost method. And it integrates seamlessly with TurboTax when it is time to file a tax return. Currently, the app costs $7.50 per month ($12 per month when combined with TurboTax).
- **Stride Drive (stridehealth.com/drive)** is a free mileage and expense tracking app that records your mileage by running in the background as you drive. You can start and stop recording your mileage for each trip by tapping the start button when you leave home, or in some versions of the app, you can set it up to record automatically. You also can use Stride Drive to log your receipts and expense records, so all your business deductions are in one place at tax time. The app includes preloaded categories and explanations (many geared toward rideshare drivers) that help identify which expenses to log (and what percentage of them you can deduct).

9-4 Travel Expenses

LO.3

Describe how travel expenses are treated.

9-4a Definition of Travel Expenses

A deduction is allowed for business travel expenses. **Travel expenses** include transportation expenses, meals and lodging, and incidental expenses while working away from home. In general, the reason for allowing a travel expense deduction is to alleviate the duplication of living expenses (where the taxpayer incurs expenses while at home and while working away from home).

Transportation expenses (discussed previously) are deductible even if the taxpayer is *not* away from home. Meals cannot be lavish or extravagant. Examples of incidental expenses include laundry, baggage fees and/or tips, and ATM fees. A deduction for travel expenses, however, is only allowed if the taxpayer is away from their tax home.

9-4b Away-from-Home Requirement

The crucial test for the deductibility of travel expenses is whether the taxpayer is away from home overnight. "Overnight" need not be a 24-hour period, but it must be a period substantially longer than an ordinary day's work and must require rest, sleep, or a relief-from-work period.[11] A one-day business trip normally does not warrant travel status; therefore, meals and lodging for such a trip are not deductible.

Temporary Assignments

The taxpayer must be away from home for a temporary period. If a taxpayer relocates to a new area for an indefinite period of time, that new location becomes the taxpayer's tax home. *Temporary* indicates that the assignment's termination is expected within a reasonably short period of time. The position of the IRS is that the tax home is the business location of the taxpayer. As a result, travel expenses are not deductible if a taxpayer is reassigned for an indefinite period and does not move their place of residence to the new location.

Temporary Becomes Permanent

Example 11

Malcolm maintains a consulting practice in Los Angeles. Due to new client responsibilities, Malcolm decided to open a new office in San Diego. Malcolm worked out of the new office for three months to train a new manager and to assist in setting up the new office. He tried commuting from his home in Los Angeles for a week and decided that he could not continue driving several hours a day. He rented an apartment in San Diego, where he lived during the week. He spent weekends with his wife and children at their home in Los Angeles.

Malcolm's rent, meals, laundry, incidentals, and automobile expenses in San Diego are deductible. To the extent that Malcolm's transportation expense related to his weekend trips home exceeds what his cost of meals and lodging would have been, the excess is personal and nondeductible.

Example 12

Assume that Malcolm in Example 11 decided that he was the best person to manage the new office in San Diego and so decided to move there permanently. His wife and children continued to live in Los Angeles until the end of the school year.

Malcolm is no longer "away from home" because the assignment is not temporary. His travel expenses are not deductible.

To curtail controversy in this area, the Code specifies that a taxpayer "*shall not* be treated as *temporarily* away from home during any period of employment if such period exceeds 1 year."[12]

Determining the Tax Home

In most situations, determining the location of a taxpayer's tax home is not difficult. The tax home is the area in which the taxpayer works.

It is possible for a taxpayer never to be away from their tax home. In other words, the tax home follows the taxpayer. In this situation, all meals and lodging remain personal and are not deductible.

---

[11] *U.S. v. Correll*, 68–1 USTC ¶9101, 20 AFTR 2d 5845, 88 S.Ct. 445 (1967); Rev.Rul. 75–168.

[12] § 162(a).

Example 13

Jim is single and works full-time as a long-haul truck driver. He lists his mother's home as his address and stays there during holidays. However, he contributes nothing toward its maintenance.

Because Jim has no regular place of duty or place where he regularly lives, his tax home is where he works (i.e., on the road). As an itinerant (transient), he is never away from home, and all of his meals and lodging while on the road are personal and not deductible.

The result reached in Example 13 is justified on the grounds that there is no duplication of living expenses in the case of itinerant taxpayers.[13]

When a taxpayer has more than one place of business or work, the main one is considered to be the tax home. This is determined by considering the time spent, the level of activity involved, and the income earned at each job.

Example 14

Art, a physical therapist, lives with his family in Lancaster, Pennsylvania. For seven months each year, he is employed by the New Orleans Saints football team at a salary of $150,000. During this period, he rents an apartment in New Orleans. In the off-season, he works for the Lancaster YMCA at a salary of $15,000.

Art's tax home is clearly New Orleans and not Lancaster. Consequently, his living expenses while in New Orleans (i.e., food and lodging) are not deductible.

9-4c Restrictions on Travel Expenses

The possibility always exists that taxpayers will attempt to treat vacation or pleasure travel as deductible business travel. To prevent such practices, the law contains restrictions on certain travel expenses.

Conventions

For travel expenses to be deductible, a convention must be directly related to the taxpayer's trade or business.[14] Compare Examples 15 and 16.

Type of Convention

Example 15

Dr. Hill, a pathologist who works for a hospital in Ohio, travels to Las Vegas to attend a two-day session on recent developments in estate planning. No deduction is allowed for Dr. Hill's travel expenses.

Example 16

Assume the same facts as in Example 15, except that the convention deals entirely with recent developments in pathology. Now a travel deduction is allowed.

The taxpayer must attend convention sessions along with other participants in order to claim a deduction. Attendance does not include watching or listening to sessions at a later date that are recorded (e.g., a taxpayer cannot vacation during the convention sessions and watch the videos later). However, a deduction will be allowed for costs (other than travel, meals, and entertainment) of renting or using recorded materials related to business.

[13] Rev.Rul. 73–529 and *James O. Henderson*, 70 TCM 1407, T.C.Memo. 1995–559, *aff'd* by 98–1 USTC ¶50,375, 81 AFTR 2d 98–1748, 143 F.3d 497 (CA–9).

[14] § 274(h)(1).

Example 17

A CPA is unable to attend a convention at which current developments in taxation are discussed. She pays $300 to stream the recorded sessions and views them at home later. The $300 is a deduction *for* AGI if the CPA is self-employed. If the CPA is an employee, the $300 is a miscellaneous itemized deduction (and not allowed from 2018 through 2025).

The Code places stringent restrictions on the deductibility of travel expenses of the taxpayer's spouse or dependent.[15] Generally, there must be a business reason for the spouse or dependent to attend, and the expenses must be otherwise deductible.

Example 18

Assume the same facts as in Example 16 with the additional fact that Dr. Hill is accompanied by her husband, Mr. Hill. Mr. Hill is not employed, but possesses secretarial skills and takes notes during the proceedings. No deduction is allowed for Mr. Hill's travel expenses.

If, however, Mr. Hill is a medical professional trained in pathology and is employed by Dr. Hill as her assistant, his travel expenses become deductible.

Education

Travel as a form of education is not deductible.[16] If, however, the education qualifies as a deduction, the travel involved is allowed. Compare Examples 19 and 20.

Education Travel

Example 19

Greta, a German teacher, travels to Germany to maintain general familiarity with the language and culture. No travel expense deduction is allowed.

Example 20

Jean-Claude, a scholar of French literature, travels to Paris to do specific library research that cannot be done elsewhere and to take courses that are offered only at the Sorbonne. The travel costs are deductible, assuming that the other requirements for deducting education expenses (discussed later in the chapter) are met.

9-4d Combined Business and Pleasure Travel

To be deductible, travel expenses need not be incurred in the performance of specific job functions.

Domestic Travel for Business and Pleasure

In order to limit the possibility of a taxpayer claiming a tax deduction for what is essentially a personal vacation, several rules were created to handle deductions associated with combined business and pleasure trips. If the business/pleasure trip is entirely within the United States, the transportation expenses are deductible only if the trip is *primarily for business*.[17] Meals, lodging, and other expenses are allocated between business and personal days. If the trip is primarily for pleasure, no transportation expenses qualify as a deduction. Compare Examples 21 and 22.

[15] § 274(m)(3).

[16] § 274(m)(2).

[17] Reg. § 1.162–2(b)(1).

Meeting the Primary Business Purpose Requirement

Example 21

In 2022, Hana travels from Seattle to New York primarily for business. She spends five days conducting business and three days sightseeing and attending shows. Her plane and taxi fare amounts to $1,160. Her meals (all at local restaurants) amount to $200 per day, and lodging and incidental expenses are $350 per day.

She can deduct the transportation charges of $1,160, because the trip is primarily for business (five days of business versus three days of sightseeing). Meals are limited to five days and are not subject to a 50% reduction since they were consumed at local restaurants (see text Section 9-6c). Her meals deduction will be $1,000 (5 days × $200), and other expenses are limited to $1,750 (5 days × $350).

Example 22

Assume that Hana goes to New York for a two-week vacation. While there, she spends several hours renewing acquaintances with people in her company's New York office. Her transportation expenses are not deductible.

Foreign Travel for Business and Pleasure

When the trip is *outside the United States*, different rules apply. Transportation expenses must be allocated between business and personal unless:

1. The taxpayer is away from home for seven days or less, *or*
2. Less than 25 percent of the time was for personal purposes.

No allocation is required if the taxpayer has no substantial control over arrangements for the trip or the desire for a vacation is not a major factor in taking the trip. If the trip is primarily for pleasure, no transportation charges are deductible. Days devoted to travel are considered business days. Weekends, legal holidays, and intervening days are considered business days, provided both the day before and the day after were business days.[18] Compare Examples 23 and 24.

The Amount of Nonbusiness Time Permitted

Example 23

In 2022, Robert takes a trip from New York to Japan primarily for business purposes. He is away from home from June 10 through June 19. He spends three days vacationing and seven days (including two travel days) conducting business. His airfare is $4,000, his meals amount to $200 per day (all at local restaurants), and lodging and incidental expenses are $300 per day. Because Robert is away from home for more than seven days and more than 25% of his time is devoted to personal purposes, only 70% (7 days business/10 days total) of the transportation is deductible. His deductions are as follows:

Transportation (70% × 4,000)	$2,800
Lodging ($300 × 7)	2,100
Meals ($200 × 7); see text Section 9-6c	1,400
Total	$6,300

Example 24

Assume the same facts as in Example 23. Robert is gone the same period of time but spends only two days (rather than three) vacationing.

Now no allocation of transportation is required. Because the pleasure portion of the trip is less than 25% of the total, all of the airfare qualifies for the travel deduction.

[18] § 274(c) and Reg. § 1.274–4. For purposes of the seven-days-or-less exception, the departure travel day is not counted.

Record-Keeping Requirements

Distinguishing between business and personal expenses can be difficult (and somewhat subjective). As a result, the tax law includes specific provisions that require the taxpayer to maintain specific, written, contemporaneous records for travel expenses.[19] These records, which assist the IRS and courts in reaching a fair determination of the legitimacy of the expenses, must include the amount, time (or dates), place, and business purpose behind the expenses.

LO.4

Differentiate between deductible and nondeductible education expenses.

9-5 Education Expenses

9-5a General Requirements

In general, a self-employed taxpayer can deduct **education expenses** provided the expenses are:

- To meet the specific legal requirements to keep their job, or
- To maintain or improve existing skills required in the present job.

Education expenses are *not* deductible if the education is:

- To meet the minimum educational standards for qualification in the taxpayer's existing job.
- To qualify the taxpayer for a new trade or business.[20]

A deduction is generally allowed for education related to new duties if the new duties involve the same general work. For example, the IRS has ruled that a practicing dentist's education expenses incurred to become an orthodontist are deductible.[21] Fees incurred for professional qualification exams (the bar exam, for example) and fees for review courses (such as a CPA review course) are not deductible.[22] From 2018 through 2025, employees incurring education expenses that are not reimbursed by the employer may not deduct these expenses (they are employee business expenses and miscellaneous itemized deductions).

9-5b Legal Requirements to Keep a Job

Taxpayers can deduct education expenses if the education is required by law. If, however, the required education is the minimum degree required for the job, no deduction is allowed. So a taxpayer classified as a staff accountant who went back to school to obtain a bachelor's degree in accounting was not allowed to deduct the expenses, since a bachelor's degree was the minimum requirement for his job.[23] Education required by law for various professions also qualifies for a deduction.

Example 25

To satisfy the State Board of Public Accountancy rules for maintaining her CPA license, Nancy takes an auditing course sponsored by a local college. The cost of the education is deductible.

[19] § 274(d). Corroborating evidence (e.g., receipt from a hotel or an airline ticket) also is required. In general, approximations and estimates are not sufficient. If a taxpayer is unable to substantiate expenses, courts use the Cohan rule to estimate the deductible amount [*Cohan v. Commissioner*, 39 F.2d 540 (CA–2, 1930)].

[20] Reg. §§ 1.162–5(b)(2) and (3).

[21] Rev.Rul. 74–78.

[22] Reg. § 1.212–1(f) and Rev.Rul. 69–292.

[23] Reg. § 1.162–5(b)(2)(iii) Example (2); *Collin J. Davidson*, 43 TCM 743, T.C.Memo. 1982–119.

9-5c Maintaining or Improving Existing Skills

The "maintaining or improving existing skills" requirement has been difficult for both taxpayers and the courts to interpret. For example, a business consultant may be permitted to deduct the costs of obtaining an advanced degree on the grounds that the advanced management education is undertaken to maintain and improve existing management skills. The consultant also can deduct the costs of specialized, nondegree management courses that maintain or improve existing skills. Expenses incurred by a self-employed accountant to obtain a law degree are not deductible, however, because the education constitutes training for a new trade or business.[24]

The conditions required for the regular education expense deduction are summarized in Concept Summary 9.2.

Concept Summary 9.2

Conditions for Deducting Regular Education Expenses

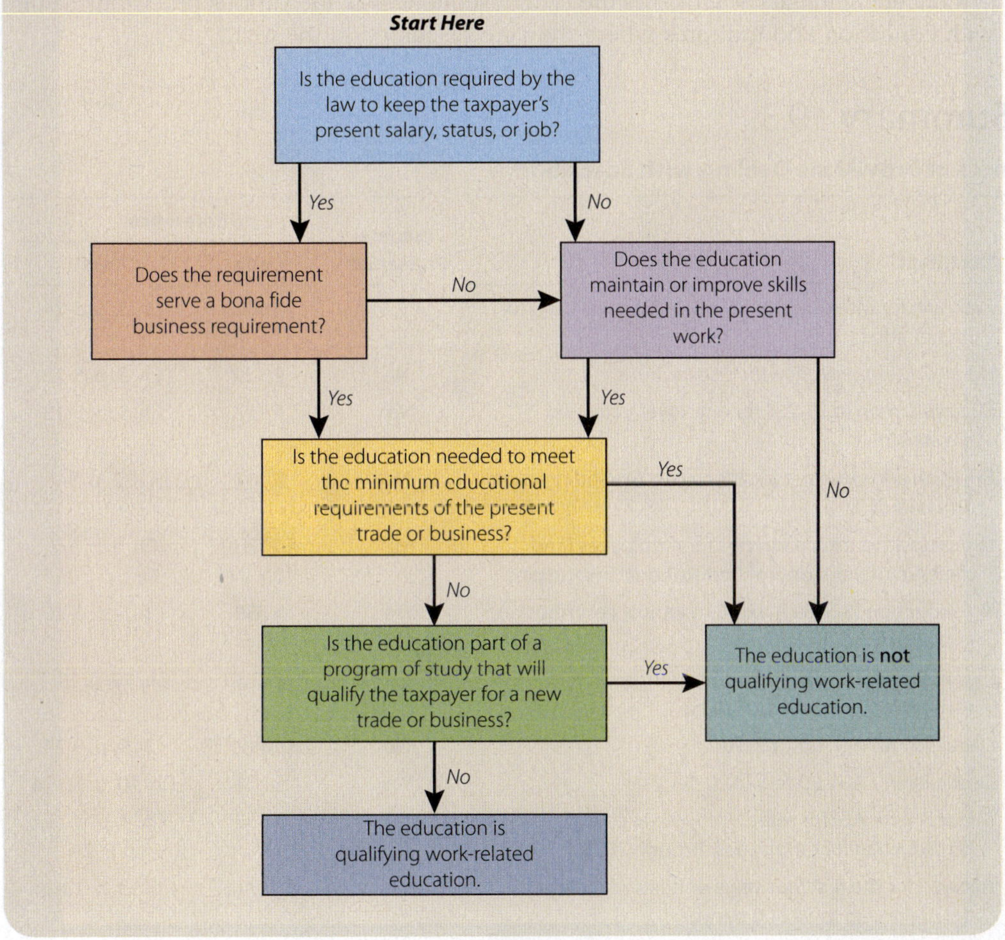

9-5d What Expenses Are Allowed?

Education expenses include tuition, books and supplies, and transportation (e.g., from the office to school) and travel (e.g., meals and lodging while away from home at an executive education training program).

---

[24]Reg. § 1.162–5(b)(3)(ii) Example (1).

The Big Picture

Example 26

Return to the facts of *The Big Picture* on p. 9-1. After starting her new job, Morgan enrolls in the evening master's degree program in child development at a local university and begins attending classes.

Although Morgan believes that the master's degree would be useful, it is not a requirement of ECCC and it is not needed to maintain or improve existing skills in her current job. As a result, none of her education expenses are deductible.[25] However, the tuition and fees (but not any expenses for books and supplies) will qualify for the lifetime learning credit (see text Section 13-4e).

9-5e Other Provisions Dealing with Education

Although this chapter deals with employment-related expenses, a wide variety of tax provisions deal with education. Because the encouragement of education is a desirable social goal, Congress continues to enact laws that provide tax incentives. The incentives come in the form of income exclusions, deductions (both *for* AGI and *from* AGI), and various credits.

Concept Summary 9.3 reviews the tax consequences of the various provisions dealing with education and indicates where they are discussed in the text.

Concept Summary 9.3

Tax Consequences of Provisions Dealing with Education

Provision	Tax Effect	Income Phaseout[a]	Reference: Code	Reference: Text
Educational savings bonds	*Exclusion* for interest on U.S. Series EE bonds used for higher education	Yes	§ 135	Ch. 5, p. 5-24
Qualified tuition program	No deduction; *exclusion* for distributions	No	§ 529	Ch. 5, p. 5-25
Educational assistance plans	*Exclusion* of up to $5,250 for employer-provided assistance	No[b]	§ 127	Ch. 5, p. 5-15
Scholarships	*Exclusion* allowed for education costs (excluding room and board)	No	§ 117	Ch. 5, p. 5-7
Qualified tuition reduction plan	*Exclusion* as to tuition waivers for employees (and dependents) of nonprofit educational institutions	No[b]	§ 117(d)	Ch. 5, p. 5-7
Coverdell education savings account (CESA)	No deduction ($2,000 maximum annual contribution); *exclusion* for distributions	Yes[c]	§ 530	Ch. 5, p. 5-25
Early distributions from IRAs	If used for qualified higher education, income recognized but penalty waived	—	§ 72(t)	Ch. 19, p. 19-7
Educator expenses	*Deduction for* AGI; up to $300	No	§ 62(a)(2)(D)	Ch. 9, p. 9-24
Interest on student loans	*Deduction for* AGI; up to $2,500 per year	Yes	§ 221	Ch. 10, p. 10-14
Job-related education expenses	*Deduction for* AGI for self-employed taxpayer; *no deduction* for employees through 2025	No	§ 162	Ch. 9, p. 9-14; p. 9-24
American Opportunity credit	Allowed for the first four years of postsecondary education; up to $2,500 per year	Yes	§ 25A(i)	Ch. 13, p. 13-18
Lifetime learning credit	20% of qualifying expenses (not to exceed $10,000 per year)	Yes	§ 25(A)(c)	Ch. 13, p. 13-18

[a]The phaseout of benefits occurs when income reaches a certain level. The phaseout amounts vary widely, depend on filing status (i.e., single or married filing jointly), and are based on MAGI (modified AGI).

[b]The availability of the benefit cannot be discriminatory (i.e., cannot favor higher-income taxpayers).

[c]The phaseout begins once AGI reaches $190,000 (married taxpayers) or $95,000 (unmarried taxpayers).

[25]*Steven Galligan*, 83 TCM 1859, T.C.Memo. 2002–150.

9-6 Other Business Expenses

LO.5

Identify other business expenses.

9-6a Office in the Home

Most expenses for personal use assets are not deductible. Except for certain expenses (primarily interest and taxes), this is the case with a personal residence. However, self-employed individuals are allowed a deduction for **office in the home expenses** if a portion of the residence is used *exclusively* on a *regular basis* as either:

- The principal place of business for any trade or business of the taxpayer, or
- A place of business used by clients, patients, or customers.

From 2018 through 2025, employees are not allowed an office in the home deduction because these expenses are employee business expenses (and miscellaneous itemized deductions).

The term *principal place of business* includes a place of business that satisfies the following requirements:[26]

- The office is used by the taxpayer to conduct administrative or management activities of a trade or business, and
- There is no other fixed location of the trade or business where the taxpayer conducts these activities.

Example 27

Josh Butler is a self-employed anesthesiologist. During the year, he spends 30 to 35 hours per week administering anesthesia and postoperative care to patients in three hospitals, none of which provides him with an office. He also spends two or three hours per day in a room in his home that he uses exclusively as an office. He does not meet patients there, but he performs a variety of tasks related to his medical practice (e.g., contacting surgeons, doing bookkeeping, and reading medical journals).

A deduction will be allowed because Dr. Butler uses the office in the home to conduct administrative or management activities of his trade or business and there is no other fixed location where these activities can be carried out.

The exclusive use requirement means that part of the home must be used *solely* for business purposes. An exception allows mixed use (both business and personal) of the home if a licensed day-care business is involved.

Exclusive Use Requirement

Example 28

Trisha is self-employed and maintains an office in her home for business purposes. The office also is used by her spouse to pay the family bills and by their children to do homework assignments. The exclusive use requirement is not met, and no office in the home deduction is allowed.

[26] § 280A(c)(1).

Exclusive Use Requirement

Example 29

Muriel operates a licensed day-care center in her home. The children use the living room as a play area during the day, and Muriel and her family use it for personal purposes in the evening and on weekends. Even though the living room is used for both business and personal purposes, Muriel can claim an office in the home deduction.

The office in the home deduction can be determined in either of two ways: the Regular (actual expense) Method or the Simplified (safe harbor) Method.

Regular Method

When using the Regular Method, relevant expenses must be categorized as direct or indirect. Direct expenses benefit only the business part of the home (e.g., repainting the office) and are deducted in full. Indirect expenses are for maintaining and operating the home (e.g., utilities and insurance). Because indirect expenses benefit both business and personal use, an allocation between the two is necessary. The allocation is made based on the floor space involved, dividing the business area by the total home area to arrive at the business percentage.

The allowable home office expenses cannot exceed the gross income from the business less all other business expenses (i.e., this deduction cannot create a loss). And the home office expenses that are allowed as itemized deductions anyway (e.g., mortgage interest and real estate taxes) must be deducted first.

Home office expenses of a self-employed individual are trade or business expenses and are deductible *for* AGI. Any disallowed home office expenses are *carried forward* and used in future years subject to the same limitations.

Example 30

Luis is a certified public accountant employed by a regional CPA firm as a tax manager. He operates a separate furniture refinishing business that he operates out of his home. For this business, he uses two rooms in the basement exclusively and regularly. The floor space of the two rooms is 240 square feet, which is 10% of the total floor space of his 2,400-square-foot residence. Gross income from the business totals $8,000. Expenses of the business (other than home office expenses) are $6,500. Luis incurs the following home office expenses:

Real property taxes on residence	$ 4,000
Interest expense on residence	7,500
Operating expenses of residence (including homeowners insurance)	2,000
MACRS cost recovery on residence (based on 10% business use)	350

Luis's deductions are determined as follows:

Business income		$ 8,000
Less: Other business expenses		(6,500)
Net income from the business (before the office in the home deduction)		$ 1,500
Less: Allocable taxes ($4,000 × 10%)	$400	
Allocable interest ($7,500 × 10%)	750	(1,150)
		$ 350
Allocable operating expenses of the residence ($2,000 × 10%)		(200)
		$ 150
Allocable MACRS cost recovery ($350, limited to remaining income)		(150)
		$ -0-

Luis has a carryover of $200 (the unused excess MACRS cost recovery). Because he is self-employed, the allocable taxes and interest ($1,150), the other deductible office expenses ($200 + $150), and $6,500 of other business expenses are deductible *for* AGI.

As noted in Example 30, the office in the home deduction includes an allocable portion of the cost recovery on the personal residence. To arrive at this cost recovery, taxpayers use the MACRS percentage for 39-year nonresidential real property (see Chapter 8). Except for the first and last years (i.e., 1 and 40), the applicable percentage is 2.564 percent—see Exhibit 8.8. Cost recovery for office equipment and furnishings is computed using the MACRS rules for personal property—see Exhibits 8.1 and 8.3. These assets also can be expensed under § 179; bonus depreciation is also available.

An office in the home deduction is also available to those who rent (rather than own) their home. In this case, the business use percentage is applied to the rent being paid.

If the Regular Method is used, the office in the home deduction is claimed using Form 8829 (Expenses for Business Use of Your Home).

Simplified Method

Because of the record keeping and calculations involved in using the Regular Method, the IRS established an optional Simplified Method for the office in the home deduction.[27] If the Simplified Method is used, Form 8829 is not required. Taxpayers using the Simplified Method are allowed a deduction of $5 per square foot of space devoted to the office. However, since no more than 300 square feet can be counted, the maximum deduction is limited to $1,500.

The various rules governing the use of the Simplified Method are summarized below.

- No depreciation on the residence can be claimed.
- Actual expenses of maintaining and operating the home (e.g., qualified residence interest, property taxes, homeowners insurance, utilities) are ignored. Expenses that are deductible elsewhere on the tax return (e.g., qualified residence interest, property taxes) can be claimed in full without any reduction due to a home office deduction being claimed.
- Office in the home deductions in excess of the net income from the business *cannot* be carried over to a future year. An unused Regular Method deduction from a prior year *cannot* be carried to a Simplified Method year.

Taxpayers can choose between the Regular Method and the Simplified Method each year. However, once a choice is made, that choice cannot be changed for that year. Care should be taken in making the choice because the Simplified Method may yield a smaller deduction.

Example 31

Assume the same facts as in Example 30, except that Luis chooses the Simplified Method. This choice results in the following deduction:

Net income from the business (before the office in the home deduction)	$ 1,500
Simplified Method office in the home deduction ($5 × 240 square feet)	(1,200)
Net income from the business	$ 300

In comparing the results of Examples 30 and 31, note that the use of the Simplified Method left Luis with $500 less in deductions (counting the $200 unused carryover). However, Luis can now use the property taxes ($400) and interest ($750) allocated to the office in the home deduction under the Regular Method as itemized deductions on Schedule A.

[27] Rev.Proc. 2013–13.

Which Method to Use

The availability of the Simplified Method presents an annual decision for the taxpayer. In choosing which method to use, here are some factors to consider:

- Both methods require exclusive and regular use of the home office.
- The Simplified Method requires fewer calculations and less record keeping.
- Because no depreciation is allowed, the Simplified Method will avoid the 25 percent tax on real estate gains when the home is sold (see Chapter 17).
- Even though the Simplified Method frees up certain home-related expenses (e.g., qualified residence interest, property taxes, homeowners insurance, utilities), not all of these expenses are deductible. Some are (property taxes), and some are not (homeowners insurance). But even the expenses that are deductible (property taxes) may be subject to other itemized deduction limitations (see Chapter 10).
- With a maximum deduction of $1,500, the Simplified Method, in most cases, will result in a smaller deduction than the Regular Method.
- Under the Simplified Method, a taxpayer is not allowed to carry over unused deductions.
- Once a taxpayer has made a choice for a year, the choice cannot be changed.

Example 32

Tyler, a calendar year taxpayer, prepared and filed his own tax return for 2021. Being in a hurry, he decided to use the Simplified Method of computing his home office deduction. In March 2023, Tyler seeks tax advice and learns how much he could have saved by using the Regular Method. Tyler cannot file an amended return for 2021, but he can switch to the Regular Method for 2022.

The Big Picture

Example 33

Return to the facts of *The Big Picture* on p. 9-1. Morgan is using her apartment's second bedroom as a home office. Her apartment has 1,200 square feet; the second bedroom has 200 square feet. Her home office is, therefore, one-sixth of her apartment (200 square feet ÷ 1,200 square feet). During 2022, her apartment expenses include:

Rent ($1,250 per month)	$15,000
Utilities	2,600
Renter's insurance	1,100
Total	$18,700

In addition, she purchases various supplies and software for her tutoring ($700) and freelance driving ($75), as well as office furniture ($100 for a file cabinet to store her business records, $400 for a table, $250 for chairs, and $50 for a lamp; $800 total). The office furniture, which she can expense immediately under § 179, will be allocated to her freelance businesses based on total revenues.

Income from her tutoring amounts to $6,795, and she earned $8,305 from her freelance driving. She also has documented her business mileage for the year (630 for tutoring and 5,400 for freelance driving) and has receipts for freeway tolls of $175 (all related to her freelance driving). Morgan uses the automatic mileage method for her business miles (see Example 9).

continued

Using the Simplified Method, Morgan's home office deduction would be $1,000 (200 square feet × $5 per square foot). Morgan will be better off using the Actual Cost Method, where her deduction will be $3,117 ($18,700 total apartment expenses × ⅙). This deduction will be allocated to her freelance businesses (tutoring and freelance driving), based on total revenues.

	Tutoring	Freelance Driving	Total
Revenues	$ 6,795	$ 8,305	$15,100
Expenses:			
Business mileage:			
630 × $0.585/mile	(369)		(369)
5,400 × $0.585/mile		(3,159)	(3,159)
Business tolls		(175)	(175)
Supplies/Software	(700)	(75)	(775)
Office furniture ($800)	(360)	(440)	(800)
Home office	(1,403)	(1,714)	(3,117)
Net income	$ 3,963	$ 2,742	$ 6,705

Note: This example assumes that Morgan meets the "exclusive use" requirement for her home office (see text Section 9-6a and Examples 27, 28, and 29). As discussed there, the "exclusive use" requirement is a significant constraint. What would happen if on *one day* during the year Morgan went into the home office, opened her laptop computer, and spent *one hour* responding to her personal e-mails?

Answer: The "exclusive use" test would not be met, and Morgan would lose the home office deduction. Further, proving a negative is difficult (how does one document that the home office was *never* used for personal purposes?). But Morgan needs to understand the standard and ensure that she complies with it. In our example, that means when she wants to use her laptop for personal purposes, she needs to use it somewhere other than the office.

9-6b Moving Expenses

The deduction for moving expenses has been suspended from 2018 through 2025. However, during this period, the moving expense deduction is retained for members of the Armed Forces (or their spouse or dependents) on active duty who move because of a military order that relates to a permanent change of station.[28] The rules providing for exclusions of amounts attributable to in-kind moving and storage expenses (and reimbursements or allowances for these expenses) also remain in place for these individuals.

9-6c Entertainment and Meal Expenses

Many businesses incur entertainment and meal expenses. Although such expenses can help build business activity, a personal element also is involved in these activities. As a result, Congress decided to limit these deductions. *No deduction* is allowed with respect to:

1. An activity generally considered to be entertainment, amusement, or recreation;
2. Membership dues with respect to any club organized for business, pleasure, recreation, or other social purposes; or
3. A facility (or portion thereof) used in connection with any of the above items.

[28] § 217(k).

However, taxpayers still may deduct some or all of the *food and beverage expenses* associated with operating their trade or business (e.g., a business meal with a current or potential client, or meals consumed by employees on work travel). In general, only *50 percent* of food and beverage expenses can be deducted.[29] However, given the impact of the COVID-19 pandemic on restaurants, Congress provided a temporary 100 percent deduction for meals and beverages provided by a restaurant in 2021 and 2022.[30]

Subsidized Eating Facilities and *De Minimis* Fringe Benefits

Prior to 2018, additional exceptions to the 50% rule applied to meals and entertainment in a subsidized eating facility or where the *de minimis* fringe benefit rule applied to food and beverages provided to employees (see Chapter 5). From 2018 through 2025, the 50 percent limitation is applied to these items.[31] Beginning in 2026, the deduction for these items will be eliminated.

Subsidized Eating Facilities and *De Minimis* Fringe Benefits

Example 34

General Hospital has an employee cafeteria on the premises for its doctors, nurses, and other employees. The cafeteria operates at cost. The 50% rule applies to the employee cafeteria costs of General Hospital.

Example 35

Canary Corporation provides coffee and sometimes doughnuts to employees in the breakroom. This is a *de minimis* fringe benefit that is not taxable to the employees. Canary may deduct only 50% of the cost of this food.

Exceptions to the 50% Rule

The 50% rule has a number of exceptions.[32] One exception covers the case where the full value of the meals is included in the compensation of the employee (or independent contractor). Expenses directly related to business meetings of employees also are not subject to the 50% rule (and are fully deductible). A similar exception applies to employer-paid recreational or social activities for employees (e.g., the annual holiday party or spring picnic). In addition, businesses that have retreats and/or other off-site training events are generally allowed to deduct 100 percent of the meals provided to participants at those sites.[33]

Example 36

Myrtle wins an all-expense-paid trip to Europe for selling the most insurance for her company during the year. Her employer treats this trip as additional compensation to Myrtle. The 50% rule does not apply to the employer.

---

[29] § 274; Reg. § 1.274–11.

[30] § 274(n)(2)(D). The expenses must be paid or incurred after December 31, 2020, and before January 1, 2023. The statutory language does not provide a definition of the term *restaurant*. Taxpayers may treat the meal portion of a *per diem* allowance (see text Section 9-9a) as if it were provided by a restaurant (Notice 2021–63).

[31] We do not know whether a subsidized eating facility is a "restaurant" for purposes of the 100% food and beverages deduction in 2021 and 2022.

[32] §§ 274(e) and (n).

[33] *Jacobs*, 148 T.C. No. 4 (6/26/17).

Business Meals

A business meal is deductible only if all of the following conditions are met:[34]

- The expense is reasonable (i.e., not lavish or extravagant).
- The taxpayer (or an employee) is present at the meal.
- The food and beverages are provided to a current or potential business customer or client.
- If combined with entertainment, the meal and beverages cost is separately itemized on the bill or receipt.

Business Meals

Example 37

During 2022, Lance submits a proposed consulting contract to a local business. He invites the two business owners to dinner at a local restaurant and pays for the meal. During the meal, Lance discusses and answers questions about the proposed contract. Lance can deduct 100% of this qualified business meal.

Example 38

Assume the same facts as Example 37, except that Lance buys dinner for the two business owners but does not attend the dinner. Since Lance was not present at the meal, no deduction is allowed.

If the taxpayer is in travel status, any meal expenses can be deducted, subject to the 50% rule (100% in 2021 and 2022 for restaurant meals).

Example 39

During 2022, Liang travels to San Francisco for a business convention. She pays for her meals at a local restaurant and is reimbursed by her employer. Liang's employer can deduct 100% of the cost of her meals.

Ethics & Equity **Your Turn or Mine?**

Natalie (a CPA), Mathew (an attorney), Jacob (a banker), and Shanice (an insurance agent) all live and work in the same community. They have been friends since college. Every Friday, they have lunch together and make it a point to discuss some business matters. They take turns paying for the group's lunches, and each deducts the amount they paid for the lunch as an entertainment expense. Presuming that one of the four is audited, do you anticipate any difficulty with the IRS? Explain.

[34] § 274(k); Reg. § 1.274–12.

Business Gifts

Although not subject to the 50 percent limit on meals, business gifts are deductible only to the extent of $25 per donee per year.[35] Incidental costs such as engraving, gift-wrapping, mailing, and delivery also are allowed (in addition to the $25 maximum). Gifts costing $4 or less (e.g., pens with the employee's or company's name on them) or promotional materials are not subject to the $25 limit. Records must be maintained to substantiate business gifts.

Business Gifts

Example 40

In December, Prism Associates purchases framed prints from a local artist and mails one to each of its clients. Each print costs $70; packaging and shipping costs are $10 per print. Prism may deduct $35 for each print sent ($25 gift maximum plus $10 for packaging and shipping).

Example 41

Assume the same facts as Example 40. In addition to the framed prints, Prism also encloses a coffee mug imprinted with its name and logo. Each mug costs $3.

The coffee mug is considered a promotional item, and its cost also is allowed as a deduction.

Record-Keeping/Documentation Requirements

Proper documentation of meal expenses is essential because of the strict record-keeping requirements that must be met. For example, documentation that consists solely of credit card receipts and canceled checks may be inadequate to substantiate the business purpose and business relationship.[36] Taxpayers should maintain detailed records of amounts, time, place, business purpose, and business relationships. A credit card receipt details the place, date, and amount of the expense. A notation made on the receipt of the names of the person(s) attending, the business relationship, and the topic of discussion should be sufficient.

9-6d Miscellaneous Employee Expenses

Miscellaneous employee expenses include costs that are job-related, not reimbursed by the employer, and not covered elsewhere in the tax law. Expenses related to maintaining job status make up a significant category of miscellaneous expenses. They include union dues; membership dues to professional organizations; subscriptions to trade publications and professional journals; special clothing (e.g., uniforms, protective shoes, and safety glasses); and various license fees paid to government agencies and other regulatory bodies. As mentioned previously, the deduction for miscellaneous itemized deductions (including employee business expenses) has been suspended from 2018 through 2025.

Educator Expenses

Many teachers pay for professional development courses or purchase school supplies for classroom use and are not reimbursed by their employer. These expenses are miscellaneous itemized deductions (i.e., *from* AGI deductions) and are not deductible from 2018 through 2025 (see text Section 9-10a).

Modest relief is provided though for elementary and secondary school educators, allowing them to claim up to $300 ($250 for 2021) of these expenses as a deduction *for* AGI.[37] Eligible educators must work at least 900 hours during a school year as a teacher, an instructor, a counselor, a principal, or an aide. Covered costs include unreimbursed expenses for

[35] § 274(b)(1). Multiple gifts to members of the same customer's family are consolidated (so only one $25 deduction will be allowed). Gifts to an employer (or an employee's superior) are not deductible.

[36] *Kenneth W. Guenther*, 54 TCM 382, T.C.Memo. 1987–440.

[37] § 62(a)(2)(D).

professional development courses, books, supplies, computer and other equipment, and supplementary materials used in the classroom. Personal protective equipment, disinfectant, and other supplies used to prevent the spread of COVID-19 also qualify.[38]

Example 42

Ron is a full-time teacher at Hoover Elementary. During 2022, he spends $1,200 for school supplies for his fourth-grade class. Under an accountable plan (see text Section 9-9a), Hoover reimburses him for $400 of these supplies. As to the $800 balance, Ron may claim $300 as a deduction *for* AGI. The remaining expenses ($500) are miscellaneous itemized deductions (and not allowed from 2018 through 2025).

9-7 The Deduction for Qualified Business Income

LO.6

Determine a taxpayer's deduction for qualified business income.

With the reduction in the corporate income tax rate to 21 percent in 2018, Congress needed to provide a means of reducing the taxes on businesses that operate in different business forms (e.g., sole proprietors, partnerships, and S corporations). Congress accomplished this with the creation of the **deduction for qualified business income** (§ 199A), which applies to *noncorporate taxpayers*.[39]

In general, the deduction for qualified business income is 20 percent of qualified business income (QBI). As you would suspect, however, the deduction is subject to a variety of limitations. The focus of the materials that follow is on the implications of the deduction for qualified business income for *sole proprietors* (although the deduction is available to any noncorporate taxpayer).[40] We begin by discussing the general rules, defining key terms, and providing some basic examples. Then we turn our attention to the various limitations that apply to higher-income taxpayers, illustrate the reporting requirements related to the qualified business income deduction (**QBI deduction**), and conclude with a discussion of some other rules related to this deduction.

9-7a General Rule

At its most basic level, § 199A permits an individual to deduct 20 percent of the qualified business income generated through a sole proprietorship, a partnership, or an S corporation.[41] As will quickly become apparent, § 199A uses the word *qualified* to modify many phrases. For example, to determine the "qualified business income deduction," one has to understand the definition of a "qualified trade or business" and "qualified business income." But let's begin with the basics. In general, the deduction for qualified business income is the *lesser of*:[42]

1. 20 percent of qualified business income (QBI),[43] or
2. 20 percent of modified taxable income.[44]

Effectively, the QBI deduction—a *from* AGI deduction—is the last deduction taken in determining taxable income.[45] Further, the deduction is available whether a taxpayer uses the standard deduction or itemizes deductions.[46]

There are *three limitations* on the QBI deduction: an overall limitation (based on modified taxable income), another that applies to high-income taxpayers, and a third that applies to certain types of services businesses. The second and third limitations

[38]Consolidated Appropriations Act, 2021 § 275 (P.L. 116-260). Applies to items purchased after March 12, 2020.

[39]§ 199A(a).

[40]For a discussion of the deduction for qualified business income as it relates to partners and S corporation shareholders, see Chapter 2 of *South-Western Federal Taxation: Corporations, Partnerships, Estates and Trusts* (Cengage Learning).

[41]§§ 199A(a), (b)(1)(A), and (b)(2)(A).

[42]§ 199A(a).

[43]If the taxpayer has more than one qualified trade or business, the qualified business income deduction is determined for each business independently [§ 199A(b)(1)(A)]. These are then combined [into the "combined qualified business income amount" of § 199A(a)(1)(A)] and compared to the modified taxable income limitation.

[44]In addition, taxpayers are allowed a deduction for 20% of qualified REIT dividends and 20% of qualified publicly traded partnership income [§ 199A(b)(1)(B)].

[45]See the last sentence of § 62(a) and § 63(b)(3).

[46]§ 63(d)(3).

only apply when taxable income before the QBI deduction exceeds, in 2022, $340,100 (married taxpayers filing a joint return) or $170,050 (single and head-of-household taxpayers).[47] We'll discuss these two limitations later.

9-7b The Overall Limitation: Modified Taxable Income

In all cases, the § 199A deduction may not exceed 20 percent of the taxpayer's modified taxable income. Modified taxable income is taxable income *before* the deduction for qualified business income[48] reduced by any net capital gain.[49] In computing modified taxable income, the term *net capital gain* includes both a net capital gain [the excess of a long-term capital gain over a short-term capital loss; § 1222(11)] plus any qualified dividend income.[50]

9-7c What Is Qualified Business Income?

Qualified business income[51] (QBI) is defined as the ordinary income less ordinary deductions a taxpayer earns from a "qualified trade or business" conducted in the United States by the taxpayer (e.g., from a sole proprietorship).[52] It also includes the distributive share of these amounts from each partnership or S corporation interest held by the taxpayer.

In determining QBI, all deductions attributable to a trade or business are taken into account.[53] Relevant deductions include the self-employment tax deduction [§ 164(f)], the self-employed health insurance deduction [§ 162(l)], and any deduction for contributions to qualified retirement plans [§ 404].[54]

Example 43

Vicki's sole proprietorship reports $54,000 of net income [on Schedule C (Form 1040)]. As a result, Vicki's self-employment tax liability is $7,630 ($54,000 × 0.9235 × 15.3%). She is allowed a *for* AGI deduction for one-half of her self-employment tax liability ($3,815; $7,630 × ½). Vicki's QBI is $50,185 ($54,000 − $3,815).

Qualified business income does not include certain types of investment income, such as:[55]

- Capital gains or capital losses (including any net § 1231 gain included in capital gain and loss computations);[56]
- Dividends;
- Interest income (unless "properly allocable" to a trade or business, such as lending); or
- Certain other investment items.

Nor does qualified business income include:[57]

- The "reasonable compensation" paid to the taxpayer with respect to any qualified trade or business; or
- Guaranteed payments made to a partner for services rendered.

As noted above, the § 199A Regulations indicate that a net § 1231 gain for a taxable year that is treated as a long-term capital gain is *excluded* from the computation of qualified business income. The Regulations also note that if the result of § 1231 netting is a *loss*, the ordinary loss will *reduce* qualified business income for that year. The Regulations are silent regarding what to do if there are multiple qualified trades or businesses and each has § 1231 gains and losses.

[47] In 2022, married taxpayers filing separately (MFS) have a threshold amount of $170,050. We have not included MFS taxpayers in the text discussion. In 2021, the threshold amounts were $329,800 (married taxpayers filing a joint return), $164,925 (married taxpayers filing separately), and $164,900 (single and head-of-household taxpayers).

[48] § 199A(e)(1).

[49] § 199A(a)(2)(B).

[50] § 199A(a)(2)(B) and Reg. § 1.199A–1(b)(3); § 199A relies on the definition of "net capital gain" in § 1(h).

[51] § 199A(c).

[52] § 199A(c)(3)(A). As a result, foreign trade or business income does not qualify for the deduction. Certain Puerto Rico activities qualify for the deduction.

[53] § 199A(c)(3)(A).

[54] Reg. § 1.199A–3(b)(1)(vi).

[55] § 199A(c)(3)(B).

[56] Reg. § 1.199A–3(b)(2)(ii).

[57] § 199A(c)(4).

9-7d What Is a Qualified Trade or Business?

For taxpayers who fall below critical taxable income thresholds established under § 199A (in 2022, $340,100 for married taxpayers filing jointly; $170,050 for single and head-of-household taxpayers), the scope of a **qualified trade or business** (QTB) is broad. In general, it includes any trade or business other than providing services as an employee.[58]

As a result, the deduction is available to sole proprietors, independent contractors, and noncorporate owners of S corporations, partnerships, and LLCs. But as discussed below, this otherwise broad application has some considerable restrictions for high-income taxpayers who are engaged in businesses involving the performance of services in certain "specified" fields.

Basic QBI Deduction Computation

Example 44

Sanjay, a married taxpayer, operates a candy store as a sole proprietor. The business has no employees (Sanjay provides all services to customers). During 2022, Sanjay's qualified business income is $210,000 [this is his Schedule C (Form 1040) net income reduced by his self-employment tax deduction]. Sanjay's AGI is $275,900, which includes wages earned by his spouse, but no other income. He and his spouse claim the standard deduction ($25,900). Sanjay's modified taxable income is $250,000 ($275,900 − $25,900).

Sanjay's QBI deduction is $42,000, the *lesser of*:

1. 20% of qualified business income ($42,000; $210,000 × 20%), or
2. 20% of modified taxable income ($50,000; $250,000 × 20%).

Sanjay's taxable income is $208,000 ($250,000 of taxable income before the QBI deduction less his $42,000 QBI deduction).

Example 45

Assume that Abby is a single taxpayer who does not itemize deductions and operates a sole proprietorship. During 2022, her business generates $140,000 of business income, $40,000 of deductible business expenses (including her self-employment tax deduction), and $2,950 of interest income from her business deposits. She has no other sources of income. Abby's AGI is $102,950.

Abby has $100,000 of qualified business income ($140,000 − $40,000). The interest income does not qualify for the QBI deduction. Her modified taxable income is $90,000 ($102,950 AGI − $12,950 standard deduction).

Abby's QBI deduction is $18,000, the *lesser of*:

1. 20% of qualified business income ($20,000; $100,000 × 20%), or
2. 20% of modified taxable income ($18,000; $90,000 × 20%).

Abby's taxable income is $72,000 ($90,000 of taxable income before the QBI deduction less her $18,000 QBI deduction).

Example 46

Assume the same facts as in Example 45, except that Abby has no interest income, but $2,950 of qualified dividend income. Abby's AGI remains $102,950, and her taxable income before the QBI deduction remains $90,000 ($102,950 AGI – $12,950 standard deduction).

However, Abby's modified taxable income is now $87,050 [$90,000 taxable income before the QBI deduction less $2,950 of "net capital gain" (the qualified dividend income)].

Abby's QBI deduction is $17,410, the *lesser of*:

1. 20% of qualified business income ($20,000; $100,000 × 20%), or
2. 20% of modified taxable income ($17,410; $87,050 × 20%).

Abby's taxable income is $72,590 ($90,000 of taxable income before the QBI deduction less her $17,410 QBI deduction).

---

[58] § 199A(d)(1)(B).

"Trade or Business" Under § 199A

What is a "trade or business" for purposes of § 199A? Reg. § 1.199A–1(b)(14) interprets the term *trade or business* by looking at the meaning of this phrase under § 162(a). With no formal definition of that phrase in § 162, the Supreme Court[59] has determined that to be "engaged in a trade or business, the taxpayer must be involved in the activity with continuity and regularity and that the taxpayer's primary purpose for engaging in the activity must be for income or profit." Ultimately, this is a "facts and circumstances" test.[60] The § 199A Regulations acknowledge that multiple businesses might be contained in a single entity, but emphasize that this determination depends on "all the facts and circumstances." At a minimum, for § 199A to apply to each business, separate books and records must be maintained for each business.

Does a rental activity qualify as a "trade or business"? Only if its activities rise to the level of those seen in a non-rental business. Here, the courts have based their decisions on a variety of factors, including the type of property (commercial real property versus a residential condominium versus personal property), the number of properties rented, the nature of the owner's involvement [handling matters directly (or through an agent) versus a triple net lease arrangement], and the rental period (short-term versus long-term).[61]

Rental Real Estate Safe Harbor A rental real estate activity (or multiple rentals if the taxpayer chooses to combine them) will be treated as a trade or business for purposes of § 199A if the following conditions are met:[62]

- Separate books and records are maintained for each rental activity (or the combined enterprise if grouped together).
- At least 250 hours of "rental services" are performed per year for the activity (or combined enterprise). Rental services include time spent on maintenance, repairs, collecting rent, paying bills, providing services to tenants, supervising contractors and employees, and efforts to rent the property (including advertising and negotiating and executing a lease). The work does not have to be performed by the taxpayer (owner). It also can be performed by employees, agents, or contractors of the property owner.
- The taxpayer maintains contemporaneous records, including time reports or similar documents, supporting the services performed (including hours, dates, description of services, and who performed the services).
- A statement is attached to the timely filed return indicating the taxpayer is using the safe harbor, describing the properties, and acknowledging that the requirements for the safe harbor are met.

A taxpayer can't use the safe harbor for the rental of any residence that the taxpayer uses as a personal residence for more than 14 days during the year (e.g., a vacation home). In addition, the taxpayer must own the rental property directly (rather than, for example, as a partner in a partnership). Finally, triple net leases are excluded from the safe harbor (these are leases where the landlord passes on the responsibility for paying real estate taxes, insurance, and maintenance to the tenant).

If property owners do not satisfy the safe harbor conditions, they still might find that their real estate rental is a trade or business under § 162 as defined in case law and the specific court cases that have considered whether rental properties constitute a trade or business.

[59] *Groetzinger v. Comm.*, 85–2 USTC ¶9622, 56 AFTR 2d 85–5683, 771 F.2d 269 (CA–7), *aff'd* in 87–1 USTC ¶9191, 59 AFTR 2d 87–532, 107 S.Ct. 980. Performing services as an employee is *not* a "trade or business."

[60] *Higgins v. Comm.*, 41–1 USTC ¶9233, 25 AFTR 1160, 61 S.Ct. 475.

[61] See, for example, *Alvary v. U.S.*, 62–1 USTC ¶9493, 9 AFTR 2d 1633, 302 F.2d 790 (CA–2), *Edwin R. Curphey*, 73 T.C. 766 (1980), *Gilford v. Comm.*, 201 F.2d 735 (CA–2), *Murtaugh*, 74 TCM 75, T.C.Memo. 1997–319, and *Victoria Balsamo*, 54 TCM 608, T.C.Memo. 1987–477.

[62] Rev.Proc. 2019–38.

Taxpayers with Multiple Businesses

The deduction for qualified business income must be determined separately for each qualified trade or business.[63] These independent calculations are then aggregated [becoming the "combined qualified business income amount" identified in § 199A(a)(1)(A)]. This combined amount is then compared to the overall modified taxable income limit.

9-7e Limitations on the QBI Deduction

The basic application of § 199A becomes more complex once a taxpayer reaches certain taxable income thresholds. These taxable income thresholds—determined without regard to the QBI deduction—are $340,100 for married taxpayers filing jointly and $170,050 for single and head-of-household taxpayers in 2022.[64] In 2021, these amounts were $329,800 and $164,900.

Once these thresholds are reached, § 199A imposes two *independent* limitations:

1. The QBI deduction is capped based on the percentage of the W–2 wages paid by the business (i.e., wages paid to its employees) *or* based on a smaller percentage of W–2 wages paid by the business and a percentage of the cost of its depreciable property used to produce QBI.[65]
2. The QBI deduction generally is *not available* for income earned from "specified service" businesses.[66] "Specified service" businesses include doctors, dentists, lawyers, accountants, consultants, investment advisers, entertainers, and athletes (among others), but not engineers and architects.

These limitations, discussed in more detail below, are fully phased in once taxable income (before the QBI deduction) exceeds $440,100 for married taxpayers filing jointly and $220,050 for single and head-of-household taxpayers. Within the phase-in ranges ($100,000 for married taxpayers filing jointly; $50,000 for all other taxpayers), each limitation is applied by comparing the amount of taxable income that exceeds the threshold amount to the appropriate phase-in range.[67]

Because the "specified services" limitation can be more complex (due to incorporating the "wages and capital investment" limitation after the "specified services" limitation), the wages and capital investment limitation is discussed first, followed by the "specified services" limitation.

Remember that in all cases, the QBI deduction can never exceed 20 percent of the taxpayer's modified taxable income (taxable income before the QBI deduction reduced by any net capital gain, including qualified dividend income). To help navigate this "thicket," Concept Summary 9.4 provides a flowchart to assist in applying these rules.

9-7f Limitation Based on Wages and Capital Investment

The **W–2 Wages/Capital Investment Limit**, which does not apply to taxpayers below the taxable income thresholds mentioned previously and is phased in as a taxpayer's income exceeds those thresholds, limits the 20 percent QBI deduction to the *greater of*:

1. 50 percent of the "W–2 wages" paid by the QTB, or
2. 25 percent of the "W–2 wages" paid by the QTB *plus* 2.5 percent of the taxpayer's share of the unadjusted basis immediately after acquisition of all tangible depreciable property (including real estate) used in the QTB that has not been fully depreciated prior to the close of the taxable year.

W–2 Wages Limit

"W–2 wages" includes the total amount of wages subject to income tax withholding, compensation paid into qualified retirement accounts, and certain other forms of deferred compensation paid to the employees of the business.[68] For labor-intensive businesses, 50 percent of the W–2 wages paid by the business will likely be the relevant limit on the QBI deduction.

---

[63] § 199A(b)(2).

[64] § 199A(e)(2). Married taxpayers filing separately have a taxable income threshold of $170,050 in 2022 ($164,925 in 2021).

[65] § 199A(b)(2)(B).

[66] § 199A(d)(2).

[67] §§ 199A(b)(3)(B) and (d)(3).

[68] § 199A(b)(4).

Concept Summary 9.4

An Overview of the 2022 Qualified Business Income Deduction

How to Use the Concept Summary: ***First,*** identify all qualified trades or businesses (QTB) of the taxpayer and the related qualified business income (QBI). ***Then*** for each QTB, move through the flowchart to determine the QBI amount for each QTB. Once this process is complete, combine all of the QBI amounts (this is the "combined qualified business income amount"). ***Finally,*** apply the *overall limitation* (based on modified taxable income). The QBI deduction is the *lesser of:*

1. The combined "qualified business income (QBI) amount," or
2. 20% of modified taxable income.*

* Modified taxable income is taxable income *before* the QBI deduction less any "net capital gain" (including any qualified dividend income).

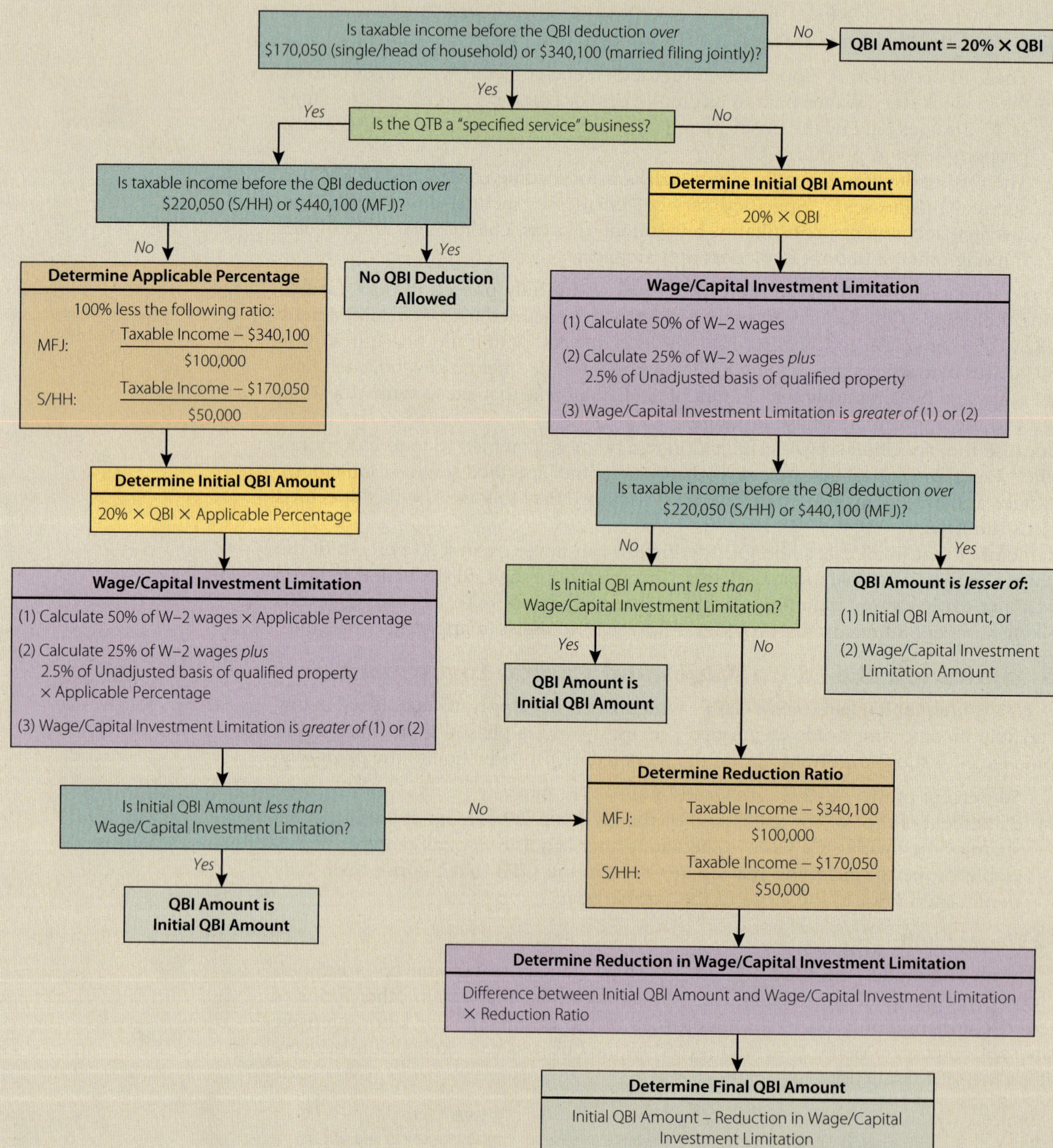

W–2 Wages Limit

Example 47

Simone, a married taxpayer, operates a business as a sole proprietor. The business has one employee, who is paid $80,000 during 2022. Assume that the business has no significant assets. During 2022, Simone's qualified business income is $230,000, and her modified taxable income is $250,000 (this is also her taxable income before the QBI deduction).

Since Simone's taxable income before the QBI deduction is below the income threshold for married taxpayers filing a joint return ($340,100), the W–2/Capital Investment Limitation does not apply. As a result, Simone's QBI deduction is $46,000, the *lesser of*:

1. 20% of qualified business income ($46,000; $230,000 × 20%), or
2. 20% of modified taxable income ($50,000; $250,000 × 20%).

Example 48

Assume the same facts as in Example 47, except that Simone's qualified business income is $500,000 and her modified taxable income is $600,000 (this is also her taxable income before the QBI deduction). Because Simone's taxable income before the QBI deduction exceeds $440,100, the W–2/Capital Investment Limitation fully applies. As a result, Simone's QBI deduction is $40,000, the *lesser of*:

1. 20% of qualified business income ($100,000; $500,000 × 20%), or
2. 50% of W–2 wages ($40,000; $80,000 × 50%).

And *no more than*:

3. 20% of modified taxable income ($120,000; $600,000 × 20%).

W–2 Wages/Capital Investment Limit

For capital-intensive businesses (e.g., real estate), an alternate limit exists. It begins with 25 percent of W–2 wages paid by the QTB and adds to this amount 2.5 percent of the unadjusted basis (immediately after acquisition) of "qualified property."

Qualified property includes depreciable tangible property—real or personal—that is used by the QTB during the year and whose "depreciable period" has not ended before the end of the taxable year.[69] Land and intangible assets are *not* qualified property. The "depreciable period" for "qualified property" under § 199A is a minimum of 10 years.[70]

Example 49

Tom and Eileen are married and file a joint return for 2022. Their taxable income before the QBI deduction is $500,000 (this is also their modified taxable income). Tom has $400,000 in QBI from a restaurant he owns (a sole proprietorship). Tom employed four individuals (cook, bartender, and wait staff) during the year and paid them $150,000 in W–2 wages. Tom owns the building in which the restaurant is located. He bought the building (and its furniture and fixtures) four years ago for $600,000, and the land was worth $100,000, so the unadjusted acquisition basis of the building (and its furniture and fixtures) is $500,000.

Since their taxable income before the QBI deduction exceeds the $440,100 threshold, the W–2 Wages/Capital Investment Limit comes into play. Their QBI deduction is $75,000, computed as follows:

1. 20% of qualified business income ($400,000 × 20%)		$ 80,000
2. But no more than the *greater of*:		
• 50% of W–2 wages ($150,000 × 50%), or		$ 75,000
• 25% of W–2 wages ($150,000 × 25%) *plus*	$37,500	
• 2.5% of the unadjusted basis of qualified property ($500,000 × 2.5%)	12,500	$ 50,000
And *no more than*:		
3. 20% of modified taxable income ($500,000 × 20%)		$100,000

[69] § 199A(b)(6)(A).

[70] § 199A(b)(6)(B).

Many owners of pass-through businesses, especially landlords, have no employees. As a result, the 25 percent of W–2 wages plus 2.5 percent of the unadjusted basis of qualified property is most likely to affect them.

Example 50

Jiaxiu, a single taxpayer, owns a five-unit apartment building that he purchased five years ago. His unadjusted basis in the building (purchase price minus the value of the land) is $500,000. He has taxable income before the QBI deduction of $250,000 during 2022 (this is also his modified taxable income). He has no employees in his business, and his QBI is $220,000.

Since his taxable income before the QBI deduction exceeds the $220,050 threshold, the W–2 Wages/Capital Investment Limit comes into play. His QBI deduction is $12,500, computed as follows:

1. 20% of qualified business income ($220,000 × 20%)		$44,000
2. But no more than the *greater of*:		
• 50% of W–2 wages ($0 × 50%), or		$ -0-
• 25% of W–2 wages ($0 × 25%) *plus*	$ -0-	
• 2.5% of the unadjusted basis of qualified property ($500,000 × 2.5%)	12,500	$12,500
And *no more than*:		
3. 20% of modified taxable income ($250,000 × 20%)		$50,000

Phase-In of W–2 Wages/Capital Investment Limit

The W–2 Wages/Capital Investment Limit does not apply to taxpayers with taxable income before the QBI deduction less than the threshold amount ($340,100 for married taxpayers filing jointly; $170,050 for singles and heads of household). And if taxable income before the QBI deduction exceeds the threshold amount by more than $100,000 (married filing jointly) or $50,000 (all other taxpayers), the W–2 Wages/Capital Investment Limit must be used.

If, however, the taxpayer's taxable income before the QBI deduction is between these two amounts *and the W–2 Wages/Capital Investment portion of the QBI deduction is capping the deduction*, then the general 20 percent QBI amount is used, but reduced as follows:

1. Determine difference between the general 20 percent QBI deduction amount and the W–2 Wages/Capital Investment amount.[71]
2. Determine the Reduction Ratio:[72]

$$\textbf{Reduction Ratio} = \frac{\textbf{Taxable income before the QBI deduction} - \textbf{Threshold amount}}{\textbf{\$100,000 (married filing jointly); \$50,000 (others)}}$$

3. Determine the Reduction in the W–2 Wages/Capital Investment Limit:

$$\text{Reduction} = \text{Difference [from (1)]} \times \text{Reduction ratio [from (2)]}$$

4. Determine QBI amount:

$$\text{20\% QBI deduction} - \text{Reduction [from (3)]}$$

[71]This is the "excess amount" in § 199A(b)(3)(B)(iii).

[72]§ 199A(b)(3)(B)(ii).

Example 51

Return to the facts of Example 49, but assume that Tom and Eileen's taxable income before the QBI deduction is $380,100 (this is also their modified taxable income), QBI is $320,000, and W–2 wages are $100,000. Their unadjusted property basis remains at $500,000. Tom and Eileen's initial calculation yields a qualified business income amount of $50,000, computed as follows:

1. 20% of qualified business income ($320,000 × 20%)		$ 64,000
2. But no more than the *greater of*:		
• 50% of W–2 wages ($100,000 × 50%), or		$ 50,000
• 25% of W–2 wages ($100,000 × 25%) *plus*	$25,000	
• 2.5% of the unadjusted basis of qualified property ($500,000 × 2.5%)	12,500	$ 37,500
And *no more than*:		
3. 20% of modified taxable income ($380,100 × 20%)		$ 76,020

Since Tom and Eileen's taxable income before the QBI deduction exceeds $340,100 but is less than $440,100 and *the W–2 Wages/Capital Investment portion of the computation is capping the deduction*, the general 20% QBI amount is used but reduced as follows:

1. Determine the difference between the general 20% QBI deduction amount and the W–2 Wages/Capital Investment amount:

General 20% QBI deduction amount	$ 64,000
Less: The W–2 Wages/Capital Investment Limit	(50,000)
Excess	$ 14,000

2. Determine the Reduction Ratio:

$$\text{Reduction Ratio} = \frac{\$40{,}000\ (\$380{,}100 - \$340{,}100)}{\$100{,}000} = 40\%$$

3. Determine the Reduction in the W–2 Wages/Capital Investment Limit:

Excess ($14,000) × Reduction ratio (40%) = $5,600

4. Determine Final QBI Amount:

General 20% QBI deduction amount	$64,000
Less: Reduction in the W–2 Wages/Capital Investment Limit	(5,600)
Final QBI amount	$58,400

Since the QBI amount ($58,400) is less than 20% of their modified taxable income ($76,020; $380,100 × 20%), they will be allowed a $58,400 deduction for qualified business income.

9-7g Limitation for "Specified Services" Businesses

For high-income taxpayers (in 2022, $440,100 for married taxpayers filing jointly; $220,050 for single and head-of-household taxpayers), § 199A excludes any "specified service trade or business" from the definition of a qualified trade or business.[73] A **specified service trade or business** includes those involving:[74]

- The performance of services in certain fields, including health, law, accounting, actuarial science, performing arts, consulting, athletics, financial services, and brokerage services;
- Services consisting of investing and investment management, trading or dealing in securities, partnership interests, or commodities; and
- Any trade or business where the business's principal asset is the reputation of one or more of its employees or owners.

Architects and engineers are specifically excluded from this definition.[75]

---

[73] §§ 199A(d)(1)(A) and (d)(2).

[74] § 199A(d)(2); see also § 1202(e)(3)(A).

[75] § 199A(d)(2)(A).

According to the legislative history of § 199A, the taxable income thresholds where the QBI deduction is phased out for "specified service" businesses were set by Congress "to deter high-income taxpayers from attempting to convert wages or other compensation for personal services to income eligible for the 20 percent deduction under the provision." However, the phaseout rules operate without regard to the taxpayer's specific motivation.

Example 52

In Example 44, Sanjay operated a sole proprietorship that generated QBI of $210,000 and he was able to claim a QBI deduction of $42,000.

But if his spouse had a salary of $300,000 (instead of $64,000), Sanjay would not be able to claim a QBI deduction since their taxable income before the QBI deduction exceeds $440,100 [$210,000 (QBI) + $300,000 (spouse's wages) − $25,900 (standard deduction) = $484,100]. Sanjay did not attempt to "convert wages to . . . income eligible for the (QBI) deduction." The *income of his spouse* triggered the limitation.

Example 52 illustrates a crucial fact. The QBI deduction phaseout for a "specified services" business is based on *taxable income* before the QBI deduction (*not* on QBI). *Any* income that contributes to taxable income can cause the "specified services" QBI deduction to be reduced.

"Specified Services" Under the § 199A Regulations

The § 199A Regulations provide specific guidance for each of the "specified services" fields identified in § 199A.[76] Exhibit 9.1 provides an overview of this guidance.

A series of examples in the Regulations illustrate these concepts.[77]

"Specified Services" Businesses

Example 53

Surgery Centers LLC (SC) operates specialty surgical centers that provide outpatient medical procedures (none of which require the patient to stay overnight). The company owns a number of facilities throughout the country. For each facility, SC ensures compliance with Federal and state laws and manages each facility's operations and performs all administrative functions. SC does not employ physicians, nurses, and medical assistants. Rather, it enters into agreements with medical professionals and other medical organizations to perform the procedures and provide all needed medical care. Patients are billed by SC for the facility costs related to their procedure; they are billed separately by the health care professional (or the medical organization) for the costs of the procedure performed by the physician and medical support team.

SC is *not* engaged in a "specified services" business (health) because it is not providing the medical services (the medical professionals using the centers are operating businesses in the field of health).

Example 54

Abby, a singer, records a song. Abby is paid a mechanical royalty when the song is licensed or streamed. She is also paid a performance royalty when the recorded song is played publicly.

Abby is engaged in a "specified services" business (performing arts).

[76] Reg. § 1.199A–5(b)(2).

[77] Reg. § 1.199A–5(b)(3).

Exhibit 9.1 **"Specified Services"**

Field	"Specified Services"	Not "Specified Services"
Health	Doctors, pharmacists, nurses, dentists, veterinarians, physical therapists, psychologists, and other similar health care professionals.	Those who provide services that may improve the health of the recipient (e.g., the operator of a health club or spa) or the research, testing, and sale of pharmaceuticals or medical devices.
Law	Lawyers, paralegals, legal arbitrators, and mediators.	Those who provide services not unique to law, like printing, stenography, or delivery services.
Accounting	Accountants, enrolled agents, return preparers, financial auditors, bookkeepers, and similar professionals (whether or not licensed by a state).	Businesses that provide payment processing and billing analysis.
Actuarial Science	Actuaries and similar professionals.	Services provided by analysts, economists, mathematicians, and statisticians not engaged in analyzing or assessing the financial costs of risk or uncertainty of events.
Performing Arts	Actors, singers, musicians, entertainers, directors, and similar professionals (including screenwriters and composers) who provide services that lead to the creation of performing arts.	Those who broadcast or disseminate video or audio to the public and those who maintain or operate equipment or facilities used in the performing arts.
Consulting	Those who provide professional advice and counsel to clients to assist in achieving goals and solving problems, including government lobbyists.	Salespeople and those who provide training or educational courses. Services provided in the fields of architecture or engineering.
Athletics	Athletes, coaches, and team managers.	Broadcasters or those who maintain or operate equipment used in an athletic event; services related to the maintenance and operation of equipment or facilities for use in athletic events.
Financial Services	Those who provide financial services to clients, including managing wealth, developing retirement or transition plans, providing advisory services related to mergers and acquisitions (including restructurings, raising capital, underwriting, and other valuation services). In summary, financial advisers, investment bankers, wealth planners, and retirement advisers.	Banking services (e.g., taking deposits or making loans).
Brokerage Services	A broker who arranges *securities* transactions.	Real estate agents and brokers.
Investment Management	Persons who receive fees for providing investing, asset management, or investment management services.	Real estate managers.
Trading	Persons who trade in securities, commodities, or partnership interests.	A farmer or manufacturer who engages in hedging transactions as part of his or her trade or business.
Reputation of One or More Employees or Owners	Any trade or business that consists of any of the following (or any combination of them): (1) Receiving fees, compensation, or other income for endorsing products or services; (2) Licensing or receiving fees, compensation, or other income for the use of an individual's image, likeness, name, signature, voice, trademark, or any other symbols associated with the individual's identity; and (3) Receiving fees, compensation, or other income for appearing at an event or on radio, television, or another media format.	Persons not covered by this narrowly crafted definition (and not in another "specified services" field). Examples include authors and personal trainers.

"Specified Services" Businesses

Example 55

Ravi is a partner in RoundballSports (RS), which owns and operates a professional basketball team. RS employs athletes and sells tickets to the public to attend games in which its basketball team competes.

RS is engaged in a "specified services" business (athletics).

Example 56

Christian is in the business of providing services that assist unrelated entities in making their personnel structures more efficient. Christian studies a variety of client organizations and structures and compares each to peers in its industry. He then makes recommendations and provides advice to clients regarding possible changes to their personnel structure, including the use of temporary workers.

Christian is engaged in a "specified services" business (consulting).

Example 57

Danielle is in the business of licensing software to customers. As part of her business, she evaluates a customer's software needs and discusses alternatives with her customers. She advises the customer on the particular software products her business licenses. Danielle is paid a flat price for the software license. After a customer licenses the software, Danielle helps to implement it.

Danielle is engaged in the trade or business of licensing software and is *not* engaged in a "specified services" business.

Example 58

Krystal is in the business of providing services to assist clients with their finances. Krystal generally studies a particular client's financial situation, including the client's present income, savings and investments, and anticipated future economic and financial needs. Based on this study, she then assists the client in making decisions and plans regarding the client's financial activities. This planning includes the design of a personal budget to assist the client in monitoring the client's financial situation, the adoption of investment strategies tailored to the client's needs, and other similar services.

Krystal is engaged in a "specified services" business (financial services).

Example 59

Emeril is a well-known chef and the sole owner of multiple restaurants, each of which is an LLC. Due to his skill and reputation as a chef, Emeril receives an endorsement fee of $5,000,000 for the use of his name on a line of cooking utensils and cookware.

Emeril is in the trade or business of being a chef and owning restaurants—*neither* is a "specified services" business. However, he is also in the trade or business of receiving endorsement income. This business—consisting of endorsement fees for Emeril's skill and/or reputation—is a "specified services" business.

Example 60

Jennifer is a well-known actor. Jennifer entered into a partnership with Shoe Company in which she contributed her likeness and the use of her name to the partnership in exchange for a 50% interest in the partnership and a guaranteed payment.

Jennifer's trade or business consisting of the receipt of the partnership interest and guaranteed payment for use of her likeness and name is a "specified services" business.

De Minimis Rule

The § 199A Regulations contain a *de minimis* rule providing that a trade or business will *not* be considered a "specified services" business merely because it provides a small amount of services in a "specified service" activity.[78]

- If a business has gross receipts of $25 million or less and *less than 10 percent* of its receipts relates to a "specified service," the business will *not* be a "specified services" business.
- If the business has gross receipts greater than $25 million, the test is *less than 5 percent* (rather than less than 10 percent).

Example 61

Computer Company has annual revenue of $20,000,000 ($18,500,000 of the revenue is related to the sales of computers and peripheral equipment; the remaining $1,500,000 relates to consulting, installation, and training services).

Because its consulting services revenues are less than 10% of Computer Company's total revenues, those services are ignored for purposes of determining whether Computer Company is a "specified services" business. As a result, Computer Company is *not* a "specified services" business.

Although the *de minimis* rules offer relief to a business with both service and non-service income, what happens if the "specified services" income is more than *de minimis*? Is the entire business tainted (or just the "specified services" portion of the business)? The § 199A Regulations provide two examples to illustrate the consequences.

"Specified Services" *De Minimis* Rule

Example 62

Landscape LLC sells lawn care and landscaping equipment. It also provides advice and counsel on landscape design for large office parks and residential buildings. The landscape design services include advice on the selection and placement of trees, shrubs, and flowers (these are "consulting services" under § 199A).

Landscape LLC separately invoices for its landscape design services and does not sell the trees, shrubs, or flowers it recommends for use in the landscape design. Landscape LLC maintains one set of books and records and treats the equipment sales and design services as a *single trade or business*. Landscape LLC has gross receipts of $2,000,000; $250,000 of the gross receipts relates to the landscape design services.

Because the gross receipts from the consulting services exceed 10% of Landscape LLC's total gross receipts, the entirety of Landscape LLC's business is considered a "specified services" business.

Example 63

Animal Care LLC provides veterinary services performed by licensed staff. It also develops and sells its own line of organic dog food at its veterinarian clinic and online. The veterinary services are in the field of health (a "specified service"). Animal Care LLC separately invoices for its veterinarian services and the sale of its organic dog food. Animal Care LLC maintains separate books and records for its veterinarian clinic and its development and sale of its dog food. Animal Care LLC also has separate employees who are unaffiliated with the veterinary clinic and who only work on the formulation, marketing, sales, and distribution of the organic dog food products.

continued

[78]Reg. § 1.199A–5(c)(1).

Animal Care LLC treats its veterinary practice and the dog food development and sales as *separate trades or businesses*. Animal Care LLC has gross receipts of $3,000,000; $1,000,000 of the gross receipts relates to the veterinary services. Although the gross receipts from the veterinary services exceed 10% of Animal Care LLC's total gross receipts, the dog food development and sales business is *not* considered a "specified services" business. Animal Care LLC has chosen to treat each business separately, so the veterinarian services business is a "specified services" business, while the dog food business is not.

As you can see, two factors led to the favorable result in Example 63. First, the taxpayer keeps separate books and records for each business. Second, each business has separate employees. As discussed previously, it is possible for a single entity to have multiple trades or businesses. However, whether multiple businesses exist depends on "all the facts and circumstances." At a minimum, separate books and records must be maintained; the § 199A Regulations imply (via the outcome in Example 63) that separate employees with separate books and records means separate businesses. But the differing outcomes of Examples 62 and 63 do mean that without separate books and records, multiple businesses in a single entity are not possible. And in that case, if the "specified services" revenue becomes more than *de minimis*, the entire entity is tainted.

Phase-In of the "Specified Services" Limit

In computing the qualified business income with respect to a "specified services" business, the taxpayer takes into account only the "applicable percentage" of QBI *and* the components of the W–2 Wages/Capital Investment Limit.[79]

$$\text{Applicable percentage} = 100\% - \frac{\text{Taxable income before the QBI deduction} - \text{Threshold amount}}{\$100{,}000 \text{ (married filing jointly); } \$50{,}000 \text{ (others)}}$$

Example 64

In 2022, a single taxpayer has modified taxable income of $200,050, of which $150,000 is attributable to an accounting sole proprietorship that pays wages of $100,000 to employees.

The taxpayer has an applicable percentage of 40%, computed as follows:

$$\text{Applicable percentage} = 100\% - \frac{\$30{,}000\ (\$200{,}050 - \$170{,}050)}{\$50{,}000} = 40\%$$

In determining includible qualified business income, the taxpayer takes into account 40% of $150,000, or $60,000. In determining the includible W–2 wages, the taxpayer takes into account 40% of $100,000, or $40,000.

A second complication exists if a taxpayer has a "specified services" business with taxable income before the QBI deduction in the phaseout range. Here, in addition to the amount of QBI, W–2 wages and unadjusted basis of property being subject to a limitation, the W–2 Wages/Capital Investment Limitation also might apply (provided the 20 percent QBI deduction is greater than the W–2 Wages/Capital Investment Limit). The following example illustrates the complexity.

[79] § 199A(d)(3)(B).

"Specified Services" Limit

Example 65

In 2022, Jenna and Paul have taxable income before the QBI deduction (and modified taxable income) of $380,100, and Jenna is a part-time financial adviser (a "specified service trade or business") with QBI of $75,000. Jenna pays $20,000 in wages to employees and has qualified business property of $90,000.

Normally, Jenna and Paul would be entitled to a QBI deduction of $15,000 ($75,000 × 20%). But since their taxable income exceeds the threshold for married taxpayers ($340,100), their QBI deduction is limited to $7,800, computed as follows:

1. Determine Applicable Percentage:

$$\text{Applicable percentage} = 100\% - \frac{\$40{,}000\ (\$380{,}100 - \$340{,}100)}{\$100{,}000} = 60\%$$

2. Determine QBI deduction:

a. 20% of qualified business income ($75,000 × 20%)		$15,000
× Applicable percentage		× 60%
		$ 9,000
b. But no more than the *greater of*:		
• 50% of W–2 wages ($20,000 × 50% × 60%), or		$ 6,000
• 25% of W–2 wages ($20,000 × 25% × 60%) *plus*	$3,000	
• 2.5% of the unadjusted basis of qualified property ($90,000 × 2.5% × 60%)	1,350	$ 4,350

Since Jenna and Paul's taxable income before the QBI deduction exceeds $340,100 but is less than $440,100 and *the W–2 Wages/Capital Investment portion of the computation is capping the deduction*, the general 20% QBI amount is used, but reduced as follows:

1. Determine the difference between the general 20% QBI deduction amount and the W–2 Wages/Capital Investment amount:

General 20% QBI deduction amount	$ 9,000
Less: The W–2 Wages/Capital Investment Limit	(6,000)
Excess	$ 3,000

2. Determine the Reduction Ratio:

$$\text{Reduction Ratio} = \frac{\$40{,}000\ (\$380{,}100 - \$340{,}100)}{\$100{,}000} = 40\%$$

3. Determine the Reduction in the W–2 Wages/Capital Investment Limit:

Excess ($3,000) × Reduction Ratio (40%) = $1,200

4. Determine Final QBI Amount:

General 20% QBI deduction amount	$ 9,000
Less: Reduction in the W–2 Wages/Capital Investment Limit	(1,200)
Final QBI amount	$ 7,800

Since the QBI amount ($7,800) is less than 20% of their modified taxable income ($76,020; $380,100 × 20%), they will be allowed a $7,800 deduction for qualified business income.

Example 66

Assume the same facts as Example 65, except that Jenna and Paul's taxable income before the QBI deduction is $450,000.

Because their modified taxable income exceeds the $440,100 threshold for married taxpayers and their only QBI is from a "specified services" business, Jenna and Paul are not allowed a QBI deduction.

"Specified Services" Limit

Example 67

Now assume the same facts as Example 65, except that Jenna's business is a flower and gift shop (*not* a "specified services" business). As before, Jenna and Paul have modified taxable income of $380,100 and Jenna has QBI of $75,000, pays $20,000 in wages to employees, and has qualified business property of $90,000. Their QBI deduction is $13,000, computed as follows:

1. 20% of qualified business income ($75,000 × 20%)		$15,000
2. But no more than the *greater of*:		
• 50% of W–2 wages ($20,000 × 50%), or		$10,000
• 25% of W–2 wages ($20,000 × 25%) *plus*	$5,000	
• 2.5% of the unadjusted basis of qualified property ($90,000 × 2.5%)	2,250	$ 7,250
And *no more than*:		
3. 20% of modified taxable income ($380,100 × 20%)		$76,020

Since Jenna and Paul's modified taxable income exceeds $340,100 but is less than $440,100 and *the W–2 Wages/Capital Investment portion of the computation is capping the deduction*, the general 20% QBI amount is used, but reduced as follows:

1. Determine the difference between the general 20% QBI deduction amount and the W–2 Wages/Capital Investment amount:

General 20% QBI deduction amount	$ 15,000
Less: The W–2 Wages/Capital Investment Limit	(10,000)
Excess	$ 5,000

2. Determine the Reduction Ratio:

$$\text{Reduction Ratio} = \frac{\$40{,}000\ (\$380{,}100 - \$340{,}100)}{\$100{,}000} = 40\%$$

3. Determine the Reduction in the W–2 Wages/Capital Investment Limit:

Excess ($5,000) × Reduction Ratio (40%) = $2,000

4. Determine Final QBI Amount:

General 20% QBI deduction amount	$ 15,000
Less: Reduction in the W–2 Wages/Capital Investment Limit	(2,000)
Final QBI amount	$ 13,000

Since the QBI amount ($13,000) is less than 20% of their modified taxable income ($76,020; $380,100 × 20%), they will be allowed a $13,000 deduction for qualified business income.

A comparison of Examples 65 and 67 demonstrates the implications (and disadvantages) of having a "specified services" business.

An even more complex setting is having multiple businesses—some "specified services" and others not. Here, a QBI deduction is determined for each business and then combined. This "combined qualified business income amount" is then compared to the overall modified taxable income limitation.

Example 68

Chaz and Abby Klein are involved in two activities during 2022. Chaz is a management consultant. Chaz's consulting business is an LLC (and a "specified services" business), which he reports as a sole proprietorship. The proprietorship generates qualified business income of $230,000, Chaz pays W–2 wages of $50,000 to an employee, and he has $100,000 of qualified property. Chaz and his wife, Abby, also own and operate rental properties. The couple report $161,000 of net income from their rental real estate (three rental properties that they manage; they meet the rental real estate safe harbor requirements for these rentals). They pay no wages with respect to the rental properties, and they have $450,000 of qualified property. They have no other income or deductions (and will use the standard deduction).

Their modified taxable income is $365,100 (AGI of $391,000 less their $25,900 standard deduction); this is also taxable income before the QBI deduction. The maximum QBI deduction they can claim

continued

is \$73,020 (\$365,100 × 20%). Because their modified taxable income is more than \$340,100 and less than \$440,100, both of the QBI deduction limitations apply.

Consulting ("Specified Services") Business

1. Determine Applicable Percentage:

$$\text{Applicable percentage} = 100\% - \frac{\$25{,}000\ (\$365{,}100 - \$340{,}100)}{\$100{,}000} = 75\%$$

2. Determine QBI deduction:

a. 20% of qualified business income (\$230,000 × 20%)		\$46,000
× Applicable percentage		× 75%
		\$34,500
b. But no more than the *greater of*:		
• 50% of W–2 wages (\$50,000 × 50% × 75%), or		\$18,750
• 25% of W–2 wages (\$50,000 × 25% × 75%) *plus*	\$ 9,375	
• 2.5% of the unadjusted basis of qualified property (\$100,000 × 2.5% × 75%)	1,875	\$11,250

Since their taxable income before the QBI deduction exceeds \$340,100 but is less than \$440,100 and *the W–2 Wages/Capital Investment portion of the computation is capping the deduction*, the general 20% QBI amount is used, but reduced as follows:

1. Determine the difference between the general 20% QBI deduction amount and the W–2 Wages/Capital Investment amount:

General 20% QBI deduction amount	\$ 34,500
Less: The W–2 Wages/Capital Investment Limit	(18,750)
Excess	\$ 15,750

2. Determine the Reduction Ratio:

$$\text{Reduction Ratio} = \frac{\$25{,}000\ (\$365{,}100 - \$340{,}100)}{\$100{,}000} = 25\%$$

3. Determine the Reduction in the W–2 Wages/Capital Investment Limit:

Excess (\$15,750) × Reduction Ratio (25%) = \$3,938

4. Determine Final QBI Amount:

General 20% QBI deduction amount	\$ 34,500
Less: Reduction in the W–2 Wages/Capital Investment Limit	(3,938)
Final QBI amount	\$ 30,562

Rentals

1. General QBI Deduction Computation:

a. 20% of qualified business income (\$161,000 × 20%)		\$32,200
b. But no more than the *greater of*:		
• 50% of W–2 wages (\$0 × 50%), or		\$ –0–
• 25% of W–2 wages (\$0 × 25%) *plus*	\$ –0–	
• 2.5% of the unadjusted basis of qualified property (\$450,000 × 2.5%)	11,250	\$11,250

Since their taxable income before the QBI deduction exceeds \$340,100 but is less than \$440,100 and *the W–2 Wages/Capital Investment portion of the computation is capping the deduction*, the general 20% QBI amount is used, but reduced as follows:

1. Determine the difference between the general 20% QBI deduction amount and the W–2 Wages/Capital Investment amount:

General 20% QBI deduction amount	\$ 32,200
Less: The W–2 Wages/Capital Investment Limit	(11,250)
Excess	\$ 20,950

continued

2. Determine the Reduction Ratio:

$$\text{Reduction Ratio} = \frac{\$25{,}000\ (\$365{,}100 - \$340{,}100)}{\$100{,}000} = 25\%$$

3. Determine the Reduction in the W–2 Wages/Capital Investment Limit:

Excess ($20,950) × Reduction Ratio (25%) = $5,238

4. Determine Final QBI Amount:

General 20% QBI deduction amount	$32,200
Less: Reduction in the W–2 Wages/Capital Investment Limit	(5,238)
Final QBI amount	$26,962

So for Chaz and Abby, the "combined qualified income amount" is $57,524, computed as follows:

QBI amount from consulting business	$30,562
+ QBI amount from rental business	26,962
Combined qualified business income amount	$57,524

Since the combined QBI amount ($57,524) is *less than* 20% of their modified taxable income ($73,020; $365,100 × 20%), they will be allowed a $57,524 deduction for qualified business income. Their final taxable income is $307,576 ($365,100 − $57,524).

9-7h Reporting the Qualified Business Income Deduction

The IRS has developed a series of forms and schedules to determine and report the QBI deduction.

- **Form 8995 (Qualified Business Income Deduction Simplified Computation)** is used when taxable income before the QBI deduction is below the limitation thresholds for the year (in 2021, $329,800 for married taxpayers filing jointly and $164,900 for single and head-of-household taxpayers; $340,100 and $170,050, respectively, in 2022).
- **Form 8995–A (Qualified Business Income Deduction)** is used by taxpayers whose taxable income before the QBI deduction exceeds the limitation thresholds. A series of schedules supplement the Form 8995–A: Schedule A (Specified Service Trades or Businesses), Schedule B (Aggregation of Business Operations), Schedule C (Loss Netting and Carryforward), and Schedule D (Patrons of Agricultural or Horticultural Cooperatives).

We will use the taxpayers in Example 68 (Chaz and Abby Klein) and their 2021 information to illustrate Form 8995–A and Schedule A (Form 8995–A).

Example 69

Chaz and Abby Klein (see Example 68) provide you with the following information for 2021 on their two businesses. Chaz's proprietorship (Chaz Management Consulting LLC; EIN 32-4567890) generated qualified business income of $230,000, he paid W–2 wages of $50,000 to an employee, and he has $100,000 of qualified property. The couple reported $149,900 of net income from their real estate rentals (Abby/Chaz Real Estate Management; EIN 32-0987654). They own and manage three rental properties (meeting the rental real estate safe harbor); they pay no wages, and they have $450,000 of qualified property.

They have no other income or deductions (and will use the standard deduction). Their modified taxable income is $354,800 (AGI of $379,900 less their $25,100 standard deduction); this is also taxable income before the QBI deduction. The maximum QBI deduction they can claim is $70,960 ($354,800 × 20%). Because their 2021 modified taxable income is more than $329,800 and less than $429,800, both of the QBI deduction limitations apply. Based on the various QBI deduction limitations, their 2021 QBI deduction is $55,859 ($30,562 for Chaz's consulting business and $25,297 from their rental real estate).

Consult the completed Form 8995–A and Schedule A (Form 8995–A) to see how their QBI deduction was determined. Form 8995–A, Part I provides a summary of the Kleins' qualified trades or businesses. As indicated in Part I, taxpayers must complete any appropriate schedules before completing Form 8995–A.

Because Chaz has a "specified service" business, the Kleins must begin by completing Schedule A (Form 8995–A). On Schedule A, the "applicable percentage" for Chaz's business is determined on lines 5 through 10. It is then applied to the business's QBI, W–2 wages and qualified property. The resulting figures (on lines 11 through 13) are then transferred to Form 8995–A (Part II, Column A, lines 2, 4, and 7).

continued

The determination of their QBI deduction now continues on Form 8995–A. The Kleins' rental real estate information is added in Column B. The remainder of Part II computes the QBI deduction for each business (including, in Part III, the phase-in reductions required because the Kleins' taxable income before the QBI deduction is greater than $329,800 but less than $429,800 in 2021). The Kleins' "combined qualified business income amount" is reported on line 16 of Part II. Part IV completes the QBI deduction determination by applying the overall limitation (based on modified taxable income). Because the Kleins are using the rental real estate safe harbor to treat their rentals as a business for § 199A purposes, they also must attach a statement to their return indicating that they are using this safe harbor.

Compare the completed forms to the computational structure of the QBI deduction contained in Example 68 to see how the forms implement these computations.

9-7i Aggregation of Qualified Trades or Businesses under the § 199A Regulations

In general, each trade or business conducted by an individual or a "relevant pass-through entity" (e.g., a partnership or an S corporation; RPE) is a separate trade or business under § 199A. However, under the § 199A Regulations, taxpayers may aggregate businesses if the following requirements are met:[80]

1. There must be control. The same person or a group of persons must own, directly or indirectly, *50 percent or more* of each business to be aggregated.[81]
   - For S corporations, ownership is measured by reference to the outstanding stock.
   - For partnerships, ownership is measured by reference to the interest in capital or profits in the partnership.
2. Control is met for the "majority" of the tax year (which must include the last day of the tax year).
3. The businesses share the same tax year.
4. None of the businesses are "specified services" businesses.
5. The businesses to be aggregated must satisfy two of the following three factors:
   - They must provide products or services that are the same or customarily offered together.
   - They must share facilities or significant centralized business elements, such as personnel, accounting, legal, manufacturing, purchasing, human resources, or information technology resources.
   - The businesses are operated in coordination with or reliance upon one or more of the businesses in the aggregated group.

Aggregation can be done by either an owner or an RPE.[82] If an RPE chooses to aggregate, the owners of the RPE are bound by that aggregation.[83] If an RPE does not aggregate, the RPE owners need not aggregate in the same manner. As a result, one owner may choose to aggregate that business with another business while a second owner may not choose to do so.

Aggregation is optional and generally cannot be changed once businesses are aggregated.[84] An individual (or RPE) may add a newly created (or acquired) business to the aggregation provided all of the requirements (above) are met.[85] If, in a subsequent year, there is a change in facts and circumstances indicating that a prior aggregation is no longer allowed, the aggregation is terminated and the taxpayer must reapply the aggregation rules to see if aggregation is allowed.

[80] Reg. § 1.199A–4(b).

[81] The § 267(b) or § 707(b) attribution rules are used for this purpose.

[82] Reg. § 1.199A–4(b)(2).

[83] Reg. § 1.199A–4(b)(2)(ii).

[84] Reg. § 1.199A–4(a). According to Reg. §§ 1.199A–4(c)(2) and (4), if aggregation occurs, an individual must attach a statement to his or her income tax return *each year* identifying each aggregated trade or business (an RPE must attach this statement to each owner's Schedule K–1). Failure to disclose this information may result in the IRS not permitting the aggregation.

[85] Reg. §§ 1.199A–4(c) (1) and (3).

Form **8995-A**

Department of the Treasury
Internal Revenue Service

Qualified Business Income Deduction

▶ Attach to your tax return.

▶ Go to *www.irs.gov/Form8995A* for instructions and the latest information.

OMB No. 1545-2294

2021

Attachment Sequence No. **55A**

Name(s) shown on return	Your taxpayer identification number
Chaz and Abby Klein	*123-45-6789*

Note: *You can claim the qualified business income deduction* ***only*** *if you have qualified business income from a qualified trade or business, real estate investment trust dividends, publicly traded partnership income, or a domestic production activities deduction passed through from an agricultural or horticultural cooperative. See instructions.*

Use this form if your taxable income, before your qualified business income deduction, is above $164,900 ($164,925 if married filing separately; $329,800 if married filing jointly), or you're a patron of an agricultural or horticultural cooperative.

Part I Trade, Business, or Aggregation Information

Complete Schedules A, B, and/or C (Form 8995-A), as applicable, before starting Part I. Attach additional worksheets when needed. See instructions.

1	(a) Trade, business, or aggregation name	(b) Check if specified service	(c) Check if aggregation	(d) Taxpayer identification number	(e) Check if patron
A	*Chaz Management Consulting LLC*	☑	☐	*32-4567890*	☐
B	*Abby/Chaz Real Estate Management*	☐	☐	*32-0987654*	☐
C		☐	☐		☐

Part II Determine Your Adjusted Qualified Business Income

			A	B	C
2	Qualified business income from the trade, business, or aggregation. See instructions	2	*172,500*	*149,900*	
3	Multiply line 2 by 20% (0.20). If your taxable income is $164,900 or less ($164,925 if married filing separately; $329,800 if married filing jointly), skip lines 4 through 12 and enter the amount from line 3 on line 13	3	*34,500*	*29,980*	
4	Allocable share of W-2 wages from the trade, business, or aggregation	4	*37,500*	*-0-*	
5	Multiply line 4 by 50% (0.50)	5	*18,750*	*-0-*	
6	Multiply line 4 by 25% (0.25)	6	*9,375*	*-0-*	
7	Allocable share of the unadjusted basis immediately after acquisition (UBIA) of all qualified property	7	*75,000*	*450,000*	
8	Multiply line 7 by 2.5% (0.025)	8	*1,875*	*11,250*	
9	Add lines 6 and 8	9	*11,250*	*11,250*	
10	Enter the greater of line 5 or line 9	10	*18,750*	*11,250*	
11	W-2 wage and UBIA of qualified property limitation. Enter the smaller of line 3 or line 10	11	*18,750*	*11,250*	
12	Phased-in reduction. Enter the amount from line 26, if any	12	*30,562*	*25,297*	
13	Qualified business income deduction before patron reduction. Enter the greater of line 11 or line 12	13	*30,562*	*25,297*	
14	Patron reduction. Enter the amount from Schedule D (Form 8995-A), line 6, if any. See instructions	14	*-0-*	*-0-*	
15	Qualified business income component. Subtract line 14 from line 13	15	*30,562*	*25,297*	
16	Total qualified business income component. Add all amounts reported on line 15 ▶	16	*55,859*		

Form 8995-A (2021) Page **2**

Part III Phased-in Reduction

Complete Part III only if your taxable income is more than $164,900 but not $214,900 ($164,925 and $214,925 if married filing separately; $329,800 and $429,800 if married filing jointly) and line 10 is less than line 3. Otherwise, skip Part III.

					A	B	C
17	Enter the amounts from line 3			17	34,500	29,980	
18	Enter the amounts from line 10			18	18,750	11,250	
19	Subtract line 18 from line 17			19	15,750	18,730	
20	Taxable income before qualified business income deduction	20	354,800				
21	Threshold. Enter $164,900 ($164,925 if married filing separately; $329,800 if married filing jointly)	21	329,800				
22	Subtract line 21 from line 20	22	25,000				
23	Phase-in range. Enter $50,000 ($100,000 if married filing jointly)	23	100,000				
24	Phase-in percentage. Divide line 22 by line 23	24	25%				
25	Total phase-in reduction. Multiply line 19 by line 24			25	3,938	4,683	
26	Qualified business income after phase-in reduction. Subtract line 25 from line 17. Enter this amount here and on line 12, for the corresponding trade or business			26	30,562	25,297	

Part IV Determine Your Qualified Business Income Deduction

27	Total qualified business income component from all qualified trades, businesses, or aggregations. Enter the amount from line 16	27	55,859		
28	Qualified REIT dividends and publicly traded partnership (PTP) income or (loss). See instructions	28	-0-		
29	Qualified REIT dividends and PTP (loss) carryforward from prior years	29	( )		
30	Total qualified REIT dividends and PTP income. Combine lines 28 and 29. If less than zero, enter -0-	30	-0-		
31	REIT and PTP component. Multiply line 30 by 20% (0.20)	31	-0-		
32	Qualified business income deduction before the income limitation. Add lines 27 and 31 ▶			32	55,859
33	Taxable income before qualified business income deduction	33	354,800		
34	Net capital gain. See instructions	34	-0-		
35	Subtract line 34 from line 33. If zero or less, enter -0-			35	354,800
36	Income limitation. Multiply line 35 by 20% (0.20)			36	70,960
37	Qualified business income deduction before the domestic production activities deduction (DPAD) under section 199A(g). Enter the smaller of line 32 or line 36 ▶			37	55,859
38	DPAD under section 199A(g) allocated from an agricultural or horticultural cooperative. Don't enter more than line 33 minus line 37			38	-0-
39	Total qualified business income deduction. Add lines 37 and 38 ▶			39	55,859
40	Total qualified REIT dividends and PTP (loss) carryforward. Combine lines 28 and 29. If zero or greater, enter -0-			40	(-0-)

Form **8995-A** (2021)

SCHEDULE A (Form 8995-A)

Department of the Treasury
Internal Revenue Service

Specified Service Trades or Businesses

► Attach to Form 8995-A.
► Go to *www.irs.gov/Form8995A* for instructions and the latest information.

OMB No. 1545-2294
2021
Attachment Sequence No. **55B**

Name(s) shown on return	Your taxpayer identification number
Chaz and Abby Klein	*123-45-6789*

Complete Schedule A only if your trade or business is a specified service trade or business (see instructions) and your taxable income is more than $164,900 but not $214,900 ($164,925 and $214,925 if married filing separately; $329,800 and $429,800 if married filing jointly). If your taxable income isn't more than $164,900 ($164,925 if married filing separately; $329,800 if married filing jointly) and you're not a patron of an agricultural or horticultural cooperative, don't file this form; instead, file Form 8995, Qualified Business Income Deduction Simplified Computation. Otherwise, complete Schedule D (Form 8995-A) before beginning Schedule A. If your taxable income is more than $214,900 ($214,925 if married filing separately; $429,800 if married filing jointly), your specified service trade or business doesn't qualify for the deduction. If you have more than three trades or businesses, attach as many Schedules A as needed. See instructions.

Part I Other Than Publicly Traded Partnerships (PTP)

See instructions before completing Parts I and II.

					A	B	C
1a	Trade or business name			1a	*Chaz Management Consulting LLC*		
b	Taxpayer identification number			1b	*32-4567890*		
2	Qualified business income or (loss) from the trade or business			2	*230,000*		
3	Allocable share of W-2 wages from the trade or business			3	*50,000*		
4	Allocable share of the unadjusted basis immediately after acquisition (UBIA) of all qualified property			4	*100,000*		
5	Taxable income before qualified business income deduction	5	*354,800*				
6	Threshold. Enter $164,900 ($164,925 if married filing separately; $329,800 if married filing jointly)	6	*329,800*				
7	Subtract line 6 from line 5	7	*25,000*				
8	Phase-in range. Enter $50,000 ($100,000 if married filing jointly)	8	*100,000*				
9	Divide line 7 by line 8	9	*25%*				
10	Applicable percentage. Subtract line 9 from 100%	10	*75%*				
11	Applicable percentage of qualified business income or (loss). Multiply line 2 by line 10. Enter this amount on Schedule C (Form 8995-A) or on Form 8995-A, line 2, for the corresponding trade or business, as appropriate			11	*172,500*		
12	Applicable percentage of W-2 wages. Multiply line 3 by line 10. Enter this amount on Form 8995-A, line 4, for the corresponding trade or business, as appropriate			12	*37,500*		
13	Applicable percentage of the UBIA of qualified property. Multiply line 4 by line 10. Enter this amount on Form 8995-A, line 7, for the corresponding trade or business, as appropriate			13	*75,000*		

Part II Publicly Traded Partnership

			A	B	C
14	Trade or business name	14			
15	Taxpayer identification number	15			
16	Qualified PTP income or (loss)	16			

17	Total PTP specified service trade or business (SSTB) income or (loss). Combine all amounts on line 16	17	
18	Taxable income before qualified business income deduction	18	
19	Threshold. Enter $164,900 ($164,925 if married filing separately; $329,800 if married filing jointly)	19	
20	Subtract line 19 from line 18	20	
21	Phase-in range. Enter $50,000 ($100,000 if married filing jointly)	21	
22	Divide line 20 by line 21	22	
23	Applicable percentage. Subtract line 22 from 100%	23	%
24	Applicable percentage of qualified PTP income or (loss). Multiply line 17 by line 23. Include this amount on Form 8995-A, line 28	24	

If businesses are aggregated, the taxpayer determines his or her share of qualified business income, W–2 wages, and property basis for the aggregated businesses before computing the QBI deduction.

Aggregating QTBs

Example 70

Anita wholly owns and operates a catering business and a restaurant through separate entities. The catering business and the restaurant share centralized purchasing to obtain volume discounts and a centralized accounting office that performs all of the bookkeeping, tracks and issues statements on all of the receivables, and prepares the payroll for each business. Anita maintains a website and print advertising materials that reference both the catering business and the restaurant. She uses the restaurant kitchen to prepare food for the catering business. The catering business employs its own staff and owns equipment and trucks that are not used by the restaurant.

Because the restaurant and catering business are held in separate entities, Anita will be treated as operating each of these businesses directly. Both businesses offer prepared food to customers. The two businesses share the same kitchen facilities in addition to centralized purchasing, marketing, and accounting. As a result, Anita may choose to treat the catering business and restaurant as a single trade or business in determining her QBI deduction.

Example 71

Assume the same facts as in the previous example. However, the catering and restaurant businesses are operated in separate partnerships with Anita, Ben, Carole, and David each owning a 25% interest in the capital and profits of each partnership. The partners are unrelated.

Because Anita, Ben, Carole, and David together own more than 50% of the capital and profits in each of the partnerships, *each* may choose to treat the catering business and the restaurant as a single trade or business in determining their QBI deduction. Further, if Anita chooses to aggregate the businesses, her decision has no effect on what Ben, Carole, and David may (independently) choose to do.

Example 72

Wanda owns a 75% interest in Sunshine, Inc. (a clothing manufacturer operating as an S corporation) and a 75% interest in PetFriendly (a retail pet food store operating as a partnership). Wanda manages both businesses, but they operate in separate facilities, with no overlap of business operations, and do not coordinate or rely on each other.

As a result, Wanda must treat the two businesses separately for purposes of determining the QBI deduction.

Here is a key point: The owner does not have to own more than 50 percent of each business directly; rather, the owner must simply establish that a group of persons owns 50 percent or more of all of the entities the owner wants to aggregate.

Example 73

Frank owns a 75% interest and Geoff owns a 5% interest in each of five partnerships. Helen owns a 10% interest in only two of the partnerships. Each partnership operates a restaurant, each restaurant is a trade or business, and there is centralized management across the restaurants (Geoff is the executive chef of all of the restaurants, and he creates the menus and orders all of the food and related supplies).

Frank may choose to aggregate all five partnerships. Geoff may do the same even though he only owns a 5% interest in each partnership (Geoff can show that Frank owns 50% or more of each of the partnerships; as a result, they are "commonly controlled"). Helen may only aggregate the two partnerships in which she has an interest.

In order to include a business within an aggregated group, the activity must rise to the level of a trade or business under § 162.

Example 74

Jasmine owns a majority interest in a sailboat racing team; she also owns an interest in JB Marina (a partnership that operates a marina). JB Marina is a trade or business under § 162, but the operations of the sailboat racing team are not sufficient to establish a trade or business under § 162.

As a result, Jasmine has only one trade or business for purposes of § 199A and cannot aggregate her interest in the sailboat racing team with her interest in JB Marina.

9-7j Treatment of Losses

If a taxpayer has a qualified business loss in one year, no QBI deduction is allowed, and the loss is carried over to the next year to reduce QBI (but not below zero).[86] Further, the statute indicates that if a taxpayer has more than one QTB and the net results of all businesses create a loss, the net loss is carried forward to the following year. Here is an example from the TCJA of 2017 Conference Report.

Example 75

A taxpayer has QBI of $20,000 from qualified business A and a qualified business loss of $50,000 from qualified business B in 2021. The taxpayer is not permitted a deduction for 2021 and has a carryover qualified business loss of $30,000 to 2022.

In 2022, the taxpayer has QBI of $20,000 from qualified business A and QBI of $50,000 from qualified business B. To determine the deduction for 2022, the taxpayer reduces the 20% deductible amount determined for the QBI of $70,000 from qualified businesses A and B by 20% of the $30,000 carryover qualified business loss.

The result is that the taxpayer has a QBI deduction in 2022 of $8,000 [($20,000 + $50,000) − $30,000 = $40,000 × 20% = $8,000].

The statute and Conference Report provided no guidance, however, on what happens when there is a loss from one QTB and net income from another QTB that nets to a *positive amount*. Fortunately, the § 199A Regulations provide the guidance needed.[87] The Regulations begin by restating the general rule of § 199A(c)(2): if the net amount of all positive and negative QBI is a loss, no § 199A deduction is allowed in the current year and the net loss is carried forward to the next year. The Regulations also indicate that the § 199A loss limitation has no effect on the availability of the loss for other purposes (e.g., reducing taxable income and/or creating a net operating loss). The Regulations make clear, however, that no W–2 wages or capital investment amounts carry forward—only the loss.

Where a taxpayer's netting of all positive and negative QBI is positive, and at least one business produces negative QBI, an "adjusted QBI" is determined by allocating the negative QBI among all of the businesses that produce QBI in proportion to their respective amounts of QBI. Only after this allocation and netting takes place are the W–2 wages and capital investment limitations applied, and no part of the W–2 wages or capital investment amounts related to the loss are used by the businesses with positive QBI.[88]

[86] § 199A(c)(2).

[87] Reg. § 1.199A–1(d)(2)(iii).

[88] Reg. § 1.199A–1(d)(2)(iii)(A).

By requiring the allocation of the loss across all of the businesses that generate QBI, the § 199A Regulations prevent taxpayers from selectively allocating the loss to businesses that will have limited (or no) QBI deduction (e.g., taxpayers above the threshold amount with businesses that pay no W–2 wages).

Multiple Businesses and Negative QBI

Example 76

Erica, who is single, operates three sole proprietorships that generate the following information in 2022 (none are "specified services" businesses):

Business	QBI	W–2 Wages	Capital Investment
A	$200,000	$60,000	$–0–
B	100,000	–0–	–0–
C	20,000	40,000	–0–

Erica chooses not to aggregate the businesses. She also earns $250,000 of wages from an unrelated business, and her modified taxable income (before any QBI deduction) is $520,000.

Because Erica's taxable income is above the threshold amount, her QBI deduction is subject to the W–2 Wages/Capital Investment limitations. These limitations must be applied on a business-by-business basis. None of the businesses own "qualified property." As a result, only the "W–2 Wages" limitation applies.

Because QBI from each business is positive, Erica applies the limitation by determining the lesser of 20% of QBI and 50% of W–2 wages for each business.

Business	QBI × 20%	W–2 Wages × 50%	Lesser
A	$40,000	$30,000	$30,000
B	20,000	–0–	–0–
C	4,000	20,000	4,000

Erica's "combined qualified business income amount" is $34,000 ($30,000 + $0 + $4,000). Since this amount is less than 20% of Erica's modified taxable income ($104,000; $520,000 × 20%), Erica's QBI deduction is $34,000 and her taxable income is $486,000.

Example 77

Assume the same facts as in Example 76, except that Business C generates a loss that results in $(90,000) of negative QBI.

Business	QBI	W–2 Wages	Capital Investment
A	$200,000	$60,000	$–0–
B	100,000	–0–	–0–
C	(90,000)	40,000	–0–

Erica chooses not to aggregate the businesses. Erica also earns $250,000 of wages from an unrelated business, and her modified taxable income (before any QBI deduction) is $410,000.

Absent the rules provided by the § 199A Regulations, Erica would allocate the Business C negative QBI to Business B. Why? Since Erica's income is over the threshold amount and Business B pays no wages, Business B will not generate a QBI deduction. By offsetting Business C's negative QBI against Business B's positive QBI, Erica maximizes her QBI deduction on Business A.

continued

However, under the § 199A Regulations, Erica is not allowed to choose where to allocate Business C's negative QBI. Erica must allocate Business C's negative QBI to Business A and Business B in proportion to their positive QBI amounts ($200,000 for Business A and $100,000 for Business B). As a result, the negative QBI from Business C is apportioned 66.66% to Business A and 33.33% to Business B. So $(60,000) is apportioned to Business A and $(30,000) to Business B.

Business	Adjusted QBI	W-2 Wages	Capital Investment
A	$140,000 ($200,000 − $60,000)	$60,000	$-0-
B	$70,000 ($100,000 − $30,000)	-0-	-0-
C	$-0- [($90,000) + $90,000]	40,000	-0-

Erica now applies the "W-2 Wages" limitation by determining the lesser of 20% of QBI and 50% of W-2 wages for each business.

Business	QBI × 20%	W-2 Wages × 50%	Lesser
A	$28,000 ($140,000 × 20%)	$30,000	$28,000
B	$14,000 ($70,000 × 20%)	-0-	-0-
C	$-0-	20,000	-0-

Erica's "combined qualified business income amount" is $28,000 ($28,000 + $0 + $0). Since this amount is less than 20% of Erica's modified taxable income ($82,000; $410,000 × 20%), her QBI deduction is $28,000 and her taxable income is $382,000. There is no carryover of any loss into the following taxable year for purposes of § 199A (the Business C negative QBI was completely used).

Example 78

Assume the same facts as in Example 77, except that Businesses A, B, and C meet the aggregation requirements of Reg. § 1.199A-4 and Erica chooses to aggregate the three businesses.

Because Erica's taxable income is above the threshold amount, her QBI deduction is subject to the W-2 wages and capital investment limitations. Because the businesses are aggregated, these limitations are applied on an *aggregated* basis.

Business	QBI	W-2 Wages	Capital Investment
A	$200,000	$ 60,000	$-0-
B	100,000	-0-	-0-
C	(90,000)	40,000	-0-
Total	$210,000	$100,000	$-0-

None of the businesses own "qualified property." As a result, only the "W-2 Wages" limitation applies. Erica's "combined qualified income amount" is $42,000, the lesser of 20% of the QBI from the aggregated businesses ($42,000; $210,000 × 20%) or 50% of W-2 wages from the aggregated businesses ($50,000; $100,000 × 50%).

Erica then applies the overall limitation, comparing her "combined qualified income amount" ($42,000) to 20% of her modified taxable income ($82,000; $410,000 × 20%). Erica's QBI deduction is $42,000 (the lesser of $42,000 or $82,000).

Note that by aggregating her businesses, Erica has increased the amount of her QBI deduction.

9-7k Other Items in the § 199A Regulations

Employee Turned Independent Contractor

The § 199A Regulations indicate that the status of an individual as an employee or independent contractor is determined by common law and statutory rules.[89] However, under the Regulations, an individual who was an employee of an employer and becomes an independent contractor while providing substantially the same services (either directly or indirectly through another entity) is presumed, for a three-year period, still to be an employee.[90] This presumption may be overturned if it can be demonstrated—using common law and statutory rules—that the individual is *not* an employee.

Example 79

Corbin is an attorney employed as an associate with LegalEagles LLP (LE). Corbin and the other associates in LE have taxable income below the threshold amount. LE terminates its employment relationship with Corbin and its other associates, allowing Corbin and the other former associates to form a new partnership, LegalBeagles LLP (LB). LB then contracts to perform services to LE. Corbin continues to provide substantially the same services to LE and its clients through LB.

The goal, obviously, is for Corbin (and the other associates) to convert wage income into pass-through income from LB that is eligible for the QBI deduction (even though LB is a "specified services" business, Corbin is below the taxable income threshold).

Because Corbin was formerly an employee of LE and continues to provide substantially the same services to LE, Corbin is presumed to be an employee of LE. Unless the presumption is rebutted, Corbin's distributive share of income from LB will be treated like wages for purposes of § 199A for a period of three years and will not be treated as qualified business income.

What if LB, instead, provides contractual services to a *different* law firm? Now the QBI deduction is available (again assuming that Corbin is below the taxable income threshold).

Determination of "W–2 Wages"

In general, the term *W–2 wages* includes the total amount of wages [as defined in § 3401(a)] plus the total amount of elective compensation deferrals (under § 457) plus the amount of designated Roth contributions (§ 402A).[91]

A business can take into account any W–2 wages paid by another business provided that the W–2 wages were paid to "common law employees or officers" of that business.[92] This means that a business using a professional employer organization (PEO) to manage parts of its business (e.g., human resources) or to lease employees can use an allocable portion of the PEO's W–2 wages in determining its total W–2 wages. Of course, this also means that the business that actually paid and reported the W–2 wages must reduce its § 199A wages by the same amount.

Determination of Unadjusted Basis Immediately after Acquisition (UBIA)

For purchased or produced property, UBIA generally will be the property's cost (under § 1012) when the property is placed in service. An addition or improvement to qualified property already placed in service is treated as *separate qualified property* on the date the addition or improvement is placed in service.[93] For purposes of the QBI deduction, property is *not* qualified property if it is acquired within 60 days of the end of the tax year and disposed of within 120 days without having been used in a trade or business for at least 45 days prior to disposition, unless the taxpayer demonstrates that the principal purpose of the acquisition and disposition was other than increasing the QBI deduction.[94]

[89] See, for example, Rev.Rul. 87–41 and Reg. §§ 31.3121(d)–1, 31.3306(i)–1, and 31.3401(c)–1.

[90] Reg. § 1.199A–5(d)(3).

[91] Reg. § 1.199A–2(b)(2). Notice 2018–64 and Rev.Proc. 2019–11 provide detailed guidance about calculating "W–2 wages" for purposes of the QBI deduction.

[92] Reg. § 1.199A–2(b)(2)(ii).

[93] Reg. § 1.199A–2(c)(1)(ii).

[94] Reg. § 1.199A–2(c)(1)(iv).

The Big Picture

Example 80

Refer back to Example 33. Morgan reports net income from her tutoring of $3,963 and her freelance driving of $2,742. Assume that Morgan's modified taxable income for 2022 is $52,000.

Her tutoring business might be classified as a "specified services" business since the "principal asset of the business is the reputation" of Morgan. Is her freelance driving business also a "specified services" business? One might argue that her driving ability (and therefore the reputation of this business) makes it a "specified services" business. Although this seems less likely (most freelance driving companies do not allow the customer to choose the driver; the driver is assigned by the company), it remains a possibility.

However, because neither activity generated a loss and her taxable income before the QBI deduction is less than the $170,050 income limit in 2022, neither the W–2 Wage/Capital Investment Limit nor the Specified Services Limit applies to her. As a result, her QBI deduction for 2022 is $1,341, computed as follows:

1. 20% of qualified business income:

Tutoring: $3,963 × 20%	$ 793
Freelance driving: $2,742 × 20%	548
Combined qualified business income amount	$ 1,341

2. 20% of modified taxable income:

$52,000 × 20%	$10,400

Since Morgan's combined qualified business income amount ($1,341) is less than 20% of her modified taxable income ($10,400; $52,000 × 20%), her QBI deduction in 2022 is $1,341. Her taxable income is $50,659 ($52,000 of taxable income before the QBI deduction less her $1,341 QBI deduction).

LO.7

Compare various deductions for contributions to retirement accounts.

9-8 Contributions to Retirement Accounts

Retirement planning is critical for employees. As noted in Chapter 1, using the tax law to provide retirement security for employees can be justified on both economic and social grounds. Although Social Security provides some retirement income, it is not sufficient for most recipients. As a result, the private sector must fill the need. Congress has enacted a variety of laws that provide significant tax advantages for retirement plans. These plans fall into two major classifications: those available to employees and those available to self-employed persons. Since Chapter 19 provides significant coverage of deferred compensation and retirement planning, only a brief discussion occurs here.

9-8a Employee IRAs

Pension plans covering employees follow one of two income tax approaches. Most plans allow an *exclusion* for the contributions the employee makes to the plan. The employee's income tax return shows nothing regarding the contribution—no income, exclusion, or deduction. This is the case even if the contribution is funded entirely (or partially) by means of a salary reduction.[95]

The other income tax approach is followed by the **traditional IRA**. Here, the contributing employee is allowed a deduction *for* AGI. The amount, a maximum of $6,000 in 2022 and 2021 ($7,000 in 2022 and 2021 for those age 50 and older), is reported as a deduction on Form 1040.[96] Under either approach (contribuion exclusion or contribution deduction), nothing is taxed to the employee-participant until distributions from the traditional IRA occur. Consequently, all of these types of retirement plans carry the advantage of deferring the taxation of income. As described in Chapter 19, all retirement plans are subject to various rules regarding coverage requirements, degree of vesting,

[95] See, for example, §§ 401(k), 403(b), and 457.

[96] §§ 219 and 408.

excessive contributions, and premature distributions. Generally, these rules are less stringent for traditional IRAs.

An alternative to the traditional IRA is the **Roth IRA**, which takes a radically different tax approach. No tax benefit (i.e., exclusion or deduction) results from the initial contribution to a Roth IRA. Instead, later distributions (including postcontribution earnings) are recovered tax-free.[97]

9-8b Self-Employed Keogh (H.R. 10) Plans

Self-employed taxpayers also can participate in retirement plans with tax-favored benefits. Known as Keogh (or H.R. 10) plans, these arrangements follow the deduction approach of traditional IRAs.[98] The amount contributed under a plan is a deduction *for* AGI and is reported on Form 1040. The plan established by a self-employed taxpayer who has employees must meet stringent requirements to ensure that it provides similar retirement benefits for the group. The law is structured to ensure that employees share an owner-employer's ability to defer taxes.

Retirement plans for self-employed taxpayers and other small businesses are not restricted to H.R. 10 plans. Other options include solo or individual § 401(k) plans, simplified employee pension (SEP) plans, and savings incentive match plans for employees (SIMPLEs).[99] The operational rules governing all of these plans are covered in Chapter 19.

9-9 Classification of Employee Expenses

LO.8

Demonstrate the difference between accountable and nonaccountable employee plans.

The classification of employee expenses depends on whether the expenses are reimbursed by the employer under an accountable plan. If so, neither the reimbursement nor the expense is reported by the employee. In effect, this result is equivalent to treating the expenses as deductions *for* AGI. If the expenses are reimbursed under a nonaccountable plan or are not reimbursed at all, then they are classified as deductions *from* AGI and are classified as miscellaneous itemized deductions.[100] Given that the TCJA of 2017 suspends the deduction of miscellaneous itemized deductions from 2018 through 2025, understanding the difference between accountable and nonaccountable plans is important.

9-9a Accountable Plans

An **accountable plan** requires the employee to satisfy these two requirements:

- *Substantiate the Expenses*. An employee provides an *adequate accounting* by submitting a record (e.g., completing an employer-provided travel expense reimbursement form), with receipts and other substantiation, to the employer.[101]
- *Return Any Excess Reimbursement or Allowance*. An "excess reimbursement or allowance" is any amount the employee does not adequately account for as an ordinary and necessary business expense.

Substantiation

No deduction is allowed for any travel, entertainment, business gift, or listed property (e.g., automobiles and computers) expenses unless properly substantiated by adequate records. The records should contain the following information:[102]

- The amount of the expense.
- The time and place of travel or entertainment (or date of gift).

---

[97] § 408A.

[98] § 401(c).

[99] The relevant Code Sections are § 408(k) for SEPs and § 408(p) for SIMPLEs.

[100] The employment-related expenses of performing artists are allowed as *for* AGI deductions; § 62(b).

[101] Reg. § 1.162–17(b)(4).

[102] § 274(d).

- The business purpose of the expense.
- The business relationship of the taxpayer to the person entertained (or receiving the gift).

As a result, the taxpayer must keep records (e.g., in a calendar or by other means) to document these expenses. Documentary evidence, such as itemized receipts, is required to support any lodging expenses while traveling away from home and for any other expenditure of $75 or more. If a taxpayer fails to keep adequate records, a written or oral statement of the exact details of the expense will be required, along with other corroborating evidence.[103]

Inadequate Substantiation

Example 81

Ben has travel expenses substantiated only by canceled checks. The checks establish the date, place, and amount of the expenditure. Because neither the business relationship nor the business purpose is established, the deduction is disallowed.[104]

Example 82

Mohammed has travel and entertainment expenses substantiated by a digital diary showing the time, place, and amount of the expenditure. He is able to provide information about the business relationship and business purpose orally. However, because he has no receipts, any expenditures of $75 or more are disallowed.[105]

Deemed Substantiation

Instead of reimbursing actual expenses for travel away from home, many employers reduce their paperwork by adopting a policy of reimbursing employees with a *per diem* allowance, a flat dollar amount per day of business travel. Of the substantiation requirements listed previously, the *amount* of the expense is proved, or *deemed substantiated*, by using such a per diem allowance or reimbursement procedure. The amount of expenses that is deemed substantiated is equal to the lesser of the per diem allowance or the amount of the Federal per diem rate.

The regular Federal per diem rate is the highest amount the Federal government will pay to its employees for lodging, meals, and incidental expenses[106] while traveling. The rates are different for different locations.[107]

The use of the standard Federal per diem rates for meals and incidental expenses also constitutes an adequate accounting. Employees and self-employed persons can use these standard allowances instead of deducting the actual cost of daily meals and incidental expenses, even if not reimbursed.

Only the amount of the expense is considered substantiated under the deemed substantiated method. Records must be maintained for the other items: place, date, business purpose of the expense, and the business relationship of the parties involved.

9-9b Nonaccountable Plans

A **nonaccountable plan** is a plan where an adequate accounting or return of excess amounts, or both, is not required. All expense reimbursements are included as wages on the employee's Form W–2. Any allowable expenses are deductible in the same manner as unreimbursed expenses.

[103] Reg. § 1.274–5T(c)(3).

[104] *William T. Whitaker*, 56 TCM 47, T.C.Memo. 1988–418.

[105] *W. David Tyler*, 43 TCM 927, T.C.Memo. 1982–160.

[106] For this purpose, incidental expenses include tips and fees to porters, bellhops, hotel maids, etc. These expenses are expected to be relatively small and typically paid out in cash.

[107] *Per Diem Rates* (IRS Publication 1542) contains the list and amounts for the year. This publication is available only on the internet at **irs.gov**. Links to per diem rates also can be found at **gsa.gov**.

Unreimbursed Employee Expenses

Unreimbursed employee business expenses (including 50 percent of any meals) are treated as miscellaneous itemized deductions and not deductible from 2018 through 2025 (see text Section 9-10). If the employee could have received but did not seek reimbursement for whatever reason, none of the employment-related expenses are deductible.

Failure to Comply with Accountable Plan Requirements

An employer may have an accountable plan and require employees to return excess reimbursements or allowances, but an employee may fail to follow the rules of the plan. In that case, the expenses and reimbursements are subject to nonaccountable plan treatment.

9-10 Limitations on Itemized Deductions

LO.9

Recognize the limitations on miscellaneous itemized deductions.

Many itemized deductions (*from* AGI deductions) are subject to limitations based on a taxpayer's AGI. For example, only those medical expenses in excess of 7.5 percent of AGI are deductible (this is often called a "floor") and charitable contributions made in cash are normally limited to a maximum of 60 percent of a taxpayer's AGI (this is often called a "ceiling"). These limitations are discussed in Chapter 10.

Miscellaneous itemized deductions (including employee business expenses) are also subject to limitations. From 2018 through 2025, the deduction for miscellaneous itemized deductions subject to the 2%-of-AGI floor has been suspended (these items are discussed in text Section 9-10a). Other miscellaneous itemized deductions are not subject to the 2%-of-AGI floor and remain deductible as a *from* AGI deduction (these items are discussed in text Section 9-10b).

9-10a Miscellaneous Itemized Deductions Subject to the 2%-of-AGI Floor

Certain miscellaneous itemized deductions, including most *unreimbursed employee business expenses*, are subject to a 2%-of-AGI floor. These expenses, which are listed below, are not deductible from 2018 through 2025.[108]

- All § 212 expenses, except expenses of producing rent and royalty income (see Chapter 6).
- All unreimbursed employee business expenses, after the 50 percent limit for meals, if applicable.
- Professional dues and subscriptions.
- Union dues and work uniforms.
- Employment-related education expenses.
- Expenses of job hunting (including employment agency fees and résumé-writing expenses).
- Home office expenses of an employee or outside salesperson.
- Legal, accounting, and tax return preparation fees.
- Hobby expenses, up to hobby income (see Chapter 6).
- Investment expenses, including investment counsel fees, subscriptions, and safe deposit box rental.
- Custodial fees relating to income-producing property or a traditional IRA or a Keogh plan.
- Appraisal fees paid to determine a casualty loss or charitable contribution.

[108] § 67(g).

9-10b Miscellaneous Itemized Deductions Not Subject to the 2%-of-AGI Floor

Certain miscellaneous itemized deductions, including the following, are *not* subject to the 2%-of-AGI floor and remain deductible *from* AGI:

- Impairment-related work expenses of individuals with a disability.
- Amortizable premium on taxable bonds.
- Losses from Ponzi-type investment schemes.
- Gambling losses to the extent of gambling winnings.
- Unrecovered investment in an annuity.

LO.10

Identify tax planning ideas related to employee and self-employed business expenses.

9-11 Tax Planning

9-11a Employment Status

When considering the merits of employee or independent contractor status, much depends on which party is involved. Earlier in the chapter, we discussed some of the employer implications of this choice. If it is the worker, being self-employed carries the obvious advantage of a deduction *for* AGI category of work-related expenses and the avoidance of the limitations related to employee business expenses.

However, a self-employed individual may have other costs, such as local gross receipts taxes, license fees or taxes, franchise fees, personal property taxes, and occupation taxes. In addition, the record-keeping and filing requirements can be quite burdensome.

One of the most expensive considerations is the Social Security tax versus the self-employment tax. For an employee in 2022, for example, the Social Security tax applies at a rate of 6.2 percent on a base amount of wages of $147,000 ($142,800 in 2021) and the Medicare tax applies at a rate of 1.45 percent with no limit on the base amount. Further, a 0.9 percent additional Medicare tax applies to certain high earners. For self-employed persons, the Social Security and Medicare tax rates *double* (to 12.4 percent and 2.9 percent, respectively). Even though a deduction *for* AGI is allowed for part of the self-employment tax paid, an employee and a self-employed individual are not in the same tax position on equal amounts of earnings. The self-employment tax is explained in Chapter 13. For the applicability of these taxes to employees, see Chapter 1.

9-11b Implications of Misclassifying Workers

The Affordable Care Act (ACA) places specific compliance burdens (both financial and reporting) on employers regarding the provision of health care coverage for their employees. The rules are complex and vary according to the size of the employer (large or small) and the status of the employee (full- or part-time).[109] Because the ACA does not apply to independent contractors and part-time employees, employers may be more likely to misclassify workers. To discourage this from happening, penalties are levied on those employers who wrongfully categorize workers as independent contractors.

There are many reasons to favor classifying workers as independent contractors rather than as employees. Besides avoiding payroll taxes and income tax withholdings, the employer circumvents a myriad of state and local laws. Examples include vacation pay obligations, unemployment tax and workers' compensation requirements,

[109] Large employers are those with 50 or more full-time or full-time equivalent employees. Part-time employees work less than 30 hours per week.

and overtime and minimum wage restrictions. Because complying with these rules is costly and burdensome, some employers are motivated to misclassify their workers as independent contractors.

In the event of misclassification, two remedies are available regarding Federal employment taxes—one legislative and one administrative. The legislative option, known as Section 530 relief, absolves the employer of the employment taxes that should have been paid.[110] To obtain Section 530 relief, *all* three of the following requirements must be met:

1. The employer has a reasonable basis for *not* treating the workers as employees. Reasonable basis means reliance on any of the following:
   - A court case, a published IRS ruling, or IRS technical advice.
   - A past IRS audit that resulted in no employment tax assessment.
   - A long-standing practice of independent contractor status in the same industry.
2. The employer has consistently treated the workers as independent contractors.
3. The employer filed a Form 1099–NEC (Nonemployee Compensation) for each worker (when required).

A Federal administrative remedy for employers who are misclassifying workers is the Voluntary Classification Settlement Program (VCSP).[111] A type of amnesty arrangement, the VCSP allows the applicant to be absolved from all employment taxes that should have been paid plus any interest and penalties that would be due. To be accepted, Form 8952 [Application for Voluntary Classification Settlement Program (VCSP)] must be filed with the IRS and certain conditions met.[112] A major condition is the payment of 10 percent of the employment taxes that are usually due when workers are reclassified.

9-11c Transportation and Travel Expenses

Adequate detailed records of all transportation and travel expenses should be kept. Because the automatic (standard) mileage method applies to all automobiles in the same manner, a new, expensive automobile used primarily for business may generate a higher deduction using the actual cost method. Once a method is chosen, a later change may be possible. Switching from the automatic mileage method to the actual cost method is allowed if a basis adjustment is made for depreciation deemed taken (see Example 7). Switching from the actual cost method to the automatic mileage method is possible only if the taxpayer has not used the MACRS statutory percentage method and has not claimed § 179 limited expensing.

If an automobile has mixed use (i.e., both personal and business), maintaining a record of business miles driven is critical. Further, the business use portion should be realistic under the circumstances. Although a 95 percent business use allocation for a one-car family living in the suburbs is possible, the IRS might question this allocation (i.e., does the 5 percent allocated to personal use reasonably account for commuting to work, trips to the grocery store and mall, soccer practice, and dance lessons?).

If a taxpayer wants to sightsee or vacation on a business trip, scheduling business on both the Friday and Monday surrounding the weekend turns the weekend into business days for allocation purposes. It is especially crucial to schedule appropriate business days when foreign travel is involved.

[110] This safe harbor for withholding purposes originated in Section 530 of the Revenue Act of 1978. See IRS *Headliner*, vol. 152 (March 27, 2006). Section 530 relief does not absolve an employer of any Affordable Care Act penalties.

[111] Announcement 2011–64.

[112] The conditions to be met are identified in the instructions for Form 8952. Many of these conditions are the same as those required for Section 530 relief.

Refocus on The Big Picture

The First Job

ISTOCK.COM/SVETIKD

The first issue that might arise as a result of Morgan's new job is the dependency exemption possibility. If Morgan was living at home and accepted the job late in the year, she could qualify as a dependent of her parents. If so, they also might be able to claim the qualified tuition deduction (or the lifetime learning credit). If, however, her employment began early in the year, she could not be a qualifying child (due to the self-supporting limitation) or a qualifying relative (due to the gross income limitation)—see Chapter 3.

Morgan can claim an office in the home deduction because she is using her second bedroom exclusively for her tutoring and freelance driving businesses. She can use either the Regular (actual expense) Method or the Simplified (safe harbor) Method. Under the Regular Method, the deduction would include a portion of the rent, utilities, and insurance paid. The Simplified Method would allow Morgan $5 per square foot for business space, but not more than 300 square feet, or $1,500. Since her second bedroom is 200 square feet, the Simplified Method produces a $1,000 deduction (see Example 33). Under either method, she also would be allowed to deduct other business expenses, including her software, supplies, and depreciation (or expensing) of office equipment and furnishings (e.g., computer, copier, desk, file cabinet). She must be careful, however, not to violate the "exclusive use" restriction (see Examples 28, 30, and 31) regardless of which method she uses. Morgan will use the Regular Method, since it results in a larger deduction ($3,117; see Example 33).

In addition to commuting between her apartment and her job at ECCC, Morgan also will use her car for her freelance businesses (see Example 5). Normally, she would need to make a choice between the automatic mileage method and the actual cost method. However, because she is using a car given to her by her parents (see Example 9), she will use the automatic mileage method.

In addition to her automobile expenses, Morgan should document any meal expenses she incurs while driving for Uber and other companies. However, any meals are subject to the 50 percent limitation. These expenses will be *for* AGI deductions. Morgan's QBI deduction in 2022 is $1,341 (see Example 80).

Any expenses she incurs related to her job with Enrichment Child Care Center will be classified as employee business expenses. The total of all employment-related expenses is a miscellaneous itemized deduction (a *from* AGI deduction) and not deductible in 2022 (and through 2025).

Morgan must maintain adequate records regarding all of these transactions. Detailed records are particularly important in arriving at her office in the home deduction (if the Regular Method is used) and the business use of her car (for her freelancing jobs).

Key Terms

Accountable plan, 9-53
Automatic mileage method, 9-6
Deduction for qualified business income, 9-25
Education expenses, 9-14
Independent contractor, 9-2
Nonaccountable plan, 9-54
Office in the home expenses, 9-17
QBI deduction, 9-25
Qualified business income, 9-26
Qualified trade or business, 9-27
Roth IRA, 9-53
Specified service trade or business, 9-33
Statutory employees, 9-5
Traditional IRA, 9-52
Transportation expenses, 9-5
Travel expenses, 9-9
W–2 Wages/Capital Investment Limit, 9-29

Discussion Questions

1. **LO.1** Mason performs services for Isabella. In determining whether Mason is an employee or an independent contractor, comment on the relevance of each of the factors listed below.
   a. Mason performs services only for Isabella and does not work for anyone else.
   b. Mason sets his own work schedule.
   c. Mason reports his job-related expenses on a Schedule C.
   d. Mason obtained his job skills from Isabella's training program.
   e. Mason performs the services at Isabella's business location.
   f. Mason is paid based on time worked rather than on task performed.

2. **LO.2** Milton is a resident of Mobile (Alabama) and is employed by Scaup Corporation. Because Scaup closed its Mobile office, Milton no longer has any nondeductible commuting expenses although he continues to work for Scaup. Explain why. *Critical Thinking*

3. **LO.2** In 2020, Emma purchased an automobile, which she uses for both business and personal purposes. Although Emma does not keep records as to operating expenses (e.g., gas, oil, and repairs), she can prove the percentage of business use and the miles driven each year. In March 2022, Emma seeks your advice as to what income tax benefit, if any, she can derive from the use of her automobile. What would you suggest? *Critical Thinking, Planning*

4. **LO.3** Dr. Werner is a full-time professor of accounting at Pelican University. During the year, he teaches continuing education programs for CPA groups in several cities. He also serves as an expert witness in numerous lawsuits involving accounting fraud. Comment on the possible tax treatment of Dr. Werner's job-related expenses. *Critical Thinking*

5. **LO.4, 9** Jamie has an undergraduate degree in finance and has an established financial planning practice (a single-member LLC). To expand her knowledge base and serve her clients better, she decides to pursue a master's degree in quantitative finance at a local university. Is the full cost of this education deductible to her?

6. **LO.5** In each of the following situations, indicate whether the 50% reduction for meals applies. Assume the year is 2023.
   a. Each year, the employer awards its top salesperson an all-expense-paid trip to Jamaica.
   b. The employer has a cafeteria for its employees where meals are furnished at cost.
   c. The employer sponsors an annual Labor Day picnic for its employees.
   d. Every Christmas, the employer gives each employee a fruitcake.
   e. The taxpayer gives business gifts to her clients at Christmas.

7. **LO.5** In connection with the office in the home deduction, comment on the following:
   a. The exclusive use requirement.
   b. The distinction between *direct* and *indirect* expenses.
   c. The effect of the taxpayer's work status (i.e., employed or self-employed) on the deduction.
   d. The ownership status of the residence (i.e., owned or rented).
   e. The tax treatment of office furnishings (e.g., desk, chairs, and file cabinets).
   f. The treatment of expenses that exceed the gross income from the business.

Communications

8. **LO.5** Review the advantages and disadvantages of the Simplified Method for determining the office in the home deduction. Create a brief summary of your findings, and e-mail it to your instructor.

9. **LO.6** Who can claim the qualified business income (QBI) deduction?

10. **LO.6** What are the general rules surrounding the QBI deduction? How is it computed?

11. **LO.6** Define each of the following terms, and explain how it is used in determining the QBI deduction:
    a. Modified taxable income.
    b. Qualified business income.
    c. Qualified trade or business.
    d. "Specified services" business.

12. **LO.6** Identify the requirements that must be met in order to aggregate businesses for purposes of the QBI deduction.

13. **LO.6** Paul wholly owns and operates an office supplies business and a printing/shipping business through separate entities. The office supplies business and printing/shipping business share centralized purchasing to obtain volume discounts and share a centralized accounting office that performs all necessary accounting for both businesses (including preparing financial statements, paying bills, collecting receivables, and preparing payrolls for both businesses). Paul maintains a website that promotes both businesses. The businesses operate in separate spaces in the same building (next to each other), but share an office and a shipping/receiving space at the rear of the building and an opening in the shared inside wall that allows customers to move between the businesses without going outside. Each business owns its own equipment and employs its own staff. May Paul aggregate these businesses for purposes of the QBI deduction? Explain.

14. **LO.7** Regarding the tax implications of various retirement plans, comment on the following:
    a. The difference between Keogh (H.R. 10) and traditional deductible IRA plans.
    b. The difference between traditional IRA and Roth IRA plans.

15. **LO.8** What tax return reporting procedures must be followed by an employee under the following circumstances?
    a. Expenses and reimbursements are equal under an accountable plan.
    b. Reimbursements at the appropriate Federal per diem rate exceed expenses, and an adequate accounting is made to the employer.
    c. Expenses exceed reimbursements under a nonaccountable plan.

Computational Exercises

16. **LO.2** Lara uses the standard mileage method for determining auto expenses. During 2022, she used her car as follows: 9,000 miles for business, 2,000 miles for personal use, 2,500 miles for a move to a new job, 1,000 miles for charitable purposes, and 500 miles for medical visits. Presuming that all the mileage expenses are allowable (i.e., not subject to percentage limitations), what is Lara's deduction for:
    a. Business?
    b. Charitable?
    c. Medical?

17. **LO.3** Tyler, a self-employed taxpayer, travels from Denver to Miami primarily on business. He spends five days conducting business and two days sightseeing. His expenses are $400 (airfare), $150 per day (meals at local restaurants), and $300 per night (lodging). What are Tyler's deductible expenses if the year is 2022? 2023?

18. **LO.3** In November 2022, Kortney (who is a self-employed management consultant) travels from Chicago to Barcelona (Spain) on business. She is gone 10 days (including 2 days of travel) during which time she spends 5 days conducting business and 3 days sightseeing. Her expenses are $1,500 (airfare), $200 per day (meals at local restaurants), and $400 per night (lodging). Because Kortney stayed with relatives while sightseeing, she only paid for 5 nights of lodging. What is Kortney's deduction for:
    a. Airfare?
    b. Meals?
    c. Lodging?

19. **LO.4** Samantha was recently employed by an accounting firm. During the year, she spends $2,500 for a CPA exam review course and begins working on a law degree in night school. Her law school expenses were $4,200 for tuition and $450 for books (which are not a requirement for enrollment in the course). Assuming no reimbursement, how much of these expenses can Samantha deduct?

20. **LO.5** In 2022, Robert takes four key clients and their spouses out to dinner at a local restaurant. Business discussions occurred over dinner. Expenses were $700 (drinks and dinner) and $140 (tips to servers). If Robert is self-employed, how much can he deduct for this event?

21. **LO.5** In 2022, the CEO of Crimson, Inc., entertains seven clients at a skybox in Memorial Stadium for a single athletic event during the year. Substantive business discussions occurred at various times during the event. The box costs $2,000 per event and seats 10 people. (The cost of a regular seat at Memorial ranges from $55 to $100.) Refreshments served during the event cost $700 (the refreshments were obtained from a local restaurant and were separately itemized on the bill Crimson received). How much of these costs may Crimson deduct?

22. **LO.5** Andrew sends Godiva chocolates to 10 of his key clients at Christmas. The chocolates cost $50 a box not including $4 for gift wrapping and shipping. How much can Andrew deduct?

23. **LO.5** Jayda maintains an office in her home that comprises 8% (200 square feet) of total floor space. Gross income for her business is $42,000, and her residence expenses are as follows:

Real property taxes	$2,400
Interest on mortgage	4,000
Operating expenses	2,200
Depreciation (based on 8% business use)	450

What is Jayda's office in the home deduction based on:

a. The Regular Method?

b. The Simplified Method?

24. **LO.6** In 2022, Meghann, a single taxpayer, has QBI of $110,000 and modified taxable income of $78,000 (this is also her taxable income before the QBI deduction). Given this information, what is Meghann's QBI deduction?

25. **LO.6** In 2021, Henry Jones (Social Security number 123-45-6789) works as a freelance driver, finding customers using various platforms like Uber and Grubhub. He is single and has no other sources of income. In 2021, Henry's qualified business income from driving is $61,200.

a. Compute Henry's QBI deduction and his tax liability for 2021.

b. Complete Henry's 2021 Form 8995 (Qualified Business Income Deduction Simplified Computation).

26. **LO.9** In 2022, Ava, an employee, has AGI of $58,000 and the following itemized deductions:

Home office expenses	$1,200
Union dues and work uniforms	350
Unreimbursed employee expenses	415
Gambling losses to the extent of gambling winnings	890

What is Ava's total itemized deduction related to these items?

Problems

27. **LO.2** Jackson, a self-employed taxpayer, uses his automobile 90% for business and during 2022 drove a total of 14,000 business miles. Information regarding his car expenses is listed below.

Business parking	$ 140
Auto insurance	1,300
Auto club dues (includes towing service)	180
Toll road charges (business-related)	200
Oil changes and engine tune-ups	210
Repairs	160
Depreciation allowable	2,850
Fines for traffic violations (incurred during business use)	320
Gasoline purchases	2,800

What is Jackson's deduction in 2022 for the use of his car if he uses:

a. The actual cost method?

b. The automatic mileage method?

c. What records must Jackson maintain?

28. **LO.2** On July 1, 2018, Brent purchases a new automobile for $40,000. He uses the car 80% for business and drives the car for business purposes as follows: 8,000 miles in 2018, 19,000 miles in 2019, 20,000 miles in 2020, and 15,000 miles in 2021. Determine Brent's basis in the business portion of the auto as of January 1, 2022, under the following assumptions:
    a. Brent uses the automatic mileage method.
    b. Brent uses the actual cost method. [Assume that no § 179 expensing is claimed and that 200% declining-balance cost recovery with the half-year convention is used—see Chapter 8. The recovery limitation for an auto placed in service in 2018 is as follows: $10,000 (first year), $16,000 (second year), $9,600 (third year), and $5,760 (fourth year).]

29. **LO.3** Kristen, an independent management consultant, is based in Atlanta. During March and April of 2022, she is contracted by a national hardware chain to help implement revised human resource policies in Jackson (Mississippi) temporarily. During this period, Kristen flies to Jackson on Sunday night, spends the week at the district office, and returns home to Atlanta on Friday afternoon. The cost of returning home is $550, and the cost of spending the weekend in Jackson would have been $490.
    a. Presuming no reimbursement for these expenses, how much, if any, of these weekend expenses may Kristen deduct?
    b. Would your answer in part (a) change if the amounts involved were reversed (i.e., the trip home would have cost $490; staying in Jackson would have been $550)? Explain.

30. **LO.3, 5** In June 2022, Enrique and Denisse Espinosa traveled to Denver to attend a three-day conference sponsored by the American Society of Implant Dentistry. Denisse, a self-employed practicing oral surgeon, participated in scheduled technical sessions dealing with the latest developments in surgical procedures. On two days, Enrique attended group meetings where various aspects of family tax planning were discussed. On the other day, he went sightseeing. Enrique does not work for his wife, but he prepares their tax returns and handles the family investments. Expenses incurred in connection with the conference are summarized below.

Airfare (two tickets)	$2,000
Lodging (single and double occupancy are the same rate—$250 each day)	750
Meals at local restaurants ($200 × 3 days)*	600
Conference registration fee (includes $120 for Family Tax Planning sessions)	620
Car rental	300

*Split equally between Enrique and Denisse Espinosa.

How much, if any, of these expenses can the Espinosas deduct?

31. **LO.1, 3, 5** Kim works for a clothing manufacturer as a dress designer. During 2022, she travels to New York City to attend five days of fashion shows and then spends three days sightseeing. Her expenses are as follows:

Airfare	$1,500
Lodging (8 nights)	1,920
Meals at local restaurants (8 days)	1,440
Airport transportation	120

[Assume that lodging/meals are the same amount for the business and personal portion of the trip ($240 per day for lodging and $180 per day for meals).]
    a. Presuming no reimbursement, how much can Kim deduct as to the trip?
    b. Would the tax treatment of Kim's deduction differ if she was an independent contractor (rather than an employee)? Explain.

32. **LO.3** On Thursday, Justin flies from Baltimore (where the office for his sole proprietorship is located) to Cadiz (Spain). He conducts business on Friday and Tuesday; vacations on Saturday, Sunday, and Monday (a legal holiday in Spain); and returns to Baltimore on Thursday. Justin was scheduled to return home on Wednesday, but all flights were canceled due to bad weather. As a result, he spent Wednesday watching floor shows at a local casino.
   a. For tax purposes, what portion of Justin's trip is regarded as being for business?
   b. Suppose Monday was not a legal holiday. Would this change your answer to part (a)? Explain.
   c. Under either part (a) or (b), how much of Justin's airfare qualifies as a deductible business expense?

Critical Thinking
Decision Making

33. **LO.3** Monica, a self-employed taxpayer, travels from her office in Boston to Lisbon, Portugal, on business. Her absence of 13 days was spent as follows:

Thursday	Depart for and arrive at Lisbon
Friday	Business transacted
Saturday and Sunday	Vacationing
Monday through Friday	Business transacted
Saturday and Sunday	Vacationing
Monday	Business transacted
Tuesday	Depart Lisbon and return to office in Boston

   a. For tax purposes, how many days has Monica spent on business?
   b. What difference does it make?
   c. Could Monica have spent more time than she did vacationing on the trip without loss of existing tax benefits? Explain.

34. **LO.5** During 2022, Stork Associates paid $60,000 for a 20-seat skybox at Veterans Stadium for eight professional football games. Regular seats to these games range from $80 to $250 each. At one game, an employee of Stork entertained 18 clients. Stork furnished food and beverages for the event (provided by a local restaurant) at a cost of $1,300. The game was preceded by a bona fide business discussion, and all expenses are adequately substantiated. How much may Stork deduct for this event?

35. **LO.5** During 2022, José, a self-employed technology consultant, made gifts in the following amounts:

To Haley (José's personal assistant) at Christmas	$36
To Darryl (a key client)—$3 was for gift wrapping	53
To Darryl's wife (a homemaker) on her birthday	20
To Veronica (José's office manager) at Christmas	30

In addition, on professional assistants' day, José takes Haley to lunch at a local restaurant at a cost of $82. Presuming that José has adequate substantiation, how much can he deduct?

36. **LO.5** Melanie is employed full-time as an accountant for a national hardware chain. She recently started a private consulting practice, which provides tax advice and financial planning to the general public. For this purpose, she maintains an office in her home. Expenses relating to her home for 2022 are as follows:

Real property taxes	$3,600
Interest on home mortgage	3,800
Operating expenses of home	900

Melanie's residence cost $350,000 (excluding land) and has living space of 2,000 square feet, of which 20% (400 square feet) is devoted to business. The office was placed in service in February 2021, and under the Regular Method, Melanie had an unused office in the home deduction of $800 for 2021. Presuming sufficient net income from her consulting practice, what is Melanie's office in the home deduction under the:

a. Regular Method?

b. Simplified Method?

37. **LO.5** Christine is a full-time fourth-grade teacher at Vireo Academy. During 2022, she spends $1,400 for classroom supplies. On the submission of adequate substantiation, Vireo reimburses her for $500 of these expenses—the maximum reimbursement allowed for supplies under school policy. [The reimbursement is not shown as income (Box 1) of Form W–2 given to Christine by Vireo.] What are the income tax consequences of the $1,400 if Christine:

a. Itemizes her deductions *from* AGI?

b. Chooses the standard deduction?

38. **LO.6** Shelly has $200,000 of QBI from her local jewelry store (a sole proprietorship). Shelly's proprietorship paid $30,000 in W–2 wages and has $20,000 of qualified property. Shelly's spouse earned $75,900 of wages as an employee, they earned $20,000 of interest income during the year, and they will be filing jointly and using the standard deduction. Based solely on this information, what is their QBI deduction for 2022?

39. **LO.6** Peter owns and manages his single-member LLC that provides a wide variety of financial services to his clients. He is married and will file a joint tax return with his spouse, Marta. His LLC reports $300,000 of qualified business income, W–2 wages of $120,000, and assets with an unadjusted basis of $75,000. Their taxable income before the QBI deduction is $285,000 (this is also their modified taxable income). Determine their QBI deduction for 2022.

40. **LO.6** Ashley (a single taxpayer) is the owner of ABC LLC. The LLC (which reports as a sole proprietorship) generates QBI of $900,000 and is not a "specified services" business. ABC paid total W–2 wages of $300,000, and the total unadjusted basis of property held by ABC is $30,000. Ashley's taxable income before the QBI deduction is $740,000 (this is also her modified taxable income). What is Ashley's QBI deduction for 2022?

41. **LO.6** Donald (a married taxpayer filing jointly) owns a wide variety of commercial rental properties held in a single-member LLC. Donald's LLC reports rental income of $1,500,000. The LLC pays no W–2 wages; rather, it pays a management fee to an S corporation that Donald controls. The management company pays W–2 wages but reports no income (or loss). Donald's total unadjusted basis of the commercial rental property is $10,000,000. Donald's taxable income before the QBI deduction (and his modified taxable income) is $2,000,000. What is Donald's QBI deduction for 2022?

42. **LO.6** Scott and Laura are married and will file a joint tax return. Scott has a sole proprietorship (not a "specified services" business) that generates qualified business income of $300,000. The proprietorship pays W–2 wages of $40,000 and holds property with an unadjusted basis of $10,000. Laura is employed by a local school district. Their taxable income before the QBI deduction is $400,100 (this is also their modified taxable income). Critical Thinking

a. Determine Scott and Laura's QBI deduction, taxable income, and tax liability for 2022.

b. After providing you with the original information in the problem, Scott finds out that he will be receiving a $6,000 bonus in December 2022 (increasing their taxable income before the QBI deduction by this amount). Redetermine Scott and Laura's QBI deduction, taxable income, and tax liability for 2022.

c. What is the marginal tax rate on Scott's bonus?

43. **LO.6** Stella Watters is a CPA who operates her own accounting firm (Watters CPA LLC). As a single-member LLC, Stella reports her accounting firm operations as a sole proprietor. Stella has QBI from her accounting firm of $540,000, she reports W–2 wages of $156,000, and the unadjusted basis of property used in the LLC is $425,000. Stella is married and will file a joint tax return with her spouse. Their taxable income before the QBI deduction is $475,000, and their modified taxable income is $448,000. Determine Stella's QBI deduction for 2022.

44. **LO.6** Ben and Molly are married and will file jointly. Ben generates $300,000 of qualified business income from his single-member LLC (a law firm). He reports his business as a sole proprietorship. Wages paid by the law firm amount to $40,000; the law firm has no significant property. Molly is employed as a tax manager by a local CPA firm. Their modified taxable income is $400,100 (this is also their taxable income before the deduction for qualified business income). Determine their QBI deduction for 2022.

45. **LO.6** Tristan, who is single, operates three sole proprietorships that generate the following information in 2022 (none are "specified services" businesses).

Business	QBI	W–2 Wages	Capital Investment
A	$300,000	$90,000	$–0–
B	(135,000)	60,000	–0–
C	150,000	–0–	–0–

Tristan chooses not to aggregate the businesses. She also earns $150,000 of wages from an unrelated business, and her modified taxable income (before any QBI deduction) is $380,000.

a. What is Tristan's QBI deduction?

b. Assume that Tristan can aggregate these businesses. Determine her QBI deduction if she decides to aggregate the businesses.

Critical Thinking
Decision Making
Planning

46. **LO.5, 8, 9, 10** Ava recently graduated from college and is interviewing for a position in marketing. Gull Corporation has offered her a job as a sales representative that will require extensive travel and entertainment but provide valuable experience. Under the offer, she has two options: she receives a salary of $53,000, and she absorbs all expenses; she receives a salary of $39,000, and Gull reimburses for all expenses. Gull assures Ava that the $14,000 difference in the two options will be adequate to cover the expenses incurred. What issues should have an impact on Ava's choice?

47. **LO.1, 2, 5, 9** Complete the following table by classifying each of the independent expenditures (assume that no reimbursement takes place and that employee business expenses are not deductible).

Expense Item	Deductible *for* AGI	Deductible *from* AGI	Not Deductible
a. Tax return preparation fee incurred by an employed plumber	_____	_____	_____
b. Safety glasses purchased by an employed pipefitter	_____	_____	_____
c. Dues to auto club (e.g., AAA) for taxpayer who uses the automatic mileage method	_____	_____	_____
d. Nursing refresher course for taxpayer who retired from nursing five years ago	_____	_____	_____
e. Gambling loss not in excess of gambling gain by a self-employed architect	_____	_____	_____

	Expense Item	Deductible *for* AGI	Deductible *from* AGI	Not Deductible
f.	Contribution to Roth IRA by a self-employed attorney	____	____	____
g.	Business travel expenses by a statutory employee	____	____	____
h.	Job hunting expense by an elementary school teacher seeking a position as an elementary school principal	____	____	____
i.	Cost of bar exam review course taken by a recent law school graduate	____	____	____

Tax Return Problems

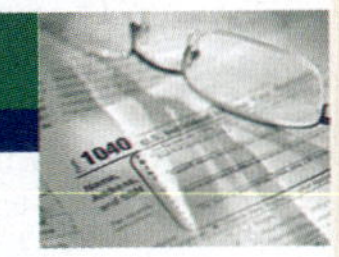

Communications
Critical Thinking
Tax Forms Problem

ProConnect™ Tax

48. David R. and Ella M. Cole (ages 39 and 38, respectively) are husband and wife who live at 1820 Elk Avenue, Denver, CO 80202. David is a self-employed consultant specializing in retail management, and Ella is a dental hygienist for a chain of dental clinics.

- David earned consulting fees of $145,000 in 2021. He maintains his own office and pays for all business expenses. The Coles are adequately covered by the medical plan provided by Ella's employer but have chosen not to participate in its § 401(k) retirement plan.

  David's employment-related expenses for 2021 are summarized below.

Airfare	$8,800
Lodging	4,835
Meals from restaurants (during travel status)	2,400
Entertainment	3,600
Ground transportation (e.g., limos, rental cars, and taxis)	800
Business gifts	900
Office supplies (includes postage, overnight delivery, and copying)	1,500

  The entertainment involved taking clients to sporting and musical events. The business gifts consisted of $50 gift certificates to a national restaurant. These were sent by David during the Christmas holidays to 18 of his major clients.

  In addition, David drove his 2019 Ford Expedition 11,000 miles for business and 3,000 for personal use during 2021. He purchased the Expedition on August 15, 2018, and has always used the automatic (standard) mileage method for tax purposes. Parking and tolls relating to business use total $340 in 2021.

- When the Coles purchased their present residence in April 2018, they devoted 450 of the 3,000 square feet of living space to an office for David. The property cost $440,000 ($40,000 of which is attributable to the land) and has since appreciated in value. Expenses relating to the residence in 2021 (except for mortgage interest and property taxes; see below) are as follows:

Insurance	$2,600
Repairs and maintenance	900
Utilities	4,700
Painting office area; area rugs and plants (in the office)	1,800

In terms of depreciation, the Coles use the MACRS percentage tables applicable to 39-year nonresidential real property. As to depreciable property (e.g., office furniture), David tries to avoid capitalization and uses whatever method provides the fastest write-off for tax purposes.

- Ella works at a variety of offices as a substitute when a hygienist is ill or on vacation or when one of the clinics is particularly busy (e.g., prior to the beginning of the school year). Besides her transportation, she must provide and maintain her own uniforms. Her expenses for 2021 appear below.

Uniforms	$690
State and city occupational licenses	380
Professional journals and membership dues in the American Dental Hygiene Association	340
Correspondence study course (taken online) dealing with teeth whitening procedures	420

Ella's salary for the year is $42,000, and her Form W–2 for the year shows income tax withholdings of $4,000 (Federal) and $1,000 (state) and the proper amount of Social Security and Medicare taxes.

- Besides the items already mentioned, the Coles had the following receipts during 2021.

Interest income—		
State of Colorado general purpose bonds	$2,500	
IBM bonds	800	
Wells Fargo Bank	1,200	$ 4,500
Federal income tax refund for year 2020		510
Life insurance proceeds paid by Eagle Assurance Corporation		200,000
Inheritance of savings account from Sarah Cole		50,000
Sales proceeds from two ATVs		9,000

For several years, the Coles' household has included David's divorced mother, Sarah, who has been claimed as their dependent. In late December 2020, Sarah unexpectedly died of a heart attack in her sleep. Unknown to Ella and David, Sarah had a life insurance policy and a savings account (with David as the designated beneficiary of each). In 2020, the Coles purchased two ATVs for $14,000. After several near mishaps, they decided that the sport was too dangerous. In 2021, they sold the ATVs to their neighbor.

- Additional expenditures for 2021 include:

Funeral expenses for Sarah		$ 4,500
Taxes—		
Real property taxes on personal residence	$6,400	
Colorado state income tax due (paid in April 2021 for tax year 2020)	310	6,710
Mortgage interest on personal residence (Rocky Mountain Bank)		6,600
Contributions to traditional IRAs for Ella and David ($6,000 + $6,000)		12,000

In 2021, the Coles made quarterly estimated tax payments of $6,000 (Federal) and $500 (state) for a total of $24,000 (Federal) and $2,000 (state).

Using the appropriate forms and schedules, compute the Coles' Federal income tax for 2021. Disregard the alternative minimum tax (AMT) and various education credits since these items are not discussed until later in the text (Chapters 12 and 13). Relevant Social Security numbers are:

David Cole	123-45-6788
Ella Cole	123-45-6787

The Coles have never owned or used any virtual currency. The Coles received the appropriate coronavirus recovery rebates (economic impact payments); related questions in ProConnect Tax should be ignored. They do not want to contribute to the Presidential Election Campaign Fund. Also, the Coles want any overpayment of tax refunded to them and *not* applied toward next year's tax liability. David will have a self-employment tax liability; refer to Exhibit 13.9 in Chapter 13 to compute this liability. Suggested software: ProConnect Tax.

49. Saanvi Patel (Social Security number 123-45-6785), single and age 32, lives at 3218 Columbia Drive, Spokane, WA 99210. She is employed as a regional sales manager by VITA Corporation, a manufacturer and distributor of vitamins and food supplements. During 2022, Saanvi is paid an annual salary of $83,000 and a separate travel allowance of $30,000. In order to access the travel allowance, VITA requires adequate accounting by Saanvi. Tax Computation Problem

- Saanvi participates in VITA's contributory health and § 401(k) plans. During 2022, she paid $4,500 for her share of the medical insurance and contributed $11,000 to the § 401(k) retirement plan.
- Saanvi uses her automobile 70% for business and 30% for personal. The automobile, a Toyota Avalon, was purchased new on June 30, 2020, for $37,000 (no trade-in was involved). Depreciation has been claimed using the MACRS 200% declining-balance method, and no § 179 election was made in the year of purchase. (For depreciation information, see text Section 8-3d.) During 2022, Saanvi drove 15,000 miles and incurred and paid the following expenses relating to the automobile:

Gasoline	$3,100
Insurance	2,900
Auto club dues	240
Interest on car loan	1,100
Repairs and maintenance	1,200
Parking (during business use)	600
Traffic fines (during business use)	500

- Because VITA does not have an office in Spokane, the company expects Saanvi to maintain one in her home. Out of 1,500 square feet of living space in her apartment, Saanvi has set aside 300 square feet as an office. Expenses for 2022 that relate to her home office are listed below.

Apartment rent	$18,000
Apartment utilities	4,000
Apartment insurance (renter's casualty and theft coverage)	1,600
Carpet replacement (office area only)	1,200

- Saanvi's employment-related expenses for 2022 (except for the trip to Korea; discussed next) are summarized below.

Airfare	$4,100
Lodging	3,200
Meals (at local restaurants during travel)	2,800
Transportation (taxis and airport limos)	300
Business gifts	540
Continuing education	400
Professional journals	140

Most of Saanvi's business trips involve visits to retail outlets in her region. Store managers and their key employees, as well as some suppliers, were the parties entertained. The business gifts were boxes of candy costing $30 ($25 each plus $5 for wrapping and shipping) sent to 18 store managers at Christmas. The continuing education was a noncredit course dealing with improving management skills that Saanvi took online.

- In July 2022, Saanvi traveled to Korea to investigate a new process that is being developed to convert fish parts to a solid consumable tablet form. She spent one week checking out the process and then took a one-week vacation tour of the country. The round-trip airfare was $3,600, and her expenses relating to business were $2,100 for lodging ($300 each night), $1,470 for meals, and $350 for transportation. Upon returning to the United States, Saanvi sent her findings about the process to her employer. VITA was so pleased with her report that it gave her an employee achievement award of $10,000. The award was sent to Saanvi in January 2023.
- Besides the items already mentioned, Saanvi had the following receipts in 2022:

Interest income—		
City of Tacoma general purpose bonds	$ 350	
Olympia State Bank	400	$ 750
Proceeds from property sales—		
City lot	$13,000	
Sailboat	18,000	31,000
Cash found at airport		5,000

Regarding the city lot (located in Vancouver), Saanvi purchased the property in 2007 for $16,000 and held it as an investment. Unfortunately, the neighborhood where the lot was located deteriorated, and property values declined. In 2022, Saanvi decided to cut her losses and sold the property for $13,000. The sailboat was used for pleasure and was purchased in 2018 for $16,500. Saanvi sold the boat because she purchased a new and larger model (see below). While at the Spokane airport, Saanvi found an unmarked envelope containing $5,000 in $50 bills. Because no mention of any lost funds was noted in the media, Saanvi kept the money.

- Saanvi's expenditures for 2022 (not previously noted) are summarized below.

Medical (not covered by insurance)	$6,000
State and local general sales tax	3,300
Church pledge (2022 and 2023)	5,600
Fee paid for preparation of 2021 income tax return	500
Contribution to mayor's reelection campaign fund	200
Contribution to a Coverdell education savings account (on behalf of a favorite nephew)	2,000

Saanvi keeps careful records regarding sales taxes. In 2022, the sales tax total was unusually high due to the purchase of a new sailboat. In 2022, Saanvi decided to pay her church pledge for both 2022 and 2023. The insurance premium was on a policy covering her father's life. (Saanvi is the designated beneficiary under the policy.)

Saanvi's employer withheld $8,600 for Federal income tax purposes, and she applied her $600 overpayment for 2021 toward the 2022 tax liability.

Compute Saanvi's Federal income tax payable (or refund) for 2022. In making the calculation, use the Tax Rate Schedule and disregard the application of the alternative minimum tax (AMT), which is not discussed until Chapter 12.

Research Problems

Note: Solutions to the Research Problems can be prepared by using the Thomson Reuters Checkpoint™ online tax research database, which accompanies this textbook. Solutions can also be prepared by using research materials found in a typical tax library.

the answer company™ THOMSON REUTERS®

Research Problem 1. Aaron, a resident of Minnesota, has been a driver for Green Delivery Service for the past six years. For this purpose, he leases a truck from Green, and his compensation is based on a percentage of the income resulting from his pickup and delivery services. Green allows its drivers to choose their 10-hour shifts and does not exercise any control on how these services are carried out (e.g., the route to be taken or the order in which parcels are delivered or picked up). Under Green's operating agreement with its drivers, Green can terminate the arrangement after 30 days' notice. In practice, however, Green allows its truckers to quit immediately without giving advance notice. The agreement also identifies the drivers as independent contractors. Green maintains no health or retirement plans for its drivers, and each year it reports their income by issuing Forms 1099–NEC (and not Forms W–2). Green requires its drivers to maintain a commercial driver's license and be in good standing with the state highway law enforcement division.

Citing the employment tax Regulations in §§ 31.3121(d)–1(c)(2) and 31.3306(i)–1(b), an IRS agent contends that Aaron is an independent contractor and, therefore, is subject to the self-employment tax. Based on *Peno Trucking, Inc.* (93 TCM 1027, T.C.Memo. 2007–66), Aaron disagrees and contends that he is an employee (i.e., not self-employed). Who is correct? Why?

Research Problem 2. Your client, a large construction firm organized as a C corporation, allows certain employees (including the president of the corporation) to use its company-owned airplane for nonbusiness flights. The employees include the value of the flights in their income. Your client is uncertain about how to treat the expenses related to these nonbusiness flights. In certain situations, the expenses of operating the plane are more than the income imputed to the employees, and in certain circumstances, the expenses are less. In doing some of its own research, your client found *Sutherland Lumber-Southwest, Inc.* [114 T.C. 197 (2000)], which suggests that as long as the employee imputes income, the full amount of the related expenses can be deducted. [The decision in the case was affirmed on appeal, *Sutherland Lumber-Southwest, Inc. v. Comm.*, 2001–2 USTC ¶50,503, 88 AFTR 2d 2001–5026, 255 F.3d 495 (CA–8).] Should your client follow the approach in *Sutherland*? Explain.

Research Problem 3. Rick Beam has been an independent sales representative for various textile manufacturers for many years. His products consist of soft goods, such as tablecloths, curtains, and drapes. Rick's customers are clothing store chains, department stores, and smaller specialty stores. The employees of these companies who are responsible for purchasing merchandise are known as buyers. These companies generally prohibit their buyers from accepting gifts from manufacturers' sales representatives. Communications

Each year, Rick gives cash gifts (never more than $25) to most of the buyers who are his customers. Generally, he cashes a large check in November and gives the money personally to the buyers around Christmas. Rick says, "This is one of the ways I maintain my relationship with my buyers." He maintains adequate substantiation of all of the gifts.

Rick's deductions for these gifts have been disallowed by the IRS based on § 162(c)(2). Rick is confused and comes to you, a CPA, for advice.

a. Write a letter to Rick concerning his tax position on this issue. Rick's address is 948 Octavia Street, Baton Rouge, LA 70821.

b. Prepare a memo for your files supporting the advice you have given.

Use internet tax resources to address the following questions. Look for reliable websites and blogs of the IRS and other government agencies, media outlets, businesses, tax professionals, academics, think tanks, and political outlets.

Communications **Research Problem 4.** Prepare a blog post for the "Online Tutor Match Company" to explain to its freelancers the tax implications of their work. Topics should include (1) what records to keep (both for income and expenses), (2) what unique situations freelancers face (e.g., home office deductions; self-employment status), and (3) what tax forms must be filed and (briefly) how to prepare those forms [e.g., Schedule C (Form 1040)].

Communications **Research Problem 5.** Download IRS Form 1099–K and its instructions from the IRS website. What is the purpose of the form, and when is it used? Go to the Square, Inc. website (**squareup.com**), and search for information about this form. Summarize what you discover in an e-mail to your instructor.

Research Problem 6. Analyze S. 700 (116th Congress) introduced by Senator John Thune to provide a new approach to provide freelance ("gig") workers independent contractor status. Also see his press release of March 7, 2019, at **thune.senate.gov/public/index.cfm/2019/3/thune-reintroduces-bill-to-add-certainty-to-worker-classification-rules**.

Compare the legislation against the current IRS rules (discussed in text Section 9-1 and Concept Summary 9.1) and against the AICPA's *Guiding Principles of Good Tax Policy* (discussed in text Section 1-3c).

Research Problem 7. Download IRS Form 8919 (Uncollected Social Security and Medicare Tax on Wages) from the IRS website. According to the instructions, who should file this form?

Becker CPA Review Questions

Becker

1. In the current year, Barlow moved from Chicago to Miami to start a new job, incurring costs of $1,200 to move household goods and $2,500 in temporary living expenses. Barlow was not reimbursed for any of these expenses. What amount should Barlow deduct as an itemized deduction for moving expense?

   a. $0
   b. $1,200
   c. $2,500
   d. $3,700

2. Bob and Nancy are married and file a joint return in 2022. They are both under age 50 and employed, with wages of $50,000 each. Their total AGI is $117,000. Neither of them is an active participant in a qualified plan. What is the maximum traditional IRA deduction they can take for the current year?

   a. $0
   b. $6,000
   c. $9,600
   d. $12,000

3. Where is the deduction for qualified business income (QBI) applied in the individual tax formula?
   a. As an adjustment to arrive at adjusted gross income
   b. As an itemized deduction
   c. As an alternative to the standard deduction
   d. As a deduction from adjusted gross income separate from the standard deduction and itemized deductions

4. Which of the following is considered a specified service trade or business (SSTB) for purposes of the qualified business income deduction?
   a. Accounting firm
   b. Manufacturing company
   c. Engineering firm
   d. Architectural services

5. What is the basic deduction calculation for the qualified business income deduction?
   a. 30% × Qualified business income (QBI)
   b. 20% × W–2 wages
   c. 20% × Qualified business income (QBI)
   d. 30% × W–2 wages

6. Which of the following is the overall limitation to the qualified business income (QBI) deduction?
   a. Lesser of 50% of combined QBI or 20% of the taxpayer's taxable income in excess of net capital gain
   b. Lesser of combined QBI or 20% of the taxpayer's taxable income in excess of net capital gain
   c. Lesser of 50% of W–2 wages or 25% of W–2 wages plus 2.5% of the unadjusted basis of qualified property
   d. Taxable income limitations based on filing status

7. Calculate the taxpayer's 2022 qualified business income deduction for a qualified trade or business:

Filing status:	Single
Taxable income:	$100,000
Net capital gains:	$0
Qualified business income (QBI):	$30,000
W–2 wages:	$10,000

   a. $5,000　　c. $20,000
   b. $70,000　　d. $6,000

8. Calculate the taxpayer's 2022 qualified business income deduction for a qualified trade or business:

Filing status:	Single
Taxable income:	$180,000
Net capital gains:	$0
Qualified business income (QBI):	$80,000
W–2 wages:	$20,000

   a. $16,000　　c. $2,700
   b. $10,000　　d. $14,806

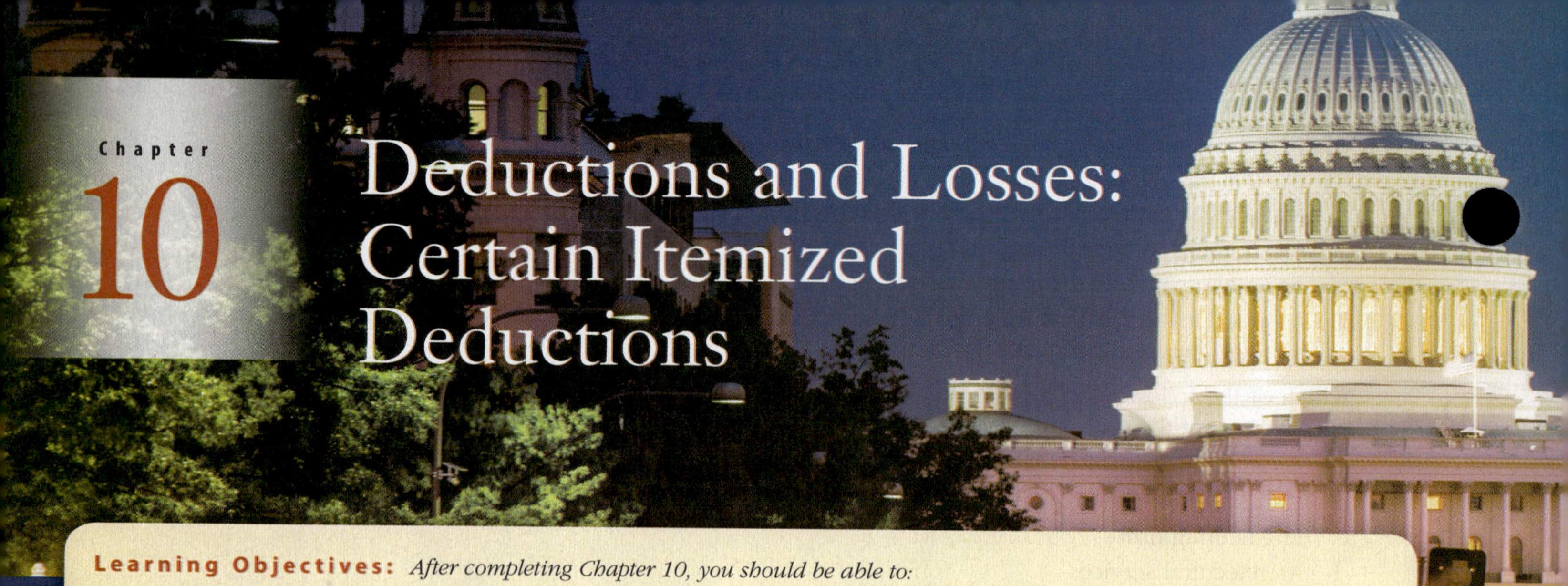

Chapter

10 Deductions and Losses: Certain Itemized Deductions

Learning Objectives: *After completing Chapter 10, you should be able to:*

- **LO.1** Distinguish between deductible and nondeductible personal expenses.
- **LO.2** Define medical expenses and compute the medical expense deduction.
- **LO.3** Contrast deductible taxes with nondeductible fees, licenses, and other charges.
- **LO.4** Explain the Federal income tax treatment of property taxes, state and local income taxes, and sales taxes.
- **LO.5** Distinguish between deductible and nondeductible interest and apply the appropriate limitations to deductible interest.
- **LO.6** Recognize charitable contributions and identify their related measurement problems and percentage limitations.
- **LO.7** List the expenses that are deductible as other itemized deductions.
- **LO.8** Identify tax planning strategies that can maximize the benefit of itemized deductions.

Chapter Outline

10-1 Medical Expenses, 10-3
- 10-1a Medical Expenses Defined, 10-3
- 10-1b Capital Expenditures for Medical Purposes, 10-4
- 10-1c Medical Expenses Incurred for Spouse and Dependents, 10-5
- 10-1d Transportation, Meal, and Lodging Expenses for Medical Treatment, 10-6
- 10-1e Amounts Paid for Medical Insurance Premiums, 10-6
- 10-1f Year of Deduction, 10-7
- 10-1g Reimbursements, 10-7
- 10-1h Health Savings Accounts, 10-8
- 10-1i Affordable Care Act Provisions, 10-10

10-2 Taxes, 10-10
- 10-2a Deductibility as a Tax, 10-10
- 10-2b Property Taxes, 10-11
- 10-2c State and Local Income Taxes and Sales Taxes, 10-13

10-3 Interest, 10-14
- 10-3a Allowed and Disallowed Items, 10-14
- 10-3b Restrictions on Deductibility and Timing Considerations, 10-17
- 10-3c Classification of Interest Expense, 10-17

10-4 Charitable Contributions, 10-18
- 10-4a Criteria for a Gift, 10-18
- 10-4b Qualified Organizations, 10-20
- 10-4c Time of Deduction, 10-20
- 10-4d Record-Keeping and Valuation Requirements, 10-21
- 10-4e Limitations on Charitable Contribution Deduction, 10-22

10-5 Timing of Payments to Maximize Deductions, 10-26

10-6 Other Itemized Deductions, 10-27

10-7 Comprehensive Example of Schedule A, 10-27

10-8 Tax Planning, 10-29
- 10-8a Maximizing the Medical Deduction, 10-29
- 10-8b Ensuring the Charitable Contribution Deduction, 10-29
- 10-8c Planning to Avoid Nondeductible Treatment, 10-31

ISTOCK.COM/IZUSEK

The Big Picture

Impact of Itemized Deductions on Major Purchases

John and Kiara Williamson, a young professional couple, have been renting an apartment in Atlanta, Georgia, since they were married. Their income has grown as they've become more established in their careers, and they now believe the time has come to purchase their own home. In addition, their desire to buy a home now may be coming at a good time, because John's mother, Martha, needs to move in with them due to her declining health and their current apartment is too small to accommodate her. John and Kiara's current monthly rent is $2,000, but they are willing to spend up to $2,600 per month on an after-tax basis for their first home.

After months of house hunting, they have found the perfect home, but they are concerned it may be too expensive. If they acquire a standard mortgage to finance the purchase of the home, the total cash outlay during the first year of ownership will be $43,000 ($2,000 principal payments, $37,000 interest payments, and $4,000 real estate taxes). Alternatively, if they use their retirement and taxable investments to secure the home financing, they can qualify for a lower interest rate and thereby reduce the interest charge from $37,000 to $35,000. They expect their Federal AGI to be about $200,000 and their taxable income to range between $170,000 and $185,000 for the year. John and Kiara have not itemized their deductions in prior years because the amount of their qualifying expenses has been just below the standard deduction amount. Assume that the Willliamsons face a 6 percent state income tax rate (after any Federal tax benefit).

Can John and Kiara Williamson afford to pursue their dream of home ownership?

Read the chapter and formulate your response.

Framework 1040 **Tax Formula for Individuals**

This chapter covers the boldfaced portions of the Tax Formula for Individuals that was introduced in Concept Summary 3.1 on p. 3-3. Below those portions are the sections of Form 1040 where the results are reported.

Income *(broadly defined)*	$xx,xxx
Less: Exclusions	(x,xxx)
Gross income	$xx,xxx
Less: Deductions *for* adjusted gross income	**(x,xxx)**

FORM 1040 (Schedule 1)

13	Health savings account deduction. Attach Form 8889
17	Self-employed health insurance deduction
21	Student loan interest deduction

Adjusted gross income	$xx,xxx
Less: The greater of total itemized deductions *or* the standard deduction	**(x,xxx)**

FORM 1040 (p. 1)

12a	**Standard deduction or itemized deductions** (from Schedule A)

Charitable contributions if you take the standard deduction*	(xxx)
Personal and dependency exemptions**	(x,xxx)
Deduction for qualified business income***	(x,xxx)
Taxable income	$xx,xxx
Tax on taxable income *(see Tax Tables or Tax Rate Schedules)*	$ x,xxx
Less: Tax credits *(including income taxes withheld and prepaid)*	(xxx)
Tax due (or refund)	$ xxx

* For 2021, married taxpayers may claim up to $600 of cash charitable donations ($300 if unmarried).

** Exemption deductions are not allowed from 2018 through 2025.

*** Only applies from 2018 through 2025.

LO.1

Distinguish between deductible and nondeductible personal expenses.

As a general rule, personal expenses are not deductible (see § 262 of the Code). However, Congress has chosen to allow certain personal expenses to be deducted as itemized deductions. Personal expenses that are deductible as itemized deductions include medical expenses, certain taxes, mortgage interest, and charitable contributions. These (and other) personal expenses allowed as itemized deductions are covered in this chapter. Although certain exceptions exist (e.g., certain alimony and traditional IRA contributions are deductible *for* AGI), personal expenses not specifically allowed as itemized deductions by the tax law are nondeductible.

Certain business and investment expenses are also deductible, like interest expense on loans to acquire investment assets (e.g., publicly traded securities) and state income taxes on business and investment income. These rules are covered in this chapter and Chapter 11.

Allowable itemized deductions are deductible *from* AGI in arriving at taxable income if the taxpayer *elects* to itemize. A taxpayer will elect to itemize when total itemized deductions exceed the standard deduction based on the taxpayer's filing status.[1]

Itemized deductions are reported on Schedule A (Form 1040) and filed with an individual's Federal income tax return (Form 1040).

The Big Picture

Example 1

Return to the facts of *The Big Picture* on p. 10-1. John and Kiara Williamson will discover that with the purchase of a home, they will be able to itemize their deductions for the first time instead of claiming the standard deduction. Assuming that the home mortgage interest expense and real estate taxes meet the requirements discussed in this chapter, they can be deducted *from* AGI because their total will

continued

[1]See §§ 63(c) and (d), respectively, for the definitions of the terms *standard deduction* and *itemized deductions.*

exceed the amount of the standard deduction for a married couple filing a joint return. Other qualifying expenses, including up to $10,000 of state and local taxes as well as charitable contributions, also will be deductible as itemized deductions. All of these items provide a tax benefit to the Williamsons.

10-1 Medical Expenses

LO.2

Define medical expenses and compute the medical expense deduction.

Medical expenses paid for the care of the taxpayer, spouse, and dependents are allowed as an itemized deduction to the extent the expenses are not reimbursed. The **medical expense** deduction is limited to the amount by which these expenses *exceed* 7.5 percent of the taxpayer's AGI.[2]

The threshold percentage, sometimes referred to as a "floor," is used to restrict deductions, because expenses below the floor are not deductible. Here, the floor is significant. Only medical expenses *in excess* of the "7.5%-of-AGI floor" are deductible. As a result, a medical expense deduction is rare (especially for high-income taxpayers).

The Big Picture

Example 2

Return to the facts of *The Big Picture* on p. 10-1. If, as expected, the Williamsons' AGI for the year is $200,000, to receive a tax benefit from any unreimbursed medical expenses, they must itemize their deductions and have more than $15,000 ($200,000 × 7.5%) of those expenses.

If they accumulate $27,000 of unreimbursed medical expenses during the year and itemize their deductions, their total itemized deductions will increase by only $12,000 ($27,000 unreimbursed medical expenses − $15,000 AGI floor).

10-1a Medical Expenses Defined

The term *medical care* includes expenses incurred for the "diagnosis, cure, mitigation, treatment, or prevention of disease, or for the purpose of affecting any structure or function of the body."[3] A *partial* list of deductible and nondeductible medical items appears in Exhibit 10.1.

Exhibit 10.1 Examples of Deductible and Nondeductible Medical Expenses Paid by Taxpayer

Deductible	Nondeductible
Medical (including dental, mental, and hospital) care	Funeral, burial, or cremation expenses
Prescription drugs and insulin	Over-the-counter medicines (except insulin)
Personal protective equipment to prevent spread of COVID-19; COVID-19 home testing kit	Bottled water
Special equipment:	Toiletries, cosmetics
• Wheelchairs	Diaper service, maternity clothes
• Crutches	Programs for the *general* improvement of health:
• Artificial limbs	• Weight reduction
• Eyeglasses (including contact lenses)	• Health spas
• Hearing aids	• Social activities (e.g., dancing and swimming lessons)
Transportation for medical care	Unnecessary cosmetic surgery
Medical and hospital insurance premiums	
Long-term care insurance premiums (subject to limitations)	
Cost of alcohol and drug rehabilitation	
Certain costs to stop smoking	
Weight reduction programs related to obesity	

[2] § 213(a).

[3] § 213(d)(1)(A).

A medical expense does not have to relate to a particular ailment to be deductible. Because the definition of medical care is broad enough to cover preventive measures, the cost of periodic physical and dental exams qualifies even for a taxpayer in good health.

Amounts paid for unnecessary *cosmetic surgery* are not deductible medical expenses. Cosmetic surgery is necessary—and, therefore, deductible—when it improves the effects of (1) a deformity arising from a congenital abnormality, (2) a personal injury, or (3) a disfiguring disease.[4]

Example 3

Jacob, age 75, paid $21,000 to a plastic surgeon for a face-lift. Jacob merely wanted to improve his appearance. The $21,000 does not qualify as a medical expense because the surgery was unnecessary.

In contrast, Marge's face is disfigured as a result of a serious automobile accident. Here, the cost of restorative cosmetic surgery is deductible as a medical expense.

The cost of care in a *nursing home or home for the aged*, including meals and lodging, is a deductible medical expense if the primary reason for being in the home is to get medical care. If the primary reason for being there is personal, any costs for medical or nursing care are deductible medical expenses, but the cost of meals and lodging must be excluded.[5]

Example 4

Norman has a chronic heart ailment. In October, his family decides to place Norman in a nursing home equipped to provide medical and nursing care. Total nursing home expenses amount to $80,000 during the year. Of this amount, $50,000 is directly attributable to medical and nursing care.

Because Norman is in need of significant medical and nursing care and is placed in the facility primarily for this purpose, all $80,000 of the nursing home costs are deductible (subject to the AGI floor, explained earlier).

Tuition expenses of a dependent at a special school for a mentally or physically handicapped individual may be deductible as a medical expense. The deduction is allowed if a principal reason for sending the individual to the school is the school's special resources for alleviating the infirmities. In this case, the cost of meals and lodging, in addition to the tuition, are deductible medical expenses.[6]

Example 5

Jason's daughter Jasmine attended public school through the seventh grade. Because Jasmine was a poor student, she was examined by a psychiatrist who concluded that Jasmine has dyslexia. Acting on the psychiatrist's recommendation, Jason enrolls Jasmine in a private school so that she can receive individual attention. The school specializes in students with learning disabilities and has a program of study designed to help students with dyslexia (including a staff of educational and psychological professionals who have developed the specialized curriculum).

The expense related to Jasmine's attendance is deductible as a medical expense. The cost of any psychiatric care also qualifies as a medical expense.[7]

10-1b Capital Expenditures for Medical Purposes

When capital expenditures are incurred for medical purposes, they must be deemed medically necessary by a physician and used primarily by the patient. In addition, their costs must be reasonable. Examples include dust elimination systems,[8] elevators,[9] and vans specially designed for wheelchair-bound taxpayers. Other expenditures that may qualify

[4]§ 213(d)(9)(A).

[5]Reg. § 1.213–1(e)(1)(v). In general, medical care is required if a taxpayer is deemed to be chronically ill and under a prescribed plan of care. A taxpayer is chronically ill if he or she cannot perform at least two daily living tasks (dressing, eating, bathing, toileting, moving from one place to another, continence) for 90 days or more [§ 7702B(c)].

[6]Reg. § 1.213–1(e)(1)(v)(a). See *Donald R. Pfeifer*, 37 TCM 816, T.C.Memo. 1978–189, *aff'd* 79–2 USTC ¶9518 (CA–10). Also see Rev.Rul. 78–340. Based on recent rulings, the IRS is allowing a deduction where there is a diagnosis of a neurologically based learning disability or other handicap, leading to a recommendation of and attendance at an institution specially equipped to help the student overcome the handicap.

[7]Ltr.Rul. 200521003.

[8]Ltr.Rul. 7948029.

[9]*Riach v. Frank*, 62–1 USTC ¶9419, 9 AFTR 2d 1263, 302 F.2d 374 (CA–9).

are swimming pools (if the taxpayer does not have access to a neighborhood pool) and air conditioners if they do not become permanent improvements (e.g., window units).[10]

Both a capital expenditure for a permanent improvement and related operating and maintenance costs may qualify as medical expenses. The allowable costs are deductible in the year incurred. Although depreciation is required for most other capital expenditures, it is not required for those qualifying for medical purposes (in other words, the entire cost of a qualifying capital expenditure is immediately deductible).

A permanent capital improvement that ordinarily would not have a medical purpose qualifies as a medical expense if it is directly related to prescribed medical care (e.g., an elevator in a personal residence). Here, the cost is deductible to the extent it *exceeds* the increase in value of the related property. Appraisal costs related to capital improvements are not medical expenses. Instead, these costs are classified as miscellaneous itemized deductions (expenses incurred in the determination of the taxpayer's tax liability).[11] However, the deduction for miscellaneous itemized deductions has been suspended from 2018 through 2025 (see text Section 10-6).

Example 6

Fred is afflicted with heart disease. His physician advises him to install an elevator in his residence so that he will not be required to climb the stairs. The cost of installing the elevator is $10,000, and the increase in the value of the residence is determined to be only $4,000.

Therefore, $6,000 ($10,000 − $4,000) is treated as a medical expense. Additional utility costs to operate the elevator and maintenance costs are also medical expenses as long as the medical reason for the capital expenditure continues to exist.

The full cost of certain home-related capital expenditures incurred to enable a *physically handicapped* individual to live independently and productively qualifies as a medical expense. Qualifying costs include expenditures for constructing entrance and exit ramps to the residence, widening hallways and doorways to accommodate wheelchairs, installing support bars and railings in bathrooms and other rooms, and adjusting electrical outlets and fixtures.[12] These expenditures are only subject to the AGI floor; the increase in the home's value is deemed to be zero.

10-1c Medical Expenses Incurred for Spouse and Dependents

In computing the medical expense deduction, a taxpayer may include medical expenses for a spouse and for a person who was a dependent at the time the expenses were paid or incurred. Of the requirements that normally apply in determining dependency status, neither the gross income nor the joint return test applies in determining dependency status for medical expense deduction purposes.[13]

Example 7

William (age 22) is married and a full-time student at a university. During the year, William incurred medical expenses that were paid by Sheba (William's mother). She provided more than half of William's support for the year.

Even if William files a joint return with his wife, Sheba may claim the medical expenses she paid for him. Sheba would combine William's expenses with her own before applying the AGI floor.

For *divorced persons* with children, a special rule applies to the noncustodial parent. The noncustodial parent may claim any medical expenses paid even though the children are not the noncustodial parent's dependents.

Example 8

Sam and Joan were divorced last year, and Joan was awarded custody of their child, Keith. During the current year, Sam pays $2,500 of Keith's medical bills. Together, Sam and Joan provide more than half of Keith's support.

Even though Keith is Joan's dependent, Sam can combine the $2,500 of medical expenses that he pays for Keith with his own when calculating his medical expense deduction.

---

[10] Reg. § 1.213–1(e)(1)(iii).

[11] § 212(3).

[12] For a complete list of the items that qualify, see Rev.Rul. 87–106.

[13] §§ 213(a) and (d)(5). Refer to text Section 3-4 for discussion of the dependency requirements.

10-1d Transportation, Meal, and Lodging Expenses for Medical Treatment

Payments for transportation to and from a point of treatment for medical care are deductible as medical expenses (subject to the AGI floor). These costs include bus, taxi, train, or plane fare; charges for ambulance service; and out-of-pocket expenses for the use of an automobile. A mileage allowance of 18 cents per mile for 2022 may be used instead of actual out-of-pocket automobile expenses.[14] Whether the taxpayer chooses to claim out-of-pocket automobile expenses or the 18 cents per mile automatic mileage option, related parking fees and tolls also can be deducted. Also included are transportation expenditures for someone like a family member or nurse who must accompany the patient. The cost of meals while en route to obtain medical care is not deductible.

A deduction is allowable for lodging while away from home for medical care if the following requirements are met:[15]

- The lodging is primarily for and essential to medical care.
- Medical care is provided by a physician in a licensed hospital or a similar medical facility (e.g., a clinic).
- The lodging is not lavish or extravagant.
- There is no significant element of personal pleasure in the travel.

The deduction for lodging expenses cannot exceed $50 *per* night for *each* person. The lodging deduction is allowed not only for the patient but also for anyone who must travel with the patient.

The Big Picture

Example 9

Return to the facts of *The Big Picture* on p. 10-1. John's mother, Martha, eventually moves in with the Williamsons because of her declining health, and she becomes their dependent. Later, John is advised by Martha's physician that she needs specialized treatment for her heart condition. Consequently, John and Martha fly to Cleveland, Ohio, where Martha receives the therapy at a heart clinic on an outpatient basis. Expenses in connection with the trip are as follows:

Round-trip airfare ($250 each)	$500
Lodging in Cleveland for two nights ($120 each per night)	480

Assuming that the Williamsons itemize their deductions (including medical expenses), the medical expense deduction for transportation is $500 and the medical expense deduction for lodging is $200 ($50 per night per person). Because of the severity of Martha's health condition, it is assumed that John's accompanying her is justified.

No deduction is allowed for the cost of meals unless they are part of the medical care and are furnished at a medical facility. If deductible, these meals are not subject to the 50 percent limit applicable to business meals (see text Section 9-6).

10-1e Amounts Paid for Medical Insurance Premiums

Medical insurance premiums (including Medicare insurance costs withheld from a Social Security recipient's monthly benefits) are included with other medical expenses subject to the AGI floor. Premiums paid by the taxpayer under a group plan or an individual plan are included as medical expenses. If an employer pays all or part of the taxpayer's medical insurance premiums, the amount paid by the employer is not included in the employee's gross income (and these amounts are not deductible by the employee). However, the medical insurance premiums paid by the employer are deductible as business expenses on the employer's tax return.

[14] This amount is adjusted periodically; see Notice 2022-3. In 2021, the allowance was 16 cents per mile.

[15] § 213(d)(2).

If a taxpayer is *self-employed*, insurance premiums paid for medical coverage are deductible as a *business* expense (*for* AGI).[16] The deduction *for* AGI is allowed for premiums paid for the taxpayer, the taxpayer's spouse, and dependents of the taxpayer. However, this deduction is not allowed if the taxpayer (or taxpayer's spouse) is eligible to participate in an employer-provided health plan.

The Big Picture

Example 10

Return to the facts of *The Big Picture* on p. 10-1. John Williamson is the sole practitioner in his unincorporated accounting practice. During the year, he paid health insurance premiums of $12,000 for his own coverage and $8,000 for coverage for his wife, Kiara. John can deduct $20,000 as a business deduction (*for* AGI) in computing their taxable income.

Taxpayers also may include premiums paid on qualified long-term care insurance contracts in medical expenses, subject to limitations based on the age of the insured. For 2022, the per-person limits range from $450 for taxpayers age 40 and under to $5,640 for taxpayers over age 70.[17]

10-1f **Year of Deduction**

Regardless of a taxpayer's method of accounting, medical expenses are deductible only in the year *paid*. In effect, individual taxpayers are on a cash basis for the medical expense deduction. One exception, however, is allowed for deceased taxpayers. If the medical expenses are paid within one year from the day following the day of death, they can be treated as being paid at the time they were *incurred*. As a result, these expenses may be reported on the final income tax return of the decedent or on earlier returns if incurred before the year of death.

No current deduction is allowed for payment for medical care to be rendered in the future unless the taxpayer is under an obligation to make the payment. Whether an obligation to make the payment exists depends on the policy of the physician or the institution furnishing the medical care.

Example 11

Upon the recommendation of his regular dentist, in December 2022, Terrell consults Dr. Smith, a prosthodontist, who specializes in crown and bridge work. Dr. Smith tells Terrell that he can do the necessary restorative work for $12,000 and that he requires all new patients to prepay 40% of the total cost of the procedure. Accordingly, Terrell pays $4,800 in December 2022. The balance of $7,200 is paid when the work is completed in January 2023.

Under these circumstances, the qualifying medical expense deductions are $4,800 for 2022 and $7,200 in 2023. The result would be the same even if Terrell prepaid the full $12,000 in 2022.

10-1g **Reimbursements**

If medical expenses are reimbursed in the same year as paid, the reimbursement merely reduces the amount that would otherwise qualify for the medical expense deduction. But what happens if the reimbursement occurs in a later year than the expenditure? In computing casualty losses, any reasonable prospect of recovery must be considered (refer to text Section 7-3). For medical expenses, however, any expected reimbursement is disregarded in measuring the amount of the deduction. Instead, the reimbursement is accounted for separately in the year in which it occurs.

Under the *tax benefit rule*, a taxpayer who receives an insurance reimbursement for medical expenses deducted in a previous year must include the reimbursement in income up to the amount of the deductions that decreased taxable income in the earlier

[16] § 162(l).

[17] The amounts for 2021 were also $450 for taxpayers age 40 and under and $5,640 for taxpayers over age 70. See IRS Publication 502, *Medical and Dental Expenses*, for details relating to requirements for deducting costs associated with qualified long-term care insurance contracts.

year. A taxpayer who did not itemize deductions in the year the expenses were paid did not receive a tax benefit and is *not* required to include a reimbursement in gross income.

Example 12

Daniel had AGI of $45,000 for 2022. He was injured in a car accident and paid $4,300 for hospital expenses and $1,700 for doctor bills. Daniel also incurred medical expenses of $600 for his dependent child. In 2023, Daniel was reimbursed $950 by his insurance company for the medical expenses attributable to the car accident. His deduction for medical expenses in 2022 is computed as follows:

Hospitalization	$ 4,300
Bills for doctor's services	1,700
Medical expenses for dependent	600
Total	$ 6,600
Less: Medical expense floor (7.5% of $45,000)	(3,375)
Medical expense deduction (assuming that Daniel itemizes his deductions)	$ 3,225

Assume that Daniel would have elected to itemize his deductions even if he had no medical expenses in 2022. If the reimbursement for medical care had occurred in 2022, the medical expense deduction would have been only $2,275 [$6,600 (total medical expenses) − $950 (reimbursement) − $3,375 (floor)] and Daniel would have paid more income tax.

Because the reimbursement was made in a subsequent year, Daniel will include $950 in gross income for 2023. If Daniel had not itemized in 2022, he would *not* have included the $950 reimbursement in 2023 gross income because he would have received no tax benefit for the medical expenses in 2022.

10-1h Health Savings Accounts

Qualifying individuals may make deductible contributions to a **Health Savings Account (HSA)**.[18] A taxpayer can use an HSA in conjunction with a high-deductible medical insurance policy to help reduce the overall cost of medical coverage. Converting from a low-deductible to a high-deductible plan generally can save an individual a considerable amount in premiums. The high-deductible policy provides coverage for extraordinary medical expenses (in excess of the deductible), and expenses not covered by the policy can be paid with funds withdrawn tax-free from the HSA.

Example 13

Antonio, who is married and has three dependent children, carries a high-deductible medical insurance policy with a deductible of $4,400. He establishes an HSA and contributes the maximum allowable amount to the HSA in 2022.

During 2022, Antonio's family incurs medical expenses of $7,000. The high-deductible policy covers $2,600 of the expenses ($7,000 expenses − $4,400 deductible). Antonio may withdraw $4,400 from the HSA to pay the medical expenses not covered by the high-deductible policy.

High-Deductible Plans

High-deductible policies are less expensive than low-deductible policies, so taxpayers with low medical costs can benefit from the lower premiums and use funds from the HSA to pay costs not covered by the high-deductible policy. A plan must meet two requirements to qualify as a high-deductible plan.[19]

1. The annual deductible in 2022 is not less than $1,400 for self-only coverage ($2,800 for family coverage).
2. The annual limit in 2022 on total out-of-pocket costs (excluding premiums) under the plan does not exceed $7,050 for self-only coverage ($14,100 for family coverage).

[18] § 223(a). An HSA is a qualified trust or custodial account administered by a qualified HSA trustee, which can be a bank, an insurance company, or another IRS-approved trustee. § 223(d).

[19] § 223(c)(2) and Rev. Proc. 2021–25. In 2021, the annual deductible limits were $1,400 (self-only coverage) and $2,800 (family coverage), and the annual out-of-pocket cost limits were $7,000 (self-only coverage) and $14,000 (family coverage).

Tax Treatment of HSA Contributions and Distributions

To establish an HSA, a taxpayer contributes funds to a custodial account.[20] As illustrated in the preceding example, funds can be withdrawn from an HSA to pay medical expenses that are not covered by the high-deductible policy. The following general tax rules apply to HSAs:

1. Contributions made by the taxpayer to an HSA are a deduction *for* AGI (i.e., the contributions reduce gross income in arriving at AGI). As a result, the taxpayer does not need to itemize to take the deduction.
2. Earnings on HSAs are not subject to taxation unless distributed, in which case taxability depends on the way the funds are used.[21]
   - Distributions from HSAs are excluded from gross income if they are used to pay for medical expenses not covered by the high-deductible policy.
   - Distributions that are not used to pay for medical expenses are included in gross income and are subject to an additional 20 percent penalty if made before age 65, death, or disability. Any distributions made by reason of death or disability and distributions made after the HSA beneficiary becomes eligible for Medicare are taxed but not penalized.

HSAs have at least two other attractive features. First, an HSA is portable. Taxpayers who switch jobs can take their HSAs with them. Second, anyone under age 65 who has a high-deductible plan and is not covered by another policy that is not a high-deductible plan can establish an HSA.

Deductible Amount

The annual deduction for contributions to an HSA is limited to an amount that depends on whether the taxpayer has self-only coverage or family coverage. The annual limit for an individual who has self-only coverage in 2022 is $3,650, and the annual limit for an individual who has family coverage in 2022 is $7,300. These amounts are subject to annual cost-of-living adjustments.[22] An eligible taxpayer who has attained age 55 by the end of the tax year may make an additional annual contribution in 2022 of up to $1,000. This additional amount is referred to as a *catch-up* contribution. A deduction is not allowed after the individual becomes eligible for Medicare coverage.

Determining the Maximum HSA Contribution Deduction

Example 14

Liu (age 45), who is married and self-employed, carries a high-deductible medical insurance policy with family coverage and an annual deductible of $4,000. In addition, he has established an HSA. Liu's maximum annual deductible contribution to the HSA in 2022 is $7,300.

Example 15

During 2022, Adam, who is self-employed, made 12 monthly payments of $1,200 for an HSA contract that provides medical insurance coverage with a $3,600 deductible. The plan covers Adam, his wife, and two children. Of the $1,200 monthly fee, $675 was for the high-deductible policy and $525 was deposited into an HSA.

Because Adam is *self-employed*, he can deduct $8,100 of the amount paid for the high-deductible policy ($675 per month × 12 months) as a deduction *for* AGI (refer to Example 10 and related discussion). In addition, he can deduct the $6,300 ($525 × 12) paid to the HSA as a deduction *for* AGI. Note that the $6,300 HSA deduction does not exceed the $7,300 annual ceiling.

[20] § 223(d).

[21] § 223(f).

[22] § 223(b)(2). See Rev.Proc. 2021–25. The annual limits were $3,600 and $7,200 in 2021.

10-1i Affordable Care Act Provisions

Information about the tax provisions of the Affordable Care Act can be found in an online appendix to the text.

LO.3

Contrast deductible taxes with nondeductible fees, licenses, and other charges.

10-2 Taxes

A deduction is allowed for *certain* state and local taxes paid or accrued by a taxpayer.[23]

10-2a Deductibility as a Tax

It is important to understand the difference between a tax and a fee, because fees are not deductible unless incurred as a business expense or as an expense in the production of income. Here is the IRS definition of a tax:

> The word *taxes* has been defined as an enforced contribution, exacted pursuant to legislative authority in the exercise of taxing power, and imposed and collected for the purpose of raising revenue to be used for public or governmental purposes and not as payment for some special privilege granted or service rendered.[24]

As a result, fees for dog licenses, automobile inspections, automobile titles and registration, hunting and fishing licenses, bridge and highway tolls, driver's licenses, parking meter deposits, and postage are not taxes.

Not all taxes are deductible. For example, Federal income taxes are not deductible. Other taxes are not deductible by individuals if they relate to personal activities (rather than business activities). An example is excise taxes included in the cost of purchasing gasoline. Deductible and nondeductible taxes are summarized in Exhibit 10.2.

State and Local Taxes—*For* AGI versus *From* AGI

State and local taxes imposed directly on business or rental property are deductible *for* AGI. For example, real property taxes imposed on the buildings or personal property taxes imposed on the equipment used by a sole proprietor are deductible as a business expense [*for* AGI; reported on Schedule C (Form 1040)]. Real property taxes imposed on an individual's rental property are also deductible *for* AGI [reported on Schedule E (Form 1040)].

In contrast, real property taxes imposed on an individual's personal residence are only deductible if the individual itemizes deductions [i.e., *from* AGI; reported on Schedule A (Form 1040)]. Additionally, real property taxes imposed on investment property (e.g., undeveloped land held for investment) are deductible as an itemized deduction (and not subject to the annual cap on state and local taxes discussed below).

Generally, state and local *income* taxes are considered to be only indirectly imposed on an individual's business and investment activity. Consider a sole proprietor with income who is operating in a state that imposes an income tax. This business owner pays state income taxes on this business income. The calculation of this state income tax, though, depends on other income and deductions of the sole proprietor as well as filing status and tax credits. As a result, the income tax is *not* directly imposed on the sole proprietorship business income (unlike property taxes that *are* directly imposed on the property used by the business). Since the income tax is *not* directly imposed on the business income, the state income tax is only deductible *from* AGI.

Changes made by Congress in 2017 make more relevant the distinction between state and local taxes *directly* imposed on a business versus those taxes *indirectly* imposed, as explained next.[25]

---

[23]Most deductible taxes are listed in § 164, and nondeductible items are included in § 275.

[24]Rev.Rul. 81–191.

[25]Rev.Rul. 58–25 and Rev.Rul. 81–288.

Exhibit 10.2 Deductible and Nondeductible Taxes

Deductible	Nondeductible
State, local, and foreign real property taxes	Federal income taxes
State and local personal property taxes	FICA taxes imposed on employees
State and local income taxes *or* sales/use taxes	Employer FICA taxes paid on domestic household workers
Foreign income taxes	Estate, inheritance, and gift taxes
	Federal, state, and local excise taxes (e.g., gasoline, tobacco, and spirits)
	Foreign income taxes if the taxpayer chooses the foreign tax credit option
	Taxes on real property to the extent these taxes are to be apportioned and treated as imposed on another taxpayer

Overall Limit on State and Local Taxes

From 2018 through 2025, the deduction for state and local taxes (including property taxes and either income taxes or sales taxes) is limited to a maximum of $10,000 per year ($5,000 if married filing separately). This limit applies to the taxes deductible *from* AGI that are *not directly imposed* on business and investment activity or property.[26]

Example 16

Adam owns and operates a dry cleaning business as a sole proprietorship. During 2022, Adam paid $7,000 of real property taxes on the building used in the business and $1,200 of personal property taxes on the equipment used in the business. In calculating and paying estimated state income taxes of $5,600 for 2022, Adam included the profit from his sole proprietorship, his investment income, and his itemized deductions and claimed a state tax credit for solar panels he installed on his home.

The $8,200 of property taxes imposed on his business ($7,000 + $1,200) is deductible *for* AGI [on Schedule C (Form 1040)], but his state income taxes are deductible *from* AGI [on Schedule A (Form 1040)]. Only the $5,600 of state income taxes is subject to the $10,000 limit on state and local taxes, not the $8,200.

Now assume that in addition to his state income taxes, Adam paid $6,000 of property taxes on his personal residence in 2022. His total state and local taxes are $11,600 ($5,600 + $6,000), and his Federal itemized deduction for state and local taxes is limited to $10,000.

10-2b Property Taxes

LO.4

Explain the Federal income tax treatment of property taxes, state and local income taxes, and sales taxes.

State, local, and foreign taxes on real property are generally deductible only by the person upon whom the tax is imposed. Foreign real property taxes are not deductible from 2018 through 2025 unless the taxes relate to an individual's business or investment property. Deductible personal property taxes must be *ad valorem* (assessed in relation to the value of the property). So a motor vehicle tax based on weight, model, year, and horsepower is not deductible. However, a tax based on value and other criteria will be partially deductible.

[26]§ 164(b)(6). Foreign income taxes also are included in this limit. This limitation is sometimes referred to as the "SALT cap." SALT is an acronym for *state and local taxes*. Notice 2020–75 provides that if a state imposes an income tax on a partnership or an S corporation, it is treated as an entity-level tax even if the entity's owners receive a partial or full deduction or credit for the tax for state income tax purposes. The benefit to the owners is that the income tax paid by the entity is not subject to the $10,000 SALT cap for the individual owners. About 22 states impose such a tax.

The Big Picture

Example 17

Return to the facts of *The Big Picture* on p. 10-1. Assuming that the Williamsons proceed with the purchase of a home, the real estate taxes they pay will be deductible *from* AGI (subject to the aggregate $10,000 limit) because they qualify to itemize their deductions. They also should review their annual registration statement for their car because a portion of it may represent personal property tax (if based on the value of the car).

For example, assume that in their state, the government imposes a motor vehicle registration tax on 2% of the value of the vehicle plus 40 cents per hundredweight. The Williamsons own a car having a value of $20,000 and weighing 3,000 pounds. They pay an annual registration fee of $412. Of this amount, $400 (2% × $20,000 of value) is deductible as a personal property tax (subject to the aggregate $10,000 annual limit). The remaining $12, based on the weight of the car, is not deductible. Any other amount included in the annual fee (e.g., processing charges) is not a tax.

Assessments for Local Benefits

As a general rule, real property taxes do not include taxes assessed for local benefits if the assessments increase the value of the property (e.g., special assessments for streets, sidewalks, curbing, and other similar improvements).[27] Instead of being deductible, these assessments are added to the basis of the taxpayer's property. Assessments included for personal benefit (e.g., trash removal and tree trimming) are not deductible and do not affect the basis of the property.

Apportionment of Real Property Taxes between Seller and Purchaser

Real estate taxes for the entire year are apportioned between the buyer and seller on the basis of the number of days the property was held by each during the real property tax year. This apportionment is required whether the tax is paid by the buyer or the seller or is prorated according to the purchase agreement. The apportionment determines who is entitled to deduct the real estate taxes in the year of sale. The required apportionment prevents the shifting of the deduction for real estate taxes from the buyer to the seller or vice versa. In making the apportionment, the assessment date and the lien date are disregarded.[28]

Example 18

A county's real property tax year runs from January 1 to December 31. Sara, the owner on January 1 of real property located in the county, sells the real property to Bob on June 30. Bob owns the real property from June 30 through December 31. The tax for the real property tax year, January 1 through December 31, is $3,650.

Assuming that this is not a leap year, the portion of the real property tax treated as imposed upon Sara, the seller, is $1,800 [(180/365) × $3,650, January 1 through June 29], and $1,850 of the tax [(185/365) × $3,650, June 30 through December 31] is treated as imposed upon Bob, the buyer.

If the actual real estate taxes are not prorated between the buyer and seller as part of the purchase agreement, adjustments are required. The adjustments are necessary to determine the amount realized by the seller and the basis of the property to the buyer. If the buyer pays the entire amount of the tax, the buyer has, in effect, paid the seller's portion of the real estate tax and has therefore paid more for the property than the

[27] Reg. § 1.164–4(a); see *Erie H. Rose*, 31 TCM 142, T.C.Memo. 1972–39, where a taxpayer was denied a deduction for the cost of a new sidewalk in front of his personal residence, even though the construction was required by the city and the sidewalk may have provided an incidental benefit to public welfare.

[28] For most years, the apportionment is based on a 365-day year. However, in a leap year (i.e., a year that is evenly divisible by 4, like 2024), the taxes are prorated over 366 days. In making the apportionment, the date of sale counts as a day the property is owned by the buyer. § 164(d).

actual purchase price. As a result, the amount of real estate tax that is apportioned to the seller (for Federal income tax purposes) and paid by the buyer is added to the buyer's basis. The seller must increase the amount realized on the sale by the same amount.

Example 19

Seth sells real estate on October 3 for $400,000. The buyer, Barbara, pays the real estate taxes of $3,650 for the calendar year, which is the real estate property tax year.

Assuming that this is not a leap year, $2,750 (for 275 days) of the real estate taxes is apportioned to and is deductible by the seller, Seth, and $900 (for 90 days) of the taxes is deductible by Barbara.

Barbara has, in effect, paid Seth's real estate taxes of $2,750 and has therefore paid $402,750 for the property. Barbara's basis is increased to $402,750, and the amount realized by Seth from the sale is increased to $402,750.

The opposite result occurs if the seller (rather than the buyer) pays the real estate taxes. In this case, the seller reduces the amount realized from the sale by the amount that has been apportioned to the buyer. The buyer is required to reduce the basis by a corresponding amount.

10-2c State and Local Income Taxes and Sales Taxes

The position of the IRS is that state and local income taxes imposed upon an individual are deductible only as itemized deductions, even if the taxpayer's sole source of income is from a business, rents, or royalties.

Cash basis taxpayers are entitled to deduct state income taxes in the year *payment is made*. This includes taxes withheld by the employer, amounts paid with the state income tax return when filed, and estimated state income tax payments.[29] If the taxpayer overpays state income taxes, any refund received is included in gross income in the year received to the extent the deduction reduced taxable income in the prior year. See text Section 5-15 for a discussion of how the tax benefit rule applies to state income tax refunds when the overall $10,000 limit on state and local taxes applied in the prior year.

Example 20

Leona, a cash basis, unmarried taxpayer, had $800 of state income tax withheld from her paychecks during 2022. Also in 2022, Leona paid $100 that was due when she filed her 2021 state income tax return and made estimated payments of $300 toward her 2022 state income tax liability. When Leona files her 2022 Federal income tax return in April 2023, she elects to itemize deductions, which amount to $15,500, including the $1,200 of state income tax payments and withholdings, all of which reduce her taxable income.

As a result of overpaying her 2022 state income tax, Leona receives a refund of $200 early in 2023. She will include this amount in her 2023 gross income in computing her Federal income tax. It does not matter whether Leona received a check from the state for $200 or applied the $200 toward her 2023 state income tax.

Individuals can elect to deduct *either* their state and local income taxes *or* their sales/use taxes paid as an itemized deduction. This election is intended to provide equity to taxpayers living in states that do not impose a state income tax (but do have sales taxes). Taxpayers making this election can deduct either actual sales/use tax payments *or* an amount from an IRS table (available on the IRS website). The IRS table amount can be increased by sales tax paid on the purchase of motor vehicles, boats, and other specified items.

[29]Rev.Rul. 71–190. See also Rev.Rul. 82–208, where a deduction is not allowed when the taxpayer cannot, in good faith, reasonably determine that there is additional state income tax liability.

LO.5

Distinguish between deductible and nondeductible interest and apply the appropriate limitations to deductible interest.

10-3 Interest

A deduction for interest has been allowed since the income tax law was enacted in 1913. However, despite its long history, the interest deduction has been a controversial area for tax policy. Should all interest be allowed as a deduction? If not, what limits should apply? Should an interest deduction be allowed for only the taxpayer's principal residence (or all residences)? What about interest on credit cards and student loans? Lawmakers and taxpayers continue to raise these questions (and others).

Personal (consumer) interest is not deductible. This includes credit card interest, interest on car loans, and other types of personal interest. However, interest on qualified student loans, qualified residence (home mortgage) interest, and investment interest are deductible, subject to the limits discussed on the following pages.[30]

10-3a Allowed and Disallowed Items

The Supreme Court has defined *interest* as compensation for the use of money.[31] The general rule permits a deduction for interest paid or accrued within the taxable year on indebtedness.

Interest on Qualified Student Loans

Taxpayers who pay interest on a qualified student loan may be able to deduct the interest as a deduction *for* AGI. The deduction is allowed if the proceeds of the loan are used to pay qualified education expenses. These payments must be made to qualified educational institutions.[32]

The maximum annual deduction for qualified student loan interest is $2,500. However, in 2022, the deduction is phased out for taxpayers with modified AGI (MAGI) between $70,000 and $85,000 ($145,000 and $175,000 on joint returns). The interest expense deduction is phased out by applying the following formula:

$$\textbf{Education interest expense} \times \frac{\textbf{Modified AGI} - \textbf{AGI phaseout floor}}{\textbf{\$15,000 (\$30,000 for married filing jointly)}}$$

The deduction is not allowed for taxpayers who are claimed as dependents or for married taxpayers filing separately.[33]

Example 21

In 2022, Curt and Rita, who are married and file a joint return, paid $3,000 of interest on a qualified student loan. Their MAGI was $152,500. Their maximum potential deduction for qualified student loan interest is $2,500, but it must be reduced by $625 as a result of the phaseout rules.

$$\$2,500 \text{ interest} \times \frac{\$152,500 \text{ (MAGI)} - \$145,000 \text{ (AGI phaseout floor)}}{\$30,000 \text{ (phaseout range)}} = \$625 \text{ reduction}$$

Curt and Rita are allowed a student loan interest deduction of $1,875 ($2,500 maximum deduction − $625 reduction = $1,875 deduction *for* AGI).

Qualified Residence Interest

Qualified residence interest is interest paid or accrued during the taxable year on indebtedness (subject to limitations) *secured* by a qualified residence of the taxpayer. Qualified residence interest falls into two categories: (1) interest on acquisition indebtedness and (2) interest on home equity loans.[34]

[30] As discussed in Chapter 6, interest expense paid or incurred in a trade or business also is deductible (§ 162; a *for* AGI deduction).

[31] *Old Colony Railroad Co. v. Comm.*, 3 USTC ¶880, 10 AFTR 786, 52 S.Ct. 211 (1932).

[32] §§ 62(a)(17) and 221. See IRS Publication 970, *Tax Benefits for Education*, for details.

[33] §§ 221(c) and (e)(2). See § 221(b)(2)(C) for the definition of MAGI. The 2021 MAGI threshold amounts were $70,000 and $85,000 ($140,000 and $170,000 on joint returns).

[34] § 163(h)(3).

A *qualified residence* includes the taxpayer's principal residence and one other residence of the taxpayer or spouse. The *principal residence* meets the requirement for nonrecognition of gain upon sale under § 121 (see text Section 15-4). The *one other residence*, or second residence, is used as a residence if not rented or, if rented, meets the requirements for a personal residence under the rental of vacation home rules (refer to Chapter 6). A taxpayer who has more than one second residence can choose the qualified second residence each year (i.e., the taxpayer can select a different second residence each year). A residence includes a house, a cooperative apartment, a condominium, and mobile homes and boats that have living quarters (sleeping, bathroom, and cooking facilities).

Although in most cases interest paid on a home mortgage is fully deductible, there are limitations.[35] A deduction is allowed for interest paid or accrued during the tax year on aggregate **acquisition indebtedness**. *Acquisition indebtedness* refers to amounts incurred in acquiring, constructing, or substantially improving the taxpayer's qualified residence that serves as security for that indebtedness. The amount of acquisition indebtedness is limited based on when the debt was incurred. If the debt is incurred after December 15, 2017, and before January 1, 2026, acquisition indebtedness is limited to $750,000 ($375,000 for married taxpayers filing separate returns). Debt incurred on or before December 15, 2017, is limited to $1 million ($500,000 for married taxpayers filing separate returns). These higher debt limits will apply to all homeowners after 2025, regardless of the date of borrowing.

The Big Picture

Example 22

Return to the facts of *The Big Picture* on p. 10-1. Given that John and Kiara Williamson will need to borrow at least a portion of the purchase price of a new home, a standard mortgage likely will qualify as acquisition indebtedness because the borrowed funds are used to acquire a principal residence. However, the interest on the acquisition indebtedness will be fully deductible only if the amount of the mortgage is $750,000 or less (assuming that John and Kiara file a joint return) and the mortgage is secured by the home, which is the typical case.

Recall that the Williamsons also are considering what appears to be a less expensive route of using their retirement and taxable investments to secure the debt. If they choose this alternative, the interest will not be deductible as qualified residence interest because the loan would not be acquisition indebtedness (i.e., the loan would not be secured by the home).

From 2018 through 2025, interest on **home equity loans** is not deductible unless the funds are used to improve the principal residence (and the total acquisition debt and home equity debt is $750,000 or less). Home equity loans utilize the personal residence of the taxpayer as security, typically in the form of a second mortgage. If the funds from home equity loans are used for personal purposes (e.g., auto purchases, vacations, medical expenses), the related interest expense is not deductible.[36]

Example 23

Larry owns a personal residence with a fair market value of $600,000 and an outstanding first mortgage of $420,000. Therefore, his equity in his home is $180,000 ($600,000 − $420,000). Larry borrows $75,000 that is secured by a second mortgage on his home to put an addition on his home.

All of Larry's interest is deductible; both loans are secured by his residence, and the total of the loans ($420,000 + $75,000) does not exceed $750,000 or the value of his residence. If Larry used the home equity loan proceeds to buy a new car and boat, the home equity loan interest would not be deductible.

[35] § 163(h)(3).

[36] § 163(h)(3)(F). Interest on home equity loans prior to 2018 was deductible only on the portion of a home equity loan that did not exceed the lesser of (1) the fair market value of the residence reduced by any acquisition indebtedness or (2) $100,000 ($50,000 for married persons filing separate returns). Proceeds from these home equity loans could be used for any purpose without impairing the interest deductibility. From 2018 through 2025, the treatment of interest expense on an equity debt that was not used to improve the home is determined using the interest tracing rules of Temp. Reg. § 1.163–8T and Reg. § 1.163–15.

Mortgage insurance premiums paid by the taxpayer on a qualified residence are deductible (and treated as qualified residence interest). The amount allowed is subject to a phaseout based on AGI; the deduction expired at the end of 2021 but might be extended by Congress.[37]

Interest Paid for Services

Mortgage loan companies commonly charge a fee, often called a loan origination fee, for finding, placing, or processing a mortgage loan. Loan origination fees are typically nondeductible amounts included in the basis of the acquired property. Other fees, sometimes called **points** and expressed as a percentage of the loan amount, are paid to reduce the interest rate charged over the term of the loan. Essentially, the payment of points is a prepayment of interest and is considered compensation to a lender for the use of money.[38]

In general, points are capitalized and are amortized and deductible ratably over the life of the loan. However, the purchaser of a principal residence can deduct qualifying points in the year of payment.This exception also covers points paid to obtain funds for improvements to a principal residence.[39]

Points paid to *refinance* acquisition indebtedness (i.e., an existing home mortgage) must be capitalized and amortized as an interest deduction over the life of the new loan.[40]

Example 24

Sandra purchased her residence many years ago, obtaining a 30-year mortgage at an annual interest rate of 6%. In the current year, Sandra refinances the mortgage to reduce the interest rate to 4%. To obtain the refinancing, she has to pay points of $2,600.

The $2,600, which is considered prepayment of interest, must be capitalized and amortized over the life of the mortgage.

Points paid by the seller for a buyer are, in effect, treated as an adjustment to the price of the residence, and the buyer is treated as having used cash to pay the points that were paid by the seller. A buyer may deduct seller-paid points in the tax year in which they are paid if certain conditions are met.[41]

Prepayment Penalty

When a mortgage or loan is paid off in full in a lump sum before its term (early), the lending institution may require an additional payment (normally, a specific percentage of the loan balance). This is known as a prepayment penalty and is considered to be interest (e.g., personal, qualified residence, or investment) in the year paid. The general rules for deductibility of interest also apply to prepayment penalties.

Investment Interest

Taxpayers sometimes borrow funds to acquire investment assets (e.g., stock). Congress, however, has limited the deductibility of interest on funds borrowed to purchase or hold investment property. The deduction for investment interest expense is limited to the net investment income for the year and is only deductible if the taxpayer itemizes deductions. A complete discussion of investment interest occurs in text Section 11-4.

Tax-Exempt Securities

No deduction is allowed for interest on debt incurred to purchase or hold tax-exempt securities.[42] Refer to text Section 6-3l for further discussion of this topic.

[37]§§ 163(h)(3)(E). In 2021, the deduction phases out for taxpayers with AGI in excess of $100,000 ($50,000 for married taxpayers filing separately) and is fully phased out when AGI exceeds $109,000 ($54,500 for married taxpayers filing separately).

[38]Rev.Rul. 69–188. To be deductible, points must be in the nature of interest and cannot be a form of service charge or payment for specific services.

[39]§ 461(g)(2).

[40]Rev.Rul. 87–22.

[41]Refer to Rev.Proc. 94–27 for a complete list of these conditions and additional aspects of this arrangement.

[42]§ 265(a)(2).

10-3b Restrictions on Deductibility and Timing Considerations

Even if interest expense is deductible (e.g., qualified residence interest), a current deduction still may not be available unless certain additional conditions described below are met.

Taxpayer's Obligation

Allowed interest is deductible if the related debt represents a bona fide obligation of the taxpayer.[43] For interest to be deductible, both the debtor and the creditor must intend for the loan to be repaid. Intent of the parties can be especially crucial between related parties (e.g., family members or a shareholder and a closely held corporation).

In addition, an individual may not deduct interest paid on behalf of another taxpayer. For example, a shareholder may not deduct interest paid by the corporation on the shareholder's behalf.[44] Likewise, a husband may not deduct interest paid on his wife's property if he files a separate return, except in the case of qualified residence interest. If both husband and wife consent in writing, either the husband or the wife may deduct the allowed interest on the principal residence and one other residence.

Time of Deduction

Under the cash method, interest must be paid to secure a deduction. Under the accrual method, interest is deductible ratably over the life of the loan.

Example 25

On November 1, 2022, Ramon borrows $2,000 to purchase computers for his consulting business. The loan is payable in 90 days at 6% interest. On the due date in late January 2023, Ramon pays the $2,000 note and interest amounting to $30.

Ramon can deduct the accrued portion ($\frac{2}{3} \times \$30 = \$20$) of the interest in 2022 only if he is an accrual basis taxpayer. Otherwise, the entire amount of interest ($30) is deductible in 2023.

Prepaid Interest

The accrual method treatment must be used by cash basis taxpayers for interest prepayments that extend beyond the end of the taxable year.[45] These payments must be allocated to the tax years to which the interest payments relate. This provision prevents cash basis taxpayers from creating tax deductions before the end of the year by prepaying interest.

10-3c Classification of Interest Expense

Whether interest is deductible *for* AGI or as an itemized deduction (*from* AGI) depends on whether the indebtedness has a business, investment, or personal purpose. If the debt proceeds are used for a business expense (other than performing services as an employee) or for an expense for an activity for the production of rent or royalty income, the interest is deductible *for* AGI. Business expenses appear on Schedule C of Form 1040, and expenses related to rents or royalties are reported on Schedule E.

If the indebtedness produces qualified residence interest, any deduction allowed is taken *from* AGI and is reported on Schedule A of Form 1040 (the taxpayer must itemize deductions to get any benefit). Recall, however, that interest on a limited amount of student loans is a deduction *for* AGI. If the taxpayer is an employee who incurs debt in relation to the taxpayer's employment, the interest is considered to be personal interest and is not deductible. Debt proceeds used for personal purposes (e.g., to pay for a vacation or personal credit card bills) produce nondeductible personal interest expense.

See Concept Summary 10.1 for a summary of the interest deduction rules.

[43] *Arcade Realty Co.*, 35 T.C. 256 (1960), *acq.* 1961–2 C.B. 3.

[44] *Continental Trust Co.*, 7 B.T.A. 539 (1927).

[45] § 461(g)(1).

Concept Summary 10.1

Deductibility of Personal, Student Loan, Mortgage, and Investment Interest

Type	Deductible	Comments
Personal (consumer) interest	No	Includes any interest that is not qualified residence interest, qualified student loan interest, investment interest, or business interest. Examples include interest on car loans and credit card debt.*
Qualified student loan interest	Yes	Deduction *for* AGI; subject to limitations.
Qualified residence interest (acquisition indebtedness)	Yes	Deductible as an itemized deduction; limited to indebtedness of $750,000 (up to $1 million if incurred on or before December 15, 2017).
Qualified residence interest (home equity indebtedness)	No	In general, not deductible from 2018 through 2025.* Prior to 2018 and after 2025, deductible as an itemized deduction; limited to indebtedness equal to the lesser of $100,000 or the FMV of residence minus acquisition indebtedness.
Investment interest (*not* related to rental or royalty property)	Yes	Itemized deduction; limited to net investment income for the year; disallowed interest can be carried over to future years (see text Section 11-4).*
Investment interest (related to rental or royalty property)	Yes	Deduction *for* AGI; limited to net investment income for the year; disallowed interest can be carried over to future years (see text Section 11-4).*

* The classification rules for interest expense are provided by Temp.Reg. § 1.163–8T, Reg. § 1.163–15, and Notice 89–35.

LO.6

Recognize charitable contributions and identify their related measurement problems and percentage limitations.

10-4 Charitable Contributions

Code § 170 allows individuals and corporations to deduct contributions made to qualified *domestic* organizations. Contributions to qualified charitable organizations serve certain social welfare needs and thus relieve the government of the cost of providing these needed services to the community.

The **charitable contribution** provisions are among the most complex in the tax law. To determine the amount deductible as a charitable contribution, several important questions must be answered:

- What constitutes a charitable contribution?
- Was the contribution made to a qualified organization?
- When is the contribution deductible?
- What record-keeping and reporting requirements apply to charitable contributions?
- How is the value of donated property determined?
- What special rules apply to contributions of property that has increased in value?
- What percentage limitations apply to the charitable contribution deduction?
- What rules apply to amounts in excess of percentage limitations (carryovers)?

These questions are addressed in the sections that follow.

10-4a Criteria for a Gift

A *charitable contribution* is defined as a gift of property made to a qualified organization. The major elements needed to qualify a contribution as a gift are a donative intent, the absence of consideration, and acceptance by the donee. Consequently, the taxpayer has the burden of establishing that the transfer was made from motives of *disinterested generosity* as established by the courts.[46] This test is quite subjective and has led to problems of interpretation (refer to the discussion of gifts in text Section 5-2).

Benefit Received Rule

When a donor derives a tangible benefit from a contribution, the donor cannot deduct the value of the benefit.

[46] *Comm. v. Duberstein*, 60–2 USTC ¶9515, 5 AFTR 2d 1626, 80 S.Ct. 1190.

Example 26

Jacob purchases a ticket at $100 for a special performance of the local symphony (a qualified charity). If the price of a ticket to a symphony concert is normally $35, Jacob is allowed only $65 as a charitable contribution. Even if Jacob does not attend the concert, the deduction is limited to $65.

If, however, Jacob does *not* accept the ticket from the symphony (or returns it prior to the event), he can deduct the full $100.

Contributions in Exchange for State and Local Tax Credits

Several states provide a state or local tax credit to taxpayers who donate to specified state or local funds or public charities. Primarily due to concerns that state and local governments might expand the availability of these programs to help taxpayers "work around" the $10,000 state and local tax deduction limit, the IRS issued rules limiting the Federal tax benefits of these "contributions." Under these rules, if taxpayers receive a state or local tax credit greater than 15 percent of the payments made, the taxpayers must reduce their charitable contribution deduction by the amount of that credit.[47]

Example 27

In 2022, Prisha, a resident of State G, donated $5,000 to State G's Scholar Program. This donation provides Prisha with a 60% state income tax credit [$3,000 ($5,000 × 60%)] that can be used to reduce her overall state income tax liability. By making this contribution, Prisha is attempting to convert a state income tax payment (with an overall limit of $10,000 per year) into a charitable contribution (with a 50%-of-AGI limit).

On Prisha's 2022 Federal return, she must reduce this charitable contribution by $3,000 because the credit she received was more than 15% of the payment made. As a result, Prisha's charitable contribution deduction for this $5,000 donation is reduced to only $2,000 ($5,000 payment − $3,000 state income tax credit).

Contribution of Services

No deduction is allowed for a contribution of one's services to a qualified charitable organization. However, unreimbursed expenses related to the services rendered may be deductible. For example, the cost of a uniform (without general utility) that is required to be worn while performing services may be deductible. In addition, deductions are permitted for out-of-pocket transportation costs, reasonable expenses for lodging, and the cost of meals while away from home that are incurred in performing the donated services. In lieu of these out-of-pocket costs for an automobile, a standard mileage rate of 14 cents per mile is allowed.[48] The travel expenses are not deductible if the travel involves a significant element of personal pleasure, recreation, or vacation.[49]

Example 28

Grace, a delegate representing her church in Miami, Florida, travels to a two-day national meeting in Denver, Colorado, in February. After the meeting, Grace spends two weeks at a nearby ski resort.

Under these circumstances, none of the transportation, meals, or lodging is deductible because the travel involved a significant element of personal pleasure, recreation, or vacation.

Nondeductible Items

In addition to the benefit received rule and the restrictions placed on contributions of services, the following items may *not* be deducted as charitable contributions:

- Dues, fees, or bills paid to country clubs, lodges, fraternal orders, or similar groups.
- Cost of raffle, bingo, or lottery tickets.
- Cost of tuition.
- Payment for the right to purchase tickets for seating at an athletic event in a university stadium.[50]

---

[47] Reg. § 1.170A–1(h)(3). Reg. § 1.162–15 allows a C corporation making contributions to such funds to treat the portion of the contribution for which a credit is earned as a business expense (§ 162). If the business is a pass-through entity and the credit applies to a tax imposed directly on the business (e.g., a property tax), the payment is treated as a business deduction. Reg. § 1.164–3(j) allows an individual with state and local taxes below the $10,000 cap to treat the disallowed charitable contribution amount as a state tax deduction (but not to exceed the $10,000 cap).

[48] § 170(i).

[49] § 170(j).

[50] § 170(l).

- Value of blood given to a blood bank.
- Donations to homeowners associations.
- Gifts to individuals.
- Rental value of property used by a qualified charity.

10-4b **Qualified Organizations**

To be deductible, a contribution must be made to one of the following organizations:[51]

- A state or possession of the United States (or any subdivision).
- A corporation, trust, community chest, fund, or foundation located in the United States and organized and operated exclusively for religious, charitable, scientific, literary, or educational purposes or for the prevention of cruelty to children or animals.
- A veterans' organization.
- A fraternal organization operating under the lodge system.
- A cemetery company.

It is commonly understood that contributions to a church, a synagogue, or another religious organization are allowed. But for less well-known recipients, taxpayers can consult an IRS list of organizations that have applied for and received tax-exempt status under § 501 of the Code.[52]

Gifts made to needy individuals are not deductible (e.g., a needy family or a homeless individual). A deduction is allowed only if the gift is made to a qualified organization.

Example 29

Sarah's neighbor is very ill and has been in the hospital for several weeks. Her insurance won't cover all of her medical bills. A neighborhood friend set up a crowdfunding website, allowing people to contribute money to help Sarah's neighbor with her medical bills. Sarah transfers $700 to this crowdfunding campaign.

Sarah may not treat the $700 as a charitable contribution because it is a nondeductible gift [i.e., for the benefit of an individual rather than a charitable (qualified) organization].

Ethics & Equity **An Indirect Route to a Contribution Deduction**

In July, a plane crashed into a residential community in Middleboro, destroying and damaging many homes. Chloe's church, a qualified charitable organization, initiated a fund-raising drive to help the Middleboro citizens whose homes had been affected. Chloe donated $50,000 to First Middleboro Church and suggested to the pastor that $25,000 of her contribution should be given to her sister, Rebecca, whose home had suffered extensive damage. The pastor appointed a committee to award funds to needy citizens. The committee solicited applications from the community and awarded Rebecca $15,000. Discuss whether Chloe is justified in deducting $50,000 as a charitable contribution.

10-4c **Time of Deduction**

A charitable contribution generally is deducted in the year the payment is made. This rule applies to both cash and accrual basis individuals. A contribution ordinarily is deemed to have been made on the delivery of the property to the donee. For example, if a gift of common stock is made to a qualified charitable organization, the gift is considered complete on the day of delivery or mailing. However, if the donor delivers the stock certificate to the bank or broker or to the issuing corporation, the gift is considered complete on the date the stock is transferred on the books of the corporation.

A contribution made by check is considered delivered on the date of mailing. Thus, a check mailed on December 31, 2022, is deductible on the taxpayer's 2022 tax return. If the contribution is charged on a credit card, the date the charge is made determines the year of deduction.

[51] § 170(c).

[52] Although this *Cumulative List of Organizations*, IRS Publication 78, may be helpful, not all organizations that qualify are listed in this publication. The IRS maintains a searchable database at **irs.gov/charities-non-profits/tax-exempt-organization-search**.

10-4d Record-Keeping and Valuation Requirements

Recall that income tax deductions allowed by law are a matter of legislative grace, but a taxpayer still bears the burden of showing that the taxpayer is entitled to claim the deduction. Not surprisingly, the tax law provides specific documentation requirements that must be met to claim a charitable contribution deduction.

Record-Keeping Requirements

In order to claim a charitable contribution deduction, the taxpayer must have appropriate documentation. The specific type of documentation required depends on the amount of the contribution and whether the contribution is made in cash or noncash property.[53] In addition, special rules may apply to gifts of certain types of property (e.g., used cars or boats) where Congress noted taxpayer abuse in the past. In addition, for certain gifts of noncash property, Form 8283 (Noncash Charitable Contributions) must be attached to the taxpayer's return.

The taxpayer must have the required documentation by the date the tax return is filed for the year the contribution is claimed (and no later than the due date, including extensions, of that tax return). Failure to comply with the reporting rules typically results in disallowance of the charitable contribution deduction. In addition, substantial penalties may apply if the taxpayer significantly overvalues any contributed property.

Common documentation and substantiation requirements are summarized in Concept Summary 10.2.

Concept Summary 10.2

Documentation and Substantiation Requirements for Charitable Contributions

Cash gifts	• A deduction is allowed only if the taxpayer has a proper receipt (e.g., a canceled check or written statement from the charity) showing the name of the charitable organization and the date and amount of the contribution. • A written statement from the charity is required if a payment is for more than $75 and is partly a contribution and partly for goods or services. The statement must provide an estimate of the value of the goods and services received by the donor.
Noncash gifts (e.g., household items)	• A receipt from the charity must be kept for any gift of property other than money. Clothes or other household items are deductible if they are in "good used condition or better" at the time of the gift. • If an item is not in good used condition or better and its value exceeds $500, a deduction is allowed if a "qualified appraisal" is included with the return.
Used cars, boats, or airplanes	• The deduction is generally limited to the amount the charity receives on the sale of the car, boat, or airplane. The taxpayer should obtain a statement from the charity documenting the sales price. Form 1098–C (Contributions of Motor Vehicles, Boats, and Airplanes) must be attached to the return if the taxpayer claims a deduction in excess of $500.
Cash or noncash gifts (including out-of-pocket expenses) of $250 or more	• A contemporaneous written acknowledgment (CWA) from the charity (as well as certain payroll records in the case of gifts made by payroll deductions) is required to deduct a single cash or property contribution of $250 or more. A CWA also is required for a donation of $250 or more of out-of-pocket expenses a donor might incur in providing services to a charity. The CWA must include the amount of money and a description of any other property contributed, whether the charity provided any goods or services in return for the contribution, and a description and estimated value of the goods or services provided. Contemporaneous means that the donor must have the CWA by the earlier of (1) the date the tax return is filed for the year of the donation or (2) the due date (including extensions) for the tax return.
Noncash gifts of more than $500	• Additional substantiation (e.g., how the property was acquired and its basis) is required on the tax return if donated noncash property is valued at more than $500. Qualified appraisals may be required if noncash contributions exceed $5,000 in value.
Antiques, paintings, jewelry, and other "tangible personal property"	• The deduction is equal to the property's appreciated FMV only if the charity puts the property to "a use related to its tax-exempt purpose." Otherwise, the deduction is limited to the property's cost. The taxpayer should obtain a statement from the charity documenting the property's use.

[53] The specific documentation thresholds and requirements are provided in § 170(f).

Global Tax Issues — Choose the Charity Wisely

Eleonora, a U.S. citizen of Italian descent, was distressed by the damage caused by a major earthquake in central Italy. She donated $100,000 to the Earthquake Victims' Relief Fund, an Italian charitable organization that was set up to help victims of the earthquake. Stefano, also a U.S. citizen of Italian descent, donated $100,000 to help with the relief effort. However, Stefano's contribution went to his church, which sent the proceeds of a fund drive to the Earthquake Victims' Relief Fund in Italy. Eleonora's contribution is not deductible, but Stefano's is. Why? Contributions to charitable organizations are not deductible unless the organization is a U.S. charity.

Valuation Requirements

Property donated to a charity is generally valued at fair market value at the time the gift is made. The Code provides very little guidance on the measurement of the fair market value. The Regulations provide this definition:[54] "The fair market value is the price at which the property would change hands between a willing buyer and a willing seller, neither being under any compulsion to buy or sell and both having reasonable knowledge of relevant facts."

Generally, charitable organizations do not provide the fair market value of the donated property. Nevertheless, as noted in Concept Summary 10.2, the taxpayer must obtain written evidence of the donation from the charity and value the donation appropriately.

10-4e Limitations on Charitable Contribution Deduction

The charitable contribution deduction is the total of all donations made during the year, both money and property. However, the charitable contribution deduction is subject to a number of limitations (based on the taxpayer's AGI, the type of property contributed, and the charity receiving the property). In general:

- If the qualifying contributions for the year total 20 percent or less of AGI, they are fully deductible.
- If the qualifying contributions are more than 20 percent of AGI, the deductible amount may be limited to 20 percent, 30 percent, 50 percent, or 60 percent of AGI, depending on the type of property given and the type of organization to which the donation is made.
- In any case, the maximum charitable contribution deduction may not exceed 60 percent of AGI for the tax year (100 percent in 2020 and 2021).

If a taxpayer's contributions for the year exceed the limitations, the excess contributions may be carried forward and deducted during a five-year carryover period.

To understand the complex rules for computing the amount of a charitable contribution deduction, it is necessary to understand the distinction between ordinary income property and capital gain property. In addition, it is necessary to understand when the various limitations apply. These topics are discussed in the sections that follow.

Ordinary Income Property

Ordinary income property is any property that, if sold, will result in the recognition of ordinary income. The term includes inventory for sale in the taxpayer's trade or business, a work of art created by the donor, and a manuscript prepared by the donor. It also includes, *for purposes of the charitable contribution calculation*, a capital asset held by the donor for a year or less (this is the holding period for short-term capital gain treatment; see text Section 16-4). If a business contributes depreciable property, it is ordinary income property to the extent of any depreciation recapture that would have been recognized had the

[54] Reg. § 1.170A–1(c)(2).

property been sold. Ordinary income property also includes personal use and investment assets that have declined in value (i.e., the fair market value is *less than* the taxpayer's basis). Used clothing contributed to the Salvation Army would fit this description.[55]

If ordinary income property is contributed, the deduction is equal to the fair market value of the property less the amount of ordinary income that would have been reported if the property were sold. In most instances, the deduction is limited to the basis of the property to the donor.

Example 30

Tim donates stock in White Corporation to a university on May 1, 2022. Tim had purchased the stock for $2,500 on March 3, 2022, and the stock had a value of $3,600 when he made the donation. Because he had not held the property long enough to meet the long-term capital gain requirement, Tim would have recognized a short-term capital gain of $1,100 if he had sold the property.

Because short-term capital gain property is treated as ordinary income property for charitable contribution purposes, Tim's charitable contribution deduction is limited to the property's basis of $2,500 ($3,600 − $1,100).

Assume, instead, that the stock had a fair market value of $2,300 (rather than $3,600) when Tim donated it to the university. Because the fair market value now is less than the basis, the charitable contribution deduction is $2,300.

Capital Gain Property

Capital gain property is any property that would have resulted in the recognition of long-term capital gain or § 1231 gain if the property had been sold by the donor.[56] As a general rule, the deduction for a contribution of capital gain property is equal to the fair market value of the property.

Two common exceptions disallow the deductibility of the appreciation on capital gain property. The first exception relates to the contribution of *tangible personalty*. Tangible personalty is all property that is not realty (land and buildings) and does not include intangible property (e.g., stock or securities). If tangible personalty is contributed to a public charity (e.g., a museum, church, or university) and the property is put to an *unrelated use*, the charitable deduction is limited to the property's basis (rather than its fair market value). The term *unrelated use* means a use that is unrelated to the exempt purpose or function of the charitable organization. For example, artwork donated to the American Red Cross is unlikely to be put to a related use. Instead, the Red Cross would likely sell the art to generate funds that would then be used to support its mission of providing assistance to individuals who have been struck by disasters.

Knowing this, taxpayers usually specify how their contributed property will be used and target donors appropriately (i.e., giving artwork to a museum rather than the Red Cross). As a result, this reduction will not apply if the property is put to a related use or if, at the time of the contribution, it was reasonable to anticipate that the property would not be put to an unrelated use by the donee.[57]

Example 31

Emma contributes a Picasso painting, for which she paid $20,000, to a local museum. She had owned the painting for four years. It had a value of $30,000 at the time of the donation. The museum displays the painting for five years and subsequently sells it for $50,000.

The charitable contribution is $30,000. It is not reduced by the unrealized appreciation because the painting is not put to an unrelated use even though it is later sold by the museum.

The second exception relates to certain private foundations. Private foundations are organizations that traditionally do not receive their funding from the general public (e.g., the Bill and Melinda Gates Foundation). Generally, foundations fall into two categories: operating and nonoperating. A private *operating* foundation spends substantially all of its income in the active conduct of its charitable purposes. Other private foundations are

[55]Depreciation recapture rules are discussed in Chapter 17. For a more complete discussion of the difference between ordinary income and capital gain property, see Chapter 16.

[56]See text Section 16-4 for a discussion of holding periods.

[57]§ 170(e)(1)(B)(i) and Reg. § 1.170A–4(b)(3)(ii)(b).

nonoperating foundations. Often, only the private foundation knows its status (operating or nonoperating) for sure, and the status can change from year to year.

If capital gain property is contributed to a private *nonoperating* foundation, the taxpayer must reduce the contribution by the long-term capital gain that would have been recognized if the property had been sold at its fair market value. The effect of this provision is to limit the deduction to the property's basis.[58]

Example 32

Ten years ago, Walter purchased land for $8,000 and has held it as an investment since then. This year, when the land is worth $20,000, he donates it to a private *nonoperating* foundation. Walter's charitable contribution is $8,000 ($20,000 − $12,000), the land's basis.

If, instead, Walter had donated the land to either a public charity or a private *operating* foundation, his charitable contribution would have been $20,000, the fair market value of the land.

Fifty Percent Ceiling

Contributions made to public charities may not exceed 50 percent of an individual's AGI for the year. Given that this ceiling is quite high, most taxpayers making contributions never have their charitable contributions limited. The 50 percent ceiling on contributions applies to public charities (e.g., churches; schools; hospitals; and Federal, state, or local governmental units). The 50 percent ceiling also applies to contributions to private operating foundations and certain private nonoperating foundations.

In the remaining discussion of charitable contributions, public charities and private foundations (both operating and nonoperating) that qualify for the 50 percent ceiling will be referred to as *50 percent organizations*.

Example 33

During the year, Tom and Emma Waters contribute $8,000 to their church, donate $500 to the Salvation Army, and give used clothes to Goodwill Industries (cost of $1,000; fair market value of $200). The clothes are ordinary income property, and the charitable contribution deduction is limited to the fair market value. Their AGI for the year is $125,000.

Tom and Emma's charitable contribution deduction is $8,700 ($8,000 + $500 + $200). Their charitable contribution deduction is not limited, since $8,700 is less than 50% of their AGI ($62,500; $125,000 × 50%).

Temporary Sixty Percent Ceiling

From 2018 through 2025, the deduction limit for *cash donations* to 50 percent organizations is 60 percent of AGI (rather than 50 percent of AGI). Congress was concerned that the combination of the increased standard deduction and the scaling back of many individual itemized deductions during this period would reduce the tax incentive to make charitable contributions. Most policy organizations believe that the increased ceiling will have little, if any, effect on the expected decline in individual donations to charities.

Thirty Percent Ceiling

A 30 percent ceiling applies to contributions of cash and ordinary income property to private nonoperating foundations that are not 50 percent organizations. The 30 percent ceiling also applies to contributions of appreciated capital gain property to 50 percent organizations.[59]

In the event the contributions for any one tax year involve both 50 percent and 30 percent property, the allowable deduction comes first from the 50 percent property.

---

[58] § 170(e)(1)(B)(ii).

[59] Under a special election, a taxpayer may choose to permanently forgo a deduction of the appreciation on capital gain property. Referred to as the reduced deduction election, this enables the taxpayer to move from the 30% limitation to the 50% limitation. See § 170(b)(1)(C)(iii).

Example 34

During the year, Lisa makes the following donations to her church: cash of $2,000 and unimproved land worth $30,000. Lisa had purchased the land four years ago for $22,000 and held it as an investment. Therefore, it is capital gain property. Lisa's AGI for the year is $60,000. Disregarding percentage limitations, Lisa's potential deduction is $32,000 [$2,000 (cash) + $30,000 (fair market value of land)].

In applying the percentage limitations, however, the *current* deduction for the land is limited to $18,000 [30% (limitation applicable to capital gain property) × $60,000 (AGI)]. Thus, the total current deduction is $20,000 ($2,000 cash + $18,000 land). Note that the total deduction does not exceed $30,000, which is 50% of Lisa's AGI.

Twenty Percent Ceiling

A 20 percent ceiling applies to contributions of appreciated capital gain property to private nonoperating foundations that are not 50 percent organizations.

Special Rules for 2020 and 2021

Several unique rules apply to the 2020 and 2021 tax years due to COVID-19-related legislation. First, in both 2020 and 2021, the deduction limit for cash contributions is increased to 100 percent of AGI (rather than 60 percent of AGI).[60] Second, in 2020, individuals who did not itemize were allowed to claim a deduction *for* AGI of up to $300 for charitable contributions made in cash.[61] Third, in 2021, individuals who do not itemize are allowed to claim a *from* AGI deduction of up to $300 for charitable contributions made in cash ($600 for married couples filing jointly); this deduction is in addition to the taxpayer's standard deduction.[62]

Concept Summary 10.3 summarizes the limitations on the deductibility of charitable contributions by individuals.

Concept Summary 10.3

Determining the Deduction for Contributions by Individuals

If the Type of Property Contributed Is:	And the Property Is Contributed to:	The Contribution Is Measured by:	But the Deduction Is Limited to:
1. Capital gain property (see Example 34)	A 50% organization	Fair market value of the property	30% of AGI
2. Ordinary income property (see Example 30)	A 50% organization	The basis of the property*	50% of AGI
3. Capital gain property (and the property is tangible personal property put to an unrelated use by the donee; see Example 31)	A 50% organization	The basis of the property*	50% of AGI
4. Capital gain property (see Example 32)	A private nonoperating foundation that is not a 50% organization	The basis of the property*	The lesser of: 1. 20% of AGI 2. 50% of AGI minus other contributions to 50% organizations
5. Cash	A 50% organization	Amount of cash	60% of AGI (100% for 2020 and 2021)

*If the fair market value of the property is less than the basis (i.e., the property has declined in value instead of appreciating), the fair market value is used.

Contribution Carryovers

Contributions that exceed the percentage limitations for the current year can be carried over for five years. In the carryover process, these contributions do not lose their identity for limitation purposes. Thus, if the contribution originally involved 30 percent property, the carryover will continue to be classified as 30 percent property in the carryover year.

[60] CARES Act § 2205(a) [P.L. 116–136]; Consolidated Appropriations Act, 2021 §213 [P.L. 116–260]

[61] §§ 62(a)(22) and (f).

[62] § 170(p).

Example 35

Assume the same facts as in Example 34. Because only $18,000 of the $30,000 value of the land is deducted in the current year, the balance of $12,000 may be carried over to the following year. But the carryover still will be treated as capital gain property and is subject to the 30%-of-AGI limitation in the carryover year.

In applying the percentage limitations, current charitable contributions must be claimed first before any carryovers can be considered. If carryovers involve more than one year, they are utilized in a first-in, first-out order.

10-5 Timing of Payments to Maximize Deductions

Because an individual may use the standard deduction in one year and itemize deductions in another year, maximum benefits can be obtained by shifting itemized deductions from one year to another. For example, if a taxpayer's itemized deductions and the standard deduction are approximately the same for each year of a two-year period, the taxpayer should use the standard deduction in one year and shift itemized deductions (to the extent permitted by law) to the other year. The individual could, for example, prepay a church pledge for a particular year to shift the deduction to the current year or avoid paying end-of-the-year medical expenses to shift the deduction to the following year.

It is sometimes possible to defer or accelerate the payment of certain deductible items (e.g., state taxes and charitable contributions) to maximize deductions when itemized deductions are close to the standard deduction. For instance, the final installment of estimated state income tax is generally due in mid-January (after the end of a given tax year). Accelerating the payment of the final installment to December could result in larger itemized deductions for the current year.

Timing to Maximize Deductions

Example 36

Jenny, who is single, expects to have itemized deductions of $11,600 in 2022 and $8,000 in 2023. She needs to pay $1,900 as the final installment on her 2022 estimated state income tax, which is due on January 15, 2023. The standard deduction for 2022 is $12,950 for single taxpayers. If Jenny pays the final installment of her 2022 state taxes in 2022, she increases her itemized deductions. If instead she pays it in January 2023 when she knows she will be claiming the standard deduction in 2023, she obtains no tax benefit for that payment.

As a result, making the final installment payment in 2022 is good tax planning. If Jenny pays the final installment in December 2022, and assuming that her state and local tax deduction is not limited, her itemized deductions will be $13,500 ($11,600 + $1,900) in 2022 and she will benefit from itemizing.

Example 37

Juan and Lisa Garcia are married and file a joint tax return. Their state income and real estate taxes are greater than $10,000 each year. They do not have a mortgage, and their health insurance typically covers all of their medical expenses. They usually make charitable contributions of about $10,000 each year. With these facts, the Garcias will claim the standard deduction ($25,900 in 2022) rather than itemize their deductions.

If the Garcias change the timing of their charitable contributions to make them every other year (or every third year), they can increase their deductions over that period of time. For example, if they opt to make no charitable contributions in 2022, they will claim the $25,900 standard deduction. If in 2023 they make $20,000 of charitable contributions, representing what they otherwise would have contributed in 2022 and 2023, they will claim itemized deductions of $30,000 (which will likely exceed their 2023 standard deduction). They can repeat this pattern to maximize their *from AGI* deductions over time.

10-6 Other Itemized Deductions

LO.7

List the expenses that are deductible as other itemized deductions.

In general, no deduction is allowed for personal, living, or family expenses.[63] However, a number of other expenses and losses are allowed as itemized deductions on Schedule A (Form 1040):

- Gambling losses up to the amount of gambling winnings.
- Impairment-related work expenses of a handicapped person.
- Federal estate tax on income in respect of a decedent.
- Deduction for repayment of amounts under a claim of right (but only if more than $3,000; discussed in text Section 18-1e).
- The unrecovered investment in an annuity contract when the annuity ceases by reason of death, discussed in text Section 4-4c.

Prior to 2018, certain other personal expenses were deductible to the extent, in total, they exceeded 2 percent of the taxpayer's AGI (and only if the taxpayer itemized deductions instead of claiming the standard deduction). These **miscellaneous itemized deductions** included unreimbursed employee business expenses, certain investment expenses, tax return preparation fees (other than for portions of the return related to business), and expenses related to hobby income (refer to text Section 6-3e). From 2018 through 2025, these expenses are not deductible.

10-7 Comprehensive Example of Schedule A

Jean Brown is single and had the following transactions for 2021:

Medicines that required a prescription	$ 830
Doctor and dentist bills paid and not reimbursed	3,120
Medical insurance premium payments	9,200
Contact lenses	370
Transportation for medical purposes on March 1, 2021 (388 miles × 16 cents per mile + $10.00 parking)	72
State income tax withheld (This amount exceeds the sales tax from the sales tax table.)	7,900
Real estate taxes	6,580
Interest paid on qualified residence mortgage (acquisition indebtedness)	4,340
Qualifying charitable contributions paid by check; proper documentation exists	2,160
Transportation in performing charitable services (800 miles × 14 cents per mile + $7.00 parking and tolls)	119
Unreimbursed employee expenses	1,870
Tax return preparation	450
Safe deposit box (used for keeping investment documents and tax records)	170

Jean's AGI is $120,000. The total of her itemized deductions is $21,211 (see the completed 2021 Schedule A on the following page). This amount is greater than her standard deduction of $12,550.[64]

[63] § 262.

[64] Jean's unreimbursed employee expenses, tax return preparation fee, and safe deposit box rental cost are miscellaneous itemized deductions. From 2018 through 2025, the deduction for these items has been suspended. In 2026, the total of these expenses ($2,490) will be deductible to the extent they exceed 2% of Jean's AGI.

SCHEDULE A (Form 1040) Department of the Treasury Internal Revenue Service (99)	**Itemized Deductions** ▶ Go to *www.irs.gov/ScheduleA* for instructions and the latest information. ▶ Attach to Form 1040 or 1040-SR. **Caution:** If you are claiming a net qualified disaster loss on Form 4684, see the instructions for line 16.	OMB No. 1545-0074 **2021** Attachment Sequence No. **07**

Name(s) shown on Form 1040 or 1040-SR	Your social security number
Jean Brown	*123-45-6789*

Section	Line	Description	Box	Amount	Line	Total
Medical and Dental Expenses		**Caution:** Do not include expenses reimbursed or paid by others.				
	1	Medical and dental expenses (see instructions)	1	*13,592*		
	2	Enter amount from Form 1040 or 1040-SR, line 11 [2] *120,000*				
	3	Multiply line 2 by 7.5% (0.075)	3	*9,000*		
	4	Subtract line 3 from line 1. If line 3 is more than line 1, enter -0-			4	*4,592*
Taxes You Paid	5	State and local taxes.				
	a	State and local income taxes or general sales taxes. You may include either income taxes or general sales taxes on line 5a, but not both. If you elect to include general sales taxes instead of income taxes, check this box ▶ ☐	5a	*7,900*		
	b	State and local real estate taxes (see instructions)	5b	*6,580*		
	c	State and local personal property taxes	5c			
	d	Add lines 5a through 5c	5d	*14,480*		
	e	Enter the smaller of line 5d or $10,000 ($5,000 if married filing separately)	5e	*10,000*		
	6	Other taxes. List type and amount ▶	6			
	7	Add lines 5e and 6			7	*10,000*
Interest You Paid **Caution:** Your mortgage interest deduction may be limited (see instructions).	8	Home mortgage interest and points. If you didn't use all of your home mortgage loan(s) to buy, build, or improve your home, see instructions and check this box ▶ ☐				
	a	Home mortgage interest and points reported to you on Form 1098. See instructions if limited	8a	*4,340*		
	b	Home mortgage interest not reported to you on Form 1098. See instructions if limited. If paid to the person from whom you bought the home, see instructions and show that person's name, identifying no., and address ▶	8b			
	c	Points not reported to you on Form 1098. See instructions for special rules	8c			
	d	Mortgage insurance premiums (see instructions)	8d			
	e	Add lines 8a through 8d	8e			
	9	Investment interest. Attach Form 4952 if required. See instructions	9			
	10	Add lines 8e and 9			10	*4,340*
Gifts to Charity **Caution:** If you made a gift and got a benefit for it, see instructions.	11	Gifts by cash or check. If you made any gift of $250 or more, see instructions	11	*2,160*		
	12	Other than by cash or check. If you made any gift of $250 or more, see instructions. You **must** attach Form 8283 if over $500	12	*119*		
	13	Carryover from prior year	13			
	14	Add lines 11 through 13			14	*2,279*
Casualty and Theft Losses	15	Casualty and theft loss(es) from a federally declared disaster (other than net qualified disaster losses). Attach Form 4684 and enter the amount from line 18 of that form. See instructions			15	
Other Itemized Deductions	16	Other—from list in instructions. List type and amount ▶			16	
Total Itemized Deductions	17	Add the amounts in the far right column for lines 4 through 16. Also, enter this amount on Form 1040 or 1040-SR, line 12a			17	*21,211*
	18	If you elect to itemize deductions even though they are less than your standard deduction, check this box ▶ ☐				

For Paperwork Reduction Act Notice, see the Instructions for Forms 1040 and 1040-SR. Cat. No. 17145C **Schedule A (Form 1040) 2021**

10-8 Tax Planning

LO.8

Identify tax planning strategies that can maximize the benefit of itemized deductions.

10-8a Maximizing the Medical Deduction

When a taxpayer anticipates that medical expenses will be close to the percentage floor for a year, the taxpayer should consider accelerating other medical expenses into the year. Any of the following techniques can help build a deduction by the end of the year:

- Incur the obligation for needed dental work or have needed work carried out.[65]
- Have elective remedial surgery that may have been postponed from prior years.
- Incur the obligation for capital improvements to the taxpayer's personal residence recommended by a physician (e.g., an air filtration system to alleviate a respiratory disorder).

The use of credit cards is deemed to be payment for purposes of timing the deductibility of charitable and medical expenses.

Example 38

On December 13, 2022, Mary (a calendar year taxpayer) purchases two pairs of prescription contact lenses and one pair of prescribed orthopedic shoes for a total of $850. These purchases are charged separately to Mary's credit card. On January 6, 2023, Mary receives her statement containing these charges and makes payment shortly thereafter.

The purchases are deductible as medical expenses in the year charged (2022) rather than in the year the account is settled (2023).

Recognizing which expenses qualify for the medical deduction also may be crucial to exceeding the percentage limitations.

Example 39

Ethan employs Leah (an unrelated party) to care for his incapacitated and dependent mother. Leah is not a trained nurse but spends approximately one-half of the time performing nursing duties (e.g., administering injections and providing physical therapy) and the rest of the time doing household chores. An allocable portion of Leah's wages that Ethan pays (including the employer's portion of FICA taxes) qualifies as a medical expense.

10-8b Ensuring the Charitable Contribution Deduction

For a charitable contribution deduction to be available, the recipient must be a qualified charitable organization. Sometimes the mechanics of how the contribution is carried out can determine whether a deduction results.

Example 40

Fumiko wants to donate $5,000 to her church's mission in Kobe, Japan. In this regard, she considers three alternatives:

1. Send the money directly to the mission.
2. Give the money to her church in Charlotte with the understanding that it is to be passed on to the mission.
3. Give the money directly to the missionary in charge of the mission who is currently in the United States on a fund-raising trip.

If Fumiko wants to obtain a deduction for the contribution, she should choose alternative 2. A direct donation to the mission (alternative 1) is not deductible because the mission is a foreign charity. A direct gift to the missionary (alternative 3) does not comply because an individual cannot be a qualified charity for income tax purposes.[66]

[65] Prepayment of medical expenses does not generate a current deduction unless the taxpayer is under an obligation to make the payment.

[66] *Thomas E. Lesslie*, 36 TCM 495, T.C.Memo. 1977–111.

When making noncash donations, the type of property chosen can have significant implications in determining the amount, if any, of the deduction.

Example 41

Sam wants to give $60,000 in value to his church in some form other than cash. In this connection, he considers four alternatives:

1. Stock held for two years as an investment with a basis of $100,000 and a fair market value of $60,000.
2. Stock held for five years as an investment with a basis of $10,000 and a fair market value of $60,000.
3. The rent-free use for a year of a building that normally leases for $5,000 a month.
4. A valuable stamp collection held as an investment and owned for 10 years with a basis of $10,000 and a fair market value of $60,000. The church plans to sell the collection if and when it is donated.

Alternative 1 is ill-advised as the subject of the gift. Even though Sam would obtain a deduction of $60,000, he would forgo the potential loss of $40,000 that would be recognized if the property were sold.[67]

Alternative 2 makes good sense because the deduction still is $60,000 and none of the $50,000 of appreciation that has occurred must be recognized as income.

Alternative 3 yields no deduction at all and is not a wise choice.

Alternative 4 involves tangible personalty that the church plans to sell. As a result, the amount of the deduction is limited to $10,000, the stamp collection's basis.[68]

For property transfers (particularly real estate), the ceiling limitations on the amount of the deduction allowed in any one year (50 percent, 30 percent, or 20 percent of AGI, as the case may be) could be a factor to take into account. With proper planning, donations can be controlled to stay within the limitations and avoid the need for a carryover of unused charitable contributions.

Example 42

Andrew wants to donate to Eastern University (a qualified charitable organization) a tract of unimproved land held as an investment. The land has been held for six years and has a current fair market value of $300,000 and a basis to Andrew of $50,000. Andrew's AGI for the current year is estimated to be $200,000, and he expects much the same for the next few years. In the current year, he deeds (transfers) an undivided one-fifth interest in the real estate to the university.

What has Andrew in Example 42 accomplished for income tax purposes? In the current year, he will be allowed a charitable contribution deduction of $60,000 ($\frac{1}{5}$ × $300,000), which will be within the applicable AGI limitation (30% × $200,000). Presuming no other charitable contributions for the year, Andrew has avoided the possibility of a carryover. In future years, Andrew can follow the same pattern. The only difficulty with this approach is the need to revalue the real estate each year before the donation, because the amount of the deduction is based on the fair market value of the interest contributed at the time of the donation.

The rules on documenting charitable contributions are crucial to the deduction. Thus, it is important for individuals who itemize their deductions to have and retain this documentation.

Example 43

Karen made several charitable contributions this year. She wrote 10 checks of $500 each to different charitable organizations. In addition, she donated some of her furniture with an estimated value of $1,200.

Karen may claim only the $5,000 of cash donations if she has the canceled checks (or other proof of payment). In addition, because each donation was $250 or more, she must have a contemporaneous written acknowledgment from the charity before she files her return.

continued

[67] *LaVar M. Withers*, 69 T.C. 900 (1978).

[68] No reduction of appreciation is necessary in alternative 2 because stock is intangible property and not tangible personalty.

Because Karen donated noncash items valued at over $500, she must complete a Form 8283, documenting the date each item was acquired, how it was acquired, the basis (generally, cost) and fair market value of each item, and how that value was determined. A contemporaneous written acknowledgment also is required for these items (since the donation was valued at $250 or more).

Karen can only claim a charitable contribution deduction for those items for which she has the required documentation.

10-8c Planning to Avoid Nondeductible Treatment

Many personal expenditures are not deductible (e.g., tax return preparation fees and unreimbursed employee business expenses). Consideration should be given to whether any of these nondeductible items can become deductible with planning and knowledge of the tax law. For example, if an individual has a sole proprietor business, the tax return preparation fees can be split between the nondeductible personal portion and the deductible portion related to the business and reported on Schedule C (Form 1040).[69]

Employees who must incur expenses for work (e.g., continuing education classes and uniform cleaning) should encourage their employer to reimburse them for these expenses. If the employer establishes an accountable plan, the expenses are deductible by the employer and not treated as income to the employee.[70]

Refocus on The Big Picture

Impact of Itemized Deductions on Major Purchases

Because the Federal tax law provides that qualified residence interest and real estate taxes are deductible by individual taxpayers, the after-tax cost of a home purchase will be reduced by the tax savings associated with these itemized tax deductions (see Example 1). Given the Williamsons' projected taxable income, they are in the 24 percent Federal income tax bracket and the 6 percent state income tax bracket (i.e., aggregate marginal tax bracket of 30 percent). As a result, the after-tax cost of financing the purchase of the home will be:

Nondeductible principal payments	$ 2,000
Deductible qualified residence interest and real estate taxes [($37,000 + $4,000) × (1 − 0.30)]	28,700
Total	$30,700
After-tax monthly cost ($30,700 ÷ 12)	$ 2,558

Because the Williamsons will be able to itemize their deductions if they purchase a new home and will be able to deduct most of their monthly house payment, the home purchase will be affordable (see Examples 17 and 22).

What If?

What if the Williamsons use the less expensive route to finance the purchase of their home by using their retirement and taxable portfolio as security for the loan? What may at first appear to be a cost-effective approach ends up being more costly when considering the impact of the tax law. With this approach, the interest expense is not deductible because it is not qualified residence interest (see Example 22); further, it is not deductible as investment interest (see text Section 11-4). Therefore, the after-tax cost of financing the home using this approach makes the home more expensive, and perhaps unaffordable, for the Williamsons.

Nondeductible principal and interest payments ($2,000 + $35,000)	$37,000
Deductible real estate taxes [$4,000 × (1 − 0.30)]	2,800
Total	$39,800
After-tax monthly cost ($39,800 ÷ 12)	$ 3,317

ISTOCK.COM/IZUSEK

[69] Rev.Rul. 92–29.

[70] Reg. § 1.62–2.

Key Terms

Acquisition indebtedness, 10-15
Capital gain property, 10-23
Charitable contribution, 10-18
Health Savings Account (HSA), 10-8
Home equity loans, 10-15
Medical expense, 10-3
Miscellaneous itemized deductions, 10-27
Ordinary income property, 10-22
Points, 10-16
Qualified residence interest, 10-14

Discussion Questions

1. **LO.1, 2** Dan, a self-employed individual taxpayer, prepared his own income tax return for the past year and has asked you to check it for accuracy. Your review indicates that Dan failed to claim certain business meals expenses. Will the correction of this omission affect the amount of medical expenses Dan can deduct? Explain.

2. **LO.2** Ángel was in an accident and required cosmetic surgery for injuries to his nose. He also had the doctor do additional surgery to reshape his chin, which had not been injured. Will the cosmetic surgery to Ángel's nose qualify as a medical expense? Will the cosmetic surgery to Ángel's chin qualify as a medical expense? Explain.

3. **LO.2, 8** Jerry and Elaine are comparing their tax situations. Both are paying all of the nursing home expenses of their parents. Jerry can include the expenses in computing his medical expense deduction, but Elaine cannot. What explanation can you offer for the difference?

Critical Thinking
Planning

4. **LO.2** Cheryl incurred $8,700 of medical expenses in November 2022. On December 5, the clinic where she was treated mailed her the insurance claim form it had prepared for her with a suggestion that she sign and return the form immediately to receive her reimbursement from the insurance company by December 31. What tax issues should Cheryl consider in deciding whether to sign and return the form in December 2022 or January 2023?

5. **LO.2** David, a sole proprietor of a bookstore, pays a $7,500 premium for medical insurance for him and his family. Joan, an employee of a small firm that doesn't provide her with medical insurance, pays medical insurance premiums of $8,000 for herself. How does the tax treatment differ for David and Joan?

6. **LO.2** Jayden, a calendar year taxpayer, paid $16,000 in medical expenses and sustained a $20,000 casualty loss in 2022 (the loss occurred in a Federally declared disaster area). He expects $12,000 of the medical expenses and $14,000 of the casualty loss to be reimbursed by insurance companies in 2023. Before considering any limitations on these deductions, how much can Jayden include in determining his itemized deductions for 2022?

7. **LO.2** Jacob, a self-employed taxpayer, is married and has two children. He has asked you to explain the tax and nontax advantages of creating a Health Savings Account (HSA) for him and his family.

Critical Thinking
Decision Making
Planning

8. **LO.5, 8** Michaela owns a principal residence in Georgia, a townhouse in San Francisco, and a yacht in Cape Cod. All of the properties have mortgages on which Michaela pays interest. What are the limitations on Michaela's mortgage interest deduction? What strategy should Michaela consider to maximize her mortgage interest deduction?

9. **LO.5, 8** Mason Gregg's car was destroyed by a flood that occurred in a Federally declared disaster area. Unfortunately, his insurance had lapsed two days before he incurred the loss. Mason uses his car for both business and personal use. Mason, who is self-employed, does not have adequate savings to replace the car and must borrow money to purchase a new car. He is considering using his credit card, at a 12% interest rate, to obtain funds for the purchase. Margaret, his wife, would prefer to sell some of their stock in Bluebird, Inc., to raise funds to purchase the new car. Mason does not want to sell the stock because it has declined in value since they purchased it and he is convinced that its price will increase in the next two years. Mason has suggested that they obtain conventional financing for the purchase from their bank, which charges 7% interest on car loans. Identify the tax issues and planning considerations related to each of the three alternatives for Mason and Margaret. Critical Thinking Planning

10. **LO.5** Commercial Bank has initiated an advertising campaign that encourages customers to take out loans secured by their home to pay for purchases of automobiles. Are there any tax advantages related to this type of borrowing? Explain.

11. **LO.5** Thomas purchased a personal residence from Monique. To sell the residence, Monique agreed to pay $5,500 in points related to Thomas's mortgage. Discuss the deductibility of the points.

12. **LO.6** The city of Lawrence recently was hit by a tornado, leaving many families in need of food, clothing, shelter, and other necessities. Betty contributed $500 to a family whose home was completely destroyed by the tornado. Jack contributed $700 to the family's church, which gave the money to the family. Discuss the deductibility of these contributions.

13. **LO.6** Mike purchased four $100 tickets to a fund-raising dinner and dance sponsored by the public library, a qualified charitable organization. In its advertising for the event, the library indicated that the cost of the tickets would be deductible for Federal income tax purposes. Comment on the library's assertion.

14. **LO.6, 8** William, a high school teacher, earns about $50,000 each year. In December 2022, he won $1,000,000 in the state lottery. William plans to donate $100,000 to his church. He has asked you, his tax adviser, whether he should donate the $100,000 in 2022 or 2023. Identify the tax issues related to William's decision. Critical Thinking Planning

Computational Exercises

15. **LO.2** Barbara incurred the following expenses during 2022: $840 dues at a health club she joined at the suggestion of her physician to improve her general physical condition, $240 for multiple vitamins and antioxidant vitamins, $3,500 for a smoking cessation program, $250 for nonprescription nicotine gum, $2,600 for insulin, and $7,200 for funeral expenses for her mother who passed away in June. Barbara's AGI for 2022 is $54,000. What is Barbara's medical expense deduction for 2022?

16. **LO.3, 4** Tabitha sells real estate on March 2 for $260,000. The buyer, Ramona, pays the real estate taxes of $5,200 for the calendar year, which is the real estate property tax year. Assume that this is *not* a leap year.
    a. Determine the real estate taxes apportioned to and deductible by the seller, Tabitha, and the amount of taxes deductible by Ramona.
    b. Calculate Ramona's basis in the property and the amount realized by Tabitha from the sale.

17. **LO.4** Pierre, a cash basis, unmarried taxpayer, had $1,400 of state income tax withheld during 2022. Also in 2022, Pierre paid $455 that was due when he filed his 2021 state income tax return and made estimated payments of $975 toward his 2022 state income tax liability. When Pierre files his 2022 Federal income tax return in April 2023, he elects to itemize deductions, which amount to $15,650, including the state income tax payments and withholdings, all of which reduce his taxable income.
    a. What is Pierre's 2022 state income tax deduction?
    b. As a result of overpaying his 2022 state income tax, Pierre receives a refund of $630 early in 2023. The standard deduction for single taxpayers for 2022 was $12,950. How much of the $630 will Pierre include in his 2023 gross income?

18. **LO.4** Derek, a cash basis, unmarried taxpayer, had $610 of state income tax withheld during 2022. Also in 2022, Derek paid $50 that was due when he filed his 2021 state income tax return and made estimated payments of $100 toward his 2022 state income tax liability. When Derek files his 2022 Federal income tax return in April 2023, he elects to take the standard deduction, which reduced his taxable income. As a result of overpaying his 2022 state income tax, Derek receives a refund of $435 early in 2023. How much of the $435 will Derek include in his 2023 gross income?

19. **LO.5** Miller owns a personal residence with a fair market value of $195,000 and an outstanding first mortgage of $157,500, which was used entirely to acquire the residence. This year, Miller gets a home equity loan of $10,000 to purchase a new fishing boat for personal use. How much of this mortgage debt is treated as qualified residence indebtedness?

20. **LO.6** Donna donates stock in Chipper Corporation to the American Red Cross on September 10, 2022. She purchased the stock for $18,100 on December 28, 2021, and it had a fair market value of $27,000 when she made the donation.
    a. What is Donna's charitable contribution deduction?
    b. Assume instead that the stock had a fair market value of $15,000 (rather than $27,000) when it was donated to the American Red Cross. What is Donna's charitable contribution deduction?
    c. What documentation should you request from Donna to confirm the amount of her charitable contribution deduction?

21. **LO. 5, 8** The Wilmoths plan to purchase a house but want to determine the after-tax cost of financing its purchase. Given their projected taxable income, the Wilmoths are in the 24% Federal income tax bracket and the 8% state income tax bracket (i.e., an aggregate marginal tax bracket of 32%). Assume that the Wilmoths will benefit from itemizing their deductions for both Federal and state purposes. The total cash outlay during the first year of ownership will be $23,400 ($1,200 principal payments, $22,200 qualified residence interest payments). Determine the initial year after-tax cost of financing the purchase of the home.

Problems

Communications

22. **LO.2** Emma Doyle is employed as a corporate attorney. For calendar year 2022, she had AGI of $75,000 and paid the following medical expenses:

Medical insurance premiums	$3,700
Doctor and dentist bills for Bob and April (Emma's parents)	6,800
Doctor and dentist bills for Emma	5,200
Prescription medicines for Emma	400
Nonprescription insulin for Emma	350

Bob and April would qualify as Emma's dependents except that they file a joint return. Emma's medical insurance policy does not cover them. Emma filed a claim for reimbursement of $2,800 of her own expenses with her insurance company in

December 2022 and received the reimbursement in January 2023. What is Emma's maximum allowable medical expense deduction for 2022? Prepare a memo for your firm's tax files in which you document your conclusions.

23. **LO.2** Reba is a single taxpayer. Lawrence, Reba's 84-year-old dependent grandfather, lived with Reba until this year, when he moved to Lakeside Nursing Home because he needs specialized medical and nursing care. During the year, Reba made the following payments on behalf of Lawrence:

Room at Lakeside	$11,000
Meals for Lawrence at Lakeside	2,200
Doctor and nurse fees at Lakeside	1,700
Cable TV service for Lawrence's room at Lakeside	380
Total	$15,280

Lakeside has medical staff in residence. Disregarding the AGI floor, how much, if any, of these expenses qualifies for a medical expense deduction by Reba?

24. **LO.2** Paul suffers from emphysema and severe allergies and, upon the recommendation of his physician, has a dust elimination system installed in his personal residence. In connection with the system, Paul incurs and pays the following amounts during 2022:

Doctor and hospital bills	$ 4,500
Dust elimination system	10,000
Increase in utility bills due to the system	450
Cost of certified appraisal	300

In addition, Paul pays $750 for prescribed medicines.

The system has an estimated useful life of 20 years. The appraisal was to determine the value of Paul's residence with and without the system. The appraisal states that his residence was worth $350,000 before the system was installed and $356,000 after the installation. Paul's AGI for the year was $50,000. How much is Paul's medical expense deduction in 2022?

25. **LO.2** For calendar year 2022, Giana was a self-employed consultant with no employees. She had $80,000 of net profit from consulting and paid $7,000 in medical insurance premiums on her policy covering 2022. How much of these premiums may Giana deduct as a deduction *for* AGI? How much may she deduct as an itemized deduction (subject to the AGI floor)?

26. **LO.2** During 2022, Susan incurred and paid the following expenses for Beth (her daughter), Ed (her father), and herself:

Surgery for Beth	$4,500
Red River Academy charges for Beth:	
Tuition	5,100
Room, board, and other expenses	4,800
Psychiatric treatment	5,100
Doctor bills for Ed	2,200
Prescription drugs for Susan, Beth, and Ed	780
Insulin for Ed	540
Nonprescription drugs for Susan, Beth, and Ed	570
Charges at Heartland Nursing Home for Ed:	
Medical care	5,000
Lodging	2,700
Meals	2,650

Beth qualifies as Susan's dependent, and Ed also would qualify except that he receives $7,400 of taxable retirement benefits from his former employer. Beth's psychiatrist recommended Red River Academy because of its small classes and specialized psychiatric treatment program that is needed to treat Beth's illness. Ed, who is a paraplegic and diabetic, entered Heartland in October. Heartland offers the type of care that he requires.

Upon the recommendation of a physician, Susan has an air filtration system installed in her personal residence. She suffers from severe allergies. In connection with this equipment, Susan incurs and pays the following amounts during the year:

Filtration system and cost of installation	$6,500
Increase in utility bills due to the system	700
Cost of certified appraisal	360

The system has an estimated useful life of 10 years. The appraisal was to determine the value of Susan's residence with and without the system. The appraisal states that the system increased the value of Susan's residence by $2,200. Ignoring the AGI floor, what is the total of Susan's expenses that qualifies for the medical expense deduction?

Critical Thinking

27. **LO.2** In May, Rebecca's daughter, Isabella, sustained a serious injury that made it impossible for her to continue living alone. Isabella, who is a novelist, moved back into Rebecca's home after the accident. Isabella has begun writing a novel based on her recent experiences. To accommodate Isabella, Rebecca incurred significant remodeling expenses (widening hallways, building a separate bedroom and bathroom, and making kitchen appliances accessible to Isabella). In addition, Rebecca had an indoor swimming pool constructed so that Isabella could do rehabilitation exercises prescribed by her physician.

In September, Isabella underwent major reconstructive surgery in Denver. The surgery was performed by Dr. Rama Patel, who specializes in treating injuries of the type Isabella sustained. Rebecca drove Isabella from Champaign, Illinois, to Denver, a total of 1,100 miles, in Isabella's specially equipped van. They left Champaign on Tuesday morning and arrived in Denver on Thursday afternoon. Rebecca incurred expenses for gasoline, highway tolls, meals, and lodging while traveling to Denver. Rebecca stayed in a motel near the clinic for eight days while Isabella was hospitalized. Identify the relevant tax issues based on this information, and prepare a list of questions you would need to ask Rebecca and Isabella to advise them as to the resolution of any issues you have identified.

28. **LO.2** In the current year, Roger pays a $3,000 premium for high-deductible medical insurance for him and his family. In addition, he contributed $2,600 to a Health Savings Account.

    a. How much may Roger deduct if he is self-employed? Is the deduction *for* AGI or *from* AGI?

    b. How much may Roger deduct if he is an employee? Is the deduction *for* AGI or *from* AGI?

29. **LO.3, 4** Alicia sold her personal residence to Rick on June 30 for $300,000. Before the sale, Alicia paid the real estate tax of $4,380 for the calendar year. For income tax purposes, the deduction is apportioned as follows: $2,160 to Alicia and $2,220 to Rick. What is Rick's basis in the residence?

30. **LO.4** Nichole, who is single and uses the cash method of accounting, lives in a state that imposes an income tax. In April 2022, she files her state income tax return for 2021 and pays an additional $1,000 in state income taxes. During 2022, her withholdings for state income tax purposes amount to $7,400, and she pays

estimated state income tax of $700. In April 2023, she files her state income tax return for 2022, claiming a refund of $1,800. Nichole receives the refund in August 2023. Nichole has no other state or local tax expenses.

a. Assuming that Nichole itemized deductions in 2022, how much may she claim as a deduction for state income taxes on her Federal return for calendar year 2022 (filed April 2023)?

b. Assuming that Nichole itemized deductions in 2022 (which totaled $20,000), how will the refund of $1,800 that she received in 2023 be treated for Federal income tax purposes?

c. Assume that Nichole itemized deductions in 2022 (which totaled $20,000) and that she elects to have the $1,800 refund applied toward her 2023 state income tax liability. How will the $1,800 be treated for Federal income tax purposes?

d. Assuming that Nichole did not itemize deductions in 2022, how will the refund of $1,800 received in 2023 be treated for Federal income tax purposes?

31. **LO.5** This year, Amy purchased a personal residence at a cost of $1,000,000. She borrowed $800,000 secured by the home to make the purchase. This year, she paid interest expense on this mortgage of $12,000. How much may she deduct?

32. **LO.6** This year, Nadia donates $4,000 to Eastern University's athletic department. The payment guarantees that Nadia will have preferred seating at football games near the 50-yard line. Assume that Nadia subsequently buys four $100 game tickets. How much can she deduct as a charitable contribution to the university's athletic department?

33. **LO.6** Liz had AGI of $130,000 in 2022. She donated Bluebird Corporation stock with a basis of $10,000 to a qualified charitable organization on July 5, 2022.

a. What is the amount of Liz's deduction assuming that she purchased the stock on December 3, 2021, and the stock had a fair market value of $17,000 when she made the donation?

b. Assume the same facts as in part (a), except that Liz purchased the stock on July 1, 2019.

c. Assume the same facts as in part (a), except that the stock had a fair market value of $7,500 (rather than $17,000) when Liz donated it to the charity.

34. **LO.6, 8** Ramon had AGI of $180,000 in 2023. He is considering making a charitable contribution this year to the American Heart Association, a qualified charitable organization. Determine the current allowable charitable contribution deduction in each of the following independent situations, and indicate the treatment for any amount that is not deductible currently. Identify any planning ideas to minimize Ramon's tax liability.

Critical Thinking
Decision Making
Planning

a. A cash gift of $95,000.

b. A gift of OakCo stock worth $95,000 on the contribution date. Ramon had acquired the stock as an investment two years ago at a cost of $84,000.

c. A gift of a painting worth $95,000 that Ramon purchased three years ago for $60,000. The charity has indicated that it would sell the painting to generate cash to fund medical research.

d. Ramon has decided to make a cash gift to the American Heart Association of $113,000. However, he is considering delaying his gift until the following year when his AGI will increase to $300,000 and he will be in the 32% income tax bracket, an increase from his 2023 income tax bracket of 24%. Ramon asks you to determine the tax savings from the tax deduction in present value terms if he were to make the gift this year rather than delay the gift until next year. See Appendix E for the present value factors, and assume a 6% discount rate.

35. **LO.6** On December 27, 2022, Roberta purchased four tickets to a charity ball sponsored by the city of San Diego for the benefit of underprivileged children. Each ticket cost $200 and had a fair market value of $35. On the same day as the purchase, Roberta gave the tickets to the minister of her church for personal use by his family. At the time of the gift of the tickets, Roberta pledged $4,000 to the building fund of her church. The pledge was satisfied by a check dated December 31, 2022, but not mailed until January 3, 2023.
    a. Presuming that Roberta is a cash basis and calendar year taxpayer, how much can she deduct as a charitable contribution for 2022?
    b. Would the amount of the deduction be any different if Roberta was an accrual basis taxpayer? Explain.

Communications
Critical Thinking
Planning

36. **LO.6, 8** In December of each year, Eleanor Young contributes 10% of her gross income to the United Way (a 50% organization). Eleanor, who is in the 24% marginal tax bracket, is considering the following alternatives for satisfying the contribution.

	Fair Market Value
(1) Cash donation	$23,000
(2) Unimproved land held for six years ($3,000 basis)	23,000
(3) Blue Corporation stock held for eight months ($3,000 basis)	23,000
(4) Gold Corporation stock held for two years ($28,000 basis)	23,000

Eleanor has asked you to help her decide which of the potential contributions listed above will be most advantageous taxwise. Evaluate the four alternatives, and write a letter to Eleanor to communicate your advice to her. Her address is 2622 Bayshore Drive, Berkeley, CA 94709.

Communications
Critical Thinking
Planning

37. **LO.2, 3, 4, 5, 7, 8** Bart and Elizabeth Forrest are married and have no dependents. They have asked you to advise them whether they should file jointly or separately in 2022. Bart incurred some significant medical expenses during the year related to an unexpected surgery. They present you with the following information:

	Bart	Elizabeth	Joint
Salary (Bart)	$38,000		
Salary (Elizabeth)		$110,000	
Interest income	400	1,200	$2,200
Deductions *for* AGI	2,400	14,000	
Medical expenses	10,427	3,358	
State income tax	900	11,800	
Real estate tax			5,800
Mortgage interest			4,200
Unreimbursed employee expenses	1,200		

If they file separately, Bart and Elizabeth will split the real estate tax and mortgage interest deductions equally. Write Bart and Elizabeth a letter in which you make and explain a recommendation on filing status for 2022. Bart and Elizabeth reside at 2003 Highland Drive, Durham, NC 27707.

38. **LO.2, 3, 4, 5, 6, 7** Evan is single and has AGI of $277,300 in 2022. His potential itemized deductions before any limitations for the year total $52,300 and consist of the following:

Medical expenses (before the 7.5%-of-AGI limitation)	$31,000
Interest on home mortgage	8,700
State income taxes	9,500
Real estate taxes	3,600
Charitable contributions	2,500

After all necessary adjustments are made, what is the amount of itemized deductions Evan may claim?

39. **LO.2, 3, 4, 5, 6, 7** Linda, who files as a single taxpayer, had AGI of $280,000 for 2022. She incurred the following expenses and losses during the year:

Medical expenses (before the 7.5%-of-AGI limitation)	$33,000
State and local income taxes	4,800
State sales tax	1,300
Real estate taxes	6,000
Home mortgage interest	5,000
Automobile loan interest	750
Credit card interest	1,000
Charitable contributions	7,000
Casualty loss (before the 10%-of-AGI limitation but after the $100 floor; not in a Federally declared disaster area)	34,000
Unreimbursed employee business expenses	7,600

Calculate Linda's allowable itemized deductions for the year.

40. **LO.2, 3, 4, 5, 6, 7** For calendar year 2022, Stuart and Pamela Gibson file a joint return reflecting AGI of $350,000. Their itemized deductions are as follows:

Casualty loss in a Federally declared disaster area (not covered by insurance; before the 10%-of-AGI limitation but after the $100 floor)	$48,600
Home mortgage interest (loan qualifies as acquisition indebtedness)	19,000
Credit card interest	800
Property taxes on home	16,300
Charitable contributions	28,700
State income tax	18,000
Tax return preparation fees	1,200

Calculate the amount of itemized deductions the Gibsons may claim for the year.

Tax Return Problems

Decision Making

Planning

Tax Forms Problem

ProConnect™ Tax

41. Alice J. and Bruce M. Byrd are married taxpayers who file a joint return. Their Social Security numbers are 123-45-6784 and 111-11-1113, respectively. Alice's birthday is September 21, 1974, and Bruce's is June 27, 1973. They live at 473 Revere Avenue, Lowell, MA 01850. Alice is the office manager for Lowell Dental Clinic, 433 Broad Street, Lowell, MA 01850 (Employer Identification Number 98-7654321). Bruce is the manager of a Super Burgers fast-food outlet owned and operated by Plymouth Corporation, 1247 Central Avenue, Hauppauge, NY 11788 (Employer Identification Number 11-1111111).

The following information is shown on their Wage and Tax Statements (Form W–2) for 2021.

Line	Description	Alice	Bruce
1	Wages, tips, other compensation	$58,000	$62,100
2	Federal income tax withheld	4,500	5,300
3	Social Security wages	58,000	62,100
4	Social Security tax withheld	3,596	3,850
5	Medicare wages and tips	58,000	62,100
6	Medicare tax withheld	841	900
15	State	Massachusetts	Massachusetts
16	State wages, tips, etc.	58,000	62,100
17	State income tax withheld	2,950	3,100

The Byrds provide over half of the support of their two children, Cynthia (born January 25, 1997, Social Security number 123-45-6788) and John (born February 7, 2001, Social Security number 123-45-6780). Both children are full-time students and live with the Byrds except when they are away at college. Cynthia earned $6,200 from a summer internship in 2021, and John earned $3,800 from a part-time job. Both children received scholarships covering tuition and materials.

During 2021, the Byrds provided 60% of the total support of Bruce's widower father, Sam Byrd (born March 6, 1945, Social Security number 123-45-6787). Sam lived alone and covered the rest of his support with his Social Security benefits. Sam died in November, and Bruce, the beneficiary of a policy on Sam's life, received life insurance proceeds of $1,600,000 on December 28.

The Byrds had the following expenses relating to their personal residence during 2021:

Property taxes	$5,000
Qualified interest on home mortgage (acquisition indebtedness)	8,700
Repairs to roof	5,750
Utilities	4,100
Fire and theft insurance	1,900

The Byrds had the following medical expenses for 2021:

Medical insurance premiums	$4,500
Doctor bill for Sam incurred in 2020 and not paid until 2021	7,600
Operation for Sam	8,500
Prescription medicines for Sam	900
Hospital expenses for Sam	3,500
Reimbursement from insurance company, received in 2021	3,600

The medical expenses for Sam represent most of the 60% that Bruce contributed toward his father's support.

Other relevant information follows:

- When they filed their 2020 state return in 2021, the Byrds paid additional state income tax of $900.
- During 2021, Alice and Bruce attended a dinner dance sponsored by the Lowell Police Disability Association (a qualified charitable organization). The Byrds paid $300 for the tickets. The cost of comparable entertainment would normally be $50.
- The Byrds contributed $5,000 to Lowell Presbyterian Church and gave used clothing (cost of $1,200 and fair market value of $350) to the Salvation Army. All donations are supported by receipts, and the clothing is in very good condition.
- Via a crowdfunding site (gofundme.com), Alice and Bruce made a gift to a needy family who lost their home in a fire ($400). In addition, they made several cash gifts to homeless individuals downtown (estimated to be $65).
- In 2021, the Byrds received interest income of $2,750, which was reported on a Form 1099–INT from Second National Bank, 125 Oak Street, Lowell, MA 01850 (Employer Identification Number 98-7654322).
- The home mortgage interest was reported on Form 1098 by Lowell Commercial Bank, P.O. Box 1000, Lowell, MA 01850 (Employer Identification Number 98-7654323). The mortgage (outstanding balance of $425,000 as of January 1, 2021) was taken out by the Byrds on May 1, 2017.
- Alice's employer requires that all employees wear uniforms to work. During 2021, Alice spent $850 on new uniforms and $566 on laundry charges.

- Bruce paid $400 for an annual subscription to the *Journal of Franchise Management* and $741 for annual membership dues to his professional association.
- Neither Alice's nor Bruce's employer reimburses for employee expenses.
- The Byrds do not keep the receipts for the sales taxes they paid and had no major purchases subject to sales tax.
- This year, the Byrds gave each of their children $2,000, which was then deposited into their Roth IRAs.
- Alice and Bruce paid no estimated Federal income tax, and they did not engage in any virtual currency transactions during the year. Neither Alice nor Bruce wants to designate $3 to the Presidential Election Campaign Fund. The Byrds received the appropriate recovery rebates (economic impact payments); related questions in ProConnect Tax should be ignored.

Part 1—Tax Computation
Compute net tax payable or refund due for Alice and Bruce Byrd for 2021, and complete their 2021 Federal tax return using appropriate forms and schedules. If they have overpaid their taxes, they want the amount to be refunded to them. Suggested software: ProConnect Tax.

Part 2—Tax Planning
Alice and Bruce are planning some significant changes for 2022. They have provided you with the following information and asked you to project their taxable income and tax liability for 2022.

The Byrds will invest the $1,600,000 of life insurance proceeds in short-term certificates of deposit (CDs) and use the interest for living expenses during 2022. They expect to earn total interest of $32,000 on the CDs.

Bruce has been promoted to regional manager, and his salary for 2022 will be $88,000. He estimates that state income tax withheld will increase by $4,000 and the Social Security tax withheld will be $5,456.

Alice, who has been diagnosed with a serious illness, will take a leave of absence from work during 2022, so she will not receive a salary or incur any work-related expenses during the year. The estimated cost for her medical treatment is $15,400, of which $6,400 will be reimbursed by their insurance company in 2022. Their medical insurance premiums will increase to $9,769. Property taxes on their residence are expected to increase to $5,100. The Byrds' home mortgage interest expense and charitable contributions are expected to be unchanged from 2021.

John will graduate from college in December 2021 and will take a job in New York City in January 2022. His starting salary will be $46,000.

Assume that all of the information reported in 2021 will be the same in 2022 unless other information has been presented above.

42. Paul and Donna Decker are married taxpayers, ages 44 and 42, respectively, who file a joint return for 2022. The Deckers live at 1121 College Avenue, Carmel, IN 46032. Paul is an assistant manager at Carmel Motor Inn, and Donna is a teacher at Carmel Elementary School. They present you with W–2 forms that reflect the following information: Tax Computation Problem

	Paul	Donna
Salary	$68,000	$56,000
Federal tax withheld	6,770	6,630
State income tax withheld	1,400	1,100
FICA (Social Security and Medicare) withheld	5,202	4,284
Social Security numbers	111-11-1112	123-45-6789

Donna is the custodial parent of two children from a previous marriage who reside with the Deckers throughout the school year. The children, Larry and Jane Parker, reside with their father, Bob, during the summer. Relevant information for the children follows:

	Larry	Jane
Age	16	18
Social Security numbers	123-45-6788	123-45-6787
Months spent with Deckers	9	9

Under the divorce decree, Bob pays child support of $150 per month per child during the nine months the children live with the Deckers. Bob says that he spends $200 per month per child during the three summer months they reside with him. Donna and Paul can document that they provide $2,000 support per child per year. The divorce decree is silent as to which parent can claim the exemptions for the children.

In August, Paul and Donna added a suite to their home to provide more comfortable accommodations for Hannah Snyder (123-45-6786), Donna's mother, who had moved in with them in February 2021 after the death of Donna's father. Not wanting to borrow money for this addition, Paul sold 300 shares of Acme Corporation stock for $50 per share on May 3, 2022, and used the proceeds of $15,000 to cover construction costs. The Deckers had purchased the stock on April 29, 2017, for $25 per share. They received dividends of $750 on the jointly owned stock a month before the sale.

Hannah, who is 66 years old, received $7,500 in Social Security benefits during the year, of which she gave the Deckers $2,000 to use toward household expenses and deposited the remainder in her personal savings account. The Deckers determine that they have spent $2,500 of their own money for food, clothing, medical expenses, and other items for Hannah. They do not know what the rental value of Hannah's suite would be, but they estimate it would be at least $300 per month.

Interest paid during the year included the following:

Home mortgage interest (paid to Carmel Federal Savings & Loan)	$7,890
Interest on an automobile loan (paid to Carmel National Bank)	1,660
Interest on Citibank Visa card	620

In July, Paul hit a submerged rock while boating. Fortunately, he was uninjured after being thrown from the boat and landing in deep water. However, the boat, which was uninsured, was destroyed. Paul had paid $25,000 for the boat in June 2021, and its value was appraised at $18,000 on the date of the accident.

The Deckers paid doctor and hospital bills of $12,700 and were reimbursed $2,000 by their insurance company. They spent $640 for prescription drugs and medicines and $5,904 for premiums on their health insurance policy. They have filed additional claims of $1,200 with their insurance company and have been told they will receive payment for that amount in January 2023. Included in the amounts paid for doctor and hospital bills were payments of $380 for Hannah and $850 for the children.

Additional information of potential tax consequence follows:

Real estate taxes paid	$6,850
Sales taxes paid (per table)	1,379
Contributions to church	4,600
Appraised value of books donated to public library	740
Refund of state income tax for 2021 (the Deckers itemized on their 2021 Federal tax return, their total state and local taxes were less than $10,000, and their total itemized deductions exceeded their standard deduction by $5,400)	1,520

Compute net tax payable or refund due for the Deckers for 2022.

Research Problems

the answer company™
THOMSON REUTERS®

Note: Solutions to the Research Problems can be prepared by using the Thomson Reuters Checkpoint™ online tax research database, which accompanies this textbook. Solutions can also be prepared by using research materials found in a typical tax library.

Research Problem 1. Jane suffers from a degenerative spinal disorder. Her physician said that swimming could help prevent the onset of permanent paralysis and recommended the installation of a swimming pool at her residence for her use. Jane's residence had a market value of approximately $500,000 before the swimming pool was installed. The swimming pool was built, and an appraiser estimated that the value of Jane's home increased by $98,000 because of the addition.

The pool cost $194,000, and Jane claimed a medical expense deduction of $96,000 ($194,000 − $98,000) on her tax return. Upon audit of the return, the IRS determined that an adequate pool should have cost $70,000 and would increase the value of her home by only $31,000. Thus, the IRS claims that Jane is entitled to a deduction of only $39,000 ($70,000 − $31,000).

a. Is there any ceiling limitation on the amount deductible as a medical expense? Explain.

b. Can capital expenditures be deductible as medical expenses? Explain.

c. What is the significance of a "minimum adequate facility"? Should aesthetic or architectural qualities be considered in the determination? Why or why not?

Research Problem 2. Ken and Mary Jane Blough, your neighbors, have asked you for advice after receiving correspondence in the mail from the IRS. You learn that the IRS is asking for documentation in support of the itemized deductions the Bloughs claimed on a recent tax return. The Bloughs tell you that their income in the year of question was $75,000. Because their record-keeping habits are poor, they felt justified in claiming itemized deductions equal to the amounts that represent the average claimed by other taxpayers in their income bracket. These averages are calculated and reported by the IRS annually based on actual returns filed in an earlier year. Accordingly, they claimed medical expenses of $7,102, taxes of $6,050, interest of $10,659, and charitable contributions of $2,693. What advice do you give the Bloughs?

Partial list of research aids:
Cheryl L. de Werff, T.C. Summary Opinion, 2011–29.

Research Problem 3. Marcia, a shareholder in a corporation with stores in five states, donated stock with a basis of $10,000 to a qualified charitable organization in 2021. Although the stock of the corporation was not traded on a public stock exchange, many shares had been sold over the past several years. Based on the average selling price for the stock in 2021, Marcia deducted $95,000 on her 2021 tax return. Marcia received a notice from the IRS that the $95,000 deduction had been reduced to $10,000 because she had not obtained a qualified appraisal or attached a summary of her appraisal to her tax return. Marcia has asked you to advise her on this matter. Write a letter containing your conclusions to Ms. Marcia Meyer, 1311 Santos Court, San Bruno, CA 94066. Communications

Partial list of research aids:
Reg. § 1.170A–13(c)(2).

Research Problem 4. On March 5, 2017, the Hortons borrowed $100,000 against the equity in their personal residence with the loan secured by that home. In 2017, they were able to deduct the interest expense on this loan as home equity interest expense [an itemized deduction on Schedule A (Form 1040)]. The Tax Cuts and Jobs Act of 2017 disallows this interest expense deduction for 2018 through 2025. The Hortons'

CPA has asked them to review their financial records for February and March of 2017. They discover that they sold Disney stock on February 20, 2017, and used the proceeds to purchase Microsoft stock. Why is their CPA asking them for this information? How might this stock purchase in March 2017 help them obtain a deduction for all or part of the interest paid in 2018 and later on this home equity loan?

Partial list of research aids:
Temp.Reg. § 1.163–8T and Reg. § 1.163–15.

Use internet tax resources to address the following questions. Look for reliable websites and blogs of the IRS and other government agencies, media outlets, businesses, tax professionals, academics, think tanks, and political outlets.

Research Problem 5. The Federal government incurs a cost for every item that is deductible in the computation of taxable income. These costs, which take the form of forgone tax revenue, are often referred to as "tax expenditures." The Joint Committee on Taxation regularly estimates the current and projected tax expenditures associated with a long list of provisions in the tax law. Locate the Joint Committee on Taxation's most recent analysis, and identify the current tax expenditure associated with the deductions for medical expenses, interest on student loans, mortgage interest, and charitable contributions. How are these costs expected to change over the next five years? How is the concept of tax expenditures helpful to tax policy analysts?

Research Problem 6. Look for reliable data on how many individuals are affected by the $10,000 SALT cap. Use that data to make an argument for or against the cap.

Becker CPA Review Questions

Becker

1. In the current year, Wells paid the following expenses:

Premiums on an insurance policy against loss of earnings due to sickness or accident	$3,000
Physical therapy after spinal surgery	2,000
Premium on an insurance policy that covers reimbursement for the cost of prescription drugs	500

In the current year, Wells recovered $1,500 of the $2,000 that she paid for physical therapy through insurance reimbursement from a group medical policy paid for by her employer. Disregarding the adjusted gross income percentage threshold, what amount could be claimed on Wells's current-year income tax return for medical expenses?

a. $4,000
b. $3,500
c. $1,000
d. $500

2. Jordan Johnson is single and has adjusted gross income of $50,000 in the current year. Additional information is as follows:

State income taxes paid	$2,000
Mortgage interest on her personal residence	9,000
Points paid on purchase of her personal residence	1,000
Deductible contributions to her IRA	3,000
Uninsured realized casualty loss (in a Federal disaster area)	6,000
Tax preparation fees for her prior year income tax return	400

What amount may Jordan claim as itemized deductions on her current-year income tax return?

a. $12,000
c. $13,300
b. $12,900
d. $15,900

3. Sydney, a single taxpayer who itemizes deductions, had $80,000 in adjusted gross income in year 2. During the year, she contributed $15,000 to her church. She also had a $17,000 contribution carryover from her year 1 church contributions. What is the maximum amount of charitable deduction that Sydney may claim on her year 2 income tax return?

a. $40,000
c. $19,200
b. $32,000
d. $15,000

4. Kurstie received an $800 state income tax refund this year. Kurstie deducted $3,000 of state income taxes paid in the prior year as part of her itemized deductions. Which of the following statements regarding the taxability of Kurstie's refund is true?

a. If Kurstie's itemized deductions exceeded the standard deduction by $200, then the $800 refund is included in gross income.
b. If Kurstie's itemized deductions exceeded the standard deduction by $200, then $200 of the refund is included in gross income.
c. If Kurstie claimed the standard deduction instead, then the $800 refund is taxable.
d. Kurstie must include $3,000 in gross income in the current year.

5. Which of the following would preclude a taxpayer from deducting student loan interest expense?

a. The total amount paid is $1,000.
b. The taxpayer is single with AGI of $55,000.
c. The taxpayer is married filing jointly with AGI of $120,000.
d. The taxpayer is a dependent of another taxpayer.

6. Which of the following may *not* be claimed as a deduction by a taxpayer who claims the standard deduction?

a. Interest penalty on early withdrawal of savings
b. Self-employed health insurance
c. State income tax paid
d. IRA contribution

7. Chandler's home was damaged by a hurricane in a Federally declared disaster area. The fair market value of his home before the hurricane was $300,000. After the hurricane, the fair market value of the home dropped to $250,000. Damage to his home was estimated at $75,000. The adjusted basis of Chandler's home before the hurricane was $150,000. Chandler received an insurance payment for the damage in the amount of $30,000. Chandler's AGI is $90,000. What is Chandler's deductible casualty loss?

a. $65,900
c. $35,900
b. $49,900
d. $10,900

Chapter 11

Investor Losses

Learning Objectives: *After completing Chapter 11, you should be able to:*

- **LO.1** **Explain the tax shelter problem and the reasons for the at-risk and passive activity loss limitations.**
- **LO.2** **Explain the at-risk limitation.**
- **LO.3** **Describe how the passive activity loss rules limit deductions for losses and identify the taxpayers subject to these restrictions.**
- **LO.4** **Define passive activity and describe the rules for identifying an activity.**
- **LO.5** **Identify the tests for material participation.**
- **LO.6** **Describe the nature of rental activities under the passive activity loss rules.**
- **LO.7** **Determine the relationship between the at-risk and passive activity loss limitations.**
- **LO.8** **Recognize the special treatment available to certain real estate activities.**
- **LO.9** **Determine the proper tax treatment on the disposition of a passive activity.**
- **LO.10** **Identify restrictions placed on the deductibility of investor losses and deductions, including those that apply to investment interest.**
- **LO.11** **Suggest tax planning strategies to minimize the effect of the passive activity loss and investment interest limitations and recognize the general impact of the additional tax on net investment income.**

Chapter Outline

11-1 The Tax Shelter Problem, 11-2

11-2 At-Risk Limits, 11-4

11-3 Passive Activity Loss Limits, 11-5
- 11-3a Classification and Tax Treatment of Passive Activity Income and Losses, 11-5
- 11-3b Taxpayers Subject to the Passive Activity Loss Rules, 11-9
- 11-3c Rules for Determining Passive Activities, 11-10
- 11-3d Interaction of the At-Risk and Passive Activity Loss Limits, 11-15
- 11-3e Special Passive Activity Rules for Real Estate Activities, 11-16
- 11-3f Dispositions of Passive Activities, 11-20

11-4 Investment Interest Limitation, 11-21
- 11-4a Limitation Imposed, 11-21
- 11-4b Computation of Allowable Deduction, 11-23

11-5 Other Investment Losses, 11-23

11-6 Tax Planning, 11-24
- 11-6a Minimizing the Impact of the Passive Activity Loss Limits, 11-24
- 11-6b Maximizing the Investment Interest Deduction, 11-26
- 11-6c Effect of the Additional Tax on Net Investment Income, 11-26

RIDO/SHUTTERSTOCK.COM

The Big Picture

Investor Loss Limitations Affect the Viability of Certain Investment Opportunities

Ana and Jim Lopez are considering ways to enhance their financial security. In fact, they are willing to borrow a substantial sum so that they can make an appropriate investment.

Currently, Ana and Jim's sole sources of income are their salaries, totaling $180,000, from their full-time jobs. Their most significant asset is their personal residence (fair market value of $500,000 with a mortgage of $350,000). Each has a retirement plan at work; both are fully funding those plans as allowed by the law. The Lopezes' financial planner suggests that they borrow $50,000 at 4 percent and use the proceeds to make *one* of the following investments:

- A high-growth, low-yield portfolio of marketable securities. The portfolio's value is expected to grow 8 percent each year.
- An interest in a limited partnership that owns and operates orange groves in Florida. The limited partnership interest is expected to generate tax losses of $12,000 in each of the next five years, after which profits are expected. Assuming the losses are deductible when incurred, their financial planner predicts that the Lopezes would average an annual 8 percent return over a 10-year period.
- An interest in a local general partnership that owns and rents apartments to college students. This partnership interest also would generate losses of $12,000 per year for five years, after which profits would follow. Assuming the losses are deductible when incurred, these expected profits and losses would produce an average annual total return of 8 percent over a 10-year period.

Ana and Jim want to choose the alternative that produces the best after-tax return over a 10-year planning horizon. They are aware, however, that tax restrictions may limit the advantages of some of these investment options. In this connection, evaluate each option.

Read the chapter and formulate your response.

Framework 1040 **Tax Formula for Individuals**

This chapter covers the boldfaced portions of the Tax Formula for Individuals that was introduced in Concept Summary 3.1 on p. 3-3. Below those portions are the sections of Form 1040 where the results are reported.

Income *(broadly defined)*	$ xx,xxx
Less: Exclusions	(x,xxx)
Gross income	**$xx,xxx**

FORM 1040 (p. 1)

7	Capital gain or (loss). Attach Schedule D if required, If not required, check here ▶ ☐

FORM 1040 (Schedule 1)

3	Business income or (loss). Attach Schedule C
4	Other gains or (losses). Attach Form 4797
5	Rental real estate, royalties, partnerships, S corporations, trusts, etc. Attach Schedule E

Less: Deductions *for* adjusted gross income	**(x,xxx)**
Adjusted gross income	$ xx,xxx
Less: The greater of total itemized deductions *or* the standard deduction	**(x,xxx)**

FORM 1040 (p. 1)

12a	**Standard deduction or itemized deductions** (from Schedule A)

Charitable contributions if you take the standard deduction*	(xxx)
Personal and dependency exemptions**	(x,xxx)
Deduction for qualified business income***	(x,xxx)
Taxable income	$ xx,xxx
Tax on taxable income *(see Tax Tables or Tax Rate Schedules)*	$ x,xxx
Less: Tax credits *(including income taxes withheld and prepaid)*	(xxx)
Tax due (or refund)	$ xxx

*For 2021, married taxpayers may claim up to $600 of cash charitable donations ($300 if unmarried).

**Exemption deductions are not allowed from 2018 through 2025.

***Only applies from 2018 through 2025.

As discussed in Chapter 6, a tax deduction for an expense or a loss is not allowed unless specifically permitted by Congress. For example, losses can be recognized and deducted in the case of certain unprofitable investments only because the Code allows them. These losses can arise from the operation of an activity *or* on its sale. For most individual taxpayers, deductible investor losses come within the scope of § 165(c)(2) relating to transactions entered into for profit.[1] But what happens if the investment is mostly motivated by the tax loss it generates? Or what if the investment generates expenses that offset ordinary income and it later is expected to produce appreciation taxed at capital gain rates? This chapter addresses these tax minimization strategies and the rules put in place to restrict their use.

LO.1

Explain the tax shelter problem and the reasons for the at-risk and passive activity loss limitations.

11-1 The Tax Shelter Problem

Before Congress passed laws to reduce their effectiveness, **tax shelters** provided a popular way to avoid or defer taxes, since they could generate deductions and other benefits to offset income from other sources. Because of the tax avoidance potential of many tax shelters, they were attractive to wealthy taxpayers in high-income tax brackets. Many tax shelters merely provided an opportunity for "investors" to obtain tax deductions and credits (and some had no profit motive).

[1]If the losses are incurred in connection with a trade or business, § 165(c)(1) applies.

Although it may seem odd that a taxpayer would intentionally invest in an activity designed to produce losses, there is a logical explanation. The typical tax shelter took advantage of accelerated deductions related to an activity (e.g., accelerated cost recovery or depletion). These deductions generated ordinary losses in the activity's early years that could offset the investor's other sources of income (e.g., salary, interest, and dividends) and deferred the recognition of the economic profits (if any) until the activity was sold. Depending on the activity, any gain recognized on the sale might be taxed at lower capital gains rates. In addition, many tax shelters were financed with *nonrecourse debt*, which posed no risk of loss to the investor.[2] This meant that the expenditures generating the deductions were paid with borrowed funds, while the related debt produced interest deductions. Finally, many tax shelters were operated as limited partnerships, attracting multiple investors who were not required (or allowed) to actively participate in the activity (and protected from the risks related to participation). The following example illustrates what was possible *before* Congress stepped in to curb tax shelter abuses in the 1980s.

Example 1

Bob, who earned a salary of $400,000 as a business executive and dividend income of $15,000, invested $20,000 for a 10% interest in a cattle-breeding tax shelter. Through the use of $800,000 of nonrecourse financing and available cash of $200,000, the partnership acquired a herd of an exotic breed of cattle costing $1,000,000. Depreciation, interest, and other deductions related to the activity resulted in a loss of $400,000, of which Bob's share was $40,000. Bob was allowed to deduct the $40,000 loss even though he had invested and stood to lose only $20,000 if the investment became worthless.

The net effect of the $40,000 deduction from the partnership was that a portion of Bob's salary and dividend income was "sheltered" (i.e., offset or neutralized by the deduction), and as a result, he was required to calculate his tax liability on only $375,000 of income [$415,000 (salary and dividends) − $40,000 (deduction)] rather than $415,000. If this deduction were available under current law and if Bob was in a combined Federal and state income tax bracket of 40%, this deduction would generate a tax savings of $16,000 ($40,000 × 40%) in the first year alone!

A review of Example 1 shows that the taxpayer claimed a *two-for-one* write-off ($40,000 deduction, $20,000 investment). Tax shelter promoters often promised tax deductions for the investor well in excess of the amount invested.

The first major law change aimed at tax shelters was the **at-risk limitation**. Its objective is to limit a taxpayer's deductions to the amount "at risk," which is the amount the taxpayer stands to lose if the investment becomes worthless. So in Example 1, the at-risk rule limits Bob's deductible loss to $20,000—the amount he invested.

The second major legislative attack on tax shelters came with the passage of the **passive activity loss** rules. The passive activity loss rules require the taxpayer to segregate all income and losses into three categories: active, portfolio, and passive (these categories are defined in text Section 11-3). In general, the passive activity loss rules disallow the deduction of passive activity losses against *active or portfolio income* even when the taxpayer is at risk to the extent of the loss. In general, passive activity losses can only offset passive activity income.

So in Example 1, the passive activity loss rules disallow a current deduction for any of the loss. The loss from the tax shelter is a passive activity loss because Bob does not "materially participate" in the activity (see text Section 11-3c). As a result, the $20,000 loss that is allowed under the at-risk rules is disallowed under the passive activity loss rules. Why? Because Bob does not report any passive activity income for the year—he reports only active and portfolio income. Consequently, Bob's current-year income only includes his nonpassive activity income of $415,000. As explained later in the chapter, the disallowed $20,000 passive activity loss is suspended and may be deducted in a future year under certain conditions.

The nature of the at-risk limits and the passive activity loss rules and their impact on investors are discussed in the pages that follow. Because of these rules, investors now

[2] Nonrecourse debt is an obligation for which the borrower is not personally liable. An example of nonrecourse debt is a liability on real estate acquired by a partnership without the partnership or any of the partners assuming any liability for the mortgage. The acquired property generally is pledged as collateral for the loan.

focus primarily on the economics of the investment instead of the tax benefits or tax avoidance possibilities that an investment may generate.

LO.2

Explain the at-risk limitation.

11-2 At-Risk Limits

The at-risk rules limit the deductibility of losses from business and income-producing activities. These rules, which apply to individuals and closely held corporations, are designed to prevent taxpayers from deducting losses in excess of their actual economic investment in an activity. In the case of an S corporation or a partnership, the at-risk limits apply at the owner level. Under the at-risk rules, a taxpayer's deductible loss from an activity for any taxable year is limited to the amount the taxpayer has at risk at the end of the taxable year (the amount the taxpayer could actually lose in the activity).

Although the amount at risk usually changes over time, the initial "at-risk" amount includes the following:[3]

- The amount of cash and the adjusted basis of property contributed to the activity by the taxpayer, and
- Any amounts borrowed for use in the activity for which the taxpayer is personally liable or has pledged as security property not used in the activity.

This amount generally is increased each year by the taxpayer's share of income and is decreased by the taxpayer's share of deductible losses and withdrawals from the activity. In addition, because general partners are jointly and severally liable for recourse debts of the partnership, their at-risk amounts are increased when the partnership increases its debt and are decreased when the partnership reduces its debt. However, a taxpayer generally is *not* considered at risk with respect to borrowed amounts if:

- The taxpayer is not personally liable for repayment of the debt (e.g., nonrecourse debt), or
- The lender has an interest (other than as a creditor) in the activity.

An important exception provides that in the case of an activity that holds real property, a taxpayer's share of any *qualified nonrecourse financing* that is secured by real property used in the activity is considered at risk.[4]

A taxpayer may deduct a loss as long as the at-risk amount is positive (but the passive activity loss rules still may apply to limit the deduction). However, once the at-risk amount is exhausted, any remaining loss cannot be deducted until a later year. Any losses disallowed for any given taxable year by the at-risk rules may be deducted when there is, and to the extent of, a positive at-risk amount.

The Big Picture

Example 2

Return to the facts of *The Big Picture* on p. 11-1. In addition to the three investment options presented to the Lopezes, in 2022, they invest $20,000 in an oil partnership that incurs a first-year net loss, of which $30,000 is their share. Assume that the Lopezes' interest in the partnership is subject to the at-risk limits but is not subject to the passive activity loss limits.

Because the Lopezes have only $20,000 of capital at risk, they cannot deduct more than $20,000 against their other income and must reduce their at-risk amount to zero ($20,000 at-risk amount − $20,000 loss deducted). The nondeductible loss of $10,000 ($30,000 loss generated − $20,000 loss allowed) can be carried over to 2023.

[3] § 465(b)(1).

[4] *Qualified nonrecourse financing* is defined in § 465(b)(6).

The Big Picture

Example 3

Continue with the facts of the previous example. In 2023, the Lopezes have taxable income of $15,000 from the oil partnership and invest an additional $10,000 in the venture. Their at-risk amount is now $25,000 ($0 beginning balance + $15,000 taxable income + $10,000 additional investment). This enables them to deduct the $10,000 carryover loss and reduces their at-risk amount to $15,000 ($25,000 at-risk amount − $10,000 carryover loss allowed).

Complicating the at-risk rule is the fact that previously allowed losses must be recaptured to the extent the at-risk amount falls below zero.[5] Under this rule, taxpayers must recognize income to bring the at-risk amount up to zero. Typically, this rule is triggered when the taxpayer receives a distribution or when the status of indebtedness changes from recourse to nonrecourse.

Calculation of at-risk amount is reviewed in Concept Summary 11.1.

Concept Summary 11.1

Calculation of At-Risk Amount

Increases to a taxpayer's at-risk amount:

- Cash and the adjusted basis of property contributed to the activity.
- Amounts borrowed for use in the activity for which the taxpayer is personally liable or has pledged as security property not used in the activity.
- Taxpayer's share of amounts borrowed for use in the activity that are qualified nonrecourse financing.
- Taxpayer's share of the activity's income.

Decreases to a taxpayer's at-risk amount:

- Withdrawals from the activity.
- Taxpayer's share of the activity's deductible loss.
- Taxpayer's share of any reductions of debt for which recourse against the taxpayer exists or any reductions of qualified nonrecourse debt.

11-3 Passive Activity Loss Limits

LO.3

Describe how the passive activity loss rules limit deductions for losses and identify the taxpayers subject to these restrictions.

This section identifies and explains the key issues that apply to the passive activity loss limits. Here are some key points:

- The limits apply only to passive activity losses incurred by certain types of taxpayers.
- Losses are limited under these rules only if they are generated by a passive activity.
- Special rules exist for interests in real estate activities.
- Any suspended losses are generally allowed when a passive activity is sold.

11-3a Classification and Tax Treatment of Passive Activity Income and Losses

The passive activity loss rules (§ 469) operate by requiring taxpayers to classify their income and losses into three categories: active, portfolio, or passive. Then the rules limit the extent to which losses in the passive category can be used to offset income in the other categories.

[5] § 465(e).

Classification

The passive activity loss rules require income and losses to be classified as active, portfolio, or passive.

Active income includes:

- Wages, salary, commissions, bonuses, and other payments for services rendered by the taxpayer.
- Profit from a trade or business in which the taxpayer is a material participant (material participation is described in text Section 11-3c).
- Gain on the sale or other disposition of assets used in an active trade or business.
- Income from intangible property if the taxpayer's personal efforts significantly contributed to the creation of the property.

Portfolio income includes:

- Interest, dividends, annuities, and royalties not derived in the ordinary course of a trade or business.
- Gain or loss from the disposition of property that produces portfolio income or is held for investment purposes.

Passive activity income or loss arises from activities that are treated as passive, which include:

- Any trade or business or income-producing activity in which the taxpayer does not materially participate.
- Subject to certain exceptions (discussed in text Section 11-3e), all rental activities whether the taxpayer materially participates or not.

General Impact

Losses or expenses generated by passive activities can be deducted only to the extent of income from the taxpayer's passive activities. Any excess passive activity loss may not be used to offset active income or portfolio income. Instead, any unused passive activity losses are suspended and carried forward to future years to offset passive activity income generated in those years. Any remaining suspended losses may be used only when a taxpayer disposes of the *entire interest* in an activity. When that occurs, generally all current and suspended passive activity losses related to the activity may offset active and portfolio income.

The Big Picture

Example 4

Return to the facts of *The Big Picture* on p. 11-1. In addition to their salaries of $180,000 from full-time jobs, assume that the Lopezes receive $5,000 in dividends and interest from various portfolio investments. Further, assume that they decide to invest $50,000 in the orange grove limited partnership, which is a passive activity that produces a $12,000 loss for the Lopezes this year.

Because their at-risk basis in the partnership is $50,000, the current $12,000 loss is not limited by the at-risk rules. However, because the loss is a passive activity loss, it is not deductible against their other income. The loss is suspended and carried over to the future.

If the Lopezes have passive activity income from this investment or from other passive activities in the future, they can offset the suspended loss against that passive activity income. If they do not have passive activity income to offset this suspended loss in the future, they will be allowed to offset the loss against other types of income when they eventually dispose of their investment in the passive activity.

Impact of Suspended Passive Activity Losses

When a taxpayer disposes of the entire interest in a passive activity, the actual economic gain or loss from the investment, including any suspended losses, can finally be determined. As a result, under the passive activity loss rules, when a fully taxable disposition occurs, any overall loss realized from the taxpayer's activity is recognized and can offset any income.

A *fully taxable disposition* generally involves a sale of the property to a third party at arm's length. This would imply that the sales price is equal to the property's fair market value. As presented in the following example, a gain recognized on the sale of a passive activity generally is treated as passive and is first offset by the suspended passive activity losses from that activity.

Example 5

Chloe sells an apartment building, a passive activity, with an adjusted basis of $500,000 for $580,000. In addition, she has suspended passive activity losses of $60,000 associated with the building. Her total gain, $80,000, and her taxable gain, $20,000, are calculated as follows:

Net sales price	$ 580,000
Less: Adjusted basis	(500,000)
Total gain	$ 80,000
Less: Suspended passive activity losses	(60,000)
Taxable gain (passive)	$ 20,000

As highlighted in Example 5, gain recognized on the sale of a passive activity generally is treated as passive and is first offset by any suspended passive activity losses from that activity. This accomplishes the purpose of determining the true economic gain or loss from the activity.

But what happens if the suspended losses exceed the gain recognized or the sale results in a loss? In this case, the excess loss is allowed to offset other income in the following order:

1. Net passive activity income or gains (if any), and
2. Nonpassive income or gains (active or portfolio).

Example 6

Dean sells an apartment building, a passive activity, with an adjusted basis of $600,000 for $650,000. In addition, he has current and suspended passive activity losses of $60,000 associated with the building and has no other passive activities. His total gain of $50,000 and his deductible loss of $10,000 are calculated as follows:

Net sales price	$ 650,000
Less: Adjusted basis	(600,000)
Total gain	$ 50,000
Less: Suspended passive activity losses	(60,000)
Deductible loss (not passive)	($ 10,000)

The $10,000 deductible loss offsets Dean's active and portfolio income.

What would be the outcome if Dean sold the building for $590,000? In this case, there would be a loss on the sale of $10,000 and an overall deductible loss of $70,000. This total loss, including the suspended passive activity losses, is deductible as a nonpassive activity loss.

Carryovers of Suspended Passive Activity Losses

The preceding examples assumed that the taxpayer had an interest in only one passive activity; as a result, the suspended loss was related exclusively to the activity that was sold. However, taxpayers may own interests in more than one activity, in which case any suspended losses must be allocated among those passive activities that generated losses. The allocation to an activity is made by multiplying the disallowed passive activity loss from all activities using the following fraction:

$$\frac{\textbf{Loss from one passive activity}}{\textbf{Sum of losses for taxable year from all passive activities having losses}}$$

Example 7

Diego has investments in three passive activities with the following income and losses for 2021:

Activity A	($30,000)
Activity B	(20,000)
Activity C	25,000
Net passive activity loss	($25,000)
Net passive activity loss of $25,000 allocated to:	
Activity A ($25,000 × $30,000 ÷ $50,000)	($15,000)
Activity B ($25,000 × $20,000 ÷ $50,000)	(10,000)
Total suspended passive activity losses	($25,000)

Suspended losses are carried over indefinitely and are offset in the future first against any passive activity income from the activities to which they relate and then against passive activity income from other passive activities.[6] Taxpayers subject to the passive activity loss limitation rule must maintain records to track the suspended losses and the activities to which they belong.

Example 8

Assume that the facts are the same as in Example 7 and that in 2022, Activity A produces $10,000 of income. Diego may use $10,000 of Activity A's suspended loss of $15,000 from 2021 to offset the $10,000 income from this activity.

If Diego sells Activity A in early 2023, the remaining $5,000 suspended loss is used to offset any income from the activity reported by Diego in 2023 and to determine his final gain or loss.

Passive Activity Credits

Credits (such as the low-income housing credit and rehabilitation credit—discussed in Chapter 13) that arise from passive activities are limited in much the same way as passive activity losses. Passive activity credits can be used only against regular tax attributable to passive activity income,[7] which is calculated by comparing the tax on all income (including passive activity income) with the tax on income excluding passive activity income.

Example 9

Sam owes $50,000 of tax, disregarding net passive activity income, and $80,000 of tax, considering both net passive activity and other taxable income (disregarding the credits in both cases). The amount of tax attributable to the passive activity income is $30,000.

In the preceding example, Sam can claim a maximum of $30,000 of passive activity credits; the excess credits are carried over. These passive activity credits can be used only against the *regular* tax attributable to passive activity income. If a taxpayer has a net loss from passive activities during a given year, no credits can be used.

Carryovers of Passive Activity Credits

Tax credits related to passive activities can be carried forward indefinitely much like suspended passive activity losses. Unlike passive activity losses, however, passive activity credits are permanently lost when the activity is disposed of in a taxable transaction where a *loss* is recognized. Credits are allowed on dispositions only when there is sufficient tax on passive activity income to absorb them.

Use of Passive Activity Credits on Disposition of an Activity

Example 10

Alicia sells a passive activity for a gain of $10,000. The activity had suspended losses of $40,000 and suspended credits of $15,000. The $10,000 gain is offset by $10,000 of the suspended losses, and the remaining $30,000 of suspended losses is deductible against Alicia's active and portfolio income. The suspended credits are permanently lost because the sale of the activity did not generate any tax.

[6] § 469(b).

[7] § 469(d)(2).

Use of Passive Activity Credits on Disposition of an Activity

Example 11

If Alicia in Example 10 had realized a $100,000 gain on the sale of the passive activity, the suspended credits could have been used to the extent of the regular tax related to the net passive activity income.

Gain on sale	$100,000
Less: Suspended passive activity losses	(40,000)
Taxable gain	$ 60,000

If the tax related to the taxable gain of $60,000 is $15,000 or more, the entire $15,000 of suspended credits can be used. If the tax related to the gain is less than $15,000, the excess of the suspended credits over the tax related to the gain is lost.

When a taxpayer has a sufficient regular tax liability from passive activities to trigger the use of suspended credits, the credits lose their character as passive activity credits. They are reclassified as regular tax credits and made subject to the same limits as other credits (discussed in Chapter 13).

Passive Activity Changes to Active

If a passive activity becomes an active one, suspended passive activity losses are allowed to the extent of income from the now active business.[8] If any of the suspended loss remains, it continues to be treated as a loss from a passive activity. The excess suspended loss can be deducted from passive activity income or carried over to the next tax year and deducted to the extent of income from the now active business in the succeeding year(s). The activity must continue to be the same activity.

Example 12

For several years, Rebecca has owned an interest in a passive activity that has produced losses of $80,000 during that period. Because she did not have passive activity income from other sources, she could not deduct any of the activity's passive activity losses.

In the current year, she has become a material participant in the activity (i.e., the passive activity is now an active business) and her share of the business profits total $25,000. As a result, she may use $25,000 of the suspended passive activity loss to offset the current business profits. Rebecca's remaining suspended passive activity loss from the activity is $55,000 ($80,000 − $25,000), which is carried over to future years and used to offset income from the formerly passive activity or income from other passive activities.

11-3b Taxpayers Subject to the Passive Activity Loss Rules

The passive activity loss rules apply to individuals, estates, trusts, personal service corporations, and closely held C corporations.[9] Passive activity income or loss from investments in partnerships or S corporations (see Chapter 20) flows through to the owners, and the passive activity loss rules are applied at the owner level.

Personal Service Corporations

Application of the passive activity loss limitations to personal service corporations is intended to prevent taxpayers from sheltering personal service income by creating personal service corporations and acquiring passive activities at the corporate level.

Example 13

Two tax accountants who earn an aggregate of $200,000 a year in their individual practices agree to work together in a newly formed personal service corporation. Shortly after its formation, the corporation invests in a passive activity that produces a $200,000 loss during the year. Because the passive activity loss rules apply to personal service corporations, the corporation may not deduct the $200,000 passive activity loss against the $200,000 of active income.

[8] § 469(f).

[9] § 469(a).

Determination of whether a corporation is a **personal service corporation** is based on rather broad definitions. A personal service corporation is a regular (or C) corporation that meets *both* of the following conditions:

- The principal activity is the performance of personal services.
- Such services are substantially performed by employee-owners.

Generally, personal service corporations include those in the fields of health, law, engineering, architecture, accounting, actuarial science, performing arts, and consulting.[10] A corporation is treated as a personal service corporation if more than 10 percent of the stock (by value) is held by employee-owners.[11] An employee is treated as an employee-owner if the employee owns stock on *any day* during the taxable year.[12] For these purposes, shareholder status and employee status do not have to occur on the same day.

Closely Held C Corporations

Application of the passive activity loss rules to closely held (nonpersonal service) C corporations also is intended to prevent individuals from incorporating to avoid the passive activity loss limitations. A corporation is classified as a **closely held corporation** if at any time during the taxable year more than 50 percent of the value of its outstanding stock is owned, directly or indirectly, by or for five or fewer individuals. Closely held C corporations (other than personal service corporations) may use passive activity losses to offset *active* income but not portfolio income.

Example 14

Silver Corporation, a closely held (nonpersonal service) C corporation, has $475,000 of passive activity losses from a rental activity, $400,000 of active income, and $100,000 of portfolio income. The corporation may offset $400,000 of the $475,000 passive activity loss against the $400,000 of active business income but may not offset the remainder against the $100,000 of portfolio income. As a result, $75,000 of the passive activity loss is suspended ($475,000 passive activity loss − $400,000 offset against active income).

Applying the passive activity loss limitations to closely held C corporations eliminates a benefit to taxpayers from transferring their portfolio investments (e.g., stocks and bonds) to these corporations.

LO.4

Define passive activity and describe the rules for identifying an activity.

11-3c Rules for Determining Passive Activities

As noted earlier, the following types of activities are treated as passive:

- Any trade or business or income-producing activity in which the taxpayer does not materially participate.
- All rental activities, subject to certain exceptions pertaining to real estate (discussed in text Section 11-3e).

To understand the meaning of the term *passive activity* and the impact of the rules, one must address the following issues, each of which is the subject of statutory or administrative guidance:

- What constitutes an *activity*?
- What is meant by *material participation*?
- When is an activity a *rental activity*?

Even though guidance is available to help the taxpayer deal with these issues, their resolution is anything but simple.

[10] § 448(d)(2)(A).

[11] § 469(j)(2).

[12] § 269A(b)(2).

Identification of an Activity

Identifying what constitutes an activity is the first step in applying the passive activity loss rules. Taxpayers who are involved in complex business operations need to determine whether a given segment of their overall business operations constitutes a separate activity or is to be treated as part of a larger activity. Proper treatment is necessary to determine whether income or loss from an activity is active or passive.

Treatment as a Component of an Activity or as a Separate Activity

Example 15

Ben owns a business with two separate departments. Department A generates net income of $120,000, and Department B generates a net loss of $95,000. Ben participates 700 hours in the operations of Department A and 100 hours in Department B. If Ben is allowed to treat the departments as components of a single activity, he can offset the $95,000 loss from Department B against the $120,000 of income from Department A.

Example 16

Assume the same facts as in the previous example. If Ben is required to treat each department as a separate activity, the tax result is not as favorable. Because he is a material participant in Department A (having devoted 700 hours to it), the $120,000 profit is active income. Assuming that Ben is not considered a material participant in Department B, the $95,000 loss is a passive activity loss. As a result, Ben cannot offset the $95,000 passive activity loss from Department B against the $120,000 of active income from Department A. (A discussion of the material participation rules follows.)

On the disposition of a passive activity, a taxpayer is allowed to offset suspended losses from the activity against other types of income. As illustrated in the next example, identifying what constitutes an activity is of crucial importance for this purpose too.

Example 17

Jasmine owns a business with two departments. Department A has a net loss of $125,000 in the current year, and Department B has a $70,000 net loss. She sells Department B at the end of the year.

Assuming that Jasmine is allowed to treat the two departments as separate passive activities, she can offset the passive activity loss from Department B against other types of income in the following order: gain from disposition of the passive activity, other passive activity income, and nonpassive activity income. This treatment leaves her with a suspended loss of $125,000 from Department A.

If, however, Departments A and B are treated as components of the same activity, when Department B is sold, its $70,000 net loss would be suspended along with the other $125,000 of suspended loss of the activity (from Department A).

Treasury Regulations provide guidelines for identifying activities subject to the passive activity loss rules.[13] These guidelines indicate, in general, that a taxpayer can treat one or more trade or business activities or rental activities as a single activity if those activities form an *appropriate economic unit* for measuring gain or loss. In making this decision, all of the relevant facts and circumstances must be considered. Taxpayers may use any reasonable method in applying the facts and circumstances. The following example, adapted from the Regulations, illustrates the application of the general rules for grouping activities.[14]

Example 18

Taj owns a men's clothing store and a brewpub in Chicago. He also owns a men's clothing store and a brewpub in Milwaukee. Reasonable methods of applying the facts and circumstances test may result in any of the following groupings:

- All four activities may be grouped into a single activity because of common ownership and control.

continued

[13]Reg. § 1.469–4.

[14]Reg. § 1.469–4(c)(3).

- The clothing stores may be grouped into an activity, and the brewpubs may be grouped into a separate activity.
- The Chicago activities may be grouped into an activity, and the Milwaukee activities may be grouped into a separate activity.
- Each of the four activities may be treated as a separate activity.

Regrouping of Activities Taxpayers should consider all tax factors carefully when deciding how to group their activities. Once activities have been grouped, they cannot be regrouped unless the original grouping was clearly inappropriate or there has been a material change in the facts and circumstances. The Regulations allow the IRS to regroup activities when *both* of the following conditions exist:[15]

- The taxpayer's grouping fails to reflect one or more appropriate economic units.
- One of the primary purposes of the taxpayer's grouping is to avoid the passive activity loss limitations.

Special Grouping Rules for Rental Activities Two rules deal specifically with the grouping of rental activities. These rules are designed to prevent taxpayers from grouping rental activities, which are generally passive, with other businesses in a way that result in a tax advantage.

First, a rental activity may be grouped with a trade or business activity only if one activity is insubstantial in relation to the other. That is, the rental activity must be insubstantial in relation to the trade or business activity, or the trade or business activity must be insubstantial in relation to the rental activity. The Regulations provide no clear guidelines as to the meaning of "insubstantial."[16]

Example 19

Schemers, a CPA firm, owns a building in Washington, D.C., in which it conducts its public accounting practice. The firm also rents space on the street level of the building to several retail establishments, which generally is considered a passive activity. Of the total revenue generated by the firm, 95% is associated with the public accounting practice and 5% is related to the rental operation.

It is likely that the rental activity would be considered insubstantial relative to the accounting practice and the two ventures could be grouped as one nonrental activity. This grouping could be advantageous to the firm, particularly if the rental operation generates a loss, since the rental loss could be used to offset any income from the public accounting practice.

Alternatively, treating the rental operation as a *separate* activity may be advantageous if this operation produces (passive activity) income. The passive activity income could then be used to absorb otherwise nondeductible passive activity losses.

Second, taxpayers generally may not treat an activity involving the rental of real property and an activity involving the rental of personal property as a single activity.

LO.5

Identify the tests for material participation.

Material Participation

If an individual taxpayer *materially participates* in a nonrental trade or business activity, any loss from that activity is treated as an active loss that can offset active or portfolio income. If a taxpayer does not materially participate, the loss is treated as a passive activity loss, which can offset only passive activity income. As a result, controlling whether a particular activity is treated as active or passive is an important part of the tax strategy of a taxpayer who owns an interest in one or more businesses. Consider the following examples.

[15] Reg. § 1.469–4(f).

[16] Reg. § 1.469–4(d).

Implications of Material Participation Status

Example 20

Noah, a corporate executive, earns a salary of $600,000 per year. In addition, he owns a separate business in which he participates. The business produces a loss of $100,000 during the year. If Noah materially participates in the business, the $100,000 loss is an active loss that may offset his active income from his corporate employer.

If he does not materially participate, the loss is passive and is suspended unless he has other passive activity income. Noah may use the suspended passive activity loss in the future only when he has passive activity income or disposes of the activity.

Example 21

Junghee, an attorney, earns $350,000 a year in her law practice. In addition, she owns interests in two activities, A and B, in which she participates. Activity A, in which she does *not* materially participate, produces a loss of $50,000. Activity B produces income of $80,000. However, Junghee has not yet met the material participation standard, described below, for Activity B. But Junghee can meet the material participation standard if she spends an additional 50 hours in Activity B during the year. Should Junghee attempt to meet the material participation standard for Activity B?

If she continues working in Activity B and becomes a material participant, the $80,000 of income from the activity is *active*, and the $50,000 passive activity loss from Activity A must be suspended. A more favorable tax strategy is for Junghee *not to meet* the material participation standard for Activity B, thus making the income from that activity passive. This enables her to offset the $50,000 passive activity loss from Activity A against most of the passive activity income from Activity B.

It is possible to devise numerous scenarios in which the taxpayer could control the tax outcome by increasing or decreasing participation in different activities. Examples 20 and 21 demonstrate some of the possibilities. In most analyses of this type, taxpayers will benefit by having profitable activities classified as passive so that any passive activity losses can be used to offset that passive activity income. If the activity produces a loss, however, the taxpayer will benefit if it is classified as active so that the loss is not subject to the passive activity loss limitations.

A nonrental trade or business in which a taxpayer owns an interest must be treated as a passive activity unless the taxpayer materially participates. A material participant is one who has "a significant nontax economic profit motive" for taking on activities and selects them for their economic value.[17] In contrast, a passive investor mainly seeks a return from a capital investment (including a possible reduction in taxes) as a supplement to an ongoing source of livelihood.

Even if the concept of being a material participant is clear, the precise meaning of the term **material participation** can be vague. As enacted, § 469 requires a taxpayer to participate on a *regular*, *continuous*, and *substantial* basis to be a material participant. In many situations, however, it is difficult or impossible to gain any assurance that this nebulous standard is met.

In response to this dilemma, Temporary Regulations[18] provide seven tests that serve to determine when material participation is achieved. Material participation is achieved by meeting any *one* of the tests. These tests are listed in Concept Summary 11.2 and can be divided into the following three categories:

- Tests based on current participation.
- Tests based on prior participation.
- Test based on facts and circumstances.

[17] *General Explanation of the Tax Reform Act of 1986* ("Blue Book"), prepared by The Staff of the Joint Committee on Taxation, May 4, 1987, H.R. 3838, 99th Cong., p. 212.

[18] Temp.Reg. § 1.469–5T(a).

Concept Summary 11.2

Tests to Determine Material Participation

Tests Based on Current Participation

1. The individual participates in the activity for more than 500 hours during the year.
2. The individual's participation in the activity for the taxable year constitutes substantially all of the participation in the activity of all individuals (including nonowner employees) for the year.
3. The individual participates in the activity for more than 100 hours during the year, and this participation is not less than that participation of any other individual (including nonowner employees) for the year.
4. The activity is a **significant participation activity** (where the person's participation *exceeds* 100 hours during the year), and the hours for all significant participation activities during the year is more than 500 hours.

Tests Based on Prior Participation

5. The individual materially participated in the activity for any 5 taxable years during the 10 taxable years that immediately precede the current taxable year.
6. The activity is a personal service activity, and the individual materially participated in the activity for any 3 preceding taxable years.

Test Based on Facts and Circumstances

7. Based on all of the facts and circumstances, the individual participates in the activity on a regular, continuous, and substantial basis during the year.

Participation Defined Participation generally includes any work done by an individual in an activity that the individual owns. Participation does not include work of a type not customarily done by owners *and* if one of the principal purposes for the work is to avoid the disallowance of passive activity losses or credits. Also, work done in an individual's capacity as an investor (e.g., reviewing financial reports in a nonmanagerial capacity) is not counted in applying the material participation tests. Participation by an owner's spouse counts as participation by the owner.[19]

Example 22

Emma, who is a partner in a CPA firm, owns a computer store that operated at a loss during the year. To offset this loss against the income from her CPA practice, Emma would like to avoid having the computer business classified as a passive activity. During the year, she worked 480 hours in the business participating in management and sales activities and 30 hours doing janitorial chores. In addition, Emma's spouse participated 40 hours as a salesperson.

It is likely that Emma's 480 hours of participation in management and sales activities will count as participation in work customarily done by owners, but the 30 hours spent doing janitorial chores will not. In addition, the 40 hours of participation by her spouse also will count.

Assuming that none of the participation's principal purposes is to avoid the disallowance of passive activity losses or credits, Emma will qualify as a material participant under the more-than-500-hour rule (480 + 40 = 520).

Limited Partners A *limited* partner is a partner whose liability to third-party creditors of the partnership is limited to the amount the partner has invested in the partnership and who has no ability to participate in the management of the partnership. Such a partnership must have at least one *general* partner who is fully liable in an individual capacity for the debts of the partnership to third parties.

Generally, a *limited partner* is not considered a material participant unless the limited partner qualifies under Test 1, 5, or 6 as shown in Concept Summary 11.2. However, a *general partner* may qualify as a material participant by meeting any of the seven tests. If a general partner also owns a limited interest in the same limited partnership, all interests are treated as a general interest.[20]

[19] § 469(h)(5) and Temp.Reg. § 1.469–5T(f)(3).

[20] § 469(h)(2) and Temp.Reg. § 1.469–5T(e)(3)(ii).

Rental Activities Defined

LO.6

Describe the nature of rental activities under the passive activity loss rules.

Subject to certain exceptions, all rental activities are treated as passive activities.[21] A **rental activity** is defined as any activity where payments are received principally for the use of tangible (real or personal) property.[22] Importantly, an activity that is classified as a rental activity is subject to the passive activity loss rules even if the taxpayer involved is a material participant.

Example 23

Sarah owns a fleet of automobiles that are held for rent, and she spends an average of 60 hours a week in the activity. Assuming that her automobile business is classified as a rental activity, it is *automatically* subject to the passive activity rules even though Sarah spends more than 500 hours a year in its operation.

Certain rentals of real and personal property might be classified under the passive activity loss rules as *nonrental* activities.[23] In these situations, assuming that the activity is a trade or business, the material participation tests shown in Concept Summary 11.2 must be applied to determine whether the activity is a passive activity. Consider the following example.

Example 24

Arturo owns a bicycle rental business at a nearby resort. Because the average period of customer use is seven days or less, Arturo's business is not treated as a rental activity.

Example 24 illustrates an exception to the definition of a rental activity. This exception is based on the presumption that a person who rents property for seven days or less is generally required to provide significant services to the customer. Providing these services supports a conclusion that the person is engaged in a service business rather than a rental business. Other examples of this exception include most hotels or motels and businesses that rent tools, tuxedos, or cars.[24]

This result, however, does not mean that Arturo's business is a nonpassive activity. Instead, it is treated as a trade or business activity subject to the material participation standards listed in Concept Summary 11.2. If Arturo is a material participant, the business is treated as active. If he is not a material participant, it is treated as a passive activity.

11-3d Interaction of the At-Risk and Passive Activity Loss Limits

LO.7

Determine the relationship between the at-risk and passive activity loss limitations.

The determination of whether a loss is suspended under the passive activity loss rules is made *after* application of the at-risk rules, as well as other rules relating to the measurement of taxable income. A loss that is not allowed for the year because of the at-risk rules is suspended under those rules, not under the passive activity loss rules. Further, a taxpayer's at-risk basis is reduced by the losses (but not below zero) even if the deductions are not currently usable because of the passive activity loss rules. The following examples illustrate these points.

At-Risk and Passive Activity Loss Interactions

Example 25

Jack's adjusted basis in a passive activity is $10,000 at the beginning of 2020. His loss from the activity in 2020 is $4,000. Because Jack has no passive activity income, the $4,000 cannot be deducted. At year-end, Jack has an adjusted basis and an at-risk amount of $6,000 in the activity and a suspended passive activity loss of $4,000.

[21] § 469(c)(2).

[22] § 469(j)(8).

[23] Temp.Reg. § 1.469–1T(e)(3).

[24] For additional discussion of the rental exceptions, see IRS Publication 925 (*Passive Activity and At-Risk Rules*).

At-Risk and Passive Activity Loss Interactions

Example 26

Jack in Example 25 has a loss of $9,000 in the activity in 2021. Because the $9,000 exceeds his at-risk amount ($6,000) by $3,000, that $3,000 loss is disallowed by the at-risk rules. If Jack has no passive activity income, the remaining $6,000 is suspended under the passive activity rules. At year-end, he has:

- A $3,000 loss suspended under the at-risk rules.
- $10,000 of suspended passive activity losses ($4,000 from 2020 and $6,000 from 2021).
- An adjusted basis and an at-risk amount in the activity of zero.

Example 27

Jack in Example 26 realizes $1,000 of passive activity income from the activity in 2022. Because the $1,000 increases his at-risk amount, $1,000 of the $3,000 unused loss from 2021 is reclassified as a passive activity loss. If he has no other passive activity income, the $1,000 income is offset by $1,000 of suspended passive activity losses. At the end of 2022, Jack has:

- No taxable passive activity income.
- $2,000 ($3,000 − $1,000) of suspended losses under the at-risk rules.
- $10,000 of (reclassified) suspended passive activity losses ($10,000 + $1,000 of reclassified suspended at-risk losses − $1,000 of passive activity losses offset against passive activity income).
- An adjusted basis and an at-risk amount in the activity of zero.

Example 28

In 2023, Jack has no gain or loss from the activity in Example 27. He contributes $5,000 more to the passive activity. Because the $5,000 increases his at-risk amount, the $2,000 of losses suspended under the at-risk rules is reclassified as passive. Jack gets no passive activity loss deduction in 2023. At year-end, he has:

- No suspended losses under the at-risk rules.
- $12,000 of suspended passive activity losses ($10,000 + $2,000 of reclassified suspended at-risk losses).
- An adjusted basis and an at-risk amount of $3,000 ($5,000 additional investment − $2,000 of reclassified losses).

The Big Picture

Example 29

Return to the facts of *The Big Picture* on p. 11-1. If the Lopezes invest in the orange grove limited partnership, the at-risk rules will not limit the deductibility of the $12,000 losses until after year 4. Sufficient at-risk basis will exist until the close of that year (i.e., the at-risk basis is reduced from $50,000 by $12,000 over each of the first four years of the investment).

However, the passive activity loss rules prohibit deductions for the losses in the first four years of the investment (assuming that the Lopezes do not have passive activity income from other sources). Based on the facts provided, none of the suspended losses would be deductible until year 6, when the orange grove is expected to begin producing profits.

Concept Summary 11.3 illustrates the interactions of the at-risk and passive activity limits.

LO.8

Recognize the special treatment available to certain real estate activities.

11-3e Special Passive Activity Rules for Real Estate Activities

The passive activity loss limits contain two exceptions related to real estate activities. The first exception allows certain rental real estate activities to avoid automatic classification as a passive activity. The second exception allows all or part of real estate rental losses to offset active or portfolio income even though the activity otherwise is defined as a passive activity.

Concept Summary 11.3

Treatment of Losses Subject to the At-Risk and Passive Activity Loss Limitations

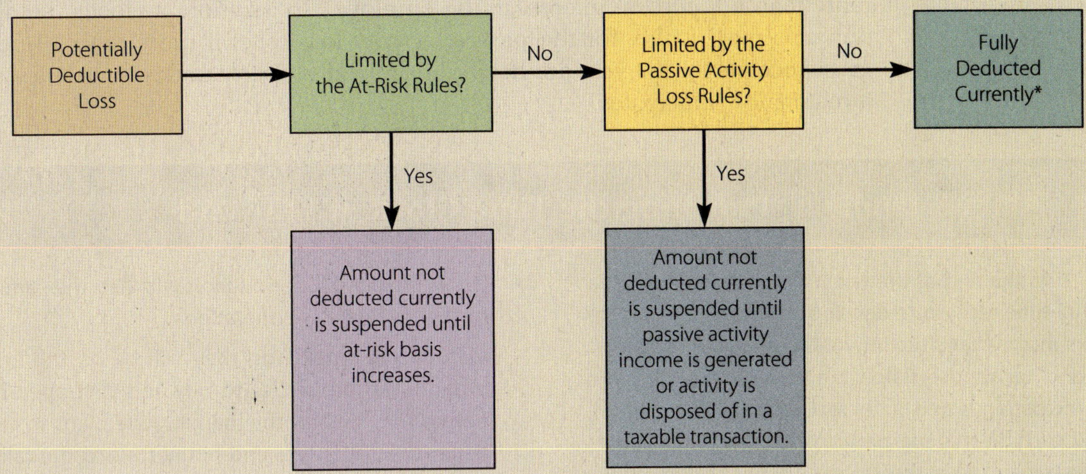

* Individuals also must determine whether the excess business loss rules of § 461(l) apply. These rules, effective for tax years 2021 through 2026, are discussed in text Section 7-5.

Material Participation in a Real Property Rental Trade or Business

The first exception to the passive activity loss rules provides relief to real estate professionals.[25] Under this exception, taxpayers meeting specific requirements are allowed to apply one of the seven material participation tests to their rental real estate activities (i.e., these *rental activities* are *not* automatically treated as passive activities). To qualify for this exception, a taxpayer must satisfy *both* of the following requirements:

- More than half of the personal services that the taxpayer performs in trades or businesses are performed in real property trades or businesses in which the taxpayer materially participates.
- The taxpayer performs more than 750 hours of services in real property trades or businesses in which the taxpayer materially participates.

Taxpayers who do not satisfy the above requirements must continue to treat income and losses from real estate rental activities as passive activity income and losses.

Example 30

During the current year, Della performs personal service activities as follows: 900 hours as a personal financial planner, 550 hours in a real estate development business, and 600 hours in a rental real estate activity. Any loss Della incurs in either real estate activity will not be subject to the passive activity loss rules.

- Being a nonrental business, the real estate development business is deemed active under the more-than-500-hour material participation test.
- Della may apply a material participation test to the real estate rental activity because (1) more than 50% of Della's personal services are devoted to real property trades or businesses (i.e., the development and rental businesses) in which she materially participates *and* (2) she has over 750 hours in real property trades or businesses in which she materially participates.
- As a result, any loss from Della's rental real estate activity can offset active and portfolio sources of income because she meets the over-500-hour material participation test for that rental activity and she qualifies as a real estate professional. Likewise, any income from this activity would be nonpassive (active) income.

As discussed earlier, a spouse's work is taken into consideration in satisfying the material participation requirement. However, the hours worked by a spouse are *not* taken into account when evaluating whether a taxpayer spent more than 50 percent of personal services in real property trades or businesses in which the taxpayer materially

[25] § 469(c)(7).

participates or has worked for more than 750 hours in these real property trades or businesses during the year.[26] Services performed by an employee are not treated as related to a real property trade or business unless the employee performing the services owns more than a 5 percent interest in the employer. In addition, a closely held C corporation also may qualify for the passive activity loss relief if more than 50 percent of its gross receipts for the year are derived from real property trades or businesses in which it materially participates.

Ethics & Equity Punching the Time Clock at Year-End

As the end of the tax year approaches, Julie, a successful full-time real estate developer and investor, recognizes that her income tax situation for the year could be bleak. Unless she and her spouse, Ralph, are able to generate more hours of participation in one of her real estate rental activities, they will not reach the material participation threshold. Consequently, the tax losses from the venture will not be deductible. To ensure deductibility, Julie suggests the following plan:

- She will document the time she spends "thinking" about her rental activities.
- During the week, Ralph will visit the apartment building to oversee (in a management role) the operations of the rentals.
- On weekends, she and Ralph will visit the same units to further evaluate the operations.
- Also on the weekends, they will be on the lookout for other rental properties to buy and visit open houses of homes they find on the market. Julie plans to count both her and Ralph's weekend hours toward the tally of total participation.

Julie contends that the law clearly allows the efforts of one's spouse to count for purposes of the material participation tests. Likewise, nothing in the tax law requires taxpayers to be efficient in their hours of participation. How do you react?

Real Estate Rental Activities with Active Participation

The second exception to the passive activity loss limits is more significant in that it is *not* restricted to real estate professionals. This exception allows individuals to deduct up to $25,000 of losses from real estate rental activities against active and portfolio income each year.[27] The potential annual $25,000 deduction is reduced by 50 percent of the taxpayer's AGI in excess of $100,000. As a result, the entire deduction is phased out at $150,000 of AGI. If married individuals file separately, the $25,000 deduction is reduced to zero unless they lived apart for the entire year. In this case, the loss amount is $12,500 each and the phaseout begins at $50,000 of AGI.[28]

To qualify for the $25,000 exception, a taxpayer must meet *both* of the following requirements:[29]

- *Actively participate* in the real estate rental activity, and
- Own 10 percent or more (in value) of all interests in the activity during the entire taxable year (or shorter period during which the taxpayer held an interest in the activity).

The difference between *active participation* and *material participation* is that the active participation threshold can be satisfied *without* regular, continuous, and substantial involvement in operations. The active participation standard is met if the taxpayer participates in making management decisions in a significant and bona fide sense. Approving new tenants, deciding on rental terms, and approving capital or repair expenditures meet this test.

[26] § 469(c)(7)(B) and Reg. § 1.469–9. In *Frank Aragona Trust*, 142 T.C. 165 (2014), the Tax Court found that a trust also could qualify for the real estate professional rule.

[27] § 469(i).

[28] In general, AGI for purposes of the phaseout is calculated without regard to IRA deductions, Social Security benefits, interest deductions on education loans, and net losses from passive activities. See § 469(i)(3)(F).

[29] § 469(i)(6).

The Big Picture

Example 31

Return to the facts of *The Big Picture* on p. 11-1. If the Lopezes invest in the apartment rental partnership, which is a passive activity, a portion (or all) of their $12,000 loss will be deductible under the real estate rental activities exception (the deductible loss will depend on their AGI and the loss phaseout that applies once AGI exceeds $100,000). This also assumes that they actively participate and own at least a 10% interest in the partnership.

The loss will be deductible in each of the first four years of their investment before their at-risk basis has been exhausted even if they do not have passive activity income from other sources (as explained earlier, the Lopezes' original at-risk basis of $50,000 plus their share of the partnership's qualified nonrecourse financing will be reduced to $0 over four years).

The $25,000 allowance is available after all active participation rental losses and gains are netted and applied to other passive activity income. If a taxpayer has a real estate rental loss in excess of the amount that can be deducted under the real estate rental exception, that excess is treated as a passive activity loss, usable in future years.

Example 32

Brad has $90,000 of AGI before considering rental activities. Brad also has $85,000 of losses from a real estate rental activity in which he actively participates. He also actively participates in another real estate rental activity from which he has $30,000 of income. He has other passive activity income of $36,000.

Of the net rental loss of $55,000 ($30,000 − $85,000), $36,000 offsets the passive activity income, leaving $19,000 that can be deducted against active or portfolio income because of the availability of the $25,000 allowance.

The $25,000 allowance is an aggregate of both deductions and the "deduction equivalent" of tax credits. The deduction equivalent of a passive activity credit is the amount of deductions that reduces the tax liability for the taxable year by an amount equal to the credit.[30] A taxpayer with $2,200 of credits and a tax bracket of 22 percent would have a deduction equivalent of $10,000 ($2,200 ÷ 22%).

If the total deduction and deduction equivalent exceed $25,000, the taxpayer must allocate the allowance on a pro rata basis, first among the losses (including real estate rental activity losses suspended in prior years) and then to credits in the following order: (1) credits other than rehabilitation and low-income housing credits, (2) rehabilitation credits, and (3) low-income housing credits.

Deduction Equivalent Considerations

Example 33

Kevin is an active participant in a real estate rental activity that produces $8,000 of income, $26,000 of deductions, and $1,500 of credits. Kevin is a single taxpayer with $98,000 of AGI before considering this rental activity and is in the 22% tax bracket. As a result, he may deduct the net passive activity loss of $18,000 ($8,000 − $26,000).

After deducting the loss, he has an available deduction equivalent of $7,000 ($25,000 − $18,000 passive activity loss). Because the actual credits produce a $6,818 deduction equivalent ($1,500 ÷ 22% = $6,818) and this amount is less than $7,000, Kevin may claim the entire $1,500 credit.

Example 34

Kelly is an active participant in three separate real estate rental activities. Kelly is a single taxpayer with $92,000 of AGI before considering these rental activities and is in the 22% tax bracket. The relevant tax results for each activity are as follows:

- Activity A: $20,000 of losses.
- Activity B: $10,000 of losses.
- Activity C: $1,100 of credits.

continued

[30] § 469(j)(5).

Kelly's deduction equivalent from the credits is $5,000 ($1,100 ÷ 22%). As a result, the total passive activity losses and deduction equivalents are $35,000 ($20,000 + $10,000 + $5,000), which exceeds the maximum allowable amount of $25,000. Consequently, Kelly must allocate the $25,000 allowance on a pro rata basis, first from among losses and then from among credits. Deductions from losses are limited as follows:

- Activity A {$25,000 × [$20,000 ÷ ($20,000 + $10,000)]} = $16,667
- Activity B {$25,000 × [$10,000 ÷ ($20,000 + $10,000)]} = $8,333

Because the amount of passive activity losses exceeds the $25,000 maximum, the remaining losses of $5,000 and passive activity credits of $1,100 must be carried forward. Kelly's suspended losses and credits by activity are as follows:

		Activity		
	Total	**A**	**B**	**C**
Allocated losses	$ 30,000	$ 20,000	$10,000	$ –0–
Allocated credits	1,100	–0–	–0–	1,100
Utilized losses	(25,000)	(16,667)	(8,333)	–0–
Suspended losses	5,000	3,333	1,667	–0–
Suspended credits	1,100	–0–	–0–	1,100

LO.9

Determine the proper tax treatment on the disposition of a passive activity.

11-3f Dispositions of Passive Activities

If a taxpayer disposes of an entire interest in a passive activity, any suspended losses (and in certain cases, suspended credits) may be used when calculating the final economic gain or loss on the investment. In addition, if there is an overall loss from the disposition, that loss can offset other types of income. However, the tax consequences may be different if the activity is disposed of in transactions that are not fully taxable (e.g., a transfer at death or by gift or an installment sale). The following sections discuss these types of dispositions.

Disposition of a Passive Activity at Death

When a transfer of a taxpayer's interest occurs because of a taxpayer's death, suspended losses are allowed (to the decedent) only to the extent they exceed the amount, if any, of the allowed increase (step-up) in basis.[31] Suspended losses that are equal to or less than the amount of the basis increase are, however, lost. The losses allowed generally are reported on the final return of the deceased taxpayer.

Disposition of Suspended Passive Activity Losses at Death

Example 35

Alyson dies with passive activity property having an adjusted basis of $40,000, suspended losses of $10,000, and a fair market value at the date of her death of $75,000. The increase (step-up) in basis is $35,000 (fair market value at date of death in excess of adjusted basis).

None of the $10,000 suspended loss is deductible on Alyson's final return or by the beneficiary. The suspended losses ($10,000) are lost because they do not exceed the step-up in basis ($35,000).

Example 36

Assume the same facts as in the previous example, except that the property's fair market value at the date of Alyson's death is $47,000.

Because the step-up in basis is only $7,000 ($47,000 − $40,000), the suspended losses allowed are limited to $3,000 ($10,000 suspended loss at time of death − $7,000 increase in basis). The $3,000 loss available to Alyson is reported on her final income tax return.

[31] § 469(g)(2); the basis of inherited property is generally the fair market value on the date of death (see Chapter 14).

Disposition of a Passive Activity by Gift

If a taxpayer's interest in a passive activity is transferred by gift, the suspended losses are added to the donee's basis of the property.[32] As a result, the donor will see no benefit from any suspended losses. However, a tax *benefit* may be available to the donee. Due to the increase in the property's basis, greater depreciation deductions can result, and there will be less gain (or more loss) on a subsequent sale of the property. The benefits of increased basis do not materialize if the recipient is a charity, as such organizations generally are not subject to income taxation.

Example 37

Carlton makes a gift to Maddie of passive activity property having an adjusted basis of $40,000, suspended losses of $10,000, and a fair market value at the date of the gift of $100,000. Carlton cannot deduct the suspended losses in the year of the disposition. However, the suspended losses transfer with the property and are added to the adjusted basis of the property, which becomes $50,000 in Maddie's hands.

Assuming that Maddie is able to sell the property for $105,000 soon after she receives the gift, her taxable gain will be $55,000 ($105,000 − $50,000), which reflects the benefit from the increased basis.

Installment Sale of a Passive Activity

An installment sale of a taxpayer's entire interest in a passive activity triggers recognition of the suspended losses.[33] The losses are allowed each year as payments are received on the installment obligation in the ratio that the gain recognized in each year bears to the total gain on the sale.

Example 38

Lucas sells his entire interest in a passive activity for $100,000. His adjusted basis in the property is $60,000. If he uses the installment method, his gross profit ratio is 40% ($40,000 gross profit ÷ $100,000 sales proceeds). If Lucas receives a $20,000 down payment, he will recognize a gain of $8,000 (40% of $20,000). If the activity has a suspended loss of $25,000, Lucas will deduct $5,000 [($8,000 ÷ $40,000) × $25,000] of the suspended loss in the first year.

This pattern will continue as Lucas receives installment payments. So, for example, if Lucas receives a $10,000 installment payment in the following year, he will recognize gain of $4,000 and can deduct $2,500 of the suspended loss in that year.

The general rules relating to passive activity losses are reviewed in Concept Summary 11.4.

11-4 Investment Interest Limitation

LO.10

Identify restrictions placed on the deductibility of investor losses and deductions, including those that apply to investment interest.

Another way investors previously used the tax law to create wealth involved the interest expense deduction. By borrowing to purchase investments that would appreciate over time, the interest on the debt was claimed as an ordinary deduction when paid. Later, when the asset was sold at a gain, only a capital gains tax was due on the appreciation. In addition to the "mismatch" of ordinary deductions leading to capital gains, the time value of money also played a role in these decisions (current deductions leading to lower taxes today; capital gains at lower rates at some point in the future).

11-4a Limitation Imposed

In response, Congress has limited the deductibility of **investment interest** for noncorporate taxpayers. Investment interest is interest paid on debt borrowed for the purpose

[32] § 469(j)(6).

[33] § 469(g)(3).

Concept Summary 11.4

Passive Activity Loss Rules: Key Issues and Answers

What is the fundamental passive activity rule?	Passive activity losses may be deducted only against passive activity income and gains. Losses not allowed are suspended and used in future years.
Who is subject to the passive activity rules?	Individuals.
	Estates.
	Trusts.
	Personal service corporations.
	Closely held C corporations.
What is a passive activity?	Trade or business or income-producing activity in which the taxpayer does not materially participate during the year or rental activities, subject to certain exceptions, regardless of the taxpayer's level of participation.
What is an activity?	One or more trade or business or rental activities that comprise an appropriate economic unit.
How is an appropriate economic unit determined?	Based on a reasonable application of the relevant facts and circumstances.
What is material participation?	In general, the taxpayer participates on a regular, continuous, and substantial basis. More specifically, when the taxpayer meets the conditions of one of the seven tests provided in the Regulations.
What is a rental activity?	In general, an activity where payments are received for the use of tangible property. Special rules apply to rental real estate.

of purchasing or continuing to hold investment property. The deduction for investment interest allowed during the tax year is limited to the lesser of the investment interest paid or net investment income.[34]

The Big Picture

Example 39

Return to the facts of *The Big Picture* on p. 11-1. If the Lopezes invest in the high-growth, low-yield portfolio of marketable securities, most of the investment return will consist of appreciation, which will not be taxed until the securities are sold. Relatively little of the current return will consist of currently taxable interest and dividend income.

Assume that the interest and dividend income for the year from these securities equals $1,500 and that all of it is treated as investment income. If the investment interest expense on the $100,000 loan is $4,000, only $1,500 of this interest will be deductible this year (i.e., the deduction for the investment interest is limited to the $1,500 of net investment income).

Net Investment Income

Net investment income, which serves as the ceiling on the deductibility of investment interest, is the excess of investment income over investment expenses. **Investment income** includes gross income from interest, annuities, and royalties not derived in the ordinary course of a trade or business.[35] However, investment income does not include any income taken into account when calculating income or loss from a passive activity.

Investment expenses are those deductible expenses directly connected with the production of investment income, such as property taxes on investment holdings. Investment expenses do not include interest expense and, from 2018 through 2025, any expenses that are miscellaneous itemized deductions (e.g., brokerage charges and investment counsel fees).

[34] § 163(d)(1).

[35] § 163(d)(4)(B). Investment income also includes net capital gains and qualified dividends to the extent the taxpayer elects to give up the preferential tax rates that apply to these items; see text Section 11-6b.

11-4b Computation of Allowable Deduction

After net investment income is determined, the allowable deductible investment interest expense is calculated.

Example 40

Ethan's financial records for the year reflect the following:

Interest income from bank savings account	$10,000
Taxable annuity receipts	5,500
Local ad valorem property tax on investments	200
Investment interest expense	17,000

Ethan's investment income amounts to $15,500 ($10,000 + $5,500), and investment expenses total $200. As a result, his net investment income is $15,300 ($15,500 − $200). Consequently, the investment interest deduction is limited to $15,300 (the lesser of investment interest expense or net investment income).

The amount of investment interest disallowed is carried over to future years. In Example 40, the amount that is carried over to the following year is $1,700 ($17,000 investment interest expense − $15,300 deduction allowed). No limit is placed on the length of the carryover period.[36] The investment interest expense deduction is determined by completing Form 4952 (Investment Interest Deduction).

11-5 Other Investment Losses

The investment activities summarized below are discussed elsewhere in this text as shown in Concept Summary 11.5.

- Sales of securities held as investments for less than basis result in capital losses. These losses can offset capital gains. In the case of individual taxpayers, excess losses are applied against ordinary income up to $3,000 per year (§ 1211). Any remaining excess capital losses are carried over for use in future years (§ 1212).
- Losses on small business stock (i.e., stock that qualifies under § 1244) are treated as ordinary losses up to a maximum of $100,000. As a result, the limitations placed on capital losses (see above) are avoided.
- Vacation homes that are rented for part of the year may generate investment losses depending on the extent of the rental period as compared to time devoted to personal use (§ 280A). If sufficient rental activity takes place, the vacation home may be treated as rental property. As a result, any losses could be subject to the passive activity loss rules.
- Securities held as an investment that become worthless produce capital losses. The losses are usually long term because they are treated as occurring on the last day of the year in which the securities become worthless [§ 165(g)(1)]. Because the securities must be completely worthless, determining the year this takes place is often difficult.

[36] § 163(d)(2).

Concept Summary 11.5

Common Investment Loss Limitation Rules

Item	Refer to Chapter	General Nature of Limitation
At-risk rules	11	Losses in excess of the at-risk basis are not deducted in the current year. Losses not deducted are suspended and used in future years when the at-risk basis increases.
Capital losses	16	Individuals may offset capital gains by capital losses realized. Up to $3,000 of realized net capital losses may offset ordinary income per year. Remaining excess capital losses are carried over to future years.
Investment interest	11	The deduction of investment interest is limited to the taxpayer's net investment income. Excess investment interest is deductible in future years.
Passive activity loss limitations	11	Generally, passive activity losses are deducted only to the extent of passive activity income. Excess passive activity losses are suspended and used in future years.
Small business (§ 1244) stock	7	Losses from the disposition of small business stock are given ordinary treatment up to a maximum of $100,000 per year.
Vacation homes	6	The deductibility of losses from vacation homes may be limited depending on the relative number of rental use days and personal use days of the property.
Worthless securities	7	Losses arising from investment securities that become worthless are treated as occurring on the last day of the tax year.

LO.11

Suggest tax planning strategies to minimize the effect of the passive activity loss and investment interest limitations and recognize the general impact of the additional tax on net investment income.

11-6 Tax Planning

11-6a Minimizing the Impact of the Passive Activity Loss Limits

Perhaps the biggest challenge individuals face with the passive activity loss rules is to recognize the potential impact of the rules and then to structure their affairs to minimize this impact. If a taxpayer does invest in an activity that produces losses subject to the passive activity loss rules, the following discussion describes strategies that may help minimize the loss of current deductions.

Taxpayers who have passive activity losses should adopt a strategy of buying an interest in an activity that is generating passive activity income that can be offset (or sheltered) by the existing passive activity losses. From a tax perspective, it would be foolish to buy a loss-generating passive activity unless (1) the taxpayer has other passive activity income to shelter, (2) the activity is rental real estate that can qualify for the $25,000 exception, or (3) the activity qualifies for the exception available to real estate professionals.

If money is borrowed to finance the purchase of a passive activity, the associated interest expense is generally treated as part of any passive activity loss. Consequently, by using more available (i.e., not borrowed) cash to purchase the passive investment, the investor will need less debt and will incur less interest expense. By incurring less interest expense, a possible suspended passive activity loss deduction is reduced.

As explained earlier, unusable passive activity losses often accumulate and provide no current tax benefit because the taxpayer has no passive activity income. When the taxpayer disposes of the entire interest in a passive activity, however, any suspended losses from that activity are used to reduce the taxable gain. If any taxable gain still remains, it can be offset by losses from other passive activities. As a result, the taxpayer should carefully select the year in which to dispose of a passive activity. It is to the taxpayer's advantage to wait until sufficient passive activity losses have accumulated to offset any gain recognized on the asset's disposition.

Example 41

Bill, a calendar year taxpayer, owns interests in two passive activities: Activity A, which he plans to sell in December of this year at a gain of $100,000, and Activity B, which he plans to keep indefinitely. Current and suspended passive activity losses associated with Activity B total $60,000, and Bill expects losses from the activity to be $40,000 next year.

If Bill sells Activity A this year, the $100,000 gain can be offset by the current and suspended losses of $60,000 from Activity B, producing a net taxable gain of $40,000. However, if Bill delays the sale of Activity A until January of next year, the $100,000 gain will be fully offset by the $100,000 of losses generated by Activity B ($60,000 current and prior losses + $40,000 next year's loss). Consequently, by postponing the sale by one month, he could avoid recognizing $40,000 of gain that would otherwise result.

Taxpayers with passive activity losses should consider the level of their involvement in all other trades or businesses in which they have an interest. If they do not materially participate in a profitable activity, the activity becomes a passive activity. Any income generated by the profitable business then could be sheltered by current and suspended passive activity losses. Family partnerships in which certain members do not materially participate would qualify. The silent partner in any general partnership engaged in a trade or business also would qualify.

Example 42

Naya has an investment in a limited partnership that produces annual passive activity losses of approximately $25,000. She also owns a newly acquired interest in a convenience store where she works. Her share of the store's income is $35,000. If she works enough to be classified as a material participant, her $35,000 share of income is treated as active income. This results in $35,000 being subject to tax every year, whereas her $25,000 loss is suspended.

However, if Naya reduces her involvement at the store so that she is not a material participant, the $35,000 of income receives passive activity treatment. Consequently, the $35,000 of passive activity income can be offset by the $25,000 passive activity loss, resulting in only $10,000 being subject to tax. By reducing her involvement, Naya ensures that the income from the profitable trade or business receives passive activity treatment and can then be used to absorb passive activity losses from other passive activities.

The impact of the passive activity loss rules often extends to other seemingly unrelated Code sections. For example, because of the restrictive nature of the passive activity loss rules, it may be advantageous for a taxpayer to use a vacation home enough to convert it to a second residence. This would enable qualified interest and real estate taxes to be deducted (subject to the limitations discussed in Chapter 10). However, this strategy would lead to the loss of other deductions, such as repairs, maintenance, and insurance. See text Section 6-3f for a discussion of the vacation home rental rules.

The passive activity loss rules can have a dramatic effect on a taxpayer's ability to claim passive activity losses currently. As a result, it is important to keep accurate records of all sources of income and losses, particularly any suspended passive activity losses and credits and the activities to which they relate, so that their potential tax benefit will not be lost.

11-6b Maximizing the Investment Interest Deduction

The term *investment income* includes net capital gain and qualified dividend income only if the taxpayer *elects* to treat them as such. For this purpose:

- Net capital gain includes gain attributable to property held for investment.
- Qualified dividend income includes dividends that are taxed at the same marginal rate that is applicable to a net capital gain.

By electing to include net capital gain and qualified dividend income as components of investment income, the amount of investment interest deductible for the year likewise increases. Form 4952 is used to make such an election. However, the election comes with a cost and is available only if the taxpayer agrees to reduce amounts qualifying for the preferential tax rates that otherwise apply to net capital gain (see Chapter 16) and qualified dividends (refer to Chapter 4) by an equivalent amount.[37]

Example 43

Olivia incurred $13,000 of interest expense related to her investments during the year. Her investment income included $4,000 of interest, $2,000 of qualified dividends, and a $5,000 net capital gain on the sale of investment securities.

If Olivia does not make the election to include the net capital gain and qualified dividends in investment income, her investment income for purposes of computing the investment income limitation is $4,000 (interest income). If she does make the election, her investment income is $11,000 ($4,000 interest + $2,000 qualified dividends + $5,000 net capital gain). In that case, $11,000 of her interest expense, rather than $4,000, is deductible currently. However, her net capital gain and qualified dividends will be taxed at ordinary tax rates.

Should Olivia in the previous example make the election to include the additional $7,000 of qualified dividends and net capital gain as investment income? By doing so, the current-year investment interest deduction increases by $7,000, and the investment interest deduction potentially carried forward to future years is reduced by the same amount. That is, the election allows for an acceleration of the investment interest deduction. As Olivia evaluates her decision, she should consider the following points:

- The election would make sense only if her marginal ordinary income tax rate exceeded the applicable capital gains rate.
- Using present value concepts, she should compare the tax cost of postponing the interest deduction to a subsequent year with the impact of losing the benefit from the preferential capital gains rate. In performing this analysis, consideration should be given to the length of the deferral of the investment interest deduction and the current and future years' tax brackets.

11-6c Effect of the Additional Tax on Net Investment Income

As if the passive activity loss and investment interest limitations are not complicated enough, individuals, estates, and trusts also are subject to an additional 3.8 percent tax on net investment income.[38] Net investment income *for this purpose* generally includes amounts such as interest, dividends, long- and short-term capital gains, royalties, rents, and income from passive activities.

The tax is levied at the flat 3.8 percent rate on the lesser of the taxpayer's net investment income or the excess of modified AGI over a threshold amount. The threshold amounts for individuals are $250,000 for surviving spouses and taxpayers filing a joint return, $125,000 for married taxpayers filing separate returns, and $200,000 for all other individual taxpayers. As a result, this tax is aimed at higher-income taxpayers and can potentially increase the marginal capital gain tax rate to 23.8 percent (from 20 percent) and the marginal ordinary income tax rate to 40.8 percent (from 37 percent). See text Section 13-5c for a discussion of this tax.

[37] Reg. § 1.163(d)–1.

[38] § 1411.

Refocus on The Big Picture

Investor Loss Limitations Can Affect Investment Returns

RIDO/SHUTTERSTOCK.COM

The objective for most investors should be to maximize after-tax wealth from among investment alternatives. This requires an understanding of the relevant tax restrictions that apply to certain expenses and losses arising from various investment choices. The after-tax returns from the three alternatives the Lopezes are considering may be affected by the at-risk, passive activity, and investment interest limitations.

The high-growth, low-yield portfolio is expected to generate very little, if any, current interest and dividend income (i.e., investment income). Nonetheless, if the financial planner's prediction is correct, the market value of the securities will grow by approximately 8 percent a year. However, the annual $2,000 of interest expense on the debt incurred to purchase the securities is not deductible as investment interest to the extent there is no investment income. Unless investment income is generated from this or some other source, the interest will not be deductible until the securities are sold (see Example 39). In addition, to the extent that any capital gain from the portfolio's sale is treated as investment income, the gain will not be subject to preferential capital gains rates (see Example 43). As a result, the net after-tax return will be impaired because of the investment interest limitation.

The net returns from the other two investment choices will be diminished by the at-risk and passive activity loss rules in addition to the investment interest limitation. The projected 8 percent return is apparently contingent on the investors being able to use the current tax losses as they arise. These benefits will be deferred because the at-risk and passive activity loss rules delay the timing of the deductions. For example, in the case of the orange grove investment, although the Lopezes are at-risk for $100,000, none of the passive activity losses are deductible until year 6, when the investment is expected to produce passive activity income (see Example 29). In the real estate rental venture, the Lopezes are similarly limited by the at-risk and the passive activity loss rules. The Lopezes cannot deduct the passive activity loss under the exception for rental real estate for the first four years, because their AGI is too high (see Example 31); the at-risk rules would limit any additional losses in year 5 to the at-risk amount. Consequently, because the at-risk and passive activity loss rules limit the tax losses flowing to the Lopezes, the after-tax return will not be nearly as high as their financial planner predicts.

What If?

If the Lopezes decide that the investment in marketable securities is their best option, could they modify their plan so that they avoid the restriction imposed by the investment interest limitation? The Lopezes' net after-tax return would improve if the interest cost of financing their investment could be deducted as incurred. A viable strategy prior to 2018 would have been to finance their investment by borrowing up to $100,000 against the equity in their home. Using this strategy would have made the interest on the home equity loan fully deductible and increased the after-tax return from their investment. Currently, however, home equity loan interest generally is not deductible. As a result, the investment interest limitation continues to negatively impact the after-tax return from an investment in marketable securities.

Key Terms

Active income, 11-6
At-risk limitation, 11-3
Closely held corporation, 11-10
Investment income, 11-22
Investment interest, 11-21
Material participation, 11-13
Net investment income, 11-22
Passive activity loss, 11-3
Personal service corporation, 11-10
Portfolio income, 11-6
Rental activity, 11-15
Significant participation activity, 11-14
Tax shelters, 11-2

Discussion Questions

Communications

1. **LO.1, 2, 3** Identify two rules designed to limit the tax benefits a taxpayer may obtain from a tax shelter investment. In an e-mail to your instructor, describe how these rules reduce or defer the recognition of tax losses.

Planning

2. **LO.2** List some events that increase or decrease an investor's at-risk amount. What are some strategies that a taxpayer can employ to increase the at-risk amount to claim a higher deduction for losses?

3. **LO.2, 3** Roberto invested $18,000 in a chicken production operation. Using nonrecourse notes, the business purchases $120,000 worth of grain to feed the chickens. If Roberto's share of the expense is $26,000, how much can he deduct?

4. **LO.3** Explain the meaning of the terms *active income, portfolio income*, and *passive activity income.*

5. **LO.3** Carlos owns an interest in an activity that produces a $100,000 loss during the year. Would he prefer to have the activity classified as active or passive? Explain.

6. **LO.3** Kim owns an interest in an activity that produces $100,000 of income during the year. Would Kim prefer to have the activity classified as active or passive? Discuss.

7. **LO.3** On a taxable disposition of a passive activity, the taxpayer can use any suspended losses and credits related to that activity. Do you agree? Explain.

8. **LO.3** Discuss whether the passive activity loss rules apply to the following: individuals, closely held C corporations, S corporations, partnerships, and personal service corporations.

9. **LO.3** Bronze Corporation has $100,000 of active income, $55,000 of portfolio income, and a $55,000 passive activity loss. Under what circumstances is Bronze prohibited from deducting the loss? Allowed to deduct the loss?

10. **LO.4** Discuss what constitutes a passive activity.

11. **LO.5** What is the significance of the term *material participation*? Why is the extent of a taxpayer's participation in an activity important in determining whether a loss from the activity is deductible or nondeductible?

12. **LO.5** How many hours must a participant work in a nonrental activity to be guaranteed material participation status?

Decision Making
Planning

13. **LO.5** Suzanne owns interests in a bagel shop, a lawn and garden store, and a convenience store. Several full-time employees work at each of the enterprises. As of the end of November of the current year, Suzanne has worked 150 hours in the bagel shop, 250 hours at the lawn and garden store, and 70 hours at the convenience store. In reviewing her financial records, you learn that she has no passive investments that are generating income and that she expects these three ventures

collectively to produce a loss. What recommendation would you offer Suzanne as she plans her activities for the remainder of the year?

14. **LO.5, 11** Jesse, an engineer, operates a separate business that he acquired eight years ago. If he participates 85 hours in the business and it incurs a loss of $34,000, under what circumstances can Jesse claim an active loss?

15. **LO.2, 3, 5** Rita retired from public accounting after a long and successful career of 45 years. As part of her retirement package, she continues to share in the profits and losses of the firm, albeit at a lower rate than when she was working full-time. Because Rita wants to stay busy during her retirement years, she has invested and works in a local hardware business, operated as a partnership. Unfortunately, the business has recently gone through a slump and has not been generating profits. Identify relevant tax issues for Rita. Critical Thinking

16. **LO.5** Some types of work are counted in applying the material participation standards, and some types are not counted. Discuss and give examples of each type.

17. **LO.5** Last year Alan's accountant informed him that he could not claim any of his passive activity losses on his income tax return because of his lack of material participation. To circumvent the tax problem this year, Alan tells his spouse that she may have to put in some time at the various businesses. Identify the tax issues that Alan faces. Critical Thinking

18. **LO.5** Sean, a limited partner in Ivy Nursery, is informed that his portion of the entity's current loss is $18,000. As a limited partner, can Sean assume that his share of the partnership loss is a passive activity loss? Explain.

19. **LO.6** Explain why some non-real estate rental activities may not be *treated* as such under the passive activity loss rules.

20. **LO.3, 4, 5, 6, 8, 11** Odette owns a beach home that she converted to rental use last year. A company manages the property, and rentals are primarily on weekends. Since the average period of customer use is seven days or less, this is not a rental activity. As a result, Odette cannot use up to $25,000 of losses annually with the special active participation rule. What might Odette do next year to be able to apply this rule given that her income is below the threshold for this special loss provision? Critical Thinking Planning

21. **LO.8** What is a *real estate professional?* Why could qualifying for this status be beneficial under the passive activity loss rules?

22. **LO.8** Caroline owns a real estate rental activity that produces a loss of $65,000 during the current year. Under what circumstances can Caroline treat the entire loss as nonpassive?

23. **LO.8** Since his college days, Charles has developed an entrepreneurial streak. After working in his family's grocery business, he starts several ventures on his own. Even though Charles is independently wealthy, he is looking forward to working in each of the ventures. He plans to "drop in" on the businesses from time to time between personal trips to Europe and the Caribbean. As of the end of the year, he has established computer software stores in Dayton (Ohio), Austin, and Seattle; bagel bakeries in Albany, Athens (Georgia), and Tallahassee; and mountain bike and ski rental shops in small towns in Vermont, West Virginia, Colorado, and California. Identify the tax issues that Charles faces. Critical Thinking

24. **LO.8** Bailey owns a small rental townhouse complex that generates a loss during the year. Under what circumstances can Bailey deduct a loss from the rental activity? What limitations apply? Planning

25. **LO.8** In connection with passive activities, what is a *deduction equivalent* and how is it computed?

26. **LO.10** What is *investment interest expense*? Describe the basic rules that may limit its deductibility.

Computational Exercises

27. **LO.2** In the current year, Ming invests $30,000 in an oil partnership. He has taxable income for the current year of $2,000 from the oil partnership and withdraws $10,000. What is Ming's at-risk amount at the end of the year?

28. **LO.3** Lucy sells her partnership interest, a passive activity, with an adjusted basis of $305,000 for $330,000. In addition, she has current and suspended losses of $28,000 associated with the partnership and has no other passive activities. Calculate Lucy's total gain and her current deductible loss. Describe the type of income that the deductible loss may offset.

29. **LO.4, 5** Zhou owns a nonrental business with two separate departments. Department A generates net income of $70,000, and Department B generates a net loss of $58,000. Zhou participates 800 hours in the operations of Department A and 300 hours in the operations of Department B. If Zhou is allowed to treat the departments as components of a single activity, calculate the amount of the Department B loss that can be offset against the income from Department A in the current year.

30. **LO.7** Rhonda has an adjusted basis and an at-risk amount of $7,500 in a passive activity at the beginning of the year. She also has a suspended passive activity loss of $1,500 carried over from the prior year. During the current year, she has a loss of $12,000 from the passive activity. Rhonda has no passive activity income from other sources this year. Determine the following items relating to Rhonda's passive activity as of the end of the year.
    a. Adjusted basis and at-risk amount in the passive activity.
    b. Loss suspended under the at-risk rules.
    c. Suspended passive activity loss.

31. **LO.8** Noah Yobs, who has $62,000 of AGI (solely from wages) before considering rental activities, has $70,000 of losses from a real estate rental activity in which he actively participates. He also actively participates in another real estate rental activity from which he has $33,000 of income. He has other passive activity income of $20,000.
    a. What amount of rental loss can Noah use to offset active or portfolio income in the current year?
    b. Compute Noah's AGI on Form 1040 [pages 1 and 2; also complete Schedule 1 (Form 1040)] for the current year. His Social Security number is 123-45-6789.

32. **LO.9** Rose dies with passive activity property having an adjusted basis of $65,000, suspended losses of $13,000, and a fair market value at the date of her death of $90,000. Of the $13,000 suspended loss existing at the time of Rose's death, how much is deductible on her final return or by the beneficiary?

33. **LO.10** Troy's financial records for the year reflect the following:

Interest income from bank savings account	$ 900
Taxable annuity receipts	1,800
City ad valorem property tax on investments	125
Investment interest expense	3,200

Calculate Troy's net investment income and his current investment interest deduction. How is a deduction for any potential excess investment interest treated?

Problems

34. **LO.2** In 2021, Fred invested $50,000 in a general partnership. Fred's interest is not considered to be a passive activity. If his share of the partnership losses is $35,000 in 2021 and $25,000 in 2022, how much can he deduct in each year?

35. **LO.2** In the current year, Bill Parker (54 Oak Drive, St. Paul, MN 55164) is considering making an investment of $60,000 in Best Choice Partnership. If Bill makes the investment, he will participate in the business operated by Best Choice (and will meet one of the material participation tests). As a result, it will not be a passive activity. Bill's share of the entity's loss in the current year will likely be $40,000, whereas his share of the partnership loss next year will probably be $25,000. Write a letter to Bill in which you indicate how the losses would be treated for tax purposes in the current year and the following year. Communications

36. **LO.2, 11** Heather wants to invest $40,000 in a relatively safe venture and has discovered two alternatives that would produce the following reportable ordinary income and loss over the next three years: Critical Thinking Decision Making Planning

Year	Alternative 1 Income (Loss)	Alternative 2 Income (Loss)
1	($20,000)	($48,000)
2	(28,000)	32,000
3	72,000	40,000

She is interested in the after-tax effects of these alternatives over a three-year horizon. Assume that Heather's investment portfolio produces sufficient passive activity income to offset any potential passive activity loss that may arise from these alternatives, that her cost of capital is 6%, that she is in the 24% tax bracket, that each investment alternative possesses equal growth potential, and that each alternative exposes her to comparable financial risk. In addition, assume that in the loss years for each alternative, there is no cash flow from or to the investment (i.e., the loss is due to depreciation), whereas in those years when the income is positive, cash flows to Heather equal the amount of the income.

a. Based on these facts, compute the present value of these two investment alternatives and determine which option Heather should choose. Refer to Appendix E for the present value factors.

b. Prepare your solution using spreadsheet software such as Microsoft Excel.

37. **LO.1, 3** Dorothy acquired a 100% interest in two passive activities: Activity A in January 2017 and Activity B in 2018. Through 2020, Activity A was profitable, but it produced losses of $200,000 in 2021 and $100,000 in 2022. Dorothy has passive activity income from Activity B of $20,000 in 2021 and $40,000 in 2022. After offsetting passive activity income, how much of the net losses may she deduct?

38. **LO.1, 3** A number of years ago, Kayla acquired an interest in a partnership in which she is not a material participant. Kayla's basis in her partnership interest at the beginning of 2021 is $40,000. Kayla's share of the partnership loss is $35,000 in 2021, and her share of the partnership income is $15,000 in 2022. How much may Kayla deduct in 2021 and 2022, assuming that she owns no other passive activities?

39. **LO.3** Mike, an attorney, earns $200,000 from his law practice and receives $45,000 in dividends and interest during the year. In addition, he incurs a loss of $50,000 from an investment in a passive activity acquired three years ago. What is Mike's net income for the current year after considering the passive investment?

40. **LO.3, 11** Emily has $100,000 that she wants to invest and is considering the following two options: Critical Thinking Decision Making Planning

- Option A: Investment in Redbird Mutual Fund, which is expected to produce interest income of $8,000 per year.

- Option B: Investment in Cardinal Limited Partnership (buys, sells, and operates wine vineyards). Emily's share of the partnership's ordinary income and loss over the next three years will be as follows:

Year	Income (Loss)
1	($ 8,000)
2	(2,000)
3	34,000

Emily is interested in the after-tax effects of these alternatives over a three-year horizon. Assume that Emily's investment portfolio produces ample passive activity income to offset any passive activity losses that may be generated. Her cost of capital is 8%, and she is in the 32% tax bracket. The two investment alternatives possess equal growth potential and comparable financial risk.

a. Based on these facts, compute the present value of these two investment alternatives and determine which option Emily should choose. Refer to Appendix E for the present value factors.

b. Prepare your solution using spreadsheet software such as Microsoft Excel.

41. **LO.3** Seojun acquired an activity several years ago, and in the current year, it generates a loss of $50,000. Seojun has AGI of $140,000 before considering the loss from the activity. If the activity is a bakery and Seojun is not a material participant, what is his AGI?

Decision Making
Planning

42. **LO.3, 9, 11** Jorge owns two passive investments, Activity A and Activity B. He plans to sell Activity A in the current year or next year. Juanita has offered to buy Activity A this year for an amount that would produce a taxable passive activity gain to Jorge of $115,000. However, if the sale, for whatever reason, is not made to Juanita, Jorge believes that he could find a buyer who would pay about $7,000 less than Juanita. Passive activity losses and gains generated (and expected to be generated) by Activity B follow:

Two years ago	($35,000)
Last year	(35,000)
This year	(8,000)
Next year	(30,000)
Future years	Minimal profits

All of Activity B's losses are suspended. Should Jorge close the sale of Activity A with Juanita this year, or should he wait until next year and sell to another buyer? Jorge is in the 32% tax bracket.

43. **LO.3, 9** Sarah has investments in four passive activity partnerships purchased several years ago. Last year the income and losses were as follows:

Activity	Income (Loss)
A	$ 30,000
B	(30,000)
C	(15,000)
D	(5,000)

In the current year, she sold her interest in Activity D for a $10,000 gain. Activity D, which had been profitable until last year, had a current loss of $1,500. How will the sale of Activity D affect Sarah's taxable income in the current year?

44. **LO.3, 9** Leon sells his interest in a passive activity for $100,000. Determine the tax effect of the sale based on each of the following independent facts:

a. Adjusted basis in this investment is $35,000. Losses from prior years that were not deductible due to the passive activity loss restrictions total $40,000.

b. Adjusted basis in this investment is $75,000. Losses from prior years that were not deductible due to the passive activity loss restrictions total $40,000.

c. Adjusted basis in this investment is $75,000. Losses from prior years that were not deductible due to the passive activity loss restrictions total $40,000. In addition, suspended credits total $10,000.

45. **LO.3** Ash, Inc., a closely held personal service corporation, has $100,000 of passive activity losses. In addition, Ash has $80,000 of active business income and $20,000 of portfolio income. How much of the passive activity loss may Ash use to offset the other types of income?

46. **LO.3** In the current year, White, Inc., earns $400,000 from operations and receives $36,000 of interest income from various portfolio investments. White also pays $150,000 to acquire a 20% interest in a passive activity that produces a $200,000 loss.

a. Assuming that White is a personal service corporation, how will these transactions affect its taxable income?

b. Same as part (a), except that White is closely held but not a personal service corporation.

47. **LO.2, 3, 7, 11** Kristin Graf (123 Baskerville Mill Road, Jamison, PA 18929) is trying to decide how to invest a $10,000 inheritance. One option is to make an additional investment in Rocky Road Excursions in which she has an at-risk basis of $0, suspended losses under the at-risk rules of $7,000, and suspended passive activity losses of $1,000. If Kristin makes this investment, her share of the expected profits this year will be $8,000. If her investment stays the same, her share of profits from Rocky Road Excursions will be $1,000. Another option is to invest $10,000 as a limited partner in the Ragged Mountain Winery; this investment will produce passive activity income of $9,000. Write a letter to Kristin to review the tax consequences of each alternative. Kristin is in the 24% tax bracket.

Communications
Critical Thinking
Decision Making
Planning

48. **LO.2, 3, 7, 11** The end of the year is approaching, and Maxine has begun to focus on ways of minimizing her income tax liability. Several years ago she purchased an investment in Teal Limited Partnership, which is subject to the at-risk and the passive activity loss rules. (Last year Maxine sold a different investment that was subject to these rules and that produced passive activity income.) She believes that her investment in Teal has good long-term economic prospects. However, it has been generating tax losses for several years in a row. In fact, when she was discussing last year's income tax return with her tax accountant, he said that unless "things change" with respect to her investments, she would not be able to deduct losses this year.

Decision Making
Planning

a. What was the accountant referring to in his comment?

b. You learn that Maxine's current at-risk basis in her investment is $1,000 and that her share of the current loss is expected to be $13,000. Based on these facts, how will her loss be treated?

c. After reviewing her situation, Maxine's financial adviser suggests that she invest at least an additional $12,000 in Teal to ensure a full loss deduction in the current year. How do you react to his suggestion?

d. What would you suggest Maxine consider as she attempts to maximize her current-year deductible loss?

49. **LO.2, 3, 7** A number of years ago, Lee acquired a 20% interest in the BlueSky Partnership for $60,000. The partnership was profitable through 2021, and Lee's amount at risk in the partnership interest was $120,000 at the beginning of 2022. BlueSky incurred a loss of $400,000 in 2022 and reported income of $200,000 in 2023. Assuming that Lee is not a material participant, how much of his loss from BlueSky Partnership is deductible in 2022 and 2023? Consider the at-risk and passive activity loss rules, and assume that Lee owns no other passive investments.

50. **LO.2, 3, 5, 7** Grace acquired an activity four years ago. The loss from the activity is $50,000 in the current year (at-risk basis of $40,000 as of the beginning of the year). Without considering the loss from the activity, she has gross income of $140,000. If the activity is a convenience store and Grace is a material participant, what is the effect of the activity on her taxable income?

51. **LO.2, 3, 5, 7** Jonathan, a physician, earns $200,000 from his practice. He also receives $18,000 in dividends and interest from various portfolio investments. During the year, he pays $45,000 to acquire a 20% interest in a partnership that operates a retail store and has no debt. The partnership produces a $300,000 loss this year. Compute Jonathan's AGI assuming that:

a. He does not participate in the operations of the partnership.

b. He is a material participant in the operations of the partnership.

52. **LO.2, 3, 7** Five years ago Gerald invested $150,000 in a passive activity, his sole investment venture. On January 1, 2021, his amount at risk in the activity was $30,000. His shares of the income and losses were as follows:

Year	Income (Loss)
2021	($40,000)
2022	(30,000)
2023	50,000

Gerald holds no suspended at-risk or passive activity losses at the beginning of 2021. How much can Gerald deduct in 2021 and 2022? What is his taxable income from the activity in 2023? Consider the at-risk rules as well as the passive activity loss rules.

Communications

53. **LO.3, 8** Several years ago Benny Jackson (125 Hill Street, Charleston, WV 25311) acquired an apartment building that currently generates a loss of $60,000. Benny's AGI is $130,000 before considering the loss. The apartment building is in an exclusive part of the city, and Benny is an active participant. Write a letter to Benny explaining what effect the loss will have on his AGI.

54. **LO.3, 5, 8** This year Maria works 1,200 hours as a computer consultant, 320 hours in a real estate development business, and 400 hours in real estate rental activities. Juan, her spouse, works 250 hours in the real estate development business and 180 hours in the real estate rental business. Maria earns $80,000 as a computer consultant, and she and Juan lost $18,000 in the real estate development business and $26,000 in the real estate rental business. How should they treat the losses?

Decision Making
Planning

55. **LO.3, 8, 11** Bonnie and Jake (ages 35 and 36, respectively) are married with no dependents and live in Montana (not a community property state). Because Jake has large medical expenses, they seek your advice about filing separately to save taxes. Their income and expenses for 2022 are as follows:

Bonnie's salary	$ 42,500
Jake's salary	26,000
Interest income (joint)	1,500
Rental loss from actively managed rental property	(23,000)
Jake's unreimbursed medical expenses	8,500
All other itemized deductions:*	
Bonnie	19,000
Jake	6,400

*None subject to limitations

Determine whether Bonnie and Jake should file jointly or separately for 2022.

Decision Making

56. **LO.3, 8, 11** Mary and Charles have owned a beach cottage on the New Jersey shore for several years and have always used it as a family retreat. When they acquired the property, they had no intentions of renting it. Because family

circumstances have changed, they are considering using the cottage for only one week a year and renting it for the remainder of the year. Their AGI approximates $100,000 per year, they are in the 30% tax bracket (combined Federal and state), and their total itemized deductions exceed the standard deduction amount. Interest and real estate taxes total $8,000 per year and are expected to continue at this level in the foreseeable future. If Mary and Charles rent the property, their *incremental* revenue and expenses are projected to be:

Rent income	$ 22,000
Rental commissions	(4,000)
Maintenance expenses	(9,000)
Depreciation expense	(10,000)

If the cottage is converted to rental property, they plan to be actively involved in key rental and maintenance decisions. Given the tax effects of converting the property to rental use, would the cash flow from renting the property be enough to meet the $12,000 annual mortgage payment? Explain.

57. **LO.3, 8** During the current year, Gene, a CPA, performs services as follows: 1,800 hours in his tax practice and 50 hours in an apartment leasing operation in which he has a 15% interest. Because of his oversight duties, Gene is considered to be an active participant. He expects that his share of the loss realized from the apartment leasing operation will be $30,000 and that his tax practice will show a profit of approximately $80,000. Gene is single and has no other income. Discuss the character and treatment of the income and losses generated by these activities.

58. **LO.3, 8** Mandy, who has AGI of $80,000 before considering rental activities, is active in three separate real estate rental activities and is in the 22% tax bracket. She has $12,000 of losses from Activity A, $18,000 of losses from Activity B, and income of $10,000 from Activity C. She also has $2,100 of tax credits from Activity A. Calculate the deductions and credits she is allowed and the suspended losses and credits.

59. **LO.8** Jiu has $105,000 of losses from a real estate rental activity in which she actively participates. She has other rental income of $25,000 and other passive activity income of $32,000. Her AGI before considering these items of income and loss is $95,000. How much rental loss can Jiu deduct against active and portfolio income (ignoring the at-risk rules)? Does she have any suspended losses to carry over? Explain.

60. **LO.9** At death, Francine owns an interest in a passive activity property (adjusted basis of $160,000, suspended losses of $16,000, and fair market value of $170,000). What is deductible on Francine's final income tax return?

61. **LO.9** In the current year, Abe gives an interest in a passive activity to his daughter, Andrea. The value of the interest at the date of the gift is $25,000, and its adjusted basis to Abe is $13,000. During the time that Abe owned the investment, losses of $3,000 could not be deducted because of the passive activity loss limitations. What is the tax treatment of the suspended passive activity losses to Abe and Andrea?

62. **LO.9** Tonya sells a passive activity in the current year for $150,000. Her adjusted basis in the activity is $50,000, and she uses the installment method of reporting the gain. The activity has suspended losses of $12,000. Tonya receives $60,000 in the year of sale. What is her gain? How much of the suspended losses can she deduct?

63. **LO.10, 11** In 2022, Kathleen Tweardy incurs $30,000 of interest expense related to her investments. Her investment income includes $7,500 of interest, $6,000 of qualified dividends, and a $12,000 net capital gain on the sale of securities. Kathleen asks you to compute the amount of her deduction for investment interest, taking into consideration any options she might have. In addition, she wants your

Communications
Decision Making
Planning

suggestions as to any tax planning alternatives that are available. Write a letter to her that contains your advice. Kathleen lives at 11934 Briarpatch Drive, Midlothian, VA 23113.

64. **LO.10** Helen Derby borrowed $150,000 to acquire a parcel of land to be held for investment purposes. During the current year, she reported AGI of $90,000 and paid interest of $12,000 on the loan. Other items related to Helen's investments include the following:

Interest and annuity income	$11,000
Long-term capital gain on sale of stock	3,500
Real estate tax on the investment land	800

a. Determine Helen's investment interest deduction for the current year.

b. Discuss the treatment of the portion of Helen's investment interest that is disallowed for the current year.

c. Complete Helen's Form 4952 for the current year. For this purpose, assume that she chooses not to include the long-term capital gain as investment income. Her Social Security number is 123-45-6789.

Research Problems

the answer company™ THOMSON REUTERS®

Note: Solutions to the Research Problems can be prepared by using the Thomson Reuters Checkpoint™ online tax research database, which accompanies this textbook. Solutions can also be prepared by using research materials found in a typical tax library.

Research Problem 1. Carol is a successful physician who owns 100% of her incorporated medical practice. She and her spouse, Jordan, are considering the purchase of a commercial office building located near the local community hospital. If they purchase the building, Carol will move her medical practice to the new location and rent space for an arm's length price. The rent income Carol and Jordan receive will be available to absorb passive activity losses generated by other passive activities they own. The net effect of this arrangement is a reduction in their income tax liability. Will Carol and Jordan's plan work? Why or why not?

Research Problem 2. Five years ago Bridget decided to purchase a limited partnership interest in a fast-food restaurant conveniently located near the campus of Southeast State University. The general partner of the restaurant venture promised her that the investment would prove to be a winner. During the process of capitalizing the business, $2,000,000 was borrowed from Northside Bank; however, each of the partners was required to pledge personal assets as collateral to satisfy the bank loan in the event that the restaurant defaulted. Bridget pledged shares of publicly traded stock (worth $200,000, basis of $75,000) to satisfy the bank's requirement.

The restaurant did a good business until just recently, when flagrant health code violations were discovered and widely publicized by the media. As a result, business has declined to a point where the restaurant's continued existence is doubtful. In addition, the $2,000,000 loan is now due for payment. Because the restaurant cannot pay, the bank has called for the collateral provided by the partners to be used to satisfy the debt. Bridget sells the pledged stock for $200,000 and forwards the proceeds to the bank. Bridget believes that her share of the restaurant's current and suspended passive activity losses can offset the $125,000 gain from the stock sale. As a result, after netting the passive activity losses against the gain, none of the gain is subject to tax.

How do you react to Bridget's position?

Research Problem 3. Ida Ross has decided to purchase a new home in a retirement community for $400,000. She has $50,000 in cash for the down payment but needs to borrow the remaining $350,000 to finance the purchase. Her financial adviser, Marc, suggests that rather than seeking a conventional mortgage, she should borrow the funds from State Bank using her portfolio of appreciated securities as collateral. Selling the securities to generate $350,000 in cash would lead to a substantial tax on the capital gain recognized. As a result, a better strategy would be to borrow against her securities and then claim a deduction for the interest paid on the loan. How do you react to the financial adviser's strategy? Planning

Partial list of research aids:
Temp.Reg. § 1.163–8T(c) and Reg. § 1.163–15.

Use internet tax resources to address the following questions. Look for reliable websites and blogs of the IRS and other government agencies, media outlets, businesses, tax professionals, academics, think tanks, and political outlets.

Research Problem 4. Since the first bitcoin transaction in 2009, the number of virtual currencies has grown to over 4,000 and some taxpayers trade the currencies multiple times each day (i.e., like a day trader). Find a reliable article on investment strategies for virtual currency and a software tool that can help the investor track the basis, fair market value, and dates of the trades. Send an e-mail to your professor that details your findings (including an investment strategy, the name of a software tool that can help with tax record keeping, and its capability of producing the necessary tax reporting form for the investor and their tax adviser). Communications Planning

Research Problem 5. Oil and gas ventures operating as publicly traded partnerships typically attract sophisticated investors who purchase limited partnership interests. Investments in these types of publicly traded partnerships are subject to a restrictive set of passive activity loss rules. Identify two publicly traded oil and gas partnerships that are currently marketed to investors, describe the benefits the promoters claim will result from such investments, and briefly review the basic nature of the unique passive activity loss restrictions placed on such investments.

Research Problem 6. Investment interest is incurred when taxpayers borrow money that is used to purchase investment property. Using *IRS Tax Statistics* for the most recent year available (**www.irs.gov/statistics**), determine (a) the number of taxpayers who claimed a deduction for investment interest expense, (b) the aggregate amount deducted by all taxpayers, and (c) the amount not deducted because of the net investment income limitation. Also determine the percentage of the total investment interest deduction claimed across various ranges of AGI. Data Analytics

Becker CPA Review Questions

Becker

1. Which of the following statements regarding passive activity losses is true?
   a. A net passive activity loss may be deducted against wages.
   b. Losses on rental property are always considered passive.
   c. A passive activity is one in which the taxpayer does not materially participate.
   d. Expenses related to passive activities may be deducted from passive activity income and portfolio income.

2. Michael owns a rental house that generated a $10,000 loss this year. Michael manages the rental property but does not meet the standards for material participation. Michael is a college professor and has wages of $60,000 and $5,000 in dividend income. How is the $10,000 rental real estate loss treated on Michael's tax return?
   a. $5,000 of the loss is deductible against the passive dividend income.
   b. The rental loss is not deductible because Michael does not have any passive income.
   c. $10,000 loss is not deductible because Michael does not materially participate in the rental activity.
   d. $10,000 loss is deductible under the rental real estate exception because Michael actively participates in the rental activity.
3. What is the correct order of applying the loss limitation rules?
   a. Passive loss limits, tax basis, at-risk amount
   b. Tax basis, at-risk amount, passive loss limits
   c. At-risk amount, tax basis, passive loss limits
   d. Passive loss limits, at-risk amount, tax basis
4. Sam rents his second home. During the current year, he reported a $40,000 net loss from the rental. Assume that Sam actively participates in the rental activity and no phase-out limitations apply. What is the greatest amount of the rental loss that Sam can deduct against ordinary income in the current year?
   a. $0
   b. $5,000
   c. $25,000
   d. $40,000
5. Sally recently invested $10,000 (tax basis) in a limited partnership interest. Her at-risk amount is also $10,000. The partnership lost $6,000 this year, and Sally's share of the loss is $2,000. Sally has $40,000 in wage income and $2,000 of dividend income. In addition, Sally's share of income from a different limited partnership is $1,000. Sally does not meet the tests for material participation for either of her partnership interests. How much of Sally's $2,000 loss from the limited partnership can she deduct this year?
   a. $2,000
   b. $0
   c. $1,000 because she has $2,000 of dividend income
   d. $1,000 because she has $1,000 income from another limited partnership
6. Thomas is an active participant in the rental condominium property he owns. During the year, the property generates a $15,000 loss. If Thomas has $120,000 of salary, $5,000 of long-term capital gains, $6,000 of dividends, and no additional sources of income or deductions, how much loss can Thomas deduct? Assume that Thomas has sufficient tax basis and at-risk basis to absorb the loss.
   a. $25,000
   b. $15,000
   c. $9,500
   d. $0

Part 4

Special Tax Computation Methods, Tax Credits, and Payment Procedures

Chapter 12
Alternative Minimum Tax

Chapter 13
Tax Credits and Payment Procedures

Part 4 presents several topics that relate to the theme of tax liability determination. The taxpayer must calculate the tax liability first using the basic tax formula, and then using the alternative minimum tax (AMT) formula. The basic tax formula was presented in Part 1; the AMT formula is covered here. A wide variety of tax credits can be used to reduce the tax liability. However, these credits are not always available and are subject to various limitations. As part of arriving at overall tax liability, payroll taxes (including the self-employment tax) must be taken into account. The specific procedures related to payment of the tax liability are also covered. Part 4 concludes with a discussion of additional Medicare taxes imposed on high-income individuals.

Chapter 12

Alternative Minimum Tax

Learning Objectives: *After completing Chapter 12, you should be able to:*

- **LO.1** **Explain the rationale for the alternative minimum tax (AMT).**
- **LO.2** **Explain the formula for computing the AMT for individuals.**
- **LO.3** **Identify the adjustments made in calculating AMTI.**
- **LO.4** **Identify the preferences that are included in calculating AMTI.**
- **LO.5** **Compute the AMT.**
- **LO.6** **Describe the role of the AMT credit in the alternative minimum tax structure.**
- **LO.7** **Identify tax planning opportunities to minimize the AMT.**

Chapter Outline

12-1 The AMT Calculation Generally, 12-2

12-1a AMT Formula: Alternative Minimum Taxable Income (AMTI), 12-3

12-1b AMT Formula: Other Components, 12-4

12-2 AMT Adjustments and Preferences, 12-6

12-2a Adjustments, 12-6

12-2b Preferences, 12-18

12-2c Illustration of the AMT Computation, 12-21

12-3 AMT Credit, 12-21

12-4 Tax Planning, 12-22

12-4a Avoiding Preferences and Adjustments, 12-22

12-4b Controlling the Timing of Preferences and Adjustments, 12-24

12-4c Other AMT Tax Planning Strategies, 12-24

WAVEBREAKMEDIA/SHUTTERSTOCK.COM

The Big Picture

The Presence or Absence of the AMT

Caroline and Mateo, single taxpayers, are friends who work for different employers in the tech industry. Their base salaries are comparable, but a significant difference in their incomes is the form in which their annual bonus is paid. Mateo receives an annual cash bonus from his employer, while Caroline receives an annual grant of an incentive stock option (ISO) from her employer (Gold Corporation). For 2022, Caroline reports taxable income of $150,000 and Mateo reports taxable income of $200,000. The employment compensation is their sole source of income and the standard deduction is their only deduction. During 2022, Caroline exercised an ISO (granted in 2018) that allowed her to acquire 2,000 shares of Gold Corporation stock for $20 per share. The fair market value of the stock at the date of exercise was $60 per share.

Over lunch one day, Caroline and Mateo discuss their Federal income tax liabilities. Caroline is dismayed to learn that she and Mateo will pay almost the same amount of Federal income tax for 2022. Her employer had explained to her that choosing to receive her bonus in the form of ISOs was an appealing alternative because such options did not create regular income tax consequences. Thus, when Caroline estimated her Federal income tax liability without consideration of her option grants or the exercise of those options, she determined that her tax liability would be substantially less than that of Mateo.

Shortly after their discussion, Caroline arranges to meet with her tax return preparer to better understand why she and Mateo have comparable Federal income tax liabilities. Should Caroline and Mateo have comparable Federal income tax liabilities for 2022? If so, what explanation can you offer Caroline for this result?

Read the chapter and formulate your response.

Framework 1040 **Tax Formula for Individuals**

This chapter covers the boldfaced portions of the Tax Formula for Individuals that was introduced in Concept Summary 3.1 on p. 3-3. Below those portions are the sections of Form 1040 where the results are reported.

Income *(broadly defined)*	$xx,xxx
Less: Exclusions	(x,xxx)
Gross income	$xx,xxx
Less: Deductions *for* adjusted gross income	(x,xxx)
Adjusted gross income	$xx,xxx
Less: The greater of total **itemized deductions** *or* the standard deduction	(x,xxx)
Charitable contributions if you take the standard deduction*	(xxx)
Personal and dependency exemptions**	(x,xxx)
Deduction for qualified business income***	(x,xxx)
Taxable income	$xx,xxx
Tax on taxable income *(see Tax Tables or Tax Rate Schedules)*	**$ x,xxx**
Less: Tax credits *(including income taxes withheld and prepaid)*	(xxx)
Tax due (or refund)	$ xxx

FORM 1040 (Schedule 2)

1	Alternative minimum tax. Attach Form 6251 . . . .

* For 2021, married taxpayers may claim up to $600 of cash charitable donations ($300 if unmarried).
** Exemption deductions are not allowed from 2018 through 2025.
*** Only applies from 2018 through 2025.

LO.1

Explain the rationale for the alternative minimum tax (AMT).

The tax law always has included incentives intended to influence the economic and social behavior of taxpayers (see text Sections 1-6b and 1-6c). As a result, some taxpayers are able to take advantage of these incentives to significantly minimize or entirely avoid any Federal income tax liability in a particular year. In such circumstances, although taxpayers are legally minimizing their tax liabilities, concerns arise about the inequity that results when taxpayers with substantial economic incomes avoid paying income tax because they are able to utilize a variety of special tax deductions, exclusions, and credits. The **alternative minimum tax (AMT)** was enacted to address this inequity and ensure that all taxpayers with more than modest economic incomes pay some minimum amount of tax.

In 2017, approximately 5 million individual taxpayers incurred an AMT liability, resulting in $37.7 billion in revenue for the U.S. Treasury. However, changes made by the Tax Cuts and Jobs Act (TCJA) of 2017, particularly the $10,000 SALT cap (text Section 10-2a), significantly reduced the number of taxpayers subject to the AMT. For instance, IRS data show that only $2.6 billion in revenue was collected from the individual AMT for the 2019 tax year.[1]

Currently, the AMT applies to individuals, trusts, and estates.[2] This chapter presents a detailed discussion of the individual AMT; the AMT provisions for trusts and estates are not addressed in this chapter.

LO.2

Explain the formula for computing the AMT for individuals.

12-1 The AMT Calculation Generally

In theory, all individual taxpayers subject to the Federal income tax are subject to the AMT. As explained in this chapter, whether a taxpayer has an AMT liability depends on a number of factors, including the taxpayer's income, geographic location, and family situation as well as the exclusions, deductions, and credits utilized in the calculation of their regular Federal income tax liability.

[1] **irs.gov/statistics/soi-tax-stats-individual-income-tax-returns#prelim**.

[2] The TCJA eliminated the corporate AMT for tax years beginning after 2017. See Chapter 20 of *South-Western Federal Taxation: Corporations, Partnerships, Estates & Trusts* for a discussion of the estate and trust AMT provisions.

12-1a AMT Formula: Alternative Minimum Taxable Income (AMTI)

The tax base used to determine AMT liability is referred to as the alternative minimum taxable income (AMTI) amount (Exhibit 12.1). The calculation of AMTI does not follow the direct approach taken in the calculation of a taxpayer's regular taxable income.[3] Rather than having a taxpayer recalculate the components of their individual taxable income using a different set of AMT rules, the calculation of AMTI *begins* with regular taxable income as shown in Exhibit 12.1. In other words, the AMT calculation requires a taxpayer to reconcile taxable income to AMTI, thus taking an indirect approach to the calculation.

Part of the reason for this indirect approach is that many items of income and expense are treated the same way for both regular tax and AMT purposes. For example, a taxpayer's salary is included in computing taxable income and also is included in AMTI. Some itemized deductions, such as charitable contributions and medical expenses, also are allowed for both regular tax and AMT purposes.

Whereas many amounts are left unchanged, certain income and expense items are treated differently for regular tax and AMT purposes. For example, interest income from bonds issued by state, county, and local governments is excluded in computing taxable income. However, if such bonds are private activity bonds, the interest income earned is included in AMTI. Under the indirect approach taken in the AMTI calculation, this means that private activity bond interest is added back to the taxable income starting point of the AMTI calculation.

In other cases, the income or expense item is included in both the regular tax and AMT computations, but the amount differs. For example, the completed contract method can be used to report income from some long-term contracts for regular tax purposes, but the percentage of completion method is required for AMT purposes. Thus, in the tax year, the amount of income from the contract included in taxable income will differ from the amount included in AMTI. Similarly, passive activity losses, to the extent of passive income, are deductible in calculating both taxable income and AMTI, but the AMT passive loss may differ from the regular tax passive loss as a result of other AMT provisions.[4] In situations like these, the indirect approach requires that an adjustment be made to the amount included in the taxable income starting point of the AMTI calculation.

As shown in Exhibit 12.1, differences between regular tax and AMT amounts are categorized as either adjustments or preferences. Most adjustments relate to timing

Exhibit 12.1 Alternative Minimum Tax Formula for Individuals

Taxable income (increased by any standard deduction taken)
Plus or minus: Adjustments
Plus: Preferences
Equals: Alternative minimum taxable income (AMTI)
Minus: Exemption
Equals: Alternative minimum tax (AMT) base
Multiplied by: 26% or 28% rate
Equals: Tentative minimum tax before foreign tax credit
Minus: AMT foreign tax credit
Equals: Tentative minimum tax (TMT)
Minus: Regular tax liability (less any foreign tax credit)
Equals: AMT (if TMT > regular tax liability)

[3] A "direct approach" means that in calculating regular taxable income, gross income is reduced by deductions to arrive at taxable income.

[4] § 58(b).

differences that arise because of different regular tax and AMT treatment. Adjustments that are caused by timing differences will eventually reverse; positive adjustments will be offset by negative adjustments in the future and vice versa.[5]

Depreciation provides a good example of a timing difference. In general, AMT depreciation methods are slower than regular tax depreciation methods. Initially then, there will be less depreciation for AMT purposes than for regular tax purposes. This difference will result in positive timing differences until AMT depreciation is larger than regular tax depreciation, when the timing difference will become negative. However, over time, the same amount of depreciation will be deducted for regular tax and AMT purposes because the asset's basis for regular tax and AMT depreciation is the same.

In contrast to adjustments, preferences represent permanent differences between the regular tax treatment and the AMT treatment of an amount.[6] Certain deductions and exclusions allowed to taxpayers for regular tax purposes provide significant tax savings. AMT preferences are designed to take back part or all of the tax benefit derived from the use of these deductions and exclusions. This is why preference items serve only to increase the taxable income amount that is the starting point of the AMTI calculation. The effect of adding back these preference items is to disallow them for AMT purposes. Examples of preferences include percentage depletion in excess of the property's adjusted basis and excess intangible drilling costs. Both adjustments and preferences are discussed in more detail later in the chapter.

Ethics & Equity **Who Will Pay the AMT?**

Changes made by the TCJA of 2017 significantly reduced the number of individual AMT filers. For comparison purposes, in 2017, slightly more than 5 million individual income tax returns included an AMT liability; approximately 150,000 returns included such a liability in 2019.

The large drop in the number of AMT filers can be explained by a variety of factors. First, the TCJA increased AMT exemption amounts significantly. Thus, a larger base amount of AMTI is sheltered from the TMT. Second, the TCJA also increased the phaseout amount for the AMT exemption. As a result, taxpayers with significant amounts of AMTI who would not have benefited from the exemption prior to the TCJA will benefit from the exemption post-TCJA. Third, the TCJA eliminated a number of regular tax deductions that triggered AMT adjustments. Changes to the state and local tax itemized deduction, personal and dependency exemptions, and depreciation methods reduce the likelihood of an AMT liability for many taxpayers.

These changes seem to redirect the AMT toward its stated goal of ensuring that taxpayers with significant amounts of economic income pay some minimum amount of tax. However, most of the TCJA's individual income tax provisions are set to expire at the end of 2025. With the expiration of those provisions, it is estimated that over 7 million individuals will owe AMT in 2026. What considerations should policymakers evaluate in determining whether to allow the AMT to revert back to its pre-TCJA form or to make the TCJA changes permanent?

Source: Based on **taxpolicycenter.org/taxvox/fixing-tcja-how-should-congress-treat-alternative-minimum-tax** and **irs.gov/statistics/soi-tax-stats-individual-income-tax-returns**.

12-1b **AMT Formula: Other Components**

Calculating AMTI is the first step in the determination of whether a taxpayer will have an alternative minimum tax liability. To complete the AMT calculation, as shown in Exhibit 12.1, the exemption, rates, credit, and regular tax liability must all be considered.

Exemption Amount

After calculating AMTI, the taxpayer determines the AMT **exemption amount**. The purpose of the AMT exemption is to ensure that taxpayers with minimal positive adjustments and preferences are not subject to an AMT liability.

[5] § 56.

[6] § 57.

The exemption amounts for 2022 are presented below. These exemption amounts are phased out at a rate of 25 cents on the dollar when AMTI exceeds certain threshold amounts (see Example 1).[7] The exemption and phaseout threshold amounts are tied to a taxpayer's filing status.

		Phaseout	
Status	**Exemption**	**Begins at**	**Ends at**
Married, joint	$118,100	$1,079,800	$1,552,200
Single or head of household	75,900	539,900	843,500
Married, separate	59,050	539,900	776,100

Once AMTI equals the end of the phaseout range, a taxpayer's exemption amount will equal zero. Example 1 explains the calculation of the phaseout of the AMT exemption.

Example 1

Harry, who is single, records AMTI of $680,000 for the year. His $75,900 exemption amount is reduced by $35,025 [($680,000 − $539,900) × 25% phaseout rate]. Harry's AMT exemption is $40,875 ($75,900 exemption – $35,025 reduction).

AMT Liability

After the exemption is calculated, a taxpayer's AMT liability can be determined. As shown in Exhibit 12.1, AMTI less the exemption equals the AMT base. This base amount is multiplied by the tax rate and reduced by any credits that are allowed, resulting in the tentative minimum tax (TMT).

The relationship between the regular tax liability and the TMT is key to the AMT calculation. If the regular tax liability exceeds the TMT, the taxpayer's AMT liability is zero. However, if the TMT exceeds the regular tax liability, the excess is the taxpayer's AMT liability. Technically, the AMT is a surtax; both tax law and the Form 6251 categorize any excess of TMT over the taxpayer's regular tax liability as the AMT amount.[8] For practical purposes, the taxpayer pays whichever tax liability is greater—that calculated using the regular tax rules or that calculated using the AMT rules.

A graduated, two-tier AMT rate schedule applies in calculating the TMT. In 2022, a 26 percent rate applies to the first $206,100 ($103,050 for married filing separately) of the AMT base and a 28 percent rate applies to any remaining AMT base.[9] Any net capital gain or qualified dividend income included in the AMT base is taxed at the favorable tax rates for such amounts rather than at the AMT rates. See the discussion of the tax treatment of capital gains in text Section 16-5.

Example 2

Anna, an unmarried individual, reports regular taxable income of $650,000. Anna itemizes deductions; she has positive adjustments of $70,000 and preferences of $65,000. Anna's regular tax liability for 2022 is $203,455. Her AMT in 2022 is calculated as follows.

Taxable income	$650,000
Plus: Adjustments	70,000
Plus: Preferences	65,000
Equals: AMTI	$785,000
Minus: AMT exemption [$75,900 − 25%($785,000 − $539,900)]	14,625
Equals: AMT base	$770,375
TMT [($206,100 × 26%) + ($770,375 − $206,100) × 28%]	$211,583
Minus: Regular tax liability	203,455
Equals: AMT	$ 8,128

Anna will pay the IRS a total of $211,583, consisting of her regular tax liability of $203,455 plus AMT of $8,128.

[7] The exemption and phaseout threshold amounts are indexed annually for inflation. § 55(d)(4).

[8] § 55(a).

[9] §§ 55(b)(1)(A) and (d)(4)(B).

Credits against regular tax liability (see Chapter 13) are allowed to some taxpayers depending on their economic circumstances or the type of business activity in which they engage. Personal nonrefundable credits (e.g., Adoption Credit, Lifetime Learning Credit, and Saver's Credit) can offset an AMT liability as well as the regular tax liability.[10]

Example 3

Michael records total personal nonrefundable credits of $11,000, regular tax liability of $133,000, and tentative minimum tax of $126,000. The entire $11,000 credit is available to offset Michael's $133,000 tax liability.

12-2 AMT Adjustments and Preferences

Adjustments and preferences are the mechanisms by which the AMT accomplishes the objective of taxing economic income. These amounts are added to (adjustments *and* preferences) or subtracted from (adjustments only) regular taxable income in order to arrive at a taxpayer's AMTI. The following sections explain the most common adjustments and preferences and demonstrate their calculation.

LO.3

Identify the adjustments made in calculating AMTI.

12-2a Adjustments

As discussed previously, **adjustments** relate to timing differences that arise because of differences in how an item is treated for regular tax and AMT purposes. As a result, it is necessary to determine both the amount of an adjustment and whether the adjustment is positive or negative.

Remember that the AMTI calculation begins with the taxpayer's regular taxable income amount before any standard deduction taken by the taxpayer (see Exhibit 12.1). Where the regular tax and AMT treatment of a deduction (or an item of expense) differ, the direction of the adjustment is determined as follows.

Regular tax deduction > **AMT deduction** = **Positive AMT adjustment**

Regular tax deduction < **AMT deduction** = **Negative AMT adjustment**

Conversely, the direction of an adjustment attributable to an income (or revenue) item can be determined as follows.

Regular tax income > **AMT income** = **Negative AMT adjustment**

Regular tax income < **AMT income** = **Positive AMT adjustment**

The remainder of this section discusses specific AMT adjustments.

Depreciation of Real Property

As discussed in text Section 8-2b, for regular tax purposes, real property is depreciated using the straight-line method. The cost of residential real property is recovered over 27.5 years, and the cost of all other real property is recovered over 39 years.[11] Whether an AMT adjustment is required for real property depreciation depends on when the property was placed in service.

For real property placed in service after 1986 (MACRS property) and before 1999, AMT depreciation is computed using the straight-line method, but the longer alternative depreciation system (ADS) recovery period is used. As a result, an AMT adjustment may be required.

For real property placed in service after 1998, no AMT adjustment is required.[12] After 1998, real property depreciation is the same for both AMT and regular tax purposes (see Exhibit 8.8 in Chapter 8). Thus, an AMT adjustment is not necessary.

[10] § 26(a)(2).

[11] The 39-year life generally applies to nonresidential real property placed in service on or after May 13, 1993.

[12] § 56(a)(1)(A).

Depreciation of Personal Property

Historically, AMT depreciation of tangible personal property was slower than regular tax depreciation. However, the differences between regular tax and AMT depreciation for such property have decreased over time. In many cases, the regular tax depreciation provisions also apply for AMT purposes. For instance, no AMT adjustment is required for any part of the cost of property that is expensed under § 179 (see text Section 8–3a).[13] Changes made by the TCJA of 2017 to the bonus depreciation provision (also known as additional first-year depreciation) further reduce the need for AMT depreciation adjustments for tangible personal property.

As discussed in text Section 8-3b, until December 31, 2022, taxpayers are eligible to deduct immediately 100 percent of the cost of qualified property placed in service for regular tax purposes. The bonus depreciation percentage is reduced by 20 percent for each tax year after 2022 and is completely phased out for property placed in service after 2026. For example, only 80 percent of the cost of qualified property placed in service in 2023 will be eligible for bonus depreciation.

In general, qualified property is broadly defined to include property with a recovery period of 20 years or less; software amortized over 36 months; water-utility property; qualified films, television and live theatrical productions; qualified improvement property; certain self-constructed assets; and plants and vines bearing fruits and nuts. Both new and used assets are eligible for bonus depreciation.[14]

For AMT purposes, a depreciation adjustment is not required when the cost of an asset is expensed under the bonus depreciation provision.[15] This is true both in the year the asset is placed in service and in all succeeding years in which the asset is depreciated for regular tax purposes (which would occur where the bonus depreciation percentage is less than 100 percent). In addition, a taxpayer may elect not to take bonus depreciation on an asset for regular tax purposes. However, as long as the asset was *eligible for* bonus depreciation, no AMT depreciation adjustment is required, again, either in the year placed in service or in any succeeding year.[16] As a result of these provisions and the applicability of bonus depreciation to used property, the AMT depreciation amount for most tangible personal property is the same as the asset's regular tax depreciation amount. The following examples illustrate these ideas.

Bonus Depreciation and AMT Depreciation

Example 4

Elison owns and operates a small after-school tutoring business. In early 2022, he purchased and placed in service furniture costing $18,000. Rather than depreciate the furniture, Elison deducts bonus depreciation of 100% of the cost of the furniture for regular tax purposes. No AMT depreciation adjustment is required in 2022 because bonus depreciation applies for both regular tax and AMT purposes.[17]

Example 5

Assume the same facts as in Example 4, except that Elison elects not to take bonus depreciation on the furniture and instead utilizes MACRS depreciation for regular tax purposes. He believes that his business will be more profitable in the future and would like to ensure that he has tax deductions available to offset this future income.

In 2022, Elison's regular tax depreciation deduction for the furniture is $2,572 ($18,000 × 0.1429). Even though the furniture is being depreciated for regular tax purposes, no AMT depreciation adjustment is needed because the property was *eligible* for bonus depreciation.

Where AMT depreciation adjustments are required (e.g., for public utility property and certain property owned by car dealerships ineligible for bonus depreciation), the amount

[13] S.Rept. No. 313, 99th Cong., 2d Sess. 522 (note 5) (1986).

[14] § 168(k).

[15] § 168(k)(2)(G).

[16] Rev.Proc. 2017–33.

[17] Assume instead that the furniture is placed in service in 2023, when the bonus depreciation percentage is 80%. If Elison deducted bonus depreciation of 80% of the cost of the furniture ($14,400) and then depreciated the remaining 20% ($3,600), his total depreciation deduction for regular tax purposes would be $14,914 [$14,400 + $514 ($3,600 × 0.1429)]. Since the depreciation of property subject to bonus depreciation is the same for both regular tax and AMT purposes, no adjustment would be required in 2023.

and direction of the adjustment is driven by a difference in the accelerated-depreciation percentage for regular tax and AMT purposes. For personal property, the MACRS recovery period and convention (see text Section 8-2a) are used to calculate regular tax depreciation as well as AMT depreciation. However, where the depreciation deduction for regular tax purposes is calculated using the 200 percent declining-balance method, AMT depreciation is calculated using the 150 percent declining-balance method.[18] (See Exhibit 8.6 in Chapter 8.) Example 6 illustrates the adjustment calculation.

Example 6

Sawyer placed an $8,000 asset ineligible for bonus depreciation in service in year 1. The MACRS recovery period for such an asset is three years. Annual regular tax (using 200% declining balance) and AMT depreciation (using 150% declining balance) amounts are as follows.

Tax Year	Regular Income Tax Deduction	AMT Deduction	AMT Adjustment
1	$2,666	$2,000	$ 666
2	3,556	3,000	556
3	1,185	2,000	(815)
4	593	1,000	(407)

As shown in Example 6, the same conventions are used for regular tax and AMT depreciation. Thus, the asset is fully depreciated over four years for both regular tax and AMT purposes because the same recovery period and the half-year convention are applied in both calculations. The AMT depreciation deduction is initially smaller because of the lesser declining balance percentage used for AMT purposes. As a result, the adjustments in year 1 and year 2 are positive; the taxable income starting point of the AMTI calculation is increased by these amounts to include the correct amount of depreciation in AMTI. In the last two years of the asset's life, the AMT adjustments are negative. The taxable income starting point of the AMTI calculation will be decreased by these amounts to include the correct amount of depreciation in AMTI. In total, the same amount of depreciation is taken for both regular tax and AMT purposes.

All personal property is taken into consideration in computing one net AMT depreciation adjustment, regardless of the date placed in service. Using this netting process, the AMT adjustment for a tax year is the difference between the total regular tax depreciation for all personal property and the total depreciation computed for that property for AMT purposes. In other words, the same principles that apply in Example 6 apply in aggregate.

Pollution Control Facilities

To encourage private industry to abate pollution, tax law provides beneficial amortization provisions for certified pollution control facilities in lieu of depreciation. For regular tax purposes, a taxpayer may elect to amortize the cost of certified facilities over 60 months. For AMT purposes, such an election is not allowed. Instead, the cost of certified pollution control facilities is recovered through depreciation.

Depreciation for AMT purposes is calculated using the straight-line method over the recovery period that would be used for regular tax (MACRS) purposes.[19] The AMT adjustment is equal to the difference between the regular tax amortization deduction and the AMT depreciation amount. The adjustment may be positive or negative. For example, the AMT deduction would be greater than the regular tax deduction after the 60-month regular tax amortization period ended. Thus, in these years, a negative AMT adjustment would be required.

Circulation Expenditures

Circulation expenditures are expenses incurred to establish, maintain, or increase the circulation of a newspaper, a magazine, or another periodical. For regular tax purposes, circulation expenditures, other than those the taxpayer elects to charge to a

[18] §§ 56(a)(1)(A) and 168(g).

[19] § 56(a)(5).

capital account, may be expensed in the year incurred.[20] For AMT purposes, circulation expenditures are not deductible in the year incurred. In computing AMTI, these expenditures must be capitalized and amortized ratably over the three-year period beginning in the year the expenditures were made.[21]

The AMT adjustment for circulation expenditures is calculated by comparing the amount expensed for regular tax purposes with the amount that can be amortized for AMT purposes. In general, in the year the circulation expenditures are incurred, the adjustment will be positive; more circulation expenditures are deducted for regular tax purposes than are allowed for AMT purposes. In the second and third years, the adjustment will be negative; a deduction is allowed for AMT purposes that was taken in the first year for regular tax purposes.

Example 7

In year 1, Lindsay's sole proprietorship incurred $30,000 of circulation expenditures. These expenditures were deducted in full in year 1 for regular tax purposes but amortized over three years for AMT purposes. Thus, in year 2, Lindsay will not have a regular tax deduction for circulation expenditures but will deduct $10,000 of circulation expenditures for AMT purposes. As a result, a negative AMT adjustment is required in year 2.

Year 2 taxable income (prior to standard deduction)		$ 95,000
Plus or minus: AMT adjustments		
Circulation expenditures deducted for regular tax purposes	$ -0-	
Circulation expenditures allowed for AMT purposes	(10,000)	
Negative adjustment		(10,000)
Plus: AMT preferences		-0-
AMTI		$ 85,000

In Example 7, the allowable AMT deduction is $10,000 more than the allowable regular tax deduction. Therefore, AMTI is $10,000 less than regular taxable income. This result is obtained by making a negative AMT adjustment of $10,000.

A taxpayer can avoid an AMT adjustment for circulation expenditures by electing to write off the expenditures over a three-year period for regular tax purposes.[22]

Expenditures Requiring 10-Year Write-Off for AMT Purposes

Certain expenditures that may be deducted earlier for regular tax purposes are written off over a 10-year period for AMT purposes. These rules apply to (1) mine exploration and development costs and (2) research and experimental expenditures.

In computing taxable income, taxpayers are allowed to deduct expenditures paid or incurred during the taxable year for exploration (ascertaining the existence, location, extent, or quality of a deposit or mineral) and for development of a mine or other natural deposit, other than an oil or gas well.[23] Mine development expenditures are expenses paid or incurred after the existence of ores and minerals in commercially marketable quantities has been discovered.

For AMT purposes, however, mine exploration and development costs must be capitalized and amortized ratably over a 10-year period.[24] The calculation of the adjustment for mine exploration and development costs is similar in spirit to that for circulation expenditures, apart from the difference in recovery period. The AMT adjustment is calculated by comparing the amount of mine exploration and development costs expensed (if any) for regular tax purposes with the amount required to be amortized for AMT purposes. In general, the adjustment will be positive in the year these expenses are incurred and negative thereafter.

[20] § 173(a).
[21] § 56(b)(2).
[22] § 59(e)(2)(A).
[23] §§ 617(a) and 616(a).
[24] § 56(a)(2).

Example 8

In the current year, Audrey incurs and deducts $150,000 of mine exploration expenditures for regular tax purposes. For AMT purposes, these mine exploration expenditures must be amortized over a 10-year period. Audrey makes a positive AMT adjustment of $135,000 ($150,000 deduction allowed for regular tax − $15,000 for AMT) for this year (i.e., the year in which the expenses were incurred). For AMT purposes, in each of the next nine years, Audrey makes a negative adjustment of $15,000 ($0 deduction allowed for regular tax − $15,000 for AMT).

To avoid the AMT adjustments for mine exploration and development costs, a taxpayer may elect to write off the expenditures over a 10-year period for regular tax purposes.[25]

Similarly, for regular tax purposes, research and experimental expenditures incurred after 2021 are capitalized and amortized ratably over the five-year period beginning with the midpoint of the year in which the costs are incurred. For AMT purposes, however, such costs must be amortized ratably over a 10-year period unless the taxpayer materially participates in the activity generating these expenditures. An AMT adjustment (positive or negative) may be required for the difference between the two amortization amounts.[26]

Completed Contract Method of Accounting

For a long-term contract, taxpayers are required to use the percentage of completion method for AMT purposes.[27] However, in limited circumstances, taxpayers can use the completed contract method for regular tax purposes.[28] Thus, where the percentage of completion method is not used for regular tax purposes, a taxpayer recognizes a different amount of income for regular tax purposes than for AMT purposes. The resulting AMT adjustment is equal to the difference between income reported under the percentage of completion method and the amount reported using the completed contract method. The adjustment can be either positive or negative depending on the amount of income recognized under the different methods.

Similar to some of the other adjustments discussed previously, a taxpayer can avoid an AMT adjustment on long-term contracts by using the percentage of completion method for regular tax purposes.

Incentive Stock Options

Like other compensatory options, **incentive stock options (ISOs)** are granted by employers to motivate employees to work harder to increase the value of the company. In return, employees should benefit from the increased compensation that a higher stock price brings. However, the exercise of an ISO is one of the more common triggers of an AMT liability.

At the time an ISO is granted, the option typically has a zero value. As a result, no gross income is recognized at the date of grant for regular tax purposes, and no adjustment is required for AMT purposes. If the value of the stock increases during the option period, the employee can obtain shares at a favorable price by exercising the option. For regular tax purposes, the exercise of an ISO does not increase taxable income.[29] However, for AMT purposes, the excess of the fair market value of the stock over the exercise price (the *spread* or the *bargain element*) is treated as an adjustment in the taxable year in which the option is exercised.[30]

[25] §§ 59(e)(2)(D) and (E).

[26] § 56(b)(2). Compare §§ 174(a) and 56(b)(2)(A)(ii). Research and experimental expenditures incurred before 2022 generally are amortized for regular tax purposes over a 60-month period beginning with the month in which benefits were realized from the expenses. Similar to mine exploration and development costs, the AMT adjustment for research and experimental expenditures can be avoided by electing to deduct such costs over a 10-year period for regular tax purposes. § 59(e).

[27] § 56(a)(3).

[28] See text Section 18-3b for a detailed discussion of the completed contract and percentage of completion methods of accounting.

[29] § 421(a).

[30] § 56(b)(3).

The Big Picture

Example 9

Return to the facts of *The Big Picture* on p. 12-1. For regular tax purposes, Caroline recognizes no gross income in either 2018, when the ISO is granted, or 2022, when the ISO is exercised. However, for AMT purposes, a positive adjustment is required for the bargain element in the year an ISO is exercised.

Because of the ISO exercised during the year, Caroline has a positive adjustment of $80,000 ($120,000 fair market value − $40,000 exercise price) for 2022.

As a result of this adjustment, the regular tax basis of the stock acquired through the exercise of ISOs is different from the AMT basis. The regular tax basis of the stock is equal to its cost, the exercise price of the option, whereas the AMT basis is equal to the fair market value of the stock on the date the option is exercised. Consequently, the amount of any gain or loss upon disposition of the stock likely will differ for regular tax and AMT purposes.

The Big Picture

Example 10

Return to the facts of *The Big Picture* on p. 12-1. Assume that Caroline sells the stock acquired with the option for $130,000 in December 2023. Her gain for regular tax purposes is $90,000 ($130,000 amount realized − $40,000 regular tax basis). For AMT purposes, the gain is $10,000 ($130,000 amount realized − $120,000 AMT basis). Therefore, Caroline will make a negative $80,000 adjustment in computing AMT in 2023.

Because the gain on sale was $80,000 larger for regular tax purposes ($90,000 regular tax gain − $10,000 AMT gain), a negative adjustment of $80,000 is required to reflect the $10,000 AMT gain. Note that this $80,000 negative adjustment upon disposition offsets the $80,000 positive adjustment made in the year of exercise.

An employee may be restricted as to when they can dispose of stock acquired with an ISO. In other words, the stock acquired with the option may not be freely transferable until some specified period has passed (see text Section 19-5a for further discussion of ISOs). If there were some restriction, then the employee would not make the AMT adjustment until the stock was freely transferable.

The Big Picture

Example 11

Return to the facts of *The Big Picture* on p. 12-1. Assume that the stock acquired with the exercise of the ISO is not freely transferable until 2023, when the fair market value was $65 per share.

Because the stock is not freely transferable until 2023, there is no AMT adjustment in 2022, the year of exercise. Instead, Caroline will make a positive adjustment of $90,000 ($130,000 fair market value − $40,000 exercise price) in 2023. The option contract does not affect regular taxable income in any tax year.

If the taxpayer exercises the ISO and disposes of the stock in the same tax year (a disqualifying disposition), compensation income is reported for regular tax purposes, which means that an AMT adjustment is not required for that option exercise.

Adjusted Gain or Loss

When property is sold or disposed of during the year, gain or loss reported for regular tax purposes may differ from gain or loss determined for AMT purposes. This difference occurs because the adjusted basis of the property for AMT purposes must reflect any current and prior AMT adjustments for the following.[31]

- Depreciation.
- Circulation expenditures.
- Research and experimental expenditures.

[31] § 56(a)(6).

- Mine exploration and development costs.
- Certified pollution control facility amortization.
- Bargain element, where stock is acquired with an ISO.

Remember that the AMT calculation begins with regular taxable income. Thus, any gain or loss adjustment should reflect the difference between the regular tax and AMT gain or loss amount. A negative gain or loss adjustment is required if:

- The gain for AMT purposes is less than the gain for regular tax purposes,
- The loss for AMT purposes is more than the loss for regular tax purposes, or
- A loss is computed for AMT purposes and a gain is computed for regular tax purposes.

Where the relationship between the regular tax and the AMT amount is reversed, the AMT gain or loss adjustment is positive.

Example 12

Return to the facts in Example 6. Sawyer sells the asset he placed in service in year 1 on September 1 of year 3 for $12,500. In the year of sale, two AMT adjustments result: the depreciation adjustment for year 3 and any gain (or loss) adjustment resulting from the sale.

The regular tax depreciation for year 3 is $593 [$8,000 cost × 14.81% (Chapter 8, Exhibit 8.3) × 0.5]. AMT depreciation for that year is $1,000 [$8,000 × 25% (Chapter 8, Exhibit 8.6) × 0.5]. Sawyer's negative AMT adjustment for year 3, reflecting the additional depreciation for AMT purposes, is $407 ($593 regular tax depreciation − $1,000 AMT depreciation).

In computing gain (or loss) as a result of the sale, the adjusted basis in the asset is different for regular tax and AMT purposes because of depreciation. The adjusted basis for each purpose is determined as follows.

	Regular Income Tax	AMT
Cost	$ 8,000	$ 8,000
Less: Depreciation for prior tax years (see Example 6)	(6,222)	(5,000)
Depreciation for year 3	(593)	(1,000)
Adjusted basis	$ 1,185	$ 2,000

Having determined the adjusted basis, the recognized gain for regular tax and AMT purposes is calculated as follows.

	Regular Income Tax	AMT
Amount realized	$12,500	$12,500
Adjusted basis	(1,185)	(2,000)
Recognized gain	$11,315	$10,500

Because the regular tax gain is greater than the AMT gain on the sale of the asset, Sawyer has a negative AMT adjustment of $815 ($11,315 regular tax gain − $10,500 AMT gain). Note that this negative adjustment offsets the prior and current-year adjustments for depreciation.

Passive Activity Losses

Losses on passive activities are not deductible in computing either regular taxable income or AMTI. However, the rules for computing taxable income differ from the rules for computing AMTI. It follows then that the rules for computing passive losses for regular tax purposes differ from the AMT rules for computing such losses. For example, where a passive activity involves circulation expenditures, if the amount of such expenditures differs for regular tax and AMT purposes, the amount of loss disallowed for AMT purposes will differ from the amount of the loss disallowed for regular tax purposes. Therefore, any *passive activity loss* computed for regular tax purposes may differ from the passive activity loss computed for AMT purposes.[32]

[32]See text Section 11-3.

Example 13

Matt acquired two passive activities this year. He received net passive income of $10,000 from Activity A and had no AMT adjustments or preferences in connection with the activity. Activity B produced gross income of $27,000 and operating expenses (not affected by AMT adjustments or preferences) of $19,000. In the current year, Matt claimed $30,000 of circulation expenditures related to Activity B. As a result, for AMT purposes, a positive $20,000 adjustment for circulation expenditures would be required for Activity B. In addition, Matt deducted $10,000 of percentage depletion in excess of basis (an AMT preference) for Activity B. The following comparison illustrates the differences in the computation of the passive activity loss for regular tax and AMT purposes for Activity B.

	Regular Income Tax	AMT
Gross income	$ 27,000	$ 27,000
Deductions		
Operating expenses	(19,000)	(19,000)
Circulation expenditures	(30,000)	(10,000)
Depletion	(10,000)	–0–
Passive activity loss	($ 32,000)	($ 2,000)

Because of the $20,000 adjustment for circulation expenditures and the preference for depletion (see the discussion of AMT preferences later in the chapter), the regular tax passive activity loss of $32,000 for Activity B is reduced, resulting in a passive activity loss of $2,000 for AMT purposes.

For regular tax purposes, Matt would offset the $10,000 of net passive income from Activity A with $10,000 of the passive loss from Activity B. For AMT purposes, he would offset the $10,000 of net passive income from Activity A with the $2,000 passive loss allowed from Activity B, resulting in passive activity income of $8,000. Thus, in computing AMTI, Matt makes a positive passive activity loss adjustment of $8,000 [$10,000 (passive activity loss allowed for regular tax) − $2,000 (passive activity loss allowed for AMT)].

To avoid duplication, the AMT adjustment for circulation expenditures and the AMT preference for depletion are *not* reported separately in the AMTI calculation; they are accounted for in determining the passive activity loss adjustment. Also note that differences in regular tax and AMT passive activity loss amounts in the current year will affect the amount of suspended passive activity losses carried forward to future tax years.

Example 14

Assume the same facts as in the previous example. For regular tax purposes, Matt reports a suspended passive activity loss of $22,000 [$32,000 (amount of loss) − $10,000 (loss used this year)]. This suspended passive activity loss can offset passive activity income in the future, or it may offset active or portfolio income when Matt disposes of the loss activity (see text Section 11-3f). For AMT purposes, Matt's suspended passive activity loss is $0 [$2,000 (amount of loss) − $2,000 (loss used this year)].

Alternative Tax Net Operating Loss Deduction

In computing taxable income, taxpayers can deduct net operating losses (NOLs) created in prior years (see text Section 7-6). Although the NOL deduction is allowed for AMT purposes, the regular tax NOL must be modified to compute AMTI correctly.

The starting point in computing the **alternative tax NOL deduction (ATNOLD)** is the NOL computed for regular tax purposes. The regular tax NOL is modified for AMT adjustments and tax preferences to arrive at the ATNOLD. Preferences and adjustment items benefited the taxpayer in computing the regular tax NOL. As a result, the adjustments made in calculating AMTI adjust the regular tax NOL amount; preferences that increase the regular tax NOL amount are added back in calculating the ATNOLD. This means that the taxpayer's regular tax NOL and ATNOLD will not be the same.[33]

Example 15

In 2022, Bianca incurred a regular tax NOL of $400,000. In 2021, she incurred mine exploration and development expenditures of $100,000; no additional expenditures were incurred in 2022. For AMT purposes, in 2022, Bianca will expense (make a negative AMT adjustment of) $10,000 related to the 2021 expenditures; this amount increases the ATNOLD. Bianca's deductions also include tax preferences of $80,000; this amount reduces the ATNOLD.

Bianca's ATNOLD carryforward to 2023 is $330,000 [$400,000 regular tax NOL − $80,000 tax preferences deducted in computing the NOL + $10,000 mine exploration and development costs adjustment].

In Example 15, if the regular tax NOL was allowed in full for AMT purposes, the $80,000 of tax preference items would have the effect of reducing AMTI in the year (or years) the 2022 NOL was utilized. Given that these preferences are disallowed in the calculation of AMTI, such an outcome is contradictory to the purpose of the AMT.

Finally, in keeping with the goal of ensuring that taxpayers with economic income pay some minimum amount of tax, a ceiling exists on the amount of the ATNOLD that can be deducted. The deduction is limited to 90 percent of AMTI (before the ATNOLD) in the year in which the NOL deduction is utilized.[34]

Example 16

Assume the same facts as in the previous example and that Bianca's AMTI (before the ATNOLD) in 2023 is $190,000. Therefore, of the $330,000 ATNOLD carryforward, only $171,000 ($190,000 × 90%) can be used in calculating the 2023 AMT. The unused $159,000 of 2022 ATNOLD will next be carried forward to 2024 for use in calculating that year's AMT.

In general, the regular tax NOL carryover provisions apply for purposes of the AMT. For instance, NOLs generated after 2020 are carried forward indefinitely (refer to text Section 7-6a) for both regular tax and AMT purposes.[35] Also note that a taxpayer who has an ATNOLD carryforward is considered to have utilized that ATNOLD in the calculation of the carryforward year's AMTI even if the taxpayer is not subject to the AMT in such year. This can result in the loss of an ATNOLD even when the taxpayer does not have an AMT liability.

Example 17

Emily's ATNOLD for 2023 (carried forward from 2022) is $10,000. AMTI in 2023, before considering the ATNOLD, is $25,000. If Emily's regular tax liability exceeds her TMT, the AMT does not apply. Nevertheless, Emily's ATNOLD of $10,000 is "used up" in 2023 and is not available for carryover to a later year.

---

[33] § 56(a)(4).

[34] § 56(d)(1)(A)(i)(II).

[35] § 172(b)(1).

Global Tax Issues — A Global Minimum Tax

The TCJA of 2017 eliminated the AMT provisions for C corporations. However, a corporate minimum tax continues to be a part of tax policy discussions both in the United States and around the world.

In January 2021, the Organization for Economic Cooperation and Development (OECD) announced that 130 countries had agreed to a proposal for a global corporate minimum tax. The goal of the proposed tax is to ensure that a multinational corporation pays a minimum amount of tax on its global income, regardless of that corporation's headquarters or home country.

What is the OECD's rationale for a corporate minimum tax? The concern shared by many governments is that multinationals with significant revenues from digital business activity are able to shift income across jurisdictions to minimize tax liability. In contrast to a brick-and-mortar economy, in the digital economy, value generally is created from a combination of algorithms, user data, sales functions, and technical knowledge. For example, a user contributes to value creation by sharing their preferences (e.g., liking a page) on a social media platform. This data will later be used by the multinational corporation to generate revenue from targeted advertising. However, the profits earned by the corporation are not always taxed in the user's country of residence. Such profits might be taxed in the country where the advertising algorithm was developed or where the royalty income was collected. As a result, the user's contribution to the multinational's profits is not considered in calculating the multinational's tax liability.

The problem the OECD is trying to solve arises because most current corporate tax systems were designed for a manufacturing economy; such systems are not as effective when revenue is earned from the sale, transfer, or use of intangible assets. Many governments believe that digital-economy multinationals either are not paying enough tax or are not paying tax in the "right" places.

Despite the consensus by these 130 countries that a corporate minimum tax is theoretically a good idea, designing and implementing such a tax will not be easy. All of the countries involved have different economic and development goals, and a handful currently have a corporate tax rate that might be lower than the proposed minimum tax rate.

In July 2021, the OECD announced that an agreement had been reached, in principle, on an outline for the minimum tax rules, with an expectation of enactment by 2023. The tax would apply to companies with more than €750 million in revenues. The end result of the plan would be that large companies would pay more tax in countries where they have customers and somewhat less in countries where their headquarters, employees, and operations were located. Additionally, the agreement includes a proposed global minimum tax rate of 15 percent, which would increase taxes on companies with earnings in low-tax jurisdictions.

The implementation of a corporate minimum tax is conditional on the enactment of such provisions by each OECD member country into its own tax law system. As a result, the successful implementation of a corporate minimum tax remains uncertain.

Source: Based on **oecd.org/newsroom/130-countries-and-jurisdictions-join-bold-new-framework-for-international-tax-reform.htm**, **europa.eu/rapid/press-release MEMO-18-2141 en.htm**, and **taxfoundation.org/global-tax-agreement/**.

Itemized Deductions

Most of the itemized deductions that are allowed for regular tax purposes are allowed for AMT purposes. As discussed next, for AMT purposes, the itemized deductions for certain taxes as well as interest expense require adjustment.

Taxes Any state and local sales, income, or property taxes (up to $10,000) deducted by an individual taxpayer in the calculation of regular taxable income are not allowed as a deduction in computing AMTI.[36] Thus, a positive AMT adjustment equal to the amount of such taxes deducted (up to $10,000) is required.

Also remember that under the tax benefit rule, a tax refund is included in regular taxable income to the extent the taxpayer obtained a tax benefit by deducting the tax in a prior year. If the taxpayer's gross income includes the recovery of any tax deducted as an itemized deduction for regular tax purposes, a negative AMT adjustment in the amount of the recovery is allowed. For example, state income taxes can be deducted for regular tax purposes but cannot be deducted in computing AMTI. Because of this, any refund of such taxes from a prior year that would be included in the calculation of regular taxable income is not included in AMTI.[37]

[36] § 56(b)(1)(A).

[37] § 56(b)(1)(C).

Example 18

Asma, age 35, is a resident of Minnesota. In 2021, her Federal taxable income included an itemized deduction of $4,200 for Minnesota income taxes. In February 2022, Asma received a Federal income tax refund of $5,800 and a Minnesota income tax refund of $600.

In 2022, Asma makes a negative AMT adjustment of $600 for the state tax refund. The $600 refund is included in 2022 regular taxable income because the deduction for state taxes reduced her prior year Federal income tax liability. However, the $600 refund is excluded from her 2022 AMTI because the deduction for state taxes was not allowed for AMT purposes.

Asma's Federal income tax refund does not create an AMT adjustment because Federal income taxes never are deducted in the calculation of regular taxable income or AMTI.

Interest in General In computing regular taxable income, taxpayers who itemize deductions can deduct qualified residence interest and they can deduct investment interest to the extent of net investment income (refer to text Section 10-3).

The AMT deduction allowed for interest expense includes only qualified housing interest[38] and investment interest,[39] to the extent of net investment income included in AMTI (as compared to regular taxable income). Any interest deducted in calculating regular taxable income that is not permitted in calculating AMTI is treated as a positive adjustment. The AMT adjustments for these amounts are discussed next.

Housing Interest Taxpayers who itemize deductions can deduct *qualified residence interest* on up to two residences. The deduction is limited to interest on acquisition indebtedness up to $750,000 ($375,000 for married taxpayers filing separately).[40] Acquisition indebtedness is debt that is incurred in acquiring, constructing, or substantially improving a qualified residence of the taxpayer and is secured by the residence.

The mortgage interest deduction for AMT purposes is limited to *qualified housing interest* rather than *qualified residence interest*. Qualified housing interest includes only interest incurred to acquire, construct, or substantially improve the taxpayer's principal residence and one other qualified dwelling used for personal purposes.

When additional mortgage interest is incurred (e.g., a mortgage refinancing), interest paid is deductible as qualified housing interest for AMT purposes only if:

- The proceeds are used to acquire or substantially improve a qualified residence,
- Interest on the prior loan was qualified housing interest, and
- The amount of the loan is not increased.

An AMT adjustment for mortgage interest likely will arise where interest is incurred on a second residence that is not a *qualified dwelling*. For instance, a houseboat can be considered a qualified residence but not a qualified dwelling. Thus, interest on a loan incurred to acquire a houseboat can be categorized as qualified residence interest but not qualified housing interest. A positive AMT adjustment would be required in the amount of any houseboat qualified residence interest allowed as an itemized deduction for regular tax purposes.

Investment Interest Investment interest is deductible for regular tax purposes and for AMT purposes to the extent of net investment income. However, an adjustment is required if the amount of investment interest deductible for regular tax purposes differs from the amount deductible for AMT purposes. For AMT purposes, net investment income must be computed taking into consideration AMT adjustment and preference provisions. For instance, the interest on private activity bonds usually is a tax preference for AMT purposes (see text Section 12-2b). Such interest also can affect the calculation of net investment income for AMT purposes.

[38] § 56(b)(1)(B)(i). Qualified housing interest is defined in § 56(e).

[39] § 56(b)(1)(B)(iii).

[40] § 163(h)(3)(F). For loans entered into prior to December 15, 2017, a $1,000,000 ($500,000 for married taxpayers filing separately) limit applies.

To determine the AMT adjustment for investment interest expense, it is necessary to compute the investment interest expense deduction for both regular tax and AMT purposes.

Example 19

Tom earned $20,000 interest income from corporate bonds and received $5,000 interest from private activity bonds. He reported the following amounts of investment income for regular tax and AMT purposes.

	Regular Income Tax	AMT
Corporate bond interest	$20,000	$20,000
Private activity bond interest	–0–	5,000
Net investment income	$20,000	$25,000

Tom incurred investment interest expense of $10,000 related to the corporate bonds. He also incurred $1,000 interest on a loan, the proceeds of which were used to purchase the private activity bonds. For regular tax purposes, this $1,000 is not deductible. His *investment* interest expense for regular tax and AMT purposes is computed below.

	Regular Income Tax	AMT
To carry corporate bonds	$10,000	$10,000
On loan to carry private activity bonds	–0–	1,000
Total investment interest expense	$10,000	$11,000

Investment interest expense is deductible to the extent of net investment income. Because the amount deductible for regular tax purposes ($10,000) differs from the amount deductible for AMT purposes ($11,000), an AMT adjustment is required.

AMT deduction for investment interest expense	$ 11,000
Regular tax deduction for investment interest expense	10,000
Negative AMT adjustment	$ 1,000

Medical Expenses Itemized medical expenses are subject to a 7.5%-of-AGI floor for all taxpayers, irrespective of age, for both regular tax and AMT purposes. Thus, no AMT adjustment for medical expenses is required.[41]

Computations and Elections Unlike some other AMT adjustments, a taxpayer cannot mitigate the effect of the itemized deduction adjustments by electing to treat the amounts in the same way for regular tax and AMT purposes. In addition, a taxpayer who elects the standard deduction for regular tax purposes cannot claim itemized deductions for AMT purposes.[42]

Other Adjustments

The standard deduction is not allowed in the calculation of AMTI. Thus, the standard deduction also gives rise to an AMT adjustment.[43] However, this adjustment enters the AMTI calculation indirectly by adjusting the taxable income amount that begins the AMTI calculation. If a taxpayer itemizes deductions, then the starting point for the AMTI

[41] § 213(a).

[42] SCA 200103073.

[43] § 56(b)(1)(E).

calculation is adjusted gross income (AGI) less itemized deductions. If, instead, a taxpayer takes the standard deduction, the starting point for the AMTI calculation is AGI. As discussed earlier in this chapter, a separate exemption (see Exemption Amount) is allowed for AMT purposes.

Example 20

Michael is single and has no dependents. He earned a salary of $225,000 in 2022, and his itemized deductions are less than the $12,950 standard deduction. Based on this information, Michael's taxable income for 2022 is $212,050 ($225,000 − $12,950 standard deduction). However, Michael's taxable income starting point for the AMTI calculation would be $225,000 since the adjustment for the standard deduction is made to the taxable income amount that starts the AMTI calculation. Any remaining adjustments (or preferences, discussed next) are made in the AMTI calculation.

Concept Summary 12.1

Summary of AMT Adjustment Provisions

1. Adjustments that reflect *timing differences* can be either positive or negative.
2. Apart from adjustments related to itemized deductions, some adjustments *can be avoided* if the taxpayer adopts the same tax treatment for regular tax purposes as is required for AMT purposes.
3. *Not all* itemized deductions trigger adjustments.
4. Where an asset is eligible for bonus depreciation or an asset is fully expensed in the year placed in service, *no depreciation adjustment* is required for the asset either in that year or in subsequent years in which depreciation is claimed.
5. The adjustment for the standard deduction *enters the AMT calculation indirectly* by adjusting the taxable income amount that begins the AMTI computation.

LO.4

Identify the preferences that are included in calculating AMTI.

12-2b Preferences

Unlike adjustments, which can be positive or negative, AMT **preferences** always are positive. In other words, preferences are added back to the taxable income starting point of the AMTI calculation.

Percentage Depletion

Congress enacted the percentage depletion rules to provide taxpayers with incentives to invest in the development of certain natural resources. Percentage depletion is computed by multiplying a rate specified in the Code by the gross income from the property (see text Section 8-6b).[44] The rate is based on the type of mineral involved. Generally, the basis of the property is reduced by the amount of depletion taken until the basis reaches zero. However, because percentage depletion is based on gross income rather than the investment in the property, taxpayers are allowed to continue taking percentage depletion deductions even after the basis of the property reaches zero. Thus, over the life of the property, depletion deductions may greatly exceed the cost of the property.

The percentage depletion preference is equal to the excess of the regular tax deduction for percentage depletion over the adjusted basis of the property at the end of the taxable year.[45] Note that the end-of-year basis is determined without regard to the depletion deduction for the taxable year. This preference is calculated separately for each mineral property owned by the taxpayer.[46] As a result, a taxpayer cannot use basis in one property to reduce the preference for excess depletion on another property.

---

[44] § 613(a).

[45] § 57(a)(1). The preference does not include percentage depletion on oil and gas wells of independent producers or royalty owners, as defined in § 613A(c).

[46] § 614(a).

Example 21

Kim owns a mineral property that qualifies for a 22% depletion rate. The basis of the property at the beginning of the year, prior to any current-year depletion deduction, is $10,000. Gross income from the property for the year is $100,000. For regular tax purposes, Kim's percentage depletion deduction (assume that the deduction is not limited by taxable income from the property) is $22,000. For AMT purposes, Kim has a tax preference of $12,000 ($22,000 − $10,000).

Intangible Drilling Costs

In computing regular taxable income, taxpayers can deduct certain intangible drilling and development costs in the year incurred, although such costs are normally capital in nature (see text Section 8-6a). The deduction is allowed for costs incurred in connection with oil and gas wells and geothermal wells.

For AMT purposes, excess intangible drilling costs (IDC) for the year are treated as a preference.[47] The IDC preference is computed separately for oil and gas wells and geothermal wells. The excess IDC preference is computed as follows.

IDC expensed in the year incurred
Minus: Deduction if IDC were capitalized and amortized over 10 years
Equals: Excess of IDC expense over amortization
Minus: 65% of net oil and gas or geothermal income
Equals: Preference amount

Example 22

Ben incurred IDC of $50,000 during the year and elected to expense that amount for regular tax purposes. His net oil and gas income for the year was $60,000. Ben has no income from geothermal wells in the current year. Ben's preference for IDC is $6,000 [($50,000 IDC − $5,000 amortization) − (65% × $60,000 income)].

A taxpayer can avoid the preference for IDC by electing to write off the expenditures over a 10-year period for regular tax purposes.

Interest on Private Activity Bonds

Like interest income earned on other municipal bonds, income from private activity bonds is not included in regular taxable income, and expenses related to carrying such bonds are not deductible for regular tax purposes. However, interest on private activity bonds is considered a preference in computing AMTI. As a result, expenses incurred in carrying the bonds are offset against the interest income in computing the preference amount.[48] Interest on private activity bonds issued in 2009 or 2010 is not treated as a preference.

In general, **private activity bonds** are issued by states or municipalities where more than 10 percent of the proceeds are for private business use.[49] For example, a state or local government seeking to attract jobs to a particular region might issue tax-exempt bonds to finance the construction of a factory for a privately owned business. Such a municipal bond would be a private activity bond.

The majority of tax-exempt bonds issued by states and municipalities are not classified as private activity bonds. Therefore, the interest income from such bonds does not regularly create a preference for AMT purposes.

Example 23

In the current year, Luisa has $3,000 of interest income from private activity bonds issued in 2018. The interest is excluded from gross income in computing regular taxable income but treated as a $3,000 preference in computing AMTI.

---

[47] § 57(a)(2).
[48] § 57(a)(5).
[49] § 141.

Example 24

In the current year, Danae earned $8,300 of interest income, comprised of:

10-year Treasury bond (issued in 2014)	$4,000
10-year municipal bond (issued in 2015)	2,500
10-year private activity bond (issued in 2018)	1,800

All of the bonds were purchased on their issuance date. Danae's preference for interest is $1,800, the interest on the private activity bond. Treasury bond interest is included in both regular taxable income and AMTI; the interest from the non-private activity municipal bond is not included in either regular taxable income or AMTI.

Exclusion for Certain Small Business Stock

Gain on the sale of certain small business stock that is owned for more than five years is excluded from gross income for regular tax purposes if that stock was acquired after September 27, 2010.[50] When claimed for regular tax, the small business stock exclusion generally does not create an AMT preference.[51]

Ethics & Equity Incentive Stock Options and the AMT

From a tax perspective, incentive stock options (ISOs) are an advantageous form of compensation. Such options do not create regular tax consequences either on the date of grant or the date of exercise as long as the holding period and certain additional requirements are met. However, as discussed in text Section 12-2a, the difference between the fair market value and the exercise price of an ISO creates an AMT adjustment in the year of exercise.

The AMT adjustment for this difference (i.e., the bargain element) is required unless a taxpayer sells the shares acquired with the ISO in the year of exercise. This is known as a disqualifying disposition. Where the price of the stock acquired with the ISO has declined since the exercise of the option, a disqualifying disposition is usually a good idea. For example, assume that a taxpayer exercises an ISO to purchase 500 shares of her employer's stock in March. The exercise price is $10, and the fair market value on the date of exercise is $50. Thus, the exercise of the ISO creates an AMT adjustment of $20,000 [($50 − $10) × 500] for that year. If by the end of the year the stock's value has declined to $16, the AMT adjustment still will be required even though the shares have declined in value and the taxpayer may not be confident that their value will increase over time. Thus, it would make sense for the taxpayer to make a disqualifying disposition before the end of the year, avoid the AMT adjustment, and pay (regular) tax on compensation income. In this example, the taxable amount would be $3,000 [($16 − $10) × 500 shares)].

However, where the stock's price increases in value in the year of exercise, a disqualifying disposition is usually best avoided. That is, in the example above, assume that the fair market value of the stock had increased to $65 near the end of the year. The AMT adjustment would be unchanged. Assuming that the taxpayer was in AMT, this adjustment would generate an AMT liability of $5,200 [$20,000 adjustment × 26% AMT rate]. A disqualifying disposition in that year would eliminate the necessity of the AMT adjustment but would trigger regular tax consequences. In this example, the taxpayer would have compensation income of $20,000 [($50 − $10) × 500] plus a short-term capital gain of $7,500 [($65 − $50) × 500]. As long as the taxpayer is in a regular tax bracket above the 26 percent or 28 percent AMT rates, the AMT adjustment has a lower tax cost than a disqualifying disposition.

Two additional considerations can be used to evaluate the above analysis. First, in the case where the stock's price increased after exercise, what if the taxpayer was leery of holding on to the stock acquired with the ISO because of concern that the employer's stock price would decline in value over time, perhaps due to some inside information the employee holds? Should a disqualifying disposition be made in that situation? Second, in the case where the stock's price declined after exercise, how does the increase in the AMT exemption and phaseout amounts affect the decision to undertake a disqualifying disposition?

[50] § 1202(a)(4). Different percentages for the excluded gain applied prior to this date. See §§ 1202(a)(1)–(3).

[51] An AMT preference equal to 7% of the exclusion applies to stock acquired before September 28, 2010. §§ 57(a)(7) and 1202(a)(4)(C).

12-2c Illustration of the AMT Computation

LO.5

Compute the AMT.

The computation of the AMT is illustrated in the following example.

Example 25

Molly Seims is single and age 56. She resides in Houston, Texas. Molly recorded taxable income for 2022 as follows.

Salary		$292,000
Interest on corporate bonds		18,000
Adjusted gross income		$310,000
Less itemized deductions:		
Medical expenses (do not exceed AGI threshhold)	$ -0-	
State income taxes	9,500	
Interest[a]		
Home mortgage (for qualified housing)	20,000*	
Investment interest	6,300*	
Charitable contributions (cash)	15,000*	
Casualty loss ($48,000 – 10% of AGI)[b]	17,000*	(67,800)
Taxable income		$242,200

[a]In this illustration, all interest is deductible in computing AMTI. Qualified housing interest is deductible without adjustment. Investment interest ($6,300) is deductible to the extent of net investment income for both regular taxable income and AMTI. Net investment income is $18,000 (corporate bond interest) for regular tax and $28,000 [$18,000 corporate bond interest plus $10,000 private activity bond interest (see below)] for AMTI. Investment interest ($6,300) is therefore fully deductible for both regular tax and AMT purposes.

[b]The casualty loss is the result of flooding that occurred in a Federally declared disaster area. Per § 165(h)(A), such losses are deductible subject to the $100 floor and the 10%-of-AGI limit. The $48,000 loss amount is after the $100 floor.

Deductions marked with an asterisk are allowed for AMT purposes. Thus, an adjustment is required for state income taxes; the remaining itemized deductions are allowed in calculating both regular taxable income and AMT.

In addition, Molly earned $10,000 of interest income on private activity bonds issued in 2015. She also exercised ISOs in 2022. The option spread (the difference between the exercise price and the fair market value on the date of exercise) was $65,000. Molly's regular tax liability in 2022 is $58,523. AMTI is computed as follows.

Taxable income	$242,200
Plus: Adjustments	
State income taxes	9,500
Incentive stock options	65,000
Plus: Preference (interest on private activity bonds)	10,000
Equals: AMTI	$326,700
Minus: AMT exemption	(75,900)
Equals: Minimum tax base	$250,800
TMT [($206,100 × 26%) + ($44,700 × 28%)]	$ 66,102
Minus: Regular tax liability	(58,523)
Equals: AMT	$ 7,579

12-3 AMT Credit

LO.6

Describe the role of the AMT credit in the alternative minimum tax structure.

As was illustrated in several of the examples in this chapter, timing differences that give rise to AMT adjustments eventually reverse. To provide equity for taxpayers, a tax credit is created in a year in which a taxpayer pays AMT as a result of these timing differences.[52]

This credit is known as the **alternative minimum tax credit**, and it is created only by the portion of the AMT liability that results from timing differences.[53] A credit is not

[52]§ 53.

[53]S.Rept. No. 313, 99th Cong., 2d Sess. 536 (1986).

created or increased by AMT items that create permanent differences between the regular tax liability and the AMT, including:

- The standard deduction.
- Itemized deductions not allowable for AMT purposes, including state and local taxes and certain interest expense.
- Excess percentage depletion.
- Tax-exempt interest on private activity bonds.

Example 26

Patrick, who is single, reports zero taxable income for 2022. He incurs positive AMT timing adjustments of $600,000 and a preference for excess percentage depletion of $300,000. Because of the amount of his AMTI, the AMT exemption is phased out completely and his AMT base is $900,000. Patrick's TMT is $247,878 [($206,100 × 26%) + ($693,900 × 28%)].

To determine the amount of AMT credit to carry over, the AMT must be recomputed to reflect only the effect of timing differences.

Example 27

Assume the same facts as in the previous example. If there had been no positive timing adjustments for the year, Patrick's AMT base would have been $224,100 ($300,000 AMTI − $75,900 exemption), and his TMT would have been $58,626 [($206,100 × 26%) + ($18,000 × 28%)]. Patrick carries over an AMT credit of $189,252 ($247,878 actual TMT − $58,626 TMT not related to timing differences) to 2023 and subsequent years.

Where a taxpayer generates an AMT credit, the credit can be utilized only in a year in which the taxpayer is not subject to the AMT. In addition, as demonstrated in the following example, the amount of the credit that can be used is equal to the excess of the taxpayer's regular tax liability over their tentative minimum tax liability. Finally, although the AMT credit cannot be carried back, the credit is carried forward indefinitely.

Example 28

Cho holds a $11,600 AMT credit from 2016. In 2022, prior to consideration of the AMT credit, Cho's regular tax liability is $60,000 and her tentative minimum tax is $54,000. In this situation, Cho can use $6,000 of the AMT credit from 2016 to reduce her 2022 regular tax liability. Thus, Cho's tax liability in 2022 is $54,000. The remaining $5,600 AMT credit is carried forward to future tax years.

Concept Summary 12.2

Summary of AMT Preference Provisions

1. Preferences are *always* positive in amount. A preference reflects a permanent difference between the regular tax and the AMT treatment of an amount.
2. With the exception of the IDC preference, preferences *cannot be avoided* by adopting the same tax treatment for regular tax and AMT purposes. In general, preferences can be avoided by not engaging in the activity that causes the preference, which may not be economically rational.
3. On occasion, Congress changes the tax code to stimulate economic activity. To the extent that an AMT preference could hinder this economic goal, the *preference also may be modified* (e.g., private activity bond interest, small business stock gain).

LO.7

Identify tax planning opportunities to minimize the AMT.

12-4 Tax Planning

12-4a Avoiding Preferences and Adjustments

One strategic approach to managing AMT liabilities is to avoid preference and adjustment amounts where possible.

- A taxpayer who expects to be subject to the AMT should not invest in private activity bonds unless doing so makes good investment sense. Any AMT triggered by interest on private activity bonds reduces the yield on an investment in such bonds.
- A taxpayer could be better off taking itemized deductions even when those deductions are less than the standard deduction if the itemized deductions do not require AMT adjustments. For example, a taxpayer with itemized deductions comprised of charitable contributions (that were less than the standard deduction) would not make an AMT adjustment for such contributions but would be required to make an adjustment for the standard deduction, which could contribute to an AMT liability.
- Neither personal property taxes nor real property taxes are deductible for AMT if they are categorized as itemized deductions. However, taxes deductible as a part of business operations or rental activities are allowed for AMT purposes. Therefore, a taxpayer who could qualify for a home office deduction would be able to deduct a portion of their home's real estate taxes as business expenses rather than as an itemized deduction potentially subject to the $10,000 limit.

Concept Summary 12.3

AMT Adjustments and Preferences for Individuals

Adjustments	**Positive**	**Negative**	**Both***
Adjusted gain or loss on property dispositions			X
Alternative tax NOL deduction (ATNOLD)			X
Circulation expenditures			X
Completed contract method			X
Depreciation of personal property			X
Depreciation of real property (placed in service before 1999)			X
Incentive stock options	X**		
Itemized deductions:			
Private activity bond interest that is AMT investment interest		X	
Property tax on personalty	X		
Property tax on realty	X		
Qualified residence interest that is AMT investment interest		X	
Qualified residence interest that is not qualified housing interest	X		
State income taxes	X		
Tax benefit rule for state income tax refund		X	
Mine exploration and development costs			X
Passive activity losses			X
Pollution control facilities			X
Research and experimental expenditures			X
Standard deduction	X		
Preferences			
Intangible drilling costs	X		
Percentage depletion in excess of adjusted basis	X		
Private activity bond interest income	X***		

*Timing differences.

**Although the adjustment is positive, the AMT basis for the stock acquired is increased by the amount of the positive adjustment.

***Interest on private activity bonds issued in 2009 or 2010 is not treated as a tax preference.

12-4b Controlling the Timing of Preferences and Adjustments

If preference and adjustment amounts cannot be avoided, the timing of these amounts may help to mitigate AMT liabilities.

- The AMT exemption often keeps items of tax preference from being subject to the AMT. To use the AMT exemption effectively, taxpayers should attempt to manage the timing of preference items in consideration of the exemption amount.
- In a year a taxpayer expects to be subject to the AMT, real estate or fourth-quarter estimated state tax payments should be paid in the following year. Any current-year benefit received from the regular tax deduction for these amounts will be offset by the AMT adjustment made.

12-4c Other AMT Tax Planning Strategies

A potential AMT liability can be reduced by decreasing adjusted gross income (AGI). Certain contributions to qualified retirement savings plans are excluded from gross income, which would result in a decreased AGI amount. Where a taxpayer participates in a § 401(k) or § 457(b) plan, or a SIMPLE IRA (see text Sections 19-1e and 19-2c), the maximum allowable salary deferral contributions to such a plan would reduce AGI, which is beneficial for both regular tax and AMT purposes, as well as for retirement planning.

Whereas the lower tax rates for long-term capital gains apply for both regular tax and AMT purposes, such long-term capital gains increase AGI and AMTI and could trigger the phaseout of some or all of the AMT exemption available to a taxpayer. In a year that a taxpayer expects to be subject to the AMT, the taxpayer should evaluate how the recognition of long-term capital gains affects AMTI and consider, where possible, whether the recognition of such gains should be deferred to a future year.

Crucial in properly calculating AMT (including in years when AMT is not owed) is good record keeping. For example, individuals need to track their passive activity income and loss annually for both regular tax and AMT purposes. This record keeping is also helpful in planning.

Refocus on The Big Picture

The Presence or Absence of the AMT

WAVEBREAKMEDIA/SHUTTERSTOCK.COM

Caroline meets with her tax return preparer to better understand the calculation of her tax liability as compared to Mateo's tax liability. The preparer explains that her employer was correct, but incomplete, in the description of the tax consequences of ISOs. While ISOs benefit from favorable regular tax treatment, there are AMT consequences associated with the exercise and sale of stock acquired with an ISO. The exercise of the ISO results in a positive adjustment of $80,000 (see Example 9) in the determination of Caroline's 2022 AMT.

The 2022 Federal income tax liabilities for Caroline and Mateo are computed as follows:

	Caroline	Mateo
Regular taxable income	$150,000	$200,000
Plus: Standard deduction	12,950	12,950
Plus: Adjustments	80,000	-0-
Equals: AMTI	$242,950	$212,950
Minus: AMT exemption	75,900	75,900
Equals: AMT base	$167,050	$137,050
TMT (26%)	$ 43,433	$ 35,633
Minus: Regular tax liability (2022 Single Tax Rate Schedule, Appendix A)	29,836	44,232
Equals: AMT	$ 13,597	$ -0-

continued

For 2022, Caroline's tax liability of $43,433 ($29,836 regular tax + $13,597 AMT) is comparable to Mateo's tax liability of $44,232 ($44,232 regular tax + $0 AMT). The reason for this result is Caroline's AMT liability arising from the exercise of the ISO. While the exercise of the ISO created an AMT liability in 2022, more favorable tax consequences may result in future years. Caroline's basis in the stock acquired in the exercise of the ISO will be $40,000 for regular tax purposes but $120,000 for AMT purposes. Thus, Caroline's AMT calculation in the year the stock is sold will include an $80,000 negative adjustment to reflect the different tax basis (see Example 10). In addition, Caroline has an AMT credit of $13,597 from 2022 that she can carry forward to offset regular tax in future years (see Example 28).

Key Terms

Adjustments, 12-6
Alternative minimum tax (AMT), 12-2
Alternative minimum tax credit, 12-21
Alternative tax NOL deduction (ATNOLD), 12-14
Exemption amount, 12-4
Incentive stock options (ISOs), 12-10
Preferences, 12-18
Private activity bonds, 12-19

Discussion Questions

1. **LO.1** Kelly was promoted and received a substantial raise that includes compensation in the form of incentive stock options. She talks to her tax adviser about potential tax ramifications. After making some projections, her adviser welcomes her to the AMT club. Kelly is surprised to learn that her promotion will be rewarded with an additional tax in the form of the AMT. Explain to Kelly the purpose of the AMT and why it applies to her.

2. **LO.2** How could the AMT be calculated without using regular taxable income as a starting point?

3. **LO.2** AMT liability results if the tentative minimum tax (TMT) exceeds the regular tax liability. What happens if the regular tax liability exceeds the TMT? Does this create a negative AMT amount that can be carried to other years? Explain.

4. **LO.2** Alfred is single, and his AMTI of $1,850,000 consists of the following amounts. What tax rates are applicable in calculating Alfred's TMT?

Ordinary income	$1,750,000
Long-term capital gains	70,000
Qualified dividends	30,000

5. **LO.2** Can any nonrefundable credits, other than the foreign tax credit, reduce the regular tax liability below the amount of the TMT? Explain.

6. **LO.3** How might a taxpayer who cannot avoid engaging in activities that generate AMT adjustments minimize or eliminate such adjustments?

7. **LO.3, 4** In a popular press article about the AMT, the author of the article indicated that he was not going to distinguish between preferences and adjustments because "… irrespective of the label, both items increase AMTI." What does the author's statement overlook?

8. **LO.3** Evaluate the validity of the following statement: In a year in which depreciable personal property is sold at a gain, the amount of the AMT gain will differ from the regular tax gain.

9. **LO.3** Evaluate the validity of the following statements: If the stock purchased with an incentive stock option (ISO) is sold in the year of exercise, no AMT adjustment is required. If the stock is sold in a later year, an AMT adjustment will be required.

10. **LO.3** In 2008, Malik purchased an office building for $500,000 to be used in his business. He sells the building in the current tax year. Explain whether his recognized gain or loss for regular tax purposes will be different from his recognized gain or loss for AMT purposes.

11. **LO.3** Paola exercised an incentive stock option on March 1, 2022. She acquired 2,000 shares of stock at an exercise price of $3 per share when the fair market value of the stock was $15 per share. However, Paola was concerned that the stock was overvalued, so she sold all of the stock acquired with the option on December 21, 2022, for $17 per share.

    Will Paola incur an AMT adjustment in 2022 as a result of the exercise of the option or the sale of the shares? Explain.

12. **LO.3, 5** How is it possible that a taxpayer could have an alternative tax NOL deduction (ATNOLD) larger than their alternative minimum taxable income (AMTI) yet still have a positive tentative minimum tax (TMT) amount?

Critical Thinking
Planning

13. **LO.3, 4, 7** Matt, who is single, always has elected to itemize deductions rather than take the standard deduction. In prior years, his itemized deductions exceeded the standard deduction by a substantial amount. Based on recent tax law changes and the fact that he recently paid off his home mortgage, he projects that his itemized deductions for 2022 will not exceed the standard deduction by very much, if at all. Matt anticipates that the amount of his itemized deductions will remain about the same in the foreseeable future.

    Matt's AGI is $850,000. He is investing the amount of his former mortgage payment each month in private activity municipal bonds. A friend recommends that Matt buy a beach house to increase his itemized deductions with the mortgage interest deduction. What are the relevant tax issues for Matt?

Critical Thinking
Planning

14. **LO.3** Amee moved to the San Francisco Bay Area to work for a technology startup 25 years ago. The startup eventually went public, and Amee is now one of the company's most senior and successful employees.

    Amee has owned a house in Nob Hill for the past 20 years. While the house has increased in value significantly during the time she has owned it, her property tax bill also has increased substantially. Given the $10,000 maximum regular tax deduction for state and local taxes and the fact that her property taxes create an AMT adjustment, Amee has decided that she would save a significant amount in AMT if she moved to a state with lower property taxes.

    Identify the flaw in Amy's logic with respect to the interaction of the $10,000 state and local tax deduction for regular tax purposes and the related AMT adjustment.

15. **LO.2, 3** In the calculation of AMTI, where is the adjustment for the standard deduction made and what is the reason for the adjustment?

Critical Thinking
Planning

16. **LO.4** During the year, Rachel earned $18,000 of interest income on private activity bonds that she had purchased in 2017. She also incurred interest expense of $7,000 in connection with amounts borrowed to purchase the bonds. How do these amounts affect Rachel's taxable income? Could there be a related beneficial effect in calculating AMTI? Explain.

Computational Exercises

17. **LO.2** Compute the 2022 AMT exemption for the following taxpayers.
    a. Bristol, who is single, reports AMTI of $650,000.
    b. Marley and Naila are married and file a joint tax return. Their AMTI is $1,528,000.

18. **LO.3** In March 2022, Serengeti exercised an ISO that had been granted by his employer, Thunder Corporation, in December 2019. Serengeti acquired 5,000 shares of Thunder stock for the exercise price of $65 per share. The fair market value of the stock at the date of exercise was $90 per share.
   What is Serengeti's 2019 AMT adjustment related to the ISO? What is the 2022 adjustment?

19. **LO.3** Brennen sold a machine used in his business for $180,000. The machine was purchased eight years ago for $340,000. Depreciation up to the date of the sale for regular tax purposes was $210,000 and $190,000 for AMT purposes.
   What, if any, AMT adjustment arises as a result of the sale of the machine?

20. **LO.4** Dimitri owns a gold mine that qualifies for a 15% percentage depletion rate. The basis of the property at the beginning of the year, prior to any current-year depletion deduction, is $21,000. Gross income from the property for the year is $200,000, and taxable income before depletion is $65,000.
   What is Dimitri's AMT depletion preference?

21. **LO.4** Kiki incurred intangible drilling costs (IDC) of $94,000 during the year and deducted that amount for regular tax purposes. Her net oil and gas income for the year was $110,000. Currently, Kiki has no income from geothermal wells.
   Kiki has calculated her current-year IDC preference to be $9,400. Is this the correct preference amount? Explain.

22. **LO. 2, 3, 5** Yanni, who is single, provides you with the following information for 2022.

Salary	$250,000
State income taxes	25,000
Mortgage interest expense on principal residence ($480,000 mortgage)	21,600
Charitable contributions	18,000
Interest income	13,000

   a. What is Yanni's 2022 taxable income?
   b. What is Yanni's 2022 AMT base?
   c. What is Yanni's 2022 TMT?

23. **LO.6** Elijah is single. He has a $12,000 AMT credit from 2021. In 2022, his regular tax liability is $28,000 and his tentative minimum tax is $24,000.
   Does Elijah owe AMT in 2022? How much (if any) of the AMT credit can Elijah use in 2022?

Problems

24. **LO.2, 3, 4, 5** Use the following data to calculate Chiara's AMT base in 2022. Chiara will itemize deductions and will file as a single taxpayer.

Taxable income	$248,000
Positive AMT adjustments	73,000
Negative AMT adjustments	25,000
AMT preferences	30,000

25. **LO.2, 3, 4, 5** Arthur Wesson, an unmarried individual who is age 58, reports taxable income of $510,000 in 2022. He records positive AMT adjustments of $80,000 and preferences of $35,000. Arthur itemizes his deductions, and his regular tax liability in 2022 is $152,253. Communications
   a. What is Arthur's AMT?
   b. What is the total amount of Arthur's tax liability?
   c. Draft an e-mail to Arthur explaining why he must pay tax in excess of the regular tax liability. Arthur's e-mail address is AWesson@FederalWest.com.

26. **LO.3, 4** In the current year, Dylan earned interest from the following investments.

Investment	Interest Income
10-year municipal bond (issued in 2009)	$1,300
10-year private activity bond (issued in 2010)	1,600
10-year Treasury bond (issued in 2015)	2,000
10-year private activity bond (issued in 2021)	900
Savings account	1,100

Dylan purchased all of the bonds on their issuance date. In addition, Dylan borrowed funds with which to purchase the 2010 private activity bond and incurred interest expense of $350 on that loan in the current year.

a. How much interest income will Dylan recognize for regular tax purposes in the current year?

b. What is her current-year AMT preference or adjustment for interest?

27. **LO.2, 3, 4** Calculate the exemption amount for the following cases in 2022 for a married taxpayer filing jointly and for a married taxpayer filing separately. In addition, use Microsoft Excel to express your solutions for the taxpayer who is married filing jointly. Place any parameter that could change annually in a separate cell, and incorporate the cell references into the formula.

Case	AMTI
1	$ 350,000
2	1,200,000
3	1,800,000

28. **LO.2** Jun records nonrefundable Federal income tax credits of $65,000 for the year. Her regular tax liability before credits is $190,000, and her TMT is $150,000.

a. What is Jun's AMT?

b. What is Jun's regular tax liability after credits?

Decision Making
Planning

29. **LO.2, 3, 7** Angela, who is single, incurs circulation expenditures of $270,000 during 2022. She is deciding whether to deduct the entire $270,000 or to capitalize the expenses and deduct them over a three-year period.

Angela is in the 37% bracket for regular tax purposes this year; she reports regular taxable income of $1,200,000 before considering the circulation expenses and has no AMT adjustments other than the circulation expenditures. Angela expects to be in the highest regular tax bracket in 2023 and 2024 as well. Advise Angela on how to treat the expenditures in 2022. Take the time value of money into consideration when calculating the tax savings of one alternative over another. Use the tables in Appendix E for this purpose, and assume that the pertinent discount rate is 4%.

30. **LO.3** Archie runs a small mineral exploration business (as a sole proprietorship). In 2020, he purchased land (for $68,000) where he suspected a magnesium deposit was located. He incurred $18,000 of exploration costs related to the development of the magnesium mine in 2020 and an additional $22,000 of exploration costs in 2021. Archie elected to deduct these expenditures for regular tax purposes in both 2020 and 2021.

In 2022, given a decline in magnesium prices, Archie sold the property for $66,000 rather than bring the mine to production.

What AMT adjustments are required in 2022 related to mine exploration expenditures and the sale of the land?

31. **LO.3, 7** In March 2022, Helen Carlon acquired used equipment for her business at a cost of $300,000. The equipment is five-year property for regular tax depreciation purposes. Communications Decision Making Planning
   a. If Helen depreciates the equipment using the method that will produce the greatest deduction for 2022 for regular tax purposes, what is the amount of the AMT adjustment?
   b. Draft an e-mail to Helen regarding the choice of depreciation methods. Helen's e-mail address is HCarlon@FederalWest.com.

32. **LO.3, 7** In 2022, Geoff incurred $900,000 of mine and exploration expenditures. He elects to deduct the expenditures as quickly as the tax law allows for regular tax purposes. Decision Making Planning
   a. How will Geoff's treatment of mine and exploration expenditures affect his regular tax and AMT computations for 2022?
   b. How can Geoff avoid having AMT adjustments related to the mine and exploration expenditures?
   c. What factors should Geoff consider in deciding whether to deduct the expenditures in the year incurred?

33. **LO.3** David is the sole proprietor of a real estate construction business. The business uses the completed contract method on a particular contract that requires 16 months to complete. The contract is for $500,000, with estimated costs of $300,000. At the end of 2021, $180,000 of costs had been incurred. The contract is completed in 2022, with the total cost being $295,000. Determine the AMT adjustments for 2021 and 2022.

34. **LO.3** In 2022, Reya exercised an incentive stock option that had been granted to her in 2019 by her employer, Weather Corporation. Reya acquired 100 shares of Weather stock for the option price of $190 per share. The fair market value of the stock at the date of exercise was $250 per share. Reya sells the stock for $340 per share in 2024.
   a. What is the amount of Reya's AMT adjustment in 2022? What is her recognized gain on the sale for regular tax and for AMT purposes in 2024?
   b. How would your answers in part (a) change if Reya had sold the stock in 2022 rather than 2024?

35. **LO.3** Andee is the sole proprietor of a small software development business. In 2022, the business incurred $250,000 of research and experimental expenditures. For regular tax purposes, Andee capitalizes and amortizes the expenses ratably over the applicable 5-year period.
   a. What is Andee's AMT adjustment for research and experimental expenditures in 2028?
   b. How would your answer to part (a) change if instead of owning and operating the software development business, Andee was a passive investor in the business?
   c. How would your answer to part (b) change if Andee had made the election to amortize the expenses for regular tax purposes over a 10-year period?

36. **LO.3** Wolfgang, who is age 33, records AGI of $125,000. He incurs the following itemized deductions for 2022.

Medical expenses [$11,875 − (7.5% × $125,000)]	$2,500
State income taxes	4,200
Charitable contributions	5,000
Home mortgage interest on his personal residence	6,000

   a. Calculate Wolfgang's itemized deductions for AMT purposes.
   b. What is the total amount of his AMT adjustments from these items?

37. **LO.3** Walter, who is single, owns a personal residence in the city. He also owns a cabin near a ski resort in the mountains. He uses the cabin as a vacation home. In the current year, he borrowed $60,000 on a home equity loan and used the proceeds to reduce credit card obligations and other debt. During the year, he paid the following amounts of interest.

On his personal residence	$16,000
On the cabin	7,000
On the home equity loan	2,500
On credit card obligations	1,500
On the purchase of an SUV	1,350

What amount, if any, must Walter recognize as an AMT adjustment for interest expense?

38. **LO.3, 4** During the current year, Yoon earned $10,000 in interest on corporate bonds and incurred $13,000 of investment interest expense related to the bond holdings. Yoon also earned $5,000 interest on private activity bonds that were issued in 2017 and incurred interest expense of $3,500 in connection with the bonds.
    a. How much investment interest expense can Yoon deduct for regular tax purposes for the year?
    b. What AMT adjustments and preferences arise as a result of the private activity bond interest income and expense?

39. **LO.3, 4** Gabriel, age 40, and Emma, age 33, are married with two dependents. They recorded AGI of $250,000 in 2022 that included net investment income of $3,000 and gambling winnings of $2,500.

    In itemizing deductions for regular tax purposes, the couple incurred the following expenses during the year.

Medical expenses (before 7.5%-of-AGI floor)	$12,000
State income taxes	5,800
Real estate tax	9,100
Interest on personal residence	18,600
Interest on home equity loan (proceeds were used to remodel the couple's kitchen)	9,800
Investment interest expense	4,500
Charitable contribution (cash)	14,200

    a. What is Gabriel and Emma's AMT adjustment for itemized deductions in 2022? Is it positive or negative?
    b. Gabriel and Emma also earned interest of $5,000 on private activity bonds that were issued in 2017. They borrowed money to buy these bonds and paid interest of $3,900 on the loan. Determine the effect on AMTI.

40. **LO.3** Anh is single, has no dependents, and itemizes deductions. In the current year for regular tax purposes, she records $60,000 of income and $105,000 of deductions and losses, primarily from business activities. Included in the losses are $30,000 of AMT preferences. Given this information, what are Anh's regular tax and alternative tax NOL amounts?

41. **LO.3, 4** Emily owns a silver mine (basis of $12,000 at the beginning of the year) that qualifies for a 15% depletion rate. Gross income from the property was $140,000, and net income before the percentage depletion deduction was $60,000. What is Emily's tax preference for excess depletion?

42. **LO.4** Amos incurred and expensed intangible drilling costs (IDC) of $70,000. His net oil and gas income was $60,000. What is the amount of Amos's preference for IDC?

43. **LO.4** Christopher regularly invests in technology company stocks, hoping to become wealthy by making an early investment in the next high-tech phenomenon. In 2014, Christopher purchased 3,000 shares of FlicksNet, a content streaming service, for $15 per share shortly after the company went public. Because Christopher purchased the shares in their initial offering, the shares are qualified small business stock.

In 2022, Christopher sold 800 of the shares (at $325 per share). What regular tax consequences and AMT consequences arise for Christopher as a result of the sale of these shares?

44. **LO.2, 3, 4, 5** Jane and Robert Brown are married and have eight children, all of whom are considered dependents for Federal income tax purposes. Robert earns $250,000 working as senior manager in a public accounting firm, and Jane earns $78,000 as a second-grade teacher. Given their large family, they live in a frugal manner. The Browns maintain a large garden and fruit trees from which they get most of their produce, and the children take family and consumer science classes so that they can help make the family's clothing and make household repairs.

The Browns record no gross income other than their salaries (all of their investment income is earned from qualified retirement savings), and their itemized deductions are less than the standard deduction. In addition, they incur no additional adjustments or preferences for AMT purposes.

a. What is the couple's 2022 regular tax liability?

b. What is the couple's 2022 AMT?

c. Express the calculation of the couple's AMT for 2022 as a Microsoft Excel formula. Place any parameter that could change annually in a separate cell, and incorporate the cell references into the formula.

45. **LO.2, 3, 4, 5** Pat is 40, is single, and has no dependents. She received a salary of $390,000 in 2022. She earned interest income of $11,000, dividend income of $15,000, gambling winnings of $14,000, and interest income from private activity bonds (issued in 2018) of $40,000. The dividends are not qualified dividends. The following additional information is relevant. Compute Pat's tentative minimum tax for 2022.

State income taxes	$ 8,100
Real estate taxes	4,000
Mortgage interest on principal residence	13,100
Investment interest expense	3,800
Gambling losses	5,100

46. **LO.2, 3, 4, 5** Renee and Sanjeev Patel, who are married, reported taxable income of $1,008,000 for 2022. They incurred positive AMT adjustments of $75,000 and tax preference items of $67,500. The couple itemizes their deductions.

a. Compute the Patels' AMTI for 2022.

b. Compute their tentative minimum tax for 2022.

47. **LO.2, 3, 4, 5** Farr is single, has no dependents, and does not itemize her deductions. She reports the following items on her 2022 tax return.

Bargain element from the exercise of an ISO (no restrictions apply to the stock)	$ 45,000
MACRS depreciation on shopping mall building acquired in 2017	49,000
Percentage depletion in excess of property's adjusted basis	50,000
Taxable income for regular tax purposes	221,000
Regular tax liability	51,103

a. Determine Farr's AMT adjustments and preferences for 2022.

b. Calculate Farr's AMT for 2022.

48. **LO.2, 3, 4, 5** Lynn, age 45, is single and has no dependents. Her income and expenses for 2022 are reported as follows.

Income—	
Salary	$233,000
Taxable interest on corporate bonds	13,700
Business income	64,000
Expenditures—	
Home office expense deduction	3,200
State income taxes	6,000
Real estate taxes	8,500
Mortgage (qualified housing) interest	9,200
Home equity loan interest	2,500
Investment interest	15,500
Cash contributions to various charities	2,900

The $64,000 business income is from Apex Office Supplies Company, a sole proprietorship that Lynn owns and operates from a home office. Lynn's self-employment tax deduction related to the Apex business income is $814. Lynn received interest of $30,000 on City of Pensacola private activity bonds that were issued in 2016.

Based on the information presented above, compute Lynn's AMT for 2022.

49. **LO.5, 6** Bonnie, who is single and itemizes deductions, reports a zero taxable income for 2022. She incurs positive timing adjustments of $200,000 and AMT exclusion items of $100,000 for the year. What is Bonnie's AMT credit carryover to 2023?

Tax Return Problems

Critical Thinking
Decision Making
Tax Forms Problem
ProConnect™ Tax

50. Robert A. Kliesh, age 41, is single and has no dependents. Robert's Social Security number is 111-11-1115. His address is 727 Big Horn Avenue, Sheridan, WY 82801. He does not contribute to the Presidential Election Campaign fund on his Form 1040.

Robert works as a financial analyst and is well regarded in his field. This year his salary totaled $1,250,000. His professional success has allowed him to purchase investments in real estate and corporate stocks and bonds. He also spends time volunteering with organizations that help people develop financial literacy skills. Examination of Robert's financial records provides the following information for 2021.

a. On January 16, Robert sold 1,000 shares of stock for a loss of $12,000. The stock was acquired 14 months ago for $17,000 and sold for $5,000. On February 15, he sold 400 shares of stock for a gain of $13,100. That stock was acquired in 2013 for $6,000 and sold for $19,100.
b. He received $100,000 of interest on private activity bonds that he purchased in 2017. He also received $40,000 of interest on tax-exempt bonds that are not private activity bonds.
c. Robert received rent income of $190,000 from an apartment complex he owns. He qualifies as an active participant in the activity. The property is located at 355 North Milward, Jackson, WY 83001.
d. Expenses related to the apartment complex, acquired in 2012, were $225,000.
e. Robert earns no taxable interest income. Because he invests only in growth stocks, he receives no dividend income.
f. He won $60,000 in the Wyoming lottery.
g. Robert was the beneficiary of an $800,000 life insurance policy on the life of his uncle Jake. He received the proceeds in October.

h. In February, Robert exercised an incentive stock option that was granted by his employer in 2018. The strike price of the option was $5 per share. On the date of exercise, the fair market value of the stock was $175 per share. Robert purchased 1,800 shares with the option; as of the end of the year, he still owns the stock (current FMV $138 per share).

i. Robert incurred the following potential itemized deductions.

- $5,200 fair market value of stock contributed to the Red Cross ($3,000 stock basis). He had owned the stock for two years. Robert also made cash contributions of $18,000 to qualified organizations during the year.
- $4,200 interest on consumer purchases.
- $18,900 state and local property taxes.
- $15,000 of medical expenses that he paid on behalf of his administrative assistant, who unexpectedly took ill.
- $8,000 paid for lottery tickets associated with playing the state lottery.
- $750 contribution to the campaign of the Green Party candidate for governor of Wyoming.
- Because Robert lived in Wyoming, he paid no state income tax.

Robert's W–2 shows Federal income tax withheld of $420,000 and Medicare tax withheld of $27,525. Robert also made estimated Federal income tax payments of $35,000. Robert did not engage in any virtual currency transactions, and he was covered by health insurance for the entire tax year. Additionally, he did not qualify for any coronavirus recovery rebates (economic impact payments); related questions in ProConnect Tax should be ignored.

Compute Robert Kliesch's 2021 net tax payable (including AMT), and complete his 2021 tax return using the appropriate forms and schedules. Suggested software: ProConnect Tax.

51. Jacob, age 42, and Jane Brewster, age 44, are married and file a joint return in 2022. The Brewsters have two dependent children, Lukas and Alexa, 14-year-old twins. Unless otherwise noted, all of the income and expense amounts in the problem relate to the 2022 tax year.

Critical Thinking
Decision Making
Tax Computation Problem

Jacob works as a data analyst; he earned $155,000. Jane is a computer systems analyst; she earned $160,000. In addition to their salaries, they recorded the following items of income.

Interest income (Carmel Sanitation District Bonds)	$22,000 (a)
Interest income (Carmel National Bank)	8,500
Qualified dividend income (Able Computer Corporation)	12,000
Gambling winnings	6,500
Inheritance (cash) received by Jane	35,000 (b)
"Citizen of the Year" award (Jane)	10,000 (c)
Gain on land sale	34,000 (d)

a. The Carmel Sanitation District Bonds are private activity bonds and were originally issued in April 2018.

b. Jane's uncle passed away early in the year. The executor divided his estate among his eight nieces and nephews. The $35,000 is Jane's share of the estate.

c. Jane was selected "Citizen of the Year" by the Carmel City Council. She used the award proceeds to pay down the family's credit card debt.

d. The Brewsters sold five acres of land to a real estate developer on October 12 for $120,000. They had acquired the land on May 15, 2012, for $86,000.

On April 1, Jane exercised an incentive stock option granted by her employer. At the date of exercise, the fair market value of the stock was $18 per share and the exercise price was $10 per share. Jane purchased 500 shares with the ISO exercise. As of December 31, the stock's fair market value was $25 per share.

The Brewsters incurred the following expenses during the year.

Charitable contributions (cash)	$ 9,500 (e)
Gambling losses	6,800
Investment interest expense	3,500
Mortgage interest—personal residence (reported on Form 1098)	8,600
Mortgage interest—home equity loan	1,800 (f)
Real property tax on personal residence	8,100
Supplies, professional organization memberships, continuing education for Jacob and Jane's work	15,800

e. In addition to their cash charitable contributions, the Brewsters contributed stock in Ace Corporation, which they acquired on February 9, 2008, at a cost of $6,500, to the Carmel Salvation Army, a qualifying charity. The fair market value of the stock was $11,000 on November 1, the date of the contribution.

f. The home equity loan was used to purchase the family's new minivan.

Taking into consideration the above amounts, the Brewsters' AGI is $386,000 and their taxable income is $338,800.

The following is a first draft of the Brewsters' 2022 AMTI calculation.

Taxable income prior to standard deduction	$364,700
Adjustments and preferences	
Citizen of the Year award	(10,000)
Real property taxes	(10,000)
Home equity interest	1,800
Charitable contribution of stock (difference between basis and FMV)	4,500
Incentive stock option exercise	7,500
Gambling loss disallowed for regular tax purposes	(300)
Supplies, professional organization memberships, etc.	4,220
AMTI	$362,420
Exemption amount	(75,900)
AMTI base	$286,520

Review the AMTI calculation, and prepare a list, including explanations, of any errors in the calculation. An error could include a missing amount or an amount that should not have been included, an amount that enters the calculation in the wrong direction, or a figure that enters the calculation in the wrong amount. You can presume that the Brewsters' AGI and taxable income amounts for the year are calculated correctly.

Research Problems

the answer company™ THOMSON REUTERS®

Note: Solutions to the Research Problems can be prepared by using the Thomson Reuters Checkpoint™ online tax research database, which accompanies this textbook. Solutions can also be prepared by using research materials found in a typical tax library.

Research Problem 1. Jaimee and Mike live in Austin, Texas. They married early in January 2021. They had saved a significant amount of money for their wedding, but instead decided to elope.

The couple used the money they had saved for the wedding to buy some vacant, unimproved land just outside Austin's city limits. Given the economic growth forecast for the area, they thought that the land was close enough to the city that it would eventually attract the attention of a property developer.

Jaimee and Mike's realtor told them that although their investment property was not currently generating any income, the investment would provide them with additional property tax deductions. However, Jaimee and Mike don't think that their itemized deductions will exceed the standard deduction. They also would prefer not to have any additional AMT adjustments. A significant portion of Jaimee's compensation consists of incentive stock options, and they are careful to manage any potential AMT liabilities.

For regular tax purposes, do Jaimee and Mike have any alternative to deducting the property taxes incurred on the investment property? If so, what impact would such an alternative have on their AMTI calculation?

Research Problem 2. On his 2021 Federal income tax return, Rigved deducted state income taxes of $8,000 for amounts withheld and estimated tax payments made in 2021. When he filed his 2021 state income tax return in April 2022, he discovered that he had overpaid his state income taxes by $1,500. Rather than having the $1,500 refunded to him, he rolled it forward as a 2022 estimated tax payment. Rigved was not subject to AMT in 2021. Critical Thinking

In preparing his 2022 Federal income tax return, Rigved is confused about how he should treat the $1,500. He knows that under the tax benefit rule, he should include the $1,500 in gross income in calculating his regular taxable income. However, because he will be subject to the AMT, he is uncertain as to how he should treat the $1,500 in calculating AMT. He thinks that the amount could be treated as a negative adjustment in converting taxable income to AMTI if 2021 had been an AMT year for him. Because it was not, Rigved is unsure of the treatment.

Advise Rigved on the appropriate treatment of the $1,500 in calculating his 2022 Federal income tax liability.

Use internet tax resources to address the following questions. Look for reliable websites and blogs of the IRS and other government agencies, media outlets, businesses, tax professionals, academics, think tanks, and political outlets.

Research Problem 3. The TCJA of 2017 repealed the corporate AMT provisions. However, any unused AMT credits a corporation had at that point in time were allowed to be used over four tax years, beginning in 2018. The 2020 Coronavirus Aid Relief and Economic Security Act (CARES Act) changed the treatment of corporate AMT credit carryforwards. Using the Thomson Reuters Checkpoint™ online tax research database, search in "Federal Tax Updates" and prepare an outline describing the CARES Act changes to the corporate AMT credit carryforward. E-mail your outline to your instructor. Communications

Research Problem 4. Use *IRS Tax Statistics* (**irs.gov/statistics/soi-tax-stats-individual-income-tax-returns**) to determine how many individual income tax returns reported an AMT liability from 2014 to 2019. What percentage of returns filed in this time period report an AMT liability? What percentage of tax revenues collected in that same period does the AMT comprise? Communications Data Analytics

Summarize your findings in a series of graphs to share with your classmates. Use the information gathered to discuss whether the tax revenues collected from the AMT justify the additional compliance costs imposed on taxpayers.

Research Problem 5. What would you expect the relationship to be between a taxpayer's AGI and AMT liability? In *IRS Tax Statistics* (**irs.gov/statistics/soi-tax-stats-individual-income-tax-returns**), find Table 1 in the preliminary data for individual income tax returns. Use the information in this table to explain the relationship between AGI and AMT liability across time. Summarize the relationship in visual form, and be prepared to discuss the directionality of the relationship and any other information the data provides. Communications Critical Thinking Data Analytics

Becker CPA Review Questions

Becker

1. Anthony entered into a long-term construction contract in year 3. The total profit of the contract is $80,000 and does not change over the life of the contract. The contract will be completed in year 5. The contract is 20% and 70% complete at the end of years 3 and 4, respectively. What is the alternative minimum tax adjustment required in year 4?

   a. $16,000
   b. $40,000
   c. $56,000
   d. $80,000

2. How is the alternative minimum tax credit applied in the calculation of the tentative minimum tax (TMT)?

   a. It is carried forward indefinitely and applied to regular tax only.
   b. It is carried back five years and applied to regular tax only.
   c. It is carried forward indefinitely and can be applied to regular tax or AMT.
   d. It is carried forward five years and applied to regular tax only.

3. Carol reports taxable income of $48,000. Included in that calculation are the following items.

Real estate taxes on her home	$2,000
Mortgage interest on acquisition indebtedness	1,200
Charitable contribution	550

   Carol also had excluded municipal bond interest income of $8,000, $3,000 of which was deemed to be private activity bond interest. What are Carol's total alternative minimum tax (AMT) adjustments?

   a. $1,200
   b. $2,000
   c. $3,000
   d. $6,750

4. Which of the following statements is most correct?

   a. Tax preference items for the alternative minimum tax are always added back to regular taxable income.
   b. Itemized deductions that are added back to regular taxable income for the alternative minimum tax are preference items.
   c. Tax preference items for the alternative minimum tax can be an increase or a decrease to regular taxable income.
   d. All taxpayers are able to deduct the full exemption in the calculation of the alternative minimum tax.

5. Betty is age 34 and has AGI of $50,000. The following items may qualify as itemized deductions for Betty:

Qualified medical expenses (before 7.5% AGI floor)	$6,000
Real estate tax	1,200
State income tax	800
Charitable contributions	600
Mortgage interest on acquisition indebtedness	2,000
Home equity interest on a loan used to improve the home	300

   What is the itemized deduction add-back for the AMT?

   a. $2,000
   b. $2,800
   c. $3,800
   d. $8,800

6. Betty is age 34 and has AGI of $50,000 and regular taxable income of $35,000. The following items may qualify as itemized deductions for Betty:

Qualified medical expenses (before percentage of AGI floor)	$3,000
Real estate tax	1,200
State income tax	800
Charitable contributions	600
Mortgage interest on acquisition indebtedness	2,000
Home equity interest on a loan used to improve the home	300

What is the alternative minimum taxable income (AMTI)?

a. $35,000

b. $37,500

c. $37,000

d. $52,800

Chapter 13

Tax Credits and Payment Procedures

Learning Objectives: *After completing Chapter 13, you should be able to:*

- **LO.1** Explain how tax credits are used to achieve social, economic, or environmental objectives or to promote equity among taxpayers.
- **LO.2** Distinguish between refundable and nonrefundable credits and understand the order in which they can be used by taxpayers.
- **LO.3** Describe various business-related tax credits.
- **LO.4** Describe various tax credits that are available primarily to individual taxpayers.
- **LO.5** Describe the tax withholding and payment procedures applicable to employers.
- **LO.6** Explain and illustrate the payment procedures applicable to self-employed persons.
- **LO.7** Explain the additional Medicare taxes assessed on high-income individuals.
- **LO.8** Identify tax planning opportunities related to tax credits and payment procedures.

Chapter Outline

13-1 Tax Policy Considerations, 13-3

13-2 Overview and Priority of Credits, 13-4
- 13-2a Refundable versus Nonrefundable Credits, 13-4
- 13-2b General Business Credit, 13-5
- 13-2c Treatment of Unused General Business Credits, 13-5

13-3 Specific Business-Related Tax Credits, 13-6
- 13-3a Tax Credit for Rehabilitation Expenditures, 13-6
- 13-3b Work Opportunity Tax Credit, 13-7
- 13-3c Research Activities Credit, 13-7
- 13-3d Low-Income Housing Credit, 13-9
- 13-3e Disabled Access Credit, 13-10
- 13-3f Credit for Small Employer Pension Plan Startup Costs, 13-11
- 13-3g Credit for Employer-Provided Child Care, 13-11
- 13-3h Credit for Employer-Provided Family and Medical Leave, 13-12

13-4 Other Tax Credits, 13-12
- 13-4a Earned Income Credit, 13-12
- 13-4b Foreign Tax Credit, 13-14
- 13-4c Child and Dependent Tax Credits, 13-15
- 13-4d Credit for Child and Dependent Care Expenses, 13-15
- 13-4e Education Tax Credits, 13-18
- 13-4f Energy Credits, 13-19
- 13-4g Credit for Certain Retirement Plan Contributions, 13-19

13-5 Payment Procedures, 13-23
- 13-5a Employers, 13-23
- 13-5b Self-Employed Taxpayers, 13-25
- 13-5c Additional Medicare Taxes on High-Income Individuals, 13-29

13-6 Tax Planning, 13-31
- 13-6a Credit for Child and Dependent Care Expenses, 13-31
- 13-6b Adjustments to Increase Withholding, 13-32
- 13-6c Adjustments to Avoid Overwithholding, 13-33

YELLOW DOG PRODUCTIONS/GETTY IMAGES

The Big Picture

Education Tax Credits

Tom and Jennifer Snyder have two children in college. Lora is a freshman, and her tuition and required fees in 2022 total $14,000. Lora has a partial scholarship amounting to $6,500, and the Snyders paid the balance of her tuition ($7,500), plus room and board of $8,500. Sam is a junior, and the Snyders paid $8,100 for his tuition, plus $7,200 for his room and board. Both students qualify as Tom and Jennifer's dependents.

The Snyders have AGI of $158,000. They would like to know what tax options are available to them related to these educational expenses. They have heard about education tax credits, but they believe that their income is too high for them to get any benefit. Are they correct?

Read the chapter and formulate your response.

Framework 1040 **Tax Formula for Individuals**

This chapter covers the boldfaced portions of the Tax Formula for Individuals that was introduced in Concept Summary 3.1 on p. 3-3. Below those portions are the sections of Form 1040 where the results are reported.

Income *(broadly defined)*	$xx,xxx
Less: Exclusions	(x,xxx)
Gross income	$xx,xxx
Less: Deductions *for* adjusted gross income	(x,xxx)
Adjusted gross income	$xx,xxx
Less: The greater of total **itemized deductions** *or* the standard deduction	(x,xxx)
Charitable contributions if you take the standard deduction*	(xxx)
Personal and dependency exemptions**	(x,xxx)
Deduction for qualified business income***	(x,xxx)
Taxable income	$xx,xxx
Tax on taxable income *(see Tax Tables or Tax Rate Schedules)*	$ x,xxx
Less: Tax credits *(including income taxes withheld and prepaid)*	(xxx)

FORM 1040 (2021 p. 2)

Line	Description		
16	**Tax** (see instructions). Check if any from Form(s): 1 ☐ 8814 2 ☐ 4972 3 ☐		16
17	Amount from Schedule 2, line 3		17
18	Add lines 16 and 17		18
19	Nonrefundable child tax credit or credit for other dependents from Schedule 8812		19
20	Amount from Schedule 3, line 8		20
21	Add lines 19 and 20		21
22	Subtract line 21 from line 18. If zero or less, enter -0-		22
23	Other taxes, including self-employment tax, from Schedule 2, line 21		23
24	Add lines 22 and 23. This is your **total tax** ▶		24
25	Federal income tax withheld from:		
a	Form(s) W-2	25a	
b	Form(s) 1099	25b	
c	Other forms (see instructions)	25c	
d	Add lines 25a through 25c		25d
26	2021 estimated tax payments and amount applied from 2020 return		26
27a	Earned income credit (EIC) (If you have a qualifying child, attach Sch. EIC.)	27a	
	Check here if you were born after January 1, 1998, and before January 2, 2004, and you satisfy all the other requirements for taxpayers who are at least age 18, to claim the EIC. See instructions ▶ ☐		
b	Nontaxable combat pay election 27b		
c	Prior year (2019) earned income 27c		
28	Refundable child tax credit or additional child tax credit from Schedule 8812	28	
29	American opportunity credit from Form 8863, line 8	29	
30	Recovery rebate credit. See instructions	30	
31	Amount from Schedule 3, line 15	31	
32	Add lines 27a and 28 through 31. These are your **total other payments and refundable credits** ▶		32
33	Add lines 25d, 26, and 32. These are your **total payments** ▶		33

Tax due (or refund)	$ xxx

* For 2021, married taxpayers may claim up to $600 of cash charitable donations ($300 if unmarried).

** Exemption deductions are not allowed from 2018 through 2025.

*** Only available from 2018 through 2025.

As explained in Chapter 1, Federal tax law often serves purposes besides merely raising revenue for the government. Evidence of equity, social, and economic considerations is found throughout the tax law, including in the area of **tax credits**. Consider the following examples.

Example 1

Paul and Peggy, husband and wife, are both employed outside the home. Their combined salaries are $50,000. However, after paying for child care expenses of $2,000 on behalf of their daughter, Polly, the net economic benefit from both spouses working is $48,000. The child care expenses are, in a sense, business-related because they would not have been incurred if both spouses did not work outside the home. If no tax benefits are associated with the child care expenses, $50,000 is subject to tax.

Another couple, Alicia and Diego, also have a child, John. Diego stays home to care for John (the value of those services is $2,000) while Alicia earns a $48,000 salary. Because the value of Diego's services rendered is not subject to tax, only Alicia's earnings of $48,000 are subject to tax.

The *credit for child and dependent care expenses* helps to mitigate the costs incurred by working taxpayers who must pay for child care services to work outside the home.

Example 2

Consider two taxpayers, Graham and Addison, both of whom incur the same economic income in 2022.

Graham, age 66, is a retired taxpayer who receives $18,000 of Social Security benefits as his only source of income. His Social Security benefits are excluded from gross income. As a result, Graham's income tax is $0.

Addison, a single taxpayer 66 years of age, has, as her sole source of income, $18,000 from a pension plan funded by her former employer. Assuming that Addison has no itemized deductions or deductions *for* AGI, her income tax (before credits) is computed as follows.

Pension plan benefits	$18,000
Less: Basic standard deduction	(12,950)
Additional standard deduction	(1,750)
Taxable income	$ 3,300
Income tax (at 10%)	$ 330

The *tax credit for elderly or disabled taxpayers* was enacted to mitigate the perceived inequity of some taxpayers with equal incomes paying different amounts of Federal income tax.

Example 3

Jane is a single parent who depends on the government's "safety net" for survival—she receives benefits under the Temporary Assistance to Needy Families program in the amount of $15,000 per year. However, she very much wants to work. Jane has located a job that will pay $15,500 per year and has found an individual to care for her child at no cost. But with the $1,185.75 ($15,500 × 7.65% tax rate) withholding for Social Security and Medicare taxes, the economic benefit from working is less than remaining reliant on the government ($14,314.25 versus $15,000).

The *earned income credit* helps offset the effect of Social Security and Medicare taxes on wages of the working poor and provides an incentive to work.

The tax credits available to individuals and other taxpayers are a major focus of this chapter. Tax credits are categorized as being either refundable or nonrefundable; this distinction may affect the taxpayer's ability to enjoy a tax benefit from a particular credit. The chapter continues with a discussion of the credits available to businesses and to individual taxpayers, and the ways in which credits enter into the calculation of the tax liability.

The Federal income tax system largely is based on the pay-as-you-go concept. That is, taxpayers or their employers are required to make deposits with the Federal government during the year related to the annual tax liability. These deposits are, in effect, refundable credits. The chapter concludes with a brief discussion of employer withholding procedures; special rules encountered by self-employed persons; penalties imposed on underpayments; and an overview of two tax provisions that are part of the Affordable Care Act—the premium tax credit and additional Medicare taxes on high-income individuals.

13-1 Tax Policy Considerations

LO.1

Explain how tax credits are used to achieve social, economic, or environmental objectives or to promote equity among taxpayers.

Congress generally uses tax credits to achieve social, economic, or environmental objectives or to promote equity among different types of taxpayers. For example, the disabled access credit was enacted to accomplish a social objective: to encourage taxpayers to renovate older buildings so that they would be in compliance with the Americans with Disabilities Act. The research activities credit encourages high-tech and energy research in the United States. The use of tax credits as a policy tool continues to evolve as economic and political circumstances change.

A tax credit is much different from an income tax deduction. Income tax deductions reduce a taxpayer's tax base; tax credits reduce a taxpayer's tax liability. As a result, the tax benefit received from a tax deduction depends on the tax rate; a tax credit is not affected by the tax rate of the taxpayer.

Example 4

Assume that Congress wants to encourage a certain type of activity. One way to accomplish this objective is to allow a tax credit of 25% for any expenses paid related to this activity. Another way is to allow an itemized deduction for the expenses. Abby's tax rate is 12%, Bill's tax rate is 35%, and they both itemize their deductions. Carmen does not incur enough qualifying expenses to itemize deductions. The following tax benefits are available to each taxpayer for a $1,000 payment.

	Abby	Bill	Carmen
Tax benefit if a 25% credit is allowed	$250	$250	$250
Tax benefit if an itemized deduction is allowed	120	350	-0-

As these results indicate, tax credits provide benefits on a more equitable basis than do tax deductions—all three taxpayers reduce their tax liabilities by the same amount. Equally apparent is that the deduction approach in this case benefits only taxpayers who itemize deductions, while the credit approach benefits all taxpayers who make the specified payments.

LO.2

Distinguish between refundable and nonrefundable credits and understand the order in which they can be used by taxpayers.

13-2 Overview and Priority of Credits

13-2a Refundable versus Nonrefundable Credits

Exhibit 13.1 identifies some of the more common refundable and nonrefundable credits. **Refundable credits** are paid to the taxpayer even if the amount of the credit (or credits) exceeds the taxpayer's tax liability.

Exhibit 13.1 Partial Listing of Refundable and Nonrefundable Credits

Refundable Credits

Taxes withheld on wages
Child tax credit*
Earned income credit
Affordable Care Act premium tax credit (covered in online ACA appendix)

Nonrefundable Credits

General business credit, which includes:

- Tax credit for rehabilitation expenditures
- Work opportunity tax credit
- Research activities credit
- Low-income housing credit
- Disabled access credit
- Credit for small employer pension plan startup costs
- Credit for employer-provided child care
- Credit for employer-provided family and medical leave

Credit for elderly and disabled
Foreign tax credit
Adoption expenses credit
Dependent tax credit
Credit for child and dependent care expenses**
Education tax credits***
Energy credits
Credit for certain retirement plan contributions
Small employer health insurance credit

*In 2021, the child tax credit was fully refundable. In 2022, the child tax credit is refundable to the extent of 15% of the taxpayer's earned income in excess of $2,500 (limited to a maximum of $1,500). Parents with three or more qualifying children compute the refundable portion using an alternative method.

**Refundable in 2021.

***Forty percent of the American Opportunity credit is refundable.

Example 5

Ted, who is single, had taxable income of $22,000 in 2022. His income tax from the 2022 Tax Rate Schedule is $2,435. During 2022, Ted's employer withheld income tax of $3,200. Ted is entitled to a refund of $765, because the credit for tax withheld on wages is a refundable credit.

Nonrefundable credits are not paid if they exceed the taxpayer's tax liability.

Example 6

Tina is single, age 67, and retired. Her taxable income for 2022 is $1,320, and the tax on this amount is $132. Tina's tax credit for the elderly is $225. This nonrefundable credit can be used to reduce her net tax liability to zero, but it will not result in a refund, even though the credit ($225) exceeds Tina's tax liability ($132).

Some nonrefundable credits, like the general business credit, can be "carried over" to other tax years if they exceed the credit allowed in a given year. Other nonrefundable credits, like the lifetime learning credit, simply are lost if they cannot be used in the tax year. Because some credits are refundable and others are not and because some credits are subject to carryover provisions and others are not, the order in which credits are offset against the tax liability can be important.

13-2b General Business Credit

The **general business credit** is composed of a number of other credits, each of which is computed separately under its own set of rules.[1] The general business credit combines these credits into one amount to limit the amount of business credits that can be used to offset a taxpayer's income tax liability.

For any tax year, the general business credit is limited to the taxpayer's *net income tax* reduced by the greater of:[2]

- The *tentative minimum tax*. See Exhibit 12.1.
- 25 percent of *net regular tax liability* that exceeds $25,000.[3]

Net regular tax liability is the regular tax liability reduced by certain nonrefundable credits (e.g., credit for child and dependent care expenses and foreign tax credit).

Example 7

Aleshia's general business credit for the current year is $70,000. Her net income tax is $150,000, tentative minimum tax is $130,000, and net regular tax liability is $150,000. She has no other tax credits. Aleshia's general business credit allowed for the tax year is computed as follows.

Net income tax	$ 150,000
Less: The greater of	
$130,000 (tentative minimum tax)	
$31,250 [25% × ($150,000 − $25,000)]	(130,000)
Amount of general business credit allowed for tax year	$ 20,000

Aleshia then has $50,000 ($70,000 − $20,000) of unused general business credits that may be carried back or forward as discussed below.

13-2c Treatment of Unused General Business Credits

Unused general business credits are initially carried back one year and are applied to reduce the tax liability during that year. As a result, the taxpayer may receive a tax refund as a result of the carryback. Any remaining unused credits are then carried forward 20 years.[4]

[1] The separate credits are listed in § 38(b).

[2] § 38(c).

[3] This amount is $12,500 for married taxpayers filing separately unless one of the spouses is not entitled to the general business credit.

[4] § 39(a)(1).

A FIFO method is applied to the carrybacks, carryovers, and utilization of credits earned during a particular year. By using the oldest credits first, the FIFO method minimizes the potential for loss of a general business credit benefit due to the expiration of credit carryovers.

Example 8

This example illustrates the use of general business credit carryovers.

General business credit carryovers		
2019	$ 4,000	
2020	6,000	
2021	2,000	
Total carryovers	$12,000	
2022 general business credit		$ 40,000
Total credit allowed in 2022 (based on tax liability)	$50,000	
Less: Utilization of carryovers		
2019	(4,000)	
2020	(6,000)	
2021	(2,000)	
Remaining credit allowed in 2022	$38,000	
Applied against		
2022 general business credit		(38,000)
2022 unused amount carried forward to 2023		$ 2,000

LO.3

Describe various business-related tax credits.

13-3 Specific Business-Related Tax Credits

Each component of the general business credit is determined separately under its own set of rules. Some of the more important credits that make up the general business credit are explained here in the order listed in Exhibit 13.1.

13-3a Tax Credit for Rehabilitation Expenditures

The **rehabilitation expenditures credit** is intended to discourage businesses from moving from older, economically distressed areas to newer locations while encouraging the preservation of historic structures. The credit is 20 percent of qualified rehabilitation expenditures related to a certified historic structure (either residential or nonresidential).[5] The 20 percent credit is taken ratably over a five-year period starting with the year the rehabilitated building is placed in service. When taking the credit, the basis of a rehabilitated building must be reduced by the full rehabilitation credit allowed.[6]

Example 9

In the current year, Juan spent $100,000 to rehabilitate a certified historic structure (adjusted basis of $40,000). He is allowed a $20,000 (20% × $100,000) credit for rehabilitation expenditures. The credit will be spread equally over five years ($4,000 per year). Juan then increases the basis of the building by a net amount of $80,000 [an increase of $100,000 (rehabilitation expenditures) and a decrease of $20,000 (credit allowed)].

To qualify for the credit, *certified historic structures* must be substantially rehabilitated during a 24-month period. A building has been *substantially rehabilitated* if qualified rehabilitation expenditures exceed the greater of:

- The adjusted basis of the property before the rehabilitation expenditures, or
- $5,000.

[5] § 47.

[6] § 50(c).

Qualified rehabilitation expenditures do not include the cost of acquiring a building, the cost of facilities related to a building (such as a parking lot), and the cost of enlarging an existing building.

13-3b Work Opportunity Tax Credit

The **work opportunity tax credit** encourages employers to hire individuals from one or more of a number of targeted and economically disadvantaged groups.[7] Examples include long-term unemployed individuals (those unemployed for at least 27 weeks), qualified ex-felons, high-risk youths, participants in the Federal Supplemental Nutrition Assistance Program (SNAP), veterans, summer youth employees, and long-term family assistance recipients.

Computation of the Work Opportunity Tax Credit: General

The credit is generally equal to 40 percent of the first $6,000 of wages (per eligible employee) for the first 12 months of employment. In general, the credit is not available for any wages paid to an employee after the *first year* of employment. If the employee's first year overlaps two of the employer's tax years, however, the employer may take the credit over two tax years. If the credit is taken, the employer's tax deduction for wages is reduced by the amount of the credit.

For an employer to qualify for the 40 percent credit, the employee must (1) be certified by a designated local agency as being a member of one of the targeted groups and (2) have completed at least 400 hours of service to the employer. If an employee meets the first condition but not the second, the credit rate is reduced to 25 percent provided the employee has completed a minimum of 120 hours of service to the employer.

Work Opportunity Credit Calculation

Example 10

In January 2022, Green Company hires four individuals who are certified to be members of a qualifying targeted group. Each employee works 800 hours and is paid wages of $8,000 during the year. Green Company's work opportunity credit is $9,600 [($6,000 × 40%) × 4 employees].

If the tax credit is taken, Green must reduce its deduction for wages paid by $9,600. No credit is available for wages paid to these employees after their first year of employment.

Example 11

On June 1, 2022, Maria, a calendar year taxpayer, hires Joe, a certified member of a targeted group. During the last seven months of 2022, Joe is paid $3,500 for 500 hours of work. Maria is allowed a credit of $1,400 ($3,500 × 40%) for 2022. Joe continues to work for Maria in 2023 and is paid $7,000 through May 31, 2023.

Because up to $6,000 of first-year wages are eligible for the credit, Maria is allowed a 40% credit on $2,500 [$6,000 − $3,500 (wages paid in 2022)] of wages paid in 2023. The credit is $1,000 ($2,500 × 40%). None of Joe's wages paid after May 31, 2023, the end of the first year of Joe's employment, are eligible for the credit.

13-3c Research Activities Credit

To encourage business-related research and experimentation, also termed research and development (R&D), a credit is allowed for certain qualifying expenditures paid or incurred by a taxpayer. The **research activities credit** is the *sum* of three components: an incremental research activities credit, a basic research credit, and an energy research credit.[8]

[7] § 51. The credit is available for qualifying employees who start work before 2026.

[8] § 41. An eligible small business ($50 million or less in gross receipts) can use the credit to reduce its alternative minimum tax (AMT) liability. In addition, a qualified startup company (less than $5 million in gross receipts) can offset the credit against its payroll tax liability.

Incremental Research Activities Credit

The incremental research activities credit is equal to 20 percent of the *excess* of qualified research expenses for the taxable year over the base amount.[9]

In general, *research expenditures* qualify if the research relates to discovering technological information that is intended for use in the development of a new or improved business component of the taxpayer. If the research is performed in-house (by the taxpayer or employees), all of the expenses qualify. If the research is contracted to others outside the taxpayer's business, only 65 percent of the amount paid qualifies for the credit.[10]

Example 12

Javiera incurs the following research expenditures.

In-house wages, supplies, computer time	$50,000
Payment to Cutting Edge Scientific (a contractor)	30,000

Javiera's qualified research expenditures are $69,500 [$50,000 + ($30,000 × 65%)].

The incremental research credit is *not* allowed for:[11]

- Research conducted once commercial production begins.
- Surveys and studies such as market research, testing, or routine data collection.
- Research conducted *outside* the United States, Puerto Rico, or U.S. possessions.
- Research in the social sciences, arts, or humanities.

Determining the *base amount* involves a complex series of computations meant to approximate recent historical levels of research activity by the taxpayer. As a result, the credit is allowed only for increases in research expenses.

Example 13

Jack, a calendar year taxpayer, incurred qualifying research expenditures of $200,000 at the beginning of 2021. Assuming that the base amount of qualified expenditures was $100,000, the incremental research activities credit was $20,000 [($200,000 − $100,000) × 20%].

In addition to qualifying for the research credit, research expenditures also can be capitalized and amortized or, in years beginning before 2022, immediately deducted in the year incurred.[12] To prevent taxpayers from receiving multiple benefits from the same expenditures, taxpayers claiming the research credit must make one of the following adjustments:

1. Reduce any immediate deduction otherwise allowable by the full amount of the credit taken,
2. If the credit exceeds the amount that would be allowable as an immediate deduction for the year, reduce any amount capitalized and amortized by the full amount of any credit taken,[13] or
3. Instead of reducing the amount of expenditures immediately deducted or capitalized and amortized, reduce the credit by the product of the full credit times the highest corporate tax rate (currently 21 percent).[14]

[9] An alternative simplified credit procedure is available. See §§ 41(c)(4) and (5).

[10] In the case of payments to a qualified research consortium, § 41(b)(3)(A) provides that 75% of the amount paid qualifies for the credit. In contrast, for amounts paid to an energy research consortium, § 41(b)(3)(D) allows the full amount to qualify for the credit.

[11] § 41(d). See also Reg. §§ 1.41–1 through 1.41–7.

[12] § 174. Also refer to the discussion in text Section 7-4. Although the immediate deduction for research and experimental expenditures expired at the end of 2021, it might be extended by Congress.

[13] § 280C(c)(1).

[14] § 280C(c)(2).

Example 14

Assume the same facts as in Example 13, which shows that Jack's potential 2021 incremental research activities credit was $20,000. Jack must choose between the following options:

	Credit Amount	Deduction Amount
1. Take the full credit and a reduced deduction		
$20,000 − $0	$20,000	
$200,000 − $20,000		$180,000
2. Take the full credit and capitalize and amortize the costs over 60 months		
$20,000 − $0	20,000	
($200,000 ÷ 60) × 12		40,000
3. Take a reduced credit and a full deduction		
$20,000 − [(100% × $20,000) × 21%]	15,800	
$200,000 − $0		200,000

Note that if the expenditures were incurred in 2022, no immediate deduction would be available and the taxpayer must choose between (1) taking the full credit and reducing the amount capitalized and amortized or (2) capitalizing and amortizing the full amount of the expenditures and reducing the credit by the product of the full credit times the highest corporate tax rate.

Basic Research Credit

Corporations (other than S corporations or personal service corporations) are allowed an additional 20 percent credit for basic research payments made in *excess* of a base amount. *Basic research* is defined generally as any original investigation for the advancement of scientific knowledge not having a specific commercial objective. Basic research conducted outside the United States and in the social sciences, arts, or humanities does not qualify. This reflects the intent of Congress to use the credit to encourage domestic high-tech research.

The basic research credit calculation is complex and is based on expenditures in excess of a specially defined base amount. The portion of the basic research expenditures not in excess of the base amount qualifies for the incremental research activities credit.

Example 15

Orange Corporation pays $75,000 to a university for basic research. Orange's base amount for the basic research credit is $50,000. The basic research activities credit allowed is $5,000 [($75,000 − $50,000) × 20%]. The $50,000 of basic research expenditures that equal the base amount also can be treated as research expenses for purposes of the regular incremental research activities credit.

Energy Research Credit

This component of the research credit encourages taxpayers to support an exempt organization conducting energy research called an energy research consortium. The credit is equal to 20 percent of payments made to these organizations.

13-3d Low-Income Housing Credit

To encourage the development of affordable housing for low-income individuals, a credit is available to owners of qualified low-income housing projects.[15]

More than any other credit, the **low-income housing credit** is influenced by nontax factors. For example, these credits are distributed nationally to various state and local agencies. So the property must be approved by the appropriate agency authorized to provide low-income housing credits.

[15] § 42.

The credit is based on the number of units rented to low-income tenants. Tenants are low-income tenants if their income does not exceed a specified percentage of the area median gross income. The amount of the credit is determined by multiplying the qualified basis by a credit rate.[16]

Generally, first-year credits are prorated based on the date the project is placed in service. A full year's credit is taken in each of the next nine years, and any remaining first-year credit is claimed in the eleventh year. The credit is claimed over a 10-year period if the property continues to meet the required conditions.

Example 16

Sarah spends $1,000,000 to build a qualified low-income housing project that is completed on January 1 of the current year. The entire project is rented to low-income families. Assume that the credit rate for property placed in service during January is 7.25%. Sarah may claim a credit of $72,500 ($1,000,000 × 7.25%) in the current year and in each of the following nine years.

If Sarah only made 75% of the project's units available to low-income families, her credit would be $54,375 [($1,000,000 × 75%) × 7.25%].

Recapture of a portion of the credit may be required if certain events occur (e.g., if the number of low-income tenant units falls below a minimum threshold or if the taxpayer sells the property).

13-3e Disabled Access Credit

The **disabled access credit** encourages eligible small businesses to make their facilities accessible to disabled individuals. The credit is 50 percent of the eligible expenditures that exceed $250 but do not exceed $10,250. As a result, the maximum credit is $5,000 ($10,000 × 50%).[17]

An *eligible small business* is a business that during the previous year either had gross receipts of $1 million or less or had no more than 30 full-time employees. An eligible business can include a sole proprietorship, a partnership, a regular corporation, or an S corporation.

Eligible expenditures include reasonable and necessary amounts that are paid or incurred to make older buildings accessible (only buildings first placed in service before November 6, 1990, qualify). Qualifying projects include installing ramps, widening doorways, and adding raised markings on elevator control buttons. Costs to assist hearing- or visually-impaired employees or customers who interact with the business also qualify. These costs can include both personnel (e.g., an interpreter) or equipment (e.g, audio or visual equipment or modifications to existing equipment).

The property's tax basis is reduced by the amount of the credit.

Example 17

This year, Red, Inc., an eligible small business, makes $11,000 of capital improvements to a building that had been placed in service in June 1990. The improvements make Red's business more accessible to the disabled and are eligible expenditures for purposes of the disabled access credit.

The amount of the credit is $5,000 [($10,250 − $250) × 50%]. Although $11,000 of eligible expenditures are incurred, only $10,000 qualifies for the credit. The capital improvements have a depreciable basis of $6,000 [$11,000 (cost) − $5,000 (amount of the credit)].

[16] The qualified basis is the property's cost times the percentage of units made available to low-income tenants; the rate is subject to adjustment every month by the IRS.

[17] § 44.

13-3f Credit for Small Employer Pension Plan Startup Costs

Small businesses are entitled to a nonrefundable credit for administrative costs associated with establishing and maintaining certain qualified retirement plans (primarily, plans for non-highly compensated employees).[18] Although these costs (e.g., payroll system changes, retirement-related education programs, and consulting fees)[19] are deductible as ordinary and necessary business expenses, the credit lowers the after-tax cost of establishing a qualified retirement program and encourages eligible employers to offer retirement plans for their employees.

The **credit for small employer pension plan startup costs** is 50 percent of qualified startup costs. An eligible employer is one with fewer than 100 employees who have earned at least $5,000 of compensation. In general, the maximum credit is the *lesser* of (1) $5,000 or (2) $250 times the number of non-highly compensated employees. However, the minimum credit is $500. The deduction for the startup costs incurred is reduced by the amount of the credit. The credit can be claimed for qualifying costs incurred in each of the three years beginning with the tax year in which the retirement plan becomes effective.

Example 18

Maple Company decides to establish a qualified retirement plan for its non-highly compensated employees. In the process, it pays consulting fees of $21,200 to a firm that will provide educational seminars to Maple's eligible employees and will assist the payroll department in making necessary changes to the payroll system. Maple has 65 non-highly compensated employees who are eligible to participate in the plan.

Maple claims a credit for the pension plan startup costs of $5,000 [the *lesser* of $5,000 or $16,250 ($250 × 65 non-highly compensated employees)]. Its deduction for these expenses is reduced to $16,200 ($21,200 − $5,000).

13-3g Credit for Employer-Provided Child Care

An employer's expenses to provide for the care of employee children is a deductible business expense. Alternatively, employers may claim a credit for providing child care facilities to their employees during normal working hours.[20]

The **credit for employer-provided child care**, limited annually to $150,000, is composed of the aggregate of two components: 25 percent of qualified child care expenses and 10 percent of qualified child care resource and referral services. *Qualified child care expenses* include the costs of acquiring, constructing, rehabilitating, expanding, and operating a child care facility. *Child care resource and referral services* include amounts paid or incurred under a contract to provide child care resource and referral services to an employee.

Any qualifying expenses otherwise deductible by the taxpayer are reduced by the amount of the credit. In addition, the taxpayer's basis for any property acquired or constructed and used for qualifying purposes is reduced by the amount of the credit. If within 10 years of being placed in service a child care facility ceases to be used for a qualified use, the taxpayer must recapture a portion of the credit previously claimed.[21]

Example 19

During the year, Tan Company constructed a child care facility for $400,000. The facility will be used by Tan employees who have preschool-aged children in need of child care services while their parents are at work. In addition, Tan incurred $100,000 of salaries for child care workers and other administrative costs associated with the facility.

As a result, Tan's credit for employer-provided child care is $125,000 [($400,000 + $100,000) × 25%]. Correspondingly, the basis of the facility is reduced to $300,000 ($400,000 − $100,000), and the deduction for salaries and administrative costs is reduced to $75,000 ($100,000 − $25,000).

[18] § 45E. A highly compensated employee is one who owns 5% of the business in the current or prior year or in the prior year earned more than $135,000 (if 2022 is the prior year; $130,000 for 2021). In addition to this credit, a $500 credit is available to small employers who include an automatic enrollment provision in retirement plans they offer (§ 45T).

[19] §§ 45E(c)(1) and (d)(1).

[20] § 45F.

[21] § 45F(d). Such a rule, often referred to as a *clawback*, is an accountability measure to help ensure that tax incentives are used as intended.

13-3h Credit for Employer-Provided Family and Medical Leave

Employers can claim a general business credit equal to 12.5 percent of the wages paid to qualifying employees while they are on family and medical leave.[22] To claim the **credit for employer-provided family and medical leave**, employers must pay a minimum of 50 percent of the wages normally paid to an employee during the leave. If the wages paid during the leave *exceed* 50 percent of normal wages, the credit is increased by 0.25 percentage point for each percentage point above 50 percent. For example, if the employer pays 60 percent of the usual wages, then the credit is 15 percent [12.5 percent + (0.25 × 10)].

The credit is capped at 25 percent of wages paid (this would be allowed if the employer paid 100 percent of the employee's wages during the leave). The credit is limited to 12 weeks of leave per employee during any taxable year.

An employer must have a written policy in place that allows all qualifying full-time employees no less than two weeks of annual paid family and medical leave (non-full-time employees must be offered leave on a pro rata basis). Wages paid as vacation leave, personal leave, or other medical or sick leave are not considered to be family and medical leave. The credit applies to wages paid in taxable years beginning after 2017 and before 2026.

LO.4

Describe various tax credits that are available primarily to individual taxpayers.

13-4 Other Tax Credits

13-4a Earned Income Credit

The **earned income credit** provides income tax equity to the working poor. In addition, the credit helps to offset other Federal taxes, such as the gasoline tax, that impose a relatively larger burden on low-income taxpayers. Further, the credit encourages economically disadvantaged individuals to become contributing members of the workforce.

The earned income credit is determined by multiplying a maximum amount of earned income by the appropriate credit percentage (see Exhibit 13.2). Generally, earned income includes employee compensation and net earnings from self-employment; it excludes items such as interest, dividends, pension benefits, nontaxable employee compensation, and alimony.[23] If a taxpayer has children, the credit percentage used in the calculation depends on the number of qualifying children.

In 2022, the maximum earned income credit for a taxpayer with one qualifying child is $3,733 ($10,980 × 34%), $6,164 ($15,410 × 40%) for a taxpayer with two qualifying children, and $6,935 ($15,410 × 45%) for a taxpayer with three or more qualifying children. However, the maximum earned income credit is phased out completely if the taxpayer's earned income or AGI exceeds certain thresholds, as shown in Exhibit 13.2.[24]

To the extent that the greater of earned income or AGI exceeds $26,260 in 2022 for married taxpayers filing a joint return ($20,130 for other taxpayers), the difference, multiplied by the appropriate phaseout percentage, is subtracted from the maximum earned income credit.

[22] § 45S; "family and medical leave" is as defined by the Family and Medical Leave Act of 1993.

[23] § 32. Due to the COVID-19 pandemic and resultant decreases in earned income, taxpayers were allowed to use either 2019 or 2021 earned income in calculating their 2021 earned income credit. The earned income credit is not available if the taxpayer's unearned income (e.g., interest and dividends) exceeds $10,300 in 2022 ($10,000 in 2021). See § 32(i).

[24] § 32(a)(2)(B). A married taxpayer filing a separate return (and living apart from his or her spouse for the last six months of the year) can claim the earned income credit provided the taxpayer lives with a qualifying child for more than half of the year.

Exhibit 13.2 Earned Income Credit and Phaseout Percentages

Tax Year	Number of Qualifying Children	Earned Income Base Amount	Credit Percentage	Maximum Credit	Phaseout Base	Phaseout Percentage	Phaseout Ends at Income of
2022	*Married, Filing Joint*						
	No children	$ 7,320	7.65	$ 560	$15,290	7.65	$22,610
	One child	10,980	34.00	3,733	26,260	15.98	49,622
	Two children	15,410	40.00	6,164	26,260	21.06	55,529
	Three or more children	15,410	45.00	6,935	26,260	21.06	59,187
	Other Taxpayers						
	No children	$ 7,320	7.65	$ 560	$ 9,160	7.65	$16,480
	One child	10,980	34.00	3,733	20,130	15.98	43,492
	Two children	15,410	40.00	6,164	20,130	21.06	49,399
	Three or more children	15,410	45.00	6,935	20,130	21.06	53,057
2021	*Married, Filing Jointly*						
	No children	$ 9,820	15.30	$1,502	$17,560	15.30	$27,380
	One child	10,640	34.00	3,618	25,470	15.98	48,108
	Two children	14,950	40.00	5,980	25,470	21.06	53,865
	Three or more children	14,950	45.00	6,728	25,470	21.06	57,414
	Other Taxpayers						
	No children	$ 9,820	15.30	$1,502	$11,610	15.30	$21,430
	One child	10,640	34.00	3,618	19,520	15.98	42,158
	Two children	14,950	40.00	5,980	19,520	21.06	47,915
	Three or more children	14,950	45.00	6,728	19,520	21.06	51,464

Example 20

In 2022, Grace Brown, who is married, files a joint return and otherwise qualifies for the earned income credit. Grace receives wages of $28,000, and she and her husband earn no other income. The Browns have one qualifying child. The couple's current earned income credit is $3,455, their maximum earned income credit of $3,733 ($10,980 × 34%) reduced by $278 [($28,000 − $26,260) × 15.98%].

If, instead, the Browns have three or more qualifying children, the calculation produces a credit of $6,569, their maximum earned income credit of $6,935 ($15,410 × 45%) reduced by $366 [($28,000 − $26,260) × 21.06%].

Earned Income Credit Table and Earned Income Tax Credit Assistant

It is not necessary to compute the credit as shown in Example 20. To simplify the compliance process, the IRS issues an Earned Income Credit Table for the determination of the appropriate amount of the credit. This table and a worksheet are included in IRS Publication 596 at **irs.gov**. In addition, the IRS has created an Earned Income Tax Credit Assistant to help taxpayers compute their credit (**apps.irs.gov/app/eitc/**).

Eligibility Requirements

Eligibility for the credit may depend not only on the taxpayer meeting the earned income and AGI thresholds but also on whether the taxpayer has a qualifying child. The term *qualifying child* generally has the same meaning here as it does for purposes of determining who qualifies as a dependent (see text Section 3-4a).

In addition to being available for taxpayers with qualifying children, the earned income credit also is available to certain *workers without children*. In general, the credit is available only to taxpayers ages 25 through 64 who cannot be claimed as a dependent on another taxpayer's return [for 2021, the minimum age to claim the credit was reduced to 19 (except for certain full-time students) and the maximum age is eliminated]. As shown in Exhibit 13.2, the credit for 2022 is calculated on a maximum earned income of $7,320 times 7.65 percent and reduced by 7.65 percent of earned income over $9,160 ($15,290 for married taxpayers filing a joint return).

Example 21

Walt, who is single, is 28 years of age, is a U.S. citizen, and is not claimed as a dependent on anyone else's return, earns $12,000 during 2022. Even though he does not have any qualifying children, he qualifies for the earned income credit. Walt's credit is $343, the maximum earned income credit of $560 ($7,320 × 7.65%) reduced by $217 [($12,000 − $9,160) × 7.65%].

If, instead, Walt's earned income is $9,100, his earned income credit is $560. Here, there is no phaseout of the maximum credit because his earned income does not exceed $9,160.

13-4b Foreign Tax Credit

Individual taxpayers and corporations may claim a tax credit for foreign income tax paid on income earned and subject to income tax in another country or a U.S. possession.[25] Alternatively, a taxpayer can claim a deduction instead of a credit.[26] In most instances, the **foreign tax credit (FTC)** is advantageous because it provides a direct offset against the tax liability.

The FTC is designed to mitigate double taxation because income earned in a foreign country is subject to both U.S. and foreign income taxes. However, the FTC is subject to an overall limitation. This limitation may result in some form of double taxation on income where the applicable U.S. tax rates are lower than those of the countries in which the income is earned.

Computation

The FTC allowed is the lesser of the foreign taxes paid or incurred, or the overall limitation computed as follows.[27]

$$\frac{\text{Foreign-source taxable income}}{\text{Worldwide taxable income}} \times \text{U.S. tax before FTC}$$

Example 22

In 2022, Ian, a calendar year taxpayer, records $10,000 of income from Country Y, which imposes a 15% tax, and $20,000 from Country Z, which imposes a 50% tax. He reports taxable income of $60,000 from within the United States and is married filing a joint return. Ian's worldwide taxable income is $90,000 ($10,000 + $20,000 + $60,000). Assume that Ian's U.S. tax before the credit is $11,034. The overall limitation is computed as follows.

$$\frac{\text{Foreign-source taxable income}}{\text{Worldwide taxable income}} \times \frac{\$30{,}000}{\$100{,}000} \times \$11{,}034 = \$3{,}310$$

In this case, $3,310 is allowed as the FTC because this amount is less than the $11,500 of foreign taxes imposed [$1,500 (Country Y) + $10,000 (Country Z)].

As a result, the overall limitation may result in some of the foreign income being subjected to double taxation. Unused FTCs [e.g., the $8,190 ($11,500 − $3,310) from Example 22] can be carried back 1 year and forward 10 years.[28]

---

[25] Code § 27 provides for the credit, but the qualifications and calculation procedure for the credit are contained in §§ 901–908.

[26] § 164.

[27] § 904. For individual taxpayers, worldwide taxable income is computed before personal and dependence exemptions are deducted. The exemption amount is zero through 2025.

[28] § 904(c) and Reg. § 1.904–2(g), Example 1.

Only income taxes, war profits taxes, and excess profits taxes (or taxes paid in lieu of such taxes) qualify for the credit.[29] Value added taxes (VAT), severance taxes, property taxes, and sales taxes do not qualify for the FTC because they are not taxes on income.

13-4c Child and Dependent Tax Credits

A **child tax credit** and **dependent tax credit** are provided to individual taxpayers based on the *number* of their qualifying children and dependents. These credits are two of several "family-friendly" provisions in the Federal income tax law. To be eligible for the child tax credit, the child must be under age 17 at the end of the year (under age 18 in 2021), must be a U.S. citizen, and must be a dependent of the taxpayer. The dependent tax credit is available for each dependent of the taxpayer (other than a qualifying child).

The child tax credit is $2,000 per child, and the dependent tax credit is $500 per non-child dependent. The credits phase out as AGI exceeds $400,000 (married filing jointly) or $200,000 (other taxpayers). These credits are phased out by $50 for each $1,000 (or fraction thereof) of AGI above the $400,000 (or $200,000) amount.

Due to the COVID-19 pandemic, Congress provided a temporary increase in the child tax credit. For 2021, the amount of the child tax credit was increased to $3,000 ($3,600 for a qualifying child under age 6 at the end of the year).

The portion of the child tax credit in excess of $2,000 ($1,600 per child under age 6 and $1,000 per child age 6 and older) is subject to its own phaseout rule. The additional child tax credit is phased out as AGI exceeds $150,000 (married, filing jointly), $112,500 (head of household), or $75,000 (other taxpayers). The credit is reduced by $50 for each $1,000 (or fraction thereof) of AGI over the applicable threshold amount. This phaseout does not reduce the $2,000 child tax credit amount (which has its own phaseout rule, noted above).

In 2021, the child tax credit was fully refundable. In 2022, the child tax credit is partially refundable (up to $1,500 per child, but no more than 15 percent of earned income in excess of $2,500). The dependent tax credit is not refundable. See text Section 3-4e for a complete discussion of these credits.

13-4d Credit for Child and Dependent Care Expenses

The **credit for child and dependent care expenses** mitigates the costs of child care services incurred by taxpayers to work outside the home.[30] The credit is a specified percentage of child and dependent care expenses. The credit percentage varies based on the taxpayer's AGI, and expenses are capped at a maximum of $6,000 in 2022 ($16,000 in 2021).

Eligibility

To be eligible for the credit, an individual must have either:

- A dependent under age 13, or
- A dependent or spouse who is physically or mentally incapacitated and who lives with the taxpayer for more than one-half of the year.

Generally, married taxpayers must file a joint return to obtain the credit.

Eligible Employment-Related Expenses

Eligible expenses include amounts paid for household services and care of a qualifying individual that are incurred to enable the taxpayer to be employed. The care can be provided in the home (e.g., by a nanny) or outside the home (e.g., at a day-care center).

Out-of-the-home expenses incurred for an older dependent or spouse who is physically or mentally incapacitated qualify for the credit if that person regularly spends at least eight hours each day in the taxpayer's household. This makes the credit available to taxpayers who keep handicapped older children and relatives who are 65 years and older in the home instead of institutionalizing them.

Child care payments to a relative are eligible for the credit unless the relative is a child (under age 19) of the taxpayer.

---

[29] Reg. § 1.901–1(a)(3)(i).

[30] § 21.

Example 23

Wilma is an employed mother of an 8-year-old child. She pays her mother, Rita, $1,500 per year to care for the child after school. Wilma pays her daughter Eleanor, age 17, $900 for the child's care during the summer. Of these amounts, only the $1,500 paid to Rita qualifies as employment-related child care expenses.

Earned Income Ceiling

Qualifying employment-related expenses are limited to an individual's earned income. For married taxpayers, this limitation applies to the spouse with the *lesser* amount of earned income. Special rules are provided for taxpayers with nonworking spouses who are disabled or are full-time students. Here, the nonworking spouse is *deemed* to have earned income of $250 per month if there is one qualifying individual in the household or $500 per month if there are two or more qualifying individuals in the household. In the case of a student-spouse, only months when the student is enrolled on a full-time basis are counted.[31]

Calculation of the Credit

Due to the increased need for child and dependent care during the COVID-19 pandemic, Congress increased the amount of expenses qualifying for the credit, increased the credit rate, and changed the income eligibility rules for 2021 (allowing more taxpayers to claim the credit at its highest rate). In 2022, these items returned to their previous levels.

In general, the credit is equal to a percentage of *unreimbursed* employment-related expenses up to $3,000 for one qualifying individual ($8,000 in 2021) and $6,000 for two or more individuals ($16,000 in 2021). The credit rate starts at 35 percent and decreases to 20 percent as AGI increases (50 percent to 0 percent in 2021); see Exhibits 13.3 and 13.4.

Example 24

During 2022, Nancy worked full-time while her spouse, Ron, was attending college for 10 months during the year. The couple has two children under age 13. Nancy earned $82,000 and incurred $6,200 of child care expenses. Ron is deemed to have earned $500 for each of the 10 months (or a total of $5,000).

Because Nancy and Ron report AGI of $82,000, they are allowed a credit rate of 20%. Nancy and Ron's $6,200 of qualified child care expenses are limited to $5,000 (Ron's deemed earned income). As a result, they are entitled to a child care credit of 1,000 (20% × $5,000; see Exhibit 13.3).

If, instead, the year was 2021, Nancy and Ron would receive a child care credit of $2,500 (50% × Ron's deemed income of $5,000; see Exhibit 13.3).

Exhibit 13.3 2021 Child and Dependent Care Credit Rates

Adjusted Gross Income		Credit	Adjusted Gross Income		Credit
Over	**But Not Over**	**Rate**	**Over**	**But Not Over**	**Rate**
$ 0	$125,000	50%	$155,000	$157,000	34%
125,000	127,000	49%	157,000	159,000	33%
127,000	129,000	48%	159,000	161,000	32%
129,000	131,000	47%	161,000	163,000	31%
131,000	133,000	46%	163,000	165,000	30%
133,000	135,000	45%	165,000	167,000	29%
135,000	137,000	44%	167,000	169,000	28%
137,000	139,000	43%	169,000	171,000	27%
139,000	141,000	42%	171,000	173,000	26%
141,000	143,000	41%	173,000	175,000	25%
143,000	145,000	40%	175,000	177,000	24%
145,000	147,000	39%	177,000	179,000	23%
147,000	149,000	38%	179,000	181,000	22%
149,000	151,000	37%	181,000	183,000	21%
151,000	153,000	36%	183,000	400,000	20%
153,000	155,000	35%	400,000	*	*

*The 20% rate phases out for taxpayers with AGI over $400,000. Specifically, a 1% reduction occurs for each additional $2,000 of AGI in excess of $400,000. As a result, the credit percentage is zero once AGI exceeds $498,000.

[31] § 21(d).

Exhibit 13.4 2022 Child and Dependent Care Credit Rates

Adjusted Gross Income		
Over	**But Not Over**	**Applicable Rate of Credit**
$ 0	$15,000	35%
15,000	17,000	34%
17,000	19,000	33%
19,000	21,000	32%
21,000	23,000	31%
23,000	25,000	30%
25,000	27,000	29%
27,000	29,000	28%
29,000	31,000	27%
31,000	33,000	26%
33,000	35,000	25%
35,000	37,000	24%
37,000	39,000	23%
39,000	41,000	22%
41,000	43,000	21%
43,000	No limit	20%

Ethics & Equity Is This the Right Way to Use the Credit for Child and Dependent Care Expenses?

During 2023, your friends, Tim and Shia, hired a child care provider (Rebecca) to come into their home while they are at work to care for their two children. Rebecca charges $4,500 for her services for the year. Tim and Shia have discovered that up to $6,000 of qualifying expenses will generate a credit for child and dependent care expenses and that qualifying expenses can include payments for housecleaning services.

As a result, they ask Rebecca whether she would be interested in working several hours more per week, after Tim returns from work, for the sole purpose of cleaning the house. The couple offers to pay Rebecca $1,500 for the additional work. The net cost of the additional services would be only $1,200 [$1,500 − ($1,500 × 20%)] due to the availability of the credit for child and dependent care expenses.

You learn of Tim and Shia's opportunity but think it is unfair. If you hired someone to perform similar housecleaning services at the same price, your net cost would be $1,500, not $1,200, because you do not qualify for the credit. You are troubled by this inequity. Is this the way the income tax law should work? Explain.

Dependent Care Assistance Program

A taxpayer is allowed an exclusion from gross income for a limited amount of employer-reimbursed child or dependent care expenses; see text Section 5-8a. If this occurs, the applicable ceilings for allowable child and dependent care expenses are reduced dollar for dollar by the amount of the employer's reimbursement.[32]

Example 25

Assume the same facts as in Example 24, except that of the $6,200 paid for child care, Nancy was reimbursed $2,500 by her employer under a qualified dependent care assistance program. Under the employer's plan, the reimbursement reduces Nancy's taxable wages. As a result, Nancy and Ron have AGI of $79,500 ($82,000 − $2,500).

In this case, the child care expense ceiling of $6,000 is reduced by the $2,500 reimbursement to $3,500. Their out-of-pocket child care expenses are $3,700 ($6,200 − $2,500), resulting in a credit of $700 ($3,500 × 20%).

If, instead, the year was 2021, the child care ceiling of $16,000 is reduced by the $2,500 reimbursement to $13,500. Their out-of-pocket child care expenses are $3,700 ($6,200 − $2,500). Because this amount is below both the $13,500 ceiling and Ron's $5,000 deemed income, their tax credit is $1,850 ($3,700 × 50%).

[32] § 21(c).

13-4e Education Tax Credits

The **American Opportunity credit** and the **lifetime learning credit**[33] are available to help qualifying low- and middle-income individuals defray the cost of higher education. The credits are available for qualifying tuition and related expenses incurred by students pursuing undergraduate or graduate degrees or vocational training. Books and other course materials are eligible for the American Opportunity credit (but not the lifetime learning credit).[34] Room and board are ineligible for both credits.

Maximum Credit

The American Opportunity credit permits a maximum credit of $2,500 per year (100 percent of the first $2,000 of tuition expenses plus 25 percent of the next $2,000 of tuition expenses) for the *first four years* of postsecondary education. The lifetime learning credit permits a credit of 20 percent of qualifying expenses (up to $10,000 per year) incurred in a year in which the American Opportunity credit is not claimed. Generally, the lifetime learning credit is used for individuals who are beyond the first four years of postsecondary education.

Eligible Individuals

Both education credits are available for qualified expenses incurred by a taxpayer, taxpayer's spouse, or taxpayer's dependent. The American Opportunity credit is available per eligible student, while the lifetime learning credit is calculated per taxpayer. To be eligible for the American Opportunity credit, a student must take at least one-half the full-time course load for at least one academic term at a qualifying educational institution. No comparable requirement exists for the lifetime learning credit. So taxpayers who are seeking new job skills or maintaining existing skills through graduate training or continuing education are eligible for the lifetime learning credit. Taxpayers who are married must file a joint return to claim either education credit.

Income Limitations and Refundability

Both education credits are phased out beginning when the taxpayer's AGI (modified for this purpose) reaches $80,000 ($160,000 for married taxpayers filing jointly).[35] The credits are reduced proportionally over a $10,000 phaseout range ($20,000 for married taxpayers filing jointly). As a result, each credit is eliminated when modified AGI reaches $90,000 ($180,000 for married taxpayers filing jointly).

Forty percent of the American Opportunity credit is refundable, and it can offset a taxpayer's alternative minimum tax (AMT) liability. The lifetime learning credit is neither refundable nor an AMT liability offset.[36]

The Big Picture

Example 26

Return to the facts of *The Big Picture* on p. 13-1. Recall that Tom and Jennifer Snyder are married; file a joint tax return; have modified AGI of $158,000; and have two children, Lora and Sam. The Snyders paid $7,500 of tuition and $8,500 for room and board for Lora (a freshman) and $8,100 of tuition plus $7,200 for room and board for Sam (a junior). Both Lora and Sam are full-time students and are Tom and Jennifer's dependents.

Lora's tuition and Sam's tuition are qualified expenses for the American Opportunity credit. For 2022, Tom and Jennifer may claim a $2,500 American Opportunity credit for both Lora's and Sam's expenses [(100% × $2,000) + (25% × $2,000)]; in total, they qualify for a $5,000 American Opportunity credit.

---

[33]§ 25A.

[34]§ 25A(i)(3).

[35]These amounts are not adjusted for inflation.

[36]If the credit is claimed for a taxpayer subject to § 1(g) (the "kiddie tax," discussed in text Section 3-6c), the credit is not refundable.

The Big Picture

Example 27

Return to the facts of *The Big Picture* on p. 13-1. Now assume that Tom and Jennifer's 2022 modified AGI is $172,000 instead of $158,000. In this case, Tom and Jennifer can claim a $2,000 American Opportunity credit for 2022 (rather than a $5,000 credit).

The credit is reduced because the taxpayers' modified AGI exceeds the $160,000 limit for married taxpayers. The reduction is the amount by which modified AGI exceeds the limit, expressed as a percentage of the phaseout range. In this case, the reduction is 60%, computed as [($172,000 − $160,000) ÷ $20,000]. Therefore, the maximum available credit for 2022 is $2,000 ($5,000 × 40% allowable portion).

The Big Picture

Example 28

Return to the facts of *The Big Picture* on p. 13-1. Now assume that Tom is going to school on a part-time basis to complete a graduate degree and pays qualifying tuition and fees of $4,000 during 2022.

Tom's qualifying tuition and fees are eligible for the lifetime learning credit. The potential lifetime learning credit of $800 ($4,000 × 20%) is reduced because the Snyders' modified AGI exceeds the $160,000 limit for married taxpayers. As modified AGI exceeds the $160,000 limit by $12,000 and the phaseout range is $20,000, the couple's lifetime learning credit is reduced by 60%.

As a result, the Sndyers' lifetime learning credit for 2022 is $320 ($800 × 40%), and their total education credits are $2,320 ($2,000 American Opportunity credit and $320 lifetime learning credit).

Restrictions on Double Tax Benefit

Taxpayers who claim an education credit may not deduct the expenses (see text Section 9-5), nor may they claim the credit for amounts that are otherwise excluded from gross income (e.g., scholarships and employer-paid educational assistance; see text Sections 5-4 and 5-8a).

13-4f Energy Credits

The Internal Revenue Code contains a variety of credits for businesses and individuals to encourage the conservation of natural resources and the development of energy sources other than oil and gas. The **energy tax credits** include incentives to:

- Install energy-efficient windows, insulation, and heating and cooling equipment;
- Purchase solar and other energy-efficient water heaters; and
- Install equipment in a business to produce electricity using solar, wind, or geothermal sources.

Credit amounts and expiration dates differ for the various provisions. Exhibit 13.5 provides a brief summary of several energy tax credits.

13-4g Credit for Certain Retirement Plan Contributions

Taxpayers may claim a nonrefundable **credit for certain retirement plan contributions** based on eligible contributions of up to $2,000 to certain qualified retirement plans, like traditional and Roth IRAs and § 401(k) plans.[37] This credit, sometimes referred to as the "saver's credit," encourages lower- and middle-income taxpayers to contribute to qualified retirement plans. If a taxpayer (and/or spouse) contributes to and receives distributions from a qualifying plan, these amounts must be netted. Distributions in the tax year, in the two prior tax years, and during the period prior to the due date of the return are used in this netting process.

[37] § 25B.

Exhibit 13.5 Energy Credits Summary

Residential Energy Tax Credits
Consumers who purchase and install specific products, such as energy-efficient windows, insulation, doors, roofs, and heating and cooling equipment, in the home can receive a tax credit of up to $1,500 for property placed in service before January 1, 2022 (§ 25C). In addition, consumers who purchase photovoltaic, fuel cell, and/or solar water heating property can receive a credit equal to 22% of the purchase price. Improvements must be made to the taxpayer's principal residence and must be completed before January 1, 2023 (§ 25D).

Plug-in Electric Drive Motor Vehicles
Consumers who purchase new plug-in electric drive motor vehicles before January 1, 2022, can qualify for a credit of $2,500 plus $417 for each kilowatt hour of battery capacity in excess of 5 kilowatt hours. The maximum credit is $7,500 (§ 30D).

Business Energy Tax Credits
Businesses are eligible for tax credits for producing alternative fuels, constructing energy-efficient buildings, producing energy-efficient products, and producing energy using alternative means.

- *Biodiesel/Alternative Fuels—Small Producer Biofuel (§ 40) and Biodiesel Credit (§ 40A).* Small agri-biodiesel producers are provided a tax credit measured in varying cents per gallon for producing these fuels (with varying maximums per year). The credits are available for sales through December 31, 2021 (§ 40) and 2022 (§ 40A).
- *Credit for Business Installation of Qualified Fuel Cells, Stationary Microturbine Power Plants, Solar, and Small Wind Energy Equipment.* A tax credit—based on the purchase price—is provided for installing qualified solar, fuel cell, small wind, microturbine, combined heat and power systems, geothermal heap pump property, and qualifying stationary microturbine power plants and geothermal heat pumps. The credits (which vary from 10% to 26%, with some subject to reduction over time) apply to property placed in service before January 1, 2026; construction must start before January 1, 2024 (§ 48).
- *Credit for Building Energy-Efficient New Homes.* A $2,000 tax credit is provided to eligible contractors for each qualified new energy-efficient home constructed through December 31, 2021 ($5,000 for homes certified as "zero energy ready"). The credit applies to manufactured homes meeting ENERGY STAR® criteria and other homes (§ 45L).
- *Energy Credit for Producing Electricity via Wind, Solar, Geothermal, and Other Property.* A tax credit is provided for producing energy via qualified wind, solar, geothermal, and other property. The tax credit—based on the number of kilowatt-hours of electricity produced—applies to production through the end of 2021 (§ 45).

Note: It is likely that many of the expired (or expiring) credits will be extended and expanded via legislation over the next year.

The credit rate applied to the eligible contributions depends on the taxpayer's AGI[38] and filing status as shown in Exhibit 13.6. However, the maximum credit allowed to an individual is $1,000 ($2,000 × 50%). Once AGI exceeds the upper end of the applicable range, no credit is available. To qualify for the credit, the taxpayer must be at least 18 years of age and cannot be a dependent of another taxpayer or a full-time student.

Example 29

Esau and Mandy, married taxpayers, each contribute $2,500 to § 401(k) plans offered through their employers. AGI reported on their joint return is $45,000. The eligible retirement plan contributions for purposes of the credit are limited to $2,000 for Esau and $2,000 for Mandy.

As a result, Esau and Mandy may claim a $400 retirement plan contributions credit [($2,000 × 2) × 10%]. They would not qualify for the credit if their AGI had exceeded $68,000.

[38]The AGI thresholds are indexed annually for inflation. For purposes of this credit, the AGI thresholds are modified to include certain excluded income items. See § 25B(e).

Exhibit 13.6 **"Saver's" Credit Rate and AGI Thresholds (2022)**

Joint Return		Head of Household		All Others		Applicable Percentage
Over	**Not Over**	**Over**	**Not Over**	**Over**	**Not Over**	
$ 0	$41,000	$ 0	$30,750	$ 0	$20,500	50%
41,000	44,000	30,750	33,000	20,500	22,000	20%
44,000	68,000	33,000	51,000	22,000	34,000	10%
68,000		51,000		34,000		0%

Concept Summary 13.1 provides an overview of the tax credits discussed in this chapter.

Concept Summary 13.1

Tax Credits

Credit	Computation	Comments
Tax withheld on wages (§ 31)	Amount is reported to employee on Form W–2.	Refundable credit.
Earned income (§ 32)	Amount is determined by reference to Earned Income Credit Table published by IRS. Computations of underlying amounts in Earned Income Credit Table are illustrated in Example 20.	Refundable credit. A form of negative income tax to assist low-income taxpayers. Earned income and AGI must be less than certain threshold amounts. Generally, one or more qualifying children must reside with the taxpayer.
Child and dependent care (§ 21)	Rate ranges from 50% to 0% depending on AGI in 2021 (35% to 20% in prior and subsequent years). In 2021, maximum base for credit is $8,000 for one qualifying individual, $16,000 for two or more ($3,000 and $6,000 in prior and subsequent years).	Nonrefundable personal credit (fully refundable in 2021). No carryback or carryforward. Benefits taxpayers who incur employment-related child or dependent care expenses in order to work or seek employment. Eligible taxpayers must have a dependent under age 13 or a dependent (any age) or spouse who is physically or mentally incapacitated.
Elderly or disabled (§ 22)	15% of sum of base amount minus reductions for (1) Social Security and other nontaxable benefits and (2) AGI in excess of base amount ($5,000 single, $7,500 head of household, $10,000 married filing jointly).	Nonrefundable personal credit. No carryback or carryforward. Provides relief for taxpayers not receiving substantial tax-free retirement benefits.
Adoption expenses (§ 23)	Up to $14,890 of costs incurred to adopt an eligible child qualify for the credit. Taxpayer claims the credit in the year qualified expenses were paid or incurred if they were paid or incurred during or after year in which adoption was finalized. For expenses paid or incurred in a year prior to when adoption was finalized, credit must be claimed in tax year following the tax year during which the expenses are paid or incurred.	Nonrefundable credit. The credit is phased out ratably over a $40,000 range once AGI exceeds $223,410. Unused credit may be carried forward five years. Purpose is to assist taxpayers who incur nonrecurring costs associated with the adoption process.
Child and Dependent (§ 24)	Credit is based on *number* of qualifying children under age 17 (under age 18 in 2021) and dependents. In general, credit is $2,000 per child and $500 per dependent (additional child tax credits are available in 2022 and 2021). Credits are phased out for higher-income taxpayers.	Child tax credit is partially refundable (up to $1,500), but limited to 15% of earned income in excess of $2,500 (the child tax credit was fully refundable in 2021). Dependent tax credit is not refundable. Purpose is to assist families with children or dependents.
Education (§ 25A)	American Opportunity credit is available for qualifying education expenses of students in first four years of postsecondary education. Maximum credit is $2,500 per year per eligible student. Credit is phased out for higher-income taxpayers.	Credit is partially refundable. Credit is designed to help defray costs of first four years of higher education for low- to middle-income families.

continued

Tax Credits—(Continued)

Credit	Computation	Comments
	Lifetime learning credit permits a credit of 20% of qualifying expenses (up to $10,000 per year) provided American Opportunity credit is not claimed with respect to those expenses. Credit is calculated per taxpayer, not per student, and is phased out for higher-income taxpayers.	Nonrefundable credit. Credit is designed to help defray costs of higher education beyond first four years and of costs incurred in maintaining or improving existing job skills for low- to middle-income taxpayers.
Credit for certain retirement plan contributions (§ 25B)	Calculation is based on amount of contribution multiplied by a percentage that depends on the taxpayer's filing status and AGI.	Nonrefundable credit. Purpose is to encourage contributions to qualified retirement plans by low- and middle-income taxpayers.
Foreign tax credit (§ 27)	Lesser of (1) the tax paid to the foreign country or (2) the ratable share of U.S. income tax liability related to foreign-source income.	Nonrefundable credit. Taxpayer instead can deduct the taxes paid. Unused credit may be carried back 1 year and then forward 10 years. Purpose is to mitigate the double taxation that may arise when income is taxed in more than one country.
General business (§ 38)	May not exceed net income tax minus the greater of tentative minimum tax or 25% of net regular tax liability that exceeds $25,000.	Nonrefundable credit. Components include tax credit for rehabilitation expenditures, work opportunity tax credit, research activities credit, low-income housing credit, disabled access credit, credit for small employer pension plan startup costs, credit for employer-provided child care, and credit for employer-provided medical and family leave. Unused credit may be carried back 1 year and forward 20 years. FIFO method applies to carrybacks, carryovers, and credits earned during current year.
Rehabilitation expenditures (§ 47)	Qualifying expenditures times 20% rate for certified historic structures.	Nonrefundable credit. Part of general business credit and therefore subject to same carryback, carryover, and FIFO rules. Purpose is to discourage businesses from moving from economically distressed areas to newer locations.
Research activities (§ 41)	Incremental credit is 20% of excess of computation year expenditures over the base amount. Basic research credit is allowed to certain corporations for 20% of cash payments to qualified organizations that exceed a specially calculated base amount. Energy research credit also available.	Nonrefundable credit. Part of general business credit and therefore subject to same carryback, carryover, and FIFO rules. Purpose is to encourage high-tech and energy research in the United States.
Low-income housing (§ 42)	Appropriate rate times eligible basis (portion of project attributable to low-income units). Credit is available each year for 10 years. Recapture may apply.	Nonrefundable credit. Part of general business credit and therefore subject to same carryback, carryover, and FIFO rules. Purpose is to encourage construction of housing for low-income individuals.
Disabled access (§ 44)	Credit is 50% of eligible access expenditures that exceed $250 but do not exceed $10,250. Maximum credit is $5,000. Available only to eligible small businesses.	Nonrefundable credit. Part of general business credit and therefore subject to same carryback, carryover, and FIFO rules. Purpose is to encourage small businesses to become more accessible to disabled individuals.
Credit for small employer pension plan startup costs (§ 45E)	Credit equals 50% of qualified startup costs incurred by eligible employers. Maximum annual credit is $500. Deduction for related expenses is reduced by the amount of the credit.	Nonrefundable credit. Part of general business credit and therefore subject to same carryback, carryover, and FIFO rules. Purpose is to encourage small employers to establish qualified retirement plans for their employees.

Tax Credits—(Continued)

Credit	Computation	Comments
Credit for employer-provided child care (§ 45F)	Credit is equal to 25% of qualified child care expenses plus 10% of qualified expenses for child care resource and referral services. Maximum credit is $150,000. Deduction for related expenses or basis must be reduced by the amount of the credit.	Nonrefundable credit. Part of general business credit and therefore subject to same carryback, carryover, and FIFO rules. Purpose is to encourage employers to provide child care for their employees' children during normal working hours.
Credit for employer-provided family and medical leave (§ 45S)	Credit is equal to 12.5% of wages paid to qualifying employees while they are on family and medical leave (limited to 12 weeks per employee per year). Employers must pay a minimum of 50% of the wages normally paid; if wages paid during the leave *exceed* 50% of normal wages, the credit is increased by 0.25% for each percentage point above 50% to a maximum credit of 25%.	Nonrefundable credit. Part of general business credit and therefore subject to same carryback, carryover, and FIFO rules. Purpose is to encourage employers to provide leave to their employees for family and medical purposes (e.g,, birth of a child; care for a sick child, spouse, or parent).
Work opportunity (§ 51)	Credit is limited to 40% of the first $6,000 of wages paid to each eligible employee.	Nonrefundable credit. Part of the general business credit and therefore subject to the same carryback, carryover, and FIFO rules. Purpose is to encourage employment of individuals in specified groups.

13-5 Payment Procedures

LO.5

Describe the tax withholding and payment procedures applicable to employers.

The tax law contains elaborate "pay-as-you-go" rules that require the prepayment of various Federal taxes. In addition, these rules carry penalties for any lack of compliance.[39] Prepayment procedures fall into two major categories: those applicable to employers and those applicable to self-employed persons. For employers, both payroll taxes (FICA and FUTA) and income taxes may be involved. With self-employed taxpayers, the focus is on the income tax and the self-employment tax.

13-5a Employers

Employment taxes include FICA (Federal Insurance Contributions Act; commonly known as Social Security) and FUTA (Federal Unemployment Tax Act). The employer usually is responsible for withholding the employee's share of FICA and appropriate amounts for income taxes. In addition, the employer must match the FICA portion withheld and fully absorb the cost of FUTA. Employers are required to pay these amounts to the IRS on a regular basis (usually weekly or monthly).

The key to employer compliance in this area involves the following.

- Identifying which employees and wages are covered by employment taxes and are subject to withholding for income taxes.
- Determining the amount to be paid and/or withheld.
- Reporting and paying employment taxes and income taxes withheld to the IRS on a timely basis through the use of proper forms and procedures.

IRS Publication 15, *Employer's Tax Guide* (Circular E), is a key resource for employers.

[39]See, for example, § 3403 (employer liable for any taxes withheld and not paid over to the IRS), § 6656 (penalty on amounts withheld and not paid over), and § 6654 (penalty for failure by an individual to pay estimated income taxes).

Amount of FICA Taxes

The FICA tax has two components: Social Security tax (old age, survivors, and disability insurance) *and* Medicare tax (hospital insurance). The tax rates and wage base under FICA have increased substantially over the years. The base amount is adjusted each year for inflation. Exhibit 13.7 shows the base amounts for both the Social Security and Medicare taxes and the related employee tax rates. The employer must match the employee's portion, so the total Social Security tax rate is 12.4 percent and the total Medicare tax rate is 2.9 percent.

Employee withholdings continue until the maximum base amount is reached. In 2022, for example, FICA withholding for the Social Security portion (6.2 percent) ends once the employee has earned $147,000 of wages. However, the employer will continue to withhold Medicare taxes on wages above $147,000 since there is no limit on this portion of the FICA tax.

Example 30

In 2022, Keshia earned a salary of $155,000 from her employer. As a result, FICA taxes withheld from her salary are $9,114.00 ($147,000 × 6.2%) plus $2,247.50 ($155,000 × 1.45%) for a total of $11,361.50. In addition to paying the amount withheld from Keshia's salary to the Federal government, her employer also must pay $11,361.50.

In at least two situations, changing jobs during the year or having multiple jobs at the same time, it is possible for an employee to have paid excess FICA taxes during a tax year.

Excess FICA Taxes Withheld

Example 31

During 2022, Kevin changed employers in the middle of the year and earned $75,000 (all of which was subject to FICA) from each job. As a result, each employer withheld $5,737.50 [(6.2% × $75,000) + (1.45% × $75,000)] for a total of $11,475.00.

Although each employer acted properly, Kevin's total FICA tax liability for the year is only $11,289 [(6.2% × $147,000) + (1.45% × $150,000)]. As a result, Kevin has overpaid his share of FICA taxes by $186 [$11,475 (amount paid) − $11,289 (amount of correct liability)]. Kevin can claim this amount as a tax credit when filing his 2022 income tax return.

Example 32

During 2022, Lori earned $115,000 from her regular job and $35,000 from a part-time job (all of which was subject to FICA). As a result, one employer withheld $8,797.50 [(6.2% × $115,000) + (1.45% × $115,000)] while the other employer withheld $2,677.50 [(6.2% × $35,000) + (1.45% × $35,000)], for a total withheld for Lori of $11,475.00.

Lori's total FICA tax liability for the year is only $11,289 [(6.2% × $147,000) + (1.45% × $150,000)]. As a result, Lori has overpaid her share of FICA taxes by $186 [$11,475 (amount paid) − $11,289 (amount of correct liability)]. Lori can claim this amount as a tax credit when filing her 2022 income tax return.

Exhibit 13.7 **FICA Rates and Base**

	Social Security Tax				Medicare Tax				
	Percent	×	Base Amount	+	Percent	×	Base Amount	=	Maximum Tax
2020	6.20%	×	137,700	+	1.45%**	×	Unlimited	=	Unlimited
2021	6.20%	×	142,800	+	1.45%**	×	Unlimited	=	Unlimited
2022	6.20%	×	147,000	+	1.45%**	×	Unlimited	=	Unlimited
2023	6.20%	×	*	+	1.45%**	×	Unlimited	=	Unlimited

*Not yet determined.
**Does not include the additional Medicare taxes on high-income individuals (see text Section 13-6b).

The FICA tax must be paid for an individual employed by their spouse. No tax is collected for children under the age of 18 who are employed in the parent's trade or business.

Amount of Income Tax Withholding

To ensure that sufficient Federal income taxes are withheld from their wages, employees complete Form W–4, Employee's Withholding Certificate. As part of this process, employees are encouraged to use an IRS-developed application to determine the appropriate amount of withholding (**apps.irs.gov/app/tax-withholding-estimator**). In addition, the employee can provide information about any available child and dependent tax credits. Once completed, the Form W–4 is provided to (and used by) the employer to support the amount of Federal income taxes withheld.[40] The form is retained by the employer as part of its payroll records.

Reporting and Payment Procedures

Employers devote a significant amount of time and expense in complying with the various employment tax and income tax withholding rules. Among the Federal forms that must be filed are the following.

Tax Form	Title
W–2	Wage and Tax Statement
940 or 940 EZ	Employer's Annual Federal Unemployment (FUTA) Tax Return
941	Employer's Quarterly Federal Tax Return

Form W–2 furnishes essential information to employees concerning wages paid, FICA, and income tax withholdings. This form (reporting information for the previous calendar year) must be furnished to an employee not later than January 31. Employees then report the relevant amounts on the appropriate lines of their Form 1040. These amounts also typically are used on the state and/or local tax return.

Form 940 (or Form 940 EZ) is the employer's annual accounting of its FUTA liability. Generally, it is due one month after the end of the calendar year (i.e., no later than January 31, 2023, for the 2022 calendar year) and must include any remaining FUTA due.

Employers make deposits of employment taxes, usually weekly or monthly,[41] and they pay any outstanding amounts at the end of every quarter, using Form 941.

Backup Withholding

Some payments made to individuals by banks or businesses are subject to backup withholding to ensure that income tax is collected on interest income and other payments reported on a Form 1099. Backup withholding is required if the taxpayer does not give their Social Security number to the business or bank when required.[42] If backup withholding applies, the payor withholds 24 percent of the gross amount.

13-5b Self-Employed Taxpayers

LO.6 **Explain and illustrate the payment procedures applicable to self-employed persons.**

Although the following discussion largely centers on self-employed taxpayers, employed taxpayers may be required to pay estimated tax if they have income other than wages that is not subject to withholding (e.g., investment income, or a second trade or business in a self-employment capacity).

[40] The withholding provisions are contained in §§ 3401 and 3402. IRS Publication 15, *Employer's Tax Guide* (Circular E), contains detailed information about the income tax withholding process.

[41] Deposit requirements are specified in IRS Publication 15, *Employer's Tax Guide* (Circular E).

[42] § 3406(a). The backup withholding rate is the fourth lowest tax rate for single filers.

Estimated Tax for Individuals

Estimated tax is the amount of tax (including AMT and self-employment tax) an individual expects to owe for the year after subtracting tax credits and income tax withheld. Any individual who has estimated tax of $1,000 or more *and* whose withholding does not equal or exceed the required annual payment (discussed below) must make quarterly payments.[43] If these payments are not made, a penalty may be assessed. No quarterly payments are required (and no penalty will apply) if the taxpayer's estimated tax is under $1,000. In addition, no penalty will apply if the taxpayer had a zero tax liability for the prior tax year, provided the prior tax year was 12 months (i.e., not a short year) *and* the taxpayer was a citizen or resident for that entire year.

The required annual payment must be computed first. This is the *smaller* of the following amounts.

- Ninety percent of the tax shown on the current year's return.
- One hundred percent of the tax shown on the preceding year's return (the return must cover the full 12 months of the preceding year). If the AGI on the preceding year's return exceeds $150,000 ($75,000 if married filing separately), the 100 percent requirement is increased to 110 percent.

In general, one-fourth of this required annual payment is due on April 15, June 15, and September 15 of the tax year and January 15 of the following year.

An equal part of withholding is deemed paid on each due date. So if $10,000 has been withheld during the year, $2,500 is applied to each quarter. If the quarterly estimates are determined to be $3,000, then $500 ($3,000 − $2,500) must be paid each quarter. Payments are submitted with the payment voucher for the appropriate quarter from Form 1040–ES.

Penalty on Underpayments

A nondeductible penalty is imposed on any estimated tax underpayment. The penalty rate is adjusted quarterly to reflect changes in the average prime rate.

An *underpayment* occurs when any installment (the sum of estimated tax paid and income tax withheld) is less than 25 percent of the required annual payment. The penalty is applied to the amount of the underpayment for the period of the underpayment.[44]

Example 33

Marta made the following payments of estimated Federal income tax for 2022. Marta had no Federal income tax withheld.

April 15, 2022	$1,400
June 15, 2022	2,300
September 15, 2022	1,500
January 17, 2023	1,800

Marta's actual tax for 2022 is $8,000, and her tax in 2021 was $10,000. As a result, each installment should have been at least $1,800 [($8,000 × 90%) × 25%]. Of the payment on June 15, $400 will be credited to the unpaid balance of the first quarterly installment due on April 15, effectively stopping the underpayment penalty for the first quarter.[45] Of the remaining $1,900 payment on June 15, $100 is credited to the September 15 payment, resulting in this third quarterly payment being $200 short.

Then $200 of the January 17 payment is credited to the September 15 shortfall, ending the underpayment period for that amount. The January 17, 2023 installment is now underpaid by $200, and a penalty will apply from January 17, 2023, to April 17, 2023 (unless some tax is paid sooner). Marta's estimated tax underpayments for the various periods are as follows:

1st installment	$400 from April 15 to June 15, 2022
2nd installment	Paid in full
3rd installment	$200 from September 15, 2022, to January 17, 2023
4th installment	$200 from January 17, 2023, to April 17, 2023

[43] §§ 6654(c)(1) and 6654(e)(1).

[44] § 6654(b)(2).

[45] Payments are credited to unpaid installments in the order in which the installments are required to be paid. § 6654(b)(3).

Exhibit 13.8 **Self-Employment Tax: Social Security and Medicare Portions**

Year		Tax Rate	Ceiling Amount
2022	Social Security portion	12.4%	$147,000
	Medicare portion	2.9%	Unlimited
	Aggregate rate	15.3%	
2021	Social Security portion	12.4%	$142,800
	Medicare portion	2.9%	Unlimited
	Aggregate rate	15.3%	

If a possible underpayment of estimated tax is indicated, Form 2210 is filed to compute the penalty due or to justify that no penalty applies.

Self-Employment Tax

The tax on self-employment income is levied to provide Social Security and Medicare benefits (old age, survivors, and disability insurance and hospital insurance) for self-employed individuals. Individuals with net earnings of $400 or more from self-employment are subject to the **self-employment tax**.[46] For 2022, the self-employment tax is 15.3 percent of self-employment income up to $147,000 and 2.9 percent of self-employment income in excess of $147,000 (see Exhibit 13.8).

Net earnings from self-employment includes gross income from a trade or business less allowable trade or business deductions, the distributive share of any partnership income or loss derived from a trade or business activity, and net income from rendering personal services as an independent contractor. This amount includes profits from sales of inventory.

Self-employed taxpayers are allowed a deduction from net earnings from self-employment, at one-half of the self-employment rate, for purposes of determining self-employment tax[47] *and* an income tax deduction (normally, one-half of the self-employment tax liability).[48]

Determining the amount of self-employment tax to be paid for 2022 involves completing the steps in Exhibit 13.9. The result of step 3 or 4 is the amount of self-employment tax to be paid. For *income tax purposes*, the amount to be reported is net earnings from self-employment before the deduction for the self-employment tax. Then the taxpayer is allowed a deduction *for* AGI of the appropriate amount of the self-employment tax.

Exhibit 13.9 **2022 Self-Employment Tax Worksheet**

1. Net earnings from self-employment. ______
2. Multiply line 1 by 92.35%. ______
3. If the amount on line 2 is $147,000 or less, multiply the line 2 amount by 15.3%. This is the self-employment tax. ______
4. If the amount on line 2 is more than $147,000, multiply line 2 by 2.9% and add $18,228. This is the self-employment tax. ______

Note: $18,228 is the maximum Social Security contribution in 2022 ($147,000 × 12.4%).

[46] § 6017.

[47] § 1402(a)(12).

[48] § 164(f).

Example 34

In 2022, Nathan and Terry report net earnings from self-employment of $55,000 and $165,000, respectively. Using the format in Exhibit 13.9, determine their self-employment tax.

Nathan's Self-Employment Tax Worksheet	
1. Net earnings from self-employment.	$55,000.00
2. Multiply line 1 by 92.35%.	$50,792.50
3. If the amount on line 2 is $147,000 or less, multiply the line 2 amount by 15.3%. This is the self-employment tax.	$ 7,771.25
4. If the amount on line 2 is more than $147,000, multiply line 2 by 2.9% and add $18,228. This is the self-employment tax.	

Terry's Self-Employment Tax Worksheet	
1. Net earnings from self-employment.	$165,000.00
2. Multiply line 1 by 92.35%.	$152,377.50
3. If the amount on line 2 is $147,000 or less, multiply the line 2 amount by 15.3%. This is the self-employment tax.	
4. If the amount on line 2 is more than $147,000, multiply line 2 by 2.9% and add $18,228. This is the self-employment tax.	$ 22,646.95

For income tax purposes, Nathan has net earnings from self-employment of $55,000 and a deduction *for* AGI of $3,885.63 ($7,771.25 × 50%). Terry has net earnings from self-employment of $165,000 and a deduction *for* AGI of $11,323.48 ($22,646.95 × 50%).

If an individual also receives wages subject to the FICA tax, the ceiling amount of the Social Security portion on which the self-employment tax is computed is reduced. However, a combination of FICA wages and self-employment earnings will not reduce the Medicare component of the self-employment tax, because there is no ceiling on this component of the tax.

Example 35

In 2022, Kelly reported $86,000 of net earnings from a data imaging services business she owns. During the year, she also received wages of $71,700 as an employee of an accounting firm. The amount of Kelly's self-employment income subject to the Social Security portion (12.4%) is $75,300 ($147,000 − $71,700), producing a tax of $9,337.20 ($75,300 × 12.4%); her Social Security ceiling amount ($75,300) is less than her net self-employment income ($79,421).

	Social Security Portion
Ceiling amount	$147,000
Less: FICA wages	(71,700)
Net ceiling	$ 75,300
Net self-employment income ($86,000 × 92.35%)	$ 79,421
Lesser of net ceiling or net self-employment income	$ 75,300

Although there is a limit on Social Security taxes ($147,000 maximum base in 2022), no such limit exists for the Medicare portion of the self-employment tax. As a result, all of Kelly's net self-employment income ($86,000 × 0.9235 = $79,421) is subject to the 2.9% Medicare portion of the self-employment tax. The self-employment tax on this portion is $2,303.21 ($79,421 × 2.9%). In total, Kelly's self-employment tax liability is $11,640.41 [$9,337.20 (Social Security) + $2,303.21 (Medicare)].

If Kelly's wages were only $50,000, then the net ceiling in the table above would be $97,000. Because her net self-employment income ($79,421) is less than this amount, she computes her self-employment tax using the format in Exhibit 13.9.

Exhibit 13.10 **2021 Self-Employment Tax Worksheet**

1. Net earnings from self-employment. ________
2. Multiply line 1 by 92.35%. ________
3. If the amount on line 2 is $142,800 or less, multiply the line 2 amount by 15.3%. This is the self-employment tax. ________
4. If the amount on line 2 is more than $142,800, multiply line 2 by 2.9% and add $17,707.20. This is the self-employment tax. ________

Note: $17,707.20 is the maximum Social Security contribution in 2021 ($142,800 × 12.4%).

For 2021, the self-employment tax computations use the 2021 Social Security ceiling amount (see Exhibit 13.10).

13-5c Additional Medicare Taxes on High-Income Individuals

LO.7

Explain the additional Medicare taxes assessed on high-income individuals.

High-income taxpayers are required to pay two types of additional Medicare taxes: (1) an additional 0.9 percent tax on *wages* received in excess of specified amounts and (2) an additional 3.8 percent tax on *unearned income.*

Additional Tax on Wages

An additional 0.9 percent Medicare tax is imposed on wages received in excess of $250,000 for married taxpayers filing a joint return ($125,000 if married filing separately) and $200,000 for all other taxpayers.[49] Unlike the general 1.45 percent Medicare tax on wages, the additional tax on a joint return is based on the *combined* wages of the employee and the employee's spouse. As a result, the Medicare tax rate is:

1. 1.45 percent on the first $200,000 of wages ($125,000 on a married filing separate return; $250,000 of combined wages on a married filing joint return), and
2. 2.35 percent (1.45% + 0.9%) on wages in excess of $200,000 ($125,000 on a married filing separate return; $250,000 of combined wages on a married filing joint return).

Additional Medicare Tax on Wages

Example 36

Jenna, who is single, earns wages of $500,000 in 2022. Jenna will pay $2,900 of Medicare taxes on the first $200,000 of her wages ($200,000 × 1.45%) and $7,050 of Medicare taxes on her wages in excess of $200,000 ($300,000 × 2.35%). In total, her Medicare tax is $9,950, of which $2,700 ($300,000 × 0.9%) represents Jenna's additional Medicare tax.

Example 37

Patrick and Paula file a joint return in 2022. During the year, Patrick earns wages of $125,000, and Paula earns wages of $175,000—so their total wages are $300,000. Patrick and Paula will pay total Medicare taxes of $4,800 ($250,000 × 1.45% plus $50,000 × 2.35%), of which $450 ($50,000 × 0.9%) represents Patrick and Paula's additional Medicare tax.

Employers must withhold the additional 0.9 percent Medicare tax on wages paid in excess of $200,000.[50] An employer is not responsible for determining wages earned by an employee's spouse (and the implications of those wages on the total Medicare tax to be paid).

[49] § 3101(b)(2). The base amounts are not indexed for inflation.

[50] § 3102(f).

Example 38

Return to the facts of Example 37. In 2022, neither Patrick's nor Paula's employer will withhold the additional Medicare tax since both wage amounts are less than $200,000. Therefore, Paula will have $2,537.50 of Medicare tax withheld ($175,000 × 1.45%), and Patrick will have $1,812.50 of Medicare tax withheld ($125,000 × 1.45%). Total Medicare tax withheld is $4,350.00 ($2,537.50 + $1,812.50). Patrick and Paula pay an additional $450.00 of Medicare taxes when they file their return.[51]

The additional Medicare tax also applies to self-employed individuals—with net earnings from self-employment being used for the threshold computations. As a result, the tax rate for the Medicare tax on self-employment income will be:

1. 2.9 percent on the first $200,000 of net earnings from self-employment ($125,000 on a married filing separate return; $250,000 on a married filing joint return); and
2. 3.8 percent (2.9% + 0.9%) on net earnings from self-employment in excess of $200,000 ($125,000 on a married filing separate return; $250,000 on a married filing joint return).

For married taxpayers, one of whom has wages and one of whom has self-employment income, the thresholds are reduced (but not below zero) by the amount of wages taken into account in determining the additional 0.9 percent Medicare tax on wages.[52] Although self-employed individuals are allowed an income tax deduction for part of the self-employment tax, this additional 0.9 percent Medicare tax will *not* create a deduction (i.e., the deduction is determined without regard to this additional tax).[53]

Additional Tax on Unearned Income (Net Investment Income Tax)

An additional 3.8 percent Medicare tax is imposed on the unearned income of individuals, estates, and trusts.[54] The net investment income tax (NIIT) is 3.8 percent of the lesser of:[55]

1. Net investment income, or
2. The excess of modified adjusted gross income over $250,000 for married taxpayers filing a joint return ($125,000 if married filing separately) and $200,000 for all other taxpayers.[56]

In general, "net investment income" includes interest, dividends, annuities, royalties, rents, income from passive activities, and net gains from the sale of investment property less deductions allowed in generating that income.[57] Modified adjusted gross income (MAGI) is adjusted gross income (AGI) increased by any foreign earned income exclusion.[58] For individuals who don't incur any excluded foreign earned income, MAGI is the same as AGI.

Additional Medicare Tax on Unearned Income

Example 39

In 2022, Xinran earns net investment income of $50,000 and MAGI of $180,000 and files as a single taxpayer. Since Xinran's MAGI does not exceed $200,000, she need not pay the additional Medicare tax on unearned income.

[51] Couples in this situation might need to make estimated tax payments to account for the additional Medicare taxes.

[52] § 1401(b)(2)(B).

[53] § 164(f).

[54] § 1411.

[55] § 1411(a)(1).

[56] § 1411(b). The base amounts are not indexed for inflation.

[57] § 1411(c). Certain types of income, including qualified retirement plan distributions, tax-exempt income, and untaxed gain from the sale of a principal residence, are excluded from this definition.

[58] § 1411(d).

Additional Medicare Tax on Unearned Income

Example 40

Assume the same facts as in Example 39, except that Xinran reports net investment income of $85,000 and MAGI of $220,000.

In this case, she pays a Medicare tax on the lesser of (1) $85,000 (her net investment income) or (2) $20,000 (the amount by which her MAGI exceeds the $200,000 threshold). As a result, Xinran's additional Medicare tax on unearned income is $760 ($20,000 × 3.8%).

Example 41

Assume the same facts as Example 40, except that Xinran's MAGI is $290,000.

Because her MAGI exceeds the threshold amount by $90,000, she pays a Medicare tax on the entire $85,000 of net investment income. As a result, Xinran's additional Medicare tax on unearned income is $3,230 ($85,000 × 3.8%).

The 3.8 percent additional Medicare tax on unearned income is *in addition to* the additional 0.9 percent Medicare tax on wages or self-employment income. Taxpayers who have both high wages (or self-employment income) *and* high investment income may be subject to both taxes.

Example 42

Assume the same facts as Example 41, except that Xinran reports MAGI of $325,000 (including $240,000 of wages and $85,000 of net investment income).

In this case, Xinran must pay an additional Medicare tax on wages of $360 ($40,000 × 0.9%, her wages in excess of $200,000). In total, Xinran pays $3,590 in additional Medicare taxes ($3,230 on unearned income and $360 on wages).

13-6 Tax Planning

LO.8

Identify tax planning opportunities related to tax credits and payment procedures.

13-6a Credit for Child and Dependent Care Expenses

A taxpayer may incur employment-related expenses that also qualify as medical expenses (e.g., a nurse is hired to provide in-home care for an incapacitated dependent parent, allowing the adult child to go to work). These expenses may be either deducted as medical expenses (generally subject to the 7.5%-of-AGI limitation) or used in determining the child and dependent care credit. If the child and dependent care credit is chosen and the employment-related expenses exceed the limitation (in 2021, $8,000, $16,000, or earned income; in 2022, $3,000, $6,000, or earned income), the excess will qualify as a medical expense. If, however, the taxpayer chooses to deduct qualified employment-related expenses as medical expenses, any portion that is not deductible because of the percentage limitation may not be used in computing the credit for child and dependent care expenses.

Example 43

Alicia reports the following information for 2022:

Adjusted gross income		$60,000
Potential itemized deductions *from* AGI—		
Other than medical expenses	$ 4,500	
Medical expenses	12,900	$17,400

All of Alicia's medical expenses were incurred to provide nursing care for her disabled father while she was working. Alicia's father lives with her and qualifies as her dependent.

What should Alicia do in this situation? One approach would be to use $3,000 of the nursing care expenses to obtain the maximum child and dependent care credit allowed of $600 (20% × $3,000). The remaining expenses should be claimed as medical expenses. After a reduction of 7.5 percent of AGI, this would produce a medical expense deduction of $5,400 [$9,900 (remaining medical expenses) − (7.5% × $60,000)].

Another approach would be to claim the full $12,900 as a medical expense in lieu of any child and dependent care credit. After applying the 7.5%-of-AGI floor of $4,500 (7.5% × $60,000), a deduction of $8,400 remains.

The choice, then, is between a credit of $600 plus a deduction of $5,400 or a credit of $0 plus a deduction of $8,400. The relative tax savings involved then depend on Alicia's marginal tax rate and whether she itemizes her deductions.

One of the traditional goals of *family tax planning* is to minimize the present value of the total tax burden of the family unit. With proper planning and implementation, the child and dependent care credit can be used to help achieve this goal. For example, payments to certain relatives for the care of qualifying dependents and children qualify for the credit if the care provider is *not* a child (under age 19) of the taxpayer. So if the care provider is in a lower tax bracket than the taxpayer, the following benefits result.

- Income is shifted to a lower-bracket family member.
- The taxpayer qualifies for the credit for child and dependent care expenses.

In addition, the goal of minimizing the family income tax liability can be enhanced in some other situations, but only if the credit's limitations are recognized and avoided. For example, tax savings may be enjoyed even if the qualifying expenses incurred by a cash basis taxpayer have reached the annual ceiling ($3,000 or $6,000). To the extent that any additional payments can be shifted into future tax years, the benefit from the credit may be preserved on these excess expenses.

Example 44

Andre, a calendar year and cash basis taxpayer, has spent $3,000 by December 1 on qualifying child care expenses for his dependent 11-year-old son. The $250 that is due the care provider for child care services rendered in December does not generate a tax credit benefit if the amount is paid in the current year because the $3,000 ceiling has been reached. However, if the payment can be delayed until the next year, the total credit over the two-year period for which Andre is eligible may be increased.

A similar shifting of expenses to the next year may be wise if this nonrefundable credit was limited by the tax liability.

13-6b Adjustments to Increase Withholding

The penalty for underpayment of estimated tax by individuals is computed for each quarter of the tax year. A taxpayer can play *catch-up* to a certain extent. Each quarterly payment is credited to the unpaid portion of any previous required installment. As a result, the penalty stops on that portion of the underpayment for the previous quarter. However, because income tax withheld is assumed to have been paid evenly throughout the year and is allocated equally among the four installments in computing any penalty, a taxpayer who otherwise would be subject to a penalty for underpayment should increase withholdings late in the year. This can be done by modifying the Form W–4 or by making a special arrangement with the employer to increase the amount withheld.

13-6c Adjustments to Avoid Overwithholding

If a taxpayer has unusually large itemized deductions, deductions *for* AGI, net losses from Schedules C, D, E, and F, or tax credits, the IRS Withholding Calculator (**apps.irs.gov/app/tax-withholding-estimator**) should be used to determine the correct amount of withholding. Net operating loss carryovers also may be considered in the computation. Based on this calculation, the taxpayer can file a revised Form W–4 with the employer.

Refocus on The Big Picture

Education Tax Credits

YELLOW DOG PRODUCTIONS/GETTY IMAGES

The American Opportunity tax credit provides some relief for Tom and Jennifer Snyder.

Lora and Sam qualify for the American Opportunity credit in 2022 because they are both in their first four years of postsecondary education. Lora and Sam both qualify for a $2,500 credit (100 percent of the first $2,000 and 25 percent of the next $2,000 of qualified expenses).

These credits phase out over a range of $20,000 once married taxpayers' AGI exceeds $160,000. Since the Snyders' AGI ($158,000) is less than this amount, the total education credits available to them amount to $5,000, and they may claim this amount as a credit on their 2022 income tax return (see Example 26). In addition, this credit may be used to offset any AMT liability, and 40 percent ($2,000) is refundable to the Snyders.

What If?

What if the Snyders' AGI is $188,000? In 2022, the Snyders would not qualify for any education credits (their income exceeds the limits for both the American Opportunity and the lifetime learning credits).

Key Terms

American Opportunity credit, 13-18
Child tax credit, 13-15
Credit for certain retirement plan contributions, 13-19
Credit for child and dependent care expenses, 13-15
Credit for employer-provided child care, 13-11
Credit for employer-provided family and medical leave, 13-12
Credit for small employer pension plan startup costs, 13-11
Dependent tax credit, 13-15
Disabled access credit, 13-10
Earned income credit, 13-12
Employment taxes, 13-23
Energy tax credits, 13-19
Estimated tax, 13-26
Foreign tax credit (FTC), 13-14
General business credit, 13-5
Lifetime learning credit, 13-18
Low-income housing credit, 13-9
Nonrefundable credits, 13-5
Refundable credits, 13-4
Rehabilitation expenditures credit, 13-6
Research activities credit, 13-7
Self-employment tax, 13-27
Tax credits, 13-2
Work opportunity tax credit, 13-7

Discussion Questions

1. **LO.1** Would an individual taxpayer receive greater benefit from deducting an expense or from taking a credit equal to 25% of the expense? How would your response change if the item would only be deductible *from* AGI?

Critical Thinking

2. **LO.2** Clint, a self-employed engineering consultant, is contemplating purchasing an old building for renovation. After the work is completed, Clint plans to rent out two-thirds of the floor space to businesses and to live and work in the remaining portion. Identify the relevant tax issues for Clint.

Critical Thinking

3. **LO.3** Sonja is considering the purchase and renovation of an old building. She has heard about the tax credit for rehabilitation expenditures but does not know the specific rules applicable to the credit. Explain the most important and relevant provisions for her.

4. **LO.3** Explain the purpose of the disabled access credit, and identify several examples of the type of structural changes to a building that qualify for the credit.

5. **LO.4** Is the earned income credit a form of negative income tax? Why or why not?

Critical Thinking

6. **LO.4** Tim recently was called into the partner's office and offered a two-year assignment in his public accounting firm's Shanghai office. Realizing that Tim will face incremental expenses while in Shanghai, such as foreign income taxes and rent, the firm will try to make him "whole" from a financial perspective by increasing his salary to help offset the expenses he will incur while living overseas. If Tim takes the assignment, he likely will rent his U.S. personal residence and sell several major tangible assets such as his personal automobile. Identify the relevant Federal income tax issues.

Critical Thinking

7. **LO.4** Mark and Lisa are approaching an exciting time in their lives as their oldest son, Austin, graduates from high school and moves on to college. What are some of the tax issues Mark and Lisa should consider as they think about paying for Austin's college education?

Critical Thinking

8. **LO.5** Elaborate rules exist that require employers to prepay various types of Federal taxes. Summarize the major issues that an employer must resolve if it is to comply with the requirements.

9. **LO.5** Kathy, a sole proprietor, owns and operates a grocery store. Kathy's husband and her 16-year-old daughter work in the business and are paid wages. Will the husband and daughter be subject to FICA? Explain.

10. **LO.6** Describe the exposure (i.e., wage base and tax rate) of a self-employed individual to the self-employment tax for 2022.

11. **LO.7** Describe the two additional Medicare taxes that are assessed on high-income taxpayers.

Computational Exercises

12. **LO.2** Carlson's general business credit for the current year is $84,000. His net income tax is $190,000, tentative minimum tax is $175,000, and net regular tax liability is $185,000. He has no other Federal income tax credits. Determine Carlson's general business credit allowed for the year and any amounts that can be carried back and forward.

13. **LO.3** Emily spent $135,000 to rehabilitate a certified historic building (adjusted basis of $90,000) that originally had been placed in service in 1935. What is Emily's rehabilitation expenditures tax credit?

14. **LO.3** During 2022, Lincoln Company hires seven individuals who are certified to be members of a qualifying targeted group. Each employee works in excess of 600 hours and is paid wages of $7,500 during the year. Determine the amount of Lincoln's work opportunity credit.

15. **LO.3** Alison incurs the following research expenditures.

In-house wages	$60,000
In-house supplies	5,000
Payment to ABC, Inc., for research	80,000

a. Determine the amount of qualified research expenditures.

b. Assuming that the base amount is $60,000, determine Alison's incremental research activities credit.

16. **LO.4** Samuel and Annamaria are married, file a joint return, and have three qualifying children. In 2022, they earn wages of $34,000 and no other income. Determine the amount of their earned income credit for 2022.

17. **LO.4** In 2022, Henri, a U.S. citizen and calendar year taxpayer, reports $30,000 of income from France, which imposes a 10% income tax, and $50,000 from Italy, which imposes a 40% tax. In addition, Henri reports taxable income of $90,000 from within the United States.

Henri is married filing a joint return, and his U.S. tax before the foreign tax credit is $28,634. Determine the amount of Henri's foreign tax credit.

18. **LO.4** In 2022, Santiago and Amy are married and file a joint tax return. They have three dependent children, ages 12, 14, and 19. All parties are U.S. citizens. The couple's AGI is $140,000. Determine any available child tax credit and dependent tax credit.

19. **LO.4** In 2022, Ivanna, who has three children under age 13, worked full-time while her spouse, Sergio, was attending college for nine months during the year. Ivanna earned $47,000 and incurred $6,400 of child care expenses. Determine Ivanna and Sergio's child and dependent care credit.

20. **LO.4, 8** Ava and her husband, Leo, file a joint return and are in the 24% tax bracket in 2022. Ava's employer offers a child and dependent care reimbursement plan that allows up to $5,000 of qualifying expenses to be reimbursed in exchange for a $5,000 reduction in the employee's salary (Ava's salary is $75,000). Because Ava and Leo have two minor children requiring child care that costs $5,800 each year, Ava is wondering if she should sign up for the program instead of taking advantage of the credit for child and dependent care expenses.

Critical Thinking
Decision Making
Planning

Analyze the effect of the two alternatives. How would your answer differ if Ava's salary was $30,000, their AGI was $25,000, and their marginal tax rate was 10%?

21. **LO.4** Paola and Isidora are married; file a joint tax return; report modified AGI of $148,000; and have one dependent child, Dante. The couple paid $12,000 of tuition and $10,000 for room and board for Dante (a freshman). Dante is a full-time student. Determine the amount of the American Opportunity credit for 2022.

22. **LO.4** Rafael and Lucy, married taxpayers, each contribute $2,900 to their respective § 401(k) plans offered through their employers. The AGI reported on the couple's joint return is $42,000. Determine their credit for retirement plan contributions (the Saver's Credit).

23. **LO.5** In 2022, Bianca earned a salary of $164,000 from her employer. Determine the amount of FICA taxes and Medicare taxes withheld from her salary.

24. **LO.6** In 2022, Miranda records net earnings from self-employment of $168,500. She has no other income. Determine the amount of Miranda's self-employment tax and her *for* AGI income tax deduction.

25. **LO.7** Determine the additional Medicare taxes for these individuals.
    a. Mario, who is single, earns wages of $440,000.
    b. George and Shirley are married and file a joint return. During the year, George earns wages of $138,000, and Shirley earns wages of $210,000.
    c. Simon has net investment income of $38,000 and MAGI of $223,000 and files as a single taxpayer.

Problems

26. **LO.2** Adelyn has a tentative general business credit of $42,000 for the current year. Adelyn's net regular tax liability before the general business credit is $107,000, and her tentative minimum tax is $88,000. Compute Adelyn's allowable general business credit for the year.

27. **LO.2** Oak Corporation has the following general business credit carryovers.

2018	$ 5,000
2019	15,000
2020	6,000
2021	19,000
Total carryovers	$45,000

If the general business credit generated by activities during 2022 equals $36,000 and the total credit allowed during the current year is $60,000 (based on tax liability), what amounts of the current general business credit and carryovers are utilized against the 2022 income tax liability? What is the amount of unused credit carried forward to 2023?

Communications
Critical Thinking
Decision Making
Planning

28. **LO.3, 8** In the current year, Paul Chaing (4522 Fargo Street, Geneva, IL 60134) acquires a qualifying historic structure for $350,000 (excluding the cost of the land) and plans to substantially rehabilitate the structure. He is planning to spend either $320,000 or $380,000 on rehabilitation expenditures.

    Write a letter to Paul and a memo for the tax files explaining, for the two alternative expenditures, (1) the computation that determines the rehabilitation expenditures tax credit available to Paul, (2) the impact of the credit on Paul's adjusted basis in the property, and (3) the cash-flow differences as a result of the tax consequences related to his expenditure choice.

29. **LO.3** Green Corporation hires six individuals on January 4, 2022, all of whom qualify for the work opportunity credit. Three of these individuals receive wages of $8,500 during 2022, and each individual works more than 400 hours during the year. The other three individuals work 300 hours and receive wages of $5,000 during the year.
    a. Calculate the amount of Green's work opportunity credit for 2022.
    b. If Green pays total wages of $140,000 to its employees during the year, how much of this amount is deductible in 2022 assuming that the work opportunity credit is taken?

30. **LO.3, 8** Tom, a calendar year taxpayer, informs you that in 2021, he incurred expenditures of $40,000 that qualify for the incremental research activities credit. In addition, it is determined that his base amount for the year is $32,800. Decision Making

a. Determine Tom's incremental research activities credit for 2021.

b. Tom is in the 24% tax bracket. Determine which approach to the research expenditures and the research activities credit (other than capitalization and subsequent amortization) would provide the greater tax benefit to Tom.

31. **LO.3** Ahmed Zinna (16 Southside Drive, Charlotte, NC 28204), one of your clients, owns two retail establishments in downtown Charlotte and has come to you seeking advice concerning the tax consequences of complying with the Americans with Disabilities Act. He understands that he needs to install various features at his stores (e.g., ramps, doorways, and restrooms that are accessible) to make them more accessible to disabled individuals. He asks whether any tax credits will be available to help offset the cost of the necessary changes. He estimates the cost of the planned changes to his facilities as follows. Communications

Location	Projected Cost
Calvin Street	$22,000
Stowe Avenue	8,500

He reminds you that the Calvin Street store was constructed in 2004 and the Stowe Avenue store is in a building that was constructed in 1947. Ahmed operates his business as a sole proprietorship and has approximately eight employees at each location. Write a letter to Ahmed in which you summarize your conclusions concerning the tax consequences of his proposed capital improvements.

32. **LO.4** Which of the following individuals qualifies for the earned income credit for 2022?

a. Thomas is single, is 21 years of age, and has no qualifying children. His income consists of $9,000 in wages.

b. Shannon, who is 27 years old, maintains a household for a dependent 11-year-old son and is eligible for head-of-household tax rates. Her income consists of $16,050 of salary and $50 of taxable interest (Shannon's AGI is $16,100).

c. Keith and Susan, both age 30, are married and file a joint return. Keith and Susan have no dependents. Their combined income consists of $28,500 of salary and $100 of taxable interest (their AGI is $28,600).

d. Colin is a 26-year-old self-supporting, single taxpayer. He has no qualifying children and generates earnings of $14,000.

33. **LO.4** Jason, a single parent, lives in an apartment with his three minor children, whom he supports. Jason earned $27,400 during 2022 and uses the standard deduction. Calculate the amount, if any, of Jason's earned income credit.

34. **LO.4, 8** Joyce, a single parent, lives in an apartment with her two minor children (ages 8 and 10), whom she supports. Joyce earns $33,000 during 2022. She uses the standard deduction and files as a head of household. Critical Thinking Decision Making Planning

a. Calculate the amount, if any, of Joyce's earned income credit.

b. During the year, Joyce is offered a new job that has greater future potential than her current job. If she accepts the job offer, her earnings for the year will be $39,000; however, she is afraid she will not qualify for the earned income credit. Using after-tax cash-flow calculations, determine whether Joyce should accept the new job offer. Since the child tax credit will be the same under either scenario, you can ignore it for purposes of this analysis.

Decision Making
Planning

35. **LO.4** Kim, a U.S. citizen and resident, owns and operates a novelty goods business. During 2022, Kim reports taxable income of $115,000: $50,000 from foreign sources and $65,000 from U.S. sources. In calculating taxable income, the standard deduction is used. The income from foreign sources is subject to foreign income taxes of $17,500. For 2022, Kim files a joint return with her spouse.
    a. Assuming that Kim chooses to claim the foreign taxes as an income tax credit, what is her net Federal income tax payable for 2022?
    b. Recently, Kim has become disenchanted with the location of her business and is considering moving her offshore operation to a different country. Based on her research, if she moved her business to her country of choice, all relevant revenues and costs would remain approximately the same, except that the income taxes payable to that country would be only $7,000. Given that any foreign income taxes paid are available to offset the U.S. tax liability (whether she operates in a high-tax or low-tax jurisdiction), what effect will this have on her decision regarding the potential move?

36. **LO.4** Blue Sky, Inc., a U.S. corporation, is a manufacturing concern that sells most of its products in the United States. It also conducts some business in the European Union through various branches. During the current year, Blue Sky reports taxable income of $700,000, of which $500,000 is U.S.-sourced and $200,000 is foreign-sourced. Foreign income taxes paid amounted to $35,000. Blue Sky's U.S. income tax liability is $147,000. What is its U.S. income tax liability net of the allowable foreign tax credit?

37. **LO.4** In 2022, Joshua and Ellen are married and file a joint return. Three individuals qualify as their dependents: their two children, ages 5 years and 6 months, and Ellen's son from a previous marriage, age 19. All parties are U.S. citizens. Joshua and Ellen's combined AGI is $68,000. Compute their child tax credit and dependent tax credit.

38. **LO.4** Paul and Karen Kent are married, and both are employed (Paul earns $44,000 and Karen earns $9,000 during 2022). Paul and Karen have two dependent children, both under the age of 13 (Samuel and Joy). So that they can work, Paul and Karen pay $3,800 ($1,900 for each child) to Sunnyside Day Care Center (422 Sycamore Road, Fort Worth, TX 76028; Employer Identification Number: 11-2345678) to care for their children while they are working. Assuming that Paul and Karen file a joint return, what, if any, is their tax credit for child and dependent care expenses?

39. **LO.4** Jim and Mary Jean are married and have two dependent children under the age of 13. Both parents are gainfully employed and during 2022 earn salaries as follows: $130,000 (Jim) and $5,200 (Mary Jean). To care for their children while they work, they pay Eleanor (Jim's mother) $5,600. Eleanor does not qualify as a dependent of Jim and Mary Jean. Assuming that Jim and Mary Jean file a joint tax return, what, if any, is their credit for child and dependent care expenses?

Communications

40. **LO.4, 8** Jenna, a longtime client of yours, is employed as an architect and is the president of the local Rotary chapter. To keep up to date with developments in her profession, she attends continuing education seminars offered by the architecture school at State University. During 2022, Jenna spends $2,000 on course tuition to attend these seminars. She spends another $400 on architecture books during the year.

    Jenna's daughter, Caitlin, is a senior majoring in engineering at the University of the Midwest. During the 2022 calendar year, Caitlin incurs the following expenses: $8,200 for tuition ($4,100 per semester) and $750 for books and course materials. Caitlin, who

Jenna claims as a dependent, lives at home while attending school full-time. Jenna is married, files a joint return, and reports a combined AGI with her spouse of $121,000.

a. Calculate the couple's education tax credits for 2022.

b. Calculate the couple's education tax credits if combined AGI was $162,000.

c. In her capacity as president of the local Rotary chapter, Jenna has asked you to prepare a 30- to 45-minute speech outlining the different ways the tax law helps defray (1) the cost of higher education and (2) the cost of continuing education once someone is in the workforce. Prepare an outline of possible topics for presentation. A tentative title for your presentation is "How Can the Tax Law Help Pay for College and Continuing Professional Education?"

41. **LO.4** Kathleen and Glenn decide that this is the year to begin getting serious about saving for their retirement by participating in their employers' § 401(k) plans. As a result, they each have $3,000 of their salary set aside in their qualified plans.

a. Calculate the maximum credit for these retirement plan contributions available to Kathleen and Glenn if the AGI on their joint return is $35,000.

b. Kathleen and Glenn persuade their dependent 15-year-old son, Joel, to put $500 of his part-time earnings into a Roth IRA during the year. What is the credit available to Joel for this contribution? His AGI is $7,000.

42. **LO.5** In each of the following independent situations, determine the amount of FICA that should be withheld from the employee's 2022 salary by the employer.

a. Harry earns a $50,000 salary and files a joint return.

b. Hazel earns a $115,000 salary and files a joint return.

c. Tracy earns a $190,000 salary and files a joint return.

d. Alicia's 17-year-old son, Carlos, earns $10,000 at the family sole proprietorship.

43. **LO.5** During 2022, Greg Cruz (1401 Orangedale Road, Troy, MI 48084) works for Maple Corporation and Gray Company. He earns $96,000 at Maple Corporation, where he is a full-time employee. Greg also works part-time for Gray Company for wages of $54,000. Communications

a. Did Greg experience an overwithholding of FICA taxes? Write a letter to Greg and a memo for the tax files in which you explain your conclusion.

b. Did Maple Corporation and Gray Company overpay the employer's portion of FICA? Explain.

44. **LO.6** Julie, a self-employed individual, is required to make estimated payments of her tax liability for the year. Her tax liability for 2021 was $25,000, and her AGI was less than $150,000. For 2022, Julie ultimately determines that her income tax liability is $18,000. During the year, however, she made the following payments, totaling $13,000.

April 15, 2022	$ 4,500
June 15, 2022	2,800
September 15, 2022	4,100
January 17, 2023	1,600
Total paid	$13,000

Because Julie prepaid so little of her ultimate income tax liability, she now realizes that she may be subject to the penalty for underpayment of estimated tax.

a. Determine Julie's estimated tax underpayment for each installment period, if any.

b. Instead, assume that Julie's tax liability for 2021 was $15,960.

45. **LO.6** a. In 2022, Maria records self-employed earnings of $135,000. Using the format illustrated in the text, compute Maria's self-employment tax liability and the allowable income tax deduction for the self-employment tax paid.

b. Express the calculation of the 2022 self-employment tax as a Microsoft Excel formula.

Tax Return Problems

Planning

Tax Forms Problem

ProConnect™ Tax

46. Beth R. Jordan lives at 2322 Skyview Road, Mesa, AZ 85201. She is a tax accountant with Mesa Manufacturing Company, 1203 Western Avenue, Mesa, AZ 85201 (employer identification number 11-1111111). She also writes computer software programs for tax practitioners and has a part-time tax practice. Beth is single and has no dependents. Beth was born on July 4, 1975, and her Social Security number is 123-45-6785. She did not engage in any vitual currency transactions during the year, and she wants to contribute $3 to the Presidential Election Campaign Fund. Beth received the appropriate coronavirus recovery rebates (economic impact payments); related questions in ProConnect Tax should be ignored.

    The following information is shown on Beth's Wage and Tax Statement (Form W–2) for 2021.

Line	Description	Amount
1	Wages, tips, other compensation	$65,000.00
2	Federal income tax withheld	9,500.00
3	Social Security wages	65,000.00
4	Social Security tax withheld	4,030.00
5	Medicare wages and tips	65,000.00
6	Medicare tax withheld	942.50
15	State	Arizona
16	State wages, tips, etc.	65,000.00
17	State income tax withheld	1,954.00

During the year, Beth received interest of $1,300 from Arizona Federal Savings and Loan and $400 from Arizona State Bank. Each financial institution reported the interest income on a Form 1099–INT. She received qualified dividends of $800 from Blue Corporation, $750 from Green Corporation, and $650 from Orange Corporation. Each corporation reported Beth's dividend payments on a Form 1099–DIV.

Beth received a $1,100 income tax refund from the state of Arizona on April 29, 2021. On her 2020 Federal income tax return, she used the standard deduction.

Fees earned from her part-time tax practice in 2021 totaled $3,800. She paid $600 to have the tax returns processed by a computerized tax return service.

On February 8, 2021, Beth bought 500 shares of Gray Corporation common stock for $17.60 a share. On September 12, 2021, Beth sold the stock for $14 a share.

On January 2, 2021, Beth acquired 100 shares of Blue Corporation common stock for $30 a share. She sold the stock on December 19, 2021, for $55 a share. Both stock transactions were reported to Beth on Form 1099–B; basis was not reported to the IRS.

Beth bought a used sport utility vehicle for $6,000 on June 5, 2021. She purchased the vehicle from her brother-in-law, who was unemployed and was in need of cash. On November 2, 2021, she sold the vehicle to a friend for $6,500.

During the year, Beth records revenues of $16,000 from the sale of a software program she developed. Beth incurred the following expenses in connection with her software development business.

Cost of personal computer	$7,000
Cost of printer	2,000
Furniture	3,000
Supplies	650
Fee paid to computer consultant	3,500

Beth elected to expense the maximum portion of the cost of the computer, printer, and furniture allowed under the provisions of § 179. These items were placed in service on January 15, 2021, and used 100% in her business.

Although her employer suggested that Beth attend an in-person conference on current developments in corporate taxation, Beth was not reimbursed for the travel expenses of $1,420 she incurred in attending the meeting. The $1,420 included $200 for the cost of meals.

During the year, Beth paid $300 for prescription medicines and $2,875 for doctor bills and hospital bills. Medical insurance premiums were paid by her employer. Beth paid real property taxes of $1,766 on her home. Interest on her home mortgage (Valley National Bank) was $3,845, and credit card interest was $320. Beth contributed $2,080 in cash to various qualifying charities during the year. Professional dues and subscriptions totaled $350.

Beth paid estimated taxes of $1,000.

Part 1—Tax Computation
Compute Beth Jordan's 2021 Federal income tax payable (or refund due), and complete her 2021 tax return using appropriate forms and schedules. Suggested software: ProConnect Tax.

Part 2—Tax Planning
Beth is anticipating significant changes in her life in 2022, and she has asked you to estimate her taxable income and tax liability for 2022.

Beth just received word that she has been qualified to adopt a two-year-old daughter. Beth expects that the adoption will be finalized in 2022 and that she will incur approximately $2,000 of adoption expenses. In addition, she expects to incur approximately $3,500 of child and dependent care expenses relating to the care of her new daughter, which will enable her to keep her job at Mesa Manufacturing Company. However, with the additional demands on her time because of her daughter, she has decided to discontinue her two part-time jobs (i.e., the part-time tax practice and her software business), and she will cease making estimated income tax payments.

In your computations, assume that all other 2022 income and expenses will be the same as 2021 amounts.

47. Tim and Sarah Lawrence are married and file a joint return. Tim's Social Security number is 123-45-6789, and Sarah's Social Security number is 111-11-1111. They reside at 100 Olive Lane, Covington, LA 70434. They have two dependent children, Sean and Debra, ages 12 and 16, respectively. Sean's Social Security number is 123-45-6788, and Debra's Social Security number is 123-45-6787. Tim is a self-employed businessperson (sole proprietor of an unincorporated business), and Sarah is a corporate executive. Tim has the following income and expenses from his business in 2022. Tax Computation Problem

Gross income	$325,000
Business expenses	201,000

Records related to Sarah's employment provide the following information.

Salary	$130,000
Unreimbursed travel expenses (including $200 of meals)	1,600

Other pertinent information for the tax year includes the following.

Proceeds from sale of stock acquired on July 15, 2022 (cost of $12,000), and sold on August 1, 2022	$ 9,800
Proceeds from sale of stock acquired on September 18, 2021 (cost of $5,000), and sold on October 5, 2022	3,800
Wages paid to full-time domestic worker for housekeeping and child supervision	10,000
Interest income received	7,000
Total itemized deductions (not including any potential deductions above)	27,900
Federal income tax withheld	28,850
Estimated Federal income tax payments	20,000

Compute the Lawrences' net Federal income tax payable or refund due for 2022.

Research Problems

the answer company™
THOMSON REUTERS®

Note: Solutions to the Research Problems can be prepared by using the Thomson Reuters Checkpoint™ online tax research database, which accompanies this textbook. Solutions can also be prepared by using research materials found in a typical tax library.

Research Problem 1. Ashby and Curtis, married professionals, have a two-year-old son, Jason. Curtis works full-time as an electrical engineer, but Ashby has not worked outside the home since Jason was born. Because Jason is getting older, Ashby thinks that he would benefit from attending nursery school several times a week, which would give her an opportunity to reinvigorate her love of painting at a nearby art studio. Ashby thinks that if she is lucky, the proceeds from the sale of her paintings will pay for the nursery school tuition.

Ashby plans to claim the credit for child and dependent care expenses, because the care provided Jason at the nursery school is required for her to pursue her art career. Can Ashby and Curtis claim the credit for child and dependent care expenses for the nursery school expense? Why or why not?

Critical Thinking

Research Problem 2. During a recent Sunday afternoon excursion, Miriam, an admirer of early twentieth-century architecture, discovers a 1920s-era house in the countryside outside Mobile, Alabama. She wants not only to purchase and renovate the house but also to move the structure into Mobile so that her community can enjoy its architectural features. Being aware of the availability of the tax credit for rehabilitation expenditures, she wants to maximize her use of the provision, if it is available in this case, once the renovation work begins in Mobile.

Miriam informs you that she will pursue the purchase, relocation, and renovation of the house only if the tax credit is available. Comment on Miriam's decision and on whether any renovation expenditures incurred will qualify for the tax credit for rehabilitation expenditures.

Partial list of research aids:

George S. Nalle III v. Comm., 93–2 USTC ¶50,468, 72 AFTR 2d 93–5705, 997 F.2d 1134 (CA–5, 1993).

Communications
Critical Thinking
Data Analytics

Research Problem 3. Which tax credits are most often claimed by individual taxpayers? Do the credits claimed vary by size of income (AGI)? To answer these questions, go to the IRS Tax Statistics page (**irs.gov/statistics**) and download the Microsoft Excel spreadsheet for the most recent tax year that documents tax liability, tax credits, and tax payments. You can find this in the Individual Income Tax Return (Form 1040) Statistics section of the site; click on the "by Size of Adjusted Gross Income" link. Scroll down this page until you find "All Returns: Tax Liability, Tax Credits, and Tax Payments."

Evaluate the credits claimed (both nonrefundable and refundable) by size of AGI. Analyze the data by clustering it into the following AGI classes: $25,000 or less; $25,000 to $50,000; $50,000 to $100,000; $100,000 to $500,000; $500,000 or more. Present your findings in a visual depiction (e.g., bar chart), summarize your findings in a one-page memo, and send your graphic and memo to your instructor.

Communications

Research Problem 4. Taxpayers who purchase health insurance coverage through the Health Insurance Marketplace may be eligible for the premium tax credit under § 36B. Use the IRS website to determine which taxpayers are eligible for the credit. Send a one-page summary of your findings to your instructor.

Communications

Research Problem 5. The IRS provides a web-based tool to help taxpayers determine whether they are eligible for the earned income tax credit. Locate the EITC Assistant at the IRS website. Then apply the facts related to Walt in Example 21 for either 2022 or 2021. Determine whether the earned income credit is available for Walt and save the results as a pdf. In an e-mail to your instructor, report the estimated credit amount and attach your pdf.

Becker CPA Review Questions

1. Which of the following statements regarding the self-employment tax is true?
   a. Income and expenses from self-employment are reported on Schedule D (Form 1040).
   b. Self-employment income is subject to both Federal income tax and self-employment tax.
   c. One half of self-employment tax is deductible as an itemized deduction.
   d. All self-employment income is subject to both Medicare and Social Security tax.

2. Which of the following credits is considered "refundable"?
   a. Child and dependent care credit
   b. Retirement plan contribution credit
   c. Child tax credit
   d. Credit for the elderly or permanently disabled

3. Jim spent four years earning his undergraduate degree at a local university. He began his first year of law school in January of the current year. Assuming he is under the phaseout limitation, what education tax credit is Jim eligible for in the current year?
   a. American Opportunity credit
   b. Earned income credit
   c. Lifetime learning credit
   d. Professional education and training credit

4. Disregarding any small business exceptions, for the current year, which of the following situations will result in a taxpayer owing a penalty for underpayment of taxes?
   a. A married filing joint taxpayer had AGI of $160,000 and total tax of $35,000 in the prior year. For the current year, AGI is $175,000 and total tax is $40,000. They had no withholding in the current year and paid a total of $35,000 in estimated taxes.
   b. The taxpayer owes $950 in taxes after his withholding was applied to his current year's tax return.
   c. The taxpayer had AGI of $75,000 and total tax of $15,000 in the prior year. For the current year, his AGI is $62,000 and total tax is $12,500. He had no withholding in the current year and paid a total of $11,500 in estimated taxes.
   d. The taxpayer had AGI of $100,000 and total tax of $20,000 in the prior year. For the current year, his AGI is also $100,000, but his total tax is $15,000. His withholding amounted to $10,000, and he paid $6,000 in estimated taxes.

5. In 2022, Madison and Nick Koz have two children, ages 8 and 10. Both children meet the definition of qualifying child. The Koz family has adjusted gross income of $300,000. What is the amount of the child tax credit on the couple's income tax return?
   a. $1,000
   b. $2,000
   c. $3,000
   d. $4,000

6. Which of the following individual tax credits can result in a carryback and/or carryforward?
   a. Earned income credit
   b. Child and dependent care credit
   c. Credit for the elderly or permanently disabled
   d. Foreign tax credit

Part 5

Property Transactions

Chapter **14**
Property Transactions: Determination of Gain or Loss and Basis Considerations

Chapter **15**
Property Transactions: Nontaxable Exchanges

Chapter **16**
Property Transactions: Capital Gains and Losses

Chapter **17**
Property Transactions: § 1231 and Recapture Provisions

Part 5 covers the tax treatment of sales, exchanges, and other dispositions of property. Included here are the rules used to determine the realized gain or loss, whether the realized gain or loss is recognized, and the characterization of any recognized gain or loss as capital or ordinary. The topic of basis is evaluated both in terms of its effect on the calculation of the gain or loss and how the basis of any property acquired as part of the transaction is determined.

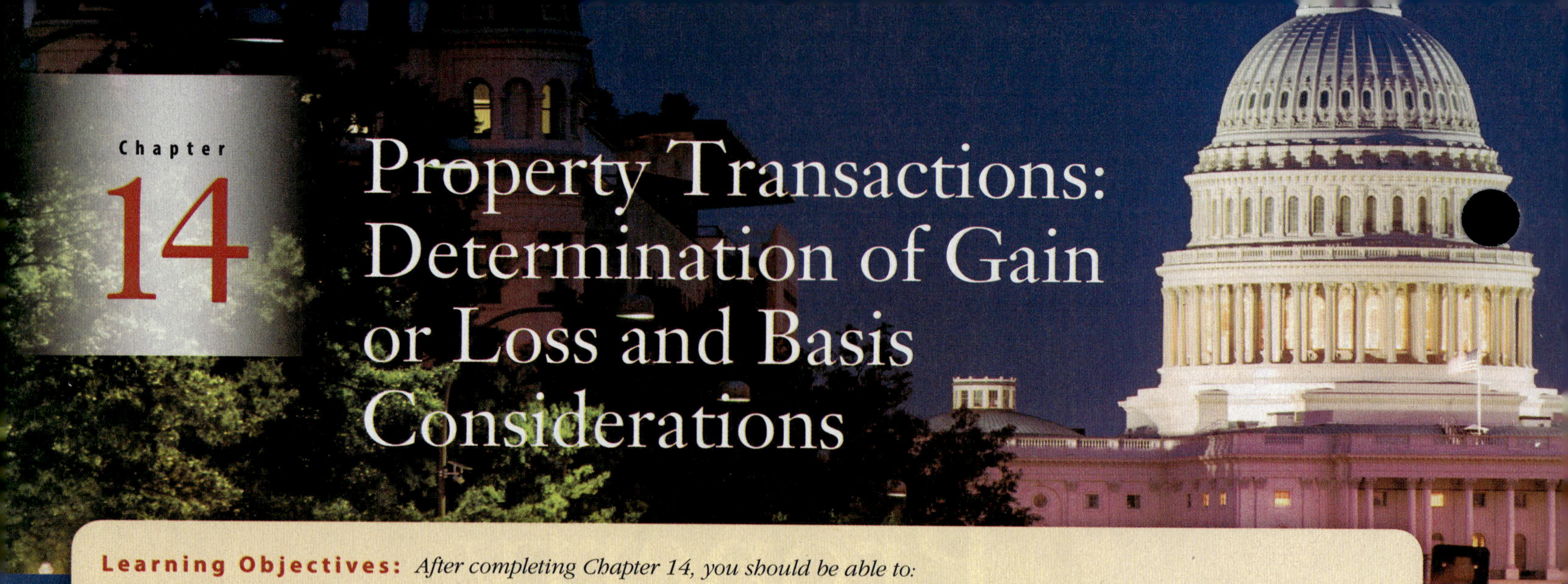

Chapter 14

Property Transactions: Determination of Gain or Loss and Basis Considerations

Learning Objectives: *After completing Chapter 14, you should be able to:*

- **LO.1** Explain the computation of realized gain or loss on property dispositions.
- **LO.2** Distinguish between realized and recognized gain or loss.
- **LO.3** Illustrate how basis is determined for various methods of asset acquisition.
- **LO.4** Describe various loss disallowance provisions.
- **LO.5** Identify tax planning opportunities related to selected property transactions.

Chapter Outline

14-1 Determination of Gain or Loss, 14-2

- 14-1a Realized Gain or Loss, 14-3
- 14-1b Recognized Gain or Loss, 14-8
- 14-1c Nonrecognition of Gain or Loss, 14-9

14-2 Basis Considerations, 14-9

- 14-2a Determination of Cost Basis, 14-9
- 14-2b Gift Basis, 14-12
- 14-2c Inherited Property, 14-13
- 14-2d Disallowed Losses, 14-15
- 14-2e Property Converted from Personal Use to Business or Income-Producing Use, 14-19
- 14-2f Summary of Basis Adjustments, 14-20

14-3 Tax Planning, 14-22

- 14-3a Cost Identification and Documentation Considerations, 14-22
- 14-3b Selection of Property for Making Gifts, 14-22
- 14-3c Selection of Property to Pass at Death, 14-22
- 14-3d Disallowed Losses, 14-23

ISTOCK.COM/MIKESPICS

The Big Picture

Proposed Sale of a House and Other Property Transactions

Alice owns a house that she received from her mother, Paula, seven months ago. Paula paid $275,000 for the house. Alice is considering selling the house to her favorite nephew, Dan, for $275,000. Alice anticipates that she will have no gain or loss on the transaction. She comes to you for advice. As Alice's tax adviser, you need answers to the following questions.

- You are aware that Paula died around the time Alice received the house from her mother. Did Alice receive the house by gift prior to her mother's death, or did she inherit it after her mother's death? What was Paula's adjusted basis for the house, and when did she buy it? What was the fair market value of the house on the date of Paula's death? Answers to these questions will help you determine Alice's basis in the house.
- Is the house Alice's principal residence? If so, when did it become her principal residence (before or after she received it from Paula)?
- To help determine the tax consequences of Alice's potential sale of the house to Dan, you need answers to these questions: What is the current fair market value of the house? Does Alice intend for the transaction with Dan to be a sale or part sale and part gift? What does Alice intend to do with the sale proceeds?

Alice also would like to know the tax consequences of selling her boat, which she purchased for $22,000 four months ago. She has been using it exclusively for personal use but is disappointed with its layout and capacity. Because it is a new model, there is significant demand for the boat, and based on listings in her area, she anticipates that she can sell it for $20,000 to $23,000.

While you are talking, Alice mentions that earlier this year, she sold some stock in Green Corporation at a loss. A few days later, after hearing Green's quarterly earnings report, she decided to buy back the shares. To determine the tax effects of these transactions, you ask her to provide additional information.

Read the chapter and formulate your response.

Framework 1040 Tax Formula for Individuals

This chapter covers the boldfaced portions of the Tax Formula for Individuals that was introduced in Concept Summary 3.1 on p. 3-3. Below those portions are the sections of Form 1040 where the results are reported.

Income *(broadly defined)*	$xx,xxx
Less: Exclusions	(x,xxx)
Gross income	**$xx,xxx**

FORM 1040 (p. 1)

7	Capital gain or (loss). Attach Schedule D if required. If not required, check here ▶ ☐

FORM 1040 (Schedule 1)

3	Business income or (loss). Attach Schedule C
4	Other gains or (losses). Attach Form 4797

Less: Deductions *for* adjusted gross income	**(x,xxx)**
Adjusted gross income	$xx,xxx
Less: The greater of total **itemized deductions** *or* the standard deduction	(x,xxx)
Charitable contributions if you take the standard deduction*	(xxx)
Personal and dependency exemptions**	(x,xxx)
Deduction for qualified business income***	(x,xxx)
Taxable income	$xx,xxx
Tax on taxable income *(see Tax Tables or Tax Rate Schedules)*	$ x,xxx
Less: Tax credits *(including income taxes withheld and prepaid)*	(xxx)
Tax due (or refund)	$ xxx

* For 2021, married taxpayers may claim up to $600 of cash charitable donations ($300 if unmarried).
** Exemption deductions are not allowed from 2018 through 2025.
*** Only applies from 2018 through 2025.

This and the following three chapters explain the income tax consequences of property transactions (the *sale or other disposition* of property).

- Is there a realized gain or loss?
- If so, is the gain or loss recognized?
- If the gain or loss is recognized, is it ordinary or capital?
- What is the basis of any replacement property that is acquired?

Chapters 14 and 15 discuss the determination of realized and recognized gain or loss and the basis of property. Chapters 16 and 17 cover the classification of any recognized gain or loss as ordinary or capital.

14-1 Determination of Gain or Loss

LO.1

Explain the computation of realized gain or loss on property dispositions.

As discussed in Chapter 4, taxpayers do not recognize gross income until there has been a realization. "Realization events" include the sale or other disposition of property.

Property includes both tangible assets (property having a physical existence, like land, a building, or equipment) and intangible assets (like investments and goodwill). Tangible assets include both real property (e.g., land or a building) and personal property (e.g., equipment, furniture, or a car). These property *types* do not change from taxpayer to taxpayer. However, how that property is *used* (e.g., for business, investment, or personal purposes) can vary by taxpayer. How property dispositions are taxed depends on the type of property involved and how it is used.

Realization events related to property involve a significant change in ownership rights, and once a realization event has occurred, a realized gain or loss must be determined. Many, but not all, *realized* gains and losses also are *recognized* (i.e., included in the determination of taxable income) at the time of the realization event. So realization is an accounting concept, and recognition is a tax concept. These matters are discussed in more depth in this section.

14-1a Realized Gain or Loss

Realization Events

Realization events include the *sale or other disposition* of property (i.e., transactions in which taxpayers change, in a meaningful way, their ownership interest in an asset). A *sale* is the most common realization event involving property. The term *other disposition* is defined broadly in the tax law and includes a wide variety of realization events including exchanges, barter transactions, trade-ins, condemnations, and bond retirements. This term also applies when the taxpayer identifies a change in property (or property rights) even if they do not receive anything on the "disposition" (e.g., a casualty, theft, the expiration of an option, or certain assets becoming worthless).

Identifying a specific economic event (e.g., a sale) is a key factor in determining whether a disposition has occurred.[1] A change in the value of the property is *not* sufficient.[2]

Example 1

Lori owns Tan Corporation stock that she bought for $3,000. The stock has appreciated in value and is now worth $5,000. Lori has no realized gain because a change in value is not an identifiable event for tax purposes. Here, Lori has an *unrealized gain* of $2,000 ($5,000 − $3,000).

The same is true if the stock had declined in value to $1,000. Because there was no identifiable event, there is no realized loss. Here, Lori would have an *unrealized loss* of $2,000 ($1,000 − $3,000).

Computation of Realized Gain or Loss

Realized gain or loss is the difference between the amount realized from the sale or other disposition of property and the property's adjusted basis on the disposition date. If the amount realized exceeds the property's adjusted basis, the result is a **realized gain**. On the other hand, if the property's adjusted basis exceeds the amount realized, the result is a **realized loss**.[3]

Example 2

Carl sells Swan Corporation stock with an adjusted basis of $3,000 for $5,400. Carl's realized gain is $2,400 ($5,400 − $3,000). If Carl had sold the stock for $1,750, he would have had a realized loss of $1,250 ($1,750 − $3,000).

Concept Summary 14.1 summarizes this calculation. The various terms used in Concept Summary 14.1 are discussed on the following pages.

Concept Summary 14.1

Realized Gain or Loss

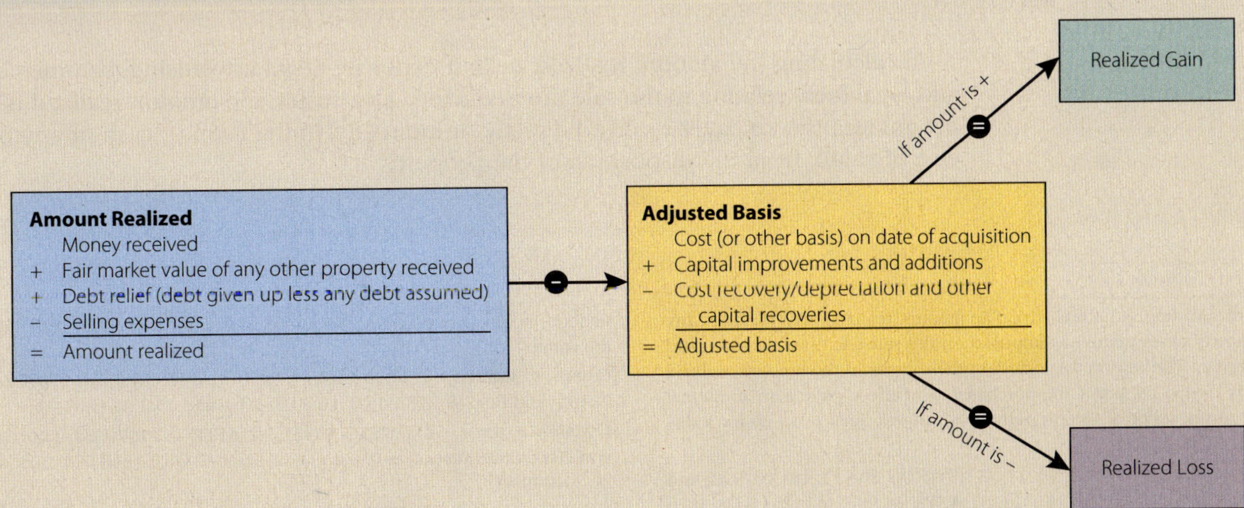

[1] Reg. § 1.1001–1(c)(1). See Chapter 7 for a discussion of casualties, thefts, and worthless securities; see Chapter 15 for a discussion of condemnations.

[2] *Lynch v. Turrish*, 1 USTC ¶18, 3 AFTR 2986, 38 S.Ct. 537 (USSC, 1918).

[3] § 1001(a) and Reg. § 1.1001–1(a).

Amount Realized

The **amount realized** from a sale or other disposition of property is a measure of the economic value received for property given up. In general, it is the sum of any money received (which includes any debt relief) plus the fair market value of other property received.[4]

Debt relief includes any liability (e.g., a mortgage) assumed by the buyer when the property is sold. Debt relief also occurs if property is sold subject to the mortgage (i.e., the seller remains liable for the debt even though the buyer will be making the payments). In addition, debt relief is not limited by the fair market value of the property.[5]

Amount Realized

Example 3

Juan sells a machine used in his landscaping business to Peter for $20,000 cash plus four acres of property that Peter owns in a nearby town with a fair market value of $36,000. Juan's amount realized on this sale is $56,000 ($20,000 cash + $36,000 land).

Example 4

Barry owns property on which there is a mortgage of $20,000. He sells the property to Cole for $50,000 cash and Cole's agreement to assume the mortgage. Barry's amount realized from the sale is $70,000 ($50,000 cash + $20,000 debt relief).

In a property transaction, the **fair market value** of property received is the price determined by a willing seller and a willing buyer when neither is compelled to sell or buy and both have reasonable knowledge of relevant facts.[6] All of the relevant factors must be considered,[7] and if the fair market value of the property received cannot be determined, the value of the property given up by the taxpayer is assumed to be equivalent and may be used.[8]

Example 5

Return to the facts of Example 3. There are several ways one can determine the fair market value of the land Juan is receiving.

- An appraiser can be paid to provide an appraisal of the land.
- City or county property tax assessment information also may be helpful; the city or county assessor determines the fair market value of property so that property taxes are levied appropriately.
- If the exchange is between a willing buyer and seller, determining the fair market value of Juan's landscaping machine could answer the question (i.e., given the facts of the case, it should be worth $56,000).

In calculating the amount realized, selling expenses (e.g., advertising, commissions, and legal fees) relating to the sale are deducted. As a result, the amount realized is the net amount the taxpayer received directly or indirectly, in the form of cash or anything else of value, from the disposition of the property.

[4] § 1001(b) and Reg. § 1.1001–1(b). The amount realized also includes any real property taxes treated as imposed on the seller that are actually paid by the buyer. The reason for including these taxes in the amount realized is that by paying the taxes, the purchaser is, in effect, paying an additional amount to the seller of the property. Refer to text Section 10-2b for a discussion of this subject.

[5] *Crane v. Comm.*, 47–1 USTC ¶9217, 35 AFTR 776, 67 S.Ct. 1047 (USSC) and *Comm. v. Tufts*, 83–1 USTC ¶9328, 51 AFTR 2d 83–1132, 103 S.Ct. 1826 (USSC). Although a legal distinction exists between the direct assumption of a mortgage and the taking of property subject to a mortgage, the Federal income tax consequences in calculating the amount realized are the same.

[6] *Comm. v. Marshman*, 60–2 USTC ¶9484, 5 AFTR 2d 1528, 279 F.2d 27 (CA–6) and Reg. §§ 1.737–1(b), 20.2031–1(b), and 25.2512–3(a).

[7] *O'Malley v. Ames*, 52–1 USTC ¶9361, 42 AFTR 19, 197 F.2d 256 (CA–8) and *Alan Baer Revocable Trust v. U.S.*, 2010–1 USTC ¶60,590, 105 AFTR 2d 2010–1544.

[8] *U.S. v. Davis*, 62–2 USTC ¶9509, 9 AFTR 2d 1625, 82 S.Ct. 1190 (USSC).

The calculation of the amount realized may appear to be one of the least complex areas associated with property transactions. However, because numerous positive and negative adjustments may be required, this calculation can be complex and confusing. In addition, determining the fair market value of the items received by the taxpayer can be difficult.

Example 6

Ridge sells an office building and the associated land on October 1, 2022. Under the terms of the sales contract, Ridge is to receive $600,000 in cash. The purchaser is to assume Ridge's mortgage of $300,000 on the property. To assist the purchaser, Ridge agrees to pay $15,000 of the purchaser's closing costs (a "closing cost credit"). The broker's commission on the sale is $45,000. The amount realized by Ridge is determined as follows.

Selling price:		
Cash	$600,000	
Mortgage assumed by purchaser	300,000	
		$900,000
Less:		
Broker's commission	$ 45,000	
Closing cost credit provided by Ridge	15,000	(60,000)
Amount realized		$840,000

Adjusted Basis

The **adjusted basis** of property disposed of is the property's original basis adjusted to the date of disposition.[9] Original basis is the cost or other basis of the property on the date acquired by the taxpayer. *Capital additions* increase and *capital recoveries* decrease the original basis.[10] As a result, adjusted basis is determined as follows.

Cost (or other adjusted basis) on date of acquisition
\+ Capital additions
− Capital recoveries
= Adjusted basis on date of disposition

A taxpayer's original basis also includes any liability incurred to acquire the property.

Example 7

Veronica purchased a residence for $250,000. Whether Veronica uses $250,000 from her personal assets to pay for the residence or uses $50,000 from her personal assets and borrows the remaining $200,000, her basis in the residence is $250,000. It does not matter whether Veronica borrows from the seller (via a land contract) or from a local bank or any other lender (via a mortgage).

Many assets are acquired without purchasing them (e.g., via gift or inheritance). We'll discuss how to determine basis for these assets later in the chapter.

Capital Additions

Capital additions include the cost of improvements made to the property that lengthen its useful life or increase its production capacity or efficiency. These costs are different from repair and maintenance expenses, which are neither capitalized nor added to the original basis (refer to text Section 6-3i). Repair and maintenance expenses are deductible in the current taxable year if they are related to business or income-producing property.

[9] § 1011(a) and Reg. § 1.1011–1.

[10] § 1016(a) and Reg. § 1.1016–1.

Any liability on property that is assumed by the buyer also is included in the buyer's original basis of the property. The same rule applies if property is acquired subject to a liability. Amortization of the discount on bonds increases the adjusted basis of the bonds.[11]

Capital Recoveries

Capital recoveries decrease the adjusted basis of property.

Depreciation and Cost Recovery The original basis of depreciable property is reduced by any cost recovery or depreciation allowed while the property is held by the taxpayer. The amount subtracted annually from the original basis is the greater of the *allowed* or *allowable* cost recovery or depreciation.[12]

Example 8

Refer back to Example 3. The machine Juan sold was acquired four years ago for $100,000. It was 7-year MACRS property, and Juan did not take either an immediate expense deduction (§179) or bonus depreciation on the property. Juan's adjusted basis is computed as follows.

Original cost		$100,000
Cost recovery:		
Year 1 ($100,000 × 0.1429)	$14,290	
Year 2 ($100,000 × 0.2449)	24,490	
Year 3 ($100,000 × 0.1749)	17,490	
Year 4 ($100,000 × 0.1249 × ½)	6,245	
Total cost recovery		(62,515)
Adjusted basis		$ 37,485

Since Juan's amount realized on the sale was $56,000, his realized gain is $18,515.

Amount realized	$ 56,000
– Adjusted basis	(37,485)
Realized gain (loss)	$ 18,515

Casualties and Thefts A casualty or theft may result in the reduction of the adjusted basis of property.[13] Adjusted basis is reduced by the amount of the *deductible* loss. In addition, adjusted basis is reduced by the amount of insurance proceeds received. However, the receipt of insurance proceeds may result in a recognized gain rather than a deductible loss. The gain increases the adjusted basis of the property.[14]

Capital Recoveries: Casualties and Thefts

Example 9

An insured truck that Marvin used in his trade or business is destroyed in an accident. At the time of the accident, the adjusted basis of the truck was $8,000, and its fair market value was $6,500. Marvin receives insurance proceeds of $6,500.

The amount of the casualty loss is $1,500 ($6,500 insurance proceeds − $8,000 adjusted basis). The truck's adjusted basis is reduced by the $1,500 casualty loss and the $6,500 of insurance proceeds received ($8,000 basis before casualty − $1,500 casualty loss − $6,500 insurance proceeds = $0 adjusted basis).

[11]See text Section 16-3b for a discussion of bond discount and the related amortization.

[12]§ 1016(a)(2) and Reg. § 1.1016–3(a)(1)(i). In most cases, these amounts are the same (refer to text Section 8-1c).

[13]Refer to text Section 7-3 for a discussion of casualties and thefts. In general, personal casualty losses are deductible only if they occur in a Federally declared disaster area; personal thefts are not deductible.

[14]Reg. § 1.1016–6(a).

Capital Recoveries: Casualties and Thefts

Example 10

How would your answer to Example 9 change if the basis of the truck was $6,000, its fair market value was $9,000, and Marvin received a $9,000 insurance settlement?

Now Marvin records a casualty gain of $3,000 ($9,000 insurance proceeds − $6,000 adjusted basis). The truck's adjusted basis is increased by the $3,000 casualty gain and is reduced by the $9,000 of insurance proceeds received ($6,000 basis before casualty + $3,000 casualty gain − $9,000 insurance proceeds = $0 adjusted basis).

Corporate Distributions A nontaxable corporate distribution is treated as a return of capital, and it reduces the shareholder's stock basis.[15] Corporations typically disclose this information to shareholders. Once the basis of the stock is reduced to zero, the amount of any subsequent distributions is recorded as a capital gain if the stock is a capital asset. These rules are illustrated in text Section 20-4a.

Amortizable Bond Premium The basis in a bond purchased at a premium is reduced by the amortizable portion of the bond premium.[16] Investors in taxable bonds may *elect* to amortize the bond premium, with an interest deduction allowed for the amount of the amortized premium.[17] So the election enables the taxpayer to take an annual interest deduction to offset ordinary income in exchange for a larger capital gain or smaller capital loss on the disposition of the bond. The amortization deduction is allowed for taxable bonds because the premium is viewed as a cost of earning the taxable interest from the bonds.

Unlike taxable bonds, the premium on tax-exempt bonds *must be* amortized (and the basis is reduced even though the amortization is not allowed as a deduction). No amortization deduction is permitted on tax-exempt bonds because the interest income is exempt from tax and the amortization of the bond premium merely represents an adjustment of the tax-exempt income earned on the bond.

Example 11

Antonio purchases Eagle Corporation taxable bonds with a face value of $100,000 for $110,000, paying a premium of $10,000. The annual interest rate is 7%, and the bonds mature 10 years from the date of purchase. The annual interest income is $7,000 (7% × $100,000).

If Antonio elects to amortize the bond premium, the $10,000 premium is deducted over the 10-year period. Antonio's basis for the bonds is reduced each year by the amount of the amortization deduction.

If the bonds were tax-exempt, amortization of the bond premium and the basis adjustment would be mandatory. However, no deduction would be allowed for the amortization.

Easements An easement is the legal right to use another's land for a special purpose. Easements typically are used to obtain rights-of-way for utility lines, roads, and pipelines. In recent years, grants of conservation easements have become a popular means of obtaining charitable contribution deductions and reducing the value of real estate for transfer tax (i.e., estate and gift) purposes. For example, a conservation easement on property containing a rare wildlife habitat might prohibit any development; one on a farm might allow continued farming and the building of additional agricultural structures but no other development. Although a conservation

[15] § 1016(a)(4) and Reg. § 1.1016–5(a).

[16] § 1016(a)(5) and Reg. § 1.1016–5(b). The accounting treatment of bond premium amortization is the same as that for tax purposes. The amortization results in a decrease in the bond investment account.

[17] § 171(c).

easement can be sold, typically it is donated to a charitable organization (like the Nature Conservancy). If donated, the difference between the value of the land with and without the easement would be a charitable contribution. Likewise, scenic easements (granted to protect open spaces or scenic views) are used to reduce the value of land as assessed for property tax purposes.

The amount received for granting an easement is subtracted from the basis of the property. If the taxpayer does not retain any right to the use of the land, all of the basis is assigned to the easement. However, if the use of the land is only partially restricted, an allocation of some of the basis to the easement is appropriate. If, however, it is impossible or impractical to separate the basis of the part of the property on which the easement is granted, the basis of the whole property is reduced by the amount received. If the amount received for the easement exceeds the basis, a taxable gain results.[18]

LO.2

Distinguish between realized and recognized gain or loss.

14-1b Recognized Gain or Loss

Recognized gain is the amount of the realized gain that is included in the taxpayer's gross income.[19] A **recognized loss**, on the other hand, is the amount of a realized loss that is deductible for tax purposes.[20] As a general rule, the entire amount of a realized gain or loss is recognized.[21]

Concept Summary 14.2 summarizes the realized gain or loss and recognized gain or loss concepts.

Concept Summary 14.2

Realized and Recognized Gain or Loss

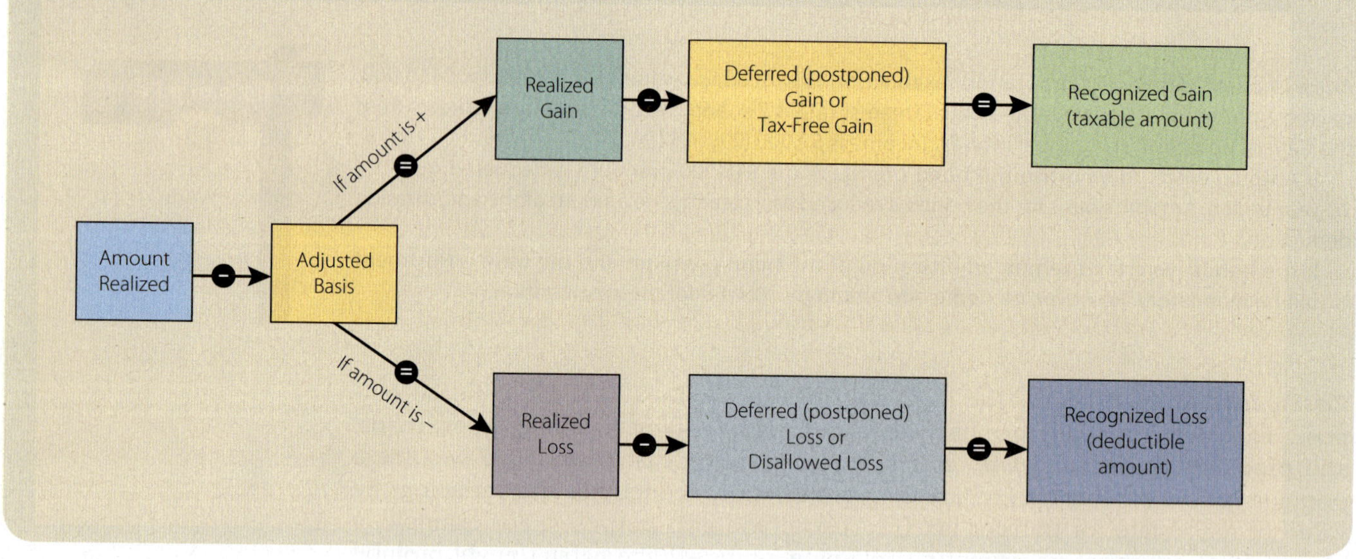

[18]See Rev.Rul. 68–291 and Rev.Rul. 77–414.

[19]§ 61(a)(3) and Reg. § 1.61–6(a).

[20]§ 165(a) and Reg. § 1.165–1(a).

[21]§ 1001(c) and Reg. § 1.1002–1(a).

14-1c Nonrecognition of Gain or Loss

In certain cases, a realized gain or loss on a property disposition is not recognized. Like-kind exchanges, covered in text Section 15-2, are one example. Others include losses realized on the sale, exchange, or condemnation of personal use assets (as opposed to business or income-producing property) and gains realized on the sale of a residence (see text Section 15-4). In addition, realized losses from the sale or exchange of business or income-producing property between certain related parties are not recognized.[22]

Sale, Exchange, or Condemnation of Personal Use Assets

A realized loss from the sale, exchange, or condemnation of personal use assets (e.g., a personal residence or an automobile used only for personal purposes) is not recognized for Federal income tax purposes. An exception exists for certain casualty or theft losses from personal use assets (see text Section 7-3). On the other hand, gains realized from the sale or other disposition of personal use assets generally are fully taxable.

The Big Picture

Example 12

Return to the facts of *The Big Picture* on p. 14-1. Assume that Alice sells the boat, which she has held exclusively for personal use, for $23,000. Recall that her adjusted basis of the boat is $22,000. Alice records a realized and recognized gain of $1,000 ($23,000 − $22,000).

Example 13

Assume that Alice sells the boat in Example 12 for $20,000. She records a realized loss of $2,000 ($20,000 − $22,000), but the loss is not recognized because the boat is a personal use asset.

14-2 Basis Considerations

LO.3 **Illustrate how basis is determined for various methods of asset acquisition.**

A key element in calculating gain or loss from a property transaction is the asset's basis at the time of the transaction. Various methods for determining basis apply, depending on how the asset was acquired.

14-2a Determination of Cost Basis

As noted earlier, the basis of property generally equals the property's cost. Cost is the amount paid for the property in cash or other property.[23]

A *bargain purchase* of property is an exception to the general rule for determining basis. A bargain purchase results, for instance, when an employer transfers property to an employee at less than the property's fair market value (as compensation), or when a corporation transfers property to a shareholder at less than the property's fair market value (a dividend).

In these cases, the amount included in gross income as either compensation for services or dividend income is the difference between the bargain purchase price and the property's fair market value. The basis of property acquired in a bargain purchase is the property's fair market value.[24] If the basis of the property were not increased by the bargain amount, the taxpayer would be taxed on this amount again at disposition.

[22] § 267(a)(1).

[23] § 1012 and Reg. § 1.1012–1(a).

[24] Reg. §§ 1.61–2(d)(2)(i) and 1.301–1(j). See text Section 5-8d for a discussion of the circumstances under which what appears to be a taxable bargain purchase is an excludible qualified employee discount.

Example 14

Wade buys land from his employer for $10,000 on December 30. The fair market value of the land is $15,000.

Wade must include in his gross income the $5,000 difference between the cost and the fair market value of the land. The bargain element represents additional compensation to Wade. His basis for the land is $15,000, the land's fair market value.

Identification Problems

Cost identification problems are frequently encountered in securities transactions. For example, the Regulations require that the taxpayer identify the particular shares of stock that have been sold (specific identification).[25] A problem arises when the taxpayer has purchased separate lots of stock on different dates or at different prices and cannot specifically identify the shares of stock being sold. If that is the case, the stock is presumed to come from the earliest shares purchased (a first-in, first-out presumption).[26] Brokers must provide investors with an annual report on the cost basis of stock sold during the year (this information is included on Form 1099–B and reported to the IRS).

Example 15

Polly purchases 100 shares of Olive Corporation stock on July 1, 2020, for $5,000 ($50 a share) and another 100 shares of Olive stock on July 1, 2021, for $6,000 ($60 a share). She sells 50 shares of the stock on January 2, 2022.

In determining gain or loss, the cost of the stock sold, assuming that Polly cannot adequately identify the shares, is $50 a share, or $2,500. If Polly was able to specifically identify the shares sold as the shares purchased in 2021, the cost basis would be $60 a share and the holding period (see text Section 16-4) would be short term.

Allocation Problems

When a taxpayer acquires *multiple assets in a lump-sum purchase*, the total cost must be allocated among the individual assets.[27] Allocation is necessary for several reasons.

- Some of the assets acquired may be depreciable (e.g., buildings), but others are not (e.g., land).
- If one of the assets acquired is sold, its basis must be known to compute realized gain or loss.
- Some of the assets may be capital or § 1231 assets that receive special tax treatment when sold in the future.

The lump-sum cost is allocated on the basis of the fair market values of the individual assets acquired.

Example 16

Harry purchases a building and land for $800,000. Because of the depressed nature of the industry in which the seller was operating, Harry was able to negotiate a favorable purchase price. Appraisals of the individual assets indicate that the fair market value of the building is $600,000, and that of the land is $400,000.

Harry's basis for the building is $480,000 [($600,000 ÷ $1,000,000) × $800,000], and his basis for the land is $320,000 [($400,000 ÷ $1,000,000) × $800,000].

If a business is purchased and **goodwill** is involved, a special allocation rule applies. Initially, the purchase price is allocated among the assets acquired, other than goodwill, based on their fair market value. Goodwill then is assigned the residual amount of the purchase price. This allocation applies to both the buyer and the seller.[28]

[25] Reg. § 1.1012–1(c)(1).

[26] *Kluger Associates, Inc.*, 69 T.C. 925 (1978).

[27] Reg. § 1.61–6(a).

[28] § 1060. The classification of the seller's recognized gain associated with the goodwill is discussed in text Section 16-7b.

Example 17

Kwame sells his business to Renata. An independent appraisal indicates that the business assets, other than goodwill, have the following fair market values.

Inventory	$ 50,000
Building	500,000
Land	200,000

After negotiations, Kwame and Renata agree on a sales price of $1,000,000. Applying the residual method with respect to goodwill results in the following allocation of the $1,000,000 purchase price.

Inventory	$ 50,000
Building	500,000
Land	200,000
Goodwill	250,000

The residual method requires that the excess of the purchase price over the fair market value of the assets other than goodwill ($1,000,000 − $750,000 = $250,000) be allocated to goodwill.

In the case of *nontaxable stock dividends*, the allocation depends on whether the dividend is a common stock dividend on common stock or a preferred stock dividend on common stock. If the stock dividend is common stock on common, the cost of the original common shares is allocated to the total shares owned after the dividend.[29]

Example 18

Susan owns 100 shares of Sparrow Corporation common stock for which she paid $1,100. She receives a 10% common stock dividend, giving her a new total of 110 shares. Before the stock dividend, Susan's basis was $11 per share ($1,100 ÷ 100 shares). The basis of each share after the stock dividend is $10 ($1,100 ÷ 110 shares).

If the nontaxable stock dividend is preferred stock on common, the cost of the original common shares is allocated between the common and preferred shares on the basis of their relative fair market values on the date of distribution.[30]

Example 19

Fran owns 100 shares of Cardinal Corporation common stock for which she paid $1,000. She receives a nontaxable stock dividend of 50 shares of preferred stock on her common stock. The fair market values on the date of distribution of the preferred stock dividend are $30 a share for common stock and $40 a share for preferred stock.

Fair market value of common ($30 × 100 shares)	$3,000
Fair market value of preferred ($40 × 50 shares)	2,000
	$5,000
Basis of common: 3/5 × $1,000	$ 600
Basis of preferred: 2/5 × $1,000	$ 400

The basis per share for the common stock is $6 ($600 ÷ 100 shares). The basis per share for the preferred stock is $8 ($400 ÷ 50 shares).

The holding period for a nontaxable stock dividend, whether received in the form of common stock or preferred stock, includes the holding period of the original shares.[31] The significance of the holding period for capital assets is discussed in text Section 16-4.

[29] §§ 305(a) and 307(a).

[30] Reg. § 1.307–1(a).

[31] § 1223(5) and Reg. § 1.1223–1(e).

14-2b Gift Basis

When a taxpayer receives property as a gift, the donee (recipient) of the gift has paid nothing to take ownership of the asset. As a result, under the cost basis provision, the donee's basis would be zero. However, this would violate the intent of the law that gifts not be subject to Federal income tax.[32] With a zero basis, if the donee sold the property, all of the amount realized would be treated as realized gain. As a result, a basis is assigned to the property received depending on:

- The date of the gift.
- The basis of the property to the donor.
- The amount of Federal gift tax paid.
- The fair market value of the property.

Gift Basis Rules, in General

The basis rules for gifts of property include the following.

- If the fair market value of the property on the date of the gift exceeds (or is equal to) the donor's basis, then the recipient's (donee's) basis is the same as the donor's (i.e., a carryover basis).[33]

Example 20

Melissa purchased stock in 2021 for $10,000. In 2022, she gave the stock to her son, Joe, when the fair market value was $15,000. Joe subsequently sells the property for $18,000. Joe's basis is $10,000, and he has a realized gain of $8,000 ($18,000 − $10,000).

If Joe sold the stock for $12,000, he would have a realized gain of $2,000 ($12,000 − $10,000). If Joe sold the stock for $7,000, he would have a realized loss of $3,000 ($7,000 − $10,000).

- If the fair market value of the property on the date of the gift is less than the donor's basis, then special *dual basis* rules apply. Here, the donee has one basis for measuring a gain and a different basis for measuring a loss. This special rule is in place to prevent the shifting of losses (typically among family members) to the individual who would receive the greatest benefit. Under this rule, the donee's *gain basis* is the donor's adjusted basis; the donee's *loss basis* is the fair market value of the property.

Example 21

Burt purchased stock in 2021 for $10,000. In 2022, he gave the stock to his son, Cliff, when the fair market value was $7,000. Cliff later sells the stock for $6,000.

Cliff's basis is $7,000 (fair market value is less than donor's adjusted basis of $10,000), and the realized loss from the sale is $1,000 ($6,000 amount realized − $7,000 basis).

The amount of the loss basis will *differ* from the amount of the gain basis only if, at the date of the gift, the adjusted basis of the property exceeds the property's fair market value. The loss basis rule prevents the donee from receiving a tax benefit from a decline in value that occurred while the donor held the property.

So in Example 21, Cliff records a loss of only $1,000 rather than a loss of $4,000 ($6,000 − $10,000). The $3,000 difference represents the decline in value that occurred while Burt held the property. In contrast, however, the donee may be subject to income tax on the appreciation that occurred while the donor held the property, as illustrated in Example 20.

If the amount realized from a sale is *between* the donee's loss basis and gain basis, no gain or loss is realized; here, the basis is deemed to be the same as the amount realized.

---

[32] § 102(a).

[33] § 1015(a) and Reg. § 1.1015–1(a)(1). See Reg. § 1.1015–1(a)(3) for rules where the facts necessary to determine the donor's adjusted basis are unknown. Refer to Example 23 for the effect of depreciation deductions by the donee.

Example 22

Assume the same facts as in Example 21, except that Cliff sells the stock for $8,000. Application of the gain basis rule produces a loss of $2,000 ($8,000 − $10,000). Application of the loss basis rule produces a gain of $1,000 ($8,000 − $7,000).

Because the amount realized is between the gain basis and the loss basis, Cliff recognizes neither a gain nor a loss.

Adjustment for Federal Gift Tax Paid

If Federal gift taxes are paid by the donor on the transfer, a rare occurrence, the portion of the gift tax paid that is related to any appreciation is taken into account in determining the donee's gain basis.[34]

Holding Period

The **holding period** for property acquired by gift begins on the date the donor acquired the property if the gain basis rule applies.[35] The holding period starts on the date of the gift if the loss basis rule applies.[36]

Basis for Depreciation

The basis for depreciation on depreciable gift property is the donee's gain basis.[37] This rule is applicable even if the donee later sells the property at a loss and uses the loss basis rule in calculating the amount of the realized loss.

Example 23

Vito gave a machine (a MACRS 5-year asset) to Tina in 2022. At that time, the adjusted basis was $32,000 (cost of $40,000 less accumulated depreciation of $8,000) and the fair market value was $26,000. No Federal gift tax was paid. Tina's gain basis at the date of the gift is $32,000, and her loss basis is $26,000. During 2022, Tina deducts depreciation (cost recovery) of $6,400 ($32,000 × 20%). At the end of 2022, Tina's gain basis and loss basis are:

	Gain Basis	Loss Basis
Donor's basis or fair market value	$32,000	$26,000
Less: Depreciation (cost recovery)	(6,400)	(6,400)
	$25,600	$19,600

14-2c Inherited Property

Special basis rules apply for inherited property (property acquired from a decedent). Typically, these rules are favorable to the taxpayer receiving this property.

General Rules

The basis of inherited property almost always is the property's fair market value at the date of death.[38]

[34] § 1015(d)(6) and Reg. § 1.1015–5(c)(2). Examples illustrating these rules can be found in Reg. § 1.1015–5(c)(5) and IRS Publication 551 (*Basis of Assets*), p. 9.

[35] § 1223(2) and Reg. § 1.1223–1(b).

[36] Rev.Rul. 59–86.

[37] § 1011 and Reg. §§ 1.1011–1 and 1.167(g)–1.

[38] §§ 1014(a) and 1022. See *South-Western Federal Taxation: Corporations, Partnerships, Estates & Trusts*, Chapter 19, for additional information.

The Big Picture

Example 24

Return to the facts of *The Big Picture* on p. 14-1. Alice and various other family members inherited property from Paula, who died in 2021. At the date of death, Paula's basis for the property Alice inherited—Paula's house—was $275,000. The house's fair market value at the date of death was $475,000.

Alice's basis for income tax purposes is $475,000. This commonly is referred to as a *stepped-up basis*.

Example 25

Assume the same facts as in Example 24, except that the house's fair market value at the date of Paula's death was $260,000.

Alice's basis for income tax purposes is $260,000. This commonly is referred to as a *stepped-down basis*.

An *alternate valuation amount* is available to estates for which a Federal estate tax return must be filed [generally, estates with a valuation in excess of $12.06 million for deaths in 2022 ($11.7 million in 2021)]. If elected by the estate's executor, the property's basis is the fair market value *six months after the date of death*.[39] The alternate valuation date can be elected *only if*, as a result of the election, both the value of the gross estate and the estate tax liability are lower than they would have been if the primary valuation date had been used.[40]

Income in Respect of a Decedent

Income in respect of a decedent (IRD) usually exists when a cash basis taxpayer dies and, on the date of death, is entitled to some form of income (e.g., compensation, interest, or dividends) but has yet to receive it. IRD most frequently is received by decedents using the cash basis of accounting. IRD includes most post-death distributions from retirement plans, including traditional IRAs and § 401(k) plans.

IRD is included in the gross estate at its fair market value (on the appropriate valuation date). Because IRD is not subject to the step-up or step-down rules applicable to property passed by death, the income tax basis of the decedent transfers to the estate or heirs.[41] Furthermore, the recipient of IRD must classify it in the same manner (e.g., ordinary income or capital gain) as the decedent would have.[42]

Example 26

George, age 58, was entitled to a salary payment of $18,000 and a bonus of $20,000 at the time of his death. In addition, George had been contributing to a traditional IRA for over 20 years. The IRA has a basis of $83,000 (due to some nondeductible contributions over the years) and a current value of $560,000. George's estate collects the salary and bonus payments, and George's wife Maria (his only beneficiary) cashes in the IRA.

continued

[39] § 2032(a)(1) and Rev.Rul. 56–60. For any property distributed by the executor during the six-month period preceding the alternate valuation date, the adjusted basis to the beneficiary is the fair market value on the date of distribution.

[40] § 2032(c); this provision prevents the alternate valuation election from being used to increase the basis of the property to the beneficiary for income tax purposes without simultaneously increasing the estate tax liability (because of estate tax deductions or credits).

[41] § 1014(c).

[42] § 691(a)(3).

Both the estate and Maria have received income in respect of a decedent (IRD) and must include ordinary income in their computation of taxable income for the year. The estate has IRD of $38,000 (salary of $18,000 + bonus of $20,000), and Maria recognizes IRD of $477,000 ($560,000 proceeds − $83,000 basis).[43]

Survivor's Share of Property

Both the decedent's share and the survivor's share of *community property* have a basis equal to the fair market value on the date of the decedent's death.[44] This occurs because the decedent's share of the community property is included in the estate and assumes a fair market value basis, whereas the surviving spouse's share is treated as if it were received from the decedent at its fair market value.

Example 27

Andrew and LaTonya own, as community property, 200 shares of Biltmore Company stock acquired in 1991 for $100,000. Andrew dies in 2022, when the securities are valued at $300,000. One-half of the Biltmore stock is included in Andrew's estate. If LaTonya inherits Andrew's share of the community property, the basis for gain or loss is $300,000.

LaTonya's one-half of the community property (stepped up from $50,000 to $150,000 due to Andrew's death)	$150,000
Andrew's one-half of the community property (stepped up from $50,000 to $150,000 due to inclusion in his gross estate)	150,000
LaTonya's new basis	$300,000

In a *common law* state, only one-half of jointly held property of spouses (tenants by the entirety or joint tenants with rights of survivorship) is included in the estate.[45] In such a case, no adjustment of the basis is permitted for the surviving spouse's share of the asset.

Example 28

Assume the same facts as in Example 27, except that the property is jointly held by Andrew and LaTonya who reside in Indiana, a common law state. Andrew purchased the property and made a gift of one-half of the property to LaTonya when the stock was acquired. No Federal gift tax was paid.

Only one-half of the Biltmore stock is included in Andrew's estate. LaTonya's basis for determining gain or loss in the excluded half is not adjusted upward for the increase in value to date of death. As a result, LaTonya's basis is $200,000.

LaTonya's one-half of the jointly held property (carryover basis of $50,000)	$ 50,000
Andrew's one-half of the jointly held property (stepped up from $50,000 to $150,000 due to inclusion in his gross estate)	150,000
LaTonya's new basis	$200,000

Holding Period of Inherited Property

The holding period of inherited property is *deemed to be long term* (held for the required long-term holding period). This rule applies regardless of whether the property is disposed of at a gain or at a loss.[46]

14-2d Disallowed Losses

LO.4 **Describe various loss disallowance provisions.**

In certain situations, realized losses are not recognized. Transactions between related parties and wash sales are two of these situations.

[43] See *South-Western Federal Taxation: Corporations, Partnerships, Estates & Trusts*, Chapter 19, for additional information.

[44] § 1014(b)(6). The community property states are listed in text Section 4-3d.

[45] § 2040(b).

[46] § 1223(9).

Related Taxpayers

Realized losses from sales or exchanges of property, directly or indirectly, between certain related parties are not recognized. This loss disallowance rule applies to several types of related-party transactions. The most common involve (1) members of a family and (2) an individual and a corporation (where the individual owns, directly or indirectly, more than 50 percent in value of the corporation's outstanding stock.)[47]

The loss disallowance rules (1) prevent a taxpayer from directly transferring an unrealized loss to a related taxpayer in a higher tax bracket who could receive a greater tax benefit from recognition of the loss and (2) eliminate a substantial administrative burden on the IRS (there is no need to determine whether the selling price is equal to the asset's fair market value). The rules governing these relationships are discussed in text Section 6-3j.

If income-producing or business property is transferred to a related taxpayer and a loss is disallowed, the related-party buyer's basis is equal to the amount paid (i.e., its cost). However, if the related-party buyer later sells the property and realizes a gain, the gain is reduced by the loss that previously was disallowed.[48] This *right of offset* is not applicable if the original sale involved the sale of a personal use asset (e.g., the sale of a personal residence between related taxpayers). Furthermore, the right of offset is available only to the original transferee (the related-party buyer).[49]

Example 29

Pedro sells business property with an adjusted basis of $50,000 to his daughter, Josefina, for its fair market value of $40,000. Pedro's realized loss of $10,000 ($40,000 − $50,000) is not recognized.

- How much gain does Josefina recognize if she sells the property for $52,000? Josefina recognizes a $2,000 gain. Her realized gain is $12,000 ($52,000 less her basis of $40,000), but she can offset Pedro's $10,000 loss against the gain.
- How much gain does Josefina recognize if she sells the property for $48,000? Josefina recognizes no gain or loss. Her realized gain is $8,000 ($48,000 less her basis of $40,000), but she can offset $8,000 of Pedro's $10,000 loss against the gain. The balance of Pedro's disallowed loss ($2,000) disappears and cannot be used. Note that Pedro's loss can only offset Josefina's gain. It cannot create a loss for Josefina.
- How much loss does Josefina recognize if she sells the property for $38,000? Josefina recognizes a $2,000 loss, the same as her realized loss ($38,000 less $40,000 basis). Pedro's loss does not increase Josefina's loss. His loss only can offset a gain. Because Josefina recorded no realized gain, Pedro's loss cannot be used and never is recognized. Note that if the property was a personal use asset (not business), her $2,000 loss would be personal and would not be recognized.

The holding period of the buyer for the property is not affected by the holding period of the seller; the *holding period* includes only the period of time the buyer held the property.[50]

Wash Sales

The **wash sale** rules are designed to eliminate the opportunity to sell stock at a loss, recognize the loss for tax purposes, but replace the stock sold by buying back identical shares shortly before or after the sale. If the wash sale rule applies, a realized loss on the sale or exchange of stock or securities is not recognized. Recognition of the loss is disallowed because the taxpayer is considered to be in substantially the same economic position after the sale and repurchase as before the sale and repurchase.

[47] § 707 provides a similar disallowance provision where the related parties are a partner and a partnership in which the partner owns, directly or indirectly, more than 50 percent of the capital interests or profits interests in the partnership.

[48] § 267(d) and Reg. § 1.267(d)–1(a).

[49] The loss disallowance rules are applicable even where the selling price is equal to the fair market value and can be validated (e.g., listed stocks).

[50] §§ 267(d) and 1223(2) and Reg. § 1.267(d)–1(c)(3).

The wash sale rule applies if a taxpayer sells or exchanges stock or securities at a loss and within 30 days before *or* after the date of the sale or exchange acquires substantially identical stock or securities.[51] Concept Summary 14.3 provides an overview of these rules.

The wash sale rules are triggered only when the investor buys back a "substantially identical" investment to the one that was sold for a loss. According to the IRS, "stocks or securities of one corporation are not considered substantially identical to stocks or securities of another corporation."[52] However, an option to purchase substantially identical securities is treated the same as actually buying the stock. So, for instance, selling Ford and buying back Ford (or Ford call options) would trigger the wash sale rules, but selling Ford and buying General Motors or selling Dell and buying Hewlett-Packard (in the same industry, but clearly a different company) would avoid the wash sale rules. Corporate bonds and preferred stock normally are not considered substantially identical to the corporation's common stock.[53]

Although the application of the "substantially identical" rule is fairly settled when dealing with individual stocks or bonds, there is more uncertainty when dealing with mutual funds or exchange-traded funds. For example, Vanguard's Windsor fund and Fidelity's Value Discovery fund have similar investment objectives (both are large cap, value funds). Not surprisingly, there is some overlap in their stock holdings. So would the "substantially identical" rule apply if 30 percent of their holdings were identical? 50 percent? Unfortunately, there is little authoritative guidance on this issue. The lack of clear direction from the Treasury Department and the courts has led many investment

Concept Summary 14.3

Wash Sale Rules

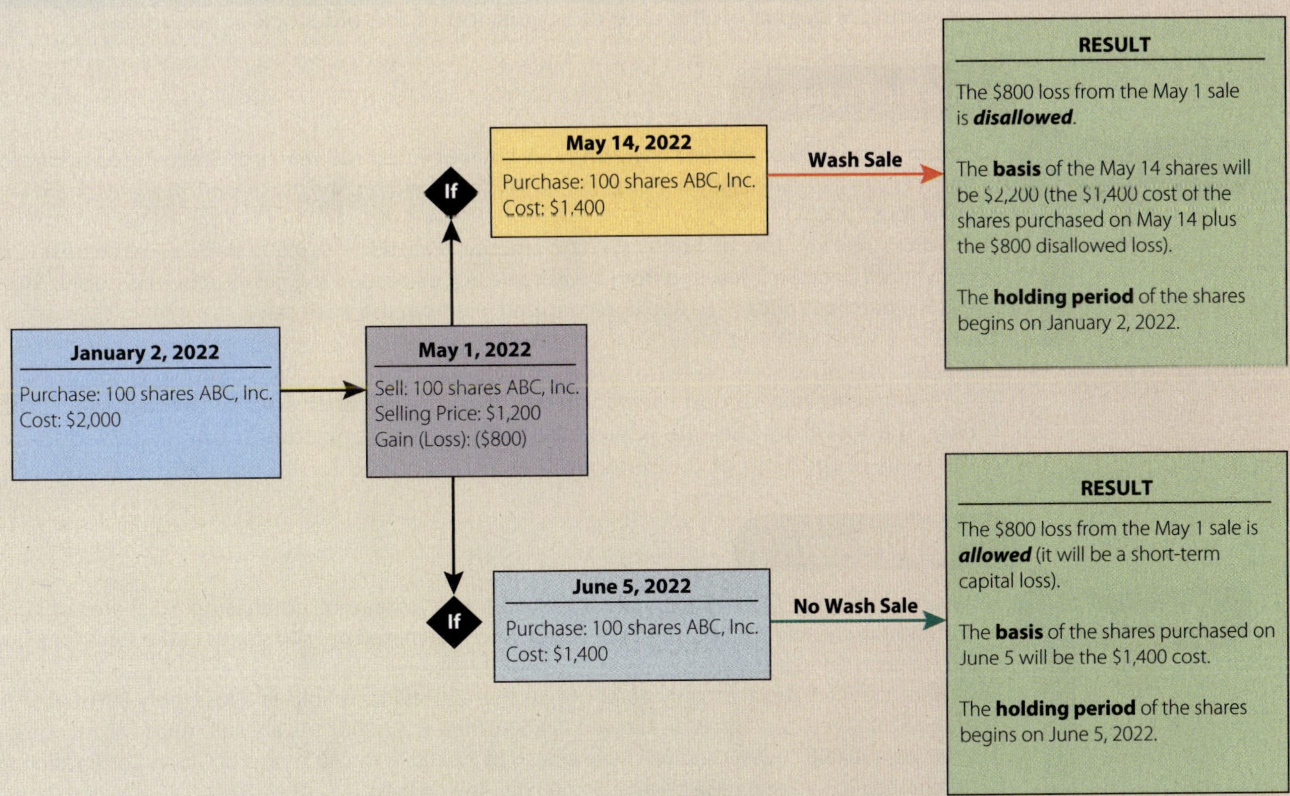

[51] § 1091(a) and Reg. §§ 1.1091–1(a) and (f).

[52] IRS Publication 550 (Investment Income and Expenses), p. 56.

[53] Rev.Rul. 56–406. However, if the bonds and preferred stock are convertible into common stock, they may be considered substantially identical.

advisers to develop a working list of transactions that are generally considered to be acceptable under the wash sale rules.[54]

For example, a tax-loss swap from one S&P 500 Index fund to another S&P 500 Index fund managed by a different fund company may result in scrutiny from the IRS. However, if the new fund tracks another large capitalization index, such as the Russell 1000, the tax loss should be allowed. These mutual fund transactions generally fall outside the wash sale rules, despite the lack of a concrete definition of what is a "substantially identical" security.

1. Sell one index fund and buy another index fund provided that the indexes of the two funds differ (e.g., S&P 500 for the Russell 1000).
2. Sell one actively managed fund and buy a fund at another company with different portfolio managers.
3. Sell an index fund and buy an actively managed fund regardless of the fund company.
4. Sell an actively managed fund and buy an index fund regardless of the fund company.

Attempts to avoid the application of the wash sales rules by having a related taxpayer repurchase the securities have been unsuccessful.[55]

Realized loss that is not recognized under the wash sale rule is added to the *basis* of the substantially identical stock or securities whose acquisition resulted in the nonrecognition of loss.[56] In other words, the basis of the replacement stock or securities is increased by the amount of the unrecognized loss. If the loss were not added to the basis of the newly acquired stock or securities, the taxpayer never would recover the entire basis of the old stock or securities.

The basis of the new stock or securities includes the unrecovered portion of the basis of the formerly held stock or securities. As a result, the *holding period* of the new stock or securities begins on the date of acquisition of the old stock or securities.[57]

The Big Picture

Example 30

Return to the facts of *The Big Picture* on p. 14-1. Alice owned 100 shares of Green Corporation stock (basis of $20,000). She sold 50 shares for $8,000. Ten days later, she purchased 50 shares of the same stock for $7,000.

Alice's realized loss of $2,000 ($8,000 amount realized − $10,000 basis of 50 shares) is not recognized because it resulted from a wash sale. Alice's basis in the newly acquired stock is $9,000 ($7,000 purchase price + $2,000 unrecognized loss from the wash sale).

A taxpayer may acquire fewer shares than the number sold in a wash sale. In this case, the loss from the sale is prorated between recognized and unrecognized loss on the basis of the ratio of the number of shares acquired to the number of shares sold.[58]

The Big Picture

Example 31

Assume the same facts as Example 30, except that instead of purchasing 50 shares of Green Corporation stock for $7,000 ($140 per share), Alice purchased only 40 shares of the stock for $5,600 (40 shares × $140 per share).

Because Alice replaced only 40 of the 50 shares previously sold at a loss, only 80% (40 ÷ 50) of the $2,000 realized loss is disallowed ($1,600; 80% × $2,000). As a result, Alice will recognize a $400 loss ($2,000 × 20%) and will have a basis of $7,200 in the 40 shares of Green Corporation she purchased ($5,600 purchase price + $1,600 disallowed loss).

[54] See, for example, "Keeping Transactions Clean from the Wash Sale Rules," Kevin Trout, *Journal of the American Association of Independent Investors* (December 2014) and "Tax Loss Harvesting: The Re-Balancing Act," Lee C. McGowen, *Journal of Financial Planning* (December 2008).

[55] *McWilliams v. Comm.*, 47–1 USTC ¶9289, 35 AFTR 1184, 67 S.Ct. 1477 (USSC).

[56] § 1091(d) and Reg. § 1.1091–2(a).

[57] § 1223(3) and Reg. § 1.1223–1(d).

[58] § 1091(b) and Reg. § 1.1091–1(c).

The wash sale rules do *not* apply to taxpayers engaged in the business of buying and selling securities.[59] In addition, the wash sales provisions do *not* apply to gains. As a result, taxpayers with capital losses (or capital loss carryovers from prior years) can sell an appreciated asset and then reacquire it, using the gain to offset the capital losses. Because the basis of the replacement stock will be the purchase price, the taxpayer gets an increased basis for the stock while using the capital gain to offset otherwise nondeductible capital losses.

Ethics & Equity **Washing a Loss Using an IRA**

Ajit owns 1,500 shares of Eagle, Inc. stock that he purchased over 10 years ago for $80,000. Although the stock has a current market value of $52,000, Ajit still views the stock as a solid long-term investment. He has sold other stock during the year with overall gains of $30,000, so he would like to sell the Eagle stock and offset the $28,000 loss against these gains but somehow keep his Eagle investment.

Ajit has devised a plan to keep his Eagle investment by using funds in his traditional IRA to purchase 1,500 Eagle shares immediately after selling the shares he currently owns. Evaluate Ajit's treatment of these stock transactions. Can his plan work?

14-2e **Property Converted from Personal Use to Business or Income-Producing Use**

As discussed previously, losses from the sale of personal use assets are not recognized for tax purposes, but losses from the sale of business and income-producing assets are deductible. Can a taxpayer convert a personal use asset that has declined in value to business or income-producing use and then sell the asset to recognize a business or income-producing loss?

The tax law prevents this practice by specifying that the *original basis for loss* on personal use assets converted to business or income-producing use is the *lower* of the property's adjusted basis or fair market value on the date of conversion.[60] The *gain basis* for converted property is the property's adjusted basis on the date of conversion. The tax law is not concerned with gains on converted property because gains are recognized regardless of whether property is business, income-producing, or personal use.

Example 32

Diane's personal residence has an adjusted basis of $175,000 and a fair market value of $160,000. Diane converts the personal residence to rental property. Her basis for loss is $160,000 (lower of $175,000 adjusted basis and fair market value of $160,000). The $15,000 decline in value is a personal loss and never is recognized for tax purposes. Diane's basis for gain is $175,000.

The basis for loss is also the *basis for depreciating* the converted property.[61] This is an exception to the general rule that the basis for depreciation is the gain basis (e.g., property received by gift). This exception prevents the taxpayer from recovering a personal loss indirectly through depreciation of the higher original basis. After the property is converted, both its basis for loss and its basis for gain are adjusted for depreciation deductions from the date of conversion to the date of disposition. These rules apply only if a conversion from personal to business or income-producing use has actually occurred.

---

[59] Reg. § 1.1091–1(a).

[60] Reg. § 1.165–9(b)(2).

[61] Reg. § 1.167(g)–1.

Example 33

At a time when his personal residence (adjusted basis of $140,000) is worth $150,000, Keith converts one-half of it to rental use. The property will be depreciated using the straight-line method, has an estimated useful life of 20 years, and has no salvage value. As a result, annual depreciation will be $3,500 ($70,000 ÷ 20 years).

After renting the converted portion for five years, Keith sells the property for $144,000. All amounts relate only to the building; assume that the land has been accounted for separately. Keith has a $2,000 realized gain from the sale of the personal use portion of the residence and a $19,500 realized gain from the sale of the rental portion.

	Personal Use	Rental
Original basis for gain and loss—adjusted basis on date of conversion (fair market value is *greater than* the adjusted basis)	$70,000	$ 70,000
Depreciation—five years	(–0–)	(17,500)
Adjusted basis—date of sale	$70,000	$ 52,500
Amount realized	72,000	72,000
Realized gain	$ 2,000	$ 19,500

Keith may be able to exclude the $2,000 realized gain from the sale of the personal use portion of the residence (see text Section 15-4). If the exclusion applies, only $17,500 (equal to the depreciation deducted) of the $19,500 realized gain from the rental portion is recognized.

Example 34

Assume the same facts as in Example 33, except that the fair market value on the date of conversion is $130,000 and the sales proceeds are $90,000. Keith has a $25,000 realized loss from the sale of the personal use portion of the residence and a $3,750 realized loss from the sale of the rental portion.

	Personal Use	Rental
Original basis for loss—fair market value on date of conversion (fair market value is *less than* the adjusted basis)	$70,000*	$ 65,000
Depreciation—five years	(–0–)	(16,250)**
Adjusted basis—date of sale	$70,000	$ 48,750
Amount realized	45,000	45,000
Realized loss	($25,000)	($ 3,750)

* Not applicable; use one-half of adjusted basis ($140,000 × 50%).
** ($65,000 ÷ 20) × 5.

The $25,000 loss from the sale of the personal use portion of the residence is not recognized. The $3,750 loss from the rental portion is recognized.

14-2f Summary of Basis Adjustments

Some of the more common items that either increase or decrease the basis of an asset appear in Concept Summary 14.4.

There are a number of techniques for determining basis for tax purposes, with the method dependent on the manner in which the asset was acquired. In summary, the basis of an asset can be determined by reference to any of the following.

- The asset's cost.
- The basis of another asset.
- The asset's fair market value.
- The basis of the asset to another taxpayer.

Concept Summary 14.4

Adjustments to Basis

Item	Effect	Refer to Chapter	Explanation
Amortization of bond discount	Increase	16	Amortization is mandatory for certain taxable bonds and elective for tax-exempt bonds.
Amortization of bond premium	Decrease	14	Amortization is mandatory for tax-exempt bonds and elective for taxable bonds.
Amortization of covenant not to compete	Decrease	8	Covenant must be for a definite and limited time period. The amortization period is a statutory period of 15 years.
Amortization of intangibles	Decrease	8	Intangibles are amortized over a 15-year period.
Assessment for local benefits	Increase	10	To the extent not deductible as taxes (e.g., assessment for streets and sidewalks that increase the value of the property versus one for maintenance or repair or for meeting interest charges).
Bad debts	Decrease	7	Only the specific charge-off method is permitted.
Capital additions	Increase	14	Certain items, at the taxpayer's election, can be capitalized or deducted (e.g., selected medical expenses).
Casualty	Decrease	7	For a casualty loss, the amount of the adjustment is the sum of the deductible loss and the insurance proceeds received. For a casualty gain, the amount of the adjustment is the insurance proceeds received reduced by the recognized gain.
Condemnation	Decrease	15	Same as for Casualty.
Cost recovery	Decrease	8	§ 168 is applicable to tangible assets placed in service after 1980 whose useful life is expressed in terms of years; includes additional first-year (bonus) depreciation.
Depletion	Decrease	8	Use the greater of cost or percentage depletion. Percentage depletion still can be deducted when the basis is zero.
Depreciation	Decrease	8	§ 167 is applicable to tangible assets placed in service before 1981 and to tangible assets not depreciated in terms of years.
Easement	Decrease	14	If the taxpayer does not retain any use of the land, all of the basis is allocable to the easement transaction. However, if only part of the land is affected by the easement, only part of the basis is allocable to the easement transaction.
Expensing under § 179	Decrease	8	Occurs only if the taxpayer elects § 179 treatment.
Improvements by lessee to lessor's property	Increase	1	Adjustment occurs only if the lessor is required to include the fair market value of the improvements in gross income under § 109.
Imputed interest	Decrease	18	Amount deducted is not part of the cost of the asset.
Inventory: lower of cost or market	Decrease	18	Not available if the LIFO method is used.
Medical capital expenditure permitted as a medical expense	Decrease	10	Adjustment is the amount of the deduction (the effect on basis is to increase it by the amount of the capital expenditure net of the deduction).
Real estate taxes: apportionment between the buyer and seller	Increase or decrease	10	To the extent the buyer pays the seller's pro rata share, the buyer's basis is increased. To the extent the seller pays the buyer's pro rata share, the buyer's basis is decreased.
Rebate from manufacturer	Decrease		Because the rebate is treated as an adjustment to the purchase price, it is not included in the buyer's gross income.
Stock dividend	Decrease	14	Adjustment occurs only if the stock dividend is nontaxable. Although the basis per share decreases, the total stock basis does not change.
Stock rights	Decrease	14	Adjustment to stock basis occurs only for nontaxable stock rights and only if the fair market value of the rights is at least 15% of the fair market value of the stock or, if less than 15%, the taxpayer elects to allocate the basis between the stock and the rights.
Theft	Decrease	7	Same as for Casualty.

LO.5

Identify tax planning opportunities related to selected property transactions.

14-3 Tax Planning

14-3a Cost Identification and Documentation Considerations

When multiple assets are acquired in a single transaction, the contract price must be allocated for several reasons. First, some of the assets may be depreciable but others are not. Here, the buyer and the seller may have different tax perspectives that will need to be reconciled. The seller will likely prefer a high allocation for nondepreciable assets (see Chapters 16 and 17); the purchaser likely will prefer a high allocation for depreciable assets subject to cost recovery. Second, the seller must be able to characterize gains and losses appropriately as capital or ordinary. Allocating the price among the assets sold allows this to happen. For example, an allocation to goodwill or to a covenant not to compete (see Chapters 8, 16, and 17) produces different tax consequences to the seller. Third, the buyer must identify the adjusted basis of each asset to be able to determine cost recovery, amortization, or depletion (if available) and to calculate the realized gain or loss if an asset is sold.

14-3b Selection of Property for Making Gifts

A donor can achieve several tax advantages by making gifts of appreciated property. The donor avoids income tax on the unrealized gain that would have occurred had the property been sold. And if the donee is in a lower tax bracket than the donor, there will be tax savings if the property is sold. Any increase in value after the gift also is taxed at a lower rate. Such gifts of appreciated property can be an effective tool in family tax planning.

Taxpayers generally should not make gifts of property that has decreased in value; the donor does not receive an income tax deduction for the unrealized loss element. In addition, the donee receives no benefit from this unrealized loss upon the subsequent sale of the property because of the loss basis rule. If the donor anticipates that the donee will sell the property upon receiving it, the donor should sell the property and take any loss deduction. The donor can then give the proceeds from the sale to the donee.

14-3c Selection of Property to Pass at Death

A taxpayer generally should distribute appreciated property via his or her will. Doing so enables both the decedent and the heir to avoid income tax on the unrealized gain; the recipient takes a fair market value basis.

Taxpayers generally should not distribute property at death that, if sold, would produce a realized loss; the decedent does not receive an income tax deduction for the unrealized loss. In addition, the heir will receive no benefit from this unrealized loss upon the subsequent sale of the property.

Example 35

On the date of her death, Marta owned land held for investment purposes. The land had an adjusted basis of $130,000 and a fair market value of $100,000. If Marta had sold the property before her death, the recognized loss would have been $30,000.

If, instead, Roger inherits the property and later sells it for $90,000, the recognized loss is $10,000 (the decline in value since Marta's death). In addition, regardless of the period of time Roger holds the property, the holding period is long term.

From an income tax perspective, it is better to transfer appreciated property as an inheritance rather than as a gift. Why? Because inherited property receives a step-up in basis but property received by gift has a carryover basis to the donee. However, in making this decision, any nontax and estate tax effects of the inheritance should be weighed against the gift tax results.

14-3d Disallowed Losses

Disallowed Losses

Taxpayers should avoid transactions that trigger the related-party loss disallowance rules. Even with the ability of the related-party buyer to offset any realized gain by the related-party seller's disallowed loss, several inequities exist. First, any tax benefit associated with the disallowed loss is shifted to the related-party buyer (the related-party seller receives no tax benefit). Second, the tax benefit of this offset is delayed until the related-party buyer sells the property. Third, if the property does not appreciate during the time period the related-party buyer holds it, part or all of the disallowed loss is permanently lost. Fourth, the right of offset is available only to the original transferee (the related-party buyer); use of the disallowed loss is eliminated permanently if the original transferee transfers the property by gift or inheritance.

Example 36

Tim sells property with an adjusted basis of $35,000 to Wes, his brother, for $25,000, the fair market value of the property. The $10,000 realized loss to Tim is disallowed by § 267.

If Wes subsequently sells the property to an unrelated party for $37,000, he records a recognized gain of $2,000 (realized gain of $12,000 reduced by disallowed loss of $10,000). As a result, from the perspective of the family unit, the original $10,000 realized loss ultimately is recognized.

However, if Wes sells the property for $29,000, he reports a recognized gain of $0 (realized gain of $4,000 reduced by disallowed loss of $4,000 necessary to offset the realized gain). From the perspective of the family unit, $6,000 of the realized loss of $10,000 is permanently lost ($10,000 realized loss − $4,000 offset permitted).

Refocus on The Big Picture

Proposed Sale of a House and Other Property Transactions

ISTOCK.COM/MIKESPICS

As Alice's tax adviser, you asked a number of questions to advise her on her proposed transaction for the house. Alice provided the following answers (refer to Example 24).

- Alice inherited the house from her mother, Paula. The fair market value of the house at the date of Paula's death, based on an appraisal, was $475,000. According to several real estate agents, the house likely is worth $485,000. Paula lived in the house for 38 years; her adjusted basis for the house was $275,000.
- As a child, Alice lived in the house for 10 years. She has not lived there during the 25 years she has been married.
- The house has been vacant during the seven months Alice has owned it. She has been trying to decide whether she should sell it for its fair market value or sell it to her nephew for $275,000. Alice has suggested a $275,000 price for the sale to Dan because she believes this is the amount at which she will have no gain or loss.
- Alice intends to invest the $275,000 in stock.

You advise Alice that her adjusted basis for the house is the $475,000 fair market value on the date of Paula's death. If Alice sells the house for $485,000 (assuming no selling expenses), she would have a recognized gain of $10,000 ($485,000 amount realized − $475,000 adjusted basis). The house is a capital asset, and Alice's holding period is long term because she inherited the house. As a result, the gain would be classified as a long-term capital gain. If, instead, Alice sells the house to

continued

her nephew for $275,000, she will have a part sale and part gift. In that case, the entire realized gain on the sale is recognized.

Amount realized	$ 275,000
Less: Adjusted basis	(269,330)*
Realized gain	$ 5,670
Recognized gain	$ 5,670

*[($275,000 ÷ $485,000) × $475,000] = $269,330.

The gain is classified as a long-term capital gain. Alice then is deemed to have made a gift to Dan of $210,000 ($485,000 − $275,000). With this information, Alice can make an informed selection between the two options.

See Examples 12 and 13 for the tax consequences associated with Alice's questions regarding selling the boat. See Examples 30 and 31 for the tax consequences associated with Alice's questions regarding the wash sale of the stock.

Key Terms

Adjusted basis, 14-5
Amount realized, 14-4
Fair market value, 14-4
Goodwill, 14-10
Holding period, 14-13
Realized gain, 14-3
Realized loss, 14-3
Recognized gain, 14-8
Recognized loss, 14-8
Wash sale, 14-16

Discussion Questions

1. **LO.1** On the sale or other disposition of property, what four questions should be considered for income tax purposes?

Critical Thinking

2. **LO.1** Isabelle invests in land, and Grace invests in taxable bonds. The land appreciates by $8,000 each year, and the bonds earn interest of $8,000 each year. After holding the land and bonds for five years, Isabelle and Grace sell them. There is a $40,000 realized gain on the sale of the land and no realized gain or loss on the sale of the bonds. Are the tax consequences to Isabelle and Grace the same for each of the five years? Explain.

3. **LO.1, 2** Suki and Dave each purchase 100 shares of stock of Burgundy, Inc., a publicly owned corporation, in July for $10,000 each. Suki sells her stock on December 31 for $8,000. Because Burgundy's stock is listed on a national exchange, Dave can ascertain that his shares are worth $8,000 on December 31. Does the Federal income tax law treat the decline in value of the stock differently for Suki and Dave? Explain.

4. **LO.1** If a taxpayer sells property for cash, the amount realized consists of the net proceeds from the sale. For each of the following, indicate the effect on the amount realized if:
   a. The property is sold on credit.
   b. A mortgage on the property is assumed by the buyer.
   c. A mortgage on the property is assumed by the seller.
   d. The buyer acquires the property subject to a mortgage of the seller.
   e. Stock that has a basis to the purchaser of $6,000 and a fair market value of $10,000 is received by the seller as part of the consideration.

5. **LO.1** Taylor is negotiating to buy some land. Under the first option, Taylor will give Ella $150,000 and assume her mortgage on the land for $100,000. Under the second option, Taylor will give Ella $250,000; Ella will pay off the mortgage immediately. Taylor wants his basis for the land to be as high as possible. Given this objective, which option should Taylor select? Explain. Decision Making

6. **LO.1** Lee owns land and a building (held for investment) with an adjusted basis of $75,000 and a fair market value of $250,000. The property is subject to a mortgage of $400,000. Because Lee is in arrears on the mortgage payments, the creditor is willing to accept the property in return for canceling the amount of the mortgage.
   a. How can the adjusted basis of the property be less than the amount of the mortgage?
   b. If the creditor's offer is accepted, what are the effects on the amount realized, the adjusted basis, and the realized gain or loss for Lee?

7. **LO.1** On July 16, 2022, Logan acquires land and a building for $500,000 to use in his sole proprietorship. Of the purchase price, $400,000 is allocated to the building, and $100,000 is allocated to the land. Cost recovery of $4,708 is deducted in 2022 for the building (nonresidential real estate).
   a. What is the adjusted basis for the land and the building at the acquisition date?
   b. What is the adjusted basis for the land and the building at the end of 2022?

8. **LO.1** Auralia owns stock in Orange Corporation and Blue Corporation. She receives a $10,000 distribution from both corporations. Information from Orange states that the $10,000 is a dividend. Blue states that the $10,000 is not a dividend. What could cause the instructions to differ as to the Federal income tax consequences?

9. **LO.1** On July 1, 2022, Katrina purchased tax-exempt bonds (face value of $75,000) for $82,000. The bonds mature in five years, and the annual interest rate is 3%. Discuss the tax reporting implications of this transaction.

10. **LO.2** Wanda is considering selling two personal use assets that she owns. One has appreciated in value by $20,000, and the other has declined in value by $17,000. Wanda believes that she should sell both assets in the same tax year so that the loss of $17,000 can offset the gain of $20,000. Decision Making
    a. Advise Wanda regarding the tax consequences of her plan.
    b. Could Wanda achieve better tax results by selling the assets in different tax years? Explain.

11. **LO.2** Ron sold his sailboat for a $5,000 loss in the current year because he was diagnosed with skin cancer. His spouse wants him to sell his Harley-Davidson motorcycle because her brother broke his leg while riding his motorcycle. Because Ron no longer has anyone to ride with, he is seriously considering his wife's advice. Critical Thinking

    Because the motorcycle is a classic model, Ron has received two offers. Each offer would result in a $5,000 gain. Joe would like to purchase the motorcycle before Christmas, and Jeff would like to purchase it after New Year's. Identify the relevant tax issues Ron faces in making his decision.

12. **LO.1, 2, 3, 5** Simon owns stock that has declined in value since acquired. He will either give the stock to his nephew, Fred, or sell it and give Fred the proceeds. If Fred receives the stock, he then will sell it to obtain the proceeds. Simon is in the 12% Federal income tax bracket, and Fred's bracket is 22%. In either case, the holding period for the stock will be short term. Critical Thinking

    Identify the tax issues relevant to Simon in deciding whether to give the stock or the sale proceeds to Fred.

13. **LO.3** Robin inherits 1,000 shares of Walmart stock from her aunt Julieta in 2022. According to the information received from the executor of Julieta's estate, Robin's adjusted basis for the stock is $55,000. Albert, Robin's fiancé, receives 1,000 shares of Walmart stock from his uncle Roberto as a gift in 2022. Roberto tells Albert that his adjusted basis for the Walmart stock is $7,000. What could cause the substantial difference in the adjusted basis for Robin's and Albert's respective 1,000 shares of Walmart stock?

14. **LO.3** Thelma inherited land from Sadie on June 7, 2022. The land appreciated in value by 100% during the six months Sadie owned it. The value has remained stable during the three months Thelma has owned it, and she expects it to continue to do so in the near future. Although she would like to sell the land now, Thelma has decided to postpone the sale for another three months. The delay is undertaken to enable the recognized gain to qualify for long-term capital gain treatment. Evaluate Thelma's understanding of the tax law.

Decision Making

15. **LO.4** Marilyn owns land that she acquired three years ago as an investment for $250,000. Because the land has not appreciated in value as she anticipated, she sells it to her brother, Amos, for its fair market value of $180,000. Amos sells the land two years later for $240,000.

a. Explain why Marilyn's realized loss of $70,000 ($180,000 amount realized – $250,000 adjusted basis) is disallowed at the time of the sale to her brother.

b. Explain why Amos records neither a recognized gain nor a recognized loss on his sale of the land.

c. How does the related-party disallowance rule affect the total gain or loss recognized by the family unit?

d. Which party wins and which party loses, in a Federal income tax sense?

e. How could Marilyn have avoided the loss disallowance on her sale of the land?

Decision Making

16. **LO.4, 5** Comment on the following transactions.

a. Mort owns 500 shares of Pear, Inc. stock with an adjusted basis of $22,000. On July 28, 2022, he sells 100 shares for $3,000. On August 16, 2022, he purchases another 100 shares for $3,400. Explain why Mort's realized loss of $1,400 ($3,000 − $4,400) on the July 28 sale is not recognized and his adjusted basis for the 100 shares purchased on August 16 is $4,800.

b. Explain how and why your answer in part (a) would change if Mort purchased the 100 shares on December 27, 2022, rather than on August 16, 2022.

Computational Exercises

17. **LO.1, 2** Sally owns real property for which the annual property taxes are $9,000. She sells the property to Kate on March 9, 2022, for $550,000. Kate pays the real property taxes for the entire year on October 1, 2022.

a. How much of the property taxes can be deducted by Sally and how much by Kate?

b. What effect does the property tax apportionment have on Kate's adjusted basis in the property?

c. What effect does the apportionment have on Sally's amount realized from the sale?

d. How would the answers in parts (b) and (c) differ if Sally paid the taxes?

18. **LO.1** Melba purchases land from Adrian. Melba gives Adrian $225,000 in cash and agrees to pay Adrian an additional $400,000 one year later plus interest at 5%.

a. What is Melba's adjusted basis for the land at the acquisition date?

b. What is Melba's adjusted basis for the land one year later?

19. **LO.3** Luciana, a nonshareholder, purchases a condominium from her employer for $85,000. The fair market value of the condominium is $120,000. What is Luciana's basis in the condominium and the amount of any income as a result of this purchase?

20. **LO.3** Sebastian purchases two pieces of equipment for $100,000. Appraisals of the equipment indicate that the fair market value of the first piece of equipment is $72,000 and that of the second piece of equipment is $108,000. What is Sebastian's basis in these two assets?

21. **LO.3** Heather owns 400 shares of Diego Corporation common stock for which she paid $4,000. She receives a nontaxable stock dividend of 20 shares of preferred stock on her common stock. The fair market values on the date of distribution of the preferred stock dividend are $20 a share for common stock and $100 a share for preferred stock. What is Heather's basis in the common and preferred shares?

22. **LO.3** Juliana purchased land three years ago for $50,000. She made a gift of the land to Tom, her brother, in the current year, when the fair market value was $70,000. No Federal gift tax is paid on the transfer. Tom subsequently sells the property for $63,000.
    a. What is Tom's basis in the land? What is his realized gain or loss on the sale?
    b. Assume, instead, that the land has a fair market value of $45,000 on the date of the gift, and that Tom sold the land for $43,000. Now what is Tom's basis in the land, and what is his realized gain or loss on the sale?

23. **LO.3** Ashley inherited all of the property of her aunt Elena, who died last year. Elena's adjusted basis for the property at the date of death was $1,200,000. The property's fair market value was $4,500,000 at the date of death and $4,800,000 six months after the date of death. What is Ashley's adjusted basis of the property?

24. **LO.4** Lisa sells business property with an adjusted basis of $130,000 to her son, Alfred, for its fair market value of $100,000.
    a. What is Lisa's realized and recognized gain or loss?
    b. What is Alfred's recognized gain or loss if he subsequently sells the property for $138,000? For $80,000?

25. **LO.4** Juan owned 200 shares of Circle Corporation stock (adjusted basis of $30,000). He sold 100 shares for $12,000. Twenty days later he purchased 100 shares of the same stock for $8,500. What is Juan's realized and recognized loss? What is his basis in the newly acquired shares?

26. **LO.4** Arianna's personal residence has an adjusted basis of $230,000 and a fair market value of $210,000. Arianna converts the personal residence to rental property. What is Arianna's gain basis? What is her loss basis?

27. **LO.4** Peyton sells an office building and the associated land on May 1 of the current year. Under the terms of the sales contract, Peyton is to receive $1,600,000 in cash. The purchaser is to assume Peyton's mortgage of $950,000 on the property. To enable the purchaser to obtain adequate financing, Peyton is to pay the $9,000 in points charged by the lender. The broker's commission on the sale is $75,000. What is Peyton's amount realized?

Problems

28. **LO.1** Anne sold her home for $290,000 in 2022. Selling expenses were $17,400. She purchased it in 2016 for $200,000. During the period of ownership, Anne did the following.

- Deducted $50,500 office-in-home expenses, which included $4,500 in depreciation. (Refer to text Section 9-6a).
- Deducted a casualty loss in 2018 for residential trees destroyed by a hurricane (her county was declared a Federal disaster area). The total loss was $19,000 (after the $100 floor and the 10%-of-AGI floor), and Anne's insurance company reimbursed her for $13,500. (Refer to text Section 7-3.)
- Paid street paving assessment of $7,000 and added sidewalks for $8,000.
- Installed an elevator for medical reasons. The total cost was $20,000, and Anne deducted $13,000 as medical expenses. (Refer to text Section 10-1b.)

What is Anne's realized gain?

29. **LO.1** Kareem bought a rental house in March 2017 for $300,000, of which $50,000 is allocated to the land and $250,000 to the building. Early in 2019, he had a tennis court built in the backyard at a cost of $7,500. Kareem has deducted $30,900 for depreciation on the house and $1,300 for depreciation on the court. In January 2022, he sells the house and tennis court for $330,000 cash.

a. What is Kareem's realized gain or loss?

b. If an original mortgage of $80,000 is still outstanding and the buyer assumes the mortgage in addition to the cash payment, what is Kareem's realized gain or loss?

c. If the buyer takes the property subject to the $80,000 mortgage rather than assuming it, what is Kareem's realized gain or loss?

30. **LO.1** Norm is negotiating the sale of a tract of his land to Pat. Use the following classification scheme to classify each of the items contained in the proposed sales contract.

Legend		
DARN	=	Decreases amount realized by Norm
IARN	=	Increases amount realized by Norm
DABN	=	Decreases adjusted basis to Norm
IABN	=	Increases adjusted basis to Norm
DABP	=	Decreases adjusted basis to Pat
IABP	=	Increases adjusted basis to Pat

a. Norm is to receive cash of $50,000.

b. Norm is to receive Pat's note payable for $25,000, payable in three years.

c. Pat assumes Norm's mortgage of $5,000 on the land.

d. Pat agrees to pay the realtor's sales commission of $8,000.

e. Pat agrees to pay the property taxes on the land for the entire year. If each party paid their respective share, Norm's share would be $1,000 and Pat's share would be $3,000.

f. Pat pays legal fees of $500.

g. Norm pays legal fees of $750.

31. **LO.1** Nissa owns a building (adjusted basis of $600,000 on January 1, 2022) that she rents to Len, who operates a restaurant in the building. The city closed the restaurant for three months during 2022 because of health code violations. Under MACRS, the cost recovery deduction for 2022 would be $20,500. However, Nissa deducted cost recovery only for the nine months the restaurant was open because she waived the rent income during the three-month period the restaurant was closed.
    a. What is the amount of the cost recovery deduction Nissa should report on her 2022 income tax return?
    b. Calculate the adjusted basis of the building at the end of 2022.

32. **LO.1, 2** Liam owns a personal use boat that has a fair market value of $35,000 and an adjusted basis of $45,000. Liam's AGI is $100,000. Calculate the realized and recognized gain or loss if:
    a. Liam sells the boat for $35,000.
    b. Liam exchanges the boat for another boat worth $35,000.
    c. The boat is stolen and Liam receives insurance proceeds of $35,000.
    d. Would your answer in part (a) change if the fair market value and the selling price of the boat were $48,000?

33. **LO.1** Ricky owns stock in Dove Corporation. His adjusted basis for the stock is $90,000. During the year, he receives a distribution from the corporation of $75,000 that is a return of capital (i.e., Dove has no earnings and profits).
    a. Determine the tax consequences to Ricky.
    b. Assume instead that the amount of the distribution is $150,000. Determine the tax consequences to Ricky.
    c. Assume instead in part (a) that the $75,000 distribution is labeled a taxable dividend (i.e., Dove has earnings and profits of at least $75,000).

34. **LO.1, 2** Zoe purchases Tan, Inc. bonds for $108,000 on January 2, 2022. The face value of the bonds is $100,000; the maturity date is December 31, 2026; and the annual interest rate is 5%. Zoe will amortize the premium only if she is required to do so. Zoe sells the bonds on July 1, 2024, for $106,000.
    a. Determine the interest income Zoe should report for 2022.
    b. Calculate Zoe's recognized gain or loss on the sale of the bonds in 2024.

35. **LO.1, 2** Which of the following results in a recognized gain or loss?
    a. Kay sells her vacation cabin (adjusted basis of $100,000) for $150,000.
    b. Hernan sells his personal residence (adjusted basis of $150,000) for $100,000.
    c. Carl's personal residence (adjusted basis of $65,000) is condemned by the city. He receives condemnation proceeds of $55,000.
    d. Olga's land is worth $40,000 at the end of the year. She had purchased the land six months earlier for $25,000.
    e. Vera's personal vehicle (adjusted basis of $22,000) is stolen. She receives $23,000 from the insurance company and does not plan to replace the automobile.
    f. Jerry sells used clothing (adjusted basis of $500) to a thrift store for $50.

36. **LO.1, 2** Yancy's personal residence is condemned as part of an urban renewal project. His adjusted basis for the residence is $480,000. He receives condemnation proceeds of $460,000 and invests the proceeds in stocks and bonds.
    a. Calculate Yancy's realized and recognized gain or loss.
    b. If the condemnation proceeds are $505,000, what are Yancy's realized and recognized gain or loss?
    c. What are Yancy's realized and recognized gain or loss in part (a) if the house was rental property?

Communications

37. **LO.3** Brent Morgan is a real estate agent for Coastal Estates, a residential real estate development. Because of his outstanding sales performance, Brent is permitted to buy a lot for $300,000 that normally would sell for $500,000. Brent is the only real estate agent for Coastal Estates who is permitted to do so.
    a. Does Brent recognize gross income from the transaction? Explain.
    b. What is Brent's adjusted basis for the land?
    c. Write a letter to Brent informing him of the income tax consequences of his acquisition of the lot. His address is 100 Tower Road, San Diego, CA 92182.

38. **LO.1, 2, 3** Karen Samuels (Social Security number 123-45-6789) makes the following purchases and sales of stock.

Transaction	Date	Number of Shares	Company	Price per Share
Purchase	1-1-2020	300	MDG	$ 75
Purchase	6-1-2020	150	GRU	300
Purchase	11-1-2020	60	MDG	70
Sale	12-3-2020	200	MDG	80
Purchase	3-1-2021	120	GRU	375
Sale	8-1-2021	90	GRU	330
Sale	1-1-2022	150	MDG	90
Sale	2-1-2022	75	GRU	500

Assuming that Karen is unable to identify the specific lots that are sold with the original purchase, determine the recognized gain or loss on each type of stock:
    a. As of July 1, 2020.
    b. As of December 31, 2020.
    c. As of December 31, 2021.
    d. As of July 1, 2022.
    e. Form 8949 and Schedule D (Form 1040) are used to report sales of capital assets (which include stock sales). Go to the IRS website, and download the most current Form 8949 and Schedule D (Form 1040). Then complete the forms for part (c) of this problem, assuming that the brokerage firm did *not* report Karen's basis to the IRS [complete Schedule D (Form 1040) through line 16].

39. **LO.1, 2, 3** Mahan purchases 1,000 shares of Bluebird Corporation stock on October 3, 2022, for $300,000. On December 12, 2022, Mahan purchases an additional 750 shares of Bluebird stock for $210,000. According to market quotations, Bluebird stock is selling for $285 per share on December 31, 2022. Mahan sells 500 shares of Bluebird stock on March 1, 2023, for $162,500.
    a. What is the adjusted basis of Mahan's Bluebird stock on December 31, 2022?
    b. What is Mahan's recognized gain or loss from the sale of Bluebird stock on March 1, 2023, assuming that the shares sold are from the shares purchased on December 12, 2022?
    c. What is Mahan's recognized gain or loss from the sale of Bluebird stock on March 1, 2023, assuming that Mahan cannot adequately identify the shares sold?

40. LO.1, 2, 3 Rod Clooney purchases Kayla Mitchell's sole proprietorship for $990,000 on August 15, 2022. The assets of the business are: Communications

Asset	Kayla's Adjusted Basis	FMV
Accounts receivable	$ 70,000	$ 70,000
Inventory	90,000	100,000
Equipment	150,000	160,000
Furniture and fixtures	95,000	130,000
Building	190,000	250,000
Land	25,000	75,000
Total	$620,000	$785,000

a. Calculate Kayla's realized and recognized gain.

b. Determine Rod's basis for each of the assets.

c. Write a letter to Rod informing him of the income tax consequences of the purchase. His address is 300 Riverview Drive, Delaware, OH 43015.

41. LO.3 Donna owns 800 shares of common stock in Macaw Corporation (adjusted basis of $40,000). She receives a 5% stock dividend when the stock is selling for $60 per share.

a. How much gross income must Donna recognize because of the stock dividend?

b. What is Donna's basis for her 840 shares of stock?

42. LO.1, 2, 3 Roberto has received various gifts over the years and has decided to dispose of several of these assets. What is the recognized gain or loss from each of the following transactions, assuming that no Federal gift tax was paid when the gifts were made?

a. In 1987, he received land worth $32,000. The donor's adjusted basis was $35,000. Roberto sells the land for $95,000 in 2022.

b. In 1992, he received stock in Gold Company. The donor's adjusted basis was $19,000. The fair market value on the date of the gift was $34,000. Roberto sells the stock for $40,000 in 2022.

c. In 1998, he received land worth $15,000. The donor's adjusted basis was $20,000. Roberto sells the land for $9,000 in 2022.

d. In 2019, he received stock worth $30,000. The donor's adjusted basis was $42,000. Roberto sells the stock for $38,000 in 2022.

e. Build a spreadsheet-based solution that provides the solution to parts (a) through (d) above and uses only the donor's basis, the fair market value at the time of the gift, and the selling price as inputs. You may want to use the IF and AND functions together.

43. LO.1, 2, 3, 4 Nicky receives a car from Sam as a gift. Sam paid $48,000 for the car. Sam had used it for business purposes and had deducted $10,000 for depreciation up to the time she gave the car to Nicky. The fair market value of the car is $33,000.

a. Assuming that Nicky uses the car for business purposes, what is her basis for depreciation?

b. Assume that Nicky deducts depreciation of $6,500 and then sells the car for $32,500. What is her recognized gain or loss?

c. Assume that Nicky deducts depreciation of $6,500 and then sells the car for $20,000. What is her recognized gain or loss?

44. LO.3 Margo receives a gift of real estate with an adjusted basis of $175,000 and a fair market value of $100,000. The donor paid gift tax of $15,000 on the transfer. If Margo later sells the property for $110,000, what is her recognized gain or loss?

45. **LO.3** On September 18, 2022, Gerald received land and a building from Lei as a gift. No gift tax was paid on the transfer. Lei's records show the following.

Asset	Adjusted Basis	FMV
Land	$100,000	$212,000
Building	80,000	100,000

a. Determine Gerald's adjusted basis for the land and building.

b. Assume instead that the fair market value of the land was $87,000 and that of the building was $65,000. Determine Gerald's adjusted basis for the land and building.

Communications
Critical Thinking

46. **LO.1, 2, 3, 5** Tyler Meade is planning to make a charitable contribution to the Girl Scouts. He will contribute Crystal, Inc. stock worth $20,000. The stock has an adjusted basis of $15,000. A friend has suggested that Tyler sell the stock and contribute the $20,000 in proceeds rather than contribute the stock.

a. Should Tyler follow the friend's advice? Why or why not?

b. Assume that the fair market value is only $13,000. In this case, should Tyler follow the friend's advice? Why or why not?

c. Rather than make a charitable contribution to the Girl Scouts, Tyler is going to make a gift to Melissa, his niece. Advise Tyler regarding parts (a) and (b).

d. Write a letter to Tyler regarding whether in part (a) he should sell the stock and contribute the cash or contribute the stock. He has informed you that he purchased the stock six years ago. Tyler's address is 500 Ireland Avenue, DeKalb, IL 60115.

47. **LO.3** As sole heir, Nadia receives all of Mary's property (adjusted basis of $11,400,000 and fair market value of $13,820,000). Six months after Mary's death, the fair market value is $13,835,000.

a. Can the executor of Mary's estate elect the alternate valuation date and amount? Explain.

b. What is Nadia's basis for the property?

c. Assume instead that the fair market value six months after Mary's death is $13,800,000. Respond to parts (a) and (b).

48. **LO.3** Dan bought a hotel for $2,600,000 in January 2018. In May 2022, he died and left the hotel to Ed. While Dan owned the hotel, he deducted $289,000 of cost recovery. The fair market value in May 2022 was $2,800,000. The fair market value six months later was $2,850,000. Assume that an estate tax return (Form 706) is not required to be filed.

a. What is the basis of the property to Ed?

b. What is the basis of the property to Ed if the fair market value six months later was $2,500,000 (not $2,850,000) and the objective of the executor was to minimize the estate tax liability?

Communications

49. **LO.3** Ella and Emma are twin sisters who live in Louisiana and Mississippi, respectively. Ella is married to Frank, and Emma is married to Richard. Frank and Richard are killed in an auto accident in 2022 while returning from a sporting event.

Ella and Frank jointly owned some farmland in Louisiana, a community property state (value of $940,000, cost of $450,000). Emma and Richard jointly owned some farmland in Mississippi, a common law state (value of $940,000, cost of $450,000). Assume that all of Frank's and Richard's property passes to their surviving wives.

a. Calculate Ella's basis in the land.

b. Calculate Emma's basis in the land.

c. What causes the difference? Summarize your answer in a one-paragraph e-mail to your instructor.

50. **LO.3, 4** Sheila sells land to Elaine, her sister, for the fair market value of $40,000. Six months later when the land is worth $45,000, Elaine gives it to Jacob, her son. (No gift tax resulted.) Shortly thereafter, Jacob sells the land for $48,000.
    a. Assuming that Sheila's adjusted basis for the land is $24,000, what are Sheila's and Jacob's recognized gain or loss on the sales?
    b. Assuming that Sheila's adjusted basis for the land is $60,000, what are Sheila's and Jacob's recognized gain or loss on the sales?

51. **LO.1, 2, 3, 4** Louis owns three pieces of land with an adjusted basis as follows: parcel A, $75,000; parcel B, $125,000; and parcel C, $175,000. Louis sells parcel A to his uncle for $50,000, parcel B to his partner for $120,000, and parcel C to his mother for $150,000.
    a. What is the recognized gain or loss from the sale of each parcel?
    b. If Louis's uncle eventually sells his land for $90,000, what is his recognized gain or loss?
    c. If Louis's partner eventually sells his land for $130,000, what is his recognized gain or loss?
    d. If Louis's mother eventually sells her land for $165,000, what is her recognized gain or loss?

52. **LO.1, 2, 3, 4** Thania inherited 1,000 shares of Aqua, Inc. stock from Joe. Joe's basis in the stock was $35,000, and the fair market value of the stock on July 1, 2022 (the date of Joe's death) was $45,000. The shares were distributed to Thania on July 15, 2022. Thania sold the stock on July 29, 2023, for $33,000. After giving the matter more thought, she decides that Aqua is a good investment and purchases 1,000 shares for $30,000 on August 19, 2023.

    Decision Making
    Planning

    a. What is Thania's basis for the 1,000 shares purchased on August 19, 2023?
    b. Could Thania have obtained different tax consequences in part (a) if she had sold the 1,000 shares on December 27, 2022, and purchased the 1,000 shares on January 5, 2023? Explain.

53. **LO.1, 2, 4** On December 28, 2022, Kramer sells 150 shares of Lavender, Inc. stock for $77,000. On January 10, 2023, he purchases 100 shares of the same stock for $82,000.

    Critical Thinking

    a. Assuming that Kramer's adjusted basis for the stock sold is $65,000, what is his recognized gain or loss? What is his basis for the new shares?
    b. Assuming that Kramer's adjusted basis for the stock sold is $89,000, what is his recognized gain or loss? What is his basis for the new shares?
    c. Advise Kramer on how he can avoid any negative tax consequences encountered in part (b).

54. **LO.1, 2, 4** Abby's home had a basis of $360,000 ($160,000 attributable to the land) and a fair market value of $340,000 ($155,000 attributable to the land) when she converted 70% of it to business use by opening a bed-and-breakfast. Four years after the conversion, Abby sells the home for $500,000 ($165,000 attributable to the land).
    a. Calculate Abby's basis for gain, loss, and cost recovery for the portion of her personal residence that was converted to business use.
    b. Calculate the cost recovery deducted by Abby during the four-year period of business use, assuming that the bed-and-breakfast is opened on January 1 of year 1 and the house is sold on December 31 of year 4.
    c. What is Abby's recognized gain or loss on the sale of the business use portion?

Communications
Critical Thinking

55. **LO.4, 5** Surendra's personal residence originally cost $340,000 (ignoring the value of the land). After living in the house for five years, he converts it to rental property. At the date of conversion, the fair market value of the house is $320,000. As to the rental property, calculate Surendra's basis for:

a. Loss.

b. Depreciation.

c. Gain.

d. Could Surendra have obtained better tax results if he had sold his personal residence for $320,000 and then purchased another house for $320,000 to hold as rental property? Explain.

e. Summarize your answer to this problem in an e-mail to your instructor.

Communications
Critical Thinking

56. **LO.3, 5** Ichiro, age 93, has accumulated substantial assets during his life. Among his many assets are the following, which he is considering giving to Koji, his grandson.

Asset	Adjusted Basis	Fair Market Value
Silver Corporation stock	$900,000	$700,000
Red Corporation stock	70,000	71,000
Emerald Corporation stock	200,000	500,000

Ichiro has been in ill health for the past five years. His physician has informed him that he probably will not live for more than six months. Which of the stocks should be transferred as gifts and which as inheritances? Summarize your answer in a two- to three-paragraph e-mail to your instructor.

Tax Return Problems

Tax Forms Problem

ProConnect™ Tax

57. Alton Newman, age 67, is married and files a joint return with his wife, Clair, age 65. Alton and Clair are both retired, and during 2021, they received Social Security benefits of $10,000. Both Alton and Clair are covered by Medicare. Alton's Social Security number is 111-11-1119, and Clair's is 123-45-6786. They reside at 210 College Drive, Columbia, SC 29201. The Newmans received the appropriate coronavirus recovery rebates (economic impact payments); related questions in ProConnect Tax should be ignored.

Alton, who retired on January 1, 2021, receives benefits from a qualified pension plan of $2,750 a month for life. His total contributions to the plan (none of which were deductible) were $168,250. In January 2021, he received a bonus of $2,000 from his former employer for service performed in 2020. No Federal or state income taxes were withheld on this bonus by his former employer (Amalgamated Industries, Inc.; EIN 12-3456789; 114 Main Street, Columbia, SC 29201). Although Amalgamated Industries, Inc., accrued the bonus in 2020, it was not paid until 2021.

Clair, who retired on December 31, 2020, started receiving benefits of $1,400 a month on January 1, 2021. Her contributions to the qualified pension plan (none of which were deductible when made) were $74,100.

On September 27, 2021, Alton and Clair received a pro rata 10% stock dividend on 600 shares of stock they owned. They had bought the stock on March 5, 2014, for $20 a share. On December 16, 2021, they sold the 60 dividend shares for $55 a share.

On October 10, 2021, Clair sold the car she had used in commuting to and from work for $17,000. She had paid $31,000 for the car in 2015.

On July 14, 2013, Alton and Clair received a gift of 1,000 shares of stock from their son, Thomas. Thomas's basis in the stock was $35 a share (fair market value at the date of gift was $25). No gift tax was paid on the transfer. Alton and Clair sold the stock on October 8, 2021, for $24 a share.

On May 1, 2021, Clair's mother died, and Clair inherited her personal residence. In February 2021, her mother had paid the property taxes for 2021 of $2,100. The residence had a fair market value of $235,000 and an adjusted basis to the mother of $160,000 on the date of her death. Clair listed the house with a real estate agent, who estimated it was worth $240,000 as of December 31, 2021.

Clair received rent income of $6,000 on a beach house she inherited three years ago from her uncle Charles. She had rented the property for one week during the July 4 holiday and one week during the Thanksgiving holiday. Charles's adjusted basis in the beach house was $150,000, and its fair market value on the date of his death was $240,000. Clair and Alton used the beach house for personal purposes for 56 days during the year. Expenses associated with the house were $3,700 for utilities, maintenance, and repairs; $2,200 for property taxes; and $800 for insurance. There are no mortgages on the property.

Clair and Alton paid estimated Federal income tax of $2,000 and had itemized deductions of $6,800 (excluding any itemized deductions associated with the beach house). They did not engage in any virtual currency transactions during the year. If they have overpaid their Federal income tax, they want the amount refunded. Both Clair and Alton want $3 to go to the Presidential Election Campaign Fund.

Compute their 2021 Federal income tax payable or refund due and complete their 2021 tax return using appropriate forms and schedules. Suggested software: ProConnect Tax.

58. John Benson, age 40, is single. His Social Security number is 111-11-1111, and he resides at 150 Highway 51, Tangipahoa, LA 70465.

Communications
Critical Thinking
Decision Making
Planning
Tax Computation Problem

John has a 7-year-old child, Kendra, who lives with her mother, Katy. As a result of his divorce in 2016, John pays alimony of $6,000 per year to Katy and child support of $12,000. The $12,000 of child support covers 65% of Katy's costs of rearing Kendra. Kendra's Social Security number is 123-45-6789, and Katy's is 123-45-6788.

John's mother, Sally, lived with him until her death in early September 2022. He incurred and paid medical expenses for her of $12,900 and other support payments of $11,000. Sally's only sources of income were $5,500 of interest income on certificates of deposit and $5,600 of Social Security benefits, which she spent on her medical expenses and on maintenance of John's household. Sally's Social Security number was 123-45-6787.

John is employed by the Highway Department of the State of Louisiana in an executive position. His salary is $95,000. The appropriate amounts of Social Security tax and Medicare tax were withheld. In addition, $9,500 was withheld for Federal income taxes and $4,000 was withheld for state income taxes.

In addition to his salary, John's employer provides him with the following fringe benefits.

- Group term life insurance with a maturity value of $95,000; the cost of the premiums for the employer was $295.
- Group health insurance plan; John's employer paid premiums of $5,800 for his coverage. The plan paid $2,600 for John's medical expenses during the year.

On the death of his aunt Josie in December 2021, John, her only recognized heir, inherited the following assets.

Asset	Josie's Adjusted Basis	FMV at Date of Death
Car	$35,000	$ 19,000
Land—300 acres	90,000	175,000
IBM stock	15,000	40,000
Cash	10,000	10,000

Three months prior to her death, Josie made a gift to John of a mountain cabin. Her adjusted basis for the mountain cabin was $120,000, and the fair market value was $195,000. No Federal gift taxes were paid.

During the year, John reported the following transactions.

- On February 1, 2022, he sold for $45,000 Microsoft stock that he inherited from his father four years ago. His father's adjusted basis was $49,000, and the fair market value at the date of the father's death was $41,000.
- The car John inherited from Josie was destroyed in an accident on October 1, 2022. He had loaned the car to Katy to use for a two-week period while the engine in her car was being replaced. Fortunately, neither Katy nor Kendra was injured. John received insurance proceeds of $16,000, the fair market value of the car on October 1, 2022.
- On December 28, 2022, John sold the 300 acres of land to his brother, James, for its fair market value of $160,000. James planned on using the land for his dairy farm.

Other sources of income for John are:

Dividend income (qualified dividends)	$ 3,500
Interest income:	
Guaranty Bank	1,000
City of Kentwood water bonds	2,000
Award from State of Louisiana for outstanding suggestion for highway beautification	10,000

Potential itemized deductions for John, in addition to items already mentioned, are:

State and local property taxes paid on his residence and cabin	$ 7,000
State property taxes paid on personalty	3,500
Estimated Federal income taxes paid	3,000
Charitable contributions	4,500
Mortgage interest on his residence	7,200
Orthodontic expenses for Kendra	4,000

Part 1—Tax Computation

Compute John's net tax payable or refund due for 2022.

Part 2—Tax Planning

Assume that rather than selling the land to James, John is considering leasing it to him for $12,000 annually with the lease beginning on October 1, 2022. James would prepay the lease payments through December 31, 2022. Thereafter, he would make monthly lease payments at the beginning of each month. What effect would this have on John's 2022 tax liability? What potential problem might John encounter? Write a letter to John in which you advise him of the tax consequences of leasing versus selling.

Research Problems

the answer company™ THOMSON REUTERS®

Note: Solutions to the Research Problems can be prepared by using the Thomson Reuters Checkpoint™ online tax research database, which accompanies this textbook. Solutions can also be prepared by using research materials found in a typical tax library.

Research Problem 1. Terry owns real estate with an adjusted basis of $600,000 and a fair market value of $1,100,000. The amount of the nonrecourse mortgage on the property is $2,500,000. Because of substantial past and projected future losses associated with the real estate development (occupancy rate of only 37% after three years), Terry deeds the property to the creditor.

a. What are the tax consequences to Terry?
b. Assume that the data are the same, except that the fair market value of the property is $2,525,000. As a result, when Terry deeds the property to the creditor, she also receives $25,000 from the creditor. What are the tax consequences to Terry?

Research Problem 2. Ruth Ames died on January 10, 2022. In filing the estate tax return, her executor, Melvin Sims, elects the primary valuation date and amount (fair market value on the date of death). On March 12, 2022, Melvin invests $30,000 of cash that Ruth had in her money market account in acquiring 1,000 shares of Orange, Inc. ($30 per share). On January 10, 2022, Orange was selling for $29 per share. The stock is distributed to a beneficiary, Annette Rust, on June 1, 2022, when it is selling for $33 per share. Communications

Melvin wants you to determine the amount at which the Orange shares should appear on the Federal estate tax return and the amount of Annette's adjusted basis for the stock. Write a letter to Melvin in which you respond to his inquiry, and prepare a memo for the tax files. His address is 100 Center Lane, Miami, FL 33124.

Use internet tax resources to address the following questions. Look for reliable websites and blogs of the IRS and other government agencies, media outlets, businesses, tax professionals, academics, think tanks, and political outlets.

Research Problem 3. How are transactions using bitcoin (or another virtual currency) treated under U.S. tax law? Locate the current IRS guidance on this question. Some background on bitcoin can be found at **bitcoin.org/en/faq**. In addition, locate the American Institute of CPAs comment letter on virtual currency (issued in May 2018). After reading these materials, provide a one-page written summary for your instructor. Communications

Research Problem 4. How do U.S. individuals generate their income? Does it vary by size of income (AGI)? Go to the IRS tax statistics website (**irs.gov/statistics**), and download a recent tax year's information on "sources of income." Compare the following types of income by size of AGI: (1) wages, (2) capital gain distributions, (3) sales of capital assets, and (4) sales of property other than capital assets. Cluster the data into no more than six AGI categories. Present your findings in a visual (e.g., bar chart), and summarize your findings in a one-page memo to your instructor. Communications Data Analytics

Research Problem 5. Many see the "step-up in basis at death" rule as an expensive tax loophole enjoyed by the wealthy. Communications

a. Find the latest estimates of the revenue loss to the U.S. Treasury that is attributable to this rule.
b. How does Canada's tax law determine the basis of property acquired from a decedent?
c. Send an e-mail to a member of the House Ways and Means Committee expressing a preference for retaining or eliminating the "step-up in basis" rule.

Research Problem 6. The specific identification method is important when one invests in mutual funds. When taxpayers sell part of their holdings, the basis of the surrendered shares can be difficult to compute. Go to the site of an investment adviser or a mutual fund to find instructions on how to compute the basis of the shares sold. What options are available to the taxpayer according to this information? Illustrate each of the alternatives.

Becker CPA Review Questions

Becker

1. Jasmin purchased 100 shares of Pinkstey Corporation (publicly traded company) on January 1 of year 1 for $5,000. The FMV of the shares at the end of year 1 was $6,000. On January 1 of year 4, Pinkstey Corporation declared a 2-for-1 stock split when the fair market value of the stock was $65 per share. On January 1 of year 5, Jasmin sold all of her Pinkstey Corporation stock when the fair market value was $40 per share. Which of the following statements is true?
   a. Jasmin reports $6,500 in gross income for the 2-for-1 stock split in year 4.
   b. Jasmin's basis in the Pinkstey Corporation stock at the end of year 4 is $65 per share.
   c. Jasmin has no taxable income for the Pinkstey Corporation stock in year 4.
   d. Jasmin owns 100 shares in Pinkstey Corporation stock at the end of year 4.

2. Alice gifted stock to her son, Bob, in year 5. Alice bought the stock in year 1 for $8,300. The value of the stock on the date of gift was $6,400. Bob sold the stock in year 7 for $15,800. What is Bob's recognized gain or loss on the sale in year 7?
   a. $0
   b. $7,500 gain
   c. $9,400 gain
   d. $15,800 gain

3. Jerry inherits an asset from his uncle, who purchased the asset five days before he died. Which of the following statements is correct?
   a. If Jerry sells the asset a few days after receiving it, any gain or loss on the sale will be short term.
   b. Jerry's basis in the asset is the carryover basis from his uncle.
   c. Jerry's basis is the FMV on the alternate valuation date or date it is distributed to him.
   d. Jerry's basis is the FMV on his uncle's date of death.

4. Which of the following statements is *not* correct?
   a. The basis of an asset that is purchased must be adjusted for depreciation allowable.
   b. The general rule for the basis of property acquired by gift is a carryover of basis from the donor.
   c. If an asset is acquired by gift and the FMV on the date of gift is lower than the donor's carryover basis, the recipient's basis cannot be determined until the asset is disposed of.
   d. The basis of property acquired from a decedent is always the FMV on the date of death.

5. Rick purchased 100 shares of XYZ stock on April 4, year 4, for $8,600. He sold 50 shares on February 8, year 5, for $3,000. He then bought another 50 shares of XYZ on March 1, year 5, for $3,200. How much loss will Rick realize in year 5?
   a. $0
   b. $1,300
   c. $3,000
   d. $5,600

6. Agnes sold 50 shares of ABC stock to her son, Steve, in year 4 for $42,000. She bought the stock eight years ago for $50,000. Steve sold the stock to an unrelated party in year 6 for $60,000. How much gain will Steve recognize from the sale in year 6?
   a. $0
   b. $10,000
   c. $18,000
   d. $60,000

7. On February 1 of the current year, Duffy learned that he was bequeathed 1,000 shares of common stock under his father's will. Duffy's father had paid $12,500 for the stock 20 years ago. Fair market value of the stock on February 1 of the current year, the date of his father's death, was $14,000 and had increased to $15,500 six months later. The executor of the estate elected the alternative valuation date for estate tax purposes. Duffy sold the stock for $14,500 on June 1 of the current year, the date that the executor distributed the stock to him. How much income should Duffy include in his current-year individual income tax return for the inheritance of the 1,000 shares of stock that he received from his father's estate?

   a. $5,500
   b. $4,000
   c. $2,500
   d. $0

8. On January 25, year 10, Mother Hall gave her daughter, Nadyne, 500 shares of common stock of XYZ, Corp. The fair market value of the stock on January 25 was $2,000. Mother Hall had paid $4,000 for the stock three years earlier. Nadyne decided a month after receiving the stock that she doesn't want to hold it and sold it for $1,000, the fair market value at the time of the sale. How much income (loss) must Nadyne include in her tax return for year 10 in regards to the sale of the stock?

   a. $0
   b. ($1,000)
   c. ($2,000)
   d. ($3,000)

9. In early year 8, Alice sold Tom, her son, 20 shares of common stock for $20,000. Alice had paid $25,000 for the stock in year 2. In late year 8, Tom sold the stock to an unrelated third party for $35,000. How much gain must Tom report in his year 8 tax return for the sale of the stock?

   a. $0
   b. $5,000
   c. $10,000
   d. $15,000

Chapter 15

Property Transactions: Nontaxable Exchanges

Learning Objectives: *After completing Chapter 15, you should be able to:*

- **LO.1** **Explain the rationale for nonrecognition (postponement) of gain or loss in certain property transactions.**
- **LO.2** **Apply the nonrecognition provisions and basis determination rules for like-kind exchanges.**
- **LO.3** **Explain the nonrecognition provisions available on the involuntary conversion of property.**
- **LO.4** **Describe the provision for the permanent exclusion of gain on the sale of a personal residence.**
- **LO.5** **Apply various tax planning opportunities related to the nonrecognition provisions discussed in the chapter.**

Chapter Outline

15-1 Nontaxable Exchanges, 15-2

15-2 Like-Kind Exchanges—§ 1031, 15-3
- 15-2a Like-Kind Property, 15-4
- 15-2b Exchange Requirement, 15-4
- 15-2c Boot, 15-6
- 15-2d Basis and Holding Period of Property Received, 15-7
- 15-2e Reporting Considerations, 15-10

15-3 Involuntary Conversions—§ 1033, 15-10
- 15-3a Involuntary Conversion Defined, 15-12
- 15-3b Computing the Amount Realized, 15-12
- 15-3c Replacement Property, 15-13
- 15-3d Time Limitation on Replacement, 15-14
- 15-3e Nonrecognition of Gain, 15-15
- 15-3f Reporting Considerations, 15-16

15-4 Sale of a Residence—§ 121, 15-16
- 15-4a Principal Residence, 15-17
- 15-4b Requirements for Exclusion Treatment, 15-17
- 15-4c Calculating the Exclusion, 15-19
- 15-4d Exceptions to the Two-Year Rules, 15-20

15-5 Tax Planning, 15-22
- 15-5a Like-Kind Exchanges, 15-22
- 15-5b Involuntary Conversions, 15-23
- 15-5c Sale of a Principal Residence, 15-23

IAIN MASTERTON/ALAMY STOCK PHOTO

The Big Picture

Alternative Uses of Property

Recall the situation introduced in *The Big Picture* in Chapter 14. After 11 months, Alice has changed her mind about selling the house to her nephew. Several weeks ago, it was announced that the development Alice's inherited house is in will be expanding to include a PGA-sponsored 72-hole golf course, a new conference facility, and a variety of other amenities. As a result, the appraised value of Alice's inherited house has increased to $800,000. Alice has decided that she needs to do something with the house other than let it remain vacant. She is considering the following options and has come to you for advice.

- Sell the house for approximately $800,000 using the services of a real estate agent. The real estate commission rate is 5 percent, and her inherited basis is $475,000.
- Convert the house to a vacation home (100 percent personal use by Alice and her family); then sell it in two years.
- Convert the house to a vacation home (projected 40 percent rental use and 60 percent personal use); then sell it in two years.
- Sell her current home and move into the inherited house. She has owned and lived in her current home for 15 years, and her realized gain on the sale would be about $200,000. Because she is nearing retirement, she would live in the inherited house for only the required period to ensure any tax benefits on its sale and then sell it.

Alice, who currently faces a 24 percent marginal tax rate, expects the inherited house to continue to appreciate in value by about 5 percent per year. She plans on retiring from her job in two years and moving to a warmer climate. Until then, she is neutral as to which house she lives in. What advice can you offer Alice?

Read the chapter and formulate your response.

Framework 1040 Tax Formula for Individuals

This chapter covers the boldfaced portions of the Tax Formula for Individuals that was introduced in Concept Summary 3.1 on p. 3-3. Below those portions are the sections of Form 1040 where the results are reported.

Income *(broadly defined)*	$ xx,xxx
Less: Exclusions	(x,xxx)
Gross income	**$xx,xxx**

FORM 1040 (p. 1)

7 Capital gain or (loss). Attach Schedule D if required. If not required, check here ▶ ☐

FORM 1040 (Schedule 1)

3 Business income or (loss). Attach Schedule C.

4 Other gains or (losses). Attach Form 4797.

Less: Deductions *for* adjusted gross income	**(x,xxx)**
Adjusted gross income	$ xx,xxx
Less: The greater of total itemized deductions *or* the standard deduction	(x,xxx)
Charitable contributions if you take the standard deduction*	(xxx)
Personal and dependency exemptions**	(x,xxx)
Deduction for qualified business income***	(x,xxx)
Taxable income	$ xx,xxx
Tax on taxable income *(see Tax Tables or Tax Rate Schedules)*	$ x,xxx
Less: Tax credits *(including income taxes withheld and prepaid)*	(xxx)
Tax due (or refund)	$ xxx

* For 2021, married taxpayers may claim up to $600 of cash charitable donations ($300 if unmarried).
** Exemption deductions are not allowed from 2018 through 2025.
*** Only applies from 2018 through 2025.

Chapter 14 was the first of a four-chapter sequence dealing with property transactions. In Chapter 14, we explained the sale or exchange concept along with how basis is determined. As shown in Concept Summary 14.2, the intermediate result is realized gain or loss. What happens to the realized gain or loss depends on the nature of the sale or exchange. Some or all of the gain or loss may be recognized, deferred, or even untaxed. Chapter 15 concentrates on several types of sales or exchanges where the usual result is deferral or avoidance of recognition of a realized gain or loss.

LO.1

Explain the rationale for nonrecognition (postponement) of gain or loss in certain property transactions.

15-1 Nontaxable Exchanges

A taxpayer who is going to replace a business asset (e.g., land and building) may decide to sell the old asset and purchase a new asset. In this case, any realized gain or loss on the asset sold is recognized and the basis of the new asset is its cost. Alternatively, the taxpayer may be able to trade the old asset (e.g., land and building) for a new asset (e.g., a large parcel of land on which the taxpayer will construct a new manufacturing plant) in an exchange that might qualify for nontaxable exchange treatment.

The tax law allows deferral or avoidance of gain/loss recognition when there is a change in the *form* but not in the *substance* of the taxpayer's relative economic position. Effectively, the replacement property received in the exchange is viewed as a continuation of the old investment.[1] In addition, a nontaxable exchange can result when the transaction does not provide the taxpayer with the *wherewithal to pay* the tax on any realized gain that would be recognized (i.e., the taxpayer does not have the cash that would have been received in a sale).

[1]Reg. § 1.1002–1(c).

In a **nontaxable exchange**, realized gains or losses are not recognized. Instead, the recognition of gain or loss is *postponed* (deferred) until the property received in the nontaxable exchange is subsequently sold in a taxable transaction. This "deferral" is accomplished by assigning a carryover basis to the replacement property.

Example 1

Debra completes a *nontaxable exchange* of property with an adjusted basis of $10,000 and a fair market value of $12,000 for property with a fair market value of $12,000.

Debra has a realized gain of $2,000 ($12,000 amount realized − $10,000 adjusted basis). Her recognized gain is $0. Her basis in the replacement property is a carryover basis of $10,000.

Assume that the replacement property is nondepreciable and that Debra subsequently sells it for $12,000. Her realized and recognized gain will be the $2,000 gain that was postponed (deferred) in the nontaxable transaction. If the replacement property is depreciable, the carryover basis of $10,000 is used in calculating depreciation.

In some nontaxable exchanges, only part of the property involved in the transaction qualifies for nonrecognition treatment. If the taxpayer receives cash or other nonqualifying property, part or all of the realized gain from the exchange is recognized; the taxpayer has the wherewithal to pay tax. Here, the basis of the replacement property is adjusted to reflect any deferred gain (gain realized but not recognized).

It is important to distinguish between a nontaxable disposition, as the term is used in the statute, and a tax-free transaction. The term *nontaxable* refers to postponement of recognition via a carryover basis. In a *tax-free* transaction, the nonrecognition is permanent. Here, the basis of any property acquired does not depend on the basis of the property sold by the taxpayer. In this chapter, we discuss two nontaxable transactions (like-kind exchanges and involuntary conversions) and one tax-free transaction (sale of a personal residence).

15-2 Like-Kind Exchanges—§ 1031

LO.2

Apply the nonrecognition provisions and basis determination rules for like-kind exchanges.

Code § 1031 requires nontaxable treatment if the following **like-kind exchange** requirements are satisfied.[2]

- The property is *like-kind* property (only *real property* qualifies).[3]
- The form of the transaction is an *exchange*.
- Both the property given up and the property received are either "used in a trade or business" *or* "held for investment."

Business and investment personal property (i.e., non-real property), inventory, any property held for personal use, domestic property exchanged for foreign property, and partnership interests (both limited and general) do *not* qualify under the like-kind exchange rules. In addition, transactions involving financial instruments (e.g., stock, bonds, or a note) do *not* qualify for like-kind exchange treatment even though they are held for investment.

If a taxpayer exchanges like-kind property *solely* for like-kind property, gain or loss realized is not recognized (it is deferred), and the basis and holding period from the old property attaches (carries over) to the new property.[4]

[2] § 1031(a) and Reg. § 1.1031(a)–1(a).

[3] Prior to 2018, business and investment *personalty* also qualified for like-kind exchange treatment. Personalty includes machines, equipment, furniture and fixtures, trucks, and automobiles.

[4] Subject to certain exceptions, related parties can engage in tax-free like-kind exchanges, but a two-year holding period applies to both the relinquished property and the replacement property [§ 1031(f)].

Example 2

During the current year, Andy exchanged 40 acres of unimproved land in Illinois (fair market value $200,000; basis $70,000) for 10 acres of unimproved land in California (fair market value $200,000).

Although Andy has a realized gain of $130,000 on this transaction ($200,000 amount realized − $70,000 basis), none of the gain is recognized; the transaction qualifies as a like-kind exchange. Andy's basis in the new property is $70,000. This carryover basis reflects the realized gain that is deferred ($200,000 California property fair market value − $130,000 gain deferred). The like-kind exchange rules acknowledge that Andy—after the exchange—would not have the wherewithal to pay tax if the realized gain were recognized.

If Andy were to sell the California property for its market value, he would have a realized and recognized gain of $130,000.

The nonrecognition provision for like-kind exchanges is *mandatory* rather than elective. A taxpayer who wants to recognize a realized gain or loss must structure the transaction in a way that fails the like-kind exchange requirements. For example, a taxpayer may want to avoid like-kind treatment so that a realized loss can be recognized, or a taxpayer might want to recognize a gain so that capital loss carryovers can be used. We discuss this more in the Tax Planning section of the chapter.

Example 3

During the current year, Stephanie exchanged her rental condo in Vail, worth $250,000 (basis of $325,000), plus $80,000 of cash for a rental condo in Malibu worth $330,000. Although Stephanie has a realized loss of $75,000 on this transaction ($250,000 amount realized − $325,000 basis), none of the loss is recognized since the transaction qualifies as a like-kind exchange.

Stephanie would likely be better off for tax purposes by selling her Vail condo (and recognizing the loss) and then buying the Malibu property.

The like-kind exchange rules are applied independently to each taxpayer in the exchange; one taxpayer may qualify for like-kind treatment, and the other may not.

15-2a **Like-Kind Property**

The term *like-kind* is intended to be interpreted very broadly.[5] *Real property* (or realty) includes rental buildings, office and store buildings, manufacturing plants, warehouses, and land. It is immaterial whether realty is improved or unimproved. As a result, an exchange of unimproved land for an apartment house can involve like-kind property. Real property held primarily for sale (i.e., inventory) does *not* qualify as like-kind property.[6]

If the exchange transaction involves multiple business assets (e.g., a television station for another television station), the determination of whether the assets qualify as like-kind property are not made at the business level.[7] Instead, the underlying assets are evaluated, and only the real property that is part of the exchange would qualify for like-kind exchange treatment.

15-2b **Exchange Requirement**

The transaction must involve a direct *exchange* of property to qualify as a like-kind exchange. The sale of old property and the purchase of new property, even though like-kind, is not an exchange. However, if the two transactions are mutually dependent, the IRS may treat them as a like-kind exchange.[8]

[5] Reg. § 1.1031(a)–1(b).
[6] § 1031(a)(2).
[7] Reg. § 1.1031(j)–1.
[8] Rev.Rul. 61–119.

Time Limitations

Like-kind exchanges of real estate can be complex. Further, it can be extremely difficult to coordinate a simultaneous transaction if the properties being exchanged are located in different counties or states. As a result, delayed (nonsimultaneous) exchanges can qualify, subject to time limits.

In a delayed like-kind exchange (often called a *Starker exchange*[9]), one party does not take immediate title to the new property because it has not yet been identified. The Code provides that the delayed swap—often made with the assistance of a qualified intermediary—will qualify as a like-kind exchange if the following requirements are satisfied (see Concept Summary 15.1).[10]

- *Identification period.* The new property must be identified within 45 days of the date when the old property was transferred to the qualified intermediary.
- *Exchange period.* The new property must be received:[11]
    - Within 180 days of the date when the old property was transferred to the qualified intermediary (usually a bank or broker), or
    - If *earlier*, by the due date (including extensions) for the tax return covering the year of the transfer.

Concept Summary 15.1

Delayed § 1031 Exchange

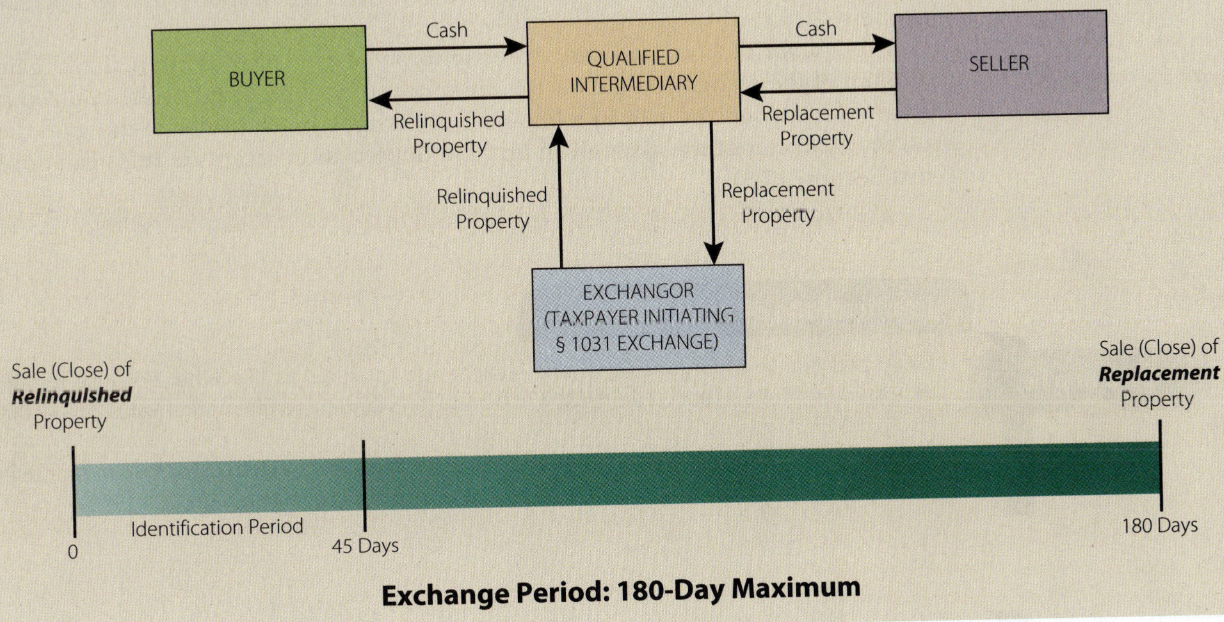

[9]*T. J. Starker v. U.S.*, 79–2 USTC ¶9541, 44 AFTR2d 79–5525, 602 F.2d 1341 (CA–9). This decision first allowed deferred like-kind exchanges.

[10]§ 1031(a)(3).

[11]In general, the IRS allows *no deviation* from either the identification period or the exchange period even when events outside the taxpayer's control preclude strict compliance. However, see Rev.Proc. 2010–14; here, the IRS allowed an exception where the qualified intermediary defaulted due to bankruptcy.

Example 4

Phil owns a store in downtown Plano. Adjacent to his store is a commercial parking lot owned by Sally (fair market value of $175,000). Phil would like to acquire the parking lot, which would allow him to expand his store, but Sally does not want to sell the lot due to the large gain she would recognize (her basis in the lot is only $3,000).

Phil agrees to purchase any "like-kind" property worth $175,000 that is acceptable to Sally if Sally agrees to transfer the parking lot to Phil immediately. Sally agrees to the plan, and the commercial lot is transferred to Phil on October 1 of the current year.

Later that month, Sally identifies a townhouse worth $175,000 and directs Phil to buy it for her. Phil negotiates the sale, which closes on December 12, and transfers the property to Sally.

This is a like-kind exchange since the replacement property was identified within 45 days of the parking lot being transferred to Phil and the townhouse was transferred to Sally within 180 days of the original transfer date. In effect, Sally sold the parking lot to Phil for $175,000 and then reinvested the proceeds in another piece of real estate without having to pay tax on the realized gain. Her basis in the townhouse ($3,000) reflects the realized gain that is deferred.

15-2c Boot

It is unusual to find like-kind transactions where the value of the property given up is exactly equal to the value of the property received. In most situations, one party normally provides some other property (e.g., cash) to "even out" the exchange. When a taxpayer in a like-kind exchange gives or receives some property that is *not* like-kind property, gain or loss recognition may occur. Property that is not like-kind, including cash, is referred to as **boot**. Although the term *boot* does not appear in the Code, tax practitioners commonly use it rather than saying "property that is not like-kind property."

The *receipt* of boot will trigger recognition of gain if there is realized gain. The amount of the recognized gain is the *lesser* of the boot received or the realized gain. If a taxpayer recognizes gain in a like-kind exchange, the character of the gain depends on the character of the asset given up (and depreciation recapture rules can apply; see text Section 17-3).

Implications of Boot Received

Example 5

Emily and Fran exchange land, and the exchange qualifies as like kind. Because Emily's land (adjusted basis of $20,000) is worth $24,000 and Fran's land has a fair market value of $19,000, Fran also gives Emily cash of $5,000.

Emily's recognized gain is $4,000, the lesser of the realized gain ($24,000 amount realized – $20,000 adjusted basis) or the fair market value of the boot received ($5,000).

Example 6

Assume the same facts as in the previous example, except that Fran's land is worth $21,000 (not $19,000). Under these circumstances, Fran gives Emily cash of $3,000 to make up the difference.

Emily's recognized gain is $3,000, the lesser of the realized gain of $4,000 ($24,000 amount realized – $20,000 adjusted basis) or the fair market value of the boot received of $3,000.

Realized Gain (Loss)		
	Amount realized ($900,000 + $300,000)	$1,200,000
−	Adjusted basis of building	(400,000)
=	Realized gain	$ 800,000
Boot Received		
	Cash	$ 300,000
Recognized Gain		
	Lesser of realized gain or boot received	$ 300,000
Basis of New Land (Simplified Method)		
	Fair market value of property received	$ 900,000
−	Postponed gain ($800,000 less $300,000)	(500,000)
=	Basis of like-kind property received	$ 400,000
Basis of New Land (Alternative Method)		
	Adjusted basis of property given up	$ 400,000
+	Adjusted basis of boot given	–0–
+	Gain recognized	300,000
−	Fair market value of boot received	(300,000)
−	Loss recognized	–0–
=	Basis of like-kind property received	$ 400,000

Example 13

Assume the same facts as Example 12, except that Vicki's building has a fair market value of $300,000 and she provides $600,000 cash to the seller as part of the exchange.

Realized Gain (Loss)		
	Amount realized (FMV of new land)	$ 900,000
−	Adjusted basis ($400,000 building + $600,000 cash)	(1,000,000)
=	Realized loss	($ 100,000)
Boot Received		$ –0–
Recognized Loss		$ –0–
Basis of New Land (Simplified Method)		
	Fair market value of property received	$ 900,000
+	Postponed loss	100,000
=	Basis of like-kind property received	$1,000,000
Basis of New Land (Alternative Method)		
	Adjusted basis of property given up	$ 400,000
+	Adjusted basis of boot given	600,000
+	Gain recognized	–0–
−	Fair market value of boot received	–0–
−	Loss recognized	–0–
=	Basis of like-kind property received	$1,000,000

If the taxpayer assumes a liability (or takes property subject to a liability) in the exchange, the amount of the liability is treated as boot given. For the taxpayer whose liability is assumed (or whose property is taken subject to the liability), the amount of the liability is treated as boot received.

Example 14

Jill Rodriguez and Rick Thompson exchange real estate investments. Jill gives up property with an adjusted basis of $250,000 (fair market value of $420,000) that is subject to a mortgage of $80,000 (assumed by Rick). In return for this property, Jill receives property with a fair market value of $340,000 (Rick's adjusted basis in the property is $200,000). Jill's and Rick's realized and recognized gains and their basis in the like-kind property received are computed as follows.[14]

	Jill	Rick
Compute Realized Gain (Loss)		
FMV of like-kind property received	$ 340,000	$ 420,000
+ FMV of other property received		
+ Cash received		
+ Debt relief	80,000	
− Cash paid		
− Debt assumed		(80,000)
= Net Consideration Received	$ 420,000	$ 340,000
− Adjusted basis of property given	(250,000)	(200,000)
= Realized Gain (Loss)	$ 170,000	$ 140,000
Compute Boot Received		
Debt relief	$ 80,000	$ –0–
+ Cash received		
+ FMV of other property received		
= Boot Received	$ 80,000	$ –0–
Compute Recognized Gain		
Lesser of realized gain or boot received	$ 80,000	$ –0–
Compute Basis for New Property (Other Than Cash)		
Adjusted Basis of Property Given	$ 250,000	$ 200,000
+ Boot given (cash paid; debt assumed)	–0–	80,000
+ Gain recognized	80,000	–0–
− Boot received	(80,000)	–0–
= Basis of New Property	$ 250,000	$ 280,000

15-2e Reporting Considerations

Code § 1031 transactions are reported on Form 8824 (Like-Kind Exchanges). Part III of Form 8824 is shown below, based on the information provided for Jill Rodriguez's exchange (Example 14).

This form must be filed even though the like-kind exchange transaction results in no recognized gain or loss. It is filed with the regular return for the tax year when the like-kind exchange occurs.

LO.3

Explain the nonrecognition provisions available on the involuntary conversion of property.

15-3 Involuntary Conversions—§ 1033

In most cases, taxpayers sell property (or exchange it) when they need to do so. There are times, however, when the taxpayer *involuntarily* (i.e., outside the taxpayer's control) disposes of property. When this happens, the taxpayer usually receives some sort of compensation (e.g., insurance proceeds or a condemnation award). Code § 1033 provides that a taxpayer who experiences an involuntary conversion of property may postpone recognition of *gain* realized from the conversion. As a result, this provision provides relief to a taxpayer who has experienced an involuntary conversion and does not have the *wherewithal to pay* the tax on any gain realized as a result of the conversion.

[14]Example (2) of Reg. § 1.1031(d)–2 illustrates a special situation where both the buyer and the seller transfer liabilities that are assumed by the other party (or both parties acquire property that is subject to a liability).

Form 8824 (2021) Page **2**

Name(s) shown on tax return. Do not enter name and social security number if shown on other side.	**Your social security number**

Part III **Realized Gain or (Loss), Recognized Gain, and Basis of Like-Kind Property Received**

Caution: If you transferred **and** received **(a)** more than one group of like-kind properties, or **(b)** cash or other (not like-kind) property, see ***Reporting of multi-asset exchanges*** in the instructions.

Note: Complete lines 12 through 14 **only** if you gave up property that was not like-kind. Otherwise, go to line 15.

Line	Description				
12	Fair market value (FMV) of other property given up. See instructions	12			
13	Adjusted basis of other property given up	13			
14	Gain or (loss) recognized on other property given up. Subtract line 13 from line 12. Report the gain or (loss) in the same manner as if the exchange had been a sale			14	
	Caution: If the property given up was used previously or partly as a home, see ***Property used as home*** in the instructions.				
15	Cash received, FMV of other property received, plus net liabilities assumed by other party, reduced (but not below zero) by any exchange expenses you incurred. See instructions			15	*80,000*
16	FMV of like-kind property you received			16	*340,000*
17	Add lines 15 and 16			17	*420,000*
18	Adjusted basis of like-kind property you gave up, net amounts paid to other party, plus any exchange expenses **not** used on line 15. See instructions			18	*250,000*
19	**Realized gain or (loss).** Subtract line 18 from line 17			19	*170,000*
20	Enter the smaller of line 15 or line 19, but not less than zero			20	*80,000*
21	Ordinary income under recapture rules. Enter here and on Form 4797, line 16. See instructions			21	*0*
22	Subtract line 21 from line 20. If zero or less, enter -0-. If more than zero, enter here and on Schedule D or Form 4797, unless the installment method applies. See instructions			22	*80,000*
23	**Recognized gain.** Add lines 21 and 22			23	*80,000*
24	Deferred gain or (loss). Subtract line 23 from line 19. If a related party exchange, see instructions			24	*90,000*
25	**Basis of like-kind property received.** Subtract line 15 from the sum of lines 18 and 23. See instructions			25	*250,000*

Realized gain is postponed to the extent that the taxpayer *reinvests* the amount realized (e.g., insurance proceeds) in replacement property. The rules for nonrecognition of gain are as follows.

- If the amount reinvested in replacement property *equals or exceeds* the amount realized, realized gain is *not recognized.*
- If the amount reinvested in replacement property is *less than* the amount realized, realized gain *is recognized* to the extent of the deficiency.

Involuntary Conversions: General Rules

Example 15

Jason operates a charter fishing business in Panama City, Florida, taking customers out in the Gulf of Mexico on daylong fishing trips. Unfortunately, his boat was completely destroyed when Hurricane Bonnie hit the Florida coast. His boat had a basis of $78,000 ($120,000 cost − $42,000 of accumulated depreciation). Fortunately, Jason had marine insurance (which included a replacement cost rider). He filed an insurance claim shortly after his boat was destroyed and received $175,000 in insurance proceeds three weeks later.

Jason has a realized gain of $97,000, computed as follows.

Amount realized (insurance proceeds)	$175,000
Less: Adjusted basis	(78,000)
Realized gain	$ 97,000

Jason can defer the entire realized gain, provided that he uses all of the insurance proceeds to purchase a new boat.

Example 16

Refer to the facts of Example 15, and assume that Jason buys a new boat for $180,000. He uses the entire insurance settlement as part of the purchase.

In this case, Jason's $97,000 realized gain is deferred, and the basis of his new boat must reflect that deferral. As a result, his new boat's basis is $83,000 ($180,000 cost − $97,000 deferred gain).

Involuntary Conversions: General Rules

Example 17

Continuing with the facts of Example 15, assume that Jason is able to negotiate an excellent price for his new boat. In fact, he is able to replace his old boat for only $168,000 and uses the $7,000 remaining from the insurance settlement to pay for other business expenses.

Jason recognizes a gain of $7,000, the difference between the $175,000 insurance settlement and the amount he paid for the new boat ($168,000; the amount of the insurance proceeds he reinvested in replacement property).

The balance of the realized gain is deferred, and the basis of his new boat must reflect that deferral. As a result, his new boat's basis is $78,000 ($168,000 cost − $90,000 deferred gain).

If an involuntary conversion results in a *loss*, § 1033 does not change the normal loss recognition rules. If a realized loss would otherwise be recognized, § 1033 does not change the result.

Example 18

Refer to the facts of Example 15, but assume that Jason had only partial coverage on his boat and his insurance settlement is only $50,000. In this case, Jason has a loss of $28,000, computed as follows.

Amount realized (insurance proceeds)	$50,000
Less: Adjusted basis	(78,000)
Realized loss	($28,000)

No tax deferral applies; Jason's realized loss of $28,000 is recognized.

15-3a Involuntary Conversion Defined

An **involuntary conversion** results from the destruction (complete or partial), theft, seizure, condemnation, or sale or exchange under threat of condemnation (e.g., a city seizing property under its right of eminent domain) of the taxpayer's property.[15] A voluntary act (e.g., a taxpayer destroying the property by arson) is *not* an involuntary conversion.[16]

Government seizures are unique events, and as a result, a unique set of rules have developed. In general, the government entity must have made a decision to acquire the property for public use, and the taxpayer must have reasonable grounds to believe the property will be taken.[17]

15-3b Computing the Amount Realized

The amount realized from an involuntary conversion typically includes any insurance proceeds received. In the case of the condemnation of property, the amount realized usually includes only the amount received as compensation for the property.[18]

Any amount received that is designated as severance damages by both the government and the taxpayer is *not* included in the amount realized. *Severance awards* usually occur when only a portion of the property is condemned (e.g., a strip of land is taken to build a highway). Severance damages are awarded because the value of the taxpayer's remaining property has declined as a result of the condemnation. In general, severance damages are a tax-free recovery of capital and reduce the basis of the property.

[15] § 1033(a) and Reg. §§ 1.1033(a)–1(a) and –2(a).

[16] Rev.Rul. 82–74.

[17] Rev.Rul. 63–221 and *Joseph P. Balistrieri*, 38 TCM 526, T.C.Memo. 1979–115.

[18] *Pioneer Real Estate Co.*, 47 B.T.A. 886 (1942), *acq.* 1943 C.B. 18.

Example 19

The government condemns a portion of Ron's farmland to upgrade a highway for driverless vehicles. Because the project denies his cattle access to a pond and some grazing land, Ron receives severance damages in addition to the condemnation proceeds for the land taken.

Ron must reduce the basis of the property by the amount of the severance damages. If the amount of the severance damages received exceeds the adjusted basis, Ron recognizes gain.

15-3c Replacement Property

The requirements for replacement property generally are more restrictive than those for like-kind property. The basic requirement is that the replacement property be *similar or related in service or use* to the involuntarily converted property.[19]

Different interpretations of the phrase *similar or related in service or use* apply depending on whether the involuntarily converted property is held by an *owner-user* (e.g., in a business or by an individual) or by an *owner-investor* (e.g., lessor). For an owner-investor, the *taxpayer use* test applies, and for an owner-user, the *functional use test* applies. In most cases, the functional use test is more restrictive than the taxpayer use test. In addition, a special rule applies in the case of involuntary conversions that result from condemnations.

Taxpayer Use Test

The taxpayer use test for owner-investors provides much more flexibility in terms of what qualifies as replacement property. Essentially, the properties must be used by the owner-investor in similar endeavors. For example, rental property held by an owner-investor qualifies if replaced with other rental property, regardless of the type of rental property involved. For example, the test is met if the owner-investor of a building being rented to a manufacturing business replaces the facility with a building rented to a business using the facility as a grocery warehouse.[20] The replacement of a rental residence with a personal residence does *not* meet the test.[21]

Functional Use Test

The functional use test applies to owner-users. Under this test, the taxpayer's use of the replacement property and of the involuntarily converted property must be the same. A manufacturer whose manufacturing plant is destroyed by fire must replace the plant with another facility of similar functional use. Replacing a manufacturing plant with an office building (both used in the same business) does *not* meet this test. The manufacturing plant would have to be replaced with another manufacturing plant. Replacing a rental residence with a personal residence also does not pass the test.

Special Rule for Condemnations

If business real property or investment real property is *condemned*, the broader replacement rules for like-kind exchanges can be used instead of the narrower involuntary conversion replacement rules. This gives the taxpayer substantially more flexibility in selecting replacement property. For example, improved real property can be replaced with unimproved real property.

---

[19] § 1033(a) and Reg. § 1.1033(a)–1.

[20] *Loco Realty Co. v. Comm.*, 62–2 USTC ¶9657, 10 AFTR 2d 5359, 306 F.2d 207 (CA–8).

[21] Rev.Rul. 70–466.

The rules concerning the nature of replacement property relative to involuntary conversions are illustrated in Concept Summary 15.2.

Concept Summary 15.2

Involuntary Conversions: Replacement Property Tests

Type of Property and User	Taxpayer Use Test	Functional Use Test	Special Rule for Condemnations*
An investor's rented shopping mall is destroyed by fire; the mall may be replaced with other rental properties (e.g., an apartment building).	X		
A manufacturing plant is destroyed by fire; replacement property must consist of another manufacturing plant that is functionally the same as the property converted.		X	
Personal residence of a taxpayer is condemned by a local government authority; replacement property must consist of another personal residence.		X	
Land used by a manufacturing company is condemned by a local government authority.			X
Apartment and land held by an investor are sold due to the threat or imminence of condemnation.			X

*Uses the like-kind exchange rules.

15-3d Time Limitation on Replacement

In general, the taxpayer must acquire replacement property within two years after the close of the taxable year in which gain is realized.[22] Typically, gain is realized when insurance proceeds or damages are received.

Example 20

Megan's building is destroyed by fire on December 16, 2021. The adjusted basis is $325,000. Megan receives $400,000 from the insurance company on February 2, 2022. She is a calendar year and cash method taxpayer.

The latest date for replacement is December 31, 2024 (the end of the taxable year in which realized gain occurred plus two years). The critical date is not the date the involuntary conversion occurred, but rather the date of gain realization.

In the case of a condemnation of real property used in a trade or business or held for investment, a three-year period is used.

Example 21

Assume the same facts as in the previous example, except that Megan's building is condemned. Megan receives notification of the future condemnation on November 1, 2021. The condemnation occurs on December 16, 2021, with the condemnation proceeds being received on February 2, 2022.

The latest date for replacement is December 31, 2025 (the end of the taxable year in which realized gain occurred plus three years).

The *earliest date* for replacement typically is the date the involuntary conversion occurs. However, if the property is condemned, it is possible to replace the condemned property before this date. In this case, the earliest date is the date of the threat of condemnation of the property. This rule allows the taxpayer to make an orderly replacement of the condemned property.

[22]§§ 1033(a)(2)(B) and (g)(4) and Reg. § 1.1033(a)–2(c)(3). The two-year period is extended to a four-year period if the property is located in a Federally declared disaster area. The taxpayer can apply for an extension of this time period anytime before its expiration [Reg. § 1.1033(a)–2(c)(3)]. The period for filing the application for extension also can be extended if the taxpayer shows reasonable cause for the delay.

Example 22

Assume the same facts as in Example 21. The earliest date that Megan can replace the building is November 1, 2021, which is the date of an official notice regarding the condemnation of the building.

15-3e Nonrecognition of Gain

Nonrecognition of gain can be either mandatory or elective, depending on whether the conversion is direct (into replacement property) or indirect (into money).

Direct Conversion

If the conversion is directly into replacement property rather than into money, nonrecognition of realized gain is *mandatory*. In this case, the basis of the replacement property is the same as the adjusted basis of the converted property. Direct conversion is rare in practice and usually involves condemnations.

Example 23

Lupe's property, with an adjusted basis of $20,000, is condemned by the state. Lupe receives property with a fair market value of $50,000 as compensation for the property taken.

Because the nonrecognition of realized gain is mandatory for direct conversions, Lupe's realized gain of $30,000 is not recognized and the basis of the replacement property is $20,000 (adjusted basis of the condemned property).

Conversion into Money

If the conversion is into money, the realized gain is recognized only to the extent the amount realized from the involuntary conversion exceeds the cost of the qualifying replacement property.[23] This is the usual case, and nonrecognition (postponement) is *elective*. If the election is not made, the realized gain is recognized.

The basis of the replacement property is the property's cost less any postponed (deferred) gain.[24] If the election to postpone gain is made, the holding period of the replacement property includes the holding period of the converted property.

Code § 1033 applies *only to gains* and *not to losses*. Losses from involuntary conversions are recognized if the property is held for business or income-producing purposes. Certain personal casualty losses are recognized (the limitations are discussed in text Section 7-3), but condemnation losses related to personal use assets (e.g., a personal residence) are neither recognized nor postponed.

Involuntary Conversion Gain or Loss

Example 24

Walt's building (used in his trade or business), with an adjusted basis of $50,000, is destroyed by fire on October 5, 2022. Walt is a calendar year taxpayer. On November 17, 2022, he receives an insurance reimbursement of $100,000 for the loss. Walt invests $80,000 in a new building and uses the other $20,000 of insurance proceeds to pay off credit card debt.

- Walt has until December 31, 2024, to make the new investment and qualify for the nonrecognition election.
- Walt's realized gain is $50,000 ($100,000 insurance proceeds received − $50,000 adjusted basis of old building).
- Assuming that the replacement property qualifies as similar or related in service or use, Walt's recognized gain is $20,000. Because he reinvested $20,000 less than the insurance proceeds received ($100,000 proceeds − $80,000 reinvested), his realized gain is recognized to that extent.
- Walt's basis in the new building is $50,000. This is the building's cost of $80,000 less the postponed gain of $30,000 (realized gain of $50,000 − recognized gain of $20,000).

[23] § 1033(a)(2)(A) and Reg. § 1.1033(a)–2(c)(1).

[24] § 1033(b).

Involuntary Conversion Gain or Loss

Example 25

Assume the same facts as in the previous example, except that Walt receives only $45,000 in insurance proceeds. He has a realized and recognized loss of $5,000. The basis of the new building is the building's cost of $80,000.

If the destroyed building in Example 25 had been held for personal use, the recognized loss would have been subject to the casualty loss limitations.[25] Personal casualty losses are deductible only if they occur in a Federally declared disaster area. In that case, the loss of $5,000 would have been limited to the decline in fair market value of the property, and the amount of the loss would have been reduced first by $100 and then by 10 percent of adjusted gross income (see text Section 7-3d).

15-3f Reporting Considerations

In general, taxpayers elect whether to defer any gain realized from an involuntary conversion. Normally, the election is made by not reporting any gain on the tax return. However, the tax return filed for the year of conversion must include detailed information related to the involuntary conversion.[26] This requirement usually is satisfied with a statement attached to the return detailing the involuntary conversion and the replacement property acquired.

What if the taxpayer intends to acquire qualifying replacement property but has not done so by the time the tax return is filed? The taxpayer should elect involuntary conversion treatment and report all details of the transaction on a statement attached to the return. When the qualifying replacement property is acquired, the taxpayer attaches a statement to the later tax return that contains relevant information for the replacement property.

An amended return must be filed if qualified replacement property is not acquired during the replacement time period. An amended return also is required if the cost of the replacement property is less than the amount realized from the involuntary conversion. In this case, the return would recognize the portion of the realized gain that no longer can be deferred.

LO.4

Describe the provision for the permanent exclusion of gain on the sale of a personal residence.

15-4 Sale of a Residence—§ 121

A taxpayer's **personal residence** is a personal use asset. Therefore, a realized loss from the sale of a personal residence is not recognized.[27]

A realized gain from the sale of a personal residence is recognized. However, taxpayers meeting the **§ 121 exclusion** requirements are allowed to exclude up to $250,000 of realized gain on the sale of a principal residence.[28] Any gain in excess of this amount normally qualifies as a long-term capital gain (subject to preferential tax rates).

Example 26

Tom and Eileen Atwood bought their home in 2013 for $525,000 and have used it as their principal residence since that time. In July 2022, they sell their home for $670,000. The Atwoods have a realized gain of $145,000 on the sale ($670,000 − $525,000), and the entire gain is excluded as a result of § 121.

What if the Atwoods sold their home for $500,000? In this case, since their home is a personal use asset, they would have a $25,000 realized loss that would not be recognized.

[25] § 165(c)(3) and Reg. § 1.165–7.

[26] Reg. § 1.1033(a)–2(c)(2).

[27] § 165(c).

[28] § 121(b).

15-4a Principal Residence

Whether property is the taxpayer's principal residence "depends upon all of the facts and circumstances in each case." According to the Regulations, the most important factor is where the taxpayer spends most of his or her time.[29] A residence does not have to be a house. For example, a houseboat, a house trailer, or a motor home can qualify.[30] The principal residence includes the land on which a home sits (so any gain on the land also qualifies for exclusion). An adjacent lot can qualify if it is regularly used by the owner as part of the residential property.

Example 27

Mitch graduates from college and moves to Boston, where he is employed. He decides to rent an apartment in Boston because of its proximity to his office. He purchases a beach condo in the Cape Cod area that he occupies most weekends. Mitch does not intend to live at the beach condo except on weekends. The apartment in Boston is his principal residence.

15-4b Requirements for Exclusion Treatment

To qualify for exclusion treatment, at the date of the sale, the residence must have been *owned* and *used* by the taxpayer as the principal residence for at least two years during the five-year period ending on the date of the sale.[31]

Example 28

Melissa sells her principal residence on September 18, 2022. She had purchased it on July 5, 2020, and lived in it since then. The sale of Melissa's residence qualifies for the § 121 exclusion.

The ownership and use requirements are *two separate tests*. Although in most situations ownership and use overlap (as in Example 28), there is no requirement that they do so for purposes of § 121. Further, the law does not require that the two-year periods be continuous.[32]

Ownership and Use Tests

Example 29

Kayla purchased a home in San Diego in May 2007 and lived in it until she took a new job in Los Angeles on January 1, 2018. From January 2018 until she sold the house on July 31, 2022, she only used the home occasionally since she lived in an apartment near her job in downtown Los Angeles. Because the house was sold on July 31, 2022, the five-year window runs from August 1, 2017, to the date of sale.

In determining whether the § 121 exclusion is available, Kayla meets the ownership test because she owned the house for two of the five years prior to its sale. However, she fails the use test. During the five-year window, she used the house as her principal residence for only five months (from August 1, 2017, to December 31, 2017).

---

[29] Other factors include the address listed on a driver's license and/or voter registration card, the location of the taxpayer's employer, and the mailing address used for bills and correspondence. Regulation § 1.121–1(b)(2) includes the complete list of factors to be considered.

[30] Reg. § 1.121–1(b)(1); Reg. § 1.1034–1(c)(3)(i).

[31] § 121(a). Code § 121(d)(10) provides that exclusion treatment does not apply if the residence was acquired in a like-kind exchange within the prior five years of the sale of the residence.

[32] According to Reg. § 1.121–1(c)(1), taxpayers must document 730 days (365 × 2) of ownership and use during the five-year period that ends on the sale date.

Ownership and Use Tests

Example 30

Charles lives in a townhouse that he rents from 2015 through January 17, 2019. On January 18, 2019, he purchases the townhouse. On February 1, 2020, due to a decline in health, Charles moves into his daughter's home. On May 25, 2022, while still living in his daughter's home, Charles sells his townhouse.

The § 121 exclusion applies because Charles *owned* the townhouse for at least two years out of the five years preceding the sale (from January 19, 2019, until May 25, 2022)[33] and he *used* the townhouse as his principal residence for at least two years during the five-year period preceding the sale [from May 25, 2017 (the beginning of the five-year window) until February 1, 2020].

Example 31

Aaron has owned and used his house as his principal residence since 2005. On January 31, 2019, Aaron moves to another state. Aaron rents his house to tenants from that date until April 18, 2021, when he sells it.

Aaron is eligible for the § 121 exclusion because he has owned and used the house as his principal residence for at least two of the five years preceding the sale.

The five-year window enables the taxpayer to qualify for the § 121 exclusion even though the property is not his or her principal residence at the date of the sale. In applying the use test, short absences (i.e., vacation or other seasonal absence) are counted as periods of use. In addition, any short-term rental of the property is ignored.[34]

Example 32

Benjamin sells his former principal residence on August 16, 2022. He had purchased it on April 1, 2014, and lived in it until July 1, 2021, when he converted it to rental property.

Even though the property is rental property on August 16, 2022, rather than Benjamin's principal residence, the sale qualifies for the § 121 exclusion.[35] During the five-year period from August 16, 2017, to August 16, 2022, Benjamin owned and used the property as his principal residence for at least two years.

In addition to the ownership and use requirements, § 121 can be used by a taxpayer only once every two years.[36] This rule restricts taxpayers who might be tempted to make liberal use of the § 121 exclusion as a means of speculating when the price of residential housing is rising. Without any time restriction on its use, § 121 would permit the exclusion of realized gain on multiple sales of principal residences.

Example 33

Miguel sells his principal residence (the first residence) in June 2021 for $150,000 (realized gain of $60,000). He then buys and sells the following (all of which qualify as principal residences).

	Date of Purchase	Date of Sale	Purchase/Sales Price
Second residence	July 2021		$160,000
Second residence		April 2022	180,000
Third residence	May 2022		200,000

Because multiple sales have taken place within a period of two years, § 121 does not apply to the sale of the second residence. As a result, Miguel's realized gain of $20,000 [$180,000 (selling price) − $160,000 (purchase price)] must be recognized.

[33]As discussed in text Section 16-4a, the holding period begins the day after acquisition date and includes the disposition date.

[34]Reg. § 1.121–1(c)(2)(i).

[35]However, any realized gain on the sale that is attributable to depreciation is not eligible for the § 121 exclusion. See Example 40.

[36]§ 21(b)(3) denies the application of the § 121 exclusion to sales occurring within two years of its last use.

15-4c Calculating the Exclusion

General Rule

The § 121 exclusion available on the sale of a principal residence is $250,000.[37] If the realized gain does not exceed $250,000, there is no recognized gain.

Realized gain is calculated in the normal manner. The *amount realized* is the selling price less any selling expenses (e.g., real estate broker commissions, advertising expenses, and legal fees). Repairs and maintenance costs to aid in selling the property are personal expenses and not deductible (and they do not increase the home's basis).

The Big Picture

Example 34

Return to the facts of *The Big Picture* on p. 15-1. Recall that one of Alice's options is to sell her current house and move into the inherited house. Assume that Alice sells her current personal residence (adjusted basis of $130,000) for $348,000. She has owned and lived in the house for 15 years. Her selling expenses are $18,000. Three weeks prior to the sale, Alice pays a carpenter and a painter $1,000 to make some repairs and paint two rooms. If Alice is single, her recognized gain is $0.

Amount realized ($348,000 − $18,000)	$ 330,000
Adjusted basis	(130,000)
Realized gain	$ 200,000
§ 121 exclusion	(200,000)
Recognized gain	$ -0-

Since the available § 121 exclusion of $250,000 exceeds Alice's realized gain of $200,000, her recognized gain is $0.

The Big Picture

Example 35

Continue with *The Big Picture* and the facts of Example 34, but the selling price is $490,000. Since the realized gain of $342,000 exceeds the § 121 exclusion amount of $250,000, Alice's recognized gain is $92,000.

Amount realized ($490,000 − $18,000)	$ 472,000
Adjusted basis	(130,000)
Realized gain	$ 342,000
§ 121 exclusion	(250,000)
Recognized gain	$ 92,000

Married Couples

If a married couple files a joint return, the $250,000 amount is increased to $500,000 if the following requirements are met.[38]

- Either spouse meets the at-least-two-years *ownership* requirement.
- Both spouses meet the at-least-two-years *use* requirement.
- Neither spouse sold a principal residence within the prior two years and used the § 121 exclusion.

[37] § 121(b)(1).

[38] § 121(b)(2).

Example 36

Margaret sells her personal residence (adjusted basis of $150,000) for $650,000. She has owned and lived in the residence for six years. Her selling expenses are $40,000. Margaret is married to Ted, and they file a joint return. Ted has lived in the residence since they were married two and one-half years ago.

Amount realized ($650,000 − $40,000)	$ 610,000
Adjusted basis	(150,000)
Realized gain	$ 460,000
§ 121 exclusion	(460,000)
Recognized gain	$ -0-

Because the realized gain of $460,000 is less than the available § 121 exclusion amount of $500,000, no gain is recognized.

A surviving spouse can use the $500,000 exclusion amount on the sale of a personal residence for the two years following the deceased spouse's death. If the sale occurs in the year of death, a joint return must be filed by the surviving spouse.

15-4d Exceptions to the Two-Year Rules

The two-year ownership and use requirements and the "only once every two years" rule could create a hardship for taxpayers in certain situations that are beyond their control. As a result, under the following special circumstances, the requirements are waived.[39]

- Change in place of employment,
- Health issues, or
- Other unforeseen circumstances.

Treasury Department guidance on these three exceptions is discussed in the sections that follow.[40] Each of these exceptions provides a *partial* exclusion. The calculation of the partial exclusion is discussed after each of the exceptions is reviewed.

Change in Place of Employment

For this exception to apply, the taxpayer measures the distance (in miles) between (1) the taxpayer's *old residence* and *old job location* and (2) the taxpayer's *old residence* and *new job location*. The exception applies if (2) exceeds (1) by at least 50 miles. The location of the new residence does not matter for this purpose.

In addition, the house being sold must be used as the principal residence of the taxpayer when the employment change happens. The exception applies whether the taxpayer takes a job with a new employer; is transferred by the current employer; or, if self-employed, moves the proprietorship to a new location.

Example 37

Assume the same facts as in Example 33, except that in March 2022, Miguel's employer transfers him to a job in another state that is 400 miles away.

As a result, the sale of the second residence and the purchase of the third residence were due to relocation of employment. Consequently, the § 121 exclusion is partially available on the sale of the second residence.

Health Issues

The health exception uses either a general facts and circumstances approach or a safe harbor established in the Regulations. If a physician recommends a change of location due to health issues (or to obtain specialized care), the safe harbor is met. A sale that is merely beneficial to the general health or well-being of the individual will not qualify.

[39] § 121(c)(2)(B).

[40] See Reg. § 1.121–3 and IRS Publication 523 (*Selling Your Home*) for further details and illustrations.

Unforeseen Circumstances

In these cases, the primary reason for the sale or exchange of the residence must be an event the taxpayer did not anticipate before purchasing and occupying the residence. The Regulations allow a safe harbor approval in any of the following instances. If none of the listed opportunities applies, the taxpayer can claim that the general facts and circumstances justify the exception.

- Involuntary conversion of the residence;
- Natural or human-made disasters or acts of war or terrorism resulting in a casualty to the residence;
- Death of a qualified individual;
- Cessation of employment, resulting in eligibility for unemployment compensation;
- Change in employment or self-employment that results in the taxpayer being unable to pay housing costs and reasonable basic living expenses for the taxpayer's household;
- Divorce or legal separation; or
- Multiple births resulting from the same pregnancy.

Example 38

Maria and Raji are engaged and buy a house (sharing the mortgage payments), living in it as their personal residence. Eighteen months after the purchase, they cancel their wedding plans, and Raji moves out of the house. Because Maria cannot afford to make the payments alone, they sell the house.

Although the sale does not fit under the safe harbor events, the broken engagement is an unforeseen event; it qualifies using the "facts and circumstances" approach.[41]

Partial § 121 Exclusion

When one of the exceptions applies, a partial § 121 exclusion is allowed. The exclusion amount ($250,000 or $500,000) is multiplied by a fraction, the numerator of which is the number of qualifying months and the denominator of which is 24 months. The resulting amount is the excluded gain.[42]

Example 39

On October 1, 2021, Rich and Audrey, who file a joint return and live in Chicago, sell their personal residence, which they have owned and lived in for eight years. The realized gain of $325,000 is excluded under § 121. They purchase another personal residence for $525,000 on October 2, 2021. Audrey's employer transfers her to the Denver office in August 2022. Rich and Audrey sell their Chicago residence on August 2, 2022, and they purchase a residence in Denver shortly thereafter. The realized gain on the sale is $300,000.

The $325,000 gain on the first Chicago residence is excluded under § 121. The sale of the second Chicago residence is within the two-year window of the prior sale, but because it resulted from a change in employment, Rich and Audrey can qualify for partial exclusion treatment.

Realized gain	$ 300,000
§ 121 exclusion:	
$\frac{10 \text{ months}}{24 \text{ months}} \times \$500,000$	(208,333)
Recognized gain	$ 91,667

[41] Reg. § 1.121–3(e)(4), Example (6).

[42] § 121(c)(1).

Basis of New Residence

Because § 121 is an exclusion provision (rather than a deferral of gain provision), the basis of a new residence is its cost.[43]

Implications of Renting or Using as a Home Office

The residence does not have to be the taxpayer's principal residence at the date of sale to qualify for the § 121 exclusion. During part of the five-year period, it could have been rental property (e.g., as a vacation home), or the taxpayer might have used part of the principal residence as a qualifying home office.

In either of these circumstances, the taxpayer may have claimed deductions for the expenses attributable to the rental or business use. What effect, if any, do such deductions have on a later sale of the residence? Will the sales proceeds still qualify for nonrecognition of gain treatment under § 121?

As long as the various § 121 requirements are met, an income exclusion will be available. However, if the taxpayer deducted depreciation, any realized gain is recognized to the extent of the depreciation deductions.[44]

Example 40

On December 5, 2022, Amanda sells her principal residence, which qualifies for the § 121 exclusion. Her realized gain is $190,000. From January through November 2021, she was temporarily out of town on a job assignment in another city and rented the residence to a college student. For this period, she deducted MACRS cost recovery of $7,000.

Without the depreciation provision, Amanda could exclude the $190,000 realized gain. However, the depreciation taken requires her to recognize $7,000 of the realized gain.

LO.5

Apply various tax planning opportunities related to the nonrecognition provisions discussed in the chapter.

15-5 Tax Planning

15-5a Like-Kind Exchanges

Because the like-kind exchange provisions are mandatory rather than elective, in certain instances, it may be preferable to avoid qualifying for § 1031 nonrecognition. For example, immediate recognition of gain (which also will result in a higher basis for the newly acquired asset) may be preferable if the taxpayer has unused capital loss carryovers. If so, the taxpayer can structure the transaction so that at least one of the § 1031 like-kind exchange requirements is failed.

Example 41

Alicia sells land and a building (used in her business) with an adjusted basis of $300,000 for $400,000. She also acquires a new building and land for $900,000. Alicia has a $125,000 capital loss carryover.

If § 1031 applies, the $100,000 realized gain is not recognized and the basis of the new land and building is reduced by $100,000 (from $900,000 to $800,000). Assuming no other capial asset transactions, Alicia can deduct only $3,000 of her capital loss carryover.

If § 1031 does not apply, a $100,000 gain is recognized and can be used to offset her $125,000 capital loss carryover. In addition, the basis of the new land and building is $900,000 rather than $800,000 because the entire gain was recognized (allowing for a larger depreciation deduction on the new building).

The like-kind exchange rules also should be avoided when a realized loss exists (adjusted basis exceeds the fair market value).

[43] § 1012.

[44] § 121(d)(6).

Example 42

Assume the same facts as in the previous example, except that the fair market value of the land and building is $250,000. If § 1031 applies, the $50,000 realized loss is not recognized.

To recognize the loss, Alicia should sell the old land and building and purchase the new one. The purchase and sale transactions should be with different taxpayers.

Tax planning for exchanges must consider the present value of tax deferrals and the possibility of future changes in tax rates. Taxpayers may prefer to pay no more than 20 percent today (the maximum tax rate on long-term capital gains) if they believe that tax rates will go up in the future. Although turning down a tax deferral may sound like a strange strategy, it fits the notion of "pay a tax today to avoid a higher tax tomorrow."

15-5b Involuntary Conversions

In certain cases, a taxpayer may prefer to recognize gain from an involuntary conversion. This is a possibility because involuntary conversion treatment generally is an elective provision.

Example 43

Ahmad has a $40,000 realized gain from the involuntary conversion of an office building. He reinvests the entire proceeds of $450,000 in a new office building. He does not elect to postpone gain under § 1033, however, because a net operating loss carryforward offsets the gain.

Because Ahmad did not elect gain postponement, his basis in the replacement property is the property's cost of $450,000 rather than $410,000 ($450,000 reduced by the $40,000 realized gain).

15-5c Sale of a Principal Residence

Waiving the Exclusion

The § 121 exclusion automatically applies if the taxpayer is eligible (i.e., the taxpayer need not make an election). However, a taxpayer can waive the § 121 exclusion.[45]

Example 44

George owns two personal residences that satisfy the two-year ownership and use test with respect to the five-year window. The Elm Street residence has appreciated by $25,000, and the Maple Street residence has appreciated by $230,000. He intends to sell both of them and move into a rental property. He sells the Elm Street residence in December 2022 and expects to sell the Maple Street residence early next year.

Unless George elects not to apply the § 121 exclusion to the sale of the Elm Street residence, he will exclude the $25,000 realized gain on that residence in 2022. In 2023, however, he recognizes a gain of $230,000 on the sale of the Maple Street residence.

If George elects to waive the exclusion on the Elm Street residence sale, he will report a recognized gain of $25,000 on this sale in 2022. But by using the § 121 exclusion in 2023, he will eliminate the recognized gain of $230,000 on the sale of the Maple Street residence.

Qualification for § 121 Exclusion

The key requirement for the § 121 exclusion is that the taxpayer must have *owned* and *used* the property as a principal residence for at least two years during the five-year window. As taxpayers advance in age, they frequently make decisions related to their personal residence(s).

[45] § 121(f).

- Sell the principal residence and buy a smaller residence or rent a principal residence.
- Sell vacation homes they own.
- Sell homes they are holding as rental property.

These properties may have experienced substantial appreciation while owned by the taxpayers. Proper planning can make it possible for multiple properties to qualify for the exclusion. Although this strategy may require taxpayers to be flexible about where they live, it can result in substantial tax savings.

Example 45

Eleanor and David, residents of Virginia, are approaching retirement. They have substantial appreciation on their principal residence (in Richmond) and on a house they own in Virginia Beach (about two hours away). After retirement, they plan to move to Florida. They have owned and lived in the principal residence for 28 years and have owned the beach house for 9 years.

If they sell their principal residence, it qualifies for the § 121 exclusion. At retirement, they could move into their beach house for two years and make it eligible for the exclusion before they relocate to Florida.

If the beach house were close enough to things they needed to do in Richmond currently (e.g., charitable work), they could sell the principal residence now and move into the beach house to start the running of the two-year use period. As noted above, any realized gain on the beach house attributable to depreciation is not eligible for the § 121 exclusion. In addition, a reduction in the § 121 exclusion for prior use as a vacation home is required.[46]

Refocus on The Big Picture

Alternative Uses of Property

IAIN MASTERTON/ALAMY STOCK PHOTO

Alice needs to be aware of the different tax consequences of her proposals and whether there are any limits to these consequences.

- *Sale of the inherited house.* This is by far the simplest transaction for Alice. Based on the facts, her recognized gain would be:

Amount realized ($800,000 − $40,000*)	$ 760,000
Adjusted basis	(475,000)
Recognized gain	$ 285,000

* $800,000 × 5% sales commission.

Because the sale of the house is not eligible for the § 121 exclusion, the entire gain would be included in Alice's taxable income. Given her marginal Federal income tax rate, the capital gain would be taxed at 15 percent, so her tax liability would be $42,750 ($285,000 × 15%). As a result, Alice's net cash flow increase is $717,250 ($760,000 − $42,750).

- *Conversion into a vacation home with only personal use.* With this alternative, the only tax benefit Alice would receive is the deduction for property taxes as an itemized deduction (subject to the $10,000 limit on state and local taxes). She would continue to incur upkeep costs (e.g., repairs, utilities, and insurance). At the end of the two-year period, the sale will result in a taxable gain (the sale of the house would not be eligible for the § 121 exclusion).

continued

[46] Additional information and examples can be found in IRS Publication 523 (*Selling Your Home*).

- *Conversion into a vacation home with partial personal use and partial rental use.* In this case, Alice would be able to deduct 40 percent of costs such as property taxes, the agent's management fee, depreciation, maintenance and repairs, utilities, and insurance. However, this amount cannot exceed the rent income generated. The remaining 60 percent of the property taxes can be claimed as an itemized deduction (subject to the $10,000 limit on state and local taxes).

  At the end of the two-year period, the sale would result in a taxable gain. In determining recognized gain, adjusted basis must be reduced by the amount of the depreciation claimed. The sale of the house would not be eligible for the § 121 exclusion.
- *Current sale of present home with sale of inherited home in two years.* The present sale of her current principal residence and the future sale of her inherited residence would enable Alice to qualify for the § 121 exclusion on each sale (see Example 34). She would satisfy the two-year ownership requirement, the two-year use requirement, and the availability of the exclusion only once every two years.

Alice must be careful to occupy the inherited residence for at least two years. If Alice is married, the occupancy requirements (the *use* test) apply to her spouse as well. Further, the period between the sales of the first and second houses must be greater than two years.

With this information, Alice can make an informed choice. In all likelihood, she probably will select the strategy of selling her current house now and the inherited house in the future. A noneconomic benefit of this option is that she will have to sell only one house at the time of her retirement.

Key Terms

Boot, 15-6

Involuntary conversion, 15-12

Like-kind exchange, 15-3

Nontaxable exchange, 15-3

Personal residence, 15-16

Section 121 exclusion, 15-16

Discussion Questions

1. **LO.1** In most nontaxable exchanges, is the nonrecognition of the realized gain or loss temporary or permanent? Explain.
2. **LO.1** Distinguish between a loss that is not recognized on a nontaxable exchange and a loss that is not recognized on the sale or exchange of a personal use asset.
3. **LO.2** Which of the following qualify as like-kind exchanges under § 1031?
   a. Improved for unimproved real estate.
   b. Rental house for personal residence.
   c. Business land for rental house (held for investment).
   d. Warehouse for office building (both used for business).
   e. Truck for computer (both used in business).
   f. Rental house for land (both held for investment).
   g. Office furniture for office equipment (both used in business).
   h. Unimproved land in Jackson, Mississippi, for unimproved land in Toledo, Spain.
   i. General partnership interest for a general partnership interest.

Critical Thinking

4. **LO.2** Melissa owns a residential lot in Spring Creek, Louisiana, that has appreciated substantially in value. She holds the lot for investment. She is considering exchanging the lot for a residential lot located in Paris, France, that she also will hold for investment. Identify the relevant tax issues for Melissa.

Critical Thinking

5. **LO.2** Ross would like to dispose of some land he acquired five years ago because he believes it will not continue to appreciate. Its value has increased by $50,000 over the five-year period. He also intends to sell stock that has declined in value by $50,000 during the eight-month period he has owned it.

   Ross has four offers to acquire the stock and land. Identify the tax issues relevant to Ross in disposing of this land and stock.

Buyer 1:	Exchange land.
Buyer 2:	Purchase land for cash.
Buyer 3:	Exchange stock.
Buyer 4:	Purchase stock for cash.

6. **LO.2** Edith exchanges a building and land used in her business for land and stock of Teal, Inc. If Edith had sold her land and building, she would have had a realized gain. Explain why the new land will have a different holding period than the stock.

7. **LO.2** Mortgaged real estate may be received in a like-kind exchange. If the taxpayer's mortgage is assumed, what effect does the mortgage have on the recognition of realized gain? On the basis of the real estate received?

8. **LO.3** Sheila's appreciated property is involuntarily converted. She receives insurance proceeds equal to the fair market value of the property. What is the minimum amount Sheila must reinvest in qualifying property to defer recognition of realized gain?

9. **LO.3** Vera owns an office building that she leases to tenants. If the building is destroyed by a tornado, is the *functional use test* or the *taxpayer use test* applied as to replacement property? Explain the differences between the two tests.

10. **LO.3** Reba, a calendar year taxpayer, owns an office building that she uses in her business. The building is involuntarily converted on November 15, 2022. On January 5, 2023, Reba receives enough proceeds to produce a realized gain. What is the latest date she can replace the building and qualify for § 1033 postponement treatment if the conversion event is:

    a. A flood?

    b. A condemnation?

    c. A tornado?

11. **LO.3** Bob is notified by the city public housing authority on May 3, 2022, that his apartment building is going to be condemned as part of a commercial development project. On June 1, 2022, Stella offers to buy the building from Bob. Bob sells the building to Stella on June 30, 2022. Condemnation occurs on September 1, 2022, and Stella receives the condemnation proceeds from the city. Both Bob and Stella are calendar year taxpayers.

    a. What is the earliest date on which Bob can dispose of the building and qualify for involuntary conversion treatment?

    b. Does the sale to Stella qualify as an involuntary conversion? Why or why not?

    c. What is the latest date on which Stella can acquire qualifying replacement property and qualify for postponement of the realized gain?

    d. What type of property will be qualifying replacement property?

12. LO.3 A warehouse owned by Martha and used in her business (i.e., to store inventory) is being condemned by the city to provide a right-of-way for a highway. The warehouse has appreciated by $180,000 based on Martha's estimate of its fair market value. In the negotiations, the city is offering $35,000 less than what Martha believes the property is worth. Critical Thinking

Alan, a real estate broker, has offered to purchase Martha's property for $20,000 more than the city's offer. Martha plans to invest the proceeds she will receive in an office building she will lease to various tenants.

a. Identify the relevant tax issues for Martha.

b. Would the answer in part (a) change if Martha's warehouse was property being held for investment rather than being used in her business? Explain.

13. LO.4 To qualify for exclusion treatment on the sale of a principal residence, the residence must have been owned and used by the taxpayer for at least two years during the five-year period ending on the date of the sale. Are there any exceptions to this provision? Explain.

Computational Exercises

14. LO.2, 5 Vijay owns land (adjusted basis of $40,000) that he uses in his business. He exchanges the land and $20,000 in cash for a different parcel of land worth $50,000. May Vijay avoid like-kind exchange treatment to recognize his realized loss of $10,000? Explain.

15. LO.2 In June 2022, Sue exchanges a sport-utility vehicle (adjusted basis of $16,000; fair market value of $19,500) for cash of $2,000 and a pickup truck (fair market value of $17,500). Both vehicles are held for business use. Sue believes that her basis for the truck is $17,500. Is Sue correct? Why or why not? As part of your response, compute Sue's realized gain or loss (and any recognized gain or loss) on the exchange.

16. LO.2 Logan and Jonathan exchange land, and the exchange qualifies as like kind under § 1031. Because Logan's land (adjusted basis of $85,000) is worth $100,000 and Jonathan's land has a fair market value of $80,000, Jonathan also gives Logan cash of $20,000.

a. What is Logan's recognized gain?

b. Assume instead that Jonathan's land is worth $90,000 and he gives Logan $10,000 cash. Now what is Logan's recognized gain?

17. LO.2 Mandy and Theo exchange real property in a like-kind exchange. Mandy receives real property with a fair market value of $78,000 and transfers real property worth $70,000 (adjusted basis of $28,000) and cash of $8,000. What is Mandy's realized and recognized gain?

18. LO.3 On June 5, 2022, Brown, Inc., a calendar year taxpayer, receives cash of $750,000 from the county upon condemnation of its warehouse building (adjusted basis of $500,000 and fair market value of $750,000).

a. What must Brown do to qualify for § 1033 postponement of gain treatment?

b. How would your advice to Brown differ if the adjusted basis was $795,000?

19. LO.3 Camilo's property, with an adjusted basis of $155,000, is condemned by the state. Camilo receives property with a fair market value of $180,000 as compensation for the property taken.

a. What is Camilo's realized and recognized gain?

b. What is the basis of the replacement property?

20. **LO.3** On February 24, 2022, Allison's building, with an adjusted basis of $1,300,000 (and used in her trade or business), is destroyed by fire. On March 31, 2022, she receives an insurance reimbursement of $1,650,000 for the loss. Allison invests $1,550,000 in a new building and buys stock with the balance of insurance proceeds. Allison is a calendar year taxpayer.
    a. By what date must Allison make the new investment to qualify for the nonrecognition election?
    b. Assuming that the replacement property qualifies as similar or related in service or use, what are Allison's realized gain, recognized gain, and basis in the replacement building?

21. **LO.4, 5** Gary, who is single, sells his principal residence (owned and occupied by him for seven years) in November 2022 for a realized gain of $148,000. He had purchased a more expensive new residence eight months prior to the sale. He anticipates that he will occupy this new house as his principal residence for only about 18 additional months. He expects it to appreciate substantially while he owns it.

    Gary would like to recognize the realized gain on the 2022 sale to offset a large investment loss from the sale of stock. Can he recognize the realized gain of $148,000 on the sale of his principal residence in 2022? Explain.

22. **LO.4** Omar, who is single, sold his principal residence on April 10, 2022, and excluded the realized gain under § 121 (exclusion on the sale of a principal residence). On April 12, 2022, he purchased another principal residence, which he sells on January 12, 2023, for a realized gain of $80,000. Can Omar exclude the $80,000 realized gain on the January 2023 sale if his reason for selling was:
    a. His noisy neighbors? Explain.
    b. A job transfer to another city? Explain.

23. **LO.4** Constanza, who is single, sells her current personal residence (adjusted basis of $165,000) for $450,000. She has owned and lived in the house for 30 years. Her selling expenses are $22,500. What is Constanza's realized and recognized gain?

24. **LO.4** On August 31, 2021, Nolan and Lei, who file a joint return and live in Charleston, South Carolina, sell their personal residence, which they have owned and lived in for 10 years. The realized gain of $292,000 was excluded under § 121. They purchased another personal residence in Charleston for $480,000 on September 1, 2021.

    In 2022, Nolan's employer transfers him to Houston, Texas. The couple sells the Charleston home on February 28, 2022, and purchases a new home in Houston. The realized gain on the second sale is $180,000. What is Nolan and Lei's recognized gain on the second sale?

Problems

25. **LO.2** Katrina owns undeveloped land with an adjusted basis of $300,000. She exchanges it for undeveloped land worth $750,000.
    a. What are Katrina's realized and recognized gain or loss?
    b. What is Katrina's basis in the undeveloped land she receives?
    c. Would the answers in parts (a) and (b) change if Katrina exchanged the undeveloped land for land and a building? Explain.

Communications
Critical Thinking

26. **LO.2** Daniela Fletcher owns undeveloped land (adjusted basis of $80,000 and fair market value of $92,000) on the East Coast. On January 4, 2022, she exchanges it with Lisa Martin (an unrelated party) for undeveloped land on the West

Coast and $3,000 cash. Lisa has an adjusted basis of $72,000 for her land, and its fair market value is $89,000. Because the real estate market on the East Coast is thriving, on September 1, 2023, Lisa sells the land she acquired for $120,000.

a. What are Daniela's recognized gain or loss and adjusted basis for the West Coast land on January 4, 2022?

b. What are Lisa's recognized gain or loss and adjusted basis for the East Coast land on January 4, 2022?

c. What is Lisa's recognized gain or loss from the September 1, 2023 sale?

d. What effect does Lisa's 2023 sale have on Daniela?

e. Write a letter to Daniela advising her of the Federal income tax consequences of this exchange. Her address is The Corral, El Paso, TX 79968.

27. **LO.2** Katie exchanges a building and land (used in her business) for Tyler's land and building and some equipment (used in his business).

	Adjusted Basis	Fair Market Value
Katie's real property	$120,000	$300,000
Tyler's real property	60,000	220,000
Equipment	50,000	80,000

a. What are Katie's recognized gain or loss and basis for the land and building and equipment acquired from Tyler?

b. What are Tyler's recognized gain or loss and basis for the land and building acquired from Katie?

28. **LO.2, 5** In two unrelated transactions, Laura exchanges property that qualifies for like-kind exchange treatment. In the first exchange, Laura gives up land purchased in May 2020 (adjusted basis of $20,000; fair market value of $17,000) in exchange for a different parcel of land (fair market value of $15,000) and $2,000 cash. Critical Thinking Planning

In the second exchange, Laura receives a parking garage (to be used in her business) with a fair market value of $50,000 in exchange for a plot of land she had held for investment. The land was purchased in April 2014 for $12,000 and has a current fair market value of $48,000. In addition to transferring the land, Laura pays an additional $2,000 to the other party.

a. What is Laura's adjusted basis for the new parcel of land?

b. When does the holding period begin for the land?

c. What is Laura's adjusted basis for the parking garage?

d. When does the holding period begin for the garage?

e. How could Laura structure either of the transactions differently to produce better tax consequences?

29. **LO.2** Suni owns land (adjusted basis of $90,000; fair market value of $125,000) that she uses in her business. She exchanges it for another parcel of land (worth $100,000) and stock (worth $25,000). Determine Suni's:

a. Realized and recognized gain or loss on the exchange.

b. Basis in the new land.

c. Basis in the stock she received.

30. **LO.2** Ed owns investment land with an adjusted basis of $35,000. Polly has offered to purchase the land from Ed for $175,000 for use in a real estate development. The amount offered by Polly is $10,000 in excess of what Ed perceives as the fair market value of the land. Ed would like to transfer the land to Polly but does not want to incur the tax liability that would result. He identifies an office building

with a fair market value of $175,000 that he would like to acquire. Polly purchases the office building and then exchanges the office building for Ed's land.

a. Calculate Ed's realized and recognized gain on the exchange and his basis for the office building.

b. Calculate Polly's realized and recognized gain on the exchange and her basis in the land.

31. **LO.2** What is the basis of the received property in each of the following exchanges?

a. Apartment building held for investment (adjusted basis of $145,000) for office building to be held for investment (fair market value of $225,000).

b. Land and building used as a barbershop (adjusted basis of $190,000) for land and building used as a grocery store (fair market value of $350,000).

c. Office building (adjusted basis of $45,000) for bulldozer (fair market value of $42,000), both held for business use.

d. IBM common stock (adjusted basis of $20,000) for ExxonMobil common stock (fair market value of $28,000).

e. Rental house (adjusted basis of $90,000) for mountain cabin to be held for rental use (fair market value of $225,000).

f. General partnership interest (adjusted basis of $400,000) for a limited partnership interest (fair market value of $580,000).

32. **LO.2, 5** Steve owns real estate (adjusted basis of $12,000 and fair market value of $15,000), which he uses in his business. Steve sells the real estate for $15,000 to Aubry (a dealer) and then purchases a new parcel of land for $15,000 from Joan (also a dealer). The new parcel of land would normally qualify as like-kind property.

a. What are Steve's realized and recognized gain on the sale of the land he sold to Aubry?

b. What is Steve's basis for the land he purchased from Joan?

c. What factors would motivate Steve to sell his land to Aubry and purchase the land from Joan rather than exchange one parcel of land for the other?

d. Assume that the adjusted basis of Steve's original parcel of land is $15,000 and the fair market value of both parcels of land is $12,000. Respond to parts (a) through (c).

Communications
Critical Thinking
Planning

33. **LO.2, 5** Tom Howard and Frank Pérez are good friends (and former college roommates). Each owns investment property in the other's hometown (Tom lives in Kalamazoo, MI; Frank lives in Austin, TX). To make their lives easier, they decide to exchange the investment properties. Under the terms of the exchange, Frank will transfer realty (20 acres of unimproved land; adjusted basis of $52,000; fair market value of $80,000) and Tom will exchange realty (25 acres of unimproved land; adjusted basis of $60,000; fair market value of $92,000). Tom's property is subject to a mortgage of $12,000 that will be assumed by Frank.

a. What are Frank's and Tom's recognized gains?

b. What are their adjusted bases?

c. As an alternative, Frank has proposed that, rather than assuming the mortgage, he will transfer cash of $12,000 to Tom. Tom would use the cash to pay off the mortgage. In an e-mail, advise Tom on whether this alternative would be beneficial to him from a tax perspective.

d. Assuming that Tom and Frank proceed with the original exchange [rather than the alternative in part (c)], complete Form 8824 (Parts I and III) for Tom. Assume that the exchange occurs on September 16, 2021 (Tom acquired his 25-acre parcel on February 15, 2013). Tom's Social Security number is 123-45-6789.

Communications
Critical Thinking

34. **LO.2** Determine the realized, recognized, and postponed gain or loss and the new basis for each of the following like-kind exchanges.

	Adjusted Basis of Old Asset	Cash Boot Given	Fair Market Value of New Asset	Boot Received
a.	$ 7,000	$ -0-	$12,000	$4,000
b.	14,000	2,000	15,000	-0-
c.	3,000	7,000	8,000	500
d.	15,000	-0-	29,000	-0-
e.	10,000	-0-	11,000	1,000
f.	17,000	-0-	14,000	-0-

g. Create a Microsoft Excel spreadsheet that—by entering the fair market value and basis of property given up and the fair market value of property received—will compute (1) realized gain or loss, (2) boot received, (3) boot given, (4) gain (loss) recognized, (5) gain (loss) deferred, and (6) the basis of like-kind property received. In separate tabs, the spreadsheet should apply the "simplified method" and the "alternative method." Ignore the implications of debt and depreciation.

Test your spreadsheet using the data in this problem (and Problem 31). E-mail your spreadsheet to your instructor along with a brief summary of how you built the spreadsheet.

35. **LO.3** Quentin's roadside vegetable stand (adjusted basis of $275,000) is destroyed by a tractor-trailer accident. He receives insurance proceeds of $240,000. Quentin immediately uses the proceeds plus additional cash of $45,000 to build another roadside vegetable stand at the same location. What are the Federal income tax consequences?

36. **LO.3** Albert owns 100 acres of land on which he grows spruce trees. His adjusted basis for the land is $100,000. He receives condemnation proceeds of $10,000 when the city's new beltway takes 5 acres along the eastern boundary of his property. He also receives a severance award of $6,000 associated with the possible harmful effects of exhaust fumes on his trees. Albert invests the $16,000 in a growth mutual fund. Determine the tax consequences to Albert of the:

a. Condemnation proceeds.

b. Severance award.

37. **LO.3** For each of the following involuntary conversions, indicate whether the property acquired qualifies as replacement property, any resulting recognized gain, and the basis for the property acquired.

a. Krystal owns a warehouse that is destroyed by a tornado. The space in the warehouse was rented to various tenants. The adjusted basis was $470,000. Krystal uses all of the insurance proceeds of $700,000 to build a shopping mall in a neighboring community where no property has been damaged by tornadoes. The shopping mall is rented to various tenants.

b. Javier owns a warehouse that he uses in his business. The adjusted basis is $300,000. The warehouse is destroyed by fire. Because of economic conditions in the area, Javier decides not to rebuild the warehouse. Instead, he uses all of the insurance proceeds of $400,000 to build a warehouse to be used in his business in another state.

c. Bailey's personal residence is condemned as part of a local government project to widen the highway from two lanes to four lanes. The adjusted basis is $170,000. Bailey uses all of the condemnation proceeds of $200,000 to purchase another personal residence.

d. Juanita owns a building that she uses in her retail business. The adjusted basis is $250,000. The building is destroyed by a hurricane. Because of an economic downturn in the area caused by the closing of a military base, Juanita decides to rent space for her retail outlet rather than replace the building. She uses all of the insurance proceeds of $300,000 to buy a four-unit apartment building in another city. A real estate agent in that city will handle the rental of the apartments for her.

e. Susan and Rick's personal residence is destroyed by a tornado. They had owned it for 15 months. The adjusted basis was $170,000. Because they would like to travel, they decide not to acquire a replacement residence. Instead, they invest all of the insurance proceeds of $200,000 in a duplex, which they rent to tenants.

f. Alec and Meghann's personal residence (adjusted basis of $245,000) is destroyed in a flood. They had owned it for 18 months. Of the insurance proceeds of $350,000, they reinvest $342,000 in a replacement residence four months later.

38. **LO.3** Mitchell, a calendar year taxpayer, is the sole proprietor of a fast-food restaurant. His adjusted basis for the building and the related land is $450,000. On March 12, 2022, state authorities notify Mitchell that his property is going to be condemned so that the highway can be widened. On June 20, Mitchell's property is officially condemned, and he receives an award of $625,000. Because Mitchell's business was successful in the past, he would like to reopen the restaurant in a new location.

a. What is the earliest date Mitchell can acquire a new restaurant and qualify for gain postponement?

b. On June 30, Mitchell purchases land and a building for $610,000. Assuming that he elects the maximum postponement amount, what is his recognized gain?

c. What is Mitchell's adjusted basis for the new land and building?

d. If he does not elect § 1033, what are Mitchell's recognized gain and adjusted basis?

e. Suppose he invests the $625,000 condemnation proceeds in the stock market on June 30. What is Mitchell's recognized gain?

39. **LO.3** Emily's warehouse (adjusted basis of $450,000) is destroyed by a hurricane in October 2022. Emily, a calendar year taxpayer, receives insurance proceeds of $525,000 in January 2023. Calculate Emily's realized gain or loss, recognized gain or loss, and basis for the replacement property if she:

a. Acquires a new warehouse for $550,000 in January 2023.

b. Acquires a new warehouse for $500,000 in January 2023.

c. Does not acquire replacement property.

Critical Thinking
Planning

40. **LO.3, 5** Cabel's warehouse, which has an adjusted basis of $380,000 and a fair market value of $490,000, is condemned by an agency of the Federal government to make way for a highway interchange. The initial condemnation offer is $425,000. After substantial negotiations, the agency agrees to transfer to Cabel a surplus warehouse that is worth $490,000. Cabel is a calendar year taxpayer. The condemnation and related asset transfer occur during September 2022.

a. What are the recognized gain or loss and the basis of the replacement warehouse if Cabel's objective is to recognize as much gain as possible?

b. Advise Cabel regarding what he needs to do by what date to achieve his objective.

41. **LO.3** What are the *maximum* postponed gain or loss and the basis for the replacement property for the following involuntary conversions?

	Property	Type of Conversion	Amount Realized	Adjusted Basis	Amount Reinvested
a.	Drugstore (business)	Casualty	$160,000	$130,000	$110,000
b.	Apartments (investment)	Condemned	100,000	125,000	175,000
c.	Grocery store (business)	Casualty	400,000	300,000	450,000
d.	Residence (personal)	Casualty*	16,000	18,000	17,000
e.	Vacant lot (investment)	Condemned	240,000	160,000	220,000
f.	Residence (personal)	Casualty*	20,000	18,000	19,000
g.	Residence (personal)	Condemned	18,000	20,000	26,000
h.	Apartments (investment)	Condemned	150,000	100,000	200,000

* Casualty occurred in a Federally declared disaster area.

42. **LO.3, 5** Wanda, a calendar year taxpayer, owned a building (adjusted basis of $250,000) in which she operated a bakery that was destroyed by fire in December 2022. She receives insurance proceeds of $290,000 for the building the following March. Wanda is considering two options regarding the investment of the insurance proceeds. First, she could purchase a local building (suitable for a bakery) that is for sale for $275,000. Second, she could buy a new home for $290,000 and go back to college and finish her degree. Decision Making Planning

a. To minimize her tax liability, which of these alternatives should Wanda choose?

b. What is the latest date on which Wanda can replace the involuntarily converted property to qualify for § 1033?

c. What is the latest date on which Wanda can replace the involuntarily converted property to qualify for § 1033 if the involuntary conversion is a condemnation?

43. **LO.4, 5** Karl purchased his residence on January 2, 2021, for $260,000, after having lived in it during 2020 as a tenant under a lease with an option to buy clause. On August 1, 2022, Karl sells the residence for $315,000. On June 13, 2022, Karl purchases a new residence for $367,000. Critical Thinking Planning

a. What is Karl's recognized gain? His basis for the new residence?

b. Assume instead that Karl purchased his original residence on January 2, 2020 (rather than January 2, 2021). What is Karl's recognized gain? His basis for the new residence?

c. In part (a), what could Karl do to minimize his recognized gain?

44. **LO.4** Taylor has owned and occupied her personal residence (adjusted basis of $190,000) for four years. In April 2022, she sells the residence for $300,000 (selling expenses are $20,000). On the same day as the sale, Taylor purchases another house for $350,000. Because of noisy neighbors, she sells the new house after just 10 months. The selling price is $483,000 (selling expenses are $18,000).

a. What is Taylor's recognized gain on the sale of the first residence?

b. What is Taylor's basis for her second residence?

c. What is Taylor's recognized gain on the sale of the second residence?

d. Assume instead that the sale of the second residence was due to Taylor's job transfer to another state. What is her recognized gain on the sale of the second residence?

45. **LO.4** Wesley, who is single, listed his personal residence with a real estate agent on March 3, 2022, at a price of $390,000. He rejected several offers in the $350,000 range during the summer. Finally, on August 16, 2022, he and the purchaser signed a contract to sell for $363,000. The sale (i.e., closing) took place on September 7, 2022. The closing statement showed the following disbursements.

Real estate agent's commission	$ 21,780
Appraisal fee	600
Exterminator's certificate	300
Recording fees	800
Mortgage to First Bank	305,000
Cash to seller	34,520

Wesley's adjusted basis for the house is $200,000. He owned and occupied the house for seven years. On October 1, 2022, Wesley purchases another residence for $325,000.

a. Calculate Wesley's recognized gain on the sale.

b. What is Wesley's adjusted basis for the new residence?

c. Assume instead that the selling price is $800,000. What is Wesley's recognized gain? His adjusted basis for the new residence?

46. **LO.4** Pedro, age 57, is the sole owner of his principal residence, which he has owned and occupied for 10 years. Maria, his spouse, has lived there with Pedro for the full 10 years. He sells the house for a realized gain of $340,000.

a. Can Pedro use the § 121 exclusion if he and Maria file a joint return? If so, what are the available amount of the exclusion and the recognized gain?

b. Can Pedro use the § 121 exclusion if he files a separate return? If so, what are the available amount of the exclusion and the recognized gain?

c. Assume instead that the realized gain is $550,000 and a joint return is filed.

d. Assume instead that the realized gain is $550,000 and separate returns are filed.

e. Assume instead that Maria and Pedro have been married for only 18 months and that she has lived in his house only since their marriage. They file a joint return.

Communications

47. **LO.4** Nell, Nina, and Nora Potter, who are sisters, sell their principal residence (owned as tenants in common) in which they have lived for the past 25 years. The youngest of the sisters is age 60. The selling price is $960,000, selling expenses and legal fees are $63,000, and the adjusted basis is $120,000 (the fair market value of the residence when inherited from their parents 25 years ago; they made no capital improvements during the time they held the residence). The sisters plan to move into rental housing and not acquire another residence. Nell has contacted you on behalf of the Potters regarding the tax consequences of the sale.

a. Write a letter to Nell advising her of the tax consequences and how taxes can be minimized. Nell's address is 100 Oak Avenue, Billings, MT 59101.

b. Prepare a memo for the tax files discussing your approach to the situation.

Critical Thinking

48. **LO.4, 5** Ramesh owns a beach house (four years) and a cabin in the mountains (six years). His adjusted basis is $300,000 in the beach house and $315,000 in the mountain cabin. Ramesh also rents a townhouse in the city where he is employed. During the year, he occupies each of the three residences as follows.

Townhouse	135 days
Beach house	155 days
Mountain cabin	75 days

The beach house is close enough to the city that he can commute to work during the spring and summer. Although this level of occupancy may vary slightly from year to year, it is representative during the time period that Ramesh has owned the two residences.

Because Ramesh plans to retire in several years, he sells both the beach house and the mountain cabin. The mountain cabin is sold on March 3, 2022, for $540,000 (related selling expenses of $35,000). The beach house is sold on December 10, 2022, for $700,000 (related selling expenses of $42,000).

a. Calculate Ramesh's least allowable recognized gain on the sale of the two residences.

b. Assume instead that both residences satisfy the two-year ownership and use tests as Ramesh's principal residence. Because the mountain cabin is sold first, can Ramesh apply the § 121 exclusion to the sale of the beach house? Explain.

49. **LO. 3, 4, 5** Cisco, a calendar year taxpayer who is age 63, owns a residence in which he has lived for 21 years. The residence is destroyed by fire on August 8, 2022. The adjusted basis is $190,000, and the fair market value is $320,000. Cisco receives insurance proceeds of $320,000 for the residence on September 1, 2022. He is deciding whether to purchase a comparable house. He anticipates that he will retire in two years and will move to a warmer climate, where he will rent a home. Critical Thinking

a. Advise Cisco of the tax consequences of replacing versus not replacing the residence.

b. Which do you recommend to him?

c. How would your answer in part (a) change if the fair market value and insurance proceeds received were $510,000?

50. **LO.4, 5** Missy, age 30, has owned her principal residence (adjusted basis of $225,000) for five years. During the first three years of ownership, she occupied it as her principal residence. During the past two years, she was in graduate school and rented the residence. After graduate school, Missy returned to the same location where she previously worked. At this point, she purchased another residence for $400,000 and listed her old residence for sale at $340,000. Due to a slow real estate market, 11 months later Missy finally receives an offer of $330,000. Critical Thinking Planning

a. What is Missy's recognized gain if she immediately accepts the $330,000 offer (i.e., 11 months after the listing date)? Selling expenses are $20,000.

b. What is Missy's recognized gain if she rejects the $330,000 offer and accepts another offer of $340,000 three months later (i.e., 14 months after the listing date)? Selling expenses are $20,000.

c. Advise Missy on which offer she should accept. She is in the 24% Federal income tax bracket.

Tax Return Problems

51. Devon Bishop, age 45, is single. He lives at 1507 Rose Lane, Albuquerque, NM 87131. His Social Security number is 111-11-1117. Devon did not engage in any virtual currency transactions during the year, and he does not want $3 to go to the Presidential Election Campaign Fund. Devon received the appropriate coronavirus recovery rebates (economic impact payments); related questions in ProConnect Tax should be ignored. Tax Forms Problem **ProConnect™ Tax**

Devon's wife, Ariane, passed away in 2017. Devon's son, Tom, who is age 18, resides with Devon. Tom's Social Security number is 123-45-6788.

Devon owns a sole proprietorship for which he uses the accrual method of accounting and maintains no inventory; the business operates as Devon's Copy Shop, 422 E. Main Street, Albuquerque, NM 87131, IRS business activity code: 453990. His revenues and expenses for 2021 are as follows.

Sales revenue	$740,000
Cost of goods sold (based on purchases for the year)	405,000
Salary expense	88,000
Rent expense	30,000
Utilities	8,000
Telephone	6,500
Advertising	4,000
Bad debts	5,000
Depreciation*	21,000
Health insurance**	26,000
Accounting and legal fees	7,000
Supplies	1,000

* New office equipment ($21,000); Devon uses the immediate expense election.

** $18,000 for employees and $8,000 for Devon.

Other income received by Devon includes the following.

Dividend income (qualified dividends):	
Swan, Inc.	$10,000
Wren, Inc.	2,000
Interest income:	
First National Bank	11,000
Second City Bank	2,500
County of Santa Fe, NM bonds	17,000

During the year, Devon and his sole proprietorship were involved in the following property transactions. Stock transactions were reported to Devon on Form 1099–B; basis was not reported to the IRS.

a. Sold Blue, Inc. stock for $45,000 on March 12, 2021. He had purchased the stock on September 5, 2018, for $50,000.

b. Received an inheritance of $300,000 from his uncle, Henry. Devon used $200,000 to purchase Green, Inc. stock on May 15, 2021, and invested $100,000 in Gold, Inc. stock on May 30, 2021.

c. Received Orange, Inc. stock worth $9,500 as a gift from his aunt, Jane, on June 17, 2021. Her adjusted basis for the stock was $5,000. No Federal gift taxes were paid on the transfer. Jane had purchased the stock on April 1, 2015. Devon sold the stock on July 1, 2021, for $22,000.

d. On July 15, 2021, Devon sold one-half of the Green, Inc. stock for $40,000.

e. Devon was notified on August 1, 2021, that Yellow, Inc. stock he purchased from a colleague on September 1, 2020, for $52,500 had become worthless. Although he understood that investing in Yellow was risky, Devon did not anticipate that the corporation would declare bankruptcy.

f. On August 15, 2021, Devon received a parcel of land in Phoenix worth $220,000 in exchange for a parcel of land he owned in Tucson. Because the Tucson parcel was worth $245,000, he also received $25,000 cash. Devon's adjusted basis for the Tucson parcel was $210,000. He originally purchased it on September 18, 2018.

g. On December 1, 2021, Devon sold the condominium in which he had been living for the past 20 years (1844 Lighthouse Lane, Albuquerque, NM 87131) and moved into a rented townhouse. The sales price was $480,000, selling expenses were $28,500, and repair expenses related to the sale were $9,400. Devon purchased the condominium for $180,000.

Devon's potential itemized deductions, exclusive of the aforementioned information, are as follows.

Medical expenses (before the 7.5%-of-AGI floor)	$ 9,500
Property taxes on residence	5,800
State income taxes	4,000
Charitable contributions	10,000
Mortgage interest on residence (First National Bank)	9,900
Sales taxes paid	5,000

During the year, Devon makes estimated Federal income tax payments of $35,000.

Compute Devon's Federal income tax payable or refund due for 2021 (assuming that he makes any available elections that will reduce the tax), and complete his tax return using appropriate forms and schedules. Suggested software: ProConnect Tax.

52. Tom and Alice Honeycutt, ages 45 and 46, respectively, live at 101 Glass Road, Delton, MI 49046. Tom is a county employee, and Alice is a self-employed accountant. Tom's Social Security number is 111-11-1111; Alice's Social Security number is 123-45-6789. The income and expenses associated with Alice's accounting practice for 2022 are as follows.

Communications
Critical Thinking
Planning
Tax Computation Problem

Revenues (cash receipts during 2022)		$185,000
Expenses		
Salaries	$ 45,000	
Office supplies	3,200	
Postage	2,900	
Depreciation of equipment	42,000	
Telephone	800	
	$ 93,900	

Because Alice is a cash method taxpayer, she does not record her receivables as revenue until she receives cash payment. At the beginning of 2022, her accounts receivable were $48,000, and the balance had decreased to $8,000 by the end of the year.

Alice used one room in their 10-room house as the office for her accounting practice (400 square feet out of a total square footage of 4,000). They paid the following expenses related to the house during 2022.

Utilities	$4,500
Insurance	2,100
Property taxes	5,200
Repairs	3,500

Tom and Alice purchased the house on September 1, 2021, for $400,000 (exclusive of land cost).

Tom received a salary of $52,000 during 2022. The appropriate amounts of Social Security tax and Medicare tax were withheld. In addition, $4,000 of Federal income taxes and $2,000 of state income taxes were withheld.

Tom and Alice's allowable itemized deductions during 2022, excluding any itemized deductions related to the house, were $22,600. They made estimated Federal income tax payments of $20,000.

Part 1—Tax Computation
Compute Tom and Alice's Federal income tax payable or refund due for 2022.

Part 2—Tax Planning
Tom and Alice own 30 acres of prime farmland that they inherited from Tom's father several years ago. At that time, the fair market value of the land was $150,000 (which became their basis in the land). The Honeycutts have been holding the land as an investment. The property recently was appraised for $190,000, and there is an outstanding mortgage on the land of $28,000. They are considering trading this land for property in the mountains of southern Colorado. The Colorado property owner—who has significant land holdings in the area—has provided two options to Tom and Alice (in both cases, the Colorado property owner would assume the mortgage as part of the exchange).

1. 15 acres of property with a fair market value of $135,000 plus $27,000 of cash, or
2. 10 acres of property with a fair market value of $160,000 plus $2,000 of cash

The Honeycutts have come to you for advice, believing either transaction to be a like-kind exchange that will allow them to defer any gain. Assume that Tom and Alice expect their 2023 taxable income to be about the same as in 2022 (with any net capital gain taxed at a 15% rate). Write a letter to Tom and Alice that contains your advice on the proposed transactions.

Research Problems

the answer company™ THOMSON REUTERS®

Note: Solutions to the Research Problems can be prepared by using the Thomson Reuters Checkpoint™ online tax research database, which accompanies this textbook. Solutions can also be prepared by using research materials found in a typical tax library.

Communications

Research Problem 1. Charlene and Alton Dutro had lived in their home for two and one-half years when they decided to enlarge and remodel the house. However, their architect advised them that more stringent building and permit restrictions had been imposed since the house was built 10 years earlier. So the Dutros decided to demolish the house and rebuild on the same site. Rather than occupying the new house, however, the Dutros sold it for a realized gain in excess of $500,000.

In calculating the recognized gain on their Federal income tax return, the Dutros reduced the realized gain of more than $500,000 by the $500,000 exclusion of § 121. The IRS has issued an income tax deficiency notice on the grounds that the Dutros did not satisfy the two-out-of-five-years requirement of § 121(a).

Who is correct? Explain in an e-mail to your tax manager.

Partial list of research aids:
§ 121(a)(1).
David A. Gates, 135 T.C. 1 (2010).

Critical Thinking

Research Problem 2. Randall owns an office building (adjusted basis of $250,000) that he has been renting to a group of physicians. During negotiations over a new seven-year lease, the physicians offer to purchase the building for $900,000. Randall accepts the offer with the stipulation that the sale be structured as a delayed § 1031 transaction. Consequently, the sales proceeds are paid to a qualified third-party intermediary on the closing date of September 30, 2022.

On October 2, 2022, Randall properly identifies an office building that he would like to acquire. Unfortunately, on November 10, 2022, the property Randall selected is withdrawn from the market. Working with the intermediary, on November 12, 2022, Randall identifies another office building that meets his requirements. The purchase of this property closes on December 15, 2022, and the title is transferred to Randall.

Randall treats the transaction as a like-kind exchange. Even though the original office building identified was not acquired, Randall concludes that in substance, he has satisfied the 45-day rule. He identified the acquired office building as soon as the negotiations ceased on his first choice. Should the IRS accept Randall's attempt to comply? Explain.

Communications

Research Problem 3. Yanling owns a 150-unit motel that was constructed in the late 1960s. It is located on 10 acres on the main highway leading into the city. Yanling renovated the motel three years ago.

Yanling's motel is condemned by the city, which is going to use 2 of the 10 acres for a small park. Yanling will sell the other 8 acres to a time-share developer who intends to build 400 units on the property. The developer already has secured approval from the city planning commission.

Yanling's attorney advises her not to contest the condemnation of the 2 acres for the park. Under the eminent domain provision, the city does have the right to take "private property for public use." However, the attorney advises Yanling to contest the condemnation of the remaining property. According to the attorney, the city does not have the right to take "private property for private use."

The city's position is that the condemnation will result in a substantial number of new jobs and additional tax revenue for the city.

Will Yanling be successful if she follows her attorney's advice? Summarize your findings in a two- to three-paragraph e-mail to your instructor.

Use internet tax resources to address the following questions. Look for reliable web-sites and blogs of the IRS and other government agencies, media outlets, businesses, tax professionals, academics, think tanks, and political outlets.

Research Problem 4. Locate the most recent data available from the IRS on Form 8824 filings (**irs.gov/statistics**). In a Microsoft Excel spreadsheet, use this information to provide a summary of these transactions through time [e.g., the number of like-kind exchanges that have been reported (in total and by entity type), the total amount of property being exchanged (i.e., the fair market value of property received), and the proportion of realized gains recognized]. Communications Critical Thinking Data Analytics

Present your findings in one or more visuals, and submit these to your instructor along with a one-page written summary of your findings.

Research Problem 5. Find two stories online about transactions to which you believe the involuntary conversion rules could apply. Do not limit your search to individual taxpayers. In an e-mail to your instructor, describe the transactions and explain whether the §1033 election is available. Communications

Research Problem 6. In general, the 45-day identification period and the 180-day exchange period for like-kind exchanges cannot be extended. Does this rule change if the like-kind property or the taxpayer involved in the exchange is located in a Federally declared disaster area? If so, to what extent? Use the IRS's website (**irs.gov**) to find the answer.

Becker CPA Review Questions

Becker

1. Susie purchased her primary residence on March 15, year 4, for $550,000. She sold it on October 15, year 7, for $240,000. What amount of loss from the sale is recognized on her year 7 income tax return?

   a. $0
   b. $60,000
   c. $250,000
   d. $310,000

2. Chad owned an office building that was destroyed in a tornado. The area was declared a Federal disaster area. The adjusted basis of the building at the time was $890,000. After the deductible, Chad received an insurance check for $850,000. He used the $850,000 to purchase a new building that same year. How much is Chad's recognized loss, and what is his basis in the new building?

	Recognized Loss	New Basis
a.	$0	$850,000
b.	$0	$890,000
c.	$40,000	$850,000
d.	$40,000	$890,000

3. Chad owned an office building that was destroyed in a tornado. The adjusted basis of the building at the time was $890,000. After the deductible, Chad received an insurance check for $950,000. He used $900,000 of the insurance proceeds to purchase a new building that same year. How much is Chad's recognized gain, and what is his basis in the new building?

	Recognized Gain	New Basis
a.	$0	$890,000
b.	$0	$900,000
c.	$50,000	$890,000
d.	$60,000	$900,000

4. Marsha exchanged land used in her business in Florida with an FMV of $72,700 and an adjusted basis of $40,000 for land used in her business in Iowa with an FMV of $57,700. Marsha also assumed a $5,000 liability on the land received in the transaction and was relieved of a $20,000 liability on the land that was given up. What is Marsha's recognized gain on the transaction?

   a. $0
   b. $15,000
   c. $20,000
   d. $32,700

5. Marsha exchanged land held for investment in Florida with an FMV of $52,700 and an adjusted basis of $60,000 for land held for investment in Iowa with an FMV of $57,700. Marsha also paid $5,000 cash in the transaction. What is Marsha's basis in the land received?

   a. $55,000
   b. $57,700
   c. $60,000
   d. $65,000

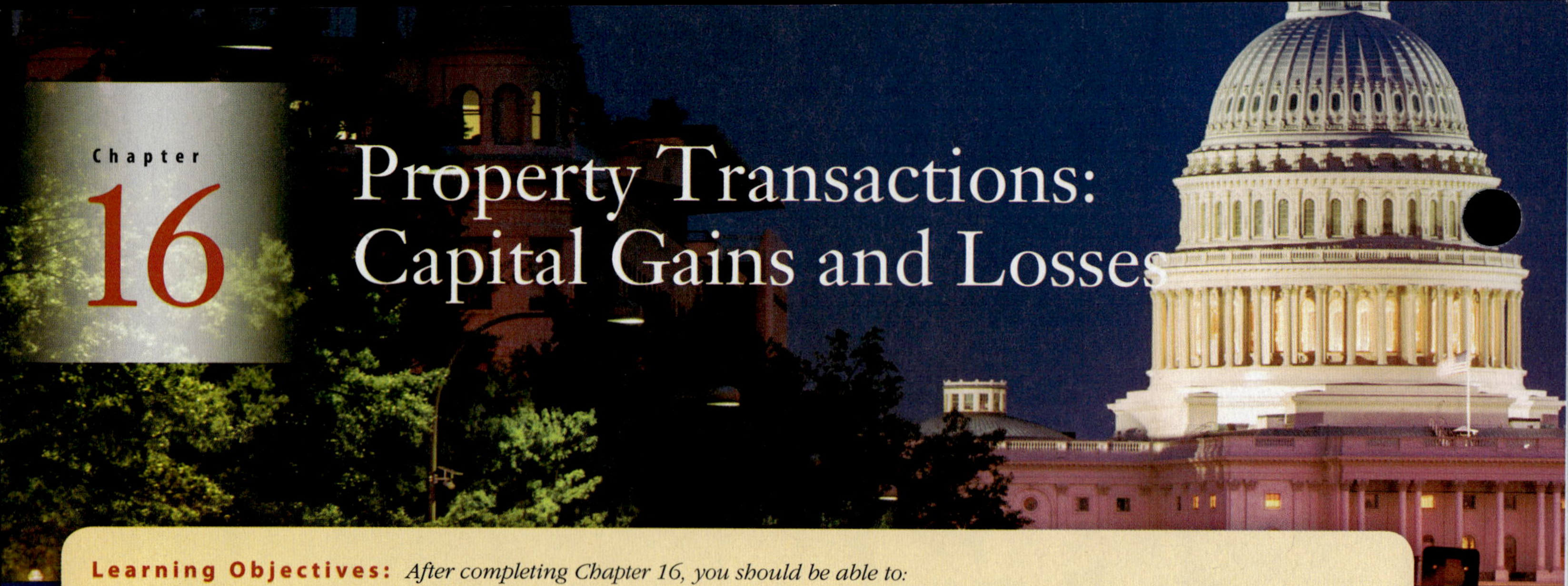

Chapter 16

Property Transactions: Capital Gains and Losses

Learning Objectives: *After completing Chapter 16, you should be able to:*

LO.1 Explain the general scheme of taxation for capital gains and losses.

LO.2 Distinguish capital assets from ordinary assets.

LO.3 Explain the relevance of a sale or exchange to classification as a capital gain or loss and apply the special rules for the capital gain or loss treatment of the retirement of corporate obligations, options, patents, franchises, and lease cancellation payments.

LO.4 Determine whether the holding period for a capital asset is long term or short term.

LO.5 Describe the beneficial tax treatment for capital gains and the detrimental tax treatment for capital losses for noncorporate taxpayers.

LO.6 Describe the tax treatment for capital gains and the detrimental tax treatment for capital losses for corporate taxpayers.

LO.7 Identify tax planning opportunities arising from the sale or exchange of capital assets.

Chapter Outline

16-1 General Scheme of Taxation, 16-3

16-2 Capital Assets, 16-3
- 16-2a Definition of a Capital Asset (§ 1221), 16-4
- 16-2b Effect of Judicial Action, 16-6
- 16-2c Statutory Expansions, 16-7

16-3 Sale or Exchange, 16-8
- 16-3a Worthless Securities and § 1244 Stock, 16-8
- 16-3b Retirement of Corporate Obligations, 16-9
- 16-3c Options, 16-9
- 16-3d Patents, 16-11
- 16-3e Franchises, Trademarks, and Trade Names (§ 1253), 16-12
- 16-3f Lease Cancellation Payments, 16-14

16-4 Holding Period, 16-15
- 16-4a General Rules, 16-15
- 16-4b Special Holding Period Rules, 16-15
- 16-4c Special Rules for Short Sales, 16-16

16-5 Tax Treatment of Capital Gains and Losses of Noncorporate Taxpayers, 16-19
- 16-5a Capital Gain and Loss Netting Process, 16-19
- 16-5b Qualified Dividend Income, 16-23
- 16-5c Alternative Tax on Net Capital Gain and Qualified Dividend Income, 16-24
- 16-5d Treatment of Net Capital Losses, 16-27
- 16-5e Reporting Procedures, 16-28

16-6 Tax Treatment of Capital Gains and Losses of Corporate Taxpayers, 16-29

16-7 Tax Planning, 16-35
- 16-7a Importance of Capital Asset Status, 16-35
- 16-7b Planning for Capital Asset Status, 16-35
- 16-7c Effect of Capital Asset Status in Transactions Other Than Sales, 16-36
- 16-7d Stock Sales, 16-37
- 16-7e Maximizing Benefits, 16-37
- 16-7f Year-End Planning, 16-37

AUREMAR/SHUTTERSTOCK.COM

The Big Picture

Managing Capital Asset Transactions

Maurice has come to you for tax advice regarding his investments. He inherited $500,000 from his uncle, Joe. A financial adviser suggested that he make the following investments, which he did nine months ago.

- $5,000 for 100 shares of Eagle Company stock.
- $50,000 for a 50 percent interest in a patent that Kevin, a college roommate who is an unemployed inventor, obtained for a special battery he developed to power green cars. To date, Kevin has been unable to market the battery to an auto manufacturer or supplier, but he has high hopes of doing so in the future.
- $95,000 to invest in a franchise from Orange, Inc.
- $200,000 in the stock of Purple, Inc., a publicly held bank that follows a policy of occasionally paying dividends. At one time, the stock appreciated to $300,000, but now it is worth only $210,000. Maurice is considering selling this stock.
- $50,000 in tax-exempt bonds. The interest rate on the bonds is only 3 percent. Maurice is considering moving this money into taxable bonds that pay 3.5 percent.
- $100,000 for a 10 percent ownership interest as a limited partner in a real estate development. Lots in the development are selling well.

Maurice read an article that discussed the beneficial tax rates for capital assets and dividends. He really liked the part about "costless" capital gains, although he did not understand it.

Maurice has retained his job as a toll booth supervisor at the municipal airport. His annual compensation is $35,000. He likes the job and has met some interesting people there.

Respond to Maurice's request for tax advice.

Read the chapter and formulate your response.

Framework 1040 Tax Formula for Individuals

This chapter covers the boldfaced portions of the Tax Formula for Individuals that was introduced in Concept Summary 3.1 on p. 3-3. Below those portions are the sections of Form 1040 where the results are reported.

Income *(broadly defined)*	$ xx,xxx
Less: Exclusions	(x,xxx)
Gross income	**$ xx,xxx**
Less: Deductions *for* adjusted gross income	**(x,xxx)**

FORM 1040 (p. 1)

7 Capital gain or (loss). Attach Schedule D if required. If not required, check here ▶ ☐

FORM 1040 (Schedule 1)

3 Business income or (loss). Attach Schedule C . . . .

4 Other gains or (losses). Attach Form 4797 . . . .

Adjusted gross income	$ xx,xxx
Less: The greater of total itemized deductions *or* the standard deduction	(x,xxx)
Charitable contributions if you take the standard deduction*	(xxx)
Personal and dependency exemptions**	(x,xxx)
Deduction for qualified business income***	(x,xxx)
Taxable income	$ xx,xxx
Tax on taxable income *(see Tax Tables or Tax Rate Schedules)*	$ x,xxx

FORM 1040 (p. 2)

16 **Tax** (see instructions). Check if any from Form(s): **1** ☐ 8814 **2** ☐ 4972 **3** ☐ ______

Less: Tax credits *(including income taxes withheld and prepaid)*	(xxx)
Tax due (or refund)	$ xxx

* For 2021, married taxpayers may claim up to $600 of cash charitable donations ($300 if unmarried).

** Exemption deductions are not allowed from 2018 through 2025.

*** Only applies from 2018 through 2025.

Fourteen years ago, a taxpayer purchased 100 shares of IBM stock for $17 a share. This year, the taxpayer sells the shares for $125 a share. Should the $108 per-share gain receive any special tax treatment? The $108 gain has built up over 14 years, so it may not be fair to tax it the same as income that was all earned this year.

What if the stock had been purchased for $125 per share and sold for $17 a share? Should the $108 loss be fully deductible? The tax law has an intricate approach to answering these investment activity-related questions.

Property transactions involve the *disposition* of *assets*. The sale of the IBM stock was the disposition of an investment-related asset. As you study this chapter, keep in mind that how investment-related gains and losses are taxed can dramatically affect whether taxpayers make investments and which investments are made. Except for a brief discussion in Chapter 3, earlier chapters dwelt on how to determine the amount of gain or loss from a property disposition, but did not discuss the classification of gains and losses. This chapter will focus on that topic.

The tax law requires **capital gains** and **capital losses** to be separated from other types of gains and losses. There are two reasons for this treatment. First, long-term capital gains may be taxed at a lower rate than ordinary gains. Second, a net capital loss is subject to deduction limitations. For noncorporate taxpayers, a net capital loss is only deductible up to $3,000 per year. Any excess loss over the annual limit carries over and may be deductible in a future tax year.

For these reasons, capital gains and losses must be distinguished from other types of gains and losses. This chapter and the next chapter describe:

- The intricate rules needed to determine what *type* of gains and losses the taxpayer has,

- How those gains and losses are intermingled among themselves,
- How the result of that intermingling then is integrated with the other items on the taxpayer's tax return, and
- How those gains and losses are taxed as part of the taxpayer's taxable income.

As a result of the need to distinguish and separately match capital gains and losses, the individual tax forms include very extensive reporting requirements for capital gains and losses. This chapter explains the rules underlying the forms and illustrates them with an example at the end of the chapter.

16-1 General Scheme of Taxation

LO.1

Explain the general scheme of taxation for capital gains and losses.

Recognized gains and losses must be *classified* properly. Proper classification depends on three characteristics:

- The tax *status* of the property (capital, § 1231, or ordinary).
- The manner of the property's *disposition* (sale, exchange, casualty, theft, or condemnation).
- The *holding period* of the property (*short-term*: one year or less; *long-term*: more than one year).

The major focus of this chapter is capital gains and losses. Chapter 17 discusses § 1231 assets. Both chapters discuss ordinary gains and losses.

16-2 Capital Assets

LO.2

Distinguish capital assets from ordinary assets.

Personal use assets and investment assets are the most common capital assets owned by individual taxpayers. Personal use assets usually include things like a residence, furniture, clothing, recreational equipment, and automobiles. Investment assets usually include stocks, bonds, and mutual funds. Remember, however, that losses from the sale or exchange of personal use assets are not recognized.

The crux of capital asset determination hinges on whether the asset is held for personal use (capital asset), investment (capital asset), or business (ordinary asset). How a taxpayer uses the property typically answers this question.

Example 1

David buys an expensive painting.

- If David purchased the painting for personal use (as a decoration in his home) and it is not of investment quality, it is a capital asset; however, any loss on its sale is not usable, whereas gain from its sale is taxable. Investment quality generally means that the painting is expected to appreciate in value.
- If the painting is used to decorate David's business office and is of investment quality, the painting is not depreciable and, therefore, is a capital asset.
- If David's business is buying and selling paintings, the painting is inventory and, therefore, an ordinary asset.
- If the painting is not of investment quality and the business did not purchase it for investment, the painting is an ordinary asset and it is depreciable even though it serves a decorative purpose in David's office. If David depreciates the painting, that is evidence that the painting is held for use in his business (and not being held for investment or as inventory). As a result, it is not a capital asset.

Since capital assets receive preferential tax treatment, taxpayers prefer capital gains rather than ordinary gains. So the definition of a capital asset is critically important. As discussed next, this definition has been the subject of many court cases and rulings.

16-2a Definition of a Capital Asset (§ 1221)

Capital assets are not directly defined in the Code. Instead, § 1221(a) defines what is *not* a capital asset. In general, a **capital asset** is property *other than* inventory, accounts and notes receivable, supplies, and most fixed assets of a business.

Specifically, the Code defines a capital asset as property held by the taxpayer (when it is connected with the taxpayer's business) that is *not* any of the following:

- Inventory or property held primarily for sale to customers in the ordinary course of a business.
- Accounts and notes receivable generated from the sale of goods or services in a business.
- Depreciable property or real estate used in a business.
- A patent, an invention, a model, or a design (whether or not patented); a secret formula or process; certain copyrights; literary, musical, or artistic compositions; or letters, memoranda, or similar property created by or for the taxpayer.
- Certain U.S. government publications.
- Supplies used in a business.

Often, the only business asset that is a capital asset is "self-generated" goodwill (purchased goodwill is a § 1231 asset). The following discussion provides further detail on each part of the capital asset definition.

Inventory

What constitutes inventory is determined by the taxpayer's business.

Inventory Determination

Example 2

Green Company buys and sells used cars. Its cars are inventory. Its gains from the sale of the cars are ordinary income.

Example 3

Soong sells her personal use automobile at a $500 gain. The automobile is a personal use asset and, therefore, a capital asset. The gain is a capital gain.

No asset is inherently capital or ordinary. If Soong (Example 3) sells her "capital asset" automobile to Green Company (Example 2), that same automobile loses its capital asset status, because the automobile is inventory to Green Company. Whether an asset is capital or ordinary, therefore, depends entirely on the relationship of the asset to the taxpayer who sold it. This classification dilemma is but one feature of capital asset treatment that makes this area so confusing and complicated.

Accounts and Notes Receivable

Accounts and notes receivable are often created as part of a business transaction. These assets may be collected by the creditor, be sold by the creditor, or become completely or partially worthless. Also, the creditor may be on the accrual or cash basis of accounting.

Collection of an *accrual basis* account or note receivable does not result in a gain or loss because the amount collected equals the receivable's basis. If sold, an ordinary gain or loss is generated if the receivable is sold for more or less than its basis (the receivable is an ordinary asset). If the receivable is partially or wholly worthless, the creditor has a "bad debt," which may result in an ordinary deduction (see text Section 7-1).

Collection of a *cash basis* account or note receivable does not result in a gain or loss because the amount collected is ordinary income. In addition, a cash basis receivable has a zero basis since no revenue is recorded until the receivable is collected. If sold, an ordinary gain is generated (the receivable is an ordinary asset). There is no bad debt deduction for cash basis receivables because they have no basis. See text Section 16-3 for more details on "sale or exchange."

Example 4

Oriole Company has accounts receivable of $100,000. Because Oriole needs working capital, it sells the receivables for $83,000 to a financial institution.

If Oriole is an *accrual basis taxpayer*, it has a $17,000 ordinary loss. Revenue of $100,000 would have been recorded, and a $100,000 basis would have been established when the receivable was created.

If Oriole is a *cash basis taxpayer*, it has $83,000 of ordinary income because it would not have recorded any revenue earlier; as a result, the receivable has no tax basis.

Business Fixed Assets

Depreciable personal property and real estate (both depreciable and nondepreciable) used by a business are *not* capital assets. The tax law related to this property is very complex; most of these rules are discussed in Chapter 17. Although business fixed assets are not capital assets, a long-term capital gain can sometimes result from their sale. Chapter 17 discusses the potential capital gain treatment for business fixed assets under § 1231. Another rule—real property subdivided for sale (§ 1237)—is discussed in text Section 16-2c.

Inventions and Processes

A patent, an invention, a model, or a design (whether or not patented) and a secret formula or process are excluded from being a capital asset. These are *ordinary* assets. The assets may be held either by the taxpayer who created the property or by a taxpayer who received the asset from the taxpayer who created the property. As a result, gains or losses from the sale or exchange of these assets do *not* receive capital gain treatment. In limited circumstances, patents (even though they are *not* capital assets) may be *treated* as capital assets. Those special rules are discussed in text Section 16-3d.

Example 5

Abigail invents a multifunctional case for a popular brand of cell phones. She has a manufacturer produce them for her and sells them via the internet. Her cost is $2.30 per case, and she sells each one for $10. To her surprise, she quickly achieves $45,000 in total sales. She has not capitalized any of the costs of developing the invention and has not patented it.

She sells all of her rights to the invention for $350,000 to a company that is in the business of producing cell phone cases. Her profit from sales of the cases is ordinary income because the cases are inventory. The $350,000 gain from selling the rights to the invention is an ordinary gain because the invention is not a capital asset.

Copyrights and Creative Works

Generally, the person whose efforts led to the copyright or creative work has an ordinary asset, not a capital asset. *Creative works* include the works of authors, composers, and artists. Also, the person for whom a letter, a memorandum, or another similar property was created has an ordinary asset. Finally, a person receiving a copyright, creative work, a letter, a memorandum, or similar property by gift from the creator or the person for whom the work was created has an ordinary asset. A taxpayer may elect to treat the sale or exchange of a musical composition or a copyright of a musical work as the disposition of a capital asset.

Creative Works

Example 6

Wanda is a part-time music composer. A music publisher purchases one of her songs for $5,000.

Wanda has a $5,000 ordinary gain from the sale of an ordinary asset unless she elects to treat the gain as a capital gain.

Example 7

Ed received a letter from the President of the United States in 1982. In the current year, Ed sells the letter to a collector for $300.

Ed has a $300 ordinary gain from the sale of an ordinary asset (because the letter was created for Ed).

Example 8

Isabella gives her son a song she composed. The son sells the song to a music publisher for $5,000.

The son has a $5,000 ordinary gain from the sale of an ordinary asset unless he elects to treat the gain as a capital gain.

If the son inherits the song from Isabella, his basis for the song is its fair market value at Isabella's death. In this situation, the song is a capital asset because the son's basis is not related to Isabella's basis for the song.

Ethics & Equity **Sculpture as a Capital Asset**

Cynthia is a successful sculptor who created a work that is now worth $400,000 and has no tax basis. Cynthia forms a corporation and contributes the sculpture to it in exchange for the corporation's shares. Fourteen months later, she sells all the stock for $400,000. She wants to treat the sale of the stock as a long-term capital gain. Evaluate the propriety of Cynthia's actions.

U.S. Government Publications

U.S. government publications received from the U.S. government (or its agencies) for a reduced price are *not* capital assets. This prevents a taxpayer from later donating the publications to charity and claiming a charitable contribution deduction equal to the fair market value of the publications. Normally, the charitable contribution of an ordinary asset provides a deduction equal to the asset's basis. If the taxpayer received the property at no cost, its basis is equal to zero. If this property is given to someone else, it retains its ordinary asset status (see text Section 10-4e for more about property contributions).

16-2b Effect of Judicial Action

Because the Code only lists categories of what are *not* capital assets, judicial interpretation is sometimes required to determine whether a specific item fits into one of those categories. The Supreme Court follows a literal interpretation of the categories. For instance, because corporate stock is not mentioned in § 1221, it is *usually* a capital asset. However, what if corporate stock is purchased for resale to customers? Then it is *inventory* (and not a capital asset) because inventory is one of the categories in § 1221.

Intent also matters. What happens when a taxpayer who normally does not acquire stock for resale to customers acquires stock but intends to resell it? The Supreme Court decided that because the stock was not acquired primarily for sale to customers (the taxpayer did not sell the stock to its regular customers), the stock was a capital asset.[1]

Because of the uncertainty associated with capital asset status, Congress has enacted several Code Sections to clarify its definition. These clarifications are discussed next.

[1] *Arkansas Best v. Comm.*, 88–1 USTC ¶9210, 61 AFTR 2d 88–655, 108 S.Ct. 971 (USSC).

16-2c Statutory Expansions

In several instances, Congress has clarified its general definition of what is *not* a capital asset.

Dealers in Securities

As a general rule, securities (stocks, bonds, and other financial instruments) held by a dealer are considered to be inventory and, therefore, are not subject to capital gain or loss treatment. A *dealer in securities* is a merchant (e.g., a brokerage firm) that regularly engages in the purchase and resale of securities to customers.

The dealer must identify any securities being held for investment. Generally, if a dealer clearly identifies certain securities as held for investment purposes by the close of business on the acquisition date, gain from the securities' sale will be capital gain. However, the gain will not be capital gain if the dealer ceases to hold the securities for investment prior to the sale. Losses are capital losses if at any time the securities have been clearly identified by the dealer as held for investment.

Example 9

Tracy is a securities dealer. She purchases 100 shares of Swan stock. If Tracy takes no further action, the stock is inventory and an ordinary asset.

If she designates in her records that the stock is held for investment, the stock is a capital asset. Tracy must designate the investment purpose by the close of business on the acquisition date. If Tracy maintains her investment purpose and later sells the stock, the gain or loss is capital gain or loss.

If Tracy redesignates the stock as held for resale (inventory) and then sells it, any gain is ordinary, but any loss is capital loss.

Real Property Subdivided for Sale (§ 1237)

Substantial real property development activities may result in the owner being considered a dealer for tax purposes. If so, ordinary income will result from any lots sold. However, § 1237 allows real estate investors capital gain treatment if they engage *only* in *limited* development activities. To be eligible for § 1237 treatment, the following requirements must be met:

- The taxpayer may not be a corporation.
- The taxpayer may not be a real estate dealer.
- No substantial improvements may be made to the lots sold. *Substantial* generally means more than a 10 percent increase in the value of a lot. Shopping centers and other commercial or residential buildings are considered substantial improvements, but filling, draining, leveling, and clearing operations are not.
- The taxpayer must have held the lots sold for at least 5 years, except for inherited property. The substantial improvements test is less stringent if the property is held at least 10 years.

If these requirements are met, all gain is capital gain until the tax year in which the *sixth* lot is sold. Sales of contiguous lots to a single buyer in the same transaction count as the sale of one lot. Beginning with the tax year the *sixth* lot is sold, 5 percent of the revenue from lot sales is potential ordinary income. That potential ordinary income is offset by any selling expenses from the lot sales. Since sales commissions often are at least 5 percent of the sales price, typically none of the gain is treated as ordinary income.

Code § 1237 does not apply to losses. A loss from the sale of subdivided real property is an ordinary loss unless the property qualifies as a capital asset under § 1221. The following example illustrates the application of § 1237.

Example 10

Jack owns a large tract of land and subdivides it for sale. Assume that Jack meets all of the requirements of § 1237 and during the tax year sells the first 10 lots to 10 different buyers for $10,000 each. Jack's basis in each lot sold is $3,000, and he incurs total selling expenses of $4,000 ($400 for each lot) on the sales. Jack's gain is computed as follows:

Selling price (10 × $10,000)	$100,000	
Less: Selling expenses (10 × $400)	(4,000)	
Amount realized		$ 96,000
Basis (10 × $3,000)		(30,000)
Realized and recognized gain		$ 66,000
Classification of recognized gain:		
Ordinary income		
Five percent of selling price (5% × $100,000)	$ 5,000	
Less: Selling expenses	(4,000)	
Ordinary gain		1,000
Capital gain		$ 65,000

A portion of the gain is given ordinary treatment because the *sixth* lot is sold in the current year.

Nonbusiness Bad Debts

A loan not made in the ordinary course of business is classified as a nonbusiness receivable. In the year the receivable becomes completely worthless, it is a *nonbusiness bad debt*, and the bad debt is treated as a short-term capital loss. Even if the receivable was outstanding for more than one year, the loss is still a short-term capital loss. Chapter 7 discusses nonbusiness bad debts more thoroughly (see text Section 7-1b).

LO.3

Explain the relevance of a sale or exchange to classification as a capital gain or loss and apply the special rules for the capital gain or loss treatment of the retirement of corporate obligations, options, patents, franchises, and lease cancellation payments.

16-3 Sale or Exchange

Recognition of capital gain or loss usually requires a sale or exchange of a capital asset. The Code uses the term **sale or exchange** but does not define it. Generally, a property *sale* involves the receipt of money by the seller and/or the assumption by the purchaser of the seller's liabilities. An *exchange* involves the transfer of property for other property. So an involuntary conversion (casualty, theft, or condemnation) is not a sale or exchange.

In several situations, Congress has created rules that specifically provide for sale or exchange treatment. For example, assume that the expiration of a right to personal property (other than stock) that would be a capital asset in the hands of the taxpayer results in a recognized gain or loss. This is a capital gain or loss.[2] Several of these special rules are discussed below, including worthless securities, the retirement of corporate obligations, options, patents, franchises, and lease cancellation payments.

16-3a Worthless Securities and § 1244 Stock

Occasionally, securities such as stock and especially bonds may become worthless due to the insolvency of their issuer. If such a security is a capital asset, the loss is deemed to have occurred as the result of a sale or exchange on the *last day* of the tax year.[3] This last-day rule may have the effect of converting what otherwise would have been a short-term capital loss into a long-term capital loss. Code § 1244 allows an ordinary deduction on disposition of stock at a loss. The stock must be that of a small business corporation, and the ordinary deduction is limited to $50,000 ($100,000 for married taxpayers filing jointly) per year. See Chapter 7 (and text Sections 7-2a and 7-2b) for a more complete discussion of these rules.

[2] § 1234A.

[3] § 165(g)(1).

16-3b Retirement of Corporate Obligations

A debt obligation (e.g., a bond or note payable) may have a tax basis in excess of or less than its redemption value because it may have been acquired at a premium or discount. Consequently, the collection of the redemption value may result in a loss or gain. Generally, the collection of a debt obligation is *treated* as a sale or exchange.[4] Therefore, any loss or gain can be a capital loss or capital gain because a sale or exchange has taken place.

Example 11

Fran acquires $1,000 of Osprey Corporation bonds for $980 in the open market. If the bonds are held to maturity, the $20 difference between Fran's collection of the $1,000 redemption value and her cost of $980 is treated as capital gain.

Original Issue Discount (§§ 1272–1288)

The benefit of the sale or exchange exception that allows a capital gain from the collection of certain obligations is reduced when the obligation has original issue discount. **Original issue discount (OID)** arises when the issue price of a debt obligation is less than the maturity value of the obligation. OID must generally be amortized over the life of the debt obligation using the effective interest method. The OID amortization increases the basis of the bond.

Most new publicly traded bond issues do not carry OID because the stated interest rate is set to make the market price on issue the same as the bond's face amount. In addition, even if the issue price is less than the face amount, the difference is not considered to be OID if the difference is less than one-fourth of 1 percent of the redemption price at maturity multiplied by the number of years to maturity.[5]

In the case where OID does exist, it may or may not have to be amortized depending upon the date the obligation was issued. When OID is amortized, the amount of gain upon collection, sale, or exchange of the obligation is correspondingly reduced. The obligations covered by the OID amortization rules and the method of amortization are presented in §§ 1272–1275. Similar rules for other obligations can be found in §§ 1276–1288.

Example 12

Jerry purchases $10,000 of newly issued White Corporation bonds for $6,000. The bonds have OID of $4,000. Jerry must amortize the discount over the life of the bonds. The OID amortization *increases* his interest income. (The bonds were selling at a discount because the market rate of interest was greater than the bonds' stated interest rate.) After Jerry has amortized $1,800 of OID, he sells the bonds for $8,000. Jerry has a capital gain of $200 [$8,000 − ($6,000 cost + $1,800 OID amortization)].

The OID amortization rules prevent him from converting ordinary interest income into capital gain. Without the OID amortization, Jerry would have capital gain of $2,000 ($8,000 − $6,000 cost).

16-3c Options

Frequently, a potential buyer of property wants some time to make the purchase decision but wants to control the sale and/or the sale price in the meantime. **Options** are used to achieve these objectives. The potential purchaser (grantee) pays the property owner (grantor) for an option on the property. The grantee then becomes the option holder. The option, which usually sets a price at which the grantee can buy the property, expires after a specified period of time.

Exercise of Options by Grantee

If the option is exercised, the amount paid for the option is added to the optioned property's selling price. This increases the gain (or reduces the loss) to the grantor resulting from the sale of the property. The grantor's gain or loss is capital or ordinary depending on the tax status of the property. The grantee adds the cost of the option to the basis of the property purchased.

[4] § 1271.

[5] § 1273(a)(3).

Sale of an Option

A grantee may sell or exchange the option rather than exercising it or letting it expire. Generally, the grantee's sale or exchange of the option results in capital gain or loss if the option property is (or would be) a capital asset to the grantee.[6]

Example 13

Rosa wants to buy some vacant land for investment purposes. However, she cannot afford the full purchase price at the present time. Instead, Rosa (grantee) pays the landowner (grantor) $3,000 to obtain an option to buy the land for $100,000 anytime in the next two years. The option is a capital asset for Rosa because if she actually purchased the land, the land would be a capital asset.

Three months after purchasing the option, Rosa sells it for $7,000. She has a $4,000 ($7,000 − $3,000) short-term capital gain on this sale because she held the option for one year or less.

Failure to Exercise Options

If an option holder (grantee) fails to exercise the option, the lapse of the option is considered a sale or exchange on the option expiration date. As a result, the loss is a capital loss if the property subject to the option is (or would be) a capital asset in the hands of the grantee.

The grantor of an option on *stocks, securities, commodities, or commodity futures* receives short-term capital gain treatment upon the expiration of the option. Options on property *other than* stocks, securities, commodities, or commodity futures (for instance, vacant land) result in ordinary income to the grantor when the option expires.

For example, an individual investor who owns certain stock (a capital asset) may sell a call option, entitling the buyer of the option to acquire the stock at a specified price higher than the value at the date the option is granted. The writer of the call receives a premium (e.g., 10 percent) for writing the option. If the price of the stock does not increase during the option period, the option will expire unexercised. When the option expires, the grantor must recognize short-term capital gain (whereas the grantee recognizes a loss, the character of which depends on the underlying asset). These rules do not apply to options held for sale to customers (the inventory of a securities dealer).

The Big Picture

Example 14

Return to the facts of *The Big Picture* on p. 16-1. On February 1, 2022, Maurice purchases 100 shares of Eagle Company stock for $5,000. On April 1, 2022, he writes a call option on the stock, giving the grantee the right to buy the stock for $6,000 during the following six-month period. Maurice (the grantor) receives a call premium of $500 for writing the call.

- If the call is exercised by the grantee on August 1, 2022, Maurice has $1,500 ($6,000 + $500 − $5,000) of short-term capital gain from the sale of the stock. The grantee has a $6,500 ($500 option premium + $6,000 purchase price) basis for the stock.
- Investors sometimes get nervous and want to "lock in" gains or losses.
  - Assume that Maurice, prior to exercise of the grantee's call, decides to sell his stock for $6,000 and enters into a closing transaction by purchasing a call on 100 shares of Eagle Company stock for $5,000.
  - Because the Eagle stock is selling for $6,000, Maurice must pay a call premium of $1,000.
  - He recognizes a $500 short-term capital loss [$500 (call premium received) − $1,000 (call premium paid)] on the closing transaction.
  - On the actual sale of the Eagle stock, Maurice has a short-term capital gain of $1,000 [$6,000 (selling price) − $5,000 (cost)].

continued

[6] § 1234(a) and Reg. § 1.1234–1(a)(1). Stock options are discussed in Chapter 19.

- The original grantee is not affected by Maurice's closing transaction. The original option is still in existence, and the grantee's tax consequences depend on what action the grantee takes—exercising the option, letting the option expire, or selling the option.
- Assume that the original option expired unexercised. Maurice has a $500 short-term capital gain equal to the call premium received for writing the option. This gain is not recognized until the option expires. The grantee has a loss from expiration of the option. The nature of the loss will depend upon whether the option was a capital asset or an ordinary asset.

Concept Summary 16.1 summarizes the consequences of various transactions involving options to both the grantor and grantee.

Concept Summary 16.1

Options: Consequences to the Grantor and Grantee

	Effect on	
Event	**Grantor**	**Grantee**
Option is granted.	Receives value and has a contract obligation (a liability).	Pays value and has a contract right (an asset).
Option is exercised.	Amount received for option increases proceeds from sale of the option property.	Amount paid for option becomes part of the basis of the option property purchased.
Option is sold or exchanged by grantee.	Result depends upon whether option later expires or is exercised (see above).	Could have gain or loss (capital gain or loss if option property would have been a capital asset for the grantee).
Option expires.	Has a short-term capital gain if the option property is stocks, securities, commodities, or commodity futures. Otherwise, gain is ordinary income.	Has a loss (capital loss if option property would have been a capital asset for the grantee).

16-3d Patents

Transfer of a **patent** is treated as the sale or exchange of a long-term capital asset when *all substantial rights* to the patent are transferred by a *holder*.[7] The transferor/holder may receive payment in virtually any form, including contingent payments based on the transferee/purchaser's productivity, use, or disposition of the patent. If the transfer meets these requirements, any gain or loss is *automatically a long-term* capital gain or loss. Whether the asset was a capital asset for the transferor, whether a sale or exchange occurred, and how long the transferor held the patent are not relevant.

Substantial Rights

To receive favorable capital gain treatment, *all substantial rights* to the patent must be transferred. The sale of a partial interest qualifies if the sale places no restrictions on the use of the patent by the purchaser. All substantial rights have not been transferred when the transfer is limited geographically within the issuing country or when the transfer is for a period less than the remaining life of the patent. All the facts and circumstances of the transaction, not just the language of the transfer document, are examined when making this determination.[8]

Example 15 illustrates the special treatment for patents.

[7] § 1235.

[8] Reg. § 1.1235–2(b)(1).

The Big Picture

Example 15

Return to the facts of *The Big Picture* on p. 16-1. Shortly after your conversation with Maurice, Green Battery Company offers to buy the patent developed by Kevin for $2,000,000 plus $0.50 for each battery sold. Kevin and Maurice agree to sell the patent.

Since Maurice transferred all his remaining rights, he automatically has a long-term capital gain from both his 50% share of the lump-sum payment ($1,000,000) and the $0.50 per battery royalty to the extent those proceeds exceed his basis for the patent.

Whether Maurice gets long-term capital gain treatment depends upon whether Maurice is a *holder*. See the following discussion and Example 16.

Holder Defined

The *holder* of a patent must be an *individual*. Usually, this is the invention's creator or an individual who purchases the patent rights from the creator before the patented invention is put into production ("reduced to practice"). So if the creator's employer has all rights to an employee's inventions, the employer is *not* eligible for long-term capital gain treatment. The employer will normally have an ordinary asset because the patent was developed as part of its business.

The Big Picture

Example 16

Return to the facts of *The Big Picture* on p. 16-1. Continuing with the facts of Example 15, Kevin is clearly a holder of the patent because he is the inventor and was not an employee when he invented the battery. When Maurice purchased a 50% interest in the patent nine months ago, he became a *holder* because the patent was not being used to manufacture batteries at the time of the purchase (i.e., it had not been "reduced to practice").

Since Maurice is also a holder, he will have an automatic long-term capital gain or loss if he transfers all substantial rights in his 50% interest to Green Battery Company. Maurice's basis for his share of the patent is $50,000, and his proceeds equal $1,000,000 plus $0.50 for each battery sold; Maurice has a long-term capital gain even though he has not held his interest in the patent for more than one year.

Compare the results here to those in Example 5. There, Abigail sold all substantial rights, but she had no patent and the invention had been "reduced to practice" because it was being manufactured and sold.

16-3e Franchises, Trademarks, and Trade Names (§ 1253)

A mode of operation, a widely recognized brand name (trade name), and a widely known business symbol (trademark) are all valuable assets. These assets may be licensed (commonly known as franchising) by their owner for use by other businesses. Many fast-food restaurants (such as McDonald's and Taco Bell) are franchises. The franchisee usually pays the owner (franchisor) an initial fee plus a contingent fee. The contingent fee is often based upon the franchisee's sales volume.

For Federal income tax purposes, a **franchise** is an agreement that gives the franchisee the right to distribute, sell, or provide goods, services, or facilities within a specified area.[9] A franchise transfer includes the grant of a franchise, a transfer by one franchisee to another person, or the renewal of a franchise.

Code § 1253 provides that a transfer of a franchise, trademark, or trade name is not a transfer of a capital asset when the transferor retains any significant power, right, or continuing interest in the property transferred.

Significant Power, Right, or Continuing Interest

In most franchising operations, the transferor retains some powers or rights. As a result, the transaction is *not* a capital asset transfer. *Significant powers, rights, or continuing interests* include control over franchise assignment, quality of products and services, sale

[9] § 1253(b)(1).

or advertising of products or services, the requirement that substantially all supplies and equipment be purchased from the transferor, and the right to terminate the franchise.

In the unusual case where the transferor does not retain any significant power, right, or continuing interest, a capital gain or loss may occur. For capital gain or loss treatment to be available, the asset transferred must qualify as a capital asset.

The Big Picture

Example 17

Return to the facts of *The Big Picture* on p. 16-1. Maurice sells for $210,000 to Mauve, Inc., the franchise purchased from Orange, Inc., nine months ago. The $210,000 received by Maurice is not contingent, and all significant powers, rights, and continuing interests are transferred.

The $115,000 gain ($210,000 proceeds − $95,000 basis) is a short-term capital gain because Maurice has held the franchise for only nine months.

Franchise Payments

In most franchise settings, when the transferor retains significant power or rights, both contingent (e.g., based on sales) and noncontingent payments occur.

Noncontingent Payments Any noncontingent payments made by the franchisee to the franchisor are ordinary income to the franchisor. The franchisee capitalizes the payments and amortizes them over 15 years. If the franchise is sold, the amortization is subject to recapture under § 1245.[10]

Example 18

Grey Company signs a 10-year franchise agreement with DOH Donuts. Grey (the franchisee) makes payments of $3,000 per year for the first 8 years of the franchise agreement—a total of $24,000. Grey cannot deduct $3,000 per year as the payments are made. Instead, Grey may amortize the $24,000 total over 15 years. As a result, Grey may deduct $1,600 per year for each of the 15 years of the amortization period.

The same result would occur if Grey made a $24,000 lump-sum payment at the beginning of the franchise period. Assuming that DOH Donuts (the franchisor) retains significant powers, rights, or a continuing interest, it will have ordinary income when it receives the payments from Grey.

Contingent Payments Any contingent franchise payments are ordinary income for the franchisor and an ordinary deduction for the franchisee. Contingent payments must meet the following requirements:

- The payments are made at least annually throughout the term of the transfer agreement.
- The payments are substantially equal in amount or are payable under a fixed formula.

Example 19

TAK, a spicy chicken franchisor, transfers an eight-year franchise to Phyllis. TAK retains a significant power, right, or continuing interest. Phyllis, the franchisee, agrees to pay TAK 15% of sales. This contingent payment is ordinary income to TAK and a business deduction for Phyllis as the payments are made.

Sports Franchises

Professional sports franchises (e.g., the Detroit Tigers) are subject to § 1253. Player contracts are usually one of the major assets acquired with a sports franchise. These contracts last only for the time stated in the contract. By being classified as § 197 intangibles, the player contracts and other intangible assets acquired in the purchase of the sports franchise are amortized over a statutory 15-year period.[11]

Concept Summary 16.2 reviews the effects of transactions involving franchises on both the franchisor and franchisee.

[10]See Chapter 17 for a discussion of the recapture rules.

[11]§ 197(a).

Concept Summary 16.2

Franchises: Consequences to the Franchisor and Franchisee

Event	**Effect on Franchisor**	**Effect on Franchisee**
Franchisor Retains Significant Powers and Rights		
Noncontingent payment	Ordinary income.	Capitalized and amortized over 15 years as an ordinary deduction; if franchise is sold, amortization is subject to recapture under § 1245.
Contingent payment	Ordinary income.	Ordinary deduction.
Franchisor Does *Not* Retain Significant Powers and Rights		
Noncontingent payment	Ordinary income if franchise rights are an ordinary asset; capital gain if franchise rights are a capital asset (unlikely).	Capitalized and amortized over 15 years as an ordinary deduction; if the franchise is sold, amortization is subject to recapture under § 1245.
Contingent payment	Ordinary income.	Ordinary deduction.

16-3f Lease Cancellation Payments

The tax treatment of payments received for canceling a lease depends on whether the recipient is the **lessor** or the **lessee** and whether the lease is a capital asset.

Lessee Treatment

Lease cancellation payments received by a lessee are treated as an exchange.[12] The treatment of these payments depends on the underlying use of the property and how long the lease has existed.[13]

- If the property was used personally (e.g., an apartment used as a residence), the payment results in a capital gain (and long term if the lease existed for more than one year).
- If the property was used for business and the lease existed for one year or less, the payment results in ordinary income.
- If the property was used for business and the lease existed for more than one year, the payment results in a § 1231 gain.

Example 20

Mark owns an apartment building that he is going to convert into an office building. Vicki is one of the apartment tenants and receives $1,000 from Mark to cancel the lease.

Vicki has a capital gain of $1,000 (which is long term or short term depending upon how long she has held the lease). Mark has an ordinary deduction of $1,000.

Lessor Treatment

Payments received by a lessor for a lease cancellation are always ordinary income because they are considered to be in lieu of rental payments.[14]

Example 21

Darnell owns an apartment building near a university campus. Hui-Fen is one of the tenants. Hui-Fen is graduating early and offers Darnell $800 to cancel the apartment lease. Darnell accepts the offer.

Darnell has ordinary income of $800. Hui-Fen has a nondeductible payment because the apartment was personal use property.

[12] § 1241 and Reg. § 1.1241–1(a).

[13] Reg. § 1.1221–1(b) and PLR 200045019.

[14] Reg. § 1.61–8(b).

16-4 Holding Period

LO.4

Determine whether the holding period for a capital asset is long term or short term.

16-4a General Rules

Property must be held *more than one year* to qualify for long-term capital gain or loss treatment.[15] Property held for one year or less results in short-term capital gain or loss. To compute the **holding period**, start counting on the day *after* the property was acquired and include the day of disposition.

The Big Picture

Example 22

Return to the facts of *The Big Picture* on p. 16-1. Assume that Maurice purchased the Purple stock on January 15, 2022. If he sells it on January 16, 2023, Maurice's holding period is more than one year and the gain or loss is long term.

If, instead, Maurice sells the stock on January 15, 2023, the holding period is exactly one year and the gain or loss is short term.

An asset's holding period is based on calendar months and fractions of calendar months (not the number of days). It does not matter that different months have different numbers of days.[16]

Example 23

Leo purchases a capital asset on February 28, 2022. If Leo sells the asset on February 28, 2023, the holding period is one year and Leo will have a short-term capital gain or loss.

If Leo sells the asset on March 1, 2023, the holding period is more than one year and he will have a long-term capital gain or loss.

16-4b Special Holding Period Rules

There are several special holding period rules.[17] The application of these rules depends upon the type of asset and how it was acquired.

Nontaxable Exchanges

The holding period of property received in a like-kind exchange includes the holding period of the former asset if the property that has been exchanged is a capital asset or a § 1231 asset. In these settings, the holding period of the former property is *tacked on* to the holding period of the newly acquired property.

Example 24

On April 22, 2022, Alejandra exchanges a business building she acquired on March 15, 2019, for another business building in a qualifying like-kind exchange.

The holding period of the replacement building begins March 15, 2019, because the holding period of the building given up in the exchange *tacks* to the holding period of the replacement building.

Gifts

When a gift occurs, if the donor's basis carries over to the recipient, the donor's holding period is *tacked on* to the recipient's holding period. This will occur when the property's fair market value at the date of the gift is greater than the donor's adjusted basis. These transactions are discussed in Chapter 14.

Carryover Basis

Example 25

Kareem acquires 100 shares of Robin Corporation stock for $1,000 on December 31, 2018. He transfers the shares by gift to Megan on December 31, 2021, when the stock is worth $2,000. Kareem's basis of $1,000 becomes the basis for determining gain or loss on a subsequent sale by Megan. Megan's holding period begins with the date the stock was acquired by Kareem.

---

[15] § 1222(3).

[16] Rev.Rul. 66–7.

[17] § 1223.

Carryover Basis

Example 26

Assume the same facts as in Example 25, except that the fair market value of the shares is only $800 on the date of the gift. The holding period begins on the date of the gift if Megan sells the stock for a loss. The value of the shares on the date of the gift is used in the determination of her basis for loss. If she sells the shares for $500 on April 1, 2022, Megan has a $300 recognized capital loss and the holding period is from December 31, 2021, to April 1, 2022 (as a result, the loss is short term).

Certain Disallowed Loss Transactions

Under several Code provisions, realized losses are disallowed. When a loss is disallowed, there is no carryover of holding period. Losses can be disallowed under § 267 (sale or exchange between related taxpayers) and § 262 (sale or exchange of personal use assets) as well as other Code Sections. Taxpayers who acquire property in a disallowed loss transaction will have a new holding period begin and will have a basis equal to the purchase price.

Example 27

Janet sells her personal automobile at a loss. She may not deduct the loss because it arises from the sale of personal use property. Janet purchases a replacement automobile for more than the selling price of her former automobile. Janet has a basis equal to the cost of the replacement automobile, and her holding period begins when she acquires the replacement automobile.

Inherited Property

The holding period for inherited property is treated as long term no matter how long the property is actually held by the heir. The holding period of the decedent or the decedent's estate is not relevant for the heir's holding period.

Example 28

Shonda inherits Blue Company stock from her father, who died in 2022. She receives the stock on April 1, 2022, and sells it on November 1, 2022. Even though Shonda did not hold the stock more than one year, she receives long-term capital gain or loss treatment on the sale.

16-4c Special Rules for Short Sales

General

The Code provides special holding period rules for short sales.[18] A **short sale** occurs when a taxpayer sells borrowed property and repays the lender with substantially identical property either held on the date of the sale or purchased after the sale. The repayment of the lender "closes" the short sale.

Short sales usually involve corporate stock. The seller's objective is to make a profit in anticipation of a decline in the stock's price. If the price declines, the seller in a short sale recognizes a profit equal to the difference between the sales price of the borrowed stock and the price paid for the replacement stock.

Example 29

Chris does not own any shares of Brown Corporation. However, Chris sells 30 shares of Brown. The shares are borrowed from Chris's broker and must be replaced within 45 days. Chris has a short sale because he was short the shares he sold. He will close the short sale by purchasing Brown shares and delivering them to his broker.

If the original 30 shares were sold for $10,000 and Chris later purchased 30 shares for $8,000, he would have a gain of $2,000. Chris's hunch that the price of Brown stock would decline was correct. Chris would be able to profit from selling high and buying low.

If Chris had to purchase Brown shares for $13,000 to close the short sale, he would have a loss of $3,000. In this case, Chris would have sold low and bought high—not the result he wanted. Chris would be making a short sale against the box if he borrowed shares from his broker to sell and then closed the short sale by delivering other Brown shares he owned at the time he made the short sale.

[18] § 1233.

Concept Summary 16.3 summarizes the short sale rules. These rules are intended to prevent the conversion of short-term capital gains into long-term capital gains and long-term capital losses into short-term capital losses.

In most settings, short sale gain or loss results in a capital gain or loss. The gain or loss is not recognized until the short sale is closed. Generally, the holding period of the short sale property is determined by how long the property used to close the short sale was held. However, when *substantially identical property* (e.g., other shares of the same stock) is held by the taxpayer, the holding period is determined as follows:

- The short sale *gain or loss* is *short term* when, on the short sale date, the substantially identical property has been held *short term* (i.e., for one year or less). (See Examples 30 and 31.)
- The short sale *gain* is *long term* when, on the short sale date, the substantially identical property has been held *long term* (i.e., for more than one year) *and* is used to close the short sale. If the long-term substantially identical property is not used to close the short sale, the short sale gain is *short term*. (See Example 32.)
- The short sale *loss* is *long term* when, on the short sale date, the substantially identical property has been held *long term* (i.e., for more than one year).
- The short sale *gain or loss* is *short term* if the substantially identical property is acquired *after* the short sale date and on or before the closing date. (See Example 33.)

Concept Summary 16.3

Short Sales of Securities

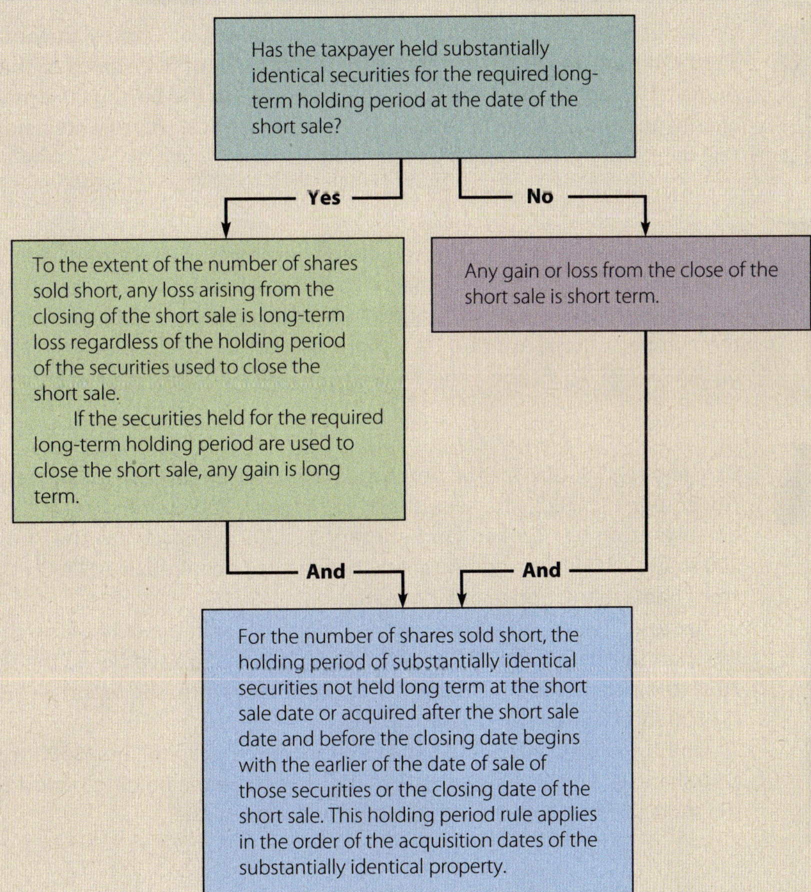

Disposition Rules for Short Sales against the Box

A *short sale against the box* occurs when the stock is borrowed from a broker by a seller and the seller already owns substantially identical securities on the short sale date or acquires them before the closing date.[19] To remove the taxpayer's flexibility as to when the short sale gain must be reported, a constructive sale approach is used. If the taxpayer has not closed the short sale by delivering the short sale securities to the broker *before* January 31 of the year following the short sale, the short sale is deemed to have been closed on the *earlier* of two events:

- On the short sale date if the taxpayer owned substantially identical securities at that time.
- On the date during the year of the short sale that the taxpayer acquired substantially identical securities.[20]

The basis of the shares in the deemed transfer of shares is used to compute the gain or loss on the short sale. As Examples 32 and 33 illustrate, when shares are *actually* transferred to the broker to close the short sale, there may be a gain or loss because the shares transferred will have a basis equal to the short sale date price and the value at the *actual* short sale closing date may be different from the short sale date price.

Illustrations

The following examples illustrate the treatment of short sales and short sales against the box.

Short Sales and Short Sales Against the Box

Example 30

On January 4, 2022, Caden purchases five shares of Osprey Corporation common stock for $100. On April 14, 2022, he engages in a short sale of five shares of the same stock for $150. On August 15, Caden closes the short sale by repaying the borrowed stock with the five shares purchased on January 4. Because his substantially identical shares were held short term as of the short sale date, Caden's $50 capital gain is short term.

Example 31

Assume the same facts as in the previous example, except that Caden closes the short sale on January 28, 2023, by repaying the borrowed stock with five shares purchased on January 27, 2023, for $200. Because Caden's substantially identical property (purchased on January 4, 2022) was short-term property at the April 14, 2022 short sale date, his $50 capital loss ($200 cost of stock purchased on January 27, 2023, and a short sale selling price of $150) is short term.

Example 32

On January 18, 2021, Rita purchases 200 shares of Owl Corporation stock for $1,000. On November 11, 2022, she sells short, for $1,300, 200 shares of Owl Corporation stock that she borrows from her broker. On February 10, 2023, Rita closes the short sale by delivering the 200 shares of Owl Corporation stock that she had acquired in 2021. On that date, Owl Corporation stock had a market price of $3 per share.

Because Rita owned substantially identical stock on the date of the short sale and did not close the short sale before January 31, 2023, she is *deemed* to have closed the short sale on November 11, 2022 (the date of the short sale). On her 2022 tax return, she reports a $300 long-term capital gain ($1,300 short sale price − $1,000 basis).

On February 10, 2023, Rita has a $700 short-term capital loss [$600 short sale closing date price (200 shares × $3 per share) − $1,300 basis] because the holding period of the shares used to close the short sale commences with the date of the short sale.

[19] The "box" refers to the safe deposit box that stock owners routinely used to keep physical stock certificates safe. Although today shares of stock typically are held electronically (rather than physically), the terminology *short sale against the box* is still used.

[20] § 1259.

Short Sales and Short Sales Against the Box

Example 33

Assume the same facts as in Example 32, except that Rita did not own any Owl Corporation stock on the short sale date and acquired the 200 shares of Owl Corporation stock for $1,000 on December 12, 2022 (after the November 11, 2022 short sale date).

The *deemed* closing of the short sale is December 12, 2022, because Rita held substantially identical shares at the end of 2022 and did not close the short sale before January 31, 2023. Her 2022 short sale gain is a *short-term* gain of $300 ($1,300 short sale price – $1,000 basis), and she still has a short-term capital loss of $700 on February 10, 2023.

16-5 Tax Treatment of Capital Gains and Losses of Noncorporate Taxpayers

LO.5

Describe the beneficial tax treatment for capital gains and the detrimental tax treatment for capital losses for noncorporate taxpayers.

All taxpayers net their capital gains and losses. Short-term gains and losses (if any) are netted against one another, and long-term gains and losses (if any) are netted against one another. The results will be net short-term gain or loss and net long-term gain or loss. If these two net positions are of opposite sign (one is a gain and one is a loss), they are netted against each other.

Six possibilities exist for the result after all possible netting has been completed.

1. A net long-term capital gain (NLTCG).
2. A net short-term capital gain (NSTCG).
3. Both NLTCG and NSTCG.
4. A net long-term capital loss (NLTCL).
5. A net short-term capital loss (NSTCL).
6. Both NLTCL and NSTCL.

Net long-term capital gains of noncorporate taxpayers are eligible for an alternative tax calculation that normally results in a lower tax liability. Neither NLTCLs nor NSTCLs are treated as ordinary losses. Treatment as an ordinary loss generally is preferable to capital loss treatment because ordinary losses are deductible in full but the deductibility of capital losses is subject to certain limitations. An individual taxpayer may deduct a maximum of $3,000 of net capital losses for a taxable year.[21]

16-5a Capital Gain and Loss Netting Process

Net short-term capital gain is not eligible for any special tax rate. It is taxed at the same rate as the taxpayer's other taxable income.

Net long-term capital gain is eligible for one or more of *five* alternative tax rates: 0 percent, 15 percent, 20 percent, 25 percent, and 28 percent. The 25 percent and 28 percent rates are used only in unique circumstances. The net long-term capital gain components are referred to as the *0%/15%/20% gain*, the *25% gain*, and the *28% gain*.

The *25% gain* is called the **unrecaptured § 1250 gain** and is related to gain from disposition of § 1231 assets (discussed in Chapter 17). Here, the discussion focuses only on how the *25% gain* is taxed and not how it is determined. The *28% gain* relates to collectibles and small business stock gain (both discussed later in this section). As discussed in text Section 16-5c, the *0%/15%/20%* rates are applied at various ranges of taxable income based on the taxpayer's filing status (see also Exhibit 16.1).

When the long-term capital gain exceeds short-term capital loss, a **net capital gain (NCG)** exists.[22] Net capital gain qualifies for beneficial alternative tax treatment (see the coverage later in the chapter).

[21] § 1211(b).

[22] § 1222(11).

Because there are both short- and long-term capital gains and losses and because the long-term capital gains may be taxed at various rates, an *ordering procedure* is required. The ordering procedure, which ensures that any long-term capital gain is taxed at the lowest preferential rate possible, includes the following steps:

Step 1. Group all gains and losses into four groups: short term, and 28%, 25%, and 0%/15%/20% long term.

Step 2. Net the gains and losses within each group.

Step 3. Offset the net 28% and net 25% amounts if they are of opposite sign.

Step 4. Offset the results after step 3 against the 0%/15%/20% amount if they are of opposite sign. If the 0%/15%/20% amount is a loss, offset it against the *highest-taxed gain first*. After this step, there is a net long-term capital gain or loss. If there is a net long-term capital gain, it may consist of only *28% gain*, only *25% gain*, only *0%/15%/20% gain* or some combination of all of these gains. If there is a net long-term capital loss, it is simply a net long-term capital loss.

Step 5. Offset the net short-term amount against the long-term results of step 4 if they are of opposite sign. The netting rules offset net short-term capital loss against the *highest-taxed gain first*. So a net short-term capital loss first offsets any *28% gain*, then any *25% gain*, and finally any *0%/15%/20% gain*.

If the result of step 5 is *only* a short-term capital gain, the taxpayer is not eligible for a reduced tax rate. If the result of step 5 is a loss, the taxpayer may be eligible for a *capital loss deduction* (discussed later in this chapter). If there was no offsetting in step 5 because the short-term and step 4 results were both gains or if the result of the offsetting is a long-term gain, a net capital gain exists and the taxpayer may be eligible for a reduced tax rate. The net capital gain may consist of *28% gain*, *25% gain*, and/or *0%/15%/20% gain*.

As you might suspect, this *ordering procedure* can produce many different results. The following series of examples illustrates some of these outcomes.

Capital Gain and Loss Netting Process

Example 34

This example shows how a *net short-term capital gain* may result from the netting process.

		Long-Term Gains and Losses			
Step	**Short Term**	**28%**	**25%**	**0%/15%/20%**	**Comment**
1	$13,000	$ 12,000		$ 3,000	
	(2,000)	(20,000)			
2	$11,000	($ 8,000)		$ 3,000	
3					No 28%/25% netting because no opposite sign.
4		3,000	⟵	(3,000)	Netted because of opposite sign.
		($ 5,000)		$ -0-	
5	(5,000) ⟵	5,000			The net short-term capital gain is taxed as ordinary income.
	$ 6,000	$ -0-			
	Net short-term capital gain				

Capital Gain and Loss Netting Process

Example 35

This example shows how a *net long-term capital gain* may result from the netting process.

Step	Short Term	Long-Term Gains and Losses: 28%	25%	0%/15%/20%	Comment
1	$ 3,000	$15,000	$4,000	$ 3,000	
	(5,000)	(7,000)		(8,000)	
2	($ 2,000)	$ 8,000	$4,000	($ 5,000)	
3					No 28%/25% netting because no opposite sign.
4		(5,000)	←	5,000	Netted because of opposite sign. Net 0%/15%/20% loss is netted against *28% gain* first.
		$ 3,000			
				$ –0–	
5	2,000 →	(2,000)			The net short-term capital loss is netted against *28% gain* first. The net long-term capital gain is $5,000 ($1,000 + $4,000).
	$ –0–	$ 1,000	$4,000		
		Net *28% gain*	Net *25% gain*		

Example 36

This example shows how a *net long-term capital loss* may result from the netting process.

Step	Short Term	Long-Term Gains and Losses: 28%	25%	0%/15%/20%	Comment
1	$ 3,000	$ 1,000		$ 3,000	
				(8,000)	
2	$ 3,000	$ 1,000		($ 5,000)	
3					No 28%/25% netting because no opposite sign.
4		(1,000)	→	1,000	Netted because of opposite sign.
		$ –0–		($ 4,000)	
5	(3,000)	→	→	3,000	The net short-term capital gain is netted against the net long-term capital loss, and the remaining loss is eligible for the capital loss deduction.
	$ –0–			($ 1,000)	
				Net long-term capital loss	

Use of Capital Loss Carryovers

A short-term capital loss carryover to the current year retains its character as short term and is combined with the short-term items of the current year. A net long-term capital loss carries over as a long-term capital loss and is combined with the current-year long-term loss. The total long-term loss is first offset with *28% gain* of the current year, then *25% gain*, and then *0%/15%/20% gain* until it is absorbed.

Example 37

In 2022, Abigail has a $4,000 short-term capital gain, a $36,000 28% long-term capital gain, and a $13,000 0%/15%/20% long-term capital gain. She also has a $3,000 short-term capital loss carryover and a $2,000 long-term capital loss carryover from 2021.

As a result, in 2022, Abigail has a $1,000 net short-term capital gain ($4,000 − $3,000), a $34,000 net 28% long-term capital gain ($36,000 − $2,000), and a $13,000 net 0%/15%/20% long-term capital gain.

Definition of Collectibles

Capital assets that are collectibles, even though they are held long term, are not eligible for the *0%/15%/20%* alternative tax rate. Instead, a 28 percent alternative tax rate applies.

For capital gain or loss purposes, **collectibles** include:[23]

- Any work of art.
- Any rug or antique.
- Any metal or gem.
- Any stamp.
- Any alcoholic beverage.
- Most coins.
- Any historical objects (documents, clothes, etc.).

Small Business Stock

A special *exclusion* is available to noncorporate taxpayers who derive capital gains from the sale or exchange of **qualified small business stock**.[24] Any amount not excluded from income is taxed at a maximum rate of 28 percent (as noted earlier). The exclusion amount varies depending on when the qualified small business stock was acquired.

- 100 percent of the gain is excluded for qualified stock acquired after September 27, 2010.
- 75 percent of the gain is excluded for qualified stock acquired after February 17, 2009, and before September 28, 2010.
- 50 percent of the gain is excluded for qualified stock acquired before February 18, 2009.

As a result, the maximum effective tax rate on gains from the sale of qualified small business stock is 0 percent (28% × 0%), 7 percent (28% × 25%), or 14 percent (28% × 50%).

Example 38

In March 2022, Yolanda realized a $100,000 gain on the sale of qualified small business stock that she acquired in 2008. Yolanda's marginal tax rate is 32% without considering this gain. Since the stock was acquired before February 18, 2009, $50,000 of this gain (50%) is excluded from gross income, and the other $50,000 is taxed at the maximum rate of 28%. As a result, Yolanda owes Federal income tax of $14,000 on the stock sale ($50,000 × 28%), an effective tax rate of 14% on the entire $100,000 gain.

If, instead, Yolanda acquired the stock any time after September 27, 2010, she would exclude 100% of the gain.

Given this very favorable treatment, Congress wanted to ensure that the gain exclusion only applied in very specific situations. As a result, they imposed the following restrictions:

- The stock must have been newly issued *after* August 10, 1993, by a regular corporation, not a Subchapter S corporation.
- The taxpayer selling the stock must not be a corporation (either regular or Subchapter S).
- The taxpayer must have held the stock *more than five years*.
- The issuing corporation must use at least 80 percent of its assets, determined by their value, in the *active conduct* of a trade or business.
- When the stock was issued, the issuing corporation's assets must not have exceeded $50 million at adjusted basis, including the proceeds of the stock issuance.
- The corporation does not engage in banking, financing, insurance, investing, leasing, farming, mineral extraction, hotel or motel operations, restaurant operations, or any business whose principal asset is the *reputation or skill* of its employees (such as accounting, architecture, health, law, engineering, or financial services).

[23] § 408(m)(2) and Reg. § 1.408–10(b).

[24] § 1202(a).

Even if each of these requirements is met, the amount of gain eligible for the exclusion is limited to the *greater* of 10 times the taxpayer's basis in the stock or $10 million per taxpayer per company,[25] computed on an aggregate basis.

Example 39

Rachel purchased $100,000 of qualified small business stock when it was first issued in October 2005. In 2022, she sold the stock for $4,000,000. Her gain is $3,900,000 ($4,000,000 − $100,000). Although this amount exceeds 10 times her basis ($100,000 × 10 = $1,000,000), it is *less* than $10,000,000. As a result, the entire $3,900,000 gain is eligible for a 50% exclusion.

Transactions that fail to satisfy *any one* of the applicable requirements are taxed as capital gains (and losses) realized by noncorporate taxpayers generally.

Gains are also eligible for *nonrecognition* treatment if the sale proceeds are invested in other qualified small business stock within 60 days.[26] Any gain postponed reduces the basis of the stock purchased. To the extent that the sale proceeds are not so invested, gain is recognized, but the exclusion still applies. To be eligible for this treatment, the stock sold must have been held more than six months.

Example 40

Assume the same facts as in the preceding example, except that Rachel sold her stock in January 2023 and used $3,500,000 of the $4,000,000 sale proceeds to purchase other qualified small business stock one month later. Rachel's gain is recognized to the extent that the sale proceeds were not reinvested—namely, $500,000 ($4,000,000 sale proceeds − $3,500,000 reinvested). A 50% exclusion will apply, however, to the $500,000.

Rachel's basis for the stock purchased in February 2023 is $100,000 ($3,500,000 purchase price − $3,400,000 postponed gain; the postponed gain is the $3,900,000 original gain less the $500,000 gain recognized in 2023).

16-5b Qualified Dividend Income

Dividends paid by domestic and certain foreign corporations are eligible to be taxed at the 0%/15%/20% long-term capital gain rates if they are **qualified dividend income (QDI)** (see the discussion of QDI in text Section 4-3b). Here, the discussion focuses on how the qualified dividend income is taxed.

The Big Picture

Example 41

Return to the facts of *The Big Picture* on p. 16-1. After holding the Purple stock for 10 months, Maurice receives $350 of dividends. If Purple is a domestic or qualifying foreign corporation, these are qualified dividends eligible for the 0%/15%/20% tax rate.

After the net capital gain or loss has been determined, the QDI is added to the net long-term capital gain portion of the net capital gain and is taxed as *0%/15%/20% gain*. If there is a net capital loss, the net capital loss is still deductible *for* AGI up to $3,000 per year with the remainder of the loss (if any) carrying forward. In this case, the QDI is still eligible to be treated as *0%/15%/20% gain* in the alternative tax calculation (it is *not* offset by the net capital loss).

Example 42

Refer to Example 35, but assume that there is qualified dividend income (QDI) of $2,500 in addition to the items shown. The QDI is not netted against the capital gains and losses. Instead, the taxpayer has $1,000 of *28% gain*, $4,000 of *25% gain*, and $2,500 of QDI taxed at 0%/15%/20%.

Refer to Example 36, but assume that there is QDI of $2,500 in addition to the items shown. The QDI is not netted against the net capital loss. The taxpayer has a $1,000 capital loss deduction and $2,500 of QDI taxed at 0%/15%/20%.

[25] For married persons filing separately, the limitation is $5 million.

[26] § 1045(a).

16-5c Alternative Tax on Net Capital Gain and Qualified Dividend Income

Code § 1 contains the rules that enable the *net capital gain* to be taxed at special rates (0, 15, 20, 25, and 28 percent). This calculation is referred to as the **alternative tax** on net capital gain.[27] The alternative tax applies only if taxable income includes some long-term capital gain (there is net capital gain) and/or qualified dividend income (QDI). Taxable income includes *all* of the net capital gain and/or QDI unless taxable income is less than the net capital gain and/or QDI. In addition, the net capital gain and/or QDI is taxed *last*, after other taxable income (including any short-term capital gain).

The *0%/15%/20%* rates are applied to any net capital gain and qualified dividend income based on the taxpayer's filing status and taxable income (see Exhibit 16.1). The taxable income ranges are adjusted for inflation each year.

Example 43

Joan, a single taxpayer, has taxable income of $118,000, including a $10,000 net capital gain and $2,000 QDI. The last $12,000 of her $118,000 taxable income is the layer related to the net capital gain and/or QDI. The first $106,000 ($118,000 − $12,000) of her taxable income is her other taxable income and is not subject to any special tax rate, so it is taxed using the regular tax rates.

Because the net capital gain and/or QDI may be made up of various *rate layers*, it is important to know in what order those layers are taxed. (Review the five-step ordering procedure discussed in text Section 16-5a and the related examples.) For *each* of the layers, the taxpayer compares the regular tax rate on that layer of income and the alternative tax rate on that portion of the net capital gain and/or QDI and uses the lower of those rates.

The layers are taxed in the following order:

- Any *25% gain*,
- Any *28% gain*,
- The 0 percent portion of the *0%/15%/20% gain* and/or QDI,
- The 15 percent portion of the *0%/15%/20% gain* and/or QDI, and then
- The 20 percent portion of the *0%/15%/20% gain* and/or QDI.

Exhibit 16.1 Alternative Tax Rates on Net Capital Gains (NCG) (Based on Filing Status and Taxable Income)

2022: FILING STATUS

Single		Married, Filing Jointly		Married, Filing Separately		Head of Household		NCG Tax Rate
Taxable Income		Taxable Income		Taxable Income		Taxable Income		
Greater Than	No More Than	Greater Than	No More Than	Greater Than	No More Than	Greater Than	No More Than	
$ –0–	$ 41,675	$ –0–	$ 83,350	$ –0–	$ 41,675	$ –0–	$ 55,800	0%
41,675	459,750	83,350	517,200	41,675	258,600	55,800	488,500	15%
459,750		517,200		258,600		488,500		20%

2021: FILING STATUS

Single		Married, Filing Jointly		Married, Filing Separately		Head of Household		NCG Tax Rate
Taxable Income		Taxable Income		Taxable Income		Taxable Income		
Greater Than	No More Than	Greater Than	No More Than	Greater Than	No More Than	Greater Than	No More Than	
$ –0–	$ 40,400	$ –0–	$ 80,800	$ –0–	$ 40,400	$ –0–	$ 54,100	0%
40,400	445,850	80,800	501,600	40,400	250,800	54,100	473,750	15%
445,850		501,600		250,800		473,750		20%

[27] § 1(h). Note: Examples 44, 45, and 46 use the 2022 Tax Rate Schedules rather than the 2022 Tax Tables (which are not yet available) to calculate the tax on the non-long-term capital gain portion of taxable income. This approach is used to better illustrate the concepts under discussion. The actual tax on the non-long-term portion of taxable income would be calculated using the Tax Tables because that income is less than $100,000.

As a result of this layering:

- The taxpayer benefits from the 0 percent portion of the net capital gain and/or QDI if the taxpayer is still in the 10 percent or 12 percent regular tax bracket after taxing other taxable income and the 25 percent and 28 percent portions of the net capital gain. Depending on the taxpayer's filing status, however, a portion of income in the taxpayer's 12 percent tax bracket is subject to the 15 percent alternative tax rate. In 2022, the 0 percent alternative tax rate applies only through $83,350 of taxable income for married taxpayers filing jointly or surviving spouses, $41,675 for single taxpayers, $55,800 for heads of household, and $41,675 for married taxpayers filing separately. These "break points" for the alternative tax rates do *not* correspond with the normal tax bracket "break points" (see the 2022 Tax Rate Schedules in Appendix A, and compare the maximum amounts in each of the 12 percent tax brackets to the maximum amounts subject to the 0 percent alternative tax rate). This means that in 2022, the last $200 (married, filing jointly and surviving spouses), $100 (single), $100 (heads of household), and $100 (married, filing separately) in the 12 percent bracket is subject to the 15 percent alternative tax rate. Since the normal tax rate (12 percent) is less than the alternative tax rate (15 percent), for these small ranges, any net capital gain or QDI will be taxed at 12 percent (rather than 15 percent).
- The taxpayer benefits from the 15 percent portion of the net capital gain and/or QDI if the taxpayer is in the 22 percent, 24 percent, and 32 percent brackets or a portion of the 35 percent regular rate bracket after taxing other taxable income and the 25 percent, 28 percent, and 0 percent portions of the net capital gain and/or QDI. In 2022, the 15 percent tax rate applies until taxable income exceeds $517,200 for married taxpayers filing jointly or surviving spouses, $459,750 for single taxpayers, $488,500 for heads of household, and $258,600 for married taxpayers filing separately.
- The taxpayer benefits from the 20 percent portion of the net capital gain and/or QDI when taxable income exceeds the maximum taxable income thresholds for the 15 percent alternative tax rate.

Concept Summary 16.4 summarizes the alternative tax computation.

Concept Summary 16.4

Income Layers for Alternative Tax on Capital Gain Computation

Compute tax on:		Other taxable income (including net short-term capital gain) using the regular tax rates.
Compute tax on:		Each of the layers below using the *lower* of the alternative tax rate or the regular tax rate for that layer (or portion of a layer) of taxable income.
	+	25% long-term capital gain (unrecaptured § 1250 gain) portion of taxable income
	+	28% long-term capital gain
	+	0% long-term capital gain [portion of *0%/15%/20% gain* and/or qualified dividend income (QDI) that is taxed at 0%; available only if other taxable income plus 25% and 28% capital gain layers do not put the taxpayer above specified thresholds in the 12% regular tax bracket*; 0% rate is no longer available once income, including the portion of the gain and/or QDI taxed at 0%, puts the taxpayer above these thresholds]
	+	15% long-term capital gain (portion of *0%/15%/20% gain* and/or QDI that is taxed at 15%; available only if other taxable income plus the 25%, 28%, and 0% layers put the taxpayer above the 12% regular tax bracket and only until other taxable income plus the 25%, 28%, 0%, and 15% layers put the taxpayer at or below specified thresholds in the 35% regular tax rate bracket)**
	+	20% long-term capital gain (portion of *0%/15%/20% gain* and/or QDI that is taxed at 20%; available when other taxable income plus the 25%, 28%, 0%, and 15% layers put the taxpayer above the specified thresholds in the 35% regular tax rate bracket)
	=	Alternative tax on taxable income

* See Exhibit 16.1 for the taxable income ranges where the *0%/15%/20%* rates apply. In 2022, the last $200 (married filing jointly and surviving spouse), $100 (single), $100 (heads of household), and $100 (married filing separately) of the 12% bracket is subject to the 15% alternative tax rate. Since the normal tax rate of 12% is less than the alternative tax rate of 15%, any *0%/15%/20% gain* or QDI in these ranges will be taxed at 12%.

** See Exhibit 16.1 for the taxable income amounts where the 20% rate begins to apply.

Alternative Tax on Net Capital Gain

Example 44

In Example 43, Joan had $118,000 taxable income. Now assume that Joan's $10,000 net capital gain is made up of $7,000 *25% gain* and $3,000 *0%/15%/20% gain*. In addition, she has $2,000 of QDI. Examination of the 2022 tax rates reveals that $106,000 ($118,000 − $12,000) of other taxable income for a single individual puts Joan at a marginal tax rate of 24%. Consequently, she uses the alternative tax on the $7,000 gain, the $3,000 gain, and the $2,000 QDI.

Her alternative tax liability is $21,706.

$19,276 (tax on $106,000 of other taxable income)
\+ 1,680 ($7,000 × 0.24; 24% rate on *25% gain*)
\+ 450 ($3,000 × 0.15; 15% rate on *0%/15%/20% gain*)
\+ 300 ($2,000 × 0.15; 15% rate on QDI)
= $21,706 Alternative Tax Liability

Since her marginal tax rate is still 24% after taxing the $106,000 other taxable income, she uses the 24% regular tax rate rather than the 25% alternative tax rate on the $7,000 *25% gain*. As the combination of the $106,000 other taxable income and her $7,000 *25% gain* puts her above the 12% regular tax bracket, none of the $3,000 *0%/15%/20% gain* or $2,000 QDI is taxed at 0%.

Her regular tax liability on $118,000 is $22,156. As a result, Joan saves $450 ($22,156 − $21,706) by using the alternative tax calculation. Since Joan's taxable income is $459,750 or less, none of her *0%/15%/20% gain* or QDI is taxed at the 20% alternative tax rate.

Example 45

Assume that Joan, a single taxpayer, has 2022 taxable income of $25,000. Of this amount, $11,000 is net capital gain, $1,000 is QDI, and $13,000 is other taxable income. The $11,000 net capital gain is made up of $8,300 of *25% gain* and $2,700 of *0%/15%/20% gain*.

Her alternative tax liability is $2,351.

$1,355 (tax on $13,000 of other taxable income)
\+ 996 (tax on $8,300 *25% gain* at 12%)
\+ 0 (tax on $2,700 *0%/15%/20% gain* at 0%)
\+ 0 (tax on $1,000 QDI at 0%)
= $2,351 Alternative Tax Liability

Because her marginal rate is still 12% after taxing the $13,000 of other taxable income, she uses the 12% regular tax rate rather than the 25% alternative tax rate on the $8,300 *25% gain*. After taxing the $13,000 and the $8,300, a total of $21,300 of the $25,000 taxable income has been taxed. Because her remaining taxable income ($3,700) remains in the 12% tax bracket (and her total taxable income does not exceed $41,675), she uses the 0% alternative rate for the $2,700 of *0%/15%/20% gain* and $1,000 QDI.

Joan's regular tax liability on $25,000 is $2,795. As a result, she saves $444 ($2,795−$2,351) by using the alternative tax calculation.

The alternative tax computation allows the taxpayer to receive the *lower of* the regular tax or the alternative tax on *each layer* of net capital gain and/or QDI or *portion of each layer* of net capital gain and/or QDI.

Example 46

Assume the same facts as in Example 45, except that Joan's 2022 taxable income is $44,000, consisting of $11,000 of net capital gain (made up of $8,300 of *25% gain* and $2,700 of *0%/15%/20% gain*), $1,000 of QDI, and $32,000 of other taxable income.

Not all of the combined *0%/15%/20% gain* and QDI ($3,700; $2,700 + $1,000) is taxed at 0% because Joan's taxable income exceeds $41,675, taking her out of the 0% alternative tax. Consequently, the last $2,325 ($44,000 − $41,675) of the $3,700 is taxed at 12% and 15% rather than 0%.

Her tax liability using the alternative tax computation is $4,977.

$3,635 (tax on $32,000 of other taxable income)
\+ 996 (tax on $8,300 25% *gain* at 12%)
\+ 0 (tax on $1,375 of the $3,700 combined *0%/15%/20% gain* and QDI at 0%)
\+ 12 (tax on $100 of the $3,700 combined *0%/15%/20% gain* and QDI at 12%)
\+ 334 (tax on $2,225 of the $3,700 combined *0%/15%/20% gain* and QDI at 15%)
= $4,977 Alternative Tax Liability

Joan's regular tax liability on $44,000 is $5,297. As a result, she saves $320 ($5,297 − $4,977) by using the alternative tax calculation.

16-5d Treatment of Net Capital Losses

Computation of Net Capital Loss

A **net capital loss (NCL)** results if capital losses exceed capital gains for the year. An NCL may be all long term, all short term, or part long and part short term.[28] The characterization of an NCL as long or short term is important in determining the capital loss deduction (discussed next).

Example 47

Three different individuals have the following capital gains and losses during the year:

	Short Term			Long Term			Combined	
Taxpayer	STCG	STCL	Net Short Term	LTCG	LTCL	Net Long Term	Combined Short Term and Long Term	Description of Result
Paulina	$1,000	($ 500)	$ 500	$1,000	($2,800)	($1,800)	($1,300)	NLTCL
Carlos	1,000	(2,800)	(1,800)	1,000	(500)	500	(1,300)	NSTCL
Anibal	500	(1,200)	(700)	400	(1,200)	(800)	(1,500)	NSTCL ($700) NLTCL ($800)

Paulina's NCL of $1,300 is all long term. Carlos's NCL of $1,300 is all short term. Anibal's NCL is $1,500, $700 of which is short term and $800 of which is long term.

Capital Loss Deduction

A net capital loss is deductible *for* AGI, but limited to no more than $3,000 per tax year.[29] So although a net capital gain receives favorable tax treatment, there is *unfavorable* treatment for capital losses due to the $3,000 annual limitation. If the NCL includes both long-term and short-term capital loss, the short-term capital loss is counted first toward the $3,000 annual limitation.

Example 48

Burt has an NCL of $5,500, of which $2,000 is STCL and $3,500 is LTCL. Burt has a capital loss deduction of $3,000 ($2,000 of STCL and $1,000 of LTCL). He has an LTCL carryforward of $2,500 ($3,500 − $1,000).

Carryovers

Taxpayers are allowed to carry over unused capital losses indefinitely. The short-term capital loss (STCL) retains its character as STCL. Likewise, the long-term capital loss retains its character as LTCL.

Example 49

In 2022, Jake incurred $1,000 of STCL and $11,000 of LTCL. In 2023, Jake has a $400 LTCG.

- Jake's NCL for 2022 is $12,000. Jake deducts $3,000 ($1,000 STCL and $2,000 LTCL). He has $9,000 of LTCL carried forward to 2023.
- Jake combines the $9,000 LTCL carryforward with the $400 LTCG for 2023. He has an $8,600 NLTCL for 2023. Jake deducts $3,000 of LTCL in 2023 and carries forward $5,600 of LTCL to 2024.

[28] Code § 1222(10) defines a net capital loss as the net loss after the capital loss deduction. However, that definition confuses the discussion of net capital loss. Therefore, net capital loss is used here to mean the result after netting capital gains and losses and before considering the capital loss deduction.

[29] § 1211(b)(1). Married taxpayers filing separate returns are limited to a $1,500 deduction per tax year. When a taxpayer has both a capital loss deduction and negative taxable income, a special computation of the capital loss carryover is required. See § 1212(b).

Concept Summary 16.5 summarizes the rules for noncorporate taxpayers' treatment of capital gains and losses.

Concept Summary 16.5

Final Results of the Capital Gain and Loss Netting Process and How They Are Taxed

Result	Maximum Tax Rate	Comments
Net short-term capital loss	—	Eligible for capital loss deduction ($3,000 maximum per year).
Net long-term capital loss	—	Eligible for capital loss deduction ($3,000 maximum per year).
Net short-term capital loss *and* net long-term capital loss	—	Eligible for capital loss deduction ($3,000 maximum per year). Short-term capital losses are counted first toward the deduction.
Net short-term capital gain	10%–37%	Taxed as ordinary income.
Net long-term capital gain	0%–28%	The net long-term capital gain may have as many as five tax rate components: 25%, 28%, and 0%/15%/20%.
• The net long-term capital gain is the *last* portion of taxable income.		The components are taxed in the following order: 25%, 28%, 0%, 15%, 20%. They are taxed *after* the non-long-term capital gain portion of taxable income has been taxed. The 0%/15%/20% component may include qualified dividend income.
• Each net long-term capital gain component of taxable income is taxed at the *lower* of the regular tax on that component or the alternative tax.		The alternative tax on net long-term capital gain can never increase the tax on taxable income, but it can reduce the tax on taxable income.
Net short-term capital gain *and* net long-term capital gain	10%–37% on net short-term capital gain; 0%–28% on net long-term capital gain	The net short-term capital gain is taxed as ordinary income; the net long-term capital gain is taxed as discussed above for just net long-term capital gain.

16-5e Reporting Procedures

The following example is used to discuss and illustrate the tax forms used for reporting (2021 forms are used because the 2022 tax forms are not yet available).

Example 50

During 2021, Maria Rapson (Social Security number 123-45-6789) had the following sales of capital assets. In addition, she has $300 of qualified dividend income and $65,700 of other taxable income. Maria is single and has no dependents.

Description	Acquired On	Date Sold	Sales Price	Tax Basis	Gain or Loss	Character
100 shares Blue stock	1/21/21	11/11/21	$11,000	$17,000	($ 6,000)	STCL
100 shares Yellow stock	9/12/16	10/12/21	36,000	20,000	16,000	LTCG
100 shares Purple stock	3/14/19	10/12/21	14,000	12,000	2,000	LTCG

Maria has a net capital gain of $12,000 ($16,000 *0%/15%/20% gain* + $2,000 *0%/5%/20% gain* − $6,000 short-term capital loss). Consequently, all of the net capital gain is composed of *0%/15%/20% gain*. Maria's $78,000 taxable income includes $65,700 of other taxable income, a $12,000 net capital gain, and $300 qualified dividend income.

Maria's stockbroker reported total stock sales to her on Form 1099-B, which showed the sales proceeds and adjusted basis for each of her transactions. She had no investments in qualified opportunity funds. Following a discussion of the reporting rules, Maria's completed forms and a related worksheet are presented.

Capital gains and losses are reported on Schedule D of Form 1040 (Capital Gains and Losses). Part I of Schedule D is used to report short-term capital gains and losses. Part II of Schedule D is used to report long-term capital gains and losses. The information shown in Parts I and II comes from Form 8949 (Sales and Other Dispositions of Assets). Form 8949 is used to accumulate gains and losses from three sources:

- Capital gain and loss transactions for which a Form 1099–B (Proceeds from Broker and Barter Exchange Transactions) has been received and the provider of the form had information on the sales proceeds *and* the tax basis of the assets disposed of.
- Capital gain and loss transactions for which a Form 1099–B has been received and the provider of the form had information on the sales proceeds *but did not* have information on the tax basis of the assets disposed of.
- Capital gain and loss transactions for which a Form 1099–B was not received.

Part III of Form 1040 Schedule D summarizes the results of Parts I and II and indicates whether the taxpayer has a net capital gain or a net capital loss. Part III then helps determine which alternative tax worksheet is used to calculate the alternative tax on long-term capital gains and qualified dividends.

- If the taxpayer has a net long-term capital gain that does *not* include any 28% or 25% long-term capital gain, then the alternative tax is calculated using the Qualified Dividends and Capital Gain Worksheet from the Form 1040 instructions.
- If the taxpayer has a net long-term capital gain that includes 28% and/or 25% long-term capital gain, then the alternative tax is calculated using the Schedule D Tax Worksheet from the Schedule D instructions.

These worksheets do not have to be filed with the tax return, but are kept for the taxpayer's records.

16-6 Tax Treatment of Capital Gains and Losses of Corporate Taxpayers

LO.6

Describe the tax treatment for capital gains and the detrimental tax treatment for capital losses for corporate taxpayers.

The treatment of a corporation's net capital gain or loss differs from the rules for individuals. Briefly, the differences are as follows:

- There is no NCG alternative tax rate.
- Capital losses offset only capital gains. No deduction of capital losses is permitted against other taxable income (whereas a $3,000 deduction is allowed to individuals).[30]
- Corporations may carry back net capital losses (whether long-term or short-term) as short-term capital losses for three years; if losses still remain after the carryback, the remaining losses may be carried forward five years.[31] Individuals may carry forward unused capital losses indefinitely, but there is no carryback.

Example 51

Sparrow Corporation has a $15,000 NLTCL for the current year and $57,000 of other taxable income. Sparrow may not offset the $15,000 NLTCL against its other income by taking a capital loss deduction.

The $15,000 NLTCL becomes a $15,000 STCL for carryback and carryover purposes. This amount may be offset against capital gains in the three-year carryback period or, if not absorbed there, offset capital gains in the five-year carryforward period. Any amount remaining after this carryforward period expires is permanently lost.

The rules applicable to corporations are discussed in greater detail in Chapter 20.

[30] § 1211(a).

[31] § 1212(a)(1).

SCHEDULE D (Form 1040)

Department of the Treasury Internal Revenue Service (99)

Capital Gains and Losses

▶ Attach to Form 1040, 1040-SR, or 1040-NR.
▶ Go to *www.irs.gov/ScheduleD* for instructions and the latest information.
▶ Use Form 8949 to list your transactions for lines 1b, 2, 3, 8b, 9, and 10.

OMB No. 1545-0074

2021

Attachment Sequence No. **12**

Name(s) shown on return: *Maria Rapson*

Your social security number: *123-45-6789*

Did you dispose of any investment(s) in a qualified opportunity fund during the tax year? ☐ **Yes** ☐ **No**
If "Yes," attach Form 8949 and see its instructions for additional requirements for reporting your gain or loss.

Part I Short-Term Capital Gains and Losses—Generally Assets Held One Year or Less (see instructions)

See instructions for how to figure the amounts to enter on the lines below. This form may be easier to complete if you round off cents to whole dollars.	**(d)** Proceeds (sales price)	**(e)** Cost (or other basis)	**(g)** Adjustments to gain or loss from Form(s) 8949, Part I, line 2, column (g)	**(h) Gain or (loss)** Subtract column (e) from column (d) and combine the result with column (g)
1a Totals for all short-term transactions reported on Form 1099-B for which basis was reported to the IRS and for which you have no adjustments (see instructions). However, if you choose to report all these transactions on Form 8949, leave this line blank and go to line 1b .				
1b Totals for all transactions reported on Form(s) 8949 with **Box A** checked	*11,000*	*17,000*		*(6,000)*
2 Totals for all transactions reported on Form(s) 8949 with **Box B** checked				
3 Totals for all transactions reported on Form(s) 8949 with **Box C** checked				

4 Short-term gain from Form 6252 and short-term gain or (loss) from Forms 4684, 6781, and 8824 . .	**4**	
5 Net short-term gain or (loss) from partnerships, S corporations, estates, and trusts from Schedule(s) K-1	**5**	
6 Short-term capital loss carryover. Enter the amount, if any, from line 8 of your **Capital Loss Carryover Worksheet** in the instructions	**6**	( )
7 **Net short-term capital gain or (loss).** Combine lines 1a through 6 in column (h). If you have any long-term capital gains or losses, go to Part II below. Otherwise, go to Part III on the back	**7**	*(6,000)*

Part II Long-Term Capital Gains and Losses—Generally Assets Held More Than One Year (see instructions)

See instructions for how to figure the amounts to enter on the lines below. This form may be easier to complete if you round off cents to whole dollars.	**(d)** Proceeds (sales price)	**(e)** Cost (or other basis)	**(g)** Adjustments to gain or loss from Form(s) 8949, Part II, line 2, column (g)	**(h) Gain or (loss)** Subtract column (e) from column (d) and combine the result with column (g)
8a Totals for all long-term transactions reported on Form 1099-B for which basis was reported to the IRS and for which you have no adjustments (see instructions). However, if you choose to report all these transactions on Form 8949, leave this line blank and go to line 8b .				
8b Totals for all transactions reported on Form(s) 8949 with **Box D** checked	*50,000*	*32,000*		*18,000*
9 Totals for all transactions reported on Form(s) 8949 with **Box E** checked				
10 Totals for all transactions reported on Form(s) 8949 with **Box F** checked.				

11 Gain from Form 4797, Part I; long-term gain from Forms 2439 and 6252; and long-term gain or (loss) from Forms 4684, 6781, and 8824	**11**	
12 Net long-term gain or (loss) from partnerships, S corporations, estates, and trusts from Schedule(s) K-1	**12**	
13 Capital gain distributions. See the instructions	**13**	
14 Long-term capital loss carryover. Enter the amount, if any, from line 13 of your **Capital Loss Carryover Worksheet** in the instructions	**14**	( )
15 **Net long-term capital gain or (loss).** Combine lines 8a through 14 in column (h). Then, go to Part III on the back	**15**	*18,000*

For Paperwork Reduction Act Notice, see your tax return instructions. Cat. No. 11338H **Schedule D (Form 1040) 2021**

Schedule D (Form 1040) 2021 Page **2**

Part III Summary

16	Combine lines 7 and 15 and enter the result	**16**	*12,000*
	• If line 16 is a **gain,** enter the amount from line 16 on Form 1040, 1040-SR, or 1040-NR, line 7. Then, go to line 17 below. • If line 16 is a **loss,** skip lines 17 through 20 below. Then, go to line 21. Also be sure to complete line 22. • If line 16 is **zero,** skip lines 17 through 21 below and enter -0- on Form 1040, 1040-SR, or 1040-NR, line 7. Then, go to line 22.		
17	Are lines 15 and 16 **both** gains? ☑ **Yes.** Go to line 18. ☐ **No.** Skip lines 18 through 21, and go to line 22.		
18	If you are required to complete the **28% Rate Gain Worksheet** (see instructions), enter the amount, if any, from line 7 of that worksheet . . . . ▶	**18**	*0*
19	If you are required to complete the **Unrecaptured Section 1250 Gain Worksheet** (see instructions), enter the amount, if any, from line 18 of that worksheet . . . . ▶	**19**	*0*
20	Are lines 18 and 19 both zero or blank and are you not filing Form 4952? ☑ **Yes.** Complete the **Qualified Dividends and Capital Gain Tax Worksheet** in the instructions for Forms 1040 and 1040-SR, line 16. **Don't** complete lines 21 and 22 below. ☐ **No.** Complete the **Schedule D Tax Worksheet** in the instructions. **Don't** complete lines 21 and 22 below.		
21	If line 16 is a loss, enter here and on Form 1040, 1040-SR, or 1040-NR, line 7, the **smaller** of: • The loss on line 16; or • ($3,000), or if married filing separately, ($1,500) } . . . . **Note:** When figuring which amount is smaller, treat both amounts as positive numbers.	**21**	( )
22	Do you have qualified dividends on Form 1040, 1040-SR, or 1040-NR, line 3a? ☐ **Yes.** Complete the **Qualified Dividends and Capital Gain Tax Worksheet** in the instructions for Forms 1040 and 1040-SR, line 16. ☐ **No.** Complete the rest of Form 1040, 1040-SR, or 1040-NR.		

Schedule D (Form 1040) 2021

Form **8949**

Department of the Treasury
Internal Revenue Service

Sales and Other Dispositions of Capital Assets

▶ Go to *www.irs.gov/Form8949* for instructions and the latest information.

▶ File with your Schedule D to list your transactions for lines 1b, 2, 3, 8b, 9, and 10 of Schedule D.

OMB No. 1545-0074

2021

Attachment Sequence No. **12A**

Name(s) shown on return	Social security number or taxpayer identification number
Maria Rapson	*123-45-6789*

Before you check Box A, B, or C below, see whether you received any Form(s) 1099-B or substitute statement(s) from your broker. A substitute statement will have the same information as Form 1099-B. Either will show whether your basis (usually your cost) was reported to the IRS by your broker and may even tell you which box to check.

Part I **Short-Term.** Transactions involving capital assets you held 1 year or less are generally short-term (see instructions). For long-term transactions, see page 2.

Note: You may aggregate all short-term transactions reported on Form(s) 1099-B showing basis was reported to the IRS and for which no adjustments or codes are required. Enter the totals directly on Schedule D, line 1a; you aren't required to report these transactions on Form 8949 (see instructions).

You *must* check Box A, B, *or* C below. Check only one box. If more than one box applies for your short-term transactions, complete a separate Form 8949, page 1, for each applicable box. If you have more short-term transactions than will fit on this page for one or more of the boxes, complete as many forms with the same box checked as you need.

☑ **(A)** Short-term transactions reported on Form(s) 1099-B showing basis was reported to the IRS (see **Note** above)

☐ **(B)** Short-term transactions reported on Form(s) 1099-B showing basis **wasn't** reported to the IRS

☐ **(C)** Short-term transactions not reported to you on Form 1099-B

1 (a) Description of property (Example: 100 sh. XYZ Co.)	(b) Date acquired (Mo., day, yr.)	(c) Date sold or disposed of (Mo., day, yr.)	(d) Proceeds (sales price) (see instructions)	(e) Cost or other basis. See the **Note** below and see *Column (e)* in the separate instructions	Adjustment, if any, to gain or loss. If you enter an amount in column (g), enter a code in column (f). **See the separate instructions.** (f) Code(s) from instructions	(g) Amount of adjustment	(h) **Gain or (loss).** Subtract column (e) from column (d) and combine the result with column (g)
100 Shares Blue Stock	*01/21/21*	*11/11/21*	*11,000*	*17,000*			*(6,000)*
2 Totals. Add the amounts in columns (d), (e), (g), and (h) (subtract negative amounts). Enter each total here and include on your Schedule D, **line 1b** (if **Box A** above is checked), **line 2** (if **Box B** above is checked), or **line 3** (if **Box C** above is checked) ▶			*11,000*	*17,000*			*(6,000)*

Note: If you checked Box A above but the basis reported to the IRS was incorrect, enter in column (e) the basis as reported to the IRS, and enter an adjustment in column (g) to correct the basis. See *Column (g)* in the separate instructions for how to figure the amount of the adjustment.

For Paperwork Reduction Act Notice, see your tax return instructions. Cat. No. 37768Z Form **8949** (2021)

Form 8949 (2021) Attachment Sequence No. **12A** Page **2**

Name(s) shown on return. Name and SSN or taxpayer identification no. not required if shown on other side	**Social security number or taxpayer identification number**

Before you check Box D, E, or F below, see whether you received any Form(s) 1099-B or substitute statement(s) from your broker. A substitute statement will have the same information as Form 1099-B. Either will show whether your basis (usually your cost) was reported to the IRS by your broker and may even tell you which box to check.

Part II **Long-Term.** Transactions involving capital assets you held more than 1 year are generally long-term (see instructions). For short-term transactions, see page 1.

Note: You may aggregate all long-term transactions reported on Form(s) 1099-B showing basis was reported to the IRS and for which no adjustments or codes are required. Enter the totals directly on Schedule D, line 8a; you aren't required to report these transactions on Form 8949 (see instructions).

You *must* check Box D, E, *or* F below. Check only one box. If more than one box applies for your long-term transactions, complete a separate Form 8949, page 2, for each applicable box. If you have more long-term transactions than will fit on this page for one or more of the boxes, complete as many forms with the same box checked as you need.

☑ **(D)** Long-term transactions reported on Form(s) 1099-B showing basis was reported to the IRS (see **Note** above)

☐ **(E)** Long-term transactions reported on Form(s) 1099-B showing basis **wasn't** reported to the IRS

☐ **(F)** Long-term transactions not reported to you on Form 1099-B

1 (a) Description of property (Example: 100 sh. XYZ Co.)	(b) Date acquired (Mo., day, yr.)	(c) Date sold or disposed of (Mo., day, yr.)	(d) Proceeds (sales price) (see instructions)	(e) Cost or other basis. See the **Note** below and see *Column (e)* in the separate instructions	Adjustment, if any, to gain or loss. If you enter an amount in column (g), enter a code in column (f). **See the separate instructions.** (f) Code(s) from instructions	(g) Amount of adjustment	(h) **Gain or (loss).** Subtract column (e) from column (d) and combine the result with column (g)
100 Shares Yellow Stock	*09/12/16*	*10/12/21*	*36,000*	*20,000*			*16,000*
100 Shares Purple Stock	*03/14/19*	*10/12/21*	*14,000*	*12,000*			*2,000*
2 Totals. Add the amounts in columns (d), (e), (g), and (h) (subtract negative amounts). Enter each total here and include on your Schedule D, **line 8b** (if **Box D** above is checked), **line 9** (if **Box E** above is checked), or **line 10** (if **Box F** above is checked) ▶			*50,000*	*32,000*			*18,000*

Note: If you checked Box D above but the basis reported to the IRS was incorrect, enter in column (e) the basis as reported to the IRS, and enter an adjustment in column (g) to correct the basis. See *Column (g)* in the separate instructions for how to figure the amount of the adjustment.

Form **8949** (2021)

Qualified Dividends and Capital Gain Tax Worksheet—Line 16

Keep for Your Records

Before you begin: √ See the earlier instructions for line 16 to see if you can use this worksheet to figure your tax.
√ Before completing this worksheet, complete Form 1040 or 1040-SR through line 15.
√ If you don't have to file Schedule D and you received capital gain distributions, be sure you checked the box on Form 1040 or 1040-SR, line 7.

1.	Enter the amount from Form 1040 or 1040-SR, line 15. However, if you are filing Form 2555 (relating to foreign earned income), enter the amount from line 3 of the Foreign Earned Income Tax Worksheet			**1.**	*78,000*	
2.	Enter the amount from Form 1040 or 1040-SR, line 3a*	**2.**	*300*			
3.	Are you filing Schedule D?* ☑ **Yes.** Enter the **smaller** of line 15 or 16 of Schedule D. If either line 15 or 16 is blank or a loss, enter -0-. ☐ **No.** Enter the amount from Form 1040 or 1040-SR, line 7.	**3.**	*12,000*			
4.	Add lines 2 and 3	**4.**	*12,300*			
5.	Subtract line 4 from line 1. If zero or less, enter -0-			**5.**	*65,700*	
6.	Enter: $40,400 if single or married filing separately, $80,800 if married filing jointly or qualifying widow(er), $54,100 if head of household.			**6.**	*40,400*	
7.	Enter the smaller of line 1 or line 6			**7.**	*40,400*	
8.	Enter the smaller of line 5 or line 7			**8.**	*40,400*	
9.	Subtract line 8 from line 7. This amount is taxed at 0%			**9.**	*0*	
10.	Enter the smaller of line 1 or line 4			**10.**	*12,300*	
11.	Enter the amount from line 9			**11.**	*0*	
12.	Subtract line 11 from line 10			**12.**	*12,300*	
13.	Enter: $445,850 if single, $250,800 if married filing separately, $501,600 if married filing jointly or qualifying widow(er), $473,750 if head of household.			**13.**	*445,850*	
14.	Enter the smaller of line 1 or line 13			**14.**	*78,000*	
15.	Add lines 5 and 9			**15.**	*65,700*	
16.	Subtract line 15 from line 14. If zero or less, enter -0-			**16.**	*12,300*	
17.	Enter the smaller of line 12 or line 16			**17.**	*12,300*	
18.	Multiply line 17 by 15% (0.15)				**18.**	*1,845*
19.	Add lines 9 and 17			**19.**	*12,300*	
20.	Subtract line 19 from line 10			**20.**	*0*	
21.	Multiply line 20 by 20% (0.20)				**21.**	*0*
22.	Figure the tax on the amount on line 5. If the amount on line 5 is less than $100,000, use the Tax Table to figure the tax. If the amount on line 5 is $100,000 or more, use the Tax Computation Worksheet				**22.**	*10,208*
23.	Add lines 18, 21, and 22				**23.**	*12,053*
24.	Figure the tax on the amount on line 1. If the amount on line 1 is less than $100,000, use the Tax Table to figure the tax. If the amount on line 1 is $100,000 or more, use the Tax Computation Worksheet				**24.**	*12,914*
25.	**Tax on all taxable income.** Enter the **smaller** of line 23 or 24. Also include this amount on the entry space on Form 1040 or 1040-SR, line 16. If you are filing Form 2555, don't enter this amount on the entry space on Form 1040 or 1040-SR, line 16. Instead, enter it on line 4 of the Foreign Earned Income Tax Worksheet				**25.**	*12,053*

* *If you are filing Form 2555, see the footnote in the Foreign Earned Income Tax Worksheet before completing this line.*

Global Tax Issues **Capital Gain Treatment in the United States and Other Countries**

The United States currently requires a very complex tax calculation when taxable income includes net long-term capital gain. However, the alternative tax on net long-term capital gain can generate tax savings even when the taxpayer is in the lowest regular tax bracket (10 percent) because there is an alternative tax rate of 0 percent. Many other countries also have an alternative tax rate on long-term capital gains. Consequently, even though the U.S. system is complex, it may be preferable because of the lower tax rates and because the lower rates are available to taxpayers in all tax brackets.

16-7 Tax Planning

LO.7

Identify tax planning opportunities arising from the sale or exchange of capital assets.

16-7a Importance of Capital Asset Status

Why is capital asset status important? Because of the alternative tax on net capital gain. Individuals who receive income in the form of long-term capital gains or qualified dividend income have an advantage over taxpayers who cannot receive income in these forms.

If a net capital loss results, the maximum deduction is $3,000 per year. Consequently, capital gains and losses must be segregated from other types of gains and losses and must be reported separately on Schedule D of Form 1040.

16-7b Planning for Capital Asset Status

Capital asset status often is a question of objective evidence. Property that is not a capital asset to one person may qualify as a capital asset to another person.

Example 52

Mila, a real estate dealer, transfers by gift a tract of land to Jeff, her son. The land was recorded as part of Mila's inventory (it was held for resale) and was therefore not a capital asset to her. Jeff, however, treats the land as an investment. The land is a capital asset in Jeff's hands, and any later taxable disposition of the property by him will yield a capital gain or loss.

With proper tax planning, even a dealer may obtain long-term capital gain treatment on the sale of property normally held for resale.

Example 53

Jim, a real estate dealer, segregates Tract A from the real estate he regularly holds for resale and designates the property as being held for investment purposes. The property is not advertised for sale and is disposed of several years later. The negotiations for the subsequent sale were initiated by the purchaser and not by Jim. Under these circumstances, it would appear that any gain or loss from the sale of Tract A should be a capital gain or loss.[32]

When a business is being sold, one of the major decisions usually concerns whether a portion of the sales price is for goodwill. For the seller, goodwill generally represents the disposition of a capital asset. Goodwill has no basis and represents a residual portion of the selling price that cannot be allocated reasonably to the known assets. As a result, the amount of goodwill represents capital gain.

From a legal perspective, the buyer may prefer that the residual portion of the purchase price be allocated to a covenant not to compete (a promise that the seller will

[32] *Toledo, Peoria & Western Railroad Co.*, 35 TCM 1663, T.C.Memo. 1976–366.

not compete against the buyer by conducting a business similar to the one the buyer has purchased). Both purchased goodwill and a covenant not to compete are § 197 intangibles. As a result, both must be capitalized and can be amortized over a 15-year statutory period.

To the seller, a covenant produces ordinary income. So the seller would prefer that the residual portion of the selling price be allocated to goodwill—a capital asset. If the buyer does not need the legal protection provided by a covenant, the buyer is neutral regarding whether the residual amount be allocated to a covenant or to goodwill. Because the seller would receive a tax advantage from labeling the residual amount as goodwill, the buyer should factor this into the negotiation of the purchase price.

Example 54

Marcia is buying Jack's dry cleaning proprietorship. An appraisal of the assets indicates that a reasonable purchase price would exceed the value of the known assets by $30,000. If the purchase contract does not specify the nature of the $30,000, the amount will be for goodwill and Jack will have a long-term capital gain of $30,000. Marcia will have a 15-year amortizable $30,000 asset.

If Marcia is paying the extra $30,000 to prevent Jack from conducting another dry cleaning business in the area (a covenant not to compete), Jack will have $30,000 of ordinary income. Marcia will have a $30,000 deduction over the statutory 15-year amortization period rather than over the actual life of the covenant (e.g., 5 years).

16-7c Effect of Capital Asset Status in Transactions Other Than Sales

The nature of an asset (capital or ordinary) is important in determining the tax consequences that result when a sale or exchange occurs. It may, however, be just as significant in circumstances other than a taxable sale or exchange. When a capital asset is disposed of, the result is not always a capital gain or loss. Rather, in general, the disposition must be a sale or exchange. Collection of a debt instrument having a basis less than the face value results in a capital gain if the debt instrument is a capital asset. The collection is a sale or exchange. Sale of the debt shortly before the due date for collection will produce a capital gain.[33] If selling the debt in such circumstances could produce a capital gain but collecting could not, the consistency of what constitutes a capital gain or loss would be undermined. Another illustration of the sale or exchange principle involves a donation of certain appreciated property to a qualified charity. Recall that in certain circumstances, the measure of the charitable contribution is fair market value when the property, if sold, would have yielded a long-term capital gain (refer to the discussion of contributions of capital gain property in Chapter 10).

Example 55

Sharon wants to donate a tract of unimproved land (basis of $40,000 and fair market value of $200,000) held for the required long-term holding period to State University (a qualified charitable organization). However, Sharon currently is under audit by the IRS for capital gains she reported on certain real estate transactions during an earlier tax year. Although Sharon is not a licensed real estate broker, the IRS agent conducting the audit is contending that she has achieved dealer status by virtue of the number and frequency of the real estate transactions she has conducted.

Under these circumstances, Sharon would be well advised to postpone the donation to State University until her status is clarified. If she has achieved dealer status, the unimproved land may be inventory (refer to Example 53 for another possible result) and Sharon's charitable contribution deduction would be limited to $40,000. If not and if the land is held as an investment, Sharon's deduction is $200,000 (the fair market value of the property).

[33] § 1271(b).

16-7d Stock Sales

The following rules apply in determining the date of a stock sale:

- The date the sale is executed is the date of the sale. The execution date is the date the broker completes the transaction on the stock exchange.
- The settlement date is the date the cash or other property is paid to the seller of the stock. This date is *not* relevant in determining the date of sale.

Example 56

Lupe, a cash basis taxpayer, sells stock that results in a gain. The sale was executed on December 29, 2021. The settlement date is January 2, 2022. The date of sale is December 29, 2021 (the execution date). The holding period for the stock sold ends with the execution date.

16-7e Maximizing Benefits

Ordinary losses generally are preferable to capital losses because of the limitations imposed on the deductibility of net capital losses and the requirement that capital losses be used to offset capital gains. The taxpayer may be able to convert what would otherwise have been capital loss to ordinary loss. For example, business (but not nonbusiness) bad debts, losses from the sale or exchange of small business investment company stock, and losses from the sale or exchange of small business corporation stock all result in ordinary losses.[34]

Although capital losses can be carried over indefinitely, *indefinite* becomes definite when a taxpayer dies. Any loss carryovers not used by the taxpayer are permanently lost. That is, no tax benefit can be derived from the carryovers subsequent to death.[35] Therefore, the potential benefit of carrying over capital losses diminishes when dealing with older taxpayers.

It is usually beneficial to spread gains over more than one taxable year. In some cases, this can be accomplished through the installment sales method of accounting.

16-7f Year-End Planning

The following general rules can be applied for timing the recognition of capital gains and losses near the end of a taxable year:

- If the taxpayer already has recognized more than $3,000 of capital loss, sell assets to generate capital gain equal to the excess of the capital loss over $3,000.

Example 57

Kevin has already incurred a $7,000 STCL. Kevin should generate $4,000 of capital gain. The gain will offset $4,000 of the loss. The remaining loss of $3,000 can be deducted against ordinary income.

- If the taxpayer already has recognized capital gain, sell assets to generate capital loss equal to the capital gain. The gain will not be taxed, and the loss will be fully *deductible* against the gain.
- Generally, if the taxpayer has a choice between recognizing short-term capital gain or long-term capital gain, long-term capital gain should be recognized because it is subject to a lower tax rate.

[34] §§ 166(d), 1242, and 1244. Refer to the discussion in Chapter 7.

[35] Rev.Rul. 74–175.

Refocus on The Big Picture

Managing Capital Asset Transactions

You explain to Maurice that your area of expertise is tax, so you are providing tax advice and not investment advice. From an overall perspective, he is correct that certain capital gains and dividends are eligible for either a 0 percent, a 15 percent, or a 20 percent tax rate rather than the regular income tax rates that go as high as 37 percent. You then discuss the potential tax consequences of each of his investments.

- *Purple stock and Eagle stock.* To qualify for the beneficial tax rate, the holding period for the stock must be longer than one year. From a tax perspective, Maurice should retain his stock investments for at least an additional three months and a day. To be eligible for the "costless" capital gains (i.e., capital gains taxed at 0%), his taxable income should not exceed $41,675 for 2022. The dividends received on the Purple stock are "qualified dividends" eligible for the *0%/15%/20%* alternative tax rate.
- *Patent.* Because he is a "holder" of the patent, it will qualify for the beneficial capital gain rate regardless of the holding period if the patent should produce income in excess of his $50,000 investment. However, if he loses money on the investment, he will be able to deduct only $3,000 of the loss per year against his ordinary income (assuming that there are no offsetting capital gains).
- *Tax-exempt bonds.* The after-tax return on the taxable bonds would be less than the 3 percent on the tax-exempt bonds. In addition, the interest on the taxable bonds would increase his taxable income, possibly moving it out of the desired 12 percent marginal tax rate into the 22 percent marginal tax rate.
- *Franchise rights.* The franchise rights purchased from Orange, Inc., probably require the payment of a franchise fee based upon the sales in the franchise business. Maurice should either start such a business or sell the franchise rights.
- *Partnership interest.* Whether Maurice receives capital or ordinary treatment associated with his partnership interest depends on whether he is reporting his share of profits or losses (ordinary income or ordinary loss) or is reporting recognized gain or loss from the sale of his partnership interest (capital gain or capital loss).

You conclude your tax advice to Maurice by telling him that whatever he does regarding his investments should make economic sense. There are no 100 percent tax rates. For example, disposing of the bank stock in the current market could be the wise thing to do.

AUREMAR/SHUTTERSTOCK.COM

Key Terms

Alternative tax, 16-24
Capital asset, 16-4
Capital gains, 16-2
Capital losses, 16-2
Collectibles, 16-22
Franchise, 16-12
Holding period, 16-15
Lessee, 16-14
Lessor, 16-14
Net capital gain (NCG), 16-19
Net capital loss (NCL), 16-27
Options, 16-9
Original issue discount (OID), 16-9
Patent, 16-11
Qualified dividend income (QDI), 16-23
Qualified small business stock, 16-22
Sale or exchange, 16-8
Short sale, 16-16
Unrecaptured § 1250 gain, 16-19

Discussion Questions

1. **LO.2, 4, 5** Sheila inherited 300 shares of stock, 100 shares of Magenta and 200 shares of Purple. She has a stockbroker sell the shares for her, uses the proceeds for personal expenses, and thinks nothing further about the transactions. What issues does she face when she prepares her Federal income tax return? *Critical Thinking*

2. **LO.2** An individual taxpayer sells some used assets at a garage sale. Why are none of the proceeds taxable in most situations? *Critical Thinking*

3. **LO.2, 4** Alison owns a painting that she received as a gift from her aunt 10 years ago. The aunt created the painting. Alison has displayed the painting in her home and has never attempted to sell it. Recently, a visitor noticed the painting and offered Alison $5,000 for it. If Alison decides to sell the painting, what tax issues does she face? *Critical Thinking*

4. **LO.2** Is a note receivable that arose in the ordinary course of the taxpayer's retail business a capital asset? Why or why not?

5. **LO.2** Anwar owns vacant land that he purchased many years ago as an investment. After getting approval to subdivide it into 35 lots, he made minimal improvements and then sold the entire property to a real estate developer. Anwar's recognized gain on the sale was $1,200,000. Is this transaction eligible for the "real property subdivided for sale" rules? Why or why not?

6. **LO.3** Hubert purchases all of the rights in a patent from the inventor who developed the patented product. After holding the patent for two years, Hubert sells all of the rights in the patent for a substantial gain. What issues does Hubert face if he wants to treat the gain as a long-term capital gain? *Critical Thinking*

7. **LO.3** Blue Corporation and Fuchsia Corporation are engaged in a contract negotiation over the use of Blue's trademarked name, DateSiteForSeniors. For a one-time payment of $45,000, Blue licensed Fuchsia to use the name DateSiteForSeniors, and the license requires that Fuchsia pay Blue a royalty every time a new customer signs up on Fuchsia's website. Blue is a developer of "website ideas" that it then licenses to other companies such as Fuchsia. Did Fuchsia purchase a franchise right from Blue, or did Fuchsia purchase the name DateSiteForSeniors from Blue?

8. **LO.4** At the date of a short sale, Sylvia has held substantially identical securities for more than 12 months. What is the nature of any gain or loss from the close of her short sale?

9. **LO.5** After netting all of her short-term and long-term capital gains and losses, Misty has a net short-term capital loss and a net long-term capital loss. Can she net these against each other? Why or why not?

10. **LO.2, 5** Charlie sells his antique farm tractor collection at a loss. He had acquired all of the tractors for his personal pleasure and sold all of them for less than he paid for them. What is the tax status of the tractors? Is his loss a 28% collectibles loss? Explain.

11. **LO.2, 5, 7** Near the end of 2022, Byron realizes that he has a net short-term capital loss of $13,000 for the year. Byron has taxable income (not including the loss) of $123,000 and is single. He owns numerous stocks that could be sold for a long-term capital gain. What should he do before the end of 2022? *Critical Thinking* *Planning*

Computational Exercises

12. **LO.2** Dexter owns a large tract of land and subdivides it for sale. Assume that Dexter meets all of the requirements of § 1237 and during the tax year sells the first eight lots to eight different buyers for $22,000 each. Dexter's basis in each lot sold is $15,000, and he incurs total selling expenses of $900 on each sale. What is the amount of Dexter's capital gain and ordinary income? Formulate your answer by constructing a spreadsheet using a format similar to that found in Example 10.

13. **LO.3** Sheila purchases $50,000 of newly issued Gingo Corporation bonds for $45,000. The bonds have original issue discount (OID) of $5,000. After Sheila amortized $2,300 of OID and held the bonds for four years, she sold the bonds for $48,000. What is the amount and character of her gain or loss?

14. **LO.3** Olivia wants to buy some vacant land for investment purposes. She cannot afford the full purchase price. Instead, Olivia pays the landowner $8,000 to obtain an option to buy the land for $175,000 anytime in the next four years. Fourteen months after purchasing the option, Olivia sells the option for $10,000. What is the amount and character of Olivia's gain or loss?

15. **LO.3** On May 9, 2022, Glenna purchases 500 shares of Ignaz Company stock for $7,500. On June 30, 2022, she writes a call option on the stock, giving the grantee the right to buy the stock for $9,000 during the following 12-month period. Glenna receives a call premium of $750 for writing the call. The call is exercised by the grantee on December 15, 2022.
    a. What is the amount and character of Glenna's gain or loss?
    b. Assume that the original option expired unexercised. What is the amount and character of Glenna's gain or loss?

16. **LO.4** Shen purchased corporate stock for $20,000 on April 10, 2020. On July 14, 2022, when the stock was worth $12,000, Shen died and his son, Mijo, inherited the stock. Mijo sold the stock for $14,200 on November 12, 2022. What is the amount and character of Mijo's gain or loss?

17. **LO.5** Coline has the following capital gain and loss transactions for 2022:

Short-term capital gain	$ 5,000
Short-term capital loss	(2,100)
Long-term capital gain (28%)	6,000
Long-term capital gain (15%)	2,000
Long-term capital loss (28%)	(10,500)

After the capital gain and loss netting process, what is the amount and character of Coline's gain or loss?

18. **LO.5** Elliott has the following capital gain and loss transactions for 2022:

Short-term capital gain	$ 1,500
Short-term capital loss	(3,600)
Long-term capital gain (28%)	12,000
Long-term capital gain (25%)	4,800
Long-term capital gain (15%)	6,000
Long-term capital loss (28%)	(4,500)
Long-term capital loss (15%)	(9,000)

After the capital gain and loss netting process, what is the amount and character of Elliott's gain or loss?

Problems

19. **LO.2, 5** During the year, Eugene had the four property transactions summarized below. Eugene is a collector of antique glassware and occasionally sells a piece to get funds to buy another. What are the amount and nature of the gain or loss from each of these transactions?

Property	Date Acquired	Date Sold	Adjusted Basis	Sales Price
Antique vase	06/18/11	05/23/22	$37,000	$42,000
Blue Growth Fund (100 shares)	12/23/13	11/22/22	22,000	38,000
Orange bonds	02/12/14	04/11/22	34,000	42,000*
Green stock (100 shares)	02/14/22	11/23/22	11,000	13,000

*The sales price included $750 of accrued interest.

20. **LO.2, 5** Rennie owns a video game arcade. He buys vintage video games from estates, often at much less than the retail value of the property. He usually installs the vintage video games in a special section of his video game arcade that appeals to players of "classic" video games. Recently, Rennie sold a classic video game that a customer "just had to have." Rennie paid $11,250 for it, owned it for 14 months, and sold it for $18,000. Because Rennie had suspected that this particular classic video game would be of interest to collectors, he had it refurbished, put it on display in his video arcade, and listed it for sale on the internet. No customers in the arcade had played it other than those testing it before considering it for purchase. Rennie would like the gain on the sale of the classic video game to be a long-term capital gain. Did he achieve that objective? Why or why not?

Critical Thinking
Decision Making
Planning

21. **LO.2** George is the owner of numerous classic automobiles. His intention is to hold the automobiles until they increase in value and then sell them. He rents the automobiles for use in various events (e.g., antique automobile shows) while he is holding them. In 2022, he sold a classic automobile for $1,500,000. He had held the automobile for five years, and it had a tax basis of $750,000.
    a. Was the automobile a capital asset? Why or why not?
    b. Assuming a rate of return of 7%, how much would he have had to invest five years ago (instead of putting $750,000 into the car) to have had $1,500,000 this year? See Appendix E for the present value factors.

22. **LO.2, 4, 5** Barbella purchased a wedding ring for $15 at a yard sale in May. She thought the ring was costume jewelry, but it turned out to be a real diamond ring. She is not in the business of buying and selling anything. She researched the ring on the internet and discovered that it was worth at least $1,000. She sold it on an internet auction site for $1,100 in July. Was the ring a capital asset? What were the amount and nature of the gain or loss from its sale by Barbella? Prepare your answer in the form of an e-mail communication between you as a staff person of the Fuchsia CPA Firm LLP and your boss, Maria Hernandez, CPA. Assume that her e-mail address is *mhernandez@fuchsiacpas.com*. Maria referred the situation to you and is aware of the facts and the questions you should answer.

Communications

23. **LO.2** Pebble Securities is a corporation that buys and sells financial assets. It purchases notes receivable from manufacturers that need cash immediately and cannot wait to collect the notes. Pebble pays about 88% of the face value of the receivables and then collects them. Because of the quality of the notes, Pebble

collected less than it paid for some of the notes. Does Pebble have a capital loss when it collects the receivables for less than it paid for them? Explain.

Communications
Planning

24. **LO.2** Faith Godwin is a dealer in securities. She has spotted a fast-rising company and would like to buy and hold its stock for investment. The stock is currently selling for $2 per share, and Faith thinks it will climb to $40 a share within two years. Faith's coworkers have told her that there is "no way" she can get long-term capital gain treatment when she purchases stock because she is a securities dealer. Faith has asked you to calculate her potential gain and tell her whether her coworkers are right. Draft a letter to Faith responding to her request. Her address is 200 Catamon Drive, Great Falls, MT 59406.

25. **LO.2** Maria meets all of the requirements of § 1237 (subdivided realty). In 2022, she begins selling lots and sells four separate lots to four different purchasers. She also sells two contiguous lots to another purchaser. The sales price of each lot is $30,000. Maria's basis for each lot is $15,000. Selling expenses are $500 per lot.
   a. What are the realized and recognized gain?
   b. Explain the nature of the gain (i.e., ordinary income or capital gain).
   c. Would your answers change if, instead, the lots sold to the fifth purchaser were not contiguous? If so, how?

Critical Thinking
Decision Making

26. **LO.2, 3, 5** Melaney has had a bad year with her investments. She lent a friend $8,000; the friend did not repay the loan when it was due and then declared bankruptcy. The loan is totally uncollectible. Melaney also was notified by her broker that the Oak corporate bonds she owned became worthless on October 13, 2022. She had purchased the bonds for $22,000 on November 10, 2021. Melaney also had a $60,000 loss on the disposition of § 1244 corporate stock that she purchased several years ago. Melaney is single.
   a. What are the nature and amount of Melaney's losses?
   b. What is Melaney's AGI for 2022 assuming that she has $65,000 of ordinary gross income from sources other than those discussed?
   c. What are the nature and amount of Melaney's loss carryforwards?

27. **LO.2, 3** Benny purchased $400,000 of Peach Corporation face value bonds for $320,000 on November 13, 2021. The bonds had been issued with $80,000 of original issue discount because Peach was in financial difficulty in 2021. On December 3, 2022, Benny sold the bonds for $283,000 after amortizing $1,000 of the original issue discount. What are the nature and amount of Benny's gain or loss?

Critical Thinking
Decision Making
Planning

28. **LO.3** Fred is an investor in vacant land. When he thinks he has identified property that would be a good investment, he approaches the landowner, pays the landowner for a "right of first refusal" to purchase the land, records this right in the property records, and then waits to see if the land increases in value. The right of first refusal is valid for four years. Fourteen months ago, Fred paid a landowner $9,000 for a right of first refusal. The land was selected as the site of a new shopping center, and the landowner was offered $1,000,000 for the land. In its title search on the land, the buyer discovered Fred's right of first refusal and involved him in the purchase negotiations. Ultimately, the landowner paid Fred $220,000 to give up his right of first refusal; the landowner then sold the land to the buyer for $1,220,000. Fred has a marginal tax rate of 37%.
   a. What difference does it make whether Fred treats the right of first refusal as an option to purchase the land?
   b. What difference does it make whether Fred is a "dealer" in land?

29. **LO.3** Carla was the owner of vacant land that she was holding for investment. She paid $2,000,000 for the land in 2019. Raymond was an investor in vacant land.

He thought Carla's land might be the site of an exit ramp from a new freeway. Raymond gave Carla $836,000 for an option on her land in 2020. The option was good for two years and gave Raymond the ability to purchase Carla's land for $4,765,000. The freeway was not approved by the government, and Raymond's option expired in 2022. Does Carla have $836,000 of long-term capital gain upon the expiration of the option? Explain.

30. **LO.2, 3** Hilde purchased all of the rights to a patent on a new garden tool developed by a friend of hers who was an amateur inventor. The inventor had obtained the patent rights, set up a manufacturing company to produce and sell the garden tool, and produced substantial quantities of the tool, but he then became discouraged when no large garden company would agree to distribute the tool for him. Hilde purchased the patent rights (but not the manufacturing company) for $120,000 on October 24, 2021. Hilde had never engaged in such a transaction before, but she is a salesperson in the garden industry and thought she could succeed where her friend had failed. On June 27, 2022, she sold all of the patent rights to Garden Tool Company for $1,233,000. Garden Tool will manufacture the tool in its own factory and sell it to its customers. What is the nature of Hilde's gain from this transaction?

31. **LO.2, 3, 4, 7** Mac, an inventor, obtained a patent on a chemical process to clean old aluminum siding so that it can be easily repainted. Mac has a $50,000 tax basis in the patent. Mac does not have the capital to begin manufacturing and selling this product, so he has done nothing with the patent since obtaining it two years ago. Now a group of individuals has approached him and offered two alternatives. Under one alternative, they will pay Mac $600,000 (payable evenly over the next 15 years) for the exclusive right to manufacture and sell the product. Under the other, they will form a business and contribute capital to it to begin manufacturing and selling the product; Mac will receive 20% of the company's shares of stock in exchange for all of his patent rights. Discuss which alternative is better for Mac.

Critical Thinking
Decision Making
Planning

32. **LO.3** Freys, Inc., sells a 12-year "stuffed potato" franchise to Reynaldo. The franchise contains many restrictions on how Reynaldo may operate his store. For instance, Reynaldo cannot use less than Grade 10 Idaho potatoes; must bake the potatoes at a constant 410 degrees; must dress store personnel in Freys-approved uniforms; and must have a Freys sign that meets detailed specifications on size, color, and construction. When the franchise contract is signed, Reynaldo makes a noncontingent $160,000 payment to Freys. During the same year, Reynaldo pays Freys $300,000—14% of Reynaldo's sales. How does Freys treat each of these payments? How does Reynaldo treat each of the payments?

33. **LO.3** Angie owns numerous strip malls. A major tenant of one of the strip malls wanted to cancel its lease because it was moving to another city. After lengthy negotiations, the tenant paid Angie $60,000 to cancel its obligations under the lease. If the tenant had fulfilled the lease terms, Angie would have received rent of $700,000. What factors should Angie consider to determine the amount and character of her income from these circumstances?

Critical Thinking

34. **LO.3** Consuela was a tenant in a campus apartment. She is a student at State University. Her lease began on August 1, 2022, and was due to expire on July 31, 2023. However, her landlord sold the building, and the new owner wanted to demolish it to build a retail building. Consuela's landlord paid her $1,000 to cancel the lease. Consuela received the $1,000 on November 30, 2022, moved out, and rented another apartment. How should Consuela treat the $1,000?

35. **LO.4** Aliya held vacant land that qualified as an investment asset. She purchased the vacant land on April 10, 2018. She exchanged the vacant land for a rental house in a qualifying like-kind exchange on January 22, 2022. Aliya was going to hold the house for several years and then sell it. However, she got an "offer she

could not refuse" and sold it on November 22, 2022, for a substantial gain. What was Aliya's holding period for the house?

36. **LO.4** Roger inherited 100 shares of Periwinkle stock when his mother, Emily, died. Emily had acquired the stock for a total of $60,000 on November 15, 2018. She died on August 10, 2022, and the shares were worth a total of $55,000 at that time. Roger sold the shares for $36,000 on December 22, 2022. How much gain or loss does Roger recognize? What is the nature of that gain or loss?

37. **LO.4** Sarah received a gift of farmland from her father. The land was worth $4,000,000 at the date of the gift, had been farmed by her father for 40 years, and had a tax basis for her father of $30,000. Sarah never farmed the land and sold it eight months after receiving it from her father for $4,200,000. What is Sarah's holding period for the farmland? What is the nature of the gain from its disposition?

38. **LO.4** Dennis sells short 100 shares of ARC stock at $20 per share on January 15, 2022. He buys 200 shares of ARC stock on April 1, 2022, at $25 per share. On May 2, 2022, he closes the short sale by delivering 100 of the shares purchased on April 1.
    a. What are the amount and nature of Dennis's loss upon closing the short sale?
    b. When does the holding period for the remaining 100 shares begin?
    c. If Dennis sells (at $27 per share) the remaining 100 shares on January 20, 2023, what will be the nature of his gain or loss?

Communications

39. **LO.5** Liana Amiri (single with no dependents) has the following transactions in 2022:

AGI (exclusive of capital gains and losses)	$540,000
Long-term capital gain	22,000
Long-term capital loss	(8,000)
Short-term capital gain	19,000
Short-term capital loss	(23,000)

What is Liana's net capital gain or loss? Draft a letter to Liana describing how the net capital gain or loss will be treated on her tax return. Note that Liana's income from other sources puts her in the 37% tax bracket. Liana's address is 300 Ireland Avenue, Shepherdstown, WV 25443.

Communications

40. **LO.3, 5** In 2022, Beth Jarow had a $28,000 loss from the sale of a personal residence. She also purchased a patent on a rubber bonding process from an individual inventor for $7,000 (and resold it in two months for $18,000). The patent had not yet been reduced to practice. Beth purchased the patent as an investment. In addition, she had the following capital gains and losses from stock transactions:

Long-term capital loss	($ 6,000)
Long-term capital loss carryover from 2021	(12,000)
Short-term capital gain	21,000
Short-term capital loss	(7,000)

What is Beth's net capital gain or loss? Draft a letter to Beth explaining the tax treatment of the sale of her personal residence. Assume that Beth's income from other sources puts her in the 24% bracket. Bertha's address is 1120 West Street, Ashland, OR 97520.

Critical Thinking
Planning

41. **LO.2, 4, 5, 7** Bridgette is known as the "doll lady." She started collecting dolls as a child, always received one or more dolls as gifts on her birthday, never sold any dolls, and eventually owned 600 dolls. She is retiring and moving to a small apartment and has decided to sell her collection. She lists the dolls on an internet auction site and, to her great surprise, receives an offer from another doll collector of $45,000 for the entire collection. Bridgette sells the entire collection, except for five dolls she purchased during the last year. She had owned all of the dolls sold

for more than a year. What tax factors should Bridgette consider in deciding how to report the sale?

42. **LO.5** Phil and Susan Hammond are married taxpayers filing a joint return. The couple have two dependent children. Susan has wages of $34,000 in 2021. Phil does not work due to a disability, but he is a buyer and seller of stocks. He generally buys and holds for long-term gain but occasionally gets in and out of a stock quickly. The couple's 2021 stock transactions are detailed below. In addition, they have $2,300 of qualifying dividends.
    a. What is Phil and Susan's AGI?

Item	Date Acquired	Date Sold	Cost	Sales Price
Blue stock (10 shares)	11/10/20	03/12/21	$ 3,000	$ 6,000
Purple stock (100 shares)	12/13/19	05/23/21	36,000	32,000
Beige stock (50 shares)	12/14/16	07/14/21	13,000	14,500
Red stock (100 shares)	06/29/20	05/18/21	26,000	27,000
Black stock (100 shares)	05/15/20	10/18/21	67,000	67,800
Gray stock (100 shares)	04/12/19	10/18/21	89,000	88,200

    b. Complete a 2021 Form 8949 for the Hammonds (Phil's Social Security number is 123-45-6789). Assume that the stock sale information was reported to the Hammonds on a Form 1099–B and that basis information was provided to the IRS.

43. **LO.5** Paul has the following long-term capital gains and losses for 2022: $62,000 28% gain, $21,000 28% loss, $18,000 25% gain, and $64,000 0%/15%/20% gain. He also has a $53,000 short-term loss and a $5,000 short-term gain. What is Paul's AGI from these transactions? If he has a net long-term capital gain, what is its makeup in terms of the alternative tax rates?

44. **LO.5** Helena has the following long-term capital gains and losses for 2022: $65,000 28% gain, $53,000 28% loss, $28,000 25% gain, and $24,000 0%/15%/20% loss. She also has a $33,000 short-term loss and a $65,000 short-term gain. What is Helena's AGI from these transactions? If she has a net long-term capital gain, what is its makeup in terms of the alternative tax rates?

45. **LO.5** For 2022, Maddie has gross income of $38,350 and a $5,000 long-term capital loss. She claims the standard deduction. Maddie is 35 years old and unmarried with two dependent children. How much of Maddie's $5,000 capital loss carries over to 2023?

46. **LO.5** Jane and Blair are married taxpayers filing jointly and have 2022 taxable income of $107,000. The taxable income includes $5,000 of gain from a capital asset held five years, $2,100 of gain from a capital asset held seven months, and $13,000 of gain from a capital asset held four years. All of the capital assets were stock in publicly traded corporations. Jane and Blair also have qualified dividend income of $3,000. What is the couple's tax on taxable income and the related tax savings from the alternative tax computation (if any)?

47. **LO.5** For 2022, Wilma has properly determined taxable income of $36,000, including $3,000 of unrecaptured § 1250 gain and $8,200 of 0%/15%/20% gain. Wilma qualifies for head-of-household filing status. Compute Wilma's tax liability and the tax savings from the alternative tax on net capital gain.

48. **LO.5** Asok's AGI for 2022 is $133,250. Included in this AGI is a $45,000 25% long-term capital gain and a $13,000 0%/15%/20% long-term capital gain. Asok is single and uses the standard deduction. Compute his taxable income, the tax liability, and the tax savings from the alternative tax on net capital gain.

Planning

49. **LO.6** Gray, Inc., a C corporation, has taxable income from operations of $1,452,000 for 2022. It also has a net long-term capital loss of $355,000 from the sale of a subsidiary's stock. The year 2022 is the first year in the last 10 years that Gray has not had at least $500,000 per year of net long-term capital gains. What is Gray's 2022 taxable income? What, if anything, can it do with any unused capital losses?

Critical Thinking
Decision Making

50. **LO.2, 3, 7** Harriet, who is single, is the owner of a sole proprietorship. Two years ago, Harriet developed a process for preserving doughnuts that gives the doughnut a much longer shelf life. The process is not patented or copyrighted, and only Harriet knows how it works. Harriet has been approached by a company that would like to buy the process. Harriet insists that she receive a long-term employment contract with the acquiring company as well as be paid for the rights to the process. The acquiring company offers Harriet a choice of two options: (1) $650,000 in cash for the process and a 10-year covenant not to compete at $65,000 per year or (2) $650,000 in cash for a 10-year covenant not to compete and $65,000 per year for 10 years in payment for the process. Which option should Harriet accept? What is the tax effect on the acquiring company of each approach?

Tax Return Problems

Tax Forms Problem

ProConnect™ Tax

51. Ashley Panda lives at 1310 Meadow Lane, Wayne, OH 43466, and her Social Security number is 123-45-6777. Ashley is single and has a 20-year-old son, Bill. His Social Security number is 111-11-1112. Bill lives with Ashley, and she fully supports him. Bill spent 2021 traveling in Europe and was not a college student. He had gross income of $4,655 in 2021. Bill paid $4,000 of lodging expenses that Ashley reimbursed after they were fully documented. Ashley paid the $4,000 to Bill using a check from her sole proprietorship. That amount is not included in the items listed below. Ashley had substantial health problems during 2021, and many of her expenses were not reimbursed by her health insurance.

Ashley owns Panda Enterprises, LLC (98-7654321), a data processing service that she reports as a sole proprietorship. Her business is located at 456 Hill Street, Wayne, OH 43466. The business activity code is 514210. Her 2021 Form 1040, Schedule C for Panda Enterprises shows revenues of $315,000, office expenses of $66,759, employee salary of $63,000, employee payroll taxes of $4,820, business meal expenses of $11,000 (all at restaurants), and rent expense of $34,000. The rent expense includes payments related to renting an office ($30,000) and payments related to renting various equipment ($4,000). There is no depreciation because all depreciable equipment owned has been fully depreciated in previous years. No fringe benefits are provided to the employee. Ashley personally purchases health insurance on herself and Bill. The premiums are $23,000 per year.

Ashley has an extensive stock portfolio and has prepared the following analysis:

Stock	Number of Shares	Date Purchased	Date Sold	Per-Share Cost	Per-Share Selling Price	Total Dividends
Beige	10	10/18/20	10/11/21	$80	$ 74	$30
Garland	30	10/11/14	10/11/21	43	157	70
Peach	15	3/10/21	8/11/21	62	33	45

Note: Ashley received a Form 1099–B from her stockbroker that included the adjusted basis and sales proceeds for each of her stock transactions. The per-share cost includes commissions, and the per-share selling price is net of commissions. Also, the dividends are the actual dividends received in 2021, and these are both ordinary dividends and qualified dividends.

Ashley had $800 of interest income from State of Ohio bonds and $600 of interest income on her Wayne Savings Bank account. She paid $25,000 of alimony to her former husband (divorce finalized in June 2017). His Social Security number is 123-45-6788.

Ashley itemizes her deductions and provides the following information, which may be relevant to her return:

Item	Amount	Comment
Unreimbursed medical expenses for Ashley	$9,748	Does not include health insurance premiums.
State income taxes paid	1,830	
Real property taxes on personal residence	3,230	
Interest paid on home mortgage (Form 1098)	8,137	The loan is secured by the residence and was incurred when the home was purchased.
Charitable contributions	1,399	$940 cash payments to Ashley's church and $459 cash payments made to homeless persons for whom she felt sorry. She can document all the expenditures.
Sales taxes	619	Amount per sales tax table.

Ashley paid $27,000 in estimated Federal income taxes, did not engage in any virtual currency transactions during the year, does not want any of her taxes to finance presidential elections, has no foreign bank accounts or trusts, and wants any refund to be applied against her 2022 taxes. Ashley received the appropriate coronavirus recovery rebates (economic impact payments); related questions in ProConnect Tax should be ignored.

Compute Ashley's net tax payable or refund due for 2021, and complete her 2021 Federal tax return using appropriate forms and schedules. Ashley qualifies for the § 199A deduction for qualified business income. Be sure to include that in your calculations. Suggested software: ProConnect Tax.

52. Anthony Barrone is a graduate student at State University. His 10-year-old son, Jamie, lives with him, and Anthony is Jamie's sole support. Anthony's wife died in 2021, and Anthony has not remarried. Anthony received $320,000 of life insurance proceeds (related to his wife's death) in early 2022 and immediately invested the entire amount as shown below.

Communications
Planning
Tax Computation Problem

Item	Date Acquired	Cost	Date Sold	Selling Price	Dividends/ Interest
1,000 shares Blue	01/23/22	$ 14,000	12/03/22	$ 3,500	$ -0-
400 shares Magenta	01/23/22	23,000			750
600 shares Orange	01/23/22	230,000			2,300
100 shares Brown	06/23/16	2,800	01/23/22	14,000	-0-
Green bonds	01/23/22	23,000			1,200
Gold money market account	01/23/22	30,000			600

Anthony had $42,000 of taxable graduate assistant earnings from State University and received a $10,000 scholarship. He used $8,000 of the scholarship to pay his tuition and fees for the year and $2,000 for Jamie's day care. Jamie attended Little Kids Day-care Center, a state-certified child care facility. Anthony received a statement related to the Green bonds saying that there was $45 of original issue discount amortization during 2022. Anthony maintains the receipts for the sales taxes he paid of $735.

Anthony lives at 1610 Cherry Lane, Bradenton, FL 34212, and his Social Security number is 111-11-1111. Jamie's Social Security number is 123-45-6789. The university withheld $2,000 of Federal income tax from Anthony's salary. Anthony is not itemizing his deductions.

Part 1—Tax Computation

Compute Anthony's lowest tax liability for 2022.

Part 2—Tax Planning

Anthony is concerned because the Green bonds were worth only $18,000 at the end of 2022, $5,000 less than he paid for them. He is an inexperienced investor and wants to know if this $5,000 is deductible. The bonds had original issue discount of $2,000 when he purchased them, and he is curious about how that affects his investment in the bonds. The bonds had 20 years left to maturity when he purchased them. Draft a brief letter to Anthony explaining how to handle these items. Also prepare a memo for Anthony's tax file.

Research Problems

the answer company™ THOMSON REUTERS®

Note: Solutions to the Research Problems can be prepared by using the Thomson Reuters Checkpoint™ online tax research database, which accompanies this textbook. Solutions can also be prepared by using research materials found in a typical tax library.

Research Problem 1. Your client, Ali, has a "basis" issue he needs help with. Ali owns 100 shares of Brown Corporation stock. He purchased the stock at five different times and at five different prices per share as indicated.

Share Block	Number of Shares	Per-Share Price	Purchase Date
A	10	$60	10/10/02
B	20	20	8/11/03
C	15	15	10/24/04
D	35	30	4/23/05
E	20	25	7/28/05

On April 28, 2022, Ali will sell 40 shares of Brown stock for $40 per share. All of Ali's shares are held by his stockbroker. The broker's records track when the shares were purchased. May Ali designate the shares he sells? If so, which shares should he sell? Assume that Ali wants to maximize his gain because he has a capital loss carryforward.

Research Problem 2. Your long-time tax client, Clyde, has a major "classification" problem he needs help with. Clyde had worked for many years as the chief executive of Red Industries, Inc., and had been a major shareholder. Clyde and the company had a falling out, and Clyde was terminated. Clyde and Red executed a document under which Clyde's stock in Red would be redeemed and Clyde would agree not to compete against Red in its geographic service area. After extensive negotiations between the parties, Clyde agreed to surrender his Red stock in exchange for $600,000. Clyde's basis in his shares was $143,000, and he had held the shares for 17 years. The agreement made no explicit allocation of any of the $600,000 to Clyde's agreement not to compete against Red. How should Clyde treat the $600,000 payment on his 2022 tax return?

Research Problem 3. Siva, a new client of yours, owns various plots of land in Fulton County, Georgia. He acquired the land at various times during the last 20 years. About every fourth year, Siva subdivides into lots one of the properties he owns. He then has water, sewer, natural gas, and electricity hookups put in each lot and paves new streets. Siva has always treated his sales of such lots as sales of capital assets. His previous tax returns were prepared by an accountant whose practice you recently purchased. Has the proper tax treatment been used on the prior tax returns? Explain.

Partial list of research aids:
§§ 1221 and 1237 and *Jesse W. and Betty J. English*, 65 TCM 2160, T.C.Memo. 1993–111.

Use internet tax resources to address the following questions. Look for reliable websites and blogs of the IRS and other government agencies, media outlets, businesses, tax professionals, academics, think tanks, and political outlets.

Research Problem 4. Perform a Google search to find information about capital gains tax rates worldwide (and across U.S. states). Try searching for "capital gains rate by country (state)." What jurisdiction has the highest capital gains tax rate? What U.S. states have high capital gains tax rates?

Research Problem 5. Find a website, other than the IRS website, that discusses the taxation of short sales of securities.

Data Analytics

Research Problem 6. Using the *IRS Tax Statistics* that can be found at **irs.gov/statistics**, based on adjusted gross income for the most recent year available, determine the amount of net long-term capital gain taxpayers reported. Use the search function to look for a table related to "capital gain."

Becker CPA Review Questions

Becker

1. A gain on the sale of which of the following assets will *not* result in a capital gain?
   a. Stock in a public company
   b. A home used as a personal residence
   c. Goodwill of a corporation
   d. Inventory of a corporation

2. Conner purchased 300 shares of Zinco stock for $30,000 in year 1. On May 23, year 6, Conner sold all the stock to his daughter Alice for $20,000, its then fair market value. Conner realized no other gain or loss during year 6. On July 26, year 6, Alice sold the 300 shares of Zinco for $25,000. What was Alice's recognized gain or loss on her sale?
   a. $0
   b. $5,000 long-term gain
   c. $5,000 short-term loss
   d. $5,000 long-term loss

3. Brad and Angie are married and file a joint return. For year 14, they had income from wages in the amount of $100,000 and had the following capital transactions to report on their income tax return:

Carryover of capital losses from year 13	$200,000
Loss on sale of stock purchased in March year 14, sold on October 10, year 14, and repurchased on November 2, year 14	20,000
Gain on the sale of stock purchased 5 years ago and sold on March 14, year 14	15,000
Gain on the sale of their personal residence (all qualifications have been met for the maximum allowable gain exclusion)	675,000
Loss on the sale of their personal automobile	10,000
Gain on the sale of their personal furniture	5,000
Loss on the sale of investment property (land only)	150,000

   What is the amount of capital loss carryover to year 15?
   a. ($155,000)
   b. ($152,000)
   c. ($132,000)
   d. ($125,000)

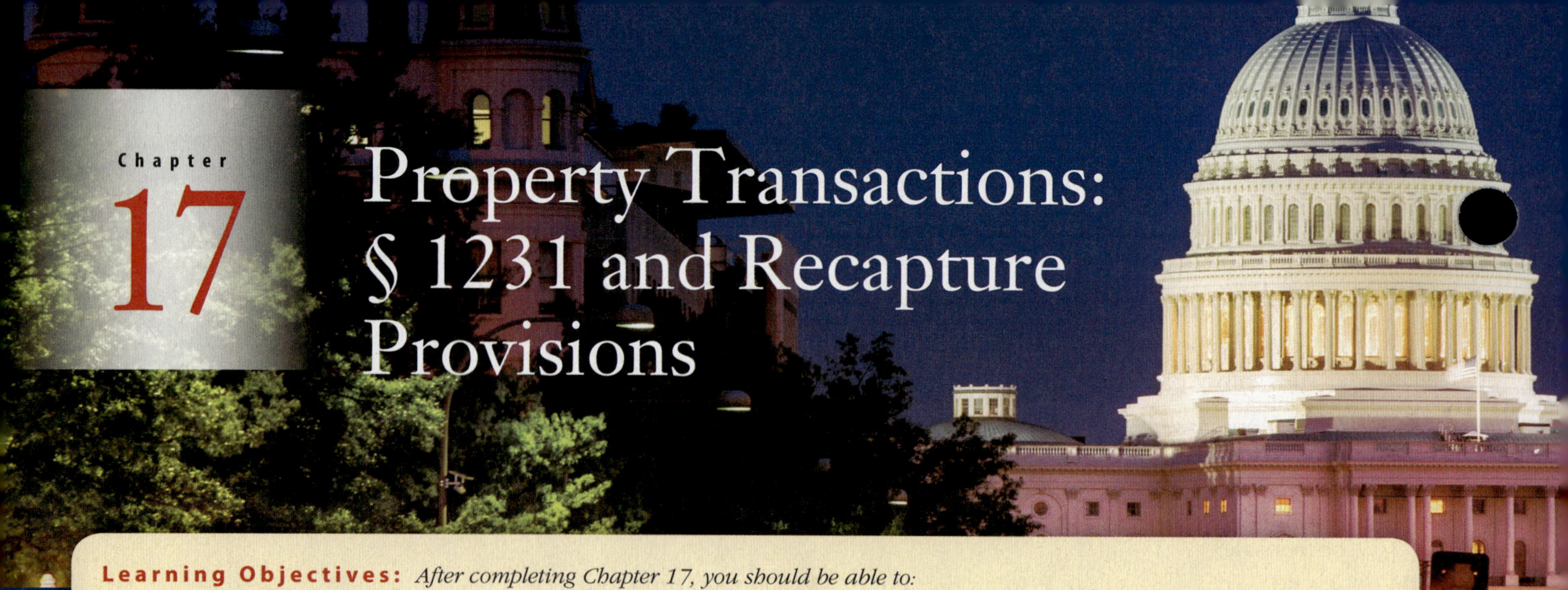

Chapter 17

Property Transactions: § 1231 and Recapture Provisions

Learning Objectives: *After completing Chapter 17, you should be able to:*

LO.1 State the rationale for and the nature and treatment of gains and losses from the disposition of business assets.

LO.2 Distinguish § 1231 assets from ordinary assets and capital assets and calculate the § 1231 gain or loss.

LO.3 Determine when § 1245 recapture applies and how it is computed.

LO.4 Determine when § 1250 recapture applies.

LO.5 Identify considerations common to §§ 1245 and 1250.

LO.6 Recognize special recapture provisions that are part of the tax law.

LO.7 Apply the reporting procedures for §§ 1231, 1245, and 1250.

LO.8 Identify tax planning opportunities associated with §§ 1231, 1245, and 1250.

Chapter Outline

17-1 Section 1231 Assets, 17-3
- 17-1a Relationship to Capital Assets, 17-3
- 17-1b Property Included, 17-4
- 17-1c Property Excluded, 17-4
- 17-1d Special Rules for Certain § 1231 Assets, 17-4
- 17-1e General Procedure for § 1231 Computation, 17-6

17-2 Section 1245 Recapture, 17-10
- 17-2a Section 1245 Property, 17-12
- 17-2b Observations on § 1245, 17-12

17-3 Section 1250 Recapture, 17-13
- 17-3a Section 1250 Recapture Situations, 17-13
- 17-3b Unrecaptured § 1250 Gain (Real Estate 25% Gain), 17-14

17-4 Considerations Common to §§ 1245 and 1250, 17-16
- 17-4a Exceptions, 17-16
- 17-4b Other Applications, 17-17

17-5 Special Recapture Provisions, 17-19
- 17-5a Special Recapture for Corporations, 17-19
- 17-5b Gain from Sale of Depreciable Property between Certain Related Parties, 17-19
- 17-5c Intangible Drilling Costs, 17-19

17-6 Reporting Procedures, 17-20

17-7 Tax Planning, 17-27
- 17-7a Timing of § 1231 Gain, 17-27
- 17-7b Timing of Recapture, 17-27
- 17-7c Postponing and Shifting Recapture, 17-28
- 17-7d Avoiding Recapture, 17-28

RL PRODUCTIONS/DIGITALVISION/GETTY IMAGES

The Big Picture

Depreciation Recapture

Hazel Brown (a sole proprietor filing a Form 1040 Schedule C) owns and operates a retail arts and crafts store. She has some four-year-old snow removal equipment with a $1,000 tax basis. Next to her store is a small lot that she bought several years ago for $15,000 to expand the store's parking lot. In 2019, she remodeled the store and replaced the store's equipment (counters, display racks, etc.), at a cost of $450,000, with used equipment that she bought from a competitor. The equipment is 7-year MACRS property. That year, she claimed $250,000 of § 179 expense on it and depreciated the balance. She did not expense the entire $450,000 (the maximum § 179 deduction in 2019 was $1,020,000) because she expected to be in a higher tax bracket in later years and wanted to "save" some of the depreciation. As of June 30, 2022, the equipment has an adjusted basis of $74,960 ($450,000 cost − $250,000 § 179 expense − $125,040 of regular MACRS depreciation). Now Hazel is again planning to replace the store's equipment, and she has determined that she can sell all of the existing equipment for $128,000.

If Hazel completes this transaction, what will be the impact on her 2022 tax return?

Read the chapter and formulate your response.

Framework 1040 **Tax Formula for Individuals**

This chapter covers the boldfaced portions of the Tax Formula for Individuals that was introduced in Concept Summary 3.1 on p. 3-3. Below those portions are the sections of Form 1040 where the results are reported.

Income *(broadly defined)*	$ xx,xxx
Less: Exclusions	(x,xxx)
Gross income	**$xx,xxx**
Less: Deductions *for* adjusted gross income	**(x,xxx)**

FORM 1040 (p. 1)

7 Capital gain or (loss). Attach Schedule D if required. If not required, check here ▶ ☐

FORM 1040 (Schedule 1)

3 Business income or (loss). Attach Schedule C. . . . .

4 Other gains or (losses). Attach Form 4797 . . . .

Adjusted gross income	$ xx,xxx
Less: The greater of total itemized deductions *or* the standard deduction	(x,xxx)
Charitable contributions if you take the standard deduction*	(xxx)
Personal and dependency exemptions**	(x,xxx)
Deduction for qualified business income***	(x,xxx)
Taxable income	$ xx,xxx
Tax on taxable income *(see Tax Tables or Tax Rate Schedules)*	**$ x,xxx**

FORM 1040 (p. 2)

16 **Tax** (see instructions). Check if any from Form(s): 1 ☐ 8814 2 ☐ 4972 3 ☐ ______

Less: Tax credits *(including income taxes withheld and prepaid)*	(xxx)
Tax due (or refund)	$ xxx

* For 2021, married taxpayers may claim up to $600 of cash charitable donations ($300 if unmarried).

** Only applies from 2018 through 2025.

*** Only applies from 2018 through 2025.

Generic Manufacturing LLC (a limited liability company) sold machinery, office furniture, and unneeded production plants for $100 million last year. The company's disposition of these assets resulted in $60 million of gains and $13 million of losses. How are these gains and losses treated for tax purposes? Do any special tax rules apply? Could any of the gains and losses receive capital gain or loss treatment?

This chapter answers these questions by explaining how to *classify* gains and losses from the disposition of assets that are used in the business rather than held for resale. Chapter 8 discussed how to *depreciate* such assets. Chapters 14 and 15 discussed how to determine the *adjusted basis* and the *amount* of gain or loss from their disposition.

A long-term capital gain was defined in Chapter 16 as the recognized gain from the sale or exchange of a capital asset held for the required long-term holding period.[1] Long-term capital assets are capital assets held more than one year.

This chapter is concerned with classification under § 1231, a very complex Code section, but one that impacts many transactions involving business assets. These transactions generally involve depreciable assets and land. Taxpayers that are affected by § 1231 are involved in a business (sole proprietors, partnerships, corporations, and some trusts) and taxpayers owning rental property.

In general, § 1231 applies to the sale or exchange of business properties and to certain involuntary conversions. These properties are *not* capital assets because they are depreciable and/or real property used in business or for the production of income.[2] Nonetheless, these business properties may be held for long periods of time and may be sold at a gain.

[1] § 1222(3).

[2] § 1221(a)(2).

Congress decided many years ago that § 1231 assets deserved *limited* capital gain-type treatment. Capital gain treatment sometimes gives too much tax advantage when assets are eligible for depreciation (or cost recovery). As a result, depreciation recapture rules were created to prevent capital gain treatment when gains are realized on § 1231 assets. This chapter covers the recapture rules that treat a portion (or all) of the gain as ordinary income (even though the gain might otherwise qualify for long-term capital gain treatment).

17-1 Section 1231 Assets

LO.1

State the rationale for and the nature and treatment of gains and losses from the disposition of business assets.

17-1a Relationship to Capital Assets

Because depreciable property and real property used in business are not capital assets, the recognized gains from the disposition of this property would appear to be ordinary income rather than capital gain. Due to § 1231, however, *net gain* from the disposition of this property is sometimes *treated as long-term capital gain*. In order for this to occur:

- A long-term holding period requirement must be met (held for *more than* a year);
- The disposition must generally be from a sale, exchange, or involuntary conversion; and
- Certain recapture provisions must be satisfied.

Code § 1231 also may apply to involuntary conversions of capital assets even though such a disposition, which is not a sale or exchange, normally would not result in a capital gain.

If the disposition of depreciable property and real property used in business results in a *net loss*, § 1231 *treats* the *loss* as an *ordinary loss* rather than as a capital loss. Ordinary losses are fully deductible *for* adjusted gross income (AGI). Capital losses are offset by capital gains, and if any loss remains, the loss is deductible to the extent of $3,000 per year for individuals and currently is not deductible at all by regular corporations.

In general, § 1231 provides the *best* of both potential results: net gain may be treated as long-term capital gain, and net loss is treated as ordinary loss; note the results in Examples 1 and 2.

The Big Picture

Example 1

Return to the facts of *The Big Picture* on p. 17-1. If Hazel sells the parking lot for $18,000, she will have disposed of a § 1231 asset because it was property used in a trade or business and held for the long-term holding period (more than one year).

Hazel's gain will be $3,000 ($18,000 selling price − $15,000 adjusted basis). Because the asset is a § 1231 asset, all of the gain is § 1231 gain, and it *may* be treated as long-term capital gain (depending on its netting with any other § 1231 gains or losses during the year).

The Big Picture

Example 2

Return to the facts of *The Big Picture* on p. 17-1. Assume that Hazel sells the snow removal equipment for $100, generating a $900 loss, and the parking lot for $15,700, generating a $700 gain.

Both properties were held for use in her business for the long-term holding period and, therefore, are § 1231 assets. Hazel's net § 1231 loss is $200, and that net loss is an ordinary loss.

The rules regarding § 1231 treatment do *not* apply to *all* business property. Code § 1231 has specific holding period requirements and, in general, requires that the property be either depreciable property or real estate used in business. As a result, neither inventory nor receivables are § 1231 assets. Nor is § 1231 necessarily limited to business property. Transactions involving certain capital assets may fall into the § 1231 category.

As discussed in Chapter 16, long-term capital gains receive beneficial tax treatment. Code § 1231 requires netting of **§ 1231 gains and losses**. If the result is a gain, it may be treated as a long-term capital gain. The net gain is added to the "real" long-term capital gains (if any) and netted with capital losses (if any). As a result, the net § 1231 gain may eventually be eligible for beneficial capital gain treatment or help avoid the deduction limitations that apply to a net capital loss. If the § 1231 gain and loss netting results in a loss, it is an ordinary loss. Finally, § 1231 assets are treated the same as capital assets for purposes of the appreciated property charitable contribution provisions (refer to Chapter 10).

LO.2

Distinguish § 1231 assets from ordinary assets and capital assets and calculate the § 1231 gain or loss.

17-1b Property Included

Section 1231 property generally includes the following assets if they are held for more than one year:

- Depreciable or real property used in business or for the production of income (principally machinery and equipment, buildings, and land).
- Timber, coal, or domestic iron ore.
- Livestock held for draft, breeding, dairy, or sporting purposes.
- Unharvested crops on land used in business.
- Certain *purchased* intangible assets (such as patents and goodwill) that are eligible for amortization.

These assets are ordinary assets until they have been held for more than one year. Only then do they become § 1231 assets.

17-1c Property Excluded

Code § 1231 property generally does *not* include the following:

- Property not held for the long-term holding period.[3]
- Nonpersonal use property where casualty losses exceed casualty gains for the taxable year (if a taxpayer has a net casualty loss, the individual casualty gains and losses are treated as ordinary gains and losses).
- Inventory and property held primarily for sale to customers.
- A patent, invention, model, or design (whether or not patented); a secret formula or process; certain copyrights; literary, musical, or artistic compositions; and certain U.S. government publications.
- Accounts receivable and notes receivable arising in the ordinary course of the trade or business.

17-1d Special Rules for Certain § 1231 Assets

A rather diverse group of assets is included under § 1231. The following discussion summarizes the special rules for some of those assets.

Timber

In order to encourage reforestation of timberlands, Congress has provided preferential treatment relative to the natural growth value of timber, which takes a relatively long time to mature. If timber is held for investment, the timber is a capital asset. If timber is used in a business, it will be a § 1231 asset if held for more than a year. But if the timber is inventory, an ordinary gain or loss will normally result. If the timber is inventory, the taxpayer can *elect* to treat the cutting of timber as a sale or exchange and, if the election is made, to treat the sale as the disposition of a § 1231 asset.[4]

The recognized § 1231 gain or loss is determined at the time the timber is cut and is equal to the difference between the timber's fair market value as of the *first day* of the taxable year and the adjusted basis for depletion. If a taxpayer sells the timber for

[3]Because the benefit of § 1231 is long-term capital gain treatment, the holding period must correspond to the more-than-one-year holding period that applies to capital assets. Livestock must be held at least 12 months (24 months in some cases). Unharvested crops do not have to be held for the required long-term holding period, but the land must be held for the long-term holding period.

[4]§ 631(a) and Reg. § 1.631–1. To receive § 631 treatment, the holding period for the timber must be greater than one year.

more or less than the fair market value as of the first day of the taxable year in which it is cut, the difference is ordinary income or loss.

Example 3

Several years ago Tom, a timber dealer, purchased a tract of land with a substantial stand of trees on it. The land cost $40,000, and the timber cost $100,000. On the first day of 2022, the timber was appraised at $250,000. In August 2022, Tom cut the timber and sold it for $265,000. Tom elects to treat the cutting as a sale or exchange under § 1231. He has a $150,000 § 1231 gain ($250,000 − $100,000) and a $15,000 ordinary gain ($265,000 − $250,000).

What if the timber had been sold for $235,000? Tom would still have a $150,000 § 1231 gain, but he also would have a $15,000 ordinary loss. The price for computing § 1231 gain is the price at the beginning of the tax year. Any difference between that price and the sales price is ordinary gain or loss. Here, because the price declined by $15,000, Tom has an ordinary loss in that amount.

Livestock

Cattle and horses must be held 24 months or more and other livestock must be held 12 months or more to qualify under § 1231.[5] Poultry is *not* livestock for purposes of § 1231.

Section 1231 Assets Disposed of by Casualty or Theft

When § 1231 assets are disposed of by casualty or theft, a special netting rule is applied. For simplicity, the term *casualty* is used to mean both casualty and theft dispositions. First, the casualty gains and losses from § 1231 assets *and* the casualty gains and losses from **long-term nonpersonal use capital assets** are determined.[6] A nonpersonal use capital asset might be art held as an investment or a baseball card collection held by a nondealer.

Next, the § 1231 asset casualty gains and losses and the nonpersonal use capital asset casualty gains and losses are netted together (see Concept Summary 17.1 later in the chapter).

- If the result is a *net loss*, the § 1231 casualty gains and the nonpersonal use capital asset casualty gains are treated as ordinary gains, the § 1231 casualty losses are deductible *for* AGI, and the nonpersonal use capital asset casualty losses are deductible *from* AGI as miscellaneous itemized deductions (which are not deductible from 2018 through 2025).
- If the result of the netting is a *net gain*, the net gain is treated as a § 1231 gain.

As a result, a § 1231 asset disposed of by casualty may or may not get § 1231 treatment, depending on whether the netting process results in a gain or a loss. Also, a nonpersonal use capital asset disposed of by casualty may get § 1231 treatment or ordinary treatment, but it will not get capital gain or loss treatment.

Casualties, thefts, and condemnations are *involuntary conversions*. Involuntary conversion gains may be deferred if conversion proceeds are reinvested; involuntary conversion losses are recognized currently (refer to Chapter 15) regardless of whether the conversion proceeds are reinvested. Thus, the special netting process discussed previously for casualties and thefts would not include gains that are not currently recognizable because the insurance proceeds are reinvested.

The special netting process for casualties and thefts also does not include condemnation gains and losses. Consequently, a § 1231 asset disposed of by condemnation will receive § 1231 treatment. This variation between recognized casualty and condemnation gains and losses sheds considerable light on what § 1231 is all about. Code § 1231 has no effect on whether *realized* gain or loss is recognized. Instead, § 1231 merely dictates how such *recognized* gain or loss is *classified* (ordinary, capital, or § 1231) under certain conditions.[7]

[5] Note that the holding period is "12 months or more" and not "more than 12 months." Congress enacted this rule due to considerable litigation over whether the livestock was inventory or a § 1231 asset.

[6] *Personal use property casualty* losses (unless they arise in a Federal disaster area) are not usable except to the extent they offset casualty gains. *Personal use property net casualty gains* are treated as long-term capital gains.

[7] *Personal use property condemnation* gains and losses are not subject to the § 1231 rules. The gains are capital gains (because personal use property is a capital asset), and the losses are nondeductible because they arise from the disposition of personal use property.

17-1e General Procedure for § 1231 Computation

Most of the time, § 1231 gains and losses result from the sale of business assets. However, as we have already discussed, disposition by casualty and/or theft also can be part of the § 1231 discussion. Consequently, the tax treatment of § 1231 gains and losses depends on the results of a complex *netting* procedure. When there are no casualties and/or thefts (the usual case), step 1 below can be skipped and the procedure is much simpler. Here are the steps that need to be followed:

Step 1: Casualty Netting

Net all recognized long-term gains and losses from casualties of § 1231 assets and nonpersonal use capital assets. Casualty gains result when insurance proceeds exceed the adjusted basis of the property. These are gains remaining after any *depreciation recapture* (discussed later in text Sections 17-2 and 17-3). This casualty netting is beneficial because if there is a net gain, the gain may receive long-term capital gain treatment. If there is a net loss, it receives ordinary loss treatment.

a. If the casualty gains exceed the casualty losses, add the excess to the other § 1231 gains for the taxable year.
b. If the casualty losses exceed the casualty gains, exclude all casualty losses and gains from further § 1231 computation. If this is the case, all casualty gains are ordinary income. Code § 1231 asset casualty losses are deductible *for* AGI. Other casualty losses may be deductible *from* AGI.

Step 2: § 1231 Netting

After adding any net casualty gain from step 1a to the other § 1231 gains and losses (including recognized § 1231 asset condemnation gains and losses), net all § 1231 gains [gains remaining after any *depreciation recapture* (discussed later in text Sections 17-2 and 17-3)] and losses.

a. If the gains exceed the losses, the § 1231 "lookback" provision must be applied (see step 3).
b. If the losses exceed the gains, all gains are ordinary income. Code § 1231 asset losses are deductible *for* AGI. Other casualty losses may be deductible *from* AGI.

Step 3: § 1231 Lookback Provision

The net § 1231 gain from step 2a is offset by the nonrecaptured net § 1231 losses for the five preceding taxable years (the **§ 1231 lookback** provision). For transactions in 2022, the lookback years are 2017, 2018, 2019, 2020, and 2021.

a. To the extent of the nonrecaptured net § 1231 loss, the current-year net § 1231 gain is ordinary income. The *nonrecaptured* net § 1231 losses are losses that have not already been used to offset net § 1231 gains.
b. Only the net § 1231 gain exceeding this net § 1231 loss carryforward is given long-term capital gain treatment.

Step 4: Ordinary Income or Capital Gain Treatment

a. Include the portion (if any) of step 3a that is an ordinary gain in the taxpayer's gross income.
b. Include the portion (if any) of step 3b that is net § 1231 gain in the capital gain and loss netting process (see text Section 16-5).

Concept Summary 17.1 summarizes the § 1231 computation procedure. Examples 4 and 5 illustrate its application without the § 1231 lookback provision. Examples 6 and 7 illustrate its application with the § 1231 lookback provision.

Concept Summary 17.1

Section 1231 Netting Procedure

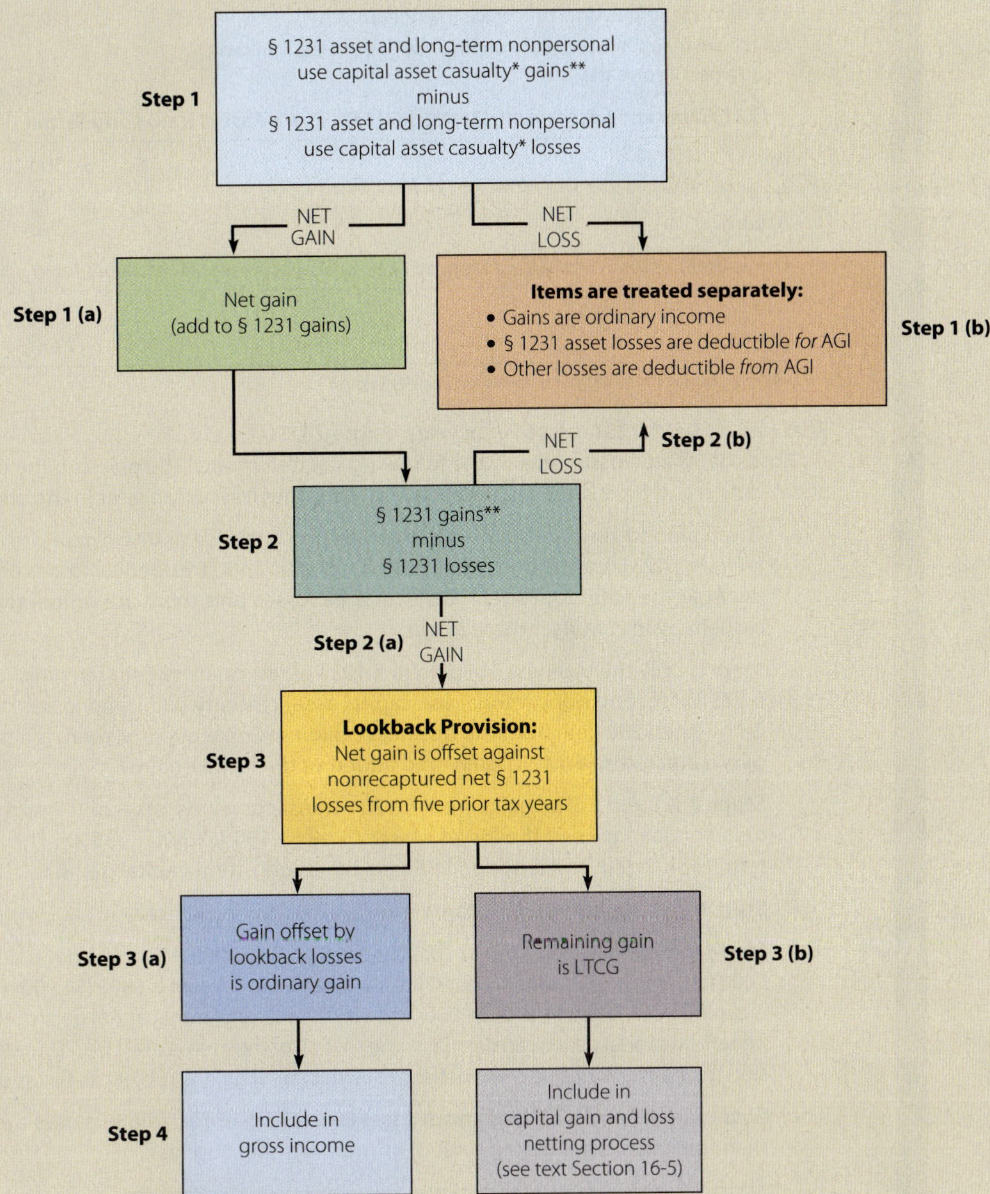

*Includes casualties and thefts.
**Gains after depreciation recapture.

Section 1231 Computations

Example 4

During 2022, Ross had $125,000 of AGI before considering the following recognized gains and losses:

Capital Gains and Losses	
Long-term capital gain	$3,000
Long-term capital loss	(400)
Short-term capital gain	1,000
Short-term capital loss	(200)

continued

Casualties	
Theft of diamond ring (owned four months)	($800)*
Fire damage to personal residence (owned 10 years)	(400)*
Gain from insurance recovery on fire loss to business building (owned two years)	200
§ 1231 Gains and Losses from Depreciable Business Assets Held Long Term	
Asset A	$ 300
Asset B	1,100
Asset C	(500)
Gains and Losses from Sale of Depreciable Business Assets Held Short Term	
Asset D	$ 200
Asset E	(300)

*As adjusted for the $100 floor on personal casualty losses.

Ross had no net § 1231 losses in tax years before 2022.

Ross's gains and losses receive the following tax treatment. [The gains on the business building and Assets A and B are *after* any depreciation recapture (discussed later in the chapter)].

- The diamond ring and the residence are personal use assets. Therefore, these casualties are not § 1231 transactions. The $800 (ring) plus $400 (residence) losses are not deductible because they are not Federal disaster area losses and there are no personal use property casualty gains to offset these losses.
- **Step 1:** Only the business building (a § 1231 asset) casualty gain remains. The netting of the § 1231 asset and nonpersonal use capital asset casualty gains and losses contains only one item—the $200 gain from the business building. Consequently, there is a net gain, and that gain is treated as a § 1231 gain (and added to the § 1231 gains).
- **Steps 1 (a) and 2:** The gains from § 1231 transactions (Assets A and B and the § 1231 asset casualty gain) exceed the losses (Asset C) by $1,100 ($1,600 − $500). This excess is a long-term capital gain and is added to Ross's other long-term capital gains.
- **Step 3:** Not applicable since there is no § 1231 lookback loss.
- **Step 4 (b):** Ross's net long-term capital gain is $3,700 ($3,000 + $1,100 from § 1231 transactions − $400 long-term capital loss). Ross's net short-term capital gain is $800 ($1,000 − $200). The result is capital gain net income of $4,500. The $3,700 net long-term capital gain portion is eligible for beneficial capital gain treatment [assume that all of the gain is *0%/15%/20% gain* (see the discussion in Chapter 16)]. The $800 net short-term capital gain is subject to tax as ordinary income.[8]
- Ross treats the gain and loss from Assets D and E (depreciable business assets held for less than the long-term holding period) as ordinary gain and loss.

Results of the Gains and Losses on Ross's Tax Computation	
NLTCG	$ 3,700
NSTCG	800
Ordinary gain from sale of Asset D	200
Ordinary loss from sale of Asset E	(300)
AGI from other sources	125,000
AGI	$129,400

- Ross will have personal use property casualty losses of $1,200 [$800 (diamond ring) + $400 (personal residence)]. The $1,200 is not deductible because the losses are not Federal disaster area losses and there are no personal use property casualty gains to offset these losses.

[8]Ross's taxable income (unless his itemized deductions are extremely large) will put him in at least the 24% bracket. Thus, the alternative tax computation will yield a lower tax. See Example 44 in Chapter 16.

Section 1231 Computations

Example 5

Assume the same facts as in Example 4, except that the loss from Asset C was $1,700 instead of $500.

- The treatment of the casualty losses is the same as in Example 4.
- **Step 1 (b):** The losses from § 1231 transactions now exceed the gains by $100 ($1,700 − $1,600). As a result, the gains from Assets A and B and the § 1231 asset casualty gain are ordinary income, and the loss from Asset C is a deduction *for* AGI (a business loss). The same result can be achieved by simply treating the $100 net loss as a deduction *for* AGI.
- **Steps 2 and 3:** Not applicable since there is no net § 1231 gain.
- **Step 4 (b):** Since there is no net § 1231 gain in step 3, the capital gain and loss netting process does not include any such gain. Capital gain net income is $3,400 ($2,600 long term + $800 short term). The $2,600 net long-term capital gain portion is eligible for beneficial capital gain treatment, and the $800 net short-term capital gain is subject to tax as ordinary income.

Results of the Gains and Losses on Ross's Tax Computation	
NLTCG	$ 2,600
NSTCG	800
Net ordinary loss on Assets A, B, and C and § 1231 casualty gain	(100)
Ordinary gain from sale of Asset D	200
Ordinary loss from sale of Asset E	(300)
AGI from other sources	125,000
AGI	$128,200

- The $1,200 of personal casualty losses is not deductible because the losses are not Federal disaster area losses and there are no personal use property casualty gains to offset these losses.

Example 6

Assume the same facts as in Example 4, except that Ross has a $700 nonrecaptured net § 1231 loss from 2021.

- The treatment of the casualty losses is the same as in Example 4.
- **Step 3 (a):** The 2022 net § 1231 gain of $1,100 is treated as ordinary income to the extent of the 2021 nonrecaptured § 1231 loss of $700.
- **Step 3 (b):** The remaining $400 net § 1231 gain is a long-term capital gain and is added to Ross's other long-term capital gains.
- **Step 4 (b):** Ross's net long-term capital gain is $3,000 ($3,000 + $400 from § 1231 transactions − $400 long-term capital loss). Ross's net short-term capital gain is still $800 ($1,000 − $200). The result is capital gain net income of $3,800. The $3,000 net long-term capital gain portion is eligible for beneficial capital gain treatment, and the $800 net short-term capital gain is subject to tax as ordinary income.

Results of the Gains and Losses on Ross's Tax Computation	
NLTCG	$ 3,000
NSTCG	800
Ordinary gain from recapture of § 1231 losses	700
Ordinary gain from sale of Asset D	200
Ordinary loss from sale of Asset E	(300)
AGI from other sources	125,000
AGI	$129,400

- The $1,200 of personal casualty losses is not deductible because the losses are not Federal disaster area losses and there are no personal use property casualty gains to offset these losses.

Section 1231 Computations

Example 7

Assume the same facts as in Example 4, except that Ross had a net § 1231 loss of $2,700 in 2020 and a net § 1231 gain of $300 in 2021.

- The treatment of the casualty losses is the same as in Example 4.
- **Step 3 (a):** The 2020 net § 1231 loss of $2,700 will have carried over to 2021 and been offset against the 2021 net § 1231 gain of $300. Thus, the $300 gain will have been classified as ordinary income, and $2,400 of nonrecaptured 2020 net § 1231 loss will carry over to 2022. The 2022 net § 1231 gain of $1,100 will be offset against this loss, resulting in $1,100 of ordinary income. The nonrecaptured net § 1231 loss of $1,300 ($2,400 − $1,100) carries over to 2023.
- **Step 4 (b):** Since there is no net § 1231 gain in step 3, the capital gain and loss netting process does not include any such gain. Capital gain net income is $3,400 ($2,600 net long-term capital gain + $800 net short-term capital gain). The $2,600 net long-term capital gain portion is eligible for beneficial capital gain treatment, and the $800 net short-term capital gain is subject to tax as ordinary income.

Results of the Gains and Losses on Ross's Tax Computation	
NLTCG	$ 2,600
NSTCG	800
Ordinary gain from recapture of § 1231 losses	1,100
Ordinary gain from sale of Asset D	200
Ordinary loss from sale of Asset E	(300)
AGI from other sources	125,000
AGI	$129,400

- The $1,200 of personal casualty losses is not deductible because the losses are not Federal disaster area losses and there are no personal use property casualty gains to offset these losses.

LO.3

Determine when § 1245 recapture applies and how it is computed.

17-2 Section 1245 Recapture

Now that the basic rules of § 1231 have been introduced, it is time to add some complications. The Code contains two major *recapture* provisions—§§ 1245 and 1250.[9] These provisions cause *gain* to be treated *initially* as ordinary gain. Thus, what may appear to be a § 1231 gain is ordinary gain instead. This recapture phenomenon applies exclusively to § 1231 gains; § 1231 assets generating losses are unaffected by these recapture provisions.

These recapture provisions also may cause a gain in a nonpersonal use casualty to be *initially* ordinary gain rather than casualty gain. Classifying gains (and losses) properly is important; improper initial classification may lead to incorrect mixing and matching of gains and losses. We begin by discussing the § 1245 recapture rules; the § 1250 recapture rules are discussed in text Section 17-3.

Code § 1245 requires taxpayers to treat all gain as ordinary gain unless the property is disposed of for more than its original cost. This result is accomplished by requiring that all gain be treated as ordinary gain to the extent of the depreciation taken on the property disposed of. The excess of the sales price over the original cost is § 1231 gain. Code § 1245 applies *primarily* to non-real-estate property like machinery, trucks, and office furniture. Code § 1245 does not apply if property is disposed of at a loss. Generally, the loss will be a § 1231 loss unless the form of the disposition is a casualty.

The Big Picture

Example 8

Refer to the facts of *The Big Picture* on p. 17-1. Hazel purchased the equipment for $450,000 and has deducted $375,040 of depreciation ($250,000 § 179 expense + $125,040 regular MACRS depreciation). As a result, the equipment's adjusted basis is $74,960.

continued

[9]Due to the passage of time, § 1250 is largely ineffective, but is still important in certain situations.

If Hazel sells the equipment for $128,000, she will have a gain of $53,040 ($128,000 − $74,960). If it were not for § 1245, the $53,040 gain would be § 1231 gain. Section 1245 prevents this potentially favorable result by treating as ordinary income (not as § 1231 gain) any gain to the extent of depreciation taken. In this example, the entire $53,040 gain would be ordinary income.

If, instead, Hazel sold the equipment for $485,000, she would have a gain of $410,040 ($485,000 − $74,960 adjusted basis). The § 1245 gain would be $375,040 (equal to the depreciation taken), and the § 1231 gain would be $35,000 (equal to the excess of the sales price over the $450,000 original cost).

Section 1245 recapture provides, in general, that the portion of recognized gain from the sale or other disposition of § 1245 property that represents depreciation is *recaptured* as ordinary income.[10] As a result, in Example 8, $53,040 of the $375,040 depreciation taken is recaptured as ordinary income when the business equipment is sold for $128,000. Only $53,040 is recaptured rather than $375,040 because Hazel is only required to recognize § 1245 recapture ordinary gain equal to the *lower* of the depreciation taken or the gain recognized.

The method of depreciation (e.g., accelerated or straight-line) does not matter. All depreciation taken is potentially subject to recapture. For this reason, § 1245 recapture often is referred to as *full recapture.* Any remaining gain after subtracting the amount recaptured as ordinary income usually will be § 1231 gain.

If the property is disposed of in a casualty event, however, the remaining gain will be casualty gain. If the business equipment in Example 8 had been disposed of by casualty and the $128,000 received had been an insurance recovery, Hazel still would have a gain of $53,040 and the gain still would be recaptured by § 1245 as ordinary gain. The § 1245 recapture rules apply before there is any casualty gain. Because all of the $53,040 gain is recaptured, no casualty gain arises from the casualty.

The following examples illustrate the general application of § 1245.

Section 1245 Recapture Computations

Example 9

In the current year, Santiago sold for $13,000 a machine acquired several years ago for $12,000. He had taken $10,000 of depreciation on the machine.

- The recognized gain from the sale is $11,000. This is the amount realized of $13,000 less the adjusted basis of $2,000 ($12,000 cost − $10,000 depreciation taken).
- Depreciation taken is $10,000. Therefore, because § 1245 recapture gain is the lower of depreciation taken or gain recognized, $10,000 of the $11,000 recognized gain is ordinary income, and the remaining $1,000 gain is § 1231 gain.
- The § 1231 gain of $1,000 also is equal to the excess of the sales price over the original cost of the property ($13,000 − $12,000 = $1,000 § 1231 gain).

Example 10

Assume the same facts as in the previous example, except that the asset is sold for $9,000 instead of $13,000.

- The recognized gain from the sale is $7,000. This is the amount realized of $9,000 less the adjusted basis of $2,000.
- Depreciation taken is $10,000. Therefore, because the $10,000 depreciation taken exceeds the recognized gain of $7,000, the entire $7,000 recognized gain is ordinary income.
- The § 1231 gain is zero. There is no § 1231 gain because the selling price ($9,000) does not exceed the original purchase price ($12,000).

[10] The term *depreciation* includes § 167 depreciation, § 168 cost recovery, § 179 immediate expensing, § 168(k) additional first-year depreciation, and § 197 amortization.

Section 1245 Recapture Computations

Example 11

Assume the same facts as in Example 9, except that the asset is sold for $1,500 instead of $13,000.

- The recognized loss from the sale is $500. This is the amount realized of $1,500 less the adjusted basis of $2,000.
- Because there is a loss, there is no depreciation recapture. All of the loss is § 1231 loss.

If § 1245 property is disposed of in a transaction other than a sale, exchange, or involuntary conversion, the maximum amount recaptured is the excess of the property's fair market value over its adjusted basis. See the discussion under Considerations Common to §§ 1245 and 1250 in text Section 17-4.

17-2a Section 1245 Property

Generally, **§ 1245 property** includes all depreciable personal property (e.g., machinery and equipment), including livestock. Buildings and their structural components generally are not § 1245 property. The following property is *also* subject to § 1245 treatment:

- Amortizable personal property such as goodwill, patents, copyrights, and leaseholds of § 1245 property.
- Professional baseball and football player contracts.
- Certain depreciable tangible real property (other than buildings and their structural components) employed as an integral part of certain activities such as manufacturing and production (e.g., a natural gas storage tank where the gas is used in the manufacturing process).
- Pollution control facilities, railroad grading and tunnel bores, on-the-job training, and child care facilities.
- Single-purpose agricultural and horticultural structures and petroleum storage facilities (e.g., a greenhouse or silo).
- Fifteen-year, 18-year, and 19-year nonresidential real estate for which accelerated cost recovery is used (this property, known as ACRS property, would have been placed in service after 1980 and before 1987).

Example 12

Steve acquired nonresidential real estate on December 1, 1986, for $100,000. He used the required ACRS accelerated method to compute the cost recovery. He sells the asset on January 15, 2022, for $120,000. The amount and nature of Steve's gain are computed as follows:

Amount realized		$120,000
Adjusted basis		
Cost	$ 100,000	
Less cost recovery: 1986–2005	(100,000)	
2006–2022	(–0–)	
January 15, 2022 adjusted basis		(–0–)
Gain realized and recognized		$120,000

The gain of $120,000 is treated as ordinary income to the extent of *all* depreciation taken because the property is 19-year nonresidential real estate for which accelerated depreciation was used. As a result, Steve reports ordinary income of $100,000 and § 1231 gain of $20,000 ($120,000 − $100,000).

17-2b Observations on § 1245

- In most instances, the total depreciation taken will exceed the recognized gain. Therefore, the disposition of § 1245 property usually results in ordinary income rather than § 1231 gain. No § 1231 gain will occur unless the § 1245 property is disposed of for more than its original cost. Refer to Examples 9 and 10.

- Recapture applies to the total amount of depreciation allowed or allowable regardless of the depreciation method used.
- Recapture applies regardless of the holding period of the property. If the property is held for less than the long-term holding period, the entire recognized gain is ordinary income because § 1231 does not apply.
- Section 1245 does not apply to losses, which receive § 1231 treatment.
- Gains from the disposition of § 1245 assets also may be treated as passive activity gains (see Chapter 11).

17-3 Section 1250 Recapture

LO.4

Determine when § 1250 recapture applies.

Generally, **§ 1250 property** is depreciable real property (principally buildings and their structural components) that is not subject to § 1245.[11] Intangible real property, such as leaseholds of § 1250 property, also is included.

Section 1250 recapture rarely applies because only the amount of *additional depreciation* (depreciation *in excess* of straight-line depreciation) is subject to recapture. Straight-line depreciation is not recaptured (except for property held one year or less). Because the straight-line depreciation method is required for depreciable real property placed in service after 1986, usually there will be *no § 1250 depreciation recapture* on such property. Finally, § 1250 does not apply if the real property is sold at a loss.

Although there is no depreciation recapture on § 1250 property, the gain from this property may be subject to a special 25 percent tax rate. See the discussion of Unrecaptured § 1250 Gain (Real Estate 25% Gain) in text Section 17-3b.

Example 13

Sanjay acquires a residential rental building on January 1, 2021, for $300,000. He receives an offer of $450,000 for the building in 2022 and sells it on December 23, 2022.

- Sanjay takes {($300,000 × 0.03485) + [$300,000 × 0.03636 × (11.5/12)] = $20,909} of total depreciation for 2021 and 2022, and the adjusted basis of the property is $279,091 ($300,000 − $20,909).
- Sanjay's recognized gain is $170,909 ($450,000 − $279,091).
- All of the gain is § 1231 gain.

17-3a Section 1250 Recapture Situations

In addition to residential real estate acquired before 1987 and nonresidential real estate acquired before 1981, accelerated depreciation may be taken on other types of real property. The § 1250 recapture rules apply to the following property for which accelerated depreciation was used:

- Any immediate expense deduction (§ 179) and/or additional first-year depreciation [§ 168(k)] exceeding straight-line depreciation taken on leasehold improvements and qualified improvement property.
- Real property used predominantly outside the United States.
- Certain government-financed or low-income housing.[12]

Concept Summary 17.2 compares and contrasts the § 1245 and § 1250 depreciation recapture rules.

[11] As noted above, in one limited circumstance, § 1245 does apply to nonresidential real estate. If the nonresidential real estate was placed in service after 1980 and before 1987 and accelerated depreciation was used, the § 1245 recapture rules would apply (rather than the § 1250 recapture rules).

[12] Described in § 1250(a)(1)(B).

Concept Summary 17.2

Comparison of § 1245 and § 1250 Depreciation Recapture

	§ 1245	§ 1250
Property affected	All depreciable personal property, but also nonresidential real property acquired after December 31, 1980, and before January 1, 1987, for which accelerated cost recovery was used. Also includes miscellaneous items such as § 179 expense and § 197 amortization of intangibles such as goodwill, patents, and copyrights.	Nonresidential real property acquired after December 31, 1969, and before January 1, 1981, on which accelerated depreciation was taken. Residential rental real property acquired after December 31, 1975, and before January 1, 1987, on which accelerated depreciation was taken.
Depreciation recaptured	Potentially all depreciation taken. If the selling price is greater than or equal to the original cost, all depreciation is recaptured. If the selling price is between the adjusted basis and the original cost, only some depreciation is recaptured.	Normally, there is no depreciation recapture, but in the special situations listed above, there can be § 1250 depreciation recapture of additional depreciation (the excess of accelerated cost recovery over straight-line cost recovery or the excess of accelerated depreciation over straight-line depreciation).
Limit on recapture	Lower of depreciation taken or gain recognized.	Lower of additional depreciation or gain recognized.
Treatment of gain exceeding recapture gain	Usually § 1231 gain.	Usually § 1231 gain.
Treatment of loss	No depreciation recapture; loss is usually § 1231 loss.	No depreciation recapture; loss is usually § 1231 loss.

17-3b Unrecaptured § 1250 Gain (Real Estate 25% Gain)

Any **unrecaptured § 1250 gain** is subject to a 25 percent tax rate. This gain, which relates to the sale of depreciable real estate, is used in the alternative tax computation for net capital gain discussed in Chapter 16. Unrecaptured § 1250 gain (*25% gain*) is some or all of the § 1231 gain that is treated as long-term capital gain.

The maximum amount of this *25% gain* is the depreciation taken on real property sold at a recognized gain. That maximum amount is computed in one or more of the following ways:

- The recognized gain from disposition is more than the depreciation taken. The *25% gain* is equal to the depreciation taken. Refer to Example 13. The depreciation taken was $20,909, but the recognized gain was $170,909. Consequently, *some* of the recognized gain is potential *25%* § 1231 gain.
- The recognized gain from disposition is less than or equal to the depreciation taken. In this case, the *25% gain* is all of the recognized gain. Refer to Example 13, but assume that the building sales price is $285,000. The recognized gain is $5,909 ($285,000 − $279,091), all of this gain is a § 1231 gain, and it is entirely a *25%* § 1231 gain.
- There is § 1245 depreciation recapture because the property is nonresidential real estate acquired in 1981–1986 on which accelerated depreciation was taken. No *25%* § 1231 gain will be left because § 1245 will recapture all of the depreciation or the recognized gain, whichever is less. Refer to Example 12. Depreciation of $100,000 was taken, but all of it was recaptured as ordinary income by § 1245. Thus, there is no remaining potential *25%* § 1231 gain. The entire $20,000 § 1231 gain in Example 12 is potential *0%/15%/20% gain*.
- Section 1231 loss from disposition of other § 1231 assets held long term reduces the gain from real estate.
- Section 1231 lookback losses convert some or all of the potential *25%* § 1231 gain to ordinary income.

Special 25% Gain Netting Rules

Where there is a § 1231 gain from real estate and that gain includes both potential *25% gain* and potential *0%/15%/20% gain*, any § 1231 loss from disposition of other § 1231 assets *first offsets* the *0%/15%/20%* portion of the § 1231 gain and then offsets the *25% gain* portion of the § 1231 gain. Also, any § 1231 lookback loss *first recharacterizes* the *25% gain* portion of the § 1231 gain and then recharacterizes the *0%/15%/20%* portion of the § 1231 gain as ordinary income.

Net § 1231 Gain Limitation

The amount of unrecaptured § 1250 gain may not exceed the net § 1231 gain that is eligible to be treated as long-term capital gain. The unrecaptured § 1250 gain is the *lesser of* the unrecaptured § 1250 gain or the net § 1231 gain that is treated as capital gain. Thus, if there is a net § 1231 gain but it is all converted to ordinary income by the five-year § 1231 lookback loss provision, there is no surviving § 1231 gain or unrecaptured § 1250 gain.

Refer to Example 6. There was $200 of § 1231 gain from the building fire that also would be potential *25% gain* if at least $200 of depreciation was taken. The net § 1231 gain was $1,100 including the $200 building gain. (The $500 loss from Asset C would offset the potential *0%/15%/20%* § 1231 gain and not the potential *25% gain*, so all of the potential *25% gain* of $200 is in the $1,100 net § 1231 gain.) However, the $700 of § 1231 lookback losses would *first* absorb the $200 building gain, so the $400 of § 1231 gain that is treated as long-term capital gain includes no *25% gain*.

Section 1250 Property for Purposes of the Unrecaptured § 1250 Gain

Section 1250 property includes any real property (other than § 1245 property) that is or has been depreciable. Land is *not* § 1250 property because it is not depreciable.

Example 14

Bridget is a single taxpayer with 2022 taxable income of $120,000 composed of:

- $100,000 ordinary taxable income,
- ($3,000) short-term capital loss,
- $15,000 long-term capital gain from sale of stock, and
- $8,000 § 1231 gain that is all unrecaptured § 1250 gain (the actual unrecaptured gain was $11,000, but net § 1231 gain is only $8,000).

Bridget's net capital gain is $20,000 [$15,000 long-term capital gain + $8,000 unrecaptured (§ 1250 gain/net § 1231 gain) − $3,000 short-term capital loss]. The $3,000 short-term capital loss is offset against the $8,000 unrecaptured § 1250 gain, reducing that gain to $5,000 (see the discussion in Chapter 16 concerning netting of capital losses). Bridget's adjusted net capital gain is $15,000 ($20,000 net capital gain − $5,000 unrecaptured § 1250 gain).

Bridget's total tax (using the alternative tax calculation discussed in Chapter 16) is $21,286 [$17,836 (tax on $100,000 other taxable income) + $1,200 ($5,000 unrecaptured § 1250 gain × 24%) + $2,250 ($15,000 adjusted net capital gain × 15%)]. Bridget uses the regular 24% tax rate on the $5,000 unrecaptured § 1250 gain because it is less than the 25% alternative tax rate on the gain.

Ethics & Equity The Sale of a "Cost-Segregated" Building

Many taxpayers have "cost-segregated" their buildings. This means that an engineering study is done to determine whether some of a building's cost can be segregated into tangible personal property (generally a 5-year or 7-year MACRS life with accelerated depreciation) rather than real property (a 27.5-year or 39-year MACRS life with straight-line depreciation). The faster depreciation for the tangible personal property yields significant tax savings. A CPA is determining the gain or loss from disposition of an office building. A sale document details the selling price of the land and building. However, the building was cost-segregated and the CPA finds records of cost and related depreciation for the tangible personal property that was part of the cost segregation. No mention of this tangible personal property was made in the sale agreement, but the building and all of its contents were sold. What should the CPA do?

LO.5

Identify considerations common to §§ 1245 and 1250.

17-4 Considerations Common to §§ 1245 and 1250

17-4a Exceptions

Gifts

Depreciation recapture potential carries over to the donee.[13]

Example 15

Wade gives his daughter, Helen, § 1245 property with an adjusted basis of $1,000. The amount of recapture potential is $700. Helen uses the property in her business and claims further depreciation of $100 before selling it for $1,900.

Helen's recognized gain is $1,000 ($1,900 amount realized − $900 adjusted basis), of which $800 is recaptured as ordinary income ($100 depreciation taken by Helen + $700 recapture potential carried over from Wade). The remaining gain of $200 is § 1231 gain. Even if Helen used the property for personal purposes, the $700 recapture potential would still be carried over.

Death

Although not a very attractive tax planning approach, death eliminates all recapture potential.[14] Any depreciation recapture potential is eliminated when property passes from a decedent to an estate or heir.

Example 16

Assume the same facts as in Example 15, except that Helen receives the property as a result of Wade's death. The $700 recapture potential from Wade is extinguished. Helen has a basis for the property equal to the property's fair market value at Wade's death (assume that the FMV is $1,700).

Helen will have a $300 gain when the property is sold because the selling price ($1,900) exceeds the property's adjusted basis of $1,600 ($1,700 original basis to Helen − $100 depreciation) by $300. Because of § 1245, $100 is ordinary income. The remaining gain of $200 is § 1231 gain.

Charitable Transfers

If depreciable property is contributed to a charity, the contribution deduction (normally fair market value) must be reduced by any ordinary gain that would have resulted had the property been sold (e.g., from depreciation recapture).[15]

The Big Picture

Example 17

Return to the facts of *The Big Picture* on p. 17-1. If instead of selling the old equipment Hazel gives it to a charity, her charitable contribution will be $74,960.

If the equipment had been sold for its fair market value, the realized gain would have been $53,040 [the equipment's $128,000 fair market value less its adjusted basis of $74,960 ($450,000 cost less $375,040 accumulated depreciation)]. All of this gain would have been ordinary (due to § 1245 depreciation recapture). This $53,040 ordinary gain reduces the charitable contribution allowed.

So Hazel's charitable contribution is $74,960 (the equipment's $128,000 fair market value less the $53,040 ordinary gain due to depreciation recapture that would have resulted had the equipment been sold). Effectively, Hazel's contribution is limited to the equipment's adjusted basis ($74,960).

Certain Nontaxable Transactions

In certain transactions, the transferor's adjusted basis of property carries over to the transferee.[16] If this is the case, any depreciation recapture potential also carries over to the transferee.[17] Included in this category are the following transfers of property:

- Nontaxable incorporations under § 351.
- Certain subsidiary liquidations under § 332.
- Nontaxable contributions to a partnership under § 721.
- Nontaxable reorganizations.

---

[13] §§ 1245(b)(1) and 1250(d)(1) and Reg. §§ 1.1245–4(a)(1) and 1.1250–3(a)(1).

[14] §§ 1245(b)(2) and 1250(d)(2).

[15] § 170(e)(1)(A) and Reg. § 1.170A–4(b)(1). In certain circumstances, § 1231 gain also reduces the amount of the charitable contribution. See § 170(e)(1)(B).

[16] §§ 1245(b)(3) and 1250(d)(3) and Reg. §§ 1.1245–4(c) and 1.1250–3(c).

[17] Reg. §§ 1.1245–2(a)(4) and −2(c)(2) and 1.1250–2(d)(1) and (3) and −3(c)(3).

Gain may be recognized in these transactions if boot is received. If gain is recognized, it is treated as ordinary income to the extent of the recapture potential or recognized gain, whichever is lower.[18]

Like-Kind Exchanges (§ 1031) and Involuntary Conversions (§ 1033)

Realized gain is recognized to the extent of boot received in a like-kind exchange. Realized gain also will be recognized to the extent the proceeds from an involuntary conversion are not reinvested in similar property. Any recognized gain is subject to recapture as ordinary income under §§ 1245 and 1250. However, since only real property can be the subject of a like-kind exchange, §1245 recapture is not likely because it generally only applies to tangible personal property. Code § 1250 recapture also is not likely because it infrequently applies to dispositions of real property. On the other hand, unrecaptured § 1250 gain (25% gain) is likely to be present if depreciable real property was the subject of the exchange. As a result, if gain is recognized on the exchange, there is likely some *25% gain*. The remaining recapture potential, if any, carries over to the property received in the exchange. Realized losses are not recognized in like-kind exchanges but are recognized in involuntary conversions (see Chapter 15).

The Big Picture

Example 18

Refer to the facts of *The Big Picture* on p. 17-1. Sometimes transactions structured as exchanges do not qualify as § 1031 like-kind exchanges. Rather than sell the equipment, assume that Hazel exchanges it by "trading it in" on replacement property. If the equipment received in the exchange was worth $150,000, Hazel would have to pay $22,000 of cash ($150,000 − value of the equipment given up in the exchange) to acquire the replacement property. Hazel, however, would not have a § 1031 like-kind exchange because this was not an exchange of real property.

Instead, her realized and recognized ordinary gain is $53,040 ($128,000 fair market value of the equipment given up − $74,960 adjusted basis of the equipment given up). All of the gain is recaptured by § 1245 because it is less than $375,040 depreciation taken.

The remaining recapture potential of $322,000 ($375,040 − $53,040) is extinguished, and the basis of the replacement equipment is its fair market value, $150,000.

17-4b Other Applications

The §§ 1245 and 1250 recapture rules *override* all other Code sections.[19] Special applications include installment sales and property dividends.

Installment Sales

Recapture gain is recognized in the year of the sale regardless of whether gain is otherwise recognized under the installment method.[20] All gain is ordinary income until the recapture potential is fully absorbed. Nonrecapture (§ 1231) gain is recognized under the installment method as cash is received.

Gain also is recognized on installment sales in the year of the sale in an amount equal to the § 179 (immediate expensing) deduction taken with respect to the property sold, because § 179 immediate expensing is depreciation subject to recapture.

The Big Picture

Example 19

Return to the facts of *The Big Picture* on p. 17-1. Assume that Hazel could sell the used equipment for $28,000 down, with the $100,000 balance received in five yearly installments of $20,000 plus interest.

Helen would have to recognize her entire $53,040 gain ($128,000 sales price − $74,960 adjusted basis) in 2022. All of the gain is § 1245 depreciation recapture gain because the $375,040 depreciation taken exceeds the $53,040 recognized gain.

Property Dividends

A corporation generally recognizes gain if it distributes appreciated property as a dividend. Recapture under §§ 1245 and 1250 applies to the extent of the *lower* of the recapture potential or the excess of the property's fair market value over the adjusted basis.[21]

[18] §§ 1245(b)(3) and 1250(d)(3) and Reg. §§ 1.1245–4(c) and 1.1250–3(c). Some of these special corporate problems are discussed in Chapter 20. Partnership contributions also are discussed in Chapter 20.

[19] §§ 1245(d) and 1250(i).

[20] § 453(i). The installment method of reporting gains on the sale of property is discussed in Chapter 18.

[21] § 311(b) and Reg. §§ 1.1245–1(c) and −6(b) and 1.1250–1(a)(4), −1(b)(4), and −1(c)(2).

Example 20

Emerald Corporation distributes § 1245 property as a dividend to its shareholders. The amount of the recapture potential is $300, and the excess of the property's fair market value over the adjusted basis is $800. Emerald recognizes $300 of ordinary income and $500 of § 1231 gain.

Concept Summary 17.3 integrates the depreciation recapture rules with the § 1231 netting process. It is an expanded version of Concept Summary 17.1.

Concept Summary 17.3

Depreciation Recapture and § 1231 Netting Procedure

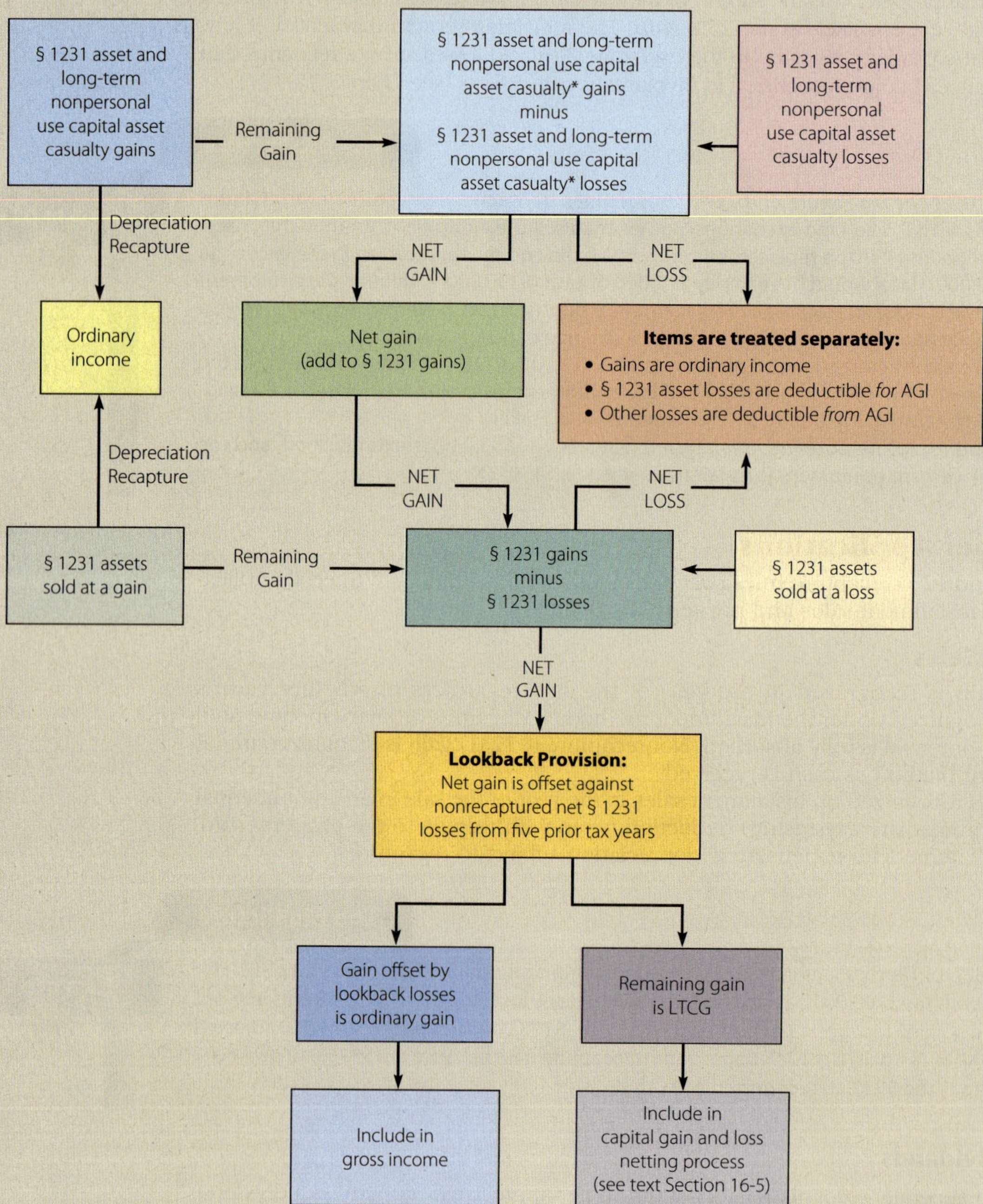

*Includes casualties and thefts.

Global Tax Issues — Depreciation Recapture in Other Countries

The rules for dispositions of depreciated property are more complex in the United States than in any other country. Most countries treat the gain or loss from the disposition of business depreciable assets as ordinary income or loss. Consequently, although the U.S. rules are more complex, they can be more beneficial than those of other countries because at least some gains from the disposition of depreciable business property may be taxed at the lower capital gain rates.

17-5 Special Recapture Provisions

LO.6 **Recognize special recapture provisions that are part of the tax law.**

17-5a Special Recapture for Corporations

Corporations selling depreciable real estate may have ordinary income in addition to that required by § 1250.[22] Under this provision, corporations selling depreciable real property are required to recapture as ordinary income the smaller of two amounts: (1) 20 percent of the recognized gain or (2) 20 percent of the depreciation taken. See the discussion of this topic in Chapter 20.

17-5b Gain from Sale of Depreciable Property between Certain Related Parties

If related parties sell or exchange property that is depreciable in the hands of the *transferee* (principally machinery, equipment, and buildings, but not land), any gain recognized by the *transferor* is ordinary income.[23] This rule applies to both direct and indirect sales or exchanges. A **related party** is defined as an individual and his or her controlled corporation or partnership or a taxpayer and any trust in which the taxpayer (or the taxpayer's spouse) is a beneficiary.

Example 21

Isabella sells a personal use automobile (therefore nondepreciable) to her controlled corporation. The automobile, which was purchased two years ago, originally cost $5,000 and is sold for $7,000. The automobile is to be used in the corporation's business.

If the related-party provision did not exist, Isabella would realize a $2,000 long-term capital gain. The income tax consequences would be favorable because Isabella's controlled corporation is entitled to depreciate the automobile based on the purchase price of $7,000. Under the related-party provision, Isabella's $2,000 gain is ordinary income.

17-5c Intangible Drilling Costs

Taxpayers may elect to either *expense or capitalize* intangible drilling and development costs for oil, gas, or geothermal properties.[24] **Intangible drilling and development costs (IDCs)** include operator (one who holds a working or operating interest in any tract or parcel of land) expenditures for wages, fuel, repairs, hauling, and supplies. These expenditures must be incident to and necessary for the drilling of wells and preparation of wells for production. In most instances, taxpayers elect to expense IDCs to maximize tax deductions during drilling.

Intangible drilling and development costs are subject to § 1254 recapture when the property is sold. Any gain realized on the disposition is recognized as ordinary income to the extent of IDCs expensed (but limited to the realized gain).

[22] § 291(a)(1).

[23] § 1239.

[24] § 263(c).

LO.7

Apply the reporting procedures for §§ 1231, 1245, and 1250.

17-6 Reporting Procedures

Noncapital gains and losses are reported on Form 4797 (Sales of Business Property). However, before Form 4797 is filled out, Part B of Form 4684 (Casualties and Thefts) must be completed to determine whether any casualties will enter into the § 1231 computation procedure. Recall that recognized gains from § 1231 asset casualties may be recaptured by § 1245 or § 1250. These gains will not appear on Form 4684. The § 1231 gains and nonpersonal use long-term capital gains are netted against § 1231 losses and nonpersonal use long-term capital losses on Form 4684 to determine if there is a net gain to transfer to Form 4797, Part I.

Because 2022 tax forms are not yet available, 2021 tax forms are used for the remainder of the discussion.

Form 4797 is divided into four parts; each part's function is summarized below.

Part	Function
I	To report regular § 1231 gains and losses [including recognized gains and losses from certain involuntary conversions (condemnations)].
II	To report ordinary gains and losses.
III	To determine the portion of the gain that is subject to recapture (e.g., §§ 1245 and 1250 gain).
IV	Computation of recapture amounts under §§ 179 and 280F when business use of depreciable property drops to 50% or less.

Generally, the best approach to completing Form 4797 is to start with Part III. Once the recapture amount has been determined, it is transferred to Part II. Any gain remaining after the recapture has been accounted for is transferred from Part III to Part I. Also transferred to Part I is any net gain from certain casualties and thefts as reported on Form 4684, Part B (refer to the beginning of this section and Chapter 15). If the netting process in Form 4797, Part I results in a gain, it is reduced by the nonrecaptured net § 1231 losses from prior years (line 8 of Part I). Any remaining gain is shifted to Schedule D (Capital Gains and Losses) of Form 1040. If the netting process in Part I of Form 4797 results in a loss, the loss moves to Part II to be treated as an ordinary loss.

The complex rules for the alternative tax on net capital gain for individuals, estates, and trusts affect the reporting of gains and losses from the disposition of business and rental assets. For example, a partnership or an S corporation that uses Form 4797 must provide information to its partners or shareholders related to the gain surviving Form 4797, Part I. Although this gain is a § 1231 gain, it goes to the partner's or shareholder's Form 4797 Part I. There it must again survive the § 1231 netting process to be treated as a long-term capital gain on the partner's or shareholder's return. The flow-through entity must identify what portion of this gain is *28% gain, 25% gain*, or *0%/15%/20% gain*.

The process followed in Example 22 is based on an analysis of Form 1040, Schedule D, and Form 4797 and their instructions. Here are some key points.

- All gains and losses treated as ordinary gains and losses (those that end up in Part II of Form 4797) are not eligible for any of the special tax rates for net capital gain.
- The net § 1231 gain goes from Part I of Form 4797 to line 11 of Schedule D (as a long-term capital gain).
- The *25% gain* (if any) from Form 4797 is part of the Schedule D, line 11, gain. *Nothing on the face of Form 4797 or Schedule D identifies this gain.* Only when the alternative tax on net capital gain is computed is the *25% gain* portion of the Form 4797 net gain specifically mentioned (see Schedule D, line 19).
- Section 1231 assets are assets held more than one year. Therefore, no gain or loss is reportable on Form 4797, Part I or Part III, unless that holding period requirement is satisfied. Instead, gains and losses from these assets are reported directly in Form 4797, Part II.

Example 22

For 2021, Troy Williams, a single taxpayer (Social Security number 111-11-1111), has taxable income of $133,000 *including* the following recognized gains and losses (assume that Troy has no nonrecaptured § 1231 losses from prior years).

Sale of Depreciable Business Assets Held Long Term	
Asset A (Note 1)	$36,500
Asset B (Note 2)	20,126
Asset C (Note 3)	(880)
Sale of Depreciable Business Assets Held Short Term	
Asset D (Note 4)	($ 600)
Capital Assets	
Long-term gain (Note 5)	$ 3,000
Short-term loss (Note 6)	(200)

Note 1. Asset A was acquired on June 23, 2018, for $50,000. It was 5-year MACRS property, and four years' cost recovery totaled $38,480. The property was sold for $48,020 on August 31, 2021.

Note 2. Asset B was purchased on May 10, 2011, for $37,000. It was 27.5-year residential rental real estate, and straight-line depreciation totaled $14,126. Asset B was sold for $43,000 on November 10, 2021.

Note 3. Asset C was purchased on December 9, 2018, for $16,000. It was 5-year MACRS property, and four years' cost recovery totaled $12,314. The property was sold for $2,806 on December 30, 2021.

Note 4. Asset D was purchased for $7,000 on July 27, 2021. It was 5-year MACRS property but proved unsuitable to Troy's business. Troy sold it for $6,400 on November 3, 2021.

Note 5. The LTCG resulted from the sale of 100 shares of Orange Corporation stock purchased for $10,000 on April 5, 2019. The shares were sold on October 21, 2021, for $13,223. Expenses of sale were $223.

Note 6. The STCL resulted from the sale of 50 shares of Blue Corporation stock purchased for $350 on March 14, 2021. The shares were sold for $170 on August 20, 2021. Expenses of sale were $20.

Reporting Consequences

Form 4797

Part III. The sales of Assets A and B are reported here because both generated gains.

- ***Asset A (§ 1245 Recapture Potential).*** The sale of Asset A results in the recapture of cost recovery (depreciation) deductions. Here, the depreciation recapture potential ($38,480) is greater than the realized gain. So all of the gain is depreciation recaptured under § 1245 (and ordinary income). That recapture is shown on line 25b and is carried to line 31.
- ***Asset B (§ 1250 Recapture Potential).*** Since straight-line cost recovery was used on Asset B, there is no § 1250 recapture. The $20,126 gain from the sale of Asset B is included on lines 30 and 32 and then carried from line 32 to Part I, line 6.

Part I. Gains and losses from § 1231 assets not appearing in Part III are reported here. In addition, the § 1231 netting process occurs here (on lines 7 to 9).

- ***Asset C.*** The loss from Asset C is reported on line 2.
- ***§ 1231 Netting.*** The § 1231 gains and losses are netted and appear on line 7. Given that Troy has no nonrecaptured net § 1231 losses from prior years (these would be reported on line 8), the net gain on line 7 is transferred to Schedule D, line 11.

Part II. Any ordinary gains and losses are accumulated here.

- ***Asset D.*** The loss from Asset D is reported on line 10.
- The depreciation recapture from Part III, line 31 appears on line 13.
- The net gain on line 18 is ordinary income and is transferred to Schedule 1 (Form 1040), line 4.

continued

Schedule D (Form 1040)

Part I. Short-Term Capital Gains and Losses.

- ***Blue Corporation Stock.*** The short-term capital loss from the Blue Corporation stock is reported on line 1a. It is assumed that the sale of the Blue Corporation stock was reported to Troy on a Form 1099–B that showed the adjusted basis and selling price of the stock. If not, a Form 8949 would be required.

Part II. Long-Term Capital Gains and Losses.

- ***Orange Corporation Stock.*** The long-term capital gain from the Orange Corporation stock is reported on line 8a. It is assumed that the sale of the Orange Corporation stock was reported to Troy on a Form 1099–B that showed the adjusted basis and selling price of the stock. If not, a Form 8949 would be required.
- ***Net § 1231 Gain.*** The net § 1231 gain transferred from Form 4797 appears on line 11.

Part III. Summary.

- The combination of short-term and long-term capital gains and losses appears on line 16. In this case, the amount is a net capital gain. The *net capital gain* is then carried to line 7 of Form 1040.

Tax Computation

- In 2021, five alternative tax rates applied: 25%, 28%, and 0%/15%/20%.
- On Form 4797, Part III, the $20,126 § 1231 gain from Asset B is made up of $14,126 of potential *25% gain* (equal to the depreciation taken) and $6,000 of potential *0%/15%/20% gain.*
  - The $880 § 1231 loss from Form 4797, Part I, line 2 offsets the potential *0%/15%/20%* portion of the $20,126 § 1231 gain on Form 4797, Part I, line 6.
  - Consequently, the $19,246 § 1231 gain that goes from Form 4797, Part I, line 7 to Schedule D, line 11 is made up of (1) $14,126 *25% gain* and (2) $5,120 *0%/15%/20% gain.*
- Schedule D, Part III, line 19 shows an unrecaptured § 1250 gain of $13,926. A worksheet in the Form 1040 Schedule D instructions must be used to determine this amount. This gain results from the $14,126 *25% gain* being reduced by the $200 short-term capital loss from Schedule D, line 7.
- Troy's 2021 tax liability is $25,024, computed as follows:

$20,464	Tax on other taxable income of $110,954 ($133,000 taxable income − $22,046 net long-term capital gain)
+ 3,342	Tax on the *25% gain* ($13,926 × 24%; the 24% regular tax rate is less than the 25% alternative tax rate)
+ 1,218	Tax on the *0%/15%/20% gain* ($8,120 × 15%)
$25,024	

The 2021 tax form solution for Example 22 appears on the following pages.

Ethics & Equity Incorrect Depreciation and Recognized Gain

A staff accountant for a large international company is calculating the tax gain from a disposition of business equipment. The equipment was 7-year MACRS property and has been fully depreciated for tax purposes. The staff accountant notices that the equipment was used in Germany, not the United States, although it is listed as an asset of the U.S. company for which the staff accountant works. Because the property was used outside the United States, it should have been depreciated using straight-line over a nine-year life. Consequently, the tax depreciation has been overstated, and the tax basis should be greater than zero, causing a smaller gain. What should the staff accountant do?

Form **4797**

Department of the Treasury
Internal Revenue Service

Sales of Business Property

(Also Involuntary Conversions and Recapture Amounts Under Sections 179 and 280F(b)(2))

▶ Attach to your tax return.

▶ Go to *www.irs.gov/Form4797* for instructions and the latest information.

OMB No. 1545-0184

2021

Attachment Sequence No. **27**

Name(s) shown on return	Identifying number
Troy Williams	*111-11-1111*

1a	Enter the gross proceeds from sales or exchanges reported to you for 2021 on Form(s) 1099-B or 1099-S (or substitute statement) that you are including on line 2, 10, or 20. See instructions	**1a**	
b	Enter the total amount of gain that you are including on lines 2, 10, and 24 due to the partial dispositions of MACRS assets	**1b**	
c	Enter the total amount of loss that you are including on lines 2 and 10 due to the partial dispositions of MACRS assets	**1c**	

Part I **Sales or Exchanges of Property Used in a Trade or Business and Involuntary Conversions From Other Than Casualty or Theft—Most Property Held More Than 1 Year** (see instructions)

2 (a) Description of property	(b) Date acquired (mo., day, yr.)	(c) Date sold (mo., day, yr.)	(d) Gross sales price	(e) Depreciation allowed or allowable since acquisition	(f) Cost or other basis, plus improvements and expense of sale	(g) Gain or (loss) Subtract (f) from the sum of (d) and (e)
Asset C	*12/09/18*	*12/30/21*	*2,806*	*12,314*	*16,000*	*(880)*

3	Gain, if any, from Form 4684, line 39	**3**	
4	Section 1231 gain from installment sales from Form 6252, line 26 or 37	**4**	
5	Section 1231 gain or (loss) from like-kind exchanges from Form 8824	**5**	
6	Gain, if any, from line 32, from other than casualty or theft	**6**	*20,126*
7	Combine lines 2 through 6. Enter the gain or (loss) here and on the appropriate line as follows	**7**	*19,246*
	Partnerships and S corporations. Report the gain or (loss) following the instructions for Form 1065, Schedule K, line 10, or Form 1120-S, Schedule K, line 9. Skip lines 8, 9, 11, and 12 below.		
	Individuals, partners, S corporation shareholders, and all others. If line 7 is zero or a loss, enter the amount from line 7 on line 11 below and skip lines 8 and 9. If line 7 is a gain and you didn't have any prior year section 1231 losses, or they were recaptured in an earlier year, enter the gain from line 7 as a long-term capital gain on the Schedule D filed with your return and skip lines 8, 9, 11, and 12 below.		
8	Nonrecaptured net section 1231 losses from prior years. See instructions	**8**	
9	Subtract line 8 from line 7. If zero or less, enter -0-. If line 9 is zero, enter the gain from line 7 on line 12 below. If line 9 is more than zero, enter the amount from line 8 on line 12 below and enter the gain from line 9 as a long-term capital gain on the Schedule D filed with your return. See instructions	**9**	

Part II **Ordinary Gains and Losses** (see instructions)

10 Ordinary gains and losses not included on lines 11 through 16 (include property held 1 year or less):

(a)	(b)	(c)	(d)	(e)	(f)	(g)
Asset D	*07/27/21*	*11/03/21*	*6,400*	*0*	*7,000*	*(600)*

11	Loss, if any, from line 7	**11**	( )
12	Gain, if any, from line 7 or amount from line 8, if applicable	**12**	
13	Gain, if any, from line 31	**13**	*36,500*
14	Net gain or (loss) from Form 4684, lines 31 and 38a	**14**	
15	Ordinary gain from installment sales from Form 6252, line 25 or 36	**15**	
16	Ordinary gain or (loss) from like-kind exchanges from Form 8824	**16**	
17	Combine lines 10 through 16	**17**	*35,900*
18	For all except individual returns, enter the amount from line 17 on the appropriate line of your return and skip lines a and b below. For individual returns, complete lines a and b below.		
a	If the loss on line 11 includes a loss from Form 4684, line 35, column (b)(ii), enter that part of the loss here. Enter the loss from income-producing property on Schedule A (Form 1040), line 16. (Do not include any loss on property used as an employee.) Identify as from "Form 4797, line 18a." See instructions	**18a**	
b	Redetermine the gain or (loss) on line 17 excluding the loss, if any, on line 18a. Enter here and on Schedule 1 (Form 1040), Part I, line 4	**18b**	*35,900*

Form 4797 (2021) Page **2**

Part III Gain From Disposition of Property Under Sections 1245, 1250, 1252, 1254, and 1255 (see instructions)

19	(a) Description of section 1245, 1250, 1252, 1254, or 1255 property:	(b) Date acquired (mo., day, yr.)	(c) Date sold (mo., day, yr.)
A	*Asset A*	*06/23/18*	*08/31/21*
B	*Asset B*	*05/10/11*	*11/10/21*
C			
D			

	These columns relate to the properties on lines 19A through 19D. ▶		Property A	Property B	Property C	Property D
20	Gross sales price (**Note:** *See line 1a before completing.*)	20	*48,020*	*43,000*		
21	Cost or other basis plus expense of sale	21	*50,000*	*37,000*		
22	Depreciation (or depletion) allowed or allowable	22	*38,480*	*14,126*		
23	Adjusted basis. Subtract line 22 from line 21	23	*11,520*	*22,874*		
24	Total gain. Subtract line 23 from line 20	24	*36,500*	*20,126*		
25	**If section 1245 property:**					
a	Depreciation allowed or allowable from line 22	25a	*38,480*			
b	Enter the **smaller** of line 24 or 25a	25b	*36,500*			
26	**If section 1250 property:** If straight line depreciation was used, enter -0- on line 26g, except for a corporation subject to section 291.					
a	Additional depreciation after 1975. See instructions	26a				
b	Applicable percentage multiplied by the **smaller** of line 24 or line 26a. See instructions	26b				
c	Subtract line 26a from line 24. If residential rental property **or** line 24 isn't more than line 26a, skip lines 26d and 26e	26c				
d	Additional depreciation after 1969 and before 1976	26d				
e	Enter the **smaller** of line 26c or 26d	26e				
f	Section 291 amount (corporations only)	26f				
g	Add lines 26b, 26e, and 26f	26g		*0*		
27	**If section 1252 property:** Skip this section if you didn't dispose of farmland or if this form is being completed for a partnership.					
a	Soil, water, and land clearing expenses	27a				
b	Line 27a multiplied by applicable percentage. See instructions	27b				
c	Enter the **smaller** of line 24 or 27b	27c				
28	**If section 1254 property:**					
a	Intangible drilling and development costs, expenditures for development of mines and other natural deposits, mining exploration costs, and depletion. See instructions	28a				
b	Enter the **smaller** of line 24 or 28a	28b				
29	**If section 1255 property:**					
a	Applicable percentage of payments excluded from income under section 126. See instructions	29a				
b	Enter the **smaller** of line 24 or 29a. See instructions	29b				

Summary of Part III Gains. Complete property columns A through D through line 29b before going to line 30.

30	Total gains for all properties. Add property columns A through D, line 24	30	*56,626*
31	Add property columns A through D, lines 25b, 26g, 27c, 28b, and 29b. Enter here and on line 13	31	*36,500*
32	Subtract line 31 from line 30. Enter the portion from casualty or theft on Form 4684, line 33. Enter the portion from other than casualty or theft on Form 4797, line 6	32	*20,126*

Part IV Recapture Amounts Under Sections 179 and 280F(b)(2) When Business Use Drops to 50% or Less (see instructions)

			(a) Section 179	(b) Section 280F(b)(2)
33	Section 179 expense deduction or depreciation allowable in prior years	33		
34	Recomputed depreciation. See instructions	34		
35	Recapture amount. Subtract line 34 from line 33. See the instructions for where to report	35		

Form **4797** (2021)

SCHEDULE D (Form 1040)

Department of the Treasury Internal Revenue Service (99)

Capital Gains and Losses

▶ Attach to Form 1040, 1040-SR, or 1040-NR.
▶ Go to *www.irs.gov/ScheduleD* for instructions and the latest information.
▶ Use Form 8949 to list your transactions for lines 1b, 2, 3, 8b, 9, and 10.

OMB No. 1545-0074

2021

Attachment Sequence No. **12**

Name(s) shown on return: *Troy Williams*

Your social security number: *111-11-1111*

Did you dispose of any investment(s) in a qualified opportunity fund during the tax year? ☐ **Yes** ☐ **No**
If "Yes," attach Form 8949 and see its instructions for additional requirements for reporting your gain or loss.

Part I Short-Term Capital Gains and Losses—Generally Assets Held One Year or Less (see instructions)

See instructions for how to figure the amounts to enter on the lines below. This form may be easier to complete if you round off cents to whole dollars.	(d) Proceeds (sales price)	(e) Cost (or other basis)	(g) Adjustments to gain or loss from Form(s) 8949, Part I, line 2, column (g)	(h) Gain or (loss) Subtract column (e) from column (d) and combine the result with column (g)
1a Totals for all short-term transactions reported on Form 1099-B for which basis was reported to the IRS and for which you have no adjustments (see instructions). However, if you choose to report all these transactions on Form 8949, leave this line blank and go to line 1b .	*170*	*370*		*(200)*
1b Totals for all transactions reported on Form(s) 8949 with **Box A** checked				
2 Totals for all transactions reported on Form(s) 8949 with **Box B** checked				
3 Totals for all transactions reported on Form(s) 8949 with **Box C** checked				

Line			Amount
4	Short-term gain from Form 6252 and short-term gain or (loss) from Forms 4684, 6781, and 8824 . .	4	
5	Net short-term gain or (loss) from partnerships, S corporations, estates, and trusts from Schedule(s) K-1	5	
6	Short-term capital loss carryover. Enter the amount, if any, from line 8 of your **Capital Loss Carryover Worksheet** in the instructions	6	( )
7	**Net short-term capital gain or (loss).** Combine lines 1a through 6 in column (h). If you have any long-term capital gains or losses, go to Part II below. Otherwise, go to Part III on the back	7	*(200)*

Part II Long-Term Capital Gains and Losses—Generally Assets Held More Than One Year (see instructions)

See instructions for how to figure the amounts to enter on the lines below. This form may be easier to complete if you round off cents to whole dollars.	(d) Proceeds (sales price)	(e) Cost (or other basis)	(g) Adjustments to gain or loss from Form(s) 8949, Part II, line 2, column (g)	(h) Gain or (loss) Subtract column (e) from column (d) and combine the result with column (g)
8a Totals for all long-term transactions reported on Form 1099-B for which basis was reported to the IRS and for which you have no adjustments (see instructions). However, if you choose to report all these transactions on Form 8949, leave this line blank and go to line 8b .	*13,223*	*10,223*		*3,000*
8b Totals for all transactions reported on Form(s) 8949 with **Box D** checked				
9 Totals for all transactions reported on Form(s) 8949 with **Box E** checked				
10 Totals for all transactions reported on Form(s) 8949 with **Box F** checked.				

Line			Amount
11	Gain from Form 4797, Part I; long-term gain from Forms 2439 and 6252; and long-term gain or (loss) from Forms 4684, 6781, and 8824	11	*19,246*
12	Net long-term gain or (loss) from partnerships, S corporations, estates, and trusts from Schedule(s) K-1	12	
13	Capital gain distributions. See the instructions	13	
14	Long-term capital loss carryover. Enter the amount, if any, from line 13 of your **Capital Loss Carryover Worksheet** in the instructions	14	( )
15	**Net long-term capital gain or (loss).** Combine lines 8a through 14 in column (h). Then, go to Part III on the back	15	*22,246*

For Paperwork Reduction Act Notice, see your tax return instructions. Cat. No. 11338H **Schedule D (Form 1040) 2021**

Part III Summary

16	Combine lines 7 and 15 and enter the result	**16**	*22,046*
	• If line 16 is a **gain,** enter the amount from line 16 on Form 1040, 1040-SR, or 1040-NR, line 7. Then, go to line 17 below. • If line 16 is a **loss,** skip lines 17 through 20 below. Then, go to line 21. Also be sure to complete line 22. • If line 16 is **zero,** skip lines 17 through 21 below and enter -0- on Form 1040, 1040-SR, or 1040-NR, line 7. Then, go to line 22.		
17	Are lines 15 and 16 **both** gains? ☑ **Yes.** Go to line 18. ☐ **No.** Skip lines 18 through 21, and go to line 22.		
18	If you are required to complete the **28% Rate Gain Worksheet** (see instructions), enter the amount, if any, from line 7 of that worksheet ▶	**18**	*0*
19	If you are required to complete the **Unrecaptured Section 1250 Gain Worksheet** (see instructions), enter the amount, if any, from line 18 of that worksheet ▶	**19**	*13,926*
20	Are lines 18 and 19 both zero or blank and are you not filing Form 4952? ☐ **Yes.** Complete the **Qualified Dividends and Capital Gain Tax Worksheet** in the instructions for Forms 1040 and 1040-SR, line 16. **Don't** complete lines 21 and 22 below. ☑ **No.** Complete the **Schedule D Tax Worksheet** in the instructions. **Don't** complete lines 21 and 22 below.		
21	If line 16 is a loss, enter here and on Form 1040, 1040-SR, or 1040-NR, line 7, the **smaller** of: • The loss on line 16; or • ($3,000), or if married filing separately, ($1,500) **Note:** When figuring which amount is smaller, treat both amounts as positive numbers.	**21**	( )
22	Do you have qualified dividends on Form 1040, 1040-SR, or 1040-NR, line 3a? ☐ **Yes.** Complete the **Qualified Dividends and Capital Gain Tax Worksheet** in the instructions for Forms 1040 and 1040-SR, line 16. ☐ **No.** Complete the rest of Form 1040, 1040-SR, or 1040-NR.		

17-7 Tax Planning

LO.8

Identify tax planning opportunities associated with §§ 1231, 1245, and 1250.

17-7a Timing of § 1231 Gain

Although § 1245 recaptures much of the gain from the disposition of business property, sometimes § 1231 gain is still substantial. For instance, land held as a business asset will generate either § 1231 gain or § 1231 loss. If the taxpayer already has a capital loss for the year, the sale of land at a gain should be postponed so that the net § 1231 gain is not netted against the capital loss. The capital loss deduction will therefore be maximized for the current tax year, and the capital loss carryforward (if any) may be offset against the gain when the land is sold. If the taxpayer already has a § 1231 loss, § 1231 gains might be postponed to maximize the ordinary loss deduction this year. However, the carryforward of unrecaptured § 1231 losses will make some or all of the § 1231 gain next year an ordinary gain.

In the examples below, the 2022 and 2023 long-term capital gain rates are assumed to be the same.

Section 1231 Planning

Example 23

Mark has a $2,000 net STCL for 2022. He could sell business land held 27 months for a $3,000 § 1231 gain. He will have no other capital gains and losses or § 1231 gains and losses in 2022 or 2023. He has no nonrecaptured § 1231 losses from prior years. Mark is in the 24% tax bracket in 2022 and will be in the 22% bracket in 2023. If he sells the land in 2022, he will have a $1,000 net LTCG ($3,000 § 1231 gain − $2,000 STCL) and will pay a tax of $150 ($1,000 × 15%).

If Mark sells the land in 2023, he will have a 2022 tax savings of $480 ($2,000 capital loss deduction × 24% tax rate on ordinary income). In 2023, he will pay tax of $450 ($3,000 × 15%).

By postponing the sale by a year, Mark gets the use of $630 ($480 + $150) of tax savings until he has to pay $450 in 2023, for a net savings of $180 between the two years without considering the time value of money and other factors.

Example 24

Beth has a $15,000 § 1231 loss in 2022. She could sell business equipment held 30 months for a $20,000 § 1231 gain and a $12,000 § 1245 gain. Beth is in the 24% tax bracket in 2022 and will be in the 22% bracket in 2023. She has no nonrecaptured § 1231 losses from prior years. If she sold the equipment in 2022, she would have a $5,000 net § 1231 gain and $12,000 of ordinary gain. Her tax would be $3,630 [($5,000 § 1231 gain × 15%) + ($12,000 ordinary gain × 24%)].

If Beth postponed the equipment sale until 2023, she would have a 2022 ordinary loss of $15,000 and tax savings of $3,600 ($15,000 × 24%). In 2023, she would have $5,000 of § 1231 gain (the 2022 § 1231 loss carries over and recaptures $15,000 of the 2023 § 1231 gain as ordinary income) and $27,000 of ordinary gain. Her tax would be $6,690 [($5,000 § 1231 gain × 15%) + ($27,000 ordinary gain × 22%)].

By postponing the sale of the § 1231 property until 2023. Beth gets the use of $7,230 ($3,600 + $3,630) of tax savings until she has to pay $6,690 in 2023, for a net savings of $540 between the two years without considering the time value of money and other factors.

17-7b Timing of Recapture

Because recapture is usually not triggered until the property is sold or disposed of, it may be possible to plan for recapture in low tax bracket or loss years. If a taxpayer has net operating loss (NOL) carryovers, the recognition of ordinary income from recapture may be advisable to absorb the loss carryovers.

Example 25

Ahmad has a $15,000 NOL carryover. He owns a machine that he plans to sell in the early part of next year. The expected gain of $17,000 from the sale of the machine will be recaptured as ordinary income under § 1245. Ahmad sells the machine before the end of this year and uses the $15,000 NOL carryover to offset $15,000 of the ordinary income.

17-7c **Postponing and Shifting Recapture**

It is also possible to postpone recapture or to shift the burden of recapture to others. For example, recapture is postponed and shifted on the exchange of a § 1231 asset if the taxpayer exchanges the property for stock in a § 351 nontaxable incorporation. In this instance, the recapture potential is shifted to the corporation.

Recapture can be shifted to others through the gratuitous transfer of § 1245 or § 1250 property to family members. A subsequent sale of such property by the donee will trigger recapture to the donee rather than the donor (refer to Example 15). This procedure would be advisable only if the donee was in a lower income tax bracket compared with the donor.

17-7d **Avoiding Recapture**

The immediate expensing election (§ 179) and additional first-year (bonus) depreciation [§ 168(k)] are subject to § 1245 recapture. If the elections are not made, the § 1245 recapture potential will accumulate more slowly (refer to Chapter 8). Because using the immediate expense election and/or additional first-year depreciation deduction complicates depreciation and book accounting for the affected asset(s), not taking these deductions may make sense even though the time value of money might indicate that they should be taken.

Refocus on The Big Picture

Depreciation Recapture

RL PRODUCTIONS/DIGITALVISION/GETTY IMAGES

Even though Hazel did not maximize her depreciation deductions when she acquired the store equipment in 2019, she still has ordinary income when she sells the equipment in 2022. She has a basis lower than the store equipment's value due to the § 179 immediate expense deduction she took and the rapid 7-year MACRS depreciation. Section 1245 "recaptures" this gain as ordinary income.

Hazel cannot avoid currently recognizing the $53,040 ($128,000 sale price − $74,960 adjusted basis) by exchanging the property because that is not a qualifying like-kind exchange (see Example 18). The only way she can avoid the ordinary gain is by not disposing of the equipment.

Key Terms

Intangible drilling and development costs (IDCs), 17-19

Long-term nonpersonal use capital assets, 17-5

Related party, 17-19

Section 1231 gains and losses, 17-3

Section 1231 lookback, 17-6

Section 1231 property, 17-4

Section 1245 property, 17-12

Section 1245 recapture, 17-11

Section 1250 property, 17-13

Section 1250 recapture, 17-13

Unrecaptured § 1250 gain, 17-14

Discussion Questions

1. **LO.1, 2** Harriet, an organic farmer, has owned depreciable farm equipment for several years. Is the equipment a capital asset? Why or why not? Critical Thinking

2. **LO.1** If there is a net loss from the sale of depreciable business property held long term, what is the character of the loss? How is it deducted (*for or from* AGI)?

3. **LO.1, 2** Bernice, a sole proprietor, sold two business assets during the year. As a result, she has an ordinary loss and a § 1231 gain. The loss asset was office furniture that was held for eight months, and the gain asset is land that was held for five years. Why doesn't the ordinary loss offset the § 1231 gain? Critical Thinking

4. **LO.1, 2** Hakim's rental building (a § 1231 asset) was not insured when it was destroyed by a hurricane. His adjusted basis for the building was substantial but was less than he had paid for the building in 2017. The building was Hakim's only asset that was damaged by the hurricane. How should Hakim handle this situation? Critical Thinking

5. **LO.2** An individual taxpayer had a net § 1231 loss in 2022. Could any of this loss be treated as a long-term capital loss? Why or why not?

6. **LO.2** Steven established a sole proprietorship in 2016. He sold § 1231 assets at a loss in 2020 and 2021. He had only sold § 1231 assets at a gain before 2020. In 2022, he could sell a § 1231 asset at a gain and would like to have the gain taxed as a long-term capital gain. What issue is Steven facing? Critical Thinking Planning

7. **LO.2** Review Examples 4 and 6 in the text. In both examples, the taxpayer's AGI is $129,400 even though in Example 6 there is $700 of nonrecaptured § 1231 loss from 2021. Explain why the two AGI amounts are the same.

8. **LO.3** A depreciable business dump truck has been owned for four years and is no longer useful to the taxpayer. What would have to be true for the disposition of the dump truck to generate at least some § 1231 loss?

9. **LO.1, 3** If depreciable equipment used in a business is sold at a recognized gain on July 10, 2022, and it was purchased on August 21, 2021, does § 1245 depreciation recapture apply to the asset? Explain.

10. **LO.3** A professional football player's contract is sold at a gain after it has been held for two years. What issues should the team consider in determining the nature of this gain? Critical Thinking

11. **LO.3** A retailer's store is destroyed by a tornado but is insured for its replacement cost. Consequently, the retailer has a $40,000 gain after receiving the insurance proceeds. The store is not replaced because the retailer spends the insurance proceeds on additional inventory. What is the nature of the gain if the building originally cost $100,000 three years ago and had an adjusted basis of $82,000 at the time of its destruction? Prepare an e-mail to your supervisor, Sharon Regan, summarizing your answer. E-mail this response to your instructor. Communication

12. **LO.4** In the current year, an individual taxpayer has net long-term capital gain from disposition of capital assets and has unrecaptured § 1250 gain. What would the circumstances have to be for the unrecaptured § 1250 gain to be taxed at 25%?

13. **LO.3, 5** Mary receives tangible personal property as a gift. The property was depreciated by the donor, and Mary also will depreciate it. At the date of the gift, the property was worth more than the donor's adjusted basis. What is the impact of these facts on Mary when she sells the property at a gain several years after she acquired it?

14. **LO.3, 5** Thomas receives tangible personal property as an inheritance from a decedent who died in 2022. The property was depreciated by the deceased, and Thomas also will depreciate it. At the date of the deceased's death, the property was worth more than the deceased's adjusted basis. What is the impact of these facts on Thomas when he sells the property at a gain several years after he acquired it?

15. **LO.3, 5** Dino contributes to charity some tangible personal property that he had used in his business and depreciated. At the date of the donation, the property has a fair market value greater than its adjusted basis but less than the original cost. What is the impact of these facts on Dino's charitable contribution?

16. **LO.3, 5** A corporation distributes a truck it has owned for three years to its sole shareholder. The shareholder will use the truck for personal use activity. The truck's fair market value at the time of the distribution is greater than its adjusted basis but less than its original cost. Does the corporation recognize a gain? If so, what is the character of the gain?

17. **LO.6** A corporation distributes a truck it has owned for three years to its sole shareholder. The shareholder will use the truck for business activity. The truck's fair market value at the time of the distribution is greater than its adjusted basis but less than its original cost. Does the corporation recognize a gain? If so, what is the character of the gain?

18. **LO.6** Complete the following statements regarding special recapture provisions.
    a. Corporations selling depreciable real property are required to recapture as ordinary income the ____________ of two amounts: (1) ____________% of the recognized gain or (2) ____________% of the depreciation taken.
    b. When the sale or exchange of property, which in the hands of the transferee is depreciable property, is between certain related parties, ____________ recognized is ordinary income.
    c. Intangible drilling and development costs are subject to ____________ recapture when the property is disposed of.

19. **LO.7** Refer to Form 4797 near the end of this chapter. Where would a § 1231 loss be entered on the form?

20. **LO.7** Refer to Form 4797 near the end of this chapter. Where would a § 1231 gain on the disposition of business land be entered on the form?

Computational Exercises

21. **LO.1** Lena is a sole proprietor. In April of this year, she sold equipment purchased four years ago for $26,000 with an adjusted basis of $15,500 for $17,000. Later in the year, Lena sold another piece of equipment purchased two years ago with an adjusted basis of $8,200 for $5,500. What is the amount and character of Lena's gain or loss?

22. **LO.2** Several years ago Nicolas, a timber dealer, purchased a tract of land with a substantial stand of trees on it. The land cost $8,000, and the timber cost $250,000. On the first day of 2022, the timber was appraised at $325,000. In August 2022, Nicolas cut the timber and sold it for $360,000. Nicolas elects to treat the cutting as a sale or exchange under § 1231. What is the amount and character of Nicolas's gain or loss?

23. **LO.3** Renata Corporation purchased equipment in 2020 for $180,000 and has taken $83,000 of regular MACRS depreciation. Renata Corporation sells the equipment in 2022 for $110,000. What is the amount and character of Renata's gain or loss?

24. **LO.3** Jacob purchased business equipment for $56,000 in 2019 and has taken $35,000 of regular MACRS depreciation. Jacob sells the equipment in 2022 for $26,000. What is the amount and character of Jacob's gain or loss?

25. **LO.1, 2, 3** Shannon owns two items of business equipment. Both were purchased in 2018 for $100,000, both have a 7-year MACRS recovery period, and both have an adjusted basis of $37,490. Shannon is considering selling these assets in 2022. One of them is worth $60,000, and the other is worth $23,000. Because both items were used in her business, Shannon simply assumes that the loss on one will be offset against the gain from the other and that the net gain or loss will increase or reduce her business income. What is the amount and character of Shannon's gain or loss? Planning

26. **LO.4** An apartment building was acquired in 2013. The depreciation taken on the building was $123,000, and the building was sold for a $34,000 gain. What is the maximum amount of *25% gain*?

27. **LO.4** An individual taxpayer has $25,000 of § 1231 gain from the disposition of nonresidential real estate. Straight-line depreciation of $43,000 was deducted on the real estate. The taxpayer also has a § 1231 loss of $56,000 from the sale of equipment. How much of the § 1231 gain is taxed as unrecaptured § 1250 gain?

28. **LO.4** Enzo is a single taxpayer with the following gains and losses for 2022:
    - $2,100 short-term capital loss.
    - $24,000 long-term capital gain from sale of stock.
    - $14,000 § 1231 gain that is all unrecaptured § 1250 gain.

    What is the amount and character of Enzo's gain or loss?

29. **LO.5** In a § 1031 like-kind exchange, Rafael exchanges a business building that originally cost $200,000. On the date of the exchange, the building given up has an adjusted basis of $85,000 and a fair market value of $110,000. Rafael pays $15,000 and receives a building with a fair market value of $125,000. What is the amount and character of Rafael's gain or loss?

30. **LO.5** Gaston Corporation distributes § 1245 property as a dividend to its shareholders. The property's fair market value is $580,000, and the adjusted basis is $560,000. In addition, the amount of the recapture potential is $55,000. What is the amount and character of Gaston's gain or loss?

Problems

31. **LO.1, 2** Jenny purchased timber on a 100-acre tract of land in South Dakota in March 2020 for $100,000. On January 1, 2022, the timber had a fair market value of $145,000. Because of careless cutting in November 2022, when the fair market value was $158,000, the wood was sold on January 30, 2023, for $98,000.
    a. What gain (loss) was recognized in 2021, 2022, and 2023 if Jenny elected to treat the cutting as a sale?
    b. What was the nature of the gains (losses) in part (a)?
    c. Does the answer change if the timber was sold in December 2022? Why or why not?
    d. If the timber was worth only $58,000 on January 1, 2022, was cut in November when it was worth $33,000 and was sold in December for $59,000, how would the answers to parts (a) and (b) change?

32. **LO.2** Bob owns a farming sole proprietorship. During the year, Bob sold a milk cow that he had owned for 15 months and a workhorse that he had owned for 66 months. The cow had an adjusted basis of $38,000 and was sold for $55,000. The horse had an adjusted basis of $750 and was sold for $4,000. Bob also has a $200 long-term capital loss from the sale of corporate stock. He has $55,000 of other AGI (not associated with the items above) for the year. He has $4,000 nonrecaptured § 1231 losses from the previous five years. What is the nature of the gains or losses from the disposition of the farm animals? What is Bob's AGI for the year?

Communications

33. **LO.2** A sculpture that Korliss Kane held for investment was destroyed in a flood. The sculpture was insured, and Korliss had a $60,000 gain from this casualty. He also had a $17,000 loss from an uninsured antique vase that was destroyed by the flood. The vase also was held for investment. Korliss had no other property transactions during the year and has no nonrecaptured § 1231 losses from prior years. Both the sculpture and the vase had been held more than one year when the flood occurred (i.e., both are long-term nonpersonal use capital assets). Compute Korliss's net gain or loss, and identify how it would be treated. Also write a letter to Korliss, explaining the nature of the gain or loss. Korliss's address is 2367 Meridian Road, Hannibal, MO 63401.

34. **LO.2** Keshara has the following net § 1231 results for each of the years shown. What would be the nature of the net gains in 2021 and 2022?

Tax Year	Net § 1231 Loss	Net § 1231 Gain
2017	$18,000	
2018	33,000	
2019	42,000	
2020		$41,000
2021		30,000
2022		41,000

Critical Thinking
Decision Making

35. **LO.2, 8** Jinjie owns two parcels of business land (§ 1231 assets). One parcel can be sold at a loss of $60,000, and the other parcel can be sold at a gain of $70,000. Jinjie has no nonrecaptured § 1231 losses from prior years. The parcels could be sold at any time because potential purchasers are abundant. Jinjie has a $35,000 short-term capital loss carryover from a prior tax year and no capital assets that could be sold to generate long-term capital gains. Both land parcels have been held more than one year. What should Jinjie do based upon these facts? (Assume that tax rates are constant, and ignore the present value of future cash flow.)

36. **LO.1, 2, 3** Siena Industries (a sole proprietorship) sold three § 1231 assets during 2022. Data on these property dispositions are as follows:

Asset	Cost	Acquired	Accumulated Depreciation	Sold for	Sold on
Rack	$100,000	10/10/18	$62,000	$86,000	10/10/22
Forklift	35,000	10/16/19	23,000	4,000	10/10/22
Bin	87,000	03/12/21	34,000	60,000	10/10/22

a. Determine the amount and the character of the recognized gain or loss from the disposition of each asset.

b. Assuming that Siena has no nonrecaptured net § 1231 losses from prior years, analyze these transactions and determine the amount (if any) that will be treated as a long-term capital gain.

37. **LO.2, 3** Amber Industries (a sole proprietorship) sold three § 1231 assets during 2022. Data on these property dispositions are as follows:

Asset	Cost	Acquired	Accumulated Depreciation	Sold for	Sold on
Rack	$100,000	10/10/18	$100,000	$145,000	10/10/22
Forklift	35,000	10/16/19	23,000	3,000	10/10/22
Bin	87,000	03/12/21	31,000	60,000	10/10/22

a. Determine the amount and the character of the recognized gain or loss from the disposition of each asset.

b. Assuming that Amber has $5,000 nonrecaptured net § 1231 losses from the five prior years, analyze these transactions and determine the amount (if any) that will be treated as a long-term capital gain.

38. LO.2, 3 Copper Industries (a sole proprietorship) sold three § 1231 assets during 2022. Data on these property dispositions are as follows:

Asset	Cost	Acquired	Accumulated Depreciation	Sold for	Sold on
Rack	$110,000	10/10/19	$70,000	$55,000	10/10/22
Forklift	45,000	10/16/18	21,000	15,000	10/10/22
Bin	97,000	03/12/21	31,000	60,000	10/10/22

a. Determine the amount and the character of the recognized gain or loss from the disposition of each asset.

b. Assuming that Copper has $6,000 nonrecaptured net § 1231 losses from prior years, analyze these transactions and determine the amount (if any) that will be treated as a long-term capital gain.

39. LO.2, 3 On December 1, 2020, Lavender Manufacturing Company (a corporation) purchased another company's assets, including a patent. The patent was used in Lavender's manufacturing operations; $49,500 was allocated to the patent, and it was amortized at the rate of $275 per month. On July 30, 2022, Lavender sold the patent for $95,000. Twenty months of amortization had been taken on the patent. What are the amount and nature of the gain Lavender recognizes on the disposition of the patent? Prepare your solution using Microsoft Excel (or a similar program). Write a letter to Lavender, discussing the treatment of the gain. Lavender's address is 6734 Grover Street, Boothbay Harbor, ME 04538. The letter should be addressed to Bill Cubit, Controller. Communications

40. LO.2, 4 On June 1, 2018, Skylark Enterprises (a calendar year LLC reporting as a sole prorietorship) acquired a retail store building for $500,000 (with $100,000 being allocated to the land). The store building was 39-year real property, and the straight-line cost recovery method was used. The property was sold on June 21, 2022, for $385,000.

a. Compute the cost recovery and adjusted basis for the building using Exhibit 8.8 from Chapter 8.

b. What are the amount and nature of Skylark's gain or loss from disposition of the property? What amount, if any, of the gain is unrecaptured § 1250 gain?

41. LO.2, 3, 4 On May 2, 1992, Hannah Weather (Social Security number: 111-22-3333) acquired residential rental real estate for $450,000. Of the cost, $100,000 was allocated to the land and $350,000 to the building. On August 20, 2021, the building, which then had an adjusted basis of $0, was sold for $545,000 and the land for $200,000.

a. Determine the amount and character of the recognized gain from the sale of the building.

b. Determine the amount and character of the recognized gain from the sale of the land.

c. Complete a 2021 Form 4797 for these transactions. Assume that there are no § 1231 lookback losses.

42. LO.2, 3, 4 Javier is the sole proprietor of a sporting goods business. During 2022, the following transactions occurred:

- Unimproved land adjacent to Javier's store was condemned by the city on February 1. The condemnation proceeds were $15,000. The land, acquired in 1989, had an allocable basis of $40,000. Javier has additional parking across the street and plans to use the condemnation proceeds to build his inventory.
- A delivery truck used in Javier's business was sold on January 2 for $3,500. The truck was purchased on January 2, 2018, for $6,000. On the date of sale, the adjusted basis was zero.
- Javier sold a rowing machine at an auction. Net proceeds were $4,900. The rowing machine was purchased as used equipment 17 years ago for $5,200 and is fully depreciated.

- Javier sold an apartment building for $300,000 on September 1. The property was purchased on September 1, 2019, for $150,000 and was being depreciated over a 27.5-year life using the straight-line method. At the date of sale, the adjusted basis was $124,783. Javier actively managed the property as a trade or business.
- Javier's personal yacht was stolen on September 5. The yacht had been purchased in August at a cost of $25,000. The fair market value immediately preceding the theft was $19,600. Javier was insured for 50% of the original cost, and he received $12,500 on December 1.
- Javier sold a Buick on May 1 for $9,600. The vehicle had been used exclusively for personal purposes. It was purchased on September 1, 2018, for $20,800.
- A trampoline stretching machine (owned two years and used in Javier's business) was stolen on May 5, but the business's insurance company will not pay any of the machine's value because Javier failed to pay the insurance premium. The machine had a fair market value of $8,000 and an adjusted basis of $6,000 at the time of theft.
- Javier had AGI of $102,000 from sources other than those described above.
- Javier has no nonrecaptured § 1231 lookback losses.

a. For each transaction, what are the amount and nature of recognized gain or loss?

b. What is Javier's 2022 AGI?

Communications
Planning

43. **LO.2, 4** On January 1, 2013, Stephanie Bridges acquired depreciable real property for $50,000. She used straight-line depreciation to compute the asset's cost recovery. The asset was sold for $96,000 on January 3, 2022, when its adjusted basis was $38,000.

a. What are the amount and nature of the gain if the real property was residential?

b. Stephanie is curious about how the recapture rules differ for tangible personal property and for residential rental real estate acquired in 1987 and thereafter. Write a letter to Stephanie, explaining the differences. Her address is 2345 Westridge Street #23, Edna, KS 67342.

Critical Thinking
Decision Making
Planning

44. **LO.2, 3, 5, 8** Hana is in the 24% tax bracket and owns depreciable business equipment that she purchased several years ago for $135,000. She has taken $100,000 of depreciation on the equipment, and it is worth $55,000. Hana's niece, Michelle, is starting a new business and is short of cash. Michelle has asked Hana to gift the equipment to her so that Michelle can use it in her business. Hana no longer needs the equipment. Identify the alternatives available to Hana if she wants to help Michelle and the tax effects of those alternatives. (Assume that all alternatives involve the business equipment in one way or another, and ignore the gift tax.)

45. **LO.2, 3, 5** Anna received tangible personal property with a fair market value of $65,000 as a gift in 2020. The donor had purchased the property for $77,000 and had taken $77,000 of depreciation. Anna used the property in her business. Anna sells the property for $23,000 in 2022. What are the tax status of the property and the nature of the recognized gain when she sells the property?

46. **LO.2, 3, 5** Miguel receives tangible personal property as an inheritance in 2020. The property was depreciated by the deceased (Miguel's father), and Miguel also will depreciate it. At the date of the deceased's death, the property was worth $532,000. The deceased had purchased it for $900,000 and had taken $523,000 of depreciation on the property. Miguel takes $223,000 of depreciation on the property before selling it for $482,000 in 2022. What are the tax status of the property and the nature of the recognized gain when Miguel sells the property?

47. **LO.5** David contributes to charity some tangible personal property that he had used in his business and depreciated. At the date of the donation, the property has a fair market value of $233,000 and an adjusted basis of zero; it was originally acquired for $400,000. What is the amount of David's charitable contribution?

48. **LO.2, 3, 5** Dedriea contributes to her wholly owned corporation some tangible personal property she had used in her sole proprietorship business and depreciated. She had acquired the property for $566,000 and had taken $431,000 of depreciation on it before contributing it to the corporation. At the date of the contribution, the property had a fair market value of $289,000. The corporation took $100,000 of depreciation on the property and then sold it for $88,000 in 2022. What are the tax status of the property to the corporation and the nature of the recognized gain or loss when the corporation sells the property?

49. **LO.2, 3, 6** Tan Corporation purchased depreciable tangible personal property for $100,000 in 2020 and immediately expensed the entire cost under § 179. In 2022, when the property was worth $80,000, Tan distributed it as a dividend to the corporation's sole shareholder. What was the tax status of this property for Tan? What is the nature of the recognized gain or loss from the distribution of the property?

50. **LO.5** Jasmine owned rental real estate that she sold to her tenant in an installment sale. Jasmine acquired the property in 2010 for $400,000; took $178,000 of depreciation on it; and sold it for $210,000, receiving $25,000 immediately and the balance (plus interest at a market rate) in equal payments of $18,500 for 10 years.

    a. What is the nature of the recognized gain or loss from this transaction?
    b. Assuming that the interest rate on the installment contract is 5%, what is the present value of the installment payments? See Appendix E for present value factors.

51. **LO.4, 7** Sasha and Tara are married, filing jointly. Their correctly determined 2022 taxable income is $127,000. This taxable income includes a $5,000 § 1231 gain from the sale of business land that was included in their $22,000 of net long-term capital gain. None of the net long-term capital gain was from collectibles.

    a. In addition to their Form 1040, what tax forms related to their property transactions would the couple include in their income tax return?
    b. Calculate the couple's tax on taxable income using the alternative tax on net capital gain method.

52. **LO.7** On August 10, 2020, Jasper purchased business equipment for $40,000. On his 2020 tax return, $40,000 of § 179 immediate expense was taken on the equipment. On July 14, 2021, Jasper sold the equipment for $12,000. What is the nature of disposition gain or loss? Where is it reported on the 2021 Form 4797?

53. **LO.7** Adrian has a 2021 Form 4797, line 9 gain of $56,000. He also has one transaction on his 2021 Form 1040 Schedule D, Part I—a loss of $58,000. What is Adrian's AGI from these events?

54. **LO.7** Theresa has a 2021 Form 1040 Schedule D, line 16 gain of $45,000. There is also a $45,000 gain on the form's line 19. What is the nature of the gain? What alternative tax rate applies to it?

55. **LO.3, 8** Jay sold three items of business equipment for a total of $300,000. None of the equipment was appraised to determine its value. Jay's cost and adjusted basis for the assets are as follows:

Critical Thinking
Decision Making
Planning

Asset	Cost	Adjusted Basis
Skidder	$230,000	$ 40,000
Driller	120,000	60,000
Platform	620,000	–0–
Total	$970,000	$100,000

Jay has been unable to establish the fair market values of the three assets. All he can determine is that combined they were worth $300,000 to the buyer in this arm's length transaction. How should Jay allocate the sales price and figure the gain or loss on the sale of the three assets?

Tax Return Problems

Tax Forms Problem

ProConnect™ Tax

56. Justin Stone was an employee of DataCare Services, Inc. His salary was $45,000 through November 10, 2021, when he was laid off. DataCare Services provided medical insurance for Justin and his family during his employment and agreed to continue this coverage through the end of 2021. He received $7,000 of unemployment compensation from November 11, 2021, through December 31, 2021. FICA withholdings were as follows: Social Security of $2,790 ($45,000 × 6.2%) and Medicare of $653 ($45,000 × 1.45%). Justin lives at 112 Green Road, Crown City, OH 45623. His Social Security number is 111-11-1118. Justin owned an apartment building until November 22, 2021, when he sold it for $200,000 (the apartment building's address is 4826 Orange Street, Crown City, OH 45623; the related land was sold for $10,000). For 2021, he had rent revenue of $33,000. He incurred and paid expenses as follows: $4,568 of repairs, $12,000 of mortgage interest, $10,000 of real estate taxes, and $1,000 of miscellaneous expenses. He purchased the building on January 2, 2015, for $125,000 (the related land was purchased for $10,000). The building generated an operating profit each year that Justin owned it. Justin received $13,000 in cash as a gift from his mother to help "tide him over" while he was unemployed. He also withdrew $10,000 from his checking account. He "invested" $300 in lottery tickets during the year but had no winnings.

    Other relevant tax information for Justin follows:

    - On November 22, 2021, Justin sold for $3,500 equipment that had been used for repairing various items in the apartments. The equipment was purchased for $25,000 on July 10, 2014, and was fully depreciated prior to 2021.
    - Justin has $3,000 of unrecaptured § 1231 losses from prior years.
    - Justin is age 38; is single; is divorced; and has custody of his 9-year-old son, Flint. Justin provides more than 50% of Flint's support. Flint's Social Security number is 123-45-6788.
    - Justin had $1,000 interest income from Blue Corporation bonds.
    - Justin had $1,500 interest income from a State Bank certificate of deposit.
    - Justin had a $2,000 *0%/15%/20%* long-term capital gain distribution from the Brown Stock Investment Fund.
    - Justin had the following itemized deductions: $4,600 real estate taxes on his home; $8,900 mortgage interest on his home; $4,760 charitable contributions (all in cash, all properly documented, and no single contribution exceeding $25); $4,300 state income tax withholding during 2021; $2,000 state estimated income tax payments during 2021; and $2,600 sales taxes paid.
    - Justin did not engage in any virtual currency transactions during the year, and he does not want to donate to the Presidential Election Campaign Fund. Justin received the appropriate recovery rebates (economic impact payments); related questions in ProConnect Tax should be ignored.
    - He had $10,000 of Federal income tax withholding during 2021 and made total Federal estimated income tax payments of $12,000 during 2021.

    Compute Justin's 2021 net tax payable or refund due, and complete his 2021 Federal tax return using appropriate forms and schedules. Ignore the § 199A deduction for qualified business income (if applicable). Suggested software: ProConnect Tax.

Communications

Tax Computation Problem

57. Glen and Diane Okumura (both age 48) are married, file a joint return, and live at 39 Kaloa Street, Honolulu, HI 96815. Glen's Social Security number is 111-11-1111, and Diane's is 123-45-6789. The Okumuras have two dependent children, Amy (age 15) and John (age 9). Amy's Social Security number is 123-45-6788, and John's Social Security number is 123-45-6787. Glen works for the Hawaii Public Works Department, and Diane works in a retail dress shop. Glen's employer provided medical insurance to Glen and his family during 2022. The Okumuras had the following transactions during 2022:

    a. Glen earned $57,000 in wages and had Federal income tax withholding of $2,000.

b. Diane earned $38,000 in wages from the dress shop and had Federal income tax withholding of $1,000.

c. The Okumuras sold a small apartment building for $89,980 on November 15, 2022. The building was acquired in October 2016 for $200,000; cost recovery was $66,820.

d. The Okumuras received $3,000 in qualified dividends on various domestic corporation stocks they own.

e. The Okumuras sold stock on November 5 for a $23,000 long-term capital gain and other stock on December 10 at a $2,000 short-term capital loss.

f. The Okumuras had the following itemized deductions: $14,790 unreimbursed medical expenses, $10,500 personal use real property taxes, $8,000 qualified residence interest, $1,500 of Glen's unreimbursed employee business expenses, $535 of investment-related expenses, $2,700 of state income taxes paid, and $1,061 of sales taxes from the sales tax table.

g. The Okumuras spent $3,000 on qualifying child care expenses during the year.

Compute the Okumuras' 2022 net tax payable or refund due. Also write a letter to the Okumuras, describing how the sale of the apartment building affects their return.

Research Problems

Note: Solutions to the Research Problems can be prepared by using the Thomson Reuters Checkpoint™ online tax research database, which accompanies this textbook. Solutions can also be prepared by using research materials found in a typical tax library.

the answer company™ THOMSON REUTERS®

Research Problem 1. Walter, your "real estate entrepreneur" client has a tax question for you. Walter is both a real estate developer and the owner and manager of residential rental real estate. Walter is retiring and is going to sell both the land he is holding for future development and the rental properties he owns. Straight-line depreciation was used to depreciate the rental real estate. The rental properties will be sold at a substantial loss, and the development property will be sold at a substantial gain. What is the nature of these gains and losses?

Partial list of research aids:
§§ 1221 and 1231.
Zane R. Tollis, 65 TCM 1951, T.C.Memo. 1993–63.

Research Problem 2. Your client, Alternate Fuel, Inc. (a regular corporation), has a problem and needs your help. It owns three sandwich shops in the Philadelphia area. In 2019, the year Alternate Fuel incorporated, it acquired land on the outskirts of Philadelphia with the hope of someday farming the land to cultivate humanely harvested meat and grow organic fruits and vegetables to use in its sandwich shops. In 2021, Alternate Fuel drew up plans for the farm and began consulting with agricultural experts about the best locations for crops and the number of animals that could be sustained on the acreage. After reviewing those plans, Alternate Fuel's CEO decided that the plans are not currently financially feasible and would like to sell the land in 2022. The land has appreciated substantially in value, and the company could use the cash infusion. Given that the land has not been used in the business, will any gain realized be categorized as a § 1231 gain or as a long-term capital gain? Explain.

Research Problem 3. Your supervisor at your CPA firm has questioned whether the depreciation taken on a building under § 168(k) is subject to § 1250 depreciation recapture. Find a discussion in the Form 4797 instructions confirming that this depreciation is subject to § 1250 recapture.

Use internet tax resources to address the following questions. Look for reliable websites and blogs of the IRS and other government agencies, media outlets, businesses, tax professionals, academics, think tanks, and political outlets.

Research Problem 4. Search for the phrase "mortgage and real estate fraud" on the IRS's website (**irs.gov**). Read the articles you find, and explain why this type of fraud is often unearthed by the IRS.

Research Problem 5. Find a state website that has tax forms and instructions for the state. Call that state "X." Find a discussion in those sources that reveals whether state X taxes gains from the sale of real estate that is located in state Y when the taxpayer is an individual and is a full-time resident of state X.

Research Problem 6. Using information from the IRS Tax Stats website (**irs.gov/statistics**), find a statistic for partnerships that indicates how much total noncapital gain there was in the latest year for which data are available.

Becker CPA Review Questions

Becker

1. A piece of depreciable machinery is sold. It has been held for three years and qualifies as § 1231 property. The selling price is greater than the adjusted basis but less than the original purchase price. Which statement below is correct?
   a. All of the gain will be subject to § 1245 recapture.
   b. Only a portion of the gain will be subject to § 1245 recapture.
   c. None of the gain will be subject to § 1245 recapture.
   d. Section 1245 recapture will not apply because there is a loss on the sale.

2. Jerry uses a building for business purposes. The building was purchased on April 1, year 3, for $124,000. It was sold on October 3, year 6, for $200,000. Accumulated depreciation as of the date of sale was $14,000, $4,000 of which was in excess of straight line. How much of the gain in year 6 is recaptured as ordinary under § 1250?
   a. $4,000
   b. $10,000
   c. $14,000
   d. $100,000

3. Jerry uses a building for business purposes. The building was purchased on April 1, year 3, for $124,000. It was sold on October 3, year 6, for $200,000. Accumulated depreciation as of the date of sale was $14,000, $4,000 of which was in excess of straight line. How much of the gain in year 6 is unrecaptured § 1250 gain?
   a. $4,000
   b. $10,000
   c. $14,000
   d. $100,000

4. Wally, Inc., sold the following three personal property assets in year 6:

Asset	Purchase Date	Cost	Accumulated Depreciation	Selling Price
A	5/1/year 3	$5,000	$3,000	$2,300
B	8/13/year 4	1,200	500	2,000
C	2/18/year 4	3,800	1,800	1,500

   What is Wally's net § 1231 gain or loss in year 6?
   a. $500 loss
   b. $300 gain
   c. $800 gain
   d. $1,600 gain

5. Wally, Inc., sold the following three personal property assets in year 6:

Asset	Purchase Date	Cost	Accumulated Depreciation	Selling Price
A	5/1/year 3	$5,000	$3,000	$1,300
B	8/13/year 4	1,200	500	1,100
C	2/18/year 4	3,800	1,800	1,500

What is Wally's net § 1231 gain or loss in year 6?

a. $500 loss
b. $700 loss
c. $1,200 loss
d. $1,200 gain

6. Wally, Inc., sold the following three personal property assets in year 6:

Asset	Purchase Date	Cost	Accumulated Depreciation	Selling Price
A	5/1/year 3	$5,000	$3,000	$2,300
B	8/13/year 4	1,200	500	2,000
C	2/18/year 6	3,800	1,800	1,500

What is Wally's net § 1231 gain or loss in year 6?

a. $500 loss
b. $300 gain
c. $800 gain
d. $1,600 gain

7. Wally, Inc., sold the following three personal property assets in year 6:

Asset	Purchase Date	Cost	Accumulated Depreciation	Selling Price
A	5/1/year 3	$5,000	$3,000	$2,300
B	8/13/year 4	1,200	500	2,000
C	2/18/year 6	3,800	1,800	1,500

What is Wally's § 1245 recapture in year 6?

a. $500 loss
b. $300 gain
c. $800 gain
d. $1,600 gain

8. Net § 1231 losses are:
   a. Deducted as a capital loss against other capital gains and nothing against ordinary income.
   b. Deducted as a capital loss against other capital gains and up to $3,000 against ordinary income.
   c. Not allowed as a deduction.
   d. Deducted as an ordinary loss.

9. Section 1245 recapture applies to which of the following?
   a. Section 1231 real property sold at a gain with accumulated depreciation in excess of straight line.
   b. Section 1231 personal property sold at a gain with accumulated depreciation.
   c. Section 1231 real property sold at a gain with accumulated depreciation equal to straight-line depreciation.
   d. Section 1231 personal property sold at a loss.

10. Section 1250 recapture applies to which of the following?
   a. Section 1231 real property sold at a gain with accumulated depreciation in excess of straight line.
   b. Section 1231 personal property sold at a gain with accumulated depreciation.
   c. Section 1231 real property sold at a gain with accumulated depreciation equal to straight-line depreciation.
   d. Section 1231 personal property sold at a loss.

Part 6

Accounting Periods, Accounting Methods, and Deferred Compensation

Chapter 18
Accounting Periods and Methods

Chapter 19
Deferred Compensation

Part 6 provides a comprehensive exploration of the accounting periods and accounting methods that were introduced in Part 2. A discussion of special accounting methods related to installment sales and long-term contracts is also included. Part 6 concludes with an analysis of the tax consequences of deferred compensation.

Chapter 18

Accounting Periods and Methods

Learning Objectives: *After completing Chapter 18, you should be able to:*

- **LO.1** Explain the relevance of the accounting period concept, accounting period options, and limitations on their use.
- **LO.2** Apply the cash method, accrual method, and hybrid method of accounting.
- **LO.3** Explain the procedure for changing accounting methods.
- **LO.4** Determine when the installment method of accounting applies and its effect on taxable income.
- **LO.5** Recognize the methods of accounting for long-term contracts.
- **LO.6** Recognize when accounting for inventories must occur and the key tax accounting methods for inventory.
- **LO.7** Identify tax planning opportunities related to accounting periods and accounting methods.

Chapter Outline

18-1 Accounting Periods, 18-2
- 18-1a Specific Provisions for Partnerships, S Corporations, and Personal Service Corporations, 18-3
- 18-1b Selecting the Tax Year, 18-6
- 18-1c Changes in the Accounting Period, 18-6
- 18-1d Taxable Periods of Less Than One Year, 18-7
- 18-1e Mitigation of the Annual Accounting Period Concept, 18-8

18-2 Accounting Methods, 18-10
- 18-2a Permissible Methods, 18-10
- 18-2b Cash Receipts and Disbursements Method, 18-11
- 18-2c Accrual Method, 18-13
- 18-2d Hybrid Method, 18-16
- 18-2e Change of Method, 18-17

18-3 Special Accounting Methods, 18-19
- 18-3a Installment Method, 18-19
- 18-3b Long-Term Contracts, 18-25

18-4 Inventories, 18-28
- 18-4a Determining Inventory Cost, 18-29
- 18-4b The LIFO Election, 18-33
- 18-4c Special Inventory Methods Relating to Farming and Ranching, 18-34
- 18-4d Inventory of Small Taxpayers, 18-34

18-5 Tax Planning, 18-35
- 18-5a Taxable Year, 18-35
- 18-5b Cash Method of Accounting, 18-35
- 18-5c Installment Method, 18-35
- 18-5d Inventories, 18-36

TETRA IMAGES/GETTY IMAGES

The Big Picture

Accounting Period and Method

Belinda (an individual), Pearl, Inc. (a C corporation), and Tweety, Inc. (an S corporation) are going to form a partnership (Silver Partnership). The ownership interests and tax years of the partners are as follows:

Partner	Partnership Interest	Tax Year Ends
Belinda	25%	December 31
Pearl, Inc.	35%	November 30
Tweety, Inc.	40%	June 30

The partnership expects to begin business on April 1, 2022. The partners have several issues they would like you to address.

- A potential conflict exists among the partners regarding when the tax year should end for Silver. Belinda and Pearl would like a year-end close to their own year-ends, and Tweety would like to have a June 30 year-end. Is this a decision Tweety can make because it owns more of the partnership than either of the other two partners? Is this a decision Belinda and Pearl can make because collectively they own more of the partnership than Tweety owns?
- Because Silver will begin business on April 1, 2022, will the first tax year be a "short" tax year? Will annualization of the net income of the partnership be required?
- How will the partners know when their share of Silver's net income or net loss should be reported on their respective income tax returns?
- Belinda is a cash basis taxpayer, and the other partners use the accrual method to report their incomes. What accounting method must be used to compute Belinda's share of the partnership income?

Read the chapter and formulate your response.

Framework 1040 **Tax Formula for Individuals**

This chapter covers the boldfaced portions of the Tax Formula for Individuals that was introduced in Concept Summary 3.1 on p. 3-3. Below those portions are the sections of Form 1040 where the results are reported.

Income *(broadly defined)*	$xx,xxx
Less: Exclusions	(x,xxx)
Gross income	$xx,xxx

FORM 1040 (Schedule 1)

3	Business income or (loss). Attach Schedule C.

Less: Deductions *for* adjusted gross income	**(x,xxx)**
Adjusted gross income	$xx,xxx
Less: The greater of total itemized deductions *or* the standard deduction	(x,xxx)
Charitable contributions if you take the standard deduction*	(xxx)
Personal and dependency exemptions**	(x,xxx)
Deduction for qualified business income***	(x,xxx)
Taxable income	$xx,xxx
Tax on taxable income *(see Tax Tables or Tax Rate Schedules)*	$ x,xxx
Less: Tax credits *(including income taxes withheld and prepaid)*	(xxx)
Tax due (or refund)	$ xxx

* For 2021, married taxpayers may claim up to $600 of cash charitable donations ($300 if unmarried).
** Exemption deductions are not allowed from 2018 through 2025.
*** Only applies from 2018 through 2025.

Tax professionals must determine *when* items of income and expense are recognized as well as *whether* the items are includible in taxable income. Earlier chapters discussed the types of income subject to tax (gross income and exclusions) and allowable deductions (the *whether* issue).[1] This chapter focuses on the related issue of the periods in which income and deductions are reported (the *when* issue).

Generally, a taxpayer's income and deductions must be assigned to identified 12-month periods—calendar years or fiscal years. Accounting methods also are important for determining when costs are part of inventory and cost of sales, as well as the basis of fixed assets.

Income and deductions are placed within tax years through the use of tax accounting methods. The basic tax accounting methods are the cash receipts and disbursements method, the accrual method, and a hybrid method. Other special purpose methods, such as the installment method and the methods used for long-term construction contracts, are available for specific circumstances or types of transactions.

Over the long run, the accounting period and tax accounting methods used by a taxpayer will not affect the aggregate (or lifetime) amount of reported taxable income. However, taxable income for a given tax year may vary significantly due to the use of a particular accounting method. This chapter discusses the taxpayer's alternatives for accounting periods and accounting methods. The focus is on business entities, including sole proprietors, rather than individuals; most individuals report taxable income using a calendar year and use the cash method of accounting.

18-1 Accounting Periods

LO.1

Explain the relevance of the accounting period concept, accounting period options, and limitations on their use.

Generally, an individual or a corporation that keeps adequate books and records may elect a **fiscal year**, a 12-month period ending on the *last day* of a month other than December, for the **accounting period**. Otherwise, a *calendar year* must be used.[2] Frequently, corporations can satisfy the record-keeping and other requirements and

[1] See Chapters 4, 5, and 6.

[2] § 441(c) and Reg. § 1.441–1(b)(1)(ii).

elect to use a fiscal year.[3] Often, the fiscal year conforms to a natural business year (e.g., a summer resort's fiscal year may end on September 30, after the close of the season). Individuals seldom use a fiscal year because they do not maintain the necessary books and records to do so and because common reporting forms they receive such as Forms W–2 and 1099 report income based on the calendar year.

Generally, a tax year may not exceed 12 calendar months. However, if certain requirements are met, a taxpayer may elect to use an annual period that varies from 52 to 53 weeks.[4] In that case, the year-end must be on the same day of the week (e.g., the Tuesday falling closest to September 30, or the last Tuesday in September). The day of the week selected for ending the tax year may depend upon business considerations. For example, a retail business that is not open on Sundays may end its tax year on a Sunday so that it can take an inventory without interrupting business operations.

Example 1

Wade, Inc., is in the business of selling farm supplies. Its natural business year terminates at the end of October with the completion of harvesting. At the end of the fiscal year, Wade must take an inventory, which is most easily accomplished on a Friday. Therefore, Wade could adopt a 52- to 53-week tax year ending on the Friday closest to October 31.

If the company selects this approach, the year-end date may fall in the following month if that Friday is closer to October 31, or the beginning date may fall in the same month as the ending date. The tax year ending in 2022 will contain 52 weeks beginning on Saturday, October 30, 2021, and ending on Friday, October 28, 2022. The tax year ending in 2023 will have 52 weeks beginning on Saturday, October 29, 2022, and ending on Friday, October 27, 2023.

18-1a Specific Provisions for Partnerships, S Corporations, and Personal Service Corporations

When a partner and the partnership have different tax years, the partner may enjoy a deferral of income. This results because partners report their share of the partnership's income and deductions for the partnership's tax year ending within or with the partner's tax year.[5] For example, if the tax year of the partnership ends on January 31, a calendar year partner will not report partnership profits for the first 11 months of the partnership tax year until the following year (that is, on the partner's tax year that includes the January 31 partnership year-end). To minimize abuse of this arrangement, the tax law provides special tax year requirements.

In general, the partnership tax year must be the same as the tax year of the majority interest partners. The **majority interest partners** are the partners who together own a greater-than-50-percent interest in the partnership capital and profits and share the same tax year-end. If there is no majority interest tax year, the partnership must adopt the same tax year that is shared by all of its principal partners. A **principal partner** is a partner with a 5 percent or more interest in the partnership capital or profits.[6]

Example 2

The RST Partnership is owned equally by Rose Corporation, Sunflower Corporation, and Tom. The partners use the following tax years.

	Partner's Tax Year Ending
Rose Corporation	June 30
Sunflower Corporation	June 30
Tom	December 31

The partnership's tax year must end on June 30 because Rose and Sunflower together have a greater-than-50% interest in the partnership. If Sunflower's and Tom's tax years both end on December 31, the partnership must adopt a calendar year.

[3]Reg. § 1.441–1(e)(2).
[4]§ 441(f).
[5]Reg. § 1.706–1(a).
[6]§§ 706(b)(1)(B) and 706(b)(3).

If all of the principal partners do not use the same tax year and no majority of partners have the same tax year, the partnership must adopt a year that results in the *least aggregate deferral* of income.[7] Under the **least aggregate deferral method**, the different tax years of the principal partners are tested to determine which produces the least aggregate taxable income deferral. This is calculated by first multiplying the combined percentages of the principal partners with the same tax year by the months of deferral for the test year. Once this is done for each set of principal partners with the same tax year, the resulting products are summed to produce the aggregate deferral. After the aggregate deferral is calculated for each of the test years, the year with the smallest total (the least aggregate deferral) becomes the tax year for the partnership.

The Big Picture

Example 3

Return to the facts of *The Big Picture* on p. 18-1. The partnership's tax year must end on November 30, because using that year-end results in the least aggregate deferral of partnership income.

Test for Tax Year Ending December 31

		1	2	1 × 2
	Partner's Year-End	**Profit Percentage**	**Months Income Deferred**	**Aggregate Months of Deferral**
Belinda	12/31	25%	0	0
Pearl, Inc.	11/30	35%	11	3.85
Tweety, Inc.	6/30	40%	6	2.40
				6.25

Test for Tax Year Ending November 30

	Partner's Year-End	**Profit Percentage**	**Months Income Deferred**	**Aggregate Months of Deferral**
Belinda	12/31	25%	1	0.25
Pearl, Inc.	11/30	35%	0	0
Tweety, Inc.	6/30	40%	7	2.80
				3.05

Test for Tax Year Ending June 30

	Partner's Year-End	**Profit Percentage**	**Months Income Deferred**	**Aggregate Months of Deferral**
Belinda	12/31	25%	6	1.50
Pearl, Inc.	11/30	35%	5	1.75
Tweety, Inc.	6/30	40%	0	0
				3.25

[7] Reg. § 1.706–1(b)(3).

Generally, S corporations must adopt a calendar year.[8] However, partnerships and S corporations may *elect* an otherwise impermissible year under either of the following conditions.

- A business purpose for the year can be demonstrated.[9]
- The partnership or S corporation makes a timely election to use a taxable year that results in a deferral of not more than three months' taxable income, and the entity agrees to make required tax payments that relate to this deferral.[10]

Business Purpose

The only business purpose for a fiscal year the IRS has acknowledged is the need to conform the tax year to the natural business year of a company.[11] Generally, only seasonal businesses have a natural business year. For example, the natural business year for a retailer may end on January 31, after holiday sales returns have been processed and clearance sales have been completed.

Required Tax Payments

When required payments are to be made, a tax payment is due from a fiscal year partnership or S corporation by May 15 of each tax year.[12] The amount due is computed by multiplying an estimate of the deferral period income by the highest individual Federal income tax rate plus 1 percentage point. The deferral period runs from the close of the fiscal year to the end of the required year. Estimated income for this period is based on the average monthly earnings for the previous fiscal year. The amount due is reduced by the required tax payment for the previous year.[13]

Example 4

Brown, Inc., an S corporation, timely elected a fiscal year ending September 30. Bob is the only shareholder and is a calendar year taxpayer. The "required" tax year ends on December 31, 2022, the major shareholder's year-end, and the deferral period is the maximum of three months. For the fiscal year ending September 30, 2022, Brown earned $100,000. The required tax payment for the previous year was $5,000. The corporation must pay $4,500 by May 15, 2023.

$$(\$100{,}000 \times 3/12 \times 38\%^{*}) - \$5{,}000 = \$4{,}500$$

*Maximum individual tax rate 37% + 1%.

Ethics & Equity Who Benefits from the Change in Tax Year?

Ajit, a public accounting sole practitioner, has reached a breaking point. All of his clients use the calendar year to report income. Many of the clients are S corporations and partnerships. Ajit's workload the first four months of the year is so heavy that it is putting the quality of his work at risk.

Ajit is considering telling his clients that any new partnership or S corporation that is formed must timely elect, under the required tax payments system, to use a fiscal year ending September 30 (assuming that the required year would otherwise be a calendar year). Although the shareholders and partners would be subject to the required tax payments rule, Ajit will sell the plan to them by promising better service. Evaluate the plan proposed by Ajit.

[8] §§ 1378(a) and (b).

[9] §§ 706(b)(1)(C) and 1378(b)(2).

[10] § 444. See Form 8716.

[11] Rev.Proc. 2006–46. Also see the following discussion in text Section 18-1c.

[12] § 444(c) and Reg. § 1.7519–2T(a)(4)(ii). No payment is required if the calculated amount is $500 or less. See Form 8752.

[13] § 7519(b).

Personal Service Corporations

A **personal service corporation (PSC)** is a corporation whose shareholder-employees provide personal services (e.g., medical, dental, legal, accounting, engineering, actuarial, consulting, or performing arts). Generally, a PSC must use a calendar year.[14] However, a PSC can *elect* a fiscal year under either of the following conditions.

- A business purpose for the year can be demonstrated.
- The PSC year results in a deferral of not more than three months' income, the corporation pays the shareholder-employee's salary during the portion of the calendar year after the close of the fiscal year, and the salary for that period is at least proportionate to the shareholder-employee's salary received for the preceding fiscal year.[15]

Example 5

Nancy's corporation paid her a salary of $120,000 during its tax year ending September 30, 2022. The corporation cannot satisfy the business purpose test for a fiscal year. The corporation can continue to use its non-calendar tax year for Federal income tax purposes, provided Nancy receives at least $30,000 [(3 months/12 months) × $120,000] of salary during the period October 1 through December 31, 2022.

If the salary test is not satisfied, the PSC can retain the fiscal year, but the corporation's deduction for salary may be limited. Any amount not deductible is carried over to the next year.

18-1b Selecting the Tax Year

A taxpayer elects to use a calendar year or, if eligible, a fiscal year by the timely filing of the initial tax return. For all subsequent tax years, the taxpayer must use this same year-end unless approval for change is obtained from the IRS.[16]

18-1c Changes in the Accounting Period

A taxpayer must obtain consent from the IRS before changing its tax year.[17] The IRS issues administrative guidelines that must be met by taxpayers who want to change their accounting period. An application for permission to change tax years must be made on Form 1128. Generally, the application must be filed by the due date (including extensions) for the short taxable period that results from the change.[18]

Example 6

Beginning in 2022, Gold Corporation, a calendar year taxpayer, would like to switch to a tax year ending March 31. This change results in a short-period return encompassing January 1 to March 31, 2022. The extended due date for this short period return is January 15, 2023, which is also the due date for the Form 1128.

[14] § 441(i).
[15] §§ 444 and 280H.
[16] Reg. §§ 1.441–1(b)(3) and 1.441–1(b)(4).
[17] § 442. Under certain conditions, corporations are allowed to change tax years without obtaining IRS approval. See Reg. § 1.442–1(c)(1); Rev.Proc. 2006–45, modified by Rev.Proc. 2007–64.
[18] Reg. § 1.442–1(b)(1), Rev.Proc. 2006–45, and Form 1128 instructions.

The IRS will not grant permission for the change unless the taxpayer can establish a substantial nontax business purpose for the request. One substantial business purpose is to change to a tax year that coincides with the *natural business year* (the completion of an annual business cycle). The IRS applies an objective gross receipts test to determine whether the entity has a natural business year. At least 25 percent of the entity's gross receipts for the 12-month period must be realized in the final two months of the 12-month period for three consecutive years.[19]

Example 7

Oceanside, a Virginia Beach motel, would like to know if it can move to a tax year that ends on August 31. It reported the following gross receipts.

	2020	2021	2022
July–August receipts	$ 300,000	$250,000	$ 325,000
September 1–August 31 receipts	1,000,000	900,000	1,250,000
Receipts for final 2 months divided by receipts for 12 months	30.0%	27.8%	26.0%

Because it satisfies the natural business year test, Oceanside can use a tax year ending August 31.

18-1d Taxable Periods of Less Than One Year

A **short taxable year** (or **short period**) is a period of less than 12 calendar months. A taxpayer may have a short year for its first or last income tax return or when there is a change in the tax year.

If the short period results from a change in the taxpayer's annual accounting period, the taxable income for the period is annualized in calculating tax liability for the short period. With a flat Federal corporate income tax rate, annualization is not needed for C corporations. However, as shown in Example 8, annualization is required to calculate state income taxes if the state has a progressive tax rate structure.

The calculations to determine the annualized tax for a short tax period resulting from change in accounting period follow.

1. Annualize the short-period income.

$$\text{Short-period income} \times \frac{12}{\text{Number of months in the short period}} = \text{Annualized income}$$

2. Compute the tax on the annualized income.
3. Convert the tax on the annualized income to a short-period tax.

$$\text{Tax on annualized income} \times \frac{\text{Number of months in the short period}}{12} = \text{Short-period tax}$$

[19] Rev.Proc. 2006–46, Rev.Rul. 87–57, and Rev.Proc. 2002–39.

Example 8

Gray Corporation, a retailer that is not an S corporation, obtained permission to change from a calendar year to a fiscal year ending September 30, beginning in 2023. For the short period January 1 through September 30, 2023, the corporation's taxable income was $48,000. Gray does business in State X. The relevant tax rates in X and the resulting short-period tax are:

Amount of Taxable Income	Tax Rates
$1–$50,000	5% of taxable income
Over $50,000	$2,500 plus 7% of taxable income in excess of $50,000

Calculation of Short-Period Tax

Annualized income $48,000 × 12/9 = $64,000

Tax on annualized income $2,500 + 7%($64,000 − $50,000) = $3,480

Short-period tax due to State X: $3,480 × 9/12 = $2,610

Tax with annualizing	$ 2,610
Tax without annualizing (5% × $48,000)	(2,400)
State income tax increase due to annualizing	$ 210

Gray's Federal income tax for the short period is $10,080 (21% × $48,000). Because of the flat corporate rate, no annualization is required to compute Gray's Federal income tax liability for the short tax year.

Some other tax rules require annualization of short-period information. For example, for the average annual gross receipts test explained in text Section 18-2, the gross receipts of any prior short period must be annualized.

Often, the short year counts as a full year for purposes of the carryback and carryforward rules for various losses and credits.[20]

18-1e Mitigation of the Annual Accounting Period Concept

Several provisions in the Code are designed to give the taxpayer relief from the seemingly harsh results that may occur due to the combined effects of an arbitrary accounting period and the progressive rate structure that applies to individuals. For example, under the NOL carryover rules, a loss in one year can be carried forward and applied against taxable income in subsequent years.[21] In addition, the Code provides special relief provisions for casualty losses arising from a Federally declared disaster and for the reporting of insurance proceeds from destruction of crops.[22]

[20] Reg. §§ 1.172–4(a)(2), 1.46–2(k), and 1.904–2(e). Certain farm losses can be carried back two years. If one of those carryback years is a short year, it counts as one of the carryback years.

[21] § 172. Refer to text Section 7-6c.

[22] §§ 165(i) and 451(d).

Farm Relief

Farmers and fishermen often are subject to income fluctuations across years, some of which are due to the weather. Congress has provided these taxpayers with a special method of computing their tax. In the high-income years, these taxpayers can elect to compute their tax on income from farming or fishing as though it were earned equally in the three previous years.[23] Thus, the tax on the farming or fishing income for the year is the sum of the additional tax that would have been due in the three previous years if one-third of the income had been earned in each of those years. This averaging system enables the taxpayer to avoid the higher marginal tax rates associated with a large amount of income received in one year.

The income pattern for farmers also can be disrupted by natural disasters that are covered by insurance. The disaster may occur and the **crop insurance proceeds** may be received in a year before the income from the crop would have been realized. Under these circumstances, the farmer can defer reporting the gross income from the insurance proceeds until the year following the disaster. Similar relief is available when livestock must be sold due to drought or other weather-related conditions.[24]

Restoration of Amounts Received under a Claim of Right

The court-made **claim of right doctrine** applies when the taxpayer receives property as income and it is under the taxpayer's control but a dispute arises over the taxpayer's rights to the income.[25] According to the doctrine, the taxpayer must include the amount as income in the year of receipt. The rationale for the doctrine is that the Federal government cannot await the resolution of all disputes before exacting a tax. As a corollary to the doctrine, if the taxpayer is required to repay the funds later, a deduction generally is allowed in the year of repayment.[26]

Example 9

In 2022, Pedro received a $5,000 bonus computed as a percentage of profits. In 2023, Pedro's employer determined that the 2022 profits had been computed incorrectly, and Pedro was required to refund the $5,000 in 2023. Pedro must include the $5,000 in his 2022 gross income, but he can claim a $5,000 deduction in 2023.

In Example 9, the transactions were a wash; that is, the income and deduction were the same ($5,000). Suppose, however, that Pedro was in the 35 percent tax bracket in 2022 but in the 22 percent bracket in 2023. Without any kind of relief provision, the mistake would be costly to Pedro. He paid a $1,750 tax in 2022 (35% × $5,000), but the deduction reduced his tax liability in 2023 by only $1,000 (22% × $5,000).

The Code does provide relief in such cases. Under § 1341, when income that has been taxed under the claim of right doctrine later must be repaid, the taxpayer can use the tax rate of the year that produces the greatest tax benefit. As a result, in Example 9, the repayment in 2023 would reduce Pedro's 2023 tax liability by $1,750 [the higher 2022 rate (35%) applied to the $5,000 deduction in 2023]. However, relief is provided only in cases where the tax is significantly different, (i.e., when the deduction for the amount previously included in income exceeds $3,000).

[23] § 1301. The tax is calculated on Schedule J.

[24] §§ 451(f) and (g). Also see IRS Publication 225.

[25] *North American Consolidated Oil Co. v. Burnet*, 3 USTC ¶943, 11 AFTR 16, 52 S.Ct. 613 (1932).

[26] *U.S. v. Lewis*, 51–1 USTC ¶9211, 40 AFTR 258, 71 S.Ct. 522.

Ethics & Equity **Special Tax Relief**

A taxpayer who reports gross income in one year but must repay the income in a subsequent year is granted special tax relief. If the taxpayer is in a lower marginal tax bracket in the year the income is repaid than in the year it was received, the deduction reduces the tax for the year of repayment by using the higher tax rate that applied to the income when it was received.

In contrast, if a taxpayer takes a deduction in one year and receives a refund of the amount giving rise to the deduction in a subsequent year, the refund is taxed at the marginal tax rate in the year of refund. This is true even though the taxpayer's marginal tax rate in the year of receipt is higher than that in the year of the deduction.

Should adjustments to income and adjustments to deductions receive the same tax relief? Or should neither situation be granted special relief? Discuss.

LO.2

Apply the cash method, accrual method, and hybrid method of accounting.

18-2 Accounting Methods

18-2a Permissible Methods

Code § 446 requires the taxpayer to compute taxable income using the method of accounting regularly employed in keeping the corresponding financial accounting records ("the books"), provided the method clearly reflects income. The Code recognizes the following as generally permissible **accounting methods**.

- The cash receipts and disbursements method.
- The accrual method.
- A hybrid method (a combination of cash and accrual).

The Regulations refer to these alternatives as *overall methods* and add that the term *method of accounting* includes not only the taxpayer's overall method of accounting but also the accounting treatment of any item.[27]

Generally, any of the three overall methods of accounting may be used if the method is consistently employed and clearly reflects income. However, certain taxpayers whose average annual gross receipts (computed over the three preceding years) exceed $27 million are required to use the accrual method.

In general, taxpayers that maintain inventory for sale to customers are required to use the accrual method of accounting for determining sales and cost of goods sold. However, taxpayers with average annual gross receipts of $27 million or less for the most recent three-year period can use the cash method to account for inventories, as long as inventories are not a material income-producing factor.[28] No more than 2 percent of all U.S. businesses report average gross receipts in excess of $27 million.

A taxpayer who has more than one trade or business may use a different method of accounting for each trade or business unless the taxpayer is required to use the accrual method. Furthermore, a taxpayer may use one method of accounting to determine income from a trade or business and use another method to compute nonbusiness items of income and deductions.[29]

The Code grants the IRS broad powers to determine whether the taxpayer's accounting method *clearly reflects income*. Thus, if the method employed does not meet this requirement, the IRS can prescribe the method to be used by the taxpayer.[30]

[27] Reg. § 1.446–1(a)(1).

[28] Reg. § 1.446–1(a)(4)(i), Reg. § 1.446–1(c)(2)(i), § 448, and § 471(c). Special methods are permitted for installment sales, long-term construction contracts, and farmers, as discussed in subsequent sections of this chapter.

[29] § 446(d) and Reg. § 1.446–1(c)(1)(iv)(b).

[30] § 446(b), as limited by § 471(c)(1)(B).

18-2b Cash Receipts and Disbursements Method

Most individuals and many businesses use the cash basis to report income and deductions. The popularity of this method can largely be attributed to its simplicity and flexibility.

Under the **cash method**, income is not recognized until the taxpayer actually receives, or constructively receives, cash or its equivalent (e.g., the receipt of accounts receivable does not trigger income until collected). Cash is constructively received if it is available to the taxpayer.[31] Generally, a cash equivalent is any business asset with a fair market value, including any goods or services received in a barter transaction and a note receivable from a customer.

The Big Picture

Example 10

Return to the facts of *The Big Picture* on p. 4-1 in Chapter 4. Recall that Dr. Cliff Payne opened a dental practice as a sole proprietorship and does not accept credit cards. In the second year of business, he adopts a new policy of requiring that his patients either pay cash at the time the services are performed or give him a note receivable with interest at the market rate. Generally, the notes can be sold to the local banks for 95% of their face amount.

At the end of the second year, Dr. Payne holds $60,000 in notes receivable from patients. The notes receivable are a cash equivalent and have a fair market value of $57,000 ($60,000 × 95%). As a result, Dr. Payne must include $57,000 in his gross income for this year.

Deductions generally are permitted in the year of payment under the cash method. Thus, year-end accounts payable and accrued expenses are not deducted in the determination of taxable income.

In many cases, a taxpayer using the cash method can choose the year in which a deduction is claimed simply by postponing or accelerating the payment of expenses. For fixed assets, however, the cash basis taxpayer claims deductions through depreciation or amortization, as does an accrual basis taxpayer. In addition, prepaid expenses must be capitalized and amortized if the life of the asset extends substantially beyond the end of the tax year.[32]

The Regulations provide a **12-month rule for prepaid expenses** that permits the taxpayer to deduct expenditures for benefits that do not extend beyond the earlier of (1) 12 months after the first date on which the taxpayer realizes the benefit or (2) the end of the tax year following the year of payment. Both cash basis and accrual basis taxpayers can use the 12-month rule.[33]

Example 11

On December 1, 2022, Elm Corporation, a calendar year taxpayer, paid $20,000 for a 12-month property insurance policy with coverage starting on February 1, 2023. Elm's benefit under this policy ends on January 31, 2024. Because this date extends beyond the earlier of (1) 12 months after February 1, 2023, or (2) the end of the next tax year (December 31, 2023), the 12-month rule does not apply. As a result, Elm must deduct its prepayment over the term of the policy rather than when paid in 2022.

If instead, the policy coverage began on December 15, 2022, and ended on December 14, 2023, the 12-month rule would apply, and Elm would deduct the entire payment in 2022. In this scenario, the benefit of the payment does not extend beyond the earlier of (1) December 14, 2023, or (2) December 31, 2023. Instead, the benefit ends on December 14, 2023.

Restrictions on Use of the Cash Method

The cash method could distort income from a merchandising or manufacturing operation, because the cost of goods sold would be a function of when payments for the goods were made rather than when they were sold. Thus, the Regulations require use of the accrual method to measure sales and cost of goods sold if inventories

[31] Reg. § 1.451–1(a). Refer to text Section 4-2c for a discussion of constructive receipt.

[32] Reg. § 1.461–1(a)(1).

[33] Reg. § 1.263(a)–4(f). See text Section 6-2d for additional examples of the 12-month rule.

are material to the business. This targeted prohibition on the use of the cash method for taxpayers with inventories is intended to ensure that annual taxable income is clearly reflected.[34]

The following taxpayers may not use the cash method (and must use the accrual method) for Federal income tax purposes regardless of whether inventories are material: (1) a corporation (other than an S corporation), (2) a partnership with a corporate partner (that is not an S corporation), and (3) a tax shelter. This accrual method requirement of § 448 has three exceptions, each of which allows the cash method to be used.

- A farming business (other than certain corporations).
- A *qualified personal service corporation* (a corporation that performs services in health, law, engineering, architecture, accounting, actuarial science, performing arts, or consulting and whose employees own substantially all of the stock) regardless of gross receipts level.
- A corporation, or a partnership with a corporate partner, whose average annual gross receipts for the prior three-year period do not exceed $27 million.

None of the exceptions apply to an entity that meets the definition of a tax shelter. A tax shelter must use the accrual method regardless of the amount of its gross receipts.[35]

Overall Accounting Method Rules

Example 12

Estrella and Estrella, CPAs, is a C corporation owned by ten CPAs that provides accounting and tax services. Its average annual gross receipts are $30,000,000. Because this entity is a qualified personal service corporation and has no inventory, it may use the cash method of accounting.

Example 13

Fit Corporation is a C corporation that operates several fitness centers. Its average annual gross receipts are $30,000,000. Fit must use the accrual method; it is a C corporation and its average annual gross receipts for the prior three-year period exceed $27,000,000. If its average annual gross receipts in the prior three-year period were $27,000,000 or less, it could use the cash method.

If Fit were a sole proprietorship, a partnership without a C corporation partner, or an S corporation, it would be allowed to use the cash method regardless of its gross receipts level, because it is not subject to the required accrual method rule of § 448 and has no inventory.

Special Rules for Farmers

The tax accounting rules include several special rules and exceptions for farmers. Generally, farmers with average annual gross receipts in the prior three-year period of $27 million or less may use the cash method.

Farmers with average annual gross receipts greater than $27 million may be required to use the accrual method. However, exceptions exist based on the type of entity.[36] For example, a partnership without a corporate partner generally can use the cash method. In this regard, whether certain costs related to production of products must be capitalized depends on the type of product.[37]

Farmers who produce crops that take more than a year from planting to harvesting (e.g., pineapples) can elect to use the crop method to report the income. Under the **crop method**, the costs of raising the crop are capitalized as those costs are incurred and then deducted in the year the income from the crop is realized.[38] This method is analogous to the completed contract method, discussed in text Section 18-3b.

[34]Reg. § 1.446–1(a)(4)(i).

[35]§§ 448(a) and 448(b). For this purpose, the hybrid method of accounting is considered the same as the cash method. Also see § 447. *Tax shelter* is defined at § 448(d)(3).

[36]See §§ 447(c), 448(b), and 464.

[37]§ 263A(d).

[38]Reg. §§ 1.61–4 and 1.162–12(a).

Generally, a cash basis farmer must capitalize the purchase price of an animal, whether it is acquired for sale or for breeding. However, costs to raise the animal generally can be deducted immediately.[39]

18-2c Accrual Method

The tax rules governing when an accrual method taxpayer reports income or claims deductions include an "all events test." The timing rules for deductions also include an "economic performance" requirement. These timing rules for income and deductions of accrual method taxpayers are explained below.

All Events Test for Income

Under the **accrual method**, an item generally is included in gross income for the year in which it is earned, regardless of when the income is collected. An item of income is earned when (1) all of the events have occurred to fix the taxpayer's right to receive the income and (2) the amount of income (the amount the taxpayer has a right to receive) can be determined with reasonable accuracy.[40] However, generally, the income cannot be deferred beyond the tax year in which it is included in the taxpayer's applicable financial statement.[41]

Example 14

Andre Corporation, a calendar year taxpayer that uses the accrual basis of accounting, was to receive a bonus equal to 6% of Blue Corporation's net income for its fiscal year ending each June 30. For the fiscal year ending June 30, 2022, Blue reported net income of $240,000. For the six months ending December 31, 2022, its net income was $150,000.

Andre includes gross income of $14,400 (6% × $240,000) for 2022 because its right to the amount became fixed when Blue's tax year closed. However, Andre would not accrue income based on Blue's profits for the last six months of 2022, because its right to the income does not accrue until the close of Blue's tax year.

An accrual basis taxpayer's amount of income and the tax year the income is recognized are based on its right to receive the income. Thus, unlike the case of a cash basis taxpayer, the fair market value of a receivable is irrelevant.

Example 15

Marcey Corporation, an accrual basis taxpayer, has provided services to clients and has the right to receive $60,000. The clients have signed notes receivable to Marcey that have a face value of $60,000 but a fair market value of $57,000. The corporation must include gross income of $60,000, the amount it has the right to receive, rather than the fair market value of the notes of $57,000.

If an accrual basis taxpayer receives advance payments for services, goods, or licensing of software, it should consider adopting a special deferral method.[42] Under this method, in the year the advance payment is received, the taxpayer reports on its tax return the same amount from its financial statement. In the subsequent year, the balance of the advance payment is included in gross income, regardless of how much is reported on the financial statement for that year (see text Section 4-2d).

[39] Reg. § 1.162–12(a).

[40] § 451(b) and Reg. § 1.451–1(a). Refer to text Section 4-2 for further discussion of the accrual method.

[41] § 451(b). *Applicable financial statement* is defined at § 451(b)(3) and generally is a statement prepared in accordance with Generally Accepted Accounting Principles and certified as such, or per international reporting standards, or is required by a regulatory or government body.

[42] Prior to the change to § 451(c) by the TCJA of 2017, the deferral method for advance payments for services, goods, and licensing of intellectual property was provided at Rev.Proc. 2004–34. For tax years beginning on or after January 1, 2021, Rev.Proc. 2004–34 is obsolete and the new deferral method rules are at Reg. § 1.451–8; they are similar to the 2004 methods.

Example 16

Troy Corporation is an accrual method, calendar year taxpayer that has adopted the deferral method for advance payments. Troy sells computers and two-year service contracts on the computers. On November 1, 2022, Troy sold a 24-month service contract and received $240. For financial reporting purposes, Troy reports $20 of gross income for 2022, $120 for 2023, and $100 for 2024. For Federal income tax purposes, Troy reports $20 of income for 2022 (same as for financial reporting) and $220 of income for 2023 (the balance of the advance payment).

Prepaid rental income, prepaid interest income, warranty or guarantee contracts, insurance premiums, and payments with respect to certain financial instruments must be recognized in the year of receipt and may not be deferred.[43]

In a situation where the accrual method taxpayer's right to income is contested and the income has not yet been collected, generally, no income is recognized until the dispute has been settled.[44] Before the settlement, "all of the events have not occurred that fix the right to receive the income."

All Events and Economic Performance Tests for Deductions

A three-part test is applied to determine when an accrual method taxpayer considers a liability as either an expense or a capital expenditure: (1) the **all events test**, (2) whether the amount is determinable with reasonable accuracy, and (3) the **economic performance test**. The all events test is met when all events have occurred to establish the fact that a liability exists (that is, the taxpayer legally owes money to another party).[45]

As to when economic performance is met, that depends on the nature of the liability. For example, if an accrual method taxpayer owes money to another entity that provided services to it, economic performance is met as the services are provided. Concept Summary 18.1 lists common types of liabilities covered by the economic performance Regulations, and when the test for economic performance is met for each liability.

Concept Summary 18.1

Accruals Under the Economic Performance Test (Reg. § 1.461–4)

Event	Example	When Economic Performance Is Satisfied
The taxpayer's use of the owner's property	Rent	Ratably over the period used
Specific property provided to the taxpayer	A company's office supplies are purchased	When the taxpayer receives the supplies
Specific services provided to the taxpayer	The taxpayer contracts for repairs to be made to its equipment	When the repairs are made
Services to be provided for a specific time period	The taxpayer purchases a service contract, such as for cleaning services	Ratably over the contract period
Property or services provided by the taxpayer	A manufacturer provides a warranty on items sold to customers	When the manufacturer incurs costs in fixing the customer's item covered by the warranty
Rebates	Manufacturer rebates based on quantity of purchases	When the rebate is paid
Tort claims	Customers are awarded claims for harm caused by the taxpayer's product	When payment is made to the injured party; not eligible for the recurring item exception
State income tax	Taxes due when filing the return	When payment is made

[43] § 451(c)(4)(B).

[44] *Burnet v. Sanford & Brooks Co.*, 2 USTC ¶636, 9 AFTR 603, 51 S.Ct. 150 (1931).

[45] § 461 and Reg. § 1.461–1(a)(2).

Economic Performance

Example 17

An accrual basis calendar year taxpayer, JAB, Inc., promoted a boxing match held in the company's arena on December 31, 2022. CLN, Inc., was contracted to clean the arena for $5,000 but did not actually perform the work until January 1, 2023. JAB paid the $5,000 on January 3, 2023 (once CLN had completed its work).

Although financial accounting rules would require JAB to accrue the $5,000 cleaning expense in 2022 to match the revenues from the fight, the economic performance test was not satisfied until 2023, when CLN performed the service. Thus, JAB deducts the expense in 2023.

Example 18

Agmax Corporation farms land owned by an individual. Agmax's contract to use the land is for three years, and at the end of three years, Agmax agreed to apply lime to the farmland. The contract term expired in 2022, and Agmax applied the lime in 2023. The all events test was satisfied at the end of 2022. However, Agmax did not provide the lime until 2023. Agmax was obligated to provide property (lime) and services. The deduction is not permitted until 2023, when Agmax incurs costs in fulfilling its obligation.[46]

The economic performance requirement is accelerated, allowing year-end accruals to be deducted, if the following four conditions are met. This is known as the *recurring item exception*.

1. The all events test is met, and the amount of the liability can be determined with reasonable accuracy.
2. Economic performance occurs on or before the earlier of the date the taxpayer files the return (including extension) or 8½ months after the close of the taxable year.
3. The item is recurring in nature.
4. The item either is not material in amount or accruing it results in a better matching of revenues and expenses.

Example 19

Green Corporation often sells goods that are on hand but cannot be shipped for another week. The all events test for the sale is satisfied; therefore, gross income is recognized although the goods have not been shipped at year-end.

Green is obligated to pay shipping costs. Although the company's obligation for shipping costs can be determined with reasonable accuracy, economic performance is not satisfied until Green (or its agent) actually delivers the goods. However, accruing shipping costs on sold items will better match expenses with revenues for the period. Therefore, the company should accrue the shipping costs on items sold but not shipped at year-end.

The economic performance test detailed in the Code does not address all possible accrued expenses. That is, in some cases, the taxpayer has a liability (owes money for something) even though no property or services were received. In these instances, economic performance generally is not satisfied until the liability is paid. The following liabilities illustrate situations where payment is the only means of satisfying economic performance.[47]

1. Workers' compensation.
2. Torts.
3. Breach of contract.
4. Violation of law.
5. Rebates and refunds.
6. Awards, prizes, and jackpots.
7. Insurance, warranty, and service contracts.[48]
8. Taxes.

[46]Reg. § 1.461–4.

[47]Reg. §§ 1.461–4(g)(2)–(6) and 1.461–5(c).

[48]This item applies to contracts that taxpayers enter into for their own protection rather than the taxpayer's liability as insurer, warrantor, or service provider.

Financial Disclosure Insights Tax Deferrals from Reserves

The tax law generally applies the all events and economic performance tests in determining when an expense is deductible. Accordingly, the use of reserves for financial accounting purposes does not carry over to the tax return. When a business creates a reserve, for example, to account for warranty obligations to customers or vacation pay for employees, book expenses are allowed, but the corresponding tax deduction usually is delayed until an expenditure is actually incurred. The temporary book-tax difference typically creates or adds to a deferred tax asset on the entity's balance sheet.

On a GAAP balance sheet, all deferred tax assets are deemed to be noncurrent.

Example 20

Yellow Corporation sold defective merchandise that injured a customer. Yellow admitted liability in 2022 but did not pay the claim until January 2023. The customer's tort claim cannot be deducted by Yellow until it is paid to the customer.

Items (5) through (8) above are eligible for the recurring item exception.

Example 21

Pelican Corporation, a calendar year taxpayer, filed its 2022 state income tax return in March 2023 and its 2022 Federal return on September 15, 2023. At the time the state return was filed, Pelican was required to pay an additional $5,000. The state taxes are eligible for the recurring item exception. Thus, the $5,000 of state income taxes can be deducted on the corporation's 2022 Federal tax return. The deduction is allowed because all of the events had occurred to fix the liability as of the end of 2022, the payment was made by the earlier of the return filing date or 8½ months after the end of the tax year, the item is recurring in nature, and allowing the deduction in 2022 results in a better matching of revenues and expenses.

Reserves

Generally, the all events and economic performance tests prevent the income tax use of reserves (e.g., for product warranty expense) frequently used in financial accounting to match expenses with revenues. However, small banks can use a bad debt reserve.[49] In addition, an accrual basis taxpayer in a service business may be allowed to not accrue revenue that appears uncollectible based on experience. In effect, this approach indirectly allows a tax reserve.[50]

18-2d Hybrid Method

A **hybrid method** of accounting involves the use of more than one overall method. For example, a taxpayer who uses the accrual basis to report sales and cost of goods sold but uses the cash basis to report other items of income and expense is employing a hybrid method. The Code permits the use of a hybrid tax accounting method provided the taxpayer's income is clearly reflected.[51] A taxpayer who uses the accrual method for business expenses must also use the accrual method for business income.

[49] § 585.

[50] § 448(d)(5).

[51] § 446(c)(3).

Example 22

The Loyal Pet Clinic boards animals, provides veterinarian services, and sells pet supplies and medicines (inventory). The clinic's gross receipts are approximately $4,000,000 per year, and 40% of the receipts are from sales of pet supplies. Under its hybrid method of accounting, the clinic uses the accrual method for the sales of supplies and medicines, because inventories are a material income-producing factor. The services income is reported using the cash method.

Businesses with average annual gross receipts in the prior three-year period of $27,000,000 or less are not required to use the accrual method. As a result, Loyal Pet Clinic should consider a change in its method from hybrid to cash and treat its inventory as deductible when purchased (and paid for) or as nonincidental supplies (further discussed in text Section 18-4).

18-2e Change of Method

LO.3 **Explain the procedure for changing accounting methods.**

The taxpayer, in effect, makes an election to use a particular accounting method when its initial tax return is filed using that method. Once chosen, the taxpayer must obtain the permission of the IRS to change its accounting method. The request for change is made on Form 3115, generally to be filed within the taxable year of the desired change.[52]

As previously mentioned, the term *accounting method* encompasses not only the overall accounting method used by the taxpayer (the cash or accrual method) but also the treatment of any material item of income or deduction.[53] For example, a change in the method of deducting property taxes from a cash basis to an accrual basis that results in a deduction for taxes in a different year constitutes a change in an accounting method. Another example of an accounting method change is a change involving the method or basis used in the valuation of inventories.

A change in treatment resulting from a change in the underlying facts does not constitute a change in the taxpayer's method of accounting.[54] For example, a change in employment contracts so that an employee accrues one day of vacation pay for each month of service rather than 12 days of vacation pay for a full year of service is a change in the underlying facts and is not an accounting method change.

Correction of an Error

A change in accounting method is not the same as the *correction of an error*. The taxpayer can correct an error (by filing amended returns) without permission of the IRS, and the IRS simply adjusts the taxpayer's liability if an error is discovered on audit of the return. Some examples of errors are incorrect postings, errors in the calculation of tax liability or tax credits, deductions of business expense items that are actually personal, and omissions of income and deductions.[55] Unless the taxpayer or the IRS corrects the error within the statute of limitations (in general, three years after a tax return is filed), the taxpayer's total lifetime taxable income is overstated or understated by the amount of the error.

Change from an Incorrect Method

An *incorrect accounting method* is the consistent (for at least two tax returns) use of an incorrect rule to report an item of income or expense. The incorrect accounting method will not affect the taxpayer's total lifetime income (unlike the error). That is, an incorrect method has a self-balancing mechanism. For example, deducting freight on inventory in the year the goods are purchased rather than when the inventory is sold

[52] See Rev.Proc. 2015–13 for the method change procedures and Rev.Proc. 2019–43, as modified by Rev. Proc. 2021–34, for the list of automatic method changes. Generally, for an automatic method change, Form 3115 is due when the tax return for the year of change is filed, including extension.

[53] Reg. § 1.446–1(a)(1).

[54] Reg. § 1.446–1(e)(2)(ii).

[55] Reg. § 1.446–1(e)(2)(ii)(b).

is an incorrect accounting method. The total cost of goods sold over the life of the business is not affected, but the year-to-year income is incorrect.[56]

If a taxpayer is employing an incorrect method of accounting, permission must be obtained from the IRS to change to a correct method. An incorrect method cannot be corrected merely by filing an amended tax return.

The tax return preparer as well as the taxpayer will be subject to penalties if the tax return is prepared using an incorrect method of accounting and permission for a change to a correct method was not requested.[57]

Net Adjustments Due to Change in Method of Accounting

In the year of a change in accounting method, an adjustment generally is required to prevent the omission or duplication of income or expense items.

Example 23

White, a C corporation, operates a web platform that allows bookkeepers and accountants to offer their services to companies and individuals. It operates similar to Uber, TaskRabbit, and similar freelancing or gig platforms. Its gross receipts have increased significantly every year since it began operations in 2016.

For 2022, White determines that its average annual gross receipts for the prior three years crossed the $27,000,000 threshold. As a result, White must change its accounting method from cash to accrual starting in 2022 (*the year of change*). It also must calculate a "net § 481(a) adjustment" to be sure that no income or expense is omitted from income (or duplicated) when it makes this method change. White reports the following information.

Accounts receivable at December 31, 2021	$1,100,000
Accounts payable at December 31, 2021	860,000

Because White used the cash method of accounting for tax purposes, the $1,100,000 of receivables was not yet reported in taxable income. Similarly, the $860,000 of payables has not yet been claimed as a deduction. When White changes from the cash method to the accrual method starting with its 2022 tax year, it will behave as if it was always using the accrual method. As a result, when it collects the $1,100,000 of receivables in 2022, White will not report any gross income because, if White had always been using the accrual method, that income would have been reported earlier when earned. Similarly, when White pays the payables in 2022, it will not claim a deduction because if White had always used the accrual method, the payables would have been deducted earlier when incurred.

To avoid omission of the $1,100,000 of income, White has a positive "§ 481(a) adjustment" of $1,100,000 (meaning it increases White's taxable income). To avoid omission of the $860,000 of deductions, White has a negative "§ 481(a) adjustment" of $860,000. These amounts are combined to yield a "net positive § 481(a) adjustment" of $240,000.

Reporting the Net § 481(a) Adjustment

Required changes in tax accounting methods can result from an IRS examination. Generally, if the IRS finds that a taxpayer is using an incorrect method of accounting, a change is imposed, but on less favorable terms than if the taxpayer had corrected the erroneous method on its own. For example, the IRS may require the taxpayer to correct the method for the earliest year open under the statute of limitations and record any positive § 481 adjustment entirely in that year (rather than over four years allowed for a voluntary change in method). Additional tax and interest then may be due.[58]

[56] But see *Korn Industries v. U.S.*, 76–1 USTC ¶9354, 37 AFTR 2d 76–1228, 532 F.2d 1352 (Ct.Cls.).

[57] § 446(f).

[58] § 481(b). Guidance on IRS-initiated method changes can be found in Rev.Proc. 2002–18.

To encourage taxpayers to *voluntarily* change from incorrect methods (rather than wait for an IRS audit resulting in a required change) and to facilitate changes from one correct method to another, the IRS generally allows the taxpayer to spread a positive adjustment into future years. One-fourth of the adjustment is applied to the year of the change, and one-fourth of the adjustment is applied to each of the next three taxable years. A negative adjustment is deducted in the year of the change.[59]

Example 24

White Corporation in Example 23 must add $60,000 ($\frac{1}{4}$ × $240,000 net positive adjustment) to its 2022, 2023, 2024, and 2025 income.

Ethics & Equity **Change in Accounting Method**

The IRS faces a difficult choice when it deals with taxpayers who use incorrect accounting methods. On the one hand, the taxpayer who has used an incorrect accounting method may be just as culpable as a person who has omitted income or taken an improper deduction. On the other hand, it often is difficult to discover that a taxpayer is using an incorrect accounting method. Therefore, the IRS relies to some extent on self-reporting by taxpayers. The Service encourages voluntary changes in incorrect accounting methods by waiving penalties for an underpayment of prior years' taxes, thus permitting the taxpayer, in effect, to pay the related taxes over a four-year period. Is this equitable treatment? Discuss the reasons underlying your position.

18-3 Special Accounting Methods

LO.4 **Determine when the installment method of accounting applies and its effect on taxable income.**

The tax law provides special accounting methods for certain installment sales and long-term contracts. These special methods were enacted, in part, to ensure that the tax will be due when the taxpayer is best able to pay the tax.

18-3a Installment Method

Under the general rule for computing the gain or loss from the sale of property, the taxpayer recognizes the entire amount of gain or loss upon the sale or other disposition of the property.

Example 25

Mark sells property to Pooja for $10,000 cash plus Pooja's note (fair market value and face amount of $90,000). Mark's basis for the property was $15,000. Gain or loss is computed under either the cash or accrual basis as follows.

Selling price	
Cash down payment	$ 10,000
Note receivable	90,000
	$100,000
Basis in the property	(15,000)
Realized gain	$ 85,000

[59] Rev.Proc. 2015–13.

In Example 25, the general rule for recognizing gain or loss requires Mark to pay a substantial amount of tax on the gain in the year of sale even though he received only $10,000 cash. Congress enacted the installment sales provisions to prevent this sort of hardship by allowing the taxpayer to spread the gain from installment sales over time as payments are made, when the taxpayer perhaps is best able to pay the tax. The installment method is an important planning tool because it creates tax deferral possibilities.

Eligibility and Calculations

The **installment method** applies to *gains* (but not losses) from the sale of property by a taxpayer who will receive at least one payment *after* the year of sale. However, the installment method cannot be used for:[60]

- Gains on property held for sale in the ordinary course of business, with limited exceptions.
- Depreciation recapture amounts.
- Gains on stocks or securities traded on an established market.

The Mandatory Aspect

As a general rule, eligible sales *must* be reported by the installment method unless the taxpayer elects not to apply this rule.[61]

Computing the Gain for Each Year Payments Are Received

The gain reported on each sale is computed using the following formula.

$$\frac{\text{Total gain}}{\text{Contract price}} \times \text{Payments received during the tax year} = \text{Gain recognized in the tax year}$$

1. *Total gain* is the selling price reduced by selling expenses and the adjusted basis of the property. The selling price is the total consideration received by the seller, including notes receivable from the buyer and the seller's liabilities assumed by the buyer.
2. *Contract price* is the selling price less the seller's liabilities that are assumed by the buyer. Generally, the contract price is the amount, other than interest, the seller will receive from the purchaser.
3. *Payments received* are the collections on the contract price received in each tax year. This generally is equal to the cash received less the interest income collected for the period. If the buyer pays any of the seller's expenses, the seller regards the amount paid as a payment received.[62]

[60] §§ 453(b), (i), and (l).

[61] §§ 453(a) and (d).

[62] The gain is reported on Form 6252.

Example 26

Gonzalo, not a dealer, reports the following for a sale of investment land.

Sales price		
Cash down payment	$ 1,000	
Seller's mortgage assumed by the buyer	3,000	
Notes payable to the seller	13,000	$ 17,000
Selling expenses		(500)
Seller's basis		(10,000)
Total gain		$ 6,500

The contract price is $14,000 ($17,000 − $3,000). Assuming that the $1,000 is the only payment in the year of sale, the recognized gain in that year is:

$$\frac{\$6{,}500 \text{ (total gain)}}{\$14{,}000 \text{ (contract price)}} \times \$1{,}000 = \$464 \text{ (gain recognized in year of sale)}$$

As previously noted, any depreciation recapture amounts generate gain recognized in the year of sale, and the installment sale gain is any remaining amount.

Example 27

Olaf sold equipment for $50,000 cash and a $75,000 note due in two years. Olaf's cost of the property was $90,000, and he had deducted depreciation of $65,000. Thus, the basis in the property was $25,000 ($90,000 − $65,000).

Olaf's realized gain is $100,000 ($125,000 − $25,000), and the $65,000 depreciation recapture gain must be recognized in the year of sale. Of the $35,000 remaining § 1231 gain, $14,000 must be recognized in the year of sale.

$$\frac{\S\,1231 \text{ gain}}{\text{Contract price}} \times \text{Payment received} = \frac{\$125{,}000 - \$25{,}000 - \$65{,}000}{\$125{,}000} \times \$50{,}000$$

$$= \frac{\$35{,}000}{\$125{,}000} \times \$50{,}000 = \$14{,}000$$

The remaining § 1231 gain of $21,000 ($35,000 − $14,000) is recognized as the $75,000 note is collected.

Imputed Interest

If a deferred payment contract for the sale of property with a selling price greater than $3,000 does not contain a reasonable interest rate, a reasonable rate is imputed by the tax law.[63] The imputing of interest effectively restates the selling price of the property to the sum of the payments at the date of the sale and the discounted present value of the future payments. The difference between the present value of a future payment and the payment's face amount is taxed as interest income.

In this way, the **imputed interest** rules prevent sellers of capital assets from increasing the selling price to reflect the equivalent of unstated interest on deferred payments, thereby converting ordinary (interest) income into long-term capital gains. The imputed interest rules create gross income for every tax year when there is deferred tax liability from installment sales.

Generally, if the contract does not charge at least the Federal rate, interest is imputed at that rate. The Federal rate is the interest rate the Federal government pays on new borrowing and is published monthly by the IRS.[64]

[63] §§ 483 and 1274.

[64] § 1274(d)(1). There are three pertinent Federal rates: short-term (not over three years), midterm (over three years but not over nine years), and long-term (over nine years). For example, see Rev.Rul. 2021–21.

As a general rule, the buyer and seller must account for interest on the accrual basis with semiannual compounding.[65] The use of the accrual method ensures that the seller's interest income and the buyer's interest expense are reported in the same tax year.

Example 28

Peggy, a cash basis taxpayer, sold land on January 1, 2022, for $200,000 cash and $6,000,000 due on December 31, 2023, with 2% interest payable December 31, 2022, and December 31, 2023. At the time of the sale, the applicable Federal rate was 4% (compounded semiannually). Because Peggy did not charge interest at least equal to the Federal rate, interest is imputed at 4%.

Date	Payment	Present Value (at 4%) on 1/1/2022	Imputed Interest
12/31/2022	$ 120,000	$ 115,384	$ 4,616
12/31/2023	6,120,000	5,658,284	461,716
	$6,240,000	$5,773,668	$466,332

As a result, the selling price is restated to $5,973,668 ($200,000 + $5,773,668) rather than $6,200,000 ($200,000 + $6,000,000). Peggy will recognize interest income, computed as follows.

	Beginning Balance	Interest (at 4%)*	Received	Ending Balance
2022	$5,773,668	$230,947	$ 120,000	$5,884,615
2023	5,884,615	235,385	6,120,000	–0–

*Compounded semiannually.

Related-Party Sales of Nondepreciable Property

If the Code did not contain special rules, a taxpayer could make an installment sale of property to a related party (e.g., a family member) as part of a tax deferral plan. Then the purchasing family member could immediately sell the property to an unrelated party for cash with no recognized gain or loss (because the amount realized would equal the basis in the sold asset). The related-party purchaser would not pay the installment note to the selling family member until a later year. The net result would be that the family has the cash, but no taxable gain is recognized until the purchasing family member makes payments on the installment note.

Under special rules designed to address the scheme described above, the proceeds from the subsequent sale (the second sale) by the purchasing family member are treated as though they were used to pay the installment note due the selling family member (the first sale). As a result, the recognition of gain from the original sale between the related parties is accelerated.[66]

However, even with these special rules, Congress did not eliminate the benefits of all related-party installment sales.

- Related parties include only the first seller's brothers, sisters, ancestors, lineal descendants, controlled corporations, and partnerships, trusts, and estates in which the seller has an interest.[67]
- There is no acceleration if the second disposition occurs more than two years after the first sale.[68]

As a result, if the taxpayer can sell the property to an "unrelated" family member (like a cousin) or a "patient" family member, the intrafamily installment sale still is a powerful tax planning tool.[69]

[65]§§ 1274(a), 1273(a), and 1272(a).

[66]§ 453(e).

[67]§ 453(f)(1), cross-referencing §§ 267(b) and 318(a). Although spouses are related parties, the exclusion of gains between spouses (§ 1041) overrides the second-disposition rules when the first sale was between spouses.

[68]§ 453(e)(2). But see § 453(e)(2)(B) for extensions of the two-year period.

[69]Other exceptions also can be applied in some circumstances. See §§ 453(e)(6) and (7).

Related-Party Sales of Depreciable Property

The installment method cannot be used to report a gain on the sale of depreciable property to a controlled entity. The purpose of this rule is to prevent the seller from deferring gain (until collections are received) while the related purchaser is enjoying a stepped-up basis for depreciation purposes.[70]

The prohibition on the use of the installment method applies to sales between the taxpayer and a partnership or corporation in which the taxpayer holds a more-than-50-percent interest. Constructive ownership rules are used in applying the ownership test (e.g., the taxpayer is considered to own stock owned by a spouse and certain other family members).[71] However, if the taxpayer can establish that tax avoidance was not a principal purpose of the transaction, the installment method can be used to report the gain.

Example 29

Alan purchased an apartment building from his controlled corporation, Emerald Corporation. Alan was short of cash at the time of the purchase (December 2022) but was to collect a large cash payment in January 2023. The agreement required Alan to pay the entire arm's length price in January 2023. Alan had nontax business reasons for acquiring the building.

Emerald should be able to show that tax avoidance was not a principal purpose for the installment sale, because of Alan's cash flow issues. Emerald reports all of the gain in the year following the year of sale, and Alan depreciates the building over 27.5 years (the cost recovery period for residential real estate).

Interest on Deferred Tax

The installment method allows the seller to defer the payment of taxes on the gain from the sale of property until payments are received from the buyer (borrower). Congress was concerned that this deferral in addition to the seller earning interest on the receivable was too significant of a benefit. To address this concern, sellers are required to pay interest on the deferred taxes if *both* of the following requirements are met.

- The installment obligation arises from the sale of property (other than farming property) for more than $150,000.
- The taxpayer's total installment obligations outstanding at the close of the tax year exceed $5 million.[72]

Disposition of Installment Obligations

Generally, a taxpayer must recognize the deferred profit from an installment sale when the obligation is transferred to another party or is otherwise relinquished. The rationale for accelerating the gain is that the deferral should continue for no longer than the taxpayer owns the installment obligation.[73]

The gift or cancellation of an installment note is treated as a taxable disposition by the donor. This discourages attempts to shift income among family members. The amount realized from the cancellation is the face amount of the note if the parties (obligor and obligee) are related to each other.[74]

[70] § 453(g).

[71] §§ 1239(b) and (c).

[72] § 453A and IRS Publication 537. This amount is not indexed for inflation.

[73] § 453B(a).

[74] § 453B(f)(2).

Example 30

Liz cancels a note issued by Ting (Liz's daughter) that arose in connection with the sale of property. At the time of the cancellation, the note had a basis to Liz of $10,000, a face amount of $25,000, and a fair market value of $20,000. Presuming that the initial sale by Liz qualified as an installment sale, the cancellation results in gain of $15,000 ($25,000 − $10,000) to Liz.

Certain exceptions to the recognition of gain provisions are provided for transfers of installment obligations to the transferor's 80 percent controlled corporation, contributions of capital to a partnership, certain corporate liquidations, transfers due to the taxpayer's death, and transfers between spouses or incident to divorce.[75] In such situations, the deferred profit is shifted to the transferee, who is responsible for the payment of tax on the subsequent collections of the installment obligations. But in the case of a transfer of installment obligations to a partnership by a partner, the transferor partner is taxed on the income when the partnership collects on the installment receivables.

The Big Picture

Example 31

Return to the facts of *The Big Picture* on p. 18-1. Assume that Belinda's capital contribution to the partnership in 2022 was an installment obligation with a basis of $40,000 and a face amount of $100,000. In 2023, the partnership collected the $100,000. The transfer in 2022 was not a taxable disposition, but in 2023 when the receivable is collected, Belinda recognizes a gain of $60,000.

Electing Out of the Installment Method

While the installment method is mandatory when it applies, a taxpayer can *elect not to use* it. The election is made by reporting the entire recognized gain on the seller's timely filed return.[76] Taxpayers and their tax advisers must be careful not to report the entire gain in the year of sale if the taxpayer did not want to elect out of installment sale treatment.

The election frequently is applied to year-end sales by taxpayers who expect to be in a higher tax bracket in the following year. Permission of the IRS is required to revoke an election not to use the installment method.[77]

Example 32

On December 31, 2022, Kurt sold investment land to Jodie for $20,000 (fair market value). He had owned the land for seven years. Jodie will pay Kurt $20,000 in cash on January 4, 2023. Kurt is a cash basis taxpayer, and his basis in the land is $8,000. As a result, he realizes a $12,000 capital gain from the sale. Kurt has a marginal tax rate of 12% in 2022. He expects his tax rate to increase to 35% in 2023.

The transaction constitutes an installment sale because a payment will be received in a tax year after the tax year of disposition. Jodie's promise to pay Kurt is an installment obligation, and under the Regulations, the value of the installment obligation is equal to the value of the property sold ($20,000). If Kurt elects out of the installment method, he will shift the $12,000 capital gain from the expected higher capital gains rate in 2023 of 15% to the 0% rate for long-term capital gains in 2022. The expected tax savings based on the rate differential may exceed the benefit of the tax deferral available with the installment method.

[75] §§ 453B(c), (d), and (g). See Chapter 20 for a discussion of some of these transactions.

[76] § 453(d) and Reg. § 15a.453–1(d).

[77] § 453(d)(3) and Reg. § 15a.453–1(d)(4).

18-3b Long-Term Contracts

LO.5

Recognize the methods of accounting for long-term contracts.

A **long-term contract** is a building, installation, construction, or manufacturing contract that is entered into but not completed within the same tax year.[78] However, a *manufacturing* contract is long term *only* if the contract is to manufacture (1) a unique item not normally carried in finished goods inventory or (2) items that normally require more than 12 calendar months to complete.[79] An item is *unique* if it is designed to meet the customer's needs and is not suitable for use by others. A contract to perform services (e.g., auditing or legal services) cannot qualify as a long-term contract.

Example 33

Rocky, a calendar year taxpayer, entered into two contracts during the year.

One contract was to construct a building foundation. Work was to begin in October 2022 and was to be completed by June 2023. The contract is long term because it will not be entered into and completed in the same tax year. The fact that the contract requires fewer than 12 calendar months to complete is not relevant because the contract is not for manufacturing.

The second contract was for architectural services to be performed over two years. Payments for these services do not qualify for long-term contract treatment.

Generally, the taxpayer must accumulate all of the direct and indirect costs incurred under a contract. This means that the production costs must be accumulated and allocated to individual contracts. Furthermore, mixed services costs (costs that benefit contracts as well as the general administrative operations of the business) must be allocated between production and general administration on a rational basis. Exhibit 18.1 lists the types of costs that must be accumulated and allocated to contracts.[80]

Example 34

Falcon, Inc., uses detailed cost accumulation records to assign labor and materials to its contracts in progress. The total cost of fringe benefits is allocated to a contract on the following basis.

$$\frac{\text{Labor on the contract}}{\text{Total salaries and labor}} \times \text{Total cost of fringe benefits}$$

Similarly, storage and handling costs for materials are allocated to contracts on the following basis.

$$\frac{\text{Contract materials}}{\text{Material purchases}} \times \text{Storage and handling costs}$$

The cost of the personnel operations, a mixed services cost, is allocated between production and general administration based on the number of employees in each function. The personnel cost allocated to production is allocated to individual contracts on the basis of the formula used to allocate fringe benefits.

The accumulated costs are deducted when the revenue from the contract is recognized. Generally, two methods of accounting are used in varying circumstances to determine when the revenue from a contract is recognized.[81]

- The completed contract method.
- The percentage of completion method.

[78]Special rules apply when the Federal government is a party to the contract. §§ 460(c) and (d).

[79]§ 460(f) and Reg. § 1.460–2(a).

[80]Reg. §§ 1.460–5(b) and 1.263A–1(e).

[81]§ 460.

Exhibit 18.1 Contract Costs, Mixed Services Costs, and Current Expense Items for Contracts

	Contracts Eligible for the Completed Contract Method	Other Contracts
Contract costs:		
Direct materials (a part of the finished product).	Capitalize	Capitalize
Indirect materials [consumed in production but not in the finished product (e.g., grease and oil for equipment)].	Capitalize	Capitalize
Storage, handling, and insurance on materials.	Expense	Capitalize
Direct labor (worked on the product).	Capitalize	Capitalize
Indirect labor [worked in the production process but not directly on the product (e.g., a construction supervisor)].	Capitalize	Capitalize
Fringe benefits for direct and indirect labor (e.g., vacation, sick pay, unemployment, and other insurance).	Capitalize	Capitalize
Depreciation on production facilities:		
For financial statements.	Capitalize	Capitalize
Tax depreciation in excess of financial statements.	Expense	Capitalize
Depreciation on idle facilities.	Expense	Expense
Property taxes, insurance, rent, and maintenance on production facilities.	Capitalize	Capitalize
Interest to finance real estate construction.	Capitalize	Capitalize
Interest to finance personal property:		
Production period of one year or less.	Expense	Expense
Production period exceeds one year, and costs exceed $1 million.*	Capitalize	Capitalize
Production period exceeds two years.*	Capitalize	Capitalize
Mixed services costs:		
Personnel operations.	Expense	Allocate
Data processing.	Expense	Allocate
Selling, general, and administrative expenses (including an allocated share of mixed services).	Expense	Expense

*The production period does not include the aging period for beer, wine, and certain distilled spirits, for interest paid or accrued before 2020.

The *completed contract method may be used* for (1) home construction contracts (contracts in which at least 80 percent of the estimated costs are for dwelling units in buildings with four or fewer units) and (2) certain other real estate construction contracts. Other real estate contracts can qualify for the completed contract method if both of the following requirements are satisfied.

- The contract is expected to be completed within the two-year period beginning on the commencement date of the contract.
- The contract is performed by a taxpayer whose average annual gross receipts for the three taxable years preceding the taxable year in which the contract is entered into do not exceed $27 million.

The percentage of completion method must be used for all other contracts.

Completed Contract Method

Under the **completed contract method**, no revenue from the contract is recognized until the contract is completed and accepted. Generally, the contract is completed when it is accepted by the customer as finished or when the customer begins using the subject of the contract.[82]

In some situations, the original contract price may be disputed, or the buyer may want additional work to be done on a long-term contract. If the disputed amount is substantial (it is not possible to determine whether a profit or loss will ultimately be realized on the contract), no amount of income or loss is recognized until the dispute is resolved. In all other cases, the profit or loss (reduced by the amount in dispute) is recognized in the current period upon completion of the contract. However, additional work may need to be performed with respect to the disputed contract. When the amount in dispute is less than the net profit on the contract before the estimated additional cost, the taxpayer must report in the year of completion the applicable profit, reduced by the estimated additional cost.[83]

Example 35

Ted, a calendar year taxpayer using the completed contract method of accounting, constructed a building for Brad under a long-term contract. The gross contract price was $500,000. Ted finished construction in 2022 at a cost of $475,000. When Brad examined the building, he insisted that the building be repainted or that the contract price be reduced. The estimated cost of repainting is $10,000.

Under the terms of the contract, Ted is assured a profit of at least $15,000 ($500,000 − $475,000 − $10,000) even if the dispute is ultimately resolved in Brad's favor. As a result, Ted must include $490,000 ($500,000 − $10,000) in gross income and is allowed deductions of $475,000 for 2022.

In 2023, Ted and Brad resolve the dispute, and Ted repaints certain portions of the building at a cost of $6,000. Ted must include $10,000 in 2023 gross income and may deduct the $6,000 expense in that year.

If the net profit less the estimated additional cost results in a loss, the loss is deferred until the dispute is resolved.

Example 36

Assume the same facts as in the previous example, except that the estimated cost of repainting the building is $50,000. Because the resolution of the dispute completely in Brad's favor would mean a net loss on the contract for Ted ($500,000 − $475,000 − $50,000 = $25,000 loss), Ted does not recognize any income or loss until the year the dispute is resolved.

Percentage of Completion Method

Under the **percentage of completion method**, a portion of the gross contract price is included in income during each period as the work progresses. The revenue accrued each period (except for the final period) is:[84]

$$\frac{C}{T} \times P$$

Where C = Contract costs incurred during the period
T = Estimated total cost of the contract
P = Contract price

[82] Reg. § 1.460–1(c)(3).

[83] Reg. §§ 1.451–3(d)(2)(ii)–(vii), Example 2.

[84] § 460(b)(1)(A).

All of the costs allocated to the contract during the period are deductible from the accrued revenue.[85] The revenue reported in the final period is any remaining revenue from the contract. Because T in this formula is an estimate that frequently differs from total actual costs (which are not known until the contract has been completed), the profit on a contract for a particular period may be overstated or understated (such that related income taxes may be overpaid or underpaid).

Example 37

Tan, Inc., entered into a contract that was to take two years to complete, with an estimated cost of $2,250,000. The contract price was $3,000,000. Costs of the contract for 2021, the first year, totaled $1,350,000. The gross profit reported by the percentage of completion method for 2021 was $450,000 {[($1,350,000 ÷ $2,250,000) × $3,000,000] − $1,350,000}.

The contract was completed at the end of 2022 at a total cost of $2,700,000. In retrospect, the 2021 profit should have been $150,000 {[($1,350,000 ÷ $2,700,000) × $3,000,000] − $1,350,000}. As a result, taxes were overpaid for 2021.

Under a *de minimis* rule, if less than 10 percent of the estimated contract costs have been incurred by the end of the taxable year, the taxpayer can elect to defer the recognition of income and the related costs until the taxable year in which at least 10 percent of total costs are incurred.[86]

Lookback Provision

In the year a contract is completed, a *lookback* provision requires the recalculation of annual profits reported on the contract under the percentage of completion method. Interest is paid to the taxpayer if taxes were overpaid, and interest is payable by the taxpayer if there was an underpayment.[87] For a corporate taxpayer, the lookback interest paid by the taxpayer is deductible, but for an individual taxpayer, it is nondeductible personal interest associated with a tax liability.

Example 38

Assume that Tan, Inc., in Example 37, was in the 21% tax bracket in both years and the relevant interest rate was 5%. For 2021, the company paid excess taxes of $63,000 [($450,000 − $150,000) × 21%]. When the contract is completed at the end of 2022, Tan should receive interest of $3,150 ($63,000 × 5%) for one year on the tax overpayment.

LO.6

Recognize when accounting for inventories must occur and the key tax accounting methods for inventory.

18-4 Inventories

The use of inventories is necessary to clearly reflect income of any business engaged in the production, purchase, or sale of merchandise. Inventories might not be required for small taxpayers, defined for this purpose as those with average annual gross receipts for the prior three-year period of $27 million or less.[88] Generally, when a taxpayer is required to account for inventories for Federal income tax purposes, tax accounting and financial accounting for inventories are much the same.

- The use of inventories is necessary to clearly reflect the income of any business engaged in the production and sale or purchase and sale of goods.[89]
- The inventories should include all finished goods, goods in process, and raw materials and supplies that will become part of the product (including containers).

[85] Reg. § 1.451–3(c)(3).

[86] § 460(b)(5).

[87] §§ 460(b)(2) and (6). The taxpayer can elect not to apply the lookback method in situations where the cumulative taxable income as of the close of each prior year is within 10% of the correct income for each prior year.

[88] Reg. § 1.471–1.

[89] § 471(a) and Reg. §§ 1.471–1 and −2.

- Inventory rules must give effect to the *best accounting practice* of a particular trade or business, and the taxpayer's method should be followed consistently from year to year.
- All items included in inventory should be valued at either (1) cost or (2) the lower of cost or market value.

The reason for the similarities between tax and financial accounting for inventories is that § 471 establishes a two-prong test. Under this provision, "inventories shall be taken . . . on such basis . . . as conforming as nearly as may be to the *best accounting practice* in the trade or business and as most *clearly reflecting the income*." The best accounting practice is synonymous with generally accepted accounting principles (GAAP). However, the IRS determines whether an inventory method clearly reflects income.

In *Thor Power Tool Co. v. Comm.*, there was a conflict between the two tests.[90] The taxpayer's method of valuing obsolete parts was in conformity with GAAP. The IRS, however, successfully argued that the clear reflection of income test was not satisfied because the taxpayer's procedures for valuing its inventories were contrary to the Regulations. Under the taxpayer's method, inventories for parts in excess of estimated future sales were expensed, although the parts were kept on hand and their asking prices were not reduced. [Under Reg. § 1.471–4(b), inventories cannot be written down unless the selling prices also are reduced.] The taxpayer contended that conformity to GAAP creates a presumption that the method clearly reflects income.

The Supreme Court disagreed, concluding that the clear reflection of income test was paramount. Moreover, the Court indicated that the IRS position controls in determining whether the method of inventory clearly reflects income. As a result, the best accounting practice test was rendered meaningless by this decision: the taxpayer's method of inventory must strictly conform to the Regulations, regardless of what GAAP may require.

18-4a Determining Inventory Cost

For merchandise purchased, cost is the invoice price less trade discounts plus freight and other handling charges.[91] Cash discounts approximating a fair interest rate can be deducted or capitalized as the taxpayer elects, provided the method used is consistently applied.

Uniform Capitalization (UNICAP)

For inventory and property produced by the taxpayer, "(A) the direct cost of such property, and (B) such property's share of those indirect costs (including taxes) part or all of which are allocable to such property" must be capitalized. The UNICAP rules apply to all types of businesses: contractors, manufacturers, farmers, wholesalers, and retailers.[92] The procedures are known as the **uniform capitalization (UNICAP) rules**, and many practitioners refer to the rules as a *super-full absorption costing system*.

Taxpayers with average annual gross receipts of $27 million or less (for the previous three years) are not required to apply the UNICAP rules. Special rules exempt certain farming property as well as deductible research expenditures from UNICAP.[93]

The UNICAP rules may result in some costs being capitalized for Federal income tax purposes but not for financial accounting purposes. For example, a wholesaler's or manufacturer's storage costs generally are expensed for financial reporting purposes but are capitalized for tax purposes. The taxpayer may capitalize straight-line depreciation of production equipment for financial accounting purposes, but tax depreciation amounts are capitalized for UNICAP.

[90] 79-1 USTC ¶9139, 43 AFTR 2d 79–362, 99 S.Ct. 773. See text Section 4-1d for the Court's discussion of the differences between tax and financial accounting.

[91] Reg. § 1.471–3(b).

[92] § 263A. H. Rep. 99–841, 99th Cong., 2nd Sess., 1986, pp. 302–309. See also Reg. § 1.263A–1(a).

[93] §§ 263A(d) and (e)(3).

To value inventory under the UNICAP rules, a *producer* must first classify all of its costs into three categories:[94]

(1) production,
(2) general administration (nonproduction), and
(3) mixed services [activities that benefit both category (1) and (2) activities, such as the legal and human resources departments].

Next, the producer needs to perform two allocations using the methods of accounting it has adopted for these purposes.

(1) Separate mixed services costs between production and general administration (nonproduction).
(2) Allocate the production costs (that now include the mixed service costs allocated to production) between the cost of goods sold and the ending inventory.

Exhibit 18.1 (see the "Other Contracts" column) lists typical items that are included in the three classes of costs. The mixed services costs should be allocated to production on a rational basis. For example, the costs of operating the human resources department may be allocated between production and general administration (e.g., based on the number of applications processed or the number of employees). In lieu of allocating each mixed services cost, the taxpayer can elect a *simplified method* whereby the total of all mixed services costs is allocated to production in this manner.[95]

$$MSP = \frac{TP}{TC} \times TMS$$

Where MSP = Mixed services costs allocated to production
TP = Total production costs other than interest and mixed services
TC = Total costs other than interest; state, local, or foreign income taxes; and mixed services costs
TMS = Total mixed services costs

Traditional cost accounting techniques (e.g., average cost per equivalent unit) can be used to allocate the costs between the cost of goods sold and the ending inventory. Alternatively, the producer can elect to allocate mixed services costs to production on the basis of labor charges only (production labor as a percentage of total labor costs).

The costs included in the inventory of *wholesalers and retailers* are comparable to those of the producer. However, many of these costs are captured in the price these taxpayers pay for the goods. The following additional costs are capitalized by these taxpayers.

- All storage costs for wholesalers.
- Off-site storage costs for retailers.
- Purchasing costs (e.g., buyers' wages or salaries).
- Handling, processing, assembly, and repackaging.
- The portion of mixed services costs allocable to these functions.
- Interest expense on loans related to production of inventory must be capitalized if (1) the estimated production period exceeds one year and the costs exceed $1 million or (2) the estimated production period exceeds two years.[96]

Mixed services costs are allocated to off-site storage, purchasing, and packaging on the basis of direct labor costs of these departments pro rata to total payroll.

[94] Reg. § 1.263A–1(c).
[95] Reg. § 1.263A–1(h)(5).
[96] § 263A(f). The $1 million amount is not indexed for inflation.

Lower of Cost or Market

Except for those taxpayers who use the LIFO method, inventories may be valued at the **lower of cost or market (replacement cost)**.[97] Any write-down of damaged or shopworn merchandise and goods that otherwise are unsalable at normal prices is not considered to be an application of the lower of cost or market method. Such items are valued at bona fide selling price less direct cost of disposal.[98]

In the case of excess inventories (as in *Thor Power Tool Co.*, discussed previously), the goods can be written down only to the taxpayer's offering price. If the offering price on the goods is not reduced, the goods are valued at cost.

Example 39

Cardinal Publishing Company invested $50,000 in printing 10,000 copies of a book. Although only 7,000 copies were sold in the first 3 years and none in the next 5 years, management is convinced that the book will become a classic in 20 years. Cardinal leaves the cover price the same as it was when the book was first distributed ($38 per copy). The remaining 3,000 books are valued at cost ($15,000). In this way, the tax law provides an incentive for the taxpayer to destroy or abandon its excess inventory and obtain an immediate deduction rather than wait for the event of future sales.

In applying the lower of cost or market method, *each* item included in the inventory must be valued at the lower of its cost or market value.[99]

Example 40

Information related to a taxpayer's ending inventory follows. Under the lower of cost or market method, the inventory is valued at $7,500 rather than $9,500.

Item	Cost	Market	Lower of Cost or Market
A	$5,000	$ 4,000	$4,000
B	3,000	2,000	2,000
C	1,500	6,000	1,500
	$9,500	$12,000	$7,500

Inventory Shrinkage

The difference between the inventory per physical count and the company's records is referred to as *inventory shrinkage*. Inventory shrinkage usually is the result of accidents, theft, and errors in recording. Many companies take physical inventories at times other than the last day of the tax year and adjust their inventory per books to agree with the physical count. In addition, companies often adjust the ending inventory, to be used in deriving cost of goods sold, for the estimated shrinkage that has occurred between the date of the physical inventory and the last day of the tax year. The adjustment often is based on the historical relationship between inventory shrinkage and sales.[100]

[97] Reg. § 1.472–4.
[98] Reg. § 1.471–2(c).
[99] Reg. § 1.471–4(c).
[100] § 471(b).

Determining Cost—Specific Identification, FIFO, and LIFO

In some cases, it is feasible to determine the cost of the particular item sold. For example, an automobile dealer can determine the specific cost of each automobile that has been sold. However, in most businesses, it is necessary to resort to a flow of goods assumption such as *first in, first out (FIFO), last in, first out (LIFO)*, or an *average cost* method. A taxpayer may use any of these methods provided the method selected is consistently applied from year to year.

During a period of rising prices, LIFO generally produces a lower ending inventory valuation, resulting in a greater cost of goods sold than would be obtained under the FIFO method and lower gross income amounts.

Example 41

On January 1, 2022, the taxpayer opened a retail store to sell refrigerators. At least 10 refrigerators must be carried in inventory to satisfy customer demands. The initial investment in the 10 refrigerators is $5,000. During the year, 10 refrigerators were sold at $750 each and were replaced at a cost of $6,000 ($600 each). Gross profit under the LIFO and FIFO methods is computed as follows.

		FIFO		LIFO
Sales 10 × $750		$ 7,500		$ 7,500
Beginning inventory	$ 5,000		$ 5,000	
Purchases	6,000		6,000	
	$11,000		$11,000	
Ending inventory				
10 × $600	(6,000)			
10 × $500			(5,000)	
Cost of goods sold		(5,000)		(6,000)
Gross profit		$ 2,500		$ 1,500

Dollar-Value LIFO

In the previous example, the taxpayer was buying and selling a single product, a particular model of a refrigerator. The taxpayer employed the specific goods LIFO technique. Under the specific goods approach, if the identical items are not on hand at the end of the period, the LIFO inventory is depleted and all of the deferred profit is recognized. Thus, taxpayers who frequently change the items carried in inventory might realize little benefit from LIFO. The dollar-value LIFO technique can address this problem.

Under **dollar-value LIFO**, each inventory item is assigned to a pool. A *pool* is a collection of similar items and is treated as a separate inventory. Determining whether items are similar involves considerable judgment. In general, however, the taxpayer would prefer broad pools so that when a particular item is sold out, it can be replaced with increases in other items in the same pool. Generally, all products manufactured at a particular plant can be treated as a pool.[101] An automobile dealer may have separate pools for new cars, lightweight trucks, heavy-duty trucks, and car and truck parts.

At the end of the period, ending inventory is valued at the current-year prices and then at the LIFO base period (the year LIFO was adopted). The ratio of the ending inventory at current prices to the ending inventory at base period prices is the *LIFO index*. If the total current inventory at base period prices is greater than the base period inventory at base period prices, a LIFO layer must be added. The LIFO index is applied to the LIFO layer to convert it to current prices.

[101] See, generally, Reg. § 1.472–8.

Example 42

Black Company adopted LIFO effective January 1, 2022. The base LIFO inventory (from December 31, 2021) was $1,000,000. On December 31, 2022, the inventory was $1,320,000 at end-of-2022 prices and $1,200,000 at end-of-2021 (the base period) prices. As a result, Black added a 2022 LIFO layer of $200,000 ($1,200,000 − $1,000,000). The layer must be converted to 2022 prices.

$$\text{LIFO index} = \$1{,}320{,}000 \div \$1{,}200{,}000 = 1.10$$

$$\text{2021 layer} \times \text{LIFO index} = \$200{,}000 \times 1.10 = \$220{,}000$$

Therefore, the 2022 ending inventory is $1,000,000 + $220,000 = $1,220,000.

The inventory on December 31, 2023, is $1,325,000 using 2022 prices and $1,250,000 using base period prices. The 2023 LIFO layer is $50,000 ($1,250,000 − $1,200,000), and the 2023 LIFO index is $1,325,000 ÷ $1,250,000 = 1.06. The LIFO inventory on December 31, 2023, is computed as follows.

	Base Period Cost	LIFO Index	LIFO Layers
Base inventory	$1,000,000	1.00	$1,000,000
2022 layer	200,000	1.10	220,000
2023 layer	50,000	1.06	53,000
	$1,250,000		$1,273,000

Ethics & Equity **Preserving the LIFO Reserve**

Blanch Corporation has been using the dollar-value LIFO inventory method for 20 years. The company maintains one inventory pool that includes raw materials, goods in process, and finished goods. The LIFO deferral is several million dollars. At the end of the current year, the corporation's inventory of finished goods was almost depleted because the company's major competitor had to recall a substantial portion of its products.

Blanch's management is aware that if the inventory is not replenished, the corporation will recognize gross income that has been deferred for 20 years. Blanch's controller has suggested that the company buy sufficient raw materials to substitute for the depleted finished goods. This will require having on hand at the end of the year the raw materials required for the next 18 months; ordinarily the company has only a three-month supply on hand. The controller argues that the cost of carrying the additional inventory is much less than the additional taxes that will be due if the inventories are allowed to decrease.

The operations manager has suggested that the company buy the raw materials before the end of the year and have the supplier store the materials. Furthermore, the supplier would act as Blanch's agent to sell the excess materials. This would minimize the actual investment in inventory. Do you think the corporation should follow either proposal? Explain.

18-4b The LIFO Election

A taxpayer may adopt LIFO by merely using the method for the year of the change and attaching Form 970 to the tax return (i.e., a taxpayer is assured IRS approval for the change). Once the election is made, it cannot be revoked. A change from LIFO to any other inventory method can be made only if the consent of the IRS is obtained.[102] In making the election, the taxpayer must establish that it is using no inventory method other than LIFO.

The beginning inventory valuation for the first LIFO year is computed by the costing method used in the preceding year. As a result, the beginning LIFO inventory generally equals the closing inventory for the preceding year. Because lower of cost or market methods cannot be used in conjunction with LIFO, previous write-downs to market for items included in the beginning inventory must be restored to income. The amount by which the inventories are written up is an adjustment due to a change in accounting method.[103] The taxpayer can spread the adjustment ratably over the year of the change and the two succeeding years.[104]

[102] Reg. §§ 1.472–3(a) and 1.472–5.

[103] Reg. § 1.472–2(c). In Rev.Rul. 76–282, the IRS required the restoration of write-downs for damaged and shopworn goods when the taxpayer switched to LIFO.

[104] § 472(d).

Example 43

In 2021, Pablo used the lower of cost or market FIFO inventory method. The FIFO cost of his ending inventory was $30,000, and the market value of the inventory was $24,000. As a result, the ending inventory for 2021 was $24,000.

Pablo switched to LIFO in 2022 and was required to write up the beginning inventory to $30,000. Pablo must add $2,000 ($6,000 ÷ 3) to his gross income in 2022, 2023, and 2024.

Once the LIFO election is made for tax purposes, the taxpayer's financial reports to owners and creditors also must be prepared using LIFO.[105] The *LIFO conformity rule* matching financial reports to tax returns is strictly enforced by the IRS; the LIFO election is lost if a different method is used in financial reporting.

18-4c Special Inventory Methods Relating to Farming and Ranching

Farmers who do not use the cash method may elect to account for inventories using the **farm price method** or the **unit-livestock-price method** rather than one of the inventory methods discussed previously. Under the farm price method, the inventory is valued at its market price less disposition costs (e.g., transportation and selling expenses).[106] If the taxpayer uses the unit-livestock-price method, the animals are valued at a standard cost, which is based on the average cost of raising an animal that is similar to those included in the ending inventory.[107]

18-4d Inventory of Small Taxpayers

Small taxpayers, defined as those with average annual gross receipts of $27 million or less in the prior three-year period, may use the cash method of accounting, and they can choose one of three methods to account for inventory.[108]

1. Treat inventory as nonincidental materials and supplies. Under this method, the taxpayer deducts the cost of the inventory when it is used (i.e., when it is sold to the customer). Because the taxpayer is using the cash method, it may only deduct the inventory if it has not only sold it but also paid for it.
2. If the taxpayer has an *applicable financial statement* (generally a certified GAAP financial statement), it may treat the inventory as it does in the financial statements.
3. If the taxpayer does not have an applicable financial statement, it may deduct the inventory in the same manner as it reports the inventory on its internal books and records.

Example 44

Jain is a sole proprietor selling widgets online. Her gross receipts average $2,700,000 per year. She buys her goods on credit, usually paying the bills when received (about 30 days after purchase). Jain uses the cash method and treats her inventory as nonincidental supplies.

In 2022, Jain recorded beginning inventory of $30,000 (cost), purchases of $1,800,000, and ending inventory of $20,000 (cost). She held outstanding payables for inventory purchases of $50,000 (including for the ending inventory). Jain's records show that all of the beginning inventory was paid for in 2021 and sold in 2022.

The 2022 inventory deduction is:

Beginning inventory paid for in 2021 but not sold until 2022	$ 30,000
Inventory purchased during the year less $50,000 not paid by year-end (including the ending inventory)	1,750,000
Inventory deduction for 2022	$1,780,000

[105] § 472(d).
[106] Reg. § 1.471–6(d).
[107] Reg. § 1.471–6(e). See also IRS Publication 225, p. 7.
[108] § 471(c) and Reg. § 1.471–1(b).

18-5 Tax Planning

LO.7

Identify tax planning opportunities related to accounting periods and accounting methods.

18-5a Taxable Year

Under the general rules for tax years, partnerships and S corporations frequently must use a calendar year. However, if the partnership or S corporation can demonstrate a business purpose for a fiscal year, it can use that year. The advantage to a fiscal year is that the calendar year partners and S corporation shareholders may be able to defer from tax the income earned from the close of the fiscal year until the end of the calendar year. Tax advisers for these entities should apply the IRS's gross receipts test to determine whether permission for the fiscal year will be granted.[109]

18-5b Cash Method of Accounting

The cash method of accounting gives the taxpayer considerable control over the recognition of expenses and some control over the recognition of income. This method can be used by proprietorships, partnerships without a C corporation partner, S corporations, qualified personal service corporations, small C corporations, and small partnerships with a C corporation partner (annual gross receipts of $27 million or less over the prior three-year period). Most farmers also can use the cash method.

18-5c Installment Method

Unlike the cash and accrual methods, the installment method often results in an interest-free loan (i.e., of deferred taxes) from the government. When eligible property is sold, the installment method can allow the seller to defer gain and attain a higher interest rate than from alternative investments. These benefits must be weighed against the risks of nonpayment by the buyer.

Advance Payments from Customers

If a business receives a significant amount of advance payments from customers, it should consider using the accrual method even if it is a small taxpayer allowed to use the cash method. An accrual method taxpayer receiving advance payments can adopt the deferral method of § 451(c) and Reg. § 1.451–8 to obtain limited deferral of all or a portion of each advance payment received from customers.

Electing Out of the Installment Method

While deferral of the reporting of gain from an installment sale generally produces favorable after-tax results, electing out of such treatment can be advantageous under circumstances such as the following.

- The seller expects tax rates to increase in future years.
- The seller has tax credits that will expire soon.
- The seller has a loss carryforward equal to or greater than the gain from the property sale.
- The installment note causes the seller to have installment obligations at year end greater than $5 million, making the seller subject to interest payments on the deferred tax amount.

Related Parties

Intrafamily installment sales can be a useful family tax planning tool. If the related party holds the property more than two years, a subsequent sale will not accelerate the gain from the first disposition. Patience and forethought are rewarded with this tax planning device.

---

[109] Rev.Proc. 2006–46.

Disposition of Installment Obligations

A disposition of an installment obligation can produce disadvantageous income tax results, accelerating the recognition of gross income to the seller. In each instance where transfers of installment obligations are contemplated, the tax adviser should analyze thoroughly the related tax and nontax consequences.

18-5d Inventories

An ending inventory valuation can be minimized and thus taxable income reduced by electing advantageous accounting methods.

- Purchase prices can be stated net of cash discounts (the net invoice method).
- The lower of cost or market method may be applied.
- The LIFO method can be adopted during periods of significantly rising prices.

Refocus on The Big Picture

Accounting Period and Method

TETRA IMAGES/GETTY IMAGES

Selection of a Tax Year

An entity's tax form will govern the rules for determining the entity's tax year. Because Silver is a partnership, Tweety's 40 percent ownership interest in Silver is not sufficient to enable it to control the selection of the partnership's tax year. Likewise, Belinda and Pearl's collective controlling interest will not allow them to control the selection of the tax year for the partnership.

The partnership applies rules in the following sequence to determine its tax year-end.

- *Majority interest tax year.* The tax year of the partners who have a common year-end and collectively own a greater-than-50-percent interest in the partnership capital and profits.
- *Principal partners' tax year.* The common tax year of all of the principal partners (5 percent or greater interest in capital or profits).
- *Least aggregate deferral tax year.* The tax year of the principal partners (grouped by a common year-end) that produces the least aggregate deferral of gross income.

Alternatively, the partnership can select its tax year based on a business purpose for the tax year selected. However, this requires the approval of the IRS, which is unlikely to be granted. The only business purpose the IRS has acknowledged is the need to conform the tax year to the entity's natural business year.

Therefore, Silver will determine its Federal income tax year by using the least aggregate deferral method. Based on this method, Silver's tax year ends on November 30 (as in Example 3).

Short Tax Year

Silver's short tax year begins on April 1, 2022, and ends on November 30, 2022, as determined by the least aggregate deferral method.

continued

What If?

If Silver Partnership's average annual gross receipts for the prior three-year period exceed $27 million, it must use the accrual method to compute its taxable income because one of the partners is a C corporation. Belinda is a cash basis taxpayer, but her share of the partnership income is computed using the accrual method.

Key Terms

Accounting methods, 18-10
Accounting period, 18-2
Accrual method, 18-13
All events test, 18-14
Cash method, 18-11
Claim of right doctrine, 18-9
Completed contract method, 18-27
Crop insurance proceeds, 18-9
Crop method, 18-12
Dollar-value LIFO, 18-32
Economic performance test, 18-14
Farm price method, 18-34
Fiscal year, 18-2
Hybrid method, 18-16
Imputed interest, 18-21
Installment method, 18-20
Least aggregate deferral method, 18-4
Long-term contract, 18-25
Lower of cost or market (replacement cost), 18-31
Majority interest partners, 18-3
Percentage of completion method, 18-27
Personal service corporation (PSC), 18-6
Principal partner, 18-3
Short period, 18-7
Short taxable year, 18-7
12-month rule for prepaid expenses, 18-11
Uniform capitalization (UNICAP) rules, 18-29
Unit-livestock-price method, 18-34

Discussion Questions

1. **LO.1** Would a calendar or fiscal year be more suitable for a ski lodge? Why?

2. **LO.1** Assume that a partnership is profitable and that its tax year ends on December 31 but one of the partners' tax year ends on September 30. Does the partner enjoy a tax benefit or detriment from the partnership's use of a December 31 tax year-end? Explain. Critical Thinking

3. **LO.1** A law practice was incorporated on January 1, 2022, and expects to earn $25,000 per month before deducting attorney Shonda's salary. Shonda owns 100% of the stock in the practice. The corporation and Shonda both use the cash method of accounting. The corporation does not need to retain any of the earnings in the business; thus, the salary of Shonda (a calendar year taxpayer) is the corporation's net income before salary expense. Critical Thinking

   If the corporation could choose any tax year and pay Shonda's salary at the time that would be most tax-efficient (but at least once every 12 months), what tax year should the corporation choose? When should the salary be paid each year? Be specific.

4. **LO.1** Art Funkel started his incorporated medical practice on June 1 of the current year. He immediately made an S election for the corporation. Art would like the corporation to adopt a tax year ending May 31 so that a full 12 months of income would be included in the first tax year. Can the corporation elect a fiscal year ending May 31? Explain.

5. **LO.1** Fred, a cash basis taxpayer, received a $15,000 bonus from his employer in 2022. The bonus was based on the company's profits for 2021. In 2023, the company discovered that its 2021 profits were computed incorrectly. As a result, Fred received an additional $10,000 with respect to 2021 profits. Fred's marginal tax rate in 2022 was 12%, and it was 35% in 2023.

   Sue, also a cash basis taxpayer, received a $35,000 bonus in 2022 that was based on 2021 profits. In 2023, the company discovered that it had overstated its profits in 2022. As a result, Sue was required to repay $10,000 of her bonus in 2023. Sue was in the 35% marginal tax bracket in 2022 and in the 12% marginal bracket in 2023.

   What special tax treatment is available to Fred and Sue as a result of their employer's errors?

Planning

6. **LO.2** Under what conditions would the cash method of accounting be preferred to the accrual basis?

7. **LO.2** In December 2022, Nell, Inc., an accrual basis taxpayer, paid $12,000 for insurance premiums for the 2023 calendar year. How much of the premiums can Nell, Inc., deduct in 2022?

8. **LO.2** In 2022, the taxpayer became ineligible to use the cash method of accounting. At the beginning of the year, accounts receivable totaled $240,000, accounts payable for merchandise totaled $80,000, and inventory on hand totaled $320,000. What is the Federal income tax adjustment due to the change in accounting method?

9. **LO.2** Osprey Corporation, an accrual basis taxpayer, reported taxable income for 2022 and paid $40,000 on its estimated state income tax for the year. During 2022, the company received a $4,000 refund upon filing its 2021 state income tax return. The company filed its 2022 state income tax return in August 2023 and paid the $7,000 state income tax due for 2022.

   In December 2022, Osprey received a notice from the state tax commission that an additional $6,000 of income tax was due for 2020 because of an error on the return. The company acknowledged the error in December 2022 and paid the additional $6,000 tax in February 2023. What is Osprey's 2022 Federal income tax deduction for state income taxes?

10. **LO.2** Compare the results of using cash and accrual methods of accounting for the following events.
    a. Purchased new equipment, paying $50,000 cash and giving a note payable for $30,000 due next year.
    b. Paid $3,600 for a three-year service contract on the new equipment.
    c. Collected $1,800 for services to be provided in the current and following years.
    d. Received a $3,000 note from a customer for services provided in the current year. The market value of the note was $2,400.

Critical Thinking

11. **LO.2** Edgar uses the cash method to report the income from his software consulting business. A publicly held corporation has offered to invest in Edgar's business as a limited partner. What tax accounting complications would be created if Edgar and the corporation became partners?

12. **LO.2** Samantha, a cash basis taxpayer, subscribes to a service that updates a database used in her business. In December 2022, Samantha paid the $120,000 subscription fee for the period January 2023 through December 2023. What is Samantha's deduction for 2022?

13. LO.2 Findley Motors is an automobile dealer. The controller consults with you about the type of accounting used for a special offer to its new car customers. Findley has offered to provide at no charge to the customer the first four recommended service visits (i.e., at 3,000, 6,000, 9,000, and 12,000 miles). It is a virtual certainty that all customers will exercise their rights to the service, and the cost of the services can be estimated accurately. The controller reasons that the estimated cost should be accrued when the sale of an automobile is made, so that all of the costs of the sale can be matched with the revenue. How would you respond to the controller?

14. LO.4, 7 Irene has made Sari an offer on the purchase of a capital asset. Irene will pay (1) $200,000 cash or (2) $50,000 cash and a 6% installment note for $150,000 guaranteed by City Bank of New York. If Sari sells for $200,000 cash, she will invest the after-tax proceeds in certificates of deposit yielding 6% interest. Sari's cost of the asset is $25,000. Why would Sari prefer the installment sale? Decision Making Planning

15. LO.4 Arnold gave land to his son, Bruce. Arnold's basis in the land was $100,000, and its fair market value at the date of the gift was $150,000. Bruce borrowed $130,000 from a bank; he used the funds to improve the property. He sold the property to Della for $360,000. Della paid Bruce $90,000 in cash, assumed his $120,000 mortgage, and agreed to pay $150,000 in two years. Bruce's selling expenses were $10,000. Della is going to pay adequate interest. What is Bruce's installment sale gain in the year of sale?

16. LO.4, 7 On June 1, 2020, Father sold land to Son for $300,000. Father reported the gain by the installment method, with the gain to be spread over five years. In May 2022, Son received an offer of $400,000 for the land, to be paid over three years. What would be the tax consequences of Son's sale? How could the tax consequences be improved? Critical Thinking

17. LO.4, 7 In December 2022, Soraya Corporation sold land it held as an investment. The corporation received $50,000 in 2022 and a note payable (with adequate interest) for $150,000 to be paid in 2024. Soraya's cost of the land was $80,000. The corporation has a $90,000 net capital loss carryover that will expire in 2022. Should Soraya report the sale in 2022 or use the installment method to report the income as payments are received? Planning

18. LO.2, 5 What are the similarities between the crop method used for farming and the completed contract method used for long-term construction? Critical Thinking

19. LO.5 Nathan uses the percentage of completion method to report income from his real estate construction contracts. A contract was begun in 2022 and completed in 2023. In 2022, Nathan reported gross income from the partial completion of the contract. In 2023, however, costs had increased above the original estimate. The contract was completed with the actual profit on the contract being less than the income from the contract reported in 2022. What mechanism should be used to correct for the overpayment of tax in 2022? Be specific.

20. LO.5 Neal uses the percentage of completion method to report his gross income from long-term contracts that were to begin in 2022. In 2023, he completes a contract for more than the estimate of total costs that was used in the prior year. What are the tax accounting implications of the incorrect estimate?

21. LO.5 The Hawk Corporation builds yachts. The vessels it currently produces are practically identical and are completed in approximately 8 months. A customer has approached Hawk about constructing a larger yacht that would take approximately 15 months to complete. What are the tax implications of accepting the contract proposal? Critical Thinking

Critical Thinking

22. **LO.6** Largo Company is an engineering consulting business that uses the accrual method of accounting for its services. Mango Company is a manufacturer of nuts and bolts that also uses the accrual method to account for its sales. Each company has a personnel department. How should the cost of personnel operations be treated by each of the two companies? *Hint:* Consider whether the UNICAP rules apply.

Critical Thinking

23. **LO.6** Amber Auto Parts adopted the dollar-value LIFO inventory method. The company has consistently used a retail price index when it should have used a producer's index. As a result, its LIFO layers have been consistently undervalued. Why is the company's error exacerbated by the fact that the company uses the LIFO method instead of the FIFO method?

Critical Thinking

24. **LO.6** Opal, Inc., is about to make its first attempt to borrow from a local bank. The company uses LIFO for tax purposes, solely to defer taxes, and it believes that income computed using the FIFO method would better reflect its income. The company also uses the double-declining balance method of depreciation for tax purposes even though the straight-line method better reflects the actual depreciation.

    The company would like to present its financial position in the most favorable light. Therefore, Opal's CEO intends to provide the bank with an income statement prepared using the FIFO inventory method and straight-line depreciation. What problems will presenting the income statement to the bank in this fashion cause for Opal?

Critical Thinking

25. **LO.6** Blue is a retailer that uses the FIFO inventory method. Blue always takes its physical inventory at the end of the last day of its tax year, December 31. This practice is very unpopular with its employees, who do not like working on New Year's Eve. The company is considering taking the inventory at the end of November and adjusting for sales and purchases in the last month of the year. However, the CFO has raised the issue that by taking the inventory at the end of November, loss from theft and breakage in December will not be taken into account until the physical inventory is taken in the following year. Is the CFO's concern valid? Explain.

Computational Exercises

26. **LO.2** Gaffney Corporation is a wholesale distributor of auto parts and uses the cash method of accounting. The company's sales have been about $20,000,000 per year for the last few years. However, Gaffney has the opportunity to acquire an unincorporated competitor with annual sales of $10,000,000. What would be the tax accounting implications of acquiring the competitor?

27. **LO.1** In 2022, Aurora received a $25,000 bonus computed as a percentage of profits. In 2023, Aurora's employer determined that the 2022 profits had been incorrectly computed, and Aurora had to refund the $8,000 in 2023. Assume that Aurora was in the 35% tax bracket in 2022 but in the 12% bracket in 2023.
    a. In 2022, how much is Aurora required to include in gross income?
    b. In 2023, what is the amount of the deduction Aurora can claim? What is the reduction in taxes for 2023 as a result of the deduction?

28. **LO.2** In 2022, Chaya Corporation, an accrual basis, calendar year taxpayer, provided services to clients and earned $25,000. The clients signed notes receivable to Chaya that have a fair market value of $22,000 at year-end. In addition, Chaya sold a 36-month service contract on June 1, 2022, and received payment in full of $12,000.

    How much gross income does Chaya report from these transactions in 2022?

29. **LO.3** For 2022, Essence Company, a calendar year taxpayer, will change from the cash method for tax purposes to the accrual method. At the end of 2021, Essence showed the following items.

Accounts receivable	$200,000
Accounts payable	135,000
Bank loan	100,000

What is the § 481(a) adjustment for this change in accounting method? Be sure to state whether it is positive or negative.

30. **LO.4** On December 30, 2022, Whitney sold a piece of property for $85,000. Her basis in the property was $40,000, and she incurred $1,200 in selling expenses. The buyer paid $5,000 down with the balance payable in $10,000 installments over the next eight years. In addition, the buyer assumed a $15,000 mortgage on the property.

Under the installment sales method, what is the total contract price, the total gain on the sale, and the amount of gain reported in 2022? Round any division to four decimal places, and use that amount in subsequent computations.

31. **LO.4** In 2022, Skylar sold equipment for $20,000 cash and a $300,000 note due in two years. Skylar's cost of the property was $250,000, and he had deducted depreciation of $150,000.

a. Under the installment sales method, what is Skylar's total realized gain?

b. In the year of sale, how much § 1245 gain does Skylar recognize? How much gain can be deferred under the installment sale method?

32. **LO.4** Farhad canceled a note issued by Emma (Farhad's niece) that arose in connection with the sale of property. At the time of the cancellation, the note had a basis to Farhad of $30,000, a face amount of $55,000, and a fair market value of $42,000. Presuming that the initial sale by Farhad qualified as an installment sale, how much gain does the cancellation result in for Farhad?

33. **LO.5** Jebali Corporation, a calendar year taxpayer utilizing the completed contract method of accounting, constructed a building for Samson, Inc., under a long-term contract. The gross contract price was $2,300,000. Jebali finished construction in 2022 at a cost of $2,100,000. However, Samson insisted that Jebali redo the doorway; otherwise, the contract price would be reduced. The estimated cost of redoing the doorway is $80,000. In 2023, the dispute is settled and Jebali fixed the doorway at a cost of $65,000.

a. How much must Jebali include in gross income for these items? What amount of deductions is Jebali allowed for 2022?

b. In 2023, how much must Jebali include in gross income? What expenses can Jebali deduct in that year?

34. **LO.5** Shumpert, Inc., entered into a contract that was to take two years to complete, with an estimated cost of $900,000. The contract price was $1,300,000. Costs of the contract for 2021, the first year, totaled $675,000.

a. What was the gross profit reported by the percentage of completion method for 2021?

b. After the contract was completed at the end of 2022 at a total cost of $950,000, what was the gross profit reported by the percentage of completion method for 2022?

35. **LO.6** Lakota's ending inventory is stated as follows. Under the lower of cost or market method, what is the Federal income tax value of Lakota's inventory?

Item	Cost	Market
Rakes	$8,100	$7,900
Shovels	$3,800	$4,300
Hoes	$6,000	$6,250

36. **LO.6** Shondee Corporation uses the lower of cost or market and FIFO inventory methods. At the end of 2021, the FIFO cost of the ending inventory was $181,000, and the market value of the inventory was $160,000. The corporation switched to LIFO in 2022. As a result, how much must Shondee add to its gross income for each of the years 2022, 2023, and 2024?

Problems

37. **LO.1** Red, White, and Blue are unrelated corporations engaged in real estate development. The three corporations formed a joint venture (treated as a partnership) to develop a tract of land. Assuming that the venture does not have a natural business year, what tax year must the joint venture adopt under the following circumstances?

		Tax Year Ending	Interest in Joint Venture
a.	Red	March 31	60%
	Blue	June 30	20%
	White	October 31	20%
b.	Red	October 31	30%
	White	September 30	40%
	Blue	January 31	30%

Decision Making
Planning

38. **LO.1, 7** The Cardinal Wholesale Company is an S corporation that began business on March 1, 2022. Robert, a calendar year taxpayer, owns 100% of the Cardinal stock. He has $400,000 taxable income from other sources each year. Robert will work approximately 30 hours a week for the corporation. Cardinal sells swimming pool supplies, and its natural business year ends in September. Approximately 80% of Cardinal's gross receipts occur in June through September.

   a. What tax year should Cardinal elect, assuming that Robert anticipates the company producing a net profit for all years?

   b. What tax year should Cardinal elect, assuming that it will lose $10,000 a month for the first 12 months and an average of $5,000 a month for the next 12 months? In the third year, the corporation will earn taxable income.

39. **LO.1** In 2021, Juan entered into a contract to write a book. The publisher advanced Juan $50,000, which was to be recovered out of future royalties. If the book was not completed by the end of 2022, however, Juan would be required to repay the publisher for the advance. Juan did not complete the book in 2022, and in accordance with the agreement, he repaid the $50,000 to the publisher in 2023. Juan is a cash basis taxpayer. What are the tax consequences to Juan of the repayment under the following assumptions?

   a. Juan's marginal tax rate was 15% in 2021 and 35% in 2023.

   b. Juan's marginal tax rate was 35% in 2021 and 12% in 2023.

40. **LO.2** Gold, Inc., is an accrual basis taxpayer. In 2022, an employee accidentally spilled hazardous chemicals on leased property. The chemicals destroyed trees on neighboring property, resulting in $30,000 of damages. In 2022, the owner of the property sued Gold, Inc., for the $30,000. Gold's attorney believes that it is liable and that the only issue is whether the neighbor will seek punitive damages that could be as much as three times the actual damages. Communications

In addition, as a result of the spill, Gold was in violation of its lease and was therefore required to pay the landlord $15,000. However, the amount due for the lease violation is not payable until the termination of the lease in 2024. None of these costs were covered by insurance.

Jeff Stuart, the president of Gold, Inc., is generally familiar with the accrual basis tax accounting rules and is concerned about when the company can deduct the amounts the company is required to pay as a result of this environmental disaster. Write Mr. Stuart a letter explaining these issues. Gold's address is 200 Elm Avenue, San Jose, CA 95192.

41. **LO.2** Compute Mary's income or deductions for 2022 using (1) the cash basis and (2) the accrual basis for each of the following.

a. In May 2022, Mary paid a license fee of $1,200 for the period June 1, 2022, through May 31, 2023.

b. In December 2022, Mary collected $10,000 for January 2023 rents. In January 2022, Mary collected $2,000 for December 2022 rents.

c. In June 2022, Mary paid $7,200 for an office equipment service contract for the period July 1, 2022, through December 31, 2023.

d. In June 2022, Mary purchased office furniture for $273,000. She paid $131,000 in cash and gave a $142,000 interest-bearing note for the balance. The office furniture has a MACRS cost recovery period of seven years. Mary did not make the § 179 election and elected not to take additional first-year depreciation.

42. **LO.2, 5** Which accounting method (cash or accrual) would you recommend for the following businesses? Critical Thinking

a. A gift shop with average annual gross receipts of $900,000.

b. An accounting partnership with average annual gross receipts of $12,000,000.

c. A drywall subcontractor who works on residences and records annual gross receipts of $3,000,000.

d. An incorporated insurance agency with average annual gross receipts of $28,000,000.

e. A sole proprietor operating a retail clothing store with average annual gross receipts of $12,000,000.

f. A sole proprietor operating a widget manufacturing plant with average annual gross receipts of $28,000,000.

43. **LO.2** Blue Company, an architectural firm, maintains a cash receipts and disbursements journal. At the end of the year (2022), the company hires you to convert the cash receipts and disbursements into accrual basis revenues and expenses. The total cash receipts are summarized as follows. Critical Thinking

Cash sales	$150,000
Collections on accounts receivable	350,000
Bank loan	90,000
Total cash receipts	$590,000

The accounts receivable from customers at the end of the year are $120,000. You note that the accounts receivable at the beginning of the year were $190,000. The cash sales included $30,000 of prepayments for services to be provided over the period January 1, 2022, through December 31, 2024.

a. Compute the company's accrual basis gross income for 2022.

b. Would you recommend that Blue use the cash method or the accrual method for Federal income tax reporting? Why?

c. The company does not maintain an allowance for uncollectible accounts. Would you recommend that such an allowance be established for Federal income tax purposes? Explain.

44. **LO.2** How do the all events and economic performance requirements apply to the following transactions by an accrual basis taxpayer?

a. The company guarantees its products for six months. At the end of 2022, customers had made valid claims under the guarantee for $600,000 that were not paid until 2023. The company estimates that another $400,000 in claims from 2022 sales will be filed and paid in 2023.

b. The accrual basis taxpayer reported $200,000 in corporate taxable income for 2022. The state income tax rate was 6%. The corporation paid $7,000 in estimated state income taxes in 2022 and paid $2,000 on 2021 state income taxes when it filed its 2021 state income tax return in March 2022. The company filed its 2022 state income tax return in March 2023 and paid the remaining $5,000 of its 2022 state income tax liability.

c. An employee was involved in an accident while making a sales call. The company paid the employee $15,000 in 2022 and agreed to pay her $15,000 a year for each of the next nine years.

45. **LO.3** Ross Company is a C corporation providing property management services. Ross has used the cash method since inception because its gross receipts did not exceed $27,000,000. This year its average annual gross receipts for the prior three years crossed the $27,000,000 mark, requiring Ross to change from the cash method to the accrual method. At the end of its prior year, Ross had accounts receivable of $850,000 and accounts payable of $540,000.

a. Compute and explain the adjustment to taxable income that Ross must make due to the change in accounting method.

b. When must Ross include this adjustment in its income?

Decision Making

46. **LO.2, 3** Raven Finance Company experiences bad debts of about 3% of its outstanding loans. At the end of the year, the company had outstanding receivables of $18,000,000. This balance included $2,000,000 of accrued interest receivable. Raven's loan loss reserve for the year was computed as follows.

Balance, January 1, 2022	$500,000
Accounts written off as uncollectible	
Loans made in 2022	(20,000)
Loans made in prior years	(40,000)
Collections on loans previously written off	15,000
Adjustment to required balance	85,000
Balance, December 31, 2022	$540,000

a. Determine the effects of the above on Raven's taxable income for 2022.

b. Assume that Raven has used bad debt reserves in computing its taxable income for the 10 years the company has been in existence. In 2022, you begin preparing Raven's tax return. What should be done on the return with regard to the reserve?

Communications

47. **LO.2, 3, 6** Jeffrey Boyd, the president of Eagle Furniture Company (average annual gross receipts of $30,000,000), has prepared the company's financial statements and income tax returns for the past 15 years. In July 2023, however,

he hires you to prepare the 2022 corporate income tax return because he has not studied taxes for over 20 years and suspects that the rules may have changed. Eagle uses the accrual method of accounting. Based on an initial examination of Eagle's trial balance and some account analyses, you have determined that the following items may require adjustments.

- The company uses the FIFO inventory method, as valued at cost. However, all freight expenses on incoming merchandise have been expensed for the 15 years the company has been in business.
- The company experiences inventory shrinkage (due to breakage and theft) of about 1% of sales each year. The shrinkage is not taken into account until the company takes a physical inventory each October, but the corporation's fiscal year ends January 31.
- The company has used an allowance for uncollectible accounts, which has a balance of $60,000. In the past, the company has been able to predict its actual bad debt expense accurately.
- The company sells a three-year service contract on its appliances. The company treats $\frac{1}{36}$ of the contract price as earned each month. At the beginning of the year, the company had $120,000 in its account for unearned revenues from the service contracts.
- The company deducts its state income tax in the year paid. Thus, the 2022 state income tax expense includes the estimated taxes paid in 2022 and the additional amount paid in 2022 on 2021 taxes.

Write a letter to Mr. Boyd, explaining what adjustments will be required and how they will be implemented. The address of Eagle Furniture Company is 1000 East Maryland Street, Evansville, IL 47722.

48. **LO.4, 7** Floyd, a cash basis taxpayer, has received an offer to purchase his land. The cash basis buyer will pay him either $100,000 at closing or $50,000 at closing and $56,000 two years after the date of closing. If Floyd recognizes the entire gain in the current year, his marginal tax rate will be 25% (combined Federal and state rates). However, if he spreads the gain over the two years, his combined marginal tax rate on the gain will be only 20%. Floyd does not consider the buyer a credit risk, and he understands that shifting the gain to next year with an installment sale will save taxes. Still, he realizes that the deferred payment will, in effect, earn only $6,000 for waiting two years for the other $50,000. Decision Making Planning

Floyd believes he can earn a 10% before-tax rate of return on his after-tax cash. Floyd's adjusted basis for the land is $25,000, the buyer also is a cash basis taxpayer, and the short-term Federal rate is 4%. Floyd has asked you to evaluate the two alternatives on an after-tax basis.

49. **LO.4, 7** Jamal purchased equipment and used materials to develop a patent. The development costs were deducted on prior returns. The bases and fair market values of the assets are presented below. Decision Making

Assets	Fair Market Value		Basis
Equipment	$350,000	Cost	$ 350,000
		Less: Depreciation	(250,000)
Patent	250,000		-0-
	$600,000		$ 100,000

Sarah has made an offer to purchase the assets. Under one plan, she would pay $200,000 now and $400,000 plus interest at 5% (the Federal rate) in one year. Alternatively, Jamal would incorporate the assets and then sell the stock to Sarah.

Incorporating the assets would not be a taxable event to Jamal, and his basis in the stock would equal his basis in the assets of $100,000. The corporation's basis in the assets also would be $100,000, the same as Jamal's basis for the stock.

Because the corporation would have a basis in the assets of less than the fair market value (and therefore, there would be less depreciation and amortization than with an asset sale by Jamal), Sarah would pay $200,000 in the current year but only $350,000, plus interest at 5%, in one year. Jamal's combined Federal and state marginal tax rate is 35% and his combined capital gain tax rate is 20%.

a. What is Jamal's gain in the year of sale from the installment sale of his assets?

b. Assuming that Jamal's time value of money is 5%, would he prefer the sale of the assets or the sale of the stock? Why?

50. **LO.4** Kay, who is not a real estate dealer, sold an apartment house to Parra during the current year (2022). The closing statement for the sale is as follows.

Total selling price		$ 190,000
Add: Parra's share of property taxes (six months) paid by Kay		3,000
Less: Kay's 8% mortgage assumed by Parra	$55,000	
Parra's refundable binder ("earnest money") paid in 2021	1,000	
Parra's 8% installment note given to Kay	99,000	
Kay's real estate commissions and attorney's fees	8,000	(163,000)
Cash paid to Kay at closing		$ 30,000
Cash due from Parra = $30,000 + $8,000 expenses		$ 38,000

During 2022, Kay collected $9,000 in principal on the installment note and $2,000 of interest. Kay's basis in the property was $110,000 [$125,000 − $15,000 (depreciation)]. The Federal rate is 6%.

a. Compute the following.
   1. Total gain.
   2. Contract price.
   3. Payments received in the year of sale.
   4. Recognized gain in the year of sale and the character of such gain.

   (*Hint:* Before you begin your computations, think about the manner in which the property taxes are handled.)

b. Same as parts (a)(2) and (3), except that Kay's basis in the property was $35,000.

Critical Thinking
Planning

51. **LO.4** On June 30, 2022, Kelly sold property for $240,000 cash and a $960,000 note due on September 30, 2023. The note pays 6% interest, which is higher than the Federal rate. Kelly's cost of the property was $400,000. She is concerned that Congress may increase the tax rate that will apply for the year when the note is collected. Kelly's after-tax rate of return on investments is 6%.

a. What can Kelly do to avoid the expected higher tax rate?

b. Assuming that Kelly's marginal combined Federal and state tax rate is 25% in 2022, how much would the tax rates need to increase to make the option identified in part (a) advisable?

Planning

52. **LO.4** On December 30, 2021, Maud sold land to her son, Charles, for $50,000 cash and a 7% installment note for $350,000, payable over 10 years. Maud's cost of the land was $150,000. In October 2023, after Charles had paid $60,000 on the principal of the note, he received an offer to sell the land for $500,000 cash. How can Charles minimize the present value of the tax liability for himself and Maud?

53. **LO.4** George sold land to an unrelated party in 2021. His basis in the land was $45,000, and the selling price was $120,000—$30,000 payable at closing and $30,000 (plus 10% interest) due January 1, 2022, 2023, and 2024. What would be the tax consequences of the following? [Treat each part independently, and assume that (1) George did not elect out of the installment method and (2) the installment obligations have values equal to their face amounts. Ignore interest rates in your calculations.]

   a. In 2022, George borrowed $40,000 from the bank. The loan was partially secured by the installment notes, but George was personally liable for the loan.

   b. In 2022, George gave to his daughter the right to collect all future payments on the installment obligations.

   c. On December 31, 2022, George received the payment due on January 1, 2023. On December 15, 2023, George died, and the remaining installment obligation was transferred to his estate. The estate collected the amount due on January 1, 2024.

54. **LO.5** The Wren Construction Company reports its Federal taxable income by the completed contract method. At the end of 2022, the company completed a contract to construct a building at a total cost of $800,000. The contract price was $1,200,000, and the customer paid Wren $900,000. However, the customer refused to accept the work and would not pay anything else on the contract because they claimed that the roof did not meet specifications. Wren's engineers estimated that it would cost $140,000 to bring the roof up to the customer's standards.

   In 2023, the dispute was settled in the customer's favor; the roof was improved at a cost of $150,000, and the customer accepted the building and paid the remaining $300,000.

   a. What would be the effects of the above on Wren's taxable income for 2022 and 2023?

   b. Same as part (a), except that Wren had incurred $1,100,000 of accumulated costs under the contract at the end of 2022.

55. **LO.5** Rust Company is a real estate construction company. Rust uses the completed contract method, and the contracts require 18 months to complete. Communications

   a. Which of the following costs would be allocated to construction in progress by Rust?

      1. The payroll taxes on direct labor.
      2. The current services pension costs for employees whose wages are included in direct labor.
      3. Accelerated depreciation on equipment used on contracts.
      4. Freight charges on materials assigned to contracts.
      5. The past service costs for employees whose wages are included in direct labor.
      6. Bidding expenses for contracts awarded.

   b. Assume that Rust generally builds commercial buildings under contracts with the owners and reports the income using the completed contract method. The company is considering building a series of similar stores for a retail chain. The gross profit margin would be a low percentage, but the company's gross receipts would triple. Write a letter to your client, Rust Company, explaining the tax accounting implications of entering into these contracts. Rust's mailing address is P.O. Box 1000, Harrisonburg, VA 22807.

56. **LO.5** On March 31, 2020, Big Boats Company entered into a contract with Vacations Unlimited to produce a state-of-the-art cruise ship to be completed within three years. Big Boats estimated the total cost of building the ship at $300,000,000. The contract price was $400,000,000. The ship was completed on February 15, 2023.

a. What tax accounting method must Big Boats use for the contract? Why?

b. Using the financial data provided relating to the contract's performance, complete the following schedule.

Date	Total Costs Incurred to Date	Total Percentage of Contract Completed	Current-Year Revenue Accrued	Current-Year Costs Deductible
12/31/20	$ 90,000,000	______	______	______
12/31/21	150,000,000	______	______	______
12/31/22	270,000,000	______	______	______
12/31/23	360,000,000	N/A	______	______

c. What are the consequences of the total cost of $360,000,000 exceeding the estimated total cost of $300,000,000?

57. **LO.5** Ostrich Company makes gasoline storage tanks. Everything produced is under contract (that is, the company does not produce any tanks until it gets a contract for a product). Ostrich makes three basic models. However, the tanks must be adapted to each individual customer's location and needs (e.g., the location of the valves and the quality of the materials and insulation). Discuss the following issues relative to Ostrich's operations.

a. An examining IRS agent contends that each of the company's contracts is to produce a "unique product." What difference does it make whether the product is unique or an "off-the-shelf item"?

b. Producing one of the tanks takes over one year from start to completion, and the total cost is in excess of $1,000,000. What costs must be capitalized for this contract that are not subject to capitalization for a contract with a shorter duration and lower cost?

c. What must Ostrich do with the costs of bidding on contracts?

d. Ostrich frequently makes several cost estimates for a contract, using various estimates of materials costs. These costs fluctuate almost daily. Assuming that Ostrich must use the percentage of completion method to report the income from the contract, what will be the Federal income tax consequence if the company uses the highest estimate of a contract's cost and the actual cost is closer to the lowest estimated cost?

Communications
Planning

58. **LO.5, 7** Swallow Company is a large real estate construction company that has made an S election. The company reports its income using the percentage of completion method. In 2023, the company completed a contract at a total cost of $4,800,000. The contract price was $7,200,000. At the end of 2022, the year the contract was begun, Swallow estimated that the total cost of the contract would be $5,400,000. Total accumulated cost on the contract at the end of 2022 was $1,800,000. The relevant tax rate is 35%, and the relevant Federal interest rate is 5%. Assume that all income tax returns were filed and taxes were paid on March 15 following the end of the calendar tax year.

a. Compute the gross profit on the contract for 2022 and 2023.

b. Compute the lookback interest due or receivable with the 2023 tax return. Assume the relevant interest rate is 5%.

c. Before bidding on a contract, Swallow generally makes three estimates of total contract costs: (1) optimistic, (2) pessimistic, and (3) most likely (based on a blending of optimistic and pessimistic assumptions). The company has asked you to write a letter explaining which of these estimates should be used for percentage of completion purposes.

In writing your letter, you should consider the fact that Swallow is incorporated and has made an S election. Therefore, the income and deductions flow through to the shareholders, who all are individuals in the 35% marginal tax bracket. The relevant Federal interest rate is 5%. Swallow's mailing address is 400 Front Avenue, Ashland, OR 97520.

59. **LO.6** Grouse Company is a furniture retailer whose average annual gross receipts for the three preceding years exceeded $27,000,000. In the current tax year, the company purchased merchandise with an invoice price of $15,000,000, less a 2% discount for early payment. However, the company had to borrow on a bank line of credit and paid $150,000 interest to take advantage of the discount for early payment. Freight on the merchandise purchased totaled $360,000. For September, Grouse agreed to pay the customer's freight on goods sold. The total cost of this freight-out was $70,000.

The company has three stores and operates a warehouse where it stores goods. The cost of operating the warehouse was $240,000, including labor, depreciation, taxes, and insurance on the building. The cost of the purchasing operations totaled $420,000. The jurisdiction where the company operates imposes a tax on inventories on hand as of January 1. The inventory tax for this year is $24,000. The invoice cost of goods on hand at the end of the year is $3,000,000.

Compute Grouse's ending inventory using the FIFO method.

60. **LO.6, 7** Lavender Manufacturing Company began business in the current year. The company uses the simplified method to allocate mixed services costs to production. The company's costs and expenses for the year were as follows. Decision Making

Direct labor	$ 3,000,000
Direct materials	4,000,000
Factory supervision	800,000
Property tax on factory	100,000
Personnel department	400,000
Computer operations	250,000
General administration	550,000
Marketing	800,000
State income tax	200,000
	$10,100,000

a. Determine Lavender's total production costs for the year.

b. Assume that the hourly pay for direct labor is much lower than the hourly pay for employees in general administration. Moreover, employee turnover is much higher for production employees than for general administration employees. How should these facts affect the company's decision to use the simplified mixed services method to allocate mixed services costs to production?

61. **LO.3, 6** In 2022, Gail changed from the lower of cost or market FIFO method to the LIFO inventory method. The ending inventory for 2021 was:

Item	FIFO Cost	Replacement Cost	Lower of Cost or Market
A	$26,000	$15,000	$15,000
B	52,000	55,000	52,000
C	30,000	7,000	7,000
			$74,000

Item C was damaged goods, and the replacement cost used was actually the estimated selling price of the goods. The actual cost to replace item C was $32,000.

a. What is the correct beginning inventory for 2022 under the LIFO method?

b. What immediate tax consequences (if any) will result from the switch to LIFO?

Communications
Planning

62. **LO.4, 7** Your client, Bob Garcia, is negotiating a sale of investment real estate for $12,000,000. Bob believes that the buyer would pay cash of $8,000,000 and a note for $4,000,000 or $3,000,000 cash and a note for $9,000,000. The notes will pay interest at slightly above the market rate. Bob realizes that the second option involves more risks of collection, but he is willing to accept that risk if the tax benefits of the installment sale are substantial.

Write a letter to Bob advising him of the tax consequences of choosing the lower down payment and larger note balance, assuming that he has no other installment receivables. Bob's address is 200 Jerdone, Gettysburg, PA 17325.

63. **LO.2, 4** Ven Company is a retailer. In 2022, its before-tax net income for financial reporting purposes was $600,000. This included a $150,000 gain from the sale of land held for several years as a possible plant site. The cost of the land was $100,000, the contract price for the sale was $250,000, and the company collected $120,000 in the year of sale. The income per books also included $90,000 from a 24-month service contract entered into in July 2021 (the customer paid $180,000 in advance for this contract). The addition to the allowance for uncollectible accounts for the year was $70,000, and the actual accounts written off totaled $40,000.

Make the necessary adjustments to the before-tax net income per books to compute Ven's taxable income for the year.

Research Problems

the answer company™ THOMSON REUTERS®

Note: Solutions to the Research Problems can be prepared by using the Thomson Reuters Checkpoint™ online tax research database, which accompanies this textbook. Solutions can also be prepared by using research materials found in a typical tax library.

Research Problem 1. You recently engaged with a new client that operates a chain of convenience stores that sell food and vehicle fuel. You notice that the company uses a customer card program where customer purchases of fuel are entered on the card. For each gallon purchased, the customer is allowed a $0.05 discount per gallon purchased within the next three months. The client treats the $0.05 discount as "earned" by the customer (and deductible by the store) when the purchase is made, which gives the customer the right to the discount. The client justifies this as clearly reflecting the company's income because an obligation arises when the gasoline is purchased and the right to the future discount is earned. Is the client's tax accounting method correct? Explain.

Research Problem 2. Your client, Vernon Jones, is a self-employed attorney. Vernon uses the cash method of accounting. In reviewing his accounting records to get ready to prepare his tax return for the current year, you find an entry in December about a lost check. In discussing this with Vernon, you learn that a client wrote him a check for $82,000 for services Vernon provided. Unfortunately, Vernon lost the check and still is waiting for a replacement check from the client. Communications

Is the $82,000 gross income in the year Vernon received the check that he lost, or is it taxed in the subsequent year when he receives the replacement check? Summarize your findings in an e-mail to your instructor.

Research Problem 3. In 2022, your client, Clear Corporation, changed from the cash to the accrual method of accounting for its radio stations. The company had a positive § 481 adjustment of $2,400,000 as a result of the change and began amortizing the adjustment in 2022.

In 2023, Clear received an offer to purchase the assets of the radio station business (this would be considered a sale of a trade or business under § 1060). If the offer is accepted, Clear plans to use the proceeds to purchase a satellite television business. Clear has asked you to explain the consequences of the sale of the radio station operation on the amortization of the § 481 adjustment.

Use internet tax resources to address the following questions. Look for reliable websites and blogs of the IRS and other government agencies, media outlets, businesses, tax professionals, academics, think tanks, and political outlets.

Research Problem 4. The U.S. tax system allows many businesses to use the cash method of accounting. Find another country that allows some businesses to use the cash method, and explain how that system compares to the U.S. system. E-mail your answer to your instructor, also noting the country and the references you used. Communications

Research Problem 5. More than one U.S. president and others have called for repeal of the LIFO method for Federal income tax purposes. Find technical arguments for and against such legislation. Summarize these arguments and e-mail this document to your instructor. Provide citations for the items that you found. Communications

Becker CPA Review Question

1. Paula has sales that qualify to be reported on the installment basis. In year 2, installment sales were $40,000 with a cost of $30,000. In year 3, installment sales were $50,000 with a cost of $25,000. Collections in year 2 were in the amount of $30,000. Collections in year 3 were $10,000 on the year 2 sales and $30,000 on the year 3 sales. How much deferred gross profit exists as of the end of year 2?

   a. $2,500
   b. $5,000
   c. $7,500
   d. $10,000

Chapter

19 Deferred Compensation

Learning Objectives: *After completing Chapter 19, you should be able to:*

- **LO.1** Distinguish between qualified (defined contribution and defined benefit) and nonqualified compensation arrangements.
- **LO.2** Identify qualification requirements for qualified plans.
- **LO.3** Discuss tax consequences of qualified plans.
- **LO.4** Calculate limitations on contributions to and benefits from qualified plans.
- **LO.5** Explain the qualified plans available to a self-employed person.
- **LO.6** Describe benefits of the different types of Individual Retirement Accounts (IRAs).
- **LO.7** Review the rationale for nonqualified deferred compensation plans and the related tax treatment.
- **LO.8** Differentiate the tax treatment of qualified and nonqualified stock options.
- **LO.9** Identify tax planning opportunities available with deferred compensation.

Chapter Outline

19-1 Qualified Pension, Profit Sharing, Stock Bonus, and Cash Balance Plans, 19-2
- 19-1a Types of Plans, 19-2
- 19-1b Qualification Requirements, 19-4
- 19-1c Tax Consequences to the Employee and Employer, 19-8
- 19-1d Limitations on Contribitions to and Benefits from Qualified Plans, 19-9
- 19-1e Section 401(k) Plans, 19-10

19-2 Retirement Plans for Self-Employed Individuals, 19-11
- 19-2a Keogh (H.R. 10) Plans, 19-11
- 19-2b Solo § 401(k) Plans, 19-12
- 19-2c Savings Incentive Match Plan for Employees (SIMPLE Plans), 19-12
- 19-2d Simplified Employee Pension Plans (SEPs), 19-12

19-3 Individual Retirement Accounts (IRAs), 19-13
- 19-3a General Rules, 19-13
- 19-3b Taxation of Benefits, 19-16
- 19-3c Rollovers and Conversions, 19-17

19-4 Nonqualified Deferred Compensation Plans, 19-18
- 19-4a Underlying Rationale for Tax Treatment, 19-18
- 19-4b Tax Treatment to the Employer and Employee, 19-18

19-5 Stock Options, 19-19
- 19-5a Incentive Stock Options, 19-19
- 19-5b Nonqualified Stock Options, 19-22

19-6 Tax Planning, 19-23
- 19-6a Qualified Plans, 19-23
- 19-6b Self-Employed Retirement Plans, 19-23
- 19-6c Individual Retirement Accounts, 19-23
- 19-6d Comparison of § 401(k) Plan with IRA, 19-24
- 19-6e Nonqualified Deferred Compensation (NQDC) Plans, 19-24
- 19-6f Stock Options, 19-25
- 19-6g Liquidating Retirement Assets, 19-26

FIZKES/SHUTTERSTOCK.COM

The Big Picture

A Taxpayer Who Saves

Maggie is a junior finance major at State University. Recently, Dr. Sanchez, the professor in her finance class, delivered a lecture on retirement savings that emphasized the need for a long-term savings horizon and multiple retirement plans. Near the end of the lecture, Dr. Sanchez mentioned that she has four different retirement plans. Maggie was surprised to hear this because she knows that her father has only a single retirement plan that is provided by his employer (an automobile manufacturer).

Maggie drops in on the professor during office hours. Her goal is to find out more about how someone can participate in multiple retirement plans. What are some facts that would be helpful for Maggie to consider?

Read the chapter and formulate your response.

Personnel retirement considerations are an essential feature of any compensation arrangement. From a tax policy perspective, providing retirement security for employees can be justified on both economic and social grounds. Because the public sector pension (i.e., Social Security) typically will not provide sufficient funding for many recipients, the private sector might be called upon to fill the need.

Thus, Congress has incentivized private long-term savings by enacting various measures that provide significant tax advantages for creating and funding employee retirement plans. Almost $40 trillion are invested in private retirement accounts that benefit individuals.

When the appropriate retirement plans are used by employers and employees, the Federal income tax advantages are substantial and include the following.

- Plan contributions that are deductible by the corporation, with individuals not taxed on these contributions until they take distributions,
- Income earned on the contributions that is not subject to tax until distributed (thus growing at a pretax rate of return), and
- Employer contributions to and benefits payable under qualified plans that generally are not subject to payroll taxes.

Although a wide variety of **deferred compensation** plans exist, this chapter focuses on the most popular qualified retirement plans: (1) pension, profit-sharing, and § 401(k) plans; (2) Individual Retirement Accounts (available to any person who has earned income); and (3) plans available to self-employed individuals, including Keogh plans (also known as H.R. 10 plans), Solo § 401(k) plans, Saving Incentive Match Plans for Employees (SIMPLE) plans, and Simplified Employee Pension (SEP) plans. See Concept Summary 19.1.

LO.1

Distinguish between qualified (defined contribution and defined benefit) and nonqualified compensation arrangements.

19-1 Qualified Pension, Profit Sharing, Stock Bonus, and Cash Balance Plans

To ensure that retirees will not be dependent solely on government programs later in life, the tax law incentivized private pension and profit sharing plans. Federal tax law provides substantial tax benefits for plans that meet certain requirements (*qualified plans*). The major requirement for qualification is that a plan not discriminate in favor of highly compensated employees.

19-1a Types of Plans

Pension Plans

A **pension plan** is a deferred compensation arrangement that provides for systematic payments of definite and determinable retirement benefits to employees who meet the requirements of the plan. Employer contributions to a qualified pension plan must *not* depend on profits. A pension plan normally must pay out benefits as lifetime annuities to provide on-going income for retired employees.

Qualified retirement plans generally are constructed as *defined benefit plans* or *defined contribution plans*.

A **defined benefit plan** includes a formula that defines the *benefits* employees are to receive.[1] Benefits generally are measured by and based on such factors as years of service and employee compensation. Under such a plan, an employer must make annual contributions based upon actuarial computations that will be sufficient to fund the retirement benefits. If permitted by the plan, employees may make their own contributions to the pension fund. A separate account is not maintained for the employer's contributions on behalf of each participant.

A defined benefit plan provides some sense of security for employees because the future payments may be expressed in fixed dollar amounts. In a defined benefit plan, the employer (not the employee) assumes all market risk because the employer promises to pay fixed benefits.

[1] § 414(j).

A **defined contribution pension plan** (or money purchase plan) defines the amount the employer is required to *contribute* (e.g., a flat dollar amount, an amount based on a special formula, or an amount equal to a certain percentage of compensation).[2] A separate account is maintained for each participant. Benefits are based solely on (1) the amount contributed and (2) income from the fund that accrues to the participant's account.[3] Consequently, actuarial calculations are not required to determine the employer's annual contribution. Upon retirement, an employee's payment amount depends on the value in the account. The plan may require or permit employee contributions to the fund.

Example 1

The qualified pension plan of Rose Company calls for both the employer and the employee to contribute annually to the pension trust an amount equal to 5% of the employee's compensation. Because the employer's rate of contribution is fixed, this is a defined contribution plan. If the plan called for contributions sufficient to provide retirement benefits equal to 30% of the employee's average salary for the last five years of employment, it is a defined benefit plan.

Concept Summary 19.1 compares and contrasts a defined benefit plan and a defined contribution plan.

Concept Summary 19.1

Defined Benefit Plan and Defined Contribution Plan Compared

Defined Benefit Plan	Defined Contribution Plan
Determinable benefits based upon years of service and average compensation. Benefits calculated by a formula.	An account for each participant. Ultimate benefits depend upon contributions and investment performance.
Maximum annual *benefits* payable may not exceed the smaller of (1) $245,000 (in 2022)* or (2) 100% of the participant's average earnings in the three highest years of employment.	Maximum annual *contribution* to an account may not exceed the smaller of (1) $61,000** (in 2022) or (2) 100% of the participant's compensation (25% for a profit sharing plan, money purchase plan, or stock bonus plan).
Employer bears the investment risk and reward.	Employee bears the investment risk and reward.
Forfeitures must reduce subsequent funding costs and cannot increase the benefits any participant can receive under the plan.	Forfeitures may be allocated to the accounts of remaining participants.
Subject to minimum funding requirement to avoid penalties.	Exempt from funding requirements.
Greater administrative and actuarial costs and greater reporting requirements.	Costs and reporting requirements less burdensome.
More favorable to employees who are older when plan is adopted because it is possible to fund higher benefits over a shorter period.	More favorable to younger employees because over a longer period, higher benefits may result.
*This amount is subject to indexing annually in $5,000 increments.	**This amount is subject to indexing annually in $1,000 increments.

Profit Sharing Plans

A **profit sharing plan** is a deferred compensation arrangement established and maintained by an employer to provide for employee participation in the company's profits. Contributions are paid from the employer to a trustee, commingled in a single trust fund; a separate account is maintained for each participant.[4] Annual employer contributions are not required.

Stock Bonus Plans

A **stock bonus plan** is another form of deferred compensation. The employer establishes and maintains the plan, to which it contributes shares of its own stock. The contributions need not be dependent on the employer's profits.[5]

[2]The majority of employee pension plans today are defined contribution plans.

[3]§ 414(i).

[4]Reg. §§ 1.401–1(b) and 1.401–4(a)(1)(iii).

[5]Reg. § 1.401–1(b)(1)(iii).

Cash Balance Plans

A **cash balance plan** is a hybrid form of a defined benefit plan that is funded by the employee. Like a defined contribution plan, a cash balance plan accrues benefits to individual accounts, and the benefits for an employee depend on how much builds up over time in the employee's account.

Ethics & Equity **Switching from Defined Benefit to Defined Contribution Pension Plans**

Over the years, there has been a major switch from the defined benefit to the defined contribution plan by corporate employers. This trend was initiated largely to reduce the costs of providing retirement income to employees. The trend shifts the longevity and investment risks from the employer to the employee.

Longevity risk refers to the risk that an employee will outlive their retirement funds. How ethical is it for employers to shift important investment risks to the employee through this unilateral change in the type of plan offered? Are employees aware of and able to make investment decisions in an effective manner under this arrangement? Because employees have different abilities in making investment decisions, is the likelihood now greater that a typical employee will "outlive their assets"?

LO.2

Identify qualification requirements for qualified plans.

19-1b Qualification Requirements

To be *qualified*, and thereby to receive favorable tax treatment, a plan generally must satisfy all of the following requirements.

- Nondiscrimination requirements.
- Participation and coverage requirements.
- Vesting requirements.
- Distribution requirements.
- Minimum funding requirements.

Nondiscrimination Requirements

Contributions and benefits under a plan must *not discriminate* in favor of highly compensated employees. A plan is not considered discriminatory merely because contributions and benefits are proportional to compensation.[6] For example, a pension plan that provides for the allocation of employer contributions based upon a flat 3 percent of each employee's compensation would not be discriminatory solely because highly paid employees receive greater benefits.

Participation and Coverage Requirements

A qualified plan must provide, at a minimum, that all employees in the covered group who are 21 years of age be eligible to participate after completing one year of service. A year of service generally is defined as the completion of 1,000 hours of service within a measuring period of 12 consecutive months. As an alternative, where the plan provides that 100 percent of an employee's accrued benefits will be vested upon entering the plan, the employee's participation may be postponed until the later of age 21 or two years from the date of employment. Part-time employees may participate if they have worked either 1,000 hours in one year or 500 hours in three consecutive years.

Once the age and service requirements are met, an employee must be allowed to participate no later than the *earlier* of:

- The first day of the first plan year beginning after the date on which the requirements were satisfied.
- Six months after the date on which the requirements were satisfied.[7]

[6] §§ 401(a)(4) and (5).

[7] §§ 410(a)(1)(A) and (B) and 410(a)(4).

Example 2

Coffee Corporation offers a calendar year retirement plan covering its employees. The corporation adopts the most restrictive eligibility rules permitted. Melanie, age 21, is hired on January 31, 2021, and meets the service requirement over the next 12 months (completes at least 1,000 hours by January 31, 2022). Melanie must be included in this plan no later than July 31, 2022, because the six-month limitation would be applicable. If the company had adopted the two-year participation rule, Melanie must be included in the plan no later than July 31, 2023.

Because a qualified plan must operate primarily for the benefit of employees and be nondiscriminatory, the plan must cover a reasonable percentage of the company employees. A plan will be qualified only if it satisfies one of the following tests.[8]

- The plan benefits a percentage of non-highly compensated employees equal to at least 70 percent of the percentage of highly compensated employees benefiting under the plan (the *ratio percentage test*). In other words, the plan must benefit a percentage of the non-highly paid employees, equal to at least 70 percent of the highly paid employees who benefit under the same plan.
- The plan meets the *average benefits test*, described below.

If a company has no highly compensated employees, the retirement plan automatically is nondiscriminatory.

Example 3

Singh Corporation has 2 highly paid employees (HPEs) and 20 non-highly paid employees (NHPEs). If this plan covers both of the HPEs, for the NHPEs to qualify, the plan must cover at least 14 of them (70% × 20). If the plan covers only one of the HPEs, the plan must cover at least 7 of the NHPEs (70% × 50% = 35% × 20).

To satisfy the *average benefits test*, the nondiscriminatory plan must benefit any employees who qualify under a classification set up by the employer. In addition, the average benefit percentage for non-highly compensated employees must be at least 70 percent of the average benefit percentage for highly compensated employees. The *average benefit percentage*, with respect to any group of employees, is the average of the benefit percentages calculated separately for each employee in the group. The *benefit percentage* includes the employer-provided contributions or benefits of an employee under all qualified plans of the employer, expressed as a percentage of that employee's compensation.

An employee is a **highly compensated employee** if, at any time during the year or the preceding year, the employee satisfies *either* of the following tests.[9]

- Was a 5 percent owner of the company.
- Received more than $135,000 (in 2022) in annual compensation from the employer *and* was a member of the top-paid group of the employer.[10] An employee whose compensation is in the top 20 percent of all of the employees is a member of the top-paid group.

An additional *minimum participation test* also must be met for some plans. A plan must cover at least 40 percent of all employees or, if fewer, at least 50 employees on one representative day of the plan year. For this purpose, nonresident aliens, certain union members, and employees not fulfilling the minimum age or years-of-service requirement of the plan may be excluded.[11]

Example 4

Assume that Rust Corporation's retirement plan meets the 70% test (the ratio percentage test) because 70% of all non-highly compensated employees benefit. The company has 100 employees, but only 38 of these employees are covered by the plan. The Rust retirement plan does not meet the minimum participation requirement.

---

[8] § 410(b).

[9] §§ 401(a)(4) and 414(q).

[10] The threshold amount can be adjusted annually in $5,000 increments.

[11] §§ 401(a)(26) and 410(b)(3) and (4). § 7701(b) defines a nonresident alien as an individual who is neither a citizen nor a resident of the United States.

Vesting Requirements

The **vesting requirements** protect an employee who has worked a reasonable period of time for an employer from losing employer contributions and net investment gains because of being fired or changing jobs. An employee's right to accrued benefits derived from their own contributions to a defined benefit plan must be nonforfeitable from the date of contribution. The accrued benefits derived from employer contributions must be nonforfeitable in accordance with one of *two alternative minimum vesting schedules* or any more generous customized vesting schedule.

To satisfy the *first alternative*, a participant must have a nonforfeitable right to 100 percent of their accrued benefits derived from employer contributions upon completion of not more than five years of service (five-year or cliff vesting). The *second alternative* is satisfied if a participant has a nonforfeitable right at least equal to a percentage of the accrued benefits derived from employer contributions as depicted in Exhibit 19.1 (graded vesting).

Example 5

Terrell has six years of service completed as of February 2, 2022, his employment anniversary date. If his defined benefit plan has a five-year (cliff) vesting schedule, 100% of Terrell's accrued benefits are vested. If the plan uses the graded vesting rule, Terrell's nonforfeitable percentage is 80%.

Defined contribution plans also must satisfy one of the following minimum vesting schedules: two- to six-year graded vesting as shown in Exhibit 19.2, three-year cliff vesting, or any more generous vesting schedule.

Example 6

Minh has five years of service completed as of February 2, 2022, her employment anniversary date. If her defined contribution plan uses three-year cliff vesting, Minh must be 100% vested. Under a two- to six-year vesting plan, Minh must be 80% vested.

Exhibit 19.1 Three- to Seven-Year Vesting for Defined Benefit Plans

Years of Service	Nonforfeitable Percentage
3	20%
4	40%
5	60%
6	80%
7 or more	100%

Exhibit 19.2 Two- to Six-Year Vesting for Defined Contribution Plans

Years of Service	Nonforfeitable Percentage
2	20%
3	40%
4	60%
5	80%
6 or more	100%

Distribution Requirements

Required minimum distribution (RMD) rules exist for all qualified defined benefit and defined contribution plans, traditional Individual Retirement Accounts (IRAs), and certain other qualified plans. Distributions to a participant must begin by April 1 of the calendar year following *the later* of (1) the calendar year in which the employee attains age 72 or (2) the calendar year in which the employee retires. Beginning with the second distribution, the withdrawal must be made by December 31.[12]

The RMD amount is determined by taking the account balance at the end of the prior year and dividing that amount by the number of years left in the owner's life expectancy, using a table provided by the IRS. The table is updated over time as changes in overall life expectancies are observed. An updated table is in effect for distributions starting in 2022. See Exhibit 19.3.

[12] § 401(a)(9). Age 70½ is used if the taxpayer was born before July 1, 1949. These distribution requirements do not apply to Roth IRAs.

Exhibit 19.3 Selected RMD Factors from IRS Table

Age of Recipient	Distributions Prior to 2022	Distribution after 2021
74	23.8	25.5
75	22.9	24.6
76	22.0	23.7
77	21.2	22.9
78	20.3	22.0
79	19.5	21.1

The RMD amount is determined by the individual every year. The provision is designed so that the income tax deferral afforded by the retirement plan comes to an end later in one's life, as distributions must be made.

Example 7

Singh is age 79, and the balance in his traditional IRA account is $240,000 at the end of the prior year. The distribution occurs for 2022, so the pertinent RMD factor is 21.1. Singh must withdraw $11,374.41 ($240,000 ÷ 21.1) from the IRA for this year.

Failure to make a required minimum distribution results in a *50 percent nondeductible excise tax* on the excess in any taxable year of the amount that should have been distributed over the amount that actually was distributed. This tax is imposed on the individual required to take the distribution (the payee).[13] The IRS can waive the tax for a given taxpayer year if the taxpayer is able to establish that the shortfall is due to reasonable error and that reasonable steps are being taken to remedy the shortfall.

Inherited IRAs When an individual dies before distributing the entire IRA balance, an "inherited IRA" is created, allowing a further deferral of the gross income caused by distributions from the account. The heir to the account must withdraw the full balance from the inherited IRA by the end of the tenth anniversary of the decedent's death, with no limitations on the dates or amounts of these distributions. If the heir is the decedent's surviving spouse, the distributions can be made using the Exhibit 19.3 table over the remainder of their own life. The ability to extend the deferral of gross income from an inherited IRA causes some advisers to call the heir's account a "stretch IRA."

Example 8

Deb dies on December 31, 2022, when the balance in her IRA is $300,000. Nico is the heir to the IRA and retitles the account in his own name. If Nico was Deb's husband, he could take RMDs using the Exhibit 19.3 table over his own life expectancy. If Nico was not the surviving spouse, he must take distributions so that the account balance is zero by December 31, 2032.

Penalties for Early Distribution If a taxpayer receives an *early distribution* from a qualified retirement plan, a 10 percent additional tax is levied on the full amount of any distribution includible in gross income.[14] The following distributions, however, are *not* treated as early distributions.

- Distributions made on or after the date the employee attains age 59½.
- Distributions made to a beneficiary (or the estate of an employee) on or after the death of the employee.
- Distributions attributable to the employee's being disabled.
- Distributions made as part of a scheduled series of substantially equal periodic payments (made not less frequently than annually) for the life of the participant (or the joint lives of the participant and the participant's beneficiary).
- Distributions made to an employee after separation from service because of early retirement under the plan after attaining age 55. This exception does not apply to a traditional IRA.

[13] § 4974(a).

[14] § 72(t). See Ltr.Rul. 8837071.

Ethics & Equity **Vesting and Withdrawal Rules**

Employees are changing jobs more often, and there is less loyalty from companies to their employees and employees to their companies. Should the vesting periods be shortened, so as not to penalize someone who "job hops"?

If a taxpayer receives early distributions from a qualified retirement plan, there is a 10 percent additional tax on the total amount of the distribution includible in gross income.

Are such severe penalties relative to retirement distributions fair, especially considering that members of minorities have shorter life expectancies than do other individuals?

- Distributions used to pay deductible medical expenses (whether or not the taxpayer itemizes deductions).
- IRA distributions that are used to pay qualified higher education expenses of the taxpayer, the spouse, or any child or grandchild of the taxpayer or the taxpayer's spouse.
- IRA distributions up to $10,000 that are used to pay expenses incurred by qualified first-time homebuyers.

LO.3

Discuss tax consequences of qualified plans.

19-1c Tax Consequences to the Employee and Employer

Although employer contributions to qualified plans generally are deductible immediately, these amounts are not subject to taxation until distributed to employees.[15] When benefits are distributed to employees or paid with respect to an employee, the employer does not receive another deduction.

The tax benefit to the employee amounts to a substantial tax deferral and may be viewed as an interest-free loan from the government to the plan. Another advantage of a qualified plan is that any income earned by the plan is not taxable when earned.[16] Employees, in effect, are taxed on such earnings when they receive the retirement benefits.

The taxation of amounts received by employees in periodic or installment payments generally follows the annuity rules (see text Section 4-4c). Alternatively, a taxpayer may (1) receive the distribution in a lump-sum payment or (2) roll over the benefits into an IRA or another qualified retirement plan.

Lump-Sum Distributions from Qualified Plans

A **lump-sum distribution** occurs when an employee receives an entire payout from a qualified plan in a single payment rather than receiving the amount in installments. All such payments are taxed in the distribution year. Because lump-sum payments have been accumulated over a number of years, bunching retirement benefits into one taxable year may impose a high Federal income tax burden.

Rollover Treatment

A taxpayer who receives a distribution can avoid current income taxation by rolling the distribution into another qualified employer retirement plan or into an IRA.[17] The taxation of the distribution is deferred until distributions are made from the recipient's qualified employer retirement plan or IRA. See text Section 19-3c.

A rollover can be *direct* with the balance in the account going directly from a qualified employer retirement plan to another qualified employer retirement plan or an IRA (sometimes called a conversion). The rollover can be *indirect* with the proceeds going to the taxpayer, who then has 60 days to transfer the proceeds into another qualified employer retirement plan or an IRA. One can use an indirect rollover to borrow from an IRA, but the "loan" must be fully reinvested in another retirement plan or IRA within the 60-day window so that the amount will not be taxable. An indirect rollover is subject to a 20 percent withholding requirement.[18]

[15] § 402(a)(1).

[16] § 501(a).

[17] § 402(c).

[18] § 3405(c).

19-1d Limitations on Contributions to and Benefits from Qualified Plans

LO.4

Calculate limitations on contributions to and benefits from qualified plans.

The annual limitations on contributions to and benefits from qualified plans may affect the amount the employer is willing to contribute to the plan; the plan is not allowed a deduction for the amount that exceeds these limitations.[19]

Defined Contribution Plans

Under a *defined contribution plan*, the annual addition to an employee's account cannot exceed the lesser of $61,000 (in 2022) or 100 percent of the employee's compensation.[20] However, the employer's deduction limit cannot exceed 25 percent of eligible compensation for all participants.[21]

Defined Benefit Plans

Under a *defined benefit plan*, the annual benefit payable to an employee is limited to the smaller of $245,000 (in 2022)[22] or 100 percent of the employee's average compensation for the highest three years of employment. This benefit limit is subject to a $10,000 *de minimis* floor. The $245,000 limitation is reduced actuarially if the benefits begin before the Social Security normal retirement age (age 66 for taxpayers born from 1942 through 1954); it is increased actuarially if the benefits begin after the Social Security normal retirement age. The dollar limit on annual benefits is reduced by one-tenth for each year of *participation* under 10 years by the employee. The 100 percent of compensation limitation and the $10,000 *de minimis* floor similarly are reduced proportionately for a participant who has less than 10 years of service with the employer.[23]

The Big Picture

Example 9

Return to the facts of *The Big Picture* on p. 19-1. The university has offered Maggie's professor, Dr. Sanchez, a choice between a defined benefit pension plan and a defined contribution plan. Dr. Sanchez expects to work at a number of universities during her career. A colleague has recommended that Dr. Sanchez choose the defined contribution plan because of its portability (i.e., she can take the plan with her to a new job). So she needs to decide if the portability factor is significant in making her choice, and how much she can contribute annually to a defined contribution plan.

Defined Benefit Limitations

Example 10

Adam's average compensation for the highest three years of employment is $87,000. The defined benefit plan will not qualify if the plan provides for benefits in excess of the smaller of (1) $87,000 or (2) $245,000 for Adam in 2022.

Example 11

Peggy has participated for four years in a defined benefit plan and has six years of service with her employer. Her average compensation for the three highest years is $60,000. Her four years of participation reduce her maximum dollar benefit to $98,000 ($245,000 × 4/10). Her six years of service reduce her 100% of compensation limitation to 60%. Therefore, her limit on annual benefits is $36,000 ($60,000 × 60%).

When calculating the average of the three highest years of compensation, the annual compensation that may be taken into account under any plan is limited to $305,000 (in 2022).[24] Thus, the benefits that highly compensated individuals receive may be smaller as a percentage of their pay than those received by non-highly compensated employees.

---

[19] § 404(j).

[20] §§ 415(c) and (d).

[21] § 415(d)(4). This amount is indexed (in $1,000 increments).

[22] This amount is indexed annually in $5,000 increments.

[23] § 415(b).

[24] §§ 401(a)(17) and 404(l). This amount is indexed in $5,000 increments.

Example 12

Swan Corporation has adopted a defined contribution plan with 10% annual contributions. An employee earning less than $305,000 in 2022 would not be affected by this includible compensation limitation (the contribution limit is $30,500 = $305,000 × 10%).

However, an employee earning $488,000 in 2022 would have only 6.25% of compensation allocated to their account because of the limit on includible compensation (6.25% × $488,000 = $30,500).

Although its contributions are deductible in the tax year such amounts are allocated or credited to the pension plan, the employer may defer the actual payment of the contributions until its Federal income tax return filing date, including extensions.[25]

A 10 percent excise tax is imposed on nondeductible contributions. The tax is levied on the employer making the contribution. The tax applies to nondeductible contributions for the current year and any nondeductible contributions for the preceding year that have not been eliminated by the end of the current year (as a carryover or by being returned to the employer in the current year).[26]

19-1e Section 401(k) Plans

A **§ 401(k) plan** is offered by many businesses to provide retirement assets for their employees. The plans are popular and make up about 20 percent of all retirement assets, or more than $7 trillion. About 60 million individuals participate in a § 401(k) plan.

Both employers and employees can contribute to a § 401(k) plan. A participant can elect either to receive up to $20,500 in 2022[27] in cash (taxed currently) or to have a contribution made on their behalf to the retirement plan. Many employers encourage their personnel to contribute to the § 401(k) plan by providing a full or partial match of any funds contributed by the employee; a match like this increases the employee's total compensation and encourages a long-term investment in their future well-being.

Any employee-elected § 401(k) contributions are excluded from gross income in the year of the deferral; they are 100 percent vested on behalf of the employee. Like employer plan contributions, employee contributions are tax-deferred until distributed, as are earnings on those contributions. The qualified plan vesting provisions apply to employer contributions and investment earnings.

Most employees are covered when a § 401(k) plan is in place. An employer can exclude from participation in the § 401(k) plan an employee who has not reached age 21, has not completed one year of service, or who has not completed 1,000 hours of service for the year. A long-time part-time employee (i.e., one who has worked at least 500 hours for three consecutive years) must be allowed to participate in the plan.

Example 13

Alejandro participates in the § 401(k) plan of his employer. The plan permits the participants to choose between a full salary or a reduced salary where the reduction becomes a pretax contribution to a retirement plan. Alejandro elects to contribute 10% of his annual compensation of $40,000 to the plan. Current-year income taxes are paid by Alejandro only on $36,000. No income taxes are paid on the $4,000 until it is distributed from the plan to Alejandro. In this way, the § 401(k) plan allows Alejandro to shift a portion of his income to a later taxable year.

Elective contributions in excess of the maximum limitation are taxable in the year of deferral. These amounts may be refunded from the plan tax-free before April 15 of the following year. Annual elective contributions also are limited by nondiscrimination requirements designed to encourage participation by non-highly compensated employees and by the general defined contribution plan limitations.

A person who has attained age 50 by the end of 2022 can make annual catch-up contributions of an additional $6,500.[28]

A qualified automatic enrollment arrangement allows employers to enroll employees automatically in a § 401(k) plan, with a prescribed contribution (not to

[25] §§ 404(a)(1) and (6).

[26] § 4972.

[27] §§ 402(g)(1) and (4). This amount was $19,500 in 2021 and 2020 and $19,000 in 2019.

[28] The catch-up contribution amount is indexed in $500 increments.

exceed 10 percent) of the employee's pay withdrawn from each paycheck (unless the employee elects to "opt out"). This contribution percentage must be applied uniformly to all eligible employees. A small employer may receive a tax credit for establishing a new qualified retirement plan that includes automatic enrollment; see text Section 13-3f.

19-2 Retirement Plans for Self-Employed Individuals

LO.5

Explain the qualified plans available to a self-employed person.

A wide variety of retirement plans are available to self-employed individuals. These parties can establish a Keogh plan (also known as an H.R. 10 plan), a Solo § 401(k) plan, a Savings Incentive Match Plan for Employees (SIMPLE plan), or a Simplified Employee Pension plan (SEP).

19-2a Keogh (H.R. 10) Plans

Keogh plans are the self-employed equivalent of corporate pension plans. A Keogh plan covers the self-employed party, and it can extend to other employees of the business. These plans must be administered by an independent trustee, but if an individual elects to make all investment decisions for the plan, a *self-directed Keogh plan* is established. In such a case, the individual may prefer to invest the funds with a financial institution such as a broker, bank, or mutual fund. Investment in most collectibles is not allowed in a self-directed Keogh plan.

Contribution Limitations

A self-employed individual may contribute annually to a *defined contribution* Keogh plan the smaller of $61,000 in 2022 ($58,000 in 2021) or 100 percent of earned income.[29] Under a *defined benefit* Keogh plan, the annual benefit payable to an employee or a self-employed person is limited to the smaller of $245,000 in 2022 ($230,000 in 2021) or 100 percent of the individual's average compensation for the three highest years of employment.[30]

Earned income equals one's net earnings from self-employment[31] (i.e., the gross income derived from a trade or business less appropriate deductions).[32] Earned income is reduced by contributions to a Keogh plan on the individual's behalf and by 50 percent of any self-employment tax.[33]

Example 14

Pat, a sole proprietor, has earned income of $150,000 in 2022 (after the deduction for one-half of self-employment tax). The maximum contribution Pat may make to a defined contribution Keogh plan is $61,000, the lesser of $150,000 or $61,000.

Although a Keogh plan must be established before the end of the year in question, contributions may be made up to the tax return filing date for that year. Self-employed individuals who hire employees may want to choose a different retirement plan, since a Keogh plan must provide retirement benefits to all employees on a nondiscriminatory basis (i.e., the sole proprietor's employees also must be covered by the Keogh plan). This requirement could be a substantial cost to the owner. Thus, a sole proprietor with few or no employees is an ideal candidate for a Keogh plan.

The Big Picture

Example 15

Return to the facts of *The Big Picture* on p. 19-1. Maggie's professor, Dr. Sanchez, has a forensic consulting practice in addition to her position at the university. Sanchez also receives book royalties from a textbook. Because Sanchez is self-employed (she will report her earnings on a Schedule C), she can establish a Keogh plan with respect to these earnings.

[29] § 415(c)(1).

[30] § 415(b)(1). This amount is indexed annually.

[31] § 401(c)(2).

[32] § 1402(a).

[33] §§ 401(c)(2)(A)(v) and 164(f).

19-2b Solo § 401(k) Plans

A Solo § 401(k) plan is designed for self-employed individuals with no employees. Because the compensation deferred as part of a § 401(k) plan does not count toward the 20 percent limit for Keogh plans, the proprietor can defer the maximum amount of compensation under the § 401(k) plan and contribute an additional 20 percent of self-employment income to the Keogh plan.[34]

Example 16

Dan is 35 years old and is a sole proprietor. His net earnings from self-employment in 2022 are $100,000. Dan sets up a Solo § 401(k) plan for his retirement. Dan can contribute $20,000 (20% of $100,000) to a Keogh plan and make a § 401(k) elective deferral contribution up to $20,500 for 2022. As a result, Dan can make total retirement contributions of $40,500 ($20,000 + $20,500, which is less than the maximum combined amount allowed of $61,000).

19-2c Savings Incentive Match Plan for Employees (SIMPLE Plans)

Employers with 100 or fewer employees who do not maintain another qualified retirement plan may establish a *savings incentive match plan for employees* (SIMPLE plan).[35] The plan can be in the form of a § 401(k) plan or an IRA. A SIMPLE § 401(k) plan is not subject to the nondiscrimination rules that usually apply to § 401(k) plans.

All employees who received at least $5,000 in compensation from the employer during any two preceding years and who reasonably expect to receive at least $5,000 in compensation during the current year must be eligible to participate in the plan. The decision to participate is that of the employee.

The contributions made by the employee (a salary-reduction approach) must be expressed as a percentage of compensation, not as a fixed dollar amount. The SIMPLE plan must not permit the SIMPLE elective employee contribution for the year to exceed $14,000 in 2022 ($13,500 in 2021).[36] The SIMPLE elective deferral limit is increased under the catch-up provision for employees age 50 and over. The catch-up amount is $3,000 in 2022 (the same as in 2021).[37]

Generally, the employer must either match elective employee contributions up to 3 percent of the employee's compensation or provide nonmatching contributions of 2 percent of compensation.

No other contributions may be made to the plan other than the employee elective contribution and the required employer matching contribution (or nonmatching contribution under the 2 percent rule). All contributions are fully vested on behalf of the employee.

19-2d Simplified Employee Pension Plans (SEPs)

Simplified Employee Pensions—referred to as SEPs or SEP-IRAs—are retirement plans that allow the proprietor to deduct up to 20 percent of self-employment income.[38]

As with Keogh and Solo § 401(k) plans, the maximum deduction allowed is $61,000 in 2022 ($58,000 in 2021). SEPs are simple to establish and administer, and costs are minimal. Overall, SEPs are as easy to administer as deductible IRAs but have a higher annual contribution limit. See Concept Summary 19.2.

[34] Reg. § 1.401(k)–1(a)(6)(ii).

[35] § 408(p).

[36] The $14,000 statutory amount is indexed for inflation in $500 increments; § 408(p)(2)(E)(i). As a result, the maximum amount that may be contributed to the plan for an employee under age 50 for 2022 is $23,150 [$14,000 employee contributions + $9,150 ($305,000 compensation ceiling × 3%) employer match].

[37] The catch-up amount is indexed for inflation in $500 increments.

[38] § 408; employees can contribute 25% of earned income up to the annual maximum.

Concept Summary 19.2

Keogh Plan and SEP Compared

	Keogh	SEP
Establishment	By end of year.	By extension due date of employer.
Type of plan	Qualified.	Qualified.
Contributions to plan	By extension due date.	By extension due date of employer.
Vesting rules	Qualified plan rules.	100% immediately.
Deduction limitation	Varies.*	Smaller of $61,000 (in 2022) or 25% of earned income.**
Self as trustee	Yes.	No.

*For a defined contribution pension plan, the limit is the smaller of $61,000 (in 2022) or 100% of self-employment income (after one-half of self-employment tax is deducted). A defined contribution profit sharing plan has a 25% deduction limit. A defined benefit Keogh plan's limit is the smaller of $245,000 (in 2022) or 100% of the employee's average compensation for the highest three years of employment.

**Only $305,000 of income can be considered.

19-3 Individual Retirement Accounts (IRAs)

LO.6

Describe benefits of the different types of Individual Retirement Accounts (IRAs).

19-3a General Rules

Employees not covered by another qualified plan can establish their own tax-deductible **Individual Retirement Accounts (IRAs)**. IRAs are a popular device for retirement savings; almost 50 million individuals own some type of IRA, with about $12 trillion invested in these vehicles.

The investor contributes to the IRA, selecting the dates and amounts of those transfers. For 2022, the annual IRA contribution ceiling is the smaller of $6,000 ($12,000 for spousal IRAs, discussed later) or 100 percent of compensation.[39] The contribution ceiling applies to all types of IRAs (traditional deductible, traditional nondeductible, and Roth). An individual who attains the age of 50 by the end of the tax year can make an additional catch-up IRA contribution of $1,000 for the year.

The amount accumulated in an IRA can be substantial. For example, if each spouse of a married couple contributes just $4,000 annually to an IRA from ages 25–65 and earns an average of 6 percent annually on the investment, the two account balances will approximate $1.4 million at age 65.

If the taxpayer is an *active participant* in another qualified plan, the traditional IRA deduction limitation is phased out *proportionately* between certain AGI ranges, as shown in Exhibit 19.4.[40] If AGI is above the phaseout range, no IRA deduction is allowed. There is a $200 floor on the IRA deduction for individuals whose AGI is not above the phaseout range.

Exhibit 19.4 Phaseout of IRS Deduction of an Active Participant in 2022

Filing Status (AGI Phaseout)	Phaseout Begins*	Phaseout Ends
Single and head of household	$ 68,000	$ 78,000
Married, filing joint return	109,000	129,000
Married, filing separate return	–0–	10,000

*These amounts are indexed annually for inflation.

[39] §§ 219(b)(1) and (c)(2). The limit is adjusted annually for inflation in $500 increments.

[40] § 219(g).

IRA Deduction Calculation

Example 17

Dan, who is single and age 45, earns compensation income of $74,000 in 2022 and is an active participant in his employer's qualified retirement plan. He contributes $6,000 to a traditional IRA. The deductible amount is reduced by $3,600 because of the phaseout.

$$\frac{\$6{,}000 \text{ amount into phaseout range}}{\$10{,}000 \text{ phaseout range}} \times \$6{,}000 \text{ contribution} = \$3{,}600 \text{ reduction}$$

As a result of the $6,000 contribution, Dan can deduct only $2,400 ($6,000 – $3,600).

Example 18

Aaron, an unmarried individual who is age 45, is an active participant in his employer's qualified retirement plan in 2022. With AGI of $77,800, he normally would have an IRA deduction limit of $120 ($6,000 – {[($77,800 – $68,000) ÷ $10,000] × $6,000}). However, because of the floor amount, Aaron is allowed a $200 IRA deduction.

An individual is not considered an active participant in a qualified plan merely because the individual's spouse is an active participant in such a plan for any part of a plan year. Thus, even when filing jointly, the nonparticipating individual may take a full $6,000 deduction regardless of the participation status of the spouse unless the couple has AGI above $204,000. If their AGI is above $204,000, the phaseout of the deduction begins at $204,000 and ends at $214,000 (phaseout over the $10,000 range) rather than beginning and ending at the phaseout amounts in Exhibit 19.4.[41]

Example 19

Nell is covered by a qualified employer retirement plan at work. Her husband, Nick, is not an active participant in a qualified plan. If Nell and Nick's combined AGI is $135,000, Nell cannot make a deductible IRA contribution because she exceeds the income threshold for an active participant in Exhibit 19.4.

However, because Nick is not an active participant and their combined AGI does not exceed $204,000, he can make a deductible contribution of $6,000 to his own IRA.

To the extent that an individual is ineligible to make a deductible contribution to an IRA, *nondeductible contributions* can be made to the account.[42] The nondeductible contributions are subject to the same dollar limits as deductible contributions ($6,000 of earned income, $12,000 for a spousal IRA). Income in the account accumulates tax-free until distributed. Only the account earnings are taxed upon distribution; the individual's account basis equals the contributions made.

A taxpayer may be entitled to a nonrefundable credit for contributions to an IRA or elective deferrals for a § 401(k) plan (see text Section 13-4f). Distributions to a traditional IRA holder must begin no later than April 1 of the calendar year following the year in which the IRA holder reaches 72.[43]

Roth IRAs

A **Roth IRA** is a *nondeductible* alternative to the traditional deductible IRA. Earnings inside a Roth IRA are not taxable to the investor, and all qualified distributions from a Roth IRA are tax-free.[44] The maximum allowable annual contribution to a Roth IRA for 2022 is the lesser of $6,000 ($12,000 for spousal IRAs) or 100 percent of the individual's

[41] § 219(g)(7).
[42] § 408(o).
[43] § 401(a)(9).
[44] § 408A.

compensation for the year. Contributions to a Roth IRA must be made by the due date (excluding extensions) of the taxpayer's tax return. Roth IRAs are not subject to the minimum distribution rules that apply to traditional IRAs.

A taxpayer can make tax-free withdrawals from a Roth IRA after an initial five-year holding period if any one of the following requirements is satisfied.

- The distribution is made on or after the date on which the participant attains age 59½.
- The distribution is made to a beneficiary (or the participant's estate) on or after the participant's death.
- The participant becomes disabled.
- The distribution is used to pay for qualified first-time homebuyer's expenses (statutory ceiling of $10,000).

Example 20

Amy establishes a Roth IRA at age 42 and contributes $5,000 per year for 20 years. The account is now worth $149,400, consisting of $100,000 of nondeductible contributions and $49,400 in accumulated earnings that have not been taxed. Amy may withdraw the $149,400 tax-free from the Roth IRA because she is over age 59½ and has met the five-year holding period requirement.

If the taxpayer receives a distribution from a Roth IRA and does not satisfy the aforementioned requirements, the distribution may be taxable to the extent of the plan's accumulated earnings. Distributions are treated as first made from the individual's contributions (i.e., as a return of capital).

Example 21

Assume the same facts as in the previous example, except that Amy is age 50 and receives a distribution of $55,000. Because her adjusted basis for the Roth IRA is $100,000 (contributions made), the distribution is tax-free, and her adjusted basis is reduced to $45,000 ($100,000 − $55,000).

Roth IRAs are subject to income limits. In 2022, the maximum annual contribution of $6,000 is phased out beginning at AGI of $129,000 for single taxpayers and $204,000 for married couples who file a joint return. The phaseout range is $10,000 for married filing jointly and $15,000 for single taxpayers. For a married taxpayer filing separately, the phaseout begins with AGI of $0 and is phased out over a $10,000 range.[45]

Example 22

Ben, a gig worker who is single, would like to contribute $6,000 to his Roth IRA in 2022. However, his AGI is $139,000, so his contribution is limited to $2,000 ($6,000 − $4,000).

$$\frac{\$10{,}000 \text{ amount into phaseout range}}{\$15{,}000 \text{ phaseout range}} \times \$6{,}000 \text{ contribution} = \$4{,}000 \text{ reduction}$$

The Big Picture

Example 23

Return to the facts of *The Big Picture* on p. 19-1. Maggie's professor, Dr. Sanchez, also contributes annually to a traditional IRA. She would prefer a Roth IRA, but her AGI exceeds the phaseout limit.

[45]The income limits for Roth IRA contributions are indexed annually for inflation.

Spousal IRAs

For a married couple, each spouse may establish an IRA individually and deduct contributions of up to $6,000 if the combined compensation of the spouses is at least equal to the total contributed amount. Thus, if only one spouse is employed or if both are employed but one has compensation of less than $6,000, each of them may contribute a maximum of $6,000 if their combined compensation is at least $12,000.

For the spousal IRA provision to apply, a joint return must be filed.[46] The spousal IRA deduction is reduced proportionately for active participants whose AGI exceeds the above target ranges.

Spousal IRAs

Example 24

Tony, who is married, is eligible to establish an IRA. He received $130,000 in compensation in 2022, and his spouse Lita does not work outside the home. Tony can contribute up to $12,000 to two IRAs to be divided in any manner between the two spouses, with no more than $6,000 allocated to either spouse.

Example 25

Assume the same facts as in the previous example, except that Lita has compensation income of $2,200. Without the spousal IRA provision, Tony could contribute $6,000 to his IRA, and Lita could contribute only $2,200 to her IRA. With the spousal IRA provision, they both can contribute $6,000 to their IRAs.

Timing of Contributions

Contributions (both deductible and nondeductible) can be made to an IRA anytime before the due date of the individual's tax return.[47] For example, an individual can establish and contribute to an IRA through April 15, 2023 (the 2022 individual tax return due date), and deduct this amount on the 2022 tax return. IRA contributions that are made during a tax return extension period do not satisfy the requirement of being made by the return due date.[48]

19-3b Taxation of Benefits

A participant has a zero basis in the *deductible* contributions of a traditional IRA because the contributions were deducted.[49] Therefore, all withdrawals from a deductible IRA are taxed as ordinary income in the year of receipt. They are not eligible for the 10-year averaging allowed for certain lump-sum distributions.

A participant has a basis equal to the contributions made for a *nondeductible* traditional IRA. As a result, only the earnings component of withdrawals is included in gross income. Such amounts are taxed as ordinary income in the year of receipt.

In addition to being included in gross income, payments from IRAs made to a participant before age 59½ are subject to a nondeductible 10 percent penalty tax on such payments.[50] However, an individual may make penalty-free withdrawals to pay for medical expenses in excess of 10 percent of AGI, to pay for qualified higher-education expenses, and to pay for qualified first-time homebuyer expenses (up to $10,000). Further, an individual who has received unemployment compensation for at least 12 consecutive weeks may use IRA withdrawals to pay for their own health insurance, and for insurance on a spouse or dependent, without incurring the 10 percent penalty tax.[51]

[46] § 219(c).
[47] § 219(f)(3).
[48] § 404(h)(1)(B).
[49] § 408(d)(1).
[50] § 72(t). There are limited exceptions to the penalty on early distributions.
[51] §§ 72(t)(2)(B), (D), (E), and (F).

19-3c Rollovers and Conversions

An IRA may be the recipient of a rollover from another qualified plan, including another IRA. Such a distribution from a qualified plan is not included in gross income if it is transferred within 60 days of receipt to an IRA or to another qualified plan.

Example 26

Ruth withdraws $15,000 from a traditional IRA on May 2, 2022 (closing the account). She deposits these funds into a different traditional IRA on June 5, 2022. This situation is a qualified rollover and will not result in any gross income for Ruth during 2022.

Taxpayers are allowed only one traditional IRA rollover per 12-month period regardless of how many IRAs they have.[52] A Roth IRA may be rolled over tax-free into another Roth IRA.[53]

Unlike a traditional IRA, which requires withdrawals at age 72, there are no required withdrawals from a Roth IRA.[54] Such savings can be accumulated over the taxpayer's lifetime and then passed to heirs without incurring Federal income or estate taxes.[55]

Example 27

Frank has both traditional IRAs and Roth IRAs. A rollover between his traditional IRA to a Roth IRA (a conversion) is not subject to the one-per-year rule. However, a rollover between his Roth IRAs will preclude a separate rollover within the one-year period between his traditional IRAs (including SEP and SIMPLE IRAs) and vice versa.

Concept Summary 19.3

Comparison of IRAs

	Traditional		
	Deductible IRA	**Nondeductible IRA**	**Roth IRA**
Maximum contribution (per year)	$6,000*	$6,000*	$6,000*
Tax-deductible contribution	Yes	No	No
Tax-free growth of income	Yes	Yes	Yes
Beginning of AGI phaseout for active participant (2022)	$68,000 single, $109,000 joint	N/A	$129,000 single, $204,000 joint
Income tax on distributions	Yes, for entire distribution	Yes, for the earnings portion	No, if satisfy 5-year holding period**
50% excise tax: age 72 insufficient distributions	Yes	Yes	No
10% early withdrawal penalty (before age 59½)	Yes, with exceptions†	Yes, with exceptions†	Yes, with exceptions†

*The total of deductible, nondeductible, and Roth IRA contributions may not exceed $6,000 per year.

**In addition, the distribution must satisfy one of the following: made after age 59½, used for qualified first-time homebuyer expenses, made to participant who is disabled, or made to a beneficiary on or after the participant's death.

†Qualified education and first-time homebuyer costs (up to $10,000) avoid the 10% penalty.

[52] *Bobrow v. Commissioner,* T.C.Memo. 2014–21; IRS Announcements 2014–15 and 2013–32.

[53] § 408A(c)(3)(B).

[54] § 408A(c)(4).

[55] Additional details on traditional and Roth IRAs can be found in IRS Publication 590, *Individual Retirement Accounts (IRAs).*

LO.7

Review the rationale for nonqualified deferred compensation plans and the related tax treatment.

19-4 Nonqualified Deferred Compensation Plans

19-4a Underlying Rationale for Tax Treatment

Nonqualified deferred compensation (NQDC) plans provide a flexible way for taxpayers, particularly those in high tax brackets, to defer Federal income taxes on distributions until a potentially lower tax bracket year. Most NQDC plans need not meet the discrimination, funding, coverage, and other requirements of qualified plans.

19-4b Tax Treatment to the Employer and Employee

A nonqualified deferred compensation arrangement occurs when an employee receives compensation after the 2½-month period following the end of an employer's tax year in which services were performed.[56] An employer's deduction of its contribution to the NQDC is delayed to match the employee's recognition of income, regardless of the employer's method of accounting.[57]

Example 28

Beige, Inc., a calendar year employer, has an accrued NQDC liability for employee Pérez of $300,000 on December 31, 2021. During 2022, the company accrues another $60,000 of NQDC. On February 13, 2023, the company pays the entire $360,000 to Pérez. Because the $60,000 was paid within 2½ months after the end of 2022, only $300,000 counts as deferred compensation. The entire $360,000 is deducted by Beige only in the year ending December 31, 2023 (i.e., when Pérez receives the cash and recognizes the related gross income).

Golden Parachute Arrangements

Golden parachute arrangements promise monetary benefits to key employees if they lose their jobs as a result of a change in ownership of the corporation. In essence, these are unfunded NQDC plans that do not vest until the change in ownership. The term **golden parachute payments**, as used in the Code, can be seen as *excess severance pay*; they are disfavored by the tax law.

The Code denies a deduction to an employer who makes a payment of cash or property to an employee or independent contractor that satisfies both of the following conditions.

- The payment is contingent on a change in ownership of a corporation through a stock or asset acquisition.
- The aggregate present value of the payment equals or exceeds three times the employee's (or independent contractor's) average annual compensation.[58]

The disallowed amount is the excess of the payment over a statutory base amount (a five-year average of taxable compensation). Further, a 20 percent excise tax is imposed on the recipient upon the receipt of these parachute payments; the tax is withheld at the time of payment.[59]

---

[56] § 404(a)(5); Reg. § 1.404(a)–12(b)(1).

[57] Reg. § 1.409A–1(b)(4).

[58] § 280G.

[59] § 4999.

Example 29

Nia, an executive, receives a golden parachute payment of $380,000 from her employer. Her average annual compensation for the most recent five tax years is $120,000. The corporation is denied a deduction for $260,000 ($380,000 payment − $120,000 base amount). Nia's excise tax is $52,000 ($260,000 × 20%).

Golden parachute payments do not include payments to or from qualified pension, profit sharing, stock bonus, annuity, or simplified employee pension plans. Any amount of the payment that represents reasonable compensation for personal services actually rendered or to be rendered similarly is not a golden parachute payment.

Generally, corporations that do not have stock that is readily tradable on an established securities market or elsewhere are exempt from these rules.

Ethics & Equity **The Ethics of Sustainable Investing**

Some investors, especially millennials, are investing solely in environmental, social, and governance (ESG) investments or socially responsible investments (SRI). ESG and SRI investments can over- or underperform when compared to other stock investments.

Some studies show that ESG and SRI investments produce lower returns than found in the rest of the market. Is it ethical for an adviser to encourage investing in these types of securities?

19-5 Stock Options

LO.8 **Differentiate the tax treatment of qualified and nonqualified stock options.**

Various equity types of stock option programs are available for an employee's compensation package. Some observers believe that some form of *equity kicker* is needed to attract new management; convert key officers into *partners* by giving them a share of the business; and retain the services of executives, product developers, or sales representatives who might otherwise leave for higher pay elsewhere. Encouraging employees to take a proprietary interest in the successful operation of their business should provide executives with a key motive to expand the company and improve its profits. In addition, under certain conditions, stock options may fall outside the $1 million limitation on the salaries of the top five executives of publicly traded companies, as discussed in text Section 6-3c. Sometimes an executive's stock option income far exceeds total cash salaries and bonuses.

A **stock option** gives an individual the right to purchase a stated number of shares of stock from a corporation at a certain price within a specified period of time. The optionee must be under no obligation to purchase the stock, and the option may be revocable by the corporation. The option must be in writing, and its terms must be clearly expressed.[60]

19-5a Incentive Stock Options

An **incentive stock option (ISO)** is an option to purchase stock of a corporation granted to an individual for any reason connected with their employment that meets specific qualification requirements.[61] The option is granted by the employer-corporation or by a parent or subsidiary corporation of the employer-corporation.

[60] Reg. §§ 1.421–1(a)(1) and −7(a)(1).

[61] § 422(b).

Financial Disclosure Insights **Share-Based Compensation**

The Financial Accounting Standards Board (FASB) requires equity-based compensation to be expensed, which lowers the company's earnings. ASC 718 applies to equity-based compensation (e.g., illiquid stock options and restricted stock) where a company acquires employee services by issuing stock, granting stock options, or providing other equity instruments to their employees. The FASB's position is that a company should determine the accounting for the cost of the employee's services based on the fair value of any compensation paid. The International Financial Reporting Standards (IFRS) also require companies to recognize share-based compensation.

A company must measure the fair value of options on the grant date and then expense the cost equally over the vested period of the options. If an option grant has a vested schedule of four years, four years is considered to be the economic life over which to expense the options. A Black-Scholes formula often is used to calculate a company's expense, taking into account the value of the common stock, exercise price, option's term, risk-free rate, and volatility.

There are no tax consequences for either the issuing corporation or the recipient when an ISO is granted. However, the *spread* (the excess of the fair market value of the share at the date of exercise over the option price)[62] is an adjustment item to the recipient for purposes of the alternative minimum tax; see text Section 12-2a.

After the option is exercised and when the stock is sold, any gain from the sale is taxed as a long-term capital gain if certain holding period requirements are met. To qualify for long-term capital gain treatment, the employee must not dispose of the stock within two years after the option is granted or within one year after the stock is acquired.[63] If the employee meets the holding period requirements, none of these transactions generate a deduction for the employer.[64] If the employee pays for the option and does not later exercise it, the purchase amount is recognized as a capital loss.

The Big Picture

Example 30

Return to the facts of *The Big Picture* on p. 19-1. Dr. Sanchez is on the board of directors of a medium-sized company, Wren Corporation. Wren granted an ISO for 100 shares of its stock to Dr. Sanchez on March 18, 2021, for service rendered. The option price was $100 and the fair market value was $100 on the date of the grant. Dr. Sanchez exercised the option on April 1, 2021, when the fair market value of the stock was $200 per share. She sells the stock on April 6, 2022, for $300 per share.

Dr. Sanchez did not recognize any ordinary income on the date of the grant or the exercise date because the option qualified as an ISO. Wren received no compensation deduction relative to the option. Dr. Sanchez has a $10,000 positive AMT adjustment on the exercise date. She has a long-term capital gain of $20,000 [($300 − $100) × 100] on the sale of the stock in 2022, because the one-year holding period and other requirements have been met.

The ISO holder must be an employee of the issuing corporation from the date the option is granted until at least 3 months (12 months if disabled) before the date of exercise. The holding period and the employee-status rules (the one-year, two-year, and three-month requirements) are waived in the case of the death of an employee.[65]

---

[62] §§ 56(b)(3), 421(a)(1), 422(a), and 1234(a)(1) and (2).

[63] § 422(a)(1).

[64] § 421(a)(2).

[65] §§ 422(a)(2) and (c)(3). Exceptions are made for parent and subsidiary situations, corporate reorganizations, and liquidations. In certain situations involving an insolvent employee, the holding period rules are modified.

The Big Picture

Example 31

Return to the facts in the previous example, except that Dr. Sanchez was not a service provider (or employee) of Wren Corporation for six months before the date she exercised the options. Dr. Sanchez must recognize $10,000 [($200 − $100) × 100] of ordinary income on the exercise date, to the extent of the spread, because she was not an employee of Wren at all times during the period beginning on the grant date and ending three months before the exercise date. Wren is allowed a deduction at the same time Dr. Sanchez reports the ordinary income.

The difference between the amount realized for the stock and the value of the stock at the date of exercise is short-term or long-term capital gain depending on the holding period of the stock itself. The employer is allowed a deduction equal to the amount recognized by the employee as ordinary income. The employee does not report an AMT adjustment.

If the holding period requirements are not satisfied but all other conditions are met, the tax still is deferred to the point of the sale. However, the difference between the option price and the value of the stock at the date the option was exercised is treated as ordinary income.

The Big Picture

Example 32

Assume the same facts as in the previous example, except that Dr. Sanchez sells the stock on March 22, 2022, for $290 per share. Because Dr. Sanchez did not hold the stock for more than one year, $10,000 of the gain is treated as ordinary income in 2022 and Wren Corporation is allowed a $10,000 compensation deduction in 2022. The remaining $9,000 is a short-term capital gain ($29,000 − $20,000) for Sanchez.

Qualification as an Incentive Stock Option

For an option to qualify as an ISO, the terms of the option must identify it as an ISO and meet the following conditions.

- The plan must be approved by the shareholders of the corporation within 12 months before or after the plan is adopted, specifying who is eligible and how the options are assigned.
- The option must be granted within 10 years of the date the plan is adopted or of the date the plan is approved by the shareholders, whichever date is earlier.
- The option must be exercisable only within 10 years of the date it is granted.
- The option price must equal or exceed the fair market value of the stock at the time the option is granted. This requirement is deemed satisfied if there has been a good-faith attempt to value the stock accurately, even if the option price is less than the stock value.
- The option is nontransferable other than at death and must be exercisable during the employee's lifetime only by the employee.

Financial Disclosure Insights **Executive Compensation**

Payments to qualified retirement plans are limited in amount and timing, but other "IOUs" are made available to managers, typically as unfunded but enforceable promises to make large payments or stock transfers, for example, after the executive retires or works for the firm for a certain number of years.

Bonus and retirement arrangements like these create a book-tax difference, because they represent compensation expenses for GAAP purposes, but no tax deduction is allowed until the compensation is paid or becomes fully funded and vested. Some firms do fund the deferred payments—no book-tax difference or deferred tax asset amount would result in that case.

- The employee must not, immediately before the option is granted, own stock representing more than 10 percent of the voting power or value of all classes of stock in the employer-corporation or its parent or subsidiary. However, the stock ownership limitation is waived when the option price is at least 110 percent of the fair market value (at the time the option is granted) of the stock subject to the option, and the option is not exercisable more than five years from the date it is granted.[66]

An overall limitation is imposed on the amount of ISOs that can be first exercisable in one year by an employee. This limit is set at $100,000 per year based on the value of the stock determined at the time the option is granted. For example, an ISO plan may permit acquisition of up to $600,000 worth of stock if it provides that the options are exercisable in six installments, each of which becomes exercisable in a different year and does not exceed $100,000.

An ISO plan may permit an employee to use company stock to pay for the exercise of the option (i.e., the employee collects the value of the stock at exercise date minus the "cost" of buying the stock at its issue-date price).

19-5b Nonqualified Stock Options

A **nonqualified stock option (NQSO)** does not satisfy the statutory requirements for ISOs, but it still is offered to employees as a fringe benefit. If the NQSO has a readily ascertainable fair market value (e.g., the option is traded on an established exchange), the value of the option is included in the employee's gross income at the date of the grant. Thereafter, capital gain or loss is recognized only when the optioned stock is sold. The employee's basis is the amount paid for the stock plus any amount reported as ordinary income. The employer obtains a corresponding tax deduction at the same time, to the extent that ordinary income is recognized by the employee.[67]

If an NQSO does not have a readily ascertainable fair market value, an employee does not recognize income at the grant date. However, as a general rule, ordinary income then is reported in the year of exercise (the difference between the fair market value of the stock at the exercise date and the option price).[68] The amount paid by the employee for the stock plus the amount reported as ordinary income becomes the basis of the shares. Any appreciation above that basis is taxed as a capital gain upon disposition. The corporation receives a corresponding tax deduction at the same time, to the extent that ordinary income is recognized by the employee.

[66] § 422(c)(5).

[67] Reg. §§ 1.421–6(c), (d), (e), and (f); Reg. § 1.83–7.

[68] Reg. § 1.83–7(a); Reg. § 1.421–6(d).

Example 33

On February 3, 2020, Maria was granted an NQSO for 100 shares of common stock at $10 per share. On the date of the grant, there was no readily ascertainable fair market value for the option. Maria exercised the options on January 3, 2021, when the stock was selling for $15 per share. She sold one-half of the shares on April 15, 2021, and the other half on September 17, 2022. The sale price on both dates was $21 per share.

Maria recognizes no gross income on the grant date (February 3, 2020), but she would recognize $500 ($1,500 − $1,000) of ordinary income on the exercise date (January 3, 2021). She would recognize a short-term capital gain of $300 on the sale of the first half in 2021 and a $300 long-term capital gain on the sale of the second batch of stock in 2022 [½ ($2,100 − $1,500)].

19-6 Tax Planning

LO.9 **Identify tax planning opportunities available with deferred compensation.**

19-6a Qualified Plans

Qualified plans provide maximum tax benefits for employers, because the employer receives an immediate tax deduction for contributions to a plan, and the income that is earned on the contributions is not taxable to the employer. The employer's contributions and any investment earnings are not taxed to the employees until those funds are made available to them.

Qualified plans are most appropriate where it is desirable to provide benefits for a cross section of employees. In some closely held corporations, the primary objective is to provide benefits for the officer-shareholder group and other highly paid personnel. The nondiscrimination requirements that must be met in a qualified plan may prevent such companies from attaining these objectives. Thus, a nonqualified arrangement may be needed as a supplement to, or used in lieu of, the qualified plan.

Cash balance plans are better for younger, mobile employees, and the employer saves money by reducing pension payouts for older and longer-service employees. If a participant moves or retires, they can roll over the lump-sum payment into an IRA or another qualified plan.

19-6b Self-Employed Retirement Plans

A Keogh or traditional deductible IRA participant may make a deductible contribution for a tax year up to the time prescribed for filing the individual's tax return. A Keogh plan must have been established by the end of the tax year (e.g., December 31) to obtain a current deduction for the contribution made in the subsequent year. An individual can establish an IRA after the end of the tax year and still receive a current deduction for the contribution made in the subsequent year. However, because the deductibility of contributions to IRAs are restricted for many middle-income and upper-income taxpayers, Keogh plans may be more attractive.

19-6c Individual Retirement Accounts

Unlike a traditional IRA, which defers taxes on the entire account, a Roth IRA allows investment earnings to accumulate completely tax-free. Ordinary income and capital gains earned inside a Roth IRA never are subject to Federal income tax (assuming that the five-year holding period provision is satisfied). Thus, a Roth IRA can run contrary to the general principle that it is usually better for a taxpayer to postpone the payment of any tax.

In many situations, a retirement plan participant will earn more wealth with a Roth IRA than with a traditional IRA. This potential for tax-free growth is so advantageous that taxpayers who have substantial traditional IRA balances and are eligible should evaluate converting at least some of their traditional IRA balances into a Roth IRA. A taxpayer does need to assess such a move in present-value after-tax terms, though, because there can be a "big hit" of gross income in the year of conversion, equal to the value of the converted traditional IRA balance.

19-6d Comparison of § 401(k) Plan with IRA

Most employees will find a § 401(k) plan more attractive than an IRA. Probably the biggest limitation of an IRA is the $6,000 maximum shelter in 2022 (ignoring the catch-up provision). Under § 401(k), employees are permitted to shelter compensation up to $20,500 (in 2022). The restrictions on deducting contributions to IRAs for many middle-income and upper-income taxpayers also encourages many employees to utilize § 401(k) plans more frequently.

The § 401(k) plan also is attractive because many employers "match or partially match" employee elective deferrals with employer contributions. Concept Summary 19.4 compares a § 401(k) plan with an IRA.

19-6e Nonqualified Deferred Compensation (NQDC) Plans

Nonqualified deferred compensation arrangements can be useful to attract executive talent or to provide substantial retirement benefits for executives. Such plans may discriminate in favor of officers and other highly paid employees. The employer, however, does not receive a tax deduction until the employee is required to include the deferred compensation in income (upon the lapse of the restrictions).

The principal advantage of NQDC plans over current compensation is that the employee can defer the recognition of income to future periods when their income tax bracket may be lower (e.g., during retirement years). The time-value-of-money benefits from the deferral of income also should be considered.

The principal disadvantage of NQDC plans could be the bunching effect that takes place on the expiration of the period of deferral. In some cases, planning can alleviate this result.

Example 34

During 2022, Khalid, an executive, enters into an agreement to postpone a portion of his payment for current services until retirement. The deferred amount is not segregated from the company's general assets and is subject to normal business risk. The entire payment, not the after-tax amount, is invested in securities and variable annuity contracts.

Khalid is not taxed on the payment in 2022, and the company receives no deduction in 2022. If Khalid receives the deferred payment in a lump sum when he retires, the tax rates might be higher and more progressive than in 2022. Thus, Khalid may want to arrange for payments to be made to him or a designated beneficiary over a number of years.

Other disadvantages may be apparent. Nonqualified plans usually are unfunded, which means that an employee has no assurance that funds ultimately will be available to pay the benefits. In effect, the deferred amounts are recorded as a liability on the company's books, and the employee is an unsecured creditor in the event of the firm's bankruptcy.

Concept Summary 19.4

Section 401(k) Plan and IRA Compared

	§ 401(k) Plan	IRA
Contribution limitation	Smaller of $20,500 (in 2022) or approximately 100% of total earnings. Limited by antidiscrimination requirements of § 401(k)(3).	$6,000 or 100% of compensation.
Distributions	Early withdrawal possible to take early retirement (55 or over) or to pay medical expenses.	10% penalty for early withdrawals, except for withdrawals to pay for certain medical expenses and health insurance, qualified education expenses, and qualified first-time homebuyer expenses.
Effect on gross income	Gross salary reduction.	No effect.
Employer involvement	Employer must keep records; monitor for compliance with antidiscrimination test.	Minimal.
Timing of contribution	Within 30 days of plan year-end or due date of employer's return.*	Up to due date of tax return (not including extensions).
Loans from plan allowed	Yes.	No.

*Elective contributions must be made to the plan no later than 30 days after the end of the plan year and nonelective contributions no later than the due date of the tax return (including extensions).

19-6f Stock Options

Rather than paying compensation in the form of corporate stock, a corporation may issue options to purchase stock at a specific price to an employee. Stock option plans are used more frequently by publicly traded companies than by closely held companies, often because of the problems of determining the value of the stock of a company that is not publicly held.

Most plans use nonqualified stock options. Nonqualified stock options (NQSOs) are more flexible and less restrictive than incentive stock options (ISOs). For example, the holding period for an NQSO is not as long as that for an ISO. However, the option price of an NQSO cannot be less than the fair market value of the stock at the time the option is granted.

An NQSO creates an employer deduction that lowers the cost of the NQSO to the employer. The employee recognizes capital gain income after selling the shares, but ordinary income is recognized on the grant or exercise date, without producing cash with which to pay the resulting tax.

Both the employer and the employee may be better off by combining NQSOs with additional cash payments rather than using ISOs. See Concept Summary 19.5.

Concept Summary 19.5

Incentive Stock Options and Nonqualified Stock Options Compared

	ISO	NQSO
Granted at any price	No	Yes
May have any duration	No	Yes
Spread subject to alternative minimum tax	Yes	No
Deduction to employer for spread	No	Yes
Available for independent contractors	No	Yes
Statutory ($100,000) limit on exercise	Yes	No
When employee taxed	Date of sale*	Ordinary income on exercise date** LTCG on sale
When employer deducts	None***	When employee recognizes ordinary income

*Spread is AMT adjustment.
**If no readily ascertainable FMV.
***If employee meets holding period requirements.

Stock options are an effective compensation device as long as share prices are rising. When stock prices fall, the options become unexercisable and possibly worthless.

19-6g **Liquidating Retirement Assets**

If a person has funds from sources other than retirement assets, which retirement assets should an individual acquire first? The most tax-efficient result usually is to postpone any Federal income tax obligation for as long as possible. Generally, retirement assets should be taken from assets or accounts in the following order so that the tax-deferred growth continues for the longest period.

- **First** — Taxable accounts
- **Second** — § 401(k) plans (e.g., for early retirement)
- **Third** — Traditional IRAs (e.g., at age 59½)
- **Fourth** — Roth IRAs (e.g., since no minimum distributions required)

Refocus on The Big Picture

A Taxpayer Who Saves

FIZKES/SHUTTERSTOCK.COM

From her discussion with Dr. Sanchez, Maggie learns that her professor has the following retirement plans.

- *Defined contribution plan*. The university offered its faculty members a choice between a defined benefit pension plan and a defined contribution plan. Dr. Sanchez expects to work at a number of universities during her career, so she chose the defined contribution plan because of its portability. The maximum annual contribution the university could make to the plan was $61,000 for 2022.
- *Keogh (H.R. 10) plan*. In addition to her position at the university, Dr. Sanchez has various outside earnings sources. Thus, she can establish a Keogh defined contribution plan. She contributes 20 percent of her net earnings from the consulting practice to the plan.
- *IRA*. Dr. Sanchez also contributes annually to a traditional IRA. She would prefer a Roth IRA, but her AGI exceeds the $144,000 phaseout limit. Likewise, she cannot deduct her contribution of $6,000 (the maximum) because of the amount of her AGI. Because she can make only nondeductible contributions, her basis in the IRA is the summation of her contributions. The $15,000 that Dr. Sanchez withdrew from her traditional IRA is not subject to current taxation and does not reduce her basis for the IRA, since she successfully completed a tax-free rollover (i.e., recontributed the $15,000 to her IRA within 60 days).

Dr. Sanchez explains that she wants to travel after retirement, so her goal is to retire by age 62 while she is still in good health. She anticipates that these plans will enable her to do so.

Key Terms

Cash balance plan, 19-4
Deferred compensation, 19-2
Defined benefit plan, 19-2
Defined contribution pension plan, 19-3
Golden parachute payments, 19-18
Highly compensated employee, 19-5
Incentive stock option (ISO), 19-19
Individual Retirement Accounts (IRAs), 19-13
Keogh plans, 19-11
Lump-sum distribution, 19-8
Nonqualified deferred compensation (NQDC), 19-18
Nonqualified stock option (NQSO), 19-22
Pension plan, 19-2
Profit sharing plan, 19-3
Roth IRA, 19-14
Section 401(k) plan, 19-10
Stock bonus plan, 19-3
Stock option, 19-19
Vesting requirements, 19-6

Discussion Questions

1. **LO.1** Determine whether each of the following independent statements best describes a defined contribution plan *(DCP)*, a defined benefit plan *(DBP)*, both *(B)*, or neither *(N)*.
   a. The amount to be received at retirement depends on actuarial calculations.
   b. Forfeitures can be allocated to the remaining participants' accounts.
   c. Requires greater reporting requirements and more actuarial and administrative costs.
   d. May exclude employees who begin employment within five years of normal retirement age.
   e. Annual addition to each employee's account may not exceed the smaller of $61,000 or 100% of the employee's salary.
   f. The final benefit to a participant depends upon investment performance.

2. **LO.2, 3, 6** Penny plans to retire this year at age 70. Identify any issues that Penny faces with respect to distributions from her qualified retirement plan. *Critical Thinking* *Planning*

3. **LO.3** Which of the following would be considered a tax benefit or advantage of a qualified retirement plan?
   a. Certain distributions may be subject to capital gain treatment.
   b. Employer contributions are deductible by the employer in the year of contribution.
   c. Employee contributions are deductible by the employee in the year of contribution.
   d. The qualified plan is tax-deferred as to all income.

4. **LO.6, 9** Should a 31-year-old self-employed single woman likely establish a traditional deductible IRA, a traditional nondeductible IRA, or a Roth IRA? She has two children, ages 10 and 8. *Critical Thinking*

5. **LO.6** Joey, who is single, is not covered by another qualified retirement plan and earns $131,000 at his job in 2022. How much can he contribute to a traditional IRA in 2022? To a Roth IRA?

6. **LO.4, 5** Sanjay Henry calls you and asks about setting up a savings incentive match plan for his employees (SIMPLE). Prepare a memo for the tax files with your response. *Communications*

7. **LO.6** Suppose an individual is 55 years old. How much of an additional catch-up IRA contribution can the person make?

8. **LO.7, 9** During his senior year in college, Sandy is drafted by the Los Angeles Dodgers. When he graduates, he expects to sign a five-year contract in the range of $1,700,000 per year. In planning for post-graduation, identify some tax benefits of a nonqualified deferred compensation plan for Sandy, which the Dodgers are offering in addition to his salary. *Planning*

9. **LO.7** What conditions cause the golden parachute rules to apply?

10. **LO.8** What is the "spread" with respect to an incentive stock option? How is it treated under the Federal income tax law?

Computational Exercises

11. **LO.2** Determine the pertinent vesting percentage for the following employees. See Exhibits 19.1 and 19.2.
    a. Jun has five years of service completed as of September 23, her employment anniversary date. If her *defined benefit plan* has a five-year cliff vesting schedule, what percent of Jun's accrued benefits are vested? If the plan uses the graded vesting rule, what is Jun's nonforfeitable percentage?
    b. Cybil has four years of service completed as of July 5, her employment anniversary date. If her *defined contribution plan* uses a two- to six-year vesting plan, what is her nonforfeitable percentage?

12. **LO.4** Sergio has participated for eight years in a defined benefit plan and has nine years of service with his employer. His average compensation for the three highest years is $160,000. What is Sergio's dollar limit on annual benefits received?

13. **LO.4** Joanna, age 44, defers $25,000 in a qualified Solo § 401(k) plan in 2022.
    a. What amount must be returned to Joanna and by what date?
    b. In what year will the amount be taxed?
    c. What occurs if excess contributions are made by the employer and not returned? By what date must the funds be returned?

14. **LO.5** Zack, a sole proprietor, has earned income of $85,000 in 2022 (after the deduction for one-half of self-employment tax). What is the maximum contribution Zack may make to a *defined contribution* Keogh plan?

15. **LO.2, 4, 5** Jadeveon, a self-employed attorney, uses a defined contribution Keogh plan with a contribution rate of 15% of compensation. His earned income after the deduction of one-half of self-employment tax but before the Keogh contribution is $304,750. What is the maximum amount of Jadeveon's contribution?

16. **LO.6** Myers, who is single, has compensation income of $75,000 in 2022. He is an active participant in his employer's qualified retirement plan. Myers contributes $6,000 to a traditional IRA. Of the $6,000 contribution, how much can Myers deduct?

Planning

17. **LO.6** Meredith, who is single, would like to contribute $6,000 annually to her Roth IRA. Her AGI is $130,000.
    a. What is the maximum amount that Meredith can contribute? Show your calculations using Microsoft Excel.
    b. Assume that Meredith's AGI is $100,000. She plans to put $6,000 each year into her Roth IRA, hoping to earn 6% annually. What amount will accumulate in her Roth IRA at the end of 20 years? *Hint:* Use the time value of money tables found in text Appendix E.
    c. In part (b), instead assume that Meredith puts the $6,000 into the Roth IRA for 15 years at 6%. How much will accumulate at the end of this period?

18. **LO.6** Mina, who is single, would like to contribute $6,000 to her Roth IRA. Her AGI is $135,000. What is the maximum amount that Mina can contribute to the plan this year? Show your answer in Microsoft Excel.

19. **LO.5, 6** In 2022, Cao's compensation before his employer's contribution to a SEP is $66,000. What is the maximum amount that Cao's employer can contribute and deduct in 2022?

20. **LO.7** Robin, an executive, receives a golden parachute payment of $600,000 from his employer. His average annual compensation for the five most recent tax years is $150,000.
    a. For what amount will the corporation be denied a deduction?
    b. What is Robin's excise tax triggered by the payment?

21. **LO.6** The AGI of the Newtons, a married couple, is $207,000 this year. They would like to contribute to a Roth IRA.
    a. What is the maximum amount this couple can contribute to a Roth IRA? Show your calculations using Microsoft Excel.
    b. Now suppose that the Newtons will report AGI of less than $201,000 and put $12,000 each year into their Roth IRA for 20 years, earning an annual return of 5%. What future value will accumulate in their Roth IRA at the end of this period? *Hint:* Use the time value of money tables found in text Appendix E.

22. **LO.8, 9** Zaire Corporation granted an ISO for 250 shares of its stock to Bruno on July 20, 2021, for services rendered. The option price was $130 and the fair market value was $130 on the date of the grant. Bruno exercised the option on September 1, 2021, when the fair market value of the stock was $225 per share. He sells the stock on November 30, 2022, for $350 per share.
    a. What is the amount of the AMT adjustment item that Bruno incurs on the exercise date?
    b. What is Bruno's long-term capital gain on the sale of the stock in 2022?

23. **LO.8, 9** On April 5, 2020, Gustavo was granted an NQSO for 200 shares of common stock at $50 per share. On the date of the grant, there was no ascertainable fair market value for the option. Gustavo exercised the options on March 31, 2021, when the stock was selling for $60 per share. He sold the shares on December 1, 2022, for $75 per share.
    a. What amount and type of income, if any, will Gustavo record on the exercise date?
    b. What amount and type of income, if any, will Gustavo incur on the date of the sale?

Problems

24. **LO.2** Sparrow, Inc., uses a three- to seven-year graded vesting approach in its retirement plan. Calculate the nonforfeitable percentage for each of the following participants based upon the years of service completed.

Participant	Years of Service
Mary	2
Sam	4
Pedro	6
Jaya	7

25. **LO.2** Mauve, Inc., uses a two- to six-year graded vesting approach in its retirement plan. Calculate the nonforfeitable percentage for each of the following participants based upon the years of service completed.

Participant	Years of Service
Chin	3
Daniel	4
Sloane	5
Ryan	7

26. **LO.2** Cheng is age 77, and the balance in her traditional IRA account at the end of December of the prior year is $231,000. Using Exhibit 19.3, calculate Cheng's required minimum distribution for 2022. Construct an Excel solution using the XLOOKUP function.

27. **LO.2** Lee inherits a traditional IRA at the end of 2022.
    a. If Lee inherits the IRA from her spouse when the value is $231,050, how must the balance be distributed to her?
    b. If Lee inherits the IRA from her brother, how must the balance be distributed to her?

Decision Making 28. **LO.2** Chee has worked for Yellow Corporation for four and one-half years, but she has an offer to move to Red Corporation for a moderate increase in salary. Her average salary for Yellow has been $210,000, and she receives a 2% benefit for each year of service in her retirement plan. The company uses a five-year vesting schedule. Advise Chee as to this possible switch in jobs.

29. **LO.4** Heather has been an active participant in a defined benefit plan for 19 years. During her last 6 years of employment, Heather earned $42,000, $48,000, $56,000, $80,000, $89,000, and $108,000, respectively (representing her highest-income years).

a. Calculate Heather's maximum allowable benefits from her qualified plan (assume that there are fewer than 100 participants).

b. Assume that Heather's average compensation for her three highest years is $199,700. Calculate her maximum allowable benefits.

30. **LO.4** Determine the maximum annual benefits payable to a participant from a defined benefit plan in the following independent situations.

a. Frank, age 66, has been a participant for 17 years, and his highest average compensation for 3 years is $127,300.

b. Ellen, age 65, has been a participant for 9 years (11 years of service), and her highest average compensation for 3 years is $102,600.

Planning 31. **LO.4, 9** Amber's employer, Lavender, Inc., uses a § 401(k) plan that permits salary deferral elections by its employees. Amber's salary is $99,000, her marginal tax rate is 24%, and she is 42 years old.

a. What is the maximum amount Amber can elect for salary deferral treatment for 2022?

b. If Amber elects salary deferral treatment for the amount in part (a), how much can she save in Federal income taxes?

c. What amount would you recommend that Amber elect for salary deferral treatment for 2022, considering only the Federal income tax effects?

32. **LO.4, 5** Shyam is a participant in a SIMPLE § 401(k) plan. He elects to contribute 4% of his $40,000 compensation to the account, and his employer contributes 3%. What amount will not vest immediately, if any?

33. **LO.2, 4, 5, 6** In 2022, Megan's sole proprietorship earns $300,000 of self-employment net income (after the deduction for one-half of self-employment tax).

a. Calculate the maximum amount that Megan can deduct for contributions to a defined contribution Keogh plan.

b. Suppose Megan contributes more than the allowable amount to the Keogh plan. What are the consequences to her?

c. Can Megan retire and begin receiving Keogh payments at age 58 without incurring a penalty? Explain.

34. **LO.5** Harvey is a self-employed accountant with earned income from the business of $120,000 (after the deduction for one-half of his self-employment tax). He uses a defined contribution Keogh plan. What is the maximum amount Harvey can contribute to his retirement plan in 2022?

35. **LO.4, 5, 6** Jong, age 29, is unmarried and an active participant in a qualified retirement plan. Her modified AGI is $70,000 in 2022.

a. Calculate the amount Jong can contribute to a traditional IRA and the amount that she can deduct.

b. Assume instead that Jong is a participant in a SIMPLE IRA and that she elects to contribute 4% of her compensation to the account and her employer contributes 3%. What amount will be contributed for 2022? What amount will be vested?

36. **LO.4, 5, 6** Answer the following independent questions for 2022.

a. Govind, age 31, earns a salary of $26,000 and is not an active participant in any other qualified plan. His wife Olga reports $600 of compensation income. What is the maximum total deductible contribution to their IRAs?

b. Danos is a participant in a SIMPLE § 401(k) plan. He contributes 6% of his salary of $42,000, and his employer contributes 3%. What amount will be contributed for the year? What amount will be vested?

c. Nancy wants to contribute $8,000 at the end of each year into a § 401(k) plan for 20 years with the expectation of an annual 6% interest earned. If the first contribution occurs at year-end, what amount will be in her § 401(k) in 20 years? *Hint:* Use the time value of money tables found in text Appendix E.

37. **LO.5, 6** Answer the following independent questions with respect to traditional IRA contributions for 2022.

a. Juan, age 41, earns a salary of $28,000 and is not an active participant in any other qualified plan. His wife, Agnes, generates no earned income. What is the maximum total deductible contribution to their IRAs?

b. Abby, age 29, reports earned income of $25,000, and her husband, Sam, records earned income of $2,600. They are not active participants in any other qualified plan. What is the maximum contribution to their IRAs?

c. Leo's employer makes a contribution of $3,500 to Leo's simplified employee pension plan. If Leo is single, he reports earned income of $32,000, and his AGI is $29,000, what amount, if any, can he contribute to an IRA?

38. **LO.6** Jimmy establishes a Roth IRA at age 47 and contributes $89,600 over 18 years. The account is now worth $112,000. How much of these funds may Jimmy withdraw tax-free?

39. **LO.6** Carri and Dane, ages 34 and 32, respectively, have been married for 11 years, and both are active participants in employer qualified retirement plans. Their total AGI in 2022 is $207,000, and they earn salaries of $89,000 and $95,000, respectively. What amount may Carri and Dane:

a. Contribute to regular IRAs?

b. Deduct for their contributions in part (a)?

c. Contribute to Roth IRAs?

d. Deduct for their contributions in part (c)?

40. **LO.5, 6** Louis is a participant in the SIMPLE IRA of his employer Brown, Inc. During 2022, he contributes 8% of his salary of $63,000, and his employer contributes 3%. What is the total amount that will be vested in his account at the end of 2022?

41. **LO.6** Gabriella, age 34, and Dev, age 32, have been married for nine years. Gabriella, who is a college student, works part-time and earns $1,500. Dev is a high school teacher and earns a salary of $64,000.

a. What is the maximum amount Gabriella can contribute to an IRA in 2022?

b. What is the maximum amount Dev can contribute to an IRA in 2022?

42. **LO.6** Samuel, age 32, loses his job in a corporate downsizing. As a result of his termination, he receives a distribution of the balance in his § 401(k) account of $20,000 ($25,000 − $5,000 Federal income tax withholding) on May 1, 2022. Samuel's marginal tax rate is 24%. Decision Making Planning

a. What effect will the distribution have on Samuel's gross income and tax liability if he invests the $20,000 received in a mutual fund?

b. Same as part (a), except that Samuel invests the $20,000 received in a traditional IRA within 60 days of the distribution.

c. Same as part (a), except that Samuel invests the $20,000 received in a Roth IRA within 60 days of the distribution.

d. How could Samuel have received better tax consequences?

43. **LO.7** Dan, a professional basketball player, is to receive a bonus of $2,000,000 for signing an employment contract. An NQDC plan is established to postpone the income beyond Dan's peak income years. In 2022, his employer transfers the bonus to an escrow agent, who then invests the bonus in mutual funds. The funds are subject to the claims of the employer's creditors. The bonus is deferred for 10 years and becomes payable gradually in years 11 through 15. When is the bonus taxable to Dan and deductible by the employer?

44. **LO.7** Grace is an officer of a local bank that merges with a national bank, resulting in a change of ownership. She loses her job as a result of the merger, but she receives a cash settlement of $590,000 from her employer under her golden parachute. Her average annual compensation for the past five tax years was $200,000.
    a. What are the tax consequences to Grace and the bank of the $590,000 payment?
    b. Assume instead that Grace's five-year average annual compensation was $110,000 and that she receives $390,000 in the settlement. What are the tax consequences to Grace and the bank?
    c. Construct a table in Microsoft Excel that produces the correct answers for Grace and the bank in parts (a) and (b).

45. **LO.8, 9** Rosa exercises ISOs for 100 shares of Copper Corporation common stock at the option price of $100 per share on May 21, 2022, when the fair market value is $120 per share. She sells the 100 shares of common stock three and one-half years later for $140.
    a. Calculate the long-term capital gain and the ordinary income on the sale.
    b. Assume that Rosa holds the stock only seven months and sells the shares for $140 per share. Calculate the capital gain and ordinary income on the sale.
    c. In part (b), what amount can Copper Corporation deduct? When?
    d. Assume instead that Rosa holds the stock for two years and sells the shares for $115 per share. Calculate any capital gain and ordinary income that results.
    e. In part (a), assume that the options are nonqualified stock options with a nonascertainable fair market value on the date of the grant. Calculate the long-term capital gain and ordinary income on the date of the sale.
    f. In part (e), assume that each option has an ascertainable fair market value of $10 on the date of the grant and that no substantial risk of forfeiture exists. Calculate the long-term capital gain and the ordinary income on the date of the sale.
    g. Construct a table in Microsoft Excel that produces the correct answers for the above alternatives.

46. **LO.8, 9** On November 19, 2020, Rex is granted a nonqualified stock option to purchase 100 shares of Tan Company. On that date, the stock is selling for $8 per share, and the option price is $9 per share. Rex exercises the option on August 21, 2021, when the stock is selling for $10 per share. Five months later Rex sells the shares for $11.50 per share. The nonqualified stock option has no ascertainable fair market value.
    a. What amount is taxable to Rex in 2020?
    b. What amount is taxable to Rex in 2021?
    c. What amount and type of gain are taxable to Rex in 2022?
    d. What amount, if any, is deductible by Tan Company in 2021?
    e. What amount, if any, is recognized by Rex in 2021 if the stock is sold for $9.50 per share?
    f. Construct a table in Microsoft Excel that produces the correct answers for the above alternatives.

47. **LO.4, 5, 9** Sari Reid, age 35, is the owner of a small business. She is trying to decide whether to use a § 401(k) plan or a simplified employee pension plan. She is not interested in a SIMPLE § 401(k) plan. Her 2022 salary will be approximately $45,000, and she will have no employees. *Communications* *Decision Making* *Planning*

Sari asks you to provide her with information on the advantages and disadvantages of both types of plans and to give your recommendation. Draft a letter to Sari that contains your response. Her address is 1414 Canal Street, New Orleans, LA 70148.

48. **LO.2, 9** Zoe owns the retirement assets listed below. She plans to retire and start withdrawing amounts with which to meet her living expenses. Rank the accounts in the order from which she should make withdrawals so that tax deferral is maximized. Show your recommendation as a timeline in a Powerpoint slide to submit to your instructor. *Planning*

Roth IRA	$923,408
Traditional IRA	118,120
§ 401(k) plan	837,010

Research Problems

Note: Solutions to the Research Problems can be prepared by using the Thomson Reuters Checkpoint™ online tax research database, which accompanies this textbook. Solutions can also be prepared by using research materials found in a typical tax library.

the answer company™ THOMSON REUTERS®

Research Problem 1. Pedro comes to your office and indicates that he received $61,000 from a qualified retirement plan in 2022 before he was 59½ years old. He is not disabled or eligible for any of the other statutory exceptions to avoid the additional 10% early withdrawal tax under § 72(t). *Communications* *Critical Thinking*

Pedro wants you to help him prepare an argument that this additional 10% tax violates the equal protection component of the Due Process Clause of the Fifth Amendment to the U.S. Constitution, because of the age and disability classification exception in § 72(t)(2). Prepare a position paper answering Pedro, and e-mail the paper to your instructor.

Research Problem 2. Using the chart below, determine the appropriateness of the type of retirement plan for the four types of entities. Use the following notations: H: highly appropriate, M: moderately appropriate, L: lightly or not appropriate, NA: not applicable. In addition to information in this chapter, also review resources at the IRS website and other reliable websites.

Plan	Sole Proprietorship	Small or S Corporation	Large Corporation	Nonprofit Entity
IRA	______	______	______	______
SIMPLE IRA	______	______	______	______
Roth IRA	______	______	______	______
SEP	______	______	______	______
Keogh	______	______	______	______
SIMPLE § 401(k)	______	______	______	______
§ 401(k) (no employees)	______	______	______	______
§ 401(k) (with employees)	______	______	______	______
Defined Contribution Plan	______	______	______	______
Defined Benefit Plan	______	______	______	______

Use internet tax resources to address the following questions. Look for reliable websites and blogs of the IRS and other government agencies, media outlets, businesses, tax professionals, academics, think tanks, and political outlets.

Communications

Research Problem 3. Jacob Patterson is limited from making a fully deductible $6,000 IRA contribution because of his income level. Instead, he makes a $3,500 nondeductible IRA contribution to his traditional IRA. Determine how Jacob reports this investment on his return, and complete the appropriate tax form that he should attach to his Form 1040. E-mail these items to your instructor.

Communications
Critical Thinking
Data Analytics

Research Problem 4. Locate IRS data about taxable IRA distributions, specifically reporting the annual number of returns with distributions and their amounts. Comment about the data for the most recent three years, using $500,000 AGI ranges up to $5,000,000. E-mail your graph and some interpretive comments to your instructor.

Communications

Research Problem 5. Prepare two PowerPoint slides for each of the following items to present to your school's Accounting Club.

a. What is an inherited IRA?
b. If you inherit an IRA, can you make additional contributions to it?
c. Do an inherited IRA's funds remain tax-deferred?
d. Can a spouse beneficiary transfer the balance of an inherited IRA to his or her own IRA?
e. For an inherited IRA, who is a Designated Beneficiary? What rules apply to that person?

Research Problem 6. Find the full IRS RMD table, and compute the 2022 required minimum distribution in each of the following situations.

a. Anya's IRA balance is $215,000, and she is 76 years old.
b. Anya is 78 years old, and her IRA balance is $196,000.
c. Anya, age 72, is the surviving spouse of an inherited IRA with a balance of $172,000.
d. Anya, age 75, is the nonspouse beneficiary of an inherited IRA with a balance of $197,500.

Communications

Research Problem 7. Prepare no more than five Powerpoint slides on the topic "Should a Millennial Establish a Roth IRA and Contribute to It?" for a talk with your school's Investment Club. For a hypothetical taxpayer, graph the difference in account balances for Roth versus traditional IRAs given a starting date of age 25 and retirement dates of ages 65 and 70.

Becker CPA Review Questions

Becker

1. On March 1 of year 0, Judy was granted an incentive stock option (ISO) to purchase 50 shares of her employer's stock for $10 per share. The FMV of the stock on the date of the grant was $12 per share. On May 1 of year 1, Judy exercised her option when the stock was selling for $15 per share. On July 1 of year 2, Judy sold all of the shares for $20 per share. What amount and character of income does Judy recognize in year 2?

   a. $0
   b. $500, ordinary
   c. $500, long-term capital gain
   d. $600, ordinary

2. On February 1 of year 0, John received a nonqualified stock option to purchase 100 shares of his employer's stock for $10 per share. At the time John received the option, it was selling for $5 per share on an established exchange. On September 1 of year 1, John exercised the options when the stock was selling for $19 per share. On December 1 of year 2, John sold all of the shares for $30 per share. What is the amount and character of income that John must report in year 0?

   a. $0
   b. $500, ordinary
   c. $500, capital
   d. $1,000, ordinary

Part 7

Corporations and Partnerships

Chapter 20
Corporations and Partnerships

This text is primarily focused on basic tax concepts and the individual taxpayer. Although many of these tax concepts also apply to corporations and partnerships, other tax provisions apply specifically to these entities. Part 7 presents an overview of these provisions. Comprehensive coverage of these topics appears in *South-Western Federal Taxation: Corporations, Partnerships, Estates & Trusts.*

Chapter

20 Corporations and Partnerships

Learning Objectives: *After completing Chapter 20, you should be able to:*

LO.1 **Describe the nontax characteristics that are important for entity choice.**

LO.2 **Identify entities treated as corporations for Federal income tax purposes.**

LO.3 **Contrast the income tax treatment of individuals with that applicable to corporations.**

LO.4 **Compute the tax deductions available only to corporations.**

LO.5 **Calculate corporate tax liability and comply with various procedural and reporting requirements.**

LO.6 **Describe the tax rules governing the formation of corporations.**

LO.7 **Explain the tax rules governing the operation of corporations.**

LO.8 **Assess the utility and effect of the S election.**

LO.9 **Describe the tax consequences of forming and operating a partnership.**

LO.10 **Identify the advantages and disadvantages of the various forms used for conducting a business.**

Chapter Outline

20-1 Choice of Entity, 20-2
- 20-1a Nontax Considerations, 20-2
- 20-1b General Tax Consequences of Different Forms of Business Entities, 20-4
- 20-1c Check-the-Box Election, 20-5

20-2 Corporations, 20-6
- 20-2a Legal Status, 20-6
- 20-2b Individuals and Corporations Compared—An Overview, 20-6
- 20-2c Specific Provisions Compared, 20-8
- 20-2d Deductions Available Only to C Corporations, 20-12
- 20-2e Determination of Corporate Tax Liability, 20-14
- 20-2f Corporate Filing Requirements, 20-15
- 20-2g Reconciliation of Corporate Taxable Income and Accounting Income, 20-15

20-3 Forming the Corporation, 20-18
- 20-3a Transfers to Controlled Corporations, 20-18
- 20-3b Capital Contributions, 20-20

20-4 Distributions to Shareholders, 20-21
- 20-4a Dividend Distributions, 20-21
- 20-4b Constructive Dividends, 20-22

20-5 S Corporations, 20-23
- 20-5a Qualification for S Status, 20-23
- 20-5b Operational Rules, 20-25

20-6 Partnerships, 20-28
- 20-6a Nature of Partnership Taxation, 20-28
- 20-6b Partnership Formation and Basis, 20-29
- 20-6c Partnership Operations, 20-31

20-7 Tax Planning, 20-33
- 20-7a Corporate versus Noncorporate Forms of Business Organization, 20-33
- 20-7b C Corporation versus S Status, 20-35
- 20-7c Income Shifting to Reduce the Family Income Tax Burden, 20-35

GARY WOODS/ALAMY STOCK PHOTO

The Big Picture

Choice of Business Entity

The Todd sisters have decided to begin a catering business to handle private parties, weddings, anniversaries, and other large social events. Since their parents previously owned several restaurants, the sisters are familiar with food service operations. All of them will participate in the operation of the business and will provide the funds for capital acquisitions (e.g., delivery trucks, kitchen equipment, and food preparation facilities) and working capital needs. Due to the cost of the premiums, the sisters plan on minimal liability insurance coverage.

In the first few years of operation, the Todds anticipate losses. When and if the business becomes profitable, however, they would consider expansion. Any such expansion would require obtaining additional capital from outside sources.

With what type of entity should the Todd sisters conduct the business?

Read the chapter and formulate your response.

Up to this point, we have concentrated on the Federal income taxation of individual taxpayers. Individuals operating a business often do so as a sole proprietorship. Although simple and straightforward—it could be that only a Schedule C included with the Form 1040 is required—this may not be the best choice in achieving the individual's financial goals. Other forms of business organization are available and should be considered. Besides the sole proprietorship, the most popular choices include the following.

- C corporation.
- S corporation.
- Limited liability company (LLC).
- Partnership.

To make an informed choice as to what type of entity to select, familiarity with operational rules, nontax characteristics, and the tax consequences of each alternative is necessary. This chapter starts with an overview of the considerations involved when choosing a business form; then it considers each of the above entity choices.

LO.1

Describe the nontax characteristics that are important for entity choice.

20-1 Choice of Entity

The "choice of entity" question generally arises when a business is first formed. An entity choice can arise again as a business grows or ownership changes. For example, a business started as a sole proprietorship may grow, needing additional capital, such that the owner may consider converting the business to a corporation. In addition to tax matters, a careful consideration of legal and nontax factors such as responsibility for liabilities, the ability to raise capital through equity and debt, treatment under state law, and the relative rights and responsibilities of owners are all issues that should be analyzed prior to making the entity choice.

20-1a Nontax Considerations

The choice of entity decision involves nontax considerations such as the legal attributes of the business entities available. For the corporate form, key legal attributes include limited liability, continuity of life, free transferability of interests, and centralized management. Many, if not all, of these attributes also could be obtained through the use of a **limited liability company (LLC)**. When nontax considerations are evaluated, close attention must be paid to applicable state law. Many states, for example, place restrictions on the use of corporations to practice certain professions (e.g., medicine and law). Likewise, the legal attributes of an LLC may vary from one state to another and may not be identical to those of corporations.

In most states, a choice of the best business entity is driven by state law. For example, most states require organizational documentation to be filed with the state for a corporation (e.g., articles of incorporation), generally filed with the state's Secretary of State's office. Corporations also require other formalities, such as the appointment of a board of directors, adoption of bylaws, issuance of shares, minutes of board meetings, and corporate resolutions. Partnerships and LLCs often use similar documents, like a partnership agreement, to document the owners' rights and responsibilities.

One key consideration for many owners is the protection of limited personal liability due to their involvement with a business. For years, this advantage was only available for the corporate form of entity. A corporation is able to take on liabilities separate from the shareholders, thus insulating shareholders from whatever debts might befall the business. However, if there is no real separation between the corporation and its owners, the courts may "pierce the corporate veil" and look through to the owners to pay liabilities ordinarily left at the corporate level.

Example 1

Annette operates her business under the corporate form; however, after filing the initial articles of incorporation with the state, Annette failed to follow any of the corporate formalities required under state law (annual meetings, bylaws, issuance of shares). In addition, Annette paid personal expenses out of the corporate entity and paid corporate expenditures from her personal account. Finally, when Annette established the corporation, she did not capitalize (invest in the equity of the corporation) at the level that would be reasonable given the expected liabilities and activities of the corporation; thus, it was never likely that the corporation could stand on its own. As a result, the courts would pierce the corporate veil and hold Annette personally responsible for the actions and liabilities of the corporation.

The owners (or "members") of an LLC generally also are shielded from the liabilities of the business. Thus, an LLC can be seen as an entity that is a hybrid of a partnership and a corporation.

Sole proprietorships and partnerships, on the other hand, can expose owners to personal liability in situations where the business cannot cover its liabilities. A sole proprietorship is not an entity separate from its owner. Thus, the individual owner is fully liable for business liabilities, although this exposure can be mitigated through the use of insurance. Partners are fully liable for partnership liabilities that cannot be satisfied by the entity. Even for a limited partnership, at least one partner must be responsible for entity liabilities (the general partner). Like corporate investors, the limited partners typically are liable only to the extent of their capital investment in the entity.

Another important nontax aspect of entity choice relates to how the owners' rights can differ among entities. The rigidity of the corporate structure does not permit much flexibility with regard to how owners share their rights of ownership of the property and earnings of the business.

Partnerships and LLCs, however, offer a great deal of flexibility through the partnership or LLC agreements. They represent a contract between the owners wherein terms such as the sharing of income and losses, the sharing of debts, and the distribution of property can be negotiated as part of the agreement between the owners. Such flexibility has caused the tax law to include sometimes complex rules to prevent taxpayers from taking advantage of the distribution of taxable income and losses among owners to shift tax liabilities or harm government revenue.

Finally, for a thriving entrepreneur, a corporation is the most likely form to be used when the business is preparing to enter into its initial public offering (IPO). Corporations operate under a centralized management beholden to the board of directors and not directly to the shareholders. The IPO can help raise the necessary capital to expand the business; however, the limited management rights of owners under the corporate form makes that entity the optimal one for preventing wayward shareholders from interfering with the day-to-day operations of the business, since shareholder involvement generally is limited to voting for board members and other corporate resolutions. In addition, the corporate form often lends itself to free transferability of ownership, allowing shareholders to buy and sell shares with lower transaction costs (e.g., on a stock exchange).

An S corporation is a corporation formed under state law that has made an "S" election under the Federal tax law. A corporation that has not made an S election is referred to as a **C corporation**. When a corporation elects to be an S corporation, the tax law prescribes some requirements that affect the nontax characteristics of an S corporation. For example, an S corporation may not have more than 100 owners, may not have a non-U.S. owner, and is not permitted to have different classes of stock. An S corporation is treated somewhat like a partnership for Federal income tax purposes, but the same corporate formalities such as articles of incorporation, bylaws, and director meetings must be followed.

Concept Summary 20.1

Nontax Characteristics of Business Entities

	Sole Proprietor	C Corporation	S Corporation	General Partnership	LLC
Organization documents required to be filed with state	No	Yes	Yes	No	Yes
Corporate formalities required	No	Yes	Yes	No	No
Govern and control	Individual owner	Board of directors	Board of directors	Partners	Manager
Liabilities	Owner	Entity	Entity	Owners	Entity
Ability to arrange ownership rights and responsibilities	n/a	Inflexible	Inflexible	Flexible	Flexible
Type of owners allowed	Individual owner	Flexible	Some restrictions	Flexible	Flexible
Management	Individual owner	Centralized	Centralized	Decentralized	Centralized or decentralized

20-1b General Tax Consequences of Different Forms of Business Entities

A business operation may be conducted as a sole proprietorship, a partnership, an LLC, a corporation, or a qualified joint venture.

- Sole proprietorships are not separate taxable entities. The owner of the business reports all business transactions on his or her individual income tax return.

Example 2

Fred operates a bookstore selling rare books. The business is operated as a sole proprietorship. His bookstore generates income of $45,000 during the year. Fred will prepare a Schedule C to report his bookstore's gross income and expenses, a Schedule SE to report his self-employment tax, and any other schedules or forms required to support deductions on his Schedule C (such as Form 4562 to report depreciation and Form 8995 to report his qualified business income deduction). The net earnings from Fred's bookstore business reported on Schedule C are included on his individual income tax Form 1040.

- Partnerships are not subject to the income tax. Under the conduit concept, the various tax attributes of the partnership's operations flow through to the partners, to be reported on their income tax returns.

Example 3

Janice and Dave are siblings who operate an auto repair shop. Because they initially wanted to go into business together, they formed a partnership to operate the business. Janice and Dave share all of the income and expenses of the business equally according to the partnership agreement they both entered into. Although the partnership will prepare a tax return for informational purposes (Form 1065), each sibling's share of income or losses is reported on their individual income tax forms. Thus, tax on the business income is paid by the partners.

- The tax treatment of limited liability companies (LLCs) usually follows that applicable to partnerships.
- The C corporation is subject to the Federal corporate income tax. The corporation is recognized as a separate taxpaying entity apart from its shareholders. Income

is taxed to the corporation as earned and taxed again to the shareholders when it is distributed as dividends.

Example 4

Sarah operates a construction equipment rental business. Because of the risks associated with this type of business, Sarah wants limited liability and structures her business as a corporation under state law. As a separate entity, the corporation prepares its own tax return. Sarah only includes the earnings of the corporation on her individual tax return when the corporation makes a taxable distribution to her.

- A C corporation may elect to be taxed as an S corporation if certain requirements are met. The conduit concept applies, similar (although not identical) to the partnership rules. Income tax generally is avoided at the corporate level, and shareholders are taxed currently on the earnings of the S corporation.

Example 5

Maria starts a new business with her four brothers. They want limited liability for themselves. They expect to operate at a loss for the first few years. To provide an opportunity to allow the losses to flow into the other income of the siblings, they agree to form a corporation and make an S election. The S corporation is required to complete an informational tax return (Form 1120S), and the losses flow through to the owner's individual tax returns. Maria and her brothers could have considered a limited liability company to achieve the same income tax results.

Because they follow the conduit concept as to the treatment of their tax attributes, partnerships, LLCs, and S corporations often are referred to as **pass-through entities**. Not only does the income pass through to owners in the current year, but the items of income generally retain the character of the original transactions. For example, if a partnership, an LLC, or an S corporation generates long-term capital gains, when passed through to the partners, the income retains that tax-favored character. If a C corporation generates long-term capital gains, the gains and all other income generally are treated as dividend income when paid to owners.

The Big Picture

Example 6

Return to the facts of *The Big Picture* on p. 20-1. It appears that the Todd sisters should consider a C or S corporation, or an LLC, to obtain limited liability for their catering business. On the other hand, the conduit effect of an S corporation or a partnership is needed to enable the sisters to take advantage of the initial losses anticipated for the business. Using one of those entities, such losses could be deducted on their individual income tax returns.

20-1c Check-the-Box Election

The IRS has issued its so-called **Check-the-box Regulations**[1] to enable taxpayers to classify a business entity for tax purposes without regard to its corporate (or noncorporate) characteristics under pertinent state law. Under the rules, an entity with more than one owner can elect to be classified as either a partnership or a corporation. An entity with only one owner can elect to be classified as a corporation or a sole proprietorship. Most joint ventures are taxed as partnerships.[2] If no election is made, unincorporated entities with multiple owners are classified as partnerships and single-person businesses as sole proprietorships.

[1] Reg. §§ 301.7701–1 through –4 and –7.

[2] § 7701(a)(2).

The Check-the-box election is not available to entities that are incorporated under state law. Eligible entities make the election as to tax status by filing Form 8832 (Entity Classification Election). A reelection is allowed after a Check-the box election is withdrawn, but only after a 60-month waiting period.

Joint ventures usually are taxed as partnerships. However, at the election of the taxpayers, certain joint ventures between spouses can avoid partnership classification. Known as a qualified joint venture, spouses report their share of the business activities from a joint venture as sole proprietors (using two Schedule C forms).[3]

20-2 Corporations

LO.2

Identify entities treated as corporations for Federal income tax purposes.

20-2a Legal Status

As described in text Section 20-1, corporations must comply with the specific requirements for corporate status under state law. But a corporation qualifying under state law may be disregarded as a taxable entity if it is lacking in economic substance.[4] The key consideration is the degree of business activity conducted at the corporate level.

Corporate Activities

Example 7

Gene and Mina are joint owners of a tract of unimproved real estate they want to protect from future creditors. Gene and Mina form Falcon Corporation and transfer the land to it in return for all of the corporation's stock. The corporation merely holds title to the land and conducts no other activities. In all respects, Falcon meets the legal requirements of a corporation under applicable state law. Nevertheless, assuming these facts, Falcon might not be recognized as a separate entity for corporate tax purposes.

Example 8

Assume the same facts as in Example 7. In addition to holding title to the land, Falcon Corporation leases the property, collects rents, and pays the property taxes. Falcon probably would be treated as a corporation for Federal income tax purposes because of the scope of its activities.

In some instances, the IRS has attempted to disregard (or collapse) a corporation to make the income taxable directly to the shareholders.[5] In other cases, the IRS has asserted that the corporation is a separate taxable entity, to assess tax at the corporate level and to tax corporate distributions to shareholders as dividend income (double taxation).[6]

Can an organization not qualifying as a corporation under state law still be treated as such for Federal income tax purposes? Yes. The tax law defines a corporation as including "associations, joint stock companies, and insurance companies."[7] Since the Code contains no definition of an "association," the issue constitutes the subject of litigation.[8]

LO.3

Contrast the income tax treatment of individuals with that applicable to corporations.

20-2b Individuals and Corporations Compared—An Overview

Similarities between Corporate and Individual Tax Rules

The gross income of a C corporation is determined in much the same manner as for individuals. Both individuals and corporations are entitled to exclusions from

[3] § 761(f). For further information, see **tinyurl.com/elect-hw**.

[4] See *Paymer v. Comm.*, 150 F.2d 334 (CA–2).

[5] *Floyd Patterson*, 25 TCM 1230, T.C.Memo. 1966–239, *aff'd* in 68–2 USTC ¶9471, 22 AFTR 2d 5810 (CA–2).

[6] *Elot H. Raffety Farms Inc. v. U.S.*, 511 F.2d 1234 (CA–8).

[7] § 7701(a)(3).

[8] See, for example, *U.S. v. Kintner*, 216 F.2d 418 (CA–5).

gross income, such as interest on municipal bonds. Gains and losses from property transactions are treated similarly. For example, whether a gain or loss is capital or ordinary depends on the nature and use of the asset rather than the type of taxpayer. Upon the sale or other taxable disposition of depreciable personalty, the recapture rules of § 1245 make no distinction between corporate and noncorporate taxpayers. In the case of the recapture of depreciation on real property (§ 1250), however, corporate taxpayers experience more severe tax consequences. As discussed in text Section 17-5a, corporations recognize as additional ordinary income 20 percent of the excess of the amount that would be recaptured under § 1245 over the amount recaptured under § 1250.[9]

In cases involving nontaxable exchanges and certain transactions allowing the deferral of gain recognition, both individuals and corporations can utilize the like-kind exchange provisions of § 1031 and the deferral allowed by § 1033 for involuntary conversions. In contrast, the § 121 exclusion for gain from the sale of a principal residence is a relief measure available only to individual taxpayers.

The business deductions of C corporations mostly parallel those available to individuals. Corporate deductions are allowed for all ordinary and necessary expenses paid or incurred in carrying on a trade or business. Corporations may deduct interest, certain taxes, losses, bad debts, depreciation, cost recovery, charitable contributions (subject to different corporate limitation rules), net operating losses, and other items.

Many of the tax credits available to individuals, such as the energy credit, can be claimed by C corporations. Not available to corporations are certain credits that are personal in nature, such as the credit for child and dependent care expenses.

Most C corporations enjoy greater flexibility in the selection of a tax year than do other business entity types. For example, C corporations usually can have different tax years from those of their shareholders. A newly formed corporation generally can choose any permissible accounting period without having to obtain the consent of the IRS. However, **personal service corporations** and S corporations are subject to restrictions on the use of a fiscal year.[10]

C corporations and partnerships with a partner that is a C corporation generally must use the accrual method of accounting.[11] However, there are exceptions to this rule.

- Corporations and partnerships with a C corporation partner, with average annual gross receipts in the prior three-year period that do not exceed $27 million.
- Certain farming businesses.[12]
- A C corporation that is a qualified personal service corporation (QPSC).[13]

These businesses (and sole proprietorships, S corporations, and partnerships without a C corporation partner) generally can use either the cash or accrual method of accounting. Businesses with average annual gross receipts in the prior three-year period of $27 million or less may use the cash method even if they have inventory. An exception exists if the entity meets the definition of a tax shelter. This entity must use the accrual method and account for inventory regardless of its gross receipts level.[14]

---

[9] § 291.

[10] §§ 441(i) and 1378.

[11] § 448(a)

[12] § 447.

[13] See § 448(d)(2). A QPSC is a corporation where substantially all of its activities involve services in the fields of health, law, engineering, architecture, accounting, actuarial science, performing arts, or consulting.

[14] See text Sections 4-2 and 18-2 for a discussion of the cash and accrual methods of accounting.

Gross Receipts Test

Example 9

Sheila's Plumbing, a plumbing contractor not organized as a corporation, records gross receipts of $12 ,000,000. Sheila's plumbing is a small business under the inventory exception rules because gross receipts do not exceed $27,000,000. This business may use the cash method for tax purposes.

Example 10

Howe Plumbing Inc. (a C corporation), a plumbing contractor, reports gross receipts of $19,000,000. Howe is eligible for the $27,000,000 small business exception to using the accrual method and accounting for inventory.

Example 11

Blue Corporation is an S corporation. It records gross receipts of $31,000,000. If Blue has no inventory, it is not required to use the accrual method of accounting. If inventory is an income-producing factor for Blue, then it must use the accrual method for inventory; it does not meet the inventory exception for small businesses.

If Blue were instead a C corporation or a partnership with a C corporation as a partner, it would be required to use the accrual method of accounting due to its gross receipts level.

Dissimilarities

Individual taxpayers are subject to progressive income tax rates. The rates are 10, 12, 22, 24, 32, 35, and 37 percent. The rate for corporations is a flat 21 percent.

As discussed in Chapter 16, qualified dividends received by individual shareholders are subject to preferential tax rates. Rates of 0, 15, or 20 percent can apply, depending on the taxable income of the individual. C corporations do not benefit from such preferential rates, but as discussed later, corporations that own stock in other corporations may claim the dividends received deduction.

There is no alternative minimum tax for corporations. The determination of adjusted gross income, so essential for individuals, has no relevance to corporations. Corporations need not be concerned with classifying deductions into deduction *for* and *from* categories.

The similarities and dissimilarities between individuals and C corporations as to tax attributes are outlined in Concept Summary 20.2.

20-2c Specific Provisions Compared

Capital Gains and Losses

Both corporate and noncorporate taxpayers aggregate gains and losses from the taxable sale or exchange of capital assets. Refer to text Section 16-5a for a description of the netting process that takes place after the aggregation has been completed.

For long-term capital gains (including gains from collectibles and unrecaptured § 1250 gain), individuals use preferential tax rates. The maximum applicable tax rate is 28 percent for collectibles, 25 percent for unrecaptured § 1250 gain, and 20 percent for other capital gains. For C corporations, all capital gains are taxed as ordinary income. Therefore, the net long-term capital gain of a corporation is taxed at 21 percent.

Example 12

Rose reports taxable income of $80,000, not including a long-term capital gain of $10,000. If Rose is an individual, the tax on the capital gain is $1,500 ($10,000 × 15%). If Rose is a C corporation, the tax becomes $2,100 ($10,000 × 21%).

Significant differences between corporations and individuals exist in the treatment of capital losses for Federal income tax purposes. Individuals, for example, can deduct up to $3,000 per year of net capital losses against ordinary income. If an individual generates both net short-term and net long-term capital losses, the short-term capital losses are used first in arriving at the $3,000 ordinary loss deduction.

C corporations may not use net capital losses to offset ordinary income, but they may use net capital losses to offset past or future capital gains.[15] Unlike individuals, C corporations are not allowed an unlimited carryover period for capital losses. Instead, they may carry back excess capital losses to the three preceding years, applying the losses initially to the earliest year. If not exhausted by the carryback, remaining unused capital losses may be carried forward for a period of five years from the year of the loss.[16]

When carried back or forward, *both* short-term capital losses and long-term capital losses are treated as short-term capital losses by corporate taxpayers. For noncorporate taxpayers, carryovers of capital losses retain their identity as short or long term.

Example 13

Hawk Corporation, a calendar year taxpayer, incurs a long-term net capital loss of $5,000 for 2022. None of the capital loss may be deducted in 2022. Hawk may, however, carry the loss back to years 2019, 2020, and 2021 (in this order) and offset any capital gains recognized in these years. If the carryback does not exhaust the loss, the loss may be carried forward to 2023, 2024, 2025, 2026, and 2027 (in this order). Such capital loss carrybacks or carryovers are treated as short-term capital losses.

Recapture of Depreciation

Under § 291, C corporations incur ordinary income equal to 20 percent of the excess of the § 1245 recapture potential over the § 1250 recapture. The § 1231 gain is reduced by the additional recapture.

Under § 1250, the excess of accelerated depreciation over straight-line depreciation is recaptured as ordinary income as to real property. See text Section 17-3.

Example 14

Condor Corporation purchases residential real property on November 3, 2008, for $300,000. Straight-line cost recovery is taken in the amount of $143,624 (see Exhibit 8.8 in Chapter 8) before the property is sold on January 6, 2022, for $250,000. (Neither the purchase nor selling price includes any amount attributable to the land.)

First, determine the recognized gain.

Sales price		$ 250,000
Less adjusted basis:		
Cost of property	$ 300,000	
Less cost recovery	(143,624)	(156,376)
Recognized gain		$ 93,624

Second, determine the § 1245 recapture potential. This is the lesser of $93,624 (recognized gain) or $143,624 (cost recovery claimed).

Third, determine the § 1250 recapture amount.

Cost recovery taken	$ 143,624
Less straight-line cost recovery	(143,624)
§ 1250 ordinary income	$ –0–

continued

[15] §§ 1211(a) and (b).

[16] § 1212(a).

Fourth, because the taxpayer is a C corporation, determine the additional § 291 amount.

§ 1245 recapture potential	$ 93,624
Less § 1250 recapture amount	(–0–)
Excess § 1245 recapture potential	$ 93,624
Apply § 291 percentage	× 20%
Additional ordinary income under § 291	$ 18,725

Condor's recognized gain of $93,624 is:

Ordinary income under § 1250	$ –0–
Ordinary income under § 291	18,725
§ 1231 gain	74,899
Total recognized gain	$ 93,624

Charitable Contributions

Generally, a charitable contribution deduction is allowed only for the tax year in which the payment is made. However, for C corporations, the deduction may be claimed in the tax year *preceding* payment if the following conditions are satisfied.

- The contribution is authorized by the board of directors by the end of that tax year, *and*
- The contribution is paid on or before the fifteenth day of the fourth month of the next tax year.[17]

Example 15

On December 26, 2022, the board of directors of Dove Corporation, a calendar year, accrual basis taxpayer, authorizes a $20,000 donation to a qualified charity. The donation is paid on April 15, 2023. Dove may claim all or a portion of the $20,000 donation as a deduction for 2022. As an alternative, Dove may claim the deduction in 2023 (the year of payment).

Like individuals, corporations are not permitted an unlimited charitable contribution deduction. In any one year, a corporate taxpayer is limited to 10 percent of taxable income computed without regard to the charitable contribution deduction, any net operating loss carryback or capital loss carryback, or the dividends received deduction (discussed later in this chapter).[18] Any contributions in excess of the 10 percent limitation are carried forward to the five succeeding tax years. A carryover is added to subsequent contributions and is subject to the 10 percent limitation. In applying the limitation, the most recent contributions are deducted first.[19]

Carryover Situations

Example 16

During 2023, Eagle Corporation (a calendar year taxpayer) reported the following income and expenses.

Income from operations	$140,000
Expenses from operations	110,000
Dividends received	10,000
Charitable contributions made in 2023	5,000

For purposes of the 10% limitation only, Eagle's taxable income is $40,000 ($140,000 − $110,000 + $10,000). Consequently, the allowable charitable contribution deduction for 2023 is $4,000 (10% × $40,000). The $1,000 unused portion of the contribution is carried forward to 2024, 2025, 2026, 2027, and 2028 (in that order) until exhausted.

[17] § 170(a)(2).

[18] § 170(b)(2). For 2020 and 2021, the threshold was 25% of taxable income for cash contributions by corporations (P.L. 116–136, 3/27/20; P.L. 116–260, 12/27/20).

[19] § 170(d)(2).

Carryover Situations

Example 17

Assume the same facts as in Example 16. In 2024, Eagle Corporation records taxable income (after adjustments) of $50,000 and makes a charitable contribution of $4,800. The maximum charitable contribution deduction allowed for 2024 is $5,000 (10% × $50,000). The first $4,800 of the allowed deduction must be allocated to the 2024 contribution, and the $200 excess is allocated to the carryover from 2023. The remaining $800 of the 2023 contribution is carried over to 2025, etc.

As noted in text Section 10-4e, the deduction for charitable contributions of ordinary income property is limited to the lesser of the fair market value or the adjusted basis of the property. A special rule permits a corporation to contribute inventory (ordinary income property) to certain charitable organizations, and to deduct an amount equal to the adjusted basis plus one-half of any appreciation in value over the basis. In no event, however, may the deduction exceed twice the adjusted basis of the property. To qualify for this exception, the inventory must be used by the charity as part of its exempt purpose for the care of children, the ill, or the needy.[20]

Example 18

Robin Company (a retail clothier) donates sweaters and overcoats to Sheltering Arms (a qualified charity caring for the homeless). The clothing is inventory and has a basis of $10,000 and a fair market value of $14,000. If Robin is a C corporation, the charitable contribution that results is $12,000 [$10,000 (basis) + $2,000 (50% of the appreciation of $4,000)]. Otherwise, the charitable contribution is limited to $10,000 (basis).

Net Operating Losses

A net operating loss (NOL) is the excess of deductions over gross income for the taxable year. Modifications are then required to this amount in deriving the NOL.[21] Individuals are subject to more modifications than are C corporations. For example, individuals must adjust the NOL to remove certain itemized deductions (see text Section 7-6).

For both individuals and C corporations, the deduction for an NOL generated after 2020 is limited to 80 percent of the current year's taxable income [without regard to the NOL deduction (NOLD)] when used. (NOLs generated prior to 2021 could be used to offset up to 100 percent of taxable income, necessitating tracking of different NOL periods.) NOLs generated after 2020 may only be carried forward, but the carryforward period is indefinite.[22] A 2-year carryback and 20-year carryforward rule applied for NOLs generated prior to 2018. For NOLs generated in 2018, 2019, or 2020, a special 5-year carryback applied, with an indefinite carryforward period.

Net Operating Loss

Example 19

In its current tax year, both Desire Corporation and Amy, a sole proprietor, recorded gross income of $120,000 and allowable business deductions of $170,000. Amy reported no other gross income, but her itemized deductions (other than a casualty or theft loss) totaled $23,000. Amy's NOL does not include the itemized deductions. Thus, her NOL is $50,000. Desire's NOL also is $50,000.

Example 20

In 2022, Rusty Corp., a calendar year corporation, has a net operating loss of $10,000. Rusty must carry this loss forward to 2023. In 2023, Rusty generates taxable income of $12,000. Rusty's use of the NOL is limited to 80% of the 2023 taxable income, or $9,600 ($12,000 × 80%). Rusty's 2023 taxable income after the NOL is $2,400 ($12,000 − $9,600). Rusty may carry forward the remaining $400 NOL indefinitely.

[20] § 170(e)(3).

[21] §§ 172(c) and (d).

[22] §§ 172 (a) and (b).

LO.4

Compute the tax deductions available only to corporations.

20-2d Deductions Available Only to C Corporations

Dividends Received Deduction

The purpose of the **dividends received deduction** is to prevent a possible triple taxation of a dollar of taxable income. Without the deduction, income paid to a corporation in the form of a dividend would be subject to taxation for a second time (after being taxed first to the distributing corporation) with no corresponding deduction to the distributing corporation. A third level of tax would be assessed on the shareholders if the recipient corporation distributed the income to its shareholders. Because the dividends received deduction may be less than 100 percent, the law may provide only partial relief.

The amount of the dividends received deduction depends on the percentage of ownership the recipient corporate shareholder holds in the corporation making the dividend distribution.[23] For dividends received or accrued, the *deduction percentage* is:

Percentage of Ownership by Corporate Shareholder	Deduction Percentage
Less than 20%	50%
20% or more (but less than 80%)	65%
80% or more	100%

The dividends received deduction may be limited to a percentage of the taxable income of a corporation computed without regard to the NOLD, the dividends received deduction, or any capital loss carryback. The percentage of taxable income limitation corresponds to the deduction percentage. Thus, if a corporate shareholder owns less than 20 percent of the stock in the distributing corporation, the dividends received deduction is limited to 50 percent of taxable income (as previously defined). However, this limitation does not apply if the DRD creates negative taxable income for the current taxable year.[24] The DRD usually is available only to dividends received from domestic corporations.

Steps to compute DRD:

1. Multiply the dividends received by the deduction percentage.
2. Multiply the taxable income (as previously defined) by the deduction percentage.
3. The deduction is limited to the lesser of step 1 or step 2, unless subtracting the amount derived from step 1 from taxable income (as previously defined) generates a negative number. If so, the amount derived in step 1 is used.

If a corporation incurs an NOL before any dividends received deduction is claimed, the full dividends received deduction (as calculated in step 1) is allowed.

Example 21

Crane, Osprey, and Gull, three unrelated calendar year C corporations, incur the following transactions for 2022.

	Crane Corporation	Osprey Corporation	Gull Corporation
Gross income from operations	$ 400,000	$ 320,000	$ 210,000
Expenses from operations	(340,000)	(340,000)	(340,000)
Dividends received from domestic corporations (less than 20% ownership)	200,000	200,000	200,000
Taxable income before the dividends received deduction	$ 260,000	$ 180,000	$ 70,000

continued

[23]§ 243(a).

[24]§ 246(b).

In determining the dividends received deduction, use the step procedure just described.

	Crane Corporation	Osprey Corporation	Gull Corporation
Step 1: (50% × $200,000)	$ 100,000	$ 100,000	$ 100,000
Step 2:			
50% × $260,000 (taxable income)	$ 130,000		
50% × $180,000 (taxable income)		$ 90,000	
50% × $70,000 (taxable income)			$ 35,000
Step 3:			
Lesser of step 1 or step 2	$ 100,000	$ 90,000	
Generates an NOL			$ 100,000

Osprey Corporation is subject to the 50 percent of taxable income limitation. It does not qualify for the loss rule treatment because subtracting $100,000 (step 1) from $180,000 yields a positive result. Gull Corporation qualifies for the loss rule treatment because subtracting $100,000 (step 1) from $70,000 yields a negative number.

Deduction of Organizational Expenditures

A corporation may elect to amortize organizational expenses over a period of 15 years starting in the taxable year in which the corporation begins business. A special exception, similar to the expensing of startup expenditures discussed in text Section 6-3d, allows the corporation to immediately expense the first $5,000 of these costs in addition to the first year's amortization amount.[25] The exception, however, is phased out on a dollar-for-dollar basis when these expenses exceed $50,000.

Example 22

Kingbird Corporation, a calendar year taxpayer, is formed on February 1, 2022, and begins business on June 1, 2022. In connection with its formation, it incurs organizational expenditures of $52,000. Kingbird's deduction for organizational expenditures for 2022, is:

$$\text{Expense: } \$5{,}000 - (\$52{,}000 - \$50{,}000) = \$3{,}000$$

$$\text{Amortization: } \frac{\$52{,}000 - \$3{,}000}{180 \text{ months}} \times 7 \text{ (months)} = \$1{,}906$$

Kingbird deducts a total of $4,906 ($3,000 + $1,906) for 2022.

The election to amortize is deemed made unless the corporation clearly indicates on its first tax return that it chooses to capitalize all such expenses.[26]

Organizational expenditures include the following.

- Legal services incident to organization (e.g., drafting the corporate charter, bylaws, minutes of organizational meetings, and terms of original stock certificates).
- Necessary accounting services.

[25] § 248.

[26] § 248(c). If the choice not to amortize is made, the expenditures cannot be deducted until the corporation ceases to conduct business and liquidates. The election covers all qualifying expenses.

- Expenses of temporary directors and of organizational meetings of directors and shareholders.
- Fees paid to the state of incorporation.

Expenditures connected with issuing or selling shares of stock or other securities (e.g., commissions, professional fees, printing costs) or with transferring assets to a corporation do not qualify for the deduction. These expenditures generally are added to the capital account and are not subject to amortization.

Interest Expense Deduction Limitation

Business interest expense in excess of 30 percent of adjusted taxable income (ATI) may not be deducted but is carried forward to a future year.[27] For tax years through 2021, the following are added back to business taxable income in arriving at ATI: business interest income and expense; net operating loss deduction; the qualified business income deduction (i.e., the 20 percent deduction under § 199A); and deductions allowable for depreciation, amortization, or depletion. After 2021, depreciation, amortization, and depletion are not added back to ATI, causing less interest expense to be deductible in the current year for an entity subject to this limitation rule.

The interest deduction limitation generally does not apply to businesses with average annual gross receipts for the prior three-year period of $27 million or less.

20-2e Determination of Corporate Tax Liability

LO.5

Calculate corporate tax liability and comply with various procedural and reporting requirements.

Income Tax Rates

Prior to 2018, corporate tax rates were progressive with marginal rates as low as 15 percent, increasing up to 35 percent. For tax years beginning after 2017, the corporate tax rate is a flat 21 percent.[28]

Example 23

A calendar year C corporation reports taxable income of $400,000 for 2022. The Federal income tax liability is $84,000, determined as $400,000 × 21%.

Alternative Minimum Tax

Prior to 2018, C corporations were subject to an alternative minimum tax (AMT) similar to that applicable to individuals.[29] The corporate AMT no longer applies.

[27] § 163(j)(1).

[28] § 11(b).

[29] § 55.

20-2f Corporate Filing Requirements

A C corporation must file a Federal income tax return whether or not it records taxable income.[30] A corporation that was not in existence throughout an entire annual accounting period must file a return for the fraction of the year during which it did exist. A C corporation is relieved of filing returns once it ceases to conduct business and dissolves.

The corporate return is filed on Form 1120. Corporations making the S election (discussed in text Section 20-5) file using Form 1120S.

Corporations with less than $250,000 of gross receipts and less than $250,000 in assets need not complete Schedule L (balance sheet) and Schedules M–1 and M–2 (see the next section) of Form 1120. Similar relief is allowed for Form 1120S. These rules can ease the compliance burden on small business.

Form 1120 is due on the fifteenth day of the fourth month following the close of the corporation's tax year.[31] Corporations can receive an automatic extension of six months for filing the return, using Form 7004.

A C corporation must make payments of estimated tax unless its tax liability reasonably is expected to be less than $500. The payments must equal the lesser of 100 percent of the corporation's final tax or 100 percent of the last year's tax.

Estimated tax payments may be made electronically in four installments, due on or before the fifteenth day of the fourth, sixth, ninth, and twelfth months of the corporate taxable year. The full amount of the unpaid tax is due on the date of the return. Failure to make the required estimated tax payments triggers a nondeductible penalty unless an exception applies.[32]

20-2g Reconciliation of Corporate Taxable Income and Accounting Income

Taxable income and accounting net income seldom equal the same amount. For example, a difference may arise if the corporation uses accelerated depreciation for tax purposes and straight-line depreciation for accounting purposes.

Many items of income for accounting purposes, such as proceeds from a life insurance policy on the death of a corporate officer and interest on municipal bonds, may not be includible in calculating taxable income. Some expense items for accounting purposes, such as expenses to produce tax-exempt income, estimated warranty reserves, a net capital loss, and Federal income taxes, are not deductible for tax purposes.

Schedule M–1 of Form 1120 is used to reconcile accounting net income (net income after Federal income taxes) with taxable income (as computed on the corporate tax return before the deduction for an NOL and the dividends received deduction). A two-column format is used.

[30] § 6012(a)(2).

[31] § 6072(a).

[32] § 6655.

Example 24

During the current year, Crow Corporation reported the following transactions.

Net income per books (after tax)	$89,400
Taxable income	50,000
Federal income tax liability (21% × $50,000)	10,500
Interest income from tax-exempt bonds	5,000
Interest paid on loan, the proceeds of which were used to purchase the tax-exempt bonds	500
Life insurance proceeds received as a result of the death of a key employee	50,000
Premiums paid on key employee life insurance policy	2,600
Excess of capital losses over capital gains	2,000

For book and tax purposes, Crow determines depreciation under the straight-line method. Crow's Schedule M–1 for the current year follows.

Schedule M-1 Reconciliation of Income (Loss) per Books With Income per Return
Note: The corporation may be required to file Schedule M-3. See instructions.

1	Net income (loss) per books	*89,400*	7	Income recorded on books this year not included on this return (itemize): Tax-exempt interest $ *5,000* *Life insurance proceeds on key employee $50,000*	*55,000*
2	Federal income tax per books	*10,500*			
3	Excess of capital losses over capital gains	*2,000*			
4	Income subject to tax not recorded on books this year (itemize):				
5	Expenses recorded on books this year not deducted on this return (itemize):		8	Deductions on this return not charged against book income this year (itemize):	
a	Depreciation $		a	Depreciation $	
b	Charitable contributions $		b	Charitable contributions $	
c	Travel and entertainment $ *Prem.–life ins. $2,600; Int.–exempt bonds $500*	*3,100*	9	Add lines 7 and 8	*55,000*
6	Add lines 1 through 5	*105,000*	10	Income (page 1, line 28)—line 6 less line 9	*50,000*

Schedule M–2 of Form 1120 reconciles accounting retained earnings at the beginning of the year with retained earnings at year-end.

Example 25

Assume the same facts as in Example 24. Crow Corporation's beginning balance in unappropriated retained earnings is $125,000, and Crow distributed a cash dividend of $30,000 to its shareholders during the year. Based on these further assumptions, Crow has the following Schedule M–2 for the current year.

Schedule M-2 Analysis of Unappropriated Retained Earnings per Books (Schedule L, Line 25)

1	Balance at beginning of year	*125,000*	5	Distributions: a Cash	*30,000*
2	Net income (loss) per books	*89,400*		b Stock	
3	Other increases (itemize):			c Property	
			6	Other decreases (itemize):	
			7	Add lines 5 and 6	*30,000*
4	Add lines 1, 2, and 3	*214,400*	8	Balance at end of year (line 4 less line 7)	*184,400*

Concept Summary 20.2

Summary of Income Tax Consequences: Individuals Compared with C Corporations

	Individuals	C Corporations
Computation of gross income	§ 61.	§ 61.
Computation of taxable income	§§ 62, 63(b) through (h).	§ 63(a). Concept of AGI has no relevance.
Deductions	Trade or business (§ 162); nonbusiness (§ 212); some personal and employee expenses (generally deductible as itemized deductions).	Trade or business (§ 162).
Deduction for qualified business income (§ 199A)	Generally allowed for qualified business income (see text Section 9-7).	Not allowed for corporations.
Charitable contributions	Limited in any tax year to 50% of AGI (60% for cash contributions); 30% for long-term capital gain property unless election is made to reduce fair market value of gift; 20% for long-term capital gain property contributed to private nonoperating foundations.	Limited in any tax year to 10% of taxable income computed without regard to the charitable contribution deduction, net operating loss or capital loss carryback, and dividends received deduction.
	Time of deduction—year in which payment is made.	Time of deduction—year in which payment is made unless accrual basis taxpayer. Accrual basis corporation may take deduction in year preceding payment if contribution was authorized by board of directors by end of that year and contribution is paid by fifteenth day of fourth month of following year.
	Contribution of ordinary income property is limited to the lesser of adjusted basis or fair market value.	Contribution of certain ordinary income property can include one-half of any appreciation on the property.
	Excess charitable contributions can be carried over for a period of up to five years.	Excess charitable contributions can be carried over for a period of up to five years.
Casualty losses	Nondeductible unless casualty is associated with recognized federal disaster.	Deductible in full.
Depreciation recapture for § 1250 property	Recaptured to extent accelerated depreciation exceeds straight-line.	20% of excess of amount that would be recaptured under § 1245 over amount recaptured under § 1250 is additional ordinary income under § 291.
Net operating loss	Adjusted for nonbusiness deductions over nonbusiness income and for personal and dependency exemptions.	Generally no adjustments.
Dividends received	Qualified dividends are taxed at the same rate applicable to net long-term capital gains.	Deduction allowed (50%, 65%, or 100%) as to dividends received.
Long-term capital gains	Generally taxed at a rate no higher than 15% (20% for certain high-income taxpayers and 0% for certain low-income taxpayers).	Taxed using regular corporate rates.

continued

Summary of Income Tax Consequences—(Continued)

	Individuals	C Corporations
Capital losses	Only $3,000 of capital loss can offset ordinary income; loss is carried forward indefinitely to offset capital gains or ordinary income up to $3,000; carryovers of short-term losses remain short term; long-term losses carry over as long term.	Can offset only capital gains; carried back three years and forward five years; carrybacks and carryovers are treated as short-term losses.
Passive activity losses	Generally deductible only against income from passive activities.	No limitation on deductibility. Personal service corporations and certain closely held corporations, however, are subject to same limitations as imposed on individuals. A closely held corporation is a corporation where five or fewer individuals own more than 50% of the stock either directly or indirectly.
Alternative minimum tax	Applied at a graduated rate schedule of 26% and 28% to AMT base (taxable income as modified by certain adjustments plus preference items minus exemption amount).	No corporate AMT.
Tax rates	Progressive with seven rates of 10%, 12%, 22%, 24%, 32%, 35%, and 37%.	Flat 21% rate.
Filing due dates	Fifteenth day of the *fourth* month following the close of the individual's tax year.	Generally same as for individuals.
Medicare Surtax on Net Investment Income (§1411)	Applies to high-income individuals with net investment income (see text Section 13-5c).	Does not apply.

Certain corporations must file **Schedule M–3**.[33] This schedule is filed in lieu of Schedule M–1 when the assets reported on Schedule L of Form 1120 total or exceed $10 million.[34] Because it reveals differences between book and taxable income in more detail, Schedule M–3 enables the IRS to identify potential audit areas.

LO.6

Describe the tax rules governing the formation of corporations.

20-3 Forming the Corporation

20-3a Transfers to Controlled Corporations

Without special provisions in the Code, a transfer of property to a corporation in exchange for its stock would be a sale or exchange of property and would constitute a taxable transaction to the transferring shareholder. Code § 351 provides for the nonrecognition of gain or loss upon such transfers of property if the transferors are in

[33]Rev.Proc. 2004–45. Schedule M–3 satisfies some of the disclosure requirements set forth in Reg. § 1.6011–4 when significant booktax differences occur.

[34]C corporations and partnerships with more than $10 million of assets but less than $50 million of assets need not complete all parts of Schedule M–3.

control of the corporation immediately after the transfer. Gain or loss is postponed in a manner similar to a like-kind exchange (see text Section 15-2).

To qualify under § 351, the transferors must be in control of the corporation immediately after the exchange. *Control* is defined as ownership of at least 80 percent of the total combined voting power of all classes of stock entitled to vote and at least 80 percent of the total number of shares of all other classes of stock.[35]

Realized gain (but not loss) is recognized to the extent the transferors receive property other than stock. Such nonqualifying property often is referred to as *boot.* If the requirements of § 351 are satisfied and no boot is involved, nonrecognition of gain or loss is *mandatory*.

Basis Considerations and Computation of Gain

The nonrecognition of gain or loss is accompanied by a carryover of basis. The basis of stock received in a § 351 transfer is determined as follows.

- Start with the adjusted basis of the property transferred by the shareholder.
- Add any gain recognized by the shareholder as a result of the transfer.
- Subtract the fair market value of any boot received by the shareholder from the corporation.[36]

Shareholders who receive noncash boot take a basis in the property equal to the fair market value. The basis of properties received by the corporation is the basis in the hands of the transferor increased by the amount of any gain recognized to the transferring shareholder.[37]

Basis Determination

Example 26

Ann and Lori form Bluejay Corporation. Ann transfers property with an adjusted basis of $30,000 and a fair market value of $60,000 for 50% of the stock. Lori transfers property with an adjusted basis of $40,000 and a fair market value of $60,000 for the remaining 50% of the stock. The realized gain ($30,000 for Ann and $20,000 for Lori) is not recognized on the transfer because the transfer qualifies under § 351. The basis of the stock to Ann is $30,000, and the basis of the stock to Lori is $40,000. Bluejay takes a basis of $30,000 in the property transferred by Ann and a basis of $40,000 in the property transferred by Lori.

Example 27

Mike and John form Condor Corporation with the following investments: Mike transfers property (adjusted basis of $30,000 and fair market value of $70,000), and John transfers cash of $60,000. Each receives 50 shares of the Condor stock, but Mike also receives $10,000 in cash. Each share of the Condor stock is worth $1,200. Mike's realized gain is determined as follows.

Value of the Condor stock received [50 (shares) × $1,200 (value per share)]	$ 60,000
Cash received	10,000
Amount realized	$ 70,000
Less basis of property transferred	(30,000)
Realized gain	$ 40,000

continued

[35]§ 368(c).

[36]§ 358(a).

[37]§ 362(a).

Mike's recognized gain is $10,000, the lesser of the realized gain ($40,000) or the fair market value of the boot received ($10,000). Mike's basis in the Condor stock is $30,000.

Basis in the property transferred	$ 30,000
Plus recognized gain	10,000
	$ 40,000
Less boot received	(10,000)
Basis to Mike of the Condor stock	$ 30,000

Condor's basis in the property transferred by Mike is $40,000 [$30,000 (basis of the property to Mike) + $10,000 (gain recognized by Mike)]. John neither realizes nor recognizes gain or loss and takes a basis of $60,000 in the Condor stock.

The receipt of stock for the performance of *services* always results in ordinary income to the transferring shareholder. An example might be an attorney who does not charge a fee for incorporating a business but instead receives the value equivalent in stock of the newly formed corporation. The basis of stock received for the performance of services is equal to the fair market value of the services.

20-3b Capital Contributions

The receipt of money or property in exchange for capital stock produces neither recognized gain nor loss to the recipient corporation.[38] Gross income of a corporation does not include shareholders' contributions of money or property to the capital of the corporation.[39] Generally, capital contributions by nonshareholders are included in the gross income of the corporation.[40]

Example 28

A city donates land worth $900,000 to Cardinal Corporation as an inducement for it to locate in the city. The receipt of the land represents gross income to Cardinal. The land's basis to the corporation is $900,000.

Thin Capitalization

The advantages of capitalizing a corporation with debt may be substantial. Interest on debt is deductible by the corporation, while dividend payments are not. Further, the shareholders are not taxed on repayments of loan principal unless the payments exceed basis.

With many small corporations, particularly nonmanufacturing personal service corporations, the corporation may have a minimum investment in stock as required under applicable state law.

In certain instances, the IRS will claim **thin capitalization** by holding that debt is really an equity interest and deny the shareholders the tax advantages of debt financing. If the debt instrument has too many similarities to stock, it may be treated as a form of stock, with principal and interest payments treated as dividends.[41]

[38] § 1032.

[39] § 118(a).

[40] §§ 61 and 118(b).

[41] § 385 lists several factors that might be used to determine whether a debtor-creditor relationship or a shareholder-corporation relationship exists.

The Big Picture

Example 29

Return to the facts of *The Big Picture* on p. 20-1. Suppose the Todd sisters decide to conduct their catering business in the corporate form—either a C or S corporation. In forming the corporation, they should probably limit their capital investment to whatever state law requires. The sisters should consider acquiring the capital assets needed to operate the business (e.g., delivery trucks, kitchen equipment, location for food preparation) on their own and leasing them to the corporation. This would allow the sisters to claim the appropriate depreciation and provide the corporation with a deduction for the rent paid.

Ethics & Equity **Selective Incorporation**

Miguel, a cash basis taxpayer, owns and operates a home renovation business that he decides to incorporate. In forming the corporation, he transfers *most* of the business, which includes unrealized receivables and inventory items. However, he retains in his own name the land and building and the trade accounts payable.

For Federal income tax purposes, what is Miguel trying to accomplish by being selective in terms of what he transfers to the corporation? Explain.

20-4 Distributions to Shareholders

LO.7 **Explain the tax rules governing the operation of corporations.**

20-4a Dividend Distributions

Corporate distributions of cash or property to shareholders are treated as dividend income to the extent the corporation has accumulated *and/or* current earnings and profits (E & P).[42] In determining the source of the distribution, a dividend is deemed to have been made initially from current E & P.

Qualified dividend income is taxed like a net long-term capital gain.[43] Consequently, the tax rate on such income cannot exceed 20 percent (0 or 15 percent for individual shareholders in the lower tax brackets).[44]

Example 30

As of the beginning of the tax year, Teal Corporation reports a deficit in accumulated E & P of $300,000. For the current tax year, it has current E & P of $100,000 and distributes $50,000 to its shareholders. The $50,000 distribution is treated as a dividend because it is deemed to have been made from current E & P. This is the case even though Teal's accumulated E & P at the end of the year is negative before accounting for the distribution.

If a corporate distribution is not made from E & P (either current or accumulated), the shareholder subtracts the amount of the distribution from the basis of the stock investment, and the distribution represents a nontaxable return of capital. Any amount received in excess of the stock basis is classified as a capital gain (if the stock is a capital asset in the hands of the shareholder).

[42] § 316. E & P is defined in the next section.

[43] Qualified dividend income is defined in § 1(h)(11)(B), and its taxation is discussed in text Section 16-5b.

[44] § 1(h)(1). See the discussion in text Section 3-9d.

Example 31

When Mallard Corporation has a zero balance in E & P (either current or accumulated), it distributes cash of $300,000 to its sole shareholder, Helen. The basis of Helen's stock investment is $200,000.

Return of capital (nontaxable)	$200,000
Capital gain	100,000
Total amount of distribution	$300,000

After the distribution, Helen has a basis of zero in the Mallard stock.

Earnings and Profits

The term **earnings and profits** is not defined in the Code, but § 312 addresses certain transactions that affect E & P. Although E & P and the accounting concept of retained earnings have certain similarities, they differ in numerous respects. For example, a nontaxable stock dividend is treated as a capitalization of retained earnings for accounting purposes, yet it does not decrease E & P for tax purposes. Taxable dividends do reduce E & P but cannot produce a deficit. Referring to Example 31, after the distribution, Mallard Corporation's E & P remains zero rather than being a negative amount.

Accumulated E & P is the sum of the corporation's prior current E & P that has not been distributed as dividends.

Noncash Dividends

A distribution of property other than cash to a shareholder is measured by the fair market value of the property on the date of distribution. The fair market value also becomes the shareholder's basis in the property.[45]

Example 32

Drake Corporation reports E & P of $60,000. It distributes land with a fair market value of $50,000 (adjusted basis of $30,000) to its sole shareholder, Art. Art records a taxable dividend of $50,000 and basis in the land of $50,000.

A corporation that distributes appreciated property to its shareholders as a dividend must recognize the amount of the appreciation as a gain.[46]

Example 33

Assume the same facts as in Example 32. Drake Corporation must recognize a gain of $20,000 on the distribution it made to Art.

However, if the property distributed has a basis in excess of its fair market value, the distributing corporation cannot recognize any loss.

20-4b Constructive Dividends

In a closely held corporation, a shareholder may direct the corporation to make certain payments to a shareholder that are not intended to be classified as a dividend (e.g., rent or salary). Depending on the reasonableness of the payment and the corporation's dividend history, the IRS may reclassify the payment as a **constructive dividend**,

[45] § 301.

[46] § 311.

thus converting the payment into a dividend for tax purposes. The following are examples of constructive dividends.

- Salaries paid to shareholder-employees that are not reasonable (refer to Example 7 in Chapter 6).
- Interest on debt owed by the corporation to shareholders that is reclassified as equity because the corporation is thinly capitalized (refer to the earlier discussion in this chapter).
- Excessive rent paid by a corporation for the use of shareholder property. The arm's length standard is used to test whether the rent is excessive (refer to Example 30 in Chapter 1).
- Advances to shareholders that are not bona fide loans.
- Interest-free (or below-market) loans to shareholders. In this situation, the dividend component is the difference between the interest provided for, if any, and that calculated using the market rate.
- Shareholder use of corporate property for less than an arm's length rate.
- Payment by the corporation of a shareholder's personal expenses.
- Bargain purchase of corporate property by shareholders.

Like other dividends, constructive dividends create dividend income for the shareholders only if they are made from E & P. As noted previously, however, constructive dividends need not be made available to all shareholders on a pro rata basis.

The Big Picture

Example 34

Return to the facts of *The Big Picture* on p. 20-1. Also recall the suggestions made in Example 29. If they choose to operate in the corporate form, the Todd sisters will need to take the following into account.

- Any salaries the sisters pay themselves should satisfy the reasonableness test.
- Rent charged to the corporation for the use of assets owned by the sisters should meet the arm's length standard.
- Loans made to the corporation for working capital purposes should provide for a market rate of interest to be charged.

Although the constructive dividend issue will not arise until the corporation becomes profitable (and has generated E & P), these procedures should be structured at the outset so that the parties will be prepared for a possible future challenge by the IRS.

20-5 S Corporations

LO.8

Assess the utility and effect of the S election.

The S election enables certain taxpayers to use the corporate form for conducting a business without being taxed under the Federal income tax rules applicable to a C corporation.

20-5a Qualification for S Status

To achieve S corporation status, the corporation must meet certain requirements and make an effective election.

Qualifying for the Election

To qualify for **S corporation** status, the corporation must be a **small business corporation**. This includes any corporation that has the following characteristics.

- It is a domestic corporation.
- There are no more than 100 shareholders.[47]
- Its shareholders are only individuals, estates, and certain trusts.
- Every shareholder must be a citizen or resident of the United States.
- It has only one class of stock outstanding.

These characteristics must continue to be met if an electing S corporation is to maintain its S status.

Example 35

Harry, a shareholder in an S corporation, dies. Under his will, Harry's stock is distributed among three children and eight grandchildren. As family members, the 11 new owners are treated as one shareholder for purposes of the 100-shareholder limitation.

Making the Election

The election is made by filing Form 2553, and *all* shareholders must consent. It is important to determine who needs to sign the form. For example, if a married couple owns the stock as community property, both spouses must sign the consent even though they count as a single shareholder.

To be effective for the current year, the election must be filed anytime during the preceding taxable year or on or before the fifteenth day of the third month of the current year.[48]

Example 36

Heron, a calendar year taxpayer, is a U.S. corporation that wants to elect S status for 2023. If the election is filed anytime from January 1, 2022, up to and including March 15, 2023, it will be effective for 2022.

Loss of the Election

The S election may be terminated *voluntarily* (a majority of the shareholders file to revoke the election) or *involuntarily*. An involuntary termination may occur in *either* of the following ways.

- The corporation ceases to qualify as a small business corporation (e.g., the number of shareholders exceeds 100 or a partnership becomes a shareholder).
- The corporation incurs passive investment income (e.g., interest and dividends) in excess of 25 percent of gross receipts for a period of three consecutive years. This restriction applies only if the corporation holds E & P (e.g., because it previously was a C corporation).[49]

If the holders of a *majority* of the shares consent to a voluntary revocation of S status, the election to revoke must be made on or before the fifteenth day of the third month of the tax year to be effective for that year.

[47]Family members who own stock are treated as a single shareholder. Members of a family include all lineal descendants (e.g., children, grandchildren) of a shareholder and spouse (or ex-spouse) and the spouses (or ex-spouses) of such lineal descendants. § 1361(c)(1).

[48]§ 1362.

[49]§ 1362(d)(3)(a)(i).

Example 37

The shareholders of Stork Corporation, a calendar year S corporation, elect to revoke the election on January 4, 2022. Assuming that the election is duly executed and timely filed, Stork will become a C corporation for calendar year 2022. If the election to revoke is not made until June 2022, Stork will not become a C corporation until calendar year 2023.

If the shareholders file the election to revoke on January 4, 2022, but state on the election that the effective date is January 1, 2023, then Stork loses its S status as of January 1, 2023.

In the case where S status is lost because of a disqualifying act (involuntarily), the loss of the election takes effect as of the date on which the event occurs.

Example 38

Crow Corporation has been a calendar year S corporation for several years. On August 12, 2022, one of its shareholders sells her stock to Kite Corporation. Because Crow no longer satisfies the definition of an S corporation (it has another corporation as a shareholder), the election has been involuntarily terminated. For calendar year 2022, therefore, Crow is an S corporation through August 11 and a C corporation from August 12 through December 31, 2022.

Barring certain exceptions, the loss of an S election means that the corporation must wait five years before S status can be reelected.

20-5b Operational Rules

The S corporation is primarily a tax-reporting rather than a taxpaying entity. In this respect, the entity is taxed much like a partnership.[50] Under the conduit concept, the taxable income and losses of an S corporation flow through to the shareholders who report them on their personal income tax returns on a per-share and per-day of stock ownership basis.[51]

Separately Stated Items

Following are some of the items that keep their identity as they pass through the S corporation and are reported as though the shareholder itself had incurred them. The items are stated separately because each may lead to a different tax result when combined with a particular shareholder's other transactions.

- Tax-exempt income.
- Long-term and short-term capital gains and losses.
- Section 1231 gains and losses.
- Charitable contributions.
- Qualified dividend income.
- Intangible drilling costs.
- Investment interest, income, and expenses.
- Certain portfolio income.
- Qualified business income (§ 199A) information.
- Passive activity gains, losses, and credits.
- AMT adjustments and tax preferences.

[50] A Federal income tax applies to an S corporation in rare situations.

[51] § 1366.

Example 39

Arnold and Jean are equal shareholders in Lark (an S corporation). For the current calendar year, each must account for one-half of Lark's short-term capital gain of $6,000. Arnold has no other capital asset transactions, and Jean reports a short-term capital loss of $3,000 from the sale of stock in Starbucks. Jean offsets the Lark gain with the $3,000 short-term capital loss from her stock sale. For Arnold, the short-term capital gain results in a $3,000 increase in his taxable income.

Taxable Income

After the separately stated items have been removed, the balance represents the ordinary taxable income of the S corporation. The dividends received deduction and the NOL deduction are not allowed, but an S corporation can amortize its organizational expenditures.

Once ordinary taxable income has been determined, this amount passes through to each shareholder as of the last day of the S corporation's tax year, proportionate to their stock holdings.

Computing S Corporation Income

Example 40

Harrier Corporation, a calendar year S corporation, incurred the following transactions during the current year.

Sales		$ 400,000
Cost of goods sold		(230,000)
Other income		
*Tax-exempt interest	$ 3,000	
*Long-term capital gain	5,000	8,000
Other expenses		
*Charitable contributions	$ 4,000	
Advertising expense	15,000	
Other operating expenses	20,000	
*Short-term capital loss	1,500	(40,500)
Net income per books		$ 137,500

The items that are to be separately stated [those preceded by an asterisk (*)] pass through proportionately to the shareholders. The shareholders also are taxed on their shares of Harrier's ordinary taxable income.

Sales		$ 400,000
Cost of goods sold		(230,000)
Other expenses		
Advertising expense	$15,000	
Other operating expenses	20,000	(35,000)
Ordinary taxable income		$ 135,000

Example 41

If Oscar owned 10% of the stock in Harrier Corporation (refer to Example 40) during all of the current year, he must account for the following.

Separately stated items	
Tax-exempt interest	$ 300
Long-term capital gain	500
Charitable contributions	400
Short-term capital loss	150
Ordinary taxable income (10% of $135,000)	13,500

Treatment of Losses

As previously noted, separately stated loss items (e.g., capital losses and § 1231 losses) flow through to the shareholders. Their treatment by a shareholder depends on the shareholder's individual income tax position. If the S corporation's taxable income determination results in an operating loss, it also passes through to the shareholders. As is the case with separately stated items, the amount of the loss assigned to each shareholder depends on the stock ownership during the year.

Example 42

In the current tax year, Oriole (a calendar year S corporation) incurred an operating loss of $365,000. During the period (not a leap year), Jason's ownership in Oriole was 20% for 200 days and 30% for 165 days. Jason's share of the loss is determined as follows.

[$365,000 × (200/365)] × 20% =	$40,000
[$365,000 × (165/365)] × 30% =	49,500
Total loss for Jason	$89,500

The Big Picture

Example 43

Return to the facts of *The Big Picture* on p. 20-1. Recall that the Todd sisters anticipate losses in the early years of their catering business. If they form a C corporation, such losses will be of no benefit to the new corporation—no carryback will be available, and there will be only a potential for a delayed carryover, with the losses "trapped" in the C corporation. With an S election, however, losses pass through currently so that the sisters secure limited liability for their business and the immediate tax benefit of any losses (assuming that they materially participate in the S corporation activity; see text Section 11-3).

Stock Basis Determination

A shareholder's *basis* in the stock of an S corporation, like that of a C corporation, is the original investment plus additional capital contributions less return of capital distributions. At this point, however, the symmetry disappears. Generally, basis in S stock is increased by the income items passed through (including those separately stated) and decreased by the loss items passed through (including those separately stated).[52]

Example 44

In the current tax year, Warbler Corporation is formed with an investment of $500,000, of which Janice contributed $100,000 for a 20% stock interest. A timely S election is made, and for the current tax year, Warbler earns taxable income of $50,000. Janice's basis in her stock investment now is $110,000 [$100,000 (original capital contribution) + $10,000 (the 20% share of the corporation's taxable income assigned to Janice)].

Distributions by an S corporation cannot reduce stock basis below zero. If the amount of a distribution exceeds the stock basis, the excess typically receives capital gain treatment.

As previously noted, operating losses of an S corporation pass through to the shareholders and reduce the basis in their stock investment. Once the basis of the stock reaches zero, any excess loss reduces the basis of loans the shareholder has made to the corporation.

[52] § 1367.

Example 45

Flamingo Corporation, a calendar year S corporation, incurs an operating loss of $60,000 for 2022. Norman, a 50% shareholder, has an adjusted basis of $25,000 in the Flamingo stock and has made loans to the corporation of $5,000. Norman deducts the $30,000 loss (50% of $60,000) on his 2022 individual income tax return. Norman's basis in the stock and the loans must be reduced accordingly, and both will be zero after the pass-through.

In the event the basis limitation precludes an operating loss from being deducted, the loss can be carried forward and claimed when there is stock basis to offset.

Example 46

Assume the same facts as in Example 45, except that Norman had not made any loans to Flamingo Corporation. Further assume that Flamingo reports taxable income of $15,000 in the following year (2023). Thus, Norman's unabsorbed loss of $5,000 from 2022 carries over to 2023 and is applied against the $7,500 of ordinary income for that year.

Ordinary loss for 2022 (limited to stock basis)	$25,000
Income to be reported in 2023 (50% of $15,000)	7,500
Restoration of stock basis in 2023 (50% of $15,000)	7,500
Loss allowed for 2023 carried over from 2020 ($30,000 – $25,000)	5,000
Basis in stock after 2023 ($7,500 – $5,000)	2,500

S corporation shareholders who report a loss from the entity must attach Form 7203 (S Corporation Shareholder Stock and Debt Basis Limitations) with their Form 1040. The IRS recommends that shareholders maintain this form in their records (even for years with positive S corporation income) to help track the shareholders' basis.

Ethics & Equity **Income Tax Basis That Does Not Change?**

In 2006, Howard purchased stock in Green, a C corporation, for $100,000. In 2012, Green made a valid S election. In 2022, Howard sells his stock in Green for $120,000. Because he paid $100,000 for the stock, Howard plans to recognize a long-term capital gain of $20,000 as a result of the sale. Do you agree with Howard's proposed reporting? Explain.

Distributions

Because the income and losses of an S corporation are passed through to the owners, later distributions to shareholders from an S corporation generally are excluded from gross income to the extent of the shareholder's stock basis. If the distribution is greater than the shareholder's basis, the amount in excess of basis usually constitutes a capital gain. However, in the rare case that the S corporation had been converted from a C corporation that held earnings and profits, a different set of rules would apply to create dividend income for distributions from E & P generated before the conversion.

A comparison of the various tax attributes of C and S corporations appears in Concept Summary 20.3.

LO.9

Describe the tax consequences of forming and operating a partnership.

20-6 Partnerships

20-6a Nature of Partnership Taxation

Unlike corporations, partnerships are not considered separate taxable entities. Each member of a partnership is subject to income tax on the partner's distributive share of the partnership's income even if an actual distribution is not made. The tax return (Form 1065) required of a partnership serves only to provide information necessary in determining the character and amount of each partner's distributive share of the partnership's income and expense.

Because a partnership acts as a conduit, items that pass through to the partners do not lose their income tax identity. For example, tax-exempt income earned by a partnership is picked up by the partners as tax-exempt income. In this regard, partnerships function in much the same fashion as S corporations, which also serve as conduits.

Concept Summary 20.3

A Comparison of Some of the Tax Attributes of S and C Corporations

Attribute	S Corporations	C Corporations
Number of shareholders	Limited to 100 with spouses counted as one. Can elect to count certain related shareholders as one.	Generally no limit.
Types of shareholders	Not most trusts, corporations, or partnerships. An individual must be a U.S. citizen or resident.	No restriction.
Tax year	Restricted to calendar year unless IRS approves a different year for business purposes or other exceptions apply.	Unrestricted selection allowed at time of filing first tax return, except for personal service corporations.
Due date of return	Fifteenth day of the *third* month following the close of the corporation's tax year.	Usually the fifteenth day of the *fourth* month following the close of the corporation's tax year.
Treatment of gains		
Tax incidence.	Generally not taxed to entity but passed through to shareholders.	Subject to the corporate income tax.
Nature of gain.	Items such as capital gains and tax-exempt income do not lose their identity.	Identity lost. When later passed through to shareholders, treated as dividend income.
Timing of taxation to shareholders.	Taxed to shareholders as of the last day of the corporation's tax year.	Not taxed to shareholders until distributed as dividends.
Treatment of losses		
Tax incidence.	Not deductible to the entity but passed through to shareholders.	Deductible by the corporation.
Nature of loss.	Items such as capital losses do not lose their identity.	Capital losses are deducted only to extent of capital gains.
Timing of taxation to shareholders.	Passed through to shareholders as of last day of the corporation's tax year. Deduction limited to shareholder's stock basis plus any loans made to corporation.	Not passed through to shareholders.
Shareholder's basis in stock	Original investment *plus* gains passed through *less* losses passed through *and* distributions from corporation.	Original investment *plus* additional capital contributions *less* return of capital distributions.

A partnership is considered a separate taxable entity in making various elections and selecting its taxable year, method of depreciation, and accounting methods. A partnership also is treated as a separate legal entity under civil law, with the right to own property in its own name.

20-6b Partnership Formation and Basis

Recognition of Gain or Loss

The general rule is that no gain or loss is recognized by a partnership or any of its partners on the contribution of property in exchange for a capital interest in the partnership.[53] This rule also applies to all subsequent contributions of property.

There are certain exceptions to the nonrecognition of gain or loss rule, including the following.

- If a partner transfers property to the partnership and receives money or other consideration (boot) as a result, realized gain is recognized to the extent of the fair market value of the boot received.

[53] § 721.

- If a partnership interest is received in exchange for services rendered or to be rendered by the partner to the partnership, the fair market value of the transferred capital interest is regarded as compensation for services. The recipient of the capital interest recognizes the amount as ordinary income in the year actually or constructively received.
- If property that is subject to a liability in excess of its basis is contributed to a partnership, the contributing partner may recognize gain equal to the excess amount.

Basis of a Partnership Interest

The contributing *partner's basis* in the partnership interest received is the sum of money contributed plus the adjusted basis of any other property transferred to the partnership.[54]

Example 47

In return for the contribution of property (with a basis of $50,000 and a fair market value of $80,000) and cash of $10,000 to the Brown Partnership, Marcia receives a 10% capital interest worth $90,000. Although Marcia has a realized gain of $30,000 ($90,000 − $60,000) on the transfer, none of the gain is recognized. The basis of her interest in the entity is $60,000 [$50,000 (basis of property contributed) + $10,000 (cash contribution)].

A partner's basis in the partnership interest is determined without regard to any amount reflected on the partnership's books as capital, equity, or a similar account.

Example 48

Marge and Diego form the equal Blue Partnership with a cash contribution of $300,000 from Marge and a property contribution (adjusted basis of $180,000 and fair market value of $300,000) from Diego. Although the books of the entity may reflect a credit of $300,000 to each partner's capital account, only Marge has a tax basis of $300,000 in her partnership interest. Diego's tax basis in his partnership interest is $180,000, the amount of his tax basis in the property contributed to the partnership.

After its initial determination, the basis of a partnership interest is increased by additional capital contributions, and by the sum of the owner's current and prior years' distributive share of:

- Taxable income of the partnership, including capital gains.
- Tax-exempt income of the partnership.
- The excess of the deductions for depletion over the basis of the partnership's property subject to depletion.[55]

Similarly, the basis of a partner's interest is decreased, but not below zero, by distributions of partnership property (including cash) and by the sum of the current and prior years' distributive share of:

- Partnership losses, including capital losses.
- Partnership expenditures that are not deductible in computing taxable income or loss and that are not capital expenditures.

Changes in the liabilities (including accounts payable and bank loans) of a partnership also affect the basis of a partnership interest. A partner's basis is increased by his or her assumption of partnership liabilities, and by his or her pro rata share of liabilities incurred by the partnership. Likewise, the partner's basis is decreased by the amount of any personal liabilities assumed by the partnership, and by the pro rata share of any decreases in the liabilities of the partnership.

[54] § 722.

[55] § 705(a).

Effect of Liability on Basis

Example 49

Tony, Martha, and Carolyn form the Orange Partnership with the following contributions: cash of $100,000 from Tony for a 50% interest in capital and profits, cash of $50,000 from Martha for a 25% interest, and property valued at $66,000 from Carolyn for a 25% interest. The property contributed by Carolyn has an adjusted basis of $30,000 and is subject to a mortgage of $16,000, which is assumed by the partnership. Carolyn's basis in her interest in the Orange Partnership is:

Adjusted basis of Carolyn's contributed property	$ 30,000
Less portion of mortgage assumed by Tony and Martha and treated as a distribution of money to Carolyn (75% of $16,000)	(12,000)
Basis of Carolyn's interest in Orange Partnership	$ 18,000

Example 50

Assuming the same facts as in Example 49, Tony and Martha have a basis in their partnership interests of $108,000 and $54,000, respectively.

	Tony	Martha
Cash contribution	$100,000	$50,000
Plus portion of mortgage assumed and treated as an additional cash contribution:		
(50% of $16,000)	8,000	
(25% of $16,000)		4,000
Basis of interest in Orange Partnership	$108,000	$54,000

Partnership's Basis in Contributed Property

The *basis of property* contributed to a partnership by a partner is the adjusted basis of the property to the contributing partner at the time of the contribution.[56] In addition, the holding period of the property for the partnership includes the period during which the property was held by the contributing partner (sometimes referred to as "tacking on" the holding period). This is logical because the partnership's basis in the property is the same basis the property had in the hands of the partner.[57]

Example 51

In 2022, Rico contributed equipment with an adjusted basis of $100,000 and fair market value of $300,000 to the Red Partnership in exchange for a one-third interest in the partnership. No gain or loss is recognized by Rico. The entity's basis in the equipment is $100,000. If Rico had acquired the equipment in 2016, the partnership's holding period would include the period from 2016 through 2022.

20-6c Partnership Operations

Measuring and Reporting Partnership Income

Although a partnership is not subject to Federal income taxation, it is required to determine its taxable income and file an income tax return for information purposes.[58] The tax return, Form 1065, is due on the fifteenth day of the *third* month following the close of the taxable year of the partnership.

[56] § 723.

[57] § 1223(2).

[58] § 6031.

Similar to S corporations in measuring and reporting partnership income, certain transactions must be reported separately on the partnership return. Items such as charitable contributions, capital gains and losses, and qualified dividend income are excluded from partnership taxable income and allocated separately to the partners.[59] These items are treated separately because they affect the computation of various exclusions, deductions, and credits at the partner level.[60]

Example 52

Alyssa, Madison, and Rodrigo are equal partners in the Yellow Partnership. All parties use the calendar year for tax purposes. Among other transactions, Yellow reported the following separately stated items: $3,000 of qualified dividends, $15,000 in long-term capital gains, and $6,000 in charitable contributions.

The pass-through of these items could generate different results for each partner: For example, Alyssa is subject to the 3.8% net investment income tax on high-income taxpayers and reports her share of the dividend income on Form 8960 (Net Investment Income Tax—Individuals, Estates, and Trusts), Madison's $5,000 long-term capital gain is not subject to tax (i.e., she is in a 15% or lower tax bracket), and Rodrigo cannot benefit from his $2,000 share of the charitable contribution because he does not itemize (i.e., he claims the standard deduction).

A second step in the measurement and reporting process is the computation of the partnership's ordinary income or loss. The taxable income of a partnership is computed in the same manner as that of an individual taxpayer. However, a partnership is not allowed the following deductions.[61]

- Taxes paid to foreign countries or possessions of the United States.
- Charitable contributions.
- Net operating losses.

The partnership's ordinary income or loss and each of the items requiring separate treatment are reported in the partnership's information return and allocated to the partners in accordance with their ownership shares.

Limitation on Partner's Share of Losses

A partner's deduction of their share of partnership losses (including capital losses) could be limited. The limitation is the adjusted basis of the partnership interest at the end of the partnership year in which the losses were incurred.

The limitation for partnership loss deductions is similar to that applicable to losses of S corporations. Partnership losses may be carried forward by the partner and utilized against future increases in the basis of the partnership interest. Such increases might result from additional capital contributions to the partnership, from a net increase in partnership liabilities, or from future partnership income. Unlike S corporations, however, loans to the entity cannot be utilized by a partner to absorb the pass-through of losses.

Loss Limitation and Utilization

Example 53

Florence and Donald do business as the Green Partnership, sharing profits and losses equally. All parties use the calendar year for tax purposes. As of January 1, 2022, Florence's basis in her partnership interest is $25,000. The partnership sustained an operating loss of $80,000 in 2022 and earned a profit of $70,000 in 2023. For the calendar year 2022, Florence may claim only $25,000 of her $40,000 distributive share of the partnership loss (one-half of the $80,000 loss). As a result, the basis in her partnership interest is reduced to zero as of January 1, 2023, and she must carry forward the remaining $15,000 of partnership losses.

[59] § 702(a).

[60] Review Schedule K–1 (Form 1065) to see what tax attributes are reported separately.

[61] § 703(a).

Loss Limitation and Utilization

Example 54

Assuming the same facts as in Example 53, what are the income tax consequences for Florence in 2023? Because the partnership earned a profit of $70,000 for the calendar year 2023, Florence reports income from the partnership of $20,000 ($35,000 distributive share of income for 2023 less the $15,000 loss not allowed for 2022). The adjusted basis of her partnership interest now becomes $20,000.

Guaranteed Payments

Payments made by a partnership to one of its partners for services rendered or for the use of capital, to the extent they are determined without regard to the income of the partnership, referred to as **guaranteed payments**, generally are deductible by the partnership as a business expense.[62] The payments must be reported as ordinary income by the receiving partner and do not affect the partner's basis in the partnership interest.

Example 55

Under the terms of the Silver Partnership agreement, Kim is entitled to a fixed annual salary of $60,000 without regard to the income of the partnership. He is also to share in the profits and losses of the partnership as a one-third partner. After deducting the guaranteed payment, the partnership has $300,000 of ordinary income. Kim must include $160,000 as ordinary income on his income tax return ($60,000 guaranteed payment + $100,000 one-third distributive share of partnership income).

Limited Liability Companies

Limited liability companies (LLCs) generally are treated as partnerships for Federal income tax purposes. An LLC differs from a partnership in a few significant ways. Generally, an LLC is required to file articles of organization with the state. Unlike general partners in a partnership, LLC members (the entity's owners) are not personally responsible for the debts of the LLC. In addition, an LLC can be formed with only one member. The operations of a single-member LLC are treated as a sole proprietorship for tax purposes.

Qualified Joint Ventures

For Federal tax purposes, an unincorporated business operated by spouses is considered a partnership. As a result, a business co-run by spouses generally must comply with filing and record-keeping requirements for partnerships and partners.

Married co-owners who want to avoid the burden of partnership documentation can form a **qualified joint venture**. The election to do so is made by reporting each spouse's share of income, losses, gains, and deductions on a Schedule C (along with other related forms). To qualify for joint venture treatment, the only members of the joint venture can be spouses filing a joint return; both spouses must materially participate in the business, and both spouses must elect not to be treated as a partnership. The business must be operated by the spouses as co-owners and not as a separate entity under state law.

20-7 Tax Planning

20-7a Corporate versus Noncorporate Forms of Business Organization

LO.10 **Identify the advantages and disadvantages of the various forms used for conducting a business.**

Because of the wide range of applicable tax rates (10 to 37 percent for individuals and 21 percent for corporations), effective income tax planning can occur. For example, the corporate form is appealing since any taxable income will be taxed at 21 percent,

[62] § 707(c).

probably lower than the individual's applicable rate. But do not overlook the potential effect of state and local income taxes for individuals and corporations.

Unless an S election is made, operating as a corporation yields a potential double tax result. Corporation income may be taxed twice—once as earned by the corporation and again when distributed to the shareholders. The payment of a dividend does not result in a deduction to the corporation, and the receipt of a dividend generally results in gross income to a shareholder. In the case of closely held corporations, therefore, a strong incentive exists to avoid the payment of dividends.

Moreover, a premium is put on distributing profits in some manner that is deductible by the corporation. This can be accomplished by categorizing the distributions as salaries, interest, or rents. If not properly structured, however, these devices can generate a multitude of problems, including the loss of the related deductions. Excessive debt, for example, can lead to its reclassification as equity (under the thin capitalization doctrine) with a resulting disallowance of any interest deduction. Large salaries could fail the reasonableness test, and rent payments must meet an arm's length standard to avoid treatment as a constructive dividend.

S corporations, partnerships, and LLCs are eligible for a 20 percent deduction on their qualified business income (QBI). This helps to create parity with the Federal income rate for C corporations; see text Section 9-7. In its simplest form, the QBI deduction allows a reduction in the tax rate for the individual reporting the pass-through income.

Example 56

Elena and Theo own a 50% interest in the Hoover Partnership. Hoover generates $40,000 of qualified business income and thus allocates $20,000 each to Elena and Theo. Elena is in the 35% marginal tax bracket. The 20% QBI deduction lowers her tax rate to 28%.

	No QBI deduction	QBI deduction
Partnership income	$20,000	$20,000
QBI deduction	0	(4,000)
Taxable pass-through income	20,000	16,000
Marginal tax rate	35%	35%
Tax	7,000	5,600
Effective tax rate	35%	28%

Theo is in the 24% marginal tax rate. His effective rate on the pass-through income is 24% × (1 – 0.20), or 19.2%.

Qualified dividends are taxed at the same rate as for net long-term capital gain.[63] Thus, the maximum rate for an individual cannot exceed 20 percent.[64] In light of this preferential treatment of qualified dividends, effective planning involves the best placement of the tax benefit. If it is the corporation, try to pay out profits in a deductible form (i.e., interest, salaries, and rents). If it is the shareholder, distribute the profits as qualified dividends.[65]

Other tax considerations concerning entity choice include:

- Shareholders are treated as employees for tax purposes if they render services to the corporation. This status may make available a number of tax-effective fringe

[63]§ 1(h)(3)(B).

[64]The net investment income tax (see text Section 13-5c) can increase the maximum rate on high-income earners to 23.8 percent. For lower-income earners, the rate can be as low as 0 percent).

[65]The 20% rate is applicable only to high-income taxpayers. Most middle-income taxpayers are subject to a 15% rate. See text Section 16-5.

benefits (e.g., group term life insurance). See text Sections 5-6 through 5-8. Partners and sole proprietors are not employees, so the entity cannot deduct payments for these benefits.

- Gross income loses its identity as it passes through a C corporation to the shareholders. Thus, items possessing preferential tax treatment (e.g., interest on municipal bonds) are not taxed as such to the shareholders.
- It may be difficult for shareholders to recover some or all of their investment in the C corporation without receiving taxable dividends: most corporate distributions are treated as dividends to the extent of the corporation's E & P. Structuring the capital of the corporation to include debt is a partial solution to this problem. Thus, the shareholder-creditor could recoup part of his or her investment through deductible interest or the tax-free payment of principal.
- Corporate losses cannot be passed through to C corporation shareholders.

20-7b **C Corporation versus S Status**

S status generally avoids Federal income tax at the corporate level, bringing the individual income tax into play. As noted, the differential between the rates for noncorporate and corporate taxpayers makes this a factor to be considered. The S election enables a business to operate in the corporate form; avoid the corporate income tax; and, depending on taxable income, possibly take advantage of both the lower rates usually applicable to individuals and the qualified business income deduction. S corporation losses incurred at the corporate level pass through to the shareholders, who can utilize them on their individual returns.

Electing S status can present several problems, however. First, some corporations do not meet the requirements to make an S election. Second, a few states do not recognize S status for purposes of state and local taxation, or they subject them to income tax at both the entity and shareholder levels.

20-7c **Income Shifting to Reduce the Family Income Tax Burden**

One objective of tax planning is to keep the income from a business within the family unit and disperse it in such a manner as to minimize the overall tax burden. To the extent feasible, income often should be shifted from higher-bracket to lower-bracket family members.

Income from property cannot be shifted to another taxpayer without also transferring an interest in the underlying assets. If, for example, a mother wants to assign income from her sole proprietorship to her children, she must form a partnership or incorporate the business. In either case, the transfer of the interest may be subject to the Federal gift tax, but any potential gift tax can be eliminated or controlled by using the annual exclusion, the election to split gifts (for married donors), and the exemption equivalent (see text Section 1-4d).

Consequently, the first problem to be resolved becomes which form of business organization will best fit the objective of income shifting. For the partnership form, one major obstacle arises. Family partnership rules preclude the assignment of income to a family member who does not contribute substantial or vital services.[66]

[66] § 704(e).

Income shifting through the use of a partnership, therefore, may be ineffectual, especially if the children are minors. The use of a C corporation usually involves no such impediment. Regardless of the nature of the business, a gift of stock carries with it the attributes of ownership. Thus, C corporation dividends paid are taxed to the owner of the stock.

What if the corporate form is utilized and the S election is made? A new hurdle arises. The Code authorizes the IRS to make adjustments where shareholders are not adequately compensated for the value of their services or capital provided to an S corporation in a family setting.[67] Thus, an S corporation suffers from the same vulnerability that exists with family partnerships.

Further, the kiddie tax applies to all children under age 19 *and* to those who are full-time students under age 24. As a result, shifting investment income (or capital gains) to a child provides no Federal income tax benefit to the extent the income is subject to the parent's marginal tax rate; see text Section 3-6c.

Refocus on The Big Picture

Choice of Business Entity

GARY WOODS/ALAMY STOCK PHOTO

A principal entity-choice concern of the Todd sisters is limited liability. A food preparation business involves a high risk in terms of potential liability (e.g., litigation resulting from food poisoning). This hazard is further magnified by the sisters' intention to carry minimal liability insurance coverage. To obtain limited liability, therefore, the choice of entity cannot be a general partnership—it must be a C or S corporation or a limited liability company (LLC). (Example 1)

The next concern is the pass-through of losses to the sisters in the early years of the business. This cannot be achieved with a C corporation and is only available with an S corporation or an LLC. (Examples 1 and 43)

In making the choice between a corporation and an LLC, the future must be considered. If the business is successful, the sisters can expand their operations. This is more easily accomplished with a corporation than an LLC. A corporation can raise additional capital for expansion by issuing more stock—even going public if necessary. Issuing additional stock may cause the S corporation election to be lost, but by then, S status will have served its tax-planning purpose (i.e., pass-through of losses).

When forming the corporation, the sisters should consider the following.

- Key assets (e.g., food preparation facilities) might better be purchased by the sisters and leased to the corporation. This approach can trigger a rent deduction for the corporation. (Example 29)
- A viable salary structure should be established for the services the sisters perform to secure a salary deduction for the corporation. (Example 34)
- Interest must be charged for the funds the sisters loan to the corporation. This yields an interest deduction for the corporation.
- Federal payroll and Medicare taxes, state and local income taxes, and local property and sales/use taxes should be factors in the decision.

[67] § 1366(e).

Key Terms

C corporation, 20-3
Check-the-box Regulations, 20-5
Constructive dividend, 20-22
Dividends received deduction, 20-12
Earnings and profits, 20-22
Guaranteed payments, 20-33
Limited liability company (LLC), 20-2
Organizational expenditures, 20-13
Pass-through entities, 20-5
Personal service corporation, 20-7
Qualified joint venture, 20-33
S corporation, 20-24
Schedule M–1, 20-15
Schedule M–3, 20-18
Small business corporation, 20-24
Thin capitalization, 20-20

Discussion Questions

1. **LO.1** Describe a situation in which a corporation will not be treated as such under Federal income tax law.

2. **LO.1** Sylvia and Trang want to enter into business together and are unsure what type of entity to form (if any). They are concerned about the complexity of the paperwork required, the protection of personal assets from business creditors, and flexibility of sharing income and losses. Explain how a corporation, a partnership, or some other arrangement may differ with respect to their areas of concern. *Critical Thinking* *Planning*

3. **LO.1** Explain why partnerships and S corporations are considered "pass-through" entities, and present an example of how the pass-through works.

4. **LO.1, 10** What are the primary tax and nontax advantages of limited liability companies? *Planning*

5. **LO.1, 2, 10** The Orosco brothers have obtained financing to start a new venture. The business will be high-risk as to potential liability and is expected to incur losses before becoming profitable. What business entities should the Oroscos consider in crafting a Federal income tax strategy? *Planning*

6. **LO.3, 4, 5, 10** Contrast the income taxation of individuals and C corporations as to:
   a. Alternative minimum tax.
   b. Dividend income.
   c. Qualified business income deduction of 20 percent.
   d. Use of the cash method of accounting.
   e. Accounting period used for tax purposes.
   f. Applicable tax rates.
   g. Due date of the tax return.

7. **LO.3, 8, 9** The taxpayer has generated excess capital losses (both short-term and long-term) for the current year. Discuss the income tax ramifications of the losses if the taxpayer is:
   a. An individual.
   b. A C corporation.
   c. An S corporation.
   d. A partnership.

8. **LO.3** In late December 2022, Gray (a calendar year C corporation) pledges a $50,000 donation to a local relief agency formed to fight AIDS in Africa. Although Gray's board of directors authorized the donation in 2022, the payment is not made until April 2023. What Federal income tax issues are involved? *Critical Thinking*

9. **LO.3** If a C corporation donates ordinary income property to a qualified charity, the measure of the amount of the deduction is the adjusted basis of the property. Do you agree with this statement? Explain.

10. **LO.3** Golf Corporation generates a $40,000 net operating loss in 2022. Leo Trees, the Golf CEO, expects to offset all of the 2023 taxable income with the NOL. Explain to Leo whether that is possible.

11. **LO.3** Kite, a calendar year C corporation, incurred a net operating loss in 2022. Explain Kite's Federal income tax treatment of this NOL.

Critical Thinking 12. **LO.4** The dividends received deduction does not always eliminate the taxation of dividend income at the shareholder level. Explain.

Critical Thinking 13. **LO.4** Two small C corporations have invested in the stock of Tesla Corporation. Although they own the same number and type of shares, one corporation is able to claim a larger dividends received deduction than the other. Explain why this could be possible.

Critical Thinking 14. **LO.4** Mallard Corporation was formed in December 2022 and plans to use the cash basis of accounting. Mallard incurred one-half of its organizational expenses in December 2022 and one-half in January 2023. The payment of these expenses also occurred in these two months. Mallard began business in February 2023. Explain the income tax treatment of these expenses.

Critical Thinking 15. **LO.5** Corporations are subject to a flat income tax rate of 21%; individuals have graduated rates from 10% to 37%. Does this make the corporate entity a better entity choice for Federal income tax purposes? Explain.

Planning 16. **LO.6, 7** Small, closely held corporations often are formed with a minimum of capital investment. Key assets used in the business then are leased to the corporation by the shareholders. What are the advantages of this approach?

Decision Making 17. **LO.6** Chang and some associates want to form a corporation to develop and operate an industrial park. Chang is to contribute the land, which has significantly appreciated in value. She would like to recognize *some* of this gain to offset losses from other sources. Considering the rules of § 351, what do you suggest?

18. **LO.7** When a corporation distributes property as a dividend, what are the tax effects on the corporation and its shareholders if:
    a. The property has declined in value.
    b. The property has appreciated in value.

19. **LO.8** A calendar year corporation has an S election in effect. What will be the effect, if any, of the following events on its S status?
    a. The board of directors of the corporation revokes its S election in March of the current year.
    b. A shareholder who is a citizen of Mexico and works in San Antonio retires and moves back to Mexico.
    c. The corporation acquires an interest in a partnership.
    d. Because of bequests after the death of a shareholder, the total number of shareholders increases from 98 to 101.
    e. A shareholder transfers her stock to a newly formed LLC.

Critical Thinking 20. **LO.8** Carlotta and Doug are equal shareholders in Penguin, a calendar year S corporation. At the end of the current tax year, Penguin has an operating loss. Although Carlotta and Doug have the same basis in their Penguin stock, Carlotta can deduct all of her share of the corporation's loss but Doug cannot. How can this occur?

21. **LO.9** Indicate whether each of the following will increase (+), decrease (−), or have no effect *(NE)* on a partner's basis in a partnership interest.
    a. Operating loss of the partnership.
    b. Capital gains of the partnership.
    c. Tax-exempt income of the partnership.
    d. Partnership expenditures that are not deductible in computing taxable income.

e. Bank loans made to the partnership.
f. The partnership pays off a mortgage on property it owns.
g. Withdrawals by a partner that *are not* guaranteed payments.
h. Withdrawals by a partner that *are* guaranteed payments.

22. **LO.9** Blaine, Cassie, and Kirstin are equal partners in the Maize Partnership. During the year, Maize incurs qualified dividends and a charitable contribution deduction. Explain how the following could happen. Critical Thinking
a. Blaine pays less tax than Cassie and Kirstin on his share of the qualified dividends.
b. Cassie cannot deduct any of her share of the charitable contributions.

Computational Exercises

23. **LO.3** Green Corporation, a calendar year taxpayer, reports ordinary income of $10,000 and a long-term capital loss of $12,000 in 2022. Green incurred a long-term capital gain of $2,500 in 2019 and a long-term capital gain of $5,000 in 2021.
a. How much of the long-term capital loss can be deducted in 2022?
b. Carried back to prior years?
c. Carried forward to future years?
d. What is the nature (long- or short-term) of any carrybacks or carryforwards?

24. **LO.3** Purple Corporation purchases residential rental property for $1,000,000 (disregarding any allocation to the land) on March 9, 2019. Straight-line cost recovery of $130,295 is taken before the property is sold on October 23, 2022, for $1,000,000.
a. What is Purple's recognized gain?
b. How much of this gain is taxed under § 1250.
c. Section 291?
d. Section 1231?

25. **LO.4** Gold and Silver are two unrelated calendar year corporations. For the current year, both entities incurred the following transactions.

	Gold	Silver
Income from operations	$220,000	$260,000
Expenses from operations	225,000	340,000
Dividends received from domestic corporations (15% ownership)	100,000	130,000
Taxable income before dividends received deduction	$ 95,000	$ 50,000

What is the dividends received deduction for:
a. Gold Corporation?
b. Silver Corporation?

26. **LO.4** Ming Corporation (a calendar year taxpayer) was formed on April 1, 2022. Calculate the maximum deduction for organizational expenses for 2022 if these costs were:
a. $4,000.
b. $24,000.
c. $54,000.
d. $64,000.
e. Using spreadsheet software such as Microsoft Excel, build a template that will calculate the first year's maximum deduction for organization expenses using only the input of the date the business started and the total amount of organizational costs. Your spreadsheet should be constructed to calculate parts (a) through (d) above with no manual intervention other than input of the total costs.

27. **LO.6** Noah and Olivia form Globe Corporation with the following investments.

	FMV
Noah—	
Cash	$180,000
Olivia—	
Property (basis of $140,000)	200,000

Noah and Olivia both receive 1,000 shares of Globe stock, but Olivia also receives cash of $20,000. (Each share of stock is worth $180.)

a. What is Olivia's recognized gain?

b. Her basis in the Globe stock?

c. What is Globe's basis in the property?

28. **LO.7** In 2022, Emily receives a distribution of $125,000 from her wholly owned calendar year corporation. As of January 1, 2022, the corporation has accumulated E & P of $15,000 and for 2022 has current E & P of $65,000. Emily's basis in her stock is $35,000. What is the character of the distribution to Emily?

29. **LO.7** At a time when Emerald Corporation has E & P of $200,000, it distributes land (adjusted basis of $95,000 and fair market value of $180,000) to its sole shareholder, Sofia.

a. What is Sofia's dividend income?

b. Basis in the land?

c. What are Emerald's tax consequences?

30. **LO.8** Drab, a calendar year S corporation, incurred the following results this year. What is Drab's ordinary business income?

Sales	$1,500,000
Cost of goods sold	700,000
Long-term capital gain	10,000
Short-term capital loss	5,000
Political lobbying expenditures	5,000
Amortization of organizational expenditures	2,000
Salary expense	100,000
Rent expense	140,000
Tax-exempt interest	10,000
Dividends paid to shareholders	45,000

31. **LO.8** Kim is a 40% shareholder in Taupe, a calendar year S corporation. During 2022, Taupe had an operating loss of $200,000. If Kim has a basis of $50,000 in his stock and has made a loan to Taupe of $20,000, how much of the loss can he deduct for 2022?

32. **LO.9** Dev and Mia form the CM Partnership, each receiving a 50% capital interest. Dev contributed property worth $200,000 (adjusted basis of $230,000), while Mia contributed property worth $210,000 (subject to a mortgage of $20,000 that is assumed by CM) with an adjusted basis of $150,000.

a. How much gain (or loss) do the parties recognize?

b. What is Mia's basis in her partnership interest?

Problems

33. LO.3, 4, 5 Using the legend provided below, classify each statement under 2022 Federal income tax law.

Legend
I = Applies *only* to the income taxation of individuals
C = Applies *only* to the income taxation of C corporations
B = Applies to the income taxation of *both* individuals and C corporations
N = Applies to the income taxation of *neither* individuals nor C corporations

a. A child care credit is available.
b. The deduction of charitable contributions is subject to percentage limitation(s).
c. Excess charitable contributions can be carried forward for five years.
d. On the contribution of inventory to charity, the full amount of any appreciation can be claimed as a deduction.
e. Excess capital losses can be carried forward indefinitely.
f. Excess capital losses cannot be carried back.
g. A net short-term capital gain is subject to the same tax rate as ordinary income.
h. The deduction for qualified business income may be available.
i. A dividends received deduction is available.
j. The like-kind exchange provisions of § 1031 are available.
k. A taxpayer with a fiscal year of May 1–April 30 has a due date for filing a Federal income tax return of July 15.
l. Estimated Federal income tax payments may be required.

34. LO.3 Garnet incurs the following capital asset transactions during the year.

Long-term capital gain	$8,000
Short-term capital gain	3,000

Further, Garnet has an excess capital loss carryforward of $6,000 from last year.

a. What are the tax consequences of these transactions if the $6,000 loss is long term and Garnet is an individual? Garnet is a C corporation?
b. What are the tax consequences of these transactions if the $6,000 loss is short term and Garnet is an individual? Garnet is a C corporation?

35. LO.3, 8 Citron, a calendar year taxpayer, began business in January 2021. It had a long-term capital gain of $5,000 in 2021 and a long-term capital loss of $10,000 in 2022. For both years, Citron had an operating profit in excess of $100,000. How are these capital gain and loss transactions handled for income tax purposes if Citron is:

a. An individual?
b. A C corporation?
c. An S corporation?

36. LO.3 Terri, a calendar year taxpayer, incurs a long-term capital loss of $4,000 and a short-term capital loss of $4,000. How are these items handled for Federal income tax purposes if Terri is:

a. An individual?
b. A C corporation?

37. **LO.3, 8** Robin incurred the following capital transactions in 2022.

LTCG	$10,000
LTCL	8,000
STCG	2,000
STCL	–0–

Robin also reported a net long-term capital loss in 2021 of $2,000, which it could not use, and ordinary income of $13,000. What are the Federal income tax consequences in 2022 if Robin is:

a. An individual.

b. A C corporation.

c. An S corporation.

38. **LO.3** On December 6, 2022, Kestrel Company (a calendar year taxpayer) authorizes a cash donation of $50,000 to the Memphis Public Library. The pledge is carried out as follows: $15,000 on December 12, 2022; $25,000 on February 13, 2023; and $10,000 on May 10, 2023. What are the alternatives for the year of the charitable contribution deduction if Kestrel is:

a. An accrual basis partnership?

b. An accrual basis C corporation?

c. What is the result under parts (a) and (b) if Kestrel is a cash basis taxpayer?

39. **LO.3** During 2023, Siskin (a C corporation) entered into the following transactions.

Income from operations	$500,000
Expenses from operations	425,000
Dividends from domestic corporations (less than 20% ownership)	45,000
Dividends received deduction (50% × $45,000)	22,500
Unused short-term capital loss from 2021 (there are no capital gains in 2022 and 2023)	2,500
NOL carryover from 2022	40,000

In June 2023, Siskin made a contribution to a qualified charitable organization of $10,500 in cash (not included in any of the items listed above).

a. How much, if any, of the contribution can be claimed as a deduction for 2023?

b. What happens to any portion of the gift that is not deductible for 2023?

40. **LO.3** Aurora Company manufactures and sells furnishings for hospitals (e.g., special needs bathroom fixtures). In the current year, it donates some of its inventory to a newly constructed hospice. The hospice is adjacent to a cancer treatment center and is intended to care for indigent and terminal patients.

The donated property has an adjusted basis of $40,000 and a fair market value of $90,000. What is the amount of the charitable contribution deduction if Aurora is a:

a. Sole proprietorship?

b. C corporation?

c. Would your answer to part (b) change if the fair market value of the property was $121,000 (not $90,000)? Explain.

41. **LO.4** Determine the dividends received deduction for each of the following independent situations. Assume that the percentage of stock owned in the corporation paying the dividend is 30% for Green Corporation and less than 20% for Red Corporation and Blue Corporation. Prepare an Excel spreadsheet to compute your answers.

	Red Corporation	Blue Corporation	Green Corporation
Income from operations	$3,000,000	$4,500,000	$8,000,000
Expenses of operations	2,700,000	4,800,000	8,400,000
Qualified dividends received	600,000	150,000	2,000,000

42. **LO.4** Puffin Corporation started business on July 1 of the current tax year and incurred qualifying organizational expenditures. It uses a calendar tax year and wants to accelerate any deductions that are available. What is Puffin's deduction for the current year if its organizational expenditures are:
    a. $3,000?
    b. $46,000?
    c. $52,000?
    d. $77,000?

43. **LO.5** Three C corporations reported the following results for the calendar tax year 2022.
    a. Determine each corporation's Federal income tax liability.
    b. Construct a single Microsoft Excel formula that will produce the correct answer for all of the entities in part (a).

Corporation	Taxable Income
Sparrow	$45,000*
Warbler	68,000**
Scaup	80,000

*Does not include a net short-term capital gain of $3,000.
**Does not include a net long-term capital loss of $4,000.

44. **LO.5** Puce, a calendar year C corporation, reported the following Schedule M–1 transactions on its Form 1120 for the current year. What is Puce's net income per books for the current year?

Taxable income	$100,000
Federal income tax	21,000
Excess capital losses over capital gains	4,000
Life insurance proceeds received on the death of Puce's vice president	100,000
Premiums paid on life insurance policy	1,000
Interest on tax-exempt bonds	10,000

45. **LO.6, 10** Dee, Walt, and Pat form Swan Corporation with the following investments.

	Basis to Transferor	Fair Market Value	Number of Shares Issued
From Dee—cash	$200,000	$200,000	200
From Walt—equipment	400,000	300,000	300
From Pat—land	550,000	600,000	500

In addition to the 500 shares of stock, Pat receives $100,000 in cash from Swan Corporation. Assume that each share of Swan stock is worth $1,000.
    a. How much loss does Walt realize? Recognize?
    b. What is Walt's basis in the Swan stock?

c. What is Swan Corporation's basis in the equipment?

d. How much gain does Pat realize? Recognize?

e. What is Pat's basis in the Swan stock?

f. What is Swan's basis in the land?

g. In terms of the answers to parts (a) through (f), does it matter whether Swan is formed as a C corporation or as an S corporation? Explain.

46. **LO.6** Elton, Neil, Courtney, and Zelma form Ecru Corporation with the following investments.

	Basis to Transferor	Fair Market Value	Number of Shares Issued
From Elton—cash	$ 200,000	$ 200,000	200
From Neil—inventory	230,000	270,000	260
From Courtney—machinery and equipment	400,000	370,000	350
From Zelma—land and building	1,270,000	1,300,000	1,200

In addition to its stock, Ecru distributes cash as follows: $10,000 to Neil, $20,000 to Courtney, and $100,000 to Zelma. Assume that each share of Ecru stock is worth $1,000. Regarding these transactions, provide the following information.

a. Neil's realized and recognized gain (or loss).

b. Neil's basis in the Ecru stock.

c. Ecru's basis in the inventory.

d. Courtney's realized and recognized gain (or loss).

e. Courtney's basis in the Ecru stock.

f. Ecru's basis in the machinery and equipment.

g. Zelma's realized and recognized gain (or loss).

h. Zelma's basis in the Ecru stock.

i. Ecru's basis in the land and building.

47. **LO.7** Ling is the sole shareholder of Crimson Corporation (a C corporation). At a time when Crimson has a deficit in accumulated E & P of $90,000 and current E & P of $65,000, it distributes a cash dividend of $85,000. If Ling's basis in her stock is $15,000, what are the tax consequences of the distribution to:

a. Ling?

b. Crimson Corporation?

Critical Thinking

48. **LO.7** Harold, Marcia, and Davante are equal shareholders in Pelican Corporation, a calendar year C corporation. During the current year, Pelican makes a $150,000 distribution to its three shareholders. Of the $50,000 that each shareholder receives, the tax result is as follows. How can these different results occur?

- $10,000 of dividend income to Harold.
- $10,000 of dividend income and $20,000 capital gain to Marcia.
- $10,000 dividend income and $40,000 capital gain to Davante.

Communications
Decision Making
Planning

49. **LO.7, 10** The stock of Estevez Corporation is held equally by Barney and Faye. The shareholders would like to receive, as a dividend, value of $800,000 each. The corporation owns the following assets that it no longer uses.

Asset	Adjusted Basis to Estevez Corporation	Fair Market Value
Unimproved land	$1,040,000	$800,000
Chevron stock	480,000	800,000

Both assets are held as investments. Estevez holds a capital loss carry-over from the previous year of $80,000 and has accumulated E & P in excess of $2,000,000.

Barney and Faye have come to you for advice. Suggest an attractive tax plan to carry out what the parties want. Write a letter (addressed to Estevez Corporation at PO Box 940, Rochester, NY 14692) describing your plan and its Federal income tax consequences.

50. **LO.8** During the current year, Thrasher (a calendar year, accrual basis S corporation) records the following transactions.

Sales	$1,500,000
Cost of goods sold	900,000
Long-term capital gain	11,000
Short-term capital gain	5,000
Salaries	210,000
Qualified dividends from stock investments	30,000
Rent expense	170,000
Advertising expense	20,000
Interest expense on business loan	15,000
§ 1231 gain	25,000
Organizational expenditures	3,000
Charitable contributions	5,000
Bad debt (trade account receivable deemed to be uncollectible)	10,000
Cash dividend distributed to shareholders	120,000

a. Determine Thrasher's separately stated items for the current year.

b. Determine Thrasher's ordinary business income for the current year.

51. **LO.8** Assume the same facts as in Problem 50. Ana Turner is a 20% shareholder in Thrasher Corporation. She is aware of the tax consequences of the various items listed on the Schedule K–1 (Form 1120S) she received but does not understand their effect on basis. She is considering selling her stock and wants to estimate the gain or loss that will result. Communications Planning

In response to Ana's request for assistance, write a letter to her (1120 Garden Way, Elizabeth, NJ 07207), summarizing the changes to stock basis that the current-year transactions caused.

52. **LO.8, 10** Jim Oza owns all of the stock in Drake, a calendar year S corporation. For calendar year 2022, Drake anticipates an operating loss of $160,000 and could, if deemed worthwhile, sell a stock investment that would generate a $10,000 long-term capital loss. Jim has an adjusted basis of $100,000 in the Drake stock. For the year, he has already realized a short-term capital gain of $7,000. He anticipates no other capital asset transactions and expects to be in the 35% tax bracket in 2022. Communications Planning

Write a letter to Jim (470 Bay Avenue, Bedford, MA 01730), suggesting a course of action that could reduce his Federal income taxes.

53. **LO.8** Jenna owns 30% of the stock in Mockingbird, a calendar year S corporation. Her basis in the stock as of January 1, 2022, is $130,000. Mockingbird has an operating loss of $500,000 in 2022 and an operating profit of $600,000 in 2023. Jenna withdraws $70,000 in cash from the corporation in 2023.

a. What are Jenna's tax consequences in 2022?

b. 2023?

c. What is Jenna's basis in her Mockingbird stock as of January 1, 2023?

d. January 1, 2024?

54. **LO.9** Guy, Alma, and Kara form the Ivory Partnership. In exchange for a 30% capital interest, Guy transfers property (basis of $200,000; fair market value of $400,000) subject to a liability of $100,000. The liability is assumed by the partnership. Alma transfers property (basis of $350,000; fair market value of $300,000) for a 30% capital interest. Kara invests cash of $400,000 for the remaining 40% capital interest. Concerning these transactions, determine:
    a. Guy's recognized gain.
    b. Guy's basis in the partnership interest.
    c. Alma's recognized loss.
    d. Alma's basis in the partnership interest.
    e. Kara's basis in the partnership interest.
    f. Ivory Partnership's basis in the property transferred by Guy and Alma.

55. **LO.9** The Pheasant Partnership reported the following items in the current year.

Operating income		$700,000
Cost of goods sold		400,000
Capital gains—		
Long-term	$20,000	
Short-term	10,000	30,000
Salaries		60,000
Guaranteed payments to Partner A		20,000
Tax-exempt interest income		2,000
Rent		24,000
Dividend from P&G stock investment		3,000
Utilities		8,000
Charitable contribution to Greenpeace		1,000
Contribution to governor's reelection campaign		500

   a. What is Pheasant's ordinary income (or loss)?
   b. What are Pheasant's separately stated items?

56. **LO.9** Aiden holds a 35% capital interest in the Oro Partnership and is entitled to a yearly guaranteed payment of $40,000. As of January 1, 2022, Aiden's basis in the partnership interest is $87,000. During tax year 2022, Oro recorded the following transactions.

Operating profit (after consideration of guaranteed payment)	$410,000
Interest income on City of Seattle bonds	20,000
Short-term capital loss	5,000
Long-term capital gain	7,000
Funds borrowed from bank to provide working capital	30,000

During 2022, Aiden withdrew cash of $70,000 from Oro to help cover his living expenses. What is Aiden's basis in his partnership interest as of January 1, 2023?

Planning

57. **LO.9, 10** As of January 1, 2022, Norman has a basis of $85,000 in his 30% capital interest in the Plata Partnership. He and the partnership use the calendar year for tax purposes. The partnership incurs an operating loss of $440,000 for 2022 and a profit of $285,000 for 2023.
    a. How much, if any, loss may Norman recognize for 2022?
    b. How much income must Norman recognize for 2023?
    c. What basis will Norman have in his partnership interest as of January 1, 2023?
    d. What basis will Norman have in his partnership interest as of January 1, 2024?
    e. What year-end 2022 tax planning would you suggest to ensure that a partner could deduct all of his or her share of any partnership losses?

58. **LO.4, 5** Del Mar Corporation (EIN 33-1234567) was formed and began operations on January 1, 2022. The corporate address is 463 E. Pershing Blvd. Cheyenne, WY 82001. Del Mar uses the accrual basis of accounting. The corporation's 12/31/2022 trial balance is presented below.

	General Ledger Account Balance	
Account Name	**Debit**	**Credit**
Cash in checking	$ 25,000	
Accounts receivable	20,000	
GAAP reserve for bad debts		$ 7,000
Inventory (at cost)	87,000	
Investments	1,000	
Organization expense	–0–	
Equipment	90,000	
Accumulated depreciation—equipment		10,000
Land	–0–	
Other intangible assets	4,000	
Accounts payable		14,000
Accrued income taxes		(910)
Accrued interest		3,400
Notes payable		85,000
Common stock		80,000
Additional paid-in capital		–0–
Retained earnings		–0–
Revenues		260,000
Sales returns and allowances	–0–	
Investment income		20,000
Gain (loss) on sale of assets	–0–	–0–
Purchase returns and allowances		–0–
Cost of goods sold	105,000	
Advertising	5,000	
Amortization	–0–	
Bad debt expense, addition to GAAP reserve	7,000	
Charitable contributions	–0–	
Depreciation	10,000	
Dues and subscriptions	–0–	
Interest expense	3,400	
Miscellaneous	–0–	
Payroll taxes	10,000	
Professional fees	–0–	
Repairs	3,000	
Utilities	–0–	
Wages	105,000	
Income taxes	3,090	
Totals	**$478,490**	**$478,490**

Additional pertinent facts include the following.

- Investment income is dividends received from a 10% owned domestic corporation.
- Wages include $75,000 of compensation to Marion Ore, CEO and 100% owner of Del Mar Corp. Her Social Security number is 456-78-0123. She devotes 100% of her time to Del Mar.
- Book depreciation was recorded to match tax depreciation.

- Del Mar made $4,000 of estimated tax payments during 2022. These were debited to the accrued income taxes account.
- An election was made to expense the maximum amount of organization costs for tax.

a. Compute Del Mar's taxable income and Federal income tax liability for 2022.
b. How much is Del Mar's first estimated tax payment, and when is it due?

Research Problems

the answer company™ THOMSON REUTERS®

Note: Solutions to the Research Problems can be prepared by using the Thomson Reuters Checkpoint™ online tax research database, which accompanies this textbook. Solutions can also be prepared by using research materials found in a typical tax library.

Communications

Research Problem 1. Tyler and Travis Best are brothers and are equal shareholders in Moreno Corporation, a calendar year C corporation. This year they incurred travel and transportation expenses on behalf of the entity. Because Moreno was in a precarious financial condition, the brothers decided not to seek reimbursement for these expenditures. Instead, each brother deducted on his individual return (Form 1040) what he had spent on travel and transportation expenses on behalf of the corporation.

Upon an audit of the returns filed by Tyler and Travis, the IRS disallowed these expenditures. Write a letter to Travis (140 Ridgeland Drive, Waynesburg, PA 15370), indicating whether he should challenge the IRS action. Explain your conclusions using nontechnical language.

Communications

Research Problem 2. During 2022, Jaden Steele received a distribution of $24,000 on stock he owns in Razorbill Corporation. He had planned to report this amount as dividend income until he talked to his mother-in-law, Sylvia. According to Sylvia, who had examined Razorbill's financial statements, the company suffered an operating loss for the year. Consequently, Sylvia thinks that the distribution is a nontaxable return of capital.

Jaden is confused and seeks a second opinion from you. Write a letter to Jaden (1260 Pike Street, Eagle, ID 83616), explaining the possibilities involved.

Partial list of research aids:
Jason Michael Juba, 103 TCM 1338, T.C.Memo. 2012–68.

Research Problem 3. Scott and Brooke are the sole shareholders of Tananger Company, a calendar year S corporation. After several loss years, in December 2022, Tananger is forced to borrow $300,000 for working capital purposes. Robin State Bank makes the loan to Tananger, but only after Scott and Brooke personally guarantee the debt.

Scott and Brooke deduct Tananger's $200,000 operating loss for 2022 on their individual income tax returns. Although they have a zero basis in their stock investment, they consider the guarantee of the bank loan to be debt within the meaning of § 1366(d)(1)(B).

Are Scott and Brooke correct in their reasoning? Explain.

Partial list of research aids:
Regs. §1.1366–2(a)(2)(ii)
Milton T. Raynor, 50 T.C. 762 (1968).
William H. Maloof, 89 TCM 1022, T.C.Memo. 2005–75.

Use internet tax resources to address the following questions. Look for reliable websites and blogs of the IRS and other government agencies, media outlets, businesses, tax professionals, academics, think tanks, and political outlets.

Research Problem 4. Does your state impose income tax on an S corporation in addition to imposing tax on the shareholders? Elaborate.

Research Problem 5. To report its transactions for the year, a partnership must file a Form 1065 with the IRS.

a. When is this return due?

b. As is the case with individuals and C corporations, can a partnership obtain an automatic extension for filing the Form 1065?

c. Must a partnership include a Schedule M–3 with its Form 1065? Explain.

d. What is the due date for partnership returns in your state? Is the partnership subject to any tax in your state?

Research Problem 6. Send your instructor a graph for tax years 2001 and every five years thereafter that shows the number of tax returns filed by C corporations, S corporations, and partnerships/LLCs. Include in your graph the results for the latest tax year for which information is available. Make two observations about your findings (e.g., concerning the filing trends seen in the data).

Communications
Data Analytics

Research Problem 7. Construct a graph with data from the latest year made available by the IRS for C corporations. Show the percentage of taxable income that is deducted as a gift to charity, divided into three groups by size of the entity's total assets. Send this graph to your instructor with at least two observations about the data. *Hint:* Start your work at **irs.gov/pub/irs-pdf/p16.pdf**.

Data Analytics

Research Problem 8. Can chatbot technology be used by a CPA firm to help clients and potential clients understand the similarities and differences among business entity types? How would this work, what are the benefits, and what cautions should the firm note for users?

Becker CPA Review Questions

Becker

1. On January 1, year 5, Olinto Corp., an accrual basis, calendar year C corporation, had $35,000 in accumulated earnings and profits. For year 5, Olinto had current earnings and profits of $15,000 and made two $40,000 cash distributions to its shareholders—one in April and one in September of year 5. What amount of the year 5 distributions is classified as dividend income to Olinto's shareholders?

a. $15,000 c. $50,000

b. $35,000 d. $80,000

2. Adams, Beck, and Carr organized Flexo Corp. with authorized voting common stock of $100,000. Adams received 10% of the capital stock in payment for the organizational services that he rendered for the benefit of the newly formed corporation. Adams did not contribute property to Flexo and was under no obligation to be paid by Beck or Carr. Beck and Carr transferred property in exchange for stock as follows.

	Adjusted Basis	Fair Market Value	Percentage of Flexo Stock Acquired
Beck	$ 5,000	$20,000	20%
Carr	60,000	70,000	70%

What amount of gain did Carr recognize from this transaction?

a. $40,000 c. $10,000

b. $15,000 d. $0

3. Village Corp., a calendar year corporation, began business in year 1. Village made a valid S corporation election on December 5, year 4, with the unanimous consent of its shareholders. The eligibility requirements for S status continued to be met throughout year 5. On what date did Village's S status become effective?
   a. January 1, year 4
   b. January 1, year 5
   c. December 5, year 4
   d. December 5, year 5
4. The Matthew Corporation, an S corporation, is equally owned by three shareholders, Emily, Alejandra, and Kristina. The corporation is on the calendar year basis for tax and financial purposes. On April 1 of the current year, Emily sold her one-third interest in the Matthew Corporation equally to the other two shareholders. For the current year, the corporation had nonseparately stated ordinary income of $900,000. For the current year, how much ordinary income should be allocated to Kristina on her Schedule K–1?
   a. $25,000
   b. $75,000
   c. $337,500
   d. $412,500
5. Barker acquired a 50% interest in Kode Partnership by contributing $20,000 cash and a building with an adjusted basis of $26,000 and a fair market value of $42,000. The building was subject to a $10,000 mortgage, which was assumed by Kode. The other partners contributed cash only. The basis of Barker's interest in Kode is:
   a. $36,000
   b. $41,000
   c. $52,000
   d. $62,000
6. Peter, a 25% partner in Gold & Stein Partnership, received a $20,000 guaranteed payment in the current year for deductible services rendered to the partnership. Guaranteed payments were not made to any other partner. Gold & Stein's current-year partnership income consisted of:

Net business income before guaranteed payments	$80,000
Net long-term capital gains	10,000

   What amount of income should Peter report from Gold & Stein Partnership on his current-year tax return?
   a. $37,500
   b. $27,500
   c. $22,500
   d. $20,000
7. The dividends received deduction (DRD) is a tax deduction that may be taken by which of the following?
   a. An individual
   b. An S corporation
   c. A partnership
   d. A C corporation
8. After a corporation's status as an S corporation is revoked or terminated, how many years is the corporation required to wait before making a new S election, in the absence of IRS consent to an earlier election?
   a. 1
   b. 3
   c. 5
   d. 10
9. Pedro, a 25% partner in Gold & Stein Partnership, received a $20,000 guaranteed payment in the current year for deductible services rendered to the partnership. Guaranteed payments were not made to any other partner. Gold & Stein's current year partnership income consisted of:

Net business income before guaranteed payments	$80,000
Net long-term capital gains	10,000

   What amount of gross income should Pedro report from Gold & Stein Partnership on his current year tax return?
   a. $37,500
   b. $27,500
   c. $22,500
   d. $20,000

Appendix A

Tax Formulas, Tax Rate Schedules, and Tables

Tax Formula for Individuals A-2

Basic Standard Deduction Amounts A-2

Amount of Each Additional Standard Deduction A-2

Personal and Dependency Exemption A-2

Income Tax Rate Schedules—Individuals (2021 and 2022) A-3

Individual Income Tax Tables (2021) A-4

Individual Optional Sales Tax Tables (2021) A-16

Tax Formula for Corporations A-23

Income Tax Rates—C Corporations (2018 and After) A-23

Income Tax Rates—Estates and Trusts (2021 and 2022) A-23

Unified Transfer Tax Rates (For Gifts Made and for Deaths After 2012) A-24

Valuation Tables, Excerpts—Table S A-25

Valuation Tables, Excerpts—Table B A-27

AMT Formula for Individuals A-28

AMT Exemption and Phaseout Amounts for Individuals (2021 and 2022) A-28

(The 2022 Individual Income Tax Tables and the 2022 Individual Optional Sales Tax Tables can be accessed at the IRS website when released: **irs.gov**)

Tax Formula for Individuals

Income (broadly defined)	$xx,xxx
Less: Exclusions	(x,xxx)
Gross income	$xx,xxx
Less: Deductions *for* adjusted gross income	(x,xxx)
Adjusted gross income	$xx,xxx
Less: The greater of— Total itemized deductions *or* standard deduction	(x,xxx)
Less: Personal and dependency exemptions*	(x,xxx)
Deduction for qualified business income**	(x,xxx)
Taxable income	$xx,xxx
Tax on taxable income	$ x,xxx
Less: Tax credits (including Federal income tax withheld and prepaid)	(xxx)
Tax due (or refund)	$ xxx

*Exemption deductions are not allowed from 2018 through 2025.
**Only applies from 2018 through 2025.

Note: For 2021, individuals using the standard deduction may also subtract *from* adjusted gross income, cash charitable contributions of up to $300 ($600 if married, filing jointly).

Basic Standard Deduction Amounts

Filing Status	2021	2022
Single	$12,550	$12,950
Married, filing jointly	25,100	25,900
Surviving spouse	25,100	25,900
Head of household	18,800	19,400
Married, filing separately	12,550	12,950

Amount of Each Additional Standard Deduction

Filing Status	2021	2022
Single	$1,700	$1,750
Married, filing jointly	1,350	1,400
Surviving spouse	1,350	1,400
Head of household	1,700	1,750
Married, filing separately	1,350	1,400

Personal and Dependency Exemption

2021	2022
$4,300	$4,400

Note: Exemption deductions have been suspended from 2018 through 2025. However, the personal and dependency exemption amount is used for other purposes (including determining whether a "qualifying relative" is a taxpayer's dependent).

2021 Tax Rate Schedules

Single—Schedule X

If taxable income is: Over—	But not over—	The tax is:	of the amount over—
$ 0	$ 9,950	.........10%	$ 0
9,950	40,525	$ 995.00 + 12%	9,950
40,525	86,375	4,664.00 + 22%	40,525
86,375	164,925	14,751.00 + 24%	86,375
164,925	209,425	33,603.00 + 32%	164,925
209,425	523,600	47,843.00 + 35%	209,425
523,600	....	157,804.25 + 37%	523,600

Head of household—Schedule Z

If taxable income is: Over—	But not over—	The tax is:	of the amount over—
$ 0	$ 14,200	.........10%	$ 0
14,200	54,200	$ 1,420.00 + 12%	14,200
54,200	86,350	6,220.00 + 22%	54,200
86,350	164,900	13,293.00 + 24%	86,350
164,900	209,400	32,145.00 + 32%	164,900
209,400	523,600	46,385.00 + 35%	209,400
523,600	....	156,355.00 + 37%	523,600

Married filing jointly or Qualifying widow(er)—Schedule Y-1

If taxable income is: Over—	But not over—	The tax is:	of the amount over—
$ 0	$ 19,900	.........10%	$ 0
19,900	81,050	$ 1,990.00 + 12%	19,900
81,050	172,750	9,328.00 + 22%	81,050
172,750	329,850	29,502.00 + 24%	172,750
329,850	418,850	67,206.00 + 32%	329,850
418,850	628,300	95,686.00 + 35%	418,850
628,300	....	168,993.50 + 37%	628,300

Married filing separately—Schedule Y-2

If taxable income is: Over—	But not over—	The tax is:	of the amount over—
$ 0	$ 9,950	.........10%	$ 0
9,950	40,525	$ 995.00 + 12%	9,950
40,525	86,375	4,664.00 + 22%	40,525
86,375	164,925	14,751.00 + 24%	86,375
164,925	209,425	33,603.00 + 32%	164,925
209,425	314,150	47,843.00 + 35%	209,425
314,150	....	84,496.75 + 37%	314,150

2022 Tax Rate Schedules

Single—Schedule X

If taxable income is: Over—	But not over—	The tax is:	of the amount over—
$ 0	$ 10,275	.........10%	$ 0
10,275	41,775	$ 1,027.50 + 12%	10,275
41,775	89,075	4,807.50 + 22%	41,775
89,075	170,050	15,213.50 + 24%	89,075
170,050	215,950	34,647.50 + 32%	170,050
215,950	539,900	49,335.50 + 35%	215,950
539,900	....	162,718.00 + 37%	539,900

Head of household—Schedule Z

If taxable income is: Over—	But not over—	The tax is:	of the amount over—
$ 0	$ 14,650	.........10%	$ 0
14,650	55,900	$ 1,465.00 + 12%	14,650
55,900	89,050	6,415.00 + 22%	55,900
89,050	170,050	13,708.00 + 24%	89,050
170,050	215,950	33,148.00 + 32%	170,050
215,950	539,900	47,836.00 + 35%	215,950
539,900	....	161,218.50 + 37%	539,900

Married filing jointly or Qualifying widow(er)—Schedule Y-1

If taxable income is: Over—	But not over—	The tax is:	of the amount over—
$ 0	$ 20,550	.........10%	$ 0
20,550	83,550	$ 2,055.00 + 12%	20,550
83,550	178,150	9,615.00 + 22%	83,550
178,150	340,100	30,427.00 + 24%	178,150
340,100	431,900	69,295.00 + 32%	340,100
431,900	647,850	98,671.00 + 35%	431,900
647,850	....	174,253.50 + 37%	647,850

Married filing separately—Schedule Y-2

If taxable income is: Over—	But not over—	The tax is:	of the amount over—
$ 0	$ 10,275	.........10%	$ 0
10,275	41,775	$ 1,027.50 + 12%	10,275
41,775	89,075	4,807.50 + 22%	41,775
89,075	170,050	15,213.50 + 24%	89,075
170,050	215,950	34,647.50 + 32%	170,050
215,950	323,925	49,335.50 + 35%	215,950
323,925	....	87,126.75 + 37%	323,925

2021 Tax Table

CAUTION

See the instructions for line 16 to see if you must use the Tax Table below to figure your tax.

Example. Mr. and Mrs. Brown are filing a joint return. Their taxable income on Form 1040, line 15, is $25,300. First, they find the $25,300-25,350 taxable income line. Next, they find the column for married filing jointly and read down the column. The amount shown where the taxable income line and filing status column meet is $2,641. This is the tax amount they should enter in the entry space on Form 1040, line 16.

Sample Table

At Least	But Less Than	Single	Married filing jointly*	Married filing sepa-rately	Head of a house-hold
		Your tax is—			
25,200	25,250	2,828	2,629	2,828	2,743
25,250	25,300	2,834	2,635	2,834	2,749
25,300	25,350	2,840	2,641	2,840	2,755
25,350	25,400	2,846	2,647	2,846	2,761

If line 15 (taxable income) is—		And you are—			
At least	But less than	Single	Married filing jointly *	Married filing sepa-rately	Head of a house-hold
		Your tax is—			
0	5	0	0	0	0
5	15	1	1	1	1
15	25	2	2	2	2
25	50	4	4	4	4
50	75	6	6	6	6
75	100	9	9	9	9
100	125	11	11	11	11
125	150	14	14	14	14
150	175	16	16	16	16
175	200	19	19	19	19
200	225	21	21	21	21
225	250	24	24	24	24
250	275	26	26	26	26
275	300	29	29	29	29
300	325	31	31	31	31
325	350	34	34	34	34
350	375	36	36	36	36
375	400	39	39	39	39
400	425	41	41	41	41
425	450	44	44	44	44
450	475	46	46	46	46
475	500	49	49	49	49
500	525	51	51	51	51
525	550	54	54	54	54
550	575	56	56	56	56
575	600	59	59	59	59
600	625	61	61	61	61
625	650	64	64	64	64
650	675	66	66	66	66
675	700	69	69	69	69
700	725	71	71	71	71
725	750	74	74	74	74
750	775	76	76	76	76
775	800	79	79	79	79
800	825	81	81	81	81
825	850	84	84	84	84
850	875	86	86	86	86
875	900	89	89	89	89
900	925	91	91	91	91
925	950	94	94	94	94
950	975	96	96	96	96
975	1,000	99	99	99	99

If line 15 (taxable income) is—		And you are—			
At least	But less than	Single	Married filing jointly *	Married filing sepa-rately	Head of a house-hold
		Your tax is—			
1,000					
1,000	1,025	101	101	101	101
1,025	1,050	104	104	104	104
1,050	1,075	106	106	106	106
1,075	1,100	109	109	109	109
1,100	1,125	111	111	111	111
1,125	1,150	114	114	114	114
1,150	1,175	116	116	116	116
1,175	1,200	119	119	119	119
1,200	1,225	121	121	121	121
1,225	1,250	124	124	124	124
1,250	1,275	126	126	126	126
1,275	1,300	129	129	129	129
1,300	1,325	131	131	131	131
1,325	1,350	134	134	134	134
1,350	1,375	136	136	136	136
1,375	1,400	139	139	139	139
1,400	1,425	141	141	141	141
1,425	1,450	144	144	144	144
1,450	1,475	146	146	146	146
1,475	1,500	149	149	149	149
1,500	1,525	151	151	151	151
1,525	1,550	154	154	154	154
1,550	1,575	156	156	156	156
1,575	1,600	159	159	159	159
1,600	1,625	161	161	161	161
1,625	1,650	164	164	164	164
1,650	1,675	166	166	166	166
1,675	1,700	169	169	169	169
1,700	1,725	171	171	171	171
1,725	1,750	174	174	174	174
1,750	1,775	176	176	176	176
1,775	1,800	179	179	179	179
1,800	1,825	181	181	181	181
1,825	1,850	184	184	184	184
1,850	1,875	186	186	186	186
1,875	1,900	189	189	189	189
1,900	1,925	191	191	191	191
1,925	1,950	194	194	194	194
1,950	1,975	196	196	196	196
1,975	2,000	199	199	199	199

If line 15 (taxable income) is—		And you are—			
At least	But less than	Single	Married filing jointly *	Married filing sepa-rately	Head of a house-hold
		Your tax is—			
2,000					
2,000	2,025	201	201	201	201
2,025	2,050	204	204	204	204
2,050	2,075	206	206	206	206
2,075	2,100	209	209	209	209
2,100	2,125	211	211	211	211
2,125	2,150	214	214	214	214
2,150	2,175	216	216	216	216
2,175	2,200	219	219	219	219
2,200	2,225	221	221	221	221
2,225	2,250	224	224	224	224
2,250	2,275	226	226	226	226
2,275	2,300	229	229	229	229
2,300	2,325	231	231	231	231
2,325	2,350	234	234	234	234
2,350	2,375	236	236	236	236
2,375	2,400	239	239	239	239
2,400	2,425	241	241	241	241
2,425	2,450	244	244	244	244
2,450	2,475	246	246	246	246
2,475	2,500	249	249	249	249
2,500	2,525	251	251	251	251
2,525	2,550	254	254	254	254
2,550	2,575	256	256	256	256
2,575	2,600	259	259	259	259
2,600	2,625	261	261	261	261
2,625	2,650	264	264	264	264
2,650	2,675	266	266	266	266
2,675	2,700	269	269	269	269
2,700	2,725	271	271	271	271
2,725	2,750	274	274	274	274
2,750	2,775	276	276	276	276
2,775	2,800	279	279	279	279
2,800	2,825	281	281	281	281
2,825	2,850	284	284	284	284
2,850	2,875	286	286	286	286
2,875	2,900	289	289	289	289
2,900	2,925	291	291	291	291
2,925	2,950	294	294	294	294
2,950	2,975	296	296	296	296
2,975	3,000	299	299	299	299

(Continued)

* This column must also be used by a qualifying widow(er).

2021 Tax Table — *Continued*

If line 15 (taxable income) is—		And you are—			
At least	But less than	Single	Married filing jointly *	Married filing sepa-rately	Head of a house-hold
		Your tax is—			
3,000					
3,000	3,050	303	303	303	303
3,050	3,100	308	308	308	308
3,100	3,150	313	313	313	313
3,150	3,200	318	318	318	318
3,200	3,250	323	323	323	323
3,250	3,300	328	328	328	328
3,300	3,350	333	333	333	333
3,350	3,400	338	338	338	338
3,400	3,450	343	343	343	343
3,450	3,500	348	348	348	348
3,500	3,550	353	353	353	353
3,550	3,600	358	358	358	358
3,600	3,650	363	363	363	363
3,650	3,700	368	368	368	368
3,700	3,750	373	373	373	373
3,750	3,800	378	378	378	378
3,800	3,850	383	383	383	383
3,850	3,900	388	388	388	388
3,900	3,950	393	393	393	393
3,950	4,000	398	398	398	398
4,000					
4,000	4,050	403	403	403	403
4,050	4,100	408	408	408	408
4,100	4,150	413	413	413	413
4,150	4,200	418	418	418	418
4,200	4,250	423	423	423	423
4,250	4,300	428	428	428	428
4,300	4,350	433	433	433	433
4,350	4,400	438	438	438	438
4,400	4,450	443	443	443	443
4,450	4,500	448	448	448	448
4,500	4,550	453	453	453	453
4,550	4,600	458	458	458	458
4,600	4,650	463	463	463	463
4,650	4,700	468	468	468	468
4,700	4,750	473	473	473	473
4,750	4,800	478	478	478	478
4,800	4,850	483	483	483	483
4,850	4,900	488	488	400	488
4,900	4,950	493	493	493	493
4,950	5,000	498	498	498	498
5,000					
5,000	5,050	503	503	503	503
5,050	5,100	508	508	508	508
5,100	5,150	513	513	513	513
5,150	5,200	518	518	518	518
5,200	5,250	523	523	523	523
5,250	5,300	528	528	528	528
5,300	5,350	533	533	533	533
5,350	5,400	638	538	538	538
5,400	5,450	543	543	543	543
5,450	5,500	548	548	548	548
5,500	5,550	553	553	553	553
5,550	5,600	558	558	558	558
5,600	5,650	563	563	563	563
5,650	5,700	568	568	568	568
5,700	5,750	573	573	573	573
5,750	5,800	578	578	578	578
5,800	5,850	583	583	583	583
5,850	5,900	588	588	588	588
5,900	5,950	593	593	593	593
5,950	6,000	598	598	598	598
6,000					
6,000	6,050	603	603	603	603
6,050	6,100	608	608	608	608
6,100	6,150	613	613	613	613
6,150	6,200	618	618	618	618
6,200	6,250	623	623	623	623
6,250	6,300	628	628	628	628
6,300	6,350	633	633	633	633
6,350	6,400	638	638	638	638
6,400	6,450	643	643	643	643
6,450	6,500	648	648	648	648
6,500	6,550	653	653	653	653
6,550	6,600	658	658	658	658
6,600	6,650	663	663	663	663
6,650	6,700	668	668	668	668
6,700	6,750	673	673	673	673
6,750	6,800	678	678	678	678
6,800	6,850	683	683	683	683
6,850	6,900	688	688	688	688
6,900	6,950	693	693	693	693
6,950	7,000	698	698	698	698
7,000					
7,000	7,050	703	703	703	703
7,050	7,100	708	708	708	708
7,100	7,150	713	713	713	713
7,150	7,200	718	718	718	718
7,200	7,250	723	723	723	723
7,250	7,300	728	728	728	728
7,300	7,350	733	733	733	733
7,350	7,400	738	738	738	738
7,400	7,450	743	743	743	743
7,450	7,500	748	748	748	748
7,500	7,550	753	753	753	753
7,550	7,600	758	758	758	758
7,600	7,650	763	763	763	763
7,650	7,700	768	768	768	768
7,700	7,750	773	773	773	773
7,750	7,800	778	778	778	778
7,800	7,850	783	783	783	783
7,850	7,900	788	788	788	788
7,900	7,950	793	793	793	793
7,950	8,000	798	798	798	798
8,000					
8,000	8,050	803	803	803	803
8,050	8,100	808	808	808	808
8,100	8,150	813	813	813	813
8,150	8,200	818	818	818	818
8,200	8,250	823	823	823	823
8,250	8,300	828	828	828	828
8,300	8,350	833	833	833	833
8,350	8,400	838	838	838	838
8,400	8,450	843	843	843	843
8,450	8,500	848	848	848	848
8,500	8,550	853	853	853	853
8,550	8,600	858	858	858	858
8,600	8,650	863	863	863	863
8,650	8,700	868	868	868	868
8,700	8,750	873	873	873	873
8,750	8,800	878	878	878	878
8,800	8,850	883	883	883	883
8,850	8,900	888	888	888	888
8,900	8,950	893	893	893	893
8,950	9,000	898	898	898	898
9,000					
9,000	9,050	903	903	903	903
9,050	9,100	908	908	908	908
9,100	9,150	913	913	913	913
9,150	9,200	918	918	918	918
9,200	9,250	923	923	923	923
9,250	9,300	928	928	928	928
9,300	9,350	933	933	933	933
9,350	9,400	938	938	938	938
9,400	9,450	943	943	943	943
9,450	9,500	948	948	948	948
9,500	9,550	953	953	953	953
9,550	9,600	958	958	958	958
9,600	9,650	963	963	963	963
9,650	9,700	968	968	968	968
9,700	9,750	973	973	973	973
9,750	9,800	978	978	978	978
9,800	9,850	983	983	983	983
9,850	9,900	988	988	988	988
9,900	9,950	993	993	993	993
9,950	10,000	998	998	998	998
10,000					
10,000	10,050	1,004	1,003	1,004	1,003
10,050	10,100	1,010	1,008	1,010	1,008
10,100	10,150	1,016	1,013	1,016	1,013
10,150	10,200	1,022	1,018	1,022	1,018
10,200	10,250	1,028	1,023	1,028	1,023
10,250	10,300	1,034	1,028	1,034	1,028
10,300	10,350	1,040	1,033	1,040	1,033
10,350	10,400	1,046	1,038	1,046	1,038
10,400	10,450	1,052	1,043	1,052	1,043
10,450	10,500	1,058	1,048	1,058	1,048
10,500	10,550	1,064	1,053	1,064	1,053
10,550	10,600	1,070	1,058	1,070	1,058
10,600	10,650	1,076	1,063	1,076	1,063
10,650	10,700	1,082	1,068	1,082	1,068
10,700	10,750	1,088	1,073	1,088	1,073
10,750	10,800	1,094	1,078	1,094	1,078
10,800	10,850	1,100	1,083	1,100	1,083
10,850	10,900	1,106	1,088	1,106	1,088
10,900	10,950	1,112	1,093	1,112	1,093
10,950	11,000	1,118	1,098	1,118	1,098
11,000					
11,000	11,050	1,124	1,103	1,124	1,103
11,050	11,100	1,130	1,108	1,130	1,108
11,100	11,150	1,136	1,113	1,136	1,113
11,150	11,200	1,142	1,118	1,142	1,118
11,200	11,250	1,148	1,123	1,148	1,123
11,250	11,300	1,154	1,128	1,154	1,128
11,300	11,350	1,160	1,133	1,160	1,133
11,350	11,400	1,166	1,138	1,166	1,138
11,400	11,450	1,172	1,143	1,172	1,143
11,450	11,500	1,178	1,148	1,178	1,148
11,500	11,550	1,184	1,153	1,184	1,153
11,550	11,600	1,190	1,158	1,190	1,158
11,600	11,650	1,196	1,163	1,196	1,163
11,650	11,700	1,202	1,168	1,202	1,168
11,700	11,750	1,208	1,173	1,208	1,173
11,750	11,800	1,214	1,178	1,214	1,178
11,800	11,850	1,220	1,183	1,220	1,183
11,850	11,900	1,226	1,188	1,226	1,188
11,900	11,950	1,232	1,193	1,232	1,193
11,950	12,000	1,238	1,198	1,238	1,198

(Continued)

* This column must also be used by a qualifying widow(er).

2021 Tax Table — *Continued*

If line 15 (taxable income) is—		And you are—			
At least	But less than	Single	Married filing jointly *	Married filing separately	Head of a household
		Your tax is—			
12,000					
12,000	12,050	1,244	1,203	1,244	1,203
12,050	12,100	1,250	1,208	1,250	1,208
12,100	12,150	1,256	1,213	1,256	1,213
12,150	12,200	1,262	1,218	1,262	1,218
12,200	12,250	1,268	1,223	1,268	1,223
12,250	12,300	1,274	1,228	1,274	1,228
12,300	12,350	1,280	1,233	1,280	1,233
12,350	12,400	1,286	1,238	1,286	1,238
12,400	12,450	1,292	1,243	1,292	1,243
12,450	12,500	1,298	1,248	1,298	1,248
12,500	12,550	1,304	1,253	1,304	1,253
12,550	12,600	1,310	1,258	1,310	1,258
12,600	12,650	1,316	1,263	1,316	1,263
12,650	12,700	1,322	1,268	1,322	1,268
12,700	12,750	1,328	1,273	1,328	1,273
12,750	12,800	1,334	1,278	1,334	1,278
12,800	12,850	1,340	1,283	1,340	1,283
12,850	12,900	1,346	1,288	1,346	1,288
12,900	12,950	1,352	1,293	1,352	1,293
12,950	13,000	1,358	1,298	1,358	1,298
13,000					
13,000	13,050	1,364	1,303	1,364	1,303
13,050	13,100	1,370	1,308	1,370	1,308
13,100	13,150	1,376	1,313	1,376	1,313
13,150	13,200	1,382	1,318	1,382	1,318
13,200	13,250	1,388	1,323	1,388	1,323
13,250	13,300	1,394	1,328	1,394	1,328
13,300	13,350	1,400	1,333	1,400	1,333
13,350	13,400	1,406	1,338	1,406	1,338
13,400	13,450	1,412	1,343	1,412	1,343
13,450	13,500	1,418	1,348	1,418	1,348
13,500	13,550	1,424	1,353	1,424	1,353
13,550	13,600	1,430	1,358	1,430	1,358
13,600	13,650	1,436	1,363	1,436	1,363
13,650	13,700	1,442	1,368	1,442	1,368
13,700	13,750	1,448	1,373	1,448	1,373
13,750	13,800	1,454	1,378	1,454	1,378
13,800	13,850	1,460	1,383	1,460	1,383
13,850	13,900	1,466	1,388	1,466	1,388
13,900	13,950	1,472	1,393	1,472	1,393
13,950	14,000	1,478	1,398	1,478	1,398
14,000					
14,000	14,050	1,484	1,403	1,484	1,403
14,050	14,100	1,490	1,408	1,490	1,408
14,100	14,150	1,496	1,413	1,496	1,413
14,150	14,200	1,502	1,418	1,502	1,418
14,200	14,250	1,508	1,423	1,508	1,423
14,250	14,300	1,514	1,428	1,514	1,429
14,300	14,350	1,520	1,433	1,520	1,435
14,350	14,400	1,526	1,438	1,526	1,441
14,400	14,450	1,532	1,443	1,532	1,447
14,450	14,500	1,538	1,448	1,538	1,453
14,500	14,550	1,544	1,453	1,544	1,459
14,550	14,600	1,550	1,458	1,550	1,465
14,600	14,650	1,556	1,463	1,556	1,471
14,650	14,700	1,562	1,468	1,562	1,477
14,700	14,750	1,568	1,473	1,568	1,483
14,750	14,800	1,574	1,478	1,574	1,489
14,800	14,850	1,580	1,483	1,580	1,495
14,850	14,900	1,586	1,488	1,586	1,501
14,900	14,950	1,592	1,493	1,592	1,507
14,950	15,000	1,598	1,498	1,598	1,513
15,000					
15,000	15,050	1,604	1,503	1,604	1,519
15,050	15,100	1,610	1,508	1,610	1,525
15,100	15,150	1,616	1,513	1,616	1,531
15,150	15,200	1,622	1,518	1,622	1,537
15,200	15,250	1,628	1,523	1,628	1,543
15,250	15,300	1,634	1,528	1,634	1,549
15,300	15,350	1,640	1,533	1,640	1,555
15,350	15,400	1,646	1,538	1,646	1,561
15,400	15,450	1,652	1,543	1,652	1,567
15,450	15,500	1,658	1,548	1,658	1,573
15,500	15,550	1,664	1,553	1,664	1,579
15,550	15,600	1,670	1,558	1,670	1,585
15,600	15,650	1,676	1,563	1,676	1,591
15,650	15,700	1,682	1,568	1,682	1,597
15,700	15,750	1,688	1,573	1,688	1,603
15,750	15,800	1,694	1,578	1,694	1,609
15,800	15,850	1,700	1,583	1,700	1,615
15,850	15,900	1,706	1,588	1,706	1,621
15,900	15,950	1,712	1,593	1,712	1,627
15,950	16,000	1,718	1,598	1,718	1,633
16,000					
16,000	16,050	1,724	1,603	1,724	1,639
16,050	16,100	1,730	1,608	1,730	1,645
16,100	16,150	1,736	1,613	1,736	1,651
16,150	16,200	1,742	1,618	1,742	1,657
16,200	16,250	1,748	1,623	1,748	1,663
16,250	16,300	1,754	1,628	1,754	1,669
16,300	16,350	1,760	1,633	1,760	1,675
16,350	16,400	1,766	1,638	1,766	1,681
16,400	16,450	1,772	1,643	1,772	1,687
16,450	16,500	1,778	1,648	1,778	1,693
16,500	16,550	1,784	1,653	1,784	1,699
16,550	16,600	1,790	1,658	1,790	1,705
16,600	16,650	1,796	1,663	1,796	1,711
16,650	16,700	1,802	1,668	1,802	1,717
16,700	16,750	1,808	1,673	1,808	1,723
16,750	16,800	1,814	1,678	1,814	1,729
16,800	16,850	1,820	1,683	1,820	1,735
16,850	16,900	1,826	1,688	1,826	1,741
16,900	16,950	1,832	1,693	1,832	1,747
16,950	17,000	1,838	1,698	1,838	1,753
17,000					
17,000	17,050	1,844	1,703	1,844	1,759
17,050	17,100	1,850	1,708	1,850	1,765
17,100	17,150	1,856	1,713	1,856	1,771
17,150	17,200	1,862	1,718	1,862	1,777
17,200	17,250	1,868	1,723	1,868	1,783
17,250	17,300	1,874	1,728	1,874	1,789
17,300	17,350	1,880	1,733	1,880	1,795
17,350	17,400	1,886	1,738	1,886	1,801
17,400	17,450	1,892	1,743	1,892	1,807
17,450	17,500	1,898	1,748	1,898	1,813
17,500	17,550	1,904	1,753	1,904	1,819
17,550	17,600	1,910	1,758	1,910	1,825
17,600	17,650	1,916	1,763	1,916	1,831
17,650	17,700	1,922	1,768	1,922	1,837
17,700	17,750	1,928	1,773	1,928	1,843
17,750	17,800	1,934	1,778	1,934	1,849
17,800	17,850	1,940	1,783	1,940	1,855
17,850	17,900	1,946	1,788	1,946	1,861
17,900	17,950	1,952	1,793	1,952	1,867
17,950	18,000	1,958	1,798	1,958	1,873
18,000					
18,000	18,050	1,964	1,803	1,964	1,879
18,050	18,100	1,970	1,808	1,970	1,885
18,100	18,150	1,976	1,813	1,976	1,891
18,150	18,200	1,982	1,818	1,982	1,897
18,200	18,250	1,988	1,823	1,988	1,903
18,250	18,300	1,994	1,828	1,994	1,909
18,300	18,350	2,000	1,833	2,000	1,915
18,350	18,400	2,006	1,838	2,006	1,921
18,400	18,450	2,012	1,843	2,012	1,927
18,450	18,500	2,018	1,848	2,018	1,933
18,500	18,550	2,024	1,853	2,024	1,939
18,550	18,600	2,030	1,858	2,030	1,945
18,600	18,650	2,036	1,863	2,036	1,951
18,650	18,700	2,042	1,868	2,042	1,957
18,700	18,750	2,048	1,873	2,048	1,963
18,750	18,800	2,054	1,878	2,054	1,969
18,800	18,850	2,060	1,883	2,060	1,975
18,850	18,900	2,066	1,888	2,066	1,981
18,900	18,950	2,072	1,893	2,072	1,987
18,950	19,000	2,078	1,898	2,078	1,993
19,000					
19,000	19,050	2,084	1,903	2,084	1,999
19,050	19,100	2,090	1,908	2,090	2,005
19,100	19,150	2,096	1,913	2,096	2,011
19,150	19,200	2,102	1,918	2,102	2,017
19,200	19,250	2,108	1,923	2,108	2,023
19,250	19,300	2,114	1,928	2,114	2,029
19,300	19,350	2,120	1,933	2,120	2,035
19,350	19,400	2,126	1,938	2,126	2,041
19,400	19,450	2,132	1,943	2,132	2,047
19,450	19,500	2,138	1,948	2,138	2,053
19,500	19,550	2,144	1,953	2,144	2,059
19,550	19,600	2,150	1,958	2,150	2,065
19,600	19,650	2,156	1,963	2,156	2,071
19,650	19,700	2,162	1,968	2,162	2,077
19,700	19,750	2,168	1,973	2,168	2,083
19,750	19,800	2,174	1,978	2,174	2,089
19,800	19,850	2,180	1,983	2,180	2,095
19,850	19,900	2,186	1,988	2,186	2,101
19,900	19,950	2,192	1,993	2,192	2,107
19,950	20,000	2,198	1,999	2,198	2,113
20,000					
20,000	20,050	2,204	2,005	2,204	2,119
20,050	20,100	2,210	2,011	2,210	2,125
20,100	20,150	2,216	2,017	2,216	2,131
20,150	20,200	2,222	2,023	2,222	2,137
20,200	20,250	2,228	2,029	2,228	2,143
20,250	20,300	2,234	2,035	2,234	2,149
20,300	20,350	2,240	2,041	2,240	2,155
20,350	20,400	2,246	2,047	2,246	2,161
20,400	20,450	2,252	2,053	2,252	2,167
20,450	20,500	2,258	2,059	2,258	2,173
20,500	20,550	2,264	2,065	2,264	2,179
20,550	20,600	2,270	2,071	2,270	2,185
20,600	20,650	2,276	2,077	2,276	2,191
20,650	20,700	2,282	2,083	2,282	2,197
20,700	20,750	2,288	2,089	2,288	2,203
20,750	20,800	2,294	2,095	2,294	2,209
20,800	20,850	2,300	2,101	2,300	2,215
20,850	20,900	2,306	2,107	2,306	2,221
20,900	20,950	2,312	2,113	2,312	2,227
20,950	21,000	2,318	2,119	2,318	2,233

* This column must also be used by a qualifying widow(er).

(Continued)

2021 Tax Table — *Continued*

If line 15 (taxable income) is—		And you are—			
At least	But less than	Single	Married filing jointly *	Married filing separately	Head of a household
		Your tax is—			
21,000					
21,000	21,050	2,324	2,125	2,324	2,239
21,050	21,100	2,330	2,131	2,330	2,245
21,100	21,150	2,336	2,137	2,336	2,251
21,150	21,200	2,342	2,143	2,342	2,257
21,200	21,250	2,348	2,149	2,348	2,263
21,250	21,300	2,354	2,155	2,354	2,269
21,300	21,350	2,360	2,161	2,360	2,275
21,350	21,400	2,366	2,167	2,366	2,281
21,400	21,450	2,372	2,173	2,372	2,287
21,450	21,500	2,378	2,179	2,378	2,293
21,500	21,550	2,384	2,185	2,384	2,299
21,550	21,600	2,390	2,191	2,390	2,305
21,600	21,650	2,396	2,197	2,396	2,311
21,650	21,700	2,402	2,203	2,402	2,317
21,700	21,750	2,408	2,209	2,408	2,323
21,750	21,800	2,414	2,215	2,414	2,329
21,800	21,850	2,420	2,221	2,420	2,335
21,850	21,900	2,426	2,227	2,426	2,341
21,900	21,950	2,432	2,233	2,432	2,347
21,950	22,000	2,438	2,239	2,438	2,353
22,000					
22,000	22,050	2,444	2,245	2,444	2,359
22,050	22,100	2,450	2,251	2,450	2,365
22,100	22,150	2,456	2,257	2,456	2,371
22,150	22,200	2,462	2,263	2,462	2,377
22,200	22,250	2,468	2,269	2,468	2,383
22,250	22,300	2,474	2,275	2,474	2,389
22,300	22,350	2,480	2,281	2,480	2,395
22,350	22,400	2,486	2,287	2,486	2,401
22,400	22,450	2,492	2,293	2,492	2,407
22,450	22,500	2,498	2,299	2,498	2,413
22,500	22,550	2,504	2,305	2,504	2,419
22,550	22,600	2,510	2,311	2,510	2,425
22,600	22,650	2,516	2,317	2,516	2,431
22,650	22,700	2,522	2,323	2,522	2,437
22,700	22,750	2,528	2,329	2,528	2,443
22,750	22,800	2,534	2,335	2,534	2,449
22,800	22,850	2,540	2,341	2,540	2,455
22,850	22,900	2,546	2,347	2,546	2,461
22,900	22,950	2,552	2,353	2,552	2,467
22,950	23,000	2,558	2,359	2,558	2,473
23,000					
23,000	23,050	2,564	2,365	2,564	2,479
23,050	23,100	2,570	2,371	2,570	2,485
23,100	23,150	2,576	2,377	2,576	2,491
23,150	23,200	2,582	2,383	2,582	2,497
23,200	23,250	2,588	2,389	2,588	2,503
23,250	23,300	2,594	2,395	2,594	2,509
23,300	23,350	2,600	2,401	2,600	2,515
23,350	23,400	2,606	2,407	2,606	2,521
23,400	23,450	2,612	2,413	2,612	2,527
23,450	23,500	2,618	2,419	2,618	2,533
23,500	23,550	2,624	2,425	2,624	2,539
23,550	23,600	2,630	2,431	2,630	2,545
23,600	23,650	2,636	2,437	2,636	2,551
23,650	23,700	2,642	2,443	2,642	2,557
23,700	23,750	2,648	2,449	2,648	2,563
23,750	23,800	2,654	2,455	2,654	2,569
23,800	23,850	2,660	2,461	2,660	2,575
23,850	23,900	2,666	2,467	2,666	2,581
23,900	23,950	2,672	2,473	2,672	2,587
23,950	24,000	2,678	2,479	2,678	2,593
24,000					
24,000	24,050	2,684	2,485	2,684	2,599
24,050	24,100	2,690	2,491	2,690	2,605
24,100	24,150	2,696	2,497	2,696	2,611
24,150	24,200	2,702	2,503	2,702	2,617
24,200	24,250	2,708	2,509	2,708	2,623
24,250	24,300	2,714	2,515	2,714	2,629
24,300	24,350	2,720	2,521	2,720	2,635
24,350	24,400	2,726	2,527	2,726	2,641
24,400	24,450	2,732	2,533	2,732	2,647
24,450	24,500	2,738	2,539	2,738	2,653
24,500	24,550	2,744	2,545	2,744	2,659
24,550	24,600	2,750	2,551	2,750	2,665
24,600	24,650	2,756	2,557	2,756	2,671
24,650	24,700	2,762	2,563	2,762	2,677
24,700	24,750	2,768	2,569	2,768	2,683
24,750	24,800	2,774	2,575	2,774	2,689
24,800	24,850	2,780	2,581	2,780	2,695
24,850	24,900	2,786	2,587	2,786	2,701
24,900	24,950	2,792	2,593	2,792	2,707
24,950	25,000	2,798	2,599	2,798	2,713
25,000					
25,000	25,050	2,804	2,605	2,804	2,719
25,050	25,100	2,810	2,611	2,810	2,725
25,100	25,150	2,816	2,617	2,816	2,731
25,150	25,200	2,822	2,623	2,822	2,737
25,200	25,250	2,828	2,629	2,828	2,743
25,250	25,300	2,834	2,635	2,834	2,749
25,300	25,350	2,840	2,641	2,840	2,755
25,350	25,400	2,846	2,647	2,846	2,761
25,400	25,450	2,852	2,653	2,852	2,767
25,450	25,500	2,858	2,659	2,858	2,773
25,500	25,550	2,864	2,665	2,864	2,779
25,550	25,600	2,870	2,671	2,870	2,785
25,600	25,650	2,876	2,677	2,876	2,791
25,650	25,700	2,882	2,683	2,882	2,797
25,700	25,750	2,888	2,689	2,888	2,803
25,750	25,800	2,894	2,695	2,894	2,809
25,800	25,850	2,900	2,701	2,900	2,815
25,850	25,900	2,906	2,707	2,906	2,821
25,900	25,950	2,912	2,713	2,912	2,827
25,950	26,000	2,918	2,719	2,918	2,833
26,000					
26,000	26,050	2,924	2,725	2,924	2,839
26,050	26,100	2,930	2,731	2,930	2,845
26,100	26,150	2,936	2,737	2,936	2,851
26,150	26,200	2,942	2,743	2,942	2,857
26,200	26,250	2,948	2,749	2,948	2,863
26,250	26,300	2,954	2,755	2,954	2,869
26,300	26,350	2,960	2,761	2,960	2,875
26,350	26,400	2,966	2,767	2,966	2,881
26,400	26,450	2,972	2,773	2,972	2,887
26,450	26,500	2,978	2,779	2,978	2,893
26,500	26,550	2,984	2,785	2,984	2,899
26,550	26,600	2,990	2,791	2,990	2,905
26,600	26,650	2,996	2,797	2,996	2,911
26,650	26,700	3,002	2,803	3,002	2,917
26,700	26,750	3,008	2,809	3,008	2,923
26,750	26,800	3,014	2,815	3,014	2,929
26,800	26,850	3,020	2,821	3,020	2,935
26,850	26,900	3,026	2,827	3,026	2,941
26,900	26,950	3,032	2,833	3,032	2,947
26,950	27,000	3,038	2,839	3,038	2,953
27,000					
27,000	27,050	3,044	2,845	3,044	2,959
27,050	27,100	3,050	2,851	3,050	2,965
27,100	27,150	3,056	2,857	3,056	2,971
27,150	27,200	3,062	2,863	3,062	2,977
27,200	27,250	3,068	2,869	3,068	2,983
27,250	27,300	3,074	2,875	3,074	2,989
27,300	27,350	3,080	2,881	3,080	2,995
27,350	27,400	3,086	2,887	3,086	3,001
27,400	27,450	3,092	2,893	3,092	3,007
27,450	27,500	3,098	2,899	3,098	3,013
27,500	27,550	3,104	2,905	3,104	3,019
27,550	27,600	3,110	2,911	3,110	3,025
27,600	27,650	3,116	2,917	3,116	3,031
27,650	27,700	3,122	2,923	3,122	3,037
27,700	27,750	3,128	2,929	3,128	3,043
27,750	27,800	3,134	2,935	3,134	3,049
27,800	27,850	3,140	2,941	3,140	3,055
27,850	27,900	3,146	2,947	3,146	3,061
27,900	27,950	3,152	2,953	3,152	3,067
27,950	28,000	3,158	2,959	3,158	3,073
28,000					
28,000	28,050	3,164	2,965	3,164	3,079
28,050	28,100	3,170	2,971	3,170	3,085
28,100	28,150	3,176	2,977	3,176	3,091
28,150	28,200	3,182	2,983	3,182	3,097
28,200	28,250	3,188	2,989	3,188	3,103
28,250	28,300	3,194	2,995	3,194	3,109
28,300	28,350	3,200	3,001	3,200	3,115
28,350	28,400	3,206	3,007	3,206	3,121
28,400	28,450	3,212	3,013	3,212	3,127
28,450	28,500	3,218	3,019	3,218	3,133
28,500	28,550	3,224	3,025	3,224	3,139
28,550	28,600	3,230	3,031	3,230	3,145
28,600	28,650	3,236	3,037	3,236	3,151
28,650	28,700	3,242	3,043	3,242	3,157
28,700	28,750	3,248	3,049	3,248	3,163
28,750	28,800	3,254	3,055	3,254	3,169
28,800	28,850	3,260	3,061	3,260	3,175
28,850	28,900	3,266	3,067	3,266	3,181
28,900	28,950	3,272	3,073	3,272	3,187
28,950	29,000	3,278	3,079	3,278	3,193
29,000					
29,000	29,050	3,284	3,085	3,284	3,199
29,050	29,100	3,290	3,091	3,290	3,205
29,100	29,150	3,296	3,097	3,296	3,211
29,150	29,200	3,302	3,103	3,302	3,217
29,200	29,250	3,308	3,109	3,308	3,223
29,250	29,300	3,314	3,115	3,314	3,229
29,300	29,350	3,320	3,121	3,320	3,235
29,350	29,400	3,326	3,127	3,326	3,241
29,400	29,450	3,332	3,133	3,332	3,247
29,450	29,500	3,338	3,139	3,338	3,253
29,500	29,550	3,344	3,145	3,344	3,259
29,550	29,600	3,350	3,151	3,350	3,265
29,600	29,650	3,356	3,157	3,356	3,271
29,650	29,700	3,362	3,163	3,362	3,277
29,700	29,750	3,368	3,169	3,368	3,283
29,750	29,800	3,374	3,175	3,374	3,289
29,800	29,850	3,380	3,181	3,380	3,295
29,850	29,900	3,386	3,187	3,386	3,301
29,900	29,950	3,392	3,193	3,392	3,307
29,950	30,000	3,398	3,199	3,398	3,313

(Continued)

* This column must also be used by a qualifying widow(er).

2021 Tax Table — *Continued*

If line 15 (taxable income) is—		And you are—			
At least	But less than	Single	Married filing jointly *	Married filing sepa-rately	Head of a house-hold
		Your tax is—			
30,000					
30,000	30,050	3,404	3,205	3,404	3,319
30,050	30,100	3,410	3,211	3,410	3,325
30,100	30,150	3,416	3,217	3,416	3,331
30,150	30,200	3,422	3,223	3,422	3,337
30,200	30,250	3,428	3,229	3,428	3,343
30,250	30,300	3,434	3,235	3,434	3,349
30,300	30,350	3,440	3,241	3,440	3,355
30,350	30,400	3,446	3,247	3,446	3,361
30,400	30,450	3,452	3,253	3,452	3,367
30,450	30,500	3,458	3,259	3,458	3,373
30,500	30,550	3,464	3,265	3,464	3,379
30,550	30,600	3,470	3,271	3,470	3,385
30,600	30,650	3,476	3,277	3,476	3,391
30,650	30,700	3,482	3,283	3,482	3,397
30,700	30,750	3,488	3,289	3,488	3,403
30,750	30,800	3,494	3,295	3,494	3,409
30,800	30,850	3,500	3,301	3,500	3,415
30,850	30,900	3,506	3,307	3,506	3,421
30,900	30,950	3,512	3,313	3,512	3,427
30,950	31,000	3,518	3,319	3,518	3,433
31,000					
31,000	31,050	3,524	3,325	3,524	3,439
31,050	31,100	3,530	3,331	3,530	3,445
31,100	31,150	3,536	3,337	3,536	3,451
31,150	31,200	3,542	3,343	3,542	3,457
31,200	31,250	3,548	3,349	3,548	3,463
31,250	31,300	3,554	3,355	3,554	3,469
31,300	31,350	3,560	3,361	3,560	3,475
31,350	31,400	3,566	3,367	3,566	3,481
31,400	31,450	3,572	3,373	3,572	3,487
31,450	31,500	3,578	3,379	3,578	3,493
31,500	31,550	3,584	3,385	3,584	3,499
31,550	31,600	3,590	3,391	3,590	3,505
31,600	31,650	3,596	3,397	3,596	3,511
31,650	31,700	3,602	3,403	3,602	3,517
31,700	31,750	3,608	3,409	3,608	3,523
31,750	31,800	3,614	3,415	3,614	3,529
31,800	31,850	3,620	3,421	3,620	3,535
31,850	31,900	3,626	3,427	3,626	3,541
31,900	31,950	3,632	3,433	3,632	3,547
31,950	32,000	3,638	3,439	3,638	3,553
32,000					
32,000	32,050	3,644	3,445	3,644	3,559
32,050	32,100	3,650	3,451	3,650	3,565
32,100	32,150	3,656	3,457	3,656	3,571
32,150	32,200	3,662	3,463	3,662	3,577
32,200	32,250	3,668	3,469	3,668	3,583
32,250	32,300	3,674	3,475	3,674	3,589
32,300	32,350	3,680	3,481	3,680	3,595
32,350	32,400	3,686	3,487	3,686	3,601
32,400	32,450	3,692	3,493	3,692	3,607
32,450	32,500	3,698	3,499	3,698	3,613
32,500	32,550	3,704	3,505	3,704	3,619
32,550	32,600	3,710	3,511	3,710	3,625
32,600	32,650	3,716	3,517	3,716	3,631
32,650	32,700	3,722	3,523	3,722	3,637
32,700	32,750	3,728	3,529	3,728	3,643
32,750	32,800	3,734	3,535	3,734	3,649
32,800	32,850	3,740	3,541	3,740	3,655
32,850	32,900	3,746	3,547	3,746	3,661
32,900	32,950	3,752	3,553	3,752	3,667
32,950	33,000	3,758	3,559	3,758	3,673

If line 15 (taxable income) is—		And you are—			
At least	But less than	Single	Married filing jointly *	Married filing sepa-rately	Head of a house-hold
		Your tax is—			
33,000					
33,000	33,050	3,764	3,565	3,764	3,679
33,050	33,100	3,770	3,571	3,770	3,685
33,100	33,150	3,776	3,577	3,776	3,691
33,150	33,200	3,782	3,583	3,782	3,697
33,200	33,250	3,788	3,589	3,788	3,703
33,250	33,300	3,794	3,595	3,794	3,709
33,300	33,350	3,800	3,601	3,800	3,715
33,350	33,400	3,806	3,607	3,806	3,721
33,400	33,450	3,812	3,613	3,812	3,727
33,450	33,500	3,818	3,619	3,818	3,733
33,500	33,550	3,824	3,625	3,824	3,739
33,550	33,600	3,830	3,631	3,830	3,745
33,600	33,650	3,836	3,637	3,836	3,751
33,650	33,700	3,842	3,643	3,842	3,757
33,700	33,750	3,848	3,649	3,848	3,763
33,750	33,800	3,854	3,655	3,854	3,769
33,800	33,850	3,860	3,661	3,860	3,775
33,850	33,900	3,866	3,667	3,866	3,781
33,900	33,950	3,872	3,673	3,872	3,787
33,950	34,000	3,878	3,679	3,878	3,793
34,000					
34,000	34,050	3,884	3,685	3,884	3,799
34,050	34,100	3,890	3,691	3,890	3,805
34,100	34,150	3,896	3,697	3,896	3,811
34,150	34,200	3,902	3,703	3,902	3,817
34,200	34,250	3,908	3,709	3,908	3,823
34,250	34,300	3,914	3,715	3,914	3,829
34,300	34,350	3,920	3,721	3,920	3,835
34,350	34,400	3,926	3,727	3,926	3,841
34,400	34,450	3,932	3,733	3,932	3,847
34,450	34,500	3,938	3,739	3,938	3,853
34,500	34,550	3,944	3,745	3,944	3,859
34,550	34,600	3,950	3,751	3,950	3,865
34,600	34,650	3,956	3,757	3,956	3,871
34,650	34,700	3,962	3,763	3,962	3,877
34,700	34,750	3,968	3,769	3,968	3,883
34,750	34,800	3,974	3,775	3,974	3,889
34,800	34,850	3,980	3,781	3,980	3,895
34,850	34,900	3,986	3,787	3,986	3,901
34,900	34,950	3,992	3,793	3,992	3,907
34,950	35,000	3,998	3,799	3,998	3,913
35,000					
35,000	35,050	4,004	3,805	4,004	3,919
35,050	35,100	4,010	3,811	4,010	3,925
35,100	35,150	4,016	3,817	4,016	3,931
35,150	35,200	4,022	3,823	4,022	3,937
35,200	35,250	4,028	3,829	4,028	3,943
35,250	35,300	4,034	3,835	4,034	3,949
35,300	35,350	4,040	3,841	4,040	3,955
35,350	35,400	4,046	3,847	4,046	3,961
35,400	35,450	4,052	3,853	4,052	3,967
35,450	35,500	4,058	3,859	4,058	3,973
35,500	35,550	4,064	3,865	4,064	3,979
35,550	35,600	4,070	3,871	4,070	3,985
35,600	35,650	4,076	3,877	4,076	3,991
35,650	35,700	4,082	3,883	4,082	3,997
35,700	35,750	4,088	3,889	4,088	4,003
35,750	35,800	4,094	3,895	4,094	4,009
35,800	35,850	4,100	3,901	4,100	4,015
35,850	35,900	4,106	3,907	4,106	4,021
35,900	35,950	4,112	3,913	4,112	4,027
35,950	36,000	4,118	3,919	4,118	4,033

If line 15 (taxable income) is—		And you are—			
At least	But less than	Single	Married filing jointly *	Married filing sepa-rately	Head of a house-hold
		Your tax is—			
36,000					
36,000	36,050	4,124	3,925	4,124	4,039
36,050	36,100	4,130	3,931	4,130	4,045
36,100	36,150	4,136	3,937	4,136	4,051
36,150	36,200	4,142	3,943	4,142	4,057
36,200	36,250	4,148	3,949	4,148	4,063
36,250	36,300	4,154	3,955	4,154	4,069
36,300	36,350	4,160	3,961	4,160	4,075
36,350	36,400	4,166	3,967	4,166	4,081
36,400	36,450	4,172	3,973	4,172	4,087
36,450	36,500	4,178	3,979	4,178	4,093
36,500	36,550	4,184	3,985	4,184	4,099
36,550	36,600	4,190	3,991	4,190	4,105
36,600	36,650	4,196	3,997	4,196	4,111
36,650	36,700	4,202	4,003	4,202	4,117
36,700	36,750	4,208	4,009	4,208	4,123
36,750	36,800	4,214	4,015	4,214	4,129
36,800	36,850	4,220	4,021	4,220	4,135
36,850	36,900	4,226	4,027	4,226	4,141
36,900	36,950	4,232	4,033	4,232	4,147
36,950	37,000	4,238	4,039	4,238	4,153
37,000					
37,000	37,050	4,244	4,045	4,244	4,159
37,050	37,100	4,250	4,051	4,250	4,165
37,100	37,150	4,256	4,057	4,256	4,171
37,150	37,200	4,262	4,063	4,262	4,177
37,200	37,250	4,268	4,069	4,268	4,183
37,250	37,300	4,274	4,075	4,274	4,189
37,300	37,350	4,280	4,081	4,280	4,195
37,350	37,400	4,286	4,087	4,286	4,201
37,400	37,450	4,292	4,093	4,292	4,207
37,450	37,500	4,298	4,099	4,298	4,213
37,500	37,550	4,304	4,105	4,304	4,219
37,550	37,600	4,310	4,111	4,310	4,225
37,600	37,650	4,316	4,117	4,316	4,231
37,650	37,700	4,322	4,123	4,322	4,237
37,700	37,750	4,328	4,129	4,328	4,243
37,750	37,800	4,334	4,135	4,334	4,249
37,800	37,850	4,340	4,141	4,340	4,255
37,850	37,900	4,346	4,147	4,346	4,261
37,900	37,950	4,352	4,153	4,352	4,267
37,950	38,000	4,358	4,159	4,358	4,273
38,000					
38,000	38,050	4,364	4,165	4,364	4,279
38,050	38,100	4,370	4,171	4,370	4,285
38,100	38,150	4,376	4,177	4,376	4,291
38,150	38,200	4,382	4,183	4,382	4,297
38,200	38,250	4,388	4,189	4,388	4,303
38,250	38,300	4,394	4,195	4,394	4,309
38,300	38,350	4,400	4,201	4,400	4,315
38,350	38,400	4,406	4,207	4,406	4,321
38,400	38,450	4,412	4,213	4,412	4,327
38,450	38,500	4,418	4,219	4,418	4,333
38,500	38,550	4,424	4,225	4,424	4,339
38,550	38,600	4,430	4,231	4,430	4,345
38,600	38,650	4,436	4,237	4,436	4,351
38,650	38,700	4,442	4,243	4,442	4,357
38,700	38,750	4,448	4,249	4,448	4,363
38,750	38,800	4,454	4,255	4,454	4,369
38,800	38,850	4,460	4,261	4,460	4,375
38,850	38,900	4,466	4,267	4,466	4,381
38,900	38,950	4,472	4,273	4,472	4,387
38,950	39,000	4,478	4,279	4,478	4,393

(Continued)

* This column must also be used by a qualifying widow(er).

2021 Tax Table — *Continued*

If line 15 (taxable income) is—		And you are—			
At least	But less than	Single	Married filing jointly *	Married filing sepa-rately	Head of a house-hold
		Your tax is—			
39,000					
39,000	39,050	4,484	4,285	4,484	4,399
39,050	39,100	4,490	4,291	4,490	4,405
39,100	39,150	4,496	4,297	4,496	4,411
39,150	39,200	4,502	4,303	4,502	4,417
39,200	39,250	4,508	4,309	4,508	4,423
39,250	39,300	4,514	4,315	4,514	4,429
39,300	39,350	4,520	4,321	4,520	4,435
39,350	39,400	4,526	4,327	4,526	4,441
39,400	39,450	4,532	4,333	4,532	4,447
39,450	39,500	4,538	4,339	4,538	4,453
39,500	39,550	4,544	4,345	4,544	4,459
39,550	39,600	4,550	4,351	4,550	4,465
39,600	39,650	4,556	4,357	4,556	4,471
39,650	39,700	4,562	4,363	4,562	4,477
39,700	39,750	4,568	4,369	4,568	4,483
39,750	39,800	4,574	4,375	4,574	4,489
39,800	39,850	4,580	4,381	4,580	4,495
39,850	39,900	4,586	4,387	4,586	4,501
39,900	39,950	4,592	4,393	4,592	4,507
39,950	40,000	4,598	4,399	4,598	4,513
40,000					
40,000	40,050	4,604	4,405	4,604	4,519
40,050	40,100	4,610	4,411	4,610	4,525
40,100	40,150	4,616	4,417	4,616	4,531
40,150	40,200	4,622	4,423	4,622	4,537
40,200	40,250	4,628	4,429	4,628	4,543
40,250	40,300	4,634	4,435	4,634	4,549
40,300	40,350	4,640	4,441	4,640	4,555
40,350	40,400	4,646	4,447	4,646	4,561
40,400	40,450	4,052	4,453	1,662	4,567
40,450	40,500	4,658	4,459	4,658	4,573
40,500	40,550	4,664	4,465	4,664	4,579
40,550	40,600	4,675	4,471	4,675	4,585
40,600	40,650	4,686	4,477	4,686	4,591
40,650	40,700	4,697	4,483	4,697	4,597
40,700	40,750	4,708	4,489	4,708	4,603
40,750	40,800	4,719	4,495	4,719	4,609
40,800	40,850	4,730	4,501	4,730	4,615
40,850	40,900	4,741	4,507	1,741	4,621
40,900	40,950	4,752	4,513	4,752	4,627
40,950	41,000	4,763	4,519	4,763	4,633
41,000					
41,000	41,050	4,774	4,525	4,774	4,639
41,050	41,100	4,785	4,531	4,785	4,645
41,100	41,150	4,796	4,537	4,796	4,651
41,150	41,200	4,807	4,543	4,807	4,657
41,200	41,250	4,818	4,549	4,818	4,663
41,250	41,300	4,829	4,555	4,829	4,669
41,300	41,350	4,840	4,561	4,840	4,675
41,350	41,400	4,851	4,567	4,851	4,681
41,400	41,450	4,862	4,573	4,862	4,687
41,450	41,500	4,873	4,579	4,873	4,693
41,500	41,550	4,884	4,585	4,884	4,699
41,550	41,600	4,895	4,591	4,895	4,705
41,600	41,650	4,906	4,597	4,906	4,711
41,650	41,700	4,917	4,603	4,917	4,717
41,700	41,750	4,928	4,609	4,928	4,723
41,750	41,800	4,939	4,615	4,939	4,729
41,800	41,850	4,950	4,621	4,950	4,735
41,850	41,900	4,961	4,627	4,961	4,741
41,900	41,950	4,972	4,633	4,972	4,747
41,950	42,000	4,983	4,639	4,983	4,753
42,000					
42,000	42,050	4,994	4,645	4,994	4,759
42,050	42,100	5,005	4,651	5,005	4,765
42,100	42,150	5,016	4,657	5,016	4,771
42,150	42,200	5,027	4,663	5,027	4,777
42,200	42,250	5,038	4,669	5,038	4,783
42,250	42,300	5,049	4,675	5,049	4,789
42,300	42,350	5,060	4,681	5,060	4,795
42,350	42,400	5,071	4,687	5,071	4,801
42,400	42,450	5,082	4,693	5,082	4,807
42,450	42,500	5,093	4,699	5,093	4,813
42,500	42,550	5,104	4,705	5,104	4,819
42,550	42,600	5,115	4,711	5,115	4,825
42,600	42,650	5,126	4,717	5,126	4,831
42,650	42,700	5,137	4,723	5,137	4,837
42,700	42,750	5,148	4,729	5,148	4,843
42,750	42,800	5,159	4,735	5,159	4,849
42,800	42,850	5,170	4,741	5,170	4,855
42,850	42,900	5,181	4,747	5,181	4,861
42,900	42,950	5,192	4,753	5,192	4,867
42,950	43,000	5,203	4,759	5,203	4,873
43,000					
43,000	43,050	5,214	4,765	5,214	4,879
43,050	43,100	5,225	4,771	5,225	4,885
43,100	43,150	5,236	4,777	5,236	4,891
43,150	43,200	5,247	4,783	5,247	4,897
43,200	43,250	5,258	4,789	5,258	4,903
43,250	43,300	5,269	4,795	5,269	4,909
43,300	43,350	5,280	4,801	5,280	4,915
43,350	43,400	5,291	4,807	5,291	4,921
43,400	43,450	5,302	4,813	5,302	4,927
43,450	43,500	5,313	4,819	5,313	4,933
43,500	43,550	5,324	4,825	5,324	4,939
43,550	43,600	5,335	4,831	5,335	4,945
43,600	43,650	5,346	4,837	5,346	4,951
43,650	43,700	5,357	4,843	5,357	4,957
43,700	43,750	5,368	4,849	5,368	4,963
43,750	43,800	5,379	4,855	5,379	4,969
43,800	43,850	5,390	4,861	5,390	4,975
43,850	43,900	5,401	4,867	5,401	4,981
43,900	43,950	5,412	4,873	5,412	4,987
43,950	44,000	5,423	4,879	5,423	4,993
44,000					
44,000	44,050	5,434	4,885	5,434	4,999
44,050	44,100	5,445	4,891	5,445	5,005
44,100	44,150	5,456	4,897	5,456	5,011
44,150	44,200	5,467	4,903	5,467	5,017
44,200	44,250	5,478	4,909	5,478	5,023
44,250	44,300	5,489	4,915	5,489	5,029
44,300	44,350	5,500	4,921	5,500	5,035
44,350	44,400	5,511	4,927	5,511	5,041
44,400	44,450	5,522	4,933	5,522	5,047
44,450	44,500	5,533	4,939	5,533	5,053
44,500	44,550	5,544	4,945	5,544	5,059
44,550	44,600	5,555	4,951	5,555	5,065
44,600	44,650	5,566	4,957	5,566	5,071
44,650	44,700	5,577	4,963	5,577	5,077
44,700	44,750	5,588	4,969	5,588	5,083
44,750	44,800	5,599	4,975	5,599	5,089
44,800	44,850	5,610	4,981	5,610	5,095
44,850	44,900	5,621	4,987	5,621	5,101
44,900	44,950	5,632	4,993	5,632	5,107
44,950	45,000	5,643	4,999	5,643	5,113
45,000					
45,000	45,050	5,654	5,005	5,654	5,119
45,050	45,100	5,665	5,011	5,665	5,125
45,100	45,150	5,676	5,017	5,676	5,131
45,150	45,200	5,687	5,023	5,687	5,137
45,200	45,250	5,698	5,029	5,698	5,143
45,250	45,300	5,709	5,035	5,709	5,149
45,300	45,350	5,720	5,041	5,720	5,155
45,350	45,400	5,731	5,047	5,731	5,161
45,400	45,450	5,742	5,053	5,742	5,167
45,450	45,500	5,753	5,059	5,753	5,173
45,500	45,550	5,764	5,065	5,764	5,179
45,550	45,600	5,775	5,071	5,775	5,185
45,600	45,650	5,786	5,077	5,786	5,191
45,650	45,700	5,797	5,083	5,797	5,197
45,700	45,750	5,808	5,089	5,808	5,203
45,750	45,800	5,819	5,095	5,819	5,209
45,800	45,850	5,830	5,101	5,830	5,215
45,850	45,900	5,841	5,107	5,841	5,221
45,900	45,950	5,852	5,113	5,852	5,227
45,950	46,000	5,863	5,119	5,863	5,233
46,000					
46,000	46,050	5,874	5,125	5,874	5,239
46,050	46,100	5,885	5,131	5,885	5,245
46,100	46,150	5,896	5,137	5,896	5,251
46,150	46,200	5,907	5,143	5,907	5,257
46,200	46,250	5,918	5,149	5,918	5,263
46,250	46,300	5,929	5,155	5,929	5,269
46,300	46,350	5,940	5,161	5,940	5,275
46,350	46,400	5,951	5,167	5,951	5,281
46,400	46,450	5,962	5,173	5,962	5,287
46,450	46,500	5,973	5,179	5,073	5,293
46,500	46,550	5,984	5,185	5,984	5,299
46,550	46,600	5,995	5,191	5,995	5,305
46,600	46,650	6,006	5,197	6,006	5,311
46,650	46,700	6,017	5,203	6,017	5,317
46,700	46,750	6,028	5,209	6,028	5,323
46,750	46,800	6,039	5,215	6,039	5,329
46,800	46,850	6,050	5,221	6,050	5,335
46,850	46,900	6,061	5,227	6,061	5,341
46,900	46,950	0,072	5,233	6,072	5,347
46,950	47,000	6,083	5,239	6,083	5,353
47,000					
47,000	47,050	6,094	5,245	6,094	5,359
47,050	47,100	6,105	5,251	6,105	5,365
47,100	47,150	6,116	5,257	6,116	5,371
47,150	47,200	6,127	5,263	6,127	5,377
47,200	47,250	6,138	5,269	6,138	5,383
47,250	47,300	6,149	5,275	6,149	5,389
47,300	47,350	6,160	5,281	6,160	5,395
47,350	47,400	6,171	5,287	6,171	5,401
47,400	47,450	6,182	5,293	6,182	5,407
47,450	47,500	6,193	5,299	6,193	5,413
47,500	47,550	6,204	5,305	6,204	5,419
47,550	47,600	6,215	5,311	6,215	5,425
47,600	47,650	6,226	5,317	6,226	5,431
47,650	47,700	6,237	5,323	6,237	5,437
47,700	47,750	6,248	5,329	6,248	5,443
47,750	47,800	6,259	5,335	6,259	5,449
47,800	47,850	6,270	5,341	6,270	5,455
47,850	47,900	6,281	5,347	6,281	5,461
47,900	47,950	6,292	5,353	6,292	5,467
47,950	48,000	6,303	5,359	6,303	5,473

(Continued)

* This column must also be used by a qualifying widow(er).

2021 Tax Table — *Continued*

If line 15 (taxable income) is—		And you are—			
At least	But less than	Single	Married filing jointly *	Married filing sepa-rately	Head of a house-hold
		Your tax is—			
48,000					
48,000	48,050	6,314	5,365	6,314	5,479
48,050	48,100	6,325	5,371	6,325	5,485
48,100	48,150	6,336	5,377	6,336	5,491
48,150	48,200	6,347	5,383	6,347	5,497
48,200	48,250	6,358	5,389	6,358	5,503
48,250	48,300	6,369	5,395	6,369	5,509
48,300	48,350	6,380	5,401	6,380	5,515
48,350	48,400	6,391	5,407	6,391	5,521
48,400	48,450	6,402	5,413	6,402	5,527
48,450	48,500	6,413	5,419	6,413	5,533
48,500	48,550	6,424	5,425	6,424	5,539
48,550	48,600	6,435	5,431	6,435	5,545
48,600	48,650	6,446	5,437	6,446	5,551
48,650	48,700	6,457	5,443	6,457	5,557
48,700	48,750	6,468	5,449	6,468	5,563
48,750	48,800	6,479	5,455	6,479	5,569
48,800	48,850	6,490	5,461	6,490	5,575
48,850	48,900	6,501	5,467	6,501	5,581
48,900	48,950	6,512	5,473	6,512	5,587
48,950	49,000	6,523	5,479	6,523	5,593
49,000					
49,000	49,050	6,534	5,485	6,534	5,599
49,050	49,100	6,545	5,491	6,545	5,605
49,100	49,150	6,556	5,497	6,556	5,611
49,150	49,200	6,567	5,503	6,567	5,617
49,200	49,250	6,578	5,509	6,578	5,623
49,250	49,300	6,589	5,515	6,589	5,629
49,300	49,350	6,600	5,521	6,600	5,635
49,350	49,400	6,611	5,527	6,611	5,641
49,400	49,450	6,622	5,533	6,622	5,647
49,450	49,500	6,633	5,539	6,633	5,653
49,500	49,550	6,644	5,545	6,644	5,659
49,550	49,600	6,655	5,551	6,655	5,665
49,600	49,650	6,666	5,557	6,666	5,671
49,650	49,700	6,677	5,563	6,677	5,677
49,700	49,750	6,688	5,569	6,688	5,683
49,750	49,800	6,699	5,575	6,699	5,689
49,800	49,850	6,710	5,581	6,710	5,695
49,850	49,900	6,721	5,587	6,721	5,701
49,900	49,950	6,732	5,593	6,732	5,707
49,950	50,000	6,743	5,599	6,743	5,713
50,000					
50,000	50,050	6,754	5,605	6,754	5,719
50,050	50,100	6,765	5,611	6,765	5,725
50,100	50,150	6,776	5,617	6,776	5,731
50,150	50,200	6,787	5,623	6,787	5,737
50,200	50,250	6,798	5,629	6,798	5,743
50,250	50,300	6,809	5,635	6,809	5,749
50,300	50,350	6,820	5,641	6,820	5,755
50,350	50,400	6,831	5,647	6,831	5,761
50,400	50,450	6,842	5,653	6,842	5,767
50,450	50,500	6,853	5,659	6,853	5,773
50,500	50,550	6,864	5,665	6,864	5,779
50,550	50,600	6,875	5,671	6,875	5,785
50,600	50,650	6,886	5,677	6,886	5,791
50,650	50,700	6,897	5,683	6,897	5,797
50,700	50,750	6,908	5,689	6,908	5,803
50,750	50,800	6,919	5,695	6,919	5,809
50,800	50,850	6,930	5,701	6,930	5,815
50,850	50,900	6,941	5,707	6,941	5,821
50,900	50,950	6,952	5,713	6,952	5,827
50,950	51,000	6,963	5,719	6,963	5,833
51,000					
51,000	51,050	6,974	5,725	6,974	5,839
51,050	51,100	6,985	5,731	6,985	5,845
51,100	51,150	6,996	5,737	6,996	5,851
51,150	51,200	7,007	5,743	7,007	5,857
51,200	51,250	7,018	5,749	7,018	5,863
51,250	51,300	7,029	5,755	7,029	5,869
51,300	51,350	7,040	5,761	7,040	5,875
51,350	51,400	7,051	5,767	7,051	5,881
51,400	51,450	7,062	5,773	7,062	5,887
51,450	51,500	7,073	5,779	7,073	5,893
51,500	51,550	7,084	5,785	7,084	5,899
51,550	51,600	7,095	5,791	7,095	5,905
51,600	51,650	7,106	5,797	7,106	5,911
51,650	51,700	7,117	5,803	7,117	5,917
51,700	51,750	7,128	5,809	7,128	5,923
51,750	51,800	7,139	5,815	7,139	5,929
51,800	51,850	7,150	5,821	7,150	5,935
51,850	51,900	7,161	5,827	7,161	5,941
51,900	51,950	7,172	5,833	7,172	5,947
51,950	52,000	7,183	5,839	7,183	5,953
52,000					
52,000	52,050	7,194	5,845	7,194	5,959
52,050	52,100	7,205	5,851	7,205	5,965
52,100	52,150	7,216	5,857	7,216	5,971
52,150	52,200	7,227	5,863	7,227	5,977
52,200	52,250	7,238	5,869	7,238	5,983
52,250	52,300	7,249	5,875	7,249	5,989
52,300	52,350	7,260	5,881	7,260	5,995
52,350	52,400	7,271	5,887	7,271	6,001
52,400	52,450	7,282	5,893	7,282	6,007
52,450	52,500	7,293	5,899	7,293	6,013
52,500	52,550	7,304	5,905	7,304	6,019
52,550	52,600	7,315	5,911	7,315	6,025
52,600	52,650	7,326	5,917	7,326	6,031
52,650	52,700	7,337	5,923	7,337	6,037
52,700	52,750	7,348	5,929	7,348	6,043
52,750	52,800	7,359	5,935	7,359	6,049
52,800	52,850	7,370	5,941	7,370	6,055
52,850	52,900	7,381	5,947	7,381	6,061
52,900	52,950	7,392	5,953	7,392	6,067
52,950	53,000	7,403	5,959	7,403	6,073
53,000					
53,000	53,050	7,414	5,965	7,414	6,079
53,050	53,100	7,425	5,971	7,425	6,085
53,100	53,150	7,436	5,977	7,436	6,091
53,150	53,200	7,447	5,983	7,447	6,097
53,200	53,250	7,458	5,989	7,458	6,103
53,250	53,300	7,469	5,995	7,469	6,109
53,300	53,350	7,480	6,001	7,480	6,115
53,350	53,400	7,491	6,007	7,491	6,121
53,400	53,450	7,502	6,013	7,502	6,127
53,450	53,500	7,513	6,019	7,513	6,133
53,500	53,550	7,524	6,025	7,524	6,139
53,550	53,600	7,535	6,031	7,535	6,145
53,600	53,650	7,546	6,037	7,546	6,151
53,650	53,700	7,557	6,043	7,557	6,157
53,700	53,750	7,568	6,049	7,568	6,163
53,750	53,800	7,579	6,055	7,579	6,169
53,800	53,850	7,590	6,061	7,590	6,175
53,850	53,900	7,601	6,067	7,601	6,181
53,900	53,950	7,612	6,073	7,612	6,187
53,950	54,000	7,623	6,079	7,623	6,193
54,000					
54,000	54,050	7,634	6,085	7,634	6,199
54,050	54,100	7,645	6,091	7,645	6,205
54,100	54,150	7,656	6,097	7,656	6,211
54,150	54,200	7,667	6,103	7,667	6,217
54,200	54,250	7,678	6,109	7,678	6,226
54,250	54,300	7,689	6,115	7,689	6,237
54,300	54,350	7,700	6,121	7,700	6,248
54,350	54,400	7,711	6,127	7,711	6,259
54,400	54,450	7,722	6,133	7,722	6,270
54,450	54,500	7,733	6,139	7,733	6,281
54,500	54,550	7,744	6,145	7,744	6,292
54,550	54,600	7,755	6,151	7,755	6,303
54,600	54,650	7,766	6,157	7,766	6,314
54,650	54,700	7,777	6,163	7,777	6,325
54,700	54,750	7,788	6,169	7,788	6,336
54,750	54,800	7,799	6,175	7,799	6,347
54,800	54,850	7,810	6,181	7,810	6,358
54,850	54,900	7,821	6,187	7,821	6,369
54,900	54,950	7,832	6,193	7,832	6,380
54,950	55,000	7,843	6,199	7,843	6,391
55,000					
55,000	55,050	7,854	6,205	7,854	6,402
55,050	55,100	7,865	6,211	7,865	6,413
55,100	55,150	7,876	6,217	7,876	6,424
55,150	55,200	7,887	6,223	7,887	6,435
55,200	55,250	7,898	6,229	7,898	6,446
55,250	55,300	7,909	6,235	7,909	6,457
55,300	55,350	7,920	6,241	7,920	6,468
55,350	55,400	7,931	6,247	7,931	6,479
55,400	55,450	7,942	6,253	7,942	6,490
55,450	55,500	7,953	6,259	7,953	6,501
55,500	55,550	7,964	6,265	7,964	6,512
55,550	55,600	7,975	6,271	7,975	6,523
55,600	55,650	7,986	6,277	7,986	6,534
55,650	55,700	7,997	6,283	7,997	6,545
55,700	55,750	8,008	6,289	8,008	6,556
55,750	55,800	8,019	6,295	8,019	6,567
55,800	55,850	8,030	6,301	8,030	6,578
55,850	55,900	8,041	6,307	8,041	6,589
55,900	55,950	8,052	6,313	8,052	6,600
55,950	56,000	8,063	6,319	8,063	6,611
56,000					
56,000	56,050	8,074	6,325	8,074	6,622
56,050	56,100	8,085	6,331	8,085	6,633
56,100	56,150	8,096	6,337	8,096	6,644
56,150	56,200	8,107	6,343	8,107	6,655
56,200	56,250	8,118	6,349	8,118	6,666
56,250	56,300	8,129	6,355	8,129	6,677
56,300	56,350	8,140	6,361	8,140	6,688
56,350	56,400	8,151	6,367	8,151	6,699
56,400	56,450	8,162	6,373	8,162	6,710
56,450	56,500	8,173	6,379	8,173	6,721
56,500	56,550	8,184	6,385	8,184	6,732
56,550	56,600	8,195	6,391	8,195	6,743
56,600	56,650	8,206	6,397	8,206	6,754
56,650	56,700	8,217	6,403	8,217	6,765
56,700	56,750	8,228	6,409	8,228	6,776
56,750	56,800	8,239	6,415	8,239	6,787
56,800	56,850	8,250	6,421	8,250	6,798
56,850	56,900	8,261	6,427	8,261	6,809
56,900	56,950	8,272	6,433	8,272	6,820
56,950	57,000	8,283	6,439	8,283	6,831

(Continued)

* This column must also be used by a qualifying widow(er).

2021 Tax Table — *Continued*

If line 15 (taxable income) is—		And you are—			
At least	But less than	Single	Married filing jointly *	Married filing sepa-rately	Head of a house-hold
		Your tax is—			
57,000					
57,000	57,050	8,294	6,445	8,294	6,842
57,050	57,100	8,305	6,451	8,305	6,853
57,100	57,150	8,316	6,457	8,316	6,864
57,150	57,200	8,327	6,463	8,327	6,875
57,200	57,250	8,338	6,469	8,338	6,886
57,250	57,300	8,349	6,475	8,349	6,897
57,300	57,350	8,360	6,481	8,360	6,908
57,350	57,400	8,371	6,487	8,371	6,919
57,400	57,450	8,382	6,493	8,382	6,930
57,450	57,500	8,393	6,499	8,393	6,941
57,500	57,550	8,404	6,505	8,404	6,952
57,550	57,600	8,415	6,511	8,415	6,963
57,600	57,650	8,426	6,517	8,426	6,974
57,650	57,700	8,437	6,523	8,437	6,985
57,700	57,750	8,448	6,529	8,448	6,996
57,750	57,800	8,459	6,535	8,459	7,007
57,800	57,850	8,470	6,541	8,470	7,018
57,850	57,900	8,481	6,547	8,481	7,029
57,900	57,950	8,492	6,553	8,492	7,040
57,950	58,000	8,503	6,559	8,503	7,051
58,000					
58,000	58,050	8,514	6,565	8,514	7,062
58,050	58,100	8,525	6,571	8,525	7,073
58,100	58,150	8,536	6,577	8,536	7,084
58,150	58,200	8,547	6,583	8,547	7,095
58,200	58,250	8,558	6,589	8,558	7,106
58,250	58,300	8,569	6,595	8,569	7,117
58,300	58,350	8,580	6,601	8,580	7,128
58,350	58,400	8,591	6,607	8,591	7,139
58,400	58,450	8,602	6,613	8,602	7,150
58,450	58,500	8,613	6,619	8,613	7,161
58,500	58,550	8,624	6,625	8,624	7,172
58,550	58,600	8,635	6,631	8,635	7,183
58,600	58,650	8,646	6,637	8,646	7,194
58,650	58,700	8,657	6,643	8,657	7,205
58,700	58,750	8,668	6,649	8,668	7,216
58,750	58,800	8,679	6,655	8,679	7,227
58,800	58,850	8,690	6,661	8,690	7,238
58,850	58,900	8,701	6,667	8,701	7,249
58,900	58,950	8,712	6,673	8,712	7,260
58,950	59,000	8,723	6,679	8,723	7,271
59,000					
59,000	59,050	8,734	6,685	8,734	7,282
59,050	59,100	8,745	6,691	8,745	7,293
59,100	59,150	8,756	6,697	8,756	7,304
59,150	59,200	8,767	6,703	8,767	7,315
59,200	59,250	8,778	6,709	8,778	7,326
59,250	59,300	8,789	6,715	8,789	7,337
59,300	59,350	8,800	6,721	8,800	7,348
59,350	59,400	8,811	6,727	8,811	7,359
59,400	59,450	8,822	6,733	8,822	7,370
59,450	59,500	8,833	6,739	8,833	7,381
59,500	59,550	8,844	6,745	8,844	7,392
59,550	59,600	8,855	6,751	8,855	7,403
59,600	59,650	8,866	6,757	8,866	7,414
59,650	59,700	8,877	6,763	8,877	7,425
59,700	59,750	8,888	6,769	8,888	7,436
59,750	59,800	8,899	6,775	8,899	7,447
59,800	59,850	8,910	6,781	8,910	7,458
59,850	59,900	8,921	6,787	8,921	7,469
59,900	59,950	8,932	6,793	8,932	7,480
59,950	60,000	8,943	6,799	8,943	7,491

If line 15 (taxable income) is—		And you are—			
At least	But less than	Single	Married filing jointly *	Married filing sepa-rately	Head of a house-hold
		Your tax is—			
60,000					
60,000	60,050	8,954	6,805	8,954	7,502
60,050	60,100	8,965	6,811	8,965	7,513
60,100	60,150	8,976	6,817	8,976	7,524
60,150	60,200	8,987	6,823	8,987	7,535
60,200	60,250	8,998	6,829	8,998	7,546
60,250	60,300	9,009	6,835	9,009	7,557
60,300	60,350	9,020	6,841	9,020	7,568
60,350	60,400	9,031	6,847	9,031	7,579
60,400	60,450	9,042	6,853	9,042	7,590
60,450	60,500	9,053	6,859	9,053	7,601
60,500	60,550	9,064	6,865	9,064	7,612
60,550	60,600	9,075	6,871	9,075	7,623
60,600	60,650	9,086	6,877	9,086	7,634
60,650	60,700	9,097	6,883	9,097	7,645
60,700	60,750	9,108	6,889	9,108	7,656
60,750	60,800	9,119	6,895	9,119	7,667
60,800	60,850	9,130	6,901	9,130	7,678
60,850	60,900	9,141	6,907	9,141	7,689
60,900	60,950	9,152	6,913	9,152	7,700
60,950	61,000	9,163	6,919	9,163	7,711
61,000					
61,000	61,050	9,174	6,925	9,174	7,722
61,050	61,100	9,185	6,931	9,185	7,733
61,100	61,150	9,196	6,937	9,196	7,744
61,150	61,200	9,207	6,943	9,207	7,755
61,200	61,250	9,218	6,949	9,218	7,766
61,250	61,300	9,229	6,955	9,229	7,777
61,300	61,350	9,240	6,961	9,240	7,788
61,350	61,400	9,251	6,967	9,251	7,799
61,400	61,450	9,262	6,973	9,262	7,810
61,450	61,500	9,273	6,979	9,273	7,821
61,500	61,550	9,284	6,985	9,284	7,832
61,550	61,600	9,295	6,991	9,295	7,843
61,600	61,650	9,306	6,997	9,306	7,854
61,650	61,700	9,317	7,003	9,317	7,865
61,700	61,750	9,328	7,009	9,328	7,876
61,750	61,800	9,339	7,015	9,339	7,887
61,800	61,850	9,350	7,021	9,350	7,898
61,850	61,900	9,361	7,027	9,361	7,909
61,900	61,950	9,372	7,033	9,372	7,920
61,950	62,000	9,383	7,039	9,383	7,931
62,000					
62,000	62,050	9,394	7,045	9,394	7,942
62,050	62,100	9,405	7,051	9,405	7,953
62,100	62,150	9,416	7,057	9,416	7,964
62,150	62,200	9,427	7,063	9,427	7,975
62,200	62,250	9,438	7,069	9,438	7,986
62,250	62,300	9,449	7,075	9,449	7,997
62,300	62,350	9,460	7,081	9,460	8,008
62,350	62,400	9,471	7,087	9,471	8,019
62,400	62,450	9,482	7,093	9,482	8,030
62,450	62,500	9,493	7,099	9,493	8,041
62,500	62,550	9,504	7,105	9,504	8,052
62,550	62,600	9,515	7,111	9,515	8,063
62,600	62,650	9,526	7,117	9,526	8,074
62,650	62,700	9,537	7,123	9,537	8,085
62,700	62,750	9,548	7,129	9,548	8,096
62,750	62,800	9,559	7,135	9,559	8,107
62,800	62,850	9,570	7,141	9,570	8,118
62,850	62,900	9,581	7,147	9,581	8,129
62,900	62,950	9,592	7,153	9,592	8,140
62,950	63,000	9,603	7,159	9,603	8,151

If line 15 (taxable income) is—		And you are—			
At least	But less than	Single	Married filing jointly *	Married filing sepa-rately	Head of a house-hold
		Your tax is—			
63,000					
63,000	63,050	9,614	7,165	9,614	8,162
63,050	63,100	9,625	7,171	9,625	8,173
63,100	63,150	9,636	7,177	9,636	8,184
63,150	63,200	9,647	7,183	9,647	8,195
63,200	63,250	9,658	7,189	9,658	8,206
63,250	63,300	9,669	7,195	9,669	8,217
63,300	63,350	9,680	7,201	9,680	8,228
63,350	63,400	9,691	7,207	9,691	8,239
63,400	63,450	9,702	7,213	9,702	8,250
63,450	63,500	9,713	7,219	9,713	8,261
63,500	63,550	9,724	7,225	9,724	8,272
63,550	63,600	9,735	7,231	9,735	8,283
63,600	63,650	9,746	7,237	9,746	8,294
63,650	63,700	9,757	7,243	9,757	8,305
63,700	63,750	9,768	7,249	9,768	8,316
63,750	63,800	9,779	7,255	9,779	8,327
63,800	63,850	9,790	7,261	9,790	8,338
63,850	63,900	9,801	7,267	9,801	8,349
63,900	63,950	9,812	7,273	9,812	8,360
63,950	64,000	9,823	7,279	9,823	8,371
64,000					
64,000	64,050	9,834	7,285	9,834	8,382
64,050	64,100	9,845	7,291	9,845	8,393
64,100	64,150	9,856	7,297	9,856	8,404
64,150	64,200	9,867	7,303	9,867	8,415
64,200	64,250	9,878	7,309	9,878	8,426
64,250	64,300	9,889	7,315	9,889	8,437
64,300	64,350	9,900	7,321	9,900	8,448
64,350	64,400	9,911	7,327	9,911	8,459
64,400	64,450	9,922	7,333	9,922	8,470
64,450	64,500	9,933	7,339	9,933	8,481
64,500	64,550	9,944	7,345	9,944	8,492
64,550	64,600	9,955	7,351	9,955	8,503
64,600	64,650	9,966	7,357	9,966	8,514
64,650	64,700	9,977	7,363	9,977	8,525
64,700	64,750	9,988	7,369	9,988	8,536
64,750	64,800	9,999	7,375	9,999	8,547
64,800	64,850	10,010	7,381	10,010	8,558
64,850	64,900	10,021	7,387	10,021	8,569
64,900	64,950	10,032	7,393	10,032	8,580
64,950	65,000	10,043	7,399	10,043	8,591
65,000					
65,000	65,050	10,054	7,405	10,054	8,602
65,050	65,100	10,065	7,411	10,065	8,613
65,100	65,150	10,076	7,417	10,076	8,624
65,150	65,200	10,087	7,423	10,087	8,635
65,200	65,250	10,098	7,429	10,098	8,646
65,250	65,300	10,109	7,435	10,109	8,657
65,300	65,350	10,120	7,441	10,120	8,668
65,350	65,400	10,131	7,447	10,131	8,679
65,400	65,450	10,142	7,453	10,142	8,690
65,450	65,500	10,153	7,459	10,153	8,701
65,500	65,550	10,164	7,465	10,164	8,712
65,550	65,600	10,175	7,471	10,175	8,723
65,600	65,650	10,186	7,477	10,186	8,734
65,650	65,700	10,197	7,483	10,197	8,745
65,700	65,750	10,208	7,489	10,208	8,756
65,750	65,800	10,219	7,495	10,219	8,767
65,800	65,850	10,230	7,501	10,230	8,778
65,850	65,900	10,241	7,507	10,241	8,789
65,900	65,950	10,252	7,513	10,252	8,800
65,950	66,000	10,263	7,519	10,263	8,811

(Continued)

* This column must also be used by a qualifying widow(er).

2021 Tax Table — *Continued*

If line 15 (taxable income) is—		And you are—			
At least	But less than	Single	Married filing jointly *	Married filing sepa-rately	Head of a house-hold
		Your tax is—			
66,000					
66,000	66,050	10,274	7,525	10,274	8,822
66,050	66,100	10,285	7,531	10,285	8,833
66,100	66,150	10,296	7,537	10,296	8,844
66,150	66,200	10,307	7,543	10,307	8,855
66,200	66,250	10,318	7,549	10,318	8,866
66,250	66,300	10,329	7,555	10,329	8,877
66,300	66,350	10,340	7,561	10,340	8,888
66,350	66,400	10,351	7,567	10,351	8,899
66,400	66,450	10,362	7,573	10,362	8,910
66,450	66,500	10,373	7,579	10,373	8,921
66,500	66,550	10,384	7,585	10,384	8,932
66,550	66,600	10,395	7,591	10,395	8,943
66,600	66,650	10,406	7,597	10,406	8,954
66,650	66,700	10,417	7,603	10,417	8,965
66,700	66,750	10,428	7,609	10,428	8,976
66,750	66,800	10,439	7,615	10,439	8,987
66,800	66,850	10,450	7,621	10,450	8,998
66,850	66,900	10,461	7,627	10,461	9,009
66,900	66,950	10,472	7,633	10,472	9,020
66,950	67,000	10,483	7,639	10,483	9,031
67,000					
67,000	67,050	10,494	7,645	10,494	9,042
67,050	67,100	10,505	7,651	10,505	9,053
67,100	67,150	10,516	7,657	10,516	9,064
67,150	67,200	10,527	7,663	10,527	9,075
67,200	67,250	10,538	7,669	10,538	9,086
67,250	67,300	10,549	7,675	10,549	9,097
67,300	67,350	10,560	7,681	10,560	9,108
67,350	67,400	10,571	7,687	10,571	9,119
67,400	67,450	10,582	7,693	10,582	9,130
67,450	67,500	10,593	7,699	10,593	9,141
67,500	67,550	10,604	7,705	10,604	9,152
67,550	67,600	10,615	7,711	10,615	9,163
67,600	67,650	10,626	7,717	10,626	9,174
67,650	67,700	10,637	7,723	10,637	9,185
67,700	67,750	10,648	7,729	10,648	9,196
67,750	67,800	10,659	7,735	10,659	9,207
67,800	67,850	10,670	7,741	10,670	9,218
67,850	67,900	10,681	7,747	10,681	9,229
67,900	67,950	10,692	7,753	10,692	9,240
67,950	68,000	10,703	7,759	10,703	9,251
68,000					
68,000	68,050	10,714	7,765	10,714	9,262
68,050	68,100	10,725	7,771	10,725	9,273
68,100	68,150	10,736	7,777	10,736	9,284
68,150	68,200	10,747	7,783	10,747	9,295
68,200	68,250	10,758	7,789	10,758	9,306
68,250	68,300	10,769	7,795	10,769	9,317
68,300	68,350	10,780	7,801	10,780	9,328
68,350	68,400	10,791	7,807	10,791	9,339
68,400	68,450	10,802	7,813	10,802	9,350
68,450	68,500	10,813	7,819	10,813	9,361
68,500	68,550	10,824	7,825	10,824	9,372
68,550	68,600	10,835	7,831	10,835	9,383
68,600	68,650	10,846	7,837	10,846	9,394
68,650	68,700	10,857	7,843	10,857	9,405
68,700	68,750	10,868	7,849	10,868	9,416
68,750	68,800	10,879	7,855	10,879	9,427
68,800	68,850	10,890	7,861	10,890	9,438
68,850	68,900	10,901	7,867	10,901	9,449
68,900	68,950	10,912	7,873	10,912	9,460
68,950	69,000	10,923	7,879	10,923	9,471
69,000					
69,000	69,050	10,934	7,885	10,934	9,482
69,050	69,100	10,945	7,891	10,945	9,493
69,100	69,150	10,956	7,897	10,956	9,504
69,150	69,200	10,967	7,903	10,967	9,515
69,200	69,250	10,978	7,909	10,978	9,526
69,250	69,300	10,989	7,915	10,989	9,537
69,300	69,350	11,000	7,921	11,000	9,548
69,350	69,400	11,011	7,927	11,011	9,559
69,400	69,450	11,022	7,933	11,022	9,570
69,450	69,500	11,033	7,939	11,033	9,581
69,500	69,550	11,044	7,945	11,044	9,592
69,550	69,600	11,055	7,951	11,055	9,603
69,600	69,650	11,066	7,957	11,066	9,614
69,650	69,700	11,077	7,963	11,077	9,625
69,700	69,750	11,088	7,969	11,088	9,636
69,750	69,800	11,099	7,975	11,099	9,647
69,800	69,850	11,110	7,981	11,110	9,658
69,850	69,900	11,121	7,987	11,121	9,669
69,900	69,950	11,132	7,993	11,132	9,680
69,950	70,000	11,143	7,999	11,143	9,691
70,000					
70,000	70,050	11,154	8,005	11,154	9,702
70,050	70,100	11,165	8,011	11,165	9,713
70,100	70,150	11,176	8,017	11,176	9,724
70,150	70,200	11,187	8,023	11,187	9,735
70,200	70,250	11,198	8,029	11,198	9,746
70,250	70,300	11,209	8,035	11,209	9,757
70,300	70,350	11,220	8,041	11,220	9,768
70,350	70,400	11,231	8,047	11,231	9,779
70,400	70,450	11,242	8,053	11,242	9,790
70,450	70,500	11,253	8,059	11,253	9,801
70,500	70,550	11,264	8,065	11,264	9,812
70,550	70,600	11,275	8,071	11,275	9,823
70,600	70,650	11,286	8,077	11,286	9,834
70,650	70,700	11,297	8,083	11,297	9,845
70,700	70,750	11,308	8,089	11,308	9,856
70,750	70,800	11,319	8,095	11,319	9,867
70,800	70,850	11,330	8,101	11,330	9,878
70,850	70,900	11,341	8,107	11,341	9,889
70,900	70,950	11,352	8,113	11,352	9,900
70,950	71,000	11,363	8,119	11,363	9,911
71,000					
71,000	71,050	11,374	8,125	11,374	9,922
71,050	71,100	11,385	8,131	11,385	9,933
71,100	71,150	11,396	8,137	11,396	9,944
71,150	71,200	11,407	8,143	11,407	9,955
71,200	71,250	11,418	8,149	11,418	9,966
71,250	71,300	11,429	8,155	11,429	9,977
71,300	71,350	11,440	8,161	11,440	9,988
71,350	71,400	11,451	8,167	11,451	9,999
71,400	71,450	11,462	8,173	11,462	10,010
71,450	71,500	11,473	8,179	11,473	10,021
71,500	71,550	11,484	8,185	11,484	10,032
71,550	71,600	11,495	8,191	11,495	10,043
71,600	71,650	11,506	8,197	11,506	10,054
71,650	71,700	11,517	8,203	11,517	10,065
71,700	71,750	11,528	8,209	11,528	10,076
71,750	71,800	11,539	8,215	11,539	10,087
71,800	71,850	11,550	8,221	11,550	10,098
71,850	71,900	11,561	8,227	11,561	10,109
71,900	71,950	11,572	8,233	11,572	10,120
71,950	72,000	11,583	8,239	11,583	10,131
72,000					
72,000	72,050	11,594	8,245	11,594	10,142
72,050	72,100	11,605	8,251	11,605	10,153
72,100	72,150	11,616	8,257	11,616	10,164
72,150	72,200	11,627	8,263	11,627	10,175
72,200	72,250	11,638	8,269	11,638	10,186
72,250	72,300	11,649	8,275	11,649	10,197
72,300	72,350	11,660	8,281	11,660	10,208
72,350	72,400	11,671	8,287	11,671	10,219
72,400	72,450	11,682	8,293	11,682	10,230
72,450	72,500	11,693	8,299	11,693	10,241
72,500	72,550	11,704	8,305	11,704	10,252
72,550	72,600	11,715	8,311	11,715	10,263
72,600	72,650	11,726	8,317	11,726	10,274
72,650	72,700	11,737	8,323	11,737	10,285
72,700	72,750	11,748	8,329	11,748	10,296
72,750	72,800	11,759	8,335	11,759	10,307
72,800	72,850	11,770	8,341	11,770	10,318
72,850	72,900	11,781	8,347	11,781	10,329
72,900	72,950	11,792	8,353	11,792	10,340
72,950	73,000	11,803	8,359	11,803	10,351
73,000					
73,000	73,050	11,814	8,365	11,814	10,362
73,050	73,100	11,825	8,371	11,825	10,373
73,100	73,150	11,836	8,377	11,836	10,384
73,150	73,200	11,847	8,383	11,847	10,395
73,200	73,250	11,858	8,389	11,858	10,406
73,250	73,300	11,869	8,395	11,869	10,417
73,300	73,350	11,880	8,401	11,880	10,428
73,350	73,400	11,891	8,407	11,891	10,439
73,400	73,450	11,902	8,413	11,902	10,450
73,450	73,500	11,913	8,419	11,913	10,461
73,500	73,550	11,924	8,425	11,924	10,472
73,550	73,600	11,935	8,431	11,935	10,483
73,600	73,650	11,946	8,437	11,946	10,494
73,650	73,700	11,957	8,443	11,957	10,505
73,700	73,750	11,968	8,449	11,968	10,516
73,750	73,800	11,979	8,455	11,979	10,527
73,800	73,850	11,990	8,461	11,990	10,538
73,850	73,900	12,001	8,467	12,001	10,549
73,900	73,950	12,012	8,473	12,012	10,560
73,950	74,000	12,023	8,479	12,023	10,571
74,000					
74,000	74,050	12,034	8,485	12,034	10,582
74,050	74,100	12,045	8,491	12,045	10,593
74,100	74,150	12,056	8,497	12,056	10,604
74,150	74,200	12,067	8,503	12,067	10,615
74,200	74,250	12,078	8,509	12,078	10,626
74,250	74,300	12,089	8,515	12,089	10,637
74,300	74,350	12,100	8,521	12,100	10,648
74,350	74,400	12,111	8,527	12,111	10,659
74,400	74,450	12,122	8,533	12,122	10,670
74,450	74,500	12,133	8,539	12,133	10,681
74,500	74,550	12,144	8,545	12,144	10,692
74,550	74,600	12,155	8,551	12,155	10,703
74,600	74,650	12,166	8,557	12,166	10,714
74,650	74,700	12,177	8,563	12,177	10,725
74,700	74,750	12,188	8,569	12,188	10,736
74,750	74,800	12,199	8,575	12,199	10,747
74,800	74,850	12,210	8,581	12,210	10,758
74,850	74,900	12,221	8,587	12,221	10,769
74,900	74,950	12,232	8,593	12,232	10,780
74,950	75,000	12,243	8,599	12,243	10,791

(Continued)

* This column must also be used by a qualifying widow(er).

2021 Tax Table — *Continued*

If line 15 (taxable income) is—		And you are—			
At least	But less than	Single	Married filing jointly *	Married filing sepa-rately	Head of a house-hold
		Your tax is—			
75,000					
75,000	75,050	12,254	8,605	12,254	10,802
75,050	75,100	12,265	8,611	12,265	10,813
75,100	75,150	12,276	8,617	12,276	10,824
75,150	75,200	12,287	8,623	12,287	10,835
75,200	75,250	12,298	8,629	12,298	10,846
75,250	75,300	12,309	8,635	12,309	10,857
75,300	75,350	12,320	8,641	12,320	10,868
75,350	75,400	12,331	8,647	12,331	10,879
75,400	75,450	12,342	8,653	12,342	10,890
75,450	75,500	12,353	8,659	12,353	10,901
75,500	75,550	12,364	8,665	12,364	10,912
75,550	75,600	12,375	8,671	12,375	10,923
75,600	75,650	12,386	8,677	12,386	10,934
75,650	75,700	12,397	8,683	12,397	10,945
75,700	75,750	12,408	8,689	12,408	10,956
75,750	75,800	12,419	8,695	12,419	10,967
75,800	75,850	12,430	8,701	12,430	10,978
75,850	75,900	12,441	8,707	12,441	10,989
75,900	75,950	12,452	8,713	12,452	11,000
75,950	76,000	12,463	8,719	12,463	11,011
76,000					
76,000	76,050	12,474	8,725	12,474	11,022
76,050	76,100	12,485	8,731	12,485	11,033
76,100	76,150	12,496	8,737	12,496	11,044
76,150	76,200	12,507	8,743	12,507	11,055
76,200	76,250	12,518	8,749	12,518	11,066
76,250	76,300	12,529	8,755	12,529	11,077
76,300	76,350	12,540	8,761	12,540	11,088
76,350	76,400	12,551	8,767	12,551	11,099
76,400	76,450	12,562	8,773	12,562	11,110
76,450	76,500	12,573	8,779	12,573	11,121
76,500	76,550	12,584	8,785	12,584	11,132
76,550	76,600	12,595	8,791	12,595	11,143
76,600	76,650	12,606	8,797	12,606	11,154
76,650	76,700	12,617	8,803	12,617	11,165
76,700	76,750	12,628	8,809	12,628	11,176
76,750	76,800	12,639	8,815	12,639	11,187
76,800	76,850	12,650	8,821	12,650	11,198
76,850	76,900	12,661	8,827	12,661	11,209
76,900	76,950	12,672	8,833	12,672	11,220
76,950	77,000	12,683	8,839	12,683	11,231
77,000					
77,000	77,050	12,694	8,845	12,694	11,242
77,050	77,100	12,705	8,851	12,705	11,253
77,100	77,150	12,716	8,857	12,716	11,264
77,150	77,200	12,727	8,863	12,727	11,275
77,200	77,250	12,738	8,869	12,738	11,286
77,250	77,300	12,749	8,875	12,749	11,297
77,300	77,350	12,760	8,881	12,760	11,308
77,350	77,400	12,771	8,887	12,771	11,319
77,400	77,450	12,782	8,893	12,782	11,330
77,450	77,500	12,793	8,899	12,793	11,341
77,500	77,550	12,804	8,905	12,804	11,352
77,550	77,600	12,815	8,911	12,815	11,363
77,600	77,650	12,826	8,917	12,826	11,374
77,650	77,700	12,837	8,923	12,837	11,385
77,700	77,750	12,848	8,929	12,848	11,396
77,750	77,800	12,859	8,935	12,859	11,407
77,800	77,850	12,870	8,941	12,870	11,418
77,850	77,900	12,881	8,947	12,881	11,429
77,900	77,950	12,892	8,953	12,892	11,440
77,950	78,000	12,903	8,959	12,903	11,451
78,000					
78,000	78,050	12,914	8,965	12,914	11,462
78,050	78,100	12,925	8,971	12,925	11,473
78,100	78,150	12,936	8,977	12,936	11,484
78,150	78,200	12,947	8,983	12,947	11,495
78,200	78,250	12,958	8,989	12,958	11,506
78,250	78,300	12,969	8,995	12,969	11,517
78,300	78,350	12,980	9,001	12,980	11,528
78,350	78,400	12,991	9,007	12,991	11,539
78,400	78,450	13,002	9,013	13,002	11,550
78,450	78,500	13,013	9,019	13,013	11,561
78,500	78,550	13,024	9,025	13,024	11,572
78,550	78,600	13,035	9,031	13,035	11,583
78,600	78,650	13,046	9,037	13,046	11,594
78,650	78,700	13,057	9,043	13,057	11,605
78,700	78,750	13,068	9,049	13,068	11,616
78,750	78,800	13,079	9,055	13,079	11,627
78,800	78,850	13,090	9,061	13,090	11,638
78,850	78,900	13,101	9,067	13,101	11,649
78,900	78,950	13,112	9,073	13,112	11,660
78,950	79,000	13,123	9,079	13,123	11,671
79,000					
79,000	79,050	13,134	9,085	13,134	11,682
79,050	79,100	13,145	9,091	13,145	11,693
79,100	79,150	13,156	9,097	13,156	11,704
79,150	79,200	13,167	9,103	13,167	11,715
79,200	79,250	13,178	9,109	13,178	11,726
79,250	79,300	13,189	9,115	13,189	11,737
79,300	79,350	13,200	9,121	13,200	11,748
79,350	79,400	13,211	9,127	13,211	11,759
79,400	79,450	13,222	9,133	13,222	11,770
79,450	79,500	13,233	9,139	13,233	11,781
79,500	79,550	13,244	9,145	13,244	11,792
79,550	79,600	13,255	9,151	13,255	11,803
79,600	79,650	13,266	9,157	13,266	11,814
79,650	79,700	13,277	9,163	13,277	11,825
79,700	79,750	13,288	9,169	13,288	11,836
79,750	79,800	13,299	9,175	13,299	11,847
79,800	79,850	13,310	9,181	13,310	11,858
79,850	79,900	13,321	9,187	13,321	11,869
79,900	79,950	13,332	9,193	13,332	11,880
79,950	80,000	13,343	9,199	13,343	11,891
80,000					
80,000	80,050	13,354	9,205	13,354	11,902
80,050	80,100	13,365	9,211	13,365	11,913
80,100	80,150	13,376	9,217	13,376	11,924
80,150	80,200	13,387	9,223	13,387	11,935
80,200	80,250	13,398	9,229	13,398	11,946
80,250	80,300	13,409	9,235	13,409	11,957
80,300	80,350	13,420	9,241	13,420	11,968
80,350	80,400	13,431	9,247	13,431	11,979
80,400	80,450	13,442	9,253	13,442	11,990
80,450	80,500	13,453	9,259	13,453	12,001
80,500	80,550	13,464	9,265	13,464	12,012
80,550	80,600	13,475	9,271	13,475	12,023
80,600	80,650	13,486	9,277	13,486	12,034
80,650	80,700	13,497	9,283	13,497	12,045
80,700	80,750	13,508	9,289	13,508	12,056
80,750	80,800	13,519	9,295	13,519	12,067
80,800	80,850	13,530	9,301	13,530	12,078
80,850	80,900	13,541	9,307	13,541	12,089
80,900	80,950	13,552	9,313	13,552	12,100
80,950	81,000	13,563	9,319	13,563	12,111
81,000					
81,000	81,050	13,574	9,325	13,574	12,122
81,050	81,100	13,585	9,334	13,585	12,133
81,100	81,150	13,596	9,345	13,596	12,144
81,150	81,200	13,607	9,356	13,607	12,155
81,200	81,250	13,618	9,367	13,618	12,166
81,250	81,300	13,629	9,378	13,629	12,177
81,300	81,350	13,640	9,389	13,640	12,188
81,350	81,400	13,651	9,400	13,651	12,199
81,400	81,450	13,662	9,411	13,662	12,210
81,450	81,500	13,673	9,422	13,673	12,221
81,500	81,550	13,684	9,433	13,684	12,232
81,550	81,600	13,695	9,444	13,695	12,243
81,600	81,650	13,706	9,455	13,706	12,254
81,650	81,700	13,717	9,466	13,717	12,265
81,700	81,750	13,728	9,477	13,728	12,276
81,750	81,800	13,739	9,488	13,739	12,287
81,800	81,850	13,750	9,499	13,750	12,298
81,850	81,900	13,761	9,510	13,761	12,309
81,900	81,950	13,772	9,521	13,772	12,320
81,950	82,000	13,783	9,532	13,783	12,331
82,000					
82,000	82,050	13,794	9,543	13,794	12,342
82,050	82,100	13,805	9,554	13,805	12,353
82,100	82,150	13,816	9,565	13,816	12,364
82,150	82,200	13,827	9,576	13,827	12,375
82,200	82,250	13,838	9,587	13,838	12,386
82,250	82,300	13,849	9,598	13,849	12,397
82,300	82,350	13,860	9,609	13,860	12,408
82,350	82,400	13,871	9,620	13,871	12,419
82,400	82,450	13,882	9,631	13,882	12,430
82,450	82,500	13,893	9,642	13,893	12,441
82,500	82,550	13,904	9,653	13,904	12,452
82,550	82,600	13,915	9,664	13,915	12,463
82,600	82,650	13,926	9,675	13,926	12,474
82,650	82,700	13,937	9,686	13,937	12,485
82,700	82,750	13,948	9,697	13,948	12,496
82,750	82,800	13,959	9,708	13,959	12,507
82,800	82,850	13,970	9,719	13,970	12,518
82,850	82,900	13,981	9,730	13,981	12,529
82,900	82,950	13,992	9,741	13,992	12,540
82,950	83,000	14,003	9,752	14,003	12,551
83,000					
83,000	83,050	14,014	9,763	14,014	12,562
83,050	83,100	14,025	9,774	14,025	12,573
83,100	83,150	14,036	9,785	14,036	12,584
83,150	83,200	14,047	9,796	14,047	12,595
83,200	83,250	14,058	9,807	14,058	12,606
83,250	83,300	14,069	9,818	14,069	12,617
83,300	83,350	14,080	9,829	14,080	12,628
83,350	83,400	14,091	9,840	14,091	12,639
83,400	83,450	14,102	9,851	14,102	12,650
83,450	83,500	14,113	9,862	14,113	12,661
83,500	83,550	14,124	9,873	14,124	12,672
83,550	83,600	14,135	9,884	14,135	12,683
83,600	83,650	14,146	9,895	14,146	12,694
83,650	83,700	14,157	9,906	14,157	12,705
83,700	83,750	14,168	9,917	14,168	12,716
83,750	83,800	14,179	9,928	14,179	12,727
83,800	83,850	14,190	9,939	14,190	12,738
83,850	83,900	14,201	9,950	14,201	12,749
83,900	83,950	14,212	9,961	14,212	12,760
83,950	84,000	14,223	9,972	14,223	12,771

(Continued)

* This column must also be used by a qualifying widow(er).

2021 Tax Table — *Continued*

If line 15 (taxable income) is— At least	But less than	And you are— Single	Married filing jointly *	Married filing separately	Head of a household
		Your tax is—			
84,000					
84,000	84,050	14,234	9,983	14,234	12,782
84,050	84,100	14,245	9,994	14,245	12,793
84,100	84,150	14,256	10,005	14,256	12,804
84,150	84,200	14,267	10,016	14,267	12,815
84,200	84,250	14,278	10,027	14,278	12,826
84,250	84,300	14,289	10,038	14,289	12,837
84,300	84,350	14,300	10,049	14,300	12,848
84,350	84,400	14,311	10,060	14,311	12,859
84,400	84,450	14,322	10,071	14,322	12,870
84,450	84,500	14,333	10,082	14,333	12,881
84,500	84,550	14,344	10,093	14,344	12,892
84,550	84,600	14,355	10,104	14,355	12,903
84,600	84,650	14,366	10,115	14,366	12,914
84,650	84,700	14,377	10,126	14,377	12,925
84,700	84,750	14,388	10,137	14,388	12,936
84,750	84,800	14,399	10,148	14,399	12,947
84,800	84,850	14,410	10,159	14,410	12,958
84,850	84,900	14,421	10,170	14,421	12,969
84,900	84,950	14,432	10,181	14,432	12,980
84,950	85,000	14,443	10,192	14,443	12,991
85,000					
85,000	85,050	14,454	10,203	14,454	13,002
85,050	85,100	14,465	10,214	14,465	13,013
85,100	85,150	14,476	10,225	14,476	13,024
85,150	85,200	14,487	10,236	14,487	13,035
85,200	85,250	14,498	10,247	14,498	13,046
85,250	85,300	14,509	10,258	14,509	13,057
85,300	85,350	14,520	10,269	14,520	13,068
85,350	85,400	14,531	10,280	14,531	13,079
85,400	85,450	14,542	10,291	14,542	13,090
85,450	85,500	14,553	10,302	14,553	13,101
85,500	85,550	14,564	10,313	14,564	13,112
85,550	85,600	14,575	10,324	14,575	13,123
85,600	85,650	14,586	10,335	14,586	13,134
85,650	85,700	14,597	10,346	14,597	13,145
85,700	85,750	14,608	10,357	14,608	13,156
85,750	85,800	14,619	10,368	14,619	13,167
85,800	85,850	14,630	10,379	14,630	13,178
85,850	85,900	14,641	10,390	14,641	13,189
85,900	85,950	14,652	10,401	14,652	13,200
85,950	86,000	14,663	10,412	14,663	13,211
86,000					
86,000	86,050	14,674	10,423	14,674	13,222
86,050	86,100	14,685	10,434	14,685	13,233
86,100	86,150	14,696	10,445	14,696	13,244
86,150	86,200	14,707	10,456	14,707	13,255
86,200	86,250	14,718	10,467	14,718	13,266
86,250	86,300	14,729	10,478	14,729	13,277
86,300	86,350	14,740	10,489	14,740	13,288
86,350	86,400	14,751	10,500	14,751	13,299
86,400	86,450	14,763	10,511	14,763	13,311
86,450	86,500	14,775	10,522	14,775	13,323
86,500	86,550	14,787	10,533	14,787	13,335
86,550	86,600	14,799	10,544	14,799	13,347
86,600	86,650	14,811	10,555	14,811	13,359
86,650	86,700	14,823	10,566	14,823	13,371
86,700	86,750	14,835	10,577	14,835	13,383
86,750	86,800	14,847	10,588	14,847	13,395
86,800	86,850	14,859	10,599	14,859	13,407
86,850	86,900	14,871	10,610	14,871	13,419
86,900	86,950	14,883	10,621	14,883	13,431
86,950	87,000	14,895	10,632	14,895	13,443

If line 15 (taxable income) is— At least	But less than	And you are— Single	Married filing jointly *	Married filing separately	Head of a household
		Your tax is—			
87,000					
87,000	87,050	14,907	10,643	14,907	13,455
87,050	87,100	14,919	10,654	14,919	13,467
87,100	87,150	14,931	10,665	14,931	13,479
87,150	87,200	14,943	10,676	14,943	13,491
87,200	87,250	14,955	10,687	14,955	13,503
87,250	87,300	14,967	10,698	14,967	13,515
87,300	87,350	14,979	10,709	14,979	13,527
87,350	87,400	14,991	10,720	14,991	13,539
87,400	87,450	15,003	10,731	15,003	13,551
87,450	87,500	15,015	10,742	15,015	13,563
87,500	87,550	15,027	10,753	15,027	13,575
87,550	87,600	15,039	10,764	15,039	13,587
87,600	87,650	15,051	10,775	15,051	13,599
87,650	87,700	15,063	10,786	15,063	13,611
87,700	87,750	15,075	10,797	15,075	13,623
87,750	87,800	15,087	10,808	15,087	13,635
87,800	87,850	15,099	10,819	15,099	13,647
87,850	87,900	15,111	10,830	15,111	13,659
87,900	87,950	15,123	10,841	15,123	13,671
87,950	88,000	15,135	10,852	15,135	13,683
88,000					
88,000	88,050	15,147	10,863	15,147	13,695
88,050	88,100	15,159	10,874	15,159	13,707
88,100	88,150	15,171	10,885	15,171	13,719
88,150	88,200	15,183	10,896	15,183	13,731
88,200	88,250	15,195	10,907	15,195	13,743
88,250	88,300	15,207	10,918	15,207	13,755
88,300	88,350	15,219	10,929	15,219	13,767
88,350	88,400	15,231	10,940	15,231	13,779
88,400	88,450	15,243	10,951	15,243	13,791
88,450	88,500	15,255	10,962	15,255	13,803
88,500	88,550	15,267	10,973	15,267	13,815
88,550	88,600	15,279	10,984	15,279	13,827
88,600	88,650	15,291	10,995	15,291	13,839
88,650	88,700	15,303	11,006	15,303	13,851
88,700	88,750	15,315	11,017	15,315	13,863
88,750	88,800	15,327	11,028	15,327	13,875
88,800	88,850	15,339	11,039	15,339	13,887
88,850	88,900	15,351	11,050	15,351	13,899
88,900	88,950	15,363	11,061	15,363	13,911
88,950	89,000	15,375	11,072	15,375	13,923
89,000					
89,000	89,050	15,387	11,083	15,387	13,935
89,050	89,100	15,399	11,094	15,399	13,947
89,100	89,150	15,411	11,105	15,411	13,959
89,150	89,200	15,423	11,116	15,423	13,971
89,200	89,250	15,435	11,127	15,435	13,983
89,250	89,300	15,447	11,138	15,447	13,995
89,300	89,350	15,459	11,149	15,459	14,007
89,350	89,400	15,471	11,160	15,471	14,019
89,400	89,450	15,483	11,171	15,483	14,031
89,450	89,500	15,495	11,182	15,495	14,043
89,500	89,550	15,507	11,193	15,507	14,055
89,550	89,600	15,519	11,204	15,519	14,067
89,600	89,650	15,531	11,215	15,531	14,079
89,650	89,700	15,543	11,226	15,543	14,091
89,700	89,750	15,555	11,237	15,555	14,103
89,750	89,800	15,567	11,248	15,567	14,115
89,800	89,850	15,579	11,259	15,579	14,127
89,850	89,900	15,591	11,270	15,591	14,139
89,900	89,950	15,603	11,281	15,603	14,151
89,950	90,000	15,615	11,292	15,615	14,163

If line 15 (taxable income) is— At least	But less than	And you are— Single	Married filing jointly *	Married filing separately	Head of a household
		Your tax is—			
90,000					
90,000	90,050	15,627	11,303	15,627	14,175
90,050	90,100	15,639	11,314	15,639	14,187
90,100	90,150	15,651	11,325	15,651	14,199
90,150	90,200	15,663	11,336	15,663	14,211
90,200	90,250	15,675	11,347	15,675	14,223
90,250	90,300	15,687	11,358	15,687	14,235
90,300	90,350	15,699	11,369	15,699	14,247
90,350	90,400	15,711	11,380	15,711	14,259
90,400	90,450	15,723	11,391	15,723	14,271
90,450	90,500	15,735	11,402	15,735	14,283
90,500	90,550	15,747	11,413	15,747	14,295
90,550	90,600	15,759	11,424	15,759	14,307
90,600	90,650	15,771	11,435	15,771	14,319
90,650	90,700	15,783	11,446	15,783	14,331
90,700	90,750	15,795	11,457	15,795	14,343
90,750	90,800	15,807	11,468	15,807	14,355
90,800	90,850	15,819	11,479	15,819	14,367
90,850	90,900	15,831	11,490	15,831	14,379
90,900	90,950	15,843	11,501	15,843	14,391
90,950	91,000	15,855	11,512	15,855	14,403
91,000					
91,000	91,050	15,867	11,523	15,867	14,415
91,050	91,100	15,879	11,534	15,879	14,427
91,100	91,150	15,891	11,545	15,891	14,439
91,150	91,200	15,903	11,556	15,903	14,451
91,200	91,250	15,915	11,567	15,915	14,463
91,250	91,300	15,927	11,578	15,927	14,475
91,300	91,350	15,939	11,589	15,939	14,487
91,350	91,400	15,951	11,600	15,951	14,499
91,400	91,450	15,963	11,611	15,963	14,511
91,450	91,500	15,975	11,622	15,975	14,523
91,500	91,550	15,987	11,633	15,987	14,535
91,550	91,600	15,999	11,644	15,999	14,547
91,600	91,650	16,011	11,655	16,011	14,559
91,650	91,700	16,023	11,666	16,023	14,571
91,700	91,750	16,035	11,677	16,035	14,583
91,750	91,800	16,047	11,688	16,047	14,595
91,800	91,850	16,059	11,699	16,059	14,607
91,850	91,900	16,071	11,710	16,071	14,619
91,900	91,950	16,083	11,721	16,083	14,631
91,950	92,000	16,095	11,732	16,095	14,643
92,000					
92,000	92,050	16,107	11,743	16,107	14,655
92,050	92,100	16,119	11,754	16,119	14,667
92,100	92,150	16,131	11,765	16,131	14,679
92,150	92,200	16,143	11,776	16,143	14,691
92,200	92,250	16,155	11,787	16,155	14,703
92,250	92,300	16,167	11,798	16,167	14,715
92,300	92,350	16,179	11,809	16,179	14,727
92,350	92,400	16,191	11,820	16,191	14,739
92,400	92,450	16,203	11,831	16,203	14,751
92,450	92,500	16,215	11,842	16,215	14,763
92,500	92,550	16,227	11,853	16,227	14,775
92,550	92,600	16,239	11,864	16,239	14,787
92,600	92,650	16,251	11,875	16,251	14,799
92,650	92,700	16,263	11,886	16,263	14,811
92,700	92,750	16,275	11,897	16,275	14,823
92,750	92,800	16,287	11,908	16,287	14,835
92,800	92,850	16,299	11,919	16,299	14,847
92,850	92,900	16,311	11,930	16,311	14,859
92,900	92,950	16,323	11,941	16,323	14,871
92,950	93,000	16,335	11,952	16,335	14,883

(Continued)

* This column must also be used by a qualifying widow(er).

2021 Tax Table — *Continued*

If line 15 (taxable income) is—		And you are—			
At least	But less than	Single	Married filing jointly *	Married filing separately	Head of a household
		Your tax is—			
93,000					
93,000	93,050	16,347	11,963	16,347	14,895
93,050	93,100	16,359	11,974	16,359	14,907
93,100	93,150	16,371	11,985	16,371	14,919
93,150	93,200	16,383	11,996	16,383	14,931
93,200	93,250	16,395	12,007	16,395	14,943
93,250	93,300	16,407	12,018	16,407	14,955
93,300	93,350	16,419	12,029	16,419	14,967
93,350	93,400	16,431	12,040	16,431	14,979
93,400	93,450	16,443	12,051	16,443	14,991
93,450	93,500	16,455	12,062	16,455	15,003
93,500	93,550	16,467	12,073	16,467	15,015
93,550	93,600	16,479	12,084	16,479	15,027
93,600	93,650	16,491	12,095	16,491	15,039
93,650	93,700	16,503	12,106	16,503	15,051
93,700	93,750	16,515	12,117	16,515	15,063
93,750	93,800	16,527	12,128	16,527	15,075
93,800	93,850	16,539	12,139	16,539	15,087
93,850	93,900	16,551	12,150	16,551	15,099
93,900	93,950	16,563	12,161	16,563	15,111
93,950	94,000	16,575	12,172	16,575	15,123
94,000					
94,000	94,050	16,587	12,183	16,587	15,135
94,050	94,100	16,599	12,194	16,599	15,147
94,100	94,150	16,611	12,205	16,611	15,159
94,150	94,200	16,623	12,216	16,623	15,171
94,200	94,250	16,635	12,227	16,635	15,183
94,250	94,300	16,647	12,238	16,647	15,195
94,300	94,350	16,659	12,249	16,659	15,207
94,350	94,400	16,671	12,260	16,671	15,219
94,400	94,450	16,683	12,271	16,683	15,231
94,450	94,500	16,695	12,282	16,695	15,243
94,500	94,550	16,707	12,293	16,707	15,255
94,550	94,600	16,719	12,304	16,719	15,267
94,600	94,650	16,731	12,315	16,731	15,279
94,650	94,700	16,743	12,326	16,743	15,291
94,700	94,750	16,755	12,337	16,755	15,303
94,750	94,800	16,767	12,348	16,767	15,315
94,800	94,850	16,779	12,359	16,779	15,327
94,850	94,900	16,791	12,370	16,791	15,339
94,900	94,950	16,803	12,381	16,803	15,351
94,950	95,000	16,815	12,392	16,815	15,363
95,000					
95,000	95,050	16,827	12,403	16,827	15,375
95,050	95,100	16,839	12,414	16,839	15,387
95,100	95,150	16,851	12,425	16,851	15,399
95,150	95,200	16,863	12,436	16,863	15,411
95,200	95,250	16,875	12,447	16,875	15,423
95,250	95,300	16,887	12,458	16,887	15,435
95,300	95,350	16,899	12,469	16,899	15,447
95,350	95,400	16,911	12,480	16,911	15,459
95,400	95,450	16,923	12,491	16,923	15,471
95,450	95,500	16,935	12,502	16,935	15,483
95,500	95,550	16,947	12,513	16,947	15,495
95,550	95,600	16,959	12,524	16,959	15,507
95,600	95,650	16,971	12,535	16,971	15,519
95,650	95,700	16,983	12,546	16,983	15,531
95,700	95,750	16,995	12,557	16,995	15,543
95,750	95,800	17,007	12,568	17,007	15,555
95,800	95,850	17,019	12,579	17,019	15,567
95,850	95,900	17,031	12,590	17,031	15,579
95,900	95,950	17,043	12,601	17,043	15,591
95,950	96,000	17,055	12,612	17,055	15,603
96,000					
96,000	96,050	17,067	12,623	17,067	15,615
96,050	96,100	17,079	12,634	17,079	15,627
96,100	96,150	17,091	12,645	17,091	15,639
96,150	96,200	17,103	12,656	17,103	15,651
96,200	96,250	17,115	12,667	17,115	15,663
96,250	96,300	17,127	12,678	17,127	15,675
96,300	96,350	17,139	12,689	17,139	15,687
96,350	96,400	17,151	12,700	17,151	15,699
96,400	96,450	17,163	12,711	17,163	15,711
96,450	96,500	17,175	12,722	17,175	15,723
96,500	96,550	17,187	12,733	17,187	15,735
96,550	96,600	17,199	12,744	17,199	15,747
96,600	96,650	17,211	12,755	17,211	15,759
96,650	96,700	17,223	12,766	17,223	15,771
96,700	96,750	17,235	12,777	17,235	15,783
96,750	96,800	17,247	12,788	17,247	15,795
96,800	96,850	17,259	12,799	17,259	15,807
96,850	96,900	17,271	12,810	17,271	15,819
96,900	96,950	17,283	12,821	17,283	15,831
96,950	97,000	17,295	12,832	17,295	15,843
97,000					
97,000	97,050	17,307	12,843	17,307	15,855
97,050	97,100	17,319	12,854	17,319	15,867
97,100	97,150	17,331	12,865	17,331	15,879
97,150	97,200	17,343	12,876	17,343	15,891
97,200	97,250	17,355	12,887	17,355	15,903
97,250	97,300	17,367	12,898	17,367	15,915
97,300	97,350	17,379	12,909	17,379	15,927
97,350	97,400	17,391	12,920	17,391	15,939
97,400	97,450	17,403	12,931	17,403	15,951
97,450	97,500	17,415	12,942	17,415	15,963
97,500	97,550	17,427	12,953	17,427	15,975
97,550	97,600	17,439	12,964	17,439	15,987
97,600	97,650	17,451	12,975	17,451	15,999
97,650	97,700	17,463	12,986	17,463	16,011
97,700	97,750	17,475	12,997	17,475	16,023
97,750	97,800	17,487	13,008	17,487	16,035
97,800	97,850	17,499	13,019	17,499	16,047
97,850	97,900	17,511	13,030	17,511	16,059
97,900	97,950	17,523	13,041	17,523	16,071
97,950	98,000	17,535	13,052	17,535	16,083
98,000					
98,000	98,050	17,547	13,063	17,547	16,095
98,050	98,100	17,559	13,074	17,559	16,107
98,100	98,150	17,571	13,085	17,571	16,119
98,150	98,200	17,583	13,096	17,583	16,131
98,200	98,250	17,595	13,107	17,595	16,143
98,250	98,300	17,607	13,118	17,607	16,155
98,300	98,350	17,619	13,129	17,619	16,167
98,350	98,400	17,631	13,140	17,631	16,179
98,400	98,450	17,643	13,151	17,643	16,191
98,450	98,500	17,655	13,162	17,655	16,203
98,500	98,550	17,667	13,173	17,667	16,215
98,550	98,600	17,679	13,184	17,679	16,227
98,600	98,650	17,691	13,195	17,691	16,239
98,650	98,700	17,703	13,206	17,703	16,251
98,700	98,750	17,715	13,217	17,715	16,263
98,750	98,800	17,727	13,228	17,727	16,275
98,800	98,850	17,739	13,239	17,739	16,287
98,850	98,900	17,751	13,250	17,751	16,299
98,900	98,950	17,763	13,261	17,763	16,311
98,950	99,000	17,775	13,272	17,775	16,323
99,000					
99,000	99,050	17,787	13,283	17,787	16,335
99,050	99,100	17,799	13,294	17,799	16,347
99,100	99,150	17,811	13,305	17,811	16,359
99,150	99,200	17,823	13,316	17,823	16,371
99,200	99,250	17,835	13,327	17,835	16,383
99,250	99,300	17,847	13,338	17,847	16,395
99,300	99,350	17,859	13,349	17,859	16,407
99,350	99,400	17,871	13,360	17,871	16,419
99,400	99,450	17,883	13,371	17,883	16,431
99,450	99,500	17,895	13,382	17,895	16,443
99,500	99,550	17,907	13,393	17,907	16,455
99,550	99,600	17,919	13,404	17,919	16,467
99,600	99,650	17,931	13,415	17,931	16,479
99,650	99,700	17,943	13,426	17,943	16,491
99,700	99,750	17,955	13,437	17,955	16,503
99,750	99,800	17,967	13,448	17,967	16,515
99,800	99,850	17,979	13,459	17,979	16,527
99,850	99,900	17,991	13,470	17,991	16,539
99,900	99,950	18,003	13,481	18,003	16,551
99,950	100,000	18,015	13,492	18,015	16,563

$100,000 or over use the Tax Computation Worksheet

* This column must also be used by a qualifying widow(er).

2021 Optional Sales Tax Tables

When Used

The election to deduct state and local general sales taxes requires that the taxpayer give up any deduction for state and local income taxes. Whether this is advisable or not depends on a comparison of the amounts involved. In making the choice, however, the outcome could be influenced by the additional sales tax incurred due to certain "big ticket" purchases that were made. For example, a taxpayer who chose to deduct state and local income taxes for 2020 might well prefer the sales tax deduction in 2021 if a new boat was purchased or home improvements were made during the year. To make the sales tax election, the taxpayer must enter the amount on Schedule A, line 5a, and check the related box.

If the sales tax election is made, the amount of the deduction can be determined by use of the *actual expense method* or *the optional sales tax tables* issued by the IRS. The actual expense method can be used only when the taxpayer has actual receipts to support the deduction claimed. In the absence of receipts (the usual case with most taxpayers), the optional sales tax tables must be used. Sales taxes related to the purchase of items used in a taxpayer's trade or business are determined separately, with this amount deducted on Schedule C (Form 1040).

Adjustments Necessary

The optional sales tax tables are based on a number of assumptions that require adjustments to be made. As the starting point for the use of the tables is AGI, nontaxable receipts have not been included. Examples of receipts that should be added include: tax-exempt interest, veterans' benefits, nontaxable combat pay, public assistance payments, workers' compensation, nontaxable Social Security, and other retirement benefits. They do not include any large nontaxable items that are not likely to be spent. For example, a $100,000 inheritance should not be added if it was invested in a certificate of deposit.

The tables represent the sales tax on the average (and recurring) expenditures based on level of income by family size and do not include exceptional purchases. Therefore, add to the table amount any sales taxes on major purchases (such as motor vehicles, aircraft, boats, and home building materials, etc.).

When the optional sales tax tables are used, special adjustments may be needed when a taxpayer has lived in more than one taxing jurisdiction (e.g., state, county, city) during the year. The adjustments involve apportionment of taxes based on days involved and are illustrated in Instructions for Schedule A (Form 1040), pages A-3 to A-7.

Local Sales Taxes

Local sales taxes (i.e., those imposed by counties, cities, transit authorities) may or may not require a separate determination. In those states where they are not imposed, no further computations are necessary. This is also the case where the local taxes are uniform and are incorporated into the state sales tax table. In other situations, another step is necessary to arrive at the optional sales tax table deduction. Depending on where the taxpayer lives, one of two procedures needs to be used. In one procedure, the local sales tax is determined by using the **state table** amount—see Example 1 and the related worksheet. In the other procedure, special **local tables** issued by the IRS for specified state and local jurisdictions are modified (if necessary) and used—see Example 2 and the related worksheet.

IRS Sales Tax Deduction Calculator

The IRS has created an online Sales Tax Deduction Calculator to assist taxpayers in making this calculation (**apps.irs.gov/app/stdc/**). The calculator includes the ability to make adjustments for large purchases and includes a local sales tax calculation.

Use Illustrated

Example 1 The Archers file a joint return for 2021 reflecting AGI of $88,000 and have three dependents. They have tax-exempt interest of $3,000, and during the year they incurred sales tax of $1,650 on the purchase of an automobile for their dependent teenage son. They live in Bellaire, Texas, where the general sales tax rates are 6.25% for state and 2% for local. Since the IRS *has not issued* optional local sales tax tables for Texas, use the Worksheet below to arrive at the Archers' general sales tax deduction of $3,035.

Sales Tax Deduction Worksheet
(To be used when *no* IRS Optional Local Sales Tax Table Available)

Adjusted Gross Income (AGI) as listed on line 11 of Form 1040		$88,000
Add nontaxable items		3,000
Table income to be used for purposes of line 1 below		$91,000
1. Use table income to determine table amount—go to state of residence and find applicable range of table income and family size column for *state* sales tax		$ 1,049
2a. Enter local general sales tax rate	2.00	
2b. Enter state general sales tax rate	6.25	
2c. Divide 2a by 2b	0.32	
2d. Multiply line 1 by line 2c for the local sales tax		336
3. Enter general sales tax on large purchases		1,650
4. Deduction for general sales tax (add lines 1 + 2d + 3) and report on line 5a of Schedule A of Form 1040		$ 3,035

Example 2 The Hardys file a joint return for 2021, reporting AGI of $42,000 and have two dependents. They received $30,000 in nontaxable pension benefits. Although the Hardys do not keep sales tax receipts, they can prove that they paid $1,185 in sales tax on the purchase of a new boat in 2021. The Hardys are residents of Georgia and live in a jurisdiction that imposes a 2% local sales tax. Since the IRS *has issued* optional local sales tax tables for Georgia, use the Worksheet below to arrive at the Hardys' general sales tax deduction of $2,121.

Sales Tax Deduction Worksheet
(To be used for Alaska, Arizona, Arkansas, Colorado, Georgia, Illinois, Louisiana, Mississippi, Missouri, New York, North Carolina, South Carolina, Tennessee, Utah, and Virginia)

Adjusted Gross Income (AGI) as listed on line 11 of Form 1040		$42,000
Add nontaxable income		30,000
Table income to be used for purposes of line 1 below		$72,000
1. Use the table income to determine *state* sales tax amount—go to table for state of residence and find applicable income range and family size column		$ 530
2a. Enter local general sales tax rate	2.0	
2b. Enter IRS *local* sales tax table amount (based on a 1% tax rate)	$203	
2c. Multiply line 2b by 2a for the local sales tax		406
3. Enter general sales tax on large purchases		1,185
4. Deduction for general sales tax (add lines 1 + 2c + 3) and report on line 5a of Schedule A of Form 1040		$ 2,121

Assume that the Hardys live in Lawrenceville, GA 30045. Use the IRS Sales Tax Deduction Calculator to confirm the calculated amount (**apps.irs.gov/app/stdc/**).

2021 Optional State Sales Tax Tables

Alabama — 1 — 4.0000%

Income At least	Income But less than	Family Size 1	2	3	4	5	Over 5
$0	$20,000	252	294	323	345	363	389
$20,000	$30,000	360	421	461	493	519	555
$30,000	$40,000	415	485	531	567	597	639
$40,000	$50,000	461	538	590	630	663	710
$50,000	$60,000	502	586	642	685	721	772
$60,000	$70,000	538	628	688	735	773	827
$70,000	$80,000	571	666	730	780	821	878
$80,000	$90,000	601	702	769	821	864	925
$90,000	$100,000	630	735	805	860	905	968
$100,000	$120,000	667	778	853	911	958	1025
$120,000	$140,000	716	835	915	976	1028	1099
$140,000	$160,000	760	887	971	1037	1091	1167
$160,000	$180,000	801	934	1023	1092	1149	1229
$180,000	$200,000	839	978	1072	1144	1204	1288
$200,000	$225,000	878	1024	1122	1198	1260	1348
$225,000	$250,000	920	1073	1176	1255	1320	1412
$250,000	$275,000	960	1119	1226	1308	1376	1472
$275,000	$300,000	997	1162	1273	1359	1430	1529
$300,000	or more	1213	1414	1549	1653	1739	1859

Arizona — 2 — 5.6000%

Income At least	Income But less than	Family Size 1	2	3	4	5	Over 5
$0	$20,000	246	280	302	319	332	352
$20,000	$30,000	363	413	445	470	491	519
$30,000	$40,000	423	481	519	548	572	605
$40,000	$50,000	475	540	582	615	641	678
$50,000	$60,000	520	591	638	674	703	744
$60,000	$70,000	561	638	688	727	758	802
$70,000	$80,000	599	681	734	775	809	856
$80,000	$90,000	634	720	777	820	856	906
$90,000	$100,000	666	757	817	863	900	952
$100,000	$120,000	709	806	870	919	959	1014
$120,000	$140,000	765	870	939	991	1034	1094
$140,000	$160,000	817	929	1002	1058	1104	1168
$160,000	$180,000	865	983	1061	1120	1169	1236
$180,000	$200,000	910	1034	1116	1178	1229	1300
$200,000	$225,000	956	1087	1173	1238	1292	1367
$225,000	$250,000	1006	1143	1234	1303	1359	1438
$250,000	$275,000	1052	1196	1291	1363	1423	1505
$275,000	$300,000	1097	1247	1346	1421	1483	1568
$300,000	or more	1358	1544	1666	1759	1835	1941

Arkansas — 2 — 6.5000%

Income At least	Income But less than	Family Size 1	2	3	4	5	Over 5
$0	$20,000	283	318	341	358	372	391
$20,000	$30,000	433	488	523	549	571	600
$30,000	$40,000	513	578	620	651	677	712
$40,000	$50,000	582	656	704	739	768	808
$50,000	$60,000	645	726	779	819	851	895
$60,000	$70,000	701	790	848	891	926	975
$70,000	$80,000	754	849	911	958	996	1048
$80,000	$90,000	802	905	971	1020	1061	1116
$90,000	$100,000	849	957	1027	1079	1122	1181
$100,000	$120,000	910	1027	1102	1158	1204	1267
$120,000	$140,000	991	1118	1199	1261	1311	1380
$140,000	$160,000	1066	1203	1291	1358	1412	1486
$160,000	$180,000	1136	1282	1376	1447	1505	1584
$180,000	$200,000	1202	1357	1456	1532	1593	1677
$200,000	$225,000	1271	1435	1541	1620	1685	1774
$225,000	$250,000	1346	1519	1631	1716	1784	1879
$250,000	$275,000	1416	1599	1717	1806	1878	1977
$275,000	$300,000	1484	1675	1799	1892	1968	2072
$300,000	or more	1887	2132	2290	2409	2506	2640

California — 3 — 7.2500%

Income At least	Income But less than	Family Size 1	2	3	4	5	Over 5
$0	$20,000	314	356	384	405	422	446
$20,000	$30,000	458	520	560	591	616	651
$30,000	$40,000	532	603	650	686	715	755
$40,000	$50,000	595	674	726	766	799	844
$50,000	$60,000	650	737	794	837	873	922
$60,000	$70,000	700	793	855	901	940	993
$70,000	$80,000	745	845	910	960	1001	1057
$80,000	$90,000	787	892	961	1014	1057	1117
$90,000	$100,000	827	937	1009	1064	1110	1172
$100,000	$120,000	879	996	1073	1131	1179	1246
$120,000	$140,000	946	1072	1155	1218	1270	1341
$140,000	$160,000	1008	1143	1231	1298	1353	1429
$160,000	$180,000	1065	1207	1300	1371	1429	1510
$180,000	$200,000	1119	1268	1366	1440	1501	1586
$200,000	$225,000	1174	1331	1433	1512	1576	1665
$225,000	$250,000	1234	1398	1506	1588	1655	1749
$250,000	$275,000	1289	1461	1574	1660	1730	1827
$275,000	$300,000	1342	1521	1638	1728	1801	1902
$300,000	or more	1652	1871	2015	2125	2215	2340

Colorado — 2 — 2.9000%

Income At least	Income But less than	Family Size 1	2	3	4	5	Over 5
$0	$20,000	127	138	144	150	154	159
$20,000	$30,000	191	208	218	226	232	241
$30,000	$40,000	225	245	257	266	273	283
$40,000	$50,000	254	276	290	301	309	320
$50,000	$60,000	280	305	320	331	341	353
$60,000	$70,000	304	330	347	359	369	383
$70,000	$80,000	325	354	372	385	396	410
$80,000	$90,000	346	376	395	409	420	435
$90,000	$100,000	364	396	416	431	443	459
$100,000	$120,000	390	424	445	461	474	491
$120,000	$140,000	422	459	483	500	514	532
$140,000	$160,000	453	493	517	536	551	571
$160,000	$180,000	481	523	550	569	585	606
$180,000	$200,000	508	552	580	601	617	640
$200,000	$225,000	535	582	612	634	651	675
$225,000	$250,000	565	614	646	669	687	713
$250,000	$275,000	593	645	678	702	721	748
$275,000	$300,000	619	674	708	733	754	782
$300,000	or more	777	846	889	921	946	981

Connecticut — 4 — 6.3500%

Income At least	Income But less than	Family Size 1	2	3	4	5	Over 5
$0	$20,000	218	237	248	257	264	273
$20,000	$30,000	337	366	384	397	408	423
$30,000	$40,000	401	435	457	473	486	503
$40,000	$50,000	457	496	521	539	553	573
$50,000	$60,000	508	551	578	598	614	636
$60,000	$70,000	554	601	631	653	670	694
$70,000	$80,000	597	648	680	703	722	747
$80,000	$90,000	637	691	725	750	771	798
$90,000	$100,000	675	733	769	795	817	845
$100,000	$120,000	726	788	827	855	878	909
$120,000	$140,000	793	861	903	934	959	993
$140,000	$160,000	856	929	974	1008	1035	1072
$160,000	$180,000	914	992	1041	1077	1106	1145
$180,000	$200,000	970	1053	1104	1142	1173	1214
$200,000	$225,000	1028	1116	1171	1211	1244	1287
$225,000	$250,000	1091	1184	1242	1285	1320	1366
$250,000	$275,000	1151	1249	1310	1356	1392	1441
$275,000	$300,000	1209	1312	1376	1423	1461	1513
$300,000	or more	1555	1688	1770	1831	1880	1946

District of Columbia — 4 — 6.0000%

Income At least	Income But less than	Family Size 1	2	3	4	5	Over 5
$0	$20,000	196	210	218	224	229	235
$20,000	$30,000	310	331	344	353	361	371
$30,000	$40,000	371	396	412	424	433	445
$40,000	$50,000	425	454	472	485	496	510
$50,000	$60,000	473	506	526	541	553	569
$60,000	$70,000	518	553	576	592	605	622
$70,000	$80,000	559	598	622	639	653	672
$80,000	$90,000	598	639	665	684	699	719
$90,000	$100,000	634	679	706	726	742	763
$100,000	$120,000	684	731	761	783	800	823
$120,000	$140,000	749	801	833	857	876	901
$140,000	$160,000	810	866	901	927	947	975
$160,000	$180,000	866	927	964	992	1014	1043
$180,000	$200,000	920	985	1025	1054	1077	1109
$200,000	$225,000	977	1046	1088	1119	1144	1177
$225,000	$250,000	1038	1111	1156	1189	1216	1251
$250,000	$275,000	1096	1173	1221	1256	1284	1322
$275,000	$300,000	1152	1233	1284	1320	1350	1389
$300,000	or more	1490	1595	1660	1708	1746	1798

Florida — 1 — 6.0000%

Income At least	Income But less than	Family Size 1	2	3	4	5	Over 5
$0	$20,000	265	301	325	343	357	378
$20,000	$30,000	394	448	483	510	532	563
$30,000	$40,000	460	524	565	597	623	659
$40,000	$50,000	517	589	635	671	700	741
$50,000	$60,000	568	646	698	737	769	814
$60,000	$70,000	614	698	754	796	831	879
$70,000	$80,000	656	746	806	851	888	940
$80,000	$90,000	694	791	854	902	941	996
$90,000	$100,000	731	832	898	949	991	1048
$100,000	$120,000	779	887	958	1012	1057	1118
$120,000	$140,000	842	959	1036	1094	1142	1208
$140,000	$160,000	900	1025	1107	1170	1221	1292
$160,000	$180,000	954	1087	1174	1240	1294	1370
$180,000	$200,000	1005	1144	1236	1306	1363	1443
$200,000	$225,000	1057	1204	1301	1374	1435	1518
$225,000	$250,000	1113	1268	1370	1448	1511	1599
$250,000	$275,000	1166	1329	1435	1517	1583	1676
$275,000	$300,000	1216	1386	1497	1582	1652	1748
$300,000	or more	1513	1724	1863	1969	2056	2176

Georgia — 2 — 4.0000%

Income At least	Income But less than	Family Size 1	2	3	4	5	Over 5
$0	$20,000	172	187	196	203	209	216
$20,000	$30,000	261	284	298	309	317	329
$30,000	$40,000	308	335	352	364	375	388
$40,000	$50,000	348	379	398	412	424	439
$50,000	$60,000	384	418	439	455	468	485
$60,000	$70,000	417	453	477	494	508	526
$70,000	$80,000	447	486	511	530	544	565
$80,000	$90,000	475	517	543	563	579	600
$90,000	$100,000	501	545	573	594	611	634
$100,000	$120,000	536	584	614	636	654	678
$120,000	$140,000	582	633	666	690	710	736
$140,000	$160,000	624	680	715	741	762	790
$160,000	$180,000	664	723	760	787	810	840
$180,000	$200,000	701	763	802	832	855	887
$200,000	$225,000	739	805	847	878	902	936
$225,000	$250,000	781	851	895	927	953	989
$250,000	$275,000	820	893	939	974	1001	1039
$275,000	$300,000	858	934	982	1018	1047	1086
$300,000	or more	1079	1176	1237	1282	1318	1368

Hawaii — 1,6 — 4.0000%

Income At least	Income But less than	Family Size 1	2	3	4	5	Over 5
$0	$20,000	275	312	336	355	370	390
$20,000	$30,000	412	468	505	532	555	586
$30,000	$40,000	483	549	592	625	652	688
$40,000	$50,000	544	619	668	705	735	776
$50,000	$60,000	599	682	735	776	809	855
$60,000	$70,000	649	738	796	840	876	925
$70,000	$80,000	694	790	852	899	938	991
$80,000	$90,000	736	838	904	954	995	1051
$90,000	$100,000	776	883	953	1006	1049	1108
$100,000	$120,000	829	943	1018	1074	1120	1184
$120,000	$140,000	897	1022	1102	1164	1214	1282
$140,000	$160,000	961	1095	1181	1247	1300	1374
$160,000	$180,000	1020	1162	1254	1323	1380	1458
$180,000	$200,000	1076	1225	1322	1396	1456	1538
$200,000	$225,000	1134	1291	1393	1471	1534	1621
$225,000	$250,000	1196	1362	1470	1552	1618	1710
$250,000	$275,000	1254	1428	1542	1628	1698	1794
$275,000	$300,000	1310	1492	1610	1700	1773	1874
$300,000	or more	1639	1868	2016	2129	2221	2347

Idaho — 1 — 6.0000%

Income At least	Income But less than	Family Size 1	2	3	4	5	Over 5
$0	$20,000	379	455	507	548	582	630
$20,000	$30,000	537	643	716	774	822	890
$30,000	$40,000	615	737	821	887	942	1020
$40,000	$50,000	682	817	909	982	1043	1129
$50,000	$60,000	740	886	986	1065	1131	1225
$60,000	$70,000	792	948	1055	1139	1210	1310
$70,000	$80,000	839	1004	1118	1207	1282	1387
$80,000	$90,000	883	1056	1176	1269	1348	1459
$90,000	$100,000	923	1105	1229	1327	1409	1525
$100,000	$120,000	977	1169	1300	1404	1490	1613
$120,000	$140,000	1046	1251	1391	1502	1594	1725
$140,000	$160,000	1109	1326	1475	1592	1690	1828
$160,000	$180,000	1167	1395	1551	1674	1777	1923
$180,000	$200,000	1221	1459	1623	1751	1859	2011
$200,000	$225,000	1277	1526	1697	1831	1943	2102
$225,000	$250,000	1336	1596	1775	1916	2033	2199
$250,000	$275,000	1391	1662	1848	1995	2117	2290
$275,000	$300,000	1444	1725	1918	2069	2196	2376
$300,000	or more	1749	2088	2320	2503	2656	2872

Illinois — 2 — 6.2500%

Income At least	Income But less than	Family Size 1	2	3	4	5	Over 5
$0	$20,000	273	313	340	361	378	402
$20,000	$30,000	402	461	501	531	556	591
$30,000	$40,000	469	537	583	618	647	688
$40,000	$50,000	525	602	653	693	725	771
$50,000	$60,000	575	659	715	759	794	844
$60,000	$70,000	620	711	771	818	856	910
$70,000	$80,000	661	758	822	872	913	970
$80,000	$90,000	700	802	870	922	966	1026
$90,000	$100,000	735	843	914	969	1015	1079
$100,000	$120,000	783	897	973	1032	1080	1148
$120,000	$140,000	844	967	1049	1113	1165	1238
$140,000	$160,000	901	1032	1120	1187	1243	1321
$160,000	$180,000	953	1092	1185	1256	1315	1397
$180,000	$200,000	1002	1148	1246	1321	1383	1469
$200,000	$225,000	1053	1207	1309	1388	1453	1544
$225,000	$250,000	1108	1269	1376	1459	1528	1623
$250,000	$275,000	1159	1327	1440	1527	1598	1698
$275,000	$300,000	1207	1383	1500	1591	1665	1769
$300,000	or more	1493	1710	1854	1966	2058	2186

Income: At least	Income: But less than	Family Size 1	2	3	4	5	Over 5	Family Size 1	2	3	4	5	Over 5	Family Size 1	2	3	4	5	Over 5
		Indiana			4		7.0000%	**Iowa**			1		6.0000%	**Kansas**			1		6.5000%
$0	$20,000	318	365	396	420	439	466	270	301	322	337	350	366	423	515	579	630	672	732
$20,000	$30,000	462	531	576	611	639	678	410	459	490	514	533	559	588	716	804	874	933	1017
$30,000	$40,000	535	615	668	708	741	787	484	542	579	607	630	661	669	815	916	995	1062	1157
$40,000	$50,000	598	687	746	791	828	879	549	614	656	688	714	749	737	897	1008	1096	1170	1274
$50,000	$60,000	653	751	815	864	905	961	606	679	726	761	789	828	796	969	1090	1184	1264	1377
$60,000	$70,000	702	808	877	930	973	1034	658	737	788	826	857	899	848	1033	1161	1262	1347	1468
$70,000	$80,000	747	860	934	990	1036	1101	707	792	846	887	920	966	896	1091	1227	1333	1423	1550
$80,000	$90,000	789	908	986	1046	1095	1163	752	842	900	944	979	1028	940	1145	1287	1398	1492	1626
$90,000	$100,000	828	953	1035	1098	1149	1220	794	890	951	997	1035	1086	980	1194	1342	1459	1557	1696
$100,000	$120,000	880	1013	1100	1167	1221	1297	851	953	1019	1069	1109	1164	1034	1259	1415	1538	1642	1789
$120,000	$140,000	947	1090	1184	1256	1314	1396	925	1036	1108	1162	1206	1265	1102	1342	1509	1640	1750	1907
$140,000	$160,000	1008	1161	1261	1338	1401	1488	994	1114	1191	1249	1296	1360	1165	1419	1595	1733	1850	2015
$160,000	$180,000	1065	1226	1332	1413	1480	1572	1057	1186	1268	1330	1380	1448	1222	1488	1673	1818	1940	2114
$180,000	$200,000	1118	1288	1399	1484	1554	1651	1118	1254	1341	1406	1459	1531	1275	1553	1746	1897	2025	2206
$200,000	$225,000	1174	1351	1468	1558	1631	1733	1181	1325	1417	1486	1542	1618	1330	1620	1821	1979	2112	2301
$225,000	$250,000	1232	1419	1542	1636	1713	1820	1249	1401	1498	1571	1631	1712	1388	1691	1900	2066	2204	2402
$250,000	$275,000	1288	1483	1611	1710	1790	1902	1313	1473	1575	1652	1715	1800	1442	1757	1974	2146	2290	2495
$275,000	$300,000	1340	1543	1677	1780	1863	1980	1375	1542	1649	1730	1795	1885	1493	1819	2045	2222	2372	2584
$300,000	or more	1647	1897	2062	2189	2292	2435	1741	1954	2090	2193	2276	2389	1788	2178	2448	2661	2840	3094

Income: At least	Income: But less than	Kentucky			4		6.0000%	Louisiana			2		4.4500%	Maine			4		5.5000%
$0	$20,000	251	274	288	298	307	318	201	228	245	259	270	285	210	237	256	270	281	297
$20,000	$30,000	395	430	453	470	483	502	297	337	363	383	399	421	303	343	369	390	406	429
$30,000	$40,000	472	515	542	562	578	601	347	393	424	447	465	492	351	397	427	450	469	496
$40,000	$50,000	539	589	620	643	662	687	389	441	475	501	522	552	391	442	476	502	523	553
$50,000	$60,000	600	655	690	716	737	765	427	484	521	550	573	605	426	482	519	548	571	603
$60,000	$70,000	656	716	754	782	805	836	460	522	563	593	618	653	458	518	558	588	613	647
$70,000	$80,000	707	772	814	844	869	902	491	557	601	633	660	697	487	551	593	625	652	688
$80,000	$90,000	755	825	869	902	928	964	520	590	636	670	699	738	514	582	626	660	688	726
$90,000	$100,000	801	875	922	957	985	1023	547	621	669	705	735	777	539	610	656	692	721	761
$100,000	$120,000	862	942	993	1030	1060	1101	583	661	712	751	783	827	572	647	697	734	765	808
$120,000	$140,000	942	1030	1085	1126	1159	1204	629	714	769	811	846	893	615	696	749	789	822	868
$140,000	$160,000	1018	1112	1172	1217	1252	1301	672	762	821	867	903	954	655	740	797	840	875	924
$160,000	$180,000	1087	1189	1253	1300	1339	1391	711	807	870	917	956	1010	691	781	840	886	923	975
$180,000	$200,000	1154	1262	1330	1380	1421	1476	748	849	915	965	1006	1063	725	819	882	929	968	1022
$200,000	$225,000	1223	1338	1410	1464	1507	1566	787	893	962	1015	1058	1118	760	859	924	974	1015	1072
$225,000	$250,000	1298	1420	1497	1554	1600	1662	828	940	1013	1068	1114	1177	797	901	970	1022	1065	1124
$250,000	$275,000	1369	1498	1579	1639	1688	1754	867	984	1060	1118	1166	1232	832	941	1013	1067	1112	1174
$275,000	$300,000	1438	1572	1658	1721	1772	1841	904	1026	1105	1166	1216	1285	866	979	1053	1110	1156	1221
$300,000	or more	1847	2022	2132	2214	2280	2369	1120	1271	1371	1446	1508	1593	1060	1198	1289	1358	1415	1494

Income: At least	Income: But less than	Maryland			4		6.0000%	Massachusetts			4		6.2500%	Michigan			4		6.0000%
$0	$20,000	245	284	310	330	347	370	241	271	291	306	319	336	253	287	309	326	339	359
$20,000	$30,000	355	411	448	477	501	535	349	393	422	443	461	486	374	424	457	482	502	531
$30,000	$40,000	411	475	518	552	579	618	404	455	488	513	533	562	436	495	533	562	586	619
$40,000	$50,000	459	530	578	615	646	689	451	507	544	572	595	626	489	555	598	631	658	695
$50,000	$60,000	500	578	630	671	704	751	492	553	594	624	649	683	537	609	656	692	721	762
$60,000	$70,000	538	621	677	720	756	807	529	595	638	671	697	734	579	657	708	747	778	822
$70,000	$80,000	572	660	720	766	804	858	563	633	678	713	742	781	618	701	755	797	831	878
$80,000	$90,000	604	697	759	808	848	905	594	668	716	753	783	824	654	742	800	843	879	929
$90,000	$100,000	633	731	796	847	890	949	623	700	751	789	821	864	688	780	841	887	925	977
$100,000	$120,000	672	776	845	899	944	1007	661	744	797	838	871	917	733	831	896	945	985	1041
$120,000	$140,000	723	834	909	966	1015	1082	711	799	857	901	937	986	791	897	967	1020	1064	1124
$140,000	$160,000	769	887	967	1028	1079	1151	757	851	912	959	997	1049	845	958	1033	1090	1136	1200
$160,000	$180,000	812	936	1020	1085	1139	1214	799	898	963	1012	1052	1107	895	1015	1093	1154	1203	1271
$180,000	$200,000	852	982	1070	1138	1195	1274	839	942	1010	1062	1104	1162	941	1068	1150	1214	1266	1337
$200,000	$225,000	893	1030	1122	1194	1253	1336	879	988	1059	1113	1157	1218	990	1123	1210	1276	1331	1406
$225,000	$250,000	938	1081	1178	1252	1314	1401	923	1037	1112	1168	1215	1279	1042	1181	1273	1343	1400	1480
$250,000	$275,000	979	1129	1229	1307	1372	1463	964	1083	1161	1220	1268	1335	1090	1237	1333	1406	1466	1549
$275,000	$300,000	1018	1174	1279	1360	1427	1521	1003	1127	1207	1269	1319	1389	1137	1289	1389	1466	1528	1615
$300,000	or more	1248	1438	1566	1665	1747	1862	1229	1381	1480	1555	1616	1701	1409	1598	1722	1817	1894	2002

Income: At least	Income: But less than	Minnesota			1		6.8750%	Mississippi			2		7.0000%	Missouri			2		4.2250%
$0	$20,000	259	283	298	309	318	330	462	556	620	671	713	772	195	226	246	262	275	293
$20,000	$30,000	402	439	462	480	493	512	650	782	872	943	1002	1086	287	332	362	385	404	431
$30,000	$40,000	479	523	551	571	588	610	743	894	998	1079	1146	1242	334	386	421	448	470	501
$40,000	$50,000	546	597	628	652	670	696	821	988	1103	1192	1267	1373	374	432	471	502	527	562
$50,000	$60,000	607	663	698	724	745	773	890	1071	1195	1292	1373	1488	409	473	516	549	577	615
$60,000	$70,000	662	723	761	790	813	843	951	1145	1277	1381	1468	1590	441	510	556	592	622	663
$70,000	$80,000	713	779	821	851	876	909	1006	1211	1352	1462	1553	1683	470	544	593	631	663	706
$80,000	$90,000	762	832	876	909	935	970	1057	1273	1420	1536	1632	1768	497	575	627	668	701	747
$90,000	$100,000	807	881	928	963	991	1028	1105	1330	1484	1605	1706	1848	523	604	659	701	736	785
$100,000	$120,000	868	948	998	1036	1065	1106	1167	1405	1568	1696	1802	1953	556	643	701	746	784	835
$120,000	$140,000	948	1035	1090	1131	1164	1208	1247	1502	1676	1812	1926	2087	600	693	756	805	845	901
$140,000	$160,000	1023	1117	1177	1221	1256	1304	1321	1591	1775	1919	2040	2211	640	740	807	859	901	961
$160,000	$180,000	1092	1193	1257	1304	1341	1392	1388	1671	1865	2017	2144	2323	677	782	853	908	953	1016
$180,000	$200,000	1159	1266	1333	1383	1423	1477	1451	1747	1950	2109	2241	2428	711	823	897	955	1002	1068
$200,000	$225,000	1228	1342	1413	1466	1508	1566	1515	1825	2037	2203	2341	2537	747	864	942	1003	1053	1122
$225,000	$250,000	1303	1424	1499	1555	1600	1661	1584	1908	2129	2303	2448	2652	786	909	991	1054	1107	1180
$250,000	$275,000	1374	1501	1581	1640	1688	1752	1648	1985	2216	2396	2547	2760	822	950	1036	1103	1158	1234
$275,000	$300,000	1442	1576	1660	1722	1771	1839	1709	2059	2298	2485	2641	2862	856	990	1080	1149	1206	1286
$300,000	or more	1852	2024	2132	2212	2276	2363	2060	2482	2770	2996	3185	3451	1057	1223	1333	1419	1489	1588

Income At least	Income But less than	Family Size 1	2	3	4	5	Over 5
Nebraska					1		5.5000%
$0	$20,000	256	291	314	332	346	366
$20,000	$30,000	376	428	462	488	509	538
$30,000	$40,000	438	499	538	569	593	627
$40,000	$50,000	490	559	603	637	665	703
$50,000	$60,000	537	612	661	698	729	771
$60,000	$70,000	579	660	713	753	786	831
$70,000	$80,000	617	704	760	803	838	887
$80,000	$90,000	653	745	805	850	887	938
$90,000	$100,000	686	783	846	894	933	986
$100,000	$120,000	730	833	901	951	993	1051
$120,000	$140,000	788	899	971	1027	1071	1133
$140,000	$160,000	841	960	1037	1096	1144	1210
$160,000	$180,000	890	1016	1098	1160	1211	1281
$180,000	$200,000	936	1068	1155	1220	1274	1348
$200,000	$225,000	983	1123	1214	1283	1339	1417
$225,000	$250,000	1034	1181	1277	1349	1409	1491
$250,000	$275,000	1082	1236	1336	1412	1474	1560
$275,000	$300,000	1128	1288	1393	1472	1537	1626
$300,000	or more	1396	1595	1725	1823	1904	2015

Income At least	Income But less than	Family Size 1	2	3	4	5	Over 5
Nevada					5		6.8500%
$0	$20,000	295	334	360	380	396	418
$20,000	$30,000	433	491	529	558	581	614
$30,000	$40,000	504	572	616	649	677	715
$40,000	$50,000	565	640	690	727	758	801
$50,000	$60,000	619	701	755	796	830	877
$60,000	$70,000	667	756	814	858	895	945
$70,000	$80,000	711	806	868	915	954	1007
$80,000	$90,000	752	852	918	968	1009	1065
$90,000	$100,000	790	895	964	1017	1060	1120
$100,000	$120,000	841	953	1026	1082	1128	1191
$120,000	$140,000	907	1027	1106	1167	1216	1284
$140,000	$160,000	967	1096	1180	1245	1298	1371
$160,000	$180,000	1023	1159	1249	1317	1372	1450
$180,000	$200,000	1076	1219	1313	1384	1443	1524
$200,000	$225,000	1130	1280	1379	1454	1516	1601
$225,000	$250,000	1188	1346	1450	1529	1594	1684
$250,000	$275,000	1243	1408	1517	1599	1667	1761
$275,000	$300,000	1295	1467	1580	1666	1737	1835
$300,000	or more	1599	1812	1952	2058	2145	2266

Income At least	Income But less than	Family Size 1	2	3	4	5	Over 5
New Jersey					4		6.6250%
$0	$20,000	246	264	276	285	292	301
$20,000	$30,000	388	418	437	451	462	477
$30,000	$40,000	465	501	524	540	554	572
$40,000	$50,000	532	574	600	619	634	655
$50,000	$60,000	593	640	669	690	708	731
$60,000	$70,000	649	700	732	756	774	800
$70,000	$80,000	701	756	791	816	836	864
$80,000	$90,000	750	809	846	873	895	924
$90,000	$100,000	796	859	898	927	950	981
$100,000	$120,000	858	926	968	999	1024	1058
$120,000	$140,000	939	1013	1060	1094	1122	1159
$140,000	$160,000	1015	1096	1146	1183	1213	1253
$160,000	$180,000	1086	1173	1227	1267	1298	1341
$180,000	$200,000	1154	1246	1303	1346	1380	1425
$200,000	$225,000	1225	1323	1384	1429	1465	1513
$225,000	$250,000	1302	1406	1471	1519	1557	1608
$250,000	$275,000	1374	1484	1553	1604	1644	1699
$275,000	$300,000	1444	1560	1632	1685	1728	1786
$300,000	or more	1866	2016	2110	2179	2235	2309

Income At least	Income But less than	Family Size 1	2	3	4	5	Over 5
New Mexico					1		5.1250%
$0	$20,000	260	285	301	313	322	335
$20,000	$30,000	400	438	462	480	495	514
$30,000	$40,000	474	519	548	569	586	610
$40,000	$50,000	538	590	622	647	666	693
$50,000	$60,000	595	653	689	716	738	767
$60,000	$70,000	648	710	750	779	803	834
$70,000	$80,000	696	764	806	837	863	897
$80,000	$90,000	742	813	858	892	919	955
$90,000	$100,000	784	860	908	943	972	1010
$100,000	$120,000	841	923	974	1012	1043	1084
$120,000	$140,000	916	1005	1060	1102	1135	1180
$140,000	$160,000	986	1081	1141	1186	1222	1270
$160,000	$180,000	1050	1152	1216	1264	1302	1354
$180,000	$200,000	1112	1219	1287	1338	1378	1433
$200,000	$225,000	1176	1290	1361	1415	1457	1515
$225,000	$250,000	1245	1365	1441	1498	1543	1604
$250,000	$275,000	1310	1437	1517	1576	1624	1688
$275,000	$300,000	1372	1505	1589	1651	1701	1769
$300,000	or more	1746	1915	2022	2101	2164	2251

Income At least	Income But less than	Family Size 1	2	3	4	5	Over 5
New York					2		4.0000%
$0	$20,000	151	156	159	162	164	166
$20,000	$30,000	243	252	257	261	264	268
$30,000	$40,000	294	305	311	315	319	323
$40,000	$50,000	340	351	358	363	367	373
$50,000	$60,000	381	394	402	407	412	418
$60,000	$70,000	419	433	441	448	453	459
$70,000	$80,000	454	469	479	485	491	498
$80,000	$90,000	487	504	514	521	527	534
$90,000	$100,000	519	537	547	555	561	569
$100,000	$120,000	562	581	592	600	607	615
$120,000	$140,000	618	639	651	660	667	677
$140,000	$160,000	671	694	707	717	725	735
$160,000	$180,000	721	745	760	770	778	789
$180,000	$200,000	769	794	810	821	830	841
$200,000	$225,000	819	846	862	874	884	896
$225,000	$250,000	873	902	919	932	942	955
$250,000	$275,000	925	955	974	987	998	1012
$275,000	$300,000	975	1007	1026	1040	1051	1066
$300,000	or more	1279	1321	1346	1364	1378	1397

Income At least	Income But less than	Family Size 1	2	3	4	5	Over 5
North Carolina					2		4.7500%
$0	$20,000	248	290	319	341	359	385
$20,000	$30,000	358	419	460	492	519	556
$30,000	$40,000	414	485	532	569	600	643
$40,000	$50,000	461	540	593	635	669	717
$50,000	$60,000	503	589	647	692	729	782
$60,000	$70,000	541	633	695	744	784	840
$70,000	$80,000	575	673	739	791	833	893
$80,000	$90,000	606	710	780	834	879	942
$90,000	$100,000	636	745	818	875	922	988
$100,000	$120,000	675	790	868	928	978	1048
$120,000	$140,000	725	849	933	997	1051	1126
$140,000	$160,000	772	903	992	1061	1118	1198
$160,000	$180,000	814	953	1047	1120	1180	1264
$180,000	$200,000	854	1000	1098	1175	1238	1326
$200,000	$225,000	895	1048	1151	1231	1298	1391
$225,000	$250,000	939	1100	1208	1292	1361	1459
$250,000	$275,000	981	1148	1261	1349	1421	1523
$275,000	$300,000	1020	1194	1311	1402	1478	1584
$300,000	or more	1248	1461	1605	1716	1809	1938

Income At least	Income But less than	Family Size 1	2	3	4	5	Over 5
North Dakota					1		5.0000%
$0	$20,000	216	249	271	288	303	323
$20,000	$30,000	314	362	395	420	440	469
$30,000	$40,000	364	420	458	486	510	544
$40,000	$50,000	407	469	511	543	570	607
$50,000	$60,000	445	513	558	594	623	664
$60,000	$70,000	479	552	601	638	670	714
$70,000	$80,000	510	587	639	680	713	760
$80,000	$90,000	538	620	675	718	753	802
$90,000	$100,000	565	651	709	753	790	842
$100,000	$120,000	600	692	753	800	840	894
$120,000	$140,000	646	744	810	861	903	962
$140,000	$160,000	689	793	863	917	962	1025
$160,000	$180,000	727	838	912	969	1016	1083
$180,000	$200,000	764	880	957	1017	1067	1137
$200,000	$225,000	802	923	1004	1068	1120	1193
$225,000	$250,000	842	969	1055	1121	1176	1253
$250,000	$275,000	880	1013	1102	1171	1228	1309
$275,000	$300,000	916	1054	1147	1219	1278	1362
$300,000	or more	1126	1295	1409	1498	1571	1673

Income At least	Income But less than	Family Size 1	2	3	4	5	Over 5
Ohio					1		5.7500%
$0	$20,000	246	271	287	299	309	322
$20,000	$30,000	379	418	443	462	477	497
$30,000	$40,000	450	496	526	548	566	591
$40,000	$50,000	511	564	598	623	644	672
$50,000	$60,000	566	625	663	691	714	745
$60,000	$70,000	616	681	722	752	777	811
$70,000	$80,000	663	732	776	809	836	872
$80,000	$90,000	706	780	827	862	891	929
$90,000	$100,000	747	825	875	912	942	983
$100,000	$120,000	801	885	939	979	1011	1055
$120,000	$140,000	872	964	1022	1066	1102	1150
$140,000	$160,000	939	1038	1101	1148	1186	1238
$160,000	$180,000	1000	1106	1173	1223	1264	1319
$180,000	$200,000	1059	1171	1242	1295	1338	1397
$200,000	$225,000	1120	1238	1314	1370	1416	1478
$225,000	$250,000	1185	1311	1391	1451	1499	1565
$250,000	$275,000	1247	1379	1464	1527	1578	1647
$275,000	$300,000	1306	1445	1534	1600	1653	1726
$300,000	or more	1661	1838	1951	2035	2104	2197

Income At least	Income But less than	Family Size 1	2	3	4	5	Over 5
Oklahoma					1		4.5000%
$0	$20,000	281	336	374	404	430	465
$20,000	$30,000	399	477	531	573	609	659
$30,000	$40,000	458	548	609	658	699	756
$40,000	$50,000	508	607	675	729	774	838
$50,000	$60,000	552	659	733	792	840	910
$60,000	$70,000	591	706	785	847	900	973
$70,000	$80,000	627	748	832	898	953	1032
$80,000	$90,000	659	787	876	945	1003	1085
$90,000	$100,000	690	824	916	988	1049	1135
$100,000	$120,000	730	872	969	1046	1110	1201
$120,000	$140,000	782	934	1038	1120	1188	1285
$140,000	$160,000	830	990	1101	1188	1260	1363
$160,000	$180,000	874	1042	1158	1250	1326	1434
$180,000	$200,000	915	1091	1212	1308	1388	1501
$200,000	$225,000	957	1141	1268	1368	1451	1569
$225,000	$250,000	1002	1195	1327	1431	1519	1642
$250,000	$275,000	1044	1245	1383	1491	1582	1711
$275,000	$300,000	1084	1292	1435	1548	1642	1775
$300,000	or more	1315	1566	1739	1875	1989	2150

Income At least	Income But less than	Family Size 1	2	3	4	5	Over 5
Pennsylvania					1		6.0000%
$0	$20,000	211	229	241	249	255	265
$20,000	$30,000	329	358	375	389	399	413
$30,000	$40,000	393	426	448	463	476	493
$40,000	$50,000	448	486	511	529	543	563
$50,000	$60,000	497	540	568	588	604	626
$60,000	$70,000	542	590	619	641	659	683
$70,000	$80,000	584	635	667	691	710	736
$80,000	$90,000	624	678	713	738	758	786
$90,000	$100,000	661	719	755	782	804	833
$100,000	$120,000	710	773	812	841	864	896
$120,000	$140,000	776	844	887	919	944	979
$140,000	$160,000	837	910	957	991	1019	1056
$160,000	$180,000	893	972	1022	1058	1088	1128
$180,000	$200,000	947	1031	1083	1123	1154	1196
$200,000	$225,000	1003	1092	1148	1190	1223	1268
$225,000	$250,000	1064	1158	1218	1262	1297	1345
$250,000	$275,000	1121	1221	1284	1330	1368	1418
$275,000	$300,000	1177	1281	1347	1396	1435	1488
$300,000	or more	1508	1643	1728	1791	1841	1910

Income At least	Income But less than	Family Size 1	2	3	4	5	Over 5
Rhode Island					4		7.0000%
$0	$20,000	293	335	362	382	399	422
$20,000	$30,000	419	479	518	548	572	605
$30,000	$40,000	483	552	597	631	659	697
$40,000	$50,000	537	613	663	701	732	775
$50,000	$60,000	584	667	722	763	797	844
$60,000	$70,000	626	716	774	818	855	905
$70,000	$80,000	665	760	822	869	908	961
$80,000	$90,000	700	800	866	915	956	1012
$90,000	$100,000	733	838	907	959	1002	1060
$100,000	$120,000	777	888	961	1016	1061	1124
$120,000	$140,000	834	953	1031	1090	1139	1206
$140,000	$160,000	886	1012	1095	1158	1210	1281
$160,000	$180,000	933	1067	1154	1220	1275	1350
$180,000	$200,000	978	1118	1209	1279	1336	1415
$200,000	$225,000	1024	1170	1266	1339	1399	1482
$225,000	$250,000	1073	1226	1327	1404	1466	1553
$250,000	$275,000	1118	1279	1384	1464	1529	1619
$275,000	$300,000	1162	1329	1438	1521	1589	1683
$300,000	or more	1415	1618	1751	1853	1935	2050

Income At least	Income But less than	Family Size 1	2	3	4	5	Over 5
South Carolina					2		6.0000%
$0	$20,000	274	314	340	359	375	398
$20,000	$30,000	396	453	491	519	543	575
$30,000	$40,000	457	524	567	600	627	665
$40,000	$50,000	510	584	632	669	699	741
$50,000	$60,000	556	637	690	730	763	809
$60,000	$70,000	597	684	741	784	820	869
$70,000	$80,000	635	727	788	834	872	924
$80,000	$90,000	670	767	831	880	920	975
$90,000	$100,000	702	804	871	923	964	1022
$100,000	$120,000	745	854	925	979	1024	1085
$120,000	$140,000	800	917	994	1052	1100	1166
$140,000	$160,000	852	976	1058	1120	1171	1241
$160,000	$180,000	898	1030	1116	1182	1235	1310
$180,000	$200,000	943	1080	1171	1240	1296	1374
$200,000	$225,000	988	1133	1228	1300	1359	1441
$225,000	$250,000	1037	1189	1288	1364	1426	1512
$250,000	$275,000	1082	1241	1345	1424	1489	1578
$275,000	$300,000	1125	1290	1399	1481	1548	1642
$300,000	or more	1377	1580	1712	1814	1896	2011

Income At least	Income But less than	1	2	3	4	5	Over 5	1	2	3	4	5	Over 5	1	2	3	4	5	Over 5
		South Dakota			1		4.5000%	**Tennessee**			2		7.0000%	**Texas**			1		6.2500%
$0	$20,000	291	338	370	394	414	442	389	458	504	540	570	612	268	301	321	337	349	367
$20,000	$30,000	430	501	548	584	614	655	561	660	727	780	823	884	410	460	492	516	535	562
$30,000	$40,000	501	584	640	682	717	766	649	763	841	901	951	1021	486	545	582	611	634	666
$40,000	$50,000	563	656	718	766	805	860	723	850	936	1004	1059	1137	551	618	661	693	720	756
$50,000	$60,000	617	720	788	840	883	944	788	927	1021	1094	1155	1240	609	684	732	768	797	837
$60,000	$70,000	666	777	851	907	954	1019	846	996	1097	1175	1240	1332	663	744	796	835	867	910
$70,000	$80,000	711	830	908	969	1019	1088	900	1058	1166	1249	1318	1416	712	799	855	897	931	978
$80,000	$90,000	753	878	962	1026	1079	1152	949	1116	1229	1317	1390	1493	758	851	911	956	992	1042
$90,000	$100,000	792	924	1012	1079	1135	1212	995	1170	1289	1381	1458	1565	801	900	963	1010	1049	1102
$100,000	$120,000	844	985	1078	1150	1210	1292	1056	1242	1368	1465	1547	1661	859	965	1033	1084	1125	1182
$120,000	$140,000	911	1063	1165	1243	1307	1396	1134	1334	1469	1574	1661	1784	935	1050	1124	1180	1225	1287
$140,000	$160,000	973	1136	1245	1328	1397	1492	1206	1419	1563	1674	1767	1897	1006	1130	1210	1270	1318	1385
$160,000	$180,000	1031	1204	1318	1407	1479	1581	1273	1497	1648	1766	1864	2002	1071	1204	1289	1353	1405	1476
$180,000	$200,000	1085	1267	1388	1481	1557	1664	1335	1570	1729	1852	1955	2099	1134	1274	1364	1432	1487	1562
$200,000	$225,000	1141	1333	1460	1558	1638	1751	1399	1646	1812	1942	2049	2200	1199	1347	1442	1514	1572	1652
$225,000	$250,000	1201	1403	1537	1640	1725	1843	1468	1726	1901	2037	2149	2308	1269	1426	1527	1603	1664	1749
$250,000	$275,000	1257	1469	1609	1717	1806	1930	1532	1802	1984	2126	2243	2409	1335	1500	1607	1687	1752	1841
$275,000	$300,000	1311	1532	1678	1791	1884	2013	1593	1873	2063	2210	2333	2505	1398	1572	1683	1767	1835	1929
$300,000	or more	1628	1902	2085	2225	2341	2502	1948	2291	2523	2703	2852	3063	1777	1999	2141	2248	2335	2454

Income At least	Income But less than	1	2	3	4	5	Over 5	1	2	3	4	5	Over 5	1	2	3	4	5	Over 5
		Utah			2		4.8500%	**Vermont**			1		6.0000%	**Virginia**			2		4.3000%
$0	$20,000	271	318	349	373	394	422	203	222	234	243	250	260	199	232	254	271	285	305
$20,000	$30,000	393	460	506	541	570	611	290	318	335	348	359	373	290	338	371	396	416	446
$30,000	$40,000	454	532	585	626	660	707	334	366	387	401	413	430	337	393	430	459	483	517
$40,000	$50,000	507	594	652	698	736	788	372	407	430	446	460	478	377	439	481	513	540	578
$50,000	$60,000	553	648	712	762	803	860	405	443	468	486	500	520	412	480	526	561	591	632
$60,000	$70,000	594	696	765	818	863	925	434	476	502	521	537	558	444	517	566	604	636	680
$70,000	$80,000	632	741	814	871	918	983	461	505	533	553	570	592	472	550	603	644	677	725
$80,000	$90,000	667	782	859	919	968	1038	486	532	561	583	601	624	499	582	637	680	716	766
$90,000	$100,000	700	820	901	964	1016	1089	509	557	588	611	629	654	524	611	669	714	751	804
$100,000	$120,000	743	870	956	1023	1078	1156	539	591	623	648	667	693	557	649	711	759	799	855
$120,000	$140,000	798	936	1028	1100	1159	1242	579	634	669	695	716	744	600	699	766	817	860	920
$140,000	$160,000	850	996	1094	1171	1234	1322	615	674	711	738	760	790	640	745	816	871	917	981
$160,000	$180,000	897	1051	1155	1235	1302	1396	648	710	749	778	801	833	676	787	862	921	969	1036
$180,000	$200,000	941	1103	1212	1296	1366	1464	679	744	785	815	840	873	710	827	906	967	1018	1089
$200,000	$225,000	987	1157	1271	1359	1433	1536	711	779	822	854	880	914	746	868	951	1015	1068	1143
$225,000	$250,000	1036	1214	1334	1427	1504	1612	745	817	862	895	922	958	783	912	999	1066	1122	1200
$250,000	$275,000	1082	1267	1393	1490	1570	1683	777	852	899	934	962	1000	819	954	1044	1115	1173	1255
$275,000	$300,000	1125	1318	1449	1550	1633	1751	808	885	934	970	999	1039	853	993	1087	1160	1221	1306
$300,000	or more	1379	1615	1775	1899	2001	2145	984	1079	1138	1183	1218	1266	1050	1222	1338	1428	1503	1608

Income At least	Income But less than	1	2	3	4	5	Over 5	1	2	3	4	5	Over 5	1	2	3	4	5	Over 5
		Washington			1		6.5000%	**West Virginia**			1		6.0000%	**Wisconsin**			1		5.0000%
$0	$20,000	281	313	334	349	362	379	250	278	297	310	321	337	218	243	260	272	281	295
$20,000	$30,000	433	483	515	540	559	586	391	437	466	487	505	529	334	372	397	416	431	451
$30,000	$40,000	514	573	612	641	664	697	468	522	557	583	604	633	395	441	470	492	510	534
$40,000	$50,000	584	652	696	729	756	792	535	598	637	667	692	725	448	500	533	559	579	607
$50,000	$60,000	647	723	771	808	838	879	596	666	710	744	771	808	495	553	590	618	641	672
$60,000	$70,000	704	787	840	880	912	957	652	728	777	813	843	883	538	602	642	672	697	730
$70,000	$80,000	757	846	903	946	981	1029	703	786	839	878	910	954	578	646	690	722	749	785
$80,000	$90,000	806	901	962	1008	1046	1097	752	840	897	939	973	1020	616	688	734	769	797	836
$90,000	$100,000	853	953	1018	1067	1106	1161	798	892	952	997	1033	1083	651	727	776	813	843	884
$100,000	$120,000	915	1023	1093	1145	1188	1246	859	961	1025	1074	1113	1167	698	780	833	872	904	948
$120,000	$140,000	996	1114	1190	1247	1294	1357	941	1052	1123	1176	1219	1278	759	849	906	949	984	1032
$140,000	$160,000	1072	1199	1281	1343	1393	1462	1017	1137	1214	1272	1318	1382	817	913	975	1021	1059	1110
$160,000	$180,000	1143	1278	1366	1431	1485	1558	1088	1217	1299	1361	1411	1479	870	973	1038	1088	1128	1183
$180,000	$200,000	1210	1353	1446	1515	1572	1650	1156	1292	1380	1446	1499	1572	920	1029	1099	1151	1193	1251
$200,000	$225,000	1279	1431	1529	1603	1663	1745	1227	1372	1465	1535	1592	1669	973	1088	1162	1217	1262	1323
$225,000	$250,000	1354	1515	1619	1698	1761	1848	1303	1458	1557	1631	1692	1774	1030	1152	1230	1288	1336	1401
$250,000	$275,000	1425	1595	1704	1787	1854	1946	1376	1540	1644	1723	1787	1874	1083	1212	1294	1356	1406	1474
$275,000	$300,000	1493	1671	1786	1872	1942	2039	1446	1618	1728	1811	1878	1969	1134	1269	1355	1420	1472	1544
$300,000	or more	1898	2125	2272	2383	2473	2596	1870	2093	2236	2343	2430	2549	1441	1612	1722	1805	1872	1963

Income At least	Income But less than	1	2	3	4	5	Over 5
		Wyoming			1		4.0000%
$0	$20,000	181	197	207	215	221	229
$20,000	$30,000	273	298	313	324	334	346
$30,000	$40,000	321	350	368	382	393	407
$40,000	$50,000	363	395	416	431	444	460
$50,000	$60,000	400	436	459	475	489	507
$60,000	$70,000	433	472	497	515	530	550
$70,000	$80,000	464	506	532	552	568	589
$80,000	$90,000	493	537	565	586	603	626
$90,000	$100,000	520	567	596	618	636	660
$100,000	$120,000	555	606	637	661	680	705
$120,000	$140,000	602	657	691	717	737	765
$140,000	$160,000	645	704	741	768	790	820
$160,000	$180,000	686	748	787	816	839	871
$180,000	$200,000	723	789	830	861	886	919
$200,000	$225,000	763	832	876	908	934	970
$225,000	$250,000	805	878	924	959	986	1023
$250,000	$275,000	845	922	970	1006	1035	1074
$275,000	$300,000	883	963	1014	1051	1082	1123
$300,000	or more	1107	1209	1272	1320	1358	1409

Note: Residents of **Alaska** do not have a state sales tax, but should follow the instructions on the next page to determine their local sales tax amount.

1. Use the Ratio Method to determine your local sales tax deduction. Your state sales tax rate is provided next to the state name.
2. Follow the instructions on the next page to determine your local sales tax deduction.
3. The California table includes the 1.25% uniform local sales tax rate in addition to the 6.00% state sales tax rate for a total of 7.25%. Some California localities impose a larger local sales tax. Taxpayers who reside in those jurisdictions should use the Ratio Method to determine their local sales tax deduction. The denominator of the correct ratio is 7.25%, and the numerator is the total sales tax rate minus 7.25%.
4. This state does not have a local general sales tax, so the amount in the state table is the only amount to be deducted.
5. The Nevada table includes the 2.25% uniform local sales tax rate in addition to the 4.60% state sales tax rate for a total of 6.85%. Some Nevada localities impose a larger local sales tax. Taxpayers who reside in those jurisdictions should use the Ratio Method to determine their local sales tax deduction. The denominator of the correct ratio is 6.85%, and the numerator is the total sales tax rate minus 6.85%.
6. The 4.0% rate for Hawaii is actually an excise tax but is treated as a sales tax for purpose of this deduction.

Which Optional Local Sales Tax Table Should I Use?

IF you live in the state of…	AND you live in…	THEN use Local Table…
Alaska	Juneau, Kenai, Ketchikan, Kodiak, Sitka, Wasilla or any locality that imposes a local sales tax	C
Arizona	Mesa, Phoenix, Tucson	A
	Chandler, Gilbert, Glendale, Peoria, Scottsdale, Tempe, Yuma or any other locality that imposes a local sales tax	B
Arkansas	Any locality that imposes a local sales tax	C
Colorado	Adams County, Arapahoe County, Aurora, Boulder County, Centennial, Colorado Springs, Denver City, El Paso County, Larimer County, Pueblo City, Pueblo County or any other locality that imposes a local sales tax	A
	Arvada, Boulder, Fort Collins, Greeley, Jefferson County, Lakewood, Longmont, Thornton or Westminster	B
Georgia	Dekalb County (excluding Atlanta)	B
	Any locality that imposes a local sales tax	C
Illinois	Arlington Heights, Bloomington, Champaign, Chicago, Cicero, Decatur, Evanston, Palatine, Peoria, Schaumburg, Skokie, Springfield or any other locality that imposes a local sales tax	A
	Aurora, Elgin, Joliet, Waukegan	B
Louisiana	East Baton Rouge Parish, Jefferson Parish	B
	Ascension Parish, Bossier Parish, Caddo Parish, Calcasieu Parish, Iberia Parish, Lafayette Parish, Lafourche Parish, Livingston Parish, Orleans Parish, Ouachita Parish, Rapides Parish, St. Bernard Parish, St. Landry Parish, St Tammany Parish, Tangipahoa Parish, Terrebonne Parish or any other locality that imposes a local sales tax	C
Mississippi	City of Jackson only	A
	City of Tupelo only	C
Missouri	Any locality that imposes a local sales tax	C
New York	Counties: Chautauqua, Chenango, Columbia, Delaware, Greene, Hamilton, Tioga Cities: New York, Norwich (Chenango County)	A
	Counties: Albany, Allegany, Broome, Cattaraugus, Cayuga, Chemung, Clinton, Cortland, Dutchess, Erie, Essex, Franklin, Fulton, Genesee, Herkimer, Jefferson, Lewis, Livingston, Madison, Monroe, Montgomery, Nassau, Niagara, Oneida, Onondaga, Ontario, Orange, Orleans, Oswego, Otsego, Putnam, Rensselaer, Rockland, St. Lawrence, Saratoga, Schenectady, Schoharie, Schuyler, Seneca, Steuben, Suffolk, Sullivan, Tompkins, Ulster, Warren, Washington, Wayne, Westchester, Wyoming or Yate Cities: Auburn, Glens Falls, Gloversville, Ithaca, Johnstown, Mount Vernon, New Rochelle, Olean, Oneida (Madison County), Oswego, Rome, Salamanca, Saratoga Springs, Utica, White Plains, Yonkers	B
	Any other locality that imposes a local sales tax	D*
North Carolina	Any locality that imposes a local sales tax	A
South Carolina	Aiken County, Anderson County, Greenwood County, Horry County, Lexington County, Myrtle Beach, Newberry County, Orangeburg County, Spartanburg County and York County	A
	Allendale County, Bamberg County, Barnwell County, Calhoun County, Charleston County, Cherokee County, Chester County, Chesterfield County, Colleton County, Darlington County, Dillon County, Edgefield County, Florence County, Hampton County, Jasper County, Kershaw County, Lancaster County, Laurens County, Lee County, Marion County, Marlboro County, McCormick County, Saluda County, Sumter County and Williamsburg County	B
	Abbeville County, Beaufort County, Berkeley County, Clarendon County, Dorchester County, Fairfield County, Pickens County, Richland County, Union County or any other locality that imposes a local sales tax	C
Tennessee	Any locality that imposes a local sales tax	C
Utah	Any locality that imposes a local sales tax	A
Virginia	Any locality that imposes a local sales tax	B

*** Note: Local Table D is just 25% of the NY State table.**

2021 Optional Local Sales Tax Tables

Income		Family Size						Family Size						Family Size						Family Size					
At least	But less than	1	2	3	4	5	Over 5	1	2	3	4	5	Over 5	1	2	3	4	5	Over 5	1	2	3	4	5	Over 5
		Local Table A						Local Table B						Local Table C						Local Table D					
$0	$20,000	42	45	48	49	50	52	53	61	65	69	72	76	65	75	82	87	91	97	38	39	40	41	41	42
20,000	30,000	64	69	72	75	76	79	78	89	96	101	106	112	94	109	118	126	132	140	61	63	64	65	66	67
30,000	40,000	75	81	85	88	90	93	90	103	111	118	123	130	109	126	137	146	153	163	74	76	78	79	80	81
40,000	50,000	85	92	96	99	102	105	101	115	125	132	138	146	122	141	153	163	171	182	85	88	90	91	92	93
50,000	60,000	94	101	106	110	113	116	111	126	136	144	151	159	133	154	167	178	186	198	95	99	101	102	103	105
60,000	70,000	102	110	115	119	122	126	119	136	147	155	162	172	143	165	180	191	200	213	105	108	110	112	113	115
70,000	80,000	109	118	123	128	131	135	127	145	157	165	173	183	152	176	192	203	213	227	114	117	120	121	123	125
80,000	90,000	116	125	131	136	139	144	134	153	165	175	183	193	161	186	202	215	225	240	122	126	129	130	132	134
90,000	100,000	122	132	138	143	147	152	141	161	174	184	192	203	169	195	212	225	236	251	130	134	137	139	140	142
100,000	120,000	131	141	148	153	157	162	150	171	185	195	204	216	179	207	225	239	251	267	141	145	148	150	152	154
120,000	140,000	142	154	161	166	170	176	161	184	199	211	220	233	193	223	242	258	270	287	155	160	163	165	167	169
140,000	160,000	152	165	173	178	183	189	172	196	212	225	234	248	205	237	258	274	288	306	168	174	177	179	181	184
160,000	180,000	162	175	183	189	194	201	182	208	225	237	248	262	217	250	273	290	304	323	180	186	190	193	195	197
180,000	200,000	171	185	194	200	205	212	191	218	236	249	260	276	228	263	286	304	319	339	192	199	203	205	208	210
200,000	225,000	180	195	204	211	217	224	201	229	248	262	274	290	239	276	300	319	335	356	205	212	216	219	221	224
225,000	250,000	190	206	216	223	229	237	211	241	260	275	288	304	251	290	315	335	351	374	218	226	230	233	236	239
250,000	275,000	200	216	227	234	240	248	221	252	272	288	301	318	262	302	329	350	367	390	231	239	244	247	250	253
275,000	300,000	209	226	237	245	251	260	230	262	284	300	313	331	272	315	343	364	382	406	244	252	257	260	263	267
300,000	or more	263	285	298	308	316	327	283	323	350	370	386	409	334	386	421	447	469	499	320	330	337	341	345	349

Tax Formula for Corporations

Income *(from whatever source)*.	$ xxx,xxx
Less: Exclusions from gross income.	– xx,xxx
Gross Income.	$ xxx,xxx
Less: Deductions.	– xx,xxx
Taxable Income.	$ xxx,xxx
Applicable tax rates.	× xx%
Gross Tax.	$ xx,xxx
Less: Tax credits and prepayments.	– x,xxx
Tax Due *(or refund)*.	$ xx,xxx

Income Tax Rates—C Corporations, 2018 and After

For all taxable income levels, the tax rate is 21%.

Income Tax Rates—Estates and Trusts

Tax Year 2021

Taxable Income		The Tax Is:	
Over—	**But not Over—**		**Of the Amount Over—**
$ 0	$ 2,650	10%	$ 0
2,650	9,550	$ 265.00 + 24%	2,650
9,550	13,050	1,921.00 + 35%	9,550
13,050	....	3,146.00 + 37%	13,050

Tax Year 2022

Taxable Income		The Tax Is:	
Over—	**But not Over—**		**Of the Amount Over—**
$ 0	$ 2,750	10%	$ 0
2,750	9,850	$ 275.00 + 24%	2,750
9,850	13,450	1,979.00 + 35%	9,850
13,450	....	3,239.00 + 37%	13,450

Unified Transfer Tax Rates

For Gifts Made and for Deaths After 2012

If the Amount with Respect to Which the Tentative Tax to Be Computed Is:	The Tentative Tax Is:
Not over $10,000	18 percent of such amount.
Over $10,000 but not over $20,000	$1,800, plus 20 percent of the excess of such amount over $10,000.
Over $20,000 but not over $40,000	$3,800, plus 22 percent of the excess of such amount over $20,000.
Over $40,000 but not over $60,000	$8,200, plus 24 percent of the excess of such amount over $40,000.
Over $60,000 but not over $80,000	$13,000, plus 26 percent of the excess of such amount over $60,000.
Over $80,000 but not over $100,000	$18,200, plus 28 percent of the excess of such amount over $80,000.
Over $100,000 but not over $150,000	$23,800, plus 30 percent of the excess of such amount over $100,000.
Over $150,000 but not over $250,000	$38,800, plus 32 percent of the excess of such amount over $150,000.
Over $250,000 but not over $500,000	$70,800, plus 34 percent of the excess of such amount over $250,000.
Over $500,000 but not over $750,000	$155,800, plus 37 percent of the excess of such amount over $500,000.
Over $750,000 but not over $1,000,000	$248,300, plus 39 percent of the excess of such amount over $750,000.
Over $1,000,000	$345,800, plus 40 percent of the excess of such amount over $1,000,000.

Valuation Tables, Excerpts

Table S: Single Life Remainder Factors Interest Rate

AGE	4.2%	4.4%	4.6%	4.8%	5.0%	5.2%	5.4%	5.6%
0	.06083	.05483	.04959	.04501	.04101	.03749	.03441	.03170
1	.05668	.05049	.04507	.04034	.03618	.03254	.02934	.02652
2	.05858	.05222	.04665	.04178	.03750	.03373	.03042	.02750
3	.06072	.05420	.04848	.04346	.03904	.03516	.03173	.02871
4	.06303	.05634	.05046	.04530	.04075	.03674	.03319	.03006
5	.06547	.05861	.05258	.04726	.04258	.03844	.03478	.03153
6	.06805	.06102	.05482	.04935	.04453	.04026	.03647	.03312
7	.07074	.06353	.05717	.05155	.04658	.04217	.03826	.03479
8	.07356	.06617	.05964	.05386	.04875	.04421	.04017	.03658
9	.07651	.06895	.06225	.05631	.05105	.04637	.04220	.03849
10	.07960	.07185	.06499	.05889	.05347	.04865	.04435	.04052
11	.08283	.07490	.06786	.06160	.05603	.05106	.04663	.04267
12	.08620	.07808	.07087	.06444	.05871	.05360	.04903	.04494
13	.08967	.08137	.07397	.06738	.06149	.05623	.05152	.04729
14	.09321	.08472	.07715	.07038	.06433	.05892	.05406	.04971
15	.09680	.08812	.08036	.07342	.06721	.06164	.05664	.05214
16	.10041	.09154	.08360	.07649	.07011	.06438	.05923	.05459
17	.10409	.09502	.08689	.07960	.07305	.06716	.06185	.05707
18	.10782	.09855	.09024	.08276	.07604	.06998	.06452	.05959
19	.11164	.10217	.09366	.08600	.07910	.07288	.06726	.06218
20	.11559	.10592	.09721	.08937	.08228	.07589	.07010	.06487
21	.11965	.10977	.10087	.09283	.08557	.07900	.07305	.06765
22	.12383	.11376	.10465	.09642	.08897	.08223	.07610	.07055
23	.12817	.11789	.10859	.10016	.09252	.08559	.07930	.07358
24	.13270	.12221	.11270	.10408	.09625	.08914	.08267	.07678
25	.13744	.12674	.11703	.10821	.10019	.09289	.08625	.08018
26	.14239	.13149	.12158	.11256	.10435	.09686	.09003	.08380
27	.14758	.13647	.12636	.11714	.10873	.10106	.09405	.08764
28	.15300	.14169	.13137	.12195	.11335	.10549	.09829	.09171
29	.15864	.14712	.13660	.12698	.11819	.11013	.10275	.09598
30	.16448	.15275	.14203	.13222	.12323	.11498	.10742	.10047
31	.17053	.15861	.14769	.13768	.12849	.12006	.11230	.10517
32	.17680	.16468	.15357	.14336	.13398	.12535	.11741	.11009
33	.18330	.17099	.15968	.14927	.13970	.13088	.12275	.11525
34	.19000	.17750	.16599	.15539	.14562	.13661	.12829	.12061

continued

Valuation Tables, Excerpts

Table S: Single Life Remainder Factors Interest Rate

AGE	4.2%	4.4%	4.6%	4.8%	5.0%	5.2%	5.4%	5.6%
35	.19692	.18423	.17253	.16174	.15178	.14258	.13408	.12621
36	.20407	.19119	.17931	.16833	.15818	.14879	.14009	.13204
37	.21144	.19838	.18631	.17515	.16481	.15523	.14635	.13811
38	.21904	.20582	.19357	.18222	.17170	.16193	.15287	.14444
39	.22687	.21348	.20105	.18952	.17882	.16887	.15962	.15102
40	.23493	.22137	.20878	.19707	.18619	.17606	.16663	.15784
41	.24322	.22950	.21674	.20487	.19381	.18350	.17390	.16493
42	.25173	.23786	.22494	.21290	.20168	.19120	.18141	.17227
43	.26049	.24648	.23342	.22122	.20982	.19918	.18922	.17990
44	.26950	.25535	.24214	.22979	.21824	.20742	.19730	.18781
45	.27874	.26447	.25112	.23862	.22692	.21595	.20566	.19600
46	.28824	.27385	.26038	.24774	.23589	.22476	.21431	.20450
47	.29798	.28349	.26989	.25712	.24513	.23386	.22326	.21328
48	.30797	.29338	.27967	.26678	.25466	.24325	.23250	.22238
49	.31822	.30355	.28974	.27674	.26449	.25294	.24206	.23179
50	.32876	.31401	.30011	.28701	.27465	.26298	.25196	.24156
51	.33958	.32477	.31079	.29759	.28513	.27335	.26221	.25168
52	.35068	.33582	.32178	.30851	.29595	.28407	.27282	.26216
53	.36206	.34717	.33308	.31974	.30710	.29513	.28378	.27301
54	.37371	.35880	.34467	.33127	.31857	.30651	.29507	.28420
55	.38559	.37067	.35652	.34308	.33032	.31820	.30668	.29572
56	.39765	.38275	.36859	.35512	.34232	.33014	.31855	.30751
57	.40990	.39502	.38086	.36739	.35455	.34233	.33068	.31957
58	.42231	.40747	.39333	.37985	.36700	.35474	.34304	.33188
59	.43490	.42011	.40600	.39253	.37968	.36740	.35567	.34446
60	.44768	.43296	.41890	.40546	.39261	.38033	.36858	.35733
61	.46064	.44600	.43200	.41860	.40578	.39351	.38175	.37048
62	.47373	.45920	.44527	.43194	.41915	.40690	.39514	.38387
63	.48696	.47253	.45870	.44544	.43271	.42049	.40876	.39749
64	.50030	.48601	.47229	.45911	.44645	.43428	.42258	.41133
65	.51377	.49963	.48603	.47295	.46037	.44827	.43662	.42540
66	.52750	.51352	.50007	.48711	.47464	.46262	.45103	.43987
67	.54144	.52765	.51436	.50154	.48919	.47727	.46578	.45468
68	.55554	.54196	.52885	.51619	.50398	.49218	.48079	.46978
69	.56976	.55640	.54349	.53102	.51896	.50731	.49603	.48513

Valuation Tables, Excerpts

Table B: Term Certain Remainder Factors Interest Rate

YEARS	4.2%	4.4%	4.6%	4.8%	5.0%	5.2%	5.4%	5.6%
1	.959693	.957854	.956023	.954198	.952381	.950570	.948767	.946970
2	.921010	.917485	.913980	.910495	.907029	.903584	.900158	.896752
3	.883887	.878817	.873786	.868793	.863838	.858920	.854040	.849197
4	.848260	.841779	.835359	.829001	.822702	.816464	.810285	.804163
5	.814069	.806302	.798623	.791031	.783526	.776106	.768771	.761518
6	.781257	.772320	.763501	.754801	.746215	.737744	.729384	.721135
7	.749766	.739770	.729925	.720230	.710681	.701277	.692015	.682893
8	.719545	.708592	.697825	.687242	.676839	.666613	.656561	.646679
9	.690543	.678728	.667137	.655765	.644609	.633663	.622923	.612385
10	.662709	.650122	.637798	.625730	.613913	.602341	.591009	.579910
11	.635997	.622722	.609750	.597071	.584679	.572568	.560729	.549157
12	.610362	.596477	.582935	.569724	.556837	.544266	.532001	.520035
13	.585760	.571339	.557299	.543630	.530321	.517363	.504745	.492458
14	.562150	.547259	.532790	.518731	.505068	.491790	.478885	.466343
15	.539491	.524195	.509360	.494972	.481017	.467481	.454350	.441612
16	.517746	.502102	.486960	.472302	.458112	.444374	.431072	.418194
17	.496877	.480941	.465545	.450670	.436297	.422408	.408987	.396017
18	.476849	.460671	.445071	.430028	.415521	.401529	.388033	.375016
19	.457629	.441256	.425498	.410332	.395734	.381681	.368153	.355129
20	.439183	.422659	.406786	.391538	.376889	.362815	.349291	.336296
21	.421481	.404846	.388897	.373605	.358942	.344881	.331396	.318462
22	.404492	.387783	.371794	.356494	.341850	.327834	.314417	.301574
23	.388188	.371440	.355444	.340166	.325571	.311629	.298309	.285581
24	.372542	.355785	.339813	.324586	.310068	.296225	.283025	.270437
25	.357526	.340791	.324869	.309719	.295303	.281583	.268525	.256096
26	.343115	.326428	.310582	.295533	.281241	.267664	.254768	.242515
27	.329285	.312670	.296923	.281998	.267848	.254434	.241715	.229654
28	.316012	.299493	.283866	.269082	.255094	.241857	.229331	.217475
29	.303275	.286870	.271382	.256757	.242946	.229902	.217582	.205943
30	.291051	.274780	.259447	.244997	.231377	.218538	.206434	.195021
31	.279319	.263199	.248038	.233776	.220359	.207736	.195858	.184679
32	.268061	.252106	.237130	.223069	.209866	.197468	.185823	.174886
33	.257256	.241481	.226702	.212852	.199873	.187707	.176303	.165612
34	.246887	.231304	.216732	.203103	.190355	.178429	.167270	.156829
35	.236935	.221556	.207201	.193801	.181290	.169609	.158701	.148512

AMT Formula for Individuals

Taxable income (increased by any standard deduction taken)
Plus or minus: Adjustments
Plus: Preferences
Equals: Alternative minimum taxable income (AMTI)
Minus: Exemption
Equals: Alternative minimum tax (AMT) base
Multiplied by: 26% or 28% rate
Equals: Tentative minimum tax before foreign tax credit
Minus: AMT foreign tax credit
Equals: Tentative minimum tax (TMT)
Minus: Regular tax liability (less any foreign tax credit)
Equals: AMT (if TMT > regular tax liability)

2021 AMT Exemption and Phaseout for Individuals

		Phaseout	
Filing Status	**Exemption**	**Begins at**	**Ends at**
Married, filing jointly	$114,600	$1,047,200	$1,505,600
Single or Head of household	73,600	523,600	818,000
Married, filing separately	57,300	523,600	752,800

2022 AMT Exemption and Phaseout for Individuals

		Phaseout	
Filing Status	**Exemption**	**Begins at**	**Ends at**
Married, filing jointly	$118,100	$1,079,800	$1,552,200
Single or Head of household	75,900	539,900	843,500
Married, filing separately	59,050	539,900	776,100

Appendix B

Tax Forms

In addition to reviewing and using the IRS tax forms in your study of taxation, also consider reviewing the comparable forms from the tax agency in your state (usually called the Department of Revenue). A list of state tax agency links is available at **aicpa.org/research/externallinks/taxesstatesdepartmentsofrevenue.html**. This can help you see some of the differences between Federal and state income tax rules, as well as similarities. More Federal tax forms can be found at **irs.gov/forms-instructions**.

Form	Title	Page
Form 1040	U.S. Individual Income Tax Return (pages 1 and 2)	B-2
Schedule 1	Additional Income and Adjustments to Income	B-4
Schedule 2	Additional Taxes	B-6
Schedule 3	Additional Credits and Payments	B-8
Schedule A	Itemized Deductions	B-10
Schedule B	Interest and Ordinary Dividends	B-11
Schedule C	Profit or Loss from Business	B-12
Schedule D	Capital Gains and Losses	B-14
Schedule E	Supplemental Income and Loss	B-16
Schedule SE	Self-Employment Tax	B-18
Form 4562	Depreciation and Amortization	B-19
Form 4797	Sales of Business Property	B-21
Form 8949	Sales and Other Dispositions of Capital Assets	B-23
Form 8995	Qualified Business Income Deduction Simplified Computation	B-25
Form 8995–A	Qualified Business Income Deduction	B-26

Form **1040** Department of the Treasury—Internal Revenue Service (99)
U.S. Individual Income Tax Return 2021
OMB No. 1545-0074 IRS Use Only—Do not write or staple in this space.

Filing Status Check only one box.
☐ Single ☐ Married filing jointly ☐ Married filing separately (MFS) ☐ Head of household (HOH) ☐ Qualifying widow(er) (QW)
If you checked the MFS box, enter the name of your spouse. If you checked the HOH or QW box, enter the child's name if the qualifying person is a child but not your dependent ▶

Your first name and middle initial	Last name	**Your social security number**
If joint return, spouse's first name and middle initial	Last name	**Spouse's social security number**

Home address (number and street). If you have a P.O. box, see instructions.			Apt. no.
City, town, or post office. If you have a foreign address, also complete spaces below.		State	ZIP code
Foreign country name	Foreign province/state/county		Foreign postal code

Presidential Election Campaign Check here if you, or your spouse if filing jointly, want $3 to go to this fund. Checking a box below will not change your tax or refund. ☐ **You** ☐ **Spouse**

At any time during 2021, did you receive, sell, exchange, or otherwise dispose of any financial interest in any virtual currency? ☐ **Yes** ☐ **No**

Standard Deduction **Someone can claim:** ☐ You as a dependent ☐ Your spouse as a dependent
☐ Spouse itemizes on a separate return or you were a dual-status alien

Age/Blindness **You:** ☐ Were born before January 2, 1957 ☐ Are blind **Spouse:** ☐ Was born before January 2, 1957 ☐ Is blind

Dependents (see instructions):
If more than four dependents, see instructions and check here ▶ ☐

(1) First name Last name	**(2)** Social security number	**(3)** Relationship to you	**(4)** ✔ if qualifies for (see instructions): Child tax credit	Credit for other dependents
			☐	☐
			☐	☐
			☐	☐
			☐	☐

Attach Sch. B if required.

1	Wages, salaries, tips, etc. Attach Form(s) W-2			1	
2a	Tax-exempt interest	2a	**b** Taxable interest	2b	
3a	Qualified dividends	3a	**b** Ordinary dividends	3b	
4a	IRA distributions	4a	**b** Taxable amount	4b	
5a	Pensions and annuities	5a	**b** Taxable amount	5b	
6a	Social security benefits	6a	**b** Taxable amount	6b	
7	Capital gain or (loss). Attach Schedule D if required. If not required, check here ▶ ☐			7	
8	Other income from Schedule 1, line 10			8	
9	Add lines 1, 2b, 3b, 4b, 5b, 6b, 7, and 8. This is your **total income** ▶			9	
10	Adjustments to income from Schedule 1, line 26			10	
11	Subtract line 10 from line 9. This is your **adjusted gross income** ▶			11	
12a	**Standard deduction or itemized deductions** (from Schedule A)	12a			
b	Charitable contributions if you take the standard deduction (see instructions)	12b			
c	Add lines 12a and 12b			12c	
13	Qualified business income deduction from Form 8995 or Form 8995-A			13	
14	Add lines 12c and 13			14	
15	**Taxable income.** Subtract line 14 from line 11. If zero or less, enter -0-			15	

Standard Deduction for—
- Single or Married filing separately, $12,550
- Married filing jointly or Qualifying widow(er), $25,100
- Head of household, $18,800
- If you checked any box under *Standard Deduction,* see instructions.

For Disclosure, Privacy Act, and Paperwork Reduction Act Notice, see separate instructions. Cat. No. 11320B Form **1040** (2021)

Form 1040 (2021) Page **2**

16	**Tax** (see instructions). Check if any from Form(s): 1 ☐ 8814 2 ☐ 4972 3 ☐ ______	16	
17	Amount from Schedule 2, line 3	17	
18	Add lines 16 and 17	18	
19	Nonrefundable child tax credit or credit for other dependents from Schedule 8812	19	
20	Amount from Schedule 3, line 8	20	
21	Add lines 19 and 20	21	
22	Subtract line 21 from line 18. If zero or less, enter -0-	22	
23	Other taxes, including self-employment tax, from Schedule 2, line 21	23	
24	Add lines 22 and 23. This is your **total tax** ▶	24	
25	Federal income tax withheld from:		
a	Form(s) W-2 — 25a		
b	Form(s) 1099 — 25b		
c	Other forms (see instructions) — 25c		
d	Add lines 25a through 25c	25d	
26	2021 estimated tax payments and amount applied from 2020 return	26	
27a	Earned income credit (EIC) — 27a		
	Check here if you were born after January 1, 1998, and before January 2, 2004, and you satisfy all the other requirements for taxpayers who are at least age 18, to claim the EIC. See instructions ▶ ☐		
b	Nontaxable combat pay election — 27b		
c	Prior year (2019) earned income — 27c		
28	Refundable child tax credit or additional child tax credit from Schedule 8812 — 28		
29	American opportunity credit from Form 8863, line 8 — 29		
30	Recovery rebate credit. See instructions — 30		
31	Amount from Schedule 3, line 15 — 31		
32	Add lines 27a and 28 through 31. These are your **total other payments and refundable credits** ▶	32	
33	Add lines 25d, 26, and 32. These are your **total payments** ▶	33	

If you have a qualifying child, attach Sch. EIC.

Refund

Direct deposit? See instructions.

34	If line 33 is more than line 24, subtract line 24 from line 33. This is the amount you **overpaid**	34	
35a	Amount of line 34 you want **refunded to you.** If Form 8888 is attached, check here ▶ ☐	35a	
▶ b	Routing number ________ ▶ c Type: ☐ Checking ☐ Savings		
▶ d	Account number ________		
36	Amount of line 34 you want **applied to your 2022 estimated tax** ▶ 36		

Amount You Owe

37	**Amount you owe.** Subtract line 33 from line 24. For details on how to pay, see instructions ▶	37	
38	Estimated tax penalty (see instructions) ▶ 38		

Third Party Designee

Do you want to allow another person to discuss this return with the IRS? See instructions ▶ ☐ **Yes.** Complete below. ☐ **No**

Designee's name ▶ | Phone no. ▶ | Personal identification number (PIN) ▶

Sign Here

Under penalties of perjury, I declare that I have examined this return and accompanying schedules and statements, and to the best of my knowledge and belief, they are true, correct, and complete. Declaration of preparer (other than taxpayer) is based on all information of which preparer has any knowledge.

Joint return? See instructions. Keep a copy for your records.

Your signature	Date	Your occupation	If the IRS sent you an Identity Protection PIN, enter it here (see inst.) ▶
Spouse's signature. If a joint return, **both** must sign.	Date	Spouse's occupation	If the IRS sent your spouse an Identity Protection PIN, enter it here (see inst.) ▶
Phone no.	Email address		

Paid Preparer Use Only

Preparer's name	Preparer's signature	Date	PTIN	Check if: ☐ Self-employed
Firm's name ▶			Phone no.	
Firm's address ▶			Firm's EIN ▶	

Go to *www.irs.gov/Form1040* for instructions and the latest information. Form **1040** (2021)

SCHEDULE 1 (Form 1040)

Department of the Treasury
Internal Revenue Service

Additional Income and Adjustments to Income

▶ Attach to Form 1040, 1040-SR, or 1040-NR.
▶ Go to *www.irs.gov/Form1040* for instructions and the latest information.

OMB No. 1545-0074

2021

Attachment Sequence No. **01**

Name(s) shown on Form 1040, 1040-SR, or 1040-NR	**Your social security number**

Part I Additional Income

1	Taxable refunds, credits, or offsets of state and local income taxes			1	
2a	Alimony received			2a	
b	Date of original divorce or separation agreement (see instructions) ▶ ________				
3	Business income or (loss). Attach Schedule C			3	
4	Other gains or (losses). Attach Form 4797			4	
5	Rental real estate, royalties, partnerships, S corporations, trusts, etc. Attach Schedule E			5	
6	Farm income or (loss). Attach Schedule F			6	
7	Unemployment compensation			7	
8	Other income:				
a	Net operating loss	8a	( )		
b	Gambling income	8b			
c	Cancellation of debt	8c			
d	Foreign earned income exclusion from Form 2555	8d	( )		
e	Taxable Health Savings Account distribution	8e			
f	Alaska Permanent Fund dividends	8f			
g	Jury duty pay	8g			
h	Prizes and awards	8h			
i	Activity not engaged in for profit income	8i			
j	Stock options	8j			
k	Income from the rental of personal property if you engaged in the rental for profit but were not in the business of renting such property	8k			
l	Olympic and Paralympic medals and USOC prize money (see instructions)	8l			
m	Section 951(a) inclusion (see instructions)	8m			
n	Section 951A(a) inclusion (see instructions)	8n			
o	Section 461(l) excess business loss adjustment	8o			
p	Taxable distributions from an ABLE account (see instructions)	8p			
z	Other income. List type and amount ▶ ________	8z			
9	Total other income. Add lines 8a through 8z			9	
10	Combine lines 1 through 7 and 9. Enter here and on Form 1040, 1040-SR, or 1040-NR, line 8			10	

Schedule 1 (Form 1040) 2021 Page **2**

Part II Adjustments to Income

11	Educator expenses	11	
12	Certain business expenses of reservists, performing artists, and fee-basis government officials. Attach Form 2106	12	
13	Health savings account deduction. Attach Form 8889	13	
14	Moving expenses for members of the Armed Forces. Attach Form 3903	14	
15	Deductible part of self-employment tax. Attach Schedule SE	15	
16	Self-employed SEP, SIMPLE, and qualified plans	16	
17	Self-employed health insurance deduction	17	
18	Penalty on early withdrawal of savings	18	
19a	Alimony paid	19a	
b	Recipient's SSN ▶		
c	Date of original divorce or separation agreement (see instructions) ▶		
20	IRA deduction	20	
21	Student loan interest deduction	21	
22	Reserved for future use	22	
23	Archer MSA deduction	23	
24	Other adjustments:		
a	Jury duty pay (see instructions)	24a	
b	Deductible expenses related to income reported on line 8k from the rental of personal property engaged in for profit	24b	
c	Nontaxable amount of the value of Olympic and Paralympic medals and USOC prize money reported on line 8l	24c	
d	Reforestation amortization and expenses	24d	
e	Repayment of supplemental unemployment benefits under the Trade Act of 1974	24e	
f	Contributions to section 501(c)(18)(D) pension plans	24f	
g	Contributions by certain chaplains to section 403(b) plans	24g	
h	Attorney fees and court costs for actions involving certain unlawful discrimination claims (see instructions)	24h	
i	Attorney fees and court costs you paid in connection with an award from the IRS for information you provided that helped the IRS detect tax law violations	24i	
j	Housing deduction from Form 2555	24j	
k	Excess deductions of section 67(e) expenses from Schedule K-1 (Form 1041)	24k	
z	Other adjustments. List type and amount ▶	24z	
25	Total other adjustments. Add lines 24a through 24z	25	
26	Add lines 11 through 23 and 25. These are your **adjustments to income.** Enter here and on Form 1040 or 1040-SR, line 10, or Form 1040-NR, line 10a	26	

SCHEDULE 2 (Form 1040)

Department of the Treasury Internal Revenue Service

Additional Taxes

▶ Attach to Form 1040, 1040-SR, or 1040-NR.

▶ Go to *www.irs.gov/Form1040* for instructions and the latest information.

OMB No. 1545-0074

2021

Attachment Sequence No. **02**

Name(s) shown on Form 1040, 1040-SR, or 1040-NR | **Your social security number**

Part I Tax

1	Alternative minimum tax. Attach Form 6251			1	
2	Excess advance premium tax credit repayment. Attach Form 8962			2	
3	Add lines 1 and 2. Enter here and on Form 1040, 1040-SR, or 1040-NR, line 17			3	

Part II Other Taxes

4	Self-employment tax. Attach Schedule SE			4	
5	Social security and Medicare tax on unreported tip income. Attach Form 4137	5			
6	Uncollected social security and Medicare tax on wages. Attach Form 8919	6			
7	Total additional social security and Medicare tax. Add lines 5 and 6			7	
8	Additional tax on IRAs or other tax-favored accounts. Attach Form 5329 if required			8	
9	Household employment taxes. Attach Schedule H			9	
10	Repayment of first-time homebuyer credit. Attach Form 5405 if required			10	
11	Additional Medicare Tax. Attach Form 8959			11	
12	Net investment income tax. Attach Form 8960			12	
13	Uncollected social security and Medicare or RRTA tax on tips or group-term life insurance from Form W-2, box 12			13	
14	Interest on tax due on installment income from the sale of certain residential lots and timeshares			14	
15	Interest on the deferred tax on gain from certain installment sales with a sales price over $150,000			15	
16	Recapture of low-income housing credit. Attach Form 8611			16	

(continued on page 2)

Schedule 2 (Form 1040) 2021 Page **2**

Part II Other Taxes *(continued)*

17	Other additional taxes:			
a	Recapture of other credits. List type, form number, and amount ▶ ________	**17a**		
b	Recapture of federal mortgage subsidy. If you sold your home in 2021, see instructions	**17b**		
c	Additional tax on HSA distributions. Attach Form 8889	**17c**		
d	Additional tax on an HSA because you didn't remain an eligible individual. Attach Form 8889	**17d**		
e	Additional tax on Archer MSA distributions. Attach Form 8853	**17e**		
f	Additional tax on Medicare Advantage MSA distributions. Attach Form 8853	**17f**		
g	Recapture of a charitable contribution deduction related to a fractional interest in tangible personal property	**17g**		
h	Income you received from a nonqualified deferred compensation plan that fails to meet the requirements of section 409A	**17h**		
i	Compensation you received from a nonqualified deferred compensation plan described in section 457A	**17i**		
j	Section 72(m)(5) excess benefits tax	**17j**		
k	Golden parachute payments	**17k**		
l	Tax on accumulation distribution of trusts	**17l**		
m	Excise tax on insider stock compensation from an expatriated corporation	**17m**		
n	Look-back interest under section 167(g) or 460(b) from Form 8697 or 8866	**17n**		
o	Tax on non-effectively connected income for any part of the year you were a nonresident alien from Form 1040-NR	**17o**		
p	Any interest from Form 8621, line 16f, relating to distributions from, and dispositions of, stock of a section 1291 fund	**17p**		
q	Any interest from Form 8621, line 24	**17q**		
z	Any other taxes. List type and amount ▶ ________	**17z**		
18	Total additional taxes. Add lines 17a through 17z		**18**	
19	Additional tax from Schedule 8812		**19**	
20	Section 965 net tax liability installment from Form 965-A	**20**		
21	Add lines 4, 7 through 16, 18, and 19. These are your **total other taxes.** Enter here and on Form 1040 or 1040-SR, line 23, or Form 1040-NR, line 23b		**21**	

SCHEDULE 3 (Form 1040) Department of the Treasury Internal Revenue Service	**Additional Credits and Payments** ▶ Attach to Form 1040, 1040-SR, or 1040-NR. ▶ Go to *www.irs.gov/Form1040* for instructions and the latest information.	OMB No. 1545-0074 **2021** Attachment Sequence No. **03**

Name(s) shown on Form 1040, 1040-SR, or 1040-NR	**Your social security number**

Part I Nonrefundable Credits

1	Foreign tax credit. Attach Form 1116 if required			1	
2	Credit for child and dependent care expenses from Form 2441, line 11. Attach Form 2441			2	
3	Education credits from Form 8863, line 19			3	
4	Retirement savings contributions credit. Attach Form 8880			4	
5	Residential energy credits. Attach Form 5695			5	
6	Other nonrefundable credits:				
a	General business credit. Attach Form 3800	6a			
b	Credit for prior year minimum tax. Attach Form 8801	6b			
c	Adoption credit. Attach Form 8839	6c			
d	Credit for the elderly or disabled. Attach Schedule R	6d			
e	Alternative motor vehicle credit. Attach Form 8910	6e			
f	Qualified plug-in motor vehicle credit. Attach Form 8936	6f			
g	Mortgage interest credit. Attach Form 8396	6g			
h	District of Columbia first-time homebuyer credit. Attach Form 8859	6h			
i	Qualified electric vehicle credit. Attach Form 8834	6i			
j	Alternative fuel vehicle refueling property credit. Attach Form 8911	6j			
k	Credit to holders of tax credit bonds. Attach Form 8912	6k			
l	Amount on Form 8978, line 14. See instructions	6l			
z	Other nonrefundable credits. List type and amount ▶ ________	6z			
7	Total other nonrefundable credits. Add lines 6a through 6z			7	
8	Add lines 1 through 5 and 7. Enter here and on Form 1040, 1040-SR, or 1040-NR, line 20			8	

(continued on page 2)

Schedule 3 (Form 1040) 2021 Page **2**

Part II Other Payments and Refundable Credits

9	Net premium tax credit. Attach Form 8962	**9**	
10	Amount paid with request for extension to file (see instructions)	**10**	
11	Excess social security and tier 1 RRTA tax withheld	**11**	
12	Credit for federal tax on fuels. Attach Form 4136	**12**	
13	Other payments or refundable credits:		
a	Form 2439 **13a**		
b	Qualified sick and family leave credits from Schedule(s) H and Form(s) 7202 for leave taken before April 1, 2021 **13b**		
c	Health coverage tax credit from Form 8885 **13c**		
d	Credit for repayment of amounts included in income from earlier years **13d**		
e	Reserved for future use **13e**		
f	Deferred amount of net 965 tax liability (see instructions) **13f**		
g	Credit for child and dependent care expenses from Form 2441, line 10. Attach Form 2441 **13g**		
h	Qualified sick and family leave credits from Schedule(s) H and Form(s) 7202 for leave taken after March 31, 2021 **13h**		
z	Other payments or refundable credits. List type and amount ▶ ______ **13z**		
14	Total other payments or refundable credits. Add lines 13a through 13z	**14**	
15	Add lines 9 through 12 and 14. Enter here and on Form 1040, 1040-SR, or 1040-NR, line 31	**15**	

Schedule 3 (Form 1040) 2021

SCHEDULE A (Form 1040)
Department of the Treasury
Internal Revenue Service (99)

Itemized Deductions

▶ Go to *www.irs.gov/ScheduleA* for instructions and the latest information.
▶ Attach to Form 1040 or 1040-SR.
Caution: If you are claiming a net qualified disaster loss on Form 4684, see the instructions for line 16.

OMB No. 1545-0074
2021
Attachment Sequence No. **07**

Name(s) shown on Form 1040 or 1040-SR | **Your social security number**

Section	Line	Description	Box	Box
Medical and Dental Expenses		**Caution:** Do not include expenses reimbursed or paid by others.		
	1	Medical and dental expenses (see instructions)	1	
	2	Enter amount from Form 1040 or 1040-SR, line 11 [2]		
	3	Multiply line 2 by 7.5% (0.075)	3	
	4	Subtract line 3 from line 1. If line 3 is more than line 1, enter -0-		4
Taxes You Paid	5	State and local taxes.		
	a	State and local income taxes or general sales taxes. You may include either income taxes or general sales taxes on line 5a, but not both. If you elect to include general sales taxes instead of income taxes, check this box ▶ ☐	5a	
	b	State and local real estate taxes (see instructions)	5b	
	c	State and local personal property taxes	5c	
	d	Add lines 5a through 5c	5d	
	e	Enter the smaller of line 5d or $10,000 ($5,000 if married filing separately)	5e	
	6	Other taxes. List type and amount ▶	6	
	7	Add lines 5e and 6		7
Interest You Paid Caution: Your mortgage interest deduction may be limited (see instructions).	8	Home mortgage interest and points. If you didn't use all of your home mortgage loan(s) to buy, build, or improve your home, see instructions and check this box ▶ ☐		
	a	Home mortgage interest and points reported to you on Form 1098. See instructions if limited	8a	
	b	Home mortgage interest not reported to you on Form 1098. See instructions if limited. If paid to the person from whom you bought the home, see instructions and show that person's name, identifying no., and address ▶	8b	
	c	Points not reported to you on Form 1098. See instructions for special rules	8c	
	d	Mortgage insurance premiums (see instructions)	8d	
	e	Add lines 8a through 8d	8e	
	9	Investment interest. Attach Form 4952 if required. See instructions	9	
	10	Add lines 8e and 9		10
Gifts to Charity Caution: If you made a gift and got a benefit for it, see instructions.	11	Gifts by cash or check. If you made any gift of $250 or more, see instructions	11	
	12	Other than by cash or check. If you made any gift of $250 or more, see instructions. You **must** attach Form 8283 if over $500	12	
	13	Carryover from prior year	13	
	14	Add lines 11 through 13		14
Casualty and Theft Losses	15	Casualty and theft loss(es) from a federally declared disaster (other than net qualified disaster losses). Attach Form 4684 and enter the amount from line 18 of that form. See instructions		15
Other Itemized Deductions	16	Other—from list in instructions. List type and amount ▶		16
Total Itemized Deductions	17	Add the amounts in the far right column for lines 4 through 16. Also, enter this amount on Form 1040 or 1040-SR, line 12a		17
	18	If you elect to itemize deductions even though they are less than your standard deduction, check this box ▶ ☐		

For Paperwork Reduction Act Notice, see the Instructions for Forms 1040 and 1040-SR. Cat. No. 17145C **Schedule A (Form 1040) 2021**

SCHEDULE B (Form 1040)

Department of the Treasury Internal Revenue Service (99)

Interest and Ordinary Dividends

▶ Go to *www.irs.gov/ScheduleB* for instructions and the latest information.
▶ Attach to Form 1040 or 1040-SR.

OMB No. 1545-0074

2021

Attachment Sequence No. **08**

Name(s) shown on return | **Your social security number**

Part I Interest

(See instructions and the Instructions for Form 1040, line 2b.)

Note: If you received a Form 1099-INT, Form 1099-OID, or substitute statement from a brokerage firm, list the firm's name as the payer and enter the total interest shown on that form.

			Amount
1	List name of payer. If any interest is from a seller-financed mortgage and the buyer used the property as a personal residence, see the instructions and list this interest first. Also, show that buyer's social security number and address ▶	1	
2	Add the amounts on line 1	2	
3	Excludable interest on series EE and I U.S. savings bonds issued after 1989. Attach Form 8815	3	
4	Subtract line 3 from line 2. Enter the result here and on Form 1040 or 1040-SR, line 2b ▶	4	

Note: If line 4 is over $1,500, you must complete Part III.

Part II Ordinary Dividends

(See instructions and the Instructions for Form 1040, line 3b.)

Note: If you received a Form 1099-DIV or substitute statement from a brokerage firm, list the firm's name as the payer and enter the ordinary dividends shown on that form.

			Amount
5	List name of payer ▶	5	
6	Add the amounts on line 5. Enter the total here and on Form 1040 or 1040-SR, line 3b ▶	6	

Note: If line 6 is over $1,500, you must complete Part III.

Part III Foreign Accounts and Trusts

Caution: If required, failure to file FinCEN Form 114 may result in substantial penalties. See instructions.

You must complete this part if you **(a)** had over $1,500 of taxable interest or ordinary dividends; **(b)** had a foreign account; or **(c)** received a distribution from, or were a grantor of, or a transferor to, a foreign trust.

		Yes	**No**
7a	At any time during 2021, did you have a financial interest in or signature authority over a financial account (such as a bank account, securities account, or brokerage account) located in a foreign country? See instructions		
	If "Yes," are you required to file FinCEN Form 114, Report of Foreign Bank and Financial Accounts (FBAR), to report that financial interest or signature authority? See FinCEN Form 114 and its instructions for filing requirements and exceptions to those requirements		
b	If you are required to file FinCEN Form 114, enter the name of the foreign country where the financial account is located ▶		
8	During 2021, did you receive a distribution from, or were you the grantor of, or transferor to, a foreign trust? If "Yes," you may have to file Form 3520. See instructions		

For Paperwork Reduction Act Notice, see your tax return instructions. Cat. No. 17146N **Schedule B (Form 1040) 2021**

SCHEDULE C (Form 1040)

Department of the Treasury Internal Revenue Service (99)

Profit or Loss From Business

(Sole Proprietorship)

▶ Go to *www.irs.gov/ScheduleC* for instructions and the latest information.

▶ Attach to Form 1040, 1040-SR, 1040-NR, or 1041; partnerships must generally file Form 1065.

OMB No. 1545-0074

2021

Attachment Sequence No. **09**

Name of proprietor | **Social security number (SSN)**

A Principal business or profession, including product or service (see instructions) | **B Enter code from instructions** ▶

C Business name. If no separate business name, leave blank. | **D Employer ID number (EIN)** (see instr.)

E Business address (including suite or room no.) ▶

City, town or post office, state, and ZIP code

F Accounting method: **(1)** ☐ Cash **(2)** ☐ Accrual **(3)** ☐ Other (specify) ▶

G Did you "materially participate" in the operation of this business during 2021? If "No," see instructions for limit on losses ☐ **Yes** ☐ **No**

H If you started or acquired this business during 2021, check here ▶ ☐

I Did you make any payments in 2021 that would require you to file Form(s) 1099? See instructions ☐ **Yes** ☐ **No**

J If "Yes," did you or will you file required Form(s) 1099? ☐ **Yes** ☐ **No**

Part I Income

1	Gross receipts or sales. See instructions for line 1 and check the box if this income was reported to you on Form W-2 and the "Statutory employee" box on that form was checked ▶ ☐	1	
2	Returns and allowances	2	
3	Subtract line 2 from line 1	3	
4	Cost of goods sold (from line 42)	4	
5	**Gross profit.** Subtract line 4 from line 3	5	
6	Other income, including federal and state gasoline or fuel tax credit or refund (see instructions)	6	
7	**Gross income.** Add lines 5 and 6 ▶	7	

Part II Expenses. Enter expenses for business use of your home only on line 30.

8	Advertising	8		18	Office expense (see instructions)	18	
9	Car and truck expenses (see instructions)	9		19	Pension and profit-sharing plans	19	
10	Commissions and fees	10		20	Rent or lease (see instructions):		
11	Contract labor (see instructions)	11		a	Vehicles, machinery, and equipment	20a	
12	Depletion	12		b	Other business property	20b	
13	Depreciation and section 179 expense deduction (not included in Part III) (see instructions)	13		21	Repairs and maintenance	21	
				22	Supplies (not included in Part III)	22	
				23	Taxes and licenses	23	
				24	Travel and meals:		
14	Employee benefit programs (other than on line 19)	14		a	Travel	24a	
15	Insurance (other than health)	15		b	Deductible meals (see instructions)	24b	
16	Interest (see instructions):			25	Utilities	25	
a	Mortgage (paid to banks, etc.)	16a		26	Wages (less employment credits)	26	
b	Other	16b		27a	Other expenses (from line 48)	27a	
17	Legal and professional services	17		b	**Reserved for future use**	27b	

28	**Total expenses** before expenses for business use of home. Add lines 8 through 27a ▶	28	
29	Tentative profit or (loss). Subtract line 28 from line 7	29	
30	Expenses for business use of your home. Do not report these expenses elsewhere. Attach Form 8829 unless using the simplified method. See instructions. **Simplified method filers only:** Enter the total square footage of (a) your home: ______ and (b) the part of your home used for business: ______. Use the Simplified Method Worksheet in the instructions to figure the amount to enter on line 30	30	
31	**Net profit or (loss).** Subtract line 30 from line 29. • If a profit, enter on both **Schedule 1 (Form 1040), line 3,** and on **Schedule SE, line 2.** (If you checked the box on line 1, see instructions). Estates and trusts, enter on **Form 1041, line 3.** • If a loss, you **must** go to line 32.	31	

32 If you have a loss, check the box that describes your investment in this activity. See instructions.

• If you checked 32a, enter the loss on both **Schedule 1 (Form 1040), line 3,** and on **Schedule SE, line 2.** (If you checked the box on line 1, see the line 31 instructions.) Estates and trusts, enter on **Form 1041, line 3.**

• If you checked 32b, you **must** attach **Form 6198.** Your loss may be limited.

32a ☐ All investment is at risk.

32b ☐ Some investment is not at risk.

For Paperwork Reduction Act Notice, see the separate instructions. Cat. No. 11334P **Schedule C (Form 1040) 2021**

Schedule C (Form 1040) 2021 Page **2**

Part III Cost of Goods Sold (see instructions)

33	Method(s) used to value closing inventory: a ☐ Cost b ☐ Lower of cost or market c ☐ Other (attach explanation)		
34	Was there any change in determining quantities, costs, or valuations between opening and closing inventory? If "Yes," attach explanation . . . ☐ Yes ☐ No		
35	Inventory at beginning of year. If different from last year's closing inventory, attach explanation . . .	35	
36	Purchases less cost of items withdrawn for personal use . . .	36	
37	Cost of labor. Do not include any amounts paid to yourself . . .	37	
38	Materials and supplies . . .	38	
39	Other costs . . .	39	
40	Add lines 35 through 39 . . .	40	
41	Inventory at end of year . . .	41	
42	**Cost of goods sold.** Subtract line 41 from line 40. Enter the result here and on line 4 . . .	42	

Part IV Information on Your Vehicle.

Complete this part **only** if you are claiming car or truck expenses on line 9 and are not required to file Form 4562 for this business. See the instructions for line 13 to find out if you must file Form 4562.

43 When did you place your vehicle in service for business purposes? (month/day/year) ► ____ / ____ / ____

44 Of the total number of miles you drove your vehicle during 2021, enter the number of miles you used your vehicle for:

a Business ________ b Commuting (see instructions) ________ c Other ________

45 Was your vehicle available for personal use during off-duty hours? . . . ☐ **Yes** ☐ **No**

46 Do you (or your spouse) have another vehicle available for personal use?. . . ☐ **Yes** ☐ **No**

47a Do you have evidence to support your deduction? . . . ☐ **Yes** ☐ **No**

b If "Yes," is the evidence written? . . . ☐ **Yes** ☐ **No**

Part V Other Expenses.

List below business expenses not included on lines 8–26 or line 30.

48 Total other expenses. Enter here and on line 27a . . . 48	

SCHEDULE D
(Form 1040)

Department of the Treasury
Internal Revenue Service (99)

Capital Gains and Losses

▶ Attach to Form 1040, 1040-SR, or 1040-NR.
▶ Go to *www.irs.gov/ScheduleD* for instructions and the latest information.
▶ Use Form 8949 to list your transactions for lines 1b, 2, 3, 8b, 9, and 10.

OMB No. 1545-0074
2021
Attachment Sequence No. **12**

Name(s) shown on return | **Your social security number**

Did you dispose of any investment(s) in a qualified opportunity fund during the tax year? ☐ **Yes** ☐ **No**
If "Yes," attach Form 8949 and see its instructions for additional requirements for reporting your gain or loss.

Part I Short-Term Capital Gains and Losses—Generally Assets Held One Year or Less (see instructions)

See instructions for how to figure the amounts to enter on the lines below. This form may be easier to complete if you round off cents to whole dollars.	**(d)** Proceeds (sales price)	**(e)** Cost (or other basis)	**(g)** Adjustments to gain or loss from Form(s) 8949, Part I, line 2, column (g)	**(h) Gain or (loss)** Subtract column (e) from column (d) and combine the result with column (g)
1a Totals for all short-term transactions reported on Form 1099-B for which basis was reported to the IRS and for which you have no adjustments (see instructions). However, if you choose to report all these transactions on Form 8949, leave this line blank and go to line 1b .				
1b Totals for all transactions reported on Form(s) 8949 with **Box A** checked				
2 Totals for all transactions reported on Form(s) 8949 with **Box B** checked				
3 Totals for all transactions reported on Form(s) 8949 with **Box C** checked				

4 Short-term gain from Form 6252 and short-term gain or (loss) from Forms 4684, 6781, and 8824 . .	**4**	
5 Net short-term gain or (loss) from partnerships, S corporations, estates, and trusts from Schedule(s) K-1	**5**	
6 Short-term capital loss carryover. Enter the amount, if any, from line 8 of your **Capital Loss Carryover Worksheet** in the instructions	**6**	( )
7 **Net short-term capital gain or (loss).** Combine lines 1a through 6 in column (h). If you have any long-term capital gains or losses, go to Part II below. Otherwise, go to Part III on the back	**7**	

Part II Long-Term Capital Gains and Losses—Generally Assets Held More Than One Year (see instructions)

See instructions for how to figure the amounts to enter on the lines below. This form may be easier to complete if you round off cents to whole dollars.	**(d)** Proceeds (sales price)	**(e)** Cost (or other basis)	**(g)** Adjustments to gain or loss from Form(s) 8949, Part II, line 2, column (g)	**(h) Gain or (loss)** Subtract column (e) from column (d) and combine the result with column (g)
8a Totals for all long-term transactions reported on Form 1099-B for which basis was reported to the IRS and for which you have no adjustments (see instructions). However, if you choose to report all these transactions on Form 8949, leave this line blank and go to line 8b .				
8b Totals for all transactions reported on Form(s) 8949 with **Box D** checked				
9 Totals for all transactions reported on Form(s) 8949 with **Box E** checked				
10 Totals for all transactions reported on Form(s) 8949 with **Box F** checked.				

11 Gain from Form 4797, Part I; long-term gain from Forms 2439 and 6252; and long-term gain or (loss) from Forms 4684, 6781, and 8824	**11**	
12 Net long-term gain or (loss) from partnerships, S corporations, estates, and trusts from Schedule(s) K-1	**12**	
13 Capital gain distributions. See the instructions	**13**	
14 Long-term capital loss carryover. Enter the amount, if any, from line 13 of your **Capital Loss Carryover Worksheet** in the instructions	**14**	( )
15 **Net long-term capital gain or (loss).** Combine lines 8a through 14 in column (h). Then, go to Part III on the back	**15**	

For Paperwork Reduction Act Notice, see your tax return instructions. Cat. No. 11338H **Schedule D (Form 1040) 2021**

Schedule D (Form 1040) 2021 Page **2**

Part III Summary

16	Combine lines 7 and 15 and enter the result	**16**	
	• If line 16 is a **gain,** enter the amount from line 16 on Form 1040, 1040-SR, or 1040-NR, line 7. Then, go to line 17 below. • If line 16 is a **loss,** skip lines 17 through 20 below. Then, go to line 21. Also be sure to complete line 22. • If line 16 is **zero,** skip lines 17 through 21 below and enter -0- on Form 1040, 1040-SR, or 1040-NR, line 7. Then, go to line 22.		
17	Are lines 15 and 16 **both** gains? ☐ **Yes.** Go to line 18. ☐ **No.** Skip lines 18 through 21, and go to line 22.		
18	If you are required to complete the **28% Rate Gain Worksheet** (see instructions), enter the amount, if any, from line 7 of that worksheet . . . . ▶	**18**	
19	If you are required to complete the **Unrecaptured Section 1250 Gain Worksheet** (see instructions), enter the amount, if any, from line 18 of that worksheet . . . . ▶	**19**	
20	Are lines 18 and 19 both zero or blank and are you not filing Form 4952? ☐ **Yes.** Complete the **Qualified Dividends and Capital Gain Tax Worksheet** in the instructions for Forms 1040 and 1040-SR, line 16. **Don't** complete lines 21 and 22 below. ☐ **No.** Complete the **Schedule D Tax Worksheet** in the instructions. **Don't** complete lines 21 and 22 below.		
21	If line 16 is a loss, enter here and on Form 1040, 1040-SR, or 1040-NR, line 7, the **smaller** of: • The loss on line 16; or • ($3,000), or if married filing separately, ($1,500)	**21**	( )
	Note: When figuring which amount is smaller, treat both amounts as positive numbers.		
22	Do you have qualified dividends on Form 1040, 1040-SR, or 1040-NR, line 3a? ☐ **Yes.** Complete the **Qualified Dividends and Capital Gain Tax Worksheet** in the instructions for Forms 1040 and 1040-SR, line 16. ☐ **No.** Complete the rest of Form 1040, 1040-SR, or 1040-NR.		

Schedule D (Form 1040) 2021

SCHEDULE E (Form 1040)

Department of the Treasury
Internal Revenue Service (99)

Supplemental Income and Loss

(From rental real estate, royalties, partnerships, S corporations, estates, trusts, REMICs, etc.)

▶ Attach to Form 1040, 1040-SR, 1040-NR, or 1041.

▶ Go to *www.irs.gov/ScheduleE* for instructions and the latest information.

OMB No. 1545-0074

2021

Attachment Sequence No. 13

Name(s) shown on return | **Your social security number**

Part I **Income or Loss From Rental Real Estate and Royalties** **Note:** If you are in the business of renting personal property, use **Schedule C.** See instructions. If you are an individual, report farm rental income or loss from **Form 4835** on page 2, line 40.

A Did you make any payments in 2021 that would require you to file Form(s) 1099? See instructions . . . . . ☐ **Yes** ☐ **No**

B If "Yes," did you or will you file required Form(s) 1099? . . . . . ☐ **Yes** ☐ **No**

1a	Physical address of each property (street, city, state, ZIP code)
A	
B	
C	

1b	Type of Property (from list below)	2 For each rental real estate property listed above, report the number of fair rental and personal use days. Check the **QJV** box only if you meet the requirements to file as a qualified joint venture. See instructions.		Fair Rental Days	Personal Use Days	QJV
A			A			☐
B			B			☐
C			C			☐

Type of Property:

1 Single Family Residence
2 Multi-Family Residence
3 Vacation/Short-Term Rental
4 Commercial
5 Land
6 Royalties
7 Self-Rental
8 Other (describe)

Income: **Properties:**		A	B	C
3 Rents received	3			
4 Royalties received	4			
Expenses:				
5 Advertising	5			
6 Auto and travel (see instructions)	6			
7 Cleaning and maintenance	7			
8 Commissions.	8			
9 Insurance	9			
10 Legal and other professional fees	10			
11 Management fees	11			
12 Mortgage interest paid to banks, etc. (see instructions)	12			
13 Other interest.	13			
14 Repairs.	14			
15 Supplies	15			
16 Taxes	16			
17 Utilities.	17			
18 Depreciation expense or depletion	18			
19 Other (list) ▶	19			
20 Total expenses. Add lines 5 through 19	20			
21 Subtract line 20 from line 3 (rents) and/or 4 (royalties). If result is a (loss), see instructions to find out if you must file **Form 6198**	21			
22 Deductible rental real estate loss after limitation, if any, on **Form 8582** (see instructions)	22	( )	( )	( )

23a Total of all amounts reported on line 3 for all rental properties	23a	
b Total of all amounts reported on line 4 for all royalty properties	23b	
c Total of all amounts reported on line 12 for all properties	23c	
d Total of all amounts reported on line 18 for all properties	23d	
e Total of all amounts reported on line 20 for all properties	23e	
24 **Income.** Add positive amounts shown on line 21. **Do not** include any losses	24	
25 **Losses.** Add royalty losses from line 21 and rental real estate losses from line 22. Enter total losses here .	25	( )
26 **Total rental real estate and royalty income or (loss).** Combine lines 24 and 25. Enter the result here. If Parts II, III, IV, and line 40 on page 2 do not apply to you, also enter this amount on Schedule 1 (Form 1040), line 5. Otherwise, include this amount in the total on line 41 on page 2 .	26	

For Paperwork Reduction Act Notice, see the separate instructions. Cat. No. 11344L **Schedule E (Form 1040) 2021**

Schedule E (Form 1040) 2021 Attachment Sequence No. **13** Page **2**

Name(s) shown on return. Do not enter name and social security number if shown on other side.	**Your social security number**

Caution: The IRS compares amounts reported on your tax return with amounts shown on Schedule(s) K-1.

Part II **Income or Loss From Partnerships and S Corporations** – **Note:** If you report a loss, receive a distribution, dispose of stock, or receive a loan repayment from an S corporation, you **must** check the box in column **(e)** on line 28 and attach the required basis computation. If you report a loss from an at-risk activity for which **any** amount is **not** at risk, you **must** check the box in column **(f)** on line 28 and attach **Form 6198.** See instructions.

27 Are you reporting any loss not allowed in a prior year due to the at-risk or basis limitations, a prior year unallowed loss from a passive activity (if that loss was not reported on Form 8582), or unreimbursed partnership expenses? If you answered "Yes," see instructions before completing this section . . . . ☐ **Yes** ☐ **No**

28	**(a)** Name	**(b)** Enter **P** for partnership; **S** for S corporation	**(c)** Check if foreign partnership	**(d)** Employer identification number	**(e)** Check if basis computation is required	**(f)** Check if any amount is not at risk
A			☐		☐	☐
B			☐		☐	☐
C			☐		☐	☐
D			☐		☐	☐

	Passive Income and Loss		**Nonpassive Income and Loss**		
	(g) Passive loss allowed (attach **Form 8582** if required)	**(h)** Passive income from **Schedule K-1**	**(i)** Nonpassive loss allowed (see **Schedule K-1**)	**(j)** Section 179 expense deduction from **Form 4562**	**(k)** Nonpassive income from **Schedule K-1**
A					
B					
C					
D					
29a Totals					
b Totals					

30	Add columns (h) and (k) of line 29a	**30**	
31	Add columns (g), (i), and (j) of line 29b	**31**	( )
32	**Total partnership and S corporation income or (loss).** Combine lines 30 and 31	**32**	

Part III **Income or Loss From Estates and Trusts**

33	**(a)** Name	**(b)** Employer identification number
A		
B		

	Passive Income and Loss		**Nonpassive Income and Loss**	
	(c) Passive deduction or loss allowed (attach **Form 8582** if required)	**(d)** Passive income from **Schedule K-1**	**(e)** Deduction or loss from **Schedule K-1**	**(f)** Other income from **Schedule K-1**
A				
B				
34a Totals				
b Totals				

35	Add columns (d) and (f) of line 34a	**35**	
36	Add columns (c) and (e) of line 34b	**36**	( )
37	**Total estate and trust income or (loss).** Combine lines 35 and 36	**37**	

Part IV **Income or Loss From Real Estate Mortgage Investment Conduits (REMICs)—Residual Holder**

38	**(a)** Name	**(b)** Employer identification number	**(c)** Excess inclusion from **Schedules Q,** line 2c (see instructions)	**(d)** Taxable income (net loss) from **Schedules Q,** line 1b	**(e)** Income from **Schedules Q,** line 3b

39	Combine columns (d) and (e) only. Enter the result here and include in the total on line 41 below	**39**	

Part V **Summary**

40	Net farm rental income or (loss) from **Form 4835.** Also, complete line 42 below			**40**	
41	**Total income or (loss).** Combine lines 26, 32, 37, 39, and 40. Enter the result here and on Schedule 1 (Form 1040), line 5 ▶			**41**	
42	**Reconciliation of farming and fishing income.** Enter your **gross** farming and fishing income reported on Form 4835, line 7; Schedule K-1 (Form 1065), box 14, code B; Schedule K-1 (Form 1120-S), box 17, code AD; and Schedule K-1 (Form 1041), box 14, code F. See instructions . .	**42**			
43	**Reconciliation for real estate professionals.** If you were a real estate professional (see instructions), enter the net income or (loss) you reported anywhere on Form 1040, Form 1040-SR, or Form 1040-NR from all rental real estate activities in which you materially participated under the passive activity loss rules	**43**			

SCHEDULE SE (Form 1040)

Department of the Treasury Internal Revenue Service (99)

Self-Employment Tax

▶ Go to *www.irs.gov/ScheduleSE* for instructions and the latest information.
▶ Attach to Form 1040, 1040-SR, or 1040-NR.

OMB No. 1545-0074

2021

Attachment Sequence No. **17**

Name of person with self-employment income (as shown on Form 1040, 1040-SR, or 1040-NR)

Social security number of person with **self-employment** income ▶

Part I Self-Employment Tax

Note: If your only income subject to self-employment tax is **church employee income,** see instructions for how to report your income and the definition of church employee income.

A If you are a minister, member of a religious order, or Christian Science practitioner **and** you filed Form 4361, but you had $400 or more of **other** net earnings from self-employment, check here and continue with Part I . . . . ▶ ☐

Skip lines 1a and 1b if you use the farm optional method in Part II. See instructions.

Line	Description			Line	Amount
1a	Net farm profit or (loss) from Schedule F, line 34, and farm partnerships, Schedule K-1 (Form 1065), box 14, code A			1a	
b	If you received social security retirement or disability benefits, enter the amount of Conservation Reserve Program payments included on Schedule F, line 4b, or listed on Schedule K-1 (Form 1065), box 20, code AH			1b	( )
	Skip line 2 if you use the nonfarm optional method in Part II. See instructions.				
2	Net profit or (loss) from Schedule C, line 31; and Schedule K-1 (Form 1065), box 14, code A (other than farming). See instructions for other income to report or if you are a minister or member of a religious order			2	
3	Combine lines 1a, 1b, and 2			3	
4a	If line 3 is more than zero, multiply line 3 by 92.35% (0.9235). Otherwise, enter amount from line 3 **Note:** If line 4a is less than $400 due to Conservation Reserve Program payments on line 1b, see instructions.			4a	
b	If you elect one or both of the optional methods, enter the total of lines 15 and 17 here			4b	
c	Combine lines 4a and 4b. If less than $400, **stop;** you don't owe self-employment tax. **Exception:** If less than $400 and you had **church employee income,** enter -0- and continue ▶			4c	
5a	Enter your **church employee income** from Form W-2. See instructions for definition of church employee income	5a			
b	Multiply line 5a by 92.35% (0.9235). If less than $100, enter -0-			5b	
6	Add lines 4c and 5b			6	
7	Maximum amount of combined wages and self-employment earnings subject to social security tax or the 6.2% portion of the 7.65% railroad retirement (tier 1) tax for 2021			7	142,800
8a	Total social security wages and tips (total of boxes 3 and 7 on Form(s) W-2) and railroad retirement (tier 1) compensation. If $142,800 or more, skip lines 8b through 10, and go to line 11	8a			
b	Unreported tips subject to social security tax from Form 4137, line 10	8b			
c	Wages subject to social security tax from Form 8919, line 10	8c			
d	Add lines 8a, 8b, and 8c			8d	
9	Subtract line 8d from line 7. If zero or less, enter -0- here and on line 10 and go to line 11 ▶			9	
10	Multiply the **smaller** of line 6 or line 9 by 12.4% (0.124)			10	
11	Multiply line 6 by 2.9% (0.029)			11	
12	**Self-employment tax.** Add lines 10 and 11. Enter here and on **Schedule 2 (Form 1040), line 4**			12	
13	**Deduction for one-half of self-employment tax.** Multiply line 12 by 50% (0.50). Enter here and on **Schedule 1 (Form 1040), line 15**	13			

Part II Optional Methods To Figure Net Earnings (see instructions)

Farm Optional Method. You may use this method **only** if **(a)** your gross farm income[1] wasn't more than $8,820, **or (b)** your net farm profits[2] were less than $6,367.

Line	Description	Line	Amount
14	Maximum income for optional methods	14	5,880
15	Enter the **smaller** of: two-thirds (2/3) of gross farm income[1] (not less than zero) **or** $5,880. Also, include this amount on line 4b above	15	

Nonfarm Optional Method. You may use this method **only** if **(a)** your net nonfarm profits[3] were less than $6,367 and also less than 72.189% of your gross nonfarm income,[4] **and (b)** you had net earnings from self-employment of at least $400 in 2 of the prior 3 years. **Caution:** You may use this method no more than five times.

Line	Description	Line	Amount
16	Subtract line 15 from line 14	16	
17	Enter the **smaller** of: two-thirds (2/3) of gross nonfarm income[4] (not less than zero) **or** the amount on line 16. Also, include this amount on line 4b above	17	

[1] From Sch. F, line 9; and Sch. K-1 (Form 1065), box 14, code B.
[2] From Sch. F, line 34; and Sch. K-1 (Form 1065), box 14, code A—minus the amount you would have entered on line 1b had you not used the optional method.
[3] From Sch. C, line 31; and Sch. K-1 (Form 1065), box 14, code A.
[4] From Sch. C, line 7; and Sch. K-1 (Form 1065), box 14, code C.

For Paperwork Reduction Act Notice, see your tax return instructions. Cat. No. 11358Z **Schedule SE (Form 1040) 2021**

Form **4562**

Department of the Treasury
Internal Revenue Service (99)

Depreciation and Amortization

(Including Information on Listed Property)

▶ **Attach to your tax return.**

▶ **Go to *www.irs.gov/Form4562* for instructions and the latest information.**

OMB No. 1545-0172

2021

Attachment Sequence No. **179**

Name(s) shown on return	Business or activity to which this form relates	Identifying number

Part I Election To Expense Certain Property Under Section 179

Note: If you have any listed property, complete Part V before you complete Part I.

1	Maximum amount (see instructions)	1	
2	Total cost of section 179 property placed in service (see instructions)	2	
3	Threshold cost of section 179 property before reduction in limitation (see instructions)	3	
4	Reduction in limitation. Subtract line 3 from line 2. If zero or less, enter -0-	4	
5	Dollar limitation for tax year. Subtract line 4 from line 1. If zero or less, enter -0-. If married filing separately, see instructions	5	

6	**(a)** Description of property	**(b)** Cost (business use only)	**(c)** Elected cost
7	Listed property. Enter the amount from line 29	7	

8	Total elected cost of section 179 property. Add amounts in column (c), lines 6 and 7	8	
9	Tentative deduction. Enter the **smaller** of line 5 or line 8	9	
10	Carryover of disallowed deduction from line 13 of your 2020 Form 4562	10	
11	Business income limitation. Enter the smaller of business income (not less than zero) or line 5. See instructions	11	
12	Section 179 expense deduction. Add lines 9 and 10, but don't enter more than line 11	12	
13	Carryover of disallowed deduction to 2022. Add lines 9 and 10, less line 12 ▶ 13		

Note: Don't use Part II or Part III below for listed property. Instead, use Part V.

Part II Special Depreciation Allowance and Other Depreciation (Don't include listed property. See instructions.)

14	Special depreciation allowance for qualified property (other than listed property) placed in service during the tax year. See instructions	14	
15	Property subject to section 168(f)(1) election	15	
16	Other depreciation (including ACRS)	16	

Part III MACRS Depreciation (Don't include listed property. See instructions.)

Section A

17	MACRS deductions for assets placed in service in tax years beginning before 2021	17	
18	If you are electing to group any assets placed in service during the tax year into one or more general asset accounts, check here ▶ ☐		

Section B—Assets Placed in Service During 2021 Tax Year Using the General Depreciation System

(a) Classification of property	**(b)** Month and year placed in service	**(c)** Basis for depreciation (business/investment use only—see instructions)	**(d)** Recovery period	**(e)** Convention	**(f)** Method	**(g)** Depreciation deduction
19a 3-year property						
b 5-year property						
c 7-year property						
d 10-year property						
e 15-year property						
f 20-year property						
g 25-year property			25 yrs.		S/L	
h Residential rental property			27.5 yrs.	MM	S/L	
			27.5 yrs.	MM	S/L	
i Nonresidential real property			39 yrs.	MM	S/L	
				MM	S/L	

Section C—Assets Placed in Service During 2021 Tax Year Using the Alternative Depreciation System

20a Class life					S/L	
b 12-year			12 yrs.		S/L	
c 30-year			30 yrs.	MM	S/L	
d 40-year			40 yrs.	MM	S/L	

Part IV Summary (See instructions.)

21	Listed property. Enter amount from line 28	21	
22	**Total.** Add amounts from line 12, lines 14 through 17, lines 19 and 20 in column (g), and line 21. Enter here and on the appropriate lines of your return. Partnerships and S corporations—see instructions	22	
23	For assets shown above and placed in service during the current year, enter the portion of the basis attributable to section 263A costs	23	

Form 4562 (2021) Page **2**

Part V **Listed Property** (Include automobiles, certain other vehicles, certain aircraft, and property used for entertainment, recreation, or amusement.)

Note: For any vehicle for which you are using the standard mileage rate or deducting lease expense, complete **only** 24a, 24b, columns (a) through (c) of Section A, all of Section B, and Section C if applicable.

Section A—Depreciation and Other Information (Caution: See the instructions for limits for passenger automobiles.)

24a Do you have evidence to support the business/investment use claimed? ☐ **Yes** ☐ **No** | **24b** If "Yes," is the evidence written? ☐ **Yes** ☐ **No**

(a) Type of property (list vehicles first)	**(b)** Date placed in service	**(c)** Business/ investment use percentage	**(d)** Cost or other basis	**(e)** Basis for depreciation (business/investment use only)	**(f)** Recovery period	**(g)** Method/ Convention	**(h)** Depreciation deduction	**(i)** Elected section 179 cost
25 Special depreciation allowance for qualified listed property placed in service during the tax year and used more than 50% in a qualified business use. See instructions .						**25**		
26 Property used more than 50% in a qualified business use:								
		%						
		%						
		%						
27 Property used 50% or less in a qualified business use:								
		%				S/L –		
		%				S/L –		
		%				S/L –		
28 Add amounts in column (h), lines 25 through 27. Enter here and on line 21, page 1 .						**28**		
29 Add amounts in column (i), line 26. Enter here and on line 7, page 1							**29**	

Section B—Information on Use of Vehicles

Complete this section for vehicles used by a sole proprietor, partner, or other "more than 5% owner," or related person. If you provided vehicles to your employees, first answer the questions in Section C to see if you meet an exception to completing this section for those vehicles.

	(a) Vehicle 1		**(b)** Vehicle 2		**(c)** Vehicle 3		**(d)** Vehicle 4		**(e)** Vehicle 5		**(f)** Vehicle 6	
30 Total business/investment miles driven during the year (**don't** include commuting miles) .												
31 Total commuting miles driven during the year												
32 Total other personal (noncommuting) miles driven												
33 Total miles driven during the year. Add lines 30 through 32												
	Yes	**No**	**Yes**	**No**	**Yes**	**No**	**Yes**	**No**	**Yes**	**No**	**Yes**	**No**
34 Was the vehicle available for personal use during off-duty hours?												
35 Was the vehicle used primarily by a more than 5% owner or related person? . .												
36 Is another vehicle available for personal use?												

Section C—Questions for Employers Who Provide Vehicles for Use by Their Employees

Answer these questions to determine if you meet an exception to completing Section B for vehicles used by employees who **aren't** more than 5% owners or related persons. See instructions.

	Yes	**No**
37 Do you maintain a written policy statement that prohibits all personal use of vehicles, including commuting, by your employees?		
38 Do you maintain a written policy statement that prohibits personal use of vehicles, except commuting, by your employees? See the instructions for vehicles used by corporate officers, directors, or 1% or more owners . .		
39 Do you treat all use of vehicles by employees as personal use?		
40 Do you provide more than five vehicles to your employees, obtain information from your employees about the use of the vehicles, and retain the information received?		
41 Do you meet the requirements concerning qualified automobile demonstration use? See instructions.		
Note: If your answer to 37, 38, 39, 40, or 41 is "Yes," don't complete Section B for the covered vehicles.		

Part VI **Amortization**

(a) Description of costs	**(b)** Date amortization begins	**(c)** Amortizable amount	**(d)** Code section	**(e)** Amortization period or percentage	**(f)** Amortization for this year
42 Amortization of costs that begins during your 2021 tax year (see instructions):					
43 Amortization of costs that began before your 2021 tax year				**43**	
44 **Total.** Add amounts in column (f). See the instructions for where to report				**44**	

Form **4797**

Department of the Treasury
Internal Revenue Service

Sales of Business Property

(Also Involuntary Conversions and Recapture Amounts Under Sections 179 and 280F(b)(2))

▶ Attach to your tax return.

▶ Go to *www.irs.gov/Form4797* for instructions and the latest information.

OMB No. 1545-0184

2021

Attachment Sequence No. **27**

Name(s) shown on return | **Identifying number**

1a	Enter the gross proceeds from sales or exchanges reported to you for 2021 on Form(s) 1099-B or 1099-S (or substitute statement) that you are including on line 2, 10, or 20. See instructions	**1a**	
b	Enter the total amount of gain that you are including on lines 2, 10, and 24 due to the partial dispositions of MACRS assets	**1b**	
c	Enter the total amount of loss that you are including on lines 2 and 10 due to the partial dispositions of MACRS assets	**1c**	

Part I Sales or Exchanges of Property Used in a Trade or Business and Involuntary Conversions From Other Than Casualty or Theft—Most Property Held More Than 1 Year (see instructions)

2	**(a)** Description of property	**(b)** Date acquired (mo., day, yr.)	**(c)** Date sold (mo., day, yr.)	**(d)** Gross sales price	**(e)** Depreciation allowed or allowable since acquisition	**(f)** Cost or other basis, plus improvements and expense of sale	**(g) Gain or (loss)** Subtract (f) from the sum of (d) and (e)

3	Gain, if any, from Form 4684, line 39	**3**	
4	Section 1231 gain from installment sales from Form 6252, line 26 or 37	**4**	
5	Section 1231 gain or (loss) from like-kind exchanges from Form 8824	**5**	
6	Gain, if any, from line 32, from other than casualty or theft	**6**	
7	Combine lines 2 through 6. Enter the gain or (loss) here and on the appropriate line as follows	**7**	
	Partnerships and S corporations. Report the gain or (loss) following the instructions for Form 1065, Schedule K, line 10, or Form 1120-S, Schedule K, line 9. Skip lines 8, 9, 11, and 12 below.		
	Individuals, partners, S corporation shareholders, and all others. If line 7 is zero or a loss, enter the amount from line 7 on line 11 below and skip lines 8 and 9. If line 7 is a gain and you didn't have any prior year section 1231 losses, or they were recaptured in an earlier year, enter the gain from line 7 as a long-term capital gain on the Schedule D filed with your return and skip lines 8, 9, 11, and 12 below.		
8	Nonrecaptured net section 1231 losses from prior years. See instructions	**8**	
9	Subtract line 8 from line 7. If zero or less, enter -0-. If line 9 is zero, enter the gain from line 7 on line 12 below. If line 9 is more than zero, enter the amount from line 8 on line 12 below and enter the gain from line 9 as a long-term capital gain on the Schedule D filed with your return. See instructions	**9**	

Part II Ordinary Gains and Losses (see instructions)

10 Ordinary gains and losses not included on lines 11 through 16 (include property held 1 year or less):

11	Loss, if any, from line 7	**11**	( )
12	Gain, if any, from line 7 or amount from line 8, if applicable	**12**	
13	Gain, if any, from line 31	**13**	
14	Net gain or (loss) from Form 4684, lines 31 and 38a	**14**	
15	Ordinary gain from installment sales from Form 6252, line 25 or 36	**15**	
16	Ordinary gain or (loss) from like-kind exchanges from Form 8824	**16**	
17	Combine lines 10 through 16	**17**	
18	For all except individual returns, enter the amount from line 17 on the appropriate line of your return and skip lines a and b below. For individual returns, complete lines a and b below.		
a	If the loss on line 11 includes a loss from Form 4684, line 35, column (b)(ii), enter that part of the loss here. Enter the loss from income-producing property on Schedule A (Form 1040), line 16. (Do not include any loss on property used as an employee.) Identify as from "Form 4797, line 18a." See instructions	**18a**	
b	Redetermine the gain or (loss) on line 17 excluding the loss, if any, on line 18a. Enter here and on Schedule 1 (Form 1040), Part I, line 4	**18b**	

Form 4797 (2021) Page **2**

Part III Gain From Disposition of Property Under Sections 1245, 1250, 1252, 1254, and 1255 (see instructions)

19	(a) Description of section 1245, 1250, 1252, 1254, or 1255 property:	(b) Date acquired (mo., day, yr.)	(c) Date sold (mo., day, yr.)
A			
B			
C			
D			

	These columns relate to the properties on lines 19A through 19D. ▶		Property A	Property B	Property C	Property D
20	Gross sales price (**Note:** *See line 1a before completing.*) .	20				
21	Cost or other basis plus expense of sale	21				
22	Depreciation (or depletion) allowed or allowable . . .	22				
23	Adjusted basis. Subtract line 22 from line 21. . . .	23				
24	Total gain. Subtract line 23 from line 20	24				
25	**If section 1245 property:**					
a	Depreciation allowed or allowable from line 22 . . .	25a				
b	Enter the **smaller** of line 24 or 25a.	25b				
26	**If section 1250 property:** If straight line depreciation was used, enter -0- on line 26g, except for a corporation subject to section 291.					
a	Additional depreciation after 1975. See instructions .	26a				
b	Applicable percentage multiplied by the **smaller** of line 24 or line 26a. See instructions.	26b				
c	Subtract line 26a from line 24. If residential rental property **or** line 24 isn't more than line 26a, skip lines 26d and 26e	26c				
d	Additional depreciation after 1969 and before 1976. .	26d				
e	Enter the **smaller** of line 26c or 26d	26e				
f	Section 291 amount (corporations only)	26f				
g	Add lines 26b, 26e, and 26f	26g				
27	**If section 1252 property:** Skip this section if you didn't dispose of farmland or if this form is being completed for a partnership.					
a	Soil, water, and land clearing expenses	27a				
b	Line 27a multiplied by applicable percentage. See instructions	27b				
c	Enter the **smaller** of line 24 or 27b	27c				
28	**If section 1254 property:**					
a	Intangible drilling and development costs, expenditures for development of mines and other natural deposits, mining exploration costs, and depletion. See instructions	28a				
b	Enter the **smaller** of line 24 or 28a.	28b				
29	**If section 1255 property:**					
a	Applicable percentage of payments excluded from income under section 126. See instructions	29a				
b	Enter the **smaller** of line 24 or 29a. See instructions .	29b				

Summary of Part III Gains. Complete property columns A through D through line 29b before going to line 30.

30	Total gains for all properties. Add property columns A through D, line 24	30	
31	Add property columns A through D, lines 25b, 26g, 27c, 28b, and 29b. Enter here and on line 13	31	
32	Subtract line 31 from line 30. Enter the portion from casualty or theft on Form 4684, line 33. Enter the portion from other than casualty or theft on Form 4797, line 6	32	

Part IV Recapture Amounts Under Sections 179 and 280F(b)(2) When Business Use Drops to 50% or Less (see instructions)

			(a) Section 179	(b) Section 280F(b)(2)
33	Section 179 expense deduction or depreciation allowable in prior years.	33		
34	Recomputed depreciation. See instructions	34		
35	Recapture amount. Subtract line 34 from line 33. See the instructions for where to report . .	35		

Form **4797** (2021)

Form **8949**

Department of the Treasury
Internal Revenue Service

Sales and Other Dispositions of Capital Assets

▶ Go to *www.irs.gov/Form8949* for instructions and the latest information.

▶ **File with your Schedule D to list your transactions for lines 1b, 2, 3, 8b, 9, and 10 of Schedule D.**

OMB No. 1545-0074

2021

Attachment Sequence No. **12A**

Name(s) shown on return	**Social security number or taxpayer identification number**

Before you check Box A, B, or C below, see whether you received any Form(s) 1099-B or substitute statement(s) from your broker. A substitute statement will have the same information as Form 1099-B. Either will show whether your basis (usually your cost) was reported to the IRS by your broker and may even tell you which box to check.

Part I **Short-Term.** Transactions involving capital assets you held 1 year or less are generally short-term (see instructions). For long-term transactions, see page 2.

Note: You may aggregate all short-term transactions reported on Form(s) 1099-B showing basis was reported to the IRS and for which no adjustments or codes are required. Enter the totals directly on Schedule D, line 1a; you aren't required to report these transactions on Form 8949 (see instructions).

You *must* check Box A, B, *or* C below. Check only one box. If more than one box applies for your short-term transactions, complete a separate Form 8949, page 1, for each applicable box. If you have more short-term transactions than will fit on this page for one or more of the boxes, complete as many forms with the same box checked as you need.

☐ **(A)** Short-term transactions reported on Form(s) 1099-B showing basis was reported to the IRS (see **Note** above)

☐ **(B)** Short-term transactions reported on Form(s) 1099-B showing basis **wasn't** reported to the IRS

☐ **(C)** Short-term transactions not reported to you on Form 1099-B

1 (a) Description of property (Example: 100 sh. XYZ Co.)	(b) Date acquired (Mo., day, yr.)	(c) Date sold or disposed of (Mo., day, yr.)	(d) Proceeds (sales price) (see instructions)	(e) Cost or other basis. See the **Note** below and see *Column (e)* in the separate instructions	**Adjustment, if any, to gain or loss.** If you enter an amount in column (g), enter a code in column (f). **See the separate instructions.** (f) Code(s) from instructions	(g) Amount of adjustment	(h) **Gain or (loss).** Subtract column (e) from column (d) and combine the result with column (g)
2 Totals. Add the amounts in columns (d), (e), (g), and (h) (subtract negative amounts). Enter each total here and include on your Schedule D, **line 1b** (if **Box A** above is checked), **line 2** (if **Box B** above is checked), or **line 3** (if **Box C** above is checked) ▶							

Note: If you checked Box A above but the basis reported to the IRS was incorrect, enter in column (e) the basis as reported to the IRS, and enter an adjustment in column (g) to correct the basis. See *Column (g)* in the separate instructions for how to figure the amount of the adjustment.

Form 8949 (2021) Attachment Sequence No. **12A** Page **2**

Name(s) shown on return. Name and SSN or taxpayer identification no. not required if shown on other side	**Social security number or taxpayer identification number**

Before you check Box D, E, or F below, see whether you received any Form(s) 1099-B or substitute statement(s) from your broker. A substitute statement will have the same information as Form 1099-B. Either will show whether your basis (usually your cost) was reported to the IRS by your broker and may even tell you which box to check.

Part II **Long-Term.** Transactions involving capital assets you held more than 1 year are generally long-term (see instructions). For short-term transactions, see page 1.

Note: You may aggregate all long-term transactions reported on Form(s) 1099-B showing basis was reported to the IRS and for which no adjustments or codes are required. Enter the totals directly on Schedule D, line 8a; you aren't required to report these transactions on Form 8949 (see instructions).

You *must* check Box D, E, *or* F below. Check only one box. If more than one box applies for your long-term transactions, complete a separate Form 8949, page 2, for each applicable box. If you have more long-term transactions than will fit on this page for one or more of the boxes, complete as many forms with the same box checked as you need.

☐ **(D)** Long-term transactions reported on Form(s) 1099-B showing basis was reported to the IRS (see **Note** above)
☐ **(E)** Long-term transactions reported on Form(s) 1099-B showing basis **wasn't** reported to the IRS
☐ **(F)** Long-term transactions not reported to you on Form 1099-B

1 (a) Description of property (Example: 100 sh. XYZ Co.)	(b) Date acquired (Mo., day, yr.)	(c) Date sold or disposed of (Mo., day, yr.)	(d) Proceeds (sales price) (see instructions)	(e) Cost or other basis. See the **Note** below and see *Column (e)* in the separate instructions	Adjustment, if any, to gain or loss. If you enter an amount in column (g), enter a code in column (f). **See the separate instructions.** (f) Code(s) from instructions	(g) Amount of adjustment	(h) **Gain or (loss).** Subtract column (e) from column (d) and combine the result with column (g)
2 Totals. Add the amounts in columns (d), (e), (g), and (h) (subtract negative amounts). Enter each total here and include on your Schedule D, **line 8b** (if **Box D** above is checked), **line 9** (if **Box E** above is checked), or **line 10** (if **Box F** above is checked) ▶							

Note: If you checked Box D above but the basis reported to the IRS was incorrect, enter in column (e) the basis as reported to the IRS, and enter an adjustment in column (g) to correct the basis. See *Column (g)* in the separate instructions for how to figure the amount of the adjustment.

Form **8995**

Department of the Treasury
Internal Revenue Service

Qualified Business Income Deduction Simplified Computation

▶ Attach to your tax return.

▶ Go to *www.irs.gov/Form8995* for instructions and the latest information.

OMB No. 1545-2294

2021

Attachment Sequence No. 55

Name(s) shown on return	Your taxpayer identification number

Note. *You can claim the qualified business income deduction* **only** *if you have qualified business income from a qualified trade or business, real estate investment trust dividends, publicly traded partnership income, or a domestic production activities deduction passed through from an agricultural or horticultural cooperative. See instructions.*

Use this form if your taxable income, before your qualified business income deduction, is at or below $164,900 ($164,925 if married filing separately; $329,800 if married filing jointly), and you aren't a patron of an agricultural or horticultural cooperative.

1	**(a)** Trade, business, or aggregation name	**(b)** Taxpayer identification number	**(c)** Qualified business income or (loss)
i			
ii			
iii			
iv			
v			

Line	Description				
2	Total qualified business income or (loss). Combine lines 1i through 1v, column (c)	2			
3	Qualified business net (loss) carryforward from the prior year	3	( )		
4	Total qualified business income. Combine lines 2 and 3. If zero or less, enter -0-	4			
5	Qualified business income component. Multiply line 4 by 20% (0.20)			5	
6	Qualified REIT dividends and publicly traded partnership (PTP) income or (loss) (see instructions)	6			
7	Qualified REIT dividends and qualified PTP (loss) carryforward from the prior year	7	( )		
8	Total qualified REIT dividends and PTP income. Combine lines 6 and 7. If zero or less, enter -0-	8			
9	REIT and PTP component. Multiply line 8 by 20% (0.20)			9	
10	Qualified business income deduction before the income limitation. Add lines 5 and 9			10	
11	Taxable income before qualified business income deduction (see instructions)	11			
12	Net capital gain (see instructions)	12			
13	Subtract line 12 from line 11. If zero or less, enter -0-	13			
14	Income limitation. Multiply line 13 by 20% (0.20)			14	
15	Qualified business income deduction. Enter the smaller of line 10 or line 14. Also enter this amount on the applicable line of your return (see instructions) ▶			15	
16	Total qualified business (loss) carryforward. Combine lines 2 and 3. If greater than zero, enter -0-			16	( )
17	Total qualified REIT dividends and PTP (loss) carryforward. Combine lines 6 and 7. If greater than zero, enter -0-			17	( )

For Privacy Act and Paperwork Reduction Act Notice, see instructions. Cat. No. 37806C Form **8995** (2021)

Form **8995-A**

Department of the Treasury
Internal Revenue Service

Qualified Business Income Deduction

▶ Attach to your tax return.

▶ Go to *www.irs.gov/Form8995A* for instructions and the latest information.

OMB No. 1545-2294

2021

Attachment Sequence No. **55A**

Name(s) shown on return | **Your taxpayer identification number**

Note: *You can claim the qualified business income deduction* **only** *if you have qualified business income from a qualified trade or business, real estate investment trust dividends, publicly traded partnership income, or a domestic production activities deduction passed through from an agricultural or horticultural cooperative. See instructions.*

Use this form if your taxable income, before your qualified business income deduction, is above $164,900 ($164,925 if married filing separately; $329,800 if married filing jointly), or you're a patron of an agricultural or horticultural cooperative.

Part I Trade, Business, or Aggregation Information

Complete Schedules A, B, and/or C (Form 8995-A), as applicable, before starting Part I. Attach additional worksheets when needed. See instructions.

1	**(a)** Trade, business, or aggregation name	**(b)** Check if specified service	**(c)** Check if aggregation	**(d)** Taxpayer identification number	**(e)** Check if patron
A		☐	☐		☐
B		☐	☐		☐
C		☐	☐		☐

Part II Determine Your Adjusted Qualified Business Income

			A	B	C
2	Qualified business income from the trade, business, or aggregation. See instructions	2			
3	Multiply line 2 by 20% (0.20). If your taxable income is $164,900 or less ($164,925 if married filing separately; $329,800 if married filing jointly), skip lines 4 through 12 and enter the amount from line 3 on line 13	3			
4	Allocable share of W-2 wages from the trade, business, or aggregation	4			
5	Multiply line 4 by 50% (0.50)	5			
6	Multiply line 4 by 25% (0.25)	6			
7	Allocable share of the unadjusted basis immediately after acquisition (UBIA) of all qualified property	7			
8	Multiply line 7 by 2.5% (0.025)	8			
9	Add lines 6 and 8	9			
10	Enter the greater of line 5 or line 9	10			
11	W-2 wage and UBIA of qualified property limitation. Enter the smaller of line 3 or line 10	11			
12	Phased-in reduction. Enter the amount from line 26, if any	12			
13	Qualified business income deduction before patron reduction. Enter the greater of line 11 or line 12	13			
14	Patron reduction. Enter the amount from Schedule D (Form 8995-A), line 6, if any. See instructions	14			
15	Qualified business income component. Subtract line 14 from line 13	15			
16	Total qualified business income component. Add all amounts reported on line 15 ▶	16			

For Privacy Act and Paperwork Reduction Act Notice, see separate instructions. Cat. No. 71661B Form **8995-A** (2021)

Form 8995-A (2021) Page **2**

Part III Phased-in Reduction

Complete Part III only if your taxable income is more than $164,900 but not $214,900 ($164,925 and $214,925 if married filing separately; $329,800 and $429,800 if married filing jointly) and line 10 is less than line 3. Otherwise, skip Part III.

				A	B	C
17	Enter the amounts from line 3		17			
18	Enter the amounts from line 10		18			
19	Subtract line 18 from line 17		19			
20	Taxable income before qualified business income deduction	20				
21	Threshold. Enter $164,900 ($164,925 if married filing separately; $329,800 if married filing jointly)	21				
22	Subtract line 21 from line 20	22				
23	Phase-in range. Enter $50,000 ($100,000 if married filing jointly)	23				
24	Phase-in percentage. Divide line 22 by line 23	24 %				
25	Total phase-in reduction. Multiply line 19 by line 24		25			
26	Qualified business income after phase-in reduction. Subtract line 25 from line 17. Enter this amount here and on line 12, for the corresponding trade or business		26			

Part IV Determine Your Qualified Business Income Deduction

27	Total qualified business income component from all qualified trades, businesses, or aggregations. Enter the amount from line 16	27			
28	Qualified REIT dividends and publicly traded partnership (PTP) income or (loss). See instructions	28			
29	Qualified REIT dividends and PTP (loss) carryforward from prior years	29	( )		
30	Total qualified REIT dividends and PTP income. Combine lines 28 and 29. If less than zero, enter -0-	30			
31	REIT and PTP component. Multiply line 30 by 20% (0.20)	31			
32	Qualified business income deduction before the income limitation. Add lines 27 and 31 ▶			32	
33	Taxable income before qualified business income deduction	33			
34	Net capital gain. See instructions	34			
35	Subtract line 34 from line 33. If zero or less, enter -0-			35	
36	Income limitation. Multiply line 35 by 20% (0.20)			36	
37	Qualified business income deduction before the domestic production activities deduction (DPAD) under section 199A(g). Enter the smaller of line 32 or line 36 ▶			37	
38	DPAD under section 199A(g) allocated from an agricultural or horticultural cooperative. Don't enter more than line 33 minus line 37			38	
39	Total qualified business income deduction. Add lines 37 and 38 ▶			39	
40	Total qualified REIT dividends and PTP (loss) carryforward. Combine lines 28 and 29. If zero or greater, enter -0-			40	( )

Form **8995-A** (2021)

Appendix C

Glossary

The key terms in this glossary have been defined to reflect their conventional use in the field of taxation. The definitions may therefore be incomplete for other purposes.

A

AAA bypass election. In the context of a distribution by an S corporation, an election made by the entity to designate that the distribution is first from accumulated earnings and profits (AEP) and only then from the accumulated adjustments account (AAA). § 1368(e)(3).

Abandoned spouse. The abandoned spouse provision enables a married taxpayer with a dependent child whose spouse did not live in the taxpayer's home during the last six months of the tax year to file as a head of household rather than as married filing separately. §§ 2(b) and 7703(b).

Accelerated cost recovery system (ACRS). A method in which the cost of tangible property is recovered (depreciated) over a prescribed period of time. This depreciation approach disregards salvage value, imposes a period of cost recovery that depends upon the classification of the asset into one of various recovery periods, and prescribes the applicable percentage of cost that can be deducted each year. A modified system is currently the default cost recovery method; it is referred to as MACRS. § 168.

Accelerated death benefits. The amount received from a life insurance policy by the insured who is terminally ill or chronically ill. Any realized gain may be excluded from the gross income of the insured if the policy is surrendered to the insurer or is sold to a licensed viatical settlement provider. § 101(g).

Acceleration rule. Treatment of an intercompany transaction on a consolidated return, when a sold asset leaves the group.

Accident and health benefits. Employee fringe benefits provided by employers through the payment of health and accident insurance premiums or the establishment of employer-funded medical reimbursement plans. Employers generally are entitled to a deduction for such payments, whereas employees generally exclude such fringe benefits from gross income. §§ 105 and 106.

Accident and health insurance benefits. See *accident and health benefits.*

Accountable plan. A type of expense reimbursement plan that requires an employee to render an adequate accounting to the employer and return any excess reimbursement or allowance. If the expense qualifies, it will be treated as a deduction *for* AGI. §§ 62(a)(2)(A) and (c).

Accounting income. The accountant's concept of income is generally based upon the realization principle. Financial accounting income may differ from taxable income (e.g., accelerated depreciation might be used for Federal income tax and straight-line depreciation for financial accounting purposes). Differences are included in a reconciliation of taxable and accounting income on Schedule M–1 or Schedule M–3 of Form 1120 for corporations.

Accounting method. The method under which income and expenses are determined for tax purposes. Important accounting methods include the cash basis and the accrual basis. Special methods are available for the reporting of gain on installment sales, recognition of income on construction projects (the completed contract and percentage of completion methods), and the valuation of inventories (last-in, first-out and first-in, first-out). Accounting methods deal with the timing of *when* income and deductions are reported. §§ 446–474.

Accounting period. The period of time, usually a year, used by a taxpayer for the determination of tax liability. Unless a fiscal year is chosen, taxpayers must determine and pay their income tax liability by using the calendar year (January 1 through December 31) as the period of measurement. An example of a fiscal year is July 1 through June 30. A change in accounting period (e.g., from a calendar year to a fiscal year) generally requires the consent of the IRS. Usually, taxpayers are free to select either an initial calendar or a fiscal year without the consent of the IRS. §§ 441–444.

Accrual method. A method of accounting that recognizes expenses as incurred and income as earned. In contrast to the cash basis of accounting, expenses need not be paid to be deductible, nor need income be received to be taxable. § 446(c)(2).

Accumulated adjustments account (AAA). An account that aggregates an S corporation's post-1982 income, loss, and deductions for the tax year (including nontaxable income and nondeductible losses and expenses). After the year-end income and expense adjustments are made, the account is reduced by distributions made during the tax year.

Accumulated E & P. Net undistributed tax-basis earnings of a corporation aggregated from March 1, 1913, to the end of the prior tax year. Used to determine the amount of dividend income associated with a distribution to shareholders. § 316 and Reg. § 1.316–2.

Accumulated earnings tax. A special 20 percent tax imposed on C corporations that accumulate (rather than distribute) their earnings beyond the reasonable needs of the business. The accumulated earnings tax and related interest are imposed on accumulated taxable income in addition to the corporate income tax. §§ 531–537.

Accuracy-related penalties. Major civil taxpayer penalties relating to the accuracy of tax return data, including misstatements stemming from taxpayer negligence and improper valuation of income and deductions, are coordinated under this umbrella term. The penalty usually equals 20 percent of the understated tax liability. § 6662.

Acquiescence. Agreement by the IRS on the results reached in certain judicial decisions; sometimes abbreviated *Acq.* or *A.*

Acquisition indebtedness. Debt incurred in acquiring, constructing, or substantially improving a qualified residence of the taxpayer. The interest on such loans is deductible as qualified residence interest. However, interest on such debt is deductible only on the portion of the indebtedness that does not exceed $750,000 ($1,000,000 for debt incurred before December 15, 2017). § 163(h)(3).

Active income. Wages, salary, commissions, bonuses, profits from a trade or business in which the taxpayer is a material participant, gain on the sale or other disposition of assets used in an active trade or business, and income from intangible property if the taxpayer's personal efforts significantly contributed to the creation of the property. The passive activity loss rules require classification of income and losses into three categories with active income being one of them.

Ad valorem taxes. A tax imposed on the value of property. The most common ad valorem tax is that imposed by states, counties, and cities on real estate. Ad valorem taxes can be imposed on personal property as well.

Additional first-year depreciation. In general, this provision provides for an additional cost recovery deduction of 100 percent for qualified property acquired and placed in service after September 27, 2017, and before January 1, 2027. (The bonus depreciation percentage is reduced by 20 percent for each tax year after 2022.) Qualified property includes most types of new and used property other than buildings. The taxpayer can elect to forgo this bonus depreciation. Different rules applied between 2008 and September 28, 2017. § 168(k).

Adjusted basis. The cost or other basis of property reduced by depreciation allowed or allowable and increased by capital improvements. Other special adjustments are provided in § 1016 and the related Regulations.

Adjusted gross estate. Used in determining eligibility for deferred payments of Federal estate tax. The gross estate less the sum allowable as deductions under § 2053 (expenses, indebtedness, and taxes) and § 2054 (casualty and theft losses during the administration of the estate). § 6166(b)(6).

Adjustments. In calculating AMTI, certain amounts (i.e., adjustments) are added to or deducted from the taxable income starting point of the AMTI calculation. These adjustments generally reflect timing differences. § 56.

Adoption expenses credit. A provision intended to assist taxpayers who incur nonrecurring costs directly associated with the adoption process, such as legal costs, social service review costs, and transportation costs. Up to $14,890 of costs incurred to adopt an eligible child qualify for the credit (unique rules apply when adopting a special needs child). A taxpayer may claim the credit in the year qualifying expenses are paid or incurred if the expenses are paid during or after the year in which the adoption is finalized. For qualifying expenses paid or incurred in a tax year prior to the year the adoption is finalized, the credit must be claimed in the tax year following the tax year during which the expenses are paid or incurred. § 23.

Affiliated group. A parent-subsidiary group of corporations that is eligible to elect to file on a consolidated basis. Eighty percent ownership of the voting power and value of all of the corporations must be achieved every day of the tax year, and an identifiable parent corporation must exist (i.e., it must own at least 80 percent of another group member without applying attribution rules). § 1504(a).

Aggregate (or conduit) concept. A perspective that regards a venture as an aggregation of its owners joined together in an agency relationship rather than as a separate entity. For tax purposes, this results in the income of the venture being taxable directly to its owners. For example, partnership income and expense, capital gains and losses, tax credits, etc., pass through the partnership (a conduit) and are subject to taxation at the partner level. Also, in an S corporation, certain items pass through and are reported on the returns of the shareholders. See also *entity concept.*

Alimony and separate maintenance payments. Alimony deductions result from the payment of a legal obligation arising from the termination of a marital relationship. Payments designated as alimony generally are included in the gross income of the recipient and are deductible *for* AGI by the payor. For divorce or separation instruments executed after December 31, 2018, alimony is neither gross income for the recipient nor deductible by the payor. § 71.

Alimony recapture. The amount of alimony that previously has been included in the gross income of the recipient and deducted by the payor that now is deducted by the recipient and included in the gross income of the payor as the result of front-loading. Alimony recapture is applicable for divorce or separation agreements executed before 2019. § 71(f).

All events test. As applied to the recognition of income, the all events test requires that income of an accrual basis taxpayer be recognized when (1) all events have occurred that fix the taxpayer's right to receive the income and (2) the amount can be determined with reasonable accuracy. Under § 451(b), an accrual method taxpayer must include amounts in income no later than for financial reporting purposes (other than for special rules such as the installment method). As applied to the recognition of expenses, the all events test prevents the recognition of a deduction by an accrual basis taxpayer until all the events have occurred that fix the taxpayer's related obligation. This can be contrasted with GAAP under which a fixed or legal obligation is not required before an expense is recognized. Reg. §§ 1.446–1(c)(1)(ii) and 1.461–1(a)(2).

Allocate. The assignment of income for various tax purposes. A multistate corporation's nonbusiness income usually is allocated to the state where the nonbusiness assets are located; it is not apportioned with the rest of the entity's income. The income and expense items of an estate or a trust are allocated between income and corpus components. Specific items of income, expense, gain, loss, and credit can be allocated to specific partners if a substantial economic nontax purpose for the allocation is established.

Alternate valuation date. Property passing from a decedent by death may be valued for estate tax purposes as of the date of death or the alternate valuation date. The alternate valuation date is six months after the date of death or the date the property is disposed of by the estate, whichever comes first. To use the alternate valuation date, the executor or administrator of the estate must make an affirmative election. The election applies to all of the estate's assets. Election of the alternate valuation date is not available unless it decreases the amount of the gross estate and reduces the estate tax liability. § 2032.

Alternative depreciation system (ADS). A cost recovery system in which the cost or other initial basis of an asset is recovered using the straight-line method over recovery periods similar to those used in MACRS. The alternative system must be used in certain instances and can be elected in other instances. § 168(g).

Alternative minimum tax (AMT). The AMT is a surtax, calculated as a percentage of alternative minimum taxable income (AMTI). AMTI generally starts with the taxpayer's taxable income, prior to any standard deduction taken. To this amount, the taxpayer (1) adds designated preference items (e.g., tax-exempt interest income on private activity bonds), (2) makes other specified adjustments (e.g., to reflect a slower cost recovery method), (3) adjusts certain AMT itemized deductions (e.g., interest incurred on housing), and (4) subtracts an exemption amount. The taxpayer must pay the greater of the resulting AMT or the regular income tax (reduced by all allowable tax credits). The AMT applies to individuals, trusts, and estates; the AMT does not apply to C corporations after 2017. AMT preferences and adjustments are assigned to partners, LLC members, and S corporation shareholders. §§ 55–59.

Alternative minimum tax credit. AMT liability can result from timing differences that give rise to positive adjustments in calculating AMTI. To provide equity for the taxpayer when these timing differences reverse, the regular tax liability may be reduced by a tax credit for a prior year's minimum tax liability attributable to timing differences. § 53.

Alternative minimum taxable income (AMTI). The base (prior to deducting the exemption amount) for computing a taxpayer's alternative minimum tax. This consists of the taxable income for the year modified for AMT adjustments and AMT preferences. § 55(b)(2).

Alternative tax. An option that is allowed in computing the tax on net capital gain. For noncorporate taxpayers, the rate is usually 15 percent (but is 25 percent for unrecaptured § 1250 gain and 28 percent for collectibles). However, the alternative tax rate is 0 percent (rather than 15 percent) for lower-income taxpayers (e.g., taxable income of $83,350 or less for married persons filing jointly). Certain high-income taxpayers (e.g., taxable income of more than $517,200 for married persons filing jointly) have an alternative tax rate of 20 percent. § 1(h).

Alternative tax NOL deduction (ATNOLD). In calculating the AMT, the taxpayer is allowed to deduct NOL carryovers following the regular tax NOL carryover provisions. The AMT NOL amount is referred to as the ATNOLD. The regular income tax NOL is modified for AMT adjustments and preferences to produce the ATNOLD. § 56(d).

American Opportunity credit. This credit applies for qualifying expenses for the first four years of postsecondary education. Qualified expenses include tuition and related expenses and books and other course materials. Room and board are ineligible for the credit. The maximum credit available per student is $2,500 (100 percent of the first $2,000 of qualified expenses and 25 percent of the next $2,000 of qualified expenses). Eligible students include the taxpayer, taxpayer's spouse, and taxpayer's dependents. To qualify for the credit, a student must take at least one-half of the full-time course load for at least one academic term at a qualifying educational institution. The credit is phased out for higher-income taxpayers. § 25A.

Amortization. The tax deduction for the cost or other basis of an intangible asset over the asset's estimated useful life. Examples of amortizable intangibles include patents, copyrights, and leasehold interests. Most purchased intangible assets (e.g., goodwill) can be amortized for income tax purposes over a 15-year period. § 197.

Amount realized. The amount received by a taxpayer upon the sale or exchange of property. Amount realized is the sum of the cash and the fair market value of any property or services received by the taxpayer plus any related debt assumed by the buyer. Determining the amount realized is the starting point for arriving at realized gain or loss. § 1001(b).

Annual exclusion. In computing the taxable gifts for the year, each donor excludes the first $16,000 (for 2022) of a gift to each donee. Usually, the annual exclusion is not available for gifts of future interests. § 2503(b).

Annuity. A fixed sum of money payable to a person at specified times for a specified period of time or for life. If the party making the payment (i.e., the obligor) is regularly engaged in this type of business (e.g., an insurance company), the arrangement is classified as a commercial annuity. A so-called private annuity involves an obligor that is not regularly engaged in selling annuities (e.g., a charity or family member).

Apportion. The assignment of the business income of a multistate corporation to specific states for income taxation. Usually, the apportionment procedure accounts for the property, payroll, and sales activity levels of the various states, and a proportionate assignment of the entity's total income is made using a statutory apportionment formula. Most states exclude nonbusiness income from the apportionment procedure; they allocate nonbusiness income to the states where the nonbusiness assets are located.

Appreciated inventory. In partnership taxation, appreciated inventory is a hot asset, and a partner's share of its ordinary income potential must be allocated to that partner. If a partner sells an interest in the partnership, ordinary income is recognized to the extent of the partner's share of the partnership's inventory and unrealized receivables. The definition of "inventory" here is broad enough to include any accounts receivable, including unrealized receivables. See also *substantially appreciated inventory*. § 751.

Arm's length. See *arm's length price*.

Arm's length price. The standard under which unrelated parties would determine an exchange price for a transaction. Suppose, for example, Cardinal Corporation sells property to its sole shareholder for $10,000. In testing whether the $10,000 is an "arm's length" price, one would ascertain the price that would have been negotiated between the corporation and an unrelated party in a bargained exchange.

ASC 740. Under Generally Accepted Accounting Principles, the rules for the financial reporting of the tax expense of an enterprise. Permanent differences affect the enterprise's effective tax rate. Temporary differences create a deferred tax asset or a deferred tax liability on the balance sheet.

ASC 740-10. An interpretation by the Financial Accounting Standards Board. When an uncertain tax return position exists, this interpretation is used to determine the financial reporting treatment, if any, for the taxpayer. If it is more likely than not (i.e., a greater than 50 percent probability) that the uncertain return position will be sustained (e.g., by the courts) on its technical merits, it must be reported on the financial statements. The amount to be reported then is computed based on the probabilities of the outcome of the technical review and the amounts at which the dispute would be resolved. If the more-likely-than-not test is failed, no current financial disclosure of the results of the return position is required.

Asset Depreciation Range (ADR) system. A system of estimated useful lives for categories of tangible assets prescribed by the IRS. The system provides a range for each category that extends from 20 percent above to 20 percent below the guideline class lives prescribed by the IRS.

Asset use test. In the context of a corporate reorganization, a means by which to determine if the continuity of business enterprise requirement is met. The acquiring corporation must continue to use the target entity's assets in the acquiror's business going forward; if this is not the case, the requirement is failed.

Assignment of income. A taxpayer attempts to avoid the recognition of income by assigning to another the property that generates the income. Such a procedure will not avoid income recognition by the taxpayer making the assignment if the income was earned at the point of the transfer. In this case, the income is taxed to the person who earns it.

At-risk limitation. Generally, a taxpayer can deduct losses related to a trade or business, S corporation, partnership, or investment asset only to the extent of the at-risk amount. The taxpayer has an amount at risk in a business or investment venture to the extent that personal assets have been subjected to the risks of the business. Typically, the taxpayer's at-risk amount includes (1) the amount of money or other property that the investor contributed to the venture for the investment, (2) the amount of any of the entity's liabilities for which the taxpayer personally is liable and that relate to the investment, and (3) an allocable share of nonrecourse debts incurred by the venture from third parties in arm's length transactions for real estate investments. § 465.

Attribution. Under certain circumstances, the tax law applies attribution (constructive ownership) rules to assign to one taxpayer the ownership interest of another taxpayer. If, for example, the stock of Gold Corporation is held 60 percent by Marsha and 40 percent by Sidney, Marsha may be deemed to own 100 percent of Gold Corporation if Marsha and Sidney are mother and child. In that case, the stock owned by Sidney is attributed to Marsha. Stated differently, Marsha has a 60 percent direct and a 40 percent indirect interest in Gold Corporation. It can also be said that Marsha is the constructive owner of Sidney's interest.

Automatic mileage method. Automobile expenses are generally deductible only to the extent the automobile is used in business or for the production of income. Personal commuting expenses are not deductible. The taxpayer may deduct actual expenses (including depreciation and insurance), or the standard (automatic) mileage rate may be used (58.5 cents per mile for 2022 and 56 cents per mile for 2021). Automobile expenses incurred for medical purposes are deductible to the extent of actual out-of-pocket expenses or at the rate of 18 cents per mile for 2022 and 16 cents per mile for 2021. For charitable activities, the rate is 14 cents per mile.

Average tax rate. The average tax rate is equal to the tax liability divided by taxable income. This rate can be useful in comparing taxpayers or a taxpayer's changed tax picture from one year to another.

B

Bad debt. A deduction is permitted if a business account receivable subsequently becomes partially or completely worthless, providing the income arising from the debt previously was included in income. Available methods are the specific charge-off method and the reserve method. However, except for certain financial institutions, TRA of 1986 repealed the use of the reserve method for 1987 and thereafter. If the reserve method is used, partially or totally worthless accounts are charged to the reserve. A nonbusiness bad debt deduction is allowed as a short-term capital loss if the loan did not arise in connection with the creditor's trade or business activities. Loans between related parties (family members) generally are classified as nonbusiness. § 166.

Balance sheet approach. The process under ASC 740 (SFAS 109) by which an entity's deferred tax expense or deferred tax benefit is determined as a result of the reporting period's changes in the balance sheet's deferred tax asset and deferred tax liability accounts.

Base Erosion and Anti-Abuse Tax (BEAT). A 10 percent minimum tax designed to prevent multinational corporations from shifting profits out of the United States to a foreign subsidiary located in a low-tax jurisdiction. § 59A.

Basis in partnership interest. The acquisition cost of the partner's ownership interest in the partnership. Includes purchase price and associated debt acquired from other partners and in the course of the entity's trade or business.

Benchmarking. The tax professional's use of two or more entities' effective tax rates and deferred tax balance sheet accounts. Used chiefly to compare the effectiveness of the entities' tax planning techniques and to suggest future tax-motivated courses of action.

Blockage rule. A factor to be considered in valuing a large block of corporate stock. Application of this rule generally justifies a discount in the asset's fair market value, because the disposition of a large amount of stock at any one time may depress the value of the shares in the marketplace.

Boot. Cash or property of a type not included in the definition of a tax-deferred exchange. The receipt of boot causes an otherwise tax-deferred transfer to become immediately taxable to the extent of the lesser of the fair market value of the boot or the realized gain on the transfer. For example, see transfers to controlled corporations under § 351(b), reorganizations under § 368, and like-kind exchanges under § 1031(b).

Built-in gains tax. A penalty tax designed to discourage a shift of the incidence of taxation on unrealized gains from a C corporation to its shareholders, via an S election. Under this provision, any recognized gain during the first five years of S status generates a corporate-level tax on a base not to exceed the aggregate untaxed built-in gains brought into the S corporation upon its election from C corporation taxable years. § 1374.

Built-in loss property. Property contributed to a corporation under § 351 or as a contribution to capital that has a basis in excess of its fair market value. An adjustment is necessary to step down the basis of the property to its fair market value. The adjustment prevents the corporation and the contributing shareholder from obtaining a double tax benefit. The corporation allocates the adjustment proportionately among the assets with the built-in loss. As an alternative to the corporate adjustment, the shareholder may elect to reduce the basis in the stock. § 362(e).

Business bad debt. A tax deduction allowed for obligations obtained in connection with a trade or business that have become either partially or completely worthless. In contrast to nonbusiness bad debts, business bad debts are deductible as business expenses. § 166.

Business purpose. A justifiable business reason for carrying out a transaction. Mere tax avoidance is not an acceptable business purpose. The presence of a business purpose is crucial in the area of corporate reorganizations and certain liquidations.

Buy-sell agreement. An arrangement, particularly appropriate in the case of a closely held corporation or a partnership, whereby the surviving owners (shareholders or partners) or the entity agrees to purchase the interest of a withdrawing owner. The buy-sell agreement provides for an orderly disposition of an interest in a business and may aid in setting the value of the interest for estate tax purposes.

Bypass amount. The amount that can be transferred by gift or at death free of any unified transfer tax. For 2022, the bypass amount is $12,060,000 for estate tax and $12,060,000 for gift tax.

Bypass election. In the context of a distribution by an S corporation, an election made by the entity to designate that the distribution is first from accumulated earnings and profits and only then from the accumulated adjustments account (AAA). § 1368(e)(3).

C

C corporation. A separate taxable entity subject to the rules of Subchapter C of the Code. This business form may create a double taxation effect relative to its shareholders. The entity is subject to the regular corporate tax and a number of penalty taxes at the Federal level.

Cafeteria plan. An employee benefit plan under which an employee is allowed to select from among a variety of employer-provided fringe benefits. Some of the benefits may be taxable, and some may be statutory nontaxable benefits (e.g., health and accident insurance and group term life insurance). The employee is taxed only on the taxable benefits selected. A cafeteria benefit plan is also referred to as a flexible benefit plan. § 125.

Capital account. The financial accounting analog of a partner's tax basis in the entity.

Capital account maintenance. Under the § 704(b) Regulations, partnership allocations will be respected only if capital accounts are maintained in accordance with those regulations. These so-called "§ 704(b) book capital accounts" are properly maintained if they reflect the partner's contributions and distributions of cash; increases and decreases for the fair market value of contributed/distributed property; and adjustments for the partner's share of income, gains, losses, and deductions. Certain other adjustments are also required. See also *economic effect test* and *Section 704(b) book capital accounts.*

Capital asset. Broadly speaking, all assets are capital except those specifically excluded from that definition by the Code. Major categories of noncapital assets include property held for resale in the normal course of business (inventory), trade accounts and notes receivable, and depreciable property and real estate used in a trade or business (§ 1231 assets). § 1221.

Capital contribution. Various means by which a shareholder makes additional funds available to the corporation (placed at the risk of the business), sometimes without the receipt of additional stock. If no stock is received, the contributions are added to the basis of the shareholder's existing stock investment and do not generate gross income to the corporation. § 118.

Capital gain property. Property contributed to a charitable organization that, if sold rather than contributed, would have resulted in long-term capital gain to the donor. § 170(e).

Capital gains. The gain from the sale or exchange of a capital asset.

Capital interest. Usually, the percentage of the entity's net assets that a partner would receive on liquidation. Typically determined by the partner's capital sharing ratio.

Capital losses. The loss from the sale or exchange of a capital asset.

Capital sharing ratio. A partner's percentage ownership of the entity's capital.

Carbon tax. A tax on fossil fuels to help reduce greenhouse gas emissions.

Carried interest. A "partnership interest held in connection with performance of services," as defined under § 1061. Long-term capital gains from such an interest are reclassified as short-term capital gains (with potential ordinary income treatment) unless the underlying asset that triggered the gain had more than a three-year holding period. This provision only applies to income and gains arising from managing portfolio investments on behalf of third-party investors, including publicly traded securities, commodities, certain real estate, or options to buy/sell such assets. Section 1061 was enacted in the TCJA of 2017 in an effort to curtail an industry practice that resulted in fund managers receiving partnership profits interests in exchange for services: these "profits partners" received long-term capital gain allocations from the fund, rather than ordinary income for the services provided in managing the fund's assets. In addition to § 1061, the IRS has, from time to time, announced that it might issue regulations (under its general "anti-abuse" authority) to expand the scope of the carried interest rules.

Cash balance plan. A hybrid form of pension plan similar in some aspects to a defined benefit plan. Such a plan is funded by the employer, and the employer bears the investment risks and rewards. But like defined contribution plans, a cash balance plan establishes allocations to individual employee accounts, and the payout for an employee depends on investment performance.

Cash method. See *cash receipts method.*

Cash receipts method. A method of accounting that reflects deductions as paid and income as received in any one tax year. However, deductions for prepaid expenses that benefit more than one tax year (e.g., prepaid rent and prepaid interest) usually are spread over the period benefited rather than deducted in the year paid. § 446(c)(1).

Casualty loss. A casualty is defined as "the complete or partial destruction of property resulting from an identifiable event of a sudden, unexpected, or unusual nature" (e.g., floods, storms, fires, auto accidents). Individuals may deduct a casualty loss only if the loss is incurred in a trade or business or in a transaction entered into for profit or arises from fire, storm, shipwreck, or other casualty or from theft. Individuals usually deduct personal casualty losses as itemized deductions subject to a $100 nondeductible amount and to an annual floor equal to 10 percent of adjusted gross income that applies after the $100 per casualty floor has been applied. Special rules are provided for the netting of certain casualty gains and losses. For tax years beginning after 2017 (and before 2026), personal casualty losses are limited to those sustained in an area designated as a disaster area by the President of the United States. §§ 165(c)(3) and (h).

Charitable contribution. Contributions made to qualified nonprofit organizations. Taxpayers, regardless of their accounting method, are generally allowed to deduct (subject to various restrictions and limitations) contributions in the year of payment. Accrual basis corporations may accrue contributions at year-end if payment is properly authorized before the end of the year and payment is made within three and one-half months after the end of the year. § 170.

Check-the-box Regulations. By using the check-the-box rules prudently, an entity can select the most attractive tax results offered by the Code, without being bound by legal forms. By default, an unincorporated entity with more than one owner is taxed as a partnership; an unincorporated entity with one owner is a disregarded entity, taxed as a sole proprietorship or corporate division. No action is necessary by the taxpayer if the legal form or default status is desired. Form 8832 is used to "check a box" and change the tax status. Not available if the entity is incorporated under state law.

Child tax credit. A tax credit based solely on the number of qualifying children under age 17. The maximum credit available is $2,000 per qualifying child. (In addition, a $500 nonrefundable credit is available for qualifying dependents other than qualifying children.) A qualifying child must be claimed as a dependent on a parent's tax return and have a Social Security number to qualify for the credit. Taxpayers who qualify for the child tax credit may also qualify for a supplemental credit. The supplemental credit is treated as a component of the earned income credit and is therefore refundable. The credit is phased out for higher-income taxpayers. (Different rules applied for 2021.) § 24. See also *dependent tax credit.*

Circuit Court of Appeals. Any of 13 Federal courts that consider tax matters appealed from the U.S. Tax Court, a U.S. District Court, or the U.S. Court of Federal Claims. Appeal from a U.S. Court of Appeals is to the U.S. Supreme Court by Certiorari.

Circular 230. A portion of the Federal tax Regulations that describes the levels of conduct at which a tax preparer must operate. Circular 230 dictates, for instance, that a tax preparer may not charge an unconscionable fee or delay the execution of a tax audit with inappropriate delays. Circular 230 requires that there be a reasonable basis for a tax return position and that no frivolous returns be filed.

Citator. A tax research resource that presents the judicial history of a court case and traces the subsequent references to the case. When these references include the citating cases' evaluations of the cited case's precedents, the research can obtain some measure of the efficacy and reliability of the original holding.

Claim of right doctrine. A judicially imposed doctrine applicable to both cash and accrual basis taxpayers that holds that an amount is includible in income upon actual or constructive receipt if the taxpayer has an unrestricted claim to the payment. For the tax treatment of amounts repaid when previously included in income under the claim of right doctrine, see § 1341.

Closely held C corporation. A regular corporation (i.e., the S election is not in effect) for which more than 50 percent of the value of its outstanding stock is owned, directly or indirectly, by five or fewer individuals at any time during the tax year. The term is relevant in identifying C corporations that are subject to the passive activity loss provisions. § 469.

Closely held corporation. A corporation where stock ownership is not widely dispersed. Rather, a few shareholders are in control of corporate policy and are in a position to benefit personally from that policy.

Closing agreement. In a tax dispute, the parties sign a closing agreement to spell out the terms under which the matters are settled. The agreement is binding on both the Service and the taxpayer. § 7121.

Collectibles. A special type of capital asset, the gain from which is taxed at a maximum rate of 28 percent if the holding period is more than one year. Examples include art, rugs, antiques, gems, metals, stamps, some coins and bullion, and alcoholic beverages held for investment. §§ 1(h)(5) and 408(m).

Combined return. In multistate taxation, a group of unitary corporations may elect or be required to file an income tax return that includes operating results for all of the affiliates, not just those with nexus in the state. Thus, apportionment data are reported for the group's worldwide or waters'-edge operations.

Community property. Arizona, California, Idaho, Louisiana, Nevada, New Mexico, Texas, Washington, and Wisconsin have community property systems. Alaska residents can elect community property status for assets. The rest of the states are common law property jurisdictions. The difference between common law and community property systems centers around the property rights possessed by married persons. In a common law system, each spouse owns whatever he or she earns. Under a community property system, one-half of the earnings of each spouse is considered owned by the other spouse. Assume, for example, that Jeff and Alice are husband and wife and that their only income is the

$50,000 annual salary Jeff receives. If they live in New York (a common law state), the $50,000 salary belongs to Jeff. If, however, they live in Texas (a community property state), the $50,000 salary is owned one-half each by Jeff and Alice.

Compensatory damages. Damages received or paid by the taxpayer can be classified as compensatory damages or as punitive damages. Compensatory damages are paid to compensate one for harm caused by another. Compensatory damages received on account of physical injuries are excludible from the recipient's gross income. § 104(a)(2).

Complete termination redemption. Sale or exchange treatment is available relative to this type of redemption. The shareholder must retire all of his or her outstanding shares in the corporation (ignoring family attribution rules) and cannot hold an interest, other than that of a creditor, for the 10 years following the redemption. § 302(b)(3).

Completed contract method. A method of reporting gain or loss on certain long-term contracts. Under this method of accounting, all gross income and expenses are recognized in the tax year in which the contract is completed. Reg. § 1.451–3.

Complex trust. Not a simple trust. Such trusts may have charitable beneficiaries, accumulate income, and distribute corpus. §§ 661–663.

Composite return. In multistate taxation, an S corporation may be allowed to file a single income tax return that assigns pass-through items to resident and nonresident shareholders. The composite or "block" return allows the entity to remit any tax that is attributable to the nonresident shareholders.

Conduit concept. A perspective taken toward a venture that regards the venture as an aggregation of its owners joined together in an agency relationship rather than as a separate entity. For tax purposes, this results in the income of the venture being taxable directly to its owners. For example, items of income and expense, capital gains and losses, tax credits, etc., realized by a partnership pass through the partnership (a conduit) and are subject to taxation at the partner level. Also, in an S corporation, certain items pass through and are reported on the returns of the shareholders.

Conduit perspective. See *conduit concept*.

Consolidated returns. A procedure whereby certain affiliated corporations may file a single return, combine the tax transactions of each corporation, and arrive at a single income tax liability for the group. The election to file a consolidated return usually is binding on future years. §§ 1501–1505 and related Regulations.

Consolidation. The combination of two or more corporations into a newly created corporation. Thus, Black Corporation and White Corporation combine to form Gray Corporation. A consolidation may qualify as a nontaxable reorganization if certain conditions are satisfied. §§ 354 and 368(a)(1)(A).

Constructive dividends. A taxable benefit derived by a shareholder from his or her corporation that is not actually initiated by the board of directors as a dividend. Examples include unreasonable compensation, excessive rent payments, bargain purchases of corporate property, and shareholder use of corporate property. Constructive dividends generally are found in closely held corporations.

Constructive liquidation scenario. The means by which recourse debt is shared among partners in basis determination.

Constructive receipt. If income is unqualifiedly available although not physically in the taxpayer's possession, it still is subject to the income tax. An example is accrued interest on a savings account. Under the constructive receipt concept, the interest is taxed to a depositor in the year available, rather than the year actually withdrawn. The fact that the depositor uses the cash basis of accounting for tax purposes is irrelevant. See Reg. § 1.451–2.

Continuity of business enterprise. In a tax-favored reorganization, the acquiring corporation must continue the historic business of the target or use a significant portion of the target's assets in the new business.

Continuity of interest. In a tax-favored reorganization, a shareholder or corporation that has substantially the same investment after an exchange as before should not be taxed on the transaction. Specifically, the target shareholders must acquire an equity interest in the acquiring corporation equal in value to at least 40 percent of all the outstanding stock of the target entity.

Control. Holding a specified level of stock ownership in a corporation. For § 351, the new shareholder(s) must hold at least 80 percent of the total combined voting power of all voting classes of stock and at least 80 percent of the shares of all nonvoting classes. Other tax provisions require different levels of control to bring about desired effects, such as 50 or 100 percent.

Controlled foreign corporation (CFC). A non-U.S. corporation in which more than 50 percent of the total combined voting power of all classes of stock entitled to vote or the total value of the stock of the corporation is owned by U.S. shareholders on any day during the taxable year of the foreign corporation. For purposes of this definition, a U.S. shareholder is any U.S. person who owns, or is considered to own, 10 percent or more of the total combined voting power of all classes of voting stock of the foreign corporation. Stock owned directly, indirectly, and constructively is used in this measure. See *U.S. shareholder*. §§ 951–965.

Controlled group. Controlled groups include parent-subsidiary groups, brother-sister groups, combined groups, and certain insurance companies. Controlled groups are required to share certain elements of tax calculations (e.g., $250,000 accumulated earnings credit) or tax credits (e.g., research credit). §§ 1561 and 1563.

Corporate liquidation. Occurs when a corporation distributes its net assets to its shareholders and ceases to be a going concern. Generally, a shareholder recognizes capital gain or loss upon the liquidation of the entity, regardless of the corporation's balance in its earnings and profits account. The liquidating corporation recognizes gain and loss on assets that it sells during the liquidation period and on assets that it distributes to shareholders in kind.

Corpus. The body or principal of a trust. Suppose, for example, Grant transfers an apartment building into a trust, income payable to Ruth for life, remainder to Shawn upon Ruth's death. Corpus of the trust is the apartment building.

Correspondence audit. An audit conducted by the IRS by the U.S. mail. Typically, the IRS writes to the taxpayer requesting the verification of a particular deduction or exemption. The remittance of copies of records or other support is requested of the taxpayer.

Cost depletion. Depletion that is calculated based on the adjusted basis of the asset. The adjusted basis is divided by the expected recoverable units to determine the depletion per unit. The depletion per unit is multiplied by the units sold during the tax year to calculate cost depletion. §§ 611 and 612.

Cost recovery. The system by which taxpayers are allowed to recover their investment in an asset by reducing their taxable income by the asset's cost or initial basis. Cost recovery methods include MACRS, § 179 expense, additional first-year deprecation, amortization, and depletion. §§ 168, 179, and 611.

Court of original jurisdiction. The Federal courts are divided into courts of original jurisdiction and appellate courts. A dispute between a taxpayer and the IRS is first considered by a court of original jurisdiction (i.e., a trial court). The four Federal courts of original jurisdiction are the U.S. Tax Court, the U.S. District Court, the U.S. Court of Federal Claims, and the Small Cases Division of the U.S. Tax Court.

Coverdell education savings account (§ 530 plan). Coverdell education savings account exempts from tax the earnings on amounts placed in a qualified account for the education expenses of a named beneficiary. Contributions are limited to $2,000 per year per beneficiary, and the proceeds can be withdrawn without tax provided the funds are used to pay qualified educational expenses for primary, secondary, or higher education. (There is an annual $10,000 per student limitation on distributions for tuition expenses for primary and secondary education.) Qualified educational expenses also include certain homeschooling expenses. The account is named for the late Senator Paul Coverdell (R-GA), who sponsored the legislation in Congress. § 530.

Credit for certain retirement plan contributions. A nonrefundable credit is available based on eligible contributions of up to $2,000 to certain qualified retirement plans, such as traditional and Roth IRAs and § 401(k) plans. The benefit provided by this credit is in addition to any deduction or exclusion that otherwise is available resulting from the qualifying contribution. The amount of the credit depends on the taxpayer's AGI and filing status. § 25B.

Credit for child and dependent care expenses. A nonrefundable tax credit ranging from 20 percent to 35 percent of employment-related expenses (child and dependent care expenses) for amounts of up to $6,000 is available to individuals who are employed (or deemed to be employed) and maintain a household for a dependent child under age 13, disabled spouse, or disabled dependent. (Different rules applied for 2021.) § 21.

Credit for employer-provided child care. A nonrefundable credit is available to employers who provide child care facilities to their employees during normal working hours. The credit, limited to $150,000, is comprised of two components. The portion of the credit for qualified child care expenses is equal to 25 percent of these expenses, while the portion of the credit for qualified child care resource and referral services is equal to 10 percent of these expenses. Any qualifying expenses otherwise deductible by the taxpayer must be reduced by the amount of the credit. In addition, the taxpayer's basis for any property used for qualifying purposes is reduced by the amount of the credit. § 45F.

Credit for employer-provided family and medical leave. A nonrefundable credit is available to employers who pay wages to employees while they are on family and medical leave. The credit is equal to 12.5 percent of wages paid to qualifying employees (limited to 12 weeks per employee per year). Employers must pay a minimum of 50 percent of the wages normally paid; if wages paid during the leave *exceed* 50 percent of normal wages, the credit is increased by 0.25 percent for each percentage point above 50 percent to a maximum of 25 percent of wages paid. The credit does not apply to wages paid in taxable years beginning after 2025. § 45S.

Credit for small employer pension plan startup costs. A nonrefundable credit available to small businesses based on administrative costs associated with establishing and maintaining certain qualified plans. While such qualifying costs generally are deductible as ordinary and necessary business expenses, the availability of the credit is intended to lower the costs of starting a qualified retirement program and therefore encourage qualifying businesses to establish retirement plans for their employees. The credit is available for eligible employers at the rate of 50 percent of qualified startup costs. The maximum credit is $500 (based on a maximum $1,000 of qualifying expenses). § 45E.

Crop insurance proceeds. The proceeds received when an insured crop is destroyed. Section 451(f) permits the farmer to defer reporting the income from the insurance proceeds until the tax year following the taxable year of the destruction.

Crop method. A method of accounting for agricultural crops that are planted in one year but harvested in a subsequent year. Under this method, the costs of raising the crop are accumulated as inventory and are deducted when the income from the crop is realized.

Cross-purchase buy-sell agreement. Under this arrangement, the surviving owners of the business agree to buy out the withdrawing owner. Assume, for example, Ron and Sara are equal shareholders in Tip Corporation. Under a cross-purchase buy-sell agreement, Ron and Sara would contract to purchase the other's interest, should that person decide to withdraw from the business.

Current distribution. A payment made by a partnership to a partner when the partnership's legal existence does not cease thereafter. The partner usually assigns a basis in the distributed property that is equal to the lesser of the partner's basis in the partnership interest (substituted basis) or the basis of the distributed asset to the partnership (carryover basis). The partner first assigns basis to any cash that he or she receives in the distribution. A cash distribution in excess of the partner's basis triggers a gain. The partner's remaining basis, if any, is assigned to the noncash assets according to their relative bases to the partnership.

Current E & P. Net tax-basis earnings of a corporation aggregated during the current tax year. A corporate distribution is deemed to be first from the entity's current earnings and profits and then from accumulated earnings and profits. Shareholders recognize dividend income to the extent of the earnings and profits of the corporation. A dividend results to the extent of current earnings and profits, even if there is a larger negative balance in accumulated earnings and profits.

Current tax expense. Under ASC 740 (SFAS 109), the book tax expense that relates to the current reporting period's net income and is actually payable (or creditable) to the appropriate governmental agencies for the current period. Also known as "cash tax" or "tax payable."

D

***De minimis* fringe.** Benefits provided to employees that are too insignificant to warrant the time and effort required to account for the benefits received by each employee and the value of those benefits. Such amounts are excludible from the employee's gross income. § 132.

***De minimis* fringe benefits.** See *de minimis fringe*.

Death benefits. A payment made by an employer to the beneficiary or beneficiaries of a deceased employee on account of the death of the employee.

Debt-financed income. Included in computations of the unrelated business income of an exempt organization, the gross income generated from debt-financed property.

Deceased spouse's unused exclusion (DSUE). In computing the Federal estate tax, the decedent uses the exclusion amount to shelter an amount of the gross estate from taxation. When the first spouse to die fails to use a portion of his/her exclusion amount, the unused portion is "portable" and becomes available to the surviving spouse. The surviving spouse can use the DSUE only of his/her last spouse to predecease. § 2010(c)(4).

Deduction for qualified business income. A deduction allowed for noncorporate taxpayers based on the qualified business income of a qualified trade or business. In general, the deduction is limited to the lesser of 20 percent of qualified business income, or 20 percent of taxable income before the qualified business income deduction less any net capital gain. There are *three limitations* on the deduction—an overall limitation (based on modified taxable income), another that applies to high-income taxpayers, and a third that applies to certain types of services businesses. § 199A.

Deductions *for* adjusted gross income. The Federal income tax is not imposed upon gross income. Rather, it is imposed upon taxable income. Congressionally identified deductions for individual taxpayers are subtracted either from gross income to arrive at adjusted gross income or from adjusted gross income to arrive at the tax base, taxable income.

Deductions *from* adjusted gross income. See *deductions for adjusted gross income*.

Deductions in respect of a decedent. Deductions accrued at the moment of death but not recognizable on the final income tax return of a decedent because of the method of accounting used. Such items are allowed as deductions on the estate tax return and on the income tax return of the estate (Form 1041) or the heir (Form 1040). An example of a deduction in respect of a decedent is interest expense accrued to the date of death by a cash basis debtor.

Deferred compensation. Compensation that will be taxed when received or upon the removal of certain restrictions on receipt and not when earned. Contributions by an employer to a qualified pension or profit sharing plan on behalf of an employee are an example. The contributions will not be taxed to the employee until the funds are made available or distributed to the employee (e.g., upon retirement).

Deferred tax asset. Under ASC 740, an asset recorded on the balance sheet to reflect the future tax benefits related to a transaction or activity which has already been reflected in the financial statements. A deferred tax asset is often the result of the deferral of a deduction or the acceleration of income for tax purposes relative to Generally Accepted Accounting Principles.

Deferred tax benefit. Under ASC 740, a reduction in the book tax expense that relates to the current reporting period's net income but will not be realized until a future reporting period. Creates or adds to the entity's deferred tax asset balance sheet account. For instance, the carryforward of a net operating loss is a deferred tax benefit.

Deferred tax expense. Under ASC 740, a book tax expense that relates to the current reporting period's net income but will not be realized until a future reporting period. Creates or adds to the entity's deferred tax liability balance sheet account. For instance, a deferred tax expense is created when tax depreciation deductions for the period are "accelerated" and exceed the corresponding book depreciation expense.

Deferred tax liability. Under ASC 740, a liability recorded on the balance sheet to reflect the future tax costs of a transaction or activity which has already been reflected in the financial statements. A deferred tax liability is often the result of the deferral of the recognition of income or the acceleration of a deduction for tax purposes relative to Generally Accepted Accounting Principles.

Defined benefit plan. Qualified plans can be dichotomized into defined benefit plans and defined contribution plans. Under a defined benefit plan, a formula defines the benefits employees are to receive. The formula usually includes years of service, employee compensation, and some stated percentage. The employer must make annual contributions based on actuarial computations that will be sufficient to pay the vested retirement benefits.

Defined contribution pension plan. Qualified plans can be dichotomized into defined benefit plans and defined contribution plans. Under a defined contribution plan, a separate account is maintained for each covered employee. The employee's benefits under the plan are based solely on (1) the amount contributed and (2) income from the fund that accrues to the employee's account. The plan defines the amount the employer is required to contribute (e.g., a flat dollar amount, an amount based on a special formula, or an amount equal to a certain percentage of compensation).

Dependency exemptions. See *personal and dependency exemptions*.

Dependent tax credit. For 2018 through 2025, the TCJA of 2017 replaced the dependency exemption with a $500 nonrefundable credit. This credit can be claimed for dependents who are not a qualifying child or under the age of 17. The dependent must be a citizen or resident of the United States. § 24(h).

Depletion. The process by which the cost or other basis of a natural resource (e.g., an oil or gas interest) is recovered upon extraction and sale of the resource. The two ways to determine the depletion allowance are the cost and percentage (or statutory) methods. Under cost depletion, each unit of production sold is assigned a portion of the cost or other basis of the interest. This is determined by dividing the cost or other basis by the total units expected to be recovered. Under percentage (or statutory) depletion, the tax law provides a special percentage factor for different types of minerals and other natural resources. This percentage is multiplied by the gross income from the interest to arrive at the depletion allowance. §§ 611–613A.

Depreciation. The system by which a taxpayer allocates for financial reporting purposes the cost of an asset to periods benefited by the asset.

Determination letter. Upon the request of a taxpayer, the IRS will comment on the tax status of a completed transaction. Determination letters frequently are used to determine whether a retirement or profit sharing plan qualifies under the Code and to determine the tax-exempt status of certain nonprofit organizations.

Disabled access credit. A tax credit designed to encourage small businesses to make their facilities more accessible to disabled individuals. The credit is equal to 50 percent of the eligible expenditures that exceed $250 but do not exceed $10,250. Thus, the maximum amount for the credit is $5,000. The adjusted basis for depreciation is reduced by the amount of the credit. To qualify, the facility must have been placed in service before November 6, 1990. § 44.

Disaster area losses. A casualty sustained in an area designated as a disaster area by the President of the United States. In such an event, the disaster loss may be treated as having occurred in the taxable year immediately preceding the year in which the disaster actually occurred. Thus, immediate tax benefits are provided to victims of a disaster. § 165(i).

Disclaimer. Rejections, refusals, or renunciations of claims, powers, or property. Section 2518 sets forth the conditions required to avoid gift tax consequences as the result of a disclaimer.

Disguised sale. When a partner contributes property to the entity and soon thereafter receives a distribution from the partnership, the transactions are collapsed and the distribution is seen as a purchase of the asset by the partnership. § 707(a)(2)(B).

Disproportionate distribution. A distribution from a partnership to one or more of its partners in which at least one partner's interest in partnership hot assets is increased or decreased. For example, a distribution of cash to one partner and hot assets to another changes both partners' interest in hot assets and is disproportionate. The intent of the disproportionate distribution rules is to ensure that each partner eventually recognizes his or her proportionate share of partnership ordinary income.

Disproportionate redemption. Sale or exchange treatment is available relative to this type of redemption. After the exchange, the shareholder owns less than 80 percent of his or her pre-redemption interest in the corporation and only a minority interest in the entity. § 302(b)(2).

Disregarded entity. The Federal income tax treatment of business income usually follows the legal form of the taxpayer (i.e., an individual's sole proprietorship is reported on the Form 1040); a C corporation's taxable income is computed on Form 1120. The check-the-box Regulations are used if the unincorporated taxpayer wants to use a different tax regime. Under these rules, a disregarded entity is taxed as an individual or a corporate division; other tax regimes are not available. For instance, a one-member limited liability company is a disregarded entity.

Distributable net income (DNI). The measure that determines the nature and amount of the distributions from estates and trusts that the beneficiaries must include in income. DNI also limits the amount that estates and trusts can claim as a deduction for such distributions. § 643(a).

Distributive share. In partnership or S corporation taxation, the distributive share is the amount of income, gain, deduction, loss, or credit allocated to a given partner or shareholder. The distributive share is the amount reported on a given line of the owner's Schedule K–1. For example, a partner's distributive share of ordinary income is the amount of income shown on that partner's Schedule K–1, Part III, line 1. For S corporations, the distributive share must be determined based on the shareholder's ownership percentage. For partnerships, the distributive share is generally determined in accordance with the partnership agreement. For both types of entities, amounts can be prorated if the ownership interest is transferred during the tax year.

Dividend. A nondeductible distribution to the shareholders of a corporation. A dividend constitutes gross income to the recipient if it is paid from the current or accumulated earnings and profits of the corporation. § 316.

Dividends received deduction. A deduction allowed a shareholder that is a corporation for dividends received from a domestic corporation. The deduction usually is 50 percent of the dividends received, but it could be 65 or 100 percent depending upon the ownership percentage held by the recipient corporation. §§ 243–246.

Divisive reorganization. A "Type D" spin-off, split-off, or split-up reorganization in which the original corporation divides its active business (in existence for at least five years) assets among two or more corporations. The stock received by the original corporation shareholders must be at least 80 percent of the other corporations.

Dock sales. A purchaser uses its owned or rented vehicles to take possession of the product at the seller's shipping dock. In most states, the sale is apportioned to the operating state of the purchaser, rather than the seller. See also *apportion* and *sales factor*.

Dollar-value LIFO. An inventory technique that focuses on the dollars invested in the inventory rather than the particular items on hand each period. Each inventory item is assigned to a pool. A pool is a collection of similar items and is treated as a separate inventory. At the end of the period, each pool is valued in terms of prices at the time LIFO was adopted (base period prices), whether or not the particular items were actually on hand in the year LIFO was adopted, to compare with current prices to determine if there has been an increase or decrease in inventories.

E

Earned income credit. A tax credit designed to provide assistance to certain low-income individuals who generally have a qualifying child. This is a refundable credit. To receive the most beneficial treatment, the taxpayer must have qualifying children. However, it is possible to qualify for the credit without having a child. See the text chapter on credits for the computation procedure required in order to determine the amount of the credit allowed. § 32.

Earnings and profits (E & P). Measures the economic capacity of a corporation to make a distribution to shareholders that is not a return of capital. Such a distribution results in dividend income to the shareholders to the extent of the corporation's current and accumulated earnings and profits.

Economic effect test. Requirements that must be met before a special allocation may be used by a partnership. The premise behind the test is that each partner who receives an allocation of income or loss from a partnership bears the economic benefit or burden of the allocation.

Economic income. The change in the taxpayer's net worth, as measured in terms of market values, plus the value of the assets the taxpayer consumed during the year. Because of the impracticality of this income model, it is not used for tax purposes.

Economic performance test. One of the requirements that must be satisfied for an accrual basis taxpayer to deduct an expense. Economic performance occurs when property or services are provided to the taxpayer, or in the case in which the taxpayer is required to provide property or services, whenever the property or services are actually provided by the taxpayer.

Education expenses. Taxpayers may deduct education expenses that are incurred either (1) to maintain or improve existing job-related skills or (2) to meet the express requirements of the employer or the requirements imposed by law to retain employment status. The expenses are not deductible if the education is required to meet the minimum educational standards for the taxpayer's job or if the education qualifies the individual for a new trade or business. The TCJA of 2017 suspended the deduction of unreimbursed employee trade or business expenses for tax years after 2017 (and through 2025). Reg. § 1.162–5.

Educational savings bonds. U.S. Series EE bonds whose proceeds are used for qualified higher educational expenses for the taxpayer, the taxpayer's spouse, or a dependent. The interest may be excluded from gross income, provided the taxpayer's adjusted gross income does not exceed certain amounts. § 135.

Effective tax rate. The financial statements for an entity include several footnotes, one of which reconciles the expected (statutory) income tax rate (e.g., 21 percent for a C corporation) with the effective tax rate. The effective tax rate is equal to taxes paid (often the tax liability) divided by the taxpayer's ability to pay (some income measure, like adjusted gross income or disposable income). For financial reporting purposes, effective tax rate generally refers to total tax expense as a percentage of pretax book income. The reconciliation often is done in dollar and/or percentage terms.

Effectively connected income. Income of a nonresident alien or foreign corporation that is attributable to the operation of a U.S. trade or business under either the asset use or the business activities test.

E-file. The electronic filing of a tax return. The filing is either direct or indirect. In direct filing, the taxpayer goes online using a computer and tax return preparation software. Indirect filing occurs when a taxpayer utilizes an authorized IRS e-file provider. The provider often is the *tax preparer*.

E-filing. See *e-file*.

Employment taxes. Taxes that an employer must pay on account of its employees. Employment taxes include FICA (Federal Insurance Contributions Act) and FUTA (Federal Unemployment Tax Act) taxes. Employment taxes are paid to the IRS in addition to income tax withholdings at specified intervals. Such taxes can be levied on the employees, the employer, or both.

Energy credits. See *energy tax credits*.

Energy tax credits. Various tax credits are available to those who invest in certain energy property. The purpose of the credit is to create incentives for conservation and to develop alternative energy sources.

Enrolled agents (EAs). A tax practitioner who has gained admission to practice before the IRS by passing an IRS examination and maintaining a required level of continuing professional education.

Entity accounting income. Entity accounting income is not identical to the taxable income of a trust or estate, nor is it determined in the same manner as the entity's financial accounting income would be. The trust document or will determines whether certain income, expenses, gains, or losses are allocated to the corpus of the entity or to the entity's income beneficiaries. Only the items that are allocated to the income beneficiaries are included in entity accounting income.

Entity buy-sell agreement. An arrangement whereby the entity is to purchase a withdrawing owner's interest. When the entity is a corporation, the agreement generally involves a stock redemption on the part of the withdrawing shareholder. See also *buy-sell agreement* and *cross-purchase buy-sell agreement*.

Entity concept. A perspective that regards a venture as an entity separate and distinct from its owners. For tax purposes, this results in the venture being directly responsible for the tax on the income it generates. The entity perspective taken toward C corporations results in the double taxation of income distributed to the corporation's owners.

Entity perspective. See *entity concept*.

Estate tax. A tax imposed on the right to transfer property by death. Thus, an estate tax is levied on the decedent's estate and not on the heir receiving the property. § 2001.

Estimated tax. The amount of tax (including alternative minimum tax and self-employment tax) a taxpayer expects to owe for the year after subtracting tax credits and income tax withheld. The estimated tax must be paid in installments at designated intervals (e.g., for a calendar year individual taxpayer, by April 15, June 15, September 15, and January 15 of the following year).

Excess business loss. The excess of aggregate deductions of the taxpayer attributable to trades or businesses of the taxpayer over the sum of aggregate gross income or gain of the taxpayer plus a threshold amount. In 2022, the threshold amount is $270,000 ($540,000 in the case of a married taxpayer filing a joint return). The threshold amount is adjusted for inflation each year. This loss limitation applies to taxpayers other than C corporations and applies after the passive activity loss limitation of § 469. § 461(l).

Excess lobbying expenditures. An excise tax is applied on otherwise tax-exempt organizations with respect to the excess of total lobbying expenditures over grass roots lobbying expenditures for the year.

Excess loss account. When a subsidiary has generated more historical losses than its parent has invested in the entity, the parent's basis in the subsidiary is zero, and the parent records additional losses in an excess loss account. This treatment allows the parent to continue to deduct losses of the subsidiary, even where no basis reduction is possible, while avoiding the need to show a negative stock basis on various financial records. If the subsidiary stock is sold while an excess loss account exists, capital gain income usually is recognized to the extent of the balance in the account.

Excise taxes. A tax on the manufacture, sale, or use of goods; on the carrying on of an occupation or activity; or on the transfer of property. Thus, the Federal estate and gift taxes are, theoretically, excise taxes.

Exclusion amount. The value of assets that is exempt from transfer tax due to the credit allowed for gifts or transfers by death. For gifts and deaths in 2022, the exclusion amount is $12,060,000. An exclusion amount unused by a deceased spouse may be used by the surviving spouse. See also *exemption equivalent amount.*

Exempt organizations. An organization that is either partially or completely exempt from Federal income taxation. § 501.

Exemption amount. An amount deducted from alternative minimum taxable income (AMTI) to determine the alternative minimum tax base. The exemption amount is adjusted for inflation and is phased out when AMTI exceeds specified threshold amounts. § 55(d).

Exemption equivalent. The maximum value of assets that can be transferred to another party without incurring any Federal gift or estate tax. See also *exemption equivalent amount.*

Exemption equivalent amount. The nontaxable amount (in 2022, $12,060,000 for gift tax and estate tax) that is the equivalent of the unified transfer tax credit allowed.

F

Fair market value. The amount at which property would change hands between a willing buyer and a willing seller, neither being under any compulsion to buy or to sell and both having reasonable knowledge of the relevant facts. Reg. §§ 1.1001–1(a) and 20.2031–1(b).

Farm price method. A method of accounting for agricultural crops. The inventory of crops is valued at its market price less the estimated cost of disposition (e.g., freight and selling expense).

Feeder organization. An entity that carries on a trade or business for the benefit of an exempt organization. However, such a relationship does not result in the feeder organization itself being tax-exempt. § 502.

FICA tax. An abbreviation that stands for Federal Insurance Contributions Act, commonly referred to as the Social Security tax. The FICA tax is comprised of the Social Security tax (old age, survivors, and disability insurance) and the Medicare tax (hospital insurance) and is imposed on both employers and employees. The employer is responsible for withholding from the employee's wages the Social Security tax at a rate of 6.2 percent on a maximum wage base and the Medicare tax at a rate of 1.45 percent (no maximum wage base). The maximum Social Security wage base for 2022 is $147,000 and for 2021 is $142,800.

Fiduciary. One who holds a legal obligation to act on another's behalf. A *trustee* and an *executor* take fiduciary relationships relative to the *grantor* and the *decedent*, respectively. The fiduciary is assigned specific duties by the principal party (e.g., to file tax returns, manage assets, satisfy debt and other obligations, and to make investment decisions). The fiduciary often possesses specialized knowledge and experience. A fiduciary must avoid conflicts of interest in which the principal's goals are compromised in some way.

Field audit. An audit conducted by the IRS on the business premises of the taxpayer or in the office of the tax practitioner representing the taxpayer.

Filing status. Individual taxpayers are placed in one of five filing statuses each year (single, married filing jointly, married filing separately, surviving spouse, or head of household). Marital status and household support are key determinants. Filing status is used to determine the taxpayer's filing requirements, standard deduction, eligibility for certain deductions and credits, and tax liability.

Final Regulations. The U.S. Treasury Department Regulations (abbreviated Reg.) represent the position of the IRS as to how the Internal Revenue Code is to be interpreted. Their purpose is to provide taxpayers and IRS personnel with rules of general and specific application to the various provisions of the tax law. Regulations are published in the *Federal Register* and in all tax services.

Financial Accounting Standards Board (FASB). See *Generally Accepted Accounting Principles (GAAP).*

Financial transaction tax. A tax imposed on some type of financial transaction, such as stock sales.

Fiscal year. A 12-month period ending on the last day of a month other than December. In certain circumstances, a taxpayer is permitted to elect a fiscal year instead of being required to use a calendar year.

Flat tax. A form of consumption tax designed to alleviate the regressivity of a value added tax (VAT). It is imposed on individuals and businesses at the same single (flat) rate.

Flexible spending plans. An employee benefit plan that allows the employee to take a reduction in salary in exchange for the employer paying benefits that can be provided by the employer without the employee being required to recognize income (e.g., medical and child care benefits). Contributions to a flexible spending plan are limited to $2,850 for 2022. § 125(i).

Flow-through entity. The entity is a tax reporter rather than a taxpayer. The owners are subject to tax. Examples are partnerships, S corporations, and limited liability companies.

Foreign-Derived Intangible Income (FDII). Income earned from sales by U.S. corporations to foreign customers from intangible assets held in the United States. § 250(b).

Foreign earned income exclusion. The Code allows exclusions for earned income generated outside the United States to alleviate any tax base and rate disparities among countries. In addition, the exclusion is allowed for housing expenditures incurred by the taxpayer's employer with respect to the non-U.S. assignment, and self-employed individuals can deduct foreign housing expenses incurred in a trade or business. The exclusion is limited to $112,000 per year for 2022 ($108,700 in 2021). § 911.

Foreign Investment in Real Property Tax Act (FIRPTA). Under the Foreign Investment in Real Property Tax Act, gains or losses realized by nonresident aliens and non-U.S. corporations on the disposition of U.S. real estate create U.S.-source income and are subject to U.S. income tax.

Foreign tax credit (FTC). A U.S. citizen or resident who incurs or pays income taxes to a foreign country on income subject to U.S. tax may be able to claim some of these taxes as a credit against the U.S. income tax. §§ 27 and 901–905.

Franchise. An agreement that gives the transferee the right to distribute, sell, or provide goods, services, or facilities within a specified area. The cost of obtaining a franchise may be amortized over a statutory period of 15 years. In general, the franchisor's gain on the sale of franchise rights is an ordinary gain because the franchisor retains a significant power, right, or continuing interest in the subject of the franchise. §§ 197 and 1253.

Franchise tax. A tax levied on the right to do business in a state as a corporation. Although income considerations may come into play, the tax usually is based on the capitalization of the corporation.

Fraud. Tax fraud falls into two categories: civil and criminal. Under civil fraud, the IRS may impose as a penalty an amount equal to as much as 75 percent of the underpayment [§ 6651(f)]. Fines and/or imprisonment are prescribed for conviction of various types of criminal tax fraud (§§ 7201–7207). Both civil and criminal fraud involve a specific intent on the part of the taxpayer to evade the tax; mere negligence is not enough. Criminal fraud requires the additional element of willfulness (i.e., done deliberately and with evil purpose). In practice, it becomes difficult to distinguish between the degree of intent necessary to support criminal, rather than civil, fraud. In either situation, the IRS has the burden of proof to show the taxpayer committed fraud.

Fringe benefits. Compensation or other benefit received by an employee that is not in the form of cash. Some fringe benefits (e.g., accident and health plans, group term life insurance) may be excluded from the employee's gross income and therefore are not subject to the Federal income tax.

Fruit and tree metaphor. The courts have held that an individual who earns income from property or services cannot assign that income to another. For example, a father cannot assign his earnings from commissions to his child and escape income tax on those amounts.

Functional currency. The currency of the economic environment in which the taxpayer carries on most of its activities and in which the taxpayer transacts most of its business.

FUTA tax. An employment tax levied on employers. Jointly administered by the Federal and state governments, the tax provides funding for unemployment benefits. FUTA applies at a rate of 6.0 percent on the first $7,000 of covered wages paid during the year for each employee. The Federal government allows a credit for FUTA paid (or allowed under a merit rating system) to the state. The credit cannot exceed 5.4 percent of the covered wages. §§ 3301–3311.

Future interest. An interest that will come into being at some future time. It is distinguished from a present interest, which already exists. Assume that Dan transfers securities to a newly created trust. Under the terms of the trust instrument, income from the securities is to be paid each year to Wilma for her life, with the securities passing to Sam upon Wilma's death. Wilma has a present interest in the trust because she is entitled to current income distributions. Sam has a future interest because he must wait for Wilma's death to benefit from the trust. The annual exclusion of $16,000 (in 2022) is not allowed for a gift of a future interest. § 2503(b).

G

General business credit. The summation of various nonrefundable business credits, including the tax credit for rehabilitation expenditures, business energy credit, work opportunity credit, research activities credit, low-income housing credit, and disabled access credit. The amount of general business credit that can be used to reduce the tax liability is limited to the taxpayer's net income tax reduced by the greater of (1) the tentative minimum tax or (2) 25 percent of the net regular tax liability that exceeds $25,000. Unused general business credits can be carried back one year and forward 20 years. § 38.

General partners. A partner who is fully liable in an individual capacity for the debts owed by the partnership to third parties. A general partner's liability is not limited to the investment in the partnership. See also *limited partners*.

General partnership (GP). A partnership that is owned by general partners (only). Creditors of a general partnership can collect amounts owed them from both the partnership assets and the assets of the partners individually.

Generally Accepted Accounting Principles (GAAP). Guidelines relating to how to construct the financial statements of enterprises doing business in the United States. Promulgated chiefly by the Financial Accounting Standards Board (FASB).

Gift tax. A tax imposed on the transfer of property by gift. The tax is imposed upon the donor of a gift and is based on the fair market value of the property on the date of the gift. § 2501.

Global Intangible Low-Taxed Income (GILTI). Income earned by a controlled foreign corporation on intellectual property or intangibles, the tax on which being designed to limit the shifting of intangible assets to countries with tax rates below the U.S. corporate rate. § 951A.

Golden parachute payments. A severance payment to employees that meets the following requirements: (1) the payment is contingent on a change of ownership of a corporation through a stock or asset acquisition and (2) the aggregate present value of the payment equals or exceeds three times the employee's average annual compensation. To the extent the severance payment meets these conditions, a deduction is disallowed to the employer for the excess of the payment over a statutory base amount (a five-year average of compensation if the taxpayer was an employee for the entire five-year period). In addition, a 20 percent excise tax is imposed on the employee who receives the excess severance pay. §§ 280G and 4999.

Goodwill. The reputation and other unidentifiable intangible assets of a company. For accounting purposes, goodwill has no basis unless it is purchased. In the purchase of a business, goodwill generally is the difference between the purchase price and the fair market value of the assets acquired. The intangible asset goodwill can be amortized for tax purposes over a 15-year period. § 197 and Reg. § 1.167(a)–3.

Grantor. A transferor of property. The creator of a trust is usually referred to as the grantor of the entity.

Grantor trust. A trust under which the grantor retains control over the income or corpus (or both) to such an extent that he or she is treated as the owner of the property and its income for income tax purposes. Income from a grantor trust is taxable to the grantor and not to the beneficiary who receives it. §§ 671–679.

Grass roots expenditures. Exempt organizations are prohibited from engaging in political activities, but spending incurred to influence the opinions of the general public relative to specific legislation is permitted by the law.

Gross estate. The property owned or previously transferred by a decedent that is subject to the Federal estate tax. The gross estate can be distinguished from the probate estate, which is property actually subject to administration by the administrator or executor of an estate. §§ 2031–2046.

Gross income. Income subject to the Federal income tax. Gross income does not include all economic income. That is, certain exclusions are allowed (e.g., interest on municipal bonds). For a manufacturing or merchandising business, gross income usually means gross profit (gross sales or gross receipts less cost of goods sold). § 61 and Reg. § 1.61–3(a).

Group term life insurance. Life insurance coverage provided by an employer for a group of employees. Such insurance is renewable on a year-to-year basis, and typically no cash surrender value is built up. The premiums paid by the employer on the insurance are not taxed to the employees on coverage of up to $50,000 per person. § 79 and Reg. § 1.79–1(b).

Guaranteed payments. Payments made by a partnership to a partner for services rendered or for the use of capital to the extent the payments are determined without regard to the income of the partnership. The payments are treated as though they were made to a nonpartner and thus are deducted by the entity. On the partnership's Schedule K and the partners' Schedules K–1, guaranteed payments are distinguished between those payments for use of the partners' capital and those paid for services provided by the partners to the partnership. The partners report the amounts as ordinary income based on the timing and amounts reported on their respective Schedules K–1. In addition to being subject to the income tax, a guaranteed payment might be subject to self-employment tax (guaranteed payment for services) or net investment income tax (guaranteed payment for capital). Guaranteed payments are not eligible for the qualified business income deduction. § 707(c).

H

Half-year convention. A cost recovery convention that assumes that property is placed in service at mid-year and thus provides for a half-year's cost recovery for that year. § 168(d).

Head of household. An unmarried individual who maintains a household for another and satisfies certain conditions set forth in § 2(b). This status enables the taxpayer to use a set of income tax rates that are lower than those applicable to other unmarried individuals but higher than those applicable to surviving spouses and married persons filing a joint return.

Health Savings Account (HSA). A medical savings account created in legislation enacted in December 2003 that is designed to replace and expand Archer Medical Savings Accounts. § 223.

Highly compensated employee. The employee group is generally divided into two categories for fringe benefit (including pension and profit sharing plans) purposes. These are (1) highly compensated employees and (2) non-highly compensated employees. For most fringe benefits, if the fringe benefit plan discriminates in favor of highly compensated employees, it will not be a qualified plan with respect, at a minimum, to the highly compensated employees.

Historic business test. In a corporate reorganization, a means by which to determine if the continuity of business enterprise requirement is met. The acquiring corporation must continue to operate the target entity's existing business(es) going forward; if this is not the case, the requirement is failed.

Hobby losses. Losses from an activity not engaged in for profit. The Code restricts the amount of losses that an individual can deduct for hobby activities so that these transactions cannot be used to offset income from other sources. The TCJA of 2017 suspended the deduction of hobby expenses for tax years after 2017 (and through 2025). § 183.

Holding period. The period of time during which property has been held for income tax purposes. The holding period is significant in determining whether gain or loss from the sale or exchange of a capital asset is long or short term. § 1223.

Home equity loans. Loans that utilize the personal residence of the taxpayer as security. The interest on such loans is deductible as qualified residence interest. However, interest is deductible only on the portion of the loan that does not exceed the lesser of (1) the fair market value of the residence, reduced by the acquisition indebtedness, or (2) $100,000 ($50,000 for married persons filing separate returns). A major benefit of a home equity loan is that there are no tracing rules regarding the use of the loan proceeds. The TCJA of 2017 suspended the deduction of interest on home equity indebtedness for tax years after 2017 (and through 2025). § 163(h)(3).

Hot assets. Unrealized receivables and substantially appreciated inventory under § 751. [For a sale of a partnership interest, "inventory" (as defined) need not be appreciated.] When hot assets are present, the sale of a partnership interest or the disproportionate distribution of the assets can cause ordinary income to be recognized.

Hybrid method. A combination of the accrual and cash methods of accounting. That is, the taxpayer may account for some items of income on the accrual method (e.g., sales and cost of goods sold) and other items (e.g., interest income) on the cash method.

I

Imputed interest. For certain long-term sales of property, under §§ 483 and 1274 the IRS can convert some of the gain from the sale into interest income if the contract does not provide for a minimum rate of interest to be paid by the purchaser. The seller recognizes less long-term capital gain and more ordinary income (interest income). Imputed interest rules also apply on certain below-market loans under § 7872.

Inbound taxation. U.S. tax effects when a non-U.S. person begins an investment or business activity in the United States.

Incentive stock options (ISOs). A type of stock option that receives favorable tax treatment. If various qualification requirements can be satisfied, stock option grants do not create taxable income for the recipient. However, the spread (the excess of the fair market value at the date of exercise over the option price) is an adjustment item for purposes of the alternative minimum tax (AMT). The gain on disposition of the stock resulting from the exercise of the stock option will be classified as long-term capital gain if certain holding period requirements are met (the employee must not dispose of the stock within two years after the option is granted or within one year after acquiring the stock). § 422.

Income. For tax purposes, an increase in wealth that has been realized.

Income in respect of a decedent (IRD). Income earned by a decedent at the time of death but not reportable on the final income tax return because of the method of accounting that appropriately is utilized. Such income is included in the gross estate and is taxed to the eventual recipient (either the estate or heirs). The recipient is, however, allowed an income tax deduction for the estate tax attributable to the income. § 691.

Income tax provision. Under ASC 740, a synonym for the book tax expense of an entity for the financial reporting period. Following the "matching principle," all book tax expense that relates to the net income for the reporting period is reported on that period's financial statements, including not only the current tax expense but also any deferred tax expense and deferred tax benefit.

Income tax treaties. See *tax treaties*.

Independent contractor. A self-employed person as distinguished from one who is employed as an employee.

Indexation. A procedure whereby adjustments are made by the IRS to key tax components (e.g., standard deduction, tax brackets, personal and dependency exemptions) to reflect inflation. The adjustments usually are made annually and are based on the change in the consumer price index.

Individual Retirement Accounts (IRAs). A type of retirement plan to which an individual with earned income can contribute a statutory maximum of $6,000 ($7,000 if age 50 or above) in 2022. IRAs can be classified as traditional IRAs or Roth IRAs. With a traditional IRA, an individual can contribute and deduct a maximum of $6,000 ($7,000 if age 50 or above) per tax year in 2022. The deduction is a deduction *for* AGI. However, if the individual is an active participant in another qualified retirement plan, the deduction is phased out proportionally between certain AGI ranges (note that the phaseout limits the amount of the deduction and not the amount of the contribution). With a Roth IRA, an individual can contribute a maximum of $6,000 ($7,000 if age 50 or above) per tax year in 2022. No deduction is permitted. However, if a five-year holding period requirement is satisfied and if the distribution is a qualified distribution, the taxpayer can make tax-free withdrawals from a Roth IRA. The maximum annual contribution is phased out proportionally between certain AGI ranges. §§ 219 and 408A.

Inheritance tax. A tax imposed on the right to receive property from a decedent. Thus, theoretically, an inheritance tax is imposed on the heir. The Federal estate tax is imposed on the estate.

Inside basis. A partnership's basis in the assets it owns.

Installment method. A method of accounting enabling certain taxpayers to spread the recognition of gain on the sale of property over the collection period. Under this procedure, the seller arrives at the gain to be recognized by computing the gross profit percentage from the sale (the gain divided by the contract price) and applying it to each payment received. § 453.

Intangible drilling and development costs (IDCs). Taxpayers may elect to expense or capitalize (subject to amortization) intangible drilling and development costs. However, ordinary income recapture provisions apply to oil and gas properties on a sale or other disposition if the expense method is elected. §§ 263(c) and 1254(a).

Intercompany transaction. A sale or exchange of goods or services between members of an *affiliated group* that files a *consolidated return*. Generally, the results of the transaction are recorded by both affiliates under general Federal income tax rules, but certain gains, losses, income, or deductions may be deferred until a later tax year.

Intermediate sanctions. The IRS can assess excise taxes on disqualified persons and organization management associated with so-called public charities engaging in excess benefit transactions. An excess benefit transaction is one in which a disqualified person engages in a non-fair market value transaction with the exempt organization or receives unreasonable compensation. Prior to the enactment of intermediate sanctions, the only option available to the IRS was to revoke the organization's exempt status.

International Accounting Standards Board (IASB). The body that promulgates International Financial Reporting Standards (IFRS). Based in London, representing accounting standard setting bodies in over 100 countries, the IASB develops accounting standards that can serve as the basis for harmonizing conflicting reporting standards among nations.

International Financial Reporting Standards (IFRS). Produced by the International Accounting Standards Board (IASB), guidelines developed since 2001 as to revenue recognition, accounting for business combinations, and a conceptual framework for financial reporting. IFRS provisions are designed so that they can be used by all entities, regardless of where they are based or conduct business. IFRS have gained widespread acceptance throughout the world, and the SEC is considering how to require U.S. entities to use IFRS in addition to, or in lieu of, the accounting rules of the Financial Accounting Standards Board.

Interpretive Regulations. A Regulation issued by the Treasury Department that purports to explain the meaning of a particular Code Section. An interpretive Regulation is given less deference than a legislative Regulation.

Inventory. Under § 1221(a)(1), a taxpayer's stock in trade or property held for resale. For partnership tax purposes, inventory is defined in § 751(d) as inventory (per the above definition) or any partnership asset other than capital or § 1231 assets. See also *appreciated inventory*.

Investment income. Consisting of virtually the same elements as portfolio income, a measure by which to justify a deduction for interest on investment indebtedness.

Investment interest. Payment for the use of funds used to acquire assets that produce investment income. The deduction for investment interest is limited to net investment income for the tax year.

Investor loss. Losses on stock and securities. If stocks and bonds are capital assets in the hands of the holder, a capital loss materializes as of the last day of the taxable year in which the stocks or bonds become worthless. Under certain circumstances involving stocks and bonds of affiliated corporations, an ordinary loss is permitted upon worthlessness.

Involuntary conversion. The loss or destruction of property through theft, casualty, or condemnation. Gain realized on an involuntary conversion can, at the taxpayer's election, be deferred for Federal income tax purposes if the owner reinvests the proceeds within a prescribed period of time in property that is similar or related in service or use. § 1033.

Itemized deductions. Personal expenditures allowed by the Code as deductions from adjusted gross income. Examples include certain medical expenses, interest on home mortgages, state income taxes, and charitable contributions. Itemized deductions are reported on Schedule A of Form 1040.

J

Joint tenants. Two or more persons having undivided ownership of property with the right of survivorship. Right of survivorship gives the surviving owner full ownership of the property. Suppose Bob and Tami are joint tenants of a tract of land. Upon Bob's death, Tami becomes the sole owner of the property. For the estate tax consequences upon the death of a joint tenant, see § 2040.

K

Keogh plans. Retirement plans available to self-employed taxpayers. They are also referred to as H.R. 10 plans. Under such plans, a taxpayer may deduct each year up to 100 percent of net earnings from self-employment or $61,000 for 2022, whichever is less. If the plan is a profit sharing plan, the percentage is 25 percent.

Kiddie tax. Passive income, such as interest and dividends, that is recognized by a child under age 19 (or under age 24 if a full-time student) is taxed according to the brackets applicable to the child's parent(s), generally to the extent the income exceeds $2,300 for 2022. The additional tax is assessed regardless of the source of the income or the income's underlying property. § 1(g).

L

Least aggregate deferral method. An algorithm set forth in the Regulations to determine the tax year for a partnership or limited liability entity with owners whose tax years differ. The tax year selected is the one that produces the least aggregate deferral of income for the owners.

Least aggregate deferral rule. See *least aggregate deferral method*.

Legislative Regulations. Some Code Sections give the Secretary of the Treasury or his delegate the authority to prescribe Regulations to carry out the details of administration or to otherwise complete the operating rules. Regulations issued pursuant to this type of authority truly possess the force and effect of law. In effect, Congress is almost delegating its legislative powers to the Treasury Department.

Lessee. One who rents property from another. In the case of real estate, the lessee is also known as the tenant.

Lessor. One who rents property to another. In the case of real estate, the lessor is also known as the landlord.

Letter ruling. The written response of the IRS to a taxpayer's request for interpretation of the revenue laws with respect to a proposed transaction (e.g., concerning the tax-free status of a reorganization). Not to be relied on as precedent by other than the party who requested the ruling.

Liabilities in excess of basis. On the contribution of capital to a corporation, an investor recognizes gain on the exchange to the extent contributed assets carry liabilities with a face amount in excess of the tax basis of the contributed assets. This rule keeps the investor from holding the investment asset received with a negative basis. § 357(c).

Life insurance proceeds. A specified sum (the face value or maturity value of the policy) paid to the designated beneficiary of the policy by the life insurance company upon the death of the insured.

Lifetime learning credit. A tax credit for qualifying expenses for taxpayers pursuing education beyond the first two years of postsecondary education. Individuals who are completing their last two years of undergraduate studies, pursuing graduate or professional degrees, or otherwise seeking new job skills or maintaining existing job skills are all eligible for the credit. Eligible individuals include the taxpayer, taxpayer's spouse, and taxpayer's dependents. The maximum credit is 20 percent of the first $10,000 of qualifying expenses and is computed per taxpayer. The credit is phased out for higher-income taxpayers. § 25A.

Like-kind exchanges. An exchange of real property held for productive use in a trade or business or for investment for other investment or trade or business real property. Unless non-like-kind property (boot) is received, the exchange is fully tax-deferred. § 1031.

Limited liability company (LLC). A legal entity in which all owners are protected from the entity's debts but which may lack other characteristics of a corporation (i.e., centralized management, unlimited life, free transferability of interests). LLCs generally are treated as partnerships (or disregarded entities if they have only one owner) for tax purposes.

Limited liability partnership (LLP). A legal entity allowed by many of the states, where a general partnership registers with the state as an LLP. All partners are at risk with respect to any liabilities arising from their own malpractice or torts or those of their subordinates. However, all partners are protected from any liabilities resulting from the malpractice or torts of other partners.

Limited partners. A partner whose liability to third-party creditors of the partnership is limited to the amounts invested in the partnership. See also *general partners* and *limited partnership (LP)*.

Limited partnership (LP). A partnership in which some of the partners are limited partners. At least one of the partners in a limited partnership must be a general partner.

Liquidating distribution. A distribution by a partnership that is in complete liquidation of the partnership trade or business activities or in complete liquidation of a partner's interest in the partnership. A liquidating distribution is generally a tax-deferred transaction if it is proportionate with respect to the partnership's hot assets. In a proportionate liquidating distribution, the partnership recognizes no gain or loss. The partner only recognizes gain if the distributed cash (and cash equivalents, such as debt relief or certain marketable securities) exceeds the partner's basis in the partnership. The partner recognizes a loss if *only* cash and hot assets are distributed and their combined inside (partnership) basis is less than the partner's basis in the partnership interest. In any case where no gain or loss is recognized, the partner's basis in the partnership interest is fully assigned to the basis of the assets received in the distribution.

Listed property. Property that includes (1) any passenger automobile; (2) any other property used as a means of transportation; (3) any property of a type generally used for purposes of entertainment, recreation, or amusement; and (4) any other property of a type specified in the Regulations. If listed property is predominantly used for business, the taxpayer is allowed to use the statutory percentage method of cost recovery. Otherwise, the straight line cost recovery method must be used. § 280F.

Lobbying expenditures. An expenditure made for the purpose of influencing legislation. Such payments can result in the loss of the exempt status of, and the imposition of Federal income tax on, an exempt organization. Lobby expenditures are not deductible. § 162(e).

Long-term care insurance. Insurance that helps pay the cost of care when the insured is unable to care for himself or herself. Such insurance is generally thought of as insurance against the cost of an aged person entering a nursing home. The employer can provide the insurance, and the premiums may be excluded from the employee's gross income. § 7702B.

Long-term contract. A building, installation, construction, or manufacturing contract that is entered into but not completed within the same tax year. A manufacturing contract is a long-term contract only if the contract is to manufacture (1) a unique item not normally carried in finished goods inventory or (2) items that normally require more than 12 calendar months to complete. The two available methods to account for long-term contracts are the percentage of completion method and the completed contract method. The completed contract method can be used only in limited circumstances. § 460.

Long-term nonpersonal use capital assets. Includes investment property with a long-term holding period. Such property disposed of by casualty or theft may receive § 1231 treatment.

Long-term tax-exempt rate. Used in deriving the yearly limitation on net operating loss and other tax benefits that carry over from the target to the acquiring when there is a more than 50-percentage-point ownership change (by value). The highest of the Federal long-term interest rates in effect for any of the last three months. § 382.

Lower of cost or market (replacement cost). An elective inventory method, whereby the taxpayer may value inventories at the lower of the taxpayer's actual cost or the current replacement cost of the goods. This method cannot be used in conjunction with the LIFO inventory method.

Low-income housing credit. Beneficial treatment to owners of low-income housing is provided in the form of a tax credit. The calculated credit is claimed in the year the building is placed in service and in the following nine years. § 42.

Lump-sum distribution. Payment of the entire amount due at one time rather than in installments. Such distributions often occur from qualified pension or profit sharing plans upon the retirement or death of a covered employee. The recipient of a lump-sum distribution may recognize both long-term capital gain and ordinary income upon the receipt of the distribution. The ordinary income portion may be subject to a special 10-year income averaging provision. § 402(c).

M

Majority interest partners. Partners who have more than a 50 percent interest in partnership profits and capital, counting only those partners who have the same taxable year. The term is of significance in determining the appropriate taxable year of a partnership. § 706(b).

Marginal tax rate. The tax rate applicable to the next dollar of income (if describing an income tax).

Marital deduction. A deduction allowed against the taxable estate or taxable gifts upon the transfer of property from one spouse to another.

Marriage penalty. The additional tax liability that results for a married couple when compared with what their tax liability would be if they were not married and filed separate returns.

Matching rule. Treatment of an intercompany transaction on a consolidated return, when a sold asset remains within the group.

Material participation. If an individual taxpayer materially participates in a nonrental trade or business activity, any loss from that activity is treated as an active loss that can be offset against active income. Material participation is achieved by meeting any one of seven tests provided in the Regulations. § 469(h).

Meaningful reduction test. A decrease in the shareholder's voting control. Used to determine whether a stock redemption qualifies for sale or exchange treatment.

Medical expenses. Medical expenses of an individual, a spouse, and dependents are allowed as an itemized deduction to the extent such amounts (less insurance reimbursements) exceed 7.5 percent of adjusted gross income. § 213.

Merger. The absorption of one corporation by another with the corporation being absorbed losing its legal identity. Flow Corporation is merged into Jobs Corporation, and the shareholders of Flow receive stock in Jobs in exchange for their stock in Flow. After the merger, Flow ceases to exist as a separate legal entity. If a merger meets certain conditions, it is not currently taxable to the parties involved. § 368(a)(1).

Mid-month convention. A cost recovery convention that assumes that property is placed in service in the middle of the month that it is actually placed in service. § 168(d).

Mid-quarter convention. A cost recovery convention that assumes that property placed in service during the year is placed in service at the middle of the quarter in which it is actually placed in service. The mid-quarter convention applies if more than 40 percent of the value of property (other than eligible real estate) is placed in service during the last quarter of the year. § 168(d).

Miscellaneous itemized deductions. A special category of itemized deductions that includes expenses such as professional dues, tax return preparation fees, job-hunting costs, unreimbursed employee business expenses, and certain investment expenses. Such expenses are deductible only to the extent they exceed 2 percent of adjusted gross income. The TCJA of 2017 suspended the deduction for these items for tax years after 2017 (and through 2025). § 67.

Modified accelerated cost recovery system (MACRS). A method in which the cost of tangible property is recovered over a prescribed period of time. Enacted by the Economic Recovery Tax Act (ERTA) of 1981 and substantially modified by the Tax Reform Act (TRA) of 1986, the method disregards salvage value, imposes a period of cost recovery that depends upon the classification of the asset into one of various recovery periods, and prescribes the applicable percentage of cost that can be deducted each year. § 168.

Multiple support agreement. To qualify for a dependency exemption, the support test must be satisfied. This requires that over 50 percent of the support of the potential dependent be provided by the taxpayer. Where no one person provides more than 50 percent of the support, a multiple support agreement enables a taxpayer to still qualify for the dependency exemption. Any person who contributed more than 10 percent of the support is entitled to claim the exemption if each person in the group who contributed more than 10 percent files a written consent (Form 2120). Each person who is a party to the multiple support agreement must meet all of the other requirements for claiming the dependency exemption. § 152(c).

Multistate Tax Commission (MTC). A regulatory body of the states that develops operating rules and regulations for the implementation of the UDITPA and other provisions that assign the total taxable income of a multistate corporation to specific states.

N

National sales tax. Intended as a replacement for the current Federal income tax. Unlike a value added tax (VAT), which is levied on the manufacturer, it would be imposed on the consumer upon the final sale of goods and services. To reduce regressivity, individuals would receive a rebate to offset a portion of the tax.

Negligence. Failure to exercise the reasonable or ordinary degree of care of a prudent person in a situation that results in harm or damage to another. A penalty is assessed on taxpayers who exhibit negligence or intentional disregard of rules and Regulations with respect to the underpayment of certain taxes. § 6662(c).

Net capital gain (NCG). The excess of the net long-term capital gain for the tax year over the net short-term capital loss. The net capital gain of an individual taxpayer is eligible for the alternative tax. § 1222(11).

Net capital loss (NCL). The excess of the losses from sales or exchanges of capital assets over the gains from sales or exchanges of such assets. Up to $3,000 per year of the net capital loss may be deductible by noncorporate taxpayers against ordinary income. The excess net capital loss carries over to future tax years. For corporate taxpayers, the net capital loss cannot be offset against ordinary income, but it can be carried back three years and forward five years to offset net capital gains. §§ 1211, 1212, and 1221(10).

Net Deemed Tangible Income Return (NDTIR). The excess of 10 percent of a controlled foreign corporation shareholder's qualified business asset investment over the amount of interest expense considered in determining net tested income of such corporation. § 951A(b)(2).

Net investment income. The excess of investment income over investment expenses. Investment expenses are those deductible expenses directly connected with the production of investment income. Investment expenses do not include investment interest. The deduction for investment interest for the tax year is limited to net investment income. § 163(d).

Net operating loss (NOL). To mitigate the effect of the annual accounting period concept, § 172 allows taxpayers to use an excess loss of one year as a deduction for certain past or future years. For NOLs incurred after 2020, an indefinite carryforward period applies, and such NOLs are subject to an 80 percent of taxable income limitation in any carryforward year. (Different carryover rules apply for NOLs incurred before 2021, and there is no limitation on an NOL deduction in such years.)

Nexus. The degree of activity that must be present before a taxing jurisdiction has the right to impose a tax on an out-of-state entity. The rules for income tax nexus are not the same as for sales tax nexus.

Ninety-day (90-day) letter. This notice is sent to a taxpayer upon request, upon the expiration of the 30-day letter, or upon exhaustion by the taxpayer of his or her administrative remedies before the IRS. The notice gives the taxpayer

90 days in which to file a petition with the U.S. Tax Court. If a petition is not filed, the IRS will demand payment of the assessed deficiency. §§ 6211–6216.

No-additional-cost service. Services the employer may provide the employee at no additional cost to the employer. Generally, the benefit is the ability to utilize the employer's excess capacity (e.g., vacant seats on an airliner). Such amounts are excludible from the recipient's gross income. § 132(b).

Nonaccountable plan. An expense reimbursement plan that does not have an accountability feature. The result is that employee expenses are not deductible.

Nonacquiescence. Disagreement by the IRS on the result reached in certain judicial decisions. *Nonacq.* or *NA*.

Nonbusiness bad debt. A bad debt loss that is not incurred in connection with a creditor's trade or business. The loss is classified as a short-term capital loss and is allowed only in the year the debt becomes entirely worthless. In addition to family loans, many investor losses are nonbusiness bad debts. § 166(d).

Nonqualified deferred compensation (NQDC). Compensation arrangements that are frequently offered to executives. Such plans may include stock options or annuities upon separation, for example. Often, an executive may defer the recognition of taxable income. The employer, however, does not receive a tax deduction until the employee is required to include the compensation in income. § 409A.

Nonqualified stock option (NQSO). A type of stock option that does not satisfy the statutory requirements of an incentive stock option. If the NQSO has a readily ascertainable fair market value (e.g., the option is traded on an established exchange), the value of the option must be included in the employee's gross income at the date of the grant. Otherwise, the employee does not recognize income at the grant date. Instead, ordinary income is recognized in the year of exercise of the option.

Nonrecourse debt. Debt secured by the property that it is used to purchase. The purchaser of the property is not personally liable for the debt upon default. Rather, the creditor's recourse is to repossess the related property. Nonrecourse debt generally does not increase the purchaser's at-risk amount.

Nonrefundable credits. A credit that is not paid if it exceeds the taxpayer's tax liability. Some nonrefundable credits qualify for carryback and carryover treatment.

Nonresident alien (NRA). An individual who is neither a citizen nor a resident of the United States. Citizenship is determined under the immigration and naturalization laws of the United States. Residency is determined under § 7701(b) of the Internal Revenue Code.

Nontaxable exchange. A transaction in which realized gains or losses are not recognized. The recognition of gain or loss is postponed (deferred) until the property received in the nontaxable exchange is subsequently disposed of in a taxable transaction. Examples are § 1031 like-kind exchanges and § 1033 involuntary conversions.

Not essentially equivalent redemption. Sale or exchange treatment is given to this type of redemption. Although various safe-harbor tests are failed, the nature of the redemption is such that dividend treatment is avoided, because it represents a meaningful reduction in the shareholder's interest in the corporation. § 302(b)(1).

Notices. A Notice is issued by the National Office of the IRS as official guidance when such information is needed before the time it takes to issue a Final Regulation. Such guidance is typically transitional until final guidance is issued. A Notice is published in an *Internal Revenue Bulletin* (I.R.B.).

O

Occupational fee. A tax imposed on various trades or businesses. A license fee that enables a taxpayer to engage in a particular occupation.

Occupational taxes. See *occupational fee*.

Offer in compromise. A settlement agreement offered by the IRS in a tax dispute, especially where there is doubt as to the collectibility of the full deficiency. Offers in compromise can include installment payment schedules as well as reductions in the tax and penalties owed by the taxpayer. § 7122.

Office audit. An audit conducted by the IRS in the agent's office.

Office in the home expenses. Employment and business-related expenses attributable to the use of a residence (e.g., den or office) are allowed only if the portion of the residence is exclusively used on a regular basis as a principal place of business of the taxpayer or as a place of business that is used by patients, clients, or customers. In computing the office in the home expenses, a taxpayer can use either the regular method or simplified method. As a general rule, the regular method requires more effort and recordkeeping but results in a larger deduction. Office in home expenses incurred by an employee are not deductible for tax years after 2017 (and through 2025). § 280A.

Operating agreement. The governing document of a limited liability company. This document is similar in structure, function, and purpose to a partnership agreement.

Optional adjustment election. See *Section 754 election*.

Options. The sale or exchange of an option to buy or sell property results in capital gain or loss if the property is a capital asset. Generally, the closing of an option transaction results in short-term capital gain or loss to the writer of the call and the purchaser of the call option. § 1234.

Ordinary and necessary. Two tests for the deductibility of expenses incurred or paid in connection with a trade or business; for the production or collection of income; for the management, conservation, or maintenance of property held for the production of income; or in connection with the determination, collection, or refund of any tax. An expense is ordinary if it is common and accepted in the general industry or type of activity in which the taxpayer is engaged. An expense is necessary if it is appropriate and helpful in furthering the taxpayer's business or income-producing activity. §§ 162(a) and 212.

Ordinary income property. Property contributed to a charitable organization that, if sold rather than contributed, would have resulted in other than long-term capital gain to the donor (i.e., ordinary income property and short-term capital gain property). Examples are inventory and capital assets held for less than the long-term holding period. A contribution of ordinary income property must generally be valued at its fair market value less the gain, if any, that would have been realized if sold. § 170(e).

Organizational expenditures. Expenditures related to the creation of a corporation or partnership. Common organizational expenditures include legal and accounting fees and state incorporation payments. Organizational expenditures exclude those incurred to obtain capital (underwriting fees) or assets (subject to cost recovery). Such expenditures incurred by the end of the entity's first year are eligible for a $5,000 limited expensing (subject to phaseout) and an amortization of the balance over 180 months. §§ 248 and 709(b).

Original issue discount (OID). The difference between the issue price of a debt obligation (e.g., a corporate bond) and the maturity value of the obligation when the issue price is less than the maturity value. OID represents interest and must be amortized over the life of the debt obligation using the effective interest method. The difference is not considered to be original issue discount for tax purposes when it is less than one-fourth of 1 percent of the redemption price at maturity multiplied by the number of years to maturity. §§ 1272 and 1273(a)(3).

Other adjustments account (OAA). Used in the context of a distribution from an S corporation. The net accumulation of the entity's exempt income (e.g., municipal bond interest), net of related nondeductible expenses. See § 1368(e)(1)(A).

Other property. In a corporate reorganization, any property in the exchange that is not stock or securities, such as cash or land. This amount constitutes boot. This treatment is similar to that in a like-kind exchange.

Outbound taxation. U.S. tax effects when a U.S. person begins an investment or business activity outside the United States.

Outside basis. A partner's basis in his or her partnership interest.

Ownership change. An event that triggers a § 382 limitation for the acquiring corporation.

P

Partial liquidation. A stock redemption where noncorporate shareholders are permitted sale or exchange treatment. In certain cases, an active business must have existed for at least five years. Only a portion of the outstanding stock in the entity is retired. §§ 302(b)(4) and (e).

Partnership. For income tax purposes, a partnership includes a syndicate, group, pool, or joint venture as well as ordinary partnerships. In an ordinary partnership, two or more parties combine capital and/or services to carry on a business for profit as co-owners. § 7701(a)(2).

Partnership agreement. The governing document of a partnership. A partnership agreement should describe the rights and obligations of the partners; the allocation of entity income, deductions, and cash flows; initial and future capital contribution requirements; conditions for terminating the partnership; and other matters.

Passive activity loss. Any loss from (1) activities in which the taxpayer does not materially participate or (2) rental activities (subject to certain exceptions). Net passive activity losses cannot be used to offset income from nonpassive activity sources. Rather, they are suspended until the taxpayer either generates net passive activity income (and a deduction of such losses is allowed) or disposes of the underlying property (at which time the loss deductions are allowed in full). One relief provision allows landlords who actively participate in the rental activities to deduct up to $25,000 of passive activity losses annually. However, a phaseout of the $25,000 amount commences when the landlord's AGI exceeds $100,000. Another relief provision applies for material participation in a real estate trade or business. § 469.

Passive investment company. A means by which a multistate corporation can reduce the overall effective tax rate by isolating investment income in a low- or no-tax state.

Passive investment income (PII). Gross receipts from royalties, certain rents, dividends, interest, annuities, and gains from the sale or exchange of stock and securities. When earnings and profits (E & P) also exist, if the passive investment income of an S corporation exceeds 25 percent of the corporation's gross receipts for three consecutive years, S status is lost.

Pass-through entities. A form of business structure for which the income and other tax items are attributed directly to the owners and generally no separate tax is levied upon the entity itself. Examples include sole proprietorships, partnerships, and S corporations. Also referred to as a flow-through entity.

Patent. An intangible asset that may be amortized over a statutory 15-year period as a § 197 intangible. The sale of a patent usually results in favorable long-term capital gain treatment. §§ 197 and 1235.

Payroll factor. The proportion of a multistate corporation's total payroll that is traceable to a specific state. Used in determining the taxable income that is to be apportioned to that state.

Pension plan. A type of deferred compensation arrangement that provides for systematic payments of definitely determinable retirement benefits to employees who meet the requirements set forth in the plan.

Percentage depletion. Depletion based on a statutory percentage applied to the gross income from the property. The taxpayer deducts the greater of cost depletion or percentage depletion. § 613.

Percentage of completion method. A method of reporting gain or loss on certain long-term contracts. Under this method of accounting, the gross contract price is included in income as the contract is completed. Reg. § 1.451–3.

Permanent differences. Under ASC 740, tax-related items that appear in the entity's financial statements or its tax return but not both. For instance, interest income from a municipal bond is a permanent book-tax difference.

Permanent establishment (PE). A level of business activity, as defined under an income tax treaty, that subjects the taxpayer to taxation in a country other than that in which the taxpayer is based. Often evidenced by the presence of a plant, an office, or other fixed place of business. Inventory storage and temporary activities do not rise to the level of a PE. PE is the treaty's equivalent to nexus.

Personal and dependency exemptions. The tax law provides an exemption for each individual taxpayer and an additional exemption for the taxpayer's spouse if a joint return is filed. An individual may also claim a dependency exemption for each dependent, provided certain tests are met. The TCJA of 2017 suspended the deduction for exemptions for tax years after 2017 (and through 2025).

Personal exemptions. See *personal and dependency exemptions.*

Personal holding company (PHC) tax. A penalty tax imposed on certain closely held corporations with excessive investment income. Assessed at a 20 percent tax rate on personal holding company income, reduced by dividends paid and other adjustments. § 541.

Personal residence. If a residence has been owned and used by the taxpayer as the principal residence for at least two years during the five-year period ending on the date of sale, up to $250,000 of realized gain is excluded from gross income. For a married couple filing a joint return, the $250,000 is increased to $500,000 if either spouse satisfies the ownership requirement and both spouses satisfy the use requirement. § 121.

Personal service corporation (PSC). A corporation whose principal activity is the performance of personal services (e.g., health, law, engineering, architecture, accounting, actuarial science, performing arts, or consulting) and where such services are substantially performed by the employee-owners. § 269A(b).

Personalty. All property that is not attached to real estate (realty) and is movable. Examples of personalty are machinery, automobiles, clothing, household furnishings, and personal effects.

Points. Loan origination fees that may be deductible as interest by a buyer of property. A seller of property who pays points reduces the selling price by the amount of the points paid for the buyer. While the seller is not permitted to deduct this amount as interest, the buyer may do so.

Portfolio income. Income from interest, dividends, rentals, royalties, capital gains, or other investment sources. Net passive activity losses cannot be used to offset net portfolio income.

Precedents. A previously decided court decision that is recognized as authority for the disposition of future decisions.

Precontribution gain or loss. Partnerships allow for a variety of special allocations of gain or loss among the partners, but gain or loss that is "built in" on an asset contributed to the partnership is assigned specifically to the contributing partner. § 704(c)(1)(A).

Preferences. In calculating alternative minimum taxable income (AMTI), preference items are added to the taxable income starting point of the AMT calculation. AMT preferences are amounts allowed in the calculation of regular taxable income but not allowed in the calculation of AMTI. For instance, interest income from certain state and local bonds (i.e., private activity bonds) is an AMT preference item. § 57.

Preferred stock bailout. A process where a shareholder used the issuance and sale, or later redemption, of a preferred stock dividend to obtain long-term capital gains, without any loss of voting control over the corporation. In effect, the shareholder received corporate profits without suffering the consequences of dividend income treatment. This procedure led Congress to enact § 306, which, if applicable, converts the prior long-term capital gain on the sale or redemption of the tainted stock to dividend income.

Premium Tax Credit (PTC). A tax credit that is refundable and available in advance of filing a return for the year. The PTC serves to reduce the cost of health coverage obtained on the Marketplace (Exchange). A PTC is available to individuals who purchase coverage on the Exchange and have household income equal to or greater than 100 percent of the Federal poverty line (FPL) and no greater than 400 percent of the FPL. Also, an individual must not have been able to obtain affordable coverage from his or her employer. If obtained in advance, the PTC is given to the insurance provider to lower the monthly premium cost to the individual. The PTC is reconciled on Form 8962 (Premium Tax Credit) filed with Form 1040 or 1040-A (not Form 1040-EZ). Individuals who obtain insurance through the Marketplace receive Form 1095-A (Health Insurance Marketplace Statement) by January 31 of the following year. This form provides information necessary to claim or reconcile the PTC, including the monthly cost of premiums and the amount of PTC received in advance each month. § 36B.

Preparer Tax Identification Number (PTIN). This number is required for individuals who are compensated for preparing or assisting in the preparation of all or substantially all of most Federal tax returns. The number must be renewed annually and reported along with the preparer's signature on the tax return to avoid imposition of a penalty. §§ 6109 and 6695.

Principal partner. A partner with a 5 percent or greater interest in partnership capital or profits. § 706(b)(3).

Private activity bonds. Interest on state and local bonds is excludible from gross income. Certain such bonds are labeled private activity bonds. Although the interest on such bonds is excludible for regular tax purposes, it is treated as a tax preference in calculating the AMT. §§ 57(a)(5) and 103.

Private foundations. An exempt organization that is subject to additional statutory restrictions on its activities and on contributions made to it, because it is not sufficiently supported by the public. Excise taxes may be levied on certain prohibited transactions, and the Code places more stringent restrictions on the deductibility of contributions to private foundations. § 509.

Probate costs. The costs incurred in administering a decedent's estate.

Probate estate. The property of a decedent that is subject to administration by the executor or administrator of an estate.

Procedural Regulations. A Regulation issued by the Treasury Department that is a housekeeping type instruction indicating information that taxpayers should provide the IRS as well as information about the internal management and conduct of the IRS itself.

Profit and loss sharing ratios. Specified in the partnership agreement and used to determine each partner's allocation of ordinary taxable income and separately stated items. Profits and losses can be shared in different ratios. The ratios can be changed by amending the partnership agreement or by using a special allocation. § 704(a).

Profit sharing plan. A deferred compensation plan established and maintained by an employer to provide for employee participation in the company's profits. Contributions are paid from the employer's current or accumulated profits to a trustee. Separate accounts are maintained for each participant employee. The plan must provide a definite, predetermined formula for allocating the contributions among the participants. It also must include a definite, predetermined formula for distributing the accumulated funds after a fixed number of years, on the attainment of a stated age, or on the occurrence of certain events such as illness, layoff, or retirement.

Profits (loss) interest. The extent of a partner's entitlement to an allocation of the partnership's operating results. This interest is measured by the profit and loss sharing ratios.

Property. Assets defined in the broadest legal sense. Property includes the unrealized receivables of a cash basis taxpayer, but not services rendered. § 351.

Property dividend. Generally treated in the same manner as a cash distribution, measured by the fair market value of the property on the date of distribution. Distribution of appreciated property causes the distributing C or S corporation to recognize gain. The distributing corporation does not recognize loss on property that has depreciated in value. §§ 311 and 1371(a).

Property factor. The proportion of a multistate corporation's total property that is traceable to a specific state. Used in determining the taxable income that is to be apportioned to that state.

Proportionate distribution. A distribution in which the partners' interests in hot assets does not change. This can happen, for instance, when no hot assets are distributed (e.g., a proportionate cash distribution) or when each partner in a partnership receives a pro rata share of hot assets being distributed. For example, a distribution of $10,000 of hot assets equally to two 50 percent partners is a proportionate distribution.

Proposed Regulations. A Regulation issued by the Treasury Department in proposed, rather than final, form. The interval between the proposal of a Regulation and its finalization permits taxpayers and other interested parties to comment on the propriety of the proposal.

Proprietorship. A business entity for which there is a single owner. The net profit of the entity is reported on the owner's Federal income tax return (Schedule C of Form 1040).

Public Law 86–272. A congressional limit on the ability of the state to force a multistate corporation to assign taxable income to that state. Under P.L. 86–272, where orders for tangible personal property are both filled and delivered outside the state, the entity must establish more than the mere solicitation of such orders before any income can be apportioned to the state.

Publicly traded partnership. A partnership the interests in which are traded on an established securities market or are readily tradable on a secondary market. Publicly traded partnerships are generally treated as corporations for tax purposes unless substantially all of their income is passive or is derived in connection with any mineral or natural resource or certain fuels. § 7704.

Punitive damages. Damages received or paid by the taxpayer can be classified as compensatory damages or as punitive damages. Punitive damages are those awarded to punish the defendant for gross negligence or the intentional infliction of harm. Such damages are includible in gross income. § 104(a)(2).

Q

QBI deduction. See *deduction for qualified business income.*

Qualified ABLE program. A state program that allows funds to be set aside for the benefit of an individual who became disabled or blind before age 26. Cash may be put into the fund annually up to the annual gift tax exclusion amount. Distributions to the designated beneficiary are not taxable provided they do not exceed qualified disability expenses for the year. § 529A.

Qualified business income (QBI). For purposes of the qualified business income deduction, it is the ordinary income less ordinary deductions a taxpayer earns from a qualified trade or business conducted in the United States by the taxpayer. Includes the distributive share of these amounts from each partnership or S corporation interest held by the taxpayer. Does not include certain types of investment income (e.g., capital gains or losses and dividends), "reasonable compensation" paid to a taxpayer with respect to any qualified trade or business, or guaranteed payments made to a partner for services rendered. § 199A(c).

Qualified business income deduction (QBID). See *deduction for qualified business income.*

Qualified business unit (QBU). A subsidiary, branch, or other business entity that conducts business using a currency other than the U.S. dollar.

Qualified dividend income (QDI). See *qualified dividends.*

Qualified dividends. Distributions made by domestic (and certain non-U.S.) corporations to noncorporate shareholders that are subject to tax at the same rates as those applicable to net long-term capital gains (i.e., 0 percent, 15 percent, or 20 percent). The 20 percent rate applies to certain high-income taxpayers. The dividend must be paid out of earnings and profits, and the shareholders must meet certain holding period requirements as to the stock. §§ 1(h)(1) and (11).

Qualified employee discount. Discounts offered employees on merchandise or services that the employer ordinarily sells or provides to customers. The discounts must be generally available to all employees. In the case of property, the discount cannot exceed the employer's gross profit (the sales price cannot be less than the employer's cost). In the case of services, the discounts cannot exceed 20 percent of the normal sales price. § 132(c).

Qualified improvement property. Any improvement to an interior portion of nonresidential real property made after the property is placed in service, including leasehold improvements. § 168(e)(6).

Qualified joint venture. At the election of the taxpayers, certain joint ventures between spouses can avoid partnership classification. Known as a qualified joint venture, the spouses generally report their share of the business activities from the venture as sole proprietors (using two Schedule C forms). This would be reported on Schedule E if the venture relates to a rental property. § 761(f).

Qualified nonrecourse financing. Debt issued on realty by a bank, retirement plan, or governmental agency. Included in the at-risk amount by the investor. In a partnership tax return, the partners' shares of qualified nonrecourse financing are reported on their Schedules K–1. § 465(b)(6).

Qualified real property business indebtedness. Indebtedness that was incurred or assumed by the taxpayer in connection with real property used in a trade or business and is secured by such real property. The taxpayer must not be a C corporation. For qualified real property business indebtedness, the taxpayer may elect to exclude some or all of the income realized from cancellation of debt on qualified real property. If the election is made, the basis of the property must be reduced by the amount excluded. The amount excluded cannot be greater than the excess of the principal amount of the outstanding debt over the fair market value (net of any other debt outstanding on the property) of the property securing the debt. § 108(c).

Qualified residence interest. A term relevant in determining the amount of interest expense the individual taxpayer may deduct as an itemized deduction for what otherwise would be disallowed as a component of personal interest (consumer interest). Qualified residence interest consists of interest paid on qualified residences (principal residence and one other residence) of the taxpayer. Debt that qualifies as qualified residence interest is limited to $1,000,000 of debt to acquire, construct, or substantially improve qualified residences (acquisition indebtedness). For acquisition indebtedness incurred after December 15, 2017, the limit is reduced to $750,000. § 163(h)(3).

Qualified small business corporation. For purposes of computing an exclusion upon the sale of *qualified small business stock*, a C corporation that has aggregate gross assets not exceeding $50 million and that is conducting an active trade or business. § 1202.

Qualified small business stock. Stock in a qualified small business corporation, purchased as part of an original issue after August 10, 1993. The shareholder may exclude from gross income 100 (or 50 or 75) percent of the realized gain on the sale of the stock if he or she held the stock for more than five years. The exclusion percentage depends on when the stock was acquired. § 1202.

Qualified terminable interest property (QTIP). Generally, the marital deduction (for gift and estate tax purposes) is not available if the interest transferred will terminate upon the death of the transferee spouse and pass to someone else. Thus, if Jim (the husband) places property in trust, life estate to Mary (the wife), and remainder to their children upon Mary's death, this is a terminable interest that will not provide Jim (or Jim's estate) with a marital deduction. If, however, the transfer in trust is treated as qualified terminable interest property (the QTIP election is made), the terminable interest restriction is waived and the marital deduction becomes available. In exchange for this deduction, the surviving spouse's gross estate must include the value of the QTIP election assets, even though he or she has no control over the ultimate disposition of the asset. Terminable interest property qualifies for this election if the donee (or heir) is the only beneficiary of the asset during his or her lifetime and receives income distributions relative to the property at least annually. For gifts, the donor spouse is the one who makes the QTIP election. For property transferred by death, the executor of the estate of the deceased spouse makes the election. §§ 2056(b)(7) and 2523(f).

Qualified trade or business. Used in determining the deduction for qualified business income (§ 199A). In general, it includes any trade or business other than providing services as an employee. In addition, a "specified services trade or business" is not a qualified trade or business. § 199A(d)(1)(B).

Qualified transportation fringes. Transportation benefits provided by the employer to the employee. If these benefits are reimbursed by the employer, they are excludible from gross income by the employee, but not deductible by the employer after 2017. Such benefits include (1) transportation in a commuter highway vehicle between the employee's residence and the place of employment, (2) a transit pass, and (3) qualified parking. Qualified transportation fringes are excludible from the employee's gross income to the extent categories (1) and (2) above do not exceed $280 per month in 2022 and category (3) does not exceed $280 per month in 2022. These amounts are indexed annually for inflation. § 132(f).

Qualified tuition program (§ 529 plan). A program that allows college tuition to be prepaid for a beneficiary. When amounts in the plan are used, nothing is included in gross income provided they are used for qualified higher education expenses. § 529.

Qualifying child. An individual who, as to the taxpayer, satisfies the relationship, abode, and age tests. To be claimed as a dependent, such individual must also meet the citizenship and joint return tests and not be self-supporting. §§ 152(a)(1) and (c).

Qualifying relative. An individual who, as to the taxpayer, satisfies the relationship, gross income, support, citizenship, and joint return tests. Such an individual can be claimed as a dependent of the taxpayer. §§ 152(a)(2) and (d).

R

Rate reconciliation. Under Generally Accepted Accounting Principles, a footnote to the financial statements often includes a table that accounts for differences in the statutory income tax rate that applies to the entity (e.g., 21 percent) and the higher or lower effective tax rate that the entity realized for the reporting period. The rate reconciliation includes only permanent differences between the book tax expense and the entity's income tax provision. The rate reconciliation table often is expressed in dollar and/or percentage terms.

Realized gain. See *realized gain or loss*.

Realized gain or loss. The difference between the amount realized upon the sale or other disposition of property and the adjusted basis of the property. § 1001.

Realized loss. See *realized gain or loss*.

Realty. Real estate.

Reasonable cause. Relief from taxpayer and preparer penalties often is allowed where reasonable cause is found for the taxpayer's actions. For example, reasonable cause for the late filing of a tax return might be a flood that damaged the taxpayer's record-keeping systems and made a timely completion of the return difficult.

Reasonable needs of the business. A means of avoiding the penalty tax on an unreasonable accumulation of earnings.

In determining the base for this tax (accumulated taxable income), § 535 allows a deduction for "such part of earnings and profits for the taxable year as are retained for the reasonable needs of the business." § 537.

Reasonableness. See *reasonableness requirement.*

Reasonableness requirement. The Code includes a reasonableness requirement with respect to the deduction of salaries and other compensation for services. The courts have expanded this requirement to all business expenses, ruling that an expense must be reasonable in order to be ordinary and necessary. What constitutes reasonableness is a question of fact. If an expense is unreasonable, the amount that is classified as unreasonable is not allowed as a deduction. The question of reasonableness generally arises with respect to closely held corporations where there is no separation of ownership and management. § 162(a)(1).

Recapitalization. A "Type E" reorganization, constituting a major change in the character and amount of outstanding equity of a corporation. Tax-free exchanges are stock for stock, bonds for bonds, and bonds for stock. For example, common stock exchanged for preferred stock can qualify as a tax-free "Type E" reorganization.

Recognized gain. See *recognized gain or loss.*

Recognized gain or loss. The portion of realized gain or loss subject to income taxation.

Recognized loss. See *recognized gain or loss.*

Recourse debt. Debt for which the lender may both foreclose on the property and assess a guarantor for any payments due under the loan. A lender also may make a claim against the assets of any general partner in a partnership to which debt is issued, without regard to whether the partner has guaranteed the debt.

Recovery of capital doctrine. When a taxable sale or exchange occurs, the seller may be permitted to recover his or her investment (or other adjusted basis) in the property before gain or loss is recognized.

Redemption to pay death taxes. Sale or exchange treatment is available relative to this type of stock redemption, to the extent of the proceeds up to the total amount paid by the estate or heir for estate/inheritance taxes and administration expenses. The stock value must exceed 35 percent of the value of the decedent's adjusted gross estate. In meeting this test, shareholdings in corporations where the decedent held at least 20 percent of the outstanding shares are combined. § 303.

Refundable credits. A credit that is paid to the taxpayer even if the amount of the credit (or credits) exceeds the taxpayer's tax liability.

Regular corporations. See *C corporation.*

Rehabilitation expenditures credit. A credit that is based on expenditures incurred to rehabilitate industrial and commercial buildings and certified historic structures. The credit is intended to discourage businesses from moving from older, economically distressed areas to newer locations and to encourage the preservation of historic structures. § 47.

Related party. Various Code Sections define related parties and often include a variety of persons within this (usually detrimental) category. Generally, related parties are accorded different tax treatment from that applicable to other taxpayers who enter into similar transactions. For instance, realized losses that are generated between related parties are not recognized in the year of the loss. However, these deferred losses can be used to offset recognized gains that occur upon the subsequent sale of the asset to a nonrelated party. Other uses of a related-party definition include the conversion of gain upon the sale of a depreciable asset into all ordinary income (§ 1239) and the identification of constructive ownership of stock relative to corporate distributions, redemptions, liquidations, reorganizations, and compensation.

Related-party transactions. The tax law places restrictions upon the recognition of gains and losses between related parties because of the potential for abuse. For example, restrictions are placed on the deduction of losses from the sale or exchange of property between related parties. In addition, under certain circumstances, related-party gains that would otherwise be classified as capital gain are classified as ordinary income. §§ 267, 707(b), and 1239.

Rental activity. Any activity where payments are received principally for the use of tangible property is a rental activity. Temporary Regulations provide that in certain circumstances, activities involving rentals of real and personal property are not to be treated as rental activities. The Temporary Regulations list six exceptions.

Reorganization. Any corporate restructuring, including when one corporation acquires another, a single corporation divides into two or more entities, a corporation makes a substantial change in its capital structure, a corporation undertakes a change in its legal name or domicile, or a corporation goes through a bankruptcy proceeding and continues to exist. The exchange of stock and other securities in a corporate reorganization can be effected favorably for tax purposes if certain statutory requirements are followed strictly. Tax consequences include the nonrecognition of any gain that is realized by the shareholders except to the extent of boot received. § 368.

Report of Foreign Bank and Financial Accounts (FBAR). FinCEN Form 114, Report of Foreign Bank and Financial Accounts (FBAR), must be filed by individuals and some businesses if they have foreign bank, brokerage, or similar accounts where at any time during the calendar year the aggregate balance exceeds $10,000. The form is filed electronically with the U.S. Department of the Treasury and is due by April 15 with an automatic extension to October 15. Significant penalties apply for failure to file the FBAR. The form is not attached to the income tax return (it is separately filed), but any interest earned by the foreign accounts is generally included in the account holder's U.S. taxable income.

Required taxable year. A partnership or limited liability company must use a required tax year as its tax accounting period, or one of three allowable alternative tax year-ends. If there is a common tax year used by owners holding a majority of the entity's capital or profits interests or if the same year-end is used by all "principal partners" (partners who hold 5 percent or more of the capital or profits interests), then that tax year-end is used by the entity. If neither of the first tests results in an allowable year-end (e.g., because there is no majority partner or because the principal partners do not have the same tax year), then the partnership uses the least aggregate deferral method to determine its tax year. § 706.

Research activities credit. A tax credit whose purpose is to encourage research and development. It consists of three components: the incremental research activities credit, the basic research credit, and the energy credit. The incremental research activities credit is equal to 20 percent of the excess qualified research expenditures over the base amount. The basic research credit is equal to 20 percent of the excess of basic research payments over the base amount. § 41.

Research and experimental expenditures. Costs incurred to develop a product or process for which there exists uncertainty regarding its viability. The Code provides three alternatives for the tax treatment of research and experimentation expenditures. They may be expensed in the year paid or incurred, deferred subject to amortization, or capitalized. If the taxpayer does not elect to expense such costs or to defer them subject to amortization (over 60 months), the expenditures must be capitalized. § 174. In general, research and experimentation expenditures paid or incurred after 2021 must be capitalized and amortized over a five-year period. Some of these expenditures may also qualify the taxpayer for the credit for increasing research activities. § 41.

Reserve method. A method of accounting whereby an allowance is permitted for estimated uncollectible accounts. Actual write-offs are charged to the reserve, and recoveries of amounts previously written off are credited to the reserve. The Code permits only certain financial institutions to use the reserve method. § 166.

Residential rental real estate. Buildings for which at least 80 percent of the gross rents are from dwelling units (e.g., an apartment building). This type of building is distinguished from nonresidential (commercial or industrial) buildings in applying the recapture of depreciation provisions. The term also is relevant in distinguishing between buildings that are eligible for a 27.5-year life versus a 39-year life for MACRS purposes. Generally, residential buildings receive preferential treatment. § 168(e)(2)(A).

Revenue Agent's Report (RAR). A Revenue Agent's Report (RAR) reflects any adjustments made by the agent as a result of an audit of the taxpayer. The RAR is mailed to the taxpayer along with the 30-day letter, which outlines the appellate procedures available to the taxpayer.

Revenue neutrality. A description that characterizes tax legislation when it neither increases nor decreases the total revenue collected by the taxing jurisdiction. Thus, any tax revenue losses are offset by tax revenue gains.

Revenue Procedures. A matter of procedural importance to both taxpayers and the IRS concerning the administration of the tax laws is issued as a Revenue Procedure (abbreviated Rev.Proc.). A Revenue Procedure is published in an *Internal Revenue Bulletin* (I.R.B.).

Revenue Rulings. A Revenue Ruling (abbreviated Rev.Rul.) is issued by the National Office of the IRS to express an official interpretation of the tax law as applied to specific transactions. It is more limited in application than a Regulation. A Revenue Ruling is published in an *Internal Revenue Bulletin* (I.R.B.).

Reversionary interest. The trust property that reverts to the grantor after the expiration of an intervening income interest. Assume that Phil places real estate in trust with income to Junior for 11 years and that upon the expiration of this term, the property returns to Phil. Under these circumstances, Phil holds a reversionary interest in the property. A reversionary interest is the same as a remainder interest, except that, in the latter case, the property passes to someone other than the original owner (e.g., the grantor of a trust) upon the expiration of the intervening interest.

Roth IRA. See *Individual Retirement Accounts (IRAs)*.

S

S corporation. The designation for a corporation that elects to be taxed similarly to a partnership. See also *Subchapter S*.

Sale or exchange. A requirement for the recognition of capital gain or loss. Generally, the seller of property must receive money or relief from debt to have sold the property. An exchange involves the transfer of property for other property. Thus, collection of a debt is neither a sale nor an exchange. The term *sale or exchange* is not defined by the Code.

Sales factor. The proportion of a multistate corporation's total sales that is traceable to a specific state. Used in determining the taxable income that is to be apportioned to that state.

Sales tax. A state- or local-level tax on the retail sale of specified property. Generally, the purchaser pays the tax, but the seller collects it, as an agent for the government. Various taxing jurisdictions allow exemptions for purchases of specific items, including certain food, services, and manufacturing equipment. If the purchaser and seller are in different states, a use tax usually applies.

Salvage value. The estimated amount a taxpayer will receive upon the disposition of an asset used in the taxpayer's trade or business. Salvage value is relevant in calculating depreciation under § 167, but is not relevant in calculating cost recovery under § 168.

Schedule K–1. A tax information form prepared for each partner in a partnership, each shareholder of an S corporation, and some beneficiaries of certain trusts. The Schedule K–1 reports the owner's share of the entity's ordinary income or loss from operations as well as the owner's share of separately stated items, along with any other information the partner, shareholder, or beneficiary needs to prepare the return.

Schedule M–1. On the Form 1120, a reconciliation of book net income with Federal taxable income. Accounts for temporary and permanent differences in the two computations, such as depreciation differences, exempt income, and nondeductible items. On Forms 1120S and 1065, the Schedule M–1 reconciles book income with the owners' aggregate taxable income.

Schedule M–3. An *expanded* reconciliation of book net income with Federal taxable income (see *Schedule M–1*). Required of C and S corporations and partnerships/LLCs with total assets of $10 million or more.

Scholarship. Scholarships are generally excluded from the gross income of the recipient unless the payments are a disguised form of compensation for services rendered. However, the Code imposes restrictions on the exclusion. The recipient must be a degree candidate. The excluded amount is limited to amounts used for tuition, fees, books, supplies, and equipment required for courses of instruction. Amounts received for room and board are not eligible for the exclusion. § 117.

Section 121 exclusion. If a residence has been owned and used by the taxpayer as the principal residence for at least two years during the five-year period ending on the date of sale, up to $250,000 of realized gain is excluded from gross income. For a married couple filing a joint return, the $250,000 is increased to $500,000 if either spouse satisfies the ownership requirement and both spouses satisfy the use requirement.

Section 179 expensing. The ability to deduct the cost of qualified property in the year the property is placed in service rather than over the asset's useful life or cost recovery period. The annual ceiling on the deduction is $1,080,000 in 2022 ($1,050,000 in 2021). However, the deduction is reduced dollar for dollar when § 179 property placed in service during the taxable year exceeds $2,700,000 ($2,620,000 in 2021). In addition, the amount expensed under § 179 cannot exceed the aggregate amount of taxable income derived from the conduct of any trade or business by the taxpayer.

Section 179 expensing election. See *Section 179 expensing*.

Section 338 election. When a corporation acquires at least 80 percent of a subsidiary within a 12-month period, it can elect to treat the acquisition of such stock as an asset purchase. The acquiring corporation's basis in the subsidiary's assets then is the cost of the stock. The subsidiary is deemed to have sold its assets for an amount equal to the grossed-up basis in its stock.

Section 382 limitation. When one corporation acquires another, the acquiring corporation's ability to use the loss and credit carryovers of the target may be limited by this anti-abuse provision. For instance, the maximum NOL deduction available to the acquiring is the value of the target when acquired times the long-term tax-exempt interest rate on that date.

Section 401(k) plan. A cash or deferred arrangement plan that allows participants to elect to receive up to $20,500 ($27,000 if age 50 or above) in 2022 in cash (taxed currently) or to have a contribution made on their behalf to a qualified retirement plan (excludible from gross income). The plan may be in the form of a salary reduction agreement between the participant and the employer.

Section 704(b) book capital accounts. Capital accounts calculated as described under Reg. § 1.704–1(b)(2)(iv). All partnerships must maintain § 704(b) book capital accounts for the partners with the intent that final liquidating distributions are in accordance with these capital account balances. Partnership allocations will not be accepted unless they are properly reflected in the partners' § 704(b) book capital accounts. These capital accounts are a hybrid of book and tax accounting methods. They reflect contributions and distributions of property at their fair market values, but the capital accounts are otherwise generally increased by the partnership's tax-basis income and decreased by tax-basis deductions (as reported on the partner's Schedule K–1). Liabilities are only reflected in these capital accounts to the extent the partnership assumes a partner's liability [reduces that partner's § 704(b) book capital account] or a partner assumes a partnership liability [increases that partner's § 704(b) book capital account]. See also *capital account maintenance* and *economic effect test*.

Section 754 election. An election that may be made by a partnership to adjust the basis of partnership assets to reflect a purchasing partner's outside basis in interest or to reflect a gain, loss, or basis adjustment of a partner receiving a distribution from a partnership. The intent of the election is to maintain the equivalence between outside and inside bases for the purchasing partner (in the case of a sale of a partnership interest) or the remaining partners in the partnership (in the case of a distribution that changes the balance of inside and outside bases). Once the election is made, the partnership must make basis adjustments for all future transactions, unless the IRS consents to revoke the election.

Section 1231 gains and losses. If the combined gains and losses from the taxable dispositions of § 1231 assets plus the net gain from business involuntary conversions (of both § 1231 assets and long-term capital assets) result in a gain, the gains and losses are treated as long-term capital gains and losses. In arriving at § 1231 gains, however, the depreciation recapture provisions (e.g., § 1245) are applied first to produce ordinary income. If the net result of the combination is a loss, the gains and losses from § 1231 assets are treated as ordinary gains and losses. § 1231(a).

Section 1231 lookback. For gain to be classified as § 1231 gain, the gain must survive the § 1231 lookback. To the extent of nonrecaptured § 1231 losses for the five prior tax years, the gain is classified as ordinary income. § 1231(c).

Section 1231 property. Depreciable assets and real estate used in trade or business and held for the required long-term holding period. § 1231(b).

Section 1244 stock. Stock issued under § 1244 by qualifying small business corporations. If § 1244 stock becomes worthless, the shareholders may claim an ordinary loss rather than the usual capital loss, within statutory limitations.

Section 1245 property. Property that is subject to the recapture of depreciation under § 1245. For a definition of § 1245 property, see § 1245(a)(3).

Section 1245 recapture. Upon a taxable disposition of § 1245 property, all depreciation claimed on the property is recaptured as ordinary income (but not to exceed any recognized gain from the disposition).

Section 1250 property. Real estate that is subject to the recapture of depreciation under § 1250. For a definition of § 1250 property, see § 1250(c).

Section 1250 recapture. Upon a taxable disposition of § 1250 property, accelerated depreciation or cost recovery claimed on the property may be recaptured as ordinary income.

Securities. Stock, debt, and other financial assets. To the extent securities other than the stock of the transferee corporation are received in a § 351 exchange, the new shareholder recognizes a gain. For purposes of corporate reorganizations, securities are generally debt with terms longer than 10 years. To the extent stock and securities are transferred in a corporate reorganization under § 368, no gain or loss is recognized.

Self-employment tax. A tax of 12.4 percent is levied on individuals with net earnings from self-employment (up to $147,000 in 2022) to provide Social Security benefits (i.e., the old age, survivors, and disability insurance portion) for such individuals. In addition, a tax of 2.9 percent is levied on individuals with net earnings from self-employment (with no statutory ceiling) to provide Medicare benefits (i.e., the hospital insurance portion) for such individuals. If a self-employed individual also receives wages from an employer that are subject to FICA, the self-employment tax will be reduced. A partial deduction is allowed in calculating the self-employment tax. Individuals with net earnings of $400 or more from self-employment are subject to this tax. §§ 1401 and 1402.

Separate foreign tax credit income categories. The foreign tax credit of a taxpayer is computed for each of several types of income sources, as specified by the Code to limit the results of tax planning. FTC income "baskets" include general and passive. The FTC for the year is the sum of the credits as computed within all of the taxpayer's separate FTC baskets used for the tax year.

Separate return limitation year (SRLY). A series of rules limits the amount of an acquired corporation's net operating loss carryforwards that can be used by the acquiror. Generally, a consolidated return can include the acquiree's net operating loss carryforward only to the extent of the lesser of the subsidiary's (1) current-year or (2) cumulative positive contribution to consolidated taxable income.

Separately stated items. Any item of a partnership or an S corporation that might be taxed differently to any two owners of the entity. These amounts are not included in the ordinary income of the entity, but are instead reported separately to the owners; tax consequences are determined at the owner level.

Severance taxes. A tax imposed upon the extraction of natural resources.

Short period. See *short taxable year*.

Short sale. A sale that occurs when a taxpayer sells borrowed property (usually stock) and repays the lender with substantially identical property either held on the date of the short sale or purchased after the sale. No gain or loss is recognized until the short sale is closed, and such gain or loss is generally short term. § 1233.

Short taxable year. A tax year that is less than 12 months. A short taxable year may occur in the initial reporting period, in the final tax year, or when the taxpayer changes tax years. Special income tax computations may be required.

Significant participation activity. Seven tests determine whether an individual has achieved material participation in an activity, one of which is based on more than 500 hours of participation in significant participation activities. A significant participation activity is one in which the individual's participation exceeds 100 hours during the year. Temp.Reg. § 1.469–5T.

Simple trust. Trusts that are not complex trusts. Such trusts may not have a charitable beneficiary, accumulate income, or distribute corpus.

Simplified employee pension (SEP) plans. An employer may make contributions to an employee's IRA in amounts not exceeding the lesser of 15 percent of compensation or $61,000 ($67,500 if age 50 or above) per individual in 2022. These employer-sponsored simplified employee pensions are permitted only if the contributions are nondiscriminatory and are made on behalf of all employees who have attained age 21 and have worked for the employer during at least three of the five preceding calendar years. § 219(b).

Small business corporation. A corporation that satisfies the definition of § 1361(b), § 1244(c), or both. Satisfaction of § 1361(b) permits an S election, and satisfaction of § 1244 enables the shareholders of the corporation to claim an ordinary loss on the worthlessness of stock.

Small business stock (§ 1244 stock). See *Section 1244 stock*.

Small Cases Division. A division within the U.S. Tax Court where jurisdiction is limited to claims of $50,000 or less. There is no appeal from this court.

Solicitation of orders. A level of activity brought about by the taxpayer within a specific state. Under Public Law 86–272, certain types of solicitation activities do not create nexus with the state. Exceeding mere solicitation, though, creates nexus.

Special allocation. Any amount for which an agreement exists among the partners of a partnership outlining the method used for spreading the item among the partners.

Special use value. Permits the executor of an estate to value, for estate tax purposes, real estate used in a farming activity or in connection with a closely held business at its current use value rather than at its most suitable or optimal use value. Under this option, a farm is valued for farming purposes even though, for example, the property might have a higher potential value as a shopping center. For the executor of an estate to elect special use valuation, the conditions of § 2032A must be satisfied.

Specific charge-off method. A method of accounting for bad debts in which a deduction is permitted only when an account becomes partially or completely worthless.

Specified service trade or business. For purposes of the deduction for qualified business income, a specified service trade or business includes those involving the performance of services in certain fields, including health, law, accounting, actuarial science, performing arts, consulting, athletics, financial services, and brokerage services; services consisting of investing and investment management, trading or dealing in securities, partnership interests, or commodities; and any trade or business where the business's principal asset is the reputation of one or more of its employees or owners. § 199A(d)(2).

Spin-off. A type of reorganization where, for example, Apple Corporation transfers some assets to Core Corporation in exchange for Core stock representing control. Apple then distributes the Core stock to its shareholders.

Split-off. A type of reorganization where, for example, Apple Corporation transfers some assets to Core Corporation in exchange for Core stock representing control. Apple then distributes the Core stock to its shareholders in exchange for some of their Apple stock. Not all shareholders need to exchange stock.

Split-up. A type of reorganization where, for example, Firefly Corporation transfers some assets to Fire Corporation and the remainder to Fly Corporation. In return, Firefly receives enough Fire and Fly stock representing control of each corporation. Firefly then distributes the Fire and Fly stock to its shareholders in return for all of their Firefly stock. Firefly then liquidates, and its shareholders now have control of Fire and Fly.

Sprinkling trust. When a trustee has the discretion to either distribute or accumulate the entity accounting income of the trust and to distribute it among the trust's income beneficiaries in varying magnitudes. The trustee can "sprinkle" the income of the trust.

Standard deduction. The individual taxpayer can either itemize deductions or take the standard deduction. The amount of the standard deduction depends on the taxpayer's filing status (single, head of household, married filing jointly, surviving spouse, or married filing separately). For 2022, the amount of the standard deduction ranges from $12,950 (for single) to $25,900 (for married, filing jointly). Additional standard deductions of either $1,400 (for married taxpayers) or $1,750 (for single taxpayers) are available if the taxpayer is blind or age 65 or over. Limitations exist on the amount of the standard deduction of a taxpayer who is another taxpayer's dependent. The standard deduction amounts are adjusted for inflation each year. § 63(c).

Startup expenditures. Expenditures paid or incurred prior to the beginning of the business that would have been deductible as an ordinary and necessary business expense if business operations had begun. Examples of such expenditures include advertising; salaries and wages; travel and other expenses incurred in lining up prospective distributors, suppliers, or customers; and salaries and fees to executives, consultants, and professional service providers. A taxpayer will immediately expense the first $5,000 (subject to phaseout) of startup expenditures and amortize the balance over a period of 180 months, unless the taxpayer elects not to do so. § 195.

Statute of limitations. Provisions of the law that specify the maximum period of time in which action may be taken concerning a past event. Code §§ 6501–6504 contain the limitation periods applicable to the IRS for additional assessments, and §§ 6511–6515 relate to refund claims by taxpayers.

Statutory employees. Statutory employees are considered self-employed independent contractors for purposes of reporting income and expenses on their tax returns. Generally, a statutory employee must meet three tests:

- It is understood from a service contract that the services will be performed by the person.
- The person does not have a substantial investment in facilities (other than transportation used to perform the services).
- The services involve a continuing relationship with the person for whom they are performed.

For further information on statutory employees, see Circular E, *Employer's Tax Guide* (IRS Publication 15).

Statutory tax rate. The statutory tax rate is the tax rate (or rates) specified in the law. For example, § 11 provides that the income tax rate for corporations is 21 percent.

Step down. See *step-down in basis.*

Step transaction. Disregarding one or more transactions to arrive at the final result. Assume, for example, Beta Corporation creates Alpha Corporation by transferring assets desired by Beta's sole shareholder, Carl. Carl then causes Alpha to liquidate to obtain the assets. Under these circumstances, the IRS may contend that the creation and liquidation of Alpha be disregarded. What really happened was a dividend distribution from Beta to Carl.

Step up. See *step-up in basis.*

Step-down in basis. A reduction in the tax basis of property. See also *step-up in basis.*

Step-up in basis. An increase in the income tax basis of property. In an estate context, a step-up in basis occurs when a decedent dies owning appreciated property. Because the estate or heir acquires a basis in the property equal to the property's fair market value on the date of death (or alternate valuation date if available and elected), any appreciation is not subject to the income tax. Thus, a step-up in basis is the result, with no immediate income tax consequences. In the partnership context, a step-up arises when a § 754 election is in effect and when one of several transactions arises: (1) a partner purchases a partnership interest for an amount that exceeds the partner's share of the partnership's inside basis, (2) the partner recognizes a gain on a distribution of cash from the partnership, or (3) a partner takes a basis in a distributed asset that is less than the partnership's basis in that asset. In the opposite situations (e.g., loss recognition or where a partner takes a basis in a distributed asset that exceeds the partnership's basis in that asset), a step-down can arise. See also *step-down in basis.*

Stock bonus plan. A type of deferred compensation plan in which the employer establishes and maintains the plan and contributes employer stock to the plan for the benefit of employees. The contributions need not be dependent on the employer's profits. Any benefits of the plan are distributable in the form of employer stock, except that distributable fractional shares may be paid in cash.

Stock dividend. Not taxable if pro rata distributions of stock or stock rights on common stock. Section 305 governs the taxability of stock dividends and sets out five exceptions to the general rule that stock dividends are nontaxable.

Stock option. The right to purchase a stated number of shares of stock from a corporation at a certain price within a specified period of time. §§ 421 and 422.

Stock redemption. A corporation buys back its own stock from a specified shareholder. Typically, the corporation recognizes any realized gain on the noncash assets that it uses to effect a redemption, and the shareholder obtains a capital gain or loss upon receipt of the purchase price.

Stock rights. Assets that convey to the holder the power to purchase corporate stock at a specified price, often for a limited period of time. Stock rights received may be taxed as a distribution of earnings and profits. After the right is exercised, the basis of the acquired share includes the investor's purchase price or gross income, if any, to obtain the right. Disposition of the right also can be taxable.

Subchapter S. Sections 1361–1379 of the Internal Revenue Code. An elective provision permitting certain small business corporations (§ 1361) and their shareholders (§ 1362) to elect to be treated for income tax purposes in accordance with the operating rules of §§ 1363–1379. S corporations usually avoid the corporate income tax, and corporate losses can be claimed by the shareholders.

Subpart F income. Certain types of income earned by a controlled foreign corporation that are included in U.S. gross income by U.S. shareholders of such an entity as they are generated, not when they are repatriated. See § 951.

Substance over form. A standard used when one must ascertain the true reality of what has occurred. Suppose, for example, a father sells stock to his daughter for $1,000. If the stock is really worth $50,000 at the time of the transfer, the substance of the transaction is probably a gift to her of $49,000.

Substantial authority. Taxpayer and tax preparer understatement penalties are waived where substantial authority existed for the disputed position taken on the return.

Substantial basis reduction. Arises when the partnership makes a liquidating distribution to a partner (under § 736) and the distributee partner recognizes a loss (or has a basis increase for the distributed assets) of at least $250,000. (The second situation would arise when the basis of the assets the liquidated partner receives must be stepped up to absorb all remaining partnership interest basis.) If there is a substantial basis reduction, the partnership is required to make a downward adjustment to the basis of its assets, even if the partnership does not have a § 754 election in effect. This adjustment is treated as a § 754 adjustment related to a distribution and so is allocated to the basis of all remaining partnership assets (except for cash). See also *substantial built-in loss* and *§ 754 election*.

Substantial built-in loss. Arises when a partner sells a partnership interest (under § 741) and the selling partner recognizes a loss on the sale of at least $250,000. In addition, a substantial built-in loss arises if the selling partner would be allocated more than a $250,000 loss if all partnership assets were sold (after considering special allocations). If there is a substantial built-in loss, the partnership is required to make a downward adjustment in the basis of its assets, even if the partnership does not have a § 754 election in effect. This adjustment is treated as a § 754 adjustment related to a sale of a partnership interest and so is allocated to the purchasing partner. See also *substantial basis reduction* and *§ 754 election*.

Substantially appreciated inventory. In partnership taxation, for purposes of the regular distribution rules and distributions under § 736, a distribution of inventory is only treated as a hot asset if it is substantially appreciated, meaning the fair market value of the inventory exceeds 120 percent of its basis. See *appreciated inventory*.

Sunset provision. A provision attached to new tax legislation that will cause such legislation to expire at a specified date. Sunset provisions are attached to tax cut bills for long-term budgetary reasons to make their effect temporary. Once the sunset provision comes into play, the tax cut is rescinded and former law is reinstated. An example of a sunset provision is contained in the Tax Relief Reconciliation Act of 2001 that related to the estate tax. After the estate tax was phased out in 2010, a sunset provision called for the reinstatement of the estate tax as of January 1, 2011.

Surviving spouse. When a husband or wife predeceases the other spouse, the survivor is known as a surviving spouse. Under certain conditions, a surviving spouse may be entitled to use the income tax rates in § 1(a) (those applicable to married persons filing a joint return) for the two years after the year of death of his or her spouse. § 2(a).

Syndication costs. Incurred in promoting and marketing partnership interests for sale to investors. Examples include legal and accounting fees, printing costs for prospectus and placement documents, and state registration fees. These items are capitalized by the partnership as incurred, with no amortization thereof allowed.

T

Tax avoidance. The minimization of one's tax liability by taking advantage of legally available tax planning opportunities. Tax avoidance can be contrasted with tax evasion, which entails the reduction of tax liability by illegal means.

Tax basis capital account. Capital accounts calculated using the tax rules by which the Form 1065 income, expenses, gains, and losses are reported. Beginning in tax year 2020, all partnerships must report partners' capital on Schedules K–1 using the tax method. These capital accounts reflect contributions and distributions of property at their tax (generally carryover) basis. Capital accounts are otherwise generally increased by the partnership's tax-basis income and decreased by tax-basis deductions. Liabilities are not included in the partners' tax basis capital accounts. See also *§ 704(b) book capital accounts*.

Tax benefit rule. A provision that limits the recognition of income from the recovery of an expense or a loss properly deducted in a prior tax year to the amount of the deduction that generated a tax saving. Assume that last year Gary had medical expenses of $4,000 and adjusted gross income of $30,000. Because of the AGI limitation, Gary could deduct only $1,000 of these expenses [$4,000 − (10% × $30,000)]. If this year Gary is reimbursed in full by his insurance company for the $4,000 of expenses, the tax benefit rule limits the amount of income from the reimbursement to $1,000 (the amount previously deducted with a tax saving).

Tax credits. Amounts that directly reduce a taxpayer's tax liability. The tax benefit received from a tax credit is not dependent on the taxpayer's marginal tax rate, whereas the benefit of a tax deduction or exclusion is dependent on the taxpayer's tax bracket.

Tax evasion. The reduction of taxes by the use of subterfuge or fraud or other nonlegal means. For example, a cash basis taxpayer tries to increase his or her charitable contribution deduction by prepaying next year's church pledge with a pre-dated check issued in the following year.

Tax haven. A country in which either locally sourced income or residents of the country are subject to a low rate of taxation.

Tax preparer. One who prepares tax returns for compensation. A tax preparer must register with the IRS and receive a special ID number to practice before the IRS and represent taxpayers before the agency in tax audit actions. The conduct of a tax preparer is regulated under Circular 230. Tax preparers also are subject to penalties for inappropriate conduct when working in the tax profession.

Tax Rate Schedules. Rate schedules that are used by upper-income taxpayers and those not permitted to use the tax table. Separate rate schedules are provided for married individuals filing jointly, heads of households, single taxpayers, estates and trusts, and married individuals filing separate returns. § 1.

Tax research. The method used to determine the best available solution to a situation that possesses tax consequences. Both tax and nontax factors are considered.

Tax shelters. The typical tax shelter generated large losses in the early years of the activity. Investors would offset these losses against other types of income and therefore avoid paying income taxes on this income. These tax shelter investments could then be sold after a few years and produce capital gain income, which is taxed at a lower rate compared to ordinary income. The passive activity loss rules and the at-risk rules now limit tax shelter deductions.

Tax Table. A table that is provided for taxpayers with less than $100,000 of taxable income. Separate columns are provided for single taxpayers, married taxpayers filing jointly, heads of households, and married taxpayers filing separately. § 3.

Tax treaties. An agreement between the U.S. Department of State and another country designed to alleviate double taxation of income and asset transfers, and to share administrative information useful to tax agencies in both countries. The United States has income tax treaties with almost 70 countries and transfer tax treaties with about 20.

Taxable estate. The taxable estate is the gross estate of a decedent reduced by the deductions allowed by §§ 2053–2057 (e.g., administration expenses, marital and charitable deductions). The taxable estate is subject to the unified transfer tax at death. § 2051.

Taxable gift. The amount of a gift that is subject to the unified transfer tax. Thus, a taxable gift has been adjusted by the annual exclusion and other appropriate deductions (e.g., marital and charitable). § 2053.

Taxable year. The annual period over which income is measured for income tax purposes. Most individuals use a calendar year, but many businesses use a fiscal year based on the natural business year. Certain entities, including S corporations, have a required taxable year. §§ 441, 706, and 1378.

Technical Advice Memoranda (TAM). TAMs are issued by the IRS in response to questions raised by IRS field personnel during audits. They deal with completed rather than proposed transactions and are often requested for questions related to exempt organizations and employee plans.

Temporary differences. Under ASC 740 (SFAS 109), tax-related items that appear in the entity's financial statements and its tax return, but in different time periods. For instance, doubtful accounts receivable often create a temporary book-tax difference, as a bad debt reserve is used to compute an expense for financial reporting purposes, but a bad debt often is deductible only under the specific write-off rule for tax purposes, and the difference observed for the current period creates a temporary difference.

Temporary Regulations. A Regulation issued by the Treasury Department in temporary form. When speed is critical, the Treasury Department issues Temporary Regulations that take effect immediately. These Regulations have the same authoritative value as Final Regulations and may be cited as precedent for three years. Temporary Regulations are also issued as proposed Regulations.

Tenants by the entirety. Essentially, a joint tenancy between husband and wife.

Tenants in common. A form of ownership where each tenant (owner) holds an undivided interest in property. Unlike a joint tenancy or a tenancy by the entirety, the interest of a tenant in common does not terminate upon that individual's death (there is no right of survivorship). Assume that Tim and Cindy acquire real estate as equal tenants in common. Upon Tim's death, his one-half interest in the property passes to his estate or heirs, not automatically to Cindy.

Terminable interests. An interest in property that terminates upon the death of the holder or upon the occurrence of some other specified event. The transfer of a terminable interest by one spouse to the other may not qualify for the marital deduction. §§ 2056(b) and 2523(b).

Theft losses. A loss from larceny, embezzlement, or robbery. It does not include misplacement of items.

Thin capitalization. When debt owed by a corporation to the shareholders becomes too large in relation to the corporation's capital structure (i.e., stock and shareholder equity), the IRS may contend that the corporation is thinly capitalized. In effect, some or all of the debt is reclassified as equity. The immediate result is to disallow any interest deduction to the corporation on the reclassified debt. To the extent of the corporation's earnings and profits, interest payments and loan repayments on the reclassified debt are treated as dividends to the shareholders.

Thirty-day (30-day) letter. A letter that accompanies an RAR (Revenue Agent's Report) issued as a result of an IRS audit of a taxpayer (or the rejection of a taxpayer's claim for refund). The letter outlines the taxpayer's appeal procedure before the IRS. If the taxpayer does not request any such procedures within the 30-day period, the IRS issues a statutory notice of deficiency (the 90-day letter).

Throwback rule. If there is no income tax in the state to which a sale otherwise would be apportioned, the sale essentially is exempt from state income tax, even though the seller is domiciled in a state that levies an income tax. Nonetheless, if the seller's state has adopted a throwback rule, the sale is attributed to the seller's state and the transaction is subjected to a state-level tax.

Traditional IRA. See *Individual Retirement Accounts (IRAs).*

Transfer pricing. The process of setting internal prices for transfers of goods and services among related taxpayers. For example, what price should be used when Subsidiary purchases management services from Parent? The IRS can adjust transfer prices when it can show that the taxpayers were attempting to avoid tax by, for example, shifting losses, deductions, or credits from low-tax to high-tax entities or jurisdictions.

Transportation expenses. Expenses that include the cost of transporting the self-employed taxpayer (or employee) from one place to another in the course of business when the taxpayer is not in travel status. For tax years beginning after 2017 and before 2026, only reimbursed transportation expenses are deductible by employees. Commuting expenses are not deductible.

Travel expenses. Expenses that include meals (generally subject to a 50 percent disallowance) and lodging and transportation expenses while away from home in the pursuit of a trade or business (including that of an employee). For tax years beginning after 2017 and before 2026, only reimbursed travel expenses are deductible by employees.

Treaty shopping. An international investor attempts to use the favorable aspects of a tax treaty to his or her advantage, often elevating the form of the transaction over its substance (e.g., by establishing only a nominal presence in the country offering the favorable treaty terms).

Twelve-month (12-month) rule for prepaid expenses. Taxpayers who use the cash method are required to use the accrual method for deducting certain prepaid expenses (i.e., must capitalize the item and can deduct only when used). If a prepayment will not be consumed or expire by the end of the tax year following the year of payment, the prepayment must be capitalized and prorated over the benefit period. Conversely, if the prepayment will be consumed by the end of the tax year following the year of payment, it can be expensed when paid. To obtain the current deduction under the one-year rule, the payment must be a required payment rather than a voluntary payment.

U

UDITPA. The Uniform Division of Income for Tax Purposes Act has been adopted in some form by many of the states. The Act develops criteria by which the total taxable income of a multistate corporation can be assigned to specific states.

Unclaimed property. A U.S. state may have the right to acquire property that has been made available to an individual or legal entity for a fixed period of time, where the claimant has not taken possession of the property after a notice period. Examples of such property that a state could acquire are an uncashed payroll check or an unused gift card.

Unearned income. Income received but not yet earned. Normally, such income is taxed when received, even for accrual basis taxpayers.

Unified transfer tax. Rates applicable to transfers by gift and death made after 1976. § 2001(c).

Unified transfer tax credit. A credit allowed against any unified transfer tax. §§ 2010 and 2505.

Uniform capitalization (UNICAP) rules. Under § 263A, the Regulations provide a set of rules that all taxpayers (regardless of the particular industry) can use to determine the items of cost (and means of allocating those costs) that must be capitalized with respect to the production of tangible property. Small businesses, defined as those with average annual gross receipts in the prior three-year period of $27 million or less, that are not a tax shelter, are not required to use the UNICAP rules.

Unitary approach. See *unitary theory.*

Unitary theory. Sales, property, and payroll of related corporations are combined for nexus and apportionment purposes, and the worldwide income of the unitary entity is apportioned to the state. Subsidiaries and other affiliated corporations found to be part of the corporation's unitary business (because they are subject to overlapping ownership, operation, or management) are included in the apportionment procedure. This approach can be limited if a waters'-edge election is in effect.

Unit-livestock-price method. A method of accounting for the cost of livestock. The livestock are valued using a standard cost of raising an animal with the characteristics of the animals on hand to the same age as those animals.

Unrealized receivables. Amounts earned by a cash basis taxpayer but not yet received. Because of the method of accounting used by the taxpayer, these amounts have a zero income tax basis. When unrealized receivables are distributed to a partner, they generally convert a transaction from nontaxable to taxable or an otherwise capital gain to ordinary income (i.e., as a "hot asset").

Unreasonable compensation. A deduction is allowed for "reasonable" salaries or other compensation for personal services actually rendered. The issue of unreasonable compensation usually is limited to closely held corporations, where the motivation is to pay out profits in some form that is deductible to the corporation. To the extent compensation is "excessive" ("unreasonable"), the distribution could be treated as a dividend, such that no deduction is allowed.

Unreasonable position. A tax preparer penalty is assessed regarding the understatement of a client's tax liability due to a tax return position that is found to be too aggressive. The penalty is avoided if there is substantial authority for the position or if the position is disclosed adequately on the tax return. The penalty equals the greater of $1,000 or one half of the tax preparer's fee that is traceable to the aggressive position.

Unrecaptured § 1250 gain. Gain from the sale of depreciable real estate held more than one year. The gain is equal to or less than the depreciation taken on such property and is reduced by § 1245 and § 1250 gain. § 1(h)(6).

Unrelated business income (UBI). Income recognized by an exempt organization that is generated from activities not related to the exempt purpose of the entity. For instance, the gift shop located in a hospital may generate unrelated business income. §§ 511 and 512.

Unrelated business income tax (UBIT). Levied on the unrelated business income of an exempt organization.

U.S. Court of Federal Claims. A trial court (court of original jurisdiction) that decides litigation involving Federal tax matters. Appeal from this court is to the Court of Appeals for the Federal Circuit.

U.S. District Court. A trial court for purposes of litigating Federal tax matters. This court allows a jury trial.

U.S. shareholder. For purposes of classification of an entity as a controlled foreign corporation, a U.S. person who owns, or is considered to own, 10 percent or more of the total combined voting power of all classes of voting stock of a foreign corporation. Stock owned directly, indirectly, and constructively is counted for this purpose. § 951(b).

U.S. Supreme Court. The highest appellate court or the court of last resort in the Federal court system and in most states. Only a small number of tax decisions of the U.S. Courts of Appeal are reviewed by the U.S. Supreme Court under its certiorari procedure. The Supreme Court usually grants certiorari to resolve a conflict among the Courts of Appeal (e.g., two or more appellate courts have assumed opposing positions on a particular issue) or when the tax issue is extremely important (e.g., due to the size of the revenue loss to the Federal government).

U.S. Tax Court. One of four trial courts of original jurisdiction that decides litigation involving Federal income, death, or gift taxes. The only trial court where the taxpayer must not first pay the deficiency assessed by the IRS. The Tax Court does not have jurisdiction over a case unless a statutory notice of deficiency (90-day letter) has been issued by the IRS and the taxpayer files the petition for hearing within the time prescribed.

U.S. trade or business. A set of activities that is carried on in a regular, continuous, and substantial manner. A non-U.S. taxpayer is subject to U.S. tax on the taxable income that is effectively connected with a U.S. trade or business.

Use tax. A use tax is designed to complement the sales tax. The use tax has two purposes: to prevent consumers from evading sales tax by purchasing goods outside the state for in-state use, and to provide an equitable taxing environment between in-state and out-of-state retailers. Purchasers of taxable goods or services who were not charged sales tax because the seller did not have *nexus* with the purchaser's state may owe use tax on the purchase.

V

Vacation homes. The Code places restrictions upon taxpayers who rent their residences or vacation homes for part of the tax year. The restrictions may result in a scaling down of expense deductions for the taxpayers. § 280A.

Valuation allowance. Under ASC 740 (SFAS 109), a tax-related item is reported for book purposes only when it is more likely than not that the item actually will be realized. When the "more likely than not" test is failed, a contra-asset account is created to offset some or all of the related deferred tax asset. For instance, if the entity projects that it will not be able to use all of its net operating loss carryforward due to a lack of future taxable income, a valuation allowance is created to reduce the net deferred tax asset that corresponds to the carryforward. If income projections later change and it appears that the carryforward will be used, the valuation allowance is reversed or "released." Creation of a valuation allowance usually increases the current tax expense and thereby reduces current book income, and its release often increases book income in the later reporting period.

Value added tax (VAT). A national sales tax that taxes the increment in value as goods move through the production process. A VAT is much used in the majority of countries but has not yet been incorporated as part of the U.S. Federal tax structure.

Vesting requirements. A qualified deferred compensation arrangement must satisfy a vesting requirement. Under this provision, an employee's right to accrued plan benefits derived from employer contributions must be nonforfeitable in accordance with one of two vesting time period schedules (or two required alternate vesting schedules for certain employer matching contributions).

Voluntary revocation. The owners of a majority of shares in an S corporation elect to terminate the S status of the entity as of a specified date. The day on which the revocation is effective is the first day of the C corporation's tax year.

W

W–2 Wages/Capital Investment Limit. A limitation on the deduction for qualified business income that caps the deduction at the greater of (1) 50 percent of the wages paid by a qualified trade or business or (2) 25 percent of the wages paid by the qualified trade or business plus 2.5 percent of the taxpayer's share of the unadjusted basis of property used in the business that has not been fully depreciated prior to the close of the taxable year. § 199A(b)(2)(B).

Wash sale. A loss from the sale of stock or securities that is disallowed because the taxpayer, within 30 days before or after the sale, has acquired stock or securities substantially identical to those sold. § 1091.

Waters' edge. A limitation on the worldwide scope of the unitary theory. If a corporate waters'-edge election is in effect, the state can consider in the apportionment procedure only the activities that occur within the boundaries of the United States.

Waters'-edge election. See *waters' edge.*

Wherewithal to pay. This concept recognizes the inequity of taxing a transaction when the taxpayer lacks the means with which to pay the tax. Under it, there is a correlation between the imposition of the tax and the ability to pay the tax. It is particularly suited to situations in which the taxpayer's economic position has not changed significantly as a result of the transaction.

Whistleblower Program. An IRS initiative that offers special rewards to informants who provide evidence regarding tax evasion activities of businesses or high-income individuals. More than $2 million of tax, interest, and penalty must be at stake. The reward can reach 30 percent of the tax recovery that is attributable to the whistleblower's information.

Work opportunity tax credit. Employers are allowed a tax credit equal to 40 percent of the first $6,000 of wages (per eligible employee) for the first year of employment. Eligible employees include certain hard-to-employ individuals (e.g., qualified ex-felons, high-risk youth, food stamp recipients, and veterans). The employer's deduction for wages is reduced by the amount of the credit taken. For qualified summer youth employees, the 40 percent rate is applied to the first $3,000 of qualified wages. The credit does not apply to any amount paid to an individual who begins work for the employer after 2025. §§ 51 and 52.

Working condition fringes. A type of fringe benefit received by the employee that is excludible from the employee's gross income. It consists of property or services provided (paid or reimbursed) by the employer for which the employee could take a tax deduction if the employee had paid for them. § 132(d).

Worthless securities. A loss (usually capital) is allowed for a security that becomes worthless during the year. The loss is deemed to have occurred on the last day of the year. Special rules apply to securities of affiliated companies and small business stock. § 165.

Writ of Certiorari. Appeal from a U.S. Court of Appeals to the U.S. Supreme Court is by Writ of Certiorari. The Supreme Court need not accept the appeal and usually does not (*cert. den.*) unless a conflict exists among the lower courts that must be resolved or a constitutional issue is involved.

Appendix D

Table of Code Sections Cited

I.R.C. Sec.	This Work Page
1	2-5, 2-37, 3-8, 16-24
1(b)	9-71
1(f)	3-33
1(g)	13-18
1(g)(2)	3-37
1(g)(7)	3-39
1(h)	9-26, 16-24
1(h)(1)	3-43, 20-1
1(h)(3)(B)	20-34
1(h)(11)	4-16
1(h)(11)(B)	20-1
1(j)	3-35, 4-16
2	2-5, 2-6, 2-7
2(a)(1)	3-31
2(a)(1)(A)	2-5
2(b)	3-31
2(b)(1)(B)	3-32
11	2-37
11(b)	20-14
12(d)	2-5
21	13-21
21(b)(3)	15-18
21(c)	13-17
21(d)	13-16
22	13-21
22(e)(3)	3-20
23	5-15, 13-21
24	13-21
24(b)	3-27
24(c)	3-26
24(d)(1)(B)(ii)	3-28
24(h)	3-26
24(h)(3)	3-27
24(h)(4)(7)	3-26
24(h)(4)(A)	3-26
24(h)(4)(B)	3-25, 3-27
24(i)(1)	3-28
24(i)(2)	3-26
24(i)(3)	3-26
24(i)(4)	3-27
25A	13-18, 13-21
25(A)(c)	9-16
25A(i)	9-16
25A(i)(3)	13-18
25B	13-19, 13-22
25B(e)	13-20
25C	13-20
25D	13-20
26(a)(2)	12-6
27	13-14, 13-22
30D	13-20
31	13-21

I.R.C. Sec.	This Work Page
32	13-12, 13-21
32(a)(2)(B)	13-12
32(i)	13-12
36B	13-42
36C	13-20
38	13-22
38(b)	13-5
38(c)	13-5
39(a)(1)	13-5
40	13-20
40A	13-20
41	7-16, 13-7, 13-22
41(b)(3)(A)	13-8
41(c)(4)	13-8
41(c)(5)	13-8
41(d)	13-8
42	13-9, 13-22
44	13-10, 13-22
45	13-20
45E	13-11, 13-22
45E(c)(1)	13-11
45E(d)(1)	13-11
45F	13-11, 13-23
45F(d)	13-11
45L	13-20
45S	13-12, 13-23
47	13-6, 13-22
48	13-20
50(c)	13-6
51	13-7, 13-23
53	12-21
55	20-14
55(a)	12-5
55(b)(1)(A)	12-5
55(d)(4)	12-5
55(d)(4)(B)	12-5
56	12-4
56(a)(1)(A)	12-6, 12-8
56(a)(2)	12-9
56(a)(3)	12-10
56(a)(4)	12-14
56(a)(5)	12-8
56(a)(6)	12-11
56(b)(1)(A)	12-15
56(b)(1)(B)(i)	12-16
56(b)(1)(B)(iii)	12-16
56(b)(1)(C)	12-15
56(b)(1)(E)	12-17
56(b)(2)	12-9

I.R.C. Sec.	This Work Page
56(b)(2)(A)(ii)	12-10
56(b)(3)	12-10, 19-20
56(d)(1)(A)(i)(II)	12-14
56(e)	12-16
57	12-4
57(a)(1)	12-18
57(a)(2)	12-19
57(a)(7)	12-20
58(b)	12-3
59(e)	7-17, 12-10
59(e)(2)(A)	12-9
59(e)(2)(D)	12-10
59(e)(2)(E)	12-10
61	2-22, 2-27, 2-37, 4-3, 4-20, 20-17, 20-20
61(a)	2-41, 3-3, 4-3
61(a)(3)	14-8
61(a)(11)	5-27
62	2-37, 6-3, 20-17
62(a)	3-4, 9-25
62(a)(1)	6-31, 7-15
62(a)(2)(A)	6-31
62(a)(2)(B)	6-31
62(a)(2)(D)	6-31, 9-16, 9-24
62(a)(3)	6-31
62(a)(4)	6-4, 6-31, 7-15
62(a)(17)	10-14
62(a)(18)	6-31
62(a)(22)	10-25
62(b)	9-53
62(f)	10-25
63(a)	20-17
63(b)	20-17
63(b) through (h)	20-17
63(b)(3)	9-25
63(c)	10-2
63(c)(1)	3-17
63(c)(4)	3-33
63(c)(5)	3-18
63(c)(6)	3-18
63(d)(3)	9-25
63(h)	20-17
66	4-20
67(b)(3)	7-15
67(g)	9-3, 9-55
71	4-20, 4-21
71(c)(2)	4-22
71(c)(3)	4-22
72(b)	4-28
72(d)	4-28

I.R.C. Sec.	This Work Page
72(t)	9-16, 19-7, 19-16, 19-33
72(t)(2)	19-33
72(t)(2)(B)	19-16
72(t)(2)(D)	19-16
72(t)(2)(E)	19-16
72(t)(2)(F)	19-16
73	4-15
74	4-29, 5-22
74(b)	4-29
74(c)	4-29
74(d)	4-29
79	5-20, 5-22, 5-37
79(d)	5-21
83(a)	4-10
85	4-29
86	4-30
91	4-20
101 through 140	5-2
101(a)	5-5
101(a)(2)	5-6
101(g)	5-5
102	5-3
102(a)	14-12
102(c)	5-4
103	6-29
103(a)	5-24
104	2-40, 5-2
104(a)(1)	5-10
104(a)(2)	5-9
104(a)(3)	5-10
105	5-11, 5-22
105(a)	5-11
105(b)	5-11
105(c)	5-11
105(h)	5-11
106	5-11, 5-22
106(d)	5-12
107	5-14
108	5-28
108(a)	5-28
108(b)	5-28
108(c)	5-28
108(e)	5-28
108(e)(5)	5-28
108(e)(6)	5-28
108(f)	5-28
108(f)(5)	5-28
108(g)	5-28
109	1-37, 14-21
111	5-29
111(a)	5-29
117	4-29, 5-2, 9-16
117(a)	5-7
117(b)	5-7, 5-8
117(d)	5-7, 9-16
118(a)	20-20
118(b)	20-20
119	5-13, 5-22
119(a)	5-13
119(d)	5-14
121	5-2, 10-15, 15-16, 15-17, 15-18, 15-19, 15-20, 15-21, 15-22, 15-23, 15-24, 20-7
121(a)	15-17, 15-38
121(a)(1)	15-38
121(b)	15-16
121(b)(1)	15-19
121(b)(2)	15-19
121(c)(1)	15-21
121(d)(6)	15-22
121(d)(10)	15-17
121(f)	15-23
125	5-16
127	5-15, 5-22, 9-16
129	5-15, 5-22
132	5-17, 5-22
132(b)	5-17
132(h)	5-17
132(j)(1)	5-20
132(j)(4)	5-15
132(m)(2)	5-20
134	5-14
135	5-24, 5-42, 9-16
137	5-15
139	5-2, 5-4
139F	5-10
141	12-19
151(d)(3)	3-33
152(b)(2)	3-25
152(b)(3)	3-25
152(c)(3)(A)	3-20
152(c)(3)(B)	3-20
152(c)(4)	3-21
152(d)	3-21
152(d)(2)(H)	3-22
152(e)	3-32
152(e)(2)	3-24
152(f)(2)	3-20

I.R.C. Sec.	This Work Page
152(f)(3)	3-22
152(f)(5)	3-20
152(f)(6)	3-20
162	2-37, 6-3, 6-4, 6-5, 6-15, 6-17, 6-31, 9-16, 9-28, 9-48, 10-14, 10-19, 20-17
162(a)	6-4, 6-31, 6-46, 9-10, 9-28
162(a)(1)	6-5
162(a)(2)	6-31
162(c)	2-23, 6-13
162(c)(2)	9-72
162(e)	6-16, 6-33
162(f)	6-13, 6-14, 6-33, 6-46, 9-8
162(f)(1)	6-13
162(g)	6-13
162(l)	6-7, 9-26, 10-7
162(m)	6-16, 6-47
162(q)	6-30
163	6-31
163(d)(1)	11-22
163(d)(2)	11-23
163(d)(3)	6-31
163(d)(4)(B)	11-22
163(h)(1)	6-31
163(h)(3)	6-31, 10-14, 10-15
163(h)(3)(E)	10-16
163(h)(3)(F)	10-15, 12-16
163(j)	6-30, 8-23
163(j)(1)	20-14
164	6-31, 10-10, 13-14
164(a)(1)	6-31
164(a)(2)	6-31
164(a)(3)	6-31
164(b)(5)	6-31
164(b)(6)	10-11
164(d)	10-12
164(f)	6-7, 9-26, 13-27, 13-30, 19-11
165	6-6
165(a)	14-8
165(c)	7-7, 15-16
165(c)(1)	6-31, 11-2
165(c)(2)	11-2
165(c)(3)	6-31, 15-16
165(g)	7-5, 7-6
165(g)(1)	11-23, 16-8
165(h)	7-10, 7-13
165(h)(A)	12-21
165(h)(2)(B)	7-13
165(h)(3)	7-12
165(h)(4)(E)	7-10
165(h)(5)	7-7
165(h)(5)(B)	7-12
165(i)	7-8, 7-11, 18-8
165(i)(5)	7-7
165(k)	7-8
166	6-31
166(a)	7-3
166(d)	7-3, 16-37
167	14-21, 17-11
168	8-2, 14-21, 17-11
168(b)	8-5, 8-9
168(b)(5)	8-8
168(c)	8-9
168(d)(1)	8-10
168(d)(3)	8-7
168(d)(4)(A)	8-6
168(e)	8-5, 8-9
168(e)(3)	8-23
168(e)(6)	8-8
168(g)	8-23, 12-8
168(g)(3)(B)	8-23
168(k)	8-14, 12-7, 17-11, 17-13
168(k)(2)(E)(ii)(I)	8-15
168(k)(2)(F)(i)	8-19
168(k)(2)(G)	12-7
170	6-31, 10-18
170(a)(2)	20-10
170(b)(1)(C)(iii)	10-24
170(b)(2)	20-10
170(c)	10-20
170(d)(2)	20-10
170(e)(1)(A)	17-16
170(e)(1)(B)	17-16
170(e)(1)(B)(i)	10-23
170(e)(1)(B)(ii)	10-24
170(e)(3)	20-11
170(f)	10-21
170(i)	10-19
170(j)	10-19
170(l)	10-19
170(p)	3-7, 10-25
171(c)	14-7
172	18-8
172(a)	7-19, 20-11
172(a)(2)	7-20
172(b)	20-11
172(b)(1)	12-14

I.R.C. Sec.	This Work Page
172(b)(1)(A)	7-20
172(b)(1)(B)(i)	7-20
172(c)	20-11
172(d)	7-20, 20-11
172(d)(8)	7-20
173(a)	12-9
174	7-15, 7-17, 13-8
174(a)	12-10
174(b)(2)	7-16
179	6-12, 8-10, 8-11, 8-12, 8-13, 8-14, 8-15, 8-16, 8-17, 8-18, 8-20, 8-21, 8-24, 8-30, 8-36, 8-37, 8-38, 8-39, 8-40, 8-41, 8-42, 8-44, 8-45, 8-46, 8-47, 9-7, 9-19, 9-20, 9-57, 9-63, 9-69, 12-7, 13-40, 14-6, 14-21, 17-1, 17-10, 17-11, 17-13, 17-14, 17-17, 17-20, 17-28, 18-43
179(b)(5)	8-20
183	6-19, 6-20, 6-32
183(b)(2)	6-19
183(d)	6-19
195	6-17, 6-31, 8-28, 8-43
195(b)	6-18
195(b)(1)(A)	8-25
195(b)(1)(B)	8-25
195(c)	8-28
195(c)(1)(A)	8-28
195(c)(1)(B)	8-28
197	6-28, 8-25, 8-39, 16-13, 16-36, 17-11, 17-14
197(a)	8-25
197(b)	8-25
197(d)	8-25
199A	6-7, 6-31, 7-21, 7-23, 9-25, 9-26, 9-27, 9-28, 9-29, 9-31, 9-33, 9-34, 9-37, 9-38, 9-43, 9-48, 9-49, 9-50, 9-51, 16-47, 20-14, 20-17
199A(a)	6-7, 9-25
199A(a)(1)(A)	9-25, 9-29
199A(a)(2)(B)	9-26
199A(b)(1)	7-23
199A(b)(1)(A)	9-25
199A(b)(1)(B)	9-25
199A(b)(2)	9-29
199A(b)(2)(A)	9-25
199A(b)(2)(B)	9-29
199A(b)(3)(B)	9-29
199A(b)(3)(B)(ii)	9-32
199A(b)(3)(B)(iii)	9-32
199A(b)(4)	9-29
199A(b)(6)(A)	9-31
199A(b)(6)(B)	9-31
199A(c)	6-7, 9-26
199A(c)(2)	7-20, 9-48
199A(c)(3)(A)	9-26
199A(c)(3)(B)	9-26
199A(c)(4)	9-26
199A(d)(1)	6-8
199A(d)(1)(A)	9-33
199A(d)(1)(B)	9-27
199A(d)(2)	6-8, 9-29, 9-33
199A(d)(2)(A)	9-33
199A(d)(3)	9-29
199A(d)(3)(B)	9-38
199A(e)(1)	9-26
199A(e)(2)	9-29
211	2-5
212	2-37, 3-6, 6-3, 6-4, 6-5, 6-29, 6-31, 9-55, 20-17
212(1)	2-5
212(3)	10-5
213	6-31, 10-25
213(a)	6-25, 10-3, 10-5, 12-17
213(a)(d)(5)	10-5
213(d)(1)(A)	10-3
213(d)(2)	10-6
213(d)(9)(A)	10-4
213(d)(10)	5-12
215	4-21
217	5-19
217(k)	6-31, 9-21
219	9-52
219(b)(1)	19-13
219(c)(2)	19-13
219(g)	19-13
219(g)(7)	19-14
221	6-31, 9-16, 10-14
221(b)(2)(C)	10-14
221(c)	10-14
221(e)(2)	10-14
222	6-31
223	5-12, 5-22
223(a)	10-8
223(b)	5-12
223(b)(2)	10-9
223(c)(2)	10-8

I.R.C. Sec.	This Work Page
223(d)	5-12, 10-8, 10-9
223(f)	10-9
243(a)	20-12
243(b)	20-12
248	20-13
248(c)	20-13
262	2-37, 6-4, 6-26, 6-31, 10-2, 10-27, 16-16
263(a)(1)	6-26
263(c)	17-19
263(e)(3)	18-29
263A	18-29
263A(d)	18-12, 18-29
263A(f)	18-30
263A(i)	4-8
265	6-29
265(a)(2)	10-16
267	2-23, 14-23
267(a)(1)	6-29, 14-9
267(b)	9-43, 18-22
267(d)	14-16
269A(b)(2)	11-10
274	2-38, 8-23, 9-22
274(a)(1)(A)	6-31
274(a)(4)	5-19, 6-30
274(b)(1)	9-24
274(c)	9-13
274(d)	8-23, 9-14, 9-53
274(e)	9-22
274(h)(1)	9-11
274(i)	8-23
274(j)	4-29
274(k)	9-23
274(m)(2)	9-12
274(m)(3)	9-12
274(n)	6-31, 9-22
274(n)(2)(D)	5-13, 9-22
275	9-25, 10-10
276	6-15
280A	2-5, 6-21, 11-23
280A through 280H	2-5
280A(c)(1)	9-17
280A(d)	6-23
280A(g)	6-22
280C(c)(1)	13-8
280C(c)(2)	13-8
280E	6-15
280F	8-18, 17-20
280F(a)(1)	8-19
280F(b)(1)	8-21
280F(b)(2)	8-21
280F(b)(3)	8-19
280F(d)(1)	8-20
280F(d)(4)(A)	8-18
280F(d)(5)	8-19
280G	19-18
280H	18-6
291	20-7, 20-9, 20-10, 20-17
291(a)(1)	17-19
301	20-2
301(c)	5-3
305(a)	5-3, 14-11
305(b)	5-3
307(a)	14-11
311(b)	17-17
312	20-2
316(a)	5-3
318	2-23
318(a)	18-22
332	17-16
351	17-16, 17-28, 20-18, 20-19, 20-38
358(a)	20-19
362(a)	20-19
385	20-20
401(a)(1)(A)	19-4
401(a)(1)(B)	19-4
401(a)(4)	19-4, 19-5
401(a)(5)	19-4
401(a)(9)	19-6, 19-14
401(a)(17)	19-9
401(a)(26)	19-5
401(c)	9-53
401(c)(2)	19-11
401(c)(2)(A)(v)	19-11
401(k)	9-52, 9-53, 9-67, 9-69, 12-24, 13-19, 13-20, 13-35, 13-39, 14-14, 19-2, 19-10, 19-11, 19-12, 19-14, 19-24, 19-26, 19-28, 19-30, 19-31, 19-32, 19-33
401(k)(3)	19-25
402(a)(1)	19-8
402(c)	19-8
402(g)(1)	19-10
402(g)(4)	19-10
402A	9-51
403(b)	9-52
404	6-7, 9-26
404(a)(1)	19-10

I.R.C. Sec.	This Work Page
404(a)(5)	19-18
404(a)(6)	19-10
404(j)	19-9
404(l)	19-9
408	9-52, 19-12
408(k)	9-53
408(m)(2)	16-22
408(o)	19-14
408(p)	9-53, 19-12
408(p)(2)(E)(i)	19-12
408A	9-53, 19-14
408A(c)(3)(B)	19-17
408A(c)(4)	19-17
410(b)	19-5
410(b)(3)	19-5
414(i)	19-3
414(q)	19-5
415(b)	19-9
415(b)(1)	19-11
415(c)	19-9
415(c)(1)	19-11
415(d)	19-9
415(d)(4)	19-9
421(a)	12-10
421(a)(1)	19-20
421(a)(2)	19-20
422(a)	19-20
422(a)(1)	19-20
422(a)(2)	19-20
422(b)	19-19
422(c)(3)	19-20
422(c)(5)	19-22
441	4-6
441(c)	18-2
441(f)	18-3
441(i)	4-6, 18-6, 20-7
442	18-6
444	18-5, 18-6
444(c)	18-5
446	18-10
446(a)	6-10
446(b)	4-7, 6-10, 18-10
446(c)(3)	18-16
446(d)	18-10
446(e)	4-7, 6-10
446(f)	18-18
447	18-12, 20-7
447(c)	18-12

I.R.C. Sec.	This Work Page
448	4-8, 6-10, 18-10, 18-12
448(a)	18-12, 20-7
448(b)	18-12
448(c)	4-9, 6-30
448(c)(1)	6-10
448(d)(2)	20-7
448(d)(2)(A)	11-10
448(d)(3)	4-8, 18-12
448(d)(5)	18-16
451(b)	4-13, 18-13
451(b)(3)	18-13
451(c)	4-14, 18-13, 18-35
451(c)(4)(B)	18-14
451(d)	18-8
451(f)	18-9
451(g)	18-9
453	4-7
453(a)	18-20
453A	18-23
453(b)	18-20
453(d)	18-20, 18-24
453(d)(3)	18-24
453(e)	18-22
453(e)(2)	18-22
453(e)(2)(B)	18-22
453(e)(6)	18-22
453(e)(7)	18-22
453(f)(1)	18-22
453(g)	18-23
453(i)	17-17, 18-20
453B(a)	18-23
453B(c)	18-24
453B(d)	18-24
453B(f)(2)	18-23
453B(g)	18-24
453(I)	18-20
453(I)(2)	18-20
454(a)	4-12
457	9-51, 9-52
457(b)	12-24
460	4-7, 18-25
460(b)(1)(A)	18-27
460(b)(2)	18-28
460(b)(5)	18-28
460(b)(6)	18-28
460(f)	18-25
461	18-14
461(g)(1)	10-17

I.R.C. Sec.	This Work Page
461(g)(2)	10-16
461(h)	6-10
461(h)(3)(A)	6-11
461(l)	7-17, 11-17
461(l)(3)	7-17
461(l)(3)(A)	7-18
461(1)(4)(A)	7-18
461(l)(5)	7-19
461(l)(6)	7-19
464	18-12
465(b)(1)	11-4
465(b)(6)	11-4
465(e)	11-5
469	7-19, 11-5, 11-13
469(a)	11-9
469(b)	11-8
469(c)(2)	11-15
469(c)(7)	11-17
469(c)(7)(B)	11-18
469(d)(2)	11-8
469(f)	11-9
469(g)(2)	11-20
469(g)(3)	11-21
469(h)(2)	11-14
469(h)(5)	11-14
469(i)	11-18
469(i)(3)(F)	11-18
469(i)(6)	11-18
469(j)(2)	11-10
469(j)(5)	11-19
469(j)(6)	11-21
469(j)(8)	11-15
471	18-29
471(a)	18-28
471(b)	18-31
471(c)	4-7, 4-8, 4-9, 18-10, 18-34
471(c)(1)(B)	18-10
472(d)	18-33, 18-34
474	2-33
481	18-18, 18-51
481(a)	18-18, 18-41, 18-51
481(b)	18-18
483	18-21
501(a)	19-8
529	5-25, 5-26, 5-27, 5-32, 5-35, 9-16
529A	5-26
530	5-25, 5-26, 5-32, 9-16

I.R.C. Sec.	This Work Page
585	18-16
611(a)	8-29
612	8-29
613(a)	8-30, 12-18
613A	8-30
613A(c)	12-18
613A(d)(4)	2-34
614(a)	12-18
616(a)	12-9
617(a)	12-9
631(a)	17-4
652(a)	4-18
662(a)	4-18
691	5-5
691(a)(3)	14-14
702(a)	20-32
703(a)	20-32
704(e)	20-35
705(a)	20-30
706	4-6
706(a)	4-18
706(b)(1)(B)	18-3
706(b)(1)(C)	18-5
706(b)(3)	18-3
707	14-16
707(b)	9-43
707(c)	20-33
721	17-16, 20-9
722	20-30
723	20-31
742	5-24
761(f)	20-6
877A	4-3
901–908	13-14
904	13-14
904(c)	13-14
911(a)	5-21
911(d)	5-22
1001(a)	14-3
1001(b)	14-4
1001(c)	14-8
1011	14-13
1011(a)	14-5
1012	9-51, 14-9, 15-22
1014(a)	14-13
1014(b)(6)	14-15
1014(c)	14-14

I.R.C. Sec.	This Work Page
1015(a)	14-12
1015(d)(6)	14-13
1016(a)	14-5
1016(a)(2)	14-6
1016(a)(4)	14-7
1016(a)(5)	14-7
1017	5-28
1022	14-13
1031	15-3, 15-5, 15-10, 15-22, 15-23, 15-25, 17-17, 20-7, 20-41
1031(a)	15-4
1031(a)(2)	15-4
1031(a)(3)	15-5
1031(f)	15-4
1032	20-20
1033	15-10, 15-12, 15-15, 15-27, 15-39, 17-17, 20-7
1033(a)	15-12, 15-13
1033(a)(2)(A)	15-15
1033(a)(2)(B)	15-14
1033(b)	15-15
1033(g)(4)	15-14
1041	4-20, 18-22
1045(a)	16-23
1060	14-10, 18-51
1091(a)	14-17
1091(b)	14-18
1091(d)	14-18
1202(a)	16-22
1202(a)(1)–(3)	12-20
1202(a)(4)	12-20
1202(a)(4)(C)	12-20
1202(e)(3)(A)	9-33
1211	11-23
1211(a)	16-29, 20-9
1211(b)	7-6, 16-19, 20-9
1211(b)(1)	16-27
1212	11-23
1212(a)	20-9
1212(a)(1)	16-29
1212(b)	16-27
1221	16-4, 16-6, 16-7, 16-48
1221(a)	16-4
1222(a)(2)	17-2
1222(1)	2-5
1222(3)	16-15, 17-2
1222(10)	16-27
1222(11)	9-26
1223	16-16
1223(1)	15-8
1223(2)	14-13, 14-16, 20-31
1223(3)	14-18
1223(5)	14-11
1223(9)	14-15
1231	9-26, 10-23, 14-10, 15-8, 16-3, 16-14, 16-19, 17-2, 17-3, 17-4, 17-5, 17-6, 17-7, 17-8, 17-9, 17-10, 17-11, 17-12, 17-13, 17-14, 17-15, 17-16, 17-17, 17-18, 17-20, 17-21, 17-27, 17-28, 18-21, 20-9
1233	16-16
1234(a)	16-10
1234(a)(1)	19-20
1234(a)(2)	19-20
1235	16-11
1237	16-5, 16-7, 16-8, 16-40, 16-48
1239	17-19
1239(b)	18-23
1239(c)	18-23
1241	16-14
1242	16-37
1244	2-29, 7-1, 7-6, 7-25, 7-26, 7-27, 7-28, 7-30, 7-33, 7-35, 11-23, 11-24, 16-8, 16-37, 16-42
1244(a)	7-6
1244(c)(3)	7-6
1244(d)(4)	7-6
1245	16-13, 16-14, 17-10, 17-11, 17-12, 17-13, 17-14, 17-15, 17-16, 17-17, 17-18, 17-20, 17-21, 17-27, 17-28, 18-41, 20-7, 20-9, 20-10, 20-17
1245(b)(1)	17-16
1245(b)(2)	17-16
1245(b)(3)	17-16, 17-17
1245(d)	17-17
1250	3-43, 16-19, 16-25, 16-38, 16-45, 17-10, 17-12, 17-13, 17-14, 17-15, 17-16, 17-17, 17-19, 17-20, 17-21, 17-22, 17-27, 17-28, 20-8, 20-9, 20-10, 20-17, 20-39
1250(a)(1)(B)	17-13
1250(d)(1)	17-16
1250(d)(2)	17-16

I.R.C. Sec.	This Work Page
1250(d)(3)	17-16, 17-17
1250(i)	17-17
1253	16-12, 16-13
1253(b)(1)	16-12
1254	17-19
1259	16-18
1271	16-9
1271(b)	16-36
1272	16-9
1272–1275	16-9
1272–1288	16-9
1272(a)	18-22
1272(a)(2)	4-11
1272(a)(3)	4-11
1273(a)	4-11, 18-22
1273(a)(3)	16-9
1274	18-21
1274(a)	18-22
1274(d)	4-23
1274(d)(1)	18-21
1276–1288	16-9
1288	16-9
1301	18-9
1341	18-9
1361(a)	4-18
1361(c)(1)	20-4
1362(d)(3)(a)(i)	20-4
1366	4-18, 20-5
1366(d)(1)(B)	20-48
1366(e)	20-36
1367	20-7
1378	4-6, 20-7
1378(a)	18-5
1378(b)	18-5
1378(b)(2)	18-5
1401(b)(2)(B)	13-30
1402(a)	7-20, 19-11
1402(a)(12)	13-27
1411	3-47, 11-26, 20-18
1411(b)	13-30
1411(c)	13-30
1411(d)	13-30
2032(a)(1)	14-14
2032(c)	14-14
2040(b)	14-15
2205(a)	10-25
3101(b)(2)	13-29
3102(f)	13-29
3121(d)(3)	9-5
3401	13-25
3401(a)	9-51
3402	3-36, 13-25
3403	13-23
3405(c)	19-8
3406(a)	13-25
3508	9-5
4064	1-13
4414(j)	19-2
4972	19-10
4974(a)	19-7
4980D	5-11
4999	19-18
6012(a)(1)	3-33
6012(a)(2)	20-15
6012(f)	3-33
6013(a)(1)	3-30
6013(d)(3)	3-30
6013(g)	3-30
6017	13-27
6031	20-31
6041(a)	9-3
6050Y	5-5
6072(a)	3-40, 20-15
6109(a)(4)	1-28
6110	2-8
6110(k)(3)	2-9
6654	3-36, 13-23
6654(b)(2)	13-26
6654(c)(1)	13-26
6654(e)(1)	13-26
6655	20-15
6662	2-25
6662(a)	2-23
6662(b)(1)	2-23
6662(c)	2-23
7463(b)	2-40
7482(a)	2-13
7482(c)	2-13
7502(f)	3-40
7519(b)	18-5
7527A	3-26
7701(a)(2)	20-5

I.R.C. Sec.	This Work Page
7701(a)(3)	20-6
7701(b)	19-5
7702B	5-12
7702B(c)	10-4
7703(b)	3-32
7703(b)(1)	3-32
7805	2-6
7805(a)	2-7
7805(e)	2-7
7852(d)	2-17
7872(a)(1)	4-23
7872(b)(2)	4-23
7872(c)	4-24
7872(c)(2)	4-25
7872(c)(3)	4-25
7872(d)	4-25
7872(f)(2)	4-23
9831(d)	5-11

Appendix E

Present Value and Future Value Tables

Present Value of $1 E-2

Present Value of an Ordinary Annuity of $1 E-2

Future Value of $1 E-3

Future Value of an Ordinary Annuity of $1 E-3

Present Value of $1

N/R	1%	2%	3%	4%	5%	6%	7%	8%	9%	10%	11%	12%
1	0.9901	0.9804	0.9709	0.9615	0.9524	0.9434	0.9346	0.9259	0.9174	0.9091	0.9009	0.8929
2	0.9803	0.9612	0.9426	0.9246	0.9070	0.8900	0.8734	0.8573	0.8417	0.8264	0.8116	0.7972
3	0.9706	0.9423	0.9151	0.8890	0.8638	0.8396	0.8163	0.7938	0.7722	0.7513	0.7312	0.7118
4	0.9610	0.9238	0.8885	0.8548	0.8227	0.7921	0.7629	0.7350	0.7084	0.6830	0.6587	0.6355
5	0.9515	0.9057	0.8626	0.8219	0.7835	0.7473	0.7130	0.6806	0.6499	0.6209	0.5935	0.5674
6	0.9420	0.8880	0.8375	0.7903	0.7462	0.7050	0.6663	0.6302	0.5963	0.5645	0.5346	0.5066
7	0.9327	0.8706	0.8131	0.7599	0.7107	0.6651	0.6227	0.5835	0.5470	0.5132	0.4817	0.4523
8	0.9235	0.8535	0.7894	0.7307	0.6768	0.6274	0.5820	0.5403	0.5019	0.4665	0.4339	0.4039
9	0.9143	0.8368	0.7664	0.7026	0.6446	0.5919	0.5439	0.5002	0.4604	0.4241	0.3909	0.3606
10	0.9053	0.8203	0.7441	0.6756	0.6139	0.5584	0.5083	0.4632	0.4224	0.3855	0.3522	0.3220
11	0.8963	0.8043	0.7224	0.6496	0.5847	0.5268	0.4751	0.4289	0.3875	0.3505	0.3173	0.2875
12	0.8874	0.7885	0.7014	0.6246	0.5568	0.4970	0.4440	0.3971	0.3555	0.3186	0.2858	0.2567
13	0.8787	0.7730	0.6810	0.6006	0.5303	0.4688	0.4150	0.3677	0.3262	0.2897	0.2575	0.2292
14	0.8700	0.7579	0.6611	0.5775	0.5051	0.4423	0.3878	0.3405	0.2992	0.2633	0.2320	0.2046
15	0.8613	0.7430	0.6419	0.5553	0.4810	0.4173	0.3624	0.3152	0.2745	0.2394	0.2090	0.1827
16	0.8528	0.7284	0.6232	0.5339	0.4581	0.3936	0.3387	0.2919	0.2519	0.2176	0.1883	0.1631
17	0.8444	0.7142	0.6050	0.5134	0.4363	0.3714	0.3166	0.2703	0.2311	0.1978	0.1696	0.1456
18	0.8360	0.7002	0.5874	0.4936	0.4155	0.3503	0.2959	0.2502	0.2120	0.1799	0.1528	0.1300
19	0.8277	0.6864	0.5703	0.4746	0.3957	0.3305	0.2765	0.2317	0.1945	0.1635	0.1377	0.1161
20	0.8195	0.6730	0.5537	0.4564	0.3769	0.3118	0.2584	0.2145	0.1784	0.1486	0.1240	0.1037

Present Value of an Ordinary Annuity of $1

N/R	1%	2%	3%	4%	5%	6%	7%	8%	9%	10%	11%	12%
1	0.9901	0.9804	0.9709	0.9615	0.9524	0.9434	0.9346	0.9259	0.9174	0.9091	0.9009	0.8929
2	1.9704	1.9416	1.9135	1.8861	1.8594	1.8334	1.8080	1.7833	1.7591	1.7355	1.7125	1.6901
3	2.9410	2.8839	2.8286	2.7751	2.7232	2.6730	2.6243	2.5771	2.5313	2.4869	2.4437	2.4018
4	3.9020	3.8077	3.7171	3.6299	3.5460	3.4651	3.3872	3.3121	3.2397	3.1699	3.1024	3.0373
5	4.8534	4.7135	4.5797	4.4518	4.3295	4.2124	4.1002	3.9927	3.8897	3.7908	3.6959	3.6048
6	5.7955	5.6014	5.4172	5.2421	5.0757	4.9173	4.7665	4.6229	4.4859	4.3553	4.2305	4.1114
7	6.7282	6.4720	6.2303	6.0021	5.7864	5.5824	5.3893	5.2064	5.0330	4.8684	4.7122	4.5638
8	7.6517	7.3255	7.0197	6.7327	6.4632	6.2098	5.9713	5.7466	5.5348	5.3349	5.1461	4.9676
9	8.5660	8.1622	7.7861	7.4353	7.1078	6.8017	6.5152	6.2469	5.9952	5.7590	5.5370	5.3282
10	9.4713	8.9826	8.5302	8.1109	7.7217	7.3601	7.0236	6.7101	6.4177	6.1446	5.8892	5.6502
11	10.3676	9.7868	9.2526	8.7605	8.3064	7.8869	7.4987	7.1390	6.8052	6.4951	6.2065	5.9377
12	11.2551	10.5753	9.9540	9.3851	8.8633	8.3838	7.9427	7.5361	7.1607	6.8137	6.4924	6.1944
13	12.1337	11.3484	10.6350	9.9856	9.3936	8.8527	8.3577	7.9038	7.4869	7.1034	6.7499	6.4235
14	13.0037	12.1062	11.2961	10.5631	9.8986	9.2950	8.7455	8.2442	7.7862	7.3667	6.9819	6.6282
15	13.8651	12.8493	11.9379	11.1184	10.3797	9.7122	9.1079	8.5595	8.0607	7.6061	7.1909	6.8109
16	14.7179	13.5777	12.5611	11.6523	10.8378	10.1059	9.4466	8.8514	8.3126	7.8237	7.3792	6.9740
17	15.5623	14.2919	13.1661	12.1657	11.2741	10.4773	9.7632	9.1216	8.5436	8.0216	7.5488	7.1196
18	16.3983	14.9920	13.7535	12.6593	11.6896	10.8276	10.0591	9.3719	8.7556	8.2014	7.7016	7.2497
19	17.2260	15.6785	14.3238	13.1339	12.0853	11.1581	10.3356	9.6036	8.9501	8.3649	7.8393	7.3658
20	18.0456	16.3514	14.8775	13.5903	12.4622	11.4699	10.5940	9.8181	9.1285	8.5136	7.9633	7.4694

Appendix F

Practice Set Assignments—Comprehensive Tax Return Problems

Problem 1

Mark R. and Suzanne N. Hauser (ages 45 and 46) are married and live at 14130 Laramie Lane, Gillette, WY 82717. Mark is a consulting engineer and Suzanne is a paralegal. They file a joint return and use the cash basis for tax purposes.

1. Trained as a mining engineer, Mark has developed considerable expertise in the treatment and disposition of waste material. He is also well versed in the Federal and state requirements for land reclamation projects. Mark operates a consulting business through which he advises clients on these matters. Mark's business activity code is 541990. Most of his clients are small and medium mine owner/operators located in Wyoming and contiguous states (e.g., Montana, Idaho, Utah). In performing his services, Mark usually visits a client's job site. He submits his recommendations in a written report to the client, which is accompanied by a billing statement for his services and reimbursement for all out-of-pocket expenses for travel to the job site.

   Mark received the following amounts from his consulting business in 2021:

Fees for services rendered		$ 92,800
Expense reimbursements:		
Airfare	$8,200	
Meals (of which $2,600 is from restaurants)	3,500	
Lodging	5,200	
Transportation (taxis, airport limos, car rentals)	920	
Subtotal for expense reimbursement		17,820
Total received		$110,620

2. Mark also provided services for three companies from his office, so there are no travel expenses. These fees are not included in the receipts listed in item 1 above.

Pierce Mining: Work done in December 2021; payment received January 2022	$5,100
Forrie Mining: Work done in December 2020; payment received January 2021	7,000
Garrett Mining: Work done in March 2021; no payment received to date	3,700

In late 2021, Mark learned that Garrett Mining is going through bankruptcy. As a result, Mark does not expect to collect any of this fee.

3. Other expenses paid by Mark in 2021 relating to his practice are listed below.

Contribution to H.R. 10 (Keogh) retirement plan	$9,000
Premiums on health insurance (covering self, spouse, and dependents)	3,800
Supplies—landscape models purchased from topographer for projects	3,200
Advertising in trade journals	2,400
Office expense	1,200
Business phone and Internet service	860
State occupation license	300
Subscriptions to trade journals	240
Membership dues to trade associations	180

4. Mark operates his consulting business out of an office in his home that measures 24 feet by 25 feet. The total living space in the home is 3,000 square feet. Mark inherited the home on Laramie Lane from his father who died on June 6, 2014. At that time, the home had a fair market value of $400,000 ($40,000 of which was allocated to the land). The Hausers moved into the home in autumn of 2014, and Mark immediately set up his home office. The home's current fair market value is $500,000 ($50,000 allocated to the land). County land records reflect that Mark's father bought the land in 1975 for $6,000 and built the house in 1979 at a cost of $60,000. Mark depreciates the business use of his home using MACRS. Additional 2021 costs related to the home are as follows:

Utilities	$4,800
Repairs and maintenance	2,900
Property/casualty insurance	2,300

The 2021 property taxes and mortgage interest on the home are listed in item 15. In addition to the repairs and maintenance noted above, Mark had the office repainted at a total cost of $1,200.

Over the years, Mark has properly deducted the cost of all the furniture and equipment used in his office either as § 179 expense or bonus depreciation in the year those assets were placed in service. On March 5, 2021, Mark purchased a heavy-duty, fire-resistant file cabinet with enhanced security features for $4,800. He made the acquisition to safeguard and maintain the privacy of client data. Consistent with past years, Mark prefers to avoid capitalizing and depreciating the cabinet if the law allows.

5. On February 4, 2020, Mark paid $41,000 (including sales tax) for an Infiniti crossover SUV (gross weight under 6,000 pounds). No trade-in was involved, and he did not claim any § 179 expense or bonus depreciation on the cost last year. Under the actual operating cost method, he depreciates the SUV using MACRS. (*Hint:* See Table 2 in the Instructions to Form 4562.) His operating expenses for the Infiniti for 2021 are as follows:

Gasoline	$3,300
Auto insurance	1,600
Repairs	240
Auto club dues	180
Oil changes and lubrication	120
License and registration	60

Mark drove the Infiniti a total of 14,500 miles during 2021, 13,050 of which were driven for business purposes. During business use, Mark received three moving traffic violations for which he paid $680 in fines. He also incurred tolls and parking charges of $440.

6. Suzanne is a licensed paralegal who is employed on a part-time basis by several local attorneys. She works in their different offices between the hours of 9 AM and 3 PM, three days a week. She commuted to work using the family Suburban a total of 813 miles and paid parking fees of $310. Her 2021 earnings and job-related expenses are summarized below.

Combined wages reported on Form W–2s from three employers	$58,000
Subscriptions and dues to professional organizations	180
Continuing education correspondence course	120
Occupational license fee	80

Since Suzanne is a part-time employee, her employers do not cover her job-related expenses. The correspondence course is required continuing education so she can retain her license. Suzanne is thinking about applying to law school, which would require her to sit for the LSAT Exam. During 2021, she spent $350 on an LSAT preparation course.

Because Suzanne is a part-time employee, she is not covered by any of her employers' medical or retirement plans. During 2021, she contributed $6,000 to a traditional IRA that she established several years ago. The Hausers use the automatic mileage method to calculate any tax deductions they are entitled to for use of the Suburban.

7. With funds received from the settlement of his father's estate, Mark purchased rental property at 6204 Aspen Court in Gillette. Of the $250,000 purchase price, $30,000 was allocated to the land. After an $80,000 renovation to the house (e.g., replaced the roof, installed new flooring throughout the house, and installed a new furnace), the property was rented beginning February 1, 2015. In 2019, the Hausers decided their investment would be more marketable if the house was fully furnished. Consequently, they spent $38,000 on new furniture, drapes, and appliances. All the furnishings were placed in service on May 1, 2019. The Hausers did not claim § 179 expense or bonus depreciation for the year in which those assets were placed in service. Under the current lease agreement, the property rents for $2,200 a month. Rent is due the first day of each month. Utilities are not included in the rent. Information regarding the property for 2021 appears below.

Rent received	$28,600
Property/casualty insurance premiums paid	3,100
Property taxes paid	2,400
Yard maintenance paid	1,200
Repairs	800

The rent received includes $2,200 for January 2022. The tenants prepaid the rent in mid-December because they went on vacation during the Christmas/New Year holidays. In addition to the property taxes listed above, Mark paid a special tax assessment of $1,300 to the City of Gillette for repaving the street in front of the property. The Hausers use MACRS to depreciate the rental home and the furnishings within it.

8. The Hausers acquired 1,000 shares of common stock in Garrett Mining on March 7, 2020, to hold for investment purposes. Mark first performed services for the company in late 2019, submitting a bill for $3,900. Because Garrett was experiencing cash flow problems at the time, Mark accepted the stock as payment for his services and recognized $3,900 of income upon receipt of the stock. Unfortunately, Garrett is currently in bankruptcy (see item 2). In late 2021, the bankruptcy

judge announced that creditors will receive a fraction of what they are owed and shareholders will recover nothing with respect to their equity investments in the company. The stock is not publicly traded.

9. On March 10, 2000, Mark's father gave the Hausers a plot of land located in Teton County as an anniversary gift. It had a value of $150,000 at the time of the gift, and no gift tax was required to be paid on the transfer. Mark's father had purchased the land on June 1, 1990, for $50,000. In December 2020, a real estate developer contacted the Hausers and made an offer to buy the property. After considerable negotiations, the Hausers agreed to transfer the Teton plot to the developer in exchange for $8,000 in cash and four city lots in Cheyenne, WY, worth $792,000. The Hausers considered the city lots to be a good investment because they are in a part of the city that is experiencing significant growth. The exchange occurred on March 4, 2021. The real estate developer paid for all closing costs and legal fees related to the exchange.

10. Mark inherited an antique gun collection from his father when he died. Although Mark has no idea what his father's cost basis was in these guns, the collection had a date-of-death value of $22,000. Concerned about the maintenance and security of the collection, Mark sold it to a dealer for $29,000 on July 10, 2021.

11. On July 12, 2007, using $50,000 she received from an aunt's life insurance policy, Suzanne purchased a plot of grazing land in Converse County, WY, to hold for investment purposes. She leased it to local ranchers over the years. However, due to drought conditions, Suzanne has not rented the land since 2019. On August 2, 2020, she sold the land to a local rancher for $75,000. Under the terms of the sale, Suzanne received a down payment of $15,000 and 10 annual notes of $6,000 each. Suzanne will also receive simple interest of 8% on the outstanding principal balance each year. Suzanne negotiated the 8% interest rate since she is taking on the risk of financing this acquisition for the rancher. Suzanne collected $10,800 on August 2, 2021, from the rancher—$6,000 on the note and interest of $4,800.

12. The Hausers had several Schedule D transactions during 2020 that netted to a short-term capital loss of $7,000. Of this loss, $3,000 was deducted in 2020, and $4,000 carried over to 2021.

13. Evelyn Olson, Suzanne's widowed mother, has lived with the Hausers for several years and has been claimed by them as a dependent. On December 30, 2020, Evelyn suffered a heart attack. After a few days in the ICU of a local hospital, Evelyn died on January 5, 2021. In early February 2021, the Hausers paid the following expenses related to Evelyn:

Funeral expenses	$17,400
Medical expenses incurred in 2020 not covered by Medicare	2,800
Medical expenses incurred in 2021 not covered by Medicare	9,700
Remainder of church pledge for 2021	900

Besides personal and household effects, Evelyn's major asset was a life insurance policy. As the sole beneficiary of the policy, Suzanne received $45,000 in death benefits on March 30, 2021.

14. In addition to the items already noted, the Hausers had the following receipts during 2021:

Interest income:	
City of Gillette general-purpose bonds	$1,900
Certificate of deposit at Wells Fargo Bank	1,100
Money market account at Bank of America	400
Yard sale proceeds	950
Qualified dividends on Meadowlark Corporation common stock	700
Jury duty pay	420

At their yard sale, the Hausers sold used furniture, books, toys, and other household goods having an estimated original cost of $1,800. In connection with her jury duty assignment in June, Suzanne drove the Suburban 40 miles and incurred expenses of $30 for parking and $45 for meals.

15. In addition to the items already noted, the Hausers had the following expenditures for 2021:

Medical and dental bills for the Hausers (other than those relating to Evelyn in item 13)	$ 7,800
Cash charitable contributions (not including Evelyn's pledge in item 13)	10,700
Ad valorem property taxes on personal residence	5,800
Interest on home equity loan used to finance the purchase of a recreational vehicle in April 2021	1,090

The Hausers drove the Suburban 420 miles to various medical and dental appointments. Wyoming has no state or local income tax but does impose a 4% general sales tax. The county in which the Hausers live imposes an additional local sales tax of 1%. Although they do not keep track of their sales taxes, the Hausers paid $1,600 of sales tax on the recreational vehicle they purchased in April 2021.

16. Besides Evelyn (see item 13), the Hausers' household includes two daughters, McKenna (age 19) and Kayleigh (age 16), and one son, Jared (age 14). McKenna graduated from high school in 2020. She earned $19,000 during 2021, all of which she put into her college savings account. She heads off to college in fall 2022. Kayleigh and Jared are full-time students in high school and middle school, respectively. Kayleigh earned $1,800 from a summer job which she put into her college savings account. During 2021, the Hausers received a $6,000 advance child tax credit payment which was reported to them in their Letter 6419 from the IRS.

17. For tax year 2020, the Hausers had a Federal income tax overpayment of $150, which they applied to their 2021 income tax. Suzanne's income tax withholdings for the year are $5,100, and the Hausers made Federal quarterly tax payments totaling $12,000 ($3,000 each installment). In addition, the Hausers received a $7,000 economic impact payment during 2021.

18. Relevant Social Security numbers are noted below.

Name	Social Security Number
Mark Hauser	111-11-1121
Suzanne Hauser	123-45-6748
Evelyn Olson	123-45-6758
McKenna Hauser	123-45-6768
Kayleigh Hauser	123-45-6778
Jared Hauser	123-45-6798

Requirements

Prepare a 2021 Federal income tax return with appropriate supporting forms and schedules for the Hausers. In doing this, follow these guidelines:

- Make necessary assumptions for information not given but needed to complete the return.
- The Hausers are preparing their own return.
- The Hausers have the necessary written substantiation (e.g., records, receipts) to support the transactions reported on their tax return.
- If the Hausers have an overpayment of tax, they want it refunded to them.
- The Hausers do not wish to contribute to the Presidential Election Campaign Fund.

Problem 2

Alejandra L. Garcia, age 37, is single and lives with her dependent mother at 12426 Euclid Avenue, Berwyn, IL 60402. Her Social Security number is 111-21-3111, and she is a cash basis taxpayer.

1. Alejandra is a licensed hairstylist. She owns and operates a salon called Belleza, located at 6520 West 22nd Street in Berwyn. Alejandra's business activity code is 812112. In addition to 10 workstations (i.e., stylist chairs) and a small reception area, the shop has display and storage areas for the products she sells (see item 2). During the year, Alejandra leased nine of the stations to other hairstylists who are considered self-employed. The IRS approved the self-employment classification for the stylists in an audit of one of Alejandra's prior tax returns. Alejandra collected $68,000 in rents from the stylists who leased the workstations. From her own station, Alejandra earned $44,000 (including tips of $8,000) for the styling services she provided to her own clients.

   Belleza is the local distributor for several beauty products (e.g., conditioners, shampoos) that cannot be purchased anywhere else. Alejandra buys these items from the manufacturers and sells them to regular patrons, walk-in customers, and other beauticians (including those who lease chairs from her). Belleza is also known for the selection and quality of its hairpieces (i.e., wigs, toupees). The shop made the following sales during 2021:

Hairpieces and wigs	$69,000
Beauty products	48,000

2. Although Alejandra operates her business using the cash method of accounting, she maintains inventory accounts for the items she sells. Relevant information about the inventories (based on lower of cost or market) is summarized below.

	Dec. 31, 2020	Dec. 31, 2021
Hairpieces and wigs	$10,700	$12,600
Beauty products	11,400	9,900

   Alejandra's purchases for 2021 were $30,500 of hairpieces and wigs and $26,100 of beauty products.

3. Belleza had the following operating expenses for 2021:

Utilities (i.e., gas, electric, telephone)		$8,900
Ad valorem property taxes:		
On realty (e.g., shop building and land)	$4,200	
On personalty (e.g., equipment, inventory)	1,800	6,000
Styling supplies (e.g., rinses, dyes, gels, hair spray)		5,700
Property insurance		4,100
Casualty insurance		4,000
Accounting services		3,800
Janitorial services		2,400
Sewer service, garbage pickup		2,300
Water		6,200
Occupation licenses (city and state)		1,500
Waiting room supplies (e.g., magazines, coffee)		1,300

4. In early 2021, Alejandra decided to renovate Belleza's waiting room. On May 10, she spent $10,400 for new chairs, a sofa, various lamps, a coffee bar, etc. Alejandra follows a policy of claiming as much depreciation as soon as possible. The old furnishings were thrown away or given to customers. For tax purposes, the old furnishings had a zero basis.

5. Belleza operates in a building Alejandra had constructed in March 2007. The shop was built for a cost of $300,000 on a lot she purchased earlier for $35,000. Except for a down payment from savings, the cost was financed by a 20-year mortgage. For tax purposes, MACRS depreciation is claimed on the building. During 2021, the following expenses were attributable to the property:

Repainting (both exterior and interior)	$8,000
Repairs (plumbing and electrical)	1,900

In May (with the accident settlement discussed in item 11), Alejandra paid the outstanding principal on the business mortgage. To do so, she incurred a prepayment penalty of $4,400. Prior to paying off the mortgage, she paid regular interest on the mortgage in 2021 of $6,000.

6. In February 2021, Belleza was cited by the city for improper disposal of certain waste chemicals. Alejandra questioned the propriety of the proposed fine of $2,000 and retained an attorney to represent her at the hearing. By pleading *nolo contendere*, the attorney was able to get the fine reduced to $500. Alejandra paid both the fine of $500 and the attorney's fee of $600 in 2021.

7. In August 2021, Alejandra saw an ad in a trade publication that caught her attention. The owner of a well-respected styling salon in Milwaukee, WI, had died, and his estate was offering the business for sale. Alejandra traveled to Milwaukee, spent several days looking over the business (including books and financial results), and met with the executor of the estate. Alejandra treated the executor to dinner and a music concert. Immediately after the concert, Alejandra made an offer to purchase the business, but the executor rejected her offer. Her expenses in connection with this trip were as follows:

Car rental	$140
Motel (August 6–7)	220
Entertainment of executor (concert)	160
Dinner with the executor at a restaurant	100
Personal meals while traveling—not at a restaurant	30

8. Rosa Lopez, one of Alejandra's best stylists, left town in March 2020 to get away from a troublesome ex-husband. In order to help Rosa establish a business elsewhere, Alejandra loaned her $7,000. Rosa signed a note dated March 3, 2020, that was payable in one year with 4% interest. On December 30, 2021, Alejandra learned that Rosa had been declared bankrupt and was awaiting trial on felony theft charges. Alejandra never received any payments from Rosa, nor did she expect to ever receive payments in the future.

9. At Christmas, Alejandra gave each of her 35 best customers a large bottle of body lotion. Each bottle had a wholesale cost to Alejandra of $12 but a retail price of $24. Alejandra also spent $3 to have each bottle gift wrapped. (*Note:* The lotion was special order merchandise and was not part of the business's inventory or purchases for the year—see item 2.) She also gave each of the nine stylists who leased chairs from her a fruit basket that cost $30 plus a $5 delivery cost.

10. In March 2021, the Illinois Department of Revenue audited Alejandra's state income tax returns for 2018 and 2019. She was assessed additional state income tax of $340 for these years. No interest was included in the assessment. Alejandra paid the back taxes in early April.

11. On a morning walk in November 2020, Alejandra was injured when she was sideswiped by a delivery truck. Alejandra was hospitalized for several days, and the driver of the truck was ticketed and charged with DUI. The owner of the truck, a national parcel delivery service, was concerned that further adverse publicity might result if the matter went to court. Consequently, the owner offered

Alejandra a settlement if she would sign a release. Under the settlement, the company paid the hospital directly for her medical expenses, and she received a cash award of $200,000. The award specified that the entire amount was for the physical pain and injuries she suffered due to the accident. Since she sustained no permanent injury, Alejandra signed the release in April 2021 and received the $200,000 settlement later that summer.

12. In January 2021, Alejandra was contacted by the state of Illinois regarding a tract of land she owned in McLean County. The state intended to convert the property into a district headquarters, barracks, and training center for its highway patrol. Alejandra had inherited the property from her father when he died on August 11, 2020. The property had a value of $140,000 on that date and had been purchased by her father on March 3, 1980, for $30,000. On July 25, 2021, after lengthy discussions which included the state's threat to initiate condemnation proceedings, she sold the tract to the state for $158,000. This transaction was not reported on a Form 1099-B. Since Alejandra is not comfortable with real estate investments, she does not plan to reinvest any of the proceeds in another piece of realty.
13. When her father died, Alejandra did not know that he had a $50,000 insurance policy on his life for which she was the sole beneficiary. She discovered the policy while sorting through her father's papers. In July 2021, Alejandra filed a claim with the carrier, Falcon Life Insurance Company. In November 2021, she received a check from Falcon for $51,500 which included $1,500 interest.
14. Upon the advice of a client who is a respected broker, Alejandra purchased 1,000 shares of common stock in Grosbeak Exploration for $40,000 on March 4, 2021. In the months following her purchase, the share value of Grosbeak plummeted. Disgusted with the unexpected erosion in the value of her investment, Alejandra sold the stock for $28,000 on December 23, 2021. This transaction was reported on Form 1099-B with Alejandra's basis correctly reported to the IRS.
15. While on her way to work in 2019, Alejandra was rear-ended by a hit-and-run driver. Thankfully, she was not injured in the accident. The damage to her Honda CRV was covered by her insurance company, General Casualty, except for the $1,000 deductible she was required to pay for the repairs. In early 2021, General Casualty located the driver who caused the accident and was reimbursed by his insurer. Consequently, Alejandra received a $1,000 refund check from General Casualty in July 2021 to reimburse her for her $1,000 deductible.
16. After her father's death, Alejandra's mother (Sofia Garcia, Social Security number 123-45-9876) moved in with her. Sofia's persistent back trouble made it difficult for her to work. So, she maintains the home for Alejandra and herself. Sofia's back trouble also made it difficult for her to climb the stairs to the second-floor bedrooms in Alejandra's house. Therefore, Alejandra had an elevator installed in her personal residence at a cost of $12,000 in January 2021. A qualified appraiser determined that the elevator increased the value of the personal residence by $5,000. The appraisal cost $400. The operation of the elevator during 2021 increased Alejandra's electric bill by $300.
17. As a favor to a long-time client who is a drama professor at a local university, Alejandra spent a weekend as a stylist for the principal actors in the annual Theater Department fund-raising event. The drama professor provided all the resources that Alejandra needed to provide her services. She estimates she would have charged $800 for the services she donated to this charitable event.

18. In addition to the items already noted, Alejandra had the following receipts during 2021:

Interest income:		
CD at Heartland Bank and Trust	$900	
City of Berwyn general-purpose bonds	490	
Money market account at BMO Harris Bank	340	$1,730
Qualified dividends on stock investments:		
General Motors	$470	
AT&T	380	850
Federal income tax refund for tax year 2020		791
Illinois state income tax refund for tax year 2020		205

Alejandra itemized deductions in 2020, claiming a deduction for state income taxes of $6,400.

19. In addition to the items already noted, Alejandra had the following expenditures for 2021:

Contribution to retirement plan		$10,000
Medical:		
Premiums on medical insurance	$ 4,800	
Dental bills	1,400	6,200
Property taxes on personal residence		5,500
Interest on home mortgage		3,200
Cash donations to qualified charities		4,500
Professional expenses:		
Subscriptions to trade journals	$ 180	
Dues to beautician trade group	140	320

The $10,000 contribution is to a § 401(k) type of plan she established in 2021. Previously, she had contributed to an H.R. 10 (Keogh) plan but found that the § 401(k) retirement arrangement provides more flexibility and is less complex. The medical insurance policy covers Alejandra and her dependent mother and was issued in the name of the business (i.e., "Belleza"). It does not cover dental work or capital modifications to a residence (see item 16).

20. During 2021, Alejandra made the following total estimated tax payments with respect to her 2021 tax returns:

Federal estimated income tax payments	$16,000
Illinois estimated income tax payments	4,200

In addition, Alejandra received a $2,800 economic impact payment during 2021.

Requirements

Prepare a 2021 Federal income tax return with appropriate supporting forms and schedules for Alejandra. In doing this, follow these guidelines:

- Make necessary assumptions for information not given but needed to complete the return.
- Alejandra is preparing her own return.
- Alejandra has the necessary written substantiation (e.g., records, receipts) to support the transactions reported in her tax return.
- Alejandra has itemized deductions ever since she became a homeowner many years ago. The sales tax option was not chosen in 2020, and Alejandra had no major purchases that qualify for the sales tax deduction in 2021.
- If Alejandra has an overpayment of tax, she wants it refunded to her.
- Alejandra does not wish to contribute to the Presidential Election Campaign Fund.

Index

A

Abandoned spouse, **3**:32–33
ABLE (Achieving a Better Life Experience)
  account, **5**:26–27
  plans, **5**:26–27
Above-the-line deductions, **3**:4
Accelerated cost recovery system (ACRS), **8**:2
  See also Modified accelerated cost recovery system (MACRS)
Accelerated death benefits, **5**:5–6
Accident and health benefits, **5**:11
Accident and health plans, employer-sponsored, **5**:11–12
  long-term care insurance benefits, **5**:12
  medical reimbursement plans, **5**:11–12
  premiums, **5**:11
  See also Employee fringe benefits
Accountability to taxpayers, tax principles, **1**:10, **1**:11
Accountable plan, **9**:53–54
  deemed substantiation, **9**:54
  substantiation, **9**:53–54
Accounting concept of income, **4**:4
Accounting income, **4**:4
  reconciliation of corporate taxable income and, **20**:15–18
Accounting methods, **4**:7–9, **6**:10, **18**:10–19
  accrual method, **18**:13–16
  cash receipts and disbursements method, **18**:11–13
  change from an incorrect method, **18**:17–18, **18**:19
  change of method, **18**:17–19
  correction of an error, **18**:17
  determined by the IRS, **18**:11
  Form 3115, Application for Change in Accounting Method, **18**:17
  gross receipts test, **20**:7–8
  hybrid method, **18**:16–17
  installment method, **18**:19–24
  long-term contracts, **18**:25–28
  net adjustments due to change in, **18**:18
  permissible methods, **18**:10
  reporting the net Section 481(a) adjustment, **18**:18–19
  special methods, **18**:19–28
  tax planning for, **18**:35–36
  See also Accrual method; Cash receipts and disbursements method; Cash receipts method; Completed contract method; Hybrid method; Installment method; Percentage of completion method
Accounting periods, **18**:2–10
  business purpose, **18**:5
  changes in, **18**:6–7
  Form 1128, Application for Change in Accounting Period, **18**:6
  IRS requirements for changes in, **18**:6–7
  mitigation of the annual accounting period concept, **18**:8–9
  personal service corporations, **18**:6
  required tax payments, **18**:5
  selecting the tax year, **18**:6
  specific provisions for partnerships, S corporations, and personal service corporations, **18**:3–6
  tax planning for, **18**:35–36
  taxable periods of less than one year, **18**:7–8
Accounting Standards Codification (ASC) 718, equity-based compensation, **19**:20
Accounting Standards Codification (ASC) 740, **1**:3
Accounts and notes receivable
  as part of the definition of a capital asset, **16**:4–5
  collection of a cash basis, **16**:5
  collection of an accrual basis, **16**:4–5
Accrual basis account receivable, collection of, **16**:4–5
Accrual basis taxpayers, special rules applicable to, **4**:13–14
  all events test and financial reporting, **4**:13
  unearned income, **4**:13–14
Accrual method, **4**:7, **4**:8–9, **18**:10, **18**:13–16
  all events test for deductions, **18**:14–16
  all events test for income, **18**:13–14
  deferral method for advance payments, **18**:13, **18**:35
  economic performance test for deductions, **18**:14–16
  exceptions, **18**:12
  requirements, timing of expense recognition, **6**:10–11
  reserves, **18**:16
Accruals under the economic performance test, **18**:14
Accumulated E & P, **20**:21–22
  dividends from, **5**:3
Accuracy-related penalty, **2**:23*ft*, **2**:25
Acquiescence ("A" or "*Acq.*"), **2**:16
Acquisition indebtedness, **10**:15, **12**:16
ACRS. *See* accelerated cost recovery system
Action on Decision, **2**:16, **2**:24
Active income, **11**:6
Active participant, qualified plan, **19**:13–14
Active participation
  difference between material participation and, **11**:18
  real estate rental activities, **11**:18–20
Actual cost method, **9**:7–9, **9**:57
Actual costs of operating an automobile, **9**:7
Ad valorem taxes, **1**:12, **10**:11
  on personal property, **1**:12–13
  on real property, **1**:12
Additional Credits and Payments, Schedule 3, Form 1040, **3**:15–16, **3**:40
Additional depreciation, **17**:13
Additional first-year depreciation, **8**:10, **8**:14–15
  depreciation of personal property, **12**:7
Additional Income and Adjustments to Income, Schedule 1, Form 1040, **3**:8, **3**:11–12, **3**:39–40
Additional Medicare taxes on high-income individuals, **13**:29–31
  additional tax on unearned income, **13**:30–31
  additional tax on wages, **13**:29–30
Additional standard deduction (age 65 or older or blind), **3**:17–18, **3**:33–34
  amounts, **3**:17
Additional tax on net investment income, tax planning for the effect of, **11**:26
Additional Taxes on Qualified Plans (Including IRAs) and Other Tax-Favored Accounts, Form 5329, **5**:25
Additional Taxes, Schedule 2, Form 1040, **3**:13–14, **3**:39–40
Adjusted basis of property, **3**:41, **14**:5
  calculation of, **14**:5
Adjusted gross income (AGI). *See* Deductions *for* AGI; Deductions *from* AGI
Adjusted gross income thresholds and saver's credit rate (2021), **13**:20
Adjusted taxable income (ATI), business interest expense limitation and, **20**:14
Adjustments, **12**:6
  summary of basis, **14**:20–21
  to basis, **14**:21
Administrative feasibility, influence of IRS, **1**:35
Administrative sources of the tax law, **2**:6–9
  assessing the validity of other, **2**:24
  letter rulings, **2**:8

Administrative sources of the tax law (*continued*)
other administrative pronouncements, **2**:8–9
Revenue Rulings, Revenue Procedures, and Notices, **2**:7–8
Treasury Department Regulations, **2**:6–7
Adoption assistance program, employee fringe benefits, **5**:15
Adoption expenses credit, **13**:21
Advance payments from customers, tax planning for, **18**:35
Affordable Care Act (ACA), **1**:19, **9**:56
provisions, **10**:10
Section 530 relief, **9**:57*ft*
Age, additional standard deduction for 65 or older, **3**:17–18, **3**:33–34
Age test, qualifying child, **3**:20
Aggregation of Business Operations, Schedule B, Form 8995–A, **9**:42
aggregation of qualified trades or businesses under the Section 199A Regulations, **9**:43, **9**:47–48
Alimony
reporting discrepancies on income taxes and, **4**:22
requirements for, **4**:21
taxation of, **4**:22
transfer of payments from payers to recipients, **4**:22
Alimony and separate maintenance payments, **4**:21
child support, **4**:22
front-loading, **4**:21
inclusion in gross income, **4**:20–23
property settlements, **4**:20–21
requirements for alimony, **4**:21
support payments, **4**:21
Alimony payments, deductions *for* AGI, **3**:5
Alimony recapture, **4**:21
All events test, **4**:13, **6**:10, **18**:14–15
and financial reporting, **4**:13
for deductions, **18**:14–16
for income, **18**:13–14
Allocation of Tax Amounts Between Certain Individuals in Community Property States, Form 8958, **3**:31*ft*
Allocation parental tax, **3**:38
Allowable cost recovery, **8**:3–4
Allowed cost recovery, **8**:3–4
Alternate valuation amount, **14**:14
Alternate valuation date, **14**:14
Alternate valuation election, **14**:14
Alternative deprecation system (ADS), **8**:6, **8**:10, **8**:23–24
alternative minimum tax (AMT) adjustment, **8**:23
class lives, **8**:23
conventions, **8**:23
depreciation of real property, **12**:6
methods, **8**:23–24
table, **8**:34, **8**:35–36
Alternative minimum tax (AMT), **12**:2
AMT adjustments, **12**:3–4, **12**:6–18
AMT preferences, **12**:3–4, **12**:18–20, **12**:22
calculation generally, **12**:2–6
corporate tax liability, **20**:14
illustration of AMT computation, **12**:21
income tax consequences of individuals compared with C corporations, **20**:18
table, **8**:34
Alternative minimum tax (AMT) adjustments, **12**:3–4, **12**:6–18
adjusted gain or loss, **12**:11–12
alternative tax net operating loss deduction (ATNOLD), **12**:13–14
circulation expenditures, **12**:8–9
completed contract method of accounting, **12**:10
depreciation of personal property, **12**:7–8
depreciation of real property, **12**:6
expenditures requiring 10-year write-off for AMT purposes, **12**:9–10
incentive stock options (ISOs), **12**:10–11, **12**:20
individuals, **12**:23
itemized deductions, **12**:15–17
passive activity losses, **12**:12–13
pollution control facilities, **12**:8
provisions, summary of, **12**:18
tax planning for avoiding, **12**:22–23
tax planning for controlling the timing of, **12**:24
Alternative minimum tax (AMT) credit, **12**:21–22
Alternative minimum tax (AMT) formula
AMT liability, **12**:5–6
AMTI, **12**:3–4
exemption amount, **12**:4–5
for individuals, **12**:3
regular tax liability, **12**:5–6
tentative minimum tax (TMT), **12**:5
Alternative minimum tax (AMT) liability, American Opportunity Act, **13**:18
Alternative minimum tax (AMT) preferences, **12**:3–4, **12**:18–20
exclusion for certain small business stock, **12**:20
individuals, **12**:23
intangible drilling costs (IDCs), **12**:19
interest on private activity bonds, **12**:19–20
percentage depletion, **12**:18–19
provisions, summary of, **12**:22
tax planning for avoiding, **12**:22–23
tax planning for controlling the timing of, **12**:24
Alternative minimum taxable income (AMTI), **12**:3–4
standard deduction and, **12**:17–18
Alternative minimum vesting schedules, **19**:6
cliff vesting, **19**:6
five-year vesting, **19**:6
graded vesting, **19**:6
Alternative tax, **16**:24, **16**:35
computation (long-term capital gains), **3**:43–44
on capital gain computation, income layers for, **16**:25
on net capital gain and qualified dividend income, **16**:24–26, **16**:35
Alternative tax NOL deduction (ATNOLD), **12**:13–14
Alternative tax rates on net capital gains (2022), **3**:43, **16**:24
Amended U.S. Individual Income Tax Return, Form 1040X, **3**:41
Amendment proof, **2**:4*ft*
American Automobile Association, **9**:8
American Federal Tax Reports (AFTR), **2**:16–17
American Institute of Certified Public Accountants (AICPA), **1**:4, **1**:10, **2**:33
ethical guidelines, **1**:28
American Opportunity credit, **13**:18–19, **13**:21
eligible individuals, **13**:18
income limitations and refundability, **13**:18–19
maximum credit, **13**:18
restrictions on double tax benefit, **13**:19
tax consequences of, **9**:16
American Rescue Plan of 2021, **2**:8, **4**:30
Americans with Disabilities Act, **13**:3
Amnesty programs, **1**:18
Amortizable bond premium, as capital recovery, **14**:6–7
Amortizable Section 197 intangibles, **8**:25
Amortizable startup expenditures, **8**:25, **8**:28
Amortization, **8**:25, **8**:28
of intangible assets, **8**:2
tax planning for, **8**:32
Amount realized, **3**:41, **14**:4–5
calculation of, **14**:5
computing in involuntary conversions, **15**:12–13
debt relief, **14**:4
fair market value, **14**:4
from sale or other disposition of property, **14**:4
in Section 121 sale, **15**:19
real property taxes, **14**:4*ft*
selling expenses, **14**:4
Analysis of Unappropriated Retained Earnings per Books, Schedule M–2, Form 1120, **20**:15, **20**:16
Annotated, commercial tax services, **2**:18
Announcements, **2**:9
Annual accounting period concept
farm relief, **18**:9
mitigating the effect of, **1**:32–33
mitigation of, **18**:8–9
restoration of amounts received under a claim of right, **18**:9
Annual exclusion per donee, **1**:16–17
Annuity, **4**:26
computing the exclusion amount, **4**:26–28
income from, **4**:26–28
number of anticipated monthly payments under the simplified method, **4**:28
simplified method for annuity distributions from qualified retirement plans, **4**:28
table, **4**:27
Annuity contracts. *See* Annuity
Annuity table, **4**:25
Appellate courts, **2**:12, **2**:24
See also Courts
Appellate process, **2**:13–14
Applicable financial statement, **18**:13*ft*, **18**:34
Application for Automatic Extension of Time to File Certain Business Income Tax, Information, and Other Returns, Form 7004, **20**:15
Application for Automatic Extension of Time to File U.S. Individual Income Tax Return, Form 4868, **3**:41

Application for Award for Original Information, Form 211, **2**:7
Application for Change in Accounting Method, Form 3115, **18**:17
Application for Change in Accounting Period, Form 1128, **18**:6
Application for Voluntary Classification Settlement Program (VCSP), Form 8952, **9**:57
Application to Use LIFO Inventory Method, Form 970, **18**:33
Appreciated property, **15**:7
Appropriate economic unit, **11**:11
Appropriate government revenues, tax principles, **1**:10, **1**:11
Arm's length concept, **1**:35–36
Asset Depreciation Range (ADR), midpoint life, **8**:5
Assets
- amortization of Section 197 intangible, **8**:25
- capital, **3**:42, **16**:3–8
- choosing for immediate expensing, **8**:16–17
- classification and use of, **8**:3
- disposition of, **16**:2
- expenditures for intangible, **6**:28
- expenditures for tangible, **6**:27
- Form 8949, Sales and Other Dispositions of Assets, **16**:29, **16**:32–33
- in a lump-sum purchase, allocation of cost among multiple, **14**:10
- intangible, **14**:2
- investment, **16**:3
- liquidating retirement, **19**:26
- ordinary, **16**:3
- personal use, **8**:3, **16**:3
- sale, exchange, or condemnation of personal use, **14**:9
- Section 1231, **16**:3, **17**:3–10
- tangible, **14**:2
- valuation of, **4**:4

Assignment of income doctrine, **4**:13, **4**:22, **4**:23
Athletic facilities, employee fringe benefits, **5**:15
Athletic scholarships, **5**:8
At-risk amount
- calculation of, **11**:5
- decreases to a taxpayer's, **11**:5
- increases to a taxpayer's, **11**:5

At-risk and passive activity loss limits
- interaction of, **11**:15–16
- treatment of losses subject to, **11**:17

At-risk limitation, **11**:3
At-risk limits, **11**:4–5
- treatment of losses subject to the passive activity and, **11**:17

At-risk rules, common investment loss limitation rules, **11**:24
AUD (Auditing and Attestation) section, CPA examination, **2**:31
Audit process, **1**:24–25, **1**:35
- selection of returns for audit, **1**:24–25
- settlement procedures, **1**:25
- types of audits, **1**:25

Auditing and Attestation (AUD) section, CPA examination, **2**:31
Authorized *e-file* provider, **3**:40
Automatic mileage method, **9**:6–9, **9**:57
- restrictions of, **9**:7

Automobiles
- actual costs of operating, **9**:7
- business and personal use of, **8**:18–23
- change from predominantly business use, **8**:21–22
- computation of expenses, **9**:6–9
- leased, **8**:22–23
- limits on cost recovery for, **8**:19–20
- not used predominantly in business, **8**:21
- passenger, **8**:19
- straight-line method and, **8**:18, **8**:21
- substantiation requirements, **8**:23
- used predominantly in business, **8**:19

Average benefit percentage, **19**:5
Average benefits test, qualified plans, **19**:5
Average cost method, **18**:32
Average rate, **3**:36
Awards, income from, **4**:29
Away-from-home requirement
- determining the tax home, **9**:10–11
- temporary assignments, **9**:10
- travel expenses, **9**:10–11

B

Backup withholding, **13**:25
Bad debt deduction, **7**:2–5
- accrual basis taxpayer versus cash basis taxpayer, **7**:2–3
- rules, **7**:5

Bad debts, **7**:2–5
- business versus nonbusiness, **7**:4
- classification of, **7**:2
- loans between related parties, **7**:5
- nonbusiness, **16**:8
- specific charge-off method, **7**:3–4

Balance Sheet per Books, Schedule L, Form 1120S, **20**:15
Bankruptcy, **2**:12, **7**:3
Bargain element, **12**:10, **12**:20
Bargain purchase, **14**:9–10
Base amount
- basic research credit, **13**:9
- incremental research activities credit, **13**:8

Basic research, **13**:9
- credit, **13**:9, **13**:22

Basic standard deduction, **3**:17–18
- amounts, **3**:17

Basis
- adjusted, **14**:5
- adjustments to, **14**:21
- for depreciating converted property, **14**:19–20
- of boot received in like-kind exchanges, **15**:7–8
- of property received in like-kind exchanges, **15**:7–10
- original, **14**:5
- partnership's basis in contributed property, **20**:31

Basis considerations, **14**:9–21
- and computation of gain, transfers to controlled corporations, **20**:19–20
- determination of cost basis, **14**:9–11
- disallowed losses, **14**:15–19
- gift basis, **14**:12–13
- inherited property, **14**:13–15
- property converted from personal use to business or income-producing use, **14**:19–20
- summary of basis adjustments, **14**:20–21

BEC (Business Environment and Concepts) section, CPA examination, **2**:31
Behavioral control, **9**:4
Below-market loans
- effect of on the lender and borrower, **4**:24
- exceptions and limitations of imputed interest on, **4**:25–26
- exceptions to the imputed interest rules for, **4**:26
- imputed interest on, **4**:23–26

Beneficiaries of estates and trusts, **4**:18
Benefit percentage, **19**:5
Benefit received rule, **10**:18–19
Bequests and inheritances, **5**:3
Betterment, **6**:27
Bitcoin, **3**:44
Black-Scholes formula, **19**:20
Blindness, additional standard deduction for, **3**:17–18
Blogs and RSS sites, tax-related, **2**:20
Bluebook, **2**:25
Board of Tax Appeals, **2**:15
Bonds, tax treatment of, **4**:12
Bonus depreciation, **1**:18, **8**:10, **8**:14–15
- and Section 179, using effectively, **8**:15–18
- depreciation of personal property, **12**:7

Boot, **15**:6–7
- given as appreciated or depreciated property, **15**:7
- giving of, **15**:7
- receipt of, **15**:6–7
- transfers to controlled corporations, **20**:19

Bracket creep, **1**:33
Bribes and kickbacks, **6**:13
Business and personal use of automobiles and other listed property, **8**:18–23
- change from predominantly business use, **8**:21–22
- leased automobiles, **8**:22–23
- limits on cost recovery for automobiles, **8**:19–20
- not used predominantly in business, **8**:21
- special limitation for sport-utility vehicles (SUVs), **8**:20–21
- substantiation requirements, **8**:23
- used predominantly in business, **8**:19

Business bad debt, **7**:2–5
Business capital gains and losses, NOL computation and, **7**:21
Business, costs of investigating, **6**:18
Business energy tax credits, **13**:20
- biodiesel/alternative fuels—small producer biofuel (Section 40) and biodiesel credit, **13**:20
- credit for building energy-efficient new homes, **13**:20
- credit for business installation of qualified fuel cells, stationary microturbine power plants, solar, and small wind energy equipment, **13**:20
- energy credit for producing electricity via wind, solar, geothermal, and other property, **13**:20

Business entities
- general tax consequences of different forms of, **20**:4–5
- nontax characteristics of, **20**:2–4

Business Entities, **2**:18
Business Environment and Concepts (BEC) section, CPA examination, **2**:31
Business expenses
  entertainment and meal expenses, **9**:21–24
  miscellaneous employee expenses, **9**:24–25
  moving expenses, **9**:21
  office in the home, **9**:17–21
Business fixed assets, as part of the definition of a capital asset, **16**:5
Business gifts, deductibility restrictions for, **9**:24
Business income, **8**:13
Business income limitation, Section 179 expensing deduction limitations, **8**:12, **8**:13
Business losses, **6**:6–7
Business meals, deductibility restrictions for, **9**:23
Business organization, tax planning for corporate versus noncorporate forms of, **20**:33–35
Business property
  loss, **7**:9–10
  Sales of Business Property, Form 4797, **17**:20–21, **17**:23–24
Business use property, **8**:3
Business year, natural, **18**:5, **18**:7

C

C corporations, **20**:3
  comparison of tax attributes of S corporations and, **20**:29
  deduction of organizational expenditures, **20**:13–14
  deductions available only to, **20**:12–14
  dividends received deduction, **20**:12–13
  estimated tax payments, **20**:15
  general tax consequences of, **20**:4–5
  interest expense deduction limitation, **20**:14
  nontax characteristics of, **20**:2–4
  tax planning for S status versus, **20**:35
Cafeteria plan, **5**:15–16
Calendar year, **4**:6, **18**:2
  personal service corporations, **18**:6
  S corporations, **18**:5
Canons (or principles) of taxation, **1**:9–10
  certainty, **1**:9
  convenience of payment, **1**:9
  economy in collection, **1**:9
  equity, **1**:9
Capital additions, **14**:5–6
Capital asset, **16**:3–8
  effect of judicial action, **16**:6
  holding period, **16**:15–19
  long-term nonpersonal use, **17**:5
  relationship to Section 1231 assets, **17**:3–4
  sale or exchange, **16**:8–14
  statutory expansions, **16**:7–8
Capital asset, definition of, **3**:42, **16**:4–6
  accounts and notes receivable, **16**:4–5
  business fixed assets, **16**:5
  copyrights and creative works, **16**:5–6
  inventions and processes, **16**:5
  inventory, **16**:4
  U.S. government publications, **16**:6
Capital asset status
  covenant not to compete, **16**:35–36
  effect of in transactions other than sales, **16**:36
  goodwill, **16**:35–36
  importance of, **16**:35
  tax planning for, **16**:35–36
Capital contributions, **20**:20–21
  thin capitalization, **20**:20–21
Capital doctrine, recovery of, **4**:3
Capital expenditures
  capitalization versus expense, **6**:27–28
  disallowance of deductions for, **6**:26–28
  examples of, **6**:26
  for medical purposes, **10**:4–5
Capital gain and loss netting process. *See* Netting process, capital gain and loss
Capital gain and loss treatment
  franchises, **16**:12–14
  lease cancellation payments, **16**:14
  nonbusiness bad debts, **16**:8
  options, **16**:9–11
  patents, **16**:11–12
  real property subdivided for sale, **16**:7–8
  retirement of corporate obligations, **16**:9
  securities, **16**:7
  short sales, **16**:17–19
  worthless securities and Section 1244 stock, **16**:8
Capital gain computation, income layers for alternative tax on, **16**:25
Capital gain property, **10**:23–24
Capital gain treatment in the United States and other countries, **16**:35
Capital gains, **16**:2
  determination of net, **3**:42
  from property transactions, **3**:42–45
  individuals and corporations compared, **20**:8–9
  long-term, **3**:43–44, **17**:2, **17**:3
  net, **16**:19
  netting process, **16**:19–23, **16**:28
  qualified dividends, **4**:16
  reporting procedures, **16**:28–34
  Schedule D, Capital Gains and Losses, **16**:29, **16**:30–31, **17**:20, **17**:22, **17**:25–26
  tax planning for maximizing benefits, **16**:37
  tax treatment of corporate taxpayers, **16**:29
  tax treatment of noncorporate taxpayers, **16**:19–29
  taxation of net, **3**:43–44
  year-end tax planning, **16**:37
  See also Long-term capital gain; Net capital gain; Net long-term capital gain; Net short-term capital gain; Short-term capital gain
Capital investment
  limit on the QBI deduction based on wages and, **6**:7–8
  QBI deduction limitation based on, **9**:29–33
Capital loss and nonbusiness deduction limits, NOL computation and, **7**:21–22
Capital loss deduction, **16**:20, **16**:27
Capital losses, **16**:2
  carryovers, **16**:21, **16**:27
  common investment loss limitation rules, **11**:24
  computation of net, **16**:27
  excess, deductions *for* AGI, **3**:5
  from property transactions, **3**:42–45
  income tax consequences of individuals compared with C corporations, **20**:18
  individuals and corporations compared, **20**:8–9
  long-term, **16**:27
  netting process, **16**:19–23, **16**:28
  reporting procedures, **16**:28–34
  Schedule D, Capital Gains and Losses, **16**:29, **16**:30–31, **17**:20, **17**:22, **17**:25–26
  short-term, **7**:2, **16**:27
  tax planning for maximizing benefits, **16**:37
  tax treatment of corporate taxpayers, **16**:29
  tax treatment of noncorporate taxpayers, **16**:19–29
  treatment of net, **16**:27–28
  worthless securities as, **7**:6
  year-end tax planning, **16**:37
  See also Long-term capital loss; Net capital loss; Net long-term capital loss; Net short-term capital loss; Short-term capital loss
Capital recoveries, **14**:5, **14**:6–8
Capital, recovery of, **4**:19
Capitalization, thin, **20**:20–21
Carbon tax, **1**:21
Carryback procedures, **1**:33
Carryover procedures, **1**:33
Carryover provision, nonrefundable credits, **13**:5
Cash balance plan, **19**:4
  See also Qualified plans
Cash basis account receivable, collection of, **16**:5
Cash basis note receivable, collection of, **16**:5
Cash basis taxpayers, special rules applicable to, **4**:9–12
  amounts received under an obligation to repay, **4**:12
  constructive receipt, **4**:9–11
  income received by an agent, **4**:11
  original issue discount, **4**:11
  Series E and Series EE bonds, **4**:11–12
Cash charitable contributions, **3**:7
  deductions *from* AGI, **3**:7
Cash equivalent, **4**:7–8, **18**:11
Cash management, relevance of taxation to accounting and finance professionals, **1**:4
Cash method, **18**:11
  requirements, timing of expense recognition, **6**:10
  restrictions on use of, **18**:11–12
  tax planning for, **18**:35
  See also Cash receipts and disbursements method
Cash receipts and disbursements method, **4**:7, **18**:10, **18**:11–13
  special rules for farmers, **18**:12–13
  See also Cash method
Cash receipts method, **4**:7–8
Casualty gain
  as capital recovery, **14**:6–7
  personal use property net, **17**:5*ft*

Casualty gains and losses, **7**:14
as capital recovery, **14**:6–7
Casualty loss, **6**:6–7, **7**:7
as capital recovery, **14**:6–7
COVID-19 pandemic, **7**:9
events that are not casualties, **7**:7
Form 4684, Casualties and Thefts, **17**:20
income tax consequences of individuals compared with C corporations, **20**:17
measuring the amount of loss, **7**:9–12
multiple losses, **7**:11–12
personal casualty gains and losses, **7**:12–14
personal use loss reductions, **7**:10–11
personal use property, **17**:5*ft*
Section 1231 assets, **17**:5
statutory framework for deducting losses of individuals, **7**:14–15
tax planning for, **7**:25
when to deduct, **7**:8–9
See also Theft losses
Casualty netting, **17**:6
Catch-up contribution, HSAs, **10**:9
CCH AnswerConnect, **2**:18
CCH IntelliConnect, **2**:18
Ceiling amount, Section 179 expensing deduction limitations, **8**:11–12
Certainty, tax principles, **1**:9, **1**:10, **1**:11
Certified historic structures, **13**:6
Change in the form but not in the substance of a taxpayer's relative economic position, nontaxable exchange, **15**:2
Charitable contribution deduction
capital gain property, **10**:23–24
contribution carryovers, **10**:25–26
determining, **10**:25
50 percent ceiling, **10**:24
individuals and corporations compared, **20**:10–11
limitations on, **10**:22–26
ordinary income property, **10**:22–23
special rules for 2020 and 2021, **10**:25
tax planning for ensuring, **10**:29–31
temporary 60 percent ceiling, **10**:24
30 percent ceiling, **10**:24–25
20 percent ceiling, **10**:25
Charitable contributions, **10**:18–26
benefit received rule, **10**:18–19
cash, **3**:7
criteria for a gift, **10**:18–20
defined, **10**:18
documentation and substantiation requirements for, **10**:21
Form 8283, Noncash Charitable Contributions, **10**:21
in exchange for state and local tax credits, **10**:19
income tax consequences of individuals compared with C corporations, **20**:17
individuals and corporations compared, **20**:10–11
nondeductible items, **10**:19–20
of services, **10**:19
qualified organizations, **10**:20, **10**:22
record-keeping requirements, **10**:21
time of deduction, **10**:20
valuation requirements, **10**:22
Charitable transfers, recapture potential of, **17**:16
Checkpoint, **2**:8, **2**:18
Check-the-box Regulations, **20**:5–6
Chief Counsel Advice (CCAs), **2**:9
Chief Counsel Notices (CCN), **2**:9
Chief executive officer (CEO), **6**:16
Chief financial officer (CFO), **6**:16
Child
personal services of, **4**:15
See also Kiddie tax
Child and dependent care
credit rates, **13**:16, **13**:17
services, employee fringe benefits, **5**:15
Child and dependent care expenses
credit for, **13**:2, **13**:15–17, **13**:21
special rule for medical expenses of noncustodial parent, **10**:5
Child care, credit for employer-provided, **13**:11
Child care resource and referral services, credit for employer-provided child care, **13**:11
Child support, **4**:22
Child tax credit, **3**:26–28, **13**:15
COVID-19 pandemic and, **3**:26
phaseout, **3**:27, **13**:15
qualifying child, **3**:20
refundable portion of, **3**:28
Children of divorced or separated parents, support test for, **3**:24
Chronically ill
accelerated death benefits and, **5**:5–6
defined, **10**:4*ft*
Circuit Court of Appeals, **2**:12, **2**:24
See also Courts
Circular E, *Employer's Tax Guide* (Publication 15), **13**:23, **13**:25*ft*
Circulation expenditures, AMT adjustments, **12**:8–9
Citations, judicial, **2**:14–17
Citator, **2**:25
Citizen-based tax system. *See* Global tax system
Citizenship test, dependents, **3**:25
Civil fraud penalty, **1**:27, **1**:35
Civil unions, filing status, **3**:30
Claim for refund, **1**:26
Claim of right doctrine, **4**:8, **18**:9
restoration of amounts received under, **18**:9
Claims Court, **2**:17*ft*
See also Courts
Claims Court Reporter (Cl.Ct), **2**:17*ft*
Class lives, for personalty and realty, **8**:4
Clawback, **13**:11*ft*
Client letter, **2**:28
Cliff vesting, **19**:6
Closely held corporation, **11**:10
reasonableness, **6**:6, **6**:16
Code of Professional Conduct, **1**:28
Collectibles, **3**:42, **16**:22
Combined business and pleasure travel, **9**:12–14
domestic travel for business and pleasure, **9**:12–13
foreign travel for business and pleasure, **9**:13
record-keeping requirements, **9**:14
Combined qualified business income amount, **9**:25*ft*
Commercial tax services, **2**:18–19
CCH AnswerConnect, **2**:18
CCH IntelliConnect, **2**:18
Checkpoint, **2**:18
Mertens Law of Federal Income Taxation, **2**:19
Parker Tax Pro Library, **2**:19
Practical Tax Expert, **2**:19
Tax Management Portfolios, **2**:19
TaxCenter, **2**:19
WestLaw, **2**:19
WestLawNext, **2**:19
Commissioner of Internal Revenue, **1**:23
Committee Reports, **2**:4
Common law employees, **9**:3
or officers, determination of W–2 wages, **9**:51
Common law property system, **1**:34, **4**:18
Common law states
married taxpayers, **3**:30
survivor's share of property, **14**:15
Community property, **4**:18–20
ramifications, tax planning for dependents, **3**:46
spouses living apart, **4**:20
survivor's share of, **14**:15
system, **1**:34
Community property states
Form 8958, Allocation of Tax Amounts Between Certain Individuals in Community Property States, **3**:31*ft*
income in, **4**:18–20
married taxpayers, **3**:30, **3**:31
taxation of income, **4**:19
Community property system, **1**:34, **4**:18
Commuter highway vehicle, **5**:19
Commuting expenses, **9**:6
See also Travel expenses
Compensation
deferred, **19**:2
equity-based, **19**:20
excessive executive, **6**:16–17
executive, **19**:22
share-based, **19**:20
Compensation for injuries and sickness, **5**:8–11
accident and health insurance benefits, **5**:10–11
damages, **5**:8–10
workers' compensation, **5**:10
wrongful incarceration, **5**:10
Compensation-related loans
effect of on the lender and borrower, **4**:24
exemption for, **4**:25
Compensatory damages, **5**:9
Compilation of Presidential Documents, **7**:25
Completed contract method, **4**:7, **18**:25–27
AMT adjustments, **12**:10
contract disputes, **18**:29
Compliance, relevance of taxation to accounting and finance professionals, **1**:3
Computer scoring, **1**:24
Conduit concept, **20**:4, **20**:5, **20**:25, **20**:28
Congress, intent of, **2**:4
Consistency, tax planning, **2**:30
Consolidated Appropriations Act, **9**:25*ft*
Constructive dividends, **20**:22–23
Constructive ownership provisions, **6**:28
Constructive ownership rules, **18**:23
Constructive receipt, **4**:9–11, **18**:11
Consumption tax, **1**:22
Content areas, Regulation (REG) section of CPA examination, **2**:32
Contingent franchise payments, **16**:13
Contract costs, **18**:26

Contract price, installment method computing of, **18**:20–21
Contracts
  contract costs, **18**:26
  current expense items for, **18**:26
  mixed services costs, **18**:26
Contributions and distributions, tax treatment of HSA, **10**:9
Contributions for IRAs, timing of, **19**:16
Control
  right to, **9**:3
  transfers to controlled corporations, **20**:19
Controlled corporations, transfers to, **20**:18–20
  basis considerations and computation of gain, **20**:19–20
Controversy, relevance of taxation to accounting and finance professionals, **1**:4
Convenience of payment, tax principles, **1**:9, **1**:10, **1**:11
Conventions
  for personalty and realty, **8**:4
  restrictions on travel expenses, **9**:11–12
Conversion. *See* Direct rollover
Conversion approach to gain or loss, tax planning, **2**:29–30
Converted property
  basis for depreciating, **14**:19–20
  cost recovery basis, **8**:4
  gain basis for, **14**:19–20
  original basis for loss on, **14**:19–20
  Section 179 expensing, **8**:14
Convertible virtual currency, **3**:44
Copyrights and creative works, as part of the definition of a capital asset, **16**:5–6
Coronavirus. *See* COVID-19 pandemic
Coronavirus Aid and Economic Security (CARES) Act, **4**:30
  excess business losses, **7**:17*ft*
Corporate distributions, **5**:3
  capital gains, **5**:3
  recovery of capital, **5**:3, **14**:7
  stock dividends, **5**:3
  Subchapter C, Corporate Distributions and Adjustments, **2**:5
Corporate income tax, **1**:3, **1**:6
Corporate obligations, retirement of, **16**:9
  original issue discount (Sections 1272–1288), **16**:9
Corporate stock, capital asset status, **16**:6
Corporate tax liability, determination of, **20**:14
  alternative minimum tax (AMT), **20**:14
  income tax rates, **20**:14
Corporate Taxation, **2**:18
Corporate taxpayers, tax treatment of capital gains and losses of, **16**:29
Corporate versus noncorporate forms of business organization, tax planning for, **20**:33–35
Corporations, **20**:6–18
  alternative minimum tax, **20**:14
  and individuals compared, **20**:6–8, **20**:8–11
  capital contributions, **20**:20–21
  determination of corporate tax liability, **20**:14
  dividend distributions, **20**:21–22
  filing requirements, **20**:15
  Form 1120, U.S. Corporation Tax Return, **20**:15
  Form 7004, Application for Automatic Extension of Time to File Certain Business Income Tax, Information, and Other Returns, **20**:15
  formation of, **20**:18–21
  income tax rates, **20**:14
  legal status, **20**:6
  nontax characteristics of, **20**:2–4
  reconciliation of corporate taxable income and accounting income, **20**:15–18
  special recapture for, **17**:19
  Subchapter C, **2**:5
  tax law definition of, **20**:6
  See also C corporations; Personal service corporations; S corporations
Corporation-shareholder loans
  effect of on the lender and borrower, **4**:24
  exceptions to the imputed interest rules, **4**:26
  exemption for, **4**:25
Correspondence audit, **1**:25
Cosmetic surgery, nondeductible medical expenses, **10**:4
Cost
  defined, **3**:41*ft*
  merchandise purchased, **18**:29
Cost basis
  allocation problems, **14**:10–11
  determination of, **14**:9–11
  identification problems, **14**:10
Cost depletion, **8**:29–30
Cost identification and documentation considerations, tax planning for, **14**:22
Cost of repairs, **7**:9
Cost recovery, **8**:2
  allowable, **8**:3–4
  allowed, **8**:3–4
  as capital recovery, **14**:6
  reporting procedures, **8**:24–25
  tables, **8**:32–36
  tax planning for, **8**:31
  See also Accelerated cost recovery system (ACRS); Modified accelerated cost recovery system (MACRS)
Cost recovery and depreciation, **8**:2–4
  allowable cost recovery, **8**:3–4
  allowed cost recovery, **8**:3–4
  cost recovery basis for personal use assets converted to business or income-producing use, **8**:4
  nature of property, **8**:2–3
  placed in service requirement, **8**:3
Cost recovery periods, MACRS personalty (and certain realty), **8**:5
Cost recovery recapture, **8**:21
Costs of investigating a business, **6**:18
Courts
  appellate courts, **2**:12, **2**:24
  Circuit Court of Appeals, **2**:12, **2**:24
  Claims Court, **2**:12*ft*, **2**:17*ft*
  Court of Appeals for the Federal Circuit, **2**:12*ft*
  Court of Claims, **2**:17*ft*
  court of original jurisdiction, **2**:10, **2**:11
  Federal Courts of Appeals, **2**:13
  influence of tax law, **1**:35–36
  trial, **2**:10, **2**:11–12, **2**:24
    appeals, **2**:12
    number of, **2**:11
    number of judges, **2**:11
    location, **2**:11
  U.S. Court of Federal Claims, **1**:25, **2**:10, **2**:11–12, **2**:13, **2**:15, **2**:17*ft*
    judicial citations of, **2**:16–17
    jurisdiction of, **2**:11
  U.S. Courts of Appeals, **2**:15
    judicial citations of, **2**:16–17
  U.S. District Courts, **1**:25, **2**:10, **2**:11–12, **2**:13, **2**:15, **2**:24
    jurisdiction of, **2**:11
  U.S. Supreme Court, **2**:13, **2**:15, **2**:24
    judicial citations of, **2**:17
  U.S. Tax Court, **1**:25, **2**:10, **2**:11–12, **2**:13–14, **2**:15
    judicial citations of, **2**:14–16
    jurisdiction of, **2**:11
    Small Cases Division of, **2**:10, **2**:14*ft*, **2**:15, **2**:16
Covenants not to compete, **8**:32, **16**:35–36
Coverdell education savings accounts (Section 530 plan), **5**:26
  tax consequences of, **9**:16
COVID-19 pandemic, **4**:3, **4**:30, **7**:9
  child tax credit, **3**:26, **13**:15
  credit for child and dependent care expenses, **13**:16
  earned income credit, **13**:12*ft*
  effect on executive compensation, **6**:33
  food and beverage expenses, **9**:22
  losses directly attributable to, **7**:9
  special rules for the deductibility of charitable contributions in 2020 and 2021, **10**:25
CPA examination, **2**:31–33
  aicpa.org/resources/toolkit/cpa-exam.html, **2**:33
  Auditing and Attestation (AUD) section, **2**:31
  Business Environment and Concepts (BEC) section, **2**:31
  evolutionofcpa.org, **2**:33
  Financial Accounting and Reporting (FAR) section, **2**:31
  preparation Blueprints, **2**:31
  Regulation (REG) section, **2**:31–33
  taxation on, **2**:31–33
  2024 modification of, **2**:33
Creative works, **16**:5
Credit for certain retirement plan contributions, **13**:19–21, **13**:22
Credit for child and dependent care expenses, **13**:2, **13**:15–17, **13**:21
  calculation of, **13**:16–17
  dependent care assistance program, **13**:17
  earned income ceiling, **13**:16
  eligible employment-related expenses, **13**:15–16
  eligibility, **13**:15
  qualifying child, **3**:20
  tax planning for, **13**:31–32
Credit for elderly or disabled taxpayers, **13**:3, **13**:21

Credit for employer-provided child care, **13**:11, **13**:23
child care resource and referral services, **13**:11
qualified child care expenses, **13**:11
Credit for employer-provided family and medical leave, **13**:12, **13**:23
Credit for small employer pension plan startup costs, **13**:11, **13**:22
Credits
carryovers of passive activity, **11**:8–9
defined for tax purposes, **1**:15*ft*
passive activity, **11**:8
See also Energy credits; Education tax credits; Tax credits
Criminal fraud penalty, **1**:27, **1**:35
Crop insurance proceeds, **18**:9
Crop method, **18**:12
Cumulative Bulletin (C.B.), **2**:8*ft*
Cumulative effect of Federal gift tax, **1**:16
Current earnings and profits (E & P), **20**:21–22
dividends from, **5**:3
Current Tax Payment Act, **1**:7
Customs duties, **1**:5
Federal, **1**:20

D

Daily Tax Reports, **2**:8
Damages, **5**:8–10
compensatory, **5**:9
personal injury, **5**:9–10
punitive, **5**:9
taxation of, **5**:9
Data analysis, relevance of taxation to accounting and finance professionals, **1**:4
De minimis floor, defined benefit plans, **19**:9
De minimis fringe benefits, **5**:18, **9**:22
De minimis rule
percentage of completion method, **18**:28
specified services under the Section 199A Regulations, **9**:37–38
De minimis safe harbor election, **6**:27
Dealers in securities, **16**:7
Death
disposition of a passive activity at, **11**:20
recapture potential of, **17**:16
tax, **1**:15
tax planning for selection of property to pass at death, **14**:22
Death benefits, **5**:4
accelerated, **5**:5–6
Debt
income from discharge of, **5**:27–28
See also Bad debts; Business debt; Nonbusiness debt
Debt relief, sale of property, **14**:4
Deductible and nondeductible medical expenses, **10**:3–10
amounts paid for medical insurance premiums, **10**:6–7
capital expenditures for medical purposes, **10**:4–5
cosmetic surgery, **10**:4
home for the aged care, **10**:4
meal and lodging expenses, **10**:6
medical care, **10**:3–4
nursing home care, **10**:4
transportation to and from treatment for medical care, **10**:6
tuition expenses, **10**:4
Deduction criteria for Section 162 and Section 212, **6**:5–6
Deduction for qualified business income, **3**:7, **6**:7–9, **9**:25–52, **20**:34
aggregation of qualified trades or businesses under the Section 199A Regulations, **9**:43, **9**:47–48
computation of, **9**:27
general rule, **9**:25–26
income tax consequences of individuals compared with C corporations, **20**:17
limitation based on wages and capital investment, **6**:7–8, **9**:29
limitation for specified services businesses, **9**:33–42
limitations on, **9**:29
modified taxable income, **6**:7, **9**:26
overall limitation, **9**:26
qualified business income (QBI) defined, **9**:26
qualified trade or business (QTB), **9**:27–29
reporting, **9**:42–43, **9**:44–46
treatment of losses, **9**:48–50
See also QBI deduction; Qualified business income (QBI) deduction
Deduction limitations, Section 179 expensing, **8**:11–13
Deductions
above-the-line, **3**:4
additional standard (age 65 or older or blind), **3**:17–18, **3**:33–34
all events and economic performance tests for, **18**:14–16
authority for, **6**:3–5
business and nonbusiness losses, **6**:6–7
classifying, **6**:3
contributions to qualified retirement plans (Section 404), **9**:26
defined for tax purposes, **1**:15*ft*
disallowance possibilities, **6**:13–30
income tax consequences of individuals compared with C corporations, **20**:17
incurred, **6**:10
itemized, **3**:6, **3**:17–18, **6**:2–3, **9**:55–56, **10**:27
limitations on charitable contribution, **10**:22–26
paid, **6**:10
personal expenses, **6**:6
reporting procedures, **6**:9
self-employed health insurance [Section 162(l)], **9**:26
self-employment tax [Section 164(f)], **9**:26
standard, **3**:7, **3**:17–19, **3**:33
timing of expense recognition, **6**:10–12
timing of payments to maximize, **10**:26
Deductions for adjusted gross income (AGI), **3**:4–5, **6**:2, **7**:2
alimony and separate maintenance payments, **4**:21
alimony payments, **3**:5
common, **6**:4
contributions to Health Savings Accounts (HSAs), **3**:5
contributions to IRAs and other retirement plans, **3**:4
educator expenses, **9**:24–25
employee contributions to Keogh (H.R. 10) plans, **9**:53
employee contributions to traditional IRAs, **9**:52
excess capital losses, **3**:5
expenses of self-employed individuals, **9**:3
Health Savings Account (HSA) contributions, **10**:9
home office expenses, **9**:18
interest, **10**:17–18
interest on student loans, **3**:5, **10**:14
legal expenses, **6**:14
medical insurance premiums of the self-employed, **10**:7
net operating loss (NOL), **7**:23–24
ordinary losses, **17**:3
part of the self-employment tax, **3**:4
recognized losses from property transactions, **3**:42
reimbursed employee expenses under an accountable plan, **9**:53
reporting procedures, **6**:9
Schedule 1, Additional Income and Adjustments to Income, Form 1040, **6**:9
Section 1231 asset casualty losses, **17**:6
Section 1231 casualty losses, **17**:5
self-employment tax, **13**:27–28
state and local taxes, **10**:10
trade or business expenses, **3**:4
Deductions from adjusted gross income (AGI), **3**:6, **6**:2
cash charitable contributions, **3**:7
casualty losses, **17**:6
educator expenses, **9**:24
employee business expenses, **9**:3
interest, **10**:17–18
itemized deductions, **10**:2
legal expenses, **6**:14
nonpersonal use capital asset casualty losses, **17**:5
personal expenses, **6**:6
qualified business income (QBI) deduction, **9**:25
reimbursed employee expenses under a nonaccountable plan, **9**:53
reporting procedures, **6**:9
Schedule A, Itemized Deductions, Form 1040, **6**:9
state and local taxes, **10**:10
unreimbursed employee expenses, **9**:53
Deemed substantiation, accountable plan for reimbursement of employee expenses, **9**:54
Defendant, **2**:11
Deferral and amortization method
research and experimental expenditures, **7**:16–17
taxable years beginning after December 21, 2021, **7**:17
taxable years beginning before January 1, 2022, **7**:16–17
Deferral of gain or loss, nontaxable exchange, **15**:2–3
Deferral of income
advance payments to accrual basis taxpayers, **4**:13–14
tax planning, **2**:29–30
U.S. government savings bonds, **4**:12

Deferred compensation, **19**:2
Individual Retirement Accounts (IRAs), **19**:13–17
nonqualified deferred compensation plans, **19**:18–19
qualified pension, profit sharing, stock bonus, and cash balance plans, **19**:2–11
retirement plans for self-employed individuals, **19**:11–13
stock options, **19**:19–23
Deferred tax, interest on, **18**:23
Deferred tax liabilities, **8**:6
depreciation and, **8**:6
Deficiency, payment of, **2**:11–12
Defined benefit Keogh plan, **19**:11
Defined benefit plan, **19**:2, **19**:9–10
compared to defined contribution plan, **19**:3
limitations on contributions to and benefits from, **19**:9–10
three- to-seven-year vesting for, **19**:6
Defined contribution Keogh plan, **19**:11
Defined contribution pension plan, **19**:3
Defined contribution plans, **19**:9
compared to defined benefit plan, **19**:3
limitations on contributions to and benefits from, **19**:9
two- to-six-year vesting for, **19**:6
Delayed like-kind exchange, **15**:5
Delayed Section 1031 exchange, **15**:5
Demonstration Cites and Metropolitan Development Act of 1966, **5**:19
Department of the Treasury, **1**:23
Dependency exemptions, **3**:7, **3**:19
Dependent care assistance program, credit for child and dependent care expenses, **13**:17
Dependent children, unearned income of, **3**:37–39
Dependent tax credit, **3**:26–28, **13**:15
phaseout, **3**:19, **3**:27
Dependents, **3**:19–28
child and dependent tax credits, **3**:26–28
citizenship test, **3**:25
comparison of categories for, **3**:25–26
filing requirements for, **3**:34
Form 8332, Release/Revocation of Release of Claim to Exemption for Child by Custodial Parent, **3**:24
joint return test, **3**:25
medical expenses incurred for, **10**:5
other rules for determining, **3**:25
qualifying child, **3**:19–21, **3**:25–26
qualifying relative, **3**:21–24, **3**:25–26
special limitations on the standard deduction for, **3**:18–19
tax planning for, **3**:45–46
tests for, **3**:26
Depletion, **8**:28–31
depletion methods, **8**:29–31
intangible drilling and development costs (IDCs), **8**:29
natural resource costs, **8**:28
of natural resources, **8**:2
operating costs, **8**:29
tangible asset costs, **8**:29
Depletion methods
cost depletion, **8**:29–30
percentage depletion, **8**:30–31
Depreciable property
recapture of gain from sale of between certain related parties, **17**:19
related-party sales of, **18**:23
Depreciation, **8**:2
additional, **17**:13
additional first-year, **8**:10, **8**:14–15
as capital recovery, **14**:6
bonus, **1**:18, **8**:10, **8**:14–15
capital expenditures for medical purposes and, **10**:5
deferred tax liabilities and, **8**:6
defined in Section 1245 recapture, **17**:10*ft*
Form 4562, Depreciation and Amortization, **8**:24–25
gift basis for, **14**:13
"luxury auto" limits, **8**:19–20
of personal property, AMT adjustments, **12**:7–8
of real property, AMT adjustments, **12**:6
of tangible assets, **8**:2
recapture of, **18**:21
recapture of, individuals and corporations compared, **20**:9–10
tax and book, **8**:6
Depreciation and Amortization, Form 4562, **8**:24–25
Depreciation and cost recovery, **8**:2–4
allowable cost recovery, **8**:3–4
allowed cost recovery, **8**:3–4
cost recovery basis for personal use assets converted to business or income-producing use, **8**:4
nature of property, **8**:2–3
placed in service requirement, **8**:3
Depreciation recapture, **17**:6, **18**:21
and Section 1231 netting procedure, **17**:18
comparison of Section 1245 and Section 1250, **17**:14
for Section 1250 property, income tax consequences of individuals compared with C corporations, **20**:17
in other countries, **17**:19
individuals and corporations compared, **20**:9–10
Section 1245, **17**:10–13, **17**:16–17
Section 1250, **17**:13–15, **17**:16–17
special provisions, **17**:19
Determination letters, **2**:9
distinction between letter rulings and, **2**:9
Dicta, **2**:11*ft*
DIF score. *See* Discriminant Function (DIF) score
Digital-economy multinational corporations, **12**:15
Direct approach, calculation of a taxpayer's regular taxable income, **12**:3
Direct expenses, Regular (actual expense) Method, **9**:18
Direct rollover, **19**:8
Direct tax, **1**:2
Disabled access credit, **13**:3, **13**:10, **13**:22
Disabled taxpayers, tax credit for, **13**:3
Disallowance possibilities
deductions for capital expenditures, **6**:26–28
excessive executive compensation, **6**:16–17
expenditures incurred for taxpayer's benefit or taxpayer's obligation, **6**:25
expenses and interest relating to tax-exempt income, **6**:29–30
hobby losses, **6**:18–21
investigation of a business, **6**:17–18
net interest expense, **6**:30
payments for qualified transportation fringe benefits, **6**:30
personal expenditures, **6**:26
political contributions and lobbying activities, **6**:15–16
public policy limitation, **6**:13–15
rental of vacation homes, **6**:21–25
settlement or payments related to sexual harassment or sexual abuse if subject to a nondisclosure agreement, **6**:30
substantiation requirements, **6**:29
transactions between related parties, **6**:28–29
Disallowed losses, **14**:15–19
holding period of certain transactions, **16**:16
related taxpayers, **14**:16
tax planning for, **14**:23
wash sales, **14**:16–19
Disaster area losses, **7**:8–9, **7**:25
Discharge of indebtedness
income from, **5**:27–28
situations subject to special exclusion treatment, **5**:28
Discriminant Function (DIF) score, **1**:24
Disinterested generosity test, **10**:18
Disposition, **14**:3
Disqualifying disposition, **12**:20
Distribution requirements, qualified plans, **19**:6–8
Distributions
and contributions, tax treatment of HSA, **10**:9
S corporation, **20**:28
taxation of income and, **4**:18
Distributions to shareholders, **20**:21–23
constructive dividends, **20**:22–23
dividend distributions, **20**:21–22
District Courts, **1**:25, **2**:10, **2**:11–12, **2**:13, **2**:15, **2**:24
judicial citations of, **2**:16–17
jurisdiction of, **2**:11
Dividend distributions
corporate, **20**:21–22
earnings and profits, **20**:22
noncash dividends, **20**:22
Dividends
constructive, **20**:22–23
income from, **4**:16–17
noncash, **20**:22
recapture potential of property, **17**:17–18
received, income tax consequences of individuals compared with C corporations, **20**:17
Dividends received deduction, **20**:12–13
Divorce agreements and decrees, tax treatment of payments and transfers pursuant to, **4**:23
Divorce, tax treatment, **4**:20–23
Divorced persons with children, special rule for medical expenses of noncustodial parent, **10**:5

Documentation and cost identification considerations, tax planning for, **14**:22
Documentation and substantiation requirements for charitable contributions, **10**:21
Dollar-value LIFO, **18**:32–33
  LIFO index, **18**:32
  pool, **18**:32
Domestic partners, filing status, **3**:30
Domestic travel for business and pleasure, **9**:12–13
Double declining-balance method, classification of property, **8**:5
Double taxation, **4**:16
  foreign tax credit (FTC) and, **13**:14–15
  global tax system, **5**:21
Drug dealers, deduction of business expenses, **6**:15
Dual basis rules, **14**:12

E

Early distribution, qualified plans, **19**:7–8
Earned income, **13**:12
Earned income ceiling, credit for child and dependent care expenses, **13**:16
Earned income credit, **13**:3, **13**:12–14, **13**:21
  and phaseout percentages, **13**:13
  COVID-19 pandemic and, **13**:12*ft*
  eligibility requirements, **13**:13–14
  qualifying child, **3**:19, **13**:13
  workers without children, **13**:14
Earned Income Credit Table, **13**:13
Earned income, Keogh (H.R. 10) plan contribution limitations, **19**:11
Earned Income Tax Credit Assistant (**apps.irs.gov/app/eitc/**), **13**:13
Earnings and profits (E & P), **20**:22
  accumulated and current, **5**:3, **20**:21–22
Easements, as capital recovery, **14**:7–8
  conservation, **14**:7–8
  scenic, **14**:8
Economic concept of income, **4**:4
Economic considerations
  control of the economy, **1**:29
  encouragement of certain activities, **1**:30
  encouragement of certain industries, **1**:30
  encouragement of small business, **1**:30
  tax law, **1**:36
Economic growth and efficiency, tax principles, **1**:10, **1**:11
Economic income, **4**:4
Economic performance test, **6**:10, **18**:14–16
  accruals under, **18**:14
  exceptions to, **6**:11
  for deductions, **18**:14–16
  recurring item exception, **18**:15–16
  requirements for, **6**:10
Economy, digital, **12**:15
Economy in collection, tax principles, **1**:9
Education
  restrictions on travel expenses, **9**:12
  tax consequences of provisions dealing with, **9**:16
Education expenses, **9**:14–16
  allowable, **9**:15–16
  condition for deducting regular, **9**:15
  general requirements, **9**:14
  legal requirements to keep a job, **9**:14
  maintaining or improving existing skills, **9**:15
  other provisions dealing with education, **9**:16
Education savings programs (Section 529 and Section 530 plans), **5**:25–26
  Coverdell education savings accounts, **5**:26
  qualified tuition program, **5**:26
Education tax credits, **13**:18–19, **13**:21–22
  eligible individuals, **13**:18
  income limitations and refundability, **13**:18–19
  maximum credit, **13**:18
  restrictions on double tax benefit, **13**:19
Educational assistance plans
  employee fringe benefits, **5**:15
  tax consequences of, **9**:16
Educational savings bonds, **5**:24–25
  tax consequences of, **9**:16
Educator expenses
  deductibility of, **9**:24–25
  tax consequences of, **9**:16
Effective rate, tax planning for taking advantage of tax rate differentials, **3**:47
Effective tax administration, tax principles, **1**:10, **1**:11
E-file, **3**:40
  Form 8453, U.S. Individual Income Tax Transmittal for an IRS *e-file* Return, **3**:40
  Form 8879, IRS *e-file* Signature Authorization, **3**:40
  irs.gov/filing/e-file-options, **3**:40
Elderly or disabled taxpayers, tax credit for, **13**:3, **13**:21
Election by a Small Business Corporation, Form 2553, **20**:24
Election to expense assets (Section 179), **8**:10–14
  conversion to personal use, **8**:14
  deduction limitations, **8**:11–13
  effect on basis, **8**:13
  mid-quarter convention, **8**:13–14
Electronic Federal Tax Payment System (EFTPS), **3**:41
Electronic (online) tax services, **2**:19
  noncommercial, **2**:19–20
Eligible expenditures, disabled access credit, **13**:10
Eligible small business
  disabled access credit, **13**:10
  research activities credit, **13**:7*ft*
Employee
  common law, **9**:3
  employer payments to, **5**:4
  Form W–4, Employee's Withholding Certificate, **13**:25, **13**:32, **13**:33
  highly compensated, **13**:11*ft*, **19**:5, **19**:9–10
  long-term part-time, **19**:10
  NQDC plans tax treatment to, **19**:18–19
  of educational institutions, housing exclusions, **5**:14
  part-time, **9**:56*ft*
  personal services of, **4**:14–15
  qualified plan tax consequences to, **19**:8
  statutory, **9**:5
Employee achievement awards, **4**:29
Employee business expenses, Tax Cuts and Jobs Act (TCJA) of 2017 and, **9**:5
Employee death benefits, **5**:4–5
Employee expenses
  accountable plans, **9**:53–54
  classification of, **9**:53–55
  miscellaneous, **9**:24–25
Employee fringe benefits, **5**:14–21, **5**:22
  cafeteria plans, **5**:15–16
  flexible spending plans, **5**:16
  general classes of excluded benefits, **5**:16–20
  nondiscrimination provisions, **5**:20
  specific benefits, **5**:15
  Tax Cuts and Jobs Act (TCJA) of 2017, **5**:20
  tax planning for, **5**:30–31
  See also Accident and health plans
Employee IRAs, **9**:52–53
Employee or independent contractor status
  Form 1099–NEC, Nonemployee Compensation, **9**:57
  Form 8952, Application for Voluntary Classification Settlement Program (VCSP), **9**:57
  Form SS–8, **9**:5
  Section 530 relief, **9**:57
  Voluntary Classification Settlement Program (VCSP), **9**:57
Employee turned independent contractor, Section 199A Regulations, **9**:51
Employee versus independent contractor, **9**:2–5
  behavioral control, **9**:4
  financial control, **9**:4
  relationship of the parties, **9**:4
Employee-employer relationship, **9**:3
Employer payments to employees, **5**:4
Employer-employee loans, exceptions to imputed interest rules, **4**:24
Employer-sponsored accident and health plans, **5**:11–12
  long-term care insurance benefits, **5**:12
  medical reimbursement plans, **5**:11–12
Employers
  amount of FICA taxes, **13**:24
  amount of income tax withholding, **13**:25
  backup withholding, **13**:25
  Form 940 or 940 EZ, Employer's Annual Federal Unemployment (FUTA) Tax Return, **13**:25
  Form 941, Employer's Quarterly Federal Tax Return, **13**:25
  large, **9**:56*ft*
  NQDC plans tax treatment to, **19**:18–19
  qualified plan tax consequences to, **19**:8
  reporting and payment procedures, **13**:25
  tax payment procedures, **13**:23–25
Employment status, tax planning for, **9**:56
Employment taxes, **1**:19–20, **13**:23
  amount of FICA taxes, **13**:24
  amount of income tax withholding, **13**:25

Employment-related expenses, credit for child and dependent care expenses, **13**:15–16
En banc decision, **2**:11, **2**:25
Energy research consortium, **13**:9
Energy research credit, **13**:9, **13**:22
Energy tax credits, **1**:30, **13**:19, **13**:20
business energy tax credits, **13**:20
plug-in electric drive motor vehicles, **13**:20
residential energy tax credits, **13**:20
summary of, **13**:20
Entertainment and meal expenses, **9**:21–24
business gifts, **9**:24
business meals, **9**:23
exceptions to the 50% rule, **9**:22
50% deduction rule, **9**:22
record-keeping/documentation requirements, **9**:24
subsidized eating facilities and *de minimis* fringe benefits, **9**:22
Entity, choice of, **20**:2–6
Check-the-box election, **20**:5–6
Form 8832, Entity Classification Election, **20**:6
general tax consequences of different forms of business entities, **20**:4–5
nontax considerations, **20**:2–4
tax planning, **2**:29–30
Entity Classification Election, Form 8832, **20**:6
Environmental, social, and governance (ESG) investments, **19**:19
Environmental, Social, and Governance (ESG) Reporting, relevance of taxation to accounting and finance professionals, **1**:3
Equity and fairness, tax principles, **1**:10, **1**:11
Equity considerations
alleviating the effect of multiple taxation, **1**:32
coping with inflation, **1**:33
mitigating the effect of the annual accounting period concept, **1**:32–33
tax law, **1**:36
wherewithal to pay concept, **1**:32
Equity kicker, stock options, **19**:19
Equity (or fairness), concept of, **1**:31–33
Equity, tax principles, **1**:9
Equity-based compensation, **19**:20
Estate Planning, **2**:18
Estate tax, **1**:15
See also Federal estate tax
Estates
beneficiaries of, **4**:18
income from, **4**:17–18
taxation of income and distributions from, **4**:18
Estimated tax, **13**:26
Form 1040–ES, Estimated Tax for Individuals, **3**:36, **13**:26
Form 2210, Underpayment of Estimated Tax by Individuals, Estates, and Trusts, **13**:27
penalty on underpayments, **13**:26–27
required annual payment, **13**:26
Ethical guidelines, American Institute of CPAs, **1**:28
Ethics & Equity
Abandoned Spouse? **3**:33
An Indirect Route to a Contribution Deduction, **10**:20
Change in Accounting Method, **18**:19
Classifying the Amount of the Claim, **5**:10
Fringe Benefits, **5**:20
Incentive Stock Options and the AMT, **12**:20
Income Tax Basis That Does Not Change? **20**:28
Incorrect Depreciation and Recognized Gain, **17**:22
Is Policy Cancellation an Escape Hatch? **7**:10
Is This the Right Way to Use the Credit for Child and Dependent Care Expenses? **13**:17
Making Good Use of Out-of-State Relatives, **1**:14
Personal or Business Expenses? **6**:26
Preserving the LIFO Reserve, **18**:33
Punching the Time Clock at Year-End, **11**:18
Reporting Tax Fraud, **2**:7
Sculpture as a Capital Asset, **16**:6
Section 179 Limitation, **8**:14
Selective Incorporation, **20**:21
Should the Tax Treatment of Government Bonds and Corporate Bonds Be Different? **4**:12
Should the Terminally Ill Pay Social Security Taxes? **5**:6
Special Tax Relief, **18**:10
State Allowed Marijuana Activity: Do Regular Business Deduction Rules Apply (or Those for Drug Dealers)? **6**:15
Switching from Defined Benefit to Defined Contribution Pension Plans, **19**:4
Tax Treatment of Damages Not Related to Physical Personal Injury, **5**:9
Tax Treatment of Unemployment Compensation, **4**:30
Taxing "Made-Up" Income, **4**:26
The Ethics of Sustainable Investing, **19**:19
The Sale of a "Cost-Segregated" Building, **17**:15
The Taxation of Alimony and the Alimony Tax Gap, **4**:22
Vesting and Withdrawal Rules, **19**:8
Washing a Loss Using an IRA, **14**:19
Who Benefits from the Change in Tax Year? **18**:5
Who Will Pay the AMT? **12**:4
Whose Qualifying Child Is He? **3**:26
Your Turn or Mine? **9**:23
Excess business loss, **7**:17–19
Coronavirus Aid, Relief, and Economic Security (CARES) Act, **7**:17*ft*
defined, **7**:17–18
losses from partnerships or S corporations, **7**:18–19
Excess business loss limitation, **7**:17–19
individual taxpayers, **7**:18
partnerships, **7**:18–19
S corporations, **7**:18–19
Section 469 passive activity loss rules, **7**:19
Excess cost recovery, **8**:21
Excess reimbursement or allowance, **9**:53
Excess severance pay, **19**:18
Excessive executive compensation, **6**:16–17
Exchange period, like-kind exchanges, **15**:5
Excise tax, **1**:2, **1**:6, **1**:13
Federal, **1**:13
space flight, **1**:23
state and local, **1**:13
Exclusion amount, income from annuities, **4**:26–28
Exclusion ratio, income from annuities, **4**:28
Exclusions versus non-income items, **5**:3
Exclusive use requirement, office in the home expenses, **9**:17–18, **9**:20–21
Execution date, stock sales, **16**:37
Executive compensation, **19**:22
deduction limits and their effect on, **6**:33
effect of COVID-19 pandemic on, **6**:33
performance-based compensation, **6**:33
Exemption amount, **3**:19, **12**:4–5
AMT formula, **12**:4–5
Exemption deduction, suspension of, **3**:19
Exemptions, **3**:19
dependency, **3**:7, **3**:19
personal, **3**:7, **3**:19
Expatriations, **4**:3
Expected return, income from annuities, **4**:27
Expenditures incurred for taxpayer's benefit or taxpayer's obligation, exception to disallowance of, **6**:25
Expenditures requiring 10-year write-off for AMT purposes, AMT adjustments
mine exploration and development costs, **12**:9–10
research and experimental expenditures, **12**:9–10
Expense method, research and experimental expenditures, **7**:16
Expenses
classification of, **6**:2–9, **6**:31, **9**:53–55
direct, Regular (actual expense) Method, **9**:18
indirect, Regular (actual expense) Method, **9**:18
investment, **11**:22
necessary, **6**:5
nonbusiness, deductions *from* AGI, **3**:6
nondeductible, **3**:7
ordinary, **6**:5
Expenses for Business Use of Your Home, Form 8829, **9**:19
Ex-dividend rate, **4**:16*ft*

F

Failure to file penalties, **1**:26–27, **1**:35
Failure to pay penalties, **1**:26–27, **1**:35
Fair market value, **14**:4
Fair Tax, **1**:22
Family and medical leave, credit for employer-provided, **13**:12
Family income tax burden, tax planning for income shifting to reduce, **20**:35–36
Family tax planning, credit for child and dependent care expenses and, **13**:32

FAR (Financial Accounting and Reporting) section, CPA examination, **2**:31
Farm price method, **18**:34
Farmers, special rules for, **18**:12–13
Farming and ranching, special inventory methods relating to, **18**:34
Federal Claims Reporter (Fed.Cl.), **2**:17
Federal Courts of Appeals, **2**:13
  See also Courts
Federal customs duties, **1**:20
Federal estate tax, **1**:13, **1**:15
Federal gift taxes, **1**:16–17
Federal income taxes, **1**:17–18
Federal Insurance Contributions Act. *See* FICA
Federal judicial system, **2**:10
  trial courts, **2**:12
Federal rates
  for loans, **4**:23–24
  long-term, **18**:21*ft*
  midpoint, **18**:21*ft*
  per diem, **9**:54
  short-term, **18**:21*ft*
Federal Register, **2**:7
Federal Supplement Second Series (F.Supp.2d), **2**:16
Federal Supplement Series (F.Supp), **2**:16*ft*
Federal Tax Articles, **2**:18
Federal Tax Coordinator 2d, **2**:18, **2**:19
Federal tax law, understanding, **1**:29–36
Federal tax revenues (estimated) in year 2022, **1**:7
Federal Third Series (F.3d), **2**:17
Federal Unemployment Tax Act. *See* FUTA
Federally declared disaster area, **7**:7*ft*
Fees, occupational, **1**:21
FICA (Federal Insurance Contributions Act), **1**:19, **13**:23–25
  rates and base, **13**:24
  tax, **1**:19–20
Field audit, **1**:25
FIFO (first in, first out) method, **18**:32
  applied to carrybacks, carryovers, and utilization of tax credits, **13**:6
FIFO presumption, cost identification problems, **14**:10
50% deduction rule, exceptions to, **9**:22
50 percent nondeductible excise tax, **19**:7
50 percent organizations, **10**:24
Filing due dates, income tax consequences of individuals compared with C corporations, **20**:18
Filing requirements, **3**:33–34
  for dependents, **3**:34
  for most taxpayers, **3**:33
Filing status, **3**:29–33
  abandoned spouse rules, **3**:32–33
  head of household, **3**:31–32
  married taxpayers, **3**:30–31
  single taxpayers, **3**:29
Final Regulations, **2**:7
Financial Accounting and Reporting (FAR) section, CPA examination, **2**:31
Financial accounting income versus taxable income, **4**:5
Financial Accounting Standards Board (FASB), **2**:26, **19**:20
Financial Disclosure Insights
  Executive Compensation, **19**:22
  Share-Based Compensation, **19**:20
  Tax and Book Depreciation, **8**:6
  Tax Deferrals from Reserves, **18**:16
  Where Does GAAP Come From? **2**:26
Financial reporting
  and the all events test, **4**:13
  relevance of taxation to accounting and finance professionals, **1**:3
Financial statement, applicable, **18**:13*ft*, **18**:34
Financial transaction tax, **1**:23
FinCEN Form 114. *See* Report of Foreign Bank and Financial Accounts (FBAR)
Fiscal year, **4**:6, **18**:2–3
  election, personal service corporations, **18**:6
Five-year vesting, **19**:6
Fixture, **1**:12
Flat tax, **1**:22
Flexible benefit plans. *See* Flexible spending plans
Flexible spending plans, **5**:16
Food and beverage expenses, 50% deduction rule, **9**:22
Foreign Corrupt Practices Act (FCPA) of 1977, **6**:14
Foreign earned income, **5**:21–23
  definition, **5**:22
Foreign earned income exclusion, **5**:21, **5**:23
Foreign housing amount exclusion, **5**:23
Foreign tax credit (FTC), **13**:14–15, **13**:22
  computation of, **13**:14–15
  double taxation and, **13**:14–15
  qualifications for, **13**:15
Foreign travel for business and pleasure, **9**:13
Form 211, Application for Award for Original Information, **2**:7
Form 461, Limitation on Business Losses, **7**:19
Form 940 or 940 EZ, Employer's Annual Federal Unemployment (FUTA) Tax Return, **13**:25
Form 941, Employer's Quarterly Federal Tax Return, **13**:25
Form 970, Application to Use LIFO Inventory Method, **18**:33
Form 1040, U.S. Individual Income Tax Return, **1**:6, **3**:8, **3**:9–10, **3**:35, **3**:39–40, **3**:45
  format of, **6**:9
  Schedule 1, Additional Income and Adjustments to Income, **3**:8, **3**:11–12, **3**:39–40
  Schedule 2, Additional Taxes, **3**:13–14, **3**:39–40
  Schedule 3, Additional Credits and Payments, **3**:15–16, **3**:40
  Schedule A, Itemized Deductions, **3**:8, **3**:40, **10**:2, **10**:17, **10**:28
  Schedule C, Profit or Loss From Business, **3**:4*ft*, **3**:40, **8**:24–25, **8**:27, **9**:3, **9**:5, **10**:17, **20**:33
  Schedule C–EZ, Net Profit From Business, **9**:3*ft*
  Schedule D, Capital Gains and Losses, **16**:29, **16**:30–31, **17**:20, **17**:22, **17**:25–26
  Schedule E, Supplemental Income or Loss, **10**:17
  Schedule SE, Self-Employment Tax, **3**:40, **9**:3*ft*
Form 1040–ES, Estimated Tax for Individuals, **3**:36, **13**:26
Form 1040SR, U.S. Tax Return for Seniors, **3**:40
Form 1040X, Amended U.S. Individual Income Tax Return, **3**:41
Form 1065, U.S. Return of Partnership Income, **4**:17, **20**:28, **20**:31
Form 1099–B, Proceeds From Broker and Barter Exchange Transactions, **14**:10, **16**:29
Form 1099–MISC, Miscellaneous Income, **13**:25
Form 1099–NEC, Nonemployee Compensation, **9**:3, **9**:57
Form 1099–Q, Payments from Qualified Education Programs, **5**:25
Form 1120, U.S. Corporation Tax Return, **20**:15
  Schedule M–1, Reconciliation of Income (Loss) per Books with Income per Return, **20**:15–16
  Schedule M–2, Analysis of Unappropriated Retained Earnings per Books, **20**:16
  Schedule M–3, Net Income (Loss) Reconciliation for Corporations With Total Assets of $10 Million or More, **20**:18
Form 1120S, U.S. Income Tax for an S Corporation, **20**:5, **20**:15
  Schedule L, Balance Sheet per Books, **20**:15
Form 1128, Application for Change in Accounting Period, **18**:6
Form 2120, Multiple Support Declaration, **3**:24
Form 2210, Underpayment of Estimated Taxes by Individuals, Estates, and Trusts, **13**:27
Form 2553, Election by a Small Business Corporation, **20**:24
Form 3115, Application for Change in Accounting Method, **18**:17
Form 3949–A, Information Referral, **2**:7
Form 4562, Depreciation and Amortization, **8**:24–25, **8**:26
Form 4684, Casualties and Thefts, **17**:20
Form 4797, Sales of Business Property, **17**:20–21, **17**:23–24
Form 4868, Application for Automatic Extension of Time to File U.S. Individual Income Tax Return, **3**:41
Form 4952, Investment Interest Deduction, **11**:23, **11**:26
Form 5329, Additional Taxes on Qualified Plans (Including IRAs) and Other Tax-Favored Accounts, **5**:25
Form 7004, Application for Automatic Extension of Time, **20**:15
Form 7203, S Corporation Shareholder Stock and Debt Basis Limitations, **20**:28
Form 8283, Noncash Charitable Contributions, **10**:21
Form 8332, Release/Revocation of Release of Claim to Exemption for Child by Custodial Parent, **3**:24
Form 8453, U.S. Individual Income Tax Transmittal for an IRS *e-file* Return, **3**:40

Form 8615, Tax for Certain Children Who Have Unearned Income, **3**:38
Form 8814, Parents' Election to Report Child's Interest and Dividends, **3**:39
Form 8824, Like-Kind Exchanges, **15**:10, **15**:11
Form 8829, Expenses for Business Use of Your Home, **9**:19
Form 8832, Entity Classification Election, **20**:6
Form 8879, IRS *e-file* Signature Authorization, **3**:40
Form 8949, Sales and Other Dispositions of Capital Assets, **16**:29, **16**:32–33
Form 8952, Application for Voluntary Classification Settlement Program (VCSP), **9**:57
Form 8958, Allocation of Tax Amounts Between Certain Individuals in Community Property States, **3**:31*ft*
Form 8960, Net Investment Income Tax—Individuals, Estates, and Trusts, **20**:32
Form 8995, Qualified Business Income Deduction Simplified Computation, **9**:42
Form 8995–A, Qualified Business Income Deduction, **9**:42, **9**:44–45
  Schedule A, Specified Service Trades or Businesses, **9**:42–43, **9**:46
  Schedule B, Aggregation of Business Operations, **9**:42
  Schedule C, Loss Netting and Carryforward, **9**:42
  Schedule D, Patrons of Agricultural or Horticultural Cooperatives, **9**:42
Form SS–8, Determination of Worker Status for Purposes of Federal Employment Taxes and Income Tax Withholding, **9**:5
Form W–2, Wage and Tax Statement, **3**:36, **13**:25
Form W–4, Employee's Withholding Certificate, **13**:25, **13**:32, **13**:33
Foundations, private operating and private nonoperating, **10**:23–24
401(k) plans, individual or solo, **9**:53
Franchise payments, **16**:13
  contingent, **16**:13
  noncontingent, **16**:13
Franchise tax, **1**:6, **1**:21
Franchise transfer, **16**:12
Franchisee, **16**:12–14
Franchises, **16**:12–14
  consequences to the franchisor and franchisee, **16**:14
  franchise payments, **16**:13
  significant power, right, or continuing interest, **16**:12–13
  sports franchises, **16**:13
Franchisor, **16**:12–14
Fraud, **1**:27, **1**:35
Fraudulent returns, **1**:26
Fringe benefits, **5**:14
  See also Employee fringe benefits
Front-loading, **4**:21
  alimony and separate maintenance payments, **4**:21
Fruit and tree metaphor, **4**:14, **4**:15
Full recapture. *See* Section 1245 recapture
Functional use test, replacement property, **15**:13–14
FUTA (Federal Unemployment Tax Act), **1**:19, **13**:25
  tax, **1**:20

G

GAAP. *See* Generally accepted accounting principles
Gain
  AMT adjustments, **12**:11–12
  determination of, **14**:2–9
  nonrecognition of, **14**:9, **15**:15–16, **20**:18–20
  realized, **3**:41–42, **14**:3–8
  recognition of by partnerships, **20**:29–30
  recognized, **3**:41–42, **14**:8
  Section 1231, **17**:3–4
  transfers to controlled corporations, basis considerations and computation of, **20**:19–20
  unrealized, **3**:4
Gain basis for converted property, **14**:19–20
Gain from sale of depreciable property between certain related parties, **17**:19
Gains from property transactions
  capital gains, **3**:42–45
  in general, **3**:41–42
Gas guzzler tax, **1**:13*ft*
General business credit, **13**:5, **13**:22
  treatment of unused, **13**:5–6
General Explanation of the Act. *See* Bluebook
General partner, material participation, **11**:14
General sales taxes, **1**:14
Generally accepted accounting principles (GAAP), **2**:26, **18**:29
  sources of, **2**:26
Gift basis, **14**:12–13
  adjustment for Federal gift tax paid, **14**:13
  basis for depreciation, **14**:13
  holding period, **14**:13
  rules, **14**:12–13
Gift loans
  effect of on the lender and borrower, **4**:24
  exceptions to the imputed interest rules, **4**:26
  exemption for, **4**:23
Gift or loan, related parties, **7**:5
Gift splitting, **1**:16–17
Gift tax, **1**:16–17
  See also Federal gift tax
Gifts
  criteria for, **5**:4, **10**:18–20
  disposition of passive activity by, **11**:21
  holding period of, **16**:15–16
  recapture potential of, **17**:16
  tax planning for selection of property for making, **14**:22
Gifts and inheritances, **5**:3–5
  employee death benefits, **5**:4–5
  employer payments to employees, **5**:4
  legislative intent, **5**:3–4
Global corporate minimum tax, **12**:15
Global Reporting Initiative (GRI) Standards, **1**:3
Global Tax Issues
  A Global Minimum Tax, **12**:15
  Benefits of the Earned Income Exclusion Are Questioned, **5**:23
  Capital Gain Treatment in the United States and Other Countries, **16**:35
  Choose the Charity Wisely, **10**:22
  Depreciation Recapture in Other Countries, **17**:19
  Filing a Joint Return, **3**:30
  From "All Sources" Is a Broad Definition, **4**:3
  Outsourcing of Tax Return Preparation, **1**:27
  Overseas Gun Sales Result in Large Fines, **6**:14
  VAT in USA? **1**:23
Global tax system, **5**:21
Golden parachute payments, **19**:18–19
Golsen rule, **2**:13–14
Goodwill, **8**:32, **14**:10–11, **16**:35–36
  taxation of interest on state and local, 5:24
  allocation of, **14**:10–11
Government bonds
  taxation of interest on U.S., **5**:24
Graded vesting, **19**:6
Graduated tax rate, **3**:36
Grantee, **16**:9–11
Grantor, **16**:9–11
Gray areas, **2**:2, **2**:12
Gross estate, **1**:15
Gross income, **3**:3–4, **4**:3–6
  computation, income tax consequences of individuals compared with C corporations, **20**:17
  economic and accounting concepts, **4**:4
  financial accounting income versus taxable income, **4**:5
  form of receipt, **4**:6
  leased automobile inclusion amount, **8**:22–23
  minimizing income included in, **4**:32
  partial list of exclusions from, **3**:4
  recovery of capital doctrine, **4**:3
  special rules related to certain items included in, **4**:20–31
  tax planning strategies for, **4**:32–35
  tax relief for repayment of, **18**:10
  timing of income recognition, **4**:6–14
  See also Income
Gross income exclusions
  compensation for injuries and sickness, **5**:8–11
  corporate distributions, **5**:3
  education savings programs (Section 529 and Section 530 plans), **5**:25–26
  educational savings bonds, **5**:24–25
  employee fringe benefits, **5**:14–21
  employer-sponsored accident and health plans, **5**:11–12
  exclusion defined, **5**:2
  foreign earned income, **5**:21–23
  gifts and inheritances, **5**:3–5
  group term life insurance, **5**:20–21
  income from discharge of indebtedness, **5**:27–28
  interest on certain state and local government obligations, **5**:23–24
  life insurance proceeds, **5**:5–7
  meals and lodging, **5**:13–14

non-income items versus, **5**:3
prizes and awards, **4**:29
qualified ABLE programs (Section 529A plans), **5**:26–27
scholarships, **5**:7–8
statutory authority, **5**:2–3
tax benefit rule, **5**:28–30
Gross income items, partial list of, **3**:5
Gross income test, qualifying relative, **3**:22–23
Gross receipts test, **20**:7–8
Group term life insurance, **5**:20–21
uniform premiums for $1,000 of protection, **5**:21
Guaranteed payments, **20**:33
Guiding Principles of Good Tax Policy: A Framework for Evaluating Tax Proposals
accountability to taxpayers, **1**:10, **1**:11
application of, **1**:11
appropriate government revenues, **1**:10, **1**:11
certainty, **1**:10, **1**:11
convenience of payment, **1**:10, **1**:11
economic growth and efficiency, **1**:10, **1**:11
effective tax administration, **1**:10, **1**:11
equity and fairness, **1**:10, **1**:11
information security, **1**:10, **1**:11
minimum tax gap, **1**:10, **1**:11
neutrality, **1**:10, **1**:11
simplicity, **1**:10, **1**:11
transparency and visibility, **1**:10, **1**:11

H

H.R. 10 plans. *See* Keogh plans
Half-year convention, **8**:6
Hall-Rabushka proposal, **1**:22
Hazard of litigation, **1**:25
Head-of-household, **3**:31–32
filing status, qualifying child, **3**:19
Health insurance. *See* Employer-sponsored accident and health plans
Health Savings Account (HSA), **5**:12, **10**:8–9
contributions to, deductions *for* AGI, **3**:5
deductible amount, **10**:9
high-deductible plans, **10**:8
qualified HSA trustee, **10**:8*ft*
tax treatment of HSA contributions and distributions, **10**:9
Highly compensated employee, **13**:11*ft*, **19**:5, **19**:9–10
Hobbies
common activities classified as, **6**:20
factors for determination of, **6**:19
versus profit-seeking activities, **6**:18–19
Hobbies/businesses with losses, common questions from the IRS concerning, **6**:20
Hobby losses, **6**:18–21
determining the amount of the deduction, **6**:20–21
general rules, **6**:19
presumptive rule of Section 183, **6**:19
tax planning for, **6**:32
Holding, **2**:11*ft*
Holding period, **14**:13, **16**:15–19
dividend income, **4**:16
for nontaxable stock dividends, **14**:11
general rules, **16**:15
gifts, **16**:15–16
nontaxable exchanges, **16**:15
of new stock or securities (wash sales), **14**:18
related taxpayers, **14**:16
requirements for incentive stock options (ISOs), **19**:20–21
short sales, **16**:16–19
special rules, **16**:15–19
Holding period of property, **16**:3
acquired by a decedent, **14**:15
acquired by gift, **14**:13
contributed in a partnership, **20**:31
inherited property, **14**:15, **16**:16
received in like-kind exchanges, **15**:7–10
Home equity loans, **10**:15
Home for the aged, deductible medical expenses, **10**:4
Home office expense, **9**:17–21
Home-related capital expenditures for a physically handicapped individual, **10**:5
Hospital insurance, **1**:19
Hotel occupancy tax, **1**:13
House of Representatives, **2**:3–4
House Ways and Means Committee, **2**:3–4, **2**:25
Housekeeping-type instructions, **2**:24
Housing exclusions, other, **5**:14
Housing interest, itemized deductions AMT adjustments, **12**:16
Hybrid method, **4**:7, **4**:9, **18**:10, **18**:16–17

I

Identification period, like-kind exchanges, **15**:5
Illegal business, deduction of expenses relating to, **6**:14–15
Immediate expense election. *See* Section 179 expensing
Immediate expensing (Section 179), **8**:10
choosing assets for, **8**:16–17
Imputed interest, **4**:23, **18**:21–22
calculation of, **4**:23–24
exceptions and limitations of, **4**:25–26
on below-market loans, **4**:23–26
Incentive stock options (ISOs), **12**:10–11, **19**:19–22
AMT adjustments, **12**:10–11, **12**:20
compared to nonqualified stock options, **19**:25
qualification as, **19**:21–22
Incidental expenses, **9**:54*ft*
Inclusion amount, leased automobiles, **8**:22–23
Income, **3**:3, **4**:4
active, **11**:6
additional Medicare tax on unearned, **13**:30–31
all events test for, **18**:13–14
alternative minimum taxable (AMTI), **12**:3–4
assignment of, **4**:14
business, **8**:13
deferral of, tax planning, **2**:29–30
dependent children's unearned, **3**:37–39
earned, **13**:12
economic and accounting concepts of gross, **4**:4
exclusions from, **3**:3
expenses and interest relating to tax-exempt, **6**:29–30
financial accounting versus taxable, **4**:5
general sources of and to whom they are taxed, **4**:14–20
gross, **4**:3–6
investment, **1**:20, **3**:37, **11**:22
least aggregate deferral method of, **18**:4
measuring and reporting partnership, **20**:31–32
net investment, **11**:22
passive activity, **11**:6
passive investment, **20**:24
portfolio, **11**:6
provisional, **4**:30–31
reconciliation of corporate taxable and accounting, **20**:15–18
recovery of capital doctrine of gross, **4**:3
shifting of, tax planning, **2**:29–30
taxable, **3**:7–8
taxation of distributions and, **4**:18
total on Form 1040, **3**:8
unearned, **1**:20, **3**:37, **4**:13–14
See also Gross income
Income earned from foreign bank and financial accounts and FBAR rules, **4**:31
Income from discharge of indebtedness, **5**:27–28
Income in community property states, **4**:18–20
Income in respect of a decedent (IRD), **5**:5, **14**:14–15
Income layers for alternative tax on capital gain computation, **16**:25
Income of certain children, tax planning for, **3**:47
Income recognition
accounting methods, **4**:7–9
special rules applicable to accrual basis taxpayers, **4**:13–14
special rules applicable to cash basis taxpayers, **4**:9–12
taxable year, **4**:6
timing of, **4**:6–14
Income shifting, **4**:34–35
from parents to children, **3**:37
tax planning, **2**:29–30, **4**:23
to reduce the family income tax burden, tax planning for, **20**:35–36
Income sources
income from partnerships, S corporations, trusts, and estates, **4**:17–18
income from property, **4**:15–17
income in community property states, **4**:18–20
personal services, **4**:14–15
Income tax, **1**:2, **1**:5, **1**:7, **1**:17–19
consequences, individuals compared with C corporations, **20**:17–18
correction of an error, **18**:17
deductibility of state and local, **10**:13
farming and fishing, **18**:9
Federal, **1**:17–18
filing status, Section 179 expensing and, **8**:11*ft*
formula for individuals, **1**:17

Income tax (*continued*)
history of, **1**:5–8
incorrect accounting method, **18**:17–18, **18**:19
local, **1**:17
state, **1**:18–19
Income tax rates, corporate, **20**:14
Income-splitting option, community property states, **3**:30
Incremental research activities credit, **13**:8–9, **13**:22
base amount, **13**:8
deduction of research expenditures, **13**:8–9
qualified research expenditures, **13**:8
Indebtedness, income from discharge of, **5**:27–28
Independent contractor, **9**:2
employee versus, **9**:2–5
Form SS–8, Determination of Worker Status for Purposes of Federal Employment Taxes and Income Tax Withholding, **9**:5
implications for misclassifying worker as, **9**:56–57
See also Self-employed individual
Independent Office of Appeals of the IRS, **1**:25
Index to Federal Tax Articles, **2**:18
Indexation, **1**:33
Indirect approach, calculation of a taxpayer's regular taxable income, **12**:3
Indirect expenses, Regular (actual expense) Method, **9**:18
Indirect rollover, **19**:8
Indirect tax, **1**:2
Individual Retirement Accounts (IRAs), **1**:30
compared to Section 401(k) plan, **19**:25
comparison of, **19**:17
contributions to, deductions *for* AGI, **3**:4
deduction of an active participant in 2021, phaseout of, **19**:13
general rules, **19**:13–16
inherited, **19**:7
rollovers and conversions, **19**:17
Roth IRAs, **9**:53, **19**:14–15
spousal IRAs, **19**:16
stretch, **19**:7
tax consequences of early distributions from, **9**:16
tax planning for, **19**:23–24
taxation of benefits, **19**:16
timing of contributions, **19**:16
traditional, **9**:52–53
Individuals and corporations compared, **20**:6–8
specific provisions compared, **20**:8–11
Individuals and taxes, **1**:6
Inflation, **1**:33
Information matching, **1**:24
Information Referral, Form 3949–A, **2**:7
Information security, tax principles, **1**:10, **1**:11
Inheritance tax, **1**:15
Inheritances. *See* Gifts and inheritances
Inherited property, **14**:13–15
alternate valuation amount, **14**:14
alternate valuation date, **14**:14
alternate valuation election, **14**:14
general rules, **14**:13–14
holding period of, **14**:15, **16**:16
income in respect of a decedent (IRD), **14**:14–15
survivor's share of property, **14**:15
tax planning for, **14**:22
Initial public offering (IPO), **20**:3
Installment method, **1**:33, **4**:7, **18**:19–24
computing the gain for each year payments are received, **18**:20–21
disposition of obligations, **18**:23–24
electing out of, **18**:24
eligibility and calculations, **18**:20
imputed interest, **18**:21–22
interest on deferred tax, **18**:23
related-party sales of depreciable property, **18**:23
related-party sales of nondepreciable property, **18**:22
tax planning for, **18**:35–36
the mandatory aspect, **18**:20
Installment obligations, tax planning for the disposition of, **18**:36
Installment sale
of a passive activity, **11**:21
recapture potential of, **17**:17
Insurance
group term life, **5**:20–21
medical premiums of the self-employed, deductibility of, **10**:7
Insurance benefits, accident and health, **5**:10–11
Intangible assets
amortization of, **8**:2, **8**:25
expenditures for, **6**:28
Intangible drilling and development costs (IDCs), **8**:28–29, **17**:19
AMT preferences, **12**:19
Intent of Congress, **2**:4
Inter vivos gifts, **5**:3
Interest, **10**:14–18
allowed and disallowed items, **10**:14–16
and penalties, **1**:26–27, **1**:35
classification of interest expense, **10**:17–18
deductible, **10**:14–18
deductibility of personal, student loan, mortgage, and investment, **10**:18
defined by U.S. Supreme Court, **10**:14
imputed, **4**:23–24, **18**:21–22
income from, **4**:15–16
investment, **10**:16, **11**:21–22
nondeductible, **10**:14–18
paid for services, **10**:16
prepaid, **10**:17
prepayment penalty, **10**:16
qualified residence interest, **10**:14–16
restrictions on deductibility and timing considerations, **10**:17
tax-exempt securities, **10**:16
taxpayer's obligation, **10**:17
time of deduction, **10**:17
Interest as business expenses, Form 1040, Schedule C, Profit or Loss From Business, **10**:17
Interest expense
deduction limitation, **20**:14
related to rents or royalties, Form 1040, Schedule E, Supplemental Income or Loss, **10**:17
Interest in general, itemized deductions, AMT adjustments, **12**:16
Interest on
certain state and local government obligations, gross income exclusions, **5**:23–24
deferred tax, **18**:23
private activity bonds, AMT preferences, **12**:19–20
Interest on qualified student loans, **10**:14
deductions *for* AGI, **3**:5
tax consequences of, **9**:16
Interest paid for services, **10**:16
Interest rates, on taxes and tax refunds, **1**:26
Internal Legal Memoranda (ILMs), **2**:9
Internal Revenue Bulletin (I.R.B.), **2**:7, **2**:8, **2**:9, **2**:16, **7**:25
Internal Revenue Code, **8**:2
arrangement of, **2**:4–5
citing, **2**:5
interpreting, **2**:23
of 1939, **1**:7, **2**:2, **2**:5*ft*
of 1954, **1**:7, **2**:2, **2**:5*ft*
of 1986, **1**:7, **2**:2, **2**:3–4, **2**:4–5, **2**:5*ft*
origin of, **2**:2
subchapter designations, **2**:5
Internal Revenue Service (IRS), **1**:2, **1**:4, **2**:8*ft*, **1**:23
assessment by, **1**:26
Circular E, *Employer's Tax Guide* (IRS Publication 15), **13**:23, **13**:25*ft*
Form 8879, IRS *e-file* Signature Authorization, **3**:40
home page, **2**:20
Independent Office of Appeals, **1**:25
influence of tax law, **1**:34–35, **1**:36
internal memoranda, **2**:9
Internal Revenue Manual, **2**:8*ft*
IRS Area Director, **2**:9
IRS Direct Pay, **3**:41
IRS Free File, **3**:40
IRS Letter Rulings Reports, **2**:8
IRS Publication 15B, *Employer's Tax Guide to Fringe Benefits*, **5**:18*ft*
IRS Publication 596, Earned Income Credit Table, **13**:13
IRS Regional Service Center (**irs.gov/filing/where-to-file-addresses-for-taxpayers-and-tax-professionals-filing-form-1040**), **3**:40*ft*
IRS Withholding Calculator (**apps.irs.gov/app/tax-withholding/estimator**), **13**:25, **13**:33
large-awards program, **2**:7
National Office of the IRS, **2**:7, **2**:8, **2**:9
small-awards program, **2**:7
website (**irs.gov**), **2**:8, **2**:20, **3**:40
International Financial Reporting Standards (IFRS), **2**:26, **19**:20
Interpretive Regulations, **2**:24
Inventions, **1**:30
Inventions and processes, as part of the definition of a capital asset, **16**:5
Inventories, **18**:28–34
as part of the definition of a capital asset, **16**:4
best accounting practice, **18**:29
clear reflection of income test, **18**:29
corporate stock, **16**:6
determining inventory cost, **18**:29–33
LIFO election, **18**:33–34
small taxpayers, **18**:34
special inventory methods relating to farming and ranching, **18**:34

Inventory cost
dollar-value LIFO, **18**:32–33
inventory shrinkage, **18**:31
lower of cost or market, **18**:31
specific identification, FIFO, and LIFO, **18**:32
uniform capitalization (UNICAP), **18**:29–30
Inventory shrinkage, **18**:31
Investigation expenses, **6**:17
Investigation of a business, expenses incurred in, **6**:17–18
Investment assets, **16**:3
Investment earnings from the reinvestment of life insurance proceeds, **5**:7
Investment expenses, **11**:22
Investment income, **1**:20, **3**:37, **11**:22, **11**:26
from annuities, **4**:27
net, **11**:22
net capital gain, **11**:26
passive, **20**:24
qualified business income (QBI) and, **9**:26
qualified dividend income, **11**:26
tax on, **1**:20
tax planning for, **5**:31
Investment interest, **10**:16, **11**:21–22
common investment loss limitation rules, **11**:24
deductibility of, **10**:18
Form 4952, Investment Interest Deduction, **11**:23, **11**:26
itemized deductions, AMT adjustments, **12**:16–17
Investment interest deduction, tax planning for maximizing, **11**:26
Investment interest limitation, **11**:21–23
computation of allowable deduction, **11**:23
Investment loss limitation rules, **11**:24
at-risk rules, **11**:24
capital losses, **11**:24
investment interest, **11**:24
passive activity loss limitations, **11**:24
small business (Section 1244) stock, **11**:24
vacation homes, **11**:24
worthless securities, **11**:24
Investment losses, **11**:23–24
Involuntary conversion, **1**:32, **15**:10–16, **17**:5
computing the amount realized, **15**:12–13
defined, **15**:12
losses, **15**:15–16
nonrecognition of gain, **15**:15–16
recapture potential of, **17**:17
replacement property, **15**:13–14
reporting considerations, **15**:16
tax planning for, **15**:23
time limitation on replacement, **15**:14–15
Involuntary revocation, S election, **20**:24–25
IRA. *See* Individual retirement account
IRs (News Releases), **2**:9
IRS. *See* Internal Revenue Service
Itemized deductions, **3**:6, **3**:17–18, **6**:2–3, **7**:2, **10**:27
AMT adjustments, **12**:15–17
charitable contributions, **10**:18–26
for adjusted gross income (AGI), **6**:3–4
Form 1040, Schedule A, Itemized Deductions, **3**:8, **3**:40, **6**:9, **10**:2, **10**:17, **10**:27–28
from adjusted gross income (AGI), **6**:3
interest, **10**:14–18
limitations on, **9**:55–56
medical expenses, **10**:3–10
miscellaneous, **10**:27
miscellaneous itemized deductions not subject to the 2%-of-AGI floor, **9**:56
miscellaneous itemized deductions subject to the 2%-of-AGI floor, **9**:55
partial list of, **3**:6
tax benefit rule, **5**:29–30
taxes, **10**:10–13

J

Job-related education expenses, tax consequences of, **9**:16
Joint and several liability, **3**:30
Joint Committee on Taxation, **2**:25
Joint Conference Committee, **2**:3–4
example of compromise in, **2**:4
Joint return test, dependents, **3**:25, **3**:45
Joint tenants with rights of survivorship, **14**:15
Jointly owned property, **4**:19
Journal of International Taxation, **2**:18
Journal of Passthrough Entities, **2**:18
Journal of Taxation, **2**:18
Journal of the American Taxation Association, **2**:18
Judicial citations, **2**:14–17
U.S. District Court, Court of Federal Claims, and Courts of Appeals, **2**:16–17
U.S. Supreme Court, **2**:17
U.S. Tax Court, **2**:14–16
Judicial concepts and doctrines relating to tax, **1**:35–36
Judicial decision reliability variables, **2**:24–25
Circuit Court decision, **2**:25
other courts' support, **2**:25
Regular or Memorandum decision, **2**:25
residence of the taxpayer, **2**:24
status on appeal, **2**:25
the level of court, **2**:24
Judicial influence on statutory provisions, **1**:36
Judicial sources of tax law, **2**:10–17
appellate courts, **2**:12
appellate process, **2**:13–14
assessing the validity of, **2**:24–25
judicial citations, **2**:14–17
judicial process in general, **2**:10–11
trial courts, **2**:11–12
Jury trial, **2**:11

K

Keogh (H.R. 10) plans, **1**:30, **9**:53, **19**:11
compared to simplified employee pension plans (SEPs), **19**:13
contribution limitations, **19**:11
Key, Internal Revenue Code, **2**:5
Kiddie tax, **3**:37–39
election to claim certain unearned income on parent's return, **3**:39
Form 8615, Tax for Certain Children Who Have Unearned Income, **3**:38
Form 8814, Parents' Election to Report Child's Interest and Dividends, **3**:39
net unearned income, **3**:38
other rules, **3**:39
tax determination, **3**:38

L

Large-awards program, Internal Revenue Service (IRS), **2**:7
Large employers, **9**:56*ft*
Lease cancellation payments, **16**:14
lessee treatment, **16**:14
lessor treatment, **16**:14
Least aggregate deferral method, **18**:4
Legal expenses incurred in defense of civil or criminal penalties, **6**:13–14
Legal foundation, tax system, **1**:6–8
Legislative process, **2**:3–4
Legislative process for tax bills, **2**:3
Legislative Regulations, **2**:24
Lessee, **16**:14
Lessor, **16**:14
Letter rulings, **2**:8
distinction between determination letters and, **2**:9
distinction between Technical Advice Memoranda (TAMs) and, **2**:9
format of, **2**:8
Life insurance proceeds, **5**:5–7, **5**:30
accelerated death benefits, **5**:5–6
general rule, **5**:5
transfer for valuable consideration, **5**:6–7
Lifetime learning credit, **13**:18–19, **13**:22
eligible individuals, **13**:18
income limitations and refundability, **13**:18–19
maximum credit, **13**:18
restrictions on double tax benefit, **13**:19
tax consequences of, **9**:16
LIFO conformity rule, **18**:34
LIFO, dollar-value, **18**:32–33
LIFO election, **18**:33–34
LIFO conformity rule, **18**:34
LIFO index, **18**:32
LIFO (last in, first out) method, **18**:32
Form 970, Application to Use LIFO Inventory Method, **18**:33
Like-kind exchanges, **15**:3–10
basis and holding period of property received, **15**:7–10
boot, **15**:6–7
exchange period, **15**:5
exchange requirement, **15**:4–6
Form 8824, Like-Kind Exchanges, **15**:10, **15**:11
identification period, **15**:5
like-kind property, **15**:4–6
recapture potential of, **17**:17
related parties, **15**:3*ft*
reporting considerations, **15**:10
time limitations, **15**:5–6
Limitation based on wages and capital investment, **9**:29, **9**:31–33
phase-in of W–2 Wages/Capital Investment Limit, **9**:32–33
W–2 Wages Limit, **9**:29, **9**:31
W–2 Wages/Capital Investment Limit, **9**:31–33

Limitation for specified services businesses, **9**:33–42
- computation of QBI amount, **9**:38–42
- phase-in of the specified services limit, **9**:38–42
- specified services under the Section 199A Regulations, **9**:34–36

Limitation on Business Losses, Form 461, **7**:19
Limitations on charitable contribution deduction, **10**:22–26
- capital gain property, **10**:23–24
- contribution carryovers, **10**:25–26
- 50 percent ceiling, **10**:24
- ordinary income property, **10**:22–23
- temporary 60 percent ceiling, **10**:24
- 30 percent ceiling, **10**:24–25
- 20 percent ceiling, **10**:25

Limitations on the QBI deduction, **9**:29
Limited liability company (LLC)
- general tax consequences of, **20**:4
- nontax characteristics of, **20**:2–4
- partnerships, **20**:33

Limited partners, material participation, **11**:14
Listed property, **8**:18
- business and personal use of, **8**:18–23
- change from predominantly business use, **8**:21–22
- more-than-50% business usage test, **8**:19
- not used predominantly in business, **8**:21
- straight-line method and, **8**:18, **8**:21
- substantiation requirements, **8**:23
- used predominantly in business, **8**:19

Livestock, as a Section 1231 asset, **17**:5
Loan origination fee, **10**:16
Loans
- below-market, effect of on the lender and borrower, **4**:24
- between related parties, **7**:5
- exceptions and limitations of imputed interest on below-market, **4**:25–26
- home equity, **10**:15
- imputed interest on below-market, **4**:23–26

Lobbying expenses, **6**:15–16
- exceptions to disallowance of, **6**:16

Local income taxes, **1**:19
Longevity risk, **19**:4
Long-term capital gain, **16**:2, **17**:2, **17**:3
- alternative tax computation, **3**:43–44
- income tax consequences of individuals compared with C corporations, **20**:17

Long-term capital loss (LTCL), **16**:27
Long-term care insurance, **5**:12
- employer-sponsored, **5**:12

Long-term contracts, **18**:25–28
- completed contract method, **18**:25–27
- lookback provisions, **18**:28
- percentage of completion method, **18**:25–26, **18**:27–28

Long-term Federal rate, **18**:21*ft*
Long-term nonpersonal use capital assets, **17**:5
Long-term unemployed individual, **13**:7
Lookback provision
- percentage of completion method, **18**:28
- Section 1231, **17**:6

Loss
- amount of, **7**:9–10
- AMT adjustments, **12**:11–12
- business and nonbusiness, **6**:6–7
- business property, **7**:9–10
- casualty, **6**:6–7
- carryovers of suspended passive activity, **11**:7–8
- common questions from the IRS concerning hobbies/businesses with, **6**:20
- complete destruction of property, **7**:9–10
- determination of, **14**:2–9
- impact of suspended passive activity, **11**:6–7
- in involuntary conversions, **15**:15–16
- in related-party transactions, **6**:29
- investment, **11**:23–24
- limitation on partner's share of, **20**:32–33
- nonrecognition of, **14**:9, **20**:18–20
- on converted property, original basis for, **14**:19–20
- ordinary, **7**:6
- partial destruction of property, **7**:9–10
- passive activity, **11**:6
- personal property, **7**:9–11
- realized, **3**:41–42, **14**:3–8
- recognition of by partnerships, **20**:29–30
- recognized, **3**:41–42, **14**:8
- rental property, **7**:9–10
- rules for determining amount of loss, **7**:9–10
- S corporation treatment of, **20**:27
- Section 1231, **17**:3–4
- tax planning for disallowed, **14**:23
- timing of expense recognition, **6**:10–12
- treatment of QBI deduction, **9**:48–50
- *See also* Capital losses; Net capital loss; Realized loss; Recognized loss

Loss limitation in partnerships, **20**:32–33
Loss Netting and Carryforward, Schedule C, Form 8995-A, **9**:42
Losses, disallowed, **14**:15–19
- related taxpayers, **14**:16
- tax planning for, **14**:23
- wash sales, **14**:16–19

Losses directly attributable to the COVID-19 pandemic, **7**:9
Losses from property transactions
- capital losses, **3**:42–45
- in general, **3**:41–42

Losses of individuals, **7**:7–15
- COVID-19 losses, **7**:9
- deductible, **7**:7
- events that are not casualties, **7**:7
- measuring the amount of loss, **7**:9–12
- nondeductible, **7**:7
- personal casualty gains and losses, **7**:12–14
- statutory framework for deducting, **7**:14–15
- theft losses, **7**:8
- when to deduct casualty losses, **7**:8–9

Losses subject to the at-risk and passive activity loss limitations, treatment of, **11**:17
Lower of cost or market (replacement cost), **18**:31
Low-income housing credit, **13**:9–10, **13**:22
- low-income tenant, **13**:10
- qualified basis, **13**:10*ft*

Lump-sum distribution, **19**:8
Lump-sum purchase, allocation problems with, **14**:10
"Luxury auto" depreciation limits, **8**:19–20

M

MACRS. *See* Modified accelerated cost recovery system
Majority interest partners, **18**:3
Manufacturing contract, **18**:25
Marginal rate, **3**:35–36
- changes in, **6**:12
- tax planning for taking advantage of tax rate differentials, **3**:46

Marijuana for medical purposes, deduction of business expenses, **6**:15
Marital deduction, **1**:15, **1**:16–17
Marriage penalty, **3**:31
Married couples, calculating the exclusion in a sale of a residence, **15**:19–20
Married taxpayers
- filing jointly, **3**:30–31
- filing separately, **3**:30–31
- filing status, **3**:30–31
- marriage penalty, **3**:31
- surviving spouse, **3**:31

Mass tax, **1**:7
Material participant, distinguishing a passive investor from, **11**:12
Material participation, **11**:12–14
- difference between active participation and, **11**:18
- in a real property rental trade or business, **11**:17–18
- limited partners, **11**:14
- participation defined, **11**:14
- Section 469, **11**:13
- tests to determine, **11**:14

Meal and entertainment expenses. *See* Entertainment and meal expenses
Meals and lodging
- for medical treatment, deductible medical expenses, **10**:6
- general rules for the exclusion, **5**:13–14

Medical deduction, tax planning for maximizing, **10**:29
Medical expenses, **10**:3–10
- amounts paid for medical insurance premiums, **10**:6–7
- capital expenditures for medical purposes, **10**:4–5
- deductible, **10**:3–10
- defined, **10**:3–4
- examples of deductible and nondeductible, **10**:3
- for a dependent, **6**:25
- health savings accounts, **10**:8–9
- incurred for spouse and dependents, **10**:5
- itemized deductions, AMT adjustments, **12**:17
- nondeductible, **10**:3–10
- reimbursements, **10**:7–8
- transportation, meal, and lodging expenses for medical treatment, **10**:6
- year of deduction, **10**:7

Medical leave, credit for employer-provided family and, **13**:12

Medical reimbursement plans, employer-sponsored, **5**:11–12
Medicare, additional taxes on high-income individuals, **13**:29–31
additional tax on unearned income, **13**:30–31
additional tax on wages, **13**:29–30
Medicare Surtax on Net Investment Income (Section 1411), income tax consequences of individuals compared with C corporations, **20**:18
Medicare tax, **1**:19, **1**:20, **13**:24
Members of the household, **3**:22
Memorandum decisions, **2**:14–16, **2**:25
Merchandise purchased, cost defined, **18**:29
Mertens Law of Federal Income Taxation, **2**:19
Method of accounting, **18**:10
Methods, for personalty and realty, **8**:4
Midterm Federal rate, **18**:21*ft*
Mid-month convention, **8**:10
Mid-quarter convention, **8**:6–8
election to expense assets (Section 179) and, **8**:13–14
Mileage tracking apps, **9**:9
MileIQ, **9**:9
Military personnel, housing exclusions, **5**:14
Millionaires' provision, **6**:16–17
covered employees, **6**:16–17
publicly held corporations and, **6**:16–17
Mine exploration and development costs, **12**:9–10
Minimum participation test, qualified plans, **19**:5
Minimum tax gap, tax principles, **1**:10, **1**:11
Miscellaneous Income, Form 1099–MISC, **13**:25
Miscellaneous itemized deductions, **10**:27
not subject to the 2%-of-AGI floor, **9**:56
subject to the 2%-of-AGI floor, **9**:55
Tax Cuts and Jobs Act (TCJA) of 2017 and, **9**:3*ft*, **9**:5, **9**:53
Mixed services costs, **18**:25, **18**:26, **18**:30
"Mixed-use" vehicle, **9**:8, **9**:57
Modified accelerated cost recovery system (MACRS), **8**:2
additional first-year depreciation, **8**:14–15
alternative depreciation system (ADS), **8**:23–24
bonus depreciation, **8**:14–15
business and personal use of automobiles and other listed property, **8**:18–23
class lives, methods, and conventions, **8**:4
deductions, deferring to future years, **8**:15–16
election to expense assets (Section 179), **8**:10–14
general rules, **8**:4–10
personalty (and certain realty), recovery periods and methods, **8**:5–9
property, AMT depreciation, **12**:6, **12**:8
realty, recovery periods and methods, **8**:9–10
special rules, **8**:10–24
straight-line method, **8**:8–9
tables, **8**:33–35
using Section 179 and bonus depreciation effectively, **8**:15–18
See also Accelerated cost recovery system (ACRS)
Modified adjusted gross income (MAGI), **1**:20, **4**:30–31, **5**:25, **13**:30
Modified taxable income, deduction for QBI, **6**:7, **9**:26
Money purchase plan, **19**:3
More-than-50% business usage test, **8**:19
Mortgage interest, deductibility of, **10**:18
Moving expenses, **9**:21
Multinational corporations
corporate minimum tax, **12**:15
digital-economy, **12**:15
Multiple assets in a lump-sum purchase, allocation of cost among, **14**:10
Multiple support agreement, **3**:24
Form 2120, Multiple Support Declaration, **3**:24
Multiple Support Declaration, Form 2120, **3**:24

N

National Association of State Boards of Accountancy (NASBA), **2**:33
National Office of the IRS, **2**:7, **2**:8, **2**:9
National sales tax, **1**:22
National Taxpayers Union, **2**:30
Natural business year, **18**:5, **18**:7
Natural resource costs, **8**:28
Natural resources, **8**:28
depletion of, **8**:2
Negligence penalty, **1**:27, **1**:35
Net capital gain (NCG), **16**:19
alternative tax on, **16**:24–26, **16**:35
alternative tax rates on, **3**:43, **16**:24
as a component of investment income, **11**:26
determination of, **3**:42
modified taxable income, **9**:26
taxation of, **3**:43–44
Net capital loss (NCL), **16**:2, **16**:27
capital loss deduction, **16**:27
computation of, **16**:27
treatment of, **3**:43, **16**:27–28
Net earnings from self-employment, **13**:27
Net gain, **17**:3, **17**:5
Net Income (Loss) Reconciliation for Corporations With Total Assets of $10 Million or More, Schedule M–3, Form 1120, **20**:18
Net income tax, **13**:5
Net investment income, **11**:22, **13**:30
tax planning for the effect of additional tax on, **11**:26
Net investment income tax, **13**:30–31
Form 8960, Net Investment Income Tax—Individuals, Estates, and Trusts, **20**:32
Net Investment Income Tax—Individuals, Estates, and Trusts, Form 8960, **20**:32
Net invoice method, **18**:36
Net long-term capital gain (NLTCG), **3**:42, **16**:19–21
Net long-term capital loss (NLTCL), **16**:19–21
Net loss, **17**:3, **17**:5
Net nonbusiness capital gains, NOL computation and, **7**:21
Net operating loss (NOL), **7**:19–24, **12**:13–14
carryback, **7**:19*ft*
carryforward only, **7**:20
carryforward provisions, **12**:14
computation of, **7**:20–23
computation of remaining NOL to carry over to future years after computation of taxable income for the initial carryforward year, **7**:24
computation of taxable income for year to which NOL is carried, **7**:23–24
deduction for qualified business income, **7**:20
deductions *for* AGI, **7**:23–24
income tax consequences of individuals compared with C corporations, **20**:17
individuals and corporations compared, **20**:11
self-employment taxes, **7**:20
Net operating loss (NOL) carryover
NOL computation and, **7**:20
recapture of, **17**:27–28
Net operating loss (NOL) deduction limit, **7**:20
Net Profit From Business, Schedule C–EZ, Form 1040, **9**:3*ft*
Net regular tax liability, **13**:5
Net Section 481(a) adjustment, **18**:18–19
reporting, **18**:18–19
Net Section 1231 gain
limitation, **17**:15
qualified business income (QBI) and, **9**:26
Net short-term capital gain (NSTCG), **16**:19–21
Net short-term capital loss (NSTCL), **3**:42, **16**:19–21
Net unearned income of a dependent child, **3**:38
Netting process, capital gain and loss, **16**:19–23
definition of collectibles, **16**:22
final results of and how they are taxed, **16**:28
net long-term capital gain, **16**:19–21
net short-term capital gain, **16**:19–21
ordering procedure, **16**:20–21
small business stock, **16**:22–23
tax rates, **16**:19–23
use of capital loss carryovers, **16**:21
Netting process, Section 1231 assets disposed of by casualty or theft, **17**:5
Neutrality, tax principles, **1**:10, **1**:11
No-additional-cost service, **5**:17
NOL. *See* Net operating loss
Nominal rates, **3**:35–36
Nonaccountable plans, **9**:54–55
failure to comply with accountable plan requirements, **9**:55
unreimbursed employee expenses, **9**:55
Nonacquiescence ("NA" or "*Nonacq.*"), **2**:16
Nonbusiness bad debt, **7**:2–5, **16**:8
capital loss treatment, **16**:8
Nonbusiness capital gains, NOL computation and, **7**:21

Nonbusiness capital losses, NOL computation and, **7**:21
Nonbusiness deductions, NOL computation and, **7**:21
Nonbusiness expenses, deductions *from* AGI, **3**:6
Nonbusiness income, NOL computation and, **7**:21
Nonbusiness losses, **6**:6–7
Noncash Charitable Contributions, Form 8283, **10**:21
Noncash dividends, **20**:22
Noncommercial electronic (online) tax services, **2**:19–20
Noncontingent franchise payments, **16**:13
Noncorporate taxpayers, tax treatment of capital gains and losses of, **16**:19–29
Noncustodial parent, deductibility of medical expenses, **10**:5
Nondeductible contributions, IRAs, **19**:14
Nondeductible expenses, **3**:7
Nondeductible items, charitable contributions, **10**:19–20
Nondepreciable property, related-party sales of, **18**:22
Nondiscrimination provisions, employee fringe benefits, **5**:20
Nondiscrimination requirements, qualified plans, **19**:4
Nonemployee Compensation, Form 1099–NEC, **9**:3, **9**:57
Nonparental source income, net unearned income, **3**:38
Nonqualified deferred compensation (NQDC), **19**:18
Nonqualified deferred compensation (NQDC) plans, **19**:18–19
  advantages and disadvantages of, **19**:24
  tax planning for, **19**:24
  tax treatment to the employer and employee, **19**:18–19
  underlying rationale for tax treatment, **19**:18
Nonqualified stock options (NQSOs), **19**:22–23
  compared to incentive stock options, **19**:25
Nonrecaptured net Section 1231 losses, **17**:6
Nonrecognition of gain, **14**:9
  conversion into money, **15**:15–16
  direct conversion, **15**:15
  under Section 351, **20**:18–20
Nonrecognition of loss, **14**:9
  sale, exchange, or condemnation of personal use assets, **14**:9
  under Section 351, **20**:18–20
Nonrecourse debt, **11**:3*ft*
Nonrecourse financing, qualified, **11**:4
Nonrefundable credits, **13**:3, **13**:4–5
  carryover provision, **13**:5
  partial listing of, **13**:4
Nonrental activity, **11**:15
Nonresident alien, **3**:18, **19**:5*ft*
Nonresidential real estate, **8**:9
  Section 1245 recapture, **17**:13*ft*
Nontax characteristics of business entities, **20**:2–4
Nontax considerations, choice of entity, **20**:2–4
Nontaxable exchanges, **15**:2–3
  holding period of, **16**:15
  involuntary conversions—Section 1033, **15**:10–16
  like-kind exchanges—Section 1031, **15**:3–10
  sale of a residence—Section 121, **15**:16–22
Nontaxable stock dividends, **14**:11
  allocation of, **14**:11
  holding period for, **14**:11
Nontaxable transactions, recapture potential of, **17**:16–17
Note receivable
  collection of a cash basis, **16**:5
  collection of an accrual basis, **16**:4–5
Notices, **2**:7–8
  citing of, **2**:8
  function of guidance, **2**:8
Nursing home care, deductible medical expenses, **10**:4

O

ObamaCare. *See* Affordable Care Act (ACA)
Obligation to repay, amounts received under, **4**:12
Obligations
  disposition of installment, **18**:23–24, **18**:36
  retirement of corporate, **16**:9
Occupational fees, **1**:19
OECD (Organization of Economic Cooperation and Development), **1**:23
Office audit, **1**:25
Office in the home expenses, **9**:17–21
  exclusive use requirement, **9**:17–18, **9**:20–21
  Form 8829, Expenses for Business Use of Your Home, **9**:19
  Regular Method, **9**:18–20
  Simplified Method, **9**:19–21
Office of Chief Counsel, **2**:9
Offset, right of, **14**:16
OID amortization rules, Sections 1272–1288, **16**:9
Oil, Gas & Energy Quarterly, **2**:18
Old age, survivors, and disability insurance, **1**:19
One other residence, **10**:15
$100-per-event floor
  Federally declared disasters, **7**:10*ft*
  reduction for, **7**:10–11
150 percent declining-balance method, classification of property, **8**:5
Online tax services, **2**:19
  noncommercial, **2**:19–20
"Only once every two years" rule, sale of a residence exclusion treatment, **15**:18
Operating costs, **8**:29
Options, **16**:9–11
  consequences to the grantor and grantee, **16**:11
  exercise of by grantee, **16**:9
  failure to exercise, **16**:10–11
  sale of, **16**:10
Ordering procedure, capital gain and loss netting process, **16**:20–21
Ordering rules for deductions, personal/rental use property, **6**:24
Ordinary and necessary, **6**:5
Ordinary and necessary expenses, **6**:5
Ordinary asset, **16**:3
Ordinary income property, **10**:22–23
Ordinary life annuities, one life—expected return multiples, **4**:27
Ordinary loss, **7**:6, **17**:3
Organization for Economic Cooperation and Development (OECD), **12**:15
Organizational expenditures, **20**:13–14
  deduction of, **20**:13–14
  election to amortize, **20**:13
Original basis, **14**:5
  for loss on converted property, **14**:19–20
Original issue discount (OID), **4**:11, **16**:9
  corporate bonds, **4**:12
  government bonds, **4**:12
Other disposition, **14**:3
Out-of-the-home expenses, credit for child and dependent care expenses, **13**:15
Outsourcing of tax return preparation, **1**:27
Owner-investor, replacement property, **15**:13
Owner-user, replacement property, **15**:13
Ownership and use tests, sale of a residence exclusion treatment, **15**:17–18

P

Parents' Election to Report Child's Interest and Dividends, Form 8814, **3**:39
Parker Tax Pro Library, **2**:19
Participation and coverage requirements, qualified plan, **19**:4–5
Partners, Subchapter K, **2**:5
Partnership, **4**:17, **20**:28–33
  Form 1065, U.S. Return of Partnership Income, **4**:17, **20**:28, **20**:31
  formation and basis of, **20**:29–31
  general tax consequences of, **20**:4
  impermissible year election, **18**:5
  income from, **4**:17–18
  losses from, excess business losses, **7**:18–19
  nature of taxation, **20**:28–29
  nontax characteristics of, **20**:2–4
  required tax payments, **18**:5
  specific provisions for, **18**:3–6
  Subchapter K, **2**:5
  tax year, **18**:3–5
  taxation of income and distributions from, **4**:18
Partnership operations, **20**:31–33
  guaranteed payments, **20**:33
  limitation on partner's share of losses, **20**:32–33
  limited liability companies, **20**:33
  measuring and reporting partnership income, **20**:31–32
  qualified joint ventures, **20**:33
Part-time employee, **9**:56*ft*
  long-term, **19**:10
Passenger automobiles, **8**:19
Passive activity
  disposition of at death, **11**:20
  disposition of by gift, **11**:21
  installment sale of, **11**:21
  regrouping of, **11**:12
  rules for determining, **11**:10–15
Passive activity credits, **11**:8
  carryovers of, **11**:8–9
  deduction equivalent of, **11**:19–20

Passive activity income, **11**:6
Passive activity income and losses
carryovers of passive activity credits, **11**:8–9
carryovers of suspended passive activity losses, **11**:7–8
classification and tax treatment of, **11**:5–9
general impact, **11**:6
impact of suspended passive activity losses, **11**:6–7
passive activity changes to active, **11**:9
passive activity credits, **11**:8
Passive activity loss, **11**:3, **11**:6
AMT adjustments, **12**:12–13
income tax consequences of individuals compared with C corporations, **20**:18
Passive activity loss limits, **11**:5–21
classification and tax treatment of passive activity income and losses, **11**:5–9
common investment loss limitation rules, **11**:24
dispositions of passive activities, **11**:20–21
interaction of the at-risk and, **11**:15–16
rules for determining passive activities, **11**:10–15
special passive activity rules for real estate activities, **11**:16–20
tax planning for minimizing the impact of, **11**:24–25
taxpayers subject to passive activity loss rules, **11**:9–10
treatment of losses subject to the at-risk and, **11**:17
Passive activity loss rules, **11**:3
closely held C corporations, **11**:10
identification of an activity, **11**:11–12
key issues and answers, **11**:22
material participation, **11**:12–14
material participation in a real property rental trade or business, **11**:17–18
nonrental activities, **11**:15
personal service corporations, **11**:9–10
real estate rental activities with active participation, **11**:18–20
rental activities, **11**:15
Passive investment income, **20**:24
Passive investor, distinguishing a material participant from, **11**:12
Passive trade or business, **7**:19
Pass-through entities, **20**:5
Patent, **16**:11–12
holder defined, **16**:12
sale of, **1**:30
substantial rights, **16**:11–12
Patient Protection and Affordable Care Act. *See* Affordable Care Act (ACA)
Patrons of Agricultural or Horticultural Cooperatives, Schedule D, Form 8995–A, **9**:42
Pay-as-you-go basis, **1**:35
Pay-as-you-go concept, **13**:3
Pay-as-you-go rules, tax payment procedures, **13**:23
Pay-as-you-go tax income tax system, **1**:7
Payments from Qualified Education Programs, Form 1099–Q, **5**:25
Payments received, installment method computing of, **18**:20–21
Payments, timing of to maximize deductions, **10**:26
Penalties
for early distribution, qualified plans, **19**:7–8
for lack of compliance, **1**:26–27, **1**:35, **13**:23
imposed on tax return preparers, **1**:28
on underpayments, self-employed taxpayers, **13**:26–27
Pension plan, **9**:52–53, **19**:2–3
employee contribution deduction, **9**:52
employee contribution exclusion, **9**:52
See also Qualified plans
Per diem allowance, **9**:54
Percentage depletion, **8**:30–31
AMT preferences, **12**:18–19
rates, **8**:30
Percentage of completion method, **4**:7, **12**:10, **18**:25–26, **18**:27–28
Performance-based compensation, **6**:33
Personal activities, **6**:4
Personal and dependency exemptions, NOL computation and, **7**:20
Personal casualty gains and losses, **7**:12–14
Personal exemptions, **3**:7, **3**:19
Personal expenditures
deduction of, **10**:2
disallowance of, **6**:26
tax planning to avoid nondeductible treatment, **10**:31
Personal expenses, deductions *from* AGI, **6**:6
Personal identification number (Self-Select PIN), **3**:40
Personal injury
damages for, **5**:9–10
nonphysical, **5**:9
physical, **5**:9
tax treatment of, **5**:9
Personal interest, deductibility of, **10**:18
Personal nonrefundable credits, AMT liability and, **12**:6
Personal property. *See* Personalty
Personal residence, **15**:16
conversion to rental property, **6**:23*ft*
Personal service corporations (PSC), **11**:9–10, **18**:6, **20**:14
calendar year, **18**:6
fiscal year election, **18**:6
qualified, **20**:7*ft*
specific provisions for, **18**:3–6
Personal services, **4**:14–15
Personal use assets, **8**:3, **16**:3
converted to business or income-producing use, cost recovery basis for, **8**:4
sale, exchange, or condemnation of, **14**:9
Personal use loss reductions, the $100-per-event and 10%-of-AGI floors, **7**:10–11
Personal use property, **8**:3
casualty losses, **17**:5*ft*
condemnation gains and losses, **17**:5*ft*
converted to business or income-producing use, **14**:19–20
net casualty gains, **17**:5*ft*
Personalty, **1**:12, **8**:2–3, **14**:2, **15**:3*ft*
class lives, **8**:4
conventions, **8**:4
loss, **7**:9–11
methods, **8**:4
tangible, **10**:23
Personalty (and certain realty), recovery periods and methods, **8**:5–9
classification of property, **8**:5–6
mid-quarter convention, **8**:6–8
qualified improvement property, **8**:8
straight-line election, **8**:8–9
Petitioner, **2**:11
"Phantom" income, **4**:26
Phaseout of IRA deduction of an active participant in 2021, **19**:13
Physical sickness, **5**:9
Piggyback approach to state income taxation, **1**:18
Plaintiff, **2**:11
Planning, relevance of taxation to accounting and finance professionals, **1**:3
Plug-in electric drive motor vehicles, energy tax credits, **13**:20
Points, **10**:16
Political considerations
political expediency situations, **1**:33–34
special interest legislation, **1**:33
state and local government influences, **1**:34
tax law, **1**:36
Political contributions, **6**:15–16
Pollution control facilities, AMT adjustments, **12**:8
Pool, **18**:32
Portfolio income, **11**:6
Practical Tax Expert, **2**:19
Practical Tax Strategies, **2**:18
Precedential authority, doctrine of, **2**:10
Precedents, **2**:13
Preferences, **12**:18
Preferential tax treatment, **1**:33
Prepaid expenses, the "12-month rule," **6**:12
Prepaid interest, **10**:17
Preparation Blueprints, CPA examination, **2**:31
Preparer Tax Identification Number (PTIN), **1**:28
Prepayment penalty, **10**:16
Preserving formalities, tax planning, **2**:29–30
Primary sources of the tax law, **2**:2, **2**:25
Principal partner, **18**:3
Principal place of business, **9**:17
Principal residence, **10**:15, **15**:17
tax planning for the sale of, **15**:23–24
Private activity bonds, **12**:19
Private nonoperating foundations, **10**:23–24
Private operating foundations, **10**:23–24
Prizes, income from, **4**:29
Procedural Regulations, **2**:24
Proceeds From Broker and Barter Exchange Transactions, Form 1099–B, **14**:10, **16**:29
Professional employer organization (PEO), determination of W–2 wages, **9**:51
Profit or Loss From Business, Schedule C, Form 1040, **3**:40, **8**:24–25, **8**:27, **9**:3, **9**:5, **10**:17, **20**:33
Profit sharing plan, **19**:3
See also Qualified plans
Progressive tax rate, **3**:36
Progressive taxes, **1**:9, **1**:31
Property, **14**:2
ad valorem taxes, **1**:12–13
adjusted basis of, **3**:41, **14**:5

Property (*continued*)
amount realized from a sale or other disposition of, **14**:4
AMT adjustments for depreciation of, **12**:6, **12**:7–8
appreciated, **15**:7
bargain purchase of, **14**:9–10
basis for depreciating converted, **14**:19–20
boot given as appreciated or depreciated, **15**:7
business and personal use of listed, **8**:18–23
business use, **8**:3
capital gain, **10**:23–24
classification and use of, **1**:12–13
conversion of personal residence to rental, **6**:23*ft*
depreciated, **15**:7
disposed by sale, exchange, casualty, theft, or condemnation, **16**:3
exchange of, **16**:8
excluded under Section 1231, **17**:4
fair market value of, **14**:4
gain basis for converted, **14**:19–20
gift basis, **14**:12–13
holding period of, **16**:3, **16**:16
included under Section 1231, **17**:4
income from, **4**:15–17
income-producing, **8**:3
involuntary conversion of, **15**:10–16
jointly owned, **4**:19
like-kind, **15**:4–6
MACRS classification of, **8**:5–6
manner of disposition, **16**:3
ordinary income, **10**:22–23
original basis for loss on converted, **14**:19–20
original basis of, **14**:5
partnership's basis in contributed, **20**:31
personal, **14**:2
personal use, **8**:3
qualified for additional first-year depreciation, **8**:14–15
qualified for bonus depreciation, **8**:14–15
real, **14**:2
related-party sales of depreciable, **18**:23
related-party sales of nondepreciable, **18**:22
replacement, **15**:13–14
sale or other disposition of, **14**:3, **16**:8
Section 179 expensing election, **8**:11
Section 1245, **17**:12
Section 1250, **17**:13
substantially identical, **16**:17
tax status of, **16**:3
Property acquired by gift, **14**:12–13
basis rules, **14**:12–13
holding period for, **14**:13
tax planning for, **14**:22
Property acquired from a decedent, **14**:13–15
alternate valuation amount, **14**:14
alternate valuation date, **14**:14
alternate valuation election, **14**:14
general rules, **14**:13–14
holding period, **14**:15
income in respect of a decedent (IRD), **14**:14–15
survivor's share of property, **14**:15
Property dispositions, **14**:2
Property dividends, recapture potential of, **17**:17–18
Property placed in service maximum, Section 179 expensing deduction limitations, **8**:11–12
Property put to an unrelated use, **10**:23
Property settlements, divorce decree, **4**:20–21
Property taxes, **1**:2, **1**:12–13, **10**:11–13
apportionment between seller and purchaser, **10**:12–13
assessments for local benefits, **10**:12
Property transactions
capital gains and losses from, **3**:42–45
gains and losses from, **3**:41–42
tax planning for, **14**:22–23
Proportional tax, **1**:31
Proposed Regulations, **2**:7
Provisional income, **4**:30–31
PTIN. *See* Preparer Tax Identification Number
Public charities, **10**:24
Public policy limitation, **6**:13–15
expenses contrary to public policy, **6**:13
expenses relating to an illegal business, **6**:14–15
justification for denying deductions, **6**:13
legal expenses incurred in defense of civil or criminal penalties, **6**:13–14
Publicly held corporations, millionaires' provision, **6**:16–17
Punitive damages, **5**:9

Q

QBI deduction, **9**:25–52
See Deduction for qualified business income; Qualified business income (QBI) deduction
Qualified ABLE program, **5**:26–27
Qualified automatic enrollment arrangement, Section 401(k) plan, **19**:10–11
Qualified basis, low-income housing credit, **13**:10*ft*
Qualified business income (QBI), **6**:7, **9**:25, **9**:26
criteria for defining, **6**:7
deduction for, **3**:7, **6**:7–9
exclusions of, **9**:26
investment income and, **9**:26
net Section 1231 gain and, **9**:26
NOLs and deduction for, **7**:20
2022 limitations, **6**:8
Qualified business income (QBI) deduction, **6**:7–9
limit based on wages and capital investment, **6**:7–8
limitations on, **9**:29
NOL computation and, **7**:20
overview of 2022, **9**:30
See also Deduction for qualified business income
Qualified Business Income Deduction, Form 8995-A, **9**:42, **9**:44–45
Qualified Business Income Deduction Simplified Computation, Form 8995, **9**:42
Qualified child, tiebreaker rules for claiming, **3**:21
Qualified child care expenses, credit for employer-provided child care, **13**:11
Qualified disaster, gross income exclusions under Section 139, **5**:2
Qualified dividend income (QDI), **4**:16, **16**:23
alternative tax on, **16**:24–26
as a component of investment income, **11**:26
Qualified Dividends and Capital Gain Tax Worksheet, **16**:29, **16**:34
Qualified domestic organization, **10**:18, **10**:22
Qualified employee discount, **5**:17–18
Qualified higher education expenses, **5**:25, **5**:26
Qualified housing interest, **12**:16
itemized deductions, AMT adjustments, **12**:16
Qualified HSA trustee, **10**:8*ft*
Qualified improvement property, **8**:8
Qualified joint venture, **20**:6, **20**:33
election to form, **20**:33
Qualified military base realignment and closure fringe, **5**:19
Qualified moving expense reimbursements, **5**:19
Qualified nonrecourse financing, **11**:4
Qualified organizations, charitable contributions, **10**:20, **10**:22
Qualified parking, **5**:19
Qualified personal service corporation, **18**:12, **20**:7*ft*
Qualified plans
distribution requirements, **19**:6–8
limitations on contributions to and benefits from, **19**:9–10
lump-sum distributions from, **19**:8
nondiscrimination requirements, **19**:4
participation and coverage requirements, **19**:4–5
qualification requirements, **19**:4–8
rollover treatment, **19**:8
Section 401(k) plans, **19**:10–11
simplified method for annuity distributions from, **4**:28
tax advantages of, **19**:2
tax consequences to the employee and employer, **19**:8
tax planning for, **19**:23
types of plans, **19**:2–4
vesting requirements, **19**:6
Qualified property, **12**:7
additional first-year depreciation, **8**:14–15
bonus depreciation, **8**:14–15
depreciable period, **9**:31
W-2 Wages/Capital Investment Limit, **9**:31–32
Qualified real property business indebtedness, **5**:28
Qualified rehabilitation expenditures, rehabilitation expenditures credit, **13**:6–7
Qualified research expenditures, incremental research activities credit, **13**:8
Qualified residence, **10**:15
one other residence, **10**:15
principal residence, **10**:15
Qualified residence interest, **10**:14–16, **12**:16
interest on acquisition indebtedness, **10**:15

itemized deductions, AMT adjustments, **12**:16
Schedule A, Form 1040, Itemized Deductions, **10**:17
Qualified retirement planning services, **5**:19
Qualified small business stock, **16**:22
Qualified startup company, research activities credit, **13**:7*ft*
Qualified trade or business (QTB), **6**:8–9, **9**:25, **9**:27–29
aggregation of under the Section 199A Regulations, **9**:43, **9**:47–48
rental real estate safe harbor, **9**:28
taxpayers with multiple businesses, **9**:29
trade or business under Section 199A, **9**:28
Qualified transportation fringes, **5**:19, **6**:30
Qualified tuition program (Section 529 plan), **5**:25–26
tax consequences of, **9**:16
Qualified tuition reduction plan, tax consequences of, **9**:16
Qualifying child, **3**:19–21
age test, **3**:20
earned income credit, **13**:13
relationship test, **3**:20
residence test, **3**:20
support test, **3**:20–21
tiebreaker rules, **3**:21
Qualifying relative, **3**:21–24
gross income test, **3**:22–23
relationship test, **3**:22
support test, **3**:23–24
Qualifying widow(er) with dependent child, **3**:31*ft*
QuickBooks Self-Employed, **9**:9

R

Rate layers, alternative tax on net capital gain and qualified dividend income, **16**:24
Ratio percentage test for qualified plans, **19**:5
Readily ascertainable fair market value, NQSO, **19**:22
Readily available income, **4**:9–10
Real estate
activities, special passive activity rules for, **11**:16–20
25% gain, **17**:14–15
Real Estate Taxation, **2**:18
Real property. *See* Realty
Real property rental trade or business, material participation in, **11**:17–18
Realization, gross income, **4**:6
Realization events, sale or other disposition of property, **14**:2, **14**:3
Realization principle, **4**:4, **4**:33
Realized gain, **3**:41–42, **14**:3–8
adjusted basis, **14**:5
amount realized, **14**:4–5
capital additions, **14**:5–6
capital recoveries, **14**:6–8
computation of, **14**:3
in involuntary conversions, **15**:15–16
original basis, **14**:5
realization events, **14**:3
Realized loss, **3**:41–42, **14**:3–8
adjusted basis, **14**:5
amount realized, **14**:4–5
capital additions, **14**:5–6
capital recoveries, **14**:6–8
computation of, **14**:3
in involuntary conversions, **15**:15–16
original basis, **14**:5
realization events, **14**:3
sale or other disposition, **14**:2–3
Realty, **1**:12, **8**:2–3, **14**:2
class lives, **8**:4
conventions, **8**:4
like-kind property, **15**:4
methods, **8**:4
recovery periods and methods, **8**:9–10
subdivided for sale, capital gain treatment, **16**:7–8
Reasonable prospect of full recovery, **7**:8
Reasonableness, **6**:5–6, **6**:16
closely held corporations and, **6**:6, **6**:16
Recapture
alimony, **4**:21
of depreciation, individuals and corporations compared, **20**:9–10
Section 1245, **17**:10–13, **17**:14
Section 1250, **17**:13–15
special provisions, **17**:19
tax planning for avoiding, **17**:28
tax planning for postponing and shifting, **17**:28
tax planning for timing of, **17**:27–28
Recapture exceptions
certain nontaxable transactions, **17**:16–17
charitable transfers, **17**:16
death, **17**:16
gifts, **17**:16
involuntary conversions (Section 1033), **17**:17
like-kind exchanges (Section 1031), **17**:17
Recognized gain, **3**:41–42, **14**:8
classification of, **16**:3
in involuntary conversions, **15**:15–16
Recognized loss, **3**:41–42, **14**:8
classification of, **16**:3
in involuntary conversions, **15**:15–16
Recognized losses from property transactions, deductions *for* AGI, **3**:42
Reconciliation of Income (Loss) per Books with Income per Return, Schedule M–1, Form 1120, **20**:15–16
Record date, **4**:17*ft*
Record-keeping/documentation requirements
charitable contributions, **10**:21
meal expenses, **9**:24
travel expenses, **9**:14
Recovery of capital, **4**:19, **5**:3
Recovery of capital doctrine, **4**:3, **8**:2, **15**:8
Recurring items, **6**:11
exception, **18**:15–16
Refund due, computation of, **3**:36–37
Refundable credits, **13**:3, **13**:4–5
partial listing of, **13**:4
Refunds, limitations on, **1**:26
REG (Regulation) section, CPA examination, **2**:31–33
content areas, **2**:32
task-based simulations (TBSs), **2**:31–33
Regressive tax, **1**:31
Regular (actual expense) Method
office in the home deduction, **9**:18
office in the home expenses, **9**:18–20
Regular decisions, **2**:14–16, **2**:25
Regular tax liability, AMT formula, **12**:5–6
Regulation (REG) section, CPA examination, **2**:31–33
content areas, **2**:32
task-based simulations (TBSs), **2**:31–33
Regulations. *See* Treasury Department Regulations
Rehabilitation expenditures credit, **13**:6–7, **13**:22
qualified rehabilitation expenditures, **13**:6–7
Related party, **6**:28, **17**:19
disallowed losses between, **14**:16
holding period, **14**:16
loans, **7**:5
recapture on gain from sale of depreciable property between, **17**:19
right of offset, **14**:16
Related-party installment sales
of depreciable property, **18**:23
of nondepreciable property, **18**:22
tax planning for, **18**:37
Related-party transactions, **6**:28–29
losses, **6**:29
relationships and constructive ownership, **6**:28
Relationship of the parties, **9**:4
Relationship test
members of the household, **3**:22
qualifying child, **3**:20
qualifying relative, **3**:22
Release/Revocation of Release of Claim to Exemption for Child by Custodial Parent, Form 8332, **3**:24
Relevant pass-through entity (RPE), **9**:43
Religious leaders, housing exclusions, **5**:14
Rent and royalty income, Form 1040, Schedule E, Supplemental Income or Loss, **6**:4
Rental activity, **11**:15
special grouping rules for, **11**:12
Rental car "surcharge," **1**:13
Rental of vacation homes, **6**:21–25
Rental property
conversion of personal residence to, **6**:23*ft*
loss, **7**:9–10
Rental real estate activities with active participation, **11**:18–20
Rental real estate safe harbor, **9**:28
Repairs, cost of, **7**:9
Replacement property
earliest and latest dates for replacement, **15**:14–15
functional use test, **15**:13–14
involuntary conversions, **15**:14
special rule for condemnations, **15**:13–14
taxpayer use test, **15**:13–14
Report of Foreign Bank and Financial Accounts (FBAR), **4**:31
Required minimum distribution (RMD), **19**:6–7
rules, qualified plans, **19**:6–7
selected factors from IRS table, **19**:7

Research activities credit, **13**:3, **13**:7–9, **13**:22
basic research credit, **13**:9, **13**:22
eligible small business, **13**:7*ft*
energy research credit, **13**:9, **13**:22
incremental research activities credit, **13**:8–9, **13**:22
qualified startup company, **13**:7*ft*
Research and development expenditures, **1**:30
Research and experimental expenditures, **7**:15–17, **12**:9–10
deferral and amortization method, **7**:16–17
expense method, **7**:16
Research expenditures, **13**:8
Reserve method, **7**:3
Reserves, **6**:11, **18**:16
tax deferrals from, **18**:16
Residence test, qualifying child, **3**:20
Residential energy tax credits, **13**:20
Residential rental real estate, **8**:9
Respondent, **2**:11
Retirement accounts, contributions to, **9**:52–53
employee IRAs, **9**:52–53
self-employed Keogh (H.R. 10) plans, **9**:53
Retirement assets, liquidating, **19**:26
Retirement plans
contributions to, deductions *for* AGI, **3**:4
simplified method for annuity distributions from qualified, **4**:28
Retirement plans for self-employed individuals, **19**:11–13
Keogh (H.R. 10) plans, **19**:11
savings incentive match plan for employees (SIMPLE plans), **19**:12
simplified employee pension plans (SEPs), **19**:12
Solo Section 401(k) plans, **19**:12
Revenue acts, **1**:6–7
of 1913, **1**:6
of 1916, **1**:15
of 1948, **1**:34
of 1978, **9**:57*ft*
Revenue Agent's Report (RAR), **1**:25
Revenue, IRS as protector of, **1**:34–35
Revenue neutrality, **1**:29
Revenue Procedures, **2**:7–8
citing of, **2**:8
commercial sources, **2**:8*ft*
function of guidance, **2**:8
Revenue Ruling 87–41, determination of employee versus independent contractor, **9**:3–4
behavioral control, **9**:4
financial control, **9**:4
relationship of the parties, **9**:4
Revenue Rulings, **2**:7–8, **2**:24
citing of, **2**:8
commercial sources, **2**:8*ft*
function of guidance, **2**:8
Revocation
involuntary, **20**:24–25
voluntary, **20**:24–25
Right of offset, **6**:29, **14**:16
Right to control, **9**:3
Rollover
direct, **19**:8
indirect, **19**:8
Rollover treatment, qualified plans, **19**:8
Rollovers and conversions, IRAs, **19**:17
Roth IRA, **9**:53, **19**:14–15
compared with traditional IRA, **19**:17

S

S corporation, **4**:18, **20**:23–28
calendar year, **18**:5
comparison of tax attributes of C corporations and, **20**:29
election, **20**:23–25
Form 1120S, U.S. Income Tax Return for an S Corporation, **20**:5, **20**:15
Schedule L, Balance Sheet per Books, **20**:15
Form 2553, Election by a Small Business Corporation, **20**:24
Form 7203, S Corporation Shareholder Stock and Debt Basis Limitations, **20**:28
general tax consequences of, **20**:5
impermissible year election, **18**:5
income from, **4**:17–18
losses from, excess business losses, **7**:18–19
nontax characteristics of, **20**:3–4
operational rules, **20**:25–28
qualification for S status, **20**:24–25
required tax payments, **18**:5
specific provisions for, **18**:3–6
Subchapter S, **2**:5
tax planning for C corporations versus S status, **20**:35
taxation of income and distributions from, **4**:18
S Corporation Shareholder Stock and Debt Basis Limitations, Form 7203, **20**:28
S election, **20**:23–25
Form 2553, Election by a Small Business Corporation, **20**:24
loss of, **20**:24–25
making, **20**:24
qualifying for, **20**:24
Safe harbor, rental real estate, **9**:28
Sale, **14**:3
Sale of a patent, **1**:30
Sale of a residence—Section 121, **15**:16–22
calculating the exclusion, **15**:19–20
exceptions to the two-year rules, **15**:20–22
principal residence, **15**:17
requirements for exclusion treatment, **15**:17–18
Sale or exchange, **16**:8–14
franchises, trademarks, and trade names (Section 1253), **16**:12–14
lease cancellation payments, **16**:14
options, **16**:9–11
patents, **16**:11–12
retirement of corporate obligations, **16**:9
worthless securities and Section 1244 stock, **16**:8
Sales and Other Dispositions of Capital Assets, Form 8949, **16**:29, **16**:32–33
Sales of Business Property, Form 4797, **17**:20–21, **17**:23–24
Sales tax, **1**:2, **1**:14
deductibility of state and local, **10**:13
holiday, **1**:14
national, **1**:22
SALT cap, **10**:11*ft*, **12**:2
SALT deduction, Tax Cuts and Jobs Act (TCJA) of 2017, **5**:29–30
Same-sex couples, filing status, **3**:30
Saver's credit, **13**:19–21
rate and AGI thresholds (2022), **13**:21
Savings incentive match plan for employees (SIMPLE plans), **9**:53, **19**:12
Schedule 1, Additional Income and Adjustments to Income, Form 1040, **3**:8, **3**:11–12, **3**:39–40
Schedule 2, Additional Taxes, Form 1040, **3**:13–14, **3**:39–40
Schedule 3, Additional Credits and Payments, Form 1040, **3**:15–16, **3**:40
Schedule A
comprehensive example of, **10**:27–28
Itemized Deductions, Form 1040, **3**:8, **3**:40, **10**:2, **10**:17, **10**:28
Specified Service Trades or Businesses, Form 8995–A, **9**:42–43, **9**:46
Schedule B, Aggregation of Business Operations, Form 8995–A, **9**:42
Schedule C
Loss Netting and Carryforward, Form 8995–A, **9**:42
Profit or Loss From Business, Form 1040, **3**:4*ft*, **3**:40, **8**:24–25, **8**:27, **9**:3, **9**:5, **10**:17, **20**:33
Schedule C–EZ, Net Profit From Business, Form 1040, **9**:3*ft*
Schedule D
Capital Gains and Losses, Form 1040, **16**:29, **16**:30–31, **17**:20, **17**:22, **17**:25–26
Patrons of Agricultural or Horticultural Cooperatives, Form 8995–A, **9**:42
Tax Worksheet, **16**:29
Schedule E, Supplemental Income or Loss, Form 1040, **6**:4, **10**:17
Schedule L, Balance Sheet per Books, Form 1120S, **20**:15
Schedule M–1, Reconciliation of Income (Loss) per Books with Income per Return, **20**:15–16
Schedule M–2, Analysis of Unappropriated Retained Earnings per Books, **20**:16
Schedule M–3, Net Income (Loss) Reconciliation for Corporations With Total Assets of $10 Million or More, Form 1120, **20**:18
Schedule SE, Self-Employment Tax, Form 1040, **3**:40, **9**:3*ft*
Scholarships, **5**:7–8
general information, **5**:7–8
tax consequences of, **9**:16
timing issues, **5**:8
Secondary sources of the tax law, **2**:2*ft*, **2**:25
Section 1, alternative tax on net capital gain, **16**:24
Section 21, credit for child and dependent care expenses, **13**:21
Section 22, credit for elderly or disabled taxpayers, **13**:21
Section 23, adoption expenses credit, **13**:21
Section 24, child and dependent tax credit, **13**:21
Section 25A, education tax credits, **13**:21–22

Section 25B, credit for certain retirement plan contributions, **13**:22
Section 27, foreign tax credit (FTC), **13**:22
Section 31, credit for tax withheld on wages, **13**:21
Section 32, earned income credit, **13**:21
Section 38, general business credit, **13**:22
Section 40(A), biodiesel tax credit, **13**:20
Section 41, research activities credit, **13**:22
Section 42, low-income housing credit, **13**:22
Section 44, disabled access credit, **13**:22
Section 45, energy credit for producing electricity via wind, solar, geothermal, and other property, **13**:20
Section 45E, credit for small employer pension plan startup costs, **13**:22
Section 45F, credit for employer-provided child care, **13**:23
Section 45S, credit for employer-provided family and medical leave, **13**:23
Section 47, rehabilitation expenditures credit, **13**:22
Section 48, credit for business installation of qualified fuel cells, stationary microturbine power plants, solar, and small wind energy equipment, **13**:20
Section 51, work opportunity credit, **13**:23
Section 61, definition of gross income, **4**:3
Section 62, deductions for adjusted gross income, **6**:3
Section 79 limited exclusion, group term life insurance, **5**:20–21
Section 105, employer-sponsored accident and health plans, **5**:11
Section 111, tax benefit rule, **5**:29
Section 119, employee meals and lodging, **5**:13
Section 121 exclusion, **15**:16
  basis of new residence, **15**:22
  implications of renting or using as a home office, **15**:22
  partial, **15**:21
  tax planning for qualification for, **15**:23–24
  tax planning for waiving, **15**:23
Section 121, sale of a residence, **15**:16–22
Section 132, general classes of excluded benefits, **5**:17
Section 139, Disaster Relief Payment, **5**:2
Section 139F, wrongful incarceration, **5**:10
Section 162, trade or business expenses, **6**:4–5, **6**:5–6, **6**:15, **9**:48
Section 162(c), Foreign Corrupt Practices Act, **2**:23
Section 162(1), self-employed health insurance deduction, **9**:26
Section 164(f), self-employment tax deduction, **9**:26
Section 165
  deduction for losses not compensated for by insurance, **6**:6
  Federally declared disasters, **7**:8*ft*
Section 165(c), losses of individuals, **7**:7
Section 168(k), additional first-year depreciation election, **17**:28
Section 170, contributions to qualified charitable organizations, **10**:18
Section 174, research and experimental expenditures, **7**:15–16
Section 179 expensing, **8**:11, **17**:17, **17**:28
  and bonus depreciation, using effectively, **8**:15–18
  conversion to personal use, **8**:14
  deduction limitations, **8**:11–13
  effect on basis, **8**:13
  Election to Expense Certain Depreciable Business Assets, **8**:10–14
  income tax filing status and, **8**:11*ft*
  mid-quarter convention, **8**:13–14
Section 183 presumptive rule, **6**:19
Section 197 intangibles, **8**:25, **16**:13
  expenditures for, **6**:28
Section 199A, deduction for qualified business income, **9**:25–52
  depreciable period for qualified property, **9**:31
Section 199A Regulations
  aggregation of qualified trades or businesses under, **9**:43, **9**:47–48
  determination of unadjusted basis immediately after acquisition (UBIA), **9**:51
  determination of W–2 wages, **9**:51
  employee turned independent contractor, **9**:51
  specified services under, **9**:34–36
  treatment of QBI deduction losses, **9**:48–50
Section 212 expenses, **6**:4, **6**:5–6
  deductions *for* AGI, **6**:4
  deductions *from* AGI, **6**:4
Section 212, investment/production of income activities, **6**:4
Section 262
  nondeductible personal expenses, **10**:2
  sale or exchange of personal use assets, **16**:16
Section 267, sale or exchange between related taxpayers, **2**:23, **16**:16
Section 274, substantiation requirements, **8**:23
Section 280A, rental property, **6**:21–22
Section 291, recapture potential of C corporations, **20**:9–10
Section 312, E & P, **20**:22
Section 318, definition of related parties for certain stock redemptions, **2**:23
Section 351, transfers of property to controlled organizations, **20**:18–20
  basis determination, **20**:19–20
Section 401(k) plan, **19**:10–11
  compared to Individual Retirement Account (IRA), **19**:25
Section 404, deduction for contributions to qualified retirement plans, **9**:26
Section 446(b), permissible accounting methods, **4**:7, **18**:10
Section 448, accrual method requirement, **18**:12
Section 469, passive activity loss rules, **7**:19, **11**:5–9, **11**:13
Section 471, best accounting practice and clear reflection of income tests for inventories, **18**:29
Section 529 plans (qualified tuition program), **5**:25–26
Section 529A plans, **5**:26–27
Section 530 plans (Coverdell education savings accounts), **5**:25–26
Section 530 relief, **9**:57
  Affordable Care Act (ACA) provisions, **9**:57*ft*
Section 604(a), independent contractors, **9**:3
Section 1031, like-kind exchanges, **15**:3–10, **17**:17
Section 1033, involuntary conversions, **15**:10–16, **17**:17
Section 1221, definition of a capital asset, **16**:4–6
Section 1231 assets, **16**:3, **17**:3–10
  condemnation gains and losses, **17**:5
  excluded property, **17**:4
  general procedure for computation, **17**:6–10
  included property, **17**:4
  relationship to capital assets, **17**:3–4
  reporting procedures, **17**:20–26
  special rules for certain, **17**:4–5
Section 1231 gains and losses, **17**:3–4, **17**:27
Section 1231 lookback provision, **17**:6
Section 1231 netting, **17**:3–4, **17**:6, **17**:7
  depreciation recapture and, **17**:18
Section 1231 property, **17**:4
Section 1237, real property subdivided for sale, **16**:7–8
Section 1244 stock, sale or exchange of, **7**:6, **7**:25, **16**:8
Section 1245 property, **17**:12
Section 1245 recapture, **16**:13, **17**:10–13, **20**:9–10
  comparison with Section 1250 recapture, **17**:14
  considerations common to Section 1250 recapture and, **17**:16–18
  depreciation defined, **17**:10*ft*
  exceptions, **17**:16–17
  nonresidential real estate, **17**:13*ft*
  other applications, **17**:17–18
  reporting procedures, **17**:20–26
Section 1250 property, **17**:13
  for purposes of the unrecaptured Section 1250 gain, **17**:15
Section 1250 recapture, **17**:13–15, **20**:9–10
  comparison with Section 1245 recapture, **17**:14
  considerations common to Section 1245 recapture and, **17**:16–18
  exceptions, **17**:16–17
  other applications, **17**:17–18
  reporting procedures, **17**:20–26
  unrecaptured gain (real estate 25% gain), **17**:14–15
Section 1253, sale or exchange, franchises, trademarks, and trade names, **16**:12–14
Section 1254 recapture, intangible drilling and development costs (IDCs), **17**:19
Section 1341, claim of right doctrine, **18**:9
Section 3403, employer liability for any taxes withheld and not paid over to the IRS, **13**:23*ft*
Section 6013(a)(1), joint returns and nonresident aliens, **3**:30
Section 6013(g), election to treat a nonqualifying spouse as a U.S. resident, **3**:30

Section 6654, penalty for failure by an individual to pay estimated income taxes, **13**:23*ft*
Section 6656, penalty on amounts withheld and not paid over, **13**:23*ft*
Section 6662, accuracy-related penalty, **2**:25
Sections 1272–1288, OID amortization rules, **16**:9
Securing Protection Against Carbon Emissions (SPACE) Tax Act proposal, **1**:23
Securities
  capital gain and loss treatment, **16**:7
  dealers in, **16**:7
  sale or exchange of worthless, **16**:8
  short sales of, **16**:17
  tax-exempt, **10**:16
  worthless, **7**:6
Securities and Exchange Commission, **6**:14
Self-directed Keogh plan, **19**:11
Self-employed and employee-related expenses
  education expenses, **9**:14–16
  in general, **9**:5
  transportation expenses, **9**:5–9
  travel expenses, **9**:9–14
Self-employed individual
  deductibility of medical insurance premiums as a business expense, **10**:7
  Form 1040, Schedule C, Profit or Loss From Business, **3**:40, **9**:3
  Form 1040, Schedule C–EZ, Net Profit From Business, **9**:3*ft*
  Form 1040, Schedule SE, Self-Employment Tax, **3**:36, **9**:3*ft*
  office in the home expenses, **9**:17–21
  tax filing requirements, **3**:34
  See also Independent contractor
Self-employed individuals, retirement plans for, **19**:11–13
  Keogh (H.R. 10) plans, **9**:53, **19**:11
  savings incentive match plan for employees (SIMPLE plans), **19**:12
  simplified employee pension plans (SEPs), **19**:12
  Solo Section 401(k) plans, **19**:12
  tax planning for, **19**:23
Self-employed taxpayers
  additional Medicare tax on unearned income, **13**:31
  additional Medicare tax on wages, **13**:30
  estimated tax for individuals, **13**:26
  Form 1040–ES, Estimated Tax for Individuals, **13**:26
  Form 2210, Underpayment of Estimated Tax by Individuals, Estates, and Trusts, **13**:27
  penalty on underpayments, **13**:26–27
  self-employment tax, **13**:27–29
  tax payment procedures, **13**:25–29
Self-employment income, **1**:19
Self-employment, net earnings from, **13**:27
Self-employment tax, **1**:20, **13**:27–29
  deductions *for* AGI, **3**:4
  Form 1040, Schedule SE, Self-Employment Tax, **3**:40, **9**:3*ft*
  NOLs and, **7**:20
  Social Security and Medicare portions, **13**:27
  worksheet for 2021, **13**:29
  worksheet for 2022, **13**:27–28
Selling price, installment method computing of, **18**:20–21
Senate, **2**:3–4
Senate Finance Committee, **2**:3–4, **2**:25
Separate home for a taxpayer's parent or parents, head of household, **3**:32
Separate qualified property, determination of UBIA, **9**:51
Separately stated items, **20**:25–26
Series E bonds, **4**:11–12
Series EE bonds, **4**:11–12, **5**:24, **5**:31
  income shifting opportunity, **4**:34–35
  tax deferral of interest income, **4**:33
Services
  contribution of, **10**:19
  interest paid for, **10**:16
  of a child, personal services, **4**:15
  of an employee, personal services, **4**:14–15
  receipt of stock for performance of, **20**:20
Settlement date, stock sales, **16**:37
7.5%-of-AGI floor, medical expenses, **10**:3, **12**:17
Severance awards, **15**:12–13
Severance taxes, **1**:14
Shareholders, distributions to, **20**:21–23
  constructive dividends, **20**:22–23
  dividend distributions, **20**:21–22
Shifting income, **4**:34–35
  from parents to children, **3**:37
  tax planning, **2**:29–30, **4**:23
Short period, **18**:7
Short sale, **16**:16
  of securities, **16**:17
  treatment illustrations, **16**:18–19
Short sale against the box, **16**:18
  disposition rules, **16**:18–19
  treatment illustrations, **16**:18–19
Short taxable year, **18**:7
Short-term capital loss (STCL), **7**:2, **16**:27
Short-term Federal rate, **18**:21*ft*
Significant participation activity, **11**:14
SIMPLE. *See* Savings incentive match plan for employees
Simplicity, tax principles, **1**:10, **1**:11
Simplified employee pension plans (SEPs), **9**:53, **19**:12
  compared to Keogh (H.R. 10) plans, **19**:13
Simplified method, **18**:30
  basis and holding period of property received, **15**:7–8
Simplified (safe harbor) Method
  office in the home deduction, **9**:18
  office in the home expenses, **9**:19–21
Simplifying America's Tax System (SATS) proposal, **1**:22–23
Single taxpayers, filing status, **3**:29
Sixteenth Amendment, ratification of, **1**:6
Small-awards program, Internal Revenue Service (IRS), **2**:7
Small business corporation, **4**:18, **7**:6, **20**:23–28
Small business, encouragement of, **1**:30
Small business stock (Section 1244 stock), **7**:6, **16**:22–23
  common investment loss limitation rules, **11**:24
  exclusion, AMT preferences, **12**:20
  losses, **7**:6
  losses, tax planning for, **7**:25
  special gain exclusion, **16**:22–23
Small Cases Division of the U.S. Tax Court, **2**:10, **2**:15
  Summary Opinions, **2**:14*ft*, **2**:16
Small taxpayers, **18**:34
Smith, Adam, **1**:10
Social considerations, tax law, **1**:36
Social Security, **13**:23
  benefits, **4**:30–31
  tax (old age, survivors, and disability insurance), **1**:19, **1**:20, **13**:24
Socially responsible investments (SRI), **19**:19
Sole proprietor
  reporting procedures, **8**:24–25
Sole proprietorship
  Form 1040, Schedule C, Profit or Loss From Business, **3**:4*ft*, **3**:40
  general tax consequences of, **20**:4
  nontax characteristics of, **20**:2–4
Solo Section 401(k) plans, **19**:12
Space flight excise tax, **1**:23
Special 25% gain netting rules, **17**:15
Specific charge-off method, **7**:3–4
  business bad debt, **7**:3
  nonbusiness bad debt, **7**:3
  tax treatment of bad debts using, **7**:4
Specific fact situations, **2**:7
Specific identification method, **18**:32
  cost identification problems, **14**:10
Specified service trade or business, **6**:8–9, **9**:29, **9**:33
Specified Service Trades or Businesses, Schedule A, Form 8995–A, **9**:42–43, **9**:46
Specified services, **9**:35
  under the Section 199A Regulations, **9**:34–38
Specified services businesses, QBI limitation for, **9**:33–42
  phase-in of specified services limit, **9**:38–42
Sports franchises, **16**:13
Spousal IRAs, **19**:16
Spouse
  abandoned spouse rules, **3**:32–33
  living apart in community property states, **4**:20
  medical expenses incurred for, **10**:5
  surviving spouse status, **3**:31
Spread, **12**:10
Spread, stock options and, **19**:20
SSTS. *See* Statements on Standards for Tax Services
Stafford Disaster Relief and Emergency Assistance Act, **7**:7*ft*
Standard deduction, **3**:7, **3**:17–19, **3**:33
  AMTI computation, **12**:17–18
  individuals not eligible for, **3**:18
  special limitations for dependents, **3**:18–19
  tax planning for maximizing the use of, **3**:45
  total, **3**:17
Standard Federal Tax Reporter, **2**:18
Standard mileage method, **9**:6, **9**:57
  restrictions of, **9**:7
Starker exchange, **15**:5
Startup expenditures, **6**:17–18, **8**:25, **8**:28
  amortization election, **8**:25, **8**:28

Startup expenses. *See* Startup expenditures
State and local excise taxes, **1**:13
State decisis, doctrine of, **2**:10, **2**:11*ft*
State income taxation
  decoupling from selected Federal tax changes, **1**:18
  piggyback approach to, **1**:18
State income taxes, **1**:18–19
State taxes on transfers at death, **1**:15
Statements on Standards for Tax Services, **1**:28
Statute of limitations, **1**:25–26
  assessment by the IRS, **1**:26
  limitations on refunds, **1**:26
Statutory authority, **5**:2–3
Statutory employees, **9**:5
  Form 1040, Schedule C, Profit or Loss From Business, **9**:5
Statutory expansions, **16**:7–8
  dealers in securities, **16**:7
  nonbusiness bad debts, **16**:8
  real property subdivided for sale (Section 1237), **16**:7–8
Statutory rates, **3**:35–36
Statutory sources of the tax law, **2**:2–5
  arrangement of the Internal Revenue Code, **2**:4–5
  citing the Code, **2**:5
  legislative process, **2**:3–4
  origin of the Internal Revenue Code, **2**:2
Stealth taxes, **1**:33–34
Stock basis determination, S corporation, **20**:27–28
Stock bonus plan, **19**:3
  See also Qualified plans
Stock, dividend income, **4**:17
Stock dividends, **5**:3
  holding period for nontaxable, **14**:11
  nontaxable, **14**:11
Stock option, **19**:19–23
  incentive stock options (ISO), **19**:19–22
  nonqualified stock options, **19**:22–23
  tax planning for, **19**:25–26
Stock sales
  execution date, **16**:37
  settlement date, **16**:37
  tax planning for, **16**:37
Straight-line cost recovery under MACRS (personalty vs. realty), **8**:9
Straight-line method, **8**:6
  automobiles and, **8**:18, **8**:21
  classification of property, **8**:5–6
  depreciation of real property, **12**:6
  listed property and, **8**:18, **8**:21
  modified accelerated cost recovery system (MACRS), **8**:8–9, **8**:18
  pollution control facilities, **12**:8
Stretch IRA, **19**:7
Stride Drive, **9**:9
Student loan interest
  deductibility of, **10**:18
  deductions *for* AGI, **3**:5, **10**:14
  tax consequences of, **9**:16
Subchapter C, Corporate Distributions and Adjustments, **2**:5
Subchapter designations, Internal Revenue Code, **2**:5
Subchapter K, Partners and Partnerships, **2**:5
Subchapter S, Tax Treatment of S Corporations and Their Shareholders, **2**:5
Subsidized eating facilities, **9**:22
Substance over form doctrine, **1**:36
Substantial authority, **2**:25
Substantial limitations or restrictions, **4**:9–11
Substantial rights, patents, **16**:11–12
Substantially identical property, **16**:17
Substantially identical stock or securities (wash sales), **14**:17–18
Substantially rehabilitated, **13**:6
Substantiation, **6**:29
Substantiation, accountable plan for reimbursement of employee expenses, **9**:53–54
Substantiation requirements, **6**:29, **8**:23
  and documentation requirements for charitable contributions, **10**:21
Sunset provision, **1**:29
Super-full absorption costing system, **18**:29
Support considerations, tax planning for dependents, **3**:46
Support payments, **4**:21
Support test
  children of divorced or separated parents, **3**:24
  multiple support agreements, **3**:24
  qualifying child, **3**:20–21
  qualifying relative, **3**:23–24
Supreme Court Reporter (S.Ct.), **2**:17
Surviving spouse, **3**:31
Suspended passive activity losses
  carryovers of, **11**:7–8
  impact of, **11**:6–7
Sustainable investing, **19**:19

T

Tables, cost recovery, **8**:32–36
Tangible asset costs, **8**:29
Tangible assets, **14**:2
  depreciation of, **8**:2
  expenditures for, **6**:27
Tangible personalty, **10**:23
Tariffs, **1**:5, **1**:20
Task-based simulations (TBSs), Regulation (REG) section of CPA examination, **2**:31–33
  Tax citation type simulation, **2**:33
  Tax form completion simulation, **2**:33
Tax administration, **1**:23–28
  audit process, **1**:24–25
  interest and penalties, **1**:26–27
  Internal Revenue Service, **1**:23
  statute of limitations, **1**:25–26
  tax practice, **1**:27–28
Tax advocacy, relevance of, to accounting and finance professionals, **1**:4
Tax and book depreciation, **8**:6
Tax avoidance, **2**:29–30, **4**:3
Tax base, **1**:8
Tax benefit rule, **5**:28–30, **10**:7–8, **12**:15
  itemized deductions, **5**:29–30
  SALT cap, **5**:29–30
  SALT deduction, **5**:29–30
  state income tax refunds, **5**:29–30
Tax bills, legislative process for, **2**:3
Tax consequences of provisions dealing with education, **9**:16
Tax conventions, **2**:17
Tax Court of the United States Reports (T.C.), **2**:14–15
Tax credits, **3**:37, **13**:2, **13**:21–23
  adoption expenses credit, **13**:21
  American Opportunity credit, **13**:18–19, **13**:21
  business energy, **13**:20
  child tax credit, **13**:15, **13**:21
  credit for certain retirement plan contributions, **13**:19–21, **13**:22
  credit for child and dependent care expenses, **13**:2, **13**:15–17, **13**:21
  credit for elderly or disabled taxpayers, **13**:3, **13**:21
  credit for employer-provided child care, **13**:11, **13**:23
  credit for employer-provided family and medical leave, **13**:12, **13**:23
  credit for small employer pension plan startup costs, **13**:11, **13**:22
  dependent tax credit, **13**:15, **13**:21
  difference between tax deductions and, **3**:37, **13**:3–4
  disabled access credit, **13**:3, **13**:10, **13**:22
  earned income credit, **13**:3, **13**:12–14, **13**:21
  education, **13**:18–19, **13**:21–22
  energy credits, **13**:19, **13**:20
  foreign tax credit (FTC), **13**:14–15, **13**:22
  general business credit, **13**:5–6, **13**:22
  lifetime learning credit, **13**:18–19, **13**:22
  low-income housing credit, **13**:9–10, **13**:22
  overview and priority of, **13**:4–6
  refundable versus nonrefundable, **13**:3, **13**:4–5
  rehabilitation expenditures credit, **13**:6–7, **13**:22
  research activities credit, **13**:3, **13**:7–9, **13**:22
  residential energy, **13**:20
  specific business-related provisions, **13**:6–12
  tax withheld on wages, **13**:21
  work opportunity tax credit, **13**:7, **13**:23
Tax Cuts and Jobs Act (TCJA) of 2017, **1**:22
  AMT and, **12**:2
  child tax credit, **2**:4
  Conference Report, example from, **9**:48
  depreciation of personal property and, **12**:7
  effect of changes to the AMT on individual taxpayers, **12**:4
  employee business expenses, **9**:5
  employee fringe benefits, **5**:20
  miscellaneous itemized deductions and, **9**:3*ft*, **9**:5, **9**:53
  qualified moving expense reimbursements, **5**:19
  qualified transportation fringes, **5**:19
  SALT deduction, **5**:29–30
  unreimbursed employee business expenses, **5**:18*ft*

Tax deductions, **3**:37
  difference between tax credits and, **3**:37, **13**:3–4
  time value of, **6**:12
Tax deferral
  bank certificates of deposit, **4**:33
  from reserves, **18**:16
  income recognition, **4**:32–34
  property transactions, **4**:32–33
  tax planning for, **4**:32–34
Tax depreciation deductions
  Federal income tax purposes, **8**:6
  generally accepted accounting principles (GAAP), **8**:6
Tax determination, **3**:34–39
  computation of net taxes payable or refund due, **3**:36–37
  kiddie tax—unearned income of dependent children, **3**:37–39
  tax rates, **3**:35–36
  unearned income of dependent children, **3**:38
Tax due (or refund), **3**:8
Tax Equity and Fiscal Responsibility Act of 1982, **2**:*3ft*
Tax evasion, **2**:30
Tax file memorandum, **2**:27
Tax for Certain Children Who Have Unearned Income, Form 8615, **3**:38
Tax formula, **3**:2–12
  basic, **1**:8–9
  components of, **3**:3–8
  correlation with Form 1040, **3**:8–12
  for individuals, **3**:3
  tax base, **1**:8
  tax rates, **1**:8–9
Tax formula components, **3**:3–8
  cash charitable contributions, **3**:7
  deduction for qualified business income, **3**:7
  deductions *for* AGI, **3**:4–5
  deductions *from* AGI, **3**:6
  dependency exemptions, **3**:7
  exclusions, **3**:3
  gross income, **3**:3–4
  income (broadly defined), **3**:3
  nondeductible expenses, **3**:7
  personal exemptions, **3**:7
  standard deduction, **3**:7
  tax due (or refund), **3**:8
  taxable income, **3**:7–8
Tax fraud, **2**:7
Tax home, determining, **9**:10–11
Tax law
  administrative sources of, **2**:6–9
  assessing the validity of judicial sources of, **2**:24–25
  assessing the validity of other administrative sources of, **2**:24
  courts influence of, **1**:35–36
  economic considerations, **1**:29–30, **1**:36
  equity considerations, **1**:31–33, **1**:36
  IRS influence of, **1**:34–35, **1**:36
  judicial sources of, **2**:10–17
  legislative process, **2**:3–4
  political considerations, **1**:33–34, **1**:36
  primary sources of, **2**:2, **2**:25
  revenue needs, **1**:29
  secondary sources of, **2**:*2ft*, **2**:25
  social considerations, **1**:30–31, **1**:36
  statutory sources of, **2**:2–5
  tax planning, **2**:28–31
  tax research, **2**:20–28
  tax research tools, **2**:18–20
  understanding the Federal, **1**:29–36
Tax law sources, **2**:2–18
  administrative, **2**:6–9
  assessing the validity of other, **2**:25
  judicial, **2**:10–17
  primary, **2**:2, **2**:25
  secondary, **2**:*2ft*, **2**:25
  statutory, **2**:2–5
  tax periodicals, **2**:18
  tax treaties, **2**:17
Tax loopholes, **1**:34
Tax Management Portfolios, **2**:19
Tax Notes, **2**:8, **2**:18
Tax Notes International, **2**:18
Tax Notes State, **2**:18
Tax on investment income, **1**:20
Tax payment procedures, **13**:23–31
  additional Medicare taxes on high-income individuals, **13**:29–31
  employers, **13**:23–25
  self-employed taxpayers, **13**:25–29
Tax periodicals, **2**:18
  Business Entities, **2**:18
  Corporate Taxation, **2**:18
  Estate Planning, **2**:18
  Journal of International Taxation, **2**:18
  Journal of Passthrough Entities, **2**:18
  Journal of Taxation, **2**:18
  Journal of the American Taxation Association, **2**:18
  Oil, Gas & Energy Quarterly, **2**:18
  Practical Tax Strategies, **2**:18
  Real Estate Taxation, **2**:18
  Tax Law Review, **2**:18
  Tax Notes, **2**:18
  Tax Notes International, **2**:18
  Tax Notes State, **2**:18
  Taxation of Exempts, **2**:18
  TAXES—The Tax Magazine, **2**:18
  The ATA Journal of Legal Tax Research, **2**:18
  The Tax Adviser (AICPA), **2**:18
  The Tax Executive, **2**:18
  Trusts & Estates, **2**:18
Tax planning
  adjustments to avoid overwithholding, **13**:33
  adjustments to increase withholding, **13**:32
  amortization, **8**:32
  avoiding nondeductible treatment, **10**:31
  avoiding preferences and adjustments, **12**:22–24
  avoiding recapture, **17**:28
  C corporation versus S status, **20**:35
  capital asset status, **16**:35–36
  cash method of accounting, **18**:35
  casualty losses, **7**:25
  comparison of Section 401(k) plan with IRA, **19**:24–25
  components of, **2**:29–30
  controlling the timing of AMT preferences and adjustments, **12**:24
  corporate versus noncorporate forms of business organization, **20**:33–35
  cost identification and documentation considerations, **14**:22
  cost recovery, **8**:31
  credit for child and dependent care expenses, **13**:31–32
  dependents, **3**:45–46
  disallowed losses, **14**:23
  effect of the additional tax on net investment income, **11**:26
  employee fringe benefits, **5**:30–31
  employment status, **9**:56
  ensuring the charitable contribution deduction, **10**:29–31
  follow-up procedures, **2**:30
  hobby losses, **6**:32
  implications of misclassifying workers, **9**:56–57
  income of certain children, **3**:47
  income shifting to reduce the family income tax burden, **20**:35–36
  individual retirement accounts, **19**:23–24
  inherited property, **14**:22
  installment method, **18**:35–36
  inventories, **18**:36
  investment income, **5**:31
  involuntary conversions, **15**:23
  life insurance, **5**:30
  like-kind exchanges, **15**:22–23
  liquidating retirement assets, **19**:26
  maximizing benefits for capital gains and losses, **16**:37
  maximizing the investment interest deduction, **11**:26
  maximizing the medical deduction, **10**:29
  maximizing use of standard deduction, **3**:45
  minimizing the impact of passive activity loss limits, **11**:24–25
  nonqualified deferred compensation (NQDC) plans, **19**:24
  nontax considerations, **2**:29
  objectives of, **2**:28
  other AMT strategies, **12**:24
  postponing and shifting recapture, **17**:28
  property transactions, **14**:22–23
  qualified plans, **19**:23
  sale of a principal residence, **15**:23–24
  selection of property for making gifts, **14**:22
  selection of property to pass at death, **14**:22
  self-employed retirement plans, **19**:23
  shifting income to other taxpayers, **4**:34–35
  small business stock (Section 1244 stock) losses, **7**:25
  stock options, **19**:25–26
  stock sales, **16**:37
  strategies, **4**:32–35
  taking advantage of tax rate differentials, **3**:46–47
  tax avoidance and tax evasion, **2**:30
  tax deferral, **4**:32–34
  taxable year, **18**:35
  timing of recapture, **17**:27–28
  timing of Section 1231 gain, **17**:27
  transportation and travel expenses, **9**:57
  vacation homes, **6**:30, **6**:32
  year-end planning for capital gains and losses, **16**:37
Tax policy considerations, **13**:3–4
Tax practice, **1**:27–28
  ethical guidelines, **1**:28
  statutory penalties imposed on tax return preparers, **1**:28

Tax principles
accountability to taxpayers, **1**:10, **1**:11
appropriate government revenues, **1**:10, **1**:11
certainty, **1**:9, **1**:10, **1**:11
convenience of payment, **1**:9, **1**:10, **1**:11
economic growth and efficiency, **1**:10, **1**:11
economy in collection, **1**:9
effective tax administration, **1**:10, **1**:11
equity, **1**:9
equity and fairness, **1**:10, **1**:11
information security, **1**:10, **1**:11
minimum tax gap, **1**:10, **1**:11
neutrality, **1**:10, **1**:11
simplicity, **1**:10, **1**:11
transparency and visibility, **1**:10, **1**:11
Tax rate differentials, tax planning for taking advantage of, **3**:46–47
Tax Rate Schedule for single taxpayers (2022), **3**:36
Tax Rate Schedule method, **3**:35–36
Tax Rate Schedules, **3**:29, **3**:35–36
Tax rates, **1**:8–9, **3**:8, **3**:35–36
corporate income, **20**:14
income tax consequences of individuals compared with C corporations, **20**:18
Tax Rate Schedule method, **3**:35–36
Tax Table method, **3**:35
Tax Reform Act (TRA) of 1986, **1**:22, **2**:2, **2**:4*ft*
Tax relief, adjustments to income and deductions, **18**:10
Tax research, **2**:20–28
arriving at the solution or at alternative solutions, **2**:25–26
assessing the validity of tax law sources, **2**:23–25
communicating, **2**:26–28
identifying the problem, **2**:21–22
locating the appropriate tax law sources, **2**:22
process, **2**:21–22
refining the problem, **2**:22
Tax research tools, **2**:18–20
commercial tax services, **2**:18–19
noncommercial electronic (online) tax services, **2**:19–20
using electronic (online) tax services, **2**:19
Tax return filing procedures, **3**:39–41
e-file approach **3**:40
modes of payment, **3**:41
selecting the proper form, **3**:39–40
when and where to file, **3**:40–41
Tax return preparation, outsourcing of, **1**:27
Tax return preparers, statutory penalties imposed on, **1**:28
Tax rules
costs of investigating a business, **6**:18
dissimilarities between corporate and individual, **20**:8
similarities between corporate and individual, **20**:6–8
Tax services, commercial, **2**:18–19
Tax shelter problem, **11**:2–4
Tax shelters, **11**:2–4
Tax system
design, **1**:8–10
global, **5**:21
primary objective, **1**:29
territorial, **5**:21
Tax Table, **3**:35
Tax Table method, **3**:35
Form 1040, U.S. Individual Income Tax Return, **3**:35
Tax treatment
of bad debts using the specific charge-off method, **7**:4
of payments and transfers pursuant to divorce agreements and decrees, **4**:23
of S Corporations and Their Shareholders, Subchapter S, **2**:5
of unemployment compensation, **4**:30
Tax treaties, **2**:2, **2**:17
Taxable estate, **1**:13
Taxable income, **1**:8, **3**:7–8
computation of, **3**:8
computation of, income tax consequences of individuals compared with C corporations, **20**:17
QBI deduction phaseout for specified services, **9**:34
reconciliation of accounting income and corporate, **20**:15–18
S corporation, **20**:26
Taxable year, **4**:6
tax planning for, **18**:35
Taxation, **1**:2–3
alleviating the effect of multiple, **1**:32
approaching the study of, **1**:2–4
defined, **1**:2
general scheme of, **16**:3
historical trends of U.S., **1**:7–8
history of U.S., **1**:5–8
of benefits for IRAs, **19**:16
of income and distributions, **4**:18
of interest on state and local government bonds, **5**:24
of interest on U.S. government bonds, **5**:24
of virtual currency, **3**:44–45
on the CPA examination, **2**:31–33
relevance of to accounting and finance professionals, **1**:3–4
transition based, **1**:4
U.S. global approach to, **3**:30
Taxation of Exempts, **2**:18
TaxCenter, **2**:19
Taxes
ad valorem, **1**:12, **10**:11
additional Medicare taxes on high-income individuals, **13**:29–31
carbon, **1**:23
consumption, **1**:22
corporate income, **1**:3, **1**:6
deductibility as, **10**:10–11
deductible and nondeductible, **10**:11
direct, **1**:2
distinguished from fees, **10**:10
Electronic Federal Tax Payment System (EFTPS), **3**:41
employment taxes, **1**:19–20
estate, **1**:15
excise, **1**:2, **1**:6, **1**:13
Fair, **1**:22
FICA, **1**:19–20
financial transaction, **1**:23
flat, **1**:22
franchise, **1**:6, **1**:21
FUTA, **1**:20
gift, **1**:16–17
in United States, overview of, **1**:21
income, **1**:2, **1**:5, **1**:7, **1**:17–19
indirect, **1**:2
individuals and, **1**:6
inheritance, **1**:15
interest on deferred, **18**:23
IRS Direct Pay, **3**:41
itemized deductions, AMT adjustments, **12**:15–16
local income, **1**:19
major types of, **1**:10–23
mass, **1**:7
Medicare, **1**:19, **1**:20
on transfers at death, **1**:15
other U.S., **1**:20–21
payment by check or money order, **3**:41
progressive, **1**:9
property, **1**:2, **1**:12–13, **10**:11–13
proportional, **1**:31
proposed U.S., **1**:22–23
regressive or progressive, **1**:31
sales, **1**:2, **1**:14, **1**:22
severance, **1**:14
Social Security, **1**:18, **1**:19, **1**:20
space flight excise, **1**:23
state and local, **1**:13, **1**:21, **10**:10, **10**:13
stealth, **1**:33–34
transaction, **1**:13–14
use, **1**:14
use of credit card to pay, **3**:41
value added, **1**:22–23
withheld on wages, **13**:21
Taxes payable, computation of net, **3**:36–37
TAXES—The Tax Magazine, **2**:18
Tax-exempt income, expenses and interest relating to, **6**:29–30
Tax-exempt securities, **10**:16
Tax-free transaction, **15**:3
Taxpayer use test, replacement property, **15**:13–14
Taxpayers, small, **18**:34
Taxpayers subject to passive activity loss rules, **11**:9–10
Taxpayers with multiple businesses, qualified trade or business (QTB), **9**:29
Tax-related blogs and RSS sites, **2**:20
Tax-related websites, **2**:20, **2**:21
TCJA of 2017. *See* Tax Cuts and Jobs Act
Technical Advice Memoranda (TAMs), **2**:9
accuracy-related penalty, **2**:9*ft*
distinction between letter rulings and, **2**:9
distinction between Technical Expedited Advice Memoranda (TEAMs) and, **2**:9*ft*
Technical Expedited Advice Memorandums (TEAMs), **2**:9
distinction between Technical Advice Memoranda (TAMs), **2**:9*ft*
Temporary assignments, travel expenses, **9**:10
Temporary Regulations, **2**:7
10%-of-AGI aggregate floor
Federally declared disasters, **7**:10*ft*
reduction for, **7**:10–11
Tenant, low-income, **13**:10
Tenants by the entirety, **14**:15
Tentative minimum tax (TMT), **12**:5, **13**:5
Term certain, income from annuities, **4**:27
Terminally ill
accelerated death benefits and, **5**:5
Social Security taxes and, **5**:6

Territorial tax system, **5**:21
Test based on
current participation, **11**:14
facts and circumstances, **11**:14
prior participation, **11**:14
Tests to determine material participation
test based on facts and circumstances, **11**:14
tests based on current participation, **11**:14
tests based on prior participation, **11**:14
The ATA Journal of Legal Tax Research, **2**:18
The Law Review, **2**:18
The Tax Adviser (AICPA), **2**:18
The Tax Executive, **2**:18
The Wealth of Nations, **1**:10
Theft losses, **7**:8
as capital recovery, **14**:6–7
personal casualty gains and losses, **7**:12–14
Section 1231 assets, **17**:5
statutory framework for deducting losses of individuals, **7**:14–15
See also Casualty loss
Thin capitalization, **20**:20–21
Third Circuit Court of Appeals, **6**:11
Tiebreaker rules
for claiming qualified child, **3**:21
qualifying child, **3**:21
Timber, as a Section 1231 asset, **17**:4–5
Time value of money, **6**:12
Time value of tax deductions, **6**:12
Timing of expense recognition, **6**:10–12
accrual method requirements, **6**:10–11
cash method requirements, **6**:10
importance of taxpayer's method of accounting, **6**:10
marginal tax rate, **6**:12
prepaid expenses—the "12-month rule," **6**:12
time value of money, **6**:12
time value of tax deductions, **6**:12
Topical, commercial tax services, **2**:18
Top-paid group, **19**:5
Total gain, installment method computing of, **18**:20–21
Total income, Form 1040, **3**:8
Total standard deduction, **3**:17
Trade names, **16**:12
Trade or business expenses
deductions *for* AGI, **3**:4
Trade or business under Section 199A, **9**:28
rental real estate activity safe harbor, **9**:28
Trademarks, **16**:12
Traditional IRA, **9**:52–53
compared with Roth IRA, **19**:17
See also Individual retirement account
Transaction taxes, **1**:13–14
Transfer for valuable consideration, life insurance proceeds, **5**:6–7
Transient occupancy tax (TOT), **1**:13
Transparency and visibility, tax principles, **1**:10, **1**:11
Transportation expenses, **9**:5–9
for medical treatment, deductible medical expenses, **10**:6
qualified expenses, **9**:5–6
tax planning for, **9**:57
Travel expenses, **9**:9–14, **9**:57
away-from-home requirement, **9**:10–11
combined business and pleasure travel, **9**:12–14
definition of travel expenses, **9**:9–10
restrictions on, **9**:11–12
Treasury Decisions (TDs), **2**:7, **2**:8–9
Treasury Department Regulations, **2**:6–7, **2**:24
assessing the validity of, **2**:23–24
Trial courts, **2**:10, **2**:11–12, **2**:24
appeals, **2**:12
number of, **2**:11
number of judges, **2**:11
See also Courts
TripLog, **9**:9
Trusts
beneficiaries of, **4**:18
income from, **4**:17–18
taxation of income and distributions from, **4**:18
Trusts and Estates, **2**:18
Tuition expenses, deductible medical expenses, **10**:4
Tuition reduction plans, **5**:7
12-month rule for prepaid expenses, **6**:12, **18**:11
2%-of-AGI floor
miscellaneous itemized deductions not subject to, **9**:56
miscellaneous itemized deductions subject to, **9**:55
Two-year rules exceptions, sale of a residence, **15**:20–22
change in place of employment, **15**:20
health issues, **15**:20
unforeseen circumstances, **15**:21

U

U.S. citizen renouncement, **4**:3
U.S. Corporation Tax Return, Form 1120, **20**:15
U.S. Court of Federal Claims, **1**:25, **2**:10, **2**:11–12, **2**:13, **2**:15, **2**:17*ft*
judicial citations of, **2**:16–17
jurisdiction of, **2**:11
See also Courts
U.S. Courts of Appeal, **2**:12, **2**:15
judicial citations of, **2**:16–17
See also Courts
U.S. District Courts, **1**:25, **2**:10, **2**:11–12, **2**:15, **2**:24
judicial citations of, **2**:16–17
jurisdiction of, **2**:11
See also Courts
U.S. global approach to taxation, **3**:30
U.S. government publications, as part of the definition of a capital asset, **16**:6
U.S. Income Tax Return for an S Corporation, Form 1120S, **20**:5, **20**:15
U.S. Individual Income Tax Return, Form 1040, **3**:8, **3**:9–10, **3**:35, **3**:39–40, **3**:45
U.S. Individual Income Tax Transmittal for an IRS *e-file* Return, Form 8453, **3**:40
U.S. Return of Partnership Income, Form 1065, **4**:17, **20**:28, **20**:31
U.S. Supreme Court, **2**:13, **2**:15, **2**:24
appeal to, **2**:14
definition of interest, **10**:14
judicial citations of, **2**:17
See also Courts
U.S. Tax Cases (USTC), **2**:16–17
U.S. Tax Court, **1**:25, **2**:10, **2**:11–12, **2**:13–14, **2**:15
judicial citations of, **2**:14–16
jurisdiction of, **2**:11
Small Cases Division of, **2**:10
website (**ustaxcourt.gov**), **2**:15
See also Courts
U.S. Tax Court Small Cases Division Summary Opinions, **2**:14*ft*, **2**:16
U.S. Tax Return for Seniors, Form 1040SR, **3**:40
Unadjusted basis immediately after acquisition (UBIA), Section 199A Regulations, determination of, **9**:51
Underpayment, estimated tax, **13**:26–27
Underpayment of Estimated Tax by Individuals, Estates and Trusts, Form 2210, **13**:27
Unearned income, **1**:20, **3**:37, **4**:13–14
additional Medicare tax on, **13**:30–31
Unearned income of dependent children, **3**:37–39
election to claim certain unearned income on parent's return, **3**:39
Form 8814, Parents' Election to Report Child's Interest and Dividends, **3**:39
net unearned income, **3**:38
other rules, **3**:39
tax determination, **3**:38
Unemployment compensation, **4**:29–30
COVID-19 pandemic, **4**:30
tax treatment of, **4**:30
Unified transfer tax credit, **1**:15, **1**:16–17
Unified transfer tax rate schedule, **1**:16
Uniform capitalization (UNICAP) rules, **18**:29–30
allocation of costs, **18**:30
classification of costs, **18**:30
inventory costs of producers, **18**:30
inventory costs of retailers, **18**:30
inventory costs of wholesalers, **18**:30
simplified method, **18**:30
Uniform Gifts to Minors Act, **4**:34
Unique item, **18**:25
Unit of property (UOP), **6**:26–27
United States Board of Tax Appeals Reports (B.T.A.), **2**:15
United States Reports, Lawyer's Edition (L.Ed.), **2**:17
United States Supreme Court Reports (U.S.), **2**:17
United States Tax Reporter, **2**:18
Unit-livestock-price method, **18**:34
Unrealized gains, **3**:4
Unrecaptured Section 1250 gain, **16**:19, **17**:14–15
net Section 1231 gain limitation, **17**:15
Section 1250 property for purposes of, **17**:15
special 25% gain netting rules, **17**:15
Unreimbursed employee business expenses, **9**:55

Unreimbursed employment-related expenses, credit for child and dependent care expenses, **13**:16
Unrelated use, **10**:23
Use or lose plans, **5**:16
Use tax, **1**:14

V

Vacation homes, **6**:21–25
common investment loss limitation rules, **11**:24
personal/rental use, **6**:23–25
primarily personal use, **6**:22–23
primarily rental use, **6**:23
rental of, **6**:21–25
tax planning for, **6**:30, **6**:32
tax treatment of, **6**:22–25
Vacation/rental home, **6**:22
Valuation requirements for charitable contributions, **10**:22
Value added tax (VAT), **1**:22–23
Vesting, **19**:6
cliff, **19**:6
five-year, **19**:6
graded, **19**:6
Vesting requirements, **19**:6
alternative minimum vesting schedules, **19**:6
qualified plans, **19**:6
Virtual currency, taxation of, **3**:44–45
convertible, **3**:44
Form 1040, U.S. Individual Income Tax Return, **3**:45
Voluntary Classification Settlement Program (VCSP), **9**:57
Voluntary revocation, S election, **20**:24–25

W

W–2 wages
defined, **9**:51
Section 199A Regulations, determination of, **9**:51
W–2 Wages Limit, QBI deduction, **9**:29, **9**:31
W–2 Wages/Capital Investment Limit, **9**:29, **9**:31–33
computation of QBI amount, **9**:32–33
phase-in of, **9**:32–33
QBI deduction, **9**:31–33
Wages
additional Medicare tax on, **13**:29–30
Form W–2, Wage and Tax Statement, **3**:36, **13**:25
limit on the QBI deduction based on capital investment and, **6**:7–8
QBI deduction limitation based on, **9**:29
Wash sale, **14**:16–19
rules, **14**:16–19
Websites, tax-related, **2**:20, **2**:21
Weight of authority, **2**:2
Westlaw, **2**:19
WestlawNext, **2**:19
Wherewithal to pay, **1**:32
involuntary conversions, **15**:10
nontaxable exchange, **15**:2
Withholding
backup, **13**:25
Form W–4, Employee's Withholding Certificate, **13**:25, **13**:32, **13**:33
tax planning for adjustments to avoid, **13**:33
tax planning for adjustments to increase, **13**:32
Work opportunity tax credit, **13**:7, **13**:23
computation of, **13**:7
targeted and economically disadvantaged groups, **13**:7
Workers without children, earned income credit, **13**:14
Workers' compensation, **5**:10
Working condition fringes, **5**:18
World Economic Forum, **1**:3
Worldwide income tax base, **4**:3
Worthless securities, **7**:6
and Section 1244 stock, sale or exchange of, **16**:8
common investment loss limitation rules, **11**:24
Writ of Certiorari, **2**:14
Wrongful incarceration, Section 139F, **5**:10

Y

Year of deduction, medical expenses, **10**:7
Year of service, qualified plans, **19**:4
Year-end planning for capital gains and losses, tax planning for, **16**:37

Z

Zero-coupon bonds, **5**:31